NATIONAL GUIDE TO FUNDING FOR THE ENVIRONMENT AND ANIMAL WELFARE

NATIONAL GUIDE TO FUNDING FOR THE ENVIRONMENT AND ANIMAL WELFARE

Seventh Edition

Edited by

Jeffrey A. Falkenstein

The Foundation Center

CONTRIBUTING STAFF

Senior Vice President for Information Resources and Publishing	Rick Schoff
Director of Foundation Database Publishing	Jeffrey A. Falkenstein
Senior Database Editor	Margaret Feczko
Contributing Editors	David Clark
	Phyllis Edelson
	David Jacobs
	Melissa Lunn
	Rebecca MacLean
	Francine Murray
Coordinator of Information Control	Yinebon Iniya
Publishing Database Administrator	Kathye Giesler
Database Operations Assistant	Emmy So
Director of Communications	Cheryl L. Loe
Production Coordinator, Publishing	Christine Innamorato
Manager of Bibliographic Services	Sarah Collins
Assistant Librarian	Jimmy Tom

The editor gratefully acknowledges the many other Foundation Center staff who contributed support, encouragement, and information that was indispensable to the preparation of this volume. Special mention should be made of the staff members of the New York, Washington, D.C., Cleveland, San Francisco, and Atlanta libraries who assisted in tracking changes in grantmaker information. We would like to express our appreciation as well to the many grantmakers that cooperated fully in updating information prior to the compilation of this volume.

CONTENTS

INTRODUCTION:
GRANTMAKER SUPPORT FOR THE ENVIRONMENT AND ANIMAL WELFARE

In 2003, over 64,000 active private and community foundations in America awarded over $30.3 billion in grants to nonprofit organizations across the country and abroad. Corporate contributions for both company-sponsored foundations (whose giving is included in the above $30.3 billion figure) and direct corporate giving programs amounted to approximately $3.5 billion. Although foundation and corporate donations represent but a small fraction of total philanthropic giving in the U.S., they are still a key source of support for many programs.

This volume is intended as a starting point for grantseekers looking for foundation, corporate, and other charitable support in environment and animal welfare. It contains a total of 3,510 entries including 2,863 grantmaking foundations, 207 direct corporate giving programs and 440 public charities (including 227 community foundations) that have shown a substantial interest in environment and animal welfare, either as part of their stated fields of interest or through the actual grants of $10,000 or more reported to the Foundation Center in the latest year of record. Grants in environment and animal welfare are listed for 297 of the foundations listed in this volume. These 7,298 grants represent almost $979 million in support for a variety of programs, including pollution control, renewable energy, and zoos and zoological societies.

Each entry in the *Guide* was carefully evaluated by Foundation Center staff to ensure that the grantmaker possesses a sufficient interest in environment and animal welfare, either stated or demonstrated. Often, a grantmaker claims interest not only programs related to environment and animal welfare but in dozens of widely diverse fields. To determine if inclusion in this *Guide* is warranted in such cases, consideration is given to the grantmaker's purpose statement, giving limitations, and, if they exist, subject-related grants. Grantseekers should be aware that inclusion does not imply that these grantmakers will consider all programs in environment and animal welfare.

Keep in mind that some grantmakers support particular programs because of their interest in a specific community or organization. Others may do so because the program relates to a highly specific subject interest of the grantmaker, such as recycling programs, environmental education, or wildlife and natural resources preservation. Still others are interested in building the capacity of nonprofit institutions by providing specific types of support such as operating costs or challenge grants. Grantseekers are therefore urged to read each foundation and corporate giving program description carefully to determine the nature of the grantmaker's interests and to note any restrictions on giving that would prevent the grantmaker from considering their proposal.

PRECISE INDEXING

Since 1989 the Foundation Center has used a Grants Classification System (GCS) based on the National Taxonomy of Exempt Entities (NTEE), a comprehensive organizational coding scheme developed by the National Center for Charitable Statistics (NCCS) that was adopted by the IRS in 1995. The GCS builds on the NTEE and is used by the Center to provide subject, types of support, and other grants information both online through two DIALOG files (a product of Knight-Ridder Information Services) and the *Foundation Directory Online,* as well as on CD-ROM through *The Foundation Grants Index on CD-ROM.*

This edition of the *National Guide to Funding for the Environment and Animal Welfare* represents a major project to utilize the more comprehensive and precise GCS terminology across all Foundation Center publications and files. This process has resulted in the Center maintaining a more unified system of classification. The enhancements to this Guide resulting from the implementation of unified indexing terms include:

1. A section in grantmaker descriptive entries identifying any international giving interests of an organization. Because of the conversion to the GCS terminology, the number of index terms describing the countries, continents, and regions in which grantmakers have giving interests has expanded

from a few dozen to over 200, providing a much greater level of specificity.

2. The full scope of the terminology used to describe a grantmaker's areas of interests has also expanded following the conversion to unified GCS subject terms. The "Fields of Interest" section of each grantmaker descriptive entry includes all indexed subject terms for the organization, rather than listing only its primary areas of giving. The "Purpose and Activities" section contains a more general statement of foundation funding priorities.

WHAT IS A FOUNDATION?

The Foundation Center defines a foundation as a nongovernmental, nonprofit organization with its own funds (usually derived from a single source, either an individual, family, or corporation) and a program managed by its own trustees and directors, which was established to maintain or aid educational, social, charitable, or other activities serving the common welfare, primarily by making grants to other nonprofit organizations.

The Internal Revenue Service code defines the category of "private foundation" only by exclusion of other nonprofit organizations, a circumstance that has led to some confusion. David Freedman, former president of the Council on Foundations, explains the Code's definition in his book *The Handbook on Private Foundations:*

> Starting with the universe of voluntary organizations described in section 501(c)(3), the Code excludes broad groups, e.g., churches, schools, hospitals, governmental units, publicly supported charities and their affiliates. Publicly supported charities are those which derive much of their general support from the public and reach out in other ways to a public constituency. All of the above kinds of excluded organizations are commonly referred to as 'public charities.' Section 501(c)(3) organizations remaining after these exclusions are, without more precise definition, 'private foundations.' One important result: organizations are included in the remainder as private foundations that are not really grantmaking foundations at all. These may include museums, homes for the aged, and libraries, among others, if they, while serving the public, happen to have been endowed by an individual or single family, or if they were established as public charities and lose that status by failing to prove they have received ongoing financial support from the general public.

A private **independent foundation** most commonly derives its assets from an individual, family, or group of individuals. The foundation may function under the voluntary direction of family members, or may bear a family name but have independent boards of trustees and

professional staffs. Typically, independent foundations have broad charters which allow a range of giving activities, but in practice most limit their giving to a few specific fields of interest and to a specific geographic area.

Operating foundations are also private foundations under tax laws, but their primary purpose is to operate research, social welfare, or other charitable programs determined by the donor or governing body. Some grants may be made outside the foundation, but the majority of the foundation's funds are expended on its own programs.

Corporations contribute through foundations, direct giving programs, or both:

Corporate or **company-sponsored** foundations are created and funded by business corporations for the purpose of making grants and performing other philanthropic activities. Legally, they are separate from the sponsoring corporation and are governed by the same federal rules and regulations as independent foundations. Company-sponsored foundations are generally managed by a board of directors that includes corporate officials but may also include individuals with no corporate affiliation. Giving programs often focus on communities where the company has operations, and on research and education in fields related to company activities.

Direct corporate giving refers to all other giving by a company, that is, money not turned over to a foundation to administer. Direct giving programs are unregulated and restricted only by the limit of taxable earnings allowed as charitable deductions. In addition to cash contributions, corporate giving may include non-cash gifts of goods and services referred to as "in-kind" giving. Donations of company products, supplies, and equipment—from computers to food—is the most common form of in-kind giving. Other types of support include technical assistance and use of office space. Direct giving programs and foundations often share the same staff, although some companies keep these functions administratively separate.

Public charities, in general, are organizations that are tax-exempt under code section 501(c)(3) and are classified by the IRS as a public charity and not a private foundation. Public charities typically derive their funding or support substantially from the general public in carrying out their social, educational, religious, or other charitable activities serving the common welfare. Some public charities engage in grantmaking activities, although most engage in direct service or other tax-exempt activities. Public charities are eligible for maximum income tax-deductible contributions from the public and are not subject to the same rules and restrictions as private foundations. Some are also referred to as "public foundations" or "publicly supported foundations" and may use the term "foundation" in their names.

Community foundations are public charities supported by and operated for a specific community or region. They receive their funds from a variety of donors; in fact, their endowments are frequently composed of a number of different trust funds, some of which bear their donors' names. Their grantmaking activities are administered by a governing body or distribution committee representative of community interests. Although community foundations may support a wide range of activities, their grants are generally restricted to charitable organizations in their city or region.

Grantseekers should be aware that an increasing number of for-profit business have also adopted "foundation" as part of their name to promote their activities. While there are no legal restrictions on the use of the word "foundation," it is important for grantseekers to understand that many of these groups do not make grants and are not governed by the same rules and regulations as private foundations or nonprofit groups.

GRANTSEEKING FROM FOUNDATIONS

Foundations receive many thousands of worthy requests each year. Most of these requests are declined because there are not enough funds to go around or because the application clearly falls outside the foundation's fields of interest. Some of the applications denied are poorly prepared and do not reflect a careful analysis of the applicant organization's needs, its credibility, or its capacity to carry out the proposed project. Sometimes the qualifications of the organization's staff are not well established; the budget or the means of evaluating the project may not be presented convincingly; or the organization may not have asked itself whether it is especially suited to make a contribution to the solution of the problem, whether it can provide the service proposed, or whether others are not already effectively engaged in the same activity.

The first step in researching foundation funding support is to analyze your own program and organization to determine the need you plan to address, the audience you will serve, and the amount and type of support you need. Become familiar with the basic facts about foundations in general and how they operate. Consider other sources of funding, such as individual contributors, government grants, earned income possibilities, and so on. Although foundations are an important source of support for nonprofit organizations, their giving represents a relatively small percentage of the total philanthropic dollars contributed annually, and an even smaller percentage of the total when government grants and earned income are included. If you are new to grantseeking, we strongly urge you to visit one of the Foundation Center's many Cooperating Collections. They provide free access to a core collection of Foundation Center publications, as well as other materials on funding sources, program planning, and fundraising.

Once you have determined the amount and type of foundation support you need and the reasons why you are seeking support, this *Guide* can help you develop an initial list of foundations that might be interested in funding your project. In determining whether or not it is appropriate to approach a particular foundation with a grant request, keep in mind the following questions:

1. Does the foundation's interest in environment and animal welfare include the specific type of service or program you are proposing?

2. Does it seem likely that the foundation will make a grant in your geographic area?

3. Does the amount of money you are requesting fit within the foundation's grant range?

4. Does the foundation have any policy prohibiting grants for the type of support you are requesting?

5. Does the foundation prefer to make grants that cover the full cost of a project or do they favor projects where other foundations or funding sources share the cost?

6. What types of organizations does the foundation tend to support?

7. Does the foundation have specific application deadlines and procedures or does it review proposals continuously?

Some of these questions can be answered from the information provided in this *Guide*, but grantseekers will almost always want to consult a few additional resources before submitting a request for funding. If the foundation issues an annual report, application guidelines, or other printed materials describing its program, it is advisable to obtain copies and study them carefully before preparing your proposal. The foundation's annual information return (Form 990-PF) includes a list of all grants paid by the foundation in addition to basic data about its finances, officers, and giving policies.

The foundations listed in this *Guide* by no means represent all of the possible foundation funding sources for programs related to environment and animal welfare. There are a number of foundations, including some 670 community foundations across the country, that support a wide variety of programs within a specific community or region. Grantseekers should learn as much as possible about the foundations in their own area, particularly when they are seeking relatively small grants for projects with purely local impact. Be sure to check any local or state directories of which the Foundation Center is currently aware. Copies of these directories are almost always available for use at your local Foundation Center cooperating library.

The Foundation Center publishes several national directories on an annual basis. *The Foundation Directory* describes the top 10,000 foundations by total giving. *The Foundation Directory Part 2* provides information on the second tier of foundations, the next 10,000 foundations by total giving. Both the *Directory* and the *Directory Part*

2 entries include a list of selected grants whenever available, providing concrete examples of a foundation's giving. The *Directory* and *Directory Part 2* are arranged by state and include a geographic index to help you identify foundations located or interested in your specific community. The Foundation Center also publishes the *Guide to U.S. Foundations, Their Trustees, Officers, and Donors*, which provides basic address and financial information on over 64,000 active grantmaking foundations in the United States, as well as fully indexed listings to all foundation trustees/directors, officers, and donors. The *Guide to U.S. Foundations* is arranged alphabetically by state. Within states, foundations are listed in descending order by annual giving amount.

For those who want more detailed information on how to identify appropriate foundation funding sources, the Center also publishes *Foundation Fundamentals*. This guide takes you step-by-step through the research strategies developed and taught by the Foundation Center, describing in the process how to gather the facts you need to best approach foundations for funding. All Foundation Center publications can be examined free of charge at Foundation Center libraries.

GRANTSEEKING FROM CORPORATIONS

The research process for corporate funding is similar to other institutional grantseeking: identifying companies that might be interested in an organization's mission and program, learning as much as possible about those companies, determining the best method of approach, and articulating program objectives so as to be in line with the company's giving rationale. It differs from researching other institutional funders, however, in that it is often more difficult to uncover the needed information. There is great diversity in method and style of giving among corporations, and companies are often looking for a quid pro quo for their giving. Because many corporations see their giving not in terms of altruism but as a responsibility or simply good business, corporate philanthropy is often considered something of an oxymoron. Soliciting support from corporations, therefore, often requires a shift in perspective, from appealing to a company's benevolence to promoting its self-interest.

Identifying corporations to approach is accomplished in several ways. Directories such as the *National Directory of Corporate Giving* describe companies with known corporate giving programs. These guides can help you identify a corporation's subject interests, geographical giving patterns, and/or the benefits it hopes to derive from its giving. General business directories aid in the search, as do the books and guides listed in the bibliography. Staff members, your organization's board, and volunteers often know or work for companies that ultimately may be able to provide funds. The telephone book is another good resource for tracking down local businesses.

After a list of likely prospects is compiled, you should continue your efforts to locate additional information about the company, its primary and secondary business activities, its officers, giving history, and any details helpful in understanding its giving rationale. Understanding why a company gives is essential, as it may point to a match of the grantseeker's programmatic goals and the corporation's giving goals. Although determining the reasons a company makes contributions can be difficult, it can be accomplished through careful research, including studying annual reports and the materials issued by other organizations the company has supported, as well as by speaking directly with company officials whenever possible.

This kind of research usually uncovers the best method for approaching a company with a request for support. Companies with formal giving programs may have guidelines and application procedures and require a written proposal, while companies with informal giving programs may be better approached through personal contacts made by board members or volunteers. Once the approach is determined, however, a written or oral presentation that articulates how your organization's programs fit into the company's giving rationale should be prepared.

Ultimately, the more you know about a company, the better your chance of obtaining support. A company should not be approached without some knowledge of its business activities or past giving history, as that may jeopardize your chances of receiving funding. This does not mean that corporations without a record of grantmaking should be ignored. Creative fundraisers have found ways of encouraging companies of all sizes, from small businesses to large corporations, to assist in their activities. Success in acquiring such support, however, is usually the result of good research and good contacts. The job of the corporate fundraiser is to be imaginative and thorough, calling on all the knowledge, people, and ideas available. It means learning where to ask, how to ask, and what to ask.

SOURCES OF INFORMATION

Foundation Center publications examine giving interests in two broad ways: what the grantmaker states as its purpose and what can be observed from a listing of its actual grants. In preparing the *National Guide to Funding for the Environment and Animal Welfare* we drew on five important tools to identify grantmakers with a specific interest in programs in religion in addition to those that make contributions for related projects as part of a broader giving program:

1. *The Foundation Directory* provides descriptions of the nation's largest foundations (the top 10,000 foundations by total giving). The statements of purpose for each foundation listed in the *Directory*

are drawn from the descriptions provided by foundations in their annual reports, informational brochures or other publications, responses to our annual questionnaire mailings, and a broad analysis of the foundation's grantmaking program over the last three years. Although some of these statements provide very specific information about the foundation's giving interests, many were developed to last for substantial periods of time and, thus, left purposely broad to allow for future shifts in emphasis. To illustrate a foundation's giving pattern, lists of up to ten selected grants are included, whenever available.

2. *The Foundation Directory Part 2* provides information on the second tier of U.S. grantmaking foundations, (the next 10,000 foundations by total giving). Like the *Directory*, the *Directory Part 2* provides lists of up to ten selected grants whenever available.

3. The *National Directory of Corporate Giving* is the source of information on corporate grantmakers. The ninth edition of the directory, published in 2003, profiles 3,211 companies making contributions to nonprofit organizations. It includes entries describing 1,359 direct corporate giving programs and 2,322 corporate foundations. The most comprehensive directory on corporate giving available, it lists only corporations that provided information to the Center or for which public documents on giving were available.

4. The Center's *Foundation Grants Index on CD-ROM* database, which records actual grants of $10,000 or more reported to the Center by approximately 1,016 major foundations, provides a more detailed picture of foundation giving interests. Each grant record includes the name and location of the organization receiving the grant, the amount of money awarded, and a brief description of the purpose for which the grant was made. Center staff analyze and index each grant by subject focus, type of organization receiving the grant, the type of support provided, and the special population group, if any, to be served by the program.

These four sources, as well as the public charities included on *FC Search: The Foundation Center's Database on CD-ROM* (see Resources of the Foundation Center for more details), provide all the information on foundations, corporate giving programs, public charities, and grants included in this *Guide.*

HOW TO USE THE *NATIONAL GUIDE TO FUNDING FOR THE ENVIRONMENT AND ANIMAL WELFARE*

When using the *Guide* to identify potential funding sources, grantseekers are urged to read each grantmaker description carefully to determine the nature of the grantmaker's interests and to note any restrictions on giving that would prevent the foundation from considering their proposal. Many grantmakers limit their giving to a particular subject field or geographic area; others are unable to provide certain types of support, such as funds for buildings and equipment or for general operating budgets. Even when a grantmaker has not provided an explicit limitations statement, restrictions on giving may exist. This is often the case with entries updated from public records. Further research into the giving patterns of these grantmakers is necessary before applying for funds.

ARRANGEMENT

The *Guide* is arranged alphabetically by state and, within states, by grantmaker name. Each descriptive entry is assigned a sequence number; references in the indexes are to these entry numbers.

WHAT'S IN AN ENTRY?

There are 36 basic data elements that could be included in a descriptive entry. The content of entries varies widely due to differences in the size, nature, and type of grantmaker and its programs and the availability of information from grantmakers. Specific data elements that could be included are:

1. The full legal **name of the grantmaker.**

2. The **former name** of the grantmaker.

3. The **street address, city, and zip code** of the grantmaker's principal office.

4. The **telephone number** of the grantmaker.

5. The name and title of the **contact person** at the grantmaker.

6. Any **additional address** (such as a separate application address) supplied by the grantmaker. Additional telephone or FAX numbers as well as E-mail and/or URL address also may be listed here.

7. **Establishment data,** including the legal form (usually a trust or corporation) and the year and state in which the grantmaker was established.

8. The **donor(s)** or principal contributor(s) to the grantmaker, including individuals, families, and corporations. If a donor is deceased, the symbol ‡ follows the name.

9. **Grantmaker type:** community foundation, company-sponsored foundation, independent fondation, operating foundation, corporate giving program, or public charity.

10. The **year-end date** of the grantmaker's accounting period for which financial data is supplied.

11. **Revenue:** The total amount of contributions and support received by the public charity, including investment income, program service revenue, net profits from sale of assets, etc.

12. **Assets:** the total value of the grantmaker's investments at the end of the accounting period. In a few instances, grantmakers that act as "pass-throughs" for annual corporate or individual gifts report zero assets.

13. **Asset type:** generally, assets are reported at market value (M) or ledger value (L).

14. **Gifts received:** the total amount of new capital received by the grantmaker in the year of record.

15. **Expenditures:** total disbursements of the grantmaker, including overhead expenses (salaries; investment, legal, and other professional fees; interest; rent; etc.) and federal excise taxes, as well as the total amount paid for grants, scholarships, and matching gifts.

16. The total amount of **qualifying distributions** made by the grantmaker in the year of record. This figure includes all grants paid, qualifying administrative expenses, loans and program-related investments, set-asides, and amounts paid to acquire assets used directly in carrying out charitable purposes.

17. **Program services expenses:** The total amount of program services expenses made by the public charity in the year of record. This figure includes all

expenses directly involved in carrying out charitable activities, including total grants paid.

18. The dollar value and number of **grants paid** during the year, with the largest grant paid (**high**) and smallest grant paid (**low**). When supplied by the grantmaker, the average range of grant payments is also indicated. Grant figures generally do not include commitments for future payment or amounts spent for grants to individuals, employee matching gifts, loans, or grantmaker-administered programs.

19. The total dollar value of **set-asides** made by the grantmaker during the year. Although set-asides count as qualifying distributions toward the grantmaker's annual payout requirement, they are distinct from any amounts listed as grants paid.

20. The total amount and number of **grants made directly to or on behalf of individuals,** including scholarships, fellowships, awards, and medical payments. When supplied by the grantmaker, high, low, and average range are also indicated.

21. The dollar amount and number of **employee matching gifts** awarded, generally by company-sponsored foundations or corporate giving programs.

22. The total dollars expended for **programs administered by the grantmaker** and the number of grantmaker-administered programs. These programs can include museums or other institutions supported exclusively by the grantmaker, research programs administered by the grantmaker, etc.

23. The dollar amount and number of **loans** made to nonprofit organizations by the grantmaker. These can include program-related investments, emergency loans to help nonprofits that are waiting for grants or other income payments, etc. When supplied by the grantmaker, high, low, and average range are also indicated.

24. The number of **loans to individuals** and the total amount loaned. When supplied by the grantmaker, high, low, and average range are also indicated.

25. The monetary value and number of **in-kind gifts.**

26. The **purpose and activities,** in general terms, of the grantmaker. This statement reflects funding interests as expressed by the grantmaker or, if no grantmaker statement is available, an analysis of the actual grants awarded by the grantmaker during the most recent two-year period for which public records exist. Many grantmakers leave statements of purpose intentionally broad, indicating only the major program areas within which they fund. More specific areas of interest can often be found in the "Fields of Interest" section of the entry.

27. The **fields of interest** reflected in the grantmaker's giving program. The terminology used in this section conforms to the Foundation Center's Grants Classification System (GCS).

28. The **international giving interests** of the grantmaker.

29. The **types of support** (such as endowment funds, support for building renovation, and equipment, fellowships, etc.) offered by the grantmaker. Definitions of the terms used to describe the forms of support available are provided at the beginning of the Types of Support Index at the back of this volume.

30. Any stated **limitations** on the grantmaker's giving program, including geographic preferences, restrictions by subject focus or type of recipient, or specific types of support the grantmaker cannot provide. It is noted here if a grantmaker does not accept unsolicited applications.

31. **Publications** or other printed materials distributed by the grantmaker that describe its activities and giving program. These can include annual or multi-year reports, newsletters, corporate giving reports, informational brochures, grant lists, etc.

32. **Application information,** including the preferred form of application, the number of copies of proposals requested, application deadlines, frequency and dates of board meetings, and the general amount of time the grantmaker requires to notify applicants of the board's decision. Some grantmakers have indicated that their funds are currently committed to ongoing projects.

33. The names and titles of **officers, principal administrators, trustees, or directors,** and members of other governing bodies. An asterisk following the individual's name indicates an officer who is also a trustee or director.

34. The number of professional and support **staff** employed by the grantmaker, and an indication of part-time or full-time status of these employees, as reported by the grantmaker.

35. **EIN:** the Employer Identification Number assigned to a foundation or public charity by the Internal Revenue Service for tax purposes. This number can be useful when accessing copies of the grantmaker's annual information return, Form 990-PF for foundations and Form 990 for public charities.

36. **Recent grants in the environment and animal welfare** awarded in 2001–2003. Entries include the name and location of the recipient, the grant amount and year awarded, and, where available, a brief description of the purpose of the grant.

INDEXES

Six indexes to the descriptive entries are provided at the back of the book to assist grantseekers and other users of this *Guide*:

1. The **Index to Donors, Officers, Trustees** is an alphabetical list of individual and corporate donors, officers, and members of governing boards whose names appear in the descriptive entries. Many grantseekers find this index helpful in determining whether current or prospective members of their own governing boards, alumni of their schools, or current contributors are affiliated with other grantmakers.

2. The **Geographic Index** references grantmaker entries by the state and city in which the grantmaker maintains its principal offices. The index includes "see-also" references at the end of each state section to indicate grantmakers that have made substantial grants in that state but are located elsewhere. Grantmakers that award grants on a national, regional, or international basis are indicated in bold type. The remaining grantmakers generally limit their giving to the state or city in which they are located.

3. The **Types of Support Index** provides access to grantmaker entries by the specific types of support the grantmaker awards. A glossary of the forms of support listed appears at the beginning of the index. Under each type of support term, entry numbers are listed by the state location and abbreviated name of the grantmaker. Grantmakers that award grants on a national, regional, or international basis are indicated in bold type. When using this index, grantseekers should focus on grantmakers located in their own state that offer the specific type of support needed, or on grantmakers listed in bold type if their program has national impact.

4. The **Index to Grantmaker by Subject** provides access to the giving interests of grantmakers based on the "Fields of Interest" sections of their entries. The terminology in the index conforms to the Foundation Center's Grants Classification System (GCS). A list of subject headings for international and foreign programs is provided at the beginning of the index. Under each subject term, entry numbers are listed by the state location and abbreviated name of the grantmaker. As in the Types of Support Index, grantmakers that award grants on a national, regional, or international basis are indicated in bold type. Again, grantseekers should focus on grantmakers located in their own state or on grantmakers listed in bold type if their program is national in scope.

5. The **Index to Grants by Subject** provides access to the individual grants included in this *Guide*. For each subject term, grants are listed first by grantmaker entry number, then by grant number within the grantmaker entry.

6. The **Grantmaker Name Index** is an alphabetical list of all grantmakers appearing in this *Guide*. Former names of grantmakers appear with "see" references to the appropriate entry numbers.

GLOSSARY

The following list includes important terms used by grantmakers and grantseekers. A number of sources have been consulted in compiling this glossary, including *The Handbook on Private Foundations,* by David F. Freeman and the Council on Foundations (New York: The Foundation Center, 1991); *The Law of Tax-Exempt Organizations,* 7th Edition, by Bruce R. Hopkins (New York: John Wiley & Sons, 1998); and the *NSFRE Fund-Raising Dictionary,* (New York, John Wiley & Sons, 1996).

Annual Report: A *voluntary* report issued by a foundation or corporation that provides financial data and descriptions of grantmaking activities. Annual reports vary in format from simple typewritten documents listing the year's grants to detailed publications that provide substantial information about the grantmaking program.

Assets: The amount of capital or principal—money, stocks, bonds, real estate, or other resources—controlled by the foundation. Generally, assets are invested and the income is used to make grants.

Beneficiary: In philanthropic terms, the donee or grantee receiving funds from a foundation or corporate giving program is the beneficiary, although society benefits as well. Foundations whose legal terms of establishment restrict their giving to one or more named beneficiaries are not included in this publication.

Bricks and Mortar: An informal term for grants for buildings or construction projects.

Capital Support: Funds provided for endowment purposes, buildings, construction, or equipment, and including, for example, grants for "bricks and mortar."

Challenge Grant: A grant awarded that will be paid only if the donee organization is able to raise additional funds from another source(s). Challenge grants are often used to stimulate giving from other donors. (*See also* **Matching Grant**)

Community Foundation: A 501(c)(3) organization that makes grants for charitable purposes in a specific community or region. Funds are usually derived from many donors and held in an endowment independently administered; income earned by the endowment is then used to make grants. Although a few community foundations may be classified by the IRS as private foundations, most are classified as public charities eligible for maximum income tax-deductible contributions from the general public. (*See also* **501(c)(3); Public Charity**)

Community Fund: An organized community program which makes annual appeals to the general public for funds that are usually not retained in an endowment but are used for the ongoing operational support of local social and health service agencies. (*See also* **Federated Giving Program**)

Company-Sponsored Foundation (also referred to as Corporate Foundation): A private foundation whose grant funds are derived primarily from the contributions of a profit-making business organization. The company-sponsored foundation may maintain close ties with the donor company, but it is an independent organization with its own endowment and is subject to the same rules and regulations as other private foundations. (*See also* **Private Foundation**)

Cooperative Venture: A joint effort between or among two or more grantmakers (including foundations, corporations, and government agencies). Partners may share in funding responsibilities or contribute information and technical resources.

Corporate Giving Program: A grantmaking program established and administered within a profit-making company. Corporate giving programs do not have a separate endowment and their annual grant totals are generally more directly related to current profits. They are not subject to the same reporting requirements as private foundations. Some companies make charitable contributions through both a corporate giving program and a company-sponsored foundation.

Distribution Committee: The board responsible for making grant decisions. For community foundations, it is intended to be broadly representative of the community served by the foundation.

Donee: The recipient of a grant. (Also known as the grantee or the beneficiary.)

Donor: The individual or organization that makes a grant or contribution. (Also known as the grantor.)

Employee Matching Gift: A contribution to a charitable organization by a company employee that is matched by a similar contribution from the employer. Many corporations have employee matching gift programs in higher education that stimulate their employees to give to the college or university of their choice.

Endowment: Funds intended to be kept permanently and invested to provide income for continued support of an organization.

Expenditure Responsibility: In general, when a private foundation makes a grant to an organization that is not classified by the IRS as a "public charity," the foundation is required by law to provide some assurance that the funds will be used for the intended charitable purposes. Special reports on such grants must be filed with the IRS. Most grantee organizations are public charities and many foundations do not make "expenditure responsibility" grants.

Family Foundation: An independent private foundation whose funds are derived from members of a single family. Family members often serve as officers or board members of the foundation and have a significant role in grantmaking decisions. (*See also* **Operating Foundation; Private Foundation; Public Charity**)

Federated Giving Program: A joint fundraising effort usually administered by a nonprofit "umbrella" organization which in turn distributes contributed funds to several nonprofit agencies. United Way and community chests or funds, the United Jewish Appeal and other religious appeals, the United Negro College Fund, and joint arts councils are examples of federated giving programs. (*See also* **Community Fund**)

501(c)(3): The section of the Internal Revenue code that defines nonprofit, charitable (as broadly defined), tax-exempt organizations; 501(c)(3) organizations are further defined as public charities, private operating foundations, and private non-operating foundations. (*See also* **Operating Foundation; Private Foundation; Public Charity**)

Form 990-PF: The annual information return that all private foundations must submit to the IRS each year and which is also filed with appropriate state officials. The form requires information on the foundation's assets, income, operating expenses, contributions and grants, paid staff and salaries, program funding areas, grantmaking guidelines and restrictions, and grant application procedures.

General Purpose Foundation: An independent private foundation that awards grants in many different fields of interest. (*See also* **Special Purpose Foundation**)

General Purpose Grant: A grant made to further the general purpose or work of an organization, rather than for a specific purpose or project. (*See also* **Operating Support Grant**)

Grantee Financial Report: A report detailing how grant funds were used by an organization. Many corporations require this kind of report from grantees. A financial report generally includes a listing of all expenditures from grant funds as well as an overall organizational financial report covering revenue and expenses, assets and liabilities.

Grassroots Fundraising: Efforts to raise money from individuals or groups from the local community on a broad basis. Usually an organization's own constituents—people who live in the neighborhood served or clients of the agency's services—are the sources of these funds. Grassroots fundraising activities include membership drives, raffles, auctions, benefits, and a range of other activities.

Independent Foundation: A grantmaking organization usually classified by the IRS as a private foundation. Independent foundations may also be known as family foundations, general purpose foundations, special purpose foundations, or private non-operating foundations. The Foundation Center defines independent foundations and company-sponsored foundations separately; however, federal law normally classifies both as private, non-operating foundations subject to the same rules and requirements. (*See also* **Private Foundation**)

In-Kind Contributions: Contributions of equipment, supplies, or other property as distinguished from monetary grants. Some organizations may also donate space or staff time as an in-kind contribution.

Matching Grant: A grant that is made to match funds provided by another donor. (*See also* **Challenge Grant; Employee Matching Gift**)

Operating Foundation: A 501(c)(3) organization classified by the IRS as a private foundation whose primary purpose is to conduct research, social welfare, or other programs determined by its governing body or establishment charter. Some grants may be made, but the sum is generally small relative to the funds used for the foundation's own programs. (*See also* **501(c)(3)**)

Operating Support Grant: A grant to cover the regular personnel, administrative, and other expenses of an existing program or project. (*See also* **General Purpose Grant**)

Payout Requirement: The minimum amount that private foundations are required to expend for charitable purposes (includes grants and, within certain limits, the administrative cost of making grants). In general, a private foundation must meet or exceed an annual payout requirement of five percent of the average market value of the foundation's assets.

Private Foundation: A nongovernmental, nonprofit organization with funds (usually from a single source, such as an individual, family, or corporation) and program managed by its own trustees or directors that was established to maintain or aid social, educational, religious, or other charitable activities serving the common welfare, primarily through the making of grants. "Private foundation" also means an organization that is tax-exempt under code section 501(c)(3) and is classified by the IRS as a private foundation as defined in the code. The code definition usually, but not always, identifies a foundation with the characteristics first described. (*See also* **501(c)(3); Public Charity**)

Program Amount: Funds that are expended to support a particular program administered internally by the foundation or corporate giving program.

Program Officer: A staff member of a foundation who reviews grant proposals and processes applications for the board of trustees. Only a small percentage of foundations have program officers.

Program-Related Investment (PRI): A loan or other investment (as distinguished from a grant) made by a foundation to another organization for a project related to the grantmaker's stated charitable purpose and interests. Program-related investments are often made from a revolving fund; the foundation generally expects to receive its money back with interest or some other form of return at less than current market rates, and it then becomes available for further program-related investments.

Proposal: A written application, often with supporting documents, submitted to a foundation or corporate giving program in requesting a grant. Preferred procedures and formats vary. Consult published guidelines.

Public Charity: In general, an organization that is tax-exempt under code section 501(c)(3) and is classified by the IRS as a public charity and not a private foundation. Public charities generally derive their funding or support primarily from the general public in carrying out their social, educational, religious, or other charitable activities serving the common welfare. Some public charities engage in grantmaking activities, although most engage in direct service or other tax-exempt activities. Public charities are eligible for maximum income tax-deductible contributions from the public and are not subject to the same rules and restrictions as private foundations. Some are also referred to as "public foundations" or "publicly supported organizations" and may use the term "foundation" in their names. (*See also* **501(c)(3); Private Foundation**)

Qualifying Distributions: Expenditures of private foundations used to satisfy the annual payout requirement. These can include grants, reasonable administrative expenses, set-asides, loans and program-related investments, and amounts paid to acquire assets used directly in carrying out exempt purposes.

Query Letter: A brief letter outlining an organization's activities and its request for funding sent to a foundation or corporation to determine whether it would be appropriate for that organization to submit a full grant proposal. Many grantmakers prefer to be contacted in this way before receiving a full proposal.

RFP: Request For Proposal. When the government issues a new contract or grant program, it sends out RFPs to agencies that might be qualified to participate. The RFP lists project specifications and application procedures. A few foundations occasionally use RFPs in specific fields, but most prefer to consider proposals that are initiated by applicants.

Seed Money: A grant or contribution used to start a new project or organization. Seed grants may cover salaries and other operating expenses of a new project.

Set-Asides: Funds set aside by a foundation for a specific purpose or project that are counted as qualifying distributions toward the foundation's annual payout requirement. Amounts for the project must be paid within five years of the first set-aside.

Special Purpose Foundation: A private foundation that focuses its grantmaking activities in one or a few special areas of interest. For example, a foundation may only award grants in the area of cancer research or child development. (*See also* **General Purpose Foundation**)

Technical Assistance: Operational or management assistance given to nonprofit organizations. It can include fundraising assistance, budgeting and financial planning, program planning, legal advice, marketing, and other aids to management. Assistance may be offered directly by a foundation or corporate staff member, or be offered in the form of a grant to pay for the services of an outside consultant. (*See also* **In-Kind Contributions**)

Trustee: A member of a governing board. A foundation's board of trustees meets to review grant proposals and make decisions. Often also referred to as a "director" or "board member."

ABBREVIATIONS

The following lists contain standard abbreviations frequently used by the Foundation Center's editorial staff. These abbreviations are used most frequently in the addresses of grantmakers and the titles of corporate and grantmaker officers.

TWO LETTER STATE AND TERRITORY ABBREVIATIONS

AK	Alaska	IL	Illinois	ND	North Dakota	SD	South Dakota
AL	Alabama	IN	Indiana	NE	Nebraska	TN	Tennessee
AR	Arkansas	KS	Kansas	NH	New Hampshire	TX	Texas
AZ	Arizona	KY	Kentucky	NJ	New Jersey	UT	Utah
CA	California	LA	Louisiana	NM	New Mexico	VA	Virginia
CO	Colorado	MA	Massachusetts	NV	Nevada	VI	Virgin Islands
CT	Connecticut	MD	Maryland	NY	New York	VT	Vermont
DC	District of Columbia	ME	Maine	OH	Ohio	WA	Washington
DE	Delaware	MI	Michigan	OK	Oklahoma	WI	Wisconsin
FL	Florida	MN	Minnesota	OR	Oregon	WV	West Virginia
GA	Georgia	MO	Missouri	PA	Pennsylvania	WY	Wyoming
HI	Hawaii	MS	Mississippi	PR	Puerto Rico		
IA	Iowa	MT	Montana	RI	Rhode Island		
ID	Idaho	NC	North Carolina	SC	South Carolina		

STREET ABBREVIATIONS

1st	First*	E.	East	N.W.	Northwest	S.W.	Southwest
2nd	Second*	Expwy.	Expressway	No.	Number	Sq.	Square
3rd	Third*	Fl.	Floor	Pkwy.	Parkway	St.	Saint
Apt.	Apartment	Ft.	Fort	Pl.	Place	St.	Street
Ave.	Avenue	Hwy.	Highway	Plz.	Plaza	Sta.	Station
Bldg.	Building	Ln.	Lane	R.R.	Rural Route	Ste.	Suite
Cir.	Circle	M.C.	Mail Code	Rd.	Road	Terr.	Terrace
Ct.	Court	M.S.	Mail Stop	Rm.	Room	Univ.	University
Ctr.	Center	Mt.	Mount	Rte.	Route	W.	West
Dept.	Department	N.	North	S.	South		
Dr.	Drive	N.E.	Northeast	S.E.	Southeast		

*Numerics used always

ABBREVIATIONS USED FOR OFFICER TITLES

Acctg.	Accounting	Corp.	Corporate, Corporation	Natl.	National
ADM.	Admiral	Co(s).	Company(s)	Off.	Officer
Admin.	Administration	Dep.	Deputy	Opers.	Operations
Admin.	Administrative	Devel.	Development	Org.	Organization
Admin.	Administrator	Dir.	Director	Plan.	Planning
Adv.	Advertising	Distrib(s).	Distribution(s)	Pres.	President
Amb.	Ambassador	Div.	Division	Prog(s).	Program(s)
Assn.	Association	Exec.	Executive	RADM.	Rear Admiral
Assoc(s).	Associate(s)	Ext.	External	Rels.	Relations
Asst.	Assistant	Fdn.	Foundation	Rep.	Representative
Bro.	Brother	Fr.	Father	Rev.	Reverend
C.A.O.	Chief Accounting Officer	Genl.	General	Rt. Rev.	Right Reverend
C.A.O.	Chief Administration Officer	Gov.	Governor	Secy.	Secretary
C.E.O.	Chief Executive Officer	Govt.	Government	Secy.-Treas.	Secretary-Treasurer
C.F.O.	Chief Financial Officer	Hon.	Judge	Sen.	Senator
C.I.O.	Chief Information Officer	Inf.	Information	Soc.	Society
C.I.O.	Chief Investment Officer	Int.	Internal	Sr.	Senior
C.O.O.	Chief Operating Officer	Intl.	International	Sr.	Sister
Capt.	Captain	Jr.	Junior	Supvr.	Supervisor
Chair.	Chairperson	Lt.	Lieutenant	Svc(s).	Service(s)
Col.	Colonel	Ltd.	Limited	Tech.	Technology
Comm.	Committee,	Maj.	Major	Tr.	Trustee
	Communications	Mfg.	Manufacturing	Treas.	Treasurer
Commo.	Commodore	Mgmt.	Management	Univ.	University
Compt.	Comptroller	Mgr.	Manager	V.P.	Vice President
Cont.	Controller	Mktg.	Marketing	VADM.	Vice Admiral
Contrib(s).	Contribution(s)	Msgr.	Monsignor	Vice-Chair.	Vice Chairperson
Coord.	Coordinator	Mt.	Mount		

ADDITIONAL ABBREVIATIONS

E-mail	Electronic mail
FAX	Facsimile
SASE	Self-Addressed Stamped Envelope
TDD, TTY	Telecommunication Device for the Deaf
Tel.	Telephone
URL	Uniform Resource Locator (World Wide Web)

Jan.	January	Sept.	September
Feb.	February	Oct.	October
Mar.	March	Nov.	November
Apr.	April	Dec.	December
Aug.	August		

BIBLIOGRAPHY OF FUNDING FOR THE ENVIRONMENT AND ANIMAL WELFARE

This selected listing is compiled from the Foundation Center's bibliographic database. Many of the items are available for free reference use in the Center's New York City, Washington, D.C., Cleveland, San Francisco, and Atlanta libraries and in many of its cooperating libraries throughout the United States. For further references on such topics as fundraising and proposal development, see *The Literature of the Nonprofit Sector Online: A Bibliography with Abstracts*, which can be accessed online at http://lnps.fdncenter.org.

Abshire, Michael. "The Environment: One Step at a Time." *Corporate Philanthropy Report,* vol. 18 (June 2003): p. 1, 4.

Wal-Mart is actively supporting environmental causes through its foundation and through corporate practices and fuel efficiency.

"Best Practices in Environmental Fundraising." *Advancing Philanthropy,* vol. 9 (March–April 2002): p. 24–7.

Posits that environmental groups need to focus on securing major gifts, as they already enjoy large membership bases.

Bray, Thomas J. "Soaring High." *Philanthropy,* vol. 18 (January–February 2004): p. 14–20.

Several environmental initiatives are profiled.

Faber, Daniel R.; Deborah McCarthy. *Green of Another Color: Building Effective Partnerships Between Foundations and the Environmental Justice Movement.* Washington, DC: Aspen Institute, 2001. iv, 79 p. (Nonprofit Sector Research Fund Working Paper Series).

An analysis of the relationship of "green politics" to philanthropy, documenting the current under-funding of the environmental justice movement, according to the authors. Begins with a brief history of the environmental justice movement, which began in 1982 as a protest against a proposed landfill in North Carolina. Profiles of numerous organizations active in the field are provided. Data showing foundation giving to environmental causes in general, and environmental justice, specifically, is given in chart form. Concludes with a discussion of exemplary grantmaking practices for the field, and ways to increase diversity. With bibliographic references.

Fine, Allison; Bruce Jacobs. *Echoes From the Field: Proven Capacity-Building Principles for Nonprofits.* Washington, DC: Innovation Network Inc, 2001. 8 p.

Nine principles that were devised in answer to the question of how technical assistance providers can best support grassroots organizations in the fulfillment of their mission. This study focused on nonprofits working in the environment and social justice areas.

Foundation Center. *Grants for Environmental Protection and Animal Welfare.* New York, NY: Foundation Center, 2003. xx, 350 p. (Grant Guide; No. 4). ISBN 1-931923-78-7

Lists 9,825 grants of $10,000 or more made by 736 foundations, mostly in 2001 and 2002, for environmental organizations including pollution abatement and control services; natural resources conservation and protection; botanical, horticultural, and landscape services; environmental education and beautification programs; wildlife preservation and protection; veterinary and other animal services; and zoos and aquariums. Grants are indexed by recipient name, location, and subject.

Greene, Stephen G. "Learning to Make Do With Less: Charities Cite Consumerism as the Cause of Many Modern Woes." *Chronicle of Philanthropy,* vol. 12 (7 September 2000): p. 1, 7–8, 10.

Article discusses the concept that proliferate consumption is at the root of environmental threats today and details how nonprofits are addressing this issue. Sidebar lists contact information for specific charities involved in altering Americans' habits.

Greene, Stephen G. "Recognizing That Small Is Beautiful." *Chronicle of Philanthropy,* vol. 12 (9 March 2000): p. 7–8, 10–11.

Profiles the New England Grassroots Environment Fund, a collaboration of community activists and ten foundations that seek to assist low-budget environmental activism efforts. To be eligible for grants, the annual budget of a group must not exceed $100,000, and it must employ no more than two paid staff members. Groups do not require nonprofit status, an office, or a bank account to be eligible for grants. Last year, the fund made 96 grants totaling $181,199. Sidebar gives a sampling of recent grants made by the New England Grassroots Environment Fund.

Greene, Stephen G. "Technology Helps Small Environmental Group Get Big Results." *Chronicle of Philanthropy,* vol. 13 (11 January 2001): p. 10.

Discusses the technological success of the Environmental Working Group, a nonprofit organization that conducts extensive research on the Internet and reports its findings on the group's Web site (http://www.ewg.org).

Gunther, Marc. "Tree Huggers, Soy Lovers, and Profits." *Fortune,* vol. 147 (23 June 2003): p. 98–100, 102, 104.

Enumerates the many corporations that are embracing sustainability and environmentally-friendly strategies and examines the extent to which these aspects of social responsibility benefit stakeholders.

Hignite, Karla B. "How Green Can You Go?" *Association Management,* vol. 54 (March 2002): p. 58–64.

Cities that can boast of having ecologically advanced convention sites are finding that they are particularly competitive in attracting conferences. The situation in Chattanooga (TN) is highlighted.

"If the Boot Fits: How L. L. Bean Helps the 'Long, Skinny Park'." *Corporate Philanthropy Report,* vol. 18 (June 2003): p. 3–4.

The L. L. Bean company is an active supporter of the Appalachian Trail as well as other conservation and environmental programs.

Kelly, Jennifer (ed.) *EMS Guide to Nonprofit Environmental Communications Organizations 2001.* Washington, DC: Environmental Media Services, 2001. 23 p.

Lewis, Nicole. "Force for Nature." *Chronicle of Philanthropy,* vol. 14 (18 April 2002): p. 9–10, 12, 14.

A profile of the Gordon E. and Betty I. Moore Foundation, which is expected to be one of the ten largest grantmakers in the United States. While mainly focusing on funding for the environment, the foundation makes grants for scientific research not usually funded by the government. Sidebar includes a sampling of grants from 2001.

London, Ted; Dennis Rondinelli. "Partnerships for Learning: Managing Tensions in Nonprofit Organizations' Alliances with Corporations." *Stanford Social Innovation Review,* vol. 1 (Winter 2003): p. 28–35.

Relates specifically to tensions that can develop when environmental projects rely on corporate giving. With bibliographical references.

New York Lawyers for the Public Interest. *Brownfields Basics: A Guide to Rebuilding Our Communities.* New York, NY: New York Lawyers for the Public Interest, Inc, 2000. 65 p plus appendices.

Richardson, Valerie. "Going to the Dogs: David Duffield's Costly Vision of a 'No-Kill' Nation." *Philanthropy,* vol. 14 (March–April 2000): p. 18–20.

Discusses David Duffield's creation of Maddie's Fund, a $200 million foundation devoted to the spread of "no-kill" animal shelters, at which no adoptable animals are euthanized. David Duffield is the founder of PeopleSoft, a Silicon Valley human resources management software company.

Rootes, Christopher. "Global Visions: Global Civil Society and the Lessons of European Environmentalism." *Voluntas,* vol. 13 (December 2002): p. 411–29.

Singletary, Loretta; Marilyn Smith; George C. Hill. "Assessing Impacts on Volunteers Who Participate in Collaborative Efforts to Manage Environmental Disputes." *Journal of Volunteer Administration,* vol. 21 (Number 2, 2003): p. 24–32.

With statistical analysis and bibliographic references.

Thiele, Corinne Szymko (ed.) *Environmental Grantmaking Foundations: 2003 Directory.* 10th ed. Cary, NC: Resources for Global Sustainability, Inc, 2003. xxiii, 1088 p. ISBN 0-9631943-9-9

Profiles 892 grantmakers, including U.S. foundations, and corporate and Canadian grantmakers. Indexed by officers, trustees, donors, and contacts; grantmaker and recipient location; activity region; emphasis; limitations; and environmental issues, topics, and activities.

Viederman, Stephen. "Don't Just Tweak the Corners." *Foundation News & Commentary,* vol. 41 (January–February 2000): p. 18–20.

Shortened version of Stephen Viederman's speech at the Environmental Grantmakers Association's 1999 fall conference. Viederman, president of the Jessie Smith Noyes Foundation, and a founding member of the

Environmental Grantmakers Association, discusses the changes in both organizations over the past 14 years in terms of increasing diversity, and the movement toward mission-based investing. In addition, Viederman makes observations regarding funder-initiated organizations, the upcoming transfer of wealth, and national vs. grassroots giving.

Whiting, Meredith Armstrong; Charles J. Bennett. *The Road to Sustainability: Business' First Steps.* New York, NY: Conference Board, 2001. 35 p. ISBN 0-8237-0758-X

A guidebook for corporations that seek to ensure that their business practices adhere to the tenets of environmental and social sustainability. Also delves into the experiences of DuPont, ABB, Procter & Gamble, and Baxter International as leading players on this issue.

Williams, Roger M. "Making Good Out of Bad." *Foundation News & Commentary,* vol. 43 (January–February 2002): p. 27–31.

This is the life story of the Virginia Environmental Endowment, a foundation created in 1977 from penalties assessed against Allied Chemical Corporation. The company was held guilty of polluting the James River (VA), and the foundation was created to fund environmental projects. Several of the philanthropy's major initiatives are discussed, and a sidebar lists some other settlement foundations.

Wondolleck, Julia M.; Steven L. Yaffee. *Making Collaboration Work: Lessons From Innovation in Natural Resource Management.* Washington, DC: Island Press, 2000. xviii, 277 p. ISBN 1-55963-462-6

Yoder, Timothy S. "Corporate Responsibility and the Environment." *Business and Society Review,* vol. 106 (Fall 2001): p. 255–72.

When the actions of corporations cause damage to the environment, who—among all the various stakeholders—is responsible? Is it the managers, the board of directors, the stockholders, or others? Yoder introduces and describes four discernible types of responsibility: causal, legal, moral, and role, and opines that all the stakeholders bear some degree of responsibility for corporate actions. With bibliographic references.

RESOURCES OF THE FOUNDATION CENTER

The Foundation Center is a national service organization founded and supported by foundations to provide a single authoritative source of information on foundation and corporate giving. The Center's programs are designed to help grantseekers select those funders which may be most interested in their projects from the more than 76,000 active U.S. grantmakers. Among its primary activities toward this end are offering searchable databases online and on CD-ROM as well as publishing print directories covering foundation and corporate philanthropy; disseminating information on grantmaking, grantseeking, and related subjects through its site on the Internet; offering educational courses and workshops; and maintaining a nationwide network of library/learning centers and cooperating collections.

Databases and publications of the Foundation Center are the primary working tools of every serious grantseeker. They are also used by grantmakers, scholars, journalists, and legislators—in short, by anyone seeking any type of factual information on philanthropy. All private foundations and a significant number of corporate grantmakers actively engaged in grantmaking, regardless of size or geographic location, are included in one or more of the Center's databases or publications.

For those who wish to access information on grantmakers and their grants electronically, *The Foundation Directory Online Basic* provides information on 10,000 of the nation's largest foundations. *The Foundation Directory Online Plus* contains the top 10,000 foundations plus a searchable database of more than 350,000 grants. *The Foundation Directory Online Premium* includes 20,000 foundations plus over 350,000 grants. *The Foundation Directory Online Platinum* includes over 76,000 grantmakers plus over 350,000 grants.

The Center also issues *FC Search: The Foundation Center's Database on CD-ROM* containing the full universe of over 76,000 grantmakers and more than 320,000 associated grants.

Foundation Center print publications are of three kinds: directories that describe specific funders, characterizing their program interests and providing fiscal and personnel data; grants indexes that list and classify by subject recent foundation and corporate awards; and guides, monographs, and bibliographies that introduce the reader to funding research, elements of proposal writing, and nonprofit management issues.

In addition, the Center's award-winning Web site features a wide array of free information about the philanthropic community.

The Foundation Center's electronic and print products may be ordered from the Foundation Center, 79 Fifth Avenue, New York, NY 10003-3076, or online at our Web site. For more information about any aspect of the Center's programs or for the name of the Center's library collection nearest you, call 1-800-424-9836, or visit us on the Web at www.fdncenter.org. Please visit our Web site for the most current information available on new products and services of the Foundation Center.

ONLINE DATABASES

THE FOUNDATION DIRECTORY ONLINE SUBSCRIPTION PLANS

The Foundation Directory Online Basic

Search for foundation funding prospects from among the nation's largest 10,000 foundations and search the index of over 64,000 names of trustees, offices, and donors. Perform searches using up to twelve search fields and print results that appear in the browser window.

Monthly subscriptions start at $19.95 per month
Annual subscriptions start at $195 per year

The Foundation Directory Online Plus

Plus service allows users to search the 10,000 largest foundations in the U.S. and the index of over 64,000 names of trustees, offices, and donors—plus over 350,000 grants awarded by major foundations.

Monthly subscriptions start at $29.95 per month
Annual subscriptions start at $295 per year

The Foundation Directory Online Premium

Research and identify more foundation funding sources online with *The Foundation Directory Online Premium.* In addition to featuring 20,000 of the nation's large and mid-sized foundations and an index of over 111,000 names of trustees, officers, and donors—*Premium* service includes a searchable database of over 350,000 grants awarded by major U.S. foundations.

Monthly subscriptions start at $59.95 per month
Annual subscriptions start at $595 per year

The Foundation Directory Online Platinum

Search our entire universe of U.S. foundations, corporate giving programs, and grantmaking public charities—76,000+ funders in all—in our most comprehensive online subscription service. In addition to more funders, you'll get access to more in-depth data and an index of over 338,000 names of trustees, officers, and donors. Only *The Foundation Directory Online Platinum* offers extensive program details for 1,500+ leading foundations; detailed application guidelines for 7,200+ foundations; and sponsoring company information for corporate givers. This service also includes a searchable file of over 350,000 grants awarded by the largest U.S. foundations.

Monthly subscriptions start at $149.95
Annual subscriptions start at $995

Foundation and grants data are updated every two weeks for the above databases. Monthly, annual, multi-user, and institution wide access subscription options are available. Please visit www.fconline.fdncenter.org to subscribe.

Foundation Grants to Individuals Online

Foundation Grants to Individuals Online features more than 6,000 foundation funding sources for individual grantseekers in education, research, arts and culture, or for special needs. Updated quarterly, users may choose from up to nine different search fields to discover prospective funders. Foundation records include current, authoritative data on the funder, including the name, address, and contact information; fields of interest; types of support; application information; and descriptions of funding opportunities for individual grantseekers.

One-month subscription: $9.95
Three-month subscription: $26.95
Annual subscription: $99.95

DIALOG

The Center's grantmaker and grants databases are also available online through The Dialog Corporation. For further information, contact The Dialog Corporation at 1-800-334-2564.

DIALOG User Manual and Thesaurus, Revised Edition

The *User Manual and Thesaurus* is a comprehensive guide that will help you retrieve essential fundraising facts quickly and easily. It will greatly facilitate your foundation and corporate giving research through our databases, offered online through Dialog.

November 1995 / ISBN 0-87954-595-X / $50

CD-ROMs

FC SEARCH: The Foundation Center's Database on CD-ROM, Version 8.0

The Foundation Center's comprehensive database of grantmakers and their associated grants can be accessed in this fully searchable CD-ROM format. *FC Search* contains the Center's entire universe of 76,000+ grantmaker records, including all known active foundations and corporate giving programs in the United States. It also includes over 320,000 newly reported grants from the largest foundations and the names of more than 338,000 trustees, officers, and donors which can be quickly linked to their foundation affiliations. Users can also link from *FC Search* to the Web sites of 4,000+ grantmakers and 2,200+ corporations.

Grantseekers and other researchers may select multiple criteria and create customized prospect lists which can be printed or saved. Basic or Advanced search modes and special search options enable users to make searches as broad or as specific as required. Up to 21 different criteria may be selected:

- grantmaker name
- grantmaker type
- grantmaker city
- grantmaker state
- geographic focus
- fields of interest
- types of support
- total assets
- total giving
- trustees, officers, and donors
- establishment date
- corporate name
- corporate location
- recipient name
- recipient city
- recipient state
- recipient type
- subject
- grant amount
- year grant authorized
- text search field

FC Search is a sophisticated fundraising research tool, but it is also user-friendly. It has been developed with both the novice and experienced researcher in mind. Assistance is available through Online Help, a *User Manual* that accompanies *FC Search*, as well as through a free User Hotline.

FC Search, *Version 8.0, March 2004 (prices include fall 2004 Update disk plus one User Manual).*
Standalone (single user) version: $1,195
Local Area Network (2–8 users in one building) version: $1,895*
Additional copies of User Manual: $19.95
New editions of FC Search are released each spring.
*Larger local area network versions, site licenses, and wide area network versions are also available. For more information, call **the Electronic Product Support Line (Mon–Fri., 9 am–5 pm EST) 1-800-478-4661.**

THE FOUNDATION DIRECTORY 1 & 2 ON CD-ROM, Version 4.0

We've combined the authoritative data found in our two print classics, *The Foundation Directory* and *The Foundation Directory Part 2*, to bring you 20,000 of the nation's largest and mid-sized foundations in this searchable CD-ROM. Search for funding prospects by choosing from 12 search fields:

- grantmaker name
- grantmaker state
- grantmaker city
- fields of interest
- types of support
- trustees, officers, and donors
- geographic focus
- grantmaker type
- total giving
- total assets
- establishment date
- text search

The CD-ROM includes links to close to 1,700 foundation Web sites, a list of sample grants in over 10,500 foundation records, and a searchable index of over 111,000 trustees, officers, and donors.

The Foundation Directory 1 & 2 on CD-ROM
(includes March 2004 release and Fall 2004 Update disk)
Standalone (single-user) version: $495
Local Area Network version (2-8 users in one building): $795

THE FOUNDATION GRANTS INDEX ON CD-ROM, Version 4.0

The same data found in our classic print publication, *The Foundation Grants Index,* is available for the first time in a fast-speed CD-ROM format. Search our database of close to 125,000 recently awarded grants by the largest 1,000 funders to help you target foundations by the grants they have already awarded. Choose from twelve search fields:

- Recipient Name
- Recipient State
- Recipient City
- Recipient Type
- Grantmaker Name
- Grantmaker State
- Geographic Focus
- Subject
- Types of Support
- Grant Amount
- Year Authorized
- Text Search

The Foundation Grants Index on CD-ROM
December 2003/ Single User / ISBN 1-931923-74-4 /$165
Call 1-800-478-4661 for network versions.

GUIDE TO GREATER WASHINGTON D.C. GRANTMAKERS ON CD-ROM, Version 3.0

Compiled with the assistance of Washington Grantmakers, an organization with a unique local perspective on the dynamics of D.C. grantmaking, this CD-ROM covers more than 2,500 grantmakers located in the D.C. region or that have an interest in D.C.-area nonprofits. It also contains close to 3,000 selected grants and a searchable index of 8,000+ trustees, officers, and donors and their grantmaker affiliations.

Users can generate prospect lists within seconds, using twelve search fields. Grantmaker portraits feature crucial information: address, phone number, contact name, financial data, giving limitations, and names of key officials. For the large foundations—those that give at least $50,000 in grants per year—the volume provides even more data, including application procedures and giving interest statements.

The CD-ROM links to more than 150 grantmaker Web sites; connects to a special Web page with resources of value to D.C. grantseekers; and offers flexible printing and saving options and the ability to mark records.

June 2004
ISBN 1-931923-97-3 / $75

GUIDE TO OHIO GRANTMAKERS ON CD-ROM

This new windows-compatible CD-ROM features profiles of over 3,400 foundations in Ohio, plus more than 400 funders outside the state that award grants in Ohio. This comprehensive searchable database provides current information on the foundations, corporate givers and public charities that make grants to Ohio-based nonprofits: crucial contact information, financial data, names of key officials, and in many cases, application procedures, giving interest statements, and a list of recent grants. *Guide to Ohio Grantmakers on CD-ROM* is produced in collaboration with the Ohio Grantmakers Forum and the Ohio Association of Nonprofit Organizations.

November 2003 / ISBN 1-931923-64-7 / $125

SYSTEM CONFIGURATIONS FOR CD-ROM PRODUCTS

- Windows-based PC
- Microsoft Windows™ ME, Windows™ 98, Windows™ 95, Windows™2000,
- Windows™NT, or Windows™ XP
- Pentium microprocessor
- 64MB memory

**Internet access and Netscape's Navigator or Communicator or Microsoft's Internet Explorer browser required to access grantmaker Web sites and Foundation Center Web site.

GENERAL RESEARCH DIRECTORIES

THE FOUNDATION DIRECTORY, 2004 Edition

The Foundation Directory has been widely known and respected in the field for more than 40 years. It includes the latest information on the 10,000 largest U.S. foundations based on total giving. The 2004 Edition includes over 1,600 foundations that are new to this edition. *Directory* foundations hold more than $380 billion in assets and award over $27 billion in grants annually.

Each *Directory* entry contains information on application procedures, giving limitations, types of support awarded, the publications of each foundation, and foundation staff. In addition, each entry features such vital data as the grantmaker's giving interests, financial data, grant amounts, address, and telephone number. This edition includes over 51,000 selected grants. The Foundation Center works closely with foundations to ensure the accuracy and timeliness of the information provided.

The *Directory* includes indexes by foundation name; subject areas of interest; names of donors, officers, and trustees; geographic location; international interests; types of support awarded; and grantmakers new to the volume. Also included are analyses of the foundation community by geography, asset and grant size, and the different foundation types.

Also available on CD-ROM and Online.
See sections on CD-ROMs and Online Databases.
March 2004
ISBN 1-931923-87-6 / $215
Published annually

THE FOUNDATION DIRECTORY PART 2, 2004 Edition

Following in the tradition of *The Foundation Directory, The Foundation Directory Part 2* brings you the same thorough coverage for the next largest set of 10,000 foundations. It includes *Directory*-level information on mid-sized foundations, an important group of grantmakers responsible for millions of dollars in funding annually. Essential data on foundations is included along with more than 45,000 recently awarded foundation grants, providing an excellent overview of the foundations' giving interests. Quick access to foundation entries is facilitated by seven indexes, including foundation name; subject areas of interest; names of donors, officers, and trustees; geographic location; international interests; types of support awarded; and grantmakers new to the volume.

March 2004 / ISBN 1-931923-88-4 / $185
Published annually

THE FOUNDATION DIRECTORY SUPPLEMENT

The Foundation Directory Supplement provides the latest-breaking information on *Foundation Directory* and *Foundation Directory Part 2* grantmakers six months after those volumes are published. Each year, thousands of policy and staff changes occur at these foundations. Fundraisers need to know about these crucial changes as rapidly as possible, as they may affect the way fundraisers prepare their grant proposals. The *Supplement* ensures that users of the *Directory* and *Directory Part 2* always have the latest addresses, contact names, policy statements, application guidelines, and financial data for the foundations they're approaching for funding.

September 2004 / ISBN 1-931923-89-2 / $125
Published annually

GUIDE TO U.S. FOUNDATIONS, THEIR TRUSTEES, OFFICERS, AND DONORS

This powerful fundraising reference tool provides fundraisers with current, accurate information on over 70,000+ private and community foundations in the U.S. The three-volume set also includes a master list of the names of the people who establish, oversee, and manage those institutions. With access to this information, fundraisers can facilitate their funding research by discovering the philanthropic connections of current donors, board members, volunteers, and prominent families in their geographic area. Because it provides a comprehensive list of U.S. foundations and the people who govern them, the *Guide to U.S. Foundations* also helps fundraisers follow up on any giving leads they may uncover. Each entry includes asset and giving amounts as well as geographic limitations, allowing fundraisers to quickly determine whether or not to pursue a particular grant source.

The *Guide to U.S. Foundations* is the only source of published data on thousands of local foundations. (It includes more than 46,000 grantmakers not covered in other print publications.) Each entry also tells you whether you can find more extensive information on the grantmaker in another Foundation Center reference work.

April 2004 / 1-931923-91-4 / $325
Published annually

THE FOUNDATION 1000

Nonprofit fundraisers and other researchers have access to annually published, comprehensive reports on the 1,000 largest foundations in the country. *The Foundation 1000* provides access to extensive and accurate information on this set of powerful funders. *Foundation 1000* grantmakers hold over $290 billion in assets and awarded close to 290,000 grants worth nearly $17 billion to nonprofit organizations nationwide.

The Foundation 1000 provides the most thorough analyses available of the 1,000 largest foundations and their extensive grant programs, including all the data fundraisers need most when applying for grants from these top-level foundations. Each multi-page foundation profile features a full foundation portrait, a detailed breakdown of the foundation's grant programs, and extensive lists of recently awarded foundation grants.

Five indexes give fundraisers the opportunity to target potential funders in a variety of ways: by subject field, type of support, geographic location, international giving, and the names of foundation officers, donors, and trustees.

October 2003 / ISBN 1-931923-60-4 / $295
Published annually

NATIONAL DIRECTORY OF CORPORATE GIVING, 9th Edition

Each year, corporations donate billions of dollars to nonprofit organizations. To help fundraisers tap into this vital source of funding, the *National Directory of Corporate Giving* offers authoritative information on over 3,600 company-sponsored foundations and direct corporate giving programs.

Fundraisers who want access to current, accurate fundraising facts on corporate philanthropies will benefit from the full range of data in this volume. The *National Directory of Corporate Giving* features detailed portraits of over 2,300 company-sponsored foundations plus over 1,300 direct corporate giving programs. Fundraisers will find essential information on these corporate grantmakers, including application information, key personnel, types of support generally awarded, giving limitations, financial data, and purpose and activities statements. Also included in the 9th Edition are over 6,500 selected grants. These grants give you the best indication of a grantmaker's funding priorities by identifying nonprofits it has already funded. The volume also provides data on the companies that sponsor foundations and direct-giving programs—essential background information for corporate grant searches. Each entry gives the company's name and address, a listing of its types of business, its financial data (complete with Forbes and Fortune ratings), a listing of its subsidiaries, divisions, plants, and offices, and a charitable-giving statement.

The *National Directory of Corporate Giving* also features an extensive bibliography to guide you to further research on corporate funding. Seven essential indexes help you target funding prospects by geographic region; international giving; types of support; subject area; officers, donors, and trustees; types of business; and the names of the corporation, its foundation, and its direct-giving program.

August 2003 / ISBN 1-931923-59-0 / $195
Published annually

DIRECTORY OF MISSOURI GRANTMAKERS, 5th Edition

The *Directory of Missouri Grantmakers* provides a comprehensive guide to grantmakers in the state or that have an interest in Missouri nonprofits—over 2,300 foundations, corporate giving programs, and public charities—from the largest grantmakers to local family foundations. The volume will facilitate your grantseeking with information-filled entries that list giving amounts, fields of interest, purpose statements, selected grants, and much more. Indexes help you target the most appropriate funders by subject interest, types of support, and names of key personnel.

June 2003 / ISBN 1-931923-46-9 / $75
Published biennially

FOUNDATION GRANTS TO INDIVIDUALS, 13th Edition

The only publication devoted entirely to foundation grant opportunities for qualified individual applicants, the 13th Edition of this volume features more than 5,500 entries, all of which profile foundation grants to individuals. Entries include foundation addresses and telephone numbers, financial data, giving limitations, and application guidelines. This volume will save individual grantseekers countless hours of research.

June 2003 / ISBN 1-931923-45-0 / $65
Published biennially

SUBJECT DIRECTORIES

The Foundation Center's National Guide to Funding series is designed to facilitate grantseeking within specific fields of nonprofit activity. Each of the directories described below performs the crucial first step of fundraising research by identifying a set of grantmakers that have already stated or demonstrated an interest in a particular field. Fact-filled entries provide access to foundation addresses, financial data, giving priorities, application procedures, contact names, and key officials. Many entries also feature recently awarded grants, the best indication of a grantmaker's funding priorities. A variety of indexes help fundraisers target potential grant sources by subject area, geographic preferences, types of support, and the names of donors, officers, and trustees.

Subject guides are published biennially.

GUIDE TO FUNDING FOR INTERNATIONAL AND FOREIGN PROGRAMS, 7th Edition

The *Guide to Funding for International and Foreign Programs* covers over 1,500 grantmakers interested in funding projects with an international focus, both within the U.S. and abroad. Program areas covered include international relief, disaster assistance, human rights, civil liberties, community development, education, and much more. The volume also includes descriptions of more than 9,500+ recently awarded grants.

May 2004 / ISBN 1-931923-95-7 / $125

NATIONAL GUIDE TO FUNDING IN AIDS, 3rd Edition

This volume covers more than 560 foundations, corporate giving programs, and public charities that support AIDS- and HIV-related nonprofit organizations involved in direct relief, medical research, legal aid, preventative education, and other programs to empower persons with AIDS and AIDS-related diseases. Over 500 recently awarded grants show the types of projects funded by grantmakers.

June 2003 / ISBN 1-931923-44-2 / $115

NATIONAL GUIDE TO FUNDING IN ARTS AND CULTURE, 8th Edition

This volume covers more than 9,600 grantmakers with an interest in funding dance companies, museums, theaters, and countless other types of arts and culture projects and institutions. The volume also includes more than 19,700 descriptions of recently awarded grants.

May 2004 / ISBN 1-931923-94-9 / $155

NATIONAL GUIDE TO FUNDING FOR THE ENVIRONMENT AND ANIMAL WELFARE, 7th Edition

This guide covers over 3,500 grantmakers that fund nonprofits involved in international conservation, ecological research, waste reduction, animal welfare, and much more. The volume includes descriptions of over 7,200 recently awarded grants.

June 2004 / ISBN 1-931923-93-0 / $125

NATIONAL GUIDE TO FUNDING IN HEALTH, 8th Edition

The *National Guide to Funding in Health* contains essential facts on nearly 10,700 grantmakers interested in funding hospitals, universities, research institutes, community-based agencies, national health associations, and a broad range of other health-related programs and services. The volume also includes descriptions of more than 16,000 recently awarded grants.

May 2003 / ISBN 1-931923-42-6 / $155

NATIONAL GUIDE TO FUNDING FOR LIBRARIES AND INFORMATION SERVICES, 7th Edition

This volume provides essential data on more than 800 grantmakers that support a wide range of organizations and initiatives, from the smallest public libraries to major research institutions, academic/research libraries, art, law, and medical libraries, and other specialized information centers. The volume also includes descriptions of over 600 recently awarded grants.

May 2003 / ISBN 1-931923-43-4 / $115

NATIONAL GUIDE TO FUNDING IN RELIGION, 7th Edition

With this volume, fundraisers who work for nonprofits affiliated with religious organizations have access to information on nearly 8,400 grantmakers that have demonstrated or stated an interest in funding churches, missionary societies, religious welfare and education programs, and many other types of projects and institutions. The volume also includes descriptions of more than 10,000 recently awarded grants.

May 2003/ ISBN 1-931923-41-8 / $155

GRANT DIRECTORIES

GRANT GUIDES

Designed for fundraisers who work within defined fields of nonprofit development, this series of guides lists actual foundation grants of $10,000 or more in 12 key areas of grantmaking.

Each title in the series affords immediate access to the names, addresses, and giving limitations of the foundations listed. The grant descriptions provide fundraisers with the grant recipient's name and location; the amount of the grant; the date the grant was authorized; and a description of the grant's intended use.

In addition, each *Grant Guide* includes three indexes, which help fundraisers target possible sources of funding by the type of organization generally funded by the grantmaker, the subject focus of the foundation's grants, and the geographic area in which the foundation has already funded projects.

Each Grant Guide also includes a concise overview of the foundation spending patterns within the specified field. The introduction uses a series of statistical tables to document such important findings as (1) the 25 top funders in your area of interest (by total dollar amount of grants); (2) the 15 largest grants reported; (3) the total dollar amount and number of grants awarded for specific types of support, recipient organization type, and population group; and (4) the total grant dollars received in each U.S. state and many foreign countries.

The *Grant Guide* series gives fundraisers the data they need to target foundations making grants in their field, to network with organizations that share their goals, and to tailor their grant applications to the specific concerns of grantmakers as expressed by the grants they have already made.

Series published annually in December /
2003 / 2004 Editions / $75 each

GUIDEBOOKS, MANUALS, AND REPORTS

ARTS FUNDING IV:
An Update on Foundation Trends

This report provides a framework for understanding trends in foundation funding for arts and culture through 2001. Based on a sample of 800+ foundations, it compares growth in arts funding with other sources of public and private support, examines changes in giving for specific arts disciplines, analyzes giving patterns by region, and explores shifts in the types of support funders award. Prepared in cooperation with Grantmakers in the Arts.

July 2003 / ISBN 1-931923-48-5 / $19.95

FAMILY FOUNDATIONS:
A Profile of Funders and Trends

Family Foundations is an essential resource for anyone interested in understanding the fastest growing segment of foundation philanthropy. The report provides the most comprehensive measurement to date of the size and scope of the U.S. family foundation community. Through the use of objective and subjective criteria, the report identifies the number of family foundations and their distribution by region and state, size, geographic focus, and decade of establishment; and includes analyses of staffing and public reporting by these funders. *Family Foundations* also examines trends in giving by a sample of larger family foundations between 1993 and 1998 and compares these patterns with independent foundations overall. Prepared in cooperation with the National Center for Family Philanthropy.

August 2000 / ISBN 0-87954-917-3 / $19.95

INTERNATIONAL GRANTMAKING II:
An Update on U.S. Foundation Trends, 2nd Edition

An update to 1997's groundbreaking *International Grantmaking* study, this report documents trends in international giving by U.S. foundations in the late 1990s. Based on a sample of over 570 foundations, *International Grantmaking II* identifies shifts in international giving priorities, types of support provided, recipients funded, and countries/regions targeted for support. The report also includes an overview of recent events and factors shaping the international funding environment; and perspectives on the changing funding climate based on a 2000 survey of more than 25 leading international grantmakers. Prepared in cooperation with the Council on Foundations.

November 2000 / ISBN 0-87954-916-5 / $35

THE FOUNDATION CENTER'S GRANTS CLASSIFICATION SYSTEM INDEXING MANUAL WITH THESAURUS, Revised Edition

A complete "how-to" guide, the *Grants Classification Manual* provides an essential resource for any organization that wants to classify foundation grants or their recipients. The *Manual* includes a complete set of all classification codes to facilitate precise tracking of grants and recipients by subject, recipient type, and population categories. It also features a completely revised thesaurus to help identify the "official" terms and codes that represent thousands of subject areas and recipient types in the Center's system of grants classification.

May 1995 / ISBN 0-87954-644-1 / $95

FOUNDATIONS TODAY SERIES, 2004 Edition

The *Foundations Today Series* provides the latest information on foundation growth and trends in foundation giving. Individual copies may be ordered separately or together at a special savings.

Foundation Giving Trends: Update on Funding Priorities—Examines 2003 grantmaking patterns of a sample of more than 1,000 larger U.S. foundations and compares current giving priorities with trends since 1980.
February 2004/ISBN 1-931923-71-X/$45

Foundation Growth and Giving Estimates: 2003 Preview—Provides a first look at estimates of foundation giving for 2003 and final statistics on actual giving and assets for 2002. Presents new top 100 foundation lists.
April 2004/ISBN 1-931923-72-8/$20

Foundation Yearbook: Facts and Figures on Private and Community Foundations—Documents the growth in number, giving, and assets of all active U.S. foundations from 1975 through 2002. *June 2004/ISBN 1-931923-96-5/$45*

Three Book Set / ISBN 1-931923-96-5 / $95

THE FOUNDATION CENTER'S GUIDE TO GRANTSEEKING ON THE WEB, 2003 Edition

Learn how to maximize use of the Web for your funding research. Packed with a wealth of information, the *Guide to Grantseeking on the Web* provides both novice and experienced Web users with a gateway to the numerous online resources available to grantseekers. Foundation Center staff experts have team-authored this guide, contributing their extensive knowledge of Web content as well as their tips and strategies on how to evaluate and use Web-based funding materials. Presented in a concise, "how-to" style, the *Guide* will introduce you to the Web and structure your funding research with a toolkit of resources. These resources include foundation and corporate Web sites, searchable databases for grantseeking, government funding sources, online journals, and interactive services on the Web for grantseekers.

September 2003 / Book / ISBN 1-931923-67-1 / $29.95
CD-ROM / ISBN 1-931923-73-6 / $29.95
Book and CD-ROM / $49.95

THE FOUNDATION CENTER'S GUIDE TO PROPOSAL WRITING, 4th Edition

The *Guide* is a comprehensive manual on the strategic thinking and mechanics of proposal writing. It covers each step of the process, from pre-proposal planning to the writing itself to the essential post-grant follow-up. The book features many extracts from actual grant proposals and also includes candid advice from grantmakers on the "do's and don't's" of proposal writing. Written by a professional fundraiser who has been creating successful proposals for more than 25 years, *The Foundation Center's Guide to Proposal Writing* offers the kind of valuable tips and in-depth, practical instruction that no other source provides.

March 2004 / ISBN 1-931923-92-2 / $34.95

GUÍA PARA ESCRIBIR PROPUESTAS

The Spanish language edition of the *Guide to Proposal Writing* (see above) includes a special appendix listing consultants and technical assistance providers who can help Spanish speakers craft proposals in English, or give advice on fundraising.

March 2003 / ISBN 1-931923-16-7 / $34.95

THE FOUNDATION CENTER'S GUIDE TO WINNING PROPOSALS

The *Guide to Winning Proposals* features twenty grant proposals that have been funded by some of today's most influential grantmakers. Each proposal—reprinted in its entirety—includes a critique by the program officer, executive director, or other funding decision-maker who granted the proposal. The accompanying commentary points to the strengths and weaknesses of each proposal and provides insights into what makes some proposals more successful than others.

To represent the diversity of nonprofits throughout the country, proposals have been selected from large and small, local and national organizations, and for many different support purposes, including basic budgetary support, special projects, construction, staff positions, and more. The *Guide to Winning Proposals* also includes actual letters of inquiry, budgets, cover letters, and vital supplementary documents needed to develop a complete proposal.

October 2003 / ISBN 1-931923-66-3 / $34.95

NEW YORK METROPOLITAN AREA FOUNDATIONS: A Profile of the Grantmaking Community

This study examines the size, scope, and giving patterns of foundations based in the eight-county New York metropolitan area. It documents the New York area's share of all U.S. foundations; details the growth of area foundations through 2000; profiles area foundations by type, size, and geographic focus; compares broad giving trends of New York area and all U.S. foundations between 1992 and 2000; and examines giving by non-New York area grantmakers to recipients in the New York area. Prepared in cooperation with the New York Regional Association of Grantmakers.

December 2002 / ISBN 1-931923-52-3 / $24.95

THE PRI DIRECTORY:
Charitable Loans and Other Program-Related Investments by Foundations, 2nd Edition

Certain foundations have developed an alternative financing approach—known as program-related investing—for supplying capital to the nonprofit sector. PRIs have been used to support community revitalization, low-income housing, microenterprise development, historic preservation, human services, and more. This directory lists leading PRI providers and includes tips on how to seek out and manage PRIs. Foundation listings include funder name and state; recipient name, city, and state (or country); and a description of the project funded. There are several helpful indexes to guide PRI-seekers to records by foundation/recipient location, subject/type of support, and recipient name, as well as an index to officers, donors, and trustees.

September 2003/ ISBN 1-931923-49-3 /$75

SOUTHEASTERN FOUNDATIONS II: A Profile of the Region's Grantmaking Community, 2nd Edition

Southeastern Foundations II provides a detailed examination of foundation philanthropy in the booming 12-state Southeast region. The report includes an overview of the Southeast's share of all U.S. foundations, measures the growth of Southeastern foundations since 1992, profiles Southeastern funders by type, size, and geographic focus, compares broad giving trends of Southeastern and all U.S. foundations in 1992 and 1997, and details giving by non-Southeastern grantmakers to recipients in the region. *Produced in cooperation with the Southeastern Council of Foundations*

November 1999 / ISBN 0-87954-775-8 / $19.95

OTHER PUBLICATIONS

AMERICA'S NONPROFIT SECTOR: A Primer, 2nd Edition
by Lester M. Salamon

In this revised edition of his classic book, Lester M. Salamon clarifies the basic structure and role of the nonprofit sector in the U.S. Moreover, he places the nonprofit sector into context in relation to the government and business sectors. He also shows how the position of the nonprofit sector has changed over time, both generally and in the major fields in which the sector is active. Illustrated with numerous charts and tables, Salamon's book is an easy-to-understand primer for government officials, journalists, and students—in short, for anyone who wants to comprehend the makeup of America's nonprofit sector.

February 1999 / ISBN 0-87954-801-0 / $14.95

BEST PRACTICES OF EFFECTIVE NONPROFIT ORGANIZATIONS: A Practitioner's Guide
by Philip Bernstein

This volume provides guidance for any nonprofit professional eager to advance your organization's goals. Philip Bernstein has drawn on his own extensive experience as a nonprofit executive, consultant, and volunteer to produce this review of "best practices" adopted by successful nonprofit organizations. The author identifies and explains the procedures which provide the foundation for social achievement in all nonprofit fields. Topics include defining purposes and goals, creating comprehensive financing plans, evaluating services, and effective communication.

February 1997 / ISBN 0-87954-755-3 / $29.95

THE BOARD MEMBER'S BOOK:
Making a Difference in Voluntary Organizations, 3rd Edition
by Brian O'Connell

The revised and expanded edition of this popular title by former Independent Sector President, Brian O'Connell, is the perfect guide to the issue, challenges, and possibilities that emerge from the interchange between a nonprofit organization and its board. O'Connell offers practical advice on how to be a more effective board member as well as on how board members can help their organizations make a difference.

March 2003 / ISBN 1-931923-17-5 / $29.95

INVESTING IN CAPACITY BUILDING:
A Guide To High-impact Approaches
by Barbara Blumenthal

This new publication by Barbara Blumenthal offers guidance to grantmakers and consultants in designing better approaches to helping nonprofits, while showing nonprofit managers how to obtain more effective assistance. Grantmakers recognize that technical assistance grants and general support have had a modest impact overall in promoting stability, effectiveness, and efficiency in the nonprofits that they support. Based on interviews with over 100 grantmakers, intermediaries, and consultants; 30 evaluations of capacity building programs; and a review of research on capacity building; *Investing in Capacity Building: A Guide to High-Impact Approaches* identifies the most successful strategies for helping nonprofits improve organizational performance.

September 2003 / ISBN 1-931923-65-5 / $34.95

CAREERS FOR DREAMERS AND DOERS: A Guide to Management Careers in the Nonprofit Sector
by Lilly Cohen and Dennis R.Young

A comprehensive guide to management positions in the nonprofit world, *Careers for Dreamers and Doers* offers practical advice for starting a job search and suggests strategies used by successful managers throughout the voluntary sector.

November 1989 / ISBN 0-87954-294-2 / $29.95

ECONOMICS FOR NONPROFIT MANAGERS
by Dennis R. Young and Richard Steinberg

Economics for Nonprofit Managers is a complete course in the economic issues faced by America's nonprofit decision-makers. Young and Steinberg treat micro-economic analysis as an indispensable skill for nonprofit managers. They introduce and explain concepts such as opportunity cost, analysis at the margin, market equilibrium, market failure, and cost-benefit analysis. This volume also focuses on issues of particular concern to nonprofits, such as the economics of fundraising and volunteer recruiting, the regulatory environment, the impact of competition on nonprofit performance, interactions among sources of revenue, and much more.

July 1995 / ISBN 0-87954-610-7 / $34.95

EFFECTIVE ECONOMIC DECISION-MAKING BY NONPROFIT ORGANIZATIONS
by Dennis R. Young

Editor Dennis R. Young offers useful, practical guidelines to support today's nonprofit managers in their efforts to maximize the effectiveness with which their organizations employ their valuable resources. Nonprofit managers and leaders must advance their mission while balancing the agendas of trustees, funders, staff, and government. In this context, this group of expert authors explores core operating decisions that face all organizations and provides solutions that are unique to nonprofits of any size. Chapters cover such key decision-making areas as pricing of services, compensation of staff, outsourcing, fundraising expenditures, and investment and disbursement of funds. Published by the National Center on Nonprofit Enterprise and the Foundation Center

December 2003 / ISBN 1-931923-69-8 / $34.95

HANDBOOK ON PRIVATE FOUNDATIONS
by David F. Freeman and the Council on Foundations

This publication provides a thorough look at the issues facing the staff and boards of private foundations in the U.S. Author David F. Freeman offers sound advice on establishing, staffing, and governing foundations and provides insights into legal and tax guidelines as well. Each chapter concludes with a useful annotated bibliography. Sponsored by the Council on Foundations.

September 1991
Softbound: ISBN 0-87954-404-X / $29.95
Hardbound: ISBN 0-87954-403-1 / $39.95

THE NONPROFIT ENTREPRENEUR: Creating Ventures to Earn Income
Edited by Edward Skloot

In a well-organized topic-by-topic approach to nonprofit venturing, nonprofit consultant and entrepreneur Edward Skloot demonstrates how nonprofits can launch successful earned-income enterprises without compromising their missions. Skloot has compiled a collection of writings by the nation's top practitioners and advisors in nonprofit enterprise. Topics covered include legal issues, marketing techniques, business planning, avoiding the pitfalls of venturing for smaller nonprofits, and a special section on museums and their retail operations.

September 1988 / ISBN 0-87954-239-X / $19.95

A NONPROFIT ORGANIZATION OPERATING MANUAL: Planning for Survival and Growth
by Arnold J. Olenick and Philip R. Olenick

This straightforward, all-inclusive desk manual for nonprofit executives covers all aspects of starting and managing a nonprofit. The authors discuss legal problems, obtaining tax exemption, organizational planning and development, and board relations; operational, proposal, cash, and capital budgeting; marketing, grant proposals, fundraising, and for-profit ventures; computerization; and tax planning and compliance.

July 1991 / ISBN 0-87954-293-4 / $29.95

PEOPLE POWER: SERVICE, ADVOCACY, EMPOWERMENT
by Brian O'Connell

Throughout his career, Brian O'Connell has broadened the impact of his own nonprofit work with thoughtful essays, speeches, and op-ed articles. *People Power,* a selection of O'Connell's most powerful writings, provides thought-provoking commentary on the nonprofit world. The 25+ essays included in this volume range from keen analyses of the role of voluntarism in American life, to sound advice for nonprofit managers, to suggestions for developing and strengthening the nonprofit sector of the future. Anyone involved in the nonprofit world will appreciate O'Connell's penetrating insights.

October 1994 / ISBN 0-87954-563-1 / $24.95

PHILANTHROPY'S CHALLENGE
Building Nonprofit Capacity Through Venture Grantmaking
by Paul B. Firstenberg

In this new book, Paul Firstenberg challenges grantors to proactively assist grantee management as the way to maximize the social impact of nonprofit programs, while showing grantseekers how the growing grantor emphasis on organizational capacity building will impact their efforts to win support. The author draws on his years of experience working within both nonprofit and for-profit organizations to explore the roles of grantor and grantee within various models of venture grantmaking. To emphasize the importance that nonprofit boards can play in this process, a full chapter is devoted to governance issues and responsibilities.

January 2003
Softbound: ISBN 1-931923-15-9 / $29.95
Hardbound: ISBN 1-931923-53-1 / $39.95

PROMOTING ISSUES AND IDEAS: A Guide to Public Relations for Nonprofit Organizations, Revised edition
by M Booth & Associates

M Booth & Associates are specialists in promoting the issues and ideas of nonprofit groups. Their book presents proven strategies that will attract the interest of the people you wish to influence and inform. Included are the "nuts-and-bolts" of advertising, publicity, speech-making, lobbying, and special events; how to write and produce informational literature that leaps off the page; public relations on a shoe-string budget; how to plan and evaluate PR efforts; the use of rapidly evolving communication technologies; and a new chapter on crisis management.

December 1995 / ISBN 0-87954-594-1 / $29.95

RAISE MORE MONEY FOR YOUR NONPROFIT ORGANIZATION: A Guide to Evaluating and Improving Your Fundraising
by Anne L. New

In *Raise More Money,* Anne New sets guidelines for a fundraising program that will benefit the incipient as well as the established nonprofit organization. The author divides her text into three sections: "The Basics," which delineates the necessary steps a nonprofit must take before launching a development campaign; "Fundraising Methods," which encourages organizational self-analysis and points the way to an effective program involving many sources of funding; and "Fundraising Resources," a 20-page bibliography that highlights the most useful research and funding directories available.

January 1991 / ISBN 0-87954-388-4 / $14.95

SECURING YOUR ORGANIZATION'S FUTURE: A Complete Guide to Fundraising Strategies, Revised Edition
by Michael Seltzer

In this completely updated edition, Michael Seltzer acts as your personal fundraising consultant. Beginners get bottom-line facts and easy-to-follow worksheets; veteran fundraisers receive a complete review of the basics plus new money-making ideas. Seltzer supplements his text with an extensive bibliography of selected readings and resource organizations. Highly recommended for use as a text in nonprofit management programs at colleges and universities.

February 2001 / ISBN 0-87954-900-9 / $34.95

SUCCEEDING WITH CONSULTANTS: Self-Assessment for the Changing Nonprofit
by Barbara Kibbe and Fred Setterberg

This inspirational book, written by Barbara Kibbe and Fred Setterberg and supported by the David and Lucile Packard Foundation, guides nonprofits through the process of selecting and utilizing consultants to strengthen their organization's operations. The book emphasizes self assessment tools and covers six different areas in which a nonprofit organization might benefit from a consultant's advice: governance, planning, fund development, financial management, public relations and marketing, and quality assurance.

April 1992 / ISBN 0-87954-450-3 / $19.95

THE 21ST CENTURY NONPROFIT
by Paul B. Firstenberg

In *The 21st Century Nonprofit,* Paul B. Firstenberg provides nonprofit managers with the know-how to make their organizations effective agents of change. *The 21st Century Nonprofit* encourages managers to adopt strategies developed by the for-profit sector in recent years. These strategies will help them to expand their revenue base by diversifying grant sources, exploit the possibilities of for-profit enterprises, develop human resources by learning how to attract and retain talented people, and explore the nature of leadership through short profiles of three nonprofit CEOs.

July 1996 / ISBN 0-87954-672-7 / $34.95

MEMBERSHIP PROGRAM

ASSOCIATES PROGRAM
A Special Membership Program

The Associates Program puts important facts and figures on your desk through an e-mail and toll-free telephone reference service, helping you to:

- identify potential sources of foundation funding for your organization; and
- gather important information to use in targeting and presenting your proposals effectively.

Your annual membership in the Associates Program gives you vital information on a timely basis, saving you hundreds of hours of research time.

- Membership in the Associates Program entitles you to important funding information, including information from:
  — foundation and corporate annual reports, brochures, press releases, grants lists, and other announcements
  — IRS 990-PF information returns for active grantmaking U.S. foundations—often the only source of information on small foundations
  — books and periodicals on the grantmaking field, including regulation and nonprofit management
- The annual fee of $995 for the Associates Program entitles you to ten free reference requests per month. Additional reference requests can be made at the rate of $30 per ten questions.
- Membership in the Associates Program allows you to request custom searches of the Foundation Center's computerized databases, which contain

information on more than 76,000 U.S. foundations and corporate givers. There is an additional cost for this service.

- Associates Program members may request photocopies of key documents. Important information from 990-PFs, annual reports, application guidelines, and other resources can be copied and either mailed or faxed to your office. Up to 50 pages per month may be requested free of charge.

- All Associates Program members receive the Associates Program quarterly newsletter, which provides news and information about new foundations, changes in boards of directors, new programs, and publications from both the Foundation Center and other publishers in the field.

- Members receive two special e-mail reports each month; one listing a minimum of 75 new or emerging foundations not yet listed in our directories or on our Web site, and a second e-mail report listing updates on current grantmaker profiles.

- Access to program services via Associates Program Online.

Thousands of professional fundraisers find it extremely cost-effective to rely on the Center's Associates Program. Put our staff of experts to work for your fundraising program. For more information call 1-800-424-9836, or visit our World Wide Web site at www.fdncenter.org.

FOUNDATION CENTER'S WEB SITE
www.fdncenter.org

Helping grantseekers succeed, helping grantmakers make a difference

The Foundation Center's Web site (www. fdncenter.org) is the premier online source of fundraising information. Updated and expanded on a daily basis, the Center's site provides grantseekers, grantmakers, researchers, journalists, and the general public with easy access to a range of valuable resources, among them:

- Personalization at the Center's Web site allows registered users to receive content tailored to their fundraising and research interests at key areas of the site, including the home page, *Philanthropy News Digest,* and the Marketplace.

- A Grantmaker Web Sites area provides annotated links to more than 2,400 grantmaker sites that can be searched by subject or geographic key words.

- Foundation Finder, our free foundation look-up tool, includes foundation contact information and brief background data, such as type of foundation, assets,

total giving, and EIN, as well as links to 990-PFs (IRS tax filings).

- *Philanthropy News Digest,* features current philanthropy-related articles abstracted from major media outlets, interviews, original content, and the "PND Talk" message board. PND is also available as a weekly listserv.

- *The Literature of the Nonprofit Sector Online,* a searchable bibliographical database, includes 22,500+ entries of works on the field of philanthropy, over 14,000 of which are abstracted.

- Our Online Library features comprehensive answers to FAQs, an online librarian to field questions about grantseeking and the Foundation Center, annotated links to useful nonprofit resources, and an online orientation to the grantseeking process.

- Our popular Virtual Classroom allows visitors to link to a Proposal Writing Short Course (in English and Spanish); Establishing a Nonprofit Organization; Demystifying the 990-PF; and more.

- Information about Center-sponsored orientations, training programs, and seminars can be found on our Library homepage and in the marketplace.

- The locations of our 200+ Cooperating Collections nationwide, and the activities and resources at our five main libraries.

- A "For Individual Grantseekers" area introduces individuals to the grantseeking process and provides tools and resources to help individuals get started.

- A special section, "For Grantmakers," offers funders the opportunity to help get the word out about their work, answers frequently asked questions, and informs grantmakers on recent developments in the field and how the Center assists grantees and applicants.

- The "For the Media" area provides journalists with current information on key developments in private philanthropy in the U.S.

- Sector Search is a search tool that continuously crawls the Web sites of thousands of private, corporate, community foundations, grantmaking public charities, and nonprofit organizations, and provides relevant, accurate search results. Search by organization type, subject, or individual's name.

All this and more is available at our Web site. The Center's publications and electronic resources can be ordered at the site's marketplace. Visit our Web site often for information on new products and services.

FOUNDATION CENTER COOPERATING COLLECTIONS   FREE FUNDING INFORMATION CENTERS

The Foundation Center is an independent national service organization established by foundations to provide an authoritative source of information on foundation and corporate giving. The New York, Washington D.C., Atlanta, Cleveland, and San Francisco reference collections operated by the Foundation Center offer a wide variety of services and comprehensive resources on foundations and grants. Cooperating Collections are libraries, community foundations, and other nonprofit agencies that make accessible a collection of Foundation Center print and electronic publications, as well as a variety of supplementary materials and education programs in areas useful to grantseekers. The collection includes:

FC SEARCH: THE FOUNDATION CENTER'S DATABASE ON
  CD-ROM
THE FOUNDATION DIRECTORY 1 AND 2, AND SUPPLEMENT
FOUNDATION FUNDAMENTALS
THE FOUNDATION 1000

FOUNDATIONS TODAY SERIES
FOUNDATION GRANTS TO INDIVIDUALS
THE FOUNDATION CENTER'S GUIDE TO GRANTSEEKING
  ON THE WEB
THE FOUNDATION CENTER'S GUIDE TO PROPOSAL WRITING

GUIDE TO U.S. FOUNDATIONS, THEIR TRUSTEES, OFFICERS,
  AND DONORS
NATIONAL DIRECTORY OF CORPORATE GIVING
NATIONAL GUIDE TO FUNDING IN. . . . (SERIES)

All five Foundation Center libraries and most Cooperating Collections have *FC: Search: The Foundation Center's Database on CD-ROM* available for public use and all provide Internet access. Increasingly, those seeking information on fundraising and nonprofit management are referring to our Web site (http://www.fdncenter.org) for a wealth of data and advice on grantseeking, including links to foundation IRS information returns (990-PFs). Because the Cooperating Collections vary in their hours, it is recommended that you call the collection in advance of a visit. To check on new locations or current holdings, call toll-free 1-800-424-9836, or visit our site at http://fdncenter.org/collections/index.html.

REFERENCE COLLECTIONS OPERATED BY THE FOUNDATION CENTER

THE FOUNDATION CENTER
2nd Floor
79 Fifth Ave.
New York, NY 10003
(212) 620-4230

THE FOUNDATION CENTER
312 Sutter St., Suite 606
San Francisco, CA 94108
(415) 397-0902

THE FOUNDATION CENTER
1627 K St., NW, 3rd floor
Washington, DC 20006
(202) 331-1400

THE FOUNDATION CENTER
Kent H. Smith Library
1422 Euclid Ave., Suite 1600
Cleveland, OH 44115
(216) 861-1933

THE FOUNDATION CENTER
Suite 150, Grand Lobby
Hurt Bldg., 50 Hurt Plaza
Atlanta, GA 30303
(404) 880-0094

ALABAMA

BIRMINGHAM PUBLIC LIBRARY
Government Documents
2100 Park Place
Birmingham 35203
(205) 226-3620

HUNTSVILLE PUBLIC LIBRARY
915 Monroe St.
Huntsville 35801
(256) 532-5940

MOBILE PUBLIC LIBRARY
West Regional Library
5555 Grelot Road
Mobile 36609-3643
(251) 340-8555

AUBURN UNIVERSITY AT
MONTGOMERY LIBRARY
74-40 East Dr.
Montgomery 36117-3596
(334) 244-3200

ALASKA

CONSORTIUM LIBRARY
3211 Providence Dr.
Anchorage 99508
(907) 786-1848

JUNEAU PUBLIC LIBRARY
292 Marine Way
Juneau 99801
(907) 586-5267

ARIZONA

FLAGSTAFF CITY-COCONINO COUNTY
PUBLIC LIBRARY
300 W. Aspen Ave.
Flagstaff 86001
(928) 779-7670

PHOENIX PUBLIC LIBRARY
Information Services Department
1221 N. Central Ave.
Phoenix 85004
(602) 262-4636

TUCSON PIMA PUBLIC LIBRARY
101 N. Stone Ave.
Tucson 87501
(520) 791-4393

ARKANSAS

UNIVERSITY OF ARKANSAS—FT. SMITH
BOREHAM LIBRARY
5210 Grand Ave.
P.O. Box 3649
Ft. Smith 72913
(479) 788-7204

CENTRAL ARKANSAS LIBRARY SYSTEM
100 Rock St.
Little Rock 72201
(501) 918-3000

CALIFORNIA

KERN COUNTY LIBRARY
Beale Memorial Library
701 Truxtun Ave.
Bakersfield 93301
(661) 868-0755

HUMBOLDT AREA FOUNDATION
Rooney Resource Center
373 Indianola
Bayside 95524
(707) 442-2993

VENTURA COUNTY COMMUNITY
FOUNDATION
Resource Center for Nonprofit Organizations
1317 Del Norte Rd., Suite 150
Camarillo 93010
(805) 988-0196

FRESNO REGIONAL FOUNDATION
Nonprofit Advancement Center
3425 N. First St., Suite 101
Fresno 93726
(559) 226-0216

CENTER FOR NONPROFIT
MANAGEMENT IN SOUTHERN
CALIFORNIA
Nonprofit Resource Library
606 South Olive St. #2450
Los Angeles 90014
(213) 623-7080

LOS ANGELES PUBLIC LIBRARY
Mid-Valley Regional Branch Library
16244 Nordhoff St.
North Hills 91343
(818) 895-3654

EAST BAY RESOURCE CENTER FOR
NONPROFIT SUPPORT
359 Frank H. Ogawa Plaza
Oakland 94612
(510) 834-1010

PHILANTHROPY RESOURCE CENTER
Flintridge Foundation
1040 Lincoln Ave, Suite 100
Pasadena 91103
(626) 449-0839

CENTER FOR NONPROFIT RESOURCES
Shasta Regional Community
Foundation's Center
Bldg. C, Suite A
2280 Benton Dr.
Redding 96003
(530) 244-1219

RICHMOND PUBLIC LIBRARY
325 Civic Center Plaza
Richmond 94804
(510) 620-6561

RIVERSIDE CITY PUBLIC LIBRARY
3581 Mission Inn Ave.
Riverside 92501
(909) 826-5201

NONPROFIT RESOURCE CENTER
Sacramento Public Library
828 I St., 2nd Floor
Sacramento 95814
(916) 264-2772

SAN DIEGO FOUNDATION
Funding Information Center
1420 Kettner Blvd., Suite 500
San Diego 92101
(619) 235-2300

COMPASSPOINT NONPROFIT SERVICES
Nonprofit Development Library
1922 The Alameda, Suite 212
San Jose 95126
(408) 248-9505

PENINSULA COMMUNITY
FOUNDATION
Peninsula Nonprofit Center
1700 S. El Camino Real, #R201
San Mateo 94402-3049
(650) 358-9392

LOS ANGELES PUBLIC LIBRARY
San Pedro Regional Branch
931 S. Gaffey St.
San Pedro 90731
(310) 548-7779

VOLUNTEER CENTER OF GREATER
ORANGE COUNTY
Nonprofit Resource Center
1901 E. 4th St., Suite 100
Santa Ana 92705
(714) 953-5757

SANTA BARBARA PUBLIC LIBRARY
40 E. Anapamu St.
Santa Barbara 93101-1019
(805) 962-7653

SANTA MONICA PUBLIC LIBRARY
1324 Fifth St.
Santa Monica 90401
(310) 458-8600

SONOMA COUNTY LIBRARY
3rd & E Sts.
Santa Rosa 95404
(707) 545-0831

SEASIDE BRANCH LIBRARY
550 Harcourt Ave.
Seaside 93955
(831) 899-8131

SIERRA NONPROFIT SUPPORT CENTER
39 No. Washington St. #F
Sonora 95370
(209) 533-1093

COLORADO

PENROSE LIBRARY
20 N. Cascade Ave.
Colorado Springs 80903
(719) 531-6333

DENVER PUBLIC LIBRARY
10 W. 14th Ave. Pkwy.
Denver 80204
(720) 865-1111

CONNECTICUT

DANBURY PUBLIC LIBRARY
170 Main St.
Danbury 06810
(203) 797-4527

GREENWICH LIBRARY
101 W. Putnam Ave.
Greenwich 06830
(203) 622-7900

HARTFORD PUBLIC LIBRARY
500 Main St.
Hartford 06103
(860) 695-6292

NEW HAVEN FREE PUBLIC LIBRARY
133 Elm St.
New Haven 06510-2057
(203) 946-7431

DELAWARE

UNIVERSITY OF DELAWARE
Hugh Morris Library
181 South College Ave.
Newark 19717-5267
(302) 831-2432

FLORIDA

BARTOW PUBLIC LIBRARY
2151 S. Broadway Ave.
Bartow 33830
(863) 534-0931

VOLUSIA COUNTY LIBRARY CENTER
City Island
105 E. Magnolia Ave.
Daytona Beach 32114-4484
(386) 257-6036

NOVA SOUTHEASTERN UNIVERSITY
Einstein Library
3100 Ray Ferrero Jr. Blvd.
Fort Lauderdale 33314
(954) 262-4613

INDIAN RIVER COMMUNITY COLLEGE
Learning Resources Center
3209 Virginia Ave.
Fort Pierce 34981-5596
(561) 462-4757

JACKSONVILLE PUBLIC LIBRARIES
Grants Resource Center
122 N. Ocean St.
Jacksonville   32202
(904) 630-2665

MIAMI-DADE PUBLIC LIBRARY
Humanities/Social Science
101 W. Flagler St.
Miami   33130
(305) 375-5575

ORANGE COUNTY LIBRARY SYSTEM
Social Sciences Department
101 E. Central Blvd.
Orlando   32801
(407) 425-4694

SELBY PUBLIC LIBRARY
Reference
1331 1st St.
Sarasota   34236
(941) 861-1100

STATE LIBRARY OF FLORIDA
R.A. Gray Building
Tallahassee 32399-0250
(850) 245-6600

HILLSBOROUGH COUNTY PUBLIC
LIBRARY COOPERATIVE
John F. Germany Public Library
900 N. Ashley Dr.
Tampa   33602
(813) 273-3652

COMMUNITY FOUNDATION OF PALM
BEACH & MARTIN COUNTIES
700 S. Dixie Hwy., Suite 200
West Palm Beach   33401
(561) 659-6800

GEORGIA

HALL COUNTY LIBRARY SYSTEM
127 Main Street Nw
Gainesville   30501
(770) 532-3311

WASHINGTON MEMORIAL LIBRARY
1180 Washington Ave.
Macon   31201
(478) 744-0828

THOMAS COUNTY PUBLIC LIBRARY
201 N. Madison St.
Thomasville   31792
(229) 225-5252

HAWAII

UNIVERSITY OF HAWAII
Hamilton Library
2550 The Mall
Honolulu   96822
(808) 956-7214

IDAHO

BOISE PUBLIC LIBRARY
Funding Information Center
715 S. Capitol Blvd.
Boise   83702
(208) 384-4024

CALDWELL PUBLIC LIBRARY
1010 Dearborn St.
Caldwell   83605
(208) 459-3242

ILLINOIS

DONORS FORUM OF CHICAGO
208 S. LaSalle, Suite 735
Chicago   60604
(312) 578-0175

EVANSTON PUBLIC LIBRARY
1703 Orrington Ave.
Evanston   60201
(847) 866-0300

ROCK ISLAND PUBLIC LIBRARY
401 19th St.
Rock Island   61201-8143
(309) 732-7323

UNIVERSITY OF ILLINOIS
AT SPRINGFIELD, LIB 140
Brookens Library
One University Plaza
Springfield   62794-9243
(217) 206-6633

INDIANA

EVANSVILLE-VANDERBURGH
PUBLIC LIBRARY
22 SE 5th St.
Evansville   47708
(812) 428-8200

ALLEN COUNTY PUBLIC LIBRARY
900 Webster St.
Ft. Wayne   36802
(260) 421-1238

INDIANAPOLIS-MARION COUNTY
PUBLIC LIBRARY
202 North Alabama
Indianapolis   46206
(317) 269-1700

VIGO COUNTY PUBLIC LIBRARY
1 Library Square
Terre Haute   47807
(812) 232-1113

IOWA

CEDAR RAPIDS PUBLIC LIBRARY
500 1st St., SE
Cedar Rapids   52401
(319) 398-5123

SOUTHWESTERN COMMUNITY
COLLEGE
Learning Resource Center
1501 W. Townline Rd.
Creston   50801
(641) 782-7081

PUBLIC LIBRARY OF DES MOINES
100 Locust
Des Moines   50309-1791
(515) 283-4152

SIOUX CITY PUBLIC LIBRARY
Siouxland Funding Research Center
529 Pierce St.
Sioux City   51101-1203
(712) 255-2933

KANSAS

PIONEER MEMORIAL LIBRARY
375 West 4th St.
Colby   67701
(785) 462-4470

DODGE CITY PUBLIC LIBRARY
1001 2nd Ave.
Dodge City   67801
(620) 225-0248

KEARNY COUNTY LIBRARY
101 East Prairie
Lakin   67860
(620) 355-6674

SALINA PUBLIC LIBRARY
301 West Elm
Salina 67401
(785) 825-4624

TOPEKA AND SHAWNEE COUNTY
PUBLIC LIBRARY
1515 SW 10th Ave.
Topeka   66604
(785) 580-4400

WICHITA PUBLIC LIBRARY
223 S. Main St.
Wichita   67202
(316) 261-8500

KENTUCKY

WESTERN KENTUCKY UNIVERSITY
Helm-Cravens Library
110 Helm Library
Bowling Green   42101-3576
(270) 745-6163

LEXINGTON PUBLIC LIBRARY
140 E. Main St.
Lexington   40507-1376
(859) 231-5520

LOUISVILLE FREE PUBLIC LIBRARY
301 York St.
Louisville   40203
(502) 574-1617

LOUISIANA

EAST BATON ROUGE PARISH LIBRARY
Centroplex Branch Grants Collection
120 St. Louis St.
Baton Rouge   70802
(225) 389-4967

BEAUREGARD PARISH LIBRARY
205 S. Washington Ave.
De Ridder   70634
(337) 463-6217

OUACHITA PARISH PUBLIC LIBRARY
1800 Stubbs Ave.
Monroe   71201
(318) 327-1490

NEW ORLEANS PUBLIC LIBRARY
Business & Science Division
219 Loyola Ave.
New Orleans   70112
(504) 596-2580

SHREVE MEMORIAL LIBRARY
424 Texas St.
Shreveport   71120-1523
(318) 226-5894

MAINE

UNIVERSITY OF SOUTHERN
MAINE LIBRARY
Maine Philanthropy Center
314 Forrest Ave.
Portland   04104-9301
(207) 780-5029

MARYLAND

ENOCH PRATT FREE LIBRARY
Social Science & History Dept.
400 Cathedral St.
Baltimore   21201
(410) 396-5320

MASSACHUSETTS

ASSOCIATED GRANT MAKERS OF
MASSACHUSETTS
55 Court St.
Room 520
Boston   02108
(617) 426-2606

BOSTON PUBLIC LIBRARY
Soc. Sci. Reference
700 Boylston St.
Boston   02116
(617) 536-5400

WESTERN MASSACHUSETTS FUNDING
RESOURCE CENTER
65 Elliot St.
Springfield   01101-1730
(413) 452-0697

WORCESTER PUBLIC LIBRARY
Grants Resource Center
3 Salem Sq.
Worcester   01608
(508) 799-1655

MICHIGAN

ALPENA COUNTY LIBRARY
211 N. 1st St.
Alpena 49707
(989) 356-6188

UNIVERSITY OF
MICHIGAN–ANN ARBOR
Graduate Library
Reference & Research Services
Department
Ann Arbor   48109-1205
(734) 763-1539

WILLARD PUBLIC LIBRARY
Nonprofit & Funding Resource
Collections
7 W. Van Buren St.
Battle Creek   49017
(269) 969-2100

HENRY FORD CENTENNIAL LIBRARY
16301 Michigan Ave.
Dearborn   48126
(313) 943-2330

WAYNE STATE UNIVERSITY
134 Purdy/Kresge Library
Detroit   48202
(313) 577-6424

MICHIGAN STATE UNIVERSITY
LIBRARIES
Main Library
Funding Center
100 Library
East Lansing   48824-1048
(517) 432-6123

FARMINGTON COMMUNITY LIBRARY
32737 W. 12 Mile Rd.
Farmington Hills   48334
(248) 553-0300

UNIVERSITY OF MICHIGAN—FLINT
Frances Willson Thompson Library
Flint   48502-1950
(810) 762-3413

GRAND RAPIDS PUBLIC LIBRARY
111 Library St. NE
Grand Rapids   49503-3268
(616) 988-5400

MICHIGAN TECHNOLOGICAL
UNIVERSITY
Harold Meese Center, Corporate Services
1400 Townsend Dr.
Houghton   49931-1295
(906) 487-2228

WEST SHORE COMMUNITY COLLEGE
LIBRARY
3000 North Stiles Road
Scottville 49454-0277
(231) 845-6211

TRAVERSE AREA DISTRICT LIBRARY
610 Woodmere Ave.
Traverse City   49686
(231) 932-8500

MINNESOTA

BRAINERD PUBLIC LIBRARY
416 South Fifth St.
Brainerd 56401
(218) 829-5574

DULUTH PUBLIC LIBRARY
520 W. Superior St.
Duluth   55802
(218) 723-3802

SOUTHWEST STATE UNIVERSITY
University Library
N. Hwy. 23
Marshall   56253
(507) 537-6108

MINNEAPOLIS PUBLIC LIBRARY
250 Marquette Ave.
Minneapolis   55401
(612) 630-6000

ROCHESTER PUBLIC LIBRARY
101 2nd St. SE
Rochester   55904-3777
(507) 285-8002

ST. PAUL PUBLIC LIBRARY
90 W. Fourth St.
St. Paul   55102
(651) 266-7000

MISSISSIPPI

LIBRARY OF HATTIESBURG, PETAL
AND FORREST COUNTY
329 Hardy St.
Hattiesburg   39401-3824
(601) 582-4461

JACKSON/HINDS LIBRARY SYSTEM
300 N. State St.
Jackson   39201
(601) 968-5803

MISSOURI

COUNCIL ON PHILANTHROPY
University of Missouri—Kansas City
Center for Business Innovation
4747 Troost, #207
Kansas City   64171-0813
(816) 235-1176

KANSAS CITY PUBLIC LIBRARY
311 E. 12th St.
Kansas City   64106
(816) 701-3541

ST. LOUIS PUBLIC LIBRARY
1301 Olive St.
St. Louis 63103
(314) 241-2288

SPRINGFIELD-GREENE
COUNTY LIBRARY
The Library Center
4653 S. Campbell
Springfield 65810
(417) 874-8110

MONTANA

MONTANA STATE UNIVERSITY—
BILLINGS
Library—Special Collections
1500 N. 30th St.
Billings 59101-0245
(406) 657-1687

BOZEMAN PUBLIC LIBRARY
220 E. Lamme
Bozeman 59715
(406) 582-2402

MONTANA STATE LIBRARY
Library Services
1515 E. 6th Ave.
Helena 59620-1800
(406) 444-3115

LINCOLN COUNTY PUBLIC LIBRARIES
Libby Public Library
220 West 6th St.
Libby 59923
(406) 293-2778

UNIVERSITY OF MONTANA
Mansfield Library
32 Campus Dr. #9936
Missoula 59812-9936
(406) 243-6800

NEBRASKA

UNIVERSITY OF NEBRASKA—
LINCOLN
225C Love Library
14th & R Sts.
Lincoln 68588-2848
(402) 472-2848

OMAHA PUBLIC LIBRARY
W. Dale Clark Library
Social Sciences Dept.
215 S. 15th St.
Omaha 68102
(402) 444-4826

NEVADA

GREAT BASIN COLLEGE LIBRARY
1500 College Parkway
Elko 89801
(775) 753-2222

CLARK COUNTY LIBRARY
1401 E. Flamingo
Las Vegas 89119
(702) 507-3400

WASHOE COUNTY LIBRARY
301 S. Center St.
Reno 89501
(775) 327-8300

NEW HAMPSHIRE

CONCORD PUBLIC LIBRARY
45 Green St.
Concord 03301
(603) 225-8670

PLYMOUTH STATE COLLEGE
Herbert H. Lamson Library
Plymouth 03264
(603) 535-2258

NEW JERSEY

CUMBERLAND COUNTY LIBRARY
800 E. Commerce St.
Bridgeton 08302
(856) 453-2210

FREE PUBLIC LIBRARY OF ELIZABETH
11 S. Broad St.
Elizabeth 07202
(908) 354-6060

NEWARK ENTERPRISE COMMUNITY
RESOURCE DEVELOPMENT CENTER
303-309 Washington St., 5th floor
Newark 07102
(973) 624-8300

COUNTY COLLEGE OF MORRIS
Learning Resource Center
214 Center Grove Rd.
Randolph 07869
(973) 328-5296

NEW JERSEY STATE LIBRARY
185 W. State St.
Trenton 08625-0520
(609) 292-6220

NEW MEXICO

ALBUQUERQUE/BERNALILLO COUNTY
LIBRARY SYSTEM
501 Copper Avenue NW
Albuquerque 87102
(505) 768-5141

NEW MEXICO STATE LIBRARY
Information Services
1209 Camino Carlos Rey
Santa Fe 87507
(505) 476-9702

NEW YORK

NEW YORK STATE LIBRARY
Humanities Reference
Cultural Education Center, 6th Fl.
Empire State Plaza
Albany 12230
(518) 474-5355

BROOKLYN PUBLIC LIBRARY
Society, Science and Technology Division
Grand Army Plaza
Brooklyn 11238
(718) 230-2122

BUFFALO & ERIE COUNTY
PUBLIC LIBRARY
Business, Science & Technology Dept.
1 Lafayette Square
Buffalo 14203-1887
(716) 858-7097

SOUTHEAST STEUBEN
COUNTY LIBRARY
300 Nasser Civic Center Plaza
Corning 14830
Phone: (607) 936-3713

HUNTINGTON PUBLIC LIBRARY
338 Main St.
Huntington 11743
(631) 427-5165

QUEENS BOROUGH PUBLIC LIBRARY
Social Sciences Division
89-11 Merrick Blvd.
Jamaica 11432
(718) 990-0700

LEVITTOWN PUBLIC LIBRARY
1 Bluegrass Ln.
Levittown 11756
(516) 731-5728

ADRIANCE MEMORIAL LIBRARY
Special Services Department
93 Market St.
Poughkeepsie 12601
(914) 485-3445

THE RIVERHEAD FREE LIBRARY
330 Court St.
Riverhead 11901
(631) 727-3228

ROCHESTER PUBLIC LIBRARY
Social Sciences
115 South Ave.
Rochester 14604
(585) 428-8120

ONONDAGA COUNTY PUBLIC LIBRARY
447 S. Salina St.
Syracuse 13202-2494
(315) 435-1900

UTICA PUBLIC LIBRARY
303 Genesee St.
Utica 13501
(315) 735-2279

WHITE PLAINS PUBLIC LIBRARY
100 Martine Ave.
White Plains 10601
(914) 422-1480

YONKERS PUBLIC LIBRARY
Riverfront Library
One Larkin Center
Yonkers 10701
(914) 337-1500

NORTH CAROLINA

PACK MEMORIAL LIBRARY
Community Foundation of Western North
Carolina
67 Haywood St.
Asheville 28802
(828) 254-4960

THE DUKE ENDOWMENT
100 N. Tryon St., Suite 3500
Charlotte 28202-4012
(704) 376-0291

DURHAM COUNTY PUBLIC LIBRARY
300 N. Roxboro St.
Durham 27702
(919) 560-0100

FORSYTH COUNTY PUBLIC LIBRARY
660 W. 5th St.
Winston-Salem 27101
(336) 727-2264

NORTH DAKOTA

BISMARCK PUBLIC LIBRARY
515 N. 5th St.
Bismarck 58501-4081
(701) 222-6410

FARGO PUBLIC LIBRARY
102 N. 3rd St.
Fargo 58102
(701) 241-1491

MINOT PUBLIC LIBRARY
516 Second Avenue SW
Minot 58701-3792
(701) 852-1045

OHIO

STARK COUNTY DISTRICT LIBRARY
715 Market Ave. N.
Canton 44702
(330) 452-0665

PUBLIC LIBRARY OF CINCINNATI &
HAMILTON COUNTY
Grants Resource Center
800 Vine St.—Library Square
Cincinnati 45202-2071
(513) 369-6000

COLUMBUS METROPOLITAN LIBRARY
Business and Technology
96 S. Grant Ave.
Columbus 43215
(614) 645-2590

DAYTON METRO LIBRARY
Grants Information Center
215 E. Third St.
Dayton 45402
(937) 227-9500

MANSFIELD/RICHLAND COUNTY
PUBLIC LIBRARY
43 W. 3rd St.
Mansfield 44902
(419) 521-3110

PORTSMOUTH PUBLIC LIBRARY
1220 Gallia St.
Portsmouth 45662
(740) 354-5688

TOLEDO–LUCAS COUNTY
PUBLIC LIBRARY
325 Michigan St.
Toledo 43612
(419) 259-5209

PUBLIC LIBRARY OF YOUNGSTOWN &
MAHONING COUNTY
305 Wick Ave.
Youngstown 44503
(330) 744-8636

OKLAHOMA

OKLAHOMA CITY UNIVERSITY
Dulaney Browne Library
2501 N. Blackwelder
Oklahoma City 73106
(405) 521-5822

TULSA CITY–COUNTY LIBRARY
400 Civic Center
Tulsa 74103
(918) 596-7977

OREGON

OREGON INSTITUTE OF TECHNOLOGY
Library
3201 Campus Dr.
Klamath Falls 97601-8801
(541) 885-1770

PACIFIC NON-PROFIT NETWORK
Southern Oregon University
1600 N. Riverside #1001
Medford 97501
(541) 552-8207

MULTNOMAH COUNTY LIBRARY
801 SW 10th Ave.
Portland 97205
(503) 988-5123

OREGON STATE LIBRARY
State Library Bldg.
250 Winter St. NE
Salem 97301-3950
(503) 378-4277

PENNSYLVANIA

NORTHAMPTON COMMUNITY
COLLEGE
The Paul and Harriet Mack Library
3835 Green Pond Rd.
Bethlehem 18017
(610) 861-5360

ERIE COUNTY LIBRARY SYSTEM
160 E. Front St.
Erie 16507
(814) 451-6927

DAUPHIN COUNTY LIBRARY SYSTEM
East Shore Area Library
4501 Ethel St.
Harrisburg 17109
(717) 652-9380

HAZLETON AREA PUBLIC LIBRARY
55 North Church St.
Hazleton 18201
Phone: (570) 454-2961

LANCASTER COUNTY LIBRARY
125 N. Duke St.
Lancaster 17602
(717) 394-2651

FREE LIBRARY OF PHILADELPHIA
Regional Foundation Center
1901 Vine St.
Philadelphia 19103-1189
(215) 686-5423

CARNEGIE LIBRARY OF PITTSBURGH
Foundation Collection
414 Wood St.
Pittsburgh 15222
(412) 281-7143

POCONO NORTHEAST
DEVELOPMENT FUND
James Pettinger Memorial Library
1151 Oak St.
Pittston 18640
(570) 655-5581

READING PUBLIC LIBRARY
100 S. 5th St.
Reading 19602
(610) 655-6355

JAMES V. BROWN LIBRARY
19 East Fourth Street
Williamsport 17701
(570) 326-0536

MARTIN LIBRARY
159 E. Market St.
York 17401
(717) 846-5300

FOUNDATION CENTER COOPERATING COLLECTIONS

RHODE ISLAND

PROVIDENCE PUBLIC LIBRARY
225 Washington St.
Providence 02906
(401) 455-8088

SOUTH CAROLINA

ANDERSON COUNTY LIBRARY
300 N. McDuffie St.
Anderson 29622
(864) 260-4500

CHARLESTON COUNTY LIBRARY
68 Calhoun St.
Charleston 29401
(843) 805-6930

SOUTH CAROLINA STATE LIBRARY
1500 Senate St.
Columbia 29211-1469
(803) 734-8666

COMMUNITY FOUNDATION OF GREATER GREENVILLE
27 Cleveland St., Suite 101
Greenville 29601
(864) 233-5925

SOUTH DAKOTA

SOUTH DAKOTA STATE LIBRARY
800 Governors Dr.
Pierre 57501-2294
(605) 773-3131
(800) 592-1841 (SD residents)

DAKOTA STATE LIBRARY
Nonprofit Grants Assistance
2505 Career Ave.
Sioux Falls 57107
(605) 782-3089

BLACK HILLS STATE UNIVERSITY
E.Y. Berry Library-Learning Center
1200 University St. Unit 9676
Spearfish 57799-9676
(605) 642-6834

TENNESSEE

UNITED WAY OF GREATER CHATTANOOGA
Center for Nonprofits
630 Market St.
Chattanooga 37402
(423) 265-0514

KNOX COUNTY PUBLIC LIBRARY
500 W. Church Ave.
Knoxville 37902
(865) 215-8751

MEMPHIS & SHELBY COUNTY PUBLIC LIBRARY
3030 Poplar Ave.
Memphis 38111
(901) 415-2734

NASHVILLE PUBLIC LIBRARY
615 Church St.
Nashville 37219
(615) 862-5800

TEXAS

AMARILLO AREA FOUNDATION
Grants Center
801 S. Filmore, Suite 700
Amarillo 79101
(806) 376-4521

HOGG FOUNDATION FOR MENTAL HEALTH
Regional Foundation Library
3001 Lake Austin Blvd., Suite 400
Austin 78703
(512) 471-5041

BEAUMONT PUBLIC LIBRARY
801 Pearl St.
Beaumont 77704-3827
(409) 838-6606

CORPUS CHRISTI PUBLIC LIBRARY
Funding Information Center
805 Comanche St.
Reference Dept.
Corpus Christi 78401
(361) 880-7000

DALLAS PUBLIC LIBRARY
Urban Information
1515 Young St.
Dallas 75201
(214) 670-1487

SOUTHWEST BORDER NONPROFIT RESOURCE CENTER
1201 W. University Dr.
Edinburgh 78539-2999
(956) 384-5920

UNIVERSITY OF TEXAS AT EL PASO
Institute for Community-Based Teaching and Learning Community Non-profit Grant Library
500 W. University, Benedict Hall, Rm. 103
El Paso 79968-0547
(915) 747-7969

FUNDING INFORMATION CENTER OF FORT WORTH
329 S. Henderson St.
Ft. Worth 76104
(817) 334-0228

HOUSTON PUBLIC LIBRARY
Bibliographic Information Center
500 McKinney
Houston 77002
(832) 393-1313

NONPROFIT MANAGEMENT AND VOLUNTEER CENTER
Laredo Public Library
1120 E. Calton Rd.
Laredo 78041
(956) 795-2400

LONGVIEW PUBLIC LIBRARY
222 W. Cotton St.
Longview 75601
(903) 237-1350

LUBBOCK AREA FOUNDATION, INC.
1655 Main St., Suite 209
Lubbock 79401
(806) 762-8061

NONPROFIT RESOURCE CENTER OF TEXAS
7404 Hwy. 90 W.
San Antonio 78212-8270
(210) 227-4333

WACO-MCLENNAN COUNTY LIBRARY
1717 Austin Ave.
Waco 76701
(254) 750-5941

NONPROFIT MANAGEMENT CENTER OF WICHITA FALLS
2301 Kell Blvd., Suite 218
Wichita Falls 76308
(940) 322-4961

UTAH

GRAND COUNTY PUBLIC LIBRARY
25 South 100 East
Moab 84532
(435) 259-5421

SALT LAKE CITY PUBLIC LIBRARY
210 E. 400 S.
Salt Lake City 84111
(801) 524-8200

VERMONT

ILSLEY PUBLIC LIBRARY
75 Main St.
Middlebury 05753
(802) 388-4095

VERMONT DEPT. OF LIBRARIES
Reference & Law Info. Services
109 State St.
Montpelier 05609
(802) 828-3261

VIRGINIA

WASHINGTON COUNTY PUBLIC LIBRARY
205 Oak Hill St.
Abingdon 24210
(276) 676-6222

HAMPTON PUBLIC LIBRARY
4207 Victoria Blvd.
Hampton 23669
(757) 727-1314

RICHMOND PUBLIC LIBRARY
Business, Science & Technology Dept.
101 E. Franklin St.
Richmond 23219
(804) 646-7223

ROANOKE CITY PUBLIC LIBRARY SYSTEM
Main Library
706 S. Jefferson
Roanoke 24016
(540) 853-2471

WASHINGTON

MID-COLUMBIA LIBRARY
1620 South Union St.
Kennewick 99338
(509) 783-7878

KING COUNTY LIBRARY SYSTEM
Redmond Regional Library
15990 NE 85th
Redmond 98052
(425) 885-1861

SEATTLE PUBLIC LIBRARY
Fundraising Resource Center
800 Pike St
Seattle 98101-3922
(206) 386-4645

SPOKANE PUBLIC LIBRARY
Funding Information Center
906 W. Main Ave.
Spokane 99201
(509) 444-5300

UNIVERSITY OF WASHINGTON TACOMA LIBRARY
1900 Commerce St.
Tacoma 98403-3100
(253) 692-4440

WENATCHEE VALLEY COLLEGE
John A. Brown Library
1300 Fifth St.
Wenatchee 98807
(509) 664-2520

WEST VIRGINIA

KANAWHA COUNTY PUBLIC LIBRARY
123 Capitol St.
Charleston 25301
(304) 343-4646

SHEPHERD COLLEGE
Ruth A. Scarborough Library
King Street
Shepherdstown 25443-3210
(304) 876-5420

WISCONSIN

UNIVERSITY OF WISCONSIN–MADISON
Memorial Library, Grants Information Center
728 State St.
Madison 53706
(608) 262-3242

MARQUETTE UNIVERSITY MEMORIAL LIBRARY
Funding Information Center
1355 W. Wisconsin Ave.
Milwaukee 53201-3141
(414) 288-1515

UNIVERSITY OF WISCONSIN— STEVENS POINT
Library—Foundation Collection
900 Reserve St.
Stevens Point 54481-3897
(715) 346-2540

WYOMING

CASPER COLLEGE
Goodstein Foundation Library
125 College Dr.
Casper 82601
(307) 268-2269

LARAMIE COUNTY COMMUNITY COLLEGE
Instructional Resource Center
1400 E. College Dr.
Cheyenne 82007-3299
(307) 778-1206

CAMPBELL COUNTY PUBLIC LIBRARY
2101 4-J Rd.
Gillette 82718
(307) 687-0115

TETON COUNTY LIBRARY
125 Virginian Ln.
Jackson 83001
(307) 733-2164

SHERIDAN COUNTY FULMER PUBLIC LIBRARY
335 West Alger St.
Sheridan 82801
(307) 674-8585

PUERTO RICO

UNIVERSIDAD DEL SAGRADO CORAZON
M.M.T. Guevara Library
Santurce 00914
(787) 728-1515

Participants in the Foundation Center's Cooperating Collections network are libraries or nonprofit information centers that provide fundraising information and other funding-related technical assistance in their communities. Cooperating Collections agree to provide free public access to a basic collection of Foundation Center publications during a regular schedule of hours, offering free funding research guidance to all visitors. Many also provide a variety of services for local nonprofit organizations, using staff or volunteers to prepare special materials, organize workshops, or conduct orientations.

A key initiative of the Foundation Center is to reach under-resourced and underserved populations throughout the United States, who are in need of useful information and training to become successful grantseekers. One of the ways we intend to accomplish this goal is by designating new Cooperating Collection libraries in regions that have the ability to serve the nonprofit communities most in need of Foundation Center resources. We are seeking proposals from qualified institutions (i.e. public, academic or special libraries) that can help us carry out this important initiative. If you are interested in establishing a funding information library in your area, or would like to learn more about the program, please contact the Coordinator of Cooperating Collections: Erika Wittlieb, The Foundation Center, 79 Fifth Avenue, New York, NY 10003 (E-mail: eaw@fdncenter.org).

DESCRIPTIVE DIRECTORY

DESCRIPTIVE DIRECTORY

ALABAMA

1
Abahac, Inc.
3850 River Run Trail
Birmingham, AL 35243-4702
Contact: Eugene B. Butler, Pres.

Established in 1988 in AL.
Donor(s): Eugene Britt Butler.
Grantmaker type: Independent foundation
Financial data (yr. ended 12/31/02): Assets,
$2,985,064 (M); gifts received, $125,000;
expenditures, $144,379; qualifying distributions,
$139,589; giving activities include $139,800 for
18 grants (high: $16,800; low: $1,000).
Purpose and activities: Giving primarily for the
environment, including streams and rivers.
Fields of interest: Environment; Legal services;
Human services; Salvation Army.
Types of support: Land acquisition.
Limitations: Applications not accepted. Giving
primarily in the southeastern U.S., with an
emphasis on AL. No grants to individuals.
Application information: Contributes only to
pre-selected organizations.
Board meeting date(s): June/July
Officers: Eugene Britt Butler, Pres.; Janice Butler
Tucker, V.P.; Robert Britt Butler, Secy.-Treas.
EIN: 570884084

2
Alabama Forestry Foundation
555 Alabama St.
Montgomery, AL 36104-4309 (334) 265-8733
Contact: Jeff Freeman, Pres.

Established in 1978.
Grantmaker type: Public charity
Financial data (yr. ended 12/31/01): Revenue,
$608,576; assets, $1,576,806; gifts received,
$500,800; expenditures, $660,884; program
services expenses, $564,480; giving activities
include $10,500 for grants to individuals.
Purpose and activities: The foundation provides
scholarships to forestry students to insure that
students receive necessary training and
education.
Fields of interest: Education; Environment,
forests; Environmental education; Environment.
Types of support: Scholarships—to individuals.
Officers and Directors:* Dean Lewis,* Chair.;
Jeff Freeman,* Pres.; Joe Rogers,* Pres.-Elect;
John McMillan,* Exec. V.P.; Dwight Harrigan,*
Secy.-Treas.; Pete Black; Mark C. Bond; Jim
Doescher; John R. Dudley, Jr.; David Helm; and
6 additional directors.

EIN: 630756161

3
AmSouth Bancorporation Foundation
c/o AmSouth Bank
P.O. Box 11426
Birmingham, AL 35202 (205) 326-5305
Contact: Ann Wells, Treas.

Established in 1997 in AL.
Donor(s): AmSouth Bancorporation.
Grantmaker type: Company-sponsored
foundation
Financial data (yr. ended 12/31/02): Assets,
$260,712 (M); gifts received, $1,512,341;
expenditures, $1,294,877; qualifying
distributions, $1,293,965; giving activities
include $1,294,127 for grants.
Purpose and activities: Provides matching gifts
to educational institutions, museums,
performing arts groups, libraries, environmental
organizations, public radio and television,
nonprofit hospitals, and health and welfare
organizations.
Fields of interest: Arts; Education; Environment;
Health care; Human services.
Types of support: Employee matching gifts.
Limitations: Giving primarily in AL, FL, GA, and
TN. No support for religious organizations for
religious purposes, alumni groups, or cultural or
social events.
Application information: Application form
required.
Deadline(s): 30 days prior to payment
schedule: Mar. 1, June 1, Sept. 1, and Dec.
1
Officers and Directors:* Stephen A. Yoder,*
Pres.; Douglas J. Jackson,* V.P.; Dale M. Herbert,
Secy.; Ann E. Wells, Treas.; Sloan D. Gibson IV;
C. Dowd Ritter.
Trustee: AmSouth Bank.
EIN: 631144265

4
Clyde B. Anderson Family Foundation
c/o Clyde B. Anderson
P.O. Box 19768
Birmingham, AL 35219

Established in 1996 in AL.
Donor(s): Clyde B. Anderson.
Grantmaker type: Independent foundation
Financial data (yr. ended 12/31/02): Assets,
$454,934 (M); gifts received, $275,784;
expenditures, $117,371; qualifying distributions,
$113,892; giving activities include $109,000 for
24 grants (high: $25,000; low: $100).
Fields of interest: Arts; Education;
Animals/wildlife; Health care; Health

organizations, association; Salvation Army;
Federated giving programs.
Limitations: Applications not accepted. Giving
primarily in Birmingham, AL. No grants to
individuals.
Application information: Contributes only to
pre-selected organizations.
Directors: Clyde B. Anderson; Lisa S. Anderson;
Terry C. Anderson.
EIN: 721368331

5
George W. Barber, Jr. Foundation
27 Inverness Center Pkwy.
Birmingham, AL 35242

Established in 1986 in AL.
Donor(s): George W. Barber, Jr.
Grantmaker type: Independent foundation
Financial data (yr. ended 12/31/01): Assets,
$6,593,339 (M); expenditures, $2,204,242;
qualifying distributions, $2,177,476; giving
activities include $2,191,000 for 11 grants (high:
$2,125,000; low: $1,000).
Purpose and activities: Giving primarily to a
museum; some giving for health care and
children's services.
Fields of interest: Museums; Arts; Education;
Natural resources; Environment;
Animals/wildlife, preservation/protection;
Health care; Health organizations, association;
Children/youth, services.
Limitations: Applications not accepted. Giving
primarily in AL. No grants to individuals.
Application information: Contributes only to
pre-selected organizations.
Officers: George W. Barber, Jr., Pres.; Russell M.
Cunningham III, Secy.; B. Austin Cunningham,
Treas.
EIN: 630941684

6
The Harry B. & Jane H. Brock Foundation
(formerly The Brock Foundation)
P.O. Box 11643
Birmingham, AL 35202 (205) 939-0236
Contact: Harry B. Brock, Jr., Pres.

Established in 1985 in AL.
Donor(s): Harry B. Brock, Jr.
Grantmaker type: Independent foundation
Financial data (yr. ended 12/31/02): Assets,
$6,797,145 (M); expenditures, $382,416;
qualifying distributions, $377,245; giving
activities include $378,508 for 41 grants (high:
$51,119; low: $400; average: $1,000–$10,000).
Purpose and activities: Primary areas of interest
include community development, community

funds, social services, and cancer treatment and research.
Fields of interest: Higher education; Education; Natural resources; Environment; Cancer; Cancer research; Recreation; Children/youth, services; Community development; Federated giving programs; Social sciences; General charitable giving.
Types of support: General/operating support; Annual campaigns; Capital campaigns; Endowments; Research.
Limitations: Giving primarily in AL. No grants to individuals.
Publications: Application guidelines.
Application information: Application form not required.
   Initial approach: Letter
   Copies of proposal: 7
   Deadline(s): Nov. 1
   Board meeting date(s): 3rd Tues. in Dec.
Officers and Directors:* Harry B. Brock, Jr.,* Pres.; Jane H. Brock,* V.P.; Carolyn F. Robertson,* Secy.; Harry B. Brock III; Stanley M. Brock; Barrett B. MacKay.
Number of staff: None.
EIN: 630926012

7
The Community Foundation of Greater Birmingham ▼
(formerly The Greater Birmingham Foundation)
2100 First Ave. N., Ste. 700
Birmingham, AL 35203 (205) 328-8641
Contact: Kate Nielsen, Pres.
FAX: (205) 328-6576; E-mail: info@foundationbirmingham.org; URL: http://www.foundationbirmingham.org

Established in 1959 in AL by resolution and declaration of trust; corporate side established in 1997.
Grantmaker type: Community foundation
Financial data (yr. ended 12/31/02): Assets, $118,000,000 (M); gifts received, $13,100,000; expenditures, $12,500,000; giving activities include $11,700,000 for 1,200 grants (high: $125,000; low: $75).
Purpose and activities: To make life better in the greater Birmingham, Alabama, area, by connecting caring people and key resources with community needs, today and tomorrow.
Fields of interest: Arts; Education; Environment; Health care; Human services; Neighborhood centers; Community development; Public affairs.
Types of support: Capital campaigns; Building/renovation; Equipment; Program development; Publication; Seed money; Curriculum development; Matching/challenge support.
Limitations: Giving from unrestricted and field-of-interest funds limited to Blount, Jefferson, Shelby, St. Clair, and Walker counties of AL. No support for religious or political purposes from unrestricted and field-of-interest funds. No grants to individuals or for scholarships, endowment funds, operating budgets, deficit reduction, national fundraising drives, conference or seminar expenses, benefits tickets, or replacement of government funding cuts.
Publications: Application guidelines, Annual report, Financial statement, Grants list, Informational brochure, Newsletter.

Application information: Please see foundation's Web site for application instructions. Agencies new to the foundation must attend an overview session prior to submitting a grant proposal. Application form not required.
   Initial approach: Letter
   Copies of proposal: 3
   Deadline(s): Check foundation's Web site; currently, Mar. 15 and Sept. 15
   Board meeting date(s): Biannually (May and Nov.) for distribution of unrestricted funds; other meetings as needed
   Final notification: June and Dec.
Officers: Cameron M. Vowell, Ph.D., Chair.; Jeffrey H. Cohn, M.D., Vice-Chair.; Kate Nielsen, Pres.
Directors: Kirkwood R. Bolton; Ralph D. Cook; Edward M. Friend III; Susan N. Haskell; Ted C. Kennedy; Thomas H. Lowder; Margaret M. Porter; Van L. Richey; Carole W. Samuelson, M.D.; William E. Smith, Jr.; Odessa Woolfolk.
Number of staff: 8 full-time professional; 3 part-time professional; 1 full-time support; 1 part-time support.
EIN: 636019864
Recent environmental and animal welfare grants:
7-1 Alabama Animal Adoption Society, Birmingham, AL, $21,000. 2001.
7-2 Alabama Environmental Council, Birmingham, AL, $10,750. 2001.
7-3 Alabama Wildlife Rehabilitation Center, Birmingham, AL, $19,050. 2001.
7-4 Aldridge Gardens, Hoover, AL, $50,000. For capital campaign to complete first phase of building and creating endowment. 2001.
7-5 Aldridge Gardens, Hoover, AL, $15,000. 2001.
7-6 Birmingham Botanical Society, Birmingham, AL, $27,500. 2001.
7-7 Cahaba River Society, Birmingham, AL, $10,550. 2001.
7-8 Emergency Animal Rescue Service (TEARS), Birmingham, AL, $21,500. 2001.
7-9 Friends of Cats and Dogs Foundation, Birmingham, AL, $20,500. 2001.
7-10 Humane Society of Greater Birmingham, Birmingham, AL, $20,550. 2001.
7-11 Humane Society of Greater Birmingham, Birmingham, AL, $15,000. To continue cruelty investigation department and for First Strike Seminar. 2001.
7-12 Humane Society of Shelby County, Columbiana, AL, $45,500. 2001.
7-13 Humane Society, Walker County, Jasper, AL, $25,000. For relocation costs and building of crematorium. 2001.
7-14 Nature Conservancy, Birmingham, AL, $24,850. 2001.
7-15 Southern Environmental Law Center, Charlottesville, VA, $51,650. 2001.

8
Community Foundation of Southeast Alabama
(formerly Wiregrass Community Foundation)
179 Honeysuckle Rd., Ste. 5
P.O. Box 1422
Dothan, AL 36302-1422 (334) 671-1059
FAX: (334) 793-0627; URL: http://www.cfsea.org

Established in 1995 in AL.

Grantmaker type: Community foundation
Financial data (yr. ended 12/31/02): Assets, $1,205,285 (M); gifts received, $837,948; expenditures, $1,840,574; giving activities include $1,667,755 for grants.
Purpose and activities: The mission of the Community Foundation of Southeast Alabama is to identify and connect caring people and their resources with community needs, today and tomorrow. The foundation administers a donor-advised fund.
Fields of interest: Arts; Education; Environment; Health care; Human services; Economic development; Religion.
Limitations: Giving limited to the five-county Wiregrass region of Henry, Houston, Coffee, Dale and Geneva counties, AL. No grants to individuals.
Officers and Trustees:* Bill Flowers,* Chair. and Treas.; Barbara Everett,* Vice-Chair. and Secy.; David C. Jamison, Pres.
Number of staff: 2 part-time professional; 2 part-time support.
EIN: 631126660

9
The G. Mack and Nancy R. Dove Foundation
(formerly The Dove Foundation)
1751 Kinsey Rd.
Dothan, AL 36302
Contact: G. Mack Dove, Pres.
Application address: P.O. Box 6827, Dothan, AL 36302, tel.: (205) 793-2284

Established in 1982 in AL.
Donor(s): G. Mack Dove, Nancy R. Dove, Reid B. Dove.
Grantmaker type: Independent foundation
Financial data (yr. ended 12/31/02): Assets, $851,449 (M); expenditures, $180,784; qualifying distributions, $180,784; giving activities include $180,784 for 18 grants (high: $75,000; low: $100).
Purpose and activities: Giving for educational and religious purposes.
Fields of interest: Arts; Education; Zoos/zoological societies; Speech/hearing centers; Health organizations, association; Youth development; American Red Cross; Children/youth, services; Christian agencies & churches.
Types of support: General/operating support; Capital campaigns.
Limitations: Giving primarily in AL. No grants to individuals.
Application information: Application form required.
   Deadline(s): None
Officers: G. Mack Dove, Pres.; Nancy R. Dove, V.P.; Charles E. Coggins, Treas.
EIN: 630836253

10
Founders Charitable Foundation, Inc.
c/o Kenneth H. Polk
2140 11th Ave. S., Ste. 400
Birmingham, AL 35205

Established in 2001 in AL.

Donor(s): Michael B. Patton, Timothy R. Smith, Carl O. Black, Marilyn S. Black, William B. Israel.
Grantmaker type: Independent foundation
Financial data (yr. ended 12/31/02): Assets, $844,199 (M); gifts received, $243,405; expenditures, $148,775; qualifying distributions, $140,442; giving activities include $140,600 for 18 grants (high: $76,000; low: $100).
Fields of interest: Environment; Health organizations, association; Human services; Children/youth, services; Christian agencies & churches.
Application information: Application form required.
  Initial approach: Letter
  Deadline(s): None
Directors: William K. Nicrosi II; Kenneth H. Polk.
EIN: 631263667

11
The Hearin-Chandler Foundation
(formerly The Chandler Foundation)
P.O. Box 81328
Mobile, AL 36689   (251) 342-3080
Contact: Luis Williams, Tr.

Established in 1963 in AL.
Donor(s): Ralph B. Chandler.‡
Grantmaker type: Independent foundation
Financial data (yr. ended 12/31/02): Assets, $18,752,715 (M); expenditures, $1,171,986; qualifying distributions, $999,474; giving activities include $962,135 for 18 grants (high: $220,000; low: $5,000).
Purpose and activities: Giving primarily to cultural institutions; giving also for education, the environment, and human services.
Fields of interest: Museums; Performing arts; Arts; Higher education; Libraries (public); Botanical gardens; Environment, beautification programs; Human services; Community development; Christian agencies & churches; Women.
Types of support: Building/renovation.
Limitations: Giving primarily in Mobile County, AL. No grants to individuals.
Application information:
  Initial approach: Letter
  Deadline(s): Nov. 30
Trustee: Luis Williams.
EIN: 636075470

12
The Mary Josephine Larkins Charitable Foundation
2862 Dauphin St.
Mobile, AL 36606

Established in 1993 in AL.
Grantmaker type: Independent foundation
Financial data (yr. ended 12/31/02): Assets, $1,845,761 (M); expenditures, $181,923; qualifying distributions, $125,405; giving activities include $125,405 for 10 grants (high: $34,000; low: $2,905).
Purpose and activities: Giving primarily for the environment and human services.
Fields of interest: Ballet; Libraries (public); Horticulture/garden clubs; Housing/shelter, development; Housing/shelter, public housing;

Boys & girls clubs; Girl scouts; Youth development, services; Day care; Human services, personal services.
Limitations: Applications not accepted. Giving primarily in AL. No grants to individuals.
Application information: Contributes only to pre-selected organizations.
Trustees: Ray Z. Cohn; Virginia Guy; Judy A. Shirk.
EIN: 631094539

13
Linn-Henley Charitable Trust
c/o Compass Bank, Asset Mgmt. Gp.
P.O. Box 10566
Birmingham, AL 35296   (205) 297-6713
Contact: Phil Rollings

Trust established in 1965 in AL.
Donor(s): Walter E. Henley.‡
Grantmaker type: Independent foundation
Financial data (yr. ended 03/31/02): Assets, $6,922,534 (M); expenditures, $435,825; qualifying distributions, $342,803; giving activities include $345,000 for 16 grants (high: $150,000; low: $1,200).
Purpose and activities: Giving primarily for higher education; support also for libraries, cultural programs, and community development.
Fields of interest: Theater; Arts; Elementary school/education; Libraries (public); Education; Zoos/zoological societies; Parks/playgrounds; Community development; Federated giving programs.
Types of support: Capital campaigns; Research; Matching/challenge support.
Limitations: Giving limited to Jefferson County, AL.
Application information:
  Initial approach: Letter
  Deadline(s): None
Trustees: Arthur C. Henley; Compass Bank.
EIN: 636051833

14
McIntosh Area Betterment Association, Inc.
P.O. Box 28
McIntosh, AL 36553-0028

Established in 1977 in AL.
Donor(s): CIBA-GEIGY Corp., Olin Corp.
Grantmaker type: Independent foundation
Financial data (yr. ended 12/31/02): Assets, $45,419 (M); gifts received, $107,500; expenditures, $90,030; qualifying distributions, $90,000; giving activities include $89,500 for 5 grants (high: $30,000; low: $10,000).
Purpose and activities: Support limited to the town of McIntosh, Alabama, for health, educational, historical, recreational, environmental and cultural activities.
Fields of interest: Arts; Education; Environment; Youth, services; Federated giving programs; Government/public administration; Christian agencies & churches.
Limitations: Giving limited to McIntosh, AL.
Application information: Application form not required.
  Initial approach: Proposal
  Deadline(s): None

Officers: J.J. McFalls, Pres.; Alan L. Hefferman, Secy.-Treas.
EIN: 630725021

15
Doris M. Schuler Foundation
200 Cahaba Park Cir., Ste. 100
Birmingham, AL 35242

Established in 1993 in AL.
Grantmaker type: Independent foundation
Financial data (yr. ended 12/31/02): Assets, $4,890,116 (M); expenditures, $275,358; qualifying distributions, $273,874; giving activities include $266,500 for 21 grants (high: $35,100; low: $100).
Fields of interest: Arts; Education; Animal welfare; Health organizations, association; Medical research, institute; Human services; Protestant agencies & churches.
Limitations: Applications not accepted. Giving primarily in AL. No grants to individuals.
Application information: Contributes only to pre-selected organizations.
Trustees: Jerry D. Hart; William M. Schuler; Mary Pride Winkenwerder.
EIN: 631090628

16
Strain Foundation
4412 Cornith Dr.
Birmingham, AL 35213
Contact: Juanelle D. Strain, Dir.

Established around 1994.
Donor(s): John T. Strain, Juanelle D. Strain.
Grantmaker type: Independent foundation
Financial data (yr. ended 10/31/02): Assets, $7,512,997 (M); expenditures, $349,270; qualifying distributions, $327,000; giving activities include $327,000 for 24 grants (high: $20,000; low: $500).
Purpose and activities: Giving for neurological research, relief and human services, and medical services.
Fields of interest: Elementary school/education; Environment; Health organizations, association; Neuroscience; Housing/shelter; American Red Cross; Protestant agencies & churches.
Limitations: Giving primarily in Birmingham, AL. No grants to individuals.
Application information:
  Initial approach: Letter
  Deadline(s): None
Directors: Janet Strain McDonald; John T. Strain; Juanelle D. Strain; Julia Strain.
EIN: 631108283

17
The Viro Fund
c/o Regions Bank, Trust Dept.
P.O. Box 2450
Montgomery, AL 36102-2450

Established in 1983 in AL.
Donor(s): Robert S. Weil.
Grantmaker type: Independent foundation
Financial data (yr. ended 12/31/02): Assets, $5,121,139 (M); expenditures, $290,641; qualifying distributions, $286,895; giving

activities include $285,850 for 33 grants (high: $30,000; low: $500).
Purpose and activities: Giving for the arts, education, hospitals, youth services, and animal welfare.
Fields of interest: Arts; Higher education; Education; Animal welfare; Hospitals (general); Youth development, centers/clubs; Human services; Jewish agencies & temples.
Limitations: Applications not accepted. Giving primarily in AL. No grants to individuals.
Application information: Contributes only to pre-selected organizations.
Trustee: Regions Bank.
Advisory Committee: Robert S. Weil; Mrs. Robert S. Weil.
EIN: 630835563

18
Vulcan Materials Company Foundation ▼
P.O. Box 385014
Birmingham, AL   35238-5014   (205) 298-3229
Contact: Mary S. Russom, Secy.-Treas.
E-mail: giving@vmcmail.com

Established in 1987 in AL.
Donor(s): Vulcan Materials Co.
Grantmaker type: Company-sponsored foundation
Financial data (yr. ended 11/30/02): Assets, $8,233,281 (M); gifts received, $351,353; expenditures, $2,531,393; qualifying distributions, $2,531,393; giving activities include $2,510,018 for 696 grants (high: $141,000; low: $50; average: $500–$10,000).
Purpose and activities: Support for educational institutions, and environmental organizations.
Fields of interest: Education, association; Early childhood education; Child development, education; Elementary school/education; Secondary school/education; Higher education; Adult/continuing education; Adult education—literacy, basic skills & GED; Libraries/library science; Reading; Education; Environment; Children/youth, services; Race/intergroup relations; Community development.
Types of support: General/operating support; Continuing support; Annual campaigns; Capital campaigns; Endowments; Program development; Seed money; Scholarship funds; Employee-related scholarships; In-kind gifts; Matching/challenge support.
Limitations: Giving primarily in regions where major company facilities are located: AL, AR, AZ, CA, FL, GA, IA, IL, IN, KS, KY, LA, MS, NC, NM, SC, TN, TX, and WI. No support for political or religious organizations, or organizations with discriminatory practices. No grants to individuals (except for employee-related scholarships).
Publications: Annual report (including application guidelines).
Application information: Application form not required.
Initial approach: 1- or 2-page letter
Copies of proposal: 1
Deadline(s): None
Board meeting date(s): Quarterly
Officers and Trustees:* D.M. James,* Chair.; W.F. Denson III,* Pres.; J.C. Phillips, V.P.; Mary S. Russom, Secy.-Treas.; G.M. Badgett III; J.W. Houston; B.C. Rosenwald; M.E. Tomkins.

Number of staff: 1 full-time professional; 1 part-time support.
EIN: 630971859

19
Walker Area Community Foundation
P.O. Box 171
Jasper, AL   35502-0171   (205) 302-0001
Contact: Carol Savage, Exec. Dir.
FAX: (205) 302-0424; E-mail: wacf@bellsouth.net; URL: http://www.walkercommunityfoundation.org/

Established in 1995 from a portion of sale of local hospital.
Grantmaker type: Community foundation
Financial data (yr. ended 12/31/02): Assets, $7,261,972 (M); gifts received, $211,539; expenditures, $370,000; giving activities include $225,657 for 50 grants (high: $25,000; low: $1,160; average: $3,000–$5,000).
Purpose and activities: The foundation provides grants to promote the community health and social welfare of citizens within the community of Walker County, Alabama. Grants may be made in the following areas: arts and humanities, children and youth, education, elder care, the environment, health and medicine, recreation, and social welfare. The foundation administers a donor-advised fund.
Fields of interest: Arts; Education; Environment; Health care; Recreation; Human services; Children/youth, services; Aging, centers/services; Community development.
Types of support: General/operating support; Management development; Capital campaigns; Building/renovation; Equipment; Program development; Curriculum development; Technical assistance; Matching/challenge support.
Limitations: Giving limited to Walker County, AL. No support for religious organizations for religious purposes. No grants to individuals, or for endowments.
Publications: Application guidelines, Annual report.
Application information: See foundation Web site for complete application guidelines and requirements. Application form required.
Copies of proposal: 1
Deadline(s): Apr. 1 and Oct. 1
Board meeting date(s): Distribution Committee meets May and Nov.
Final notification: Within 2 weeks of board meetings
Officers and Directors:* John T. Oliver, Jr.,* Pres.; J. George Mitnick,* V.P.; Pat Willingham,* Secy.-Treas.; Carol Savage, Exec. Dir.; Jack G. Allen; E.A. "Larry" Drummond; Steven "Chip" Globetti; Cristy S. Moody; Russell B. Robertson; Barbara Thorne; W. Haig Wright II.
Number of staff: 1 full-time professional; 1 part-time professional.
EIN: 631154984

20
Susan Mott Webb Charitable Trust
c/o AmSouth Bank
P.O. Box 11426
Birmingham, AL   35202   (205) 326-5382
Contact: Carla B. Gale, V.P., AmSouth Bank
E-mail: cgale@amsouth.com

Established in 1978 in AL.
Donor(s): Susan Mott Webb.‡
Grantmaker type: Independent foundation
Financial data (yr. ended 12/31/02): Assets, $15,073,834 (M); expenditures, $887,531; qualifying distributions, $803,014; giving activities include $797,200 for grants (average: $2,000–$100,000).
Purpose and activities: Emphasis on supporting charitable organizations in the Birmingham, AL, area only.
Fields of interest: Arts; Education; Animals/wildlife; Health care; Human services; Youth, services; Urban/community development; Christian agencies & churches; General charitable giving; Homeless.
Types of support: General/operating support; Continuing support; Annual campaigns; Capital campaigns; Building/renovation; Equipment; Endowments; Emergency funds; Program development; Publication; Curriculum development; Internship funds; Technical assistance.
Limitations: Giving limited to the greater Birmingham, AL, area. No grants to individuals, or for scholarships or fellowships; no loans.
Publications: Application guidelines.
Application information: Call to obtain guidelines. Application form not required.
Initial approach: Letter or proposal
Copies of proposal: 5
Deadline(s): Apr. 1 and Oct. 1
Board meeting date(s): June and Dec.
Final notification: June and Dec.
Trustees: Stewart Dansby; Suzanne Dansby Phelps; Charles B. Webb, Jr.; AmSouth Bank.
Number of staff: None.
EIN: 636112593

21
Whatley Charitable Trust
c/o Compass Bank, Asset Mgmt. Group
P.O. Box 10566
Birmingham, AL   35296   (205) 297-6947
Contact: Janet Ball

Established in 1997 in AL.
Donor(s): George B. Whatley, Willa Mae Whatley.
Grantmaker type: Independent foundation
Financial data (yr. ended 06/30/02): Assets, $1,154,851 (M); expenditures, $216,136; qualifying distributions, $200,659; giving activities include $200,000 for 13 grants (high: $25,000; low: $5,000).
Purpose and activities: Giving primarily for human services, conservation, and the arts.
Fields of interest: Arts; Natural resources; Family planning; End of life care; Human services.
Limitations: Giving on a national basis. No grants to individuals, or political activities.
Application information:
Initial approach: Letter
Deadline(s): None
Trustee: Compass Bank.

EIN: 726185747

ALASKA

22
Alaska Conservation Foundation
441 W. 5th Ave., Ste. 402
Anchorage, AK 99501-2340 (907) 276-1917
Contact: Deborah L. Williams, Exec. Dir.
FAX: (907) 274-4145; E-mail: acfinfo@akcf.org;
URL: http://www.akcf.org

Established in 1980 in AK.
Grantmaker type: Community foundation
Financial data (yr. ended 06/30/03): Assets,
$5,867,687 (M); gifts received, $4,038,842;
expenditures, $5,292,445; giving activities
include $2,178,906 for grants and $2,413,469
for foundation-administered programs.
Purpose and activities: Awards grants to protect
the integrity of Alaskan ecosystems and promote
sustainable livelihoods among Alaskan
communities and peoples; awards to honor
outstanding environmental volunteer activists
and professionals, and to sustain community
development.
Fields of interest: Environment, research;
Natural resources; Environmental education;
Environment; Animals/wildlife,
preservation/protection; Animals/wildlife,
sanctuaries; Economic development;
Community development; Social sciences,
public policy; Public affairs, information
services.
Types of support: General/operating support;
Continuing support; Equipment; Emergency
funds; Program development;
Conferences/seminars; Publication; Internship
funds; Technical assistance; Consulting services;
Program evaluation; Grants to individuals;
Scholarships—to individuals;
Matching/challenge support.
Limitations: Giving primarily in AK. No grants
for annual campaigns, deficit financing, building
funds, land acquisition, renovation projects,
general or special endowments, or exchange
programs; no student loans.
Publications: Application guidelines, Annual
report, Financial statement, Grants list,
Informational brochure, Newsletter, Program
policy statement.
Application information: Request grant
guidelines. Application form required.
  Initial approach: Letter or telephone
  Copies of proposal: 1
  Deadline(s): Varies
  Board meeting date(s): Feb., May, and Sept.
  Final notification: 2 weeks after board meeting
Officers and Trustees:* Ken Leghorn,* Chair.;
Bill Lazar,* Vice-Chair.; Eric Myers,* Secy.; Stacy
Studebaker,* Secy.; Sam Skaggs,* Treas.; David
Rockefeller, Jr., Advisor; Jonathan Blattmachr,
Counsel; Thomas A. Barron; Elvin Brudie;
Robert Bundy; Rick Caulfield; Wallace Cole;
April Crosby; Bert Fingerhut; Robert Glenn
Ketchum; Doug McConnell; Nina Heyano; Scott
Nathan; Vernita Nerdman; Helen Nienhueser;
Susan Cohn Schultz; John Siske; Ted Smith.

Number of staff: 19 full-time professional; 6
part-time professional; 2 full-time support; 1
part-time support.
EIN: 920061466

23
Sealaska Heritage Foundation
1 Sealaska Plz., Ste. 201
Juneau, AK 99801-1249 (907) 463-4844
Contact: Rosita Worl, Pres.
FAX: (907) 586-9293; URL: http://
www.sealaskaheritage.org

Established in 1980 in AK.
Donor(s): Sealaska Corp.
Grantmaker type: Public charity
Financial data (yr. ended 12/31/01): Revenue,
$1,750,334; assets, $1,009,775 (M); gifts
received, $1,710,771; expenditures,
$1,867,461; program services expenses,
$1,644,053; giving activities include $770,566
for grants to individuals.
Purpose and activities: The foundation seeks to
harness all available resources to preserve,
promote, and maintain the cultures and heritage
of the Tlingit, Haida, and Tsimshian people for
the benefit of present and future generations,
and the public; to encourage and support
cultural heritage cooperation among all tribes
and organizations; to encourage and foster the
education of Native Americans so that the
public may benefit from their talents; and to
cooperate with other heritage programs.
Fields of interest: Arts education; Arts; Business
school/education; Engineering
school/education; Environment,
management/technical aid; Natural resources;
International affairs, goodwill promotion;
Race/intergroup relations; Native
Americans/American Indians.
Types of support: Grants to individuals;
Scholarships—to individuals.
Limitations: Giving primarily in AK, although
half of giving is in lower 48 states.
Publications: Informational brochure,
Newsletter.
Application information: Application form
required.
  Initial approach: Letter or telephone
  Deadline(s): Mar. 1
Officer and Directors:* Walter A. Soboleff,
Ph.D.,* Chair.; Marlene A. Johnson,*
Vice-Chair.; Sandy Samaniego,* C.O.O. and
Devel.; Rosita Worl,* Pres.; Patrick Anderson,*
Secy.; Jayne Dangeli; Clarence Jackson, Sr.; Ethel
Lund; Marge Young.
EIN: 920081844

ARIZONA

24
A.P.S. Foundation, Inc.
P.O. Box 53999, MS 9557
Phoenix, AZ 85072-3999
Contact: Terry DeValle, Contribs. Coord.

Established in 1981 in AZ.
Donor(s): Arizona Public Service Co.

Grantmaker type: Company-sponsored
foundation
Financial data (yr. ended 12/31/02): Assets,
$22,981,752 (M); expenditures, $1,758,082;
qualifying distributions, $1,701,313; giving
activities include $1,712,968 for 230 grants
(high: $60,000; low: $63).
Purpose and activities: Giving primarily to the
arts, education, the environment, health, youth
services, minorities, and community
improvement.
Fields of interest: Arts; Education; Environment;
Hospitals (general); Children/youth, services;
Civil rights, minorities; Community
development; Economically disadvantaged.
Types of support: General/operating support;
Capital campaigns; Matching/challenge support.
Limitations: Applications not accepted. Giving
primarily in AZ. No grants to individuals.
Application information: Contributes only to
pre-selected organizations.
Officers and Directors:* William J. Post,* Pres.;
Jack E. Davis,* V.P.; Armando B. Flores,* V.P.;
James M. Levine,* V.P.; Nancy C. Loftin,*
Secy.-Treas.
Number of staff: 2 full-time professional; 1
part-time support.
EIN: 953735903

25
America West Airlines, Inc. Corporate
Giving Program
c/o Contribs. Comm.
4000 E. Sky Harbor Blvd.
Phoenix, AZ 85034
FAX: (480) 693-3715; URL: http://
www.americawest.com/aboutawa/community/
aa_mission.htm

Grantmaker type: Corporate giving program
Purpose and activities: As a complement to its
foundation, America West also makes charitable
contributions to nonprofit organizations directly.
Support is given primarily in Arizona and
Nevada.
Fields of interest: Arts; Education; Environment;
Medical care, in-patient care; Health care;
Human services; Public affairs.
Types of support: General/operating support;
Employee volunteer services; Sponsorships;
Donated products.
Limitations: Giving primarily in AZ and NV. No
support for religious, political, labor, fraternal, or
sports organizations, government-supported
organizations (over 50 percent of budget),
research organizations, or schools. No grants for
building or renovation or capital campaigns.
Application information: Proposals should be
submitted using organization letterhead. Support
is limited to 1 contribution per organization
during any given year. Telephone calls are not
encouraged. A contributions committee reviews
all requests. Application form not required.
  Initial approach: Mail or fax proposal to
   headquarters
  Copies of proposal: 1
  Deadline(s): 6 to 8 weeks prior to need
  Board meeting date(s): Weekly
  Final notification: 1 month

26
American Foundation

(formerly American Support Foundation)
4518 N. 32nd St.
Phoenix, AZ   85018-3303   (602) 955-4770
Contact: Dina Pelletier, Dir., Comm.
FAX: (602) 955-4707; E-mail:
grantinfo@americanfoundation.org; URL: http://
www.americanfoundation.org/grant_requests/

Founded in 1982 in AZ as the Interstate
Community Foundation.
Grantmaker type: Public charity
Financial data (yr. ended 12/31/01): Revenue,
$11,637; assets, $519,901 (M); gifts received,
$120; expenditures, $3,804; program services
expenses, $500; giving activities include $500
for 1 grant.
Purpose and activities: The foundation's
emphasis is on education, health, environmental
issues, religion, community development, and
the arts and sciences.
Fields of interest: Arts; Education; Environment;
Health care; Community development;
Philanthropy/voluntarism, information services;
Science; Religion.
Types of support: General/operating support;
Continuing support; Building/renovation;
Equipment; Land acquisition; Emergency funds;
Program development; Curriculum
development; Scholarship funds;
Matching/challenge support.
Limitations: Giving on a national basis. No
support for non 501(c)(3), 509(a)(1), or 509(a)(2)
organizations or for governmental or
quasi-governmental entities. No grants to
individuals or for endowment funds.
Publications: Application guidelines, Financial
statement, Grants list, Informational brochure.
Application information: See Web site for
further information. Application form required.
   Initial approach: E-mail for grant application
      information
   Copies of proposal: 1
   Deadline(s): Sept. 1
   Board meeting date(s): 4th Mon. of each
      month
   Final notification: Dec. or Jan.
Officers and Directors:* Benson L. Schaub,*
Pres. and C.E.O.; Benson S. Schaub, C.O.O.;
John F. Goodson; Robert Miller.
Number of staff: 14 full-time professional; 2
part-time professional.
EIN: 942832530

27
APS Corporate Giving Program

P.O. Box 53999, M.S. 8510
Phoenix, AZ   85072-3999   (602) 250-2257
Contact: Sandie Jones
Additional tel.: (602) 250-2259

Grantmaker type: Corporate giving program
Purpose and activities: As a complement to its
foundation, APS also makes charitable
contributions to nonprofit organizations directly.
Support is given primarily in Arizona and
northwestern New Mexico.
Fields of interest: Arts; Education; Environment;
Human services; Community development.
Types of support: General/operating support;
Capital campaigns; Employee volunteer
services; Employee matching gifts; In-kind gifts.

Limitations: Giving primarily in AZ and
northwestern NM. No support for religious,
political, or fraternal organizations. No grants to
individuals, or for travel or legislative or
lobbying efforts.
Publications: Corporate giving report (including
application guidelines).
Application information: The Community
Relations Department handles giving. The
company has a staff that only handles
contributions. Application form not required.
   Initial approach: Proposal to headquarters
   Copies of proposal: 1
   Deadline(s): None
   Final notification: 1 to 2 months
Number of staff: 2 full-time professional.

28
Arizona Association of Conservation
Districts, Inc.

3003 N. Central Ave., Ste. 800
Phoenix, AZ   85012   (602) 280-8803
Contact: Macario Herrera, Exec. Dir.
FAX: (602) 280-8779; E-mail:
aacd@az.nrcs.usda.gov; URL: http://
www.aacdonline.com

Established in 1944 in AZ as an independent
foundation.
Grantmaker type: Public charity
Financial data (yr. ended 12/31/01): Revenue,
$187,983; assets, $26,978 (M); gifts received,
$81,300; expenditures, $187,053; program
services expenses, $147,018; giving activities
include $6,477 for 8 grants.
Purpose and activities: The organization
identifies natural resource problems and
opportunities and formulates working plans to
address them.
Fields of interest: Natural resources;
Environment, water resources; Environment,
land resources.
Officers and Directors:* Johnny LaVin,* Pres.;
Frank Martinez,* 1st V.P.; Arnie Schlittenhart,*
2nd V.P.; Thomas Begay,* Secy.; Jody Latimer,*
Treas.; Macario Herrera, Exec. Dir.; Hoskie
Bryant; Herb Bundy; and 7 additional directors.
EIN: 860695025

29
Arizona Community Foundation ▼

2122 E. Highland Ave., Ste. 400
Phoenix, AZ   85016   (602) 381-1400
Contact: Sandy Doubleday, V.P., Mktg. and
Comm.
Additional tel.: (800) 222-8221; FAX: (602)
381-1575; E-mail:
rmayberry@azfoundation.com; URL: http://
www.azfoundation.org

Incorporated in 1978 in AZ.
Donor(s): L. Dilatush, Bert A. Getz, G.R.
Herberger, R. Kieckhefer, Newton Rosenzweig.
Grantmaker type: Community foundation
Financial data (yr. ended 12/31/02): Assets,
$315,133,904 (M); gifts received, $31,357,769;
expenditures, $24,852,528; giving activities
include $19,095,155 for grants.
Purpose and activities: Support for both
individual community and broader statewide
needs in a wide range of areas including the arts
and culture, public education, the environment,

youth development, community building, and
health and human services.
Fields of interest: Architecture; Performing arts;
Arts; Early childhood education; Child
development, education; Higher education;
Adult education—literacy, basic skills & GED;
Reading; Education; Natural resources;
Environment; Health care; Substance abuse,
services; Mental health/crisis services; Health
organizations, association; AIDS; AIDS research;
Legal services; Employment; Housing/shelter,
development; Human services; Children/youth,
services; Child development, services; Family
services; Homeless, human services; Rural
development; Community development;
Engineering/technology; Science;
Government/public administration; Public
affairs; Minorities; Disabled; Economically
disadvantaged; Homeless.
Types of support: General/operating support;
Continuing support; Building/renovation;
Equipment; Emergency funds; Program
development; Publication; Seed money;
Scholarship funds; Research; Technical
assistance; Matching/challenge support.
Limitations: Giving limited to AZ. No support
for religious organizations for religious purposes.
No grants to individuals (except for
scholarships), travel to or support of
conferences, fundraising campaigns and
expenses, or capital grants; generally, no loans.
Publications: Application guidelines, Annual
report, Financial statement, Informational
brochure, Newsletter, Program policy statement.
Application information: Application form
required.
   Initial approach: Letter requesting guidelines
   Copies of proposal: 15
   Deadline(s): Apr. 1 and Oct. 1
   Board meeting date(s): Semi-annually
   Final notification: 60 days
Officers and Directors:* Robert Delgado,*
Chair.; Gerald Bisgrove, Vice-Chair.; Mark
Klein,* Vice-Chair. and Treas.; Hamilton McRae
III,* Vice-Chair.; Stephen D. Mittenthal,* C.E.O.
and Pres.; Deborah Whitehurst, Exec. V.P., Ext.
Affairs; Bruce Astrein, Sr. V.P., Progs.; Sharon
Landis, Sr. V.P., Finance and Admin.; Sandy
Doubleday, V.P., Mktg. and Comm.; Kimberly C.
Kur, J.D., V.P., Professional Services; Joan P.
Lowell, V.P., Donor Svcs.; Carla Roberts, V.P.,
Affil.; Marilyn Harris,* Secy.; and 27 additional
directors.
Number of staff: 9 full-time professional; 5
full-time support.
EIN: 860348306
**Recent environmental and animal welfare
grants:**
29-1 A Grassroots Aspen Experience, Aspen,
   CO, $20,000. For grant made through Rodel
   Charitable Foundation. 2001.
29-2 Animal Aid Network, Cottonwood, AZ,
   $15,000. For grant made through Flagstaff
   Community Foundation. 2001.
29-3 Canine Companions for Independence,
   Phoenix, AZ, $16,000. For grant made
   through Ingebriston Family Foundation. 2001.
29-4 Central Arizona Land Trust, Prescott, AZ,
   $20,000. 2001.
29-5 Desert Botanical Garden, Phoenix, AZ,
   $12,000. 2001.
29-6 Grand Canyon Trust, Flagstaff, AZ,
   $78,000. For grant made through Rodel
   Charitable Foundation. 2001.

29-7 H. John Heinz III Center for Science, Economics and the Environment, DC, $10,000. For grant made through Sam and Peggy Grossman Family Foundation. 2001.

29-8 Highlands Center for Natural History, Prescott, AZ, $10,000. For grant made through Yavapai County Community Foundation. 2001.

29-9 Humane Society of Phoenix, Arizona, Phoenix, AZ, $20,000. For grant made through Stardust Charitable Fund. 2001.

29-10 Humane Society of Yavapai, Prescott, AZ, $10,000. For grant made through Yavapai County Community Foundation. 2001.

30
Arizona Horse Lovers Foundation

27202 N. 150th St.
Scottsdale, AZ 85255 (480) 471-2222
Contact: Robert C. Bohannan, Jr., Treas.
Application address (May-Oct.): 7277 Lindsay Rd., Flagstaff, AZ 86004, tel.: (520) 527-1515; (Nov.-Apr.): 27202 N. 150th St., Scottsdale, AZ 85255, tel.: (480) 471-2222

Established in 1986 in AZ.
Grantmaker type: Independent foundation
Financial data (yr. ended 12/31/02): Assets, $1,787,738 (M); expenditures, $93,442; qualifying distributions, $92,439; giving activities include $91,679 for 7 grants (high: $10,000; low: $1,000).
Purpose and activities: Funding primarily for equestrian activities in AZ.
Fields of interest: Animal welfare.
Limitations: Giving primarily in AZ.
Application information: Application form required.
   Initial approach: Letter
   Deadline(s): Oct. 1
Officers: Rick Johns, Pres.; Bill Englund, V.P.; Margaret Bohannan, Secy.; Robert C. Bohannan, Jr., Treas.
EIN: 860518824

31
Benlei Foundation Gift Annuity

(formerly Benlei Foundation)
4518 N. 32nd St.
Phoenix, AZ 85018 (800) 788-8992
Contact: Benson Schaub, Tr.

Established in 1990 in AZ.
Grantmaker type: Public charity
Financial data (yr. ended 12/31/00): Revenue, $70,108; assets, $869,852; gifts received, $1,350; expenditures, $83,053; program services expenses, $73,532; giving activities include $4,505 for 3 grants (high: $3,205; low: $600).
Purpose and activities: The foundation supports local organizations, with a focus on music, visual arts, and environmental conservation.
Fields of interest: Visual arts; Performing arts; Environment.
Limitations: Giving primarily in WI.
Trustee: Benson Schaub.
EIN: 866181471

32
Burns Family Foundation

c/o Patricia Boyd Gentry
3500 E. Lincoln Dr.
Phoenix, AZ 85018
E-mail: BoydGentry@aol.com

Incorporated in 1953 in IL.
Donor(s): Arthur E. Keating,‡ Edward Keating.
Grantmaker type: Independent foundation
Financial data (yr. ended 12/31/01): Assets, $4,594,949 (M); expenditures, $282,599; qualifying distributions, $256,989; giving activities include $240,000 for 28 grants (high: $30,000; low: $400).
Purpose and activities: Giving primarily for education.
Fields of interest: Elementary/secondary education; Higher education; Natural resources; Hospitals (general); Recreation; Children/youth, services; Family services; Christian agencies & churches.
Limitations: Applications not accepted. Giving primarily in CA. No grants to individuals.
Application information: Contributes only to pre-selected organizations.
Officers and Directors:* Patricia B. Boyd,* Pres.; Wendy B. Collins,* V.P.; Julie Ann Wrigley,* Secy.-Treas.; Lucy Keating Burns.
EIN: 366051686

33
Cadeau Foundation

c/o Vicki J. Rutter
HCR 1, Box 652
Patagonia, AZ 85624

Established in 1990 in WA.
Donor(s): Natalie Bryant.
Grantmaker type: Independent foundation
Financial data (yr. ended 12/31/01): Assets, $3,533,948 (M); expenditures, $375,179; qualifying distributions, $244,200; giving activities include $244,200 for 41 grants (high: $26,500; low: $100).
Purpose and activities: Giving primarily for education, environmental conservation, and animal welfare.
Fields of interest: Higher education; Natural resources; Animal welfare; Hospitals (general); Family planning; Human services; Community development.
Types of support: General/operating support.
Limitations: Applications not accepted. No grants to individuals.
Application information: Contributes only to pre-selected organizations.
Advisory Committee: Chris D. Mikkelsen; Vicki J. Rutter; Patrick J. West.
Trustee: Gail H. Coheen.
EIN: 911484455

34
Community Foundation for Southern Arizona

2250 E. Broadway Blvd.
Tucson, AZ 85719-6014 (520) 770-0800
Contact: Steven E. Alley, C.E.O. and Pres.
FAX: (520) 770-1500; E-mail: philanthropy@cfsoaz.org, or salley@cfsoaz.org; URL: http://www.cfsoaz.org

Established in 1980 in AZ.
Grantmaker type: Community foundation
Financial data (yr. ended 06/30/02): Assets, $68,245,200 (M); gifts received, $14,181,622; expenditures, $7,841,935; giving activities include $5,458,151 for grants.
Purpose and activities: The mission of the foundation is to work with charitably minded individuals and organizations to strengthen southern AZ communities, now and for generations to come. The foundation administers a donor-advised fund.
Fields of interest: Arts; Education; Environment; Health care; AIDS; Human services; Children/youth, services.
International interests: Mexico.
Types of support: General/operating support; Program development; Seed money; Scholarship funds; Technical assistance; Scholarships—to individuals; Matching/challenge support.
Limitations: Giving primarily in the metropolitan Tucson and southern AZ areas. No support for sectarian organizations or individual schools. No grants to individuals (except scholarships), or for capital campaign, debt retirement, research or fundraising events.
Publications: Application guidelines, Annual report, Financial statement, Informational brochure, Newsletter.
Application information: Application form required.
   Initial approach: Guidelines available by telephone or website
   Deadline(s): Varies
   Board meeting date(s): Bimonthly
Officers and Trustees:* Steven E. Alley,* C.E.O. and Pres.; Barbara Brown,* V.P., Progs.; Kerry Dufour,* V.P., Donor Relations; David Lewandowski, V.P., Fin.; Pamela Doherty, Exec. Dir.; and 31 additional trustees.
Number of staff: 6 full-time professional; 18 full-time support; 2 part-time support.
EIN: 942681765

35
Crown Foundation

P.O. Box 10790
Tempe, AZ 85284 (480) 785-7575
Contact: Eric Crown, Tr.

Established in 1999 in AZ.
Donor(s): Eric Crown, Timothy Crown.
Grantmaker type: Independent foundation
Financial data (yr. ended 12/31/01): Assets, $1,214,528 (M); gifts received, $517,400; expenditures, $175,210; qualifying distributions, $171,141; giving activities include $171,382 for 15 grants (high: $60,022; low: $100).
Purpose and activities: Giving primarily for education and medical research.
Fields of interest: Elementary/secondary education; Animal welfare; Medical research, association; YM/YWCAs & YM/YWHAs.
Types of support: General/operating support; Building/renovation.
Limitations: Giving primarily in Phoenix, AZ.
Application information:
   Initial approach: Letter
   Deadline(s): None
Trustees: Eric Crown; Timothy Crown.
EIN: 860976734

36
E. Blois du Bois Foundation, Inc.
P.O. Box 33426
Phoenix, AZ 85067
Contact: Gail B. Horne, Pres.
Scholarship inquiries: c/o Dir., Financial Aid at
Univ. of Arizona, Arizona State Univ., Northern
Arizona Univ., or any of the Arizona community
colleges

Incorporated in 1960 in AZ.
Donor(s): E. Blois du Bois.‡
Grantmaker type: Independent foundation
Financial data (yr. ended 05/31/02): Assets,
$4,245,970 (M); expenditures, $266,653;
qualifying distributions, $234,647; giving
activities include $173,000 for 3 grants (high:
$94,000; low: $3,200).
Purpose and activities: Grants primarily for
scholarship funds for students recommended by
financial aid officers of universities and
community colleges in AZ. Grants also available
for the prevention of cruelty to animals and
other humane projects.
Fields of interest: Higher education;
Scholarships/financial aid; Animal welfare.
Types of support: Scholarship funds.
Limitations: Giving limited to AZ. No grants to
individuals directly, or for endowment funds.
Application information: Scholarship inquiries:
c/o Dir., Financial Aid at Univ. of Arizona,
Arizona State Univ., Northern Arizona Univ., or
any of the Arizona community colleges.
   Initial approach: Letter
   Copies of proposal: 2
   Deadline(s): Established by various institutions
      for scholarships; none for other awards
   Board meeting date(s): As required
Officers: Gail B. Horne, Pres.; Marjorie du Bois,
V.P.; Roslyn Pine, Secy.
Director: Robert Horne.
EIN: 866052886

37
Elliott M. & Constance L. Estes Foundation
5434 E. Lincoln Dr., Ste. 44
Paradise Valley, AZ 85253

Established around 1982.
Grantmaker type: Independent foundation
Financial data (yr. ended 12/31/02): Assets,
$662,486 (M); expenditures, $107,781;
qualifying distributions, $97,808; giving
activities include $98,000 for 42 grants (high:
$13,000; low: $1,000).
Purpose and activities: Giving for the arts,
health, and human services.
Fields of interest: Arts; Higher education;
Natural resources; Hospitals (general); Christian
agencies & churches.
Limitations: Applications not accepted. Giving
primarily in AZ and MI. No grants to individuals.
Application information: Contributes only to
pre-selected organizations.
Officers and Trustees:* Constance L. Estes,*
Pres. and Treas.; Sidney W. Smith, Jr.,* Secy.;
Curtis J. Mann.
EIN: 382319855

38
The Fleischer Foundation
(formerly The M. H. Fleischer Foundation)
8910 E. Raintree Dr., Ste. 100
Scottsdale, AZ 85260 (480) 606-0820
Contact: Donna H. Fleischer, Pres.
FAX: (480) 606-0826

Established in 1987 in AZ.
Donor(s): Morton H. Fleischer, Franchise
Finance Corp. of America, FFCA Management
Co.
Grantmaker type: Independent foundation
Financial data (yr. ended 12/31/01): Assets,
$1,657,665 (M); expenditures, $228,806;
qualifying distributions, $192,249; giving
activities include $207,105 for 33 grants (high:
$50,000; low: $85).
Purpose and activities: Giving for education,
religious organizations, amateur sports, public
safety, and the prevention of cruelty to animals
and children.
Fields of interest: Arts; Education; Animal
welfare; Child abuse; Safety/disasters;
Athletics/sports, amateur leagues; Religion.
Types of support: General/operating support.
Limitations: Applications not accepted. Giving
primarily in Phoenix and Scottsdale, AZ. No
grants to individuals.
Application information: Contributes only to
pre-selected organizations.
   Board meeting date(s): Annually
Officers and Directors:* Morton H. Fleischer,*
Chair. and C.E.O.; Donna H. Fleischer,* Pres.
and Exec. Dir.; Christopher H. Volk,* V.P. and
Secy.; John R. Barravecchia,* V.P. and Treas.;
Paul E. Belitz; Jeffrey Fleischer.
Number of staff: None.
EIN: 860581168

39
Foundation Carinoso
33 N. Stone Ave., Ste. 1100
Tucson, AZ 85701-1489

Established in 1988 in AZ.
Donor(s): Thomas B. Healy, Joanne R. Healy.
Grantmaker type: Independent foundation
Financial data (yr. ended 06/30/02): Assets,
$1,572,191 (M); expenditures, $210,926;
qualifying distributions, $198,594; giving
activities include $199,000 for 30 grants (high:
$51,000; low: $500).
Purpose and activities: Giving primarily for
education, the environment, food services,
camps, the disabled, and youth services.
Fields of interest: Higher education; Education;
Environment; Food services; Camps;
Children/youth, services; Disabled.
Limitations: Applications not accepted. Giving
primarily in Tucson, AZ. No grants to individuals.
Application information: Contributes only to
pre-selected organizations.
Officers and Directors:* Thomas B. Healy, Jr.,*
Pres.; Joanne R. Healy,* V.P. and Treas.; James
M. Sakrison,* Secy.; Holly A. Donaldson;
Thomas R. Healy; W. Ross Humphreys; Francis
J. McConnell.
EIN: 860623781

40
Virginia Sugg Furrow Foundation
5025 N. Camino Escuela
Tucson, AZ 85718-5012 (520) 299-6156
Contact: Virginia S. Furrow, Pres.

Established in 1998 in AZ.
Donor(s): Virginia S. Furrow.
Grantmaker type: Independent foundation
Financial data (yr. ended 06/30/01): Assets,
$11,718 (M); gifts received, $301,922;
expenditures, $739,312; qualifying distributions,
$730,136; giving activities include $728,595 for
78 grants (high: $100,000; low: $45).
Fields of interest: Higher education; Natural
resources; Animals/wildlife,
preservation/protection; Legal services; Human
services; Christian agencies & churches.
Limitations: Giving on a national basis, with
some emphasis on Tucson, AZ. No grants to
individuals.
Application information:
   Initial approach: Letter
   Deadline(s): None
Officers: Virginia S. Furrow, Pres.; Dorothy
Smysor, V.P. and Secy.; Michael Searcy, Treas.
EIN: 860911043

41
Globe Foundation
6730 N. Scottsdale Rd., Ste. 250
Scottsdale, AZ 85253-4424 (480) 991-0500
Contact: Lynn Getz-Schmidt, Exec. Dir.
FAX: (602) 991-1912

Established in 1958 in IL.
Donor(s): Bert A. Getz, George F. Getz, Jr.‡
Grantmaker type: Independent foundation
Financial data (yr. ended 12/31/02): Assets,
$21,863,463 (M); expenditures, $1,512,365;
qualifying distributions, $1,499,618; giving
activities include $1,483,623 for 36 grants (high:
$324,720; low: $100; average:
$1,000–$100,000) and $11,734 for employee
matching gifts.
Purpose and activities: Giving primarily for
publicly supported community organizations
and institutions, with emphasis on youth,
cultural organizations, and hospitals.
Fields of interest: Museums; Arts; Environment;
Hospitals (general); Health care; Children/youth,
services; Community development; Aging.
Types of support: General/operating support;
Continuing support; Annual campaigns; Capital
campaigns; Building/renovation; Equipment;
Endowments; Program development;
Professorships; Curriculum development;
Research; Employee matching gifts;
Matching/challenge support.
Limitations: Giving on a national basis. No
support for privately supported groups. No
grants to individuals.
Application information: Application form not
required.
   Initial approach: Letter
   Copies of proposal: 1
   Deadline(s): Mar. 31 and Sept. 31
   Board meeting date(s): Apr. and Oct.
   Final notification: June 30 and Dec. 31
Officers and Directors:* Bert A. Getz,* C.E.O.
and Pres.; Lynn Getz-Schmidt,* V.P. and Exec.
Dir.; Bert A. Getz, Jr.,* V.P.; George F. Getz,*

Secy.; Michael J. Olsen, Treas.; Rock S. Edwards; James L. Johnson, Treas.
Number of staff: None.
EIN: 366054050

42

Grand Canyon National Park Foundation
(formerly Grand Canyon Fund, Inc.)
625 N. Beaver St.
Flagstaff, AZ 86001 (928) 774-1760
Contact: Deborah E. Tuck, Pres.
E-mail: info@grandcanyonfoundation.org; URL: http://www.grandcanyonfoundation.org

Incorporated in 1995 in AZ.
Grantmaker type: Public charity
Financial data (yr. ended 09/30/00): Revenue, $681,825; assets, $3,160,701; gifts received, $614,682; expenditures, $482,150; program services expenses, $225,658; giving activities include $225,658 for 5 grants (high: $89,341; low: $10,315).
Purpose and activities: The foundation is dedicated to funding projects/programs which, further the presentation, protection, and enhancement of the Grand Canyon National Park.
Fields of interest: Natural resources.
Types of support: Fellowships.
Limitations: Giving primarily in AZ.
Application information:
 Initial approach: Letter
 Deadline(s): Mar. 4
 Final notification: Mid-Apr.
Officers and Directors:* Richard A. Naille II,* Chair.; John McCain,* Co-Chair.; Deborah E. Tuck, Pres.; Robert S. Chandler,* Secy.; Jim Babbitt,* Treas.; Bill Anderson; Donald Budinger; Robert Diamond; Jack Schmidt; Richard "Dick" Snell; Thomas Tait; Steve Tedder; Curt Walters; George Woodwell.
EIN: 860805366

43

Haldan Family Charitable Foundation
P.O. Box 1074
Sedona, AZ 86339

Established in 1988 in NV.
Grantmaker type: Independent foundation
Financial data (yr. ended 12/31/01): Assets, $5,182,923 (M); expenditures, $225,660; qualifying distributions, $224,284; giving activities include $212,999 for grants.
Fields of interest: Botanical gardens; Zoos/zoological societies; Arthritis.
Limitations: Applications not accepted. Giving primarily in CA. No grants to individuals.
Application information: Contributes only to pre-selected organizations.
Officer: Ethelmae S. Haldan, Pres. and Secy.-Treas.
Trustee: Dwight S. Haldan.
EIN: 943098616

44

Arthur L. "Bud" Johnson Foundation in Memory of Elaine V. Johnson
1111 E. Bruce Ave.
Gilbert, AZ 85234 (480) 632-8693
Contact: David Hammerslag, Tr.
E-mail: ALFfoundation@ATT.net

Established in 1990 in IL.
Donor(s): Arthur L. Johnson.
Grantmaker type: Independent foundation
Financial data (yr. ended 12/31/02): Assets, $9,214,652 (M); expenditures, $474,173; qualifying distributions, $375,396; giving activities include $367,009 for 2 grants (high: $366,709; low: $300).
Fields of interest: Animals/wildlife, training; Eye diseases; YM/YWCAs & YM/YWHAs; Human services.
Limitations: No grants to individuals.
Application information: Application form not required.
 Deadline(s): None
Trustees: David Hammerslag; Hugh D. Hammerslag; Sally Hammerslag.
EIN: 363739494

45

J. W. Kieckhefer Foundation
116 E. Gurley St.
P.O. Box 1151
Prescott, AZ 86302 (928) 445-4010
Contact: Eugene P. Polk or John I. Kieckhefer, Trustees

Trust established in 1953 in AZ.
Donor(s): John W. Kieckhefer.‡
Grantmaker type: Independent foundation
Financial data (yr. ended 12/31/02): Assets, $16,605,055 (M); expenditures, $1,039,996; qualifying distributions, $959,130; giving activities include $966,501 for 59 grants (high: $250,000; low: $750; average: $1,000–$250,000).
Purpose and activities: Emphasis on medical research, hospices and health agencies; family planning and services, the handicapped, and other social services; education, including medical and other higher education; youth and child welfare agencies; ecology and conservation; community funds; and cultural programs.
Fields of interest: Arts; Higher education; Medical school/education; Education; Natural resources; Environment; Family planning; Medical care, rehabilitation; Health care; Health organizations, association; Medical research, institute; Food services; Human services; Children/youth, services; Family services; Hospices; Federated giving programs; Marine science; Public policy, research.
Types of support: General/operating support; Continuing support; Annual campaigns; Building/renovation; Equipment; Land acquisition; Endowments; Emergency funds; Program development; Conferences/seminars; Publication; Research; Matching/challenge support.
Limitations: Applications not accepted. No grants to individuals.
Application information: Contributes mostly to pre-selected organizations. Internally initiated

grants comprise virtually all of the current grantmaking of the foundation.
 Board meeting date(s): Quarterly, and as required
Trustees: John I. Kieckhefer; Eugene P. Polk.
Number of staff: None.
EIN: 866022877

46

The Kemper and Ethel Marley Foundation ▼
P.O. Box 10392
Phoenix, AZ 85064
Contact: Daniel Corrigan, V.P.

Established in 1990 in AZ.
Donor(s): Ethel Marley,‡ Kemper Marley Trust.
Grantmaker type: Independent foundation
Financial data (yr. ended 02/28/02): Assets, $95,974,039 (M); gifts received, $154,173; expenditures, $7,020,976; qualifying distributions, $5,819,429; giving activities include $5,723,551 for 35 grants (high: $550,000; low: $1,200; average: $12,000–$400,000).
Purpose and activities: Giving primarily for higher education, human service organizations, the arts, and a zoo.
Fields of interest: Museums; Historic preservation/historical societies; Higher education; Zoos/zoological societies; Youth, services.
Types of support: General/operating support.
Limitations: Applications not accepted. Giving limited to AZ. No support for animal welfare organizations. No grants to individuals.
Application information: Contributes only to pre-selected organizations.
Officers and Directors:* James Powers,* Pres.; Daniel Corrigan,* V.P.; Stephen Corrigan,* V.P.; Nancy Elitharp Ball,* Treas.
EIN: 860653091
Recent environmental and animal welfare grants:
46-1 Arizona Zoological Society, Phoenix Zoo, Phoenix, AZ, $550,000. For capital support of Animal Care Center. 2002.
46-2 Arizona Zoological Society, Phoenix Zoo, Phoenix, AZ, $75,000. For continued operating support of Zoo Lights. 2002.
46-3 Desert Botanical Garden, Phoenix, AZ, $334,000. For capital support for education building. 2002.
46-4 Phoenix Childrens Hospital, Phoenix, AZ, $300,000. For endowment of Children's Garden. 2002.

47

Margaret T. Morris Foundation
P.O. Box 592
Prescott, AZ 86302 (928) 445-4010
Contact: Eugene P. Polk, Tr.

Established in 1967.
Donor(s): Margaret T. Morris.‡
Grantmaker type: Independent foundation
Financial data (yr. ended 12/31/02): Assets, $12,753,091 (M); expenditures, $2,643,418; qualifying distributions, $2,540,018; giving activities include $2,558,307 for 88 grants (high: $225,000; low: $750; average: $1,000–$225,000).

Purpose and activities: Support for the performing arts and other cultural programs, education, with emphasis on higher education, youth and child welfare, a community foundation, family planning, medical research and education, the environment and animal welfare, and social services, primarily those benefiting the handicapped.

Fields of interest: Museums; Performing arts; Music; Arts; Higher education; Medical school/education; Education; Environment; Animal welfare; Family planning; Mental health/crisis services; Medical research, institute; Human services; Children/youth, services; Hospices; Homeless, human services; Marine science; Disabled; Economically disadvantaged; Homeless.

Types of support: General/operating support; Capital campaigns; Building/renovation; Land acquisition; Endowments; Debt reduction; Program development; Scholarship funds; Matching/challenge support.

Limitations: Applications not accepted. Giving primarily in AZ. No support for religious organizations or their agencies. No grants to individuals; no loans.

Application information: Internally initiated grants comprise virtually all of the current grantmaking of the foundation.

Board meeting date(s): Aug., Dec., and as required

Trustees: Richard L. Menschel; Eugene P. Polk; Thomas E. Polk.

Number of staff: None.

EIN: 866057798

Recent environmental and animal welfare grants:

47-1 Adventure Discovery, Flagstaff, AZ, $15,000. Toward vehicle. 2001.

47-2 Africa Rainforest and River Conservation, Jackson, WY, $10,000. For general support. 2001.

47-3 Breckenridge Outdoor Education Center, Breckenridge, CO, $15,000. For general support. 2001.

47-4 Central Arizona Land Trust, Prescott, AZ, $50,000. Toward business office and to hire professional staff. 2001.

47-5 Central Park Conservancy, New York, NY, $50,000. Toward East Meadow Restoration Project. 2001.

47-6 Grand Canyon Trust, Flagstaff, AZ, $10,000. For general support. 2001.

47-7 Nantucket Conservation Foundation, Nantucket, MA, $100,000. For endowment. 2001.

47-8 Strong Wings Adventure School, Nantucket, MA, $25,000. For mortgage reduction. 2001.

47-9 Strong Wings Adventure School, Nantucket, MA, $25,000. For operating support. 2001.

47-10 Tohono Chul Parks, Tucson, AZ, $15,000. For general support. 2001.

47-11 Transition Zone Horticultural Institute, Arboretum at Flagstaff, Flagstaff, AZ, $10,000. Toward organizational development study. 2001.

48
The Ottosen Family Foundation
105 S. 28th St.
Phoenix, AZ 85034

Donor(s): Donald R. Ottosen.

Grantmaker type: Independent foundation

Financial data (yr. ended 12/31/02): Assets, $3,822,095 (M); gifts received, $400,000; expenditures, $210,208; qualifying distributions, $201,117; giving activities include $201,750 for 22 grants (high: $75,000; low: $1,000).

Purpose and activities: Giving for education, community services, and religion.

Fields of interest: Orchestra (symphony); Higher education; Education; Botanical gardens; Health care; Human services; Salvation Army; Community development.

Limitations: Applications not accepted. Giving primarily in AZ. No grants to individuals.

Application information: Contributes only to pre-selected organizations.

Officers: Barbara J. Ottosen, Pres.; Pamela L. Perry, V.P.; Diann C. Henderson, Secy.; Donald R. Ottosen, Treas.

EIN: 860778785

49
PETsMART Charities, Inc.
19601 N. 27th Ave.
Phoenix, AZ 85027 (623) 587-2832
Contact: Patty Finch, Mgr., Charitable Giving
Additional tel.: (800) 423-7387; FAX: (623) 580-6561; E-mail: petsmartcharities@petsmart.com or pfinch@ssg.petsmartcharities.com; URL: http://www.petsmartcharities.org

Established in 1994.

Donor(s): PETsMART, Inc.

Grantmaker type: Public charity

Financial data (yr. ended 01/31/02): Revenue, $6,206,521; assets, $5,372,165; gifts received, $6,134,513; expenditures, $5,007,210; program services expenses, $3,961,966; giving activities include $3,557,442 for grants.

Purpose and activities: The organization gives grants to help homeless pets, and end euthanasia as a means to controlling the pet population.

Fields of interest: Animal welfare; Adoption.

Types of support: Equipment; Emergency funds; Program development; Conferences/seminars; Seed money; Scholarships—to individuals; Matching/challenge support.

Limitations: Giving limited to the U.S. and Canada. No support for programs in support of wildlife or endangered species. No grants for building projects, endowments, or operating expenses.

Publications: Application guidelines, Annual report, Informational brochure, Newsletter.

Application information: Sponsorship applications must be received three months prior to the event; Grant requests are reviewed three to four months after receipt; see Web site for application forms and guidelines. Application form required.

Copies of proposal: 1

Deadline(s): None

Board meeting date(s): Jan. 27, May 12, and Oct. 17

Officers and Directors:* Philip Francis,* Chair.; Bob Moran,* Pres; Kevin Groman,* Secy.; Brad Larson, Treas.; Ken Barun; Sophie Engelhard Craighead; Barbara Fitzgerald; Steve Marton; Patricia Olsen, Ph.D.; Bart Schillaci.

Number of staff: 11.

EIN: 931140967

50
David E. Reese Family Foundation
7350 E. Evans Rd., Ste. B-103
Scottsdale, AZ 85260-3128

Established in 1994 in AZ.

Donor(s): David E. Reese, Caleb F. Reese, Everett D. Reese II, Everett Reese.‡

Grantmaker type: Independent foundation

Financial data (yr. ended 12/31/02): Assets, $16,503,747 (M); expenditures, $929,135; qualifying distributions, $893,375; giving activities include $897,000 for 10 grants (high: $500,002; low: $5,000).

Purpose and activities: Emphasis on support for the United Way, a community foundation, museums, and human services.

Fields of interest: Museums (art); Arts; Higher education; Education; Environment; Animal welfare; Hospitals (general); Health care; Human services; Hospices; Homeless, human services; Foundations (community); Federated giving programs; Public policy, research.

Limitations: Applications not accepted. Giving primarily in Scottsdale and Phoenix, AZ; some giving also in Columbus, OH and also on a national basis. No grants to individuals.

Application information: Contributes only to pre-selected organizations.

Officers: David E. Reese, Pres.; Louise R. Reese, V.P. and Secy.; Everett D. Reese, Treas.

EIN: 860763892

51
Russell Charitable Trust
P.O. Box 91398
Tucson, AZ 85752-1398
Contact: Judy A. Moore, Dir.
FAX: (520) 797-6719

Established in 1960 in ME.

Donor(s): H.M. Russell.

Grantmaker type: Independent foundation

Financial data (yr. ended 07/31/02): Assets, $1,237,882 (M); expenditures, $585,965; qualifying distributions, $5,855,473; giving activities include $513,500 for 6 grants (high: $500,000; low: $2,000).

Purpose and activities: Giving to religious related institutions in the fields of higher education, medical and health-related human and animal services, media and communication which seek to promote quality human and animal services, and to institutions serving youth and the elderly.

Fields of interest: Higher education; Animals/wildlife; Health care, clinics/centers; Health care; Human services; Community development; Protestant agencies & churches; Disabled.

Types of support: General/operating support; Capital campaigns; Endowments; Seed money.

Limitations: Giving primarily in GA, NC, and SC. No grants to individuals or churches operating budgets.

Application information:

Initial approach: 1 page letter

Deadline(s): None; applications not accepted in July and Dec.

Board meeting date(s): Quarterly

Final notification: Grants are made at the beginning of each calendar quarter

Trustees: Ernest J. Arnold; Frances P. Arnold.

Director: Judy A. Moore.

EIN: 016009882

52
The W. Ford Schumann Foundation
9612 E. Vereda Solana
Scottsdale, AZ 85255

Established in 1986 in AZ.

Donor(s): W. Ford Schumann.

Grantmaker type: Independent foundation

Financial data (yr. ended 12/31/02): Assets, $447,003 (M); expenditures, $337,587; qualifying distributions, $333,160; giving activities include $326,247 for 131 grants (high: $100,000; low: $50).

Fields of interest: Museums (art); Arts; Education; Natural resources; Health organizations, association; Christian agencies & churches.

Limitations: Applications not accepted. Giving on a national basis. No grants to individuals.

Application information: Contributes only to pre-selected organizations.

Officers: W. Ford Schumann, Pres.; Susan H. Schumann, Secy.; Andrew D. Pappas, Treas.

EIN: 860553890

53
Eliot Spalding Foundation
4400 E. Broadway, Ste. 800
Tucson, AZ 85711-3524 (520) 795-6630
Contact: Peter T. Gianas, Secy.

Established in 1954 in AZ.

Grantmaker type: Independent foundation

Financial data (yr. ended 12/31/01): Assets, $3,740,795 (M); expenditures, $176,651; qualifying distributions, $139,380; giving activities include $135,000 for 13 grants (high: $74,000; low: $1,000).

Purpose and activities: Support primarily for a community fund.

Fields of interest: Botanical gardens; Human services; Federated giving programs.

Limitations: Giving primarily in Tucson, AZ. No grants to individuals.

Application information:

Initial approach: Typewritten proposal

Deadline(s): Nov. 1

Officers and Directors:* Clayton N. Niles,* Pres.; Samuel P. Goddard, Jr.,* V.P.; Clayton E. Niles,* V.P.; Peter T. Gianas,* Secy.; James M. Sakrison,* Treas.

EIN: 866050507

54
SRP Corporate Giving Program
c/o Corp. Contribs., PAB 337
P.O. Box 52025
Phoenix, AZ 85072-2025 (602) 236-2573
Tel. for employee volunteer services: (602) 236-2542; E-mail: contrib@srpnet.com; URL: http://www.srpnet.com/community/involvement.asp

Grantmaker type: Corporate giving program

Purpose and activities: SRP makes charitable contributions to nonprofit organizations involved with arts and culture, education, the environment, health and human services, and public affairs. Support is given primarily in Arizona.

Fields of interest: Arts; Education; Environment; Health care; Human services; Public affairs.

Types of support: General/operating support; Employee volunteer services; In-kind gifts.

Limitations: Giving primarily in Apache Junction, Avondale, Chandler, Fountain Hills, Glendale, Guadalupe, Mesa, Paradise Valley, Peoria, Phoenix, Queen Creek, Scottsdale, Tempe, Tolleson, and the Town of Gilbert, AZ.

Application information: Application form not required.

Initial approach: Proposal to headquarters

Copies of proposal: 1

Deadline(s): None

Final notification: Following review

55
Fred W. Stang Foundation
4971 N. Circulo Bujia
Tucson, AZ 85718 (520) 299-3680
Contact: Frank Wicks, Treas.

Established in 1997 in AZ.

Grantmaker type: Independent foundation

Financial data (yr. ended 12/31/00): Assets, $1,857,660 (M); expenditures, $261,342; qualifying distributions, $116,000; giving activities include $94,500 for 13 grants (high: $17,500; low: $1,000).

Purpose and activities: Giving primarily for children's services, and religion.

Fields of interest: Arts; Zoos/zoological societies; Human services; Children/youth, services; Jewish agencies & temples; Religion.

Limitations: Giving primarily in AZ.

Officers: Roland Earl Wicks, Pres.; Christy Lynn Hettlinger, V.P.; Nancy Lynn Hettlinger, Secy.; Franklin Redell Wicks, Treas.

EIN: 860863577

56
T & E, Inc.
P.O. Box 1498
Cortaro, AZ 85652-1498 (520) 572-0998
Contact: Thomas Wootten, Pres.
FAX: (520) 572-0962; E-mail: thwootten@earthlink.net; URL: http://www.tandeinc.com

Established in 1995 in NM.

Donor(s): Eleanor G. Wootten, Thomas H. Wootten.

Grantmaker type: Independent foundation

Financial data (yr. ended 12/31/02): Assets, $531,639 (M); gifts received, $156,213;

expenditures, $159,118; qualifying distributions, $150,071; giving activities include $150,148 for 65 grants (high: $56,219; low: $50).

Purpose and activities: Giving for the protection and management of rare plants, animals and natural communities of the southwestern United States.

Fields of interest: Animals/wildlife, management/technical aid; Animals/wildlife, research; Animals/wildlife, information services; Animals/wildlife, preservation/protection; Biological sciences.

International interests: Mexico.

Types of support: Scholarship funds; Grants to individuals.

Limitations: Giving primarily in the Southwest, with an emphasis on AZ and NM; some giving also in northern Mexico.

Application information:

Initial approach: Proposal, maximum of 5 pages

Copies of proposal: 3

Deadline(s): Mar. 1

Final notification: Apr. 15

Officers: Thomas H. Wootten, Pres.; Marianne Mershon, V.P. and Secy.; David Wootten, V.P.; Eleanor G. Wootten, V.P.

Number of staff: None.

EIN: 850424326

57
TEP Corporate Giving Program
P.O. Box 711, M.S. ID UE102
Tucson, AZ 85702 (520) 884-3740
Contact: Sharon Foltz
Application address for employee volunteer services: c/o TEP CAT Clearinghouse Subcommittee, Anna M. Cunes, P.O. Box 711, M.S. ID UE102, Tucson, AZ 85702; FAX: (520) 884-3606; E-mail: sfoltz@tucsonelectric.com; URL: http://www.tucsonelectric.com/Community/index.html

Grantmaker type: Corporate giving program

Purpose and activities: TEP makes charitable contributions to nonprofit organizations involved with education, energy conservation, environmental education, safety, economic development, and community development. Support is given primarily in Pima County and the White Mountain, Arizona, area.

Fields of interest: Education; Energy; Environmental education; Safety, education; Economic development; Community development.

Types of support: General/operating support; Capital campaigns; Employee volunteer services; In-kind gifts.

Limitations: Giving primarily in Pima County and the White Mountain, AZ, area. No support for schools, religious organizations, political organizations or candidates, fraternal, social, or veterans' organizations, individual K-12 schools, disease-specific organizations, or organizations budgeting over 10 percent of funds for services located outside of areas of company operations. No grants to individuals, or for travel, medical research, endowments, or adult sports; no electric service donations.

Application information: Proposals should be submitted using organization letterhead. Support is limited to 1 contribution per organization during any given year. An application form is required for employee volunteer services; application form available online. The Community Relations Department handles giving. A contributions committee reviews all requests for employee volunteer services.

Initial approach: Proposal to headquarters; download application form and mail or fax to application address for employee volunteer services
Deadline(s): As early as possible for employee volunteer services
Board meeting date(s): Monthly
Final notification: 1 week following committee meetings for employee volunteer services

58
The Weatherup Family Foundation
10343 E. Pinnacle Peak Rd.
Scottsdale, AZ 85255

Established in 1998 in CT.
Donor(s): Craig E. Weatherup, Constance K. Weatherup.
Grantmaker type: Independent foundation
Financial data (yr. ended 12/31/02): Assets, $6,166,843 (M); gifts received, $386,982; expenditures, $273,772; qualifying distributions, $240,572; giving activities include $243,500 for 12 grants (high: $120,000; low: $1,000).
Fields of interest: Natural resources; Animals/wildlife.
Limitations: Applications not accepted. Giving primarily in Charlotte, NC and NY. No grants to individuals.
Application information: Contributes only to pre-selected organizations.
Trustees: Constance K. Weatherup; Craig E. Weatherup.
EIN: 066469433

59
Zicarelli Foundation, Inc.
18541 Horseshoe Bend
Rio Verde, AZ 85263-7039
Contact: Mary L. Zicarelli, Pres.

Established in 1986 in AZ.
Donor(s): Robert F. Zicarelli.‡
Grantmaker type: Independent foundation
Financial data (yr. ended 12/31/02): Assets, $3,173,345 (M); expenditures, $210,590; qualifying distributions, $198,908; giving activities include $196,000 for 25 grants (high: $75,000; low: $500).
Purpose and activities: Giving primarily for education, the environment, and the arts.
Fields of interest: Museums; Education; Environment; Human services.
Types of support: General/operating support; Annual campaigns; Capital campaigns; Research.
Limitations: Applications not accepted. Giving primarily in AZ. No grants to individuals.
Application information: Contributes only to pre-selected organizations.
Officers and Directors:* Mary L. Zicarelli,* Pres.; John D. Zicarelli,* V.P. and Secy.; James R.

Zicarelli,* Treas.; David Zicarelli; Thomas Zicarelli.
Number of staff: None.
EIN: 860569257

ARKANSAS

60
Bradberry Family Foundation
1 W. Mountain St., Ste. 300
Fayetteville, AR 72701

Established in 1997 in AR.
Donor(s): Edwin G. Bradberry, Karlee Bradberry.
Grantmaker type: Independent foundation
Financial data (yr. ended 12/31/02): Assets, $962,632 (M); gifts received, $751,178; expenditures, $287,607; qualifying distributions, $268,052; giving activities include $268,095 for 9 grants (high: $211,095; low: $1,000).
Fields of interest: Higher education; Botanical gardens; Heart & circulatory diseases; Human services; Religion.
Types of support: General/operating support.
Limitations: Applications not accepted. Giving primarily in AR. No grants to individuals.
Application information: Contributes only to pre-selected organizations.
Trustees: Edwin G. Bradberry; John G. Bradberry; Karlee Bradberry; Robert W. Bradberry; William B. Bradberry; Rebecca Ann Moody; Karolyn C. Wolverton.
EIN: 626318708

61
The Ross Foundation
P.O. Box 335
Arkadelphia, AR 71923 (870) 246-9881
Contact: Ross M. Wipple, Tr.
FAX: (870) 246-9674

Established in 1966 in AR.
Donor(s): Esther C. Ross,‡ Jane Ross.‡
Grantmaker type: Independent foundation
Financial data (yr. ended 12/31/02): Assets, $50,716,110 (M); gifts received, $100,000; expenditures, $1,503,764; qualifying distributions, $769,508; giving activities include $578,135 for 119 grants (high: $325,391; low: $250).
Purpose and activities: Primary areas of interest include higher and public education, health care, conservation of natural resources, and community improvement programs.
Fields of interest: Arts; Higher education; Education; Natural resources; Health care; Mental health/crisis services; Youth, services; Community development.
Types of support: General/operating support; Building/renovation; Equipment; Endowments; Emergency funds; Program development; Publication; Seed money; Research; Consulting services; Matching/challenge support.
Limitations: Giving limited to Arkadelphia and Clark County, AR. No grants to individuals, or for scholarships or fellowships; no loans.

Publications: Application guidelines, Financial statement, Informational brochure (including application guidelines).
Application information: Application form required.
Initial approach: Letter
Copies of proposal: 6
Deadline(s): None
Board meeting date(s): 4th Tues. of Feb., May, Aug., and Nov.
Final notification: 30 days
Trustees: Peggy Clark; Toney McMillan; Robert C. Rhodes; Mary Whipple; Ross M. Whipple.
Number of staff: 4 full-time professional; 4 full-time support; 1 part-time support.
EIN: 716060574

62
Southshore Foundation
301 E. Main St.
Flippin, AR 72634
Contact: Deanna Sullivan, Tr.
Tel.: 1-(800) 775-6682, ext. 205; E-mail: dlatting@southshore.com; URL: http://www.southshore.com/foundation/

Established in 1995.
Donor(s): Northern Arkansas Telephone Co.
Grantmaker type: Independent foundation
Financial data (yr. ended 12/31/02): Assets, $212,464 (M); gifts received, $200,000; expenditures, $182,658; qualifying distributions, $182,034; giving activities include $182,061 for 20 grants (high: $75,000; low: $38).
Purpose and activities: Giving primarily to educational institutions; also awards scholarships for academic achievers in each area school district and promotes education for all ages. The foundation values the natural environment as a basis for the South Shore way of life and believes telecommunications can be employed to advance economic opportunity and community betterment.
Fields of interest: Education; Environment; Community development; Government/public administration; Transportation; Telecommunications.
Types of support: Building/renovation; Equipment; Scholarships—to individuals.
Limitations: Giving limited to the South Shore area of north central AR and south central MO. No grants to individuals (except for scholarships).
Application information: Application form can be downloaded from foundation Web site. Application form required.
Deadline(s): Jan. 1, Apr. 1, July 1 and Sept. 1
Board meeting date(s): Quarterly
Final notification: Within 30 days following board meeting
Trustees: Frank Bailey; Mike Brown; Ed Coulter; Howard Evans; Margaret Hall; Jodie Jeffrey; David Land; Steven Sanders; Betty Smith; Phyllis Speer; Deanna Sullivan; Heidi Voltrauer.
EIN: 621666363

63
Trinity Foundation
P.O. Box 7008
Pine Bluff, AR 71611-7008 (870) 534-7120
Contact: Drew Atkinson, Secy.

Incorporated about 1952 in AR.
Donor(s): Pine Bluff Sand & Gravel Co.,
McGeorge Contracting Co., Cornerstone Farm &
Gin Co., Standard Investment Co., Harvey W.
McGeorge.‡
Grantmaker type: Independent foundation
Financial data (yr. ended 09/30/02): Assets,
$18,414,314 (M); expenditures, $889,107;
qualifying distributions, $775,350; giving
activities include $775,350 for 51 grants (high:
$109,750; low: $1,000).
Purpose and activities: Giving primarily for
education, youth services, and student
scholarships.
Fields of interest: Arts; Higher education;
Scholarships/financial aid; Education;
Environment; Boys & girls clubs;
Children/youth, services.
Types of support: General/operating support;
Scholarships—to individuals.
Limitations: Giving primarily in AR. No grants to
individuals directly.
Application information: Scholarship
application information available only at
guidance offices of public high schools in Pine
Bluff, Little Rock, Benton, and Bauxite, AR.
   Deadline(s): Apr. 10 of senior year in high
      school for scholarships
Officers: Haskell Dickinson, V.P.; Scott
McGeorge, V.P.; Wallace P. McGeorge III, V.P.;
Drew Atkinson, Secy.
EIN: 716050288

64
Wal-Mart Foundation ▼
702 S.W. 8th St.
Bentonville, AR 72716-8071
URL: http://www.walmartfoundation.org

Established in 1979 in AR.
Donor(s): Wal-Mart Stores, Inc.
Grantmaker type: Company-sponsored
foundation
Financial data (yr. ended 01/31/02): Assets,
$7,597,258 (M); gifts received, $77,827,290;
expenditures, $82,631,681; qualifying
distributions, $82,622,058; giving activities
include $74,332,700 for grants, $8,022,417 for
grants to individuals and $60,790 for employee
matching gifts.
Purpose and activities: Giving for education,
health and human services, economic
involvement, and the environment. The
foundation funds six scholarship programs: 1)
Associate Scholarship Program; 2) Sam Walton
Community Scholarship Program; 3)
Distribution Center Scholarship Program; 4)
Competitive Edge Scholarship Fund; 5) the
Doyle S. Graham Intellect Scholarship Program;
and 6) the Walton Foundation Scholarship
Program.
Fields of interest: Higher education; Adult
education—literacy, basic skills & GED;
Reading; Education; Environment; Health care;
Substance abuse, services; Health organizations,
association; Alcoholism; Food services;
Safety/disasters; Children/youth, services; Aging,

centers/services; Minorities/immigrants,
centers/services; Community development;
Federated giving programs; Minorities; Aging.
Types of support: Scholarship funds; Employee
matching gifts; Scholarships—to individuals;
Matching/challenge support.
Limitations: Giving primarily in areas of
company operations. No support for cultural
performances, film and video projects, or
faith-based organizations whose projects benefit
primarily or entirely their members or adherents.
No grants to individuals (except for scholarship
programs), or for research, endowments, capital
campaigns, conferences, travel, or fundraising
dinners or galas.
Publications: Informational brochure.
Application information: Application
information for scholarship programs available
from the foundation.
   Deadline(s): Mar. 1, Assoc. Scholarship and
      Walton Fdn. Scholarship programs; Mar. 2,
      Competitive Edge Scholarship Fund; May 1,
      Distribution Center Scholarship. Contact
      high school counselors for application
      dates for Sam Walton Community
      Scholarship Program
   Board meeting date(s): Mar., May, Aug., and
      Nov.
Officer: Betsy Reithemeyer, Dir.
Trustees: Tom Coughlin; Tom Schoewe; Lee
Scott.
Number of staff: 1 full-time professional; 4
full-time support.
EIN: 716107283
**Recent environmental and animal welfare
grants:**
64-1 Desert Research Institute, Reno, NV,
   $10,000. For United Way Grand Opening.
   2002.
64-2 West Virginia, State of, Division of Natural
   Resources, Charleston, WV, $10,000. 2002.

65
Wallace Trust Foundation
209 W. Oak St.
McGehee, AR 71654 (870) 222-6660
Contact: Gibbs Ferguson, Tr.

Established in 1995 in AR.
Grantmaker type: Independent foundation
Financial data (yr. ended 12/31/01): Assets, $65
(M); gifts received, $107,195; expenditures,
$107,210; qualifying distributions, $107,195;
giving activities include $68,740 for 20 grants
(high: $30,397; low: $50) and $38,455 for 13
grants to individuals (high: $12,828; low: $293).
Purpose and activities: Awards educational
scholarships, and grants to public charities.
Fields of interest: Education; Natural resources;
Hospitals (general); Boy scouts.
Types of support: Scholarships—to individuals.
Limitations: Giving limited to AR.
Application information:
   Initial approach: Letter
   Deadline(s): None
Trustees: William Fred Denton; Gibbs Ferguson;
James Kelley.
EIN: 710754251

66
Aaroe Associates Charitable Foundation,
Inc.
2405 McCabe Way, Ste. 210
Irvine, CA 92614

Established in 1995 in CA.
Donor(s): John Aaroe & Assocs.
Grantmaker type: Independent foundation
Financial data (yr. ended 04/30/02): Assets,
$95,747 (M); gifts received, $292,219;
expenditures, $266,630; qualifying distributions,
$266,630; giving activities include $265,900 for
135 grants (high: $25,000; low: $50).
Fields of interest: Arts; Education; Natural
resources; Animals/wildlife; Rape victim
services; Health organizations, association;
Camps; Youth development; Human services.
Limitations: Applications not accepted. Giving
primarily in CA. No grants to individuals.
Application information: Contributes only to
pre-selected organizations.
Officers: Steve Games, Pres.; Nyda
Jones-Church, Secy.-Treas.
EIN: 954528536

67
Acorn Foundation
c/o Common Counsel
1221 Preservation Pkwy., Ste. 101
Oakland, CA 94612 (510) 834-2995
Contact: Elizabeth Wilcox, Exec. Dir.
FAX: (510) 834-2998; E-mail: ccounsel@igc.org;
URL: http://www.commoncounsel.org/pages/
foundation.html

Established in 1987.
Donor(s): Collier C. Kimball, Stephen C.
Kimball, William R. Kimball, Anne C. Kimball,
Jeffrey L. Kimball.
Grantmaker type: Independent foundation
Financial data (yr. ended 12/31/02): Assets,
$1,298,041 (M); gifts received, $30,025;
expenditures, $151,007; qualifying distributions,
$136,814; giving activities include $120,000 for
15 grants (high: $10,000; low: $5,000).
Purpose and activities: Support for restoration
and preservation of a healthful global
environment, including environmental justice
and indigenous rights.
Fields of interest: Environment, toxics; Natural
resources; Environment; Animals/wildlife,
preservation/protection.
Types of support: General/operating support;
Seed money.
Limitations: Giving primarily in the western U.S.
No support for government agencies. No grants
to individuals, or for capital campaigns or
organizations with budgets over $300,000 a
year.
Publications: Grants list, Informational brochure
(including application guidelines).
Application information: Consult Web site for
guidelines prior to submitting proposal.
Application form not required.
   Initial approach: Proposal
   Copies of proposal: 1

Deadline(s): Jan. 15 and June 15
Board meeting date(s): Biannually
Final notification: Within 6 months
Officers: Stephen C. Kimball, Pres.; Anne C. Kimball, Secy.; Collier C. Kimball, Treas.; William R. Kimball, Treas.; Elizabeth Wilcox, Exec. Dir.
Directors: Jeffrey L. Kimball; Julie C. Kimball.
Number of staff: 3 shared staff (shared with Abelard Foundation West, Penney Family Fund).
EIN: 942480429

68
Adobe Systems Incorporated Corporate Giving Program

c/o Community Rels., E08
345 Park Ave.
San Jose, CA 95110 (408) 536-3993
FAX: (408) 537-6313; URL: http://www.adobe.com/aboutadobe/philanthropy/main.html

Grantmaker type: Corporate giving program
Purpose and activities: Adobe makes charitable contributions to nonprofit organizations involved with arts and culture, education, the environment, hunger, disadvantaged youth, human rights, minorities, disabled people, senior citizens, economically disadvantaged people, and homeless people. Support is given primarily in San Diego and the San Jose and Silicon Valley, California, area, Washington, DC, Boston, Massachusetts, Minneapolis, Minnesota, New York, New York, the Seattle and King County, Washington, area, and the Ottawa, Canada, area. Excluding cash donations made through the Volunteer Request Program, grants are made through the Community Foundation Silicon Valley. Excluding donations made through the Software Donation Special Request Program, software donations are made through Gifts In-Kind International.
Fields of interest: Arts; Elementary/secondary education; Reading; Education; Environment; Food services; Youth, services; Civil rights; Minorities; Disabled; Aging; Economically disadvantaged; Homeless.
International interests: Canada.
Types of support: General/operating support; Employee volunteer services; Donated products.
Limitations: Giving primarily in San Diego and the San Jose and Silicon Valley, CA, area, Washington, DC, Boston, MA, Minneapolis, MN, New York, NY, the Seattle and King County, WA, area, and the Ottawa, Canada, area. No support for private foundations, political organizations, religious organizations, or discriminatory organizations. No grants to individuals, or for fundraising event entry fees.
Application information: An application form is available online. Support is limited to one contribution per organization during any given year for Software Donation Special Request Program. Unsolicited requests for employee volunteer services and cash donations from organizations located outside the San Jose and Silicon Valley, CA, Seattle and King County, WA, and Ottawa, Canada, areas are not accepted. The Community Relations Department handles giving. A contributions committee reviews all requests for Volunteer Request Program. Application form required.

Initial approach: Download application form and mail or fax to headquarters for Software Donation Special Request Program and Volunteer Request Program
Copies of proposal: 1
Deadline(s): None
Board meeting date(s): Quarterly for Volunteer Request Program

69
Agape Foundation

1095 Market St., Ste. 304
San Francisco, CA 94103 (415) 701-8707
Contact: Nina Dessart, Admin. Dir.
FAX: (415) 701-8706; E-mail: info@agapefn.org; URL: http://www.agapefn.org

Established in 1969 in CA.
Grantmaker type: Public charity
Financial data (yr. ended 12/31/02): Revenue, $875,551; assets, $498,582 (L); gifts received, $898,029; expenditures, $786,180; program services expenses, $709,594; giving activities include $696,498 for 83 grants (high: $153,100; low: $100) and $6,000 for 2 loans/program-related investments.
Purpose and activities: The foundation offers support primarily for nonviolent social change, focusing on anti-military and anti-nuclear issues, the environment, human rights, gay and lesbian rights, and women's rights.
Fields of interest: Environment; Arms control; Civil rights, women; Civil rights, gays/lesbians; Civil liberties, advocacy.
Types of support: General/operating support; Continuing support; Emergency funds; Seed money; Program-related investments/loans.
Limitations: Giving primarily in CA. No support for organizations with annual budgets exceeding $100,000 or groups that have been established for more than 5 years.
Publications: Application guidelines, Annual report.
Application information: The foundation offers an open granting session; potential recipients are invited to observe deliberations of the Board of Trustees. Application form not required.
Initial approach: Request granting guidelines
Copies of proposal: 1
Deadline(s): Feb. 1 and Aug. 1 for Board of Trustees Grants; last business day of each month for Emergency Grants and David R. Stern Memorial Fund Loans
Board meeting date(s): Monthly
Final notification: Apr. and Oct.
Officer and Trustees:* Karen Topakian, Exec. Dir.; Carol Cantwell; Victor Chavez; Don Foster; Rachel Lanzerotti; Melanie Okamoto; Christina Wilson; Dena Shupe Woolwine.
Number of staff: 2 part-time professional.
EIN: 237054694

70
Agricultural Clean Water Initiative Foundation

2300 River Plz. Dr.
Sacramento, CA 95833-3293 (916) 561-5520
Contact: William C. Pauli, Pres.

Grantmaker type: Public charity
Financial data (yr. ended 12/31/00): Revenue, $36,785; assets, $23,154; gifts received,

$36,785; expenditures, $33,132; giving activities include $32,261 for 3 grants (high: $19,511; low: $6,250).
Purpose and activities: The foundation funds programs to control agriculture nonpoint source pollution.
Fields of interest: Environment, pollution control; Water pollution; Waste management; Natural resources; Environment, water resources.
Limitations: Giving limited to Monterey, Imperial, and San Mateo counties, CA.
Officers and Directors:* William C., Pauli,* Pres.; Douglas W. Mosebar,* 1st V.P.; Paul J. Wenger,* 2nd V.P.; Joseph M. Peters,* Secy.-Treas.
EIN: 680426882

71
Winifred & Harry B. Allen Foundation

c/o Allen Properties Co.
83 Beach Rd.
Belvedere, CA 94920-2363

Established in 1963 in CA.
Donor(s): Winifred Allen,‡ Harry B. Allen.‡
Grantmaker type: Independent foundation
Financial data (yr. ended 12/31/02): Assets, $2,176,803 (M); expenditures, $95,397; qualifying distributions, $89,440; giving activities include $90,150 for 76 grants (high: $11,500; low: $200).
Purpose and activities: Giving to the arts, education, the environment and human services.
Fields of interest: Visual arts; Performing arts; Education; Natural resources; Environment; Animals/wildlife, preservation/protection; Health care; Health organizations, association; Human services; Immigrants/refugees.
Types of support: Building/renovation; Endowments.
Limitations: Applications not accepted. Giving primarily in Marin County, CA. No grants to individuals.
Application information: Funds fully committed. New applications not considered.
Board meeting date(s): Apr. 15, June 15, Sept. 15, and Dec. 15
Trustees: Andrew E. Allen; Howard B. Allen; James A. Allen; Elizabeth Straus.
Number of staff: None.
EIN: 946100550

72
Jenifer Altman Foundation

P.O. Box 29209
San Francisco, CA 94129 (415) 561-2182
Contact: Eleni Sotos, Grants Mgr.
FAX: (415) 561-6480; E-mail: info@jaf.org; URL: http://www.jaf.org

Established in 1991 in CA.
Donor(s): Jenifer Altman,‡ Pinewood Foundation.
Grantmaker type: Independent foundation
Financial data (yr. ended 06/30/02): Assets, $16,070,511 (M); gifts received, $50,000; expenditures, $1,931,366; qualifying distributions, $1,016,304; giving activities include $693,080 for 56 grants (high: $420,000; low: $1,000; average: $1,000–$10,000) and $15,000 for 3 grants to individuals of $5,000 each.

Purpose and activities: The foundation is dedicated to the vision of a socially just and ecologically sustainable future through program interests in environmental health and mind-body health.
Fields of interest: Environment; Health care; Day care; Child development, services; International economic development; Community development.
International interests: Europe; Mexico; Brazil; India.
Types of support: General/operating support; Continuing support; Program development; Conferences/seminars; Seed money.
Limitations: Giving on a local, national and international basis.
Publications: Application guidelines, Annual report, Biennial report, Grants list, Program policy statement.
Application information: Application guidelines and application cover sheet available on foundation Web site. Application form required.
  Initial approach: Letter
  Copies of proposal: 1
  Deadline(s): None
  Board meeting date(s): Fall and spring
  Final notification: Generally within 3 months
Officers and Directors:* Michael Lerner, Ph.D.,* Pres.; Thomas Silk, Secy.; Albert Wells, Treas.; Marni Rosen, Exec. Dir.; Anne Bartley; Catherine Porter.
Number of staff: 2 full-time professional; 2 part-time professional; 2 part-time support.
EIN: 943146675

73
American Honda Foundation
1919 Torrance Blvd., M.S. 100-1W-5A
Torrance, CA 90501   (310) 781-4090
Contact: Kathryn A. Carey, Mgr.
Application address: P.O. Box 2205, Torrance, CA 90509-2205; FAX: (310) 781-4270; E-mail: kathryn_carey@ahm.honda.com; URL: http://www.flstw.fsu.edu/honda.html

Established in 1984 in CA.
Donor(s): American Honda Motor Co., Inc.
Grantmaker type: Company-sponsored foundation
Financial data (yr. ended 03/31/02): Assets, $28,782,457 (M); gifts received, $1,000,000; expenditures, $1,988,137; qualifying distributions, $1,821,961; giving activities include $1,587,744 for grants.
Purpose and activities: Support for national organizations working in the areas of youth and scientific education, including private elementary and secondary schools, public and private colleges and universities, and scientific and educational organizations. Scientific education encompasses both the physical life sciences and mathematics, and environmental education.
Fields of interest: Education, association; Early childhood education; Elementary school/education; Secondary school/education; Vocational education; Higher education; Education; Natural resources; Environment; Employment, services; Employment; Human services; Children/youth, services; Minorities/immigrants, centers/services; Physical/earth sciences; Chemistry; Mathematics; Physics; Engineering/technology;

Biological sciences; Science; Economics; Minorities; Native Americans/American Indians; Economically disadvantaged.
Types of support: General/operating support; Continuing support; Program development; Seed money; Curriculum development; Matching/challenge support.
Limitations: Giving on a national basis. No support for religious, political, veterans', or fraternal organizations, private foundations, labor groups, service club activities, arts and culture, health, or welfare and social issues. No grants to individuals, or for trips, hospital operating funds, building funds, small business loans, youth recreational activities, annual fund drives, fundraising, student foreign exchange programs, sponsorships, corporate memberships, medical or educational research, conferences or seminars, disaster relief, or beauty and talent contests.
Publications: Application guidelines, Biennial report (including application guidelines), Grants list, Informational brochure (including application guidelines), Multi-year report, Program policy statement.
Application information: Proposals submitted by FAX not accepted. Application form required.
  Initial approach: Letter or telephone
  Copies of proposal: 1
  Deadline(s): Nov. 1, Feb. 1, May 1, and Aug. 1
  Board meeting date(s): Jan., Apr., July, and Oct.
  Final notification: 2 months
Officers: Hiroshi Soda, Pres.; Gary Kessler, V.P.; Tom Ross, Secy.-Treas.; Kathryn Carey, Mgr.
Board Members: Abrahm Dent; Lou Juneman; Marsha Snoddy; Wade Terry; Jeanette Tomikawa.
Number of staff: 3 full-time professional.
EIN: 953924667

74
Amerman Family Foundation
P.O. Box 479
Santa Ysabel, CA 92070

Established in 1997 in CA.
Donor(s): Jerome T. Amerman, John W. Amerman.
Grantmaker type: Independent foundation
Financial data (yr. ended 12/31/02): Assets, $4,281,066 (M); expenditures, $584,729; qualifying distributions, $497,352; giving activities include $497,352 for 10 grants (high: $98,100; low: $7,500).
Purpose and activities: Giving primarily for education, animals and wildlife, and human services.
Fields of interest: Education; Zoos/zoological societies; Animals/wildlife; Human services.
Limitations: Applications not accepted. Giving primarily in CA. No grants to individuals.
Application information: Contributes only to pre-selected organizations.
Officers: John W. Amerman, Pres.; Anne H. Thompson, Secy.; Jerome T. Amerman, Treas.
Directors: Anne J. Amerman; Garrett J. Amerman; Glenn Bozarth; John Conners.
EIN: 330757355

75
Amgen Foundation, Inc.
1 Amgen Center Dr., MIS27-4-A
Thousand Oaks, CA 91320-1799
(805) 447-1000
Contact: Elizabeth Malkerson, C.E.O. and Pres.
Additional tel.: (805) 447-4050; FAX: (805) 499-6751; URL: http://www.amgen.com/community/foundation.html

Established in 1990 in CA.
Donor(s): Amgen Inc.
Grantmaker type: Company-sponsored foundation
Financial data (yr. ended 12/31/01): Assets, $28,506,637 (M); gifts received, $5,000,000; expenditures, $5,594,536; qualifying distributions, $5,591,606; giving activities include $5,591,606 for 955 grants (high: $800,000; low: $50; average: $500–$50,000).
Purpose and activities: Giving primarily for the arts, education, and for human services.
Fields of interest: Performing arts; Arts; Education; Environment; Human services.
Types of support: General/operating support; Employee matching gifts; Grants to individuals.
Limitations: Giving limited to areas of company operations, with emphasis on Ventura County, CA. No support for religious organizations. No grants to individuals (except for Teacher Excellence Awards).
Application information: Application form not required.
  Initial approach: Letter
  Copies of proposal: 1
  Deadline(s): None
  Board meeting date(s): Quarterly
Officers and Directors:* Elizabeth Malkerson,* C.E.O. and Pres.; Barbara Gray, V.P.; Ellen L. Gams, Secy.; Barry Schehr, C.F.O.; Dennis M. Fenton; Kevin M. Sharer.
Number of staff: 1 full-time professional.
EIN: 770252898
Recent environmental and animal welfare grants:
75-1 Concerned Resource and Environmental Workers, Ojai, CA, $10,000. For general support. 2001.
75-2 Earth Share of California, San Francisco, CA, $25,175. For general support. 2001.

76
The Angelica Foundation
P.O. Box 675814
Rancho Santa Fe, CA 92067-5814
(858) 756-6756
Contact: Suzanne Brown, Pres.
FAX: (858) 756-9452; E-mail: info@angelicafoundation.org; URL: http://www.angelicafoundation.org

Established in 1994 in CA.
Grantmaker type: Independent foundation
Financial data (yr. ended 12/31/01): Assets, $6,739,431 (M); gifts received, $152,898; expenditures, $700,287; qualifying distributions, $419,351; giving activities include $121,760 for 17 grants (high: $63,500; low: $610).
Purpose and activities: Giving primarily for environmental and human service programs.
Fields of interest: Arts; Education; Environment; Human services; International human rights.
International interests: Latin America; Mexico.

Types of support: Annual campaigns.
Limitations: Giving limited to CA, CO, HI, and NM. No support for public education, political organizations, or programs promoting religious doctrines. No grants to individuals, or for academic scholarships, conferences, or fundraising events.
Publications: Application guidelines, Annual report, Informational brochure (including application guidelines), Newsletter.
Application information: Proposals submitted by FAX will not be accepted. Application form not required.
   Initial approach: Letter of intent (no more than 2 pages)
   Copies of proposal: 1
   Deadline(s): July 15
   Board meeting date(s): 1st Sat. in Dec.
   Final notification: Sept. 15
Officer: Suzanne D. Brown, Pres.
Number of staff: 1 part-time professional; 2 part-time support.
EIN: 330632647

77
Animal Protection Institute
P.O. Box 22505
Sacramento, CA 95822   (916) 447-3085
Contact: Alan H. Berger, Exec. Dir.
FAX: (916) 447-3070; E-mail:
info@api4animals.org; URL: http://www.api4animals.org/

Established in 1968.
Grantmaker type: Public charity
Financial data (yr. ended 12/31/01): Revenue, $1,473,313; assets, $3,071,006; gifts received, $1,523,206; expenditures, $2,155,012; program services expenses, $1,673,298; giving activities include $24,400 for 17 grants (high: $5,000; low: $250).
Purpose and activities: The organization advocates for the protection of animals from cruelty and exploitation.
Fields of interest: Animal welfare.
Limitations: Giving on a national basis.
Officers and Directors:* Gary Pike,* Chair.; Susan Lock,* Secy.; James Rockenbach,* Treas.; Alan H. Berger, Exec. Dir.; Duf Fischer; Kenneth E. Guerrero; Kent Robertson; Mary Mitchell Trimble.
EIN: 946187633

78
Argonaut Charitable Foundation
924 Westwood Blvd., Ste. 1060
Los Angeles, CA 90024

Established in 1926 in CA.
Grantmaker type: Independent foundation
Financial data (yr. ended 12/31/02): Assets, $1,485,964 (M); expenditures, $114,955; qualifying distributions, $101,610; giving activities include $99,300 for 39 grants (high: $15,000; low: $250).
Purpose and activities: Giving primarily for the arts and culture, education, the environment, health, social services, and federated giving programs.
Fields of interest: Arts; Libraries/library science; Education; Environment; Hospitals (general); Human services; Federated giving programs.

Limitations: Applications not accepted. Giving primarily in CA. No grants to individuals.
Application information: Contributes only to pre-selected organizations.
Trustees: Elise Marvin; William H. Mudd.
EIN: 956021227

79
Ark Foundation
P.O. Box 2244
Orinda, CA 94563   (925) 253-1260
Contact: Linda Lazare, Treas.

Established in 1983 in CA.
Donor(s): Don W. Carlson.
Grantmaker type: Independent foundation
Financial data (yr. ended 10/31/03): Assets, $62,838 (M); expenditures, $102,035; qualifying distributions, $101,370; giving activities include $101,370 for 25 grants (high: $10,000; low: $270; average: $270–$10,000).
Purpose and activities: Grants for projects in the areas of world peace, consciousness studies, and world communication.
Fields of interest: Education; Environment; Mental health/crisis services; AIDS; Youth development, citizenship; Women, centers/services; International peace/security; Civil rights; Psychology/behavioral science; Public affairs, citizen participation; Women.
Types of support: General/operating support; Equipment; Program development; Publication; Seed money; Curriculum development; Exchange programs.
Limitations: Giving primarily in Contra Costa and Alameda counties, CA. No grants to individuals.
Publications: Application guidelines, Annual report, Grants list.
Application information: Application form not required.
   Initial approach: Proposal
   Copies of proposal: 1
   Deadline(s): None
   Board meeting date(s): Quarterly
   Final notification: Generally in Oct.
Officers and Directors:* Don W. Carlson,* Pres.; Craig Comstock,* Secy.; Linda Lazare,* Treas.; Barbara Carlson; Leonard Perillo.
Number of staff: 2 full-time professional.
EIN: 942895004

80
Arntz Family Foundation
(formerly Eugene S. Arntz Foundation)
P.O. Box 10396
San Rafael, CA 94912
Contact: Nancy Rosa

Established in 1994 in CA.
Donor(s): Eugene S. Arntz,‡ K. Allan Arntz, Thomas E. Arntz, Donald M. Arntz.
Grantmaker type: Independent foundation
Financial data (yr. ended 09/30/02): Assets, $5,522,556 (M); expenditures, $382,715; qualifying distributions, $335,164; giving activities include $299,701 for 59 grants (high: $25,000; low: $50).
Fields of interest: Environment; Family planning.
International interests: Mexico; Central America.
Types of support: General/operating support; Program development.

Limitations: Applications not accepted. No grants to individuals.
Application information: Contributes only to pre-selected organizations. Unsolicited requests for funds not accepted.
   Board meeting date(s): Feb. and July
Trustees: Donald M. Arntz; K. Allen Arntz; Katherine Arntz; Thomas E. Arntz.
Number of staff: 1 part-time professional.
EIN: 686109096

81
Arques Charitable Education Trust
158 Townsend St., Ste. 950
San Francisco, CA 94107

Established in 1989 in CA.
Donor(s): Kimpton's Mental Insight Foundation, Vera Arques,‡ Tiburon Rotary Club, Rawlings Sporting Goods Company, Inc.
Grantmaker type: Independent foundation
Financial data (yr. ended 12/31/01): Assets, $3,042,260 (M); gifts received, $25,925; expenditures, $213,683; qualifying distributions, $173,945; giving activities include $101,078 for 5 grants (high: $50,000; low: $5,228) and $54,867 for 5 grants to individuals (high: $23,000; low: $4,000).
Purpose and activities: Giving primarily for grants to students of veterinary medicine, classical voice, and mechanical arts.
Fields of interest: Arts education; Opera; Music; Higher education; Veterinary medicine.
Types of support: Equipment; Scholarships—to individuals.
Limitations: Applications not accepted. Giving primarily in CA.
Application information: Unsolicited requests for funds not accepted.
Trustee: William Ziegler.
EIN: 686044627

82
Autodesk, Inc. Corporate Giving Program
c/o Community Rels. Dept.
111 McInnis Pkwy.
San Rafael, CA 94903
Contact: Julie Wilder, Mgr., Community Rels.
Application address for product donations: Gifts In Kind Intl., 333 N. Fairfax St., Alexandria, VA 22314; Tel. for product donation application form: (888) 288-4043, document no. 144; FAX: (415) 507-6138; E-mail: julie.wilder@autodesk.com

Grantmaker type: Corporate giving program
Financial data (yr. ended 01/31/03): Total giving, $746,754; giving activities include $306,350 for 147 grants, $123,962 for 780 employee matching gifts and $316,442 for in-kind gifts.
Purpose and activities: Autodesk makes charitable contributions to nonprofit organizations involved with arts and culture, education, the environment, health and human services, community development, science and technology, civic affairs, and to disabled people for product donations. Support is given on a national and international basis.
Fields of interest: Arts; Education; Environment; Health care; Human services; Community development; Science; Public affairs; Disabled.

International interests: Canada; Europe; Nigeria; Asia.

Types of support: General/operating support; Continuing support; Annual campaigns; Building/renovation; Equipment; Emergency funds; Program development; Research; Technical assistance; Employee volunteer services; Use of facilities; Sponsorships; Employee matching gifts; Grants to individuals; Donated equipment; Donated products; In-kind gifts.

Limitations: Giving on a national and international basis, including in Canada, Asia, Europe, and Nigeria, with emphasis on areas of company operations. No support for athletic teams, religious organizations, political organizations, or discriminatory organizations. No grants for sporting events or advertising.

Publications: Application guidelines, Informational brochure (including application guidelines).

Application information: Proposals should be no longer than 2 pages in length. An application form is required for product donations; application form available online. Application guidelines are available online. The Community Relations Department handles giving. The company has a staff that only handles contributions.

  Initial approach: Proposal to nearest company facility; download application form for product donations
  Deadline(s): None
  Final notification: 4 to 6 weeks
Number of staff: 1 full-time professional.

83
Gerson Bakar Foundation
1 Lombard St., Rm. 202
San Francisco, CA 94111

Established in 1984 in CA.
Donor(s): Gerson Bakar.
Grantmaker type: Independent foundation
Financial data (yr. ended 12/31/02): Assets, $33,088,614 (M); gifts received, $5,751,437; expenditures, $1,726,774; qualifying distributions, $1,575,546; giving activities include $1,558,361 for 31 grants (high: $901,300; low: $25).
Fields of interest: Museums (art); Animals/wildlife; Health organizations, association; Human services; Federated giving programs.
Limitations: Applications not accepted. Giving primarily in the San Francisco Bay Area, CA. No grants to individuals.
Application information: Contributes only to pre-selected organizations.
Officers and Directors:* Gerson Bakar, Chair.; Barbara Bass Bakar, Pres.; Richard L. Greene,* Secy.; Nalraj Goundar, Treas.; William Coblentz; Phyllis Cook; Warren Hellman.
EIN: 942949602

84
Bob Baker Foundation, Inc.
591 Camino de la Reina, Ste. 1100
San Diego, CA 92108-3113

Established in 1987 in CA.

Donor(s): Bob Baker Enterprises, Inc., and its subsidiaries, Robert H. Baker.
Grantmaker type: Company-sponsored foundation
Financial data (yr. ended 06/30/02): Assets, $1,203,265 (M); gifts received, $608,085; expenditures, $447,076; qualifying distributions, $445,932; giving activities include $427,605 for 39 grants (high: $110,350; low: $100).
Purpose and activities: Giving primarily for Roman Catholic welfare organizations and a hospital; funding also for human services.
Fields of interest: Higher education; Environment; Hospitals (general); Health care; Health organizations, association; Human services; Homeless, human services; Roman Catholic federated giving programs; Religious federated giving programs; Roman Catholic agencies & churches; Aging; Homeless.
Limitations: Giving primarily in San Diego, CA. No grants to individuals.
Application information:
  Board meeting date(s): Annually
Trustees: Michael V. Baker; Robert H. Baker; Thomas J. Solomon.
EIN: 330265135

85
Dr. Hildegard Balin Trust
c/o Wells Fargo Bank, N.A.
P.O. Box 63954
San Francisco, CA 94163

Established in 1996 in CA.
Grantmaker type: Independent foundation
Financial data (yr. ended 12/31/02): Assets, $5,941,795 (M); expenditures, $449,519; qualifying distributions, $321,662; giving activities include $290,000 for 31 grants (high: $21,000; low: $1,500).
Purpose and activities: Support for human services, especially for services benefiting the elderly and the disadvantaged; giving also for animal welfare and health.
Fields of interest: Animal welfare; Animals/wildlife; Health care; Human services; Children/youth, services; Senior continuing care; Aging, centers/services; Jewish federated giving programs; Aging; Economically disadvantaged.
Limitations: Applications not accepted. Giving primarily in CA, with emphasis on Santa Barbara County. No grants to individuals.
Application information: Contributes only to pre-selected organizations.
Trustees: David F. Horton; Wells Fargo Bank, N.A.
EIN: 776132316

86
The William C. Bannerman Foundation
9255 Sunset Blvd., Ste. 400
West Hollywood, CA 90069
Contact: Elliot Ponchick, Pres.

Established in 1958 in CA.
Grantmaker type: Independent foundation
Financial data (yr. ended 04/30/02): Assets, $9,900,378 (M); expenditures, $692,386; qualifying distributions, $538,719; giving activities include $473,200 for 49 grants (high: $35,000; low: $300).

Purpose and activities: Giving for education, women, children, and the environment.
Fields of interest: Secondary school/education; Education; Environment; Animals/wildlife, preservation/protection; Children, services; Women.
Types of support: General/operating support; Annual campaigns; Capital campaigns; Building/renovation; Program development; Seed money; Matching/challenge support.
Limitations: Giving limited to the Los Angeles, CA, area. No grants to individuals.
Publications: Application guidelines.
Application information: Application form not required.
  Initial approach: 2-page letter
  Deadline(s): Oct. 31
  Board meeting date(s): July and Mar.
  Final notification: Mar. 15
Officers and Directors:* Elliot Ponchick,* Pres.; E.T. Ponchick,* V.P. and Secy.-Treas.
Number of staff: 1 part-time professional.
EIN: 956061353

87
The Coeta and Donald Barker Foundation
(formerly The Donald R. Barker Foundation)
P.O. Box 936
Rancho Mirage, CA 92270-0936
(760) 324-2656
Contact: Nancy G. Harris, Exec. Admin.

Established in 1977 in OR.
Donor(s): Donald R. Barker.‡
Grantmaker type: Independent foundation
Financial data (yr. ended 11/30/02): Assets, $9,222,857 (M); expenditures, $369,318; qualifying distributions, $354,563; giving activities include $278,675 for 80 grants (high: $25,000; low: $200).
Purpose and activities: Giving primarily for education, conservation, health care and social services.
Fields of interest: Arts; Secondary school/education; Higher education; Natural resources; Environment; Hospitals (general); Health care; Mental health/crisis services; Health organizations, association; Heart & circulatory diseases; Medical research, institute; Heart & circulatory research; Children/youth, services; Family services; Community development; Federated giving programs; Disabled.
Types of support: General/operating support; Building/renovation; Equipment; Endowments; Program development; Scholarship funds.
Limitations: Giving limited to CA and OR. No support for sectarian religious purposes, or for agencies that rely on federal or tax dollars for their principal support. No grants to individuals, or for endowment funds, conferences, or operational deficits.
Publications: Application guidelines.
Application information: Application form required.
  Initial approach: Letter on letterhead
  Copies of proposal: 1
  Deadline(s): Mar. 1 and Aug. 1
  Board meeting date(s): May and Oct.
  Final notification: Promptly after decision
Officer and Trustees:* Coeta Barker, Chair.; John D. Brennan; Vernon Gleaves; Dana E. Newquist; Jim Richards.

Number of staff: 1 full-time support; 1 part-time support.
EIN: 930698411

88

The Barth Foundation
220 Camino Sobrante
Orinda, CA 94563

Established in 1986 in CA.
Donor(s): Worldwide Educational Svcs. of California, Eugene F. Barth.
Grantmaker type: Independent foundation
Financial data (yr. ended 09/30/02): Assets, $1,530,233 (M); expenditures, $184,708; qualifying distributions, $163,437; giving activities include $163,615 for 54 grants (high: $50,000; low: $250).
Fields of interest: Theater; College; Natural resources; Athletics/sports, school programs.
Types of support: Annual campaigns; Scholarship funds.
Limitations: Applications not accepted. Giving on a national basis. No grants to individuals.
Application information: Contributes only to pre-selected organizations. Unsolicited requests for funds not accepted.
Trustee: Eugene F. Barth.
EIN: 943025710

89

Greater Bay Bancorp Foundation
430 Cowper St., Ste. 250
Palo Alto, CA 94301 (650) 614-8913
Contact: Ervie L. Smith, Fdn. Dir.

Established in 1998 in CA.
Donor(s): Greater Bay Bancorp.
Grantmaker type: Company-sponsored foundation
Financial data (yr. ended 06/30/02): Assets, $2,149,862 (M); gifts received, $46,800; expenditures, $1,507,120; qualifying distributions, $1,361,503; giving activities include $1,405,394 for 360 grants (high: $50,000; low: $30; average: $30–$50,000), $43,891 for 130 employee matching gifts, $146,464 for foundation-administered programs and $2,056,272 for 3 loans/program-related investments.
Purpose and activities: Giving primarily for youth services.
Fields of interest: Arts; Education; Environment; Health organizations, association; Human services; Youth, services; Aging, centers/services; Human services.
Types of support: General/operating support; Endowments; Program development; Conferences/seminars; Curriculum development; Fellowships; Scholarship funds; Employee matching gifts.
Limitations: Giving primarily in the San Francisco Bay Area, CA.
Publications: Application guidelines, Annual report, Informational brochure.
Application information: Application form required.
Initial approach: Telephone
Copies of proposal: 1
Deadline(s): None
Board meeting date(s): Quarterly

Officers and Trustees:* Duncan L. Matteson,* Chair.; David L. Kalkbrenner, Pres.; Bryon A. Scordelis,* V.P.; Steve C. Smith, V.P.; Carleen Maniglia, Secy.; Shawn E. Saunders, Treas. and C.F.O.; Mark Escher, Cont.; C. Donald Allen; Lawrence A. Aufmuth; Susan B. Ford; Linda R. Meier; Donald Seiler.
Number of staff: 1 full-time professional; 1 part-time support.
EIN: 770474639

90

Beagle Charitable Foundation
c/o myCFO, Inc.
2025 Garcia Ave.
Mountain View, CA 94043
Contact: Harvey L. Armstrong, Secy.-Treas.

Established in 1999 in WA.
Donor(s): Joy D. Covey.
Grantmaker type: Independent foundation
Financial data (yr. ended 03/31/02): Assets, $8,703,961 (M); gifts received, $29,942; expenditures, $280,783; qualifying distributions, $276,365; giving activities include $246,500 for 4 grants (high: $190,000; low: $1,000).
Fields of interest: Higher education; Natural resources; Environment; Health care.
Limitations: Applications not accepted. Giving on a national basis. No grants to individuals.
Application information: Contributes only to pre-selected organizations.
Officers: Joy D. Covey, Pres.; Harvey L. Armstrong, Secy.-Treas.
EIN: 770529181

91

Bear Gulch Foundation
c/o Robert B. Flint, Jr.
185 Bear Gulch Rd.
Woodside, CA 94062

Established in 1994 in DE.
Donor(s): Lucile E. Dupont Flint,‡ Robert B. Flint, Jr.
Grantmaker type: Independent foundation
Financial data (yr. ended 12/31/02): Assets, $3,308,204 (M); expenditures, $262,610; qualifying distributions, $252,589; giving activities include $245,452 for 47 grants (high: $51,702; low: $750; average: $500–$75,000).
Purpose and activities: Giving primarily for education and the environment.
Fields of interest: Arts; Secondary school/education; Education; Environment, land resources; Environment; Family services, adolescent parents; Population studies.
Types of support: General/operating support; Continuing support; Annual campaigns; Capital campaigns; Building/renovation; Land acquisition; Seed money; Program evaluation.
Limitations: Applications not accepted. Giving primarily in northern CA. No grants to individuals.
Application information: Contributes only to pre-selected organizations.
Board meeting date(s): Varies
Officers and Directors:* Robert B. Flint, Jr.,* Pres. and Treas.; William G. Roe,* V.P.; Susan J. Flint,* Secy.; Alexis S. Flint; Katie L. Flint.
EIN: 510355031

92

Elizabeth and Stephen Bechtel, Jr. Foundation ▼
(formerly S. D. Bechtel, Jr. Foundation)
P.O. Box 193809
San Francisco, CA 94119-3809
(415) 284-8572
Contact: Stacey Carr, Asst.
FAX: (415) 284-8571; E-mail: esb@fremontgroup.com

Incorporated in 1957 in CA.
Donor(s): S.D. Bechtel, Jr., Elizabeth H. Bechtel.
Grantmaker type: Independent foundation
Financial data (yr. ended 12/31/02): Assets, $75,478,479 (M); gifts received, $882,173; expenditures, $5,200,918; qualifying distributions, $4,884,108; giving activities include $4,635,770 for 234 grants (high: $200,000; low: $1,000; average: $1,000–$50,000).
Purpose and activities: The purpose of the foundation is to support well-managed nonprofit organizations that provide quality programs and create significant sustained benefits primarily in the areas of engineering and science, conservation, youth development and education, and preventive health care programs and research. The foundation also supports civic and cultural institutions in the San Francisco Bay Area.
Fields of interest: Arts; Engineering school/education; Education; Animals/wildlife, preservation/protection; Youth development, services; Community development; Engineering/technology; Engineering; Science; Leadership development.
Types of support: General/operating support; Continuing support; Annual campaigns; Capital campaigns; Building/renovation; Land acquisition; Emergency funds; Program development; Curriculum development; Scholarship funds; Research; Program evaluation; Matching/challenge support.
Limitations: Applications not accepted. Giving primarily in the San Francisco Bay Area and northern CA. No grants to individuals, or for tenured or contract positions, endowment activities, or underwriting/sponsoring events.
Application information: Giving only to pre-selected organizations.
Officers and Directors:* S.D. Bechtel, Jr., Pres.; Nancy S. Hair, V.P. and Secy.-Treas.; Lauren B. Dachs, V.P. and Exec. Dir.; Elizabeth Hogan Bechtel,* V.P.; Alan M. Dachs; Nonie B. Ramsay.
Number of staff: 3 part-time professional; 2 part-time support.
EIN: 946066138
Recent environmental and animal welfare grants:
92-1 Audubon Society, National, Sacramento, CA, $100,000. For operating support for programs. 2001.
92-2 Big Sur Land Trust, Carmel, CA, $10,000. For operating support for programs. 2001.
92-3 California Academy of Sciences, San Francisco, CA, $20,000. For operating support for programs. 2001.
92-4 California Waterfowl Association, Sacramento, CA, $110,000. For operating support for programs. 2001.
92-5 Canine Companions for Independence, Santa Rosa, CA, $20,000. For operating support for programs. 2001.

92-6 Conservation Fund, Arlington, VA, $30,000. For operating support for programs. 2001.

92-7 Delta Waterfowl Foundation, Bismarck, ND, $55,000. For operating support for programs. 2001.

92-8 Ducks Unlimited, Rancho Cordova, CA, $40,000. For operating support for programs. 2001.

92-9 East Bay Conservation Corps, Oakland, CA, $25,000. For operating support for programs. 2001.

92-10 East Bay Zoological Society, Oakland, CA, $50,000. For capital fund. 2001.

92-11 Friends of Recreation and Parks, San Francisco, CA, $40,000. For capital support for Golden Gate Park and San Francisco Conservatory of Flowers. 2001.

92-12 Monterey Bay Aquarium, Monterey, CA, $60,000. For operating support for programs. 2001.

92-13 National Fish and Wildlife Foundation, San Francisco, CA, $20,000. For operating support for programs. 2001.

92-14 Nature Conservancy, San Francisco, CA, $25,000. For operating support for programs. 2001.

92-15 Political Economy Research Center, Bozeman, MT, $25,000. For operating support for programs. 2001.

92-16 San Francisco Zoological Society, San Francisco, CA, $55,000. For operating support for programs. 2001.

92-17 Student Conservation Association, Charlestown, NH, $10,000. For operating support for programs. 2001.

92-18 Sustainable Conservation, San Francisco, CA, $25,000. For operating support for programs. 2001.

92-19 Trust for Public Land, San Francisco, CA, $50,000. For operating support for programs. 2001.

92-20 University of California, School of Veterinary Medicine, Davis, CA, $25,000. For capital fund. 2001.

92-21 Yosemite Foundation, San Francisco, CA, $25,000. For capital support. 2001.

93
Bella Vista Foundation

(formerly Kirkwood Family Foundation)
Presidio Bldg., Ste. 300
P.O. Box 29906
San Francisco, CA 94129-0906
(415) 561-6540
Contact: Mary L. Gregory, Exec. Dir.
FAX: (415) 561-6477; URL: http://www.pacificfoundationservices.com/bellavista/index.html

Established in 1999 in CA.
Donor(s): Mrs. Morris Doyle.
Grantmaker type: Independent foundation
Financial data (yr. ended 12/31/01): Assets, $44,552,634 (M); gifts received, $15,696,450; expenditures, $723,467; qualifying distributions, $670,079; giving activities include $510,290 for 18 grants (high: $50,000; low: $790).
Purpose and activities: Maintains a two-part grantmaking focus to fund programs that address fundamental causes of societal problems, rather than programs that seek to remedy the effects of those programs. Through

its Early Childhood Development Focus Area, the foundation funds programs addressing the social, emotional, cognitive, and physical needs of children in the 45 months from conception to age three, particularly those that help parents improve their parenting/nurturing skills. Under its General Grantmaking, the foundation funds organizations 1) that serve children and families through educational opportunities or social services, and 2) that promote resource conservation.
Fields of interest: Early childhood education; Natural resources; Children, services; Child development, services; Family services, parent education.
Types of support: General/operating support; Program development.
Limitations: Giving primarily in San Francisco, Marin, San Mateo, and Santa Clara counties, CA. No support for the arts or sectarian religious purposes. No grants to individuals, or for benefit events. Generally, no grants for medical research, health care, publications, or video production (except under special circumstances and only in the early childhood development focus area).
Application information: Unsolicited requests for funds currently not accepted.
Board meeting date(s): Fall
Officers and Directors:* Robert C. Kirkwood,* Pres.; Susan K. Koe,* V.P.; John H. Kirkwood,* Secy.; Jean K. Casey,* C.F.O.; Mary L. Gregory, Exec. Dir.; Jean G. Doyle.
EIN: 943345967

94
Evelyn J. Bennett Foundation

c/o Wells Fargo Bank, N.A.
P.O. Box 63954, MAC 0103-179
San Francisco, CA 94163
Contact: Jan Ozenbaugh, Trust Off., Wells Fargo Bank, N.A.
E-mail: jozenbau@wellsfargo.com

Established in 1998 in CA.
Donor(s): Evelyn Jane Bennett.‡
Grantmaker type: Independent foundation
Financial data (yr. ended 12/21/02): Assets, $3,214,831 (M); expenditures, $130,993; qualifying distributions, $102,119; giving activities include $91,677 for 2 grants (high: $68,758; low: $22,919).
Purpose and activities: Giving primarily for wildlife population control and hospitals for children.
Fields of interest: Animal population control; Hospitals (general).
Types of support: General/operating support.
Limitations: Giving primarily in CA and FL.
Trustee: Wells Fargo Bank, N.A.
EIN: 946732943

95
Berlin Lehman Fund

1615 Mecca Dr.
La Jolla, CA 92037 (858) 454-3393
Contact: William H. Lehman, Secy.

Grantmaker type: Independent foundation
Financial data (yr. ended 12/31/01): Assets, $1,410,946 (M); expenditures, $115,079; qualifying distributions, $115,079; giving

activities include $113,971 for 25 grants (high: $25,000; low: $25).
Purpose and activities: Giving primarily for Jewish agencies.
Fields of interest: Museums (art); Education; Natural resources; Health care; Health organizations, association; Genetics/birth defects; Jewish agencies & temples; Religion; Minorities.
Types of support: General/operating support.
Limitations: Giving primarily in the San Diego, CA, area.
Application information: Application form not required.
Deadline(s): None
Officers and Directors:* Leona B. Lehman,* Pres.; William H. Lehman,* Secy.; Kenneth W. Lehman; Laura Lehman; Terry L. Miller.
EIN: 330160740

96
Bernstein Family Fund

1464 E. Valley Rd.
Santa Barbara, CA 93108

Established in 1966.
Donor(s): Philip L. Bernstein, Leslie S. Bernstein.
Grantmaker type: Independent foundation
Financial data (yr. ended 08/31/02): Assets, $632,209 (M); expenditures, $90,000; qualifying distributions, $90,000; giving activities include $90,000 for grants (high: $27,500).
Purpose and activities: Giving primarily for the arts, cancer institutes, and human services.
Fields of interest: Arts; Education; Environment; Hospitals (general); Cancer; Human services.
Limitations: Giving on a national basis.
Officer: Leslie S. Bernstein, Treas.
Trustee: Philip L. Bernstein.
EIN: 236420229

97
Betlach Family Foundation

c/o Melanie Betlach
260 29th St.
San Francisco, CA 94131

Established in 1999 in CA.
Donor(s): Charles J. Betlach.
Grantmaker type: Independent foundation
Financial data (yr. ended 12/31/00): Assets, $1,846,406 (M); expenditures, $325,449; qualifying distributions, $270,164; giving activities include $280,042 for 4 grants (high: $200,000; low: $15,000).
Purpose and activities: Support for environmental conservation and art museums.
Fields of interest: Museums (art); Natural resources.
Limitations: Applications not accepted. Giving on a national basis. No grants to individuals.
Application information: Contributes only to pre-selected organizations.
Officers: Charles J. Betlach, Pres.; Melanie C. Betlach, Secy.
EIN: 943344735

98

Birkenstock Footprint Sandals, Inc.
  Corporate Giving Program
c/o Mgr., Community Rels.
P.O. Box 6140
Novato, CA 94948
FAX: (415) 899-9117; E-mail:
donations@sales.birkenstockusa.com; URL:
http://www.birkenstock.com/our_company/
giving/community

Grantmaker type: Corporate giving program
Purpose and activities: Birkenstock makes
charitable contributions to nonprofit
organizations involved with arts and culture,
education, the environment, animals, disaster
relief, human services, and community
development. Support is given primarily in areas
of company operations.
Fields of interest: Arts; Education; Environment;
Animals/wildlife; Disasters,
preparedness/services; Human services;
Community development.
Types of support: General/operating support;
Cause-related marketing; Employee volunteer
services; Employee matching gifts; Donated
products.
Limitations: Giving primarily in areas of
company operations. No support for
discriminatory organizations, religious
organizations, political organizations, or
controversial or confrontational organizations.
Application information: Application form not
required.
  Initial approach: Mail, fax, or E-mail proposal
    to headquarters
  Copies of proposal: 1
  Final notification: Following review

99

Biszantz Charitable Foundation
P.O. Box 755
Rancho Santa Fe, CA 92067

Established in 1993 in CA.
Donor(s): Gary E. Biszantz.
Grantmaker type: Independent foundation
Financial data (yr. ended 12/31/02): Assets,
$1,679,738 (M); gifts received, $74,141;
expenditures, $1,116,760; qualifying
distributions, $1,090,471; giving activities
include $1,093,050 for 18 grants (high:
$1,000,000; low: $500).
Purpose and activities: Funding primarily for
education.
Fields of interest: Education; Animals/wildlife;
Health organizations, association;
Athletics/sports, equestrianism; Human services;
YM/YWCAs & YM/YWHAs; Children/youth,
services.
Limitations: Applications not accepted. Giving
primarily in the western U.S. No grants to
individuals.
Application information: Contributes only to
pre-selected organizations.
Trustees: Frances B. Biszantz; Gary E. Biszantz.
EIN: 330589889

100

Blue Oak Foundation
555 Portola Rd.
Portola Valley, CA 94028
Contact: Margi Gould, Exec. Dir.
FAX: (650) 851-0398

Established in 1994 in CA.
Donor(s): E. Kirk Neely, Holly E. Myers.
Grantmaker type: Independent foundation
Financial data (yr. ended 12/31/02): Assets,
$2,536,450 (M); expenditures, $165,346;
qualifying distributions, $151,132; giving
activities include $138,500 for 24 grants (high:
$15,000; low: $1,000).
Purpose and activities: Giving to support
children, youth, families and community
development.
Fields of interest: Environment; Family
planning; Children/youth, services; Community
development; International affairs;
Immigrants/refugees.
International interests: Central America.
Types of support: General/operating support;
Continuing support; Endowments; Program
development; Seed money; Research;
Matching/challenge support.
Limitations: Giving primarily in Santa Clara and
San Mateo counties, CA; some giving also in
Central America.
Publications: Application guidelines.
Application information: Application form not
required.
  Initial approach: Letter. Certified and
    registered mail not accepted
  Deadline(s): None
Officers: E. Kirk Neely, Pres.; Holly E. Myers,
Secy.-Treas.; Margi Gould, Exec. Dir.
Number of staff: 1 part-time professional.
EIN: 943214373

101

Boeing North American Employees
  Donate Once Club
(formerly North American Rockwell Employees
Donate Once Club)
2201 Seal Beach Blvd.
Seal Beach, CA 90740-1515 (562) 797-5781

Established in 1957.
Grantmaker type: Public charity
Financial data (yr. ended 12/31/01): Revenue,
$976,513; assets, $556,820; gifts received,
$953,555; expenditures, $1,208,513; program
services expenses, $1,208,513; giving activities
include $1,208,513 for 96 grants (high:
$144,187; low: $73).
Purpose and activities: The organization
supports charitable, scientific, literary, or
educational purposes and the prevention of
cruelty to children or animals.
Fields of interest: Animal welfare;
Children/youth, services.
Limitations: Giving limited to southern CA.
Committee Members: Roger Dickerson; Cheryl
Dismuke; Ann Dunbar; Bill Fumas; Nancy
Lurwig; Marc Sas; Mindy Vanderbrink; Susie
Unkeless.
EIN: 956054698

102

Booth Heritage Foundation, Inc.
201 N. Carmelina Ave.
Los Angeles, CA 90049

Established in 2000 in CA.
Donor(s): David Booth, Suzanne Deal Booth.
Grantmaker type: Independent foundation
Financial data (yr. ended 01/31/02): Assets,
$24,993 (M); gifts received, $2,500,000;
expenditures, $2,767,456; qualifying
distributions, $2,764,961; giving activities
include $2,765,035 for 46 grants (high:
$2,001,000; low: $75).
Purpose and activities: Giving primarily for
higher education.
Fields of interest: Arts; Higher education;
Education; Environment; Human services.
Limitations: Applications not accepted. Giving
primarily in CA and IL. No grants to individuals.
Application information: Contributes only to
pre-selected organizations.
Officers and Directors:* Suzanne Deal Booth,*
Pres.; David Booth,* Secy. and C.F.O.
EIN: 954785406

103

Anna & Harry Borun Foundation
c/o Wells Fargo Bank, N.A.
P.O. Box 63954, MAC 0103-179
San Francisco, CA 94163
Contact: Bessolos/Hydar
Application address: c/o Wells Fargo Bank,
N.A., 333 S. Grand Ave., Los Angeles, CA
90071, tel.: (213) 253-3156

Established in 1957 in CA.
Donor(s): Anna Borun,‡ Harry Borun.‡
Grantmaker type: Independent foundation
Financial data (yr. ended 12/31/02): Assets,
$5,839,332 (M); expenditures, $315,491;
qualifying distributions, $284,717; giving
activities include $213,000 for 26 grants (high:
$45,000; low: $400).
Fields of interest: University; Natural resources;
Jewish federated giving programs.
Limitations: Giving primarily in CA. No grants
to individuals.
Application information: Application form not
required.
  Initial approach: Letter
  Deadline(s): None
Trustee: Wells Fargo Bank, N.A.
Number of staff: None.
EIN: 956150362

104

The James G. Boswell Foundation
101 W. Walnut St.
Pasadena, CA 91103 (626) 583-3002
Contact: James A. Henry, Exec. Dir.

Incorporated in 1947 in CA.
Donor(s): James G. Boswell.‡
Grantmaker type: Independent foundation
Financial data (yr. ended 12/31/01): Assets,
$73,133,663 (M); expenditures, $4,545,900;
qualifying distributions, $4,274,286; giving
activities include $4,237,786 for 37 grants (high:
$1,500,000; low: $1,000; average:
$1,000–$50,000).

Purpose and activities: Giving primarily for education, health, youth development, agricultural education, and the environment.
Fields of interest: Higher education; Education; Environment; Hospitals (general); Health care; Health organizations, association; Agriculture; Children/youth, services.
Types of support: General/operating support; Continuing support; Annual campaigns; Scholarship funds.
Limitations: Applications not accepted. Giving primarily in CA.
Application information:
  Board meeting date(s): Feb. and as required
Officers and Trustees:* James W. Boswell,* Pres.; Susan W. Dulin,* V.P.; R. Sherman Railsback,* Secy.; James A. Henry, Exec. Dir.; James G. Boswell II; Kenneth Dulin; Rose Hall.
Number of staff: None.
EIN: 956047326

105
The Bothin Foundation
P.O. Box 29906
San Francisco, CA 94129-0906
(415) 561-6540
Contact: Lyman H. Casey, Exec. Dir.
FAX: (415) 561-6477; URL: http://www.pacificfoundationservices.com/bothin/index.html

Incorporated in 1917 in CA.
Donor(s): Henry E. Bothin,‡ Ellen Chabot Bothin,‡ Genevieve Bothin de Limur.‡
Grantmaker type: Independent foundation
Financial data (yr. ended 12/31/01): Assets, $38,027,684 (M); expenditures, $2,200,411; qualifying distributions, $1,836,750; giving activities include $1,557,117 for 96 grants (high: $150,000; low: $1,000; average: $5,000–$25,000).
Purpose and activities: Support for organizations providing direct services to low-income, at-risk children, youth and families, the elderly, and disabled. To a limited extent, grants may also be made to environmental agencies and arts organizations that serve youth predominately. The foundation prefers to make grants for capital, building, and equipment needs.
Fields of interest: Environment; Human services; Children/youth, services; Child development, services; Family services; Aging, centers/services; Homeless, human services; Disabled.
Types of support: Capital campaigns; Building/renovation; Equipment.
Limitations: Giving primarily in CA, with emphasis on San Francisco, Marin, Sonoma, San Mateo, and Santa Barbara counties. No support for religious organizations, or educational institutions (except those directly aiding the developmentally or learning disabled). No grants to individuals, or for general operating funds, endowment funds, program support, scholarships, fellowships, medical research conferences or for production or distribution of films or other media presentations; no loans.
Publications: Biennial report (including application guidelines).
Application information: Application form not required.

Initial approach: Letter containing a brief outline of the project
Copies of proposal: 1
Deadline(s): 12 weeks prior to board meeting
Board meeting date(s): Feb., May, and Oct.
Final notification: 2 to 3 months
Officers and Directors:* Genevieve di San Faustino,* Pres.; A. Michael Casey,* V.P.; Susie Pollak,* Secy.; Lyman H. Casey, Exec. Dir.; Kimberly K. Casey; Nancy R. Conner; Gordon E. Miller; Carol K. Prince.
Number of staff: None.
EIN: 941196182

106
Boudjakdji Foundation
3029 Wilshire Blvd., Ste. 200
Santa Monica, CA 90403

Established in 1997 in CA.
Donor(s): Millicent Boudjakdji.
Grantmaker type: Independent foundation
Financial data (yr. ended 09/30/02): Assets, $1,669,749 (M); expenditures, $139,071; qualifying distributions, $116,886; giving activities include $117,194 for 22 grants (high: $50,000; low: $63).
Purpose and activities: Giving primarily for education, health, and human services.
Fields of interest: Arts; Education; Animal welfare; Hospitals (general); Health organizations, association; Human services.
Limitations: Applications not accepted. No grants to individuals.
Application information: Contributes only to pre-selected organizations.
Officers: Millicent Boudjakdji, C.E.O.; Raouf Boudjakdji, Secy.; Robert Given, C.F.O.
EIN: 954664672

107
Robert C. & Lois C. Braddock Charitable Foundation
1221 Broadway, 21st Fl.
Oakland, CA 94612-1837 (510) 451-3300
Contact: Robert C. Braddock, Jr., Tr.

Classified as a private operating foundation in 1992.
Donor(s): Robert C. Braddock, Lois C. Braddock.
Grantmaker type: Operating foundation
Financial data (yr. ended 06/30/02): Assets, $5,840,562 (M); gifts received, $250,000; expenditures, $400,756; qualifying distributions, $367,911; giving activities include $331,945 for 30 grants (high: $50,000; low: $500).
Purpose and activities: Giving primarily for a public library and a business college, as well as for education, conservation and preservation, health associations, food services, human services, churches, and an aeronautical organization.
Fields of interest: Higher education; Business school/education; Libraries (public); Natural resources; Health organizations, association; Food services; Human services; Space/aviation; Christian agencies & churches.
Limitations: Giving primarily in CA.
Application information:
  Initial approach: Letter
  Deadline(s): None

Trustees: Lois C. Braddock; Robert C. Braddock, Jr.; Cheryl Lee Keemar.
EIN: 680234966

108
George and Ruth Bradford Foundation
P.O. Box 720
Ukiah, CA 95482 (707) 895-3428
Contact: Robert L. Bradford, Dir.

Established in 1985 in CA.
Donor(s): Ruth Bradford.
Grantmaker type: Independent foundation
Financial data (yr. ended 06/30/02): Assets, $2,511,157 (M); gifts received, $400; expenditures, $157,923; qualifying distributions, $157,114; giving activities include $149,350 for 39 grants (high: $50,000; low: $500).
Purpose and activities: Giving for education, youth, medical and human services.
Fields of interest: Museums; Higher education; Education; Natural resources; Health care; Eye diseases; Housing/shelter, temporary shelter; Camps; Youth development, centers/clubs; Human services; Children/youth, services; Family services.
Types of support: General/operating support; Scholarship funds.
Limitations: Giving limited to the San Francisco Bay Area, CA. No grants to individuals.
Application information:
  Initial approach: Letter
Directors: Robert Bradford; Lloyd Haefner; Myrna Oglesby.
EIN: 943015722

109
Brandes Family Foundation
P.O. Box 535
Rancho Santa Fe, CA 92067-0535
(858) 755-0297
Contact: Linda Brandes, Pres.

Established in 1996 in CA.
Donor(s): Charles Brandes, Linda Brandes.
Grantmaker type: Independent foundation
Financial data (yr. ended 12/31/00): Assets, $6,831,923 (M); gifts received, $1,446,457; expenditures, $234,517; qualifying distributions, $209,950; giving activities include $209,950 for 16 grants (high: $137,500; low: $1,000).
Purpose and activities: Giving primarily for youth and family services.
Fields of interest: Education; Animals/wildlife; Health care; Health organizations, association; Youth development; Human services; Family services.
Limitations: Giving on a national basis. No grants to individuals.
Application information:
  Initial approach: Letter
  Deadline(s): None
Officers: Linda Brandes, Pres.; Charles Brandes, Treas.
Director: Karen Nielson.
EIN: 330709977

110
Brewster West Foundation
57 Post St., Ste. 503
San Francisco, CA 94104

Established in 1994 in CA.
Donor(s): Eric Johnson.
Grantmaker type: Independent foundation
Financial data (yr. ended 12/31/02): Assets, $2,213,735 (M); expenditures, $230,201; qualifying distributions, $209,933; giving activities include $190,000 for 27 grants (high: $25,000; low: $1,500).
Purpose and activities: Giving primarily for Episcopal churches and environmental conservation organizations.
Fields of interest: Museums; Historic preservation/historical societies; Higher education; College; Libraries/library science; Natural resources; Hospices; Protestant agencies & churches.
Limitations: Applications not accepted. Giving primarily in CA. No grants to individuals.
Application information: Contributes only to pre-selected organizations.
Trustees: Mark B. Dandurand; Barbara B. Johnson; Eric L. Johnson; Martine B. Larsen; Barbara Loveless; Richard G. Malone.
EIN: 680343603

111
The Bridges/Larson Foundation
c/o R. Koblin
P.O. Box 3365
Beverly Hills, CA 90212

Established in 1993 in CA.
Donor(s): James Bridges.‡
Grantmaker type: Independent foundation
Financial data (yr. ended 12/31/02): Assets, $3,006,795 (M); expenditures, $257,464; qualifying distributions, $210,949; giving activities include $211,400 for 35 grants (high: $75,000; low: $100).
Purpose and activities: Giving primarily for higher education, arts and culture, and federated giving programs.
Fields of interest: Film/video; Television; Arts; Higher education; Animals/wildlife; AIDS; AIDS research; Federated giving programs.
Limitations: Applications not accepted. Giving primarily in CA. No grants to individuals.
Application information: Contributes only to pre-selected organizations. Unsolicited requests for funds not accepted.
Trustee: Ronald R. Koblin.
EIN: 954422320

112
Gary Broad Foundation
(formerly Gary and Sheri Broad Foundation)
10900 Wilshire Blvd., 12th Fl.
Los Angeles, CA 90024-6532

Established in 1997.
Donor(s): Gary Broad.
Grantmaker type: Independent foundation
Financial data (yr. ended 12/31/01): Assets, $1,860,383 (M); expenditures, $167,494; qualifying distributions, $162,929; giving activities include $160,000 for 8 grants (high: $25,000; low: $10,000).

Fields of interest: Natural resources; Animal welfare; Food distribution, meals on wheels; Aging, centers/services.
Limitations: Applications not accepted. Giving primarily in CA, Washington, DC, and VA. No grants to individuals.
Application information: Contributes only to pre-selected organizations.
Trustees: Gary Broad; Cindy S. Quane.
EIN: 330757689

113
Brotman Foundation of California
11845 W. Olympic Blvd., Ste. 845
Los Angeles, CA 90064 (310) 477-1400
Contact: Michael B. Sherman, Pres.

Established in 1964.
Grantmaker type: Independent foundation
Financial data (yr. ended 12/31/01): Assets, $8,179,568 (M); expenditures, $518,261; qualifying distributions, $385,431; giving activities include $325,400 for 52 grants (high: $29,000; low: $500; average: $1,000–$30,000).
Purpose and activities: Giving mainly for children, health and medical research; some support for arts, education, and environmental organizations.
Fields of interest: Arts; Education; Environment; Health care; Health organizations, association; AIDS; Medical research, institute; AIDS research; Children/youth, services.
Types of support: General/operating support; Continuing support; Conferences/seminars; Research.
Limitations: Giving primarily in southern CA. No grants to individuals.
Application information: Application form not required.
  Initial approach: Letter
  Copies of proposal: 1
  Deadline(s): None
  Board meeting date(s): 3rd Wed. of each month
Officers and Directors:* Michael B. Sherman,* Pres. and Treas.; Lowell Marks,* Secy.; Toni Brotman.
Number of staff: None.
EIN: 956094639

114
Patricia Crail Brown Foundation
3090 Bristol St., Ste. 250
Costa Mesa, CA 92626

Established in 1998 in CA.
Donor(s): Patricia A. Brown Trust.
Grantmaker type: Independent foundation
Financial data (yr. ended 12/31/02): Assets, $2,650,232 (M); expenditures, $140,288; qualifying distributions, $133,324; giving activities include $115,852 for 6 grants (high: $70,000; low: $102).
Fields of interest: Education; Animals/wildlife; Substance abuse, services; Children/youth, services.
Limitations: Giving limited to organizations located in Kern County, CA. No grants to individuals.
Application information: Application form required.
  Deadline(s): Apr. 1

Officers and Directors:* Lynn A. Brown,* Pres.; Patricia M. Soldano,* Secy.; Debra A. Wilkins,* C.F.O.
EIN: 330379373

115
Clyde D. & Betsy A. Bruhn Trust
c/o Francis B. Dillon
926 J St., Ste. 402
Sacramento, CA 95814-2786

Established in 1998 in CA.
Donor(s): Betsy A. Bruhn,‡ Clyde D. Bruhn.‡
Grantmaker type: Independent foundation
Financial data (yr. ended 12/31/02): Assets, $2,178,135 (M); expenditures, $298,237; qualifying distributions, $263,758; giving activities include $252,288 for 5 grants (high: $62,572; low: $2,000).
Purpose and activities: Giving primarily for children and youth services, including funding for a children's hospital.
Fields of interest: Animal welfare; Health care; Youth development, centers/clubs; Children/youth, services; Roman Catholic agencies & churches.
Limitations: Applications not accepted. Giving primarily in Sacramento, CA. No grants to individuals.
Application information: Contributes only to pre-selected organizations.
Trustees: Francis B. Dillon; E.M. Hulett; Stephen A. White.
Agent: Union Bank of California, N.A.
EIN: 686104896

116
Bundy Family Foundation
650 California St., 23rd Fl.
San Francisco, CA 94108
Contact: Alexandra Schwartze, Off. Mgr.

Established in 1994 in CA.
Donor(s): Frederick L. Carroll, Mrs. Frederick L. Carroll.
Grantmaker type: Independent foundation
Financial data (yr. ended 10/31/02): Assets, $3,277,967 (M); expenditures, $218,953; qualifying distributions, $200,736; giving activities include $203,000 for 7 grants (high: $130,000; low: $5,000).
Fields of interest: Museums; Higher education; Zoos/zoological societies.
Limitations: Applications not accepted. No grants to individuals.
Application information: Contributes only to pre-selected organizations.
Officers: Frederick L. Carroll, Pres.; Christina E. Carroll, Secy.-Treas.
EIN: 943215971

117
Ronald W. Burkle Foundation
10000 Santa Monica Blvd., 5th Fl.
Los Angeles, CA 90067 (310) 789-7200

Established in 1998 in CA.
Donor(s): Ronald W. Burkle.
Grantmaker type: Independent foundation

Financial data (yr. ended 12/31/01): Assets, $2,354,168 (M); gifts received, $5,296,895; expenditures, $5,586,810; qualifying distributions, $5,584,958; giving activities include $5,583,289 for 42 grants (high: $2,277,212; low: $1,000; average: $10,000–$100,000).
Purpose and activities: Giving primarily for medical research and the environment, as well as for art education and health and human services.
Fields of interest: Arts education; Environment; Health organizations, association; Medical research; Big Brothers/Big Sisters; Human services.
Limitations: Applications not accepted. Giving primarily in Los Angeles, CA. No grants to individuals.
Application information: Contributes only to pre-selected organizations.
Officer: Ronald W. Burkle, Chair.
Directors: Ken Abdalla; Naoma Nicholls-Payne.
EIN: 954664750

118
Andrew H. Burnett Foundation
114 E. De La Guerra St., Ste. 3
Santa Barbara, CA 93101 (805) 963-8822
Contact: Allen W. Finger, Pres.

Established in 1998 in CA.
Donor(s): Helen P. Burnett.
Grantmaker type: Independent foundation
Financial data (yr. ended 06/30/02): Assets, $3,449,112 (M); expenditures, $685,171; qualifying distributions, $610,728; giving activities include $564,700 for 43 grants (high: $77,000; low: $1,000).
Purpose and activities: Giving primarily for art and culture, with emphasis on music, aid for people in need, the environment, and health.
Fields of interest: Music; Arts; Environment; Health care; Human services.
Limitations: Giving limited to Santa Barbara, CA. No grants to individuals.
Application information: Application form required.
  Deadline(s): Apr. 1
Officers and Directors:* Allen W. Finger,* Pres.; Joanne S. Rapp,* Secy.; Arthur R. Gaudi,* C.F.O.
EIN: 770492768

119
Sidney S. Byers Charitable Trust
200 Manresa Ct.
Los Altos, CA 94022
Contact: Patricia H. Nelson, Tr.

Established in 1989 in CA.
Grantmaker type: Independent foundation
Financial data (yr. ended 12/31/02): Assets, $4,341,329 (M); expenditures, $346,126; qualifying distributions, $290,107; giving activities include $260,000 for 38 grants (high: $10,000; low: $5,000).
Purpose and activities: Giving primarily for the conservation and preservation of threatened and endangered wildlife and lands; some support also for the blind and hearing-impaired.
Fields of interest: Animal welfare; Animals/wildlife, preservation/protection;

Human services; Children/youth, services; Human services; Disabled.
Types of support: General/operating support; Scholarship funds; Research.
Limitations: Applications not accepted. Giving primarily in San Mateo and Santa Clara counties, CA. No grants to individuals.
Application information: Unsolicited requests for funds not accepted.
Trustees: Patricia H. Nelson; Philip S. Nelson.
EIN: 936229226

120
The Caldwell-Fisher Charitable Foundation
3620 Clay St.
San Francisco, CA 94118
Contact: John Fisher, C.E.O.
Application address: c/o Draper Fisher Assoc., 400 Seaport Ct., Ste. 250, Redwood, CA 94063

Established in 1999 in CA.
Donor(s): Jennifer Caldwell, John Fisher.
Grantmaker type: Independent foundation
Financial data (yr. ended 12/31/02): Assets, $340,814 (M); expenditures, $335,379; qualifying distributions, $329,982; giving activities include $330,000 for 4 grants (high: $250,000; low: $5,000).
Fields of interest: Education; Environment.
Limitations: Applications not accepted. Giving on a national basis. No grants to individuals.
Application information: Contributes only to pre-selected organizations.
Officers: John Fisher, C.E.O. and Secy.; Jennifer Caldwell, Pres. and V.P.
EIN: 770527966

121
California Community Foundation ▼
445 S. Figueroa St., Ste. 3400
Los Angeles, CA 90071 (213) 413-4130
Contact: Judith A. Spiegel, Sr. V.P., Progs. and Catherine Stringer, Dir., Comm.
FAX: (213) 383-2046; E-mail: info@ccf-la.org; URL: http://www.calfund.org

Established in 1915 in CA by bank resolution.
Grantmaker type: Community foundation
Financial data (yr. ended 06/30/03): Assets, $560,490,721 (M); gifts received, $54,920,641; expenditures, $63,464,509; giving activities include $54,297,438 for 5,599 grants (high: $2,000,000; low: $100), $13,000 for 85 employee matching gifts and $1,950,000 for 2 loans/program-related investments.
Purpose and activities: The mission of the foundation is to build one community out of many by matching acts of caring to community needs. In the first years of the new century, the foundation has continued to push the envelope of traditional grantmaking, investing in projects and communities with far more than grant dollars, creating initiatives that seek to radically change the foundation's approach to old problems, and developing relationships with and among donors to pool knowledge and funds for the benefit of Los Angeles's nonprofits. Acting as a leader and convener on local issues, and serving as a solution broker within L.A.'s vast and varied nonprofit landscape, are roles the community foundation undertakes with purpose and passion. The foundation has

established the following funding priorities: 1) Health - Enhance access to primary health care for the working poor and those living in poverty; 2) Early Education - To provide children from preschool through eighth grade with a solid educational base; 3) Neighborhood Revitalization - To establish communities where every individual feels they have a stake in the community's well being; and 4) Employment - To place adults into jobs that provide livable wages and ease their entry into the work force.
Fields of interest: Arts; Education; Environment; Animal welfare; Health care; AIDS; AIDS research; Domestic violence; Housing/shelter, development; Human services; Children/youth, services; Aging, centers/services; Race/intergroup relations; Community development; Public affairs; Asians/Pacific Islanders; African Americans/Blacks; Hispanics/Latinos; Native Americans/American Indians; Disabled; Aging; Women; People with AIDS (PWAs); Gays/lesbians; Immigrants/refugees; Economically disadvantaged; Homeless.
Types of support: Emergency funds; Program development; Seed money; Scholarship funds; Research; Technical assistance; Program evaluation; Program-related investments/loans; Employee matching gifts; Matching/challenge support.
Limitations: Giving limited to Los Angeles County, CA. No support for sectarian purposes. No grants to individuals (except through the Visual Arts Initiative), or for building funds, annual campaigns, equipment, endowment funds, debt reduction, operating budgets, scholarships, fellowships, films, conferences, dinners, or special events.
Publications: Application guidelines, Annual report (including application guidelines), Financial statement, Informational brochure, Informational brochure (including application guidelines), Newsletter.
Application information: Special initiatives have their own schedules and application forms. Applications received by FAX not accepted. Application form required.
  Initial approach: Request for application form
  Copies of proposal: 1
  Deadline(s): None
  Board meeting date(s): Mar., June, Sept., and Dec.
Officers: Antonia Hernandez, C.E.O. and Pres.; Joe Lumarda, Exec. V.P., Ext. Affairs; Judith A. Spiegel, Sr. V.P., Progs.; Steve Cobb, V.P. and C.F.O.
Board of Governors: Jane G. Pisano, Chair.; Vilma S. Martinez, Vice-Chair.; Bruce C. Corwin; Dorothy Avila Courtney; Jane B. Eisner; Richard M. Ferry; Ronald Gother; Paul C. Hudson; John E. Kobara; Olivia E. Mitchell; Ki Suh Park; James M. Rosser; Robert Segal; John C. Siciliano; Sheldon M. Stone; Andrea L. Van de Kamp.
Number of staff: 24 full-time professional; 18 full-time support.
EIN: 953510055
Recent environmental and animal welfare grants:
121-1 Conservation Corps of Long Beach, Long Beach, CA, $10,000. For job training classes for at-risk youth. 2002.
121-2 Los Angeles Conservation Corps, Los Angeles, CA, $20,000. For cultural programs at Good Beginnings Family Opportunities

Center, which provides child care for Corps members and low-income families in Pico-Union and South Central Los Angeles. 2002.

121-3 Pacoima Beautiful, Pacoima, CA, $68,400. To hire development director. 2002.

122
The Cameron Foundation
629 J St.
Sacramento, CA 95814
Contact: James W. Cameron, Dir.

Established in 1989.
Donor(s): James W. Cameron.
Grantmaker type: Independent foundation
Financial data (yr. ended 12/31/01): Assets, $2,056,414 (M); expenditures, $233,061; qualifying distributions, $186,887; giving activities include $187,654 for 10 grants (high: $100,000; low: $620).
Fields of interest: Radio; Education; Animal welfare; Crime/law enforcement; Philanthropy/voluntarism.
Limitations: Giving primarily in Sacramento, CA. No grants to individuals.
Application information:
Initial approach: Letter
Deadline(s): None
Director: James W. Cameron.
EIN: 680216710

123
The Capecchio Foundation
(formerly The Cortopassi Family Foundation)
11292 N. Alpine Rd.
Stockton, CA 95212

Established in 1990 in CA.
Donor(s): Dean Cortopassi, Joan Cortopassi.
Grantmaker type: Operating foundation
Financial data (yr. ended 12/31/02): Assets, $9,242,751 (M); gifts received, $5,609,600; expenditures, $671,420; qualifying distributions, $802,371; giving activities include $592,975 for 86 grants (high: $202,250; low: $100) and $1,000 for 1 grant to an individual.
Fields of interest: Performing arts; Orchestra (symphony); Historic preservation/historical societies; Arts; Secondary school/education; Reading; Education; Natural resources; Health organizations; Human services; Children/youth, services; Hospices; Federated giving programs.
Types of support: Scholarship funds.
Limitations: Applications not accepted. Giving primarily in Stockton, CA.
Application information: Unsolicited requests for funds not accepted.
Officers: Dean Cortopassi, Pres.; Donald Lenz, Secy.-Treas.
Director: Joan Cortopassi.
EIN: 680232655

124
Alan I. Casden Foundation
9090 Wilshire Blvd., 3rd Fl.
Beverly Hills, CA 90211

Donor(s): Alan I. Casden.
Grantmaker type: Independent foundation

Financial data (yr. ended 06/30/02): Assets, $2,880 (M); gifts received, $151,250; expenditures, $151,362; qualifying distributions, $151,307; giving activities include $151,250 for 8 grants (high: $35,000; low: $3,250).
Fields of interest: Education; Zoos/zoological societies; Children, services; Family services.
Limitations: Applications not accepted. Giving primarily in Los Angeles, CA. No grants to individuals.
Application information: Contributes only to pre-selected organizations.
Officers and Director:* Alan I. Casden,* Pres.; Andrew Starrels, V.P. and Treas.
EIN: 953376266

125
The Casner Family Foundation
1020 Huntington Dr.
San Marino, CA 91108
Contact: Eva Mae Casner, Pres.

Established around 1995.
Donor(s): Eva Mae Casner.
Grantmaker type: Independent foundation
Financial data (yr. ended 12/31/01): Assets, $2,894,473 (M); gifts received, $400,000; expenditures, $157,186; qualifying distributions, $149,321; giving activities include $150,500 for 27 grants (high: $37,500; low: $250).
Purpose and activities: Giving for children's services, education, family planning services, and wildlife and animal welfare.
Fields of interest: Education; Natural resources; Health organizations, association; Children/youth, services.
Limitations: Giving primarily in CA. No grants to individuals.
Application information:
Deadline(s): None
Officers: Eva Mae Casner, Pres.; Randall Kroha, V.P.; Ben H. Garrett, Secy.
EIN: 954508945

126
George V. and Rena G. Castagnola Family Foundation
2791 Sycamore Canyon Rd.
Santa Barbara, CA 93108-1916
Contact: Virginia Castagnola Hunter, Chair.

Grantmaker type: Independent foundation
Financial data (yr. ended 06/30/02): Assets, $901,362 (M); gifts received, $140,000; expenditures, $136,821; qualifying distributions, $121,236; giving activities include $117,975 for 47 grants (high: $17,200; low: $100).
Fields of interest: Museums; Performing arts; Higher education; Environment; Arms control; International affairs; Civil rights.
Types of support: Continuing support; Land acquisition; Endowments; Program development; Conferences/seminars; Publication; Seed money; Research.
Limitations: Applications not accepted. Giving limited to CA. No grants to individuals.
Application information: Contributes only to pre-selected organizations. Unsolicited requests for funds will not be considered or acknowledged.
Officers: Virginia Castagnola Hunter, Chair. and Pres.; Renee Castagnola, Secy. and C.F.O.

EIN: 770358709

127
Caufield Family Foundation
4 Embarcadero Ctr., Ste. 3620
San Francisco, CA 94111

Established in 1993 in CA.
Donor(s): Frank J. Caufield.
Grantmaker type: Independent foundation
Financial data (yr. ended 06/30/02): Assets, $3,503,902 (M); expenditures, $365,148; qualifying distributions, $317,224; giving activities include $295,657 for 62 grants (high: $112,500; low: $250).
Purpose and activities: Giving primarily for child abuse prevention, education, and the arts.
Fields of interest: Museums; Arts; Education; Environment; Health organizations; Child abuse; Human services; Children/youth, services; Civil rights, immigrants; Federated giving programs.
Limitations: Applications not accepted. Giving primarily in San Francisco, CA; some funding nationally. No grants to individuals.
Application information: Contributes only to pre-selected organizations.
Officers: Frank J. Caufield, Pres.; Frank R. Caufield, V.P.; Kirsten N. Caufield, V.P.; Kimberley R. Burke, Secy.-Treas.
EIN: 943187012

128
Center for Ecoliteracy
2522 San Pablo Ave.
Berkeley, CA 94702-2013 (510) 845-4595
Contact: Zenobia Barlow, Exec. Dir.
FAX: (510) 845-1439; E-mail: info@ecoliteracy.org; URL: http://www.ecoliteracy.org

Established in 1995 in CA.
Grantmaker type: Public charity
Financial data (yr. ended 12/31/01): Revenue, $2,027,672; assets, $753,969 (L); gifts received, $1,989,776; expenditures, $2,103,360; program services expenses, $1,719,109; giving activities include $806,900 for grants.
Purpose and activities: The center administers a donor-advised fund which is dedicated to fostering a profound understanding of the natural world, grounded in direct experience, that leads to sustainable patterns of living.
Fields of interest: Environment, public education; Environmental education.
Types of support: General/operating support; Program development; Conferences/seminars; Curriculum development; Research; Technical assistance.
Limitations: Giving primarily in the San Francisco Bay/Delta Area, CA.
Publications: Application guidelines, Grants list, Informational brochure (including application guidelines), Program policy statement.
Application information: See website for grant guidelines and other information.
Initial approach: Letter of inquiry
Copies of proposal: 4
Deadline(s): Apr. 15 and Oct. 15
Board meeting date(s): Spring and fall
Final notification: Following board meetings

Officers and Directors:* Fritjof Capra,* Chair.; Zenobia Barlow,* Exec. Dir.; Peter Buckley; Gay Hoagland; David W. Orr.
Number of staff: 6 full-time professional; 6 full-time support.
EIN: 942911417

129
Chais Family Foundation
611 N. Oakhurst Dr.
Beverly Hills, CA 90210-3530

Established in 1985.
Donor(s): Stanley Chais, Pamela Chais.
Grantmaker type: Independent foundation
Financial data (yr. ended 05/31/02): Assets, $46,442,992 (M); gifts received, $305,208; expenditures, $2,501,318; qualifying distributions, $2,462,088; giving activities include $2,465,462 for 31 grants (high: $700,000; low: $250; average: $5,000–$125,000).
Purpose and activities: Giving primarily for education, and for Jewish agencies and organizations.
Fields of interest: Theological school/education; Education; Natural resources; Jewish federated giving programs; Jewish agencies & temples.
International interests: Israel.
Limitations: Applications not accepted. Giving primarily in Los Angeles, CA, and New York, NY. No grants to individuals.
Application information: Contributes only to pre-selected organizations.
Officers and Directors:* Stanley Chais,* Chair.; Emily Chais,* V.P.; Mark Chais,* V.P.; William Chais,* V.P.; Pamela Chais,* Secy. and C.F.O.
EIN: 954017323

130
Camilla Chandler Family Foundation
2029 Century Park E., Ste. 4100
Los Angeles, CA 90067

Established in 1994 in CA.
Donor(s): Camilla Chandler Frost.
Grantmaker type: Independent foundation
Financial data (yr. ended 10/31/02): Assets, $8,643,742 (M); expenditures, $457,857; qualifying distributions, $397,159; giving activities include $380,000 for 3 grants (high: $250,000; low: $30,000).
Purpose and activities: Giving primarily for higher education and the environment.
Fields of interest: Higher education; Natural resources.
Types of support: General/operating support; Capital campaigns; Building/renovation; Equipment.
Limitations: Applications not accepted. Giving primarily in MA and WA. No grants to individuals.
Application information: Contributes only to pre-selected organizations.
Trustees: Camilla Chandler Frost; Alexander Spear; William Stinehart, Jr.
EIN: 956979804

131
Chapman Forestry Foundation
200 B St., Ste. F
Davis, CA 95616-4505

Established in 1954.
Grantmaker type: Independent foundation
Financial data (yr. ended 12/31/02): Assets, $2,100,760 (M); expenditures, $111,268; qualifying distributions, $110,160; giving activities include $96,138 for 5+ grants.
Fields of interest: Scholarships/financial aid; Education; Animals/wildlife, preservation/protection; Cemeteries/burial services.
Limitations: Applications not accepted. Giving primarily in CA and TX. No grants to individuals.
Application information: Contributes only to pre-selected organizations.
Officers: Dale Chapman, Pres.; Fred Chapman, V.P.; Christie Billing, Treas.
Directors: Alsuko Chapman; John Christie.
EIN: 626046602

132
Cheeryble Foundation
c/o Flekman, Baren & Co.
9171 Wilshire Blvd., Ste. 530
Beverly Hills, CA 90210 (310) 274-5847
Contact: Zora Charles, Pres.

Established in 1987 in CA.
Donor(s): Les Charles, Zora Charles.
Grantmaker type: Independent foundation
Financial data (yr. ended 12/31/02): Assets, $2,064,270 (M); gifts received, $500,000; expenditures, $444,480; qualifying distributions, $443,080; giving activities include $443,391 for 79 grants (high: $41,000; low: $100).
Fields of interest: Museums (art); Arts; Libraries/library science; Natural resources; Environment; Family planning; Human services; Women.
Types of support: General/operating support.
Limitations: Giving primarily in CA. No grants to individuals.
Application information: Application form not required.
  Initial approach: Letter
  Deadline(s): None
Officers: Zora Charles, Pres. and Secy.; Les Charles, C.F.O.
EIN: 954121906

133
ChevronTexaco Corporation Contributions Program
(formerly Chevron Corporation Contributions Program)
6001 Bollinger Canyon Rd., Rm. A2332
San Ramon, CA 94583-0778
Contact: David Scull, Admin., Grants
URL: http://www.chevrontexaco.com/social_responsibility

Grantmaker type: Corporate giving program
Purpose and activities: ChevronTexaco makes charitable contributions to nonprofit organizations involved with arts and culture, K-12 and higher education, the environment, health and human services, youth development, international development, and civic affairs.

Support is given on a national and international basis.
Fields of interest: Arts; Elementary/secondary education; Higher education; Natural resources; Environment; Health care; Youth development; Human services; International development; Public affairs.
Types of support: General/operating support; Scholarship funds; Employee volunteer services; Sponsorships.
Limitations: Applications not accepted. Giving on a national and international basis in areas of company operations; giving also to national organizations. No support for religious, veterans', labor, fraternal, athletic, or political organizations, United Way-supported organizations, school-related bands, or national health, medical, or human service organizations specializing in research. No grants to individuals, or for capital campaigns, conferences and seminars, sports activities, freelance films or videos, tickets, courtesy advertising, endowments, travel, or fundraising; no in-kind gifts.
Application information: Contributes only to pre-selected organizations. The Public Affairs Department handles giving. The company has a staff that only handles contributions.
Administrators: Aldo M. Caccamo, V.P., Public Affairs; David Scull, Admin., Grants.
Number of staff: 7 full-time professional; 3 full-time support.

134
Chintu Gudiya Foundation
c/o Donald Ajit Lobo
453 Lincoln Ave.
Alameda, CA 94501-3235

Established in 1999 in CA.
Donor(s): Donald Ajit Lobo.
Grantmaker type: Independent foundation
Financial data (yr. ended 06/30/02): Assets, $4,605,210 (M); expenditures, $173,190; qualifying distributions, $155,705; giving activities include $159,996 for 11 grants (high: $30,000; low: $250).
Fields of interest: Education; Natural resources; Environmental education; Domestic violence; Human services.
Limitations: Applications not accepted. No grants to individuals.
Application information: Contributes only to pre-selected organizations.
Officers and Directors:* Donald Ajit Lobo,* Pres.; Mari Grace Tilos,* Secy.-Treas.
EIN: 943315265

135
The Christensen Fund ▼
145 Addison Ave.
Palo Alto, CA 94301 (650) 462-8600
Contact: Karla Savage, Ph.D., Grants Prog. Off.
E-mail: info@christensenfund.org; *URL:* http://www.christensenfund.org/index.html

Incorporated in 1957 in CA.
Donor(s): Allen D. Christensen,‡ Carmen M. Christensen.
Grantmaker type: Independent foundation
Financial data (yr. ended 11/30/01): Assets, $118,829,935 (M); expenditures, $19,909,296;

qualifying distributions, $9,673,586; giving activities include $4,617,061 for 52 grants (high: $1,200,000; low: $305) and $14,294,805 for 19 in-kind gifts.

Purpose and activities: The fund makes grants to organizations in the areas of expressive arts and conservation science.

Fields of interest: Visual arts; Museums; Arts; Higher education; Environment, research; Natural resources; Environment.

International interests: Ethiopia; Mexico; Asia; Iran; Australia.

Types of support: Continuing support; Equipment; Program development; Seed money; Fellowships; Research; Program evaluation; Matching/challenge support.

Limitations: Giving primarily in Ethiopia, Iran, Central Asia, southwestern U.S., northern Mexico, Melanesia, and Aboriginal Northern Australia. No grants to individuals (except for scholarships), or for capital funds, or building or renovation funding; no loans.

Application information: Please refer to the fund's Web site for guidelines and program areas. Application form required.

Initial approach: Initial inquiry as outlined on Web site
Copies of proposal: 1
Deadline(s): To be decided
Board meeting date(s): Quarterly
Final notification: Following board meetings

Officers and Directors:* C. Diane Christensen,* Chair. and Pres.; Tara Diann Stein,* Secy.; Kenneth Kirshenbaum,* Treas.; Kenneth Wilson, Ph.D., Exec. Dir.; Karen K. Christensen; John Robinson; Thomas Seligman.

Number of staff: 4 full-time professional; 1 part-time support.

EIN: 946055879

Recent environmental and animal welfare grants:

135-1 American Museum of Natural History, Center for Biodiversity and Conservation, New York, NY, $30,000. For creation of tailored conservation biology curriculum to strengthen conservation capacity in Indochina. 2001.

135-2 Balboa High School, San Francisco, CA, $50,000. For Wilderness Arts and Literacy Collaborative program that uses environmental education and outdoor field experiences to integrate science, English, social studies, art, and technology in urban high schools. 2001.

135-3 California Academy of Sciences, San Francisco, CA, $179,232. For scientific and educational training of teachers and students in major biological survey of environmental changes in San Francisco Bay. 2001.

135-4 Colorados Ocean Journey, Denver, CO, $10,000. To create education outreach materials about exhibits on aquatic environments and conservation to reach larger number of K-12 students and teachers. 2001.

135-5 Conservation and Research Center Foundation, Front Royal, VA, $1,200,000. For bridge funding to support critical conservation projects including research, professional capacity building, and environmental education in the U.S. and abroad. 2001.

135-6 Diversity Initiatives, Portland, Oregon, $20,000. To create butterfly habitats in K-12

inner city schools and provide teacher training to link academic science content and outdoor lab. 2001.

135-7 Highlands Center for Natural History, Prescott, AZ, $10,000. To develop outdoor science learning center for ages 6-12 to learn about arts and natural sciences. 2001.

135-8 Hilton Pond Center for Piedmont Natural History, York, SC, $35,000. For involvement of students and teachers in Ruby-throated Hummingbird study. 2001.

135-9 Jurupa Valley High School, Mira Loma, CA, $15,215. For subsidized travel costs for student research in Galapagos Islands. 2001.

135-10 Kingfisher Public Schools, Kingfisher, OK, $25,000. For greenhouse for agricultural students to develop solutions in sustainable farming and local conservation. 2001.

135-11 Live Oak School District, Santa Cruz, CA, $80,000. For teacher training program to strengthen and expand literacy into environment and arts. 2001.

135-12 Northwest Middle School, Knoxville, TN, $17,500. For building of greenhouses to conduct research and facilitate collaboration between alternative and traditional school children to further scientific and environmental understanding. 2001.

135-13 Prince William Sound Science Center, Cordova, AK, $16,000. For cleaning and assembling of whale skeleton for local science center. 2001.

135-14 University of Missouri, International Center for Tropical Ecology, Saint Louis, MO, $1,041,250. For endowment for graduate scholars from developing countries to expand Center's geographic range and allow focus on applied conservation. 2001.

135-15 Verde Valley School, Sedona, AZ, $97,618. To subsidize high school environmental monitoring program for determining ecosystem of river and developing management plan. 2001.

135-16 Wildlife Conservation Society, Bronx, NY, $44,659. For challenge grant that supports graduate training for nationals of less developed countries, goal is long-term in-country conservation leadership. 2001.

135-17 Zoological Society of Houston, Houston, TX, $65,050. To subsidize collaborative program that involves Houston Zoo, Houston Independent School District, and Texas Southern University in developing zoo-based curriculum for teaching importance of conservation to children. 2001.

136
The Cleo Foundation
(formerly The C.A.W. Foundation)
P.O. Box 29906
San Francisco, CA 94129-0906
(415) 561-6540
Contact: Mary Gregory, Exec. Dir.
URL: http://www.pacificfoundationservices.com/cleo/index.html

Established in 1997 in CA.
Grantmaker type: Independent foundation
Financial data (yr. ended 12/31/02): Assets, $2,828,421 (M); expenditures, $170,481; qualifying distributions, $147,817; giving activities include $106,911 for 16 grants (high: $10,000; low: $111).

Fields of interest: Education; Environmental education; Health care; Substance abuse, prevention; Substance abuse, treatment; Youth development; Human services; Children/youth, services; Domestic violence; Hospices.

Types of support: General/operating support; Continuing support; Capital campaigns; Building/renovation; Program development.

Limitations: Applications not accepted. Giving primarily in San Francisco, San Benito, Mendocino and southern Monterey counties, CA; some giving also in San Luis Obispo County, CA, and Seattle, WA. No grants to individuals or religious entities, or for medical research, endowments or annual appeals.

Application information: Unsolicited requests for funds not accepted. Organizations will be invited to submit proposals.

Board meeting date(s): Usually Apr. and Oct.
Officers: Carol W. Casey, Pres.; Ann Carlie Wilmans, Secy.; Mary Gregory, Exec. Dir.
Director: Paul L. Wattis III.
EIN: 943269201

137
The Collins Family Foundation
c/o myCFO, Inc.
2029 Century Park E., Ste. 800
Los Angeles, CA 90067

Established in 1997 in CA.
Donor(s): David C. Collins, Mary C. Collins.
Grantmaker type: Independent foundation
Financial data (yr. ended 12/31/01): Assets, $6,614,436 (M); expenditures, $375,888; qualifying distributions, $352,335; giving activities include $101,991 for 9 grants (high: $25,000; low: $1,000).

Purpose and activities: Giving primarily to educational and religious organizations; funding also for a university, a heritage society, and wildlife.

Fields of interest: Historical activities; Elementary/secondary education; University; Animals/wildlife, preservation/protection.

Limitations: Applications not accepted. Giving primarily in CA. No grants to individuals.

Application information: Contributes only to pre-selected organizations.

Officers and Directors:* Mary C. Collins,* Pres.; David C. Collins,* Secy. and C.F.O.; Stephen A. Kroft.
EIN: 954618828

138
Columbia Foundation
1016 Lincoln Blvd., Ste. 205
P.O. Box 29470
San Francisco, CA 94129 (415) 561-6880
Contact: Susan Reed Clark, Exec. Dir.
FAX: (415) 561-6883; E-mail:
info@columbia.org; URL: http://www.columbia.org

Incorporated in 1940 in CA.
Donor(s): Madeleine H. Russell,‡ Christine H. Russell.
Grantmaker type: Independent foundation
Financial data (yr. ended 05/31/02): Assets, $69,871,970 (M); gifts received, $46,110; expenditures, $5,035,376; qualifying distributions, $4,349,879; giving activities

include $3,859,428 for 106 grants (high: $334,000; low: $1,000; average: $1,000–$25,000).

Purpose and activities: While the foundation's broad philanthropic purpose has given it flexibility to respond to changing social conditions, it has nevertheless maintained its long-standing interest in world peace, human rights, the environment, cross-cultural and international understanding, the quality of urban life, and the arts. Within each of these areas the board of directors sets new priorities as conditions change.

Fields of interest: Natural resources; Environment; Animals/wildlife, preservation/protection; Agriculture/food; Civil rights, advocacy; Civil liberties, advocacy; Civil liberties, right to die; Civil liberties, death penalty issues; Urban/community development.

Types of support: General/operating support; Building/renovation; Program development; Publication; Seed money; Research.

Limitations: Giving primarily in the San Francisco Bay Area, CA. Some foundation-initiated giving in the United Kingdom and other countries for the arts. No support for private foundations, institutions supported by federated campaigns or heavily subsidized by government funds, or projects in medicine or religion. No grants to individuals, or for scholarships, fellowships, ongoing programs, or operating budgets of established agencies.

Publications: Annual report (including application guidelines), Grants list.

Application information: Grants to programs based in the United Kingdom or other countries are initiated by the foundation; unsolicited proposals are not considered. Proposal sent by FAX or E-mail not considered; they should be 2-sided and reproduced on recycled paper. Application form required.

Initial approach: Letter of inquiry with application on cover sheet (no more than 4 pages)
Copies of proposal: 1
Deadline(s): Human Rights: Sept. 1; Sustainable Comm. and Econ: Dec. 1; Arts and Culture: June 1
Board meeting date(s): 4 times per year
Final notification: 10 weeks after deadline

Officers and Directors: Alice C. Russell-Shapiro,* Pres.; Christine H. Russell,* Secy.; Charles P. Russell,* Treas.; Susan Reed Clark, Exec. Dir.

Number of staff: 2 full-time professional; 2 full-time support.

EIN: 941196186

Recent environmental and animal welfare grants:

138-1 Alliance for Sustainable Jobs and the Environment, Portland, Oregon, $35,000. To bring labor, environmental and community leaders together to develop sustainable restoration economy that is ecologically-based and that will create high-skill, living-wage livelihoods and sustainable communities through landscape and watershed restoration in Humboldt County and adjacent areas in North Coast region of California. 2002.

138-2 California Academy of Sciences, San Francisco, CA, $25,000. For Annual Fund. 2002.

138-3 Center for Ecoliteracy, Berkeley, CA, $25,000. For Food Systems Project, which works with school districts and communities in Berkeley, and Marin, Sonoma, and Yolo Counties to establish and implement food policies to all students for breakfast, lunch, and snacks, to create new markets for local farmers and regional food economy by harnessing institutional buying power of schools for regional sustainable agriculture, and to establish core curriculum in classroom to teach children about connections between nutrition, food, health, and environment linked to instructional school gardens, school cafeterias, and regional sustainable farms. 2002.

138-4 Center for Urban Education About Sustainable Agriculture, Berkeley, CA, $50,000. To employ Sustainable Agriculture Education Program Director to develop and implement public education programs on sustainable agriculture and community outreach to San Francisco neighborhoods once Ferry Plaza Farmers' Market is established at new site in arcades of Ferry Building. 2002.

138-5 Ecotrust, Portland, Oregon, $100,000. To develop and distribute Section Z, newspaper information insert designed to increase public understanding about and build broader constituency for conservation economy. 2002.

138-6 Edible Schoolyard at King Middle School, Berkeley, CA, $35,000. For general operating support for environmental and health education program. 2002.

138-7 Funders for Sustainable Food Systems (FSFS), San Francisco, CA, $20,000. To educate philanthropic sector on how supporting transition to sustainable food system can effectively reduce social and environmental degradation, create sustainable regional food economies, and improve social, economic and environmental quality of life in California. 2002.

138-8 Institute for Food and Development Policy, Oakland, CA, $100,000. For continued support for Critiquing Industrial Agriculture and Genetic Engineering Program, to rebut industry misinformation concerning purported need for benefits of and lack of alternatives to genetic engineering of crops and food. 2002.

138-9 International Society for Ecology and Culture, Berkeley, CA, $50,000. To research, write, produce, and disseminate California Local Food Report and related educational materials that help inform public of social, economic, and ecological benefits of local food systems. 2002.

138-10 Materials for the Future Foundation, San Francisco, CA, $200,000. To develop nonprofit enterprises that harness potential of recycled materials (wood, building, deconstruction materials, and glass) to save natural resources, reduce pollution, and create living wage jobs in San Francisco Bay Area. 2002.

138-11 Northcoast Regional Land Trust, Eureka, CA, $75,000. To establish regional land trust for North Coast of California, with special emphasis on merging economic development and conservation strategies to protect natural resources on both working and wild lands. 2002.

138-12 Rainforest Action Network, San Francisco, CA, $25,000. To ensure implementation of corporate commitments ultimately leading to sustainable forest practices and on-the-ground protection for old growth forests worldwide. 2002.

138-13 Roots of Change Fund, San Francisco, CA, $600,000. For collaborative effort to combine significant private and public resources to fund sustainable agriculture and food systems fellowship, public policy program, and food literacy education in strategic way so that sustainable agriculture solutions to environmental and social degradation will be understood, adopted and promoted by state of California. Grant made through Canopy Institute. 2002.

139
Common Counsel Foundation

1221 Preservation Pkwy., Ste. 101
Oakland, CA 94612 (510) 834-2995
Contact: Elizabeth Wilcox, Exec. Dir.
FAX: (510)834-2998; E-mail: ccounsel@igc.org;
URL: http://www.commoncounsel.org/

Established in 1989.

Grantmaker type: Public charity

Financial data (yr. ended 12/31/00): Revenue, $397,127; assets, $112,791; gifts received, $359,706; expenditures, $372,523; program services expenses, $343,922; giving activities include $86,745 for 45 grants (high: $25,000; low: $200).

Purpose and activities: The foundation is a consortium of family foundations supporting organizations working for social, economic, and environmental justice. Through its Grantee Exchange Fund the foundation makes grants for travel to strategic planning or technical assistance workshops, conferences, etc.

Fields of interest: Environment; Community development, neighborhood development.

Types of support: Conferences/seminars; Technical assistance.

Limitations: Giving on a national basis.

Publications: Application guidelines, Biennial report, Grants list, Informational brochure.

Application information: See Web site for application forms and guidelines. Application form not required.

Initial approach: Telephone or proposal
Copies of proposal: 1
Deadline(s): Rolling
Board meeting date(s): Ongoing
Final notification: 2 weeks after receipt of proposal

Board Members: Elizabeth Wilcox, Exec. Dir.; Lina Avidan; Robert Bray; Pamela Chang; Anne Kimball; Stephen Kimball; Julie Quiroz Martinez; Albert Wells; George Wells.

Number of staff: 3 shared staff (shared with Acorn Foundation; Abelard Foundation; Penney Family Foundation).

EIN: 943214166

140
Community Foundation for Monterey County ▼
99 Pacific St., No. 155A
Monterey, CA 93940 (831) 375-9712
Contact: Todd Lueders, C.E.O. and Pres.
FAX: (831) 375-4731; E-mail: info@cfmco.org;
URL: http://www.cfmco.org

Incorporated in 1945 in CA.
Grantmaker type: Community foundation
Financial data (yr. ended 12/31/02): Assets, $63,200,000 (M); gifts received, $5,056,056; expenditures, $5,137,175; giving activities include $3,931,124 for 600 grants (high: $100,000; low: $500; average: $500–$100,000) and $591,797 for foundation-administered programs.
Purpose and activities: Support primarily for arts and cultural organizations, libraries, schools and other educational institutions, and human services organizations.
Fields of interest: Historic preservation/historical societies; Arts; Education; Environment; Health care; Health organizations, association; Human services.
Types of support: General/operating support; Continuing support; Capital campaigns; Building/renovation; Equipment; Emergency funds; Program development; Technical assistance; Consulting services; Matching/challenge support.
Limitations: Giving primarily in Monterey County, CA. No support for sectarian religious programs. No grants to individuals, or for annual campaigns, deficit financing, operating costs, general endowments, scholarships, fellowships, travel, research or publications.
Publications: Application guidelines, Annual report (including application guidelines), Informational brochure, Newsletter.
Application information: Application form required.
  Initial approach: Telephone or letter
  Copies of proposal: 2
  Deadline(s): May 1, Sept. 1, and Jan. 1
  Board meeting date(s): 3rd Tues. of each month
  Final notification: 2 1/2 months after deadline
Officers and Directors:* Robert House, Chair.; Ms. Kevin Cartwright,* Vice-Chair.; Todd Lueders, C.E.O. and Pres.; Mark Johnson,* Secy.; Warren Wayland,* Treas.; and 13 additional members.
Number of staff: 12 full-time professional.
EIN: 941615897
Recent environmental and animal welfare grants:
140-1 Monterey Bay Aquarium, Monterey, CA, $995,000. 2001.
140-2 Monterey Bay Aquarium, Monterey, CA, $100,000. 2001.
140-3 Society for the Prevention of Cruelty to Animals of Monterey County, Monterey, CA, $100,000. 2001.
140-4 Society for the Prevention of Cruelty to Animals of Monterey County, Monterey, CA, $35,330. 2001.
140-5 Society for the Prevention of Cruelty to Animals of Monterey County, Monterey, CA, $20,000. 2001.
140-6 Ventana Wilderness Sanctuary, Carmel Valley, CA, $10,000. 2001.

141
Community Foundation for Oak Park
P.O. Box 291
Agoura Hills, CA 91376
Contact: David Ross, Pres.
E-mail: cffoy@vcnet.com; URL: http://www.vcnet.com/~cffop/

Established in 1979 in CA.
Grantmaker type: Community foundation
Financial data (yr. ended 12/31/02): Assets, $300,926 (M); gifts received, $98,347; expenditures, $224,340; giving activities include $190,532 for 24 grants (high: $65,062; low: $42).
Purpose and activities: The purpose of the foundation is to improve and protect the social welfare of the residents of Oak Park, CA, with special emphasis on the cultural, educational and recreational needs of the youth of the community. The foundation administers a program of donor-advised funds.
Fields of interest: Arts; Elementary/secondary education; Libraries (public); Education; Environment; Recreation; Human services; Children/youth, services.
Limitations: Giving limited to Oak Park, CA.
Publications: Annual report (including application guidelines), Informational brochure.
Application information: No emergency requests. Application form required.
  Copies of proposal: 1
  Deadline(s): None
  Board meeting date(s): Quarterly
Officers and Trustees:* David Ross,* Pres.; Era Larson,* V.P.; Harvey Kern,* Secy.; Diane Milavetz,* Treas.; Kent Behringer; Bob Heyman; Steve Iceland; Karen Onifer; Sherwin Sammuels.
EIN: 953416510

142
The Community Foundation of Mendocino County, Inc.
(formerly Mendocino County Community Foundation, Inc.)
135 W. Gobbi St., Ste. 204
Ukiah, CA 95482-5477 (707) 468-9882
Contact: Susanne Norgard, Exec. Dir.
FAX: (707) 468-5529; E-mail: info@communityfound.org; URL: http://www.communityfound.org

Established in 1993 in CT.
Grantmaker type: Community foundation
Financial data (yr. ended 06/30/02): Assets, $3,894,662 (M); gifts received, $2,313,255; expenditures, $643,322; giving activities include $359,676 for grants.
Purpose and activities: To establish a self-sustaining source of revenue, as well as the ability for grantmaking to benefit Mendocino County, CA, for the future. The foundation administers donor-advised funds.
Fields of interest: Education; Environment; Health care; Recreation; Youth development, centers/clubs; Youth development, adult & child programs; Children/youth, services.
Types of support: Endowments; Emergency funds; Program development; Seed money; Scholarship funds; Technical assistance.
Limitations: Giving limited to Mendocino County, CA. No grants to individuals.

Publications: Application guidelines, Annual report, Newsletter.
Application information: Application form required for certain programs. Application form required.
  Initial approach: Letter of inquiry on grant programs and opportunities
  Copies of proposal: 8
  Deadline(s): Varies by program
  Board meeting date(s): 1st Tues. monthly (except for July and Dec.)
Officers: Claire Ellis, Pres.; Conrad L. Cox, V.P.; Rudolph Light, Secy.; Richard A. Bilas, Treas.
Directors: Sharon Brewer; Guilford Dye; Henry Gundling; Jim Levine; Tom Montesonti; Greg Nelson; Thomas F. Parducci; Herbert E. Pruett; Jean Slonecker; Dennis Wilson.
Number of staff: 1 full-time professional; 1 part-time professional.
EIN: 680330462

143
The Community Foundation of Santa Cruz County
(formerly Greater Santa Cruz County Community Foundation)
2425 Porter St., Ste. 17
Soquel, CA 95073-2453 (831) 477-0800
Contact: Lance Linares, Exec. Dir.
FAX: (831) 477-0991; E-mail: info@cfscc.org, or lance@cfscc.org; URL: http://www.cfscc.org

Incorporated in 1982 in CA.
Grantmaker type: Community foundation
Financial data (yr. ended 12/31/02): Assets, $19,583,420 (M); gifts received, $2,657,900; expenditures, $3,673,241; giving activities include $1,827,230 for 342 grants (high: $230,000; low: $50; average: $2,000–$50,000), $49,000 for 18 grants to individuals (high: $8,000; low: $500) and $9,000 for 1 loan/program-related investment.
Purpose and activities: The purpose of the foundation is to strengthen the community, and to inspire philanthropy and community involvement in Santa Cruz County, CA. The foundation administers a donor-advised fund.
Fields of interest: Humanities; Historic preservation/historical societies; Arts; Education; Environment; Health care; Human services; Community development.
Types of support: Continuing support; Equipment; Emergency funds; Program development; Conferences/seminars; Seed money; Scholarship funds; Technical assistance; Scholarships—to individuals; Matching/challenge support.
Limitations: Giving limited to Santa Cruz County, CA. No support for religious purposes. No grants to individuals (except for scholarships from designated funds), or for annual campaigns, deficit financing, capital campaigns, building or renovation funds, land acquisition, fellowships, or research; no student loans.
Publications: Application guidelines, Annual report, Informational brochure.
Application information: Scholarship funds for local high schools only. Guidelines available on foundation Web site. Application form required.
  Initial approach: In person, telephone, or letter
  Copies of proposal: 3
  Deadline(s): 3 times annually
  Board meeting date(s): Quarterly

Final notification: Quarterly. Management assistance grants are made monthly

Officers and Directors:* George W. Conch III,* Pres.; Jill Wilson,* Secy.; Margaret A. Leonard,* Treas.; Lance Linares, Exec. Dir.

Number of staff: 6 full-time professional; 1 part-time professional; 2 part-time support.

EIN: 942808039

144

Community Foundation Silicon Valley ▼

(formerly Community Foundation of Santa Clara County)

60 S. Market St., Ste. 1000

San Jose, CA 95113-1000 (408) 278-2200

Contact: Peter Hero, Pres.

FAX: (408) 278-0280; E-mail: info@cfsv.org; URL: http://www.cfsv.org

Established in 1954 in CA.

Grantmaker type: Community foundation

Financial data (yr. ended 06/30/02): Assets, $539,652,366 (M); gifts received, $105,716,081; expenditures, $84,420,522; giving activities include $77,103,102 for grants.

Purpose and activities: Giving primarily for education; giving also for health and social services, including programs focusing on AIDS, youth, women and minorities, and employment and housing; the fine and performing arts; community development and urban affairs; and the environment.

Fields of interest: Visual arts; Performing arts; Theater; Music; Arts; Early childhood education; Elementary school/education; Secondary school/education; Higher education; Adult education—literacy, basic skills & GED; Reading; Education; Environment; Health care; Mental health/crisis services; Health organizations, association; AIDS; AIDS research; Employment; Food services; Housing/shelter, development; Human services; Youth, services; Hospices; Women, centers/services; Minorities/immigrants, centers/services; Homeless, human services; Community development; Federated giving programs; Engineering/technology; Public affairs; Minorities; Native Americans/American Indians; Women; Homeless.

Types of support: General/operating support; Emergency funds; Program development; Seed money; Scholarship funds; Technical assistance; Consulting services; Program-related investments/loans; Matching/challenge support.

Limitations: Giving primarily in Santa Clara and southern San Mateo counties, CA. No support for religious organizations for sectarian purposes, for-profit schools, or for political activities. No grants to individuals, or for deficit financing, building funds, fundraising, endowment funds, capital campaigns, expenditures for equipment purchases, or fundamental or applied research projects.

Publications: Application guidelines, Annual report, Financial statement, Informational brochure, Newsletter.

Application information: Contact program staff at least one month prior to deadline. Application form required.

Initial approach: Telephone or letter

Copies of proposal: 1

Deadline(s): Varies

Board meeting date(s): Mar., June, Sept., and Dec.

Final notification: Within 2 weeks of board meetings

Officers and Directors:* Debra Engel,* Chair.; Gregory M. Avis,* Vice-Chair.; Peter Hero, Pres.; Leo E. Chavez,* Exec. V.P.; Karen Bradely-Follette, V.P., Devel. and Marketing; J. Michael Patterson,* Treas.; Laura K. Arrillaga; Ann Bowers; Doug Chance; M. Elizabeth Day; Kevin A. Fong; Steven Kirsch; L. Gay Krause; Barbara D. Roupe; Jeff Skoll; Boyd C. Smith; Jon D. Tompkins; Anne M. Yamamoto.

Number of staff: 18 full-time professional; 31 full-time support.

EIN: 770066922

Recent environmental and animal welfare grants:

144-1 American Society for the Prevention of Cruelty to Animals, New York, NY, $10,200. 2001.

144-2 Aquatic Outreach Institute, Richmond, CA, $22,000. 2001.

144-3 Audubon Expedition Institute, Belfast, ME, $25,000. 2001.

144-4 Audubon Society of Alaska, Anchorage, AK, $10,000. 2001.

144-5 California Coastal Protection Network, Santa Barbara, CA, $35,000. 2001.

144-6 California Trout, San Francisco, CA, $25,000. 2001.

144-7 Cheetah Conservation Fund, Ojai, CA, $352,443. 2001.

144-8 Earthome, Baldwin, MD, $10,000. 2001.

144-9 Environmental Defense, New York, NY, $10,000. 2001.

144-10 Environmental Volunteers, Palo Alto, CA, $45,250. 2001.

144-11 Friends of the Eel River, Redway, CA, $345,000. 2001.

144-12 Humane Society, Tuolumne County, Sonora, CA, $10,000. 2001.

144-13 Monterey Bay Aquarium Foundation, Monterey, CA, $18,500. 2001.

144-14 Monterey Bay Salmon and Trout Project, Aptos, CA, $25,000. 2001.

144-15 Natural Heritage Institute, San Francisco, CA, $35,000. 2001.

144-16 Natural Resources Defense Council, New York, NY, $30,600. 2001.

144-17 Nature Conservancy, Arlington, TX, $122,700. 2001.

144-18 Nature Conservancy of Hawaii, Honolulu, HI, $25,000. 2001.

144-19 Our Childrens Earth Foundation, San Francisco, CA, $393,049. 2001.

144-20 Palo Alto Junior Museum and Zoo, Friends of the, Palo Alto, CA, $37,500. 2001.

144-21 Peninsula Conservation Center Foundation, Palo Alto, CA, $51,500. 2001.

144-22 Peninsula Open Space Trust, Menlo Park, CA, $84,200. 2001.

144-23 San Francisco Bay Bird Observatory, San Jose, CA, $40,000. 2001.

144-24 San Francisco Conservation Corps, San Francisco, CA, $20,000. 2001.

144-25 San Francisco Estuary Institute, Richmond, CA, $10,000. 2001.

144-26 San Francisco Zoological Society, San Francisco, CA, $10,067. 2001.

144-27 Sempervirens Fund, Los Altos, CA, $18,350. 2001.

144-28 Sierra Club, San Francisco, CA, $101,000. 2001.

144-29 Silicon Valley Toxics Coalition, San Jose, CA, $31,133. 2001.

144-30 Singapore Environment Council, Singapore, $10,800. 2001.

144-31 Trust for Hidden Villa, Los Altos Hills, CA, $334,540. 2001.

144-32 Youth for Environmental Sanity (YES), Soquel, CA, $17,000. 2001.

145

Community Foundation Sonoma County ▼

(formerly The Sonoma County Community Foundation)

250 D St., Ste. 205

Santa Rosa, CA 95404 (707) 579-4073

Contact: Kay M. Marquet, C.E.O. and Pres.

FAX: (707) 579-4801; URL: http://www.sonomacf.org

Incorporated in 1983 in CA.

Grantmaker type: Community foundation

Financial data (yr. ended 12/31/01): Assets, $71,144,549 (M); gifts received, $5,637,936; expenditures, $16,861,305; giving activities include $14,323,125 for 475+ grants (high: $4,000,000; average: $1,000–$25,000).

Purpose and activities: Giving primarily to arts and humanities, education, the environment, and health and human services.

Fields of interest: Humanities; Arts; Education; Environment; Health care; Human services.

Types of support: General/operating support; Continuing support; Endowments; Emergency funds; Program development; Conferences/seminars; Seed money; Scholarship funds; Technical assistance; Consulting services; Program evaluation; Program-related investments/loans; Scholarships—to individuals; Matching/challenge support.

Limitations: Giving limited to Sonoma County, CA. No support for religious purposes or advocacy activities. No grants to individuals (except academic scholarships), special fundraising events, annual fund campaigns, capital campaigns, conferences, or debt retirement; no loans (except program-related investments).

Publications: Application guidelines, Annual report, Financial statement, Informational brochure, Newsletter.

Application information: Application forms and guidelines can be found at the foundation's Web site. Application form required.

Initial approach: Letter or telephone call to Prog. Off.

Deadline(s): Varies

Board meeting date(s): 1st Tues. of most months

Final notification: Varies

Officers and Directors:* Herbert M Dwight, Jr., Chair.; Kay M. Marquet, C.E.O. and Pres.; Paul Demarco, V.P., Finance and Admin.; Dan Condron, Secy.; Christopher Dobson,* Treas.; Jeannette Anglin; Demaris Brinton; Paul Elliott; Barbara Graves; Judith L. Jordan; Harry Richardon, M.D.; Jean Schulz; Ernest Shelton; Paula Thomas; Neva Turer; Francisco Vazquez, Ph.D.; Henry Wendt; Glenn Yamamoto.

Number of staff: 9 full-time professional; 3 full-time support; 1 part-time support.

EIN: 680003212

146

Compassion for Animals Foundation, Inc.
3962 Landmark St.
Culver City, CA 90232-2315
Contact: Gilbert N. Michaels, Pres.

Established in 1986 in CA.
Donor(s): Gilbert N. Michaels.
Grantmaker type: Operating foundation
Financial data (yr. ended 11/30/02): Assets, $102,151 (M); gifts received, $350,000; expenditures, $340,355; qualifying distributions, $340,355; giving activities include $339,220 for 20 grants (high: $145,000; low: $500).
Purpose and activities: Giving strictly for the protection and advancement of animal rights and the prevention of cruelty to animals, through scientific research, literary and educational efforts, and charitable activities.
Fields of interest: Animal welfare.
Types of support: General/operating support.
Limitations: Giving on a national basis.
Application information: Application form not required.
Initial approach: Letter
Deadline(s): None
Officers: Gilbert N. Michaels, Pres.; Julie Javor, Secy.; Lonnie Horn, C.F.O.
EIN: 954082225

147

Compton Foundation, Inc. ▼
535 Middlefield Rd., Ste. 160
Menlo Park, CA 94025 (650) 328-0101
Contact: Edith T. Eddy, Exec. Dir.
FAX: (650) 328-0171; E-mail:
info@comptonfoundation.org; URL: http://www.comptonfoundation.org

Incorporated in 1972 in NY as successor to the Compton Trust; reincorporated in 1992 in CA.
Donor(s): Members of the Compton family.
Grantmaker type: Independent foundation
Financial data (yr. ended 12/31/01): Assets, $85,673,417 (M); expenditures, $12,309,672; qualifying distributions, $11,783,471; giving activities include $10,902,064 for 589 grants (high: $1,000,000; low: $100; average: $5,000–$100,000).
Purpose and activities: To coordinate the family giving to community, national, and international programs in areas of its special interests, including peace and world order, population, and the environment. Other concerns include equal education opportunity, community welfare, and culture and the arts.
Fields of interest: Natural resources; Environment; Family planning; International peace/security; Arms control; Foreign policy; Population studies.
International interests: Sub-Saharan Africa; Mexico; Central America.
Types of support: General/operating support; Continuing support; Land acquisition; Program development; Fellowships; Research; Consulting services; Program-related investments/loans; Matching/challenge support.
Limitations: Giving on an international basis to U.S.-based organizations for projects in Mexico, Central America, and Sub-Saharan Africa and on a national basis for programs in peace and population and the environment. Other funding limited to areas where board members reside:

primarily San Francisco, Marin, and Santa Clara counties, CA. No grants to individuals, or for capital or building funds, no loans (except for program-related investments).
Publications: Biennial report, Informational brochure (including application guidelines).
Application information: Proposals submitted by FAX or E-mail not accepted. Application form not required.
Initial approach: Brief 3- to 4-page proposal
Copies of proposal: 1
Deadline(s): Feb. 15 and Sept. 15
Board meeting date(s): May and Dec.
Final notification: 6 months
Officers and Directors:* James R. Compton,* Chair.; Ann C. Stephens,* Vice-Chair.; Randolph O. Compton, Pres.; W. Danforth Compton, V.P. and Secy.; Richard Morrison, Treas.; Edith T. Eddy, Exec. Dir.; Rebecca DiDomenico; David W. Orr; Stephen Perry; Lee Etta Powell; Carol C. Wall.
Number of staff: 4 full-time professional; 2 part-time support.
EIN: 943142932
Recent environmental and animal welfare grants:
147-1 20/20 Vision Education Fund, DC, $13,000. For capturing moderate opinion on post-tragedy weapons issues. 2001.
147-2 Acterra: Action for a Sustainable Earth, Palo Alto, CA, $10,000. For Sustainability Project with Bay Area Action. 2001.
147-3 Adopt-A-Watershed, Hayfork, CA, $20,000. For Regional Watershed Program. 2001.
147-4 Alaska Wilderness League, DC, $40,000. For Arctic Refuge Defense Campaign as part of Alaska Coalition. 2001.
147-5 American Farmland Trust, DC, $20,000. For Farmland Protection Program. 2001.
147-6 American Indian College Fund, Denver, CO, $10,000. For Compton Foundation Natural Resource Scholars Program. 2001.
147-7 American Rivers, DC, $75,000. For Voyage of Recovery, West Campaign and California Dam Removal. 2001.
147-8 ANAI Association, Limon, Costa Rica, $40,000. For Community-centered EcoTourism as Conservation Strategy in Costa Rica. 2001.
147-9 Ancient Forest International, Redway, CA, $15,000. For protecting Forests of Rainbow Ridge, CA. 2001.
147-10 Aspen Institute, DC, $30,000. For dialogue on dams and rivers. 2001.
147-11 Audubon Society of Houston, Western Hemisphere Region, Houston, TX, $15,000. 2001.
147-12 Bay Institute of San Francisco, San Rafael, CA, $40,000. For Rivers and Delta Program's Bay Delta Program and Ecological Scorecard. 2001.
147-13 Berea College, Berea, KY, $1,000,000. For Compton Chair in Ecological Design. 2001.
147-14 California Academy of Sciences, San Francisco, CA, $15,000. For Biotic Survey of San Francisco Bay. 2001.
147-15 California Trout, San Francisco, CA, $15,000. For Cattle Grazing and Trout Habitat in California's National Forests. 2001.
147-16 California Wilderness Coalition, Davis, CA, $10,000. For report on California's Most Threatened Places. 2001.

147-17 Center for a New American Dream, Takoma Park, MD, $60,000. For environmentally preferable procurement. 2001.
147-18 Center for Ecoliteracy, Berkeley, CA, $20,000. For transition and renewal support of River of Words Awards. 2001.
147-19 Center for Environment and Population, Center for Environment and Population, Portsmouth, NH, $30,000. For Population and Water Project. Grant made through Tides Center. 2001.
147-20 Center for Watershed and Community Health, Springfield, Oregon, $10,000. For Western States Green Plan Capacity Building Initiative. 2001.
147-21 Chemical Weapons Working Group, Berea, KY, $30,000. For Legal Defense Project. Grant made through Kentucky Environmental Foundation. 2001.
147-22 Climate Solutions, Olympia, WA, $40,000. For Clean Energy Economic Opportunity. 2001.
147-23 Collective Heritage Institute, Santa Fe, NM, $16,000. For Voices of the Bioneers: Solutions and Strategies Database. 2001.
147-24 Concord Consortium, Center for a Sustainable Future, Concord, MA, $10,000. For Shaping Our Future Youth Leadership Institutes. 2001.
147-25 Conservation International, DC, $40,250. For Reproductive Health Services and Environmental Conservation in Peten Region, Guatemala. 2001.
147-26 Council of Canadians, Ottawa, Canada, $45,000. For Blue Planet Project. 2001.
147-27 Council on Economic Priorities, New York, NY, $10,000. For Corporate Environmental Research Program. 2001.
147-28 David Brower Center, San Francisco, CA, $10,000. For Brower Fellows program. 2001.
147-29 De Anza College, Cupertino, CA, $250,000. For statewide energy management program. 2001.
147-30 Development Center for Appropriate Technology (DCAT), Tucson, AZ, $50,000. For multimedia presentations on sustainability and building codes. 2001.
147-31 Earth Island Institute, Center for Safe Energy, San Francisco, CA, $25,000. For Russian-American Campaign for Plutonium Safety. 2001.
147-32 Earthjustice Legal Defense Fund, Oakland, CA, $100,000. For restoring and safeguarding the Pacific Northwest. 2001.
147-33 Ecological Design Innovation Center, Oberlin, OH, $10,000. 2001.
147-34 Ecotrust, Portland, Oregon, $40,000. For Bioregional Salmon Restoration Strategy assessment of key salmon habitats in California and Washington. 2001.
147-35 Ecumenical Project for International Cooperation, Allenspark, CO, $10,000. For biography of Gilbert White. 2001.
147-36 Environmental Defense, New York, NY, $50,000. For Colorado River Delta Restoration. 2001.
147-37 Environmental Law Institute, DC, $30,000. For National Policy Campaign to Restore Wetland Protection. 2001.
147-38 Environmental Media Services, DC, $25,000. For California Rapid Response Project. 2001.

147-39 Friends of the Earth, DC, $16,000. For community, health and environment program of sustaining agriculture by challenging genetically engineered foods. 2001.

147-40 Friends of the Earth, DC, $10,000. For Wild Salmon Project. 2001.

147-41 Friends of the River Foundation, Sacramento, CA, $60,000. For California Wild Heritage Campaign. 2001.

147-42 Friends of the River Foundation, Sacramento, CA, $40,000. For Dam Alternatives: River, Habitat, and Water Supply Solutions. 2001.

147-43 Garden Project, San Francisco, CA, $15,000. 2001.

147-44 Global Greengrants Fund, Boulder, CO, $10,000. For Grassroots Environmental Movement in Mexico, Central America, and Africa. 2001.

147-45 Grand Canyon Trust, Flagstaff, AZ, $30,000. For Greening Our Homestead. 2001.

147-46 Green Action, Kyoto, Japan, $25,000. For Changing Japan's Energy Policy and Terminate Plutonium Use. Grant made through Public Media Center. 2001.

147-47 Green Corps, Boston, MA, $17,500. For Environmental Defense Campaign, ecopledge.com. 2001.

147-48 Green Foothills Foundation, Palo Alto, CA, $10,000. For Coyote Valley Legal Efforts and Executive Director Leadership Fund. 2001.

147-49 Greenbelt Alliance, San Francisco, CA, $10,000. For Coyote Valley Legal Efforts and Executive Director Leadership Fund. 2001.

147-50 Indian Law Resource Center, Helena, MT, $15,000. For protecting Indian Ecosystems in Central America. 2001.

147-51 INFORM, New York, NY, $30,000. For Sustainable Transportation Program. 2001.

147-52 Institute for Childrens Environmental Health, Freeland, WA, $10,000. For Healthy Futures Project. Grant made through Tides Center. 2001.

147-53 Institute for Conservation and Health, Redwood Valley, CA, $23,200. For Environment Fellowship Support Services. 2001.

147-54 Institute for Conservation and Health, Redwood Valley, CA, $23,000. For Mentor Fellowship Program Support. 2001.

147-55 Institutes for Journalism and Natural Resources, Missoula, MT, $90,000. For Western Regional Institutes. 2001.

147-56 International Rivers Network, Berkeley, CA, $30,000. For Sub-Saharan Africa Project. 2001.

147-57 Izaak Walton League of America, Gaithersburg, MD, $25,000. For Sustainable Population Campaign. 2001.

147-58 Land Trust Alliance, DC, $40,000. For Pacific Program. 2001.

147-59 League to Save Lake Tahoe, South Lake Tahoe, CA, $10,000. 2001.

147-60 Low Impact Hydropower Institute, Portland, Oregon, $50,000. For Green Hydropower Certification Program. 2001.

147-61 Mountain Institute, DC, $10,000. For study of cultural and spiritual significance of mountains. 2001.

147-62 National Environmental Trust, DC, $15,000. For Energy Education Project. 2001.

147-63 National Parks Conservation Association, DC, $45,000. For National Parks Business Plan Initiative, Phase IV. 2001.

147-64 National Wildlife Federation, Reston, VA, $50,000. For capacity building for women to advance sustainable development. 2001.

147-65 National Wildlife Refuge Association, DC, $10,000. 2001.

147-66 Natural Resources Defense Council, New York, NY, $50,000. For Western Water Project. 2001.

147-67 Natural Resources Defense Council, New York, NY, $10,000. For Forest Friendly: Market-Based Approaches to Forest Conservation. 2001.

147-68 Nature Conservancy, Los Angeles, CA, $10,000. To restore ecosystems in San Joaquin River Watershed under CALFED Bay-Delta program. 2001.

147-69 Northwest Earth Institute, Portland, Oregon, $25,000. For National Outreach Project, Phase II. 2001.

147-70 Occidental Arts and Ecology Center, Occidental, CA, $12,000. For school garden teacher training and support program. 2001.

147-71 Ocean Arks International, Burlington, VT, $66,000. For Ecological Design, Living Machines and Eco-Industrial Parks. 2001.

147-72 Oregon Water Trust, Portland, Oregon, $10,000. For Defending Instream Water Rights Project. 2001.

147-73 Organization for Tropical Studies, Durham, NC, $30,000. 2001.

147-74 Pacific Forest Trust, Santa Rosa, CA, $70,000. For expanding markets for sustainability. 2001.

147-75 Pacific Forest Trust, Santa Rosa, CA, $10,000. To Protect Utility Lands in California. 2001.

147-76 Point Reyes Bird Observatory, Stinson Beach, CA, $10,000. For education center. 2001.

147-77 Population Coalition, Claremont, CA, $15,000. For Inform America, the Population Literacy Campaign. 2001.

147-78 Positive Futures Network, Bainbridge Island, WA, $20,000. For Beyond Despair: Inspiring Students to Shape a Positive Future. 2001.

147-79 Project Avary, San Rafael, CA, $10,000. For environmental education program for children. 2001.

147-80 Rails to Trails Conservancy, DC, $15,000. For general support of Founder's Fund. 2001.

147-81 Rainforest Action Network, San Francisco, CA, $25,000. For Old Growth Forest Campaign. 2001.

147-82 RAND Corporation, Santa Monica, CA, $55,145. For freshwater ecosystems and population study. 2001.

147-83 RARE Center for Tropical Conservation, Arlington, VA, $30,000. For Sustainable Livelihoods through Ecotourism in South Africa. 2001.

147-84 Redefining Progress, Oakland, CA, $10,000. For Environmental Justice and Climate Change Campaign. 2001.

147-85 River Network, Portland, Oregon, $40,000. For Clean Water Program's increasing citizen use of Clean Water Act in Oregon, Washington, and California. 2001.

147-86 Riverkeeper, Garrison, NY, $20,000. For National Fisheries and Power Plant Initiative. 2001.

147-87 Rose Foundation for Communities and the Environment, Oakland, CA, $15,000. For Environmental Fiduciary Project. 2001.

147-88 San Bruno Mountain Watch, Brisbane, CA, $10,000. For continued conservation. 2001.

147-89 San Francisco State University Foundation, Romberg Tiburon Center for Environmental Studies, San Francisco, CA, $110,000. For Sustainable Future/Solar Power Project. 2001.

147-90 San Jose Conservation Corps, San Jose, CA, $10,000. For Site Development and Classroom Construction Project. 2001.

147-91 San Jose State University Foundation, San Jose, CA, $10,000. For Environmental Business Cluster's National Alliance of Clean Energy Incubators Program. 2001.

147-92 Save Our Wild Salmon Coalition, Seattle, WA, $35,000. For Northwest Wild Salmon Media Project and Strategic Planning Process. 2001.

147-93 Scenic America, DC, $10,000. For Last Chance Landscapes Program. 2001.

147-94 Scenic Hudson, Poughkeepsie, NY, $10,000. For Generating Green Power: The Wave of Our Valley's Future. 2001.

147-95 Second Nature, Boston, MA, $100,000. For West Coast Network. 2001.

147-96 Sierra Business Council, Truckee, CA, $60,000. For Sustainable Rural Towns Initiative. 2001.

147-97 Silicon Valley Environmental Partnership, Los Altos, CA, $10,000. For Environmental Index Update. 2001.

147-98 Snake River Alliance Education Fund, Boise, ID, $25,000. For Back from the Brink Campaign Making the Case for De-Alerting Nuclear Weapons. 2001.

147-99 Sonoran Institute, Tucson, AZ, $60,000. For Community Stewardship in the Colorado River Delta. 2001.

147-100 Sustainability Institute, Plainfield, NH, $25,000. For Sustainability All Around Us. 2001.

147-101 Sustainable Careers Institute, Kingston, NY, $30,000. For Green Career Centers for Greener Campuses. Grant made through Open Space Institute. 2001.

147-102 Taxpayers for Common Sense, DC, $25,000. For Lower Snake River Dam Removal Campaign. 2001.

147-103 Tech Museum of Innovation, San Jose, CA, $10,000. For Tech Environmental Awards Program. 2001.

147-104 Tides Center, San Francisco, CA, $20,000. To help Wild Farm Alliance create Wild Farm Network. 2001.

147-105 Tides Center, Center for Public Environmental Oversight, San Francisco, CA, $20,000. For Advocacy for Sustainable Range Management. 2001.

147-106 Tides Center, Habitat Media, San Francisco, CA, $10,000. For Empty Oceans, Empty Nets with the assistance of Bay Area Video Coalition. 2001.

147-107 Tides Center, Regeneration Project, San Francisco, CA, $10,000. For Episcopal Power and Light Project. 2001.

147-108 Trust for Public Land, San Francisco, CA, $20,000. For Center for Land and People. 2001.
147-109 Trust for Public Land, San Francisco, CA, $13,500. 2001.
147-110 Tuolumne River Preservation Trust, San Francisco, CA, $10,000. For Secure Wild and Scenic Status for Clavey River. 2001.
147-111 Union of Concerned Scientists, Cambridge, MA, $25,000. For Global Security Program. 2001.
147-112 United States Public Interest Research Group Education Fund, Atlanta, GA, $40,000. For Environmental Defense Campaign. 2001.
147-113 Urban Ecology, Oakland, CA, $10,000. For Sustainable Cities Program. 2001.
147-114 WaterWatch of Oregon, Portland, Oregon, $20,000. For Klamath Basin Project. 2001.
147-115 Western Resource Advocates, Boulder, CO, $40,000. For Federal Asset Transfers Project of Western Waters Program. 2001.
147-116 Whidbey Institute, Clinton, WA, $15,000. For Power of Hope. 2001.
147-117 Wild Salmon Center, Portland, Oregon, $20,000. For Cascadia Wild Fish Sanctuary Partnership. 2001.
147-118 Wildcoast, Imperial Beach, CA, $10,000. For Sea Turtle Conservation Network of Californias. 2001.
147-119 Wilderness Society, DC, $40,000. For Defending the Roadless Area Conservation Policy. 2001.
147-120 Wilderness Society, DC, $20,000. To study land ethic as advocacy tool and unifying principle. 2001.
147-121 Wilderness Society, Nautral Trails and Waters Coalition, DC, $25,000. For Off-Road Vehicle Campaign. 2001.

148
The Conservation Land Trust
1062 Fort Cronkhite
Sausalito, CA 94965
URL: http://www.theconservationlandtrust.org

Established in 1999 in CA.
Donor(s): Douglas R. Tompkins, Kristine M. Tompkins.
Grantmaker type: Operating foundation
Financial data (yr. ended 03/31/02): Assets, $128,192,221 (M); gifts received, $7,249,500; expenditures, $1,945,051; qualifying distributions, $7,591,725; giving activities include $916,406 for 2 grants (high: $867,500; low: $48,906) and $6,592,620 for foundation-administered programs.
Purpose and activities: The trust's overarching goals are in the conservation of biodiversity and strategically important biota. Important but secondary considerations are good public access, public educational and interpretive programs, appropriate and ecologically sustainable economic activities, and tourist possibilities.
Fields of interest: Natural resources; Environment, water resources; Environment, forests.
International interests: Argentina; Chile.
Limitations: Applications not accepted. Giving primarily in Argentina and Chile. No grants to individuals.

Application information: Contributes only to pre-selected organizations.
Officers and Directors:* Douglas R. Tompkins,* Pres.; Quincey T. Imhoff,* V.P.; Debra B. Ryker,* Secy.-Treas.; Carlos Cuevas Cueto; John R. Davis; Kristine M. Tompkins.
EIN: 680245471

149
The Sirpuhe & John Conte Foundation
42-900 Bob Hope Dr., Ste. 111
Rancho Mirage, CA 92270-7139

Established in 1999 in CA.
Donor(s): John Conte, Sirpuhe Conte.
Grantmaker type: Operating foundation
Financial data (yr. ended 12/31/01): Assets, $6,548,256 (M); expenditures, $457,452; qualifying distributions, $433,764; giving activities include $341,750 for 15 grants (high: $105,750; low: $1,000).
Purpose and activities: Giving primarily for education, and to Christian organizations.
Fields of interest: Education; Animal welfare; Health care; Christian agencies & churches.
Limitations: Giving primarily in CA.
Officers: Sirpuhe Conte, Pres.; John Conte, Sr. V.P.; Louise Danelian, V.P.; Joyce Stein, V.P.; George Phillips, Secy.
EIN: 330884049

150
Corwin Family Foundation
(formerly The Bruce and Toni Corwin Foundation)
708 N. Sierra Dr.
Beverly Hills, CA 90210

Established in 1986 in CA.
Donor(s): Bruce C. Corwin, Toni Corwin.
Grantmaker type: Independent foundation
Financial data (yr. ended 12/31/02): Assets, $838,413 (M); gifts received, $50,000; expenditures, $204,092; qualifying distributions, $202,239; giving activities include $202,239 for 106 grants (high: $50,000; low: $25).
Purpose and activities: Giving primarily for Jewish organizations.
Fields of interest: Film/video; Education, association; Elementary/secondary education; Education; Animal welfare; Hospitals (general); Health care; Health organizations, association; AIDS; AIDS research; Food services; Youth development, services; Human services; Homeless, human services; Civil rights; Community development; Jewish federated giving programs; Leadership development; Public affairs; Jewish agencies & temples; Religion; Disabled; Homeless.
Types of support: General/operating support; Continuing support; Annual campaigns; Capital campaigns; Building/renovation; Endowments.
Limitations: Applications not accepted. Giving primarily in CA. No grants to individuals.
Application information: Contributes only to pre-selected organizations.
Directors: Bruce C. Corwin; Toni Corwin.
Number of staff: 1 part-time support.
EIN: 954076122

151
Country Sun Natural Foods Corporate Giving Program
c/o Corp. Contribs.
440 S. California Ave.
Palo Alto, CA 94306

Grantmaker type: Corporate giving program
Purpose and activities: Country Sun makes charitable contributions to nonprofit organizations involved with the environment, mental health, recreation, youth development, human services, and homeless people. Support is given primarily in Palo Alto, California.
Fields of interest: Environment; Mental health/crisis services; Recreation; Youth development; Human services; Homeless.
Types of support: General/operating support; Donated products.
Limitations: Giving primarily in Palo Alto, CA.
Application information: Application form not required.
Initial approach: Proposal to headquarters
Copies of proposal: 1
Final notification: Following review

152
Anthony Crabb and Barbara Grasseschi Foundation
1083 Vine St., MB 286
Healdsburg, CA 95448-3459
Contact: Anthony Crabb, V.P.

Established in 1999 in CA.
Donor(s): Barbara Grasseschi, Anthony Crabb.
Grantmaker type: Independent foundation
Financial data (yr. ended 12/31/01): Assets, $1,893,005 (M); expenditures, $99,643; qualifying distributions, $96,730; giving activities include $96,730 for 21 grants (high: $33,080; low: $250).
Fields of interest: Environment, land resources.
Limitations: Giving primarily in San Jose, CA.
Application information:
Initial approach: Letter
Deadline(s): None
Officers: Barbara Grasseschi, C.E.O. and Pres.; Anthony Crabb, V.P.
EIN: 770517537

153
The Sid and Jenny Craig Foundation
P.O. Box 675532
Rancho Santa Fe, CA 92067

Established in 1991 in CA.
Donor(s): Sid Craig, Jenny Craig.
Grantmaker type: Independent foundation
Financial data (yr. ended 12/31/01): Assets, $3,104,135 (M); expenditures, $330,337; qualifying distributions, $320,888; giving activities include $302,675 for 4 grants (high: $200,000; low: $25,000; average: $25,000–$300,000).
Purpose and activities: Support primarily for educational programs for disadvantaged children.
Fields of interest: Education; Veterinary medicine; Disasters, 9/11/01; Children, services; Economically disadvantaged.

Limitations: Applications not accepted. Giving primarily in CA. No grants to individuals.
Application information: Contributes only to pre-selected organizations.
Officers: Sid Craig, C.E.O.; Jenny Craig, V.P. and C.F.O.; Marvin Sears, Secy.
EIN: 954344841

154
Crawford Family Foundation
520 Georgian Rd.
La Canada, CA 91011

Established in 1999 in CA.
Donor(s): Gordon Crawford, Dona Crawford.
Grantmaker type: Independent foundation
Financial data (yr. ended 12/31/01): Assets, $2,172,781 (M); gifts received, $198,040; expenditures, $319,348; qualifying distributions, $316,516; giving activities include $316,664 for 25 grants (high: $95,014; low: $1,000).
Purpose and activities: Giving primarily for youth services, and health associations.
Fields of interest: Radio; Education; Natural resources; Health organizations, association; Youth development; Human services; Christian agencies & churches.
Limitations: Applications not accepted. Giving primarily in CA. No grants to individuals.
Application information: Contributes only to pre-selected organizations.
Officers: Gordon Crawford, Pres.; Dona Crawford, V.P.; Orsi Z. Crawford, Secy.; Jeffrey G. Crawford, Treas.
EIN: 954737866

155
The Mary A. Crocker Trust
233 Post St., 2nd Fl.
San Francisco, CA 94108
Contact: Barbaree Jernigan, Admin.
FAX: (415) 982-0141

Trust established in 1889 in CA.
Donor(s): Mary A. Crocker.‡
Grantmaker type: Independent foundation
Financial data (yr. ended 12/31/02): Assets, $11,461,605 (M); expenditures, $670,798; qualifying distributions, $620,967; giving activities include $486,000 for grants (average: $10,000–$20,000).
Purpose and activities: Giving primarily for precollegiate education, forestry, the environment, and community relations.
Fields of interest: Elementary school/education; Secondary school/education; Education; Natural resources; Environment; Family planning; Agriculture; Youth, services; Voluntarism promotion.
Types of support: Program development; Seed money; Matching/challenge support.
Limitations: Giving primarily in the San Francisco Bay Area, CA. No support for sectarian purposes. No grants to individuals, or for operating budgets, continuing support, annual campaigns, deficit financing, building or endowment funds, capital campaigns, land acquisition, scholarships, fellowships, or conferences; no loans.
Publications: Application guidelines, Grants list, Program policy statement.

Application information: Application form required.
  Initial approach: Letter
  Copies of proposal: 1
  Deadline(s): None
  Board meeting date(s): 2 to 3 times a year
  Final notification: 3 months
Officer: Tania W. Stepanian, Chair.
Trustees: Elizabeth Atcheson; Lucy Blake; Charles Crocker; Frederick W. Whitridge; Abigail H. Wilder.
Number of staff: 1 full-time professional.
EIN: 946051917

156
Crockett Community Foundation
P.O. Box 155
Crockett, CA 94525 (510) 787-9708
Contact: Fred Clerici, Treas.
FAX: (510) 787-1346

Established in 1994 in CA.
Grantmaker type: Community foundation
Financial data (yr. ended 12/31/01): Assets, $1,343,787 (M); gifts received, $669,379; expenditures, $613,651; giving activities include $536,591 for grants (high: $141,827).
Purpose and activities: Giving to promote and improve the quality of life in Crockett, CA. The foundation administers a donor-advised fund.
Fields of interest: Libraries/library science; Education; Environment; Safety/disasters, public policy; Recreation, community facilities; Youth development, adult & child programs; Aging, centers/services; Community development.
Types of support: General/operating support; Capital campaigns; Building/renovation; Equipment; Land acquisition; Program development; Seed money; Consulting services.
Limitations: Giving limited to Crockett, CA. No grants to individuals.
Application information: Application form required.
  Copies of proposal: 8
  Deadline(s): Sept. 30 and Mar. 31
  Board meeting date(s): 1st and 3rd Thurs. of each month
  Final notification: Dec. and June
Officers: Duane Colombo, Chair.; Paul Sizelove, Pres.; Fred Clerici, V.P.; T. Keith Hunter, Secy.; Gerald Epperson, Treas.
Directors: Harold Burnett; Ann Markus.
Number of staff: 2 shared staff (shared with East Bay Community Foundation).
EIN: 680348673

157
Roy E. Crummer Foundation
130 Newport Center Dr., Ste. 140-B
Newport Beach, CA 92660-6923

Established in 1964 in NV.
Donor(s): Jean Crummer Coburn.
Grantmaker type: Independent foundation
Financial data (yr. ended 12/31/01): Assets, $6,721,211 (M); expenditures, $434,863; qualifying distributions, $335,699; giving activities include $340,000 for 86 grants (high: $25,000; low: $120).
Fields of interest: Arts; Secondary school/education; Higher education; Animal

welfare; Health care; Health organizations, association; Human services.
Limitations: Giving primarily in CA. No grants to individuals.
Application information:
  Initial approach: Letter
  Deadline(s): Oct. 31
Officers and Trustees:* Jean Crummer Coburn,* Pres.; Margarite Brown,* Secy.-Treas.; Ian F. Gow; Lee D. Strom.
EIN: 886004422

158
Robert & Patricia Dahl Foundation
c/o Robert Dahl
119 Melody Ln.
Orinda, CA 94563

Established in 1999 in CA.
Donor(s): Robert Dahl, Patricia Dahl.
Grantmaker type: Independent foundation
Financial data (yr. ended 12/31/02): Assets, $2,526,136 (M); expenditures, $173,779; qualifying distributions, $147,485; giving activities include $147,700 for 11 grants (high: $50,000; low: $1,000).
Fields of interest: Environment; Animals/wildlife; Human services.
Limitations: Applications not accepted. Giving primarily in CA. No grants to individuals.
Application information: Contributes only to pre-selected organizations.
Directors: Patricia Dahl; Robert Dahl.
EIN: 680442961

159
Robert and Carole Daly Foundation
(formerly Robert Daly Foundation)
9460 Wilshire Blvd., Ste. 600
Beverly Hills, CA 90212

Established in 1987 in CA.
Donor(s): Robert Daly.
Grantmaker type: Independent foundation
Financial data (yr. ended 12/31/01): Assets, $3,786,148 (M); expenditures, $1,005,570; qualifying distributions, $984,127; giving activities include $984,506 for 85 grants (high: $225,000; low: $400).
Purpose and activities: Giving primarily for the arts, education, health care and human services.
Fields of interest: Film/video; Arts; Higher education; Education; Environment; Hospitals (general); Health care; Health organizations, association; Cancer research; AIDS research; Human services; Children/youth, services.
Types of support: General/operating support; Capital campaigns.
Limitations: Applications not accepted. Giving primarily in CA and NY. No grants to individuals.
Application information: Contributes only to pre-selected organizations.
Trustee: Robert Daly.
EIN: 956875322

160
Damien Foundation
P.O. Box 29903
San Francisco, CA 94129 (415) 561-6400
Contact: Kelsang Aukatsang, Admin.
FAX: (415) 561-6401

Established in 1979 in DE.
Grantmaker type: Independent foundation
Financial data (yr. ended 12/31/02): Assets,
$2,374,962 (M); expenditures, $169,119;
qualifying distributions, $143,553; giving
activities include $130,000 for 1 grant.
Purpose and activities: To empower those
whose vision for humanity and the planet is
democratic, fair and environmentally sound;
giving for grassroots organizations and projects
whose work reflects compassion, consciousness
and commitment; giving on an international
approach to grantmaking, awarding many of its
grants in South America, especially in Brazil.
The planet's delicate ecological situation is a
challenge to which the foundation responds by
directing a significant portion of our grants to
environmental projects, particularly those that
help raise awareness of the complex issues
involved. Projects organized by women or that
evoke women's transformative potential are
encouraged. Communities that nurture the
social, psychological and spiritual dimensions of
the individual are favored.
Fields of interest: Natural resources;
Environment; Women, centers/services;
Psychology/behavioral science; Women.
International interests: South America; Brazil.
Types of support: General/operating support;
Program development.
Limitations: Applications not accepted. Giving
primarily in the Southern Hemisphere, with
emphasis on Brazil; giving also in Europe. No
grants to individuals.
Publications: Informational brochure.
Application information: Contributes only to
pre-selected organizations.
   Board meeting date(s): Varies
Officers and Trustee:* Tara Lamont,* Pres.;
Humberto Mafra, Treas. and Exec. Dir.
Number of staff: None.
EIN: 133006359

161
The David Family Foundation, Inc.
10960 Wilshire Blvd., Ste. 2150
Los Angeles, CA 90024

Established in 1998 in CA.
Donor(s): Larry David, Laurie David.
Grantmaker type: Independent foundation
Financial data (yr. ended 12/31/01): Assets,
$65,447 (M); gifts received, $169,000;
expenditures, $242,446; qualifying distributions,
$242,411; giving activities include $242,411 for
28 grants (high: $100,000; low: $30).
Purpose and activities: Giving for
environmental conservation, the arts, education
and youth services.
Fields of interest: Arts; Education; Environment;
Children/youth, services.
Limitations: Applications not accepted. No
grants to individuals.
Publications: Annual report.
Application information: Contributes only to
pre-selected organizations.

Officers: Laurie David, Pres.; Larry David, Secy.;
Matt Lichtenberg, C.F.O.
EIN: 954675258

162
R. K. Davies Charitable Trust
c/o Whittier Trust Co.
1600 Huntington Dr.
South Pasadena, CA 91030-4792

Trust established in 1974 in CA.
Donor(s): Ralph K. Davies.‡
Grantmaker type: Independent foundation
Financial data (yr. ended 09/30/02): Assets,
$4,295,231 (M); expenditures, $273,912;
qualifying distributions, $243,859; giving
activities include $235,000 for 13 grants (high:
$50,000; low: $5,000).
Purpose and activities: Giving primarily for arts
and culture, education, wildlife conservation
and social services.
Fields of interest: Performing arts; Arts;
Education; Natural resources; Animals/wildlife,
preservation/protection; Health care; Human
services.
Limitations: Applications not accepted. Giving
primarily in CA, with emphasis on San
Francisco. No grants to individuals.
Application information: Contributes only to
pre-selected organizations.
Trustees: Lucy Lewis Dreyer; Maryon Davies
Lewis; Whittier Trust Company.
EIN: 237417287

163
The Barbara Delano Foundation, Inc.
(formerly The Barbara Gauntlett Foundation,
Inc.)
450 Pacific Ave., Ste. 201
San Francisco, CA 94133 (415) 834-1758
Contact: Becky Zug, Prog. Asst.
FAX: (415) 834-1759; E-mail:
bdfoundation@usa.net; URL: http://
www.bdfoundation.org

Established in 1985 in NY.
Donor(s): Barbara Gauntlett.‡
Grantmaker type: Independent foundation
Financial data (yr. ended 12/31/01): Assets,
$33,006,044 (M); expenditures, $2,485,174;
qualifying distributions, $2,278,704; giving
activities include $2,138,479 for 12 grants (high:
$1,663,979; low: $9,000).
Purpose and activities: Support for endangered
species protection in developing countries.
Fields of interest: Natural resources;
Environment, forests; Animals/wildlife,
preservation/protection; Animals/wildlife,
endangered species.
International interests: Russia; Africa; Global
programs; Developing countries; Latin America;
Asia.
Types of support: Equipment; Land acquisition;
Emergency funds; Program development;
Matching/challenge support.
Limitations: Giving on an international basis,
developing nations only. No support for private
foundations. No grants to individuals, or for
research, film projects, or conferences.
Application information: Application guidelines
available through the internet; proposals only

considered after letter of request. Application
form not required.
   Initial approach: Letter of inquiry no more
      than 2 pages
   Copies of proposal: 1
   Deadline(s): Oct. 1
   Board meeting date(s): Nov., Dec.
   Final notification: After board meeting
Officers and Directors:* Suwanna Gauntlett,*
Pres.; Christopher C. Angell,* Secy.; Charles C.
Goodfellow III,* Treas.; Jerome A. Manning;
Neal P. Myerberg.
Number of staff: 1 full-time professional; 1
part-time professional.
EIN: 115238046
**Recent environmental and animal welfare
grants:**
163-1 African Wildlife Foundation, DC,
   $50,000. For general support. 2001.
163-2 BOS-USA, Aptos, CA, $12,500. For
   general support. 2001.
163-3 Care for the Wild, Madison, WI, $50,000.
   For general support. 2001.
163-4 Environmental Investigation Agency, DC,
   $100,000. For general support. 2001.
163-5 Environmental Justice Resource Network,
   Los Angeles, CA, $106,000. For general
   support. 2001.
163-6 Fauna and Flora International, San
   Francisco, CA, $20,000. For general support.
   2001.
163-7 Marine Mammal Fund, San Francisco,
   CA, $25,000. For general support. 2001.
163-8 Phoenix Fund, Vladivostok, Russia,
   $22,000. 2001.
163-9 WildAid, San Francisco, CA, $1,663,979.
   For general support. 2001.
163-10 World Parrot Trust, Stillwater, MN,
   $40,000. For general support. 2001.

164
Leonardo DiCaprio Charitable Foundation
11766 Wilshire Blvd., Ste. 1610
Los Angeles, CA 90025

Established in 1999 in CA.
Donor(s): Leonardo DiCaprio.
Grantmaker type: Independent foundation
Financial data (yr. ended 12/31/00): Assets,
$15,330 (M); gifts received, $75,000;
expenditures, $162,476; qualifying distributions,
$161,514; giving activities include $161,514 for
5 grants (high: $79,000; low: $1,200).
Purpose and activities: Giving primarily for the
environment and education.
Fields of interest: Education; Environment.
Limitations: Applications not accepted. Giving
on a national basis. No grants to individuals.
Application information: Contributes only to
pre-selected organizations.
Officers and Directors:* Leonardo DiCaprio,*
Pres.; Irmelin DiCaprio, V.P. and C.F.O.; George
DiCaprio,* V.P.; Jeffrey Saces,* Secy.
EIN: 954743032

165
James V. & June P. Diller Family
Foundation
131 Escobar Rd.
Portola Valley, CA 94028
Contact: James V. Diller, Pres.

Established in 1998 in CA.
Donor(s): James V. Diller, June P. Diller.
Grantmaker type: Independent foundation
Financial data (yr. ended 06/30/02): Assets, $3,989,036 (M); gifts received, $23,585; expenditures, $776,887; qualifying distributions, $759,717; giving activities include $752,000 for 3 grants (high: $750,000; low: $1,000).
Purpose and activities: Giving for education, the environment, human services, and community oriented philanthropies.
Fields of interest: Education; Environment, land resources; Environment; Human services; Salvation Army; Philanthropy/voluntarism, volunteer services.
Limitations: Giving primarily in CA.
Application information:
Initial approach: Letter
Deadline(s): None
Officers and Directors:* James V. Diller,* Pres.; June P. Diller,* V.P. and Secy.-Treas.; James V. Diller, Jr.,* V.P.; Jeffrey R. Diller,* V.P.
EIN: 943314119

166
The Walt Disney Company Contributions Program
500 S. Buena Vista St.
Burbank, CA 91521-0893 (877) 282-8322
Additional application addresses: DisneyHand Teacher Awards: P.O. Box 10404, Van Nuys, CA 91410-0404, Disney Wildlife Conservation Fund: Kim Sans, Mgr., Conservation Initiatives, Walt Disney World, P.O. Box 10000, Lake Buena Vista, FL 32830, tel.: (407) 828-3417, FAX: (407) 828-2251, E-mail: kim.sans@disney.com; URL: http://disney.go.com/disneyhand

Grantmaker type: Corporate giving program
Purpose and activities: As a complement to its foundation, Disney also makes charitable contributions to nonprofit organizations and awards grants to pre-K-12 teachers directly. Support is given on a national basis.
Fields of interest: Elementary/secondary education; Natural resources; Animals/wildlife, preservation/protection.
Types of support: Continuing support; Emergency funds; Program development; Grants to individuals.
Limitations: Giving on a national basis. No grants for general operating support or tuition for Disney Wildlife Conservation Fund.
Application information: An application form is required for DisneyHand Teacher Awards and Disney Wildlife Conservation Fund Rapid Response Program; application form available online. An independent panel of judges reviews all requests for DisneyHand Teacher Awards.
Initial approach: Download application form and mail to application address for Teacher Awards; mail or E-mail letter of inquiry to application address for Conservation Fund; download application form and E-mail to application address for Rapid Response Program
Deadline(s): Postmarked by Jan. 2 for DisneyHand Teacher Awards
Final notification: Apr. for DisneyHand Teacher Awards; Dec. for Disney Wildlife Conservation Fund

167
The Walt Disney Company Foundation ▼
(formerly Disney Foundation)
500 S. Buena Vista St.
Burbank, CA 91521-0987 (818) 560-1006
Contact: Tillie J. Baptie, Exec. Dir.

Incorporated in 1951 in CA.
Donor(s): The Walt Disney Co., and its associated companies.
Grantmaker type: Company-sponsored foundation
Financial data (yr. ended 09/30/02): Assets, $718,312 (M); gifts received, $3,076,521; expenditures, $5,565,279; qualifying distributions, $5,563,083; giving activities include $4,527,273 for 64 grants (high: $500,000; low: $1,000; average: $1,000–$100,000), $700,671 for grants to individuals and $310,687 for employee matching gifts.
Purpose and activities: Emphasis on youth and child welfare agencies, health, higher education, including an arts institute, cultural programs, and community funds; scholarships for the children of employees.
Fields of interest: Music; Arts; Higher education; Hospitals (general); Health care; Health organizations, association; Human services; Children/youth, services; Federated giving programs.
Types of support: General/operating support; Continuing support; Annual campaigns; Capital campaigns; Program development; Scholarship funds; Employee-related scholarships.
Limitations: Giving primarily in areas of company operations, including Los Angeles and Orange County, CA, and Orange and Osceola counties, FL. No support for public agencies, educational institutions, nonprofit organizations supported predominantly by tax dollars, agencies receiving funds from consolidated giving programs supported by the foundation, or sectarian organizations. No grants to individuals (except for employee-related scholarships), or for endowment funds, building campaigns, seed money, research, conferences, or general fund drives; no loans.
Publications: Application guidelines.
Application information: Final action is taken by the Donations Committee at its yearly meeting held in the summer. Application form required.
Initial approach: Letter, proposal, or telephone
Copies of proposal: 1
Deadline(s): Dec. 1 for scholarships; none for others
Board meeting date(s): Annually between Jan. and May
Final notification: 20 to 30 days
Officers and Trustees:* Michael D. Eisner,* Pres.; Roy E. Disney,* V.P.; Marsha L. Reed, Secy.; Robert A. Igler, Treas.; Tillie J. Baptie, Exec. Dir.; Sanford M. Litvack; Paul S. Pressler.
Number of staff: None.
EIN: 956037079
Recent environmental and animal welfare grants:
167-1 African Wildlife Foundation, DC, $55,000. For general operating support. 2002.
167-2 American Zoo and Aquarium Association, Silver Spring, MD, $65,000. For general operating support. 2002.

167-3 Americans for Oxford, New York, NY, $31,550. For general operating support for conservation programs. 2002.
167-4 Audubon Society, National, New York, NY, $58,750. For general operating support. 2002.
167-5 BirdLife International, Cambridge, England, $10,000. For general operating support. 2002.
167-6 Conservation International, DC, $35,000. For general operating support. 2002.
167-7 Duke University, Durham, NC, $13,000. For general operating support for conservation programs. 2002.
167-8 International Crane Foundation, Baraboo, WI, $30,000. For general operating support. 2002.
167-9 International Rhinoceros Foundation, Columbus, OH, $55,000. For general operating support. 2002.
167-10 Peregrine Fund, Boise, ID, $74,750. For general operating support. 2002.
167-11 Wildlife Conservation Society, Bronx, NY, $141,850. For general operating support. 2002.

168
DJ & T Foundation
c/o Prappas Co.
9201 Wilshire Blvd., No. 204
Beverly Hills, CA 90210 (310) 278-1160
Contact: William Prappas
E-mail: WillPrappas@msn.com; URL: http://www.djtfoundation.org

Established in 1994 in CA.
Donor(s): Robert W. Barker.
Grantmaker type: Independent foundation
Financial data (yr. ended 05/31/02): Assets, $17,858,440 (M); gifts received, $2,751,996; expenditures, $1,370,706; qualifying distributions, $1,336,646; giving activities include $1,305,908 for 578 grants (high: $93,333; low: $12).
Purpose and activities: Giving only to free or low cost spay/neuter clinics or spay/neuter voucher programs.
Fields of interest: Animal population control.
Types of support: General/operating support; Continuing support; Capital campaigns; Building/renovation; Equipment; Matching/challenge support.
Limitations: Giving on a national basis. No grants to individuals.
Application information: Application form available on website. Application form required.
Initial approach: Request application
Copies of proposal: 1
Deadline(s): None
Board meeting date(s): As needed
Officers: Robert W. Barker, Pres.; Kent T. Valandra, Secy.; Robert Louis Valandra, C.F.O.
Number of staff: 1 part-time professional.
EIN: 954499239

169
Dmarlou Foundation
251 Post St., Ste. 420
San Francisco, CA 94108

Established in 1994 in CA.
Donor(s): M.J. Kaliski.

Grantmaker type: Independent foundation
Financial data (yr. ended 12/31/02): Assets, $5,187,639 (M); gifts received, $233,443; expenditures, $283,936; qualifying distributions, $231,581; giving activities include $233,028 for 8 grants (high: $63,000; low: $5,143).
Fields of interest: Animal welfare; Animals/wildlife, preservation/protection; Animals/wildlife, bird preserves.
Limitations: Applications not accepted. Giving primarily in CA. No grants to individuals.
Application information: Contributes only to pre-selected organizations.
Officers: Stanley Diamond, Pres.; Richard H. Rahl, Secy.; Felipe R. Santiago, Treas.
EIN: 680320399

170
Hans & Margaret Doe Charitable Trust

600 W. Broadway, 8th Fl.
San Diego, CA 92101 (619) 239-3444
Contact: Anton Dimitroff
FAX: (619) 232-6828

Established in 1990 in CA.
Donor(s): Doe Family Trust.
Grantmaker type: Independent foundation
Financial data (yr. ended 12/31/01): Assets, $2,781,208 (M); expenditures, $179,281; qualifying distributions, $139,281; giving activities include $38,000 for 2 grants (high: $33,000; low: $5,000) and $82,230 for 6 grants to individuals (high: $35,000; low: $7,910).
Purpose and activities: Grants are restricted to the promotion of CA water resource education. Also, scholarships for students who are children of employees of Vista Irrigation District.
Fields of interest: Environment, public education; Water pollution.
Types of support: Employee-related scholarships.
Application information: Application form not required.
Trustees: Roy Coox; Paul D. Engstrand; Maureen A. Stapleton.
EIN: 336080541

171
Thelma Doelger Charitable Trust

950 John Daly Blvd., Ste. 300
Daly City, CA 94015-3004 (650) 755-2333
Contact: D. Eugene Richard, Tr.

Established in 1995 in CA.
Grantmaker type: Independent foundation
Financial data (yr. ended 06/30/02): Assets, $12,672,096 (M); expenditures, $589,604; qualifying distributions, $424,068; giving activities include $338,500 for 14 grants (high: $50,000; low: $1,000).
Purpose and activities: Giving primarily for animal welfare, social services, a medical center, and children and youth services.
Fields of interest: Museums; Higher education; Animal welfare; Zoos/zoological societies; Hospitals (general); Boys & girls clubs; Human services; Children/youth, services.
Limitations: Giving limited to CA. No grants to individuals.
Application information: Application form required.
Deadline(s): None

Trustees: Edward M. King; Chester W. Lebsack; Howard E. Mason, Jr.; D. Eugene Richard.
EIN: 943318483

172
Thelma Doelger Trust for Animals

c/o Paul Gordon
469 9th St., Ste. 200
Oakland, CA 94607-4047

Grantmaker type: Independent foundation
Financial data (yr. ended 06/30/02): Assets, $7,726,578 (M); expenditures, $533,594; qualifying distributions, $461,988; giving activities include $377,500 for 21 grants (high: $65,000; low: $2,500).
Purpose and activities: Grants are made for the benefit of charitable organizations which are dedicated to the care and maintenance of animals, or the prevention of cruelty of animals.
Fields of interest: Animal welfare.
Limitations: Giving primarily in CA. No grants to individuals.
Application information: Application form required.
Copies of proposal: 2
Trustees: Susan Doelger; Katherine Doelger Ellis; Paul M. Gordon.
EIN: 943318485

173
The J. C. Downing Foundation

10755-F Scripps Poway Pkwy, PMB 422
San Diego, CA 92131
Contact: Stuart A. Winkelman, Dir.
E-mail: director@jcdowning.org; URL: http://www.jcdowning.org

Established in 1990 in CA.
Donor(s): John C. Downing.
Grantmaker type: Independent foundation
Financial data (yr. ended 12/31/02): Assets, $3,709,898 (M); expenditures, $204,385; qualifying distributions, $179,500; giving activities include $179,500 for 4 grants (high: $150,000; low: $2,000).
Fields of interest: Media/communications; Arts; Education; Environment, research.
Types of support: Equipment; Program development; Conferences/seminars; Seed money; Fellowships; Research; Matching/challenge support.
Limitations: Giving primarily in southern CA. No support for religious organizations, or for public schools. No grants to individuals, or for scholarships.
Application information: Guidelines available on website. Do not apply without consulting guidelines. Application form not required.
Initial approach: Query only
Copies of proposal: 1
Board meeting date(s): Quarterly
Officers: John C. Downing, Pres.; Toni Leadingham, Secy. and C.F.O.
Director: Stuart A. Winkelman.
Number of staff: 1 full-time professional; 1 full-time support; 1 part-time support.
EIN: 330445623

174
The Draper Foundation

c/o Draper Fisher Assoc.
400 Seaport Ct., Ste. 250
Redwood City, CA 94063 (650) 599-9000
Contact: Tim C. Draper, Pres.

Established in 1996 in CA.
Donor(s): William Draper, Phyllis Draper, Tim Draper, Melissa Draper, Polly Draper.
Grantmaker type: Independent foundation
Financial data (yr. ended 09/30/01): Assets, $3,459,046 (M); expenditures, $1,304,460; qualifying distributions, $1,274,572; giving activities include $1,277,722 for 67 grants (high: $281,600; low: $50).
Purpose and activities: Giving primarily for the arts, education, medical research, and children and social services.
Fields of interest: Arts; Higher education; Education; Environment; Health organizations, association; Medical research, institute; Human services; Children, services; International affairs; Federated giving programs.
Limitations: Giving on a national basis.
Application information:
Initial approach: Proposal
Deadline(s): None
Officers: Tim Draper, Pres.; Rebecca Draper, Secy.; William Draper, C.F.O.
EIN: 943256415

175
Ducommun & Gross Foundation

P.O. Box 2172
Healdsburg, CA 95448
Contact: Robert E. Ducommun, Pres.
Application address: 1155 Park Ave., New York, NY 10128

Established in 1968 in CA.
Grantmaker type: Independent foundation
Financial data (yr. ended 12/31/02): Assets, $5,420,148 (M); gifts received, $194,641; expenditures, $253,769; qualifying distributions, $251,810; giving activities include $250,000 for 20 grants (high: $85,000; low: $2,500).
Fields of interest: Media/communications; Arts; Secondary school/education; Higher education; Education; Environment, land resources; Hospitals (general); Medical research.
Limitations: Giving primarily in CA. No grants to individuals.
Application information: Application form not required.
Initial approach: Letter
Copies of proposal: 1
Deadline(s): June
Board meeting date(s): Dec.
Final notification: Dec.
Officers: Robert E. Ducommun, Pres.; Electra Ducommun de Peyster, V.P.; Frederick A. Richmand, Secy.
Advisory Directors: Courtlandt D. Gross; Anthony C. Ward.
Number of staff: None.
EIN: 956210834

176
Earthjustice Legal Defense Fund, Inc.
426 17th St., 6th Fl.
Oakland, CA 94612-2820 (510) 550-6700
Contact: Vawter "Buck" Parker, Exec. Dir.
FAX: (510) 550-6740; E-mail:
eajus@earthjustice.org; URL: http://
www.earthjustice.org/

Founded in 1971.
Grantmaker type: Public charity
Financial data (yr. ended 07/31/01): Revenue,
$21,535,260; assets, $32,427,090; gifts
received, $18,906,808; expenditures,
$22,644,603; program services expenses,
$16,578,775; giving activities include $50,000
for 1 grant.
Purpose and activities: The fund seeks to protect
people and natural resources to restore
environmental quality by enforcing and
strengthening environmental laws.
Fields of interest: Environment, legal rights;
Natural resources; Animals/wildlife.
Limitations: Giving on a national and
international basis.
Publications: Annual report.
Officers and Trustees:* Dianne Stern,* Chair.;
Cynthia Wayburn,* Vice-Chair.; R. Frederic
Fisher,* Vice-Chair., Finance Treas.; Martha
Kongsgaard,* Vice-Chair., Devel.; Louise Gund,*
Secy.; Vawter "Buck" Parker, Exec. Dir.; Andy
Andrews; Joan Bavaria; Paul G. Bower; Reginald
K. Brack, Jr.; and 18 additional trustees.
EIN: 941730465

177
The East Bay Community Foundation
DeDomenico Bldg.
200 Frank H. Ogawa Plz.
Oakland, CA 94612 (510) 836-3223
Contact: Michael M. Howe, Pres.
FAX: (510) 836-3287; E-mail:
info@eastbaycf.org or program@eastbaycf.org;
URL: http://www.eastbaycf.org

Established in 1928 in CA as The Alameda
County Community Foundation by resolution
and declaration of trust; revised in 1972 to
include Contra Costa County.
Grantmaker type: Community foundation
Financial data (yr. ended 06/30/02): Assets,
$126,951,455 (M); gifts received, $24,222,954;
expenditures, $22,405,567; giving activities
include $11,483,444 for grants.
Purpose and activities: Through its grantmaking
and other philanthropic activities, the
foundation strives to achieve sustainable
communities in the East Bay, CA, area that
maximize the capacity of individuals to reach
their full potential. Priorities in grantmaking are
children, youth, and families, cultural diversity,
empowerment, and collaboration. The
foundation administers donor-advised funds.
Fields of interest: Arts; Education; Environment;
Public health; Community development.
Types of support: General/operating support;
Management development; Program
development; Seed money; Technical
assistance; Program evaluation; Employee
matching gifts; Matching/challenge support.
Limitations: Giving limited to Alameda and
Contra Costa counties, CA. No support for
religious organizations for religious purposes.

No grants to individuals directly, or for building
and endowment funds, annual fund drives,
scholarships, deficit financing, fundraising
events and celebrations.
Publications: Application guidelines, Annual
report, Informational brochure, Newsletter,
Program policy statement.
Application information: Applications sent by
FAX not considered. Application form required.
 Initial approach: Letter or telephone
  requesting application materials, or visit
  Web site
 Copies of proposal: 1
 Deadline(s): Feb. 1 and Aug. 1
 Board meeting date(s): May and Nov.
 Final notification: Ongoing
Officers and Trustees:* Helen Pan Troxel,*
Chair.; Jill Dinwiddie,* Vice-Chair.; Craig
Lundin,* Vice-Chair.; Michael M. Howe, Pres.;
Ernest Leopold,* Treas.; Dean M. Alms; William
F. Ausfahl; Michael Bush; John Chapman;
Edward M. Downer III; Judith Epstein; Michael
Freedland; Edgar H. Grubb; Richard G. Heggie;
Stephen L. Hicks; James H. Hill; Janet
Holmgren; Cornelius L. Hopper, M.D.; Kathleen
Huston; Patricia Jones; James P. King; John
McDonnell; Karen Stevenson; Alfredo Terrazas.
Number of staff: 15 full-time professional; 1
part-time professional; 6 full-time support.
EIN: 946070996

178
**Paul & Magdalena Ecke Poinsettia
 Foundation**
5600 Avenida Encinas, No. 100
Carlsbad, CA 92008

Established around 1981 in CA.
Donor(s): Magdalena Ecke.‡
Grantmaker type: Independent foundation
Financial data (yr. ended 05/31/02): Assets,
$2,454,465 (M); expenditures, $137,875;
qualifying distributions, $123,067; giving
activities include $123,067 for 39 grants (high:
$22,500; low: $100).
Purpose and activities: Giving primarily for
botanical research.
Fields of interest: Higher education;
Botanical/horticulture/landscape services;
Hospitals (general); Cancer; Human services;
YM/YWCAs & YM/YWHAs; Children/youth,
services.
Limitations: Applications not accepted. Giving
primarily in CA. No grants to individuals.
Application information: Contributes only to
pre-selected organizations.
Officers and Directors:* Paul Ecke III,* Pres.;
Lizbeth A. Ecke,* V.P.; Barbara Ecke Winter,*
Secy.; Christopher Calkins, C.F.O. and Treas.
EIN: 953758658

179
**Edison International Corporate Giving
 Program**
(formerly SCEcorp Contributions Program)
P.O. Box 800, G.O. 1 Rm. 399
Rosemead, CA 91770 (626) 302-9853
Contact: Lucia E. Galindo, Mgr., Charitable
Contribs.
Additional tel.: (626) 302-8850; FAX: (626)
302-8114; E-mail: galindle@sce.com

Grantmaker type: Corporate giving program
Purpose and activities: As a complement to its
foundation, Edison International also makes
charitable contributions to nonprofit
organizations directly. Support is given primarily
in areas of company operations.
Fields of interest: Education; Environment;
Health care; Human services; Community
development; Public affairs.
Types of support: General/operating support;
Scholarship funds; Employee volunteer services;
Sponsorships; Employee matching gifts;
Scholarships—to individuals; In-kind gifts.
Limitations: Giving primarily in areas of
company operations.
Publications: Informational brochure (including
application guidelines).
Application information: Proposals should be
no longer than 2 pages in length. The company
has a staff that only handles contributions.
Application form not required.
 Initial approach: Proposal to headquarters
 Copies of proposal: 1
 Deadline(s): None
 Final notification: Following review
Number of staff: 3 full-time professional; 2
full-time support.

180
Eldorado Foundation
50 Lupine Ave., Apt. 3
San Francisco, CA 94118
Contact: Ava Jean Brumbaum, Secy.-Treas.

Established in 1964 in CA.
Grantmaker type: Independent foundation
Financial data (yr. ended 12/31/02): Assets,
$2,152,453 (M); expenditures, $226,946;
qualifying distributions, $220,293; giving
activities include $219,000 for 43 grants (high:
$12,000; low: $1,000).
Purpose and activities: Giving primarily for
human services. Limited funds available for
grantmaking.
Fields of interest: Arts; Education; Natural
resources; Hospitals (general); Eye research;
Human services; Christian agencies & churches;
Protestant agencies & churches.
Types of support: Continuing support; Program
development.
Limitations: Giving primarily in San Francisco,
CA. No grants to individuals.
Application information: Application form not
required.
 Initial approach: Letter
 Copies of proposal: 1
 Deadline(s): Apr. 1
 Board meeting date(s): May
Officers and Directors:* Helen D. Van Blair,*
Pres.; Bruce Dohrmann,* V.P.; Ava Jean
Brumbaum,* Secy.-Treas.; Henry K. Evers; Peggy
Merrifield.

Number of staff: None.
EIN: 946100642

181
The Endurance Fund

c/o Far West Capital Management
4749 Nicasio Valley Rd.
Nicasio, CA 94946-9743
Contact: Robert G. Schiro, Tr.
E-mail: creativephilanthropy@hotmail.com

Established in 1993 in CA.
Grantmaker type: Independent foundation
Financial data (yr. ended 12/31/02): Assets,
$2,604,118 (M); expenditures, $230,085;
qualifying distributions, $161,449; giving
activities include $161,449 for grants.
Fields of interest: Elementary school/education;
Libraries/library science; Education;
Environment; Health care.
Limitations: Giving primarily in West Marin, CA.
Application information: Application form not
required.
  Initial approach: Purpose of the grant and
    verification of the tax-exempt status of
    donees
  Deadline(s): None
Trustees: Dorene C. Schiro; Robert G. Schiro.
Number of staff: 1 part-time support.
EIN: 943170349

182
Energy Foundation ▼

1012 Torney Ave., No. 1
San Francisco, CA 94129 (415) 561-6700
Contact: Eric Heitz, Pres.
FAX: (415) 561-6709; E-mail:
energyfund@ef.org; URL: http://
www.energyfoundation.org

Established in 1991 in CA.
Donor(s): John D. and Catherine T. MacArthur
Foundation, The McKnight Foundation, Joyce
Mertz-Gilmore Foundation, The David and
Lucile Packard Foundation, The Pew Charitable
Trusts, The Rockefeller Foundation.
Grantmaker type: Independent foundation
Financial data (yr. ended 12/31/01): Assets,
$47,491,619 (M); gifts received, $24,087,955;
expenditures, $26,112,570; qualifying
distributions, $25,866,471; giving activities
include $19,385,272 for 246 grants (high:
$510,000; low: $5,000; average:
$10,000–$100,000).
Purpose and activities: To assist in a transition to
a sustainable energy future by promoting energy
efficiency and renewable energy.
Fields of interest: Energy.
International interests: China.
Types of support: Program development.
Limitations: Giving limited to the U.S. and
China. No support for sectarian or religious
purposes or political organizations. No grants to
individuals, or for endowment funds, debt
reduction, planning, renovation, maintenance,
retrofit, or purchase of buildings, equipment
purchases, land acquisition, annual fundraising
campaigns, research and development of
technology, demonstration projects or capital
construction.
Publications: Annual report (including
application guidelines), Financial statement.

Application information: Application form
required.
  Initial approach: Letter of inquiry
  Copies of proposal: 1
  Deadline(s): At least 12 weeks in advance of
    next board meeting (for inclusion in a
    specific docket)
  Board meeting date(s): 3rd week of Mar., 3rd
    week of June, and 1st week of Nov.
  Final notification: Approximately 4 weeks
Officers and Directors:* Susan F. Tierney,*
Chair.; Eric Heitz,* Pres.; Doug Ogden, Exec.
V.P. and Dir., CSEP; Robert O'Connor, V.P. and
C.F.O.; Robert Crane; Denis Hayes; James Lents;
Rose McKinney-James; Victor Rabinowitch; Phil
Sharp; Noa Staryk; Arthur Sussman; Susan
Tierney; Michael Wang; Hongjun Zhang.
Number of staff: 15.
EIN: 943126848
**Recent environmental and animal welfare
grants:**
182-1 20/20 Vision Education Fund, DC,
$25,000. To publicize new study of domestic
employment impacts of raising fuel economy
standards. 2002.
182-2 Alliance for Affordable Energy, New
Orleans, LA, $25,000. To educate Louisiana
stakeholders on benefits of energy efficiency
programs for low-income residents. 2002.
182-3 Alliance to Save Energy, DC, $400,000.
To conduct analysis and public outreach on
economic, energy, and air quality benefits of
national energy efficiency policies. 2002.
182-4 Alliance to Save Energy, DC, $200,000.
To assist states in review and adoption of
stringent building energy codes that reap high
energy, economic, and air quality benefits.
2002.
182-5 Alliance to Save Energy, DC, $180,000.
For work to increase adoption and stringency
of building codes, and appliance and
equipment standards. 2002.
182-6 Alliance to Save Energy, DC, $160,000.
To build national stakeholder and media
awareness of substantial benefits of appliance
efficiency standards, stringent building
energy codes, and market-pull programs.
2002.
182-7 Alliance to Save Energy, DC, $30,000. To
conduct focus groups and determine
endorsement label design that will encourage
consumer purchases of energy savings
products. 2002.
182-8 American Corn Growers Foundation, DC,
$50,000. To conduct outreach to farm
community on benefits of wind power. 2002.
182-9 American Council for an Energy-Efficient
Economy, DC, $500,000. To promote
appliance and equipment efficiency
standards as primary means to cut carbon
emissions and save energy at net economic
benefit. 2002.
182-10 American Council for an Energy-Efficient
Economy, DC, $180,000. For work to
advance appliance efficiency standards,
building energy codes, and national
market-pull programs. 2002.
182-11 American Council for an Energy-Efficient
Economy, DC, $160,000. To analyze and
promote state and federal utility energy
efficiency programs and policies. 2002.
182-12 American Council for an Energy-Efficient
Economy, DC, $150,000. For work to
analyze and recommend policies and

market-pull programs that increase energy
efficiency. 2002.
182-13 American Council for an Energy-Efficient
Economy, DC, $90,000. Toward work to
improve vehicle fuel efficiency through
public policy and market-based programs.
2002.
182-14 American Council for an Energy-Efficient
Economy, DC, $60,000. To analyze and
promote energy, environmental, and
economic benefits of national energy
efficiency policies, including tax incentives
for efficient cars, homes, and appliances;
increased funding for federal clean energy
programs; and efficiency performance
standards for power plants. 2002.
182-15 American Council for an Energy-Efficient
Economy, DC, $40,000. To analyze
Michigan's energy savings potential from
building efficiency standards, state
purchasing policies for efficient equipment,
and public clean energy codes, and national
market-pull programs. 2002.
182-16 American Council for an Energy-Efficient
Economy, DC, $30,000. To analyze and hold
workshop on energy efficiency programs in
key states and their impacts on electric
system reliability. 2002.
182-17 American Council for an Energy-Efficient
Economy, DC, $28,500. To bring key Chinese
government decision-makers and experts to
ACEEE Summer Study on building energy
efficiency for residential and commercial
buildings. 2002.
182-18 American Council for an Energy-Efficient
Economy, DC, $15,000. To continue to
develop and disseminate analyses of
relationships between vehicle size, weight,
design, and safety. 2002.
182-19 American Council for an Energy-Efficient
Economy, DC, $14,000. For collaborative
study with University of Michigan Physics
Department to analyze relationships between
vehicle size, fuel economy, and traffic safety.
2002.
182-20 American Council for an Energy-Efficient
Economy, DC, $10,000. To help Chinese
advocates and policymakers prepare
proposal to Global Environment Facility to
develop efficient motor systems training
program in China. 2002.
182-21 American Lung Association of
California, Oakland, CA, $125,000. To
introduce advanced, electric-drive
technology vehicles into U.S. fleets in
significant, and increasing, volumes. 2002.
182-22 American Lung Association of
California, Oakland, CA, $30,000. For efforts
to promote and implement clean distributed
generation technologies in California. 2002.
182-23 American Lung Association of New York
State, Albany, NY, $75,000. To speed
commercialization of advanced vehicle
technology by supporting New York State's
Zero-Emission Vehicle Program. 2002.
182-24 American Lung Association of San
Francisco and San Mateo Counties, Daly
City, CA, $15,000. To work with Bay Area Air
Quality Management District to develop
stringent emission standards for distributed
generation. 2002.
182-25 Americans for Equitable Climate
Solutions, DC, $75,000. To promote
auctioning carbon permits as most efficient

and equitable method of reducing carbon from electric utilities. 2002.

182-26 Beijing Center for Energy Efficiency and Environmental Technology Transfer, Beijing, China, $50,000. To analyze and develop policies to overcome barriers to small-scale cogeneration facilities in China. 2002.

182-27 Beijing Electrical Engineering Society, Beijing, China, $30,000. To establish incentive policies and management mechanisms for demand side management programs in Beijing. 2002.

182-28 Beijing Energy Efficiency Center, Beijing, China, $48,000. For completion of carbon scenarios project, to include summary for policymakers as well as full technical report documenting key assumptions and data. 2002.

182-29 Beijing Sustainable Development Center, Beijing, China, $70,000. To work with Tsinghua University to promote clean vehicle fuels and technologies as part of Beijing's Energy-Use Energy Reform Program for 2008 Olympics. 2002.

182-30 Beijing Sustainable Development Center, Beijing, China, $50,000. For analysis of total emission control mechanisms including carbon emissions reductions. 2002.

182-31 Beijing Sustainable Development Center, Beijing, China, $40,000. To support Public Benefit Fund in Beijing to finance energy efficiency and renewable energy programs. 2002.

182-32 Bluewater Network, San Francisco, CA, $100,000. For Clean Car Campaign which will advocate for strong implementation of California's new law to regulate greenhouse gases from motor vehicles. 2002.

182-33 Bluewater Network, San Francisco, CA, $45,000. To build public support for reducing petroleum use and greenhouse gas emissions in California. 2002.

182-34 Bluewater Network, San Francisco, CA, $38,000. To petition federal agencies to conduct long-term planning that accounts for impacts of climate change. 2002.

182-35 California Climate Action Registry, Los Angeles, CA, $250,000. For outreach and marketing programs of California Carbon Registry. 2002.

182-36 California Climate Action Registry, Los Angeles, CA, $225,000. To develop and execute outreach strategies with goals of recruiting new participants, develop standards for greenhouse gas accounting and reporting, and educate businesses and policymakers about functions of Registry. 2002.

182-37 CalPIRG Charitable Trust, Los Angeles, CA, $20,000. For work on California Distributed Generation Initiative. 2002.

182-38 CalPIRG Charitable Trust, Sacramento, CA, $50,000. To provide outreach, analysis, and advocacy on benefits of increased renewable energy in California. 2002.

182-39 Center for Auto Safety, DC, $29,000. Toward making information available on fuel economy and traffic safety. 2002.

182-40 Center for Clean Air Policy, DC, $115,000. For work to align Northeast and Mid-Atlantic states on climate change action. 2002.

182-41 Center for Clean Air Policy, DC, $25,000. To design utility sector carbon cap-and-trade program for New York State. 2002.

182-42 Center for Energy Efficiency and Renewable Technologies (CEERT), Sacramento, CA, $525,000. To educate policymakers and media on benefits of renewable energy procurement, renewables portfolio standard, and other clean energy policies in California. 2002.

182-43 Center for Energy Efficiency and Renewable Technologies (CEERT), Sacramento, CA, $300,000. To continue outreach, analysis, and advocacy on benefits of increased renewable energy in California. 2002.

182-44 Center for Energy Efficiency and Renewable Technologies (CEERT), Sacramento, CA, $170,000. To continue work on California Clean Distributed Generation Initiative. 2002.

182-45 Center for Energy Efficiency and Renewable Technologies (CEERT), Sacramento, CA, $110,000. For Cleaner Transportation Project, particularly work on California Zero-Emission Vehicle (ZEV) Program and pending California regulation of greenhouse gases from motor vehicles. 2002.

182-46 Center for Energy Efficiency and Renewable Technologies (CEERT), Sacramento, CA, $95,000. To promote policies that will reduce petroleum used by California's vehicle population. 2002.

182-47 Center for Energy Efficiency and Renewable Technologies (CEERT), Sacramento, CA, $50,000. To study economic and environmental alternatives to Mohave coal-fired power plant in Nevada. 2002.

182-48 Center for Public Interest Research, Boston, MA, $103,000. To provide analyses and other introductory materials on substantial state and regional benefits of state appliance standards to local stakeholders in Northeast states. 2002.

182-49 Center for Public Interest Research, Boston, MA, $50,000. For follow-up work on New England Governors/Eastern Canadian Premiers climate resolution. 2002.

182-50 Center for Public Interest Research, Boston, MA, $39,000. To develop report to educate public and policymakers on benefits and drawbacks of various kinds of distributed generation. 2002.

182-51 Center for Resource Solutions, San Francisco, CA, $225,000. To continue support of Green-e certification standards for renewable power products. 2002.

182-52 Center for Resource Solutions, San Francisco, CA, $158,695. To provide technical policy support and capacity building to Chinese policymakers in renewable energy policy development and implementation. 2002.

182-53 Center for Resource Solutions, San Francisco, CA, $46,000. For policy training for green pricing and public benefits funds programs in Beijing and Shanghai. 2002.

182-54 CERES, Boston, MA, $100,000. For Sustainable Governance Project, which posits climate change as matter of fiduciary responsibility for major companies. 2002.

182-55 China Automotive Technology and Research Center, Beijing, China, $150,000. For China's efforts to develop fuel economy policies. 2002.

182-56 China Automotive Technology and Research Center, Beijing, China, $80,000. To research policies that would promote commercialization of clean cars in China. 2002.

182-57 China Automotive Technology and Research Center, Beijing, China, $40,000. For policy analysis of China's vehicle fleet and classification of vehicles by emissions and fuel efficiency, and to provide policy recommendations for scrappage of most polluting and least efficient vehicles. 2002.

182-58 China Certification Center for Energy Conservation Products, Beijing, China, $55,000. To develop and implement Chinese government procurement policies for energy efficient products. 2002.

182-59 China Certification Center for Energy Conservation Products, Beijing, China, $25,000. To conduct focus groups and determine endorsement label design that will encourage consumer purchases of energy saving products. 2002.

182-60 China Classification Society, Beijing, China, $50,000. To assist China to develop manufacturing standards and quality certification procedures for wind turbine equipment. 2002.

182-61 China Electricity Council, Beijing, China, $40,000. For development of national electricity sector regulatory commission in order to encourage national energy efficiency and renewable energy market reforms. 2002.

182-62 China Energy Conservation Investment Corporation, Beijing, China, $40,000. For analysis of financial barriers to rapid expansion of cogeneration in China. 2002.

182-63 China Energy Research Society, Beijing, China, $65,000. To develop carbon emissions baseline statistics and policy efforts to improve China's overall energy intensity. 2002.

182-64 China Energy Research Society, Beijing, China, $45,000. For formation of financing policies to promote distributed renewable energy power generating systems in rural China. 2002.

182-65 China Energy Research Society, Beijing, China, $40,000. For journal, Energy Policy Research, aimed at improving energy efficiency and renewable energy policy coverage. 2002.

182-66 China National Institute of Standardization, Beijing, China, $80,000. To assist China to develop REACH energy efficiency standards for refrigerators and room air conditioners, such that efficiency standards are set at levels reaching best unit efficiencies available and significantly above market averages. 2002.

182-67 China National Institute of Standardization, Beijing, China, $55,000. To conduct analysis of substantial public benefits that could result from more comprehensive and rapid implementation of appliance and equipment standards in China over next ten years. 2002.

182-68 China National Institute of Standardization, Beijing, China, $50,420. To assist China in developing policy framework for mandatory energy information labels and to design those labels based on consumer and market research. 2002.

182-69 China National Institute of Standardization, Beijing, China, $40,000. Toward China's development of energy efficiency standards for color television sets. 2002.

182-70 Chinese Academy of Social Sciences, Institute of World Economics and Politics, Beijing, China, $80,000. For research on greenhouse gas emission reduction targets and long-term policy options for China's State Development Planning Commission and Ministry of Foreign Affairs. 2002.

182-71 Chinese Research Academy of Environmental Sciences, Beijing, China, $80,000. To develop policies that internalize environmental costs of electricity generation into China's electricity tariffs. 2002.

182-72 Chinese Research Academy of Environmental Sciences, Beijing, China, $40,000. To develop Generation Performance Standards in China in order to regulate thermal power plant emissions on electricity production basis at both central government and provincial levels. 2002.

182-73 Chinese Research Academy of Environmental Sciences, Beijing, China, $35,000. For development of national ethanol development plan. 2002.

182-74 Clean Air Task Force, Boston, MA, $190,000. To provide environmental and economic assessment of integrated gasification combined cycle technology combined with active carbon sequestration. 2002.

182-75 Clean Air Task Force, Boston, MA, $70,000. To study environmental concerns of water use by power plants in West and distribute study to range of target audiences. 2002.

182-76 Clean Energy Group, Montpelier, VT, $50,000. For Clean Energy Funds Network, nonprofit initiative that helps to accelerate commercialization of clean energy technologies through customized advice, information exchange, and joint projects. 2002.

182-77 Climate Neutral Network, Lake Oswego, Oregon, $135,000. For efforts to have companies eliminate their climate impact by purchasing environmentally credible emissions offsets. 2002.

182-78 Coalition for Clean Air, Los Angeles, CA, $75,000. To expand Clean Transportation Advocacy Program which promotes advanced technology vehicles and petroleum reduction policies in California. 2002.

182-79 Coalition for Clean Air, Los Angeles, CA, $45,000. To provide outreach, analysis, and advocacy on benefits of increased renewable energy in California. 2002.

182-80 Coalition for Clean Air, Los Angeles, CA, $30,000. To serve as lead organization in joint campaign to promote clean distributed generation in South Coast region of California. 2002.

182-81 Colorado Coalition for New Energy Technologies, Evergreen, CO, $75,000. To support clean energy business coalitions in Colorado, Arizona, New Mexico, and Utah. 2002.

182-82 Conservation Law Foundation, Boston, MA, $150,000. To work on energy efficiency and utility restructuring issues in Massachusetts and New England. 2002.

182-83 Conservation Law Foundation, Boston, MA, $40,000. To continue support for efforts as part of Distributed Generation Initiative. 2002.

182-84 Consumers Union of United States, San Francisco, CA, $50,000. To provide outreach, analysis, and advocacy on benefits of increased renewable energy in California. 2002.

182-85 Dakota Resource Council, Dickinson, ND, $75,000. For ongoing outreach work on wind power in North Dakota. 2002.

182-86 Dakota Rural Action, Brookings, SD, $40,000. To promote wind power as strategy for sustainable economic development in rural areas of South Dakota. 2002.

182-87 Ecoventure, Oakland, CA, $16,000. For Interfaith Appeal for Climate Justice, project of California Interfaith Power and Light, plea from religious leaders to support energy efficiency, renewable energy, and reducing emissions from automobiles. 2002.

182-88 Energy Research Institute, Beijing, China, $20,000. For second phase development of comprehensive renewable energy policy aimed at commercializing new grid-tied renewable energy technologies, to include formulating and piloting provincial policies and regulations for potential national application. 2002.

182-89 Environment Northeast, Hallowell, ME, $75,000. To support renewable energy policies in Connecticut, expand efficiency funding to natural gas utilities, and promote distributed resources as alternative to new transmission lines. 2002.

182-90 Environment Northeast, Hallowell, ME, $17,000. To promote benefits of state-focused appliance efficiency standards as means to reduce carbon emissions in Massachusetts, Connecticut, New Hampshire, and Maine. 2002.

182-91 Environmental Advocates, Albany, NY, $50,000. To develop strong Greenhouse Gas (GHG) reduction plan for New York State. 2002.

182-92 Environmental Advocates, Albany, NY, $35,000. To continue work to promote clean distributed generation in New York State. 2002.

182-93 Environmental and Energy Study Institute, DC, $60,000. To build broad-based support for federal clean bus funding during reauthorization of Transportation Equity Act of the 21st Century. 2002.

182-94 Environmental Defense, New York, NY, $140,000. To continue campaign in partnership with Environmental Defense Texas, to advance energy efficiency and renewable energy in Texas, with special emphasis on rulemaking proceedings. 2002.

182-95 Environmental Defense, New York, NY, $100,000. For work to motivate auto industry to manufacture and market significantly cleaner and more efficient passenger vehicles. 2002.

182-96 Environmental Defense, New York, NY, $90,872. For project in partnership with Environmental Defense Texas to establish emission standards for existing distributing generation units in Texas. 2002.

182-97 Environmental Law and Policy Center of the Midwest, Chicago, IL, $300,000. To continue regional efforts in Midwest to reduce air pollution and to promote development of energy efficiency and clean energy sources. 2002.

182-98 Environmental Law and Policy Center of the Midwest, Chicago, IL, $245,000. To support state and local advocacy efforts to implement clean energy programs created by 2002 Farm Bill. 2002.

182-99 Environmental Law and Policy Center of the Midwest, Chicago, IL, $80,000. To promote energy efficiency and renewable energy in transmission planning, farm policy and state policy. 2002.

182-100 Environmental Law and Policy Center of the Midwest, Chicago, IL, $70,000. To educate builders, consumers, and other stakeholders of economic, energy, and air quality benefits of statewide building energy code in Illinois. 2002.

182-101 Environmental Law and Policy Center of the Midwest, Chicago, IL, $50,000. For follow-up advocacy in Upper Midwest after release of report, Repowering the Midwest. 2002.

182-102 Environmental Media Services West, San Francisco, CA, $27,698. For media and education effort on benefits of renewables portfolio standard. 2002.

182-103 Environmental Media Services West, San Francisco, CA, $26,000. For media work on California Renewable Energy Education Campaign. 2002.

182-104 Environmental Media Services West, Environmental Media Services-West, San Francisco, CA, $38,000. For media and education effort on benefits of auto fuel efficiency. 2002.

182-105 Florida Public Interest Foundation, Monticello, FL, $17,000. To promote adoption and implementation of appliance efficiency standards for Florida. 2002.

182-106 Florida Public Interest Research Group Education Fund, Tampa, FL, $35,000. To provide information on energy, environmental, and economic benefits of state-based appliance efficiency standards in Florida. 2002.

182-107 ForestEthics, Berkeley, CA, $50,000. For project in partnership with Power Shift to work toward outreach and analysis to local governments on using revenue bonds to fund clean energy projects. 2002.

182-108 Global Environment and Technology Foundation, Annandale, VA, $85,000. To work with states to compare new methodologies that estimate air emission impacts of efficiency policies, followed by work with federal policymakers to promote best version as national model. 2002.

182-109 Global Environment and Technology Foundation, Center for Energy and Climate Solutions, Annandale, VA, $300,000. For work with businesses to save energy and money through best energy practices. 2002.

182-110 Guangdong Energy Conservation Center, Guangzhou, China, $30,000. To develop policy recommendations on implementing China's Energy Conservation Law in Guangdong Province, to include aggressive appliance standards, appliance efficiency labels, building codes, and incentive programs for energy efficiency policy compliance. 2002.

182-111 Guangdong Energy Techno-Economic Research Center, Guangzhou, China, $50,000. To develop electric power sector regulatory commission to oversee market reforms and encourage energy efficiency and renewable energy development in Guangdong Province. 2002.

182-112 Guangdong Energy Techno-Economic Research Center, Guangzhou, China, $25,000. To develop policies in support of Guangdong's wind concession pilot program. 2002.

182-113 Harvard University, John F. Kennedy School of Government, Cambridge, MA, $100,000. To continue to assess state of international research and development on technologies to abate climate change, and to recommend new research and development initiatives. 2002.

182-114 Harvard University, John F. Kennedy School of Government, Cambridge, MA, $50,000. For collaborative program aimed at developing research, development, demonstration, and deployment policies, to promote advanced vehicle technologies in China. 2002.

182-115 Illinois Public Interest Research Group Education Fund, Chicago, IL, $40,000. To promote policies that advance renewable energy in Illinois through education and outreach on economic, health, and environmental benefits of renewable energy. 2002.

182-116 International Center for Technology Assessment, DC, $50,000. To call on Environmental Protection Agency (EPA) to regulate greenhouse gas emissions from motor vehicles. 2002.

182-117 Iowa Citizen Action Network Education Foundation, Des Moines, IA, $30,000. To educate policymakers and media on renewable energy policies in Iowa, such as renewables portfolio standard. 2002.

182-118 Iowa Environmental Council, Des Moines, IA, $80,000. To educate policymakers about benefits of renewable energy efficiency in Iowa. 2002.

182-119 Izaak Walton League of America, Saint Paul, MN, $150,000. To promote renewable energy, energy efficiency, and clean distributed generation in Minnesota. 2002.

182-120 Latino Issues Forum, San Francisco, CA, $350,000. To build network of energy advocates within Latin community. 2002.

182-121 Latino Issues Forum, San Francisco, CA, $10,000. To negotiate with California public power utilities on programs implementing energy efficiency and low-income assistance. 2002.

182-122 Lawrence Berkeley Laboratory, Berkeley, CA, $170,000. To assist China in developing national commercial building code and in implementing residential building codes in hot-summer cold-winter central China climate zone. 2002.

182-123 Lawrence Berkeley Laboratory, Berkeley, CA, $140,000. For China's efforts to develop standby power energy efficiency and labeling standards for VCD and DVD players, and photocopiers. 2002.

182-124 Lawrence Berkeley Laboratory, Berkeley, CA, $140,000. For China's efforts to

develop stronger energy efficiency reach standards for refrigerators and room air-conditioners by 2004. 2002.

182-125 Lawrence Berkeley Laboratory, Berkeley, CA, $95,000. To analyze relationships between vehicle size, weight, design, and safety. 2002.

182-126 Lawrence Berkeley Laboratory, Berkeley, CA, $85,000. To assist China in developing minimum energy efficiency standard for television sets. 2002.

182-127 Lawrence Berkeley Laboratory, Berkeley, CA, $70,000. To further implement Shandong provincial sector targets pilot project, in order to demonstrate substantial energy savings in steel enterprises and to serve as national model for sector targets methodology for securing industrial energy savings. 2002.

182-128 Lawrence Berkeley Laboratory, Berkeley, CA, $52,000. For completion of carbon scenarios analysis project, to include summary for policymakers as well as full technical report. 2002.

182-129 Lawrence Berkeley Laboratory, Berkeley, CA, $40,200. Toward China's efforts to develop government procurement policies for efficient products and equipment. 2002.

182-130 Massachusetts Public Interest Research Group Education Fund, Boston, MA, $45,000. For Clean Cars Campaign, which will promote successful implementation of Low Emissions Vehicle (LEV) II motor vehicle program in Massachusetts. 2002.

182-131 Massachusetts Public Interest Research Group Education Fund, Boston, MA, $34,232. To continue outreach on establishing distributed generation air emissions standards. 2002.

182-132 Massachusetts Public Interest Research Group Education Fund, Boston, MA, $25,000. For revised Zero-Emission Vehicle (ZEV) Program in Massachusetts. 2002.

182-133 Minnesota Environmental Initiative, Minneapolis, MN, $25,000. To provide education, outreach, and organizing for clean energy businesses in Minnesota. 2002.

182-134 Minnesotans for an Energy-Efficient Economy (ME3), Saint Paul, MN, $275,000. For clean energy advocacy in Minnesota. 2002.

182-135 National Commission on Energy Policy, DC, $1,100,000. Toward establishing National Commission on Energy Policy. 2002.

182-136 National Commission on Energy Policy, DC, $400,000. Toward creation of high-level, bipartisan commission to develop environmentally and economically sound national energy policy. 2002.

182-137 National Consumer Law Center, Boston, MA, $100,000. For continued support to increase energy efficiency programs for low-income consumers. 2002.

182-138 National Environmental Trust, DC, $200,000. To conduct media and public education campaign on national energy policy. 2002.

182-139 National Environmental Trust, DC, $100,000. To continue efforts to earn coverage of clean energy solutions in business media. 2002.

182-140 National Religious Partnership for the Environment, Amherst, MA, $285,000. For

Project Director position for new Fuel Conservation and Efficiency Project. 2002.

182-141 National Religious Partnership for the Environment, Amherst, MA, $221,000. For new Fuel Conservation and Efficiency Project. 2002.

182-142 National Research Center for Science and Technology Development, Beijing, China, $50,000. For efforts to increase central government funding for energy efficiency and renewable energy technology research and development. 2002.

182-143 National Research Center for Science and Technology Development, Ministry of Agriculture, Beijing, China, $60,000. For development of financial policies aimed at removing market barriers to investment in new biomass electricity generation technologies. 2002.

182-144 National Wildlife Federation, Reston, VA, $25,000. To convene conference on impacts of coal bed methane development on wildlife in Intermountain West. 2002.

182-145 Natural Resources Council, Augusta, ME, $30,000. To support and extend California motor vehicle program in Maine. 2002.

182-146 Natural Resources Defense Council, New York, NY, $850,000. For clean energy advocacy in California, New York, New Jersey, and Pacific Northwest. 2002.

182-147 Natural Resources Defense Council, New York, NY, $350,000. To promote advanced technology vehicles and policies that reduce petroleum consumption in California and New York and in national policy. 2002.

182-148 Natural Resources Defense Council, New York, NY, $150,000. To study and recommend policies that can reinforce effectiveness of residential and commercial building codes. 2002.

182-149 Natural Resources Defense Council, New York, NY, $120,000. To continue to provide technical expertise on transmission and wholesale electric market policies that support energy efficiency and renewable resources. 2002.

182-150 Natural Resources Defense Council, New York, NY, $100,000. For continued work to promote clean distributed generation in New York and New Jersey. 2002.

182-151 Natural Resources Defense Council, New York, NY, $100,000. To provide legal defense for California Zero-Emissions Vehicle (ZEV) Program and California's new program to reduce greenhouse gases from motor vehicles. 2002.

182-152 Natural Resources Defense Council, New York, NY, $100,000. To co-fund comprehensive study of biomass as major future energy source for United States, and assess policies that could accelerate robust transition. 2002.

182-153 Natural Resources Defense Council, New York, NY, $75,000. For work on state carbon registries, and other state and regional carbon reduction policies. 2002.

182-154 Natural Resources Defense Council, New York, NY, $50,000. To co-fund comprehensive study of biomass as major future energy source for United States and assess policies that could accelerate robust transition. 2002.

182-155 Natural Resources Defense Council, New York, NY, $41,588. For continued work on California Distributed Generation Initiative. 2002.

182-156 Natural Resources Defense Council, New York, NY, $40,000. To support consideration of international experiences in demand-side management (DSM) policies and development of DSM in China. 2002.

182-157 Natural Resources Defense Council, New York, NY, $30,000. To convene stakeholders in New York State to review new analyses of energy, economic, and environmental benefits of state appliance efficiency standards. 2002.

182-158 Natural Resources Defense Council, New York, NY, $15,285. For study tour in United States for key Chinese decision-makers and electricity policy experts to learn more about successful demand-side management (DSM) policies, incentives, and program design. 2002.

182-159 Netherlands Agency for Energy and the Environment (NOVEM), Sittard, Netherlands, $34,648. To develop energy efficiency sector targets and implement regulations for China's iron and steel sector. 2002.

182-160 New Buildings Institute, Fair Oaks, CA, $100,000. To recommend modifications to national model energy codes that will improve energy efficiency performance of U.S. buildings. 2002.

182-161 New Jersey Public Interest Research Foundation, Trenton, NJ, $90,000. To support and promote clean and efficient advanced technology vehicles in New Jersey. 2002.

182-162 New Mexico Wilderness Alliance, Albuquerque, NM, $15,000. To launch public education, grassroots organizing, and media campaign to publicize results of report evaluating trade-off between energy development and natural resource conservation in Otero Mesa, New Mexico. 2002.

182-163 Northeast States for Coordinated Air Use Management Foundation, Boston, MA, $175,000. To continue support for work on reducing greenhouse gas and other toxic emissions from vehicles. 2002.

182-164 Northeast States for Coordinated Air Use Management Foundation, Boston, MA, $60,000. To develop inventories, registries, and other tools in support of New England regional Greenhouse Gas (GHG) reduction goal. 2002.

182-165 Northern Jiaotong University, Traffic and Transportation School, Beijing, China, $50,000. To develop incentive policies for commercialization of advanced technology (particularly hybrid-electric drive) vehicles for 2008 Beijing Olympic Games. 2002.

182-166 Northwest Energy Coalition, Seattle, WA, $400,000. To promote energy efficiency and renewable energy in Pacific Northwest. 2002.

182-167 Northwest Energy Coalition, Seattle, WA, $30,000. To continue Low-Income Organizing Network efforts to advance low-income energy efficiency programs in Oregon, Washington, Idaho, and Montana. 2002.

182-168 Northwest Sustainable Energy for Economic Development (SEED), Seattle, WA, $75,000. To perform outreach and education

to agricultural and rural groups on benefits of renewable energy in Washington state. 2002.

182-169 Pace Energy Center, White Plains, NY, $150,000. To promote clean energy policies in New York, including energy efficiency funding, environmental disclosure rules, and portfolio management. 2002.

182-170 Pace Energy Center, White Plains, NY, $75,000. For work on transmission policy, demand response, and energy efficiency at market operations and transmission policy forums in Northeast. 2002.

182-171 Pace Energy Center, White Plains, NY, $50,000. To advocate for model distributed generation emission rules in New York and improve state's rules on distributed generation participation in emergency demand response programs. 2002.

182-172 Pace Energy Center, White Plains, NY, $50,000. For Northeast Load Response Initiative, promoting environmentally-sound demand response programs. 2002.

182-173 PCL Foundation, Sacramento, CA, $10,000. To negotiate with California public power utilities on programs implementing energy efficiency and low-income assistance. 2002.

182-174 Physicians for Social Responsibility, Los Angeles Chapter, Los Angeles, CA, $25,800. To continue work promoting benefits of clean distributed generation technologies in the U.S. 2002.

182-175 Public Citizen Foundation, DC, $75,000. For collaboration with Texas chapter to promote clean and efficient vehicles in Texas. 2002.

182-176 Public Finance Research Institute, Fuzhou City, China, $50,000. To support local mandatory market share renewable energy policy pilot program in Fujian Province. 2002.

182-177 Public Utility Law Project of New York, Albany, NY, $40,000. To advance efforts to improve state energy policy in areas of efficiency and affordability for low-income residential consumers. 2002.

182-178 Quebec-Labrador Foundation/Atlantic Center for the Environment, Montpelier, VT, $25,000. To support Vermont's Zero-Emissions Vehicle Program and to bring clean, efficient advanced technology vehicles to Vermont consumers. 2002.

182-179 Regulatory Assistance Project, Gardiner, ME, $230,000. To provide training and other consulting services aimed at building China's capacity to develop energy efficiency and renewable energy policies in China's electric utility sector. 2002.

182-180 Regulatory Assistance Project, Gardiner, ME, $125,000. For two-part strategy of outreach and education to inform state air and utility regulators about new model rule that sets output-based emissions standards for small-scale, distributed-generation facilities. 2002.

182-181 Renewable Energy Policy Project, DC, $20,000. To work with AFL-CIO to study job impacts and economic benefits of increased renewable energy production in Nevada. 2002.

182-182 Research Institute for Standards and Norms, Beijing, China, $44,840. To establish energy-efficient windows program in China and to encourage windows industry to

participate in development and implementation of building energy codes. 2002.

182-183 Rocky Mountain Institute, Snowmass, CO, $38,000. To educate industry, environmental groups, media, and public about Hypercar technology. 2002.

182-184 Rocky Mountain Institute, Snowmass, CO, $35,000. To propose and analyze clean energy options for San Francisco energy plan. 2002.

182-185 San Juan Citizens Alliance, Durango, CO, $15,000. To disseminate biological and economic analysis of impact of energy development in Hatcher-Dyke Mountains in order to reduce energy development in area. 2002.

182-186 Shandong Environment Sciences and Planning Institute, Jinan, China, $25,000. To develop generation performance standards pollution control policies in electric power sector in Shandong Province. 2002.

182-187 Shanghai Academy of Environmental Sciences, Shanghai, China, $50,000. For low-carbon policy development framework for City of Shanghai, in order to encourage medium- and long-term municipal energy efficiency and renewable energy policies. 2002.

182-188 Shanghai Energy Conservation Supervision Center, Shanghai, China, $35,000. For policies to expand use of clean cogeneration technologies in Shanghai. 2002.

182-189 Shanghai Jiao Tong University, Shanghai, China, $35,000. For analysis of ethanol production in China, including assessment of technical feasibility and economic and environmental benefits, in order to recommend clean fuels policy development. 2002.

182-190 Shanghai Jiao Tong University, School of Mechanical and Power Engineering, Shanghai, China, $25,000. To study feasibility of promoting fuel cell scooters in Shanghai. 2002.

182-191 Shanxi Environmental Science Association, Taiyuan, China, $25,000. To develop generation performance standards pollution control policies in electric power sector in Shanxi Province. 2002.

182-192 Sichuan University, Institute for West Development, Chengdu, China, $50,000. For mandatory market share renewable energy policy pilot program in Sichuan Province. 2002.

182-193 Sierra Club Foundation, San Francisco, CA, $280,000. For efforts to build grassroots support for raising fuel economy standards. 2002.

182-194 Sierra Club Foundation, San Francisco, CA, $50,000. For Challenge to Sprawl Campaign to support development of cleaner public transportation alternatives to increased road and highway construction. 2002.

182-195 South-North Institute for Sustainable Development, Beijing, China, $60,000. To establish green pricing programs in Beijing and Shanghai such that enterprises that volunteer to pay small premium for renewable energy can provide market for new utility-scale renewable energy projects. 2002.

182-196 Southern Alliance for Clean Energy, Knoxville, TN, $100,000. To promote energy efficiency and renewable energy in Florida, Georgia, Tennessee, and North Carolina, and at Tennessee Valley Authority. 2002.

182-197 Southern Alliance for Clean Energy, Knoxville, TN, $33,000. To provide information on energy, environmental, and economic benefits of state-based appliance efficiency standards in Florida. 2002.

182-198 State Commission for Restructuring the Economic Systems, Institute of Economic System and Management, China, $50,000. To develop new national regulatory regime for China's electric power industry. 2002.

182-199 State Power Corporation, Demand-Side Management Instruction Center, Beijing, China, $50,000. To develop and implement Jiangsu provincial policy demonstration of electric utility-supported demand-side management programs. 2002.

182-200 State Power Economic Research Center, Beijing, China, $60,000. For development of demand-side management (DSM) policies and inclusion of DSM in China's electric utility reforms. 2002.

182-201 State Power Environmental Protection Institute, Nanjing, China, $25,000. To develop generation performance standards pollution control policies for Jiangsu's electric power sector. 2002.

182-202 Tides Center, San Francisco, CA, $25,000. For outreach to religious community in support of renewable energy in California, effort to mobilize faith community to buy renewable energy wherever consumers have a choice. 2002.

182-203 Tides Center, Vote Solar Initiative, San Francisco, CA, $50,000. To promote concept of solar revenue bond, educate public and media, and work with city governments to craft financially viable bond packages. 2002.

182-204 Tsinghua University Education Foundation, Beijing, China, $120,000. For graduate student fellowships that provide student research support for transportation policy analysis, including research on vehicle emissions, fuel quality, fuel economy, advanced zero-emission vehicle technology, and bus rapid transit systems. 2002.

182-205 Tsinghua University Education Foundation, Beijing, China, $20,000. For continued efforts to establish comprehensive national renewable energy policy in order to catalyze utility-scale renewable energy development over long-term. 2002.

182-206 Tsinghua University Education Foundation, Institute of Environmental Sciences and Engineering, Beijing, China, $70,000. To develop analysis of environmental and economic costs and benefits of national fuel economy standards. 2002.

182-207 Union of Concerned Scientists, Cambridge, MA, $440,000. To expand Clean Vehicle Program with emphasis on building coalition and public support for reducing greenhouse gases from motor vehicles and accelerating commercialization of clean and efficient technology vehicles. 2002.

182-208 Union of Concerned Scientists, Cambridge, MA, $350,000. To promote renewable energy policies at federal level, and in Midwest, New England, and California. 2002.

182-209 Union of Concerned Scientists, Cambridge, MA, $134,000. To conduct analysis on renewable energy and promote renewable energy through education and outreach to policymakers, agricultural community, and public. 2002.

182-210 Union of Concerned Scientists, Cambridge, MA, $45,000. To provide outreach, analysis, and advocacy on benefits of increased renewable energy in California. 2002.

182-211 United Nations Development Programme, New York, NY, $50,000. For final editing and broad distribution of book by Jose Goldemberg and several preeminent energy thinkers from around the world, who have constructed detailed analysis of world's energy situation and have looked ahead at different scenarios to build low carbon energy future. 2002.

182-212 United States Public Interest Research Group Education Fund, DC, $75,000. To advocate for higher fuel economy standards as part of Campaign to Stop Global Warming. 2002.

182-213 University of California, Berkeley, CA, $150,000. To support Energy and Resources Group as premier training ground for analysis and design of national clean energy policies. 2002.

182-214 University of Colorado Foundation, Boulder, CO, $50,000. For Colorado Business Energy Partnership, which works with Colorado-based companies on carbon reduction projects. 2002.

182-215 Utility Reform Network, San Francisco, CA, $45,000. To provide outreach, analysis, and advocacy on benefits of increased renewable energy in California. 2002.

182-216 Western Resource Advocates, Boulder, CO, $300,000. To promote clean energy policies in six-state region of Intermountain West. 2002.

182-217 Western Resource Advocates, Boulder, CO, $224,000. For Western Voices project that aims to diversify and extend participation of ranching, farming, and outdoor recreation communities in national energy policy debate. 2002.

182-218 Wilderness Society, Four Corners State Region, Denver, CO, $10,000. To conduct meetings to coordinate efforts of national environmental groups and Western states regional partners in land-use planning and natural resource management. 2002.

182-219 World Resources Institute, DC, $100,000. For Green Power Market Development Group, organization of large companies committed to large-scale, long-term renewable energy purchases. 2002.

182-220 World Resources Institute, DC, $55,200. To analyze past studies on energy efficiency, energy policy, and energy alternatives. 2002.

182-221 World Wildlife Fund/Conservation Foundation, DC, $130,000. For Climate Savers, program for companies to make industry-leading carbon dioxide reduction commitments. 2002.

182-222 Wyoming Outdoor Council, Lander, WY, $15,000. To launch public education and advocacy campaign with dissemination of Western EcoSystems Technology (WEST), Inc.'s Red Desert case study, and to work to protect Red Desert from energy development. 2002.

182-223 Zhejiang Energy Research Institute, Hangzhou, China, $30,000. For second phase of study on establishing regulatory commission to oversee electric power sector regulatory reform in China's Zhejiang Province. 2002.

182-224 Zhejiang Energy Research Institute, Hangzhou, China, $30,000. For establishment of Public Benefit Fund in Zhejiang Province to finance energy efficiency and renewable energy programs. 2002.

182-225 Zhejiang Environmental Monitoring Center, Hangzhou, China, $25,000. To develop generation performance standards pollution control policies for Zhejiang's electric power sector. 2002.

183
Environment Now Foundation
450 Newport Ctr. Dr., Ste. 450
Newport Beach, CA 92660 (949) 644-1850
Contact: Paul C. Heeschen, Secy.-Treas.

Established in 1989 in CA.
Donor(s): Frank G. Wells,‡ Luanne C. Wells.
Grantmaker type: Independent foundation
Financial data (yr. ended 12/31/01): Assets, $34,720,695 (M); gifts received, $40,000; expenditures, $2,964,486; qualifying distributions, $1,928,516; giving activities include $932,522 for 23+ grants (high: $170,000), $965,293 for 4 foundation-administered programs and $77,638 for loans/program-related investments.
Purpose and activities: Support for environmental conservation.
Fields of interest: Natural resources.
Limitations: Applications not accepted. Giving on a national basis. No grants to individuals.
Application information: Unsolicited requests for funds not considered.
Officers: Kevin Wells, Pres.; Paul C. Heeschen, Secy.-Treas.; Terry Tamminen, Exec. Dir.
Directors: Dan Emmett; Mary Nichols; Briant Wells; Luanne C. Wells.
EIN: 954247242

184
Epstein/Roth Foundation
618 Santa Barbara Rd.
Berkeley, CA 94707-1718

Established in 2000 in CA.
Donor(s): Amy Roth, Robert Epstein.
Grantmaker type: Independent foundation
Financial data (yr. ended 12/31/02): Assets, $2,687,634 (M); expenditures, $344,905; qualifying distributions, $334,832; giving activities include $336,000 for 10 grants (high: $155,000; low: $5,000).
Fields of interest: Opera; Education; Natural resources; Foundations (public); Jewish agencies & temples.
Limitations: Applications not accepted. Giving primarily in CA and NY. No grants to individuals.
Application information: Contributes only to pre-selected organizations.
Officers: Amy Roth, Pres.; Robert Epstein, Treas.
Directors: Colin Epstein; Harris Epstein.

EIN: 943357645

185
T. R. Eriksen Trust Fund
P.O. Box 806
Ukiah, CA 95482 (707) 462-3801
Contact: Joanne Lacasse, Mgr.

Established in 2000 in CA.
Grantmaker type: Independent foundation
Financial data (yr. ended 12/31/02): Assets, $4,642,608 (M); expenditures, $460,604; qualifying distributions, $272,480; giving activities include $238,150 for 21 grants (high: $36,000; low: $600).
Purpose and activities: Giving primarily for the environment and human services.
Fields of interest: Natural resources; Food banks; Boys & girls clubs; Human services; Aging, centers/services.
Types of support: General/operating support.
Limitations: Giving primarily in Mendocino County, CA. No grants to individuals.
Application information:
  Deadline(s): None
Officers and Trustees:* Joanne Lacasse,* Mgr.; Leonard J. Lacasse,* Mgr.
Grant Committee: Dorothy Jane Kelley; Larry McLeitch.
EIN: 916513400

186
The Eucalyptus Foundation
P.O. Box 29550
San Francisco, CA 94129
Contact: Stephen Schwarz, Secy.
Additional address for express mail/courier: 567 Ruger St., San Francisco, CA 94129; FAX: (415) 561-3347

Established in 1991 in CA.
Donor(s): Frances K. Geballe, Theodore H. Geballe.
Grantmaker type: Independent foundation
Financial data (yr. ended 06/30/03): Assets, $17,069,292 (M); gifts received, $1,000,000; expenditures, $1,171,603; qualifying distributions, $1,161,848; giving activities include $1,158,800 for 17 grants (high: $600,000; low: $5,000).
Purpose and activities: Giving primarily for community development and education.
Fields of interest: Adult education—literacy, basic skills & GED; Reading; Education; Environment; Human services; Children/youth, services; Community development, neighborhood development; Economically disadvantaged.
Types of support: General/operating support; Continuing support; Annual campaigns; Capital campaigns; Building/renovation; Curriculum development; Scholarship funds.
Limitations: Applications not accepted. Giving limited to River Forest, IL, Detroit, MI, Atenburg and St. Louis, MO, and Watertown WI. No grants to individuals.
Application information: Contributes only to pre-selected organizations.
  Board meeting date(s): June and as required
Officers and Directors:* Frances K. Geballe,* Pres.; Theodore H. Geballe,* V.P.; Stephen

Schwarz, Secy.; Alison F. Geballe, C.F.O.; Benjamin D. Geballe; Carol M. Geballe.
Number of staff: None.
EIN: 943148772

187
Farallon Islands Foundation
1220 Diamond Way, Ste. 100
Concord, CA 94520
Contact: Earl R. Hopkins, Treas.

Established in 1999 in CA.
Donor(s): Richard D. Spight.
Grantmaker type: Independent foundation
Financial data (yr. ended 12/31/02): Assets, $149,860 (M); gifts received, $218,196; expenditures, $108,359; qualifying distributions, $102,000; giving activities include $102,000 for 2 grants (high: $96,000; low: $6,000).
Fields of interest: Environment.
Types of support: General/operating support.
Limitations: Giving limited to the Farallon Islands, CA.
Application information: Application form not required.
  Deadline(s): None
Officers: Robert H. Sexton, Co-Pres.; Richard D. Spight, Co-Pres.; Earl R. Hopkins, Treas.
EIN: 680428790

188
Firedoll Foundation
1460 Maria Ln., Ste. 420
Walnut Creek, CA 94596 (925) 937-4560
Contact: Neil Sims, Prog. Off.
E-mail: info@firedoll.org; URL: http://www.firedoll.org

Established in 1998 in CA.
Donor(s): Straus Family Trust.
Grantmaker type: Independent foundation
Financial data (yr. ended 05/31/02): Assets, $5,683,327 (M); gifts received, $2,387,409; expenditures, $865,714; qualifying distributions, $821,711; giving activities include $819,214 for 85 grants (high: $35,000; low: $100).
Purpose and activities: The foundation offers grants to nonprofits in the areas of environmental conservation, immigrant/human rights, community development, Mid-East peace, and offers support for Bay Area non-profits servicing victims of traumatic brain injury.
Fields of interest: Natural resources; Environment; Brain disorders; Human services; International peace/security; Civil rights, immigrants; Community development, small businesses; Community development.
International interests: Middle East.
Types of support: General/operating support; Continuing support; Building/renovation; Equipment; Emergency funds; Program development; Publication; Seed money; Program evaluation; Program-related investments/loans; Matching/challenge support.
Limitations: Giving primarily in the San Francisco Bay Area, CA, with emphasis on Alameda and Contra Costa, and the East Bay counties; some giving to nationally-based organizations. No grants to individuals.
Publications: Application guidelines, Grants list, Program policy statement.

Application information: Consult application guidelines on Web site before sending proposals. Proposals not following guidelines will be returned. Application form not required.
  Initial approach: E-mail or written letter of inquiry or proposal after consulting Web site
  Copies of proposal: 1
  Deadline(s): Between Sept. 1 and Dec. 31 for Environmental Conservation and Community Development. No deadline for other areas
  Final notification: June 30
Officers: Sandor Straus, Pres. and Treas.; Faye Straus, V.P. and Secy.
Number of staff: 1 full-time professional; 1 part-time professional.
EIN: 943301999

189
Clara Helen Firth Trust
(formerly Clara Helen Firth Testamentary Trust)
c/o Wells Fargo Bank, N.A.
P.O. Box 63954
San Francisco, CA 94163 (916) 440-4449

Established in 1981.
Grantmaker type: Public charity
Financial data (yr. ended 02/28/01): Revenue, $1,362,409; assets, $6,343,933; expenditures, $292,615; program services expenses, $253,949; giving activities include $239,780 for 5 grants (high: $167,846; low: $11,989).
Purpose and activities: The trust exists for the sole benefit of the Massachusetts Society for the Prevention of Cruelty to Animals, the Humane Society of the United States, American Humane Association, the Salvation Army, and Haven Humane Society, Inc.
Fields of interest: Animal welfare; Salvation Army.
Limitations: Applications not accepted.
Application information: Contributes only to pre-selected organizations; unsolicited requests for funds not considered or acknowledged.
Trustee: Wells Fargo Bank, N.A.
EIN: 956698210

190
Flintridge Foundation
1040 Lincoln Ave., Ste. 100
Pasadena, CA 91103 (626) 449-0839
Contact: Ms. J.L. Moseley, Managing Dir.
FAX: (626) 585-0011; E-mail: Karen@flintridgefoundation.org; URL: http://www.flintridgefoundation.org

Established in 1984 in CA.
Donor(s): Francis Loring Moseley,‡ Louisa Moseley.‡
Grantmaker type: Independent foundation
Financial data (yr. ended 12/31/02): Assets, $16,264,123 (M); gifts received, $4,369; expenditures, $3,031,761; qualifying distributions, $2,298,604; giving activities include $1,332,020 for 53 grants (high: $452,948; low: $775; average: $5,000–$25,000) and $300,000 for 12 grants to individuals of $25,000 each.
Purpose and activities: The foundation currently awards grants in conservation and the arts. The conservation program is directed towards grassroots environmental organizations working

in the Pacific Northwest. The arts program has two components: visual arts - artist awards program; and theatre - focused on collaborative ensembles. The community services program is built around the foundation's Philanthropy Resource Library and includes technical assistance in the forms of resource material, workshops, and staff assistance for local nonprofits, particularly focusing on those helping families.

Fields of interest: Visual arts; Theater; Natural resources; Environment, water resources; Environment, forests; Nonprofit management; Leadership development.

Types of support: General/operating support; Continuing support; Management development; Program development; Technical assistance; Consulting services; Grants to individuals; Matching/challenge support.

Limitations: Giving primarily in CA, OR, and WA. No support for religious groups. No grants for deficit financing.

Publications: Application guidelines, Informational brochure, Newsletter.

Application information: Introductory Form available on Web site. Application form required.

Deadline(s): None

Board meeting date(s): 3 to 4 times per year

Officers and Directors:* Armando Gonzalez,* Pres.; Gordon Hamilton,* V.P.; Mona Heinze,* Secy.; Alexander Moseley,* Treas.; Judith Johnson; Ann Morris; Cassandra Moseley; David Moseley.

Number of staff: 7 full-time professional; 2 part-time professional.

EIN: 953926331

191

Flora Family Foundation ▼

2121 Sand Hill Rd., Ste. 123
Menlo Park, CA 94025 (650) 233-1335
Contact: B. Stephen Toben, V.P., Pres.
FAX: (650) 233-1340; E-mail:
info@florafamily.org; URL: http://www.Floarafamily.org

Established in 1998 in CA.

Donor(s): William Hewlett.

Grantmaker type: Independent foundation

Financial data (yr. ended 12/31/02): Assets, $87,949,132 (M); expenditures, $5,096,206; qualifying distributions, $4,555,248; giving activities include $4,145,388 for 134 grants (high: $200,000; low: $100; average: $10,000–$50,000).

Purpose and activities: Giving primarily for museums, higher education, the environment, health associations, disaster relief, children and social services, as well as services for women, philanthropy and federated giving programs.

Fields of interest: Museums; Museums (science/technology); Higher education; Education; Environment, public policy; Health care; Mental health/crisis services, public education; Health organizations, association; Health organizations; Disasters, preparedness/services; Human services; Children, services; Women, centers/services; International relief; Federated giving programs; Philanthropy/voluntarism.

Types of support: General/operating support; Continuing support; Annual campaigns; Capital

campaigns; Building/renovation; Land acquisition; Endowments; Debt reduction; Emergency funds; Program development; Conferences/seminars; Professorships; Publication; Seed money; Curriculum development; Fellowships; Internship funds; Scholarship funds; Research; Consulting services; Program evaluation; Employee matching gifts; Exchange programs; Matching/challenge support.

Limitations: Applications not accepted. No grants to individuals.

Publications: Annual report.

Application information: Contributes only to pre-selected organizations.

Board meeting date(s): Jan., April., July., Oct.

Officers and Directors:* Susan S. Briggs,* Chair.; B. Stephen Toben,* Pres.; Annette Rado, C.F.O.; Dr. Amir Ali Farman-Farma; Eleanor Gimon; Marianne Gimon; Carolyn L. Hewlett; Richard Jaffe; Herant A. Katchadourian.

Number of staff: 1 full-time professional; 1 part-time professional; 1 part-time support.

EIN: 770500183

Recent environmental and animal welfare grants:

191-1 Africa Foundation, Sandton, South Africa, $103,000. For LINCOS, Little Intelligent Communities Initiative. 2001.

191-2 Audubon Canyon Ranch, Stinson Beach, CA, $75,000. For Resource Management Fellowship. 2001.

191-3 Center for a New American Dream, Takoma Park, MD, $50,000. For general support. 2001.

191-4 Center for Holistic Resource Management, Albuquerque, NM, $40,000. For Lost Rivers Valley project. 2001.

191-5 Center of Design for an Aging Society, Portland, Oregon, $50,000. For Portland Memory Garden. 2001.

191-6 Charles Darwin Foundation for the Galapagos Islands, Falls Church, VA, $25,000. For general support. 2001.

191-7 EarthRights International, DC, $50,000. For general support. 2001.

191-8 Forest Stewardship Council, Oaxaca, Mexico, $100,000. For general support. 2001.

191-9 Institute for Local Self-Reliance, DC, $75,000. For Waste to Wealth program. 2001.

191-10 Master Peace 2001, Palo Alto, CA, $10,000. For general support. 2001.

191-11 RAFI-USA, Pittsboro, NC, $25,000. For general support. 2001.

191-12 Tides Center, San Francisco, CA, $25,000. For general support for Conserva project in Panama. 2001.

191-13 Woods Hole Research Center, Woods Hole, MA, $100,000. For new energy efficient campus. 2001.

191-14 Yosemite National Institutes, Sausalito, CA, $100,000. For Crane Flat Campus project. 2001.

192

The Foothills Foundation

P.O. Box 193809
San Francisco, CA 94119-3809

Established in 1977 in CA.

Donor(s): Gary Hogan Bechtel.

Grantmaker type: Independent foundation

Financial data (yr. ended 12/31/02): Assets, $4,499,847 (M); expenditures, $488,983; qualifying distributions, $486,246; giving activities include $483,500 for 11 grants (high: $250,000; low: $1,000).

Fields of interest: Literature; Elementary/secondary education; Secondary school/education; Education; Animal welfare; Boys & girls clubs; Human services; Children/youth, services; Jewish agencies & temples.

Types of support: General/operating support; Annual campaigns; Capital campaigns.

Limitations: Applications not accepted. Giving primarily in CA. No grants to individuals.

Application information: Contributes only to pre-selected organizations.

Officers and Directors:* Gary Hogan Bechtel,* Pres.; Jacquie L. Bechtel, V.P.; George T. Argyris,* Secy.; Nancy S. Hair, Treas.

EIN: 942412392

193

Foundation for Deep Ecology ▼

1062 Fort Cronkhite
Sausalito, CA 94965 (415) 229-9339
Contact: Lizzie Udwin, Prog. Admin.
FAX: (415) 229-9340; E-mail:
info@deepecology.org; URL: http://www.deepecology.org

Established in 1989 in CA.

Donor(s): Douglas R. Tompkins.

Grantmaker type: Independent foundation

Financial data (yr. ended 06/30/02): Assets, $52,513,101 (M); expenditures, $4,850,605; qualifying distributions, $4,391,058; giving activities include $2,702,011 for 137 grants (high: $188,500; low: $1,000; average: $5,000–$50,000) and $792,748 for 4 foundation-administered programs.

Purpose and activities: Focus on fundamental ecological issues: 1) protection of forests, aquatic ecosystems and other habitats, including wildlands philanthropy (buying land to save it), wilderness recovery (supporting the design and implementation of large-scale wilderness recovery networks), funding for activists fighting for full protection of species and ecosystems and funding for efforts to eliminate resource extraction on public lands; 2) support for alternative models of agriculture that support biodiversity, local self-reliance and healthy agrarian communities, support for efforts in the fight against industrial agriculture, and support for efforts to link conservationists with farmers and activists in order to integrate habitat preservation and restoration with diverse farming practices; 3) campaigns for effective analysis, organizing and action in response to the rapid acceleration in macroeconomic trends toward global economic integration and free trade that has shifted real political power away from citizen democracies to global corporate bureaucracies, and the further centralization of global corporate power caused by new technological innovation. Supported projects include educational programs exposing the full consequences of the global economy and new free trade agreements, technological critiques and campaigns, and groups fighting large road-building, infrastructure, and dam projects.

Fields of interest: Natural resources; Environment, land resources; Environment; Animals/wildlife, preservation/protection; Agriculture; International affairs.
International interests: South America; Argentina; Chile.
Types of support: General/operating support; Continuing support; Land acquisition; Program development; Conferences/seminars; Publication; Seed money; Grants to individuals.
Limitations: Applications not accepted. Giving primarily in South America (Chile and Argentina). No support for curriculum development or K-12 educational projects, or for businesses or debt. No grants for television, video, photography (visual arts) or film productions, research, or individual academic pursuits (including graduate work or scholarships).
Publications: Multi-year report.
Application information: Contributes only to pre-selected organizations.
Board meeting date(s): Annually
Officers and Directors:* Douglas R. Tompkins,* Pres.; Quincey Imhoff,* V.P.; Kristine Tompkins,* V.P.; Debra B. Ryker,* Secy.-Treas.
Number of staff: 3 full-time professional; 2 part-time professional; 3 full-time support.
EIN: 943106115
Recent environmental and animal welfare grants:
193-1 Adirondack Council, Elizabethtown, NY, $10,000. To preserve and protect Adirondack Park. 2002.
193-2 Adirondack Land Trust, Keene Valley, NY, $20,000. For Champlain Valley Community-based Conservation. 2002.
193-3 Amazon Watch, Malibu, CA, $15,000. To heighten awareness of environmental and social impacts of exploration and development projects. 2002.
193-4 American Lands Alliance, DC, $188,500. To protect public lands from livestock grazing. 2002.
193-5 American Lands Alliance, DC, $15,000. To promote fuel reduction activities that reflect principles of Deep Ecology. 2002.
193-6 American Lands Alliance, DC, $10,000. For public awareness of threat of invasives to forest ecosystems and biodiversity and for implementing U.S. Invasive Species Management Plan. 2002.
193-7 Asociacion Lihuen Antu, Epuyen, Argentina, $10,000. To educate public of Patagonian native forests. 2002.
193-8 Biodiversity Legal Foundation, Boulder, CO, $10,000. For general support. 2002.
193-9 California Wilderness Coalition, Davis, CA, $10,000. For public education on wilderness preservation. 2002.
193-10 Center for Biological Diversity, Tucson, AZ, $25,000. To promote curtailing and limit of grazing on public land. 2002.
193-11 Center for Biological Diversity, Tucson, AZ, $15,000. For protection of endangered species and their habitats. 2002.
193-12 Center for Food Safety, DC, $120,000. To raise public awareness about detrimental effects of industrial agriculture and promote sustainable and ecological agriculture alternatives. 2002.
193-13 Committee for Idahos High Desert, Boise, ID, $25,000. To educate public on

livestock grazing and welfare ranching on public lands. 2002.
193-14 Community Alliance with Family Farmers Foundation, Davis, CA, $25,000. For promotion of sustainable food and farming system. 2002.
193-15 Community Food Security Coalition, Venice, CA, $15,000. For education on food security and sustainable agriculture. 2002.
193-16 Consumers Association of Penang, Penang, Malaysia, $100,000. For work on climate change and sustainable development. 2002.
193-17 Defensores del Bosque, Santiago, Chile, $35,000. For protection of Chilean native forest. 2002.
193-18 Defensores del Bosque, Santiago, Chile, $15,000. For promotion of Chilean forest preservation. 2002.
193-19 Earth Island Institute, San Francisco, CA, $15,000. For public education about forest protection. 2002.
193-20 Earth Island Institute, San Francisco, CA, $10,000. To promote appropriate recreation on public lands. 2002.
193-21 Environmental Research Association, Bedford, England, $10,000. For magazine to educate public on ecological world view. 2002.
193-22 Fiscalia del Medio Ambiente (FIMA), Santiago, Chile, $10,000. To protect and conserve southern Chile's water resources. 2002.
193-23 Food and Water, Marshfield, VT, $25,000. For promotion of book on effects of industrial agriculture. 2002.
193-24 Forest Conservation Council, Santa Fe, NM, $10,000. For National Forests Programs. 2002.
193-25 Forest Guardians, Santa Fe, NM, $25,000. To promote curtailing and limit of grazing on public land. 2002.
193-26 Forest Watch, Montpelier, VT, $15,000. For land trust. 2002.
193-27 Forest Watch, Montpelier, VT, $10,000. For general support. 2002.
193-28 Friends of the Earth, DC, $10,000. For protection of biological health of public lands. 2002.
193-29 Fundacion Rodellio, Santiago, Chile, $22,000. To provide education for youth in rural communities. 2002.
193-30 Getting the Word Out, Saranac Lake, NY, $10,000. For regional newspaper to obtain support for Adirondack. 2002.
193-31 Grand Canyon Wildlands Council, Flagstaff, AZ, $10,000. For general support. 2002.
193-32 Idaho Sporting Congress, Boise, ID, $10,000. For general support. 2002.
193-33 Institute for Policy Studies, DC, $15,000. For education on environmental sustainability. 2002.
193-34 International Forum on Globalization, San Francisco, CA, $40,000. To promote book on detrimental effects of industrial agriculture and promotion of alternative sustainable ecological agriculture. 2002.
193-35 International Rivers Network, Berkeley, CA, $30,000. For education on degradation of river systems. 2002.
193-36 International Rivers Network, Berkeley, CA, $18,540. For general support. 2002.

193-37 Land Institute, Salina, KS, $60,000. For general support. 2002.
193-38 Land Stewardship Project, White Bear Lake, MN, $15,000. To promote agroecological restoration and renewal of harmonious relationship between farming and natural world. 2002.
193-39 National Campaign for Sustainable Agriculture, Pine Bush, NY, $15,000. For public awareness of a sustainable food and agriculture system. 2002.
193-40 Native Forest Network, Missoula, MT, $15,000. For Public Lands Project. 2002.
193-41 Nature Conservancy, Arlington, VA, $10,000. For regional conservation planning. 2002.
193-42 New Mexico Wilderness Alliance, Albuquerque, NM, $10,000. For general support. 2002.
193-43 Northern Appalachian Restoration Project, Lancaster, NH, $15,000. For general support. 2002.
193-44 Occidental Arts and Ecology Center, Occidental, CA, $15,000. For general support. 2002.
193-45 Occidental Arts and Ecology Center, Occidental, CA, $10,000. For education on effects of industrial agriculture. 2002.
193-46 Oregon Natural Desert Association, Bend, Oregon, $25,000. To protect Sagebrush Sea's wildlands and waterways. 2002.
193-47 Organic Consumers Association, Little Marais, MN, $37,000. For public awareness of detrimental effects of industrial agriculture and to promote alternative sustainable ecological agriculture. 2002.
193-48 Patagonia Land Trust, Sausalito, CA, $24,116. For general support. 2002.
193-49 Pesticide Action Network (PAN), North America Regional Center, San Francisco, CA, $40,000. For education of effects of industrial agriculture and use of pesticides. 2002.
193-50 POINT Foundation, Sausalito, CA, $20,000. For magazine to promote public awareness of the planet. 2002.
193-51 RAFI-USA, Pittsboro, NC, $25,000. For environmental and ecosystem analysis. 2002.
193-52 RAFI-USA, Pittsboro, NC, $20,000. To promote biodiversity and organic and sustainable agriculture. 2002.
193-53 Rainforest Action Network, San Francisco, CA, $10,000. For general support. 2002.
193-54 Red Nacional de Accion Ecologica (RENACE), Santiago, Chile, $11,000. For public education on environmental problems and alternatives for sustainable development. 2002.
193-55 Red Nacional de Accion Ecologica (RENACE), Santiago, Chile, $10,000. For public education on environmental problems and alternatives for sustainable development. 2002.
193-56 Research Foundation for Science, Technology and Ecology, New Delhi, India, $45,000. For general support. 2002.
193-57 Restore the North Woods, Concord, MA, $10,000. For general support. 2002.
193-58 Sea Shepherd Conservation Society, Venice, CA, $10,000. For general support. 2002.
193-59 Sierra Club Foundation, San Francisco, CA, $10,000. For public education on grizzly

recovery, protection of important habitat and premature removal from endangered species list. 2002.

193-60 Sky Island Alliance, Tucson, AZ, $10,000. For general support. 2002.

193-61 Southern Utah Wilderness Alliance, Salt Lake City, UT, $10,000. For general support. 2002.

193-62 Sustain, Chicago, IL, $12,000. For public awareness of advantages of organic agriculture and to support book on industrial agriculture and alternative sustainable agriculture. 2002.

193-63 Tides Center, San Francisco, CA, $15,000. For education of public about social and environmental impacts of corporate globalization. 2002.

193-64 Tides Center, San Francisco, CA, $10,000. To promote sustainable agriculture and food system in California. 2002.

193-65 Turtle Island Restoration Network, Forest Knolls, CA, $10,000. To protect sea turtle population. 2002.

193-66 Valhalla Wilderness Society, New Denver, Canada, $10,000. For protection of watersheds. 2002.

193-67 Watershed Media, Healdsburg, CA, $40,000. For book project on farming practices that are more compatible with nature. 2002.

193-68 Western Watersheds Project, Hailey, ID, $25,000. For education on and protection of public lands from livestock grazing. 2002.

193-69 Wildlands Center for Preventing Roads, Missoula, MT, $10,000. For general support. 2002.

193-70 Wildlands Project, Tucson, AZ, $55,000. For general support. 2002.

193-71 Wildlands Project, Tucson, AZ, $10,000. For wolf recovery and to restore wildness to Northeast. 2002.

193-72 Wildlands Project, Tucson, AZ, $10,000. To preserve Mexico's biological heritage. 2002.

193-73 WildLaw, Montgomery, AL, $10,000. For general support. 2002.

193-74 World Stewardship Institute, Santa Rosa, CA, $15,000. For public awareness of forest conservation. 2002.

194
The Foundation for Sustainability and Innovation

P.O. Box 149
Laguna Beach, CA 92652-0149
Contact: Ronald H. Chilcote, Dir.
Tel.: (909) 787-5037, ext.: 1571; E-mail: fsifoundation@aol.com

Established in 1998 in CA.
Grantmaker type: Independent foundation
Financial data (yr. ended 12/31/02): Assets, $1,693,560 (M); gifts received, $7,500; expenditures, $137,574; qualifying distributions, $131,749; giving activities include $131,749 for 30 grants (high: $17,500; low: $1,000).
Purpose and activities: Awards must be used for ecology-based agricultural research or education. The foundation seeks to foster environmental restoration, preservation and education with emphasis on seed money that leads to establishing demonstration projects that link rural and urban settings.

Fields of interest: Environment, research; Environment, single organization support; Environment, public education; Natural resources; Agriculture/food, single organization support; Agriculture/food, public education.
Types of support: Program development; Publication; Seed money; Curriculum development; Fellowships; Internship funds; Exchange programs; Matching/challenge support.
Limitations: Giving on a national basis.
Publications: Application guidelines, Annual report.
Application information: Application form not required.
  Initial approach: Letter requesting proposal guidelines
  Copies of proposal: 5
  Deadline(s): Apr. 15 and Oct. 15
  Board meeting date(s): May and Nov.
  Final notification: June and Nov.
Directors: Edward B. Chilcote; Frances B. Chilcote; Ronald H. Chilcote; Stephen H. Chilcote.
Number of staff: 1 part-time support.
EIN: 330785572

195
Samuel I. & John Henry Fox Foundation
(formerly John H. Fox Foundation)
c/o Union Bank of California, N.A.
P.O. Box 85404
San Diego, CA 92186
Contact: Marylou Koppel, V.P., Union Bank of California, N.A.
E-mail: marylou.koppel@uboc.com

Established in 1955 in CA.
Grantmaker type: Independent foundation
Financial data (yr. ended 03/31/02): Assets, $2,785,743 (M); expenditures, $158,086; qualifying distributions, $125,890; giving activities include $104,500 for 38 grants (high: $10,000; low: $500; average: $2,000–$5,000) and $11,000 for 1 grant to an individual.
Purpose and activities: Giving primarily for health care and the arts.
Fields of interest: Museums (natural history); Performing arts; Theater; Music; Arts; Animal welfare; Health care; Health organizations, association; Boy scouts; Girl scouts; Human services; YM/YWCAs & YM/YWHAs; Children/youth, services; Hospices; Aging, centers/services.
Types of support: General/operating support; Building/renovation; Program development; Research; Technical assistance.
Limitations: Giving limited to San Diego County, CA.
Publications: Application guidelines.
Application information: Application form not required.
  Initial approach: Letter and proposal
  Copies of proposal: 1
  Deadline(s): May 15
  Board meeting date(s): June
Trustee: Union Bank of California, N.A.
Number of staff: None.
EIN: 956010288

196
The Frankel Foundation
c/o Katz, Fram & Co.
11620 Wilshire Blvd., Ste. 580
Los Angeles, CA 90025

Established in 1988 in NY; funded in 1989.
Donor(s): Raymond Frankel.
Grantmaker type: Independent foundation
Financial data (yr. ended 12/31/02): Assets, $515,188 (M); gifts received, $104,984; expenditures, $220,662; qualifying distributions, $220,662; giving activities include $212,150 for 21 grants (high: $45,000; low: $1,000).
Purpose and activities: Giving for education, the environment, and Jewish organizations.
Fields of interest: Higher education; Libraries (academic/research); Environment; Human services; Jewish agencies & temples.
Limitations: Applications not accepted. Giving primarily in CA. No grants to individuals.
Application information: Contributes only to pre-selected organizations.
Trustees: Belinda Frankel; Maxine Frankel; Raymond Frankel; Marvin Sears.
EIN: 133187074

197
The Don and Lorraine Freeberg Foundation
801 N. Brand Blvd., No. 1010
Glendale, CA 91203 (818) 247-3681
Contact: Don Freeberg, C.E.O.

Established in 1990 in CA.
Donor(s): Donald A. Freeberg, Lorraine Freeberg.
Grantmaker type: Independent foundation
Financial data (yr. ended 03/31/02): Assets, $882,702 (M); expenditures, $467,176; qualifying distributions, $437,276; giving activities include $433,974 for 21 grants (high: $240,474; low: $500).
Purpose and activities: Giving for higher education, zoos, youth services, and legal services.
Fields of interest: Higher education; Zoos/zoological societies; Legal services; YM/YWCAs & YM/YWHAs.
Types of support: General/operating support; Scholarship funds.
Limitations: Giving primarily in CA. No grants to individuals.
Application information: Application form not required.
  Deadline(s): None
Officers: Donald Freeberg, C.E.O.; Shirley Hough, Secy.; Daniel Freeberg, C.F.O.
Directors: Lorraine Freeberg; Jim Geary; Dirk Heim; Noreen Flynn Owen.
EIN: 954307817

198
Fresno Regional Foundation
3425 N. 1st St., Ste. 101
Fresno, CA 93726 (559) 226-5600
Contact: Jesse R. Arreguin, Exec. Dir.
FAX: (559) 230-2078; E-mail: frfmaury@lightspeed.net, or info@fresnofoundation.org:; URL: http://www.fresnoregfoundation.org

Established as a trust in 1966 in CA.
Grantmaker type: Community foundation
Financial data (yr. ended 12/31/01): Assets,
$11,586,724 (M); gifts received, $1,626,114;
expenditures, $2,518,140; giving activities
include $1,754,295 for 87 grants (high:
$1,001,000; low: $38).
Purpose and activities: Interests include health,
the arts, alleviation of social problems,
education, senior citizens, character building,
conservation and beautification, religious
institutions, conservation of human and natural
resources, and local historical programs. The
foundation administers donor-advised funds.
Fields of interest: Arts; Education; Environment;
Health care; Human services;
Government/public administration.
Types of support: Continuing support;
Management development; Equipment; Seed
money; Program-related investments/loans.
Limitations: Applications not accepted. Giving
primarily in the central San Joaquin Valley, CA,
area, especially Fresno, Madera, Mariposa,
Merced, Tulare, and Kings counties. No grants to
individuals, or for endowment funds.
Application information: The foundation is not
accepting grants requests for 2003.
Officers and Governors:* Herbert John
Blossom, M.D.,* Pres.; Gloria Smith,* V.P.;
Annette LaRue,* Secy.-Treas.; Jesse R. Arreguin,
Exec. Dir.; Michael Adams, M.D.; Vernon M.
Crowder; Donald R. Fischbach; Susan J. Fisher;
Judy Ganulin; Fausto Hinojosa; Jeffery Jaech;
Morton G. Rosenstein, M.D.; Rudy L. Savala; O.
James Woodward III.
Trustee Bank: Wells Fargo Bank, N.A.
Number of staff: 3 full-time professional; 2
full-time support.
EIN: 946140207

199
Gilbert B. Friesen Foundation
770 Bonhill Rd.
Los Angeles, CA 90049

Established in 1997 in CA.
Donor(s): Gilbert B. Friesen.
Grantmaker type: Independent foundation
Financial data (yr. ended 12/31/02): Assets,
$60,171 (M); gifts received, $140,881;
expenditures, $102,420; qualifying distributions,
$98,242; giving activities include $98,242 for
17 grants (high: $46,000; low: $300).
Purpose and activities: Giving primarily for arts
and culture.
Fields of interest: Museums (art); Arts;
Education; Natural resources; Health
organizations, association; Human services;
Children, services.
Limitations: Applications not accepted. Giving
primarily in Los Angeles, CA; some giving also
in New York, NY. No grants to individuals.
Application information: Contributes only to
pre-selected organizations.
Trustees: Joel S. Ehrenkrantz; Gilbert B. Friesen.
EIN: 954632580

200
The Fullerton Family Charitable Trust
100 Drakes Landing Rd., Ste. 330
Greenbrae, CA 94904

Established in 1991 in CA.
Donor(s): Jessica Fullerton, John B. Fullerton,
Baxter Fullerton.
Grantmaker type: Independent foundation
Financial data (yr. ended 06/30/02): Assets,
$8,333,064 (M); gifts received, $140,757;
expenditures, $1,177,328; qualifying
distributions, $848,627; giving activities include
$850,365 for 29 grants (high: $220,000; low:
$500).
Purpose and activities: Giving for education,
human services, and community development.
Fields of interest: Arts; Education; Environment;
Animal welfare; Big Brothers/Big Sisters; Human
services; Federated giving programs.
Limitations: Applications not accepted. Giving
primarily in CA, CO, and OH. No grants to
individuals.
Application information: Contributes only to
pre-selected organizations.
Trustees: Jessica Fullerton; John B. Fullerton.
EIN: 680262543

201
Fund for Santa Barbara, Inc.
924 Anacapa St., Ste. 4H
Santa Barbara, CA 93101 (805) 962-9164
Contact: Geoff Green, Grants Mgr.
TDD: (800) 735-2929; *FAX:* (805) 965-0217;
E-mail: email@fundforsantabarbara.org; *URL:*
http://www.fundforsantabarbara.org/

Established in 1980 in CA.
Grantmaker type: Public charity
Financial data (yr. ended 12/31/00): Revenue,
$623,853; assets, $1,261,310 (M); gifts
received, $469,507; expenditures, $309,129;
program services expenses, $237,192; giving
activities include $154,704 for 41 grants (high:
$7,500; low: $165).
Purpose and activities: The fund supports
projects that advocate, educate, and organize in
order to examine and address the root causes of
social, economic, and environmental problems.
These projects work for issues such as: human
rights, racial equity and ethnic heritage,
protecting the environment, accessible health
care, peace and nonviolence, responsible
government, legal rights, progressive solutions,
and community organizing.
Fields of interest: Cultural/ethnic awareness;
Environment; Health care; International
peace/security; International human rights; Civil
rights; Public affairs.
Types of support: General/operating support;
Emergency funds; Seed money; Technical
assistance; Program evaluation.
Limitations: Giving limited to Santa Barbara
County, CA. No support for individual
candidates in electoral campaigns, or direct
service organizations. No grants to individuals,
or for capital ventures, building improvement, or
equipment (except for basic office supplies
equipment).
Publications: Application guidelines,
Informational brochure, Newsletter, Program
policy statement.
Application information: See Web site for
application forms and guidelines. Application
form required.
　Initial approach: Telephone or e-mail
　Copies of proposal: 14
　Deadline(s): Mar. and Sept.

Board meeting date(s): Mar. and Sept.
Final notification: Within 10 weeks
Officer and Directors:* Susan Clarke,* Pres.;
Nancy Weiss, Exec. Dir.; Britt Andreatta; Bruce
Bigenho; Vicky Blum; Sylvia Curtis; Don Harjo
Daves-Rougeaux; Dick Flacks; and 7 additional
directors.
Number of staff: 3 full-time professional; 1
part-time support.
EIN: 770070742

202
G.A.G. Charitable Corporation
132 N. El Camino Real, No. 325
Encinitas, CA 92024
Contact: Dorothy Salant, Pres.

Incorporated in 1968 in CA.
Donor(s): Dorothy Salant, George A.
Griesbach.‡
Grantmaker type: Independent foundation
Financial data (yr. ended 12/31/01): Assets,
$2,930,172 (M); expenditures, $195,291;
qualifying distributions, $169,806; giving
activities include $144,223 for 75 grants (high:
$10,000; low: $25).
Purpose and activities: Support for the
environment, human rights, food and agriculture
programs, education, and cultural organizations.
Fields of interest: Arts; Education; Natural
resources; Environment; Agriculture/food; Public
affairs.
International interests: Africa.
Types of support: General/operating support.
Limitations: Applications not accepted. Giving
primarily in CA and NY. No grants to
individuals, or for building or endowment funds,
research, scholarships, fellowships, or matching
gifts; no loans.
Publications: Financial statement, Grants list.
Application information: Contributes only to
pre-selected organizations.
　Board meeting date(s): May
Officers and Directors:* Dorothy Salant,* Pres.;
William Rybnick,* Secy.; Peter Salant,* C.F.O.;
Anthony Salant.
Number of staff: 4 part-time professional.
EIN: 952568756

203
G.T.R. & B. Charitable Foundation
132 S. Rodeo Dr.
Beverly Hills, CA 90212-2415

Established in 1993 in CA.
Donor(s): Harold A. Brown, Hermione K.
Brown, Tom R. Camp, Gregg Harrison, Jeffrey
M. Mandell, Kevin S. Marks, Donald S.
Passman, Bruce M. Ramer, Lawrence D. Rose,
Norman R. Tyre, Nancy L. Boxwell.
Grantmaker type: Independent foundation
Financial data (yr. ended 10/31/02): Assets,
$719,485 (M); gifts received, $84,614;
expenditures, $451,734; qualifying distributions,
$446,875; giving activities include $447,029 for
100 grants (high: $60,000; low: $100).
Purpose and activities: Funding primarily for
Jewish agencies, human services, education,
and the arts and culture.
Fields of interest: Arts; Education; Environment;
Animal welfare; Human services; Federated

giving programs; Jewish federated giving programs; Jewish agencies & temples.
Limitations: Applications not accepted. Giving on a national basis. No grants to individuals.
Application information: Contributes only to pre-selected organizations. Unsolicited requests for funds not accepted.
Officers and Directors:* Bruce M. Ramer,* Pres.; Nancy L. Boxwell,* V.P.; Hermione K. Brown,* Secy.
EIN: 954468911

204
Gaia Fund
235 Montgomery St., Ste. 1011
San Francisco, CA 94104 (415) 391-6943
Contact: Mark Schlesinger, Managing Tr.
FAX: (415) 391-6944; E-mail: email@gaiafundsf.org; URL: http:// www.gaiafundsf.org

Established in 1994 in CA.
Grantmaker type: Independent foundation
Financial data (yr. ended 12/31/02): Assets, $9,028,517 (M); gifts received, $607,547; expenditures, $587,732; qualifying distributions, $585,927; giving activities include $575,750 for 47 grants (high: $62,500; low: $100).
Purpose and activities: Support primarily for organizations involved with environmental programs that promote sustainable practices relative to food production, distribution, and consumption. The fund also makes grants to programs serving the Jewish community of San Francisco, CA.
Fields of interest: Environment; Jewish agencies & temples.
Types of support: General/operating support; Continuing support; Program development; Conferences/seminars.
Limitations: Giving primarily in the San Francisco Bay Area, CA. No support for Holocaust related projects, environmental education programs for children, or social service programs. No grants to individuals.
Application information: Preference given to grant requests for projects with annual budgets of less than $2 million. Application form required.
  Initial approach: Letter of inquiry
  Copies of proposal: 2
  Deadline(s): Feb. 15 and Aug. 15
  Board meeting date(s): May and Nov.
  Final notification: June 30 and Dec. 31
Officers and Directors:* Christine H. Russell,* C.E.O.; Mark L. Schlesinger,* Secy. and C.F.O.
Number of staff: None.
EIN: 943215541

205
Garen Family Foundation
c/o Quintile Wealth Mgmt.
2029 Century Park E., Ste. 400
Los Angeles, CA 90067 (310) 475-9505

Established in 1996 in CA.
Donor(s): Eric R. Garen, Nancy J. Garen.
Grantmaker type: Independent foundation
Financial data (yr. ended 12/31/02): Assets, $7,061,513 (M); expenditures, $505,334; qualifying distributions, $492,781; giving

activities include $483,578 for 31 grants (high: $183,233; low: $100).
Purpose and activities: Giving primarily to education and social services.
Fields of interest: Radio; Museums (art); Theater; Elementary/secondary education; Higher education; Engineering school/education; Natural resources; Environment; Health organizations, association; Human services.
Limitations: Applications not accepted. Giving primarily in CA, with emphasis on Los Angeles. No grants to individuals.
Application information: Contributes only to pre-selected organizations.
Trustees: Eric R. Garen; Nancy J. Garen.
EIN: 954621093

206
John Jewett & H. Chandler Garland Foundation ▼
P.O. Box 550
Pasadena, CA 91102-0550
Contact: G.E. Morrow, Mgr.

Trust established in 1959 in CA.
Donor(s): Members of the Garland family.
Grantmaker type: Independent foundation
Financial data (yr. ended 12/31/01): Assets, $1,418,662 (M); gifts received, $131,748; expenditures, $3,540,395; qualifying distributions, $3,540,395; giving activities include $3,376,231 for 93 grants (high: $950,000; low: $5,000).
Purpose and activities: Support primarily for cultural and historical programs, secondary and higher education, social services, especially for the elderly, youth agencies, hospitals, and health services.
Fields of interest: Historic preservation/historical societies; Arts; Education; Hospitals (general); Health care; Human services; Youth, services; Aging, centers/services; Homeless, human services; Aging; Homeless.
Types of support: General/operating support; Continuing support; Annual campaigns; Capital campaigns; Building/renovation; Equipment; Endowments; Debt reduction; Emergency funds; Curriculum development; Scholarship funds; Research; Matching/challenge support.
Limitations: Giving primarily in CA, with emphasis on southern CA. No grants to individuals, or for seed money.
Publications: Application guidelines.
Application information: Application form not required.
  Initial approach: Letter only; no telephone inquiries
  Copies of proposal: 1
  Deadline(s): None
  Board meeting date(s): 2 times per year
  Final notification: After each meeting
Officer and Trustees:* G.E. Morrow,* Mgr.; Ann Kelsey Babcock; Gwendolyn Garland Babcock; John Carlile Babcock; Sarah Garland Babcock; Susan Hinman Babcock; Hillary Duque Garland; William M. Garland; William May Garland III.
Number of staff: None.
EIN: 956023587
Recent environmental and animal welfare grants:

206-1 Canine Companions for Independence, Santa Rosa, CA, $10,000. For general support. 2001.
206-2 Diggers Garden Club, Pasadena, CA, $10,000. For Endowment Fund. 2001.
206-3 Humane Society of Richmond, Richmond, VA, $1,150,000. For general support, second floor walking and tract training area, construction of second floor roof garden, and Children's Exploratorium. 2001.
206-4 International Hearing Dog, Henderson, CO, $10,000. For sponsorships. 2001.
206-5 National Outdoor Leadership School, Lander, WY, $20,000. For general support. 2001.
206-6 Nature Conservancy, Arlington, VA, $40,000. For program in Big Sky Ranch in Montana. 2001.
206-7 Pasadena Humane Society, Pasadena, CA, $10,000. For general support. 2001.
206-8 Rancho Santa Ana Botanic Garden, Claremont, CA, $35,000. For general support. 2001.
206-9 Rondout Valley Animals for Adoption, Accord, NY, $10,000. For general support. 2001.
206-10 Student Conservation Association, San Francisco, CA, $15,000. For general support. 2001.

207
Gateway Foundation
(formerly Gateway 2000 Foundation, Inc.)
14303 Gateway Pl.
Poway, CA 92064-7140

Established in 1994 in SD.
Donor(s): Gateway 2000, Inc., Gateway, Inc.
Grantmaker type: Company-sponsored foundation
Financial data (yr. ended 12/31/01): Assets, $2,487,464 (M); gifts received, $1,125,192; expenditures, $974,317; qualifying distributions, $974,317; giving activities include $781,057 for 161 grants (high: $300,000; low: $25; average: $100–$25,000).
Purpose and activities: Giving primarily for medical research, human services, and education.
Fields of interest: Arts; Elementary/secondary education; Higher education; Education; Natural resources; Medical care, outpatient care; Medical research, institute; Youth development, centers/clubs; Human services; Children/youth, services.
Limitations: Applications not accepted. Giving on a national basis, with emphasis on Sioux City, IA, Kansas City, MO, Sioux Falls, SD, and Hampton and Newport News, VA. No grants to individuals.
Application information: Contributes only to pre-selected organizations.
Officers: Stephanie Heim, Secy.; Randall D. Harvey, Treas.
Directors: Glen J. Anderson; Donald McClellan.
EIN: 460434986

208
The Fred Gellert Family Foundation

361 3rd St., Ste. A
San Rafael, CA 94901 (415) 256-5433
Contact: Deborah Smith, Dir., Grant Progs.
FAX: (415) 256-5425; E-mail:
foundation@fredgellert.com; URL: http://
fdncenter.org/grantmaker/fredgellert/

Established in 1958 in CA.
Donor(s): Fred Gellert, Sr.‡
Grantmaker type: Independent foundation
Financial data (yr. ended 12/31/01): Assets,
$12,836,601 (M); expenditures, $859,420;
qualifying distributions, $648,197; giving
activities include $582,500 for 75 grants (high:
$50,000; low: $1,000).
Purpose and activities: As a result of a strategic
planning process, in 2004 the Fred Gellert
Family Foundation will focus its grantmaking in
four areas: Arts and Humanities, Environment,
Health, and Youth, Senior & Family Services.
The selection of these areas of priority will allow
us to have the greatest impact given the scope of
our resources. We will fund education-focused
grants, but not in an education program. Please
note that we will no longer consider proposals
specifically focused on K-12 school reform.
Fields of interest: Arts; Education; Natural
resources; Environment; Hospitals (general);
Family planning; Health care; Mental
health/crisis services; Human services;
Children/youth, services; Youth, pregnancy
prevention; Family services; Aging,
centers/services; Community development;
Disabled; Economically disadvantaged.
Types of support: General/operating support;
Continuing support; Equipment; Program
development; Conferences/seminars;
Publication; Curriculum development; Technical
assistance; Matching/challenge support.
Limitations: Giving on a local and national basis
for environmental grants; giving limited to San
Francisco, San Mateo, and Marin counties, CA,
for all other grants. No grants to individuals, or
for annual campaigns; no loans.
Publications: Application guidelines, Financial
statement, Grants list.
Application information: Applications will only
be considered from those grantees whose
proposals were pending in Nov. 2002 and
declined due to the economic downturn.
Application form required.
  Initial approach: Letter of request
  Copies of proposal: 1
  Deadline(s): Aug. 1 for Arts and Humanities,
    Health and Environment grants; Feb. 1 for
    Youth, Seniors & Family Service grants
  Board meeting date(s): Apr. and Nov.
  Final notification: Apr. 30 and Nov. 30
Officers and Directors:* Annette Gellert,*
Co-Chair.; Fred Gellert, Jr.,* Co-Chair.; John D.
Howard,* Secy.-Treas.
Number of staff: 1 full-time professional; 1
part-time support.
EIN: 946062859

209
Wallace Alexander Gerbode Foundation ▼

111 Pine St., Ste. 1515
San Francisco, CA 94111 (415) 391-0911
Contact: Thomas C. Layton, Pres.
FAX: (415) 391-4587; E-mail: info@gerbode.org;
URL: http://www.fdncenter.org/grantmaker/
gerbode/

Incorporated in 1953 in CA.
Donor(s): Members of the Gerbode family.
Grantmaker type: Independent foundation
Financial data (yr. ended 12/31/02): Assets,
$59,179,110 (M); gifts received, $300,000;
expenditures, $6,256,611; qualifying
distributions, $4,518,286; giving activities
include $3,986,160 for 125 grants (high:
$333,334; low: $649; average:
$5,000–$25,000).
Purpose and activities: Support for programs
and projects offering the potential for significant
impact in the areas of arts and culture, the
environment, population, reproductive rights,
citizen participation/building
communities/inclusiveness, the strength of the
philanthropic process and the nonprofit sector,
and foundation-initiated special projects.
Fields of interest: Arts; Environment;
Reproductive rights; Civil rights; Community
development; Philanthropy/voluntarism; Public
policy, research; Public affairs.
Types of support: Program development;
Technical assistance; Consulting services;
Program-related investments/loans.
Limitations: Giving primarily to programs
directly affecting residents of Alameda, Contra
Costa, Marin, San Francisco, and San Mateo
counties in CA, and HI. No support for religious
purposes or private schools. No grants to
individuals, or for direct services, deficit
budgets, general operating funds, building or
equipment funds, general fundraising
campaigns, publications, or scholarships.
Publications: Application guidelines, Annual
report (including application guidelines), Grants
list.
Application information: Application form not
required.
  Initial approach: Letter; initial contact should
    not include materials (including videotapes)
    requiring a return
  Copies of proposal: 1
  Deadline(s): None
  Board meeting date(s): 4 times per year
  Final notification: 2 to 3 months
Officers and Trustees:* Maryanna G.
Stockholm,* Chair.; Frank A. Gerbode, M.D.,*
Vice-Chair. and Secy.; Charles M. Stockholm,*
Vice-Chair. and Treas.; Thomas C. Layton,* Pres.
Number of staff: 2 full-time professional; 2
full-time support; 1 part-time support.
EIN: 946065226
**Recent environmental and animal welfare
grants:**
209-1 Bay Area Transportation and Land Use
  Coalition, San Francisco, CA, $25,000. For
  program support. 2002.
209-2 Consumers Union of United States, San
  Francisco, CA, $25,000. For California
  Energy Project. 2002.
209-3 Earthjustice Legal Defense Fund,
  Oakland, CA, $25,000. For work in Hawaii,
  generally, and work of Kapua Sproat,
  specifically. 2002.

209-4 Hawaii Nature Center, Honolulu, HI,
  $15,000. Toward organizational
  development. 2002.
209-5 Ike Aina, Honolulu, HI, $25,000. Toward
  organizational development as Native
  Hawaiian Land Trust. 2002.
209-6 Malama o Manoa, Honolulu, HI,
  $100,000. For work advocating appropriate
  energy planning Hawaii and opposition to
  additional power transmission lines being
  routed through Manoa Valley. 2002.
209-7 Natural Resources Defense Council, San
  Francisco, CA, $100,000. For Ocean
  Protection Initiative in the Pacific region.
  2002.
209-8 Orion Society, Great Barrington, MA,
  $10,000. For work involving intersection of
  environmental and cultural issues. 2002.
209-9 Pacific Institute for Studies in
  Development, Environment and Security,
  Oakland, CA, $25,000. Toward
  Environmental Indicators Project in West
  Oakland. 2002.
209-10 Pele Defense Fund, Volcano, HI,
  $10,000. For efforts to protect Wao Kele o
  Puna (Puna Rainforest). 2002.
209-11 Public Employees for Environmental
  Responsibility (PEER), DC, $25,000. For work
  in California. 2002.
209-12 Resource Renewal Institute, San
  Francisco, CA, $25,000. For project entitled,
  Public Trust Alliance. 2002.
209-13 Seacology, Berkeley, CA, $10,000. For
  program support. 2002.
209-14 Sierra Club Foundation, San Francisco,
  CA, $25,000. Toward National Education
  Project. 2002.
209-15 Snitow-Kaufman Productions, Berkeley,
  CA, $10,000. For documentary film, Thirst,
  about global scarcity and privatization of
  water. 2002.
209-16 Tides Foundation, San Francisco, CA,
  $25,000. Toward Indigenous Communities
  Mapping Initiative. 2002.
209-17 Trust for Public Land, San Francisco, CA,
  $300,000. For Hawaiian Island Program.
  2002.

210
Gerhard Family Foundation

300 Drakes Landing Rd., Ste. 290
Greenbrae, CA 94904

Established in 1991 in CA.
Donor(s): Lang Gerhard, Melissa Gerhard.
Grantmaker type: Independent foundation
Financial data (yr. ended 06/30/02): Assets,
$338,381 (M); expenditures, $301,893;
qualifying distributions, $299,498; giving
activities include $289,800 for 29 grants (high:
$50,000; low: $800).
Purpose and activities: Giving primarily for
environmental conservation and for education.
Fields of interest: Elementary/secondary
education; Education; Natural resources;
Human services.
Limitations: Applications not accepted. Giving
primarily in CA. No grants to individuals.
Application information: Contributes only to
pre-selected organizations.
Trustees: Bonnie George; Lang Gerhard.
EIN: 680262298

211
Claire Giannini Fund
P.O. Box 590297
San Francisco, CA 94159-0297
(415) 776-8181
Contact: Hilda H. Yao, Exec. Dir.

Established in 1998 in CA.
Grantmaker type: Independent foundation
Financial data (yr. ended 12/31/01): Assets, $45,373,927 (M); expenditures, $3,421,937; qualifying distributions, $2,986,381; giving activities include $3,370,000 for 53 grants (high: $600,000; low: $10,000; average: $20,000–$50,000).
Purpose and activities: Giving primarily for animals, education, human services, and arts and cultural programs.
Fields of interest: Arts; Education; Animals/wildlife; Children/youth, services.
Limitations: Applications not accepted. Giving primarily in CA. No grants to individuals.
Application information: Contributes only to pre-selected organizations.
Trustees: Donald J. Lawrence; Dorothy W. Yao; U.S. Trust.
EIN: 943297004

212
Earl B. Gilmore Foundation
P.O. Box 480314
Los Angeles, CA 90048

Incorporated in 1958 in CA.
Donor(s): A.F. Gilmore Co., Marie Dent Gilmore.‡
Grantmaker type: Independent foundation
Financial data (yr. ended 12/31/01): Assets, $2,641,513 (M); expenditures, $146,189; qualifying distributions, $142,206; giving activities include $133,225 for 91 grants (high: $11,000; low: $200).
Purpose and activities: Emphasis on social services; grants also for higher and secondary education, health agencies, and youth agencies.
Fields of interest: Arts; Secondary school/education; Higher education; Natural resources; Health care; Human services; Salvation Army; Youth, services; Religion; General charitable giving.
Limitations: Applications not accepted. Giving primarily in CA. No grants to individuals.
Application information: Contributes only to pre-selected organizations.
Officers and Directors:* Henry L. Hilty, Jr.,* Pres.; Frank W. Clark, Jr.,* V.P.; Andrew G. Hilen, Sr.,* V.P.; Frances Gilmore Hilen,* V.P.; Karl M. Samuelian,* V.P.; M.B. Hartman, Secy.-Treas.
EIN: 956029602

213
The William G. Gilmore Foundation
120 Montgomery St., Ste. 1880
San Francisco, CA 94104 (415) 546-1400
Contact: Faye Wilson, Exec. Dir.
FAX: (415) 391-8732

Incorporated in 1953 in CA.
Donor(s): William G. Gilmore,‡ Mrs. William G. Gilmore.‡
Grantmaker type: Independent foundation

Financial data (yr. ended 12/31/01): Assets, $23,234,997 (M); expenditures, $1,176,166; qualifying distributions, $1,162,750; giving activities include $1,041,100 for 140 grants (high: $50,000; low: $500; average: $500–$5,000).
Purpose and activities: Grants largely for community-based organizations, including development and urban affairs, family and social services, the elderly, child welfare and development, health services, medical education, AIDS programs, conservation, and the arts.
Fields of interest: Arts; Child development, education; Medical school/education; Education; Natural resources; Health care; Mental health/crisis services; AIDS; Human services; Children/youth, services; Child development, services; Family services; Hospices; Aging, centers/services; Homeless, human services; Community development; Public affairs; Disabled; Aging; People with AIDS (PWAs); Economically disadvantaged; Homeless.
Types of support: General/operating support; Continuing support; Annual campaigns; Capital campaigns; Building/renovation; Equipment; Emergency funds; Scholarship funds.
Limitations: Giving primarily in northern CA and OR. No grants to individuals.
Publications: Application guidelines.
Application information: Application form not required.
> *Initial approach:* Proposal
> *Copies of proposal:* 1
> *Deadline(s):* May 1 and Nov. 1
> *Board meeting date(s):* June and Dec.
> *Final notification:* 2 months
Officers and Trustees:* Robert C. Harris,* Pres.; Lee Emerson,* V.P. and Treas.; William R. Mackey,* V.P.; Faye Wilson, Exec. Dir.; Thomas B. Boklund; V. Neil Fulton.
Number of staff: 1 part-time support.
EIN: 946079493

214
Give Something Back, LLC Corporate Giving Program
7700 Edgewater Dr., Ste. 400
Oakland, CA 94621
E-mail:
communityfund@givesomethingback.com; URL: http://www.givesomethingback.com/community_giving/community_giving.html

Grantmaker type: Corporate giving program
Financial data (yr. ended 12/31/01): Total giving, $405,856; giving activities include $405,856 for grants.
Purpose and activities: Give Something Back makes charitable contributions to nonprofit organizations involved with arts and culture, education, the environment, and health and human services. Support is given primarily in areas of company operations.
Fields of interest: Arts; Education; Environment; Health care; Human services.
Types of support: General/operating support.
Limitations: Giving primarily in areas of company operations. No support for political or religious organizations.
Application information: Application form not required.

Initial approach: E-mail proposal to headquarters
Copies of proposal: 1
Deadline(s): None

215
Thornton S. Glide, Jr. and Katrina D. Glide Foundation
28120 Pierce Ranch Rd.
Davis, CA 95616 (530) 753-3803
FAX: (530) 753-3849

Established in 1997 in CA.
Donor(s): Katrina D. Glide.‡
Grantmaker type: Independent foundation
Financial data (yr. ended 12/31/02): Assets, $26,929,497 (M); expenditures, $2,082,578; qualifying distributions, $1,780,349; giving activities include $905,000 for 65 grants (high: $50,000; low: $300).
Purpose and activities: Giving includes and is limited to organizations committed to the preservation of lands in their natural state including wetlands; organizations committed to agricultural purposes; the Pacific Legal Foundation; the California Land Commission; other land and wildlife conservancy groups; animal protection organizations and opera, symphony, and other similar civic organizations.
Fields of interest: Orchestra (symphony); Opera; Arts; Environment, land resources; Animal welfare; Animals/wildlife, preservation/protection; Housing/shelter; Human services; Federated giving programs.
Limitations: Giving primarily in CA. No support for programs focused primarily on a sport; or general educational institutions, or religious organizations, (except for community social service activities). No grants to individuals; no scholarships.
Application information: Application form required.
> *Deadline(s):* June 15 through Sept. 15
Trustees: Richard D. Bruga, DVM; Yvonne LeMaitre; Russell E. White.
EIN: 943276694

216
Global Environment Project Institute, Inc.
P.O. Box 158
Pacific Palisades, CA 90272
Contact: Rampa R. Hormel, Pres. and Treas.

Established in 1986 in ID.
Donor(s): Thomas D. Hormel.
Grantmaker type: Independent foundation
Financial data (yr. ended 12/31/02): Assets, $1,402,573 (M); gifts received, $716,827; expenditures, $788,784; qualifying distributions, $783,956; giving activities include $684,200 for 13 grants (high: $100,000; low: $15,000; average: $500–$200,000).
Purpose and activities: The institute promotes the conservation of biodiversity and the sustainability of life on earth.
Fields of interest: Environment.
Types of support: General/operating support; Continuing support; Program development; Matching/challenge support.
Limitations: Applications not accepted. Giving on a national basis.
Publications: Grants list.

Application information: Unsolicited requests for funds are not accepted.
Officers and Directors:* Rampa R. Hormel,* Pres. and Treas.; Diane Ives,* Secy.; Drummond Pike.
Number of staff: None.
EIN: 820421067

217
The Godric Foundation
625 Fair Oaks Ave., Ste. 360
South Pasadena, CA 91030 (626) 441-5188
Contact: Linda J. Blinkenberg, Secy.
FAX: (626) 441-3672

Established in 1980.
Grantmaker type: Independent foundation
Financial data (yr. ended 12/31/01): Assets, $3,581,856 (M); expenditures, $128,008; qualifying distributions, $111,885; giving activities include $94,000 for 5 grants (high: $61,000; low: $1,000).
Purpose and activities: Giving to the environment.
Fields of interest: Environment.
Types of support: Program development.
Limitations: Giving primarily in Santa Barbara, CA. No grants to individuals.
Application information: Due to funding restrictions, foundation manager prefers to initiate grants. Application form not required.
  Initial approach: Letter
  Copies of proposal: 1
  Deadline(s): None
Officers and Directors:* Marcia W. Constance,* Pres.; Michael J. Casey,* V.P.; Linda J. Blinkenberg,* Secy.; Richard E. Llewellyn II,* C.F.O.; Sharon W. Bradford; Jamie Constance; Brett E. Hodges; Brian M. Hodges; Arlo G. Sorensen.
Number of staff: 4 shared staff (shared with Whittier Family Foundations).
EIN: 953500486

218
The David B. Gold Foundation
44 Montgomery St., Ste. 3750
San Francisco, CA 94104 (415) 288-9530
Contact: Steve Pridemore or Elaine Gold
FAX: (415) 288-9549

Established in 1992 in CA.
Donor(s): David B. Gold.‡
Grantmaker type: Independent foundation
Financial data (yr. ended 11/30/01): Assets, $57,679,538 (M); gifts received, $1,564,505; expenditures, $3,214,903; qualifying distributions, $2,689,459; giving activities include $2,300,683 for 105 grants (high: $500,000; low: $500; average: $5,000–$50,000).
Purpose and activities: Giving primarily to early childhood and youth development, social and human services, education, natural resource conservation and protection, democratic society and Jewish culture.
Fields of interest: Education; Natural resources; Family planning; Child abuse; Legal services; Youth development; Human services; Jewish agencies & temples.
Types of support: General/operating support; Continuing support; Capital campaigns;

Building/renovation; Land acquisition; Program development.
Limitations: Giving primarily in San Francisco, CA. No grants to individuals.
Publications: Application guidelines.
Application information: Application form required.
  Initial approach: Proposal
  Copies of proposal: 1
  Deadline(s): None
  Board meeting date(s): Quarterly
Officers and Directors:* Barbara Gold-Lurie,* Pres.; Diane Gold-Bubier,* Secy.; Steven A. Gold,* Treas.; Elaine Gold; Emily Gold.
EIN: 943169439

219
Goldman Environmental Foundation
1 Lombard St., Ste. 303
San Francisco, CA 94111 (415) 788-9090
Contact: Robert Gamble, Exec. Dir.
FAX: (415) 788-7890; E-mail: info@goldmanprize.org; URL: http://www.goldmanprize.org

Established in 1989 in CA.
Donor(s): Richard N. Goldman, Rhoda H. Goldman.‡
Grantmaker type: Independent foundation
Financial data (yr. ended 12/31/02): Assets, $33,622,406 (M); expenditures, $3,532,057; qualifying distributions, $3,254,938; giving activities include $367,000 for 39 grants (high: $30,000; low: $2,000; average: $4,000–$30,000) and $901,001 for 13 grants to individuals (high: $125,000; low: $3,000; average: $3,000–$125,000).
Purpose and activities: Support for environmental conservation, including awarding one prize annually to an individual in each of the six inhabited continents in recognition of significant achievement in the field of environmental protection.
Fields of interest: Environment.
Limitations: Applications not accepted. Giving on an international basis.
Publications: Informational brochure, Newsletter, Occasional report.
Application information: Awards to individuals are by nomination of 30 organizations and a network of environmentalists; unsolicited nominations are not considered.
  Board meeting date(s): Jan.
Officer and Directors:* Richard N. Goldman,* Pres.; Susan Gelman; Douglas E. Goldman; John D. Goldman.
Number of staff: 4 full-time professional; 2 part-time professional; 1 full-time support.
EIN: 943094857

220
Lisa and Douglas Goldman Fund
1 Daniel Burnham Ct., Ste. 330C
San Francisco, CA 94109-5460
(415) 771-1717
Contact: Nancy S. Kami, Exec. Dir.
FAX: (415) 771-1797; URL: http://fdncenter.org/grantmaker/goldman/

Established in 1992 in CA.
Grantmaker type: Independent foundation

Financial data (yr. ended 12/31/02): Assets, $9,074,967 (M); expenditures, $814,045; qualifying distributions, $814,045; giving activities include $725,000 for 184 grants (high: $50,000; low: $500; average: $500–$10,000).
Purpose and activities: To provide support for charitable organizations that enhance society, primarily to those serving the San Francisco, CA, area.
Fields of interest: Reading; Education; Environment; Health care; Human services; Children/youth, services; Public affairs; Jewish agencies & temples.
Types of support: Continuing support; Capital campaigns; Building/renovation; Program development.
Limitations: Giving primarily in the San Francisco Bay Area, CA. No grants to individuals; no support for deficit budgets, endowments, conferences, events, documentaries, films, or research.
Publications: Annual report (including application guidelines).
Application information: Does not accept unsolicited proposals from educational institutions or arts/cultural organizations. Application form not required.
  Initial approach: Brief letter of inquiry
  Copies of proposal: 1
  Deadline(s): None
  Board meeting date(s): 3 times per year
Officers and Directors:* Douglas E. Goldman,* Pres.; Lisa M. Goldman,* Secy.; Derek T. Knudsen,* Treas.; Nancy S. Kami, Exec. Dir.
Number of staff: 1 part-time professional.
EIN: 943167546

221
Richard & Rhoda Goldman Fund ▼
1 Lombard St., Ste. 303
San Francisco, CA 94111 (415) 788-1090
Contact: Robert T. Gamble, Exec. Dir.
FAX: (415) 788-7890; E-mail: info@goldmanfund.org; URL: http://www.goldmanfund.org

Incorporated in 1951 in CA.
Donor(s): Rhoda H. Goldman,‡ Richard N. Goldman.
Grantmaker type: Independent foundation
Financial data (yr. ended 12/31/02): Assets, $431,730,398 (M); gifts received, $24,123,000; expenditures, $49,442,854; qualifying distributions, $46,854,552; giving activities include $46,854,552 for 830 grants (high: $2,000,000; low: $750; average: $10,000–$200,000).
Purpose and activities: Giving primarily to programs that will have a significant positive impact in an array of fields, including: environment, population, Jewish affairs, children and youth, social and human services and the elderly.
Fields of interest: Environment; Family planning; Crime/violence prevention; Children/youth, services; Aging, centers/services; Reproductive rights; Population studies; Jewish agencies & temples.
International interests: Israel.
Types of support: General/operating support; Continuing support; Capital campaigns; Land acquisition; Program development; Seed money.

Limitations: Giving primarily in the San Francisco Bay Area, CA, and Israel. Giving nationally and internationally in the areas of population, the environment, and violence prevention. No support for unsolicited proposals from arts organizations, or from primary, secondary, or higher educational institutions. No grants to individuals, or for deficit budgets, endowment funds, documentary films, conferences, research, scholarships, fellowships, matching gifts, or general operating budgets of established organizations; no loans.

Publications: Annual report (including application guidelines), Grants list.

Application information: Applications sent by FAX or E-mail not considered. Application form not required.

Initial approach: 2-page letter (including a 1-paragraph executive summary)
Copies of proposal: 1
Deadline(s): None
Board meeting date(s): Quarterly

Officers and Directors:* Richard N. Goldman,* Pres.; Robert T. Gamble, Exec. Dir.; Michael C. Gelman; Susan R. Gelman; Douglas E. Goldman; John D. Goldman; Lisa M. Goldman; Marcia L. Goldman; Donald Seiler.

Number of staff: 7 full-time professional; 2 full-time support; 1 part-time support.

EIN: 946064502

Recent environmental and animal welfare grants:

221-1 Adopt-A-Watershed, Hayfork, CA, $25,000. 2001.

221-2 Alliance for Sustainable Jobs and the Environment, Portland, Oregon, $30,000. 2001.

221-3 Alliance to End Childhood Lead Poisoning, DC, $60,000. For Legal Remedies for Lead Poisoning Prevention. 2001.

221-4 Amazon Alliance for Indigenous and Traditional Peoples of the Amazon Basin, DC, $75,000. For working group activities. 2001.

221-5 Amazon Conservation Team, Arlington, VA, $100,000. For conservation efforts in Colombia. 2001.

221-6 Amazon Watch, Malibu, CA, $50,000. For deterring oil and gas development in the Amazon. 2001.

221-7 American Association for the Advancement of Science, DC, $150,000. For Monitoring Environmental Components of Human Rights. 2001.

221-8 American Rivers, DC, $100,000. For Rivers Unplugged Campaign. 2001.

221-9 Aquatic Outreach Institute, Richmond, CA, $15,000. 2001.

221-10 Arava Institute for Environmental Studies, Kibbutz Ketura, Israel, $50,000. To establish Arava Center for Conservation and Environmental Activism. 2001.

221-11 Asia Foundation, San Francisco, CA, $50,000. For NGO-Business Environmental Partnership to reduce industrial pollution in Asia. 2001.

221-12 Audubon Society, National, New York, NY, $100,000. For Wildlife Refuge Campaign. 2001.

221-13 Balboa High School, San Francisco, CA, $10,000. For Wilderness Arts and Literacy Collaborative. 2001.

221-14 Bay Area Ridge Trail Council, San Francisco, CA, $10,000. 2001.

221-15 Bay Institute of San Francisco, San Rafael, CA, $50,000. 2001.

221-16 Bay Nature Magazine, Berkeley, CA, $15,000. 2001.

221-17 California Academy of Sciences, San Francisco, CA, $15,000. 2001.

221-18 California Oak Foundation, Oakland, CA, $30,000. 2001.

221-19 Canadian Parks and Wilderness Society, Ottawa, Canada, $25,000. 2001.

221-20 Center for Ecosystem Survival, San Francisco, CA, $50,000. 2001.

221-21 Center for Environment and Population, Portsmouth, NH, $50,000. 2001.

221-22 City CarShare, San Francisco, CA, $50,000. 2001.

221-23 Clean Water Fund, San Francisco, CA, $75,000. For Clean and Safe Water Initiative. 2001.

221-24 Co-op America Foundation, DC, $200,000. For PAPER Project. 2001.

221-25 Coevolution Institute, San Francisco, CA, $50,000. 2001.

221-26 Communities for a Better Environment, Oakland, CA, $15,000. 2001.

221-27 Conservation Strategy Fund, Philo, CA, $40,000. For Field Economics for Tropical Forest Conservation. 2001.

221-28 Coral Reef Alliance (CORAL), San Francisco, CA, $70,000. For Marine Protected Areas Program. 2001.

221-29 Coyote Point Museum Association, San Mateo, CA, $10,000. 2001.

221-30 David Suzuki Foundation, Vancouver, Canada, $50,000. For Pacific Salmon Forests Project, to promote sustainable alternatives to logging in British Columbia. 2001.

221-31 Earth Island Institute, San Francisco, CA, $125,000. For International Marine Mammal Project. 2001.

221-32 Earth Island Institute, San Francisco, CA, $25,000. For Boreal Footprint Project. 2001.

221-33 Earth Island Institute, San Francisco, CA, $25,000. For Estuary Action Challenge (EAC). 2001.

221-34 Earthjustice Legal Defense Fund, Oakland, CA, $15,000. 2001.

221-35 EarthWays Foundation, Malibu, CA, $20,000. 2001.

221-36 East Bay Conservation Corps, Oakland, CA, $10,000. 2001.

221-37 Ecotrust, Portland, Oregon, $50,000. 2001.

221-38 Environmental Background Information Center, New York, NY, $15,000. 2001.

221-39 Environmental Defense, Oakland, CA, $15,000. 2001.

221-40 Environmental Defense, New York, NY, $250,000. For Oceans Program. 2001.

221-41 Environmental Education Associates, San Anselmo, CA, $25,000. 2001.

221-42 Environmental Grantmakers Association, New York, NY, $11,452. 2001.

221-43 Environmental Investigation Agency, DC, $75,000. For Forests for the World Campaign. 2001.

221-44 Environmental Justice Coalition on Water, Oakland, CA, $25,000. 2001.

221-45 Environmental Law Alliance Worldwide (E-LAW), Eugene, Oregon, $70,000. For Africa Project. 2001.

221-46 Environmental Leadership Program, Cambridge, MA, $75,000. For general support. 2001.

221-47 Environmental Media Services, DC, $250,000. For Global Economics and Environment Media Campaign. 2001.

221-48 Environmental Protection Information Center (EPIC), Garberville, CA, $40,000. For Litigation Program. 2001.

221-49 Environmental Research Foundation, Annapolis, MD, $30,000. 2001.

221-50 Environmental Support Center, DC, $10,000. 2001.

221-51 Environmental Traveling Companions, San Francisco, CA, $10,000. 2001.

221-52 Environmental Water Caucus, San Francisco, CA, $100,000. To restore San Francisco Bay and Delta. 2001.

221-53 Environmental Working Group, DC, $100,000. For Chemical Industry Insider Project. 2001.

221-54 Fauna and Flora International, San Francisco, CA, $30,000. 2001.

221-55 ForestEthics, Berkeley, CA, $65,000. For marketing campaign to protect British Columbia's temperate rainforest. 2001.

221-56 Friends of the Earth International, Amsterdam, Netherlands, $25,000. 2001.

221-57 Friends of the Earth-Middle East, Tel Aviv, Israel, $50,000. 2001.

221-58 Friends of the River Foundation, Sacramento, CA, $150,000. For California Wild Heritage Campaign. 2001.

221-59 Friends of the River Foundation, Sacramento, CA, $35,000. For Hydropower Relicensing Project. 2001.

221-60 Galileo Academy of Science and Technology, San Francisco, CA, $10,000. For Galileo Outdoor Adventures Program. 2001.

221-61 Global Green USA, Santa Monica, CA, $25,000. 2001.

221-62 Global Greengrants Fund, Boulder, CO, $30,000. 2001.

221-63 Global Greengrants Fund, Boulder, CO, $27,000. 2001.

221-64 Global Response, Boulder, CO, $25,000. 2001.

221-65 Grassroots Recycling Network, Athens, GA, $60,000. For general support. 2001.

221-66 Green Corps, Boston, MA, $10,000. 2001.

221-67 Greenbelt Alliance, San Francisco, CA, $40,000. 2001.

221-68 Healing Waters, San Francisco, CA, $35,000. 2001.

221-69 Health Care Without Harm, DC, $150,000. To reform environmental practices of health care industry in California. 2001.

221-70 Indian Law Resource Center, Helena, MT, $150,000. For protection of environment and human rights of indigenous people in the Americas. 2001.

221-71 Indigenous Environmental Network, Bemidji, MN, $50,000. For Indigenous Mining Campaign Project. 2001.

221-72 Institute for Agriculture and Trade Policy, Minneapolis, MN, $60,000. For Ending Industrial Aquaculture Campaign. 2001.

221-73 Institutes for Journalism and Natural Resources, Missoula, MT, $40,000. For West Coast and Alaska Institutes. 2001.

221-74 International Indian Treaty Council, San Francisco, CA, $40,000. For training indigenous communities about human rights and environment. 2001.

221-75 International Society for Ecology and Culture, Berkeley, CA, $25,000. 2001.

221-76 Israel Society for Ecology and Environmental Quality Science, Jerusalem, Israel, $20,000. 2001.

221-77 Izaak Walton League of America, Gaithersburg, MD, $75,000. For Sustainability Education Project to increase activism regarding population issues and sustainable development. 2001.

221-78 Klamath Forest Alliance, Forks of Salmon, CA, $20,000. 2001.

221-79 League to Save Lake Tahoe, South Lake Tahoe, CA, $11,500. 2001.

221-80 Life and Environment, Tel Aviv, Israel, $48,000. 2001.

221-81 Life Lab Science Program, Santa Cruz, CA, $50,000. For Garden Classroom program development. 2001.

221-82 Literacy for Environmental Justice, San Francisco, CA, $25,000. 2001.

221-83 Living Rivers, Moab, UT, $15,000. 2001.

221-84 Marine Mammal Center, Sausalito, CA, $25,000. 2001.

221-85 Materials for the Future Foundation, San Francisco, CA, $30,000. 2001.

221-86 Materials for the Future Foundation, San Francisco, CA, $25,000. 2001.

221-87 Mills College, Oakland, CA, $200,000. For Rhonda Goldman Professorship in Environmental Science. 2001.

221-88 Mission Economic Development Association, San Francisco, CA, $50,000. For Displacement and Community Sustainability Program. 2001.

221-89 Mount Shasta Bioregional Ecology Center, Mount Shasta, CA, $10,000. 2001.

221-90 Mountain Lion Preservation Foundation, Sacramento, CA, $50,000. 2001.

221-91 Mountain Mill House Outdoor Center, Calistoga, CA, $25,000. For programs for children and youth. 2001.

221-92 National Environmental Education and Training Foundation, DC, $10,000. 2001.

221-93 National Forest Protection Alliance, Missoula, MT, $20,000. 2001.

221-94 National Geographic Society, DC, $1,000,000. For Sustainable Seas Expeditions. 2001.

221-95 National Parks Conservation Association, DC, $125,000. For Marine Resources Protection Program. 2001.

221-96 National Parks Conservation Association, DC, $25,000. 2001.

221-97 Natural Heritage Institute, San Francisco, CA, $150,000. For California Global Corporate Accountability Project. 2001.

221-98 Natural Resources Defense Council, San Francisco, CA, $250,000. For Environmental Toxics Reduction Initiative. 2001.

221-99 Oregon Natural Resources Council, Portland, Oregon, $50,000. For Klamath Basin Protection Program. 2001.

221-100 Otter Project, Marina, CA, $25,000. 2001.

221-101 Outervention, San Francisco, CA, $25,000. 2001.

221-102 Ozone Action, DC, $150,000. 2001.

221-103 Pacific Crest Outward Bound, San Francisco, San Francisco, CA, $10,000. For programs for children and youth. 2001.

221-104 Pacific Forest Trust, Santa Rosa, CA, $100,000. For Conserving California's Working Forest Landscapes. 2001.

221-105 PCL Foundation, Sacramento, CA, $50,000. 2001.

221-106 Pesticide Action Network (PAN), North America Regional Center, San Francisco, CA, $75,000. For Californians for Pesticide Reform. 2001.

221-107 Physicians for Social Responsibility, DC, $75,000. For Safe Drinking Water Program. 2001.

221-108 Point Reyes Bird Observatory, Stinson Beach, CA, $100,000. For Birds Across Borders. 2001.

221-109 Presidio World College, San Francisco, CA, $30,000. 2001.

221-110 Project Underground, Berkeley, CA, $60,000. For general support. 2001.

221-111 Rachels Network, DC, $20,000. 2001.

221-112 Raincoast Conservation Foundation, Canada, $30,000. 2001.

221-113 Rainforest Alliance, New York, NY, $75,000. For Conservation Agriculture Program. 2001.

221-114 River Network, Portland, Oregon, $60,000. For Clean Water Organizing Project. 2001.

221-115 Rose Foundation for Communities and the Environment, Oakland, CA, $75,000. For Environmental Fiduciary Project. 2001.

221-116 San Francisco BayKeeper, San Francisco, CA, $25,000. For Legal Clinic. 2001.

221-117 San Francisco BayKeeper, San Francisco, CA, $25,000. 2001.

221-118 San Francisco Conservation Corps, San Francisco, CA, $30,000. For Student and Family Services of Youth in Action Program. 2001.

221-119 San Francisco Zoological Society, San Francisco, CA, $10,000. 2001.

221-120 Save San Francisco Bay Association, Oakland, CA, $250,000. For Celebrate the Bay Campaign. 2001.

221-121 Save San Francisco Bay Association, Oakland, CA, $15,000. 2001.

221-122 Save the Redwoods League, San Francisco, CA, $500,000. For Dillonwood Giant Sequoia Grove acquisition. 2001.

221-123 Sierra Fund, Nevada City, CA, $20,000. 2001.

221-124 Sierra Madre Alliance, Tucson, AZ, $10,000. 2001.

221-125 Silicon Valley Toxics Coalition, San Jose, CA, $60,000. For Bay Area High-Tech Clean Production and Best Practices Campaign. 2001.

221-126 Siskiyou Regional Educational Project, Cave Junction, Oregon, $25,000. 2001.

221-127 Slide Ranch, Muir Beach, CA, $10,000. 2001.

221-128 Smithsonian Tropical Research Institute, Panama, $100,000. For Amazon forest conservation, management, and capacity building. 2001.

221-129 Sonoran Institute, Tucson, AZ, $15,000. 2001.

221-130 South Yuba River Citizens League, Nevada City, CA, $50,000. 2001.

221-131 Stanford University, Stanford, CA, $265,000. For Center for Environmental Science and Policy. 2001.

221-132 Student Conservation Association, Charlestown, NH, $25,000. 2001.

221-133 Sustainable Conservation, San Francisco, CA, $100,000. For Dairy Project. 2001.

221-134 Sustainable Cotton Project, Oroville, CA, $75,000. For Cleaner Cotton Campaign. 2001.

221-135 Sustainable Development for the Negev, Omer, Israel, $55,000. To develop local environmental activism in Negev. 2001.

221-136 Tahoe-Baikal Institute, South Lake Tahoe, CA, $10,000. 2001.

221-137 Taxpayers for Common Sense, DC, $125,000. For California Water Project. 2001.

221-138 Tides Center, San Francisco, CA, $25,000. For Funders Forum on Environment and Education. 2001.

221-139 Tisch Family Zoological Gardens, Jerusalem, Israel, $10,000. 2001.

221-140 Tony Fitzjohn/George Adamson African Wildlife Preservation Trust, Los Angeles, CA, $20,000. 2001.

221-141 Tony La Russas Animal Rescue Foundation, Walnut Creek, CA, $25,000. 2001.

221-142 Trout Unlimited, Hillsboro, Oregon, $40,000. For California Small Water Project. 2001.

221-143 Trust for Hidden Villa, Los Altos Hills, CA, $15,000. 2001.

221-144 Tuolumne River Preservation Trust, San Francisco, CA, $30,000. For Campaign to Protect and Restore the Clavey River. 2001.

221-145 Union of Concerned Scientists, Cambridge, MA, $100,000. For Animal Antibiotics Project. 2001.

221-146 Water Watch of Oregon, Portland, Oregon, $50,000. For Western Water Project to restore habitat for coldwater fisheries. 2001.

221-147 Waterkeeper Alliance, White Plains, NY, $10,000. 2001.

221-148 Watershed Media, Healdsburg, CA, $75,000. For SimpleLife Wood Reduction Trilogy. 2001.

221-149 Wild Salmon Center, Portland, Oregon, $100,000. For Kamchatka Wild Fish Sanctuary Project in Russia. 2001.

221-150 WildAid, San Francisco, CA, $150,000. For Shark Conservation Program. 2001.

221-151 Wildlife Conservation Society, Bronx, NY, $35,000. 2001.

221-152 World Information Transfer, New York, NY, $75,000. For Breast Cancer and the Environment Education Project. 2001.

221-153 World Resources Institute, DC, $230,000. For Global Forest Watch Canada to build grassroots and indigenous capacity to monitor Canadian forests and produce independent report. 2001.

221-154 World Wildlife Fund/Conservation Foundation, DC, $250,000. For Global Toxic Chemicals Initiative. 2001.

221-155 Worldwatch Institute, DC, $100,000. For Biodiversity Program. 2001.

221-156 Yellowstone to Yukon Conservation Initiative, Canmore, Canada, $30,000. 2001.

221-157 Youth for Environmental Sanity (YES), Soquel, CA, $15,000. 2001.

222
Richard Grand Foundation

405 Davis Ct., No. 2504
San Francisco, CA 94111

Established in 1995 in CA.
Donor(s): Richard Grand, Marcia Grand, Rena Grand.‡
Grantmaker type: Independent foundation
Financial data (yr. ended 06/30/02): Assets, $12,069,575 (M); gifts received, $1,352,746; expenditures, $542,649; qualifying distributions, $503,550; giving activities include $503,550 for 85 grants (high: $50,000; low: $500).
Purpose and activities: Giving primarily for arts and culture, education, health care, and human services.
Fields of interest: Museums; Theater; Arts; Higher education; Law school/education; Education; Environment; Animal welfare; Family planning; Health organizations, association; Food banks; Human services; Children/youth, services; Human services; Jewish agencies & temples.
Limitations: Applications not accepted. Giving primarily in Tucson, AZ, San Francisco, CA, and New York, NY. No grants to individuals.
Application information: Contributes only to pre-selected organizations.
Officers: Richard Grand, Chair. and Secy.; Marcia Grand, Pres.; Cindy Grand, V.P. and C.F.O.
EIN: 943221366

223
Great Valley Center, Inc.

201 Needham St.
Modesto, CA 95354 (209) 522-5103
Contact: Denny Marshall, Dir., Fin.
FAX: (209) 522-5116; E-mail: info@greatvalley.org; URL: http://www.greatvalley.org

Established in 1997 in CA.
Grantmaker type: Public charity
Financial data (yr. ended 12/31/02): Revenue, $5,904,779; assets, $14,127,271 (M); gifts received, $5,416,247; expenditures, $5,358,834; program services expenses, $4,569,529; giving activities include $1,008,336 for 115 grants (high: $30,000; low: $800; average: $800–$30,000).
Purpose and activities: The mission of the Great Valley Center is to support activities and organizations that promote the economic, social and environmental well-being of California's Great Central Valley Region.
Fields of interest: Arts; Education; Natural resources; Human services; Community development.
Types of support: General/operating support; Income development; Program development; Publication; Curriculum development; Fellowships; Internship funds; Research; Technical assistance; Consulting services; Program evaluation; Scholarships—to individuals; In-kind gifts; Matching/challenge support.
Limitations: Giving limited to the the Central Valley, CA, area.
Publications: Application guidelines, Annual report, Grants list, Informational brochure

(including application guidelines), Newsletter, Occasional report.
Application information: Considered only during open, competitive grant period. Application form required.
Copies of proposal: 1
Deadline(s): Jan. 30
Board meeting date(s): Mar., July, and Nov.
Final notification: Apr. 30
Officers and Directors:* Carol Whiteside,* Pres.; Terry Scranton,* Secy.-Treas.; Vanessa Arellano; Kim Belshe; Mark Burrell; Bill Center; Carol Chamberlain; Mike Chrisman; Tony Coelho; Ricardo Cordova; Diane Gerard; Lon Hatamiya; Dave Koehler; Bruce Race; Steve Toben; Dan Whitehurst.
Number of staff: 14 full-time professional; 17 full-time support.
EIN: 770450770

224
Mary Jo & Hank Greenberg Animal Welfare Foundation

9903 Santa Monica Blvd.
Beverly Hills, CA 90212
Contact: Mary Jo Greenberg, Chair.

Established in 1999 in CA.
Donor(s): Mary Jo Greenberg.
Grantmaker type: Independent foundation
Financial data (yr. ended 05/31/02): Assets, $141,408 (M); gifts received, $356,771; expenditures, $344,547; qualifying distributions, $341,000; giving activities include $341,000 for 32 grants (high: $22,500; low: $2,500).
Purpose and activities: Giving primarily for animal welfare and rescue.
Fields of interest: Animals/wildlife, association; Animal welfare.
Limitations: Giving primarily in CA.
Application information:
Initial approach: Letter
Deadline(s): None
Officers and Board Members:* Mary Jo Greenberg, Chair. and Pres.; Suzie Levin,* Secy.; Susan Recht,* Treas.; Robert Furber.
EIN: 954738423

225
The Greenberg Foundation

(formerly The Mayer Greenberg Foundation)
6060 Sepulveda Blvd., No. 300
Van Nuys, CA 91411-2501

Established in 1953 in CA.
Donor(s): Daniel B. Greenberg, Aaron Masowitz Trust, Electro Rent Corp.
Grantmaker type: Independent foundation
Financial data (yr. ended 11/30/02): Assets, $5,158,560 (M); expenditures, $306,475; qualifying distributions, $302,513; giving activities include $300,380 for 124 grants (high: $125,000; low: $20).
Purpose and activities: Giving primarily for education, the arts, the environment, and health care.
Fields of interest: Arts education; Radio; Museums (art); Museums (specialized); Higher education; Law school/education; Education; Environment; Health organizations, association; Human services.

Limitations: Applications not accepted. Giving on a national basis, with emphasis on CA, Washington, DC, MA, and New York, NY. No grants to individuals.
Application information: Contributes only to pre-selected organizations.
Officers: Daniel B. Greenberg, Pres.; Ben Greenberg, V.P. and Treas.
EIN: 956037502

226
Griswold Charitable Trust

816 Arbolado Rd.
Santa Barbara, CA 93103

Established in 1996 in CA.
Grantmaker type: Independent foundation
Financial data (yr. ended 06/30/02): Assets, $10,786,222 (M); expenditures, $218,857; qualifying distributions, $151,055; giving activities include $149,651 for 5 grants (high: $47,512; low: $23,755).
Purpose and activities: Giving primarily for animal welfare, and community development.
Fields of interest: Animals/wildlife; Health organizations, public education; Health organizations, formal/general education; Community development.
Limitations: Applications not accepted. Giving primarily in CA. No grants to individuals.
Application information: Contributes only to pre-selected organizations.
Trustee: Michael C. Rodrigue.
EIN: 776135696

227
The Grousbeck Family Foundation ▼

c/o Stanford University
Graduate School of Business, Rm. L-336
Stanford, CA 94305-5015 (650) 723-0709
Contact: H. Irving Grousbeck, Pres.

Established in 1990 in CA.
Donor(s): H. Irving Grousbeck, E. Grousbeck.‡
Grantmaker type: Independent foundation
Financial data (yr. ended 11/30/01): Assets, $101,962,242 (M); expenditures, $7,202,290; qualifying distributions, $5,376,870; giving activities include $5,422,384 for 123 grants (high: $500,000; low: $134; average: $10,000–$50,000).
Purpose and activities: Grants primarily for higher education and eye research.
Fields of interest: Higher education; Eye diseases; Eye research.
Limitations: No grants to individuals.
Application information: Application form not required.
Deadline(s): None
Officers: H. Irving Grousbeck, Pres.; Susanne B. Grousbeck, V.P.; Wycliffe K. Grousbeck, Secy.-Treas.; Anne H.G. Matta, C.F.O.
Number of staff: None.
EIN: 770267061
Recent environmental and animal welfare grants:
227-1 Amazon Conservation Team, Arlington, VA, $10,000. For general support. 2001.
227-2 Asian Pacific Environmental Network (APEN), Oakland, CA, $50,000. For general support. 2001.

227-3 Bay Area Nuclear (BAN) Waste Coalition, San Francisco, CA, $30,000. For general support. 2001.

227-4 Communities for a Better Environment, Oakland, CA, $55,000. For general support. 2001.

227-5 Community Networking Resources, Albuquerque, NM, $55,000. For general support. 2001.

227-6 Cultural Conservancy, Davis, CA, $40,000. For general support. 2001.

227-7 Earth Island Institute, San Francisco, CA, $40,000. For general support for Sacred Land Film Project (SLFP). 2001.

227-8 Environmental Traveling Companions, San Francisco, CA, $30,000. For general support. 2001.

227-9 Escalante House, Escalante, UT, $20,000. For general support. 2001.

227-10 Indigenous Environmental Network, Bemidji, MN, $35,000. For general support for Seventh Generation Fund. 2001.

227-11 Nature Conservancy, Baltimore, MD, $10,000. For general support. 2001.

227-12 Peninsula Open Space Trust, Menlo Park, CA, $100,000. For general support. 2001.

227-13 People Organized in Defense of Earth and Her Resources, Austin, TX, $25,000. For general support. 2001.

227-14 People Organizing to Demand Environmental Rights, San Francisco, CA, $50,000. For general support. 2001.

227-15 Quest Scholars Program, Palo Alto, CA, $35,000. For general support. 2001.

227-16 Shundahai Network, Las Vegas, NV, $60,000. For general support. Grant made through Center for Energy Research. 2001.

227-17 Trust for Hidden Villa, Los Altos Hills, CA, $10,000. For general support. 2001.

228
Gruber Family Foundation
P.O. Box 214
Ross, CA 94957
FAX: (415) 457-2835

Established in 1987 in CA.
Donor(s): Jon D. Gruber, Linda W. Gruber.
Grantmaker type: Independent foundation
Financial data (yr. ended 12/31/02): Assets, $32,926,684 (M); expenditures, $1,331,702; qualifying distributions, $1,328,716; giving activities include $1,328,200 for 78 grants (high: $200,000; low: $500).
Purpose and activities: Primary areas of interest include education, family planning and women's issues, museums, the homeless, and social services.
Fields of interest: Museums; Arts; Education; Environment; Family planning; Abuse prevention; Human services; Youth, services; Women, centers/services; Homeless, human services; Reproductive rights; Women; Economically disadvantaged; Homeless.
Types of support: General/operating support; Continuing support; Annual campaigns; Capital campaigns; Building/renovation; Program development.
Limitations: Applications not accepted. Giving primarily in CA. No grants to individuals.
Application information: Contributes only to pre-selected organizations.

Officers: Linda W. Gruber, Pres.; Jon D. Gruber, Secy.-Treas.
Number of staff: None.
EIN: 943039716

229
Walter and Elise Haas Fund ▼
1 Lombard St., Ste. 305
San Francisco, CA 94111 (415) 398-4474
Contact: Pamela David, Exec. Dir.
E-mail: information@haassr. org; URL: http://www.haassr.org

Incorporated in 1952 in CA.
Donor(s): Walter A. Haas,‡ Elise S. Haas.‡
Grantmaker type: Independent foundation
Financial data (yr. ended 12/31/02): Assets, $179,244,560 (M); expenditures, $14,007,414; qualifying distributions, $12,793,326; giving activities include $11,533,580 for 360 grants (high: $1,250,000; low: $125; average: $1,000–$100,000) and $6,630 for 21 employee matching gifts.
Purpose and activities: The mission of the fund is to help build a healthy, just, and vibrant society in which people feel connected to and responsible for their community. The areas of focus are the arts, economic security, Jewish Life, and public education. In addition, continuing support is provided to organizations that have long established ties to the fund.
Fields of interest: Arts, ethics; Visual arts; Museums; Performing arts; Humanities; Arts; Education; Natural resources; Environment; Youth development, citizenship; Human services; Children/youth, services; Family services; Human services; Public affairs; Jewish agencies & temples.
Types of support: General/operating support; Continuing support; Capital campaigns; Building/renovation; Equipment; Land acquisition; Emergency funds; Program development; Seed money; Technical assistance; Employee matching gifts; Matching/challenge support.
Limitations: Giving primarily in San Francisco and Alameda County, CA; Jewish Life grants are awarded throughout the Bay Area. No grants to individuals, or for general fundraising, endowment campaigns, scholarships, fellowships, or for video or film production (except through the Creative Work Fund).
Publications: Application guidelines, Annual report, Program policy statement.
Application information: Grant request cover sheet must be completed and submitted with letter of inquiry. Application form required.
  Initial approach: Letter of inquiry
  Copies of proposal: 1
  Deadline(s): None
  Board meeting date(s): As required
  Final notification: 4 months
Officers and Trustees:* Peter E. Haas, Jr.,* Pres.; Pamela H. David, Exec. Dir.; Elizabeth H. Eisenhardt; Douglas E. Goldman; John D. Goldman; Peter E. Haas, Hon. Pres.; Walter J. Haas; Jennifer Haas-Dehejia.
Number of staff: 3 full-time professional; 3 part-time professional; 4 full-time support.
EIN: 946068564
Recent environmental and animal welfare grants:

229-1 Adopt-A-Watershed, Hayfork, CA, $35,000. To implement strategic plan in Bay Area, providing environmental education opportunities for children while restoring natural habitats. 2002.

229-2 American Society for the Protection of Nature in Israel, Great Neck, NY, $50,000. To continue campaign to oppose development at Haas Promenade in Jerusalem. 2002.

229-3 Coevolution Institute, San Francisco, CA, $12,000. To expand BugMobile Program to public school students and support teachers with follow-up materials. 2002.

229-4 East Bay Conservation Corps, Oakland, CA, $100,000. To start Institute for Citizenship Education and Teacher Preparation, to assist teachers in using service learning to help students become more effective citizens. 2002.

229-5 East Bay Zoological Society, Oakland, CA, $200,000. To upgrade and expand Children's Zoo. 2002.

229-6 Ecology Center, Berkeley, CA, $20,000. To expand Terrain for Schools program to assist more teachers and students in San Francisco and Oakland high schools. 2002.

229-7 Greenbelt Alliance, San Francisco, CA, $50,000. For Greenbelt 2005 project to promote livable communities and protect open space in strategic Bay Area communities. 2002.

229-8 Greenbelt Alliance, San Francisco, CA, $45,000. For Bay Area Open Space Council for outreach campaign. 2002.

229-9 San Francisco Community Power Cooperative, San Francisco, CA, $25,000. For longitudinal study of social capital changes. 2002.

229-10 Save San Francisco Bay Association, Oakland, CA, $25,000. To collaborate with San Francisco Education Fund to improve teacher support for Canoes in Sloughs. 2002.

229-11 Seacology, Berkeley, CA, $15,000. For Island Explorations, pilot environmental education program for the Bay Area. 2002.

229-12 Slide Ranch, Muir Beach, CA, $12,000. To increase percentage of disadvantaged youth participating in programs, and improve programming for these groups. 2002.

229-13 Student Conservation Association, San Francisco, CA, $20,000. For Encourage Young People With Promise, Bay Area Urban and Diversity Outreach. 2002.

229-14 Wilderness Arts and Literacy Collaborative, San Francisco, CA, $10,000. To build curricular foundation to strengthen academic program. Grant made through Tides Center. 2002.

229-15 Yosemite National Institutes, Sausalito, CA, $35,000. For Diversity Initiative at Headlands Institute providing environmental education for low-income children. 2002.

230
Harden Foundation ▼
P.O. Box 779
Salinas, CA 93902-0779 (831) 442-3005
Contact: Joseph C. Grainger, Exec. Dir.
FAX: (831) 443-1429

Established in 1963 in CA.
Donor(s): Eugene E. Harden,‡ Ercia E. Harden.‡
Grantmaker type: Independent foundation

Financial data (yr. ended 02/28/02): Assets, $58,630,754 (M); expenditures, $6,169,092; qualifying distributions, $5,300,900; giving activities include $4,751,701 for 153 grants (high: $725,000; low: $400; average: $10,000–$100,000).

Purpose and activities: The foundation supports projects that improve the well-being of young people; strengthen the family; develop individual self-reliance and health; prevent inappropriate institutionalization of individuals; improve the quality of life through cultural activities; encourage more humane treatment of animals; and eliminate duplication and improve coordination of social and community services.

Fields of interest: Arts; Environment; Animal welfare; Health care; Mental health, treatment; Agriculture/food, formal/general education; Human services; Children/youth, services; Family services; Aging, centers/services.

Types of support: General/operating support; Capital campaigns; Seed money; Matching/challenge support.

Limitations: Giving limited to Monterey County, with emphasis on the Salinas Valley, CA, area. No support for sectarian religious programs, nonagricultural related educational programs, operating foundations, or associations established for the benefit of organizations receiving substantial tax support. No grants for endowments, annual campaigns, conferences, or fundraising events.

Publications: Application guidelines, Annual report (including application guidelines).

Application information: Application form required.

Initial approach: Letter
Copies of proposal: 2
Deadline(s): Mar. 1 and Sept. 1
Board meeting date(s): June and Dec.

Officers and Directors: * Ralph L. Kokjer, Jr.,* Pres.; C. Bill Elliott,* V.P.; Thomas Merrill,* V.P.; Patricia Tynan-Chapman,* Secy.; Frank E. Ferrasci, Treas.; Joseph C. Grainger, Exec. Dir.

Number of staff: 1 full-time professional; 2 part-time professional; 2 full-time support.

EIN: 946098887

Recent environmental and animal welfare grants:

230-1 Agricultural Clean Water Initiative Foundation, Sacramento, CA, $15,000. For equipment for tracking and monitoring water quality as part of Monterey County Farm Bureau's Agricultural Water Quality Program and watershed projects. 2002.

230-2 Animal Welfare Information and Assistance, Carmel Valley, CA, $12,000. For operating support of Charity Veterinary care program and to increase Charity Spay/Neuter program. 2002.

230-3 Common Ground Monterey County, Monterey, CA, $45,000. For operating and staffing Community Education Project, which includes specific programs to provide factual information, educate public, and to foster consensus. 2002.

230-4 Save Our Shores, Santa Cruz, CA, $18,000. For Marine Education and beach cleanup programs developed in collaboration with Moss Landing Marine Laboratories Sea Lion Research Facility. 2002.

230-5 Society for the Prevention of Cruelty to Animals of Monterey County, Monterey, CA, $50,000. To repair telephone system, to

repair and replace dog runs in Animal Shelter, and to repair boiler, heat pump systems, and education building. 2002.

230-6 Ventana Wilderness Sanctuary, Carmel Valley, CA, $32,500. For operating support for Natural Science Discovery and Natural Science Adventure Camp during summer. 2002.

231
Harvego Family Foundation
2356 Gold Meadow Way, Ste. 201
Gold River, CA 95670 (916) 852-2770
Contact: Lloyd H. Harvego, Chair.

Established in 1998 in CA.

Grantmaker type: Operating foundation

Financial data (yr. ended 12/31/02): Assets, $2,395,670 (M); expenditures, $158,611; qualifying distributions, $116,966; giving activities include $108,980 for 11 grants (high: $37,000; low: $200).

Fields of interest: Theater; Arts; Zoos/zoological societies; Children, services.

Limitations: Giving primarily in Sacramento, CA. No grants to individuals.

Application information:

Initial approach: Letter or proposal
Deadline(s): Nov. 1

Officer: Lloyd H. Harvego, Chair.

Trustees: Deborah S. Harvego; Sandra J. Harvego; Terrence Harvego; Larry E. Johnson; Tamara J. H. Johnson; James A. Whillock.

EIN: 680422816

232
The Salah M. Hassanein Foundation
514 Via De La Valle, Ste. 209
Solana Beach, CA 92075 (858) 509-7979
Contact: Salah M. Hassanein, Pres.

Established in 2000 in CA.

Donor(s): Salah M. Hassanein.

Grantmaker type: Independent foundation

Financial data (yr. ended 12/31/01): Assets, $1,107,416 (M); expenditures, $174,900; qualifying distributions, $161,096; giving activities include $149,562 for 57 grants (high: $15,176; low: $25).

Fields of interest: Arts; Education; Environment; Human services.

Limitations: Giving primarily in CA and NY.

Application information:

Initial approach: Letter
Deadline(s): None

Officers: Salah M. Hassanein, Pres.; Salah V. Hassanein, V.P.; Richard C. Hassanein, Secy.; Roland G. Hassanein, Treas.

EIN: 330867251

233
The Hatfield Family Foundation
12164 Occidental Rd.
Sebastopol, CA 95472-9649

Established in 2000 in CA.

Donor(s): Michael Hatfield.

Grantmaker type: Independent foundation

Financial data (yr. ended 12/31/01): Assets, $12,110,049 (M); gifts received, $8,360,000;

expenditures, $2,558,383; qualifying distributions, $2,412,986; giving activities include $2,491,926 for 20 grants (high: $1,725,000; low: $100).

Fields of interest: College (community/junior); Housing/shelter, development; Human services.

Limitations: Applications not accepted. No grants to individuals.

Application information: Contributes only to pre-selected organizations.

Officer: Michael Hatfield, C.E.O.

EIN: 943347675

Recent environmental and animal welfare grants:

233-1 Housing Land Trust of Sonoma County, Santa Rosa, CA, $1,163,000. For general support. 2002.

234
Harold J. & Reta Haynes Family Foundation
717 Deer Valley Rd.
San Rafael, CA 94903

Established in 1999 in CA.

Donor(s): Harold J. Haynes, Reta Haynes.

Grantmaker type: Independent foundation

Financial data (yr. ended 12/31/02): Assets, $5,082,179 (M); gifts received, $1,730,432; expenditures, $363,245; qualifying distributions, $321,035; giving activities include $321,000 for 6 grants (high: $250,000; low: $1,000).

Fields of interest: Education; Natural resources; Hospitals (general).

Limitations: Applications not accepted. Giving primarily in CA. No grants to individuals.

Application information: Contributes only to pre-selected organizations.

Officer: Harold J. Haynes, Pres.

EIN: 943332186

235
Ann-Eve Hazen Foundation
c/o Mowat, Mackie & Anderson, LLP
1999 Harrison St., Ste. 750
Oakland, CA 94612

Established in 1998 in CA.

Donor(s): Ann-Eve Hazen.

Grantmaker type: Independent foundation

Financial data (yr. ended 12/31/01): Assets, $3,567,453 (M); expenditures, $2,942,248; qualifying distributions, $2,891,597; giving activities include $2,905,695 for 19 grants (high: $2,500,695; low: $500).

Purpose and activities: Giving primarily for the environment; funding also for children, family and social services.

Fields of interest: Higher education; Natural resources; Environment, land resources; Environment; Human services; Children, services; Family services.

Limitations: Applications not accepted. Giving primarily in AZ, CA, and Washington, DC. No grants to individuals.

Application information: Contributes only to pre-selected organizations.

Officers: Brandt S. Hazen, Co-Pres.; Brooke M. Hazen, Co-Pres.; Ann-Eve Hazen, Secy.

EIN: 943314990

236
Clarence E. Heller Charitable Foundation

1 Lombard St., Ste. 305
San Francisco, CA 94111-1130
(415) 989-9839
Contact: Bruce A. Hirsch, Exec. Dir.
FAX: (415) 989-1909; E-mail: info@cehcf.org;
URL: http://cehcf.org

Established in 1982 in CA.
Donor(s): Clarence E. Heller.‡
Grantmaker type: Independent foundation
Financial data (yr. ended 12/31/01): Assets,
$44,151,488 (M); expenditures, $2,923,069;
qualifying distributions, $2,494,475; giving
activities include $2,017,448 for 56+ grants
(high: $150,000; average: $10,000–$50,000).
Purpose and activities: Giving to support
research, public education, and policy
development to reduce health risks from
environmental degradation and environmental
hazards, innovative educational programs for
elementary and secondary students, sustainable
natural resource management, and programs
that promote the accessibility of symphonic and
chamber music.
Fields of interest: Music; Education;
Environment, research; Environment, public
policy; Environment, public education; Natural
resources; Agriculture.
Types of support: General/operating support;
Continuing support; Equipment; Program
development; Publication; Seed money;
Curriculum development; Scholarship funds;
Research; Technical assistance; Consulting
services; Program evaluation.
Limitations: Giving primarily in CA. No grants
to individuals.
Publications: Annual report (including
application guidelines), Grants list, Program
policy statement.
Application information: Telephone for deadline
for each funding cycle. Application form not
required.
 Initial approach: Letter of inquiry
 Copies of proposal: 1
 Deadline(s): 3 times a year
 Board meeting date(s): 3 times a year
Officers and Trustees:* Anne Heller Anderson,*
Pres.; Sarah Coade Mandell,* V.P.; Rolf Lygren,*
Secy.-Treas.; Bruce A. Hirsch, Exec. Dir.; Peter B.
Harckham; Katherine Heller; Miranda Heller;
Alan Mandell.
Number of staff: 1 full-time professional; 1
full-time support.
EIN: 942814266

237
Heller Foundation of San Diego

P.O. Box 85404
San Diego, CA 92186
Contact: Marylou Koppel, V.P., Union Bank of
California, N.A.
E-mail: marylou.koppel@uboc.com

Established in 1960 in CA.
Donor(s): Elwyn Heller,‡ Hattie Heller Marsh.‡
Grantmaker type: Independent foundation
Financial data (yr. ended 12/31/02): Assets,
$4,552,861 (M); expenditures, $295,464;
qualifying distributions, $258,101; giving
activities include $243,346 for 32 grants (high:
$35,000; low: $900; average: $5,000–$10,000).

Purpose and activities: Giving primarily for
environmental and conservation issues.
Fields of interest: Arts; Education; Natural
resources; Health care; Parks/playgrounds;
Human services; Children/youth, services.
Types of support: General/operating support;
Building/renovation; Land acquisition; Program
development; Research.
Limitations: Giving primarily in San Diego
County, CA; giving on a national basis for
environmental and conservation issues only.
Publications: Application guidelines.
Application information: Application form not
required.
 Copies of proposal: 1
 Deadline(s): Sept. 15
 Board meeting date(s): Oct.
Managers: Marylou Koppel; Skip Heller; James
Lutes.
Trustee: Union Bank of California, N.A.
Number of staff: 1 shared staff.
EIN: 956010314

238
The William and Flora Hewlett Foundation ▼

2121 Sand Hill Rd.
Menlo Park, CA 94025 (650) 234-4500
Contact: Paul Brest, Pres.
FAX: (650) 234-4501; E-mail: info@hewlett.org;
URL: http://www.hewlett.org

Incorporated in 1966 in CA.
Donor(s): Flora Lamson Hewlett,‡ William R.
Hewlett.‡
Grantmaker type: Independent foundation
Financial data (yr. ended 12/31/02): Assets,
$5,010,197,000 (M); expenditures,
$182,580,000; qualifying distributions,
$168,214,000; giving activities include
$168,214,000 for grants.
Purpose and activities: Emphasis on conflict
resolution, the environment, performing arts,
education at both the K-12 and the
college/university level, population studies,
family and community development, and
U.S.-Latin American relations.
Fields of interest: Performing arts; Dance;
Theater; Music; Arts; Elementary/secondary
education; Higher education; Libraries
(academic/research); Natural resources;
Environment; Family planning; Youth
development, services; Family services;
Urban/community development; Community
development; Population studies; International
studies; Public policy, research; Minorities.
International interests: Latin America.
Types of support: General/operating support;
Continuing support; Land acquisition;
Emergency funds; Program development; Seed
money; Employee matching gifts;
Matching/challenge support.
Limitations: Giving limited to the San Francisco
Bay Area, CA, for family and community
development programs; performing arts
primarily limited to the Bay Area; environment
programs limited to North American West. No
support for medicine and health-related
projects, law, criminal justice, and related fields,
juvenile delinquency or drug and alcohol
addiction, prevention or treatment programs,
problems of the elderly and the handicapped, or
television or radio projects. No grants to

individuals, or for building funds or capital
construction funds, basic research, equipment,
seminars, conferences, festivals, touring costs,
fundraising drives, scholarships, or fellowships;
no loans.
Publications: Application guidelines, Annual
report (including application guidelines), Grants
list, Informational brochure, Program policy
statement.
Application information: The foundation prefers
to receive letters of inquiry as documents in
Microsoft Word format, attached to messages
sent to E-mail: loi@hewlett.org. Application form
not required.
 Initial approach: Letter of inquiry
 Copies of proposal: 1
 Deadline(s): Arts: Jan. 6, music; Apr. 1,
 theater; July 1, dance, film, & video orgs.;
 Conflict: Jan. 1, theory devel. orgs. & intl.
 orgs.; July 1, promotional orgs. & consensus
 building, public participation and
 policymaking orgs.; Oct. 1, practitioner
 orgs.
 Board meeting date(s): Jan., Apr., July, and Oct.
 Final notification: 2 to 3 months
Officers and Directors:* Walter B. Hewlett,*
Chair.; Paul Brest, Pres.; Laurance Hoagland,
V.P. and C.I.O.; Nancy Strausser, Corp. Secy.;
Susan Ketcham, Treas.; Robert F. Erburu; James
C. Gaither; Eleanor H. Gimon; H. Irving
Grousbeck; Mary H. Jaffe; Herant
Katchadourian, M.D.; Richard Levin; Jean
Stromberg.
Number of staff: 20 full-time professional; 11
full-time support; 4 part-time support.
EIN: 941655673
**Recent environmental and animal welfare
grants:**
238-1 1000 Friends of New Mexico,
 Albuquerque, NM, $150,000. For general
 support. Grant made as part of Growth
 Management in Metropolitan Areas program.
 2002.
238-2 1000 Friends of Oregon, Portland,
 Oregon, $100,000. For general support.
 Grant made as part of Growth Management
 in Metropolitan Areas program. 2002.
238-3 Association for Conflict Resolution, DC,
 $75,000. For strategic planning, infrastructure
 development, and annual meeting of
 Environment/Public Policy section. 2002.
238-4 Breakthrough Technologies Institute, DC,
 $1,200,000. For Non-Road Engine
 Campaign. 2002.
238-5 California Climate Action Registry, Los
 Angeles, CA, $500,000. For general support.
 2002.
238-6 California Foundation on the
 Environment and the Economy, San
 Francisco, CA, $10,000. For roundtable
 conference on air quality and population
 growth. 2002.
238-7 Calvert Social Investment Foundation,
 Bethesda, MD, $400,000. For National Rural
 Funders Collaborative. 2002.
238-8 Calvert Social Investment Foundation,
 Bethesda, MD, $100,000. For National Rural
 Funders Collaborative. 2002.
238-9 Center for Resource Economics/Island
 Press, DC, $100,000. 2002.
238-10 Center for Science in Public
 Participation, Bozeman, MT, $100,000. For
 general support. Grant made as part of

Environmental Management in Rural Communities program. 2002.

238-11 Center for Watershed and Community Health, Springfield, Oregon, $50,000. For general support. 2002.

238-12 Centro de Derechos Humanos y Medio Ambiente, Cordoba, Argentina, $200,000. For general support. 2002.

238-13 Collins Center for Public Policy, Miami, FL, $35,000. For Funders Network for Smart Growth and Livable Communities, as part of Growth Management in Metropolitan Areas program. 2002.

238-14 Consensus Building Institute, Cambridge, MA, $50,000. For environmental justice research project. 2002.

238-15 David Suzuki Foundation, Vancouver, Canada, $250,000. For Forestry and Turning Point programs, as part of Environmental Management in Rural Communities program. 2002.

238-16 Ecotrust, Portland, Oregon, $250,000. For general support. Grant made as part of Environmental Management in Rural Communities program. 2002.

238-17 Environmental Defense, New York, NY, $300,000. For work on Rio Grande basin. 2002.

238-18 Environmental Defense, Austin, TX, $250,000. For Paso del Norte Water project. 2002.

238-19 Environmental Leadership Program, Cambridge, MA, $75,000. For creation, publication and dissemination of Diversity Storybook and Resource Guide. 2002.

238-20 Environmental Media Services, DC, $300,000. Grant made through Tides Center, as part of Environmental Management in Rural Communities program. 2002.

238-21 Florida International University, Department of Environmental Studies, Miami, FL, $300,000. For collaborative training and research with Mexican institutions. 2002.

238-22 Forest Community Research, Taylorsville, CA, $150,000. For general support. 2002.

238-23 Foundation for Self-Sufficiency (Central America), Round Rock, TX, $40,000. For La Coordinadora del Bajo Lempa in El Salvador. 2002.

238-24 Foundation for Self-Sufficiency (Central America), Round Rock, TX, $35,000. For La Coordinadora del Bajo Lempa in El Salvador. 2002.

238-25 Fundacao de Empreendimentos Cientificos e Tecnologicos (FINATEC), Brasilia, Brazil, $300,000. For Marca d'Agua project. 2002.

238-26 Grand Canyon Trust, Flagstaff, AZ, $600,000. For programs within Colorado Plateau region, as part of Environmental Management in Rural Communities. 2002.

238-27 Great Valley Center, Modesto, CA, $3,696,000. For Building Toward Sustainability program. 2002.

238-28 Greater Yellowstone Coalition, Bozeman, MT, $700,000. For general support. Grant made as part of Environmental Management in Rural Communities program. 2002.

238-29 Greater Yellowstone Coalition, Bozeman, MT, $100,000. For general support. Grant made as part of Environmental

Management in Rural Communities program. 2002.

238-30 Harvard University, Science, Technology, and Public Policy Program, Cambridge, MA, $400,000. For Energy Technology Innovation Project. 2002.

238-31 Health Effects Institute, Cambridge, MA, $500,000. For Science to Inform Worldwide Transport and Air Quality Decisions initiative. 2002.

238-32 Houston Advanced Research Center, Center for Global Studies, The Woodlands, TX, $400,000. For Paso del Norte Water project. 2002.

238-33 Initiative for Social Action and Renewal in Eurasia (ISAR), DC, $500,000. For community-based environmental protection activities in Russian Far East. 2002.

238-34 Institute for Americas Future, DC, $75,000. For initial phase of Green Growth Initiative. 2002.

238-35 Institutes for Journalism and Natural Resources, Missoula, MT, $100,000. For general support. 2002.

238-36 Instituto Tecnologico y de Estudios Superiores de Monterrey, Monterrey, Mexico, $100,000. For Rio Grande/Rio Bravo basin hydrological assessment. 2002.

238-37 Instituto Tecnologico y de Estudios Superiores de Monterrey, Centro de Calidad Ambiental, Monterrey, Mexico, $100,000. For Rio Grande/Rio Bravo basin hydrological assessment. 2002.

238-38 Johns Hopkins University, Zanvyl Krieger School of Arts and Sciences, Baltimore, MD, $50,000. For Marca d'Agua project. 2002.

238-39 Kaala Farm, Waianae, HI, $100,000. For general support. Grant made as part of Environmental Management in Rural Communities program. 2002.

238-40 Malpai Borderlands Group, Douglas, AZ, $100,000. For general support. 2002.

238-41 Missouri Botanical Garden, Saint Louis, MO, $100,000. For Center for Conservation and Sustainable Development. 2002.

238-42 Morris K. Udall Foundation, Tucson, AZ, $250,000. For U.S. Institute for Environmental Conflict Resolution. 2002.

238-43 National Commission on Energy Policy, DC, $2,000,000. For general support. 2002.

238-44 National Commission on Energy Policy, DC, $2,000,000. For general support. 2002.

238-45 National Tropical Botanical Garden, Kalaheo, HI, $100,000. For Limahuli Garden's Ahupa'a project. Grant made as part of Environmental Management in Rural Communities program. 2002.

238-46 Natural Heritage Institute, San Francisco, CA, $100,000. For Rio Grande/Rio Bravo Basin hydrological assessment. 2002.

238-47 Natural Heritage Institute, San Francisco, CA, $100,000. For Rio Grande/Rio Bravo Basin hydrological assessment. 2002.

238-48 Natural Heritage Institute, San Francisco, CA, $75,000. For general support. Grant made as part of Freshwater Management program. 2002.

238-49 Natural Resources Defense Council, San Francisco, CA, $210,000. For partnership with Silicon Valley Manufacturing Group to strengthen energy efficiency policy in Silicon Valley's high-tech world. 2002.

238-50 Natural Resources Defense Council, Climate Center, New York, NY, $300,000. To protect California Clean Air programs. 2002.

238-51 Nature Conservancy, San Francisco, CA, $1,000,000. For general support of activities in California. 2002.

238-52 New Mexico State University, Center for Latin American and Border Studies, Las Cruces, NM, $200,000. For water-policy program in collaboration with Universidad Autonoma de Ciudad Juarez and Houston Advanced Research Center. 2002.

238-53 New Mexico State University, Water Resources Research Institute, Las Cruces, NM, $100,000. For development of strategic plan and bylaws for Paso del Norte Water Task Force. 2002.

238-54 North American Institute, Santa Fe, NM, $100,000. For environmental policy programs. 2002.

238-55 Northeast States Clean Air Foundation, Boston, MA, $1,000,000. For research on strategies to reduce vehicular air pollution. 2002.

238-56 Northwest Energy Coalition, Seattle, WA, $200,000. For Citizens' Energy Plan and Campaign. 2002.

238-57 Oceans Blue Foundation, Vancouver, Canada, $375,000. For general support. 2002.

238-58 Pace University, Land Use Law Center, White Plains, NY, $200,000. For Consensus Building Alliance, land use conflict resolution program in Hudson River Valley. 2002.

238-59 Pacific Environment and Resources Center, Oakland, CA, $500,000. For regranting program to leading conservation organizations in Asian Russia. 2002.

238-60 Pacific Institute for Studies in Development, Environment and Security, Oakland, CA, $150,000. For general support. 2002.

238-61 Pacific Institute for Studies in Development, Environment and Security, Oakland, CA, $150,000. For general support. 2002.

238-62 Pacific Institute for Studies in Development, Environment and Security, Oakland, CA, $100,000. For general support. 2002.

238-63 Pro Esteros Lagunas y Marismas de las Californias, Ensenada, Mexico, $75,000. For general support. 2002.

238-64 Pronatura, Mexico, $150,000. For general support. 2002.

238-65 Pronatura, Mexico, $150,000. For general support. 2002.

238-66 Proyecto Fronterizo de Educacion Ambiental, Tijuana, Mexico, $125,000. For general support. 2002.

238-67 Proyecto Fronterizo de Educacion Ambiental, Tijuana, Mexico, $75,000. For fourth annual conference on the U.S.-Mexican border environment. 2002.

238-68 Quest Scholars Program, Palo Alto, CA, $50,000. For strategic planning. 2002.

238-69 RAND Corporation, Santa Monica, CA, $100,000. For analysis of energy resource base in Intermountain West and to examine opportunities and constraints on development. 2002.

238-70 Renewable Northwest Project, Portland, Oregon, $200,000. For general support. Grant made as part of Energy Initiative. 2002.

238-71 RESOLVE, Center for Environmental Dispute Resolution, DC, $175,000. For National Environmental Dispute Resolution Case Database project. 2002.

238-72 Resources for the Future, DC, $100,000. For project on water policy in Chile and Argentina. 2002.

238-73 Rio Grande Rio Bravo Basin Coalition, El Paso, TX, $225,000. For general support. Grant made as part of Freshwater Management program. 2002.

238-74 San Diego State University, Institute for Regional Studies of the Californias, San Diego, CA, $150,000. For freshwater management. 2002.

238-75 Save Our Wild Salmon Coalition, Seattle, WA, $200,000. For ecologically sound energy strategy. 2002.

238-76 Smart Growth British Columbia, Vancouver, Canada, $75,000. For general support. 2002.

238-77 Society of Environmental Journalists, Jenkintown, PA, $100,000. For general support. 2002.

238-78 Sonoran Institute, Tucson, AZ, $230,000. For general support and for annual gathering of national and regional environmental groups working in the West. 2002.

238-79 Tides Canada Foundation, Vancouver, Canada, $150,000. For Rain Forest Solutions project, as part of Environmental Management in Rural Communities program. 2002.

238-80 Tides Center, San Francisco, CA, $300,000. For Resources for Community Collaboration evaluation and grantee support services programs. 2002.

238-81 Tides Center, San Francisco, CA, $100,000. For California Futures Network's Civic Engagement Campaign for a Better California. 2002.

238-82 Trout Unlimited, Arlington, VA, $700,000. For Building Coalitions to Improve Public Land Conservation project. 2002.

238-83 Trust for Public Land, San Francisco, CA, $650,000. For Conservation Finance Program, as part of Environmental Management in Rural Communities. 2002.

238-84 Trust for Public Land, Boston, MA, $100,000. For Public Land Conservation Funding in the West program. 2002.

238-85 Union of Concerned Scientists, Cambridge, MA, $750,000. For Clean Vehicles Program. 2002.

238-86 United States-Mexico Foundation for Science, Oaxaca, Mexico, $300,000. For work on border-water issues. 2002.

238-87 Universidad Autonoma de Ciudad Juarez, Programa de Construccion Regional, Ciudad Juarez, Mexico, $200,000. For water policy program in collaboration with New Mexico State University and Houston Advanced Research Center. 2002.

238-88 University of California, Goldman School of Public Policy, Berkeley, CA, $75,000. For program to train local environmental authorities in Mexico. 2002.

238-89 University of California, Graduate School of Journalism, Berkeley, CA, $100,000. For Center for Environmental Journalism. 2002.

238-90 University of California, Richard and Rhonda Goldman School of Public Policy, Berkeley, CA, $75,000. For program to train local environmental authorities in Mexico. 2002.

238-91 University of California at San Diego, Center for U.S.-Mexican Studies, La Jolla, CA, $300,000. For environmental policy program. 2002.

238-92 University of Florida, Center for Latin American Studies, Gainesville, FL, $300,000. For Tropical Conservation and Development program. 2002.

238-93 University of Hawaii, International Pacific Research Center, Honolulu, HI, $25,000. For Air Pollution and Climate Change workshop. 2002.

238-94 University of Michigan, School of Natural Resources and Environment, Ann Arbor, MI, $200,000. For development of methods to evaluate collaborative ecosystem initiatives. 2002.

238-95 University of Wyoming, Laramie, WY, $75,000. For Institute for Environment and Natural Resources, as part of Environmental Management in Rural Communities program. 2002.

238-96 Vitoria Amazonica Foundation, Manaus, Brazil, $300,000. For general support. 2002.

238-97 W G B H Educational Foundation, Boston, MA, $150,000. For World in the Balance, NOVA production on global population, biodiversity and environment. 2002.

238-98 Western Resource Advocates, Boulder, CO, $415,000. For Rocky Mountain Energy Campaign. 2002.

238-99 Wilderness Society, DC, $100,000. For Natural Trails and Waters Coalition's campaign to protect wild lands of the West from damage caused by off-road vehicles. 2002.

238-100 Woods Hole Research Center, Woods Hole, MA, $150,000. For general support. 2002.

238-101 World Media Foundation, Cambridge, MA, $150,000. For Living on Earth program. 2002.

238-102 Yale University, School of Forestry and Environmental Studies, New Haven, CT, $70,000. For research on Punctuated Equilibria: A New Approach to Understanding and Promoting Policy Change. Grant made as part of Energy Initiative. 2002.

239
Hewlett-Packard Company Contributions Program

c/o Philanthropy Dept.
3000 Hanover St., M.S. 2OAH
Palo Alto, CA 94304-1112 (650) 857-3035
Application address: P.O. Box 10301, Palo Alto, CA 94303-0890; E-mail: philanthropy_ed@hp.com; URI : http://www.hp.com/hpinfo/globalcitizenship

Grantmaker type: Corporate giving program
Purpose and activities: As a complement to its foundation, Hewlett-Packard also makes charitable contributions to nonprofit organizations directly. Support is given on a national and international basis.
Fields of interest: Museums; Performing arts; Arts; Elementary/secondary education; Higher education; College (community/junior); Business school/education; Engineering school/education; Education; Environment; Hospitals (general); Health care; Biomedicine; Health organizations; Vocational rehabilitation; Housing/shelter; Human services; Business/industry; Community development; Mathematics; Engineering/technology; Science; Minorities; Disabled; Women.
International interests: Canada; Europe; United Kingdom; Asia.
Types of support: General/operating support; Equipment; Program development; Curriculum development; Employee matching gifts; Donated equipment; Donated products; In-kind gifts.
Limitations: Giving on a national basis, with emphasis on areas of company operations in CA, CO, GA, ID, NJ, OR, and WA, and on an international basis in Asia, Canada, Europe, and the United Kingdom. No support for religious or sectarian organizations or sports ventures. No grants to individuals, or for conferences, seminars, meetings, workshops, general fund drives, capital campaigns, scholarships, endowments, fundraising, or annual campaigns, dinners, memberships, or faculty chairs.
Application information: Unsolicited requests for in-kind gifts from organizations located in countries where Hewlett-Packard installation, repair, and maintenance is not available are not accepted. An application form is required for the Community College Pre-Engineering and Computer Science Grant Initiative; application form available online. Support is limited to 1 year in length. The Philanthropy Department handles giving. The company has a staff that only handles contributions. A contributions committee reviews all requests.
Initial approach: Consult Web site for initial approach; complete online application form for Community College Pre-Engineering and Computer Science Grant Initiative
Deadline(s): Varies; Feb. 1, May 1, and Oct. 1 for U.S. University Grants; Jan. 1, Apr. 1, July 1, and Oct. 1 for U.S. National Grants; Nov. 22 for Community College Pre-Engineering and Computer Science Grant Initiative
Board meeting date(s): Quarterly; 3 times per year for U.S. University Grants
Final notification: 2 to 4 weeks following committee meetings; Nov. 27 for Community College Pre-Engineering and Computer Science Grant Initiative
U.S. University Grants Staff: Faye Koester, Admin. Asst.; Nancy Levitt, Corp. Philanthropy Prog. Mgr.; Tony Napolitan, Jr., Mgr., Univ. Grants.
U.S. National Grants Staff: Kathleen Franger, Corp. Philanthropy Prog. Mgr.; Catherine Gowen, Corp. Philanthropy Prog. Mgr.; Florence Korbus, Asst.
Number of staff: 14 full-time professional; 6 full-time support.

240
The Hofmann Foundation

(formerly K. H. Hofmann Foundation)
P.O. Box 907
Concord, CA 94522
Contact: Lisa Hofmann Seeno, Secy.
Application address: 1380 Galaxy Way,
Concord, CA 94522, tel.: (925) 687-1826

Established in 1963 in CA.
Donor(s): Hofmann Construction Co., New
Discovery, Inc., Kenneth H. Hofmann.
Grantmaker type: Company-sponsored
foundation
Financial data (yr. ended 07/31/02): Assets,
$16,890,009 (M); gifts received, $1,477,000;
expenditures, $3,056,190; qualifying
distributions, $2,972,748; giving activities
include $2,984,250 for 98 grants (high:
$766,512; low: $100; average: $500–$25,000).
Purpose and activities: Support for: 1)
acquisition, preservation, and conservation of
wildlife lands, specifically the wetland
marshlands that are sanctuaries to waterfowl
and related wildlife; 2) education of the
community to its need to preserve wildlife
without undermining related sports and
recreation; 3) local educational institutions that
demonstrate a profound need to challenge and
improve the hearts and minds of its students; 4)
local cultural organizations, especially those
that demonstrate a desire to establish and create
long-lasting cultural programs and facilities; and
5) to a limited degree, local organizations that
address general welfare. Some support for local
medical and health agencies, as well as
nationally recognized medical research
agencies with local offices.
Fields of interest: Museums; Performing arts;
Elementary/secondary education; Higher
education; Natural resources; Animals/wildlife,
preservation/protection; Health care; Health
organizations, association; Biomedicine;
Medical research, institute; Human services;
Children/youth, services; Homeless, human
services; Economic development; Federated
giving programs; Christian agencies & churches;
Disabled; Homeless.
Types of support: Building/renovation;
Endowments; Emergency funds; Program
development; Research; Matching/challenge
support.
Limitations: Giving primarily in the San
Francisco Bay Area, CA, with emphasis on
Contra Costa County organizations; limited
support for national organizations. No grants to
individuals, or for general purposes, capital
funding, routine operating expenses, or
repayment of debt.
Publications: Annual report (including
application guidelines).
Application information: Application form not
required.
   Initial approach: Letter of inquiry (no more
      than 3 pages)
   Copies of proposal: 1
   Deadline(s): None
   Board meeting date(s): Quarterly
   Final notification: 3 to 4 months
Officers: Martha J. Hoffmann, C.E.O.; Lisa
Hofmann Seeno, Secy.; Dennis M. Drew, C.F.O.
Number of staff: 4.
EIN: 946108897

241
The Homeland Foundation ▼

412 N. Coast Hwy., PMB 359
Laguna Beach, CA 92651 (949) 494-0365
Contact: Glenda Menges, Admin.

Established in 1986 in CA.
Grantmaker type: Independent foundation
Financial data (yr. ended 12/31/01): Assets,
$28,093,224 (M); gifts received, $3,342,509;
expenditures, $13,342,249; qualifying
distributions, $13,223,596; giving activities
include $12,871,620 for 246 grants (high:
$1,000,000; low: $1,000; average:
$10,000–$125,000).
Purpose and activities: The Environment
Program concentrates on the conservation of
biological diversity and sustainable ecosystem
management with emphasis on marine
resources conservation; it also supports the
search for solutions to health threats caused by
toxic chemicals. The objective of the Human
Services Program is to assist women, primarily
regarding their physical, mental, and financial
health.
Fields of interest: Environment, toxics; Natural
resources; Environment, water resources;
Women, centers/services.
International interests: Mexico.
Types of support: General/operating support;
Program development.
Limitations: Giving primarily on the West Coast
of the U.S. (including Baja, CA), HI, and the
Western Pacific for the environment; funding for
women limited to Los Angeles and Orange
County, CA. No support for political campaigns.
No grants to individuals, or for scholarships,
fellowships, or film or video projects.
Publications: Application guidelines.
Application information: Contact foundation for
guidelines. Application form not required.
   Initial approach: Proposal (no more than 4
      pages)
   Copies of proposal: 1
   Deadline(s): Mar. 1, June 1, Sept. 1, and Dec.
      1
   Board meeting date(s): Quarterly
Number of staff: 2 full-time professional.
EIN: 330200133
**Recent environmental and animal welfare
grants:**
241-1 Amazon Conservation Team, Arlington,
VA, $35,000. For Colombia program. 2001.
241-2 American Oceans Campaign, Los
Angeles, CA, $25,000. For Pacific Fisheries
Habitat Protection Program. 2001.
241-3 American Oceans Campaign, Los
Angeles, CA, $25,000. For marine fish
conservation network. 2001.
241-4 American Oceans Campaign, Los
Angeles, CA, $25,000. For Pacific Fisheries
Habitat Program. 2001.
241-5 Audubon Society of Hawaii, Honolulu,
HI, $35,000. For West Pacific Fisheries. 2001.
241-6 Audubon Society, National, Los Angeles,
CA, $20,000. For Living Oceans Program.
2001.
241-7 Audubon Society, Palos Verdes Peninsula,
Palos Verdes Peninsula, CA, $10,000. For
community outreach coordinator. 2001.
241-8 Audubon Society, Sea and Sage, Laguna
Niguel, CA, $20,000. For educational
programs. 2001.

241-9 Biodiversity Project, Madison, WI,
$25,000. For public attitude survey. 2001.
241-10 Bolsa Chica Land Trust, Huntington
Beach, CA, $50,000. For land. 2001.
241-11 Bolsa Chica Land Trust, Huntington
Beach, CA, $35,000. For general support and
wetland protection activities. 2001.
241-12 Bolsa Chica Land Trust, Huntington
Beach, CA, $25,000. For land purchase.
2001.
241-13 Boy Scouts of America, Orange County
Council, Costa Mesa, CA, $10,000. For water
rake project to clean Newport Harbor. 2001.
241-14 California Coastal Protection Network,
Santa Barbara, CA, $30,000. For Coastal
Resources Projects. 2001.
241-15 CalPIRG Charitable Trust, Los Angeles,
CA, $25,000. For Californians for Pesticide
Reform. 2001.
241-16 CalPIRG Charitable Trust, Los Angeles,
CA, $10,000. For community fertilizer toxic
testing. 2001.
241-17 Canadian Environmental Law
Association, Toronto, Canada, $200,000. For
international persistent organic pollutant
elimination. 2001.
241-18 Center for Biological Diversity, Tucson,
AZ, $40,000. For Marine and Coastal
Biodiversity Projects. 2001.
241-19 Center for Health, Environment and
Justice, Falls Church, VA, $450,000. For
Health Care Without Harm Project. 2001.
241-20 Center for Independent Documentary,
Sharon, MA, $30,000. For documentary film
about PVC Industry. 2001.
241-21 Center for International Environmental
Law, DC, $50,000. For greening trade and
persistent organic pollutants. 2001.
241-22 Center for Resource Economics/Island
Press, DC, $50,000. For marine projects for
Island Press. 2001.
241-23 Center for the Support of Native Lands,
Arlington, VA, $20,000. For Marine Mapping
Projects. 2001.
241-24 Centro Ecoceanos, Santiago, Chile,
$25,000. For Chilean Sea and Lake
Protection Projects. 2001.
241-25 Centro Mexicano de Derecho
Ambiental, Mexico City, Mexico, $35,000.
For marine protection projects. 2001.
241-26 Childrens Health Environmental
Coalition, Malibu, CA, $50,000. For
children's health video. 2001.
241-27 Communities for a Better Environment,
Oakland, CA, $35,000. For community
projects in Los Angeles and San Francisco.
2001.
241-28 Consultative Group on Biological
Diversity, San Francisco, CA, $10,000. For
Health and Environmental Funders Network.
2001.
241-29 Coral Reef Alliance (CORAL), San
Francisco, CA, $30,000. For outreach
program. 2001.
241-30 David Suzuki Foundation, Vancouver,
Canada, $40,000. For salmon aquaculture.
2001.
241-31 Defenders of Wildlife, DC, $25,000. For
Endangered Species Coalition. 2001.
241-32 Dian Fossey Gorilla Fund International,
Atlanta, GA, $20,000. For Karisoke
Revitalization. 2001.
241-33 Dolphin Ecology Project, Tavernier, FL,
$10,000. For dolphin research. 2001.

241-34 Earth Action Network, Norwalk, CT, $20,000. For children's health issue of E-Magazine. 2001.

241-35 Earth Island Institute, San Francisco, CA, $30,000. For Dolphin Safe Tuna activities. 2001.

241-36 Earth Island Institute, San Francisco, CA, $25,000. For International Shrimp Action Network. 2001.

241-37 Earth Island Institute, San Francisco, CA, $25,000. For Mangrove Action Project. 2001.

241-38 Earth Trust Foundation, Malibu, CA, $20,000. For Spinner Dolphin research project. 2001.

241-39 Earthjustice Legal Defense Fund, Oakland, CA, $25,000. For Mid-Pacific Biodiversity. 2001.

241-40 Educational Broadcasting Corporation, New York, NY, $500,000. For environmental programming. 2001.

241-41 Educational Broadcasting Corporation, New York, NY, $500,000. For environmental programming. 2001.

241-42 Endangered Habitats League, Los Angeles, CA, $30,000. For Terra Peninsular Work in Baja. 2001.

241-43 Endangered Habitats League, Los Angeles, CA, $15,000. For South Orange County Biological Diversity project. 2001.

241-44 Environmental Defense, New York, NY, $125,000. For antibiotics resistance research. 2001.

241-45 Environmental Defense Center, Santa Barbara, CA, $50,000. For conservation advocacy for Channel Islands. 2001.

241-46 Environmental Investigation Agency, DC, $22,000. For marine mammal and marine ecosystem activities. 2001.

241-47 Environmental Law Alliance Worldwide (E-LAW), Eugene, Oregon, $20,000. For environmental law in Chile. 2001.

241-48 Environmental Media Services, DC, $50,000. For grant made through Tides Center. 2001.

241-49 Environmental Working Group, Oakland, CA, $350,000. For general support and Body Burden Project. 2001.

241-50 Environmental Working Group, Oakland, CA, $30,000. For environmental research. 2001.

241-51 Essential Information, DC, $150,000. For Global Anti-Incinerator Alliance. 2001.

241-52 Fiscalia del Medio Ambiente (FIMA), Santiago, Chile, $40,000. For general support and blood testing. 2001.

241-53 Foundation to Promote Sustainable Development, Fundacion Terram, Santiago, Chile, $25,000. For Chilean Salmon Aquaculture work. 2001.

241-54 Friends of the Earth, DC, $10,000. For California Green Scissors Project. 2001.

241-55 Fundacion Otway, Puerto Montt, Chile, $40,000. For land for Humboldt Penguins. 2001.

241-56 Georgia Strait Alliance, Nanaimo, Canada, $30,000. For campaign against salmon farming. 2001.

241-57 Green Seal, Palo Alto, CA, $15,000. For general support. 2001.

241-58 Green Seal, Palo Alto, CA, $15,000. For programs. 2001.

241-59 Greenpeace Fund, DC, $100,000. For whale protection. 2001.

241-60 Institute for Local Self Government, Sacramento, CA, $125,000. For PVC Phase Out Project. 2001.

241-61 International Community Foundation, San Diego, CA, $15,500. For Niparaja's environmental work in Baja California. 2001.

241-62 International Institute for Sustainable Development (IISD), Winnipeg, Canada, $20,000. For Methanex Brief. 2001.

241-63 International Marinelife Alliance, Honolulu, HI, $20,000. For fisheries management program. 2001.

241-64 International Rivers Network, Berkeley, CA, $15,000. For Yacyreta Dam. 2001.

241-65 International Sonoran Desert Alliance, Ajo, AZ, $10,000. For women's conference in Mexico. 2001.

241-66 Island Conservation and Ecology Group, Davenport, CA, $50,000. For Baja Islands. 2001.

241-67 Laguna Canyon Foundation, Laguna Beach, CA, $75,000. For Laguna Laurel. 2001.

241-68 Liberty Hill Foundation, Santa Monica, CA, $25,000. For Environmental Justice Fund. 2001.

241-69 Marine Conservation Biology Institute, Redmond, WA, $40,000. For marine conservation activities. 2001.

241-70 Moanalua Gardens Foundation, Honolulu, HI, $30,000. For Partners in Education Project. 2001.

241-71 Monitor International, Annapolis, MD, $25,000. For environmental outreach. 2001.

241-72 Montana Land Reliance, Helena, MT, $10,000. For Greater Yellowstone. 2001.

241-73 Mount Sinai School of Medicine of New York University, New York, NY, $75,000. For children's environmental health project. 2001.

241-74 National Environmental Trust, DC, $500,000. For public education on children's health issues. 2001.

241-75 National Environmental Trust, DC, $75,000. For Marine Conservation Outreach Program. 2001.

241-76 National Fish and Wildlife Foundation, DC, $75,000. For whale fund and sea turtle conservation. 2001.

241-77 National Fish and Wildlife Foundation, DC, $60,000. For Mexico Marine project. 2001.

241-78 National Religious Partnership for the Environment, Amherst, MA, $500,000. For Children's Environmental Health Project. 2001.

241-79 National Whistleblower Center, DC, $10,000. For Reform the Sludge Rule Project. 2001.

241-80 Native Planet, Seattle, WA, $10,000. For marine education program in Panama. 2001.

241-81 Natural Resources Defense Council, New York, NY, $300,000. For marine habitat protection and ocean noise regulation. 2001.

241-82 Nature Conservancy, Arlington, VA, $100,000. For Santa Cruz Island Restoration Project. 2001.

241-83 Nature Conservancy, Arlington, VA, $60,000. For Arnavon Islands in Solomon Islands. 2001.

241-84 Nature Conservancy, Arlington, VA, $30,000. For Community Conservation Network in Asia. 2001.

241-85 Nature Conservancy, Arlington, VA, $10,000. For program in Baja, Mexico. 2001.

241-86 Nature Conservancy, Arlington, VA, $10,000. For Grupo Ecologista Antares. 2001.

241-87 Nature Conservancy of Hawaii, Honolulu, HI, $125,000. For Kauai Project. 2001.

241-88 Newport Bay Naturalists and Friends, Newport Beach, CA, $15,000. For volunteer coordinator staff position. 2001.

241-89 Ocean Institute, Dana Point, CA, $100,000. For intertidal tank. 2001.

241-90 Oceana, DC, $1,000,000. For International Marine Conservation. 2001.

241-91 Orange County CoastKeeper, Newport Beach, CA, $125,000. For Orange County marine issues. 2001.

241-92 Organisation for Economic Cooperation and Development, Paris, France, $25,000. For International Energy Agency. 2001.

241-93 Pacific Cetacean Group, Marina, CA, $10,000. For Marine Conservation Education Program. 2001.

241-94 Pacific Forest Trust, Santa Rosa, CA, $15,000. For central coast forest initiative. 2001.

241-95 Pacific Marine Conservation Council, Astoria, Oregon, $25,000. For campaign coordinator. 2001.

241-96 Pesticide Action Network (PAN), North America Regional Center, San Francisco, CA, $50,000. For persistent organic pollutant elimination. 2001.

241-97 Point Reyes Bird Observatory, Stinson Beach, CA, $15,000. For Pinnipeds on Farallone Islands. 2001.

241-98 Pro Esteros, San Diego, CA, $25,000. For general support. 2001.

241-99 Public Education Center, DC, $150,000. For California Environmental Media Work. 2001.

241-100 Public Employees for Environmental Responsibility (PEER), DC, $25,000. For general support. 2001.

241-101 Public Health Foundation Enterprises, City of Industry, CA, $15,000. For British Columbia Salmon Farming. 2001.

241-102 Quail Botanical Gardens, Encinitas, CA, $10,000. For Discover Local Wildlife exhibit. 2001.

241-103 Redefining Progress, Oakland, CA, $30,000. For Precautionary Principle Project. 2001.

241-104 Reef Environmental Education Foundation, Key Largo, FL, $10,000. For West Coast Fish Survey Project. 2001.

241-105 Resources Legacy Fund, Sacramento, CA, $625,000. For Coal Canyon Phase II. 2001.

241-106 Restore Americas Estuaries, Arlington, VA, $10,000. For coastal habitat restoration. 2001.

241-107 Rockefeller Family Fund, New York, NY, $10,000. For Environmental Grantmakers Association's fall retreat. 2001.

241-108 San Diego BayKeeper, San Diego, CA, $15,000. For water monitoring project. 2001.

241-109 Santa Monica BayKeeper, Newport Beach, CA, $25,000. For Kelp Restoration Project. 2001.

241-110 School for Field Studies, Beverly, MA, $15,000. For scholarships. 2001.

241-111 Seacology, Berkeley, CA, $20,000. For West Pacific Islands. 2001.

241-112 SeaWeb, DC, $75,000. For advocacy and aquaculture work. 2001.

241-113 Sierra Club Foundation, San Francisco, CA, $15,000. For Friends of the Foothills Project in Orange County, CA. 2001.

241-114 Smithsonian Institution, DC, $20,000. For forest fragments program in Brazil. 2001.

241-115 Sonoran Institute, Tucson, AZ, $30,000. For Colorado River Delta Project. 2001.

241-116 South Coast Wilderness Sanctuary, Carmel Valley, CA, $10,000. For Ventana Wilderness Society. 2001.

241-117 South Yuba River Citizens League, Nevada City, CA, $15,000. For River Law Program. 2001.

241-118 Southwest Rivers, Flagstaff, AZ, $15,000. For Colorado River Delta Symposium. 2001.

241-119 Student Conservation Association, Charlestown, NH, $10,000. For Hawaii Internship Program. 2001.

241-120 Texas A & M Research Foundation, College Station, TX, $13,000. For dolphin research in Northern Hawaiian Islands. 2001.

241-121 Tides Foundation, San Francisco, CA, $10,000. For Global Green Grants/Earth Day. 2001.

241-122 Trust for Public Land, San Francisco, CA, $25,000. For feasibility study for Virgin Islands. 2001.

241-123 Turtle Island Restoration Network, Forest Knolls, CA, $30,000. For Longline/Gillnet Reform Project. 2001.

241-124 University of California, Berkeley, CA, $42,000. For Atrazine Research Project. 2001.

241-125 University of California, Irvine, CA, $31,000. For arboretum. 2001.

241-126 University of California, Santa Cruz, CA, $25,000. For farm and organic gardening apprenticeship. 2001.

241-127 University of California at Santa Cruz Foundation, Santa Cruz, CA, $100,000. For Center for Ocean Health. 2001.

241-128 University of Washington, School of Marine Affairs, Seattle, WA, $10,000. For Marine Protected Area (MPA) News. 2001.

241-129 Waterkeeper Alliance, White Plains, NY, $20,000. For annual meeting. 2001.

241-130 Whale Conservation Institute, Lincoln, MA, $100,000. For whale research project. 2001.

241-131 Wild Dolphin Project, Jupiter, FL, $125,000. For research of wild dolphins. 2001.

241-132 WildAid, San Francisco, CA, $75,000. For Shark Conservation Program. 2001.

241-133 WildAid, San Francisco, CA, $15,000. For Galapagos Island emergency. 2001.

241-134 Wildcoast, Imperial Beach, CA, $35,000. For conservation efforts in Baja California. 2001.

241-135 Wildlife Conservation Society, Bronx, NY, $25,000. For Turtle Conservation. 2001.

241-136 Wildlife Trust, Palisades, NY, $25,000. For sea turtle and ecosystem health program. 2001.

241-137 Windows-On-Our-Waters, Santa Monica, CA, $20,000. For Mobile Ocean Display. 2001.

241-138 Wishtoyo Foundation, Oxnard, CA, $30,000. For Chumash Indian Cultural/Environmental Project. 2001.

241-139 World Wildlife Fund/Conservation Foundation, DC, $100,000. For marine conservation in the Philippines. 2001.

241-140 World Wildlife Fund/Conservation Foundation, DC, $50,000. For Galapagos Island emergency. 2001.

241-141 Zoological Society of San Diego, San Diego, CA, $10,000. For Alakai Swamp on Kauai, Hawaii. 2001.

242
The Horn Foundation
16133 Ventura Blvd., Ste. 700
Encino, CA 91436

Established in 1989 in CA.
Donor(s): Alan F. Horn.
Grantmaker type: Independent foundation
Financial data (yr. ended 12/31/02): Assets, $1,970,851 (M); gifts received, $500,000; expenditures, $958,784; qualifying distributions, $940,845; giving activities include $933,426 for 82 grants (high: $200,000; low: $100).
Purpose and activities: Giving primarily for arts and culture, education, conservation, health associations, human services, and children and youth services.
Fields of interest: Arts; Education; Environment; Health organizations, association; Human services; Children/youth, services.
Limitations: Applications not accepted. Giving primarily in CA. No grants to individuals.
Application information: Contributes only to pre-selected organizations.
Officer: Alan F. Horn, Mgr.
EIN: 954247470

243
Ron and Cheryl Howard Family Foundation
11611 San Vicente Blvd., Ste. 740
Los Angeles, CA 90049

Established in 1998 in CA.
Donor(s): Ron Howard, Cheryl Howard.
Grantmaker type: Independent foundation
Financial data (yr. ended 12/31/00): Assets, $381,936 (M); gifts received, $325,000; expenditures, $224,233; qualifying distributions, $224,114; giving activities include $224,125 for 45 grants (high: $19,700; low: $100).
Fields of interest: Arts; Higher education; Libraries (public); Education; Animals/wildlife, preservation/protection; Hospitals (general); Health organizations, association; Medical research, institute; Safety/disasters; Human services; Children, services; Foundations (community); Federated giving programs.
Limitations: Applications not accepted. Giving on a national basis. No grants to individuals.
Application information: Contributes only to pre-selected organizations.
Officers: Ron Howard, C.E.O. and Pres.; Cheryl Howard, Secy. and C.F.O.
EIN: 954715638

244
Humane America Animal Foundation
(also known as 1-800-SAVE-A-PET.COM)
P.O. Box 7
Redondo Beach, CA 90277 (310) 263-2930
Contact: David Meyer, Exec. Dir.
Additional tel: (800) 728-3273; FAX: (310) 406-1559; E-mail: info@1-800-save-a-pet.com; URL: http://www.1-800-save-a-pet.com

Established in 1999 in CA as a private foundation.
Grantmaker type: Public charity
Financial data (yr. ended 12/31/01): Revenue, $248,436; assets, $74,127 (M); gifts received, $236,280; expenditures, $313,902; program services expenses, $217,271; giving activities include $241 for grants.
Purpose and activities: The foundation maintains a national pet adoption referral program that lowers the number of euthanasia's in Los Angeles and cities across the nation.
Fields of interest: Animal welfare.
Limitations: Giving on national basis.
Officer: David Meyer, Exec. Dir.
EIN: 954761276

245
The Impact Fund
125 University Ave.
Berkeley, CA 94710-1616
Contact: Brad Seligman, Exec. Dir.
Tel.: (510) 845-3473, ext. 304; FAX: (510) 845-3654; E-mail: impactfund@impactfund.org; URL: http://www.impactfund.org

Established in 1992 in CA.
Grantmaker type: Public charity
Financial data (yr. ended 06/30/02): Revenue, $753,852; assets, $651,130 (M); gifts received, $575,922; expenditures, $862,374; program services expenses, $732,986; giving activities include $224,717 for grants and $17,045 for 2 grants to individuals (high: $15,000; low: $2,045).
Purpose and activities: The fund supports public interest litigation in the general areas of poverty, civil rights and environmental law.
Fields of interest: Environment, public policy; Civil rights, public policy; Civil rights; Poverty studies.
Types of support: Continuing support; Annual campaigns; Research; Technical assistance.
Limitations: Giving on a national basis.
Publications: Application guidelines, Annual report, Newsletter.
Application information: See Web site for all programs and application deadlines; the fund makes quarterly grants. Application form required.
  Initial approach: Pre-application letter 1-2 pages
  Deadline(s): Spring cycle, pre-application Mar. 9, full application Mar. 16; Summer cycle, pre-application May 28, full application June 7
  Board meeting date(s): Quarterly
Directors: Brad Seligman, Exec. Dir.; Luke W. Cole; Cathy R. Dreyfuss; Theresa Fay-Bustillos; Abigail Ginzberg; Amanda Hawes; Shauna Marshall; Mari Mayeda; Arlene Mayerson; Alan Ramo; Dana Schur*; Marc Van Der Hout.

Number of staff: 4 full-time professional; 1 part-time professional; 2 full-time support.
EIN: 943161863

246
International Community Foundation
1420 Kettner Blvd., Ste. 500
San Diego, CA 92101
Contact: Marisol Lopez, Dir., Opers.
Tel.: (619) 235-2300, ext. 311; FAX: (619) 239-1710; E-mail: info@icfdn.org; URL: http://www.icfdn.org/

Established in 1990 in CA.
Grantmaker type: Public charity
Financial data (yr. ended 06/30/00): Revenue, $447,849; assets, $716,875; gifts received, $447,455; expenditures, $309,293; giving activities include $182,315 for 22 grants.
Purpose and activities: The foundation assists philanthropy across international borders in the Pacific Rim region.
Fields of interest: Arts; Education; Environment; Health care; Community development, neighborhood development; International development.
Types of support: General/operating support; Continuing support.
Limitations: Giving on an international basis, primarily in Latin America and the Pacific Rim region of Asia; recent grantmaking includes projects in Mexico, China, Ecucador, and Canada. No grants to individuals.
Publications: Annual report, Informational brochure (including application guidelines), Newsletter.
Application information: Application form not required.
  Initial approach: Letter of inquiry
  Board meeting date(s): 1st Wed. of Jan., Mar., June, Sept., and Nov.
Officers and Governors:* Augustine Gallego,* Chair.; Robert Morris,* Vice-Chair.; Yolanda Walther-Meade,* Vice-Chair.; Richard Kiy,* Pres. and C.E.O.; Jose M. Larroques,* Secy.; Leon Reinhart, Ph.D.,* Treas.; Robert Chang, Ph.D.; Robert Kelly; Jacinto Astiazaran Rosas; and 3 additional governors.
Number of staff: 3 full-time professional; 1 part-time professional; 1 part-time support.
EIN: 330457858

247
The James Irvine Foundation ▼
1 Market St.
Steuart Tower, Ste. 2500
San Francisco, CA 94105 (415) 777-2244
Contact: Kelly Martin, Grants Mgr.
FAX: (415) 777-0869; Southern CA office: 725 S. Figueroa St., Ste. 3075, Los Angeles, CA 90017-5430, tel.: (213) 236-0552, FAX: (213) 236-0537; URL: http://www.irvine.org

Incorporated in 1937 in CA.
Donor(s): James Irvine.‡
Grantmaker type: Independent foundation
Financial data (yr. ended 12/31/02): Assets, $1,132,589,948 (M); gifts received, $2,500; expenditures, $91,363,540; qualifying distributions, $83,940,551; giving activities include $73,455,310 for grants (average:

$20,000–$250,000) and $1,691,500 for foundation-administered programs.
Purpose and activities: Giving primarily for the arts, higher education, workforce development, civic culture, sustainable communities, and children, youth, and families.
Fields of interest: Multipurpose centers/programs; Cultural/ethnic awareness; Folk arts; Arts councils; Performing arts; Performing arts centers; Dance; Ballet; Theater; Orchestra (symphony); Opera; Higher education; College; University; Higher education reform; Natural resources; Employment, services; Employment, job counseling; Employment, training; Employment, retraining; Youth development, centers/clubs; Youth development, services; Race/intergroup relations; Community development, management/technical aid; Community development, volunteer services; Community development, neighborhood development; Economic development; Rural development; Nonprofit management; Philanthropy/voluntarism, association; Philanthropy/voluntarism, administration/regulation; Philanthropy/voluntarism, information services; Foundations (public); Foundations (community); Voluntarism promotion; Philanthropy/voluntarism; Public policy, research.
Types of support: General/operating support; Program development; Seed money; Technical assistance; Program evaluation; Program-related investments/loans; Employee matching gifts; Matching/challenge support.
Limitations: Giving limited to CA. No support for agencies receiving substantial government support. No grants to individuals.
Publications: Annual report, Newsletter.
Application information: Application form not required.
  Initial approach: After reviewing the foundation's annual report and/or Web site, initial contact with the foundation should be through a one-to-two page letter of inquiry. Letter can also be submitted online
  Copies of proposal: 1
  Deadline(s): None
  Final notification: 3 to 6 weeks
Officers and Directors:* Peter W. Stanley, Ph.D.,* Chair.; Gary B. Pruitt,* Vice-Chair.; James E. Canales,* C.E.O. and Pres.; John R. Jenks, C.I.O. and Treas.; Martha Campbell, V.P., Programs; Samuel H. Armacost; Greg Avis; Frank H. Cruz; Cheryl White Mason; David Mas Masumoto; Molly Munger; Patricia S. Pineda; Toby Rosenblatt; Peter J. Taylor; Kathryn L. Wheeler, Hon. Dir.
Number of staff: 25 full-time professional; 1 part-time professional; 18 full-time support.
EIN: 941236937
Recent environmental and animal welfare grants:
247-1 Action Pajaro Valley, Watsonville, CA, $250,000. For Growth Management Strategy process, to develop growth strategy to guide land use planning in Pajaro Valley region of Monterrey-Santa Cruz counties. 2002.
247-2 American Farmland Trust, DC, $150,000. To encourage preservation of prime farmland and health of urban communities through improved land use and infrastructure

investment policies at state and local levels. 2002.
247-3 Association of Community Organizations for Reform Now (ACORN), Los Angeles, CA, $105,000. To increase participation of low- and moderate-income Californians in land use policy reform. 2002.
247-4 California Center for Land Recycling, San Francisco, CA, $900,000. For project-level statewide policy work to support redevelopment of contaminated land. 2002.
247-5 California Works Foundation, Oakland, CA, $200,000. For statewide scan and analysis on opportunities to engage California labor community in land use and transportation issues. 2002.
247-6 Center on Policy Initiatives, San Diego, CA, $150,000. To assess social and economic equity in San Diego's regional land use decisions, educate labor leaders and members, and strengthen ties between labor and environmental groups. 2002.
247-7 Community Partners, Los Angeles, CA, $180,000. For Southern California Transportation and Land Use Coalition, to support public awareness of and engagement in issues of growth in Southern California, and for organizational development. 2002.
247-8 Environmental Careers Organization (ECO), Boston, MA, $340,000. For Sustainable Communities Leadership Program in California, for core support and strategic planning services. 2002.
247-9 Environmental Health Coalition, San Diego, CA, $150,000. To promote social equity in San Diego regional land use decisions by identifying opportunities for community participation and by increasing organizational capacity. 2002.
247-10 Great Valley Center, Modesto, CA, $650,000. To promote social equity and environmental concerns in Sacramento's regional land use decisions by increasing community participation and organizational capacity. 2002.
247-11 Great Valley Center, Modesto, CA, $112,500. For San Joaquin Valley Organizing Project, as part of Central Valley Partnership for Citizenship. 2002.
247-12 Urban Ecology, Oakland, CA, $150,000. To help low-income residents participate in planning for their communities, and for strategic assessment of whether community planning model should be expanded beyond Bay Area. 2002.

248
James 2:18 Foundation
527 Burlingame Ave.
Los Angeles, CA 90049

Established in 1986 in CA and DE.
Donor(s): John T. Hastings, Jr., John T. Hastings.
Grantmaker type: Independent foundation
Financial data (yr. ended 11/30/01): Assets, $1,867,383 (M); gifts received, $79,277; expenditures, $108,860; qualifying distributions, $106,821; giving activities include $102,750 for 23 grants (high: $17,270; low: $30).
Purpose and activities: Giving for the environment and Native American studies.
Fields of interest: University; Natural resources; Human services; Christian agencies & churches.

Limitations: Applications not accepted. Giving primarily in CA. No grants to individuals.
Application information: Contributes only to pre-selected organizations.
Officer and Trustee:* John T. Hastings, Jr.,* Pres.
EIN: 954080705

249
Jamieson Foundation
1 Embarcadero Ctr., Ste. 1200
San Francisco, CA 94111 (415) 732-3702
Contact: Suzanna Jamieson, Secy.
FAX: (415) 732-3710; E-mail: sannesanfr@aol.com

Established in 1986 in CA.
Donor(s): G.W. Jamieson.‡
Grantmaker type: Independent foundation
Financial data (yr. ended 11/30/02): Assets, $2,961,962 (M); expenditures, $145,406; qualifying distributions, $149,041; giving activities include $128,500 for 14 grants (high: $37,000; low: $1,500).
Fields of interest: Higher education; Environment; Hospitals (general); Recreation; Human services; Community development; Christian agencies & churches.
Types of support: General/operating support; Continuing support; Equipment; Emergency funds; Program development; Research; Technical assistance; Program-related investments/loans; In-kind gifts.
Limitations: Applications not accepted. Giving primarily in the San Francisco Bay Area, CA. No grants to individuals.
Application information: Contributes only to pre-selected organizations.
Board meeting date(s): Feb.
Officers and Directors:* D.M. Jamieson,* Pres.; G.S. Jamieson,* V.P.; S.J. Jamieson, Secy.
EIN: 943025704

250
The Stephane Janssen Art Foundation, Inc.
315 N. McCaden Pl.
Los Angeles, CA 90004 (310) 553-8800
FAX: (310) 553-8704

Established in 1993 in CA.
Donor(s): Stephane Janssen.
Grantmaker type: Independent foundation
Financial data (yr. ended 06/30/02): Assets, $1,503,802 (M); gifts received, $146,900; expenditures, $144,835; qualifying distributions, $144,835; giving activities include $101,200 for 2 grants (high: $101,000; low: $200).
Purpose and activities: Giving primarily to art museums.
Fields of interest: Arts; University; Animal welfare.
Limitations: Applications not accepted. Giving primarily in Tempe, AZ, and Santa Fe, NM. No grants to individuals.
Application information: Contributes only to pre-selected organizations.
Officers and Directors:* Maurice H. Katz,* C.E.O.; Constance Glenn,* Secy.; Stephane Janssen,* C.F.O.
Number of staff: 1 part-time professional.
EIN: 954461083

251
Adalyn Jay Foundation
19 Via Palladio
Newport Coast, CA 92657

Established in 1998 in CA.
Donor(s): William J. Ruehle, Judi A. Ruehle.
Grantmaker type: Independent foundation
Financial data (yr. ended 12/31/01): Assets, $4,330,960 (M); gifts received, $432,800; expenditures, $1,003,875; qualifying distributions, $1,002,067; giving activities include $1,002,778 for 14 grants (high: $325,150; low: $336).
Fields of interest: Animals/wildlife, special services; Health care, patient services; Parkinson's disease; Child abuse; Children/youth, services; Christian agencies & churches.
Limitations: Applications not accepted. No grants to individuals.
Application information: Contributes only to pre-selected organizations.
Directors: Michelle A. Buck; Judi A. Ruehle; William J. Ruehle.
EIN: 770487631

252
Jeangerard Foundation
c/o Robert E. Jeangerard
1930 Belmont Ave.
San Carlos, CA 94070-4731

Established in 1992 in CA.
Donor(s): Ralph W. Jeangerard.‡
Grantmaker type: Independent foundation
Financial data (yr. ended 06/30/02): Assets, $1,913,674 (M); expenditures, $109,785; qualifying distributions, $100,410; giving activities include $100,000 for 1 grant.
Fields of interest: Natural resources; Environment, forests.
Limitations: Applications not accepted. Giving primarily in CA. No grants to individuals.
Application information: Contributes only to pre-selected organizations.
Officers: Robert E. Jeangerard, Pres.; Jack J. Jeangerard, V.P.; Margie H. Jeangerard, Secy.-Treas.
EIN: 770299812

253
Marie D. Jeffrey Foundation
1683 Sage Canyon Rd.
St. Helena, CA 94574

Established in 1986 in CA.
Donor(s): Marie D. Jeffrey.
Grantmaker type: Independent foundation
Financial data (yr. ended 11/30/00): Assets, $4,522,912 (M); gifts received, $492,283; expenditures, $234,009; qualifying distributions, $133,650; giving activities include $128,625 for grants (high: $76,000).
Purpose and activities: Giving for the environment, family services, and museums.
Fields of interest: Museums; Environment; Family services.
Limitations: Applications not accepted. Giving primarily in CA. No grants to individuals.
Application information: Contributes only to pre-selected organizations.

Officer and Directors:* Richard L. Martin,* Pres.; Anne Marie Martin; Jeffrey S. Martin; Rudy P. Nodar.
EIN: 943037301

254
George Frederick Jewett Foundation
The Russ Bldg.
235 Montgomery St., Ste. 612
San Francisco, CA 94104 (415) 421-1351
Contact: Ann D. Gralnek, Sr. Advisor
FAX: (415) 421-0721; E-mail: TFBjewettf@aol.com or ADGjewettf@aol.com

Trust established in 1957 in MA.
Donor(s): George Frederick Jewett.‡
Grantmaker type: Independent foundation
Financial data (yr. ended 12/31/01): Assets, $36,837,552 (M); expenditures, $1,958,169; qualifying distributions, $1,794,930; giving activities include $1,560,500 for 84 grants (high: $50,000; low: $300; average: $5,000–$50,000).
Purpose and activities: To carry on the charitable interests of the donor to stimulate, encourage, and support activities of established, voluntary, nonprofit organizations which are of importance to human welfare. Interests include arts and culture, music, education, libraries, environment (with particular emphasis on land conservation, oceanographic studies and population), protection of environment, including population issues and scientific research, health and social services.
Fields of interest: Music; Arts; Libraries (public); Education; Environment, land resources; Environment, beautification programs; Environmental education; Environment; Health care; Human services; Science, research; Marine science.
Types of support: General/operating support; Building/renovation; Equipment; Land acquisition; Program development; Seed money; Research; Technical assistance; Matching/challenge support.
Limitations: Giving primarily in San Francisco, CA, Spokane, WA, and in geographic areas of which trustees and family members have knowledge. No support for private or operating foundations or organizations which receive support from public tax funds. No grants to individuals, or for emergency funds (except for disaster relief), purchase of tickets or support of fundraising events; no loans.
Publications: Application guidelines, Annual report (including application guidelines), Program policy statement.
Application information: Formal application by invitation only; unsolicited requests for funds not considered. Application form required.
Initial approach: Letter of inquiry
Copies of proposal: 1
Deadline(s): Quarterly: Mar., June, Sept., and Dec.
Board meeting date(s): Within the annual grant cycle and no later than mid-Dec.
Trustees: George Frederick Jewett, Jr., Chair.; Margaret Jewett Greer; William Hershey Greer, Jr.; Lucille McIntyre Jewett.
Number of staff: 1 part-time professional; 1 full-time support.
EIN: 046013832

255
Jewish Community Foundation of Greater Los Angeles
(formerly Jewish Community Foundation)
6505 Wilshire Blvd., Ste. 1200
Los Angeles, CA 90048 (323) 761-8700
Contact: Cyndi Nezik, Grants Asst.
FAX: (323) 761-8720; E-mail:
info@jewishfoundationla.org; URL: http://
www.jewishfoundationla.org

Established in 1954 in CA.
Grantmaker type: Public charity
Financial data (yr. ended 12/31/01): Revenue,
$53,263,626; assets, $268,387,149 (M); gifts
received $44,532,371; expenditures,
$32,168,440; program services expenses,
$29,009,540; giving activities include
$29,009,540 for grants.
Purpose and activities: The foundation serves as
a long-term, stable funding resource to help the
Jewish and general community of Los Angeles,
California, grow and thrive, meet emergencies,
and foster innovative responses to new
challenges.
Fields of interest: Education; Environment;
Health care; Community development; Jewish
agencies & temples.
International interests: Israel.
Types of support: Building/renovation;
Emergency funds; Program development;
Conferences/seminars; Seed money; Curriculum
development; Technical assistance; Program
evaluation.
Limitations: Giving primarily in Los Angeles
County, CA. No grants to individuals.
Publications: Application guidelines, Annual
report, Grants list, Newsletter, Program policy
statement.
Application information: See Web site for
application guidelines. Application form
required.
   Initial approach: Telephone or e-mail
   Deadline(s): Varies
Officers and Trustees:* Mark Lainer,* Chair.;
Marvin I. Schotland, Pres. and C.E.O.; Simone
Savlov, C.O.O.; Loria M. Fife,* V.P.; Bertrand I.
Ginsberg,* V.P.; Lee Hausner, Ph.D.,* V.P.;
Raymond Kurtzman,* V.P.; Howard S. Marks,*
V.P.; Cathy Siegel,* V.P.; Martin L. Kozberg,*
Secy.; Kenneth A. August,* Treas.; Usha Murthy,
C.F.O.; Martin S. Appel; Paul S. Aronzon;
Newton D. Becker, Ph.D.; Terry Bell; Leah M.
Bishop; Jonathan R. Bloch; Stuart D. Buchalter;
Victor M. Carter; Anthony Chanin; Allan B.
Cutrow; Irwin Daniels; Cliff Einstein; Max Factor
III; and 36 additional trustees.
Number of staff: 20.
EIN: 956111928

256
JL Foundation
333 S. Hope St., Ste. 52
Los Angeles, CA 90071 (213) 486-9369
Contact: Jon B. Lovelace, Pres.

Established in 1988 in CA as a public charity;
became a private, independent foundation in
2000.
Grantmaker type: Independent foundation
Financial data (yr. ended 10/31/01): Assets,
$25,530,820; expenditures, $1,421,969;
qualifying distributions, $1,333,218; giving

activities include $1,343,500 for 32 grants (high:
$250,000; low: $2,000).
Purpose and activities: Support primarily for the
arts, including arts education, public radio, and
the fine and performing arts; giving also for
education, conservation, animals and wildlife,
crime prevention, health, and international relief.
Fields of interest: Arts education; Radio; Visual
arts; Museums; Performing arts; Arts; Higher
education; Education; Natural resources;
Animals/wildlife; Health organizations;
Crime/violence prevention; International relief.
Types of support: General/operating support;
Annual campaigns; Capital campaigns;
Building/renovation; Program development;
Matching/challenge support.
Limitations: Applications not accepted. Giving
on a national basis.
Application information: Contributes only to
pre-selected organizations.
Officers and Trustees:* Jon B. Lovelace,* Pres.;
Catherine M. Ward,* Secy.-Treas.; Robert J.
Denison; William H. Kling; James B. Lovelace;
Jeffrey K. Lovelace; Robert W. Lovelace; John D.
Maguire; Gail L. Neale; Stefanie Powers.
EIN: 954129163

257
The Carl Jud Foundation
P.O. Box 10485
Marina Del Rey, CA 90295

Established in 1997 in CA.
Grantmaker type: Independent foundation
Financial data (yr. ended 12/31/01): Assets,
$1,879,956 (M); expenditures, $95,978;
qualifying distributions, $93,415; giving
activities include $89,700 for 21 grants (high:
$7,500; low: $1,000).
Fields of interest: Animal welfare;
Animals/wildlife.
Limitations: Applications not accepted. Giving
primarily in CA. No grants to individuals.
Application information: Contributes only to
pre-selected organizations.
Officers: James I. Linn, Pres.; Dale L. Payne,
Secy. and C.F.O.
EIN: 954564426

258
JWS Foundation, Inc.
19280 Bainter Ave.
Los Gatos, CA 95030

Established in 1998 in CA and NV.
Donor(s): John Holton.
Grantmaker type: Independent foundation
Financial data (yr. ended 12/31/02): Assets,
$2,200,895 (M); expenditures, $338,176;
qualifying distributions, $314,681; giving
activities include $315,000 for 10 grants (high:
$250,000; low: $500).
Fields of interest: Scholarships/financial aid;
Natural resources; Housing/shelter, aging;
Housing/shelter, repairs; Foundations
(community).
Limitations: Applications not accepted. Giving
primarily in CA. No grants to individuals.
Application information: Contributes only to
pre-selected organizations.
Officers: John Holton, Chair. and Pres.; Wanda
Kownacki, V.P. and Secy.-Treas.

EIN: 680405252

259
K.L. Felicitas Foundation
(formerly Kleissner Family Foundation)
P.O. Box 37
Los Gatos, CA 95031-0037
Contact: Lisa Kleissner, Pres.
E-mail: lisa@kleissner.com

Established in 2000 in CA.
Donor(s): Karl Kleissner, Lisa Kleissner.
Grantmaker type: Independent foundation
Financial data (yr. ended 03/31/03): Assets,
$7,570,613 (M); expenditures, $126,263;
qualifying distributions, $126,263; giving
activities include $111,900 for 8 grants (high:
$35,000; low: $5,000; average:
$1,000-$100,000).
Fields of interest: Environment; Community
development.
International interests: Canada; Austria; Brazil;
India; Nepal; Sri Lanka.
Types of support: General/operating support;
Annual campaigns; Capital campaigns;
Building/renovation; Endowments; Program
development; Seed money; Research.
Limitations: Applications not accepted. Giving
primarily in CA, Europe, South America, India,
Tibet, Sri Lanka, and Canada. No grants to
individuals.
Application information: Contributes only to
pre-selected organizations.
   Board meeting date(s): Jan. 2, June 12-13, and
   Oct. 30-31
Officers: Lisa Kleissner, Pres.; Karl Kleissner,
Secy.-Treas.
Number of staff: None.
EIN: 770539366

260
The Mitchell Kapor Foundation
P.O. Box 1080
Bolinas, CA 94924 (415) 561-2182

Established in 1997 in MA.
Donor(s): Mitchell Kapor.
Grantmaker type: Independent foundation
Financial data (yr. ended 12/31/02): Assets,
$30,645,449 (M); gifts received, $4,315,241;
expenditures, $2,235,220; qualifying
distributions, $2,002,484; giving activities
include $1,760,025 for 58 grants (high:
$302,425; low: $2,000; average:
$5,000-$25,000).
Purpose and activities: The foundation's goals
are to improve human well-being and sustain
healthy ecosystems that support all life on earth.
Two of the programs available for funding are:
the Environmental Health Program, focusing
primarily on the impact of endocrine disrupting
chemicals and other fetal contaminants on
human health and on biodiversity; the Level
Playing Field Program, focusing on
understanding and changing the ways in which
attitudes, subcultures, and processes within
educational and business environments operate
in tandem to create barriers to full participation
for disenfranchised groups based on race,
ethnicity, culture, gender, sexual orientation,
and other factors.

Fields of interest: Education; Environment, pollution control; Environment, toxics; Waste management; Environment; Health care, public policy; Human services; Community development.
Limitations: No grants to individuals.
Application information:
  Initial approach: Concept letter
  Deadline(s): None
Officers: Mitchell Kapor, Chair.; Michael Lerner, C.E.O. and Pres.; Thomas Silk, Secy.; Deborah N. Mauger, C.F.O.; Amy McDevitt, Treas.
EIN: 943330604

261
Katz Family Foundation
(formerly Springhouse Foundation)
775 E. Blithedale Ave., No. 408
Mill Valley, CA 94941
Contact: Cheryl Kurz, Grants Admin.

Established in 1986 in MA.
Donor(s): Bruce R. Katz.
Grantmaker type: Independent foundation
Financial data (yr. ended 11/30/02): Assets, $4,440,613 (M); expenditures, $133,901; qualifying distributions, $130,155; giving activities include $111,970 for grants (average: $50–$10,000).
Purpose and activities: Giving for the arts, environmental conservation, and youth services.
Fields of interest: Arts; Environment; Children/youth, services.
Types of support: Program development.
Limitations: Giving primarily on the West Coast, with emphasis on northern CA. No grants to individuals.
Application information: Contributes mainly to pre-selected organizations; funding is limited. Telephone inquiries not considered. Application form not required.
  Initial approach: Brief proposal
  Deadline(s): Oct. 1
  Board meeting date(s): Oct. 15
Officer: Tracy Barbutes, Exec. Dir.
Trustees: Bruce R. Katz; Roger Katz.
Number of staff: None.
EIN: 042947276

262
The Charles and Roberta Katz Family Foundation
P.O. Box 411
Palo Alto, CA 94302-0411

Established in 1999 in WA.
Donor(s): Charles Katz, Roberta Katz.
Grantmaker type: Independent foundation
Financial data (yr. ended 12/31/00): Assets, $4,270,940 (M); expenditures, $208,763; qualifying distributions, $153,238; giving activities include $153,960 for 7 grants (high: $55,000; low: $3,960).
Fields of interest: Arts education; Theater; Education; Animals/wildlife, preservation/protection; Philanthropy/voluntarism.
Limitations: Applications not accepted.
Application information: Contributes only to pre-selected organizations.

Officers: Charles J. Katz, Jr., Pres.; Roberta Katz, 1st V.P. and Secy.-Treas.; Sarah B. Katz, V.P.; Sydney M. Katz, V.P.
EIN: 912001806

263
Keesal, Young & Logan Charitable Foundation
P.O. Box 1730
Long Beach, CA 90801-1730

Established in 1990 in CA.
Donor(s): Keesal, Young & Logan, P.C., William H. Collier, Jr., Samuel A. Keesal, Jr., J. Stephen Young, Robert H. Logan, Michael M. Gless, Peter R. Boutin, Scott T. Pratt, Terry Ross, John D. Giffin, Phillip McLeod, Neal S. Robb, Ben Suter, and employees of Keesal, Young & Logan, P.C.
Grantmaker type: Company-sponsored foundation
Financial data (yr. ended 12/31/02): Assets, $1,648 (M); gifts received, $190,778; expenditures, $187,717; qualifying distributions, $187,687; giving activities include $187,687 for 102 grants (high: $33,610; low: $75).
Purpose and activities: Giving primarily for education and youth services.
Fields of interest: Education; Aquariums; Health care; Health organizations; Athletics/sports, Olympics; Boys & girls clubs; Human services; Children/youth, services; Community development.
Limitations: Applications not accepted. Giving primarily in CA. No grants to individuals.
Application information: Contributes only to pre-selected organizations.
Officers and Directors:* Samuel A. Keesal, Jr.,* Pres.; J. Stephen Young,* V.P. and Secy.; Robert H. Logan,* V.P. and Treas.; Michael L. Armitage, V.P.; Peter R. Boutin, V.P.; E. Beazley; Lisa M. Bertain; Robert J. Bocko; J. Cohen; William H. Collier, Jr.; D. Davis; Robert B. Ericson; Michele R. Fron; S. Garret; John D. Giffin; P. Lempriere; L. Lindh; Phillip McLeod; K. Moynihan; Albert E. Peacock III; Scott T. Pratt; H. Ray; Neal S. Robb; Terry Ross; P. Schumacher; Janet M. Simmons Stemler; Robert J. Stemler; Cameron G. Stout; Ben Suter; J. Taylor; J. Walsh; G. Young.
EIN: 330458127

264
The William C. Kenney Watershed Protection Foundation
3030 Bridgeway, Ste. 204
Sausalito, CA 94965-2810

Established in 1994 in CA.
Donor(s): William C. Kenney Trust.
Grantmaker type: Independent foundation
Financial data (yr. ended 12/31/02): Assets, $3,303,396 (M); expenditures, $273,936; qualifying distributions, $109,500; giving activities include $109,500 for 7 grants (high: $50,000; low: $1,500).
Purpose and activities: Giving to environmental programs to aid in the protection of wild rivers and ecosystem restoration in the Western U.S.
Fields of interest: Environment.
Types of support: General/operating support; Emergency funds; Program development;

Technical assistance; Consulting services; Matching/challenge support.
Limitations: Giving limited to the western U.S.
Publications: Annual report (including application guidelines).
Application information: Application form not required.
  Initial approach: 1-page letter
Officers: Jim Owens, Pres.; Mary Petterson, V.P.; Humphrey Wou, Secy.; Jay P. Kenney, Treas.
Directors: Denise Fort; Kimery Wiltshire.
EIN: 943201589

265
The Michael King Family Foundation
c/o Robert Madden
12400 Wilshire Blvd., Ste. 1170
Los Angeles, CA 90025

Established in 1999 in CA.
Donor(s): Michael King.
Grantmaker type: Independent foundation
Financial data (yr. ended 12/31/02): Assets, $7,216,805 (M); expenditures, $911,837; qualifying distributions, $905,489; giving activities include $865,883 for 44 grants (high: $100,000; low: $100).
Purpose and activities: Giving primarily for human services, human rights, and health care.
Fields of interest: Arts; Environment, formal/general education; Natural resources; Health care; Rape victim services; AIDS; Diabetes; Cancer research; Gun control; Youth development, volunteer services; Youth development, services; Domestic violence; Developmentally disabled, centers & services; Homeless, human services; International human rights; Community development, women's clubs; Foundations (community); Public affairs, political organizations; African Americans/Blacks.
Types of support: General/operating support.
Limitations: Applications not accepted. Giving on a national basis, with strong emphasis on CA. No grants to individuals.
Application information: Contributes only to pre-selected organizations.
Officers: Michael King, Pres.; Robert V. Madden, Secy.
Director: Jena Fassett King.
EIN: 954773454

266
Kinnoull Foundation
c/o Deloitte & Touche
913 Blanco Cir.
Salinas, CA 93901
Application address: c/o Vernor Miles & Noble, 5 Raymond Bldgs., Gray's Inn, London WC1R 5DD, England

Established in 1968.
Grantmaker type: Independent foundation
Financial data (yr. ended 12/31/02): Assets, $5,935,357 (M); expenditures, $238,727; qualifying distributions, $208,442; giving activities include $168,000 for 14 grants (high: $50,000; low: $2,000).
Purpose and activities: Giving primarily to further the cause of prevention of cruelty to animals; some support also toward the traditional teachings of the Catholic Church.

Fields of interest: Animal welfare; Animals/wildlife, preservation/protection; Roman Catholic agencies & churches.
Limitations: Giving on a national and international basis. No grants to individuals.
Application information: Funds currently fully committed.
Officer: J.C. Vernor Miles, Chair.
Trustees: Wilfred Vernor Miles; Gloria Taviner; Paul Williams.
EIN: 946186982

267
Steven and Michele Kirsch Foundation
c/o C.F.S.V.
60 S. Market St., Ste. 1000
San Jose, CA 95113 (408) 278-2278
Contact: Connie Padre, Exec. Asst.
FAX: (408) 278-0280; E-mail: cpadre@kirschfoundation.org, questions@kirschfoundation.org; URL: http://www.kirschfoundation.org

The foundation is a supporting organization of the Silicon Valley Community Foundation.
Grantmaker type: Public charity
Purpose and activities: The foundation is actively engaged in making grants, lobbying and advocacy activities, and educating on subjects ranging from environmental issues to medical research to philanthropy. In the year ending June 30, 2002, the foundation awarded grants totaling $3,720,056.
Fields of interest: Environment.
Types of support: Grants to individuals.
Limitations: Giving primarily in the San Francisco Bay Area, CA.
Application information: See Web site for additional guidelines and proposal deadlines.
  Initial approach: E-mail
  Deadline(s): Feb. 28 and June 28 for Environmental Grants
Officers and Directors:* Steven T. Kirsch,* Chair.; Perry Olson,* Vice-Chair.; Harry J. Saal,* Vice-Chair.; Kathleen Gwynn,* Pres., C.E.O., and C.F.O.; Peter Decourcy Hero,* Secy.
Number of staff: 6 full-time professional.
EIN: 770502997

268
David L. Klein, Jr. Foundation
(formerly David L. Klein, Jr. Memorial Foundation, Inc.)
1229 Stanyan St.
San Francisco, CA 94117-7974
Contact: Janet E. Traub, V.P.
FAX: (415) 956-4444

Incorporated in 1959 in NY.
Donor(s): David L. Klein,‡ Miriam Klein,‡ Endo Laboratories, Inc.
Grantmaker type: Independent foundation
Financial data (yr. ended 12/31/02): Assets, $12,385,951 (M); expenditures, $937,862; qualifying distributions, $875,152; giving activities include $762,000 for 59 grants (high: $75,000; low: $2,000).
Purpose and activities: Improving the quality of community life through grants to improve education and preserve natural and historic resources.

Fields of interest: Historic preservation/historical societies; Arts; Education; Natural resources; Health organizations, association; Human services; Science, research; Jewish agencies & temples.
Limitations: Applications not accepted. Giving primarily in the San Francisco Bay Area, CA, and New York, NY. No grants to individuals.
Application information: Contributes only to pre-selected organizations. Grants initiated by trustees.
Officers and Trustees:* Marjorie Traub,* Pres.; Jane Barnet,* V.P.; Janet Traub,* V.P.; Saretta Barnet,* Secy.; Geoff Barnet,* Treas.; Howard Barnet, Jr.; Peter Barnet; Nancy Chirinos; Barry Traub; Jennifer Traub.
EIN: 136085432

269
Josephine K. Knowles Trust
c/o Wells Fargo Bank
P.O. Box 63954
San Francisco, CA 94163

Established in 1971.
Grantmaker type: Public charity
Financial data (yr. ended 12/31/02): Revenue, $318,244; assets, $5,943,900 (M); expenditures, $227,756; program services expenses, $192,596; giving activities include $179,684 for 3 grants (high: $80,858; low: $26,953).
Purpose and activities: The trusts exists for the sole benefit of the University of Oregon Medical School, Berkeley Humane Society, Inc., and the Rose Resnick Lighthouse for the Blind and Visually Impaired.
Fields of interest: Medical school/education; Animal welfare; Human services; Disabled.
Limitations: Applications not accepted. Giving limited to Berkeley and San Francisco, CA, and Portland, OR.
Application information: Contributes only to pre-selected organizations; Unsolicited requests for funds not considered or acknowledged.
Trustee: Wells Fargo Bank, N.A.
EIN: 946101384

270
The Kriens Family Foundation
18974 Monte Vista Dr.
Saratoga, CA 95070

Established in 1997 in CA.
Donor(s): Joan Kriens, Scott Kriens.
Grantmaker type: Independent foundation
Financial data (yr. ended 12/31/01): Assets, $2,280,860 (M); gifts received, $5,125; expenditures, $159,198; qualifying distributions, $132,875; giving activities include $132,875 for 8 grants (high: $104,800; low: $200).
Purpose and activities: Giving primarily for children's services.
Fields of interest: Aquariums; Cancer; Human services; Children/youth, services; Christian agencies & churches.
Types of support: General/operating support.
Limitations: Applications not accepted. Giving primarily in CA. No grants to individuals.
Application information: Contributes only to pre-selected organizations.
Officers: Joan Kriens, Pres.; Scott Kriens, V.P.; Scott Carter, Secy.

EIN: 770456449

271
The La Fetra Foundation
1600 E. Euclid Ave.
Berkeley, CA 94709

Established in 1992 in CA.
Donor(s): Anthony W. La Fetra, Michael W. La Fetra.
Grantmaker type: Independent foundation
Financial data (yr. ended 12/31/02): Assets, $5,787,115 (M); expenditures, $422,025; qualifying distributions, $398,291; giving activities include $392,500 for 23 grants (high: $50,000; low: $5,000).
Purpose and activities: Giving primarily for international relief and the environment.
Fields of interest: Multipurpose centers/programs; Botanical/horticulture/landscape services; International development; Foundations (public).
Limitations: Applications not accepted. Giving primarily in CA. No grants to individuals.
Application information: Contributes only to pre-selected organizations.
Officers: Suzanne La Fetra, Pres.; Anthony W. La Fetra, C.F.O.
EIN: 954380652

272
John & Maria Laffin Trust
c/o Wells Fargo Bank, N.A.
433 N. Camden Dr., Ste. 1200
Beverly Hills, CA 90210
Contact: Derrith Chan, V.P.

Established around 1989.
Grantmaker type: Independent foundation
Financial data (yr. ended 12/31/02): Assets, $4,861,162 (M); expenditures, $195,261; qualifying distributions, $155,320; giving activities include $141,000 for 31 grants (high: $12,500; low: $628).
Fields of interest: Humanities; Higher education; Animal welfare; AIDS; Medical research, institute; AIDS research; Medical research; Children/youth, services.
Types of support: General/operating support; Scholarship funds; Research.
Limitations: Giving primarily in CA. No grants to individuals.
Publications: Application guidelines.
Application information: Application form not required.
  Copies of proposal: 1
  Deadline(s): June 15
  Board meeting date(s): June 30 and Dec. 31
Trustee: Wells Fargo Bank, N.A.
EIN: 946609731

273
The Walter Lantz Foundation
4444 Lakeside Dr., Ste. 310
Burbank, CA 91505 (818) 842-1616
Contact: Edward A. Landry

Established in 1984 in CA.
Donor(s): Grace T. Lantz,‡ Walter Lantz.‡
Grantmaker type: Independent foundation

Financial data (yr. ended 11/30/02): Assets, $13,979,993 (M); expenditures, $1,635,400; qualifying distributions, $1,273,670; giving activities include $1,277,110 for grants.
Purpose and activities: Giving primarily for higher education and the arts, including art education and visual arts; support also for health organizations and social services.
Fields of interest: Arts; Higher education; Botanical gardens; Health care; Health organizations, association; Human services; Children/youth, services.
Limitations: Giving primarily in the Los Angeles, CA, area. No grants to individuals.
Application information: Application form not required.
 Initial approach: Letter
 Copies of proposal: 1
 Deadline(s): None
Trustees: Susan J. Hazard; Peggy Jackson; Edward A. Landry.
Number of staff: 1.
EIN: 953994420

274
Herbert & Gertrude Latkin Charitable Foundation
c/o Santa Barbara Bank and Trust
P.O. Box 2340
Santa Barbara, CA 93120-2340
(805) 564-6211
Contact: Janice Gibbons
Additional address: c/o John Berryhill, 1505 E. Valley Rd., Ste. B, Santa Barbara, CA 93150

Established in 1992 in CA.
Donor(s): Herbert and Gertrude Latkin Trust.
Grantmaker type: Independent foundation
Financial data (yr. ended 12/31/02): Assets, $4,832,349 (M); expenditures, $454,085; qualifying distributions, $364,412; giving activities include $355,015 for 55 grants (high: $20,000; low: $1,000; average: $1,000–$16,000).
Purpose and activities: Giving primarily to provide assistance to and promote the welfare and health of the aged, prevent cruelty to animals, provide educational scholarships for deserving students enrolled in institutions of higher learning, provide medical assistance, supplies, and equipment for persons suffering as a result of calamity or disaster, prevent child abuse, and provide assistance to the needy.
Fields of interest: Higher education; Animal welfare; Health care, clinics/centers; Health care; Health organizations, association; Abuse prevention; Food services; Food banks; Housing/shelter, homeless; Human services; YM/YWCAs & YM/YWHAs; Children/youth, services; Family services; Hospices; Aging, centers/services; Jewish federated giving programs; Disabled.
Types of support: General/operating support; Equipment; Emergency funds; Scholarship funds.
Limitations: Giving limited to Santa Barbara County, CA.
Application information: Application form required.
 Initial approach: Letter
 Copies of proposal: 1
 Deadline(s): Apr. 1 and Oct. 1
 Board meeting date(s): May and Nov.

Trustees: John Berryhill; Pacific Capital Bank, N.A.
EIN: 776070540

275
Laurel Foundation
625 S. Fair Oaks Ave., Ste. 360
South Pasadena, CA 91030 (626) 441-5188
Contact: Linda J. Blinkenberg, Dir. of Fdns.
FAX: (626) 441-3672

Established in 1995 in CA.
Donor(s): Laure W. Kastanis.
Grantmaker type: Independent foundation
Financial data (yr. ended 12/31/02): Assets, $5,009,840 (M); gifts received, $224,046; expenditures, $288,134; qualifying distributions, $260,771; giving activities include $225,000 for 8 grants (high: $60,000; low: $10,000).
Purpose and activities: Giving for protection of animals and child education programs.
Fields of interest: Education; Animal welfare; Health care; Human services; Biological sciences.
Types of support: Program development; Scholarship funds; Matching/challenge support.
Limitations: Giving primarily in CA. No grants to individuals.
Application information: Application form not required.
 Initial approach: Letter
 Copies of proposal: 1
 Deadline(s): None
 Board meeting date(s): 2 to 3 times per year
Officers and Directors:* Laure W. Kastanis,* Pres.; David Kastanis,* V.P.; Linda J. Blinkenberg,* Secy. and Dir. of Foundations; Michael P. McShane,* C.F.O.
Number of staff: 4 shared staff (shared with Whittier Family Foundations).
EIN: 954556814

276
Richard and Ruth Lavine Family Foundation
3327 Bennett Dr.
Los Angeles, CA 90068
Contact: Ruth J. Lavine, Pres.

Established in 1990 in CA.
Donor(s): Richard A. Lavine, Ruth J. Lavine.
Grantmaker type: Independent foundation
Financial data (yr. ended 06/30/02): Assets, $4,846,033 (M); expenditures, $267,504; qualifying distributions, $227,990; giving activities include $218,972 for 20 grants (high: $35,000; low: $500).
Purpose and activities: Giving primarily for education and Jewish organizations.
Fields of interest: Orchestra (symphony); Arts; Elementary/secondary education; Law school/education; Education; Animal welfare; Family planning; Arthritis; Child abuse; Human services; Federated giving programs; Jewish federated giving programs; Jewish agencies & temples.
Limitations: Giving primarily in Los Angeles, CA. No grants to individuals.
Application information: Grantmaking funds are committed for the foreseeable future. No unsolicited proposals are desired or will be acknowledged.

Officers and Directors:* Ruth J. Lavine,* Pres.; Leonard Unger,* Secy.-Treas.; Catherine L. Unger.
EIN: 954300271

277
The Lawrence Foundation
530 Wilshire Blvd., Ste. 207
Santa Monica, CA 90401 (310) 451-1567
Contact: Lori Mitchell, Exec. Dir.
E-mail: info@thelawrencefoundation.org; URL: http://www.thelawrencefoundation.org

Established in 2000 in CA.
Donor(s): Jeff Lawrence, Diane Troth.
Grantmaker type: Independent foundation
Financial data (yr. ended 12/31/02): Assets, $2,788,012 (M); gifts received, $522,000; expenditures, $418,384; qualifying distributions, $1,461,686; giving activities include $363,744 for 21 grants (low: $500; average: $500–$100,000).
Fields of interest: Education; Environment, pollution control; Environment; Health care; Human services.
Limitations: Giving primarily in CA. No grants to individuals.
Application information: Application form not required.
 Initial approach: E-mail or letter
 Copies of proposal: 1
 Deadline(s): Feb. 1 and Aug. 1
 Board meeting date(s): Feb., Mar., Aug. and Sept.
 Final notification: June and Dec.
Officer: Lori Read Mitchell, Exec. Dir.
Trustees: Jeff Lawrence; Diane Troth.
Number of staff: 1 part-time professional.
EIN: 954804431

278
Lee-Kahn Foundation
245-M Mount Hermon Rd., Ste. 402
Scotts Valley, CA 95066-4007
Contact: Sonia Lee Kahn, Pres.

Established in 2000 in CA.
Donor(s): Sonia Lee Kahn.
Grantmaker type: Independent foundation
Financial data (yr. ended 09/30/01): Assets, $49,773 (M); gifts received, $2,704; expenditures, $483,195; qualifying distributions, $453,071; giving activities include $453,196 for 31 grants (high: $97,300; low: $500).
Fields of interest: Education; Natural resources; Animal welfare.
Limitations: Giving primarily in CA. No grants to individuals.
Application information: Application form not required.
 Deadline(s): None
Officer: Sonia Lee Kahn, Pres.
EIN: 680441700

279
The Levy-Markus Foundation, Inc.
3945 Van Noord Ave.
Studio City, CA 91604-2229

Established in 1989 in OH as a result of the merger of the Shirley and Seymour Levy Family Foundation, Inc. and the Roy & Eva Marcus Foundation, Inc.

Donor(s): Mark A. Levy, Lee M. Levy, The Eva Markus Charitable Lead Trust, The Shirley Levy Charitable Lead Trust, Members of the Levy Family.

Grantmaker type: Independent foundation

Financial data (yr. ended 07/31/02): Assets, $1,670,968 (M); gifts received, $36,922; expenditures, $188,932; qualifying distributions, $181,340; giving activities include $180,000 for 4 grants (high: $65,000; low: $25,000).

Purpose and activities: Giving primarily for education, and to Jewish causes.

Fields of interest: Education; Environment, land resources; Jewish agencies & temples.

Limitations: Applications not accepted. Giving primarily in CA and NY. No grants to individuals.

Application information: Contributes only to pre-selected organizations.

Officers: Shirley H. Levy, Pres.; Mark A. Levy, V.P. and Secy.; Lee M. Levy, V.P.

EIN: 954381108

280
Liberty Hill Foundation

2121 Cloverfield Blvd., Ste. 113
Santa Monica, CA 90404 (310) 453-3611
Contact: Torie Osborn, Exec. Dir.
FAX: (310) 453-7806; E-mail: info@libertyhill.org; URL: http://www.libertyhill.org/

Established in 1976 in CA.

Grantmaker type: Public charity

Financial data (yr. ended 06/30/02): Revenue, $5,767,148; assets, $5,978,412 (M); gifts received, $5,691,213; expenditures, $5,366,907; program services expenses, $4,719,865; giving activities include $3,721,233 for 470 grants (high: $528,602; low: $100).

Purpose and activities: The foundation offers support primarily for grassroots organizations working to effect social change. Grants target those groups which lack access to government or traditional funding sources and which seek to involve and empower the people who are most affected by the uneven distribution of economic resources and political power. Grants are made through general and donor-advised funds.

Fields of interest: Environment; AIDS; AIDS research; Housing/shelter, development; Youth, services; Minorities/immigrants, centers/services; Community development; Minorities; Disabled.

Types of support: Emergency funds; Seed money.

Limitations: Giving limited to Los Angeles County, CA.

Publications: Application guidelines, Annual report, Grants list, Informational brochure, Newsletter.

Application information: Contact foundation for application cover sheet. Application form required.

Initial approach: Application (not exceeding 10 pages)

Deadline(s): June 1 for Social Entrepreneurial Fund, Apr. 1 for the Fund for Los Angeles, Sept. 1 for Seed Fund, Nov. 1 for Environmental Justice Fund; none for all others

Final notification: Mar.

Directors: Torie Osborn, Exec. Dir.; Frank Acosta; Leo Baefsky; Barbara Cohn; Larry Gertler; Frances Jemmott; Hon. Sheila Kuehl; Paula Litt; Antonio Manning; Walter N. Marks, Jr.; Sarah Pillsbury; Jaime Regalado; Anneka Scranton; Gary Stewart; Jon Wiener; and 9 additional directors.

Number of staff: 11 full-time professional; 3 full-time support; 2 part-time support.

EIN: 510181191

281
The Lipman Family Foundation, Inc.

(formerly Howard and Jean Lipman Foundation, Inc.)
188 Favonio Rd.
Portola Valley, CA 94028
Contact: Beverly S. Lipman, Pres.

Established in 1959 in NY.

Donor(s): Howard W. Lipman,‡ Jean Lipman.‡

Grantmaker type: Independent foundation

Financial data (yr. ended 06/30/02): Assets, $14,584,082 (M); gifts received, $11,549,731; expenditures, $266,593; qualifying distributions, $266,593; giving activities include $126,222 for 15 grants (high: $25,000; low: $750; average: $750–$25,000) and $136,000 for 13 in-kind gifts.

Purpose and activities: Giving primarily for art museums, scientific research, educational institutions, and conservation organizations.

Fields of interest: Arts; Higher education; Natural resources; Health care.

Types of support: Endowments; Seed money; Matching/challenge support.

Limitations: Applications not accepted. Giving primarily in CA and NY. No grants to individuals.

Application information: Contributes only to pre-selected organizations.

Officers and Directors:* Beverly S. Lipman,* Pres.; Roger Goldman,* V.P.; Lester A. Greenberg,* Secy.; Timothy E. Lipman,* Treas.; Benjamin H. Lipman.

EIN: 136066963

282
Llagas Foundation

3470 Mount Diablo Blvd., Ste. A-210
Lafayette, CA 94549
Contact: Bobbie Adams

Established in 1980 in CA.

Grantmaker type: Independent foundation

Financial data (yr. ended 06/30/02): Assets, $3,145,256 (M); expenditures, $175,968; qualifying distributions, $166,250; giving activities include $166,500 for 56 grants (high: $25,000; low: $500).

Purpose and activities: Supports the charitable interests of the directors.

Fields of interest: Museums; Higher education; Education; Environment; Zoos/zoological societies; Hospitals (general); Human services; Children/youth, services.

Limitations: Applications not accepted. Giving primarily in CA. No grants to individuals; no loans.

Application information: Contributes only to pre-selected organizations. Unsolicited requests for funds are not considered.

Board meeting date(s): Varies

Officers and Directors:* Paul Lewis Davies III,* Pres.; Pilar H. Davies,* V.P. and Secy.; Andrew E. Zeisler, Treas.; Paul L. Davies, Jr.

Number of staff: None.

EIN: 942678807

283
The J. M. Long Foundation

(formerly Long Foundation)
2700 Ygnacio Valley Rd., Ste. 172
Walnut Creek, CA 94598 (925) 935-4138
Contact: Deborah Bland, Admin.

Established in 1966.

Donor(s): Joseph M. Long,‡ Vera M. Long.

Grantmaker type: Independent foundation

Financial data (yr. ended 12/31/01): Assets, $37,254,412 (M); expenditures, $1,840,246; qualifying distributions, $1,800,881; giving activities include $1,764,600 for 150 grants (high: $250,000; low: $1,000; average: $1,000–$50,000).

Purpose and activities: Grants primarily for colleges and universities, arts and cultural organizations, youth organizations, human services, and wildlife preservation.

Fields of interest: Multipurpose centers/programs; Museums; Performing arts; Arts; Higher education; Business school/education; Medical school/education; Animals/wildlife, preservation/protection; Pharmacy/prescriptions; Health organizations, association; Youth development, centers/clubs; Youth development; Human services; Children/youth, services.

Limitations: Giving limited to CA. No grants to individuals.

Application information:

Initial approach: Letter requesting application guidelines

Copies of proposal: 1

Deadline(s): None

Board meeting date(s): Varies

Officers and Trustees:* Robert M. Long,* Pres.; W.G. Combs,* V.P.; O.D. Jones,* Secy.; Milton Long; M.J. Souyoultzis.

Number of staff: None.

EIN: 941643626

284
The Looker Foundation

P.O. Box 1475
Summerland, CA 93067
Contact: Mary M. Looker, Pres.

Established in 1995 in CA.

Donor(s): Robert Looker, Satco., Inc., Mary M. Looker.

Grantmaker type: Independent foundation

Financial data (yr. ended 12/31/02): Assets, $3,771,309 (M); gifts received, $2,286,500; expenditures, $154,682; qualifying distributions, $150,100; giving activities include $150,100 for 21 grants (high: $17,500; low: $500).

Purpose and activities: Giving primarily for children and family services, education, the arts, and the environment.

Fields of interest: Arts; Education; Natural resources; Human services; Children/youth, services; Family services.

International interests: United Kingdom; Germany.
Types of support: Capital campaigns; Building/renovation; Equipment; Land acquisition; Endowments; Emergency funds; Program development; Curriculum development; Matching/challenge support.
Limitations: Applications not accepted. Giving in the U.S., with emphasis on CA; giving also in Germany and the U.K. No grants to individuals.
Publications: Occasional report, Program policy statement.
Application information: Unsolicited requests for funds not accepted. The foundation will not solicit requests.
  Board meeting date(s): First Mon. in Nov.
Officers and Directors:* Mary M. Looker,* Pres.; Blair Looker,* Secy.; Erin C. Looker,* C.F.O.; Amy Looker; Gina Looker; Rob Looker.
Number of staff: 1 part-time professional.
EIN: 770397495

285
Lowitz Foundation
520 N. Kenter Ave.
Los Angeles, CA   90049-1949
Contact: Barry Lowitz, Treas.

Established in 1954 in CA.
Donor(s): Barry Lowitz, Joseph Lowitz.
Grantmaker type: Independent foundation
Financial data (yr. ended 06/30/02): Assets, $1,797,946 (M); expenditures, $106,962; qualifying distributions, $96,905; giving activities include $94,600 for 31 grants (high: $25,000; low: $100).
Purpose and activities: Giving for Jewish organizations, human services, and education.
Fields of interest: Music; Arts; Education; Environment; Human services; Family services; Civil rights; Jewish federated giving programs; Jewish agencies & temples.
Limitations: Applications not accepted. Giving primarily in CA, IL, and VA.
Application information: Unsolicited requests for funds not accepted.
Officers: Raymond T. Kaiser, Pres.; Linda Lowitz, Secy.; Barry Lowitz, Treas.
Trustee: John H. Rubel.
Number of staff: None.
EIN: 956048132

286
Ludwick Family Foundation
P.O. Box 1796
Glendora, CA   91740   (626) 852-0092
Contact: Deanna Monaghan, Prog. Off.
FAX: (626) 852-0776; E-mail: ludwickfndn@ludwick.org; URL: http://www.ludwick.org

Established in 1990 in CA.
Donor(s): Arthur J. Ludwick, Sarah Lynne Ludwick.
Grantmaker type: Independent foundation
Financial data (yr. ended 12/31/02): Assets, $27,864,887 (M); gifts received, $5,840,424; expenditures, $1,377,069; qualifying distributions, $1,256,703; giving activities include $648,180 for 29 grants (high: $50,000; low: $100; average: $5,000–$50,000).

Purpose and activities: The purpose of the foundation is to assist a broad array of groups working to make a positive difference.
Fields of interest: Visual arts; Museums; Performing arts; Arts; Natural resources; Environment; Animal welfare; Food services; Housing/shelter, services; Children/youth, services; Family services; Race/intergroup relations; Community development, neighborhood development.
Types of support: Building/renovation; Equipment.
Limitations: Giving on a national basis, with emphasis on CA. No support for voter registration organizations, or to schools, universities, libraries, or hospitals (unless invited). No grants to individuals, or for salaries, general operating expenses, scholarships, endowment funds, fundraising, advertising, or for capital campaigns, travel or research.
Publications: Informational brochure (including application guidelines).
Application information: Applicant invitees chosen from initial requests. Application form required.
  Initial approach: Letter of inquiry, or online initial request form (preferred)
  Copies of proposal: 1
  Deadline(s): Aug.1 and Jan. 15, initial requests due Mar. 31 and Aug. 31
  Board meeting date(s): Oct. and Feb.
  Final notification: Oct. 31 and Mar. 1, for proposals
Officers and Directors:* Sarah Lynne Ludwick,* Pres. and Mgr.; Patrick Bushman, Exec. V.P.; Erik Arthur Ludwick,* V.P. and Mgr.; Sharon L. Warner,* Secy. and Mgr.; Arthur J. Ludwick,* C.F.O. and Mgr.; Heidi Ann Ludwick,* Mgr.
Number of staff: 2 full-time professional; 1 part-time professional; 1 full-time support; 1 part-time support.
EIN: 954296315

287
The Ludwick Family Foundation
491 Santa Rita Ave.
Palo Alto, CA   94301-3944
Contact: Andrew Ludwick, C.F.O.

Established in 1997 in CA.
Donor(s): Andrew Ludwick, Worth Z. Ludwick, Jocelyn Ludwick.
Grantmaker type: Independent foundation
Financial data (yr. ended 12/31/02): Assets, $5,948,857 (M); expenditures, $474,533; qualifying distributions, $454,724; giving activities include $457,656 for grants.
Purpose and activities: Support primarily for education, health, science, medicine, and the environment in the U.S.
Fields of interest: Education; Environment; Health care; Science.
Limitations: Applications not accepted. Giving on a national basis. No grants to individuals.
Application information: Contributes only to pre-selected organizations.
  Board meeting date(s): Quarterly
Officers: Worth Z. Ludwick, C.E.O. and Pres.; Jocelyn Ludwick, Secy.; Andrew Ludwick, C.F.O.
Directors: Christopher Ludwick; Theodore Ludwick.
EIN: 770472486

288
Lund Foundation ▼
535 N. Brand Blvd., Ste. 504
Glendale, CA   91203
Contact: Patricia Patti

Established in 1973 in CA.
Donor(s): Sharon D. Lund.‡
Grantmaker type: Independent foundation
Financial data (yr. ended 12/31/01): Assets, $97,351,715 (M); expenditures, $6,313,177; qualifying distributions, $5,636,486; giving activities include $5,499,950 for 88 grants (high: $1,250,000; low: $950; average: $25,000–$125,000).
Purpose and activities: Giving primarily for youth, arts and cultural programs, animal welfare and health.
Fields of interest: Arts; Animal welfare; Health care; Learning disorders; Children, services; Developmentally disabled, centers & services.
Types of support: General/operating support; Capital campaigns; Building/renovation; Equipment; Seed money; Scholarship funds; Matching/challenge support.
Limitations: Applications not accepted. Giving primarily in AZ and CA. No grants to individuals.
Application information: Contributes only to pre-selected organizations.
  Board meeting date(s): Quarterly
Officers: Victoria D. Lund, Pres.; Robert L. Wilson, V.P. and Secy.-Treas.; Ronald Gother; Bradford D. Lund; Michelle A. Lund.
Number of staff: 1 full-time professional.
EIN: 237306460
Recent environmental and animal welfare grants:
288-1 Amanda Foundation, Beverly Hills, CA, $15,000. 2002.
288-2 Canine Companions for Independence, Oceanside, CA, $10,000. 2002.
288-3 Helen Woodward Animal Center, Rancho Santa Fe, CA, $25,000. 2002.
288-4 Rainbow Rescue, Rosamond, CA, $15,000. 2002.

289
Luster Family Foundation, Inc.
23768 Malibu Rd.
Malibu, CA   90265
Contact: Elizabeth Luster, Pres.
Additional address: c/o Starr Ranch, 5360 Lovall Valley Rd., Sonoma, CA 95476, tel.: (707) 933-9702; FAX: (707) 933-9704; E-mail: nanadogs@aol.com

Established in 1987 in CA.
Donor(s): Elizabeth Luster.
Grantmaker type: Independent foundation
Financial data (yr. ended 12/31/00): Assets, $12,576,090 (M); gifts received, $11,334; expenditures, $1,099,875; qualifying distributions, $379,441; giving activities include $187,540 for 102 grants (high: $5,000; low: $100) and $212,042 for 1 foundation-administered program.
Purpose and activities: Giving primarily for animal welfare.
Fields of interest: Natural resources; Environment; Animal welfare; Animal population control; Animals/wildlife, preservation/protection; Family planning.
Types of support: General/operating support.

Limitations: Applications not accepted. Giving primarily in the western U.S. No grants to individuals, or for political parties or media.
Application information: Contributes only to pre-selected organizations.
Officers: Elizabeth Luster, Pres.; Andrew Luster, V.P.; Amy Luster Mueller, Secy. and C.F.O.
Number of staff: 3 full-time support; 5 part-time support.
EIN: 954100318

290
Maddie's Fund ▼
(formerly The Duffield Family Foundation)
2223 Santa Clara Ave., Ste. B
Alameda, CA 94501 (510) 337-8989
Contact: Rich Avanzino, Pres.
FAX: (510) 337-8988; E-mail: info@maddies.org;
URL: http://www.maddies.org

Established in 1994 in CA.
Grantmaker type: Independent foundation
Financial data (yr. ended 08/31/01): Assets, $181,435,997 (M); gifts received, $40,314,200; expenditures, $9,999,901; qualifying distributions, $8,776,120; giving activities include $8,277,988 for 13 grants (high: $4,798,820; low: $10,000; average: $5,000–$100,000).
Purpose and activities: The fund's mission is to revolutionize the status and well being of companion animals. They are most interested in projects demonstrating the ability to build alliances and develop collaborative community-wide projects. Successful proposals will set forth comprehensive life-saving strategies that involve the participation of cooperating animal shelters, rescue groups, volunteer foster organizations, local animal control agencies, veterinarians, and others.
Fields of interest: Animal welfare.
Limitations: Giving on a national basis. No support for government funded agencies or wildlife (except dogs and cats). No grants to individuals, or for capital building projects.
Application information: Application form required.
   Initial approach: Letter
   Copies of proposal: 2
   Deadline(s): None
   Final notification: Up to 6 months from receipt of proposal
Officers and Directors:* Amy D. Zefang,* Chair.; Richard Avanzino, Pres.; Laurie E. Peek, Secy.; Cheryl D. Duffield; David A. Duffield; Michael D. Duffield; Margaret L. Taylor.
EIN: 680339626
Recent environmental and animal welfare grants:
290-1 Alabama Veterinary Medical Association, Montgomery, AL, $305,000. For dogs and cats spay/neuter project for low-income people. 2001.
290-2 Animal Friends Connection, Lodi, CA, $77,800. For spay/neuter program. 2001.
290-3 Animal Rescue Foundation, Concord, CA, $864,957. For capital project in Walnut Creek. 2001.
290-4 Best Friends Animal Sanctuary, Kanab, UT, $1,252,553. For Utah project and supplementary support for conference. 2001.
290-5 California Veterinary Medical Association, Sacramento, CA, $4,798,820.

For cat and dog spay/neuter program for low-income people. 2001.
290-6 Dane County Veterinary Medical Association, Madison, WI, $62,000. For feral cat spay/neuter project. 2001.
290-7 Doing Things for Animals, Port Washington, NY, $10,000. For No Kill Conference. 2001.
290-8 Humane Society of Austin, Austin, TX, $439,513. For community collaboration. 2001.
290-9 Humane Society of Dane County, Madison, WI, $21,000. For operating support. 2001.
290-10 Humane Society of Nevada, Sparks, NV, $10,000. For operating support. 2001.
290-11 Seattle Animal Control, Seattle, WA, $15,000. For Help the Animals Program. 2001.
290-12 Society for the Prevention of Cruelty to Animals, East Bay, Oakland, CA, $14,782. For spay/neuter building project. 2001.
290-13 University of California, School of Veterinary Medicine, Davis, CA, $406,563. For shelter medicine program. 2001.

291
John F. Maher Family Foundation
4558 Sherman Oaks Ave., Ste. E
Sherman Oaks, CA 91403-3017
Contact: John F. Maher, Pres.

Established in 1998 in CA.
Donor(s): John F. Maher.
Grantmaker type: Independent foundation
Financial data (yr. ended 06/30/02): Assets, $1,401,427 (M); expenditures, $112,052; qualifying distributions, $97,294; giving activities include $98,200 for 13 grants (high: $30,000; low: $1,000).
Fields of interest: Arts; Education; Animals/wildlife, fisheries.
Limitations: Giving on a national basis, with some emphasis on CA, VA, and the New England region.
Application information: Application form required.
   Deadline(s): None
Officers: John F. Maher, Pres.; Helen S. Maher, Secy.-Treas.
EIN: 954650932

292
Marin Community Foundation ▼
5 Hamilton Landing, Ste. 200
Novato, CA 94949 (415) 464-2500
Contact: Fred Silverman, V.P., Comm.
FAX: (415) 464-2502; E-mail: mcf@marincf.org;
URL: http://www.marincf.org

Incorporated in 1986 in CA; the Leonard and Beryl Buck Foundation, its original donor, was established in 1973 and administered by the San Francisco Foundation through 1986.
Grantmaker type: Community foundation
Financial data (yr. ended 06/30/01): Assets, $1,150,556,205 (M); gifts received, $26,377,249; expenditures, $70,171,204; giving activities include $48,939,475 for grants (high: $3,100,000; low: $100), $1,415,163 for grants to individuals (high: $3,000; low: $1,000; average: $1,000–$3,000), $170,075 for 172

employee matching gifts and $2,100,000 for 3 loans/program-related investments.
Purpose and activities: The Marin Community Foundation is a tax-exempt charity that administers private funds for public purposes. It was established in 1986 to help improve the human condition and enhance the quality of life for all residents of the community. The foundation supports a broad array of programs, projects, and services, including fund development and management for individuals and organizations who place their philanthropic funds in its care. The foundation accepts applications for funding in seven program areas: Human Needs, Community Development, Community Recognition Awards, Education and Training, Religion, Environment, and Arts.
Fields of interest: Arts; Adult education—literacy, basic skills & GED; Education; Environment; AIDS; Legal services; Employment; Housing/shelter, development; Human services; Community development; Religion; Disabled; Aging; Homeless.
Types of support: General/operating support; Continuing support; Capital campaigns; Building/renovation; Equipment; Land acquisition; Debt reduction; Emergency funds; Program development; Conferences/seminars; Seed money; Curriculum development; Scholarship funds; Research; Technical assistance; Consulting services; Program evaluation; Program-related investments/loans; Employee matching gifts; Scholarships—to individuals; Matching/challenge support.
Limitations: Giving from Buck Trust limited to Marin County, CA; other giving on a national and international basis with emphasis on the San Francisco Bay Area. No grants for planning initiatives, research, or generally for capital projects (except those meeting criteria specified in the funding guidelines). Other limitations specific to each program area are outlined in the funding guidelines.
Publications: Application guidelines, Annual report, Informational brochure (including application guidelines), Newsletter.
Application information: Application form required.
   Initial approach: Telephone for funding policies and application guidelines or refer to foundation Web site
   Copies of proposal: 3
   Deadline(s): None
   Board meeting date(s): Monthly
   Final notification: 3 months minimum
Officers and Trustees:* Faye D'Opal, J.D.,* Chair.; Sara Barnes,* Vice-Chair.; Thomas Peters, Ph.D.,* C.E.O. and Pres.; Marsha E. Bonner, V.P., Progs.; Michael Groza, V.P., Community Outreach; Sid Hartman, V.P., Finance and Admin.; Fred Silverman, V.P., Comm.; Patrick Woods, V.P., Fund Devel.; Susan Clay, Corp. Secy.; Aileen Sweeney, Cont.; Charles H. Curley; Cassandra Flipper, J.D.; Gary T. Giacomini; Nancy U. Kamei, Pharm. D.; Lois Merriweather Moore, Ed.D.; Carlos Porrata; Larry E. Rosenberger.
Number of staff: 26 full-time professional; 6 part-time professional; 6 full-time support; 1 part-time support.
EIN: 943007979
Recent environmental and animal welfare grants:

292-1 Audubon Canyon Ranch, Stinson Beach, CA, $60,000. For Habitat Protection and Restoration Program at Bolinas Lagoon and Cypress Grove nature preserves. 2002.

292-2 Audubon Canyon Ranch, Stinson Beach, CA, $15,000. For architectural and land use plan for Bolinas Lagoon Preserve. 2002.

292-3 Audubon Society, Marin, Mill Valley, CA, $20,600. 2002.

292-4 Bay Area Alliance for Sustainable Development, Oakland, CA, $10,000. For community workshops on smart growth principles and planning efforts. 2002.

292-5 Bay Institute of San Francisco, San Rafael, CA, $135,163. For long-term marsh monitoring project. 2002.

292-6 Bay Model Association, Sausalito, CA, $212,000. For environmental education programs at Bay Model, and to enhance organizational capacity. 2002.

292-7 Bolinas Community Land Trust, Bolinas, CA, $300,000. For Gibson House Project. 2002.

292-8 Bolinas Lagoon Foundation, Stinson Beach, CA, $10,721. 2002.

292-9 Center for Ecoliteracy, Berkeley, CA, $225,000. For Project STRAW, Marin-based environmental education program. 2002.

292-10 David Brower Center, San Francisco, CA, $50,000. 2002.

292-11 Destination Conservation, San Francisco, CA, $10,000. 2002.

292-12 East Shore Planning Group, Marshall, CA, $26,600. For planning grant for improved septic pollution control in Tomales Bay. 2002.

292-13 Edible Schoolyard at King Middle School, Berkeley, CA, $50,000. For general support. 2002.

292-14 Environmental Education Council of Marin (EECOM), San Rafael, CA, $120,000. To promote integrative approaches to environmental education throughout Marin County. 2002.

292-15 Environmental Education Council of Marin (EECOM), San Rafael, CA, $120,000. To promote integrative approaches to environmental education throughout Marin County. 2002.

292-16 Golden Gate National Parks Association, San Francisco, CA, $85,000. For strategic planning process for Institute at Fort Baker. 2002.

292-17 Golden Gate National Parks Association, San Francisco, CA, $75,000. For strategic planning process for Institute at Fort Baker. 2002.

292-18 Guide Dogs for the Blind, San Rafael, CA, $11,000. 2002.

292-19 Humane Society, Marin, Novato, CA, $58,280. 2002.

292-20 Land Institute, Salina, KS, $20,000. 2002.

292-21 Last Chance Committee for the Preservation of Tiburon Open Space, Tiburon, CA, $97,250. 2002.

292-22 Marin Agricultural Land Trust, Point Reyes Station, CA, $192,067. 2002.

292-23 Marin Agricultural Land Trust, Point Reyes Station, CA, $23,000. For Summer Agricultural Institute for Marin teachers to promote agricultural literacy in the schools. 2002.

292-24 Marin Baylands Advocates, Larkspur, CA, $211,877. 2002.

292-25 Marin Organic, Point Reyes Station, CA, $30,000. For program to create sustainable farming system in County through education on sustainable farming practices. 2002.

292-26 Marin, County of, San Rafael, CA, $30,000. For BEST program to enhance energy-efficient design of affordable housing in Marin County. 2002.

292-27 Marine Mammal Center, Sausalito, CA, $88,615. For development of computerized database, strategic plan for educational programming, and expansion of youth education program. 2002.

292-28 Marine Mammal Center, Sausalito, CA, $68,789. 2002.

292-29 Mendocino Land Trust, Mendocino, CA, $397,000. 2002.

292-30 Napa County Land Trust, Napa, CA, $100,000. 2002.

292-31 Natural Step, San Francisco, CA, $350,000. 2002.

292-32 Nature Conservancy, San Francisco, CA, $12,200. 2002.

292-33 Organizacion Comunitaria Functional Yendegaia, Chile, $187,500. 2002.

292-34 Rachels Network, DC, $10,000. 2002.

292-35 Ruckus Society, Berkeley, CA, $50,000. 2002.

292-36 San Rafael, City of, San Rafael, CA, $150,000. For program that identifies safe routes to schools, provides traffic safety instruction, and creates programs providing alternative transportation to schools. 2002.

292-37 Save the Redwoods League, San Francisco, CA, $180,250. 2002.

292-38 Science Interchange, San Rafael, CA, $50,000. For Teen Environmental Media Network collaboration. 2002.

292-39 Slide Ranch, Muir Beach, CA, $620,000. For Campaign to Renew Slide Ranch. 2002.

292-40 Slide Ranch, Muir Beach, CA, $12,250. 2002.

292-41 Tides Center, San Francisco, CA, $25,000. For Trash Talk, public service radio program that provides information on reducing waste and conserving resources for sustainable living. 2002.

292-42 Trips for Kids, Mill Valley, CA, $11,668. For Re-Cyclery Program. 2002.

293
Marra Foundation
388 Market St., Ste. 400
San Francisco, CA 94111-5313
(415) 623-2777
Contact: Benita Kline, Mgr.
URL: http://www.marrafoundation.org

Established in 1999 in CA.
Donor(s): Milan Momirov, Letitia Momirov.
Grantmaker type: Independent foundation
Financial data (yr. ended 12/31/02): Assets, $982,297 (M); gifts received, $1,000,000; expenditures, $248,202; qualifying distributions, $245,326; giving activities include $216,500 for 16 grants (high: $75,000; low: $2,000).
Fields of interest: Arts; Environment; Human services; Economic development; Religion.
International interests: Africa; Central America; India.

Types of support: General/operating support; Continuing support; Program development; Seed money; Matching/challenge support.
Limitations: Applications not accepted. Giving primarily in the San Francisco Bay Area, CA, with some grantmaking in India, Africa and Central America. No grants to individuals.
Application information: Contributes only to pre-selected organizations.
Officers: Letitia Momirov, Pres.; Milan Momirov, V.P. and Treas.
Number of staff: 2 shared staff (shared with UCM Philanthropic Services).
EIN: 943347337

294
Dr. Harry Z. & Ruth M. Marx Foundation
c/o McDermand & McDermand
1545 Hotel Cir. S., Ste. 180
San Diego, CA 92108

Established in 1966 as the Harry and Helen Marx Foundation.
Donor(s): Robert F. Hendrickson.‡
Grantmaker type: Independent foundation
Financial data (yr. ended 12/31/02): Assets, $1,038,257 (M); gifts received, $50,886; expenditures, $131,627; qualifying distributions, $130,717; giving activities include $130,000 for 12 grants (high: $30,000; low: $2,000).
Purpose and activities: Giving primarily for health, human services, and youth programs.
Fields of interest: Animals/wildlife; Hospitals (general); Family planning; Cancer; Alzheimer's disease; Youth development, community service clubs; Children/youth, services; Hospices; Foundations (community).
Limitations: Applications not accepted. Giving primarily in San Diego, CA. No grants to individuals.
Application information: Contributes only to pre-selected organizations.
Officers and Trustee:* Ruth M. Marx,* Pres.; Beverly R. Grant,* V.P.; Kenneth E. Finn,* Secy.-Treas.; Renee A. Neuzil.
EIN: 237044558

295
The Materials for the Future Foundation
P.O. Box 29091
San Francisco, CA 94129-0091
(415) 561-6530
Contact: Coy Smith, Pres. and Exec. Dir.

Grantmaker type: Public charity
Financial data (yr. ended 09/30/01): Revenue, $231,212; assets, $71,913 (M); gifts received, $113,927; expenditures, $451,600; program services expenses, $345,412; giving activities include $135,842 for 1 grant.
Purpose and activities: The foundation promotes the use of tree-free fibers, and aims to expand community based development in recovered materials industry.
Fields of interest: Environment, land resources; Community development.
Officers: Dave Rymec, Chair.; Coy Smith, Pres. and Exec. Dir.; Linda Christopher, Secy.; Candy Skarlatos, Treas.
EIN: 943204662

296
Alletta Morris McBean Charitable Trust
400 S. El Camino Real, Ste. 777
San Mateo, CA 94402 (650) 558-8480
Contact: Charlene Kleiner, Asst. Secy.
FAX: (605) 558-8481; E-mail:
McBeanProperties@worldnet.att.net

Established in 1986 in CA.
Donor(s): Alletta Morris McBean.‡
Grantmaker type: Independent foundation
Financial data (yr. ended 12/31/02): Assets,
$42,168,897 (M); expenditures, $3,059,117;
qualifying distributions, $2,838,056; giving
activities include $2,760,923 for 19 grants (high:
$540,000; low: $1,250; average:
$25,000–$500,000).
Purpose and activities: To enhance the quality
of life in and around Newport and Aquidneck
Island, RI.
Fields of interest: Museums; Historic
preservation/historical societies; Environment,
land resources.
Types of support: Capital campaigns;
Building/renovation; Land acquisition;
Endowments; Matching/challenge support.
Limitations: Giving primarily in RI. No grants to
individuals.
Publications: Grants list.
Application information: Application form not
required.
  Initial approach: Letter with specific project
    identified
  Copies of proposal: 6
  Deadline(s): Feb. 28 and July 31
  Board meeting date(s): May and Oct.
Officers and Trustees:* Noreen Drexel,* Chair.;
Donald Christ,* Secy.; Harriet Reed; Gladys
Szapary; John A. van Beuren.
Number of staff: 1 part-time support.
EIN: 943019660

297
McBean Family Foundation
(formerly The Atholl McBean Foundation)
400 S. El Camino Real, Ste. 777
San Mateo, CA 94402 (650) 558-8480
Contact: Henry K. Newhall, Pres., or Charlene
C. Kleiner, Secy.
FAX: (650) 558-8481; E-mail:
McBeanProperties@worldnet.att.net

Incorporated in 1955 in CA.
Donor(s): Atholl McBean,‡ Peter McBean.‡
Grantmaker type: Independent foundation
Financial data (yr. ended 12/31/02): Assets,
$12,946,983 (M); expenditures, $1,090,351;
qualifying distributions, $996,964; giving
activities include $978,500 for 27 grants (high:
$200,000; low: $5,000; average:
$10,000–$100,000).
Purpose and activities: Giving primarily for
human services and education organizations
that have already been supported by the
foundation.
Fields of interest: Arts education; Arts;
Animals/wildlife, preservation/protection;
Nursing care; AIDS research; Alzheimer's
disease research; Children/youth, services;
Homeless, human services; Christian agencies &
churches.

Types of support: General/operating support;
Continuing support; Capital campaigns;
Research.
Limitations: Applications not accepted. Giving
primarily in northern CA, with emphasis on the
San Francisco Bay Area. No grants to
individuals, or for endowment funds,
scholarships, or fellowships; no loans.
Publications: Grants list.
Application information: The foundation only
accepts applications from organizations funded
in the past or those nominated by a board
member.
  Board meeting date(s): Nov. or Dec. and as
    required
Officers and Directors:* Henry Newhall,* Pres.;
Judith McBean,* V.P.; Charlene C. Kleiner, Secy.;
Clark Nelson, C.F.O. and Treas.; Peter Folger;
Deidra S. Head; Sheila McBean Head; Natasha
Hunt; Edith McBean; Nancy McBean.
Number of staff: 1 part-time support.
EIN: 946062239

298
McBeth Foundation
23101 Lake Center Dr., Ste. 170
Lake Forest, CA 92630
Application address: 640 Pearl Ave., Laguna
Beach, CA 92651

Established in 1989 in CA.
Donor(s): Barbara Woodruff.
Grantmaker type: Operating foundation
Financial data (yr. ended 09/30/02): Assets,
$5,155,609 (M); expenditures, $366,407;
qualifying distributions, $328,280; giving
activities include $310,000 for 16 grants (high:
$50,000; low: $5,000).
Fields of interest: Television; Arts, services;
Education; Veterinary medicine; Zoos/zoological
societies; Eye research.
Limitations: Giving primarily in CA. No grants
to individuals.
Application information:
  Initial approach: Letter
Trustee: Barbara Woodruff.
EIN: 330399736

299
Wendy P. McCaw Foundation
P.O. Box 939
Santa Barbara, CA 93102-0939

Established in 1997 in CA.
Donor(s): Craig O. McCaw.
Grantmaker type: Independent foundation
Financial data (yr. ended 12/31/02): Assets,
$36,717,765 (M); expenditures, $3,516,947;
qualifying distributions, $2,575,321; giving
activities include $2,382,061 for 20 grants (high:
$819,000; low: $1,500; average:
$25,000–$400,000).
Purpose and activities: Giving primarily for the
enhancement of the environment, and the
mitigation of the effect of development and
occupancy of land by humans on the
environment; funding also for the protection of
marine mammals and for general charitable
purposes.
Fields of interest: Environment, pollution
control; Natural resources; Environment, water

resources; Animals/wildlife,
preservation/protection.
Limitations: Applications not accepted. Giving
primarily in CA. No grants to individuals.
Application information: Contributes only to
pre-selected organizations.
Officers and Director:* Wendy P. McCaw,*
Pres.; Joseph L. Cole, V.P. and Secy.; Jon Clark,
Exec. Dir.
EIN: 770469217

300
The McConnell Foundation ▼
P.O. Box 492050
Redding, CA 96049-2050 (530) 226-6200
Contact: Lee W. Salter, C.E.O. and Pres.
FAX: (530) 226-6210; E-mail:
info@mcconnellfoundation.org; URL: http://
www.mcconnellfoundation.org

Established in 1964 in CA.
Donor(s): Carl R. McConnell,‡ Leah F.
McConnell.‡
Grantmaker type: Independent foundation
Financial data (yr. ended 12/31/02): Assets,
$302,579,597 (M); expenditures, $16,753,357;
qualifying distributions, $9,192,755; giving
activities include $9,045,544 for 44 grants (high:
$3,200,000; low: $1,000; average:
$15,000–$80,000) and $147,211 for 129
employee matching gifts.
Purpose and activities: Primary interests include
the environment, environmental education,
recreation; projects that benefit the working
poor; projects that demonstrate broad based
community support, and the promotion of
voluntarism and philanthropy.
Fields of interest: Museums; Performing arts;
Historical activities; Arts; Secondary
school/education; Environment; Health care;
Recreation; Aging, centers/services; Community
development; Voluntarism promotion.
Types of support: Capital campaigns;
Building/renovation; Equipment; Scholarship
funds; Technical assistance; Employee matching
gifts; In-kind gifts; Matching/challenge support.
Limitations: Giving limited to Shasta and
Siskiyou counties, CA; and Nepal. No support
for sectarian religious purposes. No grants to
individuals, or for endowment funds, annual
fund drives, budget deficits, or purchase or
construction of buildings.
Publications: Application guidelines, Annual
report.
Application information: Application form
required.
  Initial approach: Grant application cover sheet
  Copies of proposal: 1
  Deadline(s): First Thurs. of Feb., May, Aug.,
    and Nov.
  Board meeting date(s): Feb., Mar., June, Sept.,
    and Dec.
  Final notification: Within 60 days of deadline
Officers and Directors:* Richard J. Stimpel,*
Chair.; Lee W. Salter,* C.E.O. and Pres.; John A.
Mancasola,* Exec. V.P. and Secy.; Doreeta
Domke,* Treas.; Robert P. Blankenship; William
B. Nystrom, Dir. Emeritus.
Number of staff: 6 full-time professional; 18
full-time support; 4 part-time support.
EIN: 946102700
**Recent environmental and animal welfare
grants:**

300-1 Anderson Union High School, Anderson, CA, $120,064. For construction of school/community farm facilities and equipment. 2001.

300-2 Anderson Union High School District, Anderson, CA, $15,450. For construction of Bry Walther Memorial Farm. 2001.

300-3 Conservation Fund, Oakland, CA, $11,015. For development of environmental easements. 2001.

300-4 Institute for Sustainable Communites, Redding, CA, $201,755. For Vital Signs Community Study. 2001.

300-5 Salmon River Restoration Council, Sawyers Bar, CA, $28,767. For expansion of Watershed Center. 2001.

300-6 Shasta, County of, Redding, CA, $108,334. For Water Resource Master Plan. 2001.

300-7 Turtle Bay Museums and Arboretum on the River, Redding, CA, $5,200,000. To construct pedestrian bridge. 2001.

300-8 Turtle Bay Museums and Arboretum on the River, Redding, CA, $1,000,000. For capital campaign. 2001.

300-9 Turtle Bay Museums and Arboretum on the River, Redding, CA, $125,000. For capital campaign - endowment interest. 2001.

300-10 Turtle Bay Museums and Arboretum on the River, Redding, CA, $125,000. For capital campaign - endowment interest. 2001.

301
McElvany Family Foundation
2645 Ribera Rd.
Carmel, CA 93923

Established in 1998 in CA.
Donor(s): Doreen McElvany, James W. McElvany.
Grantmaker type: Independent foundation
Financial data (yr. ended 12/31/01): Assets, $1,925,924 (M); expenditures, $130,515; qualifying distributions, $121,799; giving activities include $119,400 for 22 grants (high: $50,000; low: $500).
Purpose and activities: Giving for the environment and religion.
Fields of interest: Natural resources; Protestant agencies & churches.
Limitations: Applications not accepted. Giving primarily in CA. No grants to individuals.
Application information: Contributes only to pre-selected organizations.
Officers and Trustees:* Doreen McElvany, Pres.; Todd Bergesen,* V.P.; James W. McElvany,* Secy. and C.F.O.
EIN: 954664807

302
The Catherine L. & Robert O. McMahan Foundation
P.O. Box 221580
Carmel, CA 93922 (831) 625-6444
Contact: Ms. Neal W. McMahan, C.E.O.

Established around 1955.
Donor(s): Robert O. McMahan.‡
Grantmaker type: Independent foundation
Financial data (yr. ended 12/31/02): Assets, $8,106,547 (M); expenditures, $663,076; qualifying distributions, $617,805; giving

activities include $622,470 for 81 grants (high: $25,000; low: $1,000).
Purpose and activities: Giving primarily for health and social services, education, and youth services; support also for cultural programs and conservation and preservation.
Fields of interest: Arts; Education; Environment; Health care; Human services; Youth, services.
Types of support: General/operating support; Continuing support; Annual campaigns; Capital campaigns; Building/renovation; Equipment; Land acquisition; Endowments; Emergency funds; Program development; Conferences/seminars; Seed money; Curriculum development; Scholarship funds; Technical assistance; Consulting services; Program-related investments/loans; Matching/challenge support.
Limitations: Giving limited to Monterey County, CA. No support for public schools or religious organizations. No grants to individuals.
Publications: Application guidelines.
Application information: Application form not required.
    Initial approach: Letter requesting guidelines
    Copies of proposal: 1
    Deadline(s): Mar. 31 and Sept. 30
    Board meeting date(s): Apr. and Oct.
    Final notification: End of Apr. and Oct.
Officers and Trustees:* Ms. Neal W. McMahan,* C.E.O.; Marsha McMahan Zelus,* Secy.; Michael L. McMahan,* C.F.O.
Number of staff: None.
EIN: 946061273

303
Giles W. and Elise G. Mead Foundation
P.O. Box 2218
Napa, CA 94558
Contact: Ms. Parry Mead, V.P.
FAX: (707) 226-2164; E-mail:
meadfoundation@aol.com; URL: http://www.gileswmeadfoundation.org

Incorporated in 1961 in CA.
Donor(s): Elise G. Mead.‡
Grantmaker type: Independent foundation
Financial data (yr. ended 10/31/02): Assets, $17,991,008 (M); expenditures, $828,664; qualifying distributions, $806,561; giving activities include $758,708 for 29 grants (high: $75,000; low: $1,750).
Purpose and activities: Giving for activities likely to enhance civilization.
Fields of interest: Natural resources; Environment.
Types of support: Equipment; Land acquisition; Program development; Conferences/seminars; Seed money; Research; Matching/challenge support.
Limitations: Giving primarily in the western U.S., with emphasis on AK, northern CA, and OR. No grants to individuals, or for general operating expenses.
Publications: Annual report (including application guidelines), Biennial report.
Application information: Application form not required.
    Initial approach: Letter or FAX
    Copies of proposal: 1
    Deadline(s): None
    Board meeting date(s): Jan., June, and Oct.
    Final notification: 2 months

Officers and Directors:* Giles W. Mead, Jr.,* Pres.; Richard N. Mackay, V.P.; Parry W. Mead,* V.P.; Calder M. Mackay,* Secy.-Treas.; Stafford R. Grady; Katherine Cone Keck; Jane W. Mead.
Number of staff: 1 part-time professional.
EIN: 956040921

304
Mellam Family Foundation
P.O. Box 610091
Redwood City, CA 94061
Tel./FAX: (650) 366-6419; E-mail:
info@mellam.org; URL: http://www.mellam.org/

Established in 1987 in NY.
Donor(s): Laura M. Mellam.‡
Grantmaker type: Independent foundation
Financial data (yr. ended 12/31/02): Assets, $14,395,856 (M); expenditures, $925,177; qualifying distributions, $888,425; giving activities include $734,191 for grants.
Purpose and activities: Giving primarily for health associations.
Fields of interest: Education; Natural resources; Health care; Medical research, institute; Human services.
Limitations: Applications not accepted. Giving on a national basis, with emphasis on CA, HI, and NY. No grants to individuals.
Application information: Contributes only to pre-selected organizations.
Officers and Directors:* Marilyn Rogers,* Pres.; Tracy Rogers,* Exec. Dir.
Number of staff: 1 full-time professional.
EIN: 136894208

305
The Mental Insight Foundation
283 2nd St. E.
Sonoma, CA 95476 (707) 938-8248
Contact: Virginia Hubbell, Admin.

Established in 1996 in CA.
Donor(s): William D. Kimpton.‡
Grantmaker type: Independent foundation
Financial data (yr. ended 12/31/01): Assets, $5,149,319 (M); gifts received, $82,830; expenditures, $729,940; qualifying distributions, $707,150; giving activities include $697,960 for 6 grants (high: $230,960; low: $5,000; average: $3,500–$200,000).
Purpose and activities: Giving to the 7 following areas: (1) Mental health-specifically traditional and alternative forms of healing depression and other mental illnesses: (2) Impoverished youth-programs targeted to reintegrating children in poverty back to society; (3) Cancer support-programs with an emphasis on reducing the sense of isolation experienced by cancer patients and their families; (4) Animal preservation-focused on spay and neuter programs, shelter for domestic and wild animals, and for programs directed to changing laws that increase the protection of domestic and wild animals and humane treatment of farm animals; (5) Arts-experimental theater, experimental emerging visual arts and new media, and programs that bring art back into the classroom; (6) Environment-direct action programs targeted on global warming and the development of renewable energy; and (7)

Indigenous people-preservation of indigenous culture and life.

Fields of interest: Arts; Environment; Animal welfare; Animals/wildlife, preservation/protection; Mental health/crisis services; Cancer; Human services; Native Americans/American Indians; Economically disadvantaged.

Types of support: General/operating support; Continuing support; Equipment; Program development; Conferences/seminars; Publication; Seed money; Research.

Limitations: Applications not accepted. Giving primarily in CA, and the metropolitan New York, NY, area. No support for religious organizations. No grants to individuals, or for endowments, operating deficits, fundraising events, capital campaigns, building renovation, or emergency funds; no loans.

Application information: Unsolicited requests for funds not accepted.

Officers: David Herskovits, Pres.; Isabelle Kimpton, Secy.; Bob Bunje, Treas.

Trustees: Barry Bunshoft; Len Dell'Amico; Jennifer Catherine Egan; Graham Lawrence Kimpton; Laura Kimpton.

Number of staff: 1 part-time professional; 2 part-time support.

EIN: 943256579

306
Metropolitan Water District of Southern California Community Partnering Program

c/o Ext. Affairs Dept., Community Partnering Prog.
P.O. Box 54153
Los Angeles, CA 90054-0153 (213) 217-7262
Contact: Christel Webb; or Toni Morehead
Application address for Innovative Conservation Prog.: c/o Water Resource Procurement Section, Bill McDonnell, P.O. Box 54153, Los Angeles, CA 90054-0153, tel.: (213) 217-7693, E-mail: bmcdonnell@mwdh2o.com; Additional tel.: (213) 217-6633, (213) 217-6103; FAX: (213) 217-6500; E-mail: cwebb@mwdh2o.com; Additional E-mail: amorehead@mwdh2o.com; URL: http://www.mwdh2o.com/mwdh2o/pages/yourwater/cpp/cpp.html; http://www.mwdh2o.com/mwdh2o/pages/conserv/icp01.html

Grantmaker type: Corporate giving program
Purpose and activities: Through the Metropolitan Water District of Southern California Community Partnering Program, Metropolitan Water District supports programs designed to encourage the discussion of water quality, water conservation, and water reliability issues important to its region through research, educational collaborations at all levels, and policy forums. Support is given primarily in the six-county Los Angeles, California, area.
Fields of interest: Environment, water resources.
Types of support: Continuing support; Program development.
Limitations: Giving primarily in the six-county Los Angeles, CA, area: giving also to statewide, regional, and national organizations. No grants for legal, lobbying, or consulting fees, equipment, office space, or travel or transportation.

Application information: An application form is available online. Multi-year funding is not automatic. Organizations receiving Innovative Conservation Program grants are asked to provide a final report. A contributions committee reviews all requests and forwards proposals to the appropriate Metropolitan Water District member agency. Application form required.
Initial approach: Complete online application form and mail proposal to headquarters for Community Partnering support; download application form and mail application form and proposal to headquarters for Innovative Conservation Program
Copies of proposal: 1
Deadline(s): Jan. 31

307
The Middleton Foundation

c/o Stenson Financial Corp.
700 Larkspur Landing, No. 105
Larkspur, CA 94939-1715

Established in 1990 in CA.
Donor(s): Fred A. Middleton, Carole Middleton.
Grantmaker type: Independent foundation
Financial data (yr. ended 12/31/02): Assets, $3,711,142 (M); gifts received, $381,000; expenditures, $261,236; qualifying distributions, $247,394; giving activities include $230,855 for 25 grants (high: $75,000; low: $60).
Purpose and activities: Giving for education and human services.
Fields of interest: Elementary/secondary education; Scholarships/financial aid; Animal welfare; Hospitals (general).
Limitations: Applications not accepted. Giving primarily in CA. No grants to individuals.
Application information: Contributes only to pre-selected organizations.
Officers: Fred A. Middleton, C.E.O.; Robert T. Stenson, Secy.; Carole Middleton, C.F.O.
EIN: 943117882

308
Margaret Mary & Owens Miller Charitable Trust

5150 E. Pacific Coast Hwy., No. 490
Long Beach, CA 90804 (562) 597-8186
Contact: Owens O. Miller, Tr.

Established in 1955 in CA.
Donor(s): W. Owens Miller.
Grantmaker type: Independent foundation
Financial data (yr. ended 07/31/02): Assets, $1,104,944 (M); gifts received, $45,000; expenditures, $402,152; qualifying distributions, $391,800; giving activities include $391,800 for 23 grants (high: $320,000; low: $100).
Purpose and activities: Giving primarily for secondary education.
Fields of interest: Arts; Education; Environment, land resources; Animals/wildlife; Health care, clinics/centers; Health organizations, association; Food distribution, groceries on wheels; Human services; Roman Catholic agencies & churches.
Limitations: Giving primarily in CA.
Application information: Application form not required.
Initial approach: Letter

Deadline(s): None
Trustees: Margaret Mary Miller; O'Malley M. Miller; Owens O. Miller.
Number of staff: None.
EIN: 956095785

309
The Mirada Habitat Foundation

1 Mirada Cir.
Rancho Mirage, CA 92270

Established in 2001 in CA.
Donor(s): MCO Properties, Inc.
Grantmaker type: Independent foundation
Financial data (yr. ended 12/31/02): Assets, $145,196 (M); gifts received, $100,181; expenditures, $116,815; qualifying distributions, $116,815; giving activities include $102,157 for 3 grants (high: $100,000; low: $350).
Fields of interest: Animals/wildlife, research.
Limitations: Applications not accepted. Giving primarily in CA. No grants to individuals.
Application information: Contributes only to pre-selected organizations.
Officers: Jay Lerner, Pres.; Charles Strother, V.P.; David Suson, Secy. and C.F.O.
EIN: 330965642

310
Mitsubishi Motors North America, Inc. Corporate Giving Progam

(formerly Mitsubishi Motor Sales of America, Inc. Corporate Giving Program)
6400 Katella Ave.
Cypress, CA 90630 (714) 372-6000
Contact: Stephanie Rico, Corp. Rels. Specialist
URL: http://www.mitsubishicars.com/company/corporate_responsibility.html

Grantmaker type: Corporate giving program
Purpose and activities: Mitsubishi makes charitable contributions to nonprofit organizations involved with the environment, automotive safety, and workplace diversity. Support is given on a national and international basis.
Fields of interest: Environment; Safety, automotive safety; Civil rights, equal rights.
International interests: Canada; Caribbean; Mexico.
Types of support: General/operating support; Seed money; Employee volunteer services; Public relations services; In-kind gifts.
Limitations: Giving on a national and international basis, including in Canada, the Caribbean, and Mexico.
Application information: The Corporate Relations Department handles giving. The company has a staff that only handles contributions. Application form not required.
Initial approach: Proposal to headquarters
Number of staff: 1.

311
MLB Foundation, Inc.

1205 Pacific Ave., Ste. 203
Santa Cruz, CA 95060

Established in 1993 in NJ.
Donor(s): David W. Mills.

Grantmaker type: Independent foundation
Financial data (yr. ended 11/30/02): Assets, $11,680 (M); gifts received, $225,000; expenditures, $224,053; qualifying distributions, $224,025; giving activities include $224,000 for 16 grants (high: $163,000; low: $1,000).
Purpose and activities: Giving primarily for wildlife and natural resources conservation.
Fields of interest: Arts; Education; Animal welfare; Animals/wildlife, preservation/protection; Arms control; Human services; Religion.
Limitations: Giving on a national basis. No grants to individuals.
Officers: Stephanie Lynn, Pres.; David W. Mills, V.P. and Treas.; Elizabeth Boggs, V.P.; Jennifer Lynn Boggs, V.P.
EIN: 223268690

312
The Mohn Family Foundation
c/o Lexington Financial Mgmt., LLC
9350 Wilshire Blvd., Ste. 250
Beverly Hills, CA 90212

Established in 2001 in CA.
Donor(s): Jarl Mohn, Pamela Mohn.
Grantmaker type: Independent foundation
Financial data (yr. ended 12/31/01): Assets, $10,093,805 (M); gifts received, $10,351,620; expenditures, $366,020; qualifying distributions, $365,334; giving activities include $366,000 for 22 grants (high: $100,000; low: $1,000).
Fields of interest: Libraries (public); Natural resources; Human services; Civil rights; Philanthropy/voluntarism.
International interests: Canada.
Limitations: Giving on a national basis, with some emphasis on CA, KY, and NY.
Officers: Jarl Mohl, Pres.; Pamela Mohn, Secy.-Treas.
EIN: 954830816

313
Moore Family Foundation ▼
P.O. Box 3099
Los Altos, CA 94024-0099

Established in 1986.
Donor(s): Betty I. Moore, Gordon E. Moore.
Grantmaker type: Independent foundation
Financial data (yr. ended 09/30/02): Assets, $33,479,091 (M); expenditures, $3,804,469; qualifying distributions, $3,621,822; giving activities include $3,571,936 for 39 grants (high: $2,125,000; low: $3,000; average: $10,000–$50,000).
Purpose and activities: Giving primarily for higher education, conservation, and science. Some giving also for social services.
Fields of interest: Higher education; Natural resources; Human services; Engineering/technology; Science.
Types of support: General/operating support; Annual campaigns; Capital campaigns; Building/renovation; Equipment; Program development.
Limitations: Applications not accepted. Giving primarily in CA. No grants to individuals.
Application information: Contributes only to pre-selected organizations.
Board meeting date(s): As needed

Trustees: Betty I. Moore; Gordon E. Moore; Kenneth G. Moore; Steven E. Moore.
Number of staff: 1 full-time professional.
EIN: 943024440
Recent environmental and animal welfare grants:
313-1 Amazon Conservation Team, Arlington, VA, $50,000. For Biocultural Conservation in Xingu Indigenous Reserve in Brazilian Amazon. 2002.
313-2 Coevolution Institute, San Francisco, CA, $20,000. For North American Pollinator Protection Campaign. 2002.
313-3 Conservation International, DC, $2,125,000. For Center for Applied Biodiversity Science. 2002.
313-4 Coyote Point Museum Association, San Mateo, CA, $20,000. For Aviary Netting Replacement Project. 2002.
313-5 EARTH University Foundation, Atlanta, GA, $136,620. For scholarships for education in Agricultural Sciences and Natural Resources, contributing to sustainable development of Humid Tropics. 2002.
313-6 Ecotrust, Portland, Oregon, $150,000. For information services program. 2002.
313-7 Environmental Volunteers, Palo Alto, CA, $15,000. For Anniversary Campaign and general support. 2002.
313-8 Global Forest Science, Banff, Canada, $50,000. For Westslope Cutthroat Trout Initiative and Indigenous Fish Conservation Project. 2002.
313-9 Idea Wild, Fort Collins, CO, $25,000. To acquire and ship equipment and supplies to conservation biologists' projects and educators in Latin America, Philippines, Madagascar, and West Africa. 2002.
313-10 International Wilderness Leadership (WILD) Foundation, Ojai, CA, $10,000. For Cheetah Conservation Fund and general operating support. 2002.
313-11 Marine Conservation Biology Institute, Redmond, WA, $50,000. For work and research to establish Marine Protected Areas. 2002.
313-12 Ocean Conservancy, DC, $50,000. For Fishery Management and Ocean Conservation projects in California, Oregon, and Washington. 2002.
313-13 Rare Species Conservatory Foundation, Loxahatchee, FL, $50,000. For Dominica Project's public environmental education program. 2002.
313-14 Seacology, Berkeley, CA, $50,000. For Islands of Polynesia Project, to protect rainforest and establish marine park. 2002.
313-15 Sinapu, Boulder, CO, $10,000. For general operating support. 2002.
313-16 Tides Center, San Francisco, CA, $10,000. For Smith River Estuary Enhancement Project in Graton, CA. 2002.
313-17 University of California, Berkeley, CA, $35,000. For Gump South Pacific Biological Research Station facilities improvement and development. 2002.
313-18 University of California at San Diego Foundation, Scripps Institution of Oceanography, La Jolla, CA, $105,716. For Fish Larval Dispersal studies in Gulf of California and Mediterranean Sea, and studies' implications for conservation. 2002.

313-19 University of California at San Diego Foundation, Scripps Institution of Oceanography, La Jolla, CA, $10,000. For annual Marine Biodiversity Conference at center for Marine Biodiversity and Conservation. 2002.
313-20 University of California at Santa Cruz Foundation, Santa Cruz, CA, $50,000. For Institute of Marine Science and Center for Ocean Health building fund. 2002.
313-21 University of California Press, Berkeley, CA, $50,000. For Ecology and Environmental publishing areas. 2002.
313-22 Wild Salmon Center, Portland, Oregon, $50,000. For Wild Fish Sanctuary Project in Kamchatka, Russia. 2002.

314
Gordon and Betty Moore Foundation
The Presidio
P.O. Box 29910
San Francisco, CA 94129-0910
(415) 561-7700
E-mail: info@moore.org; URL: http://www.moore.org/

Established in 2000 in CA.
Donor(s): Gordon E. Moore, Betty I. Moore.
Grantmaker type: Independent foundation
Financial data (yr. ended 12/31/02): Assets, $93,322,923 (M); expenditures, $109,513,519; qualifying distributions, $106,860,801; giving activities include $88,926,220 for 66 grants (high: $25,087,000; low: $285) and $617,760 for 175 employee matching gifts.
Purpose and activities: The foundation supports four major programs areas: education, scientific research, the environment, and select San Francisco Bay Area projects. The foundation strives to fund projects that will further it's mission— projects chosen through careful research, projects promising significant measurable results.
Fields of interest: Higher education; Environment; Science.
Types of support: Employee matching gifts.
Limitations: Applications not accepted. Giving on a worldwide basis, with some focus on the San Francisco, CA, area for selected projects. No grants to individuals.
Application information: Contributes only to pre-selected organizations.
Officers and Trustees:* Gordon E. Moore,* Chair, Secy., and C.F.O.; Lewis W. Coleman,* Pres.; Betty I. Moore; Kenneth G. Moore; Steven E. Moore; Kenneth F. Siebel.
EIN: 943397785
Recent environmental and animal welfare grants:
314-1 Amazon Conservation Association, DC, $649,000. For implementation of conservation concession in Peru. 2001.
314-2 Amazon Conservation Team, Arlington, VA, $407,100. For mapping in Brazil and Suriname to help protect biological diversity. 2001.
314-3 Audubon Canyon Ranch, Stinson Beach, CA, $20,000. For environmental education programs. 2001.
314-4 California Academy of Sciences, San Francisco, CA, $50,000. For exhibition, Anglers All: Humanity in Midstream. 2001.

314-5 Conservation International, DC, $12,000,000. For Global Conservation Fund, Centers for Biodiversity Conservation, and Scientific Field Stations. 2001.

314-6 Consultative Group on Biological Diversity, San Francisco, CA, $35,000. For general operating support. 2001.

314-7 Ecotrust, Portland, Oregon, $25,000. For watershed conservation strategy in Copper River ecosystem. 2001.

314-8 Field Museum of Natural History, Chicago, IL, $500,000. For protection efforts in Peru's Cordillera Azul National Park. 2001.

314-9 Global Response, Boulder, CO, $50,000. For annual international letter writing campaigns to help local communities and indigenous people preserve biological diversity in threatened ecosystems of global importance. 2001.

314-10 Henrys Fork Foundation, Ashton, ID, $50,000. For general operating support. 2001.

314-11 Nature Conservancy, Arlington, VA, $200,000. For management and organizational changes behind Conservation by Design. 2001.

314-12 Nature Conservancy, Arlington, VA, $35,000. To develop feasibility study and implementation plan for research station on Palmyra. 2001.

314-13 Peninsula Open Space Trust, Menlo Park, CA, $25,000,000. For land conservation and stewardship in San Mateo County, California. 2001.

314-14 Peregrine Fund, Boise, ID, $100,000. For scientific studies of vulture crisis in South Asia. 2001.

314-15 Rocky Mountain Institute, Snowmass, CO, $100,000. For assessment of U.S. energy policy. 2001.

314-16 University of California, Berkeley, CA, $600,000. For studies regarding range and spread of Sudden Oak Death Syndrome. 2001.

314-17 University of California, Davis, CA, $400,000. For studies regarding range and spread of Sudden Oak Death Syndrome. 2001.

314-18 Wild Salmon Center, Portland, Oregon, $475,000. To establish salmon refuges and monitoring and research biostations on Kamchatka, Russia. 2001.

314-19 Wild Salmon Center, Portland, Oregon, $75,000. To complete publication of Pacific Rim-wide survey of status of wild salmon, and to co-sponsor symposium and press conference to announce survey findings. 2001.

315
James and Rebecca Morgan Family Foundation
P.O. Box 1742
Los Altos, CA 94023-1742
Contact: Prog. Mgr.

Established in 1993 in CA.
Donor(s): James C. Morgan, Rebecca Q. Morgan.
Grantmaker type: Independent foundation
Financial data (yr. ended 12/31/01): Assets, $44,229,541 (M); gifts received, $70,000; expenditures, $2,510,099; qualifying distributions, $2,106,586; giving activities

include $2,067,951 for 4 grants (high: $1,957,951; low: $20,000; average: $20,000–$50,000).
Purpose and activities: The foundation focuses its giving on youth, education, the environment, and programs that strengthen community through collaboration and/or development of nonprofit leadership. Programs that maximize the potential of an organization and the individuals it serves are of particular interest. The majority of funding is in Santa Clara County and San Mateo County, California.
Fields of interest: Historic preservation/historical societies; Arts; Education; Environment; Youth development; Foundations (community); Leadership development.
Types of support: General/operating support; Annual campaigns; Capital campaigns; Building/renovation; Endowments; Program development; Seed money; Scholarship funds; Program evaluation; Matching/challenge support.
Limitations: Giving primarily in Santa Clara and San Mateo counties, CA. No grants to individuals.
Publications: Application guidelines, Grants list.
Application information: Unsolicited applications not accepted. Application form not required.
　Initial approach: Letter
　Copies of proposal: 1
　Deadline(s): None
Officers and Directors:* James C. Morgan,* Chair. and Treas.; Rebecca Q. Morgan,* Pres. and Secy.
Number of staff: 1 part-time professional.
EIN: 943187468

316
Morris Family Foundation
P.O. Box 282
Kentfield, CA 94914
Contact: Mary Willis, Exec. Dir.
E-mail: mff41@home.com

Established in 1997 in NV.
Grantmaker type: Independent foundation
Financial data (yr. ended 12/31/01): Assets, $2,515,150 (M); expenditures, $315,102; qualifying distributions, $248,779; giving activities include $185,205 for 16 grants (high: $47,500; low: $300) and $600 for 1 grant to an individual.
Purpose and activities: Giving for children and youth, the environment and globalization, and economic and social justice.
Fields of interest: Environment; Youth development; Children/youth, services.
Types of support: General/operating support; Continuing support; Capital campaigns; Building/renovation; Equipment; Land acquisition; Conferences/seminars; Seed money; Technical assistance; Program evaluation; Program-related investments/loans; Matching/challenge support.
Limitations: Applications not accepted.
Officer: Mary Willis, Exec. Dir.
Number of staff: 1 full-time professional.
EIN: 943287289

317
Peter A. Morton Foundation, Inc.
510 N. Robertson Blvd.
Los Angeles, CA 90048

Established in 1999 in DE.
Donor(s): Peter Morton.
Grantmaker type: Independent foundation
Financial data (yr. ended 12/31/02): Assets, $3,596 (M); gifts received, $769,189; expenditures, $768,679; qualifying distributions, $768,678; giving activities include $765,820 for 24 grants (high: $275,000; low: $200).
Purpose and activities: Giving primarily for environmental conservation, education, and medical research.
Fields of interest: Education; Natural resources; Environment; Health organizations, association; Medical research, institute; Cancer research; Human services; Children, services; Civil rights; Jewish federated giving programs.
Limitations: Applications not accepted. Giving primarily in Los Angeles, CA and New York, NY. No grants to individuals.
Application information: Contributes only to pre-selected organizations.
Officers: Peter Morton, Pres.; Brian Ogaz, Secy.
EIN: 954687071

318
Mildred E. & Harvey S. Mudd Foundation
11726 San Vicente Blvd., Ste. 625
Los Angeles, CA 90049

Grantmaker type: Independent foundation
Financial data (yr. ended 05/31/02): Assets, $18,938,861 (M); expenditures, $1,104,770; qualifying distributions, $957,646; giving activities include $918,000 for 6 grants (high: $500,000; low: $3,000).
Purpose and activities: Giving primarily for education, conservation, and museums.
Fields of interest: Museums; Education; Natural resources.
Types of support: General/operating support.
Limitations: Applications not accepted. Giving primarily in CA. No grants to individuals.
Application information: Contributes only to pre-selected organizations.
Trustees: Cynthia S. Connolly; Caryll S. Mingst; Norman F. Sprague III; William Stinehart, Jr.
EIN: 956021276

319
Namaste International Foundation
1657 Andorre Glen
Escondido, CA 92029

Established in 1999 in CA.
Donor(s): Jewel Kilcher, Lenedra Carroll.
Grantmaker type: Independent foundation
Financial data (yr. ended 11/30/01): Assets, $9,485 (M); expenditures, $230,168; qualifying distributions, $227,561; giving activities include $225,000 for 1 grant.
Purpose and activities: Giving primarily for the environment.
Fields of interest: Environment, water resources; Environment; Youth, services; Federated giving programs; Political science.
Limitations: Applications not accepted. Giving primarily in CA. No grants to individuals.

Application information: Contributes only to pre-selected organizations.
Officers: Lenedra Carrol, Chair. and Pres.; Colleen Anderson, Secy.-Treas.
EIN: 916498814

320
Naturganic Foundation

(formerly Garden of Eatin' Foundation)
5300 Santa Monica Blvd., Ste. B-14
Los Angeles, CA 90029
Contact: Al H. Jacobson, Pres.

Established in 1990 in CA.
Donor(s): Al H. Jacobson.
Grantmaker type: Independent foundation
Financial data (yr. ended 11/30/02): Assets, $93,771 (M); expenditures, $101,570; qualifying distributions, $100,593; giving activities include $97,500 for 4 grants (high: $40,000; low: $10,000).
Purpose and activities: Primary interests are environment and ecology, vegetarianism, and spirituality.
Fields of interest: Health sciences school/education; Education; Environment, plant conservation; Animal welfare; Agriculture; Nutrition.
Limitations: Giving primarily in CA.
Officers: Al H. Jacobson, Pres.; Ariel Rivera, Secy.
EIN: 954301232

321
Nissan North America, Inc. Corporate Giving Program

P.O. Box 191
Gardena, CA 90248-0191 (310) 532-3111
Contact: Kathy Bates, Community Rels. Coord.

Grantmaker type: Corporate giving program
Purpose and activities: As a complement to its foundation, Nissan also makes charitable contributions to nonprofit organizations directly. Support is given on a national basis.
Fields of interest: Arts; Education; Environment; Safety, automotive safety; Youth development; Community development; Science; General charitable giving.
Types of support: General/operating support; Employee volunteer services; Employee matching gifts.
Limitations: Giving on a national basis. No support for fraternal or veterans' organizations. No grants to individuals.
Application information: The Community Relations and Public Affairs Department handles giving. Application form not required.
Initial approach: Proposal to headquarters
Copies of proposal: 1
Deadline(s): None
Final notification: Following review

322
Andrew Norman Foundation

10960 Wilshire Blvd., Ste. 1111
Los Angeles, CA 90024 (310) 478-1213
Contact: Dan Olincy, Secy.-Treas.

Incorporated in 1958 in CA.

Donor(s): Andrew Norman.‡
Grantmaker type: Independent foundation
Financial data (yr. ended 06/30/02): Assets, $2,057,796 (M); expenditures, $225,436; qualifying distributions, $116,128; giving activities include $91,475 for 4 grants (high: $73,250; low: $225).
Purpose and activities: Emphasis on seed money for the environment, justice and the legal system, and the arts and humanities.
Fields of interest: Humanities; Arts; Environment; Crime/law enforcement.
Types of support: Program development; Seed money; Program-related investments/loans.
Limitations: Applications not accepted. Giving primarily in CA, with emphasis on the Los Angeles area. No grants to individuals, or for endowment funds, scholarships, or fellowships.
Application information: Contributes only to pre-selected organizations.
Board meeting date(s): May and as required
Officer and Trustee:* Dan Olincy,* Secy.-Treas.
Number of staff: None.
EIN: 953433781

323
Oak Tree Charitable Foundation

285 W. Huntington Dr.
Arcadia, CA 91066-6014
Contact: Sherwood C. Chillingworth, Exec. V.P., or Sue Temple, Corp. Admin.

Established in 1994 in CA.
Donor(s): Oak Tree Racing Assn.
Grantmaker type: Independent foundation
Financial data (yr. ended 05/31/02): Assets, $5,249,665 (M); expenditures, $343,185; qualifying distributions, $306,100; giving activities include $308,328 for grants.
Purpose and activities: Giving primarily for equestrian activities, health care, and children and youth services.
Fields of interest: Arts; Higher education; Environment; Animals/wildlife; Health care; Health organizations, association; Athletics/sports, equestrianism; Boys & girls clubs; Human services; Children/youth, services.
Limitations: Giving primarily in San Gabriel Valley, CA, and to thoroughbred horse racing charities. No grants to individuals.
Application information: Application form required.
Initial approach: Proposal
Copies of proposal: 1
Deadline(s): Mar. 31
Board meeting date(s): Feb., Aug. and Nov.
Final notification: July 31
Officers and Directors:* Jack K. Robbins,* Pres.; Sherwood C. Chillingworth,* Exec. V.P.; William T. Pascoe III,* V.P. and Secy.-Treas.; Rick M. Arthur,* V.P.; John H. Barr,* V.P.; Thomas R. Capehart,* V.P.
EIN: 954506950

324
Oracle Corporation Contributions Program

c/o Oracle Giving
500 Oracle Pkwy., M.S. 50P11
Redwood City, CA 94065 (650) 506-7000
Contact: Rosalie Gann, Dir., Giving and Volunteers
Application address for conference center donations: c/o Oracle Corp. Giving/Conference Center, 500 Oracle Pkwy., M.S. 50P11, Redwood City, CA 94065; E-mail for volunteer program: volunteers_ww@oracle.com; URL: http://www.oracle.com/corporate/community/index.html

Grantmaker type: Corporate giving program
Purpose and activities: Oracle makes charitable contributions to nonprofit organizations involved with K-12 education, open spaces, environmental education, endangered species protection, cancer research, AIDS research, and neuroscience research. Support is given on a national and international basis.
Fields of interest: Elementary/secondary education; Environment, beautification programs; Environmental education; Animals/wildlife, endangered species; Cancer research; AIDS research; Neuroscience research.
Types of support: General/operating support; Employee volunteer services; Use of facilities.
Limitations: Giving on a national and international basis in areas of company operations. No grants for fundraising, dinners, sporting events, or marketing brochures; no loans.
Application information: An application form is required for general operating support; application form available online. A separate application form is required for conference center donations; application form available online. Proposals should be no longer than 5 pages in length. Multi-year funding is not automatic. Support is limited to 3 years in length.
Initial approach: Download application form and mail proposal and application form to headquarters for general operating support; download application form for conference center donations; letter of inquiry or E-mail to headquarters for volunteer program
Deadline(s): Postmarked by June 1 and Dec. 1 for general operating support
Final notification: Late Aug. and late Feb. for general operating support

325
Bernard Osher Foundation ▼

909 Montgomery St., Ste. 300
San Francisco, CA 94133 (415) 861-5587
Contact: Patricia Tracy-Nagle, Sr. V.P.
FAX: (415) 677-5868; E-mail: nagle@osherfoundation.com

Established in 1977 in CA.
Donor(s): Bernard A. Osher.
Grantmaker type: Independent foundation
Financial data (yr. ended 12/31/01): Assets, $55,902,955 (M); expenditures, $19,059,476; qualifying distributions, $18,620,660; giving activities include $18,531,762 for 234 grants (high: $4,250,000; low: $500; average: $2,000–$100,000).

Purpose and activities: Giving primarily for the arts and humanities, including the fine and performing arts, education, especially higher education, and environmental education.
Fields of interest: Visual arts; Museums; Performing arts; Dance; Theater; Music; Humanities; Arts; Higher education; Education; Environmental education.
Types of support: General/operating support; Capital campaigns; Program development.
Limitations: Giving limited to Alameda and San Francisco counties, CA. No grants to individuals.
Publications: Application guidelines, Informational brochure.
Application information: Application form not required.
  Initial approach: Letter
  Copies of proposal: 1
  Deadline(s): None
  Board meeting date(s): 6 times per year
Officers and Directors:* Barbro Osher,* Pres.; Patricia Tracy-Nagle, Sr. V.P. and Secy.; Stephen Mark Dobbs, Exec. V.P.; Bernard A. Osher, Treas.; David Agger; Frederick Balderston; Judith E. Ciani; Phyllis Cook; Robert Friend; Ron Kaufman; Alfred Wilsey.
Number of staff: 1 full-time professional; 1 part-time professional.
EIN: 942506257
Recent environmental and animal welfare grants:
325-1 Bay Area Ridge Trail Council, San Francisco, CA, $15,000. 2001.
325-2 California Academy of Sciences, San Francisco, CA, $100,000. 2001.
325-3 Environmental Traveling Companions, San Francisco, CA, $25,000. 2001.
325-4 Greenbelt Alliance, San Francisco, CA, $20,000. 2001.
325-5 Marine Mammal Center, Sausalito, CA, $10,000. 2001.
325-6 Nature Conservancy, San Francisco, CA, $25,000. 2001.
325-7 Point Reyes Bird Observatory, Stinson Beach, CA, $75,000. 2001.
325-8 Point Reyes National Seashore Association, Point Reyes Station, CA, $105,691. 2001.
325-9 San Francisco Zoological Society, San Francisco, CA, $150,000. 2001.
325-10 Yosemite National Institutes, Sausalito, CA, $10,000. 2001.

326
Otter Cove Foundation
1803 6th St., Ste. B
Berkeley, CA 94720
Contact: James P. Read, Jr., Pres.

Established in 1997 in CA.
Donor(s): James P. Read, Jr.
Grantmaker type: Independent foundation
Financial data (yr. ended 12/31/00): Assets, $1,686,731 (M); gifts received, $1,000,099; expenditures, $467,494; qualifying distributions, $456,000; giving activities include $456,000 for 4 grants (high: $250,000; low: $50,000).
Purpose and activities: Giving to provide a more secure future for the well-being of humans and animals.
Fields of interest: Museums; Education; Natural resources; Environment, water resources.

Limitations: Applications not accepted. Giving primarily in CA and WA. No grants to individuals.
Application information: Contributes only to pre-selected organizations.
Officers: James P. Read, Jr., Pres.; Mark Plumley, Secy. and C.F.O.
Directors: Megan G. Lindberg; Gilan M. Reynolds.
EIN: 943287969

327
June G. Outhwaite Charitable Trust
P.O. Box 5159
Santa Barbara, CA 93150 (805) 969-1182
Contact: Marni Cooney

Established in 1998 in CA.
Donor(s): The 1994 June G. Outhwaite Revocable Trust.
Grantmaker type: Independent foundation
Financial data (yr. ended 12/31/02): Assets, $21,083,138 (M); gifts received, $6,055,982; expenditures, $1,011,117; qualifying distributions, $671,200; giving activities include $618,800 for 37 grants (high: $50,000; low: $3,000).
Fields of interest: Museums (marine/maritime); Zoos/zoological societies; Cancer; Medical research; Family services.
Types of support: General/operating support.
Limitations: Giving primarily in Santa Barbara, CA.
Application information:
  Initial approach: Letter
  Deadline(s): June 30
Trustees: C. Michael Cooney; Kent L. Englert; John S. Poucher.
EIN: 776154307

328
Pacific Life Foundation
(formerly Pacific Mutual Charitable Foundation)
700 Newport Center Dr.
Newport Beach, CA 92660-6397
(949) 219-3787
Contact: Robert G. Haskell, Pres.
FAX: (949) 219-7614; URL: http://www.pacificlife.com

Established in 1984 in CA.
Donor(s): Pacific Life Insurance Co., Pacific Mutual Holding Co.
Grantmaker type: Company-sponsored foundation
Financial data (yr. ended 12/31/02): Assets, $30,994,633 (M); gifts received, $74,630; expenditures, $2,892,128; qualifying distributions, $2,879,730; giving activities include $2,879,730 for 337 grants (high: $292,580; low: $1,000; average: $1,000–$20,000).
Purpose and activities: The foundation's grantmaking process focuses on seeking effective partnerships to address community needs.
Fields of interest: Performing arts; Arts; Education; Environment; Health care; Human services; Community development.
Types of support: Capital campaigns; Program development; Employee matching gifts; In-kind gifts.

Limitations: Giving primarily in areas of company operations in southern CA and the greater Phoenix, AZ, area. No support for political organizations, professional associations, veterans', labor, or fraternal organizations, athletic or social clubs, or sectarian or denominational religious groups, except for programs that are available to everyone. No grants to individuals, or for fundraising events, operating expenses of organizations that receive United Way funding, except under special circumstances, or advertisement sponsorship for benefit purposes.
Publications: Application guidelines, Corporate giving report (including application guidelines).
Application information: FAXED or E-mailed applications and videos are not accepted. Application form required.
  Initial approach: Proposal and Grant Application Form
  Deadline(s): July 15 through Aug. 31
  Board meeting date(s): Dec.
  Final notification: Late Dec.
Officers and Directors:* Thomas C. Sutton,* Chair.; Robert G. Haskell,* Pres.; Michele Myszka,* V.P.; Audrey L. Milfs, Secy.; Edward R. Byrd, C.F.O.; Michael T. McLaughlin, Genl. Counsel; Beth Baumann; Robert C. Hsu; Kristina Kennedy; T. Anthony Premer; James Sheridan; Bradley Sherrell.
Number of staff: 2 full-time professional; 1 full-time support.
EIN: 953433806

329
The David and Lucile Packard Foundation ▼
300 2nd St., Ste. 200
Los Altos, CA 94022 (650) 948-7658
Contact: Prog. Off. of area of interest
URL: http://www.packard.org

Incorporated in 1964 in CA.
Donor(s): David Packard,‡ Lucile Packard.‡
Grantmaker type: Independent foundation
Financial data (yr. ended 12/31/02): Assets, $4,793,893,254 (M); expenditures, $377,987,699; qualifying distributions, $423,157,893; giving activities include $349,013,818 for 1,631 grants (high: $30,000,000; low: $2,500; average: $2,500–$30,000,000), $1,034,202 for employee matching gifts, $14,956,391 for 3 foundation-administered programs and $36,805,377 for 11 loans/program-related investments.
Purpose and activities: The foundation provides grants to nonprofit organizations in the following program areas: Children, Families, and Communities; Population; and Science and Conservation; National and international grants are provided, with a special focus on the local northern California counties of San Mateo, Santa Clara, Santa Cruz, and Monterey.
Fields of interest: Performing arts; Dance; Theater; Music; Arts; Early childhood education; Natural resources; Energy; Environment; Animals/wildlife, fisheries; Family planning; Health care, insurance; Youth development, services; Human services; Children/youth, services; Day care; Child development, services; Reproductive rights; Urban/community development; Community development;

Philanthropy/voluntarism; Marine science; Engineering/technology; Science; Population studies; Economically disadvantaged.
Types of support: General/operating support; Continuing support; Capital campaigns; Equipment; Land acquisition; Emergency funds; Program development; Fellowships; Research; Technical assistance; Program evaluation; Program-related investments/loans; Employee matching gifts; Matching/challenge support.
Limitations: Giving for the arts and community development primarily in Los Altos and Santa Clara, San Mateo, Santa Cruz, and Monterey counties, CA; Pueblo, CO, and national giving for child health and development; national and international giving for population, conservation and the environment, and science. No support for religious purposes. No grants to individuals.
Application information: Application form not required.
   Initial approach: Proposal or 2- to 3-page letter of inquiry
   Copies of proposal: 1
   Deadline(s): None
   Board meeting date(s): Mar., June, Sept., and Dec.
Officers and Trustees:* Susan Packard Orr,* Chair.; Nancy Packard Burnett,* Vice-Chair.; Julie E. Packard,* Vice-Chair.; Carol S. Larson, C.E.O. and Pres.; George Vera, V.P. and C.F.O.; Barbara P. Wright, Secy.; Jane Lubchenco; Franklin M. Orr; Lewis E. Platt; William K. Reilly; Allan Rosenfield; Robert Stephens; Colburn S. Wilbur.
Number of staff: 93 full-time professional; 5 part-time professional; 62 full-time support; 4 part-time support.
EIN: 942278431
Recent environmental and animal welfare grants:
329-1 Algalita Marine Research Foundation, Long Beach, CA, $90,000. For Santa Rosalita Bay Project. 2002.
329-2 Alternare, A.C., Mexico, $100,000. For Training Center for Monarch Biosphere Reserve. 2002.
329-3 American Littoral Society, Highlands, NJ, $150,000. For Marine Fish Conservation Network. 2002.
329-4 American River Conservancy, Coloma, CA, $38,800. For fund development plan. 2002.
329-5 American Rivers, DC, $90,000. For Voyage of Recovery West. 2002.
329-6 American Rivers, DC, $38,350. For communications capacity for Northwest Regional Office. 2002.
329-7 Annual Sea Turtle Symposium, Hilton Head Island, SC, $30,000. For symposium. 2002.
329-8 Auburn University, Auburn, AL, $20,000. For sixth-year extension for graduate scholar. 2002.
329-9 Audubon Society of Hawaii, Honolulu, HI, $150,000. For Pacific Fisheries Coalition. 2002.
329-10 Audubon Society, National, Sacramento, CA, $30,000. For executive search. 2002.
329-11 Audubon Society, National, DC, $1,000,000. For 2020 Vision: Changing Face of Conservation. 2002.
329-12 Audubon Society, National, Living Oceans Program, DC, $500,000. For Seafood Lovers Initiative. 2002.

329-13 Bay Area Video Coalition, San Francisco, CA, $75,000. For Habitat Medias Video, Farming Seas. 2002.
329-14 Blue Ocean Institute, Amagansett, NY, $50,000. For general support. 2002.
329-15 Bluewater Network, San Francisco, CA, $35,000. For general support. 2002.
329-16 Border Ecology Project, Bisbee, AZ, $49,400. For technical and analytical studies for San Pedro and Sonora River Basins. 2002.
329-17 California Native Grass Association, Davis, CA, $18,950. For communications strategy. 2002.
329-18 California Native Plant Society, Sacramento, CA, $19,875. For board development and executive search. 2002.
329-19 California Rangeland Trust, Sacramento, CA, $50,000. For design of major donor campaign. 2002.
329-20 Canadian Parks and Wilderness Society, Ottawa, Canada, $25,000. For Baja California to Bering Sea Marine Conservation Initiative. 2002.
329-21 Canopy Institute, San Francisco, CA, $200,000. To launch Conservation and Community Investment Forum (CCIF) Asia. 2002.
329-22 Carmel Unified School District, Carmel, CA, $20,000. For Biological Sciences Project. 2002.
329-23 Carmel Unified School District, Carmel, CA, $11,000. For strategic planning for Biological Sciences Project at Carmel Middle School. 2002.
329-24 Carnegie Institution of Washington, DC, $1,000,000. For Department of Global Ecology at Stanford. 2002.
329-25 Center for a New American Dream, Takoma Park, MD, $150,000. For general support. 2002.
329-26 Center for Food Safety, DC, $50,000. For environmentally-sound aquaculture. 2002.
329-27 Center for Independent Documentary, Sharon, MA, $50,000. For Melting Planet. 2002.
329-28 Chefs Collaborative, Boston, MA, $75,000. For Seafood Solutions Program. 2002.
329-29 City CarShare, San Francisco, CA, $50,000. For program expansion. 2002.
329-30 Clean Air Cool Planet-A Northeast Alliance, Portsmouth, NH, $45,000. For strategic planning and fundraising strategy. 2002.
329-31 Climate Neutral Network, Lake Oswego, Oregon, $50,000. For planning and organizational redesign. 2002.
329-32 Coastal Zone Foundation, Middletown, CA, $25,000. For California and World Ocean 02 program. 2002.
329-33 Commonweal, Bolinas, CA, $500,000. For California Ocean Policy Project. 2002.
329-34 Commonweal, Bolinas, CA, $250,000. For California Nearshore Science Project. 2002.
329-35 Community Conservation Network, Honolulu, HI, $450,000. For community-based conservation in Palau. 2002.
329-36 Community Conservation Network, Honolulu, HI, $29,600. For strategic planning. 2002.

329-37 Comunidad y Biodiversidad, Guaymas, Mexico, $250,000. For community-based marine conservation in Northwest Mexico. 2002.
329-38 Congress for the New Urbanism, San Francisco, CA, $100,000. For general support. 2002.
329-39 Congress for the New Urbanism, San Francisco, CA, $32,550. For planning for new chapter structure. 2002.
329-40 Consejo Civil Mexicano para la Silvicultura Sostenible, Mexico City, Mexico, $75,000. To support and strengthen of community-based forestry in Mexico. 2002.
329-41 Consejo Nacional de Cuerpos de Conservacion Mexicanos, Merida, Mexico, $240,000. For youth participation in population and conservation issues in protected natural areas. 2002.
329-42 Conservation Biology Institute, Corvallis, Oregon, $300,000. For Science Support Program. 2002.
329-43 Conservation International, DC, $451,336. Towards zero biodiversity loss within Gulf of California. 2002.
329-44 Conservation International, DC, $160,000. For alliance of major stakeholders in Gulf of California. 2002.
329-45 Conservation of the Island Territory of Mexico, La Paz, Mexico, $70,000. For Integrated Coastal Management Strategy in Baja California Sur. 2002.
329-46 Consultative Group on Biological Diversity, San Francisco, CA, $70,000. For membership. 2002.
329-47 Consumers Choice Council, DC, $50,000. For general support. 2002.
329-48 Coral Reef Alliance (CORAL), San Francisco, CA, $300,000. For Coral Parks Program. 2002.
329-49 Discovery Institute, Seattle, WA, $50,000. For general support. 2002.
329-50 E and Co, Bloomfield, NJ, $250,000. For Clean Energy Enterprise Development in Ethiopia. 2002.
329-51 Earth Share of California, San Francisco, CA, $35,500. For executive search. 2002.
329-52 Ecologic Development Fund, Cambridge, MA, $18,000. For external communications. 2002.
329-53 Ecological Society of America, DC, $20,000. For assessment and strategic plan. 2002.
329-54 Ecotrust, Portland, Oregon, $40,000. To complete Groundfish Fleet Reduction Project. 2002.
329-55 Ecotrust Canada, Vancouver, Canada, $350,000. For Bringing Conservation Economy to Scale. 2002.
329-56 Endangered Habitats League, Los Angeles, CA, $75,000. For Terra Peninsular's Conservation of Coastal Scrub Communities of Baja California. 2002.
329-57 Endswell Foundation, Vancouver, Canada, $75,000. For Rainforest Solutions Project. 2002.
329-58 Environmental Defense, New York, NY, $450,000. For Sustainable Seafood Advertising Campaign. 2002.
329-59 Environmental Defense, New York, NY, $75,000. For Facilitating Vision for Sustainable Development. 2002.
329-60 Environmental Defense, New York, NY, $36,000. For strategic planning and

executive coaching for Ocean Wilderness Network. 2002.

329-61 Environmental Defense, New York, NY, $12,500. For Environmental Science Program Evaluation. 2002.

329-62 Environmental Flying Services, Tucson, AZ, $50,000. For general support. 2002.

329-63 Environmental Law Institute, DC, $250,000. For endangered environmental laws. 2002.

329-64 Environmental Support Center, DC, $300,000. For core operating support. 2002.

329-65 Field Trip Foundation, Woodside, CA, $20,000. For general support. 2002.

329-66 Forest Trends Association, DC, $20,000. For conference, Global Perspectives on Indigenous People's Forestry: Linking Communities, Commerce, and Conservation. 2002.

329-67 ForestEthics, Berkeley, CA, $75,000. For U.S. implementation of Forest Ethics B.C. Campaign. 2002.

329-68 Friends of the River Foundation, Sacramento, CA, $27,500. For staff development and membership development. 2002.

329-69 Global Green USA, Santa Monica, CA, $182,500. For Greening Transitional and Affordable Housing. 2002.

329-70 Global Green USA, Santa Monica, CA, $50,000. For Greater Bay Area Green Affordable Housing Initiative, Part II. 2002.

329-71 Global Greengrants Fund, Boulder, CO, $100,000. To strengthen community-based capacities to defend biodiversity in Northwest Mexico. 2002.

329-72 Greenbelt Alliance, San Francisco, CA, $25,000. For organizational assessment for Bay Area Open Space Council. 2002.

329-73 Greenway and Nature Center of Pueblo, Pueblo, CO, $35,000. For Arkansas River Corridor Legacy Project. 2002.

329-74 Harvard University, John F. Kennedy School of Government, Cambridge, MA, $250,000. For Energy Technology Policy for Greenhouse-gas Constrained World. 2002.

329-75 Harvard University, John F. Kennedy School of Government, Cambridge, MA, $145,420. For Joint Synthesis Workshop on Science and Technology for Sustainable Development. 2002.

329-76 Humane Society International, Avalon, Australia, $50,000. For Australian Toothfish Proposal. 2002.

329-77 Indiana University, Bloomington, Indiana, $1,000,000. For Life at the Edge of Hydration program. 2002.

329-78 Institute for Fisheries Resources, Eugene, Oregon, $138,000. For California Sustainable Fisheries Project. 2002.

329-79 Island Conservation and Ecology Group, Davenport, CA, $27,000. For executive search, administrative systems assessment, and board development for Mexico branch. 2002.

329-80 Land Trust Alliance, DC, $150,000. For Transportation Policy Initiative. 2002.

329-81 Land Trust Alliance, DC, $35,000. For organizational assessment and strategic planning. 2002.

329-82 Long Live the Kings, Seattle, WA, $42,945. For strategic planning. 2002.

329-83 Mahonia na Dari Research and Conservation Center, Kimbe, Papua New Guinea, $100,000. For Locally Managed Marine Areas. 2002.

329-84 Marine Aquarium Council, Honolulu, HI, $49,710. For business plan development. 2002.

329-85 Marine Conservation Biology Institute, Redmond, WA, $250,000. For Bering Sea to Baja California Conservation Areas. 2002.

329-86 Marine Conservation Biology Institute, Redmond, WA, $250,000. For general support. 2002.

329-87 Marine Stewardship Council, London, England, $245,125. For fisheries and commercial outreach work in Southeast Asia. 2002.

329-88 Marine Stewardship Council, London, England, $150,000. For acceleration of business plan. 2002.

329-89 Marine Stewardship Council, London, England, $38,000. For Information Management Assessment. 2002.

329-90 Marine Stewardship Council, Seattle, WA, $125,000. For Sustainable Fisheries Re-granting Foundation. 2002.

329-91 MBA-Nonprofit Connection, Palo Alto, CA, $50,000. For Environment Fellows Program. 2002.

329-92 Mexican Nature Conservation Fund, Mexico City, Mexico, $16,800. For advisory council to U.S. market demand for marinas in Northwest Mexico. 2002.

329-93 Monterey Bay Marine Sanctuary Foundation, Monterey, CA, $25,000. For Alliance of Communities for Sustainable Fisheries. 2002.

329-94 Mountain Park Environmental Association, Beulah, CO, $12,000. For Earth Studies Program. 2002.

329-95 Napa County Land Trust, Napa, CA, $24,000. For organizational assessment and strategic planning for Blue Ridge Berryessa Natural Area Conservation Partnership. 2002.

329-96 National Coalition for Marine Conservation, Leesburg, VA, $15,000. To conserve Pacific marine fisheries and ecosystems. 2002.

329-97 National Commission on Energy Policy, DC, $200,000. For Strategic Energy Plan. 2002.

329-98 National Council for Science and the Environment, DC, $74,500. For organizational assessment, financial management upgrade, and development planning. 2002.

329-99 National Environmental Trust, DC, $50,000. For Patagonian Toothfish: CITES Appendix II Listing. 2002.

329-100 National Environmental Trust, DC, $30,800. For Seafood Market Meeting. 2002.

329-101 National Fish and Wildlife Foundation, DC, $4,383,400. For Cargill Salt Pond Properties. 2002.

329-102 National Fish and Wildlife Foundation, Southwest Region Office, DC, $75,000. For Marine Life Protection Act Public Working Group Process. 2002.

329-103 National Geographic Society, DC, $250,000. For Oceans and Seas program. 2002.

329-104 National Oceanic and Atmospheric Administration (NOAA), Santa Cruz Laboratory, Santa Cruz, CA, DC, $250,000. For guidebook on effective management of Marine Protected Areas. 2002.

329-105 National Oceanic and Atmospheric Administration (NOAA), Santa Cruz Laboratory, Santa Cruz, CA, DC, $150,000. For tools for effective design and management of Marine Protected Areas. 2002.

329-106 Natural Resources Defense Council, New York, NY, $200,000. For Ocean Protection Initiative, Pacific Region. 2002.

329-107 Natural Resources Defense Council, New York, NY, $125,000. For Oceans Policy Project. 2002.

329-108 Nature Conservancy, Alaska Program, Arlington, VA, $30,000. For biodiversity protection and transportation planning and mitigation in Alaska. 2002.

329-109 Nature Conservancy, Asia Pacific Program, Arlington, VA, $193,000. For Marine Protected Areas in Palau. 2002.

329-110 Nature Conservancy, Asia Pacific Program, Arlington, VA, $75,000. For coral bleaching research. 2002.

329-111 Nature Conservancy, California Program, Arlington, VA, $175,000. For biodiversity protection and transportation policy. 2002.

329-112 Nature Conservancy, Mexico Program, Arlington, VA, $500,000. For Conservation by Design: Southern Gulf Coast of Baja California. 2002.

329-113 Nature Conservancy of Canada, Toronto, Canada, $40,000. To establish Taku River Conservancy. 2002.

329-114 New England Aquarium Corporation, Boston, MA, $1,500,000. For Aldo Leopold Leadership Program. 2002.

329-115 Northern Arizona University, Flagstaff, AZ, $50,000. For Seri Para-ecologist Training Program. 2002.

329-116 Ocean Conservancy, DC, $800,000. For Ocean Wilderness Challenge. 2002.

329-117 Oneill Sea Odyssey, Santa Cruz, CA, $48,000. To expand core classes. 2002.

329-118 Oregon State University, Corvallis, Oregon, $246,428. For Communicating Science of Marine Reserves. 2002.

329-119 Pacific Forest Trust, Santa Rosa, CA, $50,000. To implement Strategic Opportunities Conservation Fund. 2002.

329-120 Pacific Forest Trust, Santa Rosa, CA, $28,000. For strategic planning and board development. 2002.

329-121 Pacific Marine Conservation Council, Astoria, Oregon, $11,500. For strategic planning. 2002.

329-122 Prairie Foundation, Bozeman, MT, $100,000. For general support. 2002.

329-123 Pro Esteros, San Diego, CA, $200,000. For coastal wetland protection in Baja California and capacity building for grassroots organizations. 2002.

329-124 Pro Esteros, San Diego, CA, $50,000. For Coastal Development Campaign. 2002.

329-125 Pronatura, Mexico, $250,000. For Population-Environment Approach in Conservation Programs in Chiapas, Mexico. 2002.

329-126 Pronatura Peninsula de Baja California, Noroeste/Mar de Cortes, Ensenada, Mexico, $200,000. For Bahia De Los Angeles National Park Initiative. 2002.

329-127 Pronatura Peninsula de Baja California, Noroeste/Mar de Cortes, Ensenada, Mexico,

$35,000. For organizational assessment and strategic planning. 2002.

329-128 Pueblo Zoological Society, Pueblo, CO, $12,642. For zoo improvements. 2002.

329-129 RARE Center for Tropical Conservation, Arlington, VA, $450,000. For building support for family planning and environmental conservation in Western Pacific. 2002.

329-130 RARE Center for Tropical Conservation, Arlington, VA, $284,000. For Diploma in Conservation. 2002.

329-131 RARE Center for Tropical Conservation, Arlington, VA, $250,000. To enhance effectiveness and self-sufficiency of Mexican Protected Areas. 2002.

329-132 Redefining Progress, Oakland, CA, $40,000. For K-12 Sustainability Education Program. 2002.

329-133 Research Foundation of the State University of New York, Albany, NY, $1,000,000. For research project, Integrating Dynamics of Human Resource Use and Their Effects on Rainforests in Madagascar. 2002.

329-134 Resilience Alliance, Newton, MA, $60,000. For initial meeting of Envisioning Resilience Council. 2002.

329-135 Resource Legacy Fund Foundation, Sacramento, CA, $9,000,000. For regranting, policy development, and mentoring. 2002.

329-136 Resources Legacy Fund, Sacramento, CA, $750,000. For Marine Stewardship Council Regranting Program. 2002.

329-137 Resources Legacy Fund, Sacramento, CA, $97,400. For organizational assessment and planning for restructuring. 2002.

329-138 Resources Legacy Fund, Sacramento, CA, $50,000. To compare population, land use, and socioeconomic trends to community assets in Monterey, San Mateo, Santa Clara, and Santa Cruz Counties: Phase II. 2002.

329-139 Rockefeller Family Fund, New York, NY, $70,000. For Environmental Grantmakers Association Fall retreat. 2002.

329-140 Rockefeller Family Fund, New York, NY, $40,000. For organizational assessment of Environmental Grantmakers Association. 2002.

329-141 Round River Conservation Studies, Salt Lake City, UT, $250,000. For Taku River Wildlife Conservation Project. 2002.

329-142 San Francisco Community Power Cooperative, San Francisco, CA, $40,000. For Social Capital in Southeast San Francisco. 2002.

329-143 San Joaquin River Parkway and Conservation Trust, Fresno, CA, $42,000. For fundraising and communications strategies. 2002.

329-144 Save Our Shores, Santa Cruz, CA, $150,000. To sustain resources of Central California Coast. 2002.

329-145 Save Our Wild Salmon Coalition, Seattle, WA, $185,000. For Columbia and Snake Rivers Recovery Campaign. 2002.

329-146 Save San Francisco Bay Association, Oakland, CA, $40,000. For external communications and marketing strategy. 2002.

329-147 School for Field Studies, Beverly, MA, $130,000. For Bahia Magdalena Projects. 2002.

329-148 SeaWeb, DC, $2,100,000. For Seafood Choices Alliance, National Marine Reserves Campaign, and general support. 2002.

329-149 SeaWeb, DC, $249,816. For media workshops. 2002.

329-150 SeaWeb, DC, $131,000. For Turning Tide program. 2002.

329-151 SeaWeb, DC, $125,450. For mapping project of foundation communications practices. 2002.

329-152 SeaWeb, DC, $12,500. For Marine Reserves Public Opinion Research. 2002.

329-153 Shark Trust, Plymouth, England, $200,000. For IUCN Shark Specialist Group. 2002.

329-154 Sierra Club Foundation, San Francisco, CA, $250,000. For Global Population and Environment Program. 2002.

329-155 Sierra Club of British Columbia Foundation, Victoria, Canada, $250,000. For Coastal Forest Campaign. 2002.

329-156 Sierra Fund, Nevada City, CA, $50,000. For planning, board development, and fundraising strategy. 2002.

329-157 Sierra Legal Defence Fund, Vancouver, Canada, $26,286. For IRS withholding. 2002.

329-158 Sierra Legal Defence Fund, Vancouver, Canada, $16,600. For fund development. 2002.

329-159 Society of Environmental Journalists, Jenkintown, PA, $150,000. For general support. 2002.

329-160 South Coast Wilderness Sanctuary, Carmel Valley, CA, $27,500. For external communications. 2002.

329-161 South Pacific Regional Environment Programme (SPREP), Apia, Samoa, $35,000. For Pacific Islands Conference for Nature Conservation. 2002.

329-162 South Yuba River Citizens League, Nevada City, CA, $50,000. For strategic communications plan. 2002.

329-163 Southeast Alaska Conservation Council, Juneau, AK, $50,000. For general support. 2002.

329-164 Stanford University, Center for Environmental Science and Policy, Stanford, CA, $48,450. For Wild and Farmed Salmon Interactions in Pacific Northwest study. 2002.

329-165 Stanford University, Hopkins Marine Station, Stanford, CA, $200,000. For Tag-A-Giant Program. 2002.

329-166 Stanford University, Stanford Law School, Stanford, CA, $63,475. For Stanford Fisheries Project. 2002.

329-167 Strategies for the Global Environment, Arlington, VA, $250,000. For Pew Ocean Commission Report. 2002.

329-168 Strategies for the Global Environment, Arlington, VA, $30,000. For Report on Marine Reserves. 2002.

329-169 Surfrider Foundation, San Clemente, CA, $240,000. For California's Coast program. 2002.

329-170 Surfrider Foundation, San Clemente, CA, $150,000. For Coast and Ocean Preservation Campaign. 2002.

329-171 Sustainable Northwest, Portland, Oregon, $225,000. For program in Klamath-Siskiyou Region. 2002.

329-172 Telapak Indonesia, Bogor, Indonesia, $79,922. For Destructive Fishing Reform in Indonesia. 2002.

329-173 TERANGI, The Indonesian Coral Reef Foundation, Jakarta, Indonesia, $50,000. For Coral and Fish Trade in Indonesia. 2002.

329-174 Tides Canada Foundation, Rainforest Solutions Project, Vancouver, Canada, $780,000. To secure greater levels of protection for temperate rainforests on Central and North Coast of British Columbia. 2002.

329-175 Tides Center, San Francisco, CA, $550,000. For continued general support for Transboundary Watershed Alliance's ongoing efforts to protect ecological integrity of transboundary region. 2002.

329-176 Tides Center, San Francisco, CA, $50,000. For Environmental Media Services Northwest Office. 2002.

329-177 Tides Center, San Francisco, CA, $42,318. For strategic planning for Environmental Media Services West. 2002.

329-178 Tides Center, San Francisco, CA, $38,000. For planning for Green Media Toolshed's transition to 501(c)(3) status. 2002.

329-179 Tides Foundation, San Francisco, CA, $35,000. For Forest Stewardship Council of British Columbia. 2002.

329-180 TRAFFIC International, Cambridge, England, $200,000. For TRAFFIC Fisheries Program. 2002.

329-181 Trout Unlimited, Edmonds, WA, $250,000. For Western Water Project. 2002.

329-182 Trust for Hidden Villa, Los Altos Hills, CA, $50,000. For Environmental Internship Program: White House Renovation. 2002.

329-183 Trust for Public Land, San Francisco, CA, $25,000. For strategic planning. 2002.

329-184 Trustees for Alaska, Anchorage, AK, $19,000. For report on status of North Pacific Pollock Fisheries. 2002.

329-185 University of California, Los Angeles, CA, $115,575. For Reef Check Papua New Guinea. 2002.

329-186 University of California, Center for Sustainable Resource Development, Berkeley, CA, $215,000. For Bearhs Environmental Leadership Program: Sustainable Environmental Management. 2002.

329-187 University of California, Division of Agriculture and Natural Resources, Berkeley, CA, $18,250. For Century of California Marine Protected Areas. 2002.

329-188 University of California, Richard and Rhoda Goldman School of Public Policy, Berkeley, CA, $50,000. For Strategic Management of Environmental Policy. 2002.

329-189 University of California at San Diego, Scripps Institute of Oceanography, La Jolla, CA, $250,000. For Marine Reserve Management in Gulf of California. 2002.

329-190 University of Maryland, College Park, MD, $150,000. For National River Restoration Science Synthesis. 2002.

329-191 University of Michigan, Ann Arbor, MI, $150,000. For Population-Environment Fellows Program. 2002.

329-192 University of Rhode Island Foundation, Kingston, RI, $412,967. For Coastal Resources Center: Sustainable Development Practices for Shrimp Mariculture and Recreational Marinas. 2002.

329-193 University of Rhode Island Foundation, Kingston, RI, $25,000. For fund development, communications strategies, and development of advisory board for Coastal Resources Center. 2002.

329-194 University of Rhode Island Foundation, Coastal Resources Center, Kingston, RI, $120,000. For Integrated Coastal Resources Management. 2002.

329-195 University of the South Pacific, Suva, Fiji, $180,000. For Integrated Coastal Resources Management in Fiji. 2002.

329-196 Watershed Watch Salmon Society, Coquitlam, Canada, $50,000. For Enhancing Salmon Stewardship program. 2002.

329-197 West Coast Environmental Law Research Foundation, Vancouver, Canada, $40,000. For Forest Certification Systems in British Columbia. 2002.

329-198 Wild Salmon Center, Portland, Oregon, $210,000. For Cascadia Salmon Sanctuary Partnership. 2002.

329-199 WildAid, San Francisco, CA, $250,000. For Marine Reserve Program. 2002.

329-200 Wildlife Conservation Society, Bronx, NY, $150,000. For general support for Foundations of Success program. 2002.

329-201 Wildlife Conservation Society, South Pacific Program, Bronx, NY, $50,000. For Marine Biodiversity Research Program. 2002.

329-202 Wildlife Consultants International, The Plains, VA, $18,700. For National Marine Fisheries Commission Paper. 2002.

329-203 Woodside-Atherton Auxiliary to Lucile Salter Packard Childrens Hospital at Stanford, Menlo Park, CA, $500,000. For Allied Arts Guild renovation. 2002.

329-204 World Wide Fund for Nature-Australia, Sydney, Australia, $750,000. For Consumer Choice for Sustainable Seafood program. 2002.

329-205 World Wide Fund for Nature-Indonesia, Jakarta, Indonesia, $300,000. For MPA Certification. 2002.

329-206 World Wildlife Fund/Conservation Foundation, DC, $500,000. For Shrimp Aquaculture Certification Program. 2002.

329-207 World Wildlife Fund/Conservation Foundation, DC, $300,000. For Bering Sea Ecoregion program. 2002.

329-208 World Wildlife Fund/Conservation Foundation, DC, $196,000. To build science capacity in Melanesia. 2002.

329-209 World Wildlife Fund/Conservation Foundation, Center for Conservation Finance, DC, $80,000. For Escalera Nautica Assessment: Facilitating Conservation and Sustainable Development in Gulf of California. 2002.

329-210 World Wildlife Fund/Conservation Foundation, Center for Conservation Innovation, DC, $50,000. For strategic planning and team-building. 2002.

329-211 World Wildlife Fund/Conservation Foundation, Marine Conservation and Sustainable Commerce Program, DC, $100,000. To reduce subsidized European fishing fleets. 2002.

329-212 World Wildlife Fund/Conservation Foundation, Marine Reserves, DC, $90,000. For Outreach for Successful Marine Reserves program. 2002.

329-213 Yayasan Adi Citra Lestari, Palu, Indonesia, $75,000. For Marine Protected Area in Indonesia. 2002.

329-214 Yayasan KEHATI, Jakarta, Indonesia, $275,000. To transfer land tenure. 2002.

330
PADI Foundation
(also known as Professional Association of Diving Instructors Foundation)
9150 Wilshire Blvd., Ste. 300
Beverly Hills, CA 90212-3414
Contact: Charles P. Rettig, Pres.
FAX: (310) 859-1430; URL: http://www.padifoundation.org

Established in 1991 in CA.
Donor(s): Dept. of Justice, State of California, Capital Investments and Ventures Corp., and its subsidiaries.
Grantmaker type: Operating foundation
Financial data (yr. ended 05/31/02): Assets, $2,182,032 (M); gifts received, $202,062; expenditures, $243,607; qualifying distributions, $226,549; giving activities include $177,193 for 36 grants to individuals (high: $9,500; low: $1,000).
Purpose and activities: Encourages the preservation and understanding of the aquatic environment and encourages sensitivity to and the protection of underwater life; also promotes the understanding of sport diving physics and physiology.
Fields of interest: Natural resources; Environment; Athletics/sports, water sports.
International interests: South Africa; Brazil; Australia.
Types of support: Research; Grants to individuals.
Limitations: Giving on a national and international basis. No support for diving equipment, standard photographic equipment, or personal computers.
Publications: Application guidelines, Financial statement.
Application information: Application form not required.
  Initial approach: 3-page proposal
  Copies of proposal: 1
  Deadline(s): Feb. 15
  Board meeting date(s): Apr.
  Final notification: May 1
Officers and Directors:* Charles P. Rettig,* Pres.; Andrew Saxon, M.D.,* Secy.; Paul K. Dayton, Ph.D.; John Englander; Daniel M. Hanes, Ph.D.
EIN: 954326850

331
Pasadena Foundation
16 N. Marengo Ave., Ste. 300
Pasadena, CA 91101 (626) 796-2097
Contact: Jennifer Fleming DeVoll, Exec. Dir.
FAX: (626) 583-4738; E-mail: vkrueger@pasadenafoundation.org or pfstaff@pasadenafoundation.org; URL: http://www.pasadenafoundation.org

Established in 1953 in CA by resolution and declaration of trust.
Donor(s): Louis A. Webb,‡ Marion L. Webb,‡ Helen B. Lockett,‡ Dorothy I. Stewart,‡ Rebecca R. Anthony,‡ Lucille Crumb,‡ Cornelia Eaton,‡ Ralph Norrington,‡ Margaret Norrington,‡ Ella C. Price.‡
Grantmaker type: Community foundation
Financial data (yr. ended 12/31/02): Assets, $16,007,810 (M); gifts received, $601,032; expenditures, $2,352,043; giving activities

include $2,106,613 for 585 grants (high: $50,000; low: $50; average: $100–$50,000).
Purpose and activities: Support for nonprofit organizations that provide direct services to people in the Pasadena area in the following four categories: Children, Youth, and Families; Community Development and the Environment; Education, Arts, and Humanities; and Health and People with Special Needs. Grants are made only for or toward the acquisition of specific capital items and generally do not exceed $8,000. Major grants do not exceed $50,000.
Fields of interest: Humanities; Arts; Education; Environment; Health care; Children/youth, services; Family services; Human services; Community development; Disabled; Aging.
Types of support: Capital campaigns; Building/renovation; Equipment.
Limitations: Giving limited to the Pasadena, CA, area. No support for private foundations, organizations seeking to influence legislation, or for educational institutions or sectarian organizations (except for programs sponsored by educational institutions or sectarian organizations). No grants to individuals, or for continuing support, scholarships, general or operating support, expenses incurred in performance of program services, or elections.
Publications: Application guidelines, Annual report, Financial statement, Newsletter.
Application information: Eligible organizations must be at least 3 years old. Organizations receiving a major grant from the foundation may not apply for any other grant during the same calendar year and may not apply for another major grant for 3 years. Application form required.
  Initial approach: Grant application
  Copies of proposal: 10
  Deadline(s): Oct. 1; May 1 for major grants
  Board meeting date(s): Quarterly
  Final notification: Dec.; June for major grants
Officers and Advisory Board:* Gloria S. Pitzer,* Chair.; James D. Gamb,* Vice-Chair.; Jennifer Fleming DeVoll, Exec. Dir.; David P. Beringer; Guillermina Gutierrez Byrne; Robert E. Carlson; Betty Chin Ho; G. Arnold Mulder, M.D.; Peggy Phelps; Diane Scott.
Trustees: Citizens Business Bank.
Number of staff: 2 full-time professional; 1 part-time support.
EIN: 956047660

332
Patagonia Environmental Grants Program
P.O. Box 150
Ventura, CA 93002 (805) 643-8616
Contact: Lisa Pike, Mgr., Environmental Progs.; or Shannon Rowan, Environmental Progs. Assoc.
Additional address: 259 W. Santa Clara St., Ventura, CA 93001; FAX: (805) 667-4740; URL: http://www.patagonia.com/enviro/enviro_grants.shtml

Grantmaker type: Corporate giving program
Financial data (yr. ended 04/30/01): Total giving, $1,785,718; giving activities include $1,750,627 for grants (high: $25,000; low: $672; average: $3,000–$8,000), $35,091 for employee matching gifts and $346,000 for 5 company-administered programs.

Purpose and activities: Patagonia makes charitable contributions to nonprofit organizations involved with the environment. Support is given on a national and international basis.

Fields of interest: Natural resources; Environment.

International interests: Canada; Europe; Chile; Japan.

Types of support: General/operating support; Employee volunteer services; Loaned talent; Use of facilities; Employee matching gifts; Donated products.

Limitations: Giving on a national and international basis, including in Canada, Chile, Europe, and Japan. No grants for land acquisition, endowments, research, political campaigns, or general environmental education efforts not in direct support of a developed plan for specific action to alleviate an environmental problem.

Publications: Application guidelines, Corporate giving report, Grants list.

Application information: The Environmental Programs Department handles giving. The company has a staff that only handles contributions. A contributions committee reviews all requests. Application form not required.

Initial approach: Proposal to nearest company facility

Copies of proposal: 1

Deadline(s): Apr. 30 and Aug. 31

Final notification: Varies

Number of staff: 2 full-time professional.

333

Paws Up Foundation

275 Battery St., Ste. 1480
San Francisco, CA 94111
Contact: Maureen Youngblood

Established around 1994.

Donor(s): David E. Lipson.

Grantmaker type: Independent foundation

Financial data (yr. ended 12/31/01): Assets, $22,995 (M); gifts received, $221,401; expenditures, $315,426; qualifying distributions, $314,950; giving activities include $314,950 for 43 grants (high: $50,000; low: $200).

Purpose and activities: Giving for the arts, education, animal welfare, and human services.

Fields of interest: Arts; Higher education; Education; Animals/wildlife; Human services; Family services; Disabled.

Types of support: General/operating support; Continuing support; Annual campaigns; Capital campaigns; Endowments; Seed money; Program-related investments/loans.

Limitations: Applications not accepted. Giving on a national basis. No grants to individuals.

Application information: Contributes only to pre-selected organizations.

Officer and Directors:* David E. Lipson,* Pres. and Secy.; Laurence E. Lipson; Nadine E. Lipson.

EIN: 363946129

334

Mary R. Payden & Joseph R. Payden Foundation

c/o William R. Payden
11 Sea Colony
Santa Monica, CA 90405
Contact: Joan A. Payden, Tr.

Established in 1988 in CA.

Donor(s): Joan A. Payden.

Grantmaker type: Independent foundation

Financial data (yr. ended 12/31/02): Assets, $707,486 (M); gifts received, $100,000; expenditures, $171,364; qualifying distributions, $143,471; giving activities include $116,523 for 344 grants (high: $12,000; low: $25).

Purpose and activities: Giving for health, children's services, animal welfare and protection, religious social services, the arts, and human services.

Fields of interest: Arts; Animals/wildlife, preservation/protection; Health care; Health organizations, association; Human services; Children/youth, services; Federated giving programs; Roman Catholic agencies & churches; Religion.

Limitations: Giving primarily in CA. No grants to individuals.

Application information: Application form required.

Deadline(s): None

Trustees: Joan A. Payden; William R. Payden.

EIN: 954174573

335

Peninsula Community Foundation ▼

1700 S. El Camino Real, Ste. 300
San Mateo, CA 94402-3049 (650) 358-9369
Contact: Sterling K. Speirn, Pres.
FAX: (650) 358-9817; E-mail: inquiry@pcf.org;
URL: http://www.pcf.org

Established as a trust in 1964 in CA; incorporated in 1981.

Grantmaker type: Community foundation

Financial data (yr. ended 12/31/01): Assets, $478,503,157 (M); expenditures, $7,537,737; giving activities include $63,209,013 for grants, $9,609 for 47 grants to individuals (high: $500; low: $42), $14,652 for 78 employee matching gifts and $30,000 for loans/program-related investments.

Purpose and activities: To support local cultural, educational, social service, and health programs. Primary areas of interest include homelessness and housing, children and youth, adult services, social services, and education, including programs for minorities, the disadvantaged, and early childhood education; other interests include the environment, arts and culture, senior citizens and the needs of the aging, the disabled, civic concerns, and recreation; provides counseling services for local fund seekers. Giving includes grants to individuals as student aid, emergency assistance, and grants to local artists.

Fields of interest: Arts; Early childhood education; Child development, education; Education; Environment; Health care; Health organizations, association; Housing/shelter, development; Recreation; Human services; Children/youth, services; Child development, services; Aging, centers/services; Homeless,

human services; Government/public administration; Minorities; Disabled; Aging; Economically disadvantaged; Homeless.

Types of support: Continuing support; Emergency funds; Program development; Conferences/seminars; Seed money; Curriculum development; Internship funds; Scholarship funds; Technical assistance; Consulting services; Program-related investments/loans; Employee matching gifts; Scholarships—to individuals; Matching/challenge support.

Limitations: Giving limited to San Mateo County and northern Santa Clara County, CA. No support for fraternal organizations, religious organizations for religious purposes, or political activities. No grants for endowment funds, annual campaigns, building funds, deficit financing, land acquisition, research or fundraising events.

Publications: Application guidelines, Annual report, Financial statement, Grants list, Informational brochure, Newsletter.

Application information: Application form not required.

Initial approach: Letter of inquiry

Copies of proposal: 1

Deadline(s): None

Board meeting date(s): Distribution committee meets in Jan., Mar., May, July, Sept., and Nov.

Final notification: 2 to 3 months

Officers and Directors:* John Clinton, Jr.,* Chair.; Sterling K. Speirn, Pres.; Vera Bennett, V.P., Finance and Admin.; Ellen Clear, V.P., Comm. Progs.; Ash McNeely, V.P., Phil. Serv.; Tom Bailard; Patricia Bresee; Bernadine Chuck Fong; Susan Ford; Nylda Gemple; Charles Huggins; Rick Jones; Olivia G. Martinez; Linda Meier; Karen Van Hoesen Olson; Nancy J. Pedot; Jennifer Raiser; Gordon Russell; William Schwartz; Donald H. Seiler; Ned Spieker; Jane H. Williams.

Number of staff: 18 full-time professional; 1 part-time professional; 19 full-time support; 5 part-time support.

EIN: 942746687

Recent environmental and animal welfare grants:

335-1 Acterra: Action for a Sustainable Earth, Palo Alto, CA, $45,000. For Arastadero Preserve Stewardship Project as outlined in projected budget. 2002.

335-2 Acterra: Action for a Sustainable Earth, Palo Alto, CA, $15,000. For San Francisquito Watershed Council and San Francisquito Creek Stewardship Project. 2002.

335-3 African Wildlife Foundation, DC, $15,000. For general support. 2002.

335-4 Another Life for Animals, Half Moon Bay, CA, $25,000. For Especially for Dogs. 2002.

335-5 Audubon Society, National, Sacramento, CA, $25,000. For general support for Audubon's work in California. 2002.

335-6 California Academy of Sciences, San Francisco, CA, $25,000. For general support. 2002.

335-7 California Academy of Sciences, San Francisco, CA, $25,000. For annual fund. 2002.

335-8 California Academy of Sciences, San Francisco, CA, $10,000. For general support. 2002.

335-9 California Department of Education, California Regional Environmental

Educational Community Network, Sacramento, CA, $10,000. For part-time regional coordinator on Peninsula. 2002.

335-10 California Waterfowl Association, Sacramento, CA, $50,000. For establishing Saddleback Ranch conservation easement. 2002.

335-11 California Waterfowl Association, Sacramento, CA, $10,000. For Gold Benefactor support. 2002.

335-12 Canine Companions for Independence, Ketchum, ID, $10,000. For general support. 2002.

335-13 Cheetah Conservation Fund, Ojai, CA, $50,000. For general support. 2002.

335-14 Conservation International, DC, $10,000. For general support. 2002.

335-15 Coyote Point Museum Association, San Mateo, CA, $20,000. For Aviary Netting Replacement Project. 2002.

335-16 Coyote Point Museum Association, San Mateo, CA, $10,000. For summer camp program. 2002.

335-17 Denali Institute, Anchorage, AK, $10,000. For general support. 2002.

335-18 Environmental Defense, Oakland, CA, $60,000. To continue to encourage and help private California landowners improve conditions on their properties for endangered species. 2002.

335-19 Environmental Defense, New York, NY, $50,000. For general support. 2002.

335-20 Environmental Traveling Companions, San Francisco, CA, $20,000. For second-year support to expand wilderness program for low-income youth and youth with disabilities. 2002.

335-21 Environmental Volunteers, Palo Alto, CA, $10,000. For general support. 2002.

335-22 Environmental Volunteers, Palo Alto, CA, $10,000. For general support. 2002.

335-23 Friends of the Teton River, Driggs, ID, $25,000. For Projects for Teton River. 2002.

335-24 Gamble Garden Center, Palo Alto, CA, $10,000. For general support. 2002.

335-25 Green Foothills Foundation, Palo Alto, CA, $10,000. For educational outreach to Mid-Peninsula cities and communities. 2002.

335-26 Green Foothills Foundation, Palo Alto, CA, $10,000. For Foothills Millennium Fund. 2002.

335-27 Greenbelt Alliance, San Francisco, CA, $13,000. For general support and for Endowment Fund. 2002.

335-28 Greenbelt Alliance, San Francisco, CA, $10,000. For Smart Fill-ins Guidebook publication and distribution. 2002.

335-29 Guide Dogs for the Blind, San Rafael, CA, $10,000. For general support. 2002.

335-30 Headwaters Resource Conservation and Development Area, Butte, MT, $10,000. For general support. 2002.

335-31 Horsepower Sanctuaries, Lockwood, CA, $100,000. For general support. 2002.

335-32 Humane Society of the United States, DC, $10,000. For Especially for Dogs. 2002.

335-33 Kimya Sanctuary, San Carlos, CA, $10,000. For general support. 2002.

335-34 League to Save Lake Tahoe, South Lake Tahoe, CA, $10,000. For Americorps Volunteer Program. 2002.

335-35 Marine Science Institute, Redwood City, CA, $40,000. Toward ship project. 2002.

335-36 Marine Science Institute, Redwood City, CA, $10,000. For executive coaching. 2002.

335-37 Monterey Bay Aquarium, Monterey, CA, $1,000,000. For Jellies Exhibit. 2002.

335-38 National Disaster Search Dog Foundation, Ojai, CA, $10,000. For general support. 2002.

335-39 National Museum of Wildlife Art, Jackson, WY, $50,000. For Operating Campaign. 2002.

335-40 Natural Resources Defense Council, New York, NY, $25,000. For Oceans Initiative. 2002.

335-41 Natural Resources Defense Council, New York, NY, $10,000. For general support. 2002.

335-42 Natural Resources Defense Council, New York, NY, $10,000. For Environmental Entrepreneurs. 2002.

335-43 Natural Resources Defense Council, New York, NY, $10,000. For Ocean Initiative. 2002.

335-44 Natural Resources Defense Council, New York, NY, $10,000. For general support. 2002.

335-45 Nature Conservancy, San Francisco, CA, $1,000,000. For project in Northern Sierra. 2002.

335-46 Nature Conservancy, San Francisco, CA, $100,000. For general support. 2002.

335-47 Nature Conservancy, San Francisco, CA, $10,000. For protect Last Great Places around world. 2002.

335-48 North Carolina Outward Bound School, Asheville, NC, $10,000. For general support. 2002.

335-49 Northwest Energy Coalition, Seattle, WA, $10,000. For project: Climate Solutions. 2002.

335-50 Pacific Crest Outward Bound, San Francisco, San Francisco, CA, $25,000. For Black Tie and Tennis Shoe Dinner. 2002.

335-51 Pacific Forest Trust, Santa Rosa, CA, $25,000. For Sierra Project work. 2002.

335-52 Palo Alto Junior Museum and Zoo, Friends of the, Palo Alto, CA, $20,000. For establishment of member database system. 2002.

335-53 Palo Alto Junior Museum and Zoo, Friends of the, Palo Alto, CA, $10,000. For general support. 2002.

335-54 PCL Foundation, Sacramento, CA, $15,000. For Endowment Fund and general support. 2002.

335-55 Peninsula Humane Society, San Mateo, CA, $50,000. For specific uses, especially and primarily for dogs. 2002.

335-56 Peninsula Open Space Trust, Menlo Park, CA, $50,000. For general support. 2002.

335-57 Peninsula Open Space Trust, Menlo Park, CA, $50,000. For general support. 2002.

335-58 Peninsula Open Space Trust, Menlo Park, CA, $30,000. For Annual Support. 2002.

335-59 Peninsula Open Space Trust, Menlo Park, CA, $27,000. For operating fund and for Coastal Campaign. 2002.

335-60 Peninsula Open Space Trust, Menlo Park, CA, $25,000. For general support. 2002.

335-61 Peninsula Open Space Trust, Menlo Park, CA, $25,000. For Pigeon Point Lighthouse transfer to State of California Department of Parks and Recreation. 2002.

335-62 Pescadero Conservation Alliance, Pescadero, CA, $12,500. For general support. 2002.

335-63 Pescadero Conservation Alliance, Pescadero, CA, $10,000. For operational support. 2002.

335-64 Pets in Need, Redwood City, CA, $25,000. For general support. 2002.

335-65 Quest Scholars Program, Palo Alto, CA, $25,500. To provide resources for students to begin first year of Quest Scholars Program. 2002.

335-66 San Francisco Zoological Society, San Francisco, CA, $10,223. For environmental training in Province of Tamatave in eastern Madagascar. 2002.

335-67 San Mateo County Office of Education, Redwood City, CA, $29,323. To construct Sun House, solar classroom that will be part of Organic Garden/Sustainable Living Center at Outdoor Education Program in La Honda. 2002.

335-68 Silicon Valley Animal Rescue, Palo Alto, CA, $15,000. For free spay and neuter. 2002.

335-69 Society for the Prevention of Cruelty to Animals of San Francisco, San Francisco, CA, $25,000. For Especially for Dogs. 2002.

335-70 Sousson Foundation, Templeton, CA, $10,000. For project of planting trees by students in Sequoia National Park. 2002.

335-71 Stanford Cat Network, Palo Alto, CA, $10,000. For general support. 2002.

335-72 Stanford University, School of Business, Stanford, CA, $300,000. For Environmental Sustainability Initiative. 2002.

335-73 Sustainability Institute, Hartland, VT, $50,000. For Donella Meadows Leadership Fellows Program. 2002.

335-74 Sustainable Conservation, San Francisco, CA, $12,500. For Auto Recycling Project, program designed to reduce amount of toxic chemicals that are released into environment. 2002.

335-75 Truckee Donner Land Trust, Truckee, CA, $50,000. For Shallenberger Ridge Project. 2002.

335-76 Trust for Hidden Villa, Los Altos Hills, CA, $100,000. For general support challenge grant. 2002.

335-77 Trust for Hidden Villa, Los Altos Hills, CA, $50,000. For capital support for hostel and summer camp building at Hidden Villa. 2002.

335-78 Trust for Hidden Villa, Los Altos Hills, CA, $25,000. For general support. 2002.

335-79 Trust for Hidden Villa, Los Altos Hills, CA, $15,000. For general support. 2002.

335-80 Trust for Public Land, San Francisco, CA, $20,000. For Bridgespan Consulting Study. 2002.

335-81 Wildlife Associates, Half Moon Bay, CA, $15,000. For Wildlife Ambassadors Program. 2002.

335-82 Wildlife Conservation Network, Los Altos, CA, $50,000. For general support. 2002.

335-83 Wood River Medical Center Foundation, Sun Valley, ID, $35,000. For completion of Saint Luke's Healing Garden. 2002.

335-84 Woods Hole Research Center, Woods Hole, MA, $10,000. For general support. 2002.

335-85 World Wildlife Fund/Conservation Foundation, DC, $10,000. For conservation of life on Earth. 2002.

335-86 Yosemite Foundation, San Francisco, CA, $10,000. For Summer Intern Ranger to work this summer on Half Dome Trail Restoration Project. 2002.

335-87 Youth United for Community Action (YUCA), East Palo Alto, CA, $25,000. For second-year support for Higher Learning Program in which youth in East Palo Alto create positive community change and to develop productive community life skills through community organizing around environmental issues. 2002.

336
Peradam Foundation
c/o Robert Spertus
1813 Vine St.
Berkeley, CA 94703   (510) 527-1806

Established in 1992 in CA.
Donor(s): Robert F. Spertus, Emma Spertus, Juliette Spertus.
Grantmaker type: Independent foundation
Financial data (yr. ended 12/31/01): Assets, $1,129,724 (M); gifts received, $106,115; expenditures, $189,034; qualifying distributions, $175,500; giving activities include $175,500 for 23 grants (high: $15,000; low: $1,500).
Purpose and activities: Emphasis on wildlife and nature preservation and protection.
Fields of interest: Natural resources; Animals/wildlife, preservation/protection.
Limitations: Applications not accepted. Giving primarily in the Pacific Northwest. No grants to individuals.
Application information: Contributes only to pre-selected organizations.
Officers: Robert F. Spertus, Pres.; Anita Spertus, V.P. and Secy.-Treas.
EIN: 931099162

337
The Petco Foundation
9125 Rehco Rd.
San Diego, CA 92121-2270   (858) 453-7845
Contact: Bruce C. Hall, Pres.
E-mail: petcofoundation@petco.com; URL: http://www.petco.com/corpinfo_foundation.asp

Established in 1999.
Grantmaker type: Public charity
Financial data (yr. ended 01/31/01): Revenue, $2,485,346; assets, $1,456,852; gifts received, $2,460,717; expenditures, $2,023,661; program services expenses, $1,816,818; giving activities include $1,816,818 for grants.
Purpose and activities: The foundation supports community organizations and efforts that enhance the lives of companion animals while strengthening the bond between people and pets.
Fields of interest: Animal welfare; Disasters, 9/11/01.
Application information: See Web site for application guidelines. Application form required.
Officers and Directors:* Brian K. Devine,* C.E.O.; Bruce C. Hall,* Pres.; James M. Myers,* Sr. V.P. and Treas.; Janet D. Mitchell,* Sr. V.P. and

Secy.; Mike Woodard,* Sr. V.P.; John D. Morberg,* V.P.; Norman Dowling,* V.P., Fin.; Paul Schmitt,* V.P.; Diane L. Stewart,* Treas.; and 6 additional directors.
EIN: 330845930

338
Leon S. Peters Foundation, Inc.
4170 S. Fowler Ave.
Fresno, CA 93725-9326
Contact: Alice A. Peters, Pres.

Established in 1959 in CA.
Donor(s): Leon S. Peters.‡
Grantmaker type: Independent foundation
Financial data (yr. ended 11/30/02): Assets, $14,003,252 (M); expenditures, $635,675; qualifying distributions, $627,037; giving activities include $618,400 for 59 grants (high: $100,000; low: $1,000).
Fields of interest: Higher education; Zoos/zoological societies; Burn centers; Health care; Human services.
Types of support: General/operating support; Building/renovation; Scholarship funds.
Limitations: Giving primarily in Fresno, CA. No grants to individuals.
Application information:
   Initial approach: Letter
   Deadline(s): None
   Board meeting date(s): Feb., May, Aug., and Nov.
Officers: Alice A. Peters, Pres.; Pete P. Peters, V.P. and Secy.
Directors: Craig Apregan; Darrell Peters; Kenneth Peters; Ron Peters.
Number of staff: None.
EIN: 946064669

339
Pete P. Peters Foundation
4170 S. Fowler Ave.
Fresno, CA 93725-9326   (559) 442-3437
Contact: Pete Peters, Pres.

Established in 1980.
Donor(s): Pete P. Peters.
Grantmaker type: Independent foundation
Financial data (yr. ended 11/30/02): Assets, $5,276,763 (M); expenditures, $230,960; qualifying distributions, $228,327; giving activities include $225,694 for 35 grants (high: $101,760; low: $20).
Purpose and activities: Giving primarily for the Boy Scouts of America; some giving also for the arts, and health associations.
Fields of interest: Media/communications; Museums; Education; Environment; Zoos/zoological societies; Health organizations, association; Boy scouts; Christian agencies & churches; Protestant agencies & churches.
Limitations: Giving primarily in Fresno, CA. No grants to individuals.
Application information:
   Initial approach: Letter
   Deadline(s): None
Officers: Pete Peters, Pres.; Ronald D. Peters, Secy.-Treas.
EIN: 942738016

340
Margie & Robert E. Petersen Foundation
6420 Wilshire Blvd., 20th Fl.
Los Angeles, CA 90048-5515   (310) 640-1345
Contact: Alexandria C. Phillips, Treas.

Established in 1997 in CA.
Donor(s): Margaret M. Petersen, Robert E. Petersen.
Grantmaker type: Independent foundation
Financial data (yr. ended 12/31/02): Assets, $36,142,443 (M); gifts received, $422,343; expenditures, $1,006,317; qualifying distributions, $655,714; giving activities include $655,714 for 37 grants (high: $204,937; low: $200; average: $1,000–$40,000).
Purpose and activities: Giving primarily to medical research.
Fields of interest: Museums; Animals/wildlife, preservation/protection; Medical research, institute; Human services.
Limitations: Giving primarily in CA. No grants to individuals.
Application information:
   Initial approach: Letter
   Deadline(s): None
Officers: Robert E. Petersen, Pres.; Theodore Calleton, Secy.; Alexandria C. Phillips, Treas.
Director: Margaret M. Petersen.
EIN: 954608757

341
The Patricia Price Peterson Foundation
555 California St., 11th Fl., MC CA5-705-11-01
San Francisco, CA 94104   (415) 622-6011
Contact: R.A. Peterson, Pres.

Established about 1964.
Grantmaker type: Independent foundation
Financial data (yr. ended 12/31/00): Assets, $5,241,507 (M); expenditures, $283,748; qualifying distributions, $267,914; giving activities include $270,392 for 35 grants (high: $104,520; low: $125; average: $250–$20,000).
Purpose and activities: Giving primarily for education and for environmental programs.
Fields of interest: Education; Natural resources; Environment; Federated giving programs; Biological sciences; General charitable giving.
Limitations: Giving primarily in the San Francisco Bay Area, CA.
Application information: Application form not required.
   Initial approach: Letter
   Copies of proposal: 1
   Deadline(s): None
   Board meeting date(s): Mid-year
Officers and Directors:* R.A. Peterson,* Pres.; K.S. Smeby,* Secy.-Treas.; M.K. Bennett; S.W. Bennett; E.P. Peterson; R. Price Peterson.
Number of staff: None.
EIN: 946109098

342
George T. Pfleger Foundation
c/o W. Richard Mills
17671 Irvine Blvd., Ste. 207
Tustin, CA 92780-3129

Established in 1968 in CA.
Donor(s): George T. Pfleger, U.S. Motors Foundation.

Grantmaker type: Independent foundation
Financial data (yr. ended 12/31/01): Assets, $27,255,126 (M); expenditures, $972,948; qualifying distributions, $892,401; giving activities include $806,100 for 5 grants (high: $650,000; low: $5,000).
Purpose and activities: Primarily local giving, with emphasis on the environment, health care, and animal welfare.
Fields of interest: Natural resources; Animal welfare; Hospitals (general); Human services.
Limitations: Applications not accepted. Giving primarily in CA. No grants to individuals.
Application information: Contributes only to pre-selected organizations.
Officers and Trustees:* Thomas G. Pfleger,* Pres.; Victoria L. Cascio, Secy.-Treas.; Sandra B. Pfleger.
EIN: 952561117

343
Pfund Family Foundation
4744 Jan Dr.
Carmichael, CA 95608-1048

Established in 1993 in CA.
Grantmaker type: Independent foundation
Financial data (yr. ended 12/31/02): Assets, $2,771,609 (M); expenditures, $169,096; qualifying distributions, $146,012; giving activities include $132,000 for 33 grants (high: $10,000; low: $1,000).
Purpose and activities: Giving for art and cultural programs, children's services and education, human services, animal welfare and for services to the blind.
Fields of interest: Arts; Education; Animals/wildlife; Health organizations, association; Food services; Human services; YM/YWCAs & YM/YWHAs.
Limitations: Applications not accepted. Giving primarily in Sacramento County, CA. No grants to individuals.
Application information: Contributes only to pre-selected organizations.
Trustees: George Basye; George L. Cook; James D. Coyle III; J. Rodney Eason.
EIN: 943172761

344
PG&E Corporation Contributions Program
M.C. B32
P.O. Box 770000
San Francisco, CA 94177-0001
(415) 973-1636
Contact: Dan C. Quigley, Dir., Charitable Contribs.
Application address for in-kind gifts: c/o Non-Cash Contribs. Prog., M.C. N5F, P.O. Box 770000, San Francisco, CA 94177-0001; FAX: (415) 973-8239; E-mail: dcq1@pge.com; URL: http://www.pge.com/007_our_comm/our_community_index.shtml

Grantmaker type: Corporate giving program
Financial data (yr. ended 12/31/02): Total giving, $1,950,513; giving activities include $1,706,046 for grants (high: $25,000; low: $500; average: $500–$25,000) and $244,467 for 684 employee matching gifts.
Purpose and activities: As a complement to its foundation, PG&E also makes charitable

contributions to nonprofit organizations directly. Support is given primarily in areas of company operations.
Fields of interest: Elementary/secondary education; Higher education; Education; Natural resources; Environment; Employment, services; Economic development; Community development.
Types of support: General/operating support; Capital campaigns; Equipment; Program development; Employee volunteer services; Employee matching gifts; Donated equipment; Donated land; Donated products; In-kind gifts; Matching/challenge support.
Limitations: Giving primarily in areas of company operations in central and northern CA. No support for religious organizations not of direct benefit to the entire community, fraternal organizations, political or partisan organizations, or hospitals or medical organizations. No grants to individuals, or for debt reduction, endowments, films or videos, tickets, continuing support, sports tournaments, trips or tours, talent or beauty contests, fellowships, or conferences.
Publications: Application guidelines, Informational brochure (including application guidelines).
Application information: Proposals should be no longer than 2 to 4 pages in length. The Charitable Contributions Department handles giving. The company has a staff that only handles contributions. Application form not required.
   Initial approach: Proposal to headquarters or nearest company facility
   Copies of proposal: 1
   Deadline(s): Oct. 15
   Final notification: 3 months
Administrators: Barbara Contrevas, Coord.; Larry Goldzband, Mgr.; Dan C. Quigley, Dir., Charitable Contributions.
Number of staff: 4 full-time professional; 2 full-time support.

345
Philanthropic Ventures Foundation
1222 Preservation Pkwy.
Oakland, CA 94612-1201 (510) 645-1890
Contact: Bill Somerville, Pres. and Treas.
FAX: (510) 645-1892; E-mail: info@venturesfoundation.org; URL: http://www.venturesfoundation.org/

Established in 1991.
Grantmaker type: Public charity
Financial data (yr. ended 12/31/02): Revenue, $4,546,775; assets, $10,558,662 (L); gifts received, $4,626,020; expenditures, $4,586,633; program services expenses, $4,332,632; giving activities include $3,779,664 for 460 grants (high: $215,000; low: $15).
Purpose and activities: The foundation customizes giving programs to match donors' interests. PVF takes the investment approach to charitable giving, seeking outstanding people and opportunities whose impact in the community will be significant and bringing them to the attention of donors.
Fields of interest: Arts; Education; Environment; Human services; Economic development; Aging.

Types of support: Emergency funds; Program development; Seed money; Fellowships; Consulting services; Grants to individuals; Scholarships—to individuals.
Limitations: Applications not accepted. Giving primarily in the San Francisco Bay Area, CA, but extends nationally pursuant to donors' recommendations.
Publications: Annual report, Informational brochure, Newsletter.
Application information: Contributes only to pre-selected organizations; unsolicited requests for funds not considered or acknowledged.
   Board meeting date(s): Quarterly
Officers and Directors:* John P. Carver,* Chair.; Bill Somerville,* Pres. and Treas.; Moira C. Walsh,* Secy.; Howard H. Bell; William E. Green; Albert J. Horn; Jackie Speier; Colburn S. Wilbur; Jane Woodward.
Number of staff: 2 full-time professional; 1 full-time support; 1 part-time support.
EIN: 943136771

346
Plum Foundation
P.O. Box 1613
Studio City, CA 91604 (818) 766-8064
Contact: Pam Kaizer, Exec. Dir.
FAX: (818) 766-8064

Established in 1991 in CA.
Donor(s): Dorothy Gail Secrest.
Grantmaker type: Independent foundation
Financial data (yr. ended 08/31/02): Assets, $4,541,329 (M); expenditures, $367,810; qualifying distributions, $361,915; giving activities include $326,000 for 25 grants (high: $25,000; low: $2,500).
Purpose and activities: Giving primarily for education (with emphasis on the arts), wild animal protection, and visual and performing arts.
Fields of interest: Performing arts; Dance; Theater; Music; Arts; Elementary/secondary education; Education; Environment; Animals/wildlife, preservation/protection.
Types of support: General/operating support; Continuing support; Program development; Scholarship funds.
Limitations: Applications not accepted. Giving primarily in southern CA and TX for the arts; giving on a national basis for the environment and wildlife preservation and protection. No support for religious organizations for religious purposes, or for local animal shelters. No grants to individuals, or for land acquisition, building or endowment funds, annual fund drives of unified campaigns or capital campaigns, deficit financing, brochures, or public relations campaigns.
Publications: Informational brochure.
Application information: Contributes only to pre-selected organizations. Unsolicited requests for funds not accepted.
   Board meeting date(s): July and Dec.
Officers and Directors:* Emily Maupin, Chair.; John Montford,* Pres.; Robert Wolfe,* V.P.; Bill Baldridge, Secy.-Treas.; Pam Kaizer, Exec. Dir.; Dorothy Secrest.
Number of staff: 1 part-time professional.
EIN: 752406666

347
PowerBar Inc. Corporate Giving Program
c/o D.I.R.T. Prog., Event Sponsorship, or Team Elite Prog.
2150 Shattuck Ave.
Berkeley, CA 94704 (510) 665-2580
E-mail for Team Elite: team.elite@powerbar.com;
URL: http://www.powerbar.com/pbsports/
teamelite; http://www.powerbar.com/pbsports/
sponsorship

Grantmaker type: Corporate giving program
Purpose and activities: PowerBar makes charitable contributions to nonprofit organizations involved with natural resources conservation and protection and recreation. Support is given on a national basis.
Fields of interest: Natural resources; Recreation.
Types of support: General/operating support; Sponsorships.
Limitations: Giving on a national basis. No support for national organizations. No grants for film, video, or book projects, political campaigns, research, litigation, renovation or remodeling, or meetings or conferences.
Application information: Personal visits, telephone calls, and faxes are not encouraged. Application forms are available online. Multi-year funding for Team Elite is not automatic.
   Initial approach: Download application form for D.I.R.T.; proposal to headquarters for event sponsorships; download application form or E-mail headquarters for application form for Team Elite
   Deadline(s): June 8 for D.I.R.T.; 3 months prior to event for event sponsorships; Oct. 15 for Team Elite
   Final notification: Aug. 11 for D.I.R.T.; Jan. 15 for Team Elite

348
ProAction Foundation
4125 Hopyard Rd.
Pleasanton, CA 94588
URL: http://www.probusiness.com/
about_probusiness/community.asp

Established in 2001 in DE.
Donor(s): ProBusiness Services, Inc.
Grantmaker type: Company-sponsored foundation
Financial data (yr. ended 06/30/02): Assets, $12,494 (M); gifts received, $182,912; expenditures, $170,418; qualifying distributions, $170,418; giving activities include $167,924 for 142 grants (high: $16,375; low: $70).
Fields of interest: Education; Natural resources; Animals/wildlife; Health care; Disasters, preparedness/services; Youth, services; Community development.
Limitations: Applications not accepted. No grants to individuals.
Application information: Contributes only to pre-selected organizations.
Officers: Greg Trento, Pres.; Barbara Parkins, V.P.; Lisa Teixeira, Secy.; Alan Kaufman, Treas.
EIN: 943388199

349
Rainforest Action Network
221 Pine St., Ste. 500
San Francisco, CA 94104 (415) 398-4404
Contact: Patrick O'Heffernan, Pres.
FAX: (415) 398-2732; E-mail: rainforest@ran.org; URL: http://www.ran.org/

Established in 1985.
Grantmaker type: Public charity
Financial data (yr. ended 12/31/02): Revenue, $2,243,078; assets, $1,229,519 (M); gifts received, $1,907,267; expenditures, $2,132,810; program services expenses, $2,132,810; giving activities include $20,106 for 5 grants (high: $5,000; low: $1,000).
Purpose and activities: The organization provides public education to conserve and protect the world's natural resources, concentrating on preservation of tropical rainforests.
Fields of interest: Natural resources.
Types of support: General/operating support; Equipment; Land acquisition; Program development; Seed money.
Limitations: Giving on a national and international basis.
Publications: Annual report, Informational brochure (including application guidelines), Newsletter.
Application information: Application form not required.
   Initial approach: Proposal
   Copies of proposal: 1
   Deadline(s): None
Officers and Directors:* James D. Gollin,* Chair.; Andre Carothers,* Vice-Chair.; Randy Hayes,* Pres. and Secy.; Scott B. Price,* Treas.; Christopher Hatch, Exec. Dir.; Martha DiSario; Jodie Evans; Allan Hunt-Badiner; Michael Klein; Mike Roselle; and 5 additional directors.
Number of staff: 20 full-time professional; 3 part-time professional.
EIN: 943045180

350
The Raintree Foundation
6054 La Goleta Rd.
Goleta, CA 93117
Contact: Harold R. Frank, Secy.

Established in 1994 in CA.
Donor(s): Diana D. Frank, Harold R. Frank, H.R. Frank Family Trust.
Grantmaker type: Independent foundation
Financial data (yr. ended 12/31/02): Assets, $6,745,714 (M); gifts received, $1,232,005; expenditures, $371,124; qualifying distributions, $361,809; giving activities include $357,469 for 41 grants (high: $56,000; low: $100; average: $500–$5,000).
Purpose and activities: Giving primarily for youth services, medical research, and social services.
Fields of interest: Education; Natural resources; Medical research, institute; Youth development, centers/clubs; Human services; Children/youth, services.
Limitations: Giving primarily in Santa Barbara, CA. No grants to individuals.
Application information: Application form not required.

Initial approach: Letter on organization letterhead
Deadline(s): None
Officers: Diana D. Frank, Pres.; Harold R. Frank, Secy. and C.F.O.
Director: James A. Frank.
EIN: 770359291

351
The Robert Raskind Charitable Foundation
805 Hogan Way
Bakersfield, CA 93309 (661) 834-2883
Contact: Doris Darline Raskind, Pres.

Established in 1995 in CA.
Donor(s): Doris Darline Raskind.
Grantmaker type: Independent foundation
Financial data (yr. ended 12/31/02): Assets, $1,348,601 (M); expenditures, $110,373; qualifying distributions, $102,392; giving activities include $100,080 for 19 grants (high: $15,250; low: $200).
Fields of interest: Museums (art); Higher education; University; Nursing school/education; Animals/wildlife; Arthritis; Health organizations; Food services; Housing/shelter; Disasters, search/rescue; Human services; Homeless.
Limitations: Giving primarily in Bakersfield, CA and MT. No grants to individuals.
Application information:
   Initial approach: Proposal
   Deadline(s): Nov. 30
Officers: Doris Darline Raskind, Pres.; Susan L. Gonzales, Secy.; Novena K. Bonham, C.F.O.
Director: Carolyn M. Johnston.
EIN: 770426567

352
Will J. Reid Foundation
2801 E. Ocean Blvd.
Long Beach, CA 90803
Contact: Elizabeth Moore Westbrook, Pres.

Established in 1955 in CA.
Donor(s): Will J. Reid,‡ Virginia Reid Moore.‡
Grantmaker type: Independent foundation
Financial data (yr. ended 12/31/02): Assets, $6,293,558 (M); gifts received, $262,500; expenditures, $535,852; qualifying distributions, $490,000; giving activities include $490,000 for 57 grants (high: $70,000; low: $1,000).
Purpose and activities: Giving for art and cultural institutes, environmental organizations, and for youth and family services.
Fields of interest: Arts; Education; Natural resources; Environment; Human services; Youth, services.
Types of support: General/operating support; Continuing support; Annual campaigns; Land acquisition; Program evaluation.
Limitations: Giving primarily in southern CA. No grants to individuals.
Publications: Application guidelines.
Application information: Application form required.
   Initial approach: Letter
   Copies of proposal: 1
   Deadline(s): None
   Board meeting date(s): Annual meeting and distribution, usually in May
   Final notification: Positive responses only

Officers and Directors:* E.M. Westbrook,*
Pres.; Charlotte G. Burgess, V.P.; C.R. Moore,*
Secy.; W.J. Hancock, Treas.; W.R. Moore.
Number of staff: 1 part-time support.
EIN: 956041915

353
Resnick Family Foundation
11444 W. Olympic Blvd., 10th Fl.
Los Angeles, CA 90064

Established in 1997 in CA.
Donor(s): Lynda R. Resnick, Stewart A. Resnick.
Grantmaker type: Independent foundation
Financial data (yr. ended 09/30/01): Assets,
$475,781 (M); gifts received, $2,496,150;
expenditures, $2,394,512; qualifying
distributions, $2,393,133; giving activities
include $2,393,125 for 9 grants (high:
$1,000,000; low: $600).
Fields of interest: Museums; Education;
Disasters, 9/11/01; Human services; Jewish
federated giving programs.
Limitations: Applications not accepted. Giving
primarily in Los Angeles, CA and Washington,
DC. No grants to individuals.
Application information: Contributes only to
pre-selected organizations.
Officers and Directors:* Stewart A. Resnick,*
Co-Pres.; Lynda R. Resnick,* Co-Pres.; Peter
Gurney, Treas.
EIN: 954658095
**Recent environmental and animal welfare
grants:**
353-1 Conservation International, DC,
$500,000. For general support. 2002.

354
Adam Richter Charitable Trust
c/o Bank of America
P.O. Box 513189
Los Angeles, CA 90051-1189
Contact: Joseph Gubbrud, Trust Off., Bank of
America
Application address: 9461 Wilshire Blvd.,
Beverly Hills, CA 90212-2793, tel.: (310)
860-2505

Established in 1994 in CA.
Grantmaker type: Independent foundation
Financial data (yr. ended 09/30/02): Assets,
$2,754,632 (M); expenditures, $236,364;
qualifying distributions, $152,631; giving
activities include $140,000 for 25 grants (high:
$15,000; low: $500).
Purpose and activities: Giving for the arts,
education, the environment, health associations,
and human services.
Fields of interest: Arts; Higher education;
Environment; Animal welfare; Hospitals
(general); Health organizations, association;
Human services; Christian agencies & churches.
Limitations: Giving on a national basis.
Application information: Application form not
required.
 Deadline(s): None
Trustee: Bank of America.
EIN: 956978793

355
The Georgia B. Ridder Foundation
c/o Michael S. Whalen
553 S. Marengo Ave.
Pasadena, CA 91101-3114

Established in 2000 in CA.
Donor(s): Georgia B. Ridder.
Grantmaker type: Independent foundation
Financial data (yr. ended 12/31/01): Assets,
$362,735 (M); expenditures, $126,434;
qualifying distributions, $106,494; giving
activities include $105,500 for 16 grants (high:
$30,000; low: $1,000).
Fields of interest: Environment; Family
planning; Human services.
Limitations: Applications not accepted. Giving
primarily in CA, NY, and VA. No grants to
individuals.
Application information: Contributes only to
pre-selected organizations.
Officers and Director:* Georgia B. Ridder,*
Pres.; Michael S. Whalen, Secy. and C.F.O.
EIN: 954813547

356
Rivkin Family Foundation
(formerly The Polinsky-Rivkin Family
Foundation)
836 Prospect St., Ste. 202
La Jolla, CA 92037-4206   (619) 459-2631
Contact: Mike L. Rivkin, C.F.O.

Established in 1985 in CA.
Donor(s): Jessie W. Polinsky,‡ Jeannie P. Rivkin,
Arthur L. Rivkin, Beapol, Inc., Mike Rivkin, Bob
Rivkin, Linda Rivkin.
Grantmaker type: Independent foundation
Financial data (yr. ended 12/31/02): Assets,
$12,556,346 (M); gifts received, $99,993;
expenditures, $782,668; qualifying distributions,
$724,045; giving activities include $729,570 for
63 grants (high: $300,000; low: $118).
Fields of interest: Theater; Environment, water
resources; Children/youth, services; Human
services.
Types of support: General/operating support;
Capital campaigns; Building/renovation;
Emergency funds; Matching/challenge support.
Limitations: Giving primarily in CA. No support
for religious organizations. No grants to
individuals.
Application information: Application form not
required.
 Deadline(s): None
 Board meeting date(s): Biannually
Officers: Jeannie P. Rivkin, Pres.; Arthur L.
Rivkin, V.P.; Robert Rivkin, Secy.; Michael
Rivkin, C.F.O.
Director: Linda Rivkin.
EIN: 330072770

357
The Roberts Foundation
P.O. Box 29906
San Francisco, CA 94129-0906
(415) 561-6540
Contact: Lyman H. Casey, Exec. Dir.
FAX: (415) 561-6477; URL: http://
www.pacificfoundationservices.com/roberts/
index.html

Established in 1985 in CA.
Donor(s): George R. Roberts, Leanne B. Roberts.
Grantmaker type: Independent foundation
Financial data (yr. ended 12/31/01): Assets,
$60,350,305 (M); gifts received, $5,130,431;
expenditures, $12,317,231; qualifying
distributions, $11,571,045; giving activities
include $8,044,575 for 75 grants (high:
$1,000,000; low: $500; average:
$10,000–$100,000) and $3,403,197 for 1
foundation-administered program.
Purpose and activities: Giving primarily to
children, youth, and families, education, wildlife
preservation and animal welfare. Focus on
youth development, primarily academic
enrichment and vocational training. Within the
field of education, the foundation prefers to fund
programs for the learning disabled and
disadvantaged youth. The foundation also funds
social service projects of an entrepreneurial
nature that enable individuals to move from
positions of dependency to independence and
self-reliance. Support also for the Roberts
Enterprise Development Fund (REDF) which
creates opportunities for homeless and
low-income individuals to move out of poverty.
REDF partners with a portfolio of Bay Area
nonprofit organizations to create jobs and
training opportunities in social purpose
enterprises.
Fields of interest: Education, special; Vocational
education; Animal welfare; Animals/wildlife,
preservation/protection; Health care;
Employment; Children/youth, services; Family
services; Homeless, human services; Economic
development; Economically disadvantaged;
Homeless.
Types of support: General/operating support;
Continuing support; Program development.
Limitations: Applications not accepted. Giving
limited to northern CA, with emphasis on San
Francisco, San Mateo, Sonoma, Santa Clara, and
San Benito counties. No support for religious
organizations. No grants to individuals, or for
medical research, endowment funds, or annual
or year-end appeals.
Publications: Multi-year report.
Application information: Currently, the
foundation has suspended all grantmaking
except for that associated with the Roberts
Enterprise Development Fund. No proposals are
being accepted. If this changes, the foundation
will post new information and guidelines on it's
Web site.
 Board meeting date(s): Approximately Jan.
 and June
Officers and Directors:* Leanne B. Roberts,*
Pres. and C.E.O.; George R. Roberts,* V.P.,
Secy.-Treas., and C.F.O.; Lyman H. Casey,* V.P.
and Exec. Dir.
Number of staff: None.
EIN: 942967074

358
B. T. Rocca, Jr. Foundation
555 California St., No. 5185
San Francisco, CA 94104-1799
Contact: B.T. Rocca, Jr., Tr.

Established in 1986 in CA.
Donor(s): B.T. Rocca, Jr.
Grantmaker type: Independent foundation

Financial data (yr. ended 12/31/02): Assets, $2,646,360 (M); gifts received, $28,268; expenditures, $204,752; qualifying distributions, $162,141; giving activities include $124,800 for 56 grants (high: $5,000; low: $300).
Purpose and activities: Giving for emergency relief services, cultural institutes, health and medical services, youth services, and secondary and higher education; giving also for family services and nature conservation.
Fields of interest: Higher education; Education; Environment; Animals/wildlife, preservation/protection; Family planning; Health organizations, association; Youth development, scouting agencies (general); Human services; Federated giving programs.
Types of support: General/operating support; Continuing support; Annual campaigns; Endowments; Research.
Limitations: Applications not accepted. Giving primarily in CA. No grants to individuals.
Application information: Contributes only to pre-selected organizations.
Trustees: Marilee Johnson; B.T. Rocca, Jr.; B.T. Rocca III; Leroy H. Rocca.
Number of staff: 1 part-time professional.
EIN: 943028203

359
Romic Environmental Technologies Corp. Contributions Program
2081 Bay Rd.
East Palo Alto, CA 94303-1316
(650) 462-2315
Contact: Chris Stampolis, Dir., Community Education and Govt. Rels
E-mail: chriss@romic.com; URL: http://www.romic.com/romcomty.html

Grantmaker type: Corporate giving program
Financial data (yr. ended 12/31/02): Total giving, $34,000; giving activities include $34,000 for grants (high: $2,500; low: $350; average: $350–$2,500).
Purpose and activities: Romic makes charitable contributions to nonprofit organizations involved with education, the environment, crime prevention, children, and employment. Special emphasis is directed towards programs designed to keep children in school and build self-esteem, help people develop marketable job skills or find job opportunities, and abate drug abuse and crime. Support is given primarily in East Palo Alto, California.
Fields of interest: Education; Environment; Substance abuse, services; Crime/violence prevention; Children, services; Employment, services.
Types of support: General/operating support; Program development.
Limitations: Giving primarily in East Palo Alto, CA. No support for religious, political, or fraternal organizations. No grants to individuals, or for fundraising, advertising, or trips or tours.
Application information: The Community Relations department handles giving. A contributions committee reviews all requests. Application form required.
    Initial approach: Contact headquarters for application form
    Copies of proposal: 1
    Deadline(s): Nov. 1 and May 1
    Final notification: Following review

Number of staff: 1 full-time professional.

360
Rose Foundation for Communities and the Environment
6008 College Ave., Ste. 10
Oakland, CA 94618 (510) 658-0702
Contact: Tim Little, Exec. Dir.
FAX: (510) 658-0732; E-mail: rosefdn@earthlink.net; URL: http://www.rosefdn.org

Established in 1992 in CA.
Grantmaker type: Public charity
Financial data (yr. ended 08/31/02): Revenue, $2,045,762; assets, $1,434,046 (M); gifts received, $2,019,850; expenditures, $1,506,984; program services expenses, $1,403,110; giving activities include $1,228,509 for 63 grants (high: $162,350; low: $60), $2,000 for 2 grants to individuals of $1,000 each and $40,421 for in-kind gifts.
Purpose and activities: The foundation fosters community and environmental stewardship, improves communications between businesses and the neighbors, recognizes individual responsibility for the environmental stewardship and sustainable job creation, harnesses economic power to leverage environmental sustainability, and instills respect for the inalienable rights protected by our nation's constitution and the essential human rights to clean air, clean water and individual dignity. Some preference will be given to applicants who are bases in, or maintain operations in CA.
Fields of interest: Natural resources; Environment; Human services; Better business bureaus.
Types of support: General/operating support; Continuing support; Income development; Program development; Conferences/seminars; Seed money; Research; Technical assistance.
Limitations: Giving primarily in CA.
Publications: Application guidelines, Financial statement.
Application information: Grassroots Fund has quarterly deadlines. Please see Web site for details.
    Initial approach: Proposal (10-page maximum), or 2-page letter of inquiry if applicant is uncertain if project meets the application criteria
    Copies of proposal: 4
    Deadline(s): May 31 (for Aug. decision) and Nov. 30 (for Jan. decision)
Officers: Jill Ratner, Pres.; Kevin Hendrik, V.P.; Katie Knight, Secy.-Treas.
Directors: Marcos Cajna; Ellen Hauskens; David Michelfelder; Tom Soto.
Number of staff: 3.
EIN: 943179772

361
Rosengarten Horowitz Fund
134 The Uplands
Berkeley, CA 94705

Established in 1996 in CA.
Donor(s): Jeffrey Horowitz, Lynn Horowitz.
Grantmaker type: Independent foundation
Financial data (yr. ended 12/31/02): Assets, $7,025,302 (M); expenditures, $375,147;

qualifying distributions, $287,749; giving activities include $284,030 for 44 grants (high: $68,000; low: $100).
Purpose and activities: Giving primarily for animal welfare, education, human services, federated giving programs, and religious organizations.
Fields of interest: Media/communications; Arts; Higher education; Education; Animal welfare; Health care; Human services; Federated giving programs; Christian agencies & churches; Jewish agencies & temples.
Limitations: Applications not accepted. Giving on a national basis. No grants to individuals.
Application information: Contributes only to pre-selected organizations.
Officers and Directors:* Lynn Horowitz,* Pres.; Jeffrey Horowitz,* Secy.; Jason Briggs,* C.F.O.
EIN: 943257271

362
Sacramento Regional Foundation
555 Capitol Mall, Ste. 550
Sacramento, CA 95814 (916) 492-6510
Contact: Janice Gow Pettey, C.E.O.
FAX: (916) 492-6515; E-mail: srf@sacregfoundation.org; URL: http://www.sacregfoundation.org

Incorporated in 1983 in CA.
Grantmaker type: Community foundation
Financial data (yr. ended 12/31/01): Assets, $36,226,140 (M); gifts received, $12,187,205; expenditures, $7,549,405; giving activities include $6,438,851 for grants (high: $506,772; average: $1,000–$7,500) and $166,854 for 102 grants to individuals (average: $500–$10,000).
Purpose and activities: Primary areas of interest include the arts and humanities, education, community development, health, human services, and the environment. The foundation administers a donor-advised fund.
Fields of interest: Museums; Performing arts; Theater; Humanities; Historic preservation/historical societies; Arts; Child development, education; Elementary school/education; Higher education; Adult education—literacy, basic skills & GED; Reading; Education; Natural resources; Environment; Health care; Mental health/crisis services; Health organizations, association; AIDS; Alcoholism; Legal services; Food services; Housing/shelter, development; Youth development, services; Human services; Children/youth, services; Child development, services; Family services; Hospices; Aging, centers/services; Minorities/immigrants, centers/services; Homeless, human services; Urban/community development; Community development; Voluntarism promotion; Social sciences; Public policy, research; Government/public administration; Leadership development; Minorities; Disabled; Aging; Economically disadvantaged; Homeless.
Types of support: General/operating support; Management development; Capital campaigns; Building/renovation; Endowments; Emergency funds; Program development; Publication; Seed money; Scholarship funds; Research; Technical assistance; Program evaluation; Employee-related scholarships; Scholarships—to individuals; Matching/challenge support.

Limitations: Giving primarily focused on organizations within or those offering services to Sacramento, Yolo, Placer, and El Dorado counties, CA. No support for sectarian purposes or private foundations. No grants to individuals (except designated fund scholarships and through the Artists in Crisis Fund), or for annual campaigns, operating funds, capital campaigns, endowments, building funds, continuing support, deficit financing, foundation-managed projects, research, or land acquisition; no loans.
Publications: Annual report, Financial statement, Informational brochure, Newsletter.
Application information: Application form required.
   Copies of proposal: 10
   Deadline(s): None
   Board meeting date(s): Jan., Mar., May, July, Sept., and Nov.
Officers and Directors:* Janice Gow Pettey, C.E.O.; Steve Boutin, Pres.; Amador Bustos, V.P.; Donald C. Poole, Secy.; Ralph Andersen,* Treas.; Nick Alexander; Gerald F. Bays; Stephen A. Bradenburger; Marcy Friedman; Robert F. Gaines; Larry Gilzean; William Hegg; Oleta Lambert; David Luchetti; Melena A. Ose; Frank Ramos; Lillian Sioukas; Fred Teichert; Jesse Vaughan; Frank Whittaker.
Number of staff: 7 full-time professional; 2 full-time support.
EIN: 942891517

363
Sathya Sai Foundation of America
1220 Oaklawn Rd.
Arcadia, CA 91006

Established in 1997 in CA.
Donor(s): Rama K.R. Thumati, Narendranath A. Reddy, Choudary D. Voleti.
Grantmaker type: Independent foundation
Financial data (yr. ended 12/31/01): Assets, $36,743 (M); gifts received, $213,702; expenditures, $193,309; qualifying distributions, $180,232; giving activities include $180,234 for 10 grants (high: $121,500; low: $108).
Purpose and activities: Giving for medical supplies and for rural water development projects.
Fields of interest: Environment, water resources; Medical care, community health systems; Health care; Human services.
Limitations: Applications not accepted. No grants to individuals.
Application information: Contributes only to pre-selected organizations.
Officers: Narendranath A. Reddy, Chair.; Choudary D. Voleti, Pres.; Rama K.R. Thumati, V.P. and Secy.-Treas.
EIN: 954666929

364
San Diego Foundation for Change
3758 30th St.
San Diego, CA 92104 (619) 692-0527
Contact: Joni K. Craig, Exec. Dir.
FAX: (619) 255-3640; E-mail: info@foundation4change.org; URL: http://www.foundation4change.org

Established in 1994 in CA.
Grantmaker type: Public charity

Financial data (yr. ended 12/31/02): Revenue, $147,544; assets, $93,682 (L); gifts received, $99,518; expenditures, $205,757; program services expenses, $167,334; giving activities include $71,116 for 23 grants (high: $7,000; low: $500; average: $500–$7,000).
Purpose and activities: The foundation promotes positive, permanent change to end discrimination, lack of opportunity, poverty and environmental degradation in the San Diego/Tijuana border region by empowering small, community-based organizations with funding and technical assistance.
Fields of interest: Natural resources; Environment; Employment, equal rights; Civil rights; Public affairs, equal rights; Gays/lesbians.
Types of support: Seed money; Technical assistance.
Limitations: Giving limited to the San Diego, CA-Tijuana border region. No support for social or human service organizations that do not have a strong community organizing component; individuals; national or statewide projects unless there is a strong local focus; direct union organizing; private businesses or profit-making organizations; electoral campaigns or candidates.
Publications: Application guidelines, Grants list, Informational brochure, Newsletter.
Application information: Application form required.
   Initial approach: Letter or e-mail
   Copies of proposal: 2
   Deadline(s): Mar. 15
   Board meeting date(s): 1st Tues. of every month
   Final notification: May
Officers and Directors:* Victoria Danzig,* Founder; Kate Mayne,* Pres.; Kimberly Dark,* V.P.; Charles J. Avvampato IV,* Secy.-Treas.; Joni K. Craig, Exec. Dir.; Peter Brown; Ron L. Cummings; Felicia Eaves; Stephanie Edwards; Alan Larson; Ruth Larson; Jahida Nadi; Elizabeth Saehz-Ackerman; Sabina Widmann.
Number of staff: 1 part-time professional; 1 part-time support.
EIN: 330628755

365
The San Diego Foundation ▼
(formerly San Diego Community Foundation)
1420 Kettner Blvd., Ste. 500
San Diego, CA 92101-9693 (619) 235-2300
Contact: Robert A. Kelly, C.E.O. and Pres.
FAX: (619) 239-1710; URL: http://www.sdfoundation.org

Established in 1975 in CA.
Grantmaker type: Community foundation
Financial data (yr. ended 06/30/03): Assets, $385,898,000 (M); gifts received, $32,108,000; expenditures, $47,459,000; giving activities include $38,059,676 for 2,903+ grants (high: $2,250,000; average: $5,000–$25,000) and $9,324 for 38 employee matching gifts.
Purpose and activities: Giving to nonprofit organizations in the areas of asset building, civil society, education, environment/animal welfare, religion, scholarship, human/social services, health, arts and culture.
Fields of interest: Visual arts; Museums; Performing arts; Dance; Theater; Music; Arts; Early childhood education; Child development,

education; Elementary school/education; Secondary school/education; Vocational education; Higher education; Adult education—literacy, basic skills & GED; Reading; Education; Environment; Animal welfare; Family planning; Health care; Substance abuse, services; Mental health/crisis services; Health organizations, association; AIDS; Alcoholism; Medical research, institute; AIDS research; Crime/violence prevention, youth; Housing/shelter, development; Recreation; Human services; Children/youth, services; Child development, services; Family services; Hospices; Aging, centers/services; Women, centers/services; Homeless, human services; Community development; Voluntarism promotion; Minorities; Disabled; Aging; Women; Economically disadvantaged; Homeless.
International interests: Mexico.
Types of support: General/operating support; Continuing support; Building/renovation; Equipment; Land acquisition; Program development; Publication; Seed money; Curriculum development; Scholarship funds; Technical assistance; Program evaluation; Program-related investments/loans; Matching/challenge support.
Limitations: Giving primarily in the greater San Diego, CA, region. No support for political or religious organizations. No grants to individuals, or for annual or capital fund campaigns, endowment funds, conferences, travel, or to underwrite fundraising events and performances.
Publications: Application guidelines, Annual report (including application guidelines), Grants list, Informational brochure, Informational brochure (including application guidelines), Newsletter.
Application information: Application form required.
   Initial approach: Letter and Web site
   Copies of proposal: 3
   Deadline(s): Varies
   Board meeting date(s): Bimonthly beginning July through May
Officers and Board of Governors:* Colette Carson Royston,* Chair.; Bruce G. Blakley,* Vice-Chair.; Robert A. Kelly, C.E.O. and Pres.; Marian Diaz, Sr. V.P., Comm. Partnerships; Deborah Hoffman, V.P., Donor Rels.; Charlene Pryor, V.P., Philanthropy; Sandra Daley, M.D.,* Secy.; Raymond V. Thomas,* Treas.; Duane Drake, C.F.O.; Murray H. Hutchison; Fred Applegate; Hon. Rafael A. Arreola; Darcy C. Bingham; Robert B. Clelland; James M. Cowley; Martha Dennis, Ph.D.; John C. Raymond; Thomas N. Fat; Nova Faine, M.D.; Jerry Hoffmeister; Conny Jamison; Jerome Katzin; H. William Kuni; Denise Lew, Ph.D.; R. Michael McCraw; Paul Meyer; Barry I. Newman; Ardyth M. Shaw; Eugene L. Step; Stephen L. Weber, Ph.D.; Mary Lindenstein Walshok, Ph.D.; Carisa Wisniewski; John Wylie; Elizabeth Y. Yamada; James Ziegler.
Number of staff: 39 full-time professional; 2 part-time professional; 8 full-time support; 2 part-time support.
EIN: 952942582
Recent environmental and animal welfare grants:
365-1 Aquatic Adventures Science Education Foundation, San Diego, CA, $10,000. For Sea Series Program. 2003.

365-2 Citizens Action for Residential Environments in Saugerties (CARES), Saugerties, NY, $10,000. For Esopus Creek Conservancy Project. 2003.

365-3 Coastal Rainforest Coalition, Berkeley, CA, $20,000. For Forest Ethics. 2003.

365-4 Consensus Organizing Institute, San Diego, CA, $12,000. For Dialogue's collaborative project and Endangered Habitats League on land use planning and growth management in San Diego County. 2003.

365-5 Conservation Biology Institute, Corvallis, Oregon, $40,000. To identify binational land conservation priorities for southern San Diego County and northern Baja California that represent functional network of biogeographically important areas across border region. 2003.

365-6 Endangered Habitats League, Los Angeles, CA, $20,000. For ecosystem protection and improved land use planning for conservation in San Diego County. 2003.

365-7 Endangered Habitats League, Los Angeles, CA, $20,000. For ecosystem protection and improved land use planning for conservation in San Diego County. 2003.

365-8 Environmental Careers Organization (ECO), Boston, MA, $60,020. To recruit, place and train interns in support of San Diego Foundation's efforts to reduce and prevent environmental hazards in low-income, ethnically diverse communities in San Diego region. 2003.

365-9 Environmental Health Coalition, San Diego, CA, $39,984. To engage inter-generational and inter-cultural constituency in development issues affecting South Bay by developing corps of youth leaders educated on environmental issues. 2003.

365-10 Environmental Health Coalition, San Diego, CA, $20,000. To protect public health and environment threatened by toxic pollution. 2003.

365-11 Environmental Health Coalition, San Diego, CA, $20,000. For work of Environmental Health Coalition to eliminate environmental and public health degradation caused by toxic pollution. 2003.

365-12 Escondido Creek Conservancy, Escondido, CA, $82,700. For land purchase. 2003.

365-13 ForestEthics, Berkeley, CA, $20,000. For general support. 2003.

365-14 Guide Dogs for the Blind, San Diego, CA, $15,000. For Guide Dog Team in San Diego County. 2003.

365-15 Lakeside Conservancy, San Diego, CA, $25,000. To create flexible, community based nonprofit organization to implement Lakeside section of new San Diego River Park. 2003.

365-16 Manta Pacific Research Foundation, Kailua Kona, HI, $10,000. For general support. 2003.

365-17 North County Animal Control Shelter, Carlsbad, CA, $50,000. For North County Shelter Building Trust Fund Account. 2003.

365-18 Predator Conservation Alliance, Bozeman, MT, $10,000. For general support of wildlife conservation work. 2003.

365-19 San Diego BayKeeper, San Diego, CA, $45,000. For implementation of strategic plan. 2003.

365-20 San Diego BayKeeper, San Diego, CA, $25,000. For implementation of strategic plan. 2003.

365-21 San Diego BayKeeper, San Diego, CA, $20,000. For implementation of strategic plan. 2003.

365-22 San Diego BayKeeper, San Diego, CA, $20,000. For general operating support. 2003.

365-23 San Diego Natural History Museum, San Diego, CA, $50,000. To create plant atlas that documents San Diego's floristic diversity, and to train San Diego County residents how to identify, survey, and voucher plant specimens. 2003.

365-24 San Diego Natural History Museum, San Diego, CA, $20,000. For development of Plant Atlas for San Diego County. 2003.

365-25 San Diego State University Foundation, San Diego, CA, $50,000. To synthesize and test new non-toxic catalysts for degrading organophosphate pesticides and nerve agents. 2003.

365-26 San Diego State University Foundation, San Diego, CA, $22,000. To assess water quality in Upper San Luis Rey watershed as key indicator for environmental health at La Jolla Indian Reservation. 2003.

365-27 San Diego, City of, San Diego, CA, $16,200. For purchase of box native tree species and their installation. 2003.

365-28 San Diego, City of, San Diego, CA, $14,250. For replacement of trees lost from Red Gum Lerp Psylid. 2003.

365-29 San Diego, City of, San Diego, CA, $14,250. Toward trees for planting throughout Mission Bay Park. 2003.

365-30 San Diego, City of, San Diego, CA, $10,000. For conceptual and construction planning for pedestrian trail development in hillside section of Sunset Cliffs Natural Park. 2003.

365-31 San Diego, City of, San Diego, CA, $10,000. For concrete trash cans. 2003.

365-32 San Dieguito River Valley Land Conservancy, Del Mar, CA, $50,000. For acquisition of Bernardo Mountain. 2003.

365-33 San Dieguito River Valley Land Conservancy, Del Mar, CA, $10,000. For general support. 2003.

365-34 Scripps Institution of Oceanography, La Jolla, CA, $37,000. To determine fish metal accumulation from seafloor diet as well as from seawater. 2003.

365-35 Spay-Neuter Action Project, San Diego, CA, $15,000. For general support. 2003.

365-36 University of San Diego, San Diego, CA, $24,000. To learn how secondary organic aerosol particles form and contribute to haze formation over San Diego, environment heavily impacted by sea salt and vehicle emissions. 2003.

365-37 University of San Diego, San Diego, CA, $20,000. For Shiley Center for science and technology, Greenhouse. 2003.

365-38 Urban Corps of San Diego, San Diego, CA, $25,000. For part-time staff positions and administrative costs for Corps-to-Career education, job placement and management responsibilities. 2003.

365-39 Wildcoast, Imperial Beach, CA, $29,000. For general operating support. 2003.

365-40 Wildcoast, Imperial Beach, CA, $20,000. To protect coastal wildlife and wildlands of Baja California peninsula. 2003.

365-41 Wildcoast, Imperial Beach, CA, $16,000. For implementation of Wildcoast's strategic plan as part of its overall goal to protect coastal wildlife and wildlands of Baja California peninsula. 2003.

365-42 Wyoming Stock Growers Agricultural Land Trust, Cheyenne, WY, $10,000. For general support. 2003.

365-43 Zoological Society of San Diego, San Diego, CA, $30,900. For New Heart of Zoo Project. 2003.

365-44 Zoological Society of San Diego, San Diego, CA, $25,000. For general support. 2003.

365-45 Zoological Society of San Diego, San Diego, CA, $17,000. For printing of San Diego Habitats Brochure developed by Applied Conservation Division of CRES. 2003.

365-46 Zoological Society of San Diego, San Diego, CA, $14,850. 2003.

365-47 Zoological Society of San Diego, San Diego, CA, $10,800. For Heart of Zoo project. 2003.

365-48 Zoological Society of San Diego, San Diego, CA, $10,000. To build Asian rain forest habitat for families of siamang gibbons and orangutans. 2003.

366
San Diego Gas & Electric Company Contributions Program

c/o Corp. Community Rels.
101 Ash St.
San Diego, CA 92101 (619) 696-4297
Contact: Molly Cartmill, Dir., Corp. Community Rels.
Additional tel.: (877) 736-7729; FAX: (619) 696-1868; E-mail: sdgecommunity@sdge.com; URL: http://www.sdge.com/community/

Grantmaker type: Corporate giving program
Purpose and activities: San Diego Gas & Electric makes charitable contributions to nonprofit organizations involved with education, the environment, health and human services, community development, and public affairs. Support is given primarily in southern Orange and San Diego counties, California. Charitable contributions are also made through a separate program at Sempra Energy, the company's parent.
Fields of interest: Education; Environment; Health care; Human services; Business/industry; Community development; Public affairs.
Types of support: Program development; Conferences/seminars; Cause-related marketing; Employee volunteer services; Public relations services; Sponsorships; Employee matching gifts; Employee-related scholarships.
Limitations: Giving primarily in southern Orange and San Diego counties, CA. No support for private foundations, pass-through organizations, discriminatory organizations, sectarian or denominational organizations not of direct benefit to the entire community, sports teams or groups not of direct benefit to the

entire community, political parties or candidates or partisan political organizations, or non-educational government organizations. No grants to individuals (except for employee-related scholarships), or for general operating support, travel, debt reduction or past operating deficits, liquidation, continuing support, advertising, or sports programs or events not of direct benefit to the entire community; no gas or electric service discounts.

Publications: Application guidelines, Corporate giving report, Informational brochure (including application guidelines).

Application information: The Corporate Community Relations Department handles giving. The company has a staff that only handles contributions. A contributions committee reviews all requests. Application form not required.

> *Initial approach:* Proposal to headquarters
> *Copies of proposal:* 1
> *Deadline(s):* None
> *Board meeting date(s):* Monthly
> *Final notification:* 8 to 10 weeks

Administrators: Molly Cartmill, Dir., Corp. Community Rels.; Sammantha McDonald, Mgr.; Kelly Prasser, Mgr.; Carolyn Williams, Mgr.

Number of staff: 5 full-time professional; 4 full-time support.

367
The San Francisco Foundation ▼
225 Bush St., 5th Fl.
San Francisco, CA 94104-4224
(415) 733-8500
Contact: Sandra R. Hernandez, M.D., C.E.O. and Secy.
FAX: (415) 477-2783; E-mail: SRH@sff.org; URL: http://www.sff.org

Established in 1948 in CA by resolution and declaration of trust.

Grantmaker type: Community foundation

Financial data (yr. ended 06/30/03): Assets, $664,449,772 (M); gifts received, $53,607,137; expenditures, $75,962,915; giving activities include $65,295,022 for 4,438 grants (high: $2,187,000; low: $250) and $44,500 for 3 loans/program-related investments.

Purpose and activities: Grants principally in six categories: the arts and humanities, community health, education, environment, neighborhood and community development, and social services. Technical assistance grants also made, primarily to current recipients. The foundation serves five counties of the Bay Area.

Fields of interest: Media/communications; Performing arts; Dance; Humanities; Arts; Early childhood education; Child development, education; Elementary school/education; Adult education—literacy, basic skills & GED; Reading; Education; Natural resources; Environment; Family planning; Health care; Substance abuse, services; Mental health/crisis services; Health organizations, association; Cancer; AIDS; Alcoholism; Cancer research; AIDS research; Crime/violence prevention, youth; Legal services; Employment; Housing/shelter, development; Youth development, services; Human services; Children/youth, services; Child development, services; Family services; Aging, centers/services; Homeless, human services;

International human rights; Civil rights; Urban/community development; Community development; Voluntarism promotion; Public policy, research; Government/public administration; Leadership development; Public affairs; Minorities; Disabled; Aging; Immigrants/refugees; Economically disadvantaged; Homeless.

Types of support: General/operating support; Program development; Seed money; Fellowships; Technical assistance; Program-related investments/loans; Employee matching gifts; Scholarships—to individuals.

Limitations: Giving limited to the San Francisco Bay Area, CA, counties of Alameda, Contra Costa, Marin, San Francisco, and San Mateo. No support for religious purposes. No grants for annual campaigns, general fundraising campaigns, emergency or endowment funds, deficit financing, matching funds, or for scholarships or fellowships, except when so designated by donor.

Publications: Application guidelines, Annual report, Grants list, Informational brochure (including application guidelines), Newsletter, Program policy statement.

Application information: Application form required.

> *Initial approach:* Letter of intent (no more than 3 pages)
> *Copies of proposal:* 1
> *Deadline(s):* Mar. and Sept.
> *Board meeting date(s):* Monthly except Apr. and Aug.; applications are reviewed two times each year
> *Final notification:* 4 to 6 months

Officers and Trustees:* Leslie P. Hume,* Chair.; Sandra R. Hernandez, M.D.,* C.E.O. and Secy.; Sandi Hutchings, Cont.; Gay Plair Cobb; Stephanie DiMarco; Peter E. Haas, Jr.; Charlene Harvey; F. Warren Hellman; James C. Hormel; Tatwina Chinn Lee; Hugo Morales; Gladys Thacher.

Number of staff: 36 full-time professional; 15 full-time support; 5 part-time support.

EIN: 010679337

Recent environmental and animal welfare grants:

367-1 Alameda Center for Environmental Technologies, Alameda, CA, $25,000. To study feasibility of adding start-up companies in energy efficiency and renewable energy generation technology industries to current tenant base. 2002.

367-2 Alliance for a Clean Waterfront, San Francisco, CA, $35,000. For continued research on alternatives to San Francisco airport's proposed runway expansion plan. 2002.

367-3 Asian Pacific Environmental Network (APEN), Oakland, CA, $60,000. To build dynamic network of grassroots groups organizing around environmental and social justice issues affecting Asian Pacific Islander communities. 2002.

367-4 Asian Pacific Environmental Network (APEN), Oakland, CA, $25,000. To implement information technology plan of organization, which works on multicultural environmental justice programs in Bay Area. 2002.

367-5 Audubon Canyon Ranch, Stinson Beach, CA, $15,500. 2002.

367-6 Audubon Society, Golden Gate, Berkeley, CA, $26,000. To strengthen school-based environmental education program in East Oakland by adding Spanish-English bilingual weekend programs for family and friends of participating students. 2002.

367-7 Audubon Society, Golden Gate, Berkeley, CA, $25,000. To implement information technology plan of environmental education and conservation organization serving Bay Area. 2002.

367-8 Bay Area Ridge Trail Council, San Francisco, CA, $10,000. For Ridge Kids and Stewards environmental education program for low-income Bay Area youth. 2002.

367-9 Bay Institute of San Francisco, San Rafael, CA, $20,000. For Students and Teachers Restoring A Watershed (STRAW) environmental education program. 2002.

367-10 Bay Institute of San Francisco, San Rafael, CA, $10,000. To develop San Francisco Bay-Delta-Rivers Ecological Scorecard that will serve as tool for informing policymakers and public about how state of watershed impacts human health. 2002.

367-11 Bay Model Association, Sausalito, CA, $32,000. For continued environmental monitoring of Warm Springs Marsh in South San Francisco Bay. 2002.

367-12 Bluewater Network, San Francisco, CA, $20,000. For Clean Vessels Initiative to reduce air and water pollution in San Francisco Bay caused by fast ferries and cruise ships. 2002.

367-13 California Academy of Sciences, San Francisco, CA, $53,500. 2002.

367-14 California Environmental Trust, San Francisco, CA, $25,000. 2002.

367-15 California Exotic Pest Plant Council, Davis, CA, $60,000. To hire organization's first executive director, who will develop research and restoration program focused on protecting California's natural areas from wildland weeds. 2002.

367-16 Camp Fire, Northern California Council, Eureka, CA, $45,000. To implement Thinking Ahead, scientific-based ecology education and restoration program for youth. 2002.

367-17 Center for Environmental Health, Oakland, CA, $12,000. 2002.

367-18 Center for Urban Education About Sustainable Agriculture, Berkeley, CA, $20,000. To develop business plan for operating outdoor farmers' market, indoor produce sales area, and sustainable agriculture education center in renovated Ferry Building. 2002.

367-19 Center for Watershed and Community Health, Springfield, Oregon, $10,000. 2002.

367-20 Chez Panisse Foundation, Berkeley, CA, $31,700. 2002.

367-21 City CarShare, San Francisco, CA, $35,000. To help expand innovative and practical car sharing program that aims to reduce dependency upon automobile ownership in order to promote more sustainable Bay Area. 2002.

367-22 Communities for a Better Environment, Oakland, CA, $40,000. For low-income residents advocating for public policies that will reduce air pollution and resulting health problems in communities. 2002.

367-23 Communities for a Better Environment, Oakland, CA, $25,000. To improve environmental health conditions in West Contra Costa County by supporting collaborative partnership with Contra Costa County Public Health Department and West County Collaborative. 2002.

367-24 Connecticut Fund for the Environment, New Haven, CT, $35,000. 2002.

367-25 Conservation International, DC, $752,500. 2002.

367-26 Earth Island Institute, San Francisco, CA, $20,000. For Kids for the Bay program, classroom and hands-on environmental education for elementary school students from low-income neighborhoods in Alameda and Contra Costa Counties. 2002.

367-27 Earth Island Institute, San Francisco, CA, $12,000. For Kids for the Bay. 2002.

367-28 Earth Island Institute, San Francisco, CA, $11,000. 2002.

367-29 Earth Island Institute, San Francisco, CA, $10,000. For Bay Area Wilderness training for youth workers and teachers to enable them to lead safe and successful wilderness experiential education programs for urban youth. 2002.

367-30 Earth Team, Walnut Creek, CA, $10,000. To promote environmental learning and leadership among teens in Alameda, Contra Costa, and San Francisco Counties by linking schools with restoration projects and nonprofit and government resources. 2002.

367-31 EarthRights International, DC, $30,000. 2002.

367-32 East Bay Alliance for a Sustainable Economy, Oakland, CA, $15,000. For grassroots leadership development and multi-sector coalition building in Emeryville. 2002.

367-33 East Bay Conservation Corps, Oakland, CA, $30,000. To reduce blight in target West Oakland neighborhoods and offer local residents and crew of West Oakland Corpsmember High School students hands-on opportunities to restore and create places of natural beauty. 2002.

367-34 Ecology Center, Berkeley, CA, $10,000. To improve health of low-income Berkeley residents by increasing consumption of high quality, nutritious, and culturally appropriate fresh food while supporting sustainable agriculture. 2002.

367-35 Ecotrust, Portland, Oregon, $42,500. 2002.

367-36 Edible Schoolyard at King Middle School, Berkeley, CA, $13,000. To retrofit bungalow at Martin Luther King Jr. Middle School as permanent facility for environmental education program involving organic gardening and cooking. 2002.

367-37 Edible Schoolyard at King Middle School, Berkeley, CA, $12,700. 2002.

367-38 Environmental Defense, Oakland, CA, $81,000. 2002.

367-39 Environmental Justice Coalition on Water, Oakland, CA, $100,000. To bring concerns of low-income communities and communities of colors to attention of state and federal agencies implementing water management in California and to advocate for policies and practices that are sensitive to needs of communities. 2002.

367-40 Environmental Water Caucus, San Francisco, CA, $445,000. To promote protection and restoration of San Francisco Bay/Delta ecosystem through policy advocacy, technical analysis, and grassroots education and organizing. 2002.

367-41 Environmental Working Group, Oakland, CA, $50,000. To conduct study of Poly Brominated Dimethyl Ethers (PBDEs) in fish from San Francisco Bay in order to provide data for setting discharge standards and reducing persistent organic pollutants in food chain. 2002.

367-42 ExLoco, Sausalito, CA, $317,000. For continued support for Diversity Network Project's program. 2002.

367-43 ExLoco, Sausalito, CA, $107,500. To start Diversity Network Project, which aims to support and strengthen coalition that brings together diverse constituencies and interests to address sustainable development and social justice. 2002.

367-44 Greenaction for Health and Environmental Justice, San Francisco, CA, $15,000. For efforts to reduce pollution and ensure responsible treatment of waste generated at Bay Area medical facilities. 2002.

367-45 Greenbelt Alliance, San Francisco, CA, $21,250. 2002.

367-46 Greenpeace Foundation of America, San Francisco, CA, $16,500. 2002.

367-47 Humane Society of Michigan, Auburn Hills, MI, $10,000. 2002.

367-48 Humboldt, County of, Community Development Services Department, Eureka, CA, $30,000. To develop agriculture land protection programs for County's open space plan. 2002.

367-49 Kamehameha Schools, Honolulu, HI, $30,000. To establish ecocultural stewardship and education program for one of state's largest land holders. 2002.

367-50 Kentucky Resources Council, Frankfort, KY, $75,000. 2002.

367-51 Literacy for Environmental Justice, San Francisco, CA, $30,000. For restoration and youth stewardship programs at Heron's Head Park, wetland at base of Hunters Point power plant. 2002.

367-52 Maat Youth Academy, Richmond, CA, $25,000. For high school leadership program designed to decrease public exposure to mercury caused by eating local fish. 2002.

367-53 Marin Agricultural Land Trust, Point Reyes Station, CA, $55,658. 2002.

367-54 Marine Mammal Center, Sausalito, CA, $149,350. 2002.

367-55 Mendocino Land Trust, Mendocino, CA, $130,000. 2002.

367-56 Mendocino Land Trust, Mendocino, CA, $50,000. To help protect Big River watershed, habitat for redwoods and threatened species, by creating new California state park. 2002.

367-57 Mission Anti-Displacement Partnership, San Francisco, CA, $20,000. For inclusive community-based land-use planning process. 2002.

367-58 Monterey Bay Aquarium, Monterey, CA, $25,875. 2002.

367-59 Muir Heritage Land Trust, Martinez, CA, $60,000. To prepare restoration plan for Pacheco March, wetland at mouth of Walnut Creek Channel along Carquinez Strait in Contra Costa County. 2002.

367-60 National People of Color Environmental Leadership Summit, DC, $25,000. To enable Bay Area environmental justice activists to attend conference in Washington, DC. 2002.

367-61 Natural Heritage Institute, San Francisco, CA, $15,000. To finish developing adaptive management plan for restoring floodplain habitat in Yolo Bypass of Central California. 2002.

367-62 Natural Resources Defense Council, San Francisco, CA, $1,033,000. 2002.

367-63 Natural Resources Defense Council, San Francisco, CA, $60,000. For development, acceptance, and implementation of restoration plan for San Joaquin River, major tributary to San Francisco Bay. 2002.

367-64 Nature Conservancy, San Francisco, CA, $50,000. To restore riparian forest and protect endangered species found along Romero Creek on Mount Hamilton, as part of conservation project in Diablo range in southern Alameda and eastern Santa Clara Counties. 2002.

367-65 Nature Conservancy, San Francisco, CA, $10,750. 2002.

367-66 Nature Conservancy, Arlington, VA, $25,400. 2002.

367-67 North East Trees, Los Angeles, CA, $40,000. For Urban Stream Daylighting Program, which will map historic streams and wetlands throughout Los Angeles area as part of building support for uncovering and restoring them. 2002.

367-68 Northern California Council for the Community (NCCC), San Francisco, CA, $35,000. To produce, in cooperation with Bay Area Alliance for Sustainable Development and Bay Area Partnership, report on indicators that can be used to track region's progress towards preserving natural resources, revitalizing low-income neighborhoods, and assuring social equity. 2002.

367-69 Oceanic Society, San Francisco, CA, $10,000. 2002.

367-70 Pacific Crest Outward Bound School, Portland, Oregon, $38,000. 2002.

367-71 Pacific Rivers Council, Eugene, Oregon, $35,000. 2002.

367-72 PAL Foundation, Half Moon Bay, CA, $40,000. For Bay Area Tree Recycling Yard, which promotes highest-end uses of fallen trees through manufacture and sale of certified recycled lumber. 2002.

367-73 Peninsula Open Space Trust, Menlo Park, CA, $13,500. 2002.

367-74 People Organizing to Demand Environmental Rights, San Francisco, CA, $20,000. To develop environmental justice curriculum for elementary and middle school students in Mission District with assistance of young leaders from local community organizations. 2002.

367-75 Pets Are Wonderful Support (PAWS), San Francisco, CA, $12,500. To implement information technology plan. 2002.

367-76 Pets Unlimited, San Francisco, CA, $10,750. 2002.

367-77 Physicians for Social Responsibility, Los Angeles, CA, $30,000. To use report, In Harms Way: Toxic Threats to Child Development, in conjunction with trainings for health providers, community members, and patients on links between environmental exposure to toxins and neurodevelopmental disabilities in children. 2002.

367-78 POINT Foundation, Sausalito, CA, $10,500. 2002.

367-79 Point Reyes Bird Observatory, Stinson Beach, CA, $35,000. To develop and implement strategic communications plan to build name recognition, increase support, and develop partnerships to protect biodiversity. 2002.

367-80 Point Reyes Bird Observatory, Stinson Beach, CA, $20,000. 2002.

367-81 Rachels Network, DC, $10,000. 2002.

367-82 RARE Center for Tropical Conservation, Arlington, VA, $10,000. 2002.

367-83 Resource Renewal Institute, San Francisco, CA, $83,500. 2002.

367-84 River of Words, Berkeley, CA, $25,000. 2002.

367-85 Rocky Mountain Institute, Snowmass, CO, $25,000. To complete energy plan for City and County of San Francisco that emphasizes efficiency and renewable sources, including use of solar bonds approved by voters. 2002.

367-86 San Francisco Bay Bird Observatory, San Jose, CA, $25,000. For continued study of pollution contaminate levels in tern species and to analyze sources of exposure coming from San Francisco Bay. 2002.

367-87 San Francisco Bicycle Coalition, Transportation for a Livable City, San Francisco, CA, $25,000. To start coalition that will promote public transit, pedestrian safety, and land use practices consistent with sustainable development. 2002.

367-88 San Francisco Estuary Institute, Richmond, CA, $40,000. For regional efforts to conserve and restore wetlands by compiling and distributing data that document current and historic wetland restoration efforts in San Francisco Bay. 2002.

367-89 San Francisco Zoological Society, San Francisco, CA, $97,750. 2002.

367-90 San Mateo County Parks and Recreation Foundation, Menlo Park, CA, $25,000. For initial phase of designing environmental education program focusing on county's parks. 2002.

367-91 Satayana Institute, Boulder, CO, $30,000. 2002.

367-92 Save San Francisco Bay Association, Oakland, CA, $41,250. 2002.

367-93 Save San Francisco Bay Association, Oakland, CA, $10,000. For strategic planning. 2002.

367-94 Save the Redwoods League, San Francisco, CA, $10,000. To assist in protection of redwood forest adjacent to Jedediah Smith and Del Norte Coast Redwoods State Parks. 2002.

367-95 Seacology, Berkeley, CA, $124,000. 2002.

367-96 Seven Tepees Youth Program, San Francisco, CA, $15,000. To aid youth participants in intensive mentoring and academic enrichment program in accessing postsecondary and career opportunities. 2002.

367-97 Sierra Club Foundation, San Francisco, CA, $31,250. 2002.

367-98 Sonoma Ecology Center, Sonoma, CA, $50,000. To coordinate science education and restoration efforts around Sonoma Creek. 2002.

367-99 Sustainable Conservation, San Francisco, CA, $40,000. For Auto Recycling Project, which seeks to reduce levels of water pollution in San Francisco Bay resulting from auto dismantling. 2002.

367-100 Sustainable Conservation, San Francisco, CA, $20,000. For Partners in Restoration program in streamlining permit-seeking process for private landowners in Alameda and Marin Counties who are interested in restoring watersheds on their lands. 2002.

367-101 Sustainable Ecosystems Institute, Portland, Oregon, $25,000. 2002.

367-102 Thimmakkas Resources for Environmental Education, Oakland, CA, $20,000. For greening of South Asian restaurants in Bay Area by working with restaurant owners to promote sound waste management, organic purchasing, pollution prevention, and energy and water efficiency strategies. 2002.

367-103 Tides Center, San Francisco, CA, $15,000. For Verde Partnership Garden. 2002.

367-104 Tides Center, San Francisco, CA, $10,000. For Wilderness Arts and Literacy Collaborative, academic program using environmental education and outdoor field experiences to integrate science, English, social studies, art, and technology in schools. 2002.

367-105 Trout Unlimited, San Francisco, CA, $10,500. 2002.

367-106 Trust for Public Land, San Francisco, CA, $50,000. To add grassland habitat that harbors endangered butterflies to San Bruno Mountain State and County Park. 2002.

367-107 Trust for Public Land, San Francisco, CA, $50,000. To develop, in cooperation with Oakland Parks Coalition, city-wide stewardship program for urban parks and playgrounds that can serve as model for other communities. 2002.

367-108 Trust for Public Land, San Francisco, CA, $17,158. 2002.

367-109 University of California Cooperative Extension, Richard J. Elkus Youth Ranch, San Francisco, CA, $15,000. For new environmental science instructor to provide hands-on environmental education to Bay Area youth, including youth with special needs. 2002.

367-110 Urban Ecology, Oakland, CA, $30,000. For continued support for helping cities, community groups, and developers understand and promote sustainable land use policies. 2002.

367-111 Urban Habitat Program, Oakland, CA, $40,000. For capacity-building support during time of transition. 2002.

367-112 Visitacion Valley Greenway Project, San Francisco, CA, $25,000. To enhance capacity of organization, which is working to create urban park in Visitacion Valley. 2002.

367-113 West Oakland Community Land Trust, Oakland, CA, $10,000. To assist with community organizing support, and legal and other costs associated with fulfilling partnership responsibilities with Northern California Land Trust on the Linden Street project in West Oakland. 2002.

367-114 WestEd, San Francisco, CA, $20,000. For Bay Area activities of California Regional Environmental Education Coordinator Network, which links K-12 teachers with information, projects and resources. 2002.

367-115 Wildlife Trust, Palisades, NY, $10,250. 2002.

367-116 Woods Hole Research Center, Woods Hole, MA, $25,000. 2002.

367-117 World Wildlife Fund/Conservation Foundation, DC, $269,750. 2002.

367-118 Yosemite Foundation, San Francisco, CA, $19,500. 2002.

367-119 Youth United for Community Action (YUCA), East Palo Alto, CA, $25,000. For Fighting Injustice and Regulating Equality Fellowship and the Higher Learning program in developing young leaders in environmental and social justice movements. 2002.

368
Marian Sandercock Trust

c/o J. Donald Wheat
920 1st St. W.
Sonoma, CA 95476

Established in 1985 in CA.
Grantmaker type: Independent foundation
Financial data (yr. ended 06/30/02): Assets, $163,088 (M); expenditures, $543,534; qualifying distributions, $531,132; giving activities include $528,500 for 10 grants (high: $100,000; low: $5,000).
Fields of interest: Higher education; Animal welfare.
International interests: Central America; Belize.
Limitations: Applications not accepted. Giving primarily in Sonoma, CA; some giving also in Belize, Central America. No grants to individuals.
Application information: Contributes only to pre-selected organizations. Unsolicited requests for funds not accepted.
Trustees: Edwin C. Anderson, Jr.; J. Donald Wheat.
EIN: 686018669

369
Robert V. Sanford and Laraine M. Sanford Charitable Foundation

5476 Quail Meadows Dr.
Carmel, CA 93923
Contact: Robert V. Sanford, Pres.

Donor(s): Robert V. Sanford, Laraine M. Sanford.
Grantmaker type: Independent foundation
Financial data (yr. ended 12/31/02): Assets, $2,946,361 (M); gifts received, $3,000; expenditures, $165,158; qualifying distributions, $159,596; giving activities include $147,025 for 20 grants (high: $22,500; low: $16).
Fields of interest: Arts; Animals/wildlife, preservation/protection; Recreation.
Limitations: Giving primarily in CA.
Application information: Application form not required.
Deadline(s): None
Officers and Directors:* Robert V. Sanford,* Pres.; Laraine M. Sanford,* Secy.
EIN: 770526314

370
Santa Barbara Foundation ▼
15 E. Carrillo St.
Santa Barbara, CA 93101 (805) 963-1873
Contact: Charles O. Slosser, C.E.O. and Pres.
FAX: (805) 966-2345; E-mail:
mday@sbfoundation.org,
amyb@sbfoundation.org, or
cslosser@sbfoundation.org; URL: http://
www.sbfoundation.org

Incorporated in 1928 in CA.
Grantmaker type: Community foundation
Financial data (yr. ended 12/31/01): Assets,
$183,769,046 (M); gifts received, $3,590,447;
expenditures, $8,139,125; giving activities
include $5,049,928 for 423 grants, $205,696
for grants to individuals and $2,088,956 for
1,069 loans to individuals.
Purpose and activities: The Santa Barbara
Foundation is a community foundation
established in 1928 to enrich the lives of the
people of Santa Barbara County through
philanthropy.
Fields of interest: Arts; Education; Environment;
Health care; Human services; Children/youth,
services; Community development.
Types of support: Capital campaigns;
Building/renovation; Equipment; Land
acquisition; Emergency funds; Program
development; Scholarship funds;
Scholarships—to individuals;
Matching/challenge support; Student loans—to
individuals.
Limitations: Giving limited to Santa Barbara
County, CA. No support for religious
organizations or schools, colleges, or
universities. No grants for annual campaigns, or
for deficit financing, endowment funds,
fundraising drives, conferences, seminars,
one-time events, political lobbying or legislative
activities, scholarships, fellowships, or for
research.
Publications: Application guidelines, Annual
report, Financial statement, Informational
brochure, Newsletter, Occasional report.
Application information: Application form
required.
  Initial approach: Letter or telephone inquiry
  Deadline(s): Quarterly depending on type of
  organization
  Board meeting date(s): Monthly except July;
  decisions on grant requests made in Mar.,
  June, Sept., and Dec.
  Final notification: 3 to 4 months
Officers and Trustees:* David H. Anderson,*
Chair.; William J. Cirone,* Vice-Chair.; Shirley
Ann Hurley,* Vice-Chair.; Judith Woods
Markline,* Vice-Chair.; Charles O. Slosser,
C.E.O. and Pres.; Dinah Van Wingerden,* Secy.;
David R. Alvarado,* Treas.; Keith Berwick;
Patricia Dillon Bliss; Joyce Howerton; Joseph A.
Olivera, Jr.; Thomas Parker; Ken Saxon; Anne
Smith; Judith Cosdon Stapelmann; George
Thurlow; Hilda Zacarias.
Fund Managers: Alternative Investment
Manager; Sanford Bernstein; Capital Research &
Mgmt. Co.; Canterbury Consulting; J.L. Kaplan;
Trust Co. of the West; Wells Fargo Bank, N.A.
Number of staff: 12 full-time professional; 4
full-time support.
EIN: 951866094
**Recent environmental and animal welfare
grants:**

370-1 Animal Shelter Assistance Program of
Santa Barbara (ASAP), Santa Barbara, CA,
$10,000. For volunteer coordinator position.
2001.
370-2 Audubon Society of Santa Barbara,
Goleta, CA, $10,000. For Meet Your Wild
Neighbor Program. 2001.
370-3 Center for Urban Agriculture at Fairview
Gardens, Goleta, CA, $10,646. For
self-guided tour panels, office tilings and
furniture. 2001.
370-4 Community Environmental Council,
Santa Barbara, CA, $25,000. For staffing and
evaluator for Green Schools Program. 2001.
370-5 Environmental Defense Center, Santa
Barbara, CA, $30,000. For Central Coast
Environmental Health Project. Grant made in
partnership with The California Endowment.
2001.
370-6 Ganna Walska Lotusland Foundation,
Santa Barbara, CA, $12,000. For Elementary
School Education Outreach Program. 2001.
370-7 Goleta Beautiful, Santa Barbara, CA,
$15,000. For Goleta Beautiful Capacity
Building Program. 2001.
370-8 Growing Solutions Restoration Education
Institute, Santa Barbara, CA, $15,000. For
Healthy Habitat Program. 2001.
370-9 Land Trust for Santa Barbara County,
Santa Barbara, CA, $75,000. For acquisition
of Arroyo Hondo Ranch. 2001.
370-10 Return to Freedom, Lompoc, CA,
$10,000. For volunteer/program coordinator
position. 2001.
370-11 San Marcos Foothills Coalition, Santa
Barbara, CA, $10,000. For Education and
Outreach to Educators Program. 2001.
370-12 Santa Barbara Wildlife Care Network,
Santa Barbara, CA, $15,000. For
Rehabilitation Supervisor position. 2001.
370-13 Surfrider Foundation, San Clemente, CA,
$10,000. 2001.
370-14 Wilderness Youth Project, Carpinteria,
CA, $12,000. For Outreach Coordinator
position for Young Eagles Program. 2001.

371
Santa Cruz Island Foundation
1010 Anacapa St.
Santa Barbara, CA 93101
Contact: Marla D. Daily, Pres.

Established in 1987 in CA.
Grantmaker type: Independent foundation
Financial data (yr. ended 12/31/00): Assets,
$5,644,269 (M); gifts received, $41,226;
expenditures, $410,484; qualifying distributions,
$382,241; giving activities include $121,171 for
18 grants (high: $55,000; low: $7) and $21,043
for 3 foundation-administered programs.
Purpose and activities: Supports programs and
projects relating to the cultural and natural
history of the Channel Islands, CA.
Fields of interest: Museums; Environment.
Types of support: General/operating support;
Building/renovation.
Limitations: Giving primarily in Santa Barbara,
CA. No grants to individuals.
Application information:
  Initial approach: Letter
  Deadline(s): None

Officers: David D. Watts, Chair.; Marla D. Daily,
Pres.; Joseph Walsh, V.P.; Eric P. Hvolboll, Secy.;
Polly Goodan, Treas.
Directors: Mrs. Richard Diebenkorn; Francis J.
Weber.
EIN: 954073657

372
SANYO North America Corporation
Contributions Program
2055 SANYO Ave.
San Diego, CA 92154
Contact: Allen Foster, V.P.
URL: http://www.sanyo.com/aboutsanyo/
corp_philanthropy.cfm

Grantmaker type: Corporate giving program
Purpose and activities: SANYO makes
charitable contributions to nonprofit
organizations involved with arts and culture,
education, the environment, health, children,
and economic development. Support is given
primarily in areas of company operations.
Fields of interest: Arts; Education; Environment;
Health care; Children, services; Economic
development.
Types of support: Program development; In-kind
gifts.
Limitations: Giving primarily in areas of
company operations.
Application information: Application form not
required.
  Initial approach: Proposal to headquarters

373
The Sapling Foundation
P.O. Box 620952
Woodside, CA 94062

Established in 1995.
Donor(s): Christopher Anderson.
Grantmaker type: Independent foundation
Financial data (yr. ended 12/31/01): Assets,
$19,155,024 (M); expenditures, $1,804,526;
qualifying distributions, $1,582,487; giving
activities include $1,526,000 for 8 grants (high:
$350,000; low: $16,000).
Fields of interest: Natural resources;
Community development.
Limitations: Applications not accepted. Giving
primarily in CA and NY. No grants to individuals.
Application information: Contributes only to
pre-selected organizations.
Board Members: Christopher Anderson; Susan J.
Dawson.
EIN: 943235545

374
The Gladys W. Sargent Foundation
P.O. Box 1244
Danville, CA 94526
Contact: Lynda LaBare, Pres.
Tel./FAX: (925) 831-3716

Established in 1998 in CA.
Donor(s): Gladys W. Sargent Trust.
Grantmaker type: Independent foundation
Financial data (yr. ended 12/31/01): Assets,
$4,715,594 (M); expenditures, $355,529;

qualifying distributions, $309,389; giving activities include $305,000 for 1 grant.

Purpose and activities: The foundation supports 4 major areas of activity: 1) Animal population control through spaying and neutering; 2) Operating an animal shelter for domestic pets; 3) Acquiring unwanted domestic pets and placing them in suitable homes; 4) Education to promote kindness towards animals.

Fields of interest: Animal welfare; Animals/wildlife.

Types of support: General/operating support; Continuing support.

Limitations: Giving on a national basis. No support for religious or political organizations. No grants to individuals, or for endowments, debt reduction, scholarships, fundraising, advertising or medical/scientific research; no loans.

Application information:
Initial approach: Letter
Deadline(s): July 1

Officers: Lynda LaBare, Pres.; Virginia Handley, Secy.; Sue Molen, Treas.

Directors: Ruth Mackesey; Karen Matuska; Betty Denny Smith; Wilma Witmer.

EIN: 911843277

375
Saul Family Fund
(formerly George W. & Faye Batten Saul Family Fund)
c/o Bailard, Biehl & Kaiser
950 Tower Ln., Ste. 1900
Foster City, CA 94404-2131

Established in 1981 in CA.

Donor(s): George W. Saul, Faye E. Batten Saul, Saul Charitable Annuity Trust.

Grantmaker type: Independent foundation

Financial data (yr. ended 08/31/02): Assets, $20,168 (M); gifts received, $175,000; expenditures, $243,120; qualifying distributions, $242,990; giving activities include $243,000 for 36 grants (high: $50,000; low: $1,000).

Purpose and activities: Giving primarily to hospitals and health associations, human services and education, and wildlife conservation.

Fields of interest: Higher education; Animals/wildlife, preservation/protection; Hospitals (general); Health care; Health organizations, association; Boy scouts; Girl scouts; Human services; American Red Cross; Roman Catholic agencies & churches.

Limitations: Applications not accepted. Giving primarily in the San Francisco Bay Area, CA. No grants to individuals.

Application information: Contributes only to pre-selected organizations.

Officers: Faye E. Batten Saul, Pres. and Treas.; Jane Wynne Saul, Secy.

EIN: 942797241

376
Save-the-Redwoods League
c/o Grants Comm.
114 Sansome St., Rm. 1200
San Francisco, CA 94104-3823
(415) 362-2352
Contact: Ruskin Hartley, Conservation
FAX: (415) 362-7017; E-mail:
info@savetheredwoods.org; URL: http://www.savetheredwoods.org

Established in 1918 in CA.

Grantmaker type: Public charity

Financial data (yr. ended 03/31/01): Assets, $65,539,167 (M); expenditures, $5,790,634; giving activities include $2,774,731 for grants and $89,471 for grants to individuals.

Purpose and activities: The league works to rescue California's redwood forest from destruction and to encourage a better general understanding of the value of the primeval redwood and giant sequoia forests. It operates a number of its own programs to address issues concerning redwood conservation and to support redwood related education and research.

Fields of interest: Education; Environment, plant conservation; Environment.

Types of support: Equipment; Land acquisition; Publication; Research; Program-related investments/loans; Grants to individuals; In-kind gifts; Matching/challenge support.

Publications: Annual report, Financial statement, Informational brochure, Newsletter.

Application information: Proposals are accepted by e-mail; See Web site for grant guidelines and application forms. Application form required.
Initial approach: E-mail proposal and cover letter
Copies of proposal: 1
Deadline(s): Nov. 30 for Research; June 30 for K-12; none for Land Acquisition
Final notification: Jan. 30 for Research; July 30 for K-12

Officers and Directors:* Richard C. Otter,* Chair.; Edwin F. Claassen,* Pres.; Sandra Donnell,* V.P.; Katherine Anderton,* Secy. and Exec. Dir.; Frank W. Wentworth,* Treas.; Sarah Connick; Pete Dangermond; James Larson; Wally Mark.

Number of staff: 7 full-time professional; 9 full-time support.

EIN: 940843915

377
Schlinger Foundation
P.O. Box 1421
Santa Ynez, CA 93460-1421
Contact: Dr. Evert I. Schlinger Sr., Pres.

Established in 1986 in CA.

Donor(s): The William and E.G. Schlinger Trust.

Grantmaker type: Independent foundation

Financial data (yr. ended 12/31/01): Assets, $34,675,948 (M); expenditures, $10,075,023; qualifying distributions, $8,740,909; giving activities include $8,579,369 for 65 grants (high: $7,345,000; low: $20).

Purpose and activities: Giving primarily for arts and cultural programs, and human services.

Fields of interest: Museums (specialized); Higher education; Education; Natural resources; Animals/wildlife; Health organizations,

association; Agriculture/food; Boys & girls clubs; Human services; Biological sciences; Science.

International interests: South Africa; Chile; Fiji; New Caledonia; Australia.

Types of support: Continuing support; Annual campaigns; Equipment; Land acquisition; Endowments; Professorships; Fellowships; Scholarship funds; Research.

Limitations: Applications not accepted. Giving on a national and international basis, with emphasis on CA and Washington, DC, as well as Australia and South Africa. No grants to individuals.

Publications: Annual report.

Application information: Contributes only to pre-selected organizations.
Board meeting date(s): Varies

Officers and Director:* Evert I. Schlinger, Sr.,* Pres.; Ms. Teresa Meikel,* Secy.-Treas.; Charles Griswold; Leonard Vincent.

Number of staff: 2 part-time professional; 1 part-time support.

EIN: 944065303

378
William & Jane Schloss Family Foundation
c/o Family Investment Mgmt.
655 Deep Valley Dr., Ste. 220
Rolling Hills, CA 90274

Established in 1999 in MN.

Donor(s): Michael Flamm, Ellen Flamm, Eric Flamm, Maya Flamm.

Grantmaker type: Independent foundation

Financial data (yr. ended 12/31/02): Assets, $752,201 (M); gifts received, $90,000; expenditures, $178,127; qualifying distributions, $173,800; giving activities include $173,900 for 12 grants (high: $20,000; low: $10,000).

Fields of interest: Education; Animals/wildlife; Disasters, 9/11/01.

Limitations: Applications not accepted. Giving primarily in CA, MN, and NY. No grants to individuals.

Application information: Contributes only to pre-selected organizations.

Officers and Director:* Eric Flamm,* Pres. and Exec. Dir.; Cindi Mishkin, Secy.

EIN: 411957655

379
Marjorie Mosher Schmidt Foundation
5256 S. Mission Rd., Ste. 1010
Bonsall, CA 92003-3624
Contact: John H. Scudder, Pres.

Incorporated in 1956 in CA.

Donor(s): Marjorie Mosher Schmidt,‡ Charles L. Scudder Trust.

Grantmaker type: Independent foundation

Financial data (yr. ended 12/31/00): Assets, $3,580,489 (M); gifts received, $386,971; expenditures, $578,414; qualifying distributions, $534,858; giving activities include $531,000 for 74 grants (high: $75,000; low: $1,000).

Fields of interest: Secondary school/education; Higher education; Natural resources; Health care; Boys & girls clubs; Human services; Children/youth, services; Disabled.

Types of support: General/operating support; Continuing support; Annual campaigns; Building/renovation; Equipment; Endowments;

Program development; Conferences/seminars; Scholarship funds; Research.

Limitations: Applications not accepted. Giving primarily in southern CA. No grants to individuals.

Application information: Contributes only to pre-selected organizations.

Board meeting date(s): Nov.

Officers: John H. Scudder, Pres.; Margaret Cringle, V.P.; Craig A. Scudder, V.P.; Mark F. Scudder, V.P.; Kent M. Scudder, Secy.; John T. Kearns, Treas.

Number of staff: None.

EIN: 956047798

380
The Schow Foundation
P.O. Box 177
South Pasadena, CA 91031-0177

Established in 2000 in CA.

Donor(s): Howard Schow.

Grantmaker type: Independent foundation

Financial data (yr. ended 12/31/02): Assets, $7,731,161 (M); gifts received, $1,579,025; expenditures, $1,549,800; qualifying distributions, $1,487,355; giving activities include $1,492,500 for 12 grants (high: $500,000; low: $5,000).

Fields of interest: Higher education; Environment.

Limitations: Applications not accepted. Giving primarily in CA. No grants to individuals.

Application information: Contributes only to pre-selected organizations.

Officers: Howard Schow, Pres.; Nan Schow, Secy.-Treas.

Directors: Melanie J. Schow; Roger L. Schow; Steven Schow.

EIN: 954791558

381
The Charles Schwab Corporation Foundation ▼
101 Montgomery St., M.S.: SF120KNY-28
San Francisco, CA 94104 (877) 408-5438
Contact: Elinore Robey, Sr. Mgr.
FAX: (415) 636-3262; E-mail: CIS@Schwab.com

Established in 1993 in CA.

Donor(s): The Charles Schwab Corp.

Grantmaker type: Company-sponsored foundation

Financial data (yr. ended 06/30/02): Assets, $4,553,969 (M); gifts received, $4,948,058; expenditures, $4,207,343; qualifying distributions, $3,996,812; giving activities include $4,011,636 for 2,509 grants (high: $1,013,010; low: $13; average: $60–$2,000).

Purpose and activities: Provides cash and in-kind contributions to qualifying nonprofit organizations and institutions for services and programs that improve and enhance the quality of life in communities where Schwab employees live and work. Support for arts, education, human services, especially family services, programs for the homeless and/or hungry, AIDS programs, and youth; very limited giving for benefits or fundraisers. Most grants are unrestricted; very limited seed or capital grants; priority is given to organizations with employee involvement.

Fields of interest: Museums; Performing arts; Arts; Education; Natural resources; Health care; Employment; Youth development; Human services; Social sciences, fund raising; General charitable giving; Asians/Pacific Islanders; African Americans/Blacks; Hispanics/Latinos; People with AIDS (PWAs); Economically disadvantaged; Homeless.

Types of support: General/operating support; Annual campaigns; Internship funds; Employee matching gifts; In-kind gifts; Matching/challenge support.

Limitations: Giving primarily in the San Francisco Bay Area, CA; limited giving where company has branch locations (350 cities nationwide); state or national organizations are considered only if they serve branch communities; grants are mostly to local organizations. No support for religious purposes, athletic organizations, or single-disease organizations. No grants for advertising, scholarship funds, colleges, universities, or medical research; no challenge grants.

Publications: Application guidelines, Annual report, Informational brochure.

Application information: Prior grant does not ensure future funding unless a commitment or pledge to that effect is made by the corporate donor. Written requests from previous or current grantees are required for each new funding year.

Initial approach: Brief proposal

Copies of proposal: 1

Deadline(s): None

Final notification: Quarterly

Officers and Directors:* Charles Schwab,* Chair.; James G. Losi, Pres.; Charmel Huffman, Secy.; Dave Pottruck, Treas.; Elinore Robey, Sr. Mgr.; Larry Stupski.

Number of staff: 1 full-time professional.

EIN: 943192615

Recent environmental and animal welfare grants:

381-1 Cascade Land Conservancy, Seattle, WA, $80,500. 2002.

381-2 Humane Society of Vero Beach, Vero Beach, FL, $10,000. 2002.

382
The Ellen Browning Scripps Foundation
c/o E. Douglas Dawson
6121 Terryhill Dr.
La Jolla, CA 92037

Established in 1935 in CA.

Donor(s): Ellen Browning Scripps,‡ Robert Paine Scripps.‡

Grantmaker type: Independent foundation

Financial data (yr. ended 06/30/03): Assets, $22,093,818 (M); expenditures, $1,248,947; qualifying distributions, $1,241,944; giving activities include $1,221,957 for 45 grants (high: $281,000; low: $2,000).

Fields of interest: Arts; Education; Animals/wildlife; Health care; Human services; Hospices.

Types of support: Equipment; Scholarship funds; Research; Program-related investments/loans.

Limitations: Giving primarily in San Diego County, CA. No grants to individuals.

Application information: Foundation occasionally accepts unsolicited requests for funds. Application form not required.

Initial approach: Letter of proposal (no more than 3 pages)

Copies of proposal: 4

Deadline(s): May 1

Board meeting date(s): June

Final notification: Sept. 1

Trustees: Deborah M. Goddard; Roxanne Davis Greene; Paul K. Scripps.

Number of staff: None.

EIN: 951644633

383
Frances Seebe Trust
c/o Wells Fargo Bank, N.A.
P.O. Box 63954, MAC 0103-179
San Francisco, CA 94163

Established in 1983 in CA.

Grantmaker type: Independent foundation

Financial data (yr. ended 01/31/03): Assets, $2,715,957 (M); expenditures, $269,857; qualifying distributions, $203,466; giving activities include $175,796 for 14 grants (high: $25,000; low: $2,000).

Purpose and activities: Giving primarily to wildlife research and animal protection; support also for medical research.

Fields of interest: Animal welfare; Animals/wildlife, preservation/protection; Animals/wildlife; Cancer research; Arthritis research.

Limitations: Applications not accepted. Giving on a national basis, with emphasis on CA, particularly Los Angeles. No grants to individuals.

Application information: Contributes only to pre-selected organizations.

Trustee: Wells Fargo Bank, N.A.

EIN: 956795278

384
Barnet Segal Charitable Trust
P.O. Box S-1
Carmel, CA 93921

Established in 1986 in CA.

Grantmaker type: Independent foundation

Financial data (yr. ended 03/31/02): Assets, $16,164,121 (M); expenditures, $517,330; qualifying distributions, $369,492; giving activities include $183,000 for 25 grants (high: $70,000; low: $1,000).

Purpose and activities: Giving primarily for conservation, the arts, health care, and human services.

Fields of interest: Arts; Natural resources; Environment, land resources; Animal welfare; AIDS; Human services; Children/youth, services; Economically disadvantaged.

Types of support: General/operating support; Building/renovation.

Limitations: Applications not accepted. Giving primarily in Carmel and Monterey, CA. No grants to individuals.

Application information: Contributes only to pre-selected organizations.

Trustees: Herbert Berman; Stuart Berman; William Brodsley.

EIN: 776024786

385
Select Office Solutions Foundation
(formerly Select Copy System of Southern California Foundation)
6229 Santos Diaz St.
Irwindale, CA 91706 (626) 334-0383
Contact: Frank J. Mendicina, Pres.

Established in 1991 in CA.
Grantmaker type: Independent foundation
Financial data (yr. ended 12/31/02): Assets, $48,499 (M); gifts received, $22,545; expenditures, $149,698; qualifying distributions, $104,663; giving activities include $104,663 for grants (high: $10,000; low: $179).
Purpose and activities: Giving for education, health, youth programs, and religious organizations.
Fields of interest: Education; Animal welfare; Cystic fibrosis; Cancer; Boys & girls clubs; Youth development, services; Human services; Christian agencies & churches.
Limitations: Giving limited to southern CA. No grants to individuals.
Application information:
    Deadline(s): None
Officers: Frank J. Mendicina, Pres.; Edward D. Fulgoni, C.F.O.
EIN: 954308657

386
Sempra Energy Corporate Giving Program
c/o Corp. Community Rels. Dept.
101 Ash St., HQ15E
San Diego, CA 92101-3017 (619) 696-4297
Contact: Molly Cartmill, Dir., Corp. Community Rels.
Additional tel.: (877) SEMPRA9; FAX: (619) 696-1868; E-mail: sempracommunity@sempra.com; URL: http://www.sempra.com/community.htm

Grantmaker type: Corporate giving program
Financial data (yr. ended 12/31/02): Total giving, $8,442,000; giving activities include $8,023,000 for grants and $419,000 for 600 employee matching gifts.
Purpose and activities: Sempra Energy makes charitable contributions to nonprofit organizations involved with arts and culture, education, the environment, health and human services, community development, and civic affairs. Support is given on a national and international basis. Charitable contributions are also made through separate programs at San Diego Gas & Electric and SoCalGas, the company's subsidiaries.
Fields of interest: Arts; Education; Environment; Health care; Human services; Economic development; Business/industry; Community development; Public affairs.
International interests: Canada; Mexico; South America.
Types of support: Annual campaigns; Program development; Conferences/seminars; Cause-related marketing; Employee volunteer services; Public relations services; Sponsorships; Employee matching gifts; Employee-related scholarships.
Limitations: Giving on a national and international basis, with emphasis on central and southern CA, including Inland Empire, Los Angeles, San Diego, and Orange County, and in

Canada, Mexico, and South America. No support for private foundations, pass-through organizations, discriminatory organizations, sectarian or denominational organizations not of direct benefit to the entire community, sports teams or groups not available to the general public, political parties or candidates or partisan political organizations, or non-educational government organizations. No grants to individuals (except for employee-related scholarships), or for general operating support, travel, debt reduction, liquidation, continuing support, advertising, or sports programs or events not available to the general public; no gas or electric service discounts.
Publications: Application guidelines, Informational brochure (including application guidelines), Program policy statement.
Application information: The Corporate Community Relations Department handles giving. The company has a staff that only handles contributions. A contributions committee reviews all requests. Application form not required.
    Initial approach: Proposal to headquarters
    Copies of proposal: 1
    Deadline(s): None
    Final notification: 8 to 10 weeks
Administrators: Molly Cartmill, Dir., Corp. Community Rels.; David Jay, Mgr.; Cathy Lavin, Mgr.
Number of staff: 2 full-time professional; 3 full-time support.

387
The Seven Springs Foundation
11801 Dorthy Anne Way
Cupertino, CA 95014

Established in 1979 in CA.
Donor(s): Dorothy S. Lyddon.
Grantmaker type: Independent foundation
Financial data (yr. ended 12/31/01): Assets, $4,813,971 (M); expenditures, $358,884; qualifying distributions, $265,890; giving activities include $240,106 for 60 grants (high: $20,000; low: $500).
Fields of interest: Natural resources; Environment; Women.
Types of support: General/operating support; Continuing support; Annual campaigns; Capital campaigns; Building/renovation; Emergency funds; Program development; Conferences/seminars; Internship funds; Research; Matching/challenge support.
Limitations: Applications not accepted. Giving primarily in the San Francisco Bay Area, CA. No grants to individuals.
Application information: Unsolicited requests for funds not considered.
    Board meeting date(s): Oct.
Officers and Trustees:* Dorothy S. Lyddon,* Chair.; Martha Lyddon,* Pres.; John Lyddon,* Secy.-Treas.
Number of staff: 1 part-time professional.
EIN: 942570260

388
Seventh Generation Fund
(also known as Seventh Generation Fund for Indian Development, Inc.)
P.O. Box 4569
Arcata, CA 95518-4569 (707) 825-7640
Contact: Candice Ludlow, Proj. Asst.
FAX: (707) 825-7639; E-mail: of7gen@pacbell.net; URL: http://www.7genfund.org

Established in 1977 in CA.
Grantmaker type: Public charity
Financial data (yr. ended 06/30/02): Revenue, $1,767,198; assets, $902,861 (M); gifts received, $1,656,236; expenditures, $2,245,383; program services expenses, $2,046,241; giving activities include $237,465 for 76 grants (high: $10,000; low: $300).
Purpose and activities: The fund is a national Native American advocacy and intermediary grantmaking organization dedicated to maintaining and promoting the uniqueness of Native peoples and the distinctiveness of their nations. The fund provides an integrated program of grants, management support, training and technical assistance, and advocacy to innovative indigenous grassroots projects throughout Native communities of the U.S., Canada, and South and Central America.
Fields of interest: Natural resources; Environment; Religion; Native Americans/American Indians.
International interests: Canada; Central America; South America.
Types of support: General/operating support; Continuing support; Annual campaigns; Building/renovation; Equipment; Emergency funds; Program development; Conferences/seminars; Publication; Seed money; Technical assistance.
Limitations: Giving limited to U.S., Canada, and Central and South America.
Publications: Annual report (including application guidelines), Occasional report.
Application information: See Web site for application guidelines and cover sheet. Application form not required.
    Initial approach: Letter or telephone
    Deadline(s): None
    Board meeting date(s): Varies
Officers and Directors:* Rosalie Little Thunder,* Chair.; John Mohawk,* Pres.; Christopher Peters, Exec. Dir.; Tony Davis; Tonya Gonnella Frichner; Joann Tall; Ray Williams.
Number of staff: 2 full-time professional; 2 part-time professional; 1 full-time support; 2 part-time support.
EIN: 680027247

389
SGI Corporate Giving Program
1600 Amphitheatre Pkwy., M.S. 742
Mountain View, CA 94043-1351
(650) 933-3845
Contact: Helle Madsen, Coord., Community Rels.
Additional tel.: (650) 932-0751; FAX: (650) 932-0751; Additional FAX: (650) 932-0751; E-mail: helle@sgi.com; URL: http://www.sgi.com/company_info/community

Grantmaker type: Corporate giving program

Purpose and activities: SGI makes charitable contributions to nonprofit organizations involved with arts and culture, education, the environment, health and human services, and civic affairs. Support is given primarily in California, Minnesota, and Wisconsin.
Fields of interest: Arts; Education; Environment; Health care; Human services; Public affairs.
Types of support: General/operating support; Employee volunteer services; Use of facilities; Sponsorships; Donated equipment; In-kind gifts.
Limitations: Giving primarily in CA, MN, and WI. No support for political organizations, fraternal organizations, religious organizations, or discriminatory organizations.
Publications: Application guidelines, Corporate giving report, Informational brochure (including application guidelines).
Application information: Unsolicited requests for monetary contributions are not accepted. Proposals should be no longer than 1 page in length. The Community Relations Department handles giving. The company has a staff that only handles contributions. A contributions committee reviews all requests. Application form not required.
   Initial approach: Proposal to headquarters
   Copies of proposal: 1
   Deadline(s): July 1, Oct. 1, Jan. 1, and Apr. 1
   Board meeting date(s): Quarterly
   Final notification: Following review
Number of staff: 2 full-time professional.

390
Shaklee Corporation Contributions Program
4747 Willow Rd.
Pleasanton, CA 94588-2763 (925) 924-2000
Contact: Cheri Labadie, Mgr., Community Rels.
URL: http://www.shaklee.com/main/aboutCitizen

Grantmaker type: Corporate giving program
Purpose and activities: Shaklee makes charitable contributions to nonprofit organizations involved with arts and culture, education, the environment, health, and nutrition. Support is given primarily in areas of company operations.
Fields of interest: Performing arts; Arts; Education; Environment; Health care; Nutrition.
Types of support: General/operating support; Program development; Scholarship funds; Employee matching gifts; Donated products; In-kind gifts.
Limitations: Giving primarily in areas of company operations. No support for political organizations, labor organizations, religious organizations not of direct benefit to the entire community, or United Way-supported organizations. No grants to individuals, or for capital or building campaigns, contests or raffles, or federated giving programs.
Application information: A contributions committee reviews all requests. Application form not required.
   Initial approach: Proposal to headquarters
   Deadline(s): None
   Board meeting date(s): Quarterly

391
Shapiro Family Charitable Foundation
(formerly The Hanover Foundation)
9401 Wilshire Blvd., No. 1201
Beverly Hills, CA 90212

Established in 1983.
Donor(s): Ralph J. Shapiro, Shirley Shapiro, Flavia J. Kavanau, Earl W. Kavanau, Kihi Foundation, Knoll International Holdings, Inc.
Grantmaker type: Independent foundation
Financial data (yr. ended 01/31/02): Assets, $3,619,917 (M); gifts received, $818,408; expenditures, $1,338,585; qualifying distributions, $1,284,950; giving activities include $1,284,550 for 101 grants (high: $950,000; low: $100).
Purpose and activities: Giving primarily to United Way; also giving for education, health, human services, legal organizations and conservation.
Fields of interest: Museums; Museums (history); Arts; Higher education; Theological school/education; Libraries/library science; Education; Natural resources; Health organizations, association; Medical research, institute; Legal services; Human services; YM/YWCAs & YM/YWHAs; Children/youth, services; Foundations (community); Federated giving programs; Jewish agencies & temples; Disabled.
Types of support: General/operating support.
Limitations: Giving primarily in southern CA. No grants to individuals.
Application information: Application form not required.
   Deadline(s): None
Officers: Ralph J. Shapiro, Chair.; Shirley Shapiro, Pres.; Alison D. Shapiro, V.P.; Peter W. Shapiro, V.P.; Ava Coyne, Secy.; Floyd P. Cook, Jr., C.F.O.
EIN: 953887151

392
Shasta Regional Community Foundation
2280 Benton Dr., Bldg. C, Ste. A
Redding, CA 96003 (530) 244-1219
FAX: (530) 244-0905; *E-mail:* pam@shastarcf.org; *URL:* http://www.shastarcf.org

Established in 2000 in CA.
Grantmaker type: Community foundation
Financial data (yr. ended 06/30/02): Assets, $2,767,283 (M); gifts received, $2,777,526; expenditures, $832,413; giving activities include $409,012 for 73 grants (high: $100,000; low: $500).
Purpose and activities: The mission of the foundation is to enhance the quality of life of Shasta and Siskiyou Communities through facilitating the everlasting gift intentions of donors.
Fields of interest: Arts; Education; Environment; Health care; Human services.
Types of support: Management development; Endowments; Scholarship funds; Consulting services.
Limitations: Applications not accepted. Giving limited to nine northern CA counties, with emphasis on Shasta and Siskiyou counties.
Publications: Annual report.

Application information: Unsolicited requests for funds not accepted.
   Board meeting date(s): Monthly
Officers: Steve Baker, Chair.; Maggie John, Vice-Chair.; Angie Lidster, Secy.; Vivian Piche, Treas.; Kathy Anderson, Exec. Dir.
Number of staff: 3 full-time professional; 1 part-time professional; 1 part-time support.
EIN: 680242276

393
The Sheinberg Foundation
c/o MYCFO, Inc.
2029 Century Park E., Ste. 800
Los Angeles, CA 90067

Established in 1986 in CA.
Donor(s): Sidney J. Sheinberg, Lorraine E. Sheinberg.
Grantmaker type: Independent foundation
Financial data (yr. ended 11/30/01): Assets, $1,147,796 (M); expenditures, $928,593; qualifying distributions, $924,001; giving activities include $924,008 for 54 grants (high: $400,480; low: $100).
Purpose and activities: Giving for arts, education, health associations, and human services.
Fields of interest: Arts; Education; Natural resources; Animal welfare; Hospitals (general); Health organizations, association; Human services; Children/youth, services; Women.
Limitations: Applications not accepted. Giving primarily in CA. No grants to individuals.
Application information: Contributes only to pre-selected organizations.
Officers: Lorraine E. Sheinberg, Pres.; Lawrence Kartiganer, V.P.; Jonathon J. Sheinberg, Secy.; William D. Sheinberg, C.F.O.
Trustee: Sidney J. Sheinberg.
EIN: 954079661

394
The Thomas and Stacey Siebel Foundation
c/o First Virtual Mgmt., Inc.
2207 Bridgepointe Pkwy.
San Mateo, CA 94404 (650) 477-5379
Contact: Thomas M. Siebel, Pres.

Established in 1996 in CA.
Donor(s): Stacey Siebel, Thomas M. Siebel.
Grantmaker type: Independent foundation
Financial data (yr. ended 12/31/02): Assets, $139,504,485 (M); expenditures, $9,939,793; qualifying distributions, $9,443,956; giving activities include $9,665,505 for 19 grants (high: $2,500,000; low: $105; average: $500–$20,000).
Purpose and activities: Giving primarily to a school; giving also to the Salvation Army for programs for the homeless in San Francisco, CA, as well as for land conservation and children's scholarships and services.
Fields of interest: Education, single organization support; Elementary/secondary education; Environment, land resources; Salvation Army; Children, services; Homeless, human services.
Limitations: Giving primarily in CA.
Application information: Application form not required.
   Deadline(s): None

Officers: Thomas M. Siebel, Pres.; Stacey Siebel, Secy.
EIN: 943256331

395
The Sierra Club Foundation
85 2nd St., Ste. 750
San Francisco, CA 94105 (415) 995-1780
Contact: John DeCock, Exec. Dir.
Funding services tel.: 1-800-783-9273; FAX: (415) 995-1791; E-mail: sierraclub.foundation@sierraclub.org; URL: http://TSCF.org

Established in 1960 in CA.
Grantmaker type: Public charity
Financial data (yr. ended 12/31/02): Revenue, $23,619,830; assets, $107,733,974 (L); gifts received, $13,164,558; expenditures, $42,656,970; program services expenses, $39,272,008; giving activities include $39,198,343 for grants.
Purpose and activities: The foundation seeks to advance the preservation and protection of the natural environment by empowering the citizenry, especially democratically based grassroots organizations, with charitable resources to further the cause of environmental protection. The Sierra Club is the vehicle through which the foundation generally fulfills its charitable mission. Support is given for more than 900 volunteer-based environmental projects, primarily those of the Sierra Club working locally, regionally, nationally, and internationally to preserve the natural environment through education, research, litigation, and social services.
Fields of interest: Education; Natural resources; Environment.
Types of support: Research.
Limitations: Giving on an international basis.
Publications: Application guidelines, Annual report, Financial statement, Informational brochure.
Application information: Application form required.
  Initial approach: Telephone requesting Funding Services Guide
  Board meeting date(s): Quarterly
Officers and Trustees:* Marlene Fluharty,* Pres.; Guy Saperstein,* V.P.; Robert Perkowitz,* Secy.; Robert Flint,* Treas.; Chuck Frank,* 5th Off.; John DeCock, Exec. Dir.; and 9 additional directors.
Number of staff: 7 full-time professional; 1 part-time support.
EIN: 946069890

396
Sierra Pacific Foundation
P.O. Box 496028
Redding, CA 96049-6028
Contact: Stephanie Donham

Established in 1978 in CA.
Donor(s): Sierra Pacific Industries.
Grantmaker type: Company-sponsored foundation
Financial data (yr. ended 06/30/02): Assets, $342,244 (M); gifts received, $375,250; expenditures, $504,836; qualifying distributions, $496,729; giving activities include $236,222 for

250 grants (high: $25,000; low: $13) and $260,507 for 254 grants to individuals (high: $3,500; low: $250).
Purpose and activities: Support for higher and secondary education, including libraries; parks and recreational activities for youth; museums and other cultural programs; civic affairs, including citizens' associations and public media; wildlife and environmental preservation; social services, including women's shelters and child welfare; and hospitals, an eye bank, and other health organizations. Scholarships are restricted to dependent children of Sierra Pacific Industries employees.
Fields of interest: Media/communications; Museums; Arts; Secondary school/education; Higher education; Environment; Health care; Health organizations, association; Recreation; Human services; Children/youth, services; Women, centers/services; Government/public administration; Women.
Types of support: General/operating support; Employee-related scholarships.
Limitations: Giving primarily in CA.
Application information: Application form required.
  Initial approach: Letter requesting application
  Board meeting date(s): Mar. 31
Officers: Carolyn Emmerson Dietz, Pres.; George Emmerson, V.P.; M.D. Emmerson, Secy.
EIN: 942574178

397
The Robert M. Sinskey Foundation
233 Wilshire Blvd., Ste. 370
Santa Monica, CA 90401
Contact: Robert M. Sinskey, Pres.
Application address: 2232 Santa Monica Blvd., Santa Monica, CA 90404-2312, tel.: (310) 453-8911

Established in 1997 in CA.
Donor(s): Robert M. Sinskey.
Grantmaker type: Independent foundation
Financial data (yr. ended 12/31/00): Assets, $2,315,774 (M); gifts received, $235,175; expenditures, $131,554; qualifying distributions, $95,215; giving activities include $100,002 for 13 grants (high: $75,000; low: $37).
Fields of interest: Higher education; Natural resources; Human services.
Types of support: General/operating support.
Limitations: Giving on a national basis, with some emphasis on CA. No grants to individuals.
Application information:
  Initial approach: Letter
  Deadline(s): June 1 and Dec. 1
Officers: Robert M. Sinskey, M.D., Pres.; Jeffrey C. Lapin, Secy.
EIN: 954628223

398
L. J. Skaggs and Mary C. Skaggs Foundation
1221 Broadway, 21st Fl.
Oakland, CA 94612-1837 (510) 451-3300
Contact: Philip M. Jelley, Secy.
FAX: (510) 451-1527; E-mail: skaggs@fablaw.com

Incorporated in 1967 in CA.
Donor(s): L.J. Skaggs,‡ Mary C. Skaggs.

Grantmaker type: Independent foundation
Financial data (yr. ended 12/31/02): Assets, $1,933,307 (M); expenditures, $1,021,631; qualifying distributions, $906,797; giving activities include $1,012,720 for 69 grants (high: $125,000; low: $285; average: $5,000–$25,000).
Purpose and activities: Giving for the performing arts, specifically opera and theater, ecology programs, and projects of historic interest.
Fields of interest: Performing arts; Theater; Music; Humanities; History/archaeology; Historic preservation/historical societies; Arts; Natural resources; Environment; Animals/wildlife, preservation/protection.
International interests: United Kingdom.
Types of support: General/operating support; Continuing support; Building/renovation; Land acquisition; Program development; Conferences/seminars; Publication.
Limitations: Giving limited to northern CA for theater, ecology programs, and special projects; giving with national and international focus limited to projects of historic interest. No support for higher education, residence home programs, halfway houses, or sectarian religious purposes. No grants to individuals, or for capital funds, annual fund drives, budget deficits, scholarships, or fellowships; no loans.
Publications: Annual report, Grants list, Informational brochure (including application guidelines).
Application information: Application form not required.
  Initial approach: Letter
  Copies of proposal: 1
  Deadline(s): June 1
  Board meeting date(s): Nov.
Officers and Directors:* Mary C. Skaggs,* Pres.; Jayne C. Davis,* V.P.; Philip M. Jelley,* Secy. and Fdn. Mgr.; Joseph W. Martin, Jr.,* Treas.; Georgia A. Fulstone.
Number of staff: 1 part-time professional.
EIN: 946174113

399
The Skylark Foundation
9220 Sunset Blvd., Ste. 218
Los Angeles, CA 90069 (310) 271-9700
Contact: Barbara Schwan, Exec. Dir.
FAX: (310) 271-7036; E-mail: bschwan@skylarkfoundation.org; URL: http://www.skylarkfoundation.org

Established around 1998 in CA.
Donor(s): E. Blake Byrne.
Grantmaker type: Independent foundation
Financial data (yr. ended 12/31/01): Assets, $4,131,297 (M); expenditures, $357,836; qualifying distributions, $317,816; giving activities include $206,500 for 16 grants (high: $25,000; low: $2,500).
Purpose and activities: The foundation is interested in aviation, environmental protection, education, lesbian and gay issues, arts and humanities, broadcasting, women and the elderly.
Fields of interest: Media/communications; Humanities; Arts; Education; Natural resources; Space/aviation; Aging; Women; Gays/lesbians.
Types of support: Continuing support; Equipment; Program development; Curriculum

development; Research; Consulting services; Program-related investments/loans; Matching/challenge support.
Limitations: Giving limited to Los Angeles, CA, NC, and Portland, OR. No grants to individuals.
Publications: Application guidelines.
Application information: Application form not required.

   Initial approach: Letter, E-mail or telephone
   Deadline(s): Apr. 1
Officers: E. Blake Byrne, Chair.; John Byrne, Pres.; Charlotte Byrne, Secy.
Number of staff: 1 part-time professional.
EIN: 954525764

400
Margaret K. Sloss Foundation
818 Cherry St.
Santa Rosa, CA 95404-4207
Contact: Louis Sloss, Jr., Tr.

Established about 1958.
Donor(s): Members of the Sloss family.
Grantmaker type: Independent foundation
Financial data (yr. ended 12/31/02): Assets, $37,824 (M); gifts received, $146,678; expenditures, $149,997; qualifying distributions, $149,482; giving activities include $149,021 for 173 grants (high: $27,300; low: $25).
Purpose and activities: Giving to Jewish organizations, community foundations, the environment, and human welfare.
Fields of interest: Arts; Higher education; Environment; Family planning; Health organizations, association; Human services; International relief; International peace/security; Civil rights; Community development; Jewish agencies & temples; Economically disadvantaged.
Limitations: Applications not accepted. Giving on a national basis. No grants to individuals.
Application information: Contributes only to pre-selected organizations; unsolicited requests for funds not considered. Trustees initiate grants.
   Board meeting date(s): Annually
Trustees: Anthony Sloss; Karen Sloss; Louis Sloss, Jr.
Number of staff: None.
EIN: 946065985

401
The Small Change Foundation
19 Sutter St.
San Francisco, CA 94104-4901
(415) 546-7635
Contact: Raymond L. Mulliner, Secy.

Established in 1996 in CA.
Grantmaker type: Independent foundation
Financial data (yr. ended 10/31/02): Assets, $4,229,472 (M); expenditures, $281,767; qualifying distributions, $234,799; giving activities include $235,000 for 19 grants (high: $50,000; low: $1,000).
Purpose and activities: Giving primarily for gay and lesbian issues, as well as for human services.
Fields of interest: Museums (art); Performing arts; Environmental education; Human services; Civil rights, gays/lesbians; Asians/Pacific Islanders; People with AIDS (PWAs).

Limitations: Giving primarily in San Francisco, CA; funding also in Washington, DC, and New York, NY.
Application information:
   Initial approach: Letter
   Deadline(s): None
Officers: James C. Hormel, Pres.; Timothy Woo, V.P.; Raymond L. Mulliner, Secy.; A. Kenner Foote, Treas.
EIN: 943271247

402
Joan Irvine Smith & Athalie R. Clarke Foundation
610 Newport Ctr. Dr., Ste. 1170
Newport Beach, CA 92660
Contact: James I. Swinden, V.P. and Treas.

Established in 1991 in CA.
Donor(s): Athalie R. Clarke,‡ Joan Irvine Smith.
Grantmaker type: Independent foundation
Financial data (yr. ended 04/30/02): Assets, $21,656,457 (M); gifts received, $2,000; expenditures, $2,947,804; qualifying distributions, $2,517,119; giving activities include $2,521,000 for 20 grants (high: $1,095,000; low: $1,000; average: $5,000–$80,000).
Purpose and activities: Giving for environmental protection and the arts.
Fields of interest: Museums; Arts; Natural resources; Environment; Medical research, institute.
Types of support: Endowments; Research; Matching/challenge support.
Limitations: Applications not accepted. Giving primarily in southern CA. No grants to individuals.
Application information: Contributes only to pre-selected organizations.
Officers and Directors:* Joan Irvine Smith,* Pres.; James I. Swinden,* V.P. and Treas.; Russell G. Penniman IV,* V.P.; Brett J. Williamson,* Secy.
Number of staff: None.
EIN: 330461971

403
The Stanley Smith Horticultural Trust
720 Market St., Ste. 250
San Francisco, CA 94102
Contact: William L. Culberson
Application address: P.O. Box 51759, Durham, NC 27717-1759, tel.: (919) 660-7303, E-mail: wlc@pobox.com

Established in 1970 in CA.
Donor(s): May Smith.
Grantmaker type: Independent foundation
Financial data (yr. ended 12/31/02): Assets, $13,294,681 (M); expenditures, $952,671; qualifying distributions, $907,874; giving activities include $834,969 for 52 grants (high: $45,000; low: $4,000).
Purpose and activities: Grants to organizations for horticultural programs, including education and research.
Fields of interest: Environment, research.
Types of support: General/operating support; Equipment; Program development; Publication; Research.

Limitations: Giving primarily in North and South America. No grants to individuals, or for endowment funds.
Publications: Application guidelines.
Application information: Application form not required.
   Initial approach: Proposal
   Copies of proposal: 1
   Deadline(s): Sept. 1
   Board meeting date(s): As required
   Final notification: Early Dec.
Trustees: John P. Collins, Jr.; Ruth M. Collins; James R. Gibbs; N. Dale Matheny; May Smith.
Number of staff: 1 shared staff (shared with May and Stanley Smith Trust; May and Stanley Smith Charitable Trust).
EIN: 946209165

404
Smith-Welsh Foundation
c/o Karl Reinecker
28925 Pacific Coast Hwy., 2nd Fl.
Malibu, CA 90265-3922

Established in 1985 in CA.
Donor(s): Omer Smith Marital Trust.
Grantmaker type: Independent foundation
Financial data (yr. ended 12/31/02): Assets, $2,520,749 (M); expenditures, $186,407; qualifying distributions, $185,959; giving activities include $161,000 for 26 grants (high: $25,000; low: $1,000).
Purpose and activities: Giving primarily for the arts and for human services.
Fields of interest: Arts; Education; Environment; Human services; Federated giving programs.
Limitations: Applications not accepted. Giving primarily in the Pacific Coast states. No grants to individuals.
Application information: Contributes only to pre-selected organizations.
Officers: Nancy S. Welsh, C.E.O.; James E. Welsh, C.F.O.
EIN: 953958030

405
SoCalGas Corporate Giving Program
c/o Corp. Community Rels.
555 W. 5th St.
Los Angeles, CA 90013 (877) 736-7729
Contact: Carolyn Williams, Mgr.
E-mail: gascocommunity@socalgas.com; URL: http://www.socalgas.com/about/community

Grantmaker type: Corporate giving program
Purpose and activities: SoCalGas makes charitable contributions to nonprofit organizations involved with education, the environment, community development, and public affairs. Support is given primarily in a 12-county region of California. Charitable contributions are also made through a separate program at Sempra Energy, the company's parent.
Fields of interest: Education; Environment; Business/industry; Community development; Public affairs.
Types of support: Program development; Conferences/seminars; Cause-related marketing; Employee volunteer services; Public relations services; Sponsorships; Employee matching gifts;

Employee-related scholarships; Scholarships—to individuals.

Limitations: Giving primarily in Fresno, Imperial, Kern, Kings, Los Angeles, Orange, Riverside, Santa Barbara, San Bernardino, San Luis Obispo, Tulare, and Ventura counties, CA.

Publications: Application guidelines, Informational brochure (including application guidelines), Program policy statement.

Application information: The company has a staff that usually handles contributions. Application form not required.

   Initial approach: Proposal to headquarters
   Copies of proposal: 1
   Deadline(s): None
   Final notification: Following review

Number of staff: 2 full-time professional; 2 full-time support.

406
Richard & Mary Solari Charitable Trust
527 St. Andrews Dr.
Aptos, CA 95003

Established in 1984 in CA.

Donor(s): Richard C. Solari, Mary C. Solari.

Grantmaker type: Independent foundation

Financial data (yr. ended 09/30/02): Assets, $9,251,914 (M); gifts received, $100,000; expenditures, $620,753; qualifying distributions, $591,024; giving activities include $566,690 for 39 grants (high: $130,000; low: $500).

Purpose and activities: Giving primarily for an aquarium, education, a community foundation, and human services.

Fields of interest: Higher education; Veterinary medicine, hospital; Human services; Foundations (community); Roman Catholic agencies & churches.

Limitations: Applications not accepted. Giving primarily in CA. No grants to individuals.

Application information: Contributes only to pre-selected organizations.

Trustees: Mary C. Solari; Richard C. Solari.

EIN: 770069120

407
Solectron Corporation Contributions Program
c/o Corp. Contribs.
777 Gibraltar Dr.
Milpitas, CA 95035
URL: http://www.solectron.com/about/community.html

Grantmaker type: Corporate giving program

Purpose and activities: Solectron makes charitable contributions to nonprofit organizations involved with arts and culture, education, the environment, and human services. Support is given on an international basis.

Fields of interest: Arts; Education; Environment; Human services.

Types of support: General/operating support; Employee volunteer services.

Limitations: Giving on an international basis in areas of company operations.

Application information: Application form not required.

   Initial approach: Proposal to headquarters
   Copies of proposal: 1

Final notification: Following review

408
Sonora Area Foundation
20100 Cedar Rd., No. E
P.O. Box 577
Sonora, CA 95370-0577 (209) 533-2596
Contact: Mick Grimes, Exec. Dir.
FAX: (209) 533-2412; *E-mail:* acorn@sonora-area.org; *URL:* http://www.sonora-area.org

Established in 1989 in CA.

Grantmaker type: Community foundation

Financial data (yr. ended 12/31/02): Assets, $5,923,000 (L); gifts received, $472,369; expenditures, $936,253; giving activities include $739,455 for 175 grants (high: $70,000; average: $500–$70,000) and $29,100 for 65 grants to individuals (low: $150; average: $150–$3,600).

Purpose and activities: The foundation administers donor-advised funds.

Fields of interest: Visual arts; Performing arts; Music; Arts; Early childhood education; Child development, education; Elementary school/education; Libraries/library science; Education; Environment; Animal welfare; Hospitals (general); Health care; Substance abuse, services; Mental health/crisis services; Health organizations, association; Alcoholism; Food services; Recreation; Human services; Children/youth, services; Child development, services; Family services; Hospices; Aging, centers/services; Women, centers/services; Community development; Voluntarism promotion; Disabled; Aging; Women; Economically disadvantaged.

Types of support: General/operating support; Continuing support; Capital campaigns; Building/renovation; Equipment; Emergency funds; Program development; Conferences/seminars; Seed money; Curriculum development; Scholarship funds; Technical assistance; Consulting services; Program evaluation; Scholarships—to individuals; Matching/challenge support.

Limitations: Giving limited to Tuolumne County, CA. No support for sectarian purposes, private foundations, or political purposes. No grants for annual campaigns, endowment funds, or debt retirement.

Publications: Application guidelines, Annual report, Financial statement, Grants list, Informational brochure, Newsletter (including application guidelines), Occasional report.

Application information: Guidelines available on website. Application form required.

   Initial approach: Telephone, letter, or FAX (2-page maximum)
   Copies of proposal: 1
   Deadline(s): None
   Board meeting date(s): Monthly

Officers and Trustees:* Jim Gianelli,* Pres.; Mike Albrecht,* V.P.; Marilyn Knudson,* Secy.; Joan Bergsund,* Treas.; Mick Grimes, Exec. Dir.; Celeste Boyd; William J. Coffill; Todd Simonson.

Number of staff: 1 full-time professional; 1 full-time support; 1 part-time support.

EIN: 931023051

409
South Coast Foundation, Inc.
1563 Solano Ave., Ste. 354
Berkeley, CA 94707
Contact: Kathleen Cook, Pres.

Established in 1988 in CA as partial successor to Cook Brothers Educational Fund.

Donor(s): Howard F. Cook.‡

Grantmaker type: Independent foundation

Financial data (yr. ended 12/31/00): Assets, $2,138,404 (M); expenditures, $195,242; qualifying distributions, $143,436; giving activities include $107,575 for 20 grants (high: $14,000; low: $575).

Purpose and activities: Grants available to provide training services to South African community-based organizations in the areas of managerial and administrative skills, project and financial management, organizational development, and advocacy skills.

Fields of interest: Education; Environment; Employment, services; Human services; Child development, services.

International interests: South Africa.

Types of support: General/operating support; Continuing support; Program development.

Limitations: Applications not accepted. Giving limited to South Africa. No grants to individuals.

Application information: Contributes only to pre-selected organizations.

   Board meeting date(s): Quarterly

Officers: Kathleen M. Cook, Pres.; Franklin C. Cook, V.P.; Jason Hebel, Secy.-Treas.

Number of staff: 1 full-time professional.

EIN: 770177830

410
Spalding Family Foundation
100 Commonwealth Ave.
San Francisco, CA 94118

Established in 2000 in CA.

Donor(s): Helen M. Spalding, Richard C. Spalding.

Grantmaker type: Operating foundation

Financial data (yr. ended 12/31/01): Assets, $1,749,896 (M); expenditures, $941,862; qualifying distributions, $938,929; giving activities include $938,929 for 21 grants (high: $520,000; low: $200).

Fields of interest: Arts; Elementary/secondary education; Education; Environment; Human services.

Limitations: Applications not accepted. Giving primarily in CA. No grants to individuals.

Application information: Contributes only to pre-selected organizations.

Directors: Helen M. Spalding; Richard C. Spalding.

EIN: 943369408

411
Norman F. Sprague, Jr. Foundation
11726 San Vicente Blvd., No. 625
Los Angeles, CA 90049
Contact: Norman F. Sprague, III, Tr.

Established in 1997 in CA.

Grantmaker type: Independent foundation

Financial data (yr. ended 02/28/02): Assets, $10,063,596 (M); expenditures, $550,385;

qualifying distributions, $465,128; giving activities include $444,500 for 20 grants (high: $150,000; low: $500).
Fields of interest: Museums; Natural resources.
Limitations: Giving primarily in CA.
Trustees: Cynthia Sprague Connolly; Elizabeth Sprague Day; Caryll Sprague Mingst; Norman F. Sprague III.
EIN: 954621772

412
Springcreek Foundation
770 Tamalpais Dr., Ste. 210
Corte Madera, CA 94925

Established in 1994 in CA.
Donor(s): T. Dixon Long, Henry H. Corning, Barbara H. Young, Maud-Alison C. Long.
Grantmaker type: Independent foundation
Financial data (yr. ended 12/31/01): Assets, $15,919,700 (M); gifts received, $202,712; expenditures, $1,070,018; qualifying distributions, $816,539; giving activities include $831,483 for 178 grants (high: $25,000; low: $200).
Fields of interest: Museums; Performing arts; Theater; Orchestra (symphony); Literature; Arts; Higher education; Environment, land resources; Environment; Family planning; Human services; Children/youth, services; Community development; Philanthropy/voluntarism.
Types of support: General/operating support.
Limitations: Applications not accepted. Giving primarily in CA. No grants to individuals.
Application information: Contributes only to pre-selected organizations. Unsolicited requests for funds not accepted.
Officers and Directors:* T. Dixon Long,* Pres.; Maud-Alison Long, V.P.; Barbara H. Young,* Secy.-Treas. and C.F.O.; Henry H. Corning.
EIN: 680344778

413
The Stans Foundation
P.O. Box 1018
Arcadia, CA 91077
Contact: Steven H. Stans, Pres.
FAX: (626) 446-8286

Incorporated in 1945 in IL.
Donor(s): Maurice H. Stans,‡ Kathleen C. Stans.‡
Grantmaker type: Independent foundation
Financial data (yr. ended 12/31/01): Assets, $3,499,258 (M); expenditures, $442,827; qualifying distributions, $339,238; giving activities include $339,238 for 54 grants (high: $100,000; low: $250).
Purpose and activities: Emphasis on a restoration project, a historical society, and a museum; grants also for public service organizations, research, higher education, and church support.
Fields of interest: Museums; Education; Animal welfare; Health organizations, association; Human services; International affairs; Political science.
Types of support: General/operating support; Continuing support; Annual campaigns; Building/renovation; Equipment; Conferences/seminars; Research.
Limitations: Applications not accepted. Giving on a national basis. No grants to individuals, or

for operating budgets, endowment funds, scholarships, fellowships, or matching gifts; no loans.
Application information: Funds fully committed until 2001; applications not currently being accepted.
Board meeting date(s): Annually
Officers and Directors:* Steven H. Stans,* C.E.O., Pres., and C.O.O.; Terrell Stans Manley,* V.P. and Treas.; Walter Helmick,* V.P.; William Manley,* V.P.; Susan E. Stans, V.P.; Theodore M. Stans,* V.P.; Mary C. Elia, Secy.
Number of staff: None.
EIN: 366008663

414
Rudolf Steiner Foundation, Inc.
Presidio, Bldg. 1002B
P.O. Box 29915
San Francisco, CA 94129-0915
(415) 561-3900
Contact: John Bloom, Grants Off.
FAX: (415) 561-3919; E-mail: mail@rsfoundation.org; URL: http://www.rsfoundation.org

Established in 1936 in NY.
Grantmaker type: Public charity
Financial data (yr. ended 12/31/01): Assets, $42,126,352; expenditures, $4,108,892; giving activities include $2,551,266 for grants and $21,739,362 for loans/program-related investments.
Purpose and activities: The foundation supports initiatives in accordance with Rudolf Steiner's life mission for the self-development of each individual and the advancement of human freedom, through research and activities including, but not limited to, education and the arts, science and caring for the earth, social responsibility and mutual support, medical and religious renewal, and associative economic relationships.
Fields of interest: Arts; Education; Environment; Health care; Human services; Science.
International interests: Canada; Europe; Africa; Latin America.
Types of support: General/operating support; Continuing support; Annual campaigns; Capital campaigns; Land acquisition; Program development; Conferences/seminars; Publication; Seed money; Curriculum development; Research; Consulting services; Program evaluation; Program-related investments/loans; Grants to individuals.
Limitations: Giving on an international basis to Europe, Africa, Canada and Latin America. No grants for scholarships, travel or personal financial needs.
Publications: Application guidelines, Annual report, Financial statement, Newsletter.
Application information: Application form required.
Initial approach: Letter of intent
Copies of proposal: 1
Deadline(s): Sept. 15 and Mar. 15
Board meeting date(s): 3 times a year
Officer and Trustees:* Mark A. Finser,* Pres.; Rachel Flug,* V.P.; Philip Mees,* Secy.; Mark Censits,* Treas.; John Haenselman; Diane Bourdo; Ken Courage; Martha Daetwyler; Dominic Disalvo; Siegfried Finser; Gloria Kemp; Christopher Mann; Clemens Pietzner.

Number of staff: 15 full-time professional; 12 full-time support.
EIN: 136082763

415
Lionel Steiner Trust
c/o Wells Fargo Bank, N.A.
P.O. Box 63954, 525 Market St., Ste. 1700
San Francisco, CA 94163
Application address: c/o Roger Parodi, Acct. Admin., Wells Fargo Bank, 420 Montgomery St., 2nd Fl., San Francisco, CA 94104, tel.: (415) 396-2090

Grantmaker type: Independent foundation
Financial data (yr. ended 06/30/02): Assets, $6,925,249 (M); expenditures, $323,255; qualifying distributions, $238,302; giving activities include $223,907 for 5 grants (high: $71,457; low: $35,728).
Fields of interest: Animals/wildlife, special services; Hospitals (general); Human services; Children/youth, services; Family services; Disabled.
Limitations: Giving limited to the San Francisco Bay Area, CA.
Application information:
Initial approach: Letter
Deadline(s): None
Trustee: Wells Fargo Bank, N.A.
EIN: 946445242

416
Stephenson Foundation
3000 Sand Hill Rd., Bldg. 4, No. 280
Menlo Park, CA 94027 (650) 854-3927
Contact: Barbara Stephenson, Pres.

Established in 1999 in CA.
Donor(s): Barbara Stephenson, Thomas F. Stephenson.
Grantmaker type: Independent foundation
Financial data (yr. ended 12/31/02): Assets, $15,164,253 (M); expenditures, $896,298; qualifying distributions, $793,925; giving activities include $794,700 for 27 grants (high: $250,000; low: $100).
Purpose and activities: Giving primarily for education; funding also for the environment and children's services.
Fields of interest: Higher education; Business school/education; Education; Environment; Children, services.
Limitations: Giving primarily in CA and MA. No grants to individuals.
Application information:
Initial approach: Letter
Deadline(s): None
Officers: Barbara Stephenson, Pres.; Thomas F. Stephenson, V.P.
EIN: 943320092

417
Sidney Stern Memorial Trust
P.O. Box 893
Pacific Palisades, CA 90272 (310) 459-2117
Contact: Marvin Hoffenberg, Advisor

Trust established in 1974 in CA.
Donor(s): S. Sidney Stern.‡

Grantmaker type: Independent foundation
Financial data (yr. ended 08/31/01): Assets, $34,705,000 (M); expenditures, $2,153,332; qualifying distributions, $1,872,842; giving activities include $1,792,449 for 482 grants (high: $40,000; low: $250; average: $2,500–$8,000).
Purpose and activities: Giving primarily for higher education, social service agencies, including aid to the handicapped; youth and child welfare agencies; scientific and medical organizations, including health associations; and cultural programs.
Fields of interest: Arts; Higher education; Environment; Hospitals (general); Family planning; Health care; Health organizations, association; Legal services; Human services; Children/youth, services; Civil rights, disabled; Civil rights; Asians/Pacific Islanders; African Americans/Blacks; Hispanics/Latinos; Native Americans/American Indians; Disabled; Immigrants/refugees.
Types of support: General/operating support; Annual campaigns; Building/renovation; Equipment; Land acquisition; Endowments; Emergency funds; Program development; Scholarship funds; Research; Matching/challenge support.
Limitations: Giving primarily in CA; all funds must be used within the U.S. No grants to individuals, or for conferences or redistribution; no loans.
Publications: Application guidelines.
Application information: Application form required.
   Initial approach: Letter or proposal (1 1/2 pages describing preferred use of funds)
   Copies of proposal: 1
   Deadline(s): None
   Board meeting date(s): Monthly, except Aug.
Officers and Board of Advisors: Peter H. Hoffenberg,* Chair.; Ira E. Bilson,* Secy.; Betty S. Hoffenberg; David A. Hoffenberg; Marvin Hoffenberg; Howard O. Wilson.
Number of staff: None.
EIN: 956495222

418
The Streisand Foundation
2800 28th St., Ste. 105
Santa Monica, CA 90405   (310) 535-3767
Contact: Margery Tabankin, Exec. Dir., or Ali Berzon, Prog. Asst.
FAX: (310) 314-8396; URL: http://www.barbrastreisand.com/bio_streisand_foundation.html

Established in 1986 in NY.
Donor(s): Barbra Streisand.
Grantmaker type: Independent foundation
Financial data (yr. ended 12/31/02): Assets, $2,418,492 (M); gifts received, $6,911; expenditures, $807,153; qualifying distributions, $783,064; giving activities include $577,000 for 107 grants (high: $25,000; low: $100).
Purpose and activities: Giving primarily for civil rights, poverty, the environment, democratic values and social welfare.
Fields of interest: Environment; Children/youth, services; Voter education; Civil liberties, advocacy; Civil rights; Public affairs, citizen participation; Women.

Types of support: General/operating support; Program development.
Limitations: Giving to nationally-based groups; some local giving in Los Angeles, CA for youth organizations. No support for start-up organizations or international organizations. No grants to individuals, or for capital campaigns, documentaries or audio-visual programming, or publication of books or magazines.
Publications: Application guidelines.
Application information: See foundation Web site for full application guidelines and requirements. Application form not required.
   Initial approach: 1- to 3-page letter of inquiry
   Copies of proposal: 1
   Deadline(s): Sept. 2-Dec. 2
   Board meeting date(s): Varies
   Final notification: Following summer
Officer: Margery Tabankin, Exec. Dir.
Trustees: Richard Baskin; Marilyn Bergman; Jason Gould; Barry Hirsh; Barbra Streisand.
Number of staff: 1 part-time professional; 1 full-time support.
EIN: 132620702

419
Hadley and Marion Stuart Foundation
c/o Bogdan & Frasco, LLP
207 Powell St., Ste. 6
San Francisco, CA 94102

Established in 1988 in CA.
Donor(s): Marion Butler Stuart.
Grantmaker type: Independent foundation
Financial data (yr. ended 10/31/01): Assets, $13,522,527 (M); expenditures, $368,854; qualifying distributions, $355,027; giving activities include $355,027 for grants (high: $100,000).
Purpose and activities: Giving primarily for education and animal welfare.
Fields of interest: Natural resources; Education; Animal welfare.
Limitations: Applications not accepted. No grants to individuals.
Application information: Contributes only to pre-selected organizations.
Trustees: Brett Fullerton Stuart; Marion Butler Stuart; Nan M. Stuart.
EIN: 946607854

420
Suisun Conservation Fund
2544 Grizzly Island Rd.
Suisun City, CA 94585   (707) 425-9302
Contact: Timothy Egan, Pres.

Grantmaker type: Public charity
Financial data (yr. ended 09/30/01): Revenue, $211,921; assets, $1,063,984; gifts received, $125,000; expenditures, $73,133; program services expenses, $70,813; giving activities include $70,813 for 1 grant.
Purpose and activities: The fund exists for the sole benefit of the Suisun Resource Conservation District.
Fields of interest: Environment, single organization support.
Limitations: Applications not accepted. Giving limited to Suisun, CA.

Application information: Contributes only to a pre-selected organization; unsolicited requests for funds not considered or acknowledged.
Officers and Trustees: Timothy Egan,* Pres.; Terrance C. Connolly,* Secy.-Treas.; Gene Fromberg; George Tillotson; Tony Vaccarella.
EIN: 946109447

421
Surfrider Foundation
P.O. Box 6010
San Clemente, CA 92674-6010
(949) 492-8170
Contact: Christopher Evans, Exec. Dir.
FAX: (949) 492-8142; E-mail: info@surfrider.org; URL: http://www.surfrider.org

Established in 1984.
Grantmaker type: Public charity
Financial data (yr. ended 12/31/01): Revenue, $2,590,706; assets, $934,386 (M); gifts received, $1,816,089; expenditures, $2,455,319; program services expenses, $2,178,704; giving activities include $2,000 for 1 grant to an individual.
Purpose and activities: The foundation seeks to protect, enhance and promote the enjoyment of the world's waves and beaches for all people through conservation, research, and education.
Fields of interest: Education; Environment.
Types of support: General/operating support; Annual campaigns; Program development; Conferences/seminars; Publication; Curriculum development; Internship funds; Scholarship funds; Research; Employee matching gifts; In-kind gifts.
Limitations: Giving limited to students of Humboldt State University, CA.
Publications: Annual report, Financial statement, Informational brochure, Newsletter, Occasional report.
Application information: Application form required.
   Initial approach: Telephone or visit Humboldt State University's financial aid office for application materials
   Deadline(s): Apr. 15
   Board meeting date(s): Jan., Apr., July, and Oct.
   Final notification: May 15
Officers and Directors: Marc Chytilo,* Chair.; Tom Davis,* Vice-Chair.; Mike Orbach,* Secy.; Christopher Keys,* C.F.O.; Christopher Evans, Exec. Dir.; Jeff DuClos; Leon Richter; Mark Spaulding; Robb Waterman; and 8 additional directors.
Number of staff: 15 full-time professional; 1 full-time support; 3 part-time support.
EIN: 953941826

422
Szekely Family Foundation
(formerly Szekely Foundation for American Volunteers)
3232 Dove St.
San Diego, CA 92103
Contact: Deborah Szekely, Pres.

Established in 1986 in CA.
Donor(s): Deborah Szekely.
Grantmaker type: Independent foundation
Financial data (yr. ended 12/31/02): Assets, $4,054,727 (M); gifts received, $300,000;

expenditures, $544,020; qualifying distributions, $543,336; giving activities include $411,234 for 108 grants (high: $104,000; low: $60).

Purpose and activities: The foundation's primarily interests include 1) addressing environmental concerns for the area along the border between California and Baja California, Mexico to protect the land for future generations of Americans and Mexicans; and 2) support for the newly established Immigration Museum of New Americans, honoring those who have chosen to make new lives for themselves and their families in the United States.

Fields of interest: Environment; Immigrants/refugees.

Limitations: Applications not accepted. Giving primarily in the area along the border between CA and Baja California, Mexico. No grants to individuals.

Application information: Unsolicited requests for funds not accepted.

Board meeting date(s): As needed
Officers: Deborah Szekely, Pres.; James H. West, Secy.
Number of staff: None.
EIN: 953655645

423
S. Mark Taper Foundation ▼
12011 San Vicente Blvd., Ste. 400
Los Angeles, CA 90049   (310) 476-5413
Contact: Raymond F. Reisler, Exec. Dir.
FAX: (310) 471-4993; E-mail: rreisler@smtfoundation.org

Incorporated in 1989 in CA.
Donor(s): S. Mark Taper.‡
Grantmaker type: Independent foundation
Financial data (yr. ended 12/31/02): Assets, $110,468,509 (M); gifts received, $3,673; expenditures, $7,116,712; qualifying distributions, $6,446,502; giving activities include $6,061,337 for 56+ grants (high: $840,000; average: $15,000–$125,000).
Purpose and activities: Giving primarily to children and youth, health care, social services, employment, education, and environment.
Fields of interest: Arts; Education; Environment; Health care; Crime/violence prevention; Employment; Housing/shelter, development; Human services; Children/youth, services; Family services; Reproductive rights; Government/public administration; Disabled; Aging; Women; People with AIDS (PWAs); Economically disadvantaged; Homeless.
Types of support: General/operating support; Annual campaigns; Capital campaigns; Building/renovation; Equipment; Emergency funds; Program development; Conferences/seminars; Publication; Seed money; Curriculum development; Scholarship funds; Research; Program-related investments/loans; Matching/challenge support.
Limitations: Giving primarily in CA. No grants to individuals.
Publications: Application guidelines.
Application information: Application form required.
Initial approach: Letter
Copies of proposal: 1
Deadline(s): Sept. 1 to Feb. 28
Board meeting date(s): As required
Final notification: As needed

Officers and Directors:* Janice Taper Lazarof,* Pres.; Cynthia Taper Bolker, V.P.; Amelia Taper Stabler, Secy.; Deborah Taper Ringel, Treas.; Roy Weitz, C.F.O.; Raymond F. Reisler, Exec. Dir.
Number of staff: 3 full-time professional; 2 full-time support.
EIN: 954245076

424
The Buddy Taub Foundation
9200 Sunset Blvd., Ste. 525
Los Angeles, CA 90069

Established in 1998 in CA.
Grantmaker type: Independent foundation
Financial data (yr. ended 05/31/02): Assets, $11,916,452 (M); expenditures, $800,286; qualifying distributions, $711,860; giving activities include $633,889 for 16 grants (high: $188,350; low: $1,000).
Purpose and activities: Giving primarily for art museums; funding also for higher education, and children, youth and social services.
Fields of interest: Museums (art); Higher education; Animals/wildlife; Human services; Children/youth, services.
Limitations: Applications not accepted. Giving primarily in CA and PA. No grants to individuals.
Application information: Contributes only to pre-selected organizations.
Director: Dennis A. Roach.
EIN: 954588448

425
Teichert Foundation
3500 American River Dr.
Sacramento, CA 95864   (916) 484-3364
Contact: Frederick A. Teichert, Exec. Dir.
E-mail: info@teichertfoundation.org; URL: http://www.teichertfoundation.org

Established in 1990 in CA.
Donor(s): A. Teichert & Son, Inc., Teichert, Inc.
Grantmaker type: Company-sponsored foundation
Financial data (yr. ended 03/31/02): Assets, $5,014,416 (M); gifts received, $1,012,068; expenditures, $500,716; qualifying distributions, $491,270; giving activities include $457,858 for 71 grants (high: $255,000; low: $25).
Purpose and activities: Support for culture and the arts, education, youth and the elderly, environmental planning and preservation, transportation planning, civic improvement and historical restoration, community and social services, and rehabilitation and health services.
Fields of interest: Historic preservation/historical societies; Arts; Education; Environment; Medical care, rehabilitation; Health care; Health organizations, association; Human services; Children/youth, services; Aging, centers/services; Federated giving programs; Government/public administration; Aging.
Types of support: Employee matching gifts.
Limitations: Giving limited to Sacramento and Central Valley, CA, roughly from Truckee to Turlock. No support for religious, political, or fraternal organizations. No grants to individuals, or for national fundraising campaigns, courtesy advertising, benefits, or telephone solicitations.
Publications: Application guidelines.

Application information: Only complete proposal will be considered. Application form not required.
Initial approach: Letter of inquiry
Copies of proposal: 2
Deadline(s): Last Fri. of Feb. and Aug.
Board meeting date(s): Biannually
Officers and Directors:* Anne S. Haslam,* Secy.; Norman Eilert, C.F.O.; Frederick A. Teichert,* Exec. Dir.; Thomas J. Hammer; Judson T. Riggs; Melita M. Teichert.
Number of staff: 1 full-time professional; 1 full-time support.
EIN: 680212355

426
Tides Center
P.O. Box 29907
San Francisco, CA 94129-0907
(415) 561-6300
Contact: Willa Seldon, Exec. Dir.
FAX: (415) 561-6301; E-mail: info@tides.org; URL: http://www.tidescenter.org

Established in 1996.
Grantmaker type: Public charity
Financial data (yr. ended 12/31/02): Revenue, $71,159,042; assets, $40,887,528 (M); gifts received, $65,168,610; expenditures, $62,540,112; program services expenses, $56,664,623; giving activities include $6,389,187 for 228 grants.
Purpose and activities: Tides Center actively promotes change towards a healthy society, one which is founded on principles of social justice, broadly shared economic opportunity, a robust democratic process, and sustainable environmental practices. Tides Center believes healthy societies rely fundamentally on respect for individual rights, the vitality of communities, and a celebration of diversity.
Fields of interest: Environment; Economic development.
Types of support: Continuing support; Program development; Program evaluation.
Application information: See Web site for application guidelines. Application form required.
Initial approach: Telephone or e-mail
Officers and Directors:* Wade Rathke,* Chair.; Drummond Pike,* Pres.; Brad Luke,* Cont.; Willa Seldon, Exec. Dir.; Nao Emmett Aluli; Stephanie J. Clohesy; Jonah Martin Edelman; Ellen Friedman; Martha Jimenez; Lawrence Litvak.
EIN: 943213100

427
Tides Foundation
Presidio Main Post, Bldg. No. 37
P.O. Box 29903
San Francisco, CA 94129-0903
(415) 561-6400
Contact: Shannon Coughlin, Comm. Assoc.
FAX: (415) 561-6401; E-mail: info@tides.org; URL: http://www.tidesfoundation.org

Established in 1976.
Grantmaker type: Public charity
Financial data (yr. ended 12/31/01): Revenue, $93,224,126; assets, $161,091,756 (M); gifts received, $86,111,123; expenditures,

$84,604,356; program services expenses, $83,378,130; giving activities include $76,248,526 for grants and $117,487 for grants to individuals.

Purpose and activities: The foundation gives primarily in the areas of the environment and natural resources, international affairs, economic public policy and enterprise development, social justice, and community affairs. The foundation makes grants on the recommendation of donors.

Fields of interest: Media/communications; Natural resources; Environment; Reproductive health; AIDS; Disasters, 9/11/01; Youth development, services; International affairs; Community development, citizen coalitions; Civic centers; Economic development; Community development, economics; Public policy, research; Minorities; Native Americans/American Indians; Women; Gays/lesbians; Economically disadvantaged.

Types of support: General/operating support; Continuing support; Annual campaigns; Land acquisition; Program development; Publication; Seed money; Research; Technical assistance; Matching/challenge support.

Limitations: Giving primarily on a national basis with some international giving. No support for organizations with budgets exceeding $2 million. No grants to individuals (except for honoraria) or universities, or for capitol campaigns, endowments, or media projects.

Publications: Annual report, Informational brochure (including application guidelines).

Application information: Accepts NNG Common Application Form; see Web site for application guidelines.

　　Deadline(s): Feb. 1 and June 28

Officers and Directors:* Drummond Pike,* Pres.; Ellen Friedman, V.P.; Lauren Webster, C.F.O.; Idelisse Malave, Exec. Dir.; Joanie Bronfman; Elouise Cobell; Quinn Delaney; Andrea Kydd; John A. Powell; Wade Rathke; Charles Savitt; Joel Solomon.

Number of staff: 40 full-time professional; 1 part-time professional; 12 full-time support.

EIN: 510198509

428
Trimble Navigation Limited Corporate Giving Program
c/o Corp. Contribs. Comm.
645 N. Mary Ave.
Sunnyvale, CA 94088-3642

Grantmaker type: Corporate giving program

Purpose and activities: Trimble makes charitable contributions to nonprofit organizations involved with education, the environment, human services, and on a case by case basis. Support is given on an international basis.

Fields of interest: Education; Environment; Human services; General charitable giving.

International interests: France; Italy; United Kingdom; Spain; Germany; Hungary; Russia; Mexico; Middle East; Singapore; China; Japan; Australia; New Zealand.

Types of support: General/operating support; Donated products.

Limitations: Giving on an international basis in areas of company operations, particularly the Alameda, San Mateo, and Santa Clara counties, CA, area, and in Australia, China, France,

Germany, Hungary, Italy, Japan, Mexico, the Middle East, New Zealand, Russia, Singapore, Spain, and the United Kingdom.

Application information: A contributions committee reviews all requests. Application form not required.

　　Initial approach: Proposal to headquarters
　　Copies of proposal: 1
　　Board meeting date(s): Every 4 to 5 weeks
　　Final notification: Following review

429
Truckee Tahoe Community Foundation
P.O. Box 366
Truckee, CA 96160 (530) 587-1776
Contact: Tamara Lieberman, Prog. Off.

Established in 1998 in CA.

Grantmaker type: Community foundation

Financial data (yr. ended 06/30/03): Assets, $6,880,260 (L); gifts received, $1,721,270; expenditures, $2,714,860; giving activities include $2,345,500 for 141 grants (high: $641,896; low: $100).

Purpose and activities: Giving to enhance the quality of life in the Truckee/Tahoe, CA, area by seeking, accepting, managing, and disbursing funds for the benefit of the community.

Fields of interest: Arts; Education; Environment; Animals/wildlife, preservation/protection; Health care; Youth development; Human services; Children/youth, services; Community development.

Types of support: General/operating support; Continuing support; Income development; Management development; Equipment; Program development; Publication; Seed money; Technical assistance; Consulting services.

Limitations: Giving limited to the Truckee/North Tahoe, CA, area. No grants for capital campaigns.

Publications: Application guidelines, Grants list, Newsletter.

Application information: Application form required.

　　Copies of proposal: 12
　　Deadline(s): None
　　Board meeting date(s): Mar. 11, June 10, Sept. 9 and Dec. 9

Officers: Lisa Dobey, Pres.; Tamara Lieberman, Prog. Off.

Directors: Linda Brown; Dave Ferrari; Jim Gaither; Ernie Grossman; Kent Hoopingarner; Roger Kahn; Rob Kautz; Julie Mauer; Phil McKenney; Roz Mitchell; Jim Porter; Craig Poulsen; Nancy Richards; Scott Ryan.

Number of staff: 1 full-time support; 3 part-time support.

EIN: 680416404

430
Dorothea Tuney Foundation
c/o Leslie Batista
1959 Mendocino Blvd.
San Diego, CA 92107

Established in 2000 in CA.

Donor(s): Dorothea Tuney Trust.

Grantmaker type: Operating foundation

Financial data (yr. ended 12/31/01): Assets, $4,065,219 (M); expenditures, $155,643; qualifying distributions, $155,643; giving

activities include $151,500 for 19 grants (high: $25,000; low: $1,500).

Fields of interest: Zoos/zoological societies; Children, services; Hospices; Christian agencies & churches.

Limitations: Applications not accepted. Giving primarily in San Diego, CA. No grants to individuals.

Application information: Contributes only to pre-selected organizations.

Trustee: Leslie Batista.

EIN: 336277186

431
Alice C. Tyler Perpetual Trust
c/o Paul J. Livadary
2029 Century Park E., No. 437
Los Angeles, CA 90067

Established in 1994 in CA.

Donor(s): Alice C. Tyler,‡ Alice C. Tyler Charitable Trust.

Grantmaker type: Independent foundation

Financial data (yr. ended 12/31/01): Assets, $10,717,285 (M); expenditures, $631,872; qualifying distributions, $709,029; giving activities include $503,149 for 12 grants (high: $140,000; low: $5,000).

Purpose and activities: Giving primarily for education, environmental research, and children's services.

Fields of interest: Performing arts, education; Education; Environment, research; Human services.

Limitations: Applications not accepted. Giving primarily in CA and OR. No grants to individuals.

Application information: Contributes only to pre-selected organizations.

Trustees: Martha Appello; Allyn E. Brown; Anders M. Brown; Courtney L. Brown; John Hoag; Paul J. Livadary; Sally Ride; Nancy Sharp.

EIN: 956967787

432
Urbanek Family Foundation
75 Tuscaloosa Ave.
Atherton, CA 94027-4014

Established in 1997 in CA.

Donor(s): Lida Urbanek.

Grantmaker type: Independent foundation

Financial data (yr. ended 12/31/02): Assets, $1,223,335 (M); gifts received, $21,196; expenditures, $94,772; qualifying distributions, $90,100; giving activities include $90,100 for 23 grants (high: $41,000; low: $500).

Fields of interest: Orchestra (symphony); Higher education; Environment; Human services.

Limitations: Applications not accepted. Giving primarily in CA. No grants to individuals.

Application information: Contributes only to pre-selected organizations.

Officers and Directors:* Lida Urbanek,* Pres.; Irene Urbanek,* Secy.; Andrew Urbanek; Karel Urbanek; Matthew Urbanek.

EIN: 943267087

433
The Vadasz Family Foundation
23141 Mora Glen Dr.
Los Altos, CA 94024
Contact: Les and Judy Vadasz, Directors

Established in 1997 in CA.
Donor(s): Judy K. Vadasz, Les L. Vadasz.
Grantmaker type: Independent foundation
Financial data (yr. ended 11/30/02): Assets,
$20,417,032 (M); expenditures, $1,340,590;
qualifying distributions, $1,306,208; giving
activities include $1,188,811 for 37 grants (high:
$100,000; low: $500).
Purpose and activities: Giving for education, the
protection or preservation of the environment,
and the support of social and cultural
community needs.
Fields of interest: Arts; Education; Environment;
Health organizations, association; Human
services; Community development.
Limitations: Giving primarily in CA.
Application information: Application form not
required.
  Deadline(s): None
Officers and Directors:* Les L. Vadasz,* Pres.;
Judy K. Vadasz,* Treas.; Jeffrey E. Vadasz,* Secy.
EIN: 770469457

434
Wayne & Gladys Valley Foundation ▼
1939 Harrison St., Ste. 510
Oakland, CA 94612-3532 (510) 466-6060
Contact: Michael D. Desler, Exec. Dir.
FAX: (510) 466-6067; E-mail: info@wgvalley.org

Established in 1977 in CA.
Donor(s): F. Wayne Valley,‡ Gladys Valley.‡
Grantmaker type: Independent foundation
Financial data (yr. ended 09/30/02): Assets,
$548,512,301 (M); gifts received,
$200,972,736; expenditures, $19,272,218;
qualifying distributions, $16,167,066; giving
activities include $15,487,139 for 130 grants
(high: $850,000; low: $5,000; average:
$20,000–$250,000).
Purpose and activities: Primary areas of interest
include higher, secondary, and other education,
medicine, hospitals, youth, and local Catholic
schools and charities.
Fields of interest: Elementary/secondary
education; Higher education; Biomedicine;
Medical research, institute; Human services;
Children/youth, services; Roman Catholic
federated giving programs.
Types of support: General/operating support;
Capital campaigns; Building/renovation;
Program development; Scholarship funds;
Research; Matching/challenge support.
Limitations: Giving primarily in Alameda and
Contra Costa counties, CA. No support for
veterans, fraternal, labor, service club, military,
or similar organizations. No grants to
individuals, or for fundraising events, dinners,
advertising, or private operating foundations.
Publications: Application guidelines, Annual
report.
Application information: Application form not
required.
  Initial approach: Telephone or letter
    requesting guidelines
  Copies of proposal: 1
  Deadline(s): None

Board meeting date(s): Feb., May, Sept., and
  Nov.
  Final notification: Usually within 6 months
Officers and Directors:* Tamara Valley,* Chair.
and Pres.; Richard M. Kingsland, V.P., Secy., and
C.F.O.; Michael D. Desler, Exec. Dir.; Robert C.
Brown; Stephen M. Chandler; John P. Stock.
Number of staff: 4 full-time professional; 1
full-time support.
EIN: 953203014
**Recent environmental and animal welfare
grants:**
434-1 California Academy of Sciences, San
  Francisco, CA, $15,000. For Teacher Services
  Program. 2002.
434-2 East Bay Zoological Society, Oakland,
  CA, $2,000,000. For renovation of Children's
  Zoo. 2002.
434-3 Regional Parks Foundation, Oakland, CA,
  $30,375. For classes of grades 4-6 students
  from low-income East Bay schools to attend
  environmental programs. 2002.
434-4 University of California, School of
  Veterinary Medicine, Davis, CA, $119,550.
  For continuation of research on Equine
  Protozoal Myeloencephalitis (EPM). 2002.

435
Vanguard Public Foundation
383 Rhode Island St., Ste. 301
San Francisco, CA 94103 (415) 487-2111
Contact: Hari Dillon, Pres.
FAX: (415) 487-2124; E-mail:
grants@vanguardsf.org; URL: http://
www.vanguardsf.org/

Established in 1972 in CA.
Grantmaker type: Public charity
Financial data (yr. ended 03/31/02): Revenue,
$3,881,844; assets, $3,433,405 (L); gifts
received, $4,468,109; expenditures,
$3,563,859; program services expenses,
$3,354,737; giving activities include
$2,422,317 for 527 grants (high: $20,000; low:
$200; average: $400–$10,000) and $56,000 for
4 grants to individuals of $14,000 each.
Purpose and activities: Through grants and
donor-advised funds, the foundation funds
groups that seek to alter the underlying causes
of injustice, poverty, and disenfranchisement;
involve low-income and working-class people
in achieving self-determination; work toward a
society free from racism, sexism, homophobia,
and economic exploitation, and support the
rights of all people; and incorporate affirmative
action guidelines and practices. Among the
foundation's giving interests are groups working
on issues of civil rights, economic justice,
workers' rights, women's rights, education,
disability, health, housing, environment, cultural
activism, indigenous peoples' rights, and
international solidarity.
Fields of interest: Environment; Labor
unions/organizations; Housing/shelter; Youth
development, citizenship; Civil rights, equal
rights; Civil rights, advocacy; Civil rights,
immigrants; Civil rights, minorities; Civil rights,
women; Civil rights, gays/lesbians; Civil rights;
Public affairs, citizen participation.
Types of support: General/operating support;
Technical assistance.
Limitations: Giving limited to northern CA,
including the San Francisco Bay Area and

Fresno. No support for direct service,
educational organizations, film production
costs, or out-of-state travel. No grants for capital
campaigns, equipment, research, debt
reduction, or one-time conferences or events.
Publications: Application guidelines, Annual
report, Financial statement.
Application information: Contact foundation for
current guidelines. Application form required.
  Copies of proposal: 2
  Deadline(s): Quarterly
  Board meeting date(s): Quarterly
  Final notification: Approximately 3 months
Officers and Directors:* Walter Riley,* Chair.;
Yvette Radford,* Vice-Chair.; Hari Dillon,* Pres.;
David Matchett,* Secy.-Treas.; Janeen Antoine;
Jane Baker; Michael James; Paul Kivel; Rob
McKay; Susanna Moore; Peter Stern; and 14
additional directors.
Number of staff: 5 full-time professional; 1
part-time professional; 2 full-time support; 1
part-time support.
EIN: 942369262

436
The Vanoff Family Foundation
10960 Wilshire Blvd., Ste. 1100
Los Angeles, CA 90024

Established in 1982 in CA; funded in 1984.
Donor(s): Nicholas E. Vanoff, Felisa Vanoff.
Grantmaker type: Independent foundation
Financial data (yr. ended 12/31/02): Assets,
$169,238 (M); expenditures, $161,578;
qualifying distributions, $160,949; giving
activities include $156,520 for 77 grants (high:
$50,000; low: $10).
Purpose and activities: Giving for animal
welfare, environmental conservation, art and
cultural programs, and human services.
Fields of interest: Performing arts; Natural
resources; Environment; Animal welfare; Cancer
research; Human services.
Limitations: Applications not accepted. Giving
primarily in Los Angeles, CA. No grants to
individuals.
Application information: Contributes only to
pre-selected organizations.
Officers: Felisa Vanoff, Pres. and Treas.;
Nicholas E. Vanoff, Secy.
EIN: 953900688

437
Ventura County Community Foundation
1317 Del Norte Rd., Ste. 150
Camarillo, CA 93010 (805) 988-0196
Contact: Hugh J. Ralston, Pres.
FAX: (805) 485-5537; E-mail: vccf@vccf.org;
URL: http://www.vccf.org/

Incorporated in 1987 in CA.
Grantmaker type: Community foundation
Financial data (yr. ended 09/30/02): Assets,
$30,955,288 (M); gifts received, $5,328,732;
expenditures, $3,323,203; giving activities
include $1,867,422 for grants and $837,709 for
foundation-administered programs.
Purpose and activities: The Ventura County
Community Foundation's mission is to enrich
and enhance the quality of life in Ventura
County and to provide leadership to residents
and nonprofit organizations in building an

enduring source of funds and strengthening community participation to meet the changing needs and challenges of the community. The foundation administers donor-advised funds.
Fields of interest: Arts; Education; Natural resources; Environment; Health care; Health organizations, association; Human services; Youth, services; Family services; Hispanics/Latinos; Women; Economically disadvantaged.
Types of support: General/operating support; Management development; Building/renovation; Equipment; Emergency funds; Program development; Conferences/seminars; Seed money; Curriculum development; Scholarship funds; Technical assistance; Program evaluation; Scholarships—to individuals; Matching/challenge support.
Limitations: Giving primarily in Ventura County, CA. No grants for endowments, annual campaigns, budget deficits, or land acquisition; no program-related investments.
Publications: Application guidelines, Annual report (including application guidelines), Financial statement, Informational brochure, Newsletter.
Application information: Number of requested proposal copies may vary from 1 to 12. Application form required.
   Initial approach: Letter or telephone to get on mailing list for request for proposals (RFP)
   Deadline(s): Spring for scholarships; for all other applications, as designated by RFP
   Board meeting date(s): Bimonthly
   Final notification: June for scholarships; for all other applications, as designated by RFP
Officers and Directors:* William A. Bang,* Chair.; Hugh J. Ralston, Pres.; William Hart, M.D.,* Secy.; Ronald L. Hertel, Sr., Treas.; Denis Dupuis; Henry L. "Hank" Lacayo; Wendy Cole Lascher; Dorothy Loebl; Timothy J. McCallion; Stacy Roscoe; Scott B. Samsky; Mary Schwabauer; Robin Woodworth; Sally Yount.
Number of staff: 4 full-time professional; 1 part-time professional; 5 full-time support; 1 part-time support.
EIN: 770165029

438
Vital Spark Foundation, Inc.
942 Coral Dr.
Pebble Beach, CA 93953
Contact: Bruce Mitteldorf, Secy.
Application address: 720 Giovanetti Rd., Forestville, CA 95436, tel.: (408) 373-3694

Established in 1985 in NY.
Donor(s): A.J. Mitteldorf, Harriet M. Mitteldorf.
Grantmaker type: Independent foundation
Financial data (yr. ended 11/30/02): Assets, $2,809,863 (M); expenditures, $252,603; qualifying distributions, $155,250; giving activities include $144,000 for 18 grants (high: $20,000; low: $1,000).
Fields of interest: Theater; Arts; Higher education; Education; Animal welfare; Human services.
Limitations: Giving primarily in CA.
Application information: Application form not required.
   Deadline(s): None

Officers and Directors:* Harriet M. Mitteldorf,* Pres.; Bruce Mitteldorf,* Secy. and Mgr.; Joshua J. Mitteldorf,* Treas.
EIN: 133537545

439
Lulu May Lloyd Von Hagen Foundation
12400 Wilshire Blvd., Ste. 1180
Los Angeles, CA 90025-1030

Established in 1988 in CA.
Grantmaker type: Independent foundation
Financial data (yr. ended 12/31/00): Assets, $2,212,698 (M); expenditures, $133,657; qualifying distributions, $114,475; giving activities include $112,450 for 27 grants (high: $20,000; low: $100).
Purpose and activities: Giving primarily for education.
Fields of interest: Arts; Secondary school/education; Higher education; Natural resources; Zoos/zoological societies; Hospitals (general); Recreation; Human services.
Types of support: Endowments.
Limitations: Applications not accepted. Giving primarily in CA. No grants to individuals.
Application information: Contributes only to pre-selected organizations.
Officers: Theresa Von Hagen Bucher, Pres.; Ronald Lloyd Von Hagen, V.P.
EIN: 954194305

440
VPI Skeeter Foundation
3060 Saturn St.
Brea, CA 92822-2344 (714) 989-0555
Contact: Jack Stephens, Chair.
E-mail: Skeeter@veterinarypetins.com; URL: http://www.skeeterfoundation.com

Established in 2001 in CA.
Donor(s): Jack Stephens, Vicki Stephens.
Grantmaker type: Operating foundation
Financial data (yr. ended 12/31/02): Assets, $42,004 (M); gifts received, $164,599; expenditures, $196,554; qualifying distributions, $114,572; giving activities include $114,572 for 4 grants (high: $57,677; low: $1,000; average: $1,000–$57,677).
Purpose and activities: Giving to organizations that further the human-companion animal bond.
Fields of interest: Animals/wildlife, preservation/protection.
Types of support: Research; Scholarships—to individuals.
Limitations: Giving on a national basis, including Washington, DC. No grants to individuals (except for scholarships).
Publications: Annual report.
Application information:
   Initial approach: Letter
   Deadline(s): None
Officers and Directors:* Jack Stephens, Chair.; Rebecca Lewis, V.P.; Vicki Stephens, Secy.; Robin Itzler,* Treas.; Kathy Bacon; Elizabeth Hodgkins.
Number of staff: None.
EIN: 330906193

441
Wallis Foundation ▼
1880 Century Park East, Ste. 700
Los Angeles, CA 90067 (310) 286-9777

Established in 1957 in CA.
Donor(s): Hal B. Wallis.‡
Grantmaker type: Independent foundation
Financial data (yr. ended 06/30/02): Assets, $52,371,796 (M); expenditures, $4,306,979; qualifying distributions, $3,989,709; giving activities include $3,920,500 for 178 grants (high: $150,000; low: $500; average: $5,000–$100,000).
Purpose and activities: Giving primarily for environmental issues and human services, including Christian welfare organizations and programs for youth and families; support also for health services and the arts.
Fields of interest: Arts; Natural resources; Environment; Health care; Human services; Children/youth, services; Religious federated giving programs.
Limitations: Applications not accepted. Giving primarily in CA. No grants to individuals.
Application information: Contributes only to pre-selected organizations.
Officers and Directors:* Brent Wallis,* Pres.; Jeffrey Glassman,* Secy.; Michael Sack,* C.F.O.; Jack Baker.
EIN: 956027469
Recent environmental and animal welfare grants:
441-1 California Academy of Sciences, San Francisco, CA, $25,000. 2002.
441-2 California Coastal Protection Network, Santa Barbara, CA, $25,000. 2002.
441-3 Center for Plant Conservation, Saint Louis, MO, $30,000. 2002.
441-4 Chicago Zoological Society, Brookfield Zoo, Brookfield, IL, $65,000. 2002.
441-5 Environmental Defense Center, Santa Barbara, CA, $30,000. 2002.
441-6 Ganna Walska Lotusland, Santa Barbara, CA, $25,000. 2002.
441-7 Georges River Land Trust, Rockland, ME, $20,000. 2002.
441-8 Grand Canyon Trust, Flagstaff, AZ, $150,000. 2002.
441-9 Grand Canyon Trust, Flagstaff, AZ, $60,000. 2002.
441-10 Herring Gut Learning Center, Port Clyde, ME, $20,000. 2002.
441-11 Humane Society of Knox County, Rockland, ME, $20,000. 2002.
441-12 Injured and Orphaned Wildlife, San Jose, CA, $35,000. 2002.
441-13 International Center for Earth Concerns, Ojai, CA, $25,000. 2002.
441-14 McLaughlin Foundation, South Paris, ME, $15,000. 2002.
441-15 Natural Resources Council, Augusta, ME, $30,000. 2002.
441-16 Nature Conservancy, Brunswick, ME, $50,000. 2002.
441-17 Ohio Bird Sanctuary, Bellville, OH, $25,000. 2002.
441-18 Pets Are Wonderful Support (PAWS), San Francisco, CA, $10,000. 2002.
441-19 Pets Are Wonderful Support (PAWS), West Hollywood, CA, $35,000. 2002.
441-20 San Francisco Zoological Society, San Francisco, CA, $15,000. 2002.

441-21 Santa Barbara Botanic Gardens, Santa Barbara, CA, $45,000. 2002.
441-22 Santa Barbara Marine Mammal Center, Santa Barbara, CA, $100,000. 2002.
441-23 Surfrider Foundation, Ventura, CA, $20,000. 2002.
441-24 Trees for Life, Wichita, KS, $10,000. 2002.
441-25 Trust for Public Land, San Francisco, CA, $45,000. 2002.
441-26 Yosemite Foundation, San Francisco, CA, $50,000. 2002.

442
C. A. Webster Foundation, Inc.
P.O. Box 126
Linden, CA 95236   (209) 887-3523
Contact: William H. Williams
Application address: 8000 N. Clements Rd., Linden, CA 95326

Established in 1960 in CA.
Grantmaker type: Independent foundation
Financial data (yr. ended 12/31/01): Assets, $2,166,095 (M); expenditures, $125,245; qualifying distributions, $117,953; giving activities include $118,000 for 24 grants (high: $15,500; low: $500).
Purpose and activities: Giving to agriculture, animal welfare organizations, the arts and education.
Fields of interest: Arts; Education; Natural resources; Animal welfare; Human services.
Types of support: Scholarship funds.
Limitations: Giving primarily in the Stockton, CA, area. No grants to individuals.
Application information:
  Initial approach: Proposal
  Deadline(s): None
  Final notification: 4 months
Directors: Bethany Lunblad King; Alberta Lewallen; Webster Williams.
EIN: 946072116

443
Mandell Weiss Charitable Trust
P.O. Box 221071
San Diego, CA 92192-1071
Contact: Joseph Satz, Tr.

Established in 1994 in CA.
Grantmaker type: Independent foundation
Financial data (yr. ended 12/31/02): Assets, $8,959,735 (M); expenditures, $618,750; qualifying distributions, $526,385; giving activities include $518,500 for 41 grants (high: $50,000; low: $1,000).
Fields of interest: Museums; Dance; Ballet; Theater; Orchestra (symphony); Opera; Arts; Zoos/zoological societies; Hospitals (general); Children/youth, services.
Limitations: Applications not accepted. Giving primarily in San Diego, CA. No grants to individuals.
Application information: Contributes only to pre-selected organizations.
Trustees: George Jezek; Joseph Satz.
EIN: 336145298

444
David and Sylvia Weisz Family Philanthropic Fund
1901 Ave. of the Stars, Ste. 610
Los Angeles, CA 90067-6001   (310) 284-8856

Donor(s): Sylvia Weisz.
Grantmaker type: Independent foundation
Financial data (yr. ended 12/31/02): Assets, $4,271,610 (M); gifts received, $5,109,612; expenditures, $280,263; qualifying distributions, $236,072; giving activities include $161,500 for 44 grants (high: $10,000; low: $250).
Fields of interest: Arts; Education; Animal welfare; Human services; Jewish agencies & temples.
Application information: Application form not required.
  Initial approach: Letter
  Deadline(s): None
Officers: Sylvia Weisz, Chair. and Pres.; Jay H. Grodin, V.P. and Treas.; Judith Carroll, V.P.; Catherine Ireland, V.P.; Carey Pearlman, Secy.
Directors: Jennifer Caroll; John Caroll.
EIN: 912172529

445
Toby Wells Foundation
13495 Gregg St.
Poway, CA 92064-7135

Established in 2001 in CA.
Donor(s): Lloyd Wells, John Burnham Real Estate, Richardson Pontiac, Business Real Estate.
Grantmaker type: Independent foundation
Financial data (yr. ended 12/31/02): Assets, $78,964 (M); gifts received, $303,482; expenditures, $441,339; qualifying distributions, $420,551; giving activities include $359,512 for 24 grants (high: $200,000; low: $75).
Fields of interest: Animal welfare; Child abuse; Children, services; Developmentally disabled, centers & services.
Limitations: Applications not accepted. Giving primarily in San Diego, CA. No grants to individuals.
Application information: Contributes only to pre-selected organizations.
Officers: Lloyd D. Wells, Chair.; Lynn D. Wells, C.E.O. and Pres.; Adriene A. Castaneda, Secy.
Directors: Brian Filger; Dana Fudurich; Edward Fudurich; Sue Herndon; John Jackson; and 8 additional directors.
EIN: 330946827

446
West Marine, Inc. Corporate Giving Program
c/o Donations and Sponsorships
500 Westridge Dr.
Watsonville, CA 95076   (831) 761-4111

Grantmaker type: Corporate giving program
Purpose and activities: West Marine makes charitable contributions to nonprofit organizations involved with water conservation, boating, youth boating, and human services. Support is given primarily in areas of company operations.

Fields of interest: Environment, water resources; Athletics/sports, water sports; Youth, services; Human services.
Types of support: General/operating support; Employee volunteer services; Sponsorships; In-kind gifts.
Limitations: Giving primarily in areas of company operations.
Application information: Proposals should be no longer than 1 page in length. Proposals should be submitted using organization letterhead. Follow-up letters or telephone calls are not encouraged. Application form not required.
  Initial approach: Proposal to headquarters
  Final notification: 2 months

447
Whitecap Foundation
800 Wilshire Blvd., Ste. 1010
Los Angeles, CA 90017   (213) 624-5401
Contact: Laura Campobasso, Exec. Dir.
FAX: (213) 624-0529; E-mail: execdirector@whitecapfdn.org; URL: http://www.whitecapfdn.org

Established in 1986 in CA.
Grantmaker type: Independent foundation
Financial data (yr. ended 11/30/02): Assets, $6,706,940 (M); expenditures, $1,709,263; qualifying distributions, $1,658,865; giving activities include $1,537,029 for 58+ grants (high: $152,700; average: $10,000–$30,000).
Purpose and activities: Giving primarily directed to community-based Los Angeles organizations focusing on children, families, education, and statewide projects in CA for wildlife conservation.
Fields of interest: Adult education—literacy, basic skills & GED; Reading; Education; Environment, water resources; Employment; Children/youth, services; Family services; Family services, parent education; Hispanics/Latinos.
Types of support: Continuing support; Program development.
Limitations: Giving primarily in the Los Angeles, CA, area. No support for religious groups. No grants to individuals, or for building purchase or construction, endowment funds, or tickets for fundraising events.
Application information: Please do not send letters of inquiry with extensive attachments. If the initial review of the materials indicates a good match for the foundation, a formal proposal and site visit will be requested.
  Initial approach: Letter
  Deadline(s): None
Officers: Elizabeth Duker, Pres.; Brack Duker, C.F.O. and Secy.; Laura Campobasso, Exec. Dir.
Number of staff: 2.
EIN: 954111120

448
Lucy G. Whittier Foundation, Inc.
P.O. Box 610
Pilot Hill, CA 95664-0610

Established in 1997 in CA.
Donor(s): Lucy G. Whittier.
Grantmaker type: Independent foundation

Financial data (yr. ended 12/31/00): Assets, $59,440 (M); gifts received, $421,686; expenditures, $396,107; qualifying distributions, $334,798; giving activities include $339,000 for 5 grants (high: $150,000; low: $7,000).
Purpose and activities: Giving primarily for higher education for equine research.
Fields of interest: Higher education; Education; Animals/wildlife, research.
Limitations: Applications not accepted. Giving primarily in CA and CO. No grants to individuals.
Application information: Contributes only to pre-selected organizations.
Officers: Lucy G. Whittier, Pres.; John H. Whittier, Secy. and C.F.O.
Directors: Jacqueline W. Kubicka; Jennifer L. Miller.
EIN: 943270867

449
Brayton Wilbur Foundation
345 California St., 27th Fl.
San Francisco, CA 94104-2644

Incorporated in 1947 in CA.
Donor(s): Brayton Wilbur, Jr., Wilbur-Ellis Co.
Grantmaker type: Company-sponsored foundation
Financial data (yr. ended 12/31/01): Assets, $4,729,069 (M); gifts received, $107,950; expenditures, $248,645; qualifying distributions, $218,067; giving activities include $214,000 for 10 grants (high: $162,500; low: $1,000).
Purpose and activities: Emphasis on the arts; grants also for health and conservation.
Fields of interest: Museums (art); Arts; Natural resources; Health care.
Types of support: Continuing support; Annual campaigns; Capital campaigns; Building/renovation; Endowments.
Limitations: Applications not accepted. Giving primarily in San Francisco, CA. No grants to individuals.
Application information: Contributes only to pre-selected organizations.
Officers: Brayton Wilbur, Jr., Pres.; Carter P. Thacher, V.P.; Herbert B. Tully, Secy.-Treas.
Number of staff: None.
EIN: 946088667

450
Wilkinson Foundation
2920 Sacramento St.
San Francisco, CA 94115
Contact: Bary Wilkinson, Tr.

Established in 1986 in MI.
Donor(s): Warren S. Wilkinson.
Grantmaker type: Independent foundation
Financial data (yr. ended 01/31/03): Assets, $3,885,547 (M); gifts received, $70,000; expenditures, $198,572; qualifying distributions, $178,794; giving activities include $175,350 for 76 grants (high: $25,000; low: $500).
Purpose and activities: Giving primarily for the arts, education, health, human services, and the environment.
Fields of interest: Museums; Historical activities; Arts; Libraries/library science; Education; Natural resources; Animals/wildlife, preservation/protection; Hospitals (general);

Parks/playgrounds; Human services; Civil liberties, advocacy.
Types of support: Continuing support; Annual campaigns; Capital campaigns; Endowments; Program development; Seed money.
Limitations: Giving on a national basis.
Application information: Application form not required.
   Deadline(s): None
   Board meeting date(s): Feb., May, Aug., and Nov.
   Final notification: After board meetings
Trustees: Bary Wilkinson; Bruce Wilkinson; Guerin S. Wilkinson; Stephen Wilkinson; Todd S. Wilkinson; Warren S. Wilkinson.
Number of staff: None.
EIN: 386497639

451
The Windfall Foundation
c/o Manatt, Phelps, et al.
11355 W. Olympic Blvd.
Los Angeles, CA 90064
Application address: c/o Maryann Wlock, Joel Faden & Co., Inc., 1775 Broadway, New York, NY 10019, tel.: (212) 246-7203

Established in 1992 in CA.
Donor(s): R. Williams, M. Williams.
Grantmaker type: Independent foundation
Financial data (yr. ended 12/31/02): Assets, $1,419,374 (M); gifts received, $629,345; expenditures, $594,128; qualifying distributions, $589,468; giving activities include $592,000 for 58 grants (high: $100,000; low: $200).
Purpose and activities: Giving primarily for education, the arts, and social services.
Fields of interest: Museums; Theater; Historic preservation/historical societies; Arts; Education; Natural resources; Health care; Spine disorders; Recreation; Human services; Children/youth, services.
Limitations: Giving primarily in CA; some giving also in New York, NY. No grants to individuals.
Application information:
   Initial approach: Letter
   Deadline(s): None
Officers: Gerald Margolis, Pres.; M. Williams, V.P. and Secy.; Joel Faden, C.F.O.
EIN: 954383183

452
Witherbee Foundation
528 Arizona Ave.
Santa Monica, CA 90401

Established in 1996 in CA.
Donor(s): Victoria Witherbee.
Grantmaker type: Independent foundation
Financial data (yr. ended 12/31/01): Assets, $12,929,263 (M); expenditures, $871,456; qualifying distributions, $859,543; giving activities include $828,251 for 35 grants (high: $100,000; low: $1,000).
Purpose and activities: Giving primarily for health care and to the blind and visually impaired.
Fields of interest: Museums (specialized); Elementary/secondary education; Secondary school/education; Higher education; Animals/wildlife, preservation/protection;

Zoos/zoological societies; Hospitals (general); Eye diseases; Youth, services.
Limitations: Applications not accepted. Giving primarily in CA. No grants to individuals.
Application information: Contributes only to pre-selected organizations.
Officers and Director:* Robert Falls,* Pres.; Florita Ruskin, Secy.-Treas.
EIN: 954583560

453
Dean Witter Foundation
57 Post St., Ste. 510
San Francisco, CA 94104 (415) 981-2966
Contact: Kenneth J. Blum, Consultant
FAX: (415) 981-5218; E-mail: admin@deanwitterfoundation.org; URL: http://www.deanwitterfoundation.org

Incorporated in 1952 in CA.
Donor(s): Dean Witter,‡ Mrs. Dean Witter, Dean Witter & Co.
Grantmaker type: Independent foundation
Financial data (yr. ended 06/30/03): Assets, $14,664,007 (M); expenditures, $717,278; qualifying distributions, $717,228; giving activities include $627,979 for 23 grants.
Purpose and activities: Primary purpose is to support postgraduate research in economics and finance, with a secondary purpose to support conservation.
Fields of interest: Higher education; Natural resources; Economics.
Types of support: Equipment; Program development; Publication; Research.
Limitations: Giving for conservation projects limited to northern CA. No grants to individuals, or for endowment funds.
Publications: Annual report (including application guidelines).
Application information: Application form not required.
   Initial approach: Letter, telephone, or proposal
   Copies of proposal: 1
   Deadline(s): Submit proposal 7 weeks before board meeting
   Board meeting date(s): Jan., Apr., July, and Oct.
Officers and Trustees:* Dean Witter III,* Pres.; William D. Witter, Secy.-Treas.; Salvador O. Gutierrez; Stephen Nessier; Roland Tognazzini, Jr.; Deanne Gillette Violich; Malcolm G. Witter; William P. Witter.
Number of staff: None.
EIN: 946065150

454
Working Assets Funding Service, Inc. Corporate Giving Program
c/o Mgr., Donations
101 Market St., Ste. 700
San Francisco, CA 94105 (415) 788-0777
URL: http://www.workingassets.com/recipients.cfm

Grantmaker type: Corporate giving program
Purpose and activities: Working Assets makes charitable contributions to nonprofit organizations involved with education and freedom of expression, the environment, peace and international freedom, economic and social justice, and civil rights. Support is given to national and international organizations.

Fields of interest: Education; Environment; Arms control; International human rights; Civil rights, equal rights; Civil liberties, first amendment; Civil rights.
Types of support: General/operating support.
Limitations: Giving to national and international organizations. No support for disease-specific organizations, religious organizations, or organizations established less than a year ago.
Application information: Contributes only to organizations nominated by the company's customers. An independent foundation reviews all nominations. Application form not required.
   Initial approach: Nomination to headquarters
   Copies of proposal: 1
   Deadline(s): June 30

455
Abe Wouk Foundation, Inc.
c/o Gelfend, Rennert & Feldman
1880 Century Park E., Ste. 1600
Los Angeles, CA 90067
Contact: Suzanne Stein, Secy.
Application address: 303 Crestview Dr., Palm Springs, CA 92262

Established in 1954.
Donor(s): Betty Sarah Wouk, Herman Wouk.
Grantmaker type: Independent foundation
Financial data (yr. ended 12/31/02): Assets, $1,101,567 (M); expenditures, $157,118; qualifying distributions, $154,029; giving activities include $154,593 for 67 grants (high: $20,000; low: $100).
Purpose and activities: Giving primarily for education, the environment, and Jewish organizations.
Fields of interest: Elementary/secondary education; Higher education; Education; Environment; Animal welfare; Human services; Jewish federated giving programs; Jewish agencies & temples.
Limitations: Giving primarily in CA, Washington, DC, and New York, NY.
Application information: Application form not required.
   Deadline(s): None
Officers: Herman Wouk, Pres.; Joseph Wouk, V.P.; Suzanne Stein, Secy.; Betty Sarah Wouk, Treas.; Nathaniel Wouk, Exec. Dir.
Trustee: Charles Rembar.
EIN: 136155699

456
The Wunderkinder Foundation ▼
(formerly Max Charitable Foundation)
c/o Breslauer & Rutman, LLC
11400 W. Olympic Blvd., Ste. 550
Los Angeles, CA 90064-1551

Established in 1985 in CA.
Donor(s): Steven Spielberg.
Grantmaker type: Independent foundation
Financial data (yr. ended 11/30/01): Assets, $2,402,069 (M); gifts received, $1,765,797; expenditures, $4,552,395; qualifying distributions, $4,481,221; giving activities include $4,509,729 for 46 grants (high: $1,171,429; low: $500; average: $10,000–$200,000).
Purpose and activities: Giving primarily to the arts, education, war memorials and veterans'

organizations, and Jewish organizations; giving also for human services, with an emphasis on children and medical research.
Fields of interest: Historical activities, war memorials; Arts; Education; Natural resources; Health organizations, association; Youth development; Children/youth, services; Military/veterans' organizations; Jewish agencies & temples; Native Americans/American Indians; Gays/lesbians.
Limitations: Applications not accepted. Giving primarily in CA and NY. No grants to individuals.
Application information: Contributes only to pre-selected organizations.
Officers and Directors:* Gerald Breslauer,* Pres.; Michael Rutman,* Secy.-Treas.; Bruce Ramer.
EIN: 954016320

457
WWW Foundation
625 S. Fair Oaks Ave., Ste. 360
South Pasadena, CA 91030-2630
(626) 441-5188
Contact: Linda J. Blinkenberg, Secy.
FAX: (626) 441-3672

Established in 1983 in CA.
Donor(s): Helen W. Woodward.‡
Grantmaker type: Independent foundation
Financial data (yr. ended 07/31/02): Assets, $36,528,296 (M); gifts received, $2,128,020; expenditures, $1,507,683; qualifying distributions, $1,321,936; giving activities include $1,125,500 for 18 grants (high: $555,000; low: $2,500; average: $5,000–$50,000).
Purpose and activities: Giving primarily for an animal care center; support also for hospitals, civic affairs, and the arts.
Fields of interest: Education; Animal welfare; Hospitals (general); Medical research, institute; Human services; Children/youth, services.
Types of support: Building/renovation; Program development; Research; Matching/challenge support.
Limitations: Applications not accepted. Giving primarily in southern CA. No grants to individuals; no loans.
Application information: Unsolicited requests for funds are not accepted. The foundation prefers to initiate grants.
   Board meeting date(s): As needed
Officers and Directors:* Sharon H. Bradford,* Pres.; Bryce Rhodes, V.P.; Winifred W. Rhodes,* V.P.; Linda J. Blinkenberg,* Secy.; Arlo G. Sorensen,* C.F.O.; and 7 additional directors.
Number of staff: 5 shared staff (shared with Whittier Family Foundations).
EIN: 953694741

458
The Zilber Family Foundation
c/o Assante Business Mgmt.
10100 Santa Monica Blvd., Ste. 1300
Los Angeles, CA 90067

Established in 2002 in CA.
Grantmaker type: Independent foundation
Financial data (yr. ended 12/31/02): Assets, $206,628 (M); gifts received, $321,112; expenditures, $114,571; qualifying distributions,

$114,496; giving activities include $110,000 for 18 grants (high: $25,000; low: $500).
Fields of interest: Education; Animals/wildlife; Health care; Health organizations, association; Pediatrics; Medical research.
Limitations: Applications not accepted. No grants to individuals.
Application information: Contributes only to pre-selected organizations.
Officers: Christina Zilber, C.E.O.; Laurent Zilber, Secy.
EIN: 010617035

459
Selim K. Zilkha Foundation
750 Lausanne Rd.
Los Angeles, CA 90077
Contact: Selim K. Zilkha, Pres.

Established in 1997 in CA.
Donor(s): Selim K. Zilkha.
Grantmaker type: Independent foundation
Financial data (yr. ended 09/30/01): Assets, $13,206,868 (M); gifts received, $7,975,594; expenditures, $10,407,779; qualifying distributions, $10,402,003; giving activities include $405,356 for 18 grants (high: $260,000; low: $450).
Purpose and activities: Giving primarily for the fine and performing arts, including historic preservation; support also for education and environmental conservation.
Fields of interest: Museums; Performing arts; Historical activities; Education; Natural resources; Social sciences.
Types of support: General/operating support; Research.
Limitations: Giving primarily in CA; some giving also in Washington, DC.
Application information:
   Initial approach: Letter
   Deadline(s): None
Officers: Selim K. Zilkha, Pres.; Nadia Zilkha Wellisz, V.P.; Mary Hayley, Secy.; Michael E. Zilkha, Treas.
EIN: 954682884

COLORADO

460
Airport Business Center Foundation
303E Airport Business Ctr.
Aspen, CO 81611-3540

Established in 1986 in CO.
Donor(s): John P. McBride, John P. McBride, Jr., Katherine H. McBride, Peter McBride, Lester D. Pedicord.
Grantmaker type: Independent foundation
Financial data (yr. ended 12/31/01): Assets, $1,342,253 (M); gifts received, $40,081; expenditures, $428,478; qualifying distributions, $428,478; giving activities include $411,253 for 126 grants (high: $200,000; low: $50).
Purpose and activities: To promote the preservation of natural resources, conduct research and educational programs on world over-population and family planning, promote

amateur sports, and provide education or medical services for distressed or underprivileged communities.
Fields of interest: Education; Natural resources; Environment; Animal welfare; Family planning; Athletics/sports, winter sports; Population studies.
Limitations: Applications not accepted. Giving on a national basis. No grants to individuals.
Application information: Contributes only to pre-selected organizations.
Trustees: John P. McBride; John P. McBride, Jr.; Laurie M. McBride; Peter M. McBride; Lester D. Pedicord; Kate Puckett.
EIN: 841042661

461
American Humane Association
63 Inverness Dr. E.
Englewood, CO 80112-5117 (303) 792-9900
URL: http://www.americanhumane.org/

Founded in 1877.
Grantmaker type: Public charity
Financial data (yr. ended 06/30/03): Revenue, $9,414,404; assets, $12,574,984 (M); gifts received, $6,533,567; expenditures, $10,366,805; program services expenses, $8,405,154; giving activities include $430,242 for 119 grants (high: $135,000; low: $535; average: $535–$135,000) and $20,000 for 4 grants to individuals of $5,000 each.
Purpose and activities: The organization seeks to prevent cruelty, abuse, and neglect directed toward children and animals.
Fields of interest: Animal welfare; Children/youth, services.
Types of support: Building/renovation; Emergency funds; Program development; Curriculum development; Scholarships—to individuals.
Publications: Application guidelines, Annual report, Program policy statement.
Application information: See Web site for additional information.
Officers and Directors:* John Nobil,* Chair.; Steve Crosby,* Vice-Chair.; James Stark,* Secy.; Dan Whittemore,* Treas.; Constance Kindle; Patricia Martin.
Number of staff: 55 full-time professional; 7 part-time professional; 18 full-time support; 3 part-time support.
EIN: 840432950

462
Animal Assistance Foundation
455 Sherman St., Ste. 462
Denver, CO 80203-4405 (303) 744-8396
Contact: David L. Gies, Exec. Dir.
FAX: (303) 744-7065; E-mail: info@aaf-fd.org; URL: http://www.aaf-fd.org

Established in 1975 in CO.
Donor(s): Louise C. Harrison.‡
Grantmaker type: Independent foundation
Financial data (yr. ended 07/31/02): Assets, $23,898,587 (M); expenditures, $1,567,810; qualifying distributions, $1,263,819; giving activities include $1,081,947 for 37+ grants (high: $900,000; low: $332).
Purpose and activities: Giving for animal welfare, especially to prevent cruelty to cats and

dogs; also to promote pet population control, provide for humane treatment education, and expand scientific inquiry.
Fields of interest: Animal welfare; Animal population control.
Types of support: General/operating support; Building/renovation; Emergency funds; Program development; Conferences/seminars; Seed money; Curriculum development; Technical assistance.
Limitations: Giving limited to CO. No grants to individuals.
Publications: Annual report.
Application information: Application guidelines available on Web site. Application form required.
   Initial approach: Telephone, letter, or E-mail
   Copies of proposal: 10
   Deadline(s): Sept. 27 and Mar. 28
   Board meeting date(s): Bimonthly
   Final notification: Varies
Officers and Directors:* Jon F. Sands,* Pres.; Deborah D. Parsons,* V.P.; Alison Biggs,* Secy.; Charles D. Vail, D.V.M.,* Treas.; Susan Burgamy; Elizabeth Holtze; E. Bowman McLean; Bill Trefz, D.V.M.
Number of staff: 1 full-time professional; 1 part-time professional; 1 part-time support.
EIN: 840715412

463
Argentum Foundation
1776 Lincoln St., Ste. 1100
Denver, CO 80203-1028
Contact: Noel R. Congdon, Pres.

Established in 1984.
Donor(s): Thomas E. Congdon, Noel R. Congdon, Chelsea Congdon Brundige, Lucy Congdon Nanson.
Grantmaker type: Independent foundation
Financial data (yr. ended 05/31/02): Assets, $171,229 (M); gifts received, $129,900; expenditures, $232,298; qualifying distributions, $227,242; giving activities include $228,138 for 18 grants (high: $82,500; low: $138).
Purpose and activities: Giving primarily for education, research, and natural resources and wildlife preservation and conservation.
Fields of interest: Arts; Education; Environment; International peace/security.
Limitations: Applications not accepted. Giving primarily in CO. No grants to individuals.
Application information: Contributes only to pre-selected organizations.
Officers: Noel R. Congdon, Pres. and Treas.; Thomas E. Congdon, V.P. and Secy.
Number of staff: 5 shared staff.
EIN: 840916880

464
Barish Family Foundation
c/o Michael S. Barish
5761 E. Nassau Pl.
Englewood, CO 80111

Established in 1991 in CO.
Donor(s): Michael S. Barish.
Grantmaker type: Independent foundation
Financial data (yr. ended 12/31/02): Assets, $1,571,151 (M); expenditures, $109,646; qualifying distributions, $109,561; giving

activities include $108,902 for 44 grants (high: $20,000; low: $72).
Purpose and activities: Giving primarily to Jewish organizations and for medical research.
Fields of interest: Higher education; Animals/wildlife, preservation/protection; Medical research; Human services; Jewish federated giving programs; Jewish agencies & temples.
Limitations: Applications not accepted. Giving primarily in CO. No grants to individuals.
Application information: Contributes only to pre-selected organizations.
Directors: Brian Barish; Grant Barish; Joyce Barish; Michael S. Barish.
EIN: 841172704

465
P. Bruce and Virginia C. Benson Foundation
1422 Alamo St.
Colorado Springs, CO 80907-7302
Contact: David Benson, Secy.-Treas.

Established in 1988 in CO.
Donor(s): P. Bruce Benson.‡
Grantmaker type: Independent foundation
Financial data (yr. ended 06/30/02): Assets, $6,263,795 (M); gifts received, $744,854; expenditures, $493,232; qualifying distributions, $380,000; giving activities include $380,000 for 28 grants (high: $50,000; low: $2,500).
Purpose and activities: Giving primarily for education; some giving for health care and human services.
Fields of interest: Higher education; Education; Natural resources; Health care; Human services; Hospices; Religion.
Limitations: Giving on a national basis. No grants to individuals.
Application information: Application form not required.
   Deadline(s): None
Officers: Lucia F. Dhaens, Pres.; Polly Benson-Brown, V.P.; David Benson, Secy.-Treas.
Directors: Bruce D. Benson; Marguerite Benson.
EIN: 841090517

466
Boettcher Foundation ▼
600 17th St., Ste. 2210 S.
Denver, CO 80202 (303) 534-1937
Contact: Timothy W. Schultz, Pres.
E-mail: grants@boettcherfoundation.org; URL: http://www.boettcherfoundation.org/

Incorporated in 1937 in CO.
Donor(s): C.K. Boettcher,‡ Mrs. C.K. Boettcher,‡ Charles Boettcher,‡ Fannie Boettcher,‡ Ruth Boettcher Humphreys,‡ Mrs. Charles Boettcher II.‡
Grantmaker type: Independent foundation
Financial data (yr. ended 12/31/02): Assets, $195,018,192 (M); gifts received, $770,387; expenditures, $10,701,385; qualifying distributions, $9,871,834; giving activities include $6,336,300 for 119+ grants (high: $250,000; average: $10,000–$100,000) and $2,366,023 for 196 grants to individuals.
Purpose and activities: Grants to educational institutions, with emphasis on Boettcher Scholarship Program; community and social

services, including child welfare, women, the disadvantaged, the homeless, and urban and rural development; health, including rehabilitation and drug abuse; and civic and cultural programs, including support for the fine and performing arts.

Fields of interest: Visual arts; Museums; Performing arts; Music; Historic preservation/historical societies; Arts; Early childhood education; Higher education; Adult education—literacy, basic skills & GED; Reading; Education; Natural resources; Environment; Family planning; Medical care, rehabilitation; Health care; Substance abuse, services; Health organizations, association; Employment; Human services; Children/youth, services; Hospices; Women, centers/services; Homeless, human services; Rural development; Community development; Women; Economically disadvantaged; Homeless.

Types of support: General/operating support; Annual campaigns; Capital campaigns; Building/renovation; Land acquisition; Scholarship funds; Scholarships—to individuals; Matching/challenge support.

Limitations: Giving limited to CO. No grants to individuals (except for scholarship program), or for endowment funds.

Publications: Application guidelines, Annual report (including application guidelines).

Application information: Application form not required.

   Initial approach: Letter
   Copies of proposal: 1
   Deadline(s): None
   Board meeting date(s): Monthly
   Final notification: 2 to 3 months

Officers and Trustees:* Claudia Boettcher Merthan,* Chair.; J. William Sorensen,* Vice-Chair.; Timothy W. Schultz, Pres. and Exec. Dir.; Katie S. Kramer, V.P.; Harris D. Sherman,* Secy.; Edward D. White III,* Treas.; Marcia Z. Ashton; Pamela D. Beardsley; Paul H. Chan; James P. Craig; M. Ann Penny; Thomas Williams.

Number of staff: 4 full-time professional; 1 part-time professional; 2 full-time support.

EIN: 840404274

Recent environmental and animal welfare grants:

466-1 Cheyenne Mountain Zoological Society, Colorado Springs, CO, $200,000. Toward zoo improvements. 2002.

466-2 Greenway Foundation, Denver, CO, $30,000. 2002.

467
Boogies Diner Foundation
(formerly The Weinglass Foundation, Inc.)
P.O. Box 11509
Aspen, CO 81612

Established in 1983 in MD.
Donor(s): Leonard Weinglass.
Grantmaker type: Independent foundation
Financial data (yr. ended 12/31/02): Assets, $2,979,934 (M); expenditures, $696,853; qualifying distributions, $680,203; giving activities include $470,006 for grants and $189,107 for grants to individuals.
Purpose and activities: Support primarily for human services and Jewish temples. Some support also for community development and animal welfare.

Fields of interest: Arts; Education; Animal welfare; Recreation; Human services; Community development; Jewish agencies & temples.
Types of support: General/operating support; Building/renovation; Scholarship funds; Grants to individuals.
Limitations: Applications not accepted. Giving primarily to individuals in Aspen, CO, and Baltimore, MD.
Application information: Unsolicited requests for funds not accepted.
Officers: Leonard Weinglass, Pres.; Raymond Altman, V.P.
EIN: 521307628

468
The Botkins Foundation, Inc.
P.O. Box 101382
Denver, CO 80250

Established in 1998 in MT.
Donor(s): Leonard C. Martin.
Grantmaker type: Independent foundation
Financial data (yr. ended 12/31/01): Assets, $578 (M); gifts received, $101,550; expenditures, $126,155; qualifying distributions, $126,120; giving activities include $125,000 for 3 grants (high: $118,000; low: $2,000).
Fields of interest: Environment, forests; Animals/wildlife, sanctuaries.
Limitations: Applications not accepted. Giving on a national basis. No grants to individuals.
Application information: Contributes only to pre-selected organizations.
Officers: Christopher A. Botrin, Pres.; Myra M. Berry, Secy.; Padraic J. Dillon, Treas.
EIN: 841459663

469
Ruth H. Brown Foundation
7.5 Goose Creek Rd.
South Fork, CO 81154-9428   (719) 658-1016
Contact: Charla Brown, Treas.

Established in 1959 in CO.
Donor(s): Ruth H. Brown.
Grantmaker type: Independent foundation
Financial data (yr. ended 12/31/02): Assets, $4,830,173 (M); expenditures, $288,196; qualifying distributions, $243,620; giving activities include $240,000 for 35 grants (high: $75,000; low: $2,500).
Fields of interest: Natural resources; Environment; Animals/wildlife, preservation/protection.
Limitations: Giving on a national basis.
Application information:
   Initial approach: Letter
   Deadline(s): None
   Board meeting date(s): Aug.
Officers: Darcey Brown, Pres.; Albert Brown, V.P.; Laurene Cochran, Secy.; Charla Brown, Treas.
Number of staff: 1 part-time support.
EIN: 846023395

470
The Gayla W. Carney Family Foundation
(formerly The Gayla W. Coulter Family Foundation)
P.O. Box L-3
Aspen, CO 81612

Established in 1998 in CO and KS.
Donor(s): Gayla W. Coulter.
Grantmaker type: Independent foundation
Financial data (yr. ended 12/31/02): Assets, $155,207 (M); expenditures, $136,949; qualifying distributions, $129,632; giving activities include $129,655 for 12 grants (high: $57,500; low: $250).
Purpose and activities: Giving primarily for youth development and education.
Fields of interest: Education; Environment; Hospitals (general); Children/youth, services.
Types of support: General/operating support; Building/renovation.
Limitations: Applications not accepted. Giving primarily in Wichita, KS; some giving also in Aspen, CO. No grants to individuals.
Application information: Contributes only to pre-selected organizations.
Officers: Gayla Lynn Coulter, Pres.; Jamie J. Coulter, V.P.; Christie Somes, V.P.; Scott Somes, V.P.; Rob Gile, Secy.-Treas.
EIN: 481202350

471
Caulkins Family Foundation
c/o George P. Caulkins, Jr.
1600 Broadway, Ste. 1400
Denver, CO 80202

Established in 1993 in CO.
Donor(s): George P. Caulkins, Jr., John N. Caulkins, Mary I. Caulkins.
Grantmaker type: Operating foundation
Financial data (yr. ended 12/31/02): Assets, $3,079,118 (M); gifts received, $82,126; expenditures, $176,620; qualifying distributions, $168,314; giving activities include $168,500 for 79 grants (high: $27,000; low: $500).
Fields of interest: Arts; Elementary/secondary education; Natural resources; Food services; Boys & girls clubs; Human services.
Limitations: Applications not accepted. Giving primarily in CO. No grants to individuals.
Application information: Contributes only to pre-selected organizations.
Officers and Directors:* Eleanor N. Caulkins,* Pres.; David I. Caulkins,* V.P.; George P. Caulkins, Jr.,* V.P.; George P. Caulkins III,* V.P.; John N. Caulkins,* V.P.; Maxwell O.B. Caulkins,* Secy.; Mary I. Caulkins, Treas.
EIN: 841251441

472
The Chamberlain Foundation
c/o Shaw & Quigg, Attys.
501 N. Main St., Ste. 222
Pueblo, CO 81003   (719) 543-8596
Contact: David B. Shaw, Chair.

Established in 1979.
Donor(s): Allen G. Chamberlain, Jr.,‡ Lenore Chamberlain.‡
Grantmaker type: Independent foundation

Financial data (yr. ended 12/31/02): Assets, $5,412,414 (M); expenditures, $230,882; qualifying distributions, $228,860; giving activities include $227,705 for 19 grants (high: $114,894; low: $1,500; average: $5,000–$7,000).
Purpose and activities: Giving primarily to a historic museum and other arts groups.
Fields of interest: Museums; History/archaeology; Arts; Education; Natural resources.
Types of support: General/operating support; Equipment; Program development.
Limitations: Giving limited to Pueblo County, CO. No grants to individuals.
Publications: Application guidelines.
Application information: Application form not required.
　Initial approach: Letter
　Copies of proposal: 1
　Deadline(s): Mar. 1 and Oct. 1
　Board meeting date(s): Mar. and Oct.
Officers and Directors:* David B. Shaw, Chair.; Kay Bartecchi,* Secy.; Jeffrey C. Shaw; Katherine Vail.
Number of staff: None.
EIN: 840789794

473
Chinook Fund

2418 W. 32nd Ave.
Denver, CO 80211 (303) 455-6905
Contact: Peg Logan, Exec. Dir.
FAX: (303) 477-1617; E-mail: office@chinookfund.org; URL: http://www.chinookfund.org

Established in 1987 in CO.
Grantmaker type: Public charity
Financial data (yr. ended 06/30/03): Revenue, $498,978; assets, $900,001 (L); gifts received, $474,517; expenditures, $393,533; program services expenses, $311,325; giving activities include $130,000 for 35 grants (high: $6,500; low: $500).
Purpose and activities: The fund's primary goal is to support progressive social change organizing and activism across Colorado. The fund defines progressive social change work as efforts that challenge and attempt to alter existing economic and social relationships and institutions which are inequitable and undemocratic. This type of change requires an analysis of the root causes of social problems and their solutions, followed by action and evaluation of the effectiveness of that action. The fund supports projects that are working for progressive social change through means such as community organizing, advocacy, and coalition work.
Fields of interest: Natural resources; Environment; Civil rights, advocacy; Civil rights, gays/lesbians; Race/intergroup relations; Community development.
Types of support: General/operating support; Continuing support; Emergency funds; Program development; Seed money; Technical assistance.
Limitations: Giving limited to CO. No support for direct service organizations, pass-through agencies, organizations with wide access to traditional funding, or organizations with annual budgets exceeding $350,000. No grants to individuals.

Publications: Application guidelines, Annual report, Financial statement, Grants list, Newsletter.
Application information: Accepts Colorado Common Grant Application and NNG Common Grant form with additional information. Application form required.
　Initial approach: Telephone requesting application guidelines
　Copies of proposal: 4
　Deadline(s): Feb. 21 and Aug. 21
　Board meeting date(s): Jan., Mar., June, Aug., and Nov.
　Final notification: June and Dec.
Directors: Peg Logan, Exec. Dir.; Ana Soler; Malaika Pettigrew; and 12 additional directors.
Number of staff: 3 full-time professional; 1 full-time support.
EIN: 841076325

474
Colorado Interstate Gas Company Contributions Program

P.O. Box 1087
Colorado Springs, CO 80944 (719) 520-4235
Contact: Judy Cara, Mgr., Public Affairs and Corp. Comm.
FAX: (719) 520-4522; E-mail: judith.cara@coastalcorp.com

Grantmaker type: Corporate giving program
Purpose and activities: Colorado Interstate Gas makes charitable contributions to nonprofit organizations involved with arts and culture, education, the environment, health and human services, youth development, public affairs, and minorities. Support is given primarily in areas of company operations.
Fields of interest: Arts; Elementary/secondary education; Higher education; Education; Environment, air pollution; Environment; Health care; Youth development; Human services; Public affairs; Minorities.
Types of support: General/operating support; Annual campaigns; Capital campaigns; Scholarship funds; Employee volunteer services; Public relations services; Sponsorships; Donated equipment; In-kind gifts.
Limitations: Giving primarily in areas of company operations, particularly Colorado Springs, CO.
Publications: Informational brochure (including application guidelines).
Application information: The Public Affairs Department handles giving. A contributions committee reviews all requests. Application form not required.
　Initial approach: Letter of inquiry to headquarters
　Copies of proposal: 1
　Deadline(s): Aug. 1
　Final notification: Following review
Number of staff: 2 full-time professional.

475
Colromora Family Foundation

6042 E. Mineral Dr.
Englewood, CO 80112

Established in 1998 in CO.
Donor(s): Mary E. Collison, Steven G. Moore.
Grantmaker type: Independent foundation

Financial data (yr. ended 11/30/02): Assets, $1,080,924 (M); expenditures, $305,381; qualifying distributions, $298,825; giving activities include $301,000 for 11 grants (high: $85,000; low: $5,000).
Purpose and activities: Giving primarily to Christian ministries and schools and to a United Methodist church.
Fields of interest: Education; Environment; Christian agencies & churches; Protestant agencies & churches.
Limitations: Applications not accepted. Giving primarily in Denver, CO. No grants to individuals.
Application information: Contributes only to pre-selected organizations.
Officers: Mary E. Collison, Pres.; Steven G. Moore, V.P.
Director: Diana Green.
EIN: 841452045

476
The Community Foundation Serving Boulder County

(formerly Boulder Area Communities Foundation)
1123 Spruce St.
Boulder, CO 80302-5281 (303) 442-0436
Contact: Josie Heath, Pres.
FAX: (303) 415-1542; E-mail: info@commfound.org; URL: http://www.commfound.org

Established in 1991 in CO.
Grantmaker type: Community foundation
Financial data (yr. ended 12/31/01): Assets, $11,737,333 (L); expenditures, $1,919,765; giving activities include $1,498,038 for 229 grants (high: $500,000; low: $20; average: $500–$10,000).
Purpose and activities: Support primarily for arts and culture, education, the environment, health care, and human services.
Fields of interest: Arts; Education; Environment; Health care; Human services; Gays/lesbians.
Types of support: General/operating support; Continuing support; Annual campaigns; Capital campaigns; Building/renovation; Equipment; Endowments; Emergency funds; Program development; Conferences/seminars; Seed money; Scholarship funds; Technical assistance; Consulting services; Program-related investments/loans; Employee matching gifts; Scholarships—to individuals; In-kind gifts; Student loans—to individuals.
Limitations: Giving primarily in the Boulder County, CO, area.
Publications: Application guidelines, Annual report, Financial statement, Grants list, Informational brochure (including application guidelines), Newsletter.
Application information: Application form required.
　Initial approach: Telephone or letter of inquiry
　Copies of proposal: 1
　Deadline(s): Sept. 30
　Board meeting date(s): Monthly
　Final notification: Dec.
Officers and Directors:* Clair Beckmann,* Chair.; Josie Heath,* Pres.; Brad Bickham,* V.P.; Lindsey Delaplaine, V.P., Progs. and Admin.; Margaret Katz, V.P., Devel. and Comm.; Susan Richards,* Secy.; Patricia Nielsen,* Treas.; Amy

Batchelor; John Bohn; Steve Brett; Colleen Conant; Ann Cooper; Benita Duran; George Garcia; Dave Gilman; T.J. Heyman; Dave Hoover; Laura Hundley; Mary Lamy; Conrad Lattes; Mary Beth Lewis; Mariagnes Medrud; Bob Morehouse; John Nevile; Rick Sterling; Nancy Stevens; John Tayer; Euvaldo Valdez.
Number of staff: 2 full-time professional; 1 part-time professional; 1 full-time support.
EIN: 841171836

477
Coors Brewing Company Contributions Program
P.O. Box 4030, NH 420
Golden, CO 80401
Contact: Buck Boze, Mgr.
FAX: (303) 277-6132

Grantmaker type: Corporate giving program
Financial data (yr. ended 12/31/01): Total giving, $2,926,696; giving activities include $2,426,696 for 350 grants and $500,000 for employee matching gifts.
Purpose and activities: Coors makes charitable contributions to nonprofit organizations involved with higher education, the environment, alcohol abuse, AIDS, food distribution, business and industry, minorities, and women. Support is given primarily in Denver and Golden, Colorado, Memphis, Tennessee, and Elkton, Virginia.
Fields of interest: Higher education; Environment; Substance abuse, prevention; AIDS; Food services; Business/industry; Minorities; Women.
Types of support: Continuing support; Employee volunteer services; Sponsorships; In-kind gifts.
Limitations: Giving primarily in Denver and Golden, CO, Memphis, TN, and Elkton, VA. No support for political organizations or sports teams. No grants to individuals, or for scholarships, fundraising, races, or travel.
Publications: Application guidelines, Informational brochure (including application guidelines).
Application information: The Corporate Contributions Department handles giving. The company has a staff that only handles contributions. A contributions committee reviews all requests. Application form not required.
　Initial approach: Proposal to headquarters
　Copies of proposal: 1
　Deadline(s): 3 months prior to need
　Board meeting date(s): Monthly
　Final notification: 1 month
Number of staff: 2 full-time professional.

478
The Denver Foundation ▼
950 S. Cherry St., Ste. 200
Denver, CO 80246 (303) 300-1790
Contact: David J. Miller, C.E.O. and Pres.
FAX: (303) 300-6547; E-mail: info@denverfoundation.org; URL: http://www.denverfoundation.org

Established in 1925 in CO by resolution and declaration of trust.
Grantmaker type: Community foundation

Financial data (yr. ended 12/31/01): Assets, $198,566,572 (M); gifts received, $33,665,823; expenditures, $20,905,237; giving activities include $17,464,698 for 2,260 grants (high: $75,000).
Purpose and activities: To assist, encourage, and promote the well-being of mankind, primarily the inhabitants of metropolitan Denver. Grants primarily for education, civic, health, human services, and arts and cultural programs and strengthening neighborhoods with Small Grants Program.
Fields of interest: Arts; Education; Environment, public education; Health care; Human services; Youth, services; Community development.
Types of support: General/operating support; Building/renovation; Program development; Seed money; Technical assistance; Program-related investments/loans; Matching/challenge support.
Limitations: Giving limited to Adams, Arapahoe, Boulder, Denver, Douglas, and Jefferson counties, CO. No support for religious, political or sectarian programs, or projects supported largely by public funds. No grants to individuals, or for scholarships, debt liquidation, endowment funds, research, publications, films, travel, or conferences, symposiums, workshops, or individual health care procedures.
Publications: Annual report, Informational brochure (including application guidelines), Newsletter, Program policy statement.
Application information: Colorado Common Grant Application Form accepted including additional information. Application form not required.
　Initial approach: Letter
　Copies of proposal: 1
　Deadline(s): Feb. 3, June 2, and Oct. 1
　Board meeting date(s): Mar., June, Sept., and Dec.
　Final notification: Within 5 months
Officers and Trustees:* Dean Prina,* Chair.; Cynthia Kahn,* Vice-Chair.; Jeffrey Lee,* Vice-Chair.; David J. Miller, C.E.O. and Pres.; Rebecca Arno, V.P., Advancement; Lauren Casteel, V.P., Donor Rels.; Sarah Harrison, V.P., Comm.; Daniel Lee, V.P., Fin. and Admin.; Christine Soto, V.P., Progs.; Jeff Fard, Secy.; Mary Sissel, Treas.; Julika Ambrose; Laura Barton; Nancy Benson; Lee Palmer Everding; Marva Hammons; Anna Jo Haynes; Bill Johnson; Christine Johnson; Susan Kiely; Manuell Martinez; Barbara Neal; Bob Newman; Fred Taylor.
Number of staff: 17 full-time professional; 1 part-time professional; 9 full-time support.
EIN: 846048381
Recent environmental and animal welfare grants:
478-1 American Alpine Club, Golden, CO, $15,000. For Elizabeth Hawley Project. 2002.
478-2 Butterfly Hope, Denver, CO, $10,000. For general operating support. 2002.
478-3 Colorado Conservation Trust, Boulder, CO, $101,652. For operating support. 2002.
478-4 Colorado Conservation Trust, Boulder, CO, $25,000. For operating support. 2002.
478-5 Colorado Conservation Trust, Boulder, CO, $11,484. 2002.
478-6 Colorado Environmental Coalition, Denver, CO, $10,000. For Colorado Capacity Building Project. 2002.

478-7 Colorado Wildlife Federation, Lakewood, CO, $10,000. For Conservation Education Program. 2002.
478-8 Denver Botanic Gardens, Denver, CO, $10,000. For Fete De Fleur Fund Raiser and general operating support. 2002.
478-9 Denver Dumb Friends League-Humane Society of Denver, Denver, CO, $21,191. For general operating support. 2002.
478-10 Denver Dumb Friends League-Humane Society of Denver, Denver, CO, $15,000. For Capital Campaign to assist with reduction of interest payments. 2002.
478-11 Denver Dumb Friends League-Humane Society of Denver, Denver, CO, $11,000. For general operating support of capital campaign. 2002.
478-12 Denver Zoological Foundation, Denver, CO, $20,000. For operating support of Do At Zoo. 2002.
478-13 Denver Zoological Foundation, Denver, CO, $10,000. For Teen Zoo Crew Program. 2002.
478-14 Ducks Unlimited, Denver, CO, $10,000. For general operating support of Waterfowl Project in Northeastern Colorado. 2002.
478-15 EDUCO Colorado, Fort Collins, CO, $10,000. For program support of Peak Leadership Program. 2002.
478-16 Evergreen Animal Protection League, Evergreen, CO, $15,762. For general operating support. 2002.
478-17 FrontRange Earth Force, Denver, CO, $15,000. For general operating support. 2002.
478-18 FrontRange Earth Force, Denver, CO, $10,000. For general operating support. 2002.
478-19 Growing Gardens of Boulder County, Boulder, CO, $10,000. For general operating support. 2002.
478-20 International SeaKeepers Society, Miami, FL, $50,000. For general operating support. 2002.
478-21 James P. Beckwourth Mountain Club, Denver, CO, $18,000. For general operating support. 2002.
478-22 Meet the Wilderness, Edwards, CO, $15,000. For Capacity Building Video. 2002.
478-23 Middle Park Land Trust, Granby, CO, $15,000. For general operating support. 2002.
478-24 Middle Park Land Trust, Granby, CO, $10,000. For general operating support. 2002.
478-25 Middle Park Land Trust, Granby, CO, $10,000. For general operating support. 2002.
478-26 Nature Conservancy, Arlington, VA, $10,000. For internships and general operating support of Lake Whales Ridge Program in Babson Park, Florida. 2002.
478-27 Renewable Energy Leadership Group, Golden, CO, $25,400. For renewable energy teacher, classroom training for K-12 schools. 2002.
478-28 Rocky Mountain Nature Association, Estes Park, CO, $20,000. For land purchase. 2002.
478-29 Volunteers for Outdoor Colorado, Denver, CO, $10,000. For general operating support. 2002.

479
The Domanica Foundation
777 S. Wadsworth Blvd., Ste. 4-280
Lakewood, CO 80226-4355 (303) 985-0041
Contact: Donald V. Berlanti, Pres.

Established in 1994.
Donor(s): Donald V. Berlanti, McKenna L.
Berlanti, Matthew D. Berlanti.
Grantmaker type: Independent foundation
Financial data (yr. ended 12/31/02): Assets,
$2,171,469 (M); gifts received, $55,000;
expenditures, $196,072; qualifying distributions,
$194,500; giving activities include $194,500 for
11 grants (high: $50,000; low: $2,000).
Fields of interest: Education; Animal welfare;
Human services.
Limitations: Giving on a national basis.
Application information:
Initial approach: Letter
Officers: Donald V. Berlanti, Pres.; Karen L.
Berlanti, V.P.; McKenna L. Berlanti, Secy.;
Matthew D. Berlanti, Treas.
EIN: 521906206

480
The Dominic Foundation
777 S. Wadsworth Blvd., Ste. 4-280
Lakewood, CO 80226
Contact: Richard A. Berlanti, Pres.

Established in 1994 in PA and NM.
Donor(s): Richard A. Berlanti, Todd A. Berlanti,
Merryl A. Berlanti.
Grantmaker type: Independent foundation
Financial data (yr. ended 12/31/02): Assets,
$1,981,444 (M); expenditures, $182,482;
qualifying distributions, $181,000; giving
activities include $181,000 for 40 grants (high:
$25,500; low: $500).
Purpose and activities: Giving primarily for the
arts, and human services.
Fields of interest: Museums; Museums
(children's); Arts; Natural resources; Diabetes;
Human services; Children, services.
Limitations: Giving primarily in FL, NM, and PA.
No grants to individuals.
Application information:
Initial approach: Letter
Deadline(s): None
Officers: Richard A. Berlanti, Pres.; Merryl A.
Berlanti, V.P.; Todd A. Berlanti, Secy.-Treas.
EIN: 521905243

481
John G. Duncan Trust
c/o Wells Fargo Bank West, N.A.
1740 Broadway, MAC C7300-484
Denver, CO 80274
Contact: John G. Duncan, Tr.
Application address: c/o Yvonne Baca, Wells
Fargo Bank West, N.A., P.O. Box 5825, Denver,
CO 80217, tel.: (303) 293-5324

Trust established in 1955 in CO.
Donor(s): John G. Duncan.‡
Grantmaker type: Independent foundation
Financial data (yr. ended 12/31/02): Assets,
$6,420,041 (M); expenditures, $508,270;
qualifying distributions, $458,403; giving
activities include $445,600 for 134 grants (high:
$12,000; low: $1,000).

Purpose and activities: Giving primarily for
education, health care, including dental care
services, food services, children and youth
services, social services, including services for
people who are blind, and services for the aging.
Fields of interest: Education; Animal welfare;
Health care; Health organizations, association;
Food banks; Food distribution, meals on wheels;
Boys & girls clubs; Human services; Hospices;
Human services; Aging.
Types of support: General/operating support;
Continuing support; Annual campaigns;
Building/renovation; Equipment; Emergency
funds; Program development; Seed money;
Research.
Limitations: Giving limited to CO. No grants to
individuals, or for endowment funds,
scholarships, or fellowships; no loans.
Publications: Application guidelines.
Application information: Application form not
required.
Initial approach: Letter or proposal
Copies of proposal: 1
Deadline(s): None
Board meeting date(s): Dec.
Final notification: Dec. 31
Trustee: Wells Fargo Bank West, N.A.
Number of staff: None.
EIN: 846016555

482
**Ecumenical Project for International
Cooperation, Inc.**
(also known as EPIC)
322 Lab Rd.
P.O. Box 322
Allenspark, CO 80510-0433 (303) 747-2059
Contact: Paul T. McKay, Exec. Dir.
FAX: (303) 747-2085; E-mail: EPIC@csd.net;
URL: http://www.epicprojects.org/index.htm

Established in 1977.
Grantmaker type: Public charity
Financial data (yr. ended 12/31/00): Revenue,
$112,069; assets, $229,230; gifts received,
$84,336; expenditures, $106,279; program
services expenses, $96,917; giving activities
include $72,006 for 13 grants (high: $28,364;
low: $54) and $3,795 for 6 grants to individuals
(high: $1,215; low: $200).
Purpose and activities: The project seeks to
promote peace, human rights, sustainable
development, and preservation of the
environment through research, education and
action and by encouraging cooperation among
organizations involved in these areas.
Fields of interest: Education; Natural resources;
International development; International
peace/security; International human rights;
International affairs.
Types of support: Research.
Limitations: Giving on a national and
international basis.
Publications: Annual report.
Officers and Directors: Deborah Bauer,*
Chair.; Loren Raymond, Ph.D.,* Pres.; Penny
DeLoca; Jenny Dillon; Christie R. McKay; Mary
E. McKay; Marjorie McKinney.
EIN: 132931242

483
The Joseph Henry Edmondson Foundation
10 Lake Cir.
Colorado Springs, CO 80906 (719) 471-1241
Contact: Heather L. Carroll, Exec. Dir.

Established in 1987 in CO.
Grantmaker type: Independent foundation
Financial data (yr. ended 07/31/02): Assets,
$11,389,238 (M); gifts received, $304,130;
expenditures, $927,038; qualifying distributions,
$838,856; giving activities include $740,310 for
89 grants (high: $50,000; low: $400).
Purpose and activities: Giving limited to the
welfare of children, the ill, and the elderly, the
preservation and improvement of the
environment, and the arts in the Pikes Peak area.
Fields of interest: Arts; Environment; Health
care; Children/youth, services; Family services;
Homeless, human services.
Types of support: General/operating support;
Continuing support; Capital campaigns;
Building/renovation; Equipment; Land
acquisition; Emergency funds; Program
development; Matching/challenge support.
Limitations: Giving limited to the Colorado
Springs, CO, area. No grants to individuals; or
for debt reduction.
Publications: Application guidelines, Grants list,
Informational brochure (including application
guidelines).
Application information: Application form not
required.
Initial approach: Request guidelines
Copies of proposal: 2
Deadline(s): Dec., Mar., June, and Sept.
(Applicant should contact office for exact
deadline dates)
Board meeting date(s): Jan., Apr., July, and Oct.
Officers and Directors: Carl Donner,* Pres.
and Treas.; Bruce T. Buell,* V.P.; Christopher
Bruce Duff; Sean Duff; Sharon Higgins; Mary
Kanas; Susie Ramsay.
Number of staff: 1 full-time professional; 1
part-time support.
EIN: 841090456

484
El Pomar Foundation ▼
10 Lake Cir.
Colorado Springs, CO 80906 (719) 633-7733
Contact: William J. Hybl, Chair.
Additional tel.: (800) 554-7711; FAX: (719)
577-5702; URL: http://www.elpomar.org

Incorporated in 1937 in CO.
Donor(s): Spencer Penrose,‡ Mrs. Spencer
Penrose.‡
Grantmaker type: Independent foundation
Financial data (yr. ended 12/31/02): Assets,
$398,973,064 (M); gifts received, $202,487;
expenditures, $22,061,744; qualifying
distributions, $22,777,793; giving activities
include $13,576,565 for 723+ grants (high:
$1,700,000; low: $80; average:
$5,000–$100,000), $82,332 for 59 employee
matching gifts, $3,604,206 for 4
foundation-administered programs and
$358,823 for 39 in-kind gifts.
Purpose and activities: Grants only to nonprofit
organizations for public, educational, arts and
humanities, health, and welfare purposes,
including child welfare, the disadvantaged, and

housing; municipalities may request funds for specific projects.

Fields of interest: Media/communications; Visual arts; Museums; Performing arts; Theater; Music; Humanities; Historic preservation/historical societies; Arts; Child development, education; Elementary school/education; Secondary school/education; Vocational education; Higher education; Adult/continuing education; Adult education—literacy, basic skills & GED; Libraries/library science; Reading; Education; Natural resources; Environment; Hospitals (general); Pharmacy/prescriptions; Health care; Substance abuse, services; Health organizations, association; Employment; Food services; Nutrition; Housing/shelter, development; Recreation; Human services; Children/youth, services; Child development, services; Family services; Hospices; Aging, centers/services; Homeless, human services; Community development; Voluntarism promotion; Transportation; Minorities; Disabled; Aging; Economically disadvantaged; Homeless.

Types of support: General/operating support; Continuing support; Capital campaigns; Building/renovation; Equipment; Land acquisition; Emergency funds; Program development; Scholarship funds; Program-related investments/loans; Employee matching gifts.

Limitations: Giving limited to CO. No support for organizations that distribute funds to other grantees, religious or political organizations, primary or secondary education, or for camps or seasonal facilities. No grants to individuals, or for annual campaigns, travel, film or other media projects, conferences, deficit financing, endowment funds, research, matching gifts, seed money, or publications.

Publications: Application guidelines, Annual report (including application guidelines), Grants list, Informational brochure.

Application information: Application form not required.

Initial approach: Proposal
Copies of proposal: 1
Deadline(s): None
Board meeting date(s): 6 to 8 times a year
Final notification: 90 days

Officers and Trustees:* William J. Hybl,* Chair. and C.E.O.; R. Thayer Tutt, Jr.,* Pres. and C.I.O.; Robert J. Hilbert,* Sr. V.P., Admin. and Secy.-Treas.; David J. Palenchar,* Sr. V.P., Opers.; Susan S. Woodward, V.P., Penrose House and Awards for Excellence; Judith M. Bell; Cortlandt S. Dietler; Kent O. Olin; Brenda J. Smith; William R. Ward.

Number of staff: 40 full-time professional; 20 full-time support; 3 part-time support.

EIN: 846002373

Recent environmental and animal welfare grants:

484-1 Cheyenne Mountain Zoological Society, Colorado Springs, CO, $2,092,000. For African Rift Valley Exhibit. 2001.

484-2 Cheyenne Mountain Zoological Society, Colorado Springs, CO, $100,000. For general operating support. 2001.

484-3 Cheyenne Mountain Zoological Society, Cheyenne Mountain Zoo, Colorado Springs, CO, $15,000. For general operating support. 2001.

484-4 Colorado Cattlemens Agricultural Land Trust, Arvada, CO, $50,000. For open space preservation. 2001.

484-5 Colorado Mountain Club Foundation, Golden, CO, $15,000. For Robert V. Menary Award for Excellence in Environmental Issues. 2001.

484-6 Historic Arkansas River Project (HARP) Foundation, Pueblo, CO, $25,000. For Julie and Spencer Penrose Award to Outstanding Nonprofit Organization. 2001.

484-7 Humane Society of the Pikes Peak Region, Colorado Springs, CO, $137,000. For new shelter capital campaign. 2001.

484-8 Nature Conservancy, Boulder, CO, $10,000. For Heart of the West capital campaign. 2001.

484-9 Outward Bound West, Golden, CO, $15,000. For William Thayer Tutt Award for Excellence in Sports and Recreation. 2001.

484-10 Ridgway, Town of, Ridgway, CO, $15,000. For Uncompahgre River Restoration Project. 2001.

484-11 William J. Palmer Parks Foundation, Colorado Springs, CO, $1,320,000. To donate land for preservation. 2001.

485
Robert & Elizabeth Fergus Foundation
P.O. Box 1515
Aspen, CO 81612 (970) 925-7716
Contact: Elizabeth Fergus, Tr.

Established in 1989 in OH.
Grantmaker type: Independent foundation
Financial data (yr. ended 12/31/02): Assets, $2,107,391 (M); gifts received, $9,049; expenditures, $208,460; qualifying distributions, $169,897; giving activities include $169,522 for 73 grants (high: $10,000; low: $100).
Purpose and activities: Giving primarily for arts and culture, education, and health and human services.
Fields of interest: Arts; Education; Natural resources; Hospitals (general); Human services; Children/youth, services; Federated giving programs.
Types of support: General/operating support.
Limitations: Giving on a national basis.
Application information: Application form not required.

Initial approach: Letter
Deadline(s): None

Trustees: Corwin Fergus; Elizabeth Fergus; Sylvia Fergus; Catherine Garber.
EIN: 316087932

486
Gates Family Foundation ▼
(formerly Gates Foundation)
3575 Cherry Creek N. Dr., Ste. 100
Denver, CO 80209 (303) 722-1881
Contact: C. Thomas Kaesemeyer, Exec. Dir.
FAX: (303) 316-3038; E-mail: info@gatesfamilyfoundation.org; URL: http://www.gatesfamilyfoundation.org

Incorporated in 1946 in CO.
Donor(s): Charles C. Gates, Sr.,‡ Hazel Gates,‡ John Gates.‡
Grantmaker type: Independent foundation

Financial data (yr. ended 12/31/02): Assets, $173,119,408 (M); gifts received, $35,753,141; expenditures, $10,196,153; qualifying distributions, $9,443,149; giving activities include $8,733,861 for 91 grants (high: $1,200,000; low: $5,000; average: $10,000–$100,000).
Purpose and activities: To promote the health, welfare, and broad education of mankind, whether by means of research, grants, publications, and the foundation's own agencies and activities, or through cooperation with agencies and institutions already in existence. Grants primarily for education and youth services, including leadership development; public policy; historic preservation, humanities, and cultural affairs; health care, including cost reduction; and human services.
Fields of interest: Multipurpose centers/programs; Visual arts; Museums; Performing arts; Dance; Theater; Music; Humanities; Historic preservation/historical societies; Arts; Libraries/library science; Education; Natural resources; Health care, support services; Health care, patient services; Recreation; Youth development, services; Youth development; Human services, public policy; Human services; Youth, services; Aging, centers/services; Human services; Economics; Government/public administration; Leadership development; Aging.
Types of support: Capital campaigns; Building/renovation; Land acquisition; Fellowships; Matching/challenge support.
Limitations: Giving limited to CO, with emphasis on the Denver area, except for foundation-initiated grants. No support for private foundations, medical facilities, or individual public schools of public school districts. No grants to individuals, or for operating budgets, medical research, annual campaigns, emergency funds, deficit financing, purchase of tickets for fundraising dinners, parties, balls, or other social fundraising events, purchase of vehicles or office equipment, conferences, meetings, research, or scholarships; no loans.
Publications: Annual report (including application guidelines), Grants list.
Application information: If the summary proposal seems to dovetail with the current interests of the foundation additional information will be required. A Common Grant Application form will be provided for this purpose. Application form not required.

Initial approach: Telephone call or short summary proposal
Copies of proposal: 1
Deadline(s): Jan. 15, Apr. 1, July 1, and Oct. 1
Board meeting date(s): Approx. Apr. 1, June 15, Oct. 1, and Dec. 15
Final notification: 2 weeks following meetings

Officers and Trustees:* Charles G. Cannon,* Pres.; Valerie Gates,* V.P.; C. Thomas Kaesemeyer, Secy. and Exec. Dir.; Thomas C. Stokes,* Treas.; Christina H. Turissini, Compt.; George B. Beardsley; Charles C. Gates; William W. Grant III; Diane Gates Wallach; Mike Wilfley.
Number of staff: 4 full-time professional; 1 full-time support.
EIN: 840474837
Recent environmental and animal welfare grants:

486-1 Cheyenne Mountain Zoological Society, Colorado Springs, CO, $350,000. Toward African Rift Valley exhibit, infrastructure repairs and improvements, and to plan new education center. 2002.

486-2 Colorado Conservation Trust, Boulder, CO, $45,000. To establish Trust. 2002.

486-3 Colorado Fourteeners Initiative, Golden, CO, $70,000. For trail restoration and construction projects on heavily impacted Fourteeners. 2002.

486-4 Denver Urban Gardens, Denver, CO, $26,000. Toward construction of greenhouse at Delaney Urban Farm. 2002.

486-5 Denver Zoological Foundation, Denver, CO, $400,000. Toward Phase One capital improvements. 2002.

486-6 Freedom Service Dogs, Lakewood, CO, $25,000. For Small Operating Grant. 2002.

486-7 Healthy Mountain Communities, Basalt, CO, $17,000. Toward development of Colorado Smart Growth Scorecard. 2002.

486-8 Outward Bound West, Golden, CO, $55,000. For Leadership Scholarship Program. 2002.

486-9 Rocky Mountain National Park Associates, Estes Park, CO, $72,000. To acquire and renovate building for Field Seminar Program. 2002.

486-10 Sand Creek Regional Greenway, Denver, CO, $250,000. 2002.

486-11 Tenth Mountain Division Trail Association, Aspen, CO, $410,000. Toward construction and endowment of Sangree Mitchell Froelicher hut. 2002.

486-12 Volunteers for Outdoor Colorado, Denver, CO, $15,000. Toward construction of Dos Chappell Nature Center. 2002.

486-13 William J. Palmer Parks Foundation, Colorado Springs, CO, $36,000. For acquisition of conservation easement on Johnston Ranch. 2002.

487
Gerrish Foundation
c/o A. Gerrish
1032 Timber Ln.
Boulder, CO 80304

Established in 2000.
Donor(s): Allan M. Gerrish.
Grantmaker type: Independent foundation
Financial data (yr. ended 05/31/02): Assets, $600,215 (M); expenditures, $414,184; qualifying distributions, $374,298; giving activities include $374,500 for 22 grants (high: $100,000; low: $3,000).
Fields of interest: Education; Environment; International relief; Christian agencies & churches.
Limitations: Applications not accepted. Giving on a national basis. No grants to individuals.
Application information: Contributes only to pre-selected organizations.
Directors: Allan M. Gerrish; Gail S. Gerrish.
EIN: 841564881

488
Golden Rule, Inc.
P.O. Box 270371
Louisville, CO 80027 (303) 222-3600
Contact: Jirka Rysavy, Dir.

Established in 1997 in CO as a private foundation.
Grantmaker type: Public charity
Financial data (yr. ended 12/31/01): Revenue, $6,178; assets, $258,675 (M); gifts received, $5,053; expenditures, $2,006,319; program services expenses, $1,995,578; giving activities include $1,894,000 for 1 grant.
Purpose and activities: The organization gathers, creates, and disseminates information relating to spiritual and environmental causes and issues.
Fields of interest: Environment; Religion.
Limitations: Giving primarily in CO.
Director: Jirka Rysavy.
EIN: 841009656

489
Goodwin Foundation
c/o Wells Fargo Bank West, N.A.
P.O. Box 4010
Grand Junction, CO 81502-4010
(970) 243-1611
Contact: Joseph Skinner, Tr. Off.

Established in 1951 in CO.
Donor(s): Harry B. Goodwin.‡
Grantmaker type: Independent foundation
Financial data (yr. ended 10/31/02): Assets, $1,668,663 (M); expenditures, $108,185; qualifying distributions, $100,792; giving activities include $95,150 for 14 grants (high: $30,000; low: $750).
Purpose and activities: Support for hospitals, medical sciences, health and social services, the arts, museums, music, community development, civic affairs, the environment, and general charitable giving.
Fields of interest: Museums; Music; Arts; Environment; Hospitals (general); Health care; Health organizations, association; Biomedicine; Medical research, institute; Human services; Community development; Government/public administration; General charitable giving.
Types of support: Continuing support; Annual campaigns; Capital campaigns; Building/renovation; Land acquisition; Scholarship funds.
Limitations: Giving primarily in Mesa County and Grand Junction, CO. No grants to individuals.
Publications: Annual report.
Application information: Application form not required.
Initial approach: Letter
Copies of proposal: 1
Deadline(s): None
Board meeting date(s): Feb., Apr., Aug., and Oct.
Officer and Trustees:* William M. Ela,* Chair.; Herbert L. Bacon; Ruth H. Gormley; Wells Fargo Bank West, N.A.
Number of staff: None.
EIN: 846036758

490
Green Fund
P.O. Box 1595
Boulder, CO 80306

Established in 1993 in CO.
Donor(s): Frances M. Green, Alice K. Green.
Grantmaker type: Independent foundation
Financial data (yr. ended 12/31/02): Assets, $2,708,398 (M); expenditures, $161,908; qualifying distributions, $161,695; giving activities include $152,318 for 30 grants (high: $30,000; low: $250).
Fields of interest: Higher education; Natural resources; Human services; Federated giving programs.
Limitations: Applications not accepted. Giving primarily in Boulder, CO, and MA. No grants to individuals.
Application information: Contributes only to pre-selected organizations.
Officers and Directors:* Frances M. Green,* Pres.; Ann C. Wylie,* V.P.; Kathryn A. Porter,* Secy.
EIN: 841155083

491
Hach Company Contributions Program
c/o Public Rels. and Community Affairs
M.S. 18, P.O. Box 389
Loveland, CO 80539-0389
Contact: Teri Asmussen
E mail: hr@hach.com

Grantmaker type: Corporate giving program
Purpose and activities: Hach makes charitable contributions to nonprofit organizations involved with arts and culture, education, the environment, health and human services, and science and technology. Special emphasis is directed towards programs designed to increase student skill and ability in chemistry, science, math, and technology and increase the number of females and minorities studying chemistry and other sciences. Support is given on an international basis.
Fields of interest: Arts; Elementary/secondary education; Education; Environment; Health care; Human services; Science.
Types of support: General/operating support; Donated products.
Limitations: Giving on an international basis, particularly in Larimer County, CO. No support for sectarian or denominational religious organizations or political organizations. No grants to individuals, or for fundraising events with which Hach employees are not significantly involved, conferences, seminars, or contests, or door or raffle prizes; no product donations for use in private residences.
Application information: Monetary contributions generally do not exceed $1,500; product donations generally do not exceed $3,000 in value. Support is limited to 1 contribution per organization during any given year. Unsolicited proposals for general operating support from organizations located outside Larimer County, CO, are not accepted. A contributions committee reviews all requests. Application form required.
Initial approach: Proposal and application form to headquarters
Copies of proposal: 2

Deadline(s): Arts and culture: Mar. 30, social assistance: June 30 and Dec. 31, recreation and entertainment: Sept. 30
Board meeting date(s): 3 weeks following deadlines
Final notification: 1 week following committee meetings

492
The Frederic C. Hamilton Family Foundation
1560 Broadway, Ste. 2200
Denver, CO 80202

Established in 1997 in CO.
Donor(s): Frederic C. Hamilton, Jane Hamilton.
Grantmaker type: Independent foundation
Financial data (yr. ended 12/31/02): Assets, $17,993,476 (M); gifts received, $6,123,078; expenditures, $3,640,266; qualifying distributions, $3,494,365; giving activities include $3,558,829 for 75 grants (high: $2,011,000; low: $100).
Purpose and activities: Giving primarily for education, youth services, and conservation.
Fields of interest: Museums; Elementary/secondary education; Higher education; Natural resources; Hospitals (general); Boy scouts.
Limitations: Applications not accepted. Giving on a national basis. No grants to individuals.
Application information: Contributes only to pre-selected organizations.
Trustees: Crawford M. Hamilton; Frederic C. Hamilton; Frederic C. Hamilton, Jr.; Jane M. Hamilton; Thomas M. Hamilton; Christy Hamilton McGraw.
EIN: 841440133

493
Hawley Family Foundation, Inc.
(formerly RHW Foundation, Inc.)
32065 Castle Ct., Ste. 100
Evergreen, CO 80439
Contact: MacDonald Hawley, Pres.

Established in 1994.
Grantmaker type: Independent foundation
Financial data (yr. ended 12/31/01): Assets, $7,652,960 (M); gifts received, $823,329; expenditures, $643,782; qualifying distributions, $310,000; giving activities include $310,000 for 19 grants (high: $45,000; low: $1,000).
Purpose and activities: Giving for the arts, education, animal welfare, and hospitals.
Fields of interest: Arts; Education; Natural resources; Animals/wildlife, preservation/protection; Zoos/zoological societies; Hospitals (general).
Limitations: Giving on a national basis. No grants to individuals.
Officers and Directors:* MacDonald Hawley,* Pres. and Treas.; James M. Hawley,* V.P. and Secy.
EIN: 841224613

494
Horizon Organic Holding Corporation Contributions Program
6311 Horizon Ln.
Longmont, CO 80503 (303) 530-2711
Application address: c/o Charitable Contribs. Comm., P.O. Box 17577, Boulder, CO 80308-7577; FAX: (303) 530-6934; E-mail: webmaster@horizonorganic.com; URL: http://www.horizonorganic.com/about/corporate/index.html

Grantmaker type: Corporate giving program
Purpose and activities: Horizon Organic makes charitable contributions to nonprofit organizations involved with environmental education and preservation, family farmers and rural issues, animal welfare, and organic research, education, and promotion.
Fields of interest: Natural resources; Environmental education; Animal welfare; Agriculture/food, public education; Agriculture; Rural development; General charitable giving.
Types of support: General/operating support; Donated products.
Limitations: Giving on a national and international basis.
Application information: Proposals should be no longer than 3 pages in length. Application form required.
Initial approach: Download application form and mail application form and proposal to application address or fax or E-mail application form and proposal to headquarters
Final notification: 6 weeks

495
Mabel Y. Hughes Charitable Trust
c/o Wells Fargo Bank West, N.A.
1740 Broadway, MC 7300, No. 483
Denver, CO 80274 (720) 947-6725
Contact: Judy Dowling

Trust established in 1969 in CO.
Donor(s): Mabel Y. Hughes.‡
Grantmaker type: Independent foundation
Financial data (yr. ended 08/31/02): Assets, $11,466,325 (M); expenditures, $731,866; qualifying distributions, $631,395; giving activities include $605,800 for 40 grants (high: $60,000; low: $3,800).
Purpose and activities: Support primarily for the arts, health care and education.
Fields of interest: Museums; Opera; Education; Botanical gardens; Hospitals (general); Health organizations, association; Human services; Children, services; Federated giving programs.
Types of support: General/operating support; Continuing support; Annual campaigns; Building/renovation; Equipment; Endowments; Emergency funds; Program development; Seed money; Research.
Limitations: Giving limited to CO, with emphasis on the Denver area. No grants to individuals, or for deficit financing, scholarships, or fellowships; no loans.
Publications: Informational brochure (including application guidelines).
Application information: Application form not required.
Initial approach: Letter
Copies of proposal: 1

Deadline(s): None
Board meeting date(s): Dec.
Trustees: W. Robert Alexander; Wells Fargo Bank West, N.A.
Number of staff: None.
EIN: 846070398

496
Hunter-White Foundation
1520 S. University Blvd.
Denver, CO 80210

Established in 1998 in CO.
Donor(s): Catherine P. Cole.
Grantmaker type: Independent foundation
Financial data (yr. ended 12/31/02): Assets, $3,384,169 (M); gifts received, $45,000; expenditures, $227,777; qualifying distributions, $206,585; giving activities include $207,000 for 9 grants (high: $50,000; low: $5,000).
Purpose and activities: Giving primarily for human services, employment programs, and the environment.
Fields of interest: Natural resources; Employment; Human services.
Limitations: Applications not accepted. Giving primarily in CO. No grants to individuals.
Application information: Contributes only to pre-selected organizations.
Directors: Amy C. Berkley; Linda C. Call; Catherine P. Cole; Lisa A. Cole.
EIN: 841443958

497
Fred & Elli Iselin Foundation
P.O. Box 1145
Aspen, CO 81612 (970) 925-4290
Contact: James K. Daggs, Pres.
Application address: 715 W. Main St., Ste. 201, Aspen, CO 81611; FAX: (970) 920-4801; E-mail: daggs@rof.net

Established in 1989 in CO.
Donor(s): Elli Iselin.
Grantmaker type: Independent foundation
Financial data (yr. ended 12/31/00): Assets, $4,053,959 (M); expenditures, $326,430; qualifying distributions, $211,850; giving activities include $201,000 for 37 grants (high: $25,000; low: $500).
Purpose and activities: Giving for animal welfare groups, family and human services, and for medical research.
Fields of interest: Historic preservation/historical societies; Education; Natural resources; Animal welfare; Medical research, institute; Children/youth, services; Family services.
Limitations: Giving primarily in Aspen, CO. No grants to individuals.
Application information:
Initial approach: Letter
Deadline(s): Oct. 31
Officers: James K. Daggs, Pres.; Richard A. Knezivich, Secy.
Directors: Gae Daggs; Kristen Henry.
EIN: 742521631

498
Island Foundation
P.O. Box 5238
Englewood, CO 80155
Contact: Sally A. Ranney, V.P.

Established in 1976 in CO.
Donor(s): Ashley K. Carrithers, Catherine M. Carrithers, R. Selnick.
Grantmaker type: Independent foundation
Financial data (yr. ended 12/31/02): Assets, $938,515 (M); expenditures, $239,535; qualifying distributions, $201,774; giving activities include $160,260 for 16 grants (high: $43,500; low: $750).
Purpose and activities: Giving primarily to conservation and environmental organizations and advancement in the understanding of human consciousness.
Fields of interest: History/archaeology; Natural resources; Environmental education; Environment; Religion.
International interests: Canada; Africa; South America.
Types of support: General/operating support; Land acquisition; Seed money; Program-related investments/loans.
Limitations: Applications not accepted. Giving primarily in the Rocky Mountain region, with emphasis on western CO. No grants to individuals.
Publications: Annual report.
Application information: Contributes only to pre-selected organizations.
Officers: Ashley K. Carrithers, Pres.; Sally A. Ranney, V.P.; Walter Sedgewick, Secy.-Treas.
Number of staff: 1 part-time professional.
EIN: 840715001

499
The Janus Foundation ▼
100 Fillmore St., Ste. 300
Denver, CO 80206-4923 (720) 210-1265
Contact: Karen C. Cortese, V.P.; and Kelli Martin, Fdn. Coord.
FAX: (303) 394-7797

Established in 1994 in CO.
Donor(s): Janus Capital Corp., Janus Capital Management LLC.
Grantmaker type: Company-sponsored foundation
Financial data (yr. ended 12/31/01): Assets, $2,381,212 (M); gifts received, $5,678,769; expenditures, $5,562,370; qualifying distributions, $5,548,441; giving activities include $5,501,004 for 193 grants (high: $2,200,000; low: $496; average: $1,500–$25,000).
Purpose and activities: Giving primarily for at-risk youth through education, community service and volunteerism, and cultural institutions in the Denver, Colorado, metropolitan area.
Fields of interest: Arts; Secondary school/education; Youth development, services; Community development, service clubs; Philanthropy/voluntarism.
Types of support: Continuing support; Program development; Curriculum development; Scholarship funds.

Limitations: Giving on a national basis; support for cultural institutions in the Denver, CO, metropolitan area only.
Publications: Application guidelines.
Application information: The application form is available on the foundation's Web site. Application form required.
> *Initial approach:* Application and supporting documentation
> *Copies of proposal:* 1
> *Deadline(s):* None
> *Board meeting date(s):* 1st week of each month
> *Final notification:* Within 90 days of receipt of complete proposal
Officers and Directors:* Robin C. Beery,* Pres.; Thomas A. Early,* V.P. and Secy.; Karen C. Cortese,* V.P. and Treas.
Number of staff: 2 part-time professional.
EIN: 841271105
Recent environmental and animal welfare grants:
499-1 Denver Zoological Foundation, Denver, CO, $2,200,000. For renovations. 2001.

500
Johns Manville Fund, Inc.
(formerly Schuller Fund, Inc.)
P.O. Box 17086
Denver, CO 80217
Application Address: P.O. Box 5108, Denver, CO 80217-5108

Incorporated in 1952 in DE.
Donor(s): Schuller Corp., Johns Manville Corp.
Grantmaker type: Company-sponsored foundation
Financial data (yr. ended 12/31/02): Assets, $398,579 (M); expenditures, $171,672; qualifying distributions, $163,412; giving activities include $133,222 for 38 grants (high: $31,100; low: $500), $13,000 for 16 grants to individuals (high: $2,500; low: $250) and $17,190 for 106 employee matching gifts.
Purpose and activities: Giving primarily to those nonprofit organizations for which employees volunteer; support also for higher education and employee matching gifts to community drives, colleges and universities. Also administers a scholarship program for children of employees.
Fields of interest: Humanities; Arts; Vocational education; Higher education; Education; Environment; Health care; Health organizations, association; Housing/shelter, development; Homeless, human services; Community development; Economically disadvantaged; Homeless.
Types of support: General/operating support; Program development; Employee matching gifts; Employee-related scholarships.
Limitations: Giving primarily in areas of company operations. No support for religious, fraternal, or veterans' organizations, or groups that attempt to influence legislation.
Publications: Informational brochure (including application guidelines).
Application information: Application form required.
> *Initial approach:* Request copy of guidelines
> *Copies of proposal:* 1
> *Deadline(s):* None
> *Board meeting date(s):* Jan., Apr., Aug., and Oct.

Officers and Trustees:* M.K. Rhinehart,* Pres.; J.J. Gebert, V.P. and Treas.; R. Arant,* V.P.; D.A. Forte,* V.P.; M. Mitchell,* V.P.; W.G. Spink, Secy.
Number of staff: 1 part-time professional; 1 part-time support.
EIN: 136034039

501
Joy Family Foundation
P.O. Box 23
Aspen, CO 81612

Established in 1996 in CO.
Donor(s): Sara R. Joy, William N. Joy.
Grantmaker type: Independent foundation
Financial data (yr. ended 12/31/01): Assets, $12,414,398 (M); expenditures, $984,522; qualifying distributions, $834,540; giving activities include $834,540 for 68 grants (high: $200,000; low: $112).
Purpose and activities: Giving to art programs.
Fields of interest: Theater; Music; Higher education; Natural resources; Environment, land resources; Health organizations, association; Federated giving programs.
Limitations: Applications not accepted. Giving primarily in CO; some funding nationally. No grants to individuals.
Application information: Contributes only to pre-selected organizations.
Officers: William N. Joy, Pres.; Sara R. Joy, V.P.
Director: Ken Ransford.
EIN: 841361004

502
The KBK Foundation
(formerly The Kavadas Foundation)
c/o Judson W. Detrick
1700 Lincoln St., Ste. 4100
Denver, CO 80203-4541 (303) 861-7000

Established in 1991 in CO.
Donor(s): Kathryn B. Kavadas.
Grantmaker type: Independent foundation
Financial data (yr. ended 12/31/02): Assets, $1,105,522 (M); gifts received, $1,129; expenditures, $447,406; qualifying distributions, $429,864; giving activities include $439,000 for 22 grants (high: $100,000; low: $3,000; average: $3,000–$100,000).
Purpose and activities: Giving primarily for arts and culture, the environment, education, health care, and human services.
Fields of interest: Television; Museums; Elementary/secondary education; Higher education; Environment; Family planning; American Red Cross; Senior continuing care; Aging.
Types of support: General/operating support; Continuing support; Matching/challenge support.
Limitations: Applications not accepted. Giving primarily in the greater Boston, MA, area. No grants to individuals.
Application information: Contributes only to pre-selected organizations.
Officer and Trustees:* Kathryn B. Kavadas,* Mgr.; Judson W. Detrick; Lynn P. Hendrix; Thomas A. Richardson.
Number of staff: None.
EIN: 841186316

503
Ruth Morris Keesling Family Foundation
3801 E. Florida Ave., Ste. 100
Denver, CO 80210

Established in 1991 in CO.
Donor(s): Ruth M. Keesling, Thomas M.
Keesling.
Grantmaker type: Independent foundation
Financial data (yr. ended 12/31/01): Assets,
$737,310 (M); expenditures, $403,964;
qualifying distributions, $400,334; giving
activities include $400,449 for 13 grants (high:
$324,641; low: $30).
Fields of interest: Higher education; Animal
welfare; Animals/wildlife,
preservation/protection; Animals/wildlife,
endangered species; Zoos/zoological societies.
Limitations: Giving primarily in CO.
Application information:
  Initial approach: Letter
  Deadline(s): None
Officers: Ruth M. Keesling, Pres.; Thomas M.
Keesling, Secy.-Treas.
Directors: Frank M. Keesling; Thomas M.
Keesling, Jr.
EIN: 841163808

504
Jay P. K. Kenney Private Foundation
181 Franklin St.
Denver, CO 80218

Established in 1993 in CO.
Donor(s): Jay P.K. Kenney.
Grantmaker type: Independent foundation
Financial data (yr. ended 12/31/01): Assets,
$222,198 (M); expenditures, $189,375;
qualifying distributions, $184,872; giving
activities include $185,148 for 29 grants (high:
$60,000; low: $300).
Purpose and activities: Giving for education, the
environment, legal services, and recreation.
Fields of interest: Multipurpose
centers/programs; Elementary/secondary
education; Environment; Animals/wildlife,
preservation/protection.
Limitations: Applications not accepted. Giving
primarily in CO. No grants to individuals.
Application information: Contributes only to
pre-selected organizations.
Officers: Jay P.K. Kenney, Pres.; Thomas J.
Barrett, Jr., Secy.
EIN: 841249377

505
Kern Family Foundation
31 Albion Pl.
Castle Rock, CO 80104

Established in 1999 in CO.
Donor(s): Jerome Kern, Mary Kern.
Grantmaker type: Independent foundation
Financial data (yr. ended 12/31/02): Assets,
$5,059,545 (M); expenditures, $212,076;
qualifying distributions, $204,963; giving
activities include $206,200 for 18 grants (high:
$50,000; low: $1,000).
Fields of interest: Orchestra (symphony);
University; Environment; Mental health/crisis
services; Human services; Children, services;
Christian agencies & churches.

Limitations: Giving primarily in Denver, CO.
Officer: Jerome Kern, Pres.
EIN: 841522247

506
Koelbel Family Foundation
5291 Yale Cir.
Denver, CO 80222

Established in 1996 in CO.
Donor(s): Walter A. Koelbel.
Grantmaker type: Independent foundation
Financial data (yr. ended 12/31/00): Assets,
$2,554,058 (M); gifts received, $236,145;
expenditures, $239,701; qualifying distributions,
$203,900; giving activities include $208,900 for
49 grants (high: $100,000; low: $1,000).
Purpose and activities: Giving for education,
arts and culture, federated giving programs, and
to sports related activities and foundations.
Fields of interest: Arts; Libraries (public);
Education; Natural resources; Health
organizations, association; Athletics/sports,
winter sports; Human services; Federated giving
programs.
Limitations: Giving primarily in Denver, CO.
Officers: Walter A. Koelbel, Pres.; Gene N.
Koelbel, V.P.; Vanda N. Werner, V.P.; Thomas E.
Whyte, Secy.-Treas.
EIN: 841369773

507
The Leighty Foundation
P.O. Box 37
Cascade, CO 80809
Contact: Jane Leighty Justis, Exec. Dir.

Established in 1985.
Donor(s): H.D. Leighty, William C. Leighty.
Grantmaker type: Independent foundation
Financial data (yr. ended 08/31/02): Assets,
$5,822,829 (M); gifts received, $125,000;
expenditures, $333,212; qualifying distributions,
$206,950; giving activities include $206,950 for
117 grants (high: $7,500; low: $100).
Purpose and activities: Support for
organizations which seek to deal with today's
problems and opportunities in ways that meet
current needs without compromising the ability
of future generations to meet their needs. The
foundation concentrates its efforts in areas of
special concern to its board members. Priorities
include: peacemakers, science and the
environment, issues of poverty, spirituality,
education, human rights, population,
community service and voluntarism, and
women's issues.
Fields of interest: Education; Environment;
Health care; International peace/security;
Voluntarism promotion;
Philanthropy/voluntarism; Science; Population
studies; Religion; Women.
Types of support: General/operating support;
Annual campaigns; Building/renovation;
Equipment; Endowments; Program
development; Conferences/seminars;
Publication; Curriculum development;
Fellowships; Internship funds; Scholarship
funds; Research; Technical assistance;
Consulting services; Matching/challenge support.
Limitations: Giving primarily in AK, CO, and IA.
No grants to individuals.

Publications: Annual report, Informational
brochure (including application guidelines).
Application information: Application form
required.
  Initial approach: Letter of inquiry
  Copies of proposal: 1
  Board meeting date(s): Feb., May, and Nov.
Officers and Directors:* H.D. Leighty,* Pres.;
Nancy J. Waterman, Secy.; Jane Leighty Justis,*
Exec. Dir.; Robert F. Justis; William Clyde Leighty.
Number of staff: 1 full-time professional; 1
part-time support.
EIN: 421264476

508
Ludlow-Griffith Foundation
P.O. Box 18248
Denver, CO 80218
Contact: William G. Griffith, Treas.

Established in 1990.
Donor(s): William G. Griffith, Frances L. Griffith.
Grantmaker type: Independent foundation
Financial data (yr. ended 12/31/02): Assets,
$157,059 (M); expenditures, $4,217,997;
qualifying distributions, $4,210,723; giving
activities include $4,208,572 for 12 grants
(high: $4,149,041; low: $100).
Purpose and activities: Giving primarily for the
arts, child welfare and health.
Fields of interest: Television; Arts; Higher
education; Environment; Health organizations,
association; Children/youth, services; Christian
agencies & churches.
Limitations: Giving primarily in Denver, CO. No
grants to individuals.
Application information:
  Initial approach: Letter
  Deadline(s): May 15 and Nov. 15
Officers: William L. Schmidt, Pres.; Jeff Reder,
V.P.; Tschudy G. Schmidt, Secy.; William G.
Griffith, Treas.
EIN: 841157778

509
Jack and Marilyn MacAllister Foundation
69 Indigo Way
Castle Rock, CO 80104

Established in 1991 in CO.
Donor(s): Jack A. MacAllister, Marilyn
MacAllister.
Grantmaker type: Operating foundation
Financial data (yr. ended 12/31/02): Assets,
$1,787,287 (M); expenditures, $166,126;
qualifying distributions, $149,538; giving
activities include $150,000 for 8 grants (high:
$50,000; low: $1,000).
Purpose and activities: Giving primarily for the
arts and higher education.
Fields of interest: Higher education;
Environment; land resources.
Types of support: Scholarship funds.
Limitations: Applications not accepted. Giving
primarily in CO. No grants to individuals.
Application information: Contributes only to
pre-selected organizations.
Officers: Marilyn MacAllister, Pres.; Jack A.
MacAllister, V.P. and Secy.
EIN: 742619186

510
The Peter Lloyd MacDonald Foundation
128 Gilpin St.
Denver, CO 80218

Established in 1998 in CO.
Donor(s): Peter Lloyd MacDonald.
Grantmaker type: Independent foundation
Financial data (yr. ended 06/30/03): Assets,
$120,222 (M); expenditures, $109,459;
qualifying distributions, $108,858; giving
activities include $108,274 for 11 grants (high:
$99,024; low: $250).
Purpose and activities: Giving primarily for
education.
Fields of interest: Arts; Education; Environment;
Federated giving programs.
Types of support: General/operating support.
Limitations: Applications not accepted. Giving
primarily in CO, MA, and NH. No grants to
individuals.
Application information: Contributes only to
pre-selected organizations.
Officers: Peter Lloyd MacDonald, Pres.;
Dorothy K. Shattuck, V.P.; Vanessa N.
MacDonald, Secy.
EIN: 841496257

511
Edward Madigan Foundation
c/o Wells Fargo Bank West, N.A.
1740 Broadway, MAC C7300-484
Denver, CO 80274
Application address: Robert A. Lorentz, Trust
Off., c/o Wells Fargo Bank West, N.A., P.O. Box
5825, Denver, CO 80217

Established in 1983 in CO.
Grantmaker type: Independent foundation
Financial data (yr. ended 12/31/02): Assets,
$1,534,408 (M); expenditures, $158,924;
qualifying distributions, $141,057; giving
activities include $135,000 for 18 grants (high:
$25,000; low: $2,000).
Purpose and activities: Giving for higher
education, health and medical services, and for
youth services.
Fields of interest: Museums (specialized);
Secondary school/education; Higher education;
Education; Animals/wildlife; Hospitals (general);
Youth development; Children/youth, services;
Jewish agencies & temples.
Limitations: Giving primarily in Denver, CO. No
grants to individuals.
Application information:
   Initial approach: Letter
   Deadline(s): None
Trustee: Wells Fargo Bank West, N.A.
EIN: 846163256

512
Bob & Sharon Magness Foundation
4725 S. Holly St.
Englewood, CO 80111

Established in 1997.
Donor(s): Sharon Magness.
Grantmaker type: Independent foundation
Financial data (yr. ended 12/31/01): Assets,
$1,108,968 (M); expenditures, $559,312;
qualifying distributions, $555,658; giving
activities include $370,848 for 17 grants (high:

$105,500; low: $1,500; average:
$4,000–$26,000).
Fields of interest: Education; Aquariums;
Hospitals (general); Human services; Christian
agencies & churches; Jewish agencies & temples.
Limitations: Applications not accepted. Giving
primarily in Denver, CO. No grants to
individuals.
Application information: Contributes only to
pre-selected organizations.
Director: Sharon Magness.
EIN: 841402828

513
Maki Foundation
421D Aspen Airport Business Ctr.
Aspen, CO 81611-3551 (970) 925-3272
Contact: Patricia A. Humphry

Established in 1981 in CO.
Grantmaker type: Independent foundation
Financial data (yr. ended 12/31/02): Assets,
$4,239,747 (M); gifts received, $2,815;
expenditures, $195,683; qualifying distributions,
$190,773; giving activities include $150,500 for
43 grants (high: $5,000; low: $1,000).
Purpose and activities: Giving primarily for
wilderness and wildlands protection, river and
wetlands conservation, biological diversity
conservation, and public lands management.
Fields of interest: Natural resources;
Environment.
Types of support: General/operating support;
Program development.
Limitations: Giving limited to CO, ID, MT, NM,
UT, and WY. No support for recycling programs,
tree planting projects, toxic waste cleanup, or
wildlife rehabilitation centers. No grants for
acquisition or construction of community
recreation facilities, buildings, municipal parks,
or reservoirs; no grants for film production or
fellowships.
Publications: Application guidelines.
Application information: 2 copies of full
proposal no more than 5 pages; 5 copies of 1
page summary. Application form required.
   Initial approach: Letter or telephone
   Copies of proposal: 2
   Deadline(s): May 1
   Board meeting date(s): July
   Final notification: Sept. 1
Directors: Ruth Adams; Ann Harvey; Constance
Harvey; Mark Harvey.
Number of staff: 1 full-time professional.
EIN: 840836242

514
Manitou Foundation, Inc.
P.O. Box 118
Crestone, CO 81131
Contact: Lisa A. Cyriacks, Admin. Dir.
FAX: (719) 256-4266; *E-mail:*
Spirit@manitou.org; *URL:* http://
www.manitou.org/MF/mf_index.html

Established in 1988 in CO.
Donor(s): Maurice F. Strong, Laurance
Rockefeller.
Grantmaker type: Independent foundation
Financial data (yr. ended 12/31/00): Assets,
$687,146 (M); gifts received, $24,012;
expenditures, $253,989; qualifying distributions,

$217,637; giving activities include $174,125 for
grants.
Purpose and activities: Granting of land in
Crestone, CO. Occasional funding support for
local projects.
Fields of interest: Arts; Education; Natural
resources; Environment; Agriculture;
International peace/security; Community
development; Religion; Native
Americans/American Indians.
Types of support: General/operating support;
Equipment; Seed money; In-kind gifts.
Limitations: Applications not accepted. Giving
primarily in Crestone and San Luis Valley, CO.
No grants to individuals.
Publications: Biennial report, Informational
brochure, Program policy statement.
Application information: Contributes only to
pre-selected organizations.
Officers and Directors:* Hanne M. Strong,*
Pres.; Maurice F. Strong, V.P.; Lisa A. Cyriaks,
Admin. Dir.; Helen Davey; Dena Merriam; John
Milton.
Number of staff: 4 part-time professional.
EIN: 841102055

515
McGrath Investment Foundation
P.O. Box 2336
Englewood, CO 80150-2336
Contact: Ann Pena, Pres.
Application address: 3840 S. Jason St.,
Englewood, CO 80111, tel.: (303) 377-8900

Established in 1995 in CO.
Grantmaker type: Independent foundation
Financial data (yr. ended 12/31/01): Assets,
$2,960,111 (M); expenditures, $175,130;
qualifying distributions, $168,292; giving
activities include $169,033 for 22 grants (high:
$14,166; low: $600).
Fields of interest: Natural resources; Human
services; Roman Catholic agencies & churches.
Application information:
   Initial approach: Letter
   Deadline(s): None
Officer: Ann Pena, Pres.
Directors: Barbara L. McGrath; Bruce K.
McGrath; Tracey McGrath.
EIN: 841307861

516
Thomas M. McKee Charitable Trust
935 N. Cleveland Ave.
Loveland, CO 80537
Contact: Lynn A. Hammond, Tr.
Application address: 200 E. 7th St., Ste. 418,
Loveland, CO 80537, tel.: (970) 667-1023

Established in 1987 in CO.
Grantmaker type: Independent foundation
Financial data (yr. ended 12/31/02): Assets,
$3,646,112 (M); expenditures, $291,481;
qualifying distributions, $281,158; giving
activities include $273,857 for 9 grants (high:
$125,000; low: $500).
Fields of interest: Higher education; Education;
Animals/wildlife, special services; Health care;
Housing/shelter; Human services.
Limitations: Giving limited to Fort Collins,
Loveland, and Colorado Springs, CO.

Application information: Application form required.
Initial approach: Letter
Deadline(s): None
Trustees: Lynn A. Hammond; Home State Bank.
EIN: 846228546

517
McStain Enterprises, Inc. Corporate Giving Program
c/o Grant Comm.
75 Manhattan Dr.
Boulder, CO   80303   (303) 494-5900
Contact: Catherine Uzzalino, Chair., Grant Comm.
E-mail: ceu@mcstain.com; *URL:* http://www.mcstain.com/ecology/grants.htm

Grantmaker type: Corporate giving program
Financial data (yr. ended 12/31/00): Total giving, $40,000; giving activities include $35,000 for grants and $5,000 for 50 employee matching gifts.
Purpose and activities: McStain makes charitable contributions to nonprofit organizations involved with recycling, environmental conservation, open spaces, environmental education, and transportation. Support is given primarily in Adams, Boulder, Broomfield, Denver, and Larimer counties, Colorado.
Fields of interest: Recycling; Natural resources; Environment, beautification programs; Environmental education; Transportation.
Types of support: General/operating support; Building/renovation; Research; Employee volunteer services; Employee matching gifts.
Limitations: Giving primarily in Adams, Boulder, Broomfield, Denver, and Larimer counties, CO. No support for religious or fraternal organizations or political, labor, or lobbying organizations or political candidates. No grants for fundraising or advertising or telephone solicitation.
Publications: Corporate giving report (including application guidelines), Grants list, Newsletter.
Application information: Proposals should be no longer than 2 double-spaced pages in length. A contributions committee reviews all requests. Application form not required.
Initial approach: Proposal to headquarters
Copies of proposal: 1
Deadline(s): June 9
Board meeting date(s): Monthly
Final notification: Sept. 19
Number of staff: 1 full-time support.

518
The Merlin Foundation
545 Pearl St.
Boulder, CO   80302

Established in 1993 in CO.
Donor(s): A.G. Barron, Thomas A. Barron, F. Cabot, Mosaic Foundation.
Grantmaker type: Independent foundation
Financial data (yr. ended 11/30/02): Assets, $150,156 (M); gifts received, $267,000; expenditures, $356,140; qualifying distributions, $350,500; giving activities include $350,500 for 28 grants (high: $115,500; low: $500).
Purpose and activities: Giving primarily for land and wilderness resources.
Fields of interest: Natural resources; Environment, land resources; Environment, forests.
Limitations: Applications not accepted. No grants to individuals.
Application information: Contributes only to pre-selected organizations.
Officer: Thomas A. Barron, Pres.
Directors: Currie C. Barron; Leslie Collis Ward.
EIN: 841232001

519
Morris Animal Foundation
45 Inverness Dr. E.
Englewood, CO   80112-5480   (303) 790-2345
Contact: Robert Hilsenroth, D.V.M.
Additional tel.: (800) 243-2345; *FAX:* (303) 790-4066; *URL:* http://www.morrisanimalfoundation.org

Established in 1948.
Grantmaker type: Public charity
Financial data (yr. ended 04/30/02): Revenue, $4,369,457; assets, $57,757,740 (M); gifts received, $5,409,275; expenditures, $5,845,996; program services expenses, $4,220,026; giving activities include $3,656,278 for grants.
Purpose and activities: The foundation seeks to improve the health and well-being of companion animals and wildlife by funding humane health studies and disseminating information about these studies.
Fields of interest: Animals/wildlife.
Types of support: Research.
Publications: Annual report, Informational brochure, Newsletter (including application guidelines).
Application information: See Web site for application guidelines.
Initial approach: Pre-proposal for Research Grants
Copies of proposal: 15
Deadline(s): Nov. 1 for pre-proposals and Apr. 1 for complete proposals for Research Grants
Board meeting date(s): June
Final notification: Aug.
Officers and Trustees:* Roger Bohart,* Chair.; Cheryl Wagner,* Pres.; Allan Dewald,* V.P., Llama/Alpaca; Lester E. Fisher, D.V.M.,* V.P., Wildlife; Kathy Layton,* V.P., Equine; Jack Mara, D.V.M.,* V.P., Veterinary; Dayle P. Marsh,* V.P., Feline; Mark L. Morris, Jr., D.V.M., Ph.D.,* V.P., Scientific Activities; Harriet Vincent,* V.P., Canine; Robert Hilsenroth, D.V.M.,* Secy. and Exec. Dir.; James Meyer,* Treas.; and 11 additional trustees.
EIN: 846032307

520
Trygve E. & Victoria H. Myhren Foundation
355 Clayton St.
Denver, CO   80206

Established in 1996 in CO.
Donor(s): Trygve E. Myhren, Victoria H. Myhren.
Grantmaker type: Independent foundation

Financial data (yr. ended 12/31/02): Assets, $370,573 (M); expenditures, $205,137; qualifying distributions, $201,993; giving activities include $202,542 for 46 grants (high: $66,667; low: $250).
Purpose and activities: Giving for education, Jewish organizations, and youth programs.
Fields of interest: Education; Environment; Health care; Children/youth, services; Jewish agencies & temples.
Types of support: General/operating support; Annual campaigns; Endowments; Program development; Matching/challenge support.
Limitations: Applications not accepted. Giving primarily in CO. No grants to individuals.
Application information: Contributes only to pre-selected organizations.
Directors: Trygve E. Myhren; Victoria E. Myhren.
EIN: 311500841

521
The Aksel Nielsen Foundation
13115 N. Melody Ln.
Parker, CO   80138-8631   (303) 841-3581
Contact: Virginia N. Muse, Pres.

Established in 1956 in CO.
Grantmaker type: Independent foundation
Financial data (yr. ended 12/31/01): Assets, $3,127,575 (M); expenditures, $181,562; qualifying distributions, $166,232; giving activities include $155,800 for 28 grants (high: $30,000; low: $100).
Fields of interest: Television; Museums; Orchestra (symphony); Animal welfare; Family services; Community development; Disabled.
Types of support: General/operating support; Program development.
Limitations: Giving primarily in CO. No grants to individuals; no loans or program-related investments.
Application information: Application form not required.
Initial approach: Letter
Copies of proposal: 1
Deadline(s): None
Board meeting date(s): July and Dec.
Officers: Virginia N. Muse, Pres.; Judith M. Pemstein, V.P.; Jack M. Muse, Secy.-Treas.
Number of staff: None.
EIN: 846025711

522
Oak Lodge Foundation
c/o William O. Hunt, Jr.
P.O. Box 7951
Aspen, CO   81612

Established in 1998.
Donor(s): William O. & Jeannette P. Hunt Foundation.
Grantmaker type: Independent foundation
Financial data (yr. ended 12/31/02): Assets, $2,722,392 (M); gifts received, $22,992; expenditures, $145,049; qualifying distributions, $132,616; giving activities include $132,616 for 30 grants (high: $15,000; low: $500).
Fields of interest: Natural resources; Animals/wildlife, preservation/protection.
Limitations: Applications not accepted. Giving on a national basis. No grants to individuals.

Application information: Contributes only to pre-selected organizations.
Officers: William O. Hunt, Jr., Pres. and Treas.; Ian C. Hunt, Secy.
EIN: 311604793

523
RLC Foundation
P.O. Box 5910
Avon, CO 81620

Established in 1980 in CO.
Donor(s): Robert L. Cohen.
Grantmaker type: Independent foundation
Financial data (yr. ended 11/30/02): Assets, $909,621 (M); gifts received, $50,000; expenditures, $119,571; qualifying distributions, $107,382; giving activities include $107,500 for 5 grants (high: $50,000; low: $2,500).
Fields of interest: Museums (art); Higher education; Environment, land resources; Community development; Federated giving programs.
Types of support: General/operating support; Research.
Limitations: Applications not accepted. Giving primarily in CO. No grants to individuals.
Application information: Contributes only to pre-selected organizations.
Officers: Devra Ochs, Pres.; Stanley D. Cohen, V.P. and Secy.; Frank R. Cohen, Treas.
EIN: 742139793

524
Sterne-Elder Memorial Trust
c/o Wells Fargo Bank West, N.A.
1740 Broadway, MAC C7300-483
Denver, CO 80274
Contact: Michael J. Love, V.P., Wells Fargo Bank West, N.A.

Established in 1977 in CO.
Donor(s): Charles S. Sterne.‡
Grantmaker type: Independent foundation
Financial data (yr. ended 03/31/02): Assets, $5,683,433 (M); expenditures, $398,394; qualifying distributions, $367,231; giving activities include $357,000 for 30 grants (high: $125,000; low: $2,000).
Purpose and activities: Giving primarily for health and human service organizations in Denver, CO.
Fields of interest: Performing arts; Arts; Animal welfare; Hospitals (general); Health organizations, association; Human services; Children/youth, services; Federated giving programs.
Types of support: General/operating support; Continuing support; Annual campaigns; Capital campaigns; Endowments; Matching/challenge support.
Limitations: Applications not accepted. Giving primarily in Denver, CO. No grants to individuals.
Application information: Contributes only to pre-selected organizations.
Director: Dorothy Elder Sterne.
Trustee: Wells Fargo Bank West, N.A.
Number of staff: 1 part-time professional.
EIN: 846143172

525
The Summit Foundation
P.O. Box 4000
Breckenridge, CO 80424 (970) 453-5970
Contact: Debra A.D. Edwards, Exec. Dir.
Additional address: 108 N. French St., Breckenridge, CO 80424; FAX: (970) 453-1423; E-mail: sumfound@colorado.net; URL: http://www.summitfoundation.org

Established in 1984 in CO.
Grantmaker type: Community foundation
Financial data (yr. ended 12/31/02): Assets, $2,716,418 (M); gifts received, $1,400,996; expenditures, $1,136,508; giving activities include $766,727 for 110 grants (high: $3,600; low: $832; average: $28,650–$1,770) and $1,500 for in-kind gifts.
Purpose and activities: Giving primarily for arts and culture, health and human services, education, environment, sports, scholarships, and all projects with measurable results. The foundation administers donor-advised funds.
Fields of interest: Film/video; Visual arts; Museums; Performing arts; Theater; Music; Historic preservation/historical societies; Arts; Early childhood education; Elementary school/education; Education; Natural resources; Environment; Health care; Mental health/crisis services; Health organizations, association; Recreation; Children/youth, services; Family services; Hospices; Aging, centers/services; Disabled.
Types of support: Continuing support; Annual campaigns; Capital campaigns; Building/renovation; Equipment; Land acquisition; Program development; Conferences/seminars; Seed money; Curriculum development; Scholarship funds; Technical assistance; Program evaluation; Exchange programs; Matching/challenge support.
Limitations: Giving limited to Summit County, and the communities of Alma, Buena Vista, Fairplay, Kremmling, and Leadville, CO. No support for religious organizations or political campaigns. No grants to individuals (except for designated scholarship program), or for operating budgets.
Publications: Application guidelines, Annual report, Grants list, Informational brochure, Newsletter, Program policy statement.
Application information: Applications accepted during designated time periods only. See guidelines for number of copies of proposal necessary and other specific information. Application form required.
  Initial approach: Request guidelines after announcement of funding deadline
  Deadline(s): Mar. 19 and Aug. 20
  Board meeting date(s): 3rd Wednesday of each month
  Final notification: Within 3 to 4 months
Officers and Directors:* Marilyn Hogan,* Pres.; Nancy Follett,* V.P.; Theresa Campbell,* Secy.; Greg Finch, Treas.; Brett Barrett; David Barry; Larry Beebe; Bob Craig; Maggie Hillman; Peter Janes; Cleve Keller; John Krakauer; Meg Lass; Gary Lindstrom; Win Lockwood; Roger McCarthy; Anne Stonington; Carre Warner; Jack Wolfe.
Number of staff: 3 full-time professional; 1 full-time support.
EIN: 742341399

526
The Ruth and Vernon Taylor Foundation
518 17th St., Ste. 1670
Denver, CO 80202 (303) 893-5284
Contact: Miss Friday A. Green, Tr.

Trust established in 1950 in TX.
Donor(s): Members of the Taylor family.
Grantmaker type: Independent foundation
Financial data (yr. ended 06/30/02): Assets, $25,638,594 (M); expenditures, $1,364,073; qualifying distributions, $1,319,278; giving activities include $1,263,263 for 181 grants (high: $80,000; low: $500; average: $1,000–$20,000).
Purpose and activities: Support for education, the arts, health, human services, and conservation.
Fields of interest: Arts; Secondary school/education; Higher education; Natural resources; Environment; Hospitals (general); Medical research, institute; Human services; Youth, services.
Types of support: General/operating support; Building/renovation; Endowments; Research.
Limitations: Applications not accepted. Giving primarily in CO, IL, MT, TX, WY, and the Mid-Atlantic states. No grants to individuals.
Application information:
  Board meeting date(s): May
Trustees: Ruth Taylor Campbell; Friday A. Green; Sara Taylor Swift; James C. Taylor; Vernon F. Taylor, Jr.
Number of staff: 1 full-time professional.
EIN: 846021788

527
The Telluride Foundation
620 Mountain Village Blvd., Ste. 2B
Telluride, CO 81435 (970) 728-8717
Contact: Wynn Harris, Grants Mgr.
URL: http://www.telluridefoundation.org/

Established in 2000 in CO.
Grantmaker type: Community foundation
Financial data (yr. ended 12/31/01): Assets, $2,973,443 (M); gifts received, $2,560,110; expenditures, $1,077,065; giving activities include $691,838 for 75 grants (high: $90,000; low: $250).
Purpose and activities: The foundation is committed to preserving and enriching the quality of life of the residents, visitors and workforce of the Telluride region. It provides year-round support for local organizations involved in arts, education, athletics, charitable causes, land conservation and other community-based efforts through technical assistance, education and grantmaking.
Fields of interest: Arts; Education; Environment; Recreation; Human services; Children/youth, services; Community development.
Types of support: General/operating support; Annual campaigns; Equipment; Seed money; Technical assistance; Matching/challenge support.
Limitations: Giving primarily in San Miguel, Delta, Delores, Montrose and Ouray counties in CO.
Publications: Application guidelines, Annual report (including application guidelines), Financial statement, Grants list, Newsletter, Program policy statement.

Application information: See foundation Web site for full application guidelines and requirements, including downloadable application forms. Application form required.
Copies of proposal: 9
Deadline(s): Oct.
Board meeting date(s): Dec. and July
Officers: Ron Allred, Co-Chair.; H. Norman Schwarzkopf, Co-Chair.; Paul Major, C.E.O. and Pres.; Harmon Brown, Secy.; Stephen Wald, Treas.
Board Members: Richard Betts; Bill Carstens; Sen. Jon Corzine; Mark Dalton; Kim Day; Vern Ebert; Dave Flatt; Bunny Freidus; Tully Friedman; William Gershen; Allan Gerstle; Anne Herrick; Amb. Richard Holbrooke; Susan Saint James; Amy Levek; Sarah Lilly; Joan May; Hideo Morita; Stephen Phinny; Josh Sale; Stephen Wald; James Wear; Danforth Quayle.
Number of staff: 2 full-time professional; 1 part-time professional.
EIN: 841530768

528
Thomas Family Foundation
7105 W. 119th Pl.
Broomfield, CO   80020

Established in 1994 in CO.
Donor(s): Victor C. Thomas.‡
Grantmaker type: Independent foundation
Financial data (yr. ended 12/31/02): Assets, $1,853,117 (M); expenditures, $139,912; qualifying distributions, $90,289; giving activities include $91,500 for 16 grants (high: $20,000; low: $3,000).
Purpose and activities: Giving primarily for human services, youth services, and education.
Fields of interest: Museums (natural history); Education; Zoos/zoological societies; Chiropractic; Athletics/sports, school programs; Big Brothers/Big Sisters; Human services; Children/youth, services; Residential/custodial care; Federated giving programs.
Types of support: General/operating support; Continuing support; Scholarship funds; Grants to individuals; Scholarships—to individuals.
Limitations: Applications not accepted. Giving primarily in CO and the Rocky Mountain region.
Publications: Annual report, Financial statement, Grants list.
Application information: Unsolicited requests for funds not accepted.
Officers and Directors:* Lance M. Thomas,* Pres. and Treas.; Todd E. Thomas,* Secy.; V. Marc Thomas.
Number of staff: 1 full-time professional.
EIN: 841271157

529
George and Louise Thornton Charitable Foundation
PMB, No. 331
749 S. Lemay Ave., Ste. A3
Fort Collins, CO   80524-3251
Contact: Louise F. Thornton, Pres.

Established in 1989.
Donor(s): Kate Stamper Wilhite.‡
Grantmaker type: Independent foundation
Financial data (yr. ended 12/31/02): Assets, $1,419,490 (M); expenditures, $116,176;

qualifying distributions, $98,000; giving activities include $98,000 for 32 grants (high: $7,000; low: $1,000).
Purpose and activities: Giving for the arts, education, the environment, recreation, and human services.
Fields of interest: Arts; Secondary school/education; Environment; Athletics/sports, Olympics; Human services.
Types of support: General/operating support; Annual campaigns.
Limitations: Applications not accepted. Giving limited to Fort Collins and northern CO. No grants to individuals.
Application information: Unsolicited requests for funds not considered.
Board meeting date(s): Midyear
Officer: Louise F. Thornton, Pres.
Directors: James Cherry; Julia Cherry; Lara Tabola; Toby Tabola; Charles Thornton; Dawn Thornton; George Thornton.
EIN: 431525102

530
True North Foundation
P.O. Box 271308
Fort Collins, CO   80527-1308   (970) 223-5285
Contact: Ms. Kerry Anderson, Pres.
FAX: (970) 495-0892; E-mail: kka1119@aol.com

Established in 1986 in CO.
Grantmaker type: Independent foundation
Financial data (yr. ended 12/31/02): Assets, $26,566,888 (M); expenditures, $2,253,042; qualifying distributions, $2,036,524; giving activities include $2,036,524 for 80 grants (high: $200,000; low: $1,000).
Purpose and activities: Giving primarily for environmental programs.
Fields of interest: Natural resources; Environment; Disabled; Aging.
Types of support: General/operating support; Equipment; Program development; Conferences/seminars; Seed money; Technical assistance; Consulting services; Matching/challenge support.
Limitations: Giving primarily in AK and northern CA. No support for religious purposes, or political lobbying. No grants to individuals.
Publications: Informational brochure (including application guidelines).
Application information: Application form required.
Initial approach: Letter
Copies of proposal: 1
Deadline(s): None
Board meeting date(s): Generally bimonthly
Officer and Directors:* K. Anderson,* Pres.; S. O'Hara; K.F. Stephens.
Number of staff: 1 full-time professional.
EIN: 742421528

531
Vail Valley Foundation, Inc.
P.O. Box 309
Vail, CO   81658   (970) 949-1999
Additional tel.: (888) VVF-VAIL; FAX: (970) 949-9265; URL: http://www.vvf.org/index.cfm

Grantmaker type: Community foundation
Financial data (yr. ended 12/31/01): Assets, $18,325,143 (M); gifts received, $3,785,681;

expenditures, $10,095,445; giving activities include $244,999 for 25 grants (high: $100,000; low: $100) and $3,501,015 for foundation-administered programs.
Purpose and activities: The mission of the foundation is to provide leadership in athletic, cultural and educational endeavors to enhance the quality of life in the Vail Valley, CO, area. The foundation administers a donor-advised fund.
Fields of interest: Arts; Education; Environment; Athletics/sports, winter sports; Human services.
Limitations: Giving primarily in the Vail Valley, CO, area. No grants to individuals.
Application information:
Initial approach: Proposal
Officer and Directors:* Cecilia Folz,* Pres.; Pres. Gerald R. Ford; and 32 additional directors.
EIN: 742215035

532
The Ralph J. Wann Foundation
c/o Wells Fargo Bank West, N.A.
1740 Broadway, MAC C7300-484
Denver, CO   80274
Contact: Randy Rieck
Application address: Randy Rieck, Trust Off., c/o Wells Fargo Bank West, N.A., P.O. Box 5825, Denver, CO 80217

Grantmaker type: Independent foundation
Financial data (yr. ended 12/31/02): Assets, $4,575,668 (M); expenditures, $248,783; qualifying distributions, $219,748; giving activities include $213,063 for 1 grant.
Purpose and activities: Giving to support the Humane Society of Fremont County, and for the benefit of physically handicapped human beings in Fremont County, CO.
Fields of interest: Animal welfare; Disabled.
Limitations: Giving limited to CO.
Application information:
Initial approach: Letter
Deadline(s): None
Trustee: Wells Fargo Bank West, N.A.
EIN: 846022561

533
Weaver Family Foundation
P.O. Box 19409
Boulder, CO   80308-9409
Contact: Stephanie Schaffer, Opers. Mgr.
E-mail: info@weaverfoundation.org; URL: http://weaverfoundation.org

Established in 1999 in CO.
Donor(s): Lindsey A. Weaver, Jr., Francine Lavin Weaver.
Grantmaker type: Independent foundation
Financial data (yr. ended 12/31/02): Assets, $13,496,762 (M); expenditures, $824,816; qualifying distributions, $843,535; giving activities include $726,419 for 100 grants (high: $100,000; low: $50; average: $50–$100,000) and $120,000 for 2 loans/program-related investments.
Fields of interest: Arts; Education; Environment; Health organizations, association; Housing/shelter, development; Human services; Jewish agencies & temples.
International interests: Honduras.

Types of support: General/operating support; Continuing support; Conferences/seminars; Curriculum development; Fellowships; Consulting services; Program-related investments/loans; Matching/challenge support.
Limitations: Giving primarily in Boulder, CO, and Israel. No grants to individuals.
Application information: Contributes only to pre-selected organizations. Requests for proposals will be solicited by the foundation only.
Directors: Francine Lavin Weaver; Lindsey A. Weaver, Jr.
Number of staff: 1 full-time professional.
EIN: 841513850

534
Western Colorado Community Foundation, Inc.
P.O. Box 4334
Grand Junction, CO 81502-4334
(970) 243-3767
Contact: Anne Wenzel
FAX: (970) 243-9767; URL: http://www.wc-cf.org

Established in 1996 in CO.
Grantmaker type: Community foundation
Financial data (yr. ended 12/31/02): Assets, $2,100,000 (M); expenditures, $270,000; giving activities include $200,000 for 64 grants (high: $50,000; low: $100) and $2,000 for 2 grants to individuals of $1,000 each.
Purpose and activities: The foundation administers a donor-advised fund.
Fields of interest: Arts; Education; Environment; Health care; Human services; Community development.
Types of support: General/operating support; Seed money; Scholarships—to individuals; Matching/challenge support.
Limitations: Giving limited to western CO.
Publications: Application guidelines, Annual report, Informational brochure, Newsletter, Program policy statement.
Application information: Application form not required.
Initial approach: Letter of inquiry
Copies of proposal: 1
Deadline(s): Aug. 15
Board meeting date(s): Quarterly
Final notification: 1-2 months
Officers and Directors:* Glen Jammeson,* Chair.; Georgann Jouflas,* Vice-Chair.; Anita Cox,* Secy.; Verne Smith,* Treas.; Fid Braffett; Tom Jaskunas; Maryann McKinley; Joseph Prinster; Linda Reid; Susan Reid; Gary Wade.
Number of staff: 1 full-time professional; 1 part-time support.
EIN: 841354894

535
Wild Oats Markets, Inc. Corporate Giving Program
c/o Corp. Contribs.
3375 Mitchell Ln.
Boulder, CO 80301-2244

Grantmaker type: Corporate giving program
Purpose and activities: Wild Oats makes charitable contributions to nonprofit organizations involved with education, the environment, animal protection and welfare, health and human services, agriculture, international human rights, and community development. Support is given primarily in areas of company operations.
Fields of interest: Education; Environment; Animal welfare; Health care; Agriculture; Human services; International human rights; Community development.
Types of support: General/operating support; Employee volunteer services; Sponsorships; Donated products.
Limitations: Giving primarily in areas of company operations; giving also to regional and international organizations.
Application information: A contributions committee reviews all requests. Application form not required.
Initial approach: Proposal to headquarters
Copies of proposal: 1
Final notification: Following review

536
Yampa Valley Community Foundation
P.O. Box 774965
Steamboat Springs, CO 80477   (970) 879-8632
Contact: Linda Haltom, Staff Acct.
FAX: (970) 871-0431; E-mail: donate@yvcf.org;
URL: http://www.yvcf.org

Established in 1979 in CO.
Grantmaker type: Community foundation
Financial data (yr. ended 12/31/02): Assets, $3,681,894 (M); gifts received, $1,210,215; expenditures, $683,956; giving activities include $282,554 for 156 grants (high: $48,181; low: $250; average: $250–$20,000), $42,275 for 49 grants to individuals (high: $2,000; low: $300; average: $300–$2,000), $251,695 for foundation-administered programs and $231,674 for 96 in-kind gifts.
Purpose and activities: Giving primarily to arts and culture, education, environment, health organizations, recreation and human services. The foundation administers a donor-advised fund.
Fields of interest: Arts; Education; Environment; Health organizations, association; Recreation; Human services.
Types of support: General/operating support; Continuing support; Annual campaigns; Capital campaigns; Building/renovation; Equipment; Emergency funds; Program development; Conferences/seminars; Seed money; Curriculum development; Scholarships—to individuals; Exchange programs.
Limitations: Giving primarily in Yampa Valley, specifically Routt and Moffat counties, CO.
Publications: Application guidelines, Annual report, Grants list, Informational brochure, Newsletter.
Application information: Application forms may be downloaded from Web site. Application form required.
Initial approach: 2-page letter
Copies of proposal: 1
Deadline(s): Quarterly
Board meeting date(s): Monthly
Final notification: Within 1 month
Officers: Paula Cooper Black, Chair.; Mike Roberts, Vice-Chair.; Nick Schoewe, Vice-Chair.; Dianna Sutton, C.E.O. and Pres.; Benita Bristol, Secy.; Kathryn Crawford, Treas.

Trustees: Debbie Alpe; Barbara Barczuk; Kyle Cox; Chris Diamond; Rick Dowden; Scott Gordon; Julie Green; Linda Jensen Hamlet; Peter Kurtz; Susan Larson; Arianthe Stettner; Rob Straebel; John Vickery; Dean Vogelaar.
Number of staff: 1 full-time professional; 1 part-time professional; 2 part-time support.
EIN: 840794536

CONNECTICUT

537
The Ahn Family Foundation
106 Patterson Ave.
Greenwich, CT 06830
Contact: Alison Ahn, Tr.

Established in 1997 in CT.
Donor(s): Sangwoo Ahn, Laura Ahn.
Grantmaker type: Independent foundation
Financial data (yr. ended 12/31/01): Assets, $2,191,349 (M); gifts received, $10,000; expenditures, $112,958; qualifying distributions, $112,231; giving activities include $112,500 for 23 grants (high: $15,000; low: $1,000).
Purpose and activities: Giving for religion, human and social services, art and cultural programs and for education.
Fields of interest: Arts; Education; Natural resources; Human services; Religion.
Limitations: Giving primarily in CT, MA and NY.
Application information:
Deadline(s): None
Trustees: Alison D. Ahn; Sangwoo Ahn.
EIN: 137127169

538
Anderson-Paffard Foundation, Inc.
P.O. Box 88
New London, CT 06320

Established in 1981 in CT.
Grantmaker type: Independent foundation
Financial data (yr. ended 09/30/02): Assets, $3,200,860 (M); expenditures, $154,632; qualifying distributions, $148,250; giving activities include $148,250 for 30 grants (high: $20,000; low: $500).
Purpose and activities: Funding primarily for arts and culture, and education. Some funding also for human services.
Fields of interest: Arts; Education; Environment, land resources; Human services; Protestant agencies & churches.
Limitations: Applications not accepted. Giving primarily in southeastern CT. No support for amateur sports competitions. No grants to individuals.
Application information: Contributes only to pre-selected organizations.
Board meeting date(s): Nov.
Officers: Frederick P. Anderson, M.D., Pres.; Willa T. Schuster, V.P.; Robert P. Anderson, Jr., Secy.-Treas.
Number of staff: 1 part-time support.
EIN: 061047468

539
Arrowhead Foundation, Inc.
36 Tokeneke Trail
Darien, CT 06820
Contact: Thomas E. O'Connor, Pres.

Established in 1988 in CT.
Donor(s): Thomas E. O'Connor.
Grantmaker type: Independent foundation
Financial data (yr. ended 12/31/01): Assets, $2,579,607 (M); expenditures, $207,475; qualifying distributions, $148,395; giving activities include $148,650 for 37 grants (high: $50,000; low: $100).
Fields of interest: Television; Arts; Education; Environment; Human services; Public affairs.
Limitations: Applications not accepted. Giving primarily in CT and NY. No grants to individuals.
Application information: Contributes only to pre-selected organizations.
Officers and Directors:* Thomas E. O'Connor,* Pres.; Janet M. O'Connor,* Secy.; Thomas P. Spellane.
EIN: 223118157

540
Asea Brown Boveri Inc. Corporate Giving Program
501 Merritt 7
Norwalk, CT 06851-7000
FAX: (203) 750-7788

Grantmaker type: Corporate giving program
Purpose and activities: Asea Brown Boveri makes charitable contributions to nonprofit organizations involved with education and energy conservation. Support is given on a national basis.
Fields of interest: Education; Energy.
Types of support: General/operating support.
Limitations: Giving on a national basis.
Application information: Contributions are currently very limited.

541
The Arnold F. Baggins Foundation, Inc.
2061 Ponus Ridge Rd.
New Canaan, CT 06840

Established in 1993 in CT.
Donor(s): Robert D. Kennedy, Sally D. Kennedy.
Grantmaker type: Independent foundation
Financial data (yr. ended 12/31/02): Assets, $3,870,353 (M); gifts received, $24,981; expenditures, $292,226; qualifying distributions, $231,241; giving activities include $230,500 for 64 grants (high: $15,000; low: $500).
Fields of interest: Arts; Education; Animal welfare; Health care; Health organizations, association; Human services; Federated giving programs; Religion.
Limitations: Applications not accepted. Giving in the eastern U.S., with emphasis on CT, MA, MD, NH, NY, PA, and VA. No grants to individuals.
Application information: Contributes only to pre-selected organizations.
Officers: Robert D. Kennedy, Pres.; Sally D. Kennedy, Secy.
EIN: 061385734

542
Elinor Patterson Baker Foundation ▼
c/o Cummings & Lockwood (R.A. Beer)
P.O. Box 120
Stamford, CT 06904 (203) 869-3000
Application address: c/o Putnam Trust Co., 10 Mason St., Greenwich, CT 06830

Established in 1984 in CT.
Donor(s): Elinor Patterson Baker.‡
Grantmaker type: Independent foundation
Financial data (yr. ended 05/31/02): Assets, $45,197,823 (M); expenditures, $3,226,883; qualifying distributions, $2,987,052; giving activities include $2,639,000 for 138 grants (high: $300,000; low: $2,000; average: $5,000–$10,000).
Purpose and activities: Grants for organizations that fulfill the goals of the Humane Society of the United States.
Fields of interest: Animal welfare.
Limitations: Giving primarily in CT to organizations exempt from the state succession tax. In the case of organizations incorporated outside of CT, reciprocity must exist between CT and the state of incorporation in order for the organization to qualify for a grant.
Application information:
Deadline(s): None
Trustee: Putnam Trust Co.
EIN: 066276403
Recent environmental and animal welfare grants:
542-1 American Society for the Prevention of Cruelty to Animals, New York, NY, $25,000. For general support. 2002.
542-2 Animal Alliance, Santa Fe, NM, $10,000. For general support. 2002.
542-3 Animal Medical Center, New York, NY, $10,000. For general support. 2002.
542-4 Animal Rights Network, Baltimore, MD, $10,000. For general support. 2002.
542-5 Animal Welfare League of Benzie County, Frankfort, MI, $10,000. For general support. 2002.
542-6 Caribbean Conservation Corporation, Gainesville, FL, $30,000. For general support. 2002.
542-7 Carolina Kids Conservancy, Columbus, NC, $10,000. For general support. 2002.
542-8 Cold Mountain, Cold Rivers, Missoula, MT, $15,000. For general support. 2002.
542-9 Days End Farm Horse Rescue, Lisbon, MD, $15,000. For general support. 2002.
542-10 Delta Society, Renton, WA, $20,000. For general support. 2002.
542-11 Denver Dumb Friends League-Humane Society of Denver, Denver, CO, $97,500. For general support. 2002.
542-12 Earth Action Network, Norwalk, CT, $15,000. For general support for E Magazine. 2002.
542-13 Earth Conservation Corps, DC, $15,000. For general support. 2002.
542-14 Environmental Alliance-US-China Environmental Fund, Mount Horeb, WI, $25,000. For general support. 2002.
542-15 Greater Yellowstone Coalition, Bozeman, MT, $50,000. For general support. 2002.
542-16 Group for the South Fork, Bridgehampton, NY, $30,000. For general support. 2002.

542-17 Hornocker Wildlife Institute, Bozeman, MT, $25,000. For general support. 2002.
542-18 Humane Society for Companion Animals, Saint Paul, MN, $10,000. For general support. 2002.
542-19 Humane Society for Larimer County, Fort Collins, CO, $10,000. For general support. 2002.
542-20 Humane Society for Seattle-King County, Bellevue, WA, $10,000. For general support. 2002.
542-21 Humane Society of Chittenden County, South Burlington, VT, $10,000. For general support. 2002.
542-22 Humane Society of Jacksonville, Jacksonville, FL, $10,000. For general support. 2002.
542-23 Humane Society of Kent County, Grand Rapids, MI, $10,000. For general support. 2002.
542-24 Humane Society of Lake County, Mentor, OH, $10,000. For general support. 2002.
542-25 Humane Society of Longmont, Longmont, CO, $10,000. For general support. 2002.
542-26 Humane Society of Nevada, Sparks, NV, $10,000. For general support. 2002.
542-27 Humane Society of North Pinellas, Clearwater, FL, $10,000. For general support. 2002.
542-28 Humane Society of Oregon, Portland, Oregon, $10,000. For general support. 2002.
542-29 Humane Society of Prince Georges County, Bowie, MD, $10,000. For general support. 2002.
542-30 Humane Society of Rochester and Monroe County for the Prevention of Animal Cruelty, Fairport, NY, $10,000. For general support. 2002.
542-31 Humane Society of Taos, Taos, NM, $10,000. For general support. 2002.
542-32 Humane Society of the United States, DC, $300,000. For immunocontraception. 2002.
542-33 Humane Society of the United States, DC, $250,000. For general support. 2002.
542-34 Humane Society of the United States, DC, $250,000. For general support. 2002.
542-35 Humane Society of the United States, DC, $250,000. For general support. 2002.
542-36 Humane Society of the United States, DC, $100,000. For Wildlife Center. 2002.
542-37 Humane Society, Capital Area, Lansing, MI, $10,000. For general support. 2002.
542-38 Humane Society, Clinton, Clinton, IA, $10,000. For general support. 2002.
542-39 Humane Society, Hawaii Island, Kailua Kona, HI, $10,000. For general support. 2002.
542-40 Humane Society, Whatcom, Bellingham, WA, $10,000. For general support. 2002.
542-41 Marine Mammal Center, Sausalito, CA, $100,000. For general support. 2002.
542-42 Monitor International, Annapolis, MD, $10,000. For general support. 2002.
542-43 Music for the Earth, Litchfield, CT, $10,000. For general support. 2002.
542-44 National Education for Assistance Dog Services (NEADS), West Boylston, MA, $10,000. For general support. 2002.

542-45 Nature Center for Environmental Activities, Westport, CT, $10,000. For general support. 2002.

542-46 New England Wildlife Center, Hingham, MA, $20,000. For general support. 2002.

542-47 Ocean Futures Society, Santa Barbara, CA, $25,000. For general support. 2002.

542-48 Pelican Mans Bird Sanctuary, Sarasota, FL, $10,000. For general support. 2002.

542-49 Point Reyes Bird Observatory, Stinson Beach, CA, $30,000. For general support. 2002.

542-50 Predator Conservation Alliance, Bozeman, MT, $50,000. For general support. 2002.

542-51 Raptor Trust, Millington, NJ, $25,000. For general support. 2002.

542-52 Renew the Earth, DC, $15,000. For general support. 2002.

542-53 Saint Huberts Animal Welfare Center, Madison, NJ, $10,000. For general support. 2002.

542-54 Sea Turtle Restoration Project, Forest Knolls, CA, $10,000. For general support. 2002.

542-55 Society for the Prevention of Cruelty to Animals of Central Florida, Orlando, FL, $10,000. For general support. 2002.

542-56 Society for the Prevention of Cruelty to Animals of Pinellas County, Largo, FL, $10,000. For general support. 2002.

542-57 Society for the Prevention of Cruelty to Animals, New Hampshire, Portsmouth, NH, $10,000. For general support. 2002.

542-58 Table Mountain Animal Center Foundation, Golden, CO, $30,000. For general support. 2002.

542-59 United Activists for Animal Rights, Riverside, CA, $10,000. For general support. 2002.

542-60 Wayside Waifs, Kansas City, MO, $10,000. For general support. 2002.

542-61 Wildlife Center of Virginia, Weyers Cave, VA, $50,000. For general support. 2002.

542-62 World Society for the Protection of Animals, Boston, MA, $35,000. For general support. 2002.

543
The Baldwin Foundation
c/o D. Brandrup
57 Old Post Rd., No. 2
Greenwich, CT 06830

Established in 1980 in DE and NY.
Donor(s): Winifred B. Baldwin.‡
Grantmaker type: Independent foundation
Financial data (yr. ended 12/31/02): Assets, $6,846,298 (M); expenditures, $439,281; qualifying distributions, $410,422; giving activities include $350,000 for 12 grants (high: $100,000; low: $5,000).
Purpose and activities: Giving primarily for education; some support also for environmental conservation and animal welfare.
Fields of interest: Elementary/secondary education; Natural resources; Animals/wildlife, preservation/protection; Hospitals (general).
Types of support: General/operating support; Annual campaigns; Capital campaigns; Building/renovation; Land acquisition; Emergency funds; Matching/challenge support.

Limitations: Applications not accepted. Giving primarily in southern ME. No grants to individuals, or for scholarships.
Application information: Contributes only to pre-selected organizations.
  Board meeting date(s): July and Aug.
Officers and Directors:* Diana B. Dunnan,* Pres.; Rev. D. Stuart Dunnan,* V.P.; Winifred D. Faust,* V.P.; Joan W. Trimble,* V.P.; Douglas W. Brandrup, Secy.-Treas.
EIN: 133039728

544
The Beinecke Foundation, Inc.
8 Sound Shore Dr., Ste. 120
Greenwich, CT 06830 (203) 861-7314
Contact: John R. Robinson, Pres.

Incorporated in 1966 in NY as The Kerry Foundation, Inc. and absorbed Edwin J. Beinecke Trust, NY, in April 1985. The new name for the combined foundations was adopted in Dec. 1985.
Donor(s): Sylvia B. Robinson.‡
Grantmaker type: Independent foundation
Financial data (yr. ended 12/31/01): Assets, $61,849,227 (M); expenditures, $2,518,070; qualifying distributions, $1,994,108; giving activities include $1,528,400 for 95 grants (high: $225,000; low: $150; average: $1,000–$25,000).
Purpose and activities: Giving primarily for secondary, higher, and medical education, conservation, and Protestant church support.
Fields of interest: Secondary school/education; Higher education; Medical school/education; Natural resources; Protestant agencies & churches.
Types of support: General/operating support; Capital campaigns; Building/renovation; Equipment; Endowments; Conferences/seminars; Publication.
Limitations: Applications not accepted. Giving primarily in CT and NY. No grants to individuals; no loans.
Publications: Annual report.
Application information: Contributes only to pre-selected organizations. The foundation does not accept unsolicited requests.
  Board meeting date(s): Spring and fall
Officers and Director:* John R. Robinson,* Pres. and Treas.; Abigail Bowers, V.P. and Secy.
Number of staff: 2 full-time professional; 1 full-time support.
EIN: 136201175

545
Belgian American Educational Foundation, Inc.
195 Church St.
New Haven, CT 06510 (203) 777-5765
Contact: Emile L. Boulpaep, Ph.D., Pres.
FAX: (203) 785-4951; E-mail: emile.boulpaep@yale.edu; URL: http://www.baef.be

Incorporated in 1920 in DE.
Donor(s): The Commission for Relief in Belgium.
Grantmaker type: Public charity
Financial data (yr. ended 08/31/01): Revenue, $5,361,391; assets, $55,121,801 (M); gifts received, $1,623,642; expenditures,

$2,591,273; program services expenses, $2,338,108; giving activities include $255,184 for 2 grants (high: $251,770; low: $3,414) and $2,022,601 for 68 grants to individuals (high: $47,300; low: $4,269).
Purpose and activities: Grantmaking to promote closer relations between Belgium and the United States through graduate exchange fellowships in diverse fields and to assist higher education, scientific research, and the exchange of intellectual ideas.
Fields of interest: Film/video; Visual arts; Architecture; Performing arts; Music; History/archaeology; Arts; Child development, education; Higher education; Business school/education; Law school/education; Medical school/education; Engineering school/education; Natural resources; Environment; Health care; Health organizations; Human services; Child development, services; Foreign policy; Business/industry; Mathematics; Physics; Engineering/technology; Computer science; Engineering; Biological sciences; Science; Economics; International studies.
International interests: Belgium.
Types of support: Fellowships; Research; Grants to individuals; Scholarships—to individuals; Exchange programs.
Limitations: Giving limited to students from Belgium and the U.S. No grants for general support, endowment funds, matching gifts, or fellowships (except for Belgian and American graduate students).
Publications: Application guidelines, Financial statement, Newsletter.
Application information: Only one candidate may be nominated from each university. Application available on Web site. Application form required.
  Initial approach: Letter
  Copies of proposal: 1
  Deadline(s): Submit Graduate Fellowships proposal in Jan.; deadline Jan. 31
  Board meeting date(s): Jan., Apr., June, and Oct.
  Final notification: For Graduate Fellowships: on or about Mar. 31
Officers and Directors:* Emile L. Boulpaep, Ph.D.,* Chair. and Pres.; William Moody,* Secy.; Sherman Gray,* Treas.; Maryan Ainsworth; Gery Daeninck; Jacques de Groote; Diego du Moneeau; Susan Friberg; John H.F. Haskell, Jr.; Andre Jacques; Daniel Janssen; L. Gilles Sion; Edward H. Tuck; Luc Wauters; Jacques Willems.
Number of staff: 2 part-time support.
EIN: 131606002

546
The Bingham Trust
(formerly Mr. Bingham's Trust for Charity)
65 Parker Hill Rd. Ext.
Killingworth, CT 06419-2311
Contact: Patricia F. Davidson, Tr.

Trust established in 1935 in NY.
Donor(s): William Bingham II.‡
Grantmaker type: Independent foundation
Financial data (yr. ended 12/31/01): Assets, $56,442,793 (M); expenditures, $3,141,507; qualifying distributions, $2,797,521; giving activities include $2,577,215 for 21 grants (high: $750,000; low: $2,000; average: $5,000–$250,000).

Purpose and activities: Since its inception, the trust has confined its grants to a small group of institutions to achieve maximum philanthropic effect. Every five years it shifts its primary focus to entirely new fields of interest. Because its grant criteria are extremely narrow, all grantees are selected by invitation only after research by the trustees.

Fields of interest: Music; Early childhood education; Environment; Domestic violence.

Types of support: General/operating support; Endowments; Seed money; Research.

Limitations: Applications not accepted. No grants to individuals, or for scholarships or fellowships.

Publications: Multi-year report.

Application information:

Board meeting date(s): Quarterly

Trustees: Donald M. Barr; Patricia F. Davidson; U.S. Trust.

Number of staff: None.

EIN: 136069740

547
Bodenwein Public Benevolent Foundation
777 Main St., CTEH40222B
Hartford, CT 06115 (860) 986-7696
Contact: Marjorie Alexandre Davis

Established in 1938 in CT.

Donor(s): The Day Trust, Theodore Bodenwein.‡

Grantmaker type: Independent foundation

Financial data (yr. ended 12/31/02): Assets, $682,039 (M); gifts received, $349,759; expenditures, $293,780; qualifying distributions, $291,630; giving activities include $287,663 for 65 grants (high: $20,000; low: $579).

Purpose and activities: Giving to social service and health agencies, including AIDS support, the fine and performing arts and other cultural programs, youth and child welfare agencies, civic affairs and community development groups, education, and minority programs.

Fields of interest: Visual arts; Museums; Performing arts; Theater; Language/linguistics; Literature; Arts; Early childhood education; Child development, education; Adult/continuing education; Adult education—literacy, basic skills & GED; Libraries/library science; Reading; Education; Environment; Animal welfare; Hospitals (general); Family planning; Medical care, rehabilitation; Health care; Substance abuse, services; Mental health/crisis services; Health organizations, association; Alcoholism; Cancer research; AIDS research; Legal services; Youth development, services; Human services; Children/youth, services; Child development, services; Family services; Aging, centers/services; Women, centers/services; Minorities/immigrants, centers/services; Community development; Voluntarism promotion; Jewish federated giving programs; Engineering/technology; Science; Government/public administration; Transportation; Leadership development; Religion; Minorities; Aging; Women.

Types of support: Capital campaigns; Equipment; Program development; Publication; Seed money; Scholarship funds; Matching/challenge support.

Limitations: Giving limited to Lyme, Old Lyme, East Lyme, Waterford, New London, Montville,

Groton, Ledyard, Stonington, and North Stonington, CT.

Publications: Informational brochure (including application guidelines).

Application information: Each applicant may submit only 1 grant application per calendar year. Application form required.

Copies of proposal: 5

Deadline(s): May 15 and Nov. 15

Board meeting date(s): Jan. and July

Final notification: Feb. 1 and Aug. 1

Trustee: Fleet National Bank.

Number of staff: None.

EIN: 066030548

548
Bridgemill Foundation
9 Sawmill Ln.
Greenwich, CT 06830
Contact: John H.T. Wilson, Pres.

Established in 1992 in DE and CT.

Donor(s): John H.T. Wilson.

Grantmaker type: Independent foundation

Financial data (yr. ended 12/31/02): Assets, $5,671,527 (M); expenditures, $374,550; qualifying distributions, $336,700; giving activities include $330,250 for 65 grants (high: $50,000; low: $1,000).

Purpose and activities: Giving primarily for higher education, health associations, and children's and social services.

Fields of interest: Performing arts; Higher education; Education; Animals/wildlife; Hospitals (general); Health organizations, association; Human services; Children, services; International affairs; Foundations (community); Federated giving programs.

Limitations: Applications not accepted. Giving primarily in CT and NY. No grants to individuals.

Application information: Unsolicited requests for funds not accepted.

Officers: John H.T. Wilson, Pres.; Sandra W. Wilson, V.P.

EIN: 133671059

549
The Greater Bridgeport Area Foundation, Inc.
211 State St.
Bridgeport, CT 06604 (203) 334-7511
Contact: Cindy Kissin, C.E.O.
FAX: (203) 333-4652; URL: http://www.gbafoundation.org

Incorporated in 1967 in CT.

Grantmaker type: Community foundation

Financial data (yr. ended 12/31/02): Assets, $28,646,706 (M); gifts received, $1,849,798; expenditures, $2,058,410; giving activities include $1,011,552 for 305 grants (high: $30,000; low: $100; average: $3,000–$5,000), $176,891 for 130 grants to individuals (high: $15,000; low: $360; average: $360–$15,000) and $72,515 for foundation-administered programs.

Purpose and activities: The foundation's mission is to participate actively in shaping the well-being of the region. Giving in the form of grants and scholarships to organizations and students in the foundations community. The foundation also runs a non-profit resource

center to support the organizational development of the non-profit community. The foundation administers a designated and a donor-advised fund.

Fields of interest: Education; Environment; Health care; Human services; Economic development; Community development.

Types of support: General/operating support; Continuing support; Management development; Program development; Conferences/seminars; Scholarship funds; Technical assistance; Consulting services; Program evaluation; Scholarships—to individuals.

Limitations: Giving through competitive process for programs in Bridgeport, Easton, Fairfield, Milford, Monroe, Shelton, Stratford, Southbury, Trumbull, and Westport, CT. No support for religious purposes. No grants for deficit financing, campaigns or lobbying, annual appeals or major capital campaigns; no loans.

Publications: Application guidelines, Informational brochure.

Application information: Application form required.

Initial approach: Letter of intent

Copies of proposal: 1

Deadline(s): March 1 and Aug. 1

Board meeting date(s): Mar., June, and Nov.; distribution committee meets in June and nov.

Final notification: July and Dec.

Officers and Directors:* Mickey Herbert,* Chair.; Hon. John P. Chiota,* Vice-Chair.; Meredith Baum Reuben,* Vice-Chair.; Cindy S. Kissin, C.E.O. and Pres.; Janet M. Hansen,* Secy.; Peter F. Hurst, Jr.,* Treas.; Samuel L. Braunstein; Octavio G. Choy, M.D.; Myron I. Dworken; Fred C. Frassinelli, Jr.; Marshall Gibson; Geraldine W. Johnson; John A. Klein; Sally S. Kreitler; Robert H. Laska; Thomas Lenci; George B. Longstreth III; William A. Minter; Jan Parks; S. George Santa; Peter T. Mott; Viola J. Spinelli.

Number of staff: 7 full-time professional; 1 full-time support; 1 part-time support.

EIN: 066103832

550
The Carlson Family Foundation
59 Merrimac Dr.
Trumbull, CT 06611-1725

Established in 1994 in CT.

Donor(s): Metta R. Rehnberg,‡ Rehnberg Charitable Lead Annuity Trust, Harry A. Rehnberg Marital Trust.

Grantmaker type: Independent foundation

Financial data (yr. ended 08/31/02): Assets, $1,868,410 (M); gifts received, $112,801; expenditures, $118,047; qualifying distributions, $110,400; giving activities include $110,400 for 32 grants (high: $22,000; low: $1,000).

Purpose and activities: Giving for higher education scholarships, youth and health services, religious programs, environmental and parks conservation, historical societies and for women's services.

Fields of interest: Environment; Animals/wildlife; Human services; Religion.

Limitations: Applications not accepted. Giving primarily in CT. No grants to individuals.

Application information: Contributes only to pre-selected organizations.

Officer: Stephanie Murray, Secy.
Directors: Jennifer McCann; Harry C. Rehnberg;
Jon Rehnberg.
EIN: 133762819

551

CL&P Corporate Giving Program

107 Selden St.
Berlin, CT 06037-1616 (860) 278-8352
Contact: Jose A. Chavez, Jr., Mgr., Community
Rels.
Additional contacts: eastern CT: Carla Francis,
tel.: (860) 638-2296, western CT: Margo
Jackson, tel.: (203) 597-4350; URL: http://
www.cl-p.com/community/partners/
indexpartners.asp

Grantmaker type: Corporate giving program
Purpose and activities: CL&P makes charitable
contributions to nonprofit organizations
involved with arts and culture, education, the
environment, health and human services,
employment training, housing, community
development, public affairs, and economically
disadvantaged people. Support is given
primarily in areas of company operations.
Fields of interest: Arts; Higher education;
Education; Environment; Health care;
Employment, training; Housing/shelter; Human
services; Economic development; Community
development; Public affairs; Economically
disadvantaged.
Types of support: General/operating support;
Capital campaigns; Program development;
Employee volunteer services; Use of facilities;
Scholarships—to individuals; In-kind gifts.
Limitations: Giving primarily in areas of
company operations in CT. No support for
United Way-supported organizations, combined
health organizations, art councils, or federated
funds, private foundations, religious, fraternal, or
political organizations, or youth organizations.
No grants to individuals (except for
scholarships), or for athletic events, debt
reduction, endowments, or advertising.
Application information: An application form is
required for educational contributions and
contributions of over $1,000; application form
available online. Organizations receiving
support are asked to provide periodic progress
reports. A contributions committee reviews all
requests.
  Initial approach: Proposal to headquarters;
    complete online application form for
    educational contributions and contributions
    of over $1,000
  Final notification: Following review

552

The Community Foundation for Greater New Haven

(formerly The New Haven Foundation)
70 Audubon St.
New Haven, CT 06510 (203) 777-2386
Contact: Nancy L. Hadley, Exec. Dir.
FAX: (203) 787-6584; E-mail:
nhadley@cfgnh.org; URL: http://www.cfgnh.org

Established in 1928 in CT by resolution and
declaration of trust.
Grantmaker type: Community foundation

Financial data (yr. ended 12/31/01): Assets,
$213,699,419 (M); gifts received, $7,700,000;
expenditures, $13,241,350; giving activities
include $10,631,995 for grants.
Purpose and activities: 1) All activities should
begin with a vision of building a healthy
integrated community that controls its own
destiny over time and supports and strengthens
its commitment to children, youth, families,
neighborhoods and economic vitality. 2)
Enabling people to build the necessary skills to
take charge of their lives should be the
cornerstone of all projects for families and
individuals. Priority is given to programs that
increase access to health and social services;
support neighborhoods through technical
assistance and leadership training; and, invest in
human capital through employment/training and
family strengthening projects. 3) The foundation
gives priority to projects that promote strength
and develop potential, because prevention is
recognized to be cost-effective and to have a
long-lasting, transforming effect on the lives of
children, youth, families and individuals. 4)
Collaborative partnerships and/or projects that
capitalize on proven organizations and
resources receive high priority. 5) The
foundation seeks opportunities to support and
promote projects that fiscally and
programmatically leverage private and
government partnerships. 6) The foundation will
use specific benchmarks that identify and
measure the intended impact on individuals,
families, and institutions necessary to evaluate
projects and advocate for effective public policy.
7) The foundation occasionally will consider
supporting long-term approaches that foster and
support fundamental social change, in order to
ensure a sustaining commitment to improving
the lives of children, youth, families and the
communities in which they reside.
Fields of interest: Multipurpose
centers/programs; Environment, beautification
programs; Health care; Food services;
Housing/shelter, development; Community
development, neighborhood development;
Economic development; Business/industry.
Types of support: General/operating support;
Continuing support; Capital campaigns;
Building/renovation; Equipment; Emergency
funds; Program development;
Conferences/seminars; Seed money; Scholarship
funds; Technical assistance; Consulting services;
Program evaluation; Program-related
investments/loans; Matching/challenge support.
Limitations: Giving primarily in greater New
Haven, CT, and the lower Naugatuck River
Valley. No grants to individuals (including direct
scholarships), or for annual campaigns, deficit
financing, endowment funds, research,
fellowships, or generally for capital projects.
Publications: Application guidelines, Annual
report (including application guidelines),
Financial statement, Informational brochure
(including application guidelines), Newsletter.
Application information: Application form
required.
  Initial approach: Telephone and letter of intent
  Copies of proposal: 14
  Deadline(s): Jan., Apr., Aug., and Oct.
  Board meeting date(s): Mar., June, Sept., and
    Dec.
  Final notification: Within 1 week of decision

Officers: William W. Ginsberg, C.E.O. and
Pres.; A.F. Drew Alden, C.O.O. and C.F.O.; Etha
J. Henry, V.P., Progs.
Directors: Harold C. Donegan, Chair.; Linda K.
Lorimer, Vice-Chair.; Mary Jane Burt; John J.
Crawford; Frederick P. Leaf; Julia M. McNamara;
Jerome H. Meyer; Barbara L. Pearce; Sonia
Caban Recalde; Kenneth Schaible; Susan
Whetstone.
Trustees: BankBoston Connecticut; Fleet
National Bank; New Haven Savings Bank;
Wachovia Bank, N.A.; Webster Trust Co., N.A.
Number of staff: 18 full-time professional; 8
full-time support.
EIN: 066032106
**Recent environmental and animal welfare
grants:**
552-1 Elm City Park Conservancy, New Haven,
CT, $10,000. For Quinnipiac River Park.
2002.
552-2 Friends of the Linear Trail, Wallingford,
CT, $10,000. For land acquisition, trail
development, public outreach and
education. 2002.
552-3 New Haven Ecology Project, New
Haven, CT, $30,000. For Farm Project. 2002.
552-4 Quinnipiac River Watershed Association,
Meriden, CT, $20,000. For program support.
2002.
552-5 Solar Youth, New Haven, CT, $40,000.
For program and operating expenses. 2002.
552-6 Trust for Public Land, New Haven, CT,
$10,000. For Watershed Protection and
Smart Growth Initiative. 2002.
552-7 Upper Room Unlimited, New Haven, CT,
$23,000. For Recycling Program. 2002.
552-8 Yale University, School of Forestry and
Environmental Science, New Haven, CT,
$20,000. For four-day workshop. 2002.
552-9 Yale University, School of Forestry and
Environmental Science, New Haven, CT,
$14,500. For research project, Monitoring
Vegetation Change and Mudflat
Development. 2002.
552-10 Yale University, School of Forestry and
Environmental Science, New Haven, CT,
$10,000. For two-day course in river
processes. 2002.

553

The Community Foundation of Southeastern Connecticut

(formerly The Pequot Community Foundation,
Inc.)
147 State St.
P.O. Box 769
New London, CT 06320 (860) 442-3572
Contact: Alice F. Fitzpatrick, Pres.
FAX: (860) 442-0584; URL: http://www.cfsect.org

Established in 1982 in CT.
Donor(s): J. Martin Leatherman,‡ Beatrice G.
McEwen,‡ Dorothy Morgan,‡ Jim Smith,
members of the White Family.
Grantmaker type: Community foundation
Financial data (yr. ended 12/31/02): Assets,
$19,063,332 (L); gifts received, $1,288,945;
expenditures, $1,662,566; giving activities
include $905,649 for grants (high: $20,550;
low: $100) and $213,400 for grants to
individuals (high: $30,000; low: $500; average:
$2,500–$5,000).

Purpose and activities: The Community Foundation of Southeastern Connecticut permanently strengthens our shared community through the promotion of local philanthropy and the responsible stewardship of endowed funds. The foundation administers a donor-advised fund.
Fields of interest: Arts; Libraries/library science; Education; Natural resources; Environment; Health care; Substance abuse, services; Mental health/crisis services; Human services; Children/youth, services; Family services; Aging, centers/services; Women, centers/services; Community development; Voluntarism promotion; Disabled; Aging; Women; Economically disadvantaged.
Types of support: General/operating support; Building/renovation; Equipment; Emergency funds; Program development; Seed money; Scholarship funds; Technical assistance; Consulting services; Scholarships—to individuals.
Limitations: Giving limited to southeastern CT, including East Lyme, Groton, Ledyard, Lyme, Montville, New London, North Stonington, Old Lyme, Salem, Stonington, and Waterford. No support for sectarian or religious programs. No grants to individuals (except for scholarships awarded by nomination only), or for endowment, memorial, or building funds, deficit financing, or annual campaigns; no loans.
Publications: Application guidelines, Annual report (including application guidelines), Financial statement, Grants list, Informational brochure, Newsletter.
Application information: Application form available on foundation Web site. Application form required.
  Initial approach: Telephone or letter
  Copies of proposal: 2
  Deadline(s): Nov. 15 for grants; Apr. 1 for scholarship applications; Aug. 1 for women and girls applications
  Board meeting date(s): Jan., Mar., June, Sept., and Nov.
  Final notification: Grants are distributed in Mar.; scholarships are awarded in June; women and girls grants awarded in Oct.
Officers and Trustees:* Timothy Bates,* Chair.; Bridget Baird, Vice-Chair.; Alice F. Fitzpatrick,* Pres.; Ruth Saunders,* Secy.; Marc Ginsberg,* Treas.; and 11 additional trustees.
Number of staff: 4 full-time professional; 1 full-time support.
EIN: 061080097

554
Connecticut Energy Foundation, Inc.
10 State House Sq., 6th Fl.
P.O. Box 1500
Hartford, CT   06144-1500   (860) 727-3102
Contact: William Reis, Tr.

Established in 1984 in CT.
Donor(s): Connecticut Natural Gas Corp.
Grantmaker type: Company-sponsored foundation
Financial data (yr. ended 06/30/02): Assets, $1,236,614 (M); expenditures, $482,054; qualifying distributions, $479,453; giving activities include $480,000 for 3 grants (high: $400,000; low: $30,000).

Purpose and activities: To fund programs in the 24 towns and cities of Connecticut Natural Gas's service area that promote more efficient use of energy by low-income people, increase the availability of utility service to them, or reduce their energy costs.
Fields of interest: Natural resources; Energy; Environment; Human services; Economically disadvantaged.
Types of support: Building/renovation; Equipment; Program development; Seed money; Technical assistance; Consulting services.
Limitations: Giving limited to towns in Connecticut Natural Gas service territory, including Andover, Avon, Berlin, Bloomfield, Canton, East Hartford, Farmington, Glastonbury, Greenwich, Hartford, Hebron, Manchester, Mansfield, Marlborough, New Britain, Newington, Portland, Rocky Hill, Simsbury, South Windsor, Vernon, West Hartford, Wethersfield, and Windsor, CT.
Publications: Application guidelines.
Application information: Application form required.
  Copies of proposal: 1
  Deadline(s): None
Officer: Michael C. Stevens, Treas.
Trustees: Vincent L. Ammann; Romilda R. Anderson; John A. Dobos; Thomas J. Donohue; James P. Laurito; William Reis.
Number of staff: None.
EIN: 222546022

555
Connecticut Natural Gas Corporation Contributions Program
P.O. Box 1500
Hartford, CT   06144-1500   (203) 382-8644
Contact: John Dobis

Grantmaker type: Corporate giving program
Purpose and activities: Connecticut Natural Gas makes charitable contributions to nonprofit organizations involved with arts and culture, education, the environment, health and human services, substance abuse, disease, crime, food distribution, housing, public safety, youth development, international human rights, civil rights, community development, civic affairs, minorities, senior citizens, women, and homeless people. Support is given primarily in Greenwich, Hartford, and New Britain, Connecticut.
Fields of interest: Humanities; Historic preservation/historical societies; Arts; Elementary/secondary education; Reading; Education; Natural resources; Energy; Environment; Hospitals (general); Health care; Substance abuse, services; Health organizations, association; Health organizations; Crime/law enforcement; Food services; Housing/shelter; Safety/disasters; Youth development; Children/youth, services; Family services; Human services; International human rights; Civil rights; Urban/community development; Business/industry; Community development; Public affairs, citizen participation; Leadership development; Public affairs; Minorities; Aging; Women; Homeless.
Types of support: General/operating support; Employee volunteer services; Sponsorships; Scholarships—to individuals; In-kind gifts.

Limitations: Giving primarily in Greenwich, Hartford, and New Britain, CT. No grants to individuals (except for scholarships), or for trips.
Application information: The Charitable Contributions Department handles giving. Application form not required.
  Initial approach: Proposal to headquarters
  Board meeting date(s): Mar. and Sept.
  Final notification: 3 weeks

556
Crow Hill Foundation
c/o Thomas E. Finn, PC
35 Mason St.
Greenwich, CT   06830

Established in 1997 CT.
Donor(s): Douglas Campbell, Jr.
Grantmaker type: Independent foundation
Financial data (yr. ended 11/30/01): Assets, $2,406,501 (M); gifts received, $502,604; expenditures, $140,227; qualifying distributions, $119,643; giving activities include $122,000 for 4 grants (high: $52,000; low: $10,000).
Purpose and activities: Giving for environmental organizations.
Fields of interest: Environment.
Limitations: Applications not accepted. Giving primarily in CT, MA, and NY. No grants to individuals.
Application information: Contributes only to pre-selected organizations.
Trustee: Douglas Campbell, Jr.
EIN: 061475924

557
The Dibner Fund, Inc. ▼
P.O. Box 7575
Wilton, CT   06897   (203) 761-9904
Contact: Marci B. Sternheim, Ph.D., Exec. Dir.
FAX: (203) 761-9989; E-mail: info@dibnerfund.org

Incorporated in 1957 in CT.
Donor(s): Barbara Dibner,‡ Bern Dibner,‡ David Dibner.
Grantmaker type: Independent foundation
Financial data (yr. ended 12/31/02): Assets, $73,729,737 (M); expenditures, $4,260,469; qualifying distributions, $4,224,872; giving activities include $3,772,739 for 111 grants (high: $873,444; low: $1,000; average: $1,000–$50,000).
Purpose and activities: Support in seven particular areas: environment (emphasis on clean water and rivers); history of science and technology; humanitarian causes; Jewish heritage and culture; peaceful coexistence; science education (emphasis on support for science/math literacy and careers for minorities, and girls/women); also giving for selected community organizations.
Fields of interest: Higher education; Education; Environment; Disasters, preparedness/services; International peace/security; Engineering/technology; Science; Minorities; Native Americans/American Indians.
International interests: Europe; Israel.
Types of support: Program development; Conferences/seminars.
Limitations: Giving primarily in CT, MA, and NY. No support for religious sects or institutions,

or political parties or programs. No grants to individuals, or generally for building or endowment funds, scholarships, fellowships (except through universities, educational agencies and/or specific academic programs) capital expenditures, matching gifts or seed money; no loans.

Publications: Application guidelines, Program policy statement.

Application information: Application form not required.

Initial approach: Letter
Copies of proposal: 1
Deadline(s): None
Board meeting date(s): Quarterly

Officers and Trustees:* David Dibner,* Pres.; Brent Dibner,* V.P.; Frances K. Dibner,* V.P.; Marci B. Sternheim, Ph.D., Exec. Dir.; Michael Cohen; Daniel Dibner; Stephen D. Shapiro; Warren Shine.

Number of staff: 1 full-time professional; 2 full-time support.

EIN: 066038482

Recent environmental and animal welfare grants:

557-1 American Rivers, DC, $30,000. For general support. 2001.

557-2 Columbia University, New York, NY, $112,700. For Earth Engineering Center. 2001.

557-3 Maritime Aquarium at Norwalk, Norwalk, CT, $35,000. For general support. 2001.

557-4 Soil and Water Conservation District of Fairfield County, Fairfield, CT, $25,000. For general support. 2001.

557-5 Trust for Public Land, New Haven, CT, $25,000. For general support. 2001.

557-6 Water Environment Research Foundation, Alexandria, VA, $25,000. For general support. 2001.

558

The Educational Foundation of America ▼
35 Church Ln.
Westport, CT 06880-3515 (203) 226-6498
Contact: Diane M. Allison, Exec. Dir.
E-mail: efa@efaw.org; URL: http://www.efaw.org

Trust established in 1959 in NY.

Donor(s): Richard P. Ettinger,‡ Elsie Ettinger,‡ Richard P. Ettinger, Jr.,‡ Elaine P. Hapgood, Paul R. Andrews,‡ Virgil P. Ettinger.‡

Grantmaker type: Independent foundation

Financial data (yr. ended 12/31/01): Assets, $221,978,974 (M); gifts received, $532,917; expenditures, $17,081,561; qualifying distributions, $12,783,765; giving activities include $14,087,616 for 302 grants (high: $2,100,000; average: $10,000–$60,000).

Purpose and activities: Grants primarily for arts, education, energy and the environment, reproductive health and rights, population, and education programs benefiting Native Americans.

Fields of interest: Arts; Education; Natural resources; Energy; Environment; Family planning; Reproductive rights; Native Americans/American Indians.

Types of support: Program development; Seed money; Matching/challenge support.

Limitations: Giving limited to the U.S. No grants to individuals, annual fund-raising campaigns, or for capital or endowment funds; no loans.

Publications: Application guidelines, Annual report, Grants list.

Application information: Detailed application requirements will accompany letter of invitation to submit a full proposal. Application form not required.

Initial approach: Letter of inquiry only (no more than 2 pages). Letters must be on unbleached 100 percent post-consumer recycled paper using both sides
Copies of proposal: 2
Deadline(s): None
Board meeting date(s): Varies
Final notification: usually within 2 weeks

Officers and Directors:* Elaine P. Hapgood,* Pres.; Lynn P. Babicka,* Co-V.P. and Co-Secy.; Barbara P. Ettinger,* Co-V.P. and Co-Secy.; David L. Godfrey, Fin. Dir.; Diane M. Allison, Exec. Dir.; Jerry Babicka; Barbara Bohart; David W. Ehrenfield; Heidi P. Ettinger; Sharon W. Ettinger; Wendy W.P. Ettinger; John P. Pawers; Frances Stott, Ph.D.

Number of staff: 3 full-time professional; 2 part-time professional; 1 full-time support.

EIN: 133424750

Recent environmental and animal welfare grants:

558-1 Altamaha Riverkeeper, Darien, GA, $96,000. For Watershed Monitoring Project. 2001.

558-2 American Littoral Society, Highlands, NJ, $200,000. For Take Back the Rivers/Take Back the Bays Campaign. 2001.

558-3 As You Sow, San Francisco, CA, $30,000. For dialogue/shareholder action at Coca-Cola Company. 2001.

558-4 As You Sow, San Francisco, CA, $15,000. For investigation of shareholder action at Sysco Systems. 2001.

558-5 Ashoka Trust for Research in Ecology and the Environment, Belmont, MA, $95,000. For education and awareness for conservation, including use of information technologies, web-based instruction, and traditional methods. 2001.

558-6 Cape and Islands Self-Reliance Corporation, East Falmouth, MA, $50,000. For Green Citizens Energy Project. 2001.

558-7 Caribbean Conservation Corporation, Gainesville, FL, $150,000. For Free the Beach Campaign to reduce destruction of Florida's Coastal habitat. 2001.

558-8 Catawba River Foundation, Charlotte, NC, $50,000. For Riverkeeper Program. 2001.

558-9 Center for Health, Environment and Justice, Falls Church, VA, $130,000. For Child Proofing Our Communities. 2001.

558-10 Center for Investigative Reporting, San Francisco, CA, $50,000. For Fund for Investigative Reporting on the Environment (FIRE). 2001.

558-11 Center for Resource Economics/Island Press, DC, $200,000. For Island Press Program on Land Use and Sprawl. 2001.

558-12 Coastal Rainforest Coalition, Berkeley, CA, $50,000. For Paper and Pulp Campaign. 2001.

558-13 Columbia Land Conservancy, Chatham, NY, $500,000. For land acquisition. 2001.

558-14 Connecticut Fund for the Environment, New Haven, CT, $100,000. For Endangered Lands Project. 2001.

558-15 Conservation Law Foundation, Boston, MA, $200,000. For Seascapes Mapping Initiative for marine protected areas. 2001.

558-16 Delaware Valley Citizens Council for Clean Air, Philadelphia, PA, $35,000. For Power Scorecard Outreach Campaign. 2001.

558-17 Duke University, Nicholas School of the Environment and Earth Sciences, Durham, NC, $80,000. For Integrated Marine Conservation Program Summer Term II, Fellowships in Fisheries and Marine Conservation at Marine Laboratory, Beaufort, NC. 2001.

558-18 EarthRights International, DC, $300,000. 2001.

558-19 Environmental Defense, New York, NY, $10,000. For managing reef fish complex in Gulf of Mexico. 2001.

558-20 Fairfield University, Fairfield, CT, $40,000. For efficient controls for large grid-integrated Photovoltaics (PV) installation. 2001.

558-21 Garden Project, San Francisco, CA, $100,000. For general support. 2001.

558-22 Georgia Legal Watch, Athens, GA, $30,000. For Community Watershed Project's Map Catalogue Program. 2001.

558-23 Green Corps, Boston, MA, $100,000. For Environmental Leadership Training Program. 2001.

558-24 Illinois Stewardship Alliance, Rochester, IL, $100,000. For Campaign for Family Farms and the Environment. 2001.

558-25 Iowa Citizens for Community Improvement, Des Moines, IA, $100,000. For Campaign for Family Farms and the Environment. 2001.

558-26 Iowa Citizens for Community Improvement, Des Moines, IA, $100,000. For Campaign for Family Farms and the Environment. 2001.

558-27 Land Stewardship Project, White Bear Lake, MN, $100,000. For Campaign for Family Farms and the Environment. 2001.

558-28 Land Trust Alliance, DC, $160,000. For Land Trust National and Regional Training Project. 2001.

558-29 Meet the Wilderness, Edwards, CO, $22,500. For Adventure Education for Eagle County Schools. 2001.

558-30 Military Toxics Project, Lewiston, ME, $50,000. For Healthy Communities Campaign. 2001.

558-31 Missouri Rural Crisis Center, Columbia, MO, $100,000. For Campaign for Family Farms and Environment. 2001.

558-32 Natural Resources Defense Council, New York, NY, $30,000. For Forests for Tomorrow Initiative. 2001.

558-33 New Jersey Public Interest Research Group, Law and Policy Center, Trenton, NJ, $150,000. For Campaign for New Energy Future. 2001.

558-34 New York Botanical Garden, Bronx, NY, $120,000. For Herbal Therapies for Women's Health. 2001.

558-35 North Carolina Coastal Federation, Newport, NC, $100,000. For ShoreKeeper Program. 2001.

558-36 Northeast Sustainable Energy Association, Greenfield, MA, $25,000. For preparing for renewable energy. 2001.

558-37 Oil and Gas Accountability Project, Durango, CO, $350,000. For Western Coalbed Methane Project. 2001.

558-38 Open Space Institute, New York, NY, $200,000. For Friends of the Hudson for Hudson River Re-Industrialization Project. 2001.

558-39 Pacific Crest Outward Bound, San Francisco, San Francisco, CA, $60,000. For Pinnacle Program. 2001.

558-40 PCL Foundation, Sacramento, CA, $100,000. For Environmental Accountability Program: Increasing Citizen Influence Over Community Land Use Decisions in California. 2001.

558-41 Rainforest Action Network, San Francisco, CA, $80,000. For Old Growth Forest Campaign. 2001.

558-42 River Network, Portland, Oregon, $200,000. To build tribal capacity. 2001.

558-43 Rocky Mountain Institute, Snowmass, CO, $100,000. For Public Information Division. 2001.

558-44 Safe Energy Communication Council, DC, $240,000. For Stop the Nuclear Resurgence and Bailout Project. 2001.

558-45 Save Our Cumberland Mountains Resource Project, Lake City, TN, $120,000. For Forest Organizing Project. 2001.

558-46 Scenic Hudson, Poughkeepsie, NY, $200,000. For campaign to drive a cleanup of Hudson River polychlorinated biphenyl (PCB) contamination and to curb reindustrialization of the Hudson Valley. 2001.

558-47 Seed Savers Exchange, Decorah, IA, $200,000. To redesign, expand, and research Heritage Farm's seed databases. 2001.

558-48 Skylands CLEAN, Ringwood, NJ, $90,000. For CLEAN Membership Campaign. 2001.

558-49 Southern Environmental Law Center, Charlottesville, VA, $250,000. For Hog and Poultry Industry Project. 2001.

558-50 Stony Brook-Millstone Watershed Association, Pennington, NJ, $190,000. For Building Environmental Education Solutions. 2001.

558-51 Sustainable Cotton Project, Oroville, CA, $100,000. For Cleaner Cotton Campaign. 2001.

558-52 Sustainable Energy Advocates Network, DC, $100,000. For Project for Sustainable FERC Energy Policy. Grant made through Natural Resources Defense Council. 2001.

558-53 TreePeople, Beverly Hills, CA, $20,000. For Generation Earth service learning project. 2001.

558-54 Tufts University, Medford, MA, $25,300. To establish Database for Environmental Studies of Canine Lymphoma in Massachusetts. 2001.

558-55 United States Public Interest Research Group Education Fund, DC, $300,000. For Campaign to Cut Polluter Pork and Environmental Defense Campaign. 2001.

558-56 University of California, Santa Barbara, CA, $80,000. For El Pilar: Integrated Education in the Culture of the Maya Forest. 2001.

558-57 University of Chicago, Chicago, IL, $42,000. For Summer Environmental Research Program. 2001.

558-58 Upper Chattahoochee Riverkeeper Fund, Atlanta, GA, $60,000. For Stormwater Pollution Prevention Campaign. 2001.

558-59 Voices and Choices of the Central Carolinas, Voices and Choices of the Central Carolinas, Charlotte, NC, $200,000. For Strategic Regional Open Space Plan (SROSP). Grant made through Foundation for the Carolinas. 2001.

558-60 Western Resource Advocates, Boulder, CO, $200,000. For Southern Rockies Project. 2001.

558-61 Wheelock College, Boston, MA, $50,000. For WhaleNet Program. 2001.

558-62 Wilderness Society, Denver, CO, $150,000. For Colorado Roadless Area Protection Program. 2001.

559
The Ettinger Foundation, Inc.
35 Church Ln.
Westport, CT 06880-3515
Contact: Diane M. Allison, Secy.

Incorporated in 1949 in DE.
Donor(s): Members of the Ettinger family.
Grantmaker type: Independent foundation
Financial data (yr. ended 12/31/01): Assets, $30,817,883 (M); gifts received, $104,626; expenditures, $1,958,724; qualifying distributions, $1,809,478; giving activities include $1,778,119 for 203 grants (high: $260,000; low: $100; average: $1,000–$10,000).
Purpose and activities: Grants for art, environment, reproductive rights, Native Americans, and education.
Fields of interest: Theater; Education; Environment; Reproductive rights; Population studies; Native Americans/American Indians.
Types of support: General/operating support; Program development; Seed money; Matching/challenge support.
Limitations: Applications not accepted. Giving on a national basis. No grants to individuals, or for building or endowment funds; no loans.
Application information:
Board meeting date(s): Varies
Officers and Trustees: Elaine P. Hapgood,* Pres.; Lynn P. Babicka,* V.P.; John P. Powers,* V.P.; Diane M. Allison, Secy.; David L. Godfrey, Treas.; Barbara P. Ettinger; Heidi P. Ettinger; Sharon W. Ettinger.
Number of staff: 1 shared staff.
EIN: 066038938

560
Fairfield County Community Foundation, Inc.
(also known as FCCF)
523 Danbury Rd.
Wilton, CT 06897 (203) 834-9393
Contact: Susan M. Ross, C.E.O. Pres.
FAX: (203) 834-9996; E-mail: info@fccfoundation.org; URL: http://www.fccfoundation.org/

Established in 1992 in CT as a result of the merger of the Five Town Foundation, Danbury Community Endowment, Fairfield County Cooperative Foundation, Greenwich

Foundation for Public Giving, and Stamford Foundation.
Grantmaker type: Community foundation
Financial data (yr. ended 06/30/03): Assets, $46,812,626 (M); gifts received, $8,788,460; expenditures, $8,683,792; giving activities include $7,558,317 for 1,196 grants (high: $500,000; low: $250; average: $250–$250,000) and $195,833 for 8 loans/program-related investments.
Purpose and activities: Grants from discretionary funds primarily support program areas of children, youth and families (with a special emphasis on early childhood education and youth development), economic opportunity (including affordable housing, neighborhood and workforce development), the environment, health, nonprofit organizational effectiveness, and arts and culture. The foundation administers a donor advised fund. The foundation administers donor-advised funds.
Fields of interest: Arts; Early childhood education; Education; Environment; Health care; Housing/shelter; Youth development; Human services; Children/youth, services; Urban/community development; Nonprofit management.
Types of support: General/operating support; Management development; Equipment; Program development; Seed money; Scholarship funds; Technical assistance; Scholarships—to individuals; Matching/challenge support.
Limitations: Giving limited to the Fairfield County, CT, area from discretionary funds; giving throughout the U.S. from grants made from donor advised funds. No support for religious or political purposes, or for parochial, charter or private schools. No grants for endowments, building campaigns, deficit financing, fellowships, annual campaigns, or fundraising events.
Publications: Application guidelines, Annual report, Financial statement, Grants list, Informational brochure, Newsletter, Occasional report.
Application information: Letter of inquiry is required as first step. Full application by invitation only. Application form required.
Initial approach: Letter of inquiry
Copies of proposal: 1
Deadline(s): 3 times yearly
Board meeting date(s): Quarterly
Final notification: 2 weeks after board meeting
Officers and Directors:* Wilmot L. Harris, Jr.,* Chair.; Sheila Perrin,* Vice-Chair.; Charlotte T. Suhler,* Vice-Chair.; Susan M. Ross, C.E.O. and Pres.; Gerard E. Jones,* Secy.; Edwin A. Bescherer, Jr.,* Treas.; and 15 additional directors.
Program Committee: Sheila Perrin, Chair., Progs.
Number of staff: 3 full-time professional; 2 part-time professional; 3 full-time support; 2 part-time support.
EIN: 061083893

561
Betsy and Jesse Fink Foundation
20 Marshall St., Ste. 300
Norwalk, CT 06854-2204

Established in 1999 in CT.
Donor(s): Jesse Fink, Betsy Fink.
Grantmaker type: Independent foundation

Financial data (yr. ended 10/31/02): Assets, $9,606,637 (M); gifts received, $2,700; expenditures, $668,547; qualifying distributions, $381,152; giving activities include $355,000 for 3 grants (high: $200,000; low: $25,000).
Fields of interest: Education; Environment.
Limitations: Applications not accepted. Giving on a national basis. No grants to individuals.
Application information: Contributes only to pre-selected organizations.
Trustees: Betsy Fink; Jesse Fink.
EIN: 137219308

562
The Lawrence Flinn, Jr. Charitable Trust
2 Greenwich Plz., Rm. 150
Greenwich, CT 06830

Established in 1995 in CT.
Donor(s): Lawrence Flinn, Jr.
Grantmaker type: Independent foundation
Financial data (yr. ended 12/31/02): Assets, $18,677,637 (M); expenditures, $940,429; qualifying distributions, $880,760; giving activities include $883,873 for 75 grants (high: $200,000; low: $100).
Purpose and activities: Giving primarily for health care, the arts, education, the environment, health, youth development, community development, and federated giving programs.
Fields of interest: Arts; Education; Natural resources; Hospitals (general); Health care; Health organizations, association; Cancer; Youth development; Human services; Community development; Federated giving programs.
Limitations: Applications not accepted. Giving primarily in CT, FL, and NY. No grants to individuals.
Application information: Contributes only to pre-selected organizations.
Trustees: Lawrence Flinn, Jr.; Stephanie Flinn.
EIN: 137044737

563
Foster-Davis Foundation, Inc.
P.O. Box 1669
Greenwich, CT 06836-1669

Established about 1966.
Donor(s): Alma F. Davis Charitable Lead Trust.
Grantmaker type: Independent foundation
Financial data (yr. ended 12/31/02): Assets, $9,588,708 (M); expenditures, $853,986; qualifying distributions, $792,114; giving activities include $796,349 for 57 grants (high: $50,000; low: $500).
Purpose and activities: Giving primarily to higher education; grants also for research in mental health and biology, recreational facilities, fisheries and wildlife preservation, and health associations.
Fields of interest: Higher education; Animals/wildlife, preservation/protection; Mental health/crisis services; Health organizations, association; Recreation; Biological sciences.
Limitations: Applications not accepted. Giving primarily in CT and NY. No grants to individuals.
Application information: Contributes only to pre-selected organizations.
Board meeting date(s): 3rd week in July

Officers and Directors:* Foster Bam, Pres.; Edward F. Rodenbach,* V.P. and Secy.; Patricia S. Bam, Treas.; Howard S. Tuthill.
Number of staff: None.
EIN: 060811599

564
FSB Foundation, Inc.
c/o Farmington Savings Bank
32 Main St.
Farmington, CT 06032 (860) 677-4541
Contact: John Hangen, Treas.

Established in 1998 in CT.
Donor(s): Farmington Savings Bank.
Grantmaker type: Independent foundation
Financial data (yr. ended 12/31/02): Assets, $2,040,022 (M); gifts received, $256,000; expenditures, $255,534; qualifying distributions, $254,263; giving activities include $254,119 for 123 grants (high: $15,199; low: $100).
Fields of interest: Child development, education; Education; Environment; Family services.
Limitations: Giving limited to residents of Farmington Valley, CT.
Application information:
Initial approach: Letter
Deadline(s): None
Officers and Directors:* Bryan P. Bowerman,* Chair. and Pres.; Brenda O. Kowalski,* Secy.; John H. Hangen,* Treas.; David M. Drew; Robert F. Edmunds, Jr.
EIN: 061523804

565
Garden Homes Fund
29 Knapp St.
P.O. Box 4401
Stamford, CT 06907-1799
Contact: Joel E. Freedman, Tr.

Established in 1981 in CT.
Donor(s): Members of the Joel Freedman family.
Grantmaker type: Independent foundation
Financial data (yr. ended 12/31/02): Assets, $6,203,962 (M); expenditures, $629,211; qualifying distributions, $364,917; giving activities include $364,937 for 91 grants (high: $26,000; low: $100; average: $500–$5,000).
Purpose and activities: Giving primarily to the United Way in areas of Garden Homes Management corporate operations; support also for conservation, education, and social services in Stamford, CT.
Fields of interest: Education; Natural resources; Human services; Federated giving programs.
Types of support: Annual campaigns; Capital campaigns; Building/renovation.
Limitations: Applications not accepted. Giving primarily in CT, NJ, and NY. No grants to individuals.
Application information: Contributes only to pre-selected organizations. Unsolicited requests for funds not accepted.
Trustees: Deborah Freedman; Jane Freedman; Joel E. Freedman; Naomi K. Freedman; Richard Freedman.
Number of staff: None.
EIN: 061043730

566
GE Corporate Giving Program
c/o Corp. Contribs.
3135 Easton Tpke., Bldg. E1A
Fairfield, CT 06431 (203) 373-3216
FAX: (203) 373-3029

Grantmaker type: Corporate giving program
Purpose and activities: As a complement to its foundation, GE also makes charitable contributions to nonprofit organizations directly. Support is given on an international basis.
Fields of interest: Arts; Education; Environment; Health care; Community development; Public affairs; General charitable giving.
International interests: Canada; France; United Kingdom; Germany; Brazil; Chile; India; Japan.
Types of support: General/operating support; Employee volunteer services; Donated equipment; Donated land; Donated products; In-kind gifts.
Limitations: Giving on an international basis in areas of company operations, including in Brazil, Canada, China, France, Germany, India, Japan, and the United Kingdom. No grants to individuals.
Application information: The company has a staff that only handles contributions. Application form not required.
Initial approach: Proposal to nearest company facility
Copies of proposal: 1
Deadline(s): None
Final notification: Varies
Administrator: Robert Corcoran, Pres., GE Foundation.
Number of staff: 6 full-time professional; 4 full-time support.

567
GE Foundation ▼
(formerly GE Fund)
3135 Easton Tpke.
Fairfield, CT 06431 (203) 373-3216
Contact: Robert Corcoran, Pres.
FAX: (203) 373-3029; *E-mail:* gefoundation@ge.com; *URL:* http://www.ge.com/foundation/

Trust established in 1952 in NY.
Donor(s): General Electric Co.
Grantmaker type: Company-sponsored foundation
Financial data (yr. ended 12/31/02): Assets, $11,429 (M); gifts received, $16,215,379; expenditures, $46,352,403; qualifying distributions, $44,569,336; giving activities include $25,918,693 for 426 grants (high: $5,000,000; low: $2,000; average: $5,000–$100,000) and $18,700,233 for 1,824 employee matching gifts.
Purpose and activities: Institutional grants primarily in support of education, with emphasis on: 1) support for minority group preparation for and participation in engineering, computer science, mathematics and business administration; 2) school reform with a focus on increasing college entry and success for disadvantaged students; 3) reading, math and science education; 4) education reform through integration of the arts; 5) public issues research and analysis; and 6) matching educational contributions of employees and retirees. Grants

are directed toward specific programs authorized by the fund directors.

Fields of interest: Arts; Education, association; Education, research; Higher education; Business school/education; Engineering school/education; Environment; Disasters, 9/11/01; International affairs; Federated giving programs; Mathematics; Computer science; Engineering; Public policy, research; Public affairs; Minorities.

Types of support: Continuing support; Program development; Publication; Curriculum development; Fellowships; Scholarship funds; Research; Employee matching gifts.

Limitations: Applications not accepted. Giving on a national and international basis; grants mainly to areas where the company has a significant presence. No support for religious or political purposes. No grants to individuals, including scholarships and research grants, or for capital or endowment funds, or other special purpose campaigns; no loans or equipment donations.

Application information: Proposals reviewed by invitation only; for further details see foundation's Web site.

Board meeting date(s): Quarterly

Officers and Directors:* William J. Conaty,* Chair.; Robert Corcoran,* Pres.; Gisele N. Hill, Secy.; Michael J. Cosgrove, Treas.; Pamela Daley; Benjamin W. Heineman, Jr.; Henry A. Hubschman; Keith S. Sherin; Lloyd G. Trotter.

Number of staff: 6 full-time professional; 1 part-time professional; 4 full-time support.

EIN: 222621967

Recent environmental and animal welfare grants:

567-1 Earth Force, Alexandria, VA, $25,000. 2001.

567-2 Environmental Law Institute, DC, $50,000. 2001.

567-3 Florida Aquarium, Tampa, FL, $25,000. 2001.

567-4 Foundation for Research on Economics and the Environment (FREE), Bozeman, MT, $30,000. 2001.

567-5 Groundwork Bridgeport, Bridgeport, CT, $20,000. 2001.

567-6 Institute for Sustainable Communities, Montpelier, VT, $99,000. 2001.

567-7 Keystone Center, Keystone, CO, $30,000. 2001.

567-8 Louisville Olmsted Parks Conservancy, Louisville, KY, $20,000. 2001.

567-9 Resources for the Future, DC, $25,000. 2001.

567-10 Rio Grande Nature Center, Friends of the, Albuquerque, NM, $25,000. 2001.

567-11 Shaker Lakes Regional Nature Center, Cleveland, OH, $28,500. 2001.

567-12 SoundWaters, Stamford, CT, $20,000. 2001.

567-13 Wisconsin Society for Ornithology, Waukesha, WI, $13,000. 2001.

567-14 World Resources Institute, DC, $50,000. 2001.

567-15 Yellowstone Park Foundation, Bozeman, MT, $36,507. 2001.

568
The Goergen Foundation, Inc.

c/o Thomas E. Finn
35 Mason St.
Greenwich, CT   06830-5420

Established in 1986 in CT.

Donor(s): Robert B. Goergen.

Grantmaker type: Independent foundation

Financial data (yr. ended 12/31/01): Assets, $13,420,353 (M); expenditures, $1,425,202; qualifying distributions, $1,211,426; giving activities include $1,163,931 for grants (average: $100–$1,000).

Purpose and activities: Giving primarily for higher education and educational institutions. Support also for human services.

Fields of interest: Arts; Higher education; Business school/education; Environment; Human services; General charitable giving.

Types of support: General/operating support.

Limitations: Applications not accepted. Giving primarily in CT, NY, and PA. No grants to individuals.

Application information: Contributes only to pre-selected organizations.

Officers and Trustees:* Robert B. Goergen, Pres.; Robert B. Goergen, Jr.,* V.P.; Todd A. Goergen,* V.P.; Pamela J. Goergen, Secy.-Treas.

EIN: 061180035

569
Mabel Burchard Fischer Grant Foundation

c/o Cummings & Lockwood
P.O. Box 120
Stamford, CT   06904
Contact: Malcolm J. Edgerton, Jr. and Robert A. Beer, Trustees
Application address: c/o White & Case, 1155 Ave. of the Americas, New York, NY 10036, tel.: (212) 819-8743

Established in 1990 in CT.

Donor(s): Mabel B. Grant.‡

Grantmaker type: Independent foundation

Financial data (yr. ended 04/30/03): Assets, $4,531,119 (M); expenditures, $369,416; qualifying distributions, $291,315; giving activities include $262,075 for 59 grants (high: $10,000; low: $2,500).

Purpose and activities: Giving primarily for natural resources conservation and to a law school; funding also for the arts, children, youth and social services, and Lutheran and Roman Catholic organizations and churches.

Fields of interest: Arts; Law school/education; Natural resources; Human services; Children/youth, services; Protestant agencies & churches; Roman Catholic agencies & churches.

Limitations: Giving primarily in CT. No grants to individuals.

Application information:
Initial approach: Letter
Deadline(s): None

Trustees: Robert A. Beer; Malcolm J. Edgerton, Jr.

EIN: 066351343

570
Stewart & Constance Greenfield Foundation

279 Sturges Hwy.
Westport, CT   06880-3212

Established in 1987 in CT.

Donor(s): Stewart H. Greenfield.

Grantmaker type: Independent foundation

Financial data (yr. ended 12/31/01): Assets, $3,904,436 (M); gifts received, $320,970; expenditures, $209,024; qualifying distributions, $162,750; giving activities include $162,750 for 57 grants (high: $10,000; low: $250).

Fields of interest: Museums; Arts; College; Natural resources; Animals/wildlife, preservation/protection; Human services; Jewish agencies & temples.

Limitations: Applications not accepted. Giving on a national basis. No grants to individuals.

Application information: Contributes only to pre-selected organizations.

Officer: Stewart H. Greenfield, Mgr.

EIN: 066301506

571
The Gryphon Fund

36 Drumlin Rd.
West Simsbury, CT   06092-2906
Contact: Helen B. Kaplan, Tr.

Established in 1993 in CT.

Donor(s): Schiro Fund, Inc.

Grantmaker type: Independent foundation

Financial data (yr. ended 12/31/02): Assets, $2,087,959 (M); gifts received, $9,126; expenditures, $130,286; qualifying distributions, $124,815; giving activities include $125,100 for 77 grants (high: $5,000; low: $250).

Fields of interest: Environment; Human services.

Limitations: Giving primarily in the greater Hartford, CT, area.

Application information: Application form not required.
Initial approach: Proposal
Deadline(s): None

Trustees: David H. Kaplan; Helen B. Kaplan.

EIN: 223199039

572
Halvorsen Family Foundation

c/o Ole Andreas Halvorsen
500 Hollow Tree Ridge Rd.
Darien, CT   06820

Established in 2000 in CT.

Donor(s): Ole Andreas Halvorsen.

Grantmaker type: Independent foundation

Financial data (yr. ended 11/30/02): Assets, $2,922,858 (M); expenditures, $110,000; qualifying distributions, $110,000; giving activities include $110,000 for 14 grants (high: $25,000; low: $1,000).

Fields of interest: Higher education; Education; Environment; Hospitals (general).

Limitations: Applications not accepted. Giving primarily in CT. No grants to individuals.

Application information: Contributes only to pre-selected organizations.

Trustees: Diane K. Halvorsen; Ole Andreas Halvorsen.

EIN: 061603158

573
John and Kelly Hartman Foundation
c/o Cummings & Lockwood
185 Asylum St.
Hartford, CT 06103-3402
Contact: Paul L. Bourdeau, Tr.

Established in 1992 in FL.
Donor(s): John W. Hartman, Esther Kelly B. Hartman.
Grantmaker type: Independent foundation
Financial data (yr. ended 03/31/02): Assets, $5,510,870 (M); gifts received, $411,917; expenditures, $122,766; qualifying distributions, $90,000; giving activities include $90,000 for 5 grants (high: $30,000; low: $5,000).
Purpose and activities: Giving primarily for a museum, education and the environment.
Fields of interest: Museums; Higher education; Environment.
Limitations: Giving on a national basis. No grants to individuals.
Application information:
Initial approach: Letter
Deadline(s): None
Trustees: Larry Biehl; Paul L. Bourdeau; Esther Kelly B. Hartman; John W. Hartman.
EIN: 223139258

574
The Huisking Foundation, Inc.
P.O. Box 369
Botsford, CT 06404-0369
Contact: Frank R. Huisking, Treas.

Incorporated in 1946 in NY.
Donor(s): Claire F. Hanavan, Richard V. Huisking, Jean M. Steinschneider, Members of the Huisking family and family-related corporations.
Grantmaker type: Independent foundation
Financial data (yr. ended 12/31/02): Assets, $20,242,783 (M); expenditures, $1,109,011; qualifying distributions, $998,202; giving activities include $1,030,250 for 366 grants (high: $32,000; low: $150).
Purpose and activities: Giving primarily for arts and culture, education, the environment, animal protection, health and hospitals, human services, federated giving programs, and religious purposes.
Fields of interest: Media/communications; Museums; Performing arts; Historic preservation/historical societies; Higher education; Education; Natural resources; Animal welfare; Hospitals (general); Health organizations, association; Medical research, institute; Human services; Federated giving programs; Roman Catholic agencies & churches.
Types of support: General/operating support; Continuing support; Building/renovation; Endowments; Program development; Scholarship funds; Research.
Limitations: Giving on a national basis. No grants to individuals.
Application information: Application form not required.
Initial approach: Letter
Copies of proposal: 1
Deadline(s): Submit proposal in Feb. and Aug.
Board meeting date(s): Apr. and Nov.
Officers and Directors:* John E. Haigney,* Pres.; Richard V. Huisking, Jr.,* V.P.; William W.

Huisking, Jr.,* V.P.; Frank R. Huisking,* Treas.; Laura S. Colebank; Helen H. Crawford; Robert P. Daly; Robert P. Daly, Jr.; Claire-Marie Field; Claire F. Hanavan; Charles L. Huisking III; Paul Huisking; Jean M. Steinschneider.
Number of staff: None.
EIN: 136117501

575
International Paper Company Foundation ▼
400 Atlantic St.
Stamford, CT 06921
Contact: Phyllis Epp, Exec. Dir.
FAX: (203) 541-8309; URL: http://www.internationalpaper.com/our_world/philanthropy/index.asp

Incorporated in 1952 in NY.
Donor(s): International Paper Co.
Grantmaker type: Company-sponsored foundation
Financial data (yr. ended 12/31/02): Assets, $38,766,263 (M); gifts received, $5,343,492; expenditures, $7,524,998; qualifying distributions, $7,327,645; giving activities include $6,788,531 for 1,085 grants (high: $500,000; low: $85; average: $500–$50,000), $553,442 for 1,211 employee matching gifts and $522,637 for 800 in-kind gifts.
Purpose and activities: Grants are primarily for projects in company communities with focus on pre-college levels of education, specifically environmental, economic, and literacy. Grants are also considered for organizations where full-time employees are active volunteers.
Fields of interest: Elementary school/education; Secondary school/education; Reading; Education; Environment.
Types of support: Continuing support; Program development; Curriculum development; Employee matching gifts.
Limitations: Giving primarily in communities where there are company operations. No support for athletic organizations or religious groups. No grants to individuals, or for endowment funds or capital expenses; no loans.
Publications: Application guidelines.
Application information: Address requests from organizations in company communities to the local company contact person. Application form required.
Initial approach: Proposal with application to local facility
Copies of proposal: 1
Deadline(s): Varies among local facilities
Board meeting date(s): Sept.
Officers and Directors:* Aleesa Blum,* Pres.; Carol Tusch, Treas.; Phyllis Epp, Exec. Dir.; John Faraci; James P. Melican, Jr.; Marianne Parrs; Dennis Thomas.
Trustee: State Street Bank and Trust Co.
Number of staff: 2 full-time professional; 2 part-time professional; 1 part-time support.
EIN: 136155080
Recent environmental and animal welfare grants:
575-1 Alcorn State University, Lorman, MS, $18,750. For pre-college environmental education programs. 2001.
575-2 American Forest Foundation, DC, $20,000. For environmental education programs. 2001.

575-3 American Forest Foundation, DC, $15,000. For environmental education programs. 2001.
575-4 Atlantic Salmon Federation, Calais, ME, $50,000. For environmental programs. 2001.
575-5 Audubon Society, National, New York, NY, $25,000. For community environmental education programs. 2001.
575-6 Bruce Museum, Greenwich, CT, $10,000. For community environmental education programs. 2001.
575-7 Chesapeake Bay Foundation, Harrisburg, PA, $10,000. For pre-college environmental education programs. 2001.
575-8 Childrens Museum of the Shoals, Florence, AL, $40,000. For environmental programs. 2001.
575-9 Congressional Sportsmens Caucus Foundation, DC, $10,000. For community environmental education programs. 2001.
575-10 Conservation Fund, Arlington, VA, $20,000. For environmental programs. 2001.
575-11 Conservation Fund, Arlington, VA, $10,000. For environmental programs. 2001.
575-12 Discovery 2000, Birmingham, AL, $25,000. For community environmental education programs. 2001.
575-13 Ducks Unlimited, Memphis, TN, $10,000. For pre-college environmental education programs. 2001.
575-14 Earths Birthday Project, Santa Fe, NM, $50,000. For pre-college environmental education programs. 2001.
575-15 Empire State Forestry Foundation, Albany, NY, $20,000. For community environmental education programs. 2001.
575-16 Environmental Education Fund, Raleigh, NC, $35,000. For pre-college environmental education programs. 2001.
575-17 Florida Forestry Association, Tallahassee, FL, $10,000. For environmental education programs. 2001.
575-18 Four-H Foundation, Arkansas, Little Rock, AR, $25,000. For environmental programs. 2001.
575-19 Future Farmers of America Foundation, National, Alexandria, VA, $15,000. For pre-college environmental education programs. 2001.
575-20 Georgia Department of Transportation, Atlanta, GA, $20,000. For environmental programs. 2001.
575-21 Georgia Environmental Organization, Atlanta, GA, $11,750. For environmental education programs. 2001.
575-22 Izaak Walton League of America, Gaithersburg, MD, $10,000. For environmental programs. 2001.
575-23 Keep America Beautiful of the Midlands, Columbia, SC, $35,000. For environmental programs. 2001.
575-24 Loveland City School District, Loveland, OH, $20,513. For pre-college environmental education programs. 2001.
575-25 Maine Tree Foundation, Winslow, ME, $20,000. For community environmental education programs. 2001.
575-26 Maritime Aquarium at Norwalk, Norwalk, CT, $30,000. For community environmental education programs. 2001.
575-27 Memphis Botanic Garden Foundation, Memphis, TN, $10,000. For pre-college environmental education programs. 2001.

575-28 Memphis Museums, Memphis, TN, $31,250. For community environmental education programs. 2001.

575-29 Michigan Technological University, Houghton, MI, $25,000. For environmental education in higher education programs. 2001.

575-30 Miramichi Salmon Association, Boston, MA, $35,000. For environmental programs. 2001.

575-31 Museum of Discovery and Science, Fort Lauderdale, FL, $25,000. For environmental programs. 2001.

575-32 Nature Conservancy, Arlington, VA, $25,000. For environmental programs. 2001.

575-33 Nature Conservancy, Arlington, VA, $14,000. For environmental education programs. 2001.

575-34 North Carolina Forestry Foundation, Raleigh, NC, $10,240. For Employee Involvement Grant. 2001.

575-35 North Carolina Forestry Foundation, Raleigh, NC, $10,000. For higher education programs. 2001.

575-36 Paul D. Camp Community College, Franklin, VA, $10,000. For pre-college environmental education programs. 2001.

575-37 Resources for the Future, DC, $25,000. For environmental programs. 2001.

575-38 Smithsonian Tropical Research Institute, Panama, $25,000. For environmental programs. 2001.

575-39 Society of American Foresters, Bethesda, MD, $35,000. For higher education programs. 2001.

575-40 South Carolina Forestry Foundation, Columbia, SC, $14,000. For pre-college environmental education programs. 2001.

575-41 Syracuse Pulp and Paper Foundation at the College of Forestry, Syracuse, NY, $10,000. For environmental education in higher education programs. 2001.

575-42 Texas Forestry Association Educational Fund, Lufkin, TX, $15,000. For pre-college environmental education programs. 2001.

575-43 Texas Forestry Museum, Lufkin, TX, $15,000. For community environmental education programs. 2001.

575-44 Virginia Resource Use Education Council, Richmond, VA, $25,308. For community environmental education programs. 2001.

575-45 West Side Cultural Center, Saint Paul, MN, $10,000. For environmental programs. 2001.

575-46 World Resources Institute, DC, $15,000. For environmental initiatives. 2001.

576
The Hope Goddard Iselin Foundation
c/o Patricia F. Davidson
65 Parker Hill Ext.
Killingworth, CT 06419-2311

Established in 1972 in NY.
Donor(s): Hope Goddard Iselin.‡
Grantmaker type: Independent foundation
Financial data (yr. ended 03/31/02): Assets, $2,984,931 (M); expenditures, $207,792; qualifying distributions, $158,145; giving activities include $150,000 for 2 grants (high: $100,000; low: $50,000).

Purpose and activities: Support primarily for outdoor beautification and recreation projects.
Fields of interest: Historic preservation/historical societies; Natural resources; Environment; Recreation.
Types of support: Building/renovation; Endowments; Program development.
Limitations: Applications not accepted. Giving primarily in the eastern U.S. No grants to individuals.
Publications: Multi-year report.
Application information: Contributes only to pre-selected organizations closely allied with the donor's interests. Funds are committed four years in advance.
Trustees: Patricia F. Davidson; U.S. Trust.
Number of staff: None.
EIN: 136583545

577
Larsen Fund
2537 Post Rd., Ste. 224
Southport, CT 06890
Contact: Patricia S. Palmer

Incorporated in 1941 in NY.
Donor(s): Roy E. Larsen.‡
Grantmaker type: Independent foundation
Financial data (yr. ended 12/31/01): Assets, $12,869,339 (M); expenditures, $982,619; qualifying distributions, $791,803; giving activities include $693,233 for 108 grants (high: $67,000; low: $500).
Purpose and activities: Support for education, including medical and secondary schools, educational research, computer sciences, and social sciences; human services, including youth, family services, and family planning; hospitals and population studies; law, justice and urban affairs; intercultural relations; conservation, ecology, and wildlife preservation; and the arts.
Fields of interest: Museums; Theater; Education, research; Secondary school/education; Higher education; Medical school/education; Libraries/library science; Natural resources; Environment; Animals/wildlife, preservation/protection; Hospitals (general); Family planning; Crime/law enforcement; Children/youth, services; Family services; Race/intergroup relations; Community development; Computer science; Social sciences; Population studies; Public affairs.
Types of support: Annual campaigns; Capital campaigns; Land acquisition; Program development; Professorships; Curriculum development; Fellowships; Internship funds; Scholarship funds; Research.
Limitations: Applications not accepted. Giving primarily in CT, MA, the Minneapolis, MN, area, and the New York, NY, area. No grants to individuals.
Publications: Annual report.
Application information: Unsolicited requests for funds not accepted.
  Board meeting date(s): Beginning of June and Dec.
Officers and Directors:* Christopher Larsen,* Pres.; Jonathan Z. Larsen,* V.P.; Susan Z. Ritz,* V.P.; Ann Larsen Simonson,* V.P.; Todd H. Larsen,* Secy.; Gordon H. Ritz,* Treas.
Number of staff: 2 part-time support.
EIN: 136104430

578
The Leever Foundation, Inc.
c/o Waterbury Foundation
81 W. Main St.
Waterbury, CT 06702 (203) 753-1315
Contact: C. O'Donnell
E-mail: Codonnell@waterburyfoundation.org

Established in 1991 in CT.
Donor(s): Harold Leever,‡ Ruth Ann Leever.
Grantmaker type: Independent foundation
Financial data (yr. ended 12/31/02): Assets, $5,071,601 (M); gifts received, $376,230; expenditures, $223,185; qualifying distributions, $216,651; giving activities include $185,795 for 22 grants (high: $85,000; low: $500; average: $500–$85,000).
Fields of interest: Scholarships/financial aid; Environmental education; Health care; Youth, services; Federated giving programs.
Types of support: Capital campaigns; Seed money.
Limitations: Giving primarily in greater Waterbury, CT. No grants to individuals.
Publications: Application guidelines, Program policy statement.
Application information: Must be pre-approved to submit an application. Unsolicited requests for funds not accepted. Application form required.
  Initial approach: Letter or telephone
  Copies of proposal: 8
  Deadline(s): Generally in Feb., May and Oct.
  Board meeting date(s): Feb., May, and Oct.
  Final notification: Feb., May, and Oct.
Officer: Ruth Ann Leever, Chair.
Directors: Suzanne Leever Hart; Andrew Leever; Daniel Leever; Thomas Leever.
Number of staff: 1 shared staff (shared with Waterbury Foundation).
EIN: 223115036

579
The LittleJohn Family Foundation
648 Smith Ridge Rd.
New Canaan, CT 06840

Donor(s): Angus C. LittleJohn, Jr.
Grantmaker type: Independent foundation
Financial data (yr. ended 12/31/02): Assets, $1,495,386 (M); expenditures, $99,200; qualifying distributions, $99,200; giving activities include $98,500 for 7 grants (high: $50,000; low: $1,000).
Fields of interest: Museums (children's); Elementary/secondary education; Environment.
Limitations: Applications not accepted. Giving primarily in CT and PA. No grants to individuals.
Application information: Contributes only to pre-selected organizations.
Officer: Angus C. LittleJohn, Jr., Mgr.
EIN: 133948281

580
George A. and Grace L. Long Foundation
c/o Fleet Foundation and Philanthropic Svcs.
777 Main St., CTEH40222B
Hartford, CT 06115 (860) 952-7405
Contact: Marjorie Alexandre Davis, V.P., Fleet National Bank

Trust established in 1960 in CT.

Donor(s): George A. Long,‡ Grace L. Long.‡
Grantmaker type: Independent foundation
Financial data (yr. ended 12/31/02): Assets, $9,601,127 (M); expenditures, $701,948; qualifying distributions, $676,580; giving activities include $614,766 for 164 grants (high: $10,000; low: $750) and $6,000 for 2 employee matching gifts.
Purpose and activities: Primary areas of interest include the arts, education, health services, community development, and family services.
Fields of interest: Arts; Early childhood education; Child development, education; Adult/continuing education; Education; Environment; Hospitals (general); Health care; Health organizations, association; AIDS; AIDS research; Human services; Children/youth, services; Child development, services; Family services; Aging, centers/services; Community development; Minorities; Disabled; Aging.
Types of support: General/operating support; Continuing support; Program development; Technical assistance.
Limitations: Giving limited to CT. No grants to individuals, or for operating budgets or endowment funds; no loans.
Publications: Informational brochure (including application guidelines).
Application information: Application form required.
  Initial approach: Letter or telephone
  Copies of proposal: 2
  Deadline(s): Mar. 15 and Sept. 15
  Board meeting date(s): May and Dec.
Trustee: Alan S. Parker.
EIN: 066030953

581
Mad River Foundation
c/o Blair & Potts
P.O. Box 1214
Stamford, CT 06904-1214
Contact: Peter H. Blair, Secy.-Treas.

Incorporated in 1961 in DE.
Donor(s): Godfrey A. Rockefeller.‡
Grantmaker type: Independent foundation
Financial data (yr. ended 12/31/02): Assets, $2,377,879 (M); expenditures, $170,158; qualifying distributions, $144,590; giving activities include $144,000 for 57 grants (high: $22,000; low: $500).
Purpose and activities: Support primarily for higher and secondary education; support also for wildlife conservation and religious organizations.
Fields of interest: Secondary school/education; Higher education; Education; Animals/wildlife, preservation/protection; Christian agencies & churches.
Limitations: Applications not accepted. Giving on a national basis, with some emphasis along the East Coast. No grants to individuals.
Application information: Contributes only to pre-selected organizations.
  Board meeting date(s): Between Jan. 1 and Feb. 28
Officer and Directors:* Peter H. Blair,* Secy.-Treas.; Audrey R. Blair; Godfrey A. Rockefeller; Marion R. Stone.
EIN: 136097034

582
The McKenzie Foundation, Inc.
114 John St.
Greenwich, CT 06831 (203) 861-7525
Contact: Kathryn H. Smith, Dir.
URL: http://www.mckenziefoundation.us

Established in 1998 in CT.
Grantmaker type: Independent foundation
Financial data (yr. ended 09/30/02): Assets, $11,760,268 (M); expenditures, $530,014; qualifying distributions, $486,999; giving activities include $467,623 for 35 grants (high: $60,000; low: $623).
Purpose and activities: Giving for art and cultural programs, education, and health care.
Fields of interest: Multipurpose centers/programs; Elementary/secondary education; Scholarships/financial aid; Education; Environment.
Types of support: General/operating support; Equipment; Program development; Scholarship funds.
Limitations: Giving on a national basis.
Application information: Application form not required.
  Initial approach: Letter of inquiry
  Deadline(s): None
  Board meeting date(s): Aug.
  Final notification: Generally by Sept. 20; interim notification for smaller requests
Officers and Directors:* Richard C. McKenzie, Jr.,* Pres.; Margaret Byrne McKenzie,* Secy.-Treas.; Eileen Grace McKenzie Baylis; James Richard McKenzie; Jennifer Kathleen McKenzie; Maria Prawdzik; Kathryn H. Smith.
Number of staff: 1 part-time professional.
EIN: 061508410

583
Meek Foundation
777 Main St. CTEH4022B
Hartford, CT 06115 (860) 952-7405
Contact: Marjorie Davis, Grants Off.

Established in 1947 in CT.
Grantmaker type: Independent foundation
Financial data (yr. ended 12/31/02): Assets, $2,267,692 (M); expenditures, $174,175; qualifying distributions, $150,765; giving activities include $107,400 for 192 grants (high: $6,000; low: $150).
Purpose and activities: Giving primarily for education and environmental conservation.
Fields of interest: Education; Natural resources; Hospitals (general); Religion.
Limitations: Applications not accepted. Giving primarily in New England. No grants to individuals.
Application information: Contributes only to pre-selected organizations.
Trustees: Samuel W. Meek, Jr.; Elizabeth M.J. Peterson; Fleet National Bank.
EIN: 066033662

584
The Melville Foundation
P.O. Box 1810
8 Sound Shore Dr.
Greenwich, CT 06836-1810
Contact: Harry Burn III, Tr.

Established in 1986 in CT.
Donor(s): Harry Burn III.
Grantmaker type: Independent foundation
Financial data (yr. ended 12/31/02): Assets, $1,742,122 (M); expenditures, $190,118; qualifying distributions, $189,150; giving activities include $186,750 for 16 grants (high: $100,000; low: $5,000).
Purpose and activities: Giving for historical and environmental conservation, higher education, boys and girls clubs and Christian organizations.
Fields of interest: Higher education; Education; Environment; Children/youth, services; Christian agencies & churches.
Limitations: Applications not accepted. Giving primarily in CT and VA. No grants to individuals.
Application information: Contributes only to pre-selected organizations.
Trustees: Harry Burn III; Jean Burn.
EIN: 222777140

585
Middlesex County Community
Foundation, Inc.
211 S. Main St.
P.O. Box 25
Middletown, CT 06457-0025 (860) 347-0025
Contact: Patti Anne Vassia, Pres.
FAX: (860) 347-0029; *E-mail:* info@middlesexcountycf.org; *URL:* http://www.middlesexcountycf.org

Established in 1997 in CT.
Grantmaker type: Community foundation
Financial data (yr. ended 12/31/02): Assets, $1,699,323 (M); gifts received, $490,556; expenditures, $387,097; giving activities include $143,635 for 36 grants (high: $68,734; low: $500).
Purpose and activities: Giving to support the arts, the environment, women and girls issues, heritage advancement, community improvement, and services to help the less fortunate.
Fields of interest: Arts; Environment, pollution control; Human services; Community development; Women.
Limitations: Giving primarily in Middlesex County, CT. No grants to individuals.
Publications: Annual report, Financial statement.
Application information: Application form required.
  Initial approach: Telephone call
  Deadline(s): Fall for letter of intent
Officers: Janes S. McMillan, Funds Chair.; Ralph H. Shaw II, Board Chair.; W. Campbell Hudson III, Vice-Chair.; Patti Anne Vassia, Pres.; Sari Rosenbaum, Secy.; Patrick J. Crowley, Treas.
Directors: Marcia Bromberg; Herbert T. Clark III; Suzanne D. Kitchings; Robert L. Kirkpatrick, Jr.; Joseph G. Lombardo; Willard McRae; Elisabeth Petry; Sari A. Rosenbaum; Joan S. Young.
Number of staff: 1 full-time professional; 2 part-time professional; 1 part-time support.
EIN: 061477711

586

New Canaan Community Foundation, Inc.
P.O. Box 1285
New Canaan, CT 06840 (203) 966-0231
Contact: Judy Bentley, V.P., Distribs.
FAX: (203) 972-9671; E-mail:
cgorey@newcanaancf.org; URL: http://
www.americantowns.com/nccf

Established in 1978.
Donor(s): Alex G. Nason Foundation, Theodore and Veda Stanley Foundation.
Grantmaker type: Community foundation
Financial data (yr. ended 12/31/01): Assets, $4,682,092 (M); gifts received, $87,224; expenditures, $263,479; giving activities include $216,400 for 14 grants (high: $50,000; low: $1,500; average: $100–$50,000).
Purpose and activities: The New Canaan Community Foundation was founded in 1977 with the mission of supporting the human needs and charitable interests in New Canaan. The Foundation implements this mission by serving the community in a variety of roles, acting as a grantmaker, a steward for cost effective management of donor funds, and as a resource developer for the community. The foundation administers donor-advised funds.
Fields of interest: Museums; Historical activities; Libraries (public); Education; Environment; Health care; Parks/playgrounds; Recreation; Youth development, adult & child programs; Human services; YM/YWCAs & YM/YWHAs; Children/youth, services; Family services; Community development.
Types of support: Capital campaigns; Building/renovation; Equipment; Program development; Seed money; Program-related investments/loans.
Limitations: Giving limited to New Canaan, CT and the surrounding towns.
Publications: Annual report, Informational brochure.
Application information: Application guidelines available on Web site. Application form required.
   Initial approach: Contact foundation
   Copies of proposal: 20
   Deadline(s): Sept. 15
   Board meeting date(s): Oct. and Nov.
   Final notification: By Jan.
Officers and Directors:* Harry T. Rein,* Pres.; Vincent Ferullo, V.P., Devel.; Sherri Kielland, V.P., Develop.; Judy Bentley,* V.P., Distribs.; Timothy Throckmorton, Secy.; Jeffrey Shaw,* Treas.; Lois Anderson; Simone Demou; Joseph Dionne; Sheryl Dunleavy; Jane Fox; Wendy Hilboldt; David Kilbride; Katherine Lenoue; Donald Luke; Deborah Simpson; Hudson Stoddard.
Number of staff: 1 part-time professional.
EIN: 060970466

587

Newman's Own, Inc. Corporate Giving Program
246 Post Rd. E.
Westport, CT 06880-3615
URL: http://www.newmansown.com/5_good.html

Grantmaker type: Corporate giving program

Purpose and activities: Newman's Own makes charitable contributions to nonprofit organizations involved with arts and culture, education, the environment, hunger, affordable housing, disaster relief, children, and senior citizens. Support is given on a national and international basis.
Fields of interest: Arts; Education; Environment; Food services; Housing/shelter; Disasters, preparedness/services; Children, services; Aging.
International interests: Canada; United Kingdom; Germany; Iceland; Israel; Japan; Australia.
Types of support: General/operating support.
Limitations: Giving on a national and international basis, including in Australia, Canada, Germany, Iceland, Israel, Japan, and the United Kingdom.

588

Laura J. Niles Foundation
c/o Foundation Svcs., LLC
35 Mason St., 2nd Fl.
Greenwich, CT 06830 (203) 629-8552
FAX: (203) 629-0806; E-mail: ljn @fsllc.net;
URL: http://www.ljniles.org

Established in 1993 in CT.
Grantmaker type: Independent foundation
Financial data (yr. ended 12/31/02): Assets, $20,854,352 (M); expenditures, $1,885,310; qualifying distributions, $1,652,911; giving activities include $1,338,555 for 29 grants (high: $55,000; low: $5,000).
Purpose and activities: The foundation supports efforts that offer learning and economic growth opportunities for the motivated poor; giving also for projects that foster life enrichment through canine and other types of animal companionship.
Fields of interest: Education; Animals/wildlife; Employment; Children/youth, services.
Limitations: Giving primarily in the northeastern U.S. No grants to individuals.
Publications: Application guidelines.
Application information: Online application available on website. Application form required.
Officers and Directors:* Geoffrey M. Parkinson,* Pres.; A. Daniel D'Ambrosio,* V.P.; Leland C. Selby,* Secy.; James R. Lamb,* Treas.
EIN: 223188304

589

Northeast Utilities Foundation, Inc.
P.O. Box 5563
Hartford, CT 06102-5563 (860) 721-4117
Contact: Natalie Brown, Special Progs. Svcs. Rep.
FAX: (860) 721-4013; E-mail:
brownnm@nu.com; URL: http://www.cl-p.com/community/partners/grants/nufoundation.asp

Established in 1998 in CT.
Donor(s): The Connecticut Light and Power Co., Northeast Nuclear Energy Co., Northeast Utilities, Public Service Co. of New Hampshire, Western Massachusetts Electric Co.
Grantmaker type: Company-sponsored foundation
Financial data (yr. ended 12/31/00): Assets, $245,146 (M); gifts received, $2,057,431; expenditures, $1,543,519; qualifying

distributions, $1,543,519; giving activities include $1,471,685 for grants.
Purpose and activities: The foundation's areas of focus are: 1) Education, 2) Civic and community, including job training, economic development, and housing, 3) Human services, including social and health services and income aid, 4) Environment, and 5) Culture and the arts.
Fields of interest: Arts; Education; Environment; Health care; Employment, training; Housing/shelter; Human services; Economic development; Community development.
Limitations: Giving primarily in areas of company operations. No support for religious organizations, political groups or candidates, or fraternal or veterans' groups, unless project would benefit the community. No grants to individuals, or for fundraising or charitable events, or scholarships.
Application information: Application form can be downloaded from the foundation's Web site. Application form required.
   Initial approach: Completed application form and attachments
   Deadline(s): Jan. 5, Mar. 30, June 29, and Oct. 5
   Board meeting date(s): Feb., Apr., July, and Nov.
Officers and Directors:* John B. Keane,* Chair. and Pres.; Theresa H. Allsop, Secy. and Exec. Dir.; David R. McHale, Treas.; John H. Forsgren; Charles E. Gooley; Cheryl W. Grise; Bruce D. Kenyon; Hugh C. MacKenzie; Michael G. Morris.
EIN: 061527290

590

The October Hill Foundation
17 Taunton Ridge Rd.
Newtown, CT 06470

Established in 1994 in DE.
Donor(s): Gretchen A. Bauta.
Grantmaker type: Independent foundation
Financial data (yr. ended 12/31/02): Assets, $9,544,546 (M); expenditures, $494,777; qualifying distributions, $482,113; giving activities include $483,000 for 21 grants (high: $260,000; low: $1,000).
Purpose and activities: Giving primarily for animal welfare and environmental conservation.
Fields of interest: Natural resources; Animal welfare; Human services.
Types of support: General/operating support.
Limitations: Applications not accepted. Giving primarily in the U.S. and Canada. No grants to individuals.
Application information: Contributes only to pre-selected organizations.
Officers: Gretchen A. Bauta, Pres.; Christian Bauta, V.P. and Secy.; Humberto P. Bauta, V.P. and Treas.; Nicholas Bauta, V.P.; Pilar Bauta, V.P.
EIN: 137049883

591

Olin Corporation Charitable Trust
501 Merritt 7
P.O. Box 4500
Norwalk, CT 06856-4500 (203) 750-3301
Contact: Carmella V. Piacentini, Admin.

Trust established in 1945 in MO.

Donor(s): Olin Corp.
Grantmaker type: Company-sponsored foundation
Financial data (yr. ended 12/31/02): Assets, $64,783 (M); expenditures, $496,777; qualifying distributions, $481,514; giving activities include $369,418 for 126 grants (high: $50,000; low: $50) and $37,466 for 99 employee matching gifts.
Purpose and activities: Emphasis on science and engineering in higher education, business education, environmental studies, conservation programs, community programs in education, human services and the environment. Support also for a wide variety of programs such as precollege education, volunteerism, and environmental education. The trust matches employee gifts to education and arts and culture and awards scholarships to children of employees through the National Merit Scholarship Corporation.
Fields of interest: Secondary school/education; Higher education; Engineering school/education; Natural resources; Environmental education; Environment; Animals/wildlife, preservation/protection; Health care; Substance abuse, services; Safety/disasters; Youth, services; Civil rights; Federated giving programs; Physical/earth sciences; Chemistry; Mathematics; Engineering/technology; Engineering; Science; Economics; Minorities; African Americans/Blacks.
Types of support: General/operating support; Continuing support; Annual campaigns; Capital campaigns; Building/renovation; Equipment; Land acquisition; Emergency funds; Program development; Conferences/seminars; Seed money; Curriculum development; Fellowships; Internship funds; Scholarship funds; Research; Employee matching gifts; Matching/challenge support.
Limitations: Giving primarily in areas of company operations in AL, CT, GA, IL, IN, NY, and TN. No grants to individuals, or for endowment funds; no loans.
Application information: Application form not required.
　Initial approach: Letter or proposal
　Copies of proposal: 1
　Deadline(s): Submit proposal preferably between Jan. and Aug.; no set deadline
　Board meeting date(s): Dec.
　Final notification: 2 to 3 months
Trustees: Donald W. Griffin; Peter C. Kosche, Jr.; Wachovia Bank, N.A.
Number of staff: 1 full-time professional; 1 part-time support.
EIN: 436022750

592
Operation Fuel, Inc.
26 Wintonbury Ave.
Bloomfield, CT　06002　(860) 243-2345
Contact: Patricia J. Wrice, Exec. Dir.
URL: http://www.operationfuel.org

Established in 1997 in CT.
Grantmaker type: Public charity
Financial data (yr. ended 06/30/01): Revenue, $1,030,700; assets, $262,021; gifts received, $1,019,574; expenditures, $1,007,695; program services expenses, $875,272; giving activities

include $777,838 for 50 grants (high: $144,682; low: $25).
Purpose and activities: The organization provides emergency energy assistance to state residents who do not qualify for government assistance in their time of need.
Fields of interest: Energy; Human services.
Limitations: Giving primarily in CT.
Officers and Directors:* Carl A. Zinsser,* Chair.; Mary Hart,* Vice-Chair.; Shirley G. Dion,* Secy.; Patricia J. Wrice, Exec. Dir.; Theresa Allsop; David Asselin; Lucy Davis; Robert F. Gorman; Edythe Latney; Lucy E. Ramirez; and 4 additional directors.
EIN: 061253091

593
The Robert & Margaret Patricelli Family Foundation
22 Waterville Rd.
Avon, CT　06001-2066
Contact: Robert F. Patricelli, Chair.

Established in 1996 in CT.
Donor(s): Robert E. Patricelli, Margaret S. Patricelli.
Grantmaker type: Independent foundation
Financial data (yr. ended 06/30/02): Assets, $4,188,677 (M); expenditures, $848,523; qualifying distributions, $804,974; giving activities include $764,377 for 97 grants (high: $500,000; low: $25).
Purpose and activities: Giving primarily to the arts; also giving to higher education, social services and health care.
Fields of interest: Arts; Education, formal/general education; Higher education; Education; Natural resources; Health care; Human services.
Types of support: General/operating support; Annual campaigns; Program development; Research.
Limitations: Giving primarily in CT. No grants to individuals, or for capital campaigns.
Publications: Application guidelines.
Application information: Application form not required.
　Deadline(s): None
Officers: Robert E. Patricelli, Chair.; Margaret S. Patricelli, Pres.
Directors: Alison J. Patricelli; Thomas R. Patricelli.
Number of staff: 1 part-time professional.
EIN: 061487230

594
The Perrin Family Foundation
4 Prospect St.
Ridgefield, CT　06877-4510　(203) 438-7349
Contact: Nancy Holland
FAX: (203) 438-5062; *E-mail:* info@perrinfamilyfoundation.org; *URL:* http://www.perrinfamilyfoundation.org

Established in 1994 in CT.
Donor(s): Charles Perrin, Sheila Perrin.
Grantmaker type: Independent foundation
Financial data (yr. ended 12/31/01): Assets, $16,966,996 (M); expenditures, $774,144; qualifying distributions, $1,019,171; giving activities include $666,870 for 35 grants (high:

$50,000; low: $1,000; average: $1,000–$25,000).
Purpose and activities: Giving for education, health and cultural services for children.
Fields of interest: Arts; Education; Environment, formal/general education; Health care; Children, services; Family services.
Types of support: General/operating support; Continuing support; Program development; Seed money.
Limitations: Giving primarily in Fairfield County, CT. No grants to individuals.
Publications: Application guidelines, Informational brochure (including application guidelines).
Application information: Proposals accepted from organizations providing direct services to children. Application form required.
　Initial approach: Letter of intent
　Copies of proposal: 1
　Deadline(s): None
　Board meeting date(s): Biannually
　Final notification: Within 3 months of receiving application
Officer and Trustees:* Sheila A. Perrin,* Pres.; Charles R. Perrin; David B. Perrin; Jeffrey L. Perrin.
Number of staff: 1 part-time support.
EIN: 223309886

595
Praxair Foundation, Inc.
39 Old Ridgebury Rd.
Danbury, CT　06810-5113

Established in 1994.
Donor(s): Praxair, Inc.
Grantmaker type: Company-sponsored foundation
Financial data (yr. ended 11/30/01): Assets, $1,083,980 (M); expenditures, $1,379,365; qualifying distributions, $1,379,220; giving activities include $1,357,611 for 120 grants (high: $500,000; low: $35; average: $1,000–$50,000).
Purpose and activities: Preference is given to supporting well-defined projects in the following areas: (1) Higher education, with emphasis on science, engineering and environmental studies, including programs that encourage minority students to pursue studies in these areas; (2) community service, focused on matching employee donations to the United Way, public libraries to assist in upgrading their technology, acquiring new materials or initiating innovative programs, and employee volunteer grants; and (3) public policy and the environment.
Fields of interest: Higher education; Engineering school/education; Libraries (public); Environmental education; Environment; Community development; Federated giving programs; Science; Public policy, research; Minorities.
Types of support: Program development; Scholarship funds; Employee matching gifts.
Limitations: Giving primarily in the U.S. in areas of company operations; international giving also in countries where Praxair is expanding its presence, primarily in Asia. No grants to individuals.
Application information: See foundation Web site for funding request form. Application form required.

Officers and Directors:* Nigel D. Moir,* Pres.; Anna M. Hillman, Treas.; Robert Bassett; George P. Ristevski; S. Mark Seymour.
EIN: 061413665

596
The Prentice Foundation, Inc.
35 Church Ln.
Westport, CT 06880
Contact: Diane H. Allison, Exec. Dir.

Established in 1994 in CT.
Donor(s): Elaine P. Hapgood.
Grantmaker type: Independent foundation
Financial data (yr. ended 12/31/01): Assets, $22,879,971 (M); gifts received, $93,420; expenditures, $1,513,636; qualifying distributions, $1,366,692; giving activities include $1,347,709 for 89 grants (high: $222,000; low: $50).
Purpose and activities: Giving primarily for environmental programs.
Fields of interest: Education; Environment; Population studies; Government/public administration.
Types of support: Program development; Seed money; Matching/challenge support.
Limitations: Applications not accepted. Giving on a national basis. No grants to individuals, or for capital campaigns or endowments; no loans.
Application information: Contributes only to pre-selected organizations.
Board meeting date(s): Varies
Officers: Elaine Hopgood, Pres.; Lynn P. Babicka, V.P.; John P. Powers, V.P.
EIN: 061386173

597
Faye and Mike Richardson Charitable Trust
c/o J. Michael Richardson
33 Joshuatown Rd.
Old Lyme, CT 06371 (860) 434-3349

Established in 1994 in CT.
Donor(s): Michael Richardson.
Grantmaker type: Independent foundation
Financial data (yr. ended 06/30/03): Assets, $1,274,373 (M); expenditures, $106,526; qualifying distributions, $104,000; giving activities include $104,000 for 2 grants (high: $100,000; low: $4,000).
Fields of interest: Environment; Christian agencies & churches.
Limitations: Giving primarily in CT. No grants to individuals.
Application information: Application form required.
Initial approach: Proposal
Deadline(s): None
Trustees: Faye Richardson; J. Michael Richardson; Peter Richardson; Thomas Richardson.
EIN: 137044993

598
Lewis G. Schaeneman, Jr. Foundation, Inc.
1 Hamden Ctr.
2319 Whitney Ave.
Hamden, CT 06518

Established in 1998 in CT.
Donor(s): Lewis G. Schaeneman, Jr.‡
Grantmaker type: Independent foundation
Financial data (yr. ended 12/31/01): Assets, $8,199,703 (M); gifts received, $245,106; expenditures, $395,804; qualifying distributions, $287,330; giving activities include $151,285 for 30 grants (high: $15,000; low: $200).
Fields of interest: Education; Animals/wildlife; Human services; Children/youth, services; Roman Catholic federated giving programs.
Limitations: Applications not accepted. No grants to individuals.
Application information: Contributes only to pre-selected organizations.
Officers and Directors:* Lewis G. Schaeneman III,* Pres.; William S. Cowell,* Secy.; Laura Burrows.
EIN: 061390923

599
Robert F. & Marilyn H. Schumann Foundation
P.O. Box 813
Madison, CT 06443 (203) 245-7250
Contact: Robert F. Schumann, Tr.

Established in 1981.
Donor(s): Robert F. Schumann.
Grantmaker type: Independent foundation
Financial data (yr. ended 10/31/02): Assets, $1,130 (M); gifts received, $609,915; expenditures, $495,189; qualifying distributions, $491,128; giving activities include $496,650 for 75 grants (high: $100,000; low: $100).
Fields of interest: Higher education; Natural resources; Environment; Animals/wildlife, preservation/protection; Human services; Arms control; Federated giving programs.
Types of support: Continuing support; Capital campaigns; Program development.
Application information: Application form not required.
Initial approach: Proposal
Deadline(s): None
Trustees: Marilyn H. Schumann; Robert F. Schumann.
Number of staff: None.
EIN: 222424499

600
The Scrooby Foundation
c/o D. Ben Benoit
157 Church St., 26th Fl.
New Haven, CT 06510

Established in 1995 in MN.
Donor(s): Frederick Brewster.
Grantmaker type: Independent foundation
Financial data (yr. ended 06/30/02): Assets, $5,767,643 (M); gifts received, $500,000; expenditures, $340,457; qualifying distributions, $315,480; giving activities include $287,000 for 17 grants (high: $50,000; low: $1,000).

Purpose and activities: Giving primarily for scientific, environmental, zoological, historical, and medical research purposes.
Fields of interest: Museums; Historical activities; Elementary/secondary education; University; Natural resources; Environment; Zoos/zoological societies; Housing/shelter, development; Human services; Children, services.
Limitations: Applications not accepted. Giving on a national basis. No grants to individuals.
Application information: Contributes only to pre-selected organizations.
Officers and Directors:* Frederick Brewster,* Pres.; Priscilla Brewster,* V.P.; Marvin J. Pertzik,* Secy.-Treas.; Allison Brewster; Barbara B. Johnson; Eric L. Johnson; Edwin J. McCarthy; Susan B. McCarthy.
Agent: Fleet National Bank.
EIN: 411795397

601
Elmina B. Sewall Foundation
234 Church St., Rm. 1003
New Haven, CT 06510
Contact: William E. Curran, Treas.

Established in 1983 in ME.
Donor(s): Elmina B. Sewall.
Grantmaker type: Independent foundation
Financial data (yr. ended 09/30/02): Assets, $13,477,732 (M); expenditures, $997,711; qualifying distributions, $944,426; giving activities include $950,500 for 86 grants (high: $72,000; low: $1,000).
Purpose and activities: Giving for animal welfare, social services and youth, conservation, arts, and historical preservation.
Fields of interest: Historic preservation/historical societies; Arts; Higher education; Environment, plant conservation; Environment; Animal welfare; Animals/wildlife, preservation/protection; Human services; Children/youth, services.
Types of support: Continuing support; Annual campaigns.
Limitations: Applications not accepted. Giving primarily in New England. No grants to individuals.
Application information: Contributes only to pre-selected organizations. Unsolicited requests for funds not accepted.
Board meeting date(s): 2nd Thurs. in May and Sept.
Officers and Directors:* Elmina B. Sewall,* Pres.; Margaret Sewall Barbour,* V.P.; Harold E. Woodsum, Jr.,* Secy.; William E. Curran,* Treas.; Helen Brewster; Pamela Brewster Duffy; David E. Norris; James S. Zoldy, Jr.
Number of staff: None.
EIN: 010387404

602
Smart Family Foundation ▼
74 Pin Oak Ln.
Wilton, CT 06897-1329 (203) 834-0400
Contact: Raymond L. Smart, Pres.

Trust established in 1951 in IL.
Donor(s): David A. Smart,‡ A.D. Elden,‡ Vera Elden,‡ John Smart,‡ Edgar G. Richards,‡ Florence Richards.‡

Grantmaker type: Independent foundation
Financial data (yr. ended 12/31/01): Assets,
$168,327,786 (M); expenditures, $8,880,214;
qualifying distributions, $7,417,381; giving
activities include $7,100,001 for 100 grants
(high: $744,772; low: $3,000; average:
$10,000–$100,000).
Purpose and activities: The foundation is
primarily interested in education projects and
has, in particular, been focusing on projects that
affect primary and secondary school children.
Fields of interest: Elementary school/education;
Secondary school/education; Education.
Types of support: Seed money; Research;
Program-related investments/loans.
Limitations: No grants to individuals.
Application information: Unsolicited
applications are discouraged. Application form
not required.
   Initial approach: 1-page letter fully describing
      project and cost
   Copies of proposal: 1
   Deadline(s): Jan. 1 and June 1
   Board meeting date(s): Fall and spring
   Final notification: Within 6 weeks after board
      meetings
Officers and Directors:* Robert Feitler,* Chair.;
Raymond L. Smart,* Pres.; Mary Smart,* Secy.;
William Oswald,* Treas.; Joan Feitler; Ellen
Smart Oswald; David Stone.
Number of staff: 1 full-time professional; 1
part-time support.
EIN: 061232323
**Recent environmental and animal welfare
grants:**
602-1 Conservation International, DC,
   $114,000. For general operating support of
   programs protecting elephants. 2001.
602-2 Conservation International Brazil, Brazil,
   $111,164. For general operating support.
   2001.
602-3 New York-New Jersey Trail Conference,
   Mahwah, NJ, $75,000. For continued general
   operating support. 2001.
602-4 Peninsula Open Space Trust, Menlo Park,
   CA, $250,000. For continued general
   operating support. 2001.
602-5 Santa Barbara Botanic Gardens, Santa
   Barbara, CA, $35,000. For general operating
   support. 2001.
602-6 Save the Bay, Providence, RI, $150,000.
   For general operating support. 2001.

603
The Sontheimer Foundation, Inc.
P.O. Box 4219
Greenwich, CT   06831-0404

Established in 1988 in CT.
Donor(s): Shirley M. Sontheimer, Carl G.
Sontheimer.
Grantmaker type: Independent foundation
Financial data (yr. ended 11/30/02): Assets,
$970,672 (M); gifts received, $250,000;
expenditures, $181,731; qualifying distributions,
$181,227; giving activities include $182,080 for
67 grants (high: $30,000; low: $100).
Purpose and activities: Giving for education,
food services, disasters, human services, and
federated giving programs.
Fields of interest: Arts; Higher education;
Education; Environment; Food services;
Disasters, fire prevention/control; Human

services; Children/youth, services; Federated
giving programs.
Limitations: Giving primarily in Greenwich, CT,
and MA. No grants to individuals.
Officers: Shirley M. Sontheimer, Pres.; Albert O.
Czikowsky, V.P.
EIN: 222940503

604
Sun Hill Foundation
c/o Fred F. French Investing, LLC
Metro Ctr., 1 Station Pl.
Stamford, CT   06902   (203) 353-5320
Contact: Donald R. Milligan

Established in 1992 in CT as partial successor to
the Tudor Foundation.
Grantmaker type: Independent foundation
Financial data (yr. ended 03/31/01): Assets,
$8,830,987 (M); gifts received, $1,000,000;
expenditures, $1,695,113; qualifying
distributions, $1,562,255; giving activities
include $1,580,332 for 45 grants (high:
$666,666; low: $2,000; average:
$10,000–$50,000).
Purpose and activities: Giving primarily to
Jewish organizations, conservation programs,
and educational programs.
Fields of interest: Education; Natural resources;
Human services; Jewish agencies & temples.
Limitations: Giving primarily in the Northeast.
No grants to individuals.
Application information: Funds are currently
awarded based on recommendations and
approval of board members. Application form
not required.
   Deadline(s): None
Officers: Susan R. Malloy, Pres.; Timon J.
Malloy, Secy.; Jennifer Malloy Combs, Treas.
EIN: 061326091

605
The Wade F. B. Thompson Charitable
Foundation, Inc.
261 Old Black Point Rd.
Niantic, CT   06357
Contact: Wade F.B. Thompson, V.P.

Established in 1986 in CT.
Donor(s): Wade F.B. Thompson.
Grantmaker type: Independent foundation
Financial data (yr. ended 05/31/02): Assets,
$4,788,039 (M); gifts received, $386,480;
expenditures, $156,725; qualifying distributions,
$154,700; giving activities include $148,250 for
41 grants (high: $50,000; low: $250).
Purpose and activities: Giving for historic
preservation, arts and culture, education, the
environment and medical research, specifically
research devoted to finding a cure for prostate
cancer.
Fields of interest: Historic preservation/historical
societies; Arts; Education; Environment; General
charitable giving.
Types of support: General/operating support;
Annual campaigns; Building/renovation; Land
acquisition; Seed money.
Limitations: Applications not accepted. Giving
primarily in CT and the greater New York, NY,
area. No grants to individuals.
Application information: Contributes only to
pre-selected organizations.

Officers and Directors:* Angela E. Thompson,*
Pres.; Wade F.B. Thompson,* V.P.; Alan Siegel,
Secy.; Amanda J.T. Riegel; Charles A.Y.
Thompson.
Number of staff: None.
EIN: 061194385

606
The Leonard & Claire Tow Charitable
Trust, Inc.
c/o Citizens Communications
3 High Ridge Park
Stamford, CT   06905

Established in 1999 in CT.
Donor(s): Claire Tow, Leonard Tow.
Grantmaker type: Independent foundation
Financial data (yr. ended 12/31/02): Assets,
$303,915 (M); gifts received, $3,450,000;
expenditures, $3,396,731; qualifying
distributions, $3,395,212; giving activities
include $3,390,830 for 19 grants (high:
$140,000; low: $230).
Fields of interest: Theater; Arts; Higher
education; Botanical gardens; Environment;
Hospitals (specialty); Cancer; Health
organizations; Human services; Children,
services; Federated giving programs.
Limitations: Applications not accepted. Giving
primarily in the metropolitan NY, NJ, and CT
area. No grants to individuals.
Application information: Contributes only to
pre-selected organizations.
Officers: Leonard Tow, Chair.; Claire Tow, Pres.;
David Rosensweig, Secy.; Scott N. Schneider,
Treas.; Emily Tow Jackson, Exec. Dir.
Director: Frank Tow.
EIN: 066484045

607
Emily Hall Tremaine Foundation, Inc. ▼
290 Pratt St.
Meriden, CT   06450   (203) 639-5544
Contact: Stewart J. Hudson, Pres.
FAX: (203) 639-5545; E-mail:
info@tremainefoundation.org; URL: http://
www.tremainefoundation.org

Established in 1987 in CT.
Donor(s): Emily Hall Tremaine,‡ Burton G.
Tremaine, Sr.,‡ Burton G. Tremaine, Jr.‡
Grantmaker type: Independent foundation
Financial data (yr. ended 12/31/02): Assets,
$75,743,404 (M); expenditures, $4,329,571;
qualifying distributions, $4,039,861; giving
activities include $3,214,895 for 169 grants
(high: $150,000; low: $500; average:
$5,000–$100,000).
Purpose and activities: The foundation seeks to
fund innovative projects that advance practical
solutions to basic problems in our society. With
an overall emphasis on education principally in
the United States, it takes an active role in the
arts, the environment, and in learning
disabilities.
Fields of interest: Arts; Environment; Learning
disorders.
Types of support: General/operating support;
Continuing support; Program development;
Conferences/seminars; Publication; Seed
money; Curriculum development; Technical
assistance; Matching/challenge support.

Limitations: Applications not accepted. No grants to individuals or for building funds, research projects, or experimental demonstrations.
Publications: Biennial report.
Application information:
Board meeting date(s): 3 times a year
Officers and Directors:* Burton G. Tremaine III,* Chair and Secy.; Stewart J. Hudson,* Pres.; Atwood Collins III,* Treas.; Arthur J. Bulger, Jr.; Dorothy Tremaine Hildt; Janet Tremaine Stanley; John M. Tremaine; Sarah C. Tremaine; K. Bryant Wick, Jr.
Number of staff: 3 full-time professional; 1 part-time support.
EIN: 222533743

608
Tsunami Foundation
c/o Anson M. Beard, Jr.
241 Bedford Rd.
Greenwich, CT   06831

Established in 1993 in CT.
Donor(s): Anson McCook Beard, Jr.
Grantmaker type: Independent foundation
Financial data (yr. ended 12/31/02): Assets, $6,030,947 (M); expenditures, $449,775; qualifying distributions, $319,512; giving activities include $310,417 for 23 grants (high: $30,000; low: $17).
Fields of interest: Arts; Education; Natural resources; Hospitals (general); Parks/playgrounds; Human services.
Limitations: Applications not accepted. Giving primarily in the New England region; giving also in PA and ID.
Application information: Unsolicited requests for funds not accepted.
Trustees: Anson McCook Beard, Jr.; Jean Jones Beard.
EIN: 137019761

609
The Tyrrell Foundation, Inc.
c/o Dawson Giammalva Capital Mgmt., Inc.
354 Pequot Ave.
Southport, CT   06490
Contact: Judith A. Mack, V.P. and Secy.

Established in 1996 in CT.
Donor(s): Jonathan T. Dawson.
Grantmaker type: Independent foundation
Financial data (yr. ended 12/31/02): Assets, $16,909,412 (M); gifts received, $430,900; expenditures, $987,894; qualifying distributions, $909,497; giving activities include $812,912 for 9 grants (high: $320,000; low: $5,000).
Fields of interest: Elementary school/education; Environment, forests; Children, services.
Limitations: Applications not accepted. Giving on a national basis. No grants to individuals.
Application information: Contributes only to pre-selected organizations.
Officers and Directors:* Jonathan T. Dawson,* Pres. and Treas.; Judith A. Mack,* V.P. and Secy.
Number of staff: 1 part-time professional.
EIN: 061469527

610
The United Illuminating Company Contributions Program
157 Church St.
New Haven, CT   06506
Contact: Jean Stevenson, Grants Admin.

Grantmaker type: Corporate giving program
Purpose and activities: As a complement to its foundation, United Illuminating also makes charitable contributions to nonprofit organizations directly. Support is given primarily in Connecticut.
Fields of interest: Arts; Environment; Youth development; Community development.
Types of support: Sponsorships; Employee matching gifts; In-kind gifts.
Limitations: Giving primarily in CT.

611
Lawson Valentine Foundation
1000 Farmington Ave.
West Hartford, CT   06107   (860) 570-0728
Contact: Valentine Doyle, Prog. Off.

Established in 1989 in CT.
Donor(s): Alice P. Doyle.‡
Grantmaker type: Independent foundation
Financial data (yr. ended 12/31/02): Assets, $14,069,432 (M); expenditures, $1,250,642; qualifying distributions, $1,140,316; giving activities include $1,052,700 for 63 grants (high: $101,000; low: $1,000; average: $1,000–$10,000).
Purpose and activities: Primary areas of interest include human rights, environmental and economic justice, and food systems, including sustainable agriculture.
Fields of interest: Environment, legal rights; Agriculture, soil/water issues; Agriculture/food; International human rights; Civil rights, advocacy.
Types of support: General/operating support; Continuing support; Program development; Seed money; Technical assistance.
Limitations: Giving limited to the northeastern U.S. No support for religious activities, schools, or land trusts. No grants to individuals.
Publications: Application guidelines, Program policy statement.
Application information: Certified mail and express mail not accepted.
Initial approach: Letter
Copies of proposal: 1
Deadline(s): None
Board meeting date(s): Spring and fall
Final notification: After board meetings
Trustees: Allen Doyle; Valentine Doyle; Mark Lindeman; Lucy Miller; Paul E. Vawter; William D. Zabel.
Number of staff: 2 part-time professional.
EIN: 136920044

612
R. T. Vanderbilt Trust
c/o H.B. Vanderbilt
30 Winfield St.
Norwalk, CT   06855-1329

Trust established in 1951 in CT.
Grantmaker type: Independent foundation

Financial data (yr. ended 12/31/02): Assets, $8,161,422 (M); expenditures, $547,647; qualifying distributions, $501,980; giving activities include $473,582 for 88 grants (high: $50,000; low: $500).
Purpose and activities: Emphasis on education and conservation; support also for hospitals, cultural programs, and historic preservation.
Fields of interest: Historic preservation/historical societies; Arts; Education; Natural resources; Hospitals (general); Family planning.
Types of support: General/operating support; Building/renovation; Endowments; Program development.
Limitations: Applications not accepted. Giving primarily in CT and NY. No grants to individuals.
Application information: Contributes only to pre-selected organizations.
Board meeting date(s): Apr., June, Sept., and Dec.
Officer and Trustees:* Hugh B. Vanderbilt, Jr.,* Chair.; P. Venderbilt; R.T. Vanderbilt.
Number of staff: 2 part-time support.
EIN: 066040981

613
Vervane, Inc.
171 Cat Rock Rd.
Cos Cob, CT   06807
Contact: Josephine Merck, Pres.

Established in 1993 in CT.
Donor(s): Josephine Merck.
Grantmaker type: Independent foundation
Financial data (yr. ended 12/31/02): Assets, $7,215,405 (M); gifts received, $1,999,998; expenditures, $537,453; qualifying distributions, $482,186; giving activities include $467,000 for 16 grants (high: $15,000; low: $5,000).
Fields of interest: Arts; Environment.
Types of support: General/operating support; Land acquisition.
Limitations: Applications not accepted. Giving primarily in CT, NJ, NY, and RI. No grants to individuals.
Application information: Contributes only to pre-selected organizations.
Board meeting date(s): Dec.
Officers and Directors:* Josephine Merck,* Pres.; Tom Passios,* Secy.-Treas.; Oona Coy.
EIN: 223256829

614
The Walker Family Foundation
360 New Canaan Rd.
Wilton, CT   06897

Established in 1999 in CT.
Grantmaker type: Independent foundation
Financial data (yr. ended 03/31/02): Assets, $1,806,570 (M); expenditures, $2,560,028; qualifying distributions, $2,577,589; giving activities include $2,580,032 for 32 grants (high: $1,722,334; low: $50).
Purpose and activities: Giving primarily to higher education, nature conservation, federated giving programs, and performing arts.
Fields of interest: Higher education; Natural resources; Environment; Recreation; Human services; Federated giving programs.

Limitations: Giving in the U.S., with emphasis on New York, NY.
Application information:
Deadline(s): None
Trustees: Jeffrey Walker; Suzanne Walker.
EIN: 061543752

615
Wilmot Wheeler Foundation, Inc.
P.O. Box 429
Southport, CT 06490
Contact: Wilmot F. Wheeler, Jr., Pres.

Incorporated in 1941 in DE.
Donor(s): Wilmot F. Wheeler,‡ Hulda C. Wheeler.
Grantmaker type: Independent foundation
Financial data (yr. ended 06/30/02): Assets, $5,462,121 (M); expenditures, $440,016; qualifying distributions, $339,582; giving activities include $326,790 for 123 grants (high: $33,500; low: $100).
Purpose and activities: Giving primarily for educational and Episcopalian organizations and churches.
Fields of interest: Arts; Secondary school/education; Higher education; Environment; Animals/wildlife; Health care; Human services; Protestant agencies & churches.
Limitations: Applications not accepted. Giving primarily in CT. No grants to individuals.
Application information: Contributes only to pre-selected organizations.
Officers: Wilmot F. Wheeler, Jr., Pres.; Alexandra Wheeler, V.P.; Alexa M. Wheeler, Secy.; Halsted W. Wheeler, Treas.
EIN: 066039119

616
The David, Helen, and Marian Woodward Fund-Watertown
(also known as Marian W. Ottley Trust-Watertown)
Box 817
Watertown, CT 06795-0817
Contact: M. Heminway Merriman, Selection Comm.

Trust established in 1975 in GA.
Donor(s): Marian W. Ottley.‡
Grantmaker type: Independent foundation
Financial data (yr. ended 05/31/02): Assets, $17,737,790 (M); expenditures, $1,258,445; qualifying distributions, $1,156,303; giving activities include $1,125,567 for 39 grants (high: $100,000; low: $700).
Purpose and activities: Giving primarily for secondary, elementary, and early childhood education, social services, health services, and libraries. Support for building funds for education and hospitals.
Fields of interest: Museums; Education, fund raising; Early childhood education; Elementary school/education; Secondary school/education; Libraries/library science; Education; Environment; Hospitals (general); Medical care, rehabilitation; Health care; Health organizations, association; Human services; Youth, services; Hospices; Christian agencies & churches; Native Americans/American Indians.

Types of support: Capital campaigns; Building/renovation; Equipment; Endowments; Scholarship funds.
Limitations: Giving limited to local organizations in New England and NY. No support for institutions of higher education, or organizations lacking 501(c)(3) tax-exempt status. No grants to individuals, or for general operating funds; generally no multi-year grants.
Publications: Application guidelines.
Application information: Education awards limited to the pre-collegiate level. Application form not required.
Initial approach: 2-page letter
Copies of proposal: 3
Deadline(s): May 15
Board meeting date(s): May
Selection Committee: Anne Fitzgerald; M. Heminway Merriman; William J. Zito, M.D.
Trustee: First National Bank of Atlanta.
Number of staff: None.
EIN: 586222005

617
The Worthington Family Foundation, Inc.
P.O. Box 4231
Greenwich, CT 06831
Contact: Worthington Johnson, Jr., Treas.

Established in 1991 in CT.
Donor(s): Worthington Johnson.‡
Grantmaker type: Independent foundation
Financial data (yr. ended 12/31/02): Assets, $8,779,653 (M); gifts received, $555,000; expenditures, $480,543; qualifying distributions, $452,000; giving activities include $452,000 for 36 grants (high: $45,260; low: $1,000).
Fields of interest: Arts; Education; Animal welfare; Aquariums; Substance abuse, services; Boys & girls clubs; Children/youth, services.
Types of support: Capital campaigns; Building/renovation; Equipment.
Limitations: Giving primarily in the Northeast, with emphasis on CT and MA. No grants to individuals, or for travel, meals, or lodging for conferences or symposia.
Application information: Application form not required.
Initial approach: Proposal
Deadline(s): Oct. 1
Officers and Directors:* Marina Johnson Sutro,* Pres.; Joan Johnson Stott,* Secy.; Worthington Johnson, Jr.,* Treas.
EIN: 223100891

DELAWARE

618
Beckwith Family Foundation
c/o J.P. Morgan Svcs., Inc.
P.O. Box 6089
Newark, DE 19714-6089
Contact: John E. Trabucco, Secy.
Application address: P.O. Box 435, Murraysville, PA 15668-0435, tel.: (724) 325-9205

Established in 1999 in PA.
Donor(s): Virginia P. Beckwith.‡

Grantmaker type: Independent foundation
Financial data (yr. ended 09/30/02): Assets, $6,840,642 (M); expenditures, $431,110; qualifying distributions, $425,039; giving activities include $424,720 for 11 grants (high: $166,500; low: $220).
Purpose and activities: Giving primarily for education, and human services.
Fields of interest: Education; Botanical gardens; Hospitals (general); Human services; YM/YWCAs & YM/YWHAs.
Limitations: Giving primarily in PA. No grants to individuals.
Application information:
Initial approach: Proposal
Deadline(s): None
Officers and Trustees:* G. Nicholas Beckwith III,* Pres.; John E. Trabucco, Secy.; James S. Beckwith III,* Treas.
EIN: 311607888

619
Edward E. and Lillian H. Bishop Foundation
c/o Wilmington Trust Co.
1100 North Market St.
Wilmington, DE 19890-0001
Contact: Richard Pratt, Tr.

Trust established in 1953 in DE.
Donor(s): Lillian H. Bishop.
Grantmaker type: Independent foundation
Financial data (yr. ended 12/31/02): Assets, $5,960,754 (M); expenditures, $407,589; qualifying distributions, $376,864; giving activities include $369,010 for 34 grants (high: $288,510; low: $500).
Fields of interest: Museums; Animal welfare; Human services; Children/youth, services; Human services; Federated giving programs; Astronomy.
Types of support: General/operating support.
Limitations: Giving primarily in Manatee County, FL.
Publications: Informational brochure (including application guidelines).
Application information: Application form required.
Initial approach: Letter
Deadline(s): Nov. 15
Board meeting date(s): Dec.
Final notification: Positive responses only
Trustees: Robert Blalock; Mary Parker; Richard Pratt; Willett E. Wentzell, M.D.; Woodrow Young; Wilmington Trust Co.
EIN: 516017762

620
Lillian H. Bishop Trust A for the SPCA of Manatee County, Florida
c/o Wilmington Trust Co.
1100 N. Market St.
Wilmington, DE 19890-0001

Established in 1973 in DE.
Grantmaker type: Independent foundation
Financial data (yr. ended 12/31/02): Assets, $16,305,133 (M); expenditures, $1,011,004; qualifying distributions, $960,313; giving activities include $930,656 for 9 grants (high: $285,000; low: $20,000).

Purpose and activities: Grants primarily for animal welfare associations and a museum; support also for human services and youth groups.

Fields of interest: Museums; Animal welfare; Girls clubs; YM/YWCAs & YM/YWHAs; Community development, service clubs.

Limitations: Applications not accepted. Giving primarily in Manatee County, FL. No grants to individuals.

Application information: Contributes only to pre-selected organizations.

Trustee: Wilmington Trust Co.

EIN: 237334266

621
H. W. Buckner Charitable Residuary Trust ▼

c/o J.P. Morgan Services, Inc.
P.O. Box 6089
Newark, DE 19714-6089

Established in 1991 in DE.

Donor(s): Helen W. Buckner.‡

Grantmaker type: Independent foundation

Financial data (yr. ended 12/31/01): Assets, $10,459,744 (M); expenditures, $2,907,805; qualifying distributions, $2,861,908; giving activities include $2,859,014 for 106 grants (high: $500,000; low: $1,000; average: $5,000–$50,000).

Purpose and activities: Support primarily for education and cultural organizations.

Fields of interest: Music; Higher education; Education; Natural resources; Human services; Youth, services.

Limitations: Giving primarily in MA, NY, and RI. No grants to individuals.

Trustee: J.P. Morgan Chase Bank.

Advisory Committee: Elizabeth Buckner; Thomas W. Buckner; Walker G. Buckner, Jr.; Mary B. Shea.

Number of staff: None.

EIN: 516179860

Recent environmental and animal welfare grants:

621-1 Association for the Protection of the Adirondacks, Schenectady, NY, $10,000. For general support. 2001.

621-2 Cetacean Research Unit, Gloucester, MA, $10,000. For general support. 2001.

621-3 Damariscotta River Association, Damariscotta, ME, $10,000. For general support. 2001.

621-4 Edmund Niles Huyck Preserve, Rensselaerville, NY, $12,000. For general support. 2001.

621-5 Forest Watch, Montpelier, VT, $10,000. For general support. 2001.

621-6 Francis Small Heritage Trust, Limerick, ME, $10,000. For general support. 2001.

621-7 Green Mountain Club, Waterbury Center, VT, $212,500. For general support. 2001.

621-8 National Wildlife Federation, Montpelier, VT, $15,000. For general support. 2001.

621-9 Natural Resources Council, Augusta, ME, $10,000. For general support. 2001.

621-10 Neponset River Watershed Association, Canton, MA, $10,000. For general support. 2001.

621-11 New England Aquarium Corporation, Boston, MA, $10,000. For general support. 2001.

621-12 New England Wild Flower Society, Framingham, MA, $10,000. For general support. 2001.

621-13 Northern Appalachian Restoration Project, Lancaster, NH, $12,000. For general support. 2001.

621-14 Oyster River Bog, Rockport, ME, $10,000. For general support. 2001.

621-15 Sheepscot Wellspring Land Alliance, Freedom, ME, $25,000. For general support. 2001.

621-16 Society for the Protection of New Hampshire Forests, Concord, NH, $19,085. For general support. 2001.

621-17 Thousand Islands Land Trust, Clayton, NY, $10,000. For general support. 2001.

621-18 Trust for Public Land, Portland, ME, $15,000. For general support. 2001.

621-19 Trust for Public Land, Boston, MA, $100,000. For general support of Connecticut Headwaters Land Conservation Project in New Hampshire. 2001.

621-20 Vermont Natural Resources Council, Montpelier, VT, $10,200. For general support. 2001.

621-21 Wilderness Society, Boston, MA, $12,000. For general support. 2001.

621-22 Wildlands Project, Richmond, VT, $10,000. For general support. 2001.

621-23 Wildlands Project, Wild Earth, Richmond, VT, $11,000. For general support. 2001.

622
The Cawley Family Foundation

1100 N. King. St.
Wilmington, DE 19884-0141
Contact: Charles M. Cawley, Pres.

Established in 1997 in DE.

Donor(s): Charles M. Cawley, Julie P. Cawley.

Grantmaker type: Independent foundation

Financial data (yr. ended 12/31/00): Assets, $265,634 (M); gifts received, $2,750,000; expenditures, $3,306,308; qualifying distributions, $3,294,745; giving activities include $3,295,908 for 140 grants (high: $333,000; low: $200).

Purpose and activities: Support for the arts, education, health, the environment, youth, human services, and religion.

Fields of interest: Museums; Performing arts; Secondary school/education; Higher education; Natural resources; Health care; Youth development; Human services; Roman Catholic agencies & churches.

Types of support: General/operating support; Continuing support; Annual campaigns; Building/renovation; Debt reduction; Program development; Scholarship funds.

Limitations: Applications not accepted. Giving on a national basis, with emphasis on Washington, DC, DE, ME, MD, NJ, and PA. No grants to individuals.

Application information: Contributes only to pre-selected organizations.

Officers and Directors:* Charles M. Cawley,* Pres. and Treas.; Julie P. Cawley,* V.P. and Secy.; Charles M. Cawley III; Maureen Rhodes.

EIN: 510379108

623
Chichester duPont Foundation, Inc. ▼

3120 Kennett Pike
Wilmington, DE 19807-3045 (302) 658-5244
Contact: Gregory F. Fields, Secy.

Incorporated in 1946 in DE.

Donor(s): Lydia Chichester duPont,‡ Mary Chichester duPont Clark,‡ A. Felix duPont, Jr., Alice duPont Mills.

Grantmaker type: Independent foundation

Financial data (yr. ended 12/31/01): Assets, $53,831,614 (M); expenditures, $3,404,368; qualifying distributions, $3,037,820; giving activities include $3,000,000 for 54 grants (high: $350,000; low: $7,500; average: $10,000–$100,000).

Purpose and activities: Emphasis on child welfare, including support for a camp for handicapped children, education, health, and cultural programs; some support for conservation.

Fields of interest: Elementary/secondary education; Education; Natural resources; Health care; Human services; Children/youth, services.

Types of support: General/operating support; Building/renovation.

Limitations: Giving primarily in DE and MD. No grants to individuals.

Application information: Application form not required.

  Deadline(s): Oct. 1
  Board meeting date(s): Dec.
  Final notification: 2 weeks after meeting

Officers and Trustees:* Katharine Gahagan,* Pres.; Caroline Prickett,* V.P.; Gregory F. Fields, Secy.; Christopher duPont,* Treas.; Mary Mills Abel-Smith; Lynne L. Anderson; Allaire duPont, Sr.; Alexis D. Gahagan; Alice duPont Mills; Phyllis Mills Wyeth.

Number of staff: None.

EIN: 516011641

Recent environmental and animal welfare grants:

623-1 Brandywine Conservancy, Chadds Ford, PA, $100,000. For Environmental Management Center programs. 2001.

623-2 Delaware Nature Society, Hockessin, DE, $50,000. For renovation designed to make Ashland Nature Center handicapped accessible. 2001.

623-3 Marine Coast Heritage Trust, Brunswick, ME, $50,000. For efforts to preserve Maine's coastline. 2001.

623-4 Marion DuPont Scott Equine Medical Center, Leesburg, VA, $30,000. For research efforts. 2001.

623-5 Marshall Point Education Foundation, Rockland, ME, $125,000. To build new Herring Gut Learning Center. 2001.

623-6 Natural Resources Council, Augusta, ME, $25,000. For protection of Saint George estuary's water quality. 2001.

623-7 Peregrine Fund, Boise, ID, $20,000. For restoration of California Condor in Grand Canyon area. 2001.

623-8 Thomas Jeffersons Poplar Forest, Forest, VA, $25,000. For architectural restoration of house and gardens. 2001.

623-9 Tri-State Bird Rescue and Research, Newark, DE, $25,000. For Oil Spill Contingency program. 2001.

623-10 University of Pennsylvania, School of Veterinary Medicine, Philadelphia, PA, $100,000. For diagnostic equipment. 2001.

623-11 Vermont Institute of Natural Science, Woodstock, VT, $75,000. For construction of environmental learning center. 2001.

623-12 Virginia League of Conservation Voters Education Fund, Richmond, VA, $50,000. For voter participation program. 2001.

623-13 Virginia Outdoors Foundation, Richmond, VA, $50,000. For upgrading data management system. 2001.

623-14 Winterthur Museum, Garden & Library, Winterthur, DE, $40,000. For programming associated with 50th Anniversary exhibition. 2001.

624
Melvin S. Cohen Foundation, Inc.
c/o National Presto Industries, Inc.
P.O. Box 2105
Wilmington, DE 19899-2105
Contact: Melvin S. Cohen, Pres.
Application address: 3925 N. Hastings Way, Eau Claire, WI 54703, tel.: (715) 839-2139

Incorporated in 1963 in WI.
Donor(s): Melvin S. Cohen, Eileen F. Cohen.
Grantmaker type: Independent foundation
Financial data (yr. ended 12/31/02): Assets, $3,536,633 (M); expenditures, $170,914; qualifying distributions, $164,304; giving activities include $163,925 for 8 grants (high: $160,000; low: $100).
Purpose and activities: Giving primarily for arts and culture, higher education, natural resource conservation, health associations, social services, and Jewish federated giving programs.
Fields of interest: Arts; Education; Natural resources; Health care; Jewish federated giving programs.
Types of support: General/operating support; Scholarship funds.
Limitations: Giving primarily in northwestern WI, preferably Chippewa and Eau Claire counties. No grants to individuals.
Application information:
  Initial approach: Letter
  Deadline(s): None
Officers: Melvin S. Cohen, Pres.; Maryjo R. Cohen, V.P.; Eileen F. Cohen, Secy.-Treas.
EIN: 396075009

625
Conectiv Corporate Giving Program
(formerly Delmarva Power & Light Company Contributions Program)
P.O. Box 231
Wilmington, DE 19899
Contact: Vince Jacono, Mgr., Public Affairs

Grantmaker type: Corporate giving program
Purpose and activities: Conectiv makes charitable contributions to nonprofit organizations involved with education, the environment, public safety, and community economic development. Support is given primarily in areas of company operations.
Fields of interest: Education; Environment; Safety/disasters; Urban/community development.
Types of support: General/operating support; Annual campaigns; Scholarship funds; Research;

Employee volunteer services; Use of facilities; Donated equipment; In-kind gifts.
Limitations: Giving primarily in areas of company operations. No grants to individuals.
Publications: Informational brochure (including application guidelines).
Application information: The Corporate Communications Department handles giving. Application form required.
  Initial approach: Contact headquarters for application form
  Copies of proposal: 1
  Deadline(s): None
  Final notification: 1 month

626
Crestlea Foundation, Inc.
100 W. 10th St., Ste. 1109
Wilmington, DE 19801-1694 (302) 654-2477
Contact: Stephen A. Martinenza, Secy.-Treas.

Incorporated in 1955 in DE.
Donor(s): Henry B. duPont.‡
Grantmaker type: Independent foundation
Financial data (yr. ended 12/31/02): Assets, $31,826,003 (M); gifts received, $366,293; expenditures, $1,909,396; qualifying distributions, $1,824,538; giving activities include $1,788,530 for 67 grants (high: $1,082,785; low: $5,000; average: $5,000-$50,000).
Purpose and activities: Giving primarily to a community foundation, and for museums and education.
Fields of interest: Museums; Secondary school/education; Higher education; Natural resources; Health care; Housing/shelter, development; Human services; Community development; Federated giving programs; Public affairs.
Types of support: Annual campaigns; Capital campaigns; Building/renovation; Equipment.
Limitations: Giving primarily in the Wilmington, DE area. No grants to individuals.
Application information: Application form not required.
  Initial approach: 2-page letter
  Copies of proposal: 1
  Deadline(s): Nov. 1
  Board meeting date(s): As required
  Final notification: Dec. 31
Officers and Directors:* Otto C. Fad,* Pres.; Stephen A. Martinenza,* Secy.-Treas.
Number of staff: 1.
EIN: 516015638

627
Crystal Trust ▼
P.O. Box 39
Montchanin, DE 19710-0039 (302) 651-0533
Contact: Stephen C. Doberstein, Dir.

Trust established in 1947 in DE.
Donor(s): Irenee duPont.‡
Grantmaker type: Independent foundation
Financial data (yr. ended 12/31/01): Assets, $118,654,083 (M); expenditures, $6,718,507; qualifying distributions, $6,248,446; giving activities include $6,082,000 for 55 grants (high: $2,000,000; low: $2,000; average: $10,000-$100,000).

Purpose and activities: Giving mainly for higher and secondary education and social and family services, including youth and child welfare agencies, family planning, and programs for the aged, the disadvantaged, and the homeless; support also for the arts and cultural programs, health and hospitals, conservation programs, and historical preservation. Needs of the State of Delaware have priority.
Fields of interest: Museums; Music; Arts; Secondary school/education; Higher education; Libraries/library science; Education; Natural resources; Hospitals (general); Family planning; Health care; Health organizations, association; Food services; Housing/shelter, development; Human services; Children/youth, services; Family services; Hospices; Aging, centers/services; Homeless, human services; Aging; Economically disadvantaged; Homeless.
Types of support: Capital campaigns; Building/renovation; Equipment; Land acquisition.
Limitations: Giving primarily in DE, with emphasis on Wilmington. No grants to individuals, or for endowment funds, research, scholarships, fellowships, or matching gifts.
Publications: Informational brochure (including application guidelines).
Application information: Application form not required.
  Initial approach: Proposal
  Copies of proposal: 1
  Deadline(s): Sept. 30
  Board meeting date(s): Nov.
  Final notification: Dec. 15
Director: Stephen C. Doberstein.
Trustees: Irenee duPont, Jr.; David Greenewalt; Eleanor S. Maroney.
Number of staff: 1 part-time professional; 1 part-time support.
EIN: 516015063
Recent environmental and animal welfare grants:

627-1 Academy of Natural Sciences, Patrick Center for Environmental Research, DC, $250,000. 2002.

627-2 Brandywine Conservancy, Chadds Ford, PA, $50,000. For capital support. 2002.

627-3 Delaware Center for Horticulture, Wilmington, DE, $50,000. For technology upgrade. 2002.

627-4 Delaware Nature Society, Hockessin, DE, $100,000. For capital campaign. 2002.

627-5 Hawk Mountain Sanctuary Association, Kempton, PA, $60,000. For land acquisition. 2002.

627-6 Humane Association, Delaware, Wilmington, DE, $11,900. For computer equipment. 2002.

627-7 Nature Conservancy, Newark, DE, $25,000. For capital campaign. 2002.

627-8 Tri-State Bird Rescue and Research, Newark, DE, $10,000. For renovations. 2002.

627-9 Winterthur Museum, Garden & Library, Winterthur, DE, $25,000. For capital support. 2002.

628
Delaware Community Foundation
P.O. Box 1636
Wilmington, DE 19899 (302) 571-8004
Contact: Susan Ann Sherk, Prog. Admin.
FAX: (302) 571-1553; E-mail: info@delcf.org;
URL: http://www.delcf.org

Incorporated in 1986 in DE.
Grantmaker type: Community foundation
Financial data (yr. ended 06/30/02): Assets,
$67,185,487 (M); gifts received, $3,989,871;
expenditures, $6,414,574; giving activities
include $4,940,428 for grants (high:
$1,094,029).
Purpose and activities: The Delaware
Community Foundation is a nonprofit,
philanthropic community organization created
by and for the people of Delaware to build
community. The DCF is dedicated to inspiring
and helping people of all backgrounds and
means create lasting legacies to benefit the
people of Delaware. It enables people with
philanthropic interests to easily and effectively
support the issues they care about by
establishing a charitable fund at the Foundation
and recommending grants to nonprofit groups
they want to support. The Foundation offers
personalized service, local expertise and
community leadership. The Foundation itself
awards grants to qualified nonprofit
organizations that serve Delawareans. Program
areas include substance abuse prevention
programs and capital projects.
Fields of interest: Arts; Education; Environment;
Health care; Health organizations, association;
Child abuse; Housing/shelter, development;
Children/youth, services; Community
development.
Types of support: Continuing support; Capital
campaigns; Building/renovation; Equipment;
Seed money; Technical assistance.
Limitations: Giving limited to DE. No support
for religious or sectarian purposes, or fraternal
or veterans' groups. No grants to individuals
(except for fulfilling prior commitments), or for
annual funds, operating costs, endowments or
debt reduction.
Publications: Application guidelines, Annual
report, Informational brochure, Newsletter.
Application information: The foundation has
discontinued awarding new grants to
individuals; prior commitments will be fulfilled.
Application form required.
  Initial approach: Telephone or check Web site
  Deadline(s): Jan. 31 for Capital grants, and
  Sept. 30 for Program grants
  Board meeting date(s): Quarterly
  Final notification: After final reviews in Dec.
  and June meetings
Officers: D. Wayne Holden, Chair.; Donald R.
Kirtley, Vice-Chair.; Thomas R. Pulsifer, Secy.;
Thomas D. Croft, Treas.
Directors: David G. Burton; Linda Chick; Mary
E. Copper; William F. D'Alonzo; Katherine K.
Delapine; Israel J. Floyd; Linda J. Gilliam;
Martha Gilman; Cecil C. Gordon, Jr.; Marc A.
Ham; Paul H. Harrell, Jr.; Ann B. Holliday; Jack
B. Jacobs; Howard R. Layton; Caroline M.
Lunger; Maria M. Matos; Marcia V. Ranier;
Thomas J. Shopa; Gregory M. Sleet; Charles M.
Smith; Gilbert H. Smith; Julie Topkis-Scanlan;
Mark A. Turner.

Number of staff: 11 full-time professional; 1
part-time professional.
EIN: 222804785

629
DuPont Corporate Giving Program
c/o Corp. Contribs. Office, Public Affairs
1007 Market St.
Wilmington, DE 19898 (302) 774-2036
Application address for education: c/o DuPont
Center for Collaborative Research and
Education, P.O. Box 80030-1370, Wilmington,
DE 19880-0030

Grantmaker type: Corporate giving program
Purpose and activities: DuPont makes
charitable contributions to nonprofit
organizations involved with arts and culture,
education, the environment, health and human
services, equal opportunity and access,
intergroup and race relations, community
development, civic affairs, and economically
disadvantaged people. Support is given on a
national and international basis.
Fields of interest: Arts; Elementary/secondary
education; Higher education; Education;
Environment; Health care; Children/youth,
services; Family services; Human services; Civil
rights, equal rights; Race/intergroup relations;
Economic development; Community
development; Public affairs; Economically
disadvantaged.
Types of support: General/operating support;
Program development; Fellowships; Scholarship
funds; Employee volunteer services.
Limitations: Giving on a national and
international basis in areas of company
operations, with emphasis on Wilmington, DE.
No support for disease-specific organizations,
fraternal or veterans' organizations, political
organizations, sectarian organizations not of
direct benefit to the entire community, or
discriminatory organizations. No grants to
individuals, or for endowments, political
campaigns, curriculum development, or capital
campaigns.
Application information: Proposals should be
no longer than 2 pages in length. The Corporate
Contributions Department handles giving. A
contributions committee reviews all requests.
Application form not required.
  Initial approach: Proposal to headquarters;
  proposal to application address for
  education
  Copies of proposal: 1
  Deadline(s): None
  Board meeting date(s): May and Sept.
  Final notification: Following review

630
Ederic Foundation, Inc.
P.O. Box 4420
Wilmington, DE 19807-0420
Contact: John E. Riegel, Pres.

Incorporated in 1958 in DE.
Donor(s): John E. Riegel, Natalie R. Weymouth,
Richard E. Riegel, Jr., Mrs. G. Burton Pearson, Jr.
Grantmaker type: Independent foundation
Financial data (yr. ended 12/31/02): Assets,
$1,241 (M); gifts received, $594,768;
expenditures, $597,900; qualifying distributions,

$597,900; giving activities include $596,250 for
93 grants (high: $82,500; low: $100).
Fields of interest: Museums (marine/maritime);
Museums (natural history); Education,
association; Higher education; Education;
Natural resources; Family planning; Health
organizations, association; Disasters, fire
prevention/control; Boys & girls clubs; Human
services; Children/youth, services; Federated
giving programs; Christian agencies & churches.
Limitations: Giving primarily in DE, with
emphasis on Wilmington. No grants to
individuals.
Application information:
  Initial approach: Letter
  Deadline(s): None
Officers: John E. Riegel, Pres.; Kenneth C.
Martin, Secy.-Treas.
Trustees: Robert C. McCoy; Richard E. Riegel,
Jr.; Philip B. Weymouth, Jr.
EIN: 516017927

631
Fair Play Foundation
100 W. 10th St., Ste. 1010
Wilmington, DE 19801
Contact: Blaine T. Phillips, Pres.

Established about 1983 in DE.
Grantmaker type: Independent foundation
Financial data (yr. ended 12/31/02): Assets,
$11,753,671 (M); expenditures, $9,097,707;
qualifying distributions, $732,685; giving
activities include $628,000 for grants (average:
$20,000–$30,000).
Fields of interest: Museums; Arts; Higher
education; Environment, water resources;
Animals/wildlife, preservation/protection.
Types of support: Building/renovation;
Equipment; Land acquisition.
Limitations: Giving on a national basis. No
support for No grants to business-oriented
organizations.
Application information: Application form not
required.
  Initial approach: Letter
  Copies of proposal: 1
  Deadline(s): Oct. 1
  Board meeting date(s): Dec.
Officer and Trustees:* Blaine T. Phillips,* Pres.
and Exec. Dir.; James F. Burnett; Thomas H.
Fooks V; Milbrey R. Jacobs; Blaine T. Philips, Jr.;
W. Halsey Spruance, Jr.
Number of staff: 1 full-time professional.
EIN: 516017779

632
Farmor Foundation
c/o Wilmington Trust Co.
1100 N. Market St., Ste. 330990
Wilmington, DE 19890-0001

Established in 1994 in DE.
Donor(s): Henry A. Flint, Susan O. Flint.
Grantmaker type: Independent foundation
Financial data (yr. ended 12/31/02): Assets,
$2,698,257 (M); expenditures, $187,904;
qualifying distributions, $177,041; giving
activities include $171,000 for 4 grants (high:
$100,000; low: $1,000).
Purpose and activities: Giving primarily for
education.

Fields of interest: Education; Environment.
Limitations: Applications not accepted. Giving
primarily in CT and MA. No grants to
individuals.
Application information: Contributes only to
pre-selected organizations.
Officers: Henry A. Flint, Pres. and Treas.; Susan
O. Flint, V.P. and Secy.
EIN: 510355032

633
Four Daughters Foundation
c/o Wilmington Trust Co.
1100 N. Market St.
Wilmington, DE 19890-0900

Established in 1998 in DE.
Donor(s): John W. Milliken.
Grantmaker type: Independent foundation
Financial data (yr. ended 12/31/02): Assets,
$922,058 (M); expenditures, $152,692;
qualifying distributions, $145,794; giving
activities include $145,950 for 11 grants (high:
$47,000; low: $2,000).
Purpose and activities: Giving for education and
the environment.
Fields of interest: Arts; University; Natural
resources.
Limitations: Applications not accepted. Giving
primarily in Salt Lake City, UT. No grants to
individuals.
Application information: Contributes only to
pre-selected organizations.
Advisors: Elizabeth McCook Crile; Katharine
Murphy Crile; Ann E. Milliken; John W. Milliken.
Trustee: Wilmington Trust Co.
EIN: 516508161

634
Sumner Gerard Foundation
1209 Orange St.
Wilmington, DE 19801

Established in 1963 in DE.
Donor(s): Sumner Gerard.‡
Grantmaker type: Independent foundation
Financial data (yr. ended 04/30/02): Assets,
$3,118,974 (M); expenditures, $206,399;
qualifying distributions, $186,666; giving
activities include $162,250 for 71 grants (high:
$25,000; low: $100).
Purpose and activities: Giving primarily to
Christian aid organizations, hospitals, and
education.
Fields of interest: Historical activities; Arts;
Higher education; Education; Environment, land
resources; Health care; Human services;
Protestant agencies & churches; Roman Catholic
agencies & churches.
Limitations: Applications not accepted. Giving
on a national basis, primarily in Washington,
DC, NJ, NY and the New England states. No
grants to individuals.
Application information: Contributes only to
pre-selected organizations.
Officers: C.H. Coster Gerard, Pres.; John P.
Campbell, V.P.; Hariet C. Gerard, V.P.
EIN: 136155552

635
Jade Tree Foundation
c/o Wilmington Trust Co.
1100 N. Market St.
Wilmington, DE 19890-0001

Established in 1994 in DE.
Donor(s): Mrs. Robert B. Flint, Alice F. Roe.
Grantmaker type: Independent foundation
Financial data (yr. ended 12/31/02): Assets,
$3,144,995 (M); gifts received, $975;
expenditures, $178,022; qualifying distributions,
$155,433; giving activities include $154,500 for
23 grants (high: $50,000; low: $500).
Purpose and activities: Giving primarily for
botanical gardens, nature conservancy and
education; funding also for human services.
Fields of interest: Education; Natural resources;
Botanical gardens; Alzheimer's disease; Human
services.
Types of support: General/operating support.
Limitations: Applications not accepted. Giving
primarily in the Southwest. No grants to
individuals.
Application information: Contributes only to
pre-selected organizations.
 Board meeting date(s): Spring and fall
Officers: Alice F. Roe, Pres. and Treas.; Barbara
A. Madley, V.P.; Henry G. Roe, V.P.; William G.
Roe, Secy.
Number of staff: None.
EIN: 510355035

636
Atwater Kent Foundation, Inc.
101 Springer Bldg.
3411 Silverside Rd.
Wilmington, DE 19810 (302) 478-4383
Contact: Hope P. Annan, Pres.

Established in 1919 in DE.
Grantmaker type: Independent foundation
Financial data (yr. ended 12/31/02): Assets,
$1,979,917 (M); expenditures, $114,151;
qualifying distributions, $102,234; giving
activities include $100,000 for 98 grants (high:
$33,010; low: $50).
Purpose and activities: Giving primarily for arts
and culture, education, and human services.
Fields of interest: Museums; Arts; Education;
Natural resources; Veterinary medicine,
hospital; Hospitals (general); Health care; Health
organizations, association; Youth development;
Human services.
Limitations: Giving primarily in Palm Beach, FL
and the metropolitan Philadelphia, PA, area. No
grants to individuals, or to pass-through
organizations.
Application information: Application form not
required.
 Initial approach: Proposal
 Deadline(s): None
 Board meeting date(s): Periodically
Officers and Trustees:* Hope P. Annan,* Pres.;
A. Atwater Kent III,* V.P.; James R. Weaver,
Secy.; Christopher B. Kent,* Treas.
EIN: 510081303

637
The Kingsley Foundation
c/o Wilmington Trust Co.
1100 N. Market St.
Wilmington, DE 19890-0001

Established in 1961 in CT.
Donor(s): F.G. Kingsley, Ora K. Smith.
Grantmaker type: Independent foundation
Financial data (yr. ended 12/31/02): Assets,
$7,581,416 (M); gifts received, $112,432;
expenditures, $497,085; qualifying distributions,
$485,252; giving activities include $489,083 for
16 grants (high: $350,000; low: $500).
Purpose and activities: Giving primarily for the
arts, including the performing arts and the
opera; support also for a hospital and the
environment.
Fields of interest: Museums; Performing arts;
Opera; Arts; Environment; Hospitals (general).
Types of support: General/operating support.
Limitations: Applications not accepted. Giving
primarily in NY; some giving also in CT, MA,
and Washington, DC. No grants to individuals.
Application information: Contributes only to
pre-selected organizations.
Advisors: Lawrence Heagney; Ora R. Kingsley;
Roger Milliken; Margaret J. Smith; Ora K. Smith.
Trustee: Wilmington Trust Co.
EIN: 516163698

638
Longwood Foundation, Inc. ▼
100 W. 10th St., Ste. 1109
Wilmington, DE 19801 (302) 654-2477
Contact: Peter C. Morrow, Exec. Dir.

Incorporated in 1937 in DE.
Donor(s): Pierre S. duPont.‡
Grantmaker type: Independent foundation
Financial data (yr. ended 09/30/02): Assets,
$600,786,854 (M); expenditures, $43,108,358;
qualifying distributions, $40,117,647; giving
activities include $39,872,605 for 93 grants
(high: $12,500,000; low: $4,500; average:
$25,000–$500,000).
Purpose and activities: Primary obligation is the
support, operation, and development of
Longwood Gardens, which is open to the
public; limited grants generally to educational
institutions, to local hospitals for construction
purposes, and to social service and youth
agencies, and cultural programs.
Fields of interest: Arts; Education, fund raising;
Education; Hospitals (general); Human services;
Youth, services.
Types of support: Annual campaigns;
Building/renovation; Equipment; Land
acquisition; Endowments; Research.
Limitations: Giving limited to DE, with emphasis
on the greater Wilmington area. No grants to
individuals, or for special projects.
Application information: Application form not
required.
 Initial approach: Letter
 Copies of proposal: 1
 Deadline(s): Mar. 15 and Sept. 15
 Board meeting date(s): May and Nov.
 Final notification: At time of next board
 meeting
Officers and Trustees:* H. Rodney Sharp III,*
Pres.; Edward B. duPont,* V.P.; Irenee duPont
May,* Secy.; Henry H. Silliman, Jr.,* Treas.; Peter

C. Morrow, Exec. Dir.; Gerret van S. Copeland; David L. Craven; Pierre S. duPont IV.
Number of staff: 4 full-time professional; 1 part-time professional.
EIN: 510066734
Recent environmental and animal welfare grants:
638-1 Brandywine Conservancy, Chadds Ford, PA, $1,000,000. 2002.
638-2 Community Gardens of Chester County, Embreeville, PA, $12,000. 2002.
638-3 Delaware Center for the Inland Bays, Lewes, DE, $100,000. 2002.
638-4 Longwood Gardens, Kennett Square, PA, $7,732,300. 2002.
638-5 Partnership for the Delaware Estuary, Wilmington, DE, $50,000. 2002.

639

The Marmot Foundation
100 W. 10th St., Ste. 1109
Wilmington, DE 19801-1694 (302) 654-2477
Contact: Charles F. Gummey, Jr., Secy. (for DE organizations), or Willis H. duPont, Chair. (for FL organizations)
Application address for FL organizations: P.O. Box 2468, Palm Beach, FL 33480

Established in 1968 in DE.
Donor(s): Margaret F. duPont Trust.
Grantmaker type: Independent foundation
Financial data (yr. ended 12/31/02): Assets, $27,039,994 (M); expenditures, $1,916,998; qualifying distributions, $1,813,441; giving activities include $1,795,000 for 112 grants (high: $70,000; low: $2,000; average: $5,000–$50,000).
Purpose and activities: Support for hospitals, health, higher and secondary education, (including libraries), community funds, cultural programs, (including museums), youth agencies, social services, literacy programs, and environmental and ecological organizations.
Fields of interest: Museums; Arts; Secondary school/education; Higher education; Adult education—literacy, basic skills & GED; Libraries/library science; Reading; Natural resources; Environment; Hospitals (general); Family planning; Health care; Health organizations, association; Housing/shelter, development; Human services; Children/youth, services; Hospices; Homeless.
Types of support: Capital campaigns; Building/renovation; Equipment; Land acquisition; Research; Matching/challenge support.
Limitations: Giving primarily in DE and FL. No support for religious organizations. No grants to individuals, or for operating budgets, endowments or scholarships; no loans.
Publications: Application guidelines.
Application information: Application form not required.
Initial approach: Letter
Copies of proposal: 1
Deadline(s): Apr. 30 and Oct. 31 for DE and Oct. 31 for FL.
Board meeting date(s): May and Nov. in DE and Nov. in FL.
Final notification: 2 weeks after board meeting
Officers and Trustees:* Willis H. duPont,* Chair.; Charles F. Gummey, Secy.; Lammot

Joseph duPont; Miren duPont; Miren duPont Sanchez.
Number of staff: 1 part-time professional; 1 part-time support.
EIN: 516022487

640

The Marshall Reynolds Foundation
c/o Wilmington Trust Co.
1100 N. Market St.
Wilmington, DE 19890-0001

Established in 1986 in PA.
Donor(s): Eleanor M. Reynolds.
Grantmaker type: Independent foundation
Financial data (yr. ended 06/30/01): Assets, $20,649,700 (M); gifts received, $8,421,403; expenditures, $527,089; qualifying distributions, $373,214; giving activities include $245,400 for 19 grants (high: $25,900; low: $2,000).
Fields of interest: Higher education; Environment; Human services; YM/YWCAs & YM/YWHAs.
Limitations: Applications not accepted. Giving primarily in PA. No grants to individuals.
Application information: Contributes only to pre-selected organizations.
Trustees: Dorothea Morse; Richard A. Newman, M.D.; Jacklen E. Powell; Minturn T. Wright III.
EIN: 236869411

641

The Gerrish H. Milliken Foundation
c/o Wilmington Trust Co.
1100 N. Market St.
Wilmington, DE 19890

Established in 1962.
Grantmaker type: Independent foundation
Financial data (yr. ended 12/31/02): Assets, $7,020,168 (M); expenditures, $646,624; qualifying distributions, $638,200; giving activities include $638,200 for grants (average: $100–$100,000).
Purpose and activities: Giving for education, environmental conservation, art and cultural programs, historical preservation and research, and health and human services.
Fields of interest: Higher education; Education; Environment; Health care; Human services; Government/public administration; Protestant agencies & churches.
Types of support: General/operating support.
Limitations: Applications not accepted. Giving primarily in the northeastern U.S. No grants to individuals.
Application information: Contributes only to pre-selected organizations.
Officer: Lawrence Heagney, Treas.
Trustees: Peter Milliken; Phoebe Milliken; Roger Milliken.
EIN: 066037106

642

The Orange Tree Foundation
c/o Lucius H. Bracey, Jr.
P.O. Box 730
Wilmington, DE 19899

Established in 1987 in VA.

Donor(s): Alletta Bredin-Bell, Octavia DuPont Bredin.
Grantmaker type: Independent foundation
Financial data (yr. ended 06/30/02): Assets, $3,205,831 (M); gifts received, $101,138; expenditures, $377,956; qualifying distributions, $365,732; giving activities include $366,936 for 17 grants (high: $278,471; low: $244).
Fields of interest: Arts; Education; Environment; Crime/violence prevention; Human services.
Limitations: Applications not accepted. Giving primarily in VA. No grants to individuals.
Application information: Contributes only to pre-selected organizations.
Officers and Directors:* Alletta Bredin-Bell,* Pres.; Thomas C.T. Brokaw,* Secy.; Laura B. Hussey; Mrs. Michael M. Massie.
EIN: 541394716

643

The Mary E. Parker Foundation
c/o Wilmington Trust Co.
1100 N. Market St.
Wilmington, DE 19890-0001
Contact: Richard W. Pratt, Tr.
FAX: (941) 747-8396

Established in 1986 in FL.
Donor(s): Mary E. Parker.
Grantmaker type: Independent foundation
Financial data (yr. ended 12/31/02): Assets, $15,345,615 (M); expenditures, $1,038,844; qualifying distributions, $949,575; giving activities include $954,170 for 61 grants (high: $100,000; low: $1,000).
Purpose and activities: Giving for the arts, nursing, higher education, youth and social services, community funds, animal welfare, and guide dog training for the visually impaired.
Fields of interest: Museums; Arts; Animal welfare; Human services; Children/youth, services; Federated giving programs.
Types of support: General/operating support; Endowments.
Limitations: Giving primarily in FL.
Publications: Informational brochure (including application guidelines).
Application information: Application form required.
Initial approach: Letter
Deadline(s): Nov. 15
Board meeting date(s): Dec.
Final notification: Positive responses only
Trustees: Robert G. Blalock; Mary E. Parker; Richard W. Pratt; Willett E. Wentzell; P. Woodrow Young; Wilmington Trust Co.
EIN: 592708325

644

The Relgalf Charitable Foundation
c/o JPMorgan Services
P.O. Box 6089
Newark, DE 19714-6089
Contact: George G. Matthews, Tr.
Application address: 1925 Flagler Dr., West Palm Beach, FL 33407

Established in 1986 in FL.
Donor(s): George G. Matthews.
Grantmaker type: Independent foundation
Financial data (yr. ended 11/30/01): Assets, $4,605,592 (M); expenditures, $273,754;

qualifying distributions, $261,991; giving activities include $256,580 for 28 grants (high: $25,000; low: $1,580).
Purpose and activities: Giving for health and medical services, day schools, art organizations, and botanical gardens.
Fields of interest: Arts; Animals/wildlife, preservation/protection; Human services.
Limitations: Giving primarily in Washington, DC, West Palm Beach, FL, NC, and NY. No grants to individuals.
Application information:
  Initial approach: Proposal
  Deadline(s): None
Trustee: George G. Matthews.
EIN: 596874133

645
Rowland Foundation, Inc. ▼
c/o JP Morgan Services Inc.
P.O. Box 6089
Newark, DE 19714-6089 (302) 634-2931
Contact: Valerie Smallwood, Pres.

Incorporated in 1960 in DE.
Donor(s): Edwin H. Land,‡ Helen M. Land.
Grantmaker type: Independent foundation
Financial data (yr. ended 11/30/02): Assets, $26,935,313 (M); gifts received, $9,419; expenditures, $20,209,868; qualifying distributions, $20,179,514; giving activities include $20,159,542 for 3 grants (high: $20,000,000; low: $75,000; average: $75,000–$20,000,000).
Purpose and activities: Grants primarily for a science institute, education, including colleges and universities, social services, health, medical research, conservation, and cultural programs, including museums and historical associations.
Fields of interest: Museums; History/archaeology; Arts; Elementary/secondary education; Higher education; Natural resources; Hospitals (general); Health organizations, association; Medical research, institute; Human services; Science.
Types of support: General/operating support; Professorships; Research.
Limitations: Giving primarily in the Boston-Cambridge, MA, area. No grants to individuals, or for capital or endowment funds, or matching gifts; no loans.
Application information: Application form not required.
  Initial approach: Letter
  Copies of proposal: 1
  Deadline(s): None
  Board meeting date(s): As required
  Final notification: Varies
Officers and Trustees:* Valerie Smallwood,* Pres.; Philip DuBois,* V.P.; Joseph Haley, Secy.; Guy Smallwood,* Treas.; Daniel Drake; Edward Smallwood.
Number of staff: None.
EIN: 046046756

646
The Seraph Foundation
1105 N. Market St., Ste. 1300
Wilmington, DE 19801 (302) 661-4558
Contact: Carol M. Drummond, Admin.
FAX: (302) 661-4550

Established in 1997 in DE.
Donor(s): Edna Marion Davenport.
Grantmaker type: Independent foundation
Financial data (yr. ended 06/30/01): Assets, $48,399,815 (M); expenditures, $3,037,153; qualifying distributions, $2,767,751; giving activities include $2,764,009 for 52 grants (high: $750,000; low: $3,000; average: $5,000–$50,000).
Purpose and activities: Giving primarily for health and education.
Fields of interest: Arts; Education; Natural resources; Environment; Cancer; Hospitals (general); Medical research, association; Medical research, institute; Medical research; Human services; Protestant agencies & churches.
Types of support: Capital campaigns; Building/renovation; Equipment; Land acquisition; Endowments; Professorships; Internship funds; Scholarship funds; Research; Matching/challenge support.
Limitations: Applications not accepted. Giving primarily in the eastern and mid-U.S. No grants to individuals.
Publications: Grants list.
Application information: Contributes only to pre-selected organizations. Unsolicited requests for applications not accepted.
  Board meeting date(s): Sept., Dec., Mar., and June
Officers and Board Members:* Henry Spire,* Pres. and Treas.; Linda J. Spire,* V.P. and Secy.; William Spire.
EIN: 522030228

647
Shrieking Meadow Foundation
3801 Kennett Pike, Ste. C-200
Greenville, DE 19807

Established in 1994 in DE.
Donor(s): Lucile E. DuPont Flint, Peter H. Flint.
Grantmaker type: Independent foundation
Financial data (yr. ended 12/31/02): Assets, $3,631,568 (M); expenditures, $281,467; qualifying distributions, $193,080; giving activities include $193,080 for 12 grants (high: $45,000; low: $1,000).
Fields of interest: Theater; Music; Higher education; Natural resources.
Limitations: Applications not accepted. Giving primarily in Wilmington, DE. No grants to individuals.
Application information: Contributes only to pre-selected organizations.
Officers: Peter H. Flint, Jr., Pres.; Karen G. Flint, V.P.; Peter H. Flint, Secy.-Treas.
EIN: 510355034

648
The Paul Singer Family Foundation
(formerly The Paul & Linda Singer Foundation)
1209 Orange St., Ste. 123
Wilmington, DE 19801

Established in 1986 in DE.
Donor(s): Linda Singer, Paul E. Singer.
Grantmaker type: Independent foundation
Financial data (yr. ended 11/30/01): Assets, $15,150,465 (M); expenditures, $921,153; qualifying distributions, $907,555; giving

activities include $905,370 for 52 grants (high: $225,000; low: $100).
Purpose and activities: Giving primarily to Jewish organizations, education, the arts, particularly museums, human services, and medical organizations.
Fields of interest: Museums; Arts; Higher education; Natural resources; Health organizations; Disasters, 9/11/01; Human services; Civil rights; Jewish federated giving programs; Philanthropy/voluntarism; Jewish agencies & temples.
Limitations: Applications not accepted. Giving primarily in NJ and NY. No grants to individuals.
Application information: Contributes only to pre-selected organizations.
Officers and Directors:* Paul E. Singer,* Pres.; Andrew Singer,* V.P.; Gordon Singer,* V.P.
EIN: 222664654

649
The Starrett Foundation
c/o Wilmington Trust Co.
Rodney Sq. N., 1100 N. Market St.
Wilmington, DE 19890-0001
Contact: Patrick M. Ashley, Tr.

Established in 1980 in DE.
Donor(s): Margaretta S.B. Brokaw, Octavia Bredin.
Grantmaker type: Independent foundation
Financial data (yr. ended 11/30/02): Assets, $4,093,676 (M); gifts received, $124,872; expenditures, $208,537; qualifying distributions, $200,196; giving activities include $201,185 for 28 grants (high: $52,567; low: $100).
Purpose and activities: Giving for education, the environment, and historic preservation.
Fields of interest: Historic preservation/historical societies; Education; Natural resources; Civil rights, advocacy.
Types of support: General/operating support.
Limitations: Applications not accepted. Giving primarily in Washington, DC, DE, NY, and PA. No grants to individuals.
Application information: Contributes only to pre-selected organizations.
Officer: Margaretta S.B. Brokaw, Mgr.
Trustee: Patrick M. Ashley.
EIN: 510270831

650
Janet Upjohn Stearns Charitable Trust
c/o JPMorgan Chase Bank
P.O. Box 6089
Newark, DE 19714-6089
Application address: c/o JPMorgan Chase Bank, 345 Park Ave., 47th Fl., New York, NY 10154-1002, tel.: (212) 464-2770

Established in 1961 in NY.
Grantmaker type: Independent foundation
Financial data (yr. ended 12/31/01): Assets, $2,301,586 (M); expenditures, $162,442; qualifying distributions, $137,710; giving activities include $135,000 for 34 grants (high: $23,750; low: $500).
Purpose and activities: Giving for religion, with an emphasis on Methodism, higher education, art and cultural programs, and for health and human services.

Fields of interest: Museums; Higher education; Education; Animals/wildlife; Hospitals (general); Human services.
Limitations: Giving primarily in MA, MD, NM, NY, and VA. No grants to individuals.
Application information: Application form not required.
Deadline(s): None
Advisory Committee Members: Janet T. Beck; G.E. Eisenhardt; Janet W. Ley; Robin Munn.
Trustee: JPMorgan Chase Bank.
EIN: 136035045

651

Stroud Foundation
c/o Wilmington Trust Co.
1100 N. Market St.
Wilmington, DE 19890-0001

Trust established in 1961 in PA.
Donor(s): Joan M. Stroud.‡
Grantmaker type: Independent foundation
Financial data (yr. ended 12/31/02): Assets, $2,827,023 (M); gifts received, $9,088; expenditures, $180,402; qualifying distributions, $160,730; giving activities include $160,730 for 1 grant.
Purpose and activities: Giving primarily to an academy of nature science and social science.
Fields of interest: Higher education; Natural resources; Hospitals (general); Human services.
Types of support: Research.
Limitations: Applications not accepted. No grants to individuals, or for matching gifts; no loans.
Application information: Contributes only to pre-selected organizations.
Board meeting date(s): Annually
Trustees: Joan S. Blaine; T. Sam Means; Morris W. Stroud; W.B. Dixon Stroud; Truman Welling.
Number of staff: None.
EIN: 236255701

652

The Struthers Family Foundation
900 Old Kennett Rd.
Greenville, DE 19807-1520

Established in 1999 in DE.
Donor(s): Richard K. Struthers, Sharon M. Struthers.
Grantmaker type: Independent foundation
Financial data (yr. ended 12/31/02): Assets, $670,462 (M); gifts received, $22,100; expenditures, $308,762; qualifying distributions, $308,563; giving activities include $308,663 for 11 grants (high: $182,915; low: $2,500).
Fields of interest: Higher education; Education; Natural resources; Human services.
Types of support: General/operating support.
Limitations: Applications not accepted. Giving primarily in DE and PA. No grants to individuals.
Application information: Contributes only to pre-selected organizations.
Officers: Richard K. Struthers, Pres. and Treas.; Sharon M. Struthers, V.P. and Secy.
EIN: 510392526

653

Syngenta Corporation Contributions Program
c/o Corp. Contribs.
1800 Concord Pike
Wilmington, DE 19850

Grantmaker type: Corporate giving program
Purpose and activities: Syngenta makes charitable contributions to nonprofit organizations involved with natural resources conservation and protection and food distribution. Support is given on a national basis.
Fields of interest: Natural resources; Food services.
International interests: Canada; Mexico.
Types of support: General/operating support; Scholarship funds; Employee volunteer services; Sponsorships; Employee matching gifts.
Limitations: Giving on a national basis and in Canada and Mexico.
Application information: Application form not required.
Initial approach: Proposal to headquarters
Copies of proposal: 1
Final notification: Following review

DISTRICT OF COLUMBIA

654

Alaska Wilderness League
122 C St., N.W., Ste. 240
Washington, DC 20001 (202) 544-5205
Contact: Cindy Shogan, Exec. Dir.
FAX: (202) 544-5197; E-mail: cindy@alaskawild.org; URL: http://www.alaskawild.org

Founded in 1993 in AK.
Grantmaker type: Public charity
Financial data (yr. ended 12/31/00): Revenue, $1,038,507; assets, $641,098; gifts received, $996,649; expenditures, $704,166; program services expenses, $607,672; giving activities include $1,659 for 3 grants of $553 each.
Purpose and activities: The league seeks to further the protection of Alaska's incomparable natural endowment.
Fields of interest: Animals/wildlife, preservation/protection; Animals/wildlife.
Officer and Directors:* Hon. Robert J. Mrazek,* Chair.; Cindy Shogan, Exec. Dir.; Cindy Adams; Tom Campion; Chuck Clusen; Bruce Gitlin; Jeff Kenner; and 6 additional directors.
EIN: 521814742

655

America the Beautiful Fund
(also known as ABF)
219 Shoreham Bldg., N.W.
Washington, DC 20005 (202) 638-1649
Contact: Nanine Bilski, Pres.
Additional tel.: (800) 522-3557; FAX: (202) 204-0028; URL: http://www.america-the-beautiful.org/

Established in 1965 in DC.
Grantmaker type: Public charity

Financial data (yr. ended 06/30/02): Revenue, $3,792,292; assets, $6,855,644 (M); gifts received, $3,717,153; expenditures, $4,077,932; program services expenses, $4,006,493; giving activities include $500 for 1 grant and $2,999,805 for in-kind gifts.
Purpose and activities: The fund works to preserve our national heritage by assisting community-level programs and projects to save the natural and man-made environment and improve the quality of life.
Fields of interest: Historical activities; Historic preservation/historical societies; Natural resources; Environmental education; Community development.
Types of support: Building/renovation; Seed money; In-kind gifts.
Limitations: Giving on a national basis.
Publications: Annual report, Financial statement, Newsletter.
Application information: See web site for application form and guidelines for Operation Green Plant. Application form required.
Initial approach: Contact program director for grants information
Deadline(s): None
Board meeting date(s): Monthly
Officers and Trustees:* Thomas P. Farrell,* Chair.; Nanine Bilski,* Pres.; Jean Wallace Douglas,* V.P.; Kay Lautman,* V.P.; Daniel Schneider,* Secy.; Susan Anderson,* Treas.; Keith Argow; and 19 additional trustees.
Number of staff: 4 full-time professional; 2 part-time professional.
EIN: 520963138

656

American Gas Foundation
400 N. Capitol St. N.W., Ste. 450
Washington, DC 20001 (202) 824-7255
Contact: Kevin Hardardt, Exec. Dir.

Established in 1989 in VA.
Donor(s): American Gas Association.
Grantmaker type: Public charity
Financial data (yr. ended 12/31/00): Revenue, $11,285; assets, $100,132; gifts received, $4,620; expenditures, $100,335; program services expenses, $79,765; giving activities include $8,000 for 1 grant.
Purpose and activities: The foundation's intent is the advancement of education concerning the distribution and transmission of natural gas by providing training and educational programs and conferences, and conducting charitable and other activities.
Fields of interest: Education; Energy; Environment; Community development; Engineering/technology; Science.
Limitations: No support for fraternal, political, labor or religious organizations, United Way-supported organizations, or for organizations whose programs are local in scope; or for capital fund drives, fundraising dinners, conferences or other special events. No grants to individuals (except for Louis A. Sarkes Scholarship Program); or for general operating support.
Publications: Informational brochure.
Application information: Application form required.
Deadline(s): Jan. 1 and Aug. 1
Final notification: May 1 and Dec. 1

Officers and Trustees:* Kevin Belford,* Secy.; Joseph Martin,* Treas.; Kevin Hardardt, Exec. Dir.; Gary L. Neale; David Parker; Richard E. Terry.
EIN: 541501306

657
American Road & Transportation Builders Association Foundation

1010 Massachusetts Ave., N.W.
Washington, DC 20001-5402 (202) 289-4434
Contact: T. Peter Ruane, Pres.
FAX: (202) 289-4435 E-mail: rhaskins@artba.org; URL: http://www.artba.org

Established in 1902.
Grantmaker type: Public charity
Financial data (yr. ended 12/31/00): Revenue, $35,357; assets, $206,048; gifts received, $57,728; expenditures, $89,747; program services expenses, $89,747; giving activities include $6,500 for 5 grants to individuals (high: $2,500; low: $500).
Purpose and activities: ARTBA exclusively represents the collective interests of all sectors of U.S. transportation construction industry before the White House, congress and federal agencies. It has also become the industry's primary advocate in environmental regulatory actions and litigation. In 1999 the association gave two $5,000 scholarships.
Fields of interest: Environment; Business/industry.
Types of support: Program development; Conferences/seminars; Scholarships—to individuals.
Application information: See Web site for further information. Application form required.
  Deadline(s): May 15 for Globe Award; Mar. 15 for Scholarships; None for Young Executive; Jan. 15 for Pride in Transportation Construction Award
  Final notification: July 30 for Globe Award; May 15 for Scholarships; Feb. 15 for Pride in Transportation Construction Award
Officers and Trustees: John W. Wight,* Chair.; Jack Albert,* First Vice-Chair; Tom Hill,* C.E.O.; T. Peter Ruane,* Pres. and Secy.; Bill Toohey,* Sr. V.P.; Bill Buechner,* V.P.; James R. Madara,* Treas.; Denver Collins, Jr.; and 19 additional trustees.
EIN: 526283894

658
Bauman Family Foundation, Inc. ▼

c/o Jewett House
2040 S St., N.W.
Washington, DC 20009-1110 (202) 328-2040
Contact: Patricia Bauman, Pres.; or John L. Bryant, Jr., V.P.
FAX: (202) 328-2003

Established in 1982 in NY.
Donor(s): Lionel R. Bauman.‡
Grantmaker type: Independent foundation
Financial data (yr. ended 06/30/02): Assets, $56,107,468 (M); expenditures, $6,086,586; qualifying distributions, $5,378,922; giving activities include $4,917,455 for 74 grants (high: $500,000; low: $1,000; average: $10,000–$100,000).

Purpose and activities: Grants to local, state, or national organizations with a clear strategy for translating their projects into nationally applicable ideas, including support for issues at the intersection of the economy and the environment, e.g., reconciliation of worker and community interests in sustainable economic development, trade and the environment, and jobs and the environment; support also for fostering citizens' access to information, increasing awareness of civic rights and responsibilities, and encouraging a central role for interdisciplinary education in achieving the goals of education reform.
Fields of interest: Arts; Education; Environment; Economic development; Public policy, research.
Types of support: General/operating support; Continuing support; Program development; Conferences/seminars; Publication; Seed money; Curriculum development; Research; Technical assistance; Matching/challenge support.
Limitations: Applications not accepted. Giving on a national basis. No grants to individuals.
Application information: Only applications solicited by the foundation are accepted.
  Board meeting date(s): Quarterly
Officers and Directors:* Patricia Bauman,* Pres.; John L. Bryant, Jr.,* V.P.; Gail M. Harmon,* Secy.; Irene Crowe; Diane Ives.
Number of staff: 2 full-time professional; 1 full-time support.
EIN: 133119290
Recent environmental and animal welfare grants:
658-1 American Friends of the Hebrew University, New York, NY, $10,000. For desertification research at Multi-Disciplinary Center for Environmental Studies. 2002.
658-2 Catholic University of America, DC, $55,000. For research and related activities with respect to religion's role in environmental awareness and advocacy. 2002.
658-3 Center for Environmental Citizenship, DC, $50,000. For general support. 2002.
658-4 Center for Health, Environment and Justice, Falls Church, VA, $50,000. For general support. 2002.
658-5 Center for Independent Documentary, Sharon, MA, $10,000. For My House is Your House's film, Blue Vinyl. 2002.
658-6 Childrens Environmental Health Network, DC, $25,000. For general support. 2002.
658-7 Clean Water Fund, DC, $200,000. For general support. 2002.
658-8 Clean Water Fund, DC, $50,000. For Clean Water Fund of California. 2002.
658-9 Clean Water Fund, DC, $50,000. For Clean Water Fund of New Jersey for their right-to-know and environmental health work. 2002.
658-10 Clean Water Fund, Boston, MA, $25,000. For Precautionary Principle Project of Alliance for a Healthy Tomorrow. 2002.
658-11 Columbia University, School of Public Health, New York, NY, $50,000. For community-based outreach and education activities of Center for Children's Environmental Health. 2002.
658-12 Columbia University, School of Public Health, New York, NY, $25,000. For general support for Center for Children's Environmental Health. 2002.

658-13 Defenders of Wildlife, DC, $50,000. For State Environmental Resource Center. 2002.
658-14 Environmental Advocates, Albany, NY, $25,000. For Pesticide Right-to-Know and Reduction Project. 2002.
658-15 Environmental Defense, New York, NY, $50,000. For work on right-to-know. 2002.
658-16 Environmental Health Fund, Jamaica Plain, MA, $25,000. For general support. 2002.
658-17 Environmental Health Fund, Jamaica Plain, MA, $25,000. For Health Care Without Harm project. 2002.
658-18 Environmental Media Services, DC, $50,000. For general support. 2002.
658-19 Environmental Working Group, DC, $25,000. For general support. 2002.
658-20 Healthy Schools Network, Albany, NY, $10,000. For work on environmental health policy. 2002.
658-21 League of Conservation Voters Education Fund, DC, $250,000. For Green Voter program. 2002.
658-22 National Environmental Trust, DC, $100,000. For children's environmental health. 2002.
658-23 Natural Resources Defense Council, New York, NY, $150,000. For general support of environmental and health initiative. 2002.
658-24 Natural Resources Defense Council, New York, NY, $100,000. For general support. 2002.
658-25 Northwest Coalition for Alternatives to Pesticides, Eugene, Oregon, $15,000. For work on the right-to-know. 2002.
658-26 Partnership Project, DC, $500,000. For general support. 2002.
658-27 Partnership Project, DC, $25,000. For development consultation. 2002.
658-28 Pesticide Action Network (PAN), North America Regional Center, San Francisco, CA, $35,000. For general support for database and Web site projects. 2002.
658-29 Physicians for Social Responsibility, DC, $50,000. For Environment and Health programs. 2002.
658-30 Riddles Elephant Breeding Farm and Wildlife Sanctuary, Greenbrier, AR, $20,000. For general support. 2002.
658-31 Science and Environmental Health Network, Windsor, ND, $25,000. For general support. 2002.
658-32 Sierra Club Foundation, San Francisco, CA, $250,000. For National Education Project. 2002.
658-33 Tufts University, Global Development and Environmental Institute, Medford, MA, $50,000. For project, Priceless: Human Health, the Environment and Limits of the Market. 2002.
658-34 United States Public Interest Research Group Education Fund, DC, $175,000. For right-to-know work in New Jersey and California. 2002.
658-35 United States Public Interest Research Group Education Fund, DC, $25,000. For Working Group on Community Right-to-Know. 2002.
658-36 Washington Toxics Coalition, Seattle, WA, $15,000. For PBT Communications Project. 2002.
658-37 Waterkeeper Alliance, White Plains, NY, $10,000. For annual conference. 2002.

658-38 Womens Voices for the Earth, Missoula, MT, $10,000. For Coming Clean collaboration on chemical hazard reduction. 2002.

658-39 Work Environment Council of New Jersey, Trenton, NJ, $50,000. For general support. 2002.

658-40 World Resources Institute, DC, $50,000. For Access Initiative. 2002.

659
Bellona Foundation USA

P.O. Box 53060
Washington, DC 20009 (202) 363-6810
Contact: Thomas Jandl
E-mail: bellona@mindspring.com; URL: http://www.bellona.org

Established in 1997 in DC.
Grantmaker type: Public charity
Financial data (yr. ended 12/31/01): Revenue, $1,022; assets, $10,907; gifts received, $2,000; expenditures, $29,051; program services expenses, $20,549.
Purpose and activities: The foundation was founded in recognition of the internationalization of environmental problems and the important role the United States as the foremost political, military and economic superpower plays in bi- and multilateral environmental negotiations.
Fields of interest: Environment, pollution control; Environment; International affairs.
Limitations: Giving on an international basis.
Officers and Directors:* Stan Zimmerman,* Chair.; Siri Engesaeth; Murray Feshbach, Ph.D.; Nils Bohmer; Josh Handler; Thomas Jandl.
EIN: 521999606

660
The Butler Family Fund

One Dupont Cir., N.W., Ste. 700
Washington, DC 20036 (202) 463-8288
Contact: Martha A. Toll, Exec. Dir.
FAX: (202) 467-0790; E-mail: info@butlerfamilyfund.org; URL: http://www.butlerfamilyfund.org

Established in 1992 in DC.
Donor(s): J.E. and Z.B. Butler Foundation.
Grantmaker type: Independent foundation
Financial data (yr. ended 12/31/02): Assets, $12,232,794 (M); gifts received, $17,230; expenditures, $1,644,424; qualifying distributions, $1,509,335; giving activities include $1,346,675 for 104 grants (high: $100,000; low: $1,000; average: $1,000–$50,000).
Purpose and activities: Support for homeless families and criminal justice reform (death penalty, juvenile justice, and drug policy); also global warming.
Fields of interest: Global warming; Crime/law enforcement, reform; Housing/shelter; Civil liberties, death penalty issues; Homeless.
International interests: United Kingdom.
Types of support: General/operating support; Program development; Seed money; Program-related investments/loans.
Limitations: Applications not accepted. Giving primarily in Los Angeles, San Diego and the San Francisco Bay Area, CA, Washington, DC,

Chicago, IL, NY, Philadelphia, PA, WI, and London, England. No grants to individuals.
Publications: Grants list, Program policy statement.
Application information: Unsolicited proposals are not accepted.
Board meeting date(s): Biannually
Officers and Directors:* Alan B. Morrison,* Pres.; Anne S. Morrison, Secy.; Martha A. Toll, Exec. Dir.; Suzanne H. Binswanger; Lowell A. Blankfort; Laurence A. Gravin; Alexandra Hirsh; John B. Hirsch; Georgina Hirsh; Steven R. Hirsch; Peggy A. Horan; Rebecca Morrison; Jody Binswager Snider.
Number of staff: 1 part-time professional; 1 part-time support.
EIN: 521786778

661
The Morris and Gwendolyn Cafritz Foundation ▼

1825 K St., N.W., 14th Fl.
Washington, DC 20006 (202) 223-3100
FAX: (202) 296-7567; E-mail: info@cafritzfoundation.org; URL: http://www.cafritzfoundation.org

Incorporated in 1948 in DC.
Donor(s): Morris Cafritz,‡ Gwendolyn D. Cafritz.‡
Grantmaker type: Independent foundation
Financial data (yr. ended 04/30/02): Assets, $346,922,783 (M); expenditures, $20,502,605; qualifying distributions, $18,889,756; giving activities include $16,706,820 for 546 grants (high: $350,000; low: $51; average: $10,000–$100,000).
Purpose and activities: Giving only for programs of direct assistance, with emphasis on community service, arts and humanities, education, and health.
Fields of interest: Museums; Performing arts; Dance; Theater; Music; Arts; Education, association; Early childhood education; Child development, education; Elementary school/education; Secondary school/education; Higher education; Medical school/education; Adult/continuing education; Adult education—literacy, basic skills & GED; Natural resources; Environment; Family planning; Medical care, rehabilitation; Health care; Substance abuse, services; Mental health/crisis services; AIDS; Health organizations; AIDS research; Crime/law enforcement; Housing/shelter, development; Human services; Children/youth, services; Child development, services; Family services; Hospices; Aging, centers/services; Women, centers/services; Homeless, human services; Civil rights, immigrants; Civil rights, minorities; Civil rights, women; Civil rights, aging; Reproductive rights; Civil rights; Community development; Voluntarism promotion; Minorities; Asians/Pacific Islanders; African Americans/Blacks; Hispanics/Latinos; Disabled; Aging; Women; People with AIDS (PWAs); Immigrants/refugees; Economically disadvantaged; Homeless.
Types of support: General/operating support; Continuing support; Equipment; Program development; Seed money; Fellowships; Scholarship funds; Technical assistance; Matching/challenge support.

Limitations: Giving limited to the greater metropolitan Washington, DC, area. No grants to individuals, or for emergency funds, deficit financing, capital, endowment, or building funds, demonstration projects, or conferences; no loans (except for program-related investments).
Publications: Application guidelines, Annual report.
Application information: Uses WRAG Guidelines. Application form required.
Initial approach: Proposal
Copies of proposal: 1
Deadline(s): July 1, Nov. 1, and Mar. 1
Board meeting date(s): Generally 3 to 9 months after deadline dates
Officers and Directors:* Calvin Cafritz,* Chair., C.E.O. and Pres.; Daniel J. Callahan III,* Vice-Chair. and Treas.; John H.C. Barron, Secy.; Daniel J. Boorstin; Terence Golden; Guy T. Steuart II.
Advisory Board: Anthony Cafritz; Elliot Cafritz; Jane Cafritz; Kate D. Clark; Carolyn J. Deaver; Robert W. Deumling; Richard Hubbard Howland; Constance A. Morella; Elizabeth Peltekian; Julia Sparkman Shepard.
Number of staff: 7 full-time professional; 6 full-time support.
EIN: 526036989
Recent environmental and animal welfare grants:

661-1 American Farmland Trust, DC, $20,000. For Freshfarm Market and expanded educational activities. 2002.

661-2 Anacostia Watershed Society, Bladensburg, MD, $65,000. For general support for river restoration work and environmental education programs. 2002.

661-3 Center for Watershed Protection, Ellicott City, MD, $30,000. For Builders for the Bay, which seeks to initiate changes in local codes and ordinances of Chesapeake Bay communities and to allow for better site design. 2002.

661-4 Coalition for Smarter Growth, DC, $30,000. For general support. 2002.

661-5 Coalition for Smarter Growth, DC, $20,000. For matching grant to hire organizer in Prince George's County, Maryland. 2002.

661-6 Discovery Creek Childrens Museum, DC, $50,000. For Rolling Rainforest Initiative. 2002.

661-7 Discovery Creek Childrens Museum, DC, $25,000. For general support. 2002.

661-8 Durrin Productions, DC, $30,000. For Bombs in Our Backyard, film about toxic chemical munitions in Spring Valley neighborhood in DC. 2002.

661-9 Earth Conservation Corps, DC, $200,000. For Riverlife Expeditions, environmental and job training program focusing on Anacostia River and inner-city neighborhoods. 2002.

661-10 Echo Hill Outdoor School, Worton, MD, $10,000. To provide DC Public School children with residential outdoor experience. Grant made in memory of Hilda Taylor, teacher who died in plane that crashed into Pentagon on September 11. 2002.

661-11 Families USA Foundation, Alliance for Fairness in Reforms to Medicaid, DC, $25,000. For general support. 2002.

661-12 Friends of the Earth, DC, $20,000. For DC Environmental Network. 2002.

661-13 Garden Resources of Washington, DC, $15,000. For general support. 2002.

661-14 Garden Resources of Washington, DC, $10,000. For matching grant for general support. 2002.

661-15 Institute for Local Self-Reliance, DC, $30,000. For DC Initiative. 2002.

661-16 Low-Impact Development Center, Beltsville, MD, $10,000. For restorative landscaping to protect and improve urban water quality. 2002.

661-17 National Environmental Education and Training Foundation, DC, $35,000. To develop Watersheds and Television Weather Reporting project. 2002.

661-18 Natural Resources Defense Council, New York, NY, $40,000. For Anacostia Cleanup Initiative. 2002.

661-19 Potomac Conservancy, Annandale, VA, $45,000. For general support. 2002.

661-20 Potomac Conservancy, Annandale, VA, $15,000. For matching grant for general support. 2002.

661-21 Shaw EcoVillage Project, DC, $15,000. For general support. 2002.

661-22 Smart Growth Alliance, DC, $10,000. For start-up support for coalition of civic, environmental, business, and development organizations committed to promoting quality of life and smart growth in Washington, DC area. 2002.

661-23 Student Conservation Association, DC, $72,000. For Capital Conservation Corps which engages urban youth in conservation service learning projects and environmental education. 2002.

661-24 Sultana Projects, Chestertown, MD, $12,000. For general support of Schooner Sultana Project. 2002.

662

Naomi and Nehemiah Cohen Foundation ▼

(formerly Cohen-Solomon Family Foundation, Inc.)
P.O. Box 73708
Washington, DC 20056 (202) 234-5454
Contact: Alison McWilliams, Dir.
FAX: (202) 234-8797; E-mail: NNCF@erols.com

Incorporated in 1959 in DC.
Donor(s): Emanuel Cohen,‡ N.M. Cohen,‡ Naomi Cohen,‡ Israel Cohen,‡ Daniel Solomon, Lillian Cohen Solomon,‡ David Solomon, Stuart Brown, Diane Solomon Brown.‡
Grantmaker type: Independent foundation
Financial data (yr. ended 12/31/02): Assets, $80,337,648 (M); gifts received, $1,588,583; expenditures, $4,196,595; qualifying distributions, $4,157,745; giving activities include $4,082,500 for 120 grants (high: $100,000; low: $1,000; average: $1,000–$50,000).
Purpose and activities: The focus of the foundation is on human services, civic affairs and Jewish causes in Washington, DC and Israel.
Fields of interest: Environment; Youth development, adult & child programs; Human services; International human rights; Civil rights; Community development; Jewish agencies & temples.
International interests: Israel.

Types of support: General/operating support; Annual campaigns; Capital campaigns; Building/renovation; Program-related investments/loans; Program evaluation.
Limitations: Giving primarily in Washington, DC and Israel. No grants to individuals.
Publications: Application guidelines, Grants list.
Application information: Application form not required.
Initial approach: Letter
Board meeting date(s): Quarterly
Officers and Directors:* Daniel Solomon,* Pres.; David Solomon,* V.P.; Diane Solomon Brown,* Secy.; Stuart Brown, Treas.; Alison McWilliams, Dir.
Number of staff: 1 full-time professional.
EIN: 526054166

663

The Community Foundation for the National Capital Region ▼

(formerly The Foundation for the National Capital Region)
1201 15th St. N.W., Ste. 420
Washington, DC 20005 (202) 955-5890
Contact: Terri Lee Freeman, Pres.
FAX: (202) 955-8084; E-mail: cfncr@aol.com;
URL: http://www.cfncr.org

Incorporated in 1973 in DC.
Grantmaker type: Community foundation
Financial data (yr. ended 03/31/02): Assets, $203,765,953 (M); gifts received, $99,053,230; expenditures, $47,132,355; giving activities include $45,210,754 for 2,043+ grants (high: $1,646,155; average: $500–$100,000).
Purpose and activities: The foundation exists to foster a culture of giving in the diverse and dynamic community comprising Washington, DC, and nearby MD and VA. Through its programs and discretionary grants, the foundation works to build philanthropic capital dedicated to improving the region's quality of life, to strengthen the region's nonprofit organizations and improve their financial stability, and to fund projects and experiments offering new solutions to community needs.
Fields of interest: Arts; Education; Natural resources; Health care; Substance abuse, services; Human services; Children/youth, services; Community development; Economically disadvantaged; Homeless.
Types of support: General/operating support; Program development; Technical assistance; Program evaluation.
Limitations: Giving limited to the metropolitan Washington, DC, area. No grants to individuals (except for scholarships and fellowships), or from discretionary funds for annual campaigns, endowment funds, equipment, land acquisition, renovation projects, operating budgets, or matching gifts.
Publications: Application guidelines, Annual report, Financial statement, Program policy statement.
Application information: Accepts WG Common Grant Application Format; letter of inquiry received by FAX not accepted; Building Community Through the Arts grants does not accept unsolicited proposals. Application form required.
Initial approach: Seek guidelines for Discretionary Grants Program before

applying; letter of inquiry (no more than 3 pages)
Copies of proposal: 1
Deadline(s): June 25 and Dec. 10 for letter of inquiry; Mar. 1 and Sept. 1 for proposal (if invited)
Board meeting date(s): Quarterly
Final notification: June 1 and Dec. 1
Officers and Trustees:* Lawrence A. Hough,* Chair.; Alexine Clement Jackson,* Vice-Chair.; Terri Lee Freeman,* Pres.; Kenny Emson, V.P. and C.F.O.; Kathy A. Whelpley, V.P., Prog. and Donor Engagement; Betsy Karel, Secy.; John Schwieters, Treas.; Thomas Troyer,* Genl. Counsel; Don Beyer, Jr.; Douglas M. Bibby; Robert Boisture; Walter Fatzinger; Nancy (Bitsey) Folger; Victoria P. Sant; and 16 additional trustees.
Number of staff: 9 full-time professional; 2 part-time professional; 2 full-time support; 1 part-time support.
EIN: 237343119
Recent environmental and animal welfare grants:

663-1 Anacostia Watershed Society, Bladensburg, MD, $10,000. For general support. 2003.

663-2 Coral Reef Alliance (CORAL), San Francisco, CA, $70,000. For Coral Reef Parks Program in Mesoamerican Reef. 2003.

663-3 Discovery Creek Childrens Museum, DC, $25,000. For general support. 2003.

663-4 Discovery Creek Childrens Museum, DC, $10,000. For Rolling Rain Forest. 2003.

663-5 Indianapolis Zoological Society, Indianapolis, Indiana, $25,000. For Zoo Teen Program. 2003.

663-6 Indianapolis Zoological Society, Indianapolis, Indiana, $25,000. For corporate campaign. 2003.

663-7 LightHawk, Lander, WY, $55,000. For Biodiversity Protection in Mexico, Belize, Guatemala and Honduras project. 2003.

663-8 Marine Stewardship Council, Seattle, WA, $167,500. For improving marine fisheries management through certification around world. 2003.

663-9 Mexican Nature Conservation Fund, Mexico City, Mexico, $15,000. For implementation of donor advised grantmaking program, Integrated Population-Environment Initiative in Mexico. 2003.

663-10 National Zoo, Friends of the, DC, $15,000. 2003.

663-11 Nature Conservancy, Arlington, VA, $10,000. For general support. 2003.

663-12 Nature Conservancy, Arlington, VA, $10,000. For general support. 2003.

663-13 Operation Migration USA, Buffalo, NY, $25,000. For general support. 2003.

663-14 Population Reference Bureau, DC, $40,000. For Population, Environment and Health Program. 2003.

663-15 Sanibel-Captiva Conservation Foundation, Sanibel, FL, $25,000. For Marine Lab. 2003.

663-16 Shaw EcoVillage Project, DC, $10,000. For general support. 2003.

663-17 Toledo Institute for Development and Environment (TIDE), Punta Gorda, Belize, $37,500. For Conservation of Natural Resources in Toledo District, Belize Project. 2003.

663-18 World Resources Institute Fund, DC, $15,000. To accelerate implementation of Mesoamerican Biological Corridor Project. 2003.

663-19 World Wildlife Fund/Conservation Foundation, DC, $300,000. 2003.

664
Conservation International Foundation
1919 M St., N.W., Ste. 600
Washington, DC 20036 (202) 912-1000
Contact: Peter A. Seligmann, Chair. and C.E.O.
Additional tel.: (800) 406-2306; URL: http://www.conservation.org

Grantmaker type: Public charity
Financial data (yr. ended 06/30/02): Revenue, $222,709,275; assets, $291,910,357; gifts received, $221,423,138; expenditures, $69,024,034; program services expenses, $57,793,808; giving activities include $11,081,527 for 234 grants (high: $753,000; low: $45).
Purpose and activities: The foundation supports efforts to conserve the earth's living natural heritage, global biodiversity, and to demonstrate that human societies are able to live harmoniously with nature.
Fields of interest: Environment; Animals/wildlife, preservation/protection.
Limitations: Giving on a national and international basis.
Officers and Directors:* Peter A. Seligmann,* Chair. and C.E.O.; Meredith Auld Brokaw,* Vice-Chair.; Lewis W. Coleman,* Vice-Chair.; Harrison Ford,* Vice-Chair.; Story Clark Resor,* Vice-Chair.; Henry H. Arnhold; Skip Brittenham; Louis W. Cabot; and 22 additional directors.
EIN: 521497470

665
Shelby Cullom Davis Foundation ▼
5335 Wisconsin Ave., N.W., Ste. 440
Washington, DC 20015 (202) 686-2611
FAX: (202) 686-2614; E-mail: scdf@his.com

Incorporated in 1962 in NY.
Donor(s): Shelby Cullom Davis.‡
Grantmaker type: Independent foundation
Financial data (yr. ended 11/30/02): Assets, $72,272,309 (M); expenditures, $4,339,176; qualifying distributions, $3,509,400; giving activities include $3,509,400 for grants (average: $500–$160,000).
Purpose and activities: Giving primarily for higher education and public policy; some support for cultural programs and economic research.
Fields of interest: Arts; Higher education; Economics; Public policy, research.
Limitations: Applications not accepted. No grants to individuals.
Application information: Contributes only to pre-selected organizations.
Trustees: Andrew Adams Davis; Christopher Cullom Davis; Kathryn W. Davis; Shelby Moore Cullom Davis; Victoria Davis; Abby Moffat; Diana Davis Spencer; Kimberly F. Spencer.
Corporate Trustee: Bessemer Trust Co., N.A.
EIN: 136165382
Recent environmental and animal welfare grants:

665-1 Central Park Conservancy, New York, NY, $10,000. 2001.
665-2 Maine Coast Heritage Trust, Topsham, ME, $50,000. 2001.
665-3 Manitoga, Garrison, NY, $25,000. 2001.
665-4 Millers River Educational Cooperative, Royalston, MA, $10,000. 2001.
665-5 Natural Resources Council, Augusta, ME, $10,000. 2001.
665-6 Natural Resources Defense Council, New York, NY, $10,000. 2001.
665-7 Scenic Hudson, Poughkeepsie, NY, $330,000. 2001.

666
Environmental Support Center, Inc.
1500 Massachusetts Ave., N.W., Ste. 25
Washington, DC 20005 (202) 331-9700
Contact: Patrick Sweeney, Pres.
FAX: (202) 331-8592; URL: http://www.envsc.org/

Grantmaker type: Public charity
Financial data (yr. ended 12/31/02): Revenue, $1,644,699; assets, $2,437,136 (M); gifts received, $1,601,507; expenditures, $2,867,113; program services expenses, $2,613,969; giving activities include $754,577 for grants.
Purpose and activities: The center assists in improving the environment in the U.S. through enhancing the health and well-being of regional, state, and local organizations working on environmental issues.
Fields of interest: Environment.
Limitations: Giving on a national basis.
Application information: Application form required.
Officers and Directors:* Patrick Sweeney,* Pres.; Antonio Diaz,* V.P.; Whitlynn T. Battle,* Secy.; Brownie Carson; Lois DeBacker; Pablo Eisenberg; and 9 additional directors.
EIN: 133563949

667
Friedman-French Foundation, Inc.
2330 California St. N.W.
Washington, DC 20008-1637

Established in 1993 in DC.
Donor(s): Emanuel Friedman, Kindy French.
Grantmaker type: Independent foundation
Financial data (yr. ended 06/30/02): Assets, $856,351 (M); gifts received, $181,180; expenditures, $150,079; qualifying distributions, $138,250; giving activities include $138,250 for 17 grants (high: $56,000; low: $750).
Purpose and activities: Giving primarily for education and Jewish agencies and temples.
Fields of interest: Arts; Elementary/secondary education; Higher education; Graduate/professional education; Education; Natural resources; Human services; Protestant agencies & churches; Jewish agencies & temples.
Limitations: Applications not accepted. Giving primarily in Washington, DC, MD, NY, and VA. No grants to individuals.
Application information: Contributes only to pre-selected organizations.
Directors: Kindy French; Emanuel Friedman; Ned S. Scherer.
EIN: 521853718

668
The Gaea Foundation, Inc.
1611 Connecticut Ave. N.W., Rm. 200
Washington, DC 20009 (202) 232-0304
FAX: (202) 232-1651

Established in 1993 in DC.
Donor(s): Gaylord Neely.
Grantmaker type: Independent foundation
Financial data (yr. ended 12/31/02): Assets, $2,774,545 (M); expenditures, $806,012; qualifying distributions, $567,086; giving activities include $105,000 for 15 grants (high: $50,000; low: $1,000) and $207,764 for 2 foundation-administered programs.
Purpose and activities: Supports the establishment and early development of organizations furthering and involved with women's legal rights, and women's health issues. Also supports the environment on human health programs, fighting racism and class injustice, the international struggle for human rights, American cultural work, and the arts.
Fields of interest: Cultural/ethnic awareness; Environment; Youth development, services; Domestic violence; International human rights; Civil rights, equal rights; Civil rights, disabled; Civil rights, women; Civil rights, gays/lesbians; Race/intergroup relations; Disabled; Women.
Types of support: General/operating support; Continuing support; Emergency funds; Seed money; Program-related investments/loans; In-kind gifts.
Limitations: Applications not accepted. No grants for legal and education funds, or service-providing programs such as schools, shelters, centers, or universities.
Application information: The foundation is not accepting new grant applications at this time.
Board meeting date(s): June and Dec.
Officers and Directors:* Gaylord Neely,* Pres.; Joanne LaSalla,* V.P.; Allida Black,* Secy.
Number of staff: 1 part-time professional.
EIN: 521858609

669
Garden Resources of Washington
(also known as GROW)
1419 V St., N.W.
Washington, DC 20009 (202) 234-0591
FAX: (202) 234-0592; E-mail: GROW19@aol.com

Established in 1982.
Grantmaker type: Public charity
Financial data (yr. ended 12/31/01): Revenue, $127,220; assets, $41,718; gifts received, $125,216; expenditures, $109,871; program services expenses, $98,178; giving activities include $24,650 for 31 grants (high: $1,000; low: $200).
Purpose and activities: GROW provides technical assistance services and small grants to diverse groups in neighborhoods throughout the District of Columbia who need help starting community and youth gardens on vacant lots, at schools and after-school programs, at seniors' centers and transitional housing, at churches and social service agencies, in parks and on campuses, and at other community settings.
Fields of interest:
Botanical/horticulture/landscape services; Botanical gardens; Horticulture/garden clubs;

Environment, beautification programs; Environmental education.
Limitations: Giving limited to Washington, DC.
Officers and Board:* Ann Matikan,* Pres.; Dare Johnson,* V.P.; Peter Enchelmayer,* Secy.; Tanya Cook,* Treas.; Kathryn Enchelmayaer; Sherburne Laughlin.
EIN: 521276560

670

The German Marshall Fund of the United States

1744 R St. N.W.
Washington, DC 20009 (202) 745-3950
Contact: Phil Henderson, Dir., Programs
FAX: (202) 265-1662; European reps.: Heike MacKerron, Oranienburger Strasse 13/14, Berlin, 10178, Germany (tel.: 493-0283-4902), and Amaya Bloch-Laine - 16, Rue Paul Valery, 75016 Paris, France (tel.: 331-5628-0886); E-mail: info@gmfus.org; URL: http://www.gmfus.org

Incorporated in 1972 in DC; founded through a gift from Germany as a permanent memorial to Marshall Plan assistance.
Donor(s): Federal Republic of Germany.
Grantmaker type: Public charity
Financial data (yr. ended 05/31/03): Assets, $187,950,570 (M); expenditures, $14,219,201; program services expenses, $8,729,628; giving activities include $5,021,592 for grants.
Purpose and activities: The fund is an American public policy and grantmaking institution dedicated to promoting greater cooperation and understanding between the United States and Europe. GMF does this by supporting individuals and institutions working on transatlantic issues, by convening leaders to discuss the most pressing transatlantic themes, and by examining ways in which transatlantic cooperation can address a variety of global policy challenges. All GMF activities are organized within three principal program areas: transatlantic policy, transatlantic leadership, and wider Europe. In addition, GMF has developed a strong Central and Eastern Europe program aimed at furthering democratic consolidation and promoting integration into European and transatlantic institutions. GMF maintains a strong presence on both sides of the Atlantic.
Fields of interest: Journalism/publishing; Environment; Foreign policy.
International interests: Europe; Eastern Europe.
Types of support: Conferences/seminars; Publication; Fellowships; Research.
Limitations: Giving limited to the U.S. and Europe. No support for the arts and humanities, medicine and health, arms control, or diplomatic studies. No grants for building or operating budgets, annual campaigns, emergency funds, deficit financing, medical or scientific research, or graduate or undergraduate studies.
Publications: Annual report.
Application information: Application form only required for fellowship programs; see Web site for complete program descriptions and application guidelines. Application form required.
Initial approach: Letter (in English), or brief proposal
Copies of proposal: 1

Deadline(s): Nov. for research fellowships
Board meeting date(s): Feb., May, and Oct.
Final notification: Mar. for research fellowships
Officers and Trustees:* Guido Goldman,* Co-Chair.; Marc Leland,* Co-Chair.; Craig Kennedy,* Pres.; Jeffrey Goldstein; Lee Hamilton; David Ignatius; Robert M. Kimmitt; Scott Klug; Mara Liasson; J. Thomas Presby; Richard Roberts; John A. Ross; Steven G. Rothmeier; Barbara Shailor; Amity Shlaes; Robert M. Solow; Jenonne Walker; Leah Zell Wanger; J. Robinson West; Suzanne Woolsey.
Number of staff: 30 full-time professional; 1 part-time professional; 4 full-time support; 11 part-time support.
EIN: 520954751

671

Stephen A. and Diana L. Goldberg Foundation

c/o Mark Spisak
1615 M St., N.W., Ste. 850
Washington, DC 20036
FAX: (202) 362-8215

Established in 1994 in DE.
Grantmaker type: Independent foundation
Financial data (yr. ended 12/31/02): Assets, $1,717 (M); gifts received, $795,000; expenditures, $793,602; qualifying distributions, $792,199; giving activities include $792,199 for grants (high: $50,000).
Purpose and activities: Support primarily for children's health care and development; giving also for the arts, the environment, civil rights, and public affairs.
Fields of interest: Visual arts; Museums; Performing arts; Environment; Hospitals (specialty); Pediatrics; Health organizations; Youth development; Human services; Civil rights; Public affairs, research.
Types of support: General/operating support.
Limitations: Giving on a national basis, with some emphasis on NY, CA, MA, MI, MT, and Washington, DC.
Application information: Application form not required.
Deadline(s): None
Officers and Directors:* Stephen A. Goldberg,* Pres.; Diana L. Goldberg,* V.P.; Martin J. Kirsch,* Secy.; Brian L. Goldberg; Lauren B. Goldberg; Stuart W. Goldberg.
EIN: 510326473

672

Edith J. Goode Residuary Trust

c/o Riggs Bank, N.A.
P.O. Box 96202
Washington, DC 20090-6202
Contact: William F. Harvey
Application address: c/o Donna Pease, 700 Professional Dr., Gaithersburg, MD 20879

Established in 1972.
Donor(s): Edith J. Goode.‡
Grantmaker type: Independent foundation
Financial data (yr. ended 04/30/02): Assets, $2,231,330 (M); expenditures, $214,975; qualifying distributions, $191,614; giving activities include $173,870 for 27 grants (high: $20,000; low: $1,450).

Purpose and activities: Grants are awarded to organizations operating exclusively for the prevention of cruelty to animals.
Fields of interest: Animal welfare.
Limitations: Giving on a national basis. No grants to individuals.
Publications: Application guidelines.
Application information:
Initial approach: Letter (not more than 3 pages)
Deadline(s): None
Officers: Andrew N. Rowan, Grant Advisor; Donna Pease, Grant Admin.
Trustee: Riggs Bank, N.A.
EIN: 520950506

673

The Hanley Foundation

3201 New Mexico Ave. N.W., Ste. 350
Washington, DC 20016

Established in 1999 in DC.
Donor(s): Michael J. Hanley.
Grantmaker type: Independent foundation
Financial data (yr. ended 12/31/02): Assets, $3,496,650 (M); expenditures, $321,997; qualifying distributions, $306,982; giving activities include $308,000 for 17 grants (high: $150,000; low: $500).
Purpose and activities: Giving primarily for water resource conservation, as well as for the arts, education, community foundations, and social services, including services for people who are blind.
Fields of interest: Arts; Education; Environment, water resources; Human services; Human services; Foundations (community).
Limitations: Applications not accepted. Giving primarily in Washington, DC, and MD. No grants to individuals.
Application information: Contributes only to pre-selected organizations.
Officers: Michael J. Hanley, Pres.; Kathryn J. Hanley, V.P.; Ellen McMacken, Secy.
EIN: 522204367

674

Hill-Snowdon Foundation

1317 F St., N.W., Ste. 350
Washington, DC 20004
Contact: Richard W. Snowdon, Dir.
Application address: The Tides Foundation, P.O. Box 29903, San Francisco, CA 94129

Established in 1959.
Donor(s): Arthur B. Hill.‡
Grantmaker type: Independent foundation
Financial data (yr. ended 12/31/02): Assets, $34,151,486 (M); expenditures, $1,813,196; qualifying distributions, $1,797,794; giving activities include $1,794,000 for 16 grants (high: $1,345,000; low: $500; average: $5,000–$10,000).
Purpose and activities: Support primarily to a public foundation; giving also for secondary education, theater and other performing arts groups, environmental organizations, health and human services, and youth groups.
Fields of interest: Performing arts; Theater; Secondary school/education; Environment; Substance abuse, services; Youth development; Human services; Foundations (public); Minorities; Disabled.

Types of support: General/operating support.
Limitations: Applications not accepted. Giving on a national basis. No grants to individuals.
Application information: Contributes only to pre-selected organizations.
Directors: Edward W. Snowdon, Jr.; Marguerite H. Snowdon; Richard W. Snowdon.
EIN: 226081122

675
Paul and Annetta Himmelfarb Foundation, Inc.

4545 42nd St. N.W., Ste. 203
Washington, DC 20016 (202) 966-3795
Contact: Lillian N. Kronstadt, Treas. and Exec. Dir.

Incorporated in 1947 in DE.
Donor(s): Members of the Himmelfarb family.
Grantmaker type: Independent foundation
Financial data (yr. ended 12/31/02): Assets, $5,368,097 (M); expenditures, $380,308; qualifying distributions, $280,115; giving activities include $210,680 for 93 grants (high: $20,000; low: $45; average: $100–$20,000).
Purpose and activities: Primary areas of interest include educational and medical research, health, the elderly, human need, and Israel.
Fields of interest: Early childhood education; Education; Environment; Health care; Health organizations, association; Medical research, institute; Cancer research; AIDS research; Human services; Aging, centers/services; Homeless, human services; Jewish federated giving programs; Disabled; Aging; Homeless.
International interests: Israel.
Types of support: Continuing support; Annual campaigns; Equipment; Scholarship funds; Research; Matching/challenge support.
Limitations: Giving primarily in the Washington, DC, area; giving also in Israel. No grants to individuals.
Application information: Application form not required.
 Initial approach: Letter
 Copies of proposal: 1
 Deadline(s): None
 Board meeting date(s): Monthly
 Final notification: 3 to 6 months
Officers and Directors:* Annette Kronstadt,* Pres.; Norma Lee Naiman,* V.P.; Paul Himmelfarb, Secy.; Lillian N. Kronstadt,* Treas. and Exec. Dir.; Carole Preston.
Number of staff: 1 full-time professional; 1 part-time professional.
EIN: 520784206

676
International Life Sciences Institute
(formerly International Life Sciences Research Foundation)
1 Thomas Cir., 9th Fl.
Washington, DC 20005 (202) 659-0074
Contact: Denise Robinson, Exec. Dir.
FAX: (202) 659-3859; E-mail: ilsi@ilsi.org; URL: http://www.ilsi.org

Established in 1978 in DC.
Grantmaker type: Public charity
Financial data (yr. ended 12/31/01): Revenue, $7,294,146; assets, $6,101,088 (M); gifts received, $4,270,003; expenditures,

$6,415,933; program services expenses, $3,924,598; giving activities include $239,438 for 19 grants.
Purpose and activities: The institute promotes an understanding and resolution of nutrition and environmental issues worldwide by bringing together scientists and the public sector to solve the concerns of the general public.
Fields of interest: Environment, public policy; Environment; Nutrition.
Types of support: Conferences/seminars.
Limitations: Giving on an international basis.
Trustees: G. Harvey Anderson, Ph.D.; James R. Behnke, Ph.D.; Jon R. Blake; Fergus M. Clydesdale, Ph.D.; Jack H. Dean, Ph.D.; Howard R. Delaney; Daniel B. Dennison, Ph.D.; Yuzo Hayashi, Ph.D.; and 22 additional trustees.
EIN: 521131788

677
King Hussein Foundation
(formerly Jordan Society, Inc.)
P.O. Box 42558
Washington, DC 20015 (202) 833-4999
Contact: Jill Kassis, Exec. Dir.
FAX: (202) 833-5666; E-mail: info@khf-usa.org

Established in 1981.
Grantmaker type: Public charity
Financial data (yr. ended 12/31/01): Revenue, $2,364,667; assets, $1,658,630; gifts received, $2,355,608; expenditures, $1,278,153; program services expenses, $1,098,667; giving activities include $1,016,825 for 3 grants (high: $486,875; low: $151,930).
Purpose and activities: The foundation supports programs for community development in education, leadership, health, democracy, peace and the environment.
Fields of interest: Education; Environment; Health care; Community development, public education; Community development.
Limitations: Giving on an international basis, primarily in Amman, Jordan.
Officers and Trustees:* H.M. Queen Noor,* Chair.; Alexa Halaby,* Secy.; Jill H. Kassis, Exec. Dir.; H.R.H. Prince Firas bin Ra'ad; Zoe Baird; Hon. Lloyd Cutler; Camille Douglas; and 5 additional trustees.
EIN: 133064429

678
Landscape Architecture Foundation
636 Eye St., N.W.
Washington, DC 20001-3736 (202) 898-2444
Contact: Melinda Sippel, Exec. Asst.
FAX: (202) 898-1185; E-mail: msippel@asla.org; URL: http://www.asla.org

Established in 1966 in Washington, DC.
Grantmaker type: Public charity
Financial data (yr. ended 09/30/00): Revenue, $873,539; assets, $3,299,539; gifts received, $523,716; expenditures, $358,307; program services expenses, $312,972; giving activities include $35,100 for 9 grants to individuals (high: $15,000; low: $600).
Purpose and activities: The foundation's mission is to support the preservation, improvement, and enhancement of the quality of the environment.
Fields of interest: Environment, beautification programs.

Types of support: Annual campaigns; Scholarship funds; Scholarships—to individuals.
Application information: Applications by e-mail or FAX not accepted; see Web site for supporting material requirements for each program. Application form required.
 Initial approach: Letter
 Copies of proposal: 3
 Deadline(s): Jan. 15 for Douglas Dockery Thomas Fellowship; Aug. 1 for AILA/Yamagami/Hope Fellowship; Mar. 31 for all others
Officers and Directors:* Dennis Y. Otsuji,* Pres.; Debra L. Mitchell,* Pres.-Elect; Phillip J. Arnold,* V.P.; Kenneth E. Bassett,* V.P.; Barbara Faga,* V.P.; Susan Gottsman,* V.P.; Frederick R. Steiner, V.P.; L. Susan Everett, Exec. Dir.; and 12 additional directors.
Number of staff: 1 full-time professional; 10 part-time professional; 1 full-time support; 10 part-time support.
EIN: 526065505

679
The Leon Foundation
2134 R St. N.W.
Washington, DC 20008

Established in 1986 in VA.
Donor(s): Alan L. Wurtzel.
Grantmaker type: Independent foundation
Financial data (yr. ended 12/31/01): Assets, $65,572 (M); gifts received, $22,190; expenditures, $114,855; qualifying distributions, $114,159; giving activities include $113,385 for 67 grants (high: $15,000; low: $100).
Fields of interest: Arts; Education; Natural resources; Animals/wildlife; Health organizations, association; Gun control; Human services; Jewish agencies & temples.
Limitations: Applications not accepted. Giving primarily in Washington, DC, New York, NY, and Richmond, VA. No grants to individuals.
Application information: Contributes only to pre-selected organizations.
Officers: Alan L. Wurtzel, Pres. and Treas.; Irene R. Wurtzel, V.P.; Jacquie Coles, Secy.
Directors: Daniel H. Wurtzel; Judith H. Wurtzel; Sharon L. Wurtzel.
EIN: 541393763

680
The LWH Family Foundation
1725 I St. N.W., Ste. 300
Washington, DC 20006-5701 (202) 349-4186
FAX: (202) 349-4187

Established in 1995 in DC.
Grantmaker type: Independent foundation
Financial data (yr. ended 12/31/00): Assets, $4,409,051 (M); gifts received, $801,342; expenditures, $209,003; qualifying distributions, $185,671; giving activities include $182,500 for 10 grants (high: $37,500; low: $5,000).
Purpose and activities: Giving for foreign relations, international studies and centers, and nature conservation.
Fields of interest: Theater; Natural resources; Human services; Public policy, research.
Limitations: Applications not accepted. Giving primarily in Washington, DC, and Arlington, VA. No grants to individuals.

Application information: Contributes only to pre-selected organizations.
Trustees: Birgit Hershey; Loren W. Hershey.
EIN: 521907069

681
The Mazda Foundation (USA), Inc.
1025 Connecticut Ave. N.W., Ste. 910
Washington, DC 20036
Contact: Barbara Nocera, Prog. Dir.; and Annemarie Render, Prog. Rep.
FAX: (202) 223-6490; *E-mail:* bnocera@mazdausa.com; *URL:* http://www.mazdafoundation.org/

Established in 1990 in MI.
Donor(s): Mazda North American Opers., Mazda Motor of America, Mazda Research & Development of North America.
Grantmaker type: Company-sponsored foundation
Financial data (yr. ended 09/30/02): Assets, $8,956,518 (M); expenditures, $482,462; qualifying distributions, $432,991; giving activities include $411,138 for 9 grants (high: $90,000; low: $12,500).
Purpose and activities: Giving primarily to education for youth.
Fields of interest: Scholarships/financial aid; Reading; Education; Natural resources; Environmental education; Disasters, 9/11/01; Medical research, institute; Race/intergroup relations.
Types of support: General/operating support; Curriculum development; Scholarship funds; Research; Exchange programs.
Limitations: Giving primarily in CA, MI, and MS, as well as to national programs. No support for religious organizations. No grants to individuals, or for fundraising dinners or events, or capital building, endowments, or debt reduction drives.
Publications: Annual report.
Application information: See foundation Web site for application guidelines. Application form not required.
Initial approach: Letter
Copies of proposal: 1
Deadline(s): Aug. 15
Board meeting date(s): Oct.
Final notification: Nov.
Officers and Trustees:* Charles R. Hughes,* Chair.; Jay Amestoy,* Pres.; Richard Valenstein,* Treas.; Gordan Dickie; Steve Odell.
Number of staff: None.
EIN: 382952236

682
The McIntosh Foundation
1730 M St. N.W., Ste. 204
Washington, DC 20036-4534 (202) 338-8055

Incorporated in 1949 in NY.
Donor(s): Josephine H. McIntosh,‡ Karen McIntosh,‡ Peter McIntosh,‡ Marie Joy McIntosh.‡
Grantmaker type: Independent foundation
Financial data (yr. ended 12/31/02): Assets, $34,877,977 (M); expenditures, $2,959,636; qualifying distributions, $2,925,390; giving activities include $2,476,390 for 56 grants (high:

$1,820,000; low: $1,000) and $7,487,398 for 1 loan/program-related investment.
Purpose and activities: Giving primarily for environmental conservation.
Fields of interest: Natural resources.
Types of support: General/operating support.
Limitations: Applications not accepted. Giving limited to southeastern AK.
Application information: Due to the number of ongoing and/or permanent projects, the foundation is accepting grant applications by invitation only.
Board meeting date(s): Every 4 months
Officers and Directors:* Michael A. McIntosh,* Pres. and C.I.O.; Joan H. McIntosh,* V.P.; Winsome D. McIntosh,* V.P.; Frederick A. Terry, Jr.,* Secy.; Hunter H. McIntosh; Michael A. McIntosh, Jr.
Number of staff: 1 full-time professional; 1 part-time professional; 1 part-time support.
EIN: 136096459

683
Robert S. and Margaret C. McNamara Foundation
2412 Tracy Pl. N.W., Ste. 101
Washington, DC 20008

Established in 1954 in DC.
Donor(s): Robert S. McNamara.
Grantmaker type: Independent foundation
Financial data (yr. ended 11/30/02): Assets, $2,954,368 (M); expenditures, $212,281; qualifying distributions, $131,934; giving activities include $134,135 for 49 grants (high: $25,000; low: $50).
Purpose and activities: Giving for agricultural and other education, the arts and for public policy issues.
Fields of interest: Performing arts; Arts; Higher education; Natural resources; Parks/playgrounds; Public policy, research.
Limitations: Applications not accepted. Giving primarily in Washington, DC. No grants to individuals.
Application information: Contributes only to pre-selected organizations.
Officer: Robert S. McNamara, Pres. and Treas.
EIN: 526056486

684
Moriah Fund ▼
1 Farragut Sq. S.
1634 I St. N.W., Ste. 1000
Washington, DC 20006 (202) 783-8488
Contact: Mary Ann Stein, Pres.
FAX: (202) 783-8499; Requests in Israel: Susan Feit, P.O.Box 2788, Neve Monosson, Israel 60190; *E-mail:* info@moriahfund.org; *URL:* http://www.moriahfund.org/index.htm

Established in 1985 in IN.
Donor(s): Clarence W. Efroymson,‡ Robert A. Efroymson,‡ Ben-Ephraim Gershon Fund, Gustave Aaron Efroymson Fund.
Grantmaker type: Independent foundation
Financial data (yr. ended 12/31/02): Assets, $131,295,982 (M); gifts received, $165,592; expenditures, $12,239,388; qualifying distributions, $11,073,402; giving activities include $9,757,500 for 237 grants (high: $1,538,000; low: $1,000; average:

$20,000–$50,000) and $75,000 for 1 loan/program-related investment.
Purpose and activities: Support primarily for pluralism, democracy, and community development in Israel; human rights, civic participation and leadership of indigenous people, rural development, and social justice in Guatemala for reproductive health and conservation of biodiversity domestically and internationally; and community-based development and programs to help families overcome poverty and gain self-sufficiency in Washington, DC, only.
Fields of interest: Natural resources; Environment; Reproductive health; Family planning; Single parents; International human rights; Civil rights; Rural development; Community development; Leadership development.
International interests: Russia; Ukraine; Latin America; Guatemala; Israel.
Types of support: General/operating support; Continuing support; Program development; Seed money; Technical assistance; Program-related investments/loans; Matching/challenge support.
Limitations: Giving nationally and internationally, including Israel and Latin America; giving primarily in Washington, DC for poverty program. No support for lobbying or political campaigns, private foundations, or arts organizations. No grants to individuals, or for medical research.
Publications: Application guidelines, Annual report (including application guidelines).
Application information: All inquiries should be directed to the Washington, DC office. Application must include proposal checklist obtained from the foundation. Application form not required.
Initial approach: Letter of inquiry (not exceeding 2 to 3 pages) which must be received at least 1 month prior to application deadline. Letters are reviewed throughout the year
Copies of proposal: 1
Deadline(s): Mar. 1 and Aug. 1
Board meeting date(s): May and Nov.
Officers and Program Board:* Mary Ann Stein,* Pres.; Judith Lichtman,* 1st V.P. and Treas.; Shira Saperstein, 2nd V.P. and Prog. Dir., Women's Rights and Reprod; Karl Mathiasen,* Secy.; Geeta Rao Gupta; Noah Stein; Dorothy Stein Swamy.
Number of staff: 8 full-time professional; 6 full-time support; 1 part-time support.
EIN: 311129589
Recent environmental and animal welfare grants:
684-1 Al Aouna Fund, Beer Sheva, Israel, $20,000. For waste collection services. Grant made through New Israel Fund. 2002.
684-2 Alabama Rivers Alliance, Birmingham, AL, $20,000. For general support. 2002.
684-3 Amazon Watch, Malibu, CA, $25,000. For general support. 2002.
684-4 American Lands Alliance, DC, $20,000. For Wildlands Protection Project, for federal wildlands, defending recent gains made in forest preservation and laying groundwork for proactive agenda. 2002.
684-5 Appalachian Center for the Economy and the Environment, Lewisburg, WV, $25,000. For general support. 2002.

684-6 Appalachian Mountain Club, Boston, MA, $55,000. For Northern Forest Alliance, coalition protecting wildlands, maintaining forests, and promoting sustainable communities in region of New York, Maine, New Hampshire, and Vermont. 2002.

684-7 Appalachian Mountain Club, Boston, MA, $40,000. For Northern Forest Alliance, coalition protecting wildlands, maintaining forests, and promoting sustainable communities in region of New York, Maine, New Hampshire, and Vermont. 2002.

684-8 Appalachian Sustainable Development, Abingdon, VA, $25,000. For Sustainable Forestry and Wood Products Project, increasing public commitment in Central Appalachian region and developing markets. 2002.

684-9 Appalachian Voices, Boone, NC, $25,000. For project to promote sustainable forestry on private lands in central and southern Appalachians. 2002.

684-10 Biodiversity Project, Madison, WI, $25,000. For general support. 2002.

684-11 Center for International Environmental Law, DC, $40,000. For general support. 2002.

684-12 Center for International Environmental Law, DC, $30,000. For Campaign on Export Credit Agency Reform, expanding support system for international NGO campaign reporting agency policies, supporting Latin American NGO partner organizations joining campaign. 2002.

684-13 Center for the Support of Native Lands, Arlington, VA, $24,500. For media and outreach activities. 2002.

684-14 Coalition to Restore Coastal Louisiana, Baton Rouge, LA, $20,000. For No Time to Lose, campaign for restoration and stewardship of bays, wetlands, and estuaries. 2002.

684-15 Dogwood Alliance, Brevard, NC, $50,000. For general support. 2002.

684-16 Ecologic Development Fund, Cambridge, MA, $40,000. For Guatemala project, assisting impoverished indigenous communities. 2002.

684-17 Ecologic Development Fund, Cambridge, MA, $30,000. For operating support of EcoLogic Enterprise Ventures, green loan fund fostering biodiversity conservation and grassroots-based, socially equitable economic development. 2002.

684-18 Ecologic Development Fund, Cambridge, MA, $25,000. For Tropico Verde, Guatemalan environmental organization influencing national policy, mobilizing broad social participation in protection, and promoting rational use of ecosystem. 2002.

684-19 Ecologists Linked for Organizing Grassroots Initiatives and Action (ECOLOGIA), Middlebury, VT, $10,000. For Baltic Mini-Grants program, financing small scale environmental projects proposed by local organizations, in Estonia, Latvia, and Lithuania, stimulating increased support from in-country sources and Baltic community in U.S. 2002.

684-20 Endangered Species Coalition, DC, $40,000. For general support. 2002.

684-21 Environmental Support Center, DC, $35,000. For joint project with Institute for Conservation Leadership in southeastern U.S. 2002.

684-22 Forest Peoples Programme, Moreton-in-Marsh, England, $30,000. For project, Promoting Forest Peoples' Rights and Interests in International Forest Policy Making. 2002.

684-23 Forest Stewardship Council, DC, $35,000. For Strategic Plan for Social Involvement, strengthening and expanding implementation and promotion of social values of system of certification of forest products. 2002.

684-24 Forest Trust, Santa Fe, NM, $40,000. For Forest Stewards Guild project, national association promoting socially and environmentally responsible management. 2002.

684-25 ForestEthics, Berkeley, CA, $40,000. For Paper Campaign, obtaining commitment from office products distributor requiring suppliers to cease purchase of paper derived from ancient forests, reduce overall fiber consumption, and shift to post-consumer recycled, agricultural, and independently certified fibers, and initiating secondary campaign against additional distributor. 2002.

684-26 Friends of the Earth, DC, $40,000. For support of program reforming international financial institutions (IFIs), significant role players in determining development paths of Third World countries. 2002.

684-27 GLOBE USA, DC, $25,000. For general support. 2002.

684-28 Green Corps, Boston, MA, $40,000. For general support. 2002.

684-29 Gulf Restoration Network, New Orleans, LA, $25,000. For Wetlands Defense Campaign, advocating for reform of policies and practices of U.S. Army Corps of Engineers to stem losses. 2002.

684-30 Harrop-Procter Watershed Protection Society, Procter, Canada, $20,000. For Community Forest Project, demonstrating economically viable, community controlled, ecosystem-based forestry. 2002.

684-31 Institute for Agriculture and Trade Policy, Minneapolis, MN, $30,000. For Community Forestry Resource Center, providing outreach and technical assistance to private forest landowners and communities, establishing Forest Stewardship Council-certified cooperatives. 2002.

684-32 Institute for Conservation Leadership, Takoma Park, MD, $35,000. For joint project with Environmental Support Center in southeastern U.S. 2002.

684-33 International Rivers Network, Berkeley, CA, $30,000. For Mesoamerica Project, working with communities affected by dam projects planned under Plan Puebla Panama, helping them oppose environmentally and socially destructive mega-projects and propose alternative development plans. 2002.

684-34 Land Trust Alliance, DC, $20,000. For Southeast Land Trust Capacity-Building Program, providing training and assistance programs, promoting networking and coordination, and offering outreach. 2002.

684-35 National Environmental Education and Training Foundation, DC, $35,000. For Watersheds and Television Weather Reporting: A Prototype for the Chesapeake Bay Region project, including development of Potomac-Anacostia River-based network of watershed watchers, toward converting local television weather into broader environmental reports. 2002.

684-36 National Wildlife Federation, Reston, VA, $30,000. For Emergency Wetlands Protection Project, responding to Supreme Court ruling eliminating protection for isolated waters. 2002.

684-37 Natural Resources Council, Augusta, ME, $40,000. For North Woods project, protecting ecological systems, wild character, and sustainable timber base, focusing on remote wildland regions of ecological significance. 2002.

684-38 Natural Resources Defense Council, New York, NY, $40,000. For Clean Water Network project. 2002.

684-39 Natural Resources Defense Council, New York, NY, $40,000. For long-term initiative to mobilize consumer based market forces and public policy to make production, trade, and use of wood products environmentally sound, including advancing aspects of FSC certification movement. 2002.

684-40 Northern Forest Center, Concord, NH, $20,000. For general support. 2002.

684-41 Pacific Rivers Council, Eugene, Oregon, $30,000. For Southern Appalachian National Forest Protection Project, conserving and restoring biologically diverse Conasauga River and other endangered southern Appalachian rivers, watersheds, and native aquatic species. 2002.

684-42 Philanthropic Ventures Foundation, Oakland, CA, $30,000. For Asociacion de Servicios Comunitarios de Salud, specifically project to promote traditional medicine and ecological agriculture in indigenous communities in Guatemala. 2002.

684-43 Potomac Riverkeeper, Rockville, MD, $20,000. For general support. 2002.

684-44 Quebec-Labrador Foundation/Atlantic Center for the Environment, Ipswich, MA, $35,000. For Atlantic Center Fellows Program to Promote Land Conservation and Stewardship in Latin America and the Caribbean. 2002.

684-45 Rainforest Alliance, New York, NY, $35,000. For Ecosystems and Ecolabels: Expanding Sustainable Agriculture Certification in Latin America, green program for producers reducing environmental impacts and improving social aspects of production. 2002.

684-46 Residents Committee to Protect the Adirondacks, North Creek, NY, $30,000. For Adirondack Park Sustainable Forestry Project, making Forest Stewardship Council (FSC) certification affordable and accessible to independent, non-industrialized area forest owners, building network of certified forestlands across Adirondacks, and organizing local marketing cooperative. 2002.

684-47 Restore Americas Estuaries, Arlington, VA, $20,000. For general support. 2002.

684-48 Restore the North Woods, Concord, MA, $15,000. For Maine Woods National Park: Start the Park Project, facilitating creation of Maine Woods National Park and Preserve. 2002.

684-49 Save Our Cumberland Mountains Resource Project, Lake City, TN, $15,000. For Forest Organizing Project, promoting sustainable policies and practices at local, statewide, and regional level. 2002.

684-50 Sierra Club Foundation, DC, $30,000. For Responsible Trade Project, educating public and organizing citizens to work for environmentally supportive policies, and ensuring local and state impacts influence U.S. policymaking. 2002.

684-51 Society for Conservation Biology, Gainesville, FL, $25,000. To develop Executive Office, focusing collective voice of members to inform policy debates and solve conservation problems, and manage affairs of professional society. 2002.

684-52 Southern Environmental Law Center, Charlottesville, VA, $45,000. For Forest and Wetland Biodiversity Project in southeastern states. 2002.

684-53 Strategies for International Development, Arlington, VA, $30,000. For pilot project to help farm families in communities in Chimaltenango region to reclaim and protect watersheds and farmland while increasing their income and productivity, using effort as demonstration project in sustainable farming techniques. 2002.

684-54 Western North Carolina Alliance, Asheville, NC, $30,000. For project to increase resources for land conservation and reform of development patterns, supporting community redevelopment over sprawl in western North Carolina, working in coalition with affordable housing advocates, environmentalists, members of faith community and others. 2002.

684-55 Wild Alabama, Moulton, AL, $25,000. For general support. 2002.

684-56 WildLaw, Montgomery, AL, $20,000. For general support. 2002.

684-57 Wildlife Conservation Society, Bronx, NY, $20,000. For Community-Based Forest and Concession Management Project in Uaxactun, Guatemala, helping community generate income while conserving environment in ecologically fragile and internationally significant wildlife corridor. 2002.

684-58 World Neighbors, Oklahoma City, OK, $35,000. For Sustainable Agriculture Program in Polochic Watershed, also promoting community capacity building among Qeqchi and Pocomchi Mayan farmers in buffer zone of Sierra de las Minas protected area in Guatemala. 2002.

685
The Mountain Institute, Inc.
1828 L. St. NW, Ste. 725
Washington, DC 20036 (202) 452-1636
Contact: Catherine Nixon Cooke, Pres. and C.E.O.
FAX: (202) 452-1635; E-mail: summit@mountain.org

Founded in 1971.
Grantmaker type: Public charity
Financial data (yr. ended 12/31/00): Revenue, $2,794,481; assets, $1,691,050; gifts received, $2,266,702; expenditures, $2,833,805; program services expenses, $2,472,275; giving activities include $360,858 for 5 grants (high: $129,329; low: $250).

Purpose and activities: The organization seeks to advance mountain cultures and preserve mountain environments.
Fields of interest: Landscaping; Environment, beautification programs; Environmental education; Environment.
Limitations: Giving on a national and international basis.
Officers and Board Members:* Robert H. Whitby,* Chair.; Elsi Walker,* Vice-Chair.; Catherine Nixon Cooke,* Pres. and C.E.O.; Jim Underwood,* Secy.; Walt Coward,* Treas.; Ted Armbrecht; William W. Carter; Julius E. Coles; Henry Harmon; and 5 additional board members.
EIN: 550541323

686
Curtis & Edith Munson Foundation
1990 M St. N.W., Ste. 250
Washington, DC 20036 (202) 887-8992
Contact: C. Wolcott Henry III, Pres.
FAX: (202) 887-8987; E-mail: info@munsonfdn.org; URL: http://www.munsonfdn.org

Incorporated in 1982 in FL.
Grantmaker type: Independent foundation
Financial data (yr. ended 12/31/01): Assets, $35,758,886 (M); expenditures, $2,138,217; qualifying distributions, $2,007,458; giving activities include $1,777,500 for 105 grants (high: $125,000; low: $500; average: $2,500–$25,000).
Purpose and activities: Support for conservation of wildlife and natural resources in North America, and U.S. population and immigration issues.
Fields of interest: Natural resources; Environment, water resources; Environment; Animals/wildlife, fisheries.
Types of support: General/operating support; Program development; Seed money; Matching/challenge support.
Limitations: Giving primarily in AL and FL. No grants to individuals, or for endowment funds; no loans.
Publications: Application guidelines, Grants list.
Application information: Contributes primarily to pre-selected organizations. Application form required.
Initial approach: Letter of inquiry
Copies of proposal: 1
Deadline(s): Apr. 4 and Aug. 29
Board meeting date(s): July, Nov., and as required
Final notification: 3 weeks after meetings
Officers and Directors:* C. Wolcott Henry III,* Pres.; Bruce Reid,* Secy.; Michael C. Rausch, Treas.; Angel Braestrup, Exec. Dir.; H. Alexander Henry; Truman M. Hobbs, Jr.
Number of staff: 2 full-time professional.
EIN: 592235907

687
The National Environmental Education & Training Foundation, Inc.
(also known as N.E.E.T.F.)
1707 H St., N.W., Ste. 900
Washington, DC 20006-3915 (202) 833-2933
Contact: Deborah Sliter, V.P., Progs.
FAX: (202) 261-6464; E-mail: neetf@neetf.org; URL: http://www.neetf.org

Established in 1990 in DC by the U.S. Congress in the National Environmental Education Act.
Grantmaker type: Public charity
Financial data (yr. ended 09/30/00): Revenue, $2,727,476; assets, $2,370,404 (M); gifts received, $2,643,785; expenditures, $2,538,529; program services expenses, $2,201,808; giving activities include $472,398 for grants.
Purpose and activities: The foundation facilitates the cooperation, coordination, and contribution of public and private resources to further the development of an environmentally conscious and responsible public, a well-trained and environmentally literate workforce, and an environmentally advanced educational system. It also fosters open and effective partnerships among federal, state, and local government, business, academic institutions, and community and environmental groups.
Fields of interest: Environment, public education; Environment, water resources; Environmental education; Environment; Public health.
Types of support: Program development; Curriculum development; Technical assistance; Matching/challenge support.
Limitations: Applications not accepted. Giving on a national basis. No grants to individuals, or for land acquisition, building funds or improvements, endowments, ongoing support, multi-year grants, or basic research.
Publications: Application guidelines, Annual report, Grants list, Informational brochure, Newsletter, Occasional report.
Officers and Trustees:* Walter M. Higgins,* Chair; James R. Donnelley,* Vice-Chair.; Kevin J. Coyle,* Secy.; Dwight C. Minton,* Treas.; Brandon R. Allenby, Ph.D.; Richard C. Bartlett; Edward P. Bass; Dorothy Jacobson; Karen Bates Kress; Fred Krupp; Francis P. Pandolfi.
Number of staff: 20.
EIN: 541557043

688
National Fish and Wildlife Foundation
1120 Connecticut Ave., N.W., Ste. 900
Washington, DC 20036 (202) 857-0166
Contact: Michele Soho, Asst. Dir. Corp.
FAX: (202) 857-0162; URL: http://www.nfwf.org/

Established in 1984 in DC.
Grantmaker type: Public charity
Financial data (yr. ended 09/30/01): Revenue, $47,389,198; assets, $147,337,947 (M); gifts received, $40,178,249; expenditures, $38,607,644; program services expenses, $35,910,176; giving activities include $5,836,778 for grants and $25,116,664 for grants to individuals.
Purpose and activities: The foundation fosters cooperative partnerships between the public and private sectors to support conservation

activities. Among its goals are species habitat protection, conservation education, natural resource management, habitat and ecosystem restoration, and leadership training. Private funding for conservation is stimulated through matching grant programs.
Fields of interest: Natural resources; Environment; Animals/wildlife, preservation/protection; Animals/wildlife, bird preserves; Animals/wildlife, fisheries; Animals/wildlife.
Types of support: Equipment; Land acquisition; Program development; Conferences/seminars; Seed money; Matching/challenge support.
Limitations: Giving on a national and international basis, primarily in Latin America and Asia. No support for political advocacy or for litigation. No grants for basic research (including graduate level), administrative overhead, multi-year funding, or to cover shortfalls in government agency budgets.
Publications: Application guidelines, Annual report, Grants list, Informational brochure, Newsletter.
Application information: Full grant applications must be invited by the foundation; see Web site for additional programs, guidelines and application forms. Application form required.
  Deadline(s): Varies
  Board meeting date(s): Mar., July, and Oct.
Officer and Directors:* Steve Peet,* Chair.; Max C. Chapman, Jr.,* Vice-Chair.; Carlton Owen,* Vice-Chair.; John Berry, Exec. Dir.; Helen Campbell Alexander; Sue Anschutz-Rodgers; David G. Brown; J. Kiskwood Dupps; Patrick Durkin; Jennie Turner Garlington; Hon. Neil Goldschmidt; Victor Gonzalez; G. T. Halpin; Paul Tudor Jones II; VADM. Conrad C. Lautenbacher, Jr., U.S.N.; Sheldon Lavin; Thurgood Marshall, Jr.; Michael L. Meadows; Mark F. Rockefeller; Steve Williams; Ward W. Woods.
Number of staff: 72 full-time professional.
EIN: 521384139

689
The National Park Foundation
11 Dupont Cir., N.W., Ste. 600
Washington, DC   20036   (202) 238-4200
Contact: Wilke E. Nelson, Dir., Devel.
FAX: (202) 234-3103; E-mail: ask-npf@nationalparks.org; URL: http://www.nationalparks.org

Grantmaker type: Public charity
Financial data (yr. ended 06/30/01): Revenue, $37,815,066; assets, $79,496,701 (M); gifts received, $19,420,150; expenditures, $35,612,211; program services expenses, $32,130,667; giving activities include $23,920,511 for 70 grants (high: $5,002,102; low: $2,000).
Purpose and activities: The foundation aims to help conserve, preserve, and enhance our national parks for the benefit of the American people; support programs primarily for education and outreach, visitor information and interpretive facilities, volunteer activities, and National Park Service employees; and generate funds for grantmaking and assistance programs through gifts from private individuals, organizations, and a range of fundraising and marketing activities.

Fields of interest: History/archaeology; Natural resources; Environment; Animal welfare.
Types of support: Program development; Research.
Publications: Annual report, Newsletter.
Application information: Grants are awarded only for projects in national parks.
Officers and Directors:* Hon. Gale Norton,* Chair.; David Rockefeller, Jr.,* Vice-Chair.; Jim Maddy,* Pres.; Jill D. Nicoll, Exec. V.P. and C.O.O.; Jay Vestal, V.P., Devel.; Hon. Fran P. Mainella,* Secy.; John H. Watts, Treas.; Roger C. Altman; Ann L. Buttenweiser; John L. Colonghi; Dayton Duncan; and 15 additional directors.
EIN: 521086761

690
New Israel Fund
1101 14th St., N.W., 6th Fl.
Washington, DC   20005-5639   (202) 842-0900
Contact: Marc Breslaw, Dir., Devel.
Jerusalem office tel.: 011-972-2-672-3095; FAX: (202) 842-0991; E-mail: info@nif.org; URL: http://www.nif.org

Established in 1979 in CA.
Grantmaker type: Public charity
Financial data (yr. ended 12/31/02): Revenue, $20,797,715; assets, $15,977,880 (L); gifts received, $20,930,477; expenditures, $21,247,194; program services expenses, $17,375,107; giving activities include $12,611,032 for 350 grants (high: $804,000; low: $1,000).
Purpose and activities: The fund works to strengthen Israel's democracy and to promote freedom, justice and equality for all Israel's citizens. These principles are guaranteed in Israel's Declaration of Independence and a central element of Jewish tradition. A philanthropic partnership of Israelis, North Americans and Europeans, the fund has led the development of Israel's vibrant public interest sector, providing financial and technical support to hundreds of national and community-based organizations. The fund's focus is on fighting for civil and human rights, closing economic and social gaps and promoting religious tolerance and pluralism.
Fields of interest: Environment; Civil rights, immigrants; Civil rights; Women; Gays/lesbians.
International interests: Russia; Ethiopia; Israel; Kuwait.
Types of support: General/operating support; Continuing support; Emergency funds; Program development; Seed money; Fellowships; Technical assistance.
Limitations: Giving limited to Israel. No support for projects sponsored by universities or by municipal or national authorities, including schools or community centers. No grants to individuals or for research, conferences, publications, or cultural projects.
Publications: Annual report, Informational brochure, Newsletter.
Application information: Applications for funding only accepted from Israeli nonprofit organizations. Application form required.
  Initial approach: Telephone Jerusalem office
  Board meeting date(s): Jan. and June
Officers and Directors:* Peter Edelman,* Pres.; Israela Goldblum,* V.P., Israel; Joan Shapiro,* V.P., North America; Sanford Gallanter,* Secy.;

Robert Mnookin,* Treas.; Norman Rosenberg, Exec. Dir.; and 20 additional directors.
Number of staff: 31 full-time professional.
EIN: 942607722

691
The Cissy Patterson Foundation
c/o McKenna & Cuneo, LLP
1900 K St., N.W.
Washington, DC   20006

Established in 1993 in DC.
Donor(s): The Cissy Patterson Trust.
Grantmaker type: Independent foundation
Financial data (yr. ended 12/31/01): Assets, $6,400,115 (M); expenditures, $915,648; qualifying distributions, $883,354; giving activities include $874,500 for 53 grants (high: $100,000; low: $1,000).
Fields of interest: Natural resources; Environment; Human services; Civil rights, women.
Limitations: Applications not accepted. Giving on a national basis. No grants to individuals.
Application information: Contributes only to pre-selected organizations.
Officers: Alice Arlen, Pres.; Joseph P. Albright, V.P.; Blandina A. Rojek, Secy.; Adam Albright, Treas.
EIN: 521795554

692
H. O. Peet Foundation
P.O. Box 25613
Washington, DC   20007   (202) 915-3961

Established in 1947 in MO.
Grantmaker type: Independent foundation
Financial data (yr. ended 12/31/02): Assets, $3,856,650 (M); expenditures, $243,446; qualifying distributions, $215,227; giving activities include $206,825 for 60 grants (high: $70,000; low: $500).
Purpose and activities: Funding primarily for education, arts and culture, environmental conservation and historical preservation.
Fields of interest: Historic preservation/historical societies; Arts; Education; Natural resources; Protestant agencies & churches.
Limitations: Applications not accepted. Giving on a national basis, with some emphasis on the greater metropolitan Washington, DC, area, New York, NY, and the New England states. No grants to individuals.
Application information: Contributes only to pre-selected organizations.
Officers: Marguerite Peet Foster, Pres; Leslie K. Smith, Secy.; Rockwood H. Foster, Treas.
EIN: 446005945

693
The Marjorie Merriweather Post Foundation
c/o Riggs Bank, N.A.
P.O. Box 96202, C-7003
Washington, DC   20090-6202   (202) 835-6872
Contact: David A. McClung, Secy.

Established in 1956.

Donor(s): Marjorie Merriweather Post.‡
Grantmaker type: Independent foundation
Financial data (yr. ended 12/31/02): Assets, $5,710,733 (M); expenditures, $397,807; qualifying distributions, $315,024; giving activities include $315,000 for 45 grants (high: $20,000; low: $2,000; average: $500–$5,000).
Fields of interest: Museums (natural history); Performing arts centers; Orchestra (symphony); Historical activities; Arts; Elementary school/education; Higher education; Natural resources; Environment, forests; Hospitals (general); Human services; Roman Catholic agencies & churches.
Limitations: Giving primarily on the East Coast, with emphasis on Washington, DC. No grants to individuals.
Publications: Application guidelines.
Application information: All grants monies must be used within the territorial U.S. Application form not required.
   Initial approach: Proposal
   Copies of proposal: 1
   Deadline(s): Mar. 1 and Sept. 1
   Board meeting date(s): Spring and fall
   Final notification: Notification sent only to those organizations which are approved for grants
Officers: John A. Logan, Jr., Chair.; Spottswood P. Dudley, Vice-Chair.; Nina Craig Rumbough, Vice-Chair.; David A. McClung, Secy.; L.L. Silverstein, Treas.
Trustees: Henry A. Dudley, Jr.; George B. Hartzog, Jr.
Number of staff: None.
EIN: 526054705

694
The Prince of Wales Foundation
888 17th St., N.W., Ste. 201
Washington, DC 20006 (202) 887-8280
Contact: Geoffrey J.W. Kent, Pres.
FAX: (202) 887-8281; E-mail: princeofwalesfdn@mindspring.com

Established in 1991 in IL.
Grantmaker type: Public charity
Financial data (yr. ended 12/31/02): Revenue, $2,510,297; assets, $2,923,732 (M); gifts received, $2,376,959; expenditures, $2,678,957; program services expenses, $1,173,867; giving activities include $1,133,871 for 11 grants (high: $1,000,000; low: $50,000).
Purpose and activities: The foundation supports various projects, including those involving education, health care, disadvantaged young people, urban and rural renewal, and the environment.
Fields of interest: Arts; Education; Environment; Health care.
Limitations: Giving on a national and international basis.
Application information: Application form required.
   Initial approach: Letter or telephone
   Copies of proposal: 1
   Board meeting date(s): Biannually
Officers and Directors:* Geoffrey J.W. Kent,* Pres.; Caroline Wheeler,* Secy.; Robert Higdon,* Treas.; Mark Bolland; Christopher Forbes.
EIN: 363820023

695
Public Welfare Foundation, Inc. ▼
1200 U. St. N.W.
Washington, DC 20009-4443 (202) 965-1800
Contact: Review Comm.
FAX: (202) 265-8851; E-mail: reviewcommittee@publicwelfare.org; URL: http://www.publicwelfare.org

Incorporated in 1947 in TX; reincorporated in 1951 in DE.
Donor(s): Charles Edward Marsh.‡
Grantmaker type: Independent foundation
Financial data (yr. ended 10/31/02): Assets, $370,135,448 (M); expenditures, $25,298,630; qualifying distributions, $22,451,757; giving activities include $19,369,950 for 517 grants (high: $250,000; low: $1,000; average: $10,000–$50,000).
Purpose and activities: Grants primarily to grassroots organizations in the United States and abroad, with emphasis on the environment, health, population and reproductive health, the disadvantaged elderly, disadvantaged youth, criminal justice, human rights and global security, and community economic development and participation. Programs must serve low-income populations, with preference to short-term needs.
Fields of interest: Environment; Reproductive health; Family planning; Health care; Health organizations, association; AIDS; Crime/violence prevention; Gun control; Offenders/ex-offenders, rehabilitation; Offenders/ex-offenders, prison alternatives; Domestic violence; Legal services; Nutrition; Housing/shelter, development; Children/youth, services; Minorities/immigrants, centers/services; Homeless, human services; Arms control; International human rights; Race/intergroup relations; Civil rights; Community development; Minorities; Aging; Immigrants/refugees; Economically disadvantaged; Homeless.
International interests: Haiti; South Africa; Mexico; El Salvador.
Types of support: General/operating support; Continuing support; Program development; Seed money; Matching/challenge support.
Limitations: Giving is generally limited to the U.S. (more than 90 percent). No grants to individuals, or for building funds, capital improvements, endowments, scholarships, graduate work, foreign study, conferences, seminars, publications, research, workshops, or annual campaigns; no loans.
Publications: Annual report (including application guidelines), Grants list, Informational brochure (including application guidelines), Occasional report.
Application information: Application guidelines are available on the foundation's Web site. WRAG and NNG Common Grant Application forms accepted. Application form not required.
   Initial approach: 2-page letter of inquiry
   Copies of proposal: 1
   Deadline(s): None
   Board meeting date(s): Board (or a committee of the board) meets 8 times annually
   Final notification: 3 to 4 months
Officers and Directors:* Thomas J. Scanlon,* Chair.; Robert H. Haskell,* Vice-Chair.; Antoinette M. Haskell,* Secy.-Treas.; Larry Kressley, Exec. Dir.; Peter Edelman; Thomas Ehrlich; Juliet Villarreal Garcia; Brent L. Henry;

Myrtis H. Powell; Thomas W. Scoville; Jerome W.D. Stokes; C. Elizabeth Warner; Michael C. Williams.
Number of staff: 17 full-time professional; 5 full-time support.
EIN: 540597601
Recent environmental and animal welfare grants:
695-1 Alaska Community Action on Toxics, Anchorage, AK, $50,000. For continued general support. 2002.
695-2 Alternatives for Community and Environment (ACE), Roxbury, MA, $100,000. For general support. 2002.
695-3 American Indian Treaty Council Information Center, Minneapolis, MN, $25,000. For general support of Indigenous Trading Company environmental program. 2002.
695-4 Amigos Bravos, Taos, NM, $40,000. For general support. 2002.
695-5 Bank Information Center, DC, $120,000. For general support. 2002.
695-6 Center for Health, Environment and Justice, Falls Church, VA, $80,000. For continued general support. 2002.
695-7 Centro de Estudios Fronterizos y de Promocion de los Derechos Humanos, Reynosa, Mexico, $25,000. For continued support of Environmental Rights Project. 2002.
695-8 Childhood Lead Action Project, Providence, RI, $35,000. For continued general support. 2002.
695-9 Committee for the Rescue and Development of Vieques, Vieques, PR, $25,000. For general support. 2002.
695-10 Committee on Women, Population and the Environment, Amherst, MA, $25,000. For continued general support of international and other programs. 2002.
695-11 Concerned Citizens of Tillery, Tillery, NC, $25,000. For general support of disadvantaged elderly and other programs. 2002.
695-12 Consumers Choice Council, DC, $50,000. For continued general support of local, national, and international environmental and other programs. 2002.
695-13 DataCenter, Oakland, CA, $70,000. For continued support of Environmental Research Project. 2002.
695-14 Development Group for Alternative Policies, DC, $50,000. For continued general support. 2002.
695-15 Environmental Justice Resource Center, Atlanta, GA, $40,000. For general support. 2002.
695-16 Environmental Law Clinic, San Juan, PR, $35,000. For general support. 2002.
695-17 Families Against Incinerator Risk (FAIR), Salt Lake City, UT, $35,000. For continued general support. 2002.
695-18 Farmworker Association of Central Florida, Apopka, FL, $40,000. For continued support of Farmworker Pesticide Health and Safety Project. 2002.
695-19 Frente de Defensa de la Amazonia, Nueva Loja, Ecuador, $70,000. For continued support toward Monitoring Network. 2002.
695-20 Friends of the Earth, DC, $100,000. For continued general support. 2002.
695-21 Globalization Alternatives North and South, Albuquerque, NM, $50,000. For

continued general support of Washington, D.C., national, and international programs, including Haitian, in collaboration with Haitian Platform for Alternative Development and Convergence of Movements of the Peoples of the Americas. 2002.

695-22 Gwichin Steering Committee, Fairbanks, AK, $40,000. For continued general support. 2002.

695-23 Honor the Earth, Minneapolis, MN, $30,000. For general support. 2002.

695-24 Indigenous Environmental Network, Bemidji, MN, $120,000. For continued general support. 2002.

695-25 Institute for Energy and Environmental Research, Takoma Park, MD, $100,000. For continued general support. 2002.

695-26 Institute for Science and Interdisciplinary Studies, Amherst, MA, $90,000. For continued support of Amazon Project. 2002.

695-27 International Indian Treaty Council, San Francisco, CA, $70,000. For continued general support of Central American environmental and other programs. 2002.

695-28 Mision Industrial de Puerto Rico, San Juan, PR, $50,000. For general support. 2002.

695-29 Missouri Rural Crisis Center, Columbia, MO, $70,000. For Family Farms, Not Factory Farms: Sustainable Agriculture for the 21st Century Project. 2002.

695-30 National People of Color Environmental Leadership Summit, DC, $40,000. For general support. 2002.

695-31 Natural Resources Defense Council, New York, NY, $750,000. Toward Climate Center program. 2002.

695-32 New Mexico Environmental Law Center, Santa Fe, NM, $120,000. For continued general support. 2002.

695-33 Ohio Valley Environmental Coalition, Huntington, WV, $70,000. For general support. 2002.

695-34 Pennsylvania Environmental Network, Fombell, PA, $20,000. For continued general support. 2002.

695-35 People Organized in Defense of Earth and Her Resources, Austin, TX, $35,000. For continued general support. 2002.

695-36 Powder River Basin Resource Council, Sheridan, WY, $20,000. For continued general support. 2002.

695-37 Project Underground, Berkeley, CA, $45,000. For general support and toward programs of international partners. 2002.

695-38 Public Interest Law Center of Philadelphia, Philadelphia, PA, $50,000. For environmental project. 2002.

695-39 South African Exchange Program on Environmental Justice, Boston, MA, $70,000. For continued general support. 2002.

695-40 Southern Organizing Committee (SOC) for Economic and Social Justice, Atlanta, GA, $125,000. For continued general support of environmental and other programs. 2002.

695-41 Southwest Network for Environmental and Economic Justice, Albuquerque, NM, $130,000. For general support. 2002.

695-42 Southwest Public Workers Union, San Antonio, TX, $70,000. For continued general support of environmental and other programs. 2002.

695-43 Toxics Action Center, Boston, MA, $25,000. For general support. 2002.

695-44 West County Toxics Coalition, Richmond, CA, $25,000. For general support. 2002.

695-45 Western Shoshone Defense Project, Crescent Valley, NV, $25,000. For continued general support of environmental and other programs. 2002.

695-46 White Earth Land Recovery Project, Ponsford, MN, $25,000. For continued general support. 2002.

695-47 Woolfolk Citizens Response Group, Fort Valley, GA, $25,000. For continued general support. 2002.

695-48 Work Environment Council of New Jersey, Trenton, NJ, $35,000. For continued general support of programs in collaboration with New Jersey State Industrial Union Council, AFL-CIO. 2002.

695-49 World Foundation for Environment and Development, DC, $50,000. To reduce risk of biological weapons proliferation. 2002.

695-50 Xavier University of Louisiana, Deep South Center, New Orleans, LA, $40,000. For continued support of Mississippi River Avatar Project. 2002.

695-51 YWCA of Lincoln, Lincoln, NE, $50,000. For Survival Skills Program for youth. 2002.

696
Raiser Foundation, Inc.
3318 O St. N.W.
Washington, DC 20007

Established in 1988 in DC and DE.
Donor(s): C. Victor Raiser,‡ Mary M. Raiser.
Grantmaker type: Independent foundation
Financial data (yr. ended 12/31/02): Assets, $195,350 (M); gifts received, $100,501; expenditures, $230,875; qualifying distributions, $228,407; giving activities include $229,330 for 16 grants (high: $50,000; low: $1,000).
Purpose and activities: Giving for higher education, Christian organizations, and arts and culture.
Fields of interest: Music; Elementary/secondary education; Higher education; Education; Natural resources; Camps; Children, services; Public affairs.
Types of support: General/operating support; Annual campaigns; Scholarship funds.
Limitations: Applications not accepted. Giving primarily in Washington, DC. No grants to individuals.
Application information: Contributes only to pre-selected organizations.
Board meeting date(s): Dec.
Officers: Mary M. Raiser, Pres.; Mary van Schuyler Raiser, V.P. and Secy.; Janet L. Scribner, Treas.
Directors: John Richardson; Margaret M. Richarson; James M. Wadsworth.
Number of staff: None.
EIN: 521643511

697
The Spring Creek Foundation
P.O. Box 70263
Washington, DC 20024 (202) 547-8762
Contact: Lawrence E. Molumby, C.E.O.
FAX: (202) 547-8952; E-mail: springcreekfndtn@aol.com

Established in 1996 in DC.
Grantmaker type: Independent foundation
Financial data (yr. ended 12/31/02): Assets, $7,325,537 (M); expenditures, $606,028; qualifying distributions, $603,411; giving activities include $548,500 for 73 grants (high: $25,000; low: $1,500; average: $1,500–$25,000).
Purpose and activities: The purpose of the foundation is to fund organizations in the metropolitan Washington, DC, area, whose goals and programs benefit the human environment by providing assistance to low-income individuals and families in housing, employment, education, and emergency services, as well as organizations whose goals are the protection and enhancement of the natural environment.
Fields of interest: Education, services; Natural resources; Employment, services; Housing/shelter, services; Human services; Family services.
Types of support: General/operating support; Continuing support; Program development.
Limitations: Giving limited to the metropolitan Washington, DC, area. No grants to individuals, or for capital campaigns, real property acquisition, or construction.
Publications: Application guidelines, Grants list, Informational brochure.
Application information: Accepts WRAG Common Grant Application Form. Application form not required.
Initial approach: Telephone
Copies of proposal: 1
Deadline(s): Apr. 15 and Oct. 15
Board meeting date(s): Jan. and June
Officers and Directors:* Lawrence E. Molumby,* C.E.O. and Pres.; Maryann "Molly" Ellsworth,* V.P.; Mary M. Dwan,* Secy.; Richard Halberstein,* Treas.; James M. Didden; Ralph H. Dwan, Jr.; Kelley Ellsworth; Clyde B. Richardson; Kathryn "Kathy" Smith.
Number of staff: 1 part-time professional.
EIN: 521963479

698
The Summit Charitable Foundation, Inc. ▼
2100 Pennsylvania Ave. N.W., Ste. 525
Washington, DC 20037 (202) 912-2900
Contact: Victoria P. Sant, Pres.
FAX: (202) 912-2901; E-mail: info@summitfdn.org; URL: http://www.summitfdn.org

Established in 1991 in DE.
Donor(s): Roger W. Sant, Victoria P. Sant.
Grantmaker type: Independent foundation
Financial data (yr. ended 12/31/02): Assets, $17,665,867 (M); gifts received, $2,194,000; expenditures, $3,044,002; qualifying distributions, $2,763,172; giving activities include $738,140 for 19 grants (high: $92,140; low: $4,900) and $1,300 for 8 employee matching gifts.

Purpose and activities: Funding currently for two program areas: Conservation of the Mesoamerican Reef and Global Population & Youth Leadership.

Fields of interest: Environment, research; Natural resources; Environment; Reproductive health; Family planning; Reproductive health, fertility; Reproductive health, sexuality education; Youth development; International human rights.

International interests: Caribbean; Latin America.

Types of support: General/operating support; Continuing support; Program development; Seed money; Technical assistance; Program evaluation; Matching/challenge support.

Limitations: Applications not accepted. Giving primarily on an international basis, in the mesoamerican reef ecoregion and Atlantic Coastal Forests ecoregion, with emphasis on Latin America and the Caribbean for environmental grantmaking. No grants to individuals, or for freestanding conferences, film and video projects or basic research.

Publications: Financial statement, Grants list, Informational brochure, Program policy statement.

Application information: Unsolicited requests for funds not considered.

Board meeting date(s): 2 times a year

Officers and Trustees:* Roger W. Sant,* Chair.; Victoria P. Sant,* Pres.; Shari Sant Plummer,* Secy.; Alexis Sant,* Treas.; J. Martin Goebel; Dan Plummer; Michael Sant; Shira Saperstein.

Number of staff: 3 full-time professional.

EIN: 521743817

Recent environmental and animal welfare grants:

698-1 American Association for the Advancement of Science, DC, $19,775. To enhance dissemination of Atlas of Population and Environment via CD-ROM and the Internet. 2001.

698-2 American Oceans Campaign, DC, $10,000. To expand and enhance marine protected areas in United States. 2001.

698-3 Audubon Society of Washington State, Seattle, WA, $47,984. For Northwest Shade Coffee Campaign's initiative, The Coffee Flyway: Linking Consumer Purchases to Conservation. 2001.

698-4 Center for Environment and Population, Tides Center, Portsmouth, NH, $20,000. For dissemination of AAAS Atlas of Population and Environment. Grant made through Tides Center. 2001.

698-5 Centro Mexicano de Derecho Ambiental, Mexico City, Mexico, $309,800. To establish office in Quintana Roo to train NGOs, judges and investors on environmental legislation, provide legal advice and legally challenge destructive infrastructure projects threatening Mesoamerican Reef ecoregion. 2001.

698-6 Centro Mexicano de Derecho Ambiental, Mexico City, Mexico, $40,000. For general support for promoting compliance and effective enforcement of environmental laws and regulations. 2001.

698-7 Consumers Choice Council, DC, $60,000. For background research and development of media outreach strategies on sustainable coffee in collaboration with DDB Communications. 2001.

698-8 Earth Policy Institute, DC, $500,000. For general support. 2001.

698-9 Earthome, Baldwin, MD, $30,000. For production of documentary film, Signal Of Intention: The Work and Vision of William McDonough. 2001.

698-10 Ecologic Development Fund, Cambridge, MA, $25,000. To establish cross-border collaborative project between Guatemala and Belize along Sarstoon River. 2001.

698-11 Forest Management Trust, Gainesville, FL, $63,193. For Sustainable Forest Management in the Bayano Watershed of Panama: A Feasibility Assessment program. 2001.

698-12 Forest Stewardship Council, Oaxaca, Mexico, $210,000. To strengthen management capabilities, develop long-term fundraising strategy, conduct Board/membership meetings, and search for Executive Director. 2001.

698-13 Fundacion Futuro Latinoamericano, Quito, Ecuador, $50,000. For general support for development activities throughout Latin America in partnership with civil society organizations, national and international public entities, local communities and private sector. 2001.

698-14 INFORM, New York, NY, $100,000. For Extended Producer Responsibility Program. 2001.

698-15 League of Conservation Voters Education Fund, DC, $10,000. For general support. 2001.

698-16 LightHawk, San Francisco, CA, $150,000. To provide flight support for biodiversity protection in Mexico, Belize, Guatemala and Honduras. 2001.

698-17 Marine Stewardship Council, London, England, $600,000. To provide core and project support for raising awareness of Council and its certification labeling and building market for certified seafood. 2001.

698-18 Mexican Nature Conservation Fund, Mexico City, Mexico, $120,000. To launch donor-advised grantmaking program to support integrated population-environment initiatives. 2001.

698-19 Mexican Nature Conservation Fund, Mexico City, Mexico, $25,000. For Third General Assembly Meeting of Latin American and Caribbean Network of Environmental Funds in Angra do Reis, Brazil. 2001.

698-20 National Geographic Society, DC, $125,000. For Sustainable Seas Expedition - Islands in the Stream project. 2001.

698-21 National Wildlife Federation, Reston, VA, $10,000. For National Wildlife Productions. 2001.

698-22 Nature Conservancy, Arlington, VA, $62,000. For baseline research on availability of and demand for sustainable coffee in the US market in collaboration with Specialty Coffee Association, the Commission of Environmental Cooperation and The World Bank. 2001.

698-23 Operation Migration USA, Buffalo, NY, $50,000. For general support. 2001.

698-24 Population Communications International, New York, NY, $200,000. To initiate radio serial drama addressing population and environment themes in the Philippines, in collaboration with Conservation International. 2001.

698-25 Population Reference Bureau, DC, $250,000. For Population, Health and Environment program's efforts to provide technical assistance and networking support to strengthen research and policy work on population-environment dynamics. 2001.

698-26 Programme for Belize, Belize City, Belize, $20,000. To educate Belizean public about negative environmental and economic consequences of proposed dam, and on alternative energy sources that could satisfy growing electricity needs. 2001.

698-27 Rainforest Alliance, New York, NY, $30,000. For implementation of bilingual Web site providing information about conservation projects in Mexico and Central America, including information about funding. 2001.

698-28 RARE Center for Tropical Conservation, Arlington, VA, $11,180. For general support for Bay Islands Conservation Association. 2001.

698-29 Second Nature, Boston, MA, $300,000. To introduce sustainable design concepts into university curricula and operations. 2001.

698-30 Sociedade de Pesquisa em Vida Selvagem, Curitiba, Brazil, $30,000. For advocacy and public education campaign to close illegal road through Iguacu National Park. 2001.

698-31 Toledo Institute for Development and Environment (TIDE), Punta Gorda, Belize, $75,000. For general support. 2001.

698-32 Toledo Institute for Development and Environment (TIDE), Punta Gorda, Belize, $10,000. For emergency relief efforts to southern Belize as result of Hurricane Mitch. 2001.

698-33 World Resources Institute, DC, $600,000. For project, New Ventures: Building Entrepreneurial Leadership for Sustainability in Latin America. 2001.

698-34 World Resources Institute, DC, $50,000. To develop and present cogent critique of anti-environmental book, The Skeptical Environmentalist: Measuring the Real State of the World. 2001.

698-35 World Wildlife Fund/Conservation Foundation, DC, $133,539. For rapid ecological assessment of Barbareta Island and surrounding waters. 2001.

698-36 World Wildlife Fund/Conservation Foundation, DC, $27,780. For efforts to preserve Cuero y Salado Wildlife Refuge in Honduras, which plays important role in conservation of Mesoamerican Reef. 2001.

698-37 World Wildlife Fund/Conservation Foundation, DC, $10,000. For emergency relief efforts in Galapagos Islands, Ecuador. 2001.

699
The Summit Fund of Washington
2100 Pennsylvania Ave., NW, Ste. 525
Washington, DC 20037 (202) 912-2900
Contact: Linda Howard, Exec. Dir.
FAX: (202) 912-2901; E-mail: lhoward@summitfdn.org; URL: http://www.summitfund.org

Established in 1993 in DC; the fund is a supporting organization of the Community Foundation for the National Capital Region.
Grantmaker type: Public charity
Financial data (yr. ended 03/31/02): Revenue, $238,623; assets, $16,943,577 (M); expenditures, $3,040,212; program services expenses, $2,430,141; giving activities include $2,430,141 for 40 grants (high: $560,000; low: $500).
Purpose and activities: The fund seeks to restore and protect the Anacostia River and prevent teen pregnancy in the District of Columbia.
Fields of interest: Natural resources; Disasters, 9/11/01; Youth, pregnancy prevention.
Limitations: Giving primarily in the metropolitan Washington, DC, area.
Publications: Grants list, Informational brochure.
Application information: Application form required.
  Initial approach: Letter of inquiry
  Copies of proposal: 1
  Board meeting date(s): 4 times per year
Officers and Directors:* Roger W. Sant,* Chair.; Vicki Sant,* Pres.; Douglas Bibby,* Secy.; Linda Howard, Exec. Dir.; Carol Thompson Cole; Donald Graham; M. Charite Kruvant; Aileen B. Train; Diane Simmons Williams.
Number of staff: 1 full-time professional; 3 part-time professional.
EIN: 521799774

700
United Nations Foundation

1225 Connecticut Ave., 4th Fl.
Washington, DC 20036-1815 (202) 887-9040
Contact: David Harwood, V.P., Public Affairs
FAX: (202) 887-9021; URL: http://www.unfoundation.org

Established in 1997 in NY.
Donor(s): R.E. Turner.
Grantmaker type: Public charity
Financial data (yr. ended 12/31/01): Revenue, $99,122,687; assets, $58,010,843 (L); gifts received, $22,270,011; expenditures, $98,602,727; program services expenses, $94,739,969; giving activities include $91,790,015 for grants.
Purpose and activities: The foundation's mission is to support the goals and objectives of the United Nations and its charter in order to promote a more peaceful, prosperous, and just world, with special emphasis on economic, social, environmental, and humanitarian causes.
Fields of interest: Natural resources; Environment; Public health; Public health, communicable diseases; International development; International affairs, U.N.; International human rights; Reproductive rights; Health care, alliance; Mental health/crisis services, alliance; Housing/shelter, alliance; Community development, alliance.
Types of support: Program development; Program evaluation.
Limitations: Applications not accepted. Giving limited to pre-selected organizations on an international basis. No grants to individuals.
Application information: Contributes only to pre-selected organizations; unsolicited requests for funds not considered or acknowledged.
Officers and Directors:* R.E. Turner,* Chair.; Kathy Bushkin, C.O.O.; Timothy E. Wirth, Pres.;

Charles A. Bowsher,* V.P.; Charles Curtis,* V.P.; Virginia Davis,* V.P.; Jean-Claude Faby,* V.P.; David Harwood,* V.P.; Melinda Kimble,* V.P.; Elizabeth C. Reveal,* V.P.; Rutherford Seydel,* Secy.; Edward C. Harris,* Treas.; Ruth Cardoso; Liang Dan; Graca Machel; Emma Rothschild; Maurice Strong; Andrew Young; Muhammad Yunus.
Number of staff: 12 full-time professional; 1 part-time professional; 8 full-time support.
EIN: 582368165

701
Verizon Washington, DC Inc. Corporate Giving Program

2055 L St. N.W.
Washington, DC 20036 (202) 392-9900
Contact: Erica Warley

Grantmaker type: Corporate giving program
Purpose and activities: Verizon Washington, DC makes charitable contributions to nonprofit organizations involved with literacy, the environment, and workforce development. Support is given primarily in Washington, DC.
Fields of interest: Reading; Environment; Employment.
Types of support: General/operating support.
Limitations: Giving primarily in Washington, DC.
Application information: Application form not required.
  Initial approach: Proposal to headquarters

702
Wallace Genetic Foundation, Inc. ▼

4900 Massachusetts Ave., N.W., Ste. 220
Washington, DC 20016 (202) 966-2932
Contact: Patricia Lee, Co-Exec. Dir. or Carolyn Sand, Co-Exec. Dir.
FAX: (202) 966-3370; E-mail: president@wallacegenetic.org; URL: http://www.wallacegenetic.org

Incorporated in 1959 in NY.
Donor(s): Henry A. Wallace.‡
Grantmaker type: Independent foundation
Financial data (yr. ended 12/31/02): Assets, $77,014,820 (M); expenditures, $4,379,239; qualifying distributions, $4,031,553; giving activities include $3,896,970 for 78 grants (high: $989,970; low: $1,000; average: $25,000–$50,000).
Purpose and activities: Areas of interest are sustainable agriculture, protection of farmland near cities, plant genetic research, biodiversity protection, and environmental education.
Fields of interest: Natural resources; Environmental education; Agriculture; Public policy, research.
International interests: Soviet Union (Former); Latin America.
Types of support: General/operating support; Continuing support; Land acquisition; Program development; Seed money; Research; Matching/challenge support.
Limitations: No grants to individuals, or for scholarships, endowments, or university overhead expenses; no loans.
Publications: Grants list, Informational brochure (including application guidelines).

Application information: FAX or E-mailed proposals will not be accepted. Application form not required.
  Initial approach: 1- or 2-page letter and proposal
  Copies of proposal: 1
  Deadline(s): None
  Board meeting date(s): Monthly
  Final notification: None
Officers and Directors:* Jean W. Douglas,* Pres.; Ann D. Cornell,* V.P. and Secy.; Joan D. Murray,* V.P. and Treas.; David W. Douglas,* V.P., Research; Patricia Lee, Co-Exec. Dir.; Carolyn Sand, Co-Exec. Dir.
Number of staff: 2 part-time professional.
EIN: 136162575
Recent environmental and animal welfare grants:
702-1 America the Beautiful Fund, DC, $25,000. For general support. 2001.
702-2 American Bird Conservancy, The Plains, VA, $35,000. For Pesticides and Birds campaign. 2001.
702-3 American Farm School, New York, NY, $30,000. For Xeriscape Project. 2001.
702-4 American Farmland Trust, DC, $75,000. For Public Education Division. 2001.
702-5 American Public Information on the Environment, South Glastonbury, CT, $30,000. For 1-800 Environmental Health Line. 2001.
702-6 American Rivers, DC, $30,000. For general support. 2001.
702-7 Beyond Pesticides/NCAMP, DC, $30,000. For Center for Community Pesticide and Alternatives Information program. 2001.
702-8 Carnegie Institution of Washington, Department of Global Ecology, DC, $50,000. For global change research. 2001.
702-9 Center for Health, Environment and Justice, Falls Church, VA, $40,000. For nationwide grassroots campaign to protect children from environmental health threats. 2001.
702-10 Center for the Support of Native Lands, Arlington, VA, $25,000. For general support. 2001.
702-11 Childrens Health Environmental Coalition, Princeton, NJ, $60,000. To translate children's environmental health information into Spanish and to facilitate necessary Web enhancements. 2001.
702-12 Childrens Health Environmental Coalition, Princeton, NJ, $10,000. For general support. 2001.
702-13 Colorado Boys Ranch Foundation, La Junta, CO, $25,000. For year-round horticulture program and to purchase horticultural materials for library. 2001.
702-14 Conservation Fund, Arlington, VA, $200,000. For Rivers to the Chesapeake Initiative. 2001.
702-15 Conservation Law Foundation, Boston, MA, $25,000. For sustainable agriculture and farmland protection initiatives. 2001.
702-16 Cornell University, Lab of Ornithology, Ithaca, NY, $40,000. To design complementary multimedia, educational exhibits for new lab. 2001.
702-17 Defenders of Wildlife, DC, $20,000. For general support. 2001.
702-18 EarthMatters.org, Logan, UT, $25,000. For general support. 2001.

702-19 Hartford Food System, Hartford, CT, $20,000. For statewide farmland preservation initiative. 2001.

702-20 Healthy Schools Network, Albany, NY, $30,000. For Web site. 2001.

702-21 Initiative for Social Action and Renewal in Eurasia (ISAR), DC, $25,000. For Center for Russian Environmental Policy. 2001.

702-22 Institute for Local Self-Reliance, DC, $50,000. For Hawaii Industrial Hemp Project. 2001.

702-23 Institute for Sustainable Communities, Montpelier, VT, $15,000. For special opportunities fund. 2001.

702-24 Institute for Traditional Studies, Novato, CA, $25,000. For production of video on sustainable agriculture. 2001.

702-25 Iowa Environmental Council, Des Moines, IA, $20,000. For program promoting positive changes in Iowa's environment. 2001.

702-26 Iowa Natural Heritage Foundation, Des Moines, IA, $30,000. For general support. 2001.

702-27 Land Stewardship Project, White Bear Lake, MN, $38,000. For Farm and Rural Organizing Project. 2001.

702-28 League of Conservation Voters, DC, $15,000. For grassroots program to counter threats to environmental protection. 2001.

702-29 Marine Mammal Center, Sausalito, CA, $35,000. For Veterinary Science and Research Program. 2001.

702-30 Missouri Rural Crisis Center, Columbia, MO, $50,000. For Family Farms, Not Factory Farms Sustainable Agriculture for Twenty-First Century project. 2001.

702-31 Mount Sinai School of Medicine of New York University, Center for Children's Health and the Environment, New York, NY, $50,000. For policy work. 2001.

702-32 National Environmental Education and Training Foundation, DC, $25,000. For Pesticide Education and Practice for Pediatric Health Care Providers. 2001.

702-33 National Environmental Education and Training Foundation, DC, $10,000. For matching funds for Health Schools Network Web site. 2001.

702-34 National Park Trust, DC, $40,000. For research of Park Education Resource Center Program. 2001.

702-35 National Wildlife Federation, Reston, VA, $50,000. For conservation education work. 2001.

702-36 Natural Resources Defense Council, New York, NY, $50,000. For forest initiative. 2001.

702-37 Natural Resources Defense Council, New York, NY, $50,000. For work on climate change. 2001.

702-38 New York Botanical Garden, Bronx, NY, $25,000. For Plant Genomics Consortium. 2001.

702-39 North American Industrial Hemp Council, Madison, WI, $10,000. For general support. 2001.

702-40 Northeast Sustainable Agriculture Working Group, Belchertown, MA, $35,000. For policy education and reform and continued support for existing programs. 2001.

702-41 Northwest Coalition for Alternatives to Pesticides, Eugene, Oregon, $30,000. For Leveraging Change to Advance Sustainable Potato Farming Alternatives. 2001.

702-42 Organic Farming Research Foundation, Santa Cruz, CA, $50,000. For general support. 2001.

702-43 Persephone Productions, DC, $41,482. For production of program entitled, Coverage of School and Pesticide Issues. 2001.

702-44 Pesticide Action Network (PAN), North America Regional Center, San Francisco, CA, $25,000. For campaign on Genetic Engineering Industrial Agriculture and Sustainable Alternatives. 2001.

702-45 Rainforest Alliance, New York, NY, $25,000. For Conservation Agriculture Program. 2001.

702-46 Royal Botanic Gardens, Richmond, England, $30,000. For Millennium Seed Bank Project. 2001.

702-47 Sea Change, Marion, MA, $10,000. For planning for Drinking Water Colloquium. 2001.

702-48 Sustainable Cotton Project, Oroville, CA, $50,000. For Cleaner Cotton Campaign. 2001.

702-49 Union of Concerned Scientists, Cambridge, MA, $25,000. For Food and Environment Program. 2001.

702-50 Vetiver Network, Leesburg, VA, $45,000. For general support. 2001.

702-51 Washington Toxics Coalition, Seattle, WA, $40,000. For expansion of pesticide campaign. 2001.

702-52 Watershed Media, Healdsburg, CA, $30,000. For book entitled, Farming with the Wild Beyond Organic. 2001.

702-53 Westchester Land Trust, Bedford Hills, NY, $25,000. For Westchester Open Space Alliance. 2001.

702-54 Wilderness Society, DC, $30,000. For Eastern Network of Wild Lands project. 2001.

702-55 World Wildlife Fund/Conservation Foundation, DC, $50,000. For Wildlife and Contaminants Program. 2001.

703
Wallace Global Fund ▼
1990 M St. N.W., Ste. 250
Washington, DC 20036 (202) 452-1530
Contact: Catherine Cameron, Exec. Dir.
FAX: (202) 452-0922; E-mail: tkroll@wgf.org;
URL: http://www.wgf.org

Established in 1995.
Donor(s): Robert B. Wallace,‡ Gordon G. Wallace,‡ Henry A. Wallace,‡ Ilo B. Wallace.‡
Grantmaker type: Independent foundation
Financial data (yr. ended 12/31/02): Assets, $109,296,426 (M); expenditures, $6,104,584; qualifying distributions, $5,181,577; giving activities include $4,395,218 for 78 grants (high: $225,000; low: $5,250; average: $25,000–$100,000).
Purpose and activities: Giving primarily for environmental, population, and reproductive health issues. The foundation also funds projects that work toward global policy change in these areas.
Fields of interest: Global warming; Environment, forests; Family planning; Youth, pregnancy prevention; International economic development.
International interests: Europe.

Types of support: General/operating support; Continuing support; Program development; Matching/challenge support.
Limitations: Giving on an international basis. No grants to individuals, or for scholarships, professorships, university overhead expenses, capital campaigns, construction, debt reduction, endowment funds, land acquisition, in-kind gifts, film or video projects, travel (except project-related travel).
Publications: Financial statement, Grants list, Occasional report.
Application information: The fund recommends submission of a 3-page concept paper prior to submission of a full proposal. Application form not required.
  Initial approach: Letter of inquiry
  Board meeting date(s): 3 times a year
Officers and Directors: R. Bruce Wallace, Pres.; Catherine Cameron, Secy. and Exec. Dir.; Christy Wallace,* Treas.; Scott Fitzmorris; Jonathan Lash; H. Scott Wallace; Jackie Wallace; Randall C. Wallace; Susan Wallace.
Number of staff: 4 full-time professional; 1 full-time support.
EIN: 521918002
Recent environmental and animal welfare grants:

703-1 Center for International Environmental Law, DC, $75,000. For general operating support to strengthen international law and institutions to protect human health and the global environment and promote sustainable development. 2002.

703-2 Center for International Environmental Law, DC, $50,000. For U.S. Climate Action Network. 2002.

703-3 CERES, Boston, MA, $40,000. For CERES' Sustainable Governance Program. 2002.

703-4 Consumers Choice Council, DC, $75,000. For general support for work on promotion and protection of ecolabelling. 2002.

703-5 Environmental Defense, New York, NY, $50,000. For international program, Strengthening Environmental Performance in the Export Credit Agencies, and The World Bank Advocacy Campaign. 2002.

703-6 Environmental Defense, New York, NY, $50,000. For Combating Antibiotic Resistance in People by Curtailing Agricultural Overuse of Antibiotics. 2002.

703-7 Forest Stewardship Council, DC, $100,000. For International Secretariat. 2002.

703-8 Forest Trends Association, DC, $75,000. To promote incentives that diversifies trade in forest sector from dominance in wood products to broader range of services and products, such as ecosystem services. 2002.

703-9 Forests and the European Union Resource Network (FERN), Moreton-in-Marsh, England, $75,000. For program activities in export credit and climate. 2002.

703-10 Friends of the Earth, DC, $124,000. For groups in Netherlands, Japan, and France to participate in International Financial Institutions (IFI) Program. 2002.

703-11 Friends of the Earth, DC, $40,000. To educate policymakers on benefits of switching to energy policies that will preserve natural resources. 2002.

703-12 Friends of the Earth International, London, England, $124,000. For continued support for FOEI's International Financial

Institutions (IFI) Program, to increase control of civil society over operations of IFI's, and to replace current growth-oriented development focus with approach based on equity, human rights and recognition of limits posed by nature on all economic activity. 2002.

703-13 GLOBE USA, DC, $50,000. To educate members of Congress about major issues and their role in addressing environmental issues. 2002.

703-14 Greenpeace U.S.A., DC, $45,000. For Global Forests Campaign. 2002.

703-15 Greenpeace U.S.A., DC, $40,000. For project, Stop Global Warming: Clean Energy Now. 2002.

703-16 Ilisu Dam Campaign, Oxford, England, $26,000. For continued support. 2002.

703-17 Institute for Policy Studies, DC, $105,000. For Sustainable Energy and Economy Network (SEEN). 2002.

703-18 Izaak Walton League of America, Gaithersburg, MD, $25,000. For Sustainable Population Campaign. 2002.

703-19 League of Conservation Voters Education Fund, DC, $25,000. For Environmental Leadership Institute. 2002.

703-20 National Environmental Trust, DC, $100,000. For Global Warming Public Education Campaign. 2002.

703-21 Pacific Environment and Resources Center, Oakland, CA, $40,000. For export credit agency reform work, including ECA-Watch Web site. 2002.

703-22 Physicians for Social Responsibility, DC, $35,000. For Global Climate Change Initiative which works towards stabilization of greenhouse gas concentrations in atmosphere at levels adequate to protect human health and the environment. 2002.

703-23 Rainforest Action Network, San Francisco, CA, $25,000. To preserve ancient forests and rights of indigenous rainforest communities by shifting global forest products industry away from old growth wood. 2002.

703-24 Rainforest Alliance, New York, NY, $50,000. For core support. 2002.

703-25 Rocky Mountain Institute, Snowmass, CO, $25,000. For National Energy Policy Initiative. 2002.

703-26 Sierra Club Foundation, San Francisco, CA, $200,000. For Global Population and Environment Program. 2002.

703-27 World Resources Institute, DC, $65,000. To develop more complete and useful data on sources of greenhouse gasses for each Kyoto Treaty signatory. 2002.

703-28 World Resources Institute, DC, $35,000. To begin to describe road map to shift energy production from fossil fuels to hydrogen. 2002.

703-29 Worldwatch Institute, DC, $40,000. To serve as educator, source of research on complex problems, and inspirer of action towards more sustainable world. 2002.

704
Woodrow Wilson International Center for Scholars

1300 Pennsylvania Ave., N.W.
Washington, DC 20004-3027 (202) 691-4000
Contact: Lee Hamilton, Dir.
FAX: (202) 691-4001; E-mail: wwics@wwic.si.edu; URL: http://www.wilsoncenter.org

Established in 1968 in DC.
Grantmaker type: Public charity
Financial data (yr. ended 09/30/02): Revenue, $9,852,659; assets, $124,411,610 (M); gifts received, $9,567,476; expenditures, $16,390,024; program services expenses, $12,771,863; giving activities include $2,405,382 for grants to individuals.
Purpose and activities: The center seeks to unite the world of ideas to the world of policy by supporting pre-eminent scholarship and linking that scholarship to issues of concern to official Washington.
Fields of interest: Historical activities; Environment; Economics; Public policy, research; Public affairs.
Types of support: Fellowships; Internship funds; Research; Scholarships—to individuals.
Limitations: Giving on a national and international basis.
Application information: See Web site for application information. Application form required.
Deadline(s): Oct. 1 for Fellowships
Final notification: Early Apr. for Fellowships
Officers and Trustees:* Joseph B. Gildenhorn,* Chair.; David A. Metzner,* Vice-Chair.; Joseph A. Cari, Jr.; Carol Cartwright; Donald E. Garcia; Bruce S. Gelb; Daniel L. Lamaute; Tami Longaberger; Thomas R. Reedy; and 7 additional trustees.
EIN: 521067541

705
The Winslow Foundation

(formerly Windie Foundation)
1225 Connecticut Ave., N.W., 4th Fl.
Washington, DC 20036 (202) 833-4714
Contact: Dr. Betty Ann Ottinger, Dir.
FAX: (202) 833-4716

Established in 1987 in NJ.
Donor(s): Julia D. Winslow.‡
Grantmaker type: Independent foundation
Financial data (yr. ended 12/31/02): Assets, $26,376,498 (M); expenditures, $1,788,092; qualifying distributions, $1,375,600; giving activities include $1,375,600 for grants.
Purpose and activities: Giving primarily for the environment and population studies.
Fields of interest: Natural resources; Population studies.
Types of support: General/operating support; Continuing support; Program development; Conferences/seminars; Seed money; Research; Matching/challenge support.
Limitations: Giving on a national basis. No grants to individuals.
Publications: Application guidelines.
Application information:
Initial approach: 2-page letter of inquiry
Copies of proposal: 1
Deadline(s): None

Board meeting date(s): Varies
Officers and Directors:* Wren Winslow Wirth,* Pres.; Samuel W. Lambert III,* V.P. and Treas.; Betty Ann Ottinger.
Number of staff: 1 part-time professional; 1 part-time support.
EIN: 222778703

706
World Parks Endowment

1616 P St., N.W., Ste. 200
Washington, DC 20036 (202) 939-3808
Contact: Byron Swift, Exec. Dir.
E-mail: worldparks@worldparks.org; URL: http://www.worldparks.org/

Established in 1989.
Grantmaker type: Public charity
Financial data (yr. ended 12/31/01): Revenue, $386,772; assets, $118,509; gifts received, $386,616; expenditures, $306,487; program services expenses, $302,407; giving activities include $268,670 for 8 grants (high: $140,000; low: $500).
Purpose and activities: The organization seeks to conserve natural resources and areas of high biodiversity through international land purchases of conservation, as well as creating endowment funds for tropical protection and management.
Fields of interest: Natural resources.
Types of support: Land acquisition; Endowments.
Limitations: Giving on an international basis.
Officers and Trustees:* Dan Katz,* Pres.; Roger Pasquier,* V.P.; Robert Ridgely,* Treas.; Byron Swift, Exec. Dir.; John Mitchell; John Robinson.
Number of staff: 2.
EIN: 133500609

707
World Wildlife Fund

(formerly The Conservation Foundation)
1250 24th St., N.W.
Washington, DC 20037 (202) 293-4800
Contact: Nancy J. Dunn, V.P., Fin. and Admin. and C.F.O.
FAX: (202) 293-2239; E-mail: public.information@wwfus.org; URL: http://www.worldwildlife.org

Established in 1961 in DC.
Grantmaker type: Public charity
Financial data (yr. ended 06/30/01): Revenue, $118,144,311; assets, $148,929,295 (L); gifts received, $104,281,275; expenditures, $109,051,061; program services expenses, $88,621,812; giving activities include $25,857,808 for grants and $10,609,558 for in-kind gifts.
Purpose and activities: The fund seeks to promote the conservation of nature by focusing their work on a new priority-setting tool: the Global 200 Conservation framework. This, in turn, forms the fund's Living Planet Campaign, which seeks to combine local and global actions in a concerted, worldwide effort to save endangered species, protect important harbors of biological diversity, and encourage changes in those international markets that accelerate environmental threats.

Fields of interest: Education, public education; Animals/wildlife, endangered species.
International interests: Caribbean; Russia; Africa; Madagascar; Latin America; Asia.
Types of support: General/operating support; Equipment; Endowments; Program development; Curriculum development; Fellowships; Research; Technical assistance; Program evaluation; Grants to individuals; Scholarships—to individuals.
Limitations: Applications not accepted. Giving on an international basis.
Publications: Annual report, Informational brochure, Newsletter, Occasional report.
Application information: Contributes only to pre-selected organizations; unsolicited requests for funds not considered or acknowledged.
 Board meeting date(s): Feb., May, and Sept.
Officers and Directors:* William K. Reilly,* Chair.; Edward P. Bass,* Vice-Chair.; Kathryn S. Fuller,* Pres.; Deborah Hechinger,* Exec. V.P.; David Sandalow,* Exec. V.P.; Nancy Dunn,* V.P., Fin. and Admin., and C.F.O.; Suzanne Mink,* V.P., Devel.; Alison Richard, Secy.; Roger Sant, Treas.; Margaret Ackerley, Genl. Counsel; Janet Fesler, Dir., Board Rel.
Number of staff: 522 full-time professional; 20 part-time professional.
EIN: 521693387

FLORIDA

708
Alexander Foundation, Inc.
1200 N. Federal Hwy., Ste. 307
Boca Raton, FL 33432

Established in 1986 in FL.
Donor(s): Leslie L. Alexander.
Grantmaker type: Independent foundation
Financial data (yr. ended 12/31/01): Assets, $2,992,096 (M); expenditures, $264,036; qualifying distributions, $243,073; giving activities include $222,300 for 23 grants (high: $53,000; low: $500).
Purpose and activities: Giving primarily for animal welfare; funding also for Jewish organizations.
Fields of interest: Animal welfare; Animals/wildlife, preservation/protection; Human services; Jewish agencies & temples.
Limitations: Applications not accepted. Giving on a national basis, with emphasis on Washington, DC, FL, NC, NY, VA. No grants to individuals.
Application information: Contributes only to pre-selected organizations.
Officer: Leslie L. Alexander, Pres.
Directors: Jodi Tara Alexander; Nanci B. Alexander.
EIN: 592789197

709
Lee R. Anderson Family Foundation ▼
3054 Gordon Dr.
Naples, FL 34102

Established in 1997 in FL.

Donor(s): Katherine M. Anderson, Lee R. Anderson, Sr.
Grantmaker type: Independent foundation
Financial data (yr. ended 06/30/02): Assets, $271,194 (M); gifts received, $2,483,269; expenditures, $5,029,747; qualifying distributions, $4,932,815; giving activities include $4,964,897 for 53 grants (high: $1,500,000; low: $600; average: $1,000–$50,000).
Purpose and activities: Giving primarily to education, health associations, social services, children's services, and religion.
Fields of interest: Elementary/secondary education; Education; Animals/wildlife, preservation/protection; Health organizations, association; Medical research; Athletics/sports, school programs; Human services; Children, services; Religion.
Limitations: Applications not accepted. Giving on a national basis.
Application information: Contributes only to pre-selected organizations.
Officers: Lee R. Anderson, Sr., Pres.; Katherine M. Anderson, V.P.; Katherine E. Anderson, Secy.; Lee R. "Andy" Anderson, Jr., Treas.
EIN: 656254123
Recent environmental and animal welfare grants:
709-1 Ducks Unlimited, Memphis, TN, $27,860. 2002.
709-2 Foundation for North American Wild Sheep, Cody, WY, $200,000. 2002.
709-3 International SeaKeepers Society, Miami, FL, $100,000. 2002.

710
Archibald Foundation, Inc.
7100 Roberts Rd.
Tallahassee, FL 32309-9278
Contact: Kathy Archibald, Pres.

Established in 1996 in FL.
Donor(s): Delbert M. Archibald, Kathy Archibald.
Grantmaker type: Independent foundation
Financial data (yr. ended 12/31/02): Assets, $3,652,775 (M); expenditures, $170,796; qualifying distributions, $165,298; giving activities include $165,000 for 16 grants (high: $25,000; low: $5,000).
Fields of interest: Education; Environment; Health care; Health organizations, association; Housing/shelter, development; Children/youth, services.
Types of support: Capital campaigns; Building/renovation; Equipment; Endowments; Program development; Scholarship funds; Research; Program-related investments/loans; Matching/challenge support.
Limitations: Giving primarily in northern FL. No grants to individuals.
Application information: Application form not required.
 Initial approach: Letter to Pres.
 Deadline(s): Jan. 1 to July 31
 Board meeting date(s): Semiannually
Officer and Directors:* Kathy Archibald,* Pres.; Daniel Isaac Archibald; Delbert M. Archibald; Kenneth Cole Archibald.
Number of staff: None.
EIN: 593414615

711
AutoNation, Inc. Corporate Giving Program
(formerly Republic Industries, Inc. Corporate Giving Program)
110 S.E. 6th St.
Fort Lauderdale, FL 33301 (954) 769-7209
Contact: Gale M. Butler, V.P., Corp. Affairs

Grantmaker type: Corporate giving program
Financial data (yr. ended 12/31/02): Total giving, $2,610,000; giving activities include $2,500,000 for 500 grants (high: $200,000; low: $100; average: $100–$5,000), $10,000 for 12 employee matching gifts and $100,000 for in-kind gifts.
Purpose and activities: AutoNation makes charitable contributions to nonprofit organizations involved with arts and culture, education, the environment, youth development, families, and civic affairs. Support is given on a national basis in areas of company operations.
Fields of interest: Arts; Education; Environment; Youth development; Family services; Public affairs.
Types of support: General/operating support; Scholarship funds; Cause-related marketing; Employee volunteer services; Loaned talent; Public relations services; Use of facilities; Sponsorships; Employee matching gifts; Scholarships—to individuals; Donated equipment; Donated products; In-kind gifts.
Limitations: Giving on a national basis in areas of company operations, with emphasis on the Sunbelt states. No support for religious or fraternal organizations not of direct benefit to the entire community, political organizations, United Way- or community foundation-supported organizations, or international organizations. No grants to individuals (except for scholarships), or for travel or political campaigns.
Publications: Application guidelines.
Application information: Proposals should be no longer than 1 to 2 pages in length. Support is limited to 1 contribution per organization during any given year. Multi-year funding is not automatic. The Corporate Affairs Department handles giving. The company has a staff that only handles contributions. A contributions committee reviews all requests. Application form not required.
 Initial approach: Proposal to headquarters
 Copies of proposal: 1
 Deadline(s): Early fall
 Board meeting date(s): Quarterly
 Final notification: Following review
Number of staff: 1 full-time professional; 1 full-time support.

712
The Avellino Family Foundation, Inc.
4750 N.E. 23rd Ave.
Fort Lauderdale, FL 33308-4721

Established in 2000 in FL.
Donor(s): Frank J. Avellino.
Grantmaker type: Independent foundation
Financial data (yr. ended 12/31/02): Assets, $6,967,020 (M); expenditures, $404,789; qualifying distributions, $394,917; giving activities include $398,615 for grants.

Fields of interest: Performing arts; Arts; Education; Animals/wildlife; Health care; Human services; Children/youth, services; Christian agencies & churches.
Limitations: Applications not accepted. Giving primarily in FL, MA, NJ, and NY. No grants to individuals.
Application information: Contributes only to pre-selected organizations.
Officers: Frank J. Avellino, Pres.; Joseph Avellino, V.P.; Nancy Caroll Avellino, V.P.; Thomas Avellino, Secy.; Lorraine Avellino McEvoy, Treas.
Director: Rachel Anne Rosenthal.
EIN: 651043563

713
Bacardi Foundation
Cumberland Bldg.
800 E. Broward Blvd., Ste. 601
Fort Lauderdale, FL 33301
Contact: Roger Haagenson, Tr.

Established in 1994 in FL.
Donor(s): Hilda Bacardi.‡
Grantmaker type: Independent foundation
Financial data (yr. ended 12/31/01): Assets, $8,543,525 (M); expenditures, $905,473; qualifying distributions, $641,277; giving activities include $647,500 for 1 grant.
Fields of interest: Animals/wildlife, research.
Limitations: Giving primarily in FL.
Application information:
  Deadline(s): None
Trustees: Facundo Bacardi; Roger Haagenson; Sherry Haagenson.
EIN: 650342998

714
Bailey Family Foundation, Inc.
P.O. Box 3486
Vero Beach, FL 32964
Contact: Stephen M. Bailey, Pres.

Established in 1992.
Donor(s): Stephen M. Bailey, Lucia H. Bailey.
Grantmaker type: Independent foundation
Financial data (yr. ended 12/31/02): Assets, $3,932,913 (M); expenditures, $208,058; qualifying distributions, $200,211; giving activities include $151,725 for 125 grants (high: $16,000; low: $10).
Purpose and activities: Giving primarily to education and religion.
Fields of interest: Arts; Education; Natural resources; Hospitals (general); Human services; Christian agencies & churches.
Limitations: Applications not accepted. Giving primarily in FL. No grants to individuals.
Application information: Contributes only to pre-selected organizations. Unsolicited requests for funds not accepted.
Officers: Stephen M. Bailey, Pres. and Treas.; Lucia H. Bailey, V.P. and Secy.
EIN: 593154364

715
Constance Matheson Baker Charitable Foundation
2400 S.E. Federal Hwy., 4th Fl.
Stuart, FL 34994

Established in 2000 in FL.
Donor(s): The Constance Matheson Baker Revocable Trust.
Grantmaker type: Independent foundation
Financial data (yr. ended 12/31/01): Assets, $10,278,950 (M); gifts received, $509,932; expenditures, $428,336; qualifying distributions, $351,228; giving activities include $351,228 for 10 grants (high: $63,923; low: $15,805).
Purpose and activities: Support for Native American Indian schools, animal welfare, health care, and human services.
Fields of interest: Elementary/secondary education; Animal welfare; Health care; Roman Catholic agencies & churches; Native Americans/American Indians.
Limitations: Applications not accepted. Giving on a national basis. No grants to individuals.
Application information: Contributes only to pre-selected organizations.
Trustee: Steven J. Wood.
EIN: 656345111

716
The George T. Baker Foundation, Inc.
1111 Kane Concourse, Ste. 609
Bay Harbor Islands, FL 33154
Contact: Gladys Figueroa, Secy.-Treas.

Incorporated in 1956 in FL.
Donor(s): George T. Baker.‡
Grantmaker type: Independent foundation
Financial data (yr. ended 05/31/02): Assets, $2,319,966 (M); expenditures, $182,065; qualifying distributions, $126,481; giving activities include $127,850 for 74 grants (high: $20,000; low: $100).
Purpose and activities: Giving for higher education, hospitals, health agencies, and medical research; grants also for humane societies, social services, and children's services.
Fields of interest: Higher education; Animal welfare; Health care; Health organizations, association; Medical research, institute; Human services; Children/youth, services.
Types of support: Emergency funds.
Limitations: Applications not accepted. Giving primarily in Dade County, FL, and Blowing Rock, NC. No grants to individuals.
Application information: Contributes only to pre-selected organizations.
  Board meeting date(s): Quarterly
Officers and Trustees:* Irma Baker Lyons,* Chair.; Barbara Baker,* Pres.; Raymond Beahn,* V.P.; James F. Lyons, M.D.,* V.P.; Rev. Oscar Wilsen,* V.P.; Gladys Figueroa,* Secy.-Treas.; Patricia A. Corbett.
Number of staff: 1 full-time professional.
EIN: 596151202

717
Banbury Fund, Inc.
501 Goodlette Rd. N., D100
Naples, FL 34102
Contact: William S. Robertson, Pres.

Incorporated in 1946 in NY.
Donor(s): Marie H. Robertson,‡ Charles S. Robertson.‡
Grantmaker type: Independent foundation
Financial data (yr. ended 12/31/01): Assets, $42,687,974 (M); expenditures, $2,975,288; qualifying distributions, $2,740,958; giving activities include $2,420,000 for 88 grants (high: $185,000; low: $250; average: $1,000–$30,000).
Purpose and activities: Primary areas of interest include higher and other education and health, including cancer and other medical research.
Fields of interest: Secondary school/education; Higher education; Education; Environment; Health care; Health organizations, association; Cancer; Alcoholism; Medical research, institute; Cancer research; Crime/law enforcement; Human services; Marine science; Engineering/technology; Biological sciences; Science; Economically disadvantaged.
Types of support: General/operating support; Continuing support; Annual campaigns; Capital campaigns; Building/renovation; Equipment; Endowments; Debt reduction; Emergency funds; Seed money; Research.
Limitations: Giving primarily in NY. No grants to individuals.
Application information: Application form not required.
  Initial approach: Letter
  Copies of proposal: 3
  Deadline(s): None
Officers and Directors:* William S. Robertson,* Pres.; Walter C. Meier,* V.P.; John L. Robertson,* V.P.; Katherine R. Ernst,* Secy.; Anne R. Meier,* Treas.; Robert Ernst.
Number of staff: 4 part-time professional.
EIN: 136062463

718
Bank of America Client Foundation
(formerly Bank of America Community Foundation)
1800 2nd St., Ste. 750
Sarasota, FL 34236 (941) 957-0442
Contact: Debra Jacobs, Admin.
E-mail: djacobs@selby.org

Established in 1961 in FL as the Sarasota Bank and Trust Company Community Foundation.
Donor(s): Eileen Kroeger, Julius Brandenburg.‡
Grantmaker type: Independent foundation
Financial data (yr. ended 12/31/02): Assets, $6,031,402 (M); expenditures, $502,119; qualifying distributions, $416,693; giving activities include $416,686 for 31 grants (high: $28,000; low: $100).
Purpose and activities: Giving primarily for the arts, education, human services, natural science, and historic preservation.
Fields of interest: Film/video; Visual arts; Museums; Performing arts; Dance; Theater; Humanities; Historic preservation/historical societies; Arts; Early childhood education; Child development, education; Elementary school/education; Secondary school/education; Vocational education; Higher education; Adult education—literacy, basic skills & GED; Reading; Education; Natural resources; Environment; Family planning; Health care; Mental health/crisis services; Health organizations, association; AIDS;

Crime/violence prevention, youth; Recreation; Human services; Children/youth, services; Child development, services; Family services; Hospices; Aging, centers/services; Women, centers/services; Minorities/immigrants, centers/services; Homeless, human services; Urban/community development; Community development; Marine science; Minorities; Disabled; Aging; Women; Economically disadvantaged; Homeless.
Types of support: Building/renovation; Equipment; Program development; Matching/challenge support.
Limitations: Giving limited to organizations operating in or providing services to residents of Sarasota and Manatee counties, FL. No grants to individuals, or for endowments or general operating support.
Publications: Application guidelines.
Application information: Application form required.
Initial approach: Proposal
Copies of proposal: 7
Deadline(s): May 1 and Oct. 15
Board meeting date(s): End of June and Nov.
Final notification: Jan. 30 and July 30
Trustee: Bank of America.
Number of staff: 3 shared staff (shared with WM G. and Marie Salby Foundation).
EIN: 596142753

719
John E. and Nellie J. Bastien Memorial Foundation
440 E. Sample Rd., Ste. 209
Pompano Beach, FL 33064   (954) 942-3203
Contact: The Trustees

Trust established in 1965 in FL.
Donor(s): Nellie J. Bastien.‡
Grantmaker type: Independent foundation
Financial data (yr. ended 12/31/02): Assets, $10,397,395 (M); expenditures, $589,827; qualifying distributions, $518,052; giving activities include $417,000 for 142 grants (high: $12,500; low: $500).
Fields of interest: Performing arts; Child development, education; Higher education; Environment; Animal welfare; Hospitals (general); Health care; Substance abuse, services; Health organizations, association; Cancer; Heart & circulatory diseases; AIDS; Alcoholism; Biomedicine; Medical research, institute; Cancer research; Heart & circulatory research; AIDS research; Human services; Youth, services; Child development, services; Family services; Hospices; Aging, centers/services; Roman Catholic federated giving programs; Marine science; Religion; Aging; Economically disadvantaged.
Types of support: General/operating support; Scholarship funds.
Limitations: Giving primarily in FL.
Application information: Application form not required.
Deadline(s): None
Trustees: Carol R. Kearns; Carolyn E. Schneider; J. Wallace Wrightson.
EIN: 596160694

720
The Batchelor Foundation, Inc.
3801 P6A Blvd., Ste. 806
Palm Beach Gardens, FL 33410-5931
Contact: Daniel J. Ferraresi, Treas.

Established in 1990 in FL.
Donor(s): International Air Leases, Inc., Batchelor Enterprises, George E. Batchelor.
Grantmaker type: Company-sponsored foundation
Financial data (yr. ended 06/30/02): Assets, $137,182,925 (M); expenditures, $5,721,107; qualifying distributions, $5,459,500; giving activities include $5,459,500 for 63 grants (high: $3,000,000; low: $1,000; average: $2,000–$100,000).
Purpose and activities: Priority is given to organizations engaged in medical research, care of childhood diseases, and organizations that promote the study, preservation, and public awareness of the natural environment.
Fields of interest: Higher education; Education; Natural resources; Environment; Animals/wildlife; Hospitals (general); Health organizations, association; Medical research, institute; Housing/shelter, homeless; Human services; Children/youth, services; Foundations (community).
Limitations: Giving primarily in Miami, FL. No grants to individuals.
Application information: Application form not required.
Initial approach: Proposal
Deadline(s): None
Officers: George E. Batchelor, Chair. and Pres.; Anne O. Batchelor-Robjohns, Exec. V.P. and Secy.; Daniel J. Ferraresi, Treas.
EIN: 650188171
Recent environmental and animal welfare grants:
720-1 Audubon Society, National, Miami, FL, $200,000. For general support. 2002.
720-2 Center for Orangutan and Chimpanzee Conservation, Wauchula, FL, $10,000. For general support. 2002.
720-3 Encounters in Excellence, Miami, FL, $24,000. For general support. 2002.
720-4 McCarthys Wildlife Sanctuary, West Palm Beach, FL, $30,000. For general support. 2002.
720-5 Zoological Society of Florida, Miami, FL, $100,000. For general support. 2002.

721
Behring Foundation
2131 Hollywood Blvd., Ste. 505
Hollywood, FL 33020   (954) 920-5300
Contact: Elliot D. Stein, Tr.
FAX: (954) 922-3175

Established in 1993 in CA.
Donor(s): Kenneth E. Behring.
Grantmaker type: Independent foundation
Financial data (yr. ended 12/31/01): Assets, $11,480,853 (M); gifts received, $4,119,141; expenditures, $8,975,253; qualifying distributions, $8,509,852; giving activities include $8,055,300 for 15 grants (high: $5,000,000; low: $650) and $468,779 for 1 foundation-administered program.
Purpose and activities: Giving primarily for animal and wildlife associations, including a large grant to the Smithsonian Institute.
Fields of interest: Museums; Animals/wildlife.
Limitations: Giving primarily in CA, Washington, DC, and TN.
Application information:
Initial approach: Resume, transcripts, short statement of career options, 3 letters of reference, and an essay required for fellowships
Deadline(s): None
Trustees: David E. Behring; Kenneth E. Behring; Joel Ehrenkranz; Elliot D. Stein.
EIN: 680306096

722
Bell Family Foundation for Hope, Inc.
1500 Berille Rd., Ste. 606
Daytona Beach, FL 32114
Contact: Ron H. Bell, Pres.

Established in 1993 in FL.
Donor(s): Ron H. Bell.
Grantmaker type: Independent foundation
Financial data (yr. ended 12/31/02): Assets, $2,434,751 (M); gifts received, $20,000; expenditures, $133,694; qualifying distributions, $126,815; giving activities include $127,143 for 16 grants (high: $30,219; low: $935).
Fields of interest: University; Zoos/zoological societies; Medical care, in-patient care; Athletics/sports, Special Olympics; American Red Cross; Religion, association.
Limitations: Giving primarily in GA.
Application information: Application form not required.
Initial approach: Letter
Officer: Ron H. Bell, Pres.
EIN: 593166060

723
The Frank Stanley Beveridge Foundation, Inc.
301 Yamato Rd., Ste. 1130
Boca Raton, FL 33431   (800) 600-3723
Contact: Philip Caswell, Pres.
FAX: (561) 241-8388; E-mail: administrator@beveridge.org; URL: http://www.beveridge.org

Trust established in 1947 in MA; incorporated in 1956.
Donor(s): Frank Stanley Beveridge.‡
Grantmaker type: Independent foundation
Financial data (yr. ended 12/31/02): Assets, $34,700,502 (M); expenditures, $2,045,609; qualifying distributions, $1,857,174; giving activities include $1,537,641 for grants.
Purpose and activities: Giving primarily for higher and secondary educational institutions attended by the Beveridge family, social service and youth agencies, community development, culture, health, minorities, ecological programs, and religious organizations attended by the Beveridge family.
Fields of interest: Historic preservation/historical societies; Early childhood education; Child development, education; Adult/continuing education; Education; Animal welfare; Hospitals (general); Health care; Mental health/crisis services; Health organizations; Nutrition;

Housing/shelter, development; Human services; Youth, services; Child development, services; Family services; Hospices; Aging, centers/services; Minorities/immigrants, centers/services; Voluntarism promotion; Christian agencies & churches; Protestant agencies & churches; Religion; Minorities; Disabled; Aging.

Types of support: Annual campaigns; Capital campaigns; Building/renovation; Equipment; Land acquisition; Emergency funds; Program development; Seed money; Research; Technical assistance; In-kind gifts; Matching/challenge support.

Limitations: Giving only in Hampden and Hampshire counties, MA. No grants to individuals, or for endowment or operating funds, scholarships, or fellowships; no loans.

Application information: Application form required.

Initial approach: Web site only
Copies of proposal: 1
Deadline(s): Feb. 1 and Aug. 1
Board meeting date(s): Apr. and Oct.
Final notification: 1 month following meeting

Officers and Directors:* Philip Caswell,* Pres.; Carole S. Lenhart, V.P. and Treas.; David F. Woods,* Clerk; Ward S. Caswell; Latimer B. Eddy; Alfred L. Griggs; Ian C. Palmer; Joseph Beveridge Palmer; Frederick W. Stecher; Patsy Palmer Stecher.

Number of staff: 1 full-time professional; 1 part-time professional.

EIN: 046032164

724

Lydia H. Bickerton Charitable Trust
P.O. Box 3967
Clearwater, FL 33767
Contact: G. John Hurley, Tr.

Established in 1986 in FL.
Grantmaker type: Independent foundation
Financial data (yr. ended 06/30/02): Assets, $1,811,622 (M); expenditures, $498,041; qualifying distributions, $219,323; giving activities include $219,323 for 19 grants (high: $55,000; low: $500).
Purpose and activities: Giving primarily for the arts, animal welfare, and social services.
Fields of interest: Performing arts centers; Orchestra (symphony); Arts; Animal welfare; Health organizations, association; Recreation; Human services.
Limitations: Giving primarily in Denver, CO, and FL.
Application information: Application form not required.
Initial approach: Proposal
Deadline(s): None
Trustee: G. John Hurley.
EIN: 592745408

725

Margaret R. Binz Foundation, Inc.
1825 S. Riverview Dr.
Melbourne, FL 32901
Contact: James L. Reinman, Pres.

Established in 1981 in FL.
Donor(s): Margaret R. Binz.‡
Grantmaker type: Independent foundation

Financial data (yr. ended 12/31/02): Assets, $1,513,168 (M); expenditures, $173,670; qualifying distributions, $161,713; giving activities include $161,500 for 27 grants (high: $30,000; low: $500).
Purpose and activities: Giving to underprivileged children and the prevention of cruelty to animals.
Fields of interest: Animal welfare; Hospitals (general); Health organizations, association; Youth development; Human services; Children/youth, services.
Limitations: Giving limited to FL. No grants to individuals or for scholarships.
Application information: Application form required.
Initial approach: Letter
Deadline(s): None
Officers: James L. Reinman, Pres.; Daniel Donovan, V.P.; Henry Carnegie, Secy.-Treas.
Number of staff: None.
EIN: 591367134

726

Blank Family Foundation, Inc.
3455 N.W. 54 St.
Miami, FL 33142
Contact: Andy Blank, Tr.

Established in 1987 in FL.
Donor(s): Rose Kramer.
Grantmaker type: Independent foundation
Financial data (yr. ended 12/31/01): Assets, $20,642,948 (M); expenditures, $1,193,746; qualifying distributions, $976,700; giving activities include $976,700 for 73 grants (high: $175,000; low: $200).
Purpose and activities: Giving primarily for Jewish organizations and community service programs.
Fields of interest: Arts; Higher education; Natural resources; Animals/wildlife; Hospitals (general); Human services; Jewish federated giving programs; Jewish agencies & temples; Aging.
Limitations: Applications not accepted. Giving primarily in the Miami, FL, area. No grants to individuals.
Application information: The foundation neither accepts nor responds to unsolicited proposals.
Officers and Directors:* Jerome Blank,* Pres.; Andrew Blank,* V.P.; Mark Blank,* V.P.; Tony Blank,* V.P.; Robin Reiter.
EIN: 650060771

727

Boyer & Meyrovitz Charitable Foundation
7791 N.W. 146th St.
Miami Lakes, FL 33016-1567

Established around 1992 in FL.
Grantmaker type: Independent foundation
Financial data (yr. ended 10/31/02): Assets, $1,802,601 (M); expenditures, $146,795; qualifying distributions, $137,979; giving activities include $131,689 for 12 grants (high: $33,000; low: $1,000).
Purpose and activities: Giving for youth programs and human services.
Fields of interest: Zoos/zoological societies; Youth development, adult & child programs; Human services; Salvation Army.

Limitations: Applications not accepted. Giving primarily in FL. No grants to individuals.
Application information: Contributes only to pre-selected organizations.
Trustee: Wendell I. Nichols.
EIN: 656082311

728

Brabson Library & Educational Foundation
c/o Bank of America
P.O. Box 40200, MC FL9-100-10-19
Jacksonville, FL 32203
Application address: 9008 Natalie Ave. N.E., Albuquerque, NM 87111-3132

Established in 1990 in FL.
Grantmaker type: Independent foundation
Financial data (yr. ended 06/30/02): Assets, $2,789,419 (M); gifts received, $406,301; expenditures, $147,284; qualifying distributions, $131,870; giving activities include $125,658 for 4 grants (high: $40,000; low: $22,325).
Purpose and activities: Giving for higher education, the arts, and nature conservation.
Fields of interest: Opera; Orchestra (symphony); Higher education; Natural resources; Youth development, adult & child programs.
Types of support: General/operating support.
Limitations: Giving on a national basis. No grants to individuals.
Application information: Application form not required.
Deadline(s): None
Officers and Directors:* Margaret B. Becker,* Pres.; John Brabson,* V.P.; John Becker,* Treas.; Bennet Brabson; G. Dana Brabson, Jr.
EIN: 593021777

729

Elliot J. Brody Foundation
17556 Lake Estates Dr.
Boca Raton, FL 33496

Established around 1985.
Donor(s): Elliot J. Brody.
Grantmaker type: Independent foundation
Financial data (yr. ended 12/31/01): Assets, $800,455 (M); gifts received, $64,472; expenditures, $117,587; qualifying distributions, $108,649; giving activities include $107,461 for 38 grants (high: $80,750; low: $25).
Purpose and activities: Giving for the environment, animal welfare, health, and Jewish organizations.
Fields of interest: Environment; Animals/wildlife; Health organizations, association; Medical research, institute; Jewish federated giving programs; Jewish agencies & temples.
Limitations: Applications not accepted. No grants to individuals.
Application information: Contributes only to pre-selected organizations.
Officers: Elliot J. Brody, Pres.; Helene Brody, V.P. and Secy.
Directors: Bradley Mark Brody; Jeffrey Brody; Arnold Golieb; D. David Peshkin.
EIN: 421254812

730
William J. and Janice D. Brown Foundation
P.O. Box 157
Boca Raton, FL 33429-0157
Contact: Thomas Ehrbar, Secy.-Treas.

Established in 1996 in FL.
Grantmaker type: Independent foundation
Financial data (yr. ended 12/31/00): Assets, $171,069 (M); expenditures, $99,117; qualifying distributions, $98,295; giving activities include $97,235 for 43 grants (high: $28,027; low: $74).
Fields of interest: Animal welfare; Boy scouts; Girl scouts; Children/youth, services.
Limitations: Giving primarily in FL.
Officers: Joan Russo, Pres.; Stephen Polozie, V.P.; Thomas Ehrbar, Secy.-Treas.
EIN: 650564781

731
Edgar T. Cato Foundation, Inc.
3985 Douglas Rd.
Miami, FL 33133

Established in 1998 in FL.
Donor(s): Edgar T. Cato, Christine A. Cato Charitable Lead Annuity Trust.
Grantmaker type: Independent foundation
Financial data (yr. ended 12/31/02): Assets, $47,232 (M); gifts received, $43,488; expenditures, $310,909; qualifying distributions, $310,000; giving activities include $310,000 for 10 grants (high: $200,000; low: $2,500).
Purpose and activities: Giving primarily to a related institute for public policy, as well as to a sporting library.
Fields of interest: Libraries (special); Botanical gardens; Disasters, fire prevention/control; Public policy, research.
Limitations: Applications not accepted. Giving primarily in Washington, DC, and Middleburg, VA. No grants to individuals.
Application information: Contributes only to pre-selected organizations.
Officers and Directors:* Thomas R. Cannon,* Pres.; Christine Anne Cato,* V.P.; Aaron A. Smith, Secy.; Theresa R. Gebhardt, Treas.; Edgar T. Cato; Edgar T. Cato III.
EIN: 650450989

732
Catt Family Foundation
701 E. Camino Real, Apt. 5J
Boca Raton, FL 33432
Contact: Jacqueline C. Scheifla, Treas.

Established in 1985 in PA.
Donor(s): Anne G. Catt, Catt Charitable Lead Trust.
Grantmaker type: Independent foundation
Financial data (yr. ended 04/30/02): Assets, $1,547,503 (M); expenditures, $158,124; qualifying distributions, $149,663; giving activities include $150,000 for 16 grants (high: $40,000; low: $500).
Purpose and activities: Giving primarily for higher education, animal welfare and medical research.
Fields of interest: Education; Animal welfare; Health care, clinics/centers; Health organizations, association; Cancer; Eye research;

Boys & girls clubs; American Red Cross; Human services.
Limitations: Giving on a national basis.
Application information: Application form not required.
　　Deadline(s): May 31
Officers and Directors:* Anne C. Filer,* Pres.; Karen J. Catt,* V.P.; Joal C. Devine,* Secy.; Jacqueline C. Scheifla,* Treas.
EIN: 232351773

733
The Chingos Foundation
639 E. Ocean Ave., Ste. 307
Boynton Beach, FL 33435-5016
(561) 737-7111
Contact: William Manikas, Tr.

Established in 1985 in FL.
Grantmaker type: Independent foundation
Financial data (yr. ended 11/30/02): Assets, $3,891,997 (M); expenditures, $253,368; qualifying distributions, $180,775; giving activities include $180,775 for grants (high: $20,000).
Purpose and activities: Giving primarily for the environment and for animal and wildlife protection.
Fields of interest: Natural resources; Animals/wildlife, endangered species.
Types of support: General/operating support; Land acquisition.
Limitations: Giving primarily in FL. No support for humane societies.
Application information: Application form not required.
　　Initial approach: Proposal
　　Copies of proposal: 1
　　Deadline(s): None
Trustees: Jennifer Manikas; William Manikas; Samuel Wax.
Number of staff: 1 part-time support.
EIN: 592381901

734
The Clements Family Charitable Trust
c/o Thomas Clements III
1025 Fleming St.
Key West, FL 33040

Established in 1993 in OH.
Donor(s): Helen T. Clements.
Grantmaker type: Independent foundation
Financial data (yr. ended 12/31/01): Assets, $1,187,125 (M); expenditures, $162,285; qualifying distributions, $146,633; giving activities include $144,510 for 88 grants (high: $25,000; low: $75).
Purpose and activities: Giving to the arts, culture, education, health care, and medical research.
Fields of interest: Arts; Education; Environment; Health care; Human services.
Limitations: Applications not accepted. Giving primarily in FL, ME, and NY. No grants to individuals.
Application information: Contributes only to pre-selected organizations.
Trustees: Helen T. Clements; Robert M. Clements, Jr.; Thomas Clements III.
Number of staff: None.
EIN: 341748724

735
Cobin Charitable Foundation
(formerly Howard and Nancy Cobin Charitable Foundation)
2501 S. Tamiami Trail
Sarasota, FL 34239
Application address: c/o Howard Cobin, 483 Meadowlark Dr., Sarasota, FL 34236

Established in 1991 in MA.
Donor(s): Howard D. Cobin, Nancy Cobin.
Grantmaker type: Independent foundation
Financial data (yr. ended 12/31/01): Assets, $30,975 (M); expenditures, $102,350; qualifying distributions, $102,350; giving activities include $102,210 for 11 grants (high: $76,144; low: $60).
Purpose and activities: Giving for marine science, health organizations, and Jewish organizations.
Fields of interest: Environment, water resources; Health organizations, association.
Limitations: Giving primarily in Sarasota, FL.
Application information:
　　Initial approach: Letter
　　Deadline(s): None
Trustee: Howard D. Cobin.
EIN: 223127132

736
Nancy Y. and Martin Cohen Family Charitable Trust
3731 Toulouse Dr.
Palm Beach Gardens, FL 33410-1463

Established in 1998 in FL.
Donor(s): Louise M. Simons.‡
Grantmaker type: Independent foundation
Financial data (yr. ended 12/31/02): Assets, $2,790,778 (M); expenditures, $156,915; qualifying distributions, $155,315; giving activities include $155,315 for 83 grants (high: $20,000; low: $75).
Purpose and activities: Giving primarily in the areas of mental health, the environment, education, and the performing arts.
Fields of interest: Performing arts; Higher education; Education; Environment; Mental health/crisis services; Human services; Jewish agencies & temples.
Limitations: Applications not accepted. Giving on a national basis. No grants to individuals.
Application information: Contributes only to pre-selected organizations.
Trustees: Martin Cohen; Nancy Y. Cohen.
EIN: 526924875

737
The Cole Family Foundation, Inc.
100 Royal Palm Way, Ste. 5C
Palm Beach, FL 33480
Contact: Margaret B. Cole, Dir.

Established in 1997 in FL.
Donor(s): David C. Cole, Margaret B. Cole.
Grantmaker type: Independent foundation
Financial data (yr. ended 11/30/02): Assets, $1,302,739 (M); expenditures, $215,047; qualifying distributions, $158,428; giving activities include $158,548 for 15 grants (high: $35,000; low: $500).

Purpose and activities: Giving primarily for the environment, education, and the arts.
Fields of interest: Arts; Education; Natural resources.
Limitations: Giving primarily in Washington, DC, HI, MD, NY, and VA.
Application information: Application form not required.
  Deadline(s): None
Directors: David C. Cole; Margaret B. Cole.
EIN: 541835269

738
The Colen Foundation, Inc.
(formerly The On Top of the World Foundation, Inc.)
8447 S.W. 99th St.
Ocala, FL 34481-4547
Contact: Kenneth D. Colen, Dir.

Established in 1984.
Donor(s): Kenneth D. Colen, Sidney Colen.
Grantmaker type: Independent foundation
Financial data (yr. ended 11/30/02): Assets, $10,240,965 (M); expenditures, $511,005; qualifying distributions, $482,908; giving activities include $468,643 for 29 grants (high: $107,768; low: $375) and $3,600 for 1 grant to an individual.
Purpose and activities: The foundation makes grants to qualified charities and provides assistance to the charitable class of the aged to enable members of the class to maintain a modest standard of living in their communities during their declining years.
Fields of interest: Museums (history); Music; Elementary school/education; Higher education; Education; Horticulture/garden clubs; Developmentally disabled, centers & services; Federated giving programs; Jewish agencies & temples.
Limitations: Giving primarily in FL.
Application information: Application form required.
  Initial approach: Write for application procedure
  Deadline(s): None
Officers and Directors:* Sidney Colen,* Pres.; Kenneth D. Colen,* V.P. and Treas.; Gerald R. Colen; Ina A. Colen; Leslee R. Colen; Robert Colen.
EIN: 592474711

739
Community Foundation for Palm Beach and Martin Counties, Inc. ▼
(formerly Palm Beach County Community Foundation)
700 S. Dixie Hwy., Ste. 200
West Palm Beach, FL 33401 (561) 659-6800
Contact: Shannon G. Sadler, C.E.O.
Martin County Office: P.O. Box 2441, Stuart, FL 34995-2441, tel.: (888) 853-4438; FAX: (561) 832-6542; E-mail: info@cfpbmc.org; URL: http://www.yourcommunityfoundation.org

Incorporated in 1972 in FL.
Grantmaker type: Community foundation
Financial data (yr. ended 06/30/03): Assets, $74,434,065 (M); gifts received, $3,921,185; expenditures, $7,226,812; giving activities include $6,384,632 for grants (high: $815,220;

low: $250), $234,650 for 85 grants to individuals (high: $14,000; low: $500; average: $500–$14,000) and $8,990 for 5 in-kind gifts.
Purpose and activities: Primary areas of interest include health, social services, youth, race relations, education, arts and culture, conservation and preservation, and community development.
Fields of interest: Historic preservation/historical societies; Arts; Early childhood education; Elementary school/education; Adult education—literacy, basic skills & GED; Reading; Education; Natural resources; Environment; Health care; Health organizations, association; AIDS; Youth development, intergenerational programs; Human services; Children/youth, services; Race/intergroup relations; Economic development; Community development.
Types of support: General/operating support; Management development; Equipment; Program development; Conferences/seminars; Seed money; Scholarship funds; Technical assistance; Consulting services; Employee-related scholarships; Scholarships—to individuals; Matching/challenge support.
Limitations: Giving primarily in Palm Beach and Martin counties, FL. No support for religious organizations for religious purposes. Generally, no grants from unrestricted funds to individuals (except for the Dwight Allison Fellows Program), or for operating funds, building campaigns, endowments, annual campaigns, fundraising events, or deficit financing.
Publications: Application guidelines, Annual report (including application guidelines), Informational brochure, Newsletter.
Application information: Application form required.
  Initial approach: Telephone call followed by proposal, personal referral, professional advisor referrals
  Copies of proposal: 1
  Deadline(s): None
  Board meeting date(s): Feb., Apr., May, Sept., Oct., and Dec.
  Final notification: Within weeks of proposal
Officers and Directors:* Joy Funston,* Chair.; Allyson Dupree Smith,* Vice-Chair.; Eliot I. Snider,* Vice-Chair.; Patricia Toppel,* Vice-Chair.; Shannon G. Sadler, C.E.O. and Pres.; Beverly Pope Sears, Exec. V.P. and C.O.O.; Danielle Cameron, V.P., Donor Svcs.; Linda Raybin, V.P., Progs.; Michele Veil, V.P., Finance; Barbara Chapin,* Secy.; Mike Victor,* Treas.; Ronald Alvarez; William J. Bryant, D.D.S.; Carol Collins; Julie Cummings; Elaine Darwin; John B. Dodge; Rebecca Dunn; Danielle Hickox; Brenda S. Magee; William Matthews; Peter Matwiczyk; Deborah Pucillo; Pamela Robertson; Edward Rodgers; John Shuff.
Number of staff: 9 full-time professional; 4 full-time support.
EIN: 237181875
Recent environmental and animal welfare grants:
739-1 Assistance Dogs of America, Jupiter, FL, $15,000. 2002.
739-2 Dreher Park Zoo, West Palm Beach, FL, $10,000. 2002.
739-3 FAU/FIU Joint Center for Environmental and Urban Problems, Miami, FL, $15,000. 2002.

739-4 Humane Society of the Treasure Coast, Palm City, FL, $13,000. 2002.
739-5 Pine Jog Environmental Sciences Center, West Palm Beach, FL, $19,000. 2002.
739-6 Resource Depot, West Palm Beach, FL, $15,000. 2002.

740
Community Foundation of Broward
(formerly Broward Community Foundation, Inc.)
1401 E. Broward Blvd., Ste. 100
Fort Lauderdale, FL 33301 (954) 761-9503
Contact: Linda B. Carter, C.E.O. and Pres.
FAX: (954) 761-7102; E-mail: lcarter@cfbroward.org; URL: http://www.cfbroward.org

Incorporated in 1984 in FL.
Grantmaker type: Community foundation
Financial data (yr. ended 06/30/03): Assets, $40,307,567 (M); gifts received, $3,752,835; expenditures, $3,339,101; giving activities include $1,944,585 for 720 grants (high: $25,000; low: $1,000; average: $1,000–$10,000).

Purpose and activities: Gives priority to programs which: address emerging needs not being met by existing government or private charitable agencies or by existing revenue sources, strengthen internal management capabilities of existing organizations, reach a broad segment of the community or serve those not being adequately served by the community's resources, promote collaboration and avoid duplication of service among charitable agencies, test or demonstrate new approaches and techniques for solving problems, generate matching funds or attract contributions from other donors to the community or agency, and promote volunteer participation and citizen involvement in community affairs. The foundation administers donor-advised funds.
Fields of interest: Arts; Education; Environment; Animal welfare; Health care; AIDS; Human services; Children/youth, services; Foster care; Community development; Engineering/technology.
Types of support: Equipment; Emergency funds; Program development; Seed money; Research; Technical assistance; Scholarships—to individuals; Matching/challenge support.
Limitations: Giving limited to Broward County, FL. No grants to individuals (except for designated scholarship funds), or for annual campaigns, building funds, consulting services, continuing support, deficit financing, endowment funds, emergency funds, land acquisition, or operating budgets; no loans.
Publications: Application guidelines, Annual report, Financial statement, Informational brochure (including application guidelines), Newsletter.
Application information: Application form required.
  Initial approach: Letter or telephone
  Copies of proposal: 1
  Deadline(s): Mar. 15, June 15, Aug. 15, and Dec. 17
  Board meeting date(s): Various, 6-7 times per year
  Final notification: Jun. 29, Sept. 30, Nov. 28, and Mar. 30

Officers and Directors:* Edwin A. Huston,* Chair.; Louise F. Dill, Vice-Chair.; Linda B. Carter,* C.E.O. and Pres.; William Sullivan, Secy.; Steven H. Woods,* Treas.; Anthony Brunson; Rita Case; Barbara R. Castell; Frederick L. Hicks; David Horvitz; Steve Hyatt; Thomas Katz; Christine L. Lambertus; Mark Maller; John C. McKeon; Arlene Pecora; Carlos J. Reyes; Sally Robbins; John W. Ruffin, Jr.; Christopher L. Smith; J. Kenneth Tate.
Number of staff: 9 full-time professional.
EIN: 592477112

741
Community Foundation of Collier County
c/o Mary George
2400 Tamiami Trail, N., Ste. 300
Naples, FL   34103   (239) 649-5000
Contact: Mary Ellen Barrett, Prog. Off.
Additional tel.: 877 907-1449; FAX: (239) 649-5337; E-mail: ssuarez@cfcollier.org; URL: http://www.cfcollier.org

Incorporated in 1983 in FL.
Grantmaker type: Community foundation
Financial data (yr. ended 05/31/03): Assets, $38,230,074 (M); gifts received, $5,319,986; expenditures, $4,224,145; giving activities include $3,139,131 for 410 grants (high: $1,065,000; low: $100; average: $250–$25,000).
Purpose and activities: Support for organizations dedicated to solving community problems in the areas of health and human services, youth, education, civic affairs, the environment, and arts and culture.
Fields of interest: Arts; Education; Natural resources; Health care; Human services; Children/youth, services.
Types of support: Building/renovation; Equipment; Emergency funds; Program development; Conferences/seminars; Seed money; Internship funds; Scholarship funds; Technical assistance; Program evaluation; Matching/challenge support.
Limitations: Giving limited to Collier County, FL. No support for religious purposes. No grants to individuals, or for operating budgets, deficit financing, scholarly research, capital campaigns, conferences, or endowment funds.
Publications: Application guidelines, Annual report (including application guidelines), Newsletter.
Application information: Organization must have completed a profile on www.guidestar.com. Application form required.
  Initial approach: Proposal; see Web site for application and guidelines
  Copies of proposal: 8
  Deadline(s): Varies
  Board meeting date(s): Monthly from Oct. to May
  Final notification: Varies
Officers and Trustees:* Gordon Watson,* Chair.; Dottie Gerrity, Vice-Chair.; Alison Douglas, Secy.; Henry Albrecht; Linda C. Flewelling; Tom Ingram; Bill Laimbeer; Jim Lancaster; Phyliss Landes; Linda Malone; Ned Sachs; Mike Schroeder; Joanne Wyss.
Number of staff: 5 full-time professional; 3 full-time support; 1 part-time support.
EIN: 592396243

742
The Community Foundation of Sarasota County, Inc.
(formerly The Sarasota County Community Foundation, Inc.)
P.O. Box 49587
Sarasota, FL   34230-6587   (941) 955-3000
Contact: Stewart W. Stearns, C.E.O. and Pres.
Office address: 1800 2nd St., Ste. 103, Sarasota, FL 34236; FAX: (941) 952-1951; E-mail: sstearns@sarasota-foundation.org; URL: http://www.sarasota-foundation.org

Incorporated in 1979 in FL.
Grantmaker type: Community foundation
Financial data (yr. ended 05/31/03): Assets, $79,404,321 (M); gifts received, $14,698,911; expenditures, $6,029,240; giving activities include $4,791,464 for 820 grants (high: $317,749; low: $100) and $497,822 for 241 grants to individuals (high: $6,000; low: $500).
Purpose and activities: Giving to the arts, education, environment, animal protection, health care, human services, and religious causes. The foundation administers donor-advised funds.
Fields of interest: Arts; Education; Environment; Health care; Health organizations, association; Human services; Children/youth, services; Economically disadvantaged.
Types of support: Equipment; Emergency funds; Program development; Seed money; Scholarship funds; Scholarships—to individuals.
Limitations: Giving primarily in Sarasota County, FL, and surrounding communities. No support for fraternal or political organizations. No grants to individuals (except selected scholarships), or for annual campaigns, building campaigns, endowment funds, deficit financing, debt retirement, publications, operating expenses, travel, fundraising events, or conferences.
Publications: Application guidelines, Annual report, Grants list, Informational brochure, Newsletter, Program policy statement.
Application information: Application form required.
  Initial approach: Contact V.P. of Progs. by telephone and/or meeting prior to submitting proposal
  Copies of proposal: 1
  Deadline(s): None
  Board meeting date(s): Jan., Mar., May, July, Sept., and Nov.
  Final notification: Usually 60 days after receiving proposal
Officers: Mary Fran Carroll, Chair.; Sophia LaRusso, 1st Vice-Chair.; Edwin A. Weiller, 2nd Vice-Chair.; Stewart W. Stearns, C.E.O. and Pres.; Ronald Koepsel, Secy.; James Shedivy, Treas.
Number of staff: 4 full-time professional; 2 part-time professional; 4 full-time support.
EIN: 591956886
Recent environmental and animal welfare grants:
742-1 Animal Rescue Coalition, Sarasota, FL, $21,000. For surgical supplies for spay-neuter mobile clinic. 2002.
742-2 Marie Selby Botanical Gardens, Sarasota, FL, $11,375. For LCD projectors and laptop computer for education outreach programs. 2002.
742-3 Pet Therapy, Tallevast, FL, $15,000. For Youth Service Learning Project. 2002.

742-4 Venice Area Beautification, Venice, FL, $15,000. For playground equipment for Venetian Waterway Parkway. 2002.

743
Community Foundation of Tampa Bay, Inc.
(formerly The Community Foundation of Greater Tampa, Inc.)
4950 W. Kennedy Blvd., Ste. 250
Tampa, FL   33609-1837   (813) 282-1975
Contact: George J. Baxter, Pres.
FAX: (813) 282-3119; E-mail: gbaxter@cftampabay.org; URL: http://www.cftampabay.org

Established in 1990 in FL.
Grantmaker type: Community foundation
Financial data (yr. ended 06/30/03): Assets, $77,188,612 (M); gifts received, $7,478,828; expenditures, $5,440,523; giving activities include $4,812,495 for grants.
Purpose and activities: Primary areas of interest include the arts, family and children, elementary and higher education, and social services. The foundation administers a donor-advised fund.
Fields of interest: Visual arts; Performing arts; Historic preservation/historical societies; Arts; Elementary school/education; Higher education; Education; Environment; Health care; Medical research, institute; Housing/shelter, development; Human services; Children/youth, services; Family services; Aging, centers/services; Community development; Government/public administration; Public affairs; Religion; Aging; Homeless.
Types of support: Equipment; Emergency funds; Program development; Seed money; Curriculum development; Scholarship funds; Technical assistance; Consulting services.
Limitations: Giving limited to the Tampa Bay, FL, area. No support for lobbying or political efforts. No grants to individuals, (except for scholarships) or for operating costs of established programs, advertising, or tickets to sponsor events.
Publications: Annual report, Financial statement, Informational brochure, Newsletter.
Application information: Application form required.
  Initial approach: Letter
  Copies of proposal: 1
  Deadline(s): Sept. 1 and Mar. 1
  Board meeting date(s): Jan., Mar., May, Sept., and Nov.
  Final notification: Apr. 15 and Oct. 15
Officers and Trustees:* Joe Garcia,* Chair.; Frank J. Rice III, Vice-Chair.; George J. Baxter,* Pres.; E. Jackson Boggs, Advisory Comm. Chair.; Paul Hanna, Fund Acceptance Comm. Chair.; Gene Marshall, Grants Comm. Chair.; James Strenski, Public Information Comm. Chair.; Adelaide Sink,* Secy.; Raymond Murray, Treas.; and 18 additional trustees.
Number of staff: 3 full-time professional; 1 part-time professional; 3 full-time support; 2 part-time support.
EIN: 593001853

744
Community Foundation of the Florida Keys, Inc.
P.O. Box 162
Key West, FL 33041-0162 (305) 292-1502
Contact: Ann Storandt, Secy.
FAX: (305) 292-1598; E-mail: cffk@bellsouth.net

Established in 1996 in FL.
Grantmaker type: Community foundation
Financial data (yr. ended 06/30/02): Assets, $3,147,522 (M); gifts received, $1,291,370; expenditures, $827,887; giving activities include $714,131 for 25 grants (high: $409,579; low: $500) and $41,000 for 13 grants to individuals (high: $5,000; low: $1,500).
Purpose and activities: The foundation administers a donor-advised fund.
Fields of interest: Historic preservation/historical societies; Arts; Education; Environment; Health care; Human services.
Types of support: Program development; Conferences/seminars; Scholarship funds; Scholarships—to individuals; Matching/challenge support.
Limitations: Giving primarily in Key West, FL.
Publications: Annual report, Newsletter.
Application information: Application form required.
  Initial approach: Letter
  Copies of proposal: 5
  Board meeting date(s): 2nd Tues. monthly
Officers: Shirley Freeman, Chair.; William Andersen, Vice-Chair.; Matthew Helmerich, Vice-Chair.; Rudy Marn, Vice-Chair.; Ann Storandt, Secy. and Admin.; Thomas Clements, Treas.
Board Members: Calvin Allen; Ray Baker; Roger Emmons; Marva Green; Robert E. Highsmith; Holly Merrill; Philip Miani; Martha Robinson; Karen Sharp; Kerry Shelby; Sandra Taylor; Nicholas Trivisonno.
Number of staff: 1 part-time professional.
EIN: 650648968

745
Dade Community Foundation, Inc. ▼
(formerly Dade Foundation)
200 S. Biscayne Blvd., Ste. 505
Miami, FL 33131-2343 (305) 371-2711
Contact: Ruth Shack, Pres.
FAX: (305) 371-5342; E-mail: rshack01@bellsouth.net; URL: http://www.dadecommunityfoundation.org

Established in 1967 in FL.
Grantmaker type: Community foundation
Financial data (yr. ended 12/31/01): Assets, $68,401,730 (M); gifts received, $6,001,826; expenditures, $9,138,514; giving activities include $6,983,399 for grants (high: $505,000; low: $5; average: $1,000–$10,000) and $110,300 for grants to individuals (high: $2,500; low: $500; average: $500–$2,500).
Purpose and activities: Giving primarily to reduce cultural alienation and lack of community cohesion, and considers all grant proposals in the context of this commitment. Grants are made in broad program areas including education, health, human services, arts and culture, environment, community and economic development, social justice, and religion. In addition, field of interest and special funding initiatives have enabled significant grantmaking addressing the issues of abused and neglected children, immigrants and refugees, AIDS, homelessness, and community and affordable housing. The foundation also provides technical assistance through grant support and one-on-one consultations to build the capacity of nonprofits.
Fields of interest: Multipurpose centers/programs; Visual arts; Arts; Animal welfare; Health organizations, association; Heart & circulatory diseases; AIDS; Child abuse; Housing/shelter; Disasters, 9/11/01; Children/youth, services; Homeless, human services; Civil rights, minorities; Civil rights, gays/lesbians; Civil rights; Community development, neighborhood development; Religion; African Americans/Blacks; Aging; People with AIDS (PWAs); Gays/lesbians; Homeless.
Types of support: General/operating support; Building/renovation; Equipment; Land acquisition; Endowments; Emergency funds; Program development; Publication; Seed money; Scholarship funds; Research; Technical assistance; Consulting services; Program-related investments/loans; Scholarships—to individuals; Matching/challenge support.
Limitations: Giving limited to Dade County, FL. No grants to individuals (except through scholarship funds), or for memberships, fundraising, memorials, deficit financing, or conferences.
Publications: Application guidelines, Annual report, Newsletter, Occasional report.
Application information: Proposals by FAX not accepted. Application form not required.
  Initial approach: Letter
  Copies of proposal: 1
  Deadline(s): Submit proposal preferably in Nov.; deadline Nov. 30
  Board meeting date(s): Feb., May, Sept., and Nov.
  Final notification: 1st quarter of the year
Officers and Governors:* Hugh A. Westbrook,* Chair.; Thomas R. McGuigan,* Vice-Chair.; Ruth Shack, Pres.; Sergio M. Ganzalez, Secy.; Cynthia W. Curry, Treas.; Anthony Brunson; and 16 additional governors.
Investment Managers: Barr Rosenberg; American Century; Bank of America; Fox Asset Management; Mellon Financial Corp.; Morgan Stanley; Neuberger and Berman Trust Co.; Northern Trust Bank of Florida, N.A.; PIMCO; State Street Global Advisors; SunTrust Banks, Inc.; TIFF; Wachovia Bank, N.A.; World Asset Management.
Number of staff: 5 full-time professional; 4 full-time support; 1 part-time support.
EIN: 650350357
Recent environmental and animal welfare grants:
745-1 Fairchild Tropical Garden, Miami, FL, $46,000. 2002.
745-2 Florida International University, Miami, FL, $30,000. To use work on creating nature/historic walk on vacant land along common border shared by Allapattah and Overtown to bring together Black and Hispanic organizations and residents in communities. Grant made through Miamians Working Together. 2002.
745-3 Miami, City of, Virginia Key Beach Park Trust, Miami, FL, $30,000. To come up with plan for preserving significant civil history of Virginia Key Beach Park, ensuring environmentally sensitive recreational development and attracting people of all ethnic backgrounds to enjoy and celebrate both. Grant made through Miamians Working Together. 2002.

746
Darden Restaurants, Inc. Foundation
6100 Lake Ellenor Dr.
P.O. Box 593330
Orlando, FL 32859-3330 (407) 245-5213
Contact: Patty DeYoung, Admin.
FAX: (407) 245-4462; E-mail: pdeyoung@darden.com; URL: http://www.darden.com/community/foundation.html

Established in 1995 in FL.
Donor(s): Darden Restaurants, Inc.
Grantmaker type: Company-sponsored foundation
Financial data (yr. ended 05/31/02): Assets, $9,506,465 (M); expenditures, $4,058,042; qualifying distributions, $4,056,017; giving activities include $4,056,017 for grants.
Purpose and activities: The foundation focuses its philanthropic giving on four key areas: education, social services and nutrition, arts and culture, and preservation of natural resources.
Fields of interest: Multipurpose centers/programs; Museums (science/technology); Theater; Music; Education, fund raising; Elementary/secondary education; Secondary school/education; Higher education; Natural resources; Environment; Substance abuse, services; Crime/violence prevention; Crime/law enforcement, DWI; Food services; Housing/shelter, development; Family services; Family services, parent education; Hospices; Federated giving programs.
Types of support: General/operating support; Capital campaigns; Program development; Employee matching gifts; In-kind gifts; Matching/challenge support.
Limitations: Giving limited to central FL. No support for religious organizations for religious purposes, non-exempt international, or disease-specific organizations. No grants to individuals, or for one-time, short-term events, advertising, team sponsorships, athletic scholarships, or national conferences.
Publications: Application guidelines, Annual report.
Application information: Application form can be downloaded from foundation Web site. Application form required.
  Initial approach: Brief proposal; concept paper by E-mail or phone
  Copies of proposal: 2
  Deadline(s): None
  Board meeting date(s): Feb., May, Aug., and Nov.
Officers and Trustees:* Joe R. Lee,* Chair.; Richard J. Walsh,* V.P.; Paula J. Shives, Secy.; Clarence Otis, Jr., Treas.; Mary Darden; Blaine Sweatt III; Robert Waggoner; Greg Watson.
Number of staff: 1 full-time professional; 1 part-time professional.
EIN: 593332929

747
Frank E. Duckwall Foundation, Inc.
P.O. Box 3351
Tampa, FL 33601-3351 (813) 258-6660
Contact: Frank J. Rief, III, Tr.
FAX: (813) 258-6686

Established in 1983 in FL.
Donor(s): Frank E. Duckwall.‡
Grantmaker type: Independent foundation
Financial data (yr. ended 12/31/02): Assets, $9,272,995 (M); expenditures, $981,239; qualifying distributions, $920,037; giving activities include $919,912 for 51 grants (high: $100,000; low: $5,000).
Fields of interest: Museums; Higher education; Environment; Human services.
Types of support: Capital campaigns; Building/renovation; Equipment; Endowments; Professorships; Scholarship funds; Research; Matching/challenge support.
Limitations: Giving limited to the Tampa Bay, FL, area.
Publications: Financial statement, Informational brochure (including application guidelines), Occasional report.
Application information: Application form required.
> *Initial approach:* Letter
> *Copies of proposal:* 3
> *Deadline(s):* 2 weeks before meeting
> *Board meeting date(s):* Mar., June, Sept., and Dec.
> *Final notification:* 2 weeks after board meeting
Officer and Trustees:* James M. Kelly,* Pres.; G. Lowe Morrison; Frank J. Rief III.
Number of staff: None.
EIN: 596773462

748
Elizabeth Ordway Dunn Foundation, Inc.
P.O. Box 016309
Miami, FL 33101-6309 (305) 667-5521
Contact: Robert W. Jensen, Managing Dir.
Additional application address: c/o E. Rodman Titcomb, Jr., Managing Dir., P.O. Box 3267, Palm Beach, FL, 33480-3267, tel.: (561) 832-5826; E-mail: eodf@worldnet.att.net

Incorporated in 1984 in FL.
Donor(s): Elizabeth Ordway Dunn Charitable Lead Trust.
Grantmaker type: Independent foundation
Financial data (yr. ended 12/31/01): Assets, $1,094,987 (M); gifts received, $661,772; expenditures, $822,745; qualifying distributions, $812,675; giving activities include $682,100 for grants.
Purpose and activities: Giving for conservation, ecology, wildlife, and other environmental concerns in the state of FL.
Fields of interest: Natural resources; Environment; Animals/wildlife, preservation/protection.
Types of support: Program development; Seed money; Matching/challenge support.
Limitations: Giving primarily in FL. No support for sectarian religious activities. No grants to individuals, or for capital purposes, operating budgets, endowments, or deficit financing.
Publications: Annual report, Informational brochure (including application guidelines).

Application information: Applicants are urged to submit concept papers; if the paper is reviewed favorably, a full proposal will be requested. One copy should be sent to the main address, and one to the additional application address. Applications sent by FAX not accepted. Application form not required.
> *Initial approach:* Telephone calls to program staff encouraged
> *Copies of proposal:* 2
> *Deadline(s):* Mar. 15 and Sept. 15
> *Board meeting date(s):* May and Nov.
> *Final notification:* Following board meetings
Directors: Robert W. Jensen; Donna McKinney Lummus; E. Rodman Titcomb, Jr.
Number of staff: 2 part-time professional; 1 part-time support.
EIN: 592393843

749
Eckerd Family Foundation, Inc.
P.O. Box 5165
Clearwater, FL 33758-5165

Donor(s): Jack Eckerd.
Grantmaker type: Independent foundation
Financial data (yr. ended 12/31/01): Assets, $163,796 (M); gifts received, $3,100,000; expenditures, $3,847,489; qualifying distributions, $3,101,182; giving activities include $2,739,697 for 40 grants (high: $1,250,000; low: $263).
Fields of interest: Elementary/secondary education; Zoos/zoological societies; Aquariums; Health care, clinics/centers; Human services; YM/YWCAs & YM/YWHAs; Children, services; Family services; Women, centers/services; Community development; Foundations (community).
Types of support: Research.
Limitations: Applications not accepted. Giving primarily in FL. No grants to individuals.
Application information: Contributes only to pre-selected organizations.
Officer: Jack Eckerd, Chair.
Directors: Terrell Clark; Richard Eckerd; Ruth Eckerd; William Eckerd; Nancy Hart; Rosemary Lassiter; Kathleen Short; James Swann.
EIN: 592803659

750
The Flaherty Family Foundation
c/o William Flaherty
125 Worth Ave., Ste. 200
Palm Beach, FL 33480

Established in 1990 in NY.
Donor(s): Clementina S. Flaherty, William E. Flaherty.
Grantmaker type: Independent foundation
Financial data (yr. ended 12/31/01): Assets, $79,532 (M); gifts received, $295,730; expenditures, $247,120; qualifying distributions, $247,120; giving activities include $234,683 for 36 grants (high: $50,000; low: $25).
Purpose and activities: Giving primarily for human services.
Fields of interest: Arts; Higher education; Libraries (school); Education; Natural resources; Hospitals (general); Human services; Children/youth, services.

Limitations: Applications not accepted. Giving primarily in FL and NY. No grants to individuals.
Application information: Contributes only to pre-selected organizations.
Trustees: Clementina S. Flaherty; William E. Flaherty.
EIN: 133599123

751
Florida Power & Light Company Contributions Program
700 Universe Blvd.
Juno Beach, FL 33408
Contact: John L. Kitchens, Corp. Contribs. Admin.
E-mail: john_kitchens@fpl.com

Grantmaker type: Corporate giving program
Purpose and activities: As a complement to its foundation, Florida Power & Light also makes charitable contributions to nonprofit organizations directly. Support is given primarily in areas of company operations in Florida.
Fields of interest: Education; Environment; Public affairs.
Types of support: General/operating support; Employee matching gifts; In-kind gifts.
Limitations: Giving primarily in areas of company operations in FL. No support for religious or political organizations or United Way-supported organizations. No grants to individuals.
Publications: Application guidelines.
Application information: The External Affairs Department handles giving. The company has a staff that only handles contributions. Application form not required.
> *Initial approach:* Proposal to nearest company facility
> *Copies of proposal:* 1
> *Final notification:* Following review

752
Claiborne F. Foulds Foundation Trust
(formerly Claiborne and Ned Foulds Foundation)
c/o Bank of America
P.O. Box 40200, MC FL9-100-10-19
Jacksonville, FL 32203-0200
Application address: c/o Bank of America, Private Client Group, P.O. Box 927, Fort Myers, FL 33902

Established in 1981 in FL.
Grantmaker type: Independent foundation
Financial data (yr. ended 07/31/02): Assets, $3,426,774 (M); expenditures, $188,587; qualifying distributions, $160,666; giving activities include $150,808 for 29 grants (high: $15,000; low: $1,069).
Purpose and activities: Giving primarily for education and human services.
Fields of interest: Orchestra (symphony); Historic preservation/historical societies; Higher education; Education; Animal welfare; Human services; Children/youth, services.
Types of support: Building/renovation; Equipment.
Limitations: Giving primarily in Lee County, FL. No support for churches or religious organizations. No grants to individuals, or for administrative or operational expenses.

Application information: Application form required.

Initial approach: Letter
Copies of proposal: 1
Deadline(s): July 1
Board meeting date(s): 3rd quarter of year
Final notification: Dec. 31
Trustee: Bank of America.
Number of staff: None.
EIN: 596705105

753
FPL Group Foundation, Inc.
(formerly FPL Foundation, Inc.)
700 Universe Blvd.
Juno Beach, FL 33408-2683
Contact: John L. Kitchens, Corp. Contribs. Admin.
Application address: P.O. Box 029100, Miami, FL 33102

Established in 1987 in FL.
Donor(s): Florida Power & Light Co.
Grantmaker type: Company-sponsored foundation
Financial data (yr. ended 12/31/01): Assets, $6,177,721 (M); gifts received, $1,525,710; expenditures, $1,689,440; qualifying distributions, $1,661,255; giving activities include $1,409,389 for 59 grants (high: $262,000; low: $100; average: $500–$50,000) and $251,866 for 198 employee matching gifts.
Purpose and activities: Giving currently focused on the environment, customer satisfaction/social services, workforce readiness/organizational effectiveness, and community development/civic leadership.
Fields of interest: Visual arts; Performing arts; Arts; Higher education; Education; Energy; Environment; Health care; Health organizations, association; Human services; Aging, centers/services; Minorities/immigrants, centers/services; Race/intergroup relations; Community development; Voluntarism promotion; Minorities; African Americans/Blacks; Hispanics/Latinos; Disabled; Aging; Economically disadvantaged; Homeless.
Types of support: Capital campaigns; Endowments; Employee matching gifts.
Limitations: Giving primarily in areas of company operations, including most of the east and west coasts from Bradenton to Naples, FL. No support for religious or political groups or United Way-affiliated agencies. No grants to individuals, or for endowments, travel, or conferences.
Publications: Application guidelines.
Application information: Application form required.

Initial approach: Letter requesting application form
Copies of proposal: 1
Deadline(s): Aug.
Officers and Directors:* Lew Hay III,* Chair.; Paul J. Evanson,* Pres. and Treas.; Lawrence J. Kelleher III, V.P.; Dennis P. Coyle,* Secy.
Number of staff: 2 part-time support.
EIN: 650031452

754
Free Family Foundation Corp.
P.O. Box 2036
Clearwater, FL 33757-2036

Established in 1999 in FL.
Donor(s): Harry J. Free, Carole J. Free.
Grantmaker type: Independent foundation
Financial data (yr. ended 12/31/02): Assets, $591,364 (M); expenditures, $460,987; qualifying distributions, $460,364; giving activities include $447,350 for 33 grants (high: $170,000; low: $200).
Purpose and activities: Giving primarily for health care and for services for senior citizens; funding also for social services.
Fields of interest: Education, ESL programs; Aquariums; Hospitals (general); Health care; Human services; Aging, centers/services.
Limitations: Applications not accepted. No grants to individuals.
Application information: Contributes only to pre-selected organizations.
Officers: Harry J. Free, Pres.; Carole J. Free, V.P.; Thomas E. Free, Treas.
Director: Douglas J. Free.
EIN: 593611945

755
Alice Busch Gronewaldt Foundation, Inc.
c/o Caldwell & Pacetti
324 Royal Palm Way, Ste. 300
Palm Beach, FL 33480

Established in 1990 in FL.
Donor(s): Alice Busch Gronewaldt.‡
Grantmaker type: Independent foundation
Financial data (yr. ended 12/31/02): Assets, $9,477,506 (M); expenditures, $790,660; qualifying distributions, $674,368; giving activities include $676,500 for 81 grants (high: $70,000; low: $500).
Purpose and activities: Support primarily for education, the arts, animal welfare, and health care.
Fields of interest: Arts; Elementary/secondary education; Education; Animal welfare; Hospitals (general); Health care.
Types of support: General/operating support.
Limitations: Applications not accepted. Giving primarily in Palm Beach, FL, and Cooperstown, NY. No grants to individuals.
Application information: Contributes only to pre-selected organizations.
Officers and Directors:* Louis Busch Hager, Jr., Pres.; Alice Hager Holbrook,* V.P.; Mary Hager Thomas,* V.P.; Andrew W. Regan,* Secy.
EIN: 650212289

756
GSB Family Foundation, Inc.
301 W. Camino Gardens Blvd., Ste. 101
Boca Raton, FL 33432

Established in 1996 in FL.
Donor(s): Gary S. Bailey.
Grantmaker type: Independent foundation
Financial data (yr. ended 12/31/02): Assets, $795,667 (M); gifts received, $122,311; expenditures, $242,509; qualifying distributions, $240,690; giving activities include $239,750 for 32 grants (high: $25,000; low: $500).

Fields of interest: University; Natural resources; Hospitals (general); Christian agencies & churches.
Limitations: Applications not accepted. No grants to individuals.
Application information: Contributes only to pre-selected organizations.
Officers: Gary S. Bailey, Pres. and Treas.; Brenda M. Bailey, V.P. and Secy.
EIN: 650714038

757
Gubelmann Family Foundation, Inc.
1 N. Clematis, Ste. 320
West Palm Beach, FL 33401
Contact: H.M. Ridgely III, Treas.

Established in 1995 in FL.
Grantmaker type: Independent foundation
Financial data (yr. ended 12/31/02): Assets, $1,541,448 (M); expenditures, $123,181; qualifying distributions, $115,984; giving activities include $113,061 for 71 grants (high: $11,800; low: $100).
Fields of interest: Arts; Education; Environment, pollution control; Human services; Children/youth, services.
Types of support: General/operating support; Continuing support; Annual campaigns; Building/renovation; Research.
Limitations: Applications not accepted. Giving primarily in FL and NY. No grants to individuals.
Publications: Grants list.
Application information: Contributes only to pre-selected organizations.

Board meeting date(s): Oct.
Officers: Barton G. Gubelmann, Pres.; James B. Gubelmann, V.P.; William S. Gubelmann, V.P.; Julie Bedard, Secy.; H.M. Ridgely III, Treas.
Number of staff: None.
EIN: 650538042

758
The A. D. Henderson Foundation, Inc.
P.O. Box 14096
Fort Lauderdale, FL 33302
Contact: Barbara Monz

Established in 1969.
Grantmaker type: Independent foundation
Financial data (yr. ended 09/30/01): Assets, $67,055,398 (M); expenditures, $5,035,817; qualifying distributions, $4,404,738; giving activities include $3,925,057 for 135 grants (high: $160,000; low: $50; average: $5,000–$75,000).
Purpose and activities: Giving primarily for historic preservation, child development education, animal welfare, wildlife preservation and protection, family planning, and children and youth services.
Fields of interest: Historic preservation/historical societies; Child development, education; Animal welfare; Animals/wildlife, preservation/protection; Family planning; Children/youth, services; Child development, services.
Limitations: Giving primarily in southern FL and VT. No grants to individuals; no loans.
Application information:
Initial approach: Letter
Deadline(s): Quarterly

Officers and Trustees:* Allen Douglas
Henderson,* Pres.; Barbara K. Henderson,* V.P.;
Lucia Henderson,* V.P.; James M. Lyon,* V.P.;
Bruce D. Oberfest, Secy.-Treas.
EIN: 237047045
**Recent environmental and animal welfare
grants:**
758-1 Broward Education Foundation, Fort
Lauderdale, FL, $50,000. For BURT Urban
Institute of Environmental Studies. 2001.
758-2 Humane Society of Broward County, Fort
Lauderdale, FL, $21,000. For community
outreach coordinator. 2001.
758-3 Humane Society of Chittenden County,
South Burlington, VT, $12,500. For animal
behavior program. 2001.
758-4 Lake Champlain Basin Science Center,
Burlington, VT, $125,000. For
Science-on-the-Move. 2001.
758-5 Museum of Science, Miami, FL, $48,867.
For promoting appreciation of wildlife. 2001.
758-6 Safe Water Instruction Means Safety
Foundation, Plantation, FL, $55,120. For
Tadpole Landings. 2001.
758-7 Vermont Institute of Natural Science,
Woodstock, VT, $30,615. For Making Tracks
to Environmental Citizenship. 2001.

759
Hope Foundation
2231 Forrest Ln.
Naples, FL 34102
Contact: Philip M. Francoeur, Jr., Tr.

Established around 1969.
Donor(s): Philip M. Francoeur, Sr.‡
Grantmaker type: Independent foundation
Financial data (yr. ended 12/31/02): Assets,
$1,742,677 (M); expenditures, $104,174;
qualifying distributions, $102,392; giving
activities include $92,250 for 28 grants (high:
$12,500; low: $500).
Purpose and activities: Giving to environmental
conservation, religion and education.
Fields of interest: Higher education; Natural
resources; Health care; Mental health,
association; Human services.
Types of support: General/operating support;
Continuing support; Annual campaigns; Capital
campaigns; Building/renovation; Endowments;
Scholarship funds.
Limitations: Giving on a national basis. No
grants to individuals.
Application information: Application form not
required.
Initial approach: Letter
Copies of proposal: 1
Deadline(s): None
Trustee: Philip M. Francoeur, Jr.
Number of staff: None.
EIN: 066088319

760
Hufty Foundation
330 Island Rd.
Palm Beach, FL 33480

Established in 1953 in FL.
Grantmaker type: Independent foundation
Financial data (yr. ended 12/31/02): Assets,
$2,104,936 (M); expenditures, $130,699;
qualifying distributions, $128,312; giving

activities include $129,585 for 73 grants (high:
$12,600; low: $100).
Purpose and activities: Giving for various public
foundations with an emphasis on environmental
conservation, Christian and Jewish organizations
and churches, public affairs, research institutes,
and for education.
Fields of interest: Education; Natural resources;
Urban/community development; Foundations
(public); Christian agencies & churches; Jewish
agencies & temples.
Limitations: Applications not accepted. Giving
primarily in the eastern U.S. No grants to
individuals.
Application information: Contributes only to
pre-selected organizations.
Trustee: Frances Archbold Hufty.
EIN: 526041681

761
Huizenga Family Foundation ▼
450 E. Las Olas Blvd., Ste. 1500
Fort Lauderdale, FL 33301
Contact: H. Wayne Huizenga, Jr., Pres.

Established in 1987 in FL.
Donor(s): H. Wayne Huizenga.
Grantmaker type: Independent foundation
Financial data (yr. ended 12/31/02): Assets,
$4,139,365 (M); gifts received, $5; expenditures,
$2,892,254; qualifying distributions,
$2,864,646; giving activities include
$2,890,274 for 147 grants (high: $1,000,000;
low: $50; average: $1,000–$50,000).
Purpose and activities: Giving primarily for
social services.
Fields of interest: Education; Animal welfare;
Hospitals (general); Health care; Cancer;
Recreation; Boys & girls clubs; Human services;
Philanthropy/voluntarism; General charitable
giving.
Limitations: Applications not accepted. Giving
primarily in FL.
Application information: Contributes only to
pre-selected organizations.
Officers and Directors:* H. Wayne Huizenga,
Jr.,* Pres.; Martha Jean Huizenga,* V.P.; Steven
R. Berrard,* Secy.; Richard C. Rochon,* Treas.;
Harris W. Hudson; H. Wayne Huizenga.
EIN: 650018158

762
Jacarlene Foundation
c/o SunTrust Banks, Inc.
P.O. Box 1498
Tampa, FL 33601   (813) 224-2460

Established in 2000.
Donor(s): Jacarlene Foundation, Inc.
Grantmaker type: Independent foundation
Financial data (yr. ended 12/31/02): Assets,
$1,635,466 (M); gifts received, $23,572;
expenditures, $120,162; qualifying distributions,
$99,512; giving activities include $99,945 for
14 grants (high: $16,000; low: $3,000).
Fields of interest: Arts; Education;
Zoos/zoological societies; Animals/wildlife.
Limitations: Giving primarily in FL. No grants to
individuals.
Application information:
Initial approach: Letter
Deadline(s): None

Officers: Jacqueline Preis, Pres.; John J. Howley,
Secy.-Treas.
Director: Aileen Steinberg.
EIN: 597188681

763
Thomas A. and Mary S. James Foundation,
Inc.
880 Carillon Pkwy.
St. Petersburg, FL 33716

Established in 1994 in FL.
Donor(s): Thomas A. James.
Grantmaker type: Independent foundation
Financial data (yr. ended 12/31/02): Assets,
$4,096,819 (M); expenditures, $246,034;
qualifying distributions, $201,606; giving
activities include $202,000 for 42 grants (high:
$50,000; low: $250).
Purpose and activities: Giving primarily for arts
and culture, education, and social services.
Fields of interest: Multipurpose
centers/programs; Museums (art); Museums
(science/technology); Performing arts; Higher
education; Law school/education; Education;
Botanical gardens; Recreation, social clubs;
Federated giving programs.
Limitations: Applications not accepted. Giving
primarily in FL. No grants to individuals.
Application information: Contributes only to
pre-selected organizations.
Officers and Trustees:* Thomas A. James,* Pres.;
Mary S. James,* Secy.; Court James; Hunt James.
EIN: 593288143

764
The Jelks Family Foundation, Inc.
239 E. 4th St.
Panama City, FL 32401

Established in 1995 in FL.
Grantmaker type: Independent foundation
Financial data (yr. ended 12/31/02): Assets,
$4,271,447 (M); expenditures, $176,032;
qualifying distributions, $167,237; giving
activities include $133,054 for 138 grants (high:
$60,000; low: $100).
Fields of interest: Arts; University; Natural
resources; Health organizations, association;
Children/youth, services; Federated giving
programs.
Limitations: Applications not accepted. Giving
primarily in FL. No grants to individuals.
Application information: Contributes only to
pre-selected organizations.
Directors: Allen Jelks; Allen N. Jelks, Jr.;
Deborah Stephens Jelks; Howard L. Jelks; Lisa
Grace Jelks; Mary Jelks; Christopher B. King;
Helen J. King; Alice J. Lezcano; Edgar Lezcano.
EIN: 593270436

765
Irving S. Johnson and Alwyn N. Johnson
Family Foundation
4601 Rue Belle Mer
Sanibel, FL 33957-2707
Contact: Irving S. Johnson, Pres.

Established in 1997 in IN.
Donor(s): Alwyn N. Johnson, Irving S. Johnson.

Grantmaker type: Independent foundation
Financial data (yr. ended 12/31/02): Assets, $2,101,626 (M); expenditures, $132,990; qualifying distributions, $131,572; giving activities include $127,500 for 66 grants (high: $10,000; low: $500).
Purpose and activities: Giving primarily for religion, education and the environment.
Fields of interest: Education; Natural resources; Christian agencies & churches.
Limitations: Giving on a national basis. No grants to individuals.
Application information:
  Initial approach: Letter
  Deadline(s): None
Officers: Irving S. Johnson, Pres.; Alwyn N. Johnson, Secy.-Treas.
Board Members: Rebecca L. Johnson Brown; Bryan G. Johnson; Kevin B. Johnson.
EIN: 352017579

766
The Katcher Family Foundation, Inc.
1111 Brickell Ave., Rm. 2920
Miami, FL 33131 (305) 358-4222
Contact: Gerald Katcher, Dir.

Established in 1996 in DE and FL.
Donor(s): Gerald Katcher.
Grantmaker type: Independent foundation
Financial data (yr. ended 11/30/02): Assets, $2,104,693 (M); gifts received, $2,889,632; expenditures, $1,002,493; qualifying distributions, $990,072; giving activities include $1,000,658 for 23 grants (high: $105,000; low: $100).
Purpose and activities: Giving primarily for arts, education, and the environment.
Fields of interest: Museums; Museums (art); Arts; Education; Environment, research.
Limitations: Giving primarily in CO, FL and NY.
Application information:
  Initial approach: Letter or telephone
  Deadline(s): None
Directors: Lesley Heller; Gerald Katcher; Jane Katcher.
EIN: 650715498

767
KBR Foundation
11801 Acorn Woods Terrace
Bradenton, FL 34202

Established in 1992 in VA.
Donor(s): Margaret Dole Rust.‡
Grantmaker type: Independent foundation
Financial data (yr. ended 12/31/02): Assets, $5,528,828 (M); expenditures, $416,847; qualifying distributions, $290,131; giving activities include $270,330 for 42 grants (high: $50,000; low: $50).
Purpose and activities: Giving primarily to health associations, and human services.
Fields of interest: Education; Natural resources; Animals/wildlife, preservation/protection; Health care; Health organizations, association; Athletics/sports, Special Olympics; Human services; Children/youth, services; Biological sciences; Botany.
Limitations: Applications not accepted. Giving primarily in Washington, DC. No grants to individuals.

Application information: Contributes only to pre-selected organizations.
Directors: Joseph P. Bornstein; Lynn Harris Bornstein.
EIN: 521772480

768
The Delores Pass Kesler Foundation, Inc.
9700 Philips Hwy., Ste. 101
Jacksonville, FL 32256 (904) 996-7082
Contact: Delores Kesler, Pres.

Established in 1997 in FL.
Donor(s): Delores Kesler.
Grantmaker type: Independent foundation
Financial data (yr. ended 06/30/02): Assets, $2,350,077 (M); expenditures, $676,808; qualifying distributions, $562,784; giving activities include $442,700 for 59 grants (high: $113,000; low: $100).
Purpose and activities: Giving primarily for human services, Jewish organizations, temples, and Christian churches.
Fields of interest: Arts; Higher education; Education; Environment; Family planning; Children/youth, services; Christian agencies & churches; Jewish agencies & temples.
Limitations: Giving primarily in FL. No grants to individuals.
Application information:
  Initial approach: Proposal, maximum of 5 pages
  Deadline(s): None
Officers: Delores Kesler, Pres.; Deborah Pass, Secy.; Mark Pass, Treas.
EIN: 593391143

769
The Kirk Foundation
(formerly Landon Foundation, Inc.)
c/o Bessemer Trust Co. of Florida
801 Brickell Ave., 19th Fl.
Miami, FL 33131

Established in 1998 in FL.
Donor(s): R. Kirk Landon.
Grantmaker type: Independent foundation
Financial data (yr. ended 12/31/01): Assets, $6,635,752 (M); gifts received, $225,000; expenditures, $3,207,734; qualifying distributions, $3,160,875; giving activities include $3,155,000 for 17 grants (high: $1,250,000; low: $2,000).
Purpose and activities: Giving primarily for higher and other education, particularly to a military academy; funding also for the arts, children's services, and federated giving programs.
Fields of interest: Media/communications; Ballet; Higher education; Education; Zoos/zoological societies; Children, services; Federated giving programs.
Limitations: Applications not accepted. Giving primarily in Miami, FL, and Chatham, VA. No grants to individuals.
Application information: Contributes only to pre-selected organizations.
Officers and Directors:* R. Kirk Landon,* Pres.; Frederick H. Sandstrom, Secy.-Treas.; Gerald N. Gaston; Chris J. Landon; Kathleen A. Staley.
EIN: 311625551

770
The Kislak Family Fund, Inc.
7900 Miami Lakes Dr. W.
Miami Lakes, FL 33016-5897

Established in 1992 in FL.
Donor(s): Jay I. Kislak, J.I. Kislak, Inc.
Grantmaker type: Independent foundation
Financial data (yr. ended 12/31/02): Assets, $7,601,273 (M); expenditures, $450,655; qualifying distributions, $447,693; giving activities include $447,590 for 60 grants (high: $250,000; low: $50).
Purpose and activities: Giving primarily for human services, animal welfare, and to Jewish agencies.
Fields of interest: Museums; Museums (art); Museums (marine/maritime); Museums (specialized); Higher education; Zoos/zoological societies; Jewish agencies & temples.
Limitations: Applications not accepted. Giving primarily in FL. No grants to individuals.
Application information: Contributes only to pre-selected organizations.
Officers and Directors:* Jay I. Kislak,* Pres.; Jean Kislak,* Secy.; Philip Thomas Kislak; Paula Mangravite.
EIN: 650350930

771
Landmark Charitable Foundation, Inc.
(formerly Landmark Vineyards Foundation, Inc.)
c/o Wilomar Corp.
900 S. U.S. Hwy. 1, Ste. 205
Jupiter, FL 33477-6469

Established in 1991 in FL.
Donor(s): Damaris D.W. Ethridge.
Grantmaker type: Independent foundation
Financial data (yr. ended 12/31/02): Assets, $604,596 (M); gifts received, $1,357; expenditures, $124,418; qualifying distributions, $120,855; giving activities include $120,855 for 20 grants (high: $72,355; low: $250).
Purpose and activities: Giving for the arts, medical centers and services, nature conservation, and for education.
Fields of interest: Arts; Education; Natural resources; Environment; Hospitals (general); Federated giving programs; Christian agencies & churches.
Limitations: Applications not accepted. Giving primarily in DE and FL. No grants to individuals.
Application information: Contributes only to pre-selected organizations.
Officers and Director:* Damaris D.W. Ethridge,* Pres.; William Ethridge, Secy.-Treas.
EIN: 133604188

772
The Lastinger Family Foundation, Inc.
8342 A1A S.
St. Augustine, FL 32086

Established in 1998 in FL.
Donor(s): Allen L. Lastinger, Jr.
Grantmaker type: Independent foundation
Financial data (yr. ended 05/31/02): Assets, $5,193,946 (M); expenditures, $169,261; qualifying distributions, $145,982; giving activities include $145,000 for 3 grants (high: $100,000; low: $20,000).

Purpose and activities: Giving primarily for education.
Fields of interest: Museums (natural history); Secondary school/education; Higher education; Natural resources.
Limitations: Applications not accepted. Giving primarily in FL. No grants to individuals.
Application information: Contributes only to pre-selected organizations.
Officers: Allen L. Lastinger, Jr., Pres.; Delores T. Lastinger, V.P.; Ryan Riggs, Secy.-Treas.
Directors: Beth Lastinger; Lane Lastinger; Lindsey Riggs; Amy Vigilante; Jason Vigilante.
EIN: 593512737

773
Forrest C. Lattner Foundation, Inc. ▼
777 E. Atlantic Ave., Ste. 317
Delray Beach, FL 33483-5352 (561) 278-3781
Contact: Susan L. Lloyd, Pres., or Martha L. Connelly, Chair.

Incorporated in 1981 in FL.
Donor(s): Mrs. Forrest C. Lattner,‡ Forrest C. Lattner,‡ Frances H. Lattner.‡
Grantmaker type: Independent foundation
Financial data (yr. ended 12/31/01): Assets, $156,635,067 (M); expenditures, $8,546,338; qualifying distributions, $7,147,036; giving activities include $7,185,200 for 288 grants (high: $710,000; low: $1,000; average: $5,000–$50,000).
Purpose and activities: The foundation's primary areas of giving are research, education, conservation, health and social services, arts and humanities, and the preservation of historical, cultural, and environmental resources.
Fields of interest: Arts; Education; Natural resources; Environment; Health organizations, association.
Types of support: General/operating support; Building/renovation; Capital campaigns; Equipment; Endowments; Program development; Curriculum development; Scholarship funds; Research; Matching/challenge support.
Limitations: Giving primarily in Palm Beach County, FL, Wichita, KS, St. Louis, MO, and Westerly, RI.
Publications: Application guidelines.
Application information: Application form not required.
Initial approach: Letter stating grant request
Copies of proposal: 1
Deadline(s): Mar. 1 and Sept. 1
Board meeting date(s): June and Dec.
Officers and Directors:* Martha L. Connelly,* Chair.; Susan L. Lloyd,* Pres. and Secy.; Forrest C. Brown, M.D.; Susan Funke; Richard M. Harris; David Hollenbeck; Douglas W. Hollenbeck.
Number of staff: 1 part-time professional; 2 part-time support.
EIN: 592147657
Recent environmental and animal welfare grants:
773-1 American Oceans Campaign, DC, $15,000. 2001.
773-2 Audubon Society, National, New York, NY, $12,000. 2001.
773-3 Chez Panisse Foundation, Berkeley, CA, $25,000. 2001.

773-4 Gore Range Natural Science School, Red Cliff, CO, $25,000. 2001.
773-5 Marin Agricultural Land Trust, Point Reyes Station, CA, $10,000. 2001.
773-6 Marin Baylands Advocates, Larkspur, CA, $10,000. 2001.
773-7 National Park Trust, DC, $35,000. 2001.
773-8 Natural Step, San Francisco, CA, $25,000. 2001.
773-9 Nature Conservancy, Boulder, CO, $10,000. 2001.
773-10 Nature Conservancy, Atlanta, GA, $10,000. 2001.
773-11 Nature Conservancy, Wichita, KS, $50,000. 2001.
773-12 Nature Conservancy, Philadelphia, PA, $10,000. 2001.
773-13 Nature Conservancy of Rhode Island, Providence, RI, $10,000. 2001.
773-14 Nature Conservancy of Texas, Houston, TX, $10,000. 2001.
773-15 Organic Farming Research Foundation, Santa Cruz, CA, $110,000. 2001.
773-16 Rails to Trails Conservancy, DC, $60,000. 2001.
773-17 Saint Louis Zoo Foundation, Saint Louis, MO, $10,000. 2001.
773-18 Save Americas Forests Fund, DC, $50,000. 2001.
773-19 Surfrider Foundation, San Clemente, CA, $130,000. 2001.
773-20 Trees for Life, Wichita, KS, $25,000. 2001.
773-21 WaterKeepers Northern California, San Francisco, CA, $35,000. 2001.
773-22 Westerly Land Trust, Westerly, RI, $100,000. 2001.
773-23 Wood-Pawcatuck Watershed Association, Hope Valley, RI, $15,000. 2001.
773-24 World Wildlife Fund/Conservation Foundation, DC, $12,000. 2001.

774
The Lennar Foundation, Inc.
c/o Lennar Corp.
700 N.W. 107th Ave.
Miami, FL 33172
Contact: Marshall Ames, V.P.

Established in 1989 in FL; funded in fiscal 1990.
Donor(s): Lennar Corp.
Grantmaker type: Company-sponsored foundation
Financial data (yr. ended 11/30/02): Assets, $9,702,987 (M); gifts received, $4,357,203; expenditures, $1,989,997; qualifying distributions, $1,983,043; giving activities include $1,984,182 for 13 grants (high: $1,329,650; low: $100).
Purpose and activities: Giving primarily for education and youth organizations.
Fields of interest: Education; Zoos/zoological societies; Children/youth, services; Federated giving programs.
Types of support: General/operating support; Endowments; Curriculum development.
Limitations: Giving primarily in Miami, FL. No grants to individuals.
Application information: Application form not required.
Initial approach: Proposal
Deadline(s): None

Officers and Trustees:* Stuart A. Miller,* Pres.; Marshall Ames, V.P.; Waynewright Malcolm,* V.P.
EIN: 650171539

775
The Sumter and Ivilyn Lowry Foundation, Inc.
P.O. Box 18065
Tampa, FL 33679-8065
Contact: Ann L. Murphy, Pres.

Established in 1987 in FL.
Donor(s): Sumter Lowry,‡ Ivilyn Lowry.‡
Grantmaker type: Independent foundation
Financial data (yr. ended 12/31/02): Assets, $3,547,597 (M); gifts received, $283,319; expenditures, $245,472; qualifying distributions, $217,588; giving activities include $218,700 for 41 grants (high: $111,000; low: $500).
Purpose and activities: Giving primarily to a YMCA and to Christian organizations and churches.
Fields of interest: Education; Zoos/zoological societies; Human services; YM/YWCAs & YM/YWHAs; Children/youth, services; Christian agencies & churches.
Limitations: Giving primarily in Tampa, FL. No grants to individuals.
Application information:
Initial approach: Letter
Deadline(s): None
Officers and Directors:* Ann L. Murphy,* Pres.; David R. Murphy,* V.P.; Helen M. Brown,* Secy.-Treas.
EIN: 592824550

776
The Milton and Tamar Maltz Family Foundation, Inc.
5500 Military Trail, Ste. 22-367
Jupiter, FL 33458
Contact: David Maltz, Treas.
E-mail: maltzfoundation@aol.com

Established in 1989 in FL.
Donor(s): Milton S. Maltz, Tamar Maltz.
Grantmaker type: Independent foundation
Financial data (yr. ended 06/30/02): Assets, $7,241,070 (M); gifts received, $3,000,000; expenditures, $259,698; qualifying distributions, $232,776; giving activities include $235,000 for 8 grants (high: $175,000; low: $1,000).
Purpose and activities: Giving primarily for the arts, medical research, and human services.
Fields of interest: Arts; Natural resources; Medical research, institute; Human services; Aging, centers/services; Jewish federated giving programs.
Types of support: General/operating support; Annual campaigns; Building/renovation; Research.
Limitations: Applications not accepted. Giving on a national basis, with emphasis on FL and Cleveland, OH. No grants to individuals.
Application information: Contributes only to pre-selected organizations.
Officers: Milton S. Maltz, Pres.; Julie E. Konigsberg, V.P.; Daniel Maltz, V.P.; Tamar Maltz, Secy.; David Maltz, Treas.
Number of staff: None.

EIN: 650164300

777
Bernard A. & Chris Marden Foundation
1290 S. Ocean Blvd.
Palm Beach, FL 33480

Established in 1993 in DE and FL.
Grantmaker type: Independent foundation
Financial data (yr. ended 12/31/02): Assets, $2,016,123 (M); expenditures, $422,808; qualifying distributions, $422,388; giving activities include $419,478 for 34 grants (high: $250,000; low: $75).
Fields of interest: Opera; Arts; Natural resources; Health care, clinics/centers; Jewish federated giving programs.
Limitations: Applications not accepted. Giving primarily in Washington, DC, FL, and NY. No grants to individuals.
Application information: Contributes only to pre-selected organizations.
Officers: Bernard A. Marden, Pres.; Chris Marden, V.P.
Directors: Patrice Marden Auld; James Marden.
EIN: 650409920

778
McNulty Charitable Foundation, Inc.
c/o Pressly & Pressly
222 Lakeview Ave., Ste. 910
West Palm Beach, FL 33401

Established in 1990 in FL.
Donor(s): Patience M. Campbell.
Grantmaker type: Independent foundation
Financial data (yr. ended 12/31/02): Assets, $1,625,380 (M); expenditures, $136,361; qualifying distributions, $121,672; giving activities include $105,000 for 11 grants (high: $15,000; low: $5,000).
Purpose and activities: Giving to zoos, education, and health services.
Fields of interest: Education; Zoos/zoological societies; Eye diseases; Heart & circulatory research; Human services.
Limitations: Giving primarily in the Palm Beach, FL, area.
Application information: Application form not required.
Deadline(s): None
Directors: Kim Campbell; Rolla Campbell; Robert Harvey.
EIN: 650229961

779
Henry James and Christie M. Metz Foundation
1825 8th St. S.
Naples, FL 34102-7521

Established in 1988 in IA.
Donor(s): Henry J. Metz, Christie M. Metz.
Grantmaker type: Independent foundation
Financial data (yr. ended 12/31/02): Assets, $863,348 (M); expenditures, $139,961; qualifying distributions, $137,729; giving activities include $105,495 for 12 grants (high: $25,000; low: $500) and $32,602 for 3 grants to individuals (high: $31,045; low: $500).

Purpose and activities: Scholarships are given to students of veterinary medicine, with emphasis on those who specialize in equine medicine.
Fields of interest: Education; Animal welfare; Human services; Christian agencies & churches.
Types of support: General/operating support; Building/renovation; Endowments; Scholarships—to individuals.
Limitations: Giving primarily in Sioux City, IA.
Application information: Application form required.
Initial approach: Letter
Deadline(s): None
Trustees: Christie M. Metz; Henry J. Metz.
EIN: 421324791

780
J. Patrick Michaels, Jr. Foundation, Inc.
101 E. Kennedy Blvd., Ste. 3925
Tampa, FL 33602
Contact: Barbara Brockland

Established in 1993.
Grantmaker type: Independent foundation
Financial data (yr. ended 12/31/01): Assets, $62,546 (M); expenditures, $223,585; qualifying distributions, $192,339; giving activities include $192,339 for 38 grants (high: $50,000; low: $100; average: $100–$50,000).
Purpose and activities: Giving for health, medical research and treatment, education, relief services and institutes for culture and the humanities.
Fields of interest: Media/communications; Elementary/secondary education; Higher education; Animals/wildlife, preservation/protection; Health organizations, association; Recreation; Youth development, centers/clubs; Human services; Children/youth, services; Residential/custodial care; Hospices; Federated giving programs; Christian agencies & churches.
Types of support: General/operating support; Continuing support; Program development; Scholarship funds.
Limitations: Giving in the Tampa Bay, FL area, including Hillsborough and Pasco counties. No grants to individuals.
Application information: Application form not required.
Initial approach: Letter
Deadline(s): None
Board meeting date(s): Quarterly
Officer: Doris D. Rainey, Secy.
Directors: H. Gene Gawthrop; J. Patrick Michaels, Jr.; Kimberly L. Michaels.
Number of staff: 1 full-time professional.
EIN: 593197148

781
The John A. Moran Charitable Trust
125 Worth Ave., Ste. 202
Palm Beach, FL 33480 (561) 659-0075
Contact: John A. Moran, Tr.

Established in 1988 in FL.
Donor(s): John A. Moran.
Grantmaker type: Independent foundation
Financial data (yr. ended 12/31/02): Assets, $7,584,603 (M); expenditures, $586,884; qualifying distributions, $549,380; giving

activities include $550,121 for 5 grants (high: $500,000; low: $1,000).
Fields of interest: Historical activities, war memorials; Arts; Higher education; Environment; Hospitals (general); Cancer research; Human services.
Limitations: Giving on a national basis. No grants to individuals.
Application information: Application form not required.
Initial approach: Letter
Deadline(s): None
Trustees: Kellie Dawn Hudson; Carole O. Moran; John A. Moran; Marisa Moran Sullivan.
EIN: 650066880

782
Mote Scientific Foundation, Inc.
1600 Ken Thompson Pkwy.
Sarasota, FL 34236
Contact: Peter Hull, Pres. or Helen Pratt, Secy.

Incorporated in 1950 in NY.
Donor(s): William R. Mote,‡ T.R. Bartels,‡ Theodore R. Bartels.‡
Grantmaker type: Independent foundation
Financial data (yr. ended 11/30/02): Assets, $24,405,045 (M); gifts received, $3,352,501; expenditures, $4,098,756; qualifying distributions, $3,825,497; giving activities include $3,776,588 for 10 grants (high: $3,758,688; low: $500).
Purpose and activities: Giving mainly for oceanography; support primarily for the Mote Marine Laboratory; support also for social services.
Fields of interest: Environment; Marine science.
Types of support: General/operating support; Research.
Limitations: Applications not accepted. Giving primarily in FL. No grants to individuals.
Publications: Annual report.
Application information: Contributes only to pre-selected organizations.
Board meeting date(s): Quarterly
Officers and Trustees:* Peter Hull, Pres.; Helen Pratt, Secy.; Bill Galvano, Treas.; Kumor Manadevan; Bill Ritchie.
Number of staff: 1 part-time support.
EIN: 136117615
Recent environmental and animal welfare grants:
782-1 Mote Marine Laboratory, Sarasota, FL, $3,758,688. For general support. 2002.

783
Scott Opler Foundation
1300 North Shore Dr., N.E.
St. Petersburg, FL 33701-1426
Contact: James N. Peebles, Treas.
FAX: (727) 895-2351

Established in 1993 in MA.
Donor(s): Scott Opler.‡
Grantmaker type: Independent foundation
Financial data (yr. ended 06/30/02): Assets, $7,713,955 (M); expenditures, $985,356; qualifying distributions, $874,945; giving activities include $758,650 for 38 grants (high: $50,000; low: $150; average: $5,000–$30,000).
Purpose and activities: Primary fields of interest are: 1) scholarly study and preservation of art

and architecture; 2) nature conservation and wildlife preservation; and 3) AIDS-related services and education.

Fields of interest: Arts education; History/archaeology; Natural resources; Animals/wildlife, preservation/protection; AIDS.

International interests: Italy.

Types of support: General/operating support; Capital campaigns; Building/renovation; Equipment; Land acquisition; Endowments; Emergency funds; Conferences/seminars; Professorships; Publication; Seed money; Fellowships; Scholarship funds; Matching/challenge support.

Limitations: Giving primarily in Washington, DC, St. Petersburg, FL, Boston, MA, and Jackson, WY.

Publications: Financial statement, Informational brochure (including application guidelines).

Application information: Application form required.

> *Initial approach:* Letter
> *Copies of proposal:* 3
> *Deadline(s):* Annually
> *Board meeting date(s):* June
> *Final notification:* June

Officers and Directors:* Cathe Henry,* Pres.; C. Cabell Chinnis, Jr.,* Clerk; James N. Peebles,* Treas.

Number of staff: None.

EIN: 043201088

784

The Osiason Educational Foundation, Inc.
10500 S.W. 71st Ave.
Miami, FL 33156-3264

Established in 1989.

Grantmaker type: Independent foundation

Financial data (yr. ended 08/31/00): Assets, $4,321,696 (M); expenditures, $235,593; qualifying distributions, $183,145; giving activities include $137,971 for 9 grants (high: $50,000; low: $300).

Purpose and activities: Giving to health and human services.

Fields of interest: Zoos/zoological societies; Diabetes; Human services; Children/youth, services.

Limitations: Applications not accepted. Giving primarily in FL. No grants to individuals.

Application information: Contributes only to pre-selected organizations.

Officers: Lee J. Osiason, Pres.; Kimberly Osiason, V.P.; Marjorie Osheroff, Secy.; Robert Flannery, Treas.

EIN: 650078411

785

Peacock Foundation, Inc.
100 S.E. 2nd St., Ste. 2370
Miami, FL 33131-2127 (305) 373-1386
Contact: Joelle Allen, Exec. Dir.

Incorporated in 1947 in FL.

Donor(s): Henry B. Peacock, Jr.‡

Grantmaker type: Independent foundation

Financial data (yr. ended 11/30/02): Assets, $42,066,299 (M); expenditures, $1,814,663; qualifying distributions, $1,350,730; giving activities include $1,170,809 for 59 grants (high:

$75,000; low: $1,000; average: $5,000–$30,000).

Purpose and activities: The foundation's priorities include: supporting educational programs in the arts and the environment, as well as special education for disabled persons; contributing to medical research, health care organizations, and hospitals; and making grants to human services providers that promote youth development, assist abused or neglected children, women, and the elderly, and seek to reduce abuse, prevent homelessness, and end hunger in our prosperous community.

Fields of interest: Arts education; Education; Environmental education; Hospitals (general); Mental health/crisis services; Health organizations, association; Medical research, institute; Youth, services.

Types of support: General/operating support; Continuing support; Annual campaigns; Endowments; Program development; Research; Matching/challenge support.

Limitations: Giving primarily in the southeast FL communities located in Broward, Miami-Dade, and Monroe counties. No support for political lobbying or religious organizations unless project benefits entire community. No grants to individuals or for construction campaigns, deficit financing or debt reduction, conferences, or fundraising/special/athletic events.

Application information: Disbursements made upon selections initiated by board members. Application form not required.

> *Initial approach:* 2-page letter of inquiry
> *Copies of proposal:* 1
> *Deadline(s):* None
> *Board meeting date(s):* Quarterly

Officers and Directors:* Barbara A. Rickard,* Pres.; Thomas R. Post,* V.P.; Peter Houghton,* Secy.; Joelle Allen, Exec. Dir.

Number of staff: 1 full-time professional.

EIN: 590999759

786

Folke H. Peterson Charitable Foundation
c/o SunTrust Banks, Inc., N.A.
P.O. Box 14728
Fort Lauderdale, FL 33302
Contact: Howard Usher

Established in 1988 in FL.

Donor(s): Folke H. Peterson.‡

Grantmaker type: Independent foundation

Financial data (yr. ended 11/30/01): Assets, $21,982,590 (M); expenditures, $2,006,381; qualifying distributions, $1,740,531; giving activities include $1,740,531 for 59 grants (high: $535,449; low: $500) and $1,850,751 for foundation-administered programs.

Purpose and activities: Giving primarily for nonprofit organizations involved in the health and well-being of animals; support also for higher education.

Fields of interest: Higher education; Animal welfare.

Limitations: Giving limited to FL. No grants to individuals.

Application information: Application must be bound in a hard back 1/2 inch 3-ring binder.

> *Initial approach:* Letter
> *Copies of proposal:* 5
> *Deadline(s):* None

Trustees: Don E. Champion; Richard Kornmeier; Emily Van Vliet; Frank Van Vliet; SunTrust Banks, Inc.; Wildlife Care Center/SPCA.

EIN: 656040055

787

POLE Foundation, Inc.
(formerly Jonathan D. Lewis Foundation, Inc.)
4649 Ponce de Leon Blvd., Ste. 304
Coral Gables, FL 33146-2118 (305) 669-8990
Contact: Jonathan D. Lewis, Pres.

Donor(s): Jonathan D. Lewis.

Grantmaker type: Independent foundation

Financial data (yr. ended 12/31/01): Assets, $1,741,886 (M); expenditures, $134,455; qualifying distributions, $123,531; giving activities include $127,686 for 15 grants (high: $62,500; low: $100).

Purpose and activities: Giving primarily to arts and human services.

Fields of interest: Arts; Education; Environment, research; AIDS research; Human services; Civil rights, gays/lesbians; Religion.

Limitations: Giving primarily in Aspen, CO, FL, NY, and WA. No grants to individuals.

Application information: Application form required.

> *Deadline(s):* None

Officers: Jonathan D. Lewis, Pres.; Roberto E. Posada, V.P.; Maria R. Millares, Secy.

EIN: 650330579

788

Victor Posner Foundation, Inc.
1250 E. Hallandale Beach Blvd., Ste. 300
Hallandale, FL 33009

Established in 1974 in FL and MD.

Donor(s): Victor Posner.

Grantmaker type: Independent foundation

Financial data (yr. ended 03/31/02): Assets, $2,313,884 (M); gifts received, $165,808; expenditures, $189,603; qualifying distributions, $189,533; giving activities include $181,400 for 28 grants (high: $27,300; low: $250).

Purpose and activities: Giving primarily for religion, medical research, and human services.

Fields of interest: Higher education; Botanical gardens; Hospitals (general); Cancer; Heart & circulatory research; Federated giving programs; Christian agencies & churches; Jewish agencies & temples.

Types of support: General/operating support; Research.

Limitations: Applications not accepted. Giving primarily in FL. No grants to individuals.

Application information: Contributes only to pre-selected organizations.

Officers: Victor Posner, Chair.; Brenda Nestor, Vice-Chair.; Blanche Launer, Treas.

Number of staff: None.

EIN: 526055283

789
The Rayonier Foundation
(formerly The ITT Rayonier Foundation)
50 N. Laura St., Ste. 1900
Jacksonville, FL 32202 (904) 357-9100
Contact: Jay A. Fredericksen, V.P.

Incorporated in 1952 in NY.
Donor(s): ITT Rayonier Inc., Rayonier Inc.
Grantmaker type: Company-sponsored foundation
Financial data (yr. ended 12/31/02): Assets, $4,311,554 (M); gifts received, $979,250; expenditures, $857,674; qualifying distributions, $849,910; giving activities include $804,311 for 98 grants (high: $10,000; low: $250) and $46,904 for 72 employee matching gifts.
Purpose and activities: Created as a medium to meet civic responsibilities in the areas of company operations and to support educational institutions related to Rayonier recruitment or to forest industry specializations. Grants to educational associations for scholarships, hospitals for buildings and equipment, health agencies and community funds, the arts, and environmental organizations; scholarships to individuals residing in areas of company operations in Nassau County, FL, Wayne County, GA, and Clallam, Mason, and Grays Harbor counties, WA.
Fields of interest: Performing arts; Libraries/library science; Education; Natural resources; Hospitals (general); Medical care, rehabilitation; Substance abuse, services; Mental health/crisis services; Health organizations, association; Alcoholism; Recreation; Human services; Children/youth, services; Family services; Women, centers/services; Minorities/immigrants, centers/services; Community development; Voluntarism promotion; Federated giving programs; Engineering/technology; Science; Economics; Minorities; Disabled; Women; Economically disadvantaged.
Types of support: General/operating support; Continuing support; Annual campaigns; Capital campaigns; Building/renovation; Equipment; Land acquisition; Endowments; Debt reduction; Emergency funds; Program development; Seed money; Scholarship funds; Research; Employee matching gifts; Employee-related scholarships; In-kind gifts; Matching/challenge support.
Limitations: Giving primarily in areas of company operations in Nassau County, FL, Wayne County, GA, and Olympic Peninsula, WA. No loans.
Application information: Application form required for scholarships.
   Initial approach: Letter or proposal
   Copies of proposal: 1
   Deadline(s): Nov. 13 for scholarships
   Board meeting date(s): Feb.
   Final notification: Scholarship awards announced in Apr.
Officers and Directors:* W.L. Nutter,* Chair. and Pres.; Jay A. Fredericksen,* V.P.; Ed Frazier III, Secy.; Macdonald Auguste, Treas.; John Kublbock, Cont.; William S. Berry; J.P. O'Grady; Jill Witter.
EIN: 136064462

790
The John M. Regan, Jr. & Prudence S. Regan Foundation, Inc.
c/o R. Chapin
1201 George Bush Blvd.
Delray Beach, FL 33483-7203

Established in 1993 in FL.
Donor(s): John M. Regan, Jr., Prudence S. Regan.
Grantmaker type: Independent foundation
Financial data (yr. ended 12/31/02): Assets, $2,682,347 (M); expenditures, $394,934; qualifying distributions, $379,883; giving activities include $380,200 for 27 grants (high: $250,000; low: $100).
Purpose and activities: Giving primarily for higher education, and to Roman Catholic churches and organizations.
Fields of interest: Higher education; Education; Natural resources; Hospitals (general); Human services; Roman Catholic agencies & churches.
Limitations: Applications not accepted. Giving on a national basis. No grants to individuals.
Application information: Contributes only to pre-selected organizations.
Officers and Directors:* John M. Regan, Jr.,* Pres. and Treas.; Prudence S. Regan,* V.P.; Robert D. Chapin, Secy.; Deborah Regan Edwards; Prudence R. Hallarman; John M. Regan III; Peter M. Regan; R. Christopher Regan.
EIN: 650374592

791
River Branch Foundation
1514 Nira St.
Jacksonville, FL 32207
Contact: Judith Leroux, Trustee
Application address: 177 Fourth Ave. N., Jacksonville, FL 32250

Trust established in 1963 in NJ.
Donor(s): J. Seward Johnson 1951 and 1961 Charitable Trusts, The Atlantic Foundation.
Grantmaker type: Independent foundation
Financial data (yr. ended 12/31/01): Assets, $25,714,495 (M); expenditures, $1,656,596; qualifying distributions, $1,432,810; giving activities include $1,447,000 for 45 grants (high: $100,000; low: $1,000).
Purpose and activities: Giving primarily for human services, children's services, education, the arts and the environment.
Fields of interest: Arts; Environment; Children/youth, services.
Limitations: Giving primarily in the Jacksonville, FL, area. No grants to individuals.
Application information: Application form not required.
   Initial approach: Letter; do not telephone
   Copies of proposal: 1
   Deadline(s): None
Director: Jennifer Johnson Duke.
Trustees: Jason Gregg; Simon Gregg; Judith Leroux.
EIN: 226054887

792
J. Carlisle Rogers, Ruth G. Rogers & James Carlisle Rogers, Jr. Family Foundation, Inc.
215 N. Joanna Ave.
Tavares, FL 32778

Established in 1989 in FL.
Donor(s): Ruth Rogers Trust.
Grantmaker type: Independent foundation
Financial data (yr. ended 12/31/02): Assets, $3,748,015 (M); gifts received, $26,234; expenditures, $243,102; qualifying distributions, $206,945; giving activities include $206,945 for 14 grants (high: $50,000; low: $1,000).
Purpose and activities: Giving primarily for education and Christian agencies and churches.
Fields of interest: Education, public education; Secondary school/education; College; Libraries (public); Education; Animals/wildlife; Boys & girls clubs; Christian agencies & churches.
Limitations: Applications not accepted. Giving primarily in Leesburg, FL. No grants to individuals.
Application information: Contributes only to pre-selected organizations.
Officers: William Cauthen, Pres.; Howard Hewitt, V.P.; Phyllis Butler, Secy.-Treas.
EIN: 592969938

793
Rooms to Go Children's Fund
11540 Hwy. 92 E.
Seffner, FL 33584 (813) 623-5400
Contact: Lewis Stein, V.P.

Established in 1998 in FL.
Donor(s): Rooms To Go, Inc.
Grantmaker type: Independent foundation
Financial data (yr. ended 11/30/01): Assets, $1,808,388 (M); gifts received, $1,500,000; expenditures, $391,802; qualifying distributions, $384,676; giving activities include $382,894 for 57 grants (high: $10,000; low: $300).
Fields of interest: Zoos/zoological societies; Hospitals (general); Health care; Health organizations, association; Disasters, 9/11/01; Human services; YM/YWCAs & YM/YWHAs; Children/youth, services; Federated giving programs; Jewish agencies & temples.
Types of support: General/operating support.
Limitations: Giving primarily in FL.
Officers and Directors:* Jeffrey Seaman,* Pres.; Lewis Stein, V.P. and Secy.-Treas.; J. Michael Kettle.
EIN: 650878894

794
William J. & Tina Rosenberg Foundation
2511 Ponce De Leon Blvd., Ste. 320
Coral Gables, FL 33134 (305) 444-6121
Contact: Jack G. Admire, or Ruth S. Admire, Trustees
FAX: (305) 444-5508; E-mail: rsadmire@yahoo.com

Established in 1970 in FL.
Donor(s): Tina Rosenberg.‡
Grantmaker type: Independent foundation
Financial data (yr. ended 04/30/03): Assets, $3,685,984 (M); expenditures, $194,999;

qualifying distributions, $164,841; giving activities include $130,500 for 27 grants (high: $25,000; average: $1,000–$50,000).
Purpose and activities: Primary areas of giving include public education, the environment, the disadvantaged, social services, cultural programs, including museums, and health.
Fields of interest: Museums; Performing arts; Arts; Education; Natural resources; Environment; Family planning; Health care; AIDS; AIDS research; Crime/violence prevention, youth; Housing/shelter, development; Human services; Children/youth, services; Hospices; Homeless, human services; Civil rights, advocacy; Community development; Jewish federated giving programs; Protestant federated giving programs; Protestant agencies & churches; Disabled; Economically disadvantaged; Homeless.
Types of support: General/operating support; Emergency funds; Program development; Seed money; Matching/challenge support.
Limitations: Giving primarily in Dade County, FL. No grants to individuals.
Publications: Application guidelines.
Application information: Application form not required.
Initial approach: Proposal
Copies of proposal: 1
Deadline(s): None
Board meeting date(s): Varies
Trustees: Jack G. Admire; John G. Admire; Ruth S. Admire; John C. Sullivan, Jr.; Wachovia Bank, N.A.
Number of staff: 1 shared staff (shared with The Charles N. & Eleanor Knight Leigh Foundation, Inc., Ruth Anderson Foundation, The McIntosh Foundation).
EIN: 237088390

795
The Saunders Foundation
c/o Bank of America
P.O. Box 31813
Tampa, FL 33631-3813 (813) 225-8588
Contact: Kathleen J. Belmonte, Dir.

Established in 1970 in FL.
Donor(s): William N. Saunders,‡ Ruby Lee Saunders.‡
Grantmaker type: Independent foundation
Financial data (yr. ended 12/31/02): Assets, $13,639,208 (M); expenditures, $868,854; qualifying distributions, $793,200; giving activities include $711,400 for 33 grants (high: $250,000; low: $250).
Purpose and activities: Giving primarily for children, and for education, the arts, and historical preservation.
Fields of interest: Museums (ethnic/folk arts); Museums (science/technology); Performing arts centers; Orchestra (symphony); Historical activities; Higher education; Zoos/zoological societies; Aquariums; Health care; Children/youth, services; General charitable giving; Disabled.
Types of support: Building/renovation; Program development; Scholarship funds; Matching/challenge support.
Limitations: Giving primarily in the Tampa Bay, FL, area. No support for organizations that promote sports or athletic competition. No

grants to individuals, or for fellowships, travel projects, or operating funds.
Publications: Application guidelines.
Application information: Application form required.
Copies of proposal: 2
Deadline(s): None
Board meeting date(s): 1st Wed. of each month
Officers and Directors:* Solon F. O'Neal, Jr.,* Pres.; James M. Kelly,* V.P. and Treas.; George B. Howell III,* Secy.; Kathleen J. Belmonte.
Number of staff: None.
EIN: 596152326

796
Scaife Family Foundation ▼
West Tower, Ste. 903
777 So. Flagler Dr.
West Palm Beach, FL 33401 (561) 659-1188
Contact: Barbara M. Sloan, Exec. Dir.
URL: http://www.scaife.com

Established in 1983 in PA.
Donor(s): Sarah Mellon Scaife.‡
Grantmaker type: Independent foundation
Financial data (yr. ended 12/31/02): Assets, $75,293,495 (M); expenditures, $4,684,411; qualifying distributions, $4,382,244; giving activities include $3,982,000 for 38 grants (high: $1,000,000; low: $2,000; average: $15,000–$75,000).
Purpose and activities: Grants to support and develop programs that strengthen families, address issues surrounding the health and welfare of women and children, promote animal welfare, and that demonstrate the beneficial interaction between humans and animals; Support also for conservation, and early intervention and prevention efforts in the area of drug and alcohol addiction.
Fields of interest: Animal welfare; Health care; Substance abuse, prevention.
Types of support: General/operating support; Program development.
Limitations: No grants to individuals; no loans.
Publications: Annual report, Grants list.
Application information: Application form not required.
Initial approach: Letter
Copies of proposal: 1
Deadline(s): Grant applications are normally considered quarterly; no set deadline
Board meeting date(s): Quarterly
Final notification: Following board meetings
Officers and Trustees:* Jennie K. Scaife,* Chair.; Barbara M. Sloan, Pres. and Secy.-Treas.; Beth H. Genter,* V.P.; Mary T. Walton,* V.P.
Number of staff: 1 full-time professional; 1 full-time support.
EIN: 251427015
Recent environmental and animal welfare grants:
796-1 All Creatures Sanctuary, Palm Beach Gardens, FL, $130,000. For general support. 2002.
796-2 Animal Rescue League of Western Pennsylvania, Pittsburgh, PA, $15,000. For capital support. 2002.
796-3 Animal Rescue League of Western Pennsylvania, Pittsburgh, PA, $15,000. For general support. 2002.
796-4 Assistance Dogs of America, Swanton, OH, $30,000. For program support. 2002.

796-5 Dreher Park Zoo, West Palm Beach, FL, $100,000. For project support. 2002.
796-6 Humane Society of Florida, Jupiter, FL, $300,000. For general support. 2002.
796-7 Humane Society of Florida, Jupiter, FL, $150,000. For capital support. 2002.
796-8 Humane Society, Western Pennsylvania, Pittsburgh, PA, $50,000. For capital support. 2002.
796-9 National Police Bloodhound Association, Downers Grove, IL, $15,000. For training program. 2002.
796-10 Pets for the Elderly Foundation, Beachwood, OH, $20,000. For general support. 2002.
796-11 Puppies Behind Bars, New York, NY, $100,000. For general support. 2002.
796-12 Whispering Springs Rescue and Research, Bradford, PA, $14,800. For general support. 2002.

797
The Stephen Harold Schimmel Foundation, Inc.
c/o Rothstein, Kass & Co.
8466 N. Lockwood Ridge Rd., Ste. 248
Sarasota, FL 34243

Established in 1995 in DE.
Donor(s): Stephen Harold Schimmel, Rosalba Schimmel.
Grantmaker type: Independent foundation
Financial data (yr. ended 09/30/02): Assets, $5,426,400 (M); expenditures, $335,499; qualifying distributions, $223,531; giving activities include $221,000 for 5 grants (high: $125,000; low: $10,000).
Purpose and activities: Giving primarily for Christian organizations.
Fields of interest: Botanical gardens; Christian agencies & churches.
Limitations: Applications not accepted. Giving on a national basis. No grants to individuals.
Application information: Contributes only to pre-selected organizations.
Officers: Stephen Harold Schimmel, Pres. and Secy.; Rosalba Schimmel, V.P. and Treas.
EIN: 223386066

798
Schultz Foundation, Inc.
Schultz Bldg.
P.O. Box 1200
Jacksonville, FL 32201-1200 (904) 354-3603

Established in 1964 in FL.
Donor(s): Mae W. Schultz,‡ Genevieve S. Ayers,‡ Frederick H. Schultz, Nancy R. Schultz.
Grantmaker type: Independent foundation
Financial data (yr. ended 12/31/02): Assets, $3,279,654 (M); expenditures, $209,598; qualifying distributions, $165,817; giving activities include $165,817 for 81 grants (high: $41,992; low: $50).
Fields of interest: Museums (history); Museums (science/technology); Education, research; Education, public policy; Education; Environment, association; Water pollution; Zoos/zoological societies; Federated giving programs.
Types of support: General/operating support.

Limitations: Giving primarily in Jacksonville, FL, and GA. No grants to individuals.
Publications: Annual report.
Trustees: Clifford G. Schultz II; John R. Schultz; Nancy R. Schultz.
Number of staff: 1 part-time professional.
EIN: 591055869

799
Richard H. Simons Charitable Trust
4000 Hollywood Blvd., Ste. 485S
Hollywood, FL 33021   (954) 966-2112
Contact: Robert M. Kramer, Tr.

Established in 1996 in FL.
Grantmaker type: Independent foundation
Financial data (yr. ended 12/31/02): Assets, $5,025,287 (M); expenditures, $481,499; qualifying distributions, $413,620; giving activities include $216,909 for 33 grants (high: $101,000; low: $100).
Purpose and activities: Giving primarily for education and health and human services. 51 percent of giving goes to public education/broadcasting; cancer research/education; and rainforest preservation/research/education.
Fields of interest: Television; Radio; Higher education; Education; Environment, research; Environment, forests; Environment; Hospitals (general); Cancer; Cancer research; Human services; Jewish agencies & temples.
Limitations: Giving primarily in the Miami, FL, area.
Application information:
  Initial approach: Brief letter (not more than 2 pages)
  Deadline(s): None
Trustee: Robert M. Kramer.
EIN: 597034786

800
Les and Judy Smout Foundation, Inc.
100 N. Starcrest Dr.
Clearwater, FL 33765-3224

Established in 1989 in FL.
Donor(s): Jack Eckerd, Les Smout.
Grantmaker type: Independent foundation
Financial data (yr. ended 04/30/02): Assets, $1,299,149 (M); expenditures, $107,697; qualifying distributions, $105,135; giving activities include $105,600 for 11 grants (high: $41,000; low: $750).
Purpose and activities: Giving primarily for animal organizations, particularly a chimp farm.
Fields of interest: Museums; Museums (specialized); Higher education; Education; Animals/wildlife; Federated giving programs.
Limitations: Applications not accepted. Giving primarily in FL; some funding also in Baraboo, WI. No grants to individuals.
Application information: Contributes only to pre-selected organizations.
Officers and Directors:* Les Smout,* Pres.; Judy Smout,* V.P.; Janet Heyman,* Secy.-Treas.; Joanne Smout.
EIN: 650118624

801
Joe Sonken Charitable Trust
3300 N. 29th Ave., Ste. 102
Hollywood, FL 33020   (954) 922-2207
Contact: Gary Hacker, Tr.

Established in 1992 in FL.
Grantmaker type: Independent foundation
Financial data (yr. ended 12/31/02): Assets, $2,314,431 (M); expenditures, $362,244; qualifying distributions, $290,688; giving activities include $227,781 for 38 grants (high: $20,000; low: $2,000).
Purpose and activities: Funding primarily to benefit needy children and animals.
Fields of interest: Museums; Education; Animal welfare; Hospitals (general); Youth development, centers/clubs; Human services; Children/youth, services; Homeless, human services.
Limitations: Giving limited to FL. No grants to individuals.
Application information:
  Initial approach: Letter
  Deadline(s): Prior to board meeting
  Board meeting date(s): Feb. or Mar.
Trustees: Suzanne Barnett; Gary Hacker; Jerome S. Richman; Claran Slocum.
EIN: 656077181

802
William & Lynda Steere Foundation
c/o Kelly
2640 Golden Gate, No. 305
Naples, FL 34105-3203

Established in 1999.
Donor(s): William Steere, Jr., Lynda Steere.
Grantmaker type: Independent foundation
Financial data (yr. ended 12/31/02): Assets, $8,534,437 (M); expenditures, $1,704,074; qualifying distributions, $1,700,895; giving activities include $1,701,433 for 17 grants (high: $1,050,000; low: $600).
Fields of interest: Arts; Botanical gardens; Health care.
Limitations: Applications not accepted. Giving primarily in NY. No grants to individuals.
Application information: Contributes only to pre-selected organizations.
Trustees: Elwood B. Davis; Lynda G. Steere; William C. Steere, Jr.
EIN: 656286705

803
The David A. Stein Foundation, Inc.
(formerly Stein Family Foundation)
P.O. Drawer U
Jacksonville, FL 32203   (904) 725-4122
Contact: David A. Stein, Chair.

Established in 1949 in FL.
Donor(s): David A. Stein, Martin Stein,‡ King Provision Corp., Southern Industrial Corp.
Grantmaker type: Independent foundation
Financial data (yr. ended 12/31/02): Assets, $3,978,327 (M); gifts received, $200,000; expenditures, $467,269; qualifying distributions, $417,023; giving activities include $417,023 for 52 grants (high: $103,400; low: $100).
Fields of interest: Museums; Performing arts; Arts; Elementary/secondary education; Zoos/zoological societies; Hospitals (general);

Cancer; Heart & circulatory diseases; Youth development; Human services; Aging, centers/services; Community development, neighborhood development; Foundations (community); Federated giving programs; Jewish federated giving programs; Jewish agencies & temples.
Limitations: Giving primarily in Jacksonville, FL. No grants to individuals.
Application information: Application form not required.
  Initial approach: Letter
  Copies of proposal: 1
  Deadline(s): None
Officers: David A. Stein, Chair. and Secy.; Lois Chepenik, Vice-Chair.; Tracey Stein, Treas.
Trustees: Allison S. Robbins; Linda B. Stein.
Number of staff: None.
EIN: 596152351

804
Jerry Taylor and Nancy Bryant Foundation
1 Las Olas Cir., Ste. 1002
Fort Lauderdale, FL 33316
Contact: Nancy Bryant, Mgr.
Application address: 4200 Wisconsin Ave. N.W., Ste. 106, Washington, DC 20016

Established in 1999 in FL.
Donor(s): Galen D. Taylor Charitable Trust.
Grantmaker type: Independent foundation
Financial data (yr. ended 12/31/02): Assets, $6,596,235 (M); gifts received, $168,000; expenditures, $300,205; qualifying distributions, $242,440; giving activities include $247,400 for 22 grants (high: $40,000; low: $400).
Purpose and activities: Giving primarily for the basic needs of the poor and underprivileged.
Fields of interest: Education; Environment; Human services; Children, services.
International interests: Bahamas.
Types of support: General/operating support; Emergency funds; Program development.
Limitations: Applications not accepted. Giving primarily in Washington DC and Fort Lauderdale/Broward County, FL; some funding also in Nassau, Bahamas. No grants to individuals.
Application information: Contributes only to pre-selected organizations.
  Board meeting date(s): Nov.
Managers: Nancy Bryant; Galen D. Taylor; Gerald Taylor.
EIN: 522134053

805
The John A. and Elizabeth F. Taylor Charitable Foundation, Inc.
c/o Harrison K. Chauncey, Jr.
241 Bradley Pl.
Palm Beach, FL 33480

Established in 1989 in FL.
Donor(s): Elizabeth F. Taylor, Sandra T. Kaupe.
Grantmaker type: Independent foundation
Financial data (yr. ended 12/31/02): Assets, $268,531 (M); gifts received, $202,754; expenditures, $2,152,438; qualifying distributions, $2,100,564; giving activities include $2,100,564 for 4 grants (high: $2,050,000; low: $12,500).

Purpose and activities: Giving for higher education, and for water resources and fisheries.
Fields of interest: Education; Environment, water resources; Animals/wildlife, fisheries; Marine science.
Types of support: General/operating support; Capital campaigns; Endowments; Debt reduction; Emergency funds; Seed money; Fellowships; Internship funds; Scholarship funds; Research.
Limitations: Applications not accepted. Giving primarily in FL. No grants to individuals.
Application information: Contributes only to pre-selected organizations.
Board meeting date(s): Dec. of each year
Officers and Directors:* Elizabeth F. Taylor,* Chair.; Sandra T. Kaupe,* Pres.; Donald A. Wilson,* V.P.; Peter D. Kaupe,* Secy.-Treas.; Patrice Kaupe; Serena S. Wilson.
Number of staff: None.
EIN: 650155013

806
The Ross E. Traphagen, Jr. Fund
c/o Caler, Donton, Levine, et al.
505 S. Flagler Dr., Ste. 900
West Palm Beach, FL 33401

Established in 1976 in NY.
Donor(s): Ross E. Traphagen, Jr.
Grantmaker type: Independent foundation
Financial data (yr. ended 03/31/02): Assets, $3,142,097 (M); expenditures, $661,491; qualifying distributions, $605,665; giving activities include $605,665 for 37 grants (high: $500,000; low: $10).
Purpose and activities: Giving primarily for education, human services, and the environment.
Fields of interest: Secondary school/education; Higher education; Law school/education; Environment; Human services; Christian agencies & churches.
Limitations: Applications not accepted. Giving primarily in FL, NJ, and NY. No grants to individuals; no loans.
Application information: Contributes only to pre-selected organizations.
Trustees: Judson B. Traphagen; Ross E. Traphagen, Jr.
EIN: 132894831

807
The Vanneck-Bailey Foundation
217 West Indies Dr.
Palm Beach, FL 33480
Contact: William P. Vanneck, Treas.

Established in 1971 in NY through the consolidation of The Vanneck Foundation, incorporated in 1949 in NY, and The Frank and Marie Bailey Foundation.
Donor(s): John Vanneck,‡ Barbara Bailey Vanneck.
Grantmaker type: Independent foundation
Financial data (yr. ended 12/31/02): Assets, $6,645,359 (M); expenditures, $332,321; qualifying distributions, $322,076; giving activities include $316,000 for 71 grants (high: $35,000; low: $500).

Fields of interest: Higher education; Natural resources; Hospitals (general); Community development; Protestant agencies & churches.
Types of support: Continuing support; Research.
Limitations: Applications not accepted. Giving primarily on the East Coast. No grants to individuals.
Application information: Contributes only to pre-selected organizations.
Officers: Barbara V. May, Pres.; Jeanne M. Wiedenman, Secy.; William P. Vanneck, Treas.
EIN: 237165285

808
The Weiler Foundation, Inc.
231 Bradley Pl., Ste. 204
Palm Beach, FL 33480 (561) 659-2212
Contact: Bartlett Burnap, Pres.

Established in 1961 in CA.
Donor(s): Ralph J. Weiler.‡
Grantmaker type: Independent foundation
Financial data (yr. ended 04/30/01): Assets, $11,545,177 (M); expenditures, $741,913; qualifying distributions, $590,767; giving activities include $482,000 for 30 grants (high: $60,000; low: $1,000; average: $5,000–$25,000).
Purpose and activities: Giving primarily for education; funding also for wildlife preservation, and children's and social services.
Fields of interest: Higher education; Education; Animals/wildlife, preservation/protection; Human services; Children, services.
Limitations: Giving primarily in CA and FL; funding also in NY. No support for individual churches or religious organizations. No grants to individuals, or for capital campaigns, capital improvements, start-up funds for new organizations, or to institutions supported by state or federal funds.
Publications: Application guidelines.
Application information: Application form required.
Initial approach: Proposal
Copies of proposal: 3
Deadline(s): Mar.
Board meeting date(s): Monthly
Officers: Bartlett Burnap, Pres.; William Bullis, V.P.
Directors: Christiane Burnap; Ian Burnap.
EIN: 311475728

809
Winn Foundation Trust
c/o John Winn
12318 N.E., CR 1471
Waldo, FL 32694 (352) 468-1669

Established in 1967.
Donor(s): Mary E. Winn.
Grantmaker type: Independent foundation
Financial data (yr. ended 12/31/02): Assets, $1,446,177 (M); expenditures, $101,065; qualifying distributions, $100,585; giving activities include $98,100 for 29 grants (high: $25,000; low: $100).
Purpose and activities: Giving primarily for the environment and animal welfare.
Fields of interest: Education; Natural resources; Environment; Animal welfare; Animals/wildlife, preservation/protection.

Limitations: No grants to individuals.
Application information: Application form not required.
Initial approach: Letter
Deadline(s): None
Trustees: John C. Winn; Mary E. Winn; Mary Lou Winn; Merrill Lynch & Co., Inc.
EIN: 596194105

810
Winn-Dixie Stores, Inc. Corporate Giving Program
c/o Corp. Contribs.
P.O. Box B
Jacksonville, FL 32203-0297

Grantmaker type: Corporate giving program
Purpose and activities: As a complement to its foundation, Winn-Dixie also makes charitable contributions to nonprofit organizations directly. Support is given primarily in areas of company operations.
Fields of interest: Education; Environment; Health care; Food services; Food banks; Safety/disasters.
Types of support: General/operating support; Employee matching gifts.
Limitations: Giving primarily in areas of company operations.
Application information: Application form not required.
Initial approach: Contact nearest company store for application information
Copies of proposal: 1
Number of staff: 2 full-time professional.

GEORGIA

811
The AEC Trust
c/o Wachovia Bank, N.A.
191 Peachtree St., GA 8023
Atlanta, GA 30303
Contact: Susanna C. Adams
FAX: (404) 332-1389

Established in 1980 in IL.
Donor(s): Members of the Cofrin family.
Grantmaker type: Independent foundation
Financial data (yr. ended 12/31/01): Assets, $33,011,931 (M); expenditures, $1,869,693; qualifying distributions, $1,719,524; giving activities include $1,724,675 for 49 grants (high: $100,000; low: $8,675; average: $10,000–$50,000).
Purpose and activities: Giving primarily for the arts, educational support for pre-selected schools, environment, women's issues, and AIDS related services.
Fields of interest: Museums; Arts; Education; Environment; Women; People with AIDS (PWAs).
Types of support: General/operating support; Capital campaigns; Building/renovation; Equipment; Land acquisition; Debt reduction; Conferences/seminars; Professorships; Publication; Research; Technical assistance; Matching/challenge support.

Limitations: Giving primarily in Boulder, CO, Gainesville, FL, Amherst, MA, Green Bay, WI, and Atlanta, GA; support in Atlanta limited to organizations with offices inside the perimeter. No support for religious organizations, government agencies, affiliates of large public charities, sponsorships, or special events. No grants to individuals or for organizations with budgets over $1 million.
Publications: Application guidelines.
Application information: Proposal must be submitted in a format that can be easily photocopied. Application form not required.
  Initial approach: Letter of inquiry, 2 months. prior to deadline, asking for guidelines and briefly summarizing grantee interest
  Copies of proposal: 1
  Deadline(s): Apr. 1 and Sept. 1
  Board meeting date(s): Spring and fall
  Final notification: On a rolling basis
Advisory Committee: David A. Cofrin, Co-Chair.; Mary Ann H. Cofrin, Co-Chair.; David H. Cofrin; Edith D. Cofrin; Gladys G. Cofrin; Mary Ann P. Cofrin; Paige W. Cofrin.
Corporate Trustee: Wachovia Bank, N.A.
Number of staff: None.
EIN: 366725987

812
The AFC Foundation, Inc.
6 Concourse Pkwy., Ste. 1700
Atlanta, GA   30328   (770) 390-9500
Contact: Frank J. Belatti, Pres.
URL: http://www.afce.com/culture/foundation.html

Established in 1994.
Grantmaker type: Public charity
Financial data (yr. ended 12/31/00): Revenue, $495,941; assets, $66,959; gifts received, $491,183; expenditures, $483,989; program services expenses, $396,300; giving activities include $396,300 for grants.
Purpose and activities: The foundation supports programs that build stronger families and encourages economic development in its communities by promoting projects that support affordable housing, education, youth camps, arts, music, and the environment.
Fields of interest: Arts; Education; Environment; Housing/shelter.
Limitations: Applications not accepted. Giving on a national and international basis.
Officers and Directors:* Frank J. Belatti,* Pres.; Allan J. Tanenbaum,* Secy.; Daniel Bauer,* Treas.; Ellen Hartman; Dick R. Holbrook; Gregg Kaplan; Jon Luther; Hala Moddelmog.
EIN: 582081265

813
AGL Resources Inc. Corporate Giving Program
c/o Community Affairs Dept.
P.O. Box 4569, Location 1601
Atlanta, GA   30302-4569   (404) 584-3791
URL: http://www.aglresources.com/content/company/aglr_ourcom_cominv.html

Grantmaker type: Corporate giving program
Purpose and activities: As a complement to its foundation, AGL Resources also makes charitable contributions to nonprofit

organizations directly. Support is given primarily in areas of company operations.
Fields of interest: Historic preservation/historical societies; Arts; Elementary/secondary education; Higher education; Environment, air pollution; Natural resources; Environment, forests; Environment, beautification programs; Housing/shelter, homeless; Housing/shelter; Transportation; Leadership development; Minorities; Aging; Women; Economically disadvantaged.
Types of support: General/operating support; Employee volunteer services; Employee matching gifts; In-kind gifts.
Limitations: Giving primarily in areas of company operations in AZ, GA, TN, TX, and VA. No support for religious organizations, K-12 private schools, or sports teams. No grants to individuals, or for advertising.
Application information: Support is limited to 1 contribution per organization during any given year. The Community Affairs Department handles giving. Application form not required.
  Initial approach: Proposal to headquarters

814
AGL Resources Private Foundation, Inc.
c/o Wachovia Bank, N.A.
P.O. Box 4569, Location 1601
Atlanta, GA   30302-4569
Contact: Staci Bush, Asst. Secy.

Established in 1998 in GA.
Donor(s): Georgia Gas Co., AGL Foundation, AGL Resources Inc.
Grantmaker type: Company-sponsored foundation
Financial data (yr. ended 12/31/02): Assets, $3,685,182 (M); expenditures, $320,144; qualifying distributions, $989,098; giving activities include $280,000 for 29 grants (high: $37,500; low: $5,000).
Purpose and activities: The purpose of the foundation is to strategically work together with our internal and external stakeholders to positively impact the communities we serve. Giving energy assistance to low income families and senior citizens. Also supports education programs with an emphasis on reading, math, science and the environment.
Fields of interest: Reading; Education; Energy; Environment; Mathematics.
Limitations: Giving primarily in GA, Chattanooga, TN, Houston, TX, and VA. No support for religious organizations, or for private K-12 schools. No grants to individuals.
Application information: Application form not required.
  Initial approach: Proposal
  Copies of proposal: 1
  Board meeting date(s): Feb., May, Aug., and Nov.
Officers: Melanie A. Platt, Chair.; Drew Evans, Treas.; Harriette Watkins, Vice-Chair. and Secy.
Trustee: Wachovia Bank, N.A.
EIN: 582399946

815
Ivan Allen Furniture Co., LLC Corporate Giving Program
730 Peachtree St., Ste. 200
Atlanta, GA   30308
Application address: P.O. Box 1712, Atlanta, GA 30301

Grantmaker type: Corporate giving program
Purpose and activities: Ivan Allen makes charitable contributions to nonprofit organizations involved with arts and culture, the environment, and children. Support is given primarily in areas of company operations.
Fields of interest: Arts; Environment; Children, services.
Types of support: General/operating support.
Limitations: Giving primarily in areas of company operations. No support for religious, political, or fraternal organizations or unions. No grants to individuals.
Application information: Application form not required.
  Initial approach: Proposal to headquarters or nearest company facility
  Copies of proposal: 1
  Deadline(s): None
  Final notification: 3 weeks

816
American Camellia Society Development Fund, Inc.
1 Massee Ln.
Fort Valley, GA   31030-1217
Contact: W.C. Wyatt, Pres.

Established in 1985.
Grantmaker type: Public charity
Financial data (yr. ended 06/30/00): Revenue, $0; assets, $5,073,712; gifts received, $37,132; expenditures, $302,765; program services expenses, $119,101; giving activities include $30,000 for 1 grant.
Purpose and activities: The organization promotes the cultivation of camellias by providing grants to the American Camellia Society.
Fields of interest: Horticulture/garden clubs.
Limitations: Applications not accepted.
Officers and Directors:* W.C. Wyatt,* Pres.; Ann Walton,* Exec. Secy.; Ted Alexander; Leslie "Buddy" Cawthon; Louis Daudt; Robert E. Ehrhart; Annabelle L. Fetterman; Richard Frank; Fred G. Hahn; and 16 additional directors.
EIN: 581585989

817
Anncox Foundation, Inc.
P.O. Box 550307
Atlanta, GA   30355
Contact: Heather Baber

Incorporated in 1960 in GA.
Donor(s): Anne Cox Chambers.
Grantmaker type: Independent foundation
Financial data (yr. ended 12/31/02): Assets, $288,737 (M); gifts received, $785,167; expenditures, $1,710,169; qualifying distributions, $1,682,399; giving activities include $1,685,102 for 90 grants (high: $500,000; low: $125).

Purpose and activities: Giving primarily for museums and education, animal welfare, health, and human services.
Fields of interest: Museums; Education; Animal welfare; Animals/wildlife, preservation/protection; Health organizations, association; Human services; Federated giving programs.
Limitations: Giving primarily in GA, and the greater metropolitan New York, NY, area. No grants to individuals.
Application information:
  Initial approach: Letter
  Deadline(s): None
Officers and Trustee:* Anne Cox Chambers, Pres. and Treas.; James Cox Chambers,* V.P. and Treas.
Number of staff: 6 shared staff.
EIN: 586033966

818
The Arnold Foundation, Inc.
127 Peachtree St. N.E., Ste. 1600
Atlanta, GA 30303-1845

Established in 1999 in GA.
Grantmaker type: Independent foundation
Financial data (yr. ended 09/30/02): Assets, $1,130,932 (M); expenditures, $234,634; qualifying distributions, $218,468; giving activities include $220,625 for 23 grants (high: $53,650; low: $1,500).
Fields of interest: Orchestra (symphony); Botanical gardens; Mental health/crisis services; Health organizations, fund raising; Boys & girls clubs; Protestant agencies & churches.
Limitations: Applications not accepted. Giving primarily in GA. No grants to individuals.
Application information: Contributes only to pre-selected organizations.
Trustees: Clyde F. Anderson; David H. Flint; Drew R. Fuller.
EIN: 582450328

819
Atlanta Dogwood Festival, Inc.
20 Executive Park Dr., No. 2019
Atlanta, GA 30329 (404) 329-0501
Contact: Stephen Ficarra, Pres.
FAX: (404) 329-0509; E-mail: coordinator@dogwood.org; URL: http://www.dogwood.org

Established in 1936 in GA.
Grantmaker type: Public charity
Financial data (yr. ended 06/30/01): Revenue, $817,404; assets, $267,883; gifts received, $347,635; expenditures, $671,900; program services expenses, $544,759; giving activities include $30,050 for 2 grants (high: $30,000; low: $50).
Purpose and activities: The organization supports Camp Sunshine and Magical Garden programs and promotes environmental awareness and education.
Fields of interest: Environmental education.
Limitations: Giving primarily in Atlanta, GA.
Officers and Directors:* Dieter Kretschy,* Chair.; Stephen Ficarra,* Pres.; Diane Lewis,* Secy.; Jim Dahlby; Bill Hammer; Jim Kimbell; Carol King; Stephen LaMastra; Edward

McDonnell; Bruce Meyer; Michael Moore; Denise Paultre; John L. Sands, Jr.; Tracy Tepp.
EIN: 581787081

820
The Bancker-Williams Foundation, Inc.
c/o Beverly Kelly
11 Piedmont Ctr. N.E., Ste. 405
Atlanta, GA 30305-1738

Established in 1989 in GA.
Grantmaker type: Independent foundation
Financial data (yr. ended 06/30/02): Assets, $2,764,796 (M); expenditures, $239,928; qualifying distributions, $239,620; giving activities include $187,000 for 11 grants (high: $38,000; low: $500).
Purpose and activities: Giving to grassroots efforts on an international basis.
Fields of interest: Arts; Natural resources; Environment; Animals/wildlife, preservation/protection; Women, centers/services; Women.
Types of support: Continuing support; Program development; Seed money; Scholarship funds.
Limitations: Applications not accepted. Giving on an international basis. No grants to individuals.
Application information: Contributes only to pre-selected organizations.
Officers and Trustees:* Katharine B. Johnson,* Chair.; Elaine O. Blackmon,* Secy.-Treas.; Belitje B. Bull; Charlotte Holmes; Elizabeth O. Jackson; Dorothy B. Robertson.
EIN: 581868577

821
The Arthur M. Blank Family Foundation ▼
The Forum
3290 Northside Pkwy., N.W., Ste. 600
Atlanta, GA 30327 (404) 239-0600
Contact: Deva Hirsch, V.P.; or Elise Eplan, V.P.
FAX: (404) 442-0991; URL: http://www.blankfoundation.org

Established in 1995 in GA.
Donor(s): Arthur M. Blank.
Grantmaker type: Independent foundation
Financial data (yr. ended 12/31/01): Assets, $2,700,165 (M); gifts received, $381,898; expenditures, $30,348,122; qualifying distributions, $29,383,207; giving activities include $29,105,253 for 362 grants (high: $1,300,000; low: $100; average: $10,000–$50,000).
Purpose and activities: Giving primarily for youth development in the following six program areas: Arts and Culture, Athletics and Fitness, Education Enhancement, Environment (including Outdoor Activities), Fostering Understanding, and Organizational Effectiveness. The foundation supports gender-specific activities formerly highlighted in its Young Women and Girls program area throughout each of these program areas.
Fields of interest: Theater; Education; Youth development, services.
Types of support: General/operating support; Annual campaigns; Capital campaigns; Endowments; Program development; Seed money; Technical assistance.

Limitations: Giving primarily in Maricopa County, AZ, Atlanta, GA, Coastal, SC and New York City. No support for government agencies, municipalities, parochial or private schools, or therapeutic programs. No grants to individuals, or for events.
Publications: Application guidelines, Annual report.
Application information: Beginning in Jan. 2003, the board only considers applications submitted by current or former grant recipients that meet foundation guidelines. Application form required.
  Initial approach: Letter
  Copies of proposal: 2
  Deadline(s): Jan. 6 and Apr. 4
  Board meeting date(s): Apr. and Dec.
  Final notification: 3 to 4 months
Officers and Trustees:* Arthur M. Blank,* Chair.; Elise Eplan, V.P.; Deva Hirsch, V.P.; Danielle Blank; Dena Blank; Kenny Blank; Stephanie Blank.
Number of staff: 12 part-time professional.
EIN: 586292769
Recent environmental and animal welfare grants:
821-1 Alternatives for Community and Environment (ACE), Roxbury, MA, $30,000. 2002.
821-2 Appalachian Mountain Club, Boston, MA, $50,000. 2002.
821-3 Arizona Zoological Society, Phoenix Zoo, Phoenix, AZ, $28,500. 2002.
821-4 Atlanta Botanical Garden, Atlanta, GA, $50,000. 2002.
821-5 Atlanta Outward Bound Center of the North Carolina Outward Bound School, Decatur, GA, $40,000. 2002.
821-6 Atlanta Outward Bound Center of the North Carolina Outward Bound School, Decatur, GA, $10,000. For youth programs. Grant made through Atlanta Falcons Youth Foundation. 2002.
821-7 Bridger Outdoor Science School, Bozeman, MT, $10,000. For grant made through Mountain Sky Guest Ranch Fund. 2002.
821-8 Brooklyn Botanic Garden, Brooklyn, NY, $55,000. 2002.
821-9 Canine Assistants, Alpharetta, GA, $10,000. For youth programs. Grant made through Atlanta Falcons Youth Foundation. 2002.
821-10 Chattahoochee Oconee Forest Interpretive Association, Gainesville, GA, $15,000. 2002.
821-11 Conservation Fund, Tucker, GA, $2,150,000. 2002.
821-12 DeKalb, County of, Decatur, GA, $350,000. For South Peachtree Creek Nature Preserve. 2002.
821-13 Environmental Careers Organization (ECO), Boston, MA, $60,000. 2002.
821-14 Environmental Justice Resource Center, Atlanta, GA, $50,000. 2002.
821-15 Girls Outdoor Adventure for Leadership (GOAL), Atlanta, GA, $60,000. 2002.
821-16 Global Habitat Project, Boston, MA, $30,000. 2002.
821-17 Grant Park Conservancy, Atlanta, GA, $150,000. 2002.
821-18 Horizons for Youth, Sharon, MA, $30,000. 2002.

821-19 Humane Society of Atlanta, Atlanta, GA, $25,000. 2002.

821-20 Hurricane Island Outward Bound School, Rockland, ME, $87,000. 2002.

821-21 Land Trust Alliance, DC, $15,000. 2002.

821-22 Los Angeles Conservation Corps, Los Angeles, CA, $25,000. 2002.

821-23 Lowcountry Open Land Trust, Charleston, SC, $50,000. 2002.

821-24 Montana Conservation Corps, Bozeman, MT, $10,000. For grant made through Mountain Sky Guest Ranch Fund. 2002.

821-25 National Wildlife Federation, Atlanta, GA, $65,000. 2002.

821-26 Natural Step, San Francisco, CA, $21,000. 2002.

821-27 Nature Conservancy, Atlanta, GA, $125,000. 2002.

821-28 New York Botanical Garden, Bronx, NY, $20,000. 2002.

821-29 New York City Outward Bound Center, Long Island City, NY, $90,450. 2002.

821-30 North Carolina Outward Bound School, Asheville, NC, $70,000. 2002.

821-31 Oakhurst Community Garden Project, Decatur, GA, $27,000. 2002.

821-32 Olmstead Linear Park Alliance, Atlanta, GA, $300,000. 2002.

821-33 Outward Bound West, Golden, CO, $63,500. 2002.

821-34 Pacific Crest Outward Bound School, Portland, Oregon, $90,000. 2002.

821-35 Park Pride Atlanta, Atlanta, GA, $50,000. 2002.

821-36 PATH Foundation, Atlanta, GA, $500,000. 2002.

821-37 Peachtree Woodall Whetstone Watershed Alliance, Atlanta, GA, $1,000,000. 2002.

821-38 Piedmont Park Conservancy, Atlanta, GA, $25,000. 2002.

821-39 Rails to Trails Conservancy, DC, $30,000. 2002.

821-40 Rocking the Boat, Bronx, NY, $15,000. 2002.

821-41 South Carolina Aquarium, Charleston, SC, $100,000. 2002.

821-42 South Carolina Coastal Conservation League, Charleston, SC, $50,000. 2002.

821-43 Southern Alliance for Clean Energy, Knoxville, TN, $30,000. 2002.

821-44 Southface Energy Institute, Atlanta, GA, $30,000. 2002.

821-45 Student Conservation Association, Charlestown, NH, $35,000. 2002.

821-46 Thompson Island Outward Bound Education Center, Boston, MA, $90,000. 2002.

821-47 TreePeople, Beverly Hills, CA, $35,000. 2002.

821-48 Trees Atlanta, Atlanta, GA, $50,000. 2002.

821-49 Trust for Public Land, Atlanta, GA, $1,684,364. 2002.

821-50 Trust for Public Land, Atlanta, GA, $25,000. For support for South Carolina Chapter. 2002.

821-51 Upper Chattahoochee Riverkeeper Fund, Atlanta, GA, $20,000. 2002.

821-52 Voyageur Outward Bound School, Minneapolis, MN, $91,780. 2002.

821-53 Wave Hill, Bronx, NY, $25,000. 2002.

821-54 Wonderland Gardens, Decatur, GA, $52,000. 2002.

821-55 Zoo Atlanta, Atlanta, GA, $1,175,000. 2002.

822
The Virginia & Charles Brewer Family Foundation

(formerly The McHenry Foundation)
100 Colony Sq.
1175 Peachtree St., Ste. 400
Atlanta, GA 30361

Established in 1999 in GA.
Donor(s): Charles M. Brewer.
Grantmaker type: Independent foundation
Financial data (yr. ended 06/30/02): Assets, $4,164,053 (M); expenditures, $223,728; qualifying distributions, $195,520; giving activities include $191,825 for 26 grants (high: $20,000; low: $800).
Fields of interest: Ballet; Environment, legal rights; Environment; Animal welfare; Diabetes; Human services; Protestant agencies & churches.
Limitations: Giving primarily in Atlanta, GA; some giving also in VA.
Trustee: Charles M. Brewer.
Distribution Committee: Virginia F. Brewer.
EIN: 586396904

823
Captain Planet Foundation, Inc.

1 CNN Ctr., Ste. 1090
Atlanta, GA 30348-5366 (404) 827-4130
Contact: Sona Chambers
FAX: (404) 588-6279; E-mail:
captain.planet.foundation@turner.com; URL:
http://www.captainplanetfdn.org

Established in 1991 in GA.
Grantmaker type: Independent foundation
Financial data (yr. ended 12/31/01): Assets, $540,825 (M); gifts received, $260,115; expenditures, $307,601; qualifying distributions, $305,455; giving activities include $130,999 for grants.
Purpose and activities: Giving to elementary and secondary education, the environment, and youth services.
Fields of interest: Elementary/secondary education; Environment; Human services; Federated giving programs; General charitable giving.
Types of support: Seed money; Matching/challenge support.
Limitations: Giving on a national basis. No grants to individuals.
Publications: Application guidelines, Corporate giving report, Grants list, Informational brochure.
Application information:
   Initial approach: Proposal
   Deadline(s): None
Officers and Directors:* Barbara Pyle, Chair. and C.E.O.; Roger Mayer,* Pres.; Nick Boxer,* V.P.
EIN: 581959421

824
The Raymond M. Cash Foundation, Inc.

2451 Cumberland Pkwy., Ste. 3513
Atlanta, GA 30339-6136 (404) 799-1122
Contact: Stacie Metcalfe, Tr.
E-mail: rmcfoundation@aol.com

Established in 1996 in GA.
Donor(s): Raymond M. Cash.
Grantmaker type: Independent foundation
Financial data (yr. ended 12/31/02): Assets, $5,771,446 (M); gifts received, $260; expenditures, $303,967; qualifying distributions, $208,512; giving activities include $142,685 for 17 grants (high: $45,000; low: $905).
Purpose and activities: Giving primarily for education, children and social services, community benefit, environmental, and historic preservation.
Fields of interest: Historic preservation/historical societies; Education; Environment; Children, services.
Types of support: Annual campaigns; Fellowships; Research; Matching/challenge support.
Limitations: Giving primarily in GA. No grants to individuals.
Application information: Application form required.
   Board meeting date(s): Quarterly
Trustees: Eric Cash; Raymond M. Cash; Stacie Metcalfe; Rachel Roper; Fredna Woodall.
Number of staff: 5 part-time support.
EIN: 582271522

825
The Coca-Cola Company Contributions Program

1 Coca-Cola Plz.
Atlanta, GA 30313 (404) 676-2121
Contact: Helen Price, Exec. Dir., The Coca-Cola Fdn., Inc.
URL: http://www2.coca-cola.com/citizenship/index.html

Grantmaker type: Corporate giving program
Purpose and activities: As a complement to its foundation, Coca-Cola also makes charitable contributions to nonprofit organizations directly. Special emphasis is directed towards programs designed to address youth issues. Support is given on a national basis.
Fields of interest: Elementary/secondary education; Education; Environment; Youth development; Hispanics/Latinos; Women.
Types of support: General/operating support; Program development; Sponsorships; Employee matching gifts.
Limitations: Giving on a national basis, with emphasis on Atlanta, GA. No support for religious organizations, local chapters of national organizations, or individual schools. No grants to individuals.
Application information: Application form required.
   Initial approach: Contact headquarters for application form
   Deadline(s): None
   Final notification: 4 months

826
Colonial Pipeline Company Contributions Program

c/o Corp. Contribs.
Resurgens Plz., 945 E. Paces Ferry Rd.
Atlanta, GA 30326 (404) 841-2333
URL: http://www.colpipe.com/ab_com.asp

Grantmaker type: Corporate giving program
Purpose and activities: Colonial Pipeline makes charitable contributions to nonprofit organizations involved with the environment. Support is given primarily in areas of company operations.
Fields of interest: Environment.
Types of support: General/operating support.
Limitations: Giving primarily in areas of company operations.
Application information: Application form not required.
Initial approach: Proposal to headquarters
Copies of proposal: 1
Final notification: Following review

827
Community Foundation of Northwest Georgia, Inc.

P.O. Box 942
Dalton, GA 30722-0942 (706) 275-9117
Contact: Shawn Mashburn, Pres.
FAX: (706) 275-9118; E-mail: cfnwg@alltel.net;
URL : http://www.cfnwg.org

Established in 1998 in GA.
Grantmaker type: Community foundation
Financial data (yr. ended 12/31/02): Assets, $8,860,145 (M); gifts received, $948,645; expenditures, $854,214; giving activities include $679,030 for 74 grants (high: $157,633; low: $200; average: $500–$1,500).
Purpose and activities: To enhance the quality of life in the northwest GA region for both present and future generations by promoting philanthropy; building and maintaining permanent endowment funds to be used for the broad charitable needs of the region; serving as a leader in identifying and prioritizing needs in the community; serving as a catalyst in developing effective responses to community issues; encouraging collaboration between organizations and agencies to shape solutions; and serving as a steward of the funds in the endowment. The foundation administers a donor-advised fund.
Fields of interest: Historic preservation/historical societies; Arts; Education; Environment; Animal welfare; Health care; Human services; Children/youth, services; Community development.
Types of support: Program development; Seed money; Matching/challenge support.
Limitations: Giving limited to northwest GA.
Publications: Application guidelines, Annual report, Informational brochure.
Application information: Application form required.
Initial approach: Letter of inquiry
Copies of proposal: 2
Deadline(s): Sept. 30 and Mar. 31
Officers: Norris Little, Chair.; Jim Bethel, Vice-Chair.; John P. Neal III, Secy.; Gordon C. Morehouse, Treas.

Directors: James Brown; Norman D. Burkett, Sr.; Carl L. Griggs; James Jarrett; Mrs. Walter M. Jones; Charles D. Miller; John D. Tice; Larry Winter.
Number of staff: 1 full-time professional; 1 part-time support.
EIN: 582360356

828
Community Foundation of the Chattahoochee Valley

(formerly Chattahoochee Valley Community Foundation, Inc.)
11 10th St.
P.O. Box 1620
Columbus, GA 31902-1620 (706) 320-0027
Contact: Betsy W. Covington, Exec. Dir.
FAX: (706) 320-9331; E-mail bcovington@cfcv.com; URL: http://www.cfcv.com/

Established in 1998 in GA.
Grantmaker type: Community foundation
Financial data (yr. ended 12/31/02): Assets, $9,315,425 (M); gifts received, $2,999,836; expenditures, $2,949,406; giving activities include $2,708,595 for 127 grants (high: $181,396; low: $100).
Fields of interest: Arts; Education; Natural resources; Human services; Children/youth, services; Community development.
Types of support: Program evaluation.
Limitations: Giving limited to the Chattahoochee Valley Region in west central GA and east central AL.
Officers and Trustees:* Alan F. Rothschild, Jr.,* Pres.; Lula Lunsford,* V.P.; Alan Rothschild,* Secy.; D. Raines Jordan,* Treas.; Betsy W. Covington, Exec. Dir.; G. Tyler Talley, Jr.; W. David Varner, Jr.; J. Mike Venable.
Number of staff: 2 full-time professional.
EIN: 582381589

829
Frederick E. Cooper and Helen Dykes Cooper Charitable Foundation, Inc.

170 W. Paces Ferry Rd. N.E.
Atlanta, GA 30305

Established in 1998 in FL.
Donor(s): Frederick E. Cooper, Helen D. Cooper.
Grantmaker type: Independent foundation
Financial data (yr. ended 09/30/02): Assets, $5,897,283 (M); expenditures, $332,978; qualifying distributions, $309,841; giving activities include $313,500 for 41 grants (high: $100,000; low: $250).
Purpose and activities: Giving primarily for educational and environmental purposes and human services.
Fields of interest: Higher education; Natural resources; Animals/wildlife, preservation/protection; Medical research, institute; Disasters, 9/11/01; Human services; American Red Cross; YM/YWCAs & YM/YWHAs; Protestant agencies & churches; Economically disadvantaged.
Limitations: Giving primarily in GA and VA.
Application information:
Initial approach: Proposal
Deadline(s): None

Directors: Beckwith Archer Cooper; Frederick E. Cooper; Frederick E. Cooper, Jr.; Helen D. Cooper; Johnson Joseph Cooper; Bernard Lanigan, Jr.
EIN: 582433546

830
CRJ Foundation, Inc.

44 Wakefield Dr. N.E.
Atlanta, GA 30309

Established in 1997 in GA.
Grantmaker type: Independent foundation
Financial data (yr. ended 12/31/01): Assets, $1,007,089 (M); expenditures, $116,502; qualifying distributions, $80,520; giving activities include $89,595 for 30 grants (high: $20,000; low: $30).
Purpose and activities: Giving for education, environmental and wildlife conservation, and Christian churches and organizations.
Fields of interest: University; Environment; Scholarships/financial aid; Education; Animals/wildlife, preservation/protection; Christian agencies & churches.
Limitations: Applications not accepted. No grants to individuals.
Application information: Contributes only to pre-selected organizations.
Officers: Herron P. Weems, Chair. and Pres.; Cary W. Weems, Secy.-Treas.
EIN: 582313768

831
Foundation for Agronomic Research, Inc.

655 Engineering Dr., Ste. 110
Norcross, GA 30092-2843
Contact: T.L. Roberts, Pres. and Treas.
URL: http://www.ppi-far.org

Established in 1980 in DE.
Donor(s): U.S. Borax Inc., DowElanco, Gold Kist Inc., United Soybean Board.
Grantmaker type: Independent foundation
Financial data (yr. ended 12/31/01): Assets, $1,028,838 (M); gifts received, $834,706; expenditures, $1,090,389; qualifying distributions, $1,133,754; giving activities include $925,992 for 91 grants (high: $68,468; low: $100).
Purpose and activities: Grants primarily to North American universities and research organizations for studies of soil management and improved crop yields.
Fields of interest: Environment, plant conservation; Agriculture.
International interests: Canada.
Types of support: Research.
Limitations: Applications not accepted. Giving primarily in the U.S. and Canada. No support for profit-making organizations. No grants to individuals.
Publications: Annual report.
Application information: Unsolicited requests for funds not accepted.
Board meeting date(s): Oct.
Officers: H. Mathot, Chair.; T.L. Roberts, Pres. and Treas.; H.R. Reetz, Jr., V.P.; H.W. Fogt, Secy.
Directors: C. Adams; D. Addis; S.E. Allred; P.E. Fixen; R. Hoyum; B. Jarrett; K.D. Kunz; R.L. Moore; K. Moshanek; L. Murphy.
Number of staff: None.

EIN: 581406074

832
The Frank Family Foundation, Inc.
920 Crest Valley Dr. N.W.
Atlanta, GA 30327

Established in 1994 in GA.
Donor(s): Larry Frank.
Grantmaker type: Independent foundation
Financial data (yr. ended 12/31/00): Assets,
$2,825,224 (M); expenditures, $102,513;
qualifying distributions, $101,674; giving
activities include $101,674 for 119 grants (high:
$26,200; low: $25).
Purpose and activities: Giving primarily to
Jewish agencies and temples.
Fields of interest: Museums; Arts;
Elementary/secondary education; Higher
education; Education; Environment; Health
organizations, association; Human services;
Jewish agencies & temples.
Limitations: Applications not accepted. No
grants to individuals.
Application information: Contributes only to
pre-selected organizations.
Officers: Larry Frank, Chair.; Lois Frank, Pres.;
Adam Frank, Secy.; M. Joshua Frank, Treas.
Directors: Aaron Frank; Isaac Frank.
EIN: 582082981

833
Fund for Southern Communities
4285 Memorial Dr., Ste. G
Decatur, GA 30032 (404) 292-7600
Contact: Alice Jenkins, Exec. Dir.
FAX: (404) 292-7835; E-mail:
grants@fund4south.org; URL: http://
www.fund4south.org

Established in 1981 in GA.
Grantmaker type: Public charity
Financial data (yr. ended 06/30/01): Revenue,
$1,306,209; assets, $1,418,021 (L); gifts
received, $1,236,312; expenditures,
$1,236,312; program services expenses,
$1,165,762; giving activities include $318,000
for grants.
Purpose and activities: The fund provides
financial support and human resources to
grassroots organizations working for social and
economic justice.
Fields of interest: Environment; Labor
unions/organizations; Youth development; Civil
rights, disabled; Civil rights, women; Civil rights,
gays/lesbians; Civil rights; Community
development.
Types of support: General/operating support;
Program development; Seed money.
Limitations: Giving limited to GA, NC, and SC.
No grants to individuals.
Publications: Application guidelines, Annual
report, Grants list, Newsletter.
Application information: Application must be
typed, single-spaced, and up to 10 pages.
Application form required.
  Initial approach: Letter, telephone, or URL
  Copies of proposal: 13
  Deadline(s): Apr. 1 and Oct. 1
  Board meeting date(s): Jan., Apr., July and Oct.
  Final notification: June 30 and Dec. 31

Officer and Directors:* Lynn Cothren,* Chair.;
Wendy Brinker; Jeff Cheek; Betsy Fenhagen;
Kevin Gray; Harriet Hancock; Beni Ivey; Rabbi
Marc Kline; Kent Matlock; Ajulo Norman;
Naomi Randolph; Loneiyce Washington.
Number of staff: 3 full-time professional.
EIN: 581426028

834
Courtney Knight Gaines Foundation
70 Shipwatch Rd.
Savannah, GA 31410

Established in 1998 in GA.
Donor(s): Courtney Knight Gaines.
Grantmaker type: Independent foundation
Financial data (yr. ended 12/31/02): Assets,
$8,396,396 (M); expenditures, $589,296;
qualifying distributions, $550,971; giving
activities include $519,350 for 47 grants (high:
$100,000; low: $1,000).
Purpose and activities: Giving primarily for
education, conservation and wildlife, and health
and human services.
Fields of interest: Arts; Education; Natural
resources; Animals/wildlife,
preservation/protection; Health organizations,
association; Human services; Religion.
Limitations: Applications not accepted. Giving
primarily in GA. No grants to individuals.
Application information: Contributes only to
pre-selected organizations.
Officers: Courtney Knight Gaines, Pres.;
Christopher E. Klein, Secy.
Directors: Courtney Gaines Fetz; Ezekiel
Baldwin Gaines III; Grace Gaines Gattis.
EIN: 582398209

835
Georgia Power Company Contributions Program
241 Ralph McGill Blvd. N.E., Bin 10131
Atlanta, GA 30308-3374 (404) 506-6784
Contact: Susan Carter, Mgr., Charitable Giving
FAX: (404) 506-1485

Grantmaker type: Corporate giving program
Financial data (yr. ended 12/31/02): Total giving,
$3,446,180; giving activities include
$2,712,920 for 702 grants (high: $1,081,037;
low: $20), $138,735 for 364 employee
matching gifts and $594,525 for 12 in-kind gifts.
Purpose and activities: As a complement to its
foundation, Georgia Power also makes
charitable contributions to nonprofit
organizations directly. Support is given primarily
in Georgia.
Fields of interest: Arts; Education; Environment;
Employment, services; Human services; Civil
rights, equal rights; Minorities.
Types of support: General/operating support;
Capital campaigns; Program development;
Conferences/seminars; Scholarship funds;
Employee volunteer services; Loaned talent; Use
of facilities; Sponsorships; Employee matching
gifts; Donated equipment; Donated land.
Limitations: Giving primarily in GA. No support
for religious organizations or private schools.
No grants to individuals, or for continuing
support.

Publications: Application guidelines,
Informational brochure (including application
guidelines).
Application information: The Charitable Giving
Department handles giving. The company has a
staff that only handles contributions. A
contributions committee reviews all requests of
over $10,000. Application form not required.
  Initial approach: Proposal to nearest company
  facility
  Copies of proposal: 1
  Deadline(s): None
  Board meeting date(s): Mar., June, Sept., and
  Dec.
  Final notification: Following review
Administrators: Donna Goodman, Grant
Admin.; Nancy Landers, Prog. Admin.
Number of staff: 5 part-time professional; 4
part-time support.

836
Georgia Power Foundation, Inc. ▼
241 Ralph McGill Blvd., N.E., Bin 10131
Atlanta, GA 30308-3374 (404) 506-6784
Contact: Susan Carter, Exec. Dir.
FAX: (404) 506-1485; E-mail:
gpfoundation@southernco.com

Established in 1986 in GA.
Donor(s): Georgia Power Co.
Grantmaker type: Company-sponsored
foundation
Financial data (yr. ended 12/31/02): Assets,
$86,819,383 (M); expenditures, $7,366,273;
qualifying distributions, $6,744,127; giving
activities include $6,371,651 for 366 grants
(high: $1,546,500; low: $150; average:
$150–$1,546,500).
Purpose and activities: Support for education in
Georgia as it relates to workforce recruitment,
health and human services organizations
through the United Way and Salvation Army;
cancer prevention; environmental protection;
and diversity initiatives.
Fields of interest: Education; Environment;
Health care; Cancer; Human services.
Types of support: General/operating support;
Continuing support; Annual campaigns; Capital
campaigns; Building/renovation; Equipment;
Debt reduction; Program development;
Conferences/seminars; Curriculum
development; Scholarship funds; Employee
matching gifts.
Limitations: Giving primarily in GA. No support
for private foundations, religious organizations,
private secondary schools and non-public
charities. No grants to individuals (except for
employee-related scholarships); or multi-year
commitments.
Publications: Informational brochure (including
application guidelines).
Application information: Application form not
required.
  Initial approach: Letter with proposal
  Copies of proposal: 1
  Deadline(s): 2 weeks prior to board meeting
  Board meeting date(s): Mar., June, Sept., and
  Dec.
  Final notification: After board review
Officers and Directors:* Judy M. Anderson,*
C.E.O. and Pres.; Susan Carter, Secy. and Exec.
Dir.; Roger Steffens, Treas.; William C. Archer III;
Ronnie Bates; Mickey Brown; James K. Davis;

O. Ben Harris; Allen Leverett; Christopher Womack.
Number of staff: None.
EIN: 581709417
Recent environmental and animal welfare grants:
836-1 American Association of Blacks in Energy, Atlanta Chapter, Atlanta, GA, $15,000. For project support. 2002.
836-2 Atlanta Botanical Garden, Atlanta, GA, $25,000. For operating support. 2002.
836-3 Chattahoochee Nature Center, Roswell, GA, $15,000. For operating support. 2002.
836-4 Conservation Fund, Arlington, VA, $25,000. For project support. 2002.
836-5 Georgia Conservancy, Atlanta, GA, $25,000. For capital support. 2002.
836-6 Georgia Conservancy, Atlanta, GA, $25,000. For operating support. 2002.
836-7 Georgia Department of Natural Resources, Division of Wildlife Resources, Atlanta, GA, $50,000. For project support. 2002.
836-8 Georgia Wildlife Federation, Conyers, GA, $25,000. For project support. 2002.
836-9 Keep Georgia Beautiful Foundation, Atlanta, GA, $10,000. For project support for collaboration with Georgia Department of Community Affairs. 2002.
836-10 Nature Conservancy, Atlanta, GA, $200,000. For operating support. 2002.
836-11 Nature Conservancy, Atlanta, GA, $50,000. For project support. 2002.
836-12 Piedmont Park Conservancy, Atlanta, GA, $10,000. For operating support. 2002.
836-13 Piedmont Park Conservancy, Atlanta, GA, $10,000. For project support. 2002.
836-14 Trees Atlanta, Atlanta, GA, $10,000. For project support. 2002.
836-15 Trust for Public Land, Atlanta, GA, $25,000. For operating support. 2002.
836-16 Zoo Atlanta, Atlanta, GA, $50,000. For project support. 2002.
836-17 Zoo Atlanta, Atlanta, GA, $25,000. For project support. 2002.
836-18 Zoo Atlanta, Atlanta, GA, $10,000. For operating support. 2002.

837
Georgia-Pacific Foundation, Inc. ▼
133 Peachtree St., N.E.
Atlanta, GA 30303 (404) 652-4000
Contact: C.M. Dossman, Jr., Pres.
URL: http://www.gp.com/center/community/index.html

Incorporated in 1958 in OR.
Donor(s): Georgia-Pacific Corp., and subsidiaries.
Grantmaker type: Company-sponsored foundation
Financial data (yr. ended 12/31/01): Assets, $899,640 (M); gifts received, $3,755,000; expenditures, $4,908,479; qualifying distributions, $4,908,479; giving activities include $4,731,198 for 637 grants (high: $388,043; low: $15; average: $1,000–$50,000) and $138,000 for 68 grants to individuals.
Purpose and activities: Giving for higher and other education, including employee-related scholarships to graduating seniors in areas of major company operations; support also for

community funds, hospitals and health services, and social services and youth agencies.
Fields of interest: Higher education; Education; Hospitals (general); Health care; Human services; Youth, services; Federated giving programs.
Types of support: General/operating support; Continuing support; Annual campaigns; Capital campaigns; Building/renovation; Program development; Conferences/seminars; Internship funds; Scholarship funds; Employee matching gifts; Employee-related scholarships; Scholarships—to individuals; In-kind gifts.
Limitations: Giving limited to areas of company operations. No support for churches or religious denominations, theological schools, social, labor, veterans', alumni or fraternal organizations, athletic associations and sporting events, medical and nursing schools or social sciences or health science programs. No grants to individuals (except for scholarships and community service programs), or for bail out funds, goodwill advertising, general operating support for United Way, purchase of tickets/tables for testimonials or similar benefit events, named academic chairs, fundraising events, or trips or tours.
Publications: Application guidelines, Biennial report, Corporate giving report.
Application information: Application form not required.
  Copies of proposal: 1
  Deadline(s): None
  Board meeting date(s): As required
  Final notification: 45 to 60 days
Officers and Trustees:* James Bostic, Jr.,* Chair.; C.M. Dossman, Jr., Pres.; Kenneth F. Khoury, Secy.; Phillip M. Johnson, Treas.; Kimberly Dyslin Roundtree.
Number of staff: 5 full-time professional; 1 full-time support.
EIN: 936023726
Recent environmental and animal welfare grants:
837-1 American Forest Foundation, DC, $25,000. 2001.
837-2 American Forest Foundation, DC, $10,000. 2001.
837-3 Atlanta Botanical Garden, Atlanta, GA, $20,000. 2001.
837-4 Chattahoochee Nature Center, Roswell, GA, $20,000. 2001.
837-5 Environmental Law Institute, DC, $10,000. 2001.
837-6 Friends of South Slough Reserve, Charleston, Oregon, $10,000. 2001.
837-7 Georgia Conservancy, Atlanta, GA, $25,000. 2001.
837-8 Georgia Environmental Organization, Atlanta, GA, $25,000. 2001.
837-9 Hardman Farm at Nacoochee Valley, Gainesville, GA, $16,666. 2001.
837-10 Keystone Center, Keystone Science School, Keystone, CO, $40,500. 2001.
837-11 Lake Superior Center for Freshwater Understanding, Duluth, MN, $15,000. 2001.
837-12 Mickey Leland National Urban Air Toxics Research Center, Houston, TX, $20,000. 2001.
837-13 Nature Conservancy, Arlington, VA, $10,000. 2001.
837-14 Nature Conservancy, Arlington, VA, $10,000. 2001.

837-15 Piedmont Park Conservancy, Atlanta, GA, $25,000. 2001.
837-16 Piedmont Park Conservancy, Atlanta, GA, $25,000. 2001.
837-17 Resources for the Future, DC, $30,000. 2001.
837-18 Resources for the Future, DC, $10,000. 2001.
837-19 Southeastern Flower Show, Atlanta, GA, $10,000. 2001.
837-20 Trust for Public Land, Atlanta, GA, $25,000. 2001.
837-21 Zoo Atlanta, Atlanta, GA, $20,000. 2001.
837-22 Zoo Atlanta, Atlanta, GA, $12,000. 2001.

838
Lenora and Alfred Glancy Foundation, Inc.
c/o Alston & Bird
1201 W. Peachtree St.
Atlanta, GA 30309-3424 (404) 881-7488
Contact: Benjamin T. White

Established in 1994 in GA.
Grantmaker type: Independent foundation
Financial data (yr. ended 12/31/02): Assets, $1,461,918 (M); expenditures, $133,156; qualifying distributions, $119,537; giving activities include $108,958 for 8 grants (high: $46,458; low: $2,500).
Fields of interest: Arts; Education; Environment; Hospitals (general); Medical care, rehabilitation; Children/youth, services; Residential/custodial care; Christian agencies & churches.
Limitations: Giving primarily in GA. No grants to individuals.
Application information:
  Initial approach: Letter
  Deadline(s): None
Officer: Christopher I. Brandon, Chair. and Secy.-Treas.
EIN: 582115479

839
The John N. Goddard Foundation, Inc.
1201 W. Peachtree St., Ste. 4200
Atlanta, GA 30309

Established in 1997 in GA.
Donor(s): Mrs. Elkin G. Alston.
Grantmaker type: Independent foundation
Financial data (yr. ended 12/31/02): Assets, $3,184,458 (M); expenditures, $284,897; qualifying distributions, $232,527; giving activities include $200,000 for 9 grants (high: $100,000; low: $4,000).
Fields of interest: Natural resources; Botanical gardens.
Limitations: Applications not accepted. Giving primarily in Atlanta, GA. No grants to individuals.
Application information: Contributes only to pre-selected organizations.
Officers and Trustees:* Elkin G. Alston,* Chair.; John G. Alston,* Vice-Chair.; Elkin A. Cushman,* Vice-Chair.; B. Harvey Hill, Jr.,* Secy.-Treas.; James E. Cushman, Jr.
EIN: 582314424

840
The Hack Foundation, Inc.
4220 Dykes Dr. N.W.
Atlanta, GA 30342
Contact: Avary H. Doubleday, Secy.-Treas.

Established in 1988 in GA.
Donor(s): Avary Hack Doubleday, Gerry Doubleday, Billie S. Hack,‡ Carolyn W. Hack, Debby Hack, Frederick C. Hack, Jr., O. Byron Hack.
Grantmaker type: Independent foundation
Financial data (yr. ended 12/31/02): Assets, $1,619,044 (M); expenditures, $144,514; qualifying distributions, $142,829; giving activities include $140,000 for 7 grants (high: $100,000; low: $2,000).
Purpose and activities: Giving for arts and culture, theological schools, education, environment, youth services, and health sciences.
Fields of interest: Arts; Education; Environment; Health care; Children/youth, services; Religion; General charitable giving.
Limitations: Giving primarily in GA and SC. No grants to individuals.
Application information:
  Initial approach: Letter, including descriptive or financial information
  Deadline(s): None
Officers and Directors:* Frederick C. Hack, Jr.,* Pres.; Avary Hack Doubleday,* Secy.-Treas.; E. Gerry Doubleday; Carolyn W. Hack; Deborah S. Hack; O. Byron Hack.
EIN: 581802331

841
Hardaway Foundation, Inc.
P.O. Box 1360
Columbus, GA 31902-1360 (706) 322-3274
Contact: Fred J. Dodelin, Secy.

Established in 1966.
Grantmaker type: Independent foundation
Financial data (yr. ended 12/31/02): Assets, $1,680,251 (M); expenditures, $111,160; qualifying distributions, $97,617; giving activities include $94,295 for 23 grants (high: $15,000; low: $100) and $4,020 for 10 grants to individuals (high: $520; low: $250).
Purpose and activities: Support for historic preservation, the arts, wildlife conservation, and community development; scholarships limited to graduates of Hardaway High School.
Fields of interest: Historic preservation/historical societies; Arts; Education; Natural resources; Animals/wildlife, preservation/protection; Children/youth, services; Human services; Federated giving programs.
Types of support: General/operating support; Scholarships—to individuals.
Limitations: Giving primarily in GA.
Application information: Application form required.
  Deadline(s): Aug. 31
Officers: B.H. Hardaway III, Chair.; Mason H. Lampton, Vice-Chair.; Fred J. Dodelin, Secy.
EIN: 586033161

842
The Home Depot, Inc. Corporate Giving Program
2455 Paces Ferry Rd.
Atlanta, GA 30339-4089
Tel.: (770) 433-8211, ext. 82688

Grantmaker type: Corporate giving program
Financial data (yr. ended 12/31/00): Total giving, $18,000,000; giving activities include $18,000,000 for grants.
Purpose and activities: As a complement to its foundation, the Home Depot also makes charitable contributions to nonprofit organizations directly. Support is given on a national and international basis.
Fields of interest: Environment; Housing/shelter; Safety/disasters; Youth development.
Types of support: General/operating support; Employee volunteer services; Employee matching gifts; In-kind gifts.
Limitations: Giving on an international basis in areas of store operations. No support for religious, fraternal, political, labor, athletic, social, or veterans' organizations. No grants to individuals, or for fundraising, dinners, exhibits, conferences, sports events, advertising, or continuing support.
Publications: Application guidelines, Corporate giving report.
Application information: Application form not required.
  Initial approach: Proposal to headquarters
  Copies of proposal: 1
  Deadline(s): Jan. 1 and Mar. 15 for environmental organizations
  Final notification: 4 to 6 weeks
Number of staff: 2 full-time professional; 3 full-time support.

843
Hudgens Family Foundation, Inc.
3870 Pleasant Hill Rd., Ste. A
Duluth, GA 30096-0988

Established in 1989 in GA.
Donor(s): D. Scott Hudgens, Jr.
Grantmaker type: Independent foundation
Financial data (yr. ended 09/30/01): Assets, $6,254,467 (M); expenditures, $1,903,377; qualifying distributions, $1,893,406; giving activities include $1,897,013 for 4 grants (high: $1,097,728; low: $30,000).
Purpose and activities: Giving primarily for arts and cultural programs, the environment, federated giving programs, education, and medical research.
Fields of interest: Arts; Elementary/secondary education; Botanical gardens; Medical research, institute; Community development, business promotion; Federated giving programs; Government/public administration.
Limitations: Applications not accepted. Giving limited to GA. No grants to individuals.
Application information: Contributes only to pre-selected organizations.
Officers and Directors:* Jacqueline C. Hudgens,* V.P. and Secy.-Treas.; Marcia H. Duggan,* V.P.; Dallas S. Hudgens III,* V.P.; Mark R. Hudgens,* V.P.; Michael S. Hudgens,* V.P.
EIN: 581852073

844
The Norman & Emmy Lou Illges Foundation
P.O. Box 23024
Columbus, GA 31902

Established in 1998 in GA.
Donor(s): Emmy Lou Illges.‡
Grantmaker type: Independent foundation
Financial data (yr. ended 12/31/02): Assets, $3,983,130 (M); expenditures, $226,715; qualifying distributions, $189,441; giving activities include $191,000 for 12 grants (high: $35,000; low: $1,000).
Fields of interest: Animals/wildlife, preservation/protection; Federated giving programs.
Types of support: General/operating support.
Limitations: Applications not accepted. Giving primarily in Colombus, GA. No grants to individuals.
Application information: Contributes only to pre-selected organizations.
Trustees: Shannon I. Candler; Judith I. Harding; Susan I. Lanier; Synovus Trust Co.
EIN: 586368426

845
Interface, Inc. Corporate Giving Program
2859 Paces Ferry Rd., Ste. 2000
Atlanta, GA 30339

Grantmaker type: Corporate giving program
Purpose and activities: Interface makes charitable contributions to nonprofit organizations involved with the environment. Support is given on a national basis.
Fields of interest: Environment.
Types of support: General/operating support.
Limitations: Giving on a national basis.

846
JBS Foundation
(formerly Jocelyn Botterell Staton Foundation)
c/o SunTrust Banks, Inc.
P.O. Box 4655
Atlanta, GA 30302-4655 (404) 230-5479
Contact: Dale Welch

Established in 1995 in GA.
Grantmaker type: Independent foundation
Financial data (yr. ended 12/31/02): Assets, $5,328,817 (M); expenditures, $346,724; qualifying distributions, $329,402; giving activities include $314,500 for 16 grants (high: $75,000; low: $2,000).
Fields of interest: Arts; Education; Botanical gardens; Spine disorders; Youth development, scouting agencies (general); Human services; Federated giving programs.
Limitations: Giving primarily in GA, with emphasis on Atlanta. No grants to individuals.
Application information:
  Initial approach: Letter
  Deadline(s): None
  Board meeting date(s): Dec.
Committee Members: Louise Staton Gunn; John C. Staton, Jr.; Margaret A. Staton; Mary Staton.
Trustee: SunTrust Banks, Inc.
EIN: 586301523

847
Lacy Foundation, Inc.
6151 Powers Ferry Rd., Ste. 520
Atlanta, GA 30339
Contact: Lynda Ramseur, Treas.

Established around 1957.
Donor(s): David Lacy, Sr., B.F. Lacy.‡
Grantmaker type: Independent foundation
Financial data (yr. ended 10/31/02): Assets,
$1,788,711 (M); expenditures, $118,052;
qualifying distributions, $115,350; giving
activities include $115,500 for 7 grants (high:
$40,000; low: $500).
Purpose and activities: Giving for secondary
education, health and medical services, and
human services.
Fields of interest: Education; Animals/wildlife;
Hospitals (general); Health organizations,
association; Human services; Protestant
agencies & churches.
Limitations: Applications not accepted. Giving
primarily in Atlanta, GA. No grants to
individuals.
Application information: Contributes only to
pre-selected organizations.
Officers: David M. Lacy, Chair.; Douglas Lacy,
Vice-Chair.; William Linkous, Secy.; Lynda
Ramseur, Treas.
EIN: 586034851

848
Mills B. Lane Memorial Foundation, Inc.
c/o Bank of America
P.O. Box 9626
Savannah, GA 31412

Incorporated in 1947 in GA.
Donor(s): Members of the Lane family.
Grantmaker type: Independent foundation
Financial data (yr. ended 12/31/02): Assets,
$5,638,396 (M); expenditures, $426,397;
qualifying distributions, $405,094; giving
activities include $405,784 for 22 grants (high:
$45,000; low: $1,000).
Purpose and activities: Giving primarily for
higher education and conservation.
Fields of interest: Higher education; Education;
Environment; Animals/wildlife,
preservation/protection; Federated giving
programs.
Types of support: Building/renovation;
Equipment; Land acquisition; Endowments;
Professorships; Seed money; Fellowships;
Internship funds; Scholarship funds; Exchange
programs; Matching/challenge support.
Limitations: Giving primarily in the Savannah,
GA, area. No grants to individuals, or for
operating budgets; no loans.
Publications: Application guidelines.
Application information: Application form not
required.
Copies of proposal: 1
Deadline(s): None
Board meeting date(s): Spring and fall
Final notification: 2 weeks after board
meetings
Officers: Hugh C. Lane, Jr., Pres.; Mills Lane
Morrison, Secy.
Trustee: Charles G. Lane.
Number of staff: None.
EIN: 586033043

849
The Sartain Lanier Family Foundation, Inc.
(formerly Oxford Foundation, Inc.)
25 Puritan Mill, 950 Lowery Blvd.
Atlanta, GA 30318 (404) 564-1259
Contact: Mark B. Riley, Dir.
FAX: (404) 564-1251; E-mail:
info@lanierfamilyfoundation.org; URL: http://
www.lanierfamilyfoundation.org

Established in 1963 in GA.
Donor(s): Sartain Lanier.‡
Grantmaker type: Independent foundation
Financial data (yr. ended 12/31/01): Assets,
$62,172,193 (M); gifts received, $2,146,452;
expenditures, $2,745,602; qualifying
distributions, $3,121,129; giving activities
include $2,176,029 for 96 grants (high:
$343,333; low: $90; average:
$10,000–$50,000).
Purpose and activities: The foundation targets its
grants to the following areas with priority in the
order listed. Special consideration is given to
institutions that were supported by Mr. Lanier
during his lifetime. The target areas are: 1)
education, 2) health and human services, 3) arts
and 4) environment and community
development.
Fields of interest: Arts; Elementary/secondary
education; Education; Environment; Health care;
Human services; Community development.
Types of support: General/operating support;
Capital campaigns; Building/renovation;
Endowments; Program development;
Program-related investments/loans.
Limitations: Giving primarily in the southeastern
U.S., with primary emphasis on Atlanta, GA. No
support for churches or religious organizations
(for projects that primarily benefit their own
members). No grants to individuals; political
purposes, tickets to charitable events or dinners,
or to sponsor special events or fundraisers.
Publications: Application guidelines.
Application information: Application form not
required.
Initial approach: Letter (2 pages)
Deadline(s): Apr. 1 and Oct. 1
Board meeting date(s): May and Nov.
Director: Mark B. Riley.
Officers and Trustees:* J. Hicks Lanier,* Chair.;
Vance W. Lanier,* Vice-Chair.; George H.
Lanier,* Secy.-Treas.; Cecil D. Conlee; John B.
Ellis; Wilton D. Looney.
Number of staff: 1 part-time professional; 1
part-time support.
EIN: 586045056

850
The Martha and Wilton Looney Foundation, Inc.
4470 Sentinel Post Rd., NW
Atlanta, GA 30327 (404) 760-0246
Contact: Bruce L. Dick, Secy.-Treas.

Established in 1992 in GA.
Donor(s): Wilton D. Looney, Martha W. Looney.
Grantmaker type: Independent foundation
Financial data (yr. ended 12/31/02): Assets,
$3,973,523 (M); gifts received, $53,210;
expenditures, $203,236; qualifying distributions,
$200,075; giving activities include $199,654 for
34 grants (high: $25,000; low: $1,000).

Fields of interest: Education; Animal welfare;
Health care; Health organizations, association;
Human services; Protestant agencies & churches.
Limitations: Giving primarily in GA. No grants
to individuals.
Application information: Application form not
required.
Initial approach: Letter
Deadline(s): None
Officers: Sylvia L. Dick, Chair.; Wilton D.
Looney, Vice-Chair; Bruce L. Dick, Secy.-Treas.
Trustee: Martha W. Looney.
EIN: 582022885

851
Mattie H. Marshall Foundation Trust
(formerly Mattie H. Marshall Foundation)
c/o SunTrust Banks, Inc.
P.O. Box 4655, MC 221
Atlanta, GA 30302-4655
Contact: Danah Craft

Established in 1963 in GA.
Grantmaker type: Independent foundation
Financial data (yr. ended 12/31/02): Assets,
$6,175,080 (M); gifts received, $300,000;
expenditures, $474,003; qualifying distributions,
$446,736; giving activities include $422,000 for
22 grants (high: $100,000; low: $1,000).
Purpose and activities: Support to orphans,
hospitals, nursing for the aged, and Methodist
churches, organizations and retired ministers.
Fields of interest: Higher education; Animal
welfare; Hospitals (general); Aging,
centers/services; Protestant agencies & churches;
Aging.
Types of support: General/operating support;
Annual campaigns; Capital campaigns;
Building/renovation; Endowments; Program
development.
Limitations: Giving limited to GA, with
emphasis on Americus and southern GA. No
grants to individuals.
Publications: Application guidelines.
Application information: Application form not
required.
Initial approach: Application form
Copies of proposal: 1
Deadline(s): Nov. 15
Board meeting date(s): Dec.
Final notification: Dec. 31
Officer: Hon. Thomas O. Marshall, Chair. and
Secy.
Director: Martha M. Dykes.
Trustee: SunTrust Banks, Inc.
Number of staff: None.
EIN: 586042019

852
McAliley Endowment Fund
c/o SunTrust Banks, Inc.
P.O. Box 4655, MC 221
Atlanta, GA 30302-4655
Contact: Mark Drake, Tr. Off.

Established around 1948.
Donor(s): Louise B. Cramer.
Grantmaker type: Independent foundation
Financial data (yr. ended 12/31/02): Assets,
$1,232,070 (M); expenditures, $162,822;
qualifying distributions, $156,676; giving

activities include $151,000 for 85 grants (high: $5,000; low: $500).

Purpose and activities: Awards grants for pediatric medicine, schools, and other children-oriented concerns.

Fields of interest: Arts; Child development, education; Education; Environment, beautification programs; Pediatrics; Human services; Children, services; Federated giving programs; Christian agencies & churches.

Limitations: Giving primarily in Atlanta, GA. No loans or program-related investments.

Application information: Application form not required.

Initial approach: Letter
Copies of proposal: 1
Deadline(s): None

Trustees: Margaret R. Foreman; Rawson Foreman.

EIN: 237093919

853

McCamish Foundation
1 Buckhead Plz.
3060 Peachtree Rd., 19th Fl.
Atlanta, GA 30305-2228 (404) 261-4418
Contact: Roy M. Jones, Pres.

Established in 1988 in GA.

Donor(s): Henry F. McCamish, Jr.

Grantmaker type: Independent foundation

Financial data (yr. ended 12/31/02): Assets, $2,166,534 (M); expenditures, $1,779,843; qualifying distributions, $1,775,415; giving activities include $1,775,873 for 26 grants (high: $651,000; low: $500).

Purpose and activities: Giving for a wildlife preservation and other conservation associations and Christian based seed ministries; support also for a performing arts group and other cultural programs, international affairs, and educational associations; minor support for social services and health, especially specific disease associations.

Fields of interest: Performing arts; Arts; Education, association; Natural resources; Animals/wildlife, preservation/protection; Human services; Christian agencies & churches.

Types of support: Land acquisition; Program development; Seed money.

Limitations: Giving primarily in Atlanta and Fulton County, GA. No grants to individuals.

Publications: Application guidelines.

Application information: Application form not required.

Initial approach: Informal application
Deadline(s): None
Board meeting date(s): Twice a year

Officers and Directors:* Henry F. McCamish, Jr.,* Chair., and Treas.; Roy M. Jones, Pres.; J. Gordon Beckham, Jr.,* V.P.; H. Stephen Merlin,* Secy.; Michael Youssef.

Number of staff: 9 full-time professional.

EIN: 581808980

854

The Devereaux F. and Dorothy McClatchey Foundation, Inc.
c/o Bank South, N.A.
66 Avery Dr. N.E.
Atlanta, GA 30309-2702
Contact: J. Harvey Saunders, V.P.
Application address: 733 Liberty Hill Rd., LaGrange, GA 30240

Established in 1990 in GA.

Donor(s): Devereaux F. McClatchey, Dorothy M. McClatchey.

Grantmaker type: Independent foundation

Financial data (yr. ended 12/31/01): Assets, $3,590,105 (M); expenditures, $147,251; qualifying distributions, $125,686; giving activities include $116,006 for 44 grants (high: $84,000; low: $15).

Fields of interest: Museums (history); College (community/junior); Environment; Federated giving programs.

Types of support: General/operating support; Scholarship funds; Research.

Limitations: Giving primarily in Atlanta, GA. No grants to individuals directly.

Application information: Grants paid to organizations supporting individual applicant's research.

Initial approach: Proposal
Deadline(s): None

Officers: Dorothy M. McClatchey, Pres.; J. Harvey Saunders, V.P.; Robert B. Rountree, Secy.-Treas.

Trustees: Eileen Rhea Brown; Jane P. Harmon; Devereaux F. McClatchey IV; Eve McClatchey Saunders.

EIN: 586250115

855

McKibbon Brothers Foundation, Inc.
P.O. Box 1018
Gainesville, GA 30503

Established in 1989 in GA.

Donor(s): McKibbon Brothers, Inc.

Grantmaker type: Independent foundation

Financial data (yr. ended 06/30/02): Assets, $12,023 (M); gifts received, $185,000; expenditures, $215,821; qualifying distributions, $215,821; giving activities include $207,338 for 47 grants (high: $45,000; low: $100).

Purpose and activities: Giving to federated giving programs, the arts, education, and Protestant organizations.

Fields of interest: Higher education; Animal welfare; Human services; Federated giving programs; Protestant agencies & churches.

Types of support: Scholarship funds.

Limitations: Applications not accepted. Giving primarily in GA, and to a lesser extent, giving also in AL, FL, and TN. No grants to individuals.

Application information: Contributes only to pre-selected organizations.

Officers and Directors:* Richard M. Harris,* Pres.; John B. McKibbon III,* V.P.; Steve P. McKibbon,* Secy.-Treas.; Joseph M. McRae; Woodrow Stewart.

EIN: 581858973

856

The Jane and Randy Merrill Foundation, Inc.
4246 Sentinel Post Rd.
Atlanta, GA 30327 (404) 816-1145
Contact: T. Randolph Merrill, Chair.

Established in 1992 in GA.

Grantmaker type: Independent foundation

Financial data (yr. ended 12/31/02): Assets, $1,064,646 (M); gifts received, $3,856; expenditures, $124,169; qualifying distributions, $95,039; giving activities include $91,700 for 66 grants (high: $20,000; low: $10).

Fields of interest: Museums (art); Education; Botanical gardens; Health organizations, association; Human services; Federated giving programs; Christian agencies & churches.

Limitations: Applications not accepted. Giving limited to the Atlanta, GA, area. No grants to individuals.

Application information: Unsolicited requests for funds not accepted.

Officers and Trustees:* T. Randolph Merrill,* Chair.; Michelle Christy Merrill,* Vice-Chair.; Jane Ann Merrill,* Secy.-Treas.

EIN: 581999764

857

Money-Arenz Foundation, Inc.
c/o Wachovia Bank
191 Peachtree St., 24th Fl.
Atlanta, GA 30303 (706) 571-6594
Contact: Lydia Clements Whitman, Advisor

Established in 1993 in GA.

Grantmaker type: Independent foundation

Financial data (yr. ended 12/31/02): Assets, $967,646 (M); gifts received, $426,406; expenditures, $464,366; qualifying distributions, $443,709; giving activities include $431,500 for 82 grants (high: $47,000; low: $300).

Purpose and activities: Giving primarily for environmental and wildlife conservation.

Fields of interest: Elementary/secondary education; Higher education; Environment, research; Natural resources; Animal welfare; Human services; Children/youth, services.

Limitations: Applications not accepted. Giving on a national basis. No grants to individuals.

Application information: Contributes only to pre-selected organizations. Unsolicited requests for funds not accepted.

Officers: Betty M. Arenz, Pres.; Ronnie L. Bridges, Secy.

EIN: 582049998

858

The Montgomery Foundation, Inc.
3568 Cloudland Dr. N.W.
Atlanta, GA 30327-2906
Contact: George A. Montgomery, Pres.

Established in 1987.

Grantmaker type: Independent foundation

Financial data (yr. ended 12/31/00): Assets, $8,334,362 (M); expenditures, $521,673; qualifying distributions, $511,996; giving activities include $495,000 for 35 grants (high: $50,000; low: $5,000).

Purpose and activities: Funding primarily for education, conservation and historic

preservation. Some funding also for arts and culture.
Fields of interest: Performing arts; Historic preservation/historical societies; Elementary/secondary education; Natural resources; Christian agencies & churches.
Limitations: Applications not accepted. Giving primarily in GA. No grants to individuals.
Application information: Contributes only to pre-selected organizations.
Officers: George A. Montgomery, Pres.; Nancy T. Montgomery, V.P.
EIN: 581741652

859
Morgens West Foundation
3562 Knollwood Dr.
Atlanta, GA 30305-1022

Established around 1968.
Donor(s): Morgens West Charitable Lead Annuity Trust.
Grantmaker type: Independent foundation
Financial data (yr. ended 12/31/02): Assets, $5,228,034 (M); gifts received, $241,090; expenditures, $512,505; qualifying distributions, $448,382; giving activities include $416,200 for 16 grants (high: $96,200; low: $2,000).
Fields of interest: Museums; Higher education; Natural resources; Environment, land resources; Human services; Federated giving programs; Protestant agencies & churches.
Limitations: Applications not accepted. Giving primarily in Atlanta, GA. No grants to individuals.
Application information: Contributes only to pre-selected organizations.
Trustees: E.H. Morgens; J.H. Morgens; S.F. Morgens.
EIN: 316090957

860
Morris Communications Foundation, Inc.
(formerly Stauffer Communications Foundation)
P.O. Box 936
Augusta, GA 30903-0936
Contact: William S. Morris IV, Tr.

Established in 1976 in KS.
Donor(s): Stauffer Communications, Inc.
Grantmaker type: Company-sponsored foundation
Financial data (yr. ended 12/31/01): Assets, $1,160,241 (M); gifts received, $99,250; expenditures, $120,579; qualifying distributions, $120,579; giving activities include $116,357 for 33 grants (high: $20,000; low: $100) and $1,700 for 3 employee matching gifts.
Purpose and activities: Giving primarily for the arts, education, natural resource conservation, hospitals, housing development, and community foundations.
Fields of interest: Arts; Education, fund raising; Higher education; Natural resources; Hospitals (general); Health care; Children/youth, services; Community development; Federated giving programs.
Types of support: Capital campaigns; Building/renovation; Employee matching gifts.
Limitations: Giving limited to areas of company operations. Generally, no grants to individuals.

Application information: Application form not required.
   Deadline(s): None
   Board meeting date(s): 3rd week of Mar., June, Sept., and Dec.
Trustees: John Fish; Gregg A. Ireland; William S. Morris IV; John H. Stauffer; Stanley H. Stauffer.
Number of staff: None.
EIN: 486212412

861
The Morris Family Foundation, Inc.
(formerly The Michael A. Morris Foundation, Inc.)
2455 Paces Ferry Rd., Ste. C-21
Atlanta, GA 30339-4024

Established in 1998 in GA.
Donor(s): Bernard Marcus.
Grantmaker type: Independent foundation
Financial data (yr. ended 12/31/00): Assets, $9,069,558 (M); gifts received, $5,034,687; expenditures, $328,383; qualifying distributions, $321,242; giving activities include $304,613 for grants.
Purpose and activities: Giving primarily for Jewish organizations.
Fields of interest: Theater; Orchestra (symphony); Secondary school/education; Higher education; Zoos/zoological societies; Civil rights; Federated giving programs; Christian agencies & churches; Jewish agencies & temples.
Limitations: Applications not accepted. Giving on a national basis. No grants to individuals.
Application information: Contributes only to pre-selected organizations.
Officers: Michael Morris, Chair.; Frederick Slagle, Secy.-Treas.
Director: Belinda Morris.
EIN: 582396544

862
Katherine John Murphy Foundation ▼
50 Hurt Plz., Ste. 1210
Atlanta, GA 30303 (404) 589-8090
Contact: Brenda Rambeau, Dir., or Martin Gatins, Chair.
E-mail: info@murphyfoundation.org; URL: http://www.kjmurphyfoundation.org

Trust established in 1954 in GA.
Donor(s): Katherine Murphy Riley.‡
Grantmaker type: Independent foundation
Financial data (yr. ended 12/31/02): Assets, $19,508,164 (M); expenditures, $2,456,664; qualifying distributions, $2,355,325; giving activities include $2,046,917 for 120 grants (high: $75,000; low: $200; average: $5,000–$50,000).
Purpose and activities: Giving primarily for the arts, higher education, the environment, hospitals, and youth services.
Fields of interest: Arts; Higher education; Environment; Hospitals (general); Health care; Children/youth, services.
International interests: Latin America.
Types of support: Capital campaigns; Building/renovation; Equipment; Program development; Seed money; Scholarship funds.
Limitations: Giving primarily in Atlanta, GA. No grants to individuals, or for research, or matching gifts; no loans.

Publications: Informational brochure.
Application information: Application form not required.
   Initial approach: Letter
   Copies of proposal: 1
   Deadline(s): Mar. 30, June 30, Sept. 30, and Dec. 15
   Board meeting date(s): Jan., Apr., July, and Sept.
Officer and Trustees:* Martin Gatins,* Chair.; Dameron Black III; Phillip Gatins.
Investment Trustee: SunTrust Banks, Inc.
Number of staff: 1 full-time professional.
EIN: 586026045

863
The Newland Family Foundation, Inc.
(formerly The DSN Foundation)
230 Hampton Ct.
Athens, GA 30605-1404 (706) 543-3938
Contact: Dorothy Sams Newland, Pres.
FAX: (706) 354-6694; E-mail:
newlandfamfdninc@mindspring.com

Established in 1994 in GA.
Donor(s): Dorothy Sams Newland.
Grantmaker type: Independent foundation
Financial data (yr. ended 12/31/01): Assets, $1,525,559 (M); gifts received, $49,330; expenditures, $138,752; qualifying distributions, $122,812; giving activities include $118,084 for 17 grants (low: $1,200; average: $1,200–$15,000).
Purpose and activities: To support programs primarily in the areas of human services, education, conservation and the environment, with an emphasis on those programs within the Athens-Clarke County, GA, area.
Fields of interest: Education; Natural resources; Environment; Housing/shelter, homeless; Boys & girls clubs; Youth development; Human services; Aging, centers/services.
Types of support: General/operating support; Capital campaigns; Building/renovation; Equipment; Emergency funds; Program development; Seed money; Curriculum development; Matching/challenge support.
Limitations: Giving primarily in GA, with emphasis on Athens-Clarke County.
Publications: Application guidelines, Grants list.
Application information: Application form not required.
   Initial approach: Letter
   Copies of proposal: 1
   Deadline(s): 2nd month of each calendar quarter
   Board meeting date(s): Quarterly
Officers and Board Members:* Dorothy Sams Newland,* Pres.; Harriet Newland Hulsey,* V.P.; James L. Newland, Jr.,* V.P.; James L. Newland,* Secy.-Treas.; R. Drew Hulsey, Jr.; Tina Lowe Newland.
Number of staff: None.
EIN: 582142455

864
North Georgia Community Foundation

(formerly Gainesville Community Foundation)
P.O. Box 1583
Gainesville, GA   30503   (770) 535-7880
Contact: James E. Mathis, Jr., C.E.O. and Pres.
FAX: (770) 503-0439; E-mail: jmathis@ngcf.org;
URL: http://www.ngcf.org

Established in 1985 in GA.
Grantmaker type: Community foundation
Financial data (yr. ended 06/30/02): Assets,
$12,272,714 (M); gifts received, $3,598,124;
expenditures, $2,881,765; giving activities
include $2,515,754 for grants.
Purpose and activities: The foundation exists to
be the primary vehicle for building and
managing the community's permanent
charitable resources. The foundation administers
donor-advised funds.
Fields of interest: Arts; Education; Environment;
Health care; Human services; Economic
development; Community development;
Philanthropy/voluntarism; Religion.
Types of support: Capital campaigns; Program
development; Seed money; Scholarship funds;
Program-related investments/loans; In-kind gifts;
Matching/challenge support.
Limitations: Giving limited to the 15-county
area of northeast GA.
Publications: Application guidelines, Financial
statement, Grants list, Informational brochure
(including application guidelines), Newsletter.
Application information: Application form
required.
  Initial approach: Telephone
  Copies of proposal: 1
  Deadline(s): Mar. 31
  Board meeting date(s): 2nd Wed. monthly
  Final notification: 8-10 weeks
Officers and Directors:* J. Kenneth Nix,* Chair.;
John A. Gram,* Vice-Chair.; James E. Mathis, Jr.,
C.E.O. and Pres.; Douglas A. Carter,* Secy.;
Richard D. White,* Treas.; Charles Black; Al
Crumley; Sally B. Darden; James A. Dunlap;
Anthony W. Dye; Anderson Flen; J.C.
Highsmith, Jr.; Brent W. Hoffman; J. Russell Ivie;
Emily D. Lawson; Deborah K. Mack; James H.
Moore; John M. Nix; Antonio Rios; Lindsay B.
Robertson; Lawrence B. Schrage; John D.
Solesbee; W. David Wallace.
Number of staff: 4 full-time professional; 1
part-time professional.
EIN: 581610318

865
Oxford Industries Foundation, Inc.

222 Piedmont Ave., N.E.
Atlanta, GA   30308-3391   (404) 653-1273
Contact: Susan Bennett

Established in 1975 in GA.
Donor(s): Oxford Industries, Inc.
Grantmaker type: Company-sponsored
foundation
Financial data (yr. ended 12/31/00): Assets,
$1,241,240 (M); expenditures, $172,587;
qualifying distributions, $149,295; giving
activities include $149,295 for 66 grants (high:
$10,000; low: $45).
Purpose and activities: Giving for the arts and
education, health and medical institutes, human
services, and the economically disadvantaged.

Fields of interest: Museums; Humanities; Arts;
Child development, education; Animal welfare;
Hospitals (general); Health care; Human
services; Children/youth, services; Family
services; Homeless, human services;
Economically disadvantaged; Homeless.
Types of support: General/operating support;
Continuing support; Annual campaigns; Capital
campaigns; Employee matching gifts.
Limitations: Giving primarily in areas of
company operation, GA, MS, NY, SC, TN, and
TX. No grants to individuals, or for advertising.
Publications: Program policy statement.
Application information: Application form not
required.
  Initial approach: Proposal
  Copies of proposal: 2
  Board meeting date(s): Jan., Apr., July, and Oct.
Officer and Trustees:* J. Hicks Lanier,* Chair.
and Pres.; Tom Chubb.
EIN: 581209452

866
Abreu Patterson Endowment Trust

c/o Bank of America
22 Bull St., 2nd Fl.
Savannah, GA   31401-2618

Established in 1972.
Grantmaker type: Public charity
Financial data (yr. ended 12/31/01): Revenue,
$22,964; assets, $1,094,525; expenditures,
$52,247; program services expenses, $52,247;
giving activities include $52,247 for 1 grant.
Purpose and activities: The trust operates solely
for the benefit of Humane Society of South
Coastal Georgia, Inc.
Fields of interest: Animal welfare.
Limitations: Applications not accepted. Giving
limited to GA.
Application information: Contributes only to a
pre-selected organization; unsolicited requests
for funds not considered or acknowledged.
Trustee: Bank of America.
EIN: 586081437

867
Patterson-Barclay Memorial Foundation, Inc.

6487 Peachtree Industrial Blvd., Ste. A
Atlanta, GA   30360   (770) 458-9888
Contact: Hugh R. Powell, Jr., Secy.

Incorporated in 1953 in GA.
Donor(s): Frederick W. Patterson.‡
Grantmaker type: Independent foundation
Financial data (yr. ended 12/31/02): Assets,
$8,944,504 (M); expenditures, $748,554;
qualifying distributions, $572,451; giving
activities include $578,026 for 79 grants (high:
$40,000; low: $1,000; average: $1,000–$5,000).
Purpose and activities: Giving for Christian
organizations, hospitals, and higher secondary,
and other education; grants also for health,
social service and youth agencies, arts and
culture, and the environment.
Fields of interest: Museums; Performing arts;
Theater; Arts; Education, association; Child
development, education; Secondary
school/education; Higher education; Natural
resources; Environment; Animals/wildlife,
preservation/protection; Hospitals (general);

Medical care, rehabilitation; Health care;
Substance abuse, services; Human services;
Children/youth, services; Child development,
services; Hospices; Aging, centers/services;
Women, centers/services; Homeless, human
services; Community development;
Government/public administration; Christian
agencies & churches; Religion; Economically
disadvantaged.
Types of support: General/operating support;
Continuing support; Annual campaigns; Capital
campaigns; Building/renovation; Endowments;
Scholarship funds.
Limitations: Giving primarily in the metropolitan
Atlanta, GA, area. No grants to individuals.
Application information: Application form not
required.
  Copies of proposal: 1
  Deadline(s): Oct. 1
  Board meeting date(s): 3rd Wed. in May and
  Oct.
  Final notification: Positive responses only
Officers and Trustees:* Mrs. Lee Barclay
Patterson Allen,* Pres. and Treas.; Jack W.
Allen,* V.P.; Hugh R. Powell, Jr., Secy.; Ross
Arnold; Laurell Allen Reussow.
Number of staff: None.
EIN: 580904580

868
Pine Mountain Benevolent Foundation, Inc.

630 Hopewell Church Rd.
Pine Mountain, GA   31822   (706) 663-1000
Contact: Cason J. Callaway, Jr., Dir.

Incorporated in 1959 in GA.
Donor(s): Ida Cason Callaway Foundation,
Cason J. Callaway, Jr.
Grantmaker type: Independent foundation
Financial data (yr. ended 06/30/02): Assets,
$672,108 (M); expenditures, $141,961;
qualifying distributions, $141,239; giving
activities include $141,239 for 19 grants (high:
$31,000; low: $100).
Fields of interest: Elementary/secondary
education; Higher education; Environment;
Human services; Protestant agencies & churches.
Limitations: Giving primarily in Harris County,
GA.
Application information: Application form not
required.
  Initial approach: Letter
  Deadline(s): None
Directors: Cason J. Callaway, Jr.; Kenneth H.
Callaway; Nancy H. Callaway.
EIN: 586033162

869
Parker Poe Charitable Trust

P.O. Box 1395
Thomasville, GA   31799

Established in 1991 in GA.
Donor(s): Parker Poe.‡
Grantmaker type: Independent foundation
Financial data (yr. ended 03/31/02): Assets,
$12,020,010 (M); expenditures, $1,213,532;
qualifying distributions, $1,021,617; giving
activities include $1,020,700 for 20 grants
(high: $230,000; low: $500).

Purpose and activities: Giving primarily for education, the arts, and land preservations.
Fields of interest: Performing arts; Arts; Education; Environment, land resources; Human services; Federated giving programs.
Limitations: Applications not accepted. Giving primarily in GA. No grants to individuals.
Application information: Contributes only to pre-selected organizations.
Trustees: M.H. Allen; Kate Ireland.
EIN: 596968647

870
The Price-Campbell Foundation
900 Pineridge Dr.
Valdosta, GA 31602 (229) 242-1348

Donor(s): Mildred M. Price.‡
Grantmaker type: Independent foundation
Financial data (yr. ended 04/30/02): Assets, $2,266,647 (M); expenditures, $124,085; qualifying distributions, $113,902; giving activities include $102,000 for 9 grants (high: $21,000; low: $1,000).
Purpose and activities: Awards postgraduate scholarships in the fields of medicine and law to students at three universities in GA; support also for conservation, human services, youth, and arts.
Fields of interest: Medical school/education; Libraries (public); Natural resources; Environment; Food banks; Boy scouts; Human services.
Types of support: General/operating support; Scholarships—to individuals.
Limitations: Giving primarily in Lowndes County, GA.
Application information: Application form not required.
Initial approach: Letter or telephone for guidelines
Deadline(s): None
Trustees: Lucy Acree; John R. Bennett; Barbara K. Passmore.
EIN: 581530873

871
The Rich Foundation, Inc.
11 Piedmont Ctr., Ste. 204
Atlanta, GA 30305 (404) 262-2266
Contact: Anne Poland Berg, Grant Consultant

Incorporated in 1943 in GA.
Donor(s): Rich's, Inc.
Grantmaker type: Independent foundation
Financial data (yr. ended 01/31/03): Assets, $41,709,136 (M); expenditures, $2,341,972; qualifying distributions, $2,177,592; giving activities include $2,108,500 for 80 grants (high: $150,000; low: $2,500; average: $5,000–$100,000).
Purpose and activities: Giving primarily for the performing arts and other cultural programs, higher education, social services, including programs for the homeless and people with AIDS, youth agencies, and hospitals, including research in heart disease.
Fields of interest: Theater; Arts; Higher education; Environment; Hospitals (general); Health care; Health organizations, association; Heart & circulatory research; Human services; Children/youth, services; Homeless, human

services; Disabled; Aging; People with AIDS (PWAs); Economically disadvantaged; Homeless.
Types of support: General/operating support; Annual campaigns; Capital campaigns; Building/renovation; Equipment; Endowments; Research; Technical assistance.
Limitations: Giving limited to the Atlanta, GA, area. No support for religious, political or fraternal organizations. No grants to individuals, or for matching gifts, conferences and seminars, fundraising dinners, sporting events, and accumulated debt; no loans.
Publications: Application guidelines.
Application information: Application form required.
Initial approach: Letter
Copies of proposal: 5
Deadline(s): Dec. 15, Mar. 15, June 15, and Sept. 15
Board meeting date(s): Feb., May, Aug., and Nov.
Final notification: 2 weeks
Officers and Trustees:* Joel Goldberg,* Pres.; Thomas J. Asher,* V.P. and Secy.; Margaret S. Weiller, Treas.; David S. Baker.
Number of staff: None.
EIN: 586038037

872
The Richards Foundation, Inc.
(formerly Roy Richards, Jr. Foundation for Charitable Giving)
P.O. Box 800
Carrollton, GA 30112 (770) 832-4097
Contact: Judy W. Windom
FAX: (770) 832-5265; E-mail: Judy_Windom@southwire.com; URL: http://www.rrichards.org

Established in 1990.
Donor(s): Roy Richards, Jr.
Grantmaker type: Independent foundation
Financial data (yr. ended 12/31/02): Assets, $12,748,721 (M); expenditures, $172,843; qualifying distributions, $172,843; giving activities include $111,080 for 6 grants (high: $50,000; low: $1,000).
Purpose and activities: Giving primarily for human services.
Fields of interest: Museums (natural history); Education; Environment; Hospitals (general); Health organizations, association; Cancer research; Parks/playgrounds; Human services; Youth, services; Community development; Federated giving programs; Economically disadvantaged.
Limitations: Giving primarily in Carroll County, GA, and surrounding counties.
Application information:
Initial approach: Letter
Deadline(s): Ongoing
Directors: Robin R. Donohoe; William V. Hearnburg; Roy Richards.
EIN: 581933598

873
Rock-Tenn Company Contributions Program
c/o Corp. Giving
504 Thrasher St.
Norcross, GA 30071 (770) 448-2193
Contact: Brandy Hall

Grantmaker type: Corporate giving program
Purpose and activities: Rock-Tenn makes charitable contributions to nonprofit organizations involved with arts and culture, education, and the environment. Support is given on a national basis.
Fields of interest: Arts; Education; Environment.
Types of support: General/operating support; Employee volunteer services; Employee matching gifts.
Limitations: Giving on a national basis.
Application information: Application form not required.
Initial approach: Proposal to headquarters
Deadline(s): Sept. 30
Final notification: 2 months

874
The Sapelo Foundation, Inc.
(formerly Sapelo Island Research Foundation, Inc.)
308 Mallory St., Ste. C
St. Simons Island, GA 31522 (912) 638-6265
Contact: Phyllis Bowen, Exec. Dir.
Additional tel.: (912) 634-6209; FAX: (912) 638-6028; E-mail: sapelofoundation@mindspring.com; URL: http://www.sapelofoundation.org

Incorporated in 1949 in GA.
Donor(s): Richard J. Reynolds, Jr.‡
Grantmaker type: Independent foundation
Financial data (yr. ended 06/30/02): Assets, $33,383,616 (M); expenditures, $1,956,961; qualifying distributions, $1,800,502; giving activities include $1,537,031 for 59 grants (high: $75,000; low: $1,975; average: $10,000–$40,000).
Purpose and activities: The foundation promotes progressive social change affecting, in particular, rural communities and the natural environment.
Fields of interest: Education, reform; Environment, public policy; Environment, air pollution; Environment, toxics; Environment, water resources; Environment, forests; Animals/wildlife, preservation/protection; Legal services, public interest law; Civil liberties, due process; Civil liberties, death penalty issues; Civil rights.
Types of support: General/operating support; Annual campaigns; Program development.
Limitations: Giving limited to GA. No grants for capital, emergency, or endowment funds, deficit financing, or publications; no loans.
Application information: Visit foundation's Web site for complete application guidelines and procedures. Application form not required.
Initial approach: Phone inquiry or visit Web site
Copies of proposal: 1
Deadline(s): Mar. 1 and Sept. 1
Board meeting date(s): May and Nov.
Final notification: Within two weeks following board meeting

Officers and Trustees:* Susan Lehman Carmichael,* Pres.; Henry H. Carey,* V.P.; William K. Broker,* Secy.; Smith Bagley, Treas.; Phyllis Bowen, Exec. Dir.; Franklin D. Bobrow-Williams; Katherine R. Grant; Nan Grogan Orrock; Annemarie Reynolds; Irene Reynolds.
Number of staff: 2 full-time professional.
EIN: 580827472

875
Savannah Electric and Power Company Contributions Program

P.O. Box 968
Savannah, GA 31402
Contact: Julien Pafford; or Lee Ann Powell

Grantmaker type: Corporate giving program
Purpose and activities: Savannah Electric and Power makes charitable contributions to nonprofit organizations involved with education, the environment, health and human services, and community development. Support is given primarily in areas of company operations.
Fields of interest: Education; Environment; Health care; Human services; Economic development; Community development.
Types of support: Program development.
Limitations: Giving primarily in areas of company operations in GA. No support for athletic teams, religious organizations, or private schools. No grants to individuals.
Publications: Corporate report.
Application information: Application form not required.
  Initial approach: Proposal to headquarters
  Copies of proposal: 1
  Deadline(s): None
  Final notification: Following review

876
The SF Foundation II

c/o Phillip E. Sadler
7000 Central Pkwy., Ste. 650
Atlanta, GA 30328

Established in 1996 in GA.
Donor(s): Dorothy C. Sadler, Phillip E. Sadler.
Grantmaker type: Independent foundation
Financial data (yr. ended 12/31/02): Assets, $6,659,929 (M); expenditures, $285,206; qualifying distributions, $283,800; giving activities include $283,800 for 39 grants (high: $42,500; low: $100).
Purpose and activities: Giving primarily to education, animal welfare, health care, federated giving programs, and religious organizations.
Fields of interest: University; Animal welfare; Health care; Federated giving programs; Protestant agencies & churches.
Limitations: Applications not accepted. No grants to individuals.
Application information: Contributes only to pre-selected organizations.
Trustees: Dorothy C. Sadler; Phillip E. Sadler.
EIN: 582277136

877
Lewis Hall & Mildred Sasser Singletary Foundation, Inc.

P.O. Box 1095
Thomasville, GA 31799
Contact: Susan Izzo
FAX: (229) 226-2474

Established in 1990.
Grantmaker type: Independent foundation
Financial data (yr. ended 12/31/01): Assets, $33,534,338 (M); expenditures, $1,439,263; qualifying distributions, $1,276,364; giving activities include $1,276,364 for 52 grants (high: $225,119; low: $1,000; average: $1,000–$540,000).
Purpose and activities: Giving primarily for kids at risk mainly in the southeast and primarily in southwest GA.
Fields of interest: Elementary/secondary education; Secondary school/education; Libraries (public); Libraries (special); Environmental education; Animal welfare; Animal population control; Boy scouts; YM/YWCAs & YM/YWHAs; Adoption; International affairs; Foundations (community); Christian agencies & churches; Protestant agencies & churches.
Types of support: Capital campaigns; Seed money; Matching/challenge support.
Limitations: Giving primarily in the southeastern U.S., with emphasis on Thomas County, GA. No grants to individuals.
Publications: Application guidelines.
Application information: Application guidelines available. Application form not required.
  Initial approach: Letter
  Copies of proposal: 1
  Deadline(s): Sept. 30
  Board meeting date(s): Dec.
  Final notification: Dec.
Officers and Directors:* Karen S. Leabo,* Pres.; Richard L. Singletary,* V.P.; Richard L. Singletary, Jr.,* Treas.; Greg Hamil; Jeanne S. Hamil; J. Philip Leabo; J. Philip Leabo, Jr.; JoAnn Leabo; Julia Singletary; Karen L. Singletary; Lewis Hall Singletary II; Rebecca Singletary; Tim Singletary.
Number of staff: 1 part-time professional.
EIN: 581906094

878
Southern Partners Fund

1237 Ralph David Abernathy Blvd., S.W.
Atlanta, GA 30310 (404) 758-1983
Contact: Joan Garner, Exec. Dir.
FAX: (404) 758-2880; E-mail: info@spfund.org; URL: http://www.spfund.org

Established in 1998 in GA.
Grantmaker type: Public charity
Financial data (yr. ended 12/31/02): Revenue, $1,732,169; assets, $3,620,576 (M); gifts received, $376,603; expenditures, $2,233,005; program services expenses, $1,589,106; giving activities include $1,031,455 for grants.
Purpose and activities: The foundation supports grassroots organizations striving toward economic, social and/or environmental justice.
Fields of interest: Environment; Youth development; Civil rights, ethics; Community development.
Types of support: General/operating support; Continuing support; Seed money.

Limitations: Giving limited to the South. No support for organizations lacking 501(c)(3) designation. No grants to individuals.
Publications: Application guidelines, Annual report, Informational brochure (including application guidelines), Newsletter.
Application information:
  Initial approach: Letter
Officers and Directors:* Leroy Johnson,* Chair.; Karen Watson,* Vice-Chair.; Ann Brown,* Secy.; Peggy Matthews,* Treas.; Araceli Corona; Fernando Cuevas, Jr.; Cynthia Laramore; Kamau Marcharia; Malika Sanders.
Number of staff: 4 full-time professional; 3 full-time support.
EIN: 582409301

879
Southwire Company Contributions Program

c/o Corp. Contribs.
1 Southwire Dr.
Carrollton, GA 30119 (770) 832-4242
Additional address: P.O. Box 1000, Carrollton, GA 30119; FAX: (770) 832-4463; URL: http://www.southwire.com/community

Grantmaker type: Corporate giving program
Purpose and activities: Southwire makes charitable contributions to nonprofit organizations involved with education, the environment, health and human services, youth development, and community development. Support is given primarily in areas of company operations.
Fields of interest: Education; Environment; Health care; Youth development; Family services; Human services; Community development.
Types of support: General/operating support.
Limitations: Giving primarily in areas of company operations.
Application information:
  Initial approach: Contact headquarters for application information

880
Paul and Ferne Sticht Foundation

c/o Wachovia Bank, N.A.
191 Peachtree St., GA8023
Atlanta, GA 30303
Contact: Susanna Adams

Established in 1986 in GA.
Donor(s): Ferne C. Sticht, J. Paul Sticht.
Grantmaker type: Independent foundation
Financial data (yr. ended 12/31/02): Assets, $1,146,575 (M); expenditures, $125,387; qualifying distributions, $117,197; giving activities include $115,550 for 21 grants (high: $60,000; low: $100).
Purpose and activities: Giving for higher education, conservation, federated giving programs, health and medical services and research, and services for the elderly.
Fields of interest: Education; Environment; Health care; Medical research, institute; Federated giving programs; Aging.
Limitations: Applications not accepted. Giving primarily in the eastern U.S. No grants to individuals.

Application information: Contributes only to pre-selected organizations. Unsolicited requests for funds not considered.
Trustees: David S. Sticht; Ferne C. Sticht; J. Paul Sticht; Mark D. Sticht; Wachovia Bank, N.A.
Number of staff: None.
EIN: 581704090

881
TBS Corporate Giving Program
c/o Corp. Affairs Dept.
101 Marietta St., 15th Fl.
Atlanta, GA 30303
Contact: Kristina Christy, Mgr., Corp. Contribs.
FAX: (404) 878-6575; E-mail: corporate.contributions@turner.com

Grantmaker type: Corporate giving program
Financial data (yr. ended 12/31/02): Total giving, $1,020,000; giving activities include $1,000,000 for grants (high: $65,000) and $20,000 for employee matching gifts.
Purpose and activities: TBS makes charitable contributions to nonprofit organizations involved with arts and culture, education, and the environment. Support is given primarily in Atlanta, Georgia.
Fields of interest: Arts; Secondary school/education; Education; Environment.
Types of support: General/operating support; Program development; Employee volunteer services; Use of facilities; Program-related investments/loans; Employee matching gifts; Donated equipment; Donated products; Matching/challenge support.
Limitations: Giving primarily in Atlanta, GA; giving also to national organizations. No support for religious organizations, fraternal organizations, athletic organizations, or veterans' organizations. No grants to individuals, or for continuing support.
Application information: The Corporate Affairs Department handles giving. The company has a staff that only handles contributions. A contributions committee reviews all requests. Application form not required.
  Initial approach: Mail or fax proposal to headquarters
  Copies of proposal: 1
  Deadline(s): None
  Board meeting date(s): Monthly
  Final notification: 6 weeks
Administrators: Ronnie Gunnerson, Sr. V.P., Corp. Affairs; Kristina Christy, Mgr., Corp. Contribs.
Number of staff: 1 full-time professional.

882
Kate and Elwyn Tomlinson Foundation, Inc.
750 Hammond Dr., Bldg. 17
Atlanta, GA 30328 (404) 256-1144
Contact: Jack Fisher, Chair.

Incorporated in 1949 in GA.
Grantmaker type: Independent foundation
Financial data (yr. ended 12/31/02): Assets, $3,721,950 (M); expenditures, $266,478; qualifying distributions, $221,320; giving activities include $225,651 for 57 grants (high: $30,000; low: $100).

Purpose and activities: Giving primarily for conservation, and health and human services.
Fields of interest: Arts; Higher education; Education; Environment; Health care; Human services; Protestant agencies & churches.
Limitations: Giving primarily in GA. No grants to individuals, or for scholarships.
Application information:
  Initial approach: Letter
  Deadline(s): None
Officer: Jack Fisher, Chair.
Directors: Kathryn T. Bridges; Mark Tomlinson; Sally Tomlinson.
EIN: 580634727

883
The Tull Charitable Foundation ▼
50 Hurt Plz., Ste. 1245
Atlanta, GA 30303 (404) 659-7079
Contact: Barbara Cleveland, Exec. Dir.

Trust established in 1952 in GA as The J.M. Tull Foundation; reorganized under current name in 1984 with the Tull Charitable Foundation.
Donor(s): J.M. Tull,‡ J.M. Tull Metal and Supply Co., Inc.
Grantmaker type: Independent foundation
Financial data (yr. ended 12/31/01): Assets, $85,783,829 (M); expenditures, $5,010,114; qualifying distributions, $4,526,460; giving activities include $4,148,849 for 119 grants (high: $390,534; low: $200; average: $25,000–$50,000) and $158,340 for 157 employee matching gifts.
Purpose and activities: Support for higher and private secondary education; grants also for health and human services, youth and child welfare agencies, and culture.
Fields of interest: Arts; Secondary school/education; Higher education; Education; Environment; Health care; Health organizations, association; Housing/shelter, development; Youth development, services; Human services; Children/youth, services; Homeless, human services; Homeless.
Types of support: Capital campaigns; Building/renovation; Endowments; Professorships; Seed money; Employee matching gifts.
Limitations: Giving limited to GA. No support for projects of religious organizations that primarily benefit their own adherents. No grants to individuals, or for conferences or seminars, scientific research, purchase of tickets to benefit events, sponsorship of performances, operating support, or scholarships (except for scholarship endowments); no loans.
Publications: Informational brochure (including application guidelines).
Application information: Application form not required.
  Initial approach: Letter
  Copies of proposal: 1
  Deadline(s): 1st day of month of meeting
  Board meeting date(s): Jan., Apr., July, and Oct.
  Final notification: 1 week after board meeting, in writing
Officers and Trustees:* John McIntyre,* Chair.; Barbara Cleveland, Secy.-Treas. and Exec. Dir.; Sylvia L. Dick; Harald R. Hansen; Warren Jobe; Larry Prince; Franklin Skinner.
Agent: SunTrust Banks, Inc.

Number of staff: 1 full-time professional; 1 part-time professional.
EIN: 581687028
Recent environmental and animal welfare grants:
883-1 Canine Assistants, Alpharetta, GA, $52,000. For capital support. 2001.
883-2 Nature Conservancy, Atlanta, GA, $95,106. For grant made in form of stock. 2001.
883-3 Zoo Atlanta, Atlanta, GA, $47,886. For grant made in form of stock. 2001.

884
Turner Foundation, Inc. ▼
133 Luckie St., 2nd Fl.
Atlanta, GA 30303 (404) 681-9900
Contact: Michael Finley, Pres.
FAX: (404) 681-0172; E-mail: turnerfi@turnerfoundation.org; URL: http://www.turnerfoundation.org

Established in 1990 in GA.
Donor(s): R.E. Turner III.
Grantmaker type: Independent foundation
Financial data (yr. ended 12/31/02): Assets, $30,826,467 (M); gifts received, $51,100; expenditures, $36,858,386; qualifying distributions, $35,859,239; giving activities include $28,349,381 for 518 grants (high: $4,750,000; low: $100; average: $5,000–$150,000) and $5,892,350 for 1 foundation-administered program.
Purpose and activities: The foundation is committed to preventing damage to the natural systems-water, air, and land-on which all life depends and makes grants in the areas of the environment and population. The main components of these priorities are: protection of water and reduction of toxic impacts on the environment; improved air quality through promotion of energy efficiency and renewable and improved transportation policies and practices; protection of biodiversity through habitat preservation; and development and implementation of sound, equitable practices and policies designed to reduce population growth rates.
Fields of interest: Environment, pollution control; Water pollution; Environment, toxics; Natural resources; Energy; Environment; Animals/wildlife, preservation/protection; Family planning; Reproductive rights; Community development, neighborhood development; Public affairs, citizen participation.
International interests: Canada; Russia; Mexico; Argentina; Brazil.
Types of support: General/operating support; Continuing support; Capital campaigns; Research; Technical assistance; Matching/challenge support.
Limitations: Applications not accepted. Giving primarily in AK, CO, FL, GA, MT, NE, NM, SC, and internationally, with priority given to programs in Argentina, Brazil, Mexico, Russia, and British Columbia, Canada. No grants to individuals, or for buildings, land acquisition, endowments, start-up funds, films, books, magazines, and other specific media projects.
Publications: Annual report.
Application information: Due to a significant decline in the value of the foundation's asset base, the Board has determined it to be in the

best interest of the foundation's long-term sustainability to forgo any funding requests in 2003. The foundation also plans to implement an invitation-only process in 2004. During this time the foundation will honor all previously awarded multi-year grants. Multi-year grants require submission of progress reports. See foundation's Web site for guidelines for both final and interim reports.

Board meeting date(s): Mar./Apr., July, Sept., and Dec.

Officers and Directors:* Robert E. Turner III,* Chair.; Michael Finley,* Pres.; J. Rutherford Seydel II, Secy.; Catherine E. Mickle, Treas.; Jane Fonda; Jennie Turner Garlington; Laura Lee Turner Seydel; Reed Beauregard Turner; Rhett Lee Turner; Teddy Turner.

Number of staff: 6 full-time professional; 1 part-time professional; 5 full-time support.

EIN: 581924590

Recent environmental and animal welfare grants:

884-1 1000 Friends of Florida, Tallahassee, FL, $35,000. For legal advocacy project, designed to protect Florida's growth management legislation against legal challenges and help local governments and citizens' groups implement effective growth management. 2001.

884-2 1000 Friends of New Mexico, Albuquerque, NM, $50,000. To launch campaign opposing new loop roads in Albuquerque and to promote alternative transportation vision to control sprawling development. 2001.

884-3 1000 Friends of New Mexico, Albuquerque, NM, $10,000. To complete report outlining state water allocation problems and discussing solutions. 2001.

884-4 20/20 Vision Education Fund, DC, $50,000. For general support for public education, grassroots outreach, media and advocacy to activate people's involvement in environmental issues. 2001.

884-5 Advocacy Arts Foundation, Los Angeles, CA, $30,000. For field research and photography to produce publication about Wood-Tikchik State Park in southwest Alaska. 2001.

884-6 Alabama Rivers Alliance, Birmingham, AL, $20,000. For general support for organizing and advocacy to protect and improve ecological integrity of Alabama, Coosa, Tallapoosa and lower Chattahoochee watersheds, with particular focus on interstate water compacts and responsible hydropower. 2001.

884-7 Alaska Conservation Alliance, Anchorage, AK, $25,000. To increase impact and effectiveness of conservation community by coordinating issue groups, developing communications network, hosting conferences and offering networking and training opportunities to member groups. 2001.

884-8 Alaska Marine Conservation Council, Anchorage, AK, $20,000. For general support to reestablish and protect health and diversity of Alaska's marine ecosystem. 2001.

884-9 Alaska Wilderness League, DC, $30,000. To protect public lands, focusing on Arctic Refuge Campaign and celebrating anniversary of Alaska Lands Act. 2001.

884-10 Alliance for Nuclear Accountability, Seattle, WA, $25,000. To provide service to local, regional and national organizations monitoring U.S. nuclear weapons complex and related facilities. 2001.

884-11 Alliance for the Rio Grande Heritage, Santa Fe, NM, $25,000. To develop and implement comprehensive program to protect and restore ecological health of Rio Grande through its Upper Basin. 2001.

884-12 Alliance for the Rio Grande Heritage, Santa Fe, NM, $20,000. For planning grant for involvement and assistance with Turner Community Youth Development Initiative. 2001.

884-13 Alliance for the Wild Rockies, Missoula, MT, $100,000. For general support of campaign to protect habitat and ecosystems in Northern Rockies. 2001.

884-14 Altamaha Riverkeeper, Darien, GA, $50,000. For general support to restore and protect Altamaha River and its watershed. 2001.

884-15 Alternative Energy Resources Organization, Helena, MT, $40,000. To support Smart Growth and Transportation, and Montana FarmLink programs. 2001.

884-16 Amazon Alliance for Indigenous and Traditional Peoples of the Amazon Basin, DC, $20,000. For general support to defend rights and territories of indigenous and traditional peoples of Amazon Basin. 2001.

884-17 Amazon Watch, Malibu, CA, $20,000. For general support to investigate and publicize proposed projects in culturally and environmentally sensitive areas of the Amazon. 2001.

884-18 American Association for the Advancement of Science, DC, $30,000. To convert recently-published Atlas of Population and Environment into digital format accessible via the Internet and CD-ROMs to increase availability of information on integrated approaches to population and environment problem-solving. 2001.

884-19 American Bird Conservancy, The Plains, VA, $50,000. For general support to maintain and increase partnerships needed to address full range of threats to birds and their habitats through Policy Council, Pesticides and Birds Campaign, Cats Indoors Campaign, and international programs. 2001.

884-20 American Council for an Energy-Efficient Economy, DC, $50,000. To craft, analyze, and advocate policies to increase energy efficiency and reduce polluting emissions. 2001.

884-21 American Farmland Trust, DC, $50,000. For Southeast farm and forest protection program which will work with rural Southeastern communities threatened by sprawl. 2001.

884-22 American Lands Alliance, DC, $25,000. For invasive species and Western Fire Ecology Center programs. 2001.

884-23 American Littoral Society, Highlands, NJ, $35,000. For Florida Reefs For the Future campaign to protect coral reefs and preserve their diversity. 2001.

884-24 American Oceans Campaign, DC, $15,000. For Mobilizing Grassroots Activists in Florida project to advocate for ocean and coastal health at the federal level. 2001.

884-25 American Rivers, DC, $40,000. For organizing and advocacy campaigns focusing on wild and scenic rivers, hydropower relicensing, community riverfront redesign, dam removal, and restoration of the Missouri River. 2001.

884-26 American Rivers, DC, $20,000. For general support of work to reform national hydropower policies and achieve improvements to rivers that have been altered by hydropower dams. 2001.

884-27 American Solar Energy Society, Boulder, CO, $20,000. For general support to advocate for clean energy technologies. 2001.

884-28 American Whitewater Affiliation, Silver Spring, MD, $20,000. For Restoring Southeastern Rivers Program to use hydropower relicensing process to achieve environmental and recreational benefits by establishing dynamic flow regimes. 2001.

884-29 American Wildlands, Bozeman, MT, $25,000. For general support to conserve aquatic and terrestrial life of Northern Rocky Mountains by protecting and maintaining wildlife and maintaining wildlife habitat connectivity, key watersheds, biologically diverse wildlands and roadless areas. 2001.

884-30 Americans for Equitable Climate Solutions, DC, $60,000. For project to develop centrist approach to U.S. climate policy that is not tied directly to the Kyoto Protocol. 2001.

884-31 Amigos Bravos, Taos, NM, $35,000. For general support for research, public education, organizing and strategic litigation to protect and restore ecological health of New Mexico's rivers and the Rio Grande watershed and balance ecosystem needs of rivers with legitimate claims of New Mexico's land-based communities. 2001.

884-32 Antarctica Project, DC, $10,000. For general support to ensure effective implementation of international agreements to protect Antarctica's marine ecosystem. 2001.

884-33 Apalachicola Bay and Riverkeeper, Apalachicola, FL, $25,000. For general support of programs and activities to protect Apalachicola River and Bay, its tributaries and its watershed. 2001.

884-34 Aperture Foundation, New York, NY, $35,000. For photography project, Rivers of Life: Southwest Alaska, the Last Great Fishery, to consist of a publication, traveling exhibition and education/media campaign in support of freshwater habitat conservation in Alaska's Bristol Bay. 2001.

884-35 Arizona State University, Tempe, AZ, $50,000. For Sustainability of Mimbres Land Use Project, aimed at archaeological research on the Ladder Ranch and for school education programs. 2001.

884-36 Arizona-Sonora Desert Museum, Tucson, AZ, $53,000. For research study focused on conserving pollinators that move seasonally between southern Mexico and southwestern United States. 2001.

884-37 Artemis Wildlife Foundation, Helena, MT, $15,000. For Common Ground projects to keep family ranches intact while improving land management practices. 2001.

884-38 Atlantic Salmon Federation, Calais, ME, $50,000. To expand and enhance conservation efforts and sound management of wild Atlantic salmon and its critical habitat through research and advocacy by examining low marine survival rates and impacts of aquaculture on them. 2001.

884-39 Audubon Council of Montana, Helena, MT, $20,000. For wetland and riparian conservation efforts, including documenting effects of government permits on riprap, weir, and barbs along Yellowstone River and floodplain. 2001.

884-40 Audubon Society, National, Atlanta, GA, $15,000. For Important Bird Areas project, which seeks to determine, designate and prioritize protection of essential habitat sites for declining bird species in Georgia and to hire full-time coordinator for the project. 2001.

884-41 Audubon Society, National, New York, NY, $30,000. For project support to continue and expand advocacy and education work to provide conservation voice to committees of Platte River Cooperative Agreement and Niobrara River Council to ensure preservation of critical habitat for sandhill cranes and other wildlife. 2001.

884-42 Audubon Society, National, New York, NY, $30,000. For Campaign for America's Refuges program, which will use combination of grassroots organizing, education, advocacy and media outreach to mobilize support for National Wildlife Refuge System. 2001.

884-43 Audubon Society, National, New York, NY, $30,000. For Cuban Birds and Biodiversity Conservation project, to conduct surveys of Cuban birds, including raptors, endemic and migratory species, and establish baseline documentation for remnant population of Ivory-billed woodpeckers. 2001.

884-44 Bank Information Center, DC, $25,000. For general support to monitor World Bank's implementation of its sustainable development framework, its role in globalization and its accountability to the communities and environments most directly affected by its lending policies. 2001.

884-45 Bat Conservation International, Austin, TX, $25,000. For general support of initiatives that train wildlife managers, teach children about the benefits of bats, and help protect cave, mine and forest ecosystems. 2001.

884-46 Big Sur Land Trust, Carmel, CA, $20,000. For general support to expand donor base and increase exposure through community outreach efforts to protect natural habitat and open space in Monterey County. 2001.

884-47 Bighorn Institute, Palm Desert, CA, $25,000. For general support to conserve endangered Peninsular big horn sheep in southern California by introducing captive-reared big horn into the wild, monitoring their health, researching the causes for population decline, promoting habitat conservation by providing data to state and federal research agencies and implementing public education campaign. 2001.

884-48 Business for Social Responsibility (BSR) Education Fund, San Francisco, CA, $50,000. For Green Freight Group, a business working group to develop private sector policies and

supplier requirements that customer companies will expect their ground freight transport service providers to meet. 2001.

884-49 Canadian Parks and Wilderness Society, Ottawa, Canada, $60,000. For general support for public education and to promote efforts to increase parklands and other protected marine and terrestrial areas in northern British Columbia through Parkwatch, Northern British Columbia, Yellowstone to Yukon, Marine and Grasslands projects. 2001.

884-50 Caribbean Conservation Corporation, Gainesville, FL, $30,000. For defense of constitutional protections for sea turtles and to protect their nesting beaches from inappropriate use of coastal armoring. 2001.

884-51 Catawba-Wateree Relicensing Coalition, Charlotte, NC, $10,000. For general support to enhance and restore ecological integrity of the Catawba River Basin by promoting and supporting public participation in relicensing process for hydropower plants operated by Duke Power Company. 2001.

884-52 Center for a Sustainable Coast, Saint Simons Island, GA, $20,000. To protect natural and cultural resources of coastal Georgia through advocacy, networking, technical assistance and policy analysis. 2001.

884-53 Center for a Sustainable Economy, DC, $100,000. To bring labor and environmental groups together to support air and effective climate change policies. 2001.

884-54 Center for a Sustainable Economy, DC, $60,000. For Climate Change and the American Worker: State Impacts Supplement project. 2001.

884-55 Center for Biological Diversity, Tucson, AZ, $75,000. For litigation to obtain final critical habitat designations for animal and plant species in western U.S. 2001.

884-56 Center for Clean Air Policy, DC, $95,000. For state-level assessments of economic impacts of reducing greenhouse gas emissions. 2001.

884-57 Center for Environmental Citizenship, DC, $35,000. For Southern Outreach Project, which will feature trainings on political and organizing skills and environmental journalism. 2001.

884-58 Center for Environmental Politics, Missoula, MT, $15,000. For core program of recruiting conservation-oriented citizens for public office, and for Montana Political Accountability Project to monitor elected officials in highest statewide political offices. 2001.

884-59 Center for Health, Environment and Justice, Falls Church, VA, $100,000. For general support of programs that train and strengthen local groups working to protect their communities from environmental threats and of campaigns that promote awareness of national environmental hazards. 2001.

884-60 Center for Health, Environment and Justice, Falls Church, VA, $40,000. For campaigns to improve environmental practices of healthcare industry. 2001.

884-61 Center for Resource Solutions, San Francisco, CA, $40,000. To develop viable best practices standards for green energy programs sponsored by regulated utilities,

focusing on development and completion of a green power accreditation process for Southeast U.S. 2001.

884-62 Center for Rural Affairs, Walthill, NE, $25,000. For project to offer farmers and ranchers training and technical assistance in sustainable livestock management practices, and in securing access to organic markets. 2001.

884-63 Center for Science in Public Participation, Bozeman, MT, $20,000. For technical assistance to grassroots organizations to reverse or prevent environmental damage from mining operations. 2001.

884-64 Center for Watershed Protection, Ellicott City, MD, $20,000. For training and technical assistance to grassroots watershed organizations that advocate for improved local land use and better watershed management. 2001.

884-65 Charles Darwin Foundation for the Galapagos Islands, Falls Church, VA, $30,000. For general support for institutional strengthening to allow for continued efforts to conserve Galapagos archipelago biodiversity through research, education and training. 2001.

884-66 Chattahoochee Nature Center, Roswell, GA, $20,000. For expansion of environmental education project to teach middle and high school students about impact of commercial and residential development on Chattahoochee River watershed. 2001.

884-67 Chattahoochee Riverkeeper, Columbus, GA, $10,000. To protect, preserve and restore Chattahoochee River and its tributaries with particular focus on the middle Chattahoochee. 2001.

884-68 Chattooga Conservancy, Clayton, GA, $70,000. To protect Chattooga watershed's national forests by holding U.S. Forest Service accountable to federal laws, preventing agency abuse of resources, and continuing to oversee legal settlements. 2001.

884-69 Chattowah Open Land Trust, Alpharetta, GA, $15,000. For general support to continue developing conservation easements program to protect land in northern Georgia from unplanned, unregulated growth, forest fragmentation and unsustainable development. 2001.

884-70 Chesapeake Bay Foundation, Richmond, VA, $25,000. For Resource Protection and Restoration Project that includes campaigns aimed at restoring and sustaining the surrounding ecosystem. 2001.

884-71 Cimarron Municipal School District, Cimarron, NM, $20,000. To provide community garden and greenhouse program for local youth. 2001.

884-72 Citizens Environmental Coalition, Albany, NY, $25,000. For campaign to develop and deploy strategies for encouraging enforcement of Federal Clean Air Act's Maximum Achievable Control Technology rule. 2001.

884-73 Citizens for a Better Flathead, Kalispell, MT, $60,000. To monitor Montana Department of Transportation and organize communities in western Montana to support transportation and land use planning reforms. 2001.

884-74 Clark Fork Coalition, Missoula, MT, $20,000. For work to protect and restore water quality throughout Clark Fork basin with particular attention to Clark Fork River Superfund site and monitoring of growth in floodplains. 2001.

884-75 Clean Air Task Force, Boston, MA, $125,000. To reduce polluting emissions from power plants through litigation, negotiation, public education and technical and policy assistance to state organizations. 2001.

884-76 Clean Air Trust Education Fund, DC, $35,000. To defend Clean Air Act and to promote new policies regulating stationary and mobile emissions. 2001.

884-77 Clean Water Fund, DC, $15,000. For Clean and Safe Water Initiative to improve safe drinking water policies and to protect watershed resources through constituency building, training and technical assistance to grassroots campaigns, and policy advocacy. 2001.

884-78 Climate Institute, DC, $40,000. To develop on-line information system to monitor greenhouse gas emissions in major Western Hemisphere cities, partnerships to develop sustainable energy technologies in St. Lucia and other island countries, and to work with the G-8 Task Force on renewable energy. 2001.

884-79 Co-op America Foundation, DC, $30,000. To mobilize American individual and business consumers to reduce wood consumption and shift remaining purchases to forest-sustaining products. 2001.

884-80 Coalition for Clean Affordable Energy, Albuquerque, NM, $30,000. For support of work to improve New Mexico's energy policy for consumers to have broader range of choices and renewable energy sources that are not unfairly excluded from electricity grid. Grant made through Southwest Research Information Center. 2001.

884-81 Coast Alliance, DC, $30,000. To ensure permanent protection of Florida's undeveloped coastal lands and barrier islands through completing and disseminating studies to facilitate public acquisition of these lands and to demonstrate their economic value as undeveloped lands. 2001.

884-82 Coastal Georgia Land Trust, Savannah, GA, $15,000. For general support to preserve ecological integrity of coastal Georgia by cultivating conservation buyers, drafting conservation easements and monitoring properties placed under permanent protection. 2001.

884-83 Coastal Mountains Land Trust, Rockport, ME, $10,000. For general support. 2001.

884-84 Colorado Environmental Coalition, Denver, CO, $40,000. For Canyon Country Wilderness Campaign to permanently protect wild canyon lands through grassroots organizing, public outreach, and education activities. 2001.

884-85 Colorado Public Interest Research Foundation, Denver, CO, $40,000. For Livable Communities Project to promote land use planning and transportation policies that will lead to more managed growth. 2001.

884-86 Communities for a Better Environment, Oakland, CA, $20,000. To empower citizens to monitor and reduce toxic hazards from heavy industrial sources. 2001.

884-87 Community Networking Resources, Albuquerque, NM, $15,000. For campaign to encourage Environmental Protection Agency to increase enforcement and remediation in Southwest and pursue Title VI complaints. 2001.

884-88 Community Office for Resource Efficiency (CORE), Aspen, CO, $20,000. For general support to promote energy efficiency and renewable energy through partnering with municipal utilities, nonprofits and businesses. 2001.

884-89 Community Rights Counsel, DC, $50,000. To help communities implement and defend laws combating sprawl and protecting open space, fragile ecosystems, and critical habitat. 2001.

884-90 Concerned Citizens for Nuclear Safety, Santa Fe, NM, $35,000. For work to expose and remediate environmental impacts of research, development, testing and production of nuclear weapons, and storage and disposal of hazardous wastes generated. 2001.

884-91 ConservAmerica, Albuquerque, NM, $20,000. For public education project to identify and engage conservationist Republicans in support of environmental protections. 2001.

884-92 Conservation Fund, Eagle River, AK, $25,000. For land acquisition targeting acres of private inholding properties in state and federal conservation areas. 2001.

884-93 Conservation Fund, Tucker, GA, $750,000. To acquire an alternative site for proposed East Point elementary school, executing deal to protect tract of old-growth forest known as Connally Park. 2001.

884-94 Conservation Research Institute, Atlanta, GA, $10,000. To promote sustainable economic development in Georgia by educating decision-makers, training citizen activists, and developing broad public support for environmental criteria to be applied to state economic development projects. 2001.

884-95 Consumer Policy Institute, Yonkers, NY, $20,000. To develop comprehensive, interactive website encyclopedia on environmental labels for use by consumers, policymakers, product manufacturers, the eco-labeling industry, and citizen and environmental groups. 2001.

884-96 Consumers Choice Council, DC, $30,000. For general support to work with the government and large institutions to consider environmental and social impacts of their purchasing choices. 2001.

884-97 Container Recycling Institute, Alexandria, VA, $35,000. To study, develop and promote strategies and policies to reduce litter and waste and promote recycling, to shift pollution costs from public to private sector, and to encourage sustainable development. 2001.

884-98 Coosa River Basin Initiative, Rome, GA, $15,000. To create a cleaner, healthier and more economically viable Coosa River Basin. 2001.

884-99 Corporation for Northern Rockies Sustainable Communities, Livingston, MT, $20,000. To secure local markets for sustainably-produced agricultural products in south central Montana by identifying producers and retailers of sustainable agricultural products, facilitating contracts between producers and markets and increasing consumer demand through a communication campaign and Sustainability Fair. 2001.

884-100 David Suzuki Foundation, Vancouver, Canada, $85,000. To conserve globally significant coastal temperate rainforests of northern British Columbia by empowering small coastal communities to develop sustainable economies based on alternatives to industrial logging and commercial fisheries. 2001.

884-101 Defenders of Wildlife, DC, $425,000. To establish State Environmental Advocacy Center to shape laws, policies and programs to conserve wildlife habitat and biodiversity at state level. 2001.

884-102 Defenders of Wildlife, DC, $100,000. For Collaborative Defense Campaign, joint endeavor to educate public, media and decision-makers about threats to America's landmark environmental safeguards. 2001.

884-103 Defenders of Wildlife, DC, $70,000. For general support to maintain integrity of Endangered Species Act through education campaign to improve and add capacity to current website, increase earned media, and recruit new allies and activists. 2001.

884-104 Del Agua Institute, Silver City, NM, $10,000. To prepare water demand evaluation for Placitas area of Sandoval County. 2001.

884-105 Development Center for Appropriate Technology (DCAT), Tucson, AZ, $35,000. For general support to reduce environmental impacts of construction and development, particularly addressing how regulatory systems create barriers to sustainable practices. 2001.

884-106 Dian Fossey Gorilla Fund International, Atlanta, GA, $20,000. For general support for scientific staff and collaborator travel to conduct biological surveys on gorilla populations, determine requirements for gorilla conservation, provide training, and make conservation recommendations in key areas of Albertine Rift. 2001.

884-107 Dogwood Alliance, Brevard, NC, $30,000. To advance corporate market strategy and increase landowner outreach programs. 2001.

884-108 Ducks Unlimited, Wetlands America Trust, Memphis, TN, $160,000. For land conservation efforts: protection of wetland habitat through conservation easements in the South Carolina Lowcountry and replication of program to neighboring states, and restoration of drained wetlands and broken sod with native prairie grasses and forbs in South Dakota. 2001.

884-109 Earth Force, Alexandria, VA, $30,000. For general support to provide opportunities for youth nationwide to develop projects that contribute to lasting solutions to environmental and community problems. 2001.

884-110 Earth Island Institute, San Francisco, CA, $60,000. For general support to reduce emissions from marine vessels and to reduce groundwater contamination from fuel additive MTBE. 2001.

884-111 Earth Island Institute, San Francisco, CA, $40,000. For Climate Solutions' programs addressing climate change: rural constituency-building, the development of a public-private coalition advancing clean energy legislation, and tangible commitments to carbon reductions from utilities, businesses and local governments. 2001.

884-112 Earth Island Institute, San Francisco, CA, $25,000. For general support to continue efforts to end logging on public lands, reduce demand for forest products while promoting use of alternative fibers, and advocate for responsible stewardship of private lands. 2001.

884-113 Earth Island Institute, San Francisco, CA, $20,000. For general support to provide services to environmental activists and projects. 2001.

884-114 Earth Island Institute, International Marine Mammal Project, San Francisco, CA, $10,000. For campaign to block deployment of U.S. Navy's LFA Sonar program. 2001.

884-115 Earth Share, Bethesda, MD, $150,000. To develop unified national structure to organize workplace giving campaigns for environmental causes. 2001.

884-116 Earth Share of Georgia, Atlanta, GA, $33,000. To build infrastructure in preparation for organization's transition to Earth Share of Georgia. 2001.

884-117 Earthlife Canada Foundation, Vancouver, Canada, $20,000. To increase community understanding of relationship between land protection and economic stability, establish community-driven planning as model for forest management, and protect important fish and wildlife habitat on the island of Haida Gwaii. 2001.

884-118 Ecology Center, Missoula, MT, $80,000. For general support to restore and protect prairie ecosystems throughout Northern Great Plains and public lands in northern Rockies. 2001.

884-119 Ecotrust, Portland, Oregon, $25,000. For general support for Indigenous Community Capacity Development in Southeast Alaska project, which will build capacity of indigenous groups through mapping and technical outreach. 2001.

884-120 Ecotrust Canada, Vancouver, Canada, $30,000. For general support to work with First Nation partners to build conservation economy on British Columbia's coast. 2001.

884-121 Edmund S. Muskie Foundation, DC, $40,000. To develop network of state legislators nationwide to develop and defend progressive environmental legislation and initiatives. 2001.

884-122 Emory University, School of Law, Atlanta, GA, $115,000. To train students in environmental law and advocacy, and to expand Turner Environmental Law Clinic's caseload. 2001.

884-123 Environmental and Energy Study Institute, DC, $80,000. For Energy and Climate and the Sustainable Communities Programs, which educates members of Congress and advocates for more climate-friendly federal policies that promote managed growth, and build coalitions among

strategic constituencies and NGOs in support of these positions. 2001.

884-124 Environmental Background Information Center, New York, NY, $10,000. For general support to provide grassroots environmental and environmental justice groups with access to information and training in use of information technology tools for organizing. 2001.

884-125 Environmental Community Action (ECO-Action), Atlanta, GA, $50,000. For training program for community activists. 2001.

884-126 Environmental Defense, New York, NY, $100,000. For clean car project that is encouraging auto industry to produce cleaner vehicles, developing national criteria for evaluating environmental impact of new cars, educating public about clean car technology and developing market for hybrid vehicles. 2001.

884-127 Environmental Defense, New York, NY, $100,000. To influence implementation of national transportation and environmental laws that shape planning and investment in order to reduce air pollution, traffic congestion, sprawl, and greenhouse gas emissions. 2001.

884-128 Environmental Grantmakers Association, New York, NY, $10,000. For retreat. 2001.

884-129 Environmental Research Foundation, Princeton, NJ, $20,000. For general support to strengthen democratic decision-making by providing individuals and organizations with reliable scientific and medical information on sources and impacts of toxic pollution. 2001.

884-130 Environmental Support Center, DC, $150,000. For general support for capacity-building programs for local grassroots organizations and State Environmental Leadership Program, which works to counter negative effects of devolution by maintaining network that serves as coordination and strategy mechanism for pro-environment multi-state campaigns. 2001.

884-131 Environmental Working Group, DC, $75,000. For general support of research and public education on pesticide policy reform, the impacts of environmental toxins on women and children and the enforcement of environmental laws. 2001.

884-132 Fernbank Museum of Natural History, Atlanta, GA, $60,000. For IMAX film, Lost Worlds, Life in the Balance, and for related educational programs around this film. 2001.

884-133 First Nations Development Institute, Fredericksburg, VA, $35,000. To promote sustainable natural resource management in Native Alaskan communities through regional workshops, technical assistance, research, and public policy advocacy. 2001.

884-134 Five Valleys Land Trust, Missoula, MT, $30,000. For general support of private land conservation easements in the Missoula Valley, the Rock Creek Watershed and the Clark Fork River Corridor. 2001.

884-135 Flathead Land Trust, Kalispell, MT, $10,000. For general support to increase community involvement through outreach and membership-building programs and project development in expanded territories. 2001.

884-136 Florida Certified Organic Growers and Consumers, Gainesville, FL, $25,000. To promote environmentally- and economically-sound farming practices. 2001.

884-137 Florida Defenders of the Environment, Tallahassee, FL, $25,000. To protect and restore Ocklawaha River, its floodplain, forest, and the natural springs associated with the river valley. 2001.

884-138 Florida Stewardship Foundation, Boca Raton, FL, $20,000. To implement Resource Conservation Agreement and A New Look at Agriculture initiatives, and to broaden these programs from the state to the national level. 2001.

884-139 Florida Wildlife Federation, Tallahassee, FL, $30,000. To defend rural and natural lands in Southwest Florida from urban sprawl. 2001.

884-140 Forest Trends Association, DC, $20,000. For project support to publish, promote and distribute resource guide, The Wood Reduction Trilogy: The Guide to Tree-Free, Recycled and Certified Papers - Building With Vision and Unwrapping Packaging. 2001.

884-141 Forest Trust, Santa Fe, NM, $30,000. To increase capacity of southeastern foresters to provide private landowners with options for sustainable forest management. 2001.

884-142 ForestEthics, Berkeley, CA, $60,000. For national marketing campaign to stop purchasing from ancient and publicly-owned forests and reduce virgin wood fiber use by shifting to post-consumer, agricultural and other tree-free fibers. 2001.

884-143 Friends of Action Group on Erosion Technology and Concentration, Carrboro, NC, $35,000. For public education, legislative and regulatory advocacy, campaign coordination, and farm-based projects to promote sustainable agriculture, the conservation of agricultural biodiversity and preservation of family farms. 2001.

884-144 Friends of the Bitterroot, Hamilton, MT, $10,000. For general support of forest watch, wildland and wildlife conservation, river protection, and grassroots outreach programs. 2001.

884-145 Friends of the Earth, DC, $50,000. For general support for efforts to raise public awareness of economic-environmental linkages, build coalitions, and facilitate grassroots involvement in key policy debates and reform. 2001.

884-146 Friends of the Wild Swan, Swan Lake, MT, $10,000. For general support to restore aquatic and terrestrial ecosystems in northwest Montana. 2001.

884-147 Fund for Southern Communities, Decatur, GA, $100,000. For Environmental Justice Fund, which provides small grants to community-based groups addressing local environmental problems. 2001.

884-148 Fund for Southern Communities, Decatur, GA, $50,000. For general support to educate, inform and mobilize public about threats to environmental health of Coastal Georgia, and of performance of regulatory agencies in addressing those threats. 2001.

884-149 Fund for Southern Communities, Decatur, GA, $15,000. For work to intervene in Nuclear Regulatory Commission license application process to oppose building of prototype factory for producing mixed oxide fuel at Savannah River site in South Carolina. 2001.

884-150 Fundacion Vida Silvestre Argentina (FVSA), Buenos Aires, Argentina, $25,000. For Biodiversity Conservation in Austrocedrus Chilensis Forest project to analyze changes in biodiversity and the economic benefits of forest management and recovery alternatives. 2001.

884-151 Gallatin Valley Land Trust, Bozeman, MT, $20,000. For general support to complete land protection projects, including continued conservation easement negotiation in Yellowstone to Yukon Bozeman Pass Corridor, in riparian/wetland areas and other wildlife habitats in Greater Yellowstone ecosystem. 2001.

884-152 Garden Club of Georgia, Atlanta, GA, $20,000. For ongoing litigation against Georgia's Department of Transportation and outdoor advertisers to prevent publicly-owned, right-of-way trees from being cut for billboard visibility. 2001.

884-153 Georgia Center for Law in the Public Interest, Atlanta, GA, $75,000. For general support to promote development and enforcement of effective environmental laws in Georgia through litigation, legislative initiatives and public advocacy. 2001.

884-154 Georgia Conservancy, Atlanta, GA, $100,000. For general support to develop comprehensive strategy to address sprawl issues in northern metropolitan Atlanta, coordinate state-wide planning for protection of green space and critical habitats, and continue to enhance website and build organizing capacity. 2001.

884-155 Georgia Department of Natural Resources, Atlanta, GA, $10,000. For Celebrating Our Coastal Treasures event. 2001.

884-156 Georgia Department of Natural Resources, Atlanta, GA, $10,000. For Weekend for Wildlife event. 2001.

884-157 Georgia Forestwatch, Ellijay, GA, $20,000. For general support to protect and enhance biological diversity of North Georgia's public lands and Piedmont's Oconee National Forest through public education and protective legislation, forest planning and project monitoring. 2001.

884-158 Georgia Legal Watch, Athens, GA, $75,000. For general support of community organizing, public education, and advocacy and strategic litigation to promote governmental accountability and responsiveness, with focus on promoting enforcement of Clean Water Act provisions regarding development of and community participation in Total Maximum Daily Loads. 2001.

884-159 Georgia Organic Growers Association, Acworth, GA, $20,000. For general support to promote organic agriculture. 2001.

884-160 Georgia River Network, Atlanta, GA, $50,000. For general support to strengthen statewide network of watershed groups to expand public awareness of water and watershed threats, and to enforce accountability of regulatory agencies with responsibility for waters and watersheds. 2001.

884-161 Georgia Southern University, Statesboro, GA, $15,000. For Saint Catherine's Sea Turtle Conservation Program, effort to protect nesting sea turtles and nests through research, monitoring and environmental education. 2001.

884-162 Georgians for Clean Energy, Atlanta, GA, $35,000. To promote clean, affordable energy through coalition building, advocacy and educational road shows. 2001.

884-163 German World Population Foundation, Hannover, Germany, $75,000. For general support of advocacy and media projects to increase support for family planning and sustainable development in Germany and Europe. 2001.

884-164 Global Green USA, Santa Monica, CA, $60,000. For educational outreach and advocacy, and publications in support of green building and green power, primarily in California. 2001.

884-165 Global Green USA, DC, $50,000. For Businesses and Environmentalists Allied for Recycling project to increase national recycling rates. 2001.

884-166 Global Green USA, DC, $50,000. For Businesses and Environmentalists Allied for Recycling project to increase national recycling rates. 2001.

884-167 Grand Canyon Trust, Flagstaff, AZ, $10,000. For general support to protect and restore canyon country of Colorado Plateau in southern Utah and northwest Arizona. 2001.

884-168 Greater Yellowstone Coalition, Bozeman, MT, $100,000. For general support to protect forest ecosystems and wildlife in Greater Yellowstone ecosystem. 2001.

884-169 Green Fire Productions, Eugene, Oregon, $20,000. To provide quality video programs to strengthen western environmental groups' advocacy efforts, with focus on habitat protection issues. 2001.

884-170 Greenpeace Fund, DC, $150,000. To address global warming through public outreach and education. 2001.

884-171 Greenpeace Fund, DC, $50,000. For World Heritage Forests program to protect primary forests in Russia. 2001.

884-172 Greenpeace Fund, DC, $50,000. For Collaborative Defense Campaign, a joint endeavor to educate the public, media and decision-makers about threats to America's landmark environmental safeguards. 2001.

884-173 Groundwater Foundation, Lincoln, NE, $25,000. For project support to protect groundwater resources. 2001.

884-174 H. John Heinz III Center for Science, Economics and the Environment, DC, $100,000. For leadership forums on global climate change. 2001.

884-175 Hawkwatch International, Salt Lake City, UT, $20,000. To further conservation science strategy to address issues of powerline electrocution of raptors, wildlife poisoning from lead-based ammunition and sinkers, and habitat loss and degradation. 2001.

884-176 Headwaters Resource Conservation and Development Area, Butte, MT, $10,000. To address gaps in after-school assistance and recreational opportunities for youth in after-school computer/study club and Youth Community Volunteer Program. 2001.

884-177 Idaho Sporting Congress, Boise, ID, $10,000. For general support to litigate against illegal logging of forests on federal lands and educate public to effect sound environmental policies. 2001.

884-178 Independent Press Association, San Francisco, CA, $15,000. For PAPER Project, partnership with Co-op America and Conservatree, to advocate for and aid magazine publishers to switch to more environmentally-responsible paper products. 2001.

884-179 INFORM, New York, NY, $15,000. To persuade government agencies and public facilities to minimize procurement of products containing mercury, lead, dioxin and persistent bioaccumulative toxins. 2001.

884-180 Institute for Agriculture and Trade Policy, Minneapolis, MN, $50,000. To promote socially and ecologically sustainable development while ensuring environmental protection. 2001.

884-181 Institute for Energy and Environmental Research, Takoma Park, MD, $20,000. To build capacities of individuals and organizations concerned with production and disposal of nuclear weapons. 2001.

884-182 Institute for Policy Studies, DC, $75,000. For Sustainable Energy and Economy Network's efforts to monitor investments of World Bank and other public financial institutions in fossil fuel projects in developing countries, and to promote increased investment by these institutions in renewable energy projects. 2001.

884-183 Institutes for Journalism and Natural Resources, Missoula, MT, $35,000. For hands-on environmental education programs for journalists, and Wallace Stegner Initiative to monitor and assess quality of news coverage of environment in the West. 2001.

884-184 International Council for Local Environmental Initiatives USA, Boston, MA, $70,000. To enhance Cities for Climate Protection campaign through initiative to achieve deeper long-term reductions in greenhouse gas emissions. 2001.

884-185 International Crane Foundation, Baraboo, WI, $50,000. For general support to use ultralight aircraft to lead groups of captive-reared Whooping Cranes from Wisconsin to Florida in effort to reintroduce them to wild. 2001.

884-186 International Rivers Network, Berkeley, CA, $35,000. For general support to develop and assist global grassroots movement to protect rivers and watersheds from inappropriate and damaging uses. 2001.

884-187 International Snow Leopard Trust, Seattle, WA, $25,000. For Snow Leopard and Habitat Conservation in the Former Soviet Union project. 2001.

884-188 Izaak Walton League of America, Gaithersburg, MD, $200,000. To strengthen current power plant campaigns in Midwest and Southeast, focusing on states and issue areas where best opportunities exist for tangible progress on power plant clean-up policy. 2001.

884-189 Izaak Walton League of America, Gaithersburg, MD, $35,000. To expand Outdoor American Campaign, which seeks to involve more hunters, anglers and other political moderates in key environmental issues and ongoing implementation of Save Our Streams Program. 2001.

884-190 Jackson Hole Wildlife Film Festival, Jackson, WY, $10,000. For general support. 2001.

884-191 Kentucky Environmental Foundation, Berea, KY, $35,000. To prevent siting of chemical weapons incinerators in communities and to ensure use of clean advanced technologies for chemical weapons disposal. 2001.

884-192 Lake Allatoona Preservation Authority, Acworth, GA, $20,000. To reduce pollutant loading and sedimentation into Lake Allatoona through vegetative stabilization of critical areas of shoreline. 2001.

884-193 Land Institute, Salina, KS, $40,000. For general support to develop and disseminate new agricultural paradigm to reduce problems of soil erosion and agrochemical application. 2001.

884-194 Land Trust Alliance, DC, $150,000. For general support to increase quality, effectiveness and sustainability of land trusts and their conservation transactions, increase public's understanding of land trusts and importance of voluntary conservation, and expand land trusts' access to information and educational opportunities. 2001.

884-195 Land Trust Alliance, DC, $100,000. For Southwest Matching Grants Program to assist southwestern land trusts in building their organizational capacity and expertise. 2001.

884-196 Lawyers Committee for Civil Rights Under Law, DC, $40,000. To strengthen grassroots community groups working to address toxic contamination and protect public health. 2001.

884-197 League of Conservation Voters, DC, $400,000. To strengthen and deploy state partnership projects on key issues nationwide, and upgrade capacity of environmental leaders and organizers on front lines of shaping environmental policy at state and local level. 2001.

884-198 League of Conservation Voters Education Fund, DC, $2,278,614. To strengthen and deploy state partnership projects on key issues nationwide and enhance skills of environmental leaders and organizers at state and local levels. 2001.

884-199 Legal Environmental Assistance Foundation (LEAF), Tallahassee, FL, $70,000. To strengthen ability of Georgia, Florida and Alabama communities to protect themselves from environmental threats. 2001.

884-200 Lowcountry Open Land Trust, Charleston, SC, $45,000. For general support to increase permanent protection of South Carolina's coastal lands by conservation easements, through landowner education programs, membership development, and continued cultivation of major donors. 2001.

884-201 Lula Lake Land Trust, Chattanooga, TN, $12,000. For small budget, local land trusts in Georgia, Florida, South Carolina, Montana, New Mexico, Colorado and Nebraska that have proven track record of preserving natural landscapes. 2001.

884-202 Military Toxics Project, Lewiston, ME, $20,000. For general support to expose, confront and remediate environmental impacts of military activity. 2001.

884-203 Mineral Policy Center, DC, $95,000. For reform of mining laws and regulations, to support local campaigns against mining projects, and to improve industry performance by compelling companies to raise level of their social and environmental practices. 2001.

884-204 Montana Association of Churches, Billings, MT, $20,000. To empower voices of faith on behalf of environmental issues. 2001.

884-205 Montana Environmental Information Center, Helena, MT, $65,000. For general support of campaigns to build permanent environmental protections. 2001.

884-206 Montana Land Reliance, Helena, MT, $50,000. To aggressively pursue land conservation easements, build bridge capital and explore real estate options in order to compete against sprawl and irreversible development on threatened private lands, those owned by ranchers and farmers. 2001.

884-207 Montana State Parks Association, Billings, MT, $15,000. For Yellowstone River Conservation Forum project, a coalition of river stakeholders formed to achieve cooperative and comprehensive protection and management of Yellowstone River. 2001.

884-208 Montana State University, Department of Land Resources and Environmental Sciences, Bozeman, MT, $30,000. To investigate ecological processes that encourage invasion of exotic plant species. 2001.

884-209 Montana Wilderness Association, Helena, MT, $15,000. For Quiet Trails Campaign to protect public wildlands, wildlife, and backcounty recreation opportunities from inappropriate off-road vehicle use. 2001.

884-210 Mountain Conservation Trust of Georgia, Jasper, GA, $10,000. To purchase mountain forest in North Georgia and to complete conservation easement of forest adjacent to wilderness area. 2001.

884-211 National Alliance for Community Trees, College Park, MD, $10,000. For National Policy program which will educate Congressional members, provide testimony to House Sub-Committee on interior appropriations in support of Forest Service's Urban and Community Forest Program, educate state and federal agencies on how they can increase impact of congressionally mandated programs, and provide comments on Farm Bill to agencies and elected officials. 2001.

884-212 National Association of Conservation Districts, DC, $90,000. For expanded outreach program to conservation district officials and other farm groups on topic of agriculture and global warming, with particular emphasis on carbon sequestration through improved conservation practices. 2001.

884-213 National Campaign for Sustainable Agriculture, Pine Bush, NY, $15,000. For general support for programs and campaigns to insure environmental integrity of Farm Bill. 2001.

884-214 National Catholic Rural Life Conference, Des Moines, IA, $20,000. For general support to promote sustainable policy outcomes for Omnibus Farm Bill. 2001.

884-215 National Fish and Wildlife Foundation, DC, $80,000. For general support to expand watershed and longleaf pine conservation programs on private lands throughout Southeast. 2001.

884-216 National Fish and Wildlife Foundation, DC, $20,000. To conserve prairie dog ecosystem of northwestern Mexico, and associated species and their habitat of key grasslands areas. 2001.

884-217 National Fish and Wildlife Foundation, DC, $15,000. For general support. 2001.

884-218 National Forest Protection Alliance, Missoula, MT, $40,000. For general support toward ending commercial logging on public lands. 2001.

884-219 National Parks Conservation Association, DC, $175,000. For general support to build comprehensive program to assess and protect biological health of national parks, and project support to identify and mobilize new individuals for organization's advocacy and broader conservation movement. 2001.

884-220 National Parks Conservation Association, DC, $75,000. For Collaborative Defense Campaign, joint endeavor to educate public, media and decision-makers about threats to America's landmark environmental safeguards. 2001.

884-221 National Parks Conservation Association, DC, $10,000. For Tribute Committee Annual Award. 2001.

884-222 National Public Radio (NPR), DC, $50,000. For environmental news coverage on news magazine shows, Morning Edition, and All Things Considered. 2001.

884-223 National Religious Partnership for the Environment, Amherst, MA, $213,000. For interfaith global warming campaigns in states and to broaden public awareness of faith community's interest in this issue. 2001.

884-224 National Religious Partnership for the Environment, Amherst, MA, $125,000. For development of collaborative electronic advocacy networks serving faith community and public health community. 2001.

884-225 National Trust for Historic Preservation, DC, $50,000. To address proliferation of big-box retail stores and mega-schools, which encourage sprawling development, and to promote preservation-based alternatives. 2001.

884-226 National Wildlife Federation, Anchorage, AK, $40,000. For project support to prevent road construction and other activities from threatening Copper River Delta basin and to work with Forest Service to have portions of the basin designated as wilderness area. 2001.

884-227 National Wildlife Federation, Reston, VA, $500,000. For general support to mobilize citizen activists around state, regional and national conservation issues. 2001.

884-228 National Wildlife Federation, Reston, VA, $135,000. For Collaborative Defense Campaign, joint endeavor to educate public, media and decision-makers about threats to America's landmark environmental safeguards. 2001.

884-229 National Wildlife Refuge Association, DC, $100,000. For general support to make National Wildlife Refuge System cornerstone of ecosystem-wide efforts to improve nation's ecological health and biological integrity. 2001.

884-230 Natural Resources Defense Council, New York, NY, $666,667. For opinion research and message development to enhance campaigns against climate change. 2001.

884-231 Natural Resources Defense Council, New York, NY, $400,000. To mount technical and legal challenges to ill-conceived missile defense programs and liaise with European governments and activists on missile defense and U.S. nuclear doctrinal issues. 2001.

884-232 Natural Resources Defense Council, New York, NY, $100,000. For Clean Vehicle Fuels program, consisting of California Petroleum Reduction campaign and legal and public campaign for regulating vehicle emissions of carbon dioxide. 2001.

884-233 Natural Resources Defense Council, New York, NY, $100,000. To coordinate federally-focused clean water policy advocacy (with concentration on enforcement, feedlots, wetlands, and total maximum daily loads), and to organize a campaign focused on total maximum daily loads, pulp and paper mills, and confined animal feeding operations (CAFOs) in Florida. 2001.

884-234 Natural Resources Defense Council, New York, NY, $90,000. For Collaborative Defense Campaign, joint endeavor to educate public, media, and decision-makers about threats to America's landmark environmental safeguards. 2001.

884-235 Nature Conservancy, Atlanta, GA, $200,000. For Freshwater Initiative, an organization-wide campaign to increase protection of biological diversity of rivers and lakes in the Americas. 2001.

884-236 Nature Conservancy, Bismarck, ND, $20,000. To increase reproductive success of Great Plains population of threatened Piping Plover. 2001.

884-237 NatureServe, Arlington, VA, $30,000. For project support to provide information documenting and ranking impacts of invasive species on native plants, animals and ecological systems through Internet-based NatureServe. 2001.

884-238 Nebraska Wildlife Federation, Lincoln, NE, $30,000. For Platte River Basin project to influence development of basin management plan for Platte River. 2001.

884-239 New Mexico Environmental Law Center, Santa Fe, NM, $50,000. For general support to provide free legal representation to organizations and communities attempting to protect themselves and their environments, especially air and water, from pollution and exposure to toxins. 2001.

884-240 New Mexico Public Interest Research Group Education Fund, Albuquerque, NM, $30,000. For programs promoting renewable energy and limiting impacts of sprawl and development, encompassing research, public education, grassroots organizing and advocacy efforts. 2001.

884-241 New Mexico Wilderness Alliance, Albuquerque, NM, $20,000. To protect and restore both designated and eligible wilderness areas. 2001.

884-242 Northern Plains Resource Council, Billings, MT, $30,000. For Montana Waters Protection Project, including community organizing, public education, advocacy, and strategic litigation to protect ground and surface waters threatened by mining, waste disposal, and animal factories. 2001.

884-243 Nuclear Control Institute, DC, $15,000. To prevent use of plutonium fuel in commercial nuclear reactors in North and South Carolina and to halt plans to fabricate mixed oxide fuel (MOX) at the Savannah River site in South Carolina. 2001.

884-244 Oregon Trout, Portland, Oregon, $20,000. For Fish Refuge Program to create interconnected system of refuges for native salmon, steelhead, trout, and other aquatic species. 2001.

884-245 Ossabaw Island Foundation, Savannah, GA, $35,000. For general support of public use and environmental education programs. 2001.

884-246 Ossabaw Island Foundation, Savannah, GA, $10,000. For general support. 2001.

884-247 Pacific Environment and Resources Center, Oakland, CA, $90,000. For efforts by leading environmental organizations to protect Russian taiga by stopping large-scale resource extraction in Siberia and Russian Far East. 2001.

884-248 Pacific Primate Sanctuary, Haiku, HI, $10,000. For general support to rehabilitate traumatized Central and South American primates and maintain viable breeding colonies of New World monkeys, including threatened marmosets and tamarins. 2001.

884-249 Pacific Rivers Council, Eugene, Oregon, $25,000. For general support for effective aquatic conservation on federal and private industrial timberlands in Southern Appalachians and Northern Rockies. 2001.

884-250 Partners for DeKalb Parks, Decatur, GA, $75,000. To produce Natural Heritage Area Management Plan for Arabia Mountain in southeast Dekalb County. 2001.

884-251 Partnership Project, DC, $1,218,750. To coordinate large-scale campaigns through activating membership base of environmental groups. 2001.

884-252 Partnership Project, DC, $580,000. For large-scale coordinated communications between national environmental groups and their members. 2001.

884-253 Partnership Project, DC, $200,000. To coordinate large-scale campaigns through activating membership base of environmental groups. 2001.

884-254 PCL Foundation, Sacramento, CA, $30,000. To continue tabling campaign to defend current Zero-Emission Vehicle standards in California. 2001.

884-255 Peregrine Fund, Boise, ID, $40,000. For project support for recovery of California Condor and Aplomado Falcon. 2001.

884-256 Pesticide Action Network (PAN), North America Regional Center, San Francisco, CA, $20,000. For project to advocate for ecologically sound pest management practices. 2001.

884-257 Physicians for Social Responsibility, DC, $60,000. For Environment and Health Program that mobilizes health care providers as environmental health advocates with

particular attention to advocating for US Senate ratification of Persistent Organic Pollutants treaty. 2001.

884-258 Piedmont Park Conservancy, Atlanta, GA, $10,000. For project support for Atlanta's Green Heart Campaign, specifically to restore Lake Clara Meer in Piedmont Park. 2001.

884-259 Poseidon, New York, NY, $100,000. To establish international advocacy organization with singular mission of protecting life in the sea. 2001.

884-260 Prairie Plains Resource Institute, Aurora, NE, $10,000. For general support of Platte River Corridor Initiative to further private land restoration projects along Platte by removing invasive red cedars, establishing grassland bank, enlarging prescribed burning cooperative, and assisting private landowners in replanting native prairies. 2001.

884-261 Predator Conservation Alliance, Bozeman, MT, $30,000. For general support for conservation and public education, outreach, and organizing efforts to ensure protection and restoration of predators throughout Northern Rockies and High Plains. 2001.

884-262 Project del Rio, Las Cruces, NM, $15,000. To enhance environmental education program through conducting in-depth reflective assessment with teachers. Grant made through Tides Center. 2001.

884-263 Public Employees for Environmental Responsibility (PEER), DC, $40,000. For ongoing work to encourage professional integrity in enforcement of environmental laws at local, state, and federal agencies. 2001.

884-264 Public Lands Action Network, Albuquerque, NM, $35,000. For general support of advocacy and public education within Gila Watershed, focused primarily on opposing grazing permits on public lands. 2001.

884-265 Public Media Center, San Francisco, CA, $20,000. For project support to educate Japanese public about timber industry and health of world's forests, reduce paper consumption within Japan, propose alternative fibers and organize letter writing campaign. 2001.

884-266 Quivira Coalition, Santa Fe, NM, $20,000. For general support to teach ranchers, environmentalists, public land managers, and other members of New Mexico public that ecologically health rangeland and economically robust ranches can be compatible. 2001.

884-267 Rails to Trails Conservancy, DC, $35,000. For International Trail and Greenways Network which will catalyze development of regional green infrastructure systems by connecting individual trail and greenway projects with information and resources necessary for success. 2001.

884-268 Rainforest Action Network, San Francisco, CA, $50,000. For Old Growth Campaign to continue efforts to shift forest products industry away from old growth wood and towards sustainable alternatives through markets and grassroots pressure, and partnerships with leading retailers. 2001.

884-269 Rainforest Alliance, New York, NY, $25,000. For SmartWood Project, which promotes wood certification by making timber certification affordable and accessible to small community and indigenous groups that are currently underserved by forestry certification industry. 2001.

884-270 Reef Relief, Key West, FL, $60,000. For advocacy, education, and research programs to strengthen protection for and encourage responsible stewardship of Coral Reefs. 2001.

884-271 Reuse Development Organization, West Sand Lake, NY, $15,000. For general support of work to promote reuse as an environmentally sound, socially beneficial, and economical means for managing surplus and discarded materials. 2001.

884-272 Rio Grande Restoration, El Prado, NM, $40,000. For general support of work to restore Rio Grande to health by securing streamflow regime of improved, high quality water. 2001.

884-273 Rio Grande Rio Bravo Basin Coalition, El Paso, TX, $20,000. For general support of work to build and sustain bi-national network of organizations and citizens prepared to work together to insure long-term sustainability of Rio Grande Rio Bravo Basin. 2001.

884-274 Robert W. Woodruff Arts Center, Atlanta, GA, $20,000. To limit destructive logging on public land, restore native forests in Appalachian Range, promote non-wood alternative products, and support greater sustainable forestry movement. 2001.

884-275 Rockefeller Family Fund, New York, NY, $100,000. To strengthen implementation and enforcement of environmental laws at state level. 2001.

884-276 Rocky Mountain Elk Foundation, Missoula, MT, $50,000. For general support to establish Elk Country Legacy Program, science-based habitat conservation effort that will involve coordinated conservation planning by wide range of stakeholders in priority areas identified through habitat mapping. 2001.

884-277 Rocky Mountain Institute, Snowmass, CO, $65,000. To foster efficient and restorative use of natural and human capital by showing corporations, communities, individuals, and governments how to create more wealth and employment and enhance natural and human capital. 2001.

884-278 Safe Energy Communication Council, DC, $25,000. For Climate Change and Sustainable Energy Education project, which aims to replace policies that subsidize nuclear energy production and development with policies supporting cleaner and safer energy solutions. 2001.

884-279 Saint Johns Riverkeeper, Jacksonville, FL, $25,000. For general support to protect, preserve and restore ecological integrity of Saint John's River watershed through public education, outreach, and strategic advocacy. 2001.

884-280 San Juan Citizens Alliance, Durango, CO, $15,000. For Wild San Juans Campaign, effort to protect and restore habitat and wildlife of San Juan Mountains in southwest Colorado. 2001.

884-281 Savannah Science Museum, Savannah, GA, $10,000. For research, environmental education, and conservation efforts for threatened loggerhead sea turtles nesting on Wassaw Island. 2001.

884-282 Save the Bay, Providence, RI, $20,000. To secure an environmentally sound re-permitting of Brayton Point Power Plant and watershed-wide habitat restoration. 2001.

884-283 Save the Manatee Club, Maitland, FL, $25,000. For general support to protect, rescue, and rehabilitate manatees. 2001.

884-284 Scenic America, DC, $15,000. To promote scenic conservation by focusing public attention on scenic costs of unplanned development patterns and making connection between urban sprawl and environmental degradation. 2001.

884-285 Sea Turtle Restoration Project, Forest Knolls, CA, $30,000. For Pacific Fisheries Program to protect migratory habitats of endangered leatherback sea turtle and other marine species by addressing impacts of industrial fishing in the Pacific. 2001.

884-286 Seva Foundation, Berkeley, CA, $30,000. To establish Native Conservancy Land Trust to preserve Bering River coalfields and adjacent lands in Copper River Delta region, in addition to continued efforts to conserve and protect Copper River Delta and Prince William Sound until mutually agreed upon conservation plan is in place. 2001.

884-287 Seventh Generation Fund for Indian Development, Arcata, CA, $25,000. To defend ecological integrity of traditional Native homelands and to restore Native ecological practices. 2001.

884-288 Sierra Club Foundation, San Francisco, CA, $125,000. For Collaborative Defense Campaign, joint endeavor to educate public, media and decision-makers about threats to America's landmark environmental safeguards. 2001.

884-289 Sierra Club Foundation, San Francisco, CA, $100,000. For Fuel Economy Campaign, to educate American public, media, and policymakers about need for cleaner cars, and to build pressure on automakers to implement and exceed commitments they have made to improve SUV fuel economy. 2001.

884-290 Sierra Club Foundation, San Francisco, CA, $75,000. For Challenge to Sprawl campaign, to educate citizens about costs of sprawl and benefits of smart growth, and to empower citizens to participate in decisions about land use and transportation. 2001.

884-291 Sierra Club Foundation, San Francisco, CA, $50,000. For Southern Rockies Wolf Restoration Campaign. 2001.

884-292 Sierra Club Foundation, San Francisco, CA, $30,000. To reduce annual average of human-bear conflicts in Yellowstone regions through outreach/educational campaigns to sportsmen and recreationalists, local homeowners, businesses and others; a bear-proof dumpster purchase program in cooperation with Bridger-Teton National Forest and pepper-spray donation project in cooperation with manufacturers; and collaborative efforts to address specific problems such as garbage dumps. 2001.

884-293 Sierra Club of British Columbia Foundation, Victoria, Canada, $120,000. To protect Great Bear Rainforest by utilizing logging moratoria and increasing public and market campaign pressure to leverage an ecologically-sound land use plan that represents agreement amongst First Nations, government, and environmental community. 2001.

884-294 Sierra Legal Defence Fund, Vancouver, Canada, $40,000. For strategic litigation and comprehensive communications campaign to expose Ministry of Forest's lack of enforcement and International Forestry Products' forestry practices. 2001.

884-295 Sierra Legal Defence Fund, Vancouver, Canada, $30,000. For general support to provide free legal services to First Nations in British Columbia with goal of redressing inequities that perpetuate environmental degradation. 2001.

884-296 Sinapu, Boulder, CO, $25,000. For general support of predator restoration and protection programs in Southern Rockies, including its leadership of two national coalitions, the Southern Rockies Wolf Restoration Project and the Aerial Gunning Resistance Organizers. 2001.

884-297 Sky Island Alliance, Tucson, AZ, $20,000. For fieldwork, public outreach, and land and wildlife policy work to help implement new Sky Islands Wildlands Network Conservation Plan in southeastern Arizona, southwestern New Mexico and northwestern Mexico. 2001.

884-298 SOC Education Fund, Louisville, KY, $60,000. To assist network of grassroots groups organizing against toxic threats to low-income communities. 2001.

884-299 Society of Environmental Journalists, Jenkintown, PA, $20,000. For general support to improve quality, accuracy and visibility of environmental reporting. 2001.

884-300 Sonoran Institute, Tucson, AZ, $40,000. For Yellowstone to Yukon Community Stewardship program, which integrates community-based approaches into Y2Y Initiative's overall conservation strategy, so that ecological and human communities thrive side by side. 2001.

884-301 Soque River Watershed Association, Clarkesville, GA, $30,000. For general support of public education and advocacy to maintain and improve water quality in the Soque River, its tributaries and its watershed. 2001.

884-302 South Carolina Coastal Conservation League, Charleston, SC, $100,000. For general support to expand local land use planning efforts, to establish a permanent presence in state capitol, to employ state-of-the-art communications technology, and to develop endowment and expanded donor base. 2001.

884-303 South Carolina Environmental Law Project, Pawleys Island, SC, $60,000. For general support for programs and operations providing legal services to environmental community. 2001.

884-304 South Carolina Forest Watch, Westminster, SC, $20,000. For general support to ensure that state and federal agencies manage public forestlands according to sound ecological principles. 2001.

884-305 South Carolina Waterfowl Association (SWCA), Pinewood, SC, $10,000. To examine historic and future population trends in wood ducks and other cavity-nesting species in relation to changing human activities in South Carolina. 2001.

884-306 Southeast Alaska Conservation Council, Juneau, AK, $50,000. For general support to defend Tongass National Forest and neighboring unprotected wildlands from destructive development through watchdogging activities and efforts to increase grassroots support. 2001.

884-307 Southeast Watershed Forum, Annapolis, MD, $10,000. For general support to provide information and training to watershed groups in Southeast and to facilitate dialogue and cooperation between watershed stakeholders (NGOs, state agencies, and business interests) in the Southeast. 2001.

884-308 Southern Appalachian Biodiversity Project, Asheville, NC, $15,000. For project support for defense of natural forest ecosystems and endangered species threatened by logging activities. 2001.

884-309 Southern Environmental Law Center, Charlottesville, VA, $350,000. For continued support to clean up old coal-fired power plants in Southeast through closing loophole allowing these plants to operate despite violations of Clean Air regulations. 2001.

884-310 Southern Environmental Law Center, Charlottesville, VA, $180,000. For environmental advocacy efforts in Georgia and South Carolina. 2001.

884-311 Southern Environmental Law Center, Charlottesville, VA, $80,000. For general support to secure permanent protection for public land in Southern Appalachians. 2001.

884-312 Southern Partners Fund, Atlanta, GA, $50,000. For regranting program to support general operating expenses and training costs for environmental justice organizations in Florida. 2001.

884-313 Southern Rockies Ecosystem Project, Nederland, CO, $20,000. For general support to design and implement Southern Rockies Wildlands Network conservation plan, provide Geographic Information Systems (GIS) mapping services and data to conservation groups and advocate for protection of biodiversity and wildlands through education and outreach to general public and land managers. 2001.

884-314 Southface Energy Institute, Atlanta, GA, $60,000. To educate and organize coalition for cleaner energy in Georgia. 2001.

884-315 Southwest Community Resources, Albuquerque, NM, $20,000. To strengthen environmentally threatened communities in southwest. 2001.

884-316 Southwest Environmental Center, Las Cruces, NM, $15,000. To restore Rio Grande ecosystem by developing restoration plan, ending destructive flow management practices, strengthening water quality standards, and protecting riparian habitat and water rights along the river. 2001.

884-317 Southwest Research and Information Center, Albuquerque, NM, $30,000. To stop construction and operation of proposed uranium mines in northwestern New Mexico. 2001.

884-318 Surfrider Foundation, San Clemente, CA, $10,000. To establish and strengthen

beach water quality monitoring programs. 2001.

884-319 Sustainable Cotton Project, Oroville, CA, $40,000. For Cleaner Cotton Project to increase supply of organic cotton through farmer-to-farmer mentoring program and to increase demand for organic cotton through outreach to apparel manufacturers. 2001.

884-320 Tampa Baywatch, Saint Petersburg, FL, $20,000. For general operating support to implement area restoration activities. 2001.

884-321 Taxpayers for Common Sense, DC, $40,000. For Green Scissors Campaign, which exposes federal subsidies that harm environment. 2001.

884-322 Texas A & I University, Kingsville, TX, $20,000. For research into ecology of Black Bear populations along Mexican-United States border to determine basic population numbers, denning ecology, and dispersal patterns of this endangered species. 2001.

884-323 Texas A & M University, College Station, TX, $90,000. For Banking Bison: Tissue Culture Cells for Cloning of Bison in Case of Catastrophic Loss, a collaborative research project with goal of identifying and developing repository of bison cells that will represent as near as possible the total genetic variation that exists in modern bison herds to insure against loss of species and encourage genetic diversity among particular bison herds. 2001.

884-324 Texas Fund for Energy and Environmental Education, Austin, TX, $70,000. For Campaign ExxonMobil, including conference for corporate campaigners, and of efforts to monitor global warming plan for Texas. 2001.

884-325 Third Millennium Foundation, Henderson, NC, $60,000. To advocate for ratification of Specially Protected Areas and Wildlife (SPAW) Protocol, international agreement that provides for protection of rare and fragile Caribbean ecosystems and plants and animals they support. 2001.

884-326 Tides Center, San Francisco, CA, $75,000. To assist environmentalists through educating the media and other communications strategies. 2001.

884-327 Tides Center, San Francisco, CA, $35,000. For Climate Justice Project, which aims to link efforts of people fighting pollution from oil refineries and other fossil fuel industries in their communities with international debate on climate change. 2001.

884-328 Tides Center, San Francisco, CA, $35,000. To monitor implementation and enforcement of National Organic Standard, EPA reassessment of pesticide food tolerances, and general federal pesticide policy. 2001.

884-329 Tides Center, San Francisco, CA, $25,000. For general support of campaigns within paper industry to increase the market share of ecologically sound papers. 2001.

884-330 Tides Center, San Francisco, CA, $15,000. To engage media on behalf of air quality advocates at recent summit on Kyoto Protocol. 2001.

884-331 Tides Foundation, San Francisco, CA, $25,000. For grantmaking program that provides small grants to grassroots organizations that address environmental concerns in developing countries. 2001.

884-332 Tree New Mexico, Albuquerque, NM, $20,000. For tree planting and riparian restoration projects. 2001.

884-333 Trees, Water and People, Fort Collins, CO, $10,000. To promote formation of new watershed protection groups in Colorado and Wyoming and to strengthen new and existing watershed groups by providing technical and capacity-building assistance. 2001.

884-334 Tri-State Coalition for Responsible Investment, Newton, NJ, $15,000. To organize shareholders in support of corporate action to prevent climate change. 2001.

884-335 Trout Unlimited, Missoula, MT, $25,000. For Western Water Project to protect and restore instream flows through advocacy, public education, and strategic coalition building. 2001.

884-336 Trust for Public Land, Atlanta, GA, $700,000. For Chattahoochee Land Protection Campaign, effort to acquire river greenway on either side of the Chattahoochee River from its headwaters in Helen south to Columbus. 2001.

884-337 Trust for Public Land, Northwest Regional Office, Seattle, WA, $15,000. For research and community outreach for conservation funding initiative to generate funds for open space and rural land conservation projects throughout Gallatin County. 2001.

884-338 Trust for Public Land, Southwest Regional Office, Santa Fe, NM, $30,000. To secure public funding for land and water conservation projects at local and state levels. 2001.

884-339 Turner Endangered Species Fund, Atlanta, GA, $1,137,000. For general support to restore habitat and endangered or threatened species to private property owned by R. E. Turner. 2001.

884-340 Union of Concerned Scientists, Cambridge, MA, $100,000. To expand efforts to shape federal and state policy on vehicle tax incentives through Clean Car Pledge Campaign, web-based organizing, and increased corporate engagement with automakers. 2001.

884-341 Union of Concerned Scientists, Cambridge, MA, $90,000. For public education and outreach program focused on building support for increased investments in renewable technologies and energy efficiency in federal energy policy. 2001.

884-342 Union of Concerned Scientists, Cambridge, MA, $50,000. For Transportation Program, to reduce environmental impacts of motor vehicles through promoting cleaner technologies. 2001.

884-343 United States Public Interest Research Group Education Fund, DC, $30,000. To ensure progress in environmental policy arena. 2001.

884-344 United States Public Interest Research Group Education Fund, DC, $15,000. For general support to promote community right-to-know as an effective strategy for reducing toxic chemical hazards and increasing corporate and governmental accountability. 2001.

884-345 University of Georgia, Vinson Institute of Government, Athens, GA, $250,000. For state-wide mapping exercise detailing land cover of Georgia, to be used to make sound management decisions by both natural resource state agencies and the non-profit sector. 2001.

884-346 University of Georgia Foundation, Athens, GA, $10,000. For Red Clay Conference to promote and increase environmental awareness in legal and general communities. 2001.

884-347 University of South Carolina, Beaufort, SC, $50,000. To promote the preservation of loggerhead sea turtle through conservation and research projects on Pritchard Island and St. Philips Island. 2001.

884-348 Upper Chattahoochee Riverkeeper Fund, Atlanta, GA, $200,000. To secure protection and stewardship of Chattahoochee River. 2001.

884-349 Upper Chattahoochee Riverkeeper Fund, Atlanta, GA, $10,000. For general support. 2001.

884-350 Valhalla Wilderness Society, New Denver, Canada, $40,000. For general support to preserve biological diversity of British Columbia's inland, temperate rainforests. 2001.

884-351 Valhalla Wilderness Society, New Denver, Canada, $10,000. For general support. 2001.

884-352 W A M C Public Radio, Albany, NY, $20,000. For general support to produce and broadcast programs on population issues, sprawl, open spaces, health preservation and restoration of ecosystems. 2001.

884-353 Water Information Network (WIN), Albuquerque, NM, $15,000. For organizing work on uranium mining on Indian lands, nuclear waste siting in West Texas, and coal mining on or near Indian lands. 2001.

884-354 Waterkeeper Alliance, White Plains, NY, $50,000. To increase effectiveness of national water/bay keeper network by facilitating intra-network communications through development and expansion of a website. 2001.

884-355 Western Environmental Law Center, Eugene, Oregon, $50,000. For Rio Grande Initiative researching and prosecuting sources of pollution in southern New Mexico and Island Mountains Conservation Project representing tribal clients on environmental issues in Montana. 2001.

884-356 Western Organization of Resource Councils Education Project, Billings, MT, $20,000. For project to challenge environmentally damaging mining practices through grassroots campaigns. 2001.

884-357 Western Resource Advocates, Boulder, CO, $100,000. For Climate Change Program, which encourages western coal-based utilities to support national four-pollutant legislation to both reduce local smog pollution and mitigate global climate change. 2001.

884-358 Western Resource Advocates, Boulder, CO, $40,000. To protect and restore in-stream flows to the Middle Rio Grande River. 2001.

884-359 Western States Center, Portland, Oregon, $35,000. To build the capacity of environmental and social justice organizations to advance growth management and equity policies at state and local levels. 2001.

884-360 Western Sustainable Agriculture Working Group, Butte, MT, $15,000. For general support to promote the development of sustainable agriculture in the West. 2001.

884-361 Whale Conservation Institute, Ocean Alliance, Lincoln, MA, $40,000. For programs and operations to promote global conservation of whales and marine environment. 2001.

884-362 Whirling Disease Foundation, Bozeman, MT, $75,000. For general support to expand science coordination, outreach and education capacities, including annual whirling disease symposium and to continue research toward eliminating threat of whirling disease to native and wild trout, char, salmon and steelhead. 2001.

884-363 White Earth Land Recovery Project, Ponsford, MN, $12,000. To restore and stabilize sturgeon population as living indicator of aquatic ecosystem. 2001.

884-364 Wild Angels, Santa Fe, NM, $25,000. For efforts to protect fragile ecosystems in western U.S., with focus on New Mexico. 2001.

884-365 Wild Salmon Center, Portland, Oregon, $50,000. For project to establish salmon refuges on Russia's Kamchatka Peninsula. 2001.

884-366 Wild Things Unlimited, Bozeman, MT, $10,000. To document status of lynx, wolverines and fishers and their habitats, as well as to provide information regarding impact of human activities such as motorized recreation and timber management. 2001.

884-367 WildAid, San Francisco, CA, $35,000. For anti-poaching efforts in Russian Far East and to coordinate conservation activities of anti-poaching rangers, school administrators, scientists, and media. 2001.

884-368 Wilderness Society, DC, $40,000. For general support to limit motorized recreational vehicle abuse of public lands and waters, with specific focus on upholding snowmobile and jet ski bans in national parks and pressuring Forest Service and Bureau of Land Management to strengthen ORV regulations. 2001.

884-369 Wilderness Society, DC, $25,000. For general support of national campaign to stop damage caused by off road vehicles on public land and water. 2001.

884-370 Wilderness Watch, Missoula, MT, $10,000. For general support to ensure adoption of management plan for Frank Church/River of No Return Wilderness area and to expand organization's capacity to address wilderness management under Department of the Interior. 2001.

884-371 Wildlands Center for Preventing Roads, Missoula, MT, $25,000. For general support to limit motorized recreation and actively pressure agencies to protect and maintain roadless areas. 2001.

884-372 Wildlands Project, Tucson, AZ, $60,000. For Rewild the Rockies Campaign to restore large carnivores such as wolves, grizzly bears, and others to their natural ranges. 2001.

884-373 Wildlands Project, Tucson, AZ, $20,000. To complete analysis of protected vegetation types and to map rare species in Great Divide study area in Wyoming, Utah, Idaho and Colorado. 2001.

884-374 Wildlife Conservation Society, Bronx, NY, $48,000. For wildlife conservation program on Patagonian steppe and in Andean forests, including research on endangered and threatened wildlife of Patagonia in order to develop conservation management strategies. 2001.

884-375 Wildlife Conservation Society, Bronx, NY, $27,500. To conduct ecological research on endangered huemul of Patagonia to prepare and implement conservation plan for the species and its habitat. 2001.

884-376 Wildlife Forever, Brooklyn Center, MN, $30,000. To encourage participation of hunters and anglers in conservation issues relating to future management of fish and wildlife resources on national forests and other public lands. 2001.

884-377 Womens Voices for the Earth, Missoula, MT, $15,000. For organizing and public education targeted at women, and focused on closing medical waste incinerators and raising awareness of connections between toxic pollution and breast cancer. 2001.

884-378 World Resources Institute, DC, $75,000. For general support to build capacity and infrastructure for Global Forest Watch program to map forest development in Guyana Shield and Brazilian Amazon regions, establish local monitoring networks across the regions, and apply new information technologies to international program's monitoring work. 2001.

884-379 World Resources Institute, DC, $25,000. To assist outgoing Assistant Secretary of Energy to document knowledge gained at Department of Energy and to make recommendations for future. 2001.

884-380 World Wildlife Fund/Conservation Foundation, DC, $100,000. For Collaborative Defense Campaign, joint endeavor to educate the public, media and decision-makers about threats to America's landmark environmental safeguards. 2001.

884-381 Worldwatch Institute, DC, $150,000. For research, publishing, outreach, and capacity-building activities. 2001.

884-382 Wyoming Outdoor Council, Lander, WY, $20,000. To integrate ongoing conservation efforts in Greater Yellowstone ecosystem and its boundary areas to safeguard wildlife and habitat. 2001.

884-383 Yellowstone Park Foundation, Bozeman, MT, $40,000. To launch donor development initiative to help Project Yellowstone National Park and surrounding ecosystem. 2001.

884-384 Yellowstone to Yukon Conservation Initiative, Canmore, Canada, $50,000. For general support to protect wildlife and wildlands in Rocky Mountains in U.S. and Canada. 2001.

884-385 Yosemite Foundation, San Francisco, CA, $30,000. For project to conduct census and study of Lee Vining Canyon herd of Sierra Nevada bighorn sheep in Yosemite National Park, including in-depth DNA analysis, radio collaring of sheep and yearly monitoring. 2001.

884-386 Zoo Atlanta, Atlanta, GA, $200,000. For Save a Species: The Campaign for Giant Pandas. 2001.

885
The Edna Wardlaw Charitable Trust
c/o SunTrust Banks, Inc.
P.O. Box 4655
Atlanta, GA 30302-4655
Contact: Danah Craft

Established in 1992 in GA.
Donor(s): Edna Wardlaw.
Grantmaker type: Independent foundation
Financial data (yr. ended 12/31/02): Assets,
$21,326,959 (M); gifts received, $8,466,721;
expenditures, $390,645; qualifying distributions,
$821,360; giving activities include $794,042 for
64 grants (high: $70,642; low: $39).
Purpose and activities: Giving primarily for
children's services and environmental
conservation.
Fields of interest: Natural resources; Family
planning; Children/youth, services; Homeless,
human services; International affairs, goodwill
promotion; International peace/security;
International human rights.
Limitations: Giving on a national basis.
Application information:
  Initial approach: Letter
  Deadline(s): None
Distribution Committee: Edna Raine Coker;
Elizabeth H. Coker; Charlotte S. Hoffman; Trudie
Olavarrieta-Coker; Julia Milner Wardlaw;
William C. Wardlaw III.
Trustee: SunTrust Banks, Inc.
EIN: 586278167

886
The Edus H. and Harriet H. Warren Foundation, Inc.
2660 Peachtree Rd. N.W., Ste. 11C
Atlanta, GA 30305-3675

Established in 1997 in GA.
Grantmaker type: Independent foundation
Financial data (yr. ended 12/31/02): Assets,
$2,853,862 (M); expenditures, $146,616;
qualifying distributions, $140,958; giving
activities include $142,000 for 7 grants (high:
$96,000; low: $3,000).
Fields of interest: Education; Botanical gardens;
Community development; Foundations
(community).
Limitations: Applications not accepted. No
grants to individuals.
Application information: Contributes only to
pre-selected organizations.
Officers: Edus H. Warren, Chair. and Treas.;
Harriet H. Warren, Vice-Chair. and Secy.
EIN: 311486911

887
The Weber Family Foundation
P.O. Box 889063
Atlanta, GA 30356-9063 (404) 786-4451
Contact: Donald W. Weber, Tr.
E-mail: info@weberfoundation.org; URL: http://
www.weberfoundation.org/

Established in 1995 in GA.
Donor(s): Donald W. Weber, Rosemary Weber.
Grantmaker type: Independent foundation
Financial data (yr. ended 12/31/02): Assets,
$1,414,837 (M); gifts received, $6,070;
expenditures, $139,110; qualifying distributions,

$132,132; giving activities include $126,150 for
31 grants (high: $27,500; low: $500).
Purpose and activities: Areas of interest include
children and youth services, education, health,
human services, and arts and cultural programs.
Fields of interest: Visual arts; Museums (art);
College (community/junior); Education;
Zoos/zoological societies; Hospitals (general);
Health care, infants; Health care; Cancer; Heart
& circulatory diseases; Child abuse; Food banks;
Housing/shelter, development; Human services;
American Red Cross; Salvation Army.
Types of support: Annual campaigns; Capital
campaigns; Building/renovation; Endowments;
Emergency funds; Scholarship funds; Research.
Limitations: Giving primarily in Atlanta, GA.
Application information: Application form not
required.
  Initial approach: Letter
  Copies of proposal: 1
  Deadline(s): Jan. 1, Apr. 1, July 1, and Oct. 1
  Board meeting date(s): Quarterly
  Final notification: Mar. 15, June 15, Sept. 15,
  and Dec. 15
Trustees: Jennifer Ann Major; Christopher John
Weber; Donald W. Weber; Rosemary Weber;
Steven David Weber.
Number of staff: None.
EIN: 582101308

888
Joseph B. Whitehead Foundation
50 Hurt Plz., Ste. 1200
Atlanta, GA 30303 (404) 522-6755
Contact: Charles H. McTier, Pres.
FAX: (404) 522-7026; E-mail:
fdns@woodruff.org; URL: http://
www.jbwhitehead.org

Incorporated in 1937 in GA.
Donor(s): Joseph B. Whitehead, Jr.‡
Grantmaker type: Public charity
Financial data (yr. ended 12/31/02): Revenue,
$18,272,236; assets, $802,773,523 (M);
expenditures, $18,580,295; program services
expenses, $18,408,790; giving activities include
$18,250,000 for 18 grants (high: $3,000,000;
low: $200,000).
Purpose and activities: Principal giving interests
are focused on the following program areas:
human services, particularly for children and
youth; elementary and secondary education;
health care and education; economic
development and civic affairs; and literacy and
vocational training. Preference is given to
one-time capital projects of established private
charitable organizations.
Fields of interest: Elementary/secondary
education; Child development, education;
Education; Environment; Health care; Health
organizations, association; Children/youth,
services; Child development, services; Aging,
centers/services; Economic development;
Government/public administration; Aging.
Types of support: Capital campaigns;
Building/renovation; Equipment; Land
acquisition; Program development; Seed money.
Limitations: Giving limited to the metropolitan
Atlanta, GA, area. No grants to individuals, or
for endowment funds, research, scholarships,
fellowships, or matching gifts; generally, no
support for operating expenses; no loans.

Publications: Application guidelines, Grants list,
Informational brochure (including application
guidelines).
Application information: Grants only to past
recipients of foundation funding. Application
form not required.
  Initial approach: Letter
  Copies of proposal: 1
  Deadline(s): Feb. 1 and Sept. 1
  Board meeting date(s): Apr. and Nov.
  Final notification: Within 30 days of trustee
  meeting
Officers and Trustee:* James B. Williams,*
Chair.; James M. Sibley,* Vice-Chair.; Charles H.
McTier,* Pres.; P. Russell Hardin,* V.P. and Secy.;
J. Lee Tribble,* Treas.; Joseph W. Jones.
Number of staff: 10 shared staff (shared with
Robert W. Woodruff Foundation, Inc., Lettie
Pate Evans Foundation, Inc., Lettie Pate
Whitehead Foundation, Inc.)
EIN: 586001954

889
The Willcox-Lumpkin Foundation, Inc.
P.O. Box 77
Columbus, GA 31902

Established in 1998 in GA.
Donor(s): Frank G. Lumpkin, Jr.
Grantmaker type: Independent foundation
Financial data (yr. ended 12/31/02): Assets,
$995,656 (M); expenditures, $100,498;
qualifying distributions, $90,234; giving
activities include $90,000 for 14 grants (high:
$22,000; low: $1,000).
Purpose and activities: Giving for education and
youth programs.
Fields of interest: Higher education; Education;
Animal welfare; Boy scouts; YM/YWCAs &
YM/YWHAs; Children/youth, services.
Types of support: General/operating support.
Limitations: Applications not accepted. Giving
primarily in GA. No grants to individuals.
Application information: Contributes only to
pre-selected organizations.
Officer: Julia W. Lumpkin, Chair.
EIN: 582400489

890
Williams Family Foundation of Georgia, Inc.
P.O. Box 378
Thomasville, GA 31799
Contact: Alston P. Watt, Exec. Dir.
FAX: (229) 228-7780

Established in 1980 in GA.
Donor(s): Diane W. Parker, Marguerite N.
Williams,‡ Thomas L. Williams III, Bennie G.
Williams.‡
Grantmaker type: Independent foundation
Financial data (yr. ended 11/30/01): Assets,
$59,454,103 (M); gifts received, $500,000;
expenditures, $3,058,192; qualifying
distributions, $2,806,485; giving activities
include $2,691,972 for 79 grants (high:
$554,400; low: $125; average:
$1,000–$50,000).
Purpose and activities: The foundation gives to
religious, educational, and public charities in
the GA area.

Fields of interest: Visual arts; Museums; Performing arts; Historic preservation/historical societies; Arts; Secondary school/education; Higher education; Libraries/library science; Education; Natural resources; Environment; Animals/wildlife, preservation/protection; Family services; Community development; Government/public administration.
Types of support: General/operating support; Building/renovation; Program development; Matching/challenge support.
Limitations: Giving primarily in GA, with emphasis on Thomasville and Thomas County. No grants to individuals.
Publications: Application guidelines, Corporate giving report, Informational brochure (including application guidelines).
Application information: New contributions limited due to numerous commitments. Application form required.
Initial approach: Letter
Copies of proposal: 1
Deadline(s): Mar. 15 and Aug. 15
Board meeting date(s): May and Nov.
Final notification: June 10 and Nov. 10
Officers and Directors:* Thomas L. Williams III,* Pres.; Stephen T. Parker, V.P.; Diane W. Parker,* Secy.; Bernard Lanigan, Jr.,* Treas.; Joseph E. Beverly; Frederick E. Cooper; Lawrence A. Harmon; Thomas W. Parker; Thomas H. Vann, Jr.; Alston P. Watt.
Number of staff: 1 part-time support.
EIN: 581414850

891
Betty A. and James B. Williams Foundation, Inc.
c/o SunTrust Banks, Inc.
P.O. Box 4655, MC 221
Atlanta, GA 30302
Contact: Danah C. Craft, Off.

Established in 1996 in GA.
Donor(s): James B. Williams.
Grantmaker type: Independent foundation
Financial data (yr. ended 12/31/02): Assets, $6,671,503 (M); expenditures, $392,507; qualifying distributions, $381,015; giving activities include $381,000 for 12 grants (high: $124,742; low: $1,000).
Purpose and activities: Giving primarily for education, and to a Presbyterian church.
Fields of interest: Arts; Elementary/secondary education; Education; Natural resources; Health organizations, association; Boys & girls clubs; Boy scouts; Federated giving programs; Protestant agencies & churches.
Limitations: No grants to individuals.
Application information:
Initial approach: Letter
Deadline(s): None
Officers: Betty A. Williams, Chair.; James B. Williams, Secy.
EIN: 582302288

892
Robert W. Woodruff Foundation, Inc. ▼
(formerly Trebor Foundation, Inc.)
50 Hurt Plz., Ste. 1200
Atlanta, GA 30303 (404) 522-6755
Contact: Charles H. McTier, Pres.
FAX: (404) 522-7026; E-mail: fdns@woodruff.org; URL: http://www.woodruff.org

Incorporated in 1937 in DE.
Donor(s): Robert W. Woodruff,‡ The Acmaro Securities Corp., and others.
Grantmaker type: Independent foundation
Financial data (yr. ended 12/31/02): Assets, $2,210,193,890 (M); expenditures, $124,994,735; qualifying distributions, $123,251,987; giving activities include $122,731,185 for 68 grants (high: $41,670,000; low: $20,000; average: $50,000–$500,000).
Purpose and activities: Principal giving interests are focused on the following program areas: elementary, secondary, and higher education; health care and education; human services, particularly for children and youth; economic development and civic affairs; art and cultural activities; and conservation of natural resources and environmental protection. Preference is given to one-time capital projects of established private charitable organizations.
Fields of interest: Arts; Elementary/secondary education; Higher education; Education; Natural resources; Environment; Health care; Health organizations, association; Human services; Children/youth, services; Aging, centers/services; Economic development; Government/public administration; Public affairs; Aging.
Types of support: Capital campaigns; Building/renovation; Equipment; Land acquisition; Program development.
Limitations: Giving primarily in GA, with emphasis on the metropolitan Atlanta area. No support for churches or denominational programs. No grants to individuals, or for operating support, festivals or performances, films and documentaries, seed money, or conferences, no loans.
Publications: Application guidelines, Grants list, Informational brochure.
Application information: Application form not required.
Initial approach: Letter
Copies of proposal: 1
Deadline(s): Feb. 1 and Sept. 1
Board meeting date(s): Apr. and Nov.
Final notification: Within 30 days of trustee meeting
Officers and Trustees:* James B. Williams,* Chair.; James M. Sibley,* Vice-Chair.; Charles H. McTier, Pres.; P. Russell Hardin, V.P. and Secy.; J. Lee Tribble, Treas.; Charles B. Ginden; Joseph W. Jones, Chair., Emeritus; Wilton D. Looney.
Number of staff: 12 shared staff (shared with Joseph B. Whitehead Foundation, Lettie Pate Evans Foundation, Inc., Lettie Pate Whitehead Foundation, Inc.)
EIN: 581695425
Recent environmental and animal welfare grants:
892-1 Clean Air Campaign, Atlanta, GA, $100,000. For campaign to encourage voluntary use of transportation alternatives in metro Atlanta. 2002.

892-2 Georgia, State of, Lake Allatoona Preservation Authority, Atlanta, GA, $100,000. For stabilization of Lake Allatoona shoreline. 2002.
892-3 Ichauway, Newton, GA, $7,000,000. For capital and operating support. 2002.
892-4 Ida Cason Callaway Foundation, Pine Mountain, GA, $25,000. For replacement of roof and other improvements at John A. Sibley Horticultural Center. 2002.
892-5 Olmstead Linear Park Alliance, Atlanta, GA, $200,000. For Phase II of rehabilitation of Olmsted Linear Park. 2002.
892-6 Zoo Atlanta, Atlanta, GA, $1,000,000. For Campaign for Conservation Leadership. 2002.

893
Wormsloe Foundation, Inc.
Wormsloe Isle of Hope
Savannah, GA 31406
Contact: Craig Barrow III, Treas.
Application address: P.O. Box 8346, Savannah, GA 31412

Established in 1951.
Donor(s): Elfrida Derenne Barrow.‡
Grantmaker type: Independent foundation
Financial data (yr. ended 12/31/02): Assets, $2,684,773 (M); gifts received, $32,588; expenditures, $138,505; qualifying distributions, $112,524; giving activities include $106,013 for 11 grants (high: $55,000; low: $13).
Purpose and activities: Giving limited to the preservation and study of agriculture, horticulture, forestry, and historical sites and documents.
Fields of interest: Museums (art); History/archaeology; Historic preservation/historical societies; Higher education; Education; Natural resources; Agriculture.
Types of support: General/operating support; Scholarship funds.
Limitations: Giving primarily in GA.
Application information:
Initial approach: Letter
Deadline(s): None
Officers: Laura B. Barrow, Chair.; Craig Barrow III, Treas.
Trustees: Diane D. Barrow; Thornton D. Barrow; Malcolm Bell III; Muriel B. Bell; J. Wiley Ellis; Elfrida B. Moore.
EIN: 586034319

894
WSG Foundation, Inc.
2931 Paces Ferry Rd., NW Ste. 100
Atlanta, GA 30339-3720
Contact: John M. Millkey, Pres.

Established in 1995 in GA.
Donor(s): William S. Green.‡
Grantmaker type: Independent foundation
Financial data (yr. ended 09/30/01): Assets, $2,105,997 (M); expenditures, $203,725; qualifying distributions, $151,929; giving activities include $112,000 for 8 grants (high: $77,000; low: $1,000).
Purpose and activities: Giving for the arts, education, and the environment.

Fields of interest: Historic preservation/historical societies; Arts; Education; Environment.

Types of support: Capital campaigns; Building/renovation; Endowments; Debt reduction; Fellowships.

Limitations: Applications not accepted. Giving primarily in the southeastern U.S. No grants to individuals.

Application information: Contributes only to pre-selected organizations.

Officer and Trustees:* Linda Millkey,* V.P.; John M. Millkey.

EIN: 582213357

895
Zeist Foundation, Inc.

3715 Northside Pkwy., N.W., Ste. 3-195
Atlanta, GA 30327-2812 (404) 949-3162
Contact: Lizanne Stephenson, Exec. Dir.
FAX: (404) 949-3161; E-mail:
lstephenson@zeistfoundation.org

Established in 1989 in GA.

Donor(s): George W. Brumley, Jr.,‡ Jean S. Brumley.‡

Grantmaker type: Independent foundation

Financial data (yr. ended 12/31/01): Assets, $3,906,778 (M); gifts received, $19,730; expenditures, $2,084,277; qualifying distributions, $1,989,623; giving activities include $1,739,566 for 74 grants (high: $762,261; low: $50; average: $1,000–$25,000).

Purpose and activities: Primarily supports education, children and youth services, community building, health and the arts, the environment, and wildlife conservation.

Fields of interest: Arts; Education; Natural resources; Health organizations, association; Human services; Children/youth, services; Community development; Federated giving programs.

Types of support: General/operating support; Annual campaigns; Capital campaigns; Building/renovation; Land acquisition; Debt reduction; Conferences/seminars; Curriculum development; Internship funds; Research; Technical assistance; Consulting services; Program evaluation; Matching/challenge support.

Limitations: Applications not accepted. Giving primarily in the metropolitan Atlanta, GA, and Research Triangle, NC, areas. No grants to individuals.

Publications: Informational brochure.

Application information: Contributes only to pre-selected organizations.

Board meeting date(s): Quarterly

Officer: Lizanne Stephenson, Exec. Dir.

Directors: Nancy J. Brumley; Marie B. Foster; R. Brad Foster.

Number of staff: 1 full-time professional; 1 full-time support.

EIN: 581890927

HAWAII

896
Alexander & Baldwin Foundation

822 Bishop St.
Honolulu, HI 96813 (808) 525-6641
Contact: Linda Howe, V.P. or Kris Kobayashi
Hawaii or Pacific Area application address: P.O. Box 3440, Honolulu, HI 96801-3440; tel: (808) 525-6642, FAX: (808) 525-6677; Mainland U.S. application address: 555 12th St., Oakland, CA 94607, tel.: (707) 421-8121, FAX: (707) 421-1835; URL: http://www.alexanderbaldwin.com/abf/index.htm

Established in 1991 in HI; funded in 1992.

Donor(s): Alexander & Baldwin, Inc., A & B Properties, Inc., East Maui Irrigation Co., Ltd., Hawaiian Commercial and Sugar Co., Kahului Trucking and Storage, Kauai Coffee Co., Kauai Commerical Co., Inc., Matson Navigation Co., Inc.

Grantmaker type: Company-sponsored foundation

Financial data (yr. ended 12/31/02): Assets, $6,131,315 (M); gifts received, $2,000; expenditures, $1,697,370; qualifying distributions, $1,680,311; giving activities include $1,602,516 for 648 grants (high: $125,000; low: $25).

Purpose and activities: Support for health and human services, education, culture and the arts, community, maritime and the environment.

Fields of interest: Museums (marine/maritime); Arts; Education; Environment; Health care; Human services; Community development; Federated giving programs.

Types of support: General/operating support; Continuing support; Annual campaigns; Capital campaigns; Building/renovation; Equipment; Program development; Conferences/seminars; Seed money; Curriculum development; Employee matching gifts; Matching/challenge support.

Limitations: Giving primarily in CA and HI, primarily to benefit communities where Alexander & Baldwin companies operate or where company employees reside. No support for United Way agencies for additional operating support. No grants to individuals, or for events, travel expenses, or scholarships.

Publications: Application guidelines, Corporate giving report.

Application information: Application form required.

Initial approach: Applicants should request foundation guidelines prior to submitting proposal. Funding requests must be in writing and should be covered by grant application cover sheet

Copies of proposal: 1

Deadline(s): First of month prior to committee meeting; major capital and grant requests of $10,000 or more considered twice a year in Mar. and Sept.

Board meeting date(s): Bimonthly, in odd-numbered months

Final notification: 6 to 8 weeks, in writing

Officers and Directors:* W.A. Doane,* Pres.; J.S. Andrasick,* V.P. and Treas.; M.J. Ching,* V.P.; L.M. Howe, V.P.; M.J. Marks, V.P.; C.B.

Mulholland, V.P.; T.A. Wellman, V.P.; A.J. Nakamura, Secy.; R.S. Bliss; J.F. Gasher; G.S. Holaday; R.K. Sasaki.

Number of staff: None.

EIN: 990291942

897
Atherton Family Foundation ▼

c/o Hawaii Community Foundation
1164 Bishop St., Ste. 800
Honolulu, HI 96813 (808) 566-5524
Contact: Lissa Schiff, Private Fdn. Svcs. Off.
Additional tel.: (888) 731-3863 (Hawaii and neighbor islands only); FAX: (808) 521-6286; E-mail: Foundations@hcf-hawaii.org; URL: http://www.Athertonfamilyfoundation.org

Incorporated in 1975 in HI as successor to Juliette M. Atherton Trust established in 1915; F. C. Atherton Trust merged into the foundation in 1976.

Donor(s): Juliette M. Atherton,‡ Frank C. Atherton.‡

Grantmaker type: Independent foundation

Financial data (yr. ended 12/31/02): Assets, $73,930,944 (M); expenditures, $6,047,030; qualifying distributions, $5,119,068; giving activities include $5,119,068 for 318 grants (high: $260,000; low: $2,000; average: $5,000–$75,000).

Purpose and activities: Concerned with education, human services, culture and the arts, health, religion, and the environment. Scholarships for the postgraduate education of Protestant ministers, Protestant ministers' children for undergraduate study, and for graduate theological education at a Protestant seminary.

Fields of interest: Humanities; Arts; Theological school/education; Education; Environment; Health care; Health organizations, association; Human services; Protestant agencies & churches.

Types of support: Management development; Annual campaigns; Capital campaigns; Building/renovation; Equipment; Program development; Seed money; Research; Technical assistance; Scholarships—to individuals; Matching/challenge support.

Limitations: Giving limited to HI; student aid for HI residents only. No support for private foundations or for organizations engaged in fundraising for the purpose of distributing grants to recipients of their own choosing. No grants to individuals (except for scholarship program) or endowment funds; no loans.

Publications: Annual report.

Application information: Application form required for scholarships. Foundation also provides grants to purchase/upgrade automation equipment, usually limited to $3,000. See foundation Web site for application details. Application form required.

Initial approach: Proposal

Copies of proposal: 1

Deadline(s): 1st of Feb., Apr., Aug., Oct., and Dec., for organizations; Mar. 1 for scholarships

Board meeting date(s): Feb., Apr., June, Oct., and Dec.

Final notification: 1 to 2 months

Officers and Directors:* Robert F. Midkiff,* Pres.; Judith M. Dawson,* V.P. and Secy.; Frank

C. Atherton,* V.P. and Treas.; Pat R. Giles,* V.P.; Paul F. Morgan,* V.P.; Joan H. Rohlfing,* V.P.
Number of staff: 6 shared staff (shared with HCF Administered Cooke Foundation, Ltd.; Victoria S. and Bradley L. Geist Foundation; Fred Baldwin Memorial Foundation. George P. & Ida Tenney Castle Trust and Teresa F. hughes Estate Trust).
EIN: 510175971
Recent environmental and animal welfare grants:
897-1 Center for a Sustainable Future, Honolulu, HI, $20,000. For salary for part-time education assistant. 2001.
897-2 Five Mountains Hawaii, Kamuela, HI, $15,000. For start-up support for The Kohala Center. 2001.
897-3 Friendship Garden Foundation, Honolulu, HI, $25,000. For endowment for garden. 2001.
897-4 Hawaii Nature Center, Honolulu, HI, $15,000. For environmental field education program. 2001.
897-5 Honolulu Zoological Society, Honolulu, HI, $50,000. For construction of Discovery Center. 2001.
897-6 Maui Tomorrow Foundation, Wailuku, HI, $10,000. For start-up support for Maui Coastal Preservation Trust. 2001.
897-7 Maui Zoological Society, Kula, HI, $10,000. For salary for executive director. 2001.
897-8 Moanalua Gardens Foundation, Honolulu, HI, $10,000. For educational partnerships program. 2001.

898
Leburta Atherton Foundation
c/o Bank of Hawaii
P.O. Box 3170
Honolulu, HI   96802-3170

Established in 1997 in HI.
Grantmaker type: Independent foundation
Financial data (yr. ended 12/31/02): Assets, $5,915,254 (M); expenditures, $286,555; qualifying distributions, $268,478; giving activities include $268,000 for 12 grants (high: $100,000; low: $2,500).
Purpose and activities: Giving for education and the environment.
Fields of interest: Education; Environment.
Limitations: Applications not accepted. Giving primarily in Honolulu, HI.
Application information: Unsolicited requests for funds not accepted.
Officers and Directors:* Leburta G. Atherton,* Pres.; Marjory A. Newell,* V.P.; Frank C. Atherton,* Secy.; Balbi A. Brooks,* Treas.
Trustee: Bank of Hawaii.
EIN: 943260209

899
Bank of Hawaii Charitable Foundation
(formerly Bancorp Hawaii Charitable Foundation)
c/o Evelyn Hunter
P.O. Box 3170
Honolulu, HI   96802-3170

Established in 1981 in HI.
Donor(s): Bank of Hawaii.

Grantmaker type: Company-sponsored foundation
Financial data (yr. ended 12/31/01): Assets, $8,147,252 (M); expenditures, $2,219,079; qualifying distributions, $2,117,228; giving activities include $1,152,011 for 89 grants (average: $5,000–$25,000) and $926,304 for grants to individuals.
Purpose and activities: Giving primarily for the arts, education, natural resource conservation and protection, hospitals, human services, and religion.
Fields of interest: Arts; Secondary school/education; Higher education; Education; Natural resources; Hospitals (general); Human services; Religion.
Types of support: General/operating support; Continuing support; Annual campaigns; Building/renovation; Endowments.
Limitations: Applications not accepted. Giving limited to HI, and other Pacific areas where Bank of Hawaii has a presence.
Application information: Contributes only to pre-selected organizations.
Officers and Directors:* Lawrence M. Johnson,* Pres.; Richard J. Dahl,* V.P.; Cori Weston, Secy.; Dennis Isono, Treas.; and 17 additional directors.
Number of staff: None.
EIN: 990210467

900
Change Happens Foundation
75-5710 Mamalahoa Hwy.
Holualoa, HI   96725

Established in 2001 in CA.
Donor(s): Douglas D. Troxel.
Grantmaker type: Independent foundation
Financial data (yr. ended 12/31/02): Assets, $4,011,130 (M); gifts received, $1,231,125; expenditures, $452,704; qualifying distributions, $390,937; giving activities include $400,000 for 2 grants (high: $300,000; low: $100,000).
Fields of interest: Education; Environment.
Limitations: Applications not accepted. Giving on a national basis. No grants to individuals.
Application information: Contributes only to pre-selected organizations.
Officers: Douglas D. Troxel, Pres.; Sergei George Troxel, Secy.; Michael Douglas Troxel, C.F.O.
EIN: 990355027

901
Cooke Foundation, Ltd.
Hawaii Community Foundation
1164 Bishop St., Ste. 800
Honolulu, HI   96813   (808) 566-5524
Contact: Private Foundation Services
E-mail: foundations@hcf-hawaii.org; URL: http://www.cookefdn.org

Trust established in 1920 in HI; incorporated in 1971.
Donor(s): Anna C. Cooke.‡
Grantmaker type: Independent foundation
Financial data (yr. ended 06/30/03): Assets, $23,630,472 (M); expenditures, $1,706,389; qualifying distributions, $1,476,600; giving activities include $1,476,600 for 85 grants (high: $100,000; low: $1,500; average: $5,000–$25,000).

Purpose and activities: To assure the continuance of, as well as to expand and extend all worthy endeavors for the betterment and welfare of the Hawaii community.
Fields of interest: Humanities; Education; Environment; Health care; Health organizations, association; Human services.
Types of support: Management development; Capital campaigns; Building/renovation; Equipment; Program development; Seed money; Technical assistance; Consulting services; Program evaluation; Matching/challenge support.
Limitations: Giving limited to HI and organizations serving the people of HI. No support for churches or religious organizations, unless the trustees' missionary forebears were involved with them. No grants to individuals, or for scholarships, fellowships, general operations, or endowment funds; no loans.
Publications: Annual report (including application guidelines).
Application information: The required funding request coversheet is available on the foundation's Web site. Application form required.
   Initial approach: Telephone or proposal
   Copies of proposal: 1
   Deadline(s): July 1 for Sept. meeting; Nov. 1 for Jan. meeting; Mar. 1 for May meeting
   Board meeting date(s): 3rd Wed. in Sept., Jan., and May
   Final notification: 2 weeks after board meeting
Officers and Trustees:* Samuel A. Cooke,* Pres.; Betty P. Dunford,* V.P. and Treas.; Dale S. Bachman, V.P.; Charles C. Spalding, Jr.,* V.P.; Anna D. Blackwell,* Secy.; Lynne Johnson.
Number of staff: 6 shared staff (shared with Atherton Family Foundation, Fred Baldwin Memorial Foundation, Victoria and Bradley Geist Foundation, George P. Ida Tenney Castle Trust, Teresa F. Hughes Trust Estate).
EIN: 237120804

902
Gertrude M. Damon Trust
c/o KPMG, LLP
P.O. Box 4150
Honolulu, HI   96812-4150

Established in 1957 in HI.
Donor(s): Harriet D. Baldwin.
Grantmaker type: Independent foundation
Financial data (yr. ended 12/31/02): Assets, $2,313,722 (M); expenditures, $179,098; qualifying distributions, $175,964; giving activities include $175,000 for 1 grant.
Purpose and activities: Giving for animal welfare and youth programs.
Fields of interest: Education; Animal welfare; Youth development, adult & child programs; Big Brothers/Big Sisters.
Limitations: Applications not accepted. Giving primarily in HI. No grants to individuals.
Application information: Contributes only to pre-selected organizations.
Trustees: Harriet D. Baldwin; Michael E. Haig; Heide Snow.
EIN: 996002637

903
The Garden Club of Honolulu
3860 Manoa Rd.
Honolulu, HI 96822-1180 (808) 988-7533
Contact: Anne Swanson, Pres.
Fax: (808) 988-0462; E-mail:
info@gchonolulu.org; URL: http://
www.gchonolulu.org

Established in 1930 in HI.
Grantmaker type: Public charity
Financial data (yr. ended 06/30/02): Revenue,
$63,414; assets, $194,843 (M); gifts received,
$16,290; expenditures, $66,904; program
services expenses, $32,089; giving activities
include $22,990 for grants (high: $14,815).
Purpose and activities: The club stimulates the
knowledge and love of gardening, to educate in
horticultural and botanical subjects, aid in the
protection of native flora, to encourage the
beautification of public places and to assist
scientific and botanical research.
Fields of interest:
Botanical/horticulture/landscape services;
Horticulture/garden clubs; Landscaping;
Environmental education.
Officers and Directors:* Anne Swanson,* Pres.;
Moira Knox,* 1st V.P.; Trudie Taylor,* 2nd V.P.;
Margie Kiessling,* Corresp. Secy.; Mary Fielder,*
Rec. Secy.; Lynn Murray,* Treas.; and 29
additional directors.
EIN: 996001533

904
Hawaii Heptachlor Research & Education
Foundation
c/o Hedberg, et al.
733 Bishop St., Ste. 1220
Honolulu, HI 96813
Contact: Willis Butler, Pres.
Application address: 250 Ward Ave., Ste. 217,
Honolulu, HI 96814, tel.: (808) 589-2963

Established in 1994 in HI.
Grantmaker type: Independent foundation
Financial data (yr. ended 12/31/01): Assets,
$1,434,048 (M); expenditures, $303,673;
qualifying distributions, $290,693; giving
activities include $143,798 for 5 grants (high:
$60,000; low: $15,000; average:
$11,387–$290,000).
Fields of interest: University; Environment.
Types of support: Research.
Limitations: Giving on a national basis, with
some emphasis on CA and NC.
Application information: Application form
required.
Officers: Willis Butler, M.D., Pres.; Gail Hirota,
V.P.; Steven L. Montgomery, Ph.D., Secy.; David
Watamull, Jr., Treas.; Richard Scudder, Exec. Dir.
Directors: Joe E. Youngs; Art Mori, Ph.D.;
Helene Takemoto.
EIN: 990258945

905
Hawaiian Electric Industries Charitable
Foundation
(also known as H.E.I. Charitable Foundation)
900 Richards St.
Honolulu, HI 96813-2919
E-mail: sshirai@hei.com; URL: http://
www.hei.com/heicf/heicf.html

Established in 1984 in HI.
Donor(s): Hawaiian Electric Industries, Inc.
Grantmaker type: Company-sponsored
foundation
Financial data (yr. ended 12/31/01): Assets,
$3,231,542 (M); gifts received, $1,243,773;
expenditures, $1,040,142; qualifying
distributions, $1,028,347; giving activities
include $1,003,150 for 67 grants (high:
$338,000; low: $500; average: $500–$350,000)
and $25,080 for employee matching gifts.
Purpose and activities: Support for federated
giving programs, including the United Way,
education, family services, community
development, and environment-related
programs in HI.
Fields of interest: Education; Environment;
Family services; Community development;
Federated giving programs.
Types of support: Annual campaigns;
Building/renovation; Program development;
Employee matching gifts; Employee-related
scholarships; Matching/challenge support.
Limitations: Applications not accepted. Giving
limited to HI for direct fund programs and
projects. No support for political, religious,
veterans', or fraternal organizations. No grants
to individuals (except for employee-related
scholarships), or for operating budgets,
maintenance activities, advertising, dinners, or
tournaments; no scholarships to individuals
other than the children of employees of
Hawaiian Electric Industries, Inc.
Publications: Annual report.
Application information: Contributes only to
pre-selected organizations.
    Board meeting date(s): Dec.
Officers and Directors:* Robert F. Clarke,*
Pres.; Constance H. Lau,* V.P.; T. Michael May,*
V.P.; Peter C. Lewis,* Secy.; Curtis Y. Harada,
Treas.; Victor H. Li; Oswald K. Stender; Jeffrey
N. Watanabe.
Number of staff: 1 full-time professional; 1
full-time support.
EIN: 990230697

906
The People's Fund
(also known as Hawaii People's Fund)
810 N. Vineyard Blvd.
Honolulu, HI 96817 (808) 845-4800
Contact: Nancy Aleck, Exec. Dir.
E-mail: peoples@lava.net; URL: http://
www.peoplesfund.org

Established in 1972 in HI.
Grantmaker type: Public charity
Financial data (yr. ended 06/30/03): Revenue,
$66,897; assets, $46,348 (M); gifts received,
$66,748; expenditures, $58,940; giving
activities include $15,960 for 12 grants (high:
$2,000; low: $100).
Purpose and activities: The fund provides
financial support and technical assistance of up

to $2,000 to progressive grassroots social
change organizations, especially those
considered too small, too new, or too radical by
traditional funders. The fund invites applications
from organizations and individuals working
against discrimination based on race, sex, age,
religion, economic status, sexual orientation,
ethnic background, illness/disease, or physical
or mental disabilities; struggling for the rights of
workers; promoting self-determination in
low-income and disenfranchised communities;
creating alternative arts and media; and
promoting peace and responsible U.S. foreign
policy. Emergency grants of up to $500 are
available for response to issues that arise
unexpectedly. Does not affect eligibility for a
grant during regularly scheduled funding cycle.
Fields of interest: Environment; Employment;
equal rights; Aging, centers/services;
International peace/security; Civil rights,
gays/lesbians; Race/intergroup relations; Civil
rights; Aging.
Types of support: General/operating support;
Emergency funds; Conferences/seminars;
Publication; Seed money; Curriculum
development.
Limitations: Giving limited to HI and the Pacific
Basin. No support for groups with annual
budgets exceeding $100,000 or organizations
that have received a grant from the fund in the
previous 12 months.
Publications: Application guidelines, Biennial
report, Financial statement, Grants list,
Informational brochure, Newsletter, Occasional
report.
Application information: Application form
required.
    Initial approach: Letter or telephone
    Copies of proposal: 10
    Deadline(s): Apr. 1 and Oct. 1; none for
        emergency grants
    Board meeting date(s): Monthly
    Final notification: Late Apr. and late Oct.
Officers and Directors:* Maralyn Kurshals,*
Pres.; Lucy Witek,* V.P.; Yoon Bok-Dong,* Secy.;
Danny Li,* Treas.; Richard Rothschiller, Exec.
Dir.; Setsu Okubo; Frank Peterson; Claire
Shimabukuro; Keawe Vredenburg.
Number of staff: 1 full-time professional.
EIN: 237250803

907
The Strong Foundation
P.O. Box 3170
Honolulu, HI 96802

Established in 1995 in HI.
Grantmaker type: Independent foundation
Financial data (yr. ended 08/31/02): Assets,
$26,720,703 (M); expenditures, $1,683,162;
qualifying distributions, $1,507,653; giving
activities include $1,500,000 for 16 grants
(high: $200,000; low: $25,000).
Purpose and activities: Giving primarily for
nature conservation and for the arts. Some
giving for education.
Fields of interest: Theater; Opera; Higher
education; Education; Environment; YM/YWCAs
& YM/YWHAs; Federated giving programs.
Limitations: Applications not accepted. Giving
limited to HI. No grants to individuals.
Application information: Contributes only to
pre-selected organizations.

Officers and Trustees:* William E. Aull,* Pres.; Samuel A. Cooke,* V.P.; Marilynn Matsumoto, Secy.; Douglas Philpotts,* Treas.; S.J. Beardmore; Anne Strong Carter; Charles M. Holland; Robert H. Rath, Sr.; Henry F. Rice.
EIN: 990090807

908
S. J. Ungar - J. Shapiro Family Foundation
P.O. Box 509
Kamuela, HI 96743-0509
Contact: Joan Shapiro, Dir.

Established in 1990 in NY.
Grantmaker type: Independent foundation
Financial data (yr. ended 06/30/02): Assets, $2,545,687 (M); expenditures, $210,638; qualifying distributions, $164,804; giving activities include $158,580 for 43 grants (high: $60,000; low: $70).
Purpose and activities: Giving primarily to Jewish organizations, as well as for international affair and conflict resolution; funding also for human services.
Fields of interest: Arts; Animals/wildlife, sanctuaries; Health organizations, association; Human services; International conflict resolution; International affairs; Jewish federated giving programs; Jewish agencies & temples.
International interests: Israel.
Limitations: Giving on a national basis. No grants to individuals.
Application information:
  Initial approach: Letter on organizational letterhead
  Deadline(s): None
Director: Joan Shapiro.
EIN: 990275249

IDAHO

909
Agricultural and Environmental Research Foundation, Inc.
P.O. Box 4848
Pocatello, ID 83205

Established in 1997 in ID.
Grantmaker type: Independent foundation
Financial data (yr. ended 12/31/02): Assets, $84,754 (M); gifts received, $418,104; expenditures, $359,173; qualifying distributions, $359,173; giving activities include $358,741 for 4 grants (high: $348,811; low: $1,000).
Fields of interest: Higher education; Environment; Agriculture.
Limitations: Applications not accepted. Giving primarily in ID. No grants to individuals.
Officer: Rick D. Keller, Exec. Dir.
EIN: 820473902

910
The ALSAM Foundation ▼
P.O. Box 1760
Eagle, ID 83616   (208) 854-0414
Contact: George L. Moosman, Pres.

Established in 1984.
Donor(s): L.S. Skaggs.
Grantmaker type: Independent foundation
Financial data (yr. ended 12/31/01): Assets, $113,300,027 (M); expenditures, $10,629,810; qualifying distributions, $10,009,827; giving activities include $9,333,529 for 18 grants (high: $2,642,500; low: $2,500; average: $10,000–$500,000).
Purpose and activities: Giving primarily for education, religion, animal welfare, medical research, and human services.
Fields of interest: Arts education; Theological school/education; Scholarships/financial aid; Education; Animals/wildlife, preservation/protection; Medical research, institute; Food services; Housing/shelter; Human services; Homeless, human services; Roman Catholic federated giving programs; Science, research; Religion; General charitable giving; Economically disadvantaged; Homeless.
Types of support: Scholarship funds.
Limitations: Applications not accepted. No grants to individuals.
Application information: Contributes only to pre-selected organizations. Unsolicited requests for funds not accepted.
Officer: George L. Moosman, Pres.
Trustee: The Northern Trust Co.
Number of staff: 1 full-time professional; 1 part-time support.
EIN: 742364289
Recent environmental and animal welfare grants:
910-1 Oregon Trail History and Education Center, Boise, ID, $10,000. For programs for children at risk for behavior problems. 2002.

911
Boise Cascade Corporation Contributions Program
1111 W. Jefferson St., P.O. Box 50
Boise, ID 83728   (208) 384-7673
URL: http://www.boisecascade.com/corporate/community.html

Grantmaker type: Corporate giving program
Purpose and activities: Boise Cascade makes charitable contributions to nonprofit organizations involved with arts and culture, education, the environment, and health and human services. Support is given primarily in areas of company operations.
Fields of interest: Arts; Education; Environment; Health care; Human services.
Types of support: General/operating support; Employee volunteer services; In-kind gifts.
Limitations: Giving primarily in areas of company operations; giving also to national organizations.
Application information: Contributions are currently very limited.

912
CHC Foundation
P.O. Box 1644
Idaho Falls, ID 83403   (208) 522-2368
Contact: Ralph Isom, Pres.

Established in 1985 in ID.
Grantmaker type: Independent foundation

Financial data (yr. ended 12/31/02): Assets, $12,163,096 (M); gifts received, $31,958; expenditures, $966,221; qualifying distributions, $829,003; giving activities include $742,915 for 56 grants (high: $150,000; low: $750).
Fields of interest: Arts; Elementary/secondary education; Education; Natural resources; Human services; Children/youth, services; Aging, centers/services; Human services; Community development.
Types of support: Capital campaigns; Building/renovation; Equipment; Matching/challenge support.
Limitations: Giving limited to southeastern ID. No grants to individuals or for operating expenses.
Publications: Informational brochure (including application guidelines).
Application information: Application form required.
  Initial approach: Proposal
  Copies of proposal: 13
  Deadline(s): Mar. 1 and Sept. 1
  Board meeting date(s): 1st Wed. of the month
  Final notification: 10 weeks
Officers: Ralph Isom, Pres.; John I. Sackett, V.P.; Joan Hahn, Secy.; Forde Johnson, Treas.
Directors: Milton F. Adam; Donald R. Bjornson, M.D.; Joan C. Hahn; Deborah Jenkins; Janice C. Matthews; Charles M. Rice; Anne S. Voilleque.
Number of staff: 1 part-time support.
EIN: 820211282

913
The Christensen Family Foundation
HC 64, Box 8288
Ketchum, ID 83340

Established in 1993 in ID.
Donor(s): Ann L. Christensen, Douglas M. Christensen.
Grantmaker type: Independent foundation
Financial data (yr. ended 12/31/02): Assets, $11,677 (M); gifts received, $155,855; expenditures, $150,250; qualifying distributions, $149,631; giving activities include $149,632 for grants (high: $87,073).
Purpose and activities: Giving primarily for environmental conservation.
Fields of interest: Education; Environment; Community development.
Limitations: Applications not accepted. Giving primarily in ID. No grants to individuals.
Application information: Contributes only to pre-selected organizations.
Trustees: Aimee R. Christensen; Ann L. Christensen; Douglas M. Christensen; Eloise M. Christensen.
EIN: 820456812

914
The James & Barbara Cimino Foundation, Inc.
P.O. Box 448
Sun Valley, ID 83353   (208) 622-4556
Contact: Christine Bender, Secy.-Treas.

Established in 1995 in ID.
Donor(s): James N. Cimino, Barbara Cimino, Robert Cimino.
Grantmaker type: Independent foundation

Financial data (yr. ended 06/30/02): Assets, $1,657,789 (M); gifts received, $1,018,100; expenditures, $983,011; qualifying distributions, $918,543; giving activities include $924,100 for 21 grants (high: $840,000; low: $1,000).
Purpose and activities: Giving primarily for the arts, education, and human services.
Fields of interest: Arts; Elementary/secondary education; Higher education; University; Libraries/library science; Natural resources; Human services.
Limitations: Giving primarily in ID. No grants to individuals.
Application information:
Initial approach: Letter
Deadline(s): None
Officers and Directors:* James N. Cimino,* Pres.; James A. Cimino,* V.P.; Christine Bender,* Secy.-Treas.; David Cimino; Robert Cimino.
EIN: 820474867

915
Robert M. Golden Foundation
c/o Morley Golden
P.O. Box 286
Sun Valley, ID 83353-0286

Established in 1960.
Grantmaker type: Independent foundation
Financial data (yr. ended 12/31/02): Assets, $6,016,896 (M); expenditures, $441,076; qualifying distributions, $391,618; giving activities include $385,530 for 112 grants (high: $35,000; low: $100; average: $50).
Fields of interest: Arts; Higher education; Environment.
Limitations: Applications not accepted. Giving limited to CA and ID. No grants to individuals.
Application information: Contributes only to pre-selected organizations.
Officers: Connie Golden, Pres.; Marilyn Golden Kelley, V.P.; Morley Golden, Secy.-Treas.
Number of staff: None.
EIN: 956099985

916
The Susan and Richard Hare Family Foundation, Inc.
P.O. Box 2508
Sun Valley, ID 83353

Established in 2002 in ID.
Donor(s): Richard Hare, Susan Hare.
Grantmaker type: Independent foundation
Financial data (yr. ended 12/31/02): Assets, $1,172,223 (M); gifts received, $1,491,009; expenditures, $344,265; qualifying distributions, $344,250; giving activities include $331,750 for 24 grants (high: $178,500; low: $100).
Fields of interest: Performing arts centers; Natural resources; Human services.
Limitations: Applications not accepted. Giving primarily in ID. No grants to individuals.
Application information: Contributes only to pre-selected organizations.
Officers: Richard Hare, Pres.; Susan Hare, Secy.-Treas.
Director: Lanny McLean.
EIN: 810547042

917
Joan Leidy Foundation, Inc.
P.O. Box 989
Ketchum, ID 83340
Contact: Helen Leidy Samson, Pres.
Application address: P.O. Box 3389, Hailey, ID 83333

Established in 1993 in ID.
Donor(s): Helen Leidy Samson.
Grantmaker type: Independent foundation
Financial data (yr. ended 12/31/02): Assets, $2,838,494 (M); expenditures, $173,232; qualifying distributions, $153,999; giving activities include $155,000 for 26 grants (high: $15,000; low: $1,000).
Fields of interest: Animal welfare; Animals/wildlife; Family planning; Legal services; Housing/shelter, development; Hospices; Homeless, human services; Christian agencies & churches.
Limitations: Applications not accepted. Giving primarily in ID. No grants to individuals.
Application information: Contributes only to pre-selected organizations.
Officers: Leidy Sue Samson, Pres.; Ann Erickson, Secy.
Directors: K.C. Garrison; Ellery Samson; Meagan Samson; Earl Skeel.
EIN: 943184527

918
Margaret W. Reed Foundation
P.O. Box A
Coeur d'Alene, ID 83816
Contact: Scott W. Reed, Tr.

Established in 1976 in ID.
Donor(s): Margaret W. Reed.‡
Grantmaker type: Independent foundation
Financial data (yr. ended 12/31/01): Assets, $2,529,582 (M); expenditures, $162,420; qualifying distributions, $96,838; giving activities include $91,147 for 27 grants (high: $20,000; low: $100).
Purpose and activities: Giving for environmental conservation, education, and human services.
Fields of interest: Natural resources; Environment.
Types of support: General/operating support; Continuing support; Program development; Publication.
Limitations: Applications not accepted. Giving limited to ID. No grants to individuals.
Application information: Unsolicited requests for funds not accepted.
Trustees: Marylou Reed; Scott W. Reed; Tara Reed.
Number of staff: 1 part-time support.
EIN: 820336633

919
Troxell Fund, Inc.
827 Balsam
Boise, ID 83706
Contact: Ann T. Murdoch, Pres.

Established in 1991 in ID.
Donor(s): Robert I. Troxell, Barbara Noble Troxell, Ann T. Murdoch.
Grantmaker type: Independent foundation

Financial data (yr. ended 12/31/02): Assets, $283,405 (M); gifts received, $186,000; expenditures, $227,674; qualifying distributions, $225,837; giving activities include $226,000 for 20 grants (high: $40,000; low: $5,000).
Fields of interest: Education; Animal welfare; Human services; American Red Cross; Children/youth, services; Women.
Limitations: Giving primarily in ID. No grants to individuals.
Application information: Application form not required.
Deadline(s): None
Officers and Directors:* Ann T. Murdoch,* Pres.; Barbara Noble Troxell,* V.P.; Stephen Murdoch.
EIN: 943135977

920
Macauley & Helen Dow Whiting Foundation
P.O. Box 1980
Sun Valley, ID 83353-1980
Contact: Helen Dow Whiting, Treas.

Incorporated in 1957 in MI.
Grantmaker type: Independent foundation
Financial data (yr. ended 12/31/02): Assets, $3,458,834 (M); expenditures, $339,692; qualifying distributions, $265,250; giving activities include $265,250 for 9 grants (high: $81,000; low: $5,000).
Purpose and activities: Emphasis on higher and secondary education; support also to environmental and energy conservation organizations; grants only to institutions with which trustees are familiar.
Fields of interest: Higher education; Education; Natural resources; Hospitals (general); Recreation.
Limitations: Giving primarily in ID. No grants to individuals.
Application information: Application form not required.
Initial approach: Letter
Copies of proposal: 1
Deadline(s): None
Board meeting date(s): At least twice a year
Officers and Trustees:* Macauley Whiting,* Pres.; Mary Macauley Whiting,* Secy.; Helen Dow Whiting,* Treas.; Sara Whiting.
EIN: 237418814

ILLINOIS

921
Lester S. Abelson Foundation
30 N. LaSalle St., Ste. 2024
Chicago, IL 60602-2504

Established in 1966 in IL.
Donor(s): Lester S. Abelson,‡ and members of the Abelson family.
Grantmaker type: Independent foundation
Financial data (yr. ended 12/31/02): Assets, $1,956,011 (M); expenditures, $166,489; qualifying distributions, $146,258; giving

activities include $146,258 for 70 grants (high: $25,000; low: $30).
Purpose and activities: Support primarily for cultural programs, including music, dance, theater, museums and the fine arts; support also for environmental organizations.
Fields of interest: Visual arts; Museums; Performing arts; Dance; Theater; Music; Arts; Environment.
Limitations: Applications not accepted. Giving primarily in IL. No grants to individuals.
Application information: Contributes only to pre-selected organizations.
Officers and Directors:* Hope A. Abelson,* Pres.; Katherine A. Abelson,* V.P.
EIN: 366153888

922
Ameren Corporation Charitable Trust ▼
(formerly Union Electric Company Charitable Trust)
231 S. LaSalle St., IL1-231-14-19
Chicago, IL 60697 (314) 466-3455
Contact: Otis Cowan, Mgr., Community Rels.
Additional tel.: (314) 554-2789 (for Secy., Corp. Comm.), (217) 535-5025 (for Donna Bailey, AmerenCIPS), (309) 677-5516 (for Neal Johnson Ameren, CILCO), or (314) 554-2817 (for Susan Bell, AmerenUE); FAX: (314) 554-2888; E-mail: ocowan@ameren.com; URL: http://www.ameren.com

Trust established in 1944 in MO.
Donor(s): Union Electric Co., Ameren Corp.
Grantmaker type: Company-sponsored foundation
Financial data (yr. ended 12/31/01): Assets, $10,281,558 (M); expenditures, $2,598,397; qualifying distributions, $2,548,344; giving activities include $2,497,220 for 46 grants (high: $845,000; low: $5,000; average: $5,000–$75,000), $51,124 for 424 employee matching gifts and $27,752 for in-kind gifts.
Purpose and activities: Current emphasis is on education, services for youth and the elderly, and the environment. Giving also for community funds, social service agencies, arts and cultural programs, community development, and public policy.
Fields of interest: Arts; Higher education; Environment; Human services; Children/youth, services; Aging.
Types of support: General/operating support; Continuing support; Annual campaigns; Capital campaigns; Building/renovation; Equipment; Emergency funds; Program development; Scholarship funds; Employee matching gifts; In-kind gifts; Matching/challenge support.
Limitations: Giving limited to Ameren service areas in IL and MO. No support for religious, political, fraternal, or veterans' organizations. No grants to individuals, or for endowments or social purposes; no in-kind donations of electric or natural gas service; no loans.
Publications: Application guidelines, Annual report, Corporate giving report.
Application information: Application form not required.
   Initial approach: Letter
   Copies of proposal: 1
   Deadline(s): None
   Board meeting date(s): 2 or 3 times per year
   Final notification: 2 to 6 months

Trustees: Charles W. Mueller; Bank of America.
Number of staff: 2 full-time professional; 1 full-time support.
EIN: 436022693

923
American Floral Endowment
11 Glen-Ed Professional Park
Glen Carbon, IL 62034 (618) 692-0045
Contact: Steven F. Martinez, Exec. V.P.
FAX: (618) 692-4045; E-mail: afe@endowment.org; URL: http://www.endowment.org

Incorporated in 1961.
Grantmaker type: Public charity
Financial data (yr. ended 06/30/02): Revenue, $197,282; assets, $9,507,530 (M); gifts received, $309,247; expenditures, $1,282,547; program services expenses, $974,882; giving activities include $847,782 for grants (high: $297,782; low: $2,250) and $89,600 for 24 grants to individuals (high: $6,000; low: $1,500).
Purpose and activities: The endowment gives primarily for the support of educational and scientific research projects within the field of floriculture and environmental horticulture. Major research areas include pest management, breeding, new crops development, and post-production studies.
Fields of interest: Higher education; Environmental education; Agriculture.
Types of support: Research; Scholarships—to individuals.
Limitations: No grants to individuals (except for scholarships), or for equipment.
Publications: Application guidelines, Annual report, Informational brochure, Newsletter.
Application information: See Web site for application. Application form required.
   Copies of proposal: 30
   Deadline(s): For research grants, pre-proposals Aug. 15, invited proposals Nov. 30; all other programs, June 1
   Board meeting date(s): Jan. and July
   Final notification: July for research grants; Nov. for all other programs
Officers and Trustees:* Norman T. White,* Chair.; L. James Leider,* Vice-Chair., Projects and Grants; Wanda Weder,* Vice-Chair., Educ.; Steven F. Martinez,* Exec. V.P.; Tony Fiannaca,* Secy.-Treas.; Sten Crissey; JoLynn Gustin; Red Kennicott; H. Michael Mellano, Sr.; Gustavo Moreno; Jim Phillip, Jr.; Jack Van Namen; Charles Walton; Bob Wilkins.
Number of staff: 2 full-time professional; 4 part-time support.
EIN: 236268380

924
ARIA Foundation, Inc.
c/o Elliott M. Friedman
1313 W. 175th St.
Homewood, IL 60430

Established in 1991 in VT.
Donor(s): Adam Albright, Rachel Albright.
Grantmaker type: Independent foundation
Financial data (yr. ended 10/31/02): Assets, $17,888,626 (M); gifts received, $1,995,370; expenditures, $1,080,702; qualifying distributions, $952,156; giving activities include

$959,530 for 22 grants (high: $397,530; low: $5,000).
Fields of interest: Elementary/secondary education; Education; Natural resources; Environment; International affairs.
Limitations: Applications not accepted. Giving on a national basis. No grants to individuals.
Application information: Contributes only to pre-selected organizations.
Officers: Adam Albright, Pres.; Rachel Albright, Secy.
Trustees: Ruth S. Flynn; Elliott M. Friedman.
EIN: 133603275

925
Atwood Foundation
c/o L.B.D. Trust Co.
P.O. Box 7327
Rockford, IL 61125-7327

Incorporated in 1949 in IL.
Donor(s): members of the Atwood family, Atwood Enterprises, Inc.
Grantmaker type: Independent foundation
Financial data (yr. ended 12/31/02): Assets, $3,306,978 (M); expenditures, $190,039; qualifying distributions, $189,421; giving activities include $190,000 for 25 grants (high: $50,000; low: $500).
Purpose and activities: Emphasis on education, hospitals, conservation, arts and cultural programs, and youth and health agencies.
Fields of interest: Arts; Education; Natural resources; Hospitals (general); Human services; YM/YWCAs & YM/YWHAs.
Types of support: Capital campaigns.
Limitations: Applications not accepted. Giving primarily in Rockford, IL. No grants to individuals.
Publications: Informational brochure.
Application information: Contributes only to pre-selected organizations. Unsolicited requests for funds not considered.
   Board meeting date(s): Oct. or Nov.
Trustees: Bruce T. Atwood; Diane P. Atwood; Seth G. Atwood; Seth L. Atwood; Marlowe Holstrum.
Number of staff: None.
EIN: 366108602

926
BANK ONE Foundation ▼
(formerly First National Bank of Chicago Foundation)
1 BANK ONE Plz., Ste. 0308
Chicago, IL 60670 (312) 407-8052
Contact: James E. Donovan, Treas.

Incorporated in 1961 in IL.
Donor(s): The First National Bank of Chicago, First Chicago Equity Corp., Bank One, N.A.
Grantmaker type: Company-sponsored foundation
Financial data (yr. ended 12/31/02): Assets, $39,572,362 (M); gifts received, $17,239,207; expenditures, $32,759,440; qualifying distributions, $33,112,529; giving activities include $32,404,785 for 2,100 grants (high: $1,067,000; low: $8; average: $5,000–$100,000), $332,876 for 583 employee matching gifts and $375,365 for 3 loans/program-related investments.

Purpose and activities: Giving primarily for human services, including housing programs and race relations; community development, civic affairs, and crime and law enforcement; education, especially business and other higher education, libraries, and education building funds; and the arts and culture, including museums, music, dance, and the theater.
Fields of interest: Visual arts; Museums; Performing arts; Dance; Theater; Music; Arts; Education, fund raising; Higher education; Business school/education; Libraries/library science; Education; Natural resources; Environment; Crime/law enforcement; Housing/shelter, development; Human services; Youth, services; Minorities/immigrants, centers/services; Race/intergroup relations; Civil rights; Urban/community development; Business/industry; Community development; Federated giving programs; Government/public administration; Minorities.
Types of support: General/operating support; Continuing support; Annual campaigns; Capital campaigns; Building/renovation; Endowments; Fellowships; Employee matching gifts; In-kind gifts; Matching/challenge support.
Limitations: Giving primarily in areas of company operations in AZ, DE, IL, MI, OH, and WI, with emphasis on the metropolitan Chicago, IL, area. No support for fraternal or religious organizations, preschool, elementary, or secondary education, public agencies, or United Way/Crusade of Mercy-supported agencies. No grants to individuals, or for emergency funds, deficit financing, land acquisition, research, publications, conferences, or multi-year operating pledges; no loans (except for program-related investments).
Publications: Informational brochure (including application guidelines).
Application information: Application form not required.
Initial approach: Letter
Copies of proposal: 1
Deadline(s): None
Board meeting date(s): Mar., June, Sept., and Dec.
Final notification: 3 months
Officers and Directors:* Warren K. Chapman,* Pres.; Margaret E. O'Hara,* V.P.; Lesley D. Slavitt,* V.P.; Marie I. Jordan, Secy.; James E. Donovan, Treas.; Michael J. Cavanagh; David E. Donovan; Christine Edwards; Larry L. Helm; Norma J. Lauder; Melinda McMullen; Heidi G. Miller.
Number of staff: 2 full-time professional; 1 full-time support.
EIN: 366033828
Recent environmental and animal welfare grants:
926-1 Aullwood Audubon Center and Farm, Dayton, OH, $10,000. 2001.
926-2 Brandywine Conservancy, Chadds Ford, PA, $12,500. 2001.
926-3 Cincinnati Zoo and Botanical Garden, Cincinnati, OH, $29,150. 2001.
926-4 Columbus Zoological Park, Powell, OH, $25,000. 2001.
926-5 Dallas Arboretum and Botanical Society, Dallas, TX, $20,000. 2001.
926-6 Delta Institute, Chicago, IL, $10,000. 2001.
926-7 Denver Zoological Foundation, Denver, CO, $15,000. 2001.

926-8 Desert Botanical Garden, Phoenix, AZ, $48,000. 2001.
926-9 Detroit Zoological Society, Royal Oak, MI, $200,000. 2001.
926-10 Downtown Dayton Riverscape Fund, Dayton, OH, $50,000. 2001.
926-11 Greening of Detroit, Detroit, MI, $10,000. 2001.
926-12 Humane Society of Phoenix, Arizona, Phoenix, AZ, $20,000. 2001.
926-13 Indianapolis Zoological Society, Indianapolis, Indiana, $15,000. 2001.
926-14 Indianapolis Zoological Society, Indianapolis, Indiana, $12,500. 2001.
926-15 John Ball Zoological Society, Grand Rapids, MI, $10,000. 2001.
926-16 Lincoln Park Zoological Society, Chicago, IL, $180,000. 2001.
926-17 Longue Vue House and Gardens, New Orleans, LA, $10,000. 2001.
926-18 Louisville Zoo Foundation, Louisville, KY, $10,000. 2001.
926-19 Michigan Botanical Garden, Grand Rapids, MI, $25,000. 2001.
926-20 Nature Conservancy, Arlington, VA, $18,750. 2001.
926-21 Winterthur Museum, Garden & Library, Winterthur, DE, $30,000. 2001.

927
Bill Bartholomay Foundation
875 N. Michigan Ave., 20th Fl.
Chicago, IL 60611
Contact: William C. Bartholomay, Tr.

Established in 1989 in IL.
Donor(s): William C. Bartholomay.
Grantmaker type: Independent foundation
Financial data (yr. ended 12/31/02): Assets, $3,841,414 (M); expenditures, $283,845; qualifying distributions, $268,873; giving activities include $269,900 for 130 grants (high: $50,000; low: $100).
Fields of interest: Arts; Higher education; Education; Aquariums; Children/youth, services; Christian agencies & churches.
Limitations: Applications not accepted. Giving limited to IL. No grants to individuals.
Application information: Contributes only to pre-selected organizations.
Trustee: William C. Bartholomay.
EIN: 363679496

928
Elizabeth E. & Joseph H. Bascom Charitable Foundation
c/o Bank of America
231 S. Lasalle St.
Chicago, IL 60697
Contact: R. Scott Mosley
Application address: c/o Bank of America, P.O. Box 14737, St. Louis, MO 63178, tel.: (314) 466-0202

Established in 1957 in MO.
Grantmaker type: Independent foundation
Financial data (yr. ended 12/31/02): Assets, $2,078,198 (M); expenditures, $103,331; qualifying distributions, $93,343; giving activities include $92,000 for 34 grants (high: $15,000; low: $500).

Purpose and activities: Giving for children's and family services, nature and wildlife conservation, and for the arts.
Fields of interest: Arts; Education; Natural resources; Health care; Health organizations, association; Human services; Children/youth, services; Family services.
Limitations: Giving primarily in St. Louis, MO.
Application information:
Initial approach: Letter
Deadline(s): None
Trustees: Charles Bascom; Bank of America.
Directors: Constance B. McPheeters; John C. McPheeters.
EIN: 436024670

929
Bellebyron Foundation
c/o D.B. Smith
3600 W. Lake Ave.
Glenview, IL 60025
Contact: Stephen B. Smith, Pres.

Established in 1983 in IL.
Donor(s): Harold Byron Smith.
Grantmaker type: Independent foundation
Financial data (yr. ended 12/31/02): Assets, $6,401,339 (M); expenditures, $824,319; qualifying distributions, $819,207; giving activities include $819,207 for 10 grants (high: $130,150; low: $5,000).
Purpose and activities: Giving primarily for the arts and higher education.
Fields of interest: Film/video; Theater; Higher education; Libraries/library science; Botanical gardens; Zoos/zoological societies; Aquariums.
Limitations: Giving primarily in IL. No grants for Individuals.
Application information:
Initial approach: Letter
Deadline(s): None
Officers: Stephen B. Smith, Pres.; Christopher B. Smith, V.P.; Harold Byron Smith, Jr., Secy.; David B. Smith, Treas.
EIN: 366058056

930
The Berner Charitable and Scholarship Foundation
221 N. LaSalle St., Ste. 2900
Chicago, IL 60601-1504 (312) 782-5885
Contact: Ruben R. Vernof, Tr.

Established in 1994 in IL.
Grantmaker type: Independent foundation
Financial data (yr. ended 12/31/02): Assets, $10,023,621 (M); expenditures, $601,795; qualifying distributions, $573,595; giving activities include $471,000 for 31 grants (high: $250,000; low: $1,000) and $10,000 for 1 grant to an individual.
Purpose and activities: Giving primarily for education and health associations. Scholarships are awarded to residents of the U.S. who are attending, or who are planning to attend, any U.S. college or university. Selection shall be based on scholastic achievements, or the potential to make scholastic achievements, financial need, and demonstrated quality of leadership. Applicants who are seeking a scholarship for undergraduate degree must have graduated from high school with a "C" average

or better. Applicants who are seeking a scholarship for a graduate degree, must have graduated from college with a "C" average or better. Applicants must enroll as full-time students and carry a full-time course load.
Fields of interest: Higher education; Education; Animal welfare; Health care; Health organizations, association; Cancer research; Child abuse; Human services; Children/youth, services; Human services.
Types of support: Scholarships—to individuals.
Limitations: Giving primarily in Chicago, IL.
Trustees: Norman N. Schwartz; Ruben R. Vernof.
EIN: 363923844

931
Grace A. Bersted Foundation
c/o Bank of America
231 S. LaSalle St.
Chicago, IL 60697 (312) 828-1785
Contact: M. Catherine Ryan

Established in 1986 in IL.
Donor(s): Grace A. Bersted.‡
Grantmaker type: Independent foundation
Financial data (yr. ended 12/31/02): Assets, $7,649,740 (M); expenditures, $583,882; qualifying distributions, $527,631; giving activities include $493,000 for 15 grants (high: $80,000; low: $10,000).
Purpose and activities: Giving primarily for human services; funding also for higher education, a conservation unit, YM/YWCAs, family services, and an independent foundation.
Fields of interest: Higher education; Natural resources; Human services; YM/YWCAs & YM/YWHAs; Family services; Foundations (private independent).
Limitations: Giving limited to DuPage, Kane, Lake, and McHenry counties, IL. No grants to individuals.
Application information: Application form not required.
Initial approach: Proposal
Deadline(s): None
Trustee: Bank of America.
EIN: 366841348

932
Blair Foundation
c/o The Northern Trust Co.
50 S. LaSalle St., Ste. L-5
Chicago, IL 60675
Application address: c/o The Northern Trust Co., 4001 Tamiami Trail N., Naples, FL 34103, tel.: (239) 262-8800

Grantmaker type: Independent foundation
Financial data (yr. ended 12/31/02): Assets, $7,714,457 (M); expenditures, $495,547; qualifying distributions, $478,361; giving activities include $439,800 for 61 grants (high: $125,000; low: $1,000).
Purpose and activities: Giving primarily for conservation, animals and wildlife, as well as for education, health, human services, children and youth services, family services, and community development.
Fields of interest: Education; Natural resources; Animals/wildlife; Health care; Human services; Children/youth, services; Family services; Community development.

Limitations: Giving primarily in Washington, DC, Naples, FL, and NY. No grants to individuals.
Application information: Application form not required.
Deadline(s): None
Advisors: Dorothy S. Blair; John Graham; Robert W. Rieman, M.D.
Trustee: The Northern Trust Co.
EIN: 656072965

933
Margaret S. & Philip D. Block, Jr. Family Foundation
30 W. Monroe St.
Chicago, IL 60603-2401 (312) 346-5580
Contact: Philip D. Block, III, Secy.

Established in 1959 in IL.
Donor(s): Andrew K. Block, Margaret S. Block, Shaun C. Block, Philip D. Block III.
Grantmaker type: Independent foundation
Financial data (yr. ended 12/31/02): Assets, $3,000,297 (M); gifts received, $3,283; expenditures, $257,002; qualifying distributions, $250,597; giving activities include $247,550 for 72 grants (high: $30,000; low: $100).
Fields of interest: Arts; Education; Zoos/zoological societies; Health organizations, association.
Limitations: Giving primarily in Chicago, IL. No grants to individuals.
Application information: Application form not required.
Initial approach: Letter
Deadline(s): None
Officers: Andrew K. Block, Pres.; Philip D. Block III, Secy.
Directors: Judith S. Block; Shaun C. Block.
EIN: 366047602

934
The Boeing Company Contributions Program
100 N. Riverside
Chicago, IL 60606-1596
URL: http://www.boeing.com/companyoffices/aboutus/community/

Grantmaker type: Corporate giving program
Purpose and activities: As a complement to its foundation, Boeing also makes charitable contributions to nonprofit organizations directly. Support is given on a national and international basis.
Fields of interest: Arts; Elementary/secondary education; Higher education; Education; Environment; Health care; Substance abuse, services; Domestic violence; Human services; Public affairs; Aging.
International interests: Canada; Australia.
Types of support: Continuing support; Capital campaigns; Building/renovation; Equipment; Emergency funds; Program development; Conferences/seminars; Professorships; Seed money; Fellowships; Scholarship funds; Research; Technical assistance; Consulting services; Employee volunteer services; Loaned talent; Public relations services; Use of facilities; Sponsorships; Employee matching gifts;

Donated equipment; In-kind gifts; Matching/challenge support.
Limitations: Giving on a national and international basis in areas of company operations. No support for political candidates, committees, or organizations, religious organizations, hospital or medical research organizations, or athletic organizations. No grants to individuals, or for travel, agency-sponsored walks, runs, or golf tournaments, auction booklet printing, tickets, or one-time events.
Application information: Contact headquarters for nearest application address. Printing services are provided on an every-other year basis for educational and awareness materials. The Community and Educational Relations Department handles giving. Application form required.
Initial approach: Contact nearest company facility for application form
Copies of proposal: 1
Deadline(s): None; 6 to 8 weeks prior to need for printing services
Final notification: 1 to 2 months

935
Helen Brach Foundation ▼
55 W. Wacker Dr., Ste. 701
Chicago, IL 60601 (312) 372-4417
Contact: Toni Perille, Assoc. Dir.
FAX: (312) 372-0290

Established in 1974 in IL.
Donor(s): Helen Brach.‡
Grantmaker type: Independent foundation
Financial data (yr. ended 03/31/02): Assets, $108,346,999 (M); expenditures, $6,453,948; qualifying distributions, $5,885,870; giving activities include $5,461,620 for 439 grants (high: $150,000; low: $100; average: $10,000–$25,000).
Purpose and activities: Support for the prevention of cruelty to animals; programs that test public safety; social and family services, including programs for the prevention of cruelty to children, youth and child welfare, the homeless and housing, the disabled, and the disadvantaged; conservation of the environment; secondary, higher, and other education; and general health.
Fields of interest: Arts; Secondary school/education; Higher education; Education; Environment; Animal welfare; Health care; Housing/shelter; Youth development, services; Human services; Children/youth, services; Homeless, human services; Disabled; Economically disadvantaged.
Types of support: General/operating support; Annual campaigns; Building/renovation; Equipment; Program development; Conferences/seminars; Publication; Scholarship funds.
Limitations: Giving primarily in the Midwest, and CA, MA, OH, PA and SC, No grants outside continental U.S. No support for political organizations. No grants to individuals (except for scholarships), or to organizations with less than one year of budget history.
Publications: Application guidelines, Multi-year report (including application guidelines).
Application information: No grants under $5,000. Application form required.

Initial approach: Letter or FAX
Copies of proposal: 7
Deadline(s): Dec. 31 (earlier preferred)
Board meeting date(s): Quarterly; grants considered at Mar. meeting
Final notification: Mar. to Apr.
Officers and Directors:* Raymond F. Simon,* Pres.; James J. O'Connor,* V.P.; John J. Sheridan,* Secy.-Treas.; R. Matthew Simon; Charles A. Vorhees.
Number of staff: 3 full-time professional.
EIN: 237376427
Recent environmental and animal welfare grants:
935-1 Alley Cat Allies, DC, $20,000. To match up veterinary schools with local feral cat caretakers to create and expand free spay/neuter clinics for feral cats. 2002.
935-2 Animal Legal Defense Fund, Petaluma, CA, $25,000. For Zero Tolerance for Cruelty campaign, enforcing state anti-cruelty laws. 2002.
935-3 Anti-Cruelty Society, Chicago, IL, $20,000. For general operating support. 2002.
935-4 Canine Companions for Independence, Glenview, IL, $25,000. For continued support of North Central Regional Training Center budget, providing trained assistance dogs to people with disabilities. 2002.
935-5 Chicago Zoological Society, Brookfield Zoo, Brookfield, IL, $25,000. For general operating support. 2002.
935-6 Elephant Sanctuary in Hohenwald, Hohenwald, TN, $20,000. Toward acquiring additional acreage to expand habitat. 2002.
935-7 Farm Sanctuary, Watkins Glen, NY, $10,000. Toward promoting farm animal protection through investigations, legal advocacy and humane education campaigns. 2002.
935-8 Food Animal Concerns Trust (FACT), Chicago, IL, $40,000. For new education program, including full-time position to manage public information program. 2002.
935-9 Great Lakes Aquarium, Duluth, MN, $10,000. For traveling exhibit devoted to Lake Victoria and people and creatures inhabiting its shores. 2002.
935-10 Greyhound Friends, Hopkinton, MA, $10,000. For continued support of new kennel buildings. 2002.
935-11 Humane Society, Cen Tex, Killeen, TX, $17,000. To shelter, house, feed and give medical attention, including immunization and sterilization, to animals for adoption. 2002.
935-12 Humane Society, Clinton, Clinton, IA, $18,000. Toward expansion of shelter for homeless and abandoned animals. 2002.
935-13 Humane Society, Little Traverse Bay, Harbor Springs, MI, $15,000. For Doggie Day Care and Dog Obedience program support. 2002.
935-14 Humane Society, Western Pennsylvania, Pittsburgh, PA, $30,000. Toward ongoing campaign for new building to be used for homeless companion animals and modern veterinary clinic. 2002.
935-15 International Crane Foundation, Baraboo, WI, $10,000. For reintroduction of whooping cranes into Midwest that will migrate from Wisconsin to Florida. 2002.

935-16 International Primate Protection League, Summerville, SC, $30,000. For care and maintenance of Gibbons at sanctuary and for future construction. 2002.
935-17 Lincoln Park Zoo, Chicago, IL, $25,000. Toward operating support for Zoo Intern Program that engages underserved teenagers in summer activities. 2002.
935-18 Lowry Park Zoological Society of Tampa, Tampa, FL, $10,000. For medical equipment and to repair water-damaged cabinetry in Manatee Hospital and Aquatic Center. 2002.
935-19 Marine Mammal Center, Sausalito, CA, $25,000. For Rescue, Rehabilitation, and Release Program for marine mammals stranded on California coast. 2002.
935-20 National Wildlife Rehabilitators Association, Saint Cloud, MN, $15,000. Toward salary for Executive Director. 2002.
935-21 Orphans of the Storm, Deerfield, IL, $20,000. For general operating support. 2002.
935-22 PAWS Chicago, Chicago, IL, $15,000. For low- or no-cost sterilization and vaccinations for pets of low-income owners and humane education programs. 2002.
935-23 Performing Animal Welfare Society, Galt, CA, $50,000. Toward providing cage-free refuge for wildlife in need of safe sanctuary. 2002.
935-24 Portage County Animal Protective League, Ravenna, OH, $10,000. Toward developing and equipping medical treatment room for animals with minor injuries in new shelter. 2002.
935-25 Rocky Mountain Wildlife Conservation Center, Keenesburg, CO, $15,000. For continued support to provide expert care for unwanted exotic wildlife while addressing education on captive wildlife problems. 2002.
935-26 United Animals Nations-USA, Sacramento, CA, $20,000. For continued support of new member development through direct mail acquisition program. 2002.
935-27 United Poultry Concerns, Machipongo, VA, $10,000. For Humane Education Program with emphasis on classroom hatching projects and teacher training. 2002.
935-28 Wild Animal Orphanage, San Antonio, TX, $60,000. For continued support of new member direct mail acquisition program and to educate about plight of surplus animals. 2002.
935-29 Wilderness Society, DC, $10,000. To defend abundant wildlife on public lands in Wyoming and Montana. 2002.
935-30 World Resources Institute, DC, $50,000. For continued support of research program on global warming. 2002.

936
S. & E. Bramsen Foundation
(formerly Svend & Elizabeth Bramsen Foundation)
c/o Pedersen & Houpt
161 N. Clark St., Ste. 3100
Chicago, IL 60601-3221

Donor(s): Spraying Systems Co.
Grantmaker type: Independent foundation

Financial data (yr. ended 12/31/01): Assets, $1,596,791 (M); gifts received, $100,000; expenditures, $127,397; qualifying distributions, $118,487; giving activities include $118,500 for 20 grants (high: $35,000; low: $500).
Purpose and activities: Giving primarily for higher education and youth development.
Fields of interest: Higher education; Natural resources; Zoos/zoological societies; Youth development, adult & child programs.
Limitations: Applications not accepted. Giving primarily in IL. No grants to individuals.
Application information: Contributes only to pre-selected organizations.
Officers and Directors:* James E. Bramsen,* Pres. and Treas.; Peer Pedersen,* Secy.; Franklin Bramsen; Julia Bramsen; Sigrid Gray.
EIN: 362546470

937
Brinckman Family Foundation
c/o S. Kerrick
P.O. Box 1289
Woodstock, IL 60098-1289

Established in 1997 in IL.
Donor(s): Donald Brinckman.
Grantmaker type: Independent foundation
Financial data (yr. ended 12/31/02): Assets, $954,766 (M); expenditures, $140,081; qualifying distributions, $113,200; giving activities include $113,200 for 6 grants (high: $50,000; low: $1,000).
Purpose and activities: Giving for the arts, higher education, Christian organizations, and environmental conservation.
Fields of interest: Arts; Higher education; Natural resources; Christian agencies & churches.
Limitations: Applications not accepted. Giving primarily in IL. No grants to individuals.
Application information: Contributes only to pre-selected organizations.
Officers and Directors:* Donald Brinckman,* Pres.; Beverly Brinckman,* V.P.; Scott Brinckman; Barbara Ladd; Bonny Putney; Donna Sherman; Dawn Walters.
EIN: 364157903

938
The Brinson Foundation
737 N. Michigan Ave., Ste. 1850
Chicago, IL 60611 (312) 799-4500
Contact: Ronald P. Martinez, Exec. Dir.
FAX: (312) 799-4310; E-mail: mail@brinsonfoundation.org; URL: http://www.brinsonfoundation.org

Established in 2000 in IL.
Donor(s): Gary P. Brinson.
Grantmaker type: Independent foundation
Financial data (yr. ended 12/31/02): Assets, $39,259,812 (M); expenditures, $1,824,000; qualifying distributions, $1,047,000; giving activities include $1,047,000 for 33 grants (high: $75,000; low: $10,000).
Fields of interest: Higher education; Environment; Medical care, in-patient care; Health care.
Types of support: Continuing support; Land acquisition; Fellowships; Scholarship funds; Research.

Limitations: Giving primarily in IL. No grants to individuals, political activities, or religious promotion.
Publications: Annual report, Informational brochure (including application guidelines).
Application information: See Web site for application information. Application form required.
  Copies of proposal: 1
  Deadline(s): Feb. 28th and Aug. 31st
  Board meeting date(s): May and Oct.
Trustees: Talina Sue Boaz; Gary P. Brinson; Monique Brinson; Suzann Boaz Brinson; Ronald P. Martinez.
Number of staff: 3 full-time professional; 1 full-time support.
EIN: 367331362

939
The Bruning Foundation
c/o Larry J. Brooks
787 Berkshire Ln.
Des Plaines, IL 60016-7545

Established in 1960.
Donor(s): Herbert F. Bruning, Paul J. Bruning.
Grantmaker type: Independent foundation
Financial data (yr. ended 12/31/02): Assets, $16,371,079 (M); expenditures, $1,221,976; qualifying distributions, $1,078,900; giving activities include $1,078,900 for 111 grants (high: $140,000; low: $1,000).
Purpose and activities: Giving primarily to churches, and for education and the arts; giving also for prevention of cruelty to children and animals.
Fields of interest: Elementary/secondary education; Higher education; Animals/wildlife; Health organizations; Human services.
Types of support: General/operating support.
Limitations: Applications not accepted. Giving primarily in IL. No grants to individuals.
Application information: Contributes only to pre-selected organizations.
Officers and Directors:* Charles Bruning II,* Pres.; Kathleen Bruning, Secy.; Edwin C. Bruning,* Treas.; Larry J. Brooks, Mgr.; Charles Bruning III; John Bruning.
EIN: 366068626

940
The Brunswick Foundation, Inc.
1 N. Field Ct.
Lake Forest, IL 60045-4811   (847) 735-4467
Contact: Carol Stame, Pres.

Incorporated in 1957 in IL.
Donor(s): Brunswick Corp., Peter N. Larson.
Grantmaker type: Company-sponsored foundation
Financial data (yr. ended 12/31/02): Assets, $6,478,933 (M); expenditures, $1,733,743; qualifying distributions, $514,800; giving activities include $109,300 for 92 grants (high: $32,000; low: $150) and $405,500 for 225 grants to individuals (high: $2,000; low: $1,000).
Purpose and activities: Support primarily for higher education, welfare, and civic organizations in areas where there are high concentrations of Brunswick employees, with a preference for local (plant community)

organizations in which employees are personally involved.
Fields of interest: Multipurpose centers/programs; Higher education; Environment; Health organizations, association; Human services.
Types of support: General/operating support; Continuing support; Capital campaigns; Building/renovation; Program development; Scholarship funds; Employee matching gifts; Employee-related scholarships.
Limitations: Giving primarily in areas of company operations in AL, AZ, CT, FL, GA, IL, IN, KY, LA, MD, MI, MN, MS, NC, NE, OK, OR, SC, TN, TX, and WI. No support for religious organizations, preschools, primary or secondary schools, fraternal orders, veterans' or labor groups, or trips, tours, tickets, or advertising for benefit purposes. No grants to individuals (except for employee-related scholarships), or for endowment or capital funds; no in-kind gifts; no program-related investments; no loans.
Publications: Application guidelines.
Application information: Accepts only written requests for application guidelines; priority given to organizations that have already generated Brunswick Corp. employee involvement. Application form required.
  Initial approach: Letter
  Copies of proposal: 2
  Deadline(s): Mar. 22
  Board meeting date(s): Quarterly
  Final notification: 5 to 12 months
Officers and Directors:* B. Russell Lockridge,* Pres.; Carol Stame,* Pres.; Marschall I. Smith, V.P. and Secy.; William L. Metzger, V.P. and Treas.; Kathryn J. Chieger, V.P.; Mary Gibbard, Secy.; Geoffrey T. Smith, Treas.; George W. Buckley; Victoria J. Reich.
Number of staff: 1 full-time professional.
EIN: 366033576

941
The Buchanan Family Foundation
222 E. Wisconsin Ave.
Lake Forest, IL 60045-1701
Contact: Huntington Eldridge, Jr., Treas.

Established in 1967 in IL.
Donor(s): D.W. Buchanan, Sr.,‡ D.W. Buchanan, Jr.
Grantmaker type: Independent foundation
Financial data (yr. ended 12/31/01): Assets, $48,470,663 (M); expenditures, $2,401,922; qualifying distributions, $2,335,330; giving activities include $2,350,000 for 90 grants (high: $113,000; low: $3,000; average: $5,000–$50,000).
Purpose and activities: Emphasis on cultural programs, hospitals and health associations, education, social service agencies, community funds, and environmental associations.
Fields of interest: Arts; Elementary/secondary education; Higher education; Environment; Hospitals (general); Health organizations, association; Medical research, institute; Human services; Federated giving programs.
Limitations: Applications not accepted. Giving primarily in Chicago, IL. No grants to individuals.
Application information: Contributes only to pre-selected organizations.
  Board meeting date(s): Fall

Officers: Kenneth H. Buchanan, Pres.; G.M. Walsh, V.P. and Secy.; Huntington Eldridge, Jr., Treas.
Directors: John A. Andersen; Kent Chandler, Jr.
Number of staff: None.
EIN: 366160998

942
Buehler Family Foundation
(formerly A. C. Buehler Foundation)
c/o Bank of America
231 S. LaSalle St.
Chicago, IL 60697   (312) 828-1785
Contact: M. Catherine Ryan

Incorporated in 1972 in IL.
Donor(s): Albert C. Buehler.
Grantmaker type: Independent foundation
Financial data (yr. ended 12/31/01): Assets, $16,990,365 (M); expenditures, $2,186,353; qualifying distributions, $2,084,052; giving activities include $2,067,500 for 11 grants (high: $850,000; low: $10,000; average: $10,000–$100,000).
Purpose and activities: Emphasis on medical and health-related organizations located in the metropolitan Chicago, IL, area.
Fields of interest: Botanical gardens; Aquariums; Health care, association; Hospitals (general); Family services.
Types of support: Equipment; Research.
Limitations: Giving primarily in the metropolitan Chicago, IL, area.
Application information:
  Initial approach: Letter
  Deadline(s): None
Officers and Directors:* A.C. Buehler, Jr.,* Chair.; Dale Park, Jr.,* Secy.; M. James Termondt,* Treas.; Patricia Buehler; Pamela Varner.
EIN: 237166014

943
Howard G. Buffett Foundation
407 Southmoreland Pl.
Decatur, IL 62521

Established in 1999 in IL and NE.
Donor(s): E. Buffett, Warren Buffett.
Grantmaker type: Independent foundation
Financial data (yr. ended 12/31/02): Assets, $30,107,578 (M); expenditures, $2,156,562; qualifying distributions, $2,023,978; giving activities include $2,023,978 for 26 grants (high: $1,245,000; low: $833).
Fields of interest: Education; Environment; Animals/wildlife; Human services.
Limitations: Applications not accepted. Giving primarily in IL. No grants to individuals.
Application information: Contributes only to pre-selected organizations.
Officers and Directors:* Howard G. Buffett,* Pres.; Ronald O. Olson,* Secy.; Devon G. Buffett.
EIN: 470824756

944
D. L. and S. E. Burnham Foundation
15 Bridlewood Rd.
Northbrook, IL 60062-4707

Established in 1987 in IL.
Donor(s): Duane L. Burnham, Susan E. Burnham.
Grantmaker type: Independent foundation
Financial data (yr. ended 12/31/02): Assets, $1,373,424 (M); gifts received, $185,000; expenditures, $1,262,992; qualifying distributions, $1,262,638; giving activities include $1,262,282 for 16 grants (high: $980,350; low: $1,000).
Purpose and activities: Giving for hospitals, the performing arts, and human services.
Fields of interest: Performing arts; Historic preservation/historical societies; Higher education; Botanical gardens; Hospitals (general); Human services; Federated giving programs; Protestant agencies & churches.
Limitations: Applications not accepted. Giving primarily in IL. No grants to individuals.
Application information: Contributes only to pre-selected organizations.
Officers and Directors:* Duane L. Burnham,* Pres.; Susan E. Burnham,* V.P. and Secy.-Treas.; David L. Burnham.
EIN: 363476527

945
Tyler R. Cain Family Foundation
3 Market Sq. Ct.
Lake Forest, IL 60045
Contact: Tyler R. Cain, Pres.
Application address: P.O. Box 755, Chicago, IL 60690

Established in 1986 in IL.
Grantmaker type: Independent foundation
Financial data (yr. ended 12/31/02): Assets, $1,895,097 (M); gifts received, $4,655; expenditures, $144,812; qualifying distributions, $144,812; giving activities include $142,542 for 42 grants (high: $101,650; low: $100).
Purpose and activities: Giving for education, the environment, and Christian organizations.
Fields of interest: Education; Environment; Human services; Christian agencies & churches.
Types of support: General/operating support; Annual campaigns; Capital campaigns.
Limitations: Giving primarily in IL, including Chicago and Lake Forest; giving also in FL and NY. No grants to individuals.
Application information:
    Initial approach: Proposal in letter form
    Deadline(s): None
Officer: Tyler R. Cain, Pres.
EIN: 363496960

946
Apollos Camp and Bennet Humiston Trust
300 W. Washington St.
Pontiac, IL 61764-0710
Contact: Neil C. Bach, Chair.

Trust established in 1925 in IL.
Grantmaker type: Independent foundation
Financial data (yr. ended 04/30/02): Assets, $7,895,757 (M); expenditures, $447,210; qualifying distributions, $373,862; giving

activities include $334,226 for 21 grants (high: $69,000; low: $708).
Purpose and activities: Giving primarily for children and youth services, social services, a student health center, and a nature center.
Fields of interest: Education; Natural resources; Health care; Recreation; Boys & girls clubs; Human services; Children/youth, services; Community development.
Types of support: General/operating support; Building/renovation; Equipment.
Limitations: Giving limited to Pontiac, IL. No grants to individuals.
Application information:
    Initial approach: Proposal
    Deadline(s): None
Officer: Neil C. Bach, Chair.
Trustees: Victoria P. Glennon; David R. Harding; William C. Harris; Louis Lyons.
EIN: 370701044

947
Carney Family Foundation
10 S. Riverside Plz., No. 1600
Chicago, IL 60606

Established in 2000 in IL.
Donor(s): Peter R. Carney.
Grantmaker type: Independent foundation
Financial data (yr. ended 12/31/01): Assets, $788,332 (M); gifts received, $27,315; expenditures, $108,036; qualifying distributions, $100,314; giving activities include $100,284 for 97 grants (high: $25,000; low: $50).
Fields of interest: Orchestra (symphony); Education; Natural resources; Human services; Community development; Religion.
Limitations: Applications not accepted. Giving primarily in IL and WY. No grants to individuals.
Application information: Contributes only to pre-selected organizations.
Officers: Peter R. Carney, Pres. and Treas.; Marina G. Carney, V.P. and Secy.
Director: Aidan I. Mullett.
EIN: 364346222

948
Castaways Foundation
414 N. Orleans St., Ste. 301
Chicago, IL 60610-4466

Established around 1991.
Donor(s): Members of the Crown family.
Grantmaker type: Independent foundation
Financial data (yr. ended 12/31/02): Assets, $1,796,212 (M); expenditures, $125,407; qualifying distributions, $109,496; giving activities include $110,000 for 72 grants (high: $7,010; low: $100).
Fields of interest: Arts; Elementary/secondary education; Education; Animals/wildlife; Hospitals (general); Crime/law enforcement, police agencies; Human services.
Limitations: Applications not accepted. Giving primarily in CO and Chicago, IL. No grants to individuals.
Application information: Contributes only to pre-selected organizations.
Officers and Directors:* Donna Lynn Crown,* Pres.; Bradley D. Crown,* V.P.; Laurie J. Crown,* Secy.; Bruce A. Crown, Treas.
EIN: 363738769

949
Ceres Foundation
P.O. Box 8203
Northfield, IL 60093

Established in 1991 in IL.
Donor(s): Burton W. Hales, Daniel B. Hales, Marion J. Hales, Hales Charitable Fund, Inc.
Grantmaker type: Independent foundation
Financial data (yr. ended 12/31/01): Assets, $7,381,046 (M); expenditures, $592,442; qualifying distributions, $526,581; giving activities include $524,350 for 85 grants (high: $35,000; low: $250).
Purpose and activities: Giving primarily for the arts, education, conservation, health, human services, community foundations, and Christian and Protestant churches and organizations.
Fields of interest: Arts; Education; Botanical gardens; Hospitals (general); Health organizations, association; Human services; Children/youth, services; Foundations (community); Federated giving programs; Christian agencies & churches; Protestant agencies & churches.
Limitations: Applications not accepted. Giving primarily in IL and MI; some funding nationally. No grants to individuals.
Application information: Contributes only to pre-selected organizations.
Officers and Directors:* Burton W. Hales, Jr.,* Pres.; Daniel R.J. Hales,* V.P.; Daniel B. Hales,* Secy.; Florence H. Testa,* Treas.
EIN: 363735653

950
Harry E. Chamberlain & Adrienne S. Chamberlain Memorial Fund
c/o Bank of America
231 S. LaSalle St.
Chicago, IL 60697

Established in 1986.
Grantmaker type: Public charity
Financial data (yr. ended 04/30/02): Assets, $12,275,430 (M); expenditures, $432,454; program services expenses, $356,378; giving activities include $348,010 for 6 grants (high: $87,002; low: $34,801).
Purpose and activities: The fund exists for the six named charitable organizations.
Fields of interest: Animal welfare; Cancer; Boys clubs; Salvation Army; Children/youth, services.
Limitations: Applications not accepted. Giving limited to Charleston, Des Plaines, Chicago, and Chicago Ridge, IL, Morristown, NJ, and New York, NY. No grants to individuals.
Application information: Contributes only to pre-selected organizations; unsolicited requests for funds not considered or acknowledged.
Trustee: Bank of America.
EIN: 366836133

951
Chicago Board of Trade Foundation
141 W. Jackson Blvd., Ste. 1740-A
Chicago, IL 60604 (312) 435-3500
Contact: Julia Spraggs, Admin.

Established in 1984 in IL.
Donor(s): Chicago Board of Trade.

Grantmaker type: Company-sponsored foundation
Financial data (yr. ended 06/30/02): Assets, $3,508,029 (M); gifts received, $166,925; expenditures, $421,783; qualifying distributions, $380,778; giving activities include $381,925 for 34 grants (high: $103,463; low: $2,000).
Purpose and activities: Support for rehabilitation and the handicapped; arts and culture, including libraries and museums; education, including higher education and science and technology; youth and child development; wildlife; and media and communications.
Fields of interest: Zoos/zoological societies; Cancer; Children/youth, services; Youth, services; Christian agencies & churches.
Types of support: General/operating support; Continuing support; Annual campaigns; Capital campaigns; Endowments.
Limitations: Giving limited to Chicago, IL. No grants to individuals.
Application information: Application form not required.
   Initial approach: Letter
   Copies of proposal: 1
   Deadline(s): None
   Board meeting date(s): 1st quarter annually
   Final notification: Within 30 days
Officers: Nickolas Neubauer, Chair.; Jill A. Harley, Treas.; Ellen Paparelli, Admin.; Julia Spraggs, Admin.
Directors: Charles P. Carey; Robert Corvino; Thomas P. Cunningham; Michael Daley.
EIN: 363348469

952
Clemens Family Foundation
c/o Schiff, Hardin & Waite, Attn: T. Abendroth
6600 Sears Twr.
Chicago, IL 60606

Established in 1990 in IL.
Donor(s): George S. Clemens.
Grantmaker type: Independent foundation
Financial data (yr. ended 12/31/02): Assets, $2,500,568 (M); expenditures, $119,253; qualifying distributions, $100,000; giving activities include $100,000 for 1 grant.
Fields of interest: Environment; Animals/wildlife, preservation/protection; Reproductive health; Public health; Women.
Limitations: Applications not accepted. Giving primarily in the U.S., including programs with an international impact. No grants to individuals.
Application information: Contributes only to pre-selected organizations.
Trustees: June M. Clemens; Marshall W. Clemens; Patricia H. Clemens.
EIN: 363705143

953
Clovis Foundation
650 Dundee Rd., No. 456
Northbrook, IL 60062

Established in 1997 in IL.
Donor(s): Jonathan Green.
Grantmaker type: Independent foundation
Financial data (yr. ended 12/31/02): Assets, $1,585,640 (M); expenditures, $116,530; qualifying distributions, $104,332; giving

activities include $101,150 for 35 grants (high: $10,000; low: $1,000).
Purpose and activities: Giving primarily for health, education, and the environment.
Fields of interest: Arts; Education; Natural resources; Hospitals (general); Human services.
Limitations: Applications not accepted. No grants to individuals.
Application information: Contributes only to pre-selected organizations.
Trustees: Brenda Berry Green; Jonathan Green.
EIN: 367214742

954
ComEd Corporate Giving Program
(formerly Unicom Corporation Contributions Program)
c/o Corp. Affairs Dept., 38FNE
P.O. Box 767
Chicago, IL 60690 (312) 394-3063
Contact: Leslie Jackson, Mgr., Corp. Responsibility

Grantmaker type: Corporate giving program
Purpose and activities: ComEd makes charitable contributions to nonprofit organizations involved with higher education, environmental education, health and human services, disease, and science. Support is given primarily in areas of company operations.
Fields of interest: Higher education; Environmental education; Hospitals (general); Health care; Health organizations; Human services; Mathematics; Science.
Types of support: General/operating support; Continuing support; Capital campaigns; Building/renovation; Use of facilities; Employee matching gifts; Donated equipment; In-kind gifts.
Limitations: Giving primarily in areas of company operations, particularly northern IL. No support for religious, political, or fraternal organizations. No grants to individuals, or for advertising.
Publications: Application guidelines, Informational brochure (including application guidelines), Program policy statement.
Application information: Requests may be submitted using the Chicago Common Application Form. The Corporate Affairs Department handles giving. A contributions committee reviews all requests. Application form not required.
   Initial approach: Proposal to nearest company facility
   Copies of proposal: 1
   Deadline(s): None
   Board meeting date(s): Quarterly
   Final notification: 2 weeks following committee meetings
Number of staff: 2 part-time professional.

955
Comer Charitable Fund
c/o Lawrence Richman
2 N. LaSalle St., Ste. 2200
Chicago, IL 60602

Established in 2002.
Donor(s): Gary Comer.
Grantmaker type: Independent foundation
Financial data (yr. ended 04/30/03): Assets, $101,996,623 (M); gifts received, $45,600,000;

expenditures, $6,153,892; qualifying distributions, $4,857,995; giving activities include $4,839,343 for 85 grants (high: $800,000; low: $500).
Fields of interest: Arts; Libraries/library science; Education; Natural resources; Health organizations, association; Human services.
Limitations: Applications not accepted. Giving primarily in IL. No grants to individuals.
Application information: Contributes only to pre-selected organizations.
Officers: Gary Comer, Pres.; John Latter, V.P.; William Schleicher, V.P.
EIN: 010682597

956
The Comer Foundation ▼
c/o Neal Gerber & Eisenberg
2 N. LaSalle St.
Chicago, IL 60602
Contact: Stephanie Comer, Pres.

Established in 1986 in IL.
Donor(s): Gary C. Comer, Frances Comer.
Grantmaker type: Independent foundation
Financial data (yr. ended 12/31/02): Assets, $538,340 (M); expenditures, $1,994,355; qualifying distributions, $1,970,798; giving activities include $1,819,426 for 36 grants (high: $1,161,889; low: $300; average: $1,000–$100,000).
Purpose and activities: Giving primarily for environmental protection, medicine, arts and cultural organizations, human services, and education.
Fields of interest: Museums; Arts; Libraries/library science; Education; Natural resources; Zoos/zoological societies; Hospitals (general); Public health; AIDS; Human services; Children/youth, services.
Types of support: General/operating support; Continuing support; Program development; Internship funds; Scholarship funds.
Limitations: Applications not accepted. Giving primarily in Chicago, IL. No grants to individuals.
Application information: Contributes only to pre-selected organizations.
Officers: Stephanie Comer, Pres.; Frances Comer, V.P. and Secy.; Gary C. Comer, Treas.
Number of staff: 1 full-time professional.
EIN: 363522486

957
Community Foundation of Central Illinois
(formerly Peoria Area Community Foundation)
331 Fulton St., Ste. 310
Peoria, IL 61602 (309) 674-8730
Contact: James Sullivan
FAX: (309) 674-8754; E-mail: jim communityfoundationci.org; URL: http://www.communityfoundationci.org

Incorporated in 1987 in IL.
Grantmaker type: Community foundation
Financial data (yr. ended 06/30/02): Assets, $8,974,835 (M); gifts received, $2,029,411; expenditures, $716,305; giving activities include $441,019 for 187 grants (high: $50,000; low: $50; average: $50–$100,000) and $21,700 for 25 grants to individuals (high: $1,500; low: $250).

Purpose and activities: Primary areas of interest include community development, the arts and humanities, education, and health. The foundation administers a donor-advised fund.
Fields of interest: Visual arts; Museums; Performing arts; Dance; Humanities; Historic preservation/historical societies; Arts; Early childhood education; Child development, education; Elementary school/education; Secondary school/education; Higher education; Adult/continuing education; Adult education—literacy, basic skills & GED; Reading; Education; Natural resources; Environment; Animal welfare; Animals/wildlife, preservation/protection; Family planning; Medical care, rehabilitation; Health care; Substance abuse, services; Mental health/crisis services; Health organizations, association; Cancer; Heart & circulatory diseases; AIDS; Alcoholism; Cancer research; Heart & circulatory research; AIDS research; Crime/violence prevention, youth; Food services; Nutrition; Recreation; Youth development, services; Human services; Children/youth, services; Child development, services; Family services; Aging, centers/services; Homeless, human services; Civil rights; Urban/community development; Community development; Voluntarism promotion; Federated giving programs; Social sciences; Government/public administration; Leadership development; Minorities; Disabled; Aging; Economically disadvantaged; Homeless.
Types of support: General/operating support; Capital campaigns; Equipment; Program development; Conferences/seminars; Seed money; Scholarship funds; Employee matching gifts; In-kind gifts; Matching/challenge support.
Limitations: Giving limited to the central IL area. No support for sectarian religious purposes. No grants to individuals (except for scholarships), or for annual campaigns or endowments; no loans.
Publications: Application guidelines, Annual report (including application guidelines), Financial statement, Informational brochure, Newsletter.
Application information: Application form not required.
Initial approach: Letter
Copies of proposal: 1
Deadline(s): Jan. 15, Apr. 15 and Oct. 15
Board meeting date(s): Monthly
Final notification: May, Aug., Nov. and Feb.
Officers and Directors:* Jay Vonachen,* Pres.; Mary Dill,* Secy.; Terry Machetti,* Treas.; Deb Bowers; Laraine Bryson; Royal Coulter; Michael Cutlinan; Ellen Foster; Karl Kuppler; Michael Landwirth; James Mamer; Arthur Oakford; A.J. Rassi; Robert Stevenson III; Jan Wright-Vergon.
Number of staff: 2 full-time professional; 1 part-time professional.
EIN: 371185713

958
The Bryan & Christina I. Cressey Foundation
c/o Rosen & Cohen
555 Skokie Blvd., Ste. 260
Northbrook, IL 60062 (847) 897-8900
Contact: Bryan C. Cressey, Pres. and Treas.

Established in 1986 in IL.
Donor(s): Bryan C. Cressey, Christina I. Cressey.

Grantmaker type: Independent foundation
Financial data (yr. ended 12/31/02): Assets, $677,952 (M); gifts received, $348,000; expenditures, $231,650; qualifying distributions, $228,925; giving activities include $228,925 for 41 grants (high: $22,000; low: $500; average: $1,000–$75,000).
Purpose and activities: Giving primarily for Christian and Protestant churches, particularly Episcopal churches; funding also for education and human services.
Fields of interest: Higher education; Business school/education; Animals/wildlife; Health organizations, association; Recreation; Human services; Women, centers/services; Christian agencies & churches.
Types of support: General/operating support.
Limitations: Giving primarily in Barrington, IL. No grants to individuals.
Application information: Application form not required.
Deadline(s): None
Officers: Bryan C. Cressey, Pres. and Treas.; Christina I. Cressey, V.P. and Secy.
EIN: 363486617

959
The Danielson Foundation
410 N. Michigan Ave., Rm. 590
Chicago, IL 60611

Established in 1964 in IL.
Grantmaker type: Independent foundation
Financial data (yr. ended 11/30/02): Assets, $1,832,256 (M); gifts received, $190,000; expenditures, $252,111; qualifying distributions, $249,709; giving activities include $249,000 for 33 grants (high: $40,000; low: $2,000).
Purpose and activities: Giving for charitable, cultural, educational, health and religious purposes.
Fields of interest: Arts; Higher education; Education; Botanical gardens; Health care; Health organizations, association; Human services; Federated giving programs; Christian agencies & churches.
Limitations: Applications not accepted. Giving primarily in CA and FL. No grants to individuals.
Application information: Contributes only to pre-selected organizations.
Officers and Directors:* John Rau,* Pres.; Candida D. Burnap,* V.P.; Charles E. Schroeder,* Secy.-Treas.; Catherine Andrea Massey; Christopher Massey; Richard S. Massey.
EIN: 362540494

960
DAO Foundation
c/o Rockford Acromatic Products Co.
611 Beacon St.
Loves Park, IL 61111-5902
Contact: Patricia Olson, Tr.

Established in 1961 in IL.
Donor(s): Rockford Acromatic Products Co., Aircraft Gear Corp.
Grantmaker type: Company-sponsored foundation
Financial data (yr. ended 03/31/02): Assets, $2,892,501 (M); expenditures, $170,251; qualifying distributions, $148,840; giving

activities include $149,850 for 23 grants (high: $42,500; low: $250).
Purpose and activities: Giving primarily for Rockford, IL, area community groups and conservation causes.
Fields of interest: Arts; Higher education; Education; Natural resources; Health care; Human services; Youth, services; Community development.
Types of support: Annual campaigns; Capital campaigns; Building/renovation; Equipment.
Limitations: Giving primarily in Rockford, IL. No grants to individuals.
Publications: Application guidelines.
Application information: Application form not required.
Initial approach: Letter
Copies of proposal: 1
Deadline(s): None
Board meeting date(s): 4 times annually
Trustees: Amy Olson; Nancy N. Olson; Patricia Olson.
EIN: 366101712

961
John Deere Corporate Giving Program
1515 River Dr.
Moline, IL 61265-8098 (309) 748-7955
Contact: James H. Collins, Pres., John Deere Fdn.; or Judy A. Christison, Mgr., Contribs. and Community Rels.
E-mail: christisonjudya@johndeere.com

Grantmaker type: Corporate giving program
Financial data (yr. ended 10/31/01): Total giving, $229,000; giving activities include $229,000 for grants (high: $125,000; low: $1,000).
Purpose and activities: As a complement to its foundation, John Deere also makes charitable contributions to nonprofit organizations directly. Support is given on a national and international basis.
Fields of interest: Arts; Education; Environment; Health care; Human services; Community development; Public affairs.
Types of support: Capital campaigns; Building/renovation; Program development; Seed money; Research; Employee volunteer services; Loaned talent; Sponsorships; In-kind gifts.
Limitations: Giving on a national and international basis in areas of company operations; giving also to national organizations. No grants to individuals, or for scholarships.
Publications: Corporate giving report (including application guidelines).
Application information: The John Deere Foundation handles giving. The company has a staff that only handles contributions. Application form not required.
Initial approach: Proposal to headquarters or nearest company facility; proposal to headquarters for national organizations
Copies of proposal: 1
Deadline(s): None
Final notification: Following review
Administrators: Judy A. Christison, Mgr., Contribs. and Community Rels.; James H. Collins, Pres., John Deere Fdn.
Number of staff: 2 full-time professional; 1 part-time professional; 1 part-time support.

962
John Deere Foundation ▼
1515 River Dr.
Moline, IL 61265 (309) 748-7955
Contact: James H. Collins, Pres.
FAX: (309) 748-7953; E-mail:
ChristisonJudyA@JohnDeere.com

Incorporated in 1948 in IL.
Donor(s): Deere & Co.
Grantmaker type: Company-sponsored
foundation
Financial data (yr. ended 10/31/01): Assets,
$23,668,719 (M); gifts received, $7,982,201;
expenditures, $6,817,131; qualifying
distributions, $6,799,651; giving activities
include $5,878,725 for 422 grants (high:
$796,000; low: $500; average:
$3,000–$100,000) and $671,824 for 2
foundation-administered programs.
Purpose and activities: Grants largely for
community development, education, health and
human services, and cultural programs.
Fields of interest: Arts; Education; Health care;
Human services; Community development.
Types of support: Annual campaigns; Capital
campaigns; Building/renovation; Seed money;
Fellowships.
Limitations: Giving limited to areas where
company employees live and work. No grants to
individuals, or for endowment funds; no loans.
Publications: Corporate giving report (including
application guidelines).
Application information: Application form not
required.
   Initial approach: Letter
   Copies of proposal: 1
   Deadline(s): None
   Board meeting date(s): As required, usually
      quarterly
   Final notification: 30 days after board review
Officers and Directors:* Curtis G. Linke,*
Chair.; James H. Collins,* Pres.; Robert W.
Lane,* V.P.; Pamela Nelson, Secy.; Samuel R.
Allen; James R. Jenkins; Nathan J. Jones.
Number of staff: 2 full-time professional; 2
full-time support.
EIN: 366051024
**Recent environmental and animal welfare
grants:**
962-1 Horicon Marsh International Education
   Center, Friends of, Horicon, WI, $200,000.
   2001.
962-2 Horicon Marsh International Education
   Center, Friends of, Horicon, WI, $100,000.
   2001.
962-3 Lincoln Park Zoo, Chicago, IL,
   $3,000,000. 2001.
962-4 Lincoln Park Zoo, Chicago, IL, $250,000.
   2001.
962-5 Quad City Botanical Center Foundation,
   Rock Island, IL, $10,000. 2001.
962-6 Quad City Botanical Center Foundation,
   Rock Island, IL, $10,000. 2001.

963
Deering Foundation
410 N. Michigan Ave., Rm. 590
Chicago, IL 60611

Incorporated in 1956 in IL.
Donor(s): Barbara D. Danielson, Richard E.
Danielson, Jr., Marion D. Campbell, Miami Corp.

Grantmaker type: Independent foundation
Financial data (yr. ended 11/30/02): Assets,
$15,031,204 (M); expenditures, $580,610;
qualifying distributions, $772,255; giving
activities include $775,000 for 10 grants (high:
$200,000; low: $10,000).
Purpose and activities: Giving primarily to
affiliated foundations, the arts, and education.
Fields of interest: Arts education; Performing
arts centers; Arts; Higher education; Natural
resources; Hospitals (general); Federated giving
programs.
Types of support: General/operating support.
Limitations: Applications not accepted. Giving
primarily in FL, IL and MA. No grants to
individuals, or for scholarships or fellowships;
no loans.
Application information: Contributes only to
pre-selected organizations.
Officers and Directors:* Barbara S. Danielson,*
Pres.; Candida D. Burnap,* V.P.; Charles E.
Schroeder,* Secy.-Treas.; Charles E. Seitz;
Richard Strachan; Stephen M. Strachan; Jocelyn
D. Tennille.
EIN: 366051876

964
Delta Foundation
c/o Arthur R. O'Brien, Tr.
1249 Waukegan Rd.
Glenview, IL 60025-3077 (847) 729-8191

Established in 1994 in IL.
Donor(s): Jean F. Deal.
Grantmaker type: Independent foundation
Financial data (yr. ended 05/31/02): Assets,
$4,811,891 (M); expenditures, $356,541;
qualifying distributions, $355,240; giving
activities include $277,193 for 26 grants (high:
$25,000; low: $1,000).
Fields of interest: Education; Zoos/zoological
societies; Health care; Arthritis research;
Recreation; Human services; YM/YWCAs &
YM/YWHAs; Children, services; Community
development; Foundations (community);
Christian agencies & churches.
Limitations: Applications not accepted. Giving
primarily in IL and MI. No grants to individuals.
Application information: Contributes only to
pre-selected organizations.
Trustees: Harmon B. Deal, Jr.; Harmon B. Deal
III; Jean F. Deal; Arthur R. O'Brien; Michael
O'Brien; Nancy D. Walch.
EIN: 363917119

965
The Dick Family Foundation
273 Market Sq.
P.O. Box 312
Lake Forest, IL 60045

Established in 1979 in IL.
Grantmaker type: Independent foundation
Financial data (yr. ended 12/31/02): Assets,
$2,917,739 (M); expenditures, $137,443;
qualifying distributions, $171,912; giving
activities include $137,200 for 48 grants (high:
$13,000; low: $500).
Fields of interest: Arts; Higher education;
Education; Natural resources; Hospitals
(general); Federated giving programs.

Limitations: Applications not accepted. Giving
primarily in IL, with emphasis on Chicago and
Lake Forest. No grants to individuals.
Application information: Contributes only to
pre-selected organizations.
Officers and Directors:* John H. Dick, Pres. and
Treas.; Natalie C. Culley,* Secy.; Helen D.
Bronson; C. Mathews Dick, Jr.; Edison W. Dick;
S.H. Paige.
EIN: 366057056

966
Mary Barnes Donnelley Family Foundation
30 N. LaSalle St., Rm. 1232
Chicago, IL 60602

Established in 1986 in IL.
Grantmaker type: Independent foundation
Financial data (yr. ended 12/31/02): Assets,
$1,451,946 (M); expenditures, $124,433;
qualifying distributions, $114,249; giving
activities include $114,766 for grants.
Purpose and activities: Giving primarily for
education and wildlife conservation.
Fields of interest: Higher education; Education;
Animals/wildlife, preservation/protection.
Limitations: Applications not accepted. Giving
primarily in IL.
Application information: Contributes only to
pre-selected organizations.
Officers and Directors:* Patrick J. Herbert III,*
Pres.; Sandra L. Lake,* Secy.; Lori S.
Helmantoler,* Treas.; Laren Donnelley; Naoma
Donnelley; Reuben S. Donnelley.
EIN: 363487746

967
Gaylord and Dorothy Donnelley Foundation ▼
35 E. Wacker Dr., Ste. 2600
Chicago, IL 60601-2102 (312) 977-2700
Contact: Judith M. Stockdale, Exec. Dir.
FAX: (312) 977-1686; URL: http://www.gddf.org

Incorporated in 1952 in IL.
Donor(s): Gaylord Donnelley,‡ Dorothy Ranney
Donnelley.‡
Grantmaker type: Independent foundation
Financial data (yr. ended 12/31/01): Assets,
$84,815,281 (M); gifts received, $3,087,753;
expenditures, $4,508,673; qualifying
distributions, $4,040,152; giving activities
include $3,266,649 for 223 grants (high:
$250,000; low: $500; average:
$5,000–$25,000).
Purpose and activities: Primary areas of interest
include conservation and environment,
education, arts and culture, and short term food
and shelter programs.
Fields of interest: Arts; Education; Natural
resources; Environment; Housing/shelter,
development; Youth development.
Types of support: General/operating support;
Program development.
Limitations: Giving primarily in the Chicago, IL,
area and in the Lowcountry area of SC. No
support for religious purposes. No grants to
individuals, or for pledges, endowments, capital
campaigns, benefits, conferences, meetings,
eradication of deficits, publications, films,
videos, fundraising events, or matching gifts; no
loans.

Publications: Application guidelines, Annual report.
Application information: Telephone or FAX requests not considered. Application form required.
Initial approach: Letter requesting guidelines
Copies of proposal: 1
Deadline(s): None
Board meeting date(s): Spring, summer, and fall
Officers and Directors:* Strachan Donnelley, Ph.D.,* Chair.; Laura Donnelley-Morton,* Vice-Chair. and Treas.; Robert T. Carter,* Secy.; Judith M. Stockdale, Exec. Dir.; Gerald W. Adelmann; Elliott R. Donnelley,* Life Dir.; Shawn M. Donnelley; James B. Edwards; Ronne Hartfield; Coy Johnston; Challis M. Lowe; Jane Rishel, Life Dir.; Nancy F. Talbot; Max E. Wheeler.
Number of staff: 4 full-time professional.
EIN: 366108460

968
The Donnelley Foundation
(formerly Elliott and Ann Donnelley Foundation)
c/o Thomas E. Donnelley, II
360 N. Michigan Ave., Ste. 1009
Chicago, IL 60601-3803

Incorporated in 1954 in IL.
Donor(s): Elliott Donnelley,‡ Ann S. Hardy, Thomas E. Donnelley II, James R. Donnelley, Barbara C. Donnelley, Nina H. Donnelley, Robert G. Donnelley, Miranda S. Donnelley.
Grantmaker type: Independent foundation
Financial data (yr. ended 12/31/00): Assets, $16,043,037 (M); gifts received, $11,582,730; expenditures, $790,683; qualifying distributions, $731,856; giving activities include $725,349 for 180 grants (high: $90,000; low: $100).
Purpose and activities: Giving primarily to wildlife conservation, youth welfare, libraries, historic preservation, and educational and medical institutions with whom the foundation directors have long-term relationships and/or serve on the boards.
Fields of interest: Museums; Historic preservation/historical societies; Libraries/library science; Education; Animals/wildlife, preservation/protection; Hospitals (general); Children/youth, services.
Types of support: General/operating support; Continuing support; Annual campaigns; Capital campaigns; Building/renovation; Endowments; Seed money; Matching/challenge support.
Limitations: Applications not accepted. Giving primarily in CA, CT, IL, MT, OR, and VT. No grants to individuals.
Application information: Contributes only to pre-selected organizations.
Board meeting date(s): As required
Officers: Thomas E. Donnelley II, Pres.; James R. Donnelley, 1st V.P.; David E. Donnelley, V.P. and Secy.; Robert G. Donnelley, V.P. and Treas.
Number of staff: None.
EIN: 366066894

969
Douglass Family Foundation
c/o Bank of America
231 S. LaSalle St.
Chicago, IL 60697 (312) 828-1785
Contact: M.C. Ryan

Established in 1997 in IL.
Donor(s): Benjamin P. Douglass, Elizabeth Douglass.
Grantmaker type: Independent foundation
Financial data (yr. ended 07/31/02): Assets, $1,945,949 (M); expenditures, $142,604; qualifying distributions, $119,370; giving activities include $117,000 for 3 grants (high: $108,000; low: $4,500).
Purpose and activities: Giving to the arts, hospitals, and women's services.
Fields of interest: Zoos/zoological societies; Hospitals (general); Women, centers/services.
Limitations: Giving primarily in AZ, IL, and NY.
Application information:
Initial approach: Letter
Deadline(s): None
Trustees: Benjamin P. Douglass; Catherine J. Douglass; Bank of America.
EIN: 367190046

970
Mildred & Bernard Doyle Charitable Trust
c/o The Northern Trust Co.
50 S. LaSalle St., Ste. L-5
Chicago, IL 60675

Established in 1997 in FL.
Grantmaker type: Independent foundation
Financial data (yr. ended 05/31/02): Assets, $3,480,976 (M); expenditures, $240,555; qualifying distributions, $213,014; giving activities include $210,502 for 18 grants (high: $43,000; low: $2,500).
Purpose and activities: Giving for the arts, education, and women's services.
Fields of interest: Arts; Education; Botanical gardens; Big Brothers/Big Sisters; Salvation Army; Women.
Limitations: Applications not accepted. Giving primarily in FL. No grants to individuals.
Application information: Contributes only to pre-selected organizations.
Trustee: The Northern Trust Co.
EIN: 656232467

971
The DuPage Community Foundation
110 N. Cross St.
Wheaton, IL 60187-5318 (630) 665-5556
Contact: David M. McGowan, Exec. Dir.
FAX: (630) 665-9571; E-mail: bheydorn@dcfdn.org, nchibucos@dcfdn.org, or dmm@dcfdn.org; URL: http://www.dcfdn.org

Established in 1986 in IL as fund of Chicago Community Trust; became a separate entity in 1994.
Grantmaker type: Community foundation
Financial data (yr. ended 06/30/02): Assets, $8,292,299 (M); gifts received, $1,057,808; expenditures, $650,531; giving activities include $325,059 for grants (low: $40).
Purpose and activities: The foundation administers donor-advised funds.

Fields of interest: Arts; Education; Environment; Health care; Human services; Children/youth, services; Civic centers.
Types of support: General/operating support; Building/renovation; Equipment; Program development; Seed money; Scholarship funds; Matching/challenge support.
Limitations: Giving primarily in DuPage County, IL.
Publications: Application guidelines, Annual report (including application guidelines), Grants list, Informational brochure, Newsletter.
Application information: Application available on website. Application form required.
Initial approach: Telephone
Copies of proposal: 2
Deadline(s): Spring
Board meeting date(s): Bimonthly
Final notification: Fall
Officers and Trustees:* George N. Gilkerson, Jr.,* Pres.; Jack E. Mensching, V.P.; Irene D. Antoniou, Secy.; Charlie A. Thurston,* Treas.; David P. Aldridge; Steven J. Beaman; Norman J. Beles; Betty Bradshaw; Cleve E. Carney; Carole Cline; Will M. Gillett; Joseph F. Kindlon; Paul J. Lehman; Vincent A. Naccarato; Nancy E. Sindelar; Ralph Smykal; Mary Eleanor Wall; Carson R. Yeager.
Number of staff: 2 full-time professional; 1 part-time professional; 1 part-time support.
EIN: 363978733

972
EBR Foundation
30 N. LaSalle St., Rm. 1232
Chicago, IL 60602-2502

Established in 1987 in IL.
Donor(s): Elizabeth B. Rogers, Howard B. Simpson, Charles H. Morse IV.
Grantmaker type: Independent foundation
Financial data (yr. ended 12/31/02): Assets, $1,227,859 (M); gifts received, $26,151; expenditures, $181,746; qualifying distributions, $172,577; giving activities include $173,000 for 22 grants (high: $50,000; low: $250).
Fields of interest: Museums; Secondary school/education; University; Zoos/zoological societies; Athletics/sports, equestrianism; Human services; Children/youth, services.
Limitations: Applications not accepted. Giving primarily in IL. No grants to individuals.
Application information: Contributes only to pre-selected organizations.
Officers: Patrick J. Herbert III, Pres.; Joanne Pitman Larson, Secy.; Lori S. Helmantoler, Treas.
Directors: Jessie S. Hasler; Charles H. Morse IV; Howard B. Simpson; James Simpson IV; William M. Simpson.
EIN: 363488134

973
Evanston Community Foundation
828 Davis St., Ste. 301
Evanston, IL 60201 (847) 492-0990
Contact: Sara L. Schastok, Exec. Dir.
FAX: (847) 492-0904; E-mail: Schastok@evcommfdn.org, or info@evcommfdn.org; URL: http://www.evcommfdn.org

Established in 1986 in IL.

Grantmaker type: Community foundation
Financial data (yr. ended 12/31/02): Assets, $3,224,187 (M); gifts received, $318,739; expenditures, $477,398; giving activities include $268,100 for 16 grants (high: $10,380; low: $1,000; average: $1,000–$10,380) and $10,290 for 1 in-kind gift.
Purpose and activities: The Evanston Community Foundation is a philanthropic organization dedicated to enriching Evanston and the lives of its people, now and in the future. The Foundation builds and manages its own and other community endowments, addresses Evanston's changing needs through grantmaking, and provides leadership on important community issues. The foundation administers donor-advised funds.
Fields of interest: Arts; Early childhood education; Education; Environment; Health care; Health organizations, association; AIDS; Housing/shelter, development; Youth development, services; Human services; Children/youth, services; Family services; Aging, centers/services; Minorities/immigrants, centers/services; Homeless, human services; Community development, neighborhood development; Community development; Public affairs, citizen participation; Leadership development; Minorities; Disabled; Aging; Economically disadvantaged; Homeless.
Types of support: Income development; Management development; Program development; Seed money; Curriculum development.
Limitations: Giving limited to Evanston, IL. No grants to individuals.
Publications: Application guidelines, Annual report, Informational brochure.
Application information: Application form required.
  Initial approach: Letter
  Copies of proposal: 12
  Deadline(s): Feb. 24
  Board meeting date(s): Monthly, except Aug.
  Final notification: June 1
Officers and Directors:* Eleanor Revelle,* Chair.; Carolyn DeSwarte Gifford,* Secy.; Mark McCarville,* Treas.; Sara L. Schastok, Exec. Dir.; Marybeth Schroeder, Community Prog. Dir.; Mary Anne Cappo; and 23 additional directors.
Number of staff: 2 full-time professional; 1 part-time professional; 1 full-time support.
EIN: 363466802

974
The Excelsior! Foundation
c/o John McGovern
225 W. Wacker Dr., Ste. 2800
Chicago, IL 60606

Donor(s): Barbara Olin Taylor.
Grantmaker type: Independent foundation
Financial data (yr. ended 12/31/02): Assets, $842,503 (M); expenditures, $1,437,100; qualifying distributions, $1,427,644; giving activities include $1,386,363 for 40 grants (high: $480,933; low: $25).
Purpose and activities: Giving primarily for education and human services.
Fields of interest: Education, administration/regulation; Education, research; Higher education; Education; Natural resources; Health care; Health organizations, association;

Human services; Federated giving programs; Philanthropy/voluntarism; Christian agencies & churches.
Limitations: Applications not accepted. Giving on a national basis. No grants to individuals.
Application information: Contributes only to pre-selected organizations.
Officers and Directors:* Barbara Olin Taylor,* Pres. and Treas.; Frederick M. Taylor III, V.P.; James W. Taylor, V.P.; Spencer O. Taylor, V.P.; John E. McGovern, Jr.,* Secy.; F. Morgan Taylor, Jr.
EIN: 363812346

975
Farm Foundation
1211 W. 22nd St., Ste. 216
Oak Brook, IL 60523-2197 (630) 571-9393
Contact: Walter J. Armbruster, Pres.
FAX: (630) 571-9580; E-mail: walt@farmfoundation.org; URL: http://www.farmfoundation.org

Established in 1933 in IL.
Grantmaker type: Public charity
Financial data (yr. ended 04/30/02): Revenue, $1,296,609; assets, $22,981,364 (M); gifts received, $167,309; expenditures, $1,128,504; program services expenses, $929,887.
Purpose and activities: The foundation acts as a catalyst to increase knowledge about agricultural and rural issues; to apply that knowledge through education programs dealing with the challenges, issues, and opportunities faced by agricultural and rural people; to develop human capital; to facilitate interaction about emerging issues among agribusiness and policy leaders, government officials, and the academic community; to explore policy alternatives; and to facilitate communication about the issues and alternatives.
Fields of interest: Environment; Agriculture; Rural development; Consumer protection.
Types of support: Conferences/seminars; Publication.
Limitations: Giving on a national basis.
Publications: Annual report, Informational brochure, Occasional report, Program policy statement.
Application information: See Web site for further application information. Application form not required.
  Initial approach: Letter
  Copies of proposal: 1
  Board meeting date(s): June and Jan.
Officers and Trustees:* Ronald D. Knutson, Ph.D.,* Chair.; Roderick N. Stacey,* Vice-Chair.; Walter J. Armbruster,* Pres.; Steve A. Halbrook, V.P. and Secy.; Nicholas C. Babson; William T. Boehm; Paul G. Brower; David L. Chicoine; Drew R. Collier; Jeffrey A. Conrad; Ed Dickinson; Daniel M. Dooley; Charles Fischer; Barry L. Flinchbaugh; Richard L. Gady; and 14 additional trustees.
Number of staff: 3 full-time professional; 2 full-time support.
EIN: 362270048

976
Jamee and Marshall Field Foundation
225 W. Wacker Dr., Ste. 1500
Chicago, IL 60606 (312) 917-1823
Contact: Patricia E. Wallies, Exec. Dir.

Established in 1982 in IL.
Donor(s): Jamee J. Field, Marshall Field.
Grantmaker type: Independent foundation
Financial data (yr. ended 09/30/02): Assets, $5,187,969 (M); gifts received, $15,764; expenditures, $542,711; qualifying distributions, $474,911; giving activities include $378,500 for 43 grants (high: $55,000; low: $500) and $10,856 for employee matching gifts.
Purpose and activities: Giving primarily in the areas of conservation and environment, particularly preservation of unique natural areas, wildlife protection, and pollution abatement; and culture, for selected major cultural institutions.
Fields of interest: Arts; Natural resources; Environment; Animals/wildlife, preservation/protection.
Types of support: General/operating support; Continuing support; Annual campaigns; Capital campaigns; Building/renovation; Program development.
Limitations: Giving primarily in the metropolitan Chicago, IL, area. No support for national health agencies, political or fraternal organizations, or United Way member agencies. No grants to individuals, or for medical or scholarly research, benefits, tickets or advertisements, conferences, meetings, publications, or films or videos.
Publications: Application guidelines.
Application information: Application form not required.
  Initial approach: Proposal
  Copies of proposal: 1
  Deadline(s): Jan. 15, Apr. 15, and Aug. 15
  Board meeting date(s): Mar., June and Oct.
Officers and Directors:* Marshall Field,* Pres.; Jamee J. Field,* V.P.; Torrence K. Hammond,* Treas.; Patricia E. Wallies, Exec. Dir.
Number of staff: 1.
EIN: 363184245

977
The Field Foundation of Illinois, Inc.
200 S. Wacker Dr., Ste. 3860
Chicago, IL 60606 (312) 831-0910
Contact: Handy L. Lindsey, Jr., Pres.
URL: http://www.fieldfoundation.org

Incorporated in 1960 in IL.
Donor(s): Marshall Field IV.‡
Grantmaker type: Independent foundation
Financial data (yr. ended 04/30/02): Assets, $50,692,595 (M); expenditures, $3,246,014; qualifying distributions, $2,695,493; giving activities include $2,143,597 for 242 grants (high: $25,000; low: $592; average: $4,000–$10,000) and $42,150 for 36 employee matching gifts.
Purpose and activities: Giving in the fields of health, community welfare, primary and secondary education, cultural activities, conservation, and urban and community affairs.
Fields of interest: Museums; Arts; Early childhood education; Elementary school/education; Secondary school/education; Adult education—literacy, basic skills & GED;

Reading; Education; Natural resources; Environment; Medical care, rehabilitation; Health care; Substance abuse, services; Mental health/crisis services; Health organizations, association; AIDS; Employment; Food services; Human services; Children/youth, services; Aging, centers/services; Homeless, human services; Race/intergroup relations; Community development; Public policy, research; Public affairs; Aging; Economically disadvantaged; Homeless.

Types of support: Capital campaigns; Building/renovation; Equipment; Land acquisition; Emergency funds; Program development; Seed money; Curriculum development; Technical assistance; Employee matching gifts.

Limitations: Giving primarily in the Chicago, IL, area. No support for member agencies of community funds, national health agencies, neighborhood health clinics, small cultural groups, or religious purposes. No grants to individuals, or for endowment funds, continuing operating support, medical research, conferences, operating support of day care centers, fundraising events, advertising, scholarships, printed materials or video equipment, or fellowships; no loans.

Publications: Biennial report (including application guidelines), Informational brochure (including application guidelines), Occasional report.

Application information: Application form not required.

  Initial approach: Proposal
  Copies of proposal: 1
  Deadline(s): Jan. 15, May 15, and Sept. 15
  Board meeting date(s): 3 times per year

Officers and Directors:* Philip Wayne Hummer,* Chair.; Handy L. Lindsey, Jr.,* Pres., Treas., and Exec. Dir.; Gary H. Kline,* Secy.; Judith S. Block; Burlean Miller Burris; Marshall Field; F. Oliver Nicklin; George A. Ranney, Jr.; Christine M. Tchen.

Number of staff: 3 full-time professional; 1 part-time professional; 1 full-time support; 1 part-time support.

EIN: 366059408

978
C. W. Finkl Foundation, Inc.
2011 Southport Ave.
Chicago, IL 60614

Established in 1985 in IL.
Donor(s): Charles W. Finkl, Sarah Lee Finkl.
Grantmaker type: Independent foundation
Financial data (yr. ended 10/31/01): Assets, $397,978 (M); expenditures, $191,457; qualifying distributions, $187,743; giving activities include $170,715 for 39 grants (high: $130,000; low: $50).
Purpose and activities: Support primarily for education; some giving also to youth agencies.
Fields of interest: Vocational education, post-secondary; Natural resources; Environment; Hospitals (general); Health organizations, association; Children/youth, services.
Limitations: Applications not accepted. Giving primarily in Chicago, IL. No grants to individuals.
Application information: Contributes only to pre-selected organizations.

Officers and Directors:* Charles W. Finkl,* Pres.; Jeanne M. Rooks, Secy.; Sarah Lee Finkl,* Treas.; James B. Finkl.
Number of staff: None.
EIN: 363412118

979
Sonja and F. Conrad Fischer Foundation
1050 Crescent Ln.
Winnetka, IL 60093
Contact: F. Conrad Fischer, Tr.
Application address: c/o William Blair & Co., 222 W. Adams, Chicago, IL 60606, tel.: (312) 236-1600

Established in 1990 in IL.
Donor(s): Sylvia Fischer, F. Conrad Fischer, Sonja H. Fischer.
Grantmaker type: Independent foundation
Financial data (yr. ended 12/31/02): Assets, $1,877,694 (M); gifts received, $153,803; expenditures, $114,845; qualifying distributions, $112,465; giving activities include $112,900 for 20 grants (high: $23,500; low: $300).
Purpose and activities: Giving primarily for education and youth programs.
Fields of interest: Music; Higher education; Education; Botanical/horticulture/landscape services; Zoos/zoological societies; Children/youth, services.
Limitations: Giving on a national basis, with emphasis on Chicago, IL. No grants to individuals.
Application information:
  Initial approach: Proposal
  Deadline(s): Nov. 15
Trustees: F. Conrad Fischer; Sonja H. Fischer.
EIN: 366941059

980
Flanagan Family Foundation
c/o John R. Waters & Co.
311 S. Wacker Dr.
Chicago, IL 60606

Established in 1998 in IL.
Donor(s): Thomas Flanagan, Constance Flanagan.
Grantmaker type: Independent foundation
Financial data (yr. ended 03/31/02): Assets, $117,051 (M); gifts received, $200,000; expenditures, $124,941; qualifying distributions, $124,941; giving activities include $124,900 for 18 grants (high: $70,500; low: $250).
Fields of interest: Education; Natural resources; Roman Catholic agencies & churches; Medical research.
Types of support: General/operating support.
Limitations: Applications not accepted. Giving primarily in FL. No grants to individuals.
Officers: Thomas Flanagan, Pres.; Constance Flanagan, V.P.; James E. Murphy, Secy.-Treas.
Director: Sharon Breen.
Number of staff: None.
EIN: 364148847

981
Peter and Virginia Foreman Family Foundation
(formerly Peter and Virginia Foreman Foundation)
225 W. Washington St., Ste. 1650
Chicago, IL 60606
Contact: Peter B. Foreman, Pres.

Established in 1990 in IL.
Donor(s): Christopher Foreman, Peter Foreman.
Grantmaker type: Independent foundation
Financial data (yr. ended 06/30/02): Assets, $11,668,761 (M); expenditures, $467,690; qualifying distributions, $482,953; giving activities include $423,113 for 123 grants (high: $50,000; low: $5).
Purpose and activities: Giving primarily for the arts, education, health, and human services; also support for Jewish organizations.
Fields of interest: Museums; Theater; Arts; Higher education; Education; Natural resources; Botanical gardens; Hospitals (general); Health care; Health organizations, association; Parks/playgrounds; Human services; Children/youth, services; Women, centers/services; Community development, neighborhood development; Jewish federated giving programs.
Limitations: Giving primarily in Chicago, IL. No grants to individuals.
Application information: Application form not required.
  Initial approach: Letter
  Deadline(s): None
Officers: Peter B. Foreman, Pres.; Virginia Foreman, V.P.; Rhonda Kaysor, V.P.
Directors: Christopher Foreman; Jeffrey Foreman.
EIN: 363712587

982
Mrs. Zollie S. Frank Fund
(formerly Zollie and Elaine Frank Fund)
666 Garland Pl.
Des Plaines, IL 60016-4725
Contact: Elaine S. Frank, Pres.

Incorporated in 1953 in IL.
Donor(s): Zollie S. Frank, Elaine S. Frank, Z. Frank, Inc., Four Wheels, Inc., Wheels, Inc., Frank Consolidated Enterprises.
Grantmaker type: Independent foundation
Financial data (yr. ended 12/31/02): Assets, $5,616,313 (M); gifts received, $25,000; expenditures, $288,306; qualifying distributions, $269,470; giving activities include $269,455 for 101 grants (high: $100,250; low: $25).
Purpose and activities: Giving primarily for higher education, and Jewish federated giving programs, agencies, and temples; funding also for arts and culture, environmental conservation, hospitals, health care and health associations, children and youth services, and social services.
Fields of interest: Arts education; Arts; Higher education; Natural resources; Hospitals (general); Health care; Health organizations, association; Human services; Children/youth, services; Jewish federated giving programs; Jewish agencies & temples.
Types of support: General/operating support.

Limitations: Giving primarily in IL, with emphasis on Chicago.
Application information:
Initial approach: Letter
Deadline(s): None
Officers: Elaine S. Frank, Pres.; James S. Frank, V.P.; Laurie A. Lieberman, V.P.; Nancy Schechtman, Secy.; Charles E. Frank, Treas.
EIN: 366118400

983
Helen V. Froehlich Foundation
c/o The Northern Trust Co.
50 S. LaSalle St., L-5
Chicago, IL 60675

Established in 1993 in IL.
Grantmaker type: Independent foundation
Financial data (yr. ended 05/31/02): Assets, $33,799,266 (M); expenditures, $1,863,243; qualifying distributions, $1,858,663; giving activities include $1,819,500 for 6 grants (high: $497,000; low: $22,500; average: $25,000–$250,000).
Purpose and activities: Giving primarily for natural resource conservation.
Fields of interest: Higher education; Natural resources; Environment, water resources; Environment, land resources; Botanical gardens.
Limitations: Applications not accepted. Giving primarily in Chicago, IL, and NY. No grants to individuals.
Application information: Contributes only to pre-selected organizations.
Trustee: The Northern Trust Co.
EIN: 367033137

984
Marshall B. Front Family Charitable Foundation
c/o Front Barnett, LLC
3 First National Plz., Ste. 4920
Chicago, IL 60602

Established in 1996.
Donor(s): Marshall B. Front.
Grantmaker type: Independent foundation
Financial data (yr. ended 12/31/02): Assets, $681,967 (M); gifts received, $123,169; expenditures, $112,015; qualifying distributions, $110,850; giving activities include $110,850 for 26 grants (high: $15,000; low: $100).
Purpose and activities: Giving to the arts, culture and education.
Fields of interest: Museums; Arts; Higher education; Education; Aquariums; Human services.
Limitations: Applications not accepted. Giving primarily in Chicago, IL, with some giving in NY. No grants to individuals.
Application information: Contributes only to pre-selected organizations.
Officers: Marshall B. Front, Pres.; Laura D. Front, V.P.; Paul J. Miller, V.P.
EIN: 364121527

985
GATX Corporation Contributions Program
500 W. Monroe St.
Chicago, IL 60661-3676   (312) 621-6222
Contact: Jesse Kane, Supvr., Community Affairs
FAX: (312) 621-6698; E-mail: community@gatx.com; URL: http://www.gatx.com/common/about/community.asp

Grantmaker type: Corporate giving program
Financial data (yr. ended 12/31/02): Total giving, $1,284,713; giving activities include $1,220,484 for grants and $64,229 for employee matching gifts.
Purpose and activities: As a complement to its foundation, GATX also makes charitable contributions to nonprofit organizations directly. Support is given primarily in areas of company operations.
Fields of interest: Multipurpose centers/programs; Arts; Reading; Education; Environment, beautification programs; Environment; Health care; Health care; Substance abuse, services; Employment; Housing/shelter; Children/youth, services; Family services; Domestic violence; Family services, adolescent parents; Human services; Race/intergroup relations; Economic development; Homeless.
Types of support: General/operating support; Equipment; Program development; Seed money; Research; Employee volunteer services; Loaned talent; Employee matching gifts; Donated equipment; Donated products; In-kind gifts; Matching/challenge support.
Limitations: Giving primarily in areas of company operations, with emphasis on the Chicago, IL, neighborhoods of Englewood, Grand Boulevard, and Humboldt Park. No support for political, labor, athletic, or fraternal organizations, sectarian religious organizations, private foundations, individual public or private K-12 schools, United Way-supported organizations, or local chapters of national organizations. No grants to individuals, or for trips, tours, conferences, advertising, tickets, capital campaigns, endowments, land acquisition, debt reduction, or health research.
Publications: Grants list, Informational brochure (including application guidelines), Newsletter, Program policy statement.
Application information: The Community Affairs Department handles giving. The company has a staff that only handles contributions. A contributions committee reviews all requests. Application form required.
Initial approach: Letter of inquiry to headquarters
Copies of proposal: 1
Deadline(s): Jan. 15, Apr. 15, July 15, and Oct. 15
Board meeting date(s): Feb., May, Aug., and Nov.
Final notification: 1 month following committee meetings
Number of staff: 1 full-time professional.

986
The Getz Foundation
(formerly Emma & Oscar Getz Foundation)
111 E. Wacker Dr., Ste.2800
Chicago, IL 60601

Established in 1966 in IL.
Donor(s): Oscar Getz,‡ Emma Getz.
Grantmaker type: Independent foundation
Financial data (yr. ended 12/31/01): Assets, $12,162,899 (M); gifts received, $101,260; expenditures, $1,733,009; qualifying distributions, $1,615,992; giving activities include $1,576,655 for 111 grants (high: $150,000; low: $250).
Purpose and activities: Giving primarily for the arts, particularly a jazz festival; funding also for education, health, social services, community foundations, and Jewish organizations.
Fields of interest: Museums; Theater; Music; Arts; Elementary/secondary education; Higher education; Education; Environment, land resources; Health organizations; Medical research, institute; Human services; Foundations (community); Jewish agencies & temples.
Limitations: Applications not accepted. Giving primarily in Aspen, CO, and Chicago, IL. No grants to individuals.
Application information: Contributes only to pre-selected organizations. Unsolicited requests for funds not accepted.
Officers: William M. Getz, Pres.; Ralph D. Silver, V.P. and Secy.; H. Debra Levin, Treas.
EIN: 366150787

987
Gibbet Hill Foundation
410 N. Michigan Ave., Ste. 590
Chicago, IL 60611-4220

Established in 1976 in IL.
Donor(s): Deering Foundation, Miami Corp.
Grantmaker type: Independent foundation
Financial data (yr. ended 12/31/02): Assets, $1,929,245 (M); gifts received, $190,000; expenditures, $604,213; qualifying distributions, $290,671; giving activities include $290,000 for 8 grants (high: $90,000; low: $5,000).
Purpose and activities: Giving primarily for higher and other education; funding also for the opera, the environment, and for family planning.
Fields of interest: Opera; Higher education; Education; Environment; Family planning.
Types of support: General/operating support.
Limitations: Applications not accepted. Giving on a national basis. No grants to individuals.
Application information: Contributes only to pre-selected organizations.
Officers and Directors:* Richard Strachan,* Pres.; Stephen Strachan,* V.P.; Charles E. Schroeder,* Secy.-Treas.
EIN: 510189357

988
The John and Charlotte Gilmore Foundation
c/o Goldman Sachs
4900 Sears Tower
Chicago, IL 60606
Contact: John F. Gilmore, Jr., Tr.

Established in 1989 in IL.
Donor(s): John F. Gilmore, Jr.
Grantmaker type: Independent foundation
Financial data (yr. ended 06/30/02): Assets, $905,876 (M); expenditures, $327,770; qualifying distributions, $320,533; giving

activities include $319,965 for 30 grants (high: $200,000; low: $100).

Purpose and activities: Giving primarily for Roman Catholic churches and organizations.

Fields of interest: Education; Zoos/zoological societies; Children/youth, services; Roman Catholic agencies & churches.

Limitations: Applications not accepted. Giving primarily in Chicago, IL. No grants to individuals.

Application information: Contributes only to pre-selected organizations.

Trustees: Charlotte Gilmore; John F. Gilmore, Jr.

EIN: 133545181

989
Glore Fund

208 S. LaSalle St., Ste. 2145
Chicago, IL 60604
Contact: Robert Hixon Glore, Pres.

Established in 1985 in IL.

Donor(s): Robert Hixon Glore.

Grantmaker type: Independent foundation

Financial data (yr. ended 12/31/02): Assets, $79,878 (M); gifts received, $176,809; expenditures, $103,840; qualifying distributions, $101,273; giving activities include $102,320 for 49 grants (high: $30,000; low: $50).

Purpose and activities: Giving for the arts, hospitals, and the environment.

Fields of interest: Museums; Performing arts; Historical activities; Environment; Hospitals (general).

Limitations: Giving primarily in the Chicago, IL, area. No grants to individuals.

Application information: Application form not required.

> *Deadline(s):* None

Officers and Directors:* Robert Hixon Glore,* Pres.; Frederick H. Glore, V.P.; Maude Glore Harper, V.P.; Dorothy Thorsen,* Secy.-Treas.

EIN: 366108355

990
William and Karen Goodyear Foundation

c/o Bank of America
231 S. LaSalle St.
Chicago, IL 60697 (312) 828-1398
Contact: William M. Goodyear, Tr.

Established in 1997 in IL.

Donor(s): Karen E. Goodyear, William M. Goodyear.

Grantmaker type: Independent foundation

Financial data (yr. ended 04/30/03): Assets, $1,178 (M); gifts received, $125,000; expenditures, $190,248; qualifying distributions, $188,665; giving activities include $188,650 for 24 grants (high: $61,500; low: $250).

Purpose and activities: Giving primarily for child development, education, and arts and culture; funding also for social services.

Fields of interest: Museums (science/technology); Theater; Arts; Higher education; Libraries (public); Zoos/zoological societies; Human services; Children/youth, services; Child development, services.

Limitations: Giving primarily in Chicago, IL.

Application information: Application form not required.

> *Deadline(s):* None

Trustees: Karen E. Goodyear; William M. Goodyear.

EIN: 364157874

991
Grand Victoria Foundation ▼

60 S. Grove Ave.
Elgin, IL 60120 (847) 289-8575
Contact: Nancy Fishman, Exec. Dir.
FAX: (847) 289-8576; E-mail: info@grandvictoriafdn.org; URL: http://www.grandvictoriafdn.org

Established in 1996 in IL.

Donor(s): Grand Victoria Casino.

Grantmaker type: Company-sponsored foundation

Financial data (yr. ended 02/28/02): Assets, $69,972,875 (M); gifts received, $20,074,636; expenditures, $4,264,282; qualifying distributions, $4,150,228; giving activities include $3,631,746 for 105 grants (high: $228,000; low: $100; average: $2,000–$50,000).

Purpose and activities: The foundation's mission is to assist communities in their efforts to pursue systemic solutions to problems in specific areas of education, economic development, and the environment.

Fields of interest: Education; Environment; Employment; Housing/shelter; Community development.

Types of support: Capital campaigns; Land acquisition; Program development; Technical assistance; Consulting services; Program evaluation; Matching/challenge support.

Limitations: Giving limited to IL. No support for religious purposes or political campaigns. No grants to individuals, or for endowments, fundraising events, or debt or deficit reduction.

Publications: Application guidelines.

Application information: Application form required.

> *Initial approach:* Letter of intent
> *Deadline(s):* 2 months before board meeting
> *Board meeting date(s):* Quarterly
> *Final notification:* In writing

Officer: Nancy Fishman, Exec. Dir.

Directors: Antonio Gracias; Taffy Hoffer; Nick Pritzker; Richard Schulze; Peter Simon; Michelle Stickney-Rasmusson.

Number of staff: 2 full-time professional; 2 full-time support.

EIN: 364107162

Recent environmental and animal welfare grants:

991-1 American Farmland Trust, DC, $50,000. 2002.

991-2 Audubon Society, National, New York, NY, $25,000. 2002.

991-3 Ballard Family Nature Center, Altamont, IL, $228,000. 2002.

991-4 Canal Corridor Association, Chicago, IL, $95,000. 2002.

991-5 Center for Neighborhood Technology, Chicago, IL, $150,000. 2002.

991-6 Chicago Wilderness, Chicago, IL, $40,000. For Mighty Acorns. Grant made through Field Museum of Natural History. 2002.

991-7 Chicago Wilderness Magazine, Evanston, IL, $30,000. 2002.

991-8 Citizens for a Better Environment, Chicago, IL, $38,500. 2002.

991-9 Corporation for Open Lands (CorLands), Chicago, IL, $50,000. 2002.

991-10 Delta Institute, Chicago, IL, $150,000. 2002.

991-11 Environmental Law and Policy Center of the Midwest, Chicago, IL, $25,000. 2002.

991-12 Friends of the Chicago River, Chicago, IL, $60,000. 2002.

991-13 Garfield Park Conservatory Alliance, Chicago, IL, $12,500. 2002.

991-14 Natural Land Institute, Rockford, IL, $50,000. 2002.

991-15 Natural Land Institute, Rockford, IL, $50,000. 2002.

991-16 Nature Conservancy, Chicago, IL, $109,000. 2002.

991-17 Southwestern Illinois Resource Conservation and Development Council, Mascoutah, IL, $50,000. 2002.

991-18 Wetlands Initiative, Chicago, IL, $150,000. 2002.

991-19 Youth Conservation Corps, Deerfield, IL, $10,000. 2002.

992
David F. and Margaret T. Grohne Family Foundation

907 Lawn Ct.
Western Springs, IL 60558
Contact: David Grohne, Pres.

Established in 1995.

Donor(s): David Grohne.

Grantmaker type: Independent foundation

Financial data (yr. ended 12/31/02): Assets, $15,767,133 (M); gifts received, $1,000,000; expenditures, $1,383,455; qualifying distributions, $1,327,033; giving activities include $1,327,033 for 3 grants (high: $1,000,000; low: $77,033).

Fields of interest: Animals/wildlife, preservation/protection; Animals/wildlife, bird preserves.

Limitations: Giving primarily in MT and TN. No grants to individuals.

Application information: Application form not required.

> *Deadline(s):* None

Officers: David Grohne, Pres.; Margaret Grohne, V.P.

Director: Jeffrey Grohne.

EIN: 364061509

993
David D. & Mary F. Grumhaus Fund

197 N. Green Bay Rd.
Lake Forest, IL 60045-2137

Donor(s): David D. Grumhaus, Mary F. Grumhaus.

Grantmaker type: Independent foundation

Financial data (yr. ended 12/31/02): Assets, $1,977,157 (M); expenditures, $96,175; qualifying distributions, $96,175; giving activities include $91,825 for 75 grants (high: $14,550; low: $25).

Purpose and activities: Giving for the arts, hospitals, and youth services.

Fields of interest: Orchestra (symphony); Zoos/zoological societies; Hospitals (general); Children/youth, services.
Types of support: General/operating support; Scholarship funds.
Limitations: Applications not accepted. Giving primarily in IL, with emphasis on Chicago. No grants to individuals.
Application information: Contributes only to pre-selected organizations.
Officers: Mary F. Grumhaus, Pres.; David D. Grumhaus, V.P. and Treas.; Audrey G. Young, Secy.
Directors: Jennifer G. Daly; David D. Grumhaus, Jr.; Lisa Grumhaus; Whitney Grumhaus.
Number of staff: None.
EIN: 363225807

994
Ernest A. Grunsfeld Memorial Fund

211 E. Ontario St., Ste. 1390
Chicago, IL 60611
Contact: Ernest A. Grunsfeld, III, Pres.
FAX: (312) 202-1810

Established in 1948 in IL.
Donor(s): Ernest A. Grunsfeld, Jr.,‡ Ernest A. Grunsfeld III, Esther G. Klatz.
Grantmaker type: Independent foundation
Financial data (yr. ended 12/31/02): Assets, $979,578 (M); gifts received, $92,937; expenditures, $162,384; qualifying distributions, $159,510; giving activities include $160,000 for 5 grants (high: $125,000; low: $2,500).
Purpose and activities: Giving to higher education, music, the arts and horticulture.
Fields of interest: Architecture; Music; Arts; Higher education; Horticulture/garden clubs.
Types of support: Fellowships; Internship funds; Research.
Limitations: Applications not accepted. Giving primarily in the metropolitan Chicago, IL, area. No grants to individuals.
Application information: Contributes only to pre-selected organizations.
Board meeting date(s): As required
Officers and Directors:* Ernest A. Grunsfeld III,* Pres.; Esther G. Klatz,* Exec. V.P. and Treas.; Frank Mayer, Jr.,* Secy.
EIN: 366108523

995
The H.B.B. Foundation

400 N. Michigan Ave., Ste. 1120
Chicago, IL 60611

Established in 1964 in IL.
Grantmaker type: Independent foundation
Financial data (yr. ended 12/31/02): Assets, $7,640,188 (M); expenditures, $445,389; qualifying distributions, $417,602; giving activities include $364,000 for 53 grants (high: $45,000; low: $500).
Purpose and activities: Giving primarily for health services and the arts.
Fields of interest: Museums; Arts; Libraries (public); Education; Environment; Hospitals (general); Human services; Children/youth, services; Disabled.
Limitations: Applications not accepted. Giving in the U.S., with emphasis on IL; some giving

also in CO, MA, and VA. No grants to individuals.
Application information: Contributes only to pre-selected organizations.
Officers and Directors:* Elizabeth B. Tieken, Pres.; Theodore D. Tieken, Jr.,* V.P. and Secy.; Mark Stephenitch,* Treas.; Elizabeth Kirkpatrick; Nancy B. Tieken.
EIN: 366104969

996
Haffner Foundation

35 E. Wacker Dr., Ste. 2650
Chicago, IL 60601-2398
Contact: Charles C. Haffner III, Pres.
FAX: (312) 977-1686

Incorporated in 1952 in IL.
Donor(s): Charles C. Haffner, Jr.,‡ Mrs. Charles C. Haffner, Jr.,‡ Charles C. Haffner III.
Grantmaker type: Independent foundation
Financial data (yr. ended 12/31/02): Assets, $3,812,042 (M); expenditures, $264,403; qualifying distributions, $261,000; giving activities include $261,000 for 44 grants (high: $43,000; average: $2,000–$10,000).
Purpose and activities: To contribute to religious, charitable, and educational organizations of whose activities the foundation's officers have personal knowledge. Support largely for higher, business, secondary, and elementary education, and building funds; hospitals and health agencies; social service agencies, including programs for the handicapped; the arts, including museums; and environmental conservation and ecology.
Fields of interest: Visual arts; Museums; Performing arts; Humanities; Arts; Elementary school/education; Secondary school/education; Higher education; Natural resources; Environment; Animals/wildlife, preservation/protection; Hospitals (general); Health care; Human services; Disabled.
Types of support: General/operating support; Continuing support; Annual campaigns; Capital campaigns; Building/renovation; Equipment; Land acquisition; Endowments; Emergency funds; Seed money.
Limitations: Applications not accepted. Giving primarily in IL, MA, and WA. No grants to individuals, or for scholarships, fellowships, or matching gifts; no loans.
Application information: Contributes only to pre-selected organizations.
Board meeting date(s): May
Officers and Directors:* Charles C. Haffner III,* Pres. and Treas.; Clarissa H. Chandler,* V.P. and Secy.; Phoebe H. Andrew; Frances H. Colburn.
Number of staff: None.
EIN: 366064770

997
John R. Halligan Charitable Fund

c/o Neal, Gerber & Eisenberg
2 N. LaSalle St., Ste. 2200
Chicago, IL 60602
Contact: Norman J. Gantz, Pres.
E-mail: ngantz@ngelaw.com

Established in 1962.
Donor(s): John R. Halligan.‡
Grantmaker type: Independent foundation

Financial data (yr. ended 12/31/02): Assets, $22,205,020 (M); expenditures, $591,359; qualifying distributions, $563,500; giving activities include $563,500 for 27 grants (high: $100,000; low: $3,500).
Purpose and activities: Giving for the arts and cultural institutes.
Fields of interest: Arts; Animals/wildlife.
Types of support: Continuing support; Annual campaigns.
Limitations: Applications not accepted. Giving primarily in Honolulu, HI, and Chicago, IL. No grants to individuals.
Application information: Contributes only to pre-selected organizations.
Officers and Directors:* Norman J. Gantz,* Pres.; Norman Kellerman,* Treas.; Lawrence Richman.
Number of staff: None.
EIN: 366078591

998
Hamill Family Foundation

(formerly Happy Hollow Fund)
c/o Corwith Hamill, Chair.
P.O. Box 206
Wayne, IL 60184-0206

Established in 1963.
Donor(s): Corwith Hamill, Joan B. Hamill, Jonathan C. Hamill.
Grantmaker type: Independent foundation
Financial data (yr. ended 12/31/02): Assets, $22,266,907 (M); gifts received, $27,582,706; expenditures, $1,847,266; qualifying distributions, $1,778,002; giving activities include $1,778,000 for grants.
Purpose and activities: Giving primarily for the environment and animal welfare; giving also for education, the arts, and health and human services.
Fields of interest: Arts; Higher education; Environment; Human services; Christian agencies & churches.
Types of support: General/operating support; Continuing support; Capital campaigns; Endowments; Debt reduction; Matching/challenge support.
Limitations: Applications not accepted. Giving primarily in IL. No grants to individuals.
Application information: Contributes only to pre-selected organizations.
Officers and Directors:* Corwith Hamill,* Chair.; Joan B. Hamill,* Pres.; Elizabeth C. Bramsen,* V.P.; Nancy C.H. Winter,* V.P.; Jonathan C. Hamill,* Secy.-Treas.
Number of staff: None.
EIN: 366096808

999
Anna Emery Hanson Testamentary Charitable Trust

c/o The Northern Trust Co.
50 S. LaSalle St., Ste. L-5
Chicago, IL 60675

Established in 1986 in IL.
Donor(s): Anna Emery Hanson.‡
Grantmaker type: Independent foundation
Financial data (yr. ended 09/30/02): Assets, $3,552,004 (M); expenditures, $274,887; qualifying distributions, $246,278; giving

activities include $241,930 for 51 grants (high: $50,000; low: $500).
Purpose and activities: Giving primarily for education.
Fields of interest: Elementary/secondary education; Higher education; Environment; Hospitals (general); Health care; Human services; Children/youth, services; Family services; Community development.
Types of support: General/operating support; Endowments; Seed money; Matching/challenge support.
Limitations: Giving primarily in WI and WY. No grants to individuals.
Application information: Application form not required.
Deadline(s): None
Trustees: Marjorie Hanson Greenfield; Mary Anna Hanson MacLean; Rainer R. Weigel; The Northern Trust Co.
EIN: 366854655

1000
Philip S. Harper Foundation
c/o Harper-Wyman Co.
930 N. York Rd., Ste. 204
Hinsdale, IL 60521-2913 (630) 887-8688
Contact: Charles C. Lamar, Secy.-Treas.

Incorporated in 1953 in IL.
Donor(s): Philip S. Harper, Harper-Wyman Co.
Grantmaker type: Independent foundation
Financial data (yr. ended 09/30/02): Assets, $6,284,880 (M); expenditures, $440,134; qualifying distributions, $383,942; giving activities include $364,500 for 171 grants (high: $23,500; low: $250).
Purpose and activities: Giving primarily for the arts, education, Protestant churches and organizations, and for human services.
Fields of interest: Media/communications; Arts; Elementary/secondary education; Higher education; Natural resources; Health care; Medical research, institute; Legal services; Human services; Children/youth, services; Public affairs; Christian agencies & churches; Protestant agencies & churches.
Limitations: Giving on a national basis. No grants to individuals.
Application information:
Initial approach: Letter
Deadline(s): None
Officers: Philip S. Harper, Jr., Pres.; Lamar Harper Williams, V.P.; Charles C. Lamar, Secy.-Treas.
EIN: 366049875

1001
Harris Family Foundation
200 S. Wacker Dr., Ste. 3900
Chicago, IL 60606
Application address: 333 Skokie Blvd., Ste. 114, Northbrook, IL 60062, tel.: (847) 498-1261

Incorporated in 1957 in IL.
Donor(s): Nelson Harris.‡
Grantmaker type: Independent foundation
Financial data (yr. ended 02/28/02): Assets, $49,283,101 (M); gifts received, $451,260; expenditures, $2,331,553; qualifying distributions, $2,087,559; giving activities

include $2,087,559 for 149 grants (high: $345,250; low: $15; average: $100–$10,000).
Purpose and activities: Giving primarily for education, arts and culture, botanical gardens, zoos, hospitals and medical research, human services, children and family services, and Jewish organizations and temples.
Fields of interest: Arts; Higher education; Education; Botanical gardens; Zoos/zoological societies; Hospitals (general); Medical care, rehabilitation; Health organizations, association; Medical research, institute; Human services; Children/youth, services; Family services; Jewish federated giving programs; Jewish agencies & temples.
Types of support: General/operating support; Continuing support; Annual campaigns; Capital campaigns; Building/renovation; Conferences/seminars; Professorships; Internship funds; Scholarship funds.
Limitations: Giving primarily in the Chicago, IL, area. No grants to individuals.
Application information: Application form not required.
Initial approach: Letter
Copies of proposal: 1
Deadline(s): None
Board meeting date(s): May and Nov.
Final notification: 30 days
Officer and Directors:* Edward Schwartz,* Secy.-Treas.; Bette D. Harris; Katherine Harris; King W. Harris; Toni H. Paul.
Number of staff: None.
EIN: 366054378

1002
Lynne Cooper Harvey Foundation
1035 Park Ave.
River Forest, IL 60305-1307

Established in 1981 in IL.
Donor(s): Paul Harvey, Lynne Cooper Harvey, Paul H. Aurandt II.
Grantmaker type: Independent foundation
Financial data (yr. ended 06/30/02): Assets, $5,753,267 (M); gifts received, $250,000; expenditures, $466,268; qualifying distributions, $458,167; giving activities include $460,000 for 30 grants (high: $100,000; low: $1,000).
Purpose and activities: Giving for animal welfare and protection; funding also for higher education and to a museum.
Fields of interest: Museums (specialized); Higher education; Animal welfare; Animals/wildlife, preservation/protection; Zoos/zoological societies.
Types of support: General/operating support.
Limitations: Applications not accepted. Giving on a national basis. No grants to individuals.
Application information: Contributes only to pre-selected organizations.
Officers: Lynne Cooper Harvey, Pres.; Paul H. Aurandt II, V.P.
Director: Joseph J. Maier.
EIN: 363148657

1003
Hedberg Foundation Inc.
c/o Carla Westcott
1035 N. Sheridan
Lake Forest, IL 60045
Contact: Robert C. Zahn, C.O.O.

Established in 1991 in WI.
Donor(s): Donald D. Hedberg, Geraldine Hedberg.‡
Grantmaker type: Independent foundation
Financial data (yr. ended 12/31/02): Assets, $2,581,434 (M); expenditures, $291,578; qualifying distributions, $291,500; giving activities include $291,500 for 25 grants (high: $250,000; low: $500; average: $1,000–$25,000).
Purpose and activities: The foundation generally targets organizations dedicated to the arts and humanities, education, environment, health and safety, and other community service organizations.
Fields of interest: Humanities; Arts; Education; Natural resources; Health care; Community development.
Types of support: General/operating support; Continuing support; Annual campaigns; Capital campaigns; Building/renovation; Endowments; Seed money; Scholarship funds; Matching/challenge support.
Limitations: Giving primarily in WI. No support for religious or political organizations. No grants to individuals.
Application information: Application form not required.
Initial approach: Letter
Copies of proposal: 1
Deadline(s): None
Board meeting date(s): Late Mar., June, Sept., and Dec.
Officers and Directors:* Robert C. Zahn,* C.O.O.; Carla H. Westcott,* Pres.; Donald D. Hedberg,* V.P.; Peggy H. Stich,* Secy.-Treas.; Lara Hedberg-Deam.
Number of staff: 1 part-time professional; 1 part-time support.
EIN: 391684914

1004
Julius W. Hegeler II Foundation
1521 N. Vermilion St.
Danville, IL 61832
Contact: Julius W. Hegeler, II, Dir.

Established in 1992 in IL.
Donor(s): Julius W. Hegeler II.
Grantmaker type: Operating foundation
Financial data (yr. ended 06/30/02): Assets, $11,724,296 (M); expenditures, $415,208; qualifying distributions, $556,248; giving activities include $112,175 for 11 grants (high: $55,000; low: $75) and $447,135 for 1 foundation-administered program.
Fields of interest: Museums (specialized); Arts; Higher education; Libraries (public); Natural resources; Environment; Cerebral palsy; Parks/playgrounds; YM/YWCAs & YM/YWHAs; Community development; Federated giving programs; Disabled.
Limitations: Giving primarily in IL. No grants to individuals.
Application information: Application form not required.

Deadline(s): None
Officer and Directors:* Delores A. Roberts,*
Secy.-Treas.; F. Jay Foster; Alix S. Hegeler; Julius
W. Hegeler II.
EIN: 371302455

1005
Helios Foundation
c/o Bank of America
231 S. LaSalle St.
Chicago, IL 60697 (312) 828-8028
Contact: M.C. Ryan

Established in 1986 in WI.
Donor(s): Marjorie Klewit.
Grantmaker type: Independent foundation
Financial data (yr. ended 05/31/02): Assets,
$2,612,818 (M); expenditures, $162,146;
qualifying distributions, $143,692; giving
activities include $142,000 for 20 grants (high:
$25,000; low: $1,000).
Purpose and activities: Giving primarily for
museums and environmental conservation.
Fields of interest: Arts; Theological
school/education; Education; Natural resources;
Environment; Boys clubs.
Limitations: Giving on a national basis. No
grants to individuals.
Application information: Application form not
required.
Deadline(s): None
Directors: Barbara Alfs; John H. Buchanan;
Linda Jacob; Marjorie Kiewit; Nancy
McLoughlin.
Trustee: Bank of America.
EIN: 391532106

1006
The Henry Foundation, Inc.
102 N. Westgate Ave.
Jacksonville, IL 62650-1718
Contact: C. Wolcott Henry III, Pres.

Established in 1986 in FL.
Grantmaker type: Independent foundation
Financial data (yr. ended 12/31/02): Assets,
$10,301,180 (M); expenditures, $920,801;
qualifying distributions, $705,106; giving
activities include $596,250 for 58 grants (high:
$190,000; low: $200).
Purpose and activities: Giving primarily for
education and for animal welfare.
Fields of interest: Secondary school/education;
Higher education; Animals/wildlife,
preservation/protection; Mental health/crisis
services.
Types of support: Program development;
Conferences/seminars; Publication; Seed
money; Matching/challenge support.
Limitations: Applications not accepted. Giving
primarily in FL and the Chicago, IL, area. No
grants to individuals.
Application information: Contributes only to
pre-selected organizations.
Officers and Directors:* C. Wolcott Henry III,*
Pres. and Treas.; Nancy Cummings Henry,*
Secy.; H. Alexander Henry; Nancy H. McKelvy;
Michael C. Rausch.
EIN: 592827461

1007
The Hobbs Foundation
102 N. Westgate Ave.
Jacksonville, IL 62651-1107

Established in 1986 in AL.
Donor(s): Ioka Fund.
Grantmaker type: Independent foundation
Financial data (yr. ended 12/31/00): Assets,
$12,175,402 (M); expenditures, $366,356;
qualifying distributions, $353,266; giving
activities include $353,250 for grants.
Fields of interest: Arts; Secondary
school/education; Higher education;
Animals/wildlife; Protestant agencies & churches.
Types of support: Capital campaigns;
Building/renovation.
Limitations: Applications not accepted. Giving
primarily in Montgomery, AL. No grants to
individuals.
Officer: Truman M. Hobbs, Pres.
Directors: Joyce C. Hobbs; Truman M. Hobbs, Jr.
EIN: 630952482

1008
Hoellen Family Foundation
1940 W. Irving Park Rd., 2nd Fl.
Chicago, IL 60613-2498

Established in 1983.
Donor(s): John J. Hoellen.
Grantmaker type: Independent foundation
Financial data (yr. ended 12/31/00): Assets,
$7,190,173 (M); expenditures, $322,445;
qualifying distributions, $169,569; giving
activities include $251,500 for 23 grants (high:
$25,000; low: $1,000).
Purpose and activities: Giving primarily for
education.
Fields of interest: Museums (history); Museums
(science/technology); Historic
preservation/historical societies;
Elementary/secondary education; Secondary
school/education; University; Libraries/library
science; Zoos/zoological societies; Protestant
agencies & churches.
Limitations: Giving limited to Chicago, IL
metropolitan area.
Application information: Application form not
required.
Officers: Mary Jane Hoellen, Pres.; Rev. George
A. Rice, V.P.; Allan Pallante, Treas.
Directors: Robert B. Hoellen; Liz Ward.
EIN: 363209348

1009
Hogan-Penrith Foundation
c/o Gary Penrith
38869 Oakcrest Ln.
Wadsworth, IL 60083

Established in 1993 in Il .
Grantmaker type: Independent foundation
Financial data (yr. ended 12/31/02): Assets,
$361,698 (M); gifts received, $395,300;
expenditures, $124,475; qualifying distributions,
$104,856; giving activities include $104,856 for
55 grants (high: $25,000; low: $50).
Purpose and activities: Giving for Christian
organizations, professional organizations, and
education.

Fields of interest: Arts; Education;
Zoos/zoological societies; Disasters,
preparedness/services; Christian agencies &
churches.
Limitations: Applications not accepted. Giving
primarily in IL. No grants to individuals.
Application information: Contributes only to
pre-selected organizations.
Officers and Directors:* Gary Penrith,* Pres.;
Lynn Penrith,* Secy.-Treas.
EIN: 363866400

1010
Huizenga Foundation
20 N. Wacker Dr., Ste. 2800
Chicago, IL 60606-3194

Established in 1988 in IL.
Donor(s): Peter H. Huizenga.
Grantmaker type: Independent foundation
Financial data (yr. ended 12/31/01): Assets,
$2,610,244 (M); gifts received, $400,000;
expenditures, $510,934; qualifying distributions,
$487,590; giving activities include $487,590 for
69 grants (high: $110,000; low: $100).
Purpose and activities: Giving primarily for
Christian organizations, education, and
environmental conservation.
Fields of interest: Higher education; Theological
school/education; Environment; Christian
agencies & churches.
Limitations: Applications not accepted. Giving
primarily in IL and MI. No grants to individuals.
Application information: Contributes only to
pre-selected organizations.
Officers and Directors:* Peter H. Huizenga,*
Pres.; J.C. Huizenga,* Secy.; Heidi A.
Huizenga,* Treas.
EIN: 363582536

1011
Hunter Family Foundation
911 Woodbine Pl.
Lake Forest, IL 60045 (847) 234-0190
Contact: Thomas B. Hunter III, Tr.

Established in 1995 in IL.
Donor(s): Thomas B. Hunter III.
Grantmaker type: Independent foundation
Financial data (yr. ended 12/31/02): Assets,
$4,926,477 (M); expenditures, $268,341;
qualifying distributions, $267,526; giving
activities include $267,526 for 64 grants (high:
$50,500; low: $100).
Fields of interest: Orchestra (symphony); Arts;
Elementary/secondary education; Higher
education; Environment; Hospitals (general);
Health organizations, association; Human
services; Federated giving programs; Protestant
agencies & churches.
Limitations: Applications not accepted. Giving
primarily in IL, with emphasis on Chicago. No
grants to individuals.
Application information: Contributes only to
pre-selected organizations.
Trustees: Maxine Hunter; Thomas B. Hunter III.
EIN: 363959347

1012
The James Huntington Foundation
c/o Samuel H. Ellis
11 S. LaSalle St., Ste. 2900
Chicago, IL 60603-1305

Established in 1987 in IL.
Donor(s): Samuel H. Ellis.
Grantmaker type: Independent foundation
Financial data (yr. ended 12/31/02): Assets,
$10,303,873 (M); gifts received, $131,330;
expenditures, $494,936; qualifying distributions,
$436,405; giving activities include $440,000 for
56 grants (high: $125,000; low: $1,000).
Purpose and activities: Giving primarily for
wildlife conservation.
Fields of interest: Arts; Elementary/secondary
education; Higher education; Animals/wildlife,
preservation/protection; Hospitals (general);
Human services.
Limitations: Applications not accepted. Giving
primarily in IL. No grants to individuals.
Application information: Contributes only to
pre-selected organizations.
Trustee: Samuel H. Ellis.
EIN: 363553345

1013
Hurvis Charitable Foundation
4065 Commercial Ave.
Northbrook, IL 60062-1851
Application address: c/o Ann Verhulst, P.O. Box
1614, Northbrook, IL 60065-1614, tel.: (847)
559-2255

Established in 1990 in IL.
Donor(s): J. Thomas Hurvis.
Grantmaker type: Independent foundation
Financial data (yr. ended 12/31/02): Assets,
$111,419 (M); gifts received, $22,000;
expenditures, $127,473; qualifying distributions,
$124,015; giving activities include $124,500 for
25 grants (high: $15,000; low: $500).
Purpose and activities: Giving for education.
Fields of interest: Higher education; Education;
Environment; Youth development, adult & child
programs.
Types of support: Scholarship funds;
Scholarships—to individuals.
Limitations: Giving limited to WI.
Publications: Application guidelines.
Application information: Application form
required.
  Initial approach: Letter
  Deadline(s): Feb. 15, May 15, Aug. 15, and
    Nov. 15
Officer: Brian R. Schweigel, Mgr.
Trustees: J. Thomas Hurvis; Riaz M. Waraich.
Number of staff: None.
EIN: 363755657

1014
The IHC Group Foundation
(formerly Illinois Hydraulic Foundation)
1797 N. La Fox St.
South Elgin, IL 60177-1207

Donor(s): Illinois Hydraulic Construction Co.,
IHC Group, Inc., Thomas S. Rakow, Susan
Rakow.
Grantmaker type: Company-sponsored
foundation

Financial data (yr. ended 08/31/02): Assets,
$522,786 (M); gifts received, $200,000;
expenditures, $233,312; qualifying distributions,
$232,953; giving activities include $233,050 for
38 grants (high: $147,200; low: $100).
Purpose and activities: Giving for youth and
health programs.
Fields of interest: Animals/wildlife, association;
Hospitals (general); Human services; Federated
giving programs.
Types of support: General/operating support.
Limitations: Applications not accepted. Giving
primarily in IL. No grants to individuals.
Application information: Contributes only to
pre-selected organizations.
Officers: Susan Rakow, Pres. and Secy.; Thomas
S. Rakow, Treas.
EIN: 366069769

1015
Illinois Power Company Contributions
Program
c/o Contribs. Coord., Dept. A-16
500 S. 27th St.
Decatur, IL 62521-2200 (217) 362-6336
E-mail: ipgrants@illinoispower.com; *URL:* http://
www.illinoispower.com/ip.nsf/web/
ourcommunity

Grantmaker type: Corporate giving program
Purpose and activities: Illinois Power makes
charitable contributions to nonprofit
organizations involved with K-12 education, the
environment, health, public safety, community
development, minorities, disabled people,
senior citizens, women, and economically
disadvantaged people. Support is given
primarily in central, northern, and southern
Illinois.
Fields of interest: Elementary/secondary
education; Environment; Health care; Safety,
education; Economic development; Community
development; Minorities; Disabled; Aging;
Women; Economically disadvantaged.
Types of support: General/operating support;
Seed money; Employee volunteer services;
Grants to individuals; In-kind gifts.
Limitations: Giving primarily in central,
northern, and southern IL. No support for
political organizations, religious organizations
not of direct benefit to the entire community,
labor organizations, fraternal or veterans'
organizations, or discriminatory organizations.
No grants to individuals (except through Bright
Ideas and Classroom Grants programs), or for
memorial funds, capital campaigns, or political
campaigns.
Application information: An application form is
available online.
  Initial approach: Proposal to headquarters or
    complete online application form
  Deadline(s): None
  Final notification: Following review

1016
IMC Global Inc. Corporate Giving
Program
100 S. Saunders Rd.
Lake Forest, IL 60045
Contact: David Prichard, V.P., Investor Rels. and
Corp. Comm.

Grantmaker type: Corporate giving program
Purpose and activities: IMC Global makes
charitable contributions to nonprofit
organizations involved with the environment,
agriculture, food distribution, and geology.
Support is given on a national basis.
Fields of interest: Environment; Agriculture;
Food services; Physical/earth sciences.
Types of support: General/operating support;
Employee matching gifts; Employee-related
scholarships; In-kind gifts.
Limitations: Giving on a national basis, with
emphasis on FL, LA, and NM, and in Canada.
Application information: Application form not
required.
  Initial approach: Proposal to headquarters
  Deadline(s): None

1017
Verne G. and Judith A. Istock Foundation
100 E. Huron St., Apt. 4602
Chicago, IL 60611

Established in 2001 in IL.
Donor(s): Verne G. Istock.
Grantmaker type: Independent foundation
Financial data (yr. ended 12/31/01): Assets,
$2,439,343 (M); gifts received, $2,493,690;
expenditures, $249,702; qualifying distributions,
$249,435; giving activities include $249,435 for
2 grants (high: $200,080; low: $49,355).
Fields of interest: Environment; Federated giving
programs.
Limitations: Applications not accepted. Giving
primarily in Chicago, IL. No grants to
individuals.
Application information: Contributes only to
pre-selected organizations.
Trustees: Judith A. Istock; Verne G. Istock.
EIN: 367362355

1018
Reinhardt H. & Shirley R. Jahn Foundation
2737 Eastwood Ave.
Evanston, IL 60201-1544

Established in 1992 in IL.
Donor(s): Shirley R. Jahn, Reinhardt H. Jahn.
Grantmaker type: Independent foundation
Financial data (yr. ended 12/31/02): Assets,
$1,967,459 (M); expenditures, $638,058;
qualifying distributions, $637,883; giving
activities include $622,766 for 12 grants (high:
$394,266; low: $1,000).
Fields of interest: Arts; Botanical gardens;
Hospitals (general); Boys & girls clubs;
Protestant agencies & churches.
Limitations: Applications not accepted. Giving
primarily in IL. No grants to individuals.
Application information: Contributes only to
pre-selected organizations.
Officer and Directors:* Shirley R. Jahn,* Pres.;
Charles L. Jahn; Reinhardt E. Jahn.
EIN: 363857635

1019
Jefferson Smurfit Corporation Charitable Trust
c/o Bank of America
231 S. LaSalle St.
Chicago, IL 60697
Contact: Lyle L. Meyer, Member, Admin. Comm.
Application address: c/o Jefferson Smurfit Corp.,
P.O. Box 66820, St. Louis, MO 63166

Established in 1951.
Donor(s): Jefferson Smurfit Corp., Container
Corp. of America, Smurfit-Stone Container Corp.
Grantmaker type: Company-sponsored
foundation
Financial data (yr. ended 12/31/02): Assets,
$42,419 (M); expenditures, $2,282,806;
qualifying distributions, $2,272,279; giving
activities include $2,271,790 for 98 grants (high:
$600,000; low: $150).
Purpose and activities: Giving primarily for
federated giving programs, and health and
human services.
Fields of interest: Arts; Education; Animal
welfare; Hospitals (general); Health
organizations, association; Human services;
Children/youth, services; Federated giving
programs.
Limitations: Giving primarily in MO.
Application information:
  Initial approach: Proposal
  Deadline(s): None
Administrative Committee: J.R. Funke; Lyle L.
Meyer; J.E. Terrill.
Trustee: Bank of America.
EIN: 436023508

1020
JMR Charities, Inc.
333 W. 35th St.
Chicago, IL 60616

Donor(s): Jerry Reinsdorf.
Grantmaker type: Independent foundation
Financial data (yr. ended 12/31/02): Assets,
$5,782 (M); gifts received, $293,000;
expenditures, $309,330; qualifying distributions,
$309,325; giving activities include $309,304 for
grants.
Purpose and activities: Giving for the arts,
education, health, and Jewish organizations.
Fields of interest: Arts; Education; Animal
welfare; Health care; Health organizations,
association; Youth development; Human
services; Voluntarism promotion; Jewish
federated giving programs; Jewish agencies &
temples.
Limitations: Applications not accepted. Giving
on a national basis. No grants to individuals.
Application information: Contributes only to
pre-selected organizations.
Officers: Jerry Reinsdorf, Pres.; Allan Muchin,
Secy.
Director: Gerald Penner.
EIN: 363218989

1021
Jocarno Fund
203 N. Wabash, Ste. 1800
Chicago, IL 60601 (312) 641-5765
Contact: Iris Krieg, Admin.

Established in 1959 in IL.
Grantmaker type: Independent foundation
Financial data (yr. ended 12/31/02): Assets,
$2,132,452 (M); expenditures, $157,898;
qualifying distributions, $138,927; giving
activities include $127,000 for 76 grants (high:
$10,000; low: $100).
Purpose and activities: Giving for the arts,
education, and health and human services.
Fields of interest: Arts; Higher education;
Natural resources; Health care; Youth
development; Human services; International
peace/security; Civil rights; Foundations
(community); Federated giving programs;
Religion.
Types of support: General/operating support;
Continuing support; Annual campaigns; Land
acquisition; Emergency funds.
Limitations: Giving primarily in Chicago, IL.
Application information: Application form not
required.
  Initial approach: Proposal
  Copies of proposal: 1
  Deadline(s): None
Officer: John Schlossman, Pres.
Director: Donald Lubin.
Number of staff: 9.
EIN: 366062019

1022
C. Paul Johnson Family Charitable Foundation
233 S. Wacker Dr., Ste. 9650
Chicago, IL 60606

Established in 1988.
Donor(s): C. Paul Johnson.
Grantmaker type: Independent foundation
Financial data (yr. ended 12/31/02): Assets,
$30,708 (M); gifts received, $695,899;
expenditures, $706,017; qualifying distributions,
$689,868; giving activities include $691,823 for
grants (high: $309,927).
Purpose and activities: Giving primarily for
archaeological research and education, and
human services.
Fields of interest: Higher education; Education;
Natural resources; Human services; Science.
International interests: Israel.
Types of support: General/operating support;
Scholarship funds; Research.
Limitations: Applications not accepted. Giving
primarily in IL. No grants to individuals.
Application information: Contributes only to
pre-selected organizations.
Trustees: Adrienne Johnson; C. Paul Johnson;
Debra Johnson; Julianne Johnson; Vince
Mancuso; Rebecca Milne; Deborah Reguera.
EIN: 366891454

1023
The Joyce Foundation ▼
3 First National Plz.
70 W. Madison St., Ste. 2750
Chicago, IL 60602 (312) 782-2464
Contact: Prog. Staff
FAX: (312) 782-4160; E-mail:
info@joycefdn.org; URL: http://www.joycefdn.org

Incorporated in 1948 in IL.
Donor(s): Beatrice Joyce Kean.‡
Grantmaker type: Independent foundation

Financial data (yr. ended 12/31/02): Assets,
$653,771,733 (M); expenditures, $42,812,009;
qualifying distributions, $40,298,486; giving
activities include $36,247,720 for 320 grants
(high: $700,000; low: $5,000; average:
$20,000–$100,000) and $36,791 for employee
matching gifts.
Purpose and activities: The foundation supports
efforts to protect the natural environment of the
Great Lakes, to reduce poverty and violence in
the region, and to ensure that its people have
access to good schools, decent jobs, and a
diverse and thriving culture. It is especially
interested in improving public policies, because
public systems such as education and welfare
directly affect the lives of so many people, and
because public policies help shape private
sector decisions about jobs, the environment,
and the health of our communities. To ensure
that public policies truly reflect public rather
than private interests, the foundation supports
efforts to reform the system of financing election
campaigns.
Fields of interest: Arts; Education; Environment;
Crime/violence prevention; Gun control;
Employment; Public affairs, finance; Public
affairs, political organizations.
Types of support: Continuing support; Program
development; Employee matching gifts.
Limitations: Giving primarily in the Great Lakes
region, including IA, IL, IN, MI, MN, OH, and
WI; limited number of environment grants made
in Canada; culture grants restricted to the
metropolitan Chicago, IL, area. No support for
religious activities. No grants for endowment
campaigns, scholarships, direct service
programs, or capital proposals.
Publications: Annual report (including
application guidelines), Financial statement,
Informational brochure (including application
guidelines), Newsletter.
Application information: Program policy and
grant proposal guidelines reviewed annually in
Dec. Proposals in all program areas will be
considered at each board meeting. Applicants
are encouraged to submit their proposals for the
Mar. or July meeting, since most grant funds will
be distributed at those times. Application form
required.
  Initial approach: Contact foundation for
    application guidelines prior to submitting 2-
    to 3-page letter of inquiry
  Copies of proposal: 1
  Deadline(s): Letter of inquiry required at least
    4 to 6 weeks before proposal deadlines. For
    formal proposals: Dec. 10 (for Apr.
    meeting); Apr. 15 (for July meeting); Aug. 16
    (for Dec. meeting)
  Board meeting date(s): Apr., July, Dec.
  Final notification: 2 weeks after meeting
Officers and Directors:* John T. Anderson,*
Chair.; Richard K. Donahue,* Vice-Chair.; Ellen
S. Alberding,* Pres.; Lawrence N. Hansen, V.P.,
Secy. and Prog. Off., Money and Politics;
Deborah Gillespie, C.F.O.; Gil Sarmiento, Cont.;
Michael F. Brewer; Charles U. Daly; Anthony S.
Earl; Roger R. Fross; Howard L. Fuller; Carlton L.
Guthrie; Marion T. Hall; Valerie B. Jarrett; Daniel
P. Kearney; Paula Wolff.
Number of staff: 14 full-time professional; 1
part-time professional; 6 full-time support.
EIN: 366079185
**Recent environmental and animal welfare
grants:**

1023-1 1000 Friends of Wisconsin Land Use Institute, Madison, WI, $92,500. To create researched policy agenda for state transportation reform. 2002.

1023-2 American Council for an Energy-Efficient Economy, DC, $75,000. To promote federal energy policies that would improve automobile fuel efficiency and encourage more efficient buildings and appliances. 2002.

1023-3 Canadian Environmental Law Association, Toronto, Canada, $43,000. For activities to improve water quality in Great Lakes basin. 2002.

1023-4 Center for Clean Air Policy, DC, $100,000. For Air Quality Dialogue, which seeks to identify compromise proposal for cleaning up power plants. 2002.

1023-5 Center for Resource Solutions, San Francisco, CA, $35,000. For business-to-business workshop in Wisconsin to encourage business and institutional consumers to purchase Green Energy. 2002.

1023-6 Center for Rural Affairs, Walthill, NE, $200,000. To follow up on conservation options created by federal agriculture legislation and to document examples of conservation-based development in Midwest rural areas. 2002.

1023-7 Clean Air Task Force, Boston, MA, $150,000. For research and advocacy efforts of Clean Air Task Force, as part of larger long-term effort to reduce air pollution caused by region's older, coal-fired electric power plants. 2002.

1023-8 Coalition for Alternative Wastewater Treatment, Gloucester, MA, $20,000. For Soft Path Integrated Water Resources Workshop. Grant made through Action, Inc. 2002.

1023-9 Environmental and Energy Study Institute, DC, $250,000. For briefs of federal and state policymakers regarding follow-up and implementation of newly established federal farm policies relating to renewable energy development and other federal policies involving energy production and energy efficiency. 2002.

1023-10 Environmental Defense, New York, NY, $500,000. For follow-up efforts for funding opportunities under recent farm bill for environmental conservation. 2002.

1023-11 Environmental Defense, New York, NY, $200,000. For continued leadership of Pollution Prevention Alliance. 2002.

1023-12 Environmental Law and Policy Center of the Midwest, Chicago, IL, $700,000. For regional energy project. 2002.

1023-13 Environmental Law Institute, DC, $75,000. To build state and regional government's capacity to address proliferation of non-native invasive species. 2002.

1023-14 Environmental Support Center, DC, $21,052. To assess technical needs of Great Lakes environmental organizations. 2002.

1023-15 Great Lakes Commission, Ann Arbor, MI, $195,000. To inventory water quality monitoring programs in Great Lakes basin, including assessing impact of proposed federal and state budget changes on existing programs. 2002.

1023-16 Illinois Environmental Council Education Fund, Springfield, IL, $90,000. To

help Council rebuild after resignation of staff. 2002.

1023-17 Institute for Conservation Leadership, Takoma Park, MD, $58,000. To develop and implement advanced training program for executive directors of selected Great Lakes environmental organizations. 2002.

1023-18 Izaak Walton League of America, Minnesota Division, Saint Paul, MN, $480,000. For campaigns in Midwestern states and Ontario that inform public and policymakers about problem of air pollution from region's older coal-fired electric power plants. 2002.

1023-19 Laidlaw Foundation, Toronto, Canada, $85,000. To enable Sustainability Network to bring customized technical assistance to leaders of selected Canadian environmental organizations in Great Lakes basin. 2002.

1023-20 League of Conservation Voters Education Fund, DC, $50,000. For production of environmental briefing books targeting policymakers and opinion leaders in Illinois, Michigan, and Wisconsin. 2002.

1023-21 Michigan Environmental Council, Lansing, MI, $98,950. For activities that examine institutional issues facing Great Lakes ecosystem. 2002.

1023-22 Michigan Land Use Institute, Beulah, MI, $150,000. For efforts to reform state and local transportation policies throughout Michigan. 2002.

1023-23 Michigan Technological University, Department of Social Sciences, Houghton, MI, $80,976. To research gaps in regulation of septic systems in Great Lakes basin, with particular emphasis on Great Lakes shoreline, and to identify reasons for and recommend solutions to those gaps. 2002.

1023-24 Minnesota Center for Environmental Advocacy, Saint Paul, MN, $212,140. For continued partnership with state business interests to advocate for better state transportation policies. 2002.

1023-25 Minnesota Environmental Partnership, Saint Paul, MN, $75,000. To educate legislators about Partnerships Protect Our Water agenda, and for project helping Minnesota farmers more effectively participate in federal conservation programs established in federal farm legislation. 2002.

1023-26 Minnesotans for an Energy-Efficient Economy (ME3), Saint Paul, MN, $350,000. To promote changes in state energy, transportation, and tax policies that would encourage energy efficiency and discourage waste and pollution. 2002.

1023-27 Natural Resources Defense Council, New York, NY, $250,000. For Midwest Desk, which bridges activities involving energy policy, clean air, and electric utilities with Midwest advocacy groups and policymakers interested in those issues. 2002.

1023-28 Northeast-Midwest Institute, DC, $200,000. For ongoing support of policy work associated with Great Lakes program. 2002.

1023-29 Northeast-Midwest Institute, DC, $20,000. To enable mayors of Great Lakes shoreline communities to develop shared vision for improving Great Lakes and action plan to implement that vision. 2002.

1023-30 Ohio Environmental Council, Columbus, OH, $200,000. For continued

support of efforts to improve Ohio policies governing protection and restoration of state's rivers, streams and lakes, including Lake Erie. 2002.

1023-31 Openlands Project, Chicago, IL, $221,275. To develop database and map documenting open space and natural areas in counties in Wisconsin, Illinois, and Indiana that could become basis for natural resource protection in Lake Michigan basin. 2002.

1023-32 Pacific Institute for Studies in Development, Environment and Security, Oakland, CA, $70,500. For production of written evaluation of freshwater issues specific to Great Lakes. 2002.

1023-33 Redefining Progress, Oakland, CA, $300,000. To promote use of federal and state tax policy to address environmental problems. 2002.

1023-34 Rockefeller Family Fund, Environmental Grantmakers Association, New York, NY, $20,000. For Sustainable Agriculture and Food Systems Funders working group and for EGA general support. 2002.

1023-35 Sierra Club Foundation, San Francisco, CA, $300,000. To establish better state-level policies relating to toxic air pollution in Wisconsin and Minnesota. 2002.

1023-36 Surface Transportation Policy Project (STPP), DC, $100,000. To enable new spin-off group, Smart Growth America, to identify and promote ways in which federal and state transportation policy could help improve water quality. 2002.

1023-37 Tellus Institute for Resource and Environmental Strategies, Boston, MA, $350,000. To develop framework for reporting on environmental performance of individual facilities, primarily manufacturing plants. 2002.

1023-38 Third Way Foundation, DC, $250,000. To help state policymakers identify and adopt state and local solutions to emerging environmental threats such as climate change and reduced or polluted water supply. 2002.

1023-39 Tides Center, San Francisco, CA, $75,000. For Funder's Forum on Environment and Education Wingspread Symposium on Healthy Schools by Design. 2002.

1023-40 Union of Concerned Scientists, Cambridge, MA, $200,000. To encourage policies that would reduce use of antibiotics in animal agriculture. 2002.

1023-41 Union of Concerned Scientists, Cambridge, MA, $200,000. To promote policies supporting renewable energy resources, such as wind, solar, and energy from crops in Illinois, Iowa, Minnesota, and Wisconsin. 2002.

1023-42 University of Illinois at Urbana-Champaign, Regional Economics Applications Laboratory, Urbana, IL, $10,000. To prepare summary of publication, Repowering the Midwest, for distribution to policymakers. 2002.

1023-43 University of Michigan, School of Natural Resources and Environment, Ann Arbor, MI, $279,806. To develop Minority Environmental Leadership Development Initiative. 2002.

1023-44 World Resources Institute, DC, $200,000. To convene policymakers and experts from business and academic communities to develop blueprint for environmentally safe use of genetic engineering in agriculture. 2002.

1024
JYN Foundation
c/o Kinship Corp.
400 Skokie Blvd., Ste. 300
Northbrook, IL 60062

Established in 1999 in OR.
Donor(s): Carolynn D. Loacker, John R. Loacker.
Grantmaker type: Independent foundation
Financial data (yr. ended 12/31/00): Assets, $2,942,322 (M); expenditures, $124,431; qualifying distributions, $110,659; giving activities include $112,000 for 3 grants (high: $50,000; low: $20,000).
Fields of interest: Animals/wildlife, preservation/protection; Community development.
Limitations: Applications not accepted. Giving primarily in IL and OR. No grants to individuals.
Application information: Contributes only to pre-selected organizations.
Trustees: Carolynn D. Loacker; John R. Loacker.
EIN: 931267230

1025
Kainz Family Foundation
(formerly Joseph A. & Susan J. Kainz Foundation)
c/o KRD
1101 Perimeter Dr., No. 760
Schaumberg, IL 60173

Established in 2000 in IL.
Donor(s): Joseph A. Kainz, Susan J. Kainz.
Grantmaker type: Independent foundation
Financial data (yr. ended 06/30/03): Assets, $4,863,553 (M); expenditures, $142,663; qualifying distributions, $111,110; giving activities include $111,110 for 7 grants (high: $25,000; low: $5,000).
Fields of interest: Natural resources; Environment; Children, services.
Limitations: Applications not accepted. Giving primarily in IL. No grants to individuals.
Application information: Contributes only to pre-selected organizations.
Directors: Joseph A. Kainz; Susan J. Kainz.
EIN: 364394506

1026
Max & Yetta Karasik Family Foundation
c/o Northern Trust Bank of FL, N.A.
50 S. LaSalle St., Ste. L-5
Chicago, IL 60675

Established in 2001 in FL.
Donor(s): Marshall Karasik.‡
Grantmaker type: Independent foundation
Financial data (yr. ended 12/31/02): Assets, $4,183,784 (M); gifts received, $58,653; expenditures, $224,029; qualifying distributions, $200,553; giving activities include $183,000 for 4 grants (high: $108,000; low: $25,000).
Fields of interest: Environment; Hospitals (general); Health care; Health organizations, association.

Limitations: Applications not accepted. Giving on a national basis. No grants to individuals.
Application information: Contributes only to pre-selected organizations.
Officers: Jean Sanson, Secy.; Leslie Robbins Rudawsky, Treas.
Trustees: Lois G. Robbins; Richard Robbins.
EIN: 311667792

1027
Keller Family Foundation
c/o Northern Trust Co.
50 S. LaSalle St., Ste. L-5
Chicago, IL 60675

Established in 1997 in IL.
Donor(s): Dennis J. Keller.
Grantmaker type: Independent foundation
Financial data (yr. ended 12/31/01): Assets, $3,890,554 (M); expenditures, $1,371,042; qualifying distributions, $1,367,970; giving activities include $1,368,650 for 195 grants (high: $5,000; low: $10).
Purpose and activities: Giving primarily for education, conservation, and health and human services.
Fields of interest: Arts; Education; Environment; Animals/wildlife; Health care; Human services.
Limitations: Applications not accepted. Giving primarily in IL. No grants to individuals.
Application information: Contributes only to pre-selected organizations.
Trustees: Constance T. Keller; David M. Keller; Dennis J. Keller; Jeffrey B. Keller; John T. Keller.
EIN: 364209206

1028
Kinship Foundation
(formerly Tricord Foundation)
400 Skokie Blvd., Ste. 300
Northbrook, IL 60062 (847) 714-1702
Contact: Alison Janus, Exec. Dir.
FAX: (847) 714-1716; E-mail:
alison.janus@kinshipcorp.com

Established in 1997 in IL.
Grantmaker type: Independent foundation
Financial data (yr. ended 12/31/02): Assets, $4,000,596 (M); expenditures, $275,005; qualifying distributions, $249,369; giving activities include $250,000 for 4 grants (high: $150,000; low: $10,000).
Purpose and activities: Giving primarily for the environment and wildlife conservation, human services, and education.
Fields of interest: Education; Natural resources; Animals/wildlife, preservation/protection; Human services.
Limitations: Applications not accepted. Giving primarily in CO, IL, and MI. No grants to individuals.
Application information: Contributes only to pre-selected organizations.
Officers: Marion S. Searle, Pres.; Louise S. Klarr, V.P.; S. Gunnar Klarr, V.P.; Elizabeth S. Reichert, V.P.; James D. Reichert, V.P.; Bryan R. Dunn, Secy.; Eric A. Schreiner, Treas.; Alison Janus, Exec. Dir.
EIN: 364198123

1029
The Koldyke Family Foundation
c/o Frontenac Co.
55 W. Monroe St., Ste. 3560
Chicago, IL 60603-5077

Established in 1985 in IL.
Donor(s): Martin J. Koldyke.
Grantmaker type: Independent foundation
Financial data (yr. ended 07/31/02): Assets, $11,352 (M); gifts received, $51,374; expenditures, $300,814; qualifying distributions, $290,663; giving activities include $293,114 for 124 grants (high: $32,500; low: $100).
Purpose and activities: Giving primarily for education, the arts, and human services.
Fields of interest: Media/communications; Theater; Historic preservation/historical societies; Arts; Higher education; Teacher school/education; Education; Environment; Health organizations; Medical research, institute; Human services; Children/youth, services; Federated giving programs; Government/public administration.
Limitations: Applications not accepted. Giving primarily in IL, with emphasis on Chicago. No grants to individuals.
Application information: Contributes only to pre-selected organizations.
Officers and Directors:* Patricia B. Koldyke,* Chair.; Martin J. Koldyke,* Pres. and Treas.; Stanford J. Goldblatt,* Secy.; Rodney L. Goldstein; Martin L. Koldyke.
EIN: 363482711

1030
Kovler Family Foundation
(formerly Harry and Maribel G. Blum Foundation)
875 N. Michigan Ave., Ste. 3400
Chicago, IL 60611 (312) 664-5050
Contact: H.H. Bregar, Secy.

Established in 1967 in IL.
Donor(s): Harry Blum,‡ Everett Kovler.
Grantmaker type: Independent foundation
Financial data (yr. ended 12/31/02): Assets, $32,371,000 (M); expenditures, $2,126,349; qualifying distributions, $2,122,974; giving activities include $2,090,600 for 33 grants (high: $750,000; low: $200; average: $500–$500,000).
Purpose and activities: Giving primarily for university medical research, a Jewish welfare fund, a zoological society, and an art museum.
Fields of interest: Museums (art); Higher education; Zoos/zoological societies; Medical research, institute; Human services; Jewish federated giving programs.
Types of support: General/operating support; Research.
Limitations: Giving primarily in Chicago, IL. No grants to individuals.
Application information: Application form not required.
> *Initial approach:* Letter or proposal
> *Copies of proposal:* 1
> *Deadline(s):* None
> *Board meeting date(s):* As required
Officers and Directors:* H. Jonathan Kovler,* Pres.; H.H. Bregar,* Secy.
Number of staff: 2 full-time professional; 2 part-time professional.
EIN: 366152744

1031
Krehbiel Family Foundation
807 Chestnut Ave.
Wilmette, IL 60091

Established in 1993 in IL.
Grantmaker type: Independent foundation
Financial data (yr. ended 10/31/02): Assets,
$7,253,655 (M); expenditures, $432,272;
qualifying distributions, $416,778; giving
activities include $414,000 for 22 grants (high:
$50,000; low: $3,000).
Purpose and activities: Giving primarily for
higher education, conservation and botanical
gardens; funding also for hospitals, and
children's services, including a children's
hospital.
Fields of interest: Higher education; Botanical
gardens; Environment; Hospitals (general);
Children, services.
Limitations: Applications not accepted. Giving
primarily in IL and KS. No grants to individuals.
Application information: Contributes only to
pre-selected organizations.
Trustees: Fred A. Krehbiel; John H. Krehbiel, Jr.
EIN: 393985704

1032
Bertha Lebus Charitable Trust
c/o The Northern Trust Co.
50 S. LaSalle St., Ste. L-5
Chicago, IL 60675

Grantmaker type: Independent foundation
Financial data (yr. ended 12/31/02): Assets,
$3,983,064 (M); expenditures, $288,774;
qualifying distributions, $263,119; giving
activities include $236,211 for 37 grants (high:
$30,000; low: $1,000).
Purpose and activities: Giving primarily for
higher education; funding also for the arts,
health and human services.
Fields of interest: Museums (natural history);
Arts; Higher education; Libraries (public);
Education; Horticulture/garden clubs; Hospitals
(general); Cancer; Human services; YM/YWCAs
& YM/YWHAs; Family services.
Limitations: Applications not accepted. Giving
primarily in IL and KY.
Application information: Contributes only to
pre-selected organizations.
Directors: Sally Ann Hagan; Frazer D. Lebus, Jr.;
Jessica Robbins.
Trustee: The Northern Trust Co.
EIN: 956022085

1033
Donald Levin Family Foundation
2301 Ravine Way
Glenview, IL 60025

Established in 1984 in IL.
Donor(s): Donald Levin, DRL Enterprises.
Grantmaker type: Independent foundation
Financial data (yr. ended 09/30/02): Assets,
$1,222,414 (M); expenditures, $103,453;
qualifying distributions, $93,849; giving
activities include $94,000 for 6 grants (high:
$70,000; low: $1,000).
Purpose and activities: Giving to animal welfare
agencies, health related issues, youth services
and Jewish agencies.

Fields of interest: Education; Zoos/zoological
societies; Health care; Children/youth, services;
Jewish agencies & temples.
Limitations: Applications not accepted. Giving
on a national basis. No grants to individuals.
Application information: Contributes only to
pre-selected organizations.
Director: Donald Levin.
EIN: 363329401

1034
Stuart & Sheri Levine Family Foundation, Inc.
500 Lake Cook Rd.
Deerfield, IL 60015

Established in 1996 in IL.
Donor(s): Sheri Levine, Stuart Levine.
Grantmaker type: Independent foundation
Financial data (yr. ended 12/31/02): Assets,
$49,837 (M); gifts received, $364,230;
expenditures, $361,170; qualifying distributions,
$361,170; giving activities include $360,250 for
26 grants (high: $100,000; low: $50).
Purpose and activities: Giving primarily for
educational and Jewish religious purposes as
well as for health services.
Fields of interest: Higher education;
Zoos/zoological societies; Medical care,
in-patient care; Jewish agencies & temples.
Limitations: Applications not accepted. Giving
primarily in Chicago, IL. No grants to
individuals.
Application information: Contributes only to
pre-selected organizations.
Officers: Stuart Levine, Pres. and Treas.; Sheri
Levine, V.P. and Secy.
Director: Thomas Herskovits.
EIN: 364118537

1035
Josephine P. & John J. Louis Foundation
(formerly John J. Louis, Jr. Foundation)
c/o Frye-Louis Capital Mgmt.
225 W. Wacker Dr., Ste. 1000
Chicago, IL 60606
Contact: Jennifer M. Millhouse, Admin.

Established in 1992 in IL as partial successor to
John J. Louis Foundation.
Donor(s): John J. Louis, Jr.,‡ Josephine P. Louis,
John J. Louis Foundation.
Grantmaker type: Independent foundation
Financial data (yr. ended 12/31/02): Assets,
$3,923,002 (M); gifts received, $744,502;
expenditures, $596,126; qualifying distributions,
$531,829; giving activities include $531,829 for
52 grants (high: $115,000; low: $100).
Purpose and activities: Giving primarily for
education, health care, and religion.
Fields of interest: Arts; Elementary/secondary
education; Environment; Hospitals (general);
Human services; Government/public
administration; Religion.
International interests: United Kingdom.
Types of support: General/operating support;
Continuing support; Annual campaigns; Capital
campaigns; Building/renovation; Endowments.
Limitations: Applications not accepted. Giving
primarily in the Chicago, IL, area; limited giving
to United Kingdom organizations. No grants to
individuals, or for scholarships or fellowships.

Application information: Contributes only to
pre-selected organizations.
Board meeting date(s): Mid to late Oct.
Officers and Directors:* Josephine P. Louis,*
V.P.; J. Jeffry Louis III,* Secy.-Treas.; Tracy Louis
Merrill; Kimberly Louis Stewart.
Number of staff: None.
EIN: 363837993

1036
Edward K. Love Conservation Foundation
c/o Bank of America
231 S. LaSalle St., IL1-231-14-19
Chicago, IL 60697
Contact: Andrew S. Love, Jr., Gov.
Application address: c/o Love Realty, 515 Olive
St., Ste. 1400, St. Louis, MO 63101, tel.: (314)
621-1200

Grantmaker type: Independent foundation
Financial data (yr. ended 09/30/02): Assets,
$6,476,184 (M); expenditures, $454,645;
qualifying distributions, $398,705; giving
activities include $394,754 for 9 grants (high:
$100,000; low: $25,000).
Purpose and activities: Support is limited to
recipients who aid in the protection and
conservation of wildlife in MO.
Fields of interest: Higher education; Natural
resources; Animals/wildlife,
preservation/protection.
Limitations: Giving limited to MO.
Application information:
Initial approach: Proposal
Deadline(s): None
Trustees: Jerry Paul Combs; Samuel B. Hayes III;
Daniel Spoule Love; Bank of America.
Governor: Andrew S. Love, Jr.
EIN: 436022352

1037
The Lumpkin Family Foundation
7200 Sears Twr.
233 S. Wacker Dr.
Chicago, IL 60606
Contact: Bruce Karmazin, Exec. Dir.
Application address: 121 S. 17th St., Mattoon, IL
61938, tel.: (217) 258-8444; FAX: (217)
258-8444; E-mail:
executivedirector@lumpkinfoundation.org; URL:
http://www.lumpkinfoundation.org/

Incorporated in 1953 in IL.
Donor(s): Besse Adamson Lumpkin,‡ Mary G.
Lumpkin,‡ Richard Adamson Lumpkin,‡ Illinois
Consolidated Telephone Co., Richard Anthony
Lumpkin, Mary Lee Sparks, Margaret L. Keon,
Elizabeth Lumpkin Celio.
Grantmaker type: Independent foundation
Financial data (yr. ended 12/31/02): Assets,
$33,100,123 (M); gifts received, $201,647;
expenditures, $1,887,899; qualifying
distributions, $1,676,919; giving activities
include $1,342,927 for 157 grants (high:
$592,500; low: $25; average: $1,000–$30,000).
Purpose and activities: Giving primarily for
conservation and human services.
Fields of interest: Libraries (public); Education;
Natural resources; Human services; Children,
services.

Types of support: Annual campaigns; Program development; Seed money; Internship funds; Matching/challenge support.
Limitations: Giving primarily in central IL; giving also in the San Francisco Bay Area, CA, Albuquerque, NM, Boulder, CO, Chicago, IL, Philadelphia, PA, the Jamestown area in western NY, Gloucester, MA, and New Canaan, CT. No grants to individuals.
Publications: Application guidelines.
Application information: Application form required.
   Initial approach: Letter
   Copies of proposal: 1
   Deadline(s): Apr. 15, May 16, and Oct. 15
   Board meeting date(s): Feb., Apr., June, Sept. and Nov.
   Final notification: May, June, and Nov.
Officers and Directors:* John W. Sparks, Pres.; Elizabeth Lumpkin Celio, V.P.; S.L. Grissom, Secy.; Richard Anthony Lumpkin,* Treas.; Barbara Federico; Margaret Lumpkin Keon; Pamela Ryan Keon.
Number of staff: 2 full-time professional; 1 full-time support.
EIN: 237423640

1038
Ann and Robert H. Lurie Family Foundation
2 N. Riverside Plz., Ste. 1500
Chicago, IL 60606-2639 (312) 466-3997
Contact: Janet V. Ecker, C.A.O.

Established in 1986 in IL.
Donor(s): Robert Lurie.‡
Grantmaker type: Independent foundation
Financial data (yr. ended 12/31/01): Assets, $36,967,686 (M); gifts received, $200; expenditures, $4,475,741; qualifying distributions, $4,464,677; giving activities include $4,393,835 for 31 grants (high: $1,000,000; low: $1,000; average: $2,500–$100,000).
Purpose and activities: Giving primarily for education, human services, and health.
Fields of interest: Higher education; Environment, research; Natural resources; Health care; Health organizations, association; Children/youth, services.
Types of support: Endowments.
Limitations: Applications not accepted. Giving primarily in Chicago, IL, and MI. No grants to individuals.
Application information: Contributes only to pre-selected organizations.
Officers and Directors:* B. Ann Lurie,* Pres. and Treas.; Sheli Z. Rosenberg,* V.P. and Secy.; Andrew Lurie,* V.P.; Mark Sleazak,* V.P.; Robert M. Levin.
EIN: 363486274
Recent environmental and animal welfare grants:
1038-1 John G. Shedd Aquarium, Chicago, IL, $1,000,000. For unrestricted support. 2001.
1038-2 Windy City PAWS, Chicago, IL, $25,000. For unrestricted support. 2001.

1039
John D. and Catherine T. MacArthur Foundation ▼
140 S. Dearborn St., Ste. 1100
Chicago, IL 60603-5285 (312) 726-8000
Contact: Richard Kaplan, Asst. V.P., Institutional Research and Grants Mgmt.
FAX: (312) 920-6258; TDD: (312) 920-6285;
E-mail: 4answers@macfound.org; URL: http://www.macfound.org

Incorporated in 1970 in IL.
Donor(s): John D. MacArthur,‡ Catherine T. MacArthur.‡
Grantmaker type: Independent foundation
Financial data (yr. ended 12/31/02): Assets, $3,836,621,632 (M); expenditures, $273,276,308; qualifying distributions, $236,285,990; giving activities include $179,401,560 for 1,259 grants (high: $6,100,000; low: $2,500; average: $30,000–$250,000), $13,303,473 for 345 grants to individuals, $2,868,295 for 696 employee matching gifts and $14,342,695 for 11 loans/program-related investments.
Purpose and activities: The foundation is a private, independent grantmaking institution dedicated to helping groups and individuals foster lasting improvement in the human condition. The foundation seeks the development of healthy individuals and effective communities; peace within and among nations; responsible choices about human reproduction; and a global ecosystem capable of supporting healthy human societies. The foundation pursues this mission by supporting research, policy development, dissemination, education and training, and practice.
Fields of interest: Media/communications; Film/video; Education, public education; Early childhood education; Higher education; Natural resources; Reproductive health; Health care; Mental health/crisis services, public policy; Crime/violence prevention, youth; Gun control; International economic development; International peace/security; Foreign policy; International affairs; Community development, neighborhood development; Public policy, research.
International interests: Russia; Africa; Nigeria; Mexico; India.
Types of support: General/operating support; Program development; Fellowships; Research; Program-related investments/loans; Employee matching gifts; Grants to individuals; Matching/challenge support.
Limitations: Giving on a national and international basis, with emphasis on Chicago, IL. No support for churches or religious programs, political activities or campaigns. No grants for capital or endowment funds, equipment purchases, plant construction, conferences, publications, media productions, debt retirement, development campaigns, fundraising appeals, scholarships, or fellowships (other than those sponsored by the foundation).
Publications: Annual report, Informational brochure (including application guidelines), Newsletter.
Application information: Please do not send the letter of inquiry by FAX. Send it by mail to the office of Grants Management or by E-mail: LOI@macfound.org. Applicants should contact foundation for brochures outlining program

guidelines. Direct applications for MacArthur Fellows and Health programs not accepted. Grants increasingly initiated by the board. Application form not required.
   Initial approach: Letter of inquiry (2 to 3 pages) and one-page summary
   Copies of proposal: 1
   Deadline(s): None
   Board meeting date(s): Mar., June, Sept. and Dec.
   Final notification: 8 to 10 weeks
Officers and Directors:* Sara Lawrence-Lightfoot,* Chair.; Jonathan F. Fanton,* Pres.; Arthur Sussman, V.P. and Secy.; Lyn Hutton, V.P. and C.F.O; William E. Lowry, V.P., Human Resources; Joshua J. Mintz, V.P. and Genl. Counsel; Julia M. Stasch, V.P. Progs., Human and Community Devel.; Mitchel B. Wallerstein, V.P. Progs., Global Security and Sustainability; Marc P. Yanchura, Treas.; Sharon R. Burns, C.I.O.; Lloyd Axworthy; John Seely Brown; Drew Saunders Days III; Robert E. Denham; William H. Foege, M.D.; Jamie S. Gorelick; Mary Graham; John P. Holdren; Mario J. Molina; George A. Ranney, Jr.; Thomas C. Theobold.
Number of staff: 99 full-time professional; 88 full-time support.
EIN: 237093598
Recent environmental and animal welfare grants:
1039-1 African Wildlife Foundation, DC, $300,000. For biodiversity conservation in Virunga-Bwindi area of Albertine Rift Hotspot. 2002.
1039-2 Amazon Conservation Association, DC, $250,000. For research and conservation program in Pampas del Heath, Bolivia. 2002.
1039-3 Archbold Expeditions, Buck Island Ranch, Lake Placid, FL, $500,000. For MacArthur Agro-ecology Research Center, to evaluate effectiveness of wetland restoration on Florida ranch landscape. 2002.
1039-4 Bioresources Development and Conservation Programme, Silver Spring, MD, $50,000. For environmental law and policy work for biodiversity conservation in Niger Delta. 2002.
1039-5 Center for Resource Economics/Island Press, DC, $2,500,000. For general operating support. 2002.
1039-6 Centro Mexicano de Derecho Ambiental, Mexico City, Mexico, $150,000. For environmental law and policy activities to protect and conserve Mexico's biodiversity. 2002.
1039-7 Chicago Horticultural Society, Chicago Botanic Garden, Glencoe, IL, $500,000. For one-time public-information campaign. 2002.
1039-8 Clark University, Worcester, MA, $99,000. For Policy Integration, Technology Change, and Sustainability in East Asia. 2002.
1039-9 College of African Wildlife Management, Moshi, Tanzania, $200,000. For protected area capacity building for biodiversity conservation in Albertine Rift Hotspot. 2002.
1039-10 Columbia University, Center for United States-China Arts Exchange, New York, NY, $50,000. For biological assessment and to develop sustainable management plan for Gaoligongshan Nature Reserve in Yunnan Province. 2002.

1039-11 Community Forestry International, Santa Barbara, CA, $180,000. To develop community forestry policy framework for northeast India. 2002.

1039-12 Conservation and Research Center Foundation, Front Royal, VA, $85,000. To develop integrated conservation strategy for northeast India. 2002.

1039-13 Conservation Fund, West Palm Beach, FL, $500,000. For establishing John D. and Catherine T. MacArthur Revolving Fund for Land Conservation. 2002.

1039-14 Conservation Fund, West Palm Beach, FL, $200,000. For activities to promote smart growth in South Florida. 2002.

1039-15 Consultative Group on Biological Diversity, San Francisco, CA, $50,000. For activities to increase impact of private foundations working in biodiversity conservation. 2002.

1039-16 Coordinadora Estadal de Productores de Cafe de Oaxaca, Oaxaca, Mexico, $145,000. For training, community outreach, and market development for conservation-oriented coffee production. 2002.

1039-17 Earth Island Institute, San Francisco, CA, $50,000. For World Sustainability Hearing at Rio Plus 10 World Summit. 2002.

1039-18 Environmental Law Alliance Worldwide (E-LAW), Eugene, Oregon, $225,000. For activities to build environmental law capacity in Bolivia. 2002.

1039-19 Environmental Law and Policy Center of the Midwest, Chicago, IL, $200,000. For advocacy and public education activities related to regional transportation infrastructure. 2002.

1039-20 Environmental Law Institute, DC, $270,000. For capacity building and strengthening of legal frameworks for biodiversity conservation in Albertine Rift Hotspot. 2002.

1039-21 Field Museum of Natural History, Chicago, IL, $480,000. For activities to build national-level capacity in survey, collection, management, and analysis of biological information in Bhutan. 2002.

1039-22 Florida Atlantic University Foundation, Boca Raton, FL, $600,000. For South Florida Regional Resource Center. 2002.

1039-23 Florida Oceanographic Society, Stuart, FL, $10,000. For general operations and expansion of Coastal Center programs. 2002.

1039-24 Garfield Park Conservatory Alliance, Chicago, IL, $75,000. For general operating support. 2002.

1039-25 Global Environment Facility (GEF), DC, $50,000. To develop lessons-learned case studies for presentation at Rio Plus 10 World Summit. Grant made through International Bank for Reconstruction and Development. 2002.

1039-26 Humanitarian Project, Takoma Park, MD, $60,000. For building international linkages for sustainable development of East Timor. 2002.

1039-27 Inner Asian Conservation, Hamden, CT, $380,000. For work to increase management capacity for existing protected areas and to assist creation of new protected areas in Indian state of Arunachal Pradesh. 2002.

1039-28 Institute for Energy and Environmental Research, Takoma Park, MD, $150,000. For Global Security Project, which provides information about nuclear dangers to policymakers, activists, and journalists in countries with nuclear programs. 2002.

1039-29 Institute for Lifecycle Energy Analysis, Institute for Lifecycle Analysis, Seattle, WA, $68,000. For Critical Analysis of Hydrogen Economy. 2002.

1039-30 Institute for Policy Studies, DC, $50,000. For pilot study of ecotourism in Costa Rica to test how lessons from forest certification programs can be applied to larger tourism industry. 2002.

1039-31 International Centre for Integrated Mountain Development, Kathmandu, Nepal, $350,000. For efforts to establish natural corridors linking protected areas of eastern Nepal, Indian state of Sikkim, and western Bhutan. 2002.

1039-32 International Centre of Insect Physiology and Ecology, Nairobi, Kenya, $230,000. For biodiversity conservation project in Echuya Forest Reserve of Uganda, within Albertine Rift Hotspot. 2002.

1039-33 International Council for Science, Paris, France, $120,000. For ecosystems management training for conservationists working in Albertine Rift Hotspot. 2002.

1039-34 International Union for Conservation of Nature and Natural Resources, World Conservation Union, Gland, Switzerland, $175,000. For participation by developing countries in World Parks Congress. 2002.

1039-35 Lincoln Park Zoological Society, Lincoln Park Zoo, Chicago, IL, $150,000. For general operating support. 2002.

1039-36 Morton Arboretum, Lisle, IL, $50,000. For general operating support. 2002.

1039-37 Mountain Institute, DC, $350,000. To promote community management of Kangchenjunga Conservation Area in eastern Nepal and Indian state of Sikkim. 2002.

1039-38 Museo Nacional de Historia Natural, La Paz, Bolivia, $120,000. For applied research on fish biodiversity in Madidi National Park and Piln Lajas Biosphere Reserve. 2002.

1039-39 National Commission on Energy Policy, DC, $500,000. For general operating support. 2002.

1039-40 New York Botanical Garden, Bronx, NY, $29,000. For restoration of Haiti's national herbarium. 2002.

1039-41 Organization for Tropical Studies, Durham, NC, $50,000. For endowment campaign. 2002.

1039-42 Overseas Development Institute, Forest Policy and Environment Group, London, England, $200,000. For research about human and social dimensions of hunting and trade of wild meat from tropical forests. 2002.

1039-43 Pacific Institute for Studies in Development, Environment and Security, Oakland, CA, $150,000. For research and communications in areas of environmental security, sustainable water use, and global change. 2002.

1039-44 Pro Naturaleza-Fundacion Peruana para la Conservacion de la Naturaleza, Lima, Peru, $300,000. To develop conservation management plan for two protected areas

and to implement sustainable forestry concessions in southeastern Peru. 2002.

1039-45 Protsahan, India, $171,024. To study population dynamics in coastal communities on west coast of India. 2002.

1039-46 Rainforest Expeditions, Lima, Peru, $50,000. For ecotourism training program for native community of Infierno in Tambopata. 2002.

1039-47 Royal Society for the Protection of Nature, Thimphu, Bhutan, $180,000. For project to strengthen protection and management of Phobjikha Conservation Area. 2002.

1039-48 Sociedad para el Estudio de los Recursos Bioticos de Oaxaca, Oaxaca, Mexico, $75,000. To strengthen research and outreach capacity in high-priority biodiversity. 2002.

1039-49 Sociedad Peruana de Derecho Ambiental, Lima, Peru, $300,000. For efforts to implement laws and regulations governing biodiversity conservation. 2002.

1039-50 Tropica Rural Latinoamericana, Chetumal, Mexico, $135,000. For programs to promote conservation and sustainable resource use in community-managed forests in states of Quintana Roo and Campeche. 2002.

1039-51 Union of Concerned Scientists, Cambridge, MA, $1,000,000. For Ounce of Prevention campaign. 2002.

1039-52 Union of Concerned Scientists, Cambridge, MA, $98,000. For first international professional meeting of independent technical peace and security analysts. 2002.

1039-53 Universidad Autonoma de Yucatan, Programa de Manejo y/Conservacion de Recursos Naturales Tropicales, Merida, Mexico, $295,000. To consolidate PROTROPICO master's degree program in natural resource use and conservation and Ecological Agricultural School. 2002.

1039-54 University of Hannover, Institute of Soil Science, Hannover, Germany, $25,325. For Exporting Natural Disasters. 2002.

1039-55 University of Kentucky Research Foundation, Lexington, KY, $75,000. For Moral Economy of Water. 2002.

1039-56 Wildlife Conservation Society, Bronx, NY, $300,000. For forest conservation in protected areas within Albertine Rift countries of Uganda, Rwanda, and Democratic Republic of Congo. 2002.

1039-57 Wildlife Conservation Society, Bronx, NY, $300,000. For field-based analysis of alternative strategies to reduce hunting and wildlife trade in tropical forests. 2002.

1039-58 World Resources Institute, DC, $1,000,000. For Strategic Opportunity Fund and purchase and implementation of hardware and software technology to support special projects of such Fund. 2002.

1039-59 World Wide Fund for Nature-Eastern Africa, East Africa Regional Programme Office, Nairobi, Kenya, $300,000. For work to protect Virunga and Kibira forests in central part of Albertine Rift Hotspot. 2002.

1039-60 World Wide Fund for Nature-Eastern Africa, East Africa Regional Programme Office, Nairobi, Kenya, $300,000. For regional strategic plan and monitoring system for conservation of biodiversity in Albertine

Rift Hotspot and to strengthen local conservation groups. 2002.

1039-61 World Wildlife Fund/Conservation Foundation, DC, $600,000. To assist Royal Government of Bhutan in setting up management system for Sakteng Wildlife Sanctuary. 2002.

1039-62 World Wildlife Fund/Conservation Foundation, DC, $345,000. To assist government of Nepal in establishing and managing Kangchenjunga Conservation Area. 2002.

1040
Marquis George MacDonald Foundation, Inc.

c/o Northern Trust Bank of Florida, N.A.
50 S. LaSalle St., Ste. L-5
Chicago, IL 60675
Contact: Donna M. Bowers, Admin.

Incorporated in 1951 in NY.
Donor(s): Marquis George MacDonald.‡
Grantmaker type: Independent foundation
Financial data (yr. ended 12/31/02): Assets, $698,720 (M); expenditures, $591,104; qualifying distributions, $544,507; giving activities include $510,488 for 180 grants (high: $18,000; low: $100).
Purpose and activities: Giving for the arts, environment, higher and secondary education, church support, religious associations, hospitals, health, cancer and AIDS research, welfare funds, and organizations providing benefit to the community and serving the public interest.
Fields of interest: Media/communications; Visual arts; Museums; Performing arts; Dance; Theater; Music; Arts; Secondary school/education; Higher education; Natural resources; Environment; Animal welfare; Hospitals (general); Health care; Health organizations, association; Cancer; AIDS; Alcoholism; Cancer research; AIDS research; Food services; Human services; Aging, centers/services; Women, centers/services; Arms control; Community development; Roman Catholic agencies & churches; Jewish agencies & temples; Religion; Disabled; Aging; Women.
Types of support: Continuing support; Program development; Scholarship funds.
Limitations: Applications not accepted. Giving on a national basis, with emphasis on NY and PA. No grants to individuals, or for matching gifts; no loans.
Application information: Contributes only to pre-selected organizations.
Board meeting date(s): May 7, Aug. 6, and Dec. 10
Officer: Catherine MacDonald, Pres.
Directors: Elizabeth MacDonald; Helen MacDonald; John Lee MacDonald; Joseph MacDonald; Kevin MacDonald; Charles Shea.
Number of staff: 1 part-time professional.
EIN: 131957181

1041
MACFUND

271-0 Market Sq.
Lake Forest, IL 60045-1815 (847) 234-0260
Contact: David MacKenzie, Secy.-Treas., or Linda Martinat, Dir.
FAX: (847) 234-1903

Established in 1965.
Donor(s): Deborah W. MacKenzie, David O. MacKenzie.
Grantmaker type: Independent foundation
Financial data (yr. ended 12/31/02): Assets, $1,132,820 (M); expenditures, $120,642; qualifying distributions, $113,586; giving activities include $114,470 for 256 grants (high: $10,000; low: $20).
Purpose and activities: Giving for the arts and education.
Fields of interest: Orchestra (symphony); Environment, land resources; Human services.
Types of support: Continuing support; Annual campaigns; Endowments.
Limitations: Giving primarily in the Chicago, IL, area. No grants to individuals.
Application information: Application form not required.
Initial approach: Letter
Copies of proposal: 1
Deadline(s): Aug. 31
Board meeting date(s): Nov.
Final notification: Dec. 15
Officers: Deborah W. MacKenzie, Pres.; Marion M. Christoph, V.P.; David O. MacKenzie, Secy.-Treas.
Director: Linda Martinat.
Number of staff: 1 part-time support.
EIN: 362545433

1042
J. Edward Mahoney Foundation

2 W. Roberta St.
Lemont, IL 60439-6400
Contact: Jennifer L. Green, Exec. Dir.
E-mail: jemfound@hotmail.com

Established in 1997 in IL.
Donor(s): Mary Ann Mahoney.
Grantmaker type: Independent foundation
Financial data (yr. ended 12/31/02): Assets, $3,726,729 (M); expenditures, $390,137; qualifying distributions, $355,050; giving activities include $355,050 for 9 grants (high: $200,000; low: $10,000).
Purpose and activities: Giving primarily for education and health care.
Fields of interest: Elementary/secondary education; Secondary school/education; Libraries (public); Natural resources; Environment; Hospitals (general); Health care; Children/youth, services; Foundations (public).
Types of support: Continuing support; Building/renovation; Land acquisition; Program development; Publication; Research.
Limitations: Applications not accepted. Giving primarily in IL. No grants to individuals.
Application information: Contributes only to pre-selected organizations.
Board meeting date(s): Quarterly
Officer and Trustees:* Jennifer L. Green,* Exec. Dir.; Rosemary Duke; Juliann Geijer; John J. Gonczy; Nicole M. Gonczy; Daniel L. Hughes;

Michael D. Hughes; Mary Ann Mahoney; Margaret A. Schwartz.
Number of staff: 1 part-time professional.
EIN: 367192604

1043
Makray Family Foundation

c/o David Buckley
231 W. Main St.
Barrington, IL 60010

Donor(s): Paul Makray.
Grantmaker type: Independent foundation
Financial data (yr. ended 01/31/03): Assets, $14,310,398 (M); expenditures, $925,523; qualifying distributions, $850,000; giving activities include $850,000 for 31 grants (high: $99,000; low: $5,000).
Purpose and activities: Giving primarily for conservation.
Fields of interest: Environment; Animals/wildlife; Youth development.
Limitations: Applications not accepted. Giving primarily in IL. No grants to individuals.
Application information: Contributes only to pre-selected organizations.
Officers and Directors:* Nancy Harney,* Pres.; Christine Brownstein,* V.P.; Carol Donohoe,* V.P.; Robert Harney, Secy.; Paul Makray, Jr.,* Treas.; David P. Buckley, Jr.; Robert F. Lamping.
EIN: 364298517

1044
Malott Family Foundation

(formerly Camalott Charitable Foundation)
c/o Robert H. Malott
200 E. Randolph Dr.
Chicago, IL 60601

Established in 1989 in IL.
Donor(s): Robert H. Malott.
Grantmaker type: Independent foundation
Financial data (yr. ended 12/31/02): Assets, $24,943,315 (M); gifts received, $4,332; expenditures, $1,379,208; qualifying distributions, $1,321,710; giving activities include $1,288,801 for 65 grants (high: $400,000; low: $250).
Purpose and activities: Funding primarily for arts and culture, and education. Some funding also for human services and health care.
Fields of interest: Performing arts; Opera; Arts; Higher education; Graduate/professional education; Education; Environment; Health care; Public policy, research; General charitable giving.
Limitations: Applications not accepted. Giving primarily in IL. No grants to individuals.
Application information: Unsolicited requests for funds not considered.
Officers: Robert H. Malott, Pres.; Elizabeth Malott Pohle, Secy.
Directors: Barbara Malott Kizziah; Keith Kizziah; Jill Hammer Malott; Robert Deane Malott; Chris Pohle.
Number of staff: 1 full-time professional; 1 part-time professional.
EIN: 363680666

1045
Mason Foundation, Inc.
(formerly Mason Charitable Foundation)
180 E. Pearson, Ste. 5705
Chicago, IL 60611-2186

Established in 1980 in IL.
Donor(s): Marian Tyler.
Grantmaker type: Independent foundation
Financial data (yr. ended 01/31/02): Assets,
$3,956,156 (M); expenditures, $287,830;
qualifying distributions, $250,339; giving
activities include $251,000 for 8 grants (high:
$96,000; low: $10,000).
Fields of interest: Orchestra (symphony);
Elementary/secondary education;
Scholarships/financial aid; Environment, land
resources; Aquariums; Housing/shelter,
homeless; Human services; Domestic violence.
Limitations: Applications not accepted. Giving
primarily in IL and MI. No grants to individuals.
Application information: Contributes only to
pre-selected organizations.
Officers and Directors:* Marian Tyler,* Pres.;
Robert D. Douglass,* V.P.; William A. Anderson,
Secy.-Treas.; Kathryn Greeley.
EIN: 363101263

1046
The Anne Beverly McCormack Foundation
c/o The Northern Trust Co.
50 LaSalle St., Ste. 1
Chicago, IL 60675
Contact: Anne McCormack Jones, Pres.

Established in 1988 in NY.
Donor(s): Anne McCormack Jones.
Grantmaker type: Independent foundation
Financial data (yr. ended 12/31/01): Assets,
$684,348 (M); expenditures, $93,504;
qualifying distributions, $89,597; giving
activities include $89,500 for 11 grants (high:
$10,000; low: $6,000).
Purpose and activities: Giving for hospitals and
for animal welfare.
Fields of interest: Animal welfare;
Animals/wildlife, preservation/protection;
Hospitals (general); Human services;
Foundations (public).
Limitations: Giving primarily in New York, NY.
No grants to individuals.
Application information:
Initial approach: Typed letter
Deadline(s): None
Officers and Directors:* Anne McCormack
Jones,* Pres.; John Woods,* Treas.; Freeman
Jones.
EIN: 133458360

1047
Chauncey and Marion Deering
McCormick Foundation ▼
410 N. Michigan Ave., Rm. 590
Chicago, IL 60611-4252 (312) 644-6720

Incorporated in 1957 in IL.
Donor(s): Brooks McCormick, Brooks
McCormick Trust, Charles Deering McCormick
Trust, Roger McCormick Trust.
Grantmaker type: Independent foundation
Financial data (yr. ended 07/31/02): Assets,
$60,657,043 (M); gifts received, $2,500,000;

expenditures, $4,835,357; qualifying
distributions, $4,771,733; giving activities
include $4,777,592 for 70 grants (high:
$2,000,000; low: $2,500; average:
$5,000–$150,000).
Purpose and activities: Emphasis on higher and
secondary education, hospitals, and cultural
institutions, including an art institute and a
museum; support also for conservation and
child welfare.
Fields of interest: Museums; Arts; Higher
education; Natural resources; Zoos/zoological
societies; Hospitals (general); Children/youth,
services.
Types of support: General/operating support.
Limitations: Giving primarily in Chicago, IL. No
grants to individuals.
Application information: Application form not
required.
Officers and Trustees:* Brooks McCormick,*
Chair.; Lawson E. Whitesides,* Pres.; Charlotte
Deering McCormick,* V.P.; Charles E.
Schroeder,* Secy.-Treas.; Lisa Collins;
Christopher Hunt; Fiona M. Hunt; Ian C. Hunt;
Blair Collins Maus; Nancy C.T. McCormick;
Hilary H. McCutcheon; Abby McCormick
O'Neil.
EIN: 366054815
**Recent environmental and animal welfare
grants:**
1047-1 Canal Corridor Association, Chicago, IL,
$20,000. For unrestricted support. 2002.
1047-2 Conservation Foundation of DuPage
County, Naperville, IL, $50,000. For
unrestricted support. 2002.
1047-3 Friends of the Chicago River, Chicago,
IL, $10,000. For unrestricted support. 2002.
1047-4 International Crane Foundation,
Baraboo, WI, $50,000. For operating
support. 2002.
1047-5 Jane Goodall Institute for Wildlife
Research, Education and Conservation, Silver
Spring, MD, $15,000. For unrestricted
support. 2002.
1047-6 Lincoln Park Zoological Society,
Chicago, IL, $10,000. For unrestricted
support. 2002.
1047-7 Nature Conservancy, Chicago, IL,
$130,000. For unrestricted support. 2002.
1047-8 Openlands Project, Chicago, IL,
$125,000. For endowment. 2002.
1047-9 Openlands Project, Chicago, IL,
$15,000. For unrestricted support. 2002.

1048
McDonald's Corporation Contributions
Program
McDonald's Plz.
Oak Brook, IL 60521 (630) 623-7048
Contact: Jackie Meara, Supvr., Contribs.

Grantmaker type: Corporate giving program
Purpose and activities: McDonald's makes
charitable contributions to nonprofit
organizations involved with arts and culture,
education, the environment, health and human
services, substance abuse, disease, medical
research, employment, nutrition, civil rights,
community development, science, public
affairs, minorities, disabled people, senior
citizens, women, and economically
disadvantaged people. Support is given on a
national basis.

Fields of interest: Music; Historic
preservation/historical societies; Arts;
Elementary/secondary education; Vocational
education; Higher education; Adult
education—literacy, basic skills & GED;
Reading; Education; Natural resources;
Environment; Hospitals (general); Medical care,
rehabilitation; Health care; Substance abuse,
services; Alcoholism; Health organizations;
Medical research; Employment; Nutrition;
Youth, services; Human services; Civil rights;
Business/industry; Community development;
Mathematics; Engineering/technology; Science;
Public affairs; Minorities; Disabled; Aging;
Women; Economically disadvantaged.
Types of support: Program development; Seed
money; Employee matching gifts; In-kind gifts;
Matching/challenge support.
Limitations: Giving on a national basis,
particularly in areas of restaurant operations. No
support for fraternal, veterans', religious,
political, or sectarian organizations,
intermediary funding organizations, or United
Way-supported organizations located outside
the Chicago, IL, area. No grants to individuals,
or for capital funds, general operating support,
endowments, investment funds, advertising,
unspecified funds for specific elementary or
secondary schools, multi-year support, or
research; no loans.
Publications: Corporate report, Corporate giving
report.
Application information: The Public and
Community Affairs Department handles giving.
A contributions committee reviews all requests.
Application form not required.
Initial approach: Proposal to headquarters
Copies of proposal: 1
Deadline(s): None
Board meeting date(s): As needed
Final notification: 3 months
Administrators: Kenneth L. Barun; Jackie Meara,
Supvr., Contribs.

1049
McGraw Foundation
653 Landwehr Rd.
Northbrook, IL 60062-2309 (847) 291-9810
Contact: James F. Quilter, V.P.
FAX: (847) 291-9811; E-mail:
maxmcgraw@worldnet.att.net

Incorporated in 1948 in IL.
Donor(s): Alfred Bersted,‡ Carol Jean Root,‡
Maxine Elrod,‡ Donald S. Elrod,‡ Max
McGraw,‡ Richard F. McGraw,‡
McGraw-Edison Co., and others.
Grantmaker type: Independent foundation
Financial data (yr. ended 12/31/02): Assets,
$11,698,209 (M); expenditures, $1,331,319;
qualifying distributions, $1,329,256; giving
activities include $1,212,519 for 70+ grants
(high: $400,000; low: $25).
Purpose and activities: Primary areas of interest
include education, particularly in scientific and
environmental fields, including higher
education, social services, cultural programs,
health and medical research.
Fields of interest: Education, special; Higher
education; Environment; Medical research,
institute; Human services;
Engineering/technology; Science.

Types of support: General/operating support; Continuing support; Annual campaigns; Capital campaigns; Building/renovation; Professorships; Seed money; Scholarship funds; Research; Employee matching gifts; Matching/challenge support.
Limitations: Giving primarily in the Chicago, IL, area, and in adjoining states. No support for religious purposes. No grants to individuals.
Publications: Application guidelines, Program policy statement.
Application information: No grant proposals will be considered in 2003; 2003 grants restricted to honoring commitments already made. Application form not required.
　Initial approach: Letter
　Copies of proposal: 1
　Deadline(s): Submit proposal between Dec. 1 and Feb. 1
　Board meeting date(s): June; grant committee meets annually in Mar.
　Final notification: 30 days to 1 year
Officers and Directors:* Carol E. Moorman,* Pres.; James F. Quilter,* V.P., Secy.-Treas., and Exec. Dir.; J. Bradley Davis; Scott M. Elrod; Dennis W. Fitzgerald; Jerry D. Jones; William W. Mauritz; Kathryn B. Nelson; Bernard B. Rinella.
Number of staff: 1 full-time professional; 1 full-time support.
EIN: 362490000

1050
Max McGraw Wildlife Foundation
P.O. Box 9, Rte. 25
Dundee, IL 60118-0009 (847) 741-8000
Contact: Charles S. Potter, Exec. Dir.

Established in 1962.
Donor(s): McGraw Foundation.
Grantmaker type: Operating foundation
Financial data (yr. ended 04/30/02): Assets, $18,972,711 (M); gifts received, $1,696,111; expenditures, $3,638,149; qualifying distributions, $1,966,300; giving activities include $195,416 for 43 grants (high: $21,600; low: $54).
Purpose and activities: Funding for wildlife research projects involving upland game birds, song birds, waterfowl, fisheries, and endangered species.
Fields of interest: Higher education; Natural resources; Animals/wildlife, preservation/protection.
Types of support: Internship funds; Technical assistance.
Limitations: Giving primarily in the Midwest. No grants to individuals, directly.
Publications: Informational brochure.
Application information:
　Initial approach: Letter
　Deadline(s): None
　Board meeting date(s): Mid-June
Officers: Timothy N. Thoelecke, Pres.; John J. Brittain, V.P.; Richard T. Schroeder, V.P.; Charles S. Potter, Jr., Secy. and Exec. Dir.; Robert B. Wilson, Treas.
Directors: Frederick G. Acker; H. Grant Clark, Jr.; William J. Cullerton; J. Bradley Davis; Robert G. Donnelley; Richard A. Giesen; J. Stanley Pepper; Charles R. Tonge; Allen M. Turner.
EIN: 362519612

1051
McLamore Family Foundation
c/o Northern Trust Bank of Florida, N.A.
50 S. LaSalle St., Ste. L-5
Chicago, IL 60675

Established in 1996 in FL.
Donor(s): Burger King Corp.
Grantmaker type: Independent foundation
Financial data (yr. ended 07/31/02): Assets, $2,530,711 (M); gifts received, $50,100; expenditures, $176,204; qualifying distributions, $162,207; giving activities include $153,000 for 4 grants (high: $100,000; low: $1,500).
Purpose and activities: Giving for higher and other education.
Fields of interest: Media/communications; Higher education; Education; Horticulture/garden clubs; Federated giving programs.
Limitations: Applications not accepted. Giving primarily in Miami, FL. No grants to individuals.
Application information: Contributes only to pre-selected organizations.
Officers: Nancy N. McLamore, Chair.; S. Whitman McLamore, Pres.; Pamela M. Spence, V.P.; Lynne M. Maddux, Secy.; Susan M. McCormack, Treas.
EIN: 591896729

1052
Melvoin Foundation
966 Wildwood Ln.
Highland Park, IL 60035-4128
Contact: Hugo J. Melvoin, Pres.

Donor(s): Hugo J. Melvoin, Lois G. Melvoin.
Grantmaker type: Independent foundation
Financial data (yr. ended 12/31/02): Assets, $1,285,325 (M); gifts received, $56,886; expenditures, $117,746; qualifying distributions, $110,614; giving activities include $110,614 for 132 grants (high: $49,428; low: $25).
Purpose and activities: Giving for education, religion and public charities.
Fields of interest: Media/communications; Arts; Natural resources; Environment, water resources; Environment, forests; Botanical gardens; Animals/wildlife, fisheries; Roman Catholic agencies & churches; Jewish agencies & temples.
Limitations: Giving primarily in Chicago, IL. No grants to individuals.
Application information: Application form not required.
　Initial approach: Letter
　Deadline(s): None
Officers and Directors:* Hugo J. Melvoin,* Pres. and Treas.; Lois G. Melvoin,* V.P. and Secy.; Sonsiarae Hadley, Secy.-Treas.; Susan M. Martin; Jeffrey D. Melvoin; Richard I. Melvoin.
EIN: 366047994

1053
Meyers Charitable Family Fund
8748 W. Kells Dr.
Hickory Hills, IL 60457 (708) 598-8111
Contact: David R. Meyers, Pres.

Established in 1988 in IL.
Grantmaker type: Independent foundation

Financial data (yr. ended 12/31/02): Assets, $1,962,897 (M); expenditures, $222,519; qualifying distributions, $20,282; giving activities include $199,980 for 135 grants (high: $11,300; low: $50).
Purpose and activities: Giving for animal welfare, Christian organizations, and the arts.
Fields of interest: Arts; Education; Animals/wildlife, preservation/protection; Zoos/zoological societies; Christian agencies & churches; General charitable giving.
Limitations: Giving primarily in the greater Chicago, IL, area. No grants to individuals.
Application information: Application form not required.
　Deadline(s): None
Officers and Directors:* David R. Meyers,* Pres.; Frederick C. Meyers, Secy.-Treas.; Margery McGrew.
EIN: 363610777

1054
William H. Miner Foundation
10 S. Dearborn, Ste. 5100
Chicago, IL 60603-2279
Contact: Larry D. Berning, Tr.

Established in 1950.
Grantmaker type: Public charity
Financial data (yr. ended 12/31/01): Revenue, $7,848,301; assets, $70,972,048 (M); expenditures, $4,017,860; program services expenses, $3,261,335; giving activities include $3,231,335 for 3 grants (high: $2,949,832; low: $109,820).
Purpose and activities: The foundation exists for the sole benefit of Chazy Central Rural School, Champlain Valley Physicians Hospital Medical Center and the William H. Miner Agricultural Research Institute.
Fields of interest: Education; Natural resources; Hospitals (general).
Limitations: Applications not accepted. Giving limited to NY.
Application information: Contributes only to pre-selected organizations; unsolicited requests for funds not considered or acknowledged.
Trustees: Larry D. Berning; Joseph C. Burke; Maurie J. Miller.
EIN: 361488081

1055
Molex Foundation
2222 Wellington Ct.
Lisle, IL 60532

Established in 2000 in IL.
Donor(s): Molex Inc.
Grantmaker type: Company-sponsored foundation
Financial data (yr. ended 06/30/02): Assets, $194,385 (M); expenditures, $200,000; qualifying distributions, $200,000; giving activities include $200,000 for 2 grants of $100,000 each.
Fields of interest: Education; Environment.
Limitations: Applications not accepted. Giving primarily in IL. No grants to individuals.
Application information: Contributes only to pre-selected organizations.
Trustees: Frederick A. Krehbiel; John H. Krehbiel, Jr.; Sandra Lockhart.

EIN: 367328046

1056
The Moran Family Foundation
(formerly Everett N. McDonnell Foundation)
c/o John D. Marshall
190 S. LaSalle St.
Chicago, IL 60603-3441

Incorporated in 1946 in IL.
Donor(s): Everett N. McDonnell.‡
Grantmaker type: Independent foundation
Financial data (yr. ended 10/31/02): Assets,
$3,464,244 (M); expenditures, $278,161;
qualifying distributions, $227,672; giving
activities include $217,045 for 93 grants (high:
$27,000; low: $100).
Fields of interest: Arts; Animals/wildlife;
Hospitals (general); Health organizations,
association; Human services; Religion.
Types of support: Endowments.
Limitations: Applications not accepted. Giving
primarily in GA and IL. No grants to individuals.
Application information: Contributes only to
pre-selected organizations.
Officers and Directors:* Gwyneth O. Moran,*
Pres. and Treas.; Gwyneth M. Dennard,* V.P.;
Lee Moran, V.P.; John D. Marshall,* Secy.
EIN: 366109359

1057
Morton Family Foundation
452 Lageschulte St.
Barrington, IL 60010 (847) 381-4403
Contact: Charles Frey, Pres.

Donor(s): John B. Morton.
Grantmaker type: Independent foundation
Financial data (yr. ended 12/31/02): Assets,
$4,686,248 (M); gifts received, $2,310;
expenditures, $328,257; qualifying distributions,
$234,688; giving activities include $236,200 for
22 grants (high: $94,250; low: $500).
Purpose and activities: Giving for education, the
environment, and Christian organizations.
Fields of interest: Television; Education; Natural
resources; Christian agencies & churches.
Application information:
  Initial approach: Letter
  Deadline(s): None
Officers: Charles Frey, Pres.; William O'Keefe,
Secy.-Treas.
EIN: 363605391

1058
Mark Morton Memorial Fund
123 N. Wacker Dr.
Chicago, IL 60606-1743

Established in 1951 in IL.
Grantmaker type: Independent foundation
Financial data (yr. ended 12/31/02): Assets,
$20,407,388 (M); expenditures, $1,893,358;
qualifying distributions, $1,766,045; giving
activities include $900,000 for 5 grants (high:
$300,000; low: $50,000) and $692,233 for 177
grants to individuals (high: $32,697; low: $141).
Purpose and activities: Grants limited to
individuals who have been verifiable employees
of the Morton Salt Co. since or before June 30,

1971, to assist with hospital, medical, and
surgical expenses, as well as assistance to the
aged, blind, or disabled.
Fields of interest: Natural resources; Food
services; Domestic violence; Women,
centers/services; Disabled; Aging; Economically
disadvantaged.
Types of support: Grants to individuals.
Limitations: Giving primarily in LA and TX.
Officers and Directors:* Scott Ellwood,* Pres.;
William J. Cooney,* V.P.; John C. Hedley,* V.P.;
Davis H. Roenisch,* V.P.; Leonard E. Zak,* V.P.;
Janet E. Hutzler, Secy.-Treas.
Number of staff: 2.
EIN: 237181380

1059
James & Aune Nelson Foundation
P.O. Box 5146
Godfrey, IL 62035

Donor(s): Aune Nelson.‡
Grantmaker type: Independent foundation
Financial data (yr. ended 12/31/01): Assets,
$20,237,920 (M); expenditures, $1,307,872;
qualifying distributions, $1,284,680; giving
activities include $1,281,000 for 8 grants (high:
$335,000; low: $7,000).
Purpose and activities: Giving primarily for
conservation.
Fields of interest: Natural resources.
Limitations: Applications not accepted. Giving
primarily in IL. No grants to individuals.
Application information: Contributes only to
pre-selected organizations.
Officers: Robert Freeman, Pres.; James Struif,
V.P.; William Hoagland, Secy.; Marcus Sessel,
Treas.
Directors: Wayne Freeman; Annie Hoagland;
Paivi Pulkkinen.
EIN: 371371840

1060
Neuman Family Foundation
3711 RFD
Long Grove, IL 60047

Established in 1998 in IL.
Grantmaker type: Independent foundation
Financial data (yr. ended 12/31/02): Assets,
$4,165,210 (M); expenditures, $209,422;
qualifying distributions, $173,531; giving
activities include $175,000 for 5 grants (high:
$62,500; low: $2,500).
Purpose and activities: Giving primarily for
education, the environment, and human
services.
Fields of interest: Arts; Education; Environment;
Human services.
Limitations: Applications not accepted. Giving
primarily in Chicago, IL; some giving also in CA,
CO, and NY. No grants to individuals.
Application information: Unsolicited requests
for funds not accepted.
Trustees: Judith Neuman; Suzanne Neuman;
Werner Neuman; William Neuman.
EIN: 367234939

1061
Lawrence S. Newmark and Gloria Newmark Foundation
c/o Barry D. Elman
222 N. LaSalle St., Ste. 1900
Chicago, IL 60601

Established around 1995 in IL.
Grantmaker type: Independent foundation
Financial data (yr. ended 03/31/02): Assets,
$3,506,211 (M); expenditures, $222,920;
qualifying distributions, $179,612; giving
activities include $181,450 for 56 grants (high:
$50,000; low: $200).
Purpose and activities: Giving primarily for arts
and culture, medical research, human services
and Jewish agencies.
Fields of interest: Arts; Animal welfare;
Hospitals (general); Health organizations,
association; Medical research, institute; Human
services; Jewish federated giving programs;
Jewish agencies & temples.
Limitations: Applications not accepted. Giving
primarily in Chicago, IL. No grants to
individuals.
Application information: Contributes only to
pre-selected organizations.
Trustees: Barry D. Elman; Marvin S. Fenchel.
EIN: 363968578

1062
Norwell Fund
c/o Ravid and Bernstein
230 W. Monroe, Ste. 330
Chicago, IL 60606
Contact: Farwell Smith, Pres.

Established in 1963 in IL.
Donor(s): Farwell Smith, Nora Stone Smith.‡
Grantmaker type: Independent foundation
Financial data (yr. ended 12/31/02): Assets,
$334,154 (M); gifts received, $129,048;
expenditures, $185,996; qualifying distributions,
$182,086; giving activities include $182,289 for
67 grants (high: $42,500; low: $25).
Fields of interest: Education; Natural resources;
Environment; Animals/wildlife,
preservation/protection; Medical research,
institute.
Limitations: Giving on a national basis. No
grants to individuals.
Application information:
  Initial approach: Letter
  Deadline(s): None
Officers: Farwell Smith, Pres.; Linda McMullen,
V.P.
Director: George W. Overton.
EIN: 366063686

1063
Norwottock Charitable Trust
643 W. Arlington Pl.
Chicago, IL 60614-2611 (312) 404-5566
Contact: John L. Simmons or Adele Smith
Simmons, Trustees

Established in 1986 in MA.
Donor(s): John L. Simmons, Adele Smith
Simmons.
Grantmaker type: Independent foundation
Financial data (yr. ended 12/31/02): Assets,
$582,887 (M); gifts received, $53,945;

expenditures, $286,275; qualifying distributions, $279,133; giving activities include $274,315 for 81 grants (high: $50,000; low: $40).
Fields of interest: Museums; Higher education; Education; Environment; International peace/security; International affairs; Human services; Federated giving programs.
Limitations: Giving primarily in MA.
Application information:
Deadline(s): None
Trustees: Adele Smith Simmons; John L. Simmons.
EIN: 046561597

1064
Oberweiler Foundation
18 E. Dundee Rd., Ste. 204
Barrington, IL 60010

Established in 2000 in IL.
Donor(s): Siegfried Weiler.
Grantmaker type: Independent foundation
Financial data (yr. ended 12/31/02): Assets, $8,359,628 (M); expenditures, $638,138; qualifying distributions, $397,364; giving activities include $299,813 for 17 grants (high: $110,376; low: $100).
Fields of interest: Environment; Health organizations, association; Children/youth, services.
Limitations: Applications not accepted. Giving primarily in Chicago, IL. No grants to individuals.
Application information: Contributes only to pre-selected organizations.
Officers and Directors:* Siegfried Weiler,* Pres.; James R. Bartell,* V.P.; Anna Weiler, Secy.; Ruth S. Flynn; Ronald Ohlsen.
EIN: 364376705

1065
The Offield Family Foundation ▼
400 N. Michigan Ave., Rm. 407
Chicago, IL 60611

Incorporated in 1940 in IL.
Donor(s): Dorothy Wrigley Offield.
Grantmaker type: Independent foundation
Financial data (yr. ended 06/30/02): Assets, $93,738,656 (M); gifts received, $3,042,062; expenditures, $7,524,453; qualifying distributions, $7,204,417; giving activities include $7,089,456 for 69 grants (high: $1,007,868; low: $500; average: $5,000–$100,000).
Purpose and activities: Emphasis on hospitals, a family planning agency, education, and cultural programs.
Fields of interest: Arts; Education; Hospitals (general).
Limitations: Applications not accepted. Giving primarily in AZ, CA, the Chicago, IL, area and MI. No grants to individuals.
Application information: Contributes only to pre-selected organizations.
Officers and Directors:* Paxson H. Offield, Pres.; James S. Offield,* V.P.; Marie Larson,* Secy.; Raymond H. Drymalski,* Treas.; Chase Offield; Meighan Offield.
EIN: 366066240
Recent environmental and animal welfare grants:

1065-1 Aspen Center for Environmental Studies, Aspen, CO, $15,000. 2002.
1065-2 Aspen Valley Land Trust, Aspen, CO, $20,000. 2002.
1065-3 Billfish Foundation, Fort Lauderdale, FL, $200,000. 2002.
1065-4 Camp Daggett, Petoskey, MI, $25,000. 2002.
1065-5 Catalina Sea Bass Fund, Avalon, CA, $100,000. 2002.
1065-6 Elephant Sanctuary in Hohenwald, Hohenwald, TN, $25,000. 2002.
1065-7 Hidden Harbor Marine Environmental Project, Marathon, FL, $50,000. 2002.
1065-8 Humane Society, Little Traverse Bay, Harbor Springs, MI, $10,000. 2002.
1065-9 Little Traverse Conservancy, Harbor Springs, MI, $1,007,868. For grant made in form of stock. 2002.
1065-10 Ocean Futures Society, Santa Barbara, CA, $292,500. 2002.
1065-11 Peregrine Fund, Boise, ID, $299,382. For grant made in form of stock. 2002.
1065-12 Pfleger Institute for Environmental Research, Newport Beach, CA, $372,759. For grant made in form of stock. 2002.
1065-13 Pfleger Institute for Environmental Research, Newport Beach, CA, $120,000. 2002.
1065-14 Santa Catalina Island Conservancy, Avalon, CA, $249,485. For grant made in form of stock. 2002.
1065-15 Surfrider Foundation, San Clemente, CA, $100,000. 2002.
1065-16 Tiger Haven, Kingston, TN, $25,000. 2002.
1065-17 Tip of the Mitt Watershed Council, Petoskey, MI, $100,000. 2002.
1065-18 United Anglers of Southern California, Long Beach, CA, $50,000. 2002.
1065-19 University of Southern California, Wrigley Institute of Environmental Studies, Los Angeles, CA, $698,557. For grant made in form of stock. 2002.
1065-20 Zoological Society of San Diego, Center for the Reproduction of Endangered Species, San Diego, CA, $125,000. 2002.

1066
Katherine L. Olson Charitable Foundation
707 Skokie Blvd., Ste. 420
Northbrook, IL 60062

Established in 1986 in IL.
Donor(s): Katherine L. Olson.
Grantmaker type: Independent foundation
Financial data (yr. ended 12/31/00): Assets, $3,300,042 (M); gifts received, $300,000; expenditures, $121,664; qualifying distributions, $121,664; giving activities include $106,905 for 103 grants (high: $10,500; low: $150).
Purpose and activities: Giving for the arts, education, and health associations.
Fields of interest: Arts education; Radio; Ballet; Arts; Higher education; Education; Botanical/horticulture/landscape services; Hospitals (general); Health care; Christian agencies & churches.
Types of support: General/operating support.
Limitations: Applications not accepted. Giving primarily in Chicago, IL. No grants to individuals.

Application information: Contributes only to pre-selected organizations.
Trustee: Katherine L. Olson.
EIN: 366857384

1067
The OMC Foundation
(formerly The Ole Evinrude Foundation)
c/o Dir., Public Affairs
100 Sea Horse Dr.
Waukegan, IL 60085 (847) 689-7165

Incorporated in 1945 in WI.
Donor(s): Outboard Marine Corp.
Grantmaker type: Independent foundation
Financial data (yr. ended 09/30/02): Assets, $4,943,656 (M); expenditures, $266,649; qualifying distributions, $224,923; giving activities include $135,000 for 2 grants (high: $85,000; low: $50,000) and $89,500 for 64 grants to individuals (high: $3,000; low: $500).
Purpose and activities: Support of private higher education, especially business and engineering, in states in which the company operates, scholarship aid to children of company employees, and capital grants to hospital and cultural building projects in company locations; support also for recreation and environmental programs.
Fields of interest: Arts; Secondary school/education; Higher education; Business school/education; Engineering school/education; Environment; Hospitals (general); Recreation; Human services; Engineering.
Types of support: Continuing support; Annual campaigns; Capital campaigns; Building/renovation; Equipment; Program development; Seed money; Scholarship funds; Research; Employee matching gifts; Employee-related scholarships.
Limitations: Giving limited to areas of company operations, with emphasis on FL, GA, IL, IN, NC, SC, and WI. No support for organizations participating in local combined appeals. No grants to individuals (except for employee-related scholarships), or for endowment funds or operating expenses; no loans.
Application information: Application form not required.
Initial approach: Letter
Copies of proposal: 1
Deadline(s): Submit proposal preferably in Aug.; deadline Sept. 15
Board meeting date(s): 1st week of Dec.
Final notification: 30 days after annual meeting
Officer and Directors:* Kim Bors,* Pres.; Gordon Repp,* Secy.; Terry Ellis,* Treas.
EIN: 396037139

1068
OMRON Foundation, Inc.
c/o OMRON Electronics, Inc.
1 E. Commerce Dr.
Schaumburg, IL 60173 (847) 843-7900
Contact: Frank Newburn
FAX: (847) 240-5362

Established in 1989 in IL.

Donor(s): OMRON Systems, Inc., OMRON Management Center of America, OMRON Systems of America, Inc., OMRON Healthcare, Inc., OMRON Advanced Systems, Inc., OMRON Office Automation Products, Inc., OMRON Automotive Electronics, OMRON Electronics, Inc.
Grantmaker type: Company-sponsored foundation
Financial data (yr. ended 03/31/02): Assets, $1,130,770 (M); gifts received, $346,519; expenditures, $436,232; qualifying distributions, $433,659; giving activities include $433,843 for 165 grants (high: $50,000; low: $15).
Purpose and activities: Primary areas of interest include higher and other education, the handicapped, cultural programs, the environment, and the elderly.
Fields of interest: Museums; Performing arts; Music; Humanities; Language/linguistics; Literature; Arts; Education, fund raising; Early childhood education; Child development, education; Secondary school/education; Higher education; Adult/continuing education; Libraries/library science; Education; Natural resources; Energy; Environment; Animals/wildlife, preservation/protection; Medical care, rehabilitation; Health care; Substance abuse, services; Mental health/crisis services; Health organizations, association; Cancer; Alcoholism; Biomedicine; Medical research, institute; Cancer research; Employment; Safety/disasters; Youth development, citizenship; Human services; Children/youth, services; Child development, services; Hospices; Aging, centers/services; Women, centers/services; Minorities/immigrants, centers/services; Homeless, human services; International economic development; International peace/security; Foreign policy; International human rights; International affairs; Race/intergroup relations; Civil rights; Community development; Voluntarism promotion; Federated giving programs; Engineering/technology; Science; Population studies; Public policy, research; Public affairs, citizen participation; Public affairs; Minorities; Disabled; Aging; Women; Immigrants/refugees; Homeless.
International interests: Asia; Japan.
Types of support: General/operating support; Continuing support; Building/renovation; Scholarship funds; Employee matching gifts; Employee-related scholarships; In-kind gifts.
Limitations: Giving primarily in Chicago, IL; minor support for organizations outside IL. No grants to individuals (except for employee-related scholarships).
Publications: Application guidelines, Grants list, Informational brochure, Program policy statement.
Application information: Application form not required.
   Initial approach: Letter
   Deadline(s): None
   Board meeting date(s): Quarterly
Officers: Yoshio Tateisi, Pres.; Hideki Masuda, V.P.; Masatoshi Yajima, Secy.; Takashi Kasai, Treas.
Directors: Nicholas Hahn; Kazuo Saito; Soichi Yukawa.
EIN: 363644055

1069
The Oppenheimer Family Foundation
1501 N. State Pkwy., Ste. 11B
Chicago, IL 60610
Contact: Edward H. Oppenheimer, Pres.
Application address: P.O. Box 14471, Chicago, IL 60614; FAX: (312) 943-9472

Incorporated in 1953 in IL.
Donor(s): Seymour Oppenheimer,‡ Edward H. Oppenheimer, James K. Oppenheimer, Harry D. Oppenheimer.
Grantmaker type: Independent foundation
Financial data (yr. ended 12/31/02): Assets, $5,689,930 (M); gifts received, $950; expenditures, $749,532; qualifying distributions, $689,464; giving activities include $693,427 for 71 grants (high: $200,250; low: $400).
Purpose and activities: Support for precollegiate education, the environment, and crime prevention.
Fields of interest: Elementary school/education; Secondary school/education; Environment; Crime/violence prevention.
Limitations: Giving primarily in Chicago, IL.
Application information: Application form not required.
   Initial approach: Letter
   Copies of proposal: 1
   Deadline(s): None
Officers and Directors:* Edward H. Oppenheimer,* Pres.; Harry D. Oppenheimer,* V.P.; James K. Oppenheimer,* V.P.; William J. Garmisa,* Secy.
Number of staff: None.
EIN: 366054015

1070
Parker Family Foundation
c/o The Northern Trust Bank, N.A.
50 S. LaSalle St., Ste. L-5
Chicago, IL 60675

Established in 1999 in CA.
Donor(s): Gerald Hans Parker, Carol Ellen Parker.
Grantmaker type: Independent foundation
Financial data (yr. ended 09/30/02): Assets, $1,868,390 (M); expenditures, $130,774; qualifying distributions, $115,202; giving activities include $110,500 for 16 grants (high: $30,000; low: $1,000).
Fields of interest: Museums; Opera; Elementary/secondary education; Higher education; Natural resources; Engineering/technology.
Limitations: Applications not accepted. Giving primarily in CA. No grants to individuals.
Application information: Contributes only to pre-selected organizations.
Trustees: Carol Ellen Parker; Gerald Hans Parker; The Northern Trust Co.
EIN: 946746143

1071
Frank E. Payne and Seba B. Payne Foundation ▼
c/o Bank of America
231 S. LaSalle St.
Chicago, IL 60697 (312) 828-1785
Contact: M. Catherine Ryan, 2nd V.P., Bank of America

Trust established in 1962 in IL.
Donor(s): Seba B. Payne.‡
Grantmaker type: Independent foundation
Financial data (yr. ended 06/30/02): Assets, $124,431,458 (M); expenditures, $8,249,253; qualifying distributions, $7,614,362; giving activities include $7,631,100 for 63 grants (high: $2,300,000; low: $5,000; average: $500–$150,000).
Purpose and activities: Support for education, hospitals, and cultural and religious programs; support also for the prevention of cruelty to children or animals.
Fields of interest: Arts; Education; Animal welfare; Hospitals (general); AIDS; AIDS research; Children/youth, services.
Types of support: General/operating support; Building/renovation; Equipment.
Limitations: Giving primarily in the metropolitan Chicago, IL, area and PA. No grants to individuals, or for fellowships; generally no support for endowments; no loans.
Publications: Application guidelines.
Application information: Application form not required.
   Initial approach: Proposal
   Copies of proposal: 1
   Deadline(s): None
   Board meeting date(s): May and Nov., and as
     required
   Final notification: 4 months
Trustees: Susan Hurd Cummings; George Hurd, Sr.; Priscilla Payne Hurd; Bank of America.
Number of staff: None.
EIN: 237435471
Recent environmental and animal welfare grants:
1071-1 Adopt-A-Pet, Irwin, PA, $10,000. 2002.
1071-2 Hawk Mountain Sanctuary Association, Kempton, PA, $100,000. 2002.
1071-3 Trails End Wildlife Refuge, Martinsville, Indiana, $10,000. 2002.
1071-4 Wildlands Conservancy, Emmaus, PA, $25,000. 2002.

1072
Pioneer Foundation
(formerly Reichert Family Foundation)
c/o Clifton Gunderson, LLP
1301 W., 22nd St., Ste. 1100
Oak Brook, IL 60523

Established in 1994 in IL.
Donor(s): Elizabeth S. Reichert.
Grantmaker type: Independent foundation
Financial data (yr. ended 12/31/01): Assets, $252,281 (M); expenditures, $177,875; qualifying distributions, $175,609; giving activities include $175,705 for 5 grants (high: $100,705; low: $10,000).
Fields of interest: Elementary/secondary education; Animals/wildlife, preservation/protection.

Types of support: General/operating support; Annual campaigns; Capital campaigns.
Limitations: Applications not accepted. Giving primarily in Denver, CO, Park City, UT, and Owings Mills, MD. No grants to individuals.
Application information: Contributes only to pre-selected organizations.
Trustee: James D. Reichert.
EIN: 367093680

1073
Frederick Pitzman Fund
(formerly Pitzman Fund)
c/o Bank of America
231 S. LaSalle St.
Chicago, IL 60697
Contact: Ellen Crabtree, V.P., Bank of America
Application address: c/o Bank of America, 100 N. Broadway, St. Louis, MO 63178, tel.: (314) 466-3416

Established in 1944.
Donor(s): Frederick Pitzman.‡
Grantmaker type: Independent foundation
Financial data (yr. ended 09/30/01): Assets, $6,516,083 (M); expenditures, $269,622; qualifying distributions, $256,082; giving activities include $256,500 for 15 grants (high: $100,000; low: $500).
Purpose and activities: Giving primarily for education, health, and human services.
Fields of interest: Arts; Education; Botanical gardens; Environment; Zoos/zoological societies; Family planning; Health care; Human services; Children/youth, services; Protestant agencies & churches.
Types of support: General/operating support; Continuing support; Annual campaigns.
Limitations: Giving primarily in St. Louis, MO.
Application information: Application form not required.
Deadline(s): None
Trustees: Caroline P. Early; Gilbert Gordon Early; Bank of America.
Number of staff: None.
EIN: 436023901

1074
Ploughshares Foundation
108 W. Grand Ave.
Chicago, IL 60610 (312) 321-9700
Contact: Donald M. Ephraim, Pres.

Established in 1990 in IL.
Grantmaker type: Independent foundation
Financial data (yr. ended 12/31/02): Assets, $29,751,793 (M); expenditures, $1,963,598; qualifying distributions, $1,784,668; giving activities include $1,802,000 for 91 grants (high: $130,000; low: $2,000; average: $5,000–$100,000).
Fields of interest: Environment; AIDS; Human services; Race/intergroup relations; Homeless.
Types of support: General/operating support.
Limitations: Giving on a national basis. No grants to individuals.
Application information: Application form not required.
Initial approach: Proposal
Deadline(s): None
Officer and Directors:* Donald M. Ephraim,* Pres.; Joseph F. Coyne; Eliot S. Ephraim.

EIN: 363739577

1075
Vivian Porch Welfare League Trust
c/o Bank of America
231 S. LaSalle St.
Chicago, IL 60697-0246

Established in 1991.
Grantmaker type: Public charity
Financial data (yr. ended 08/31/02): Revenue, $241,882; assets, $5,345,461; expenditures, $208,764; program services expenses, $172,255; giving activities include $168,283 for 1 grant.
Purpose and activities: The league exists for the sole benefit of the Illinois Citizen's Animal Welfare League.
Fields of interest: Animal welfare.
Limitations: Applications not accepted. Giving limited to Chicago Ridge, IL.
Application information: Contributes only to a pre-selected organization; unsolicited requests for funds not considered or acknowledged.
Trustee: Bank of America.
EIN: 366937543

1076
Prince Charitable Trusts ▼
303 W. Madison St., Ste. 1900
Chicago, IL 60606 (312) 419-8700
Contact: Benna Wilde, Managing Dir.
FAX: (312) 419-8558; Additional address: Prince Charitable Trusts, 816 Connecticut Ave., N.W., Washington, DC 20006, Tel.: (202) 728-0646; E-mail: bwilde@prince-trusts.org (Chicago office), Kpauly@princetrusts.org (DC office); URL: http://www.fdncenter.org/grantmaker/prince/

Frederick Henry Prince Trust dated July 9, 1947 established in 1947 in IL. Frederick Henry Prince Testamentary Trust established in 1947 in RI. Abbie Norman Prince Trust established in 1949 in IL.
Donor(s): Frederick Henry Prince.‡
Grantmaker type: Independent foundation
Financial data (yr. ended 12/31/01): Assets, $172,018,698 (M); expenditures, $7,502,387; qualifying distributions, $7,379,035; giving activities include $6,537,822 for 321 grants (high: $550,000; low: $100; average: $5,000–$50,000).
Purpose and activities: Support for cultural programs, public school programming, youth organizations, social services, hospitals, hospital morale, rehabilitation, and environment.
Fields of interest: Arts; Early childhood education; Elementary school/education; Secondary school/education; Education; Natural resources; Environment; Hospitals (general); Family planning; Medical care, rehabilitation; Health care; Human services; Children/youth, services; Youth, pregnancy prevention; Family services; Minorities; Economically disadvantaged; Homeless.
Types of support: General/operating support; Continuing support; Capital campaigns; Program development; Seed money; Technical assistance; Program-related investments/loans.
Limitations: Giving limited to local groups in Washington, DC, Chicago, IL, and RI, with

emphasis on Aquidneck Island. No support for national organizations. No grants to individuals.
Publications: Application guidelines.
Application information: The DC office has its own application guidelines. All applications must include a cover sheet which can be found at the trust's Web site or by contacting the Grants Mgr. Application form not required.
Initial approach: Letter and proposal (3 to 5 pages for proposal)
Copies of proposal: 1
Deadline(s): Chicago: Jan. 13 for Health, Educ., and Soc. Svcs., June 30 for Envir., Arts and Capital; Rhode Island: June 1; Washington, DC: Feb. 1 for Envir., Arts and Capital, Sept. 1 for Health, Soc. Svcs. and Educ.
Board meeting date(s): Chicago: spring and fall; Rhode Island: summer; Washington, DC: late spring and late fall
Final notification: Within 5 months of proposal deadline
Trustees: Frederick Henry Prince IV; William Norman Wood Prince.
Number of staff: 3 full-time professional; 2 part-time professional; 1 full-time support; 1 part-time support.
Recent environmental and animal welfare grants:
1076-1 American Farmland Trust, DC, $10,000. For Virginia Rural Lands Program. 2002.
1076-2 Aquidneck Island Land Trust, Middletown, RI, $2,500,000. For easements and land on Aquidneck Island. 2002.
1076-3 Aquidneck Island Land Trust, Middletown, RI, $250,000. For operating support. 2002.
1076-4 Audubon Naturalist Society of the Central Atlantic States, Chevy Chase, MD, $30,000. For general operating support. 2002.
1076-5 Audubon Society of Chicago, Chicago, IL, $15,000. For Chicago Habitat Stewards. 2002.
1076-6 Bull Run Mountains Conservancy, Broad Run, VA, $10,000. For general operating support. 2002.
1076-7 Canal Corridor Association, Chicago, IL, $30,000. For Canal Origins Park. 2002.
1076-8 Chesapeake Bay Foundation, Annapolis, MD, $25,000. For lands program support. 2002.
1076-9 Chicago Botanic Garden, Glencoe, IL, $15,000. For School Garden Initiative. 2002.
1076-10 Clean Water Fund, DC, $20,000. For general operating support. 2002.
1076-11 Conservation Law Foundation, Boston, MA, $40,000. To establish fully staffed office of Conservation Law Foundation in Rhode Island. 2002.
1076-12 Conservation Law Foundation, Boston, MA, $10,000. For operating support. 2002.
1076-13 Discovery Creek Childrens Museum, DC, $10,000. For DC Public School Outreach. 2002.
1076-14 Earth Conservation Corps, DC, $10,000. For RiverLife Expeditions. 2002.
1076-15 Earthjustice Legal Defense Fund, DC, $25,000. For general operating support for office's transportation program. 2002.
1076-16 Environmental Defense, DC, $30,000. For transportation program. 2002.
1076-17 Environmental Law and Policy Center of the Midwest, Chicago, IL, $25,000. For operating support. 2002.

1076-18 Friends of Conservation, Oak Brook, IL, $15,000. For Kenya Rhino Management Program. 2002.

1076-19 Friends of the Chicago River, Chicago, IL, $15,000. For operating support. 2002.

1076-20 Funders Network for Smart Growth and Livable Communities, Coral Gables, FL, $15,000. For general operating support. 2002.

1076-21 Garfield Park Conservatory Alliance, Chicago, IL, $20,000. For operating support. 2002.

1076-22 George Washington University, Law School, Center on Sustainability and Regional Growth, DC, $10,000. For International Forum on Sustainable Cities. 2002.

1076-23 Grow Smart Rhode Island, Providence, RI, $35,000. For operating support. 2002.

1076-24 Lake Michigan Federation, Chicago, IL, $20,000. For southeast Chicago open space initiative. 2002.

1076-25 Land Trust Alliance, DC, $20,000. For Mid-Atlantic program support. 2002.

1076-26 Lincoln Park Zoo, Chicago, IL, $15,000. For operating support. 2002.

1076-27 National Fish and Wildlife Foundation, DC, $10,000. For general operating support. 2002.

1076-28 New England Aquarium, Boston, MA, $10,000. For operating support for Newport Exploration Center. 2002.

1076-29 Norman Bird Sanctuary, Providence, RI, $250,000. For restoration of Paradise Farm. 2002.

1076-30 Oatlands, Leesburg, VA, $25,000. For Campaign to Save Oatlands Scenic Vistas. 2002.

1076-31 Openlands Project, Chicago, IL, $30,000. For GreenNet mini-grants program. 2002.

1076-32 Openlands Project, Chicago, IL, $25,000. For Urban Greening Program. 2002.

1076-33 Piedmont Environmental Council, Warrenton, VA, $180,000. For general operating support. 2002.

1076-34 Piedmont Environmental Council, Warrenton, VA, $120,000. For Coalition for Smarter Growth. 2002.

1076-35 Piedmont Environmental Council, Warrenton, VA, $10,000. For Save the Cities and You Save the Country. 2002.

1076-36 Piedmont Environmental Council, Warrenton, VA, $10,000. For Save the Cities and You Save the Country Thank You Abe. 2002.

1076-37 Potomac Conservancy, Annandale, VA, $10,000. For operating support. 2002.

1076-38 Potomac Riverkeeper, Rockville, MD, $10,000. For general operating support. 2002.

1076-39 Potter League for Animals, Middletown, RI, $10,000. For operating support. 2002.

1076-40 Preservation Society of Newport County, Newport, RI, $25,000. For Tree and Landscape Preservation Program. 2002.

1076-41 Providence Health Foundation, DC, $41,320. For Healing Garden. 2002.

1076-42 Rhode Island Tree Council, Providence, RI, $15,000. Toward endowment for Rhode Island Tree Stewards Education Program. 2002.

1076-43 Sakonnet Preservation Association, Little Compton, RI, $10,000. For one-time grant for inventory of open space surrounding Watson Reservoir. 2002.

1076-44 Save Blithewold, Bristol, RI, $50,000. For capital campaign for Greenhouse. 2002.

1076-45 Save the Bay, Providence, RI, $650,000. Toward Explore the Bay capital campaign. 2002.

1076-46 Save the Bay, Providence, RI, $45,000. For operating support. 2002.

1076-47 Scenic America, DC, $40,000. For resources survey of Journey Through Hallowed Ground corridor. 2002.

1076-48 Sierra Club, San Francisco, CA, $20,000. For Transportation Reform Project. 2002.

1076-49 Sierra Club Foundation, DC, $20,000. For Sustainable Washington Project. 2002.

1076-50 Southeast Environmental Task Force, Chicago, IL, $10,000. For Calumet open space enhancement program. 2002.

1076-51 Southern Environmental Law Center, DC, $15,000. For Western Transportation Corridor and Piedmont Virginia issues. 2002.

1076-52 Student Conservation Association, DC, $10,000. For National Capital Region Urban and Diversity Outreach. 2002.

1076-53 University of Rhode Island, Kingston, RI, $40,000. For Aquidneck Island West Side Master Plan. 2002.

1076-54 Urban Land Institute, DC, $20,000. For Smart Growth Alliance. 2002.

1076-55 Washington Regional Network for Livable Communities, DC, $30,000. For general operating support. 2002.

1077
Pritzker Foundation ▼
200 W. Madison St., 25th Fl.
Chicago, IL 60606 (312) 750-8400
Contact: Glen Miller, V.P.

Incorporated in 1944 in IL.
Donor(s): Members of the Pritzker family, H. Group Holding, Inc. and Subsidiaries, Marmon Holdings, Inc. and Subsidiaries.
Grantmaker type: Independent foundation
Financial data (yr. ended 12/31/01): Assets, $618,823,133 (M); gifts received, $820,677; expenditures, $15,487,043; qualifying distributions, $11,249,625; giving activities include $11,155,783 for 163 grants (high: $2,000,000; low: $100; average: $1,000–$100,000).
Purpose and activities: Grants largely for higher education, including medical education, and religious welfare funds; giving also for hospitals, temple support, and cultural programs.
Fields of interest: Arts; Higher education; Medical school/education; Hospitals (general); Human services; Religious federated giving programs; Jewish agencies & temples.
Limitations: Applications not accepted. Giving on a national basis, with some emphasis on Chicago, IL. No grants to individuals.
Application information: Contributes only to pre-selected organizations.
Board meeting date(s): Dec. and as required
Officers and Directors:* Robert A. Pritzker,* Pres.; Mark Hoplamazian, V.P. and Secy.; Glen Miller, V.P. and Treas.; Nicholas J. Pritzker,* V.P.; Penny S. Pritzker,* V.P.; Thomas J. Pritzker,* V.P.

Number of staff: None.
EIN: 366058062
Recent environmental and animal welfare grants:
1077-1 Conservation International, DC, $1,000,000. For general operating support. 2001.
1077-2 Corporation for Open Lands (CorLands), Chicago, IL, $10,000. For general operating support. 2001.
1077-3 John G. Shedd Aquarium, Chicago, IL, $400,000. For general operating support. 2001.
1077-4 Lincoln Park Zoological Society, Chicago, IL, $100,000. For general operating support. 2001.
1077-5 Lincoln Park, Friends of, Chicago, IL, $33,000. For Lily Pool Restoration Project. 2001.

1078
Relations Foundation
205 N. Wabash Ave., Ste. 1800
Chicago, IL 60601 (312) 647-5765
Contact: Iris Kreig

Established in 1969 in IL.
Grantmaker type: Independent foundation
Financial data (yr. ended 12/31/01): Assets, $5,521,228 (M); gifts received, $350,000; expenditures, $898,966; qualifying distributions, $798,500; giving activities include $798,500 for 76 grants (high: $110,000; low: $1,000; average: $3,000–$6,000).
Purpose and activities: Giving primarily to Jewish causes; support also for medical research and social service agencies.
Fields of interest: Environment; Human services; Reproductive rights; Jewish agencies & temples; Women.
International interests: Israel.
Types of support: Continuing support; General/operating support; Program development; Seed money; Matching/challenge support.
Limitations: Giving primarily in the Chicago, IL, area. No grants to individuals, or for endowment funds; no loans.
Publications: Application guidelines.
Application information: Application form not required.
Initial approach: Proposal
Copies of proposal: 1
Deadline(s): Apr. 1, July 1, and Oct. 1
Board meeting date(s): May, Aug., and Dec.
Officers and Directors:* Barbara Kessler,* Pres.; Dennis L. Kessler,* V.P.; Joseph Radov,* V.P.; Sylvia M. Radov,* V.P.; David A. Weinberg,* Treas.; Jerry Newton; Lewis Weinberg.
Number of staff: 2 shared staff.
EIN: 237032294

1079
Roberts Family Foundation
c/o Bank of America
231 S. LaSalle St.
Chicago, IL 60697 (312) 828-8028
Contact: Charles Slamar, Jr.

Established in 1997 in IL.
Donor(s): Ann W. Roberts.
Grantmaker type: Independent foundation

Financial data (yr. ended 04/30/03): Assets, $2,327,701 (M); expenditures, $157,244; qualifying distributions, $137,105; giving activities include $134,500 for 55 grants (high: $8,000; low: $1,000).
Fields of interest: Museums; Performing arts; Arts; Elementary/secondary education; University; Education; Botanical gardens; Hospitals (general); Human services; Children/youth, services; Foundations (public); Protestant agencies & churches.
Limitations: Giving primarily in FL, IL, MA, and NJ.
Application information: Application form not required.
  Deadline(s): None
Managers: Ann W. Roberts; John H. Roberts.
Trustee: Bank of America.
EIN: 367186052

1080
Rohlen Foundation
1504 N. Wells St.
Chicago, IL 60610
Contact: Frances Ann Rohlen, Mgr.

Established in 1967 in IL.
Donor(s): Frances P. Rohlen,‡ Karl V. Rohlen,‡ Frances Ann Rohlen, Karl V. Rohlen, Jr., Thomas P. Rohlen.
Grantmaker type: Independent foundation
Financial data (yr. ended 12/31/01): Assets, $2,270,056 (M); expenditures, $106,725; qualifying distributions, $96,900; giving activities include $96,900 for 34 grants (high: $20,000; low: $500).
Fields of interest: Arts; Higher education; Animals/wildlife; Health organizations, association; Human services; Youth, services.
Limitations: Giving primarily in the Chicago, IL, area. No grants to individuals, or for research or scholarships.
Application information: Application form not required.
  Initial approach: Letter
  Copies of proposal: 1
  Deadline(s): None
  Board meeting date(s): Quarterly
Officers and Directors:* Frances Ann Rohlen,* Pres.; Thomas P. Rohlen,* V.P.; Karl V. Rohlen, Jr.,* Secy.
Number of staff: None.
EIN: 366161800

1081
Benjamin J. Rosenthal Foundation
P.O. Box 166037
Chicago, IL 60616-6037

Incorporated in 1922 in IL.
Donor(s): Benjamin J. Rosenthal.‡
Grantmaker type: Independent foundation
Financial data (yr. ended 12/31/02): Assets, $5,018,676 (M); expenditures, $534,200; qualifying distributions, $458,178; giving activities include $393,750 for 137 grants (high: $50,000; low: $500).
Purpose and activities: Support primarily for youth, child welfare, human services, arts and culture, and protection of animals.
Fields of interest: Arts; Scholarships/financial aid; Education; Natural resources; Animal

welfare; Animals/wildlife, preservation/protection; Human services; Children/youth, services.
Limitations: Applications not accepted. Giving on a national basis, with emphasis on Chicago, IL, and Washington, DC. No grants to individuals.
Application information: Contributes only to pre-selected organizations.
Officers: Elaine Broadhead, Chair.; Melissa Foulke, Pres. and Treas.; Walter Roth, Secy.
Trustee: Joseph Glossberg.
EIN: 362523643

1082
Rossetter Foundation
c/o Jerry D. Jones
200 W. Adams St., Ste. 2600
Chicago, IL 60606

Established in 1992.
Donor(s): Thomas B. Rossetter, Roberta B. Rossetter, Laura Rossetter.
Grantmaker type: Independent foundation
Financial data (yr. ended 12/31/02): Assets, $2,244,653 (M); expenditures, $164,765; qualifying distributions, $146,089; giving activities include $139,000 for 28 grants (high: $25,000; low: $1,000).
Purpose and activities: Giving for education, nature conservation, children and family services, health, and community services.
Fields of interest: Elementary/secondary education; Natural resources; Foundations (community); Philanthropy/voluntarism.
Limitations: Applications not accepted. Giving primarily in CO and WY. No grants to individuals.
Application information: Contributes only to pre-selected organizations.
Officers and Directors:* Thomas B. Rossetter,* Pres.; Roberta B. Rossetter,* V.P. and Secy.-Treas.; Laura Rossetter, Exec. Dir.; Ellen Jebb Kelly; David B. Rossetter; Penny R. Rossetter; Stephen M. Rossetter.
EIN: 830299674

1083
A. Frank and Dorothy B. Rothschild Fund
c/o Melvin C. Rosenberg, Topel Forman, LLC
676 N. Saint Clair St., Ste. 2200
Chicago, IL 60611 (312) 726-5808

Established in 1952 in IL.
Donor(s): Dorothy B. Rothschild.
Grantmaker type: Independent foundation
Financial data (yr. ended 12/31/02): Assets, $2,572,271 (M); expenditures, $148,644; qualifying distributions, $146,177; giving activities include $144,475 for 125 grants (high: $50,000; low: $50).
Purpose and activities: Giving primarily for health care and various medical disciplines.
Fields of interest: Arts; Education; Environment; Animals/wildlife, preservation/protection; Hospitals (general); Health organizations, association; Human services; Jewish agencies & temples.
Limitations: Applications not accepted. Giving primarily in IL, MI, and NY. No grants to individuals.

Application information: Contributes only to pre-selected organizations.
Officers and Directors:* Dorothy B. Rothschild,* Pres.; A. Frank Rothschild, Jr.,* Secy.-Treas.; Henry DeVos Lawrie, Jr.
EIN: 366049231

1084
RREEF Outreach
875 N. Michigan Ave., 41st Fl.
Chicago, IL 60611

Established in 1994 in IL.
Donor(s): RREEF AMERICA, LLP.
Grantmaker type: Independent foundation
Financial data (yr. ended 12/31/01): Assets, $15,972 (M); gifts received, $158,333; expenditures, $169,461; qualifying distributions, $167,461; giving activities include $155,043 for 100 grants (high: $21,000; low: $25).
Purpose and activities: Giving for education, social outreach and community-based programs, health and medical agencies and programs, the environment, art programs, and to organizations serving the underprivileged.
Fields of interest: Arts; College; University; Environment; Hospitals (general); Health care; Children, services; Family services; Community development; Economically disadvantaged.
Limitations: Applications not accepted. Giving on a national basis. No grants to individuals.
Application information: Contributes only to pre-selected organizations.
Officers: Janemarie Dionne King, Pres.; Teresa Broccolo, V.P.; Barbara G. Callan, V.P.; Janet Caputo, V.P.; Alison Carbone, V.P.; Susan Cook, V.P.; Kathleen T. Egan, V.P.; Cathy Gonzalez, V.P.; Janet W. Greig, V.P.; Martha Hackett, V.P.; Margaret Kachadurian, V.P.; Suzanne J. King, V.P.; Melissa Lavender, V.P.; Rose Marie Leitner, V.P.; Carol A. Navratil, V.P.; Terry C. Sowden, V.P.; Sara Steppe, V.P.; Sandra S. Thompson, V.P.; Walter M. Rebovich, Secy.; Paula Ferkull, Treas.
Directors: Patrick J. Callan; Gerald E. Egan; Donald A. King, Jr.; James D. King; Stephen M. Steppe.
EIN: 363959216

1085
Salwil Foundation
c/o William L. Searle
400 Skokie Blvd., Ste. 300
Northbrook, IL 60062

Established in 1985 in IL.
Donor(s): William L. Searle.
Grantmaker type: Independent foundation
Financial data (yr. ended 12/31/02): Assets, $3,619,996 (M); expenditures, $257,723; qualifying distributions, $244,288; giving activities include $245,000 for 3 grants (high: $200,000; low: $20,000).
Purpose and activities: Giving primarily for conservation, education and health care.
Fields of interest: Education; Environment; Animals/wildlife, preservation/protection; Hospitals (general); Christian agencies & churches.
Types of support: General/operating support; Annual campaigns; Capital campaigns.
Limitations: Applications not accepted. Giving primarily in IL. No grants to individuals.

Application information: Contributes only to pre-selected organizations.
Officers and Directors:* S. Gunnar Klar,* Pres.; Marion S. Searle,* V.P.; Elizabeth B. Searle,* Secy.-Treas.; Bryan R. Dunn; Sally B. Searle; William L. Searle.
EIN: 363377945

1086
Schiff, Hardin & Waite Foundation
233 S. Wacker Dr., Ste. 6600
Chicago, IL 60606   (312) 876-1000

Established in 1986 in IL.
Donor(s): Schiff, Hardin & Waite.
Grantmaker type: Company-sponsored foundation
Financial data (yr. ended 11/30/02): Assets, $63,562 (M); gifts received, $136,260; expenditures, $114,796; qualifying distributions, $114,796; giving activities include $111,950 for 34 grants (high: $30,000; low: $150).
Purpose and activities: Giving for higher and legal education, civil rights and legal services, health and human services, and youth programs.
Fields of interest: Performing arts; Theater; Education, fund raising; Elementary/secondary education; Higher education; Natural resources; Food banks; Big Brothers/Big Sisters; Federated giving programs; Protestant agencies & churches; Roman Catholic agencies & churches; Jewish agencies & temples.
Limitations: Applications not accepted. Giving primarily in Chicago, IL. No grants to individuals.
Application information: Contributes only to pre-selected organizations.
Directors: Marci A. Eisenstein; Peter V. Fazio, Jr.; Scott E. Pickens; Robert H. Riley; Bruce P. Weisenthal.
EIN: 363465740

1087
Robert E. Schneider Foundation
150 E. Ontario St.
Chicago, IL 60611

Established in 1968 in IL.
Donor(s): Phyllis Schneider, Melvin Schneider.
Grantmaker type: Independent foundation
Financial data (yr. ended 12/31/02): Assets, $3,305,047 (M); expenditures, $205,125; qualifying distributions, $176,309; giving activities include $177,000 for 25 grants (high: $30,000; low: $1,000).
Purpose and activities: Giving primarily for children and youth.
Fields of interest: Education; Environment, water resources; Hospitals (general); Medical research, institute; Housing/shelter, development; Children/youth, services.
Limitations: Applications not accepted. Giving primarily in FL and IL. No grants to individuals.
Application information: Contributes only to pre-selected organizations.
Officers and Directors:* Richard Schneider,* Pres.; Claudia Schneider,* V.P.; Frederic Schneider,* V.P.; Marilyn R. Moss,* Secy.-Treas.
EIN: 366212061

1088
Dr. Scholl Foundation ▼
1033 Skokie Blvd., Ste. 230
Northbrook, IL 60062   (847) 559-7430
Contact: Pamela Scholl, Pres.
URL: http://www.drschollfoundation.com

Incorporated in 1947 in IL.
Donor(s): William M. Scholl.‡
Grantmaker type: Independent foundation
Financial data (yr. ended 12/31/01): Assets, $155,694,430 (M); expenditures, $10,432,033; qualifying distributions, $9,049,937; giving activities include $8,217,241 for 469+ grants (high: $300,000; average: $5,000–$100,000).
Purpose and activities: Support for private education at all levels, including elementary, secondary, and postsecondary schools, colleges and universities, and medical and nursing institutions; general charitable programs, including grants to hospitals, and programs for children, the developmentally disabled, and senior citizens; and civic, cultural, social welfare, economic, and religious activities.
Fields of interest: Film/video; Visual arts; Museums; Performing arts; Dance; Theater; History/archaeology; Arts; Elementary/secondary education; Early childhood education; Child development, education; Elementary school/education; Secondary school/education; Higher education; Business school/education; Law school/education; Medical school/education; Adult education—literacy, basic skills & GED; Libraries/library science; Reading; Education; Natural resources; Animal welfare; Hospitals (general); Nursing care; Health care; Mental health/crisis services; Health organizations, association; Cancer; Heart & circulatory diseases; AIDS; Alcoholism; Medical research, institute; Cancer research; Heart & circulatory research; AIDS research; Crime/violence prevention, youth; Legal services; Housing/shelter, development; Human services; Children/youth, services; Child development, services; Family services; Hospices; Aging, centers/services; Minorities/immigrants, centers/services; Homeless, human services; Civil rights; Community development; Jewish federated giving programs; Engineering/technology; Computer science; Science; Economics; Government/public administration; Roman Catholic agencies & churches; Religion; Minorities; Disabled; Aging; Economically disadvantaged; Homeless.
Types of support: Building/renovation; Equipment; Endowments; Program development; Conferences/seminars; Fellowships; Research.
Limitations: Giving in the U.S., with emphasis on IL. No support for public education. No grants to individuals, or for general support, continuing support, operating budgets, deficit financing, or unrestricted purposes.
Publications: Application guidelines.
Application information: The scholarship program for the children of company employees has been discontinued. Applications sent by FAX or E-mail not accepted. Application form required.
Copies of proposal: 1
Deadline(s): Mar. 1
Board meeting date(s): Feb., May, Aug., and Oct.

Final notification: Nov.
Officers and Directors:* William H. Scholl, Chair.; Pamela Scholl,* Pres.; Jack E. Scholl,* Secy.; David L. Royalty,* Treas.; Neil Flanagan; Richard B. Patterson; Jeanne M. Scholl; Michael W. Scholl; Susan Scholl; Douglas C. Witherspoon.
Number of staff: 3 full-time professional; 3 full-time support.
EIN: 366068724
Recent environmental and animal welfare grants:
1088-1 Canine Companions for Independence, Santa Rosa, CA, $10,000. Toward outreach and follow-up program. 2001.
1088-2 Chicago Horticultural Society, Glencoe, IL, $40,000. Toward Internship Program. 2001.
1088-3 Environmental Law and Policy Center of the Midwest, Chicago, IL, $20,000. Toward environmental markets project. 2001.
1088-4 Friends of the Chicago River, Chicago, IL, $10,000. Toward Adopt-A-River program. 2001.
1088-5 Greenwood Wildlife Rehabilitation Sanctuary, Boulder, CO, $15,000. Toward wildlife treatment and education programs. 2001.
1088-6 Isle of Man Childrens Centre, Douglas, United Kingdom, $25,000. Toward Mobile Outdoor Education Resource. 2001.
1088-7 Lincoln Park Zoological Society, Chicago, IL, $20,000. Toward Research Fellows program. 2001.
1088-8 Nature Conservancy, Chicago, IL, $20,000. Toward restoration work. 2001.
1088-9 Smiles Foundation, Carrollton, IL, $10,000. Toward truck purchase. 2001.
1088-10 Youth Conservation Corps, Deerfield, IL, $10,000. Toward Executive Director/Development position. 2001.

1089
Soretta & Henry Shapiro Family Foundation, Inc.
1540 N. Lake Shore Dr.
Chicago, IL 60610
Contact: Henry Shapiro, Pres.

Established in 1970 in IL.
Donor(s): Henry Shapiro, Isaac and Fannie Shapiro Memorial Foundation.
Grantmaker type: Independent foundation
Financial data (yr. ended 12/31/00): Assets, $7,727,673 (M); expenditures, $520,692; qualifying distributions, $336,085; giving activities include $323,665 for 75 grants (high: $146,500; low: $10).
Fields of interest: Music; Arts; Higher education; Theological school/education; Natural resources; Human services; Jewish federated giving programs; Jewish agencies & temples.
Limitations: Giving primarily in Chicago, IL. No grants to individuals.
Application information:
Initial approach: Proposal
Deadline(s): None
Officers and Directors:* Henry Shapiro, Pres.; Earl Shapiro,* V.P.; James Shapiro,* V.P.; Soretta Shapiro, Secy.-Treas.
EIN: 237063846

1090
Saul & Devorah Sherman Fund
676 N. Michigan Ave., No. 2920
Chicago, IL 60611

Established in 1962 in IL.
Donor(s): Saul S. Sherman, Unit Crane and Shovel Corp.
Grantmaker type: Independent foundation
Financial data (yr. ended 09/30/02): Assets, $624,680 (M); expenditures, $91,451; qualifying distributions, $90,350; giving activities include $90,350 for 25 grants (high: $20,000; low: $100).
Purpose and activities: Giving primarily to Jewish organizations and medical associations. Funding also for education and the arts.
Fields of interest: Television; Ballet; Higher education; Environment; Health care; Health organizations, association; Human services; Jewish federated giving programs.
Limitations: Applications not accepted. Giving on a national basis, with some emphasis on Chicago, IL. No grants to individuals.
Application information: Contributes only to pre-selected organizations.
Officers and Directors:* Devorah Sherman,* Pres.; Saul S. Sherman,* V.P. and Treas.; John L. Sherman, V.P.; Robert D. Zimelis, Secy.
EIN: 366059502

1091
The Shifting Foundation
c/o Ostron, Reisin, Berk & Abrams, Ltd.
455 N. City Front Plz. Dr., Ste. 2600
Chicago, IL 60611

Established in 1982 in IL.
Donor(s): Julie Breskin, David Breskin.
Grantmaker type: Independent foundation
Financial data (yr. ended 12/31/02): Assets, $6,302,360 (M); gifts received, $198,026; expenditures, $246,554; qualifying distributions, $244,000; giving activities include $244,000 for 28 grants (high: $50,000; low: $500).
Purpose and activities: Support primarily for the economically disadvantaged, hunger relief, social services, health organizations, human and civil rights, environmental and anti-nuclear interests, and Third World development.
Fields of interest: Visual arts; Museums; Performing arts; Music; Literature; Arts; Education; Environment; Animals/wildlife, preservation/protection; Family planning; Health care; Children/youth, services; Women, centers/services; Minorities/immigrants, centers/services; Homeless, human services; International relief; International peace/security; Arms control; International human rights; Race/intergroup relations; Civil rights; Community development; Minorities; Women; Economically disadvantaged; Homeless.
Types of support: General/operating support; Continuing support; Capital campaigns; Program development.
Limitations: Applications not accepted. Giving on a national basis. No grants to individuals.
Application information: Contributes only to pre-selected organizations. The foundation has suspended grantmaking to individual artists.
Officers and Directors:* David Breskin,* Pres.; Julie Breskin,* V.P.; Ralph Segall,* Secy.
Number of staff: None.

EIN: 366108560

1092
The Siragusa Foundation ▼
875 N. Michigan Ave., Ste. 3216
Chicago, IL 60611 (312) 280-0833
Contact: Irene S. Phelps, Pres.
FAX: (312) 943-4489; E-mail: information@siragusa.org; URL: http://www.siragusa.org

Trust established in 1950 in IL; incorporated in 1980.
Donor(s): Ross D. Siragusa.‡
Grantmaker type: Independent foundation
Financial data (yr. ended 12/31/02): Assets, $30,780,906 (M); expenditures, $4,441,398; qualifying distributions, $4,004,600; giving activities include $3,726,414 for 153 grants (high: $1,500,000; low: $700; average: $5,000–$25,000) and $2,421 for employee matching gifts.
Purpose and activities: The foundation supports organizations in all areas of child development, education, medical, human services, and cultural endeavors.
Fields of interest: Humanities; Arts; Child development, education; Higher education; Education; Environment; Hospitals (general); Health care; Health organizations, association; Cancer; Heart & circulatory diseases; Arthritis; Diabetes; Medical research, institute; Cancer research; Heart & circulatory research; Brain research; Human services; Youth, services; Child development, services; Aging, centers/services; Homeless, human services; Disabled; Economically disadvantaged; Homeless.
Types of support: General/operating support; Annual campaigns; Equipment; Program development; Scholarship funds; Research; Matching/challenge support.
Limitations: Applications not accepted. Giving primarily in the Midwest, with emphasis on the metropolitan Chicago, IL, area. No grants to individuals, or for endowment funds; no loans.
Publications: Annual report.
Application information: Submit proposal only when invited. The foundation will not be accepting any unsolicited proposals in 2003.
Board meeting date(s): Apr. and Nov.
Officers and Directors:* John R. Siragusa,* Chair.; Richard D. Siragusa,* Vice-Chair. and Secy.; Irene S. Phelps, Pres.; Jennifer I. Hicks; John E. Hicks, Jr.; Melvyn H. Schneider; Alexander Siragusa; Martha P. Siragusa; Ross D. Siragusa, Jr.; Ross D. Siragusa III; Sinclair C. Siragusa; James B. Wilson.
Number of staff: 1 full-time professional; 1 part-time professional; 2 full-time support.
EIN: 363100492
Recent environmental and animal welfare grants:
1092-1 Chicago Botanic Garden, Glencoe, IL, $10,000. To help kids' maintain The Children's Garden, where creative play supports discovery and learning about plants, gardening, and nature through summer camps, local scout troops and school programs. 2002.
1092-2 John G. Shedd Aquarium, Chicago, IL, $125,000. For conservation endowment fund, which supported coral propagation project, Partnership for Marine Conservation,

iguana research in Bahamas, beluga whale cooperative breeding program, and freshwater river mussel surveys, among other projects, also for feasibility study for Center for Aquatic Conservation. 2002.
1092-3 John G. Shedd Aquarium, Chicago, IL, $10,000. For Schooling with Shedd, which provides high quality programming for children and teachers in Chicago and other area schools though distance learning courses and beluga day classroom programs and to launch new ACES Project (Aiming for CPS Excellence in Science), which gives Aquarium sustained presence in Chicago Public Schools. 2002.
1092-4 Lincoln Park Zoo, Chicago, IL, $125,000. For Farm-in-the-Zoo Design Development and Endowment to introduce visitors to variety of Midwestern Farm animals. 2002.
1092-5 Lincoln Park Zoo, Chicago, IL, $10,000. For conservation research programs that focus on both wild and captive animals, and to help Lincoln Park Zoo remain free to public. 2002.
1092-6 Loyola Academy, Wilmette, IL, $12,500. To develop Loyola West Athletic Campus that will also play a role as an outdoor science laboratory for students. 2002.

1093
Spitz-Nebenzahl Foundation, Inc.
(formerly Joel & Maxine Spitz Foundation)
135 Crescent Dr.
Glencoe, IL 60022
Contact: Jocelyn Spitz Nebenzahl, Pres.; or Kenneth Nebenzahl, Secy.-Treas.

Established in 1949 in IL.
Donor(s): Jocelyn Spitz Nebenzahl, Kenneth Nebenzahl.
Grantmaker type: Independent foundation
Financial data (yr. ended 12/31/02): Assets, $980,137 (M); expenditures, $132,141; qualifying distributions, $117,549; giving activities include $117,549 for 73 grants (high: $19,532).
Purpose and activities: Giving for scientific and educational organizations.
Fields of interest: Arts; Education; Environment; Human services; International affairs; Jewish agencies & temples.
Limitations: Giving primarily in IL. No grants to individuals.
Application information:
Initial approach: Letter
Deadline(s): None
Officers and Directors:* Jocelyn Spitz Nebenzahl,* Pres.; Kenneth Nebenzahl,* Secy.-Treas.; Patricia Nebenzahl Frish.
EIN: 366079729

1094
The Bill and Orli Staley Foundation
9450 W. Bryn Mawr Ave., Ste. 310
Rosemont, IL 60018-5272
Contact: Lynne Kaplan

Established in 1993 in IL.
Grantmaker type: Independent foundation
Financial data (yr. ended 12/31/02): Assets, $1,421,756 (M); gifts received, $233,655;

expenditures, $180,078; qualifying distributions, $163,554; giving activities include $166,100 for 24 grants (high: $25,000; low: $500).
Purpose and activities: Giving for the arts and culture.
Fields of interest: Arts education; Museums (art); Performing arts; Natural resources; Zoos/zoological societies; Philanthropy/voluntarism.
Limitations: Giving primarily in Chicago, IL. No grants to individuals.
Application information:
  Initial approach: Letter
  Deadline(s): None
Trustees: Arlene D. Staley; William D. Staley.
EIN: 363925847

1095
A. E. Staley, Jr. Foundation
c/o Soy Capital Bank & Trust Co.
455 N. Main St.
Decatur, IL 62523-1103
Contact: Ki Kim, Sr. V.P. and Trust Off., Soy Capital

Established in 1955 in IL.
Donor(s): Augustus Eugene Staley, Jr.
Grantmaker type: Independent foundation
Financial data (yr. ended 12/31/02): Assets, $4,767,873 (M); expenditures, $372,441; qualifying distributions, $251,095; giving activities include $250,225 for 40 grants (high: $80,000; low: $250).
Purpose and activities: Giving primarily for education and for health care.
Fields of interest: Higher education; Environment; Animal welfare; Hospitals (general); Health care; Federated giving programs.
Limitations: Applications not accepted. Giving primarily in IL. No grants to individuals.
Application information: Contributes only to pre-selected organizations.
Trustee: Soy Capital Bank.
EIN: 376023961

1096
Kent D. & Mary L. Steadley Memorial Trust
c/o Bank of America
231 S. LaSalle St.
Chicago, IL 60697-0001
Contact: Lareta Garnier
Application address: c/o Bank of America, P.O. Box 8300, Springfield, MO, 65801-8300, tel.: (417) 227-6237

Established in 1970.
Grantmaker type: Independent foundation
Financial data (yr. ended 12/31/02): Assets, $17,104,045 (M); expenditures, $1,013,538; qualifying distributions, $962,248; giving activities include $953,468 for 11 grants (high: $294,868; low: $3,600; average: $5,000–$100,000).
Purpose and activities: Funds shall be distributed exclusively in and near the city of Carthage, MO, to promote community well-being.
Fields of interest: Elementary/secondary education; Animal welfare; Youth development,

scouting agencies (general); Human services; Community development.
Limitations: Giving limited to the Carthage, MO, area. No grants to individuals, or for national fundraising events.
Application information: Application form required.
  Initial approach: Letter requesting application materials
  Deadline(s): None
  Final notification: Usually within 6 months
Trustee: Bank of America.
Number of staff: None.
EIN: 436120866

1097
Stewart Foundation
515 Redwood Dr.
Aurora, IL 60506-3382

Established in 1984 in IL.
Donor(s): American Livestock Insurance Co., John Alexander, Thomas S. Alexander, Alexander S. Rudolph, Geoffrey E. Rudolph, Emily H. Alexander.
Grantmaker type: Independent foundation
Financial data (yr. ended 08/31/01): Assets, $3,291,195 (M); gifts received, $45; expenditures, $2,137,800; qualifying distributions, $2,087,347; giving activities include $2,110,780 for 30 grants (high: $1,500,000; low: $1,000).
Purpose and activities: Giving primarily for higher education, wildlife conservation, and community and religious services.
Fields of interest: Performing arts; University; Education, alumni groups; Zoos/zoological societies; Aquariums; Reproductive health.
Limitations: Applications not accepted. Giving primarily in IL. No grants to individuals.
Application information: Contributes only to pre-selected organizations.
Officers and Directors:* John Alexander,* Pres.; Geoffrey E. Rudolph,* Secy.; Thomas S. Alexander,* Treas.
EIN: 363339135

1098
Clayton A. Struve Family Foundation
c/o O'Connor Partners
141 W. Jackson Blvd., 39th Fl.
Chicago, IL 60604

Established in 1996 in IL.
Donor(s): Clayton A. Struve.
Grantmaker type: Independent foundation
Financial data (yr. ended 12/31/02): Assets, $1,164,516 (M); expenditures, $92,313; qualifying distributions, $92,461; giving activities include $92,500 for 26 grants (high: $10,000; low: $500).
Fields of interest: Business school/education; Natural resources; Health organizations, association; Human services; Children/youth, services; Federated giving programs.
Limitations: Applications not accepted. Giving on a national basis, with emphasis on IL. No grants to individuals.
Application information: Contributes only to pre-selected organizations.
Trustee: Clayton A. Struve.
EIN: 367168400

1099
Sudix Foundation
c/o Wesley M. Dixon, Jr.
400 Skokie Blvd., Ste. 300
Northbrook, IL 60062

Established in 1985 in IL.
Donor(s): Wesley M. Dixon, Jr.
Grantmaker type: Independent foundation
Financial data (yr. ended 12/31/02): Assets, $1,753,309 (M); expenditures, $435,067; qualifying distributions, $424,383; giving activities include $425,000 for 8 grants (high: $200,000; low: $20,000).
Purpose and activities: Giving primarily to higher education.
Fields of interest: Arts; Higher education; Botanical gardens; Protestant agencies & churches.
Limitations: Applications not accepted. Giving primarily in IL. No grants to individuals.
Application information: Contributes only to pre-selected organizations.
Officers: Wesley M. Dixon, Jr., Pres.; Suzanne S. Dixon, V.P. and Secy.-Treas.
Director: Pamela Bolton.
EIN: 363377946

1100
Robert Swanson and Cynthia Shevlin Charitable Foundation
c/o The Northern Trust Co.
50 S. LaSalle St., Ste. L-5
Chicago, IL 60675

Established in 1998 in IL.
Donor(s): Cynthia J. Shevlin, Robert O. Swanson.
Grantmaker type: Independent foundation
Financial data (yr. ended 08/31/02): Assets, $1,854,183 (M); expenditures, $181,888; qualifying distributions, $165,142; giving activities include $165,000 for 4 grants (high: $90,000; low: $20,000).
Purpose and activities: Giving for education.
Fields of interest: Elementary/secondary education; Education; Animals/wildlife, formal/general education; Health care.
Limitations: Applications not accepted. Giving primarily in AZ, CT, IL and MA. No grants to individuals.
Application information: Contributes only to pre-selected organizations.
Trustees: Cynthia J. Shevlin; Robert O. Swanson.
EIN: 367237696

1101
Mr. & Mrs. George W. Taylor Foundation
c/o Wachovia Securities
6810 Spring Creek Rd., Ste. 2B
Rockford, IL 61104   (815) 637-6363
Contact: James Thiede, Tr.

Established in 1984 in IL.
Donor(s): Edna May Taylor.
Grantmaker type: Independent foundation
Financial data (yr. ended 12/31/02): Assets, $2,028,458 (M); gifts received, $135,565; expenditures, $184,960; qualifying distributions, $118,667; giving activities include $96,681 for 5 grants (high: $83,006; low: $1,000) and

$21,986 for 6 grants to individuals (high: $7,060; low: $1,660).

Purpose and activities: Giving primarily to museums and general charities; also awards scholarships for students in the Rockford, IL, community who are willing to participate in the engineering program at the University of Minnesota Institute of Technology.

Fields of interest: Museums; Higher education; Engineering school/education; Scholarships/financial aid; Animal welfare; Federated giving programs; Engineering.

Types of support: General/operating support; Scholarships—to individuals.

Limitations: Giving primarily in Rockford, IL.

Application information: Applications accepted only for student aid program. Application form not required.

> *Initial approach:* Letter
> *Deadline(s):* None
> *Board meeting date(s):* Quarterly; Dec. meeting for grants decisions
> *Final notification:* Dec. and Jan.

Trustees: Tim Gaffney; Edna May Taylor; James Thiede.

Number of staff: 1 part-time support.

EIN: 363321315

1102
Tellabs Foundation
1415 W. Diehl Rd., Ste. MS10
Naperville, IL 60563 (630) 798-2506
Contact: Meredith Hilt, Exec. Dir.
E-mail: meredith.hilt@tellabs.com; URL: http://www.tellabs.com

Established in 1997 in IL.
Donor(s): Tellabs, Inc.
Grantmaker type: Company-sponsored foundation
Financial data (yr. ended 12/31/01): Assets, $27,128,674 (M); gifts received, $32,520; expenditures, $1,742,255; qualifying distributions, $1,527,879; giving activities include $1,495,170 for 27 grants (high: $183,334; low: $10,000).
Purpose and activities: Giving grants for education, health, and the environment.
Fields of interest: Education; Environment; Health organizations, association.
Types of support: Building/renovation; Land acquisition; Program development; Conferences/seminars; Professorships; Seed money; Curriculum development; Fellowships; Research.
Limitations: Giving on a national basis, with emphasis on communities surrounding the 4 major U.S. Tellabs facilities in Bolingbrook and Naperville, IL, Sunrise, FL, and Ashburn, VA.
Publications: Informational brochure (including application guidelines).
Application information:
> *Initial approach:* Letter
> *Deadline(s):* None
> *Board meeting date(s):* Quarterly
Officers and Directors:* Michael Birck,* Pres. and Treas.; Denise Callarman,* V.P.; Carol Gavin,* V.P.; Stephanie P. Marshall,* V.P.; Meredith Hilt,* Secy.
EIN: 364037547

1103
The Thorson Foundation
1824 A. Wildberry Dr.
Glenview, IL 60025-1784
Contact: John C. Goodall, Jr., Pres.

Established in 1954 in IL.
Donor(s): Robert D. Thorson,‡ Reuben Thorson,‡ Dorothy W. Thorson.‡
Grantmaker type: Independent foundation
Financial data (yr. ended 12/31/02): Assets, $2,969,123 (M); expenditures, $214,049; qualifying distributions, $199,411; giving activities include $199,593 for 77 grants (high: $30,000; low: $150).
Purpose and activities: Primary areas of interest include education and the arts, including zoological societies, museums, and art institutes.
Fields of interest: Museums; Arts; Education; Natural resources; Hospitals (general); Children/youth, services.
Types of support: Continuing support; Annual campaigns; Capital campaigns.
Limitations: Applications not accepted. Giving primarily in IL. No grants to individuals.
Application information: Contributes only to pre-selected organizations.
Officers and Directors:* John C. Goodall, Jr.,* Pres.; Dana T. De Angelis,* V.P. and Treas.; John C. Goodall III,* Secy.
Number of staff: None.
EIN: 366051916

1104
U.S. Cellular Connecting With Our Communities Program
c/o Public Affairs and Comm. Dept., U.S. Cellular Connecting With Our Communities Prog.
8410 W. Bryn Mawr, Ste. 700
Chicago, IL 60631
E-mail: publicaffairs&communications@uscellular.com; URL: http://www.uscc.com/uscellular/SilverStream/Pages/a_charitable.html

Grantmaker type: Corporate giving program
Purpose and activities: U.S. Cellular makes charitable contributions to nonprofit organizations involved with arts and culture, education, the environment, health and human services, community development, and civic affairs. Support is given primarily in areas of company operations.
Fields of interest: Arts; Education; Environment; Health care; Human services; Community development; Public affairs.
Types of support: Program development; Employee matching gifts; Donated products.
Limitations: Giving primarily in areas of company operations. No support for discriminatory organizations, political organizations or candidates, lobbying organizations, or advocacy organizations, religious organizations not of direct benefit to the entire community, social, labor, alumni, or fraternal organizations not of direct benefit to the entire community, primary, secondary, or charter schools, or local athletic or sports organizations. No grants to individuals, or for endowments or memorials, construction or renovation, special occasion, goodwill, or

single-interest magazines, walk-a-thons, travel, or general operating support.
Application information: An application form is available online. Proposals should be submitted in Microsoft Word format on an IBM compatible disk. A contributions committee reviews all requests. Application form required.
> *Initial approach:* Download application form and mail proposal and application form to headquarters
> *Copies of proposal:* 1
> *Deadline(s):* None
> *Board meeting date(s):* Mar., June, Sept., and Dec.

1105
Van Nice Foundation
c/o Jeanette Hunt Van Nice
1209 N. Astor St.
Chicago, IL 60610

Established in 1998 in IL.
Donor(s): William O. & Jeannette P. Hunt Foundation.
Grantmaker type: Independent foundation
Financial data (yr. ended 12/31/02): Assets, $2,141,295 (M); gifts received, $23,117; expenditures, $133,404; qualifying distributions, $120,050; giving activities include $120,050 for 38 grants (high: $28,500; low: $300).
Fields of interest: Multipurpose centers/programs; Libraries/library science; Education; Botanical gardens; Human services.
Limitations: Applications not accepted. Giving primarily in IL, with emphasis on Chicago. No grants to individuals.
Application information: Contributes only to pre-selected organizations.
Officers: Jeanette Hunt Van Nice, Pres.; Anthony H. Van Nice, Secy.; Peter Errett Van Nice, Treas.
EIN: 311604783

1106
Warwick Foundation
135 Melrose Ave.
Kenilworth, IL 60043-1248

Established in 1986 in IL.
Donor(s): John W. Taylor, Jr., Frances B. Taylor, John W. Taylor III.
Grantmaker type: Independent foundation
Financial data (yr. ended 12/31/02): Assets, $3,100,519 (M); expenditures, $181,826; qualifying distributions, $178,278; giving activities include $181,000 for 23 grants (high: $15,000; low: $1,000).
Purpose and activities: Giving for hospitals, the arts, and education.
Fields of interest: Museums; Arts; Elementary/secondary education; University; Education; Botanical gardens; Zoos/zoological societies; Hospitals (general); Human services.
Limitations: Applications not accepted. Giving primarily in the Chicago, IL, area. No grants to individuals.
Application information: Contributes only to pre-selected organizations.
Officers: Constance T. Patterson, Chair.; John W. Taylor III, Pres.; John W. Taylor, Jr., V.P.; Kaari T. Taylor, Secy.; Donald W. Patterson, Treas.
EIN: 363499673

1107
WD Foundation
c/o Harry Drucker
2500 Greenwood Ave.
Wilmette, IL 60091

Established in 1998 in IL.
Grantmaker type: Independent foundation
Financial data (yr. ended 04/30/03): Assets,
$379,693 (M); expenditures, $99,846;
qualifying distributions, $94,375; giving
activities include $95,075 for grants.
Fields of interest: Orchestra (symphony);
Natural resources; Animals/wildlife, sanctuaries.
Types of support: General/operating support.
Limitations: Applications not accepted. Giving
primarily in IL and MI. No grants to individuals.
Application information: Contributes only to
pre-selected organizations.
Directors: Suzanne Brown; Harry Drucker;
William Drucker; Suzanne W. Frank; Ann
Gleason; Sally Stults.
EIN: 367186849

1108
**The Gerhard and Patricia Weiler Family
Foundation**
10635 Bull Valley Dr.
Woodstock, IL 60098   (847) 437-0665

Established in 2000 in IL.
Donor(s): Gerhard Weiler, Patricia Weiler.
Grantmaker type: Independent foundation
Financial data (yr. ended 05/31/02): Assets,
$2,449,274 (M); expenditures, $233,137;
qualifying distributions, $144,959; giving
activities include $145,000 for 8 grants (high:
$50,000; low: $5,000).
Fields of interest: Arts education; Performing
arts, education; Performing arts; Performing arts
centers; Natural resources; Cancer; Recreation,
centers.
Limitations: Giving primarily in Chicago, IL. No
grants to individuals.
Application information:
 Initial approach: Letter
 Deadline(s): None
Officer: Gerhard H. Weiler, Pres.
Director: Patricia A. Weiler.
EIN: 364379492

1109
Peter & Penelope West Charitable Fund
255 Overlook Dr.
P.O. Box 143
Lake Forest, IL 60045-0143

Established in 1996 in IL.
Donor(s): Penelope G. West, Peter S. West.
Grantmaker type: Independent foundation
Financial data (yr. ended 12/31/02): Assets,
$593,514 (M); expenditures, $99,395;
qualifying distributions, $89,140; giving
activities include $89,500 for 10 grants (high:
$73,000; low: $500).
Purpose and activities: Giving primarily to a
residential retreat for writers, and other artists, as
well as for education, a camp, and human
services.
Fields of interest: Orchestra (symphony); Arts,
artist's services; Higher education; Natural

resources; Camps; Youth development; Human
services.
Limitations: Applications not accepted. Giving
primarily in IL, with emphasis on Lake Forest.
No grants to individuals.
Application information: Contributes only to
pre-selected organizations.
Officers: Penelope G. West, Pres.; Philip R.
Frankfort, V.P.; Peter S. West, Secy.-Treas.
EIN: 364118034

1110
Wilemal Fund
1275 N. Greenbay Rd.
Lake Forest, IL 60045-2427

Established in 1964.
Donor(s): Elizabeth Byron Brown.
Grantmaker type: Independent foundation
Financial data (yr. ended 12/31/02): Assets,
$19,030,738 (M); expenditures, $754,552;
qualifying distributions, $686,323; giving
activities include $680,250 for 32 grants (high:
$105,000; low: $1,000).
Purpose and activities: Giving primarily for the
arts, education, social services, and Christian
churches.
Fields of interest: Arts education; Television;
Architecture; Orchestra (symphony); Arts;
Higher education; Zoos/zoological societies;
Community development; Christian agencies &
churches.
Limitations: Applications not accepted. Giving
primarily in FL, IL, with emphasis on Chicago,
and Winston-Salem, NC. No grants to
individuals.
Application information: Contributes only to
pre-selected organizations. Unsolicited requests
for funds not accepted.
Officers and Directors:* William Gardner
Brown,* Pres. and Secy.; Malcolm McDougal
Brown,* V.P. and Treas.; Solange Pezon Brown.
EIN: 366098849

1111
Anne Potter Wilson Foundation
c/o Bank of America
231 S. LaSalle St., IL1-231-14-19
Chicago, IL 60697-1411
Contact: Patrick Nelson
Application address: c/o Bank of America, 1
Bank of America Plz., Nashville, TN 37239, tel.:
(615) 749-3916

Established in 1996 in TN.
Grantmaker type: Independent foundation
Financial data (yr. ended 12/31/01): Assets,
$26,401,385 (M); expenditures, $1,556,330;
qualifying distributions, $1,422,166; giving
activities include $1,415,607 for 8 grants (high:
$1,000,000; low: $15,000).
Purpose and activities: Giving primarily for
higher education.
Fields of interest: Historic
preservation/historical societies; Higher
education; Libraries (public); Botanical gardens;
Zoos/zoological societies; Human services.
Limitations: Giving primarily in Washington,
DC and Nashville, TN. No grants to individuals.
Application information: Application form not
required.
 Initial approach: Letter

Deadline(s): None
Trustee: Bank of America.
EIN: 626306576

1112
Winona Corporation
4801 Emerson Ave., Ste. 102
Palatine, IL 60067-0504

Established in 1965 in IL.
Donor(s): Marjorie M. Kelly.‡
Grantmaker type: Independent foundation
Financial data (yr. ended 12/31/02): Assets,
$4,462,998 (M); expenditures, $205,878;
qualifying distributions, $185,015; giving
activities include $185,000 for 16 grants (high:
$60,000; low: $5,000).
Purpose and activities: Giving primarily to a
planetarium, as well as other museums, and for
land, nature, and wildlife conservation; support
also for social services.
Fields of interest: Journalism/publishing;
Museums; Museums (natural history);
Planetarium; Education; Natural resources;
Horticulture/garden clubs; Hospitals (general);
Brain research; Human services; Youth, services;
Women, centers/services.
Limitations: Applications not accepted. Giving
primarily in Chicago, IL. No grants to
individuals.
Application information: Contributes only to
pre-selected organizations.
Officers: Patricia K. Healy, Pres.; Timothy G.
Carroll, Secy.; Marjorie K. Webster, Treas.
EIN: 366132949

INDIANA

1113
Back Home Again Foundation, Inc.
2635 Foxpointe Dr., Ste. B
Columbus, IN 47203   (812) 372-2978
Contact: Randolph H. Deer, Secy.

Established in 1999 in IN.
Donor(s): Central Indiana Community
Foundation, Randall H. Deer.
Grantmaker type: Independent foundation
Financial data (yr. ended 12/31/02): Assets,
$1,706,232 (M); gifts received, $865,000;
expenditures, $903,264; qualifying distributions,
$862,232; giving activities include $759,628 for
21 grants (high: $522,000; low: $200).
Fields of interest: Museums (art); Performing
arts; Arts; Higher education; Animal welfare;
Health organizations, association; Food
services; Camps; Human services; Children,
services.
Limitations: Giving primarily in Indianapolis, IN.
Application information:
 Initial approach: Letter
 Deadline(s): None
Officers: Wayne P. Zink, Pres.; Randolph H.
Deer, Secy.-Treas.
Director: Gene E. Wilkins.
EIN: 352068199

1114
Ball Brothers Foundation ▼
P.O. Box 1408
Muncie, IN 47308 (765) 741-5500
Additional address: 222 S. Mulberry St., Muncie,
IN 47305; FAX: (765) 741-5518; E-mail:
doug.bakken@ballfdn.org

Incorporated in 1926 in IN.
Donor(s): Edmund B. Ball,‡ Frank C. Ball,‡
George A. Ball,‡ Lucius L. Ball,‡ William A.
Ball.‡
Grantmaker type: Independent foundation
Financial data (yr. ended 12/31/01): Assets,
$112,979,404 (M); expenditures, $5,301,687;
qualifying distributions, $4,669,782; giving
activities include $4,473,142 for 38 grants (high:
$2,160,672; low: $1,000; average:
$1,000–$10,000) and $1,223,263 for in-kind
gifts.
Purpose and activities: Support for the
humanities and cultural programs, higher and
other education, health and medical education,
youth, and family and social services.
Fields of interest: Museums; Humanities; Arts;
Elementary school/education; Secondary
school/education; Higher education; Medical
school/education; Adult education—literacy,
basic skills & GED; Reading; Education;
Hospitals (general); Health care; Health
organizations, association; Human services;
Children/youth, services; Family services;
Community development.
Types of support: General/operating support;
Annual campaigns; Capital campaigns;
Building/renovation; Program development;
Conferences/seminars; Professorships;
Publication; Curriculum development;
Research; Technical assistance;
Matching/challenge support.
Limitations: Giving limited to IN. No grants to
individuals.
Publications: Application guidelines,
Informational brochure.
Application information: Application form not
required.
  Initial approach: Letter and proposal
  Copies of proposal: 1
  Deadline(s): Submit proposal preferably
    before June; no set deadline
  Board meeting date(s): Quarterly and as
    necessary
  Final notification: Varies
Officers and Directors:* John W. Fisher,* Chair.
and Pres.; Frank E. Ball,* V.P.; William L.
Peterson, Secy.; Douglas J. Foy,* Treas.; Virginia
B. Ball; William M. Bracken; Lucina B. Moxley;
Judith F. Oetinger; John J. Pruis; William L.
Skinner.
Number of staff: 1 full-time professional; 1
part-time professional; 1 full-time support.
EIN: 350882856
**Recent environmental and animal welfare
grants:**
1114-1 Cardinal Greenway, Muncie, Indiana,
  $27,500. 2001.
1114-2 Minnetrista Cultural Foundation,
  Muncie, Indiana, $2,160,672. For operating
  support for Cultural Center. 2001.
1114-3 Soil and Water Conservation District,
  Delaware County, Muncie, Indiana, $10,000.
  2001.

1115
George and Frances Ball Foundation ▼
P.O. Box 1408
Muncie, IN 47308 (765) 741-5500
Contact: Joyce Beck, Admin. Asst.
Additional address: 222 S. Mulberry St., Muncie,
IN 47305; FAX: (765) 741-5518; E-mail:
jjpruis@iquest.net

Incorporated in 1937 in IN.
Donor(s): George A. Ball.‡
Grantmaker type: Independent foundation
Financial data (yr. ended 12/31/02): Assets,
$88,350,165 (M); expenditures, $4,606,815;
qualifying distributions, $4,185,643; giving
activities include $4,185,643 for 52 grants (high:
$1,400,000; low: $50; average:
$5,000–$50,000).
Purpose and activities: Emphasis on higher
education and community programs.
Fields of interest: Historic preservation/historical
societies; Arts; Higher education; Education;
Community development, neighborhood
development.
Types of support: Capital campaigns;
Building/renovation; Equipment; Program
development; Professorships;
Matching/challenge support.
Limitations: Giving primarily in Muncie and
Delaware County, IN. No grants to individuals.
Application information: Application form not
required.
  Initial approach: Letter and proposal
  Copies of proposal: 1
  Deadline(s): None
  Board meeting date(s): Varies
  Final notification: Following board review
Officers and Directors:* Frank A. Bracken,*
Pres.; John J Pruis,* Exec. V.P.; Joan H. McKee,*
Secy.; Douglas J. Foy, Treas.; Stefan S. Anderson;
Jon H. Moll; Samuel L. Reed; Robert M. Smitson.
Number of staff: 1 part-time professional; 1
part-time support.
EIN: 356033917
**Recent environmental and animal welfare
grants:**
1115-1 Leelanau Conservancy, Leland, MI,
  $60,000. For capital campaign. 2002.
1115-2 Minnetrista Cultural Foundation,
  Muncie, Indiana, $35,000. For Phase Three
  strategic planning. 2002.
1115-3 Minnetrista Cultural Foundation,
  Muncie, Indiana, $17,315. For Nature Area
  Advance. 2002.
1115-4 Minnetrista Cultural Foundation,
  Oakhurst Gardens, Muncie, Indiana,
  $993,030. 2002.
1115-5 Nature Conservancy, Indianapolis,
  Indiana, $60,000. For Geography of Hope
  Campaign. 2002.
1115-6 Red-Tail Conservancy, Muncie, Indiana,
  $10,000. For land acquisition. 2002.
1115-7 Red-Tail Conservancy, Muncie, Indiana,
  $10,000. For operating support. 2002.

1116
Brown County Community Foundation, Inc.
P.O. Box 191
Nashville, IN 47448 (812) 988-4882
Contact: James L. Brunnemer, C.E.O.
FAX: (812) 988-0299; E-mail: info atisgn
browncountycommunityfoundation.org; URL:
http://
www.browncountycommunityfoundation.org

Established in 1993 in IN.
Grantmaker type: Community foundation
Financial data (yr. ended 12/31/02): Assets,
$5,250,610 (M); gifts received, $1,845,381;
expenditures, $477,952; giving activities include
$127,444 for 55 grants (high: $17,000; low:
$10; average: $1,000–$5,000) and $185,833 for
19 grants to individuals (high: $25,000; low:
$250; average: $1,000–$10,000).
Fields of interest: Arts; Education; Environment;
Health care; Human services; Community
development.
Types of support: Continuing support; Annual
campaigns; Capital campaigns;
Building/renovation; Equipment; Land
acquisition; Seed money; Scholarship funds;
Technical assistance; Scholarships—to
individuals; Matching/challenge support.
Limitations: Giving primarily in Brown County,
IN.
Publications: Application guidelines, Annual
report, Informational brochure (including
application guidelines), Newsletter.
Application information: Application form
required.
  Initial approach: Letter
  Copies of proposal: 10
  Deadline(s): June 28
  Board meeting date(s): Monthly
  Final notification: Aug. 31
Officers and Directors:* Missy Davis,* Chair.;
David Redman,* Vice-Chair.; Jim Brunnemer,
C.E.O. and Pres.; Jay Carter,* Secy.; James
Moore, Treas.; Diane Cantrell; John Kipp; Betsy
Lease; Steve Mollo; Rachel Perry; F. Andrew
Rogers; Rick Schrimper; Judith Stewart; Robert
Wright.
Number of staff: 2 full-time professional.
EIN: 351960379

1117
Jerry L. and Barbara J. Burris Foundation, Inc.
P.O. Box 80238
Indianapolis, IN 46280-0238
Contact: Jeffrey H. Thomasson, Secy.
Application address: 11711 N. Meridian St., Ste.
600, P.O. Box 80238, Indianapolis, IN
46280-0238, tel.: (317) 843-5678

Established in 1994 in IN.
Donor(s): Jerry L. Burris.‡
Grantmaker type: Independent foundation
Financial data (yr. ended 12/31/02): Assets,
$3,073,435 (M); expenditures, $139,197;
qualifying distributions, $107,097; giving
activities include $99,000 for 25 grants (high:
$15,000; low: $1,000).
Purpose and activities: Giving for museums,
colleges, churches and hospitals.
Fields of interest: Arts; Higher education;
Zoos/zoological societies; Hospitals (general);

Health organizations, association; Youth development, centers/clubs; Big Brothers/Big Sisters; Human services; Children/youth, services; Protestant agencies & churches.
Types of support: Scholarship funds.
Limitations: Giving primarily in Indianapolis, IN.
Officers: Barbara J. Burris, Pres.; Stacey L. Burris Ice, V.P.; Jeffrey H. Thomasson, Secy.
EIN: 351914399

1118
Community Foundation of Boone County, Inc.
60 E. Cedar St.
P.O. Box 92
Zionsville, IN   46077   (317) 873-0210
Contact: Lisa Latz John, Exec. Dir.
Additional tel.: (765) 482-0024; FAX: (317) 873-0219; E-mail: cfbc@in-motion.net; URL: http://www.bccn.boone.in.us/cf/

Established in 1991 in IN.
Grantmaker type: Community foundation
Financial data (yr. ended 12/31/01): Assets, $9,301,539 (M); gifts received, $1,217,956; expenditures, $880,128; giving activities include $189,539 for grants and $244,482 for grants to individuals.
Purpose and activities: The foundation was established in order to serve as the central philanthropic vehicle to address the needs of the Boone County, IN, community. The foundation administers donor-advised funds.
Fields of interest: Arts; Education; Environment; Health care; Human services; Children/youth, services; Disabled; Aging; Economically disadvantaged.
Types of support: Emergency funds; Program development; Seed money; Scholarship funds; Technical assistance; Program-related investments/loans; Grants to individuals; Scholarships—to individuals; Matching/challenge support; Student loans—to individuals.
Limitations: Giving limited to the residents of Boone County, IN, area. No support for religious or political purposes. No grants to individuals (except for designated scholarship funds).
Publications: Application guidelines, Annual report, Informational brochure, Newsletter.
Application information: Application form not required.
Initial approach: Letter
Copies of proposal: 15
Deadline(s): Mar. 15, June 15, Sept. 15, and Dec. 15
Board meeting date(s): Monthly
Officers and Directors:* Peter Hudson,* Pres.; Ronald L. Lind,* V.P.; Lisa Latz John, Exec. Dir.; Jean Acton; Nancy Beesley; Brett Boyston; J. David Cook; Rollin M. Dick; Bill Haggstrom; Charles M. Keenan; Margaret A. Larr; Wendell McBurney; Kathleen McClanahan; Debbie Mercer; Doug Vawter; and 9 additional Directors.
Number of staff: 2 full-time professional; 1 part-time professional.
EIN: 351829585

1119
The Community Foundation of Jackson County, Inc.
P.O. Box 1231
Seymour, IN   47274   (812) 523-4483
Contact: C.W. Walther, Pres.
FAX: (812) 523-1433; E-mail: jccf@hsonline.net

Established in 1992 in IN.
Grantmaker type: Community foundation
Financial data (yr. ended 12/31/01): Assets, $6,313,411 (L); gifts received, $189,775; expenditures, $456,819; giving activities include $109,713 for 50 grants and $35,532 for 34 grants to individuals.
Purpose and activities: Grants awarded for the development and betterment of Jackson County, IN. Donations were made for the purchasing and planting of trees around the community to preserve and promote conservation, the arts, youth groups, religion, and education, including scholarships awarded to Jackson County high school students. The foundation administers a donor-advised fund.
Fields of interest: Arts; Education; Environment; Youth development; Community development.
Types of support: Building/renovation; Equipment; Endowments; Seed money; Curriculum development; Scholarship funds; Technical assistance; Consulting services; Program evaluation; Scholarships—to individuals; Matching/challenge support.
Limitations: Giving limited to Jackson County, IN. No support for sectarian programs. No grants for seminars, or for trips, endowments or equipment.
Publications: Annual report, Financial statement, Grants list, Informational brochure (including application guidelines).
Application information: Application form required.
Initial approach: Request proposal form
Copies of proposal: 10
Deadline(s): July 31
Board meeting date(s): 4th Wed. of Feb., Apr., June, Aug., Oct., and Dec.
Final notification: Oct. 31
Officers: David Windley, Chair.; Jim Potts, Vice-Chair.; C.W. Walther, Pres.; Cheryl Stuckwish, Secy.; Tom Lantz, Treas.
Directors: Andy Applewhite; Nancy Bishop; Julie Bradley; Terrye Davidson; Drew Day; Andy Denny; Mike Fleetwood; Rosemary Jenkinson; Susan Judd; Dennis Kern; Don Jay Rice; Erin Royalty; Debra Schill; Trina Tracy; Rexanne Ude; Ken Warbritton; Dennis Wayman; Larry Welker; Phyllis Zabel.
Number of staff: 2 full-time professional; 1 part-time support.
EIN: 311119856

1120
Community Foundation of Madison and Jefferson County, Inc.
410 Mulberry St.
P.O. Box 306
Madison, IN   47250-0306   (812) 265-3327
Contact: Louise Markel, Exec. Dir.
FAX: (812) 273-0181; E-mail: jeffcom@cfmjc.org; URL: http://www.cfmjc.org

Established in 1992 in IN.
Grantmaker type: Community foundation

Financial data (yr. ended 12/31/02): Assets, $10,378,000 (M); gifts received, $2,429,000; expenditures, $963,500; giving activities include $523,500 for 120 grants (high: $250,000; low: $100) and $155,500 for 52 grants to individuals (high: $25,200; low: $100).
Purpose and activities: The mission of the foundation is to assist donors to build an enduring source of charitable assets to benefit its community; to provide responsible stewardship of the gifts donated; to promote leadership in addressing community issues; to make grants in the field of community service, social service, education, health, the environment and the arts. The foundation administers donor-advised funds.
Fields of interest: Arts; Education; Environment; Health organizations, association; Human services; Community development.
Types of support: Capital campaigns; Program development; Seed money; Scholarship funds; Technical assistance; Consulting services; Scholarships—to individuals; Matching/challenge support.
Limitations: Giving limited to Jefferson County, IN.
Publications: Application guidelines, Annual report, Informational brochure, Newsletter.
Application information: Application form required.
Initial approach: Letter
Copies of proposal: 7
Deadline(s): Varies
Board meeting date(s): 1st Wed. of each month
Officers and Directors:* Matt Forrester,* Chair.; Bill Hensler,* Vice-Chair.; Nancy Underwood,* Secy.; Tony Waltz,* Treas.; Louise Markel, Exec. Dir.; and 12 additional directors.
Number of staff: 1 full-time professional; 1 full-time support.
EIN: 351847297

1121
The Community Foundation of Muncie and Delaware County, Inc.
P.O. Box 807
Muncie, IN   47308-0807   (765) 747-7181
Contact: Roni Johnson, Pres.
FAX: (765) 289-7770; E-mail: commfound@cfmdin.org; URL: http://www.cfmdin.org

Incorporated in 1985 in IN.
Grantmaker type: Community foundation
Financial data (yr. ended 12/31/02): Assets, $32,057,785 (M); gifts received, $5,484,136; expenditures, $3,308,689; giving activities include $2,848,234 for 316 grants.
Purpose and activities: Support for the improvement of the quality of life; primary areas of interest include economic development, arts and culture, education, human services, and community betterment. The foundation administers a donor-advised fund.
Fields of interest: Theater; Arts; Education, association; Libraries/library science; Education; Environment; Health care; Health organizations, association; Crime/law enforcement; Human services; Youth, services; Minorities/immigrants, centers/services; Community development; Economics; Minorities.
Types of support: General/operating support; Capital campaigns; Building/renovation; Equipment; Program development;

Conferences/seminars; Seed money; Scholarship funds; Technical assistance; Grants to individuals; Scholarships—to individuals; In-kind gifts; Matching/challenge support.
Limitations: Giving limited to Muncie and Delaware County, IN. No support for religious purposes or public agency projects. No grants for endowment support or budget deficits.
Publications: Application guidelines, Annual report, Financial statement, Informational brochure, Informational brochure (including application guidelines), Newsletter, Occasional report.
Application information: Application form required.
Initial approach: Letter
Copies of proposal: 16
Deadline(s): 2nd Fri. of Jan., Apr., July, and Oct.
Board meeting date(s): 3rd Mon. of each month
Final notification: 3rd Mon. of Feb., May, Aug., and Nov.
Officers and Trustees:* Jack Buckles,* Chair.; Beverly Pitts,* Vice-Chair.; Roni Johnson,* Pres.; Ermalene Faulkner,* Secy.; Thomas Kinghorn,* Treas.; Michael Cox; John Littler; Julie Skinner; Kelly Stanley; Charles Sursa; Terry Walker.
Number of staff: 2 full-time professional; 1 part-time professional; 2 full-time support.
EIN: 351640051

1122
Community Foundation of Southern Indiana

4104 Charlestown Rd.
New Albany, IN 47150 (812) 948-4662
Contact: Laura Hansen Dean, Pres.
Additional tel.: (888) 388-2374; FAX: (812) 948-4678; E-mail: info@cfsouthernindiana.com; URL: http://www.cfsouthernindiana.com/

Established in 1991 in IN.
Grantmaker type: Community foundation
Financial data (yr. ended 06/30/03): Assets, $23,868,575 (M); gifts received, $1,954,746; expenditures, $1,872,110; giving activities include $555,941 for grants and $174,000 for 1 in-kind gift.
Purpose and activities: The foundation uses its funds to assist and benefit people in Clark, Floyd, Harrison, and Crawford counties, IN, through funding of health, education, cultural, civic and recreational programs. The mission of the foundation is to foster philanthropy and build assets for the common good, now and forever.
Fields of interest: Arts; Education; Environment; Health care; Public affairs.
Types of support: Management development; Capital campaigns; Building/renovation; Emergency funds; Program development; Conferences/seminars; Seed money; Scholarship funds; Scholarships—to individuals; Matching/challenge support.
Limitations: Giving limited to Clark, Crawford, Floyd, and Harrison counties, IN. No grants to individuals (except for designated scholarship funds).
Publications: Annual report (including application guidelines), Financial statement, Informational brochure.

Application information: See foundation Web site for application form and guidelines. Application form required.
Initial approach: Telephone, letter or Web site
Deadline(s): None
Board meeting date(s): Bimonthly
Officers: Robert Kleehamer, Chair.; Michael Douglas, Vice-Chair.; Laura Hansen Dean, C.E.O. and Pres.; Don Day, Secy.; Douglas York, Treas.
Directors: Les Albro; Hazel Bales; Ronald F. Barnes; Paul Beckort; Joyce Brown; Bob Cadwallader; William E. Childers; Tom Lindley; Debrah Bowers More; Stanley V. Pennington; Kyle Ridout; Rita Shourds; Herbert Smith; Darrell Voelker; Barbara Williams.
Number of staff: 3 full-time professional; 5 full-time support.
EIN: 351827813

1123
Community Foundation of St. Joseph County

P.O. Box 837
South Bend, IN 46624-0837 (574) 232-0041
Contact: Angela Butiste, Prog. Off.
FAX: (574) 233-1906; E-mail: info@cfsjc.org; URL: http://www.cfsjc.org/

Established in 1991 in IN.
Grantmaker type: Community foundation
Financial data (yr. ended 06/30/03): Assets, $58,991,143 (M); gifts received, $2,582,473; expenditures, $6,243,121; giving activities include $5,431,114 for grants (average: $1,000–$5,000).
Purpose and activities: Currently, the foundation awards challenge grants, offering $1 for every $1 raised.
Fields of interest: Arts; Education; Environment; Health care; Children/youth, services; Community development, neighborhood development; Religion.
Types of support: Matching/challenge support.
Limitations: Giving limited to St. Joseph County, IN.
Publications: Application guidelines, Annual report, Financial statement, Newsletter.
Application information:
Initial approach: Telephone for guidelines
Deadline(s): Mar. 1 and Oct. 1
Board meeting date(s): Sept., Dec., and May
Final notification: Following May and Dec. board meetings
Officer: Rose Meissner, Pres.
Number of staff: 6 full-time professional; 2 full-time support.
EIN: 237365930

1124
Community Foundation of Wabash County

(formerly North Manchester Community Foundation)
218 E. Main St.
P.O. Box 98
North Manchester, IN 46962-0098
(260) 982-4824
Contact: Patty Grant, Exec. Dir.
FAX: (260) 982-8644; E-mail: patty@cfwabash.org; URL: http://www.cfwabash.org

Established in 1954 in IN as North Manchester Community Foundation; current name adopted in 1992.
Grantmaker type: Community foundation
Financial data (yr. ended 12/31/02): Assets, $17,570,485 (M); gifts received, $4,054,810; expenditures, $2,788,273; giving activities include $2,569,700 for 391 grants (high: $207,000; low: $90).
Purpose and activities: The foundation administers a donor-advised fund.
Fields of interest: Arts; Education; Environment; Health care; Recreation; Community development; Social sciences.
Types of support: General/operating support; Continuing support; Building/renovation; Equipment; Endowments; Program development; Seed money; Curriculum development; Scholarship funds; Technical assistance; Program evaluation; Matching/challenge support.
Limitations: Giving limited to Wabash County, IN. No grants to individuals.
Publications: Application guidelines, Annual report (including application guidelines), Informational brochure, Newsletter.
Application information: Application form required.
Copies of proposal: 11
Deadline(s): Mar. 1 and Sept. 1
Board meeting date(s): Quarterly
Final notification: 6 to 8 weeks after deadline
Officers: Tom Hodson, Pres.; Steve Hammer, V.P.; Sharon Beauchamp, Secy.; Ralph Naragon, Treas.
Number of staff: 3 full-time professional; 2 part-time professional; 1 part-time support.
EIN: 356019016

1125
Clarence E. Custer & Inez R. Custer Foundation, Inc.

c/o Irwin Union Bank & Trust Co.
500 Washington St.
Columbus, IN 47201
Contact: William Helmbrecht, Treas.
Application address: c/o Irwin Union Bank & Trust Co., Trust Dept., P.O. Box 929, Columbus, IN 47201, tel.: (812) 376-1718

Established in 1988 in IN.
Grantmaker type: Independent foundation
Financial data (yr. ended 12/31/02): Assets, $3,998,024 (M); expenditures, $400,382; qualifying distributions, $325,041; giving activities include $308,231 for 60 grants (high: $20,000; low: $600).
Fields of interest: Education; Zoos/zoological societies; Hospitals (general); Youth development; Human services.
Limitations: Giving primarily within a 50-mile radius of Columbus, IN. No grants to individuals.
Application information: Application form required.
Deadline(s): None
Board meeting date(s): As required
Officers and Directors:* Richard H. Willmore,* Pres. and Mgr.; James W. Holland,* Secy.; William A. Helmbrecht,* Treas.; Dianne Bardley; Max E. Carothers.
Corporate Trustee: Irwin Union Bank & Trust Co.
EIN: 311130385

1126
Dearborn Community Foundation
(formerly Dearborn County Community Foundation)
406 2nd St.
Aurora, IN 47001 (812) 926-9300
Contact: Andrea Thalheimer, Exec. Dir.
FAX: (812) 926-9700; E-mail: dcf@Suscom.net;
URL: http://www.dearborncounty.org/dccf

Established in 1997 in IN.
Donor(s): The Greater Cincinnati Foundation, Lilly Endowment, Rising Sun Regional Foundation.
Grantmaker type: Community foundation
Financial data (yr. ended 12/31/02): Assets, $8,108,222 (M); gifts received, $1,984,058; expenditures, $1,452,178; giving activities include $1,056,695 for grants (high: $50,000; low: $250) and $161,152 for 24 grants to individuals (high: $85,008; low: $500).
Purpose and activities: Giving for community and social services, education and health, the environment, the arts and scholarships to benefit the residents of Dearborn County, IN. The foundation also administers donor-advised funds.
Fields of interest: Arts; Elementary/secondary education; Education; Natural resources; Hospitals (general); Health care; Human services; Community development.
Types of support: Building/renovation; Equipment; Program development; Seed money; Scholarships—to individuals; Matching/challenge support.
Limitations: Giving limited to Dearborn County, IN.
Publications: Annual report, Informational brochure (including application guidelines), Newsletter.
Application information: Application form required.
Initial approach: Applications available at local libraries
Copies of proposal: 1
Deadline(s): None
Board meeting date(s): 4th Thurs. of every month except Dec., July, and Apr.
Officers and Committee Members:* Marie Dausch,* Chair.; Jim Helms, Pres.; Mike Hollenbeck, V.P.; Joseph Stephens,* Secy.; Kip Newman,* Treas.; Lisa DeHart Lehner, Counsel; Jim Deaton; Norman Gellert; Mike Heffelmire; Mike Kramer; Elaine Kroger; Fred McCarter; Karleen McGraw; Jane Ohlmansiek; John Reiniger.
Number of staff: 2 full-time professional; 1 full-time support.
EIN: 352036110

1127
DeKalb County Community Foundation, Inc.
704 W. 7th St.
P.O. Box 285
Auburn, IN 46706 (260) 925-0311
Contact: Wendy Oberlin, Exec. Dir.
Additional tel.: (888) 727-3834; FAX: (260) 925-0383; E-mail: woberlin@dekalbfoundation.org; URL: http://www.dekalbfoundation.org

Established in 1996 in IN.
Grantmaker type: Community foundation

Financial data (yr. ended 12/31/02): Assets, $8,406,926 (M); gifts received, $3,306,751; expenditures, $679,491; giving activities include $410,299 for 33+ grants (high: $62,598).
Purpose and activities: To be an asset builder and grantmaker whose purpose is to improve the quality of life in the DeKalb County, IN, community. The foundation administers donor-advised funds.
Fields of interest: Arts; Education; Environment; Health care; Youth development; Human services; Community development.
Types of support: Capital campaigns; Building/renovation; Equipment; Program development; Scholarships—to individuals.
Limitations: Giving limited to DeKalb County, IN.
Publications: Application guidelines, Annual report, Informational brochure, Newsletter.
Application information: Application form required.
Initial approach: Contact foundation for grant proposal guidelines
Copies of proposal: 1
Deadline(s): Varies
Board meeting date(s): Varies
Officers and Directors:* Robert Menzie, Pres.; Brian D. Ruegsegger,* V.P.; Kathryn A. McNerney,* Secy.; Robert B. Keifer,* Treas.; Don M. Allison; Donna Martin Boseker; Darla Brennan; Fred L. Brown; Sherry Crisp-Ridge; Margie A. Crow; Richard A. Dircksen; Don Farrington; J. Bryan Nugen; Christine Rowe; Gaylord Toll; Michael Tullis.
Number of staff: 1 full-time professional; 1 part-time professional; 2 part-time support.
EIN: 351992897

1128
John A. Delegan Memorial Trust
5231 Hohman Ave.
Hammond, IN 46320

Established in 2001 in IN.
Grantmaker type: Independent foundation
Financial data (yr. ended 12/31/02): Assets, $1,575,044 (M); expenditures, $167,994; qualifying distributions, $157,914; giving activities include $146,754 for 14 grants (high: $29,847; low: $5,835).
Fields of interest: Animals/wildlife.
Limitations: Applications not accepted. No grants to individuals.
Application information: Contributes only to pre-selected organizations.
Trustee: Mary T. Ciciora.
EIN: 356710464

1129
Dow AgroSciences LLC Corporate Giving Program
9330 Zionsville Rd.
Indianapolis, IN 46268 (317) 337-3000
Contact: Steve Furste

Grantmaker type: Corporate giving program
Purpose and activities: Dow AgroSciences makes charitable contributions to nonprofit organizations involved with education, the environment, health and human services, and biotechnology. Support is given primarily in areas of company operations.

Fields of interest: Education; Environment; Health care; Human services; Biological sciences.
Types of support: General/operating support; Scholarship funds; Employee volunteer services; Sponsorships; Employee matching gifts; In-kind gifts.
Limitations: Giving primarily in areas of company operations, particularly the Indianapolis, IN, area. No support for discriminatory organizations.
Application information: Application form not required.
Initial approach: Proposal to headquarters
Copies of proposal: 1
Deadline(s): None
Final notification: Following review

1130
Richard M. Fairbanks Foundation, Inc. ▼
(formerly Fairbanks Foundation, Inc.)
9292 N. Meridan St., Ste. 304
Indianapolis, IN 46260 (317) 846-7111
Contact: Betsy Bikoff, Chief Grant Making Off.
FAX: (317) 844-0167; E-mail: Bikoff@rmfairbanksfoundation.org; URL: http://www.rmfairbanksfoundation.org

Established in 1986 in IN.
Donor(s): Richard M. Fairbanks.‡
Grantmaker type: Independent foundation
Financial data (yr. ended 12/31/02): Assets, $241,202,454 (M); gifts received, $125,744,084; expenditures, $7,109,548; qualifying distributions, $6,524,341; giving activities include $6,268,600 for 48 grants (high: $1,200,000; low: $5,000; average: $5,000–$1,200,000).
Purpose and activities: Support primarily for health care, human services, education, and arts and culture.
Fields of interest: Arts; Education; Hospitals (general); Health care; Human services.
Types of support: General/operating support; Continuing support; Annual campaigns; Capital campaigns; Equipment; Endowments; Program development; Professorships; Seed money; Research; Matching/challenge support.
Limitations: Giving primarily in greater Indianapolis and central IN. No grants to individuals.
Application information: Proposals should be submitted to the foundation only upon request.
Initial approach: Telephone or letter of inquiry (2-3 pages)
Copies of proposal: 1
Deadline(s): Feb. 1 and Aug. 1
Board meeting date(s): Spring and fall
Final notification: After board meetings
Officers and Directors:* Leonard J. Betley,* Pres.; Richard M. Fairbanks III,* V.P.; Thomas H. Ristine,* Secy.; Roger S. Snowdon,* Treas.; Daniel C. Appel; Elizabeth N. Mann.
Number of staff: 2 full-time professional; 1 part-time professional; 1 part-time support.
EIN: 311189885
Recent environmental and animal welfare grants:
1130-1 Indianapolis Zoo, White River Gardens, Indianapolis, Indiana, $500,000. For general support. 2001.

1131
Fayette County Foundation
P.O. Box 844
Connersville, IN 47331 (765) 827-9966
Contact: Anna Dungan, Exec. Dir.
FAX: (765) 827-5836; E-mail:
info@fayettefoundation.com; URL: http://
www.fayettefoundation.com

Established in 1986 in IN.
Grantmaker type: Community foundation
Financial data (yr. ended 06/30/01): Assets,
$5,750,464 (M); gifts received, $875,997;
expenditures, $245,125; giving activities include
$177,578 for grants and $67,547 for grants to
individuals.
Purpose and activities: The mission of the
Fayette County Foundation is to inspire a spirit
of philanthropy in Fayette County, IN by
enhancing the quality of life through impacting
grantmaking, strategic endowment building, and
community leadership.
Fields of interest: Education; Environment;
Animal welfare; Youth development, adult &
child programs; Human services; Community
development; Religion.
Types of support: Annual campaigns;
Endowments; Conferences/seminars.
Limitations: Giving limited to Fayette County,
IN. No support for religious organizations. No
grants for deficit funding, or for salaries, annual
campaigns, repeat funding, or for travel
expenses.
Publications: Annual report.
Application information: Application guidelines
available on foundation Web site. Application
form required.
  Initial approach: Letter
  Copies of proposal: 1
  Deadline(s): None
Officers: Bruce K. Bowden, Pres.; Nancy
Stevens, Secy.; Hilton Henry, Treas.
Director: Nancy Burke.
Number of staff: 1 full-time professional; 1
part-time support.
EIN: 311185980

1132
John Anna & Martha Jane Fields Trust Foundation
(formerly Fields Foundation Trust)
c/o Wells Fargo Bank Indiana, N.A.
112 W. Jefferson Blvd.
South Bend, IN 46601 (574) 237-3475
Contact: Charles F. Nelson, V.P., Wells Fargo
Bank Indiana, N.A.

Established in 1997 in IN.
Grantmaker type: Independent foundation
Financial data (yr. ended 12/31/02): Assets,
$2,198,997 (M); expenditures, $117,159;
qualifying distributions, $103,494; giving
activities include $93,000 for 6 grants (high:
$50,000; low: $5,500).
Purpose and activities: Giving primarily to the
arts.
Fields of interest: Theater; Zoos/zoological
societies; Religion.
Limitations: Giving limited to South Bend, IN.
No grants to individuals.
Application information: Application form not
required.
  Initial approach: Letter

Copies of proposal: 8
Deadline(s): Apr. 1 and Oct. 1
Board meeting date(s): May and Nov.
Final notification: May and Nov.
Trustee: Wells Fargo Bank, N.A.
EIN: 356256726

1133
The Golden Light Foundation
(formerly NRZ Foundation)
c/o James McGrath
135 N. Pennsylvania St.
Indianapolis, IN 46204

Established in 1991 in IN.
Donor(s): Bernice R. Zink, Ned Zink.
Grantmaker type: Independent foundation
Financial data (yr. ended 12/31/02): Assets,
$485,360 (M); gifts received, $66,450;
expenditures, $115,666; qualifying distributions,
$110,382; giving activities include $110,000 for
5 grants (high: $100,000; low: $1,000).
Fields of interest: Animals/wildlife, association;
Hospitals (general); Human services.
Limitations: Applications not accepted. Giving
primarily in AZ, IN, and MD. No grants to
individuals.
Application information: Contributes only to
pre-selected organizations.
Officer and Trustees:* Ned R. Zink,* Exec. Dir.;
James R. Zink.
EIN: 351837497

1134
The W. C. Griffith Foundation
c/o National City Bank of Indiana
101 W. Washington St., Ste. 600E
Indianapolis, IN 46255 (317) 267-7262
Contact: Curt Farran

Established in 1959 in IN.
Donor(s): William C. Griffith,‡ Ruth Perry
Griffith.‡
Grantmaker type: Independent foundation
Financial data (yr. ended 11/30/02): Assets,
$10,736,540 (M); expenditures, $923,549;
qualifying distributions, $899,165; giving
activities include $861,250 for 130 grants (high:
$50,000; low: $750).
Purpose and activities: Support primarily for
hospitals, health associations, medical and
cancer research, the arts, including music and
museums, community funds and development,
higher, secondary, and other education, family
planning services, child welfare, the homeless,
the environment, libraries, and Christian
religious organizations.
Fields of interest: Museums; Music; Arts;
Secondary school/education; Higher education;
Libraries/library science; Education;
Environment; Hospitals (general); Family
planning; Health organizations, association;
Cancer; Medical research, institute; Cancer
research; Children/youth, services; Homeless,
human services; Community development;
Federated giving programs; Christian agencies &
churches; Minorities; Homeless.
Types of support: Continuing support; Capital
campaigns; Building/renovation.
Limitations: Giving primarily in Indianapolis,
IN. No grants to individuals, or for scholarships
or fellowships.

Application information: Application form not
required.
  Initial approach: Letter
  Copies of proposal: 1
  Deadline(s): None
  Board meeting date(s): June and Nov.
Advisors: Ruthelen Griffith Burns; Charles P.
Griffith, Jr.; Walter S. Griffith; William C. Griffith
III; Wendy Griffith Kortepeter.
Trustee: National City Bank of Indiana.
Number of staff: 1 part-time support.
EIN: 356007742

1135
The Hilbert Foundation
P.O. Box 90198
Indianapolis, IN 46290-0198 (317) 848-3146
Contact: Phillip S. Scheffsky

Established in 1996 in IN.
Donor(s): Stephen C. Hilbert, Tomisue S. Hilbert.
Grantmaker type: Independent foundation
Financial data (yr. ended 12/31/02): Assets,
$180,835 (M); expenditures, $834,442;
qualifying distributions, $819,732; giving
activities include $769,557 for 14 grants (high:
$502,500; low: $200; average: $10,000).
Fields of interest: Theater; Arts; Zoos/zoological
societies; Hospitals (general); Protestant
agencies & churches.
Limitations: Giving primarily in Indianapolis, IN.
Application information: Application form not
required.
  Initial approach: Proposal
  Deadline(s): None
Trustees: Stephen C. Hilbert; Tomisue S. Hilbert.
EIN: 352002703

1136
Igo Family Foundation, Inc.
2600 1 Indiana Sq.
Indianapolis, IN 46204

Established in 1993 in IN.
Donor(s): Lena M. Igo.
Grantmaker type: Independent foundation
Financial data (yr. ended 12/31/02): Assets,
$1,468,941 (M); expenditures, $112,607;
qualifying distributions, $91,847; giving
activities include $92,000 for 11 grants (high:
$35,000; low: $1,000).
Purpose and activities: Giving for education,
hospitals, and community development.
Fields of interest: Music; Orchestra (symphony);
Environment, land resources; Zoos/zoological
societies; Medical care, in-patient care;
Hospitals (general); Health care; Medical
research, institute; Children/youth, services;
Foundations (public); Protestant agencies &
churches.
Limitations: Applications not accepted. Giving
primarily in FL. No grants to individuals.
Application information: Contributes only to
pre-selected organizations.
Officers and Directors:* Myra K. Haley,* Pres.;
Eugene L. Henderson,* Secy.; John D. Haley.
EIN: 351897262

1137
Indiana Chemical Trust
c/o Old National Trust Co.
P.O. Box 1447
Terre Haute, IN 47808-1447 (812) 462-7255
Contact: Brenda Voll

Established in 1953 in IN.
Donor(s): Terre Haute Gas Corp., Indiana Gas and Chemical Corp., Tribune-Star Publishing Co.
Grantmaker type: Company-sponsored foundation
Financial data (yr. ended 12/31/02): Assets, $8,284,509 (M); expenditures, $406,521; qualifying distributions, $383,064; giving activities include $382,000 for 19 grants (high: $125,000; low: $2,000).
Purpose and activities: Grants primarily to civic, charitable, youth, and educational institutions, with emphasis on a social service agency; giving also for Roman Catholic church support, including monasteries.
Fields of interest: Education; Animals/wildlife, preservation/protection; Zoos/zoological societies; Recreation; Human services; Children/youth, services; Roman Catholic agencies & churches.
Types of support: General/operating support.
Limitations: Giving primarily in Vigo County, IN. No grants to individuals.
Application information: Application form not required.
  Deadline(s): None
  Board meeting date(s): Dec.
Committee Members: W. Curtis Brighton; Anton Hulman George; Mari Hulman George.
Trustee: Old National Trust Co.
EIN: 356024816

1138
IPALCO Enterprises, Inc. Corporate Giving Program
1 Monument Cir.
Indianapolis, IN 46204 (317) 261-8484
Contact: Linda Brown-Koch, Mgr., Community Investments
Application address: P.O. Box 1595, Indianapolis, IN 46206-1595; FAX: (317) 261-8324; E-mail: mlemons@ipalco.com (environmental grants); URL: http://www.ipalco.com/ABOUTIPALCO/Community/Community.html

Grantmaker type: Corporate giving program
Purpose and activities: IPALCO Enterprises makes charitable contributions to nonprofit organizations involved with arts and culture, education, the environment, community development, and on a case by case basis. Support is given primarily in IN.
Fields of interest: Visual arts; Dance; Theater; Music; Literature; Arts; Education; Environment; Community development; General charitable giving.
Types of support: General/operating support; Employee volunteer services; Employee matching gifts; Grants to individuals.
Limitations: Giving primarily in IN, particularly central IN and Indianapolis. No support for religious or political organizations.
Application information: The Community Relations Department handles giving. Application form not required.

Initial approach: Telephone or proposal to headquarters
Copies of proposal: 1
Deadline(s): None
Board meeting date(s): Last week in Feb. and other times
Final notification: 6 to 8 weeks

1139
The Scott A. Jones Foundation, Inc.
1150 W. 116th St.
Carmel, IN 46032

Established in 1994 in MA.
Donor(s): Scott A. Jones.
Grantmaker type: Independent foundation
Financial data (yr. ended 12/31/02): Assets, $5,730,361 (M); expenditures, $1,207,147; qualifying distributions, $1,204,531; giving activities include $1,169,033 for 12 grants (high: $750,000; low: $200).
Purpose and activities: Giving primarily for human services, the arts, and education.
Fields of interest: Museums (children's); Secondary school/education; Education; Zoos/zoological societies; Human services; Children/youth, services.
Limitations: Applications not accepted. Giving primarily in IN. No grants to individuals.
Application information: Contributes only to pre-selected organizations.
Officers: Scott A. Jones, Pres.; Thomas P. Jalkut, Clerk; Lisa Hull, Treas.
EIN: 223295174

1140
Kosciusko County Community Foundation, Inc.
102 E. Market St.
Warsaw, IN 46580 (574) 267-1901
Contact: Suzanne M. Light, Exec. Dir.
FAX: (574) 268-9780; E-mail: KCF@KCFoundation.org; URL: http://www.kcfoundation.org

Established in 1968 by the Warsaw Chamber of Commerce as the Greater Warsaw Foundation. In 1972, after reorganization to include the entire county, the name was changed. In 2002, the current name was adopted.
Grantmaker type: Community foundation
Financial data (yr. ended 06/30/03): Assets, $21,683,281 (M); gifts received, $2,321,082; expenditures, $1,311,278; giving activities include $791,497 for grants and $109,068 for grants to individuals.
Purpose and activities: The mission of the Kosciusko County Community Foundation is to encourage and serve donors and their community by building philanthropic endowments for the betterment of the people of Kosciusko County, IN, now and in the future.
Fields of interest: Arts; Education; Environment; Health care; Human services; Public affairs.
Types of support: Management development; Capital campaigns; Building/renovation; Program development; Seed money; Scholarships—to individuals; Matching/challenge support.
Limitations: Giving limited to Kosciusko County, IN. No support for sectarian or religious groups. No grants to individuals (except for

scholarships), or for operating budgets, endowment funds, or long-term funding.
Publications: Annual report (including application guidelines).
Application information: Guidelines available on Web site. Application form required.
  Initial approach: Letter or telephone
  Copies of proposal: 1
  Deadline(s): Jan. 15, May 15, and Sept. 15
  Board meeting date(s): Every 2 months
Officers and Directors:* Robert Condon,* Pres.; Grant McGuire, V.P.; Avis Gunter,* Secy.; Alan Wuthrich,* Treas.; Suzanne M. Light, Exec. Dir.; Donald C. Allen; Carolyn Anderson; Brad Bishop; Nilah Brown; James Caskey; Marsha Cook; Antony Garza; Richard Green; Maureen Hall; Beth Krull; Jean Northenor; Stanley Pequignot; Dixie Pryor; Greg Sasso; Rita Schobert; Rita Price Simpson; Rebecca Thomas; Cara Tucker; Rev. Gerald Yoder.
Number of staff: 2 full-time professional; 3 full-time support.
EIN: 356086777

1141
LaGrange County Community Foundation, Inc.
109 E. Central Ave., No. 3
LaGrange, IN 46761 (260) 463-4363
Contact: Evelyn J. Evers, Exec. Dir.
FAX: (260) 463-4856; E-mail: lccf@lccf.net; URL: http://www.lccf.net

Established in 1991 in IN.
Grantmaker type: Community foundation
Financial data (yr. ended 12/31/01): Assets, $7,626,991 (L); gifts received, $532,086; expenditures, $661,171; giving activities include $419,728 for 92 grants (high: $34,440; low: $6) and $2,500 for 24 in-kind gifts.
Purpose and activities: To encourage philanthropy and charitable giving throughout LaGrange County, IN. The foundation administers a donor-advised fund.
Fields of interest: Arts; Education; Environment; Health care; Youth development; Human services; Children/youth, services; Community development; Aging.
Types of support: General/operating support; Annual campaigns; Equipment; Land acquisition; Endowments; Emergency funds; Program development; Conferences/seminars; Seed money; Scholarship funds; Technical assistance; Consulting services; Employee-related scholarships; Grants to individuals; Scholarships—to individuals; Matching/challenge support.
Limitations: Giving limited to LaGrange County, IN.
Publications: Application guidelines, Annual report, Financial statement, Grants list, Informational brochure (including application guidelines), Occasional report.
Application information: Application form required.
  Initial approach: Letter requesting guidelines
  Copies of proposal: 1
  Deadline(s): Feb. 1, June 1, and Oct. 1
  Board meeting date(s): 3rd Thurs. of each month
  Final notification: Apr. 1, Aug. 1, and Dec. 1
Officers and Directors:* Terry Schmidt, Pres.; Laura Lemings, V.P.; Sharon Bowen,* Secy.;

Becky Yoder, Treas. and Dir. Mktg.; David Fought, Dir., Fin.; DeWayne Bontrager; Joan Bovee; William Connelly; Fred Hartz; Jan Olinger; Ned Stump; Ernie Yoder.
Number of staff: 2 full-time professional; 1 part-time professional; 1 full-time support.
EIN: 351834679

1142
Legacy Foundation, Inc.
1000 E. 80th Pl., N. Tower 420
Merrillville, IN 46410-5644 (219) 736-1880
Contact: Nancy K. Johnson, Pres.
FAX: (219) 736-1940; E-mail:
legacy1@netnitco.net; URL: http://
www.legacyfoundationlakeco.org

Established in 1992 in IN.
Grantmaker type: Community foundation
Financial data (yr. ended 06/30/03): Assets, $17,859,727 (M); gifts received, $4,866,345; expenditures, $560,902; giving activities include $1,698,233 for 362 grants (high: $213,824; low: $25) and $24,069 for 49 grants to individuals (high: $700; low: $105).
Purpose and activities: The foundation exists to encourage community philanthropy. It will seek and accept endowments from public and private sources and distribute the income for community enhancing projects and other charitable purposes.
Fields of interest: Arts; Education; Environment; Public health; Human services; Youth, services; Community development, neighborhood development; Philanthropy/voluntarism; Public affairs.
Types of support: Building/renovation; Equipment; Program development; Conferences/seminars; Seed money; Scholarship funds; Technical assistance; Scholarships—to individuals; Matching/challenge support.
Limitations: Giving primarily in Lake County, IN. No support for sectarian religious programs or basic municipal or educational functions and services. No grants to individuals (except through designated scholarship funds), or for operating budgets, endowment funds, debt reduction, continuing support, general operating expenses (except for start up), annual campaigns, fundraising events, travel grants, multi year grants or scholarly research grants.
Publications: Application guidelines, Annual report, Informational brochure, Newsletter (including application guidelines).
Application information: Application form not required.
Initial approach: Letter of inquiry
Copies of proposal: 1
Deadline(s): Rolling; The deadline for capital requests is July 1 and Jan. 1 of each year
Board meeting date(s): 1st Tues. of Feb., Apr., June, Aug., Oct., and Dec.
Officer: Nancy K. Johnson, Pres. and Exec. Dir.
Number of staff: 2 full-time professional; 1 full-time support.
EIN: 351872803

1143
Marshall County Community Foundation, Inc.
P.O. Box 716
Plymouth, IN 46563 (574) 935-5159
Contact: R. Jeffrey Honzik, Exec. Dir.
FAX: (574) 936-8040; E-mail:
info@marshallcountycf.org; URL: http://
www.marshallcountycf.org

Established in 1991 in IN.
Grantmaker type: Community foundation
Financial data (yr. ended 06/30/02): Assets, $16,844,730 (M); gifts received, $1,789,166; expenditures, $1,066,452; giving activities include $735,044 for 67 grants (high: $120,790; low: $250) and $69,120 for 63 grants to individuals (high: $4,000; low: $100).
Purpose and activities: The mission of the foundation is to assist individuals within the Marshall County, IN community in the building and administration of endowment and planned giving resulting in an enriched quality of life for all current and future citizens.
Fields of interest: Arts; Secondary school/education; Higher education; Libraries (public); Scholarships/financial aid; Animals/wildlife, preservation/protection; Hospitals (general); Parks/playgrounds; Recreation; Community development; Government/public administration; Protestant agencies & churches.
Types of support: General/operating support; Endowments; Publication; Consulting services; Grants to individuals.
Limitations: Giving limited to Marshall County, IN. No grants to individuals (except for scholarships), or for operating expenses, long-term funding or for endowments.
Publications: Application guidelines, Annual report (including application guidelines), Financial statement, Grants list, Informational brochure (including application guidelines), Newsletter, Program policy statement.
Application information: Application form available on Web site. Application form required.
Initial approach: Send request
Deadline(s): Feb. 1 and Aug. 1
Board meeting date(s): Mar. and Sept.
Officers: William Pippenger, Pres.; Bruce Jennings, V.P.; Lynn Overmyer, Secy.; Chuck Lewallen, Treas.; R. Jeffrey Honzik, Exec. Dir.
Directors: Sue Chase; Richard Leeper; Connie Lemler; Harold Louderback; Gordon Taiclet.
Number of staff: 2 full-time professional; 2 part-time professional.
EIN: 351826870

1144
The Martin Foundation, Inc.
500 Simpson Ave.
Elkhart, IN 46515 (574) 295-3343
Contact: Geraldine F. Martin, Chair. and Pres.
Application guidelines: 5051 Castello Sq., Ste. 204, Naples, FL 34103-8982

Incorporated in 1953 in IN.
Donor(s): Ross Martin,‡ Esther Martin,‡ Lee Martin, Geraldine F. Martin.
Grantmaker type: Independent foundation
Financial data (yr. ended 06/30/02): Assets, $25,877,585 (M); expenditures, $3,679,232;

qualifying distributions, $3,474,103; giving activities include $3,524,400 for 31 grants (high: $2,400,000; low: $500; average: $1,000–$25,000).
Purpose and activities: Emphasis on education and social services, including programs for women and youth, environmental and conservation organizations; support also for cultural programs, public interest programs, and international development.
Fields of interest: Media/communications; Museums; Arts; Early childhood education; Higher education; Adult/continuing education; Libraries/library science; Education; Natural resources; Environment; Animal welfare; Animals/wildlife, preservation/protection; Family planning; Medical care, rehabilitation; Mental health/crisis services; Housing/shelter, development; Human services; Youth, services; Family services; Women, centers/services; Minorities/immigrants, centers/services; International economic development; International peace/security; Community development; Federated giving programs; Population studies; Public affairs; Minorities; Women; Economically disadvantaged.
Limitations: Giving primarily in IN; limited national and international support. No grants to individuals.
Publications: Annual report (including application guidelines).
Application information: Write to the foundation for guidelines and annual report. Application form not required.
Initial approach: Letter
Copies of proposal: 1
Deadline(s): None
Board meeting date(s): As required
Final notification: 4 to 8 weeks
Officers and Directors:* Geraldine F. Martin,* Chair. and Pres.; Casper Martin,* Secy.-Treas.; Jennifer L. Martin; Lee Martin; Lisa Martin.
Number of staff: None.
EIN: 351070929

1145
The Maxon Charitable Foundation, Inc.
201 E. 18th St.
Muncie, IN 47302-4124
Contact: Jeffrey R. Lang, Secy.-Treas.
Application address: P.O. Box 2068, Muncie, IN 47307-0068

Established in 1987 in IN.
Donor(s): Maxon Corp.
Grantmaker type: Company-sponsored foundation
Financial data (yr. ended 12/31/02): Assets, $982,363 (M); expenditures, $156,963; qualifying distributions, $156,438; giving activities include $155,163 for 21 grants (high: $40,000; low: $100).
Purpose and activities: Giving primarily for community development.
Fields of interest: Education; Natural resources; Hospitals (general); Recreation; Human services; Children/youth, services; Community development; Federated giving programs.
Types of support: General/operating support; Annual campaigns; Equipment; Scholarship funds; Scholarships—to individuals.
Limitations: Giving limited to Muncie, IN.
Publications: Application guidelines.

Application information: Application form required.
>*Initial approach:* Letter
>*Deadline(s):* None
>*Board meeting date(s):* July and Dec.
>*Final notification:* 6 months

Officers: Robert M. Smitson, Chair.; Jeffrey R. Lang, Secy.-Treas.
Directors: Stefan S. Anderson; Charles N. Hetrick.
EIN: 311183770

1146
Met Foundation, Inc.
7406 N. Washington Blvd.
Indianapolis, IN 46240 (317) 259-0717
Contact: Susan M. Tolbert, Pres.

Established in 1997 in IN.
Donor(s): Sue Anne McVie.
Grantmaker type: Independent foundation
Financial data (yr. ended 12/31/02): Assets, $13,493,906 (M); expenditures, $256,753; qualifying distributions, $254,049; giving activities include $247,000 for 26 grants (high: $50,000; low: $500).
Purpose and activities: Giving for the arts, youth services, and animal welfare.
Fields of interest: Museums; Natural resources; Environment, land resources; Animals/wildlife, preservation/protection; Youth, services; Boy scouts; Protestant agencies & churches.
Limitations: Giving primarily in Indianapolis, IN.
Application information: Application form not required.
>*Deadline(s):* Dec. 31

Officers and Directors:* Susan M. Tolbert,* Pres. and Treas.; Douglas S. McVie,* V.P.; Alexander M. McVie III,* Secy.
EIN: 351995120

1147
Michigan City Community Enrichment Corporation
409 W. Kieffer Rd.
Michigan City, IN 46360
Application address: P.O. Box 9046, Michigan City, IN 46361, tel.: (219) 877-0232

Established in 1998 in IN.
Donor(s): Blue Chip Casino, Inc.
Grantmaker type: Independent foundation
Financial data (yr. ended 12/31/01): Assets, $441,864 (M); gifts received, $750,000; expenditures, $829,797; qualifying distributions, $769,348; giving activities include $665,727 for 47 grants (high: $50,000; low: $500).
Purpose and activities: Giving for children and community services.
Fields of interest: Education, services; Education, community/cooperative; Zoos/zoological societies; Health organizations, association; Parks/playgrounds; Salvation Army; Community development.
International interests: Indian Subcontinent & Afghanistan.
Limitations: Giving primarily in Michigan City, IN. No grants to individuals.
Application information: Application form required.
>*Deadline(s):* Varies

Officers: Stephanie Oberlie, Chair.; Stephen Gonzalez, V.P.; Andrea Smith, Secy.; Sue Yadavia, Treas.
Directors: Michael Brillson; Joe Doyle; Eddie Newson; Beth Nieman; Robert Rose; Nate Williams.
EIN: 352036426

1148
Montgomery County Community Foundation
P.O. Box 334
Crawfordsville, IN 47933 (765) 362-1267
Contact: L. Ann Malott, Exec. Dir.
FAX: (765) 361-0562; E-mail: ann@mc-cf.com; URL: http://www.mc-cf.org/

Established in 1991 in Crawfordsville, IN.
Grantmaker type: Community foundation
Financial data (yr. ended 12/31/01): Assets, $21,172,573 (M); expenditures, $1,399,764; giving activities include $514,614 for 99 grants (high: $65,625; low: $33) and $312,249 for 332 grants to individuals (high: $18,214; low: $100).
Purpose and activities: The foundation administers donor-advised funds.
Fields of interest: Historic preservation/historical societies; Arts; Higher education; Education; Environment; Disabled.
Types of support: Annual campaigns; Capital campaigns; Building/renovation; Equipment; Program development; Conferences/seminars; Seed money; Scholarship funds; Scholarships—to individuals; Matching/challenge support.
Limitations: Giving limited to Montgomery County, IN. No support for religious organizations. No grants to individuals (except for scholarship recipients), or for endowments, operating budgets or for special events.
Publications: Application guidelines, Annual report, Grants list, Informational brochure (including application guidelines), Newsletter.
Application information: Application form required.
>*Initial approach:* Telephone or letter or visit Web site
>*Copies of proposal:* 11
>*Deadline(s):* Jan., May and Sept.
>*Board meeting date(s):* Monthly

Officers and Directors:* Harry Siamas,* Pres.; Suanne Milligan,* V.P.; Jeannie Stevens,* Secy.; Greg Starnes,* Treas.; L. Ann Malott, Exec. Dir.; Charles Arvin; Rosalie Bambrey; Jeffrey H. Birk; Bill Degitz; Anne Ford; Elmo Gonzalez; Pat Hearson; Becky Hurt; Eric Johnson; Steve Loy; Kenneth Newnum; George Spencer; Kathleen Steele.
EIN: 351836315

1149
Namaste Foundation, Inc.
c/o Terry B. Marbach
9704 W. Raintree Dr.
Columbus, IN 47201

Established in 1990 in IN.
Donor(s): Constance Marbach, Terry Marbach.
Grantmaker type: Independent foundation
Financial data (yr. ended 12/31/02): Assets, $3,269,418 (M); gifts received, $48,750; expenditures, $168,976; qualifying distributions,

$158,575; giving activities include $153,525 for 48 grants (high: $25,000; low: $200).
Fields of interest: Environment; Family planning; Children/youth, services; Protestant agencies & churches.
Types of support: General/operating support; Capital campaigns; Land acquisition; Endowments; Seed money; Scholarship funds.
Limitations: Applications not accepted. Giving primarily in Columbus, IN. No grants to individuals.
Publications: Annual report, Financial statement.
Application information: Contributes only to pre-selected organizations.
Officers: Terry Marbach, Pres. and Treas.; Constance Marbach, V.P. and Secy.
Directors: Beth Marbach; Jill Marbach.
Number of staff: None.
EIN: 351814583

1150
Parke County Community Foundation, Inc.
P.O. Box 276
Rockville, IN 47872
E-mail: pccf@abcs.com

Established in 1993 in IN.
Grantmaker type: Community foundation
Financial data (yr. ended 06/30/02): Assets, $6,238,530 (M); gifts received, $232,946; expenditures, $545,831; giving activities include $257,040 for 105 grants (high: $101,200; low: $11) and $2,348 for 12 grants to individuals (high: $715; low: $7).
Purpose and activities: Administers various trusts set up for the benefit of the community. The foundation administers donor-advised funds.
Fields of interest: Theater; Historic preservation/historical societies; Elementary/secondary education; Higher education; Education; Animal welfare; Health organizations, association; Disasters, fire prevention/control; Human services; Community development; Protestant agencies & churches; Cemeteries/burial services.
Types of support: General/operating support; Program development; Scholarship funds; Scholarships—to individuals.
Limitations: Giving primarily in Parke County, IN.
Officers: Ray R. Lewis, Chair.; James A. Gardner, Vice-Chair.; George Leanson, Secy.; Alex B. Milligan, Treas.; Brad Bumgarnder, Exec. Dir.
Directors: John L. Asbury; Leighton M. Britton; Adrene Brown; Monti J. Byers; Sally Curley; James D. Foster; Jeffrey S. Gooch; Bob Hale; Barbara Hardesty; Jessica M. Harney-Lynk; Kathryn R. Keller; Ann McCullough; Janie Pound; Larry Rickett; Mark C. Spelbring; Laird L. Thompson.
EIN: 351881810

1151
Perelman Charitable Foundation, Inc.
8751 Jaffa Ct. E. Dr., No. 16
Indianapolis, IN 46260
Contact: Dr. Melvin Perelman, Pres.

Established in 1991 in IN.
Donor(s): Melvin Perelman.
Grantmaker type: Independent foundation

Financial data (yr. ended 12/31/02): Assets, $3,522,425 (M); gifts received, $9,639; expenditures, $191,526; qualifying distributions, $178,577; giving activities include $176,580 for 14 grants (high: $102,330; low: $100).
Purpose and activities: Giving for museums, public broadcasting, higher education, animal welfare organizations and federated giving programs.
Fields of interest: Museums; Higher education; Medical school/education; Environment; Animals/wildlife, single organization support; Zoos/zoological societies; Federated giving programs.
Limitations: Giving primarily in IN. No grants to individuals.
Application information: Application form not required.
Initial approach: Letter
Copies of proposal: 1
Deadline(s): None
Officers: Melvin Perelman, Pres. and Treas.; Joan B. Perelman, Secy.
Directors: Wendy L. Schrimper; Jeffrey H. Thomasson.
Number of staff: None.
EIN: 351838295

1152

Nina Mason Pulliam Charitable Trust ▼
135 N. Pennsylvania St., Ste. 1200
Indianapolis, IN 46204 (317) 231-6075
Contact: Mary Prince
Application address for Arizona organizations: 2201 E. Camelback Rd. Ste. 600B, Phoenix, AZ 85016, tel.: (602) 955-3000; URL: http://www.ninapulliamtrust.org

Established in 1997 in AZ and IN.
Grantmaker type: Independent foundation
Financial data (yr. ended 12/31/01): Assets, $367,393,493 (M); expenditures, $21,954,387; qualifying distributions, $20,065,070; giving activities include $17,372,003 for 238 grants (high: $1,000,000; low: $2,500).
Purpose and activities: The trust seeks to help people in need, especially women, children and families; to protect animals and nature; and to enrich community life in the metropolitan areas of Indianapolis and Phoenix.
Fields of interest: Museums; Arts; Education; Natural resources; Animal welfare; Health care; Eye diseases; Food banks; Human services; Children/youth, services; Family services; Community development; Disabled.
Types of support: Annual campaigns; Capital campaigns; Building/renovation; Equipment; Land acquisition; Endowments; Curriculum development.
Limitations: Giving primarily in Phoenix, AZ, and Indianapolis, IN. No grants to individuals, or for academic research, religion, politics, non-operating private foundations, sectarian purposes, or international activities.
Publications: Application guidelines, Annual report (including application guidelines), Grants list.
Application information: See the foundation's Web site for an application. Requests for funding are limited to one request per organization per year. Application form required.
Initial approach: Proposal
Copies of proposal: 6

Deadline(s): Jan. 15, May 15, and Sept. 15
Final notification: Feb. 28, July 1, and Oct. 31
Officers: Harriet M. Ivey, C.E.O. and Pres.; Robert L. Lowry, C.F.O.
Trustees: Frank E. Russell; Nancy M. Russell; Carol P. Schatt.
Number of staff: 9 full-time professional; 8 full-time support.
EIN: 356644088
Recent environmental and animal welfare grants:
1152-1 Animal Defense League of Arizona, Tucson, AZ, $30,000. For Spay/Neuter Program in Phoenix, Tucson, Prescott, Flagstaff and area Native American reservations and Graham County. 2002.
1152-2 Arizona Trail Association, Phoenix, AZ, $100,000. To hire initial executive director, expand education and volunteer programs, and establish Phoenix-area office to complete trail connecting Arizona to Mexico and Utah. 2002.
1152-3 Audubon Society, National, Phoenix, AZ, $100,000. To establish state office in Phoenix, Arizona, to create network of community nature education centers, particularly in Maricopa County and in other urban and underserved portions of the state. 2002.
1152-4 Audubon Society, National, Indianapolis, Indiana, $100,000. To establish state office in Indianapolis, IN, to create network of community nature education centers, particularly in Marion County and other urban and underserved portions of state. 2002.
1152-5 Cry in the Wilderness, Tonopah, AZ, $40,000. For expansion of existing medical facility to provide quarantine area and treatment room for sick and abandoned wildlife. 2002.
1152-6 Desert Foothills Land Trust, Cave Creek, AZ, $100,000. For Desert Legacy III, third phase of Go John Canyon Preserve Campaign to protect Cave Creek Watershed as part of riparian habitat. 2002.
1152-7 Environmental Management Institute, Indianapolis, Indiana, $70,000. For Citizen's Healthy Homes initiative to reduce exposure of low-income residents, in Kennedy-King Park area, to environmental hazards through training and awareness program. 2002.
1152-8 Foundation Against Companion Animal Euthanasia, Indianapolis, Indiana, $100,000. For building addition to enable clinic to increase number of low-cost spay/neuter surgeries. 2002.
1152-9 Friends of White River, Indianapolis, Indiana, $50,400. To expand executive director position from part-time to full-time. 2002.
1152-10 Grand Canyon Trust, Flagstaff, AZ, $500,000. For Land Protection Plan of the Colorado Plateau, including acquisition of Dry Lake near Flagstaff, habitat protection in the Grand Canyon Parashant National Monument, and continuation of Animal Species and Wild Lands Science Program. 2002.
1152-11 Handi-Dogs, Tucson, AZ, $26,300. To establish assistance dog training program in Phoenix to teach the deaf and hearing-impaired to train their own dogs as hearing-ear dogs. 2002.

1152-12 Indiana Canine Assistant and Adolescent Network (ICAAN), Indianapolis, Indiana, $25,000. To expand the service dog training program to increase availability of service dogs to individuals with physical disabilities in Indiana. 2002.
1152-13 Indianapolis Parks Foundation, Indianapolis, Indiana, $190,000. For Hub Naturalist Program to create environmental hubs in Marion County which will provide programs to parks, churches, and community centers. 2002.
1152-14 Malpai Borderlands Group, Douglas, AZ, $35,000. For Habitat Conservation Planning Project to conduct regionwide conservation planning for endangered and threatened wildlife species in the area. 2002.
1152-15 Native Seeds/Southwestern Endangered Arid-Land Resource Clearing House (SEARCH), Tucson, AZ, $75,000. For Tribal Crop Growout Project large-scale campaign to regenerate the most endangered and critically aged seed varieties and to increase availability of seeds to Native Americans and other farmers and gardeners. 2002.
1152-16 Nature Conservancy, Indianapolis, Indiana, $90,000. To establish office in Brown County which will develop conservation site plan for land in Brown County Hills region. 2002.
1152-17 Scottsdale Community College, Scottsdale, AZ, $97,000. For Education Outreach and Desert Restoration programs to increase awareness and appreciation of Sonoran Desert wildlife by providing opportunities for K-12 and college students to restore and preserve desert habitat using hands-on educational experiences. 2002.

1153

The Putnam County Community Foundation
2 S. Jackson St.
P.O. Box 514
Greencastle, IN 46135-0514 (765) 653-4978
Contact: M. Elaine Peck, Exec. Dir.
FAX: (765) 653-6385; E-mail: epeck@pcfoundation.org; URL: http://www.pcfoundation.org

Established in 1986 in IN.
Grantmaker type: Community foundation
Financial data (yr. ended 12/31/02): Assets, $10,673,803 (M); gifts received, $628,911; expenditures, $730,275; giving activities include $352,782 for grants.
Purpose and activities: The foundation administers a donor-advised fund.
Fields of interest: Arts; Education; Environment; Health care; Recreation; Human services; Economic development.
Types of support: Equipment; Program development; Seed money; Scholarship funds; Technical assistance; Matching/challenge support.
Limitations: Giving limited to Putnam County, IN.
Publications: Application guidelines, Annual report (including application guidelines).
Application information: Application form required.
Initial approach: 1-page letter of inquiry
Copies of proposal: 12

Deadline(s): Feb. 2, May 4, and Aug. 3
Board meeting date(s): Monthly
Officers and Directors:* James Renz,* Pres.;
Lynn Bohmer,* V.P.; Harold Spicer,* Secy.;
Ginger Scott,* Treas.; M. Elaine Peck, Exec. Dir.;
and 10 additional directors.
Number of staff: 2 full-time professional; 1
full-time support; 1 part-time support.
EIN: 311159916

1154
M. E. Raker Foundation, Inc.
6207 Constitution Dr.
Fort Wayne, IN 46804
Contact: John E. Hogan, Pres.

Established in 1984 in IN.
Donor(s): M.E. Raker.‡
Grantmaker type: Independent foundation
Financial data (yr. ended 06/30/02): Assets,
$9,703,243 (M); expenditures, $743,887;
qualifying distributions, $621,730; giving
activities include $540,445 for 64 grants (high:
$25,000; low: $1,000).
Fields of interest: Secondary school/education;
Education; Natural resources; Health care;
Health organizations, association; Human
services; Children/youth, services; Human
services; Federated giving programs; Christian
agencies & churches.
Types of support: General/operating support;
Capital campaigns; Building/renovation;
Scholarship funds.
Limitations: Giving primarily in Fort Wayne, IN.
No support for the arts. No grants to individuals.
Application information: Application form
required.
Initial approach: Letter requesting application
Deadline(s): None
Officer: John E. Hogan, Pres.
Directors: John N. Pichon; Stephen J. Williams.
EIN: 311040474

1155
Reilly Foundation
300 N. Meridian St., Ste. 1500
Indianapolis, IN 46204
Contact: Rand Brooks, Tr.

Established in 1962 in IN.
Donor(s): Reilly Tar & Chemical Corp., Reilly
Industries, Inc.
Grantmaker type: Company-sponsored
foundation
Financial data (yr. ended 12/31/02): Assets,
$809,025 (M); expenditures, $289,011;
qualifying distributions, $289,011; giving
activities include $268,350 for 49 grants (high:
$51,400; low: $500) and $12,050 for 20
employee matching gifts.
Purpose and activities: Giving primarily for
higher education, community funds, the arts,
and social service agencies; educational grants
and scholarships limited to children of company
employees.
Fields of interest: Arts; Higher education;
Medical school/education; Education;
Zoos/zoological societies; Human services;
Children/youth, services; Federated giving
programs.

Types of support: General/operating support;
Employee matching gifts; Employee-related
scholarships.
Limitations: Giving limited to areas of company
operations.
Application information:
Initial approach: Letter of intent
Deadline(s): None
Trustees: Heather Murphy; Elizabeth C. Reilly;
Michael W. Rodman; Kevin Wilhelm.
EIN: 352061750

1156
Richard and Joan Ringoen Family Trust
c/o Indiana Trust & Investment Mgmt. Co.
315 W. Adams St.
Muncie, IN 47308

Established in 1990 in IN.
Donor(s): Richard M. Ringoen.
Grantmaker type: Independent foundation
Financial data (yr. ended 12/31/02): Assets,
$1,795,939 (M); expenditures, $128,722;
qualifying distributions, $112,069; giving
activities include $112,250 for 46 grants (high:
$11,500; low: $450).
Purpose and activities: Giving for human
services and Christian organizations.
Fields of interest: Arts; Education; Natural
resources; Family planning; Youth development,
religion; Human services; Civil rights;
Foundations (community); Christian agencies &
churches; Protestant agencies & churches.
Limitations: Applications not accepted. Giving
primarily in CO. No grants to individuals.
Application information: Contributes only to
pre-selected organizations.
Trustee: Indiana Trust & Investment Mgmt. Co.
EIN: 351803115

1157
Rotary Foundation of Indianapolis, Inc.
350 N. Meridian St.
Indianapolis, IN 46204 (317) 631-3733

Grantmaker type: Public charity
Financial data (yr. ended 06/30/02): Revenue,
$431,607; assets, $5,511,699 (M); gifts received,
$59,060; expenditures, $335,063; program
services expenses, $275,650; giving activities
include $275,650 for 60 grants (high: $33,750;
low: $440).
Purpose and activities: The foundation is the
charitable arm of the Rotary Club of
Indianapolis, awarding grants in the greater
Indianapolis area and promoting the Rotary
philosophy of "service above self."
Fields of interest: Performing arts; Education;
Zoos/zoological societies; Public health; Health
care; Camps; Recreation; Boy scouts; Youth
development; Human services; Family services;
Urban/community development.
Types of support: General/operating support;
Capital campaigns; Building/renovation;
Equipment; Program development;
Matching/challenge support.
Limitations: Giving limited to the greater
Indianapolis, IN, area. No support for sectarian
and/or religious programs, other foundations, or
organizations lacking 501(c)(3) nonprofit status.

No grants to individuals, or for after-the-fact
funding requests.
Application information:
Initial approach: Letter
Deadline(s): None
Final notification: 90 to 120 days
Officers and Directors:* Eugene M. Busche,*
Pres.; Stan Hurt,* V.P.; Marsha Spring,* Secy.;
Tom Surgener,* Treas.; Robert W. Seymour, Exec.
Dir.; Ken Chapman; William Douthit; Thomas
G. Fisher; Robert Hulett; Polly Jontz; Thomas
Lugar; Robert McNamara; John Murphy.
EIN: 356043931

1158
Save the Dunes Conservation Fund
c/o Thomas Anderson
444 Barker Rd.
Michigan City, IN 46360-7426
(219) 879-3564
FAX: (219) 872-4875; E-mail:
sand@savedunes.org; URL: http://
www.savedunes.org/html/stdcfund.html

Established in 1994 in IN.
Grantmaker type: Public charity
Financial data (yr. ended 12/31/00): Revenue,
$80,535; assets, $121,128; gifts received,
$55,912; expenditures, $73,210; program
services expenses, $55,338; giving activities
include $1,050 for 3 grants to individuals (high:
$500; low: $50).
Purpose and activities: The organization seeks
to restore and protect the environment of the
Indiana Dunes.
Fields of interest: Environment.
Types of support: Grants to individuals;
Scholarships—to individuals.
Limitations: Giving primarily in IN.
Officers and Directors:* Thomas C. Serynek,*
Pres.; Dorothy Potucek,* 1st V.P.; Geof Benson,*
2nd V.P.; Ellen Firme,* Secy.; David F. Drake,*
Treas.; Carolyn Bach; Carol Cook; Gina Darnell;
Elizabeth Freese; and 7 additional directors.
EIN: 351915468

1159
Sam Shine Foundation, Inc.
P.O. Box 1407
New Albany, IN 47151-1407

Established in 1995 in IN.
Donor(s): Sam M. Shine.
Grantmaker type: Independent foundation
Financial data (yr. ended 12/31/02): Assets,
$7,551,214 (M); expenditures, $536,582;
qualifying distributions, $486,721; giving
activities include $507,021 for grants (high:
$383,869).
Purpose and activities: Giving primarily for
conservation programs.
Fields of interest: Natural resources;
Environment.
Limitations: Applications not accepted. Giving
on a national basis. No grants to individuals.
Application information: Contributes only to
pre-selected organizations.
Officer and Directors:* Sam M. Shine,* Pres.;
Dale L. Gettelfinger; Betty Shine; John Shine; J.
Robert Shine.
EIN: 351961730

1160
Unity Foundation of La Porte County, Inc.
619 Franklin St.
P.O. Box 527
Michigan City, IN 46361-0527
(219) 879-0327
Contact: Margaret Spartz, Pres.
E-mail: unity@uflc.net; URL: http://www.uflc.net

Established in 1992 in IN.
Grantmaker type: Community foundation
Financial data (yr. ended 12/31/01): Assets, $10,854,986 (M); gifts received, $1,176,189; expenditures, $1,293,108; giving activities include $587,520 for grants (average: $500–$5,000) and $254,444 for grants to individuals.
Purpose and activities: To accept and pool charitable contributions from a variety of resources, and use the proceeds to support other charitable activities and organizations to benefit the residents of La Porte County, IN. The foundation administers a donor-advised fund.
Fields of interest: Arts; Education; Environment; Human services; Children/youth, services; Community development.
Types of support: Building/renovation; Equipment; Program development; Conferences/seminars; Seed money; Scholarship funds; Technical assistance; Employee matching gifts.
Limitations: Giving limited to residents of La Porte County, IN.
Publications: Application guidelines, Annual report, Grants list, Newsletter.
Application information: Application form required.
 Initial approach: Letter
 Copies of proposal: 1
 Deadline(s): July
 Board meeting date(s): 1st Mon. of month
 Final notification: Within 90 days of grant deadline
Officers: Michael Brennan, Co-Chair.; Edward Volk, Co-Chair.; Robert Schaefer, Vice-Chair.; Margaret A. Spartz, Pres.; Romona Hay, Secy.; Arlene Dunn, Treas.
Directors: Susan Aaron; Margaret F. Hiler; Jim Jessup; Jerry Kabelin; Vidya Kora; Robert Lake; Daniel E. Lewis, Jr.; Mary Lou Linnen; C. Edward Raab; Burton B. Ruby; Robert J. Schaefer; Marti Swanson.
Number of staff: 1 full-time professional; 3 part-time support.
EIN: 351658674

1161
The White Lick Heritage Community Foundation, Inc.
5055 E. Main St., Ste. A
Avon, IN 46123 (317) 718-1200
Contact: Delynn A. Daniel, Exec. Dir.
E-mail: wlhcf@indy.net

Established in 1996 in IN.
Grantmaker type: Community foundation
Financial data (yr. ended 12/31/02): Assets, $3,797,202 (M); gifts received, $1,333,259; expenditures, $943,877; giving activities include $147,447 for grants and $560,087 for grants to individuals.
Purpose and activities: The foundation administers a donor-advised fund.

Fields of interest: Arts; Environment; Health care; Human services.
Types of support: Continuing support; Building/renovation; Equipment; Land acquisition; Emergency funds; Program development; Seed money; Curriculum development; Research; Grants to individuals; Scholarships—to individuals; Matching/challenge support.
Limitations: Giving limited to Hendricks County, IN.
Publications: Annual report, Financial statement, Informational brochure, Newsletter.
Officers: Ken Sebree, Pres.; Dick Dietz, V.P.; Judy Pingel, Secy.; Thomas Newlin, Treas.; Delynn A. Daniel, Exec. Dir.
Number of staff: 1 part-time professional; 2 part-time support.
EIN: 351878973

1162
Jerry J. Wilson Memorial Foundation, Inc.
c/o Kemper CPA Group, LLC
P.O. Box 327
Connersville, IN 47331

Established in 1998 in IN.
Donor(s): Jane T. Wilson.
Grantmaker type: Independent foundation
Financial data (yr. ended 12/31/01): Assets, $2,176,935 (M); expenditures, $1,557,964; qualifying distributions, $1,554,211; giving activities include $1,515,000 for 4 grants (high: $1,200,000; low: $5,000).
Fields of interest: Education; Natural resources; Health care, clinics/centers; Human services; Human services, gift distribution; Gays/lesbians.
Limitations: Applications not accepted. Giving primarily in Connersville, IN. No grants to individuals.
Application information: Contributes only to pre-selected organizations.
Directors: James Wilson; Jane T. Wilson; Jennifer J. Wilson; John D. Wilson; Thomas D. Wilson.
EIN: 352032589

IOWA

1163
H. Reimers Bechtel Charitable Remainder Uni-Trust
1000 Firstar Ctr.
201 W. 2nd St., Ste. 1000
Davenport, IA 52801 (563) 328-3333
Contact: R. Richard Bittner, Tr.

Established in 1987 in IA.
Grantmaker type: Independent foundation
Financial data (yr. ended 08/31/02): Assets, $2,066,763 (M); expenditures, $207,321; qualifying distributions, $189,806; giving activities include $174,000 for 13 grants (high: $30,000; low: $2,000).
Purpose and activities: Giving for youth services, high school education, and public services.

Fields of interest: Television; Higher education; Botanical gardens; Boy scouts; YM/YWCAs & YM/YWHAs; Family services; Community development; Christian agencies & churches.
Limitations: Giving primarily in IA and IL. Generally no grants to individuals, or for endowment funds, debt retirement, past operating deficit, general or continuing support, or for scholarly research in an established discipline.
Application information: Application form required.
 Initial approach: Request application form
 Deadline(s): None
Trustee: R. Richard Bittner.
EIN: 426342964

1164
F. William Beckwith & Leola I. Beckwith Charitable Foundation
P.O. Box 70
Boone, IA 50036-0070
Contact: F. William Beckwith, Pres.

Established in 1995.
Donor(s): F. William Beckwith, Leola I. Beckwith.
Grantmaker type: Operating foundation
Financial data (yr. ended 12/31/02): Assets, $3,064,425 (M); gifts received, $450,000; expenditures, $344,896; qualifying distributions, $343,733; giving activities include $342,200 for 9 grants (high: $130,000; low: $4,000).
Purpose and activities: Giving primarily for education and family services.
Fields of interest: Libraries (public); Education; Botanical gardens; Camps; Youth development, agriculture; Family services; Christian agencies & churches.
Limitations: Giving primarily in IA. No grants to individuals.
Application information:
 Initial approach: Letter
 Deadline(s): None
Officers: F. William Beckwith, Pres. and Treas.; Leola I. Beckwith, Secy.
EIN: 421448419

1165
Berman Family Foundation
504 N. 4th St., Ste. 104
Fairfield, IA 52556
Contact: Warren Berman, Pres.

Established in 1996 in IL.
Donor(s): Warren Berman.
Grantmaker type: Independent foundation
Financial data (yr. ended 12/31/02): Assets, $171,105 (M); expenditures, $1,321,891; qualifying distributions, $1,315,449; giving activities include $1,315,450 for 18 grants (high: $1,250,000; low: $100).
Purpose and activities: Giving primarily for education, including transcendental meditation programs.
Fields of interest: Arts; Education; Natural resources; Community development.
Limitations: Giving primarily in IA. No grants to individuals.
Application information:
 Initial approach: Letter

Officers and Directors:* Warren Berman,*
Pres.; Harriet Berman,* Treas.; Joseph Berman.
EIN: 421465136

1166
Myron & Jacqueline Blank Fund
(formerly The Myron and Jacqueline Blank
Charity Fund)
414 Insurance Exchange Bldg.
505 5th Ave.
Des Moines, IA 50309
Contact: Sandy Fein, Assoc.

Incorporated in 1948 in IA.
Donor(s): A.H. Blank,‡ Myron N. Blank.
Grantmaker type: Independent foundation
Financial data (yr. ended 12/31/01): Assets,
$6,583,243 (M); expenditures, $1,623,135;
qualifying distributions, $1,593,548; giving
activities include $1,595,254 for 27 grants
(high: $1,157,390; low: $100).
Purpose and activities: Giving primarily to a
zoo foundation, as well as for the arts, human
services, health, federated giving programs, and
Jewish organizations.
Fields of interest: Arts; Zoos/zoological
societies; Family planning; Health care; Human
services; Federated giving programs; Jewish
federated giving programs; Jewish agencies &
temples.
Types of support: Annual campaigns;
Building/renovation; Endowments;
Professorships.
Limitations: Applications not accepted. Giving
primarily in Des Moines, IA. No grants to
individuals.
Application information: Contributes only to
pre-selected organizations.
Officers and Directors:* Myron N. Blank,*
Pres.; Michael G. Gartner, V.P.; Jacqueline N.
Blank,* Secy.-Treas.
Number of staff: 2 part-time professional.
EIN: 237423791

1167
**The Greater Cedar Rapids Community
Foundation**
(formerly The Greater Cedar Rapids Foundation)
200 1st St. S.W.
Cedar Rapids, IA 52404 (319) 366-2862
Contact: Daniel Baldwin, C.E.O. and Pres.
FAX: (319) 366-2912; E-mail: info@gcrcf.org;
URL: http://www.gcrcf.org

Established in 1949 in IA.
Grantmaker type: Community foundation
Financial data (yr. ended 12/31/02): Assets,
$24,475,830 (M); gifts received, $4,400,856;
expenditures, $2,143,695; giving activities
include $1,700,449 for grants.
Purpose and activities: To enhance the quality
of life in the community by supporting creative
and innovative programs, current or emerging
charitable opportunities, services not presently
offered, and occasional capital projects.
Fields of interest: Historic
preservation/historical societies; Arts; Education;
Environment; Health care; AIDS; Human
services; Community development;
neighborhood development.
Types of support: Capital campaigns;
Building/renovation; Equipment; Emergency

funds; Program development;
Conferences/seminars; Publication; Seed
money; Curriculum development; Scholarship
funds; Technical assistance; Consulting services;
Matching/challenge support.
Limitations: Giving limited to the greater Cedar
Rapids and surrounding Linn County, IA, area.
No support for crisis intervention. No grants to
individuals, or for annual operating budgets;
generally no grants for deficit financing, or
after-the-fact funding.
Publications: Application guidelines, Annual
report, Informational brochure, Newsletter.
Application information: Applicants are
encouraged to telephone regarding preliminary
information prior to submitting an application.
Application form required.
Initial approach: Application
Copies of proposal: 11
Deadline(s): Feb., June and Oct.
Board meeting date(s): Bimonthly
Final notification: Apr., Aug. and Dec.
Officers and Directors:* Gilda Boyer,* Chair.;
Greg Neumeyer,* Vice-Chair.; Daniel Baldwin,
C.E.O and Pres.; Kristin C. Novak,* Secy.; Larry
Christy,* Treas.; Bill Aossey; F. James Bradley;
Katrina Garner; Dennis Green; Cathy
Gullickson; Gerald R. Hinzman; Ann Hoffman;
Kory Kazimar; Barbara Knapp; Ann Lipsky; Jay
Petersen; Paul Phelan, Jr.; Mary K. Quass;
Curran L. Rosser; John Smith; Terry Trimpe; John
Wasta.
Number of staff: 4 full-time professional; 1
part-time professional; 1 full-time support.
EIN: 426053860

1168
Fleming Family Foundation
2014 Scotch Ridge Rd.
Carlisle, IA 50047-3142

Established in 1989 in IA.
Donor(s): Ann W. Fleming, Robert J. Fleming.
Grantmaker type: Independent foundation
Financial data (yr. ended 04/30/02): Assets,
$2,141,761 (M); expenditures, $108,503;
qualifying distributions, $104,369; giving
activities include $106,200 for 33 grants (high:
$25,000; low: $200).
Purpose and activities: Giving primarily for the
arts, education, and human services.
Fields of interest: College; University; Hospitals
(general); Natural resources; Human services.
Limitations: Applications not accepted. Giving
primarily in Des Moines, IA. No grants to
individuals.
Application information: Contributes only to
pre-selected organizations.
Officers and Directors:* Robert J. Fleming,*
Pres.; Ann W. Fleming,* V.P.; Carlton T. King,*
Secy.
EIN: 421336624

1169
Gilchrist Foundation
c/o Security National Bank
P.O. Box 147
Sioux City, IA 51102

Established in 1998 in IA.
Grantmaker type: Independent foundation

Financial data (yr. ended 12/31/02): Assets,
$17,375,208 (M); expenditures, $1,270,119;
qualifying distributions, $1,123,273; giving
activities include $1,125,000 for 16 grants
(high: $100,000; low: $25,000).
Fields of interest: Arts, association; Television;
Radio; Orchestra (symphony); Arts; Natural
resources; Animal welfare; Health care,
association; American Red Cross.
Types of support: General/operating support.
Limitations: Applications not accepted. Giving
primarily in IA. No grants to individuals.
Application information: Contributes only to
pre-selected organizations.
Trustee: Security National Bank.
EIN: 426578668

1170
**Harold W. and Leone L. Godbersen
Family Foundation**
c/o Sharon Godbersen
199-121 E. Hwy. 175, Box 151
Ida Grove, IA 51445

Established in 1987 in IA.
Donor(s): Leone L. Godbersen.
Grantmaker type: Independent foundation
Financial data (yr. ended 12/31/02): Assets,
$1,412,842 (M); expenditures, $99,361;
qualifying distributions, $89,177; giving
activities include $89,625 for 3 grants (high:
$50,000; low: $1,000).
Purpose and activities: Giving for education
scholarships, community services, including fire
and medical services, and for recreation.
Fields of interest: Secondary school/education;
Education; Natural resources; Human services.
Types of support: General/operating support.
Limitations: Applications not accepted. Giving
limited to Ida Grove, IA. No grants to
individuals.
Application information: Contributes only to
pre-selected organizations.
Directors: Gary Godbersen; Sharon Godbersen;
Edward Jacobson.
EIN: 421287050

1171
**William M. & Donna J. Hoaglin
Foundation, Inc.**
800 Alter Ct.
Mount Pleasant, IA 52641-1988
Contact: Donna J. Hoaglin, Pres.
Application address: P.O. Box 791, Mount
Pleasant, IA 52641-0791

Established in 1979.
Donor(s): William M. Hoaglin, Donna J.
Hoaglin.
Grantmaker type: Independent foundation
Financial data (yr. ended 01/31/03): Assets,
$5,574,117 (M); expenditures, $250,634;
qualifying distributions, $246,773; giving
activities include $249,361 for 29 grants (high:
$50,000; low: $1,250).
Purpose and activities: Giving primarily to
promote the literary and educational welfare of
people in Henry and Van Buren counties, IA.
Fields of interest: Orchestra (symphony);
Historical activities; College; Education; Natural

resources; Human services; Federated giving programs.
Limitations: Giving primarily in Henry and Van Buren counties, IA. No grants to individuals.
Application information: Application form required.
Deadline(s): Jan. 1 and July 1
Officers: Donna J. Hoaglin, Pres.; Carmen Heaton, Secy.; David J. Carrick, Treas.
Directors: Norman Kisling; Hugh McCoy; Russell Remick; Richard Thuma.
EIN: 421121634

1172
Fred and Charlotte Hubbell Foundation
c/o Bankers Trust Co., Trust Div.
665 Locust St.
Des Moines, IA 50309
Contact: Mindy Nussbaum

Established in 1997 in IA.
Donor(s): Charlotte Hubbell, Frederick S. Hubbell.
Grantmaker type: Independent foundation
Financial data (yr. ended 12/31/02): Assets, $2,949,104 (M); expenditures, $219,524; qualifying distributions, $205,139; giving activities include $196,750 for 26 grants (high: $101,000; low: $250).
Purpose and activities: Giving for federated giving programs, educational and scientific purposes, and the arts.
Fields of interest: Performing arts centers; Higher education; Law school/education; Environment, association; Federated giving programs.
Limitations: Giving primarily in IA, with emphasis on Des Moines.
Application information:
Initial approach: Letter
Deadline(s): None
Trustee: Bankers Trust Co.
EIN: 391878112

1173
Hubbell-Waterman Foundation
c/o Wells Fargo Bank Iowa, N.A.
203 W. 3rd St.
Davenport, IA 52801

Established in 1971 in IA.
Donor(s): Mary Waterman.
Grantmaker type: Independent foundation
Financial data (yr. ended 12/31/02): Assets, $9,585,620 (M); gifts received, $685; expenditures, $534,090; qualifying distributions, $496,735; giving activities include $492,000 for 26 grants (high: $200,000; low: $1,000).
Purpose and activities: Giving primarily for the arts, with emphasis on museums, as well as for human services.
Fields of interest: Museums (natural history); Arts; Education; Natural resources; Human services; Foundations (community).
Limitations: Applications not accepted. Giving primarily in Davenport, IA. No grants to individuals.
Application information: Contributes only to pre-selected organizations.
Trustee: Wells Fargo Bank, N.A.
EIN: 426126467

1174
The Iowa Foundation for Education, Environment and the Arts
4222 Forest Ave.
Des Moines, IA 50311-2541

Established in 1992 in IA.
Donor(s): David W. Belin.
Grantmaker type: Independent foundation
Financial data (yr. ended 12/31/02): Assets, $4,662,131 (M); expenditures, $331,207; qualifying distributions, $243,264; giving activities include $244,631 for 28 grants (high: $36,000; low: $100).
Fields of interest: Museums; Arts; Education; Zoos/zoological societies; Family planning; Boys & girls clubs; Hospices; Religion.
Limitations: Applications not accepted. Giving primarily in IA. No grants to individuals.
Application information: Contributes only to pre-selected organizations.
Officers: Thomas Richard Belin, Pres.; Joy Elizabeth Belin, V.P.; James M. Belin, Secy.-Treas.
EIN: 421333063

1175
Kehl Family Foundation
P.O. Box 1234
Clinton, IA 52733-1234

Established in 1998 in NV.
Donor(s): Robert J. Kehl, Ruth A. Kehl.
Grantmaker type: Independent foundation
Financial data (yr. ended 12/31/02): Assets, $342,224 (M); gifts received, $350,559; expenditures, $335,925; qualifying distributions, $333,826; giving activities include $334,000 for 4 grants (high: $233,000; low: $25,000).
Fields of interest: College; Environment, water resources; Disabled.
Limitations: Applications not accepted. Giving primarily in IA. No grants to individuals.
Application information: Contributes only to pre-selected organizations.
Officers: Robert J. Kehl, Pres.; Ruth A. Kehl, Secy.-Treas.
Trustees: Kenneth A. Bonnet; Christina M. Kehl; Daniel J. Kehl; Kevin A. Kehl; Robert A. Kehl; Cynthia A. Winter.
EIN: 421478647

1176
The Kenneth (Ken) R. Krause Charitable Foundation
P.O. Box 41355
Des Moines, IA 50311
Contact: Brett H. Krause, Tr.

Established in 1995 in IA.
Grantmaker type: Independent foundation
Financial data (yr. ended 12/31/02): Assets, $1,062,972 (M); expenditures, $125,430; qualifying distributions, $94,250; giving activities include $94,250 for 15 grants (high: $30,000; low: $750).
Purpose and activities: Giving primarily for higher education and health.
Fields of interest: Arts; Higher education; Animals/wildlife, preservation/protection; Health care; Cancer; Housing/shelter, development; International human rights.

Limitations: Giving on a national basis.
Application information:
Initial approach: Statement of purpose, including amount to be spent on each charitable purpose
Deadline(s): None
Trustee: Brett H. Krause.
EIN: 421446789

1177
Krause Gentle Foundation
6400 Westown Pkwy, Ste. 220
West Des Moines, IA 50266

Established in 1994 in IA.
Donor(s): William A. Krause, KG Investments.
Grantmaker type: Independent foundation
Financial data (yr. ended 12/31/02): Assets, $3,561,040 (M); gifts received, $10,000; expenditures, $367,645; qualifying distributions, $318,550; giving activities include $310,550 for 68 grants (high: $100,000; low: $100).
Purpose and activities: Giving for Catholic schools, churches and organizations; giving also for youth services and programs and for higher education.
Fields of interest: Music (choral); Visual arts; Higher education; Animal welfare; Cystic fibrosis; Muscular dystrophy; Multiple sclerosis; Housing/shelter, development; Recreation, association; Camps; Boy scouts; Girl scouts; YM/YWCAs & YM/YWHAs; Youth, services; Residential/custodial care; Federated giving programs; Protestant agencies & churches; Roman Catholic agencies & churches.
Limitations: Giving on a national basis, with emphasis on IA. No grants to individuals.
Directors: Dennis Folden; William A. Krause.
EIN: 421414004

1178
Lee Foundation
215 N. Main St.
Davenport, IA 52801   (319) 383-2100
Contact: Carl Schmidt, Secy.-Treas.

Incorporated in 1962 in IA.
Donor(s): Lee Enterprises, Inc.
Grantmaker type: Company-sponsored foundation
Financial data (yr. ended 09/30/02): Assets, $5,617,813 (M); expenditures, $505,669; qualifying distributions, $502,842; giving activities include $503,123 for 60 grants (high: $50,000; low: $300).
Fields of interest: Arts; Education; Animal welfare; Child abuse.
Types of support: Capital campaigns; Building/renovation; Endowments.
Limitations: Giving primarily in areas of company operations in CA, ID, IA, IL, IN, KY, MN, MT, NE, NY, ND, OR, PA, SC, SD, WA, WI, and WY. No grants to individuals.
Application information: Initial request must be submitted to the publisher of the area. Application form not required.
Initial approach: Letter
Copies of proposal: 5
Deadline(s): None
Officers and Directors:* Mary Junck,* Pres.; Carl Schmidt,* Secy.-Treas.; Greg Schermer; Greg Veon.

Number of staff: 1 part-time support.
EIN: 426057173

1179
The F. Maytag Family Foundation
(formerly The Fred Maytag Family Foundation)
P.O. Box 366
Newton, IA 50208 (641) 791-0395
Contact: Ellen Bergeron, Secy.

Trust established in 1945 in IA.
Donor(s): Fred Maytag II,‡ and members of the Maytag family.
Grantmaker type: Independent foundation
Financial data (yr. ended 12/31/01): Assets, $36,529,784 (M); expenditures, $3,825,734; qualifying distributions, $3,501,655; giving activities include $3,527,622 for 120 grants (high: $1,000,000; low: $100; average: $1,000–$25,000).
Purpose and activities: Giving for higher and other education, arts and culture, public affairs, social services, health, including cancer research, and aid for the handicapped.
Fields of interest: Arts; Higher education; Education; Natural resources; Health care; Health organizations, association; Cancer; Cancer research; Human services; Community development; Science, research; Public affairs; Disabled.
Types of support: General/operating support; Continuing support; Annual campaigns; Capital campaigns; Building/renovation; Equipment; Land acquisition; Endowments; Emergency funds; Program development; Conferences/seminars; Professorships; Publication; Seed money; Curriculum development; Fellowships; Internship funds; Scholarship funds; Research; Technical assistance; Matching/challenge support.
Limitations: Giving primarily in Des Moines and Newton, IA. No grants to individuals, or for emergency funds, deficit financing, scholarships, fellowships, demonstration projects, or conferences; no loans.
Publications: Application guidelines.
Application information: Application form not required.
  Initial approach: Request application guidelines
  Copies of proposal: 3
  Deadline(s): None
  Board meeting date(s): N
Officer: Ellen Bergeron, Secy.
Trustees: Frederick L. Maytag III; Kenneth P. Maytag; William C. Weinsheimer, Esq.
Number of staff: 2 full-time support.
EIN: 421444870

1180
R. J. McElroy Trust
KWWL Bldg., Ste. 318
500 E. 4th St.
Waterloo, IA 50703 (319) 287-9102
Contact: Linda L. Klinger, Exec. Dir.
FAX: (319) 287-9105; E-mail: mcelroy@cedarnet.org; URL: http://www.cedarnet.org/mcelroy/index.html

Established in 1965 in IA; private foundation status attained in 1984.
Donor(s): R.J. McElroy.

Grantmaker type: Independent foundation
Financial data (yr. ended 12/31/01): Assets, $46,886,215 (M); expenditures, $3,009,928; qualifying distributions, $2,701,024; giving activities include $2,519,464 for 139+ grants (high: $200,000; low: $50; average: $1,000–$50,000) and $80,500 for 35 grants to individuals (high: $7,500; low: $1,000).
Purpose and activities: Primary emphasis on higher education, especially scholarship and loan programs; public secondary education, particularly for the disadvantaged; early childhood and elementary education and programs for minorities; and youth, including internships. Giving also for the arts, recreation, and the environment; some support through matching funds and fellowships for graduate study.
Fields of interest: Visual arts; Performing arts; Arts; Early childhood education; Child development, education; Elementary school/education; Secondary school/education; Higher education; Education; Environment; Recreation; Youth development, services; Human services; Children/youth, services; Child development, services; Leadership development; Minorities; Economically disadvantaged.
Types of support: Capital campaigns; Building/renovation; Equipment; Emergency funds; Program development; Professorships; Seed money; Fellowships; Internship funds; Scholarship funds; Research; Matching/challenge support.
Limitations: Giving primarily in the KWWL viewing area, 19 counties in northeast IA. No grants to individuals (except for fellowship program).
Publications: Application guidelines, Grants list, Informational brochure (including application guidelines), Program policy statement.
Application information: Application form not required.
  Copies of proposal: 1
  Deadline(s): Mar. 1, June 1, Sept. 1, and Dec. 1
  Board meeting date(s): Monthly
  Final notification: May 1, Aug. 1, Nov. 1, and Feb. 1
Officers and Trustees:* Ross D. Christensen,* Chair.; Linda L. Klinger, Exec. Dir.; Raleigh D. Buckmaster; James B. Waterblury; Rick Young.
Number of staff: 1 full-time professional; 1 full-time support.
EIN: 426173496

1181
Edwin T. Meredith Foundation
1716 Locust St.
Des Moines, IA 50309-3023 (515) 284-2545
Contact: E.T. Meredith III, Pres.

Incorporated in 1946 in IA.
Donor(s): Meredith Publishing Co.
Grantmaker type: Independent foundation
Financial data (yr. ended 12/31/01): Assets, $18,493,405 (M); expenditures, $1,018,185; qualifying distributions, $925,950; giving activities include $927,667 for 30 grants (high: $100,000; low: $500).
Purpose and activities: Grants largely for youth agencies, higher education, cultural programs, and a historic preservation area; some support

for hospitals and health agencies, as well as for conservation.
Fields of interest: Arts; Higher education; Natural resources; Health care; Children/youth, services.
Types of support: Annual campaigns; Capital campaigns; Building/renovation; Endowments.
Limitations: Applications not accepted. Giving primarily in IA. No grants to individuals.
Application information: Contributes only to pre-selected organizations.
  Board meeting date(s): June
Officers: E.T. Meredith III, Pres.; Katherine C. Meredith, V.P.; John Zieser, Secy.; Marilyn J. Dillivan, Treas.
Number of staff: None.
EIN: 426059818

1182
Principal Financial Group Foundation, Inc. ▼
711 High St.
Des Moines, IA 50392-0150 (515) 248-3172
Contact: Jodi Murphy
FAX: (515) 246-5475; E-mail: murphy.jodi@principal.com; URL: http://www.principal.com/about/giving

Established in 1987 in IA.
Donor(s): Principal Life Insurance Co.
Grantmaker type: Company-sponsored foundation
Financial data (yr. ended 12/31/02): Assets, $58,315,597 (M); expenditures, $6,300,346; qualifying distributions, $5,896,289; giving activities include $5,896,289 for 1,173 grants (high: $305,271; low: $1; average: $25–$50,000).
Purpose and activities: Support for health and human services, education, arts and culture, the environment, recreation and tourism, and the United Way of Central Iowa.
Fields of interest: Performing arts; Theater; Music; Arts; Early childhood education; Higher education; Business school/education; Medical school/education; Education; Environment; Health care; Health organizations, association; AIDS; Medical research, institute; AIDS research; Housing/shelter, development; Human services; Family services; Aging, centers/services; Minorities/immigrants, centers/services; Urban/community development; Community development; Public policy, research; Government/public administration; Public affairs; General charitable giving; Minorities; Aging; Economically disadvantaged.
Types of support: General/operating support; Continuing support; Annual campaigns; Capital campaigns; Building/renovation; Land acquisition; Program development; Professorships; Seed money; Curriculum development; Scholarship funds; Technical assistance; Program evaluation; Employee matching gifts; In-kind gifts.
Limitations: Giving primarily in Des Moines, and in areas of company operations in Mason City and Waterloo, IA, Wilmington, DE, Grand Island, NE, and Spokane, WA. No support for political, athletic, fraternal, sectarian, religious, denominational, or social organizations, organizations redistributing funds, private foundations, trade, industrial, or professional

associations, libraries, individual K-12 schools, organizations outside the U.S. whose activities are mainly international, or veterans' groups. No grants to individuals, or for conference or seminar attendance, goodwill ads, endowments, fellowships, festival participation, or hospital or health care capital fund drives.

Publications: Application guidelines, Biennial report, Corporate giving report.

Application information: Application form required.

 Initial approach: Proposal
 Copies of proposal: 11
 Deadline(s): Health and Human Services: Mar. 1; Education: June 1; Arts and Culture: Sept. 1; Recreation and Tourism: Dec. 1
 Board meeting date(s): Quarterly
 Final notification: 4 to 6 weeks

Officers and Directors:* J. Barry Griswell,* Chair. and C.E.O.; Mary O'Keefe,* Sr. V.P.; Libby Jacobs,* Secy.; Jed Fisk,* Treas.; John Aichenbrenner; Mike Gersie; Joyce Hoffman; Mark Movic.

Number of staff: None.

EIN: 421312301

Recent environmental and animal welfare grants:

1182-1 Animal Rescue League of Iowa, Des Moines, IA, $10,000. For human education and animal assisted therapy. 2001.

1182-2 Blank Park Zoo Foundation, Des Moines, IA, $25,000. For Habitat Heroes Discovery Center. 2001.

1182-3 Iowa Natural Heritage Foundation, Des Moines, IA, $30,000. For general support and membership challenge. 2001.

1182-4 Living History Farms, Urbandale, IA, $66,667. For Get Your Grip on History project. 2001.

1183
Sehgal Family Foundation
700 Walnut St., Ste. 1600
Des Moines, IA   50309-3899

Established in 1998 in IA.

Donor(s): Edda G. Sehgal, Surinder M. Sehgal.

Grantmaker type: Independent foundation

Financial data (yr. ended 12/31/01): Assets, $59,166,111 (M); gifts received, $1,000,000; expenditures, $2,551,278; qualifying distributions, $1,942,933; giving activities include $1,953,305 for 17 grants (high: $667,000; low: $1,000).

Fields of interest: Botanical gardens; Environment; Foundations (community).

International interests: India.

Limitations: Applications not accepted. Giving in the U.S., with some emphasis on the midwestern states of MO, KS, and IA, and internationally. No grants to individuals.

Application information: Contributes only to pre-selected organizations.

Officers: Surinder M. Sehgal, Pres. and Treas.; Edda G. Sehgal, V.P. and Secy.

Director: A.K. Bahl.

EIN: 421477858

1184
The Wallace Research Foundation
c/o RSM McGladrey, Inc.
221 3rd Ave. S.E., Ste. 300
Cedar Rapids, IA   52401
Contact: Joe Gevock

Established in 1996 in IA.

Donor(s): H.B. Wallace, Jean W. Wallace, Robert B. Wallace, Jocelyn M. Wallace, Henry D. Wallace, Linda Wallace-Gray.

Grantmaker type: Independent foundation

Financial data (yr. ended 12/31/01): Assets, $81,222,630 (M); expenditures, $4,578,781; qualifying distributions, $4,139,412; giving activities include $4,050,116 for 41 grants (high: $635,250; low: $7,200; average: $10,000–$200,000) and $42,000 for 1 loan/program-related investment.

Purpose and activities: Giving primarily for education, the environment, and medical research.

Fields of interest: Higher education; Natural resources; Environment; Skin disorders research.

Limitations: Applications not accepted. Giving primarily in Tucson, AZ. No grants to individuals.

Application information: Contributes only to pre-selected organizations.

Officers: H.B. Wallace, Pres. and Secy.-Treas.; Henry D. Wallace, V.P.; Jocelyn M. Wallace, V.P.; Linda Wallace-Gray, V.P.

EIN: 426540579

Recent environmental and animal welfare grants:

1184-1 Arizona-Sonora Desert Museum, Tucson, AZ, $11,000. 2001.

1184-2 Audubon Society of Tucson, Tucson, AZ, $15,000. 2001.

1184-3 Audubon Society, National, New York, NY, $150,000. 2001.

1184-4 Boyce Thompson Southwestern Arboretum, Superior, AZ, $13,000. 2001.

1184-5 Colorado Environmental Coalition, Denver, CO, $10,000. 2001.

1184-6 Conservation Fund, Las Vegas, NV, $10,000. 2001.

1184-7 Drylands Institute, Tucson, AZ, $110,000. 2001.

1184-8 Malpai Borderlands Group, Douglas, AZ, $44,500. 2001.

1184-9 Native Seeds/Southwestern Endangered Arid-Land Resource Clearing House (SEARCH), Tucson, AZ, $73,000. 2001.

1184-10 Nature Conservancy, Arlington, VA, $635,250. 2001.

1184-11 Northern Rockies Conservation Cooperative, Jackson, WY, $10,000. 2001.

1184-12 Sedgwick County Zoological Society, Wichita, KS, $10,000. 2001.

1184-13 Wildcoast, Imperial Beach, CA, $24,950. 2001.

1185
Izaak Walton League of America Davenport Chapter
8402 Harrison St.
Davenport, IA   52806   (563) 391-5200
Contact: Jean Lambert, Treas., or Sarah Trammel, Secy.
FAX: (563) 649-2507

Established in 1942 in IA.

Grantmaker type: Public charity

Financial data (yr. ended 08/31/00): Revenue, $47,425; assets, $23,144; gifts received, $18,416; expenditures, $46,671; program services expenses, $1,262; giving activities include $984 for 5 grants (high: $300; low: $107).

Purpose and activities: The league is a national conservation organization with several chapters. The Davenport chapter offers scholarships and small grants to local individuals and nonprofits.

Fields of interest: Natural resources.

Types of support: Program development; Scholarships—to individuals.

Limitations: Applications not accepted. Giving limited to the Davenport, IA, area.

Application information: Contributes only to pre-selected organizations and individuals; unsolicited requests for funds not considered or acknowledged.

 Board meeting date(s): Monthly

Officers and Members:* Don Passmore,* Pres.; Rodney Fink,* V.P.; Betty Ann Dickinson,* Secy.; Jean Lambert,* Treas.; and 5 additional members.

EIN: 426087943

1186
Windsor Charitable Foundation
c/o Bankers Trust Co., Trust Dept.
P.O. Box 897
Des Moines, IA   50304

Established in 1984 in IA.

Donor(s): Mary Belle H. Windsor.

Grantmaker type: Independent foundation

Financial data (yr. ended 12/31/02): Assets, $2,580,132 (M); gifts received, $3; expenditures, $146,138; qualifying distributions, $139,443; giving activities include $133,520 for 15 grants (high: $60,000; low: $520).

Purpose and activities: Giving primarily for human services, art and culture.

Fields of interest: Opera; Zoos/zoological societies; Family planning; Science.

Types of support: Building/renovation.

Limitations: Applications not accepted. Giving primarily in IA. No grants to individuals.

Application information: Contributes only to pre-selected organizations.

Trustees: Mark W. Beerman; Herbert W. Montis, Jr.; James H. Windsor IV; Bankers Trust Co.

EIN: 421227965

1187
Young Family Foundation of Waterloo, Iowa
c/o Richard C. Young
P.O. Box 1077
Waterloo, IA   50704   (319) 235-5346

Established in 1990 in IA.

Donor(s): Richard C. Young.

Grantmaker type: Independent foundation

Financial data (yr. ended 12/31/02): Assets, $4,086,497 (M); expenditures, $424,453; qualifying distributions, $202,719; giving activities include $204,995 for 13 grants (high: $50,000; low: $495).

Purpose and activities: Giving primarily for conservation and for the purchase development, operation and enhancement of the natural and recreational resources in northeast IA.

Fields of interest: Environment.

Types of support: Annual campaigns; Capital campaigns; Building/renovation; Equipment; Land acquisition; Emergency funds; Curriculum development; Internship funds; Research; Employee matching gifts.
Limitations: Giving limited to northeastern IA.
Application information: Application form not required.
  Copies of proposal: 1
  Board meeting date(s): Quarterly
Officers: Richard C. Young, Pres.; Jane Young Anglim, V.P.; Thomas A. Young, Secy.; Julie Young Dunbar, Treas.
EIN: 421356506

KANSAS

1188
Annie Foundation
1436 Spring Dr.
Wichita, KS 67208

Established in 1992 as partial successor to Garvey Kansas Foundation.
Donor(s): Ann E. Garvey, Garvey Kansas Foundation.
Grantmaker type: Independent foundation
Financial data (yr. ended 12/31/01): Assets, $384,707 (M); expenditures, $135,835; qualifying distributions, $135,058; giving activities include $134,393 for 21 grants (high: $100,000; low: $50).
Fields of interest: Performing arts; Arts; Education; Botanical gardens; Human services; Christian agencies & churches.
Types of support: General/operating support; Continuing support; Capital campaigns; Endowments; Program development; Fellowships.
Limitations: Giving primarily in KS. No grants for Individuals.
Trustee: Ann E. Garvey.
EIN: 481128251

1189
Bramlage Family Foundation
P.O. Box 1005
Junction City, KS 66441

Established in 1997 in KS.
Donor(s): Dorothy O. Bramlage, Fred C. Bramlage.
Grantmaker type: Independent foundation
Financial data (yr. ended 12/31/02): Assets, $5,006,365 (M); expenditures, $395,242; qualifying distributions, $248,316; giving activities include $249,680 for 44 grants (high: $33,000; low: $1,000).
Purpose and activities: Giving for education, scouting organizations, and for public institutes.
Fields of interest: Elementary/secondary education; Higher education; Natural resources; Mental health/crisis services, hot-lines; Youth development, centers/clubs.
Limitations: Applications not accepted. Giving primarily in KS. No grants to individuals.
Application information: Contributes only to pre-selected organizations.

Officers: Dorothy O. Bramlage, Pres.; Dorothy B. Willcoxon, Secy.; F. Robert Bramlage, Treas.
EIN: 742822314

1190
Galey Coleman Charitable Foundation
2414 N. Woodlawn St., Ste. 170
Wichita, KS 67220-3900

Established in 1990 in KS.
Donor(s): Galey Coleman,‡ Sheldon C. Coleman.
Grantmaker type: Independent foundation
Financial data (yr. ended 12/31/02): Assets, $735,738 (M); expenditures, $207,639; qualifying distributions, $196,894; giving activities include $197,050 for 7 grants (high: $148,550; low: $500).
Purpose and activities: Giving to public education, food services, and zoos.
Fields of interest: Elementary/secondary education; Higher education; Zoos/zoological societies; Food banks; Community development.
Types of support: Capital campaigns; Scholarship funds.
Limitations: Applications not accepted. Giving primarily in Wichita, KS. No grants to individuals.
Application information: Contributes only to pre-selected organizations.
Officers and Directors: * Sheldon C. Coleman,* Pres.; John M. Reiff,* V.P. and Secy.; William J. Walsh, V.P.
Number of staff: None.
EIN: 481092996

1191
Coleman Family Foundation, Inc.
610 E. Jefferson St.
Pittsburg, KS 66762
Contact: H. Richard Coleman, Pres.

Established in 2002 in KS and MO.
Donor(s): Faith P. Coleman, H. Richard Coleman.
Grantmaker type: Independent foundation
Financial data (yr. ended 12/31/02): Assets, $22,278 (M); gifts received, $159,363; expenditures, $140,260; qualifying distributions, $140,000; giving activities include $130,000 for 4 grants (high: $50,000; low: $5,000).
Fields of interest: Animal welfare; Children/youth, services; Family services.
Application information:
  Initial approach: Letter
  Deadline(s): None
Officers: H. Richard Coleman, Pres. and Treas.; Faith P. Coleman, V.P.; Marcia A. Sorrick, Secy.
EIN: 431947299

1192
Barry L. & Paula M. Downing Foundation
8907 E. Shadowridge
Wichita, KS 67226
Contact: Lisa Jackson, Tr.
Tel.: (316) 636-5050, ext. 709

Established in 1993 in KS.
Donor(s): Barry L. Downing.
Grantmaker type: Independent foundation

Financial data (yr. ended 12/31/02): Assets, $2,234,586 (M); gifts received, $2,000,000; expenditures, $1,910,498; qualifying distributions, $20; giving activities include $1,871,228 for 20 grants (high: $1,576,728; low: $500).
Purpose and activities: Giving for education, the arts, and youth services.
Fields of interest: Multipurpose centers/programs; Museums (art); Education; Animal welfare; Human services; Children/youth, services.
Limitations: Giving primarily in Wichita, KS.
Application information:
  Initial approach: Letter
  Deadline(s): None
Trustees: Barry L. Downing; Paula M. Downing; Lisa Jackson.
EIN: 481134459

1193
KGE Corporate Giving Program
120 E. 1st
Wichita, KS 67202   (316) 261-6371
Contact: Ron Holt
FAX: (316) 261-6624

Grantmaker type: Corporate giving program
Purpose and activities: KGE makes charitable contributions to nonprofit organizations involved with the environment, children and youth, community development, and senior citizens. Support is given primarily in Kansas.
Fields of interest: Environment; Children/youth, services; Community development; Aging.
Types of support: General/operating support; Employee volunteer services; Sponsorships; Employee matching gifts; In-kind gifts.
Limitations: Giving primarily in KS, particularly eastern KS.
Application information: Application form not required.
  Initial approach: Proposal to headquarters or nearest company facility
  Copies of proposal: 1
  Final notification: Following review

1194
Charles G. Koch Charitable Foundation
P.O. Box 2256
Wichita, KS 67201
Contact: Kelly Young, V.P.
Application address: 1450 G St. N.W., Ste. 445, Washington, DC 20005-2001, tel.: (202) 393-2354; FAX: (202) 393-2355

Established in 1981 in KS.
Donor(s): Charles G. Koch, Fred C. Koch Foundation, Fred C. Koch Trusts for Charity.
Grantmaker type: Independent foundation
Financial data (yr. ended 12/31/02): Assets, $27,144,920 (M); gifts received, $18,724; expenditures, $3,365,794; qualifying distributions, $3,313,808; giving activities include $3,008,000 for 18 grants (high: $400,000; low: $10,000; average: $25,000–$300,000).
Purpose and activities: Funding for academic and public policy research directed at solving significant social problems through voluntary action and free enterprise. Support for projects that find market-based solutions to problematic

social issues. For research, the foundation primarily funds institutions working with doctorate-level investigators in disciplines such as economics, history, philosophy, political science, and organizational behavior.
Fields of interest: Environment; Legal services; Economics; Public policy, research.
Types of support: General/operating support; Program development; Conferences/seminars; Seed money; Research; Program evaluation.
Limitations: No grants to individuals (except through summer fellows program).
Application information: Application form not required.
  Initial approach: 1- to 2-page letter
  Copies of proposal: 1
  Deadline(s): None
Officers and Directors:* Richard Fink,* Pres.; Kelly Young,* V.P.; Vonda Holliman, Secy.-Treas.; Charles Chase Koch; Charles G. Koch; Elizabeth B. Koch; Elizabeth Robinson Koch.
Number of staff: None.
EIN: 480918408
Recent environmental and animal welfare grants:
1194-1 Environmental Literacy Council, DC, $30,000. For general operating support. 2001.

1195
Koch Industries, Inc. Corporate Giving Program
4111 E. 37th St. N.
Wichita, KS 67220-3203
FAX: (316) 828-5739; URL: http://
www.kochind.com/community/default.asp

Grantmaker type: Corporate giving program
Purpose and activities: Koch Industries makes charitable contributions to nonprofit organizations involved with education, the environment, and human services. Support is given primarily in areas of company operations.
Fields of interest: Education; Environment; Human services.
Types of support: General/operating support.
Limitations: Giving primarily in areas of company operations.

1196
Kuehn Foundation
4350 Shawnee Mission Pkwy., Ste. 280
Fairway, KS 66205
Contact: Carrie Hoelscher

Established in 1968 in IN.
Donor(s): Nicholas E. Kuehn Trust A.
Grantmaker type: Independent foundation
Financial data (yr. ended 12/31/02): Assets, $4,341,959 (M); expenditures, $305,194; qualifying distributions, $253,090; giving activities include $238,500 for 63 grants (high: $21,000; low: $1,000).
Purpose and activities: Giving largely for higher education; support also for museums, cultural affairs, and social services.
Fields of interest: Museums; Higher education; Botanical gardens; Human services; Children/youth, services; Community development, neighborhood development.

Limitations: Applications not accepted. Giving primarily in FL, IN, KS, and MO. No grants to individuals.
Application information: Contributes only to pre-selected organizations.
  Board meeting date(s): Fall
Officers and Trustees:* Mary Catherine Powell,* Chair.; Richard K. Powell,* Secy.; Nicholas K. Powell,* Treas.; George E. Powell III; Peter E. Powell.
Number of staff: 1 part-time support.
EIN: 237021199

1197
Mark and Bette Morris Family Foundation
140 Fairlawn Rd.
Topeka, KS 66606
Contact: Mark L. Morris, Jr., Pres.
Additional address: 5500 S.W. 7th St., Topeka, KS 66606

Established in 1989 in KS.
Donor(s): Mark L. Morris, Jr., Bette M. Morris.
Grantmaker type: Independent foundation
Financial data (yr. ended 12/31/02): Assets, $19,492,688 (M); expenditures, $1,148,177; qualifying distributions, $977,682; giving activities include $993,500 for 6 grants (high: $505,000; low: $5,000).
Purpose and activities: Support only to pre-selected organizations that encourage the healthy development and well-being of persons and animals, and that are personally known by the donors.
Fields of interest: Veterinary medicine; Children/youth, services.
Limitations: Applications not accepted. Giving on a national basis. No grants to individuals.
Application information: Contributes only to pre-selected organizations that are personally known by the donors. Unsolicited requests for funds not considered.
Officers: Mark L. Morris, Jr., Pres. and Treas.; Bette M. Morris, V.P. and Secy.
Number of staff: None.
EIN: 481077121

1198
Stone Family Foundation
P.O. Box 528
El Dorado, KS 67042-0528 (316) 321-0830
Contact: Clifford W. Stone, Pres.

Established in 1997 in KS.
Donor(s): Clifford W. Stone.
Grantmaker type: Independent foundation
Financial data (yr. ended 12/31/01): Assets, $1,780,756 (M); gifts received, $414,939; expenditures, $108,401; qualifying distributions, $105,360; giving activities include $105,090 for 20 grants (high: $36,000; low: $1,000).
Purpose and activities: Giving to art and cultural programs, botanical gardens and civic projects.
Fields of interest: Multipurpose centers/programs; Museums; Performing arts; Historic preservation/historical societies; Arts; Higher education; Education; Environment; Health care; Human services; Protestant agencies & churches.
Limitations: Giving primarily in KS and MO.
Application information: Application form not required.

Initial approach: Letter
Deadline(s): None
Officers: Clifford W. Stone, Pres. and Treas.; Sue Stone Hunter, V.P.; Samuel C. Stone, V.P.; Thomas M. Higgins III, Secy.
EIN: 431773536

1199
Topeka Community Foundation
1315 S.W. Arrowhead Rd.
P.O. Box 4525
Topeka, KS 66604 (785) 272-4804
Contact: Chandler Moenius, Pres.
FAX: (785) 273-2467; E-mail:
tcf@cjnetworks.com

Incorporated in 1983 in KS.
Grantmaker type: Community foundation
Financial data (yr. ended 12/31/00): Assets, $15,950,748 (M); gifts received, $857,444; expenditures, $579,608; giving activities include $406,872 for grants.
Purpose and activities: Primary area of interest is the arts, including fine and performing arts; social services, including family services; and civic affairs. the foundation administers a donor-advised fund.
Fields of interest: Performing arts; Arts; Early childhood education; Education; Natural resources; Environment; Substance abuse, services; Human services; Children/youth, services; Family services; Homeless, human services; Community development; Government/public administration; Homeless.
Types of support: General/operating support; Continuing support; Annual campaigns; Capital campaigns; Building/renovation; Emergency funds; Program development; Seed money; Scholarship funds; Employee matching gifts; Scholarships—to individuals; In-kind gifts; Matching/challenge support.
Limitations: Giving limited to Topeka and Shawnee County, KS. No support for religious organizations for religious purposes. No grants for scientific, medical, or academic research.
Publications: Application guidelines, Annual report, Financial statement, Informational brochure, Informational brochure (including application guidelines), Newsletter.
Application information: Application form required.
  Copies of proposal: 10
  Deadline(s): Feb. 15
  Board meeting date(s): Bimonthly, last Thurs. of month
  Final notification: Apr. 15
Officers and Directors:* Jeff Ungerer,* Chair.; Alicia Salisbury,* Vice-Chair.; Chandler Moenius, Pres.; Penny Lumpkin, V.P.; Duane Bond,* Treas.; and 12 additional directors.
Number of staff: 1 full-time professional.
EIN: 480972106

1200
John K. Vanier Family Foundation
P.O. Box 1393
Salina, KS 67402 (785) 823-3794
Contact: John K. Vanier, Pres.

Established in 1993 in KS.
Donor(s): John K. Vanier, Star F, Inc.
Grantmaker type: Independent foundation

Financial data (yr. ended 12/31/02): Assets, $4,721,078 (M); expenditures, $251,834; qualifying distributions, $247,886; giving activities include $247,886 for 44 grants (high: $21,420; low: $500).
Fields of interest: Arts; Higher education; Animals/wildlife; Human services; YM/YWCAs & YM/YWHAs; Children/youth, services; Christian agencies & churches.
Limitations: Giving primarily in Salina, KS. No grants to individuals.
Application information: Application form not required.
Initial approach: Letter
Deadline(s): None
Final notification: 2 months
Officer and Trustees:* John K. Vanier,* Pres.; Donna L. Vanier; John K. Vanier II; Martha A. Vanier; Mary L. Vanier.
EIN: 481141901

1201
Kenneth J. Wagnon Foundation
3445 N. Webb Rd.
Wichita, KS 67226

Established in 1993 in KS.
Donor(s): Ken Wagnon.
Grantmaker type: Independent foundation
Financial data (yr. ended 10/31/02): Assets, $8,925 (M); gifts received, $125; expenditures, $113,065; qualifying distributions, $103,189; giving activities include $102,675 for 24 grants (high: $42,000; low: $25).
Purpose and activities: Giving primarily for the arts, social services, and education.
Fields of interest: Museums (art); Theater; Arts; Education, special; Education; Zoos/zoological societies; Human services; Children/youth, services; Human services.
Limitations: Applications not accepted. Giving primarily in KS. No grants to individuals.
Application information: Contributes only to pre-selected organizations.
Officer and Directors:* Ken Wagnon,* Pres.; Sharol Rasberry.
EIN: 481140527

1202
Westar Energy Foundation
(formerly Western Resources Foundation, Inc.)
818 Kansas Ave.
Topeka, KS 66612 (785) 575-1544
Contact: Cynthia McCarvel, Pres.
FAX: (785) 785-6399

Established in 1991 in KS; funded in 1992.
Donor(s): Western Resources, Inc., Westar Energy, Inc.
Grantmaker type: Company-sponsored foundation
Financial data (yr. ended 12/31/01): Assets, $253,355 (M); gifts received, $1,255,350; expenditures, $1,813,704; qualifying distributions, $1,806,722; giving activities include $1,806,672 for 211 grants (high: $262,770; low: $35; average: $300–$10,000).
Purpose and activities: Giving primarily for higher education and human services.
Fields of interest: Child development, education; Higher education; Environment;

Child development, services; Federated giving programs.
Types of support: General/operating support; Emergency funds; Seed money; Scholarship funds; Research; Employee matching gifts; In-kind gifts.
Limitations: Giving primarily in areas of company operations in KS. No grants to individuals.
Publications: Financial statement, Informational brochure.
Application information: Further helpful materials: other types of funding, letters of support from political or civic leaders. Application form required.
Initial approach: Proposal
Copies of proposal: 1
Deadline(s): 6 months before grant expected
Board meeting date(s): Quarterly
Officers: Cynthia McCarvel, Pres.; Greg Greenwood, V.P. and Treas.; Alice Crossen, Secy.
Directors: Larry Irick; Jim Ludwig; Bill Moore; Caroline Williams.
EIN: 481099341

1203
Wichita Community Foundation
(formerly Greater Wichita Community Foundation)
Centre City Plz.
151 N. Main, Ste. 140
Wichita, KS 67202 (316) 264-4880
Contact: James D. Moore, Exec. Dir.
FAX: (316) 264-7592

Incorporated in 1986 in KS.
Grantmaker type: Community foundation
Financial data (yr. ended 06/30/01): Assets, $103,183,530 (M); gifts received, $3,467,443; expenditures, $2,482,122; giving activities include $2,029,231 for grants.
Purpose and activities: The foundation administers a donor-advised fund.
Fields of interest: Humanities; Education; Natural resources; Environment; Health care; Human services.
Limitations: Giving limited to the greater Wichita, KS, area. No grants to individuals, or for annual operating budgets (except for seed money), capital campaigns, special events, building projects, endowments, fellowships, medical research, or travel purposes.
Publications: Application guidelines, Annual report, Financial statement, Informational brochure, Newsletter.
Application information: Application form required.
Initial approach: Proposal
Copies of proposal: 4
Deadline(s): July 31 and Jan. 31
Board meeting date(s): Oct. 24 and Apr. 16
Final notification: June 30
Officers: Nancy E. Martin, Chair. and Pres.; Sheri Dill, Secy.; Donald J. Glenn, Treas.; James D. Moore, Exec. Dir.
Directors: Clay Bastian; Vicki Bergkamp; Reginald Boothe; Daniel M. Carney; Charlie Chandler; Donald L. Cordes; Barry L. Downing; Phillip S. Frick; Chris Goebel; Ron Holt; Brent A. Mitchell; Phillip R. Neff; Michael Oatman; Thomas A. Page; Dennis L. Ross, M.D.; Jerome Williams.

Number of staff: 1 full-time professional; 1 part-time professional; 1 full-time support.
EIN: 481022361

1204
Mary Jo Williams Charitable Trust
P.O. Box 439
Garden City, KS 67846
Contact: Michael E. Collins, Tr.
Application address: 607 N. 7th St., Garden City, KS 67846, tel.: (620) 276-3203

Established in 1988 in KS.
Grantmaker type: Independent foundation
Financial data (yr. ended 12/31/02): Assets, $3,276,887 (M); expenditures, $255,589; qualifying distributions, $199,979; giving activities include $197,750 for 12 grants (high: $50,000; low: $2,000).
Purpose and activities: Giving primarily for the prevention of cruelty to children or animals.
Fields of interest: Higher education; Natural resources; Food services; Human services; Salvation Army; Federated giving programs.
Types of support: Capital campaigns; Equipment; Endowments.
Limitations: Giving primarily in Garden City, KS. No support for the funding or promotion of athletics or athletic competition. No grants to individuals.
Application information:
Initial approach: Letter
Deadline(s): None
Trustees: Michael E. Collins; Leonard Rich; Jack Williamson.
EIN: 486276428

KENTUCKY

1205
AAEP Foundation, Inc.
(also known as American Association of Equine Practitioners)
4075 Iron Works Pkwy.
Lexington, KY 40511-8462 (859) 233-0147
Contact: David L. Foley, Exec. Dir.
FAX: (859) 233-1968; E-mail: aaepoffice@aaep.org; URL: http://www.aaep.org

Established in 1954.
Grantmaker type: Public charity
Financial data (yr. ended 12/31/02): Revenue, $149,627; assets, $546,230 (M); gifts received, $108,011; expenditures, $52,425; program services expenses, $50,105; giving activities include $18,604 for 6 grants (high: $4,655; low: $1,000) and $1,500 for 1 grant to an individual.
Purpose and activities: The association seeks to improve the health and welfare of the horse, to further the professional development of its members, and to provide resources and leadership for the benefit of the equine industry.
Fields of interest: Medical school/education; Animals/wildlife, research.
Types of support: Research; Grants to individuals.
Limitations: Giving on a national basis.

Application information: See Web site for application information. Application form required.

Copies of proposal: 16
Deadline(s): Oct. 1

Officers and Directors:* Jerry B. Black, D.V.M.,* Pres.; Thomas R. Lenz, D.V.M.,* Pres.-Elect; Harry W. Werner, V.M.D., M.S.,* Treas.; David L. Foley, Exec. Dir.; Duncan Alexander; R. Reynolds Cowles, Jr., D.V.M.; and 12 additional directors.
EIN: 611259683

1206

The Abercrombie Foundation
P.O. Box 68
Versailles, KY 40383
Contact: John W. Backer, Jr., Mgr.

Established in 1988 in TX as partial successor to the J.S. Abercrombie Foundation.
Donor(s): Josephine E. Abercrombie.
Grantmaker type: Independent foundation
Financial data (yr. ended 12/31/01): Assets, $5,989,904 (M); expenditures, $1,356,018; qualifying distributions, $1,286,736; giving activities include $1,290,600 for 30 grants (high: $100,000; low: $500; average: $500–$100,000).
Purpose and activities: Support primarily for higher and secondary education, including medical education, educational research, and building funds; giving also for child welfare and drug abuse programs.
Fields of interest: Education, research; Education, fund raising; Secondary school/education; Higher education; Medical school/education; Education; Natural resources; Substance abuse, services; Children/youth, services.
Types of support: General/operating support; Building/renovation; Research.
Limitations: Giving primarily in central KY. No grants to individuals.
Application information: The foundation is currently not accepting applications. Application form not required.

Initial approach: Proposal
Copies of proposal: 1
Deadline(s): May 15 and Nov. 15
Board meeting date(s): June and Dec.

Officers and Trustees:* Josephine E. Abercrombie,* Pres.; John W. Backer, Jr., Mgr.; Alice H. Chandler; Margaret M. Patterson.
Number of staff: 2 part-time support.
EIN: 760229183

1207

Ashland Inc. Foundation
(formerly Ashland Inc. Corporate Giving Program)
P.O. Box 391
Covington, KY 41012 (859) 815-3333
Contact: Charles Whitehead, Pres., Ashland Inc. Fdn.
FAX: (859) 815-4496; URL: http://www.ashland.com/community

Grantmaker type: Corporate giving program
Financial data (yr. ended 09/30/01): Total giving, $6,611,774; giving activities include $5,568,270 for grants, $748,225 for employee matching gifts and $295,279 for in-kind gifts.

Purpose and activities: Through the Ashland Inc. Foundation, a direct corporate giving program, Ashland makes charitable contributions to nonprofit organizations involved with arts and culture, education, the environment, health and human services, and civic affairs. Support is given primarily in areas of company operations.
Fields of interest: Arts; Education; Environment; Health care; Human services; Public affairs.
Types of support: General/operating support; Annual campaigns; Cause-related marketing; Public relations services; Sponsorships; Employee matching gifts; Donated equipment; Donated products; In-kind gifts.
Limitations: Giving primarily in areas of company operations.
Publications: Informational brochure, Newsletter.
Application information: Unsolicited requests are accepted but not preferred. The Corporate Affairs Department handles giving. The company has a staff that only handles contributions. A contributions committee reviews all requests. Application form not required.

Board meeting date(s): Varies

Administrators: Deborah George, Contribs. Asst.; Martha Johnson, V.P., Ashland Inc. Fdn.; Shirley Rice, Contribs. Asst.; Charles Whitehead, Pres., Ashland Inc. Fdn.; Chris Yaudas, Mgr., Community Rels.
Number of staff: 3 full-time professional; 2 full-time support.

1208

W. L. Lyons Brown Foundation
Waterfront Plz., Ste. 1110
325 W. Main St.
Louisville, KY 40202 (502) 585-4649
Contact: Susan V. Nicholson, Admin.
E-mail: susann@cflouisville.org

Incorporated in 1962 in KY.
Donor(s): W.L. Lyons Brown,‡ Sara S. Brown.
Grantmaker type: Independent foundation
Financial data (yr. ended 12/31/02): Assets, $20,235,277 (M); expenditures, $1,619,290; qualifying distributions, $1,544,197; giving activities include $1,578,167 for 29 grants (high: $500,000; low: $5,000; average: $10,000–$100,000).
Purpose and activities: Giving primarily to organizations in KY seeking to improve quality of life, including museums, parks, educational institutions, and organizations supporting the arts.
Fields of interest: Museums; Arts; Higher education; Natural resources.
Types of support: General/operating support; Annual campaigns; Capital campaigns; Building/renovation; Land acquisition.
Limitations: Applications not accepted. Giving primarily in the metropolitan Louisville, KY, area. No support for sectarian projects. No grants to individuals, or for scholarships or annual appeals; no loans.
Application information: Unsolicited requests for funds not accepted.

Board meeting date(s): Oct.

Officers and Trustees:* Ina B. Bond,* Pres.; Mrs. W.L. Lyons Brown,* Secy.; Owsley Brown II,* Treas.; Martin S. Brown.

Number of staff: 1 shared staff (shared with The Community Foundation of Louisville, Inc.)
EIN: 610598511

1209

Brown-Forman Corporation Contributions Program
850 Dixie Hwy.
Louisville, KY 40210 (502) 774-7289
Contact: Lois Mateus
FAX: (502) 774-7189

Grantmaker type: Corporate giving program
Purpose and activities: Brown-Forman makes charitable contributions to nonprofit organizations involved with arts and culture, education, the environment, housing, and civic affairs. Support is given primarily in areas of company operations.
Fields of interest: Arts; Education; Environment; Housing/shelter; Public affairs.
Types of support: General/operating support; Employee matching gifts; In-kind gifts.
Limitations: Giving primarily in areas of company operations, with emphasis on Louisville, KY.
Application information: Application form not required.

Initial approach: Proposal to headquarters

1210

Alex G. Campbell, Jr. Foundation, Inc.
831 E. Main St.
Lexington, KY 40502
Contact: Rebecca L. Reinhold, Secy.

Established in 1997 in KY.
Donor(s): Alex G. Campbell, Jr.
Grantmaker type: Independent foundation
Financial data (yr. ended 04/30/02): Assets, $2,360,872 (M); expenditures, $214,759; qualifying distributions, $183,609; giving activities include $183,700 for 26 grants (high: $75,000; low: $100).
Purpose and activities: Funding primarily for education and health care, and horse-related services.
Fields of interest: Historic preservation/historical societies; Arts; University; Natural resources; Animal welfare; Animals/wildlife; Health care; Athletics/sports, equestrianism; Human services; YM/YWCAs & YM/YWHAs; Children/youth, services.
Limitations: Giving primarily in KY. No grants to individuals.
Application information:

Initial approach: Letter
Deadline(s): None

Officers and Directors:* Alex G. Campbell, Jr.,* Pres.; Rebecca L. Reinhold,* Secy.; Edward S. Barr,* Treas.
EIN: 311532423

1211

The Community Foundation of Louisville, Inc. ▼

(formerly Louisville Community Foundation, Inc.)
Waterfront Plz. Bldg.
325 W. Main St., Ste. 1110
Louisville, KY 40202 (502) 585-4649
Contact: C. Dennis Riggs, C.E.O. and Pres.
FAX: (502) 587-7484; E-mail:
info@cflouisville.org; URL: http://
www.cflouisville.org

Established in 1916 in KY; reorganized in 1984.
Grantmaker type: Community foundation
Financial data (yr. ended 06/30/02): Assets,
$159,432,288 (M); gifts received, $12,583,154;
expenditures, $13,466,699; giving activities
include $9,223,481 for 1,910 grants (high:
$750,000; low: $100; average: $100–$750,000).
Purpose and activities: The mission of the
foundation is to advance philanthropy by
serving the charitable interests of donors,
enabling increased charitable giving, and
improving communities by being a permanent
philanthropic resource for current and future
needs. Giving for health and human services,
arts and humanities, education, and the
environment; support also for scholarships. The
current focus of grantmaking from unrestricted
funds is to help children and families in poverty
achieve self-sufficiency.
Fields of interest: Humanities; Arts; Education;
Environment; Public health; Human services.
Types of support: General/operating support;
Continuing support; Annual campaigns; Capital
campaigns; Building/renovation; Equipment;
Endowments; Emergency funds; Program
development; Publication; Seed money;
Scholarship funds; Research; Technical
assistance; Scholarships—to individuals;
Matching/challenge support.
Limitations: Applications not accepted. Giving
primarily in Louisville and Jefferson County, KY.
No support for sectarian purposes. No grants to
individuals (except for scholarships).
Publications: Annual report, Informational
brochure, Newsletter, Program policy statement.
Application information: Grantmaking in areas
of community need as decided by board;
unsolicited requests for funds not considered.
 Board meeting date(s): Mar., June, Sept., and
 Dec.
Officers and Directors:* Michael B. Mountjoy,*
Chair.; Olivia F. Kirtley,* Vice-Chair.; C. Dennis
Riggs, C.E.O. and Pres.; Susan V. Nicholson, V.P.
and C.F.O.; Kathy B. Steward, V.P., Fund Devel.;
Kit Georgehead,* Secy.; and additional directors.
Number of staff: 10 full-time professional; 4
full-time support.
EIN: 310997017

1212

Community Foundation of West Kentucky

(formerly Paducah Area Community Foundation)
P.O. Box 7901
Paducah, KY 42002-7901 (270) 442-8622
Contact: Tony Watkins
FAX: (270) 442-8623

Established in 1998 in KY.
Grantmaker type: Community foundation

Financial data (yr. ended 12/31/01): Assets,
$946,218 (M); gifts received, $387,164;
expenditures, $255,571; giving activities
include $179,015 for grants.
Purpose and activities: The foundation supports
areas of art and culture, community
development, education, environment, health
and social needs. The foundation administers a
donor-advised fund.
Fields of interest: Cultural/ethnic awareness;
Arts; Education; Environment; Public health;
Health care; Human services; Community
development.
Types of support: General/operating support;
Annual campaigns; Capital campaigns;
Endowments; Debt reduction; Emergency funds;
Program development; Scholarship funds.
Limitations: Giving primarily in western KY. No
grants to individuals.
Publications: Application guidelines, Annual
report, Newsletter.
Application information: Application form not
required.
 Initial approach: Letter
 Copies of proposal: 1
 Board meeting date(s): Quarterly in Feb., May,
 Aug., and Nov.
Officers: George B. Shaw, Pres.; Geraldine
Montgomery, V.P.
Director: Tony Watkins.
Number of staff: 1 full-time professional; 1
full-time support; 1 part-time support.
EIN: 611304905

1213

Owsley Brown Frazier Family Foundation, Inc.

4938 Brownsboro Rd., Ste. 200
Louisville, KY 40222

Established in 1997 in KY.
Donor(s): Owsley B. Frazier.
Grantmaker type: Operating foundation
Financial data (yr. ended 12/31/02): Assets,
$1,455,682 (M); gifts received, $1,240,000;
expenditures, $1,262,193; qualifying
distributions, $1,260,005; giving activities
include $1,260,325 for grants (high: $200,000).
Purpose and activities: Giving primarily for
educational programs and organizations.
Fields of interest: Museums; Historical activities;
Arts; Elementary/secondary education; Higher
education; Zoos/zoological societies; Hospitals
(general); Human services; Federated giving
programs.
Limitations: Applications not accepted. Giving
primarily in KY. No grants to individuals.
Application information: Contributes only to
pre-selected organizations.
Officers: Owsley B. Frazier, Pres.; Laura F.
Huneke, Secy.
EIN: 311571175

1214

Friends of the Louisville Zoo, Inc.

(formerly Louisville Zoological Society, Inc.)
P.O. Box 37250
Louisville, KY 40233

Established in 1969.
Grantmaker type: Public charity

Financial data (yr. ended 06/30/02): Revenue,
$288,305; assets, $323,160; gifts received,
$48,669; expenditures, $134,265; program
services expenses, $34,101; giving activities
include $32,601 for 1 grant.
Purpose and activities: The organization exists
for the sole benefit of the Louisville Zoo
Foundation, Inc.
Fields of interest: Zoos/zoological societies.
Limitations: Applications not accepted. Giving
limited to Louisville, KY.
Application information: Contributes only to a
pre-selected organization; unsolicited requests
for funds not considered or acknowledged.
Officers and Directors:* Colin Lindsay,* Pres.;
Cheryl Parish,* 1st V.P.; Maria A. Ladd,* 2nd
V.P.; Bonnie Taylor,* Secy.; Joseph Straughan,
Jr.,* Treas.; Marisa Baker; Elizabeth S. Boland;
and 23 additional directors.
EIN: 610721682

1215

The Juilfs Foundation

1 Riverfront Pl.
Newport, KY 41071 (859) 292-7000
Contact: George C. Juilfs, Tr.

Established in 1962 in OH.
Grantmaker type: Independent foundation
Financial data (yr. ended 12/31/02): Assets,
$1,978,607 (M); expenditures, $101,001;
qualifying distributions, $96,250; giving
activities include $96,250 for 31 grants (high:
$20,000; low: $300).
Fields of interest: Museums; Zoos/zoological
societies; Parks/playgrounds; Human services;
Federated giving programs.
Types of support: Annual campaigns; Capital
campaigns.
Limitations: Giving primarily in the greater
Cincinnati, OH, area. No grants to individuals.
Application information:
 Initial approach: Letter
 Deadline(s): None
Trustees: George C. Juilfs; Howard W. Juilfs;
Kimberly K. Juilfs.
EIN: 316027571

1216

LG&E Energy Foundation, Inc.

220 W. Main St.
Louisville, KY 40202
Contact: Elaine Ashcraft, Grants Admin.
Application address: P.O. Box 32030, Louisville,
KY 40232; FAX: (502) 627-3629; URL: http://
www.lgeenergy.com/foundation/default.asp

Established in 1994 in KY.
Donor(s): LG&E Energy Corp.
Grantmaker type: Company-sponsored
foundation
Financial data (yr. ended 12/31/02): Assets,
$13,666,761 (M); expenditures, $2,415,842;
qualifying distributions, $2,158,323; giving
activities include $2,158,323 for 103 grants
(high: $453,161; low: $500; average:
$1,000–$50,000).
Purpose and activities: Giving primarily for
education; community outreach: H and W,
Diversity and civic projects; environment; and
arts.

Fields of interest: Arts; Environment; Human services; Community development.
Types of support: General/operating support; Building/renovation; Program development; Scholarship funds; Employee matching gifts; Matching/challenge support.
Limitations: Giving primarily in areas of company service in KY. No support for organizations without an IRS 501(c)(3) designation; political, fraternal, labor, or religious organizations/endeavors; athletic sponsorships; medical research, or United Way and Fund for the Arts agencies. No grants to individuals, or for capital campaigns, disease campaigns/walks, or pageants or travel expenses.
Publications: Application guidelines, Program policy statement.
Application information: Corporate Contributions Request form may be obtained from the foundation. Application form required.
   Initial approach: See the foundation's Web site for application guidelines
   Copies of proposal: 1
   Deadline(s): Varies
   Board meeting date(s): Annually
Officers and Directors:* Victor A. Stafferi,* Pres.; John R. McCall,* V.P. and Secy.; S. Bradford Rives,* V.P. and Treas.; Rudolph W. Keeling, V.P.
Number of staff: 1 full-time professional.
EIN: 611257368

1217
The Norton Foundation, Inc.
(formerly The George W. Norton Foundation, Inc.)
4350 Brownsboro Rd., Ste. 133
Louisville, KY 40207 (502) 893-9549
Contact: Lucy Crawford, Secy.-Treas.
FAX: (502) 896-9378; E-mail:
nortfound@aol.com

Incorporated in 1958 in KY.
Donor(s): Mrs. George W. Norton.‡
Grantmaker type: Independent foundation
Financial data (yr. ended 12/31/02): Assets, $15,990,605 (M); expenditures, $1,233,471; qualifying distributions, $1,041,386; giving activities include $929,112 for 34 grants (high: $100,000; low: $1,500).
Purpose and activities: The foundation's mission is to contribute to the improvement of the quality of life, and foster a favorable business climate in the company's communities in North America, consistent with and supportive of business objectives.
Fields of interest: Arts education; Early childhood education; Elementary school/education; Secondary school/education; Adult education—literacy, basic skills & GED; Reading; Education; Environment; Human services; Children/youth, services; Family services; Minorities/immigrants, centers/services; International peace/security; Minorities; Economically disadvantaged.
Types of support: General/operating support; Continuing support; Annual campaigns; Endowments; Program development; Seed money; Scholarship funds.
Limitations: Giving limited to the metropolitan Louisville, KY, area. No grants to individuals.
Publications: Application guidelines.

Application information: Application form required.
   Initial approach: Proposal
   Copies of proposal: 3
   Deadline(s): Quarterly
   Board meeting date(s): Quarterly
Officers and Directors:* Jane Norton Newton,* Pres.; Robert W. Dulaney,* V.P.; Lucy Crawford,* Secy.-Treas. and Exec. Dir.; Richard H.C. Clay.
Number of staff: 1 full-time professional.
EIN: 616024040

1218
Charlotte M. Richardt Charitable Trust
c/o Ronald G. Keeping, Tr.
P.O. Box 5
Henderson, KY 42419-0005

Established in 1996 in KY.
Donor(s): Charlotte M. Richardt.‡
Grantmaker type: Independent foundation
Financial data (yr. ended 12/31/02): Assets, $325,404 (M); expenditures, $378,821; qualifying distributions, $370,386; giving activities include $350,000 for 8 grants (high: $100,000; low: $25,000) and $18,600 for 4 grants to individuals (high: $5,000; low: $3,600).
Purpose and activities: Giving primarily to an association for blind people and a humane society; funding also for health associations and libraries. The trust also awards college scholarships to students of Central High School, in Evansville, IN.
Fields of interest: Museums (art); Libraries (public); Animal welfare; Cancer; Eye diseases; Heart & circulatory diseases; Boys & girls clubs; Human services; Federated giving programs.
Types of support: Scholarships—to individuals.
Limitations: Applications not accepted. Giving primarily in Evansville, IN.
Application information: Unsolicited requests for funds not accepted.
Trustee: Ronald G. Keeping.
EIN: 616233945

1219
Ephraim Roseman Foundation, Inc.
6302 Transylvania Beach Rd.
Prospect, KY 40059

Established in 1961 in KY.
Donor(s): Wilma S. Roseman.
Grantmaker type: Independent foundation
Financial data (yr. ended 12/31/02): Assets, $2,894,221 (M); expenditures, $226,440; qualifying distributions, $167,585; giving activities include $167,736 for 12 grants (high: $101,000; low: $1,000).
Purpose and activities: Giving for higher education, Jewish religious institutes, and for human services.
Fields of interest: Animals/wildlife, association; Human services; Jewish federated giving programs; Jewish agencies & temples.
Limitations: Applications not accepted. No grants to individuals.
Application information: Contributes only to pre-selected organizations.
Officers: Wilma S. Roseman, Pres.; Gary D. Phillips, V.P. and Secy.; Romie R. Griffey, V.P. and Treas.
EIN: 616027248

1220
Al J. Schneider Foundation Corporation
P.O. Box 16970
Louisville, KY 40256-0970 (502) 448-6351
Contact: Al J. Schneider, Pres.

Incorporated in 1957 in KY.
Donor(s): Al J. Schneider, Home Supply Co.
Grantmaker type: Independent foundation
Financial data (yr. ended 02/28/02): Assets, $244,322 (M); gifts received, $104,800; expenditures, $106,455; qualifying distributions, $106,455; giving activities include $105,524 for 40 grants (high: $30,000; low: $5; average: $1,000–$30,000).
Purpose and activities: Emphasis on a Roman Catholic convent and other religious associations, health, cultural programs, youth agencies, education, particularly higher education, and community development; minor support also to religious members of the community and other individuals.
Fields of interest: Higher education; Education; Zoos/zoological societies; Health care; Health organizations, association; Human services; Community development; Christian agencies & churches; Roman Catholic agencies & churches.
Types of support: General/operating support; Grants to individuals.
Limitations: Giving primarily in KY.
Officers: Al J. Schneider, Pres.; Robert L. Ackerson, Secy.-Treas.; Mary Moseley, Secy.
EIN: 610621591

1221
Sumner Foundation, Inc.
1930 National City Twr.
Louisville, KY 40202

Established in 1968 in KY.
Donor(s): John S. Greenebaum.
Grantmaker type: Independent foundation
Financial data (yr. ended 12/31/02): Assets, $198,659 (M); expenditures, $165,904; qualifying distributions, $153,332; giving activities include $154,017 for 44 grants (high: $20,000; low: $100).
Fields of interest: Higher education; Natural resources; Family planning; Children/youth, services; Federated giving programs.
Limitations: Applications not accepted. Giving limited to Louisville, KY. No grants to individuals.
Application information: Contributes only to pre-selected organizations.
Officers and Trustees:* John S. Greenebaum, Pres. and Treas.; Lynn H. Wangerin,* Secy.; Anastasia Greenebaum.
EIN: 237043909

1222
Lester E. Yeager Charitable Trust B
P.O. Box 964
Owensboro, KY 42302-0964 (270) 686-8254

Established in 1989 in KY.
Donor(s): Lester E. Yeager.‡
Grantmaker type: Independent foundation
Financial data (yr. ended 12/31/02): Assets, $4,970,063 (M); gifts received, $418; expenditures, $270,669; qualifying distributions,

$252,164; giving activities include $216,338 for 49 grants (high: $24,295; low: $500).
Purpose and activities: Giving primarily for health and human services.
Fields of interest: Arts; Higher education; Environmental education; Health care; Human services.
Limitations: Giving limited to areas of southern IN that are adjacent to KY, with emphasis on Daviess and Henderson counties in IN. No grants to individuals.
Application information: Application form required.
> *Initial approach:* 1-page cover letter with application
> *Copies of proposal:* 4
> *Deadline(s):* Oct. 15

Trustees: Ruth F. Adkins; Donald W. Haas; Nancy C. Kennedy.
Number of staff: 1 part-time professional.
EIN: 611159548

LOUISIANA

1223
Baton Rouge Area Foundation ▼
406 N. 4th St.
Baton Rouge, LA   70802   (225) 387-6126
Contact: John G. Davies, C.E.O. and Pres.
FAX: (225) 387-6153; E-mail: jdavies@braf.org;
URL: http://www.braf.org

Incorporated in 1964 in LA.
Grantmaker type: Community foundation
Financial data (yr. ended 12/31/01): Assets, $200,132,000 (M); gifts received, $34,366,000; expenditures, $71,150,000; giving activities include $52,387,000 for 1,000 grants (high: $402,000; low: $100).
Purpose and activities: The foundation funds programs in the areas of the arts and humanities, community development, education, the environment, human services, health and medical issues, and religion. Primary areas of interest include elementary and secondary education and health. Preference given to those projects which promise to affect a broad segment of the population or which tend to help a segment of the citizenry who are not being adequately served by the community's resources.
Fields of interest: Arts; Child development, education; Elementary school/education; Secondary school/education; Medical school/education; Nursing school/education; Education; Environment; Health care; Health organizations, association; Human services; Children/youth, services; Child development, services; Aging, centers/services; Women, centers/services; Community development; Religion; Disabled; Aging; Women; Economically disadvantaged.
Types of support: Capital campaigns; Building/renovation; Equipment; Endowments; Emergency funds; Program development; Seed money; Research; Program-related investments/loans; Matching/challenge support.
Limitations: Giving limited to the Baton Rouge, LA, area, including East Baton Rouge, West Baton Rouge, Livingston, Ascension, Iberville,

Pointe Coupee, East Feliciana, and West Feliciana parishes. No grants for continuing support, annual campaigns, deficit financing, fellowships, or operating budgets.
Publications: Application guidelines, Annual report (including application guidelines), Informational brochure, Newsletter.
Application information: Application form required.
> *Initial approach:* Telephone
> *Copies of proposal:* 1
> *Deadline(s):* Feb. 1, May 1, Aug. 1, and Nov. 1; telephone office for Manship Fund and Arbritton Fund deadlines
> *Board meeting date(s):* Mar., June, Sept., and Dec.
> *Final notification:* 3 months

Officers and Directors:* Virginia B. Noland,* Chair.; John G. Davies,* C.E.O. and Pres.; Hans Dekker, Exec. V.P.; Kevin R. Lyle, V.P.; L. Lane Grigsby, Secy.; Ralph J. Stephens, Treas.; and 17 additional directors.
Trustee Bank: Bank One, N.A.
Number of staff: 16 full-time professional.
EIN: 726030391
Recent environmental and animal welfare grants:
1223-1 Animal Welfare Society, Capital Area, Baton Rouge, LA, $13,962. 2002.
1223-2 Animal Welfare Society, Puerto Rico, Aguadilla, PR, $25,000. 2002.
1223-3 Baton Rouge Economic and Agricultural Development Alliance (BREADA), Baton Rouge, LA, $66,805. 2002.
1223-4 Baton Rouge Green, Baton Rouge, LA, $64,503. 2002.
1223-5 Nature Conservancy, Baton Rouge, LA, $43,650. 2002.

1224
The Biedenharn Foundation
P.O. Box 577
Benton, LA   71006

Established in 1985 in LA.
Donor(s): R.Z. Biedenharn.‡
Grantmaker type: Independent foundation
Financial data (yr. ended 11/30/02): Assets, $4,901,204 (M); gifts received, $32,504; expenditures, $225,762; qualifying distributions, $195,146; giving activities include $186,500 for 36 grants (high: $10,000; low: $1,000).
Purpose and activities: Giving primarily for human services and environmental conservation.
Fields of interest: Radio; Theater; Higher education; Environment; Health care, research; Human services; Hospices.
Types of support: General/operating support; Annual campaigns; Endowments; Emergency funds; Research.
Limitations: Applications not accepted. Giving on a national basis. No grants to individuals.
Application information: Unsolicited requests for funds not accepted.
Officers and Board Members:* Sydney Biedenharn Walker,* Chair.; David M. Caskey,* Vice-Chair.; David E. Tyrone,* Secy.-Treas.; Sue Brown Dykes; Mary Cobb Thompson; Randy Walker.
Number of staff: None.
EIN: 721052971

1225
The Booth-Bricker Fund
826 Union St., Ste. 300
New Orleans, LA   70112   (504) 581-2430
Contact: Gray S. Parker, Chair.

Established in 1966 in LA.
Donor(s): John F. Bricker, Nina B. Bricker.‡
Grantmaker type: Independent foundation
Financial data (yr. ended 12/31/02): Assets, $27,253,449 (M); expenditures, $2,081,204; qualifying distributions, $1,768,515; giving activities include $1,615,082 for 123 grants (high: $60,200; low: $50; average: $100–$50,000).
Purpose and activities: Giving primarily for the purpose of promoting, developing, and fostering religious, charitable, scientific, literary, and educational programs.
Fields of interest: Visual arts; Museums; Performing arts; Theater; Historic preservation/historical societies; Arts; Education, fund raising; Elementary/secondary education; Early childhood education; Child development, education; Secondary school/education; Higher education; Theological school/education; Adult education—literacy, basic skills & GED; Libraries/library science; Reading; Education; Environment; Hospitals (general); Speech/hearing centers; Health care; Mental health/crisis services; Health organizations, association; Cancer; Biomedicine; Medical research, institute; Cancer research; Crime/law enforcement; Food services; Human services; Youth, services; Child development, services; Family services; Aging, centers/services; Homeless, human services; Roman Catholic agencies & churches; Religion; Aging; Economically disadvantaged; Homeless.
Types of support: Capital campaigns; Building/renovation; Equipment; Endowments; Debt reduction; Professorships; Publication; Scholarship funds; Research; Employee matching gifts; Matching/challenge support.
Limitations: Giving primarily in LA, with emphasis on New Orleans. No grants to individuals, or for operating or maintenance costs.
Application information: Videotapes not accepted. Application form not required.
> *Initial approach:* Letter or proposal
> *Deadline(s):* None
> *Board meeting date(s):* Quarterly

Officers and Trustees:* Gray S. Parker,* Chair.; Donald J. Nalty,* Secy.; Ingrid C. Laffont, Treas.; Dorothy R. Boyle; Robert L. Goodwin; Henry N. Kuechler III; Charles B. Mayer; Nathaniel P. Phillips, Jr.; H. Hunter White, Jr.
EIN: 720818077

1226
BR & R Foundation
648 Albert Hart Dr.
Baton Rouge, LA   70808-5803

Established in 1996 in LA.
Grantmaker type: Independent foundation
Financial data (yr. ended 12/31/02): Assets, $3,368,972 (M); expenditures, $203,013; qualifying distributions, $202,289; giving activities include $101,180 for 38 grants (high: $40,000; low: $250).

Purpose and activities: Funding for human services, health care, and medical research.
Fields of interest: Media/communications; Elementary/secondary education; Environment; Cancer; Recreation; Foundations (public); Roman Catholic agencies & churches.
Limitations: Applications not accepted. Giving primarily in Baton Rouge, LA. No grants to individuals.
Application information: Contributes only to pre-selected organizations.
Officer: Randall J. Roberts, Pres.
EIN: 721340978

1227
Joe W. & Dorothy Dorsett Brown Foundation

1 Galleria Plz., Ste. 2105
Metairie, LA 70001-7509 (504) 834-3433
Contact: D.P. Spencer, Pres.

Established in 1959 in LA.
Donor(s): Joe W. Brown,‡ Dorothy Dorsett Brown.‡
Grantmaker type: Independent foundation
Financial data (yr. ended 12/31/01): Assets, $116,886,570 (M); expenditures, $3,750,222; qualifying distributions, $6,167,182; giving activities include $2,546,209 for 116 grants (high: $285,190; low: $500; average: $5,000–$25,000) and $1,931,920 for 10 loans/program-related investments.
Purpose and activities: Giving primarily to natural resources conservation and protection, hospitals, food services, human services with special emphasis on services for the homeless.
Fields of interest: Natural resources; Hospitals (general); Food services; Human services; Homeless, human services; Homeless.
Types of support: General/operating support; Continuing support; Scholarship funds; Research; Program-related investments/loans; Matching/challenge support.
Limitations: Giving primarily in southern LA and the Gulf Coast of MS. No grants to individuals.
Application information: The foundation has discontinued awarding scholarships to individuals. Application form required.
Initial approach: Proposal
Copies of proposal: 1
Deadline(s): None
Board meeting date(s): On Fridays mid-monthly
Officers: D.P. Spencer, Pres.; V.C. Rodriguez, V.P.; B.G. Spencer, V.P.; D.B. Spencer, V.P.; E.K. Hunter, Secy.; B.M. Estopinal, Treas.
Number of staff: 2 full-time professional; 2 part-time professional.
EIN: 726027232

1228
Burden Foundation

4911 Bennington Ave.
Baton Rouge, LA 70808-3153

Grantmaker type: Independent foundation
Financial data (yr. ended 12/31/02): Assets, $7,938,366 (M); expenditures, $468,493; qualifying distributions, $395,368; giving activities include $394,000 for 3 grants (high: $234,000; low: $5,000).

Fields of interest: Education; Natural resources; Community development.
Limitations: Applications not accepted. Giving limited to LA. No grants to individuals.
Application information: Contributes only to pre-selected organizations.
Officers: Paul W. Murrill, Pres.; Robert A. Hawthorne, Jr., V.P.; O. Miles Pollard, Secy.-Treas.
EIN: 726030712

1229
Cleco Corporation Contributions Program

2030 Donahue Ferry Rd.
Pineville, LA 71360-5226 (318) 484-7120
Application address: P.O. Box 5000, Pineville, LA 71361-5000; FAX: (318) 484-7192

Grantmaker type: Corporate giving program
Purpose and activities: Cleco makes charitable contributions to nonprofit organizations involved with education, the environment, public safety, human services, community development, and civic affairs. Support is given primarily in areas of company operations.
Fields of interest: Education; Environment; Safety/disasters; Human services; Community development; Public affairs.
Types of support: General/operating support; Employee volunteer services; Loaned talent; Donated products; In-kind gifts.
Limitations: Giving primarily in areas of company operations.
Application information:
Initial approach: Proposal to headquarters

1230
The Community Foundation of Shreveport-Bossier

105 Louisiana Twr.
401 Edwards St.
Shreveport, LA 71101 (318) 221-0582
Contact: Dorothy Gwin, Exec. Dir.
FAX: (318) 221-7463; E-mail: cfsb@comfoundsb.org; URL: http://www.comfoundsb.org/

Incorporated in 1961 in LA.
Grantmaker type: Community foundation
Financial data (yr. ended 12/31/02): Assets, $32,004,097 (M); gifts received, $1,063,842; expenditures, $1,952,387; giving activities include $1,564,119 for 154 grants (high: $100,000; low: $300; average: $300–$100,000).
Purpose and activities: The foundation administers donor-advised funds.
Fields of interest: Arts; Higher education; Adult education—literacy, basic skills & GED; Reading; Education; Natural resources; Health care; Health organizations, association; Human services; Youth, services; Aging, centers/services; Homeless, human services; Community development; Science; Disabled; Aging; Women; Economically disadvantaged; Homeless.
Types of support: Continuing support; Capital campaigns; Building/renovation; Equipment; Land acquisition; Emergency funds; Program development; Seed money; Curriculum development; Scholarship funds; Technical assistance; Matching/challenge support.

Limitations: Giving strictly limited to Caddo and Bossier parishes, LA. No support for agencies located outside of Caddo and Bossier parishes, LA unless specifically named, or for political or religious organizations. No grants to individuals directly.
Publications: Application guidelines, Annual report (including application guidelines), Grants list, Informational brochure (including application guidelines), Newsletter.
Application information: Application form required.
Initial approach: Inquiry prior to submitting full grant request, or telephone
Copies of proposal: 8
Deadline(s): Mar. 31 and Aug. 31
Board meeting date(s): Feb., Mar., May, and Oct.
Final notification: Immediately after board meetings in May and Oct.
Officers and Directors:* Hon. Carl Stewart,* Chair.; L. Frank Moore,* Vice-Chair.; Carolyn Q. Nelson,* Secy.; Thomas E. McElroy,* Treas.; Joe N. Averett, Jr.; Maxine Sarpy; Marion W. Weiss.
Trustee Banks: Bank One, N.A.; AmSouth Bank; Hibernia National Bank.
Number of staff: 3 full-time professional; 1 full-time support.
EIN: 726022365

1231
Coypu Foundation

c/o Whitney National Bank, Trust Dept.
P.O. Box 6120
New Orleans, LA 70161-1260

Established in 1988 in LA.
Donor(s): John S. McIlhenny.
Grantmaker type: Independent foundation
Financial data (yr. ended 12/31/00): Assets, $18,568,927 (M); gifts received, $105,451; expenditures, $1,007,278; qualifying distributions, $893,252; giving activities include $901,000 for 10 grants (high: $150,000; low: $6,000).
Purpose and activities: Giving primarily for higher education; funding also for an arboretum.
Fields of interest: Higher education; Natural resources; Environmental education; Agriculture/food.
Limitations: Applications not accepted. Giving primarily in LA. No grants to individuals.
Application information: Contributes only to pre-selected organizations.
Trustees: William Callihan; George Denegre; Chris Hale; John Hernandez; Eugine Schwartz; Whitney National Bank.
EIN: 581795856

1232
Entergy Charitable Foundation

639 Loyola Ave.
New Orleans, LA 70113
Application address: P.O. Box 61000, New Orleans, LA 70161, tel.: (504) 576-5785; URL: http://www.entergy.com/corp/community/ecf.asp

Established in 2000 in AR and LA.
Donor(s): Entergy Corp.
Grantmaker type: Company-sponsored foundation

Financial data (yr. ended 12/31/01): Assets, $2,760,249 (M); gifts received, $5,663,526; expenditures, $4,058,172; qualifying distributions, $4,058,172; giving activities include $4,045,462 for grants (high: $250,000).
Fields of interest: Arts; Education; Animals/wildlife, preservation/protection; Legal services; Food services; Housing/shelter, development; American Red Cross; Aging, centers/services; Economic development; Federated giving programs; Christian agencies & churches.
Limitations: Giving primarily in communities where Entergy customers and employees live and work. No grants to individuals, political candidates, gala events, fundraising events or for a specific religion or church; no loans.
Application information: See Web site for application form and further information. Application form required.
   Deadline(s): Feb. 1, May 1, and Aug. 1
Officers and Directors:* Horace S. Webb,* Chair. and Pres.; Kay Kelly Arnold,* Vice-Chair.; C. John Wilder,* Secy.-Treas.; Joseph F. Domino; Curt L. Hebert, Jr.; Donald C. Hintz; J. Wayne Leonard; William E. Madison; Carolyn C. Shanks; Richard J. Smith.
EIN: 710845366

1233
Entergy Corporation Contributions Program
c/o Corp. Contribs.
P.O. Box 61000, L-ENT-8A
New Orleans, LA 70161 (504) 576-6990
Contact: Deanna Rodriguez, V.P., Corp. Contribs.
Additional tel.: (877) 285-2006

Grantmaker type: Corporate giving program
Financial data (yr. ended 12/31/00): Total giving, $9,493,492; giving activities include $9,000,000 for 2,845 grants (high: $1,000,000; low: $100; average: $1,000–$15,000), $125,300 for 452 employee matching gifts, $368,192 for 315 in-kind gifts and $2,500,000 for 1 loan/program-related investment.
Purpose and activities: As a complement to its foundation, Entergy also makes charitable contributions to nonprofit organizations directly. Support is given primarily in areas of company operations.
Fields of interest: Arts; Reading; Education; Environment; Housing/shelter; Economically disadvantaged.
Types of support: Annual campaigns; Emergency funds; Scholarship funds; Employee volunteer services; Use of facilities; Employee matching gifts; Donated equipment; In-kind gifts.
Limitations: Giving primarily in areas of company operations, particularly New Orleans, LA. No support for political organizations or candidates or sectarian religious organizations. No grants for amateur sports, general operating support, or consultant fees.
Publications: Corporate giving report (including application guidelines).
Application information: The Corporate Contributions Department handles giving. The company has a staff that only handles

contributions. A contributions committee reviews all requests. Application form required.
   Initial approach: Contact nearest company facility for application form
   Copies of proposal: 1
   Board meeting date(s): Monthly
   Final notification: Following review
Number of staff: 3 full-time professional; 1 full-time support.

1234
The Ella West Freeman Foundation
P.O. Box 13218
New Orleans, LA 70185 (504) 895-1984
Contact: Louis M. Freeman, Chair.
FAX: (504) 895-1988; E-mail: info@ellawest.org;
URL: http://www.ellawest.org

Trust established about 1940 in LA.
Donor(s): Richard W. Freeman,‡ Alfred B. Freeman.‡
Grantmaker type: Independent foundation
Financial data (yr. ended 12/31/01): Assets, $28,999,998 (M); expenditures, $1,634,479; qualifying distributions, $1,626,595; giving activities include $1,602,833 for grants (average: $5,000–$150,000).
Purpose and activities: Emphasis on higher education and civic affairs; support also for a museum, historic preservation, and the environment.
Fields of interest: Historic preservation/historical societies; Arts; Higher education; Environment; Government/public administration.
Types of support: Annual campaigns; Capital campaigns; Building/renovation; Endowments; Program development; Seed money.
Limitations: Giving primarily in the greater New Orleans, LA, area. No grants to individuals.
Publications: Application guidelines.
Application information: Application form required.
   Initial approach: Proposal (no more than 3 pages)
   Copies of proposal: 2
   Deadline(s): Feb. 15 and Oct. 15
   Board meeting date(s): Biannually beginning in spring
Officer and Trustees:* Louis M. Freeman,* Chair.; Richard W. Freeman, Jr.; R. West Freeman III; Virginia Rowan; Philip Woollam; Tina F. Woollam.
Number of staff: None.
EIN: 726018322

1235
Jerome S. Glazer Foundation, Inc.
546 Corondolet St.
New Orleans, LA 70130

Established in 1961 in LA.
Donor(s): Jerome S. Glazer.‡
Grantmaker type: Independent foundation
Financial data (yr. ended 12/31/01): Assets, $7,375,605 (M); gifts received, $30,000; expenditures, $503,181; qualifying distributions, $455,989; giving activities include $411,925 for 76 grants (high: $200,000; low: $25).

Fields of interest: Arts; Scholarships/financial aid; Education; Natural resources; Hospitals (general); Human services; Jewish federated giving programs; Jewish agencies & temples.
Limitations: Applications not accepted. Giving primarily in LA and NY. No grants to individuals.
Application information: Contributes only to pre-selected organizations.
Officers: Alfred H. Moses, Chair.; Bradford A. Glazer, Pres. and Treas.; Kim Glazer Goldberg, V.P. and Secy.
EIN: 726020850

1236
Gottesman Family Foundation
P.O. Box 2370
New Orleans, LA 70176-2370

Donor(s): Charlotte S. Gottesman.
Grantmaker type: Independent foundation
Financial data (yr. ended 12/31/02): Assets, $706,945 (M); gifts received, $122,413; expenditures, $216,541; qualifying distributions, $202,625; giving activities include $202,625 for 12 grants (high: $103,000; low: $125).
Fields of interest: Education; Natural resources; Jewish agencies & temples.
Officer: Charlotte S. Gottesman, Mgr.
EIN: 581967635

1237
Live Oak Foundation
(formerly Frank & Mary Godchaux Foundation)
P.O. Box 269
Abbeville, LA 70511-0269

Donor(s): Frank A. Godchaux III, Charles R. Godchaux, Frank M. Godchaux.
Grantmaker type: Independent foundation
Financial data (yr. ended 12/31/01): Assets, $2,625,160 (M); gifts received, $246,426; expenditures, $373,340; qualifying distributions, $334,463; giving activities include $335,360 for grants (high: $67,500).
Purpose and activities: Giving primarily for nursing school education, the environment, and federated giving programs.
Fields of interest: Nursing school/education; Education; Environment; Federated giving programs; Protestant agencies & churches; Cemeteries/burial services.
Limitations: Applications not accepted. Giving on an international basis. No grants to individuals.
Application information: Contributes only to pre-selected organizations.
Officers: Charles R. Godchaux, Pres.; Frank K. Godchaux, V.P.; Leslie K. Godchaux, Secy.
EIN: 726042163

1238
The Lee Matherne Family Foundation
615 N. Landry
New Iberia, LA 70562-1410 (337) 369-1000
Contact: Lee J. Matherne, Pres.

Established in 2002 in LA.
Donor(s): Lee J. Matherne.

Grantmaker type: Independent foundation
Financial data (yr. ended 12/31/02): Assets, $297,557 (M); gifts received, $612,170; expenditures, $266,010; qualifying distributions, $260,381; giving activities include $257,243 for 17 grants (high: $60,400; low: $250).
Fields of interest: Education; Animals/wildlife, sanctuaries; Medical research, institute; Protestant agencies & churches; Roman Catholic agencies & churches.
Limitations: Giving primarily in LA.
Officer: Lee J. Matherne, Pres.
EIN: 721518380

1239
McDermott International, Inc. Corporate Giving Program
1450 Poydras St.
New Orleans, LA 70112
Contact: Louis J. Sannino, Sr. V.P., Human Resources, and Corp. Compliance Off.

Grantmaker type: Corporate giving program
Financial data (yr. ended 12/31/02): Total giving, $320,000; giving activities include $320,000 for grants.
Purpose and activities: McDermott International makes charitable contributions to nonprofit organizations involved with arts and culture, education, the environment, human services, and civic affairs. Support is given primarily in areas of company operations.
Fields of interest: Arts; Education; Environment; Human services; Public affairs.
Types of support: General/operating support; Annual campaigns; Capital campaigns; Program development; Scholarship funds; Employee volunteer services; Loaned talent; Employee-related scholarships; Scholarships—to individuals.
Limitations: Giving primarily in areas of company operations, with emphasis on Morgan City and New Orleans, LA, West Point, MS, Akron, Alliance, Barberton, Copley, and Lancaster, OH, Houston and Paris, TX, and Lynchburg, VA. No support for political or religious organizations, secondary schools, or United Way-supported organizations. No grants for advertising.
Publications: Program policy statement.
Application information: The Communications Department handles giving. A contributions committee reviews all requests. Application form not required.
Initial approach: Proposal to headquarters
Copies of proposal: 1
Final notification: Following review
Contributions Committee: Louis J. Sannino, Sr. V.P., Human Resources, and Compliance Off.; Don Washington, Dir., Comm. and Investor Rels.; Bruce Wilkinson, Chair. and C.E.O.
Number of staff: 3 full-time professional.

1240
The Frances R. McDonough Charitable Foundation
701 Poydras St., Ste. 3650
New Orleans, LA 70139

Established in 2000 in LA.
Donor(s): Frances R. McDonough.‡

Grantmaker type: Independent foundation
Financial data (yr. ended 12/31/02): Assets, $766,596 (M); gifts received, $20,024; expenditures, $118,586; qualifying distributions, $116,362; giving activities include $100,000 for 1 grant.
Fields of interest: Animal welfare.
Limitations: Applications not accepted. No grants to individuals.
Application information: Contributes only to pre-selected organizations.
Trustee: Mary Lou Voelkel.
EIN: 721436751

1241
The Reily Foundation
640 Magazine St.
New Orleans, LA 70130-3406 (504) 524-6131
Contact: H. Eustis Reily, Dir.

Established in 1962.
Donor(s): The Reily Cos.
Grantmaker type: Company-sponsored foundation
Financial data (yr. ended 12/31/00): Assets, $19,979,207 (M); gifts received, $8,000,000; expenditures, $1,786,966; qualifying distributions, $1,711,240; giving activities include $1,711,240 for 72 grants (high: $333,000; low: $500).
Purpose and activities: Giving primarily for education, the arts, federated giving programs, children and youth services, and human services.
Fields of interest: Orchestra (symphony); Higher education; Education; Natural resources; Health care; Human services; Children/youth, services; Federated giving programs.
Limitations: Giving primarily in the metropolitan New Orleans, LA, area. No grants to individuals.
Application information: Application form required.
Initial approach: Proposal
Deadline(s): None
Directors: Joan M. Coulter; H. Eustis Reily; Robert D. Reily; William B. Reily III.
EIN: 726029179

1242
William B. Wiener, Jr. Foundation
333 Texas St., Ste. 2375
Shreveport, LA 71101

Donor(s): William B. Wiener, Jr.
Grantmaker type: Independent foundation
Financial data (yr. ended 02/28/02): Assets, $3,060,999 (M); gifts received, $104,350; expenditures, $139,137; qualifying distributions, $136,413; giving activities include $135,850 for 42 grants (high: $30,000; low: $250).
Purpose and activities: Giving primarily for the environment and Jewish organizations.
Fields of interest: Environment, reform; Environment, government agencies; Natural resources; Environment; Jewish federated giving programs; Jewish agencies & temples.
International interests: Israel.
Limitations: Applications not accepted. Giving primarily in LA. No grants to individuals.
Application information: Contributes only to pre-selected organizations.

Officers: William B. Wiener, Jr., Pres.; Donald B. Wiener, V.P.; Donald P. Weiss, Secy.
Directors: David Rockefeller, Jr.; Ted Smith.
EIN: 726024398

1243
Mary Freeman Wisdom Foundation
P.O. Box 13647
New Orleans, LA 70185-3467
Contact: Adelaide Wisdom Benjamin, Pres.

Established in 1986 in LA.
Donor(s): Mary Freeman Wisdom.‡
Grantmaker type: Independent foundation
Financial data (yr. ended 04/30/02): Assets, $3,826,438 (M); expenditures, $253,356; qualifying distributions, $227,696; giving activities include $224,500 for 39 grants (high: $25,000; low: $1,000; average: $3,000–$5,000).
Purpose and activities: Giving for arts groups; support also for education, conservation, and social and legal services.
Fields of interest: Arts; Elementary/secondary education; Higher education; Education; Natural resources; Environment; Human services.
Types of support: General/operating support; Continuing support; Annual campaigns; Capital campaigns; Building/renovation; Equipment; Endowments; Program development; Conferences/seminars; Seed money; Scholarship funds; Matching/challenge support.
Limitations: Giving primarily in New Orleans, LA. No grants to individuals.
Publications: Application guidelines.
Application information: Application form required.
Copies of proposal: 2
Deadline(s): Feb. 1
Board meeting date(s): Late Apr.
Final notification: May 15
Officers and Trustees:* Adelaide Wisdom Benjamin,* Pres.; Betty Wisdom,* Secy.; Helen H. Wisdom,* Treas.; Edward Wisdom Benjamin; Stuart Minor Benjamin; Steven W. Usdin; Arthur Mitteer Wisdom; Matthew Morgan Wisdom.
Number of staff: 1 part-time support.
EIN: 726123208

1244
The Woldenberg Foundation
(formerly Dorothy & Malcolm Woldenberg Foundation)
301 Magazine St., 2nd Fl.
New Orleans, LA 70130
Contact: William Goldring, Pres.
Application address: P.O. Box 53333, New Orleans, LA 70153

Incorporated in 1959 in LA as Woldenberg Charitable and Educational Foundation.
Donor(s): Malcolm Woldenberg, Magnolia Liquor Co., Inc., Sazerac Co., Inc., Great Southern Liquor Co., Inc., Duval Spirits, Inc.
Grantmaker type: Independent foundation
Financial data (yr. ended 12/31/01): Assets, $14,781,354 (M); expenditures, $3,167,370; qualifying distributions, $3,039,249; giving activities include $3,042,613 for 52 grants (high: $600,000; low: $1,000; average: $1,000–$100,000).
Purpose and activities: Giving primarily for education, and to Jewish organizations.

Fields of interest: Museums; Arts; Zoos/zoological societies; Human services; Federated giving programs.
Limitations: Giving primarily in FL and LA. No grants to individuals.
Application information:
  Initial approach: Letter
  Deadline(s): None
Officers: William Goldring, Pres.; Mark Halpern, V.P.; Robert Steeg, Secy.-Treas.
EIN: 726022665

MAINE

1245
The Aldermere Foundation
(also known as Albert H. Chatfield, Jr. & Marion W. Chatfield Trust f/b/o The Aldermere Foundation)
c/o Acadia Trust, N.A.
145 Exchange St., Ste. 2
Bangor, ME 04401-6505 (207) 941-2495
Contact: R. Paul Pasquine, Sr. V.P., Acadia Trust, N.A.
FAX: (207) 941-2498; URL: http://www.acadiatrust.com

Established in 1977 in ME.
Grantmaker type: Independent foundation
Financial data (yr. ended 12/31/02): Assets, $4,090,629 (M); expenditures, $198,319; qualifying distributions, $184,241; giving activities include $184,241 for 23 grants (high: $122,641; low: $600).
Purpose and activities: Giving primarily for the arts, education, environmental preservation and youth programs.
Fields of interest: Arts; Natural resources; Animals/wildlife, preservation/protection; YM/YWCAs & YM/YWHAs; Youth, services.
Types of support: General/operating support.
Limitations: Giving primarily in ME. No grants to individuals.
Publications: Application guidelines.
Application information: Application form not required.
  Initial approach: Letter or telephone
  Copies of proposal: 1
  Deadline(s): Oct. 15
  Final notification: Nov.
Trustee: Acadia Trust, N.A.
EIN: 016059906

1246
The Peter Alfond Foundation
c/o Dexter Enterprises, Inc.
2 Monument Sq.
Portland, ME 04101

Established in 1993 in ME.
Donor(s): Peter G. Alfond, Berkshire Hathaway Inc.
Grantmaker type: Independent foundation
Financial data (yr. ended 12/31/01): Assets, $7,080,482 (M); gifts received, $76,313; expenditures, $269,400; qualifying distributions, $246,600; giving activities include $227,100 for 15 grants (high: $80,000; low: $100).

Purpose and activities: Giving primarily for education, social services, conservation, and federated giving programs.
Fields of interest: Secondary school/education; Higher education; Libraries (public); Education; Natural resources; Human services; Federated giving programs; Jewish agencies & temples.
Limitations: Applications not accepted. Giving primarily in MA, ME, PR, and RI. No grants to individuals.
Application information: Contributes only to pre-selected organizations.
Officer: Gregory Powell, Mgr.
Trustees: Peter G. Alfond; William Alfond.
EIN: 223267949

1247
The Baker Conservation Trust
c/o Pemaquid Advisors
9 Bristol Rd.
Damariscotta, ME 04543
Application address: c/o First National Bank of Damariscotta, Trust Dept., Main St., Damariscotta, ME 04543

Established in 1991.
Donor(s): Robert W. Baker.
Grantmaker type: Independent foundation
Financial data (yr. ended 12/31/02): Assets, $2,559,715 (M); gifts received, $200,000; expenditures, $158,538; qualifying distributions, $153,630; giving activities include $152,441 for 2 grants (high: $137,441; low: $15,000).
Purpose and activities: Giving primarily for natural resource conservation.
Fields of interest: Natural resources; Environment.
Limitations: Giving primarily in ME.
Application information: Application form not required.
  Deadline(s): None
Trustee: Pemaquid Advisors.
EIN: 226560684

1248
L. L. Bean, Inc. Corporate Giving Program
c/o Public Affairs Dept.
Casco St.
Freeport, ME 04033 (207) 865-4761
Contact: Janet Wyper, Mgr., Community Rels.
FAX: (207) 552-6821; URL: http://www.llbean.com/customerService/aboutLLBean/charitable_giving.html

Grantmaker type: Corporate giving program
Financial data (yr. ended 02/24/01): Total giving, $1,100,000; giving activities include $1,100,000 for grants.
Purpose and activities: L.L. Bean makes charitable contributions to nonprofit organizations involved with arts and culture, education, natural resources, health and human services, and recreation. Support is given primarily in Brunswick, Freeport, Lewiston, and Portland, Maine, and on a national basis for natural resources.
Fields of interest: Arts; Education; Natural resources; Health care; Recreation; Human services.
Types of support: General/operating support; Program development; Donated products.

Limitations: Giving primarily in Brunswick, Freeport, Lewiston, and Portland, ME; giving on a national basis for natural resources. No support for political, sectarian, or religious organizations. No grants to individuals, or for team sponsorships or sporting events, conferences, advertising, or television or film underwriting.
Publications: Informational brochure (including application guidelines).
Application information: Proposals should be no longer than 3 to 6 pages in length. The Community Relations Department handles giving. The company has a staff that only handles contributions. Application form not required.
  Initial approach: Proposal to headquarters
  Copies of proposal: 1
  Deadline(s): None
  Final notification: 3 weeks
Number of staff: 1 full-time professional; 2 full-time support.

1249
Margaret E. Burnham Charitable Trust
c/o H.M. Payson & Co.
1 Portland Sq., P.O. Box 31
Portland, ME 04112-0031 (207) 772-3761
Contact: Thomas M. Pierce, Tr.
URL: http://www.megrants.org/Burnham.htm

Established in 1995 in ME.
Donor(s): Margaret E. Burnham.‡
Grantmaker type: Independent foundation
Financial data (yr. ended 12/31/02): Assets, $5,833,474 (M); expenditures, $381,940; qualifying distributions, $333,666; giving activities include $335,700 for 104 grants (high: $20,000; low: $500).
Purpose and activities: Giving primarily for the arts, education, the environment, and human services.
Fields of interest: Arts; Higher education; Environment; Hospitals (general); Human services.
Types of support: Continuing support; Annual campaigns; Capital campaigns; Building/renovation; Equipment; Land acquisition; Program development; Publication; Research.
Limitations: Giving limited to ME. No grants to individuals.
Publications: Application guidelines.
Application information: Application form required.
  Initial approach: Letter
  Copies of proposal: 1
  Deadline(s): Nov. 15
  Board meeting date(s): Dec. 15
  Final notification: Dec. 31
Trustees: Thomas M. Pierce; Clifford H. Sinnett.
Selection Committee: John D. Duncan; William A. MacLeod.
EIN: 010496879

1250
Edward H. Daveis Benevolent Fund
1 Portland Sq.
P.O. Box 586
Portland, ME 04112-0586 (207) 774-4000
Contact: John D. Duncan, Tr.
FAX: (207) 774-7499; E-mail: jdd@verdan.com

Established in 1950 in ME.
Grantmaker type: Independent foundation
Financial data (yr. ended 12/31/02): Assets,
$1,730,984 (M); expenditures, $123,490;
qualifying distributions, $106,131; giving
activities include $106,000 for 31 grants (high:
$30,000; low: $1,000).
Purpose and activities: Giving primarily for the
arts and education.
Fields of interest: Museums; Theater; Higher
education; Animal welfare; Hospitals (general);
Youth development, centers/clubs; Youth,
services; Family services; Federated giving
programs; General charitable giving.
Types of support: Capital campaigns;
Building/renovation; Equipment; Land
acquisition; Endowments; Program
development; Conferences/seminars; Research.
Limitations: Giving primarily in the Portland,
ME, area. No grants to individuals.
Publications: Application guidelines.
Application information: Application form
required.
Initial approach: Proposal
Copies of proposal: 1
Deadline(s): Nov. 30
Board meeting date(s): Dec.
Final notification: Dec.
Trustees: John D. Duncan; Alden H. Sawyer, Jr.;
Frederic Thompson.
Number of staff: None.
EIN: 010473137

1251
Davis Conservation Foundation
4 Fundy Rd.
Falmouth, ME 04105-1705 (207) 781-5504
Contact: Nancy M. Winslow, Exec. Dir.

Established in 1989 in ME.
Grantmaker type: Public charity
Financial data (yr. ended 12/31/02): Assets,
$11,401,654 (M); gifts received, $186,447;
expenditures, $798,564; program services
expenses, $744,320; giving activities include
$698,406 for 61 grants (high: $40,000; low:
$800; average: $800–$40,000).
Purpose and activities: The foundation's broad
goal is the wise utilization, protection, and
advancement of our physical environment and
the different natural forms of life which inhabit
it, including wildlife, sea life, and mankind as
they are impacted by the environment. The
foundation's primary areas of interest are
projects and activities related to wildlife, wildlife
habitat, environmental protection, and outdoor
recreation. Projects which strengthen volunteer
activity and outreach/community involvement
in the above categories are of particular interest.
The major focus of grantmaking is in two broad
categories: 1) Northern New England Forests,
and 2) the Gulf of Maine.
Fields of interest: Natural resources;
Environment.

Limitations: Giving primarily in northern New
England. No grants to individuals, or for
scholarships, fellowships, loans, travel, or to
reduce deficits, support annual giving
campaigns, or make multi-year pledges.
Publications: Application guidelines, Annual
report.
Application information: Application form
required.
Initial approach: Letter or telephone
Deadline(s): Apr. 10 and Oct. 10
Board meeting date(s): May and Nov.
Officer: Nancy M. Winslow,* Exec. Dir.
Number of staff: 2 shared staff (shared with
Davis Educational Foundation; Davis Family
Foundation).
EIN: 222976811

1252
The Falcon Charitable Foundation
c/o Robert B. Gregory
P.O. Box 760
Damariscotta, ME 04543

Established in 1994 in ME.
Donor(s): Mary F. Fiore.
Grantmaker type: Independent foundation
Financial data (yr. ended 12/31/02): Assets,
$3,285,503 (M); expenditures, $352,484;
qualifying distributions, $322,761; giving
activities include $326,250 for 52 grants (high:
$30,000; low: $500).
Purpose and activities: Giving primarily for the
arts and environmental conservation; funding
also for human rights and civil liberties.
Fields of interest: Arts; Natural resources;
Hospitals (general); Human services;
International human rights; Civil liberties,
advocacy.
Limitations: Applications not accepted. Giving
primarily in ME and NY. No grants to individuals.
Application information: Contributes only to
pre-selected organizations.
Trustees: Joseph A. Fiore; Mary F. Fiore.
EIN: 223340779

1253
Fisher Charitable Foundation
(formerly Dean L. Fisher Charitable Foundation)
P.O. Box 17513
Portland, ME 04112 (207) 253-1568
Contact: Owen W. Wells, Clerk

Established in 1997 in ME.
Grantmaker type: Independent foundation
Financial data (yr. ended 12/31/02): Assets,
$5,654,621 (M); gifts received, $114,406;
expenditures, $638,164; qualifying distributions,
$594,946; giving activities include $561,600 for
49 grants (high: $25,000; low: $3,000).
Purpose and activities: Giving primarily for
education; some giving also for health care and
the arts.
Fields of interest: Arts; Education; Natural
resources; Hospitals (general); Medical research,
institute.
Limitations: Giving primarily in ME. No grants
to individuals.
Application information: Application form not
required.
Deadline(s): None

Officers and Trustees:* Alexandra Fisher Coles,*
Pres.; Owen Wells,* Clerk; Meg Baxter; A. Leroy
Greason; Henry L.P. Schmelzer.
EIN: 010512082

1254
Fore River Foundation
P.O. Box 7525
Portland, ME 04112-7525
Contact: Mary Gamage, Fdn. Mgr.

Established in 1986.
Donor(s): Kate Davis P. Quesada, Peter W.
Quesada, T. Ricardo Quesada.
Grantmaker type: Independent foundation
Financial data (yr. ended 11/30/02): Assets,
$3,965,869 (M); gifts received, $222,726;
expenditures, $389,686; qualifying distributions,
$382,317; giving activities include $388,494 for
67 grants (high: $32,000; low: $249).
Purpose and activities: Giving primarily for the
arts, education, health and human services.
Fields of interest: Historic preservation/historical
societies; Arts; Education; Natural resources;
Youth development, centers/clubs; Human
services.
Types of support: General/operating support.
Limitations: Applications not accepted. Giving
primarily in ME. No grants to individuals; no
loans or program-related investments.
Application information: Contributes only to
pre-selected organizations.
Officers and Directors:* T. Ricardo Quesada,*
Pres.; Kate Davis P. Quesada,* V.P.; Richard E.
Curran, Jr., Secy.; Peter W. Quesada,* Treas.
EIN: 010421912

1255
The Golden Rule Foundation, Inc.
P.O. Box 286
Belfast, ME 04915
Contact: Lissa Widoff, Mgr.
FAX: (207) 338-5655; E-mail:
goldenrule@prexar.com; URL: http://
www.goldrule.org

Established in 1981 in DC.
Donor(s): Jack Evans.‡
Grantmaker type: Independent foundation
Financial data (yr. ended 10/31/02): Assets,
$6,042,293 (M); expenditures, $324,494;
qualifying distributions, $296,390; giving
activities include $257,500 for 41 grants (high:
$20,000; low: $500).
Purpose and activities: Giving primarily for the
arts, environmental programs, and social
services.
Fields of interest: Arts; Education; Environment,
alliance; Environment, toxics; Natural resources;
Human services; Community development.
International interests: Mexico.
Types of support: General/operating support;
Program development; Seed money.
Limitations: Applications not accepted. Giving
primarily on the East Coast. No grants to
individuals.
Publications: Informational brochure.
Application information: Unsolicited requests
for funds not considered.
Board meeting date(s): Late Aug.

Officers and Directors:* Jean Evans,* Pres.; Gareth Evans,* Secy.; Sian Evans; Trevor Evans; Sal Messina; Tegan Stephen.
Number of staff: 1 part-time support.
EIN: 599207701

1256
Hannaford Charitable Foundation
P.O. Box 1000
Portland, ME 04104
Application address: c/o Scholarship America, Inc., 1505 Riverview Rd., P.O. Box 297, St. Peter, MN 56082, tel.: (507) 931-1682

Established in 1993 in ME.
Donor(s): Hannaford Bros. Co.
Grantmaker type: Company-sponsored foundation
Financial data (yr. ended 12/31/02): Assets, $1,542,755 (M); gifts received, $1,185,000; expenditures, $1,399,015; qualifying distributions, $1,325,282; giving activities include $1,300,550 for 77 grants (high: $221,000; low: $200; average: $1,000–$10,000).
Purpose and activities: Giving primarily to the United Way and to children's organizations. The foundation also maintains a scholarship program to assist Hannaford associates and their children who plan to pursue post-secondary education in college and vocational programs.
Fields of interest: Museums (art); Arts; Education; Natural resources; Human services; YM/YWCAs & YM/YWHAs; Federated giving programs.
Types of support: General/operating support; Capital campaigns; Scholarship funds; Exchange programs.
Limitations: Giving primarily in ME and NH. No support for veterans', fraternal, or religious organizations. No grants to individuals, or for advertising.
Application information: Application form required.
Deadline(s): Apr. 1 (for scholarships)
Final notification: May (for scholarships)
Officers: Bradford A. Wise, Pres.; Donna J. Boyce, Secy.; Garrett D. Bowne, Treas.
Directors: Shelley Broader; Beth Newlands Campbell; Mark Doiron; Andy Mayo; Bob Schools.
EIN: 010483892

1257
Kenduskeag Foundation
P.O. Box 17577
Portland, ME 04112-8577 (207) 773-5841
Contact: P. Andrews Nixon, Tr.

Established in 1955 in ME.
Donor(s): Curtis M. Hutchins,‡ Dead River Group of Cos.
Grantmaker type: Independent foundation
Financial data (yr. ended 12/31/02): Assets, $696,558 (M); expenditures, $224,916; qualifying distributions, $221,973; giving activities include $221,500 for 48 grants (high: $32,500; low: $100).
Purpose and activities: Support for local charities.
Fields of interest: Elementary/secondary education; Higher education; Environment,

pollution control; Human services; Foundations (community); Christian agencies & churches.
Types of support: Annual campaigns; Capital campaigns; Building/renovation; Program development; Scholarship funds.
Limitations: Giving limited to ME.
Application information: Application requests accepted at the Portland, ME, address only. Application form not required.
Deadline(s): None
Trustee: P. Andrews Nixon.
Number of staff: None.
EIN: 016018972

1258
Kennebunk Savings Bank Foundation
104 Main St.
P.O. Box 28
Kennebunk, ME 04043-0028

Donor(s): Kennebunk Savings Bank.
Grantmaker type: Company-sponsored foundation
Financial data (yr. ended 12/31/02): Assets, $400,376 (M); gifts received, $621,410; expenditures, $225,999; qualifying distributions, $219,691; giving activities include $218,509 for 186 grants (high: $11,197; low: $25).
Fields of interest: Arts; Education; Environment; Human services; Children/youth, services.
Limitations: Giving primarily in ME.
Application information:
Initial approach: Letter
Officers and Directors:* Andrew T. Furlong, Jr.,* Chair.; Joel W. Stevens,* Pres.; Wayne F. Manchester,* V.P.; Susan F. Hoctor, Secy.; Pamela J. Drew,* Treas.; Richard V. Bibber; James J. Keating III; Raymond E. Mailhot; Stephen A. Morris; Geofrey Titherington.
EIN: 010547392

1259
The Maine Community Foundation, Inc.
245 Main St.
Ellsworth, ME 04605 (207) 667-9735
Portland mailing address: 1 Monument Way, Ste. 200, P.O. Box 7380, Portland, ME 04112; Additional tels.: (207) 761-2440, (877) 700-6800; FAX: (207) 667-0447; E-mail: info@mainecf.org; grants@mainecf.org; URL: http://www.mainecf.org

Incorporated in 1983 in ME.
Grantmaker type: Community foundation
Financial data (yr. ended 12/31/01): Assets, $91,031,629 (M); gifts received, $12,579,759; expenditures, $8,515,130; giving activities include $6,622,920 for grants.
Purpose and activities: Primary areas of interest include the arts, child welfare and youth, the disadvantaged, education, health, community development, and sustainable development. The foundation administers donor-advised funds.
Fields of interest: Arts; Education; Natural resources; Environment; Health care; Health organizations, association; Youth development, services; Human services; Children/youth, services; Aging, centers/services; Urban/community development; Community development; Leadership development; Economically disadvantaged.

Types of support: Land acquisition; Program development; Seed money; Technical assistance; Grants to individuals; Scholarships—to individuals; Matching/challenge support.
Limitations: Giving limited to ME. No support for religious organizations for religious purposes. No grants to individuals (except for scholarship funds), or for endowment funds, equipment, or annual campaigns for regular operations or for capital campaigns.
Publications: Application guidelines, Annual report, Grants list, Informational brochure, Newsletter.
Application information: Application form required.
Initial approach: Letter, telephone, or E-mail for guidelines
Copies of proposal: 1
Deadline(s): Jan., May and Sept. (Please check Web site)
Board meeting date(s): 5 times annually
Final notification: 2-4 months after deadline
Officers and Directors:* Charles Roscoe,* Chair.; Henry Schmelzer, Pres.; James E. Geary, V.P., Fin Svcs. and C.F.O.; Ellen Pope, V.P. Dev.; Meredith Jones, V.P. for Philanthropic Services; Sarah Luck, V.P., Southern ME; Sidney St. F. Thaxter, Clerk; and 23 additional directors.
Number of staff: 15 full-time professional; 3 full-time support; 1 part-time support.
EIN: 010391479

1260
Maine Initiatives, Inc.
283 Water St., 3rd Fl.
P.O. Box 2248
Augusta, ME 04338 (207) 622-6294
Contact: Deborah Felder, Exec. Dir.
FAX: (207) 622-6295; E-mail: meinit@gwi.net; URL: http://www.maineinitiatives.org

Established in 1993 in ME.
Grantmaker type: Public charity
Financial data (yr. ended 12/31/00): Revenue, $554,113; assets, $621,226; gifts received, $538,859; expenditures, $319,212; program services expenses, $253,056; giving activities include $138,892 for 40 grants (high: $19,928; low: $500; average: $500–$20,000).
Purpose and activities: The initiative supports multi-year grants to organizations cultivating economic, environmental, and social justice at the grassroots level in Maine communities.
Fields of interest: Environment; Agriculture/food; Human services; Economic development; Social sciences, ethics; Economics.
Types of support: General/operating support; Continuing support; Program development; Seed money; Technical assistance.
Limitations: Giving primarily in ME. No support for direct services, publications, art or cultural activities, research, education, sports, recreation, or religious activities.
Publications: Application guidelines, Annual report, Grants list, Informational brochure, Newsletter.
Application information: Applications by e-mail, FAX, or Web submission not accepted. Application form required.
Initial approach: Letter
Copies of proposal: 10

Deadline(s): 1st Wed. in Nov. and 1st Wed. in Apr. for Harvest Fund; 2nd Wed. in Nov. for major grant letter of inquiry; Feb. for proposal
Board meeting date(s): 8 times a year Sept. to June
Final notification: Apr. for Major grants
Officers and Trustees:* Sarah Shed,* Pres.; Susan Hudson Glick,* V.P.; David Steven Rappoport,* Treas.; Deborah Felder, Exec. Dir.; Keith Bisson; Christine Cole; Mike Finnegan; R. Stephen Jenks; Cynthia Longstaff; and 8 additional trustees.
Number of staff: 2 full-time professional; 1 part-time professional; 1 part-time support.
EIN: 010484310

1261
The Morton-Kelly Charitable Trust
c/o Jensen Baird Gardner & Henry
10 Free St., Box 4510
Portland, ME 04112 (207) 775-7271
Contact: Michael J. Quinlan, Secy. and Clerk
FAX: (207) 775-7935; E-mail:
mquinlan@jbgh.com

Established in 1988 in ME.
Donor(s): Mildred D. Morton,‡ Joan M. Kelly.
Grantmaker type: Independent foundation
Financial data (yr. ended 12/31/02): Assets, $3,013,290 (M); expenditures, $211,936; qualifying distributions, $183,712; giving activities include $179,000 for 24 grants (high: $15,000; low: $2,000; average: $2,000–$15,000).
Purpose and activities: Giving primarily for cultural, educational, historical and environmental programs.
Fields of interest: Historic preservation/historical societies; Arts; Vocational education; Education; Environment.
Types of support: General/operating support; Continuing support; Annual campaigns; Capital campaigns; Building/renovation; Equipment; Endowments; Program development; Seed money; Internship funds; Scholarship funds; Research.
Limitations: Giving limited to ME.
Application information: Applications not accepted prior to July 1 annually. Application form not required.
  Initial approach: Letter
  Copies of proposal: 2
  Deadline(s): Nov. 1
  Board meeting date(s): Dec.
  Final notification: Jan. 15
Officers and Directors:* Joan M. Kelly,* Pres.; Michael J. Quinlan,* Secy. and Clerk; Merton G. Henry,* Treas.; Adrian Asherman.
Number of staff: None.
EIN: 010442078

1262
The Clarence E. Mulford Trust
P.O. Box 290
Fryeburg, ME 04037-0290 (207) 935-2061
Contact: David R. Hastings II, Tr.

Established in 1950 in ME.
Donor(s): Clarence E. Mulford.‡
Grantmaker type: Independent foundation

Financial data (yr. ended 12/31/01): Assets, $9,940,389 (M); expenditures, $519,362; qualifying distributions, $475,143; giving activities include $445,821 for 26 grants (high: $289,311; low: $250).
Purpose and activities: Giving primarily to churches, hospitals, and animal welfare organizations; support also for education and community service.
Fields of interest: Secondary school/education; Libraries/library science; Education; Animal welfare; Human services; Community development; Christian agencies & churches.
Limitations: Giving primarily in Fryeburg, ME, and neighboring towns. No grants to individuals, or for building or endowment funds, scholarships, fellowships, or matching gifts; no loans.
Application information: Application form not required.
  Initial approach: Letter
  Copies of proposal: 3
  Deadline(s): Preferably in June or Dec., no later than July 10 or Jan. 10
  Board meeting date(s): Jan. and July
  Final notification: Positive replies only
Trustees: David R. Hastings II; Peter G. Hastings.
EIN: 010247548

1263
Narragansett Number One Foundation
P.O. Box 779
Bar Mills, ME 04004
Contact: Patricia Wales, Pres. and Erwin Wales, V.P.
URL: http://www.nnof.org

Established in 2001 in ME.
Donor(s): Patricia M. Wales, R. Erwin Wales.
Grantmaker type: Independent foundation
Financial data (yr. ended 06/30/02): Assets, $4,672,345 (M); gifts received, $5,000,000; expenditures, $184,877; qualifying distributions, $163,665; giving activities include $163,665 for 22 grants (high: $52,106; low: $960).
Fields of interest: Historic preservation/historical societies; Education; Veterinary medicine; Human services; Community development.
Limitations: Giving primarily in Buxton, ME, and surrounding areas. No grants to individuals.
Application information: See Web site for application information and forms. Application form required.
  Initial approach: Letter
  Copies of proposal: 4
  Deadline(s): Mar. 1, 2004
Officers and Directors:* Patricia M. Wales,* Pres.; R. Erwin Wales,* V.P.; Elizabeth T. Mccandless, Secy.; Angela H. Desruisseaux,* Treas.; David Desruisseaux; Pamela H. Haines; James B. Haines, Jr.; Thomas Charles Holding; Eric P. Wales; Wendy York Wales.
EIN: 010546133

1264
North Woods Wilderness Trust
P.O. Box 10, Maynards Ln.
Rockwood, ME 04478
Contact: G.E. Fackelman, Pres.

Established in 1999 in ME.
Donor(s): The Nature Conservancy of Maine.

Grantmaker type: Independent foundation
Financial data (yr. ended 12/31/01): Assets, $71,556 (M); gifts received, $21,000; expenditures, $127,317; qualifying distributions, $125,200; giving activities include $125,200 for 2 grants (high: $125,000; low: $200).
Fields of interest: Environment, forests.
Types of support: Land acquisition.
Limitations: Giving primarily in ME. No grants to individuals.
Application information: Application form not required.
  Initial approach: Letter
  Copies of proposal: 1
  Deadline(s): Jan.
  Board meeting date(s): Semi-annually
  Final notification: Mid Mar.
Officers: G.E. Fackelman, Pres. and Secy.; Rudy Engholm, V.P. and Treas.
Directors: Jon Lund; Frank Woodward.
EIN: 010512529

1265
The Sandy River Charitable Foundation
RFD No. 3 Voter Hill
Box 7500
Farmington, ME 04938
E-mail: info@srcfoundation.org; URL: http://www.srcfoundation.org

Established in 1997 in ME.
Donor(s): Berry Charitable Trust.
Grantmaker type: Independent foundation
Financial data (yr. ended 05/31/02): Assets, $39,080,665 (M); gifts received, $779,000; expenditures, $4,593,886; qualifying distributions, $4,288,022; giving activities include $4,209,987 for 87 grants (high: $250,000; low: $1,780; average: $25,000–$250,000).
Purpose and activities: Giving primarily to disaster rehabilitation and hunger relief services; funding also for a community foundation in Ellsworth, ME, and a mountain alliance in Farmington, ME.
Fields of interest: Environment; Food services; Disasters, preparedness/services; International agricultural development; Foundations (community).
Limitations: Applications not accepted. Giving on a national basis. No grants to individuals.
Application information: Contributes only to pre-selected organizations.
Officers: Archie W. Berry, Jr., Pres.; Nathanel W. Berry, V.P. and Secy.; Jon W. Berry, Treas.
Directors: Mark Berry; Marla Berry; Nan Berry; Suphaporn V. Berry; Lillian Dox.
EIN: 522029911
Recent environmental and animal welfare grants:
1265-1 Association for Resource Conservation, Centerport, NY, $50,000. For Materials Resource Center. 2002.
1265-2 Philadelphia Zoo, Philadelphia, PA, $50,000. For MAYA Project. 2002.
1265-3 Sustainable Long Island, Huntington, NY, $125,000. For general operating support. 2002.
1265-4 Sustainable Long Island, Huntington, NY, $40,000. For general support. 2002.
1265-5 Western Mountains Alliance, Farmington, ME, $107,000. For capacity building. 2002.

1265-6 Western Mountains Alliance, Farmington, ME, $22,698. For general operating support. 2002.

1265-7 World Vision International, Federal Way, WA, $250,000. For Senegal Water Development. 2002.

1266
Robert and Patricia Switzer Foundation
(formerly Switzer Foundation)
P.O. Box 293
Belfast, ME 04915 (207) 338-5654
Contact: Lissa Widoff, Exec. Dir.
URL: http://www.switzernetwork.org/

Established in 1985 in OH.
Donor(s): Robert Switzer,‡ Patricia Switzer.
Grantmaker type: Independent foundation
Financial data (yr. ended 06/30/02): Assets, $15,626,097 (M); expenditures, $1,039,582; qualifying distributions, $1,015,675; giving activities include $844,229 for 7 grants (high: $400,000; low: $5,000).
Purpose and activities: Scholarships and research grants for work that examines ways to reduce air, water, and land pollution. Scholarships awarded only to students in California through the San Francisco Foundation and in New England through the New Hampshire Charitable Foundation.
Fields of interest: Environment.
Types of support: Scholarship funds; Research.
Limitations: Giving limited to CA, CT, MA, ME, NH, RI, and VT for scholarship program, other giving on a national basis. No grants to individuals.
Publications: Informational brochure (including application guidelines), Newsletter.
Application information: See foundation Web site for details. Application form required.
  Initial approach: Telephone call
  Copies of proposal: 1
Officers and Trustees:* Thomas K. Wessels,* Chair.; Lisa Widoff, Exec. Dir.; Ashley Boren; Kevin Carley; Cynthia R. Robinson; Mark Switzer; Patricia D. Switzer; Peter Switzer.
EIN: 341504501

1267
Tom's of Maine, Inc. Corporate Giving
Program
P.O. Box 710
Kennebunk, ME 04043 (207) 985-2944
Contact: Rosanne Chessie, Grant Leader
URL: http://www.tomsofmaine.com/about/partnerships.asp

Grantmaker type: Corporate giving program
Financial data (yr. ended 06/30/02): Total giving, $27,000; giving activities include $27,000 for 6 grants (high: $5,000; low: $500; average: $500–$5,000).
Purpose and activities: Tom's of Maine makes charitable contributions to nonprofit organizations involved with arts and culture, education, the environment, and human services. Special emphasis is directed towards programs designed to integrate at least two of the company's focus areas. Support is given on a national basis.
Fields of interest: Arts; Education; Environment; Human services.

Types of support: General/operating support; Employee volunteer services; Sponsorships; Employee matching gifts; Donated products; In-kind gifts.
Limitations: Giving on a national basis. No support for political organizations or candidates or religious organizations. No grants to individuals.
Application information: The company has a staff that only handles contributions. A contributions committee reviews all requests.
  Initial approach: Visit Web site for application information
  Deadline(s): Feb. 1
  Final notification: Apr. 15 for monetary contributions
Number of staff: 1 full-time professional.

MARYLAND

1268
The Abell Foundation, Inc. ▼
111 S. Calvert St., Ste. 2300
Baltimore, MD 21202-6174 (410) 547-1300
Contact: Robert C. Embry, Jr., Pres.
FAX: (410) 539-6579; *E-mail:* abell@abell.org;
URL: http://www.abell.org

Incorporated in 1953 in MD.
Donor(s): A.S. Abell Co., Harry C. Black,‡ Gary Black, Sr.‡
Grantmaker type: Independent foundation
Financial data (yr. ended 12/31/02): Assets, $177,561,737 (M); expenditures, $13,344,981; qualifying distributions, $12,790,766; giving activities include $9,649,220 for 271 grants (high: $592,930; low: $93; average: $5,000–$50,000), $127,626 for employee matching gifts, $228,578 for 4 foundation-administered programs and $693,602 for 7 loans/program-related investments.
Purpose and activities: Supports education with emphasis on public education, including early childhood and elementary education, educational research, and minority education; community development, including workforce development; human services, including programs for child welfare and development and health and family services; the arts and culture; conservation; and the homeless, including hunger issues.
Fields of interest: Arts; Education, research; Early childhood education; Child development, education; Elementary school/education; Natural resources; Environment; Health care; Substance abuse, services; Employment, services; Employment; Food services; Youth development, services; Children/youth, services; Family services; Community development; Leadership development; Minorities; Economically disadvantaged; Homeless.
Types of support: General/operating support; Capital campaigns; Building/renovation; Equipment; Land acquisition; Endowments; Program development; Conferences/seminars; Seed money; Curriculum development; Scholarship funds; Program-related

investments/loans; Employee matching gifts; Matching/challenge support.
Limitations: Giving limited to MD, with emphasis on Baltimore. Generally no support for medical facilities. No grants to individuals, or for operating budgets, sponsorships, memberships, sustaining funds, or deficit financing.
Publications: Application guidelines, Annual report (including application guidelines), Newsletter, Occasional report, Program policy statement.
Application information: Detailed information about what to submit with proposal should be requested. Application form required.
  Initial approach: Letter
  Copies of proposal: 1
  Deadline(s): Jan. 1, Mar. 1, May 1, Aug. 1, Sept. 1, and Nov. 1
  Board meeting date(s): Bimonthly
  Final notification: Within 1 week of board meetings
Officers and Trustees:* Gary Black, Jr.,* Chair.; Robert C. Embry, Jr.,* Pres.; Anne LaFarge Culman, V.P.; Frances Murray Keenan, V.P., Finance; Esthel M. Summerfield, Secy.; Eileen M. O'Rourke, Treas.; W. Shepherdson Abell; George L. Bunting, Jr.; Robert Garrett; Sally J. Michel; Walter Sondheim, Jr.
Number of staff: 8 full-time professional; 6 part-time professional; 3 full-time support; 1 part-time support.
EIN: 526036106
Recent environmental and animal welfare grants:
1268-1 1000 Friends of Maryland, Baltimore, MD, $27,400. For developing County Score Card to measure efforts to abate sprawl, and to publish land-use legislation guide for activists interested in political process and land use litigation. 2001.
1268-2 Baltimore City Police Foundation, Baltimore, MD, $50,000. For Environmental Crimes Unit Campaign Against Illegal Dumping, including prosecution of offenders and establishment of tip line to encourage citizens to report illegal dumping and targeting ten hot spots identified as chronic dumping sites for commercial debris and illegal contaminants. 2001.
1268-3 Baltimore Regional Partnership, Baltimore, MD, $50,000. For analysis of alternative land use, transportation, and housing scenarios for Baltimore region, helping to provide new planning tools for strategies to reduce traffic and air pollution. 2001.
1268-4 Center for Watershed Protection, Ellicott City, MD, $25,000. For Builders of the Bay program, designed to launch series of local roundtable task forces which will investigate existing building codes and ordinances and make recommendations designed to make building codes environmentally sensitive and economically feasible. 2001.
1268-5 Chesapeake Bay Foundation, Annapolis, MD, $170,000. For rewriting Turning the Tide, book on current state and outlook for recovery of Chesapeake Bay and for establishing interactive Web site to accompany publication. 2001.
1268-6 Conservation Fund, Annapolis, MD, $150,000. For technical assistance to local county officials and land trusts to facilitate

Maryland's Green Print and Legacy Programs and to produce and distribute Better Models for Development in Maryland as educational tool to encourage local officials to take more strategic approaches to land conservation. 2001.

1268-7 Earthome, Baldwin, MD, $11,500. For expenses related to production, pre-screening, and symposia on The Next Industrial Revolution, treatise on sustainable economic, environmental, and social responsibility. 2001.

1268-8 Earthspan, Baltimore, MD, $91,000. For implementation of Eye of the Falcon, an educational pilot program in math, science and wildlife conservation research within Ingenuity Project curriculum in Baltimore public middle schools, in collaboration with Conservation Research and Technology at University of Maryland Baltimore City. 2001.

1268-9 Environmental Law Institute, DC, $20,000. For continued support of Forests for the Bay Project to abate forest fragmentation and disappearance of Maryland woodlands, and to advocate voluntary landowner management of existing forestland, cooperative management of smaller parcels, re-establishment of trees in brownfields, provisions for property tax incentives for retention and stewardship of forests, expansion of programs to secure forest buffers along waterways, and better monitoring of current forest harvest practices to ensure compliance with regulations. 2001.

1268-10 International Center for Sustainable Development, Gaithersburg, MD, $300,000. For start-up costs to establish International Center for Sustainable Development in Baltimore, to focus on program to promote energy conservation, efficiency, renewable energy and sustainable development through efforts of Energy Ombudsman and convening of Sustainable Baltimore Forum of community leaders and experts to discuss local opportunities. 2001.

1268-11 Parks and People Foundation, Baltimore, MD, $190,000. For SuperKids Camp, six-week summer school educational, cultural and recreational program for inner-city public school students entering third grade who are performing below grade level. 2001.

1268-12 Parks and People Foundation, Baltimore, MD, $123,000. For Boys Middle School Soccer League for students maintaining 90 percent attendance rate and C average. 2001.

1268-13 Patterson Park Community Development Corporation, Baltimore, MD, $20,000. Toward initiative to clean streets and alleys in area surrounding Patterson Park community. 2001.

1269
Adalman-Goodwin Charitable Foundation, Inc.

(formerly Adalman Charitable Foundation, Inc.)
2224 Crest Rd.
Baltimore, MD 21209 (410) 664-1674
Contact: Douglas S. Goodwin, Pres.

Established in 1952.
Grantmaker type: Independent foundation

Financial data (yr. ended 12/31/02): Assets, $2,714,879 (M); gifts received, $744,271; expenditures, $200,461; qualifying distributions, $193,627; giving activities include $194,964 for 76 grants (high: $102,500; low: $100).
Fields of interest: Performing arts centers; Arts; Higher education; Botanical gardens; Jewish agencies & temples.
Types of support: General/operating support.
Limitations: Giving primarily in Baltimore, MD. No grants to individuals.
Application information:
Initial approach: Proposal
Officers and Directors:* Douglas S. Goodwin,* Pres.; Daniel Goodwin,* V.P.; Hilda Goodwin,* Secy.
EIN: 526045035

1270
The Adams Charitable Foundation, Inc. ▼
11049 Seven Hill Ln.
Potomac, MD 20854

Established in 1996 in MD.
Donor(s): Richard Adams.
Grantmaker type: Independent foundation
Financial data (yr. ended 12/31/01): Assets, $49,194,029 (M); expenditures, $3,019,630; qualifying distributions, $2,611,892; giving activities include $2,570,000 for 8 grants (high: $1,150,000; low: $25,000; average: $100,000–$500,000).
Purpose and activities: Support primarily for arts and culture, safety, the environment, and wildlife.
Fields of interest: Arts; Environment, pollution control; Animal welfare; Safety/disasters.
Limitations: Applications not accepted. Giving on a national basis. No grants to individuals.
Application information: Contributes only to pre-selected organizations.
Officers and Directors:* Donnalyn Frey Adams,* Pres.; Allan H. Frey,* V.P.; Richard L. Adams, Jr.,* Secy.-Treas.
EIN: 522002510
Recent environmental and animal welfare grants:
1270-1 National Zoo, Friends of the, DC, $1,150,000. 2001.

1271
American Ferret Association, Inc.
626-C Admiral Dr., PMB 255
Annapolis, MD 21401 (888) 337-7381
Contact: Tara Palaski, Secy.
FAX: (516) 908-5215; E-mail: afa@ferret.org;
URL: http://www.ferret.org

Established in 1992 in MD.
Grantmaker type: Public charity
Financial data (yr. ended 12/31/01): Revenue, $75,704; assets, $30,244 (L); gifts received, $19,914; expenditures, $51,949; program services expenses, $51,478; giving activities include $974 for 2 grants (high: $500; low: $474) and $1,000 for 1 grant to an individual.
Purpose and activities: The association seeks to promote the domestic ferret as a companion animal; protect the domestic ferret from any practice deemed to lower the health standards or survivability of the animal; and to provide

constant and up-to-date information of interest to ferret fanciers everywhere.
Fields of interest: Animals/wildlife, formal/general education; Animal welfare.
Types of support: Conferences/seminars; Grants to individuals.
Limitations: Giving on a national basis.
Publications: Informational brochure (including application guidelines), Newsletter.
Officers and Directors:* Gigi Shields,* Pres.; Mary McCarty-Houser,* V.P.; Tara Palaski,* Secy.; Sally Heber,* Treas.; Freddie Ann Hoffman; Vickie McKimmey.
EIN: 521718033

1272
The Ammerman Foundation
9013 Holly Leaf Ln.
Bethesda, MD 20817
Contact: Joy Ammerman, Tr.

Established in 1986 in MD.
Donor(s): Bruce Ammerman, Joy Ammerman, Lenell Ammerman.‡
Grantmaker type: Independent foundation
Financial data (yr. ended 12/31/02): Assets, $3,170,503 (M); gifts received, $1,682,514; expenditures, $161,900; qualifying distributions, $155,495; giving activities include $156,743 for 61 grants (high: $46,700; low: $15).
Purpose and activities: Giving primarily to education, environmental purposes, hospitals and Jewish organizations.
Fields of interest: Medical school/education; Theological school/education; Natural resources; Environment; Hospitals (general); Jewish federated giving programs; Jewish agencies & temples.
Types of support: General/operating support; Continuing support; Annual campaigns; Capital campaigns; Building/renovation; Land acquisition; Endowments; Curriculum development; Internship funds; Scholarship funds; Research; Grants to individuals.
Limitations: Giving primarily in the Washington, DC, area, including MD.
Application information:
Initial approach: Letter
Deadline(s): None
Trustees and Board Members:* Allie Ammerman; Alyssa Ammerman; Bruce Ammerman*; Joshua Ammerman; Joy Ammerman*; Lenell Ammerman*; Matthew Ammerman; Rebecca Ammerman.
EIN: 521320467

1273
The Baltimore Community Foundation
c/o Anne Ross Knoeller
2 E. Read St., 9th Fl.
Baltimore, MD 21202 (410) 332-4171
Contact: Thomas E. Wilcox, Pres.
FAX: (410) 837-4701; E-mail: knoeller@bcf.org;
URL: http://www.bcf.org

Incorporated in 1972 in MD.
Grantmaker type: Community foundation
Financial data (yr. ended 12/31/01): Assets, $95,401,101 (M); gifts received, $15,662,097; expenditures, $18,406,503; giving activities include $15,934,025 for grants (average: $1,000–$10,000).

Purpose and activities: Giving primarily for children and family, cultural, neighborhood, human services, and other community needs. Grants primarily for pilot projects, system-wide solutions, and to increase organizational effectiveness and self-sufficiency. The foundation also provides grants to help local organizations to help with capacity building. The foundation administers donor-advised funds.

Fields of interest: Arts education; Arts; Education; Environment; Health care; Mental health/crisis services; Health organizations, association; Housing/shelter, development; Human services; Youth, services; Family services; Aging, centers/services; Community development; Voluntarism promotion; Government/public administration; Aging.

Types of support: Income development; Management development; Endowments; Program development; Seed money; Scholarship funds; Technical assistance; Consulting services; Matching/challenge support.

Limitations: Giving primarily in the Baltimore, MD, area. No support for religious or sectarian purposes. No grants to individuals, or for operating support or capital campaigns.

Publications: Application guidelines, Annual report, Newsletter.

Application information: Application form not required.

> *Initial approach:* 2-page letter
> *Copies of proposal:* 1
> *Deadline(s):* Mar. 1, June 1, Sept. 1, and Dec. 1
> *Board meeting date(s):* Mar., June, Sept., and Dec.
> *Final notification:* Within 2 weeks after meetings

Officers and Trustees:* Walter D. Pinkard, Jr.,* Chair.; Calman J. Zamoiski, Jr.,* Vice-Chair.; Thomas E. Wilcox, Pres.; Cheryl Casciani,* Secy.; Richard O. Berndt,* Treas.; and 28 additional trustees.

Number of staff: 8 full-time professional; 3 part-time professional; 6 full-time support.

EIN: 237180620

1274
The Bancroft Foundation
101 W. Mount Royal Ave.
Baltimore, MD 21201 (410) 369-9308
Contact: Karen Kreisberg
FAX: (410) 752-1177; E-mail: kkreisberg@jcfb.org

Established in 1999.

Grantmaker type: Public charity

Financial data (yr. ended 12/31/02): Revenue, $95,582; assets, $1,037,001 (M); gifts received, $69,908; expenditures, $151,725; program services expenses, $143,000; giving activities include $143,000 for 11 grants (high: $30,000; low: $1,000).

Purpose and activities: The foundation funds educational efforts for children with alternative learning needs, and environmental issues for the Maryland-District of Columbia area.

Fields of interest: Education, special; Environment.

Types of support: General/operating support; Emergency funds; Program development; Seed money; Scholarship funds.

Limitations: Giving in the Washington, DC, and MD area.

Publications: Informational brochure.

Application information: Application form not required.

> *Initial approach:* Letter of interest
> *Copies of proposal:* 1
> *Board meeting date(s):* Spring and fall

Number of staff: 1 part-time professional; 1 part-time support.

EIN: 311644387

1275
Beretta U.S.A. Corp. Contributions Program
c/o Corp. Contribs.
17601 Beretta Dr.
Accokeek, MD 20607

Grantmaker type: Corporate giving program

Purpose and activities: Beretta makes charitable contributions to nonprofit organizations involved with education, natural resource conservation, and recreation. Support is given on a national basis.

Fields of interest: Education; Natural resources; Recreation.

Types of support: General/operating support; Employee volunteer services; Sponsorships.

Limitations: Giving on a national basis.

Application information: Application form not required.

> *Initial approach:* Proposal to headquarters
> *Copies of proposal:* 1
> *Deadline(s):* None
> *Final notification:* Following review

1276
BGE Corporate Giving Program
(also known as Constellation Energy Group, Inc. Corporate Giving Program)
P.O. Box 1475
Baltimore, MD 21203-1475 (888) 460-2002
Contact: Malinda B. Small, Dir., Natl.-State Affairs and Corp. Contribs.
FAX: (410) 783-3279; URL: http://www.constellation.com/about/community.asp; http://www.bge.com/cmp/CDA/section/0,1668,15,00.html

Grantmaker type: Corporate giving program

Financial data (yr. ended 12/31/02): Total giving, $1,800,695; giving activities include $1,484,255 for 853 grants (high: $100,000; low: $25), $273,190 for 439 employee matching gifts and $43,250 for 82 in-kind gifts.

Purpose and activities: As a complement to its foundation, BGE also makes charitable contributions to nonprofit organizations directly. Support is limited to areas of company operations.

Fields of interest: Education; Environment; Economic development.

Types of support: General/operating support; Continuing support; Capital campaigns; Building/renovation; Equipment; Conferences/seminars; Employee volunteer services; Sponsorships; Employee matching gifts; Donated equipment; In-kind gifts; Matching/challenge support.

Limitations: Giving limited to areas of company operations. No support for United Way member

organizations, religious organizations not of direct benefit to the entire community, sports teams, organizations posing a conflict of interest with BGE or Constellation Energy Group, or individual public schools. No grants to individuals, or for seed money.

Publications: Informational brochure (including application guidelines).

Application information: Proposals should be submitted using organization letterhead. Proposals should be no longer than 5 pages in length. The National-State Affairs and Corporate Contributions Department handles giving. The company has a staff that only handles contributions. Application form not required.

> *Initial approach:* Proposal to headquarters
> *Copies of proposal:* 2
> *Deadline(s):* May 1 to Sept. 1
> *Final notification:* 6 to 8 weeks

Administrator: Suzanne MacKenzie, Corp. Contribs. Admin.

Number of staff: 1 part-time professional; 2 full-time support.

1277
Brandywine Foundation, Inc.
c/o Richard Pridgeon
600 Baltimore Ave., Ste. 205
Baltimore, MD 21204 (410) 823-0211
Contact: Ernest D. Levering, Dir.

Established in 1960 in MD.

Donor(s): Charles E. Scarlett, Jr.

Grantmaker type: Independent foundation

Financial data (yr. ended 10/31/02): Assets, $1,789,867 (M); expenditures, $121,871; qualifying distributions, $112,200; giving activities include $112,200 for 140 grants (high: $5,000; low: $100).

Purpose and activities: Giving for the arts, education, animals and health.

Fields of interest: Arts; Elementary/secondary education; Higher education; Animals/wildlife; Hospitals (general); Health care; Roman Catholic agencies & churches.

Types of support: General/operating support.

Limitations: Giving primarily in Baltimore, MD. No grants to individuals.

Application information: Application form not required.

> *Initial approach:* Proposal
> *Deadline(s):* None

Director: Ernest D. Levering.

EIN: 526033622

1278
Alex Brown & Sons Charitable Foundation, Inc.
c/o Deutsche Banc Alex Brown Inc.
1 South St.
Baltimore, MD 21202
Contact: Margaret Preston, Secy.

Established in 1954 in MD.

Donor(s): Alex Brown & Sons Inc.

Grantmaker type: Company-sponsored foundation

Financial data (yr. ended 12/31/00): Assets, $21,763,233 (M); expenditures, $4,182,289; qualifying distributions, $4,025,202; giving activities include $4,065,521 for 106 grants

(high: $500,000; low: $500; average: $1,000–$60,000).
Purpose and activities: Giving primarily for higher education, hospitals, the arts, and human services.
Fields of interest: Museums; Humanities; Arts; Higher education; Education; Natural resources; Hospitals (general); Human services.
Types of support: General/operating support; Continuing support; Annual campaigns; Capital campaigns; Building/renovation; Endowments; Scholarship funds.
Limitations: Applications not accepted. Giving primarily in MD. No support for private schools or churches. No grants to individuals.
Application information: Contributes only to pre-selected organizations.
Officers and Trustees:* Mayo A. Shattuck III,* Pres.; Margaret Preston, Secy.; Thomas Schweizer.
Number of staff: None.
EIN: 526054236

1279
Alvin I. & Peggy S. Brown Charitable Foundation
7900 Wisconsin Ave., Ste. 403
Bethesda, MD 20814-3601 (301) 656-5998
Contact: Charles Harab, Secy.-Treas.

Established about 1963.
Donor(s): Alvin I. Brown, Peggy S. Brown.
Grantmaker type: Independent foundation
Financial data (yr. ended 03/31/03): Assets, $4,247,652 (M); gifts received, $580,000; expenditures, $635,432; qualifying distributions, $631,243; giving activities include $621,394 for 85 grants (high: $238,100; low: $15; average: $15–$238,100).
Purpose and activities: Giving primarily to Jewish agencies and temples; some giving also to education.
Fields of interest: Museums; Education; Zoos/zoological societies; Health organizations, association; Medical research, institute; Human services; Jewish federated giving programs; Social sciences; Jewish agencies & temples.
Limitations: Applications not accepted. Giving on a national basis. No grants to individuals.
Application information: Unsolicited requests for funds not accepted.
  Board meeting date(s): Varies
Officers: Alvin I. Brown, Pres.; Peggy S. Brown, V.P.; Charles Harab, Secy.-Treas.; Larry N. Gandal, Secy.
EIN: 526041735

1280
The H. Barksdale Brown Charitable Trust
c/o Mercantile-Safe Deposit & Trust Co.
766 Old Hammonds Ferry Rd.
Linthicum, MD 21090 (410) 237-5653

Established in 1965 in MD.
Grantmaker type: Independent foundation
Financial data (yr. ended 12/31/01): Assets, $1,245,912 (M); expenditures, $106,666; qualifying distributions, $97,859; giving activities include $100,000 for 21 grants (high: $12,000; low: $1,000).
Purpose and activities: Giving primarily for education and the environment.

Fields of interest: Arts; Education; Natural resources.
Limitations: Applications not accepted. Giving primarily in San Francisco Bay Area, CA, and Baltimore, MD; some giving also in MA, NM, and WI. No grants to individuals.
Application information: Contributes only to pre-selected organizations.
Trustee: Mercantile-Safe Deposit & Trust Co.
EIN: 526063083

1281
The Vaughan W. Brown Charitable Trust
c/o Mercantile-Safe Deposit & Trust Co.
766 Old Hammonds Ferry Rd.
Linthicum, MD 21090-1323
Contact: J. Michael Miller III, V.P., Mercantile-Safe Deposit & Trust Co.

Grantmaker type: Independent foundation
Financial data (yr. ended 12/31/02): Assets, $929,607 (M); expenditures, $102,461; qualifying distributions, $95,532; giving activities include $95,800 for 58 grants (high: $7,000; low: $500).
Purpose and activities: Giving primarily for education and religious organizations.
Fields of interest: Education; Environment; Human services; Christian agencies & churches.
Limitations: Applications not accepted. Giving primarily in Washington, DC, and MD; some giving also in San Francisco, CA, and Atlanta, GA. No grants to individuals.
Application information: Contributes only to pre-selected organizations.
Trustee: Mercantile-Safe Deposit & Trust Co.
EIN: 526063087

1282
The Keith Campbell Foundation for the Environment, Inc.
210 W. Pennsylvania Ave., Ste. 770
Towson, MD 21204-5338
Contact: Keith Campbell, Pres.

Established in 1998 in MD.
Donor(s): Keith Campbell.
Grantmaker type: Independent foundation
Financial data (yr. ended 12/31/00): Assets, $13,469,676 (M); gifts received, $7,000,000; expenditures, $295,134; qualifying distributions, $272,976; giving activities include $283,391 for 15 grants (high: $150,000; low: $100).
Fields of interest: Education; Environment; Medical research; Human services; Philanthropy/voluntarism.
Types of support: General/operating support.
Limitations: Giving primarily in MD. No grants to individuals.
Application information: Application form not required.
  Deadline(s): None
Officer and Director:* Keith Campbell,* Pres. and Secy.
EIN: 522136842

1283
Capital Gazette Foundation, Inc.
c/o Wilbert H. Sirota, Esq.
6225 Smith Ave.
Baltimore, MD 21209-3600

Established in 1986 in MD.
Donor(s): Capital Gazette Communications, Inc., Washington Magazine, Inc., The Washingtonian.
Grantmaker type: Independent foundation
Financial data (yr. ended 12/31/01): Assets, $311,982 (M); gifts received, $407,678; expenditures, $274,277; qualifying distributions, $273,450; giving activities include $273,450 for 32 grants (high: $15,500; low: $250).
Fields of interest: Arts; Higher education; Natural resources; Health care; Human services; Federated giving programs.
Types of support: General/operating support; Matching/challenge support.
Limitations: Applications not accepted. Giving primarily in Washington, DC and MD. No grants to individuals.
Application information: Contributes only to pre-selected organizations.
Officers: Philip Merrill, Pres.; Wilbert H. Sirota, Secy.; Eleanor Merrill, Treas.
EIN: 521490576

1284
Eugene B. Casey Foundation ▼
800 S. Frederick Ave., Ste. 100
Gaithersburg, MD 20877-4102
Contact: Betty Brown Casey, Chair.

Established in 1981 in MD.
Grantmaker type: Independent foundation
Financial data (yr. ended 08/31/02): Assets, $171,703,050 (M); expenditures, $54,387,084; qualifying distributions, $52,210,956; giving activities include $52,470,000 for 26 grants (high: $45,853,750; low: $5,000; average: $10,000–$100,000).
Purpose and activities: Support primarily for higher education and medical research; support also for the fine arts and community development.
Fields of interest: Visual arts; Performing arts; Higher education; Medical research, institute; Community development.
Types of support: General/operating support.
Limitations: Applications not accepted. Giving primarily in the greater Washington, DC, area, and MD.
Application information: Funds fully committed to 2015.
Officers and Trustees:* Betty Brown Casey,* Chair., Pres., and Treas.; Stephen N. James,* V.P. and Secy.; Douglas R. Casey; W. James Price.
EIN: 526220316
Recent environmental and animal welfare grants:
1284-1 Garden Club of America Casey Trees Endowment Fund, DC, $45,853,750. For reforestation and tree maintenance in Washington. Grant made in form of stock. 2002.
1284-2 Garden Club of America Casey Trees Endowment Fund, DC, $4,158,250. For reforestation and tree maintenance in Washington. 2002.

1285
Eugene Chaney Foundation, Ltd.
P.O. Box 548
Waldorf, MD 20604
Contact: Francis H. Chaney II, Pres.
Application address: Chaney Bldg., Waldorf,
MD 20601

Established in 1987 in MD.
Donor(s): Chaney Enterprises, LP, B.P.O.E.,
Southstar, LP.
Grantmaker type: Company-sponsored
foundation
Financial data (yr. ended 12/31/02): Assets,
$1,166,168 (M); gifts received, $428,333;
expenditures, $319,671; qualifying distributions,
$295,545; giving activities include $295,545 for
grants (high: $43,641).
Fields of interest: Education; Environment;
Health organizations, association;
Children/youth, services; Religion.
Types of support: General/operating support;
Research; Employee matching gifts.
Limitations: Giving limited to southern MD. No
grants to individuals.
Publications: Annual report.
Application information: Application form not
required.
  Initial approach: Letter
  Deadline(s): None
  Board meeting date(s): 3rd Mon. of Feb. and
  Sept.
Officers and Directors:* Francis H. Chaney II,*
Pres.; William F. Childs IV,* V.P.; Carol Jackson,*
Secy.; Bob Agee; Mary M. Chaney; Mike
Mickelton.
EIN: 521525001

1286
Chesapeake Bay Trust
60 W. St., Ste. 200-A
Annapolis, MD 21401-2400 (410) 974-2941
Contact: David J. O'Neill, Exec. Dir.
FAX: (410) 269-0387; E-mail:
postmaster@cbtrust.org; URL: http://
www.chesapeakebaytrust.org

Established in 1985 in MD.
Grantmaker type: Public charity
Financial data (yr. ended 06/30/02): Revenue,
$1,775,413; assets, $9,665,336 (M); gifts
received, $1,234,700; expenditures,
$2,223,646; program services expenses,
$2,004,481; giving activities include
$1,699,878 for 559 grants (high: $75,000; low:
$50) and $12,000 for 3 in-kind gifts.
Purpose and activities: The organization
provides financial support grants to civic and
community organizations, schools, and
volunteer groups for Chesapeake Bay restoration
and education projects in Maryland.
Fields of interest: Environment, water resources;
Environment, land resources; Environment.
Types of support: Matching/challenge support.
Limitations: Giving primarily in the Chesapeake
Bay Watershed region in MD. No support for
lobbying, or activities that advocate political
solutions. No grants to individuals, or for
fundraising, benefits, indirect costs, food items,
endowments, building campaigns, deficit
financing, annual giving, research, or capital
construction.

Publications: Application guidelines, Annual
report, Informational brochure (including
application guidelines).
Application information: Proposals for $2,000
and under are welcomed throughout the year,
and should be received at least 4-6 weeks in
advance of the project. However, applications
for grants over $2,000 must be received by the
specific application deadline date. Applicants
are encouraged to discuss project ideas and
activities with trust staff before submitting
application form. Application form required.
  Initial approach: Telephone or e-mail
  Copies of proposal: 1
  Deadline(s): Mar. 12, July 16, Sept. 17, and
  Dec. 10
  Board meeting date(s): Feb. 4, May 7, Sept. 8,
  and Nov. 10
Officers and Trustees:* Martin H. Poretsky,*
Chair.; Midgett S. Parker,* Vice-Chair.; Gary
Heath,* Secy.; Robert Hoyt,* Treas.; David J.
O'Neill, Exec. Dir.; Frances Flannigan; and 14
additional trustees.
Number of staff: 4 full-time professional; 1
part-time professional.
EIN: 521454182

1287
The Dr. Francis P. Chiaramonte Private
Foundation
7503 Surratts Rd.
Clinton, MD 20735

Established in 1998 in MD.
Donor(s): Francis P. Chiaramonte.
Grantmaker type: Independent foundation
Financial data (yr. ended 12/31/02): Assets,
$2,319,000 (M); gifts received, $1,000,000;
expenditures, $195,035; qualifying distributions,
$195,000; giving activities include $195,000 for
15 grants (high: $30,000; low: $2,500).
Fields of interest: Secondary school/education;
Environment; Boys & girls clubs; Human
services; Salvation Army.
Limitations: Applications not accepted. No
grants to individuals.
Application information: Contributes only to
pre-selected organizations.
Trustee: Francis P. Chiaramonte.
EIN: 522136769

1288
COGEMA, Inc. Corporate Giving Program
1 Bethesda Ctr.
4800 Hampden Ln., Ste. 1100
Bethesda, MD 20814 (301) 986-8585
Contact: Jean-Francois Gervais, V.P. and C.F.O.

Grantmaker type: Corporate giving program
Purpose and activities: COGEMA makes
charitable contributions to nonprofit
organizations involved with education, the
environment, and on a case by case basis.
Support is given primarily in areas of company
operations.
Fields of interest: Education; Environment;
General charitable giving.
Types of support: General/operating support;
Sponsorships.
Limitations: Giving primarily in areas of
company operations.

1289
The Columbia Foundation
10227 Wincopin Cir., G-15
Columbia, MD 21044-2624
Contact: Barbara K. Lawson, C.E.O. and Pres.
FAX: (410) 715-3043; E-mail:
info@columbiafoundation.org; URL: http://
www.columbiafoundation.org

Incorporated in 1969 in MD.
Grantmaker type: Community foundation
Financial data (yr. ended 12/31/02): Assets,
$7,427,839 (M); gifts received, $865,077;
expenditures, $977,570; giving activities
include $768,894 for grants (average:
$500–$30,000).
Purpose and activities: Grants for health and
human services, including programs for youth,
the aged, and the disabled; arts and culture,
including music, the performing arts, and
historic preservation; educational programs; and
housing. The foundation administers
donor-advised funds.
Fields of interest: Performing arts; Music;
Historic preservation/historical societies; Arts;
Education; Environment; Animals/wildlife;
Health care; Housing/shelter, development;
Human services; Children/youth, services;
Family services; Aging, centers/services;
Disabled; Aging.
Types of support: General/operating support;
Continuing support; Building/renovation;
Equipment; Emergency funds; Program
development; Conferences/seminars; Seed
money; Curriculum development; Technical
assistance; Consulting services; Program-related
investments/loans; Matching/challenge support.
Limitations: Applications not accepted. Giving
limited to Howard County, MD. No support for
projects of a sectarian religious nature. No
grants to individuals, or for annual campaigns,
deficit financing, land acquisition, medical
research, or general or special endowments.
Publications: Annual report.
Application information:
  Board meeting date(s): 3rd Wed. of each
  month
Officers and Trustees:* Malynda H. Madzel,*
Chair.; Barbara K. Lawson, C.E.O. and Pres.;
Michael Davis,* V.P.; Ilana Bittner,* Secy.; Steve
Dubin,* Treas.; and 26 additional trustees.
Number of staff: 1 full-time professional; 1
full-time support.
EIN: 520937644

1290
The Community Foundation of Frederick
County, Maryland, Inc.
312 E. Church St.
Frederick, MD 21701 (301) 695-7660
Contact: Elizabeth Y. Day, Pres.
FAX: (301) 695-7775; E-mail: info@cffredco.org;
URL: http://www.cffredco.org

Established in 1986 in MD.
Grantmaker type: Community foundation
Financial data (yr. ended 06/30/03): Assets,
$23,000,000 (M); gifts received, $2,278,943;
expenditures, $1,829,887; giving activities
include $1,200,433 for 183 grants (high:
$169,095; low: $59; average: $59–$169,095)
and $167,872 for 162 grants to individuals
(high: $5,866; low: $50; average: $50–$5,866).

Purpose and activities: To enhance the quality of life for all the people of Frederick County, MD, by serving as a community leader and a resource for philanthropy, by supporting a broad range of programs and projects, by helping people fulfill their charitable dreams, and by building permanent endowments. The foundation administers donor-advised funds, for good, forever, for Frederick County, MD.
Fields of interest: Historic preservation/historical societies; Arts; Education; Environment, pollution control; Health care; Human services; Community development.
Types of support: Capital campaigns; Building/renovation; Emergency funds; Program development; Seed money; Scholarship funds; Grants to individuals; Scholarships—to individuals.
Limitations: Giving limited to Frederick County, MD.
Publications: Application guidelines, Annual report, Newsletter.
Application information: Application information available on foundation Web site. Application form not required.
  Initial approach: Check foundation Web site
  Copies of proposal: 1
  Deadline(s): Oct. 1
  Board meeting date(s): 4th Thurs. of each month
  Final notification: mid Dec.
Officers and Trustees:* James H. Clapp,* Chair.; Gordon M. Cooley,* 1st Vice-Chair; D. Hunt Hendrickson,* 2nd Vice-Chair.; Elizabeth Y. Day, Pres.; C. Richard Miller, Jr.,* Secy.; Gail M. Fitzgerald, C.F.O.; Edmond B. "Ted" Gregory,* Treas.; Ruth Dredden; and 19 additional trustees.
Number of staff: 3 full-time professional; 2 full-time support; 1 part-time support.
EIN: 521488711

1291
Community Foundation of the Eastern Shore, Inc.
200 W. Main St.
Salisbury, MD 21803-0152 (410) 742-9911
Contact: David N. Michaud, Pres.
Additional address: P.O. Box 152, Salisbury, MD 21803; FAX: (410) 742-6638; E-mail: cfes@cfes.org; URL: http://www.cfes.org/

Established in 1984 in MD.
Grantmaker type: Community foundation
Financial data (yr. ended 06/30/02): Assets, $32,213,224 (M); gifts received, $4,049,268; expenditures, $1,593,814; giving activities include $1,175,087 for grants.
Purpose and activities: The mission of the Community Foundation of the Eastern Shore is to strengthen the community by building charitable endowments, maximizing benefits to donors, making effective grants and providing leadership to address community needs. The foundation administers donor-advised funds.
Fields of interest: Historic preservation/historical societies; Arts; Education; Environment; Health care; Human services; Community development.
Types of support: Management development; Program development; Conferences/seminars; Seed money; Scholarship funds; Technical assistance; Consulting services; Matching/challenge support.

Limitations: Giving limited to the lower Eastern Shore counties of Wicomico, Worcester, and Somerset, MD. No support for sectarian or religious purposes. No grants to individuals, or for annual campaigns, major capital campaigns, building or endowment funds, continuing support, land acquisition, long-term operating support, debt retirement or budget deficits; no program-related investments.
Publications: Application guidelines, Annual report, Financial statement, Informational brochure, Newsletter.
Application information: Application form required.
  Initial approach: Letter or telephone
  Copies of proposal: 2
  Deadline(s): Apr. 1, Aug. 1, and Dec. 1
  Board meeting date(s): June, Oct., and Feb.
  Final notification: Immediately following board decision
Officers and Directors:* Virginia B. Layfield,* Chair.; Martin T. Neat,* Vice-Chair.; David N. Michaud, Pres.; Gladys B. Goslee,* Secy.; Gregory L. Stein,* Treas.; and 21 additional directors.
Number of staff: 2 full-time professional; 2 part-time professional; 2 part-time support.
EIN: 521326014

1292
The Concordia Foundation
c/o Mercantile-Safe Deposit and Trust Co.
Two Hopkins Plz., P.O. Box 1477
Baltimore, MD 21203
Contact: Joseph Ferlise

Established in 1997 in MD.
Donor(s): John J. Roberts.
Grantmaker type: Independent foundation
Financial data (yr. ended 12/31/01): Assets, $31,430,817 (M); expenditures, $1,718,673; qualifying distributions, $1,704,125; giving activities include $1,533,230 for 48 grants (high: $200,000; low: $2,000).
Purpose and activities: Giving primarily for education, preserving the ecosystems of the Eastern Shore of MD, and supporting the work of living artists, writers and musicians.
Fields of interest: Arts; Education; Natural resources.
Types of support: General/operating support; Capital campaigns; Program development.
Limitations: Giving primarily in MD and NJ; some funding also in NY. No grants to individuals, or for matching gifts; no loans.
Application information: Application form not required.
  Initial approach: Letter
Trustees: Christopher L. Roberts; John J. Roberts; Nancy L. Roberts; Rebecca B. Roberts.
EIN: 311486126

1293
Conservation Treaty Support Fund, Inc.
3705 Cardiff Rd.
Chevy Chase, MD 20815-5943
(301) 654-3150
Contact: George A. Furness, Jr., Pres.
Additional tel.: (800) 654-3150; FAX: (301) 652-6390; E-mail: ctsf@conservationtreaty.org; URL: http://www.conservationtreaty.org/

Established in 1986.
Donor(s): Pet Industry Joint Advisory Council, H.R.H Prince Barahead of the Netherlands, Robert Bateman, N. Marshall Meyers, George A. Furness, Jr., W. Alton Jones Foundation, Mary Helsapels.
Grantmaker type: Public charity
Financial data (yr. ended 12/31/00): Revenue, $48,976; assets, $72,000; gifts received, $48,102; expenditures, $44,983; program services expenses, $40,302; giving activities include $30,600 for 4 grants (high: $10,600; low: $5,000).
Purpose and activities: The organization supports major inter-governmental treaties which conserve wild natural resources for their own sake and the benefit of people.
Fields of interest: Environment, land resources; Animals/wildlife.
Types of support: Program development; Conferences/seminars; Research; Technical assistance.
Limitations: Giving on a national and international basis. No grants to individuals.
Publications: Annual report, Biennial report.
Application information: Application form not required.
  Board meeting date(s): Once every year or two
Officers and Directors:* George A. Furness, Jr.,* Pres.; Frederick E. Morris,* V.P.; John C. Goldsmith,* V.P., Intl. Affairs; Lawrence N. Mason,* Secy.; Faith T. Campbell,* Treas.; Margarita Astralaga; Thomas P. Benjamin; Jaques Berney; Peter Dollinger; and 12 additional directors.
Number of staff: 1.
EIN: 521493562

1294
Constellation Energy Group Foundation, Inc.
(formerly Baltimore Gas and Electric Foundation, Inc.)
P.O. Box 1475
Baltimore, MD 21203 (888) 460-2002
Contact: Malinda B. Small, Dir., Corp. Citizenship and Contrib.
FAX: (410) 783-3279; URL: http://www.constellation.com

Established in 1986 in MD.
Donor(s): Baltimore Gas and Electric Co., Constellation Energy Group, Inc.
Grantmaker type: Company-sponsored foundation
Financial data (yr. ended 12/31/02): Assets, $3,153,122 (M); gifts received, $5,000,000; expenditures, $1,624,144; qualifying distributions, $1,623,194; giving activities include $2,143,194 for 25 grants (high: $777,944; low: $10,000; average: $10,000–$100,000).
Purpose and activities: Support primarily for education, economic development, and environmental initiatives.
Fields of interest: Museums; Arts; Higher education; Adult education—literacy, basic skills & GED; Reading; Education; Environment; Economic development; Community development.
Types of support: General/operating support; Continuing support; Capital campaigns;

Building/renovation; Equipment; Matching/challenge support.
Limitations: Giving primarily in areas where there is significant business interest. No support for United Way member agencies. No grants to individuals, or for endowment funds, sports, health research, hospital capital or for start-up funding.
Publications: Informational brochure (including application guidelines).
Application information: Application form required.
Copies of proposal: 2
Deadline(s): May 1 and Sept. 1
Board meeting date(s): 2 times per year
Final notification: Letter
Officers: Paul J. Allen, Pres.; Malinda B. Small, V.P.; Kathleen A. Chagnon, Secy.; Thomas E. Ruszin, Jr., Treas.
Number of staff: 3 shared staff.
EIN: 521452037

1295
Entomological Foundation
9332 Annapolis Rd., Ste. 210
Lanham, MD 20706-3115 (301) 459-9082
Contact: April Gower, Exec. Dir.
FAX: (301) 459-9084; E-mail: melodie@entfdn.org; URL: http://www.entfdn.org/

Established in 1992 in MD.
Grantmaker type: Public charity
Financial data (yr. ended 12/31/01): Revenue, $69,016; assets, $887,924; gifts received, $46,341; expenditures, $145,156; program services expenses, $131,962; giving activities include $18,864 for 13 grants to individuals (high: $4,000; low: $300).
Purpose and activities: The foundation promotes education and research in entomology through scholarships, grants, and other educational programs.
Fields of interest: Animals/wildlife, research.
Types of support: Fellowships; Research; Grants to individuals; Scholarships—to individuals.
Application information: See Web site for application guidelines. Application form required.
Initial approach: Telephone or e-mail
Deadline(s): Varies
Officers and Directors:* James Olmes, Ph.D.,* Pres.; Fred Knapp, Ph.D.,* V.P.; Frank E. Gilstrap, Ph.D.,* Secy.-Treas.; April Gower,* Exec. Dir.; Paul Borth; Paula G. Lettice; Thomas Payne; Lynn Riddiford; Patricia Zungoli.
Members: William Gimpel; Michael Ivie; Larry Larson; Z.B. Mayo, Jr.; J.E. McPherson; Sharon Quisenberry; Kathleen B. Shields.
EIN: 521756169

1296
Gretchen V. & Samuel M. Feldman Private Foundation, Inc.
27 Caveswood Ln.
Owings Mills, MD 21117

Established in 1997 in MD.
Grantmaker type: Independent foundation
Financial data (yr. ended 12/31/02): Assets, $1,953,472 (M); expenditures, $179,200; qualifying distributions, $149,549; giving

activities include $145,275 for 82 grants (high: $25,000; low: $15).
Purpose and activities: Giving for education, health, medical and community services, and for Jewish organizations.
Fields of interest: Education; Environment, land resources; Medical care, community health systems; Health care, infants; Health care; Eye diseases; Jewish agencies & temples.
Limitations: Applications not accepted. Giving primarily in MA. No grants to individuals.
Application information: Contributes only to pre-selected organizations.
Officers: Samuel M. Feldman, Chair.; Gretchen V. Feldman, Pres.; Leigh E. Feldman, V.P. and Secy.; Dene E. Feldman, V.P. and Treas.
EIN: 522034763

1297
France-Merrick Foundation ▼
The Exchange
1122 Kenilworth Dr., Ste. 118
Baltimore, MD 21204 (410) 832-5700
Contact: Robert W. Schaefer, Exec. Dir.
FAX: (410) 832-5704

Established in 1962; merged with Jacob and Annita France Foundation, Inc. and assumed current name in 1998.
Donor(s): Robert G. Merrick, Sr.,‡ Robert G. Merrick, Jr.;‡ Anne M. Merrick,‡ Jacob France,‡ Annita France.‡
Grantmaker type: Independent foundation
Financial data (yr. ended 05/31/02): Assets, $210,027,085 (M); expenditures, $12,124,606; qualifying distributions, $10,123,850; giving activities include $9,317,066 for 65 grants (high: $1,016,000; low: $500; average: $1,000–$100,000) and $416,677 for 101 employee matching gifts.
Purpose and activities: Emphasis on civic and cultural activities, historic preservation, private and higher education, public education, health, social services, and conservation and the environment.
Fields of interest: Historic preservation/historical societies; Arts; Education; Natural resources; Environment; Health care; Human services.
Types of support: General/operating support; Capital campaigns; Building/renovation; Equipment; Endowments; Program development; Seed money; Employee matching gifts; Matching/challenge support.
Limitations: Giving primarily in the metropolitan Baltimore, MD, area. No grants to individuals.
Publications: Application guidelines.
Application information: Application form not required.
Initial approach: Letter
Copies of proposal: 1
Deadline(s): None
Board meeting date(s): Mar., May, July, Oct., and Dec.
Final notification: Letter from Exec. Dir.
Officers and Directors:* Anne M. Pinkard,* Pres.; Walter D. Pinkard, Jr.,* V.P.; Robert M. Pinkard,* Secy.; Gregory C. Pinkard,* Treas.; Robert W. Schaefer, Exec. Dir.; Redmond C.S. Finney; Freeman A. Hrabowski III; Robert G. Merrick III.

Number of staff: 1 full-time professional; 2 part-time professional; 2 full-time support; 1 part-time support.
EIN: 526072964
Recent environmental and animal welfare grants:
1297-1 Conservation Fund, Arlington, VA, $40,000. 2002.
1297-2 Gunpowder Valley Conservancy, Kingsville, MD, $100,000. 2002.
1297-3 Irvine Natural Science Center, Stevenson, MD, $154,000. 2002.

1298
Gildea Foundation, Inc.
c/o Bank of America
10 Light St., MD4-302-17-06
Baltimore, MD 21202

Established in 1964 in MD.
Grantmaker type: Independent foundation
Financial data (yr. ended 12/31/02): Assets, $2,279,574 (M); expenditures, $180,001; qualifying distributions, $159,847; giving activities include $155,000 for 3 grants (high: $75,000; low: $40,000).
Purpose and activities: Giving for education, environmental conservation, and the arts.
Fields of interest: Education, government agencies; University; Botanical gardens.
Limitations: Applications not accepted. Giving on a national basis. No grants to individuals.
Application information: Contributes only to pre-selected organizations.
Officers: Ray M. Gildea, Pres.; Barry Y. Gildea, V.P.; Brian W. Gildea, V.P.; Gertrude S. Gildea, V.P.; Matthew C. Long, V.P.; Patricia Gildea Long, V.P.; Phillis A. Gildea, V.P.; Ray Y. Gildea, Jr., V.P.; George E. Thomsen, Secy.
Trustee: Bank of America.
EIN: 520811730

1299
W. R. Grace Foundation, Inc.
7500 Grace Dr.
Columbia, MD 21044 (410) 531-4000
Contact: Marihelen Johnson

Incorporated in 1996 in FL.
Donor(s): W.R. Grace & Co.
Grantmaker type: Company-sponsored foundation
Financial data (yr. ended 12/31/02): Assets, $5,128,531 (M); expenditures, $1,332,651; qualifying distributions, $819,486; giving activities include $746,794 for 145 grants (high: $100,000; low: $45) and $67,402 for employee matching gifts.
Purpose and activities: Giving primarily for arts and cultural programs, education and human services.
Fields of interest: Arts; Elementary/secondary education; Higher education; Natural resources; Health organizations, association; Human services; Children/youth, services; Government/public administration.
Limitations: Giving primarily in communities where the company has a significant employee presence.
Application information: Application form not required.
Initial approach: Letter

Deadline(s): None
Officers and Directors:* W. Brian McGowan,* Chair.; William M. Corcoran,* V.P.; Mark A. Shelnitz, Secy.; Robert M. Tarola, Treas.; Paul J. Norris.
EIN: 650630671

1300
The Homer and Martha Gudelsky Family Foundation, Inc.
11900 Tech Rd.
Silver Spring, MD 20904 (301) 622-0100
Contact: Medda Gudelsky, V.P.

Incorporated in 1968 in MD.
Donor(s): Members of the Gudelsky family, Percontee, Inc.
Grantmaker type: Independent foundation
Financial data (yr. ended 12/31/01): Assets, $26,626,320 (M); expenditures, $1,367,866; qualifying distributions, $1,348,131; giving activities include $1,345,000 for 25 grants (high: $500,000; low: $1,000).
Fields of interest: Theater; Higher education; Engineering school/education; Environment, research; Health care, information services; Health care.
Types of support: Annual campaigns; Capital campaigns; Building/renovation; Equipment; Scholarship funds; Research.
Limitations: Giving primarily in MD. No grants to individuals.
Application information: Application form not required.
Initial approach: Letter
Deadline(s): None
Officers and Directors:* John Gudelsky,* Pres.; Martha Gudelsky,* V.P.; Medda Gudelsky,* V.P.; Rita Regino,* V.P.; Holly Stone,* V.P.; Jonathan Genn,* Secy.; Joseph Yedlin,* Treas.
Number of staff: None.
EIN: 520885969

1301
The Head Family Foundation
c/o Sterling Foundation Mgmt., LLC
115 Sudbrook Ln., Ste. 210
Baltimore, MD 21208 (410) 602-0064

Established in 2000 in VA.
Donor(s): William C. Head.
Grantmaker type: Independent foundation
Financial data (yr. ended 12/31/02): Assets, $2,835,128 (M); expenditures, $151,662; qualifying distributions, $127,170; giving activities include $106,500 for 6 grants (high: $80,000; low: $1,000).
Fields of interest: Higher education; Natural resources; Health organizations, association; Orthopedics research; Christian agencies & churches.
Types of support: General/operating support.
Limitations: No grants to individuals.
Application information: Application form not required.
Deadline(s): None
Officer: William C. Head, Pres. and Secy.-Treas.
Directors: Brice W. Head; Gretchen C. Head; Rita W. Head.
EIN: 541969607

1302
The Howard and Martha Head Foundation, Inc.
(formerly The Howard and Martha Head Fund, Inc.)
901 S. Bond St.
Baltimore, MD 21231

Established around 1989 in MD.
Donor(s): Howard Head.‡
Grantmaker type: Independent foundation
Financial data (yr. ended 12/31/02): Assets, $3,185,167 (M); expenditures, $397,827; qualifying distributions, $363,012; giving activities include $359,282 for grants (average: $100–$10,000).
Purpose and activities: Giving primarily for federated giving programs, as well as for the arts, education, and human services.
Fields of interest: Arts; Higher education; Education; Zoos/zoological societies; Human services; Federated giving programs.
Types of support: Continuing support; Annual campaigns; Program development.
Limitations: Applications not accepted. Giving on a national basis, with some emphasis on Vail, CO. No grants to individuals.
Application information: Contributes only to pre-selected organizations.
Officers and Trustees:* Michael D. Hankin,* Pres.; Martha Head,* V.P.; Robin W. Denick, Secy.
EIN: 521268755

1303
The Helena Foundation
P.O. Box 625
Crownsville, MD 21032-0625

Established in 1987 in MD.
Donor(s): Margaret H. Earl.‡
Grantmaker type: Independent foundation
Financial data (yr. ended 12/31/01): Assets, $28,745,116 (M); gifts received, $68,898; expenditures, $1,417,521; qualifying distributions, $1,409,962; giving activities include $1,410,007 for 36 grants (high: $420,000; low: $1,000; average: $1,000–$5,000).
Purpose and activities: Giving primarily to colleges and universities; some support also for elementary and secondary education, the arts, and hospitals.
Fields of interest: Arts; Elementary/secondary education; Higher education; Environment, land resources; Hospitals (general).
Types of support: General/operating support; Capital campaigns; Endowments.
Limitations: Applications not accepted. Giving primarily in Boston, MA and MD. No grants to individuals.
Application information: Contributes only to pre-selected organizations.
Officers and Directors:* James A. Earl,* Pres. and Treas.; Sylvia Earl,* V.P. and Secy.
EIN: 521522573

1304
David L. Hopkins, Jr. and Suzanne B. Hopkins Private Foundation
15200 Old York Rd.
Monkton, MD 21111

Established in 1997 in MD.
Donor(s): David L. Hopkins, Jr.
Grantmaker type: Independent foundation
Financial data (yr. ended 12/31/01): Assets, $70 (M); gifts received, $62,587; expenditures, $110,549; qualifying distributions, $109,645; giving activities include $109,630 for 13 grants (high: $58,780; low: $250).
Fields of interest: Opera; Historic preservation/historical societies; Higher education; Libraries/library science; Botanical gardens; Environment; Hospitals (general); Physical/earth sciences; Religion.
Types of support: General/operating support.
Limitations: Applications not accepted. No grants to individuals.
Application information: Contributes only to pre-selected organizations.
Trustees: David L. Hopkins, Jr.; Suzanne B. Hopkins.
EIN: 522068944

1305
International Youth Foundation
(also known as IYF)
32 South St., Ste. 500
Baltimore, MD 21202 (410) 347-1500
Contact: Mary Stelletello, Dir., Partner Svcs. and Grants
FAX: (410) 347-1188; E-mail: youth@iyfnet.org; URL: http://www.iyfnet.org

Established in 1990.
Grantmaker type: Public charity
Financial data (yr. ended 12/31/01): Revenue, $17,366,617; assets, $48,273,194 (M); gifts received, $13,595,286; expenditures, $25,355,689; program services expenses, $21,294,669; giving activities include $7,859,236 for 78 grants (high: $3,540,861; low: $525).
Purpose and activities: The foundation is dedicated to the positive development of children and youth, ages 5 to 20, worldwide, enabling them to lead healthy, productive, and fulfilling lives. This goal is accomplished by identifying, strengthening, and replicating effective programs for young people; building a global network of independent, indigenous foundations committed to positive youth development; and increasing international philanthropy in support of such efforts. The foundation is interested in holistic, developmental programs related to issues such as drug and alcohol use, violence, teen pregnancy, school dropouts, vocational skills, and self-esteem. It does this by supporting programs which provide support and services in vocational training, health education, recreation, cultural tolerance, environmental awareness, and the development of leadership, conflict resolution, and decision-making skills.
Fields of interest: Vocational education; Drop-out prevention; Environment, public education; Health care; Substance abuse, services; Crime/violence prevention; Dispute resolution; Recreation; Youth development;

Children/youth, services; Youth, pregnancy prevention; Race/intergroup relations; Foundations (public).

International interests: Canada; Netherlands; Ireland; United Kingdom; Portugal; Spain; Germany; Finland; Czech Republic; Slovakia; Poland; Romania; Russia; Tanzania; South Africa; Mexico; Argentina; Brazil; Colombia; Ecuador; Paraguay; Peru; Uruguay; Venezuela; Middle East; Israel; India; Philippines; Thailand; China; Taiwan; South Korea; Japan; Australia.

Types of support: General/operating support; Program development; Conferences/seminars; Publication; Seed money; Curriculum development; Technical assistance; Program evaluation.

Limitations: Applications not accepted. Giving on an international basis, operating in 49 countries. No support for unsolicited proposals. No grants to individuals.

Application information: Most funding directed to partner foundations; limited support made available for programs outside of current partner countries which meet criteria; unsolicited proposals are not accepted.

  Board meeting date(s): 3 times each year

Officers and Directors:* David Bell,* Chair.; Rick R. Little,* Pres. and C.E.O.; William S. Reese, C.O.O.; Don Mohanlal, Exec. V.P., Global Partner Network; Par Stenbach, V.P., Europe and Middle East; Sten A. Akestam; Queen Rania Al-Abdulla; Sari Baldauf; Maria Livanos Cattaui; Arnold Langbo; Helio Mattar; Hon. Richard Schubert; Jaime Augusto Zobel de Ayala II.

Number of staff: 44 full-time professional; 12 full-time support.

EIN: 382935397

1306
The Knapp Foundation, Inc.
P.O. Box O
St. Michaels, MD   21663   (410) 745-5660
Contact: Ruth M. Capranica, V.P.

Incorporated in 1929 in NC.
Donor(s): Joseph Palmer Knapp.‡
Grantmaker type: Independent foundation
Financial data (yr. ended 12/31/02): Assets, $21,684,412 (M); expenditures, $1,859,866; qualifying distributions, $1,732,184; giving activities include $1,607,970 for 38 grants (high: $1,000,000; low: $2,500).
Purpose and activities: Grants primarily for conservation and preservation of wildlife and wildfowl, and for assistance to college and university libraries in the purchasing of reading materials and equipment to improve education.
Fields of interest: Higher education; Libraries/library science; Animals/wildlife, preservation/protection.
Types of support: Equipment; Matching/challenge support.
Limitations: Giving limited to the U.S., primarily in the eastern region, including CT, FL, GA, MA, MD, ME, NC, NH, NJ, NY, PA, RI, SC, VA, and VT. No support for foreign projects. No grants to individuals, or for endowment or building funds, operating budgets, or research.
Publications: Application guidelines.
Application information: Application form not required.
  Initial approach: Letter

Copies of proposal: 1
Deadline(s): None
  Board meeting date(s): Dec.; executive board meets quarterly
  Final notification: 90 days
Officers and Trustees:* Antoinette P. Vojvoda,* Pres.; Ruth M. Capranica,* V.P. and Secy.; Steven F. Capranica,* Treas.; Krista L. Hodgkin; Margaret P. Newcombe; Sylvia V. Penny.
Number of staff: 1 part-time professional.
EIN: 136001167

1307
Koch Family Foundation, Inc.
2661 Riva Rd., Ste. 220
Annapolis, MD   21401   (410) 573-5720
Contact: Gary W. Koch, Pres.

Established in 1993 in MD.
Donor(s): Gary W. Koch.
Grantmaker type: Independent foundation
Financial data (yr. ended 12/31/02): Assets, $557,993 (M); gifts received, $250,000; expenditures, $150,486; qualifying distributions, $150,115; giving activities include $150,115 for 20 grants (high: $20,000; low: $100).
Purpose and activities: Giving for education, animal welfare, health, and housing.
Fields of interest: Education; Animals/wildlife, preservation/protection; Health care; Health organizations, association; Housing/shelter; Human services.
Limitations: Giving primarily in AZ, MD, and TN. No grants to individuals.
Application information:
  Initial approach: Letter
  Deadline(s): None
Officers and Trustee:* Gary W. Koch,* Pres. and Treas.; Lynda R. Koch, V.P. and Secy.
EIN: 521859184

1308
The Allene & Jerome Lapides Foundation, Inc.
917 Arbutus Dr.
Annapolis, MD   21403
Contact: Jerome Lapides, Pres.

Established around 1943.
Grantmaker type: Independent foundation
Financial data (yr. ended 12/31/02): Assets, $536,996 (M); expenditures, $282,493; qualifying distributions, $266,940; giving activities include $265,900 for 40 grants.
Purpose and activities: Giving for community development, animal welfare, and the environment.
Fields of interest: Natural resources; Animal welfare; Animals/wildlife, preservation/protection; Community development.
Limitations: Giving primarily in Washington, DC, Annapolis and Baltimore, MD, and Santa Fe, NM. No grants to individuals.
Application information:
  Initial approach: Letter
  Deadline(s): None
Officers: Jerome Lapides, Pres. and Treas.; Allene Lapides, V.P.; Robert Goldman, Secy.
EIN: 237418069

1309
The Greta Brown Layton Trust
(formerly Greta Brown Layton Charitable Trust)
766 Old Hammonds Ferry Rd.
Linthicum, MD   21090

Established in 1965 in MD.
Grantmaker type: Independent foundation
Financial data (yr. ended 12/31/02): Assets, $1,855,113 (M); expenditures, $133,658; qualifying distributions, $126,298; giving activities include $126,850 for 75 grants (high: $10,000; low: $250).
Purpose and activities: Giving for federated giving programs, environmental conservation, education, health and medical services, and the arts.
Fields of interest: Museums; Arts; Education; Environment; Hospitals (general); Health care; Health organizations, association; Human services; Federated giving programs.
Limitations: Applications not accepted. Giving primarily in DE. No grants to individuals.
Application information: Contributes only to pre-selected organizations.
Trustee: Mercantile-Safe Deposit & Trust Co.
EIN: 526063086

1310
Gordon F. and Jocelyn B. Linke Foundation
c/o Gordon Linke
5115 Cammack Dr.
Bethesda, MD   20816

Established in 1997 in MD.
Grantmaker type: Independent foundation
Financial data (yr. ended 12/31/02): Assets, $4,808,092 (M); expenditures, $273,273; qualifying distributions, $245,500; giving activities include $243,830 for 92 grants (high: $24,816; low: $500).
Purpose and activities: Giving primarily for animals, education, health and human services, and to Catholic churches.
Fields of interest: Museums; Arts; Higher education; Elementary/secondary education; Environment; Animals/wildlife; Human services; Roman Catholic agencies & churches.
Limitations: Applications not accepted. Giving primarily in CA, CT, Washington, DC, MD, and NY. No grants to individuals.
Application information: Contributes only to pre-selected organizations.
Officers and Directors:* Gordon F. Linke,* Co-Pres. and Mgr.; Jocelyn B. Linke,* Co-Pres. and Mgr.; Jocelyn S. Witt,* Treas. and Mgr.
EIN: 521985801

1311
Lutheran World Relief
700 Light St.
Baltimore, MD   21230   (410) 230-2700
Contact: Kathryn F. Wolford, Pres.
FAX: (410) 230-2882; E-mail: lwr@lwr.org; URL: http://www.lwr.org

Established in 1945 in NY.
Grantmaker type: Public charity
Financial data (yr. ended 09/30/01): Revenue, $32,537,145; assets, $25,106,896 (M); gifts received, $31,730,231; expenditures, $31,846,702; program services expenses,

$30,155,419; giving activities include
$12,835,002 for grants (high: $4,829,618).
Purpose and activities: The foundation's goals
are to alleviate suffering caused by natural
disaster, conflict, or poverty; to enable
marginalized people to meet basic needs and
improve their lives; and to promote a peaceful,
just, and sustainable global community. The
foundation and its partners give assistance
regardless of gender, race, ethnicity, religion, or
political affiliation.
Fields of interest: Environment; Agriculture;
Disasters, preparedness/services; International
development; International relief; Civil rights,
advocacy; Civil liberties, advocacy; Nonprofit
management; Community development; People
with AIDS (PWAs).
International interests: Europe; Africa; Latin
America; Asia; Middle East.
Types of support: General/operating support;
Emergency funds; Program development; Seed
money; Technical assistance; Program
evaluation; In-kind gifts.
Limitations: Applications not accepted. Giving
on an international basis. No support for
U.S.-based programs. No grants to individuals.
Application information: Contributes only to
pre-selected organizations; unsolicited requests
for funds not considered or acknowledged.
Board meeting date(s): Jan., June, and Sept.
Officers and Directors:* Elizabeth Duda,*
Acting Chair.; Kathryn F. Wolford,* Pres.; Cherri
D. Waters,* V.P., Progs. and Planning; Michael
Malewicki,* V.P., Fin. and Admin.; Kirk H. Betts;
Rev. Matthew C. Harrison; Brad L. Hewitt;
Denise R. Hooks; Loretta Ishida; Rev. Bonnie L.
Jensen; Rev. April Ulring Larson; Rev. Nadine F.
Lehr; Rev. Edward F. Markquart; Vincent Peters;
Rev. Dr. Warren W. Schumacher; Myrna Sheie.
Number of staff: 24 full-time professional; 5
part-time professional; 13 full-time support; 3
part-time support.
EIN: 132574963

1312
**Morton and Sophia Macht Foundation,
Inc.**
11 E. Fayette St.
Baltimore, MD 21202-1606 (410) 539-2370
Contact: Amy Macht, Pres.
FAX: (410) 752-7813; E-mail:
mbishoff@regionalmgmt.com

Established in 1956 in MD.
Donor(s): Sophia Macht,‡ Westland Gardens Co.
Grantmaker type: Independent foundation
Financial data (yr. ended 04/30/02): Assets,
$1,640,874 (M); gifts received, $213,500;
expenditures, $380,018; qualifying distributions,
$343,611; giving activities include $344,095 for
133 grants (high: $26,349; low: $25).
Purpose and activities: Giving primarily for arts
and culture, higher education, and human
services.
Fields of interest: Arts; Higher education;
Education; Environment; Human services.
Types of support: General/operating support;
Continuing support; Annual campaigns; Capital
campaigns; Equipment; Program development;
Conferences/seminars; Publication; Seed
money; Scholarship funds; Research.
Limitations: Giving primarily in the metropolitan
Baltimore, MD, area. No grants to individuals.

Application information: Application form not
required.
Initial approach: Proposal
Copies of proposal: 1
Deadline(s): None
Final notification: By letter
Officers and Trustees:* Amy Macht,* Pres.;
Katherine Kelly Howard,* V.P. and Secy.; Jill
Gansler,* V.P. and Treas.; Bette D. Cohen,* V.P.;
William A. Goodhardt,* V.P.; Philip Macht,* V.P.;
Robert W. Mastropieri,* V.P.
Number of staff: None.
EIN: 526035753

1313
Marpat Foundation, Inc.
P.O. Box 1769
Silver Spring, MD 20915-1769
Contact: Joan F. Koven, Secy.-Treas.
E-mail: jkoven@marpatfoundation.org; URL:
http://fdncenter.org/grantmaker/marpat/

Incorporated in 1985 in MD.
Donor(s): Marvin Breckinridge Patterson.‡
Grantmaker type: Independent foundation
Financial data (yr. ended 12/31/02): Assets,
$9,770,975 (M); expenditures, $837,112;
qualifying distributions, $747,966; giving
activities include $697,500 for 96 grants (high:
$15,000; low: $2,500; average: $2–$20,000).
Purpose and activities: Grants will be made
primarily to established charitable organizations
whose activities are personally known to the
directors and based in or benefiting the greater
Washington, DC, metropolitan area. Grants will
be made to the following: organizations that
advance international understanding,
universities, museums, and libraries for the
advancement and diffusion of knowledge;
organizations and schools that sponsor
programs that advocate and encourage family
planning, or promote or provide health care;
organizations promoting or conducting scientific
programs and research projects; organizations
providing services and/or education designed to
preserve natural and historical resources, or
advance the knowledge of mankind's history
and cultural past; and organizations that
promote volunteer participation in, and citizen
involvement with such organizations.
Fields of interest: Visual arts; Museums;
Performing arts; Historic preservation/historical
societies; Arts; Higher education;
Libraries/library science; Education; Natural
resources; Environment; Family planning;
Health care; Human services; Voluntarism
promotion.
Types of support: General/operating support;
Building/renovation; Equipment; Program
development; Publication.
Limitations: Giving primarily in the metropolitan
Washington, DC, area. No support for projects
or organizations for any weapons development,
or for medical research. No grants to
individuals, or for endowment funds.
Publications: Application guidelines, Grants list.
Application information: Application form
available on Web site. Request summary sheet
from foundation. Application form required.
Initial approach: Stage one application form
Copies of proposal: 3
Deadline(s): June 1st
Board meeting date(s): Dec.

Final notification: End of June
Officers and Directors:* Isabella G.
Breckinridge, Pres.; Ellen Bozman, V.P.; Sherrill
M. Houghton, V.P.; Christine Minter-Dowd,*
V.P.; Thomas W. Richards, V.P.; Samuel N.
Stokes,* V.P.; Charles E. Yonkers, V.P.; Joan F.
Koven,* Secy.-Treas.
Number of staff: 1 part-time professional.
EIN: 521358159

1314
The Marvin Foundation
c/o Bank of America
10 Light St., MD4-302-17-06
Baltimore, MD 21202-1435
Contact: Peter M. Watts, Trust Off., Bank of
America
Application address: c/o 5550 Friendship Blvd.,
Chevy Chase, MD 20815, tel.: (301) 986-6716

Established in 1994 in WA.
Donor(s): Elaine A. Coles.
Grantmaker type: Independent foundation
Financial data (yr. ended 06/30/02): Assets,
$1,711,753 (M); expenditures, $120,105;
qualifying distributions, $110,177; giving
activities include $111,700 for 11 grants (high:
$24,000; low: $2,000).
Purpose and activities: Giving for education.
Fields of interest: Arts; Elementary/secondary
education; Animals/wildlife; Legal services;
Human services; American Red Cross; Christian
agencies & churches.
Limitations: Giving primarily in WA. No grants
to individuals.
Application information: Application form not
required.
Initial approach: Letter
Deadline(s): None
Trustees: Elaine A. Coles; Theodore Mausshardt;
Bank of America.
EIN: 526702573

1315
The Sumner T. McKnight Foundation
901 S. Bond St.
Baltimore, MD 21231

Incorporated in 1956 in MN.
Donor(s): Sumner T. McKnight, H. Turney
McKnight.
Grantmaker type: Independent foundation
Financial data (yr. ended 12/31/02): Assets,
$4,319,300 (M); expenditures, $429,220;
qualifying distributions, $394,093; giving
activities include $390,625 for 33 grants (high:
$100,000; low: $625).
Fields of interest: Natural resources;
Environment.
Limitations: Applications not accepted. Giving
primarily in MD. No support for religion. No
grants to individuals, or for endowment or
capital funds or trips or tours.
Application information: Contributes only to
pre-selected organizations.
Board meeting date(s): Apr.
Directors: Annie K. Huber; Christina McKnight
Kippen; H. Turney McKnight; Sumner T.
McKnight; Serena Miles; John T. Westrum.
Number of staff: 1.
EIN: 416022360

1316
Middendorf Foundation, Inc.
2 E. Read St.
Baltimore, MD 21202
Contact: E. Phillips Hathaway, Pres.

Incorporated in 1953 in MD.
Donor(s): J. William Middendorf, Jr.,‡ Alice C. Middendorf.‡
Grantmaker type: Independent foundation
Financial data (yr. ended 03/31/01): Assets, $32,100,226 (M); expenditures, $1,875,100; qualifying distributions, $1,699,412; giving activities include $1,675,500 for 42 grants (high: $250,000; low: $1,000).
Purpose and activities: Giving primarily for conservation, historic preservation and art museums.
Fields of interest: Museums (art); Historic preservation/historical societies; Arts; Higher education; Libraries (public); Natural resources; Health care; Human services; Hospices; Protestant agencies & churches.
Types of support: Endowments; Professorships; Matching/challenge support.
Limitations: Giving primarily in MD. No grants to individuals.
Application information:
Initial approach: Letter
Copies of proposal: 1
Deadline(s): None
Officers and Trustees:* E. Phillips Hathaway,* Pres.; Forrest F. Bramble, Jr.,* V.P.; Theresa N. Knell,* Secy.; Craig Lewis,* Treas.; Phillips Hathaway; Sealy H. Hopkinson; Benjamin F. Lucas II.
Number of staff: 2 full-time professional.
EIN: 526048944

1317
Middle Patuxent Environmental Foundation
c/o Marianne Schmitt Hellauer
6225 Smith Ave.
Baltimore, MD 21209-3600

Established in 1996 in MD.
Grantmaker type: Independent foundation
Financial data (yr. ended 12/31/02): Assets, $1,378,996 (M); expenditures, $109,844; qualifying distributions, $92,530; giving activities include $91,630 for 1 grant.
Fields of interest: University; Environment, land resources.
Limitations: Applications not accepted. Giving primarily in MD. No grants to individuals.
Application information: Contributes only to pre-selected organizations.
Officers and Trustees:* Joyce M. Kelly,* Chair.; Charles D. Rhodehamel, Vice-Chair.; Johanna G. Cote, Secy.-Treas.; Aelred Dean Geis; N. Douglas Hostetler; Joseph H. Necker; Kennedy T. Paynter, Jr.
EIN: 521981322

1318
The Morningstar Foundation
4550 Montgomery Ave., Ste. 650 N.
Bethesda, MD 20814
Contact: Michael C. Gelman, V.P.
FAX: (301) 913-9042

Established in 1982 in DC and MD.
Donor(s): Michael C. Gelman, Susan R. Gelman, Richard Goldman 1997 Charitable Lead Annuity Trust.
Grantmaker type: Independent foundation
Financial data (yr. ended 12/31/01): Assets, $12,757,452 (M); gifts received, $2,181,629; expenditures, $1,403,279; qualifying distributions, $1,287,702; giving activities include $1,232,817 for 114 grants (high: $65,000; low: $200).
Fields of interest: Arts; Education; Environment; Human services; International peace/security; Jewish agencies & temples.
International interests: Israel.
Types of support: General/operating support; Annual campaigns; Capital campaigns.
Limitations: Applications not accepted. Giving primarily in the greater Washington, DC, area. No grants to individuals.
Application information: Contributes only to pre-selected organizations. Unsolicited requests for funds not accepted.
Board meeting date(s): Quarterly
Officers: Susan R. Gelman, Pres.; Michael C. Gelman, V.P.; George P. Levendis, Secy.
Number of staff: 1 part-time support.
EIN: 521270464

1319
Mpala Wildlife Foundation, Inc.
c/o Jeffrey K. Gonya
910 Saint George Rd.
Baltimore, MD 21210-1411

Established in 1989 in MD; funded in fiscal 1990.
Donor(s): George L. Small, Princeton University.
Grantmaker type: Operating foundation
Financial data (yr. ended 06/30/02): Assets, $455,000 (M); gifts received, $351,430; expenditures, $298,783; qualifying distributions, $183,000; giving activities include $183,000 for 2 grants (high: $163,000; low: $20,000).
Purpose and activities: Giving primarily to a wildlife sanctuary and preserve, and operation of a scientific research center, as well as for the operation of a mobile clinic.
Fields of interest: Animals/wildlife, preservation/protection.
International interests: Kenya.
Limitations: Applications not accepted. Giving primarily in Nanyuki, Kenya. No grants to individuals.
Application information: Contributes only to pre-selected organizations.
Officers and Trustees:* Donald C. Graham, Chair.; Jeffrey K. Gonya,* Secy.-Treas.; Howard Ende; Dennis Keller; Michael H. Shaw; John Wreford-Smith.
EIN: 521656147

1320
The Nabit Foundation, Inc.
17 Commerce St.
Baltimore, MD 21202 (410) 727-2404
FAX: (410) 625-1531

Donor(s): Merwin J. Nabit, Charles J. Nabit.
Grantmaker type: Independent foundation
Financial data (yr. ended 06/30/02): Assets, $1,034,394 (M); gifts received, $23,400;

expenditures, $113,238; qualifying distributions, $100,323; giving activities include $100,400 for 19 grants (high: $50,000; low: $200).
Fields of interest: Arts; Higher education; Animal welfare; Lupus; Jewish agencies & temples.
Limitations: Applications not accepted. Giving primarily in Sewanee, TN. No grants to individuals.
Application information: Contributes only to pre-selected organizations.
Board meeting date(s): Periodically
Officers and Directors:* Merwin J. Nabit,* Pres.; Charles J. Nabit,* Secy.; Michael C. Hodes.
EIN: 521756376

1321
The Peck Foundation, Inc.
1651 Belfast Rd.
Sparks, MD 21152-9788

Established in 1999 in MD.
Grantmaker type: Independent foundation
Financial data (yr. ended 12/31/01): Assets, $241,782 (M); gifts received, $124,237; expenditures, $187,154; qualifying distributions, $183,696; giving activities include $185,000 for 5 grants (high: $80,000; low: $1,500).
Fields of interest: Theater; Arts; Education; Natural resources; Historic preservation/historical societies.
Limitations: Applications not accepted. No grants to individuals.
Application information: Contributes only to pre-selected organizations.
Officers: J. Stevenson Peck, Jr., Pres.; Seska Peck Ramberg, V.P.; Christine Peck, Secy.-Treas.
EIN: 522169632

1322
The Pennyghael Foundation, Inc.
4204 Underwood Rd.
Baltimore, MD 21218
Contact: Charles Goodwin, V.P. or Charlotte Goodwin, Pres.

Established in 1997 in MD.
Donor(s): Charles Goodwin, Charlotte O. Goodwin.
Grantmaker type: Independent foundation
Financial data (yr. ended 12/31/02): Assets, $1,963,826 (M); expenditures, $109,685; qualifying distributions, $104,800; giving activities include $104,800 for 69 grants (high: $10,000; low: $100).
Purpose and activities: Giving primarily for arts and culture, education, natural resource conservation, wildlife, hospitals, and social services.
Fields of interest: Arts; Elementary/secondary education; Higher education; Natural resources; Animals/wildlife; Hospitals (general); Human services.
Limitations: Giving primarily in MA and Baltimore, MD.
Application information: Application form not required.
Initial approach: Letter
Deadline(s): None
Officers and Directors:* Charlotte O. Goodwin,* Pres. and Secy.; Charles Goodwin,* V.P. and Treas.

EIN: 522026972

1323
PG&E National Energy Group Environmental Education Grants Program
c/o Environmental Education Grants Prog.
7600 Wisconsin Ave.
Bethesda, MD 20814
Contact: Amy McWethy
E-mail: grants@neg.pge.com; URL: http://
www.neg.pge.com/grantProgram.html

Grantmaker type: Corporate giving program
Purpose and activities: PG&E National Energy Group makes charitable contributions to nonprofit organizations and K-12 schools involved with environmental education. Support is directed towards programs designed to promote a greater understanding among young people of challenges facing our environment, with an emphasis on solutions improving local environmental quality. Support is given on a national basis. The program's administration and funding is shared by the PG&E Corporation Foundation.
Fields of interest: Elementary/secondary education; Environmental education.
Types of support: General/operating support.
Limitations: Giving on a national basis. No grants for capital campaigns or building/renovation, real estate purchases, scholarships or tuition assistance awarded by an organization for its own activities, one-day events, political advocacy, or travel or lodging; no grants equaling more than 25 percent of the salary of the organization's coordinator or program director; no grants equaling more than 10 percent of a speaker's honorarium.
Application information: Support is limited to 1 year in length. Organizations receiving support are asked to provide a final report. Application form required.
  Initial approach: E-mail or write to headquarters for application form
  Copies of proposal: 6
  Deadline(s): Postmarked by Sept. 30
  Final notification: Nov. 20

1324
The Rathmann Family Foundation
c/o WindCrest Mgmt., LLC
1290 Bay Dale Dr., PMB No. 352
Arnold, MD 21012 (410) 349-2376
Contact: Rick Rathmann
FAX: (410) 349-2377

Established in 1991 in WA.
Donor(s): George Rathmann, Joy Rathmann.
Grantmaker type: Independent foundation
Financial data (yr. ended 12/31/01): Assets, $55,863,055 (M); expenditures, $2,931,614; qualifying distributions, $2,753,014; giving activities include $2,559,599 for 72 grants (high: $560,000; low: $500; average: $1,000–$100,000).
Purpose and activities: The mission (or purpose) of the foundation is to promote and support innovation, development and excellence in science, technology, education and the environment. The foundation funds

organizations and programs which apply research, science, technology and education to improving lives and strengthening communities and the nation. The foundation's educational interests extend from elementary through post-secondary years and focus primarily on science, math, technology, the environment, medicine and the arts. Related areas of foundation interest include biotechnology and conservation of the environment and open spaces for low impact use, such as hiking, walking and off-leash recreation.
Fields of interest: Arts; Education; Environment; Health care; Health organizations, association; Children/youth, services; Science, research; Science, public education; Mathematics; Economically disadvantaged.
Types of support: General/operating support; Continuing support; Capital campaigns; Equipment; Endowments; Program development; Conferences/seminars; Seed money; Curriculum development; Fellowships; Internship funds; Scholarship funds; Research; Program evaluation; Program-related investments/loans; Matching/challenge support.
Limitations: Applications not accepted. Giving primarily in the San Francisco Bay Area, CA, Annapolis, MD, the metropolitan Minneapolis-St. Paul, MN, area, Philadelphia, PA, and Seattle, WA. No support for private foundations, religious organizations for religious activities, civil rights, social action, or advocacy organizations, fraternal, labor, or veterans' groups, political purposes, or mental health counseling. No grants to individuals, or for fundraising, media events, public relations, propaganda, or annual appeals.
Application information: The foundation will fund only board-initiated or solicited programs and, in selected cases, organizations and programs in which it has previously invested in 1999.
Officers and Directors:* George B. Rathmann,* Chair.; Margaret Crosby Rathmann,* Pres.; James Louis Rathmann,* V.P.; Laura Jean Rathmann,* V.P.; Richard G. Rathmann,* V.P.; Frances Joy Rathmann,* Secy.; Sally Rathmann Kadifa, M.D.,* Treas.; Suzanne E. Busta, Exec. Dir.
Number of staff: 1 shared staff.
EIN: 521757445

1325
The Frederick W. Richmond Foundation, Inc.
31 S. Harrison St.
Easton, MD 21601
Contact: Erin Knudsen, Exec. Dir.

Incorporated in 1962 in NY.
Donor(s): Frederick W. Richmond.
Grantmaker type: Independent foundation
Financial data (yr. ended 06/30/02): Assets, $3,302,782 (M); expenditures, $184,370; qualifying distributions, $175,129; giving activities include $171,700 for 42 grants (high: $25,000; low: $100).
Purpose and activities: The foundation is interested in funding pilot projects, primarily in the arts, education, health, and the environment.
Fields of interest: Arts; Education; Environment; Health care.

Types of support: Annual campaigns; Capital campaigns; Building/renovation; Program development; Professorships; Seed money; Fellowships; Scholarship funds.
Limitations: Giving primarily in Talbot County, MD; some giving also in NY. No support for non-exempt organizations. No grants to individuals.
Publications: Program policy statement.
Application information: Most grants are initiated by board members. Unsolicited inquiries are reviewed in Aug. Application form not required.
  Initial approach: 1-page letter of inquiry
  Copies of proposal: 1
  Deadline(s): None
  Board meeting date(s): Aug.
  Final notification: Following board meeting
Officers and Directors:* Timothy E. Wyman,* Pres.; Fulton P. Jeffers, Secy.; Erin Knudsen, Exec. Dir.; Elizabeth Wyman.
Number of staff: None.
EIN: 136124582

1326
James S. & Gail P. Riepe Charitable Foundation
P.O. Box 64
Butler, MD 21023-0050

Established in 1986 in MD.
Donor(s): James S. Riepe.
Grantmaker type: Independent foundation
Financial data (yr. ended 12/31/02): Assets, $4,270,822 (M); expenditures, $317,912; qualifying distributions, $306,220; giving activities include $305,750 for 48 grants (high: $125,000; low: $250).
Fields of interest: Arts; Higher education; Education; Natural resources; Human services; Federated giving programs.
Types of support: Continuing support; Annual campaigns; Capital campaigns; Building/renovation; Land acquisition; Endowments; Scholarship funds.
Limitations: Applications not accepted. Giving primarily in Baltimore, MD. No grants to individuals.
Application information: Contributes only to pre-selected organizations.
Officer and Trustees:* James S. Riepe,* Pres.; Christina N. Riepe; Gail P. Riepe; James S. Riepe, Jr.
EIN: 526287385

1327
The Anne Carter Robins and Walter R. Robins, Jr. Foundation
c/o Bank of America
10 Light St., MD4-302-17-06
Baltimore, MD 21202
Contact: Rita M. Smith, Treas.
Application address: c/o Bank of America, P.O. Box 26903, Richmond, VA 23261

Established in 1994 in VA.
Donor(s): M. Bruce Robins.
Grantmaker type: Independent foundation
Financial data (yr. ended 12/31/01): Assets, $1,470,184 (M); gifts received, $62,815; expenditures, $114,556; qualifying distributions,

$98,473; giving activities include $98,000 for 12 grants (high: $25,000; low: $1,000).
Fields of interest: Animal welfare; Community development; Federated giving programs.
Limitations: Giving primarily in VA. No grants to individuals.
Application information:
  Initial approach: Letter
  Deadline(s): None
Officers: Anne C.R. Mallory, Pres.; Betty Armentrout, V.P.; Otto B. Shreaves, Jr., V.P.; John B. O'Grady, Secy.; Rita M. Smith, Treas.
EIN: 546362175

1328
Elizabeth B. and Arthur E. Roswell Foundation, Inc.
10 E. Baltimore St., Ste.1111
Baltimore, MD 21202 (410) 347-7201
Contact: Arthur E. Roswell, Pres.
E-mail: info@blafund.org

Incorporated in 1986 in MD.
Donor(s): Elizabeth B. Roswell.
Grantmaker type: Independent foundation
Financial data (yr. ended 12/31/00): Assets, $10,291,023 (M); expenditures, $365,264; qualifying distributions, $365,264; giving activities include $334,958 for 43 grants (high: $40,000; low: $500; average: $1,000–$50,000).
Purpose and activities: Giving primarily for basic human needs and the environment.
Fields of interest: Natural resources; Food banks; Housing/shelter, development; Human services; Family services.
Types of support: General/operating support; Annual campaigns.
Limitations: Giving primarily in Baltimore, MD, NJ, and southeastern PA. No grants to individuals, or for fundraising or direct mailings; no loans.
Application information: Application form not required.
  Initial approach: Letter
  Copies of proposal: 1
  Deadline(s): None
  Board meeting date(s): Periodic
  Final notification: 1 year
Officers and Trustees:* Elizabeth B. Roswell,* Chair.; Arthur E. Roswell,* Pres.; Barbara Roswell,* V.P.; Marjorie B. Roswell,* V.P.; Robert A. Roswell,* V.P.; Judith E. Weinstein,* V.P.; Kenneth C. Weinstein,* V.P.; Lynn Wintriss, Secy.-Treas.
Number of staff: 4 shared staff (shared with Jacob & Hilda Blaustein Foundation, Barbara B. Hirschhorn Foundation, Henry & Ruth B. Rosenberg Foundation, and Morton K. & Jane Blaustein Foundation).
EIN: 521490498

1329
Schifter Family Foundation
c/o R. Philipson Co.
8601 Georgia Ave., Ste. 1001
Silver Spring, MD 20910

Established in 2000 in DC.
Donor(s): Richard P. Schifter, Jennifer Schifter.
Grantmaker type: Independent foundation
Financial data (yr. ended 12/31/02): Assets, $1,925,843 (M); expenditures, $542,548;

qualifying distributions, $369,756; giving activities include $369,800 for 33 grants (high: $200,000; low: $250).
Purpose and activities: Giving primarily for education, environmental conservation groups, and Jewish organizations.
Fields of interest: Elementary/secondary education; Higher education; Natural resources; Human services; Jewish agencies & temples.
Limitations: Applications not accepted. Giving primarily in Washington, DC. No grants to individuals.
Application information: Contributes only to pre-selected organizations.
Trustees: Jennifer Schifter; Richard P. Schifter.
EIN: 134148941

1330
The Schoeneman-Halle Foundation, Inc.
(formerly The Schoeneman-Weiler Fund, Inc.)
766 Old Hammonds Ferry Rd.
Linthicum, MD 21090
Contact: Edward A. Halle, Pres.

Established in 1946.
Grantmaker type: Independent foundation
Financial data (yr. ended 11/30/02): Assets, $1,979,392 (M); expenditures, $135,446; qualifying distributions, $108,255; giving activities include $108,796 for 62 grants (high: $25,000; low: $10).
Purpose and activities: Support primarily for arts, education, the environment, and health and human services.
Fields of interest: Museums; Arts; Education; Natural resources; Health organizations, association; Human services.
Types of support: General/operating support; Capital campaigns; Building/renovation; Research.
Limitations: Applications not accepted. Giving primarily in the greater Baltimore, MD, area. No grants to individuals.
Application information: Contributes only to pre-selected organizations.
Officers: Edward A. Halle, Pres.; Ellen W. Halle, V.P.; Jan S. Halle, V.P.; Edward A. Halle, Jr., Secy.; James S. Halle, Treas.
Number of staff: None.
EIN: 526038453

1331
Tim and Barbara Schweizer Foundation, Inc.
831 Hillside Rd.
Brooklandville, MD 21022

Established in 1999 in MD.
Donor(s): Thomas Schweizer.
Grantmaker type: Independent foundation
Financial data (yr. ended 12/31/01): Assets, $322,684 (M); gifts received, $358; expenditures, $130,392; qualifying distributions, $129,676; giving activities include $130,000 for 3 grants (high: $90,000; low: $15,000).
Purpose and activities: Giving primarily for education.
Fields of interest: Elementary/secondary education; Zoos/zoological societies; Roman Catholic agencies & churches.
Types of support: General/operating support.

Limitations: Applications not accepted. Giving primarily in Baltimore, MD. No grants to individuals.
Application information: Contributes only to pre-selected organizations.
Officers: Thomas Schweizer, Jr., Pres.; Barbara W. Schweizer, V.P. and Secy.-Treas.
Trustees: Anthony W. Schweizer; Nicholas P. Schweizer.
EIN: 522147380

1332
The Shared Earth Foundation
113 Hoffman Ln.
Chestertown, MD 21620 (410) 778-6868
Contact: Caroline D. Gabel, C.E.O.
FAX: (410) 778-9050; E-mail: sharedearth@aol.com; URL: http://www.sharedearth.org/

Established in 1999 in MD.
Donor(s): Caroline D. Gabel.
Grantmaker type: Independent foundation
Financial data (yr. ended 03/31/02): Assets, $1,325,495 (M); gifts received, $317,564; expenditures, $1,172,501; qualifying distributions, $347,641; giving activities include $341,500 for 31 grants (high: $25,000; low: $4,000).
Purpose and activities: Support for the environment, biodiversity, the protection and enhancement of the natural habitat, and the protection of wildlife and endangered species.
Fields of interest: Natural resources; Environment, land resources; Environment; Animals/wildlife, preservation/protection; Animals/wildlife, endangered species.
International interests: Canada; Mexico; Guatemala; Bolivia; Indonesia.
Types of support: General/operating support; Continuing support; Program development; Research; Technical assistance; Matching/challenge support.
Limitations: Applications not accepted. Giving on a national and international basis, with emphasis on the eastern shore of MD. No grants to individuals.
Publications: Annual report.
Application information: The foundation is currently not accepting new applications.
Officer: Caroline D. Gabel, C.E.O. and Pres.
Number of staff: None.
EIN: 522151843

1333
The Snyder Foundation for Animals, Inc.
(formerly Foundation for Animal Information & Pet Services, Inc.)
3600 Clipper Mall Rd., Ste. 224
Baltimore, MD 21211 (410) 366-0787
Contact: Lora Dean Junkin, Exec. Dir.
FAX: (410) 366-0789; URL: http://www.snyderanimals.org

Established in 1898 in MD; reorganized in 1992.
Grantmaker type: Independent foundation
Financial data (yr. ended 04/30/02): Assets, $6,903,112 (M); expenditures, $558,888; qualifying distributions, $504,004; giving activities include $206,669 for 33 grants (high: $24,358; low: $524) and $15,603 for foundation-administered programs.

Purpose and activities: Giving limited to promoting animal welfare. This includes giving for humane and environmental education, spay/neuter programs, programs dealing with pet overpopulation, wildlife rehabilitation, and animal shelters.
Fields of interest: Environment, public education; Environment; Animal welfare; Animals/wildlife, preservation/protection; Animals/wildlife.
Types of support: Building/renovation; Equipment; Emergency funds; Program development; Conferences/seminars; Publication; Curriculum development; Matching/challenge support.
Limitations: Giving limited to MD. No grants to individuals, or for personnel positions, capital campaigns, or general operating expenses.
Publications: Application guidelines, Financial statement, Program policy statement.
Application information: Unsolicited requests for funds not accepted. Application form required.
   Initial approach: Proposal
   Copies of proposal: 8
   Deadline(s): Mid Jan.
   Board meeting date(s): 4th Thurs. of each month
   Final notification: Apr. 30
Officers and Directors:* Bill W. Benson,* Pres.; Barbara Feeser,* V.P.; Paul Nastasi, Secy.-Treas.; Lora Dean Junkin, Exec. Dir.; Sharon Christie; Sharon Chup; Carolyn McElroy; Stephen Montanarelli; Maureen Pulver.
Number of staff: 3 full-time professional; 1 full-time support.
EIN: 526001538

1334
The Benjamin Spencer Fund
c/o Bond Beebe
7315 Wisconsin Ave., Ste. 200W
Bethesda, MD   20814-3208

Established in 1993 in NM and MD.
Donor(s): Benjamin M. Spencer,‡ Hope Aldrich.
Grantmaker type: Independent foundation
Financial data (yr. ended 12/31/02): Assets, $4,774,603 (M); expenditures, $4,576,625; qualifying distributions, $4,480,667; giving activities include $4,500,000 for 7 grants (high: $2,500,000; low: $50,000).
Fields of interest: Multipurpose centers/programs; Education; Natural resources; Civil liberties, advocacy.
Types of support: General/operating support; Continuing support; Annual campaigns.
Limitations: Applications not accepted. Giving on a national basis. No grants to individuals.
Application information: Contributes only to pre-selected organizations.
Trustees: Hope Aldrich; Alida R. Messinger; Phoebe Jane Winthrop.
EIN: 136968299

1335
Creston G. Tate and Betty Jane Tate Foundation, Inc.
4 Kuethe Rd. N.E.
P.O. Box 1178
Glen Burnie, MD   21060-1178
Contact: Atwood B. Tate, Dir.

Established in 1997 in MD.
Donor(s): Creston G. Tate.
Grantmaker type: Independent foundation
Financial data (yr. ended 04/30/00): Assets, $2,678,456 (M); gifts received, $405,840; expenditures, $466,653; qualifying distributions, $230,000; giving activities include $230,000 for 2 grants (high: $200,000; low: $30,000).
Purpose and activities: Giving primarily to educational and health care organizations.
Fields of interest: Secondary school/education; Environment, beautification programs; Health care.
Limitations: Giving primarily in MD, with emphasis on Glen Burnie.
Application information:
   Initial approach: Verbal
   Deadline(s): None
Director: Atwood B. Tate.
EIN: 526875523

1336
TKF Foundation
(formerly Open Spaces, Sacred Places)
410 Severn Ave., Ste. 309
Annapolis, MD   21403   (410) 263-1056
Contact: Mary F. Wyatt, Exec. Dir.
FAX: (410) 280-6765; E-mail: info@tkffdn.org; URL: http://www.tkffdn.org

Established in 1985 in IA.
Donor(s): Thomas H. Stoner, Katharine E. Stoner.
Grantmaker type: Independent foundation
Financial data (yr. ended 12/31/02): Assets, $13,318,168 (M); expenditures, $882,728; qualifying distributions, $645,182; giving activities include $642,094 for 24 grants (high: $90,150; low: $100).
Purpose and activities: To create urban greenspace, sponsor public art, and champion urban agriculture with the goals of nurturing the human spirit and fostering a sense of community. The foundation funds two programs: Open Spaces, Sacred Places, and Community Greening.
Fields of interest: Arts; Natural resources; Community development.
Types of support: Continuing support; Seed money; Technical assistance; Matching/challenge support.
Limitations: Giving limited to Washington, DC, and Annapolis and Baltimore, MD. No grants to individuals or for endowments, debt reduction, ongoing operating costs, or capital campaigns.
Publications: Annual report, Informational brochure (including application guidelines).
Application information: Association of Baltimore Area Grantmakers Common Grant Application Form required. Application form required.
   Initial approach: Screening letter
   Copies of proposal: 2
   Deadline(s): Oct. 1 for Open Spaces, Sacred Places, Community Greening deadline Aug. 1, Nov. 1 for pre-approved organizations

Board meeting date(s): Monthly
Final notification: Jan. 15 for Open Spaces, Sacred Places; Nov. 1 for Community Greening
Officers and Directors:* Thomas H. Stoner,* Pres.; Katharine E. Stoner,* V.P.; Mary F. Wyatt, Exec. Dir.
Number of staff: 1 full-time professional; 1 part-time professional; 1 part-time support.
EIN: 421263576

1337
Town Creek Foundation, Inc. ▼
121 N. West St.
Easton, MD   21601   (410) 763-8171
Contact: Christine B. Shelton, Exec. Dir.
FAX: (410) 763-8172; E-mail: info@towncreekfdn.org; URL: http://www.towncreekfdn.org

Established in 1981 in MD.
Donor(s): Edmund A. Stanley, Jr.
Grantmaker type: Independent foundation
Financial data (yr. ended 12/31/02): Assets, $50,372,171 (M); expenditures, $2,817,902; qualifying distributions, $2,545,079; giving activities include $2,377,600 for 82 grants (high: $100,000; low: $100; average: $10,000–$50,000).
Purpose and activities: The foundation seeks a healthy natural environment, an informed society, and a peaceful world and is committed to achieving its mission through public education, citizen action, and advocacy. The foundation makes grants in the following four areas: 1) Protecting the environment; 2) News and commentary; 3) Promoting peace; and 4) Talbot County.
Fields of interest: Media/communications; Natural resources; Environment; International peace/security.
Types of support: General/operating support; Continuing support; Program development; Seed money; Matching/challenge support.
Limitations: Giving nationally for major programs; support limited to Talbot County, MD, for social services. No support for primary or secondary schools, hospitals, health care institutions, or religious organizations. No support for colleges or universities except when some aspect of their work is an integral part of a program supported by the foundation. No grants to individuals, or for endowment, capital, or building fund campaigns, purchase of land or buildings, research, scholarship programs, conferences, the publication of books or periodicals, or visual or performing arts projects.
Publications: Application guidelines, Grants list.
Application information: Application guidelines available upon request; include SASE (regular business-sized envelope). Applications sent by FAX or E-mail not considered. Application form not required.
   Initial approach: Letter of inquiry, up to 2 pages, may be submitted before a full proposal. Letter may be sent by FAX or E-mail
   Copies of proposal: 1
   Deadline(s): Before Jan. 15, May 15, and Sept. 15. If those dates fall on a weekend or holiday, deadline is extended to the next business day
   Board meeting date(s): Mar., July, and Nov.

Final notification: 15 days after board meetings
Officers and Trustees:* Jennifer Stanley,* Pres.; Lisa A. Stanley, V.P.; Philip E.L. Dietz, Jr.,* Secy.-Treas.; Christine B. Shelton, Exec. Dir.; Edmund A. Stanley, Jr.; Betsy Taylor.
Number of staff: 1 full-time professional; 1 part-time professional; 1 part-time support.
EIN: 521227030

1338
Marcia Brady Tucker Foundation, Inc.
P.O. Box 1149
Easton, MD 21601
Contact: Luther Tucker, Jr., Pres.

Incorporated in 1941 in NY.
Donor(s): Marcia Brady Tucker.‡
Grantmaker type: Independent foundation
Financial data (yr. ended 12/31/00): Assets, $15,631,635 (M); expenditures, $873,192; qualifying distributions, $711,387; giving activities include $677,165 for 146 grants (high: $55,000; low: $100).
Purpose and activities: Giving primarily for the arts, education, the environment, social services, and Christian institutions.
Fields of interest: Museums; Arts; Higher education; Theological school/education; Environment; Hospitals (general); Human services; Philanthropy/voluntarism; Christian agencies & churches; Jewish agencies & temples; Religion.
Types of support: General/operating support; Continuing support; Annual campaigns; Capital campaigns; Building/renovation; Endowments; Program development; Seed money; Matching/challenge support.
Limitations: Applications not accepted. Giving primarily in CA, CO, MD, NY, and OH. No grants to individuals.
Application information: Contributes only to pre-selected organizations. Unsolicited requests for funds not accepted.
Board meeting date(s): Spring and fall
Officers and Directors:* Luther Tucker, Jr.,* Pres.; Nicholas Tucker,* V.P.; Cam Sanders III,* Secy.; Carll Tucker III,* Treas.; Marcia Boogaard; Tom Boogaard; Barbara Randell; David Randell; Elizabeth Stoehr; Naomi Stoehr; Toinette Tucker.
Number of staff: 1 part-time support.
EIN: 136161561

1339
Dorothy Wagner Wallis Charitable Trust
7 Saint Paul St., Ste. 1400
Baltimore, MD 21202-1626 (410) 347-8770
Contact: Frederick Singley Koontz, Tr.

Established in 1993.
Grantmaker type: Independent foundation
Financial data (yr. ended 12/31/02): Assets, $6,006,070 (M); expenditures, $386,326; qualifying distributions, $367,960; giving activities include $362,132 for 17 grants (high: $155,000; low: $3,667).
Purpose and activities: Giving primarily for historic preservation, art, higher education, and human services.
Fields of interest: Historic preservation/historical societies; Arts; Higher education; Animal welfare; Human services.

Limitations: Giving primarily in Baltimore, MD. No grants to individuals.
Application information:
Initial approach: Proposal
Deadline(s): None
Trustee: Frederick Singley Koontz.
EIN: 526605828

1340
Weiler-Miller Fund
(formerly Weiler-Miller Foundation)
766 Old Hammonds Ferry Rd.
Linthicum, MD 21090
Contact: J. Jefferson Miller, Pres.
Additional address: c/o Thomas Provost, Mercantile-Safe Deposit & Trust Co., 2 Hopkins Pl., Baltimore, MD 21201, tel.: (410) 237-5518

Established in 1997 in MD.
Donor(s): Josepha S. Miller Revocable Trust, Schoeneman-Halle Foundation.
Grantmaker type: Independent foundation
Financial data (yr. ended 11/30/02): Assets, $2,243,556 (M); gifts received, $15,000; expenditures, $139,925; qualifying distributions, $120,893; giving activities include $120,555 for 71 grants (high: $15,000; low: $100).
Purpose and activities: Giving primarily for the arts, education, health care, and human services.
Fields of interest: Museums; Arts; Education; Natural resources; Hospitals (general); Health organizations, association; Human services; Children/youth, services.
Types of support: Annual campaigns; Capital campaigns; Building/renovation.
Limitations: Applications not accepted. Giving primarily in Baltimore, MD. No grants to individuals.
Application information: Contributes only to pre-selected organizations.
Officers: J. Jefferson Miller, Pres.; Anne W. Miller, V.P.; Pamela Himmelrich, Secy.; Joshua M. Miller, Treas.
Number of staff: None.
EIN: 522109374

MASSACHUSETTS

1341
The Acushnet Foundation
c/o Seamark Fin. Svcs.
P.O. Box 1498
Mattapoisett, MA 02739 (508) 758-6159
Contact: William Blasdale

Trust established in 1953 in MA.
Grantmaker type: Independent foundation
Financial data (yr. ended 06/30/02): Assets, $8,432,669 (M); expenditures, $566,399; qualifying distributions, $517,549; giving activities include $502,500 for 51 grants (high: $95,000; low: $1,000).
Fields of interest: Historic preservation/historical societies; Secondary school/education; Education; Animal welfare; Hospitals (general); Boys & girls clubs; Human services; YM/YWCAs & YM/YWHAs; Children/youth, services; Family services;

Foundations (community); Federated giving programs.
Types of support: Continuing support; Annual campaigns; Capital campaigns; Building/renovation; Emergency funds; Seed money; Scholarship funds.
Limitations: Giving generally limited to the greater New Bedford, MA, area. No grants to individuals, or for endowment funds, operating budgets, deficit financing, or matching gifts.
Application information: Application form not required.
Initial approach: Letter
Copies of proposal: 1
Deadline(s): None
Board meeting date(s): As required
Final notification: 4 to 6 weeks
Trustees: R. William Blasdale; Mrs. R. William Blasdale; Graeme L. Flanders; Carl Ribeiro; Mrs. Carl Ribeiro; Richard B. Young; Mrs. Richard B. Young; William E. Young.
Number of staff: 1 part-time support.
EIN: 046032197

1342
Agape Foundation
40 Oakley Rd.
Watertown, MA 02472-1360 (617) 926-8560
Contact: Anthony Palomba, Tr.

Established in 1985 in MA.
Grantmaker type: Independent foundation
Financial data (yr. ended 09/30/02): Assets, $1,918,763 (M); gifts received, $40; expenditures, $147,056; qualifying distributions, $122,708; giving activities include $123,072 for 12 grants (high: $32,576; low: $250).
Purpose and activities: Support for survival education, a school for peace, and wildlife and wilderness conservation organizations that have been in existence for at least 5 years.
Fields of interest: Education; Natural resources; Human services; International peace/security; Law/international law.
Types of support: General/operating support; Continuing support; Program development.
Limitations: Giving primarily in New England. No grants to individuals.
Application information: Application form required.
Initial approach: Letter
Deadline(s): None
Board meeting date(s): Annually
Trustees: Holly Martin; Anthony Palomba; Loren Shumway.
EIN: 222690962

1343
American Meteorological Society
45 Beacon St.
Boston, MA 02108-3693
Contact: Melissa Weston, Exec. Off.
Tel.: (617) 227-2426, ext. 250; FAX: (617) 742-8718; Additional address: 1120 G. St., N.W., Ste. 800, Washington, DC 20005, tel.: (202) 682-9006, FAX: (202) 682-9298; E-mail: amsinfo@ametsoc.org; URL: http://www.ametsoc.org/ams

Established in 1919 in MA.
Grantmaker type: Public charity

Financial data (yr. ended 12/31/00): Revenue, $11,305,271; assets, $16,079,060; gifts received, $243,081; expenditures, $11,790,938; program services expenses, $11,466,042; giving activities include $465,000 for 58 grants to individuals.
Purpose and activities: The society develops and disseminates knowledge of the atmosphere and related oceanic and hydrologic sciences, and promotes the professional applications of this knowledge.
Fields of interest: Environmental education; Science; Marine science.
Types of support: Annual campaigns; Fellowships; Scholarships—to individuals.
Publications: Application guidelines, Annual report, Financial statement, Grants list, Informational brochure, Newsletter, Program policy statement.
Application information: Candidates must be U.S. citizens or hold permanent resident status, and should specify the program about which they are inquiring and the year of academic study they will be entering in the fall, when requesting an application. Application form required.
> *Initial approach:* Telephone or e-mail
> *Deadline(s):* Feb. 16 for Government Graduate Fellowships; Feb. 23 for Minority, Industry, and Undergraduate Scholarships; Mar. 1 for Congressional Science Fellowship; Mar. 16 for Graduate Fellowship in Science; June 12 for Macelwane Awards
> *Board meeting date(s):* 3 times a year
Officers: Richard Rosen, Pres.; Kenneth C. Spengler, Secy.-Treas.; Barry C. Mohan, Cont.; Ronald D. McPherson, Ph.D., Exec. Dir.
Number of staff: 45 full-time professional.
EIN: 042103657

1344
Analog Devices, Inc. Corporate Giving Program
c/o Contribs. Admin.
1 Technology Way, P.O. Box 9106
Norwood, MA 02062-9106   (781) 329-4700

Grantmaker type: Corporate giving program
Purpose and activities: Analog Devices makes charitable contributions to nonprofit organizations involved with arts and culture, education, the environment, human services, community development, computer science, and engineering. Support is given primarily in areas of company operations.
Fields of interest: Museums; Arts; Higher education; Education; Environment; Human services; Community development; Computer science; Engineering.
Types of support: General/operating support; Employee volunteer services; Employee matching gifts.
Limitations: Giving primarily in areas of company operations, with emphasis on the greater Boston, MA, area. No support for religious or political organizations, professional organizations or societies, national organizations, or disease-specific organizations. No grants for advertising, dinners, or fundraising.
Publications: Informational brochure, Newsletter.
Application information: Unsolicited proposals from educational organizations are not

accepted. A contributions committee reviews all requests. Application form required.
> *Initial approach:* Contact headquarters for application form
> *Copies of proposal:* 1
> *Deadline(s):* None
> *Board meeting date(s):* Quarterly
> *Final notification:* Following review
Contributions Committee: Farhad Vazehgoo, Chair.; John Alberghini; Hunt Bergen; Diane Corning; Pam LeBlanc; Mal Lemeshow; Steve Lewis; MaryAnn Naumann; Erin O'Sullivan; Marsha Terrelonge.

1345
Animal Umbrella, Inc.
P.O. Box 2675
Acton, MA 01720   (978) 731-7267
Contact: Annamarie Taylor, Pres.
E-mail: info@animalumbrella.org; URL: http://www.animalumbrella.org/

Founded in 1986 in MA.
Grantmaker type: Public charity
Financial data (yr. ended 12/31/00): Revenue, $86,057; assets, $55,231; gifts received, $69,480; expenditures, $155,390; program services expenses, $145,289; giving activities include $99,374 for 1 grant.
Purpose and activities: The organization is dedicated to the rescue, care, rehabilitation, adoption, and overall welfare of homeless cats and kittens in MA.
Fields of interest: Animal welfare.
Limitations: Giving primarily in MA.
Officers and Directors:* Annamarie Taylor,* Pres.; Linda Lachman,* Secy.; Marie Bright,* Treas.; Mary Albano; Mary Jane Kalb; Cheryl Minieri; Jamie Robredo; Justine Rudgis.
EIN: 222662445

1346
Appalachian Mountain Club
5 Joy St.
Boston, MA 02108-1433   (617) 523-0636
Contact: Laurie Burt, Pres.
FAX: (617) 523-0722; E-mail: information@outdoors.org; URL: http://www.outdoors.org

Established in 1876.
Grantmaker type: Public charity
Financial data (yr. ended 12/31/01): Revenue, $20,688,188; assets, $45,082,442; gifts received, $10,720,658; expenditures, $16,446,966; program services expenses, $13,809,860; giving activities include $31,044 for grants (high: $11,188).
Purpose and activities: The club promotes the protection, enjoyment and wise use of the mountains, rivers, and trails of the Appalachian Region.
Fields of interest: Natural resources; Recreation.
Officers and Directors:* Laurie Burt,* Pres.; William M. Hill,* V.P.; Kendal B. Price,* Secy.; Peter H. Sprayregen,* Treas.; Andrew J. Falender, Exec. Dir.; Alson D. Braley; Susan Fulford Cerullo; Woolsey S. Conover; Trudy Coxe; W.A. Devereaux; and 12 additional directors.
EIN: 046001677

1347
Arcadia Charitable Trust
c/o North American Mgmt.
10 Post Office Sq., Ste. 300
Boston, MA 02109   (617) 695-2116
Contact: Earl E. Watson III, Treas.

Established in 1997 in MA.
Donor(s): Lucy S. Moore, Marion R. Stone, Robert G. Stone, Jr.
Grantmaker type: Independent foundation
Financial data (yr. ended 12/31/02): Assets, $3,650,815 (M); gifts received, $526,662; expenditures, $285,348; qualifying distributions, $229,535; giving activities include $230,750 for 32 grants (high: $32,500; low: $1,000).
Purpose and activities: Giving primarily for education.
Fields of interest: Education; Medical research, institute; Environment; Human services.
Limitations: Giving primarily in CT and MA.
Application information: Application form required.
> *Copies of proposal:* 8
> *Deadline(s):* None
> *Board meeting date(s):* July 14 and Nov. 17
Officer: Earl E. Watson III, Treas.
Trustees: Helen Fitzgerald; Lucy S. Moore; Catherine S. Osier; Jennifer P. Stone; Marion R. Stone; Robert G. Stone, Jr.; R. Gregg Stone III; Timothy B. Stone.
Number of staff: 1 part-time professional.
EIN: 137102310

1348
Archibald Family Charitable Foundation
c/o Kirkpartrick & Lockhart, LLP
75 State St.
Boston, MA 02109
Contact: Melville Chapin, Tr.

Established in 1998 in MA.
Donor(s): Anne G. Archibald.
Grantmaker type: Independent foundation
Financial data (yr. ended 03/31/02): Assets, $296,468 (M); expenditures, $333,849; qualifying distributions, $299,322; giving activities include $299,000 for 68 grants (high: $25,000; low: $500).
Purpose and activities: Giving primarily for education; some funding for conservation, animal and wildlife protection, and health and human services.
Fields of interest: Historic preservation/historical societies; Higher education; Education; Natural resources; Animal welfare; Health care; Human services.
Limitations: Giving primarily in MA. No grants to individuals.
Application information: Application form not required.
> *Deadline(s):* None
Trustees: John L.C. Archibald; Melville Chapin; Mary A. Poor.
EIN: 043417222

1349
The Argosy Foundation
(formerly The Abele Family Charitable Trust)
c/o The Philanthropic Initiative
77 Franklin St., 9th Fl.
Boston, MA 02110
Contact: Kristen Whelan

Established in 1993 in MA.
Donor(s): John E. Abele.
Grantmaker type: Independent foundation
Financial data (yr. ended 11/30/02): Assets,
$28,831,154 (M); expenditures, $2,246,921;
qualifying distributions, $1,984,197; giving
activities include $2,024,874 for 60 grants
(high: $250,000; low: $1,500).
Purpose and activities: The foundation's mission
is to support people and programs that make
our society a better place to live. The method is
to support creative, entrepreneurial approaches
that help people to help themselves. These
programs should have the potential to become
self-sustaining whenever possible, to build
teams and communities, to be replicated, and to
motivate and inspire others to contribute in their
own ways.
Fields of interest: Music; Arts; Education;
Environment, public education; Environment;
Housing/shelter, services.
Types of support: General/operating support;
Scholarship funds.
Limitations: Applications not accepted. Giving
nationally, with emphasis on CO, VT, and WI.
No grants to individuals.
Application information: Contributes only to
pre-selected organizations.
Trustees: Alexander T. Abele; Christopher S.
Abele; Jennifer L. Abele; John E. Abele; Mary S.
Abele.
EIN: 046752868

1350
Dorothy Q. & David B. Arnold, Jr.
 Charitable Trust
c/o Hemenway & Barnes
P.O. Box 6842
Boston, MA 02102

Established in 1996 in MA.
Donor(s): Dorothy Q. Arnold, David B. Arnold,
Jr. Charitable Lead Annuity Trust.
Grantmaker type: Independent foundation
Financial data (yr. ended 12/31/01): Assets,
$1,648,080 (M); gifts received, $210,544;
expenditures, $209,361; qualifying distributions,
$188,087; giving activities include $187,837 for
44 grants (high: $25,000; low: $100).
Fields of interest: Choreography; Dance;
Orchestra (symphony); Museums (art); Animal
welfare; Animals/wildlife,
preservation/protection.
Limitations: Applications not accepted. No
grants to individuals.
Application information: Contributes only to
pre-selected organizations.
Trustees: David B. Arnold III; Timothy F. Fidgeon.
EIN: 222474779

1351
Elisha V. Ashton Trust
c/o Choate, Hall & Stewart
53 State St., Exchange Pl.
Boston, MA 02109-2804

Established in 1884 in MA.
Grantmaker type: Independent foundation
Financial data (yr. ended 10/31/02): Assets,
$17,577,610 (M); expenditures, $1,154,732;
qualifying distributions, $1,051,274; giving
activities include $1,030,400 for 23 grants of
$44,800 each.
Purpose and activities: Giving primarily for
social services, especially organizations which
aid and house the needy, indigent, aged, and
women and children; support also for hospitals
and animal welfare.
Fields of interest: Animal welfare; Hospitals
(general); Human services; Children/youth,
services; Aging, centers/services; Women,
centers/services; Aging; Women.
Limitations: Applications not accepted. Giving
primarily in the Boston, MA, area. No grants to
individuals.
Application information: Contributes only to
pre-selected organizations.
Trustees: John M. Cornish; James R. Nichols.
EIN: 046016303

1352
Ausolus Trust
c/o Putnam Funds
1 Post Office Sq.
Boston, MA 02109
Contact: George Putnam, Tr.

Established in 1997 in MA.
Donor(s): George Putnam.
Grantmaker type: Independent foundation
Financial data (yr. ended 12/31/02): Assets,
$1,524,449 (M); gifts received, $45,317;
expenditures, $97,330; qualifying distributions,
$91,509; giving activities include $90,000 for 5
grants (high: $55,000; low: $5,000).
Purpose and activities: Giving primarily for
education, historical societies, and
communications.
Fields of interest: Media/communications;
Historic preservation/historical societies; Higher
education; Education; Environment; Human
services.
Limitations: Giving primarily in Boston, MA and
ME.
Application information: Unsolicited requests
for funds not accepted. Application form not
required.
 Deadline(s): Dec. 1
Trustees: George Putnam; Nancy Putnam.
EIN: 043368079

1353
Azadoutioun Foundation
c/o Gravestar
1 Broadway
Cambridge, MA 02142
Contact: Laurie A. LeBlanc
FAX: (978) 521-9204; E-mail:
lleblanc9498C@aol.com

Established in 1985 in MA.
Donor(s): Carolyn G. Mugar.

Grantmaker type: Independent foundation
Financial data (yr. ended 12/31/00): Assets,
$5,431,446; expenditures, $214,509; qualifying
distributions, $142,000; giving activities include
$142,000 for 9 grants (high: $30,000; low:
$5,000).
Purpose and activities: Giving primarily for
education and human services.
Fields of interest: Adult education—literacy,
basic skills & GED; Reading; Environment;
Human services; International economic
development.
Types of support: General/operating support;
Program development.
Limitations: Giving on a national basis. No
grants to individuals; no loans.
Application information: Application form not
required.
 Copies of proposal: 1
 Deadline(s): None
 Board meeting date(s): Quarterly
Trustees: Janet Corpus; Carolyn G. Mugar;
Sidney Peck; Sharryn Ross.
Number of staff: 1 part-time professional; 1
part-time support.
EIN: 042876245

1354
The Paul and Edith Babson Foundation
c/o Nichols & Pratt
50 Congress St., Ste. 832
Boston, MA 02109-4017 (617) 523-8368
Contact: Elizabeth D. Nichols, Prog. Off.
FAX: (617) 523-8949; E-mail:
pebabsonfdn@babsonfoundations.org; URL:
http://www.babsonfoundations.org

Trust established in 1957 in MA.
Donor(s): Paul T. Babson.‡
Grantmaker type: Independent foundation
Financial data (yr. ended 12/31/02): Assets,
$11,252,896 (M); expenditures, $641,034;
qualifying distributions, $605,441; giving
activities include $580,158 for grants.
Purpose and activities: The competitive grant
program focuses on providing opportunities for
the people of Greater Boston through grants in
four program areas: entrepreneurship and
economic development, culture, education and
leadership development, environment and
community building, and health and social
services.
Fields of interest: Theater; Music; Arts;
Education; Environment, beautification
programs; AIDS; Domestic violence; Youth,
services; Economic development;
Urban/community development; Community
development, small businesses.
Types of support: General/operating support;
Program development; Scholarship funds.
Limitations: Giving limited to the greater
Boston, MA, area as generally defined by Route
128. No grants to individuals, or for individual
scholarships, conferences, films, fundraising, or
donor cultivations.
Publications: Application guidelines, Grants list,
Program policy statement.
Application information: Summary Sheets
available on foundation Web site. Application
form required.
 Initial approach: Two-page concept letter with
 Summary Sheet
 Copies of proposal: 2

Deadline(s): Feb. 6 and Sept. 9
Board meeting date(s): May and Nov.
Final notification: June 15 and Dec. 15
Trustees: James A. Babson; Katherine L. Babson, Jr.; James R. Nichols.
Number of staff: 2 shared staff (shared with The Susan A. and Donald P. Babson Charitable Foundation and the Harold Whitworth Pierce Charitable Trust).
EIN: 046037891

1355

Barr Foundation ▼

(formerly The Hostetter Foundation)
The Pilot House
Lewis Wharf
Boston, MA 02110 (617) 854-3500
Contact: Kerri Hurley
E-mail: khurley@pilothouse.com; URL: http://www.barrfoundation.org

Established in 1987 in MA.
Donor(s): Amos B. Hostetter, Jr.
Grantmaker type: Independent foundation
Financial data (yr. ended 11/30/02): Assets, $760,765,310 (M); gifts received, $14,776,875; expenditures, $47,646,049; qualifying distributions, $42,233,039; giving activities include $41,167,200 for 345+ grants (high: $1,000,000; average: $1,000–$1,000,000).
Purpose and activities: Giving primarily for education and the environment in the greater Boston area.
Fields of interest: Elementary school/education; Natural resources.
Types of support: General/operating support; Continuing support; Annual campaigns; Capital campaigns; Building/renovation; Land acquisition; Endowments; Emergency funds; Program development; Conferences/seminars; Research; Technical assistance; Consulting services; Program evaluation; Matching/challenge support.
Limitations: Applications not accepted. Giving primarily in the greater Boston, MA, area. No grants to individuals.
Application information: Unsolicited requests for funds not accepted.
Board meeting date(s): Quarterly
Officer: Marion Kane, Exec. Dir.
Trustees: Amos B. Hostetter, Jr.; Barbara W. Hostetter.
Number of staff: 4 full-time professional; 2 part-time professional; 1 full-time support; 2 part-time support.
EIN: 046579815
Recent environmental and animal welfare grants:
1355-1 Alternatives for Community and Environment (ACE), Roxbury, MA, $90,000. 2002.
1355-2 Alternatives for Community and Environment (ACE), Roxbury, MA, $40,000. 2002.
1355-3 American Humane Education Society, Boston, MA, $50,000. 2002.
1355-4 Antioch New England Graduate School, Antioch New England Institute, Keene, NH, $100,000. 2002.
1355-5 Boston GreenSpace Alliance, Boston, MA, $125,000. 2002.
1355-6 Boston Natural Areas Network, Boston, MA, $100,000. 2002.

1355-7 Charles River Conservancy, Newton, MA, $40,000. 2002.
1355-8 Charles River Watershed Association, Auburndale, MA, $200,000. 2002.
1355-9 Clean Water Fund, DC, $100,000. 2002.
1355-10 Coevolution Foundation, San Francisco, CA, $25,000. 2002.
1355-11 Commonwealth Zoological Corporation, Boston, MA, $10,000. 2002.
1355-12 Conservation Law Foundation, Boston, MA, $100,000. 2002.
1355-13 Ducks Unlimited, Memphis, TN, $50,000. 2002.
1355-14 Eagle Eye Institute, Somerville, MA, $10,000. 2002.
1355-15 Earthworks Projects, Jamaica Plain, MA, $90,000. 2002.
1355-16 Emerald Necklace Conservancy, Boston, MA, $20,000. 2002.
1355-17 Environmental Careers Organization (ECO), Boston, MA, $140,000. 2002.
1355-18 Environmental Leadership Program, Cambridge, MA, $50,000. 2002.
1355-19 Environmental League of Massachusetts, Boston, MA, $60,000. 2002.
1355-20 Global Habitat Project, Boston, MA, $50,000. 2002.
1355-21 Kids Institutes for Discovery, Roxbury, MA, $50,000. 2002.
1355-22 Land Trust Alliance, Saratoga Springs, NY, $100,000. 2002.
1355-23 Manomet Center for Conservation Sciences, Manomet, MA, $150,000. 2002.
1355-24 Massachusetts Horticultural Society, Boston, MA, $10,000. 2002.
1355-25 Mystic River Watershed Association, Arlington, MA, $55,000. 2002.
1355-26 Nantucket Maria Mitchell Association, Nantucket, MA, $30,000. 2002.
1355-27 Nantucket Sustainable Development Corporation, Nantucket, MA, $10,000. 2002.
1355-28 National Parks Conservation Association, DC, $25,000. 2002.
1355-29 Nature Conservancy, Boston, MA, $100,000. 2002.
1355-30 New Ecology, Cambridge, MA, $75,000. 2002.
1355-31 New Ecology, Cambridge, MA, $25,000. 2002.
1355-32 New England Aquarium Corporation, Boston, MA, $500,000. 2002.
1355-33 New England Aquarium Corporation, Boston, MA, $102,273. 2002.
1355-34 New England Aquarium Corporation, Boston, MA, $100,000. 2002.
1355-35 New England Forestry Foundation, Groton, MA, $100,000. 2002.
1355-36 New England Grassroots Environment Fund, Montpelier, VT, $75,000. 2002.
1355-37 New England Wild Flower Society, Framingham, MA, $125,000. 2002.
1355-38 New England Wild Flower Society, Framingham, MA, $100,000. 2002.
1355-39 New England Wildlife Center, Hingham, MA, $166,667. 2002.
1355-40 New England Wildlife Center, Hingham, MA, $10,000. 2002.
1355-41 Nonquit Street Neighborhood Association and Land Trust, Dorchester, MA, $30,000. 2002.
1355-42 Save the Harbor—Save the Bay, Boston, MA, $150,000. 2002.
1355-43 Save the Harbor—Save the Bay, Boston, MA, $50,000. 2002.

1355-44 Trust for Public Land, Boston, MA, $125,000. 2002.
1355-45 Trustees of Reservations, Beverly, MA, $1,000,000. 2002.
1355-46 Trustees of Reservations, Beverly, MA, $10,000. 2002.
1355-47 Tufts University, Medford, MA, $50,000. For Global Development and Environmental Institute at School of Medicine in Boston. 2002.
1355-48 Urban Ecology Institute, Chestnut Hill, MA, $100,000. 2002.
1355-49 WalkBoston, Boston, MA, $50,000. 2002.

1356

Bay State Gas Company Contributions Program

300 Friberg Pkwy.
Westborough, MA 01581 (508) 836-7000
Contact: Carol Churchhill, Dir., Comm.

Grantmaker type: Corporate giving program
Purpose and activities: Bay State Gas makes charitable contributions to nonprofit organizations involved with arts and culture, education, the environment, human services, and community development. Support is given primarily in areas of company operations.
Fields of interest: Arts; Higher education; Education; Environment; Human services; Community development.
Types of support: General/operating support.
Limitations: Giving primarily in areas of company operations, particularly southern ME, Merrimack Valley, southeastern, and western MA, and coastal NH.
Application information: The Communications Department handles giving. The company has a staff that only handles contributions. Application form not required.
Initial approach: Proposal to nearest company facility
Copies of proposal: 1
Final notification: Following review

1357

Berkshire Taconic Community Foundation ▼

(formerly Berkshire-Taconic Foundation)
271 Main St., Ste. 3
Great Barrington, MA 01230 (800) 969-2823
Contact: Jennifer Dowley, Pres.; B. Carter White, V.P.; or Maeve M. O'Dea, Prog. Off.
Additional tel.: (413) 528-8039; FAX: (413) 528-8158; E-mail: info@berkshiretaconic.org; URL: http://www.berkshiretaconic.org/

Established in 1987 in CT.
Grantmaker type: Community foundation
Financial data (yr. ended 12/31/02): Assets, $29,292,293 (M); gifts received, $9,208,923; expenditures, $6,562,259; giving activities include $6,058,163 for grants (high: $15,000).
Purpose and activities: Support primarily for education, the arts, the environment, and health and human services.
Fields of interest: Arts; Education; Environment; Health care; Human services.
Types of support: General/operating support; Equipment; Endowments; Emergency funds;

Program development; Conferences/seminars; Publication; Seed money; Curriculum development; Fellowships; Scholarship funds; Technical assistance; Consulting services; Program evaluation; Employee-related scholarships; Scholarships—to individuals; Matching/challenge support; Student loans—to individuals.

Limitations: Giving limited to northwest Litchfield County, CT, Berkshire County, MA, and northeast Dutchess and Columbia counties, NY.

Publications: Application guidelines, Annual report, Financial statement, Informational brochure (including application guidelines), Occasional report.

Application information: Application form required.

Initial approach: Telephone for application guidelines
Copies of proposal: 1
Deadline(s): Oct. 1
Board meeting date(s): Quarterly
Final notification: Dec.

Officers and Directors:* Gail L.K. Cashen,* Chair.; Mark S. Gold,* Vice-Chair.; Jennifer Dowley,* Pres.; B. Carter White, V.P.; John R.H. Blum,* Secy.; Mark Macomber, Treas.; Lo Yi Chan; Wendy C. Curtis; Joan Dunlop; Rachel G. Fletcher; David Klausmeyer; Lael Locke; Neil M. McCarthy; David McKearnan; Patrick J. Mele, Jr.; Hamilton W. Meserve; Carmi Rapport; Arthur Rosenblatt; Elizabeth T. Selkowitz; Nancy Stahl; Craig Thorn III; John Tuke; Jane Allen Waters.

Number of staff: 7 full-time professional; 10 part-time professional; 1 part-time support.
EIN: 061254469

Recent environmental and animal welfare grants:

1357-1 American Horse Trials Foundation, Annapolis, MD, $100,000. 2002.

1357-2 American Horse Trials Foundation, Annapolis, MD, $30,000. 2002.

1357-3 Ayacara International, Boulder, CO, $10,000. 2002.

1357-4 Ayacara International, Boulder, CO, $10,000. 2002.

1357-5 Berkshire Botanical Garden, Stockbridge, MA, $10,000. For annual operating fund. 2002.

1357-6 Berkshire Regional Planning Commission, Pittsfield, MA, $15,000. For Conservation Agent Program. 2002.

1357-7 New England Heritage Breeds Conservancy, Richmond, MA, $10,000. 2002.

1357-8 New England Tropical Conservatory, Bennington, VT, $25,000. 2002.

1357-9 Scenic Hudson, Poughkeepsie, NY, $10,000. 2002.

1357-10 Trustees of Reservations, Beverly, MA, $11,400. For insurance premiums. 2002.

1358
Boston Foundation for Architecture
52 Broad St.
Boston, MA 02109-4301
Contact: Richard Fitzgerald, Exec. Dir.
Tel.: (617) 951-1433, ext. 232; FAX: (617) 951-0845; E-mail: rfitzgerald@architects.org; URL: http://www.bfagrants.org

Established in 1984 in MA.
Grantmaker type: Public charity

Financial data (yr. ended 12/31/02): Assets, $650,138 (M); gifts received, $13,871; expenditures, $85,074; program services expenses, $63,950; giving activities include $63,950 for grants.

Purpose and activities: The foundation encourages, through its grantmaking program, greater public awareness of the value of well-designed public places. Support is given to projects that further the understanding of design, such as: educational programs about design, aimed especially at young people, focusing on the public realm; community forums or "charrettes" to discuss and debate public improvements to the communal environment; exhibitions of exceptional examples of public-facility design; recognition programs, awards programs, and other ways of enhancing the visibility of well-designed infrastructure and civic architecture; lecture series on topics relevant to the design of public buildings or spaces; ideas for competitions for future public buildings and improvements; historic studies of public facilities that have been especially well-designed; and infrastructure art and design in and around the Central Artery/Tunnel Project. Organizations that have existing membership bases and networks, especially those with public education experience, will be favored in order to facilitate immediate educational impact. School-based groups, which the foundation has traditionally assisted, will continue to be encouraged to seek funding.
Fields of interest: Architecture; Environment; Urban/community development; Community development; Transportation.
Types of support: General/operating support; Continuing support; Program development; Conferences/seminars; Publication; Seed money; Curriculum development; Grants to individuals; Matching/challenge support.
Limitations: Giving primarily in MA. No grants for capital expenditures or for endowments.
Publications: Application guidelines, Annual report, Grants list, Informational brochure (including application guidelines), Occasional report.
Application information: See Web site for application forms and guidelines. Application form required.

Initial approach: Telephone or Web site
Copies of proposal: 1
Deadline(s): Aug.
Board meeting date(s): Nov.
Final notification: Jan. 1

Officers and Directors:* Richard Green, F.A.I.A.,* Chair.; Rob Radloff,* Vice-Chair.; Lisa Reindorf, A.I.A.,* Secy.; Susan W. Leff,* Treas.; Richard Fitzgerald, Exec. Dir.; Ron Ancrum; Ena Fox; Roger Goldstein, F.A.I.A.; Robert Kuehn; Peter Kuttner, F.A.I.A.; Ted Landsmark, Assoc. A.I.A.; Peter Madsen, F.A.I.A.; Kyra Montagu; Sam Plimpton; Mysore Ravindra, P.E.; Linda Snyder.
Number of staff: 1 part-time professional.
EIN: 046268891

1359
Alexander H. Bright Charitable Trust
c/o The Boston Family Office
88 Broad St.
Boston, MA 02110 (617) 624-0800
Contact: Solange M. Bell

Established in 1952 in MA.
Donor(s): Alexander H. Bright.‡
Grantmaker type: Independent foundation
Financial data (yr. ended 12/31/02): Assets, $3,703,408 (M); expenditures, $266,846; qualifying distributions, $230,415; giving activities include $233,700 for 108 grants (high: $75,000; low: $100).
Purpose and activities: Support primarily for wildlife, conservation and environmental organizations; support also for education, social services, and youth.
Fields of interest: Education; Natural resources; Environment; Animals/wildlife, preservation/protection; Human services; Children/youth, services.
Types of support: General/operating support.
Limitations: Giving primarily in MA. No grants to individuals.
Application information: Application form not required.

Initial approach: Proposal
Deadline(s): Oct.
Board meeting date(s): Mar., June, Sept., and Dec.
Final notification: Jan.

Trustee: Edward W. Weld.
EIN: 046013967

1360
The Bromley Charitable Trust
299 Clapboardtree St.
Westwood, MA 02090

Established in 1994 in MA.
Donor(s): Duncan M. McFarland, Elizabeth M. McFarland, Ellen B. McFarland.
Grantmaker type: Independent foundation
Financial data (yr. ended 12/31/02): Assets, $1,665,093 (M); gifts received, $457,367; expenditures, $389,972; qualifying distributions, $378,407; giving activities include $378,407 for 43 grants (high: $211,000; low: $50).
Fields of interest: Elementary/secondary education; Natural resources; Hospitals (general); Health organizations, association; Human services; Community development.
Limitations: Applications not accepted. No grants to individuals.
Application information: Contributes only to pre-selected organizations.
Trustees: Duncan M. McFarland; Ellen B. McFarland.
EIN: 043237138

1361
Cabot Corporation Foundation, Inc.
2 Seaport Ln., Ste. 1300
Boston, MA 02210 (617) 342-6002
Contact: Dorothy L. Forbes, Exec. Dir.
Additional tel.: (617) 342-6004; E-mail: dorothy_forbes@cabot-corp.com

Incorporated in 1953 in MA.
Donor(s): Cabot Corp.

Grantmaker type: Company-sponsored foundation
Financial data (yr. ended 09/30/02): Assets, $1,360,964 (M); gifts received, $325,000; expenditures, $594,708; qualifying distributions, $728,516; giving activities include $512,228 for 42 grants (high: $50,000; low: $315) and $216,487 for 10 employee matching gifts.
Purpose and activities: Emphasis on science and technology, higher and other education, including employee matching gifts to schools, and community funds. Support also for community improvement projects and cultural programs; particular interest in strengthening the future scientific and technological capabilities of the nation. As a result, projects, organizations, and activities with a science and technology focus that cut across all program areas receive special attention.
Fields of interest: Arts; Education, research; Education, fund raising; Early childhood education; Elementary school/education; Secondary school/education; Higher education; Adult/continuing education; Education; Natural resources; Environment; Family services; Community development; Federated giving programs; Chemistry; Mathematics; Engineering/technology; Computer science; Biological sciences; Science; Economics; Disabled.
Types of support: General/operating support; Annual campaigns; Capital campaigns; Building/renovation; Equipment; Program development; Seed money; Scholarship funds; Research; Technical assistance; Employee matching gifts; In-kind gifts; Matching/challenge support.
Limitations: Giving limited to communities near Cabot corporate installations in Douglas County, IL, St. Mary Parish and Evangeline Parish, LA, Billerica, Everett, and Boston, MA, Boyertown, PA, Pampa, TX, and Waverly, WV. No support for religious institutions for religious purposes, or for political or fraternal organizations. No grants to individuals, or for advertising or dinner table sponsorship.
Publications: Annual report (including application guidelines), Occasional report.
Application information: Application form not required.
  Initial approach: Proposal (no more than 2 pages) or telephone
  Copies of proposal: 1
  Deadline(s): 1 month prior to meetings
  Board meeting date(s): Mar., June, Sept., and Dec.
  Final notification: 3 months
Officers and Directors:* Samuel W. Bodman,* Pres.; Margaret Hanratty,* V.P. and Treas.; Dorothy L. Forbes,* V.P. and Exec. Dir.; Charles A. Gray,* Secy.; Charles D. Gerlinger, Clerk; Susan Alexander; Robert Culver; Karen M. Morrissey.
Number of staff: None.
EIN: 046035227

1362
The Virginia Wellington Cabot Foundation
c/o Cabot-Wellington, LLC
70 Federal St., 7th Fl.
Boston, MA 02110 (617) 451-1744
Contact: Joan Whelton, Exec. Dir.

Established in 1992 in MA.
Donor(s): Thomas D. Cabot, Jr., Thomas D. Cabot 1986 Conduit Trust, Virginia W. Cabot Revocable Trust.
Grantmaker type: Independent foundation
Financial data (yr. ended 12/31/02): Assets, $34,806,364 (M); expenditures, $2,396,442; qualifying distributions, $2,165,973; giving activities include $1,932,758 for 139 grants (high: $100,000; low: $500; average: $1,000–$50,000).
Purpose and activities: Giving for education, the arts, youth, the environment, and women's services.
Fields of interest: Arts; Education, association; Secondary school/education; Higher education; Education; Environment; Youth development; Human services; Federated giving programs.
Application information: Application form not required.
  Deadline(s): Apr. 1, Aug. 1, and Dec. 1
Trustees: Sara Arshad; Christinia Cabot; Edmund Cabot; Elizabeth Cabot; James Cabot; Louis W. Cabot; Robert M. Cabot; Linda Cabot-Black; Laura Cabot-Carrington; Kathleen Fitzgerald; Cecily Klingman; Diane Scanlon.
EIN: 046728351

1363
Ella Lyman Cabot Trust, Inc.
c/o Palmer & Dodge, LLP
111 Huntington Ave., 19th Fl.
Boston, MA 02199
Contact: Mary Jane Gibson, Exec. Secy.
Application address: c/o Brooks Thompson, 109 Rockland St., Holliston, MA 01746

Incorporated in 1939 in MA.
Donor(s): Richard Cabot.‡
Grantmaker type: Independent foundation
Financial data (yr. ended 12/31/02): Assets, $2,099,226 (M); gifts received, $11,500; expenditures, $129,121; qualifying distributions, $115,455; giving activities include $10,000 for 1 grant and $86,104 for 10 grants to individuals (high: $21,650; low: $2,125).
Purpose and activities: Grants to individuals for projects (sometimes involving a departure from one's usual vocation or a creative extension of it) with a promise of good to others. Awards are usually made on a one-year basis and are not renewed.
Fields of interest: Music; Humanities; Arts; Child development, education; Education; Environment; Health care; Health organizations, association; Biomedicine; Medical research, institute; Crime/law enforcement; Human services; Youth, services; Child development, services; Women, centers/services; International peace/security; Civil rights; Religion; Women.
Types of support: Grants to individuals.
Limitations: No support for organizations. No grants for scholarships, fellowships, research pursued as a regular part of a profession, or salaries during sabbatical leaves.
Publications: Application guidelines.
Application information: Proposals screened before application form is issued. Application form required.
  Initial approach: Letter and proposal, not exceeding 5 pages, including detailed budget
  Copies of proposal: 1

Deadline(s): Mar.1 and Oct.1
Board meeting date(s): May and Nov.
Final notification: Usually by May 15 and Nov. 15
Officers and Trustees:* Allan L. Friedlich,* Chair.; Hon. Mary Jane Gibson,* Exec. Secy.; Jeffrey Swope,* Treas.; Hon. Robert F. Bales; Andrew G. Bodnar; P. Sidney Cabot; Dudley W. Dudley; Rev. Peter J. Gomes; Ellen Harris; Richard Hocking; Elizabeth Osborne; Leroy S. Rouner; Philip Stone; Constance Williams.
Number of staff: 1 part-time professional.
EIN: 042111393

1364
Ward M. & Mariam C. Canaday Educational and Charitable Trust
c/o Fleet Private Client Group
100 Federal St.
Boston, MA 02110

Trust established in 1945 in OH.
Donor(s): Ward M. Canaday,‡ Mariam C. Canaday.‡
Grantmaker type: Independent foundation
Financial data (yr. ended 12/31/02): Assets, $14,085,477 (M); gifts received, $68,863; expenditures, $779,074; qualifying distributions, $767,107; giving activities include $720,274 for 38 grants (high: $89,000; low: $600).
Purpose and activities: Giving primarily for education, natural resource conservation, animal and wildlife protection, and human services.
Fields of interest: Humanities; Arts; Early childhood education; Libraries (public); Natural resources; Animals/wildlife; Human services; Federated giving programs.
Limitations: Applications not accepted. Giving primarily in VT. No grants to individuals.
Application information: Contributes only to pre-selected organizations.
  Board meeting date(s): Annually
Trustee: Fleet National Bank.
Number of staff: None.
EIN: 346523619

1365
Cape Cod Five Cents Savings Bank Charitable Trust
P.O. Box 10
Orleans, MA 02653-0010 (508) 247-2223
Contact: David B. Williard, Secy.

Established in 1998 in MA.
Donor(s): Cape Cod Five Cents Savings Bank.
Grantmaker type: Company-sponsored foundation
Financial data (yr. ended 12/31/02): Assets, $6,011,236 (M); gifts received, $1,740,000; expenditures, $263,076; qualifying distributions, $261,052; giving activities include $251,103 for 151 grants (high: $17,000; low: $140).
Purpose and activities: Giving to improve the quality of life for specific townships in MA.
Fields of interest: Arts; Education; Environment; Health care; Human services; Children/youth, services.
Types of support: Continuing support; Capital campaigns; Building/renovation; Land

acquisition; Program development;
Conferences/seminars; Scholarship funds.
Limitations: Giving limited for the benefit of
MA. No support for operating expenses,
fundraisers, third party events, or field trips.
Application information: Application form
required.
Copies of proposal: 1
Board meeting date(s): Every 7 weeks
Officers: Elliott Carr, Chair.; David Williard,
Secy.; Ronald Reed, Treas.
Number of staff: None.
EIN: 043423249

1366
Cardinal Brook Trust
(formerly Karen & David Davis Charitable Fund)
95 Maple Ln.
Petersham, MA   01366

Established in 1988 in MA.
Donor(s): David Davis, Karen Davis.
Grantmaker type: Independent foundation
Financial data (yr. ended 11/30/00): Assets,
$3,894,223 (M); gifts received, $704,989;
expenditures, $314,865; qualifying distributions,
$260,579; giving activities include $271,495 for
41 grants (high: $50,000; low: $200).
Fields of interest: Elementary/secondary
education; College; Natural resources;
Environment, forests; Human services.
Limitations: Applications not accepted. Giving
primarily in MA. No grants to individuals.
Application information: Contributes only to
pre-selected organizations.
Trustees: David Davis; Karen Davis.
EIN: 043050557

1367
Carlee Charitable Trust
c/o Loring, Wolcott, & Coolidge
230 Congress St.
Boston, MA   02110   (617) 523-6531
Contact: Frederick D. Ballou, Tr.

Established in 1995 in MA.
Donor(s): Jane H. Carlee.
Grantmaker type: Independent foundation
Financial data (yr. ended 12/31/02): Assets,
$3,471,785 (M); expenditures, $270,551;
qualifying distributions, $245,681; giving
activities include $242,250 for 4 grants (high:
$100,000; low: $36,000).
Purpose and activities: Giving for the protection
and care of domestic animals, the protection of
natural wildlife species, the conservation of
areas of natural habitat and beauty, and the
preservation of historic architecture in the New
England area.
Fields of interest: Natural resources; Animal
welfare.
Types of support: Capital campaigns; Land
acquisition; Seed money.
Limitations: Giving primarily in the Nantucket,
MA area. No grants to individuals.
Application information:
Initial approach: Letter
Deadline(s): None
Trustees: Frederick D. Ballou; William H. Hays
III; Patricia H. Loring.
EIN: 046796657

1368
Charles River Laboratories Foundation, Inc.
(formerly Charles River Foundation)
251 Ballardvale St.
Wilmington, MA   01887
Contact: Dennis R. Shaughnessy, Clerk

Donor(s): Charles River Laboratories, Inc.
Grantmaker type: Company-sponsored
foundation
Financial data (yr. ended 10/31/02): Assets,
$31,602 (M); gifts received, $235,000;
expenditures, $222,563; qualifying distributions,
$222,563; giving activities include $216,250 for
28 grants (high: $50,000; low: $150) and
$4,500 for 2 grants to individuals (high: $2,500;
low: $2,000).
Purpose and activities: Grants for research in
the field of biomedical science.
Fields of interest: Animal welfare; Biomedicine
research; Medical research.
Types of support: General/operating support.
Limitations: Giving primarily in MA.
Application information: Application form not
required.
Deadline(s): None
Officers and Directors:* Gilbert M. Slater,*
Chair. and V.P.; Marilyn Brown, Pres.; Dennis R.
Shaughnessy, Clerk; James C. Foster,* Treas.;
Henry L. Foster, D.V.M.
EIN: 510188208

1369
Chelonian Research Foundation
168 Goodrich St.
Lunenburg, MA   01462   (978) 582-9668
Contact: Anders G.J. Rhodin, Dir.

Established in 1999 in MA.
Donor(s): Anders G.J. Rhodin.
Grantmaker type: Operating foundation
Financial data (yr. ended 12/31/01): Assets,
$204,488 (M); gifts received, $88,298;
expenditures, $196,146; qualifying distributions,
$107,572; giving activities include $97,081 for
4 grants (high: $93,596; low: $860), $10,500 for
10 grants to individuals (high: $1,500; low:
$1,000) and $179,694 for 4
foundation-administered programs.
Purpose and activities: Support only to
individuals who deal in some capacity with
chelonians.
Fields of interest: Animals/wildlife,
preservation/protection.
Types of support: Scholarships—to individuals.
Application information:
Initial approach: Proposal
Deadline(s): Nov. 15
Directors: Russell A.M. Mittermeier; Peter C.H.
Pritchard; Anders G.J. Rhodin.
EIN: 046705444

1370
Roberta M. Childs Charitable Foundation
P.O. Box 639
North Andover, MA   01845   (978) 685-4113
Contact: John R.D. McClintock, Tr.

Established in 1978 in MA.
Donor(s): Roberta M. Childs.‡
Grantmaker type: Independent foundation

Financial data (yr. ended 03/31/03): Assets,
$5,171,544 (M); expenditures, $318,794;
qualifying distributions, $276,808; giving
activities include $276,000 for 58 grants (high:
$25,000; low: $1,500).
Purpose and activities: Giving primarily for
education, animal welfare, hospitals, youth
services, and the homeless.
Fields of interest: Higher education;
Scholarships/financial aid; Animal welfare;
Animals/wildlife, preservation/protection;
Hospitals (general); Food banks;
Housing/shelter; Youth development,
centers/clubs; Human services; Children/youth,
services; Homeless, human services.
Types of support: General/operating support;
Continuing support.
Limitations: Giving primarily in MA. No grants
to individuals.
Application information: Application form not
required.
Initial approach: Letter
Copies of proposal: 1
Deadline(s): None
Board meeting date(s): Varies
Trustee: John R.D. McClintock.
Number of staff: None.
EIN: 042660275

1371
Clark Charitable Trust
P.O. Box 681
Lincoln, MA   01773-0681
Contact: Timothy A. Taylor, Tr.

Established in 1937 in MA.
Grantmaker type: Independent foundation
Financial data (yr. ended 12/31/01): Assets,
$5,587,972 (M); expenditures, $325,673;
qualifying distributions, $318,869; giving
activities include $259,500 for 14 grants (high:
$89,500; low: $1,000).
Purpose and activities: Support for preservation
of wildlands, animal welfare, music, food banks,
and higher education.
Fields of interest: Music; Higher education;
Animal welfare; Animals/wildlife,
preservation/protection; Food banks.
Types of support: General/operating support;
Annual campaigns; Capital campaigns;
Building/renovation; Equipment; Land
acquisition; Endowments; Scholarship funds;
Matching/challenge support.
Limitations: Giving on a national basis.
Publications: Financial statement.
Application information: Application form not
required.
Initial approach: Letter
Deadline(s): None
Trustees: Russel T. Kopp; Timothy A. Taylor.
EIN: 046037650

1372
Cogan Family Foundation
c/o Hale and Dorr, LLP
P.O. Box 9350
Boston, MA   02209

Established in 2000 in MA.
Donor(s): John F. Cogan, Jr.
Grantmaker type: Independent foundation

Financial data (yr. ended 08/31/02): Assets, $18,454,016 (M); expenditures, $686,084; qualifying distributions, $662,392; giving activities include $660,000 for 50 grants (high: $100,000; low: $1,000).
Fields of interest: Museums (art); Arts; Higher education; Libraries/library science; Education; Animals/wildlife, preservation/protection; Hospitals (general); Parkinson's disease research; Housing/shelter, development; Disasters, 9/11/01; Human services.
Limitations: Applications not accepted. Giving primarily in CA, MA, and NY. No grants to individuals.
Application information: Contributes only to pre-selected organizations.
Trustees: Gregory Cogan; John F. Cogan, Jr.; Mary Cornille; Pamela Cogan Riddle.
EIN: 046923387

1373
The Community Foundation of Cape Cod
295 Willow St.
P.O. Box 406
Yarmouth Port, MA 02675 (508) 790-3040
Contact: Elizabeth Gawron, Exec. Dir., or Lisa McNeill, Prog. Off.
Additional tel.: (800) 947-2322; FAX: (508) 790-4069; E-mail: info@capecodfoundation.org; URL: http://www.capecodfoundation.org

Established in 1989 in MA.
Grantmaker type: Community foundation
Financial data (yr. ended 12/31/02): Assets, $30,066,587 (M); gifts received, $5,765,627; expenditures, $4,186,697; giving activities include $3,848,137 for grants.
Purpose and activities: Giving primarily for the arts and human services. The foundation administers donor-advised funds.
Fields of interest: Humanities; Arts; Environment; Human services; Youth, services; Economic development; Economically disadvantaged.
Types of support: Continuing support; Management development; Endowments; Seed money; Scholarship funds; Technical assistance; Grants to individuals; Scholarships—to individuals; In-kind gifts; Matching/challenge support; Student loans—to individuals.
Limitations: Giving limited to Barnstable County, MA. No grants for general operating expenses.
Publications: Application guidelines, Informational brochure, Newsletter.
Application information: Application form required.
Initial approach: Letter or phone
Copies of proposal: 10
Deadline(s): Apr. 1 and Oct. 1
Board meeting date(s): Bimonthly; Semiannually for Grant Review meetings
Final notification: Within 60 days
Officers and Directors:* James Vaccaro,* Chair and Pres.; Joseph A. Signore,* V.P.; Brooks S. Thayer, Clerk; Roger W. Ludwig,* Treas.; Elizabeth Gawron, Exec. Dir.; Kenneth S. Brock; Mary Cotoia; George Dillon; Gene Kennedy; Bruce S. MacKilligan; Robert S. Marshall; Stuart J. Nickerson; Brian O'Connell; Jennifer S.D. Roberts; Lois Taylor.
Number of staff: 2 full-time professional; 1 full-time support; 1 part-time support.

EIN: 510140462

1374
Community Foundation of Southeastern Massachusetts
227 Union St., Ste. 609
New Bedford, MA 02740 (508) 996-8253
Contact: Anne M. Beaulieu, Pres.
FAX: (508) 996-8254; URL: http://www.cfsema.com

Established in 1995 in MA.
Grantmaker type: Community foundation
Financial data (yr. ended 12/31/02): Assets, $3,666,595 (M); gifts received, $879,713; expenditures, $647,114; giving activities include $390,845 for grants.
Purpose and activities: To support programs that improve the quality of life for residents of the 41 towns and cities in Southeastern MA. The foundation administers a donor-advised fund.
Fields of interest: Historic preservation/historical societies; Arts; Child development, education; Education; Environment; Health care; Mental health, treatment; Medical research, institute; Housing/shelter; Disasters, preparedness/services; Human services; Child development, services; Children/youth, services; Children, services; Family services; Economic development; Community development; Leadership development.
Types of support: General/operating support; Management development; Building/renovation; Emergency funds; Program development; Seed money; Scholarship funds.
Limitations: Giving primarily in southeastern MA.
Publications: Application guidelines, Financial statement, Informational brochure, Multi-year report.
Application information: Application form required.
Initial approach: Letter or telephone for application guidelines
Copies of proposal: 9
Deadline(s): None
Board meeting date(s): Monthly
Final notification: In writing
Officers and Directors:* Peter Bullard,* Chair.; Elizabeth Isherwood,* Vice-Chair.; Anne M. Beaulieu,* Pres.; Samuel McFadden,* Secy.; Mary Louise Nunes,* Treas.
Number of staff: 3 full-time professional; 1 full-time support; 1 part-time support.
EIN: 043280353

1375
Community Foundation of Western Massachusetts
1500 Main St., Ste. 2300
P.O. Box 15769
Springfield, MA 01115 (413) 732-2858
Contact: Kent W. Faerber, Pres.
FAX: (413) 733-8565; E-mail: wmass@communityfoundation.org; URL: http://www.communityfoundation.org

Established in 1991 in MA.
Grantmaker type: Community foundation
Financial data (yr. ended 03/31/03): Assets, $60,961,887 (M); gifts received, $9,354,011;

expenditures, $4,781,881; giving activities include $4,781,881 for grants.
Purpose and activities: The foundation administers a donor-advised fund.
Fields of interest: Performing arts; Historic preservation/historical societies; Arts; Education, fund raising; Adult/continuing education; Adult education—literacy, basic skills & GED; Libraries/library science; Reading; Education; Natural resources; Environment; Animals/wildlife, preservation/protection; Hospitals (general); Family planning; Medical care, rehabilitation; Health care; Substance abuse, services; Health organizations, association; Cancer; Heart & circulatory diseases; AIDS; Crime/violence prevention, youth; Crime/law enforcement; Housing/shelter, development; Safety/disasters; Recreation; Human services; Children/youth, services; Aging, centers/services; Women, centers/services; Minorities/immigrants, centers/services; Civil rights; Community development; Voluntarism promotion; Public policy, research; Public affairs; Minorities; Native Americans/American Indians; Disabled; Aging; Women; Gays/lesbians; Economically disadvantaged.
Types of support: Capital campaigns; Building/renovation; Equipment; Program development; Conferences/seminars; Publication; Seed money; Scholarship funds; Technical assistance; Scholarships—to individuals; Matching/challenge support.
Limitations: Giving limited to western MA, including on Hampden County, Hampshire County, and Franklin County. No support for political or religious organizations, private secondary or higher education. No grants to individuals directly, or for operating budgets, endowments, fundraising events, tickets for benefits, courtesy advertising, academic or medical research or multi-year funding.
Publications: Application guidelines, Annual report, Grants list, Informational brochure, Newsletter.
Application information: Application form required.
Initial approach: Telephone
Copies of proposal: 3
Deadline(s): Jan. 30, June 1 and Oct. 1
Board meeting date(s): Quarterly
Final notification: Within 3 months
Officers and Trustees:* Robert Carroll,* Chair.; Kent W. Faerber,* C.E.O. and Pres.; Nancy Reiche, V.P., Progs.; Michael Riley, C.F.O.; Robert B. Atkinson; Charles P. Barker; Bruce Brown; Marcia Burrick; Robert S. Cohn; Ruth Constantine; Helen S. Fuller; John G. Gallup; Kurt M. Hertzfeld; Orlando Isaza; M. Trish Robinson; Donna Ross; Jean Salter Roetter; William Sadowsky; David Starr; Albert E. Steiger, Jr.; Elizabeth D. Scheibel; R. Lyman Wood; Angela Wright; Richard Zilewicz.
Number of staff: 5 full-time professional; 1 part-time professional; 5 full-time support.
EIN: 223089640

1376
Conservation, Food and Health Foundation, Inc.
c/o Grant Mgmt. Assocs.
77 Summer St., 8th Fl.
Boston, MA 02110 (617) 426-7172
Contact: Prentice Zinn
FAX: (617) 426-5441; E-mail: cfhf@grantsmanagement.com; URL: http://www.grantsmanagement.com/cfhguide.html

Established in 1985 in MA.
Grantmaker type: Independent foundation
Financial data (yr. ended 12/31/01): Assets, $8,756,038 (M); expenditures, $1,440,752; qualifying distributions, $970,827; giving activities include $961,093 for grants (average: $5,000–$15,000).
Purpose and activities: Giving limited to projects of benefit to the Third World.
Fields of interest: Natural resources; Environment; Animals/wildlife, preservation/protection; Health care; Agriculture; Agriculture/food.
International interests: Developing countries.
Types of support: Program development; Seed money; Research; Technical assistance.
Limitations: Giving limited to benefit Third World countries. No support for famine, emergency relief, or for overhead expenses of large institutions. No grants to individuals (except for research efforts sponsored by organizations and institutions), or for building or land purchase, endowments, fundraising activities, or general operating support.
Publications: Application guidelines, Grants list.
Application information: FAX or E-mail proposals will not be accepted. Application guidelines available on foundation Web site. Application form required.
  Initial approach: Letter of inquiry or concept paper
  Copies of proposal: 5
  Deadline(s): Nov. 1 and May 1 for concept papers; Feb. 1 and Aug. 1 for invited proposals
  Board meeting date(s): Apr. and Oct.
  Final notification: Immediately after board meetings
Officer: Philip M. Fearnside, Pres.
Number of staff: 2 shared staff.
EIN: 222625024

1377
Copeland Family Foundation, Inc.
1183 Randolph Ave.
Milton, MA 02186 (617) 698-5980
Contact: Martha Verdone, Pres.

Established around 1983.
Grantmaker type: Independent foundation
Financial data (yr. ended 03/31/01): Assets, $41,074,735 (M); gifts received, $7,906,769; expenditures, $2,648,230; qualifying distributions, $2,141,527; giving activities include $2,175,075 for 192 grants (high: $350,000; low: $75; average: $5,000–$15,000).
Purpose and activities: Giving primarily for education, animal welfare, hospitals, health associations, human services, community development, and Christian agencies and churches.

Fields of interest: Education; Animal welfare; Hospitals (general); Health organizations, association; Human services; Community development; Christian agencies & churches.
Limitations: Giving primarily in MA, with emphasis on Milton.
Application information:
  Initial approach: Letter
  Deadline(s): None
Officers and Directors:* Martha Verdone,* Pres.; Owen M. Carle,* Clerk and Treas.; Joyce Tobin,* Clerk; John Tobin,* Treas.; A. Gladys Copeland; Gladys M. Eager; John Everets; Elizabeth Verdone.
EIN: 222474056

1378
The Ruth Covo Family Foundation
c/o Hale and Dorr, LLP
P.O. Box 9350
Boston, MA 02209

Established in 1987 in MA.
Donor(s): Ruth U. Covo.
Grantmaker type: Independent foundation
Financial data (yr. ended 12/31/02): Assets, $1,417,661 (M); expenditures, $106,365; qualifying distributions, $87,235; giving activities include $89,000 for 10 grants (high: $30,000; low: $2,000).
Purpose and activities: Giving primarily for wildlife preservation.
Fields of interest: Higher education; Natural resources; Medical specialty research.
Limitations: Applications not accepted. Giving on a national basis, with some emphasis on the greater metropolitan Washington, DC, area, Boston, MA, NY, and PA. No grants to individuals.
Application information: Contributes only to pre-selected organizations.
Trustees: Joanne Covo; Marilyn Covo; Jennifer C. Snyder.
EIN: 046584378

1379
Cox Foundation, Inc.
c/o Hemenway & Barnes
P.O. Box 6842
Boston, MA 02102
Contact: Michael J. Puzo, Dir.

Established in 1970.
Donor(s): William C. Cox, Jr.
Grantmaker type: Independent foundation
Financial data (yr. ended 12/31/01): Assets, $22,550,714 (M); gifts received, $1,000,000; expenditures, $1,463,395; qualifying distributions, $1,355,996; giving activities include $1,336,000 for grants.
Purpose and activities: Giving primarily for education, conservation, and human services.
Fields of interest: Museums; Arts; Secondary school/education; Natural resources; Environment; Hospitals (general); Medical research, institute.
Types of support: General/operating support; Continuing support; Annual campaigns; Capital campaigns; Land acquisition; Program development; Research.
Limitations: Applications not accepted. Giving primarily in FL and MA. No grants to individuals.

Application information: Contributes only to pre-selected organizations.
  Board meeting date(s): Dec.
Officers and Directors:* William C. Cox, Jr.,* Pres.; Roy A. Hammer,* Clerk; Martha W. Cox,* Treas.; Michael J. Puzo.
EIN: 237068786

1380
Crane & Co. Fund
c/o E.M. Pomeroy
30 South St.
Dalton, MA 01226
Contact: John R. Schulte, Tr.

Established in 1953 in MA.
Donor(s): Crane & Co., Inc., Byron-Weston Co.
Grantmaker type: Company-sponsored foundation
Financial data (yr. ended 12/31/02): Assets, $0 (M); gifts received, $211,620; expenditures, $211,620; qualifying distributions, $211,620; giving activities include $211,550 for 20 grants (high: $88,500; low: $100).
Purpose and activities: Giving primarily to charitable organizations in Berkshire County, MA, and to charities that benefit employees of Crane & Co.
Fields of interest: Museums; Arts; Education; Natural resources; Health care; Health organizations, association; Human services; Federated giving programs; Government/public administration.
Types of support: General/operating support; Annual campaigns; Capital campaigns.
Limitations: Giving limited to Berkshire County, MA. No grants to individuals.
Application information: Application form not required.
  Initial approach: Letter
Trustees: Lansing E. Crane; Richard D. Kendall; John R. Schulte.
EIN: 046057388

1381
Louise Crane Foundation
P.O. Box 901
Falmouth, MA 02541

Established in 1963 in NY.
Donor(s): Louise Crane.‡
Grantmaker type: Independent foundation
Financial data (yr. ended 12/31/01): Assets, $36,640,927 (M); expenditures, $2,739,260; qualifying distributions, $2,494,677; giving activities include $2,500,000 for 22 grants (high: $350,000; low: $10,000; average: $25,000–$150,000).
Purpose and activities: Giving primarily for environmental issues and health care.
Fields of interest: Arts; Environment; Hospitals (general); Health organizations, association; Community development.
Types of support: General/operating support; Continuing support; Capital campaigns.
Limitations: Applications not accepted. Giving primarily in Berkshire County, MA. No grants to individuals.
Application information: Contributes only to pre-selected organizations. Unsolicited requests for funds not considered.

Officers and Directors:* Davis C. Greene,* Pres.; Winnie C. Mackey,* V.P.; William K. Mackey,* Secy.-Treas.
Number of staff: None.
EIN: 136119886

1382
Creighton Family Foundation
c/o Peabody & Arnold
50 Rowes Wharf
Boston, MA 02110

Established in 1964 in MA.
Grantmaker type: Independent foundation
Financial data (yr. ended 12/31/01): Assets, $1,936,111 (M); expenditures, $124,859; qualifying distributions, $111,987; giving activities include $105,000 for 30 grants (high: $22,000; low: $100).
Purpose and activities: Giving for boys and girls clubs, educational purposes, medical services and public services.
Fields of interest: Television; Museums (science/technology); Environment; Hospitals (general); Boys & girls clubs; Federated giving programs.
Types of support: General/operating support.
Limitations: Applications not accepted. Giving primarily in FL, MA, and NY. No grants to individuals.
Application information: Contributes only to pre-selected organizations.
Trustees: Albert M. Creighton, Jr.; Peter M. Shapland; Benjamin Williams, Jr.
EIN: 046148712

1383
The Cricket Foundation
Exchange Pl., Ste. 2200
Boston, MA 02109-2881   (617) 570-1130
Contact: George W. Butterworth, Counsel
E-mail: gbutterworth@goodwinprocter.com

Established in 1978 in MA.
Grantmaker type: Independent foundation
Financial data (yr. ended 09/30/02): Assets, $2,523,610 (M); expenditures, $196,675; qualifying distributions, $175,202; giving activities include $160,000 for 21 grants (high: $15,000; low: $5,000).
Fields of interest: Visual arts; Museums; Performing arts; Natural resources; Environment.
Types of support: General/operating support; Capital campaigns; Building/renovation; Equipment; Land acquisition; Program development; Conferences/seminars; Publication; Seed money; Research; Matching/challenge support.
Limitations: Giving primarily in the northeastern U.S. No support for religious organizations. No grants to individuals.
Publications: Application guidelines.
Application information: Application form not required.
  Initial approach: Letter or proposal
  Copies of proposal: 1
  Deadline(s): Apr. 30 and Oct. 31
  Board meeting date(s): May and Nov.
  Final notification: June 30 and Dec. 31
Trustee: A. Joshua Sherman.
Number of staff: 1 part-time professional.
EIN: 042655735

1384
The Croll Foundation
c/o Goodwin, Proctor, LLP
Exchange Pl.
Boston, MA 02109-2881

Established in 1987 in MA.
Donor(s): David D. Croll, Victoria B. Croll.
Grantmaker type: Independent foundation
Financial data (yr. ended 10/31/02): Assets, $18,033,162 (M); expenditures, $834,066; qualifying distributions, $799,133; giving activities include $799,133 for 37 grants (high: $175,000; low: $500).
Purpose and activities: Giving primarily for the arts, higher and other education, hospitals, including a children's hospital, Christian churches and the United Way.
Fields of interest: Museums; Historic preservation/historical societies; Secondary school/education; Higher education; Business school/education; Education; Natural resources; Hospitals (general); Hospitals (specialty); Federated giving programs; Christian agencies & churches.
Types of support: Scholarship funds.
Limitations: Applications not accepted. Giving primarily in MA. No grants to individuals.
Application information: Contributes only to pre-selected organizations.
Trustees: David D. Croll; Victoria B. Croll.
EIN: 222946282

1385
Devonshire Associates
75 Federal St., Ste. 1100
Boston, MA 02110-1911

Incorporated in 1949 in MA.
Donor(s): Melita S. Howland,‡ Weston Howland, Jr., Weston Howland III, Susan H. Power.
Grantmaker type: Independent foundation
Financial data (yr. ended 12/31/02): Assets, $5,499,432 (M); expenditures, $393,850; qualifying distributions, $353,320; giving activities include $352,857 for 12 grants (high: $150,000; low: $500).
Purpose and activities: Emphasis on a college and an aquarium; support also for cultural programs, higher education, and youth agencies.
Fields of interest: Arts; Higher education; Natural resources; Children/youth, services.
Limitations: Applications not accepted. Giving primarily in MA. No grants to individuals.
Application information: Contributes only to pre-selected organizations.
Officers and Trustees:* Weston Howland, Jr.,* Pres.; Weston Howland III,* Secy.-Treas.; H.A. Tubman.
EIN: 046004808

1386
Laura Stratton Dewey Foundation
c/o John A. Tyler Assocs.
186 Alewife Brook Pkwy., Ste. 200
Cambridge, MA 02138-1121

Established in 1965 in NY.
Donor(s): Laurie Dewey.
Grantmaker type: Independent foundation

Financial data (yr. ended 12/31/01): Assets, $1,195,697 (M); gifts received, $17,026; expenditures, $131,850; qualifying distributions, $114,298; giving activities include $114,500 for 20 grants (high: $20,000; low: $1,000).
Fields of interest: Media/communications; Museums; Education; Natural resources; International affairs.
Limitations: Applications not accepted. Giving primarily in Washington, DC and MA. No grants to individuals.
Application information: Contributes only to pre-selected organizations.
Trustees: Laurie T. Dewey; Reed T. Dewey; Robert Zevin.
EIN: 166054218

1387
Paul W. DiMaura Charitable Trust
c/o Laurie E. Cutler, PC
60 State St.
Boston, MA 02109

Established in 1992 in MA.
Donor(s): Paul W. DiMaura.
Grantmaker type: Independent foundation
Financial data (yr. ended 12/31/01): Assets, $1,228,241 (M); gifts received, $11,967; expenditures, $113,478; qualifying distributions, $99,500; giving activities include $99,500 for 26 grants (high: $60,000; low: $100).
Purpose and activities: Giving for higher education, hospitals, health and medical treatment, and research.
Fields of interest: University; Environment, forests; Hospitals (general); Health organizations; Human services.
Limitations: Applications not accepted. No grants to individuals.
Application information: Contributes only to pre-selected organizations.
Trustees: Karen S. DiMaura; Paul W. DiMaura.
EIN: 046720853

1388
The Dragon Foundation, Inc.
P.O. Box 515
Rochester, MA 02770-0515
Contact: Daniel L. Clark, Pres.

Established in 1985 in ME.
Donor(s): Mariana L. Clark, Robert L. Clark.
Grantmaker type: Independent foundation
Financial data (yr. ended 11/30/02): Assets, $784,203 (M); expenditures, $167,061; qualifying distributions, $156,114; giving activities include $153,000 for 43 grants (high: $10,000; low: $250).
Purpose and activities: Giving for higher education, hospitals, health associations, and marine science.
Fields of interest: Elementary/secondary education; Higher education; Natural resources; Hospitals (general); Family planning; Nursing care; Health organizations, association; Developmentally disabled, centers & services; Women, centers/services; Marine science.
Limitations: Giving primarily in CT and ME. No grants to individuals.
Application information: Application form not required.
  Initial approach: Letter

Deadline(s): None
Officers and Directors:* Daniel L. Clark,* Pres.
and Treas.; Peter L Clark,* V.P.; Victoria Clark
Dibner,* Secy.; Christopher L. Clark; Paul E.
Clark.
EIN: 010412143

1389
The Carlton Dub Foundation
c/o CitiCorp Trust, N.A.
125 Summer St., 17th Fl.
Boston, MA 02110

Grantmaker type: Independent foundation
Financial data (yr. ended 02/28/03): Assets,
$5,252,334 (M); expenditures, $446,492;
qualifying distributions, $377,000; giving
activities include $310,000 for 10 grants (high:
$62,000; low: $7,750).
Purpose and activities: Giving primarily for
health associations, human services, and to an
Episcopal church.
Fields of interest: Animal welfare; Health
organizations, association; Human services;
Protestant agencies & churches.
Limitations: Applications not accepted. Giving
primarily in Palm Beach, FL.
Application information: Contributes only to
pre-selected organizations.
Trustee: Citibank, N.A.
EIN: 116473887

1390
The Dusky Foundation
50 Congress St., Ste. 925
Boston, MA 02109-4002
Contact: Robert S. Gulick, Tr.

Established in 1991 in MA.
Grantmaker type: Independent foundation
Financial data (yr. ended 12/31/02): Assets,
$2,568,881 (M); expenditures, $436,941;
qualifying distributions, $415,228; giving
activities include $416,500 for 27 grants (high:
$100,000; low: $1,000).
Purpose and activities: Giving primarily for
education, social, cultural, and inner-city.
Fields of interest: Music; Arts; Higher education;
Education; Natural resources.
Types of support: General/operating support;
Continuing support; Capital campaigns;
Building/renovation; Equipment.
Limitations: Giving primarily in New England,
with emphasis on Boston, MA. No grants to
individuals.
Application information: Application form not
required.
  Copies of proposal: 1
  Deadline(s): Apr. 30 (for mid-year grants) and
    Oct. 31 (for year-end grants)
  Board meeting date(s): Quarterly
Trustees: J. Linzee Coolidge; Robert S. Gulick.
EIN: 043122206

1391
Earthwatch Expeditions, Inc.
(also known as Earthwatch Institute)
3 Clock Tower Pl., Ste. 100
Maynard, MA 01754   (978) 461-0081
Contact: Beth Morris, Fellowship Prog. Off.
FAX: (978) 461-2332; E-mail:
info@earthwatch.org; URL: http://
www.earthwatch.org

Established in 1971 in MA.
Grantmaker type: Public charity
Financial data (yr. ended 09/30/01): Revenue,
$9,803,045; assets, $3,514,683; gifts received,
$8,697,907; expenditures, $8,480,142; program
services expenses, $6,576,669; giving activities
include $523,556 for grants to individuals.
Purpose and activities: The institute globally
promotes sustainable conservation of natural
resources and cultural heritage by creating
partnerships between scientists, educators and
the general public through volunteer-based
research initiatives. No monetary support is
available.
Fields of interest: Environment, research;
Natural resources.
Types of support: Fellowships; Research.
Application information: Application forms
requesting volunteers for research are available
through Earthwatch Expeditions' affiliate, the
Center for Field Research; See Web site for other
forms.
  Initial approach: Telephone
  Deadline(s): None for Research Grants; Mar. 1
    for Education Awards; Nov. 12 for Student
    Challenge Awards nomination, Jan. 3 for
    ensuing application
  Final notification: Late Mar. for Student
    Challenge Awards
Officers and Directors:* William G. Meserve,*
Chair.; William R. Moomaw, Ph.D.,*
Vice-Chair.; Chester G. Atkins; Roger V.D.
Bergen; Amy Ruth Borun Dewind; G. Keith
Funston, Jr.; Jeremy Guth; James S. Hoyte;
Francis O. Hunnewell; and 14 additional
directors.
Number of staff: 46.
EIN: 237168440

1392
Eco-Logic Development Fund
25 Mt. Auburn St., Ste. 203
Cambridge, MA 02138   (617) 441-6300
Contact: Shaun Paul, Pres. and Exec. Dir.
FAX: (617) 441-6307; E-mail: info@ecologic.org;
URL: http://www.ecologic.org/

Established in 1993 in PA.
Grantmaker type: Public charity
Financial data (yr. ended 12/31/02): Revenue,
$674,649; assets, $54,218 (M); gifts received,
$673,599; expenditures, $1,189,062; program
services expenses, $987,415; giving activities
include $818,054 for 9 grants (high: $350,000;
low: $4,248).
Purpose and activities: The fund seeks to
preserve the diversity of tropical ecosystems and
promote the well-being of local inhabitants
through small scale community-based
development in threatened areas.
Fields of interest: Environment.
International interests: Latin America.

Limitations: Applications not accepted. Giving
limited to Latin America.
Application information: Contributes only to
pre-selected organizations; unsolicited requests
for funds not considered or acknowledged.
Officers and Directors:* William Russell Grace
Byers, Jr.,* Chair.; Shaun Paul,* Pres. and Exec.
Dir.; Mark Bookman, JD,* Treas.; Elsa Chang;
David Crocker; Ronald Davenport; Marcela O.
de Rovzar; Leslie Harroun; Gert Rosenthal;
Winstead Rouse.
EIN: 251704582

1393
Elfers Foundation, Inc.
c/o Choate, Hall & Stewart
53 State St., Exchange Pl., 35th Fl.
Boston, MA 02109-2804

Established in 1970 in MA.
Donor(s): William Elfers.
Grantmaker type: Independent foundation
Financial data (yr. ended 11/30/02): Assets,
$4,962,754 (M); expenditures, $298,402;
qualifying distributions, $259,097; giving
activities include $243,650 for 68 grants (high:
$25,000; low: $100).
Purpose and activities: Giving for Christian
churches, wildlife conservation, diabetes
services and higher education.
Fields of interest: Elementary/secondary
education; Higher education; Animal welfare;
Medical research, institute; Children/youth,
services; Christian agencies & churches.
Limitations: Applications not accepted. Giving
primarily in MA. No grants to individuals.
Application information: Contributes only to
pre-selected organizations.
Officers and Directors:* Ann R. Elfers,* Chair.;
William R. Elfers,* Pres.; David E. Place,* Secy.;
William Elfers,* Treas.; Joanne Elfers; Jane Elfers
Muther.
EIN: 237090080

1394
Environmental Leadership Program, Inc.
132 Main St.
P.O. Box 446
Haydenville, MA 01039   (413) 268-0035
Contact: Paul Sabin, Exec. Dir.
Additional address: 649 Massachusetts Ave., Ste.
8, 2nd Fl., Cambridge, MA 02139, tel.: (617)
354-4052; FAX: (413) 268-0036; E-mail:
info@elpnet.org; URL: http://www.elpnet.org

Grantmaker type: Public charity
Financial data (yr. ended 12/31/01): Revenue,
$856,725; assets, $517,541; gifts received,
$844,860; expenditures, $747,551; program
services expenses, $538,056; giving activities
include $184,650 for 28 grants to individuals.
Purpose and activities: The organization
transforms public understanding of
environmental issues by training and supporting
a diverse network of visionary, action-oriented
emerging leaders.
Fields of interest: Environment.
Limitations: Giving on a national basis.
Application information: See Web site for
application information. Application form
required.
  Deadline(s): Oct. 1

Final notification: Mid Dec.
Director and Trustees: Paul Sabin, Exec. Dir.; Mary Bills; Don Chen; Katherine Dawes; Michael Dorsey; and 9 additional trustees.
EIN: 043521791

1395
ESB Charitable Trust
c/o Lowell Blake & Assoc.
141 Tremont St.
Boston, MA   02111-1209

Established in 1999 CT and MA.
Donor(s): Ellen C. Burt, Stuart D. Burt, Jr.
Grantmaker type: Independent foundation
Financial data (yr. ended 12/31/02): Assets, $2,366,628 (M); gifts received, $709,527; expenditures, $97,848; qualifying distributions, $91,798; giving activities include $90,000 for 7 grants (high: $30,000; low: $2,000).
Fields of interest: Environment.
Limitations: Applications not accepted. Giving on a national basis, with emphasis on CT, MA, and NY. No grants to individuals.
Application information: Contributes only to pre-selected organizations.
Trustees: Ellen C. Burt; John F. Burt; Laurie Burt; S. Jeffrey Burt; Stuart D. Burt.
EIN: 066487362

1396
Farm Aid
11 Ward St., Ste. 200
Somerville, MA   02143   (617) 354-2922
Contact: Ted Quaday, Prog. Dir.
Additional tel.: (800) FARM-AID; FAX: (617) 354-6992; E-mail: farmaid1@aol.com

Established in 1985.
Grantmaker type: Public charity
Financial data (yr. ended 12/31/01): Revenue, $892,017; gifts received, $661,361; expenditures, $1,019,807; program services expenses, $796,991; giving activities include $344,636 for 43+ grants.
Purpose and activities: Grants are given for five types of programs: emergency relief funds to help farm families cope in the short-term; telephone hotline programs for farmers in financial and emotional crisis; legal services for farmers; programs providing information to farmers on issues such as credit, land stewardship, and farm policy, or which provide public education on family farm systems; and funds which make it possible for organizations to build long-term solutions to the problems farmers face. The organization also has an interest in organic and sustainable agriculture.
Fields of interest: Agriculture; Agriculture, farm cooperatives; Agriculture, farmlands.
Types of support: General/operating support; Emergency funds; Program development; Scholarship funds.
Limitations: Giving limited to the U.S. No support for programs that influence legislation or elections, or personal or commercial services. No grants to individuals, or for capital campaigns, equipment purchases, endowments, deficit financing, media productions, legal defense funds, historic preservation of farms or buildings, or for conferences, publications, or

research projects not directly connected to program activities.
Publications: Application guidelines, Annual report, Informational brochure, Newsletter.
Application information: Application form not required.
    Copies of proposal: 1
    Deadline(s): Varies
Officers and Directors:* Willie Nelson,* Pres.; Lana Nelson,* Secy.; Paul English,* Treas.; Carolyn Mugar, Exec. Dir.; David Anderson; Joel Katz; Dave Matthews; John Mellencamp; Mark Rothbaum; Evelyn Shriver; Neil Young.
Number of staff: 6 full-time professional; 2 part-time professional.
EIN: 363383233

1397
The Elizabeth T. Fessenden Charitable Foundation
c/o R H & B, Inc.
50 Congress St., Ste. 1025
Boston, MA   02109

Established in 1995 in MA.
Grantmaker type: Independent foundation
Financial data (yr. ended 07/31/02): Assets, $6,253,749 (M); expenditures, $503,843; qualifying distributions, $476,791; giving activities include $470,000 for 22 grants (high: $75,000; low: $5,000).
Purpose and activities: Giving primarily for education and theater.
Fields of interest: Television; Museums (art); Orchestra (symphony); Historic preservation/historical societies; Higher education; Libraries (public); Education; Natural resources; Botanical gardens; Horticulture/garden clubs; Hospitals (general); Family planning.
Limitations: Applications not accepted. Giving limited to MA. No grants to individuals.
Application information: Contributes only to pre-selected organizations.
Trustees: Katherine C. Ferguson; Neil W. Rice; Louise C. Riemer.
EIN: 223432161

1398
Fiduciary Charitable Foundation
c/o Fiduciary Trust Co.
P.O. Box 1647
Boston, MA   02105-1647   (617) 482-5270
Contact: Rosalyn Sovie

Established in 1990.
Grantmaker type: Public charity
Financial data (yr. ended 12/31/01): Revenue, $4,583,125; assets, $151,509 (M); gifts received, $4,606,621; expenditures, $4,510,465; program services expenses, $4,510,215; giving activities include $4,510,215 for 676 grants (high: $700,000; low: $300).
Purpose and activities: The foundation supports various charitable organizations, with a focus on art, education, health care, and human services.
Fields of interest: Museums; College; University; Education; Environment; Health care; Religion.
Trustee: Fiduciary Trust Co.
EIN: 046649138

1399
Fields Pond Foundation, Inc.
5 Turner St.
P.O. Box 540667
Waltham, MA   02454-0667   (781) 899-9990
Contact: Brian H. Rehrig, V.P.
FAX: (781) 899-2819; E-mail: info@fieldspond.org; URL: http://www.fieldspond.org

Established in 1993 in MA.
Grantmaker type: Independent foundation
Financial data (yr. ended 12/31/02): Assets, $9,222,822 (M); gifts received, $4,375; expenditures, $379,173; qualifying distributions, $442,285; giving activities include $335,100 for 57 grants (high: $335,100; low: $57).
Purpose and activities: Provides assistance to nature and land conservation organizations which are community based, and which serve to increase environmental awareness by involving local residents in conservation issues.
Fields of interest: Natural resources; Environment.
Types of support: Capital campaigns; Land acquisition; Endowments; Emergency funds; Seed money; Matching/challenge support.
Limitations: Giving primarily in New England. No support for sectarian religious activities. No grants to individuals; or for deficit financing, routine operating budgets, or for funding usually supported by public subscription or through national appeals.
Publications: Application guidelines, Grants list.
Application information: Application form not required.
    Initial approach: Organizations may submit a 1-page outline before full proposal
    Copies of proposal: 2
    Deadline(s): None
    Board meeting date(s): Bimonthly
Officers and Directors:* Leon H. Cohen,* Pres. and Treas.; Brian H. Rehrig,* V.P.; Rhoda R. Cohen,* Clerk; Elizabeth S. Bercow; Nina R. Cohen; Russell A. Cohen.
Number of staff: 1 part-time professional; 1 part-time support.
EIN: 043196041

1400
Fieldstone Foundation, Inc.
(formerly Meetinghouse Foundation, Inc.)
c/o TSG Equity Partners, LLC
636 Great Rd., Ste. 202
Stow, MA   01775

Established in 1990 in MA.
Donor(s): Thomas R. Shepherd.
Grantmaker type: Independent foundation
Financial data (yr. ended 12/31/01): Assets, $5,496,437 (M); expenditures, $497,833; qualifying distributions, $402,354; giving activities include $402,800 for 43 grants (high: $25,000; low: $3,500).
Purpose and activities: Giving primarily for education and the arts.
Fields of interest: Arts; Elementary/secondary education; Early childhood education; Higher education; Environment.
Limitations: Applications not accepted. Giving primarily in MA and VT. No grants to individuals.
Application information: Contributes only to pre-selected organizations.

Officers and Directors:* Nancy Shepherd,* Pres.; Katharine S. Furney,* Clerk; Thomas R. Shepherd,* Treas.; Elizabeth R. Shepherd; Ruth H. Shepherd; T. Nathanial Shepherd.
EIN: 223111728

1401
The FIRSTFED Charitable Foundation
1 FIRSTFED Park Dr.
Swansea, MA 02777 (508) 679-8181
Contact: Stacie Charbonneau, Fdn. Coord.
E-mail: foundation@firstfedamerica.com; FAX: (508) 235-1684; URL: http://www.firstfedamerica.com/foundation/index.htm

Established in 1996 in MA.
Donor(s): FIRSTFED AMERICA BANCORP, INC.
Grantmaker type: Company-sponsored foundation
Financial data (yr. ended 03/31/02): Assets, $14,455,730 (M); expenditures, $430,426; qualifying distributions, $414,163; giving activities include $325,430 for 114 grants (high: $10,000; low: $25; average: $25–$25,000).
Purpose and activities: Making awards, grants and other distributions designed to expand home ownership opportunities in the communities in which First Federal Savings Bank of America operates, as well as to support community organizations that contribute to the quality of life in those communities. The foundation focuses on housing assistance programs, economic development, educational programs, youth enrichment programs, and arts and cultural programs.
Fields of interest: Arts; Education; Environment; Housing/shelter; Human services; Children/youth, services; Community development.
Types of support: Continuing support; Scholarship funds.
Limitations: Giving limited to Fall River and southeastern MA, and RI, where First Federal Savings Bank of America has branches. No support for schools or athletic organizations. No grants to individuals.
Publications: Application guidelines, Informational brochure.
Application information: Application form available on Web site. Application form required.
  Copies of proposal: 1
  Deadline(s): None
  Board meeting date(s): Mar., May, Aug., and Nov.
  Final notification: Rolling
Officers and Directors:* Robert F. Stoico,* Chair., C.E.O. and Pres.; Nelson J. Braga, V.P.; Joseph L. Bustin, V.P.; Philip G. Campbell, V.P.; Christine F. Chicca, V.P.; Richard M. Farmer, V.P.; David Galvin, V.P.; Robert N. Gaumont, V.P.; Timothy V. Geremia, V.P.; June Goguen, V.P.; Edward A. Hjerpe III, V.P.; Robert Hole, V.P.; Barbara L. Holt, V.P.; E.M. Hughes, V.P.; Michael R. Lacey, V.P.; Stuart A. Lawrence, V.P.; Kevin J. McGillicuddy, V.P.; Raymond D. Mountain, V.P.; Michael E. Pavia, V.P.; Sheila M. Rioux, V.P.; Eileen A. Rayan-Saeger, V.P.; Edward A. Schultz, V.P.; Frederick R. Sullivan, V.P.; Terrence M. Tyrrell, V.P.; Gary J. Vierra, V.P.; Anthony L. Weatherford, V.P.; Cecilia R. Viveiros, Corp. Secy.; Gregory Derderian, Treas.; Richard W. Cederberg; John S. Holden, Jr.; Gilbert C.

Oliveira; Paul A. Raymond; Thomas A. Rodgers, Jr.; Robert A. Skurka; Anthony L. Sylvia.
EIN: 043343529

1402
The Fleming Family Foundation
24 Wildwood Dr.
Sherborn, MA 01770

Established in 1997 in MA.
Donor(s): David D. Fleming, Margaret E. Fleming.
Grantmaker type: Independent foundation
Financial data (yr. ended 12/31/02): Assets, $389,255 (M); expenditures, $156,981; qualifying distributions, $142,717; giving activities include $142,717 for 43 grants (high: $64,546; low: $25).
Purpose and activities: Giving primarily for nature and science centers, education, health associations and social services.
Fields of interest: Higher education; Education; Natural resources; Hospitals (general); Human services; Science; Christian agencies & churches.
Limitations: Applications not accepted. Giving on a national basis, with emphasis on MA and OH. No grants to individuals.
Application information: Contributes only to pre-selected organizations.
Officer and Director:* Margaret E. Fleming,* Treas.
Trustee: David D. Fleming.
EIN: 043361641

1403
Foundation M
P.O. Box 3219
Andover, MA 01810-0804

Established in 2000 in MA.
Donor(s): Casper Martin, Martin Foundation, Inc.
Grantmaker type: Independent foundation
Financial data (yr. ended 06/30/02): Assets, $10,075,028 (M); gifts received, $9,225,044; expenditures, $138,161; qualifying distributions, $104,764; giving activities include $109,000 for 4 grants (high: $86,000; low: $3,000).
Fields of interest: Animals/wildlife, association; Human services; Women.
Limitations: Applications not accepted. No grants to individuals.
Application information: Contributes only to pre-selected organizations.
Trustees: Casper Martin; Linda Woolford.
EIN: 043559359

1404
George F. and Sybil H. Fuller Foundation ▼
730 Main St.
1-B Central St.
Boylston, MA 01505 (508) 869-6723
Contact: Russell E. Fuller, Chair.

Trust established in 1955 in MA.
Donor(s): George Freeman Fuller,‡ Sybil H. Fuller.
Grantmaker type: Independent foundation

Financial data (yr. ended 12/31/01): Assets, $68,948,313 (M); expenditures, $3,883,682; qualifying distributions, $3,804,875; giving activities include $3,731,900 for 88 grants (high: $326,300; low: $500; average: $5,000–$55,000).
Purpose and activities: Emphasis on higher education, cultural institutions, historic preservation, hospitals, community funds, and youth organizations; support also for social service agencies and schools.
Fields of interest: Museums; Arts; Higher education; University; Human services.
Types of support: Continuing support; Annual campaigns; Capital campaigns; Building/renovation; Equipment; Emergency funds; Seed money; Scholarship funds; Research; Matching/challenge support.
Limitations: Giving primarily in MA, with emphasis on Worcester. No grants to individuals, or for endowments or general operating support; no loans.
Publications: Application guidelines.
Application information: Application form not required.
  Initial approach: Telephone or letter of inquiry
  Copies of proposal: 1
  Deadline(s): One week before board meeting
  Board meeting date(s): Jan.-Mar., June-Aug., and Oct.-Dec.
  Final notification: 1 to 2 months
Officers and Trustees:* Russell E. Fuller,* Chair.; Mark W. Fuller,* Vice-Chair.; Diane H. Robbins,* Secy.; Jan Fuller; Lincoln E. Fuller; David P. Hallock.
Number of staff: 1 part-time support.
EIN: 046125606
Recent environmental and animal welfare grants:
1404-1 American Chinese Veterinary Medical Frontiers, West Boylston, MA, $50,000. 2001.
1404-2 Audubon Society of Massachusetts, Worcester, MA, $10,000. 2001.
1404-3 EcoTarium, Worcester, MA, $108,000. 2001.
1404-4 Greater Worcester Land Trust, Worcester, MA, $50,000. 2001.
1404-5 Tufts University, Medford, MA, $60,000. For Veterinary School in Grafton. 2001.
1404-6 Worcester County Horticultural Society, Boylston, MA, $130,000. 2001.

1405
The Garfield Foundation
3 Barnabas Rd.
Marion, MA 02738
Contact: Jennie McCann, Exec. Dir.
FAX: (508) 748-1976; E-mail: inquiry@garfieldfoundation.org

Established in 1980.
Grantmaker type: Independent foundation
Financial data (yr. ended 11/30/02): Assets, $55,529,458 (M); expenditures, $3,995,818; qualifying distributions, $3,266,800; giving activities include $2,928,600 for 67 grants (low: $2,500).
Purpose and activities: To stimulate systemic-level solutions to progress towards a more equitable, economically prosperous and environmentally sustainable global society. Grantmaking priorities include sustainable production and consumption, biodiversity

conservation, animal welfare and toxic metal pollutant source reduction, and community revitalization.
Fields of interest: Environment, toxics; Natural resources; Animal welfare; Youth development; Economic development; Community development.
International interests: South America.
Limitations: Applications not accepted. No grants to individuals.
Application information: Contributes only to pre-selected organizations.
Trustees: Michael Baldwin; Ronald Berman; Brian Garfield.
Number of staff: 2 full-time professional.
EIN: 222285358

1406
The Gateway Fund
c/o Welch & Forbes
45 School St.
Boston, MA 02108
Contact: Robert L.V. French, Tr.
Application address: 1086 Sugar Hill Rd., Hopkinton, NH 03229, tel.: (603) 529-2127

Established in 1997 in NH.
Donor(s): Robert L.V. French, Shirley S. French.
Grantmaker type: Independent foundation
Financial data (yr. ended 12/31/02): Assets, $1,223,683 (M); expenditures, $121,548; qualifying distributions, $106,350; giving activities include $106,350 for 7 grants (high: $50,000; low: $2,500).
Purpose and activities: Giving primarily for education.
Fields of interest: Education; Environment, land resources; Environment; Children/youth, services.
Limitations: Giving primarily in MA, NH, NY, and VT. No grants to individuals.
Application information: Application form not required.
Initial approach: Letter
Deadline(s): None
Trustees: Robert L.V. French; Shirley S. French.
EIN: 043366747

1407
GenRad Foundation
P.O. Box 444
West Groton, MA 01472-0444
(978) 448-8942
Contact: Linda B. Schuler, Tr.

Established in 1934 in MA.
Donor(s): GenRad, Inc., Henry Shaw.‡
Grantmaker type: Company-sponsored foundation
Financial data (yr. ended 12/31/01): Assets, $804,380 (M); expenditures, $160,172; qualifying distributions, $159,465; giving activities include $102,500 for 13 grants (high: $29,500; low: $2,500).
Purpose and activities: Giving primarily for family and social services, child welfare, voluntarism, hospitals and health associations, environmental conservation, higher and secondary education, and cultural programs, including museums and the fine and performing arts.

Fields of interest: Museums; Performing arts; Arts; Secondary school/education; Higher education; Education; Natural resources; Environment; Hospitals (general); Mental health/crisis services; Health organizations, association; Human services; Children/youth, services; Family services; Voluntarism promotion; Aging.
Types of support: General/operating support; Continuing support; Annual campaigns; Capital campaigns; Building/renovation; Endowments; Program development; Seed money.
Limitations: Giving primarily in the Concord, MA, area. No grants to individuals.
Publications: Application guidelines.
Application information: Application form not required.
Initial approach: Telephone; proposal limited to 5 pages
Copies of proposal: 1
Deadline(s): None
Board meeting date(s): As needed
Final notification: Generally within 3 months of receipt of proposal
Trustees: Linda B. Schuler; Barbara J. Wahler.
Number of staff: 1 full-time professional; 1 part-time support.
EIN: 046043570

1408
Grand Circle Foundation, Inc.
347 Congress St.
Boston, MA 02210 (617) 346-6398
Contact: Maury Peterson, Dir.
FAX: (617) 346-6030; E-mail: mpeterson@gct.com; URL: http://www.gct.com/gct/general

Established in 1993 in MA.
Donor(s): Grand Circle Travel, Overseas Adventure Travel.
Grantmaker type: Company-sponsored foundation
Financial data (yr. ended 12/31/01): Assets, $1,647,773 (M); gifts received, $2,557,175; expenditures, $2,011,182; qualifying distributions, $2,006,745; giving activities include $2,006,745 for 88 grants (high: $600,000; low: $50; average: $5,000–$100,000).
Purpose and activities: Support primarily for three areas of interest: the environment; international appreciation of cultures; and community projects directed towards low-income and disadvantaged children and families.
Fields of interest: Museums; Natural resources; Human services; International development.
International interests: Nepal.
Types of support: General/operating support; Continuing support; Emergency funds.
Limitations: Giving internationally where company does business and in Boston, MA. No support for religious organizations. Generally, no grants to individuals, or for advertising, dinner table sponsorship, or fundraising.
Publications: Application guidelines.
Application information:
Initial approach: 1- to 2-page proposal
Copies of proposal: 6
Deadline(s): Apr. 30, July 31, and Oct. 31
Board meeting date(s): Feb., May, Aug., and Nov.

Final notification: Oct.
Officer and Directors:* Harriet R. Lewis, Chair.; Mark Frevert; Alan E. Lewis.
Number of staff: 2 full-time professional.
EIN: 043175434

1409
Jeremy and Hannelore Grantham Charitable Trust
40 Rowes Wharf
Boston, MA 02110
Contact: Jeremy Grantham, Tr.

Established in 1997 in MA.
Donor(s): R. Jeremy Grantham.
Grantmaker type: Independent foundation
Financial data (yr. ended 12/31/02): Assets, $21,428,763 (M); gifts received, $3,250,950; expenditures, $726,798; qualifying distributions, $683,288; giving activities include $701,000 for 43 grants (high: $170,000; low: $500).
Fields of interest: Museums (specialized); Education; Natural resources; Human services; Federated giving programs.
Limitations: Applications not accepted. No grants to individuals.
Application information: Contributes only to pre-selected organizations.
Trustee: Jeremy Grantham.
EIN: 046856456

1410
Joseph M. Hamilburg Foundation
c/o Plymouth Rubber Co.
104 Revere St.
Canton, MA 02021

Established in 1963 in MA.
Donor(s): Daniel M. Hamilburg.
Grantmaker type: Independent foundation
Financial data (yr. ended 12/31/02): Assets, $1,831,786 (M); expenditures, $177,483; qualifying distributions, $137,646; giving activities include $138,185 for 36 grants (high: $50,000; low: $35).
Purpose and activities: Giving primarily to the arts, education, animal welfare, and health associations.
Fields of interest: Museums; Performing arts; Secondary school/education; Higher education; Animals/wildlife; Health organizations, association.
Limitations: Applications not accepted. Giving primarily in MA. No grants to individuals, or for loans or program-related investments.
Application information: Contributes only to pre-selected organizations.
Trustees: Joseph D. Hamilburg; Maurice J. Hamilburg.
EIN: 046128210

1411
Deborah A. Hawkins Charitable Trust
c/o Tanager Financial Svcs., Inc.
800 South St., Ste. 195
Waltham, MA 02453

Established in 1998 in MA.
Donor(s): Deborah A. Hawkins.
Grantmaker type: Independent foundation

Financial data (yr. ended 12/31/02): Assets, $50,486 (M); expenditures, $376,291; qualifying distributions, $372,904; giving activities include $372,000 for 3 grants (high: $370,000; low: $1,000).
Fields of interest: Natural resources; Health organizations, association.
Limitations: Applications not accepted. Giving primarily in New England. No grants to individuals.
Application information: Contributes only to pre-selected organizations.
Trustee: Deborah A. Hawkins.
EIN: 046834358

1412
Haymarket People's Fund
42 Seaverns Ave.
Boston, MA 02130 (617) 522-7676
Contact: Patricia Maher, Exec. Dir.
FAX: (617) 522-9580; URL: http://www.haymarket.org

Established in 1974 in MA.
Grantmaker type: Public charity
Financial data (yr. ended 06/30/01): Revenue, $2,082,316; assets, $6,894,554; gifts received, $1,635,866; expenditures, $3,012,045; program services expenses, $2,685,665; giving activities include $2,052,650 for grants.
Purpose and activities: The fund is a progressive organization that makes grants throughout New England to grassroots groups which organize for peace, equality, and economic justice. Besides providing support and resources to grassroots organizations through grants, the fund does its best to provide technical assistance and referrals as well as encouraging coalition building and networking. It strives to maintain a multicultural organization controlled by activists representing constituencies served.
Fields of interest: Environment; Health care; AIDS; AIDS research; Employment; International peace/security; Race/intergroup relations; Civil rights; Community development, citizen coalitions; Community development; Minorities; Disabled; Women; Gays/lesbians; Immigrants/refugees; Homeless.
International interests: Latin America; Middle East.
Types of support: General/operating support; Emergency funds; Program development; Program-related investments/loans.
Limitations: Giving limited to New England. No support for social service organizations, government agencies, alternative businesses, or groups receiving significant government or corporate funding. No grants to individuals.
Publications: Application guidelines, Annual report, Financial statement, Grants list, Newsletter.
Application information: Grant proposals received by FAX not accepted. Application form required.
Initial approach: Telephone
Deadline(s): Mar. 15 and Sept.15 for Sustaining Grants for MA applicants; Feb. 1 and Oct. 1 for CT, ME, NH, RI, VT applicants; Mar. 30 and Oct. 30 for New England-wide applicants (projects in 3 or more N.E. states); none for emergency grants
Board meeting date(s): Every 2 months

Final notification: Within 1 month after funding board decisions
Officers and Director:* Melinda Sulazar,* Pres.; Mikala Bembery,* Secy.; Lawrence Locke,* Treas.; Pat Maher, Exec. Dir.
Number of staff: 7 full-time professional; 2 part-time professional.
EIN: 042586725

1413
Hazard Family Foundation
23 Marlborough St.
Boston, MA 02116 (617) 912-4328
Contact: C. Michael Hazard, Tr.

Established in 1996 in MA.
Donor(s): C. Michael Hazard, Susan G. Hazard.
Grantmaker type: Independent foundation
Financial data (yr. ended 12/31/02): Assets, $2,622,252 (M); expenditures, $139,857; qualifying distributions, $114,000; giving activities include $114,000 for 15 grants (high: $40,000; low: $1,000).
Purpose and activities: Giving primarily for education, hospitals, the arts, and environmental preservation.
Fields of interest: Visual arts; Education; Environment; Hospitals (specialty).
Types of support: Annual campaigns; Capital campaigns; Land acquisition.
Limitations: Applications not accepted. Giving primarily in MA and RI.
Application information: Contributes only to pre-selected organizations.
Trustee: C. Michael Hazard.
EIN: 043338927

1414
The Henderson Family Foundation
c/o Robert P. Henderson
5 Arlington St.
Boston, MA 02116

Established in 2000 in MA.
Donor(s): Robert P. Henderson.
Grantmaker type: Independent foundation
Financial data (yr. ended 12/31/02): Assets, $1,793,526 (M); expenditures, $127,479; qualifying distributions, $103,989; giving activities include $101,000 for 12 grants (high: $25,000; low: $1,000).
Fields of interest: Multipurpose centers/programs; Arts; Education; Aquariums.
Types of support: General/operating support.
Limitations: Applications not accepted. Giving primarily in Boston, MA. No grants to individuals.
Application information: Contributes only to pre-selected organizations.
Trustees: Carol T. Henderson; Robert P. Henderson.
EIN: 043506549

1415
The Highland Street Connection ▼
P.O. Box 5209
Framingham, MA 01701
E-mail: tobydouthwright@highlandstreet.org;
URL: http://www.highlandstreet.org

Established in 1994 in MA.
Donor(s): David J. McGrath, Jr.
Grantmaker type: Independent foundation
Financial data (yr. ended 12/31/01): Assets, $174,287,765 (M); gifts received, $332,297; expenditures, $8,934,760; qualifying distributions, $7,946,067; giving activities include $7,103,623 for 188 grants (high: $500,000; low: $250; average: $1,000–$100,000) and $434,631 for 2 loans/program-related investments.
Purpose and activities: Giving primarily for education and children's mentoring programs.
Fields of interest: Arts; Education.
Limitations: Applications not accepted. Giving primarily in MA. No grants to individuals.
Application information: Contributes only to pre-selected organizations.
Board meeting date(s): June and Dec.
Trustees: Christopher R. McGrath; David J. McGrath III; Holly L. McGrath; Joann McGrath; Scott J. McGrath; Sean P. McGrath.
EIN: 043048298
Recent environmental and animal welfare grants:
1415-1 Appalachian Mountain Club, Boston, MA, $500,000. For general operating support. 2001.
1415-2 Appalachian Mountain Club, Boston, MA, $10,000. For general operating support. 2001.
1415-3 Shelburne Farms, Shelburne, VT, $20,000. For general operating support. 2001.
1415-4 Tufts University, School of Veterinary Medicine, Medford, MA, $10,000. For general operating support. 2001.
1415-5 Tufts University, School of Veterinary Medicine Development Office, Medford, MA, $300,000. For capital support. 2001.
1415-6 Worcester Natural History Society, Worcester, MA, $50,000. For youth coordinator's salary and Teen Action Science Crew (TASC) Program. 2001.

1416
The Hirschtick Family Foundation
c/o Jon and Melissa Hirschtick
10 Porter Ln.
Lexington, MA 02420

Established in 1998 in MA.
Donor(s): Jon K. Hirschtick, Melissa H. Hirschtick.
Grantmaker type: Independent foundation
Financial data (yr. ended 12/31/02): Assets, $153,382 (M); gifts received, $155,750; expenditures, $296,307; qualifying distributions, $291,523; giving activities include $292,860 for 25 grants (high: $100,000; low: $50).
Fields of interest: Television; Animal welfare; Human services; Jewish agencies & temples.
Limitations: Applications not accepted. No grants to individuals.
Application information: Contributes only to pre-selected organizations.
Trustees: Jon K. Hirschtick; Melissa H. Hirschtick.
EIN: 046868401

1417
Hoffman Family Foundation
(formerly The John Ernest Hoffman Foundation)
c/o Loring, Wolcott & Coolidge Office
230 Congress St.
Boston, MA 02110

Established in 1985 in MA.
Donor(s): Effe K.D. Hoffman.‡
Grantmaker type: Independent foundation
Financial data (yr. ended 12/31/02): Assets,
$5,354,748 (M); expenditures, $430,568;
qualifying distributions, $405,209; giving
activities include $405,500 for 28 grants (high:
$130,000; low: $2,000).
Purpose and activities: Giving primarily for the
arts, particularly a center for chamber music;
funding also for natural resource conservation,
health associations, human services, federated
giving programs, and Christian churches.
Fields of interest: Performing arts centers;
Music; Orchestra (symphony); Arts; Higher
education; Education; Natural resources;
Environment, forests; Health organizations;
Human services; Foundations (community);
Federated giving programs; Christian agencies &
churches.
Types of support: General/operating support;
Continuing support; Annual campaigns; Capital
campaigns; Building/renovation.
Limitations: Applications not accepted. Giving
primarily in MA and NH; some funding also in
CT. No grants to individuals.
Application information: Contributes only to
pre-selected organizations. Unsolicited requests
for funds not considered.
    Board meeting date(s): As needed
Trustees: John E. Hoffman, Jr.; Stephen A.
Moore; Roger M. Thomas.
Number of staff: None.
EIN: 222677966

1418
Horizon Foundation, Inc.
P.O. Box 670
Ipswich, MA 01938 (978) 356-8317
Contact: Alexander Buck, Jr., Pres.
FAX: (978) 356-8318; E-mail: horizon@nii.net;
URL: http://www.horizonfoundation.org

Established in 1997 in MA and PA.
Donor(s): Alexander K. Buck, Sr., Alexander K.
Buck, Jr., N. Harrison Buck.
Grantmaker type: Independent foundation
Financial data (yr. ended 06/30/02): Assets,
$9,840,875 (M); gifts received, $130,013;
expenditures, $262,347; qualifying distributions,
$306,154; giving activities include $242,700 for
29 grants (high: $35,000; low: $1,000).
Purpose and activities: Giving primarily for
education in the arts, history, the environment,
and leadership training for children; funding
also for community services and mentoring.
Fields of interest: Arts education;
History/archaeology; Education; Environmental
education; Leadership development.
Types of support: Equipment; Program
development; Conferences/seminars; Seed
money; Curriculum development; Internship
funds; Program evaluation; Matching/challenge
support.
Limitations: Giving limited to Barnstable, and
Essex counties, MA, Cumberland, Franklin,

Lincoln, and York counties, ME, and Mercer
County, NJ. No support for colleges and
universities, or public and private schools. No
grants to individuals, or for international or
foreign affairs, religion, state agencies, or
emergency requests.
Publications: Application guidelines, Annual
report, Grants list, Informational brochure
(including application guidelines).
Application information: Unsolicited proposals
are not considered. Application form not
required.
    Initial approach: 1-page letter of inquiry; no
    faxed letters of inquiry or proposals
    Copies of proposal: 1
    Deadline(s): Apr. 1 or Oct. 1; proposals
    arriving after deadlines are considered in
    next cycle of awards
    Board meeting date(s): May, July, and Nov.
    Final notification: June 1 and Dec. 1
Officers: Alexander K. Buck, Sr., Chair.;
Alexander K. Buck, Jr., Pres.; Nancy B. Buck,
V.P.; Sara L. Buck, V.P.; Anne E. Buck, Secy.; N.
Harrison Buck, Treas.
Number of staff: 1 part-time professional.
EIN: 232867116

1419
Henry Hornblower Fund, Inc.
P.O. Box 2365
Boston, MA 02107-2365
Contact: Nathan N. Withington, Pres.

Incorporated in 1945 in MA.
Donor(s): Hornblower & Weeks-Lothrop
Withington.
Grantmaker type: Operating foundation
Financial data (yr. ended 12/31/02): Assets,
$4,683,336 (M); expenditures, $243,143;
qualifying distributions, $239,516; giving
activities include $217,100 for 25 grants (high:
$100,000; low: $100) and $2,700 for 7
employee matching gifts.
Purpose and activities: Emphasis on higher and
secondary education, hospitals, and cultural
programs; support also for needy individuals
presently or formerly employed by Hornblower
& Weeks.
Fields of interest: Visual arts; Museums; Arts;
Secondary school/education; Higher education;
Libraries/library science; Environment, land
resources; Hospitals (general).
Types of support: General/operating support;
Capital campaigns; Endowments; Emergency
funds; Scholarship funds.
Limitations: Giving primarily in MA. No grants
to individuals directly; no loans.
Application information: Application form not
required.
    Initial approach: Letter
    Copies of proposal: 1
    Deadline(s): Dec. 31
    Board meeting date(s): June and Dec.
    Final notification: Dec. 31
Officer and Directors:* Nathan N. Withington,*
Pres.; Orin H. Meyer; Lothrop Withington III.
Number of staff: 1 part-time support.
EIN: 237425285

1420
**Houghton Mifflin Company Contributions
    Program**
222 Berkeley St.
Boston, MA 02116-3764

Grantmaker type: Corporate giving program
Purpose and activities: Houghton Mifflin makes
charitable contributions to nonprofit
organizations through employee matching gifts
only. Support is given on a national basis.
Fields of interest: Arts; Higher education;
Education; Environment; Youth, services;
Human services.
Types of support: Employee matching gifts.
Limitations: Applications not accepted. Giving
on a national basis.
Application information: Contributes only
through employee matching gifts.

1421
The Howell Family Charitable Foundation
c/o Welch & Forbes
45 School St.
Boston, MA 02108
Contact: Priscilla W. Howell, Tr.
Application address: 51 Fairview St., Rosindale,
MA 02131

Established in 1998 in MA.
Grantmaker type: Independent foundation
Financial data (yr. ended 12/31/01): Assets,
$1,702,904 (M); expenditures, $110,302;
qualifying distributions, $90,671; giving
activities include $90,000 for 10 grants (high:
$12,500; low: $2,500).
Purpose and activities: Giving primarily for
human services.
Fields of interest: Television; Adult
education—literacy, basic skills & GED;
Environment, land resources; Animals/wildlife,
bird preserves; Family planning; Mental
health/crisis services, association; Women,
centers/services; Community development,
neighborhood development.
Limitations: Giving primarily in MA, with
emphasis on Boston. No grants to individuals.
Application information:
    Deadline(s): Proposal
    Board meeting date(s): N
Trustees: Barbara W. Howell; John A. Howell;
Peter L. Howell; Priscilla W. Howell; Samuel H.
Howell.
EIN: 043425079

1422
Hurdle Hill Foundation
c/o Sagamore Partners, LLP
27 School St.
Boston, MA 02108-4303

Established in 1960 in MA.
Donor(s): Edith M. Adams, and members of the
Phippen family.
Grantmaker type: Independent foundation
Financial data (yr. ended 12/31/02): Assets,
$323,892 (M); gifts received, $305,303;
expenditures, $381,222; qualifying distributions,
$376,429; giving activities include $377,800 for
234 grants (high: $25,000; low: $50).
Fields of interest: Historic preservation/historical
societies; Arts; Education; Natural resources;

Health care; Health organizations, association; Human services; International peace/security; Christian agencies & churches.
Limitations: Applications not accepted. Giving primarily in MA. No grants to individuals.
Application information: Contributes only to pre-selected organizations.
Trustees: Henry P. Phippen; Peter D. Phippen; Richard D. Phippen; Susanne LaCroix Phippen; William LaCroix Phippen.
EIN: 046012782

1423
The Crawford Idema Family Foundation
(formerly The Crawford Idema Foundation)
100 Main St., Ste. 325
Concord, MA 01742 (978) 318-0505
Contact: Philip VanDerWilden, Exec. Dir.
FAX: (978) 318-0535

Established in 1997 in CA.
Grantmaker type: Independent foundation
Financial data (yr. ended 12/31/02): Assets, $9,009,888 (M); expenditures, $692,782; qualifying distributions, $553,718; giving activities include $450,500 for 48 grants (high: $25,000; low: $1,000).
Fields of interest: Education, reform; Natural resources; Nursing home/convalescent facility; Substance abuse, services; Substance abuse, prevention; Substance abuse, treatment; Child development, services.
Types of support: Continuing support; Equipment; Curriculum development; Research.
Limitations: Giving primarily in the Santa Barbara, CA and the greater Boston, MA areas. No grants for general fund raising drives, endowment funds, or for debt reduction.
Publications: Informational brochure, Occasional report.
Application information:
   Initial approach: Letter - no more than 2 pages
   Deadline(s): None
   Board meeting date(s): May and Nov.
Officers: Thomas Crawford, Jr., Pres.; Nancy S. Crawford, Secy. and C.F.O.
Directors: Rob Adams; Susan C. Adams; Nancy R. Crawford; Peter T. Crawford; Thomas Crawford IV; Mary-Wren VanDerWilden.
EIN: 043473310

1424
International Fund for Animal Welfare, Inc.
411 Main St.
Yarmouth Port, MA 02675

Established in 1998 in MA, founded in 1969.
Grantmaker type: Public charity
Purpose and activities: The organization seeks to motivate the public to prevent cruelty to animals and to promote animal welfare, and conservation policies that advance the well-being of both animals and people.
Fields of interest: Animal welfare; Animals/wildlife, preservation/protection; Animals/wildlife, endangered species; Animals/wildlife.
International interests: Canada; Russia; Africa; South Africa; Latin America; China; Australia.
Types of support: General/operating support; Equipment; Land acquisition; Emergency funds;

Program development; Conferences/seminars; Publication; Research; Scholarships—to individuals; In-kind gifts.
Limitations: Applications not accepted. Giving on a national and international basis.
Application information: Contributes only to pre-selected organizations; unsolicited requests for funds not considered or acknowledged.
Officers and Directors:* Anne Fitzgerald,* Chair.; Frederick O'Regan,* C.E.O.; Azzedine Downes,* C.O.O.; Christopher Tuite,* C.F.O.; Stijn Albregts; Karen Cotton; John Garamendi; Margaret Kennedy; Atherton Martin; Michael O'Connell; Gary Tabor.
EIN: 311594197

1425
Island Foundation, Inc.
589 Mill St.
Marion, MA 02738-1553 (508) 748-2809
Contact: Julie A. Early, Exec. Dir.
FAX: (508) 748-0991; E-mail: islandfdn@earthlink.net

Incorporated in 1979 in MA as Ram Island, Inc.; current entity formed in 1986 by merger with Green Island, Inc.
Donor(s): W. Van Alan Clark, Jr.‡
Grantmaker type: Independent foundation
Financial data (yr. ended 12/31/01): Assets, $36,186,988 (M); expenditures, $1,901,849; qualifying distributions, $1,688,825; giving activities include $1,590,069 for 58 grants (high: $300,000; low: $1,500).
Purpose and activities: Giving primarily for: 1) coastal water protection in New England environmental projects: right whale research, impact of toxins on wildlife-research, land use conservation in southeast MA, and 2) building the capacity of individuals and neighborhoods in the city of New Bedford, MA; and 3) alternative education programs.
Fields of interest: Education; Natural resources; Environment; Animals/wildlife, preservation/protection; Economic development; Community development; Marine science; Biological sciences; Public policy, research.
Types of support: General/operating support; Capital campaigns; Equipment; Land acquisition; Program development; Curriculum development; Internship funds; Research; Technical assistance; Program-related investments/loans; Exchange programs; Matching/challenge support.
Limitations: Giving primarily in New Bedford, MA, for economic and community development, MA, ME, and RI for environmental programs. No support for religious organizations for sectarian purposes or political organizations. No grants to individuals.
Publications: Annual report (including application guidelines).
Application information: Full proposals by invitation only. Associated Grantmakers of MA Common Proposal Format accepted. Application form not required.
   Initial approach: Telephone or letter
   Copies of proposal: 1
   Deadline(s): Rolling
   Board meeting date(s): Annually and as needed

Officers: Jo-Ann Watson, Pres.; Michael Moore, V.P.; Peter Nesbeda, Treas.; Julie A. Early, Exec. Dir.
Directors: K. Clark; Stephen Clark; Hannah Moore; Christopher Tupper; Douglas Watson.
Number of staff: 1 full-time professional.
EIN: 042670567

1426
Jacbel Foundation
21 Clifton Rd.
Newton Center, MA 02459

Established in 1995.
Grantmaker type: Independent foundation
Financial data (yr. ended 12/31/01): Assets, $4,859,162 (M); expenditures, $244,210; qualifying distributions, $218,646; giving activities include $220,000 for 24 grants (high: $30,000; low: $2,500).
Fields of interest: Education; Natural resources; Alzheimer's disease; Human services.
Limitations: Applications not accepted. Giving primarily in MA and ME. No grants to individuals.
Application information: Contributes only to pre-selected organizations.
Trustees: Jeffrey W. Stulin; Rita J. Stulin.
EIN: 046796689

1427
Janci Foundation
c/o Bruce Bettigole, Gilmore, Rees, et al.
20 Walnut St.
Wellesley, MA 02481

Established in 2000 in RI.
Donor(s): Jeffrey Weiss.
Grantmaker type: Independent foundation
Financial data (yr. ended 12/31/01): Assets, $637 (M); gifts received, $166,528; expenditures, $166,578; qualifying distributions, $150,000; giving activities include $150,000 for 4 grants (high: $80,000; low: $10,000).
Purpose and activities: Giving primarily for education.
Fields of interest: Education; Zoos/zoological societies; Food banks.
Limitations: Applications not accepted. Giving primarily in RI. No grants to individuals.
Application information: Contributes only to pre-selected organizations.
Trustees: Bruce J. Bettigole; Nancy Freeman; Jeffrey Weiss.
EIN: 043506575

1428
The Joe Lewis Jefferson Foundation, Inc.
(formerly The D'Egville Foundation, Inc.)
c/o Steven A. Branson
501 Providence Hwy.
Norwood, MA 02062

Established in 1991 in MA.
Donor(s): Mark S. Ptashne.
Grantmaker type: Independent foundation
Financial data (yr. ended 12/31/01): Assets, $2,017,469 (L); expenditures, $174,559; qualifying distributions, $129,472; giving

activities include $129,472 for 30 grants (high: $44,929; low: $50).

Purpose and activities: Giving primarily for the arts.

Fields of interest: Music; Orchestra (symphony); Arts; Higher education; Natural resources; Hospitals (general); Foundations (public).

Limitations: Applications not accepted. Giving primarily in Boston, MA. No grants to individuals.

Application information: Contributes only to pre-selected organizations.

Officer: Mark S. Ptashne, Pres.

Director: Steven A. Branson.

EIN: 223151628

1429
Edward C. Johnson Fund ▼
82 Devonshire St., S3
Boston, MA 02109-3614 (617) 563-6806
Contact: Anne-Marie Soulliere, Fdn. Dir.

Trust established in 1964 in MA.

Donor(s): Edward C. Johnson II,‡ Edward C. Johnson III.

Grantmaker type: Independent foundation

Financial data (yr. ended 12/31/01): Assets, $280,101,038 (M); gifts received, $1,637,361; expenditures, $22,490,978; qualifying distributions, $21,210,881; giving activities include $20,987,524 for 61 grants (high: $6,950,404; low: $500; average: $20,000–$200,000).

Purpose and activities: Emphasis on museums, historical societies, medical institutions, and some youth programs. Support also for the visual arts, historic preservation, higher education, elementary and secondary schools, and environmental organizations.

Fields of interest: Visual arts; Museums; Performing arts; Historic preservation/historical societies; Arts; Environment; Health care; Medical research, institute; Youth, services.

Types of support: Capital campaigns; Building/renovation; Endowments; Program development; Research.

Limitations: Giving limited to the greater Boston, MA, area. No grants to individuals, or for scholarships.

Publications: Application guidelines.

Application information:
Initial approach: Letter of inquiry
Deadline(s): Mar. 30 and Oct. 30
Board meeting date(s): June and Dec.

Officers and Directors:* Edward C. Johnson III,* Pres.; Patricia R. Hurley, Secy.; Richard Weidmann, Treas.; Anne-Marie Soulliere, Fdn. Dir.; Abigail P. Johnson; Edward C. Johnson IV; Elizabeth L. Johnson.

Number of staff: 4 shared staff (shared with Fidelity Foundation).

EIN: 046108344

Recent environmental and animal welfare grants:

1429-1 Marine Biological Laboratory, Woods Hole, MA, $20,000. 2002.

1429-2 New England Aquarium, Boston, MA, $167,775. 2002.

1429-3 Society for the Prevention of Cruelty to Animals of Massachusetts, Boston, MA, $75,000. 2002.

1430
The Gerald R. Jordan Foundation
75 State St.
Boston, MA 02109

Established in 1996 in MA.

Grantmaker type: Independent foundation

Financial data (yr. ended 12/31/02): Assets, $8,031,656 (M); expenditures, $249,518; qualifying distributions, $215,210; giving activities include $215,210 for 28 grants (high: $100,000; low: $75).

Purpose and activities: Giving primarily for the arts, education, health, and youth services.

Fields of interest: Museums; Historic preservation/historical societies; Higher education; Education; Aquariums; Hospitals (general); Health care; Cancer research; Boys & girls clubs; Federated giving programs.

Types of support: Scholarship funds.

Limitations: Applications not accepted. Giving primarily in New England. No grants to individuals.

Application information: Contributes only to pre-selected organizations.

Trustee: Gerald R. Jordan, Jr.

EIN: 043293081

1431
Kahn Charitable Foundation
(formerly JED Charitable Foundation)
c/o United Properties
1330 Boylston St.
Chestnut Hill, MA 02467

Established in 1992 in MA.

Donor(s): The Jed Trust.

Grantmaker type: Independent foundation

Financial data (yr. ended 06/30/02): Assets, $13,147,588 (M); gifts received, $291,765; expenditures, $684,552; qualifying distributions, $676,062; giving activities include $675,500 for 25 grants (high: $115,000; low: $500).

Fields of interest: Elementary/secondary education; University; Natural resources; Environment, water resources; Animal welfare.

Limitations: Applications not accepted. Giving limited to Cambridge, MA. No grants to individuals.

Application information: Contributes only to pre-selected organizations.

Trustees: Joseph Kahn; Edward I. Rudman.

EIN: 046718867

1432
Karp Family Foundation
c/o New England Development
1 Wells Ave.
Newton, MA 02459
Contact: Stephen R. Karp, Tr. or Jill E. Karp, Tr.

Established in 1994 in MA.

Donor(s): Stephen R. Karp.

Grantmaker type: Independent foundation

Financial data (yr. ended 02/28/02): Assets, $5,215,784 (M); expenditures, $912,722; qualifying distributions, $886,038; giving activities include $888,250 for 20 grants (high: $225,000; low: $2,500).

Fields of interest: Secondary school/education; College; Aquariums; Hospitals (general); Cancer;

Multiple sclerosis; Human services; Jewish agencies & temples.

Limitations: Applications not accepted. Giving primarily in MA. No grants to individuals.

Application information: Contributes only to pre-selected organizations.

Trustees: Jill E. Karp; Stephen R. Karp.

EIN: 043226725

1433
Keane Family Foundation
c/o Weston Financial Group
40 William St., Ste. 100
Wellesley, MA 02481

Established in 1993.

Donor(s): John Keane, Marilyn Keane.

Grantmaker type: Independent foundation

Financial data (yr. ended 12/31/02): Assets, $7,261,826 (M); expenditures, $482,860; qualifying distributions, $440,090; giving activities include $440,090 for 34 grants (high: $100,000; low: $180).

Fields of interest: Television; Arts; Higher education; Education; Aquariums; Health care; Federated giving programs.

Limitations: Applications not accepted. Giving primarily in MA. No grants to individuals.

Application information: Contributes only to pre-selected organizations. Unsolicited requests for funds not accepted.

Trustees: John Keane; Marilyn Keane.

EIN: 046743248

1434
Edward Bangs Kelley and Elza Kelley Foundation, Inc.
243 South St.
P.O. Drawer M
Hyannis, MA 02601 (508) 775-3117
Contact: Henry L. Murphy, Jr., Pres.

Incorporated in 1954 in MA.

Donor(s): Edward Bangs Kelley,‡ Elza deHorvath Kelley.‡

Grantmaker type: Independent foundation

Financial data (yr. ended 12/31/02): Assets, $4,863,002 (M); gifts received, $7,500; expenditures, $265,753; qualifying distributions, $241,473; giving activities include $142,000 for 26 grants (high: $25,000; low: $150) and $35,500 for 32 grants to individuals (high: $2,500; low: $250).

Purpose and activities: To promote the health and welfare of inhabitants of Barnstable County, MA; grants for higher education, including scholarships, and particularly for medical and paramedical education; support also for health and hospitals, hospices, prevention of drug and alcohol abuse, child development and youth agencies, the elderly, libraries, the environment, marine sciences, and cultural programs, including museums, fine arts, theater, and the performing arts.

Fields of interest: Visual arts; Museums; Performing arts; Theater; Arts; Child development, education; Higher education; Medical school/education; Libraries/library science; Education; Environment; Hospitals (general); Health care; Substance abuse, services; Health organizations, association; Alcoholism; Children/youth, services; Child

development, services; Hospices; Aging, centers/services; Marine science; Aging.
Types of support: General/operating support; Capital campaigns; Building/renovation; Equipment; Emergency funds; Program development; Seed money; Scholarship funds; Research; Technical assistance; Scholarships—to individuals; Matching/challenge support.
Limitations: Giving limited to Barnstable County, MA. No grants to individuals (except for scholarships), or for annual campaigns, deficit financing, land acquisition, endowment funds, exchange programs, fellowships, publications, or conferences; no loans.
Publications: Annual report (including application guidelines).
Application information: Application form required.
Initial approach: Letter, followed by proposal
Copies of proposal: 6
Deadline(s): Apr. 30 for scholarships; no deadline for grants; grants considered Apr., July, and Oct. if greater than $2,500
Board meeting date(s): Jan., Apr., July, and Oct.
Final notification: 3 weeks
Officers and Directors:* Henry L. Murphy, Jr.,* Pres. and Admin.; Mary Louise Montgomery,* V.P.; R. Bruce Hammatt, Jr., Clerk; Thomas S. Olsen,* Treas.; Doreen Bilezikion; Jocelyn Bowman; Robert B. Hirschman; Townsend Hornor; John M. Kayajan; Kenneth S. MacAffer, Jr.; Stephen W. Malaquias, M.D.; Joshua A. Nickerson, Jr.; Charles N. Robinson; Barbara H. Sheaffer; Hamilton N. Shepley.
Number of staff: 1 part-time professional; 1 part-time support.
EIN: 046039660

1435
The Henry P. Kendall Foundation ▼
176 Federal St.
Boston, MA 02110 (617) 951-2525
Contact: Theodore M. Smith, Exec. Dir.
FAX: (617) 443-1977; URL: http://www.kendall.org

Trust established in 1957 in MA.
Donor(s): Members of the Henry P. Kendall family.
Grantmaker type: Independent foundation
Financial data (yr. ended 12/31/01): Assets, $79,448,455 (M); expenditures, $4,872,797; qualifying distributions, $4,354,467; giving activities include $3,322,395 for 70 grants (high: $644,781; low: $5,000; average: $5,000–$75,000).
Purpose and activities: Emphasis on strategic environmental policies/ecosystem management.
Fields of interest: Natural resources.
International interests: Canada.
Types of support: General/operating support; Program development; Seed money; Internship funds.
Limitations: Giving primarily in northeastern and northwestern North America (U.S. and Canada) for environmental and natural resource programs. No support for waste clean-ups, toxic or air/water pollution prevention or pollution monitoring initiatives, land trusts, or species-specific preservation efforts. No grants to individuals, or for capital or endowment funds, building construction/operation, basic research, scholarships, fellowships, equipment,

debt reduction, or conference participation/travel.
Publications: Biennial report.
Application information:
Board meeting date(s): Mar., June, and Nov.
Officer: Theodore M. Smith, Exec. Dir.
Trustees: Andrew W. Kendall; David F. Kendall; John P. Kendall; Sarah K. Mitchell.
Number of staff: 4 full-time professional; 1 part-time professional.
EIN: 046029103

1436
Michael R. Kidder 1996 Charitable Trust
c/o Palmer & Dodge, LLP
111 Huntington Ave.
Boston, MA 02199

Established in 1996 in MA.
Donor(s): Michael R. Kidder.
Grantmaker type: Independent foundation
Financial data (yr. ended 08/31/02): Assets, $7,410,150 (M); expenditures, $476,069; qualifying distributions, $419,716; giving activities include $411,000 for 9 grants (high: $241,000; low: $5,000).
Fields of interest: Education; Environment; Boys & girls clubs; YM/YWCAs & YM/YWHAs.
Limitations: Applications not accepted. Giving primarily in Martha's Vineyard, MA. No grants to individuals.
Application information: Contributes only to pre-selected organizations.
Trustee: Michael R. Kidder.
EIN: 046824225

1437
Constance Killam Trust
c/o Nutter, McClennen & Fish, LLP
World Trade Ctr. W., 155 Seaport Blvd.
Boston, MA 02210-2604
Contact: Thomas P. Jalkut, Tr.

Established in 1977 in MA.
Donor(s): Constance Killam.‡
Grantmaker type: Independent foundation
Financial data (yr. ended 04/30/02): Assets, $5,880,532 (M); expenditures, $344,310; qualifying distributions, $319,430; giving activities include $290,000 for 10 grants (high: $75,000; low: $5,000).
Purpose and activities: Giving primarily to protect the environment.
Fields of interest: Arts; Higher education; Natural resources; Animals/wildlife, preservation/protection.
Limitations: Applications not accepted. Giving primarily in MA. No grants to individuals.
Application information: Contributes only to pre-selected organizations. Unsolicited requests for funds not considered or acknowledged.
Trustees: Thomas P. Jalkut; John B. Newhall.
Number of staff: None.
EIN: 046420685

1438
The King Family Foundation
(formerly Greenroad Foundation)
c/o Welch & Forbes
45 School St.
Boston, MA 02108

Established in 1984 in MA.
Donor(s): Judith S. King.
Grantmaker type: Independent foundation
Financial data (yr. ended 01/31/02): Assets, $1,887,539 (M); gifts received, $250,038; expenditures, $109,978; qualifying distributions, $99,500; giving activities include $99,500 for 21 grants (high: $12,000; low: $1,000).
Fields of interest: Museums (art); Higher education; Natural resources; Health care; Human services; Community development; Federated giving programs.
Limitations: Applications not accepted. Giving primarily in MA, with emphasis on Worcester. No grants to individuals.
Application information: Contributes only to pre-selected organizations.
Trustees: Bruce A. King; Judith S. King.
EIN: 222505794

1439
King Spruce Company
c/o Thomas E. Needham
50 Congress St., Ste. 410
Boston, MA 02109

Established in 1952.
Donor(s): M. Millicent Clapp, Eugene H. Clapp II, Maud M. Clapp.
Grantmaker type: Independent foundation
Financial data (yr. ended 05/31/02): Assets, $3,609,090 (M); expenditures, $193,225; qualifying distributions, $160,500; giving activities include $160,500 for 32 grants (high: $25,000; low: $1,000).
Purpose and activities: Giving primarily for the arts, education, and hospitals.
Fields of interest: Arts; Higher education; Education; Environment, forests; American Red Cross; Protestant agencies & churches.
Types of support: Capital campaigns; Endowments; Scholarship funds.
Limitations: Applications not accepted. Giving primarily in MA. No grants to individuals.
Application information: Contributes only to pre-selected organizations.
Officers and Trustees:* Eugene H. Clapp II,* Pres.; Nathanial P. Clapp,* V.P.; Thomas E. Needham, Clerk; Meredith P. Clapp,* Treas.
EIN: 016009168

1440
Kingsbury Road Charitable Foundation
P.O. Box 140
Mansfield, MA 02048-0140
Additional addresses: Roger B. Hunt, c/o Sullivan and Worcester, 1 Post Office Sq., Boston, MA 02109; Edward W. Weld, c/o Boston Family Office, 88 Broad St., Boston, MA 02110

Established in 1996 in MA.
Donor(s): Hamilton Osgood, G. Grandchamps Charitable Remainder Trust, R.L. Christmas Charitable Remainder Trust.

Grantmaker type: Independent foundation
Financial data (yr. ended 12/31/02): Assets, $6,357,202 (M); gifts received, $36,000; expenditures, $416,984; qualifying distributions, $387,741; giving activities include $357,500 for 17 grants (high: $47,000; low: $6,500).
Purpose and activities: Giving primarily for the arts, as well as for education, and human services.
Fields of interest: Television; Music; Orchestra (symphony); Education; Animal welfare; Human services.
Types of support: General/operating support.
Limitations: Applications not accepted. Giving primarily in MA. No grants to individuals.
Application information: Contributes only to pre-selected organizations. Unsolicited requests for funds not accepted.
Trustees: Roger B. Hunt; Edward W. Weld.
EIN: 046820320

1441
Hollis Declan Leverett Memorial Fund
c/o A. Arnold Lundwall, et al.
8 Grove St.
Wellesley, MA   02482

Grantmaker type: Independent foundation
Financial data (yr. ended 12/31/02): Assets, $1,695,017 (M); expenditures, $166,820; qualifying distributions, $151,798; giving activities include $152,530 for 7 grants (high: $40,000; low: $13,360).
Purpose and activities: Giving primarily for the promotion of the planting and upkeep of trees, shrubs and other plants, which promote and encourage desirable bird life.
Fields of interest: Natural resources.
Limitations: Applications not accepted. No grants to individuals.
Application information: Contributes only to pre-selected organizations.
Trustees: A. Arnold Lundwall; Fleet National Bank.
EIN: 311700503

1442
John and Sonia Lingos Family Foundation
32 Jacqueline Cir.
West Yarmouth, MA   02673
Contact: Tamara Lingos Utley, Dir.

Established in 1991 in MA.
Donor(s): John W. Lingos,‡ Sonia Tasha Lingos.‡
Grantmaker type: Independent foundation
Financial data (yr. ended 06/30/02): Assets, $2,034,088 (M); expenditures, $96,806; qualifying distributions, $91,750; giving activities include $91,750 for 32 grants (high: $34,500; low: $500).
Purpose and activities: Giving for education, wildlife protection, and Christian organizations.
Fields of interest: Higher education; Libraries (public); Education; Animals/wildlife, preservation/protection; Christian agencies & churches.
Types of support: General/operating support; Building/renovation; Scholarship funds.
Limitations: Applications not accepted. Giving limited to the eastern U.S., with emphasis on MA. No grants to individuals.
Publications: Annual report.

Application information: Unsolicited requests for funds not accepted.
Officers and Directors:* Sonia Tasha Lingos,* Pres.; Tamara Lingos Utley,* Treas.; Thalia Lingos Huser; Tania Lingos Webb.
Number of staff: 1 full-time professional.
EIN: 043134266

1443
The Little Family Foundation
c/o Mellon Financial Corp.
1 Boston Pl.
Boston, MA   02108

Trust established in 1946 in RI.
Donor(s): Royal Little.‡
Grantmaker type: Independent foundation
Financial data (yr. ended 12/31/00): Assets, $26,172,320 (M); expenditures, $835,576; qualifying distributions, $728,320; giving activities include $628,869 for 98 grants (high: $100,000; low: $365) and $5,000 for 1 employee matching gift.
Purpose and activities: Support for scholarship funds at designated business schools; Rhode Island Junior Achievement for programs in secondary schools; and various charities in New England, including youth agencies, cultural programs, and hospitals.
Fields of interest: Performing arts; Dance; Music; Arts; Elementary/secondary education; Business school/education; Education; Natural resources; Environment; Hospitals (general); Youth, services.
Types of support: General/operating support; Continuing support; Annual campaigns; Building/renovation; Equipment; Emergency funds; Scholarship funds; Matching/challenge support.
Limitations: Applications not accepted. Giving primarily in MA and RI in the New England region, and OR and WA in the Pacific Northwest. No grants to individuals directly, or for seed money or deficit financing; no loans.
Application information: Contributes only to pre-selected organizations.
   Board meeting date(s): Quarterly
Trustee: Mellon Financial Corp.
Number of staff: 1 part-time support.
EIN: 056016740

1444
Greater Lowell Community Foundation
169 Merrimack St., 5th Fl.
Lowell, MA   01852   (978) 970-1600
Contact: David Kronberg, Exec. Dir.
FAX: (978) 970-2444; E-mail: glcf@gis.net; URL: http://www.glcfoundation.org

Established in 1996 in MA.
Donor(s): Joe Donaghue, Richard K. Donahue, Sr., Human Svcs. Corp., Lowell Museum Corp., The Theodore Edson Parker Foundation.
Grantmaker type: Community foundation
Financial data (yr. ended 03/31/02): Assets, $5,638,612 (M); gifts received, $1,383,834; expenditures, $656,235; giving activities include $375,868 for grants.
Purpose and activities: To improve the quality of life in the greater Lowell, MA, area by attracting funds, distributing grants, making loans and striving as a catalyst and leaders among funders,

agencies and individuals to address identified and emerging community needs. The foundation administers donor-advised funds.
Fields of interest: Arts; Education; Environment; Health care; Human services; Community development.
Types of support: Income development; Management development.
Limitations: Giving limited to the greater Lowell, MA, area. No support for religious organizations. No grants to individuals, or for continuing support, operating expenses, building funds or endowment funds.
Application information:
   Deadline(s): Mar. 15
   Final notification: May
Officers and Directors:* Richard K. Donahue, Sr.,* Pres.; John E. Leggat, V.P.; Brenda Costello,* Clerk; Peter S. Stamas,* Treas.; David Kronberg,* Exec. Dir.; Kay Doyle; Winslow H. Duke; George L. Duncan; Mary Jo Leahy; Elkin McCallum; Catherine G. Quinn.
EIN: 043401997

1445
The Maurice and Anne Makepeace Family Foundation
200 Tihonet Rd.
Wareham, MA   02571   (508) 295-1429
Contact: Christopher Makepeace, Tr.

Established in 1998 in MA.
Donor(s): Maurice Makepeace.
Grantmaker type: Independent foundation
Financial data (yr. ended 12/31/02): Assets, $2,479,750 (M); expenditures, $162,487; qualifying distributions, $138,144; giving activities include $139,000 for 16 grants (high: $35,000; low: $2,000).
Purpose and activities: Giving primarily for education and social services.
Fields of interest: Museums (marine/maritime); Elementary/secondary education; Botanical gardens; Hospitals (general); Human services; YM/YWCAs & YM/YWHAs.
Application information:
   Initial approach: Proposal
   Deadline(s): None
Trustees: Joanna Bennett; Christopher Makepeace.
EIN: 046863845

1446
The Roger M. Marino Charitable Foundation
360 Woodland St., No. 5
Holliston, MA   01746

Established in 1993 in MA.
Donor(s): Roger M. Marino.
Grantmaker type: Independent foundation
Financial data (yr. ended 12/31/01): Assets, $5,413,787 (M); expenditures, $687,335; qualifying distributions, $418,404; giving activities include $315,720 for 24 grants (high: $80,000; low: $100).
Purpose and activities: Giving primarily for animal welfare and for children's services.
Fields of interest: Animal welfare; Health care, patient services; Cancer research; Children/youth, services.

Limitations: Applications not accepted. Giving primarily in MA. No grants to individuals.
Application information: Contributes only to pre-selected organizations.
Officers and Trustees:* Lauren Marino,* Mgr.; Linda Marino,* Mgr.; Michelle S. Marino; Roger M. Marino.
EIN: 046749547

1447
Mazar Family Charitable Foundation
c/o The Colony Group
199 State St.
Boston, MA 02109

Established in 1997 in MA.
Donor(s): Anne Mazar, Brian Mazar.
Grantmaker type: Independent foundation
Financial data (yr. ended 12/31/02): Assets, $3,872,898 (M); expenditures, $1,728,444; qualifying distributions, $1,724,274; giving activities include $1,724,274 for 64 grants (high: $1,500,000; low: $25).
Fields of interest: Natural resources; Health care; Human services; Children/youth, services; International development; Federated giving programs.
Limitations: Applications not accepted. Giving primarily in MA. No grants to individuals.
Application information: Contributes only to pre-selected organizations.
Trustees: Anne Mazar; Brian Mazar.
EIN: 043344681

1448
The McCance Foundation
c/o Greylock
880 Winter St.
Waltham, MA 02451
Contact: Keith S. Jennings, Tr.
Application address: c/o Beach Investment Counsel, Inc., Three Radnor Corp. Ctr., Radnor, PA 19087

Established in 1994 in MA.
Grantmaker type: Independent foundation
Financial data (yr. ended 12/31/02): Assets, $6,286,683 (M); expenditures, $389,990; qualifying distributions, $375,578; giving activities include $376,200 for 41 grants (high: $150,000; low: $100).
Fields of interest: Higher education; Animals/wildlife; Health care; Disasters, fire prevention/control; Athletics/sports, racquet sports; Human services.
Limitations: Giving primarily in MA.
Application information: Application form not required.
Initial approach: Letter
Deadline(s): None
Trustees: Keith S. Jennings; Allison J. McCance; Henry F. McCance.
EIN: 046772532

1449
Merck Family Fund
303 Adams St.
Milton, MA 02186 (617) 696-3580
Contact: Jenny Russell, Exec. Dir.
FAX: (617) 696-7262; E-mail: merck@merckff.org; URL: http://www.merckff.org

Incorporated in 1954 in NJ.
Donor(s): Members of the Merck family.
Grantmaker type: Independent foundation
Financial data (yr. ended 12/31/02): Assets, $55,774,320 (M); gifts received, $4,857,443; expenditures, $3,996,748; qualifying distributions, $3,715,425; giving activities include $3,362,916 for 107 grants (high: $489,725; low: $750; average: $1,500–$25,000).
Purpose and activities: To restore and protect the natural environment, and to strengthen the social fabric and physical landscape of the urban community. Primary areas of interest are: 1) Protecting and restoring vital eastern U.S. ecosystems and promoting sustainable economic practices; and 2) Strengthening the urban community, concentrating on green and open space programs and youth organizing in Boston, MA, Providence, RI, and New York City.
Fields of interest: Environment; Youth development; Children/youth, services; Community development, neighborhood development; Economics; Economically disadvantaged.
Types of support: General/operating support; Continuing support; Land acquisition; Program development; Conferences/seminars; Seed money; Matching/challenge support.
Limitations: Giving primarily in Boston, MA, New York, NY, and Providence, RI, for Urban Program; the Northern Forest of ME, NH, and VT, southern Appalachia, and SC coastal areas, for Eastern Ecosystems; and nationally for Economics Program. No support for sectarian or religious purposes, for-profit organizations, or for projects intended to support candidates for political office. No grants to individuals, or for endowments, debt reduction, annual fundraising campaigns, capital construction, equipment, land acquisition, or film or video projects; generally no grants for academic research or books.
Publications: Application guidelines, Annual report (including application guidelines), Grants list.
Application information: Full proposals by invitation only. Application form not required.
Initial approach: Letter of inquiry (not to exceed 2 pages); proposals should not exceed 8 pages on 100 percent recycled paper
Copies of proposal: 1
Deadline(s): Varies annually
Board meeting date(s): May and Oct.
Final notification: Within one week of board decision
Officers and Trustees:* Josephine A. Merck,* Pres.; Sharman Altshuler,* V.P.; Serena Whitridge,* Secy.; Wilhelm M. Merck,* Treas.; Jenny Russell, Exec. Dir.; Patience M. Chamberlin; Francis W. Hatch III; Antony M. Merck.
Number of staff: 2 full-time professional; 1 part-time professional.
EIN: 226063382

Recent environmental and animal welfare grants:
1449-1 Alternatives for Community and Environment (ACE), Roxbury, MA, $30,279. For Roxbury Environmental Empowerment Project (REEP), youth education and environmental justice organizing project. 2001.
1449-2 Appalachian Mountain Club, Boston, MA, $50,033. For Campaign for the Preservation of the Northern Forest. 2001.
1449-3 Arboretum Park Conservancy, Boston, MA, $10,001. For construction of gates at public transit entrances of Arnold Arboretum. 2001.
1449-4 Arts of Peace, Mainstream Media Project, Arcata, CA, $43,962. For public media campaign designed to raise awareness about consumption issues through use of radio interviews. 2001.
1449-5 Boston GreenSpace Alliance, Boston, MA, $35,611. For expansion of community outreach, membership development, and creation of Parks Education Resource Center. 2001.
1449-6 Boston GreenSpace Alliance, Boston, MA, $14,500. For data assessment, mapping, and report production on Greening of Boston Project. 2001.
1449-7 Boston Natural Areas Network, Boston, MA, $30,000. For developing greenways to Boston Harbor on the Neponset River and in East Boston. 2001.
1449-8 Brooklyn Bridge Park Coalition, Brooklyn, NY, $30,552. For community outreach, advocacy and programming for new park along Brooklyn waterfront. 2001.
1449-9 Center for a Sustainable Economy, DC, $50,000. For environmental tax reform. 2001.
1449-10 Center for Environmental Citizenship, DC, $10,000. To train young people to work in environmental advocacy field. 2001.
1449-11 Chattooga Conservancy, Clayton, GA, $30,061. To monitor activities of U.S. Forest Service and other land protection efforts. 2001.
1449-12 Chelsea Human Services Collaborative, Chelsea, MA, $25,000. For community organizing and advocacy for parks, gardens, and sustainable development in Chelsea and along Chelsea Creek. 2001.
1449-13 Conservation Fund, Tucker, GA, $500,429. For revolving loan fund for preservation of critical biological habitat and sustainably managed forests in southern Appalachians. 2001.
1449-14 Container Recycling Institute, Alexandria, VA, $39,518. For public education and research concerning bottle bills. 2001.
1449-15 Dogwood Alliance, Brevard, NC, $75,666. For southeastern forest preservation and merger with Southeast Forest Project. 2001.
1449-16 East New York Planning Group, Brooklyn, NY, $25,000. For East New York Farms, project that works with community gardeners and young people to grow food for newly established urban market. Grant made through Local Development Corporation of East New York. 2001.
1449-17 Environmental Grantmakers Association, New York, NY, $10,000. For general operating support. 2001.

1449-18 Environmental League of Massachusetts, Boston, MA, $25,957. For environmental tax-shifting in Massachusetts. 2001.

1449-19 Food Alliance, Portland, Oregon, $35,315. For expansion of eco-labeling project. 2001.

1449-20 Forest Society of Maine, Bangor, ME, $50,000. For capacity-building to hold and monitor forest easements. 2001.

1449-21 Forest Stewards Guild, Santa Fe, NM, $29,486. For Northeast chapter's work to promote sustainable forestry. Grant made through The Forest Trust. 2001.

1449-22 Friends of the Earth, DC, $35,315. For New England Tax Shifting Initiative. 2001.

1449-23 Garden Futures, Boston, MA, $25,000. To fund education, advocacy and public support for Boston's community gardens. 2001.

1449-24 Georgia Forestwatch, Ellijay, GA, $29,329. For forest protection initiatives and oversight of forest management plans. 2001.

1449-25 Global Action Plan for the Earth, Woodstock, NY, $50,422. For Sustainable Lifestyle Campaign that works with municipalities to reduce their citizens' impact on natural resources and generation of waste. 2001.

1449-26 Grassroots Recycling Network, Athens, GA, $35,220. For Zero Waste Action Campaign. 2001.

1449-27 Green Corps, Boston, MA, $35,611. For Environmental Leadership Training Program that trains youth to work with environmental campaigns. 2001.

1449-28 Green Guerillas, New York, NY, $30,489. For general support for community organizing to support garden preservation. 2001.

1449-29 Health Care Without Harm, DC, $34,741. For campaign to green health care industry. Grant made through Environmental Health Fund. 2001.

1449-30 Hubbard Brook Research Foundation, Campton, NH, $30,552. For Science Links, research and dissemination program conveying information on nitrogen pollution. 2001.

1449-31 Jordan Institute, Stratham, NH, $39,126. For NH Minimum Impact Development Partnership (NHMID) to help create ecologically-based standard for development in New Hampshire. 2001.

1449-32 Just Food, New York, NY, $24,430. For City Farms, urban agriculture project with community gardens. 2001.

1449-33 Land Trust Alliance, DC, $20,000. To establish Southeast Land Trust Capacity Building Program. 2001.

1449-34 Lowcountry Open Land Trust, Charleston, SC, $25,050. For conservation protection in coastal South Carolina. 2001.

1449-35 Magnolia Tree Earth Center of Bedford Stuyvesant, Brooklyn, NY, $27,500. For Hattie Carthan Garden Way neighborhood revitalization project and Urban Tree Crops, youth environmental education program. 2001.

1449-36 Municipal Art Society of New York, New York, NY, $25,000. For international design competition that will produce master plan for reclamation of Fresh Kills Landfill. 2001.

1449-37 Natural Resources Council, Augusta, ME, $30,000. To protect Maine's North Woods through education and advocacy. 2001.

1449-38 Neighborhood of Affordable Housing, East Boston, MA, $30,000. For efforts to increase quantity and quality of green space along Chelsea Creek in East Boston. 2001.

1449-39 New Ecology, Cambridge, MA, $35,611. For general support for sustainable development initiatives in New England. 2001.

1449-40 New England Grassroots Environment Fund, Montpelier, VT, $40,946. For general support for administration and distribution of small grants to grassroots environmental projects in New England. 2001.

1449-41 New York City Environmental Justice Alliance, New York, NY, $30,750. To create accurate maps and accompanying reports that analyze distribution of open space in community districts. 2001.

1449-42 Northern Forest Alliance, Montpelier, VT, $50,422. For protection of New England's Northern Forest. Grant made through Appalachian Mountain Club. 2001.

1449-43 Northern Forest Center, Concord, NH, $40,000. For operating support to implement conservationist approach to sustainable use and protection of Northern Forest. 2001.

1449-44 Northern Forest Center, Concord, NH, $24,430. For organizational phase of Sustainable Forest Futures, market-based forestry investment project. 2001.

1449-45 Northwest Earth Institute, Portland, Oregon, $35,809. For national network of programs that offer courses on sustainability, consumption, and environmental values. 2001.

1449-46 Pacific Rivers Council, Eugene, Oregon, $20,000. For staff in Southeast who contribute to aquatic and riparian perspectives relative to forest management planning. 2001.

1449-47 Partnerships for Parks, New York, NY, $30,000. For Bronx River Restoration Alliance, development of Bronx River Greenway, ecological restoration of river, and community education and outreach. Grant made through City Parks Foundation. 2001.

1449-48 Partnerships for Parks, New York, NY, $30,000. For outreach, coalition building, and community organizing aimed at educating New York City council and mayoral candidates to make greenspace key election issue. Grant made through City Parks Foundation. 2001.

1449-49 Point Community Development Corporation, Bronx, NY, $30,000. For open space revitalization through community planning, greenway design and implementation, and youth activism in Hunt's Point and along Bronx River. 2001.

1449-50 Prospect Park Alliance, Brooklyn, NY, $24,886. For coalition of park volunteer and advocacy groups seeking to increase level of funding for city parks. 2001.

1449-51 Providence Plan, Providence, RI, $25,427. For organizing and engaging low-income residents in Woonasquatucket River Greenway Project. 2001.

1449-52 Quebec-Labrador Foundation/Atlantic Center for the Environment, Ipswich, MA,

$30,000. For community-based programs in Northern Forest. 2001.

1449-53 Redefining Progress, Oakland, CA, $50,326. To promote Ecological Footprint model to assess countries' impacts on natural resource depletion. 2001.

1449-54 ReVision House, Boston, MA, $25,244. For general support for urban agriculture project at home for teen mothers. 2001.

1449-55 Save Our Cumberland Mountains Resource Project, Lake City, TN, $30,000. For Forest Organizing Project. 2001.

1449-56 Save the Harbor—Save the Bay, Boston, MA, $30,000. For Campaign for the Water's Edge that sponsors open space projects and public access to Boston Harbor. 2001.

1449-57 Society for the Protection of New Hampshire Forests, Concord, NH, $32,255. For improvement of forestry practices and more widespread use of ecosystem-based forest management in New Hampshire. 2001.

1449-58 South Carolina Coastal Conservation League, Charleston, SC, $100,843. For capital campaign. 2001.

1449-59 South End-Lower Roxbury Open Space Land Trust, Boston, MA, $25,000. For involvement of local communities in restoration, programming, and management of Berkeley Street Garden. 2001.

1449-60 Southern Appalachian Forest Coalition, Asheville, NC, $49,568. To support member groups. Grant made through Southern Environmental Law Center. 2001.

1449-61 Southern Environmental Law Center, Charlottesville, VA, $48,860. For Southern Forest Protection Project. 2001.

1449-62 Southside Community Land Trust, Providence, RI, $25,010. For general support for education, organizing, and technical assistance for urban agriculture and community gardens. 2001.

1449-63 Southwings, Chattanooga, TN, $35,315. For general support for conservation-based aviation service in the Southeast. 2001.

1449-64 Trust for Public Land, Charlotte, NC, $50,014. To start up Charleston, South Carolina office. 2001.

1449-65 Vermont Businesses for Social Responsibility Research and Education Foundation, South Burlington, VT, $30,000. For Vermont Tax-Shifting Project. 2001.

1449-66 Vermont Natural Resources Council, Montpelier, VT, $30,000. For Vermont Tax-Shifting Project. 2001.

1449-67 Vermont Public Interest Research Group Education Fund, Montpelier, VT, $30,000. For Vermont Tax-Shifting Project. 2001.

1449-68 Virginia Forest Watch, Charlottesville, VA, $29,329. For reforming forestry practices on private lands in Virginia. 2001.

1449-69 Watershed Media, Healdsburg, CA, $39,293. For production and distribution of resources, Building with Vision and Rethinking Packaging. 2001.

1449-70 Western North Carolina Alliance, Asheville, NC, $29,863. For general support for public forest protection and clean air standards. 2001.

1449-71 Wilderness Society, DC, $21,503. For economic analyses for wildland protection in the Northern Forest. 2001.

1449-72 Yale University, School of Forestry and Environmental Studies, New Haven, CT, $50,007. For tenure track position in sustainable forestry. 2001.

1449-73 Youth Ministries for Peace and Justice, Bronx, NY, $35,000. For RIVER, Researching and Including Youth Voices for Environmental Rights, youth organizing project. 2001.

1450
The John Merck Fund ▼
11 Beacon St., Ste. 1230
Boston, MA 02108 (617) 723-2932
Contact: Ruth G. Hennig, Exec. Dir.
FAX: (617) 523-6029; E-mail: info@jmfund.org

Established in 1970 in NY as a trust.
Donor(s): Serena S. Merck.‡
Grantmaker type: Independent foundation
Financial data (yr. ended 12/31/01): Assets, $194,017,773 (M); expenditures, $16,137,204; qualifying distributions, $13,529,090; giving activities include $12,721,977 for 235 grants (high: $400,000; low: $1,852; average: $20,000–$100,000).
Purpose and activities: Grants are made in the following areas: to medical teaching hospitals for research on developmental disabilities in children; to preserve environmental quality in rural New England and globally; to promote nonproliferation of nuclear weapons; to support reproductive health and rights initiatives; to advance international human rights; and to support job creation and training in the northeastern U.S.
Fields of interest: Natural resources; Energy; Environment; Medical research, institute; Employment, services; Employment; Arms control; International human rights; Reproductive rights.
Types of support: General/operating support; Program development; Conferences/seminars; Publication; Fellowships; Research.
Limitations: Generally, no support for large organizations with well-established funding sources. No grants to individuals, or for endowment or capital fund projects.
Publications: Grants list, Informational brochure (including application guidelines).
Application information: The fund does not encourage the submission of unsolicited applications for grants. The fund prefers to request a grant proposal after receiving preliminary written or verbal information about a project.
  Initial approach: Letter of inquiry
  Board meeting date(s): Monthly
Officers and Trustees:* Francis W. Hatch,* Chair.; Ruth G. Hennig, Secy. and Exec. Dir.; Huyler C. Held,* Treas.; David Altshuler; Judith M. Buechner; Olivia H. Farr; George W.M. Hatch; Serena M. Hatch; Arnold Hiatt; Robert M. Pennoyer; Frederica Perera.
Number of staff: 3 full-time professional.
EIN: 237082558
Recent environmental and animal welfare grants:
1450-1 20/20 Vision Education Fund, DC, $50,000. To educate public and key policymakers on national missile defense and taking nuclear weapons off alert, using monthly action cards, Internet-based

activism, partnerships with faith groups, and field organizing in target regions. 2001.

1450-2 20/20 Vision Education Fund, DC, $35,000. To educate and mobilize members, their communities, and many people now reachable through the Internet to advocate for labeling of genetically modified foods and moratorium on new genetically engineered products until they are proven safe. 2001.

1450-3 20/20 Vision Education Fund, DC, $15,000. To purchase technology to improve organization's ability to track effectiveness in reaching public with information. 2001.

1450-4 Alliance for Nuclear Accountability, Seattle, WA, $60,600. To improve internal operations of offices by upgrading technical equipment, software, and other resources; and to improve basic skills of member organizations through workshops on media, strategic planning, fundraising, and computer literacy. Grant made through Capacity-Building Pilot Program. 2001.

1450-5 Alliance for Nuclear Accountability, Seattle, WA, $40,000. To coordinate and support national network of organizations dedicated to monitoring Department of Energy nuclear weapons production complex, preventing further weapons development and encouraging environmental cleanup. 2001.

1450-6 Alliance for Nuclear Accountability, Seattle, WA, $11,000. Toward Movement for Nuclear Safety in Russia in replacing computers and equipment lost in office robbery. 2001.

1450-7 American Planning Association, Tallahassee, FL, $40,000. To educate Floridians on environmental, health, and economic harm caused by polluting power plants and benefits of and opportunities for energy efficiency and use of alternative energy sources such as solar power. 2001.

1450-8 Appalachian Mountain Club, Boston, MA, $30,000. For Upper Androscoggin Valley Community Conservation Project. 2001.

1450-9 Center for Clean Air Policy, DC, $50,000. To provide governments of Northeastern states with technical assistance, strategic advice, collaborative opportunities, and encouragement to implement programs that reduce greenhouse gas emissions and build momentum for national action to abate climate change. 2001.

1450-10 Center for Energy and Climate Solutions, Annandale, VA, $75,000. To demonstrate to Northeastern businesses, large institutions, and municipalities the financial and environmental advantages of more effective energy management. 2001.

1450-11 Center for Environmental Citizenship, DC, $40,000. To hire New England Energy and Environmental Health Issue Fellows who will implement energy and environmental health campaigns on New England campuses, and to connect students strategically to ongoing community-based campaigns in order to strengthen environmental movement. 2001.

1450-12 Center for Public Interest Research, Boston, MA, $20,000. For Genetic Engineering Action Network, coalition that addresses environmental and human health risks, as well as socioeconomic and ethical

consequences, posed by genetic engineering. 2001.

1450-13 Childrens Health Environmental Coalition, Princeton, NJ, $50,000. To inform new parents of babies born in U.S. hospitals each year about importance of reducing their infants' household toxic exposures, which have been linked to variety of long-term health problems, including asthma, learning disabilities, and cancer. 2001.

1450-14 Citizen Alert, Reno, NV, $45,000. To prevent construction of high-level nuclear waste repository at Yucca Mountain, and to stop testing of nuclear weapons components at Nevada Test Site. 2001.

1450-15 Citizens Nuclear Information Center, Tokyo, Japan, $30,000. To reverse Japanese government's plan to use plutonium for energy production, with emphasis on ending reprocessing of spent nuclear fuel. 2001.

1450-16 Clean Air Task Force, Boston, MA, $200,000. To reduce emissions of smog, soot, haze, acid rain, toxics, and greenhouse gases from nation's diesel engines by reforming state and federal policies and, where possible, achieving voluntary commitments to emissions reductions from engine and equipment manufacturers. 2001.

1450-17 Clean Air Task Force, Boston, MA, $75,000. To reduce emissions of sulfur dioxide, nitrogen oxides, toxic substances, and greenhouse gases from nation's electric power plants by reforming state and federal policies. 2001.

1450-18 Clean Energy Group, Montpelier, VT, $75,000. To conduct outreach to key industries, such as data and financial services, healthcare and medical research institutions, and manufacturers of chemicals, pharmaceuticals and semiconductors, whose need for premium, reliable power could be met with fuel cells. 2001.

1450-19 Clean Energy Group, Montpelier, VT, $50,000. To define appropriate target industries and needed outreach strategies to enlist corporations and other major institutions in collaborations that explore clean energy installations at their sites. 2001.

1450-20 Clean Water Fund, DC, $130,000. To achieve major improvements in air quality in New England by reducing pollution from region's dirtiest coal- and oil-fired power plants, in collaboration with MASSPIRG Education Fund, Natural Resources Council of Maine, and Toxics Action Center. 2001.

1450-21 Clean Water Fund, DC, $115,000. To transform Precautionary Principle from theory about safety standards required before introducing technologies and substances into environment into set of policies and decision-making processes that can be implemented by state governments to protect human health and environment. 2001.

1450-22 Clean Water Fund, DC, $90,000. To coordinate New England-wide campaign to achieve virtual elimination of mercury emissions in region by 2010. 2001.

1450-23 Clean Water Fund, DC, $50,000. To create visible consumer movement in Massachusetts and other New England states that supports removing genetically engineered ingredients from grocery store brand products. 2001.

1450-24 Concerned Citizens for Nuclear Safety, Santa Fe, NM, $25,000. To complete administrative reorganization by hiring permanent executive director; to strengthen organization's media outreach by improving website; and to monitor Department of Energy radioactive wastes and toxic emissions at Los Alamos National Laboratory. 2001.

1450-25 Conservation Law Foundation, Boston, MA, $40,000. To oppose proposed sale of Vermont Yankee Nuclear Power Facility, ensure that ratepayers do not continue to subsidize nuclear power, and create state clean energy fund in Vermont. 2001.

1450-26 Conservation Law Foundation, Boston, MA, $40,000. To defend Northeast Interstate Dairy Compact against efforts to eliminate it. 2001.

1450-27 Conservation Law Foundation, Boston, MA, $20,000. To oppose construction of Chittenden County Circumferential Highway in northwest Vermont. 2001.

1450-28 Consumer Policy Institute, Yonkers, NY, $30,000. To increase public understanding of scientific uncertainties about safety and impacts of genetically engineered food production; and to ensure that federal regulation of genetically engineered foods reflects those uncertainties. 2001.

1450-29 EarthRights International, DC, $50,000. To train Burmese leaders in human rights documentation, organizational development, and leadership skills. 2001.

1450-30 EarthRights International, DC, $25,000. For general support. 2001.

1450-31 Ecologists Linked for Organizing Grassroots Initiatives and Action (ECOLOGIA), Middlebury, VT, $40,000. For denuclearization in Seversk, closed nuclear weapons production city in Russia. 2001.

1450-32 Environmental and Energy Study Institute, DC, $30,000. To build national support for gradual elimination of diesel buses in metropolitan transit fleets in order to move bus industry away from heavily polluting diesel engines. 2001.

1450-33 Environmental League of Massachusetts, Boston, MA, $30,000. To improve implementation of Massachusetts' Toxic Use Reduction Act by improving state agency enforcement, pressuring businesses to reduce their use of toxic chemicals, and making information about toxic chemical use more readily available to citizens. 2001.

1450-34 Government Accountability Project (GAP), DC, $50,000. To reduce environmental health and safety consequences of nuclear weapons production; and to provide legal representation to nuclear workers who report illegal or unsafe activities at nuclear weapons production sites. 2001.

1450-35 Government Accountability Project (GAP), DC, $15,000. To convene strategy conference for developing responses to Columbia River's impending contamination from Hanford Nuclear Reservation's weapons production complex. 2001.

1450-36 Green Corps, Boston, MA, $75,000. For Free the Planet's efforts to educate and engage college students in public debate on climate change and genetic engineering; and

for New England Environmental Leadership Training program. 2001.

1450-37 Green House Network, Lake Oswego, Oregon, $35,000. For The Heat Is On Campaign to enable author of the book to promote awareness of hazards posed by climate change and to catalyze actions needed to stabilize global climate systems. 2001.

1450-38 Harvard University, Cambridge, MA, $50,000. For Center for Health and the Global Environment in Boston to develop local and regional solutions for reducing greenhouse gas emissions. 2001.

1450-39 Hubbard Brook Research Foundation, Campton, NH, $20,000. To increase understanding among policymakers and heighten public awareness of damaging ecosystem effects from nitrogen pollution in Northeastern United States; and to make scientific information more readily usable for non-scientists who are developing environmental policies. 2001.

1450-40 Institute for Conservation Leadership, Takoma Park, MD, $30,000. To conduct pilot program for New England's environmental organizations that improves fundraising capabilities. 2001.

1450-41 Institute for Energy and Environmental Research, Takoma Park, MD, $50,000. To provide technical support to citizen organizations working on issues relating to nuclear weapons production, including plutonium and waste management, laboratory nuclear testing, de-alerting and disassembling weapons, and environmental cleanup. 2001.

1450-42 Institute for Local Self-Reliance, DC, $50,000. To eliminate polyvinyl chloride (PVC) plastic and formaldehyde from use in construction projects. 2001.

1450-43 Intervale Foundation, Burlington, VT, $50,000. To develop sustainable solutions for Vermont's farming future through incubation projects, training, education, and advocacy. 2001.

1450-44 Izaak Walton League of America, Gaithersburg, MD, $75,000. To reduce pollution from coal-fired power plants in Midwest. 2001.

1450-45 Maine Peoples Resource Center, Portland, ME, $40,000. To strengthen citizen involvement in decision-making processes concerning mercury-contaminated Penobscot River sediments and HoltraChem site cleanup; and to increase accountability of state and federal regulatory agencies and corporate polluters for river's excessive level of mercury contamination. 2001.

1450-46 Massachusetts Breast Cancer Coalition, Waltham, MA, $20,000. To transform Precautionary Principle from theory about safety standards required before introducing technologies and substances into environment into set of policies and decision-making processes that can be implemented by state governments to protect human health and environment. 2001.

1450-47 Massachusetts Climate Action Network (MCAN), Arlington, MA, $10,000. To encourage local communities to implement measures to reduce their greenhouse gas emissions. 2001.

1450-48 Massachusetts Energy Consumers Alliance, Boston, MA, $50,000. To conduct feasibility study for aggregating Boston-area residents and members of environmental organizations into customer block for purchasing electricity from clean energy sources. 2001.

1450-49 Massachusetts Energy Consumers Alliance, Boston, MA, $35,000. To measure and highlight emerging financial and environmental benefits associated with deploying clean distributed generation technologies (solar power, fuel cells and microturbines) within transmission-constrained urban area of Greater Boston. 2001.

1450-50 Massachusetts Institute of Technology, Cambridge, MA, $60,000. To produce independent, scientific analysis of unresolved technical issues that may affect safety of proposed Yucca Mountain repository for high-level nuclear waste in Nevada. 2001.

1450-51 Massachusetts Public Interest Research Group Education Fund, Boston, MA, $20,000. To achieve major improvements in air quality in New England by reducing pollution from region's dirtiest coal- and oil-fired power plants in collaboration with Clean Water Fund, Natural Resources Council of Maine, and Toxics Action Center. 2001.

1450-52 Merck Forest and Farmland Center, Rupert, VT, $54,000. To develop comprehensive series of demonstrations that can be used to teach benefits of sustainable forest and farmland management. 2001.

1450-53 Movement for Nuclear Safety, Chelyabinsk, Russia, $38,000. To raise public awareness and understanding of nuclear nonproliferation in Russia. 2001.

1450-54 National Environmental Trust, DC, $100,000. To mount media and public education campaign to raise awareness and understanding about misguided energy policies in U.S. 2001.

1450-55 National Environmental Trust, DC, $100,000. To ensure that climate change is treated as priority by policy-makers, media, and public during critical junctures in policy developments at both international and domestic levels. 2001.

1450-56 National Wildlife Federation, Reston, VA, $35,000. To eliminate mercury as threat to people and wildlife in New England, through combined program of education, research, coalition building, and policy advocacy. 2001.

1450-57 Natural Resources Council, Augusta, ME, $30,000. To participate in New England campaign to achieve virtual elimination of mercury emission in region by 2010. 2001.

1450-58 Natural Resources Council, Augusta, ME, $15,000. To achieve major improvements in air quality in New England by reducing pollution from region's dirtiest coal- and oil-fired power plants, in collaboration with Clean Water Fund, MASSPIRG Education Fund, and Toxics Action Center. 2001.

1450-59 Natural Resources Defense Council, New York, NY, $75,000. To compel HoltraChem Manufacturing Company and Mallinckrodt Inc. to develop plan to clean up mercury-contaminated sediment in

Penobscot River and Bay caused by their chemical manufacturing facility in Orrington, ME. 2001.

1450-60 Natural Resources Defense Council, New York, NY, $50,000. To promote nuclear nonproliferation, focusing on opposing proposals for missile defense system. 2001.

1450-61 Nautilus of America, Berkeley, CA, $57,000. To promote nuclear nonproliferation in Northeast Asia, primarily through electronic information exchange. 2001.

1450-62 Nautilus of America, Berkeley, CA, $25,000. For general support. 2001.

1450-63 New England Forestry Foundation, Groton, MA, $60,000. To hire senior land protection specialist in order to meet growing demand for conservation services following successful completion of country's largest easement transaction. 2001.

1450-64 New England Grassroots Environment Fund, Montpelier, VT, $50,000. To foster and give voice to community-based environmental initiatives in New England and build vibrant and diverse grassroots network of activists across region, through small grants. 2001.

1450-65 New Hampshire Public Interest Research Group Education Fund, Concord, NH, $20,000. To participate in public education and advocacy campaign to clean up dirty power plants in New Hampshire. 2001.

1450-66 Partnership Project, DC, $300,000. For Collaborative Defense Campaign. 2001.

1450-67 Physicians for Social Responsibility, Cambridge, MA, $100,000. To educate medical, patient, and policymaking communities about links between toxic chemical exposures and children's developmental, behavioral, and learning disabilities, and to increase understanding that these exposures are preventable. 2001.

1450-68 Physicians for Social Responsibility, Cambridge, MA, $50,000. For Health Care Without Harm's Boston Sustainable Hospitals Project. 2001.

1450-69 Public Employees for Environmental Responsibility (PEER), DC, $45,000. For National PEER Activist Summit; and to enhance ability and willingness of state and federal resource agencies in New England to enforce existing environmental protection laws by amplifying voice of and protecting agency employees. 2001.

1450-70 Science and Environmental Health Network, Windsor, ND, $75,000. To continue to develop Precautionary Principle as unifying and practical tool in developing sounder, more far-sighted environmental policy. 2001.

1450-71 Snake River Alliance Education Fund, Boise, ID, $35,000. To educate decision makers and public about importance of taking nuclear weapons off high alert. 2001.

1450-72 Southern Environmental Law Center, Charlottesville, VA, $40,000. To clean up outdated coal-burning power plants in Southeast. 2001.

1450-73 STAND of Amarillo, Amarillo, TX, $40,000. To monitor Department of Energy activities at Pantex Plant in Amarillo, TX, and to encourage citizen involvement in opposing nuclear weapons production and

promoting environmental cleanup at site. 2001.

1450-74 TechRocks, San Francisco, CA, $50,000. For planning and initial development of ClimateSaver.org, which is designed to build public awareness of impact and threats posed by climate change. 2001.

1450-75 Tides Center, San Francisco, CA, $182,500. For Environmental Media Services; Minuteman Media, to generate and disseminate articles on climate and energy issues to small newspapers across U.S.; and International Human Rights Funders Group. 2001.

1450-76 Tides Center, San Francisco, CA, $40,000. For Mercury Policy Project in Montpelier, VT to participate in New England campaign to achieve virtual elimination of mercury emissions in region by 2010. 2001.

1450-77 Tides Center, Regeneration Project, San Francisco, CA, $50,000. To reduce greenhouse gas emissions and strengthen renewable energy sector by encouraging Episcopal churches and parishioners, as well as assisting other religious groups, to conserve energy or purchase green energy products where available. 2001.

1450-78 Toxics Action Center, Boston, MA, $55,000. To achieve major improvements in air quality in New England by reducing pollution from region's dirtiest coal- and oil-fired power plants, in collaboration with Clean Water Fund MASSPIRG Education Fund, and Natural Resources Council of Maine. 2001.

1450-79 Tri-Valley Communities Against a Radioactive Environment, Livermore, CA, $40,000. To mobilize citizen involvement in monitoring Department of Energy's nuclear weapons research and development activities at Lawrence Livermore National Laboratory in California. 2001.

1450-80 Union of Concerned Scientists, Cambridge, MA, $100,000. To promote nuclear nonproliferation, with specific focus on preventing deployment of U.S. national missile defense system and weaponization of space. 2001.

1450-81 Union of Concerned Scientists, Cambridge, MA, $60,000. To increase role that renewable power and energy efficiency play in New England's energy supply. 2001.

1450-82 Union of Concerned Scientists, Cambridge, MA, $50,000. To shape role of genetic engineering in quest for sustainable food system. 2001.

1450-83 United States Public Interest Research Group Education Fund, DC, $75,000. To expand public education, media, and grassroots organizing campaign on interrelated problems of climate change and energy policy, with emphasis on need for domestic action to reduce greenhouse gas emissions and increase reliance on energy efficiency and renewable energy. 2001.

1450-84 University of Massachusetts, Lowell Center for Sustainable Production, Lowell, MA, $35,000. To transform Precautionary Principle from theory about safety standards required before introducing technologies and substances into environment into set of policies and decision-making processes that can be implemented by state governments to

protect human health and environment. 2001.

1450-85 University of New Hampshire, Durham, NH, $25,000. To evaluate benefits of using sheep to control unwanted vegetation, as opposed to herbicide spraying or mechanical mowers, under power lines in southeastern New Hampshire. 2001.

1450-86 University of Vermont, Burlington, VT, $21,500. To improve income for beef producers, establish sustainable value-added markets for cattle industry, and increase land for beef enterprises in Vermont. 2001.

1450-87 University of Vermont, Center for Sustainable Agriculture, Burlington, VT, $35,000. To connect people who want to farm in Vermont with people who have available land; and to provide information and training that keeps Vermont farmland in agriculture use despite ownership transfers. 2001.

1450-88 Vermont Forum on Sprawl, Burlington, VT, $50,000. To promote greater awareness about problems that sprawl development causes, and about actions that individuals and communities can take to prevent it. 2001.

1450-89 Vermont Forum on Sprawl, Burlington, VT, $12,000. To plan Vermont Smart Growth Collaborative. 2001.

1450-90 Vermont Public Interest Research Group Education Fund, Montpelier, VT, $75,000. To eliminate or reduce contamination of Vermont's lakes, rivers, and drinking water from pesticides and chemical fertilizers used for farming, forestry, golf courses, and by individual households. 2001.

1450-91 Western Resource Advocates, Boulder, CO, $50,000. To reduce emissions at power plants in Southwest and Rocky Mountain states. 2001.

1450-92 Western States Legal Foundation, Oakland, CA, $25,000. To conduct research and analysis on U.S. nuclear weapons program, related high-technology weapons programs, and their impacts on arms control regimes; and to expose health and environmental consequences of nuclear weapons research, testing and production. 2001.

1450-93 World Information Service on Energy, Paris, France, $40,000. To raise awareness about dangers of using nuclear weapons-grade plutonium as commercial product in nuclear power generation or reprocessing in Europe and Japan. 2001.

1451
George H. & Jane A. Mifflin Memorial Fund

c/o Loring, Wolcott & Coolidge
230 Congress St.
Boston, MA 02110 (617) 523-6531
Contact: Lawrence Coolidge, Tr.

Established in 1974 in Massachusetts.
Grantmaker type: Independent foundation
Financial data (yr. ended 09/30/02): Assets, $27,412,359 (M); expenditures, $2,134,485; qualifying distributions, $1,940,123; giving activities include $1,975,000 for 104 grants (high: $65,000; low: $5,000; average: $5,000–$50,000).

Purpose and activities: Giving primarily for education. Some giving also for human services and environmental conservation.
Fields of interest: Education; Natural resources; Legal services; Human services; Economically disadvantaged.
Types of support: General/operating support; Capital campaigns; Building/renovation; Land acquisition; Scholarship funds; Matching/challenge support.
Limitations: Giving primarily in MA. No grants to individuals.
Application information: Application form not required.
Initial approach: Letter
Copies of proposal: 2
Deadline(s): Apr. 1 and Aug. 1
Board meeting date(s): May and Sept.
Final notification: Sept. 30
Trustees: John G. Brooks; Lawrence Coolidge; Peter B. Loring.
EIN: 046384983

1452
Herman and Frieda L. Miller Foundation
c/o Grants Mgt. Assoc.
77 Summer St., 8th Fl.
Boston, MA 02110-1006
Contact: Amy Segal Shorey

Established in 1997 in MA.
Donor(s): Herman Miller.‡
Grantmaker type: Independent foundation
Financial data (yr. ended 11/30/02): Assets, $37,282,317 (M); expenditures, $1,761,033; qualifying distributions, $1,653,197; giving activities include $1,647,270 for 30 grants (high: $200,000; low: $1,000).
Purpose and activities: Giving primarily for arts and cultural programs, the environment, and human services.
Fields of interest: Arts; Natural resources; Environment; Human services; Women, centers/services; Community development.
Types of support: General/operating support; Annual campaigns; Capital campaigns; Building/renovation; Matching/challenge support.
Limitations: Applications not accepted. Giving primarily in Boston, MA. No grants to individuals.
Application information: Contributes only to pre-selected organizations.
Trustee: Myron Miller.
Number of staff: 2 part-time professional; 1 full-time support.
EIN: 137131926

1453
The Martha Morse Foundation
c/o Bingham Legg Advisors
45 Milk St.
Boston, MA 02109-5105
Contact: Colin S. Marshall, Tr.
Application address: c/o Bingham Dana, LLP, 150 Federal St., Boston, MA 02110, tel.: (617) 951-8576

Established in 1997 in NC.
Grantmaker type: Independent foundation
Financial data (yr. ended 03/31/02): Assets, $2,897,215 (M); expenditures, $197,227;

qualifying distributions, $164,420; giving activities include $165,000 for 12 grants (high: $50,000; low: $5,000).
Purpose and activities: Giving primarily to wildlife organizations.
Fields of interest: Animal welfare; Animals/wildlife, preservation/protection.
Limitations: Giving in the New England area, primarily in MA, ME, and NH.
Application information: Application form not required.
Deadline(s): None
Trustee: Colin S. Marshall.
EIN: 043375373

1454
MWC Foundation, Inc.
c/o Nutter, McClennen & Fish, LLP
155 Seaport Blvd., World Trade Ctr. W.
Boston, MA 02210-2604
Contact: Thomas P. Jalkut, Clerk

Established in 1988 in MA.
Grantmaker type: Independent foundation
Financial data (yr. ended 12/31/01): Assets, $28,158,168 (M); gifts received, $1,210,000; expenditures, $2,500,156; qualifying distributions, $2,428,097; giving activities include $2,284,002 for 63 grants (high: $850,000; low: $4,000; average: $10,000–$50,000).
Purpose and activities: Giving primarily for social services.
Fields of interest: Environment; Human services; Community development.
Limitations: Applications not accepted. Giving primarily in New England. No grants to individuals.
Application information: Contributes primarily to pre-selected organizations. Due to existing commitments, very few unsolicited requests receive favorable consideration.
Officer: Thomas P. Jalkut, Clerk.
EIN: 222914691

1455
The Creighton Narada Foundation
c/o Day, Berry & Howard, LLP
260 Franklin St.
Boston, MA 02110

Established in 1994 in MA.
Donor(s): Albert M. Creighton, Jr., Charitable Lead Unitrust.
Grantmaker type: Independent foundation
Financial data (yr. ended 12/31/02): Assets, $9,018,812 (M); gifts received, $73,878; expenditures, $548,146; qualifying distributions, $531,007; giving activities include $520,000 for 17 grants (high: $175,000; low: $500).
Purpose and activities: Giving primarily for land conservation and social services.
Fields of interest: Museums; Higher education; Natural resources; Environment, land resources; Boys & girls clubs; Human services.
Limitations: Applications not accepted. Giving primarily in MA; substantial giving also in ME. No grants to individuals.
Application information: Contributes only to pre-selected organizations.

Trustees: Albert M. Creighton, Jr.; Albert M. Creighton III; Hilary H. Creighton; Peter H. Creighton.
EIN: 043243114

1456
NEB Corporate Giving Program
32 Tozer Rd.
Beverly, MA 01915-5599 (978) 927-5054
Contact: Fana Mersha, Chair.

Grantmaker type: Corporate giving program
Purpose and activities: As a complement to its foundation, NEB also makes charitable contributions to nonprofit organizations directly. Support is given primarily in the North Shore area of Massachusetts.
Fields of interest: Education; Environment; Food banks; Housing/shelter, homeless; Recreation.
Types of support: General/operating support; Donated equipment; In-kind gifts.
Limitations: Giving primarily in the North Shore area of MA.
Application information: A contributions committee reviews all requests.
Initial approach: Proposal to headquarters
Deadline(s): Apr. 1 and Nov. 1
Final notification: 1 month following deadline

1457
New England Biolabs Foundation
32 Tozer Rd.
Beverly, MA 01915 (978) 927-2404
Contact: Martine Kellett, Exec. Dir.; or Vicki Cataldo, Asst. to Exec. Dir.
FAX: (978) 921-1350; E-mail: cataldo@nebf.org, kellett@nebf.org; URL: http://www.nebf.org

Established in 1982 in MA.
Donor(s): New England Biolabs, Inc., Donald G. Combs.
Grantmaker type: Company-sponsored foundation
Financial data (yr. ended 11/30/02): Assets, $7,618,662 (M); gifts received, $203,000; expenditures, $552,808; qualifying distributions, $523,046; giving activities include $372,488 for 50 grants (high: $13,000; low: $1,000; average: $1,000–$10,000).
Purpose and activities: Giving to grassroots organizations involved in land and water (especially ocean) protection and management; emphasis on natural resource conservation and protection, biodiversity issues, marine conservation, agroforestry projects, international economic development, energy, arts and cultural programs, elementary education, and limited scientific research.
Fields of interest: Arts; Elementary school/education; Natural resources; Environment, water resources; Environment, forests; Environment; International economic development; Marine science; Science.
International interests: Caribbean; Ghana; Cameroon; Tanzania; Central America; El Salvador; Guatemala; Honduras; Nicaragua; Bolivia; Ecuador; Peru; Papua New Guinea; Philippines.
Types of support: General/operating support; Program development; Seed money; Curriculum development; Research; Matching/challenge support.

Limitations: Giving primarily in Suffolk and Essex counties, MA, and in Papua New Guinea, Cameroon, Central America, and the Caribbean. No support for religious activities, specific animal protection, services for the elderly or the handicapped, projects normally funded by major agencies, or art projects outside the immediate community. No grants for capital endowment or building funds, operating costs, fellowships, movies or videos, scholarships, or conferences.
Publications: Grants list, Informational brochure (including application guidelines).
Application information: Accepts NNG Common Grant Proposal Form. Application form not required.
Initial approach: Letter or telephone
Copies of proposal: 3
Deadline(s): Mar. 1, Sept. 1, and Dec. 1
Board meeting date(s): Jan., Apr., and Oct.
Final notification: 4 to 6 weeks after meeting
Officer: Martine Kellett, Exec. Dir.
Trustees: Mary Catherine Bateson; David Comb; Henry P. Paulus.
Number of staff: 3 part-time professional.
EIN: 042776213

1458
The New Tudor Foundation
264 N. Pleasant St., 2nd Fl.
Amherst, MA 01002 (413) 256-0349
Contact: Ada Sanchez, Exec. Dir.
FAX: (413) 256-3536

Established in 1991 in MA as the Rabinowitz Family Charitable Foundation; current name adopted in 1993.
Donor(s): Tudor Foundation, Inc.
Grantmaker type: Independent foundation
Financial data (yr. ended 12/31/01): Assets, $2,447,180 (M); expenditures, $168,970; qualifying distributions, $152,025; giving activities include $124,563 for grants (average: $5,000–$20,000).
Purpose and activities: Giving primarily for social justice, health care, and the environment.
Fields of interest: Environment; Health care; Women.
Types of support: General/operating support; Building/renovation; Equipment; Program development; Publication; Seed money; Scholarship funds; Technical assistance.
Limitations: Applications not accepted. Giving on a national basis. No support for conferences or fundraising drives. No grants to individuals.
Application information: Contributes only to pre-selected organizations; unsolicited requests for funds not considered.
Board meeting date(s): Fall
Officer: Ada Sanchez, Exec. Dir.
Trustees: Alan Rabinowitz; Andrea Rabinowitz.
Number of staff: 1 shared staff (shared with Peppercorn Foundation, CarEth Foundation).
EIN: 043125604

1459
Northeast Charitable Trust
50 Congress St., Rm. 1000
Boston, MA 02109 (888) 404-1557
Contact: William A. Oates, Jr., Tr.

Established in 1990 in MA.

Grantmaker type: Independent foundation
Financial data (yr. ended 12/31/02): Assets, $567,905 (M); expenditures, $119,021; qualifying distributions, $108,260; giving activities include $107,850 for 52 grants (high: $75,000; low: $50).
Fields of interest: Higher education; Education; Natural resources; Boys & girls clubs; Christian agencies & churches.
Limitations: Giving limited to the Northeast, primarily in MA. No grants to individuals.
Application information:
Initial approach: Letter
Deadline(s): None
Trustees: Robert B. Minturn, Jr.; Ernest E. Monrad; William A. Oates, Jr.
EIN: 043078302

1460
The Oak Foundation U.S.A. ▼
47 Winter St., 6th Floor
Boston, MA 02108
Contact: Karen Phair, Asst. to the Pres.
FAX: (617) 542-5570; E-mail: oak@oakfnd.org;
URL: http://www.oakfnd.org

Established in 1986 in DE.
Donor(s): The Oak Trust, The Forest Trust.
Grantmaker type: Independent foundation
Financial data (yr. ended 12/31/01): Assets, $241,476,885 (M); gifts received, $33,194,049; expenditures, $10,748,625; qualifying distributions, $8,557,168; giving activities include $7,616,753 for 40 grants (high: $3,200,000; low: $1,000; average: $2,000–$200,000).
Purpose and activities: To address issues of global, social, and environmental concern, particularly those that have a major impact on the lives of the disadvantaged.
Fields of interest: Global warming; Natural resources; Environment, water resources; Environment; Learning disorders; Child abuse; Housing/shelter, homeless; International human rights; Women.
International interests: Europe; Africa; Zimbabwe; Asia.
Types of support: General/operating support; Continuing support; Building/renovation; Equipment; Program development; Program evaluation; Matching/challenge support.
Limitations: Giving on a national and international basis. No grants to individuals.
Publications: Annual report (including application guidelines).
Application information: Application form required.
Copies of proposal: 1
Deadline(s): None
Officers and Directors:* Jette Parker,* Chair.; Alan M. Parker,* Vice-Chair.; William R. Cotter,* Pres.; Gary Goodman, Secy.
Number of staff: 3 full-time professional; 2 part-time professional.
EIN: 133321196
Recent environmental and animal welfare grants:
1460-1 Clean Air Cool Planet-A Northeast Alliance, Portsmouth, NH, $25,000. For general support. 2001.
1460-2 Conservation Law Foundation, Boston, MA, $70,000. For general support. 2001.

1460-3 Land Trust Alliance, DC, $105,000. For general support. 2001.
1460-4 Nature Conservancy, Arlington, VA, $75,000. For general support. 2001.
1460-5 New England Aquarium, Boston, MA, $72,554. For general support. 2001.
1460-6 Sierra Club Foundation, San Francisco, CA, $50,000. For general support. 2001.
1460-7 Wild Salmon Center, Portland, Oregon, $10,000. For general support. 2001.
1460-8 Wildlife Conservation Society, Bronx, NY, $81,000. For general support. 2001.
1460-9 Wildlife Trust, Palisades, NY, $75,000. For general support of Center for Conservation Medicine's programs in North Grafton, MA. 2001.
1460-10 World Resources Institute, DC, $251,099. For general support. 2001.

1461
The Orchard Foundation
c/o M. Gordon Ehrlich, Bingham, McCutchen
150 Federal St.
Boston, MA 02110
Contact: Brigitte L. Kingsbury, Exec. Dir.
Mailing address: P.O. Box 2587, South Portland, ME 04116-2587, tel.: (207) 799-0686, E-mail: orchard@maine.rr.com; URL: http://home.maine.rr.com/orchard/homeorchard.htm; http://www.orchardfoundation.org

Established in 1990 in MA.
Donor(s): Moose Mountain Trust, Leigh Fibers, Inc., Leigh Fibers Holdings, Inc.
Grantmaker type: Company-sponsored foundation
Financial data (yr. ended 12/31/02): Assets, $11,366,770 (M); gifts received, $700,000; expenditures, $1,099,593; qualifying distributions, $924,202; giving activities include $924,202 for 103 grants (average: $3,000–$15,000).
Purpose and activities: Primary areas of interest include the environment, including air quality, biodiversity, fresh and coastal waters, forests, toxic substances, and pollution prevention; and children, youth, and family services, especially literacy, and pregnancy prevention.
Fields of interest: Reading; Natural resources; Environment; Animals/wildlife, preservation/protection; Family planning.
Types of support: Program development; Seed money.
Limitations: Giving limited to NY and the New England states, including national groups with regional offices or projects in these areas. No support for religious programs, animal hospitals, rehabilitation centers or groups which focus on specific diseases or conditions. No grants to individuals, or for endowment funds, annual and capital campaigns, equipment, building projects, land acquisition, conferences, travel, scholarships, or fellowships; no loans.
Publications: Application guidelines, Grants list, Program policy statement.
Application information: Express mail discouraged. When possible, submit unbound double-sided materials. No "over-the-transom" proposals accepted. Application form not required.
Initial approach: Check Web site for guidelines
Copies of proposal: 1

Deadline(s): Concept letter due Mar. 1 and
Sept. 1. Invited proposals will have a
separate deadline
Board meeting date(s): June and Nov.
Final notification: Mid-June and mid-Dec.
Officer and Trustees:* Brigitte L. Kingsbury,*
Exec. Dir.; M. Gordon Ehrlich; Carl P. Lehner;
Heidi Lehner; Peter Lehner; Philip Lehner.
Number of staff: 1 part-time professional.
EIN: 046660214

1462
Osram Sylvania Inc. Corporate Giving Program

c/o Corp. Comm. Dept.
100 Endicott St.
Danvers, MA 01923 (978) 750-2895
Contact: Susan Reminger, Admin., Corp. Giving
Prog.
E-mail: susan.reminger@sylvania.com; URL:
http://www.sylvania.com/aboutus/corpgiving

Grantmaker type: Corporate giving program
Purpose and activities: Osram Sylvania makes
charitable contributions to nonprofit
organizations involved with arts and culture,
education, the environment, and health and
human services. Support is given on a national
basis.
Fields of interest: Arts; Education; Environment;
Health care; Human services.
Types of support: Program development;
Employee volunteer services; Employee
matching gifts; Employee-related scholarships;
Donated products.
Limitations: Giving on a national basis in areas
of company operations. No support for religious
organizations not of direct benefit to the entire
community, political candidates or lobbying
organizations, or fraternal, labor, or veterans'
organizations. No grants to individuals (except
for employee-related scholarships), or for
general operating support, capital campaigns,
travel, national conferences or sporting events,
sponsorships or advertising, or athletic
scholarships.
Application information: An application form is
available online. Multi-year funding is not
automatic. Application form required.
Initial approach: Complete online application
form
Copies of proposal: 1
Deadline(s): None
Final notification: Following review

1463
Edith H. Overly Foundation

c/o Choate, Hall & Stewart
53 State St., Exchange Pl.
Boston, MA 02109-2804

Established in 1990 in MA.
Donor(s): Edith H. Overly.
Grantmaker type: Independent foundation
Financial data (yr. ended 12/31/02): Assets,
$7,989,353 (M); expenditures, $610,258;
qualifying distributions, $566,100; giving
activities include $558,500 for 28 grants (high:
$30,000; low: $15,000).
Fields of interest: Media/communications;
Museums; Music; Arts; Medical
school/education; Education; Animals/wildlife,

formal/general education; Medical research,
institute; Cancer research.
Limitations: Applications not accepted. Giving
primarily in Boston, MA. No grants to
individuals.
Application information: Contributes only to
pre-selected organizations.
Trustees: F. Davis Dassori; Edith H. Overly.
EIN: 223043340

1464
The Pacer Foundation

c/o Foster Dykema Cabot & Co.
21 Milk St., 3rd Fl.
Boston, MA 02109-5408

Established in 1990 in CA.
Donor(s): Barbara Hunter Foster.
Grantmaker type: Independent foundation
Financial data (yr. ended 06/30/02): Assets,
$2,380,696 (M); gifts received, $252;
expenditures, $170,518; qualifying distributions,
$143,765; giving activities include $145,100 for
51 grants (high: $50,000; low: $100).
Purpose and activities: Giving primarily for
education.
Fields of interest: Secondary school/education;
Higher education; Education; Animal welfare;
Federated giving programs.
Limitations: Applications not accepted. Giving
on a national basis. No grants to individuals.
Application information: Contributes only to
pre-selected organizations.
Officers and Directors:* Barbara Hunter Foster,
Chair.; Hugh K. Foster, Jr.,* Pres.; Frank H.
Foster,* V.P.; Jennifer B. Foster,* V.P.; Adelaide E.
Foster,* Secy.; Elizabeth G. Woodard,* Treas.
EIN: 770233360

1465
Arthur M. & Martha R. Pappas Foundation

271 Main St., Ste. 203
Stoneham, MA 02180-3580

Established in 1988 in MA.
Donor(s): Arthur M. Pappas, Martha R. Pappas.
Grantmaker type: Independent foundation
Financial data (yr. ended 12/31/02): Assets,
$8,927,250 (M); gifts received, $8,000,000;
expenditures, $406,010; qualifying distributions,
$403,282; giving activities include $403,545 for
67 grants (high: $301,000; low: $25).
Purpose and activities: Giving for the arts,
education, the environment, health, and human
services.
Fields of interest: Arts; Education; Environment;
Health care; Health organizations, association;
Medical research; Human services; Christian
agencies & churches.
Limitations: Applications not accepted. Giving
primarily in MA. No grants to individuals.
Application information: Contributes only to
pre-selected organizations.
Trustees: Arthur M. Pappas; Martha R. Pappas.
EIN: 222967957

1466
Samuel P. Pardoe Foundation

c/o Grants Mgmt. Assoc., Inc.
77 Summer St., 8th Fl.
Boston, MA 02110 (617) 426-7080
Contact: Mary Phillips
FAX: (617) 426-7087; E-mail:
mphillips@grantsmanagement.com

Established in 1989 in DC.
Donor(s): Samuel P. Pardoe,‡ Helen P. Pardoe
Trust.
Grantmaker type: Independent foundation
Financial data (yr. ended 06/30/03): Assets,
$10,300,886 (M); expenditures, $508,278;
qualifying distributions, $450,392; giving
activities include $403,303 for 44 grants (high:
$97,225; low: $300; average: $5,000–$20,000).
Purpose and activities: Support primarily for
programs that provide educational and
economic opportunities for underprivileged
persons. Other areas of interest include health
and social services, cultural programs,
community development activities, education,
and land and resource management.
Fields of interest: Education; Environment, land
resources; Human services.
Types of support: Capital campaigns;
Building/renovation; Equipment; Program
development.
Limitations: Giving limited to the Lakes Region
of NH. No support for religious or sectarian
purposes. No grants to individuals, or for
operating expenses, endowments, scholarships,
deficit financing, advertising, special events, or
fundraising activities; no loans.
Publications: Application guidelines.
Application information: Application form
required.
Initial approach: Letter or telephone
Copies of proposal: 2
Deadline(s): Jan. 15
Board meeting date(s): Spring and fall
Final notification: Apr. 15
Officers and Directors:* Charles H. Pardoe II,*
Pres.; P. Bruce Pardoe,* V.P.; E. Spencer Pardoe
Ballou,* Secy.; Charles E. Pardoe,* Treas.
Number of staff: 3 shared staff.
EIN: 521660757

1467
The Theodore Edson Parker Foundation

c/o Grants Mgmt. Assocs., Inc.
77 Summer St., 8th Fl.
Boston, MA 02110 (617) 426-7172
Contact: Philip Hall, Admin.
FAX: (617) 426-5441; E-mail:
phall@grantsmanagement.com; URL: http://
www.grantsmanagement.com/
parkerfoundation.html

Incorporated in 1944 in MA.
Donor(s): Theodore Edson Parker.‡
Grantmaker type: Independent foundation
Financial data (yr. ended 12/31/02): Assets,
$19,406,701 (M); expenditures, $1,076,405;
qualifying distributions, $957,843; giving
activities include $823,654 for 36 grants (high:
$60,000; low: $300).
Purpose and activities: Giving in Lowell, MA,
for social services, arts, housing, community
development, and the urban environment, with

a particular interest in aiding underserved populations, particularly minorities.

Fields of interest: Arts; Education; Environment; Health care; Substance abuse, services; Employment; Housing/shelter, development; Human services; Children/youth, services; Minorities/immigrants, centers/services; Community development; Public affairs; Minorities; Economically disadvantaged.

Types of support: Building/renovation; Equipment; Program development; Seed money; Program-related investments/loans.

Limitations: Giving primarily in Lowell, MA. No grants to individuals, or for operating budgets, continuing support, annual campaigns, emergency funds, deficit financing, scholarships, or fellowships; no matching gifts.

Publications: Application guidelines, Grants list.

Application information: Application form not required.

   Initial approach: Telephone, proposal, or letter
   Copies of proposal: 1
   Deadline(s): None
   Board meeting date(s): Spring and fall
   Final notification: 4 months

Officers and Trustees:* Newell Flather,* Pres.; Andrew C. Bailey,* Secy.-Treas.; Karen H. Carpenter; Thomas E. Leggat.

Number of staff: 2 shared staff (shared with Georgina Goddard Eaton Memorial Fund, Anna B. Stearns Foundation, Clipper Ship Foundation, Foley Hoag Foundation, Herman and Frieda L. Miller Foundation, and Harold Brooks Foundation).

EIN: 046036092

1468
Amelia Peabody Charitable Fund ▼
10 P.O. Sq., North Ste. 995
Boston, MA 02109-4603   (617) 451-6178
Contact: Jo Anne Borek, Exec. Dir.

Established in 1974.

Donor(s): Amelia Peabody,‡ Eaton Foundation.

Grantmaker type: Independent foundation

Financial data (yr. ended 12/31/02): Assets, $145,657,024 (M); gifts received, $72,267; expenditures, $9,106,083; qualifying distributions, $8,288,354; giving activities include $7,877,984 for 162 grants (high: $500,018; low: $3,000; average: $10,000–$100,000).

Purpose and activities: Grants primarily for hospitals, medical research, health and family services, higher education, the environment, and culture, including museums.

Fields of interest: Museums; Arts; Higher education; Environment; Hospitals (general); Health care; Medical research, institute; Children/youth, services; Family services.

Types of support: Capital campaigns; Building/renovation; Equipment; Land acquisition; Research; Matching/challenge support.

Limitations: Giving primarily in New England with emphasis on MA. No support for tax-supported municipal or government organizations or religious groups. No grants to individuals, or for salaries or operating expenses.

Publications: Application guidelines, Grants list.

Application information: Application form not required.

   Initial approach: Letter with proposal

Copies of proposal: 3
Deadline(s): Feb. 1, June 1, and Oct. 1; if deadline falls on Sat. or Sun., the proposal is due the following Mon.
   Board meeting date(s): More than 15 times annually
   Final notification: Generally, 8 to 12 weeks from deadline

Officer and Trustees:* Jo Anne Borek,* Exec. Dir.; Richard A. Leahy; William B. Lowell; J. Elisabeth Rice; Patricia E. Rice.

Number of staff: 1 full-time professional; 1 full-time support.

EIN: 237364949

Recent environmental and animal welfare grants:

1468-1 American Chinese Veterinary Medical Frontiers, West Boylston, MA, $100,000. For research. 2001.

1468-2 Boston Natural Areas Network, Boston, MA, $24,500. For renovations of community gardens. 2001.

1468-3 Frenchman Bay Conservancy, Ellsworth, ME, $15,000. For land purchase. 2001.

1468-4 Manomet Center for Conservation Sciences, Manomet, MA, $40,000. For renovations and maintenance. 2001.

1468-5 National Education for Assistance Dog Services (NEADS), West Boylston, MA, $20,000. For wheelchair accessible van. 2001.

1468-6 Nature Conservancy, Brunswick, ME, $25,000. For land purchase. 2001.

1468-7 New England Forestry Foundation, Groton, MA, $500,000. To purchase areas of Pingree Forests. 2001.

1468-8 Outdoor Explorations, Cambridge, MA, $15,000. For equipment. 2001.

1468-9 Piscataquog Watershed Association, New Boston, NH, $15,000. For land acquisition. 2001.

1468-10 Save the Bay, Providence, RI, $150,000. For construction and infrastructure. 2001.

1468-11 Thompson Island Outward Bound Education Center, Boston, MA, $11,000. For computer technology. 2001.

1468-12 Woods Hole Research Center, Woods Hole, MA, $50,000. For construction of office and laboratory. 2001.

1469
Peace Development Fund
P.O. Box 1280
44 N. Prospect St.
Amherst, MA 01004-1280
Contact: Kazu Haga, Prog. Coord.
Tel.: (413) 256-8306, ext. 109; FAX: (413) 256-8871; E-mail: grants@peacefund.org; URL: http://www.peacedevelopmentfund.org

Established in 1981 in MA.

Grantmaker type: Public charity

Financial data (yr. ended 06/30/02): Revenue, $1,925,958; assets, $3,113,560 (L); gifts received, $1,802,464; expenditures, $1,914,147; program services expenses, $1,648,524; giving activities include $969,347 for grants.

Purpose and activities: The fund provides grants to organizations and projects working to achieve peaceful, just, and equitable relationships among people and nations. Grants

focus on three distinct types of relationships: relationships between the U.S. and peoples and countries elsewhere in the world; relationships among people and groups within the U.S.; and relationships between institutions, the power that maintains them, and the individuals whom they serve.

Fields of interest: Environment, legal rights; International peace/security; Civil rights, public education; Race/intergroup relations; Community development, citizen coalitions.

International interests: Haiti; Mexico.

Types of support: General/operating support; Continuing support; Program development; Seed money; Technical assistance.

Limitations: Giving on an international basis, primarily in the U.S., its territories, Canada, Mexico and Haiti. No support for academic institutions. No grants to individuals, or for research, conferences and other single events.

Publications: Application guidelines, Annual report, Financial statement, Grants list, Informational brochure, Newsletter.

Application information: Proposals by invitation only; 3 copies of letter of intent required; contact office for application guidelines or see Web site; applications not accepted by FAX or e-mail. Application form required.

   Initial approach: Telephone
   Copies of proposal: 8
   Deadline(s): Sept. 1 and Feb. 1
   Board meeting date(s): May and Dec.
   Final notification: 2 months after receipt of proposal

Officers and Directors:* Minh-Tram Nguyen,* Pres.; Teresa Juarez,* V.P.; Susan Balbas,* Secy.; Paul Haible,* Treas.; Aleah Bacquie Vaughn, Dir. Grants & Training; Kazu Haga, Prog. Coord.; Michelle E. Curry; Loretta M. Hobbs; Tawna Sanchez.

Number of staff: 6 full-time professional; 2 part-time professional.

EIN: 042738794

1470
The Pegasus Foundation
c/o Day, Berry & Howard
260 Franklin St.
Boston, MA 02110
Contact: David W. Fitts, Tr.
E-mail: info@pegasusfoundation.org; URL: http://www.pegasusfoundation.org/

Established in 1997 in MA.

Donor(s): Barbara U. Birdsey.

Grantmaker type: Independent foundation

Financial data (yr. ended 12/31/02): Assets, $172,331 (M); gifts received, $408,726; expenditures, $455,049; qualifying distributions, $438,155; giving activities include $240,767 for 28 grants (high: $75,000; low: $500).

Purpose and activities: Funding for wildlife and animal causes.

Fields of interest: Animal welfare; Animal population control; Animals/wildlife, preservation/protection.

International interests: Caribbean.

Types of support: Continuing support; Management development; Program development; Conferences/seminars; Program evaluation; Matching/challenge support.

Limitations: Applications not accepted. Giving primarily in FL, MA, select western states, and the Caribbean. No grants to individuals.
Publications: Annual report, Informational brochure.
Application information: Contributes only to pre-selected organizations.
Board meeting date(s): Quarterly
Officer and Trustees:* Peter A. Bender,* Exec. Dir.; David W. Fitts; George W. Malloy; Stephen Ziobrowski.
Number of staff: 3 full-time professional; 1 part-time professional.
EIN: 223487149

1471
Peppercorn Foundation
c/o Hale and Dorr, LLP
P.O. Box 9350
Boston, MA 02209

Established in 1999 in MA.
Donor(s): Alan Rabinowitz.
Grantmaker type: Independent foundation
Financial data (yr. ended 12/31/02): Assets, $4,803,422 (M); expenditures, $502,644; qualifying distributions, $456,016; giving activities include $351,000 for 9 grants (high: $51,000; low: $10,000).
Fields of interest: Higher education; Environmental education; Children/youth, services.
Limitations: Applications not accepted. Giving on a national basis. No grants to individuals.
Application information: Contributes only to pre-selected organizations.
Trustees: Jennifer Ladd; Alan Rabinowitz; Andrea Rabinowitz.
EIN: 043487843

1472
The Perfect Storm Foundation, Inc.
P.O. Box 1941
Gloucester, MA 01931-1941 (978) 283-2903
Contact: Dierdre Savage
FAX: (978) 282-9550; URL: http://www.perfectstorm.org

Grantmaker type: Public charity
Financial data (yr. ended 12/31/02): Revenue, $22,218; assets, $116,396 (M); gifts received, $19,444; expenditures, $14,450; program services expenses, $6,750; giving activities include $6,500 for grants to individuals.
Purpose and activities: The foundation provides educational and cultural opportunities through grants, scholarships, and direct programs to young people whose parents make their living in the commercial fishing industry and in working marine communities.
Fields of interest: Secondary school/education; Environment, formal/general education; Youth development.
Types of support: Grants to individuals; Scholarships—to individuals.
Limitations: Giving primarily in Gloucester, MA.
Application information: See Web site for application form and guidelines. Application form required.
Deadline(s): None
Officers and Directors:* Sebastian Junger,* Chair.; Jeanne Blake,* Pres.; Vito Calomo;

Deedee Cheveton; Chuck Dalaklis; Ann Margaret Ferrante; John Hogan; Philip Salzman; Mary Anne Shatford.
EIN: 043418631

1473
Ellis L. Phillips Foundation
233 Commonwealth Ave., Ste. 2
Boston, MA 02116 (617) 424-7607
Contact: Julie Wack, Exec. Dir.
E-mail: elpfndtn@gis.net; URL: http://www.ellislphillipsfndn.org

Incorporated in 1930 in NY.
Donor(s): Ellis L. Phillips.‡
Grantmaker type: Independent foundation
Financial data (yr. ended 06/30/02): Assets, $4,681,344 (M); expenditures, $672,686; qualifying distributions, $600,029; giving activities include $530,640 for 5 grants (high: $467,500; low: $640).
Purpose and activities: The foundation is primarily interested in strategically significant modest project grants to northern New England institutions in the following fields: informal and women's education; advanced training and institutional development in music and the visual arts; rural human services; rural historic preservation; and biodiversity conservation.
Fields of interest: Music; Historical activities; Arts; Education; Natural resources; Human services; Rural development.
Types of support: Program development.
Limitations: Applications not accepted. Giving primarily in northern New England. No support for businesses or private foundations. No grants to individuals, or for medical research, scholarships, fellowships, general operations, or matching gifts; no loans.
Application information: Unsolicited requests for funds not accepted.
Board meeting date(s): Oct., Feb., and May
Officers and Directors:* Ellis L. Phillips III,* Pres.; Ellis L. Phillips, Jr.,* V.P.; Cynthia Phillips Prosser,* Secy.; David Lloyd Brown; Cornelia Grumman; David L. Grumman; George E. McCully; Walter C. Paine; K. Noel Phillips; E. Clinton Swift.
Number of staff: 2 part-time professional.
EIN: 135677691

1474
The Harold Whitworth Pierce Charitable Trust
c/o Nichols and Pratt
50 Congress St., Ste. 832
Boston, MA 02109-4017 (617) 523-8368
Contact: Elizabeth D. Nichols, Prog. Dir.
FAX: (617) 523-8949; E-mail: piercetrust@nichols-pratt.com

Trust established in 1960 in MA.
Donor(s): Harold Whitworth Pierce.‡
Grantmaker type: Independent foundation
Financial data (yr. ended 12/31/02): Assets, $23,122,298 (M); expenditures, $1,484,901; qualifying distributions, $1,399,356; giving activities include $1,376,400 for 54 grants (high: $250,000; low: $1,000).
Purpose and activities: The Harold Whitworth Pierce Charitable Trust offers grants primarily for projects that will produce long-range benefits

through leverage of the trust's resources. Grants are made for specific programs, for seed money, and for capital projects, especially those which can reduce operating costs. Occasional grants are made for operating support. Grants are focused on institutions and programs in the Boston, MA, area.
Fields of interest: Teacher school/education; Education; Environment; Community development.
Types of support: General/operating support; Capital campaigns; Building/renovation; Endowments; Seed money; Scholarship funds; Research.
Limitations: Giving primarily in the Boston, MA, area. No grants to individuals, or for scholarships for individuals, fund-raising events, fund-raising training, films, videos, travel, or advocacy.
Publications: Grants list, Informational brochure (including application guidelines).
Application information: Concept letter and cover sheet. No more than 2 pages accepted. Proposals invited from among concept letters. Grants are occasionally made for medical research and arts education; unsolicited proposals are not accepted for these areas. Application form not required.
Initial approach: Letter or telephone
Copies of proposal: 1
Deadline(s): Mar. 1 and Sept. 15 for concept letters; Mid-Apr. and mid-Oct. for invited proposals
Board meeting date(s): Mar., June, Sept., and Nov.
Final notification: June 1 and Dec. 1
Trustees: James R. Nichols; Harold I. Pratt.
Number of staff: 2 shared staff (shared with The Paul and Edith Babson Foundation; the Susan A. and Donald P. Babson Charitable Foundation).
EIN: 046019896

1475
Quinque Foundation
c/o Philanthropic Advisors
400 Atlantic Ave., Ste. 401
Boston, MA 02110-3333 (617) 574-7707
Contact: Lauren A. Goldberg
Additional address: c/o David S. Mitchell, Conservation Fellowship Mgr., Scottish Conservation Bureau, Historic Scotland, Longmore House, Edinburgh EH9 1SH, Scotland,; URL: http://www.quinquefoundation.org

Established in 1999 in MA.
Donor(s): Helen D. Buchanan, The Royal Oak Foundation.
Grantmaker type: Operating foundation
Financial data (yr. ended 12/31/02): Assets, $5,292,125 (M); gifts received, $24,929; expenditures, $675,450; qualifying distributions, $673,795; giving activities include $380,836 for 9 grants (high: $183,590; low: $7,070).
Fields of interest: Radio; Historic preservation/historical societies; Higher education; Education; Natural resources; Botanical gardens; Zoos/zoological societies; Medical care, in-patient care; Family planning; AIDS; Federated giving programs.
Types of support: General/operating support.

Limitations: Giving on a national and international basis, with emphasis on MA, RI, and Scotland. No grants to individuals.
Application information: Application form required.
  Deadline(s): Apr. 15 for Quinque Fellows Program
  Final notification: June 30
Trustees: Fanchon M. Burnham; Helen D. Buchanan; Jane Watkins; Stephen D. Watkins.
EIN: 050508431

1476
The Radley Family Foundation
225 Country Club Rd.
Dedham, MA 02026 (781) 237-4455
Contact: James A. Radley, Tr.

Established in 1997 in MA.
Donor(s): Gail C. Radley, James A. Radley.
Grantmaker type: Independent foundation
Financial data (yr. ended 12/31/02): Assets, $74,991 (M); expenditures, $254,301; qualifying distributions, $254,285; giving activities include $254,285 for 36 grants (high: $100,000; low: $50).
Purpose and activities: Giving primarily to a children's hospital.
Fields of interest: Education; Environment, land resources; Hospitals (specialty); Health organizations, association; Human services.
Limitations: Applications not accepted. Giving primarily in MA. No grants to individuals.
Application information: Contributes only to pre-selected organizations.
Trustees: Gail C. Radley; James A. Radley.
EIN: 043371968

1477
Jerome Lyle Rappaport Charitable Foundation
c/o Rappaport Aserkoff & Geller
60 State St., Ste. 1525
Boston, MA 02109
Contact: Jerome Lyle Rappaport, Tr.
Application address: c/o Rappaport Aserkoff & Geller, 1 Longfellow Pl., Boston, MA 02114

Established in 1996 in FL.
Donor(s): Jerome Lyle Rappaport.
Grantmaker type: Independent foundation
Financial data (yr. ended 09/30/02): Assets, $6,781,650 (M); expenditures, $553,458; qualifying distributions, $494,677; giving activities include $455,375 for 26 grants (high: $200,000; low: $100).
Purpose and activities: Giving primarily for higher education and museums.
Fields of interest: Arts; Higher education; Education; Natural resources; Hospitals (general); Family planning; Jewish federated giving programs; Jewish agencies & temples.
Limitations: Giving primarily in MA. No grants to individuals.
Application information: Application form not required.
  Deadline(s): None
Trustees: Elizabeth J. Rappaport; James W. Rappaport; Jerome Lyle Rappaport; Nancy Rappaport; Phyllis E. Rappaport.
EIN: 311485041

1478
Neil & Anna Rasmussen Foundation
393 Estabrook Rd.
Concord, MA 01742-5604

Established in 1994 in MA.
Donor(s): Neil Rasmussen, Anna Rasmussen.
Grantmaker type: Independent foundation
Financial data (yr. ended 12/31/01): Assets, $6,390,984 (M); expenditures, $447,518; qualifying distributions, $360,863; giving activities include $358,405 for 20 grants (high: $100,000; low: $150).
Fields of interest: Higher education; Libraries/library science; Natural resources; Hospitals (general).
Limitations: Applications not accepted. Giving primarily in MA. No grants to individuals.
Application information: Contributes only to pre-selected organizations.
Trustees: Anna Rasmussen; Neil Rasmussen.
EIN: 046771880

1479
V. Kann Rasmussen Foundation ▼
c/o Hale and Dorr LLP
60 State St.
Boston, MA 02109 (617) 526-6610
Contact: Martin S. Kaplan, Tr.
FAX: (617) 526-5000; E-mail: martin.kaplan@haledorr.com; URL: http://www.vkrf.org/

Established in 1991 in MA.
Donor(s): The Velux Trust.
Grantmaker type: Independent foundation
Financial data (yr. ended 06/30/02): Assets, $102,218,536 (M); expenditures, $10,694,073; qualifying distributions, $9,925,371; giving activities include $8,943,096 for 67 grants (high: $554,500; low: $7,500; average: $20,000–$500,000).
Purpose and activities: Giving primarily for environmental protection, education, federated giving programs, and medical research.
Fields of interest: Elementary/secondary education; Higher education; Natural resources; Medical research, institute; Federated giving programs; General charitable giving.
Types of support: General/operating support.
Limitations: Applications not accepted. Giving primarily in Greenwood, SC. No grants to individuals.
Publications: Informational brochure.
Application information: Contributes only to pre-selected organizations.
  Board meeting date(s): Varies
Trustees: Martin S. Kaplan; Anne-Margrete Ogstrup-Pedersen; Aino Kann Rasmussen; Hans Kann Rasmussen.
Number of staff: None.
EIN: 223101266
Recent environmental and animal welfare grants:
1479-1 Americans for Equitable Climate Solutions, DC, $100,000. 2002.
1479-2 Bucknell University, Lewisburg, PA, $100,000. For forum on religion and ecology. 2002.
1479-3 Center for Clean Air Policy, DC, $50,000. 2002.
1479-4 Center for Environmental Citizenship, DC, $100,000. 2002.

1479-5 Center for International Environmental Law, DC, $150,000. 2002.
1479-6 Center for Respect of Life and Environment, DC, $175,000. 2002.
1479-7 CERES, Boston, MA, $150,000. 2002.
1479-8 Clean Air Cool Planet-A Northeast Alliance, Portsmouth, NH, $100,000. 2002.
1479-9 Clemson University Foundation, Clemson, SC, $191,120. For environmental program at Clemson University. 2002.
1479-10 Coevolution Institute, San Francisco, CA, $200,000. 2002.
1479-11 Columbia University, New York, NY, $500,000. For Center for Environmental Research and Conservation. 2002.
1479-12 Columbia University, New York, NY, $400,000. For Children's Environmental Health Center. 2002.
1479-13 Earth Force, Alexandria, VA, $25,000. 2002.
1479-14 Earth Restoration Corps, DC, $25,000. 2002.
1479-15 EcoLogic Enterprise Ventures, Cambridge, MA, $100,000. 2002.
1479-16 Environmental Health Fund, Jamaica Plain, MA, $200,000. 2002.
1479-17 Environmental Leadership Program, Haydenville, MA, $75,000. 2002.
1479-18 Environmental Literacy Council, DC, $35,000. 2002.
1479-19 Environmental Magazine, Norwalk, CT, $15,000. 2002.
1479-20 Environmental Media Services, DC, $125,000. 2002.
1479-21 Global Greengrants Fund, Boulder, CO, $75,000. 2002.
1479-22 Green House Network, Lake Oswego, Oregon, $25,000. 2002.
1479-23 Greenpeace U.S.A., DC, $306,000. 2002.
1479-24 Health Sciences Foundation for the Arthritis Research Fund, Charleston, SC, $168,350. For environmental program at Medical University of South Carolina. 2002.
1479-25 International SeaKeepers Society, Miami, FL, $50,000. 2002.
1479-26 Massachusetts Institute of Technology, Cambridge, MA, $300,000. For Alliance for Global Sustainability. 2002.
1479-27 National Environmental Education and Training Foundation, DC, $25,000. 2002.
1479-28 Natural Step, San Francisco, CA, $100,000. 2002.
1479-29 Public Education Center, DC, $50,000. For Natural Resources News Service. 2002.
1479-30 Redefining Progress, Oakland, CA, $100,000. 2002.
1479-31 Second Nature, Boston, MA, $100,000. 2002.
1479-32 Silicon Valley Toxics Coalition, San Jose, CA, $50,000. 2002.
1479-33 Sonoran Institute, Tucson, AZ, $150,000. For Yellowstone to Yukon Conservation Initiative. 2002.
1479-34 South Carolina, State of, Columbia, SC, $100,000. For environmental education. 2002.
1479-35 Tufts University, Medford, MA, $226,500. For School of Veterinary Medicine in Grafton. 2002.
1479-36 Union of Concerned Scientists, Cambridge, MA, $75,000. 2002.

1479-37 University of Miami, Coral Gables, FL, $200,000. For program on development and the environment. 2002.

1479-38 University of South Carolina, Columbia, SC, $75,000. For environmental education. 2002.

1479-39 University of South Carolina Educational Foundation, Columbia, SC, $340,530. For environmental program at the University of South Carolina. 2002.

1479-40 Upper Savannah Land Trust, Greenwood, SC, $20,000. 2002.

1479-41 Upstate Forever, Greenville, SC, $30,000. 2002.

1479-42 Wallace F. Pate Foundation for Environmental Research, Clemson, SC, $35,000. 2002.

1479-43 Wildlife Trust, Palisades, NY, $554,500. 2002.

1480
Raymond Family Foundation
306 Dartmouth St.
Boston, MA 02116-2206

Established in 1989 in MA.
Donor(s): Neil St. John Raymond.
Grantmaker type: Independent foundation
Financial data (yr. ended 12/31/01): Assets, $1,090,258 (M); expenditures, $177,917; qualifying distributions, $170,256; giving activities include $170,600 for 33 grants (high: $25,000; low: $100).
Purpose and activities: Giving primarily for theater, education and human services.
Fields of interest: Arts; Higher education; Education; Natural resources; Environment, land resources; Animals/wildlife, alliance; Human services; YM/YWCAs & YM/YWHAs.
Limitations: Applications not accepted. Giving primarily in MA. No grants to individuals.
Application information: Contributes only to pre-selected organizations.
Trustee: Neil St. John Raymond.
EIN: 043076151

1481
Raytheon Company Contributions Program
Waltham Woods
870 Winter St.
Waltham, MA 02451-1449 (781) 522-3000
Contact: Carol J. Ramsey, Dir., Corp. Contribs.
E-mail: corporatecontributions@raytheon.com;
URL: http://www.raytheon.com/community

Grantmaker type: Corporate giving program
Financial data (yr. ended 12/31/02): Total giving, $9,252,580; giving activities include $7,485,000 for 178 grants (high: $705,000; low: $250; average: $5,000–$10,000) and $1,767,580 for 5,271 employee matching gifts.
Purpose and activities: Raytheon makes charitable contributions to nonprofit organizations involved with education, the environment, and access and opportunity. Support is given on a national and international basis.
Fields of interest: Education; Environment; Civil rights, equal rights.
International interests: Brazil.

Types of support: General/operating support; Capital campaigns; Building/renovation; Endowments; Program development; Technical assistance; Employee matching gifts; Employee-related scholarships.
Limitations: Giving on a national and international basis in areas of company operations, including in Brazil. No support for United Way-supported organizations, religious, fraternal, political, athletic, or veterans' organizations, health or disease-specific organizations, private foundations, or private K-12 schools. No grants to individuals (except for employee-related scholarships), or for basic research projects or regional, national, or international competitions, conferences, tournaments, or events; no product donations or in-kind gifts.
Publications: Application guidelines.
Application information: Unsolicited requests from institutions of higher education are not accepted. Telephone calls are not encouraged. The Corporate Contributions Department handles giving. The company has a staff that only handles contributions. Application form required.
Initial approach: Contact headquarters or nearest company facility for application form
Copies of proposal: 1
Deadline(s): None
Final notification: 2 months
Number of staff: 2 full-time professional; 1 part-time support.

1482
Red Acre Farm, Inc.
P.O. Box 278
Stow, MA 01775
Contact: Carolyn Bird, Exec. Dir.

Established in 1903 in MA.
Grantmaker type: Independent foundation
Financial data (yr. ended 09/30/02): Assets, $6,529,893 (M); gifts received, $8,065; expenditures, $1,202,212; qualifying distributions, $1,098,486; giving activities include $1,084,000 for 33 grants (high: $720,000; low: $5,000).
Purpose and activities: Giving primarily to a conservation trust, for animal welfare, wildlife protection, and human and animal bond efforts.
Fields of interest: Natural resources; Animal welfare; Animals/wildlife, preservation/protection.
Limitations: Giving limited to New England, AZ and some areas in CO. No grants to individuals.
Application information: Application form required.
Initial approach: Request for proposal form
Deadline(s): Varies
Officers and Directors:* Leonard W. Johnson,* Pres.; David M. Pinkham,* V.P.; Walter M. Bird III,* Secy.; Walter M. Bird, Jr.,* Treas.; Carolyn G. Bird, Exec. Dir.; David Ayer; Helen B. Guidotti; Nathanael Shepherd; Arthur Slade.
EIN: 042119492

1483
RESIST, Inc.
259 Elm St., Ste. 201
Somerville, MA 02144 (617) 623-5110
Contact: Robin E. Carton, Dir., Grant Prog. and Fin.
E-mail: resistinc@igc.org; URL: http://www.resistinc.org

Established in 1967 in MA.
Grantmaker type: Public charity
Financial data (yr. ended 12/31/01): Revenue, $631,793; assets, $490,277 (L); gifts received, $617,497; expenditures, $619,913; program services expenses, $427,648; giving activities include $295,900 for 136 grants (high: $3,000; low: $300; average: $300–$3,000).
Purpose and activities: RESIST supports organizations that tend to fall outside of mainstream funding sources because their political perspective is considered to be too "radical." Grants and loans of up to $3,000 per year are awarded to groups with annual budgets under $125,000. Grants are given for general support, specific campaigns, or projects. RESIST is also committed to supporting projects that enable all people to participate in the movement for social justice. As such, RESIST will fund the additional costs of projects or events which will make them accessible to people with disabilities (e.g., signers for events, or wheelchair-accessible venues) for amounts up to $3,000. RESIST also provides three-year general support grants to organizations that have been funded at least two times during the preceding five years.
Fields of interest: Media/communications; Film/video; Natural resources; Youth development; International peace/security; Arms control; Civil rights, advocacy; Race/intergroup relations; Civil rights; Community development, neighborhood development; Business/industry; Native Americans/American Indians; Women; Gays/lesbians.
Types of support: General/operating support; Equipment; Emergency funds; Program development; Publication; Technical assistance.
Limitations: Giving on a national basis. No support for foreign programs, social or direct service organizations. No grants to individuals, or for production of films/videos, legal defense costs, material aid campaigns, or travel expenses.
Publications: Application guidelines, Financial statement, Grants list, Informational brochure, Newsletter.
Application information: Application form required.
Initial approach: Letter or telephone
Copies of proposal: 1
Deadline(s): Every 6 to 8 weeks
Board meeting date(s): 6 times each year
Final notification: 1 to 2 weeks following board meeting
Directors: Nakhil Aziz; Robin Carton; Pam Chamberlain; Ty Depass; Leila Farsakh; Rebecca Howes-Mischel; Kay Mathew; Marc Miller; Henry Rosemont; Carol Schachet; Abbey Scher.
Staff Members: Robin Carton, Dir., Grantmaking and Finances; Rebecca Howes-Mischel, Office Mgr. and Grant Prog. Assoc.; Carol Schachet, Dir., Devel. and Comm.
Number of staff: 2 full-time professional; 1 part-time professional.
EIN: 042433182

1484
The Robbins-De Beaumont Foundation
c/o Sullivan & Worcester, LLP
1 Post Office Sq.
Boston, MA 02109
Contact: Joseph C. Robbins, Tr.
URL: http://www.agmconnect.org/robbins.html

Established in 1992 in MA.
Donor(s): Joseph C. Robbins, Mary D. De Beaumont.
Grantmaker type: Independent foundation
Financial data (yr. ended 12/31/02): Assets, $7,531,125 (M); gifts received, $3,712,500; expenditures, $347,127; qualifying distributions, $324,882; giving activities include $311,600 for 23 grants (high: $34,600; low: $2,000).
Fields of interest: Arts; Education; Natural resources; Human services; Youth, services; Community development.
Limitations: Giving primarily in MA. No grants to individuals.
Application information: Use Associated Grantmakers of Massachusetts Common Proposal.
Deadline(s): Mar. 1 for concept paper; June 30 for grant application
Board meeting date(s): Quarterly, grant determinations usually in Nov.
Trustees: Joan Hudson Kopperl; Joseph C. Robbins.
EIN: 046719809

1485
Roehr Family Foundation, Inc.
c/o Schaefer & Lydon, LLP
185 Devonshire St., Ste. 1000
Boston, MA 02110-1000

Established in 1986 in MA.
Grantmaker type: Independent foundation
Financial data (yr. ended 06/30/02): Assets, $1,868,794 (M); expenditures, $151,123; qualifying distributions, $128,389; giving activities include $129,150 for 15 grants (high: $27,150; low: $1,000).
Purpose and activities: Giving primarily for youth services and for housing.
Fields of interest: College; Education; Natural resources; Housing/shelter, development; Human services; Children/youth, services; Women.
Limitations: Applications not accepted. Giving primarily in MA. No grants to individuals.
Application information: Contributes only to pre-selected organizations.
Officers and Directors:* Marcia A. Roehr,* Pres. and Treas.; Carolyn A. Roehr,* Clerk; Cynthia R. Anthony; Mary E. Lord.
EIN: 222777634

1486
John B. & Jane M. Ryerson Charitable Trust
c/o Citibank, N.A.
125 Summer St., 17th Fl.
Boston, MA 02110

Established in 1992 in NY.
Grantmaker type: Independent foundation
Financial data (yr. ended 02/28/02): Assets, $6,237,113 (M); expenditures, $479,140;

qualifying distributions, $308,614; giving activities include $310,250 for 10 grants (high: $62,000; low: $7,750).
Fields of interest: Animal welfare; Health organizations, association; Human services; Salvation Army; Protestant agencies & churches; Cemeteries/burial services.
Limitations: Applications not accepted. Giving limited to Palm Beach and West Palm Beach FL, and Cooperstown, NY. No grants to individuals.
Application information: Contributes only to pre-selected organizations.
Trustees: Dub Carlton; Susan Heeke; Citibank, N.A.
EIN: 166349529

1487
Sacharuna Foundation
c/o Peregrine Financial Corp.
84 State St.
Boston, MA 02109

Established in 1985 in NY.
Donor(s): Lavinia Currier, Jack Robinson.
Grantmaker type: Independent foundation
Financial data (yr. ended 12/31/00): Assets, $14,405,488 (M); expenditures, $950,523; qualifying distributions, $824,480; giving activities include $799,791 for 21 grants (high: $270,000; low: $1,000).
Purpose and activities: Giving primarily for conservation, environmental, and wildlife organizations, and international affairs, with emphasis on organizations relating to Tibet; some support for education, historic preservation and cultural programs.
Fields of interest: Elementary/secondary education; Higher education; Natural resources; Environment; Animals/wildlife, preservation/protection; International human rights.
Types of support: General/operating support.
Limitations: Applications not accepted. Giving on a national basis. No grants to individuals.
Application information: Contributes only to pre-selected organizations.
Trustee: Lavinia Currier.
EIN: 133264132

1488
Salem Five Charitable Foundation, Inc.
210 Essex St.
Salem, MA 01970 (978) 740-5772
Contact: Nicholas A. Caporale, Clerk

Established in 1996 in MA.
Donor(s): Salem Five Cents Savings Bank.
Grantmaker type: Independent foundation
Financial data (yr. ended 12/31/02): Assets, $1,101,896 (M); gifts received, $682,504; expenditures, $129,637; qualifying distributions, $128,137; giving activities include $126,587 for 210 grants (high: $10,000; low: $30).
Purpose and activities: Grants will be given to social service agencies, cultural, educational, art, community economic development and other programs that impact the needs of the Salem Five communities.
Fields of interest: Arts; Education; Animals/wildlife; Medical research, institute; Food services; Recreation; Youth development;

Human services; Federated giving programs; Jewish agencies & temples.
Limitations: Giving primarily in Salem, MA.
Application information: Application form required.
Deadline(s): Varies
Officers and Directors:* William H. Mitchelson,* C.E.O.; Nicholas A. Caporale, Clerk; Joseph M. Gibbons, Treas.; David H. Caldwell; Ping Yin Chai; Richard Gourdeau; Timothy J. Hunt; William J. Lundregan III.
EIN: 043342405

1489
Richard Saltonstall Charitable Foundation
c/o Saltonstall & Co., Inc.
50 Congress St., Rm. 800
Boston, MA 02109 (617) 227-8660
Contact: Dudley H. Willis, Tr.
Application address: P.O. Box 730, Sherborn, MA 01770

Established in 1964 in MA.
Donor(s): Richard Saltonsall.‡
Grantmaker type: Independent foundation
Financial data (yr. ended 12/31/01): Assets, $24,600,477 (M); expenditures, $1,449,706; qualifying distributions, $1,378,967; giving activities include $1,295,275 for 36 grants (high: $175,000; low: $5,000).
Fields of interest: Arts; Libraries/library science; Natural resources; Hospitals (general); Federated giving programs.
Limitations: Giving primarily in MA.
Application information: Application form not required.
Initial approach: Letter
Deadline(s): Oct. 15
Board meeting date(s): Nov. and Dec.
Final notification: Dec.
Trustees: Robert A. Lawrence; Emily S. Lewis; Dudley H. Willis; Sally S. Willis.
Number of staff: 1 full-time professional; 1 full-time support.
EIN: 046078934

1490
Saquish Foundation
c/o Hunter Office
75 Federal St., Rm. 2005
Boston, MA 02110

Donor(s): Charles M. Werly.‡
Grantmaker type: Independent foundation
Financial data (yr. ended 12/31/02): Assets, $7,168,395 (M); gifts received, $950,580; expenditures, $412,074; qualifying distributions, $341,328; giving activities include $304,000 for 46 grants (high: $20,000; low: $4,000).
Purpose and activities: Giving for the arts, education, the environment, hospitals, and youth programs.
Fields of interest: Arts; Education; Environment; Hospitals (general); Boys & girls clubs; Human services; Federated giving programs; Christian agencies & churches; Disabled.
Limitations: Applications not accepted. Giving on a national basis. No grants to individuals.
Application information: Contributes only to pre-selected organizations.
Trustees: Horace S. Nichols; John Werly.
EIN: 046136550

1491
The Schooner Foundation
(formerly Ryan Family Charitable Foundation)
c/o Schooner Capital LLC
745 Atlantic Ave., 10th Fl.
Boston, MA 02111

Established in 1996 in MA.
Donor(s): Vincent J. Ryan.
Grantmaker type: Independent foundation
Financial data (yr. ended 12/31/01): Assets,
$9,234,702 (M); gifts received, $543,750;
expenditures, $1,447,741; qualifying
distributions, $1,337,621; giving activities
include $1,348,092 for 48 grants (high:
$251,212; low: $200).
Fields of interest: Animals/wildlife, research;
International relief; International peace/security.
Limitations: Applications not accepted. Giving
on a national basis. No grants to individuals.
Application information: Contributes only to
pre-selected organizations.
Officer: Stephen D. Maiocco, Treas.
Trustee: Kimberly R. Dano; Stephanie R.
Ditenhafer; Jennifer R. Flynn; Carla E. Meyer;
Cynthia A. Ryan; Vincent J. Ryan.
EIN: 043347626

1492
Septimus Foundation II
c/o Woodstock Service Corp.
27 School St.
Boston, MA 02108-4303

Established in 1974 in MA.
Donor(s): Jeanne L. Crocker, John T. Crocker,
Suzanne C. Richey, David B. Crocker, Martha P.
Crocker, and members of the Crocker family.
Grantmaker type: Independent foundation
Financial data (yr. ended 12/31/02): Assets,
$177,396 (M); gifts received, $116,631;
expenditures, $261,477; qualifying distributions,
$225,079; giving activities include $225,263 for
30 grants (high: $55,000; low: $100).
Purpose and activities: Giving primarily for
education and human services.
Fields of interest: Television; Education;
Environment.
Limitations: Applications not accepted. Giving
primarily in MA. No grants to individuals.
Application information: Contributes only to
pre-selected organizations.
Trustees: Bigelow Crocker, Jr.; David B. Crocker;
Jeanne L. Crocker; John T. Crocker; Martha P.
Crocker; Suzanne C. Richey.
EIN: 046359030

1493
Sheehan Family Foundation
P.O. Box K
Kingston, MA 02364
Contact: Elizabeth Sheehan, Exec. Dir.
Application address: P.O. Box 2831, Duxbury,
MA 02331; E-mail: claymor22@aol.com

Established in 1993.
Donor(s): L. Knife & Son, Inc.
Grantmaker type: Independent foundation
Financial data (yr. ended 12/31/02): Assets,
$5,715,110 (M); gifts received, $1,144,646;
expenditures, $688,447; qualifying distributions,

$688,447; giving activities include $665,727 for
16 grants (high: $200,231; low: $2,000).
Purpose and activities: Giving primarily for
education, including after school programs.
Fields of interest: Early childhood education;
Education; Natural resources.
Types of support: General/operating support;
Continuing support; Land acquisition;
Conferences/seminars; Curriculum
development; Scholarship funds; Technical
assistance; Program evaluation;
Matching/challenge support.
Limitations: Applications not accepted. Giving
limited to Essex, Middlesex, Plymouth,
Barnstable, Dukes, and Nantucket counties,
MA. No grants to individuals.
Publications: Annual report.
Application information: Contributes only to
pre-selected organizations.
Board meeting date(s): Mar. and May
Officer: Elizabeth Sheehan, Exec. Dir.
Trustees: Margaret Sheehan; Timothy Sheehan.
Number of staff: None.
EIN: 043197325

1494
The Shipley Family Foundation, Inc.
c/o Nutter, McClennen & Fish, LLP
P.O. Box 51400
Boston, MA 02205

Established in 1969 in MA.
Donor(s): Charles R. Shipley, Jr., Lucia H.
Shipley.
Grantmaker type: Independent foundation
Financial data (yr. ended 12/31/02): Assets,
$11,505,197 (M); expenditures, $1,012,474;
qualifying distributions, $948,395; giving
activities include $929,010 for 7 grants (high:
$530,000; low: $2,010).
Fields of interest: Secondary school/education;
Higher education; Animals/wildlife; Hospitals
(general); Health care; Health organizations,
association; Government/public administration;
Disabled.
Limitations: Applications not accepted. Giving
primarily in MA.
Application information: Contributes only to
pre-selected organizations and individuals.
Officers: Charles R. Shipley, Jr., Pres.; William
H. MacCrellish, Jr., Clerk; Lucia H. Shipley, Treas.
Directors: Thomas P. Jalkut; Richard C. Shipley.
EIN: 237015570

1495
Sholley Foundation, Inc.
c/o State Street Bank and Trust Co.
P.O. Box 351
Boston, MA 02101
Contact: George W. Butterworth, Tr.

Established in 1945 in MA.
Donor(s): Sidney L. Sholley.‡
Grantmaker type: Independent foundation
Financial data (yr. ended 04/30/02): Assets,
$2,135,351 (M); expenditures, $129,379;
qualifying distributions, $110,496; giving
activities include $102,550 for 104 grants (high:
$10,000; low: $200).
Purpose and activities: Support primarily for
education, social services, youth, health
organizations, and community development.

Fields of interest: Education, fund raising;
Education; Natural resources; Environment;
Family planning; Health care; Health
organizations, association; Human services;
Children/youth, services; Family services;
Community development.
Types of support: General/operating support;
Continuing support; Seed money.
Limitations: Applications not accepted. Giving
primarily in MA. No grants to individuals.
Publications: Annual report.
Application information: Contributes only to
pre-selected organizations.
Board meeting date(s): June and Dec.
Officers and Trustees:* Peter B. Sholley,* Pres.;
William T. Cloney,* Secy.; Charles D. Post,*
Treas.; George W. Butterworth; Nancy F. Sholley.
EIN: 046014010

1496
The Silver Tie Fund, Inc.
c/o Wiley Osborn BDO Seidman, LLP
40 Broad St., Ste. 500
Boston, MA 02109 (617) 484-4167
Application address: c/o Paul Cohen, 38 Payson
Terrace, Belmont, MA 02178

Established in 1998 in NY.
Grantmaker type: Independent foundation
Financial data (yr. ended 12/31/01): Assets,
$1,649,886 (M); expenditures, $140,357;
qualifying distributions, $119,683; giving
activities include $120,000 for 18 grants (high:
$20,000; low: $1,000).
Purpose and activities: Giving primarily for
environmental and wildlife conservation, art
centers, and medical services.
Fields of interest: Multipurpose
centers/programs; Natural resources;
Animals/wildlife, preservation/protection; Health
care, volunteer services; Health care;
International relief.
Application information:
Initial approach: Proposal
Officer: Paul Cohen, Pres. and Secy.-Treas.
EIN: 223457088

1497
Stamps Family Charitable Foundation, Inc.
c/o Summit Partners
600 Atlantic Ave., Ste. 2800
Boston, MA 02210

Donor(s): Penelope W. Stamps, E. Roe Stamps
IV.
Grantmaker type: Independent foundation
Financial data (yr. ended 11/30/01): Assets,
$36,782,315 (M); gifts received, $4,685,735;
expenditures, $2,554,571; qualifying
distributions, $2,290,983; giving activities
include $2,339,880 for 46 grants (high:
$1,960,000; low: $100).
Purpose and activities: Giving primarily for the
arts, education and health associations.
Fields of interest: Performing arts; Arts;
Education; Botanical gardens; Health care;
Human services; Children, services; Federated
giving programs.
Limitations: Applications not accepted. Giving
primarily in MA. No grants to individuals.
Application information: Contributes only to
pre-selected organizations.

Officers: Penelope Stamps, Pres.; E. Roe Stamps IV, Treas.
EIN: 042943910

1498
Anna B. Stearns Charitable Foundation, Inc.
c/o Grants Mgmt. Assocs., Inc.
77 Summer St., 8th Fl.
Boston, MA 02110-1006 (617) 426-7172
Contact: Amy Segal Shorey, Admin., or Anna Karlsson, Fdn. Asst.
Application address for NH: New Hampshire Charitable Fdn., Stuart Cornstock-Gay, Assoc. Dir., 37 Pleasant St., P.O. Box 1335, Concord, NH 03302-1335, tel.: (603) 225-6641

Established in 1966 in MA.
Donor(s): Anna B. Stearns.‡
Grantmaker type: Independent foundation
Financial data (yr. ended 12/31/02): Assets, $16,000,563 (M); expenditures, $787,450; qualifying distributions, $726,476; giving activities include $630,175 for 43 grants (high: $75,000; low: $5,000).
Purpose and activities: Giving primarily for women, children and youth programs leading to their independence and self-sufficiency with, special interest in the healthy development of girls; support also for protection and preservation of the natural urban environment.
Fields of interest: Environment; Children/youth, services; Family services; Women, centers/services.
Types of support: General/operating support; Continuing support; Program development; Technical assistance; Matching/challenge support.
Limitations: Giving primarily in the Boston, MA, area (including Cambridge, Somerville, and Chelsea), and northern NH. No support for statewide initiatives.
Publications: Application guidelines, Grants list.
Application information: Massachusetts Common Proposal Form/cover summary sheet required; AGM Common Proposal Form may be used for application. Proposals for summer programs will only be considered in the winter round (Nov. 1 deadline). Application form not required.
Initial approach: Proposal or telephone call
Copies of proposal: 1
Deadline(s): May 1 and Nov. 1
Board meeting date(s): During 1st and 3rd quarters
Final notification: Within 1 month of board meeting
Officers and Directors:* Sylvia Simmons,* Pres.; Katherine L. Babson, Jr.,* Clerk and Treas.; Christine G. Franklin; Deborah C. Jackson; Leonard W. Johnson; Miren Uriarte.
Number of staff: 2 shared staff (shared with Clipper Ship Foundation, Theodore Edson Parker Foundation, Harold Brooks Foundation, Foundation for Financial Planning, Herman and Frieda L. Miller Foundation, and Linden Foundation).
EIN: 046144732

1499
Stearns Charitable Trust
66 Commonwealth Ave.
Concord, MA 01742
Contact: Russell S. Beede, Tr.

Trust established in 1947 in MA.
Donor(s): Russell B. Stearns.‡
Grantmaker type: Independent foundation
Financial data (yr. ended 12/31/02): Assets, $6,504,106 (M); expenditures, $429,437; qualifying distributions, $352,990; giving activities include $345,500 for 71 grants (high: $50,000; low: $500).
Purpose and activities: Emphasis on cultural programs, including a science museum; support also for libraries, community funds, the environment, an aquarium, and social services.
Fields of interest: Museums; Arts; Libraries/library science; Environment; Alcoholism; Human services; Federated giving programs.
Types of support: General/operating support; Continuing support; Annual campaigns; Capital campaigns; Building/renovation; Land acquisition; Program development.
Limitations: Applications not accepted. Giving primarily in IL, MA, and RI. No grants to individuals.
Application information: Contributes primarily to pre-selected organizations.
Board meeting date(s): As required
Trustees: Russell S. Beede; Virginia Stearns Gassel; Anne B. Jencks.
Number of staff: None.
EIN: 046036697

1500
The Abbot and Dorothy H. Stevens Foundation
P.O. Box 111
North Andover, MA 01845 (978) 688-7211
Contact: Elizabeth A. Beland, Admin.
FAX: (978) 686-1620; E-mail: 74722.2637@compuserve.com

Trust established in 1953 in MA.
Donor(s): Abbot Stevens.‡
Grantmaker type: Independent foundation
Financial data (yr. ended 12/31/02): Assets, $21,773,856 (M); expenditures, $1,255,178; qualifying distributions, $1,127,350; giving activities include $1,049,750 for grants (average: $2,000–$9,000).
Purpose and activities: Giving primarily for the arts, education, conservation and health and human services.
Fields of interest: Museums; Humanities; Historic preservation/historical societies; Arts; Medical school/education; Education; Natural resources; Health care; Health organizations, association; Domestic violence; Human services; Children/youth, services; African Americans/Blacks; Hispanics/Latinos; Disabled; Aging; Immigrants/refugees; Economically disadvantaged.
Types of support: General/operating support; Continuing support; Capital campaigns; Building/renovation; Equipment; Endowments; Program development; Seed money; Technical assistance; Program-related investments/loans; Matching/challenge support.

Limitations: Giving limited to MA, with emphasis on the greater Lawrence area. No support for national organizations, or for state or federal agencies. No grants to individuals, or for annual campaigns, deficit financing, exchange programs, internships, professorships, scholarships, or fellowships.
Publications: Application guidelines, Program policy statement.
Application information: Accepts Associated Grantmakers Common Proposal Form. Application form not required.
Initial approach: Proposal
Copies of proposal: 1
Deadline(s): None
Board meeting date(s): Monthly except July and Aug.
Final notification: 1 week following board meetings
Trustees: Phebe S. Miner; Christopher W. Rogers; Samuel S. Rogers.
Number of staff: 1 full-time professional; 1 part-time support.
EIN: 046107991

1501
The Nathaniel and Elizabeth P. Stevens Foundation
P.O. Box 111
North Andover, MA 01845 (978) 688-7211
Contact: Elizabeth A. Beland, Admin.
FAX: (978) 686-1620; E-mail: 74722,2637@compuserve.com

Trust established in 1943 in MA.
Donor(s): Nathaniel Stevens.‡
Grantmaker type: Independent foundation
Financial data (yr. ended 12/31/02): Assets, $17,300,773 (M); expenditures, $985,736; qualifying distributions, $974,781; giving activities include $916,135 for 136 grants (high: $150,000; low: $100; average: $2,000–$8,000).
Fields of interest: Museums; Historic preservation/historical societies; Arts; Medical school/education; Education; Natural resources; Hospitals (general); Health care; Health organizations, association; Domestic violence; Housing/shelter, development; Human services; Minorities/immigrants, centers/services; Minorities; African Americans/Blacks; Hispanics/Latinos; Disabled; Aging; Immigrants/refugees; Economically disadvantaged.
Types of support: General/operating support; Continuing support; Capital campaigns; Building/renovation; Equipment; Land acquisition; Endowments; Emergency funds; Program development; Conferences/seminars; Seed money; Technical assistance; Consulting services; Matching/challenge support.
Limitations: Giving limited to MA, with emphasis on the greater Lawrence and Merrimack Valley areas. No support for national organizations, or for state or federal agencies. No grants to individuals, or for deficit financing, exchange programs, internships, lectureships, research, professorships, scholarships, fellowships, or annual campaigns.
Publications: Application guidelines, Program policy statement.
Application information: Accepts Associated Grantmakers Common Proposal Form. Application form required.

Initial approach: Proposal
Copies of proposal: 1
Deadline(s): None
Board meeting date(s): Monthly except July and Aug.
Final notification: 2 months
Trustees: Joshua L. Miner IV; Phebe S. Miner; Samuel S. Rogers.
Number of staff: 2 shared staff (shared with The Abbot and Dorothy H. Stevens Foundation, The Charlotte Home).
EIN: 042236996

1502
Stevenson Family Charitable Trust

68 Fayerweather St.
Cambridge, MA 02138

Established in 1989 in MA.
Donor(s): Howard H. Stevenson.
Grantmaker type: Independent foundation
Financial data (yr. ended 12/31/01): Assets, $2,213,784 (M); expenditures, $249,195; qualifying distributions, $191,850; giving activities include $191,850 for 33 grants (high: $50,000; low: $100).
Purpose and activities: Giving primarily for education and human services.
Fields of interest: Arts; Elementary/secondary education; Higher education; Education; Natural resources; Human services.
Limitations: Applications not accepted. Giving primarily in MA. No grants to individuals.
Application information: Contributes only to pre-selected organizations.
Trustees: Fredericka O. Stevenson; Howard H. Stevenson.
EIN: 046629590

1503
The Stoddard Charitable Trust ▼

370 Main St., 12th Fl.
Worcester, MA 01608 (508) 798-8621
Contact: Warner S. Fletcher, Chair.

Trust established in 1939 in MA.
Donor(s): Harry G. Stoddard.‡
Grantmaker type: Independent foundation
Financial data (yr. ended 12/31/01): Assets, $75,741,687 (M); gifts received, $616,969; expenditures, $5,055,150; qualifying distributions, $4,792,619; giving activities include $4,774,500 for 61 grants (high: $1,500,000; low: $3,000; average: $5,000–$75,000).
Purpose and activities: Emphasis on education, cultural programs, historical associations, youth agencies, and a community fund; support also for social service agencies, environmental concerns, and health associations.
Fields of interest: History/archaeology; Historic preservation/historical societies; Arts; Education; Environment; Health organizations, association; Human services; Youth, services; Federated giving programs.
Types of support: General/operating support; Continuing support; Annual campaigns; Capital campaigns; Building/renovation; Equipment; Land acquisition; Emergency funds; Professorships; Seed money; Fellowships; Internship funds; Research; Matching/challenge support.

Limitations: Giving primarily in Worcester, MA. No grants to individuals.
Application information: Application form not required.
Initial approach: Proposal
Copies of proposal: 4
Deadline(s): Submit proposal between Jan. and Nov.; no set deadlines
Board meeting date(s): Quarterly
Final notification: 3 months
Officers and Trustees:* Warner S. Fletcher,* Chair.; Valerie S. Loring,* Secy.; Judith S. King, Treas.; Allen W. Fletcher.
Number of staff: None.
EIN: 046023791
Recent environmental and animal welfare grants:
1503-1 EcoTarium, Worcester, MA, $400,000. Toward Long-Term Capital Development Program. 2001.
1503-2 Greater Worcester Land Trust, Worcester, MA, $50,000. Toward purchase of Parcel K. 2001.

1504
Stratford Foundation ▼

High Street Tower
125 High St.
Boston, MA 02110 (617) 248-7300
Contact: Peter A. Wilson, Exec. Dir.
FAX: (617) 248-7100

Established in 1983 in MA.
Donor(s): Kenneth H. Olsen.
Grantmaker type: Independent foundation
Financial data (yr. ended 12/31/01): Assets, $58,482,880 (M); expenditures, $9,554,185; qualifying distributions, $9,054,966; giving activities include $9,010,091 for 101 grants (high: $625,000; low: $2,000; average: $5,000–$100,000).
Purpose and activities: Grants primarily to institutions closely associated with the donor and the donor's family. However, non-donor associated grants may be considered.
Limitations: No grants to individuals.
Publications: Application guidelines.
Application information: Application form required.
Initial approach: Telephone
Copies of proposal: 1
Deadline(s): None
Board meeting date(s): Periodically
Officer: Peter A. Wilson, Exec. Dir.
Trustees: Ava-Liisa Memmen; Eeva-Liisa Aulikki Olsen; Kenneth H. Olsen; Richard J. Testa.
Custodian Bank: Investors Bank & Trust Co.
Number of staff: None.
EIN: 222524023
Recent environmental and animal welfare grants:
1504-1 Appalachian Mountain Club, Boston, MA, $500,000. 2001.
1504-2 Nature Conservancy, Brunswick, ME, $515,000. 2001.
1504-3 Nature Conservancy, Boston, MA, $50,000. 2001.
1504-4 New England Wild Flower Society, Framingham, MA, $50,000. 2001.
1504-5 Rural Land Foundation of Lincoln, Lincoln, MA, $625,000. 2001.
1504-6 Zoo New England, Boston, MA, $275,000. 2001.

1505
Sudbury Foundation

278 Old Sudbury Rd.
Sudbury, MA 01776 (978) 443-0849
Contact: Derry Tanner, Exec. Dir.
FAX: (978) 443-3767; URL: http://www.agmconnect.org/sudbury1.html

Trust established in 1952 in MA.
Donor(s): Esther M. Atkinson,‡ Herbert J. Atkinson.‡
Grantmaker type: Independent foundation
Financial data (yr. ended 12/31/01): Assets, $31,915,139 (M); expenditures, $2,016,663; qualifying distributions, $1,874,129; giving activities include $1,378,200 for 75 grants (high: $325,000; low: $750; average: $10,000–$75,000) and $295,500 for 58 grants to individuals.
Purpose and activities: Scholarships to residents of Sudbury or Metrowest, MA, who are graduates of Lincoln-Sudbury Regional High School or are dependents of employees of the Town of Sudbury; support also for community building and civic issues, the environment, local social services, public elementary and secondary education, and arts and culture.
Fields of interest: Arts; Elementary school/education; Secondary school/education; Environment; Human services; Community development; Government/public administration.
Types of support: Seed money; Scholarships—to individuals; Matching/challenge support.
Limitations: Giving primarily in Sudbury, MA. No support for sectarian religious activities. No grants to individuals (except for the scholarship program), or for ongoing operating support, deficit financing, general appeals, or graduate study.
Publications: Application guidelines, Biennial report, Informational brochure, Program policy statement.
Application information: Student loan program is being phased out and replaced by the Atkinson scholarship program. Application form required.
Initial approach: Proposal
Deadline(s): Nov. 1 for scholarships; organizational grant deadline dates available on request
Board meeting date(s): Dates available on request
Final notification: Mid-Dec.
Officer: Derry Tanner, Exec. Dir.
Trustees: Richard H. Davison; John E. Taft; Fleet National Bank.
EIN: 046037026

1506
Sweet Water Trust

Faneuil Hall Marketplace
4 S. Market Bldg., 4th Fl.
Boston, MA 02109 (617) 243-7776
Contact: Nancy Smith, Exec Dir.; or Sigrid Pickering, Prog. Dir.
FAX: (617) 243-7774; E-mail: watersweet@aol.com; URL: http://www.sweetwatertrust.org

Established in 1991 in MA.
Donor(s): Walker G. Buckner, Jr., Foundation for the Needs of Others, Inc.

Grantmaker type: Independent foundation
Financial data (yr. ended 12/31/02): Assets, $20,474,309 (M); expenditures, $1,135,301; qualifying distributions, $1,130,780; giving activities include $603,800 for 11 grants (high: $250,000; low: $2,000) and $290,730 for 3 loans/program-related investments.
Purpose and activities: Support for environmental preservation through 3 programs: 1) Land Protection Program: wild land; wild water - to help purchase land and conservation easements. The trust seeks partners (land trusts, government agencies, businesses and individuals) to work toward the ecological and biotic health of New England by establishing, enlarging, and connecting reserve areas. Grants range from $1,000-$1,000,000 for land acquisition, 2) Conservation Stewardship— $1,000-$10,000 for conservation stewardship, and 3) wilderness advocacy grants; giving through this program is earmarked for nonprofits in ME, MA, NH, NY, and VT; and - Grants are awarded for projects in science and natural resource protection, ecological analysis, stewardship, endowments, management plans; projects to create more wilderness and/or to ensure areas so designated are managed as such.
Fields of interest: Natural resources; Environment, water resources; Environment, land resources; Animals/wildlife, preservation/protection; Biological sciences.
Types of support: Land acquisition; Endowments; Emergency funds; Publication; Seed money; Research; Technical assistance; Program-related investments/loans; Matching/challenge support.
Limitations: Giving generally limited to New England and upstate NY. No support for projects for the protection of farmland, timberlands, parks, and trails unless they are a small part of a reserve design of a natural area which exceeds 2,000 acres. No grants to individuals, or for operating support.
Publications: Biennial report (including application guidelines), Grants list.
Application information: After preliminary telephone interview and review of concept paper, grant application is by invitation only. Application form not required.
  Initial approach: Telephone
  Copies of proposal: 1
  Deadline(s): Varies annually
  Board meeting date(s): Monthly
  Final notification: By telephone and award letter
Trustee: Walker G. Buckner, Jr.
Number of staff: 1 full-time professional; 4 part-time professional.
EIN: 043118545

1507
Sidney A. Swensrud Foundation
(formerly Sidney A. Swensrud Charitable Trust)
88 Broad St., 2nd Fl.
Boston, MA 02110-3407

Established in 1955 in MA.
Donor(s): Jeffrey F. Swegler, Leslie R. Swensrud, S. Blake Swensrud II, Anthony S. Swensrud.
Grantmaker type: Independent foundation
Financial data (yr. ended 12/31/02): Assets, $15,861,339 (M); expenditures, $992,278; qualifying distributions, $871,535; giving

activities include $871,535 for 20 grants (high: $265,000; low: $1,000; average: $5,000-$35,000).
Purpose and activities: Giving primarily for higher education, immigration reform, population study, and environmental preservation.
Fields of interest: Higher education; Natural resources; Health care; Human services; Population studies; Immigrants/refugees.
Limitations: Applications not accepted. Giving primarily in Washington, DC, FL, MA, NY, and PA. No grants to individuals.
Application information: Contributes only to pre-selected organizations.
Trustees: Nancy S. Anthony; Stephen B. Swensrud.
EIN: 256050238

1508
The Katherine U. & Ronald W. Takvorian Charitable Foundation
c/o Rodney Hass
137 South St., 6th Fl.
Boston, MA 02111

Established in 1992 in AL.
Grantmaker type: Independent foundation
Financial data (yr. ended 12/31/02): Assets, $1,019,044 (M); expenditures, $137,883; qualifying distributions, $131,284; giving activities include $131,571 for 17 grants (high: $62,514; low: $50).
Fields of interest: Media/communications; Performing arts; Arts; Higher education; Libraries/library science; Education; Environment, land resources.
Limitations: Applications not accepted. Giving primarily in MA. No grants to individuals.
Application information: Contributes only to pre-selected organizations.
Directors: Katherine U. Takvorian; Ronald W. Takvorian; Samuel E. Upchurch.
EIN: 631083895

1509
The Taylor Foundation
c/o Taylor, Ganson & Perrin, LLP
160 Federal St.
Boston, MA 02110
Contact: Sarah V. Harrison, Tr.

Established in 1998.
Grantmaker type: Independent foundation
Financial data (yr. ended 12/31/01): Assets, $2,887,478 (M); expenditures, $196,209; qualifying distributions, $143,500; giving activities include $143,500 for 27 grants (high: $22,300; low: $1,000).
Purpose and activities: Giving primarily for arts and culture, education, and human services; funding also for animals and wildlife.
Fields of interest: Arts; Elementary/secondary education; Education; Animals/wildlife, bird preserves; Animals/wildlife; Human services.
Limitations: Applications not accepted. Giving primarily in MA. No grants to individuals.
Application information: Contributes only to pre-selected organizations.
Trustees: Sarah V. Harrison; Jonathan V. Taylor; William F. Taylor.
EIN: 046855950

1510
Towards Sustainability Foundation
c/o Eastern Bank & Trust Co.
217 Essex St.
Salem, MA 01970
Contact: Susan K. Syversen

Established in 1997 in MA.
Grantmaker type: Independent foundation
Financial data (yr. ended 09/30/02): Assets, $4,281,473 (M); expenditures, $304,915; qualifying distributions, $269,745; giving activities include $271,000 for 13 grants (high: $50,000; low: $5,000).
Purpose and activities: The foundation supports public charities that help promote the efficient use of the earth's natural resources and human capital towards a balanced carrying capacity that can support all living organisms fairly and justly.
Fields of interest: Education; Environment, association; Natural resources; Environment; Family planning; Agriculture/food, research; Agriculture/food, formal/general education; Disasters, 9/11/01.
Limitations: Giving primarily in MA, NY, and Philadelphia, PA. No grants to individuals.
Application information:
  Initial approach: Letter
  Deadline(s): None
Trustee: Eastern Bank & Trust Co.
EIN: 043397681

1511
Trust in Diversity
c/o Bingham Legg Advisers, LLC
45 Milk St.
Boston, MA 02109-5105

Established in 1994 in MA.
Donor(s): John R. Bemis, Charlotte H. Bemis.
Grantmaker type: Operating foundation
Financial data (yr. ended 07/31/02): Assets, $226,735 (M); gifts received, $203,951; expenditures, $223,869; qualifying distributions, $217,468; giving activities include $169,025 for 7 grants (high: $50,000; low: $6,000) and $48,373 for foundation-administered programs.
Fields of interest: Arts; Natural resources; Children/youth, services; International conflict resolution; Federated giving programs.
Types of support: General/operating support; Grants to individuals.
Limitations: Applications not accepted.
Application information: Unsolicited requests for funds not accepted.
Trustees: Charlotte H. Bemis; Eleanor Bemis; Gordon H. Bemis; John R. Bemis; Marjorie Bemis; Alice Bemis Bveti; Thomas E. Peckham.
EIN: 046747335

1512
The Tupancy-Harris Foundation of 1986
c/o Fiduciary Trust Co.
Box 1647
Boston, MA 02105-1647 (617) 574-3413
Contact: Robert N. Karelitz, V.P., Fiduciary Trust Co.
Application address: 175 Federal St., Boston, MA 02110, tel.: (617) 482-5270; FAX: (617) 482-2078; E-mail: karelitz@fiduciary-trust.com

Established in 1986 in MA.
Donor(s): Oswald A. Tupancy.‡
Grantmaker type: Independent foundation
Financial data (yr. ended 12/31/02): Assets,
$22,174,242 (M); expenditures, $2,403,847;
qualifying distributions, $2,228,012; giving
activities include $2,250,204 for 37 grants (high:
$838,314; low: $1,000; average:
$1,000–$75,000).
Purpose and activities: Support for the activities
of the Nantucket Conservation Foundation and
the Nantucket Historical Association.
Fields of interest: Media/communications;
Historic preservation/historical societies; Higher
education; Natural resources; Hospitals
(general); Medical research, institute; Human
services; Children/youth, services.
Types of support: Annual campaigns; Capital
campaigns; Building/renovation.
Limitations: Giving limited to Nantucket, MA.
Application information: Application form not
required.
  Initial approach: Letter
  Copies of proposal: 1
  Deadline(s): None
Trustee: Fiduciary Trust Co.
Number of staff: None.
EIN: 046547989

1513
The Elsie Procter Van Buren Foundation
c/o Bingham Legg Advisors
45 Milk St.
Boston, MA 02109-5105
Contact: Colin S. Marshall, Tr.
Application address: c/o Bingham McCutchen,
LLP, 150 Federal St., Boston MA 02110-1726,
tel.: (617) 951-8576

Established in 1994 in MA.
Grantmaker type: Independent foundation
Financial data (yr. ended 12/31/02): Assets,
$4,196,007 (M); expenditures, $235,312;
qualifying distributions, $219,624; giving
activities include $220,500 for 68 grants (high:
$25,000; low: $500).
Fields of interest: Arts; Higher education;
Education; Environment; Human services;
Foundations (private grantmaking).
Application information:
  Deadline(s): None
Trustees: Colin S. Marshall; Elsie Procter Van
Buren.
EIN: 043251802

1514
Van Sloun Foundation
Scotch Pine Ln.
P.O. Box 116
Westport, MA 02790
Contact: Neil J. Van Sloun, Tr.

Established in 1991 in MA.
Donor(s): Neil J. Van Sloun, Sylvia Van Sloun.
Grantmaker type: Independent foundation
Financial data (yr. ended 12/31/02): Assets,
$5,114,975 (M); gifts received, $654,868;
expenditures, $257,323; qualifying distributions,
$230,605; giving activities include $234,100 for
35 grants (high: $30,000; low: $200).
Purpose and activities: Giving for religious,
scientific, literary and educational purposes.

Fields of interest: Secondary school/education;
Higher education; Natural resources; Animal
welfare; Cancer; Cancer research; YM/YWCAs &
YM/YWHAs.
Limitations: Giving primarily in MA. No grants
to individuals.
Application information:
  Initial approach: Letter
  Deadline(s): None
Trustees: David B. Titus; Dennis L. Van Sloun;
Joseph Van Sloun; Neil J. Van Sloun; Sylvia Van
Sloun.
EIN: 046691809

1515
The Vingo III Trust
c/o Loring, Wolcott & Coolidge
230 Congress St.
Boston, MA 02110   (617) 434-4644

Established in 1991 in MA.
Grantmaker type: Independent foundation
Financial data (yr. ended 12/31/00): Assets,
$5,037,559 (M); expenditures, $309,607;
qualifying distributions, $245,452; giving
activities include $246,851 for 50 grants (high:
$70,000; low: $500).
Purpose and activities: Giving primarily for
education.
Fields of interest: Museums; Historic
preservation/historical societies; Higher
education; Education; Environment.
Limitations: Applications not accepted. Giving
primarily in MA. No grants to individuals.
Application information: Contributes only to
pre-selected organizations.
Trustees: David W. Fitz; Catherine C. Lastavica;
John Lastavica.
EIN: 223106692

1516
The George R. Wallace Foundation
c/o Proctor, Goodwin & Hoar
1 Exchange Pl.
Boston, MA 02109-2881
Contact: Nancy Keller-Go

Trust established in 1963 in MA.
Donor(s): George R. Wallace.‡
Grantmaker type: Independent foundation
Financial data (yr. ended 12/31/02): Assets,
$7,766,775 (M); expenditures, $728,984;
qualifying distributions, $650,932; giving
activities include $611,000 for 27 grants (high:
$25,000; low: $5,000).
Purpose and activities: Giving primarily for
education, particularly an international student
exchange; funding also for historical
preservation, social services, and Christian
agencies and churches.
Fields of interest: Television; Arts; Higher
education; Education; Natural resources; Family
planning; Human services; Aging,
centers/services; International exchange,
students; Christian agencies & churches.
Types of support: General/operating support;
Annual campaigns; Capital campaigns;
Building/renovation; Equipment; Land
acquisition; Endowments; Seed money;
Matching/challenge support.

Limitations: Giving primarily in FL and MA. No
grants to individuals, or for scholarships or
fellowships; no loans.
Application information: Application form not
required.
  Initial approach: Letter
  Copies of proposal: 1
  Deadline(s): None
  Board meeting date(s): Semiannually
  Final notification: 6 months
Officer and Trustees:* George R. Wallace III,*
Chair.; John Grado, Jr.; Henry B. Shepard, Jr.
Number of staff: None.
EIN: 046130518

1517
Weld Foundation
c/o Loring, Wolcott & Coolidge
230 Congress St.
Boston, MA 02110-2437

Trust established in 1952 in MA.
Donor(s): Mary Weld Pingree.‡
Grantmaker type: Independent foundation
Financial data (yr. ended 12/31/02): Assets,
$9,109,660 (M); expenditures, $638,054;
qualifying distributions, $595,281; giving
activities include $592,000 for 16 grants (high:
$150,000; low: $2,000).
Purpose and activities: Giving primarily for
education and museums; support also for health
and social services.
Fields of interest: Museums;
Elementary/secondary education; Secondary
school/education; Natural resources; Health
care; Religion.
Limitations: Applications not accepted. Giving
primarily in MA. No grants to individuals.
Application information: Contributes only to
pre-selected organizations.
Trustees: Frederick D. Ballou; Peter B. Loring;
Charles W. Pingree.
EIN: 046039173

1518
William P. Wharton Trust
c/o Choate, Hall & Stewart
53 State St., Exchange Pl.
Boston, MA 02109-2804   (617) 248-5000
Contact: John M. Cornish, Jr. or Pearl E. Bell, Tr.
Admin.

Established in 1976 in MA.
Grantmaker type: Independent foundation
Financial data (yr. ended 09/30/02): Assets,
$3,615,210 (M); expenditures, $263,333;
qualifying distributions, $214,670; giving
activities include $214,670 for 28 grants
(average: $2,000–$10,000).
Purpose and activities: To support projects that
directly promote the study, conservation, and
appreciation of nature. Specific objectives
include: bird and forestry research and
management, natural areas preservation, and
management techniques designed to improve
environmental quality and species diversity.
Fields of interest: Natural resources;
Environment; Animals/wildlife,
preservation/protection.
Types of support: Equipment; Land acquisition;
Program development; Publication; Research.

Limitations: Giving primarily in New England, with some emphasis on MA.
Publications: Informational brochure (including application guidelines).
Application information: Application form required.
   Initial approach: Letter requesting application form
   Copies of proposal: 6
   Deadline(s): Apr. 1 and Oct. 1
   Board meeting date(s): Apr. and Oct.
   Final notification: Within 30 days of board meeting
Trustees: John M. Cornish; Thomas H.P. Whitney, Jr.
Number of staff: None.
EIN: 046407797

1519
David P. Wheatland Charitable Trust
c/o Acadia Mgmt. Co., Inc.
111 Devonshire St., Ste. 620
Boston, MA   02109
Contact: Richard Wheatland, Tr.

Established in 1993 in MA.
Donor(s): David P. Wheatland Trust.
Grantmaker type: Independent foundation
Financial data (yr. ended 12/31/02): Assets, $6,449,739 (M); expenditures, $357,770; qualifying distributions, $354,304; giving activities include $332,790 for 6 grants (high: $100,000; low: $26,000).
Purpose and activities: Giving primarily to a museum of art, architecture and culture, as well as for a university historical science center; funding also for a marine mammal center.
Fields of interest: Museums (art); Historical activities; Animal welfare; Foundations (community).
Types of support: General/operating support.
Limitations: Giving primarily in MA. No grants to individuals.
Application information: Preference given to organizations historically supported by the donor and members of his family.
   Deadline(s): None
Trustees: Eileen M. Balthazard; Peter B. Seamans; Richard Wheatland.
EIN: 046744379

1520
Arthur Ashley Williams Foundation
379 Underwood St.
Holliston, MA   01746   (508) 429-6228
Application address: P.O. Box 6280, Holliston, MA 01746

Incorporated in 1951 in MA.
Donor(s): Arthur A. Williams.‡
Grantmaker type: Independent foundation
Financial data (yr. ended 12/31/02): Assets, $3,236,541 (M); expenditures, $200,971; qualifying distributions, $147,393; giving activities include $125,500 for 39 grants (high: $12,000; low: $500).
Purpose and activities: Giving primarily for historical and natural history societies, as well as to churches; funding also for arts and culture, animals and wildlife, health associations, food services, and women's and social services.

Fields of interest: Historic preservation/historical societies; Arts; Animals/wildlife; Health organizations, association; Food banks; Human services; Women, centers/services; Christian agencies & churches; Aging.
Types of support: Scholarship funds; Scholarships—to individuals.
Limitations: Giving primarily in CA, CT, MA, and Canaan and Plymouth, NH.
Publications: Application guidelines.
Application information: Application form required.
   Initial approach: Letter
   Copies of proposal: 1
   Deadline(s): None
   Board meeting date(s): Jan., Apr., July, and Oct.
Officers: Elbert F. Tuttle, Chair.; Martha Anderson, Clerk; Clement T. Lambert, Treas.
Trustees: Melissa W. Laverack; Polly McWherter; Nancy Rose.
Number of staff: None.
EIN: 046044714

1521
Shirley Shattuck Windsor Charitable Trust
c/o Loring, Wolcott, & Coolide
230 Congress St.
Boston, MA   02110   (617) 523-6531
Contact: Frederick D. Ballou, Tr.

Established in 1997 in MA.
Donor(s): Frederick D. Ballou, Gilbert M. Roddy, Jr.
Grantmaker type: Independent foundation
Financial data (yr. ended 12/31/02): Assets, $3,140,072 (M); expenditures, $198,458; qualifying distributions, $178,691; giving activities include $175,000 for 3 grants (high: $100,000; low: $25,000).
Purpose and activities: Giving primarily for the prevention of cruelty to animals.
Fields of interest: University; Animals/wildlife, preservation/protection; Hospitals (general); Disasters, 9/11/01; Human services.
Types of support: General/operating support.
Limitations: Giving primarily in MA. No grants to individuals.
Application information:
   Initial approach: Letter
   Deadline(s): None
Trustees: Frederick D. Ballou; Gilbert M. Roddy, Jr.
EIN: 046851595

1522
Clara B. Winthrop Trust
c/o Welch & Forbes, LLC
45 School St.
Boston, MA   02108-3204   (617) 523-1635
Contact: Richard Olney, III, Tr.

Established in 1969.
Donor(s): Clara B. Winthrop.‡
Grantmaker type: Independent foundation
Financial data (yr. ended 12/31/02): Assets, $3,058,157 (M); expenditures, $290,471; qualifying distributions, $254,360; giving activities include $251,500 for 28 grants (high: $25,000; low: $2,000).
Fields of interest: Museums; Arts; Education; Natural resources; Community development.

Types of support: General/operating support; Continuing support; Annual campaigns; Capital campaigns.
Limitations: Giving limited to MA. No grants to individuals.
Application information: Application form not required.
   Initial approach: Letter
   Deadline(s): None
   Board meeting date(s): Dec.
Trustees: Arthur C. Hodges; Richard Olney III; Oliver A. Spalding.
Number of staff: None.
EIN: 046039972

1523
Greater Worcester Community Foundation, Inc.
370 Main St., Ste. 650
Worcester, MA   01608-1738   (508) 755-0980
Contact: Ann T. Lisi, Exec. Dir.
FAX: (508) 755-3406; E-mail: atlisi@greaterworcester.org or conaghan@greaterworcester.org; URL: http://www.greaterworcester.org/

Incorporated in 1975 in MA.
Grantmaker type: Community foundation
Financial data (yr. ended 12/31/02): Assets, $75,867,937 (M); gifts received, $5,098,241; expenditures, $5,130,850; giving activities include $4,180,970 for 781 grants (high: $200,000; low: $100; average: $500–$30,000).
Purpose and activities: To support programs that improve the quality of life for residents of the greater Worcester, MA, area.
Fields of interest: Humanities; Arts; Medical school/education; Nursing school/education; Education; Environment; Health care; Health organizations, association; Medical research, institute; Abuse prevention; Housing/shelter, development; Youth development; Human services; Children/youth, services; Family services; Aging, centers/services; Homeless, human services; Community development; Government/public administration; Public affairs; African Americans/Blacks; Disabled; Aging; People with AIDS (PWAs); Economically disadvantaged; Homeless.
Types of support: Annual campaigns; Building/renovation; Program development; Conferences/seminars; Seed money; Scholarship funds; Research; Technical assistance; Consulting services; Program evaluation; Program-related investments/loans; Scholarships—to individuals; Matching/challenge support.
Limitations: Giving limited to Worcester County, MA. No grants to individuals (except for designated scholarship funds); generally no grants for general operating expenses, capital improvements, or endowment campaigns.
Publications: Application guidelines, Annual report, Newsletter.
Application information: Submit 2 copies of the foundation's Summary of Application Form and 2 copies of complete proposal. See foundation Web site for additional application information. Scholarships are for residents of Worcester County, MA, only. Scholarship applications are available at Worcester County high schools. Application form required.
   Initial approach: Telephone or letter

Copies of proposal: 2
Deadline(s): Feb. 1 and Sept. 15 for
   organizations; Mar. 14 for scholarships
Board meeting date(s): Jan., Mar., June, Sept.,
   Nov., and as required
Final notification: 3 months
Officers and Directors:* Michael D.
Brockelman,* Pres.; Robert K. "Ross" Dik,* V.P.
and Dist. Chair.; Robert Bachelder,* Clerk; James
E. Collins,* Treas.; Ann T. Lisi, Exec. Dir.; Sara
Trillo Adams; Christopher W. Bramley; P. Kevin
Condron; Allen W. Fletcher; Ramon V. Frias;
Lawrence J. Glick; Barbara E. Greenberg; Mary
Kett; Cynthia M. McMullen; Janet Wilson
Moore; Barrett Morgan; Martha R. Pappas;
Gladys Rodriguez-Parker; Paul R. Rossley.
Distribution Committee: Pamela K. Boisvert;
Ellen S. Dunlap; Susan G. Gateley; Joseph M.
Hamilton; Monica E. Lowell; Donna McGrath.
Number of staff: 6 full-time professional; 1
part-time professional; 2 full-time support; 2
part-time support.
EIN: 042572276

1524
Yawkey Foundation I
(also known as The Thomas A. Yawkey
Foundation)
990 Washington St., Ste. 315
Dedham, MA 02026-6704   (781) 329-7470
Contact: James Healey
FAX: (781) 329-8195; URL: http://
www.yawkeyfoundation.org

Established in 1976.
Grantmaker type: Public charity
Financial data (yr. ended 06/30/02): Revenue,
$4,614,744; assets, $54,008,500; gifts received,
$808,476; expenditures, $1,913,376; program
services expenses, $1,402,396; giving activities
include $1,402,396 for grants.
Purpose and activities: The foundation is
committed to organizations that focus on
conservation, education, social services, health
care, arts and culture, and amateur sports. A
portion of the net income of the foundation is
applied to the preservation, maintenance and
development of the Tom Yawkey Wildlife
Center, as well as support for the Jimmy Fund,
Tara Hall Home for Boys, and Yale University.
Fields of interest: Arts; Higher education;
Education; Natural resources; Animals/wildlife,
preservation/protection; Health care;
Athletics/sports, amateur leagues;
Athletics/sports, baseball; Recreation; Human
services; Youth, services.
Types of support: Program development;
Scholarships—to individuals.
Limitations: Applications not accepted. Giving
primarily in SC and New England.
Application information: Currently not
accepting unsolicited proposals. Check
foundation Web site for updated information.
Officer and Trustees:* John L. Harrington,*
Exec. Dir.; Eleanor S. Armstrong; William B.
Gutfarb.
EIN: 132890749

MICHIGAN

1525
James C. Acheson Foundation
600 Fort St., Ste. 101
Port Huron, MI 48060

Established in 1999 in MI.
Donor(s): James C. Acheson.
Grantmaker type: Independent foundation
Financial data (yr. ended 12/31/02): Assets,
$12,109,913 (M); gifts received, $75,000;
expenditures, $344,048; qualifying distributions,
$215,748; giving activities include $215,748 for
20 grants (high: $174,063; low: $100; average:
$1,000–$40,000).
Purpose and activities: Support for the arts,
health, the environment, human services, and
community development.
Fields of interest: Museums; Environment;
Health care; Mental health/crisis services;
Human services; American Red Cross;
Community development; Federated giving
programs.
Limitations: Applications not accepted. Giving
primarily in MI. No grants to individuals.
Application information: Contributes only to
pre-selected organizations.
Officers: James C. Acheson, Pres.; Donna M.
Niester, V.P.; Douglas R. Austin, Secy.-Treas.
EIN: 383463509

1526
Americana Foundation
28115 Meadowbrook Rd.
Novi, MI 48377-3128   (248) 347-3863
Contact: Marlene J. Fluharty, Exec. Dir.
FAX: (248) 347-3349; E-mail:
fluhartm@msue.msu.edu

Established in 1978 in MI.
Donor(s): Adolph H. Meyer,‡ Ida M. Meyer.‡
Grantmaker type: Independent foundation
Financial data (yr. ended 12/31/02): Assets,
$16,730,955 (M); expenditures, $1,115,009;
qualifying distributions, $1,045,695; giving
activities include $793,646 for 36 grants (high:
$50,000; low: $1,000; average:
$1,500–$50,000).
Purpose and activities: Support for education
and advocacy programs that address issues of
conserving agriculture and natural resources,
and the preservation of the American heritage.
Fields of interest: Historic preservation/historical
societies; Environment; Agriculture.
Types of support: General/operating support;
Building/renovation; Endowments; Program
development; Conferences/seminars;
Publication; Technical assistance;
Matching/challenge support.
Limitations: Giving primarily in MI. No support
for private foundations or for political purposes.
No grants to individuals, or for fundraising
events, tables, or scholarships.
Publications: Annual report (including
application guidelines), Grants list,
Informational brochure (including application
guidelines).

Application information: Application form not
required.
   Initial approach: Letter or telephone
   Copies of proposal: 1
   Deadline(s): Middle of Jan., Apr., July, and Oct.
   Board meeting date(s): Quarterly
Officers and Trustees:* Robert Janson,* Pres.;
Jonathan Thomas,* V.P.; Thomas F. Ranger,*
Treas.; Norman Brown; Kathryn Eckert; Barbara
Livy; Gary Rentrop.
Number of staff: 1 full-time professional; 1
part-time support.
EIN: 382269431

1527
Ann Arbor Area Community Foundation
(formerly Ann Arbor Area Foundation)
201 S. Main St., Ste. 501
Ann Arbor, MI 48104-2113   (734) 663-0401
Contact: Cheryl Elliott, C.O.O. and V.P.
Additional tel.: (734) 663-2173; FAX: (734)
663-3514; E-mail: info@aaacf.org; URL: http://
www.aaacf.org/

Incorporated in 1963 in MI.
Grantmaker type: Community foundation
Financial data (yr. ended 12/31/02): Assets,
$20,106,537 (M); gifts received, $1,464,014;
expenditures, $1,201,851; giving activities
include $487,134 for grants (high: $50,000).
Purpose and activities: The mission of the
foundation is to enrich the quality of life in the
greater Ann Arbor, MI, area through building a
permanent endowment, providing a flexible
vehicle for donors, and acting as a leader for the
philanthropic community. The foundation
administers donor-advised funds.
Fields of interest: Visual arts; Performing arts;
Theater; Arts; Higher education; Education;
Natural resources; Environment; Health care;
Health organizations, association; Domestic
violence; Human services; Children/youth,
services; Family services; Aging,
centers/services; Homeless, human services;
Community development; Aging; Homeless.
Types of support: Income development;
Management development; Emergency funds;
Program development; Conferences/seminars;
Publication; Seed money; Scholarship funds;
Research; Matching/challenge support.
Limitations: Giving limited to the Ann Arbor, MI,
area. No support for religious or sectarian
purposes, or for advocacy or political purposes.
No grants to individuals (except from designated
funds), or for operating budgets, construction
projects, computer hardware equipment,
continuing support, annual campaigns, deficit
financing, fundraising purposes, land
acquisition, endowment funds, consulting
services, technical assistance, or fellowships; no
loans or program-related investments.
Publications: Application guidelines, Annual
report (including application guidelines),
Informational brochure (including application
guidelines), Newsletter, Program policy
statement.
Application information: Guidelines available
on Web site. Application form required.
   Initial approach: Telephone
   Copies of proposal: 11
   Deadline(s): Feb., May, and Oct. for grants;
      Sept. for youth projects

Board meeting date(s): Jan., Mar., May, July, Sept., and Nov.
Final notification: 60 days
Officers and Trustees:* David Lutton,* Chair.; Norman Herbert,* Vice-Chair.; Cheryl W. Elliot, Pres.; Ellie Serras,* Secy.; Jamie Buhr,* Treas.; Dan Balbach; Deborah Bueche; Thomas Dew; D.J. Dorney; Cal Fette; Bill Kinley; John Martin; Betsy McCallister; Kevin McDonald; David Rutledge; Ingrid Sheldon; Timothy Wadhams; Sandy White.
Number of staff: 1 full-time professional; 2 part-time professional; 1 full-time support; 1 part-time support.
EIN: 386087967

1528
Arcus Foundation

(formerly Jon L. Stryker Foundation)
303 N. Rose St., Ste. 300
Kalamazoo, MI 49007-3846 (269) 373-4373
Contact: Linda May, Exec. Dir.
FAX: (269) 373-0277; E-mail: info@arcusfoundation.org; URL: http:// www.arcusfoundation.org

Established in 1997 in MI.
Donor(s): Jon L. Stryker.
Grantmaker type: Independent foundation
Financial data (yr. ended 12/31/01): Assets, $12,061,783 (M); expenditures, $4,189,555; qualifying distributions, $3,986,268; giving activities include $4,032,311 for 92 grants (high: $1,000,000; low: $15; average: $1,000–$50,000).
Purpose and activities: Support for programs that fight prejudice and discrimination and protect and defend human and civil rights, including the issues confronting the gay, lesbian, bisexual, and transgender community. Giving also for Great Apes Sanctuary and Conservation.
Fields of interest: Animals/wildlife, endangered species; Animals/wildlife, sanctuaries; Animals/wildlife, special services; Civil rights, gays/lesbians; Civil rights; Gays/lesbians.
Limitations: Giving on a national basis, with emphasis on Kalamazoo, MI for some programs. No support for religious activities. No grants to individuals.
Publications: Annual report (including application guidelines), Newsletter.
Application information: Formal proposal accepted by invitation only following letter of inquiry process. See Web site for complete formal proposal requirements.
Initial approach: Letter, no more than 2 pages
Copies of proposal: 3
Deadline(s): Apr. 1 and Sept. 1 for letter of inquiry; May 1 and Oct. 1 for invited proposals
Board meeting date(s): June and Dec.
Final notification: Within three weeks for letter of inquiry
Officers: Jon L. Stryker, Pres.; Linda May, Exec. Dir.
Number of staff: 1 full-time professional.
EIN: 383332791

1529
Asthma & Allergy Foundation of America, Michigan Chapter

17520 W. 12 Mile Rd., Ste. 102
Southfield, MI 48076-1943 (248) 557-8050
Contact: Alina Pabin, Exec. Dir.
Additional tel.: (888) 444-0333; FAX: (248) 557-8768; E-mail: aafamich@aol.com; URL: http://www.aafa.org/

Grantmaker type: Public charity
Financial data (yr. ended 12/31/02): Revenue, $78,888; assets, $71,428 (L); gifts received, $34,758; expenditures, $62,904; program services expenses, $45,557; giving activities include $11,649 for 1 grant.
Purpose and activities: The foundation seeks to improve the quality of life for individuals affected by asthma and allergic diseases and to promote awareness of these disorders.
Fields of interest: Environment, air pollution; Public health; Allergies; Asthma; Pediatrics.
Limitations: Giving primarily in MI.
Publications: Informational brochure, Newsletter.
Application information: Application form not required.
Initial approach: Telephone
Board meeting date(s): Quarterly
Officers and Directors:* Allen Sosin, M.D.,* Pres.; Clyde R. Flory, M.D.,* V.P., Medical; Karen Gray,* V.P., Progs.; Lana Hardin,* V.P., Devel.; Jean Yonke,* Secy.; Matthew Hunter,* Treas.; Alina Pabin, Exec. Dir.; Heather Davis; Sandra Gibbings; Jacqueline Moore, M.D.; Suzie Schafer; Lawrence Sweet, M.D.
Number of staff: 1 part-time professional.
EIN: 382534175

1530
James D. Azzar Foundation, Inc.

P.O. Box 1182
Grand Rapids, MI 49501

Established in 2001 in MI.
Donor(s): Azzar Industries, Inc., Patty Processing, Inc.
Grantmaker type: Independent foundation
Financial data (yr. ended 12/31/02): Assets, $130 (M); gifts received, $451,000; expenditures, $450,870; qualifying distributions, $450,870; giving activities include $450,000 for 1 grant.
Purpose and activities: Giving primarily to an animal shelter.
Fields of interest: Animal welfare.
Limitations: Applications not accepted. No grants to individuals.
Application information: Contributes only to pre-selected organizations.
Director: James D. Azzar.
EIN: 383533254

1531
James & Shirley Balk Foundation

1230 Monroe Ave. N.W.
Grand Rapids, MI 49505-4690
(616) 874-8333
Contact: James Balk II, Tr.

Established in 1984 in MI.
Donor(s): James Balk II, Shirley Balk.

Grantmaker type: Independent foundation
Financial data (yr. ended 12/31/02): Assets, $4,152,927 (M); gifts received, $174,000; expenditures, $402,165; qualifying distributions, $400,622; giving activities include $403,710 for 23 grants (high: $150,000; low: $250).
Purpose and activities: Giving primarily for Christian education; support also for the arts, churches, human services, and botanical gardens.
Fields of interest: Arts; Higher education; Education; Botanical gardens; Human services; Federated giving programs; Christian agencies & churches.
Types of support: General/operating support.
Limitations: Giving primarily in Grand Rapids, MI. No grants to individuals.
Application information:
Initial approach: Letter on organization's letterhead
Deadline(s): None
Trustees: James Balk II; Shirley Balk.
EIN: 382556356

1532
Barry Community Foundation

629 W. State St., Ste.201
Hastings, MI 49058-0644 (269) 945-0526
Contact: Bonnie Ballinger, Exec. Dir. or Jennifer Richards, Prog. Dir.
FAX: (269) 945-0826; E-mail: bonnie@barrycf.org or jen@barrycf.org; URL: http://www.barrycf.org

Established in 1996 in MI.
Grantmaker type: Community foundation
Financial data (yr. ended 01/31/02): Assets, $4,323,216 (M); gifts received, $306,483; expenditures, $312,643; giving activities include $151,790 for grants (average: $100–$50,000).
Purpose and activities: The purpose of the foundation is to identify and address current and anticipated community needs by providing services and assisting donors with their philanthropic interests; including fostering youth development and community development. The foundation administers donor-advised funds.
Fields of interest: Arts; Education; Natural resources; Hospitals (general); Human services; Children/youth, services; Community development, neighborhood development.
Types of support: Annual campaigns; Capital campaigns; Building/renovation; Equipment; Endowments; Program development; Conferences/seminars; Seed money; Curriculum development; Scholarship funds; Technical assistance; Consulting services; Program evaluation; Matching/challenge support.
Limitations: Giving limited to Barry County, MI. No grants to individuals.
Publications: Application guidelines, Annual report, Informational brochure, Newsletter.
Application information: Application form required.
Initial approach: Telephone
Copies of proposal: 22
Deadline(s): Mar. 15 and Oct. 15
Board meeting date(s): 3rd Thurs. monthly
Final notification: May 31 and Dec. 31
Officers: Maggie Coleman, Pres.; Bob Bender, V.P.; Kathy Johnson, Secy.; Jon Simpson, Treas.; Bonnie Ballingor, Exec. Dir.

Directors: Doug DeCamp; Richard Groos; Jan Hartough; Fred Jacobs; Russ Keech; Richard Shuster; and 2 additional directors.
Number of staff: 1 full-time professional; 1 full-time support.
EIN: 383246131

1533

Battle Creek Community Foundation
(formerly Greater Battle Creek Foundation)
1 Riverwalk Ctr.
34 W. Jackson St.
Battle Creek, MI 49017-3505 (269) 962-2181
Contact: Angela Graham, V.P.
FAX: (269) 962-2182; E-mail: bccf@bccfoundation.org; URL: http://www.bccfoundation.org

Established in 1974 in MI.
Grantmaker type: Community foundation
Financial data (yr. ended 03/31/02): Assets, $59,424,044 (M); gifts received, $8,384,713; expenditures, $6,184,459; giving activities include $4,087,948 for 120+ grants (high: $612,658; low: $5,000; average: $5,000–$40,000) and $91,688 for grants to individuals.
Purpose and activities: Grantmaking for programming in the Battle Creek, Michigan, area that serves the citizens of the community through education, health, human services, arts, public affairs, and community development; scholarships are also available to students residing in the greater Battle Creek area.
Fields of interest: Arts; Child development, education; Adult education—literacy, basic skills & GED; Reading; Education; Animal welfare; Hospitals (general); Health care; Health organizations, association; Children/youth, services; Child development, services; Minorities/immigrants, centers/services; Community development; Public affairs; Minorities.
Types of support: Building/renovation; Equipment; Land acquisition; Emergency funds; Program development; Conferences/seminars; Publication; Seed money; Curriculum development; Scholarship funds; Technical assistance; Program evaluation; Program-related investments/loans; Scholarships—to individuals; Matching/challenge support.
Limitations: Giving limited to the greater Battle Creek, MI, area. No grants for operating budgets, deficit financing, endowments, or research; no loans (except for program-related investments).
Publications: Application guidelines, Annual report, Biennial report (including application guidelines), Financial statement, Grants list, Informational brochure, Newsletter, Program policy statement.
Application information: Contact high school counselors for scholarship applications.
Application form required.
Initial approach: Letter or telephone
Copies of proposal: 17
Deadline(s): Quarterly
Board meeting date(s): Monthly
Final notification: 7 weeks after application deadline
Officers and Trustees:* Velma Laws-Clay,* Chair.; James P. Baldwin,* Vice-Chair.; Brenda L. Hunt, C.E.O. and Pres.; Angela Graham, V.P.;

Susan S. Day, Secy.; David E. Kinnisten, Treas.; Charles Cooper, Jr.; Roberta H. Cribbs; Stephanie M. Demarest; Annie Dunsky; David H. Eddy; James R.C. Hazel, Jr.; James F. Hettinger; Peter M. Kelley; Samir Kulkarni; David P. Lucas; Fred F. Meyer; Kathleen D. Rizor; David L. Schweitzer; Clara J. Stewart.
Number of staff: 9 full-time professional; 1 part-time professional; 3 full-time support; 1 part-time support.
EIN: 382045459
Recent environmental and animal welfare grants:
1533-1 Humane Society of Calhoun County, Battle Creek, MI, $10,000. For transitional funding for mission alignment. 2001.
1533-2 Leila Arboretum Society, Battle Creek, MI, $11,000. 2001.

1534

Bay Area Community Foundation
703 Washington Ave.
Bay City, MI 48708-5717 (989) 893-4438
Contact: Roger Merrifield, C.E.O.
Additional tel.: (800) 926-3217; FAX: (989) 893-4448; E-mail: bacfnd@bayfoundation.org; URL: http://www.bayfoundation.org

Established in 1982 in MI.
Grantmaker type: Community foundation
Financial data (yr. ended 12/31/02): Assets, $17,049,828 (M); gifts received, $1,297,322; expenditures, $1,418,433; giving activities include $899,522 for grants (high: $20,000; low: $100; average: $100–$15,000).
Purpose and activities: To fulfill a wide array of donors charitable wishes by building permanent endowment funds and to serve as a leader for community development. Priority will be given to projects that focus on the following areas: Community Vision, Arts and Recreation and Multigenerational initiatives. The foundation administers donor-advised funds.
Fields of interest: Visual arts; Performing arts; Arts; Education; Energy; Environment; Housing/shelter, development; Recreation; Human services; Children/youth, services; Community development; Science; Disabled.
Types of support: Capital campaigns; Building/renovation; Endowments; Program development; Seed money; Curriculum development; Internship funds; Scholarship funds; Research; Technical assistance; In-kind gifts.
Limitations: Giving limited to Bay and Arenac counties, MI. No support for religious purposes. No grants to individuals (excluding scholarships), or for annual fund drives, or general operating expenses.
Publications: Annual report, Financial statement, Grants list, Informational brochure (including application guidelines), Newsletter, Occasional report.
Application information: Applications sent by FAX will not be accepted. Application form required.
Initial approach: Telephone or letter requesting application
Deadline(s): Varies
Board meeting date(s): Monthly, except in June, Aug. and Dec.
Officers and Trustees:* Janalou Blecke, Chair.; Charles Curtiss, Vice-Chair.; Roger Merrifield,*

C.E.O. and Pres.; Michael Kasperski, Secy.; Jerome L. Yantz,* Treas.; Joy Baker; Gary Bosco; Mary Beth Callahan; Diane Demers; Kevin Dykema; Jane Hagen; Mike Hanisko; Ruth Jaffe; Steve Kessler; Gary Labadie; Steve Lawrence; Gary Manthey; Pamela Monastiere; Robert Monroe.
Number of staff: 1 full-time professional; 1 part-time professional; 2 full-time support.
EIN: 382418086

1535

The Julius H. and Barbara B. Beers Family Foundation
109 E. Front St.
Traverse City, MI 49684

Established in 1998 in MI.
Donor(s): Julius Beers, Barbara Beers.
Grantmaker type: Independent foundation
Financial data (yr. ended 12/31/02): Assets, $1,780,701 (M); expenditures, $116,862; qualifying distributions, $105,688; giving activities include $106,000 for 17 grants (high: $10,000; low: $1,000).
Fields of interest: University; Environment; Health care; Human services; Family services; Women, centers/services; Foundations (community); Federated giving programs; Protestant agencies & churches.
Limitations: Applications not accepted. Giving primarily in Traverse City, MI. No grants to individuals.
Application information: Contributes only to pre-selected organizations.
Officer and Director:* Barbara Beers,* Pres.
EIN: 383417343

1536

Berrien Community Foundation, Inc.
2900 S. State St., Ste. 2E.
St. Joseph, MI 49085 (269) 983-3304
Contact: Nanette Keiser, Ed.D., Exec. Dir.
FAX: (269) 983-4939; E-mail: nkeiser@qtm.net;
URL: http://www.berriencommunity.org

Incorporated in 1952 in MI.
Grantmaker type: Community foundation
Financial data (yr. ended 12/31/02): Assets, $11,619,276 (M); gifts received, $1,175,626; expenditures, $772,423; giving activities include $468,762 for 91 grants (high: $34,607; low: $35; average: $100–$469,000).
Purpose and activities: Primary areas of interest include youth, education, family issues, and general charitable giving. The foundation administers donor-advised funds.
Fields of interest: Museums; Music; Humanities; Historic preservation/historical societies; Arts; Elementary school/education; Secondary school/education; Adult education—literacy, basic skills & GED; Libraries/library science; Reading; Education; Environment; Health care; Substance abuse, services; Health organizations, association; Nutrition; Safety/disasters; Recreation; Youth development; Human services; Children/youth, services; Family services; Aging, centers/services; Homeless, human services; Community development; Voluntarism promotion; Engineering/technology; Science; Public affairs; Disabled; Aging; Homeless.

Types of support: General/operating support; Building/renovation; Equipment; Endowments; Emergency funds; Program development; Seed money; Curriculum development; Scholarship funds; Consulting services; Program evaluation; Scholarships—to individuals; In-kind gifts; Matching/challenge support.

Limitations: Giving limited to Berrien County, MI. No support for sectarian religious purposes. No grants to individuals (except for scholarships), or for consulting services, technical assistance, operating funds, deficit financing, or annual fund drives; no loans or program-related investments.

Publications: Annual report, Financial statement, Informational brochure (including application guidelines), Newsletter.

Application information: Application guidelines available on request. 20 copies of application required for youth-oriented projects only. Application form required.

   Initial approach: Telephone
   Copies of proposal: 1
   Deadline(s): Sept. 15 for winter meeting; Mar. 1 for spring meeting
   Board meeting date(s): Every 2 months
   Final notification: 10 to 14 weeks

Officers and Trustees: B. David Allen,* Pres.; Joanne Sims,* V.P.; Gregory Vaughn,* Secy.; Sharon Vargo,* Treas.; Elaine Chaudoir; Robert D. Gottlieb; Nadra Kissman; Mark Miller; Gladys Peeples-Burks, Ph.D.; Stephen Sizer.

Number of staff: 3 full-time professional; 1 part-time support.

EIN: 386057160

1537
BFK Foundation

c/o Stephen Kaplan, Pres.
1213 S. Forest Ave.
Ann Arbor, MI 48104-3922

Donor(s): Beatrice Kaplan, Rubin H. Kaplan.
Grantmaker type: Independent foundation
Financial data (yr. ended 12/31/02): Assets, $372,536 (M); gifts received, $100,000; expenditures, $91,950; qualifying distributions, $91,713; giving activities include $90,000 for 12 grants (high: $15,000; low: $5,000).
Purpose and activities: Giving primarily for environmental protection and to Jewish organizations.
Fields of interest: Natural resources; Jewish agencies & temples.
Types of support: General/operating support.
Limitations: Applications not accepted. Giving primarily in Washington, DC, MO, NY, OH, and VA. No grants to individuals.
Application information: Contributes only to pre-selected organizations.
Directors: Abram W. Kaplan; Rachel Kaplan; Stephen Kaplan.
EIN: 522069703

1538
Guido A. & Elizabeth H. Binda Foundation

124 S. Minges Rd.
Battle Creek, MI 49015
Contact: Elizabeth H. Binda, Pres.
Application address: 25 W. Michigan Ave., Ste. 1415, Battle Creek, MI 49017

Established in 1977 in MI.
Donor(s): Guido A. Binda.‡
Grantmaker type: Independent foundation
Financial data (yr. ended 06/30/02): Assets, $13,488,820 (M); expenditures, $911,666; qualifying distributions, $824,412; giving activities include $781,931 for 61 grants (high: $271,085; low: $250; average: $500–$200,000).
Purpose and activities: Giving primarily for education; support also for health care, community development, and human services.
Fields of interest: Architecture; Arts; Elementary school/education; Secondary school/education; Higher education; Adult education—literacy, basic skills & GED; Scholarships/financial aid; Reading; Education; Environment; Health care; Substance abuse, services; Human services; Community development; Minorities; Economically disadvantaged.
Types of support: Capital campaigns; Building/renovation; Emergency funds; Program development; Seed money; Curriculum development; Scholarship funds; Program-related investments/loans.
Limitations: Giving limited to Battle Creek and southwestern MI. No grants to individuals, or for endowments or capital campaigns.
Publications: Annual report.
Application information: Application form required.
   Copies of proposal: 9
   Deadline(s): Dec. 1 to May 1
   Board meeting date(s): Jan. and June
Officers and Trustees: Elizabeth H. Binda,* Pres. and Secy.; Richard Tsoumas, V.P.; E. James Swan,* Treas.; Robert Binda; LaVerne H. Boss; Norman Brown; Chris T. Christ; John Hosking; Joel Orosz.
Number of staff: 1 part-time support.
EIN: 382184423

1539
Branch County Community Foundation

2 W. Chicago St., Ste. E-1
Coldwater, MI 49036-1602   (517) 278-4517
Contact: Colleen Knight, Exec. Dir.
FAX: (517) 279-2319; *E-mail:* info@brcofoundation.org; *URL:* http://www.brcofoundation.org

Established in 1991 in MI.
Grantmaker type: Community foundation
Financial data (yr. ended 09/30/03): Assets, $3,795,327 (M); gifts received, $593,999; expenditures, $390,528; giving activities include $112,035 for 103 grants (high: $16,963; low: $50; average: $300–$600,000).
Purpose and activities: To enhance the quality of life for all Branch County, MI, citizens. The foundation does this through building a permanent endowment for grantmaking, and by serving as a catalyst and conveyor. The foundation administers donor-advised funds.
Fields of interest: Humanities; Education; Environment; Health care; Human services.
Types of support: General/operating support; Equipment; Endowments; Conferences/seminars; Scholarship funds; Technical assistance; In-kind gifts; Matching/challenge support.
Limitations: Giving limited to Branch County and Colon, MI. No grants to individuals; no loans or program-related investments.

Publications: Application guidelines, Annual report, Financial statement, Informational brochure, Newsletter, Occasional report.
Application information: See Web site for information. Application form required.
   Initial approach: Letter requesting application form
   Deadline(s): Mar. 1 and Sept. 1
   Board meeting date(s): Monthly
   Final notification: May 1 and Nov. 1
Officers and Directors: Ray Bregger,* Pres.; M. Joe Ganger,* V.P.; Nancy Hutchins,* Secy.; Remus Rigg,* Treas.; Colleen Knight, Exec. Dir.; and 7 additional directors.
Number of staff: 1 full-time professional; 1 full-time support.
EIN: 383021071

1540
Broadleaf Foundation

111 Lyon St. N.W., Ste. 900
Grand Rapids, MI 49503-2487

Established in 1998 in MI.
Donor(s): Jonathan M. Wege.
Grantmaker type: Independent foundation
Financial data (yr. ended 12/31/02): Assets, $259,976 (M); gifts received, $24,000; expenditures, $686,935; qualifying distributions, $651,666; giving activities include $659,500 for 2 grants (high: $650,000; low: $9,500).
Fields of interest: Arts; Natural resources; Nursing home/convalescent facility.
Types of support: General/operating support.
Limitations: Applications not accepted. Giving primarily in MI. No grants to individuals.
Application information: Contributes only to pre-selected organizations.
Officers: Jonathan M. Wege, Pres.; Anna C. Wege, V.P.; Jeffrey B. Power, Secy.-Treas.
EIN: 383419873

1541
Burt Foundation

c/o Erik H. Serr, Miller Canfield
101 N. Main St., 7th Fl.
Ann Arbor, MI 48104

Established in 1996 in MI.
Donor(s): Andrea L. Holmes.
Grantmaker type: Independent foundation
Financial data (yr. ended 12/31/02): Assets, $2,772,548 (M); gifts received, $45,276; expenditures, $316,416; qualifying distributions, $309,373; giving activities include $310,000 for 19 grants (high: $25,000; low: $5,000).
Purpose and activities: Giving primarily for animal welfare.
Fields of interest: Environment; Animal welfare.
Limitations: Applications not accepted. Giving primarily in MI. No grants to individuals.
Application information: Contributes only to pre-selected organizations.
Officer: Andrea L. Holmes, Pres. and Treas.
Director: Howard S. Holmes.
EIN: 383309907

1542
Samuel Higby Camp Foundation

c/o Comerica Bank, Trust Dept.
245 W. Michigan
Jackson, MI 49201
Contact: Walter R. Boris, Chair.
Application address: 145 S. Jackson St., Jackson, MI 49201, tel.: (517) 787-4100

Established in 1951 in MI.
Donor(s): Donna Ruth Camp.‡
Grantmaker type: Independent foundation
Financial data (yr. ended 12/31/01): Assets, $1,843,716 (M); expenditures, $136,025; qualifying distributions, $112,939; giving activities include $113,225 for 34 grants (high: $8,000; low: $1,000).
Purpose and activities: Giving primarily for education, including higher and business education, community development, and cultural programs.
Fields of interest: Arts; Higher education; Business school/education; Medical school/education; Libraries/library science; Education; Animal welfare; Recreation; Children/youth, services; Hospices; Community development; Biological sciences; Government/public administration.
Types of support: General/operating support; Annual campaigns; Capital campaigns; Debt reduction; Curriculum development.
Limitations: Giving primarily in south central MI, with emphasis on Jackson.
Application information: Application form not required.
> *Initial approach:* Letter or proposal
> *Copies of proposal:* 1
> *Deadline(s):* Aug. 15
> *Board meeting date(s):* As needed
> *Final notification:* Oct. or Nov.
Officers: Walter R. Boris, Chair. and Pres.; Maclay D. Gwinn, Vice-Chair.; Linda S. Sekerke, Secy.; Frederick Davies, Treas.
Number of staff: None.
EIN: 381643281

1543
Capital Region Community Foundation

6035 Executive Dr., Ste. 104
Lansing, MI 48911 (517) 272-2870
Contact: Dennis W. Fliehman, Pres. (general), or Joyce McGowan, V.P. (grants)
FAX: (517) 272-2871; E-mail: jmcgowan@crcfoundation.org (for grants), or dfliehman@crcfoundation.org (general); URL: http://www.crcfoundation.org

Established in 1987 in MI.
Grantmaker type: Community foundation
Financial data (yr. ended 12/31/02): Assets, $31,879,668 (M); gifts received, $2,239,235; expenditures, $2,916,650; giving activities include $2,026,844 for 460 grants (high: $400,000; low: $40; average: $2,000–$4,000).
Purpose and activities: The purpose of the foundation is to build the number and size of permanent endowments so that all deserving charitable needs in the Eaton, Clinton, and Ingham tri-county areas in MI, are met. The foundation administers donor-advised funds.
Fields of interest: Humanities; Education; Environment; Health care; Human services;

Children/youth, services; Community development; Public affairs.
Types of support: General/operating support; Capital campaigns; Building/renovation; Equipment; Program development; Seed money; Technical assistance; Matching/challenge support.
Limitations: Giving limited to Ingham, Clinton, and Eaton counties, MI. Generally no support for international organizations, religious programs or sectarian purposes. No grants to individuals, or for endowment funds, fundraising campaigns, annual meetings, general operating support, or for existing obligations.
Publications: Application guidelines, Annual report, Financial statement, Newsletter.
Application information: Application form required.
> *Initial approach:* Telephone for application and guidelines or see Web site
> *Copies of proposal:* 18
> *Deadline(s):* Jan. 30 (Youth Fund), Apr. 1 (all other funds)
> *Board meeting date(s):* Bimonthly
Officers and Director:* Charles Janssen,* Chair.; Dennis W. Fliehman, Pres.; Joyce McGowan, V.P., Prog.; Julia Oliver, V.P., Fin.; Suzanne Mills, Secy.; Sara Clark Pierson, Treas.
Number of staff: 3 full-time professional; 1 full-time support; 1 part-time support.
EIN: 382776652

1544
The Carls Foundation ▼

333 W. Fort St., Ste. 1940
Detroit, MI 48226-3134 (313) 965-0990
Contact: Elizabeth A. Stieg, Exec. Dir.
FAX: (313) 965-0547; URL: http://www.carlsfdn.org

Established in 1961 in MI.
Donor(s): William Carls.‡
Grantmaker type: Independent foundation
Financial data (yr. ended 12/31/02): Assets, $93,703,459 (M); expenditures, $5,200,093; qualifying distributions, $4,872,462; giving activities include $4,487,737 for 51 grants (high: $600,000; low: $1,500; average: $10,000–$100,000).
Purpose and activities: The principal purpose and mission of the foundation is: 1) Children's Welfare including: health care facilities and programs, with special emphasis on the prevention and treatment of hearing impairment, and recreational, educational, and welfare programs especially for children who are disadvantaged for economic and/or health reasons; and 2) Preservation of natural areas, open space and historic buildings and areas having special natural beauty or significance in maintaining America's heritage and historic ideals, through assistance to land trusts and land conservancies and directly related environmental educational programs.
Fields of interest: Historic preservation/historical societies; Education; Natural resources; Hospitals (general); Speech/hearing centers; Health care; Recreation; Children/youth, services.
Types of support: Capital campaigns; Program development; Seed money.

Limitations: Giving primarily in MI. No grants to individuals, or for publications, film and video, research, endowments, fellowships, travel, conferences, special event sponsorships, playground or athletic facilities, or seminars; no educational loans.
Publications: Annual report.
Application information: Use of the CMF Common Grant Application Form is optional and acceptable. Application form not required.
> *Initial approach:* Telephone
> *Copies of proposal:* 1
> *Deadline(s):* Mar. 1, July 1, and Nov. 1
> *Board meeting date(s):* Jan., May and Sept.
> *Final notification:* Notification letter sent to all applicants
Officers and Trustees:* Arthur B. Derisley,* Pres. and Treas.; Harold E. Stieg,* V.P. and Secy.; Elizabeth A. Stieg, Exec. Dir.; Henry Fleischer; Teresa R. Krieger.
Advisory Board: Brian A. Derisley; Homer E. Nye; Rev. Delayne E. Pauling; Robert A. Sajdak; Edward C. Stieg.
Number of staff: 1 full-time professional; 1 part-time professional; 1 full-time support.
EIN: 386099935

1545
Clannad Foundation

P.O. Box 587
Bloomfield Hills, MI 48304
Contact: Annie West Graham, Recording Secy.

Established in 1994 in MI.
Donor(s): Jeanne H. Graham, Ralph A. Graham.
Grantmaker type: Independent foundation
Financial data (yr. ended 10/31/02): Assets, $2,575,925 (M); expenditures, $141,084; qualifying distributions, $117,600; giving activities include $117,600 for 33 grants (high: $20,000; low: $100).
Purpose and activities: Giving for the environment and youth services.
Fields of interest: Natural resources; Food services; Human services; Children/youth, services; Human services, emergency aid; Economically disadvantaged.
Types of support: General/operating support; Continuing support; Annual campaigns; Equipment; Land acquisition; Emergency funds.
Limitations: Giving primarily in MI and NC. No grants to individuals.
Publications: Informational brochure.
Application information: Application form not required.
> *Initial approach:* Proposal
> *Copies of proposal:* 1
> *Deadline(s):* None
> *Board meeting date(s):* Three times a year
> *Final notification:* Oct. 31
Officers: Jeanne H. Graham, Pres. and Treas.; Ralph A. Graham, Exec. V.P.; David W. Laughlin, V.P.; James H. LoPrete, Secy.; Annie West Graham, Recording Secy.
Trustees: Jennifer Graham; Thomas Graham; William Graham.
Number of staff: 2 part-time support.
EIN: 383209484

1546
Community Foundation for Delta County, Michigan, Inc.

2500 7th Ave. S., Ste. 103, Box 5
Escanaba, MI 49829 (906) 786-6654
Contact: Gary LaPlant, Exec. Dir.
FAX: (906) 786-9124; E-mail:
cffdc@chartermi.net

Established in 1989 in MI.
Grantmaker type: Community foundation
Financial data (yr. ended 12/31/02): Assets,
$1,827,855 (M); gifts received, $440,638;
expenditures, $382,376; giving activities
include $195,666 for 65 grants (high: $3,100;
low: $60).
Purpose and activities: The foundation seeks to
enhance the quality of life in the Delta County,
MI, area by improving the educational, cultural,
recreational, environmental and social welfare
resources of the area, and developing youth for
community leadership. The foundation
administers donor-advised funds.
Fields of interest: Performing arts; Environment;
Health care; Health organizations; Recreation;
Human services; Family services; Hospices;
Voluntarism promotion; Government/public
administration.
Types of support: General/operating support;
Emergency funds; Seed money; Scholarship
funds; In-kind gifts; Matching/challenge support.
Limitations: Giving limited to Delta County, MI.
No grants for fundraising, exhibits, religious or
sectarian purposes, or operational funding.
Publications: Application guidelines, Annual
report, Informational brochure.
Application information: Call or write for
complete guidelines; also available on Web site.
Application form required.
   Initial approach: Letter or telephone
   Copies of proposal: 5
   Deadline(s): Feb. 1, May 1, Aug. 1 and Nov. 1
   Board meeting date(s): Monthly
   Final notification: Feb. 28, May 31, Aug. 31
      and Nov. 30
Officers and Trustees:* William Lake,* Pres.;
Karin Van Dyke, 1st V.P.; William LeMire III,*
2nd V.P.; Matt Smith, Jr.,* Secy.; David Schaaf,
Treas.; Gary LaPlant, Exec. Dir.; David Anthony;
John Beaumier; James Boes; Alice Butch;
Willard Carne, Sr.; Mary Cretens; Barbara
Hammerburg; Dennis Harrison; Rev. Richard
Hutton; Lorrayne Krans; Emily Krieg; Erin
Thomas; Robert Van Damme; David Williams.
Number of staff: 3 shared staff (shared with
Community Foundation of the Upper Peninsula
and its affiliates).
EIN: 382907795

1547
Community Foundation for Northeast Michigan

(formerly Northeast Michigan Community
Foundation)
111 Water St.
P.O. Box 495
Alpena, MI 49707 (989) 354-6881
Contact: Barbara A. Willyard, Exec. Dir.
Additional tel.: Toll free for MI and FL: (877)
354-6881; FAX: (989) 356-3319; E-mail:
bwillard@cfnem.org; URL: http://www.cfnem.org

Incorporated in 1974 in MI.

Grantmaker type: Community foundation
Financial data (yr. ended 09/30/02): Assets,
$13,970,676 (M); gifts received, $1,100,019;
expenditures, $3,370,491; giving activities
include $3,044,943 for 568 grants (high:
$1,290,000; low: $100).
Purpose and activities: Primary mission of the
foundation is to provide leadership and
resources to focus both private and public
attention on the needs of the area; to enhance
the quality of life in the area through support of
a broad range of services in such fields as
human services, health, education, the arts, the
environment, disease, and civic responsibilities;
and to stimulate the establishment of
endowments and invest them wisely to serve the
residents of northeast Michigan. The foundation
administers donor-advised funds.
Fields of interest: Humanities; Arts;
Environment; Libraries/library science;
Education; Health care; Health organizations,
association; Human services; Children/youth,
services; Government/public administration.
Types of support: Continuing support;
Building/renovation; Equipment; Program
development; Conferences/seminars;
Publication; Seed money; Scholarship funds;
Program-related investments/loans;
Matching/challenge support.
Limitations: Giving limited to Alcona, Alpena,
Cheboygan, Crawford, Iosco, Montmorency,
Ogemaw, Oscoda, Presque Isle, and Mackinow
City, MI. No grants to individuals, or for
operating needs or budget deficits.
Publications: Application guidelines, Annual
report, Financial statement, Informational
brochure, Newsletter, Program policy statement.
Application information: Application form
required.
   Initial approach: Letter or telephone
   Copies of proposal: 1
   Deadline(s): Feb. 1, Aug. 1, and Nov. 1
   Board meeting date(s): Quarterly
   Final notification: Within days of board
      meeting
Officers and Trustees:* Beach Hall,* Pres.;
George Cavin,* V.P.; Erik Nadolsley,* Secy.;
Steve Lappan, Treas.; Marcia Aten; Carolyn
Brummund; Nancy Coombs; Georgene
Hildebrand; Carl Huebner; Charles Ingle; Jennie
Kerr; Bill Maford; Vernie Nethercut; Gary
Williams; Steven Wilson.
Number of staff: 4 full-time professional; 3
part-time professional.
EIN: 237384822

1548
Community Foundation for Southeastern Michigan ▼

333 W. Fort St., Ste. 2010
Detroit, MI 48226 (313) 961-6675
Contact: Mariam C. Noland, Pres.
FAX: (313) 961-2886; E-mail: cfsem@cfsem.org;
URL: http://www.cfsem.org

Established in 1984 in MI.
Grantmaker type: Community foundation
Financial data (yr. ended 12/31/02): Assets,
$318,823,250 (M); gifts received, $24,737,503;
expenditures, $21,882,440; giving activities
include $18,843,419 for grants.
Purpose and activities: Supports projects in
areas of civic affairs, social services, arts and

culture, health, education, environment and
land use, neighborhood and regional economic
development and workforce development.
Fields of interest: Arts; Education; Health care;
Health organizations, association; Youth
development, services; Human services; Youth,
services; Race/intergroup relations; Community
development; Government/public
administration; Leadership development;
Economically disadvantaged.
Types of support: General/operating support;
Program development; Seed money;
Scholarship funds; Technical assistance.
Limitations: Giving limited to southeastern MI in
the counties of Wayne, Macomb, Oakland,
Washtendiv, Livingston, Monroe and St. Clair.
No support for sectarian religious programs. No
grants to individuals from unrestricted funds, or
for capital projects, endowments, annual
campaigns, operating budgets (except in initial
years of new ventures), conferences, computers
and computer systems, fundraising, annual
meetings, building funds, or equipment.
Publications: Application guidelines, Annual
report (including application guidelines),
Informational brochure (including application
guidelines), Newsletter.
Application information: There are separate
grantmaking guidelines for several special
grantmaking projects. These guidelines and
special application forms are available by
contacting the foundation. Application form not
required.
   Initial approach: Telephone or letter before
      submission of proposal
   Copies of proposal: 1
   Deadline(s): Mar. 1, June 1, Sept. 1 and Dec. 1
   Board meeting date(s): Mar., June, Sept., and
      Dec.
   Final notification: Three months after
      submission of proposal
Officers and Trustees:* Eugene A. Miller,*
Chair.; Max M. Fisher,* Vice-Chair.; Alfred R.
Glancy III,* Vice-Chair.; Alan E. Schwartz,*
Vice-Chair.; Mariam C. Noland, Pres.; Robin D.
Ferriby, V.P., Donor Rels.; Karen L. Leppanen,
V.P., Finance and Admin.; Mark E. Neithercut,
V.P., Prog.; Hon. Anna Diggs Taylor, Secy.; Eddie
R. Munson,* Treas.; Frederick M. Adams, Jr.;
Maggie Allesee; Penny B. Blumenstein; Julie
Fisher Cummings; Tarik S. Daoud; Paul R.
Dimond; Deborah L. Dingell; Walter E. Douglas;
Anthony F. Earley, Jr.; Irma B. Elder; W. Frank
Fountain; George F. Francis III; Yousif B. Ghafari;
Allan D. Gilmour; David Hecker; David M.
Hempstead; William M. Hermann; William K.
Howenstein; Joseph L. Hudson, Jr.; Robert C.
Larson; Ben C. Maibach III; Florine Mark; Jack
Martin; Kathleen McCree-Lewis; Heath J
Meriwether; Edward J. Miller; Michael T.
Monahan; James B. Nicholson; David K. Page;
Cynthia Pasky; William F. Pickard; Sandra E.
Pierce; John Rakolta, Jr.; Douglas J. Rasmussen,
Chair., Prog. and Distribution; Pamela Rodgers;
Howard F. Sims; Vivian Day Stroh; Gary Torgow;
Barbara C. Van Dusen; Martin B. Zimmerman.
Number of staff: 13 full-time professional; 2
part-time professional; 10 full-time support; 1
part-time support.
EIN: 382530980
**Recent environmental and animal welfare
grants:**
1548-1 Ann Arbor, City of, Ann Arbor, MI,
   $25,375. To assess feasibility of using a dam

as trail link along Border-to-Border Trail. 2001.

1548-2 Clinton Charter Township, Clinton Township, MI, $43,000. For topographical surveys needed for engineering study for placement of bike-hike pathway. 2001.

1548-3 Detroit Zoological Society, Royal Oak, MI, $35,950. 2001.

1548-4 Detroit Zoological Society, Royal Oak, MI, $10,000. For technical assistance for planned giving initiative. 2001.

1548-5 Detroit, City of, Detroit, MI, $63,000. For development of plan for hiking and biking trail linking Clark and Riverside Parks with Historic Fort Wayne. 2001.

1548-6 Flat Rock, City of, Flat Rock, MI, $200,000. For construction of trail to cross Huron river. 2001.

1548-7 Forest History Society, Durham, NC, $50,000. 2001.

1548-8 Greening of Detroit, Detroit, MI, $12,000. 2001.

1548-9 Grosse Pointe Animal Adoption Society, Grosse Pointe Farms, MI, $10,000. 2001.

1548-10 Humane Society of Livingston County, Howell, MI, $20,000. For comprehensive animal adoption and care program. 2001.

1548-11 Humane Society of Michigan, Auburn Hills, MI, $10,750. 2001.

1548-12 Indian River Land Trust, Vero Beach, FL, $11,500. 2001.

1548-13 Leader Dogs for the Blind, Rochester, MI, $10,000. For technical assistance for planned giving initiative. 2001.

1548-14 Little Traverse Conservancy, Harbor Springs, MI, $12,500. 2001.

1548-15 LocalMotion, Ann Arbor, MI, $71,750. 2001.

1548-16 Nativity of Our Lord Church, Detroit, MI, $10,000. For beautification and gardening projects. 2001.

1548-17 Northwest Detroit Neighborhood Development, Detroit, MI, $37,930. For planning Lyndon Greenway Project to connect to Eliza Howell Park. 2001.

1548-18 Nortown Community Development Corporation, Detroit, MI, $75,000. To construct Conner Creek/Milbank Greenway following Milbank Street between Van Dyke and Conner Avenue in northeast Detroit. 2001.

1548-19 Polly Ann Trailway Management Council, Leonard, MI, $240,000. To build Polly Ann Trailway in northeast Oakland County. 2001.

1548-20 Rochester Hills, City of, Rochester Hills, MI, $250,000. For purchase of abandoned Canadian Railroad right-of-way to be used as part of Clinton River Trail. 2001.

1548-21 Sylvan Lake, City of, Sylvan Lake, MI, $75,000. For purchase of abandoned Canadian railroad right-of-way to be used as part of Clinton River Trail. 2001.

1548-22 University of Michigan, Dearborn, MI, $381,750. For trail along Rouge River Gateway Pathway System. 2001.

1548-23 Van Buren Charter Township, Belleville, MI, $38,700. For development of plan for 5-mile greenway to connect to Downriver Linked Greenways network. 2001.

1548-24 WARM Training Program, Detroit, MI, $40,000. For demonstration project promoting sustainable community development in affordable housing. 2001.

1548-25 Washtenaw, County of, Ann Arbor, MI, $200,000. To construct part of Border-to-Border Trail between Ann Arbor and Ypsilanti. 2001.

1549
Community Foundation of Greater Flint
502 Church St.
Flint, MI 48502-1206 (810) 767-8270
Contact: Victor J. Papale, Pres.
FAX: (810) 767-0496; E-mail: cfgf@cfgf.org;
URL: http://www.cfgf.org/

Established in 1978 in MI.
Grantmaker type: Community foundation
Financial data (yr. ended 12/31/02): Assets, $94,312,425 (M); gifts received, $5,353,278; expenditures, $6,358,158; giving activities include $5,371,876 for 576 grants (high: $378,161; low: $63; average: $63–$378,161) and $1,735,945 for foundation-administered programs.
Purpose and activities: To respond to current or emerging needs in the Genesee County, MI, area in conservation and the environment, culture and the arts, education, health and human services, and leadership development. Interests include programs focusing on children under the age of ten and eradicating persistent and pervasive poverty. The foundation administers donor-advised funds.
Fields of interest: Arts; Education; Natural resources; Environment; Health care; Youth development, services; Human services; Children/youth, services; Leadership development; Economically disadvantaged.
Types of support: General/operating support; Income development; Management development; Capital campaigns; Building/renovation; Equipment; Land acquisition; Program development; Conferences/seminars; Seed money; Scholarship funds; Technical assistance; Consulting services; Program evaluation; Matching/challenge support.
Limitations: Giving primarily in Genesee County, MI. Generally no support for sectarian religious purposes. No grants to individuals, or for deficit reduction, routine operating expenses of existing organizations, or endowments.
Publications: Application guidelines, Annual report, Financial statement, Grants list, Informational brochure (including application guidelines), Newsletter, Occasional report, Program policy statement.
Application information: Application form required.
  Initial approach: Telephone or personal contact
  Copies of proposal: 1
  Deadline(s): Varies
  Board meeting date(s): 1st Fri. of even-numbered months
Officers and Trustees:* Diane Lindholm, Chair.; Roger Samuel, Vice-Chair.; Victor J. Papale, Pres.; Mary Ittigson, V.P., Fin.; Alice Hart, V.P., Progs.; and 17 additional trustees.
Number of staff: 7 full-time professional; 2 part-time professional; 4 full-time support; 1 part-time support.
EIN: 382190667

1550
Community Foundation of Greater Rochester
(formerly Greater Rochester Area Community Foundation)
P.O. Box 80431
Rochester, MI 48308-0431 (248) 608-2804
Contact: Peggy Hamilton, Exec. Dir.
FAX: (248) 608-2826; E-mail: cfound@cfound.org; URL: http://www.cfound.org/index.html

Incorporated in 1983 in MI.
Grantmaker type: Community foundation
Financial data (yr. ended 12/31/00): Assets, $1,823,538 (M); gifts received, $494,562; expenditures, $338,534; giving activities include $201,017 for grants (high: $31,000; low: $50) and $13,100 for 26 grants to individuals (high: $1,000; low: $150).
Purpose and activities: To enhance the quality of life for community residents within the following funding categories: arts and culture, education, youth, civic beautification, and human concerns. The foundation administers donor-advised funds.
Fields of interest: Museums; Performing arts; Music; Arts; Elementary school/education; Education; Natural resources; Environment; Youth, services; Family services; Community development; Disabled.
Types of support: General/operating support; Annual campaigns; Building/renovation; Equipment; Endowments; Emergency funds; Seed money; Scholarship funds; Scholarships—to individuals; Matching/challenge support.
Limitations: Giving limited to Macomb and Oakland counties, MI. No grants to individuals (except for designated scholarship funds) or for operating budgets.
Publications: Annual report (including application guidelines), Financial statement, Informational brochure, Newsletter.
Application information: Application form required.
  Initial approach: Letter or telephone
  Copies of proposal: 7
  Deadline(s): 30 days prior to board meeting
  Board meeting date(s): Quarterly
Officers and Trustees:* Kenneth D. Bilodeau,* Pres.; George Seifert,* V.P.; Dave Shellenbarger,* V.P.; Mary Ann Reidinger,* Secy.; Vern Pixley, Treas.; Corey Bordine; Joseph Champagne; Tom Finnerty; Michael Glass; Ed Golick; Ed McKibbon; Marty Sibert; Graham Silcox; Lawrence Ternan.
Number of staff: 1 full-time professional; 1 part-time support.
EIN: 382476777

1551
Community Foundation of Monroe County
111 E. 1st St.
P.O. Box 627
Monroe, MI 48161 (734) 242-1976
Contact: Kristyn Theisen, Exec. Dir.
FAX: (734) 242-1234; E-mail: info@cfmonroe.org; URL: http://www.cfmonroe.org

Established in 1978 in MI.
Grantmaker type: Community foundation

Financial data (yr. ended 03/31/03): Assets, $3,511,952 (M); gifts received, $618,529; expenditures, $535,145; giving activities include $264,831 for 37+ grants (high: $40,000) and $14,650 for 30 grants to individuals (high: $1,200; low: $125).
Purpose and activities: The foundation administers a donor-advised fund.
Fields of interest: Performing arts; Theater; Music; History/archaeology; Historic preservation/historical societies; Arts; Elementary school/education; Higher education; Adult education—literacy, basic skills & GED; Reading; Education; Natural resources; Environment; Health care; Substance abuse, services; Health organizations, association; Food services; Housing/shelter, development; Human services; Children/youth, services; Aging, centers/services; Minorities/immigrants, centers/services; Homeless, human services; Community development; Voluntarism promotion; Public affairs; Minorities; Disabled; Aging; Economically disadvantaged.
Types of support: General/operating support; Capital campaigns; Building/renovation; Equipment; Program development; Seed money; Scholarship funds; Technical assistance; Consulting services; Scholarships—to individuals; Exchange programs; Matching/challenge support.
Limitations: Giving primarily in Monroe County, MI. No grants to individuals (except through designated scholarship funds); no loans.
Publications: Application guidelines, Annual report, Financial statement, Grants list, Informational brochure, Newsletter.
Application information: Application form required.
    Initial approach: Letter or telephone
    Copies of proposal: 12
    Deadline(s): Jan. 15, Apr. 15, July 15 and Oct. 15
    Board meeting date(s): 4th Wed. of each month
Officers and Trustees:* Ted A. Meyer,* Pres.; Michael Heller,* V.P.; Christine Gakenheimer, Secy.; Gary Banning, Treas.; and 12 additional trustees.
Number of staff: 1 full-time professional; 1 full-time support; 2 part-time support.
EIN: 382236628

1552
The Community Foundation of the Holland/Zeeland Area
(formerly Holland Community Foundation, Inc.)
70 W. 8th St., Ste. 100
Holland, MI 49423 (616) 396-6590
Contact: William Vanderbilt, Exec. Dir.
FAX: (616) 396-3573; E-mail: cfothza@macatawa.org; URL: http://www.macatawa.org/~cfothza

Incorporated in 1951 in MI.
Grantmaker type: Community foundation
Financial data (yr. ended 12/31/02): Assets, $16,621,455 (M); gifts received, $2,667,270; expenditures, $1,847,656; giving activities include $1,500,000 for 210 grants (high: $300,000; low: $500; average: $15,000) and $64,225 for grants to individuals.
Purpose and activities: To support cultural, educational, human services, youth activities,

and the preservation and conservation of historical, environmental, and cultural resources. The foundation administers donor-advised funds.
Fields of interest: Art conservation; Historic preservation/historical societies; Arts; Education; Environment; Human services; Children/youth, services; Aging.
Types of support: Capital campaigns; Building/renovation; Equipment; Program development; Seed money; Curriculum development; Scholarship funds; Technical assistance; Program evaluation; Employee-related scholarships; Scholarships—to individuals; In-kind gifts.
Limitations: Giving limited to the Holland/Zeeland, MI, area. No grants for endowment funds, operating budgets, research, fellowships, or matching gifts, travel, or computers.
Publications: Application guidelines, Annual report, Informational brochure, Informational brochure (including application guidelines), Newsletter.
Application information: Submit 35 copies of proposal for youth-related programs. Application form required.
    Initial approach: Letter or telephone
    Copies of proposal: 14
    Deadline(s): Oct. 15
    Board meeting date(s): Feb., Apr., Aug., and Oct.
    Final notification: Apr. 27
Officers and Trustees:* Don Wassink, Chair., Fin.; John Nordstrom, Chair., Devel.; Jeff Helder, Pres.; Peter Neydon,* 1st V.P.; Melissa Kamara,* 2nd V.P.; Carla Masselink,* Secy.; Grace Van Haitsma, Treas.; Habeeb Awad; Kenneth Bing; James W.F. Brooks; Thun Champassak; Doug DeKock; Robert DenHerder; Sara Donkersloot; Frank Garcia; Jim Jurries; Hannes Meyers; Peg Padnos; Adam Rodriguez.
Number of staff: 2 full-time professional; 2 part-time professional.
EIN: 386095283

1553
Community Foundation of the Upper Peninsula
(formerly Upper Peninsula Community Foundation Alliance)
2500 7th Ave. S., Ste. 103
Escanaba, MI 49829-1176 (906) 789-5972
Contact: Gary LaPlant, Exec. Dir.
FAX: (906) 786-9214; E-mail: info@upcfa.org and cfup@chartermi.net; URL: http://www.cfup.org

Established in 1994 in MI.
Grantmaker type: Community foundation
Financial data (yr. ended 12/31/02): Assets, $2,700,156 (M); gifts received, $692,429; expenditures, $781,241; giving activities include $492,740 for 146 grants (high: $340,000; low: $40; average: $200–$1,000) and $37,919 for 25 grants to individuals (high: $1,200; low: $100; average: $100–$1,200).
Purpose and activities: To enhance the quality of life in the Upper Peninsula of MI. The foundation will provide its own U.P.-wide philanthropy and that of its geographic affiliate members through growth of permanent endowment funds from a wide range of donors.

The CFUP also provides financial, administrative, communication, and other support services to its affiliate members and to other U.P. community foundations. The foundation administers a donor-advised fund.
Fields of interest: Scholarships/financial aid; Environment; Economic development.
Types of support: Capital campaigns; Scholarship funds; Scholarships—to individuals.
Limitations: Giving limited to the Upper Peninsula, MI, area, including Gogebic County, Cedarville, Paradise, St. Ignace, Watersmeet, Schoolcraft County, Delta, Alger, and Iron County areas.
Publications: Annual report, Informational brochure, Informational brochure (including application guidelines).
Application information: Application form required.
    Copies of proposal: 8
    Deadline(s): Spring
    Board meeting date(s): Jan., Apr., July, and Oct.
    Final notification: By mail
Officers and Trustees:* William LeMire III, M.D.,* Co-Pres.; K. Gerald Marsden,* Co-Pres.; Kenneth Drenth,* Co-V.P.; William Lake,* Co-V.P.; Mary Bowerman,* Secy.; Tom Luckey,* Treas.; Gary LaPlant, Exec. Dir.; Elio Argentati; John MacFarlane III; Walter North; Francis E. Paoli; Matt Smith, Jr.; Karin Van Dyke.
Number of staff: 2 full-time professional; 1 part-time professional.
EIN: 383227080

1554
Consumers Energy Company Contributions Program
(formerly Consumers Power Company Contributions Program)
212 W. Michigan Ave.
Jackson, MI 49201 (517) 788-0432
Contact: Carolyn A. Bloodworth, Secy.-Treas., Consumers Energy Fdn.

Grantmaker type: Corporate giving program
Financial data (yr. ended 12/31/02): Total giving, $293,300; giving activities include $293,300 for 133 grants (high: $25,000; low: $100).
Purpose and activities: As a complement to its foundation, Consumers Energy also makes charitable contributions to nonprofit organizations directly. Support is given primarily in areas of company operations.
Fields of interest: Museums; Performing arts; Theater; Music; Arts; Education, fund raising; Education; Environment; Animals/wildlife, preservation/protection; Health care; Mental health/crisis services; Health organizations; Youth, services; Family services; Human services; Urban/community development; Community development; Government/public administration; Public affairs; General charitable giving; Minorities; Women.
Types of support: General/operating support; Annual campaigns; Capital campaigns; Building/renovation; Equipment; Endowments; Program development; Conferences/seminars; Publication; Seed money; Employee matching gifts; In-kind gifts; Matching/challenge support.
Limitations: Giving primarily in areas of company operations, with emphasis on MI. No support for fraternal or veterans' organizations,

churches, or K-12 schools. No grants to individuals.
Publications: Application guidelines.
Application information: The Government and Public Affairs Department handles giving. Application form not required.
   Initial approach: Proposal to headquarters
   Copies of proposal: 1
   Deadline(s): First quarter is preferred
   Final notification: 8 to 10 weeks
Number of staff: 1 full-time professional; 1 full-time support.

1555
Cook Family Foundation
P.O. Box 278
Owosso, MI 48867-0578 (989) 725-1621
Contact: Bruce L. Cook, Pres.
FAX: (989) 725-3138; E-mail: tom_cook@chartermi.net

Established in 1979 in MI.
Donor(s): Donald O. Cook,‡ Florence-Etta Cook,‡ Donald O. Cook Charitable Trust, Wolverine Sign Works.
Grantmaker type: Independent foundation
Financial data (yr. ended 12/31/02): Assets, $8,228,392; expenditures, $501,190; qualifying distributions, $469,590; giving activities include $454,356 for 39 grants (high: $75,000; low: $500).
Purpose and activities: Giving primarily for education and youth programs.
Fields of interest: Historic preservation/historical societies; Higher education; Environmental education; Children/youth, services.
Types of support: General/operating support; Annual campaigns; Capital campaigns; Building/renovation; Program development; Internship funds; Scholarship funds.
Limitations: Applications not accepted. Giving limited to MI. No grants to individuals.
Publications: Annual report, Informational brochure.
Application information: Contributes only to pre-selected organizations.
   Board meeting date(s): Quarterly
Officers: Bruce L. Cook, Pres.; Laurie Caszatt Cook, V.P.; Thomas B. Cook, Secy.-Treas.
Trustees: Jacqueline P. Cook; Paul C. Cook; Anna E. Owens.
Number of staff: 1 part-time professional.
EIN: 382283809

1556
Cronin Foundation
203 E. Michigan Ave.
Marshall, MI 49068
Contact: Ronald J. DeGraw, Secy.-Treas.

Established in 1990 in MI.
Donor(s): Elizabeth Cronin,‡ Mary Virginia Cronin.‡
Grantmaker type: Independent foundation
Financial data (yr. ended 12/31/02): Assets, $2,555,880 (M); gifts received, $204,105; expenditures, $183,407; qualifying distributions, $173,879; giving activities include $174,476 for 9 grants (high: $75,000; low: $4,000).
Purpose and activities: Giving primarily for educational, social, economic, civic, and

cultural needs of the community contained within the Marshall, MI, school district.
Fields of interest: Education; Environment; Hospitals (general); Medical care, rehabilitation; Athletics/sports, soccer; Human services; Community development.
Types of support: Building/renovation; Equipment; Program development.
Limitations: Giving limited to Marshall, MI. No grants to individuals.
Application information: Letter or telephone for guidelines.
   Initial approach: Proposal
   Deadline(s): Mar. 1, June 1, Sept. 1, and Dec. 1
   Board meeting date(s): Following application deadlines and as needed
   Final notification: Following board meeting
Officers and Directors:* Helen L. Hensick,* Pres.; John F. Miller, Jr., V.P.; Ronald J. DeGraw,* Secy.-Treas.; Monica Anderson; Robert Currie.
Number of staff: 1 part-time professional.
EIN: 382908362

1557
The Dart Foundation
(formerly Solid Waste Management Foundation)
500 Hogsback Rd.
Mason, MI 48854-9547
Contact: James D. Lammers, V.P.

Established in 1989 in MI.
Donor(s): W.A. Dart Foundation.
Grantmaker type: Independent foundation
Financial data (yr. ended 10/31/01): Assets, $3,602,557 (M); gifts received, $2,380,000; expenditures, $2,910,457; qualifying distributions, $2,902,516; giving activities include $2,169,120 for 95 grants (high: $265,000; low: $250; average: $5,000–$50,000) and $721,368 for 4 foundation-administered programs.
Purpose and activities: Giving primarily for education and youth services.
Fields of interest: Journalism/publishing; Education; Environment; Crime/law enforcement; Children/youth, services; Human services, victim aid; Mathematics; Engineering/technology; Science.
Types of support: General/operating support; Continuing support; Building/renovation; Program development; Conferences/seminars; Publication; Curriculum development; Research; Matching/challenge support.
Limitations: Giving primarily in Sarasota, FL, and central MI. No grants to individuals.
Application information: Application form not required.
   Initial approach: Letter
   Copies of proposal: 2
   Deadline(s): None
Officers and Directors:* William A. Dart,* Pres. and Secy.; Claire T. Dart,* V.P. and Treas.; Kenneth B. Dart,* V.P.; Robert C. Dart,* V.P.; James D. Lammers, V.P.
EIN: 382849841

1558
DENSO International America, Inc.
Corporate Giving Program
24777 DENSO Dr.
P.O. Box 5047, M.C. 4600
Southfield, MI 48086-5047 (248) 372-8232
Contact: John Voorhorst, V.P., Ext. Affairs
FAX: (248) 213-2550; E-mail: john_voorhorst@denso-diam.com; URL: http://www.densocorp-na.com/corporate/community.html

Grantmaker type: Corporate giving program
Financial data (yr. ended 12/31/02): Total giving, $425,274; giving activities include $286,793 for 28 grants, $400 for 6 employee matching gifts and $138,081 for 12 in-kind gifts.
Purpose and activities: As a complement to its foundation, DENSO International also makes charitable contributions to nonprofit organizations directly. Support is given primarily in areas of company operations.
Fields of interest: Higher education; Business school/education; Environment.
Types of support: Program development; Employee volunteer services; Sponsorships; Employee matching gifts; Donated equipment; Donated products.
Limitations: Giving primarily in areas of company operations, with emphasis on southeastern MI.
Publications: Application guidelines.
Application information: An application form is available online. The External Affairs Department handles giving. The company has a staff that only handles contributions. A contributions committee reviews all requests. Application form required.
   Initial approach: Complete online application form
   Copies of proposal: 1
   Deadline(s): None
   Board meeting date(s): Apr., July, Oct., and Dec.
   Final notification: Following review
Contributions Committee: John Voorhorst, Chair.; Barbara Wertheimer, Prog. Coord.
Number of staff: 1 part-time professional.

1559
The Richard C. Devereaux Foundation
39533 Woodward Ave., Ste. 200
Bloomfield Hills, MI 48304

Donor(s): Mrs. Richard C. Devereaux, S.W. Smith.
Grantmaker type: Independent foundation
Financial data (yr. ended 08/31/02): Assets, $5,807,386 (M); gifts received, $6,112,223; expenditures, $404,584; qualifying distributions, $382,668; giving activities include $370,000 for 6 grants (high: $100,000; low: $30,000).
Purpose and activities: Giving primarily for education, cancer research, and wildlife preservation.
Fields of interest: Orchestra (symphony); Higher education; Animals/wildlife, preservation/protection; Cancer; Cancer research.
Types of support: General/operating support.
Limitations: Applications not accepted. Giving primarily in Washington, DC, IL, MI, and VA. No grants to individuals.

Application information: Contributes only to pre-selected organizations.
Officers: Leslie C. Devereaux, Pres. and Treas.; Sidney W. Smith, Jr., V.P.; Curtis J. Mann, Secy.
EIN: 382638858

1560
The DeVlieg Foundation

(formerly The Charles DeVlieg Foundation)
500 Woodward Ave., Ste. 2500
Detroit, MI 48226
Contact: Curtis J. DeRoo, Secy.-Treas.
FAX: (313) 961-0388

Incorporated in 1961 in MI.
Donor(s): Charles B. DeVlieg,‡ Charles R. DeVlieg,‡ Kathryn S. DeVlieg,‡ DeVlieg Machine Co.
Grantmaker type: Independent foundation
Financial data (yr. ended 12/31/02): Assets, $5,272,401 (M); gifts received, $2,155; expenditures, $378,931; qualifying distributions, $319,693; giving activities include $267,500 for 23 grants (high: $35,000; low: $500).
Purpose and activities: Support largely for higher and other education, including grants to a university for fellowships and a scholarship program for engineering, wildlife education, youth agencies, the arts, environmental organizations, and science and technology.
Fields of interest: Arts; Higher education; Engineering school/education; Natural resources; Environment; Youth, services; Engineering/technology; Engineering; Science.
Types of support: General/operating support; Professorships; Scholarship funds.
Limitations: Giving primarily in ID, southeastern MI, and WA. No grants to individuals, or for endowment funds; no loans.
Publications: Annual report (including application guidelines).
Application information: Application form required.
Initial approach: Letter
Copies of proposal: 2
Deadline(s): None
Board meeting date(s): Semiannually
Officers and Directors:* Janet DeVlieg Pope,* Pres.; Curtis J. DeRoo,* Secy.-Treas.; Julia DeVlieg; Richard A. Jerue; Gary Stetler; Gerald Stetler.
Number of staff: 1 part-time professional.
EIN: 386075696

1561
Gary W. Dietrich Family Foundation

5810 Delta River Dr.
Lansing, MI 48906

Established in 1997 in MI.
Grantmaker type: Independent foundation
Financial data (yr. ended 01/31/02): Assets, $1,554,676 (M); expenditures, $107,704; qualifying distributions, $91,144; giving activities include $91,230 for 27 grants (high: $20,000; low: $800).
Fields of interest: Museums; College; Environment; Boys & girls clubs.
Limitations: Applications not accepted. No grants to individuals.
Application information: Contributes only to pre-selected organizations.

Officer: Gary W. Dietrich, Pres. and Secy.-Treas.
EIN: 383339852

1562
Dow Corning Corporation Contributions Program

2200 W. Salzburg Rd.
Auburn, MI 48611 (989) 496-4078
Contact: Scott Seeburger

Grantmaker type: Corporate giving program
Purpose and activities: As a complement to its foundation, Dow Corning also makes charitable contributions to nonprofit organizations directly. Support is given on an international basis.
Fields of interest: Arts; Education, reform; Environment.
International interests: United Kingdom; Wales.
Types of support: General/operating support; Capital campaigns; Curriculum development; Employee matching gifts; Donated equipment.
Limitations: Giving on an international basis in areas of company operations, particularly Carollton and Elizabethtown, KY, Bay, Midland, and Saginaw counties, MI, Greensboro, NC, and Barry, Wales, United Kingdom. No support for political, veterans', or religious organizations. No grants to individuals, or for fundraising or collegiate athletic activities.
Publications: Application guidelines.
Application information: A contributions committee reviews all requests. Application form required.
Initial approach: Telephone headquarters for application form
Copies of proposal: 1
Deadline(s): 2 weeks prior to committee meetings
Board meeting date(s): Apr. and Nov.
Final notification: 2 weeks following committee meetings

1563
Dow Corning Foundation

2200 W. Salzburg Rd., Mail No. C01112
Midland, MI 48686-0994 (989) 496-6290
Contact: Anne Deboer
URL: http://www.dowcorning.com/content/about/aboutcomm/aboutcomm_guidelines1.asp

Established in 1982 in MI.
Donor(s): Dow Corning Corp.
Grantmaker type: Company-sponsored foundation
Financial data (yr. ended 12/31/02): Assets, $13,537,200 (M); gifts received, $3,000,000; expenditures, $1,606,043; qualifying distributions, $1,669,906; giving activities include $1,618,121 for 55 grants (high: $233,300; low: $1,250).
Purpose and activities: Giving primarily for pre-college and higher education, community development, family programs, and the environment.
Fields of interest: Secondary school/education; Higher education; Environment; Housing/shelter, homeless; Athletics/sports, Special Olympics; Family services; Foundations (community).
Types of support: Capital campaigns; Building/renovation; Equipment; Endowments; Program development; Seed money.

Limitations: Giving primarily in areas of company operations, with emphasis on MI; giving also in AZ, IN, KY, SD, and VA. No support for veterans', religious, or political organizations. No grants to individuals, or for operating funds, conferences, dinners, fundraising events, or public advertisements.
Application information: Application form is provided to those meeting qualifications through initial screening. Application form required.
Initial approach: Telephone or letter
Deadline(s): None
Board meeting date(s): Grant requests are reviewed on a quarterly basis
Officers and Trustees:* Jere D. Marciniak,* Pres.; Marie Eckstein,* V.P.; Paul A. Marcela, Secy.; Brad Sauve, Treas.; Mohamed Ahmed; Barbara S. Carmichael; Scott Fuson; Thomas H. Lane; Feifei Lin; Leslie Patterson.
EIN: 382376485

1564
The Herbert H. and Grace A. Dow Foundation ▼

1018 W. Main St.
Midland, MI 48640-4292 (989) 631-3699
Contact: Margaret Ann Riecker, Pres.
FAX: (989) 631-0675; E-mail: info@hhdowfoundation.org; URL: http://www.hhdowfoundation.org

Trust established in 1936 in MI.
Donor(s): Grace A. Dow.‡
Grantmaker type: Independent foundation
Financial data (yr. ended 12/31/01): Assets, $446,011,415 (M); expenditures, $26,797,776; qualifying distributions, $23,614,229; giving activities include $22,014,708 for 107 grants (high: $195,678; low: $1,000; average: $1,000–$15,000).
Purpose and activities: Support for religious, charitable, scientific, literacy, or educational purposes for the public benefaction of the inhabitants of the city of Midland and of the people of the state of Michigan. Grants largely for education, particularly higher education, community and social services, civic improvement, conservation, scientific research, church support (only in Midland County), and cultural programs; maintains a public horticultural garden.
Fields of interest: Arts; Higher education; Libraries/library science; Education; Natural resources; Human services; Community development; Engineering/technology; Science.
Types of support: General/operating support; Building/renovation; Equipment; Endowments; Program development; Seed money; Research; Matching/challenge support.
Limitations: Giving limited to MI, with emphasis on Midland County. No support for political organizations or sectarian religious organizations or programs, other than churches in Midland County. No grants to individuals, or for travel or conferences; no loans.
Publications: Annual report (including application guidelines).
Application information: Application form not required.
Initial approach: Proposal
Copies of proposal: 1
Deadline(s): None
Board meeting date(s): Bimonthly

Final notification: 2 months
Officers and Trustees:* Herbert D. Doan,*
Chair.; Margaret Ann Riecker,* Pres.; Michael
Lloyd Dow,* V.P. and Treas.; Macauley Whiting,
Jr., Secy.; Julie Carol Arbury; Bonnie B.
Matheson; Michael D. Parker; Frank Popoff;
Margaret E. Thompson; Ruth B. Wheeler.
Number of staff: None.
EIN: 381437485
**Recent environmental and animal welfare
grants:**
1564-1 Chippewa Nature Center, Midland, MI,
$72,000. For continued operating support.
2001.
1564-2 Conservation Fund, Arlington, VA,
$50,000. For continued operating support of
Saginaw Bay Watershed Initiative Network
(WIN). 2001.
1564-3 Ducks Unlimited, Grand Rapids, MI,
$325,000. For continued support of
Geographic Information System (GIS)
proposal. 2001.
1564-4 Grand Traverse Regional Land
Conservancy, Traverse City, MI, $100,000.
For operating support. 2001.
1564-5 Inland Seas Education Association,
Suttons Bay, MI, $15,000. For operating
support. 2001.
1564-6 Little Forks Conservancy, Midland, MI,
$50,000. For operating support. 2001.
1564-7 Little Traverse Conservancy, Harbor
Springs, MI, $100,000. For operating support.
2001.
1564-8 Nature Conservancy, Arlington, VA,
$100,000. For operating support. 2001.
1564-9 Saginaw Valley Zoological Society,
Saginaw, MI, $203,134. For operating
support. 2001.

1565
DTE Energy Foundation
(formerly Detroit Edison Foundation)
2000 2nd Ave., Rm. 1046 WCB
Detroit, MI 48226-1279 (313) 235-9271
Contact: Karla Hall, Secy.
URL: http://www.dteenergy.com/community/
foundation/index.html

Established in 1986 in MI.
Donor(s): The Detroit Edison Co.
Grantmaker type: Company-sponsored
foundation
Financial data (yr. ended 12/31/01): Assets,
$21,131,377 (M); expenditures, $5,287,373;
qualifying distributions, $5,190,511; giving
activities include $4,942,405 for 356 grants
(high: $265,294; low: $500; average:
$5,000–$25,000) and $250,155 for 1,356
employee matching gifts.
Purpose and activities: Support for all levels of
education, and civic, local community, social
service, and cultural organizations, and the
United Way.
Fields of interest: Arts; Early childhood
education; Child development, education;
Elementary school/education; Higher education;
Engineering school/education; Education;
Energy; Environment; Food services; Human
services; Youth, services; Child development,
services; Homeless, human services;
Urban/community development;
Business/industry; Voluntarism promotion;

Federated giving programs; Engineering;
Government/public administration; Homeless.
Types of support: General/operating support;
Capital campaigns; Employee matching gifts.
Limitations: Giving primarily in southeast MI.
No support for political organizations or
activities, or religious organizations for religious
services. No grants to individuals, or for student
group trips.
Publications: Informational brochure (including
application guidelines), Program policy
statement.
Application information: Accepts CMF
Common Grant Application Form. Application
form not required.
  Initial approach: Letter
  Copies of proposal: 1
  Deadline(s): Apr. 15 and Aug. 15
  Board meeting date(s): 5 times per year
  Final notification: 60 to 90 days
Officers and Directors:* Frederick E. Shell,
Pres.; Karla Hall,* Secy.; Naif A. Loomans,*
Treas.; Susan M. Beale; Robert J. Buckler; James
F. Connelly; Lynne Ellyn; Stephen E. Ewing;
Michael C. Porter; Larry E. Steward; S. Martin
Taylor.
Number of staff: 1 full-time professional; 2
full-time support.
EIN: 382708636

1566
The Duffy Foundation
c/o Erik H. Serr, Miller Canfield
101 N. Main St., 7th Fl.
Ann Arbor, MI 48104

Established in 1989.
Donor(s): Howard S. Holmes, Andrea L.
Holmes, Mary B. Holmes.
Grantmaker type: Independent foundation
Financial data (yr. ended 12/31/02): Assets,
$36,541,043 (M); gifts received, $26,282,462;
expenditures, $1,724,153; qualifying
distributions, $1,631,061; giving activities
include $1,635,500 for 50 grants (high:
$100,000; low: $2,500).
Purpose and activities: Giving primarily to a
hospice, animal protection organizations,
environmental conservation, human services,
and the disabled.
Fields of interest: Arts; Natural resources;
Animal welfare; Animals/wildlife, special
services; Domestic violence; Food services;
Children/youth, services; Hospices; Disabled.
Limitations: Applications not accepted. Giving
primarily in MI. No grants to individuals.
Application information: Contributes only to
pre-selected organizations.
Officers: Mary B. Holmes, Pres.; Kathryn W.
Holmes, V.P. and Treas.
Directors: Andrea L. Holmes; Christine Holmes.
EIN: 382908719

1567
Dyer-Ives Foundation
Waters Bldg., Ste. 501-H
161 Ottawa Ave. N.W.
Grand Rapids, MI 49503 (616) 454-4502
Contact: Linda B. Patterson, Exec. Dir.
FAX: (616) 454-8545; E-mail:
dyer_ives@msn.com

Established in 1961 in MI.
Donor(s): John R. Hunting.
Grantmaker type: Independent foundation
Financial data (yr. ended 08/31/02): Assets,
$6,112,460 (M); expenditures, $500,637;
qualifying distributions, $447,126; giving
activities include $238,997 for 33 grants (high:
$31,000; low: $240) and $81,414 for 2
foundation-administered programs.
Purpose and activities: Acts primarily as a
catalyst and stimulator for small innovative
projects that encourage a sense of community in
educational, social, environmental or cultural
fields.
Fields of interest: Humanities; Arts; Education;
Environment; Employment; Housing/shelter;
Youth development, services; Human services;
Community development, neighborhood
development; Philanthropy/voluntarism.
Types of support: Program development;
Publication; Seed money; Curriculum
development; Technical assistance; Consulting
services.
Limitations: Giving limited to the central city of
Grand Rapids, MI. No grants to individuals, or
for building or endowment funds, operating
budgets, or scholarship funds.
Publications: Biennial report (including
application guidelines), Financial statement,
Grants list, Informational brochure (including
application guidelines), Multi-year report.
Application information: Application form not
required.
  Initial approach: Telephone and proposal
  Copies of proposal: 1
  Deadline(s): None
  Board meeting date(s): Monthly
  Final notification: After board meetings
Officers and Directors:* John R. Hunting,*
Chair.; John D. Hibbard, Jr.,* Vice-Chair.;
George K. Heartwell, Pres.; Carol L. Townsend,
V.P.; R. Malcolm Cumming,* Secy.; Susan
Cobb,* Treas.; Linda B. Patterson, Exec. Dir.; Lee
Nelson Weber, Prog. Dir.; George A. Bayard III;
Beverly A. Drake; Julia A. Guevara; Bradford
Mathis; Debra K. Muller; Jose L. Rayna; Mary
Banghart Therrien.
Number of staff: 2 part-time professional.
EIN: 386049657

1568
Eden Foods, Inc. Corporate Giving
Program
701 Tecumseh Rd.
Clinton, MI 49236 (517) 456-7424
Contact: James Hughes, Cont.
FAX: (517) 456-6075

Grantmaker type: Corporate giving program
Purpose and activities: Eden Foods makes
charitable contributions to nonprofit
organizations involved with the environment.
Support is given on an international basis.
Fields of interest: Environment.
Types of support: General/operating support;
Sponsorships; Donated products.
Limitations: Giving on an international basis.
Application information: Application form not
required.
  Initial approach: Proposal to headquarters
  Copies of proposal: 1
  Deadline(s): None
  Final notification: Following review

1569
Fabiano Foundation
1219 N. Mission
Mount Pleasant, MI 48858

Established in 1997 in MI.
Donor(s): Fabiano Brothers, Inc.
Grantmaker type: Company-sponsored foundation
Financial data (yr. ended 12/31/02): Assets, $815,633 (M); gifts received, $245,000; expenditures, $132,750; qualifying distributions, $132,652; giving activities include $132,750 for 12 grants (high: $75,100; low: $100).
Purpose and activities: Giving primarily for Roman Catholic education.
Fields of interest: Elementary/secondary education; Higher education; Animal welfare; Roman Catholic agencies & churches.
Limitations: Applications not accepted. No grants to individuals.
Application information: Contributes only to pre-selected organizations.
Officers: James C. Fabiano, Pres. and Treas.; James C. Fabiano II, V.P.; Joseph R. Fabiano II, V.P.; Evangeline L. Fabiano, Secy.
EIN: 383324462

1570
The Paul Farago Foundation Trust
3518 Erie Dr.
Orchard Lake, MI 48324-1522
Contact: Frank Campanale, Pres.

Established in 1998 in MI.
Grantmaker type: Independent foundation
Financial data (yr. ended 12/31/02): Assets, $2,467,803 (M); expenditures, $109,056; qualifying distributions, $95,000; giving activities include $95,000 for 4 grants (high: $25,000; low: $20,000).
Purpose and activities: Support to organizations that train dogs to assist the disabled.
Fields of interest: Animals/wildlife, special services; Disabled.
Limitations: Giving primarily in MI. No grants to individuals.
Application information:
  Initial approach: Letter on organization letterhead
  Deadline(s): None
Officer: Frank Campanale, Pres.
EIN: 383378111

1571
The Farbman Foundation
(formerly Burton and Susan Farbman Foundation)
28400 N.W. Hwy., 4th Fl.
Southfield, MI 48034-1839

Established in 1997 in MI.
Donor(s): Burton D. Farbman, Susan B. Farbman.
Grantmaker type: Independent foundation
Financial data (yr. ended 12/31/02): Assets, $40,910 (M); gifts received, $140,000; expenditures, $144,239; qualifying distributions, $144,188; giving activities include $144,200 for 13 grants (high: $50,000; low: $200).

Fields of interest: Education; Zoos/zoological societies; Cancer; YM/YWCAs & YM/YWHAs; Jewish agencies & temples.
Limitations: Applications not accepted. Giving primarily in MI. No grants to individuals.
Application information: Contributes only to pre-selected organizations.
Directors: Burton D. Farbman; Susan B. Farbman.
EIN: 383345578

1572
Mary G. & Robert H. Flint Foundation
100 W. Long Lake Rd., Ste. 100
Bloomfield Hills, MI 48304 (248) 647-5111
Contact: L. James Wilson

Established in 1985 in MI.
Donor(s): Mary G. Flint, Robert H. Flint,‡ Robert Flint Trust.
Grantmaker type: Independent foundation
Financial data (yr. ended 11/30/02): Assets, $2,795,267 (M); gifts received, $814,705; expenditures, $279,164; qualifying distributions, $253,562; giving activities include $250,000 for 3 grants (high: $100,000; low: $50,000).
Purpose and activities: Giving primarily for higher education and human services.
Fields of interest: Higher education; Animal welfare; Human services.
Limitations: Giving primarily in MI. No grants to individuals.
Application information:
  Initial approach: Letter
  Deadline(s): None
Officer: Susan E. Cooper, Pres.
EIN: 382641865

1573
Floriculture Industry Research and Scholarship Trust
(formerly Bedding Plants Foundation)
P.O. Box 280
East Lansing, MI 48826-0280 (517) 333-4617
Contact: William T. Willbrandt, J.D., Exec. Dir.
FAX: (517) 333-4494; E-mail: info@firstinfloriculture.org (general inquiries), scholarships@firstinfloriculture.org (scholarship inquiries), research@firstinfloriculture.org (research inquiries); URL: http://www.firstinfloriculture.org/

Established in 2001 through the merger of Bedding Plants Foundation and Ohio Floriculture Foundation.
Grantmaker type: Public charity
Financial data (yr. ended 03/31/02): Revenue, $795,324; assets, $1,875,838; gifts received, $864,551; expenditures, $304,557; program services expenses, $206,117; giving activities include $87,460 for 11 grants (high: $14,350; low: $2,300) and $49,250 for 38 grants to individuals (high: $3,000; low: $500).
Purpose and activities: FIRST is a leading organization for funding research and education in floriculture to improve the production and marketability of plants. The scholarship program assists the floriculture industry by helping identify, motivate and support qualified students; FIRST research grants assist the bedding plant industry by helping define vital issues and empower scientific breakthroughs.

Fields of interest: Environment, plant conservation; Horticulture/garden clubs; Environmental education; Botany.
Types of support: Research; Scholarships—to individuals.
Limitations: Giving on a national and international basis, with emphasis on U.S. and Canadian residents and organizations. No grants for overhead or travel expenses.
Application information: See foundation Web site for full application guidelines and requirements. Scholarship and research application forms can be downloaded; scholarship applicants may also apply online. Application form required.
  Deadline(s): Jan. 1 to May 1 for scholarships; Sept. 1 for research grants
Officers and Directors:* Tim Stiles,* Pres.; Justin Marotta,* V.P.; Bruce Bordine,* Treas.; William T. Willbrandt, J.D., Exec. Dir.; Diane Blazek; Judy Corfield; P.J. Ellison; Troy Lucht; Delilah Onofrey; Paul A. Thomas; Lloyd Traven; Peggy Van de Wetering; Al Zylstra.
EIN: 591975717

1574
L. H. Foley & M. H. Frischkorn Wildlife & Conservation Fund I
c/o Comerica Bank
P.O. Box 75000, MC 3302
Detroit, MI 48275 (810) 645-8951

Grantmaker type: Public charity
Financial data (yr. ended 09/30/02): Revenue, $21,084; assets, $696,998; expenditures, $33,179; program services expenses, $16,893; giving activities include $16,893 for 1 grant.
Purpose and activities: The fund exists for the sole benefit of Nature Conservancy, Inc., supporting their activities to preserve and conserve refuges and sanctuaries for wildlife.
Fields of interest: Animals/wildlife, single organization support; Animals/wildlife, preservation/protection; Animals/wildlife, sanctuaries; Animals/wildlife.
Limitations: Applications not accepted. Giving limited to Arlington, VA.
Application information: Contributes only to a pre-selected organization; unsolicited requests for funds not considered or acknowledged.
Trustees: George Stege III, Ph.D; Comerica Bank.
EIN: 386646186

1575
L. H. Foley & M. H. Frischkorn Wildlife & Conservation Fund II
c/o Comerica Bank
P.O. Box 75000, MC 3302
Detroit, MI 48275 (810) 645-8951

Grantmaker type: Public charity
Financial data (yr. ended 09/30/02): Revenue, $20,448; assets, $691,777; expenditures, $32,562; program services expenses, $16,123; giving activities include $16,123 for 1 grant.
Purpose and activities: The organization operates solely for the benefit of the North American Wildlife Foundation.
Fields of interest: Natural resources; Animals/wildlife, preservation/protection; Animals/wildlife.

Limitations: Applications not accepted.
Application information: Contributes only to a pre-selected organization; unsolicited requests for funds not considered or acknowledged.
Trustees: George Stege III, Ph.D.; Comerica Bank.
EIN: 386646185

1576
William & Lisa Ford Foundation
100 Renaissance Ctr., 34th Fl.
Detroit, MI 48243 (313) 259-7777
Contact: David M. Hempstead, Secy.

Established in 1998 in MI.
Donor(s): William Clay Ford, Jr., Lisa V. Ford.
Grantmaker type: Independent foundation
Financial data (yr. ended 12/31/02): Assets, $8,845,978 (M); gifts received, $1; expenditures, $492,509; qualifying distributions, $449,906; giving activities include $451,346 for 20 grants (high: $100,000; low: $500).
Purpose and activities: Giving primarily for children's services and higher education; funding also for human services.
Fields of interest: Museums; Higher education; Education; Environment, land resources; Health care; Human services; Children, services; Federated giving programs; Buddhism.
Limitations: Giving primarily in MI. No grants to individuals.
Application information: Awards are generally limited to charitable organizations already known and of interest to the foundation.
  Initial approach: Letter
  Deadline(s): None
Officers and Trustee:* William Clay Ford, Jr.,* Pres. and Dir.; Lisa V. Ford, V.P.; David M. Hempstead, Secy.; George A. Straitor, Treas.
EIN: 383441138

1577
William and Martha Ford Fund
100 Renaissance Ctr., 34th Fl.
Detroit, MI 48243 (313) 259-7777
Contact: David M. Hempstead, Secy.

Incorporated in 1953 in MI.
Donor(s): William Clay Ford, Martha Firestone Ford.
Grantmaker type: Independent foundation
Financial data (yr. ended 12/31/02): Assets, $9,852,270 (M); expenditures, $1,052,257; qualifying distributions, $1,005,875; giving activities include $1,002,500 for 64 grants (high: $352,500; low: $300; average: $2,500–$50,000).
Fields of interest: Museums; Arts; Higher education; Zoos/zoological societies; Hospitals (general); Health care; Substance abuse, services; Boys & girls clubs; Human services; Foundations (community); Federated giving programs.
Limitations: Giving primarily in MI; some giving nationally. No grants to individuals.
Application information: Awards generally limited to charities already favorably known to substantial contributors of the foundation.
  Initial approach: Letter
  Deadline(s): None

Officers and Trustees:* William Clay Ford,* Pres.; David M. Hempstead,* Secy.; George A. Straitor, Treas.; Martha F. Ford.
EIN: 386066335

1578
Edsel B. Ford II Fund
100 Renaissance Ctr., 34th Fl.
Detroit, MI 48243 (313) 259-7777
Contact: David M. Hempstead, Secy.

Established in 1993 in MI.
Donor(s): Edsel B. Ford II.
Grantmaker type: Independent foundation
Financial data (yr. ended 12/31/02): Assets, $5,275,036 (M); expenditures, $231,132; qualifying distributions, $221,065; giving activities include $218,004 for 33 grants (high: $30,000; low: $300).
Purpose and activities: Giving primarily for higher education, health, social services, children and youth services, particularly juvenile diabetes, federated giving programs, and a Presbyterian church.
Fields of interest: Arts; Higher education; Education; Zoos/zoological societies; Hospitals (general); Health care; Diabetes; Human services; Children/youth, services; Federated giving programs; Protestant agencies & churches.
Limitations: Giving primarily in MI. No grants to individuals.
Application information: Generally contributes to organizations already known to the donor.
  Initial approach: Letter
  Deadline(s): None
Officers and Director:* Edsel B. Ford II,* Pres.; David M. Hempstead, Secy.; George A. Straitor, Treas.
EIN: 383153050

1579
Ford Motor Company Contributions Program
1 American Rd.
P.O. Box 1899, Rm. 335
Dearborn, MI 48126-2798 (888) 313-0102
Contact: Sandra E. Ulsh, Pres., Ford Motor Co. Fund
FAX: (313) 594-7001; URL: http://www.ford.com/en/goodworks/default.htm

Grantmaker type: Corporate giving program
Financial data (yr. ended 12/31/02): Total giving, $48,300,000; giving activities include $47,100,000 for grants and $1,200,000 for in-kind gifts.
Purpose and activities: As a complement to its foundation, Ford also makes charitable contributions to nonprofit organizations directly. Support is given on a national and international basis.
Fields of interest: Journalism/publishing; Visual arts; Performing arts; Arts; Higher education; Business school/education; Education; Environment; Medical research; Youth, services; International affairs; Engineering/technology; Science; Minorities.
International interests: Asia; Australia; Canada; Europe; Mexico; South America.
Types of support: General/operating support; Building/renovation; Conferences/seminars; Technical assistance; Employee volunteer

services; Use of facilities; Sponsorships; Donated equipment; Donated land; Donated products.
Limitations: Giving on a national and international basis in areas of company operations, including in Asia, Australia, Canada, Europe, Mexico, and South America. No grants to individuals, or for capital campaigns or endowments.
Publications: Application guidelines, Corporate giving report (including application guidelines).
Application information: The Ford Motor Company Fund handles giving. The company has a staff that only handles contributions. Application form not required.
  Initial approach: Letter of inquiry to headquarters
  Copies of proposal: 1
  Deadline(s): None
  Final notification: 6 Months
Number of staff: 10 full-time professional; 7 full-time support; 2 part-time support.

1580
Ford Motor Company Fund ▼
One American Rd.
P.O. Box 1899
Dearborn, MI 48126-2798 (313) 248-4745
Contact: Sandra E. Ulsh, Pres.
Additional tel.: (888) 313-0102; URL: http://www.ford.com/en/dedication/fundingAndGrants/fordMotorCompanyFund/default.htm

Incorporated in 1949 in MI.
Donor(s): Ford Motor Co.
Grantmaker type: Company-sponsored foundation
Financial data (yr. ended 12/31/02): Assets, $103,911,785 (M); gifts received, $47,000,000; expenditures, $33,222,317; qualifying distributions, $31,760,956; giving activities include $81,150,826 for 1,454 grants (high: $5,000,000; low: $200) and $2,850,298 for employee matching gifts.
Purpose and activities: Support for education, including matching gifts for colleges and universities, the environment, health and welfare, civic affairs and public policy, and arts and humanities.
Fields of interest: Arts; Higher education; Education; Environment; Hospitals (general); Community development; Federated giving programs; Government/public administration; Public affairs; Minorities.
Types of support: General/operating support; Continuing support; Annual campaigns; Capital campaigns; Equipment; Emergency funds; Program development; Conferences/seminars; Publication; Curriculum development; Scholarship funds; Research; Employee matching gifts; In-kind gifts; Matching/challenge support.
Limitations: Giving primarily in areas where plants and offices are located and members of the community are employed, with special emphasis on Detroit, MI. No support for religious, or sectarian organizations for religous purposes, political or fraternal organizations, animal rights organizations, labor groups, private schools, profitmaking enterprises, organizations supported by the United Way, or species specific organizations. No grants to individuals, or for scholarships (except

employee-related scholarships), fellowships, endowments, debt reduction, fundraising, operating expenses, or beauty or talent contests; no loans, program-related investments or donation of vehicles.

Publications: Application guidelines, Annual report, Corporate giving report, Informational brochure.

Application information: Application form not required.

Initial approach: Letter
Copies of proposal: 1
Deadline(s): None
Board meeting date(s): Apr. and Oct.
Final notification: Within 3 months

Officers and Trustees:* Allan D. Gilmour, Chair.; Sandra E. Ulsh, Pres.; Susan M. Cischke, V.P.; Peter Sherry, Jr., Secy.; Malcom S. MacDonald, Treas.; Alfred B. Ford; Sheila Ford Hamp; Martin Zimmerman.

Number of staff: 11 full-time professional; 8 full-time support; 3 part-time support.

EIN: 381459376

Recent environmental and animal welfare grants:

1580-1 America Recycles Day, Alexandria, VA, $50,000. For Exclusive Automotive sponsor for national recycling campaign. 2001.

1580-2 American Forest Foundation, DC, $60,000. For Project Learning Tree. 2001.

1580-3 Audubon Society, National, New York, NY, $3,500,000. 2001.

1580-4 Audubon Society, National, New York, NY, $1,000,000. For National Partner Program for Birds and Biodiversity. 2001.

1580-5 Conservation Fund, Arlington, VA, $159,000. For Conservation Leadership Network. 2001.

1580-6 Conservation International, DC, $5,000,000. 2001.

1580-7 Conservation International, DC, $250,000. For annual support for Brazil project. 2001.

1580-8 Conservation International, DC, $250,000. 2001.

1580-9 Conservation International, DC, $250,000. 2001.

1580-10 Conservation International, DC, $250,000. 2001.

1580-11 Conservation International, DC, $250,000. 2001.

1580-12 Conservation Resource Alliance, Traverse City, MI, $10,000. For Ten For Ten-River Care. 2001.

1580-13 Detroit Zoological Society, Royal Oak, MI, $1,000,000. 2001.

1580-14 Detroit Zoological Society, Royal Oak, MI, $40,000. For director matching gift. 2001.

1580-15 Detroit Zoological Society, Royal Oak, MI, $10,000. For annual support for general operating support. 2001.

1580-16 Earth Day San Diego, San Diego, CA, $10,000. For general support. 2001.

1580-17 Earthwatch Expeditions, Maynard, MA, $1,000,000. For Ford Conservation Research Centers and Scholarships. 2001.

1580-18 Environmental Careers Organization (ECO), Boston, MA, $50,000. For Environmental Scholars Program. 2001.

1580-19 Four Corners School of Outdoor Education, Monticello, UT, $50,000. For Outdoor Education Project. 2001.

1580-20 Georgia Conservancy, Atlanta, GA, $11,000. For Youth Environmental Symposium. 2001.

1580-21 Georgia Tech Foundation, Atlanta, GA, $2,000,000. For Ford Motor Company Environmental Science and Technology program. 2001.

1580-22 Greening of Detroit, Detroit, MI, $50,000. For TreeKeepers Kids (TKK) program. 2001.

1580-23 Heal The Bay, Santa Monica, CA, $65,000. For Orange County CRC Beach Report Card. 2001.

1580-24 INFORM, New York, NY, $25,000. For renewal of Corporate Associates Program. 2001.

1580-25 Inland Seas Education Association, Suttons Bay, MI, $50,000. For scholarship aid. 2001.

1580-26 International Center for Journalists, DC, $125,000. For Environmental Journalism Fellowships. 2001.

1580-27 Keep America Beautiful, Stamford, CT, $20,000. For general support. 2001.

1580-28 Louisville Zoological Society, Louisville, KY, $18,000. For Zoofan. 2001.

1580-29 Louisville Zoological Society, Louisville, KY, $10,000. For Zoofair. 2001.

1580-30 National Geographic Society, DC, $400,000. For Conservation Trust. 2001.

1580-31 National Park Foundation, DC, $1,000,000. For Proud Partner program, providing transportation and environmental solutions to enable visitors to enjoy national parks. 2001.

1580-32 Nature Conservancy, East Lansing, MI, $50,000. For general support. 2001.

1580-33 Norfolk Botanical Garden Society, Norfolk, VA, $10,000. For youth educational program. 2001.

1580-34 Norfolk Rotary Charities, Norfolk, VA, $12,500. For oyster bed in Elizabeth River. 2001.

1580-35 Orange Coast Watch, Irvine, CA, $10,000. 2001.

1580-36 Our World - Underwater Scholarship Society, Chicago, IL, $50,000. For National Geographic Fellow. 2001.

1580-37 Pacific Northwest Trail Association, Mount Vernon, WA, $50,000. For education program, SKY (Service, Knowledge, and Youth). 2001.

1580-38 Princeton University, Princeton, NJ, $500,000. For Carbon Mitigation Program. 2001.

1580-39 Puerto Rico Conservation Trust Fund, San Juan, PR, $30,000. For nature trail at Haurealu La Esperanza Manail Puerto Rico. 2001.

1580-40 Resources for the Future, DC, $200,000. For anniversary symposium and gala. 2001.

1580-41 Resources for the Future, DC, $35,000. For annual support. 2001.

1580-42 Southwest Detroit Environmental Vision Project, Detroit, MI, $12,500. For general support. 2001.

1580-43 Sustainable Conservation, San Francisco, CA, $100,000. For Urban Watershed Program. 2001.

1580-44 Sustainable Development Institute, DC, $105,194. For Environmental Film Festival. 2001.

1580-45 Sustainable Development Institute, DC, $50,000. For Environmental Film Festival. 2001.

1580-46 Wayside Waifs, Kansas City, MO, $13,000. For director matching gift. 2001.

1580-47 Wilderness Inquiry, Minneapolis, MN, $10,000. For Mighty Mississippi Passport. 2001.

1580-48 Wildlife Habitat Council, Silver Spring, MD, $150,000. For Wildlife at Work Programs, Corporate Lands for Learning. 2001.

1580-49 World Resources Institute, DC, $100,000. For communicating findings. 2001.

1581
Four County Community Foundation
(formerly Four County Foundation)
231 E. Saint Clair St.
P.O. Box 539
Almont, MI 48003-0539 (810) 798-0909
Contact: Janet Bauer, Exec. Dir.
FAX: (810) 798-0908 E-mail: info@4ccf.org;
URL: http://www.4ccf.org

Established in 1987 in MI; originally converted from Community Hospital Foundation and sold to Saint Joseph Mercy of Macomb North.

Grantmaker type: Community foundation

Financial data (yr. ended 12/31/02): Assets, $5,727,879 (M); gifts received, $227,658; expenditures, $467,052; giving activities include $289,738 for grants.

Purpose and activities: The foundation is dedicated to bringing together human and financial resources to support progressive ideas in education, health, community, youth and adult programs.

Fields of interest: Education; Environment; Health care; Recreation; Health organizations, association; Children/youth, services.

Types of support: Continuing support; Program development; Seed money; Scholarship funds; Matching/challenge support.

Limitations: Giving limited to southeast Lapeer, northwest Macomb, northeast Oakland, and southwest St. Clair counties, MI. Generally no grants to individuals, or for operating expenses.

Publications: Application guidelines, Annual report, Newsletter, Program policy statement.

Application information: Application form required.

Initial approach: Letter, telephone or Web site for application
Copies of proposal: 9
Deadline(s): Jan. 1, Apr. 1, July 1, and Oct. 1
Board meeting date(s): 6 meetings per year
Final notification: Within 1 month

Officers: Shane Diehl, Pres.; Judy Czerepowicz, V.P.; Kim Jorgensen, Secy.; Charles Schiedegger, Treas.

Number of staff: 1 full-time professional; 1 part-time support.

EIN: 382736601

1582

Frey Foundation ▼
40 Pearl St., N.W., Ste. 1100
Grand Rapids, MI 49503-3028
(616) 451-0303
Contact: Milton W. Rohwer, Pres.
FAX: (616) 451-8481; E-mail:
freyfdn@freyfdn.org; URL: http://www.freyfdn.org

Established in 1974 in MI.
Donor(s): Edward J. Frey, Sr.,‡ Frances T. Frey.‡
Grantmaker type: Independent foundation
Financial data (yr. ended 12/31/02): Assets,
$102,000,000 (M); expenditures, $8,100,000;
qualifying distributions, $6,300,000; giving
activities include $5,462,485 for 242 grants
(high: $1,000,000; low: $50; average:
$50–$1,000,000) and $37,515 for 87 employee
matching gifts.
Purpose and activities: Priorities include
promoting healthy developmental outcomes for
children in their early years (0-6 years); support
for land use planning and growth management,
and protection of natural resources; stimulating
the vitality, effectiveness, and growth of
community-based arts; encouraging civic
progress and leadership; and strengthening
philanthropy.
Fields of interest: Visual arts; Performing arts;
Arts; Early childhood education; Child
development, education; Natural resources;
Environment; Animals/wildlife,
preservation/protection; Children/youth,
services; Child development, services; Family
services; Public policy, research; Minorities;
Economically disadvantaged.
Types of support: Capital campaigns; Land
acquisition; Program development; Seed money;
Research; Technical assistance; Employee
matching gifts.
Limitations: Giving primarily in Emmet,
Charlevoix, and Kent counties, MI. No support
for sectarian charitable activity. No grants to
individuals, or for endowment funds, debt
retirement, general operating expenses,
scholarships, conferences, speakers, travel, or to
cover routine, current, or emergency expenses.
Publications: Application guidelines, Annual
report.
Application information: Application form
required for all requests; accepts CMF Common
Grant Application Form. Application form
required.
   Initial approach: Letter of inquiry or telephone
   Copies of proposal: 1
   Deadline(s): Feb. 15, May 15, Aug. 15, and
      Nov. 15
   Board meeting date(s): Feb., May, Aug., and
      Nov.
Officers and Directors:* David G. Frey,* Chair.;
John M. Frey,* Vice-Chair.; Milton W. Rohwer,
Pres.; Edward J. Frey, Jr.,* Secy.-Treas.; Mary
Caroline Frey.
Number of staff: 6 full-time professional; 1
full-time support.
EIN: 237094777
**Recent environmental and animal welfare
grants:**
1582-1 Camp Daggett, Petoskey, MI, $33,000.
To construct indoor adventure and activity
center allowing for year-round adventure
programming. 2001.
1582-2 Center for Environmental Study, Grand
Rapids, MI, $22,000. For start-up support for

Neighborhood Wetland Stewards Program to
protect local wetlands and educate public of
their value. 2001.
1582-3 Coldwater River Watershed Council,
Alto, MI, $20,000. For implementation of
river protection program for scientific
monitoring, community education, and
erosion and sedimentation inventory and
repair. 2001.
1582-4 Collins Center for Public Policy, Miami,
FL, $10,000. For Funders' Network for Smart
Growth and Livable Communities. 2001.
1582-5 Detroit Renaissance Foundation,
Detroit, MI, $40,000. For Michigan Business
Roundtable Urban Sprawl and Economic
Development project. 2001.
1582-6 Frederik Meijer Gardens and Sculpture
Park, Grand Rapids, MI, $10,000. For
Gardens of Art campaign. 2001.
1582-7 Humane Society, Little Traverse Bay,
Harbor Springs, MI, $20,000. For building
fund and operating support. 2001.
1582-8 Land Conservancy of West Michigan,
Grand Rapids, MI, $35,000. To protect and
steward critical land and habitat in areas of
West Michigan through West Michigan Dune
and Savannah project. 2001.
1582-9 Land Conservancy of West Michigan,
Grand Rapids, MI, $15,000. For program for
land protection by identifying priority
conservation sites, plus challenge grant
related to annual membership campaign.
2001.
1582-10 Little Traverse Conservancy, Harbor
Springs, MI, $150,000. For challenge grant
for protection of scenic character of US-31
corridor from southern Charlevoix County to
Petoskey. 2001.
1582-11 Little Traverse Conservancy, Harbor
Springs, MI, $75,000. For purchase of
Fochtman property between Round and
Crooked Lakes. 2001.
1582-12 Michigan Economic and
Environmental Roundtable, Lansing, MI,
$14,700. For Status of Michigan Cities,
updated report on quality of life. 2001.
1582-13 Michigan Environmental Council,
Lansing, MI, $33,000. To continue Land
Stewardship Initiative, which seeks to stem
loss of rural and natural lands to urban
sprawl. 2001.
1582-14 Michigan Integrated Food and Farming
Systems (MIFFS), East Lansing, MI, $30,000.
For leadership training to establish successful
local farmland preservation programs
throughout Michigan. 2001.
1582-15 Michigan Land Use Institute, Beulah,
MI, $50,000. For support of Natural Rivers
program. 2001.
1582-16 Michigan State University, East
Lansing, MI, $76,400. To preserve Kent
County farmland and strengthen central city
Grand Rapids through United Growth
program. 2001.
1582-17 Nature Conservancy, East Lansing, MI,
$50,000. To protect and steward critical land
and habitat areas of West Michigan through
West Michigan Dune and Savannah Project.
2001.
1582-18 Northern Lakes Economic Alliance,
Boyne City, MI, $10,000. For Sustainable
Farming through Value-Added Agriculture.
2001.

1582-19 Timberland Resource Conservation and
Development Area Council, Grand Rapids,
MI, $20,000. For Regional Trails/Greenways
coordination project. 2001.
1582-20 Tip of the Mitt Watershed Council,
Petoskey, MI, $50,000. To purchase and
remodel headquarters as model for effective
stormwater management/lakefront
demonstration site at Crooked Lake. 2001.
1582-21 University of Michigan, Ann Arbor, MI,
$38,000. For public broadcasting coverage of
West Michigan environment and land use
issues through television documentaries on
urban sprawl. 2001.
1582-22 West Grand Neighborhood
Organization, Grand Rapids, MI, $30,000.
For Turner Avenue Beautification Project.
2001.

1583

The Glancy Foundation, Inc.
400 Maple Park Blvd., Ste. 405
St. Clair Shores, MI 48081 (810) 498-6600
Contact: Alfred R. Glancy III, Chair.
FAX: (810) 498-6603; E-mail:
alglancy@glancyfamily.com

Established in 1994 in GA.
Grantmaker type: Independent foundation
Financial data (yr. ended 12/31/02): Assets,
$3,006,635 (M); expenditures, $214,971;
qualifying distributions, $192,647; giving
activities include $174,025 for 22 grants (high:
$45,000; low: $500).
Purpose and activities: Giving primarily for
education, and a zoological society; support
also for the arts, natural resource conservation,
and social services.
Fields of interest: Arts; Higher education;
Education; Natural resources; Zoos/zoological
societies; Human services.
Limitations: Giving primarily in MI. No grants to
individuals.
Application information:
   Initial approach: Letter
   Deadline(s): None
Officers: Alfred R. Glancy III, Chair. and Treas.;
Ruth R. Glancy, Vice Chair. and Secy.
Trustees: Alfred R. Glancy IV; Joan C. Glancy.
EIN: 582116482

1584

Hal & Jean Glassen Memorial Foundation
533 S. Grand Ave.
Lansing, MI 48933-7159
Contact: Neil A. McLean, Pres.

Established in 1991 in MI; funded in 1993.
Donor(s): Harold Glassen.‡
Grantmaker type: Independent foundation
Financial data (yr. ended 12/31/02): Assets,
$4,653,053 (M); expenditures, $319,798;
qualifying distributions, $542,922; giving
activities include $224,409 for 12 grants (high:
$50,000; low: $1,200).
Fields of interest: Education; Environment;
Athletics/sports, fishing/hunting.
Limitations: Giving primarily in MI. No grants to
individuals.
Application information: Application form not
required.
   Deadline(s): None

Officers and Directors:* Neil A. McLean,* Pres.;
Frank W. Perrin,* V.P.; Tom Huggler,* Secy.;
Glen Miller, D.V.M.,* Treas.; C. Alan Stewatt.
EIN: 383012223

1585
Grand Haven Area Community
Foundation, Inc.
1 S. Harbor Dr.
Grand Haven, MI 49417   (616) 842-6378
Contact: Ann L. Tabor, Pres.
FAX: (616) 842-9518; E-mail: info@ghacf.org;
URL: http://www.ghacf.org/

Incorporated in 1971 in MI.
Grantmaker type: Community foundation
Financial data (yr. ended 03/31/03): Assets,
$29,488,458 (M); gifts received, $5,459,698;
expenditures, $4,574,675; giving activities
include $4,241,925 for grants.
Purpose and activities: Primary areas of interest
include: education (including technical training,
mathematics, and business and accounting
education), the environment, health, crime
prevention, and community collaboration.
Scholarship awards are limited to students of
Grand Haven, Spring Lake, Holland Christian,
Catholic Central, West Michigan Christian, West
Ottawa, and Fruitport high schools, in MI. The
foundation administers donor-advised funds.
Fields of interest: Vocational education,
post-secondary; Business school/education;
Environment; Health care; Crime/law
enforcement; Community development;
Mathematics.
Types of support: Capital campaigns;
Equipment; Program development; Seed money;
Scholarship funds; Scholarships—to individuals;
Matching/challenge support.
Limitations: Giving limited to the MI Tri-Cities
area. No support for profit-making organizations
or religious programs that serve, or appear to
serve, specific religious denominations. No
grants to individuals (except for scholarships), or
for annual campaigns, emergency or deficit
financing, operating costs or ongoing operating
support, or endowments.
Publications: Application guidelines, Annual
report (including application guidelines),
Financial statement, Informational brochure
(including application guidelines), Newsletter,
Program policy statement.
Application information: See foundation Web
site for full application guidelines and form.
Application form required.
  Initial approach: Proposal, letter, or telephone
  Copies of proposal: 12
  Deadline(s): Usually 2 weeks prior to
    distribution committee meeting
  Board meeting date(s): Distribution committee
    meets quarterly: July, Oct., Jan., and Apr.;
    board meetings are usually 2 weeks
    following the distribution committee
    meeting
  Final notification: 1 week after board meeting
Officers and Trustees:* Lynne Sherwood,*
Chair.; Mary Eagin,* Vice-Chair.; Ann Irish
Tabor, Pres.; Mary Jane Evink,* Secy.; Jim
MacLachlan,* Treas.; Don Anderson; Dennis
Dornbush; Darell Moreland; Thomas Reinsma;
Charles Rycenga.
Number of staff: 4 full-time professional.
EIN: 237108776

1586
Grand Rapids Community Foundation ▼
(formerly The Grand Rapids Foundation)
209-C Waters Bldg.
161 Ottawa Ave. N.W.
Grand Rapids, MI 49503-2757
(616) 454-1751
Contact: Diana R. Sieger, Pres.
FAX: (616) 454-6455; E-mail:
grfound@grfoundation.org; URL: http://
www.grfoundation.org

Established in 1922 in MI by resolution and
declaration of trust; Incorporated 1989.
Grantmaker type: Community foundation
Financial data (yr. ended 06/30/03): Assets,
$159,659,724 (M); gifts received, $8,839,288;
expenditures, $9,941,360; giving activities
include $7,255,119 for grants, $8,755 for 49
employee matching gifts and $14,224 for 3
foundation-administered programs.
Purpose and activities: To provide support for
projects or causes designed to benefit the
people and the quality of life in Grand Rapids,
MI, and its surrounding communities through
grants for social needs, youth agencies, cultural
programs, health, recreation, neighborhood
development, the environment, and education,
including scholarships for Kent County residents
to attend selected colleges. Grant decisions are
made according to a project's fit with the
following guiding principles: Accountability,
Collaboration, Diversity, Justice, Prevention,
Social Capital and Systems Approach.
Fields of interest: Museums; Performing arts;
Theater; Humanities; Historic
preservation/historical societies; Arts; Child
development, education; Higher education;
Reading; Education; Environment; Substance
abuse, services; Mental health/crisis services;
Health organizations, association; AIDS;
Alcoholism; Employment; Nutrition;
Housing/shelter, development; Recreation;
Youth development, services; Human services;
Children/youth, services; Child development,
services; Family services; Hospices; Aging,
centers/services; Women, centers/services;
Minorities/immigrants, centers/services;
Homeless, human services; Civil rights,
immigrants; Civil rights, minorities; Civil rights,
disabled; Civil rights, women; Civil rights, aging;
Civil rights, gays/lesbians; Reproductive rights;
Race/intergroup relations; Community
development; Voluntarism promotion;
Leadership development; Minorities;
Asians/Pacific Islanders; African
Americans/Blacks; Native Americans/American
Indians; Disabled; Aging; Women; People with
AIDS (PWAs); Gays/lesbians;
Immigrants/refugees; Economically
disadvantaged; Homeless.
Types of support: Capital campaigns;
Building/renovation; Land acquisition; Program
development; Seed money; Scholarship funds;
Technical assistance; Program-related
investments/loans; Employee matching gifts;
Employee-related scholarships; Scholarships—to
individuals; Matching/challenge support.
Limitations: Giving limited to Grand Rapids, MI,
and surrounding communities. No support for
religious organizations, hospitals, K-12 schools,
child care centers, nursing homes/retirement
facilities, or political or cause-related projects.
No grants io individuals (except for

scholarships), or for continued operating
support, annual campaigns, travel expenses,
medical or scholarly research, deficit financing,
endowment funds, computers, vehicles, films,
videos, or conferences; no student loans; no
venture capital for competitive profit-making
activities.
Publications: Application guidelines, Annual
report, Informational brochure, Newsletter.
Application information: The student loan
program has been discontinued; new loans will
not be made. Application form required.
  Initial approach: Letter of inquiry - reviewed
    every 2 weeks
  Copies of proposal: 8
  Deadline(s): Submit scholarship applications
    between Jan. 1 and Apr. 1; deadline for all
    other applications is 12 weeks preceding
    board meeting
  Board meeting date(s): 6 times a year
    (bimonthly)
  Final notification: June 15 for scholarships; 1
    month after board decision for other
    requests
Officers: Diana R. Sieger, Pres.; Lynne Black,
V.P., Fin. and Admin.; Molly Parker, V.P., Devel.;
Marcia Rapp, V.P., Progs.
Trustees: Hon. Janet Haynes, Chair.; Richard P.
Haslinger, Vice-Chair.; Brian Cloyd; Samuel M.
Cummings; Beverly A. Drake; Kevin T. Kabat;
Marilyn A. Lankfer; Mark Meijer; Juan R.
Olivarez; Margaret Sellers-Walker; Thomas L.
Stevens.
Number of staff: 12 full-time professional; 1
part-time professional; 7 full-time support.
EIN: 382877959
**Recent environmental and animal welfare
grants:**
1586-1 Aquinas College, Grand Rapids, MI,
  $100,000. For Get the Lead Out. 2002.
1586-2 Calvin College, Grand Rapids, MI,
  $100,000. For Ecosystem Interpretive Center.
  2002.
1586-3 Frederik Meijer Charitable Trust, Grand
  Rapids, MI, $34,000. 2002.
1586-4 Lowell, City of, Lowell, MI, $25,000.
  For Lowell Area Trailway. 2002.
1586-5 Michigan Land Use Institute, Beulah,
  MI, $37,500. For Enhancing Smart Growth in
  Michigan. 2002.
1586-6 Timberland Resource Conservation and
  Development Area Council, Grand Rapids,
  MI, $100,000. For West Michigan
  Trails/Greenway Coalition Project. 2002.

1587
Gratiot County Community Foundation
1131 E. Center St.
P.O. Box 310
Ithaca, MI 48847-0310   (989) 875-4222
Contact: Tina M. Travis, Exec. Dir.
Additional tel.: (517) 875-5101, ext. 248; FAX:
(989) 875-2858; E-mail: gccf@edzone.net

Incorporated in 1992 in MI; operations began in
late 1994.
Grantmaker type: Community foundation
Financial data (yr. ended 12/31/02): Assets,
$2,558,000 (M); gifts received, $187,000;
expenditures, $105,000; giving activities
include $95,000 for 48 grants (high: $8,000;
low: $100; average: $5,000).

Purpose and activities: Building endowments and making grants in the field of the arts, education, the environment and human services. The foundation administers donor-advised funds.
Fields of interest: Arts; Education; Environment; Health care; Public health; Youth development; Human services; Community development; Public affairs; Aging.
Types of support: Program development; Seed money; Internship funds; Research; Scholarships—to individuals.
Limitations: Giving limited to Gratiot County, MI.
Publications: Application guidelines, Annual report, Informational brochure, Newsletter.
Application information: Application form required.
  Initial approach: Telephone or letter
  Copies of proposal: 8
  Deadline(s): Mar. 1 and Oct. 1
  Board meeting date(s): 1st Tues. of each month
  Final notification: Apr. and Nov.
Officers and Directors:* Patrick Duffy,* Pres.; Pam Munderlah, Secy.; Linda Williams, V.P.; Brad Vibber,* Treas.; Richard Abbott, Chair., Develop. Comm.; Sheila Rummer, Chair., Dist. Comm.; Jim Wheeler, Chair., Fin. Comm.; Tina M. Travis, Exec. Dir.; Ginna Holmes,* Advisor.
Number of staff: 1 part-time professional.
EIN: 383087756

1588
Great Lakes Fishery Trust

c/o Public Sector Consultants
600 W. St. Joseph, Ste. 10
Lansing, MI 48933-2263 (517) 371-7468
Contact: Holly Madill, Asst. Mgr.
FAX: (517) 484-6549; E-mail: glft@glft.org; URL: http://www.glft.org/

Established in 1996 in MI.
Grantmaker type: Public charity
Financial data (yr. ended 12/31/02): Revenue, $3,795,315; assets, $24,597,980 (M); expenditures, $5,202,965; program services expenses, $4,812,272; giving activities include $4,812,272 for 14 grants (high: $927,576).
Purpose and activities: The trust provides funding to enhance, protect, and rehabilitate Great Lakes fishery resources and to mitigate for lost use and enjoyment of the Lake Michigan fishery resulting from the operation of the Ludington Pumped Storage Plant.
Fields of interest: Environment, research; Environment, public education; Environment, water resources; Animals/wildlife, preservation/protection; Animals/wildlife, fisheries.
Types of support: Continuing support; Equipment; Land acquisition; Program development; Conferences/seminars; Seed money; Curriculum development; Research; Matching/challenge support.
Limitations: Giving limited to MI, with Lake Michigan and its tributaries the primary geographic target for projects; secondary consideration given to projects that primarily benefit fisheries or fishing access outside the Lake Michigan watershed.
Publications: Annual report, Occasional report.
Application information: See Web site for application information. Application form required.

Copies of proposal: 1
Deadline(s): Oct. 4 for Fishing Access, Feb. 17 for Research, and Aug. 5 for Education
Board meeting date(s): Feb., May, Aug., and Nov.
Final notification: Nov. for Fishing Access and for Education, Aug. for Research
Officer and Trustees: K.L. Cool,* Chair.; Andy Buchsbaum; Mike Cox; Christine Mitchell; Sam Washington; Charles Wooley.
Number of staff: 5.
EIN: 383331471

1589
Alice Kales Hartwick Foundation

c/o Gregory V. Dicenso
840 W. Long Lake Rd., Ste. 200
Troy, MI 48098-6358
Contact: Peter A. Dow, Secy.-Treas.
Application address: 191 Ridge Rd., Grosse Pointe Farms, MI 48236, tel.: (313) 886-1424

Donor(s): Alice Kales Hartwick Unitrust.
Grantmaker type: Independent foundation
Financial data (yr. ended 12/31/02): Assets, $1,605,023 (L); gifts received, $143,668; expenditures, $335,633; qualifying distributions, $315,708; giving activities include $302,000 for 28 grants (high: $30,000; low: $3,000).
Purpose and activities: Giving primarily for arts and culture, education, and human services.
Fields of interest: Arts, association; Ceramic arts; Performing arts; Orchestra (symphony); Arts; Libraries (public); Education; Zoos/zoological societies; Human services; Community development; Federated giving programs.
Limitations: Giving primarily in Detroit, MI.
Application information: Application form not required.
  Initial approach: Proposal
  Deadline(s): None
Officers and Trustees:* Frank J. Sladen, Jr.,* Pres.; Carl M. Eckert,* V.P.; Peter A. Dow, Secy.-Treas.
EIN: 382248118

1590
Florence E. Herman Charitable Trust

c/o Fifth Third Bank
P.O. Box 3636
Grand Rapids, MI 49501-3636

Established in 1991.
Grantmaker type: Public charity
Financial data (yr. ended 06/30/02): Revenue, $90,294; assets, $1,710,517 (M); expenditures, $70,289; program services expenses, $62,089; giving activities include $62,089 for 1 grant.
Purpose and activities: The trust exists for the sole benefit of the Kalamazoo County Humane Society.
Fields of interest: Animal welfare.
Limitations: Applications not accepted. Giving limited to Kalamazoo, MI.
Application information: Contributes only to a pre-selected organization; unsolicited requests for funds not considered or acknowledged.
Trustee: Fifth Third Bank.
EIN: 386567414

1591
The Herrington-Fitch Family Foundation, Inc.

c/o Louis A. Smith
603 Bay St., P.O. Box 705
Traverse City, MI 49685-0705

Established in 1996 in MI.
Donor(s): Leslie Lee.
Grantmaker type: Independent foundation
Financial data (yr. ended 12/31/02): Assets, $2,924,028 (M); gifts received, $3,492; expenditures, $204,100; qualifying distributions, $199,891; giving activities include $200,203 for 22 grants (high: $140,000; low: $500).
Purpose and activities: Giving for art and cultural programs, education, and nature conservation.
Fields of interest: Arts; Education; Natural resources; Environment, land resources; Environment.
Types of support: General/operating support.
Limitations: Applications not accepted. Giving primarily in MI. No grants to individuals.
Application information: Contributes only to pre-selected organizations.
Officer: Leslie Lee, Pres.
EIN: 383331023

1592
Hillsdale County Community Foundation

52 E. Bacon St.
P.O. Box 276
Hillsdale, MI 49242-0276 (517) 439-5101
Contact: Sharon E. Bisher, Exec. Dir.
FAX: (517) 439-5109; E-mail: s.bisher@abouthccf.org; URL: http://www.abouthccf.org/

Established in 1991 in MI.
Grantmaker type: Community foundation
Financial data (yr. ended 09/30/02): Assets, $6,186,385 (M); gifts received, $445,338; expenditures, $730,658; giving activities include $418,221 for 90 grants (high: $37,450; low: $100).
Purpose and activities: The foundation gives to support community organizations and services in Hillsdale County, MI. The foundation also administers a scholarship program for area students. The foundation administers donor-advised funds.
Fields of interest: Visual arts; Performing arts; Theater; Arts; Education, association; Early childhood education; Child development, education; Elementary school/education; Higher education; Libraries/library science; Education; Natural resources; Environment; Animal welfare; Hospitals (general); Health care; Health organizations, association; Crime/violence prevention, youth; Crime/law enforcement; Employment; Food services; Recreation; Youth development, services; Human services; Children/youth, services; Child development, services; Family services; Hospices; Aging, centers/services; Community development; Voluntarism promotion; Biological sciences; Economics; Leadership development; Public affairs; Aging; Economically disadvantaged.
Types of support: Annual campaigns; Conferences/seminars; Publication; Seed money; Scholarship funds; Employee-related

scholarships; Scholarships—to individuals; In-kind gifts; Matching/challenge support.
Limitations: Giving limited to Hillsdale County, MI. No support for political, religious, or sectarian purposes. No grants to individuals (except for scholarships), or for new building campaigns, routine maintenance, remodeling, or capital campaigns; no loans.
Publications: Application guidelines, Annual report, Financial statement, Informational brochure (including application guidelines), Newsletter.
Application information: See foundation Web site for guidelines and downloadable application forms. Application form required.
  Initial approach: Telephone or in person
  Copies of proposal: 1
  Deadline(s): Apr. 15 and Oct. 15 for general grants; Mar. 1, July 1, and Nov. 1 for Kellogg YOUTH grants; and Apr. 1 for scholarships
  Board meeting date(s): 1st Tues. of the month
  Final notification: Within 2 months
Officers and Trustees:* James B. Parker,* Pres.; Michael Nye,* V.P.; Barry Hill,* Secy.; Thomas H. Osbourne,* Treas.; Muriel Alexandrowski; Penny Arnn; Brett Boyd; James Drews; Robert Henthorne; Eric Leutheuser; Annette Magda; Scott Menzel; Bill Smith; Stanley Smith; Kasee Stratton; Mollie Wolf.
Number of staff: 3 part-time professional; 1 part-time support.
EIN: 383001297

1593
Hunting Foundation
2820 Pioneer Club Rd. S.E.
Grand Rapids, MI 49506

Established in 1998 in MI.
Donor(s): John R. Hunting.
Grantmaker type: Independent foundation
Financial data (yr. ended 12/31/02): Assets, $1,318,633 (M); expenditures, $97,795; qualifying distributions, $89,061; giving activities include $89,300 for 37 grants (high: $18,000; low: $250).
Purpose and activities: Giving primarily for the arts and human services.
Fields of interest: Arts; Education; Environment, pollution control; Medical research, institute; Human services.
Types of support: General/operating support.
Limitations: Applications not accepted. Giving primarily in MI, IL, and MN. No grants to individuals.
Application information: Contributes only to pre-selected organizations.
Officers: Helen J. Hunting, Pres.; Allen I. Hunting, Secy.; Allen I. Hunting, Jr., Treas.
Director: Anne Hunting.
EIN: 383412588

1594
The Jackson County Community Foundation
(formerly The Jackson Community Foundation)
1 Jackson Sq., Ste. 110A
Jackson, MI 49201-1406 (517) 787-1321
Contact: Shelly Schadewald, C.E.O.
FAX: (517) 787-4333; E-mail: info@jacksoncf.org or sschadewald@jacksoncf.org; URL: http:// www.jacksoncf.org

Incorporated in 1948 in MI.
Grantmaker type: Community foundation
Financial data (yr. ended 12/31/02): Assets, $12,982,964 (M); gifts received, $429,343; expenditures, $1,057,468; giving activities include $548,107 for grants (average: $500–$18,000).
Purpose and activities: Support for community improvement and other programs for the benefit of the residents of Jackson County, MI. The foundation administers donor-advised funds.
Fields of interest: Humanities; Historic preservation/historical societies; Arts; Adult education—literacy, basic skills & GED; Reading; Education; Environment; Health care; Substance abuse, services; Human services; Children/youth, services; Community development.
Types of support: Capital campaigns; Building/renovation; Equipment; Land acquisition; Program development; Seed money; Technical assistance; Consulting services; Program-related investments/loans; Matching/challenge support.
Limitations: Giving limited to Jackson County, MI. No support for religious purposes. No grants to individuals (except through designated funds), or for endowment funds, scholarships, fellowships, publications, or conferences.
Publications: Application guidelines, Annual report (including application guidelines), Newsletter.
Application information: Application form not required.
  Initial approach: Letter or telephone
  Copies of proposal: 20
  Deadline(s): Jan. 15 for health and arts applications; Apr. 15 for human services applications; July 15 for education applications; Oct. 15 for capital campaigns and economic development, including public, safety, civic and environment applications
  Board meeting date(s): Feb., Mar., May, Aug., Nov., Dec.
  Final notification: 10 days after board meeting
Officers: Dennis A. Hill, Chair. and Secy.; Miles E. Jones, Chair., Fin. Comm.; Marty Hansen Mercer, Vice-Chair.; Shelly Schadewald, C.E.O. and Pres.; Carole A. Booms, V.P.
Trustees: Charles E. Anderson; Carl Benes; Jerry Booth; Carolyn Crocheron; Carl L. English; Georgia A. Fojtasek; Carrie Glick; James S. Grace; Aaron Kantor; Gary L. Krupa; Kevin T. Lavery, M.D.; Marty Hansen Mercer; R. Dale Moretz; Miguel L. Rodriguez; Susan J. Schaffer; Marilyn F. Stephen; Richard L. Walicki.
Number of staff: 4 full-time professional; 1 part-time professional.
EIN: 386070739

1595
Kalamazoo Community Foundation ▼
(formerly Kalamazoo Foundation)
151 S. Rose St., Ste. 332
Kalamazoo, MI 49007 (269) 381-4416
Contact: David D. Gardiner, V.P., Progs.
FAX: (269) 381-3146; E-mail: info@kalfound.org; URL: http:// www.kalfound.org/

Established in 1925; incorporated in 1930 in MI.
Grantmaker type: Community foundation
Financial data (yr. ended 12/31/02): Assets, $209,537,807 (M); gifts received, $8,948,954; expenditures, $17,051,237; giving activities include $11,690,154 for 1,877 grants (high: $1,253,167; low: $25), $1,585,145 for 451 grants to individuals (high: $11,600; low: $250; average: $250–$11,600) and $1,672,886 for 9 loans/program-related investments.
Purpose and activities: Primary areas of giving include 1) economic development, 2) education and learning, 3) community engagement and youth development and 4) individuals and families. Grants largely for capital purposes and innovative programs.
Fields of interest: Elementary/secondary education; Environment; Health care; Housing/shelter, development; Economic development.
Types of support: General/operating support; Capital campaigns; Building/renovation; Equipment; Emergency funds; Program development; Seed money; Scholarship funds; Technical assistance; Program-related investments/loans; Employee matching gifts; Scholarships—to individuals; Matching/challenge support.
Limitations: Giving limited to Kalamazoo County, MI. No grants to individuals (except for scholarships), or for endowment funds.
Publications: Application guidelines, Annual report (including application guidelines), Financial statement, Grants list, Informational brochure (including application guidelines), Newsletter.
Application information: Application form required.
  Initial approach: Telephone
  Copies of proposal: 1
  Deadline(s): Jan. 8 and July 2 for individuals and families, and economic development; April 2 and Oct. 1 for education and learning, and community engagement and youth development
  Board meeting date(s): Mar., June. Sept., and Dec.
  Final notification: 2 months
Officers, Trustees and Distribution Committee:* Jeffrey L. DeNooyer,* Chair.; Marilyn J. Schlack,* Vice-Chair.; John E. "Jack" Hopkins, C.E.O., Pres. and Secy.-Treas.; Wesley Freeland, V.P., Donor Svcs.; David D. Gardiner, V.P., Progs.; Gloria Z. Royal, V.P., Mktg. Comm.; Susan Springgate, V.P., Finance and Admin.; Karen Racette, Cont.; J. Louis Felton; David L. Hatfield; Judith Maze; Ronda E. Stryker; Donald J. Vander Kooy.
Custodian Bank: National City Bank.
Number of staff: 15 full-time professional; 3 part-time professional; 8 full-time support; 1 part-time support.
EIN: 383333202

Recent environmental and animal welfare grants:

1595-1 Downtown Tomorrow, Kalamazoo, MI, $25,000. Toward rehabilitation of Green Building. 2002.

1595-2 Habitat for Humanity, Kalamazoo Valley, Kalamazoo, MI, $24,800. To build new homes in Kalamazoo area, one of which will showcase alternative building and energy conservation technologies. 2002.

1595-3 Kalamazoo Nature Center, Kalamazoo, MI, $15,000. For Growing With Your Garden Expansion, which will combine Nature Center's Roots and Shoots and Growing With Your Garden programs to establish effective, year-round learning opportunity for children. 2002.

1595-4 Parks Foundation of Kalamazoo, Kalamazoo, MI, $50,000. To facilitate construction of pedestrian trails. 2002.

1596
The Kantzler Foundation

900 Center Ave.
Bay City, MI 48708 (989) 892-0591
Contact: Robert D. Sarow, Secy.

Incorporated in 1974 in MI.
Donor(s): Leopold J. Kantzler.‡
Grantmaker type: Independent foundation
Financial data (yr. ended 12/31/02): Assets, $4,943,712 (M); expenditures, $317,745; qualifying distributions, $301,808; giving activities include $297,514 for 14 grants (high: $50,000; low: $1,000).
Purpose and activities: To support projects and capital improvements of charitable, artistic, educational, and cultural organizations in the greater metropolitan Bay City, MI, area.
Fields of interest: Arts; Education; Natural resources; Human services; Community development; Foundations (community).
Types of support: Capital campaigns; Building/renovation; Equipment; Land acquisition; Seed money; Program development; Scholarship funds; Matching/challenge support.
Limitations: Giving limited to the greater Bay City, MI, area. No grants to individuals, or for endowment funds, operating budgets, continuing support, annual campaigns, special projects, publications, conferences, emergency funds, deficit financing, research, scholarships, or fellowships; no loans.
Publications: Financial statement, Informational brochure (including application guidelines).
Application information: Application form not required.
Initial approach: Proposal
Copies of proposal: 1
Deadline(s): 2 weeks before board meeting
Board meeting date(s): Approximately 6 times per year
Final notification: 2 months
Officers: Dominic Monastiere, Pres.; Joseph Sasiela, V.P.; Robert D. Sarow, Secy.
Trustees: Meade A. Gougeon; Linda R. Heemstra; Ruth M. Jaffe; D. Brian Law; Clifford C. Van Dyke; Jerome L. Yantz.
Number of staff: None.
EIN: 237422733

1597
The Keeler Foundation

(formerly The Miner S. & Mary Ann Keeler Fund)
200 Monroe Ave. N.W., Ste. 340
Grand Rapids, MI 49503-2213
Contact: Miner S. Keeler II, Pres., or Mary Ann Keeler, Secy.-Treas.

Incorporated in 1985 in MI as successor to the First Keeler Fund established in 1953, which transferred its assets to the new Keeler Fund in 1986.
Donor(s): Mary Ann Keeler, Miner S. Keeler II, The Keeler Fund.
Grantmaker type: Independent foundation
Financial data (yr. ended 07/31/02): Assets, $4,992,322 (M); gifts received, $2,500,022; expenditures, $1,691,085; qualifying distributions, $1,659,070; giving activities include $1,660,363 for 58 grants (high: $350,000; low: $300).
Purpose and activities: Giving primarily to organizations that are artistic or scholastic in nature.
Fields of interest: Museums; Performing arts; Arts; Secondary school/education; Higher education; Libraries (public); Environment; Human services; Roman Catholic agencies & churches.
Limitations: Giving primarily in MI, with emphasis on Grand Rapids. No grants to individuals.
Application information:
Initial approach: Letter
Deadline(s): None
Officers: Miner S. Keeler II, Pres.; Isaac S. Keeler, V.P.; Mary Ann Keeler, Secy.-Treas.
EIN: 382625402

1598
Keller Foundation

5225 33rd St. S.E.
Grand Rapids, MI 49512 (616) 949-5138
Contact: Anne Williamson, Exec. Dir.
Tel ext.: 124

Established around 1980 in MI.
Donor(s): Paragon Die & Engineering Co.
Grantmaker type: Independent foundation
Financial data (yr. ended 06/30/03): Assets, $6,005,573 (M); gifts received, $1,329,570; expenditures, $239,692; qualifying distributions, $208,989; giving activities include $185,250 for 78 grants (high: $15,000; low: $50; average: $1,000–$5,000) and $12,000 for employee matching gifts.
Purpose and activities: Giving primarily to core city youth in Grand Rapids, MI.
Fields of interest: Performing arts; Education; Botanical/horticulture/landscape services; Zoos/zoological societies; Health care; Human services; Children/youth, services; Christian agencies & churches.
Types of support: General/operating support; Continuing support; Capital campaigns; Building/renovation; Program development; Seed money; Curriculum development; Scholarship funds; Matching/challenge support.
Limitations: Giving primarily in the Grand Rapids, MI, area. No grants to individuals.
Publications: Application guidelines.
Application information: Application form required.

Initial approach: Letter of request
Copies of proposal: 1
Deadline(s): None
Board meeting date(s): June, Sept., and Dec.
Officers and Directors:* Kathleen K. Muir,* Chair.; Lorissa K. MacAllister,* Vice-Chair.; William M. Muir,* Secy.; Frederick P. Keller,* Treas.; Anne Williamson, Exec. Dir.; Bernedine J. Keller; Christina L. Keller; Fred M. Keller; Linn Maxwell Keller; Wes MacAllister; Cathy Muir; David F. Muir; Elizabeth M. Muir; William W. Muir, Jr.; Lars Whitman; Susan T.K. Whitman.
Number of staff: 1 part-time professional.
EIN: 382331693

1599
W. K. Kellogg Foundation ▼

1 Michigan Ave. E.
Battle Creek, MI 49017-4058 (269) 968-1611
Contact: Debbie Rey, Supervisor of Proposal Processing
FAX: (269) 968-0413; URL: http://www.wkkf.org

Incorporated in 1930 in MI.
Donor(s): W.K. Kellogg,‡ W.K. Kellogg Foundation Trust.
Grantmaker type: Independent foundation
Financial data (yr. ended 08/31/03): Assets, $5,729,303,302 (M); gifts received, $760,021; expenditures, $242,219,559; qualifying distributions, $176,303,269; giving activities include $173,939,946 for grants and $2,363,323 for employee matching gifts.
Purpose and activities: The W.K. Kellogg Foundation was established in 1930 to help people help themselves through the practical application of knowledge and resources to improve their quality of life and that of future generations. The foundation targets its grants toward specific focal points or areas. These include: health; food systems and rural development; youth and education; and philanthropy and voluntarism. The foundation learns from the knowledge, experiences, and lessons learned by all of its projects as they apply to leadership, information and communication technology, capitalizing on diversity, and social and economic community development. Grants are concentrated in the United States, Latin America and the Caribbean, and in the countries of Botswana, Lesotho, Mozambique, South Africa, Swaziland, and Zimbabwe.
Fields of interest: Early childhood education; Elementary school/education; Secondary school/education; Health sciences school/education; Adult/continuing education; Education; Health care, support services; Health care; Health organizations, association; Agriculture; Agriculture/food; Youth development, services; Youth, services; Aging, centers/services; Minorities/immigrants, centers/services; Community development, neighborhood development; Rural development; Community development; Voluntarism promotion; Computer science; International studies; Leadership development; Minorities; African Americans/Blacks; Aging.
International interests: Caribbean; Botswana; Lesotho; Mozambique; South Africa; Swaziland; Zimbabwe; Latin America.
Types of support: Seed money; Employee matching gifts; Matching/challenge support.

Limitations: Giving primarily in the U.S., Latin America and the Caribbean, and the south African countries of Botswana, Lesotho, South Africa, Swaziland, Zimbabwe and Mozambique. No support for religious purposes or for capital facilities. No grants to individuals (except through fellowship programs), or for endowment funds, development campaigns, films, equipment, publications, conferences, or radio and television programs unless they are an integral part of a project already being funded; no grants for operating budgets, or capital facilities.

Publications: Application guidelines, Annual report (including application guidelines), Financial statement, Informational brochure (including application guidelines), Newsletter, Occasional report, Program policy statement.

Application information: Proposals must conform to specified program priorities. Application form not required.

Initial approach: Pre-proposal letter (1 to 2 pages) or on-line application
Copies of proposal: 1
Deadline(s): None
Board meeting date(s): Monthly

Officers and Trustees:* William C. Richardson, Ph.D.,* C.E.O. and Pres.; Gregory A. Lyman, Sr. V.P. and Corp. Secy.; Anne C. Petersen, Sr. V.P., Progs.; La June J. Montgomery-Talley, V.P., Finance and Treas.; Richard M. Foster, V.P., Progs.; Marguerite Johnson, V.P., Progs.; Paul J. Lawler, V.P. and C.I.O.; Robert F. Long, V.P., Progs.; Gail D. McClure, V.P., Progs.; Shirley D. Bowser; Dorothy A. Johnson; Fred P. Keller; Hanmin Liu; Russell G. Mawby; Cynthia H. Milligan; Wenda Weekes Moore; Howard F. Sims; Joseph M. Stewart; Jonathan T. Walton.

Number of staff: 119 full-time professional; 1 part-time professional; 77 full-time support.

EIN: 381359264

Recent environmental and animal welfare grants:

1599-1 Africa Resources Trust, Johannesburg, South Africa, $200,000. To promote youth engagement in ecotourism in Bushbuckridge area of Limpopo Province. 2002.

1599-2 Alliance to End Childhood Lead Poisoning, DC, $70,000. For program support. 2002.

1599-3 Altarum Institute, Ann Arbor, MI, $200,000. To assist cyber-state.org to focus statewide agenda on digital divide and broadly increase private sector and other funding. 2002.

1599-4 Appalachian Sustainable Development, Abingdon, VA, $150,000. 2002.

1599-5 Associacao de Apoio as Comunidades do Campo do Rio Grande do Norte, Supporting Association to the Rural Communities of the North Rio Grande, Natal, Brazil, $65,923. For youth programs. 2002.

1599-6 Barnes Foundation, Merion, PA, $100,000. For capacity-building to develop partnerships and economic sustainability, including youth educational component. 2002.

1599-7 Centro de Estudios de Producciones Agroecologicas (CEPAR), Center for the Study of Agro-Ecological Production, Rosario, Argentina, $276,050. 2002.

1599-8 Centro para el Desarrollo Agropecuario y Forestal (CEDAF), Santo Domingo, Dominican Republic, $400,000. Toward

developing comprehensive models for breaking cycle of poverty by facilitating exchange of experiences through organizing traveling seminars and other networking activities. 2002.

1599-9 Centro para el Desarrollo Agropecuario y Forestal (CEDAF), Center for the Development of Agriculture and Forestry, Santo Domingo, Dominican Republic, $40,000. For continued support of Third Encounter of Foundation projects comprising Human Nutrition Initiative, promoting exchange of experiences and fostering ongoing contacts. 2002.

1599-10 Chikukwa Ecological Land Use Community Trust, Zimbabwe, $200,000. 2002.

1599-11 Collins Center for Public Policy, Miami, FL, $30,000. For continued support to promote knowledge among funders on complexity and interconnectedness of land use and urban sprawl issues through Funders' Network for Smart Growth and Livable Communities. 2002.

1599-12 Comprehensive Health Care (CHoiCe), Tzaneen, South Africa, $174,000. To strengthen capacity of Mohlanatsi community board of management, assisting in developing business plans in eco-tourism and agriculture. 2002.

1599-13 Conservation Fund, Arlington, VA, $150,000. To form key partnership alliances and networks and create communication strategies to build capacity for entrepreneurial development in West Virginia. 2002.

1599-14 Development Group for Alternative Policies, DC, $197,600. To educate Americans on international financial institutions and policies promoted in client countries, and present alternatives. 2002.

1599-15 East Bay Conservation Corps, Oakland, CA, $24,259. For evaluation activities measuring student academic, social, and emotional development in service-learning oriented charter school. 2002.

1599-16 Environmental and Development Agency, Johannesburg, South Africa, $100,000. To develop beekeeping project for Lower Telle community in Eastern Cape province. 2002.

1599-17 Environmental Defense, New York, NY, $100,000. To improve understanding of and inform changes in federal agricultural policy and related environmental impact on U.S. regions producing commodity crops in small volumes. 2002.

1599-18 Federal University of Bahia, Salvador, Brazil, $131,652. To train leaders for social programs and local sustainable development, through diploma course targeted at governmental and NGO professionals in northeast Brazil. 2002.

1599-19 Foods Resource Bank, Kalamazoo, MI, $1,406,726. 2002.

1599-20 Fundacion para la Autogestion y el Medio Ambiente, Foundation for Self-Management and the Environment, Cochabamba, Bolivia, $359,577. 2002.

1599-21 Grand Traverse Regional Land Conservancy, Traverse City, MI, $150,000. Toward developing business plan to protect shorelines and farmland adjacent to Lake Michigan. 2002.

1599-22 Greater Lansing Food Alliance, Lansing, MI, $10,000. To implement garden-based curriculum at Gunnisonville Elementary School. 2002.

1599-23 Grupo para Promover la Educacion y el Desarrollo Sustentable (GRUPEDSAC), Group for the Promotion of Education and Sustainable Development, Naucalpan, Mexico, $500,000. For continued support to enhance ability of rural promoters and small farmers to produce food through teaching concentration on written and audio-visual information in Echo Technologies. 2002.

1599-24 Haitian Christian Service, Port-au-Prince, Haiti, $195,000. To develop youth citizenship through training in reforestation and other areas on La Gonave Island. 2002.

1599-25 Harvard University, Cambridge, MA, $1,205,808. To ameliorate unhealthy living environment of public housing residents, using environmental, energy, safety, and behavioral approaches and interventions. 2002.

1599-26 Institute for Conservation Leadership, Takoma Park, MD, $785,000. 2002.

1599-27 Institutes for Journalism and Natural Resources, Missoula, MT, $300,000. To develop and implement new agriculture and rural communities program. 2002.

1599-28 Instituto de Desenvolvimento Sustentavel do Baixo Sul da Bahia, Institute of Sustainable Development of the Lower South of Bahia, Bahia, Brazil, $600,000. For continued support to involve youth as key players in regional development and leadership promotion, through offering training programs and creating opportunities for income generation in urban and rural communities. 2002.

1599-29 Instituto Ecologico para el Desarrollo, Ecological Institute for Development, Lima, Peru, $188,000. To improve living conditions of young indigenous Huancavelican women, through training program qualifying and managing traditional productive activities and developing personal skills. 2002.

1599-30 Instituto para el Desarrollo de la Mixteca, Huajuapn de Leon, Mexico, $250,000. 2002.

1599-31 International Union for Conservation of Nature, Cape Town, South Africa, $300,000. To facilitate participation of community-based organizations in World Summit on Sustainable Development and learning toward best practices in sustainable livelihood programming. 2002.

1599-32 Iowa State University, Ames, IA, $100,000. To promote food production systems encouraging local ownership, environmental stewardship, public health, and economic sustainability for farmers, processors, distributors, retailers, and consumers. 2002.

1599-33 Leila Arboretum Society, Battle Creek, MI, $200,000. For continued support to provide youth training and employment opportunities through intergenerational community gardening program. 2002.

1599-34 Michigan Land Use Institute, Beulah, MI, $150,000. To improve health of small farms and surrounding communities through introducing economic development officials to benefits of community-based food systems. 2002.

1599-35 Michigan State University, East Lansing, MI, $3,000,000. To establish Kellogg Chair in Ethics and strengthen integrated learning land-grant program through creating Sustainable Michigan Fund. 2002.

1599-36 Michigan State University, East Lansing, MI, $500,000. To improve coordination and integration of land use research and extension-outreach efforts, and develop People and Land Public Education Program. 2002.

1599-37 Mountain Association for Community Economic Development, Berea, KY, $150,000. To define alternatives for forest owners and build advocacy among organizations and individuals throughout eastern Kentucky. 2002.

1599-38 National Association of State Universities and Land Grant Colleges, DC, $200,000. To design and initiate strategic plan for increasing public and federal support of food and agricultural programs toward healthy society and environment, economically viable communities, and globally competitive food system. 2002.

1599-39 National Center for Appropriate Technology, Butte, MT, $497,574. To expand locally owned and environmentally sound farms, ranches, and food enterprises in four corners states of Southwest. 2002.

1599-40 New England Small Farm Institute, Belchertown, MA, $75,000. To assist New American Farmer Initiative in becoming financially self-sustaining in specialty vegetable and other enterprises. 2002.

1599-41 Oaxaca Community Foundation, Oaxaca, Mexico, $270,000. To improve quality of life of marginalized populations through implementation of multi-sector cooperative sustainable development processes. 2002.

1599-42 Ohio University, Athens, OH, $150,000. To define wastewater and other water infrastructure policy issues and implications for community and economic development through Mayors' Partnership for Progress. 2002.

1599-43 Public Sector Consultants, Lansing, MI, $1,500,000. For continued support to build capacity for land-use decisions in Michigan through implementation of Phase II of People and Land Cluster. 2002.

1599-44 Public Sector Consultants, Lansing, MI, $280,110. For continued support to implement Phase I of People and Land Cluster of program activity in Michigan. 2002.

1599-45 Quitman County Development Organization, Marks, MS, $100,000. To strengthen coalition of Mississippi African-American farmers, toward transition to economically viable and environmentally sustainable production. 2002.

1599-46 Rural Action, Trimble, OH, $150,000. 2002.

1599-47 Shorebank Enterprise Group Pacific, Ilwaco, WA, $691,807. 2002.

1599-48 Small Farmers Association of the Municipality of Valente, Valente, Brazil, $250,000. To teach environmentally friendly technologies. 2002.

1599-49 Soil and Water Conservation Society, Ankeny, IA, $268,396. 2002.

1599-50 Universidad Autonoma de Chapingo, Texcoco, Mexico, $200,000. To support agricultural production among small farmers and rural community leaders and family nutrition through teaching environmentally friendly technologies in Durango and Oaxaca. 2002.

1599-51 University of Wisconsin, Madison, WI, $493,603. To engage faculty and students as partners in multidisciplinary research, learning, and service activities, through establishment of learning community centered around community-owned and managed garden. 2002.

1599-52 University of Zimbabwe, Harare, Zimbabwe, $600,000. For continued support to facilitate implementation of integrated sustainable rural development policy program. 2002.

1599-53 Veld Products Research and Development, Gaborone, Botswana, $198,000. To develop micro-enterprises in Kweneng District, including honey and herbal tea production and guinea fowl rearing. 2002.

1599-54 Washington College, Chestertown, MD, $100,000. To develop Rural Communities Leadership Program for Eastern Shore counties, with focus on planning for sustainable agriculture economy. 2002.

1599-55 Waterkeeper Alliance, White Plains, NY, $20,000. To advance public and consumer education in environmentally sustainable farming. 2002.

1599-56 Watershed Agricultural Council of the New York City Watersheds, Walton, NY, $200,000. 2002.

1599-57 White Earth Land Recovery Project, Ponsford, MN, $55,086. To increase production and distribution of traditional foods to in-need on White Earth Reservation. 2002.

1599-58 Zero Regional Environment Organization, Harare, Zimbabwe, $200,000. For consolidation of Community Organizations Regional Network to serve as platform helping define and implement development initiatives in southern Africa. 2002.

1600
Kellogg's Corporate Citizenship Fund ▼
1 Kellogg Sq.
P.O. Box 3599
Battle Creek, MI 49016-3599 (269) 961-2000
Contact: Timothy R. Knowlton, Dir., Corp. Affairs
FAX: (269) 961-3494

Established in 1994 in MI.
Donor(s): Kellogg Co.
Grantmaker type: Company-sponsored foundation
Financial data (yr. ended 12/31/02): Assets, $6,168,819 (M); expenditures, $4,534,759; qualifying distributions, $4,511,994; giving activities include $3,287,372 for 184 grants (high: $677,150; low: $56; average: $5,000–$25,000) and $962,493 for 450 employee matching gifts.
Purpose and activities: Giving primarily for elementary and higher education, the arts, wildlife preservation and protection, human services, and federated giving programs.

Fields of interest: Arts; Elementary/secondary education; Higher education; Animals/wildlife, preservation/protection; Human services; Federated giving programs.
Types of support: General/operating support; Employee matching gifts.
Limitations: Giving primarily in areas of company operations.
Application information: Application form required for matching gifts program. Application form required.
  Initial approach: Letter
  Deadline(s): None
Officers and Trustees:* George A. Franklin,* Pres.; W.S. Perry,* V.P.; Dawn M. Smith, Secy.; Janice L. Perkins,* Treas.; Timothy S. Knowlton, Exec. Dir.; Celeste A. Clark; Carla R. Cooper; Janet L. Kelly; Edward Moore.
EIN: 383167772

1601
John C. & Nancy G. Kennedy Family Foundation
4070 E. Paris Ave. S.E.
Kentwood, MI 49512-3909

Established in 1993 in MI.
Donor(s): John C. Kennedy, Nancy G. Kennedy.
Grantmaker type: Independent foundation
Financial data (yr. ended 12/31/01): Assets, $514,938 (M); expenditures, $154,000; qualifying distributions, $151,158; giving activities include $151,500 for 19 grants (high: $50,000; low: $1,000).
Fields of interest: Museums; Education; Botanical gardens; Youth development, business; Human services; Federated giving programs; Philanthropy/voluntarism; Christian agencies & churches.
Types of support: General/operating support; Building/renovation; Program development.
Limitations: Applications not accepted. Giving primarily in Grand Rapids, MI. No grants to individuals.
Application information: Contributes only to pre-selected organizations.
Officers: John C. Kennedy, Pres.; Nancy G. Kennedy, V.P.
Director: Stuart F. Cheney.
EIN: 383099643

1602
Keweenaw Community Foundation
City Center, Lower Level
P.O. Box 101
Houghton, MI 49931-0101 (906) 482-9673
Contact: Mary Sue Hyslop, Exec. Dir.
FAX: (906) 482-9679; E-mail: KCF@chartermi.net; URL: http:// www.keweenaw-community-foundation.org; http://www.k-c-f.org

Established in 1994 in MI.
Grantmaker type: Community foundation
Financial data (yr. ended 03/31/03): Assets, $1,725,673 (M); gifts received, $161,719; expenditures, $164,521; giving activities include $102,107 for grants (high: $44,637) and $3,300 for in-kind gifts.
Purpose and activities: The foundation is committed to serving the residents of Houghton and Keweenaw counties, MI, by developing a

permanent endowment to provide stable local funding sources for grants to vital local programs; by increasing charitable giving to a broad range of non-profit organizations; by providing a flexible philanthropic vehicle capable of adapting to changing community needs; and by serving as a catalyst to nurture community leadership. Funding also for skiing.

Fields of interest: Arts; Education; Environment; Health care; Athletics/sports, winter sports; Human services; Community development.

Types of support: General/operating support; Endowments; Program development; Scholarship funds; Matching/challenge support.

Limitations: Giving primarily in Houghton and Keweenaw counties, MI. No grants to individuals, or for membership drives or fundraising events.

Publications: Annual report, Informational brochure, Newsletter.

Application information: Proposals submitted by FAX not accepted. Application form required.

Initial approach: Telephone for application form
Copies of proposal: 1
Deadline(s): Varies
Board meeting date(s): 3rd Wed., bimonthly beginning in Jan.

Officers and Directors:* James Bogan,* Chair.; Douglas Stuart,* Secy.; Mick Hagwell,* Treas.; Mary Sue Hyslop, Exec. Dir.; Betty Anderson; Ronald Helman; Robert Langseth; Philip Musser; Dale Penny; Trina Roulet; John Sullivan; Ann West.

Trustees: Katie Keranen; Paul Ollila; William W. Predebon; Steve Zutter.

Advisory Committee: Jim Boyce; Roger Helman; Jay Rowe.

Number of staff: 2 part-time professional; 2 part-time support.

EIN: 383223079

1603
Klopcic Family Foundation

5400 Patterson Ave. S.E.
Grand Rapids, MI 49512

Established in 1994 in MI.

Donor(s): Donald L. Klopcic, Sr., Elizabeth M. Klopcic.

Grantmaker type: Independent foundation

Financial data (yr. ended 12/31/02): Assets, $2,148,345 (M); expenditures, $105,934; qualifying distributions, $101,884; giving activities include $102,500 for 11 grants (high: $25,000; low: $1,500).

Purpose and activities: Giving primarily for education, youth programs, and recreation.

Fields of interest: Education; Zoos/zoological societies; Health care; Abuse prevention; Athletics/sports, soccer; Youth development.

Limitations: Applications not accepted. Giving limited to MI, with emphasis on Grand Rapids. No grants to individuals.

Application information: Contributes only to pre-selected organizations.

Officers: Donald L. Klopcic, Sr., Pres. and Treas.; Donald L. Klopcic, Jr., V.P.; Keith C. Klopcic, V.P.; Elizabeth M. Klopcic, Secy.

EIN: 383211779

1604
James A. and Faith Knight Foundation

c/o Carol Knight-Drain
180 Little Lake Dr., Ste. 6B
Ann Arbor, MI 48103

Established in 1999 in MI.

Donor(s): James A. McKnight Trust.

Grantmaker type: Independent foundation

Financial data (yr. ended 12/31/01): Assets, $14,906,026 (M); gifts received, $81,106; expenditures, $752,078; qualifying distributions, $644,793; giving activities include $629,260 for 20 grants (high: $90,000; low: $5,000).

Purpose and activities: Giving primarily to a humane society; support also for women's services, including domestic violence prevention.

Fields of interest: Theater; Environmental education; Animal welfare; Domestic violence; Day care; Family services; Women, centers/services; Federated giving programs; Women.

Types of support: General/operating support; Program development.

Limitations: Applications not accepted. Giving primarily in Ann Arbor and Jackson, MI. No grants to individuals.

Application information: Contributes only to pre-selected organizations.

Officers: Carol Knight-Drain, Co-Pres. and Secy.; David Knight, Co-Pres.; Scott Drain, Treas.

EIN: 383465904

1605
Harry B. & Anna Korman Foundation

c/o Larry Zietz
30445 Northwestern Hwy., Ste. 230
Farmington Hills, MI 48334
Contact: Harry B. Korman, Pres.

Established in 1956 in MI.

Donor(s): Harry B. Korman.

Grantmaker type: Independent foundation

Financial data (yr. ended 12/31/02): Assets, $1,740,052 (M); gifts received, $100,000; expenditures, $132,031; qualifying distributions, $99,959; giving activities include $100,000 for 6 grants (high: $50,000; low: $5,000).

Fields of interest: Zoos/zoological societies; Cancer.

Limitations: Giving primarily in Detroit, MI. No grants to individuals.

Application information:
Initial approach: Letter
Deadline(s): None

Officers and Directors:* Harry B. Korman, Pres.; Helen Braverman,* V.P.; Lawrence D. Zietz,* Secy.; Ingeborg Schuetz,* Treas.; Eunice Ring.

EIN: 386078083

1606
The Kresge Foundation ▼

3215 W. Big Beaver Rd.
P.O. Box 3151
Troy, MI 48007-3151 (248) 643-9630
Contact: John E. Marshall III, C.E.O. and Pres.
FAX: (248) 643-0588; URL: http://www.kresge.org

Incorporated in 1924 in MI.

Donor(s): Sebastian S. Kresge.‡

Grantmaker type: Independent foundation

Financial data (yr. ended 12/31/02): Assets, $2,164,478,054 (M); expenditures, $105,289,203; qualifying distributions, $98,974,162; giving activities include $98,583,000 for 160 grants (high: $3,164,000; low: $50,000; average: $200,000–$800,000) and $391,162 for employee matching gifts.

Purpose and activities: Challenge grants only for building construction or renovation projects, major capital equipment or an integrated system at a cost of at least $300,000 (equipment costs may include computer software if applicable) and purchase of real estate; grants generally to tax-exempt institutions involved in higher education (awarding baccalaureate and/or graduate degrees), health and long-term care, human services, science and environment, arts and humanities, and public affairs. Full accreditation is required for higher education and hospital applicants. The foundation does not grant initial funds or total project costs; grants are for a portion of the costs remaining at the time of grant approval. Special Program: The Kresge Foundation will accept applications for a challenge grant program to upgrade and endow scientific equipment and laboratories in colleges and universities, teaching hospitals, medical schools, and research institutions. For details, request a pamphlet entitled "The Kresge Foundation Science Initiative".

Fields of interest: Humanities; Arts; Higher education; Environment; Health care; Human services; Science; Public affairs.

Types of support: Capital campaigns; Building/renovation; Equipment; Land acquisition; Employee matching gifts; Matching/challenge support.

Limitations: No support for religious organizations, community colleges, private foundations, or elementary or secondary schools unless they predominantly serve individuals with physical and/or developmental disabilities. No grants to individuals, or for operating or special project budgets, furnishings, conferences, seminars, church building projects, endowment funds, student aid, scholarships, fellowships, research, debt retirement, completed projects, or general purposes; no loans.

Publications: Application guidelines, Annual report.

Application information: Application form required.

Initial approach: Letter or telephone
Copies of proposal: 1
Deadline(s): None
Board meeting date(s): Mar., June, Sept., and Dec.
Final notification: Generally within 4 to 6 months; decisions announced after each board meeting, applicants notified in writing

Officers and Trustees:* Bruce A. Kresge, M.D.,* Chair.; John E. Marshall III,* C.E.O. and Pres.; Edward M. Hunia, Sr. V.P. and Treas.; Elizabeth C. Sullivan, V.P., Prog. and Adminstration; Lee C. Bollinger; Jane L. Delgado; Steven K. Hamp; Irene Y. Hirano; Robert C. Larson; Katherine A. Lutey; Deborah E. McDowell; David K. Page; Robert D. Storey.

Number of staff: 23 full-time professional.

EIN: 381359217

Recent environmental and animal welfare grants:

1606-1 Brandywine Conservancy, Chadds Ford, PA, $750,000. For challenge grant for renovation and expansion of Brandywine River Museum and renovation and construction of support buildings. 2002.

1606-2 Cheyenne Mountain Zoological Society, Colorado Springs, CO, $650,000. For challenge grant for construction of outdoor exhibit for giraffes, antelopes, and other animals. 2002.

1606-3 Detroit Economic Growth Association, Detroit, MI, $50,000. For challenge grant for initial planning process for comprehensive redevelopment of East Riverfront area along Detroit River. 2002.

1606-4 Detroit Institute of Arts, Detroit, MI, $2,000,000. For challenge grant for comprehensive campaign to renovate museum to address environmental issues; reinstall core galleries to improve visitors' experience; create and expand new programs; and add endowment to stabilize finances. 2002.

1606-5 Detroit Riverfront Conservancy, Detroit, MI, $5,500,000. For challenge grant for planning and constructing RiverWalk, including public green spaces and pedestrian promenades along Detroit River. 2002.

1606-6 Dumb Friends League, Denver, CO, $500,000. For challenge grant for renovation and expansion of facility to provide shelter and medical treatment areas for animals. 2002.

1606-7 Environmental Defense, New York, NY, $1,500,000. For challenge grant for renovation of office facility and purchase of equipment to upgrade information technology systems as part of campaign for capital and program funds. 2002.

1606-8 Girl Scouts of the U.S.A., Golden Plains Council, Wichita, KS, $200,000. For challenge grant for construction of facilities at Starwoods Outdoor Center to provide sports pavilion, lodges, boathouse, crafts building, and science and nature center. 2002.

1606-9 Girl Scouts of the U.S.A., Tarheel Triad Council, Colfax, NC, $650,000. For challenge grant for purchase of property as part of plan to provide facilities for administration, programs, and outdoor environmental education. 2002.

1606-10 John G. Shedd Aquarium, Chicago, IL, $1,000,000. For challenge grant for construction of addition for exhibit featuring diverse coral, reef, and mangrove habitats of Philippines. 2002.

1606-11 Saint Louis Zoo, Saint Louis, MO, $1,500,000. For challenge grant for construction of exhibit for hippopotamus, black rhino, and Amazonian species as part of construction and renovation of facilities. 2002.

1606-12 Save the Bay, Providence, RI, $500,000. For challenge grant for construction of facility for environmental education organization working to protect, restore, and explore Narragansett Bay. 2002.

1606-13 Shaker Lakes Regional Nature Center, Cleveland, OH, $150,000. For challenge grant for renovation and expansion of facility for environmental and nature education programs. 2002.

1607
Patricia A. & William E. LaMothe Foundation

620 Jennings Ln.
Battle Creek, MI 49015 (269) 965-6761
Contact: Patricia A. LaMothe, Pres.

Established in 1986 in MI.
Donor(s): Patricia A. LaMothe, William E. LaMothe, Sydney McManus.
Grantmaker type: Independent foundation
Financial data (yr. ended 12/31/02): Assets, $4,054,347 (M); gifts received, $324,700; expenditures, $339,631; qualifying distributions, $324,678; giving activities include $325,009 for 93 grants (high: $26,100; low: $20).
Purpose and activities: Giving primarily for higher education, Roman Catholic organizations and conservation.
Fields of interest: Education; Natural resources; Health organizations, association; Human services; Roman Catholic agencies & churches.
Limitations: Giving primarily in Battle Creek and Kalamazoo, MI.
Application information:
 Initial approach: Letter
 Deadline(s): None
Officers and Trustees:* Patricia LaMothe,* Pres.; Alexis LaMothe,* V.P.; Sydney McManus,* Secy.; William E. LaMothe,* Treas.
EIN: 386517929

1608
Leelanau Township Community Foundation, Inc.

109 Nagonaba St.
P.O. Box 818
Northport, MI 49670 (231) 386-9000
Contact: Sue Bolde, Exec. Dir.
FAX: (231) 386-9000; E-mail: ltcf@chartermi.net

Incorporated in 1945 in MI.
Donor(s): F.H. Haserot.‡
Grantmaker type: Community foundation
Financial data (yr. ended 12/31/02): Assets, $1,885,007 (M); gifts received, $79,486; expenditures, $222,442; giving activities include $136,672 for 45 grants (high: $22,809; low: $94).
Purpose and activities: The foundation administers a donor-advised fund.
Fields of interest: Arts; Early childhood education; Education; Natural resources; Hospitals (general); Health care; Recreation.
Types of support: Capital campaigns; Building/renovation; Equipment; Endowments; Seed money; Scholarships—to individuals.
Limitations: Giving limited to Leelanau Township, MI.
Publications: Annual report, Newsletter.
Application information: Application form required.
 Initial approach: Telephone
 Copies of proposal: 2
 Deadline(s): 2 weeks prior to board meeting
 Board meeting date(s): Quarterly
Officers and Trustees:* George W. Anderson,* Chair.; Tim Sahs,* Vice-Chair.; Sue Bolde, Exec. Dir.
Number of staff: 1 part-time professional; 1 part-time support.
EIN: 386060138

1609
Jeanne McMurchy Luyckx Trust

41800 W. Eleven Mile Rd., Ste. 115
Novi, MI 48375-2572

Established as a private foundation.
Donor(s): Jeanne McMurchy Luyckx.‡
Grantmaker type: Public charity
Financial data (yr. ended 12/31/01): Revenue, $61,876; assets, $2,263,067 (M); expenditures, $61,876; program services expenses, $60,566; giving activities include $60,566 for 2 grants of $30,283 each.
Purpose and activities: The trust exists for the sole benefit of Michigan Humane Society and Michigan Anti-Cruelty Society.
Fields of interest: Animal welfare.
Types of support: General/operating support.
Limitations: Applications not accepted. Giving limited to Detroit, MI.
Application information: Contributes only to pre-selected organizations; unsolicited requests for funds not considered or acknowledged.
Trustee: David M. Fried.
EIN: 386679502

1610
Anna Main Charitable Trust

c/o Victor R. Hayes and Gerald R. Gase
18263 E. 10 Mile Rd., Ste. A
Roseville, MI 48066-5805

Established in 1998 in MI.
Donor(s): Anna Main.
Grantmaker type: Independent foundation
Financial data (yr. ended 09/30/02): Assets, $5,961,304 (M); expenditures, $227,786; qualifying distributions, $213,431; giving activities include $200,000 for 9 grants (high: $37,500; low: $5,000).
Purpose and activities: Giving primarily for handicapped and disabled children.
Fields of interest: Animal welfare; Athletics/sports, Special Olympics; Children, services; Roman Catholic agencies & churches; Disabled.
Limitations: Applications not accepted. Giving on a national basis, with emphasis on MI, OH, and KY. No grants to individuals.
Application information: Contributes only to pre-selected organizations.
Trustees: Gerald R. Gase; Victor R. Hayes.
EIN: 383336530

1611
Malloure Family Foundation

c/o Donald H. Malloure
22630 N. Nottingham Dr.
Beverly Hills, MI 48025-3523

Donor(s): D.H. Malloure.
Grantmaker type: Independent foundation
Financial data (yr. ended 09/30/02): Assets, $5,736 (M); gifts received, $162,823; expenditures, $159,735; qualifying distributions, $159,735; giving activities include $159,710 for 35 grants (high: $100,000; low: $50).
Purpose and activities: Giving primarily for higher education, as well as for social services, health associations, and federated giving programs.

Fields of interest: Higher education; Animal welfare; Health organizations, association; Human services; Family services; Federated giving programs.
Limitations: Applications not accepted. Giving primarily in MI.
Application information: Contributes only to pre-selected organizations.
Officers and Directors:* Lucille A. Malloure,* Pres.; D.H. Malloure,* Secy.; Susan L. Whitaker.
EIN: 383505870

1612
Oliver Dewey Marcks Foundation
645 Griswold St., Ste. 3180
Detroit, MI 48226-4250
Contact: John M. Chase, Jr., Pres.

Established in 1960.
Donor(s): Eula D. Marcks,‡ Oliver Dewey Marcks.‡
Grantmaker type: Independent foundation
Financial data (yr. ended 12/31/02): Assets, $9,922,231 (M); expenditures, $659,526; qualifying distributions, $628,091; giving activities include $597,140 for 32 grants (high: $119,640; low: $5,000; average: $5,000–$119,640).
Fields of interest: Arts; Education; Natural resources; Animal welfare.
Types of support: General/operating support; Program development.
Limitations: Giving limited to Detroit, MI, and surrounding communities. No grants to individuals.
Publications: Application guidelines.
Application information: Application form required.
  Initial approach: Letter, including a 1-page summary
  Copies of proposal: 4
  Board meeting date(s): May, July and Oct.
Officers and Board Members:* John M. Chase, Jr.,* Pres.; Marion Valentine,* Secy.; Michael J. Predhomme,* Treas.
Number of staff: None.
EIN: 386081311

1613
Edward & Helen Mardigian Foundation
c/o Comerica Bank
P.O. Box 75000, MC 3302
Detroit, MI 48275-3302
Contact: Edward Mardigian, Jr.
Application address: 1400 N. Woodward Ave., Ste. 225, Bloomfield Hills, MI 48304

Incorporated in 1955 in MI.
Donor(s): Edward S. Mardigian,‡ Helen Mardigian, Arman Mardigian.‡
Grantmaker type: Independent foundation
Financial data (yr. ended 12/31/02): Assets, $17,735,176 (M); gifts received, $350,000; expenditures, $997,147; qualifying distributions, $986,155; giving activities include $957,610 for 41 grants (high: $335,000; low: $100).
Purpose and activities: Giving primarily for Armenian organizations and churches in the U.S.; funding also for children, youth and social services, and health associations.
Fields of interest: Higher education; Zoos/zoological societies; Health organizations,

association; Human services; Children/youth, services; Christian agencies & churches; Orthodox Catholic agencies & churches; Minorities.
Limitations: Giving primarily in MI. No grants to individuals.
Application information:
  Initial approach: Letter
  Deadline(s): None
Officers: Helen Mardigian, Pres. and Secy.; Edward S. Mardigian, V.P. and Treas.
Directors: Robert D. Mardigian; Marilynn Varbedian.
Number of staff: None.
EIN: 386048886

1614
Mariel Foundation
P.O. Box 6461
Traverse City, MI 49696-6461

Established in 1997 in MI.
Donor(s): Carolyn T. Hoagland, James H. Hoagland, John T. Hoagland, Nancy L. Hoagland, Anne H. Magoun.
Grantmaker type: Independent foundation
Financial data (yr. ended 09/30/02): Assets, $2,048,745 (M); expenditures, $148,672; qualifying distributions, $134,281; giving activities include $132,037 for 33 grants (high: $18,000; low: $319).
Purpose and activities: Giving for general charitable giving.
Fields of interest: Arts; Environment; General charitable giving.
Limitations: Applications not accepted. Giving on a national basis. No grants to individuals.
Application information: Contributes only to pre-selected organizations.
Directors: Carolyn T. Hoagland; James H. Hoagland; John H. Hoagland; John T. Hoagland; Nancy L. Hoagland; Anne H. Magoun.
EIN: 383334050

1615
The Meijer Foundation ▼
P.O. Box 3636
Grand Rapids, MI 49501-3636

Established in 1990 in MI.
Donor(s): Frederik G.H. Meijer, Meijer, Inc.
Grantmaker type: Independent foundation
Financial data (yr. ended 09/30/02): Assets, $73,627,944 (M); gifts received, $9,000,000; expenditures, $7,092,250; qualifying distributions, $6,601,139; giving activities include $6,600,259 for 32 grants (high: $1,053,081; low: $1,690; average: $100,000–$400,000).
Purpose and activities: Giving primarily to a horticultural society, and to a charitable trust; funding also for community foundations and an art museum. The foundation administers a donor-advised fund.
Fields of interest: Museums (art); Botanical gardens; Horticulture/garden clubs; Foundations (community).
Limitations: Applications not accepted. Giving primarily in Grand Rapids, MI, some giving also in Greenville, MI. No grants to individuals.
Application information: Contributes only to pre-selected organizations.

Trustee: Frederik G.H. Meijer.
EIN: 386575227
Recent environmental and animal welfare grants:
1615-1 Frederik Meijer Charitable Trust, Grand Rapids, MI, $7,834,301. 2001.
1615-2 Frederik Meijer Gardens and Sculpture Park, Grand Rapids, MI, $7,871,206. For sculptures and other projects. 2001.
1615-3 Michigan Botanic Garden Foundation, Grand Rapids, MI, $477,908. For sculptures and other projects. 2001.

1616
Michigan Automotive Compressor, Inc. Corporate Giving Program
2400 N. Dearing Rd.
Parma, MI 49269 (517) 531-5646
Contact: Cheryl R. Norey, Community Rels. Coord.
FAX: (517) 531-1711; E-mail: noreyc@michauto.com

Grantmaker type: Corporate giving program
Purpose and activities: Michigan Automotive Compressor makes charitable contributions to nonprofit organizations involved with K-12 education and environmental education. Support is given primarily in the Parma, Michigan, area.
Fields of interest: Elementary/secondary education; Environmental education.
Types of support: General/operating support; Annual campaigns; Capital campaigns; Emergency funds; Program development; Publication; Scholarship funds; Employee volunteer services; In-kind gifts.
Limitations: Giving primarily in the Parma, MI, area.
Application information: The Community Relations Department handles giving. A contributions committee reviews all requests. Application form not required.
  Initial approach: Proposal to headquarters
  Copies of proposal: 1
  Board meeting date(s): Monthly
  Final notification: Following review
Number of staff: 1 part-time professional.

1617
Midland Area Community Foundation
(formerly Midland Foundation)
109 E. Main St.
P.O. Box 289
Midland, MI 48640 (989) 839-9661
Contact: Denise K. Spencer, C.E.O. & Pres.
FAX: (989) 839-9907; E-mail: info@midlandfoundation.com; URL: http://www.midlandfoundation.com/

Established in 1973 in MI.
Grantmaker type: Community foundation
Financial data (yr. ended 12/31/02): Assets, $33,826,858 (M); gifts received, $2,466,786; expenditures, $1,872,468; giving activities include $1,032,842 for grants and $1,000 for loans to individuals.
Purpose and activities: Supporting the charitable, cultural, educational, and scientific needs of the Midland County, Michigan, area. The foundation administers a donor-advised fund.

Fields of interest: Humanities; Arts; Adult/continuing education; Education; Energy; Human services; Youth, services; Community development.

Types of support: Building/renovation; Equipment; Seed money; Scholarship funds; Technical assistance; Consulting services; Matching/challenge support; Student loans—to individuals.

Limitations: Giving generally restricted to organizations within and serving Midland County, MI. No grants to individuals (except for student loans), or for operating budgets, continuing support, annual campaigns, deficit financing, or endowment funds.

Publications: Application guidelines, Annual report, Grants list, Newsletter.

Application information: Application form required.

> *Initial approach:* Telephone or letter requesting guidelines
> *Copies of proposal:* 1
> *Deadline(s):* 2 weeks before grants committee meeting
> *Board meeting date(s):* Feb., May, Aug., Nov., and as needed
> *Final notification:* 1 month

Officers and Trustees:* Donna Rapp,* Chair.; Carole Dennings, Vice-Chair.; Denise K. Spencer, C.E.O. and Pres.; Nicole Lomas, V.P. and C.F.O.; Sheri Constantin,* Secy.; Arthur Frock, Treas.; Linda Cline; Maureen Donken; Gordon Hall; Cliff Miles; Pat Naegele; Cindy Newman; Linda Owen; John Reder; Brian Rodgers; James Secor; Chris Velasquez.

Number of staff: 3 full-time professional; 2 full-time support.

EIN: 382023395

1618
The Mosaic Foundation of R. & P. Heydon
2394 Winewood St.
P.O. Box 7801
Ann Arbor, MI   48107-7801
Contact: Peter N. Heydon, Dir.

Established in 1990 in MI.

Donor(s): Kenneth F. Montgomery, Peter N. Heydon, Henrietta M. Heydon.

Grantmaker type: Independent foundation

Financial data (yr. ended 12/31/00): Assets, $3,094,563 (M); gifts received, $5,226; expenditures, $333,906; qualifying distributions, $354,744; giving activities include $293,238 for grants and $61,506 for 1 loan/program-related investment.

Purpose and activities: Giving primarily for the arts and education.

Fields of interest: Radio; Museums; Arts; Elementary/secondary education; Higher education; Environment; Animals/wildlife; Human services.

Limitations: Applications not accepted. Giving in the U.S., with emphasis on MI. No grants to individuals.

Application information: Contributes only to pre-selected organizations.

Directors: James R. Beuche; Henrietta M. Heydon; Peter N. Heydon.

EIN: 382910797

1619
Charles Stewart Mott Foundation ▼
Mott Foundation Bldg.
503 S. Saginaw St., Ste. 1200
Flint, MI   48502-1851   (810) 238-5651
Contact: Office of Proposal Entry
FAX: (810) 766-1753; *E-mail:* publications@mott.org or info@mott.org; *URL:* http://www.mott.org

Incorporated in 1926 in MI.

Donor(s): Charles Stewart Mott,‡ and family.

Grantmaker type: Independent foundation

Financial data (yr. ended 12/31/02): Assets, $2,011,395,991 (M); expenditures, $125,376,259; qualifying distributions, $108,659,450; giving activities include $108,659,450 for grants.

Purpose and activities: To support efforts that promote a just, equitable and sustainable society in the areas of civil society, the environment, and poverty. The foundation makes grants for a variety of purposes within these program areas, including: philanthropy and voluntarism; assisting emerging civil societies in Central/Eastern Europe, Russia and South Africa; conservation of fresh water ecosystems in North America; reform of international finance and trade; improving the outcome for children, youth and families at risk of persistent poverty; education and neighborhood and economic development. The foundation also makes grants to strengthen the capacity of local institutions in its home community of Flint, Michigan.

Fields of interest: Education; Environment, pollution control; Natural resources; Human services; Children, services; Child development, services; Family services, parent education; Race/intergroup relations; Economic development; Urban/community development; Rural development; Community development; Voluntarism promotion; Leadership development; Minorities; Economically disadvantaged.

International interests: Canada; Europe; Eastern Europe; Russia; South Africa; Latin America.

Types of support: General/operating support; Continuing support; Program development; Conferences/seminars; Seed money; Technical assistance; Program evaluation; Employee matching gifts; Matching/challenge support.

Limitations: Giving nationally and to emerging countries in Central and Eastern Europe, Russia, and South Africa. No support for religious organizations for religious purposes. No grants to individuals, or generally for building or endowment funds, research, scholarships, or fellowships.

Publications: Annual report (including application guidelines), Financial statement, Grants list, Informational brochure (including application guidelines), Newsletter, Occasional report, Program policy statement.

Application information: Applicants strongly encouraged to submit proposals during first quarter of the year. Application form not required.

> *Initial approach:* Letter of inquiry or proposal
> *Copies of proposal:* 1
> *Deadline(s):* None; grants are determined by Sept. 30th of any given year
> *Board meeting date(s):* Mar., June, Sept., and Dec.

Final notification: 60 to 90 days

Officers and Trustees:* William S. White,* Chair., C.E.O., and Pres.; William H. Piper,* Vice-Chair.; Phillip H. Peters, V.P., Admin. Group, Secy., and Treas.; Robert E. Swaney, Jr., V.P., Investments and C.I.O.; Gavin Clabaugh, V.P., Inf. Svcs.; Marilyn S. LeFeber, V.P., Comm.; Maureen H. Smyth, V.P., Progs.; A. Marshall Acuff, Jr.; Rushworth M. Kidder; Tiffany W. Lovett; Webb F. Martin; Olivia P. Maynard; John Morning; Maryanne Mott; Douglas X. Patino; John W. Porter; Marise M.M. Stewart; Claire M. White.

Number of staff: 69 full-time professional; 1 part-time professional; 31 full-time support; 2 part-time support.

EIN: 381211227

Recent environmental and animal welfare grants:

1619-1 ActionAid, London, England, $250,000. For continued support for Bretton Woods Project, which will assess current communication approaches of organizations working in many countries on reform of international financial institutions. 2002.

1619-2 Agir ici, Paris, France, $240,000. For continued support of work to reform international financial institutions as it relates to sustainable development. 2002.

1619-3 Alabama Rivers Alliance, Birmingham, AL, $225,000. For continued general support. 2002.

1619-4 Altarum Institute, Ann Arbor, MI, $400,000. For Automotive Communities Program. 2002.

1619-5 American Lands Alliance, DC, $150,000. For continued support for project, Protecting Global Forests Through International Trade and Investment Policy Reform. 2002.

1619-6 Arab Community Center for Economic and Social Services (ACCESS), Dearborn, MI, $200,090. For conference, Building Capacity Through Diversity. 2002.

1619-7 Aspen Institute, DC, $60,000. For continued support for project, Dialogue on Dams and Rivers. 2002.

1619-8 Bellagio Forum for Sustainable Development, Osnabruck, Germany, $30,000. For general support. 2002.

1619-9 Berne Declaration, Zurich, Switzerland, $200,000. For continued support for Sustainable Financial Relations Project, multilateral development bank reform efforts. 2002.

1619-10 Biodiversity Project, Madison, WI, $200,000. For continued general support. 2002.

1619-11 Border Ecology Project, Bisbee, AZ, $50,000. For Hemispheric Trade, Investment, and Integration Project. 2002.

1619-12 Cahaba River Society, Birmingham, AL, $120,000. For general support. 2002.

1619-13 Canadian Environmental Law Association, Toronto, Canada, $200,000. For continued support for Environment, Development and Trade Project, effort to raise public awareness about environmental impacts of global and regional economic integration. 2002.

1619-14 Carnegie Endowment for International Peace, DC, $300,000. For conferences and workshops to support efforts to engage U.S. policymakers on environment and development issues related to the Free Trade Area of the Americas agreement. 2002.

1619-15 Center for Economic and Policy Research, DC, $75,000. For continued support for Multilateral Economic Institutions and Sustainable Development, effort to incorporate economic analyses in proposals for environmental reform of international finance and trade institutions. 2002.

1619-16 Center for Environmental Public Advocacy, Ponicka Huta, Slovakia, $77,000. For continued general support. 2002.

1619-17 Center for International Environmental Law, DC, $250,000. For programs to reform global economic institutions including promoting greater accountability and stronger environmental policies in international trade law and institutions, reducing environmental and social impacts of the World Bank and other international financial institutions, and promoting increased corporate accountability and disclosure for private investment in developing countries. 2002.

1619-18 Center of Concern, DC, $150,000. For efforts to promote sustainable development in international trade. 2002.

1619-19 Center of Concern, DC, $25,000. For continued support for leadership of Global Financial Architecture Coalition which works to enable nongovernmental organization members to understand official proposals to reform global financial system in wake of 1998 Asian financial crisis, evaluate impact of these proposals, develop alternative proposals, share information and research, and develop strategies to promote implementation of alternative policies. 2002.

1619-20 Centro Mexicano de Derecho Ambiental, Mexico City, Mexico, $50,000. For continued support for Trade and Environment Program, effort to broaden understanding of trade and environment issues by key stakeholders within Mexico so they may begin to build positive national agenda related to those issues and to collaborate with organizations in other countries to develop and promote Sustainable Americas proposal that could be taken up by negotiators working to create hemispheric Free Trade Area of the Americas. 2002.

1619-21 Collins Center for Public Policy, Miami, FL, $50,000. For continued support for Funders' Network for Smart Growth and Livable Communities, resource and focal point for foundations, nonprofit organizations, and other partners working to solve environmental, social, and economic problems created by suburban sprawl and urban disinvestment. 2002.

1619-22 Columbia University, Initiative for Policy Dialogue, New York, NY, $200,000. For effort to create Environmental Economics Task Force to determine environmental impact of economic policies and provide developing countries with viable and environmentally sound alternatives for development. 2002.

1619-23 Conservation Fund, Arlington, VA, $2,000,000. For continued support of Great Lakes Revolving Loan Fund designed to provide short-term financing critical to conservation of coastal and freshwater sites

of exceptional ecological significance in the U.S. portion of the Great Lakes basin. Loans from fund will be used for purchase of property as well as for purchase of conservation easements. 2002.

1619-24 Consumers Choice Council, DC, $275,000. To help nongovernmental organizations and under-represented parts of government prepare for Fifth World Trade Organization (WTO) ministerial meeting. 2002.

1619-25 Council of Great Lakes Governors, Chicago, IL, $150,000. For Annex 2001 Stakeholder Engagement Process, convocation to begin negotiation and contract for targeted legal advice and policy analysis as it applies to new and uniform water management system for Great Lakes Basin. 2002.

1619-26 Czech Environmental Partnership Foundation, Brno, Czech Republic, $85,000. For community development assistance. 2002.

1619-27 Czech Union for Nature Conservation, Prague, Czech Republic, $35,000. For membership development. 2002.

1619-28 Earthjustice Legal Defense Fund, Oakland, CA, $180,000. For International Program, designed to make international trade institutions more responsive to environmental concerns and more effective in promoting sustainable development. 2002.

1619-29 Ecologic Club of Transylvania, Cluj, Romania, $49,980. To support rural sustainable development in Romania. 2002.

1619-30 Ecological Foundation, Corner House Trade, Investment and Environment Project, Bodmin, England, $25,000. For continued support toward research of environmental impacts of United Kingdom's export credit guarantees in developing countries and work with Foundation grantees in other industrial countries to promote adoption of common environmental standards for export credit agencies and provide analytical support and strategy development for developing country organizations working to promote environmental reform of the multilateral development banks, the World Trade Organization, and privately financed infrastructure development. 2002.

1619-31 Ednannia: Initiative Center to Support Social Action, Path to the Future, Kiev, Ukraine, $200,000. To build capacity, through regranting efforts, of grassroots Ukrainian nongovernmental organizations addressing local environmental and social concerns. 2002.

1619-32 Eletfa Environmental Protection Association, Eger, Hungary, $85,000. For work to strengthen nongovernmental organization (NGO) coalitions. 2002.

1619-33 Environmental Advocates, Albany, NY, $90,000. For Securing New York's Water Future. 2002.

1619-34 Environmental Law Alliance Worldwide (E-LAW), Eugene, Oregon, $250,000. For general support. 2002.

1619-35 Environmental Management and Law Association, Budapest, Hungary, $83,362. To review and improve legal framework of Hungarian nongovernmental sector and to highlight importance of sector-wide

discussions around key issues for Hungarian nongovernmental organizations. 2002.

1619-36 Environmental Support Center, DC, $200,000. For continued support for State Environmental Leadership Program. 2002.

1619-37 EURONATURA, Centre for Environmental Law and Sustainable Development, ECA-Iberia Campaign, Lisbon, Portugal, $100,000. To encourage Spanish and Portuguese export credit agencies to require environmental impact assessments of all proposed projects, disclose relevant information, and adopt environmental and social criteria for their project financing. ECAs are public or parastatal agencies that provide government-backed loans, guarantees and insurance to corporations from their home countries that seek to do business overseas in developing countries and emerging markets. 2002.

1619-38 European Natural Heritage Fund, Bonn, Germany, $80,000. For continued support for Private Finance Institutions Reform Campaign. 2002.

1619-39 Federation of Ontario Naturalists, Don Mills, Canada, $280,000. Toward continued participation in project entitled, New Opportunities: Realizing the Potential of the Forest Accord. 2002.

1619-40 Finnish Association for Nature Conservation, Helsinki, Finland, $150,000. For Finnish campaign to reform export credit agencies. 2002.

1619-41 Foundation for International Environmental Law and Development, London, England, $80,000. For Trade, Investment and Sustainable Development Program. 2002.

1619-42 Friends of the Earth, DC, $450,000. For Changing the Rules of the Global Economy, effort to reform international financial institutions and trade policies in order to preserve natural environment. 2002.

1619-43 Friends of the Earth Japan, Tokyo, Japan, $165,000. Toward reform of Japanese Export Credit Agencies. 2002.

1619-44 Genesee, County of, Flint, MI, $891,000. For Abandoned Property and Land Re-Use Plan, inter-governmental land re-use plan for Flint and Genesee County as income generating initiative. 2002.

1619-45 Georgetown University, Environmental Law and Policy Institute, DC, $45,000. For research project, Emerging International Laws of Regulatory Takings, which will provide academic analysis and research on implications for U.S. domestic law of international trade agreements, focusing on ways in which new international agreements are diverging from established domestic U.S. law. 2002.

1619-46 Georgia Center for Law in the Public Interest, Atlanta, GA, $60,000. For general support. 2002.

1619-47 Global Greengrants Fund, Boulder, CO, $500,000. For IFI Small Grants Fund, effort to strengthen global networks of nongovernmental organizations working to reform international financial institutions. 2002.

1619-48 Global Reporting Initiative, Amsterdam, Netherlands, $1,000,000. For general support. 2002.

1619-49 GLOBE USA, DC, $70,000. For continued support for efforts to educate legislators about environmental impacts of international economic policy decisions. 2002.

1619-50 GLOBE USA, DC, $60,000. To provide training and information to legislators from various countries in preparation for World Summit on Sustainable Development. 2002.

1619-51 Great Lakes United, Buffalo, NY, $300,000. For general support. 2002.

1619-52 Great Lakes United, Buffalo, NY, $38,000. For general support. 2002.

1619-53 Greenpeace Russia, Moscow, Russia, $49,000. For continued support to encourage development of philanthropy in Russia through market research, development of fundraising strategies and dissemination of information to Russian nongovernmental organizations. 2002.

1619-54 Gulf Restoration Network, New Orleans, LA, $40,000. For continued general support. 2002.

1619-55 Institute for Agriculture and Trade Policy, Minneapolis, MN, $300,000. For project, Strengthening the Voice of Civil Society in the Global Arena, effort to help nongovernmental organizations and local governments make environmental and social issues part of the international trade agenda. 2002.

1619-56 Institute for International Economics, DC, $300,000. For follow-up studies, A Policy Agenda for Economic Progress in Latin America, and NAFTA: An Eight-Year Appraisal, dealing with previous work in Latin America on economic liberalization policies, including trade (as it applies to environmental issues). 2002.

1619-57 Institute for Policy Studies, DC, $30,000. For conference and other work on sustainable energy and alternative global economic policies. 2002.

1619-58 Institute for Sustainable Communities, Montpelier, VT, $112,001. For project, Strengthening Community School Partnerships in Ukraine, effort to facilitate development of community school partnerships in two demonstration communities in Ukraine. 2002.

1619-59 Institute for Sustainable Development, Warsaw, Poland, $50,000. For general support. 2002.

1619-60 Institute for Washingtons Future, Renton, WA, $200,000. For Online Progressive Empowerment Network, organizing campaign that will link community organizing, economic development, technology access, and public policy change. 2002.

1619-61 Inter Press Service, Rome, Italy, $200,000. To hire global financial correspondent as way to increase coverage of international financial institutions and their impacts on the environment and people. 2002.

1619-62 InterAction/American Council for Voluntary International Action, DC, $25,350. To improve Inter-American Development Bank's performance on environmental and social issues. 2002.

1619-63 International Institute for Sustainable Development (IISD), Winnipeg, Canada, $70,000. For Investment Policy Workshops Project. 2002.

1619-64 International Rivers Network, Berkeley, CA, $300,000. For continued support for Strategic Opportunities for Living Rivers Project, effort to undertake follow-up work on issues related to dam construction projects in developing countries including study of the role of export credit agencies and other financial intermediaries in financing dam construction projects and publication of Citizens Guide to the World Commission on Dams and to engage in formal follow-up to World Commission on Dams. 2002.

1619-65 Justice and Witness Ministries of the United Church of Christ, DC, $50,000. To support youth involvement at National People of Color Environmental Leadership Summit. 2002.

1619-66 Kalamazoo College, Center for Policy Studies, Kalamazoo, MI, $40,000. For research project, External Liberalization, Dollarization and the Environment: Brazil, Ecuador and Mexico, study of environmental consequences of development strategy in these three countries with objective of creating ecologically friendly alternatives to structural adjustment programs, and introducing environmental macroeconomics as analysis of environmental issues in contrast to standard cost-benefit analysis on micro level. 2002.

1619-67 Kentucky Waterways Alliance, Munfordville, KY, $150,000. For general support. 2002.

1619-68 La Piana Associates, Piedmont, CA, $100,000. For project to assess NGO capacity, providing information on current organizational capacity and capacity-building needs of nonprofit organizations focused on freshwater ecosystem conservation in the Great Lakes basin and southeastern U.S. 2002.

1619-69 Lake Michigan Federation, Chicago, IL, $225,000. For continued general support. 2002.

1619-70 Legal Environmental Assistance Foundation (LEAF), Tallahassee, FL, $100,000. For continued support for Alabama Rivers Ecosystem Project. 2002.

1619-71 Mani Tese, Milan, Italy, $240,000. Toward information clearinghouse on multilateral development bank reform issues in Italy (as they relate to sustainable development) as part of Multilateral Development Bank (MDB) and Export Credit Agency (ECA) Reform Campaign. 2002.

1619-72 Michigan Suburbs Alliance, Ferndale, MI, $60,000. Toward development of Michigan Suburbs Alliance, environmental effort to advance policy solutions that will benefit established municipalities. 2002.

1619-73 Minnesota Environmental Partnership, Saint Paul, MN, $120,000. For general support. 2002.

1619-74 Mvula Trust, Johannesburg, South Africa, $150,000. For pilot project, Community-Based Organizations, Gender and Water Provision, effort to focus on developing partnerships between local government (which is responsible for delivery of water services) and local communities on water provision. 2002.

1619-75 NAACP, Detroit Branch, Detroit, MI, $190,000. For Addressing Michigan's Challenges to Regionalism Program, initiative to become more involved in growing discussion of growth management policies in Michigan by sponsoring research studies, conducting educational outreach in state, and communicating with members of state legislature, particularly members of Michigan Legislative Black Caucus. 2002.

1619-76 National Fish and Wildlife Foundation, DC, $225,000. For Lower Mississippi River Capacity Building Project. 2002.

1619-77 National Wildlife Federation, Reston, VA, $300,000. For continued support for initiative, Sustaining the Great Lakes Project, which provides efforts to improve Great Lakes water quality through policy reform and demonstation projects including reducing and eliminating toxic fallout. 2002.

1619-78 National Wildlife Federation, Reston, VA, $55,000. For continued support for efforts to improve Great Lakes water quality through policy reform and demonstation projects including reducing and eliminating toxic fallout. 2002.

1619-79 National Wildlife Federation, Reston, VA, $32,141. For Quantum Leap Project, training and capacity-building initiative to assist environmental groups in making leap beyond past efforts to influence development finance decisions of governments and multilateral lenders and develop new approaches to influence commercial banks and other international private sector institutions. Federation is in process of transitioning Project to another organization. Grant will assist with transitional activities as well as with program planning on international finance issues. 2002.

1619-80 Natural Resources Defense Council, New York, NY, $300,000. For continued support for Clean Water Network. 2002.

1619-81 Nature Conservancy, Arlington, VA, $300,000. For continued support for Advancing Freshwater Ecosystem Conservation in Priority Regions Initiative. 2002.

1619-82 North Carolina Agricultural Foundation, Natural Resources Leadership Institute, Raleigh, NC, $45,680. To conduct leadership development program to build trust, skills and shared knowledge among group of shareholders working for agreement on terms of new licenses for hydropower relicensing along the Catawba-Wateree river system in the Carolinas. 2002.

1619-83 Northeast-Midwest Institute, Great Lakes Washington Program, DC, $300,000. For work on policy issues including key appropriations to benefit the Great Lakes, water export and diversion, ecosystem restoration, Farm Bill re-authorization, and other key policy issues as they become apparent. 2002.

1619-84 Northeast-Midwest Institute, Great Lakes Washington Program, DC, $50,000. For continued support for work on policy issues including key appropriations to benefit the Great Lakes, water export and diversion, ecosystem restoration, Farm Bill re-authorization, and other key policy issues as they become apparent. 2002.

MICHIGAN—Mount Pleasant—1620

1619-85 Ohio Environmental Council, Columbus, OH, $50,000. For continued support for Lake Erie Water Quality Standards Project. 2002.

1619-86 Outward Bound Romania, Targu Mures, Romania, $35,000. For Youth Leadership Program. 2002.

1619-87 Peregrine Environmental Consulting, Takoma Park, MD, $75,000. For strategic review of International Export Credit Agencies (ECA) Reform Campaign. 2002.

1619-88 River Network, Portland, Oregon, $10,000. Toward capacity-building technical assistance services for citizen groups working for freshwater protection. 2002.

1619-89 Rockefeller Family Fund, New York, NY, $100,000. For Environmental Grantmakers Association and Funders Network on Trade and Globalization. 2002.

1619-90 Silver Water Retreat, Todd, NC, $30,000. For Entrepreneurial Skills Summer Youth Program. 2002.

1619-91 South Carolina Coastal Conservation League, Charleston, SC, $150,000. Toward efforts to carry out Protecting Freshwater Ecosystems project designed to increase public involvement in wetlands and habitat protection, slow down sprawl, and prevent pollution and physical alteration of state's aquatic systems. 2002.

1619-92 Southern Environmental Law Center, Charlottesville, VA, $350,000. For continued support for Water Quality Protection Initiative, effort to provide leadership on water quality and quantity policy issues of importance to health of freshwater ecosystems. 2002.

1619-93 Stichting Fern, Moreton-in-Marsh, England, $100,000. For EU Campaign to Reform Export Credit Agencies, effort to more actively assess work of export credit agencies throughout Europe, including research and providing input to possible reforms of Europe Investment Fund, establishing coordination strategy with reform efforts in European countries and with broader international export credit reform network. 2002.

1619-94 Texas Center for Policy Studies, Austin, TX, $50,000. For Texas/Mexico Border Environment Project which will monitor and disseminate information on U.S./Mexico border institutions created as a result of North American Free Trade Agreement, assess environmental and public health impacts of economic integration and trade along the border and provide small grants to Mexican nongovernmental organizations and community leaders working on environmental issues. 2002.

1619-95 Tides Center, San Francisco, CA, $200,000. For work by Asian Pacific Environmental Exchange (APEX) to identify need for ecological economics within organization campaigns, conduct seminars on applying ecological economics to an organization's reform work, link ecological economists to work with organizations on their campaign issues, and increase awareness on issues of ecological economics and international finance and trade. 2002.

1619-96 Tides Center, San Francisco, CA, $15,000. For Globalization Challenge Initiative, which will provide capacity-building services to academic and policy reform groups, including energy and environmental policy organizations, in order to broaden informed engagement in policymaking processes. 2002.

1619-97 Tip of the Mitt Watershed Council, Petoskey, MI, $15,000. For Great Lakes Aquatic Habitat Network and Fund, organization providing information and financial support to grassroots citizen initiatives working to protect and restore Great Lakes shorelines, inland lakes, rivers, wetlands, and other aquatic habitats in the Great Lakes Basin. 2002.

1619-98 Trout Unlimited, Arlington, VA, $175,000. To strengthen organizational capacity of state councils in Great Lakes and Southeastern regions, with particular emphasis on states of Michigan, Wisconsin, North Carolina, and Tennessee as part of New Directions in Coldwater Conservation Initiative. 2002.

1619-99 University of Maryland, College of Life Sciences, Department of Entomology, College Park, MD, $150,000. To evaluate practice of stream restoration and identify effective restoration techniques by building restoration database for stream ecosystems. 2002.

1619-100 University of Maryland Foundation, School of Public Affairs, Adelphi, MD, $100,000. For continued support for Supporting Tomorrows Leaders in Ecological Economics, project to enable two students to study with leader in the field of ecological economics. 2002.

1619-101 University of Miami, Coral Gables, FL, $200,000. To support environmental assessment and capacity building for Free Trade Area of the Americas Agreement. 2002.

1619-102 University of Michigan, Center for Applied Environmental Research, Flint, MI, $346,875. For study entitled, Build the Capacity to Respond to the Challenges of Suburban Sprawl in Genesee County, effort to explore land-use and sprawl issues in the Flint area. 2002.

1619-103 Upstate Forever, Greenville, SC, $50,000. For general support. 2002.

1619-104 Urgewald, Sassenberg, Germany, $160,000. For continued support to work for reform of Germany's multilateral aid policies and Export Credit Agencies (ECAs). 2002.

1619-105 Uruguayan Study Center of Appropriate Technologies, Montevideo, Uruguay, $120,000. For continued support for project, Democratizing Environmental Components of Latin American Integration, effort to engage citizens' groups, environmental organizations, government officials and other stakeholders in South America in environmental aspects of regional economic integration processes. 2002.

1619-106 Wisconsin Wetlands Association, Madison, WI, $135,000. For continued general support. 2002.

1619-107 Wisconsins Environmental Decade Institute, Madison, WI, $120,000. For initiative, Managing Water Resources for Today and Tomorrow, which will encourage Wisconsin environmental community's participation in Annex 2001 process, which is an amendment to Great Lakes Charter outlining new regional approach to water management. 2002.

1619-108 World Economy, Ecology and Development Association, Bonn, Germany, $200,000. For continued support for efforts to promote environmental reform of multilateral development bank polices and operations. 2002.

1619-109 World Resources Institute, DC, $450,000. To promote transparency and accountability in forest sector through Global Forest Watch. 2002.

1619-110 World Resources Institute, DC, $300,000. For World Summit on Sustainable Development with goal of promoting improved environmental governance at national and international levels. 2002.

1619-111 World Wildlife Fund/Conservation Foundation, DC, $171,000. For Southeastern Rivers and Streams Support Fund. 2002.

1620
Mount Pleasant Area Community Foundation
(formerly Mount Pleasant Community Foundation)
113 W. Broadway
P.O. Box 1283
Mount Pleasant, MI 48804-1283
(989) 773-7322
Contact: Michelle L. Gostomski, Exec. Dir., Grant Review Comm.
FAX: (989) 773-1517; E-mail: mgostomski@impact.org; URL: http://www.mpacf.org

Established in 1990 in MI.
Grantmaker type: Community foundation
Financial data (yr. ended 12/31/02): Assets, $2,986,794 (M); gifts received, $562,961; expenditures, $781,211; giving activities include $230,356 for grants.
Purpose and activities: Giving to community and civic organizations, awarding education scholarships and loans, and giving to youth and senior services. The foundation administers a donor-advised fund.
Fields of interest: Education, research; Education; Environment; Health care; Youth development; Human services.
Types of support: Capital campaigns; Equipment; Endowments; Emergency funds; Program development; Conferences/seminars; Publication; Seed money; Scholarship funds; Research; Technical assistance; Scholarships—to individuals; Matching/challenge support; Student loans—to individuals.
Limitations: Giving limited to Isabella County, MI. No support for political campaigns, or to groups seeking to influence legislature of any governmental body, or to promote religious teaching of any kind. No grants to individuals (except for scholarships).
Publications: Application guidelines, Annual report, Financial statement, Grants list, Informational brochure, Newsletter.
Application information: Complete guidelines available on Web site. Application form required.
Initial approach: Letter
Board meeting date(s): Bimonthly
Final notification: Within 1 week of board meeting
Officers and Trustees:* Robert A. Janson,* Pres.; Shirley Martin Decker,* V.P.; Kay A. Smith,*

Secy.; Susan K. Murray,* Treas.; John J. Bradac;
Mary Ann Breuer; Mark Cwiek; Doug Dodge;
Kim Ellertson; Jim Goodrich; Cindy E. Hales;
Dykstra Heinze; Chuck Hubscher; Eric R. Janes;
Dave Keilitz; Steve Martineau; Diane Morey;
Michael Rao; Dennis Riley; W. Sidney Smith;
Judith Sullivan; Robert L. Wheeler.
Number of staff: 1 full-time professional; 1
part-time support.
EIN: 382951873

1621
MPS Foundation
39533 Woodward Ave.
Bloomfield Hills, MI 48304

Established in 1997 in MI.
Grantmaker type: Independent foundation
Financial data (yr. ended 06/30/02): Assets,
$2,356,532 (M); expenditures, $193,593;
qualifying distributions, $140,302; giving
activities include $140,500 for 13 grants (high:
$88,000; low: $250).
Purpose and activities: Support primarily for
environmental conservation.
Fields of interest: Natural resources;
Animals/wildlife.
Limitations: Applications not accepted. Giving
on a national basis, with emphasis on MI. No
grants to individuals.
Application information: Contributes only to
pre-selected organizations.
Officers: Joanne N. Arbaugh, Pres. and
Secy.-Treas.; Steven L. Arbaugh, V.P.
EIN: 383421778

1622
Mukkamala Family Foundation
4545 Warwick Cir.
Grand Blanc, MI 48439 (810) 695-0188
Contact: Apparao Mukkamala, Pres.

Established in 1995 in MI.
Donor(s): Apparao Mukkamala, Sumathi
Mukkamala.
Grantmaker type: Independent foundation
Financial data (yr. ended 12/31/02): Assets,
$17,552 (M); gifts received, $163,187;
expenditures, $167,082; qualifying distributions,
$164,486; giving activities include $162,084 for
7 grants (high: $100,000; low: $101).
Purpose and activities: Giving for animal
welfare, religion, and education.
Fields of interest: Education; Animal welfare;
Human services; Religion.
Limitations: Giving on a national basis.
Application information:
   Initial approach: Letter
   Deadline(s): None
Officer: Apparao Mukkamala, Pres.
Directors: Aparna Mukkamala; Srinivas
Mukkamala; Sumathi Mukkamala.
EIN: 383224822

1623
Wanda Muntwyler Foundation For
Animals
c/o Fifth Third Bank
P.O. Box 3636
Grand Rapids, MI 49501-3636

Established in 1996 in IL.
Donor(s): Wanda Muntwyler.‡
Grantmaker type: Independent foundation
Financial data (yr. ended 12/31/02): Assets,
$1,984,280 (M); gifts received, $12,303;
expenditures, $178,844; qualifying distributions,
$121,711; giving activities include $119,551 for
23 grants (high: $22,500; low: $1,771).
Purpose and activities: Giving primarily for
animal welfare.
Fields of interest: Higher education; Animal
welfare; Veterinary medicine.
Types of support: General/operating support;
Scholarship funds.
Limitations: Applications not accepted. Giving
primarily in IL. No grants to individuals.
Application information: Contributes only to
pre-selected organizations.
Trustee: Fifth Third Bank.
EIN: 367155124

1624
Oleson Foundation
6645 N. Long Lake Rd.
Traverse City, MI 49684-9607 (231) 946-9349
Contact: John R. Spencer, M.D., Dir.

Established in 1959 in MI.
Donor(s): Gerald W. Oleson,‡ Frances M.
Oleson.‡
Grantmaker type: Independent foundation
Financial data (yr. ended 12/31/01): Assets,
$16,397,882 (M); expenditures, $1,059,261;
qualifying distributions, $754,327; giving
activities include $737,810 for 68 grants (high:
$76,000; low: $100).
Purpose and activities: Giving primarily for
education and human services.
Fields of interest: Historic preservation/historical
societies; Elementary/secondary education;
Higher education; Environment; Health care;
Youth development, centers/clubs; Human
services; Federated giving programs; Christian
agencies & churches.
Types of support: General/operating support;
Continuing support; Annual campaigns; Capital
campaigns; Building/renovation; Equipment;
Land acquisition; Curriculum development;
Matching/challenge support.
Limitations: Giving primarily in the Traverse
City, MI, area. No grants to individuals.
Application information: Application form
required.
   Initial approach: 1-page letter
   Copies of proposal: 1
   Deadline(s): Apr. 15
   Board meeting date(s): June
Officers and Directors:* Donald W. Oleson,*
Pres.; Gerald E. Oleson,* V.P.; Richard Ford,*
Secy.-Treas.; John R. Spencer, M.D.
Number of staff: 1 part-time professional.
EIN: 386083080

1625
Donald and Ann Parfet Family Foundation
259 E. Michigan Ave., Ste. 409
Kalamazoo, MI 49007-5902 (269) 349-8483
Contact: Wendy Van Peenan
FAX: (269) 349-8993; E-mail:
wvanpeenan@ameritech.net

Established in 1996 in MI.
Donor(s): Donald R. Parfet.
Grantmaker type: Independent foundation
Financial data (yr. ended 12/31/02): Assets,
$2,252,449 (M); expenditures, $365,129;
qualifying distributions, $352,356; giving
activities include $329,699 for 95 grants (high:
$85,000; low: $50; average: $50–$85,000) and
$10,500 for 2 employee matching gifts.
Purpose and activities: Giving primarily for
health, human services and religious
organizations.
Fields of interest: Arts; Education; Natural
resources; Hospitals (general); Human services;
Religion.
Types of support: General/operating support;
Continuing support; Annual campaigns; Capital
campaigns; Building/renovation; Endowments;
Emergency funds; Scholarship funds; Employee
matching gifts.
Limitations: Giving primarily in Kalamazoo, MI.
No grants to individuals.
Application information: Application form not
required.
   Initial approach: Letter with accompanying
      information
   Copies of proposal: 1
   Board meeting date(s): Nov. and Dec.
Officers and Trustees:* Ann V. Parfet,* Pres.;
Rachel E. Worgess, V.P.; Sydney E. Waldorf,
Secy.; Donald R. Parfet,* Treas.; C. MacKenzie
Waldorf; Andrew Worgess.
Number of staff: 1 part-time professional.
EIN: 383326370

1626
Preston S. Parish Foundation
244 N. Rose St., Ste. 100
Kalamazoo, MI 49007
Contact: Barbara J. Parish, V.P.

Established in 1984 in MI.
Donor(s): Preston S. Parish.
Grantmaker type: Independent foundation
Financial data (yr. ended 12/31/02): Assets,
$159,280 (M); expenditures, $249,137;
qualifying distributions, $245,261; giving
activities include $241,505 for 103 grants (high:
$50,000; low: $125).
Purpose and activities: Giving for the arts,
community development, the environment,
higher education, and Christian organizations.
Fields of interest: Arts; Higher education;
Natural resources; Health organizations,
association; Community development;
Federated giving programs; Christian agencies &
churches; Women.
Types of support: Annual campaigns; Capital
campaigns.
Limitations: Applications not accepted. Giving
primarily in Kalamazoo, MI. No grants to
individuals.
Application information: Contributes only to
pre-selected organizations.

Officers: Preston S. Parish, Pres. and Secy.; Barbara J. Parish, V.P.; Kathy A. Roschek, Treas.
Number of staff: 1 shared staff (shared with Richard U. Light Foundation).
EIN: 363249490

1627
Petoskey-Harbor Springs Area Community Foundation
616 Petoskey St., Ste. 100
Petoskey, MI 49770 (231) 348-5820
Contact: Maureen M. Nicholson, Exec. Dir.
FAX: (231) 348-5883; E-mail: phsacf@freeway.net; URL: http://www.petoskey-harborspringsfoundation.org

Established in 1991 in MI.
Grantmaker type: Community foundation
Financial data (yr. ended 03/30/03): Assets, $7,137,881 (M); gifts received, $1,015,365; expenditures, $677,448; giving activities include $378,551 for 149 grants (average: $100–$10,000).
Purpose and activities: The foundation awards grants to non-profit organizations, schools or municipalities in Emmet County, MI or to those that serve a significant number of Emmet County residents. The foundation administers donor-advised funds.
Fields of interest: Arts; Education; Environment; Health care; Youth development; Human services; Community development.
Types of support: Building/renovation; Equipment; Program development; Seed money; Scholarship funds; Technical assistance; Matching/challenge support.
Limitations: Giving limited to Emmet County, MI. No support for sectarian purposes. No grants to individuals, or for endowments or debt reduction.
Publications: Application guidelines, Annual report, Financial statement, Informational brochure.
Application information: Potential applicants should contact the foundation prior to submitting an application to discuss their project. Application form required.
  Initial approach: Letter or telephone
  Copies of proposal: 20
  Deadline(s): Apr. 1 and Oct. 1
  Board meeting date(s): Monthly
  Final notification: Summer and winter
Officers and Directors:* James T. Ramer,* Pres.; Louise T. Graham, V.P.; David T. Buzzelli, Secy.; John E. Fought,* Treas.; Maureen N. Nicholson, Exec. Dir; Sandra T. Baker; Lisa G. Blanchard; Jane T. Damschroder; Edward J. Frey, Jr.; Charles H. Gano; Elaine M. Hameister; David H. Irish; W. David Kring; Richard A. Lent; Virginia B. McCoy; Philip H. Millard.
Number of staff: 2 full-time professional; 1 full-time support.
EIN: 383032185

1628
Ralph L. and Winifred E. Polk Foundation
26955 Northwestern Hwy.
Southfield, MI 48034
Contact: Ann Hoerle, Exec. Admin.

Incorporated in 1962 in MI.
Donor(s): Ralph L. Polk,‡ Winifred E. Polk.

Grantmaker type: Independent foundation
Financial data (yr. ended 12/31/02): Assets, $2,952,344 (M); expenditures, $177,934; qualifying distributions, $166,625; giving activities include $164,000 for 37 grants (high: $15,000; low: $1,000).
Purpose and activities: Giving primarily for education and youth programs.
Fields of interest: Arts; Education; Natural resources; Zoos/zoological societies; Human services; Children/youth, services; Philanthropy/voluntarism; Christian agencies & churches.
Types of support: General/operating support; Capital campaigns.
Limitations: Applications not accepted. Giving primarily in MI, with emphasis on Detroit. No grants to individuals.
Application information: Contributes only to pre-selected organizations.
Officers and Trustees:* Winifred E. Polk,* Pres.; Stephen R. Polk,* V.P. and Treas.; Joe Walker, Secy.; Janet P. Read.
EIN: 386080075

1629
Porter Foundation
P.O. Box 6484
Grand Rapids, MI 49516-6484
Contact: Margaret Beusse, Pres. and Secy.

Established in 1966.
Donor(s): Burke E. Porter Machinery Co., Burke Porter Trust.
Grantmaker type: Independent foundation
Financial data (yr. ended 06/30/02): Assets, $4,114,414 (M); expenditures, $218,339; qualifying distributions, $215,762; giving activities include $213,070 for 45 grants (high: $20,000; low: $25).
Purpose and activities: Funding primarily for arts and culture, youth services, and education.
Fields of interest: Arts; Higher education; Education; Zoos/zoological societies; Human services.
Types of support: General/operating support; Matching/challenge support.
Limitations: Giving primarily in Grand Rapids, MI. Generally prefers programs with no religious affiliation.
Application information:
  Initial approach: Letter, including letter from school counselor
  Deadline(s): Mar. 31
  Final notification: June 30
Officers: Margaret Beusse, Pres. and Secy.; Andrew D. Murch, V.P.; Sarah Jury, Treas.
Director: Burke E. Porter.
Number of staff: None.
EIN: 386118663

1630
Ransom Fidelity Company
124 W. Allegan St., Ste. 1220
Lansing, MI 48933 (517) 482-1538
Contact: Edward B. McRee, V.P.
FAX: (517) 482-1539

Incorporated in 1915 in MI.
Donor(s): Ransom E. Olds.‡
Grantmaker type: Independent foundation

Financial data (yr. ended 12/31/02): Assets, $3,257,517 (M); expenditures, $362,310; qualifying distributions, $389,984; giving activities include $326,565 for 76 grants (high: $25,665; low: $100).
Purpose and activities: Giving primarily for education, health, social services, religion, and YWCAs.
Fields of interest: Museums (specialized); Arts; Higher education; Education; Natural resources; Hospitals (general); Health organizations; Human services; YM/YWCAs & YM/YWHAs; Hospices; Community development; Protestant agencies & churches; Roman Catholic agencies & churches.
Types of support: Annual campaigns; Capital campaigns; Building/renovation; Equipment; Endowments; Emergency funds; Conferences/seminars; Internship funds; Scholarship funds; Matching/challenge support.
Limitations: Giving in the U.S., with emphasis on MI. No grants to individuals.
Publications: Annual report, Financial statement, Grants list.
Application information: Application form required.
  Deadline(s): None
Officers: R.E. Olds Anderson, Pres.; Edward B. McRee, V.P.; Jean Hunnicutt, Secy.
Directors: Doris B. Anderson; Katrina B. Anderson-Denomy; Ron Beckwith; Deborah Stephens; Diane M. Tarpoff.
Number of staff: 2 full-time professional.
EIN: 381485403

1631
Ann & Mike Rosenthal Family Foundation
(formerly Rosenthal Family Foundation)
1225 Stuyvesant Rd.
Bloomfield Hills, MI 48301

Established in 1986 in MI.
Donor(s): Ann Rosenthal, Marvin Rosenthal.
Grantmaker type: Independent foundation
Financial data (yr. ended 10/31/02): Assets, $1,289,949 (M); expenditures, $135,283; qualifying distributions, $134,161; giving activities include $135,275 for 78 grants (high: $25,000; low: $50).
Purpose and activities: Giving to human services, health associations and youth development.
Fields of interest: Arts; Zoos/zoological societies; Health organizations, association; Human services; Federated giving programs; Jewish federated giving programs; Jewish agencies & temples.
Limitations: Applications not accepted. Giving primarily in MI. No grants to individuals.
Application information: Contributes only to pre-selected organizations.
Officers and Directors:* Ann Rosenthal,* Pres.; Rochelle Forester,* V.P.; James Rosenthal,* Secy.
EIN: 382702954

1632
Rotary Charities of Traverse City

250 E. Front St., Ste. 320
Traverse City, MI 49684-2510 (231) 941-4010
Contact: Marsha J. Smith, Exec. Dir., or Stacey
Foster, Admin. Asst.
FAX: (231) 941-4066; E-mail: rotary@gtii.com

Established in 1976.
Donor(s): Rotary Club of Traverse City.
Grantmaker type: Public charity
Financial data (yr. ended 06/30/03): Revenue,
$1,678,921; assets, $33,325,342 (M);
expenditures, $1,728,527; program services
expenses, $1,332,968; giving activities include
$1,217,393 for 43 grants (high: $200,000; low:
$5,000; average: $5,000–$200,000).
Purpose and activities: The charity focuses on
managing growth and the environment,
education, affordable housing, cultural
recreation, and strengthening families.
Fields of interest: Arts; Education; Environment,
management/technical aid; Housing/shelter,
search services; Recreation; Family services.
Types of support: Capital campaigns;
Building/renovation; Equipment; Seed money;
Technical assistance; Matching/challenge
support.
Limitations: Giving limited to Antrim, Benzie,
Grand Traverse, Kalkaska, and Leelanau
counties, MI. No support for religious activities
or programs. No grants to individuals, or for
endowment funds or ongoing support; no loans
to individuals.
Publications: Application guidelines, Annual
report (including application guidelines),
Financial statement, Grants list.
Application information: Accepts CMF
Common Grant Application Form. Application
form required.
Initial approach: Telephone
Copies of proposal: 1
Deadline(s): Sept. 1 and Mar. 1
Board meeting date(s): Monthly
Final notification: Dec. and June
Officers and Trustees:* George Bearup,* Pres.;
Edward Bagley,* V.P.; Donald Piche,* Secy.;
Henry Zuilhof,* Treas.; Marsha J. Smith, Exec.
Dir.; and 6 additional trustees.
Number of staff: 1 full-time professional; 1
full-time support.
EIN: 382170564

1633
Saddle Foundation

c/o Erik H. Serr, Miller Canfield
101 N. Main St., 7th Fl.
Ann Arbor, MI 48104-1400

Established in 1997 in MI.
Donor(s): Kathryn W. Holmes.
Grantmaker type: Independent foundation
Financial data (yr. ended 12/31/02): Assets,
$4,763,009 (M); gifts received, $138,794;
expenditures, $342,854; qualifying distributions,
$327,240; giving activities include $328,534 for
7 grants (high: $64,000; low: $50,000).
Purpose and activities: Giving primarily for arts,
higher education, and human services.
Fields of interest: Museums; Higher education;
Natural resources; Animals/wildlife,
preservation/protection; YM/YWCAs &
YM/YWHAs; Foundations (community).

Limitations: Applications not accepted. Giving
primarily in San Francisco, CA, and MI. No
grants to individuals.
Application information: Contributes only to
pre-selected organizations.
Officer: Kathryn W. Holmes, Pres.
Director: Howard "Howdy" S. Holmes.
EIN: 383347262

1634
Saginaw Community Foundation

100 S. Jefferson Ave., Ste. 201
Saginaw, MI 48607 (989) 755-0545
Contact: Lucy R. Allen, C.E.O. and Pres.
FAX: (989) 755-6524; E-mail:
staff@saginawfoundation.org; URL: http://
www.saginawfoundation.org

Incorporated in 1984 in MI.
Grantmaker type: Community foundation
Financial data (yr. ended 12/31/02): Assets,
$19,824,121 (M); gifts received, $2,265,586;
expenditures, $2,272,500; giving activities
include $1,265,698 for 432 grants (high:
$100,000; low: $100).
Purpose and activities: Support for projects not
currently being served by existing community
resources and for projects providing leverage for
generating other funds and community
resources. The foundation administers
donor-advised funds.
Fields of interest: Arts; Education; Environment;
Health care; Recreation; Human services;
Community development; General charitable
giving.
Types of support: Building/renovation;
Equipment; Emergency funds; Program
development; Publication; Seed money;
Scholarship funds; Technical assistance;
Scholarships—to individuals;
Matching/challenge support.
Limitations: Giving limited to Saginaw County,
MI. No support for churches or sectarian
religious programs. No grants to individuals
(except for designated scholarship funds), or for
operating budgets, endowment campaigns, debt
reduction, travel, or basic municipal or
educational services; generally no multi-year
grants.
Publications: Application guidelines, Annual
report (including application guidelines),
Informational brochure, Newsletter, Occasional
report, Program policy statement.
Application information: Application forms can
be downloaded from foundation Web site.
Application form required.
Initial approach: Letter
Copies of proposal: 3
Deadline(s): Feb. 1, May 1, Aug. 1, and Nov. 1
Board meeting date(s): Monthly
Final notification: 2 months after deadline
Officers and Directors:* Larry L. Preston,*
Chair.; Linda L. Sims,* Vice-Chair.; Lucy R.
Allen,* C.E.O. and Pres.; Richard T. Watson,*
Secy.; Morton E. Weldy,* Treas.; Bethany M.
Bernthal; Lucille M. Beuthin; Heidi A. Bolger;
Sally I. Cannon, Ph.D.; Hon. Terry L. Clark;
Craig Douglas, Ph.D.; Michael Elliott; Mark S.
Flegenheimer; Kim M. Gardey; Robert A.
Jarema; Richard D. Lane; Timothy M. Mackay;
Susan A. Pumford; Robert R. Rhode; Jack R.
Rummel; John Ruppel; James J. Shinners; Martin

Stark; Roma Perry Thurin; Jerry Ulrey; Richard
H. Winters.
Number of staff: 3 full-time professional.
EIN: 382474297

1635
Louis & Nellie Sieg Foundation

40700 Woodward Ave., Ste. A
Bloomfield Hills, MI 48304 (248) 642-5700
Contact: James H. LoPrete, Pres.

Established in 2000 in MI.
Donor(s): Shirley Sieg Nimcrut,‡ Shirley Sieg
Living Trust.
Grantmaker type: Independent foundation
Financial data (yr. ended 04/30/02): Assets,
$3,480,378 (M); gifts received, $706,170;
expenditures, $118,040; qualifying distributions,
$106,632; giving activities include $106,632 for
36 grants (high: $10,000; low: $300).
Fields of interest: Natural resources; Human
services.
Limitations: Giving primarily in southeast MI.
Application information: Application form not
required.
Initial approach: Letter
Copies of proposal: 1
Deadline(s): None
Board meeting date(s): Varies. Meet in Oct. or
Nov. to make most grant awards
Officers: James H. LoPrete, Pres.; Marion A.
LoPrete, V.P.; Mary M. Lyneis, Secy.; James S.
LoPrete, Treas.
Number of staff: None.
EIN: 383527097

1636
Skilling and Andrews Foundation

11720 E. Shore Dr.
Whitmore Lake, MI 48189
Contact: Ann Skilling Andrews, Pres.

Established in 1996 in MI.
Donor(s): Hazel D. Skilling,‡ Hugh H. Skilling
Trust.
Grantmaker type: Independent foundation
Financial data (yr. ended 12/31/02): Assets,
$7,337,646 (M); expenditures, $513,816;
qualifying distributions, $510,200; giving
activities include $510,200 for grants (high:
$501,100; average: $100–$501,100).
Purpose and activities: Giving primarily to aid
new secondary schools; some support also for
conservation.
Fields of interest: Secondary school/education;
Natural resources.
Limitations: Applications not accepted. Giving
primarily in central states of the U.S. No grants
to individuals.
Application information: Contributes only to
pre-selected organizations.
Board meeting date(s): Aug. and Dec.
Officers and Trustees:* Ann Skilling Andrews,*
Pres. and Treas.; Kenneth Andrews,* V.P.; Steven
Andrews,* Secy.
Number of staff: None.
EIN: 383335356

1637
Speckhard-Knight Charitable Foundation
771 Bogey Ct.
Ann Arbor, MI 48103 (734) 761-8752
Contact: Gerald Knight, Pres.
E-mail: zmjk@comcast.net; URL: http://
www.skcf.org

Established in 1999 in MI.
Donor(s): Gerald Knight.
Grantmaker type: Independent foundation
Financial data (yr. ended 12/31/02): Assets,
$4,421,165 (M); expenditures, $329,966;
qualifying distributions, $301,252; giving
activities include $292,971 for 20 grants (high:
$60,000; low: $250).
Fields of interest: Environment; Human
services; Adoption; Foster care.
Types of support: General/operating support;
Land acquisition; Program development.
Limitations: Giving primarily in MI.
Application information: Information available
on Web site or by E-mail. Application form
required.
  Initial approach: E-mail
  Copies of proposal: 1
  Deadline(s): None
Officers and Director:* Gerald Knight,* Pres.;
Maureen Knight, V.P.
EIN: 383466344

1638
St. Deny's Foundation, Inc.
(formerly Tremble Foundation, Inc.)
P.O. Box 704
Dowagiac, MI 49047
Contact: Kelly Deritter

Established in 1988 in MI.
Donor(s): Helen R. Tremble.‡
Grantmaker type: Independent foundation
Financial data (yr. ended 12/31/02): Assets,
$4,165,381 (M); expenditures, $388,370;
qualifying distributions, $311,191; giving
activities include $311,600 for 40 grants (high:
$55,300; low: $1,000).
Fields of interest: Higher education;
Environment; Animal welfare.
Types of support: General/operating support;
Program development; Scholarship funds.
Limitations: Giving primarily in MI, with
emphasis on the Dowagiac area.
Application information: Application form not
required.
  Initial approach: Proposal
  Copies of proposal: 1
  Deadline(s): Feb. 1 and Aug. 1
  Board meeting date(s): Spring and fall
  Final notification: 6 months
Officers and Directors:* Thomas Dalton,* Pres.;
Lynn Dalton, V.P.; Robert Sajdak, Secy.-Treas.;
Cara Carrabine-Dalton; Dillon Dalton; Dusty
Dalton; Jim McWilliams.
Trustee: Comerica Bank.
EIN: 382869889

1639
Steelcase Foundation ▼
P.O. Box 1967, CH-4E
Grand Rapids, MI 49501-1967
(616) 246-4695
Contact: Susan Broman, Exec. Dir.
FAX: (616) 475-2200; E-mail:
sbroman@steelcase.com

Trust established in 1951 in MI.
Donor(s): Steelcase Inc.
Grantmaker type: Company-sponsored
foundation
Financial data (yr. ended 11/30/02): Assets,
$104,743,934 (M); gifts received, $3,824,790;
expenditures, $7,609,021; qualifying
distributions, $7,355,271; giving activities
include $7,065,196 for 420 grants (high:
$673,000; low: $20; average:
$2,000–$673,000).
Purpose and activities: Support for human
services, community and economic
development, health, education, arts and
culture, and the environment. Special
consideration is given to grant requests
involving people who are disadvantaged,
disabled, young, and elderly to improve the
quality of their lives.
Fields of interest: Arts; Education; Environment;
Health care; Human services; Youth, services;
Economic development; Community
development; Disabled; Aging; Economically
disadvantaged.
International interests: Canada.
Types of support: General/operating support;
Capital campaigns; Building/renovation;
Equipment; Land acquisition; Program
development; Seed money; Scholarship funds;
Employee matching gifts; Matching/challenge
support.
Limitations: Giving limited to areas of company
operations, including Athens, AL, Orange
County, CA, Grand Rapids, MI, Asheville, NC,
and Markham, Canada. No support for
churches, or programs with substantial religious
overtones of a sectarian nature. No grants to
individuals, or for endowment funds,
conferences and seminars.
Publications: Application guidelines, Annual
report (including application guidelines).
Application information: The foundation does
not acknowledge receipt of proposals nor does
it grant interviews with applicants. Application
form required.
  Initial approach: Letter of intent
  Copies of proposal: 1
  Deadline(s): Quarterly
  Board meeting date(s): Quarterly
  Final notification: At least 90 days
Officer: Susan Broman, Exec. Dir.
Trustees: Kate Pew Wolters, Chair.; James P.
Hackett; Earl Holton; David D. Hunting, Jr.;
Mary Goodwillie Nelson; Robert C. Pew III;
Peter M. Wege; James C. Welch; Fifth Third
Bank.
Number of staff: 1 full-time professional; 1
full-time support.
EIN: 386050470

1640
Steelcase Inc. Corporate Giving Program
c/o Corp. Rels. Dept.
P.O. Box 1967, CH-4E
Grand Rapids, MI 49501-1967

Grantmaker type: Corporate giving program
Financial data (yr. ended 02/28/02): Total giving,
$659,300; giving activities include $503,800 for
108 grants and $155,500 for 99 in-kind gifts.
Purpose and activities: As a complement to its
foundation, Steelcase also makes charitable
contributions to nonprofit organizations directly.
Support is given primarily in the Athens,
Alabama, Tustin, California, Grand Rapids,
Michigan, Fletcher, North Carolina, Toronto,
Canada, and Tijuana, Mexico, areas.
Fields of interest: Arts; Higher education;
Education; Natural resources; Family planning;
Health care; Substance abuse, services; Mental
health/crisis services; AIDS; Alcoholism; Health
organizations; AIDS research; Food services;
Children/youth, services; Human services;
Community development; Public affairs;
Minorities; Disabled; Aging; Women;
Economically disadvantaged; Homeless.
International interests: Canada; Mexico.
Types of support: General/operating support;
Donated products.
Limitations: Giving primarily in the Athens, AL,
Tustin, CA, Grand Rapids, MI, Fletcher, NC,
Toronto, Canada, and Tijuana, Mexico, areas.
Publications: Informational brochure (including
application guidelines).
Application information: The Corporate
Relations Department handles giving. The
company has a staff that only handles
contributions. A contributions committee
reviews all requests. Application form required.
  Initial approach: Contact nearest company
    facility for application form
  Copies of proposal: 1
  Deadline(s): None
  Board meeting date(s): Ongoing
  Final notification: Following review
Number of staff: 4.

1641
The Helmut Stern Foundation
P.O. Box 1733
Ann Arbor, MI 48106 (734) 663-2455
Contact: Helmut F. Stern, Pres.

Established in 1983 in MI.
Donor(s): Helmut F. Stern.
Grantmaker type: Independent foundation
Financial data (yr. ended 11/30/02): Assets,
$1,958,399 (M); expenditures, $180,655;
qualifying distributions, $148,000; giving
activities include $148,000 for 8 grants (high:
$100,000; low: $1,000).
Purpose and activities: Giving primarily for
higher education; support also for social
services, museums, hospitals, and conservation.
Fields of interest: Museums; Arts; Higher
education; Medical school/education;
Education; Natural resources; Hospitals
(general); Human services; Federated giving
programs.
Types of support: Land acquisition; Fellowships;
Scholarship funds.
Limitations: Applications not accepted. Giving
primarily in MI. No grants to individuals.

Application information: Contributes only to pre-selected organizations.
Officer: Helmut F. Stern, Pres.
EIN: 382515772

1642
Margaret Jane Stoker Charitable Trust
c/o Citizens Bank, Wealth Mgmt.
101 N. Washington Ave.
Saginaw, MI 48607 (989) 776-1416
Contact: Karen McNish, Trust Off., Citzens Bank, Wealth Mgmt.

Established in 2001 in MI.
Grantmaker type: Independent foundation
Financial data (yr. ended 09/30/02): Assets, $2,128,365 (M); gifts received, $2,738,966; expenditures, $132,127; qualifying distributions, $125,075; giving activities include $120,000 for 2 grants (high: $70,000; low: $50,000).
Fields of interest: University; Zoos/zoological societies.
Limitations: Giving primarily in the Saginaw County, MI area.
Application information: Application form required.
Deadline(s): None
Trustee: Citizens Bank.
EIN: 320000318

1643
Jane Smith Turner Foundation, Inc.
500 Woodward Ave., Ste. 2500
Detroit, MI 48226

Established in 1994 in MI.
Grantmaker type: Independent foundation
Financial data (yr. ended 12/31/02): Assets, $9,294,683 (M); expenditures, $672,557; qualifying distributions, $531,407; giving activities include $547,675 for 71 grants (high: $120,000; low: $100; average: $5,000–$50,000).
Purpose and activities: Giving primarily to arts and cultural programs, education, wildlife preservation, health associations, and natural resource conservation.
Fields of interest: Arts; Education; Natural resources; Animals/wildlife, preservation/protection; Hospitals (general); Health organizations, association.
Limitations: Applications not accepted. Giving primarily in GA, NC, and SC. No grants to individuals.
Application information: Contributes only to pre-selected organizations.
Officers and Directors:* Jane Smith Turner, Pres. and Secy.; David W. Laughlin,* Treas.; Sarah Jane Turner Garlington; Laura Turner Seydel; Reed Beauregard Turner; Rhett Lee Turner; Robert E. Turner IV; John Wilson.
EIN: 383199326

1644
Harold and Grace Upjohn Foundation
Mall Plz., Ste. 90
157 S. Kalamazoo Mall
Kalamazoo, MI 49007 (269) 344-2818
Contact: Floyd L. Parks, Secy.-Treas.

Incorporated in 1958 in MI.
Donor(s): Grace G. Upjohn.‡
Grantmaker type: Independent foundation
Financial data (yr. ended 10/31/02): Assets, $11,160,860 (M); expenditures, $710,616; qualifying distributions, $638,873; giving activities include $628,150 for 33 grants (high: $61,700; low: $2,000).
Purpose and activities: Grants primarily to promote scientific research for the alleviation of human suffering; to care for the sick, aged, and helpless whose private resources are inadequate; to conduct research for and otherwise assist in the improvement of living, moral and working conditions; to promote the spread of education and to provide scholarships for deserving young men and women; to promote and aid in the mental, moral, intellectual and physical improvement, assistance and relief of the poor, indigent or deserving inhabitants of the U.S., regardless of race, color or creed.
Fields of interest: Arts; Higher education; Environment; Family services; Aging, centers/services; Community development, neighborhood development; Christian agencies & churches.
Types of support: Program development; Seed money; Scholarship funds; Research.
Limitations: Giving limited to Kalamazoo, MI. No grants to individuals, or for operating budgets or annual campaigns.
Publications: Application guidelines, Annual report, Program policy statement.
Application information: Application form required.
Initial approach: Call or write for application form and instructions
Copies of proposal: 6
Deadline(s): Apr. 1 and Sept. 1
Board meeting date(s): Spring and fall
Final notification: 30 days after board meeting
Officers: Christopher U. Light, Pres.; Janet J. Deal-Koestner, V.P.; Floyd L. Parks, Secy.-Treas.
Trustees: Mary U. Meader; Florence Upjohn Orosz; Jon L. Stryker.
EIN: 386052963

1645
Vaughan Foundation
c/o Erik H. Serr, Miller Canfield
101 N. Main St., 7th Fl.
Ann Arbor, MI 48104

Established in 1997 in MI.
Donor(s): Christine M. Holmes.
Grantmaker type: Independent foundation
Financial data (yr. ended 12/31/02): Assets, $4,506,552 (M); gifts received, $294,756; expenditures, $232,932; qualifying distributions, $223,279; giving activities include $225,000 for 14 grants (high: $30,000; low: $5,000).
Purpose and activities: Funding primarily for arts and culture, human services, and animal welfare.
Fields of interest: Arts; Animal welfare; Human services; American Red Cross; YM/YWCAs & YM/YWHAs.
Limitations: Applications not accepted. Giving primarily in MI. No grants to individuals.
Application information: Contributes only to pre-selected organizations.
Officer: Christine Holmes, Pres.

EIN: 383355160

1646
The Visteon Fund
5500 Auto Club Dr.
P.O. Box 6200
Dearborn, MI 48126
URL: http://www.visteon.com/about/community/

Established in 1999 in MI.
Donor(s): Visteon Corp.
Grantmaker type: Company-sponsored foundation
Financial data (yr. ended 12/31/01): Assets, $5,650,901 (M); gifts received, $7,000,000; expenditures, $1,470,662; qualifying distributions, $1,467,396; giving activities include $1,468,793 for 188 grants (high: $200,000; low: $500).
Purpose and activities: The goal of the fund is to enrich the lives of children and improve the environment by working on a local level in the communities where Visteon employees live, work, and volunteer.
Fields of interest: Elementary/secondary education; Higher education; Education; Natural resources; Hospitals (general); Health organizations; Food services; Disasters, 9/11/01; Youth development, scouting agencies (general); Youth development; Human services; Children/youth, services; Family services; Community development.
Types of support: General/operating support.
Limitations: Applications not accepted. Giving on a national basis in areas of company operations, with some emphasis on MI. No grants to individuals.
Application information: Contributes only to pre-selected organizations.
Trustees: Daniel R. Coulson; Stacy L. Fox; Peter Look; Peter J. Pestillo; Susan F. Skerker.
EIN: 383566029

1647
Wege Foundation ▼
P.O. Box 6388
Grand Rapids, MI 49516-6388
(616) 957-0480
Contact: Ellen Satterlee, Exec. Dir.
FAX: (616) 957-0616

Established about 1967 in MI.
Donor(s): Peter M. Wege.
Grantmaker type: Independent foundation
Financial data (yr. ended 12/31/02): Assets, $147,000,697 (M); expenditures, $15,011,275; qualifying distributions, $13,881,950; giving activities include $13,719,248 for 113 grants (high: $3,661,384; low: $395; average: $1,000–$50,000).
Purpose and activities: Giving primarily to museums, performing arts, health and human services, youth, Christian agencies, and education.
Fields of interest: Museums; Performing arts; Elementary/secondary education; Higher education; Natural resources; Hospitals (general); Human services; Children/youth, services; Community development; Christian agencies & churches.
Types of support: Annual campaigns; Capital campaigns; Building/renovation; Equipment;

Endowments; Program development; Curriculum development; Matching/challenge support.
Limitations: Giving primarily in greater Kent County, MI, with emphasis on the Grand Rapids area. No grants to individuals, or for operating budgets.
Publications: Application guidelines, Annual report.
Application information: Accepts CMF Common Grant Application Form. Application form not required.
  Initial approach: Proposal
  Copies of proposal: 1
  Deadline(s): Feb. 15 and Sept. 15
Officers and Directors: Peter M. Wege,* Pres.; Peter M. Wege II,* V.P.; W. Michael Van Haren,* Secy.; Ellen Satterlee, Treas. and Exec. Dir.; Mary Nelson; Christopher Wege; Diana Wege; Jonathan Wege.
Number of staff: 3 full-time professional.
EIN: 386124363
Recent environmental and animal welfare grants:
1647-1 Ferris State University, Big Rapids, MI, $92,241. For Muskegon River Watershed Assembly. 2002.
1647-2 Grand Valley State University, Water Research Institute, Allendale, MI, $147,000. 2002.
1647-3 Lake Michigan Federation, Chicago, IL, $25,000. 2002.
1647-4 Land Conservancy of West Michigan, Grand Rapids, MI, $21,510. 2002.
1647-5 League of Conservation Voters Education Fund, DC, $10,000. For Michigan Geographic Alliance. 2002.
1647-6 Michigan Land Use Institute, Beulah, MI, $50,000. 2002.
1647-7 National Parks Conservation Association, DC, $100,500. 2002.
1647-8 National Wildlife Federation, Reston, VA, $200,000. 2002.
1647-9 Timberland Resource Conservation and Development Area Council, Grand Rapids, MI, $20,000. 2002.
1647-10 University of Pennsylvania, Philadelphia, PA, $350,000. For Guanacaste Dry Forest Conservation Fund. 2002.
1647-11 Waterkeeper Alliance, White Plains, NY, $25,000. 2002.
1647-12 Wilderness Society, DC, $35,000. 2002.

1648
Henry E. and Consuelo S. Wenger Foundation, Inc.
8916 Gale Rd.
White Lake, MI 48386

Incorporated in 1959 in MI.
Donor(s): Consuelo S. Wenger.
Grantmaker type: Independent foundation
Financial data (yr. ended 12/31/02): Assets, $13,716,255 (M); expenditures, $697,404; qualifying distributions, $680,827; giving activities include $680,244 for 85 grants (high: $100,000; low: $100).
Purpose and activities: Support for the arts, secondary and higher education, environmental preservation, hospitals, and Christian churches.
Fields of interest: Arts; Elementary/secondary education; Higher education; Environment;

Hospitals (general); Health care; Youth development, centers/clubs; Human services; Christian agencies & churches.
Limitations: Applications not accepted. Giving primarily in IL, MI, and NY. No grants to individuals.
Application information: Contributes only to pre-selected organizations.
Officer: Diane Wenger Wilson, Pres.
EIN: 386077419

1649
Matilda R. Wilson Fund ▼
100 Renaissance Ctr., 34th Fl.
Detroit, MI 48243 (313) 259-7777
Contact: George D. Miller, Jr., Pres.

Incorporated in 1944 in MI.
Donor(s): Matilda R. Wilson,‡ Alfred G. Wilson.‡
Grantmaker type: Independent foundation
Financial data (yr. ended 12/31/01): Assets, $50,362,659 (M); expenditures, $4,716,501; qualifying distributions, $4,365,210; giving activities include $4,121,704 for 60 grants (high: $400,000; low: $5,000; average: $10,000–$100,000).
Purpose and activities: Support for the arts, youth agencies, higher education, and social services.
Fields of interest: Arts; Higher education; Hospitals (general); Human services; Youth, services.
Types of support: General/operating support; Building/renovation; Equipment; Endowments; Program development; Scholarship funds; Research; Matching/challenge support.
Limitations: Giving primarily in southeast MI. No grants to individuals; no loans.
Application information: Application form not required.
  Initial approach: Letter
  Copies of proposal: 1
  Deadline(s): None
  Board meeting date(s): Jan., June, Sept., and Dec.
Officers and Trustees: George D. Miller, Jr.,* Pres.; David M. Hempstead,* Secy.; Robert M. Surdam,* Treas.
Number of staff: None.
EIN: 386087665
Recent environmental and animal welfare grants:
1649-1 Detroit Zoological Society, Royal Oak, MI, $250,000. For capital support. 2001.
1649-2 Detroit Zoological Society, Royal Oak, MI, $250,000. For capital support. 2001.

1650
The Woodall Foundation
2525 Telegraph Rd., Ste. 102
Bloomfield Hills, MI 48302

Established in 1943 in MI.
Grantmaker type: Independent foundation
Financial data (yr. ended 12/31/02): Assets, $523,054 (M); expenditures, $125,121; qualifying distributions, $94,650; giving activities include $94,650 for 31 grants (high: $10,000; low: $450).

Purpose and activities: Giving primarily for organizations which promote the understanding of Christian Science.
Fields of interest: Arts; Education; Animal welfare; Human services; Youth, services; Religion.
Types of support: General/operating support.
Limitations: Applications not accepted. Giving in the U.S., with emphasis on MI and VA. No grants to individuals.
Application information: Contributes only to pre-selected organizations.
Trustees: Harold C. McPike; Virginia W. McPike; Barbara J. Weaver.
Number of staff: None.
EIN: 386070915

1651
Young Family Foundation
P.O. Box 5430
Plymouth, MI 48170

Established in 2001 in MI.
Donor(s): William P. Young.
Grantmaker type: Independent foundation
Financial data (yr. ended 12/31/02): Assets, $2,322,483 (M); gifts received, $1,000,000; expenditures, $580,409; qualifying distributions, $576,967; giving activities include $575,000 for 5 grants (high: $300,000; low: $25,000).
Purpose and activities: Giving primarily for higher education.
Fields of interest: Higher education; Natural resources.
Limitations: Applications not accepted. Giving primarily in Detroit, MI. No grants to individuals.
Application information: Contributes only to pre-selected organizations.
Officers and Directors: William C. Young,* Pres.; William Patrick Young,* V.P.; Tracey L. Deal,* Secy.; Amy L. Morgan,* Treas.
EIN: 300003762

MINNESOTA

1652
3M Company Contributions Program
3M Ctr., Bldg. 225-1S-23
St. Paul, MN 55144-1000 (651) 733-0144
Contact: Barbara W. Kaufmann, Mgr., Corp. Contribs., Education and Community Affairs; or Cynthia F. Kleven, Mgr., Corp. Contribs., Health and Human Svcs., Arts, and Environment, and Secy., 3M Fdn.
Additional tel.: (651) 733-1241; FAX: (651) 737-3061; E-mail: cfkleven@mmm.com; URL: http://www.3m.com/about3m/community

Grantmaker type: Corporate giving program
Financial data (yr. ended 12/31/02): Total giving, $26,117,000; giving activities include $3,225,000 for grants and $22,892,000 for in-kind gifts.
Purpose and activities: As a complement to its foundation, 3M also makes charitable contributions to nonprofit organizations directly. Support is given on a national basis.

Fields of interest: Arts; Higher education; Education; Environment; Health care; Housing/shelter, temporary shelter; Youth development, centers/clubs; Youth development; Family services; Family services, parent education; Human services.

Types of support: General/operating support; Capital campaigns; Building/renovation; Equipment; Program development; Professorships; Seed money; Fellowships; Internship funds; Scholarship funds; Technical assistance; Employee volunteer services; Use of facilities; Employee matching gifts; Donated equipment; Donated land; Donated products; In-kind gifts; Matching/challenge support.

Limitations: Giving on a national basis in areas of company operations. No support for political, fraternal, social, veterans', or military organizations, propaganda or lobbying organizations, or religious organizations not of direct benefit to the entire community. No grants to individuals, or for electronic media promotion or sponsorships, athletic events, non-3M equipment, capital campaigns or endowments, emergency funds, conferences, seminars, workshops, symposia, fundraising or testimonial events, or travel; no cause-related marketing.

Publications: Application guidelines, Corporate giving report (including application guidelines), Grants list.

Application information: Contact headquarters for nearest application address. Support is limited to 1 contribution per organization during any given year for 3 years in length. An application form will be sent following receipt of an eligible proposal. The Community Affairs Department handles giving. The company has a staff that only handles contributions. A contributions committee reviews all requests. Application form required.

   Initial approach: Proposal to nearest company facility

   Copies of proposal: 1

   Deadline(s): 2 months prior to committee meetings

   Board meeting date(s): Aug. for Health and Human Services; Mar. for Arts; Dec. for Education

   Final notification: Following review

Corporate Contributions Committee: Thomas A. Boardman, Staff V.P., Dep. Genl. Counsel, and Asst. Secy.; J.J. Fernandez, V.P., Office Supplies Div.; F. Harris, Jr., Staff V.P., Community Affairs; Jay V. Ihlenfeld, V.P., Research and Devel.; Barbara W. Kaufmann, Mgr., Corp. Contribs.; Cynthia F. Kleven, Mgr., Corp. Contribs., and Secy., 3M Fdn., Inc.; R.E. Larson, Staff V.P., Engineering Systems; W.J. Mahoney, Staff V.P., Human Resources; W. James McNerney, Jr., Chair. and C.E.O.; David W. Powell, V.P., Mktg., and Pres., 3M Fdn., Inc.; Donna M. Schorr, Recording Secy.; James B. Stake, Exec. V.P., Display and Graphics Business; P.J. Swain, Genl. Mgr., Safety and Security Systems Div.; Janet L. Yeomans, V.P., Mergers and Acquisitions.

Number of staff: 4 full-time professional; 1 part-time professional; 2 full-time support.

1653
3M Foundation ▼

(also known as Minnesota Mining and Manufacturing Foundation)
3M Ctr., Bldg. 225-1S-23
St. Paul, MN 55144-1000 (651) 733-0144
Contact: Cindy F. Kleven, Secy.
FAX: (651) 737-3061; E-mail: cfkleven1@mmm.com; URL: http://www.3M.com/about3m/community

Incorporated in 1953 in MN.

Donor(s): Minnesota Mining and Manufacturing Co., 3M Co.

Grantmaker type: Company-sponsored foundation

Financial data (yr. ended 12/31/02): Assets, $32,510,270 (M); expenditures, $18,583,815; qualifying distributions, $18,475,026; giving activities include $15,783,127 for 1,546 grants (high: $2,599,333; low: $100; average: $500–$10,000) and $1,803,204 for 779 employee matching gifts.

Purpose and activities: The foundation's goal is to help develop productive, educated and engaged citizens. The contributions program targets math, science and economics education in elementary through graduate schools. Health and social services grants target programs that strengthen families and youth, while reaching out with disaster relief to people around the world. Arts and cultural grants help foster creative expression as well as make our communities more interesting places to live. Support extends to environmental efforts that make immediate and meaningful progress toward the sustainability of the Earth's eco-systems.

Fields of interest: Arts; Early childhood education; Child development, education; Elementary school/education; Secondary school/education; Higher education; Education; Natural resources; Environment; Dental care; Human services; Youth, services; Child development, services; Family services; Family services, parent education; Residential/custodial care, half-way house; Homeless, human services; Business/industry; Community development.

Types of support: General/operating support; Capital campaigns; Building/renovation; Program development; Scholarship funds; Research; Employee matching gifts.

Limitations: Giving primarily in locations where the company has facilities in AL, AK, AR, CA, CT, DC, GA, HI, IA, IL, IN, KY, MA, MI, MN, MO, NC, NE, NJ, NY, OH, SC, SD, TX, UT, and WI. No support for projects of specific religious denominations or sects, athletic events, conduit agencies, or political, fraternal, social, veterans', hospitals, K-12 schools, or military organizations. No grants to individuals, or for capital or endowment funds, emergency operating support, advocacy and lobbying efforts, fundraising events and associated advertising, travel, publications unrelated to foundation-funded projects, seed money, purchase of equipment not manufactured by 3M, deficit financing, or conferences; no loans or investments.

Publications: Annual report, Corporate giving report (including application guidelines), Grants list, Informational brochure (including application guidelines).

Application information: Application form required.

   Initial approach: Letter of inquiry

   Copies of proposal: 1

   Deadline(s): At least 8 weeks prior to month in which board meets

   Board meeting date(s): Jan., Apr., and Aug.

   Final notification: 3 months

Officers and Directors:* David W. Powell,* Pres.; F. Harris, Jr., V.P.; Cynthia F. Kleven, Secy.; Thomas A. Boardman; J.M. Borseth; Jay V. Ihlenfeld; Barbara W. Kaufmann; Ralph E. Larson; W.J. Mahoney; W.J. McNerney; R.M. Miller; K.E. Reed; J.B. Stake; Peter J. Swain; S.K. Tokach.

Number of staff: None.

EIN: 416038262

Recent environmental and animal welfare grants:

1653-1 Alliance to Save Energy, DC, $10,000. 2001.

1653-2 Carkeek Watershed Community Action Project, Seattle, WA, $10,000. 2001.

1653-3 Chelan-Douglas Land Trust, Wenatchee, WA, $10,000. 2001.

1653-4 Fish First, Woodland, WA, $10,000. 2001.

1653-5 Keystone Center, Keystone Science School, Keystone, CO, $10,800. 2001.

1653-6 Lady Bird Johnson Wildflower Center, Austin, TX, $10,000. 2001.

1653-7 Nature Conservancy, Minnesota Chapter, Minneapolis, MN, $1,800,000. 2001.

1653-8 Pennypack Ecological Restoration Trust, Huntingdon Valley, PA, $10,000. 2001.

1653-9 Watchable Wildlife, Marine On Saint Croix, MN, $18,000. 2001.

1653-10 Whirling Disease Foundation, Bozeman, MT, $20,000. 2001.

1654
AgStar Fund for Rural America

P.O. Box 4249
Mankato, MN 56002 (507) 345-5656
Contact: Jody Bloemke, Admin.
E-mail: jbloemk@agstar.com; URL: http://www.agstar.com/about/fund.shtml

Grantmaker type: Corporate giving program

Purpose and activities: Through the AgStar Fund for Rural America, a direct corporate giving program, AgStar makes charitable contributions to nonprofit organizations involved with agriculture and rural development. Special emphasis is directed towards programs designed to educate young, beginning, or future farmers; maintain or improve the quality of the rural environment; support the advancement and utilization of technology for the benefit of farmers and rural communities; and enhance the quality of life for farmers and rural communities. Support is given primarily in Minnesota and northwestern Wisconsin.

Fields of interest: Education; Environment; Agriculture; Human services; Rural development; Science.

Types of support: General/operating support; Management development; Capital campaigns; Program development; Technical assistance.

Limitations: Giving primarily in MN and northwestern WI. No support for religious organizations not of direct benefit to the entire community, medical facilities, fraternal or veterans' organizations, arts-related facilities, or discriminatory organizations. No grants for legislative or lobbying activities, political campaigns, medical research, fundraising, sports sponsorships, recreational facility construction or maintenance, theatrical productions, books or magazines, articles, or advertising, arts-related activities, public or private school teaching positions, debt reduction, activities directly benefiting specific individuals or private businesses, or activities directly benefiting AgStar employees or directors.

Application information: An application form is available online. Additional information may be requested at a later date. A site visit may be requested. The AgStar Fund for Rural America Board of Trustees reviews all requests of over $2,500. Multi-year funding is not automatic. Organizations receiving support may be asked to provide a final report. Support is limited to 1 contribution per organization during any given year. Contributions generally do not exceed $10,000. Application form required.

Initial approach: Complete online application form
Copies of proposal: 1
Deadline(s): Nov. 30

1655
Allete, Inc. Corporate Giving Program

(formerly Minnesota Power, Inc. Corporate Giving Program)
c/o Contribs. Prog.
30 W. Superior St.
Duluth, MN 55802
Contact: Peggy Hanson, Community Rels. Admin.
Tel.: (218) 722-5642, ext. 3380; Additional tel.: (800) 228-4966; E-mail: pchanson@mnpower.com; URL: http://www.mnpower.com/community/index.htm

Grantmaker type: Corporate giving program
Purpose and activities: Allete makes charitable contributions to nonprofit organizations involved with arts and culture, education, the environment, health, community development, and civic affairs. Special emphasis is directed towards K-12 education programs designed to enhance basic skills in language arts, math, and science which help prepare students for the working world. Support is given primarily in upper Minnesota.
Fields of interest: Arts; Elementary/secondary education; Education; Environment; Health care; Community development; Public affairs.
Types of support: General/operating support; Program development.
Limitations: Giving primarily in upper MN. No support for labor, fraternal, social, or other membership organizations, religious organizations, or political organizations. No grants to individuals, or for capital campaigns or endowments, fundraising, conferences or seminars, publications, debt reduction, or research.
Publications: Application guidelines.
Application information: A contributions committee reviews all major requests. A contributions committee at each company location reviews all minor requests originating from that particular area. Proposals may be

submitted using the Minnesota Common Grant Application Form. Application form not required.
Initial approach: Proposal to headquarters
Copies of proposal: 1
Deadline(s): None
Board meeting date(s): 6 times per year for major requests; monthly for minor requests
Final notification: Following review
Number of staff: 1 full-time professional.

1656
Elmer L. & Eleanor J. Andersen Foundation

2424 Territorial Rd.
St. Paul, MN 55114 (651) 642-0127
Contact: Mari Oyanagi Eggum, Fdn. Admin.
FAX: (651) 645-4684; E-mail: eandefdn@mtn.org

Established in 1957 in MN.
Donor(s): Elmer L. Andersen, Eleanor J. Andersen, Anthony L. Andersen.
Grantmaker type: Independent foundation
Financial data (yr. ended 11/30/02): Assets, $5,817,365 (M); gifts received, $1,000; expenditures, $1,515,976; qualifying distributions, $491,286; giving activities include $440,000 for 184 grants (high: $37,500; low: $500; average: $500–$75,000).
Purpose and activities: The purpose of the foundation is to enhance the quality of the civic, cultural, educational, environmental, and social aspects of life primarily in the St. Paul, MN, area.
Fields of interest: Media/communications; Arts; Libraries/library science; Education; Environment; Human services.
Types of support: General/operating support; Continuing support; Annual campaigns; Capital campaigns; Building/renovation; Program development; Publication.
Limitations: Giving primarily in MN, with emphasis on the metropolitan St. Paul-Minneapolis area, primarily St. Paul. No support for health-related projects. No grants to individuals.
Publications: Annual report (including application guidelines).
Application information: Use MN Common Grant Application Form. Application form required.
Initial approach: Request for guidelines
Copies of proposal: 1
Deadline(s): Submit proposal by Feb. 1, May 1, Aug. 1, or Nov. 1
Board meeting date(s): Middle of month in Mar., June, Sept., and Dec.
Final notification: 21 days following board meeting
Officers and Directors:* Julian Andersen,* Pres.; Eleanor J. Andersen,* V.P.; Terry Slye, Secy.; Elmer L. Andersen,* Treas.; Amy Andersen; Tony Andersen; Charles Dayton.
Number of staff: 1 part-time professional.
EIN: 416032984

1657
Gordon & Margaret Bailey Foundation

c/o Thomas Campbell
1380 Corporate Center Curve, Ste. 317
Eagan, MN 55121
Contact: Margaret Bailey, Pres.

Established around 1991.
Grantmaker type: Independent foundation

Financial data (yr. ended 12/31/02): Assets, $2,870,610 (M); gifts received, $515,000; expenditures, $237,188; qualifying distributions, $233,794; giving activities include $228,200 for 41 grants (high: $100,000; low: $50).
Purpose and activities: Giving for Christian organizations, garden and landscape organizations, and education.
Fields of interest: Education; Botanical/horticulture/landscape services; Health care; Human services; Christian agencies & churches.
Limitations: Applications not accepted. Giving primarily in MN.
Application information: Unsolicited requests for funds not accepted.
Officer: Margaret Bailey, Pres.
Directors: Patrick Bailey; Thomas J. Campbell; Theresa McEnaney.
EIN: 411704413

1658
Bailey Nurseries Foundation

c/o John Bailey
1325 Bailey Rd.
Newport, MN 55055

Established in 1997 in MN.
Donor(s): Bailey Nurseries, Inc.
Grantmaker type: Company-sponsored foundation
Financial data (yr. ended 12/31/02): Assets, $901,456 (M); gifts received, $340,000; expenditures, $268,433; qualifying distributions, $268,258; giving activities include $268,258 for 72 grants (high: $44,300; low: $40).
Purpose and activities: Giving to organizations helping to improve the quality of life in the communities surrounding the Bailey Nurseries, Inc. areas.
Fields of interest: Arts; Education; Botanical/horticulture/landscape services; Youth development; Community development.
Limitations: Applications not accepted. Giving limited to MN. No grants to individuals.
Application information: Contributes only to pre-selected organizations.
Officers: Gordon J. Bailey, Chair.; Rodney P. Bailey, Pres.; John P. Bailey, Secy.; Theresa McEnaney, Treas.
EIN: 411890034

1659
Baker Foundation

80 S. 8th St., Ste. 4900
Minneapolis, MN 55402 (612) 332-7479
Contact: David C. Sherman, Pres.; or James W. Peter, Secy.-Treas.

Established in 1947; incorporated in 1954 in MN.
Donor(s): Morris T. Baker,‡ William M. Baker,‡ Roger L. Baker.
Grantmaker type: Independent foundation
Financial data (yr. ended 12/31/02): Assets, $4,255,447 (M); expenditures, $248,503; qualifying distributions, $201,365; giving activities include $189,365 for 70 grants (high: $24,000; low: $100).
Fields of interest: Music; Natural resources; Hospitals (general); Medical research, institute; Children/youth, services.

Types of support: General/operating support; Annual campaigns; Capital campaigns; Building/renovation.
Limitations: Giving primarily in MN. No grants to individuals.
Application information: Minnesota Common Grant Application Form is preferred.
Initial approach: Proposal
Copies of proposal: 1
Deadline(s): None
Board meeting date(s): Oct.
Officers and Directors:* David C. Sherman,* Pres.; Roger L. Baker,* V.P.; Sandra B. Sherman,* V.P.; James W. Peter,* Secy.-Treas.; Morris T. Baker III; Nancy W. Baker; Mary Baker-Philbin; Laura S. Decker; Tobias R. Philbin; Charles C. Pineo III; Linda Baker Pineo; William J. Sherman.
Number of staff: 1 part-time professional; 1 part-time support.
EIN: 416022591

1660
Bank Street Foundation
80 S. 8th St., Ste. 1910
Minneapolis, MN 55402-2111

Donor(s): David M. Winton.
Grantmaker type: Independent foundation
Financial data (yr. ended 12/31/02): Assets, $672,803 (M); expenditures, $174,485; qualifying distributions, $164,600; giving activities include $164,600 for 16 grants (high: $50,000; low: $1,000).
Fields of interest: Arts; Education; Landscaping; Federated giving programs; Civil liberties, advocacy.
Limitations: Applications not accepted. Giving primarily in Minneapolis, MN. No grants to individuals.
Application information: Contributes only to pre-selected organizations.
Trustees: David M. Winton; Sarah R. Winton.
EIN: 411858115

1661
The Beim Foundation
20450 Lakeview Ave.
Deephaven, MN 55331 (952) 470-1236
Contact: William H. Beim, Jr., Pres.
E-mail: bbeim@msn.com; URL: http://www.beimfoundation.org

Incorporated in 1947 in MN.
Donor(s): N.C. Beim,‡ Raymond N. Beim.‡
Grantmaker type: Independent foundation
Financial data (yr. ended 12/31/02): Assets, $6,899,302 (M); gifts received, $89,187; expenditures, $714,517; qualifying distributions, $659,900; giving activities include $648,500 for 134 grants (high: $50,000; low: $1,000).
Purpose and activities: Primary areas of interest include the environment, conservation, wildlife, women, and the arts.
Fields of interest: Arts; Education; Natural resources; Environment; Animals/wildlife, preservation/protection; Human services; Women, centers/services; Women.
Types of support: Capital campaigns; Building/renovation; Equipment; Land acquisition; Program development; Seed money; Program evaluation.

Limitations: Giving limited to the upper Midwest, with emphasis on MN. No grants to individuals, or for deficit financing; no loans.
Publications: Application guidelines.
Application information: Current application guidelines available on Web site. Application form not required.
Initial approach: Proposal
Copies of proposal: 1
Deadline(s): Refer to Web site
Board meeting date(s): May and Nov.
Final notification: May 31 and Nov. 30
Officers and Directors:* William H. Beim, Jr.,* Pres.; Patricia Arnold,* V.P. and Secy.; Judith McKim,* V.P. and Treas.; Jack Arnold; Andrew H. Beim; Beth Conover; Carol Nulsen; Scott Russell.
EIN: 416022529

1662
David Winton Bell Foundation
1660 South Hwy. 100, Ste. 426
St. Louis Park, MN 55416 (952) 512-1165
Contact: Randall J. Sukovich

Established in 1955 in NY.
Donor(s): Charles H. Bell, Lucy W. Bell.
Grantmaker type: Independent foundation
Financial data (yr. ended 12/31/02): Assets, $3,076,406 (M); expenditures, $173,996; qualifying distributions, $159,327; giving activities include $159,500 for 35 grants (high: $19,000; low: $1,000).
Purpose and activities: Giving primarily to programs addressing environmental preservation and education, critical social education, and human service needs in Minneapolis.
Fields of interest: Child development, education; Higher education; Education; Natural resources; Environment; Animals/wildlife, preservation/protection; Employment, services; Human services; Children/youth, services; Child development, services; Family services; Community development; Minorities; Disabled; Economically disadvantaged.
Types of support: General/operating support; Continuing support; Capital campaigns; Building/renovation; Program development; Seed money.
Limitations: Applications not accepted. Giving primarily in Minneapolis, MN.
Application information: Unsolicited requests for funds not considered.
Trustees: Charles H. Bell; John M. Hartwell; Lucy B. Hartwell; Penny B. Hatten.
Number of staff: None.
EIN: 416023104

1663
James Ford Bell Foundation
1818 Oliver Ave. S.
Minneapolis, MN 55405 (612) 377-8400
Contact: Diane B. Neimann, Exec. Dir.
FAX: (612) 377-8407; *E-mail:* general@fpadvisors.com; URL: http://www.fpadvisors.com

Established in 1955 in MN.
Donor(s): Charles H. Bell, James Ford Bell.‡
Grantmaker type: Independent foundation
Financial data (yr. ended 12/31/02): Assets, $10,524,299 (M); expenditures, $776,628;

qualifying distributions, $783,375; giving activities include $614,679 for 38 grants (high: $200,000; low: $300) and $42,386 for 12 employee matching gifts.
Purpose and activities: Emphasis on cultural programs; support also for wildlife preservation and conservation, youth agencies, and education, health and human services.
Fields of interest: Museums; Arts; Early childhood education; Child development, education; Higher education; Adult/continuing education; Adult education—literacy, basic skills & GED; Reading; Education; Natural resources; Environment; Animals/wildlife, preservation/protection; Family planning; Human services; Children/youth, services; Child development, services; Family services; Reproductive rights; Urban/community development; Community development; Biological sciences; Population studies; Minorities; Asians/Pacific Islanders; African Americans/Blacks; Hispanics/Latinos; Native Americans/American Indians; Disabled; Women; Immigrants/refugees; Economically disadvantaged.
Types of support: General/operating support; Continuing support; Capital campaigns; Building/renovation; Endowments; Program development; Seed money; Internship funds.
Limitations: Applications not accepted. Giving primarily in MN. No grants to individuals, or for fellowships, memberships, annual campaigns, or special events or fundraisers.
Publications: Annual report.
Application information: Unsolicited requests for funds not accepted.
Board meeting date(s): Spring and fall
Officers and Trustees:* Ford W. Bell,* Chair.; Diane B. Neimann, Exec. Dir.; Samuel H. Bell, Jr.; David B. Hartwell.
Number of staff: None.
EIN: 416023099

1664
The Beverly Foundation
(formerly The Beverly Deikel Foundation)
5354 Parkdale Dr., Ste. 310
Minneapolis, MN 55416 (952) 545-3000
Contact: Beverly Deikel, Pres.

Established in 1999 in MN.
Donor(s): Beverly Deikel.
Grantmaker type: Independent foundation
Financial data (yr. ended 12/31/02): Assets, $25,387,376 (M); gifts received, $10,500; expenditures, $1,434,952; qualifying distributions, $1,315,963; giving activities include $1,287,168 for 85 grants (high: $456,251; low: $100).
Fields of interest: Arts; Education; Environment; Human services; Children/youth, services.
Types of support: General/operating support; Management development; Capital campaigns; Building/renovation; Emergency funds; Program development; Consulting services; Program evaluation.
Limitations: Giving primarily in MN. No grants to individuals.
Application information: Application form not required.
Initial approach: Letter or proposal
Copies of proposal: 1
Deadline(s): None

Officer: Beverly Deikel, Pres. and Secy.-Treas.
Number of staff: 1 part-time professional; 1 part-time support.
EIN: 411958161

1665
Bush Foundation ▼
E-900 First National Bank Bldg.
332 Minnesota St.
St. Paul, MN 55101 (651) 227-0891
Contact: Anita M. Pampusch, Pres.
FAX: (651) 297-6485; E-mail:
info@bushfoundation.org; URL: http://
www.bushfoundation.org

Incorporated in 1953 in MN.
Donor(s): Archibald Granville Bush,‡ Edyth Bassler Bush.‡
Grantmaker type: Independent foundation
Financial data (yr. ended 11/30/02): Assets, $608,648,465 (M); gifts received, $900,000; expenditures, $43,695,084; qualifying distributions, $35,653,887; giving activities include $29,410,397 for 313 grants (high: $1,000,000; low: $6,000; average: $20,000–$150,000) and $2,546,923 for grants to individuals.
Purpose and activities: Support largely for education, arts and humanities, human services, delivery of health care, minority opportunity, and women and girls. Also operates the Bush Leadership Fellows Program, the Bush Artist Fellowship Program and the Bush Medical Fellows Program.
Fields of interest: Media/communications; Visual arts; Museums; Performing arts; Music; Humanities; Literature; Arts; Higher education; Education; Environment; Health care; Youth development, services; Human services; Minorities; Women; Immigrants/refugees.
Types of support: Capital campaigns; Building/renovation; Program development; Fellowships; Matching/challenge support.
Limitations: Giving primarily in MN, ND, and SD. No support for private foundations. No grants to individuals (except for fellowships), or for research in biomedical and health sciences. Generally, no grants for continuing operating support; construction of hospitals or medical facilities, church sanctuaries, individual day care centers, municipal buildings, or buildings in public colleges and universities; or for covering operating deficits or to retire mortgages or other debts; no loans.
Publications: Application guidelines, Annual report, Financial statement, Grants list, Program policy statement.
Application information: Prefers use of foundation cover sheet. Application form not required.
Initial approach: Letter of inquiry
Copies of proposal: 2
Deadline(s): Mar. 1, July 1, and Nov. 1
Board meeting date(s): Mar., Apr., July, and Nov.
Final notification: 10 days after board meetings
Officers and Directors:* William P. Pierskalla,* Chair.; Esperanza Guerrero-Anderson,* 1st Vice-Chair.; Ivy S. Bernhardson,* 2nd Vice-Chair.; Anita M. Pampusch, Pres.; Dudley Cocke,* Secy.; Kathryn H. Tunheim,* Treas.; Connie Thompson, C.F.O.; Terence Doyle,

Genl. Counsel; Wilson Bradshaw; Shirley M. Clark; Roxanne Givens Copeland; Steve Goldstein; Robert J. Jones, Ph.D.; Diana E. Murphy; Catherine V. Piersol; Gordon M. Sprenger; W. Richard West, Jr.; Ann Wynia.
Number of staff: 11 full-time professional; 6 full-time support; 2 part-time support.
EIN: 416017815
Recent environmental and animal welfare grants:
1665-1 Cannon River Watershed Partnership, Northfield, MN, $180,000. For stormwater runoff study and development of best management practices. 2002.
1665-2 Clean Up the River Environment, Montevideo, MN, $68,000. For program support. 2002.
1665-3 Clean Water Fund, Minneapolis, MN, $210,000. For grassroots development campaign in North Dakota and Minnesota. 2002.
1665-4 Dakota Rural Action, Brookings, SD, $60,000. To expand efforts to involve citizens in agricultural policy and land use practices in South Dakota. 2002.
1665-5 Farmers Legal Action Group (FLAG), Saint Paul, MN, $140,000. For Farm Preservation Advocacy Project. 2002.
1665-6 Illusion Theater and School, Minneapolis, MN, $100,000. For community-based program to prevent and reduce effects of lead poisoning among Minnesota children. 2002.
1665-7 Institute for Local Self-Reliance, Minneapolis, MN, $250,000. For New Rules Project to increase community self-reliance with focus in Minnesota and North and South Dakota. 2002.
1665-8 Izaak Walton League of America, Gaithersburg, MD, $150,000. To promote improvements to coal-fired power plants and overcome barriers to transmission improvements for wind power in Minnesota, North Dakota, and South Dakota. 2002.
1665-9 Lake Area Zoological Society, Watertown, SD, $170,000. To establish Roots and Shoots program for Northern Great Plains. 2002.
1665-10 Midtown Greenway Coalition, Minneapolis, MN, $100,000. To hire additional staff. 2002.
1665-11 Minnesota Environmental Partnership, Saint Paul, MN, $150,000. For program support. 2002.
1665-12 Minnesota Landscape Arboretum Foundation, Chanhassen, MN, $500,000. For capital campaign to construct new Visitor Center. 2002.
1665-13 Sierra Club Foundation, San Francisco, CA, $150,000. To conduct Phase II of Minnesota Air Toxics Campaign. 2002.
1665-14 Sustainable Resources Center, Minneapolis, MN, $31,500. To establish connection between community gardens and lead poisoning; implement program that educates gardeners on connection between lead and nutrition; increase lead inspections; and develop indicators of success. 2002.

1666
Patrick and Aimee Butler Family Foundation
US Bank Bldg., E-1420
332 Minnesota St.
St. Paul, MN 55101-1369 (651) 222-2565
Contact: Kerrie Blevins, Prog. Dir.
E-mail: info@butlerfamilyfoundation.org; URL: http://www.butlerfamilyfoundation.org

Incorporated in 1951 in MN.
Donor(s): Patrick Butler,‡ Aimee Mott Butler.‡
Grantmaker type: Independent foundation
Financial data (yr. ended 12/31/02): Assets, $48,729,689 (M); gifts received, $350,000; expenditures, $4,088,203; qualifying distributions, $3,820,604; giving activities include $3,809,441 for 110 grants (high: $2,621,441; low: $2,500; average: $5,000–$30,000).
Purpose and activities: Primary areas of interest include the disadvantaged, women, family and other social services, and the environment.
Fields of interest: Museums; Humanities; Arts; Environment; Substance abuse, services; Housing/shelter, development; Human services; Family services; Women, centers/services.
Types of support: General/operating support; Continuing support; Annual campaigns; Program development; Consulting services.
Limitations: Giving primarily in the St. Paul and Minneapolis, MN, area. No support for criminal justice, secondary and elementary education, health or hospitals, employment or vocational programs, music or dance programs, or economic education. No grants to individuals, or for medical research, films or videos, capital funds, or endowment funds; no loans.
Publications: Annual report (including application guidelines), Grants list.
Application information: Applicant must submit Butler Family Foundation Application Form in addition to full proposal. Application form required.
Initial approach: Letter or telephone requesting guidelines
Copies of proposal: 1
Deadline(s): Mar. and July
Board meeting date(s): June and Sept.
Final notification: July for Mar. deadline, Oct. for July deadline
Officers and Trustees:* Peter M. Butler,* Pres.; Patrick Butler,* V.P.; Shehla Tauscher, Secy.; John K. Butler,* Treas.; Brigid M. Butler; Cecelia M. Butler; Kate Butler; Patricia Butler; Paul S. Butler; Sandra K. Butler; Suzanne A. LeFevour.
Number of staff: 2 part-time professional; 1 part-time support.
EIN: 416009902
Recent environmental and animal welfare grants:
1666-1 American Rivers, DC, $15,000. To promote Ecological Design for River Communities. 2002.
1666-2 Eagle Bluff Environmental Learning Center, Lanesboro, MN, $10,000. For general operating support. 2002.
1666-3 Friends of the Mississippi River, Saint Paul, MN, $10,000. For general operating support. 2002.
1666-4 Methow Conservancy, Winthrop, WA, $10,000. For Methow Valley Recycling Project. 2002.

1666-5 Minnesota Center for Environmental Advocacy, Saint Paul, MN, $10,000. For general operating support. 2002.

1666-6 Minnesota Land Trust, Saint Paul, MN, $10,000. For general operating support. 2002.

1666-7 Oregon Water Trust, Portland, Oregon, $10,000. For general operating support. 2002.

1666-8 Pacific Crest Outward Bound School, Portland, Oregon, $10,000. For Pinnacle Scholarship Fund. 2002.

1666-9 Parks and Trails Council of Minnesota, Saint Paul, MN, $10,000. For Samuel H. Morgan land acquisition. 2002.

1666-10 Trust for Public Land, Saint Paul, MN, $15,000. For Minnesota State Office. 2002.

1666-11 Trustees of Reservations, Beverly, MA, $12,000. For general operating support. 2002.

1667
Buuck Family Foundation

c/o Lowry Hill
90 S. 7th St., Ste. 5300
Minneapolis, MN 55402
Contact: Robert E. Buuck, Pres.
Application address: 8800 Deer Ridge Ln., Bloomington, MN 55438; FAX: (612) 667-7839

Established in 1995 in MN.
Donor(s): Gail P. Buuck, Robert P. Buuck.
Grantmaker type: Independent foundation
Financial data (yr. ended 12/31/02): Assets, $8,847,257 (M); expenditures, $632,246; qualifying distributions, $589,511; giving activities include $575,500 for 83 grants (high: $70,000; low: $250; average: $250–$50,000).
Purpose and activities: Giving primarily for environmental issues and programs.
Fields of interest: Arts; Scholarships/financial aid; Environment; Protestant agencies & churches.
Types of support: General/operating support; Continuing support; Annual campaigns; Capital campaigns; Building/renovation; Land acquisition; Endowments; Emergency funds; Research.
Limitations: Applications not accepted. Giving primarily in MN. No grants to individuals.
Publications: Annual report.
Application information: Contributes only to pre-selected organizations.
Officers: Robert E. Buuck, Pres.; David A. Buuck, V.P. and Secy.; Gail P. Buuck, V.P. and Treas.; John R. Buuck, V.P.; Katherine E. Fratzke, V.P.
Number of staff: None.
EIN: 411796911

1668
Cargill, Incorporated Corporate Giving Program

c/o Citizenship Comm.
P.O. Box 5650
Minneapolis, MN 55440-5650
(952) 742-4311
Contact: Stacey Smida, Admin., Grants
Additional contact: Michelle Grogg, Sr. Prog. Off., tel.: (952) 742-2931, E-mail: michelle_grogg@cargill.com; Additional address: Cargill Office Ctr., 15407 McGinty Rd. W., Wayzata, MN 55391-2399 (express mail or messenger); FAX: (952) 742-7224; E-mail: stacey_smida@cargill.com; URL: http://www.cargill.com/commun/index.htm

Grantmaker type: Corporate giving program
Financial data (yr. ended 05/31/02): Total giving, $4,650,245; giving activities include $4,562,637 for 564 grants (high: $350,000; low: $100) and $87,608 for employee matching gifts.
Purpose and activities: Cargill makes charitable contributions to nonprofit organizations involved with K-12 and higher education, natural resources conservation and protection, food and nutrition, and economically disadvantaged youth. Support is given on a national and international basis.
Fields of interest: Elementary/secondary education; Higher education; Natural resources; Agriculture/food; Youth, services; Economically disadvantaged.
Types of support: General/operating support; Continuing support; Capital campaigns; Program development; Employee volunteer services; Employee matching gifts; Employee-related scholarships; Scholarships—to individuals; Donated land; Donated products.
Limitations: Giving on a national and international basis in areas of company operations; giving also to regional, national, and international organizations active in areas of company operations. No support for religious organizations not of direct benefit to the entire community. No grants to individuals (except for scholarships), or for research, planning, personal needs, or travel, public service or political campaigns, lobbying, political, or fraternal activities, benefit dinners, fundraising, or tickets, disease-specific activities, athletic scholarships, advertising, publications, audio-visual production, or special broadcasts, or endowments; generally, no grants for general operating support or capital campaigns.
Publications: Application guidelines, Corporate giving report, Informational brochure.
Application information: Unsolicited requests from institutions of higher education are not accepted. Proposals should be no longer than 2 to 3 pages in length. An application form is required for regional, national, and international organizations following receipt of an eligible proposal; application form available online. The company may request additional information at a later date. A site visit may be requested. The Public Affairs Department handles giving. The company has a staff that only handles contributions.
> *Initial approach:* Proposal to nearest company facility; mail or E-mail proposal to headquarters for regional, national, and international organizations; contact

headquarters for general operating support or capital campaign requests
> *Deadline(s):* None
> *Final notification:* 3 months for regional, national, and international organizations submitting application forms

Number of staff: 4 full-time professional.

1669
Carolyn Foundation

901 Marquette Ave., Ste. 2630
Minneapolis, MN 55402 (612) 596-3279
Contact: Rebecca L. Erdahl, Exec. Dir.
FAX: (612) 338-2084; E-mail: carolyn@winternet.com; URL: http://www.carolynfoundation.org

Trust established in 1964 in MN.
Donor(s): Carolyn McKnight Christian.‡
Grantmaker type: Independent foundation
Financial data (yr. ended 12/31/02): Assets, $29,000,000 (M); expenditures, $1,173,192; qualifying distributions, $1,023,072; giving activities include $745,000 for 45 grants (high: $50,000; low: $5,000; average: $5,000–$25,000) and $39,890 for 81 employee matching gifts.
Purpose and activities: Priorities include children and families, the environment, community and arts, and the disadvantaged.
Fields of interest: Arts; Education; Environment; Health care; Human services; Children/youth, services; Women; Economically disadvantaged.
Types of support: General/operating support; Annual campaigns; Capital campaigns; Building/renovation; Equipment; Land acquisition; Program development; Seed money; Curriculum development.
Limitations: Giving primarily in New Haven, CT, and Minneapolis-St. Paul, MN. No support for political or veterans' groups, fraternal societies, or religious organizations for religious purposes. No grants to individuals, or for endowment funds, annual fund drives, conferences, seminars, deficit funding, costs of litigation, or continuing support; no loans.
Application information: Application form optional. Please see foundation's Web site for the most current information regarding funding priorities, guidelines, and application process. Application form not required.
> *Initial approach:* Proposal (no more than 6 pages excluding other required documentation)
> *Copies of proposal:* 1
> *Deadline(s):* Jan. 31 and July 31
> *Board meeting date(s):* June and Dec.
> *Final notification:* June and Dec.

Officers and Trustees:* Charles C. Dobson,* Chair.; Anne T. Calabresi,* Vice-Chair.; Edwin L. Crosby, Vice-Chair.; Rebecca L. Erdahl, Secy. and Exec. Dir.; Thomas M. Crosby, Jr.,* Treas.; Guido Calabresi, Emeritus; Betsey Copp; Franklin M. Crosby III; G. Christian Crosby; Harriett Crosby; Stwart F. Crosby; Sumner McK. Crosby, Jr.; Sumner McK. Crosby III; Edmund C. Graham III; Lucy C. Mitchell.
Number of staff: 1 full-time professional; 1 part-time support.
EIN: 416044416

1670
CenterPoint Energy Minnegasco Corporate Giving Program

(formerly Reliant Energy Minnegasco Corporate Giving Program)
c/o Public Rels. Dept.
800 LaSalle Ave., P.O. Box 59038
Minneapolis, MN 55459-0038
(612) 321-4828
Contact: Patty Pederson, Assoc. Dir., Public Rels.; or Suzanne Pierazek, Sr. Public Rels. Rep.

Grantmaker type: Corporate giving program
Purpose and activities: CenterPoint Energy Minnegasco makes charitable contributions to nonprofit organizations involved with the environment, housing, and community development. Support is given primarily in areas of company operations.
Fields of interest: Environment; Housing/shelter; Community development.
Types of support: General/operating support; Employee volunteer services; Use of facilities; Sponsorships; Donated equipment; Donated products; In-kind gifts.
Limitations: Giving primarily in areas of company operations in MN. No support for United Way-supported organizations or religious or political organizations. No grants to individuals, or for travel, conferences, fundraising, capital campaigns, endowments, contingencies, reserve purposes, debt reduction, national fund drives, continuing support, or athletic activities.
Publications: Application guidelines.
Application information: The Public Relations Department handles giving. Application form required.
  Initial approach: Contact headquarters for application form
  Copies of proposal: 1
  Deadline(s): Quarterly
  Final notification: Following review
Administrators: Patty Pederson, Assoc. Dir., Public Rels.; Suzanne Pierazek, Sr. Public Rels. Rep.
Number of staff: 3 part-time professional.

1671
Central Minnesota Community Foundation

101 S. 7th Ave., Ste. 200
St. Cloud, MN 56301 (320) 253-4380
Contact: Steven R. Joul, Pres.
Toll-free tel.: (877) 253-4380; FAX: (320) 240-9215; E-mail: gstark@communitygiving.org; URL: http://www.communitygiving.org

Established in 1985 in MN.
Grantmaker type: Community foundation
Financial data (yr. ended 06/30/03): Assets, $35,661,913 (M); gifts received, $4,255,859; expenditures, $4,261,221; giving activities include $3,618,637 for grants (average: $250–$10,000).
Purpose and activities: To make a continuing relevant contribution to the present and future vitality of central MN, building the independence and interdependence of people in the development of self-capacity and fullness of life. The foundation administers donor-advised funds.

Fields of interest: Arts; Education; Environment; Youth development, services; Human services; Family services.
Types of support: Building/renovation; Equipment; Endowments; Program development; Conferences/seminars; Seed money; Scholarship funds; Technical assistance; Program-related investments/loans; Scholarships—to individuals.
Limitations: Giving primarily in Benton, Stearns, Morrison, and Sherburne counties, MN. No support for religious activities, or for political or fraternal organizations. No grants to individuals (except for designated scholarship funds), or for medical research, general operating expense, national fundraising, telephone solicitations, travel, capital campaigns, endowments or debt retirement.
Publications: Application guidelines, Annual report, Informational brochure, Newsletter.
Application information: Application guidelines and Minnesota Common Grant Application Form available on foundation Web site. Application form required.
  Initial approach: Telephone or letter requesting guidelines
  Copies of proposal: 10
  Deadline(s): June 1 and Dec. 1
  Board meeting date(s): 3rd Thurs. in Jan., Mar., May, July, and Oct.
  Final notification: 2 months after deadline date
Officers and Directors:* John Brownson,* Chair.; Jerry McCarter,* Vice-Chair.; Steven R. Joul,* Pres.; Mary Mathews,* Secy.; Loran Hall,* Treas.; Dean Anderson; Teresa Bohnen; Andy Hilger; Peter Hill; Kevin Hughes; Janet Knoblach; Shelly Bauerly Kopel; Alan Marcyes; Asha Morgan Moran; John Sullivan; Don Watkins.
Number of staff: 5 full-time professional; 2 full-time support; 1 part-time support.
EIN: 363412544

1672
The Collins Family Foundation

112 Groveland Terr.
Minneapolis, MN 55403

Established in 1994 in MN.
Donor(s): Arthur D. Collins, Anne B. Collins.
Grantmaker type: Independent foundation
Financial data (yr. ended 12/31/02): Assets, $1,550,666 (M); expenditures, $247,914; qualifying distributions, $243,692; giving activities include $245,650 for 43 grants (high: $92,000; low: $50).
Purpose and activities: Giving for family services, education and the arts.
Fields of interest: Arts; Business school/education; Education; Zoos/zoological societies; Family planning; Health organizations, association; Human services; YM/YWCAs & YM/YWHAs; Federated giving programs.
Limitations: Applications not accepted. Giving on a national basis. No grants to individuals.
Application information: Contributes only to pre-selected organizations.
Trustees: Anne B. Collins; Arthur D. Collins.
EIN: 411792606

1673
The Cote Foundation

10179 Crosstown Cir.
Eden Prairie, MN 55344
Contact: Jim Olson, Exec. Dir.

Established in 1961 in MN.
Donor(s): James Randolph Cote, Jim Olson.
Grantmaker type: Independent foundation
Financial data (yr. ended 02/28/02): Assets, $1,651,927 (M); expenditures, $528,708; qualifying distributions, $503,079; giving activities include $504,000 for 9 grants (high: $480,000; low: $1,000).
Fields of interest: Elementary/secondary education; Natural resources.
Limitations: Giving primarily in MN. No grants to individuals.
Application information:
  Initial approach: Letter
  Deadline(s): None
  Board meeting date(s): July and Jan.
Officer: Jim Olson, Exec. Dir.
Trustees: Mary C. Boos; James Randolph Cote; Robert C. Cote; Samual Ruggles Cote; Kelly Cote Jasper; Carolyn Jones.
EIN: 416022646

1674
Cottonwood Foundation

P.O. Box 10803
White Bear Lake, MN 55110-3755
(651) 426-8797
Contact: Paul Moss, Exec. Dir.
FAX: (651) 426-0320; E-mail: cottonwood@igc.org; URL: http://www.cottonwoodfdn.org/

Established in 1992 in MN.
Grantmaker type: Public charity
Financial data (yr. ended 12/31/02): Revenue, $51,468; assets, $67,737 (M); gifts received, $49,337; expenditures, $42,820; program services expenses, $40,000; giving activities include $40,000 for 40 grants of $1,000 each.
Purpose and activities: The foundation awards grants to grassroots organizations active in promoting cultural diversity, protecting the environment, empowering people to meet their basic needs, and encouraging volunteerism. Small grants, ranging from $500 to $1,000, are awarded to organizations and projects that meet all of these four criteria.
Fields of interest: Environment; International affairs; Community development; Economically disadvantaged.
Types of support: General/operating support; Continuing support; Annual campaigns; Capital campaigns; Building/renovation; Equipment; Land acquisition; Program development; Publication; Seed money; Curriculum development; Matching/challenge support.
Limitations: Giving on a national and international basis. No support for for-profit organizations, political and religious organizations, governmental agencies, or universities. No grants to individuals.
Publications: Application guidelines, Annual report, Grants list, Informational brochure, Newsletter.
Application information: Unsolicited grant applications are not accepted at this time; see Web site for additional information.

Board meeting date(s): Every other month
Officers and Directors:* Jeff Washburne,*
Chair.; Craig R. Miller,* Vice-Chair.; Karen
Grabau,* Secy.; Suzanne Wisniewski,* Treas.;
Paul Moss, Exec. Dir.; Sarah Hannigan; Karissa
Huntington; Jan Lucke; Lucinda Pepper; Paul
Schmiechen; Laura Van Tassel.
EIN: 411714008

1675
Cox Family Fund
1920 S. 1st St., Ste. 403
Minneapolis, MN 55454-1096

Incorporated in 1986 in MN.
Donor(s): David C. Cox, Vicki B. Cox.
Grantmaker type: Independent foundation
Financial data (yr. ended 12/31/00): Assets,
$5,375,224 (M); gifts received, $483,427;
expenditures, $286,707; qualifying distributions,
$274,000; giving activities include $274,000 for
44 grants (high: $25,000; low: $500).
Purpose and activities: Giving for arts and
culture, education and the environment.
Fields of interest: Arts; Education; Environment;
Human services.
Limitations: Applications not accepted. Giving
primarily in MN. No grants to individuals.
Application information: Contributes only to
pre-selected organizations.
Officers and Directors:* David C. Cox,* Pres.
and Treas.; Vicki B. Cox,* V.P. and Secy.; Philip
S. Sherburne.
EIN: 411570849

1676
Edwin W. and Catherine M. Davis
Foundation
332 Minnesota St., Ste. 2100
St. Paul, MN 55101-1394 (651) 228-0935
Contact: Bette D. Moorman, Pres.
FAX: (651) 228-0776

Incorporated in 1956 in MN.
Donor(s): Samuel S. Davis,‡ Edwin W. Davis,‡
Frederick W. Davis.‡
Grantmaker type: Independent foundation
Financial data (yr. ended 12/31/02): Assets,
$14,813,635 (M); gifts received, $3,353,182;
expenditures, $663,975; qualifying distributions,
$606,584; giving activities include $577,681 for
grants (average: $1,000–$10,000).
Purpose and activities: Concerned with the
amelioration of social problems and increasing
the opportunities available to disadvantaged
people, with particular interest in the fields of
education, social welfare, mental health, the
arts, and environmental problems. Educational
grants primarily for colleges and universities.
Fields of interest: Arts; Higher education;
Natural resources; Mental health/crisis services;
Human services; Children/youth, services.
Types of support: General/operating support;
Continuing support; Annual campaigns;
Scholarship funds.
Limitations: Giving primarily in CA and WA. No
grants to individuals, or for emergency funds,
capital outlay, building funds or equipment, or
endowments; no loans.
Publications: Annual report (including
application guidelines).

Application information: Application form not
required.
Initial approach: Letter (no more than 3 pages)
Copies of proposal: 1
Deadline(s): None
Board meeting date(s): May or June and as
required
Final notification: 4 to 6 weeks
Officers and Directors:* Bette D. Moorman,*
Pres.; Mary E. Davis,* V.P.; Fred W. Davis II,*
Secy.; Lisa M. Fremont.
Number of staff: None.
EIN: 416012064

1677
The Donaldson Foundation
1400 W. 94th St.
Bloomington, MN 55431
Contact: Norman C. Linnell, Pres.
Application address: P.O. Box 1299,
Minneapolis, MN 55440, tel.: (952) 703-4999;
E-mail:
donaldsonfoundation@mail.donaldson.com;
URL: http://www.donaldson.com/en/about/
community/foundation.html

Established in 1966 in MN.
Donor(s): Donaldson Co., Inc.
Grantmaker type: Company-sponsored
foundation
Financial data (yr. ended 07/31/02): Assets,
$2,251,448 (M); expenditures, $917,706;
qualifying distributions, $857,536; giving
activities include $841,091 for 61 grants (high:
$187,000; low: $1,000) and $16,445 for
employee matching gifts.
Fields of interest: Arts; Education, association;
Vocational education; Higher education;
Environment; Health care; Youth, services;
Community development; Federated giving
programs.
Types of support: Annual campaigns; Capital
campaigns; Building/renovation; Employee
matching gifts.
Limitations: Giving primarily in areas of
company operations, including IA, IL, IN, KY,
MN, MO, and WI. No support for religious
organizations. No grants to individuals.
Application information: Application form not
required.
Initial approach: Letter
Copies of proposal: 1
Deadline(s): None
Board meeting date(s): Feb., May, Aug., and
Nov.
Officers and Trustees:* Norm Linnell,* Pres. and
Treas.; Sandra Johnson,* Secy.; Marty Barris;
Becky Cahn; H. Young Chung; Pat Fisher; Karen
Geronime; Tim Grafe; Dennis Grigal; Jim
Martin; Jeff May; Aileen Torgeson.
EIN: 416052950

1678
Duluth-Superior Area Community
Foundation
Medical Arts Bldg.
324 W. Superior St., Ste. 212
Duluth, MN 55802-1707 (218) 726-0232
Contact: Holly C. Sampson, Pres.
FAX: (218) 726-0257; E-mail:
info@dsacommunityfoundation.com; URL: http://
www.dsacommunityfoundation.com

Established in 1982 in MN.
Grantmaker type: Community foundation
Financial data (yr. ended 12/31/02): Assets,
$29,475,130 (M); gifts received, $1,541,308;
expenditures, $1,598,753; giving activities
include $828,454 for 169 grants (high: $25,000;
low: $332; average: $332–$25,000) and
$332,656 for 155 grants to individuals (high:
$5,500; low: $170; average: $170–$5,500).
Purpose and activities: Support primarily for
welfare, including emergency relief, family
services, employment, hunger, shelter, nonprofit
capacity building, and youth and child welfare;
education, especially higher education and
programs for minorities; cultural programs,
including music and other performing and fine
arts groups; and the environment. Support also
for peace organizations and intercultural
relations, community development, and Native
Americans; also awards scholarships to
promising high school graduates, small business
entrepreneurs, and returning adult students. The
foundation administers donor-advised funds.
Fields of interest: Visual arts; Performing arts;
Music; Arts; Child development, education;
Higher education; Education; Environment;
Animal welfare; Crime/violence prevention;
Employment; Food services; Housing/shelter,
development; Human services; Children/youth,
services; Child development, services; Family
services; Homeless, human services;
International affairs, goodwill promotion;
International peace/security; Race/intergroup
relations; Economic development; Community
development; Government/public
administration; Minorities; Native
Americans/American Indians; Disabled;
Women; Economically disadvantaged;
Homeless.
Types of support: General/operating support;
Emergency funds; Program development;
Publication; Seed money; Curriculum
development; Scholarship funds; Research;
Technical assistance; Consulting services;
Program evaluation; Scholarships—to
individuals.
Limitations: Giving primarily in Douglas and
Bayfield counties, WI, and Koochiching, Itasca,
St. Louis, Lake, Cook, Carlton, and Aitkin
counties in northeastern MN. No support for
direct religious activities. Generally, no grants to
individuals (except for designated scholarship
funds or specialized one-time crisis programs),
or for capital or annual campaigns,
endowments, debt retirement, medical research,
national fundraising programs, continuing
support, deficit financing, land acquisition, or
for grants beyond single funding cycle; no loans.
Publications: Application guidelines, Annual
report, Grants list, Informational brochure
(including application guidelines), Newsletter.
Application information: Low priority given to
capital and equipment requests. Minnesota

Common Grant Application Form required.
Application form required.
Initial approach: Telephone or letter for
guidelines, E-mail request is preferred
Copies of proposal: 3
Deadline(s): Feb. 1, Apr. 1, Aug. 1, and Oct. 1
Board meeting date(s): Monthly
Final notification: 60-90 days after deadline
Officers and Trustees:* Thomas B. Wheeler,*
Chair.; Nan R. Olson,* Vice-Chair.; Holly C.
Sampson, C.E.O. and Pres.; Karen Fillenworth,*
Secy.; Abbot G. Apter, Treas.; Peter L. Boman;
Paul R. Buckley; Helena E. Jackson; Todd L.
Johnson; John P. Lawien; Ilene F. Levin; Robert
Mars, Jr.; Mary E. Millard; Lyle W. Northey;
James H. Stewart; Donald L. Wallgreen.
Number of staff: 3 full-time professional; 3
part-time professional; 1 full-time support.
EIN: 411429402

1679
Ecolab Foundation
370 Wabasha St.
St. Paul, MN 55102
Contact: Lois West Duffy, V.P.

Established in 1982 in MN.
Donor(s): Ecolab Inc.
Grantmaker type: Company-sponsored
foundation
Financial data (yr. ended 12/31/01): Assets,
$5,485,860 (M); gifts received, $3,402,584;
expenditures, $3,038,181; qualifying
distributions, $3,038,170; giving activities
include $3,108,395 for 1,079 grants (high:
$125,000; low: $10; average: $100–$50,000).
Purpose and activities: Support for youth and
education, civic and community development,
arts and culture, environment and conservation
and community based contributions.
Fields of interest: Arts; Education; Environment;
Health care; Health organizations, association;
Youth development; Community development.
Types of support: General/operating support;
Employee matching gifts; Employee-related
scholarships.
Limitations: Giving primarily in San Jose, CA,
Atlanta, GA, Joliet, IL, Huntington, IN, St. Paul,
MN, Greensboro, NC, Grand Forks, ND,
Woodbridge, NJ, Hebron, OH, Memphis, TN,
Garland, TX, Beloit, WI, and Martinsburg, WV.
No support for sectarian or denominational
religious organizations unless used for direct
community interest, disease-specific
organizations, sports and athletic programs, or
industry, trade, or professional association
memberships. No grants to individuals (except
for employee-related scholarships); no loans or
program-related investments.
Publications: Corporate giving report (including
application guidelines), Grants list.
Application information: The foundation
accepts the Minnesota Common Grant Form.
Application form required.
Initial approach: Letter of inquiry requesting
application guidelines
Copies of proposal: 1
Deadline(s): Sept. 15
Board meeting date(s): Quarterly
Final notification: Mar.
Officers and Directors:* Michael J. Monahan,*
Pres.; Lawrence T. Bell,* V.P.; Lois West Duffy,

V.P.; John G. Forsythe, V.P.; Diana D. Lewis, V.P.;
William A. Mathison, V.P.; Thomas J. Hill, Treas.
Number of staff: 1 full-time professional; 1
part-time support.
EIN: 411372157

1680
Ecotrust Foundation
c/o Wells Fargo Bank Minnesota, N.A.
90 S. 7th St., Ste. 5300
Minneapolis, MN 55402

Established in 1992 in MN.
Donor(s): V. Wurtele, Peter Vaughan.
Grantmaker type: Independent foundation
Financial data (yr. ended 12/31/02): Assets,
$2,322,933 (M); gifts received, $50,036;
expenditures, $376,235; qualifying distributions,
$357,676; giving activities include $359,785 for
61 grants (high: $106,000; low: $100).
Purpose and activities: Giving primarily for
environmental research, protection and
conservation, including population control and
family planning services.
Fields of interest: Natural resources;
Environment; Family services.
Limitations: Applications not accepted. No
grants to individuals.
Application information: Contributes only to
pre-selected organizations.
Officer: Peter Vaughan.
EIN: 411735062

1681
Fairview Foundation
P.O. Box 64713
St. Paul, MN 55164-0713

Established in 1999 in MD.
Grantmaker type: Independent foundation
Financial data (yr. ended 06/30/02): Assets,
$653,553 (M); gifts received, $13,230;
expenditures, $307,117; qualifying distributions,
$298,159; giving activities include $305,000 for
11 grants (high: $100,000; low: $5,000).
Fields of interest: Education; Environment;
Medical research, institute.
Limitations: Applications not accepted. Giving
primarily in Washington, DC. No grants to
individuals.
Application information: Contributes only to
pre-selected organizations.
Officer: Harriett Crosby, Pres.
Directors: Lester Brown; Eliza Klose.
EIN: 311633189

1682
Federated Insurance Foundation, Inc.
121 E. Park Sq.
Owatonna, MN 55060 (507) 455-8906
Contact: Brian Brose, Admin.

Established in 1972.
Grantmaker type: Independent foundation
Financial data (yr. ended 12/31/02): Assets,
$243,302 (M); gifts received, $61,031;
expenditures, $269,312; qualifying distributions,
$264,339; giving activities include $264,253 for
160 grants (high: $50,000; low: $74).

Purpose and activities: Giving primarily to
education and human services.
Fields of interest: Higher education;
Libraries/library science; Education;
Animals/wildlife, preservation/protection;
Children/youth, services; Federated giving
programs; General charitable giving.
Types of support: General/operating support.
Limitations: Giving primarily in MN.
Application information: Application form not
required.
Initial approach: Letter
Copies of proposal: 1
Deadline(s): None
Board meeting date(s): As needed
Officers: A.T. Annexstad, Pres.; H.J. Moret, V.P.;
A.D. Lewis, Secy.; R.R. Stawarz, Treas.; Greg
Stroik.
EIN: 237173646

1683
H. B. Fuller Company Contributions
Program
1200 Willow Lake Blvd.
P.O. Box 64683
St. Paul, MN 55164-0683 (612) 236-5217
Contact: Naida M. Kissner, Community Affairs
Rep.
FAX: (612) 236-5065

Grantmaker type: Corporate giving program
Financial data (yr. ended 11/29/01): Total giving,
$556,645; giving activities include $556,645 for
grants (high: $2,000; low: $50).
Purpose and activities: As a complement to its
foundation, H.B. Fuller also makes charitable
contributions to nonprofit organizations directly.
Support is given on a national and international
basis.
Fields of interest: Arts; Education; Environment;
Health care; Human services; Community
development.
International interests: Canada; Europe; Latin
America.
Types of support: General/operating support;
Employee volunteer services; In-kind gifts.
Limitations: Giving on a national and
international basis in areas of company
operations, with emphasis on Roseville, CA,
Covington and Tucker, GA, Palatine, IL,
Paducah, KY, St. Paul, MN, and in Canada,
Europe, and Latin America. No support for
religious, fraternal, or veterans' organizations
not of direct benefit to the entire community,
political or lobbying organizations,
disease-specific organizations, or programs
which appear to be the responsibility of
government which are not community-based
efforts directed at improving the delivery of
government funded services. No grants to
individuals, or for travel, basic or applied
research, courtesy or public service advertising,
capital campaigns, or endowments.
Publications: Corporate giving report (including
application guidelines).
Application information: The Community
Affairs Department handles giving. The
company has a staff that only handles
contributions. A contributions committee
reviews all requests. Application form required.
Initial approach: Contact headquarters for
application form
Copies of proposal: 1

Deadline(s): None
Board meeting date(s): Monthly
Final notification: Following review
Community Affairs Department: Naida M.
Kissner, Community Affairs Rep.; Karen P.
Muller, Dir., Community Affairs.
Number of staff: 2 full-time professional.

1684
Greycoach Foundation
505 N. Highway 169, Ste. 595
Plymouth, MN 55441 (763) 417-2981
Contact: Sid Sehlin, Asst. Secy.
FAX: (763) 417-2984; E-mail:
swaychoff@kochfamily.net

Established in 1974 in MN.
Donor(s): Barbara G. Koch, David A. Koch.
Grantmaker type: Independent foundation
Financial data (yr. ended 11/30/01): Assets,
$11,160,557 (M); expenditures, $1,310,544;
qualifying distributions, $1,248,234; giving
activities include $1,256,000 for 41 grants (high:
$250,000; low: $2,000).
Purpose and activities: The foundation was
established and is operated according to the
basic truths and principles of the Roman
Catholic church.
Fields of interest: Elementary school/education;
Higher education; Animal welfare; Girl scouts;
Protestant agencies & churches.
Types of support: General/operating support;
Annual campaigns; Capital campaigns;
Building/renovation; Endowments; Program
development; Curriculum development;
Program-related investments/loans.
Limitations: Giving primarily in the Twin Cities,
MN, area. No grants to individuals.
Application information: Application form not
required.
  Initial approach: Letter
  Copies of proposal: 1
  Deadline(s): None
Officers: David A. Koch, Pres.; Barbara G.
Koch, V.P.; Paul M. Torgerson, Secy.
Trustee: Sidney R. Sehlin.
Number of staff: None.
EIN: 237417559

1685
Mary Livingston Griggs and Mary Griggs
Burke Foundation
1400 Norwest Ctr.
55 E. 5th St.
St. Paul, MN 55101-1792 (651) 227-7683
Contact: Marvin Pertzik, Secy.-Treas.

Established in 1966 in MN.
Donor(s): Mary L. Griggs.‡
Grantmaker type: Independent foundation
Financial data (yr. ended 06/30/01): Assets,
$29,010,630 (M); expenditures, $2,628,320;
qualifying distributions, $2,539,445; giving
activities include $2,479,610 for 91 grants (high:
$458,000; low: $500; average:
$2,500–$15,000).
Purpose and activities: Support primarily for arts
and culture, including museums and an Asian
cultural society; support also for conservation,
higher education, and social services.
Fields of interest: Museums; Arts; Higher
education; Natural resources; Human services.

Types of support: General/operating support;
Continuing support; Annual campaigns; Capital
campaigns; Building/renovation; Endowments;
Scholarship funds; Matching/challenge support.
Limitations: Giving primarily in St. Paul, MN,
and New York, NY. No grants to individuals.
Application information: Application form not
required.
  Initial approach: Letter
  Copies of proposal: 1
  Deadline(s): None
  Board meeting date(s): Quarterly
  Final notification: 10 days to 3 months
Officers and Directors:* Mary Griggs Burke,*
Pres.; C.E. Bayliss Griggs,* V.P.; Marvin Pertzik,*
Secy.-Treas.; Eleanor Briggs; Gale Lansing Davis.
Number of staff: None.
EIN: 416052355

1686
Hedberg Family Charitable Foundation
c/o U.S. Bank, Tax Svcs.
P.O. Box 64713
St. Paul, MN 55164-0713

Established in 1986.
Donor(s): John Hedberg.
Grantmaker type: Independent foundation
Financial data (yr. ended 12/31/02): Assets,
$775,646 (M); gifts received, $1,200;
expenditures, $155,081; qualifying distributions,
$151,812; giving activities include $151,000 for
2 grants (high: $151,000; low: $1,000).
Purpose and activities: Giving primarily for
medical research and care, justice and freedom
through rule of law, humane care of living
creatures, and protection and care of the
environment.
Fields of interest: Environment; Medical
research, institute; Human services.
Limitations: Applications not accepted. Giving
primarily in MN. No grants to individuals.
Application information: Contributes only to
pre-selected organizations.
Trustees: Jean Hedberg; John Hedberg; Peter
Hedberg; Stephen Hedberg; Thomas Hedberg;
Carolyn Stucky.
EIN: 411543653

1687
Huss Foundation
(formerly Alvin & Miriam Huss Foundation)
332 Minnesota St., Ste. W-3070
St. Paul, MN 55101

Established in 1983 in WI.
Donor(s): Alvin J. Huss.‡
Grantmaker type: Independent foundation
Financial data (yr. ended 12/31/02): Assets,
$11,514,838 (M); expenditures, $1,266,702;
qualifying distributions, $1,148,331; giving
activities include $1,144,312 for 22 grants (high:
$300,000; low: $2,000).
Fields of interest: Arts; Elementary
school/education; Higher education;
Environment; Hospitals (general); Alcoholism;
Girl scouts; Human services; Aging,
centers/services; Christian agencies & churches;
Aging.
Types of support: Annual campaigns; Capital
campaigns; Endowments; Research.

Limitations: Applications not accepted. Giving
on a national basis, with an emphasis on the
midwestern U.S. No grants to individuals.
Application information: Contributes only to
pre-selected organizations.
Trustees: Alvin J. Huss, Jr.; Ruth S. Huss.
Number of staff: 1 part-time support.
EIN: 391474563

1688
Imation Corp. Contributions Program
c/o Employee Involvement Comm.
1 Imation Pl.
Oakdale, MN 55128-3414
FAX: (651) 704-3892; E-mail for Computer Arts
Scholarship Prog.: cas@imation.com

Grantmaker type: Corporate giving program
Purpose and activities: Imation makes
charitable contributions to nonprofit
organizations involved with arts and culture,
education, the environment, and human
services. Special emphasis is directed towards
programs designed to expand access to
technology. Support is given primarily in
Tucson, Arizona, Camarillo, California,
Minneapolis and St. Paul, Minnesota,
Wahpeton, North Dakota, Weatherford,
Oklahoma, and Menomonie and Nekoosa,
Wisconsin.
Fields of interest: Arts; Secondary
school/education; Education; Environment;
Human services.
Types of support: General/operating support;
Employee volunteer services; Scholarships—to
individuals.
Limitations: Giving primarily in Tucson, AZ,
Camarillo, CA, Minneapolis and St. Paul, MN,
Wahpeton, ND, Weatherford, OK, and
Menomonie and Nekoosa, WI; giving on a
national basis for scholarships. No support for
pass-through organizations, political or lobbying
organizations, or religious organizations. No
grants to individuals (except through Computer
Arts Scholarship Program), or for endowments,
capital campaigns, memberships, or
professional sporting events, marathons, or
fundraising.
Application information: Requests may be
submitted using the Minnesota Common Grant
Application Form. A contributions committee
reviews all requests.
  Initial approach: Mail or fax proposal to
    headquarters
  Deadline(s): None; Dec. 14 for scholarships
  Board meeting date(s): Quarterly
  Final notification: 3 months; Feb. for
    scholarships

1689
John Larsen Foundation
2416 Humbolt
Minneapolis, MN 55405
Contact: John A. Larsen, Pres.
E-mail: johnlarsen@mn.rr.com

Established in 1991 in MN.
Grantmaker type: Independent foundation
Financial data (yr. ended 12/31/02): Assets,
$3,567,154 (M); expenditures, $281,536;
qualifying distributions, $193,880; giving

activities include $188,500 for 19 grants (high: $34,500; low: $1,000).
Fields of interest: Arts; Education; Environment; Human services; International human rights.
Types of support: General/operating support; Continuing support; Management development; Capital campaigns; Building/renovation; Endowments; Curriculum development; Matching/challenge support.
Limitations: Applications not accepted. Giving primarily in MN. No grants to individuals.
Publications: Annual report.
Application information: Unsolicited requests for funds not accepted.
  Board meeting date(s): Varies
Officers: John A. Larsen, Pres.; Karen R. Larsen, V.P.; John E. Larsen, Secy.; Kristen L. Rose, Treas.
Number of staff: 1 part-time support.
EIN: 411715465

1690
Steven C. Leuthold Family Foundation
412A Butler Sq.
100 N. 6th St.
Minneapolis, MN 55403
Contact: Steven C. Leuthold, Dir.

Established in 1990 in MN.
Donor(s): Steven C. Leuthold.
Grantmaker type: Independent foundation
Financial data (yr. ended 12/31/02): Assets, $9,315,808 (M); gifts received, $1,002,146; expenditures, $781,232; qualifying distributions, $695,253; giving activities include $650,000 for 97 grants (high: $33,000; low: $1,000).
Purpose and activities: Giving primarily for historical societies, education, nature conservation, animal welfare, children's and social services, and federated giving programs.
Fields of interest: Historic preservation/historical societies; Education; Natural resources; Animal welfare; Hospitals (general); Human services; Salvation Army; Children/youth, services; Federated giving programs.
Limitations: Giving primarily in Washington, DC, ID, and MN, with emphasis on Minneapolis; some funding nationally.
Application information:
  Initial approach: Letter
  Deadline(s): None
Directors: Linda Leuthold Donerkiel; Kurt Leuthold; Michael Leuthold; Russell Leuthold; Steven C. Leuthold.
EIN: 411680986

1691
Richard Coyle Lilly Foundation
c/o U.S. Bank, N.A.
332 Minnesota St., SPFS0270
St. Paul, MN 55101 (651) 244-0939
Contact: Jeffrey T. Peterson, Secy.

Incorporated in 1941 in MN.
Donor(s): Richard C. Lilly.‡
Grantmaker type: Independent foundation
Financial data (yr. ended 12/31/02): Assets, $8,902,992 (M); expenditures, $563,574; qualifying distributions, $464,872; giving activities include $441,300 for 84 grants (high: $35,000; low: $300).

Purpose and activities: Emphasis on higher and environmental education, culture, youth, and social services.
Fields of interest: Arts; Higher education; Natural resources; Environment; Human services; Children/youth, services.
Types of support: General/operating support; Continuing support; Annual campaigns; Building/renovation; Equipment; Land acquisition; Endowments; Program development; Publication; Seed money; Research; Matching/challenge support.
Limitations: Giving primarily in St. Paul, MN. No grants to individuals, or for fellowships or scholarships; no loans.
Application information: Application form not required.
  Initial approach: Proposal or letter
  Copies of proposal: 1
  Deadline(s): Nov. 1
  Board meeting date(s): Dec.
  Final notification: 6 weeks
Officers and Directors:* David M. Lilly,* Pres.; Elizabeth M. Lilly,* V.P.; Jeffrey T. Peterson,* Secy.; Susanne Lilly Hutcheson; Bruce A. Lilly; David M. Lilly, Jr.
Number of staff: None.
EIN: 416038717

1692
The Charles A. and Anne Morrow Lindbergh Foundation
2150 3rd Ave. N., Ste. 310
Anoka, MN 55303-2200 (763) 576-1596
Contact: Marlene White, Exec. Dir.
FAX: (763) 576-1664; E-mail: info@lindberghfoundation.org

Established in 1977 in NY.
Grantmaker type: Public charity
Financial data (yr. ended 12/31/02): Revenue, $368,985; assets, $1,462,385 (M); gifts received, $185,126; expenditures, $656,668; program services expenses, $581,761; giving activities include $93,550 for 10 grants to individuals (high: $9,580; low: $1,000).
Purpose and activities: The foundation aims to further Charles A. and Anne Morrow Lindbergh's shared vision of balancing technological development and environmental preservation, and to honor the Lindbergh legacy. Giving is primarily for research and educational projects.
Fields of interest: Humanities; Waste management; Natural resources; Biomedicine research; Medical research; Agriculture; Space/aviation; Population studies.
Types of support: Research; Grants to individuals.
Limitations: Giving on an international basis. No grants for tuition, fellowships, or scholarships.
Publications: Application guidelines, Annual report, Informational brochure, Newsletter.
Application information: Application form required.
  Initial approach: Letter, including SASE
  Copies of proposal: 8
  Deadline(s): 2nd Tues. of June
  Board meeting date(s): Mar., May, and Oct.
  Final notification: Apr. 1
Officers and Directors:* Reeve Lindbergh,* Pres.; Clare Hallward,* V.P.; Kristina Lindbergh,*

V.P.; Bryan Sharratt,* Secy.; Steven Whitley,* Treas.; Kasse Andrews-Weller; and 24 additional directors.
Number of staff: 3 full-time professional; 1 part-time professional.
EIN: 132882090

1693
Marbrook Foundation
1450 U.S. Trust Bldg.
730 2nd Ave. S.
Minneapolis, MN 55402 (612) 752-1783
Contact: Conley Brooks, Jr., Exec. Dir. or Julie S. Hara, Prog. Off.
FAX: (612) 752-1780; E-mail: marbrook@brooksinc.net

Established in 1948 in MN.
Donor(s): Edward Brooks,‡ Markell C. Brooks.‡
Grantmaker type: Independent foundation
Financial data (yr. ended 12/31/02): Assets, $13,055,675 (M); expenditures, $1,006,096; qualifying distributions, $819,886; giving activities include $778,500 for 124 grants (high: $30,000; low: $1,000).
Purpose and activities: Primary areas of interest include education, the arts, the environment, social improvement, health, basic human needs and spiritual endeavors.
Fields of interest: Visual arts; Performing arts; Theater; Historic preservation/historical societies; Arts; Elementary school/education; Education; Natural resources; Environment; Health care; Health organizations, association; Employment; Housing/shelter; Human services; Children/youth, services; Community development; Federated giving programs; Religion.
Types of support: General/operating support; Continuing support; Annual campaigns; Capital campaigns; Building/renovation; Equipment; Land acquisition; Endowments; Emergency funds; Program development; Professorships; Scholarship funds; Research; Matching/challenge support.
Limitations: Giving limited to the Minneapolis-St. Paul, MN, area. No support for political purposes. No grants to individuals; or for start-up organizations, conferences, events, programs for the elderly, domestic abuse programs, disease-related organizations, or programs servicing the mentally or physically disabled.
Publications: Annual report (including application guidelines), Grants list.
Application information: Application form not required.
  Initial approach: Proposal
  Copies of proposal: 1
  Deadline(s): May 30 and Nov. 30
  Board meeting date(s): June/July and Nov./Dec.
  Final notification: 1-2 weeks after meeting
Officer and Trustees:* Conley Brooks, Jr.,* Exec. Dir.; Conley Brooks; Markell C. Brooks; Stephen B. Brooks; Markell Kiefer; Julie B. Zelle.
Number of staff: 1 part-time professional.
EIN: 416019899

1694
The William W. McGuire and Nadine M. McGuire Family Foundation
315 Woodhill Rd.
Wayzata, MN 55391-9102

Established in 1996 in MN.
Donor(s): William W. McGuire.
Grantmaker type: Independent foundation
Financial data (yr. ended 11/30/02): Assets, $7,019,360 (M); expenditures, $1,283,453; qualifying distributions, $1,167,567; giving activities include $1,167,567 for 8 grants (high: $1,000,000; low: $10,000).
Fields of interest: Arts; University; Education; Zoos/zoological societies.
Limitations: Applications not accepted. Giving primarily in Gainesville, FL and MN. No grants to individuals.
Application information: Contributes only to pre-selected organizations.
Officers and Director:* Nadine M. McGuire,* Pres.; William W. McGuire,* Secy.-Treas.
EIN: 411861103

1695
The McKnight Foundation ▼
710 Second St. S., Ste. 400
Minneapolis, MN 55401 (612) 333-4220
Contact: Rip Rapson, Pres.
FAX: (612) 332-3833; E-mail: info@mcknight.org; URL: http://www.mcknight.org

Incorporated in 1953 in MN.
Donor(s): William L. McKnight,‡ Maude L. McKnight,‡ Virginia M. Binger,‡ James H. Binger.
Grantmaker type: Independent foundation
Financial data (yr. ended 12/31/02): Assets, $1,549,715,000 (M); expenditures, $103,381,000; qualifying distributions, $87,000,000; giving activities include $86,973,190 for 813 grants and $26,810 for 66 employee matching gifts.
Purpose and activities: Emphasis on grantmaking in the areas of human and social services; has multi-year comprehensive program in the arts, environment, and housing; has multi-year program for support of projects in non-metropolitan areas of MN; supports nationwide scientific research programs in areas of: 1) neuroscience, particularly for research in memory and diseases affecting the memory; 2) collaborative crop research, with support for basic and applied research aimed at improving food crops and agricultural systems in developing countries; and 3) eating disorders.
Fields of interest: Arts; Energy; Environment; Neuroscience; Housing/shelter, development; Youth development; Human services; Children/youth, services; Child development, services; Family services; International conflict resolution; Rural development; Community development; Public affairs; Economically disadvantaged.
International interests: Tanzania; Uganda; Zimbabwe; Cambodia; Laos; Vietnam.
Types of support: General/operating support; Capital campaigns; Building/renovation; Equipment; Program development; Technical assistance; Program-related investments/loans; Matching/challenge support.

Limitations: Giving limited to organizations in MN, especially the seven-county Twin Cities, MN, area, except for programs in the environment, international aid, and research. No support for religious organizations for religious purposes. No grants to individuals (except for the Virginia McKnight Binger Awards in Human Service), or for basic research in academic disciplines (except for defined programs in crop research, neuroscience, and eating disorders), endowment funds, scholarships, fellowships, national fundraising campaigns, ticket sales, or conferences.
Publications: Application guidelines, Annual report (including application guidelines), Grants list, Informational brochure, Informational brochure (including application guidelines), Occasional report.
Application information: Application form not required.
  Initial approach: 2- to 4-page letter of inquiry
  Copies of proposal: 3
  Deadline(s): Feb. 15, May 15, Aug. 15, and Nov. 15 for human services and other general grants; Jan. 15, Apr. 15, July 15, and Oct. 15 for arts and environment
  Board meeting date(s): Feb., May, Aug., Nov.
  Final notification: 3 months
Officers and Directors:* Noa Staryk,* Chair.; Rip Rapson, Pres.; Carol Berde, Exec. V.P.; Richard J. Scott, V.P., Fin. and Admin. and Secy.; James M. Binger,* Treas.; Ben Binger; Erika Binger; Patricia S. Binger; Peggy J. Birk; Cynthia Binger Boynton; Meghan Binger Brown.
Number of staff: 20 full-time professional; 11 full-time support.
EIN: 410754835
Recent environmental and animal welfare grants:
1695-1 1000 Friends of Minnesota, Saint Paul, MN, $200,000. For capacity-building activities addressing issues in Minnesota counties. 2002.
1695-2 Angkor Participatory Development Organization (APDO), Siem Reap, Cambodia, $60,000. For community economic development activities for people living near Angkor Archaeological Park in Cambodia. 2002.
1695-3 Audubon Society, National, New York, NY, $560,000. For integrated program to protect and restore Upper Mississippi River. 2002.
1695-4 Cannon River Watershed Partnership, Northfield, MN, $100,000. For general operating support. 2002.
1695-5 Clean Water Fund, Minneapolis, MN, $60,000. For continued coordination of environmental protection strategies in rural Minnesota. 2002.
1695-6 Coalition for a Clean Minnesota River, New Ulm, MN, $14,000. For coalition to address agricultural drainage. 2002.
1695-7 Coalition to Restore Coastal Louisiana, Baton Rouge, LA, $120,000. For general operating support. 2002.
1695-8 Collins Center for Public Policy, Miami, FL, $20,000. For Funders Network for Smart Growth and Livable Communities annual conference in Minneapolis. 2002.
1695-9 Community Design Center of Minnesota, Saint Paul, MN, $121,500. For Youth, Enterprise in Food and Ecology Project, gardening, nutrition, environmental

education, and community service program. 2002.
1695-10 East Side Neighborhood Development Company, Saint Paul, MN, $80,000. For Lower Phalen Creek Project, effort to revitalize Mississippi River floodplain in St. Paul. 2002.
1695-11 Empresa Brasileira de Pesquisa Agropecuaria (EMBRAPA), Embrapa Milho e Sorgo, Sete Lagoas, Brasilia, Brazil, $880,000. For research, New Approach for Improving Phosphorus Acquisition and Aluminum Tolerance of Plants in Marginal Soils. 2002.
1695-12 Environmental Defense, New York, NY, $200,000. To promote water resource and agriculture policies that will restore Mississippi River. 2002.
1695-13 Environmental Law and Policy Center of the Midwest, Chicago, IL, $40,000. To protect and restore Upper Mississippi River basin. 2002.
1695-14 Environmental Support Center, DC, $225,000. To train and assist groups working to protect Mississippi River. 2002.
1695-15 Farm in the City, Saint Paul, MN, $80,000. For year-round gardening and arts program for youth ages 7-16. 2002.
1695-16 Foundation for Sustainable Development, Austin, TX, $120,000. To restore bottomland hardwood forest in Lower Mississippi Valley. 2002.
1695-17 Friends of the Mississippi River, Saint Paul, MN, $275,000. For general operating support. 2002.
1695-18 Gulf Restoration Network, New Orleans, LA, $90,000. To improve public policies to reduce pollution in Mississippi River that causes Gulf of Mexico's Dead Zone. 2002.
1695-19 Harvest Moon Community Farm, Scandia, MN, $25,000. For youth enrichment program focusing on agriculture, arts, and environment. 2002.
1695-20 Institute for Agriculture and Trade Policy, Minneapolis, MN, $75,000. To explore alternatives to address congestion management in navigation on Upper Mississippi River system. 2002.
1695-21 Institute for Conservation Leadership, Takoma Park, MD, $280,000. Toward building capacity of environment and conservation organizations in Mississippi River basin. 2002.
1695-22 Institute for Minnesota Archaeology, Saint Paul, MN, $90,000. For community-based initiative to conserve and interpret resources of Mississippi River watershed near Little Falls, MN. 2002.
1695-23 Institute for Minnesota Archaeology, Saint Paul, MN, $15,000. For bridge funds for Great River/Great People Resource Partnership. 2002.
1695-24 International Collaborative for Science, Education, and the Environment, Wayland, MA, $23,000. For enterprise development program and business management training program for women in Tanzania. 2002.
1695-25 Isaiah, Minneapolis, MN, $70,000. For membership mapping and analysis project involving multiple organizations working on smart growth issues. 2002.
1695-26 Izaak Walton League of America, Gaithersburg, MD, $155,000. To investigate

and publicize fish kills in Upper Mississippi River and its tributaries. 2002.

1695-27 Kentucky Waterways Alliance, Munfordville, KY, $60,000. For efforts to monitor enforcement of water quality laws and to provide effective public policy advocacy on water quality issues in Kentucky. 2002.

1695-28 Kingfield Neighborhood Association, Minneapolis, MN, $50,000. For planning and organizing along greenway connecting Minneapolis Chain of Lakes and Mississippi River. 2002.

1695-29 Kinnickinnic River Land Trust, River Falls, WI, $75,000. For capacity building. 2002.

1695-30 Land Stewardship Project, White Bear Lake, MN, $100,000. To engage farmers in increased conservation efforts through effective implementation of new Farm Bill. 2002.

1695-31 League of Conservation Voters Education Fund, DC, $40,000. For general operating support. 2002.

1695-32 Lilydale, City of, Lilydale, MN, $22,000. For bluff restoration plan to control stormwater and erosion. 2002.

1695-33 Lower Mississippi River Conservation Committee, Vicksburg, MS, $16,000. For Restoring America's Greatest River Workshop. 2002.

1695-34 Minneapolis Public Schools, Minneapolis, MN, $35,000. For Navigators program, which provides outdoors-environmental experiences for urban children after-school, on regular school holidays, and in summer. 2002.

1695-35 Minneapolis, City of, Minneapolis, MN, $100,000. For environmental interpretation at North Mississippi Regional Park. 2002.

1695-36 Minnesota Center for Environmental Advocacy, Saint Paul, MN, $395,000. To protect and improve water quality in Minnesota and Upper Mississippi River basins and to reduce impacts of regional growth. 2002.

1695-37 Minnesota Center for Environmental Advocacy, Saint Paul, MN, $25,000. For Better Blueprint Campaign, cross-sector organizing project aimed at strengthening Met Council's 2030 Regional Blueprint policies and implementation. 2002.

1695-38 Minnesota Environmental Initiative, Minneapolis, MN, $75,000. To help neighborhood organizations convert blighted properties into community assets. 2002.

1695-39 Minnesota Environmental Partnership, Saint Paul, MN, $100,000. To provide communications assistance to environmental and conservation organizations. 2002.

1695-40 Minnesota Land Trust, Saint Paul, MN, $50,000. For general operating support. 2002.

1695-41 Minnesota Landscape Arboretum Foundation, Chanhassen, MN, $36,000. For Urban Garden Program for youth in Phillips neighborhood. 2002.

1695-42 Minnesota Project, Saint Paul, MN, $60,000. For efforts to shape effective implementation of conservation programs in new Farm Bill. 2002.

1695-43 Minnesotans for an Energy-Efficient Economy (ME3), Saint Paul, MN, $200,000.

For policy and fiscal analysis projects related to Smart Growth Organizing Project. 2002.

1695-44 Minnesotans for an Energy-Efficient Economy (ME3), Saint Paul, MN, $25,000. To advance work of Smart Growth State Policy Committee. 2002.

1695-45 Mississippi River Basin Alliance, Minneapolis, MN, $325,000. For general operating support. 2002.

1695-46 Missouri Coalition for the Environment Foundation, Saint Louis, MO, $100,000. To protect Missouri's waterways and floodplains. 2002.

1695-47 Nature Conservancy, Arlington, VA, $300,000. For efforts to naturalize water flow in Upper Mississippi River. 2002.

1695-48 Parks and Trails Council of Minnesota, Saint Paul, MN, $100,000. To increase capacity of organization to advocate for better parks and trails in Mississippi, Minnesota, and St. Croix River corridors. 2002.

1695-49 Participatory Development Training Center, Vientiane, Laos, $82,000. For project that establishes microenterprise programs in rural communities in Laos. 2002.

1695-50 Prairie Rivers Network, Champaign, IL, $80,000. For general operating support. 2002.

1695-51 Public Employees for Environmental Responsibility (PEER), DC, $75,000. To improve federal agencies actions affecting Mississippi River watershed. 2002.

1695-52 Public Intervenors Network, Red Wing, MN, $35,000. To explore wind energy transmission in southwestern Minnesota. 2002.

1695-53 Resource Center of the Americas, Minneapolis, MN, $50,000. For creation of Plaza de las Americas, urban open space. 2002.

1695-54 River Action, Davenport, IA, $560,000. To improve Mississippi River greenways in Quad Cities and demonstrate stormwater management techniques. 2002.

1695-55 Rivers Council of Minnesota, Sauk Rapids, MN, $50,000. To evaluate volunteer water quality monitoring activities. 2002.

1695-56 Sierra Club Foundation, San Francisco, CA, $85,000. For citizen involvement in local land use decision making and protection of open space. 2002.

1695-57 Students Partnership Worldwide (SPW) Uganda, Jinja, Uganda, $15,000. For program that teaches sustainable organic farming methods to women in Uganda. 2002.

1695-58 Sustain, Chicago, IL, $100,000. For targeted communications program in river communities. 2002.

1695-59 Sustainable Resources Center, Minneapolis, MN, $65,000. For policy and community organizing effort to ensure green space preservation. 2002.

1695-60 Taxpayers for Common Sense, DC, $150,000. To assess and publicize wasteful Corps of Engineers water projects. 2002.

1695-61 Trailnet, Saint Louis, MO, $500,000. For implementation of Confluence Greenway along Mississippi River in Missouri and Illinois. 2002.

1695-62 Tree Trust, Saint Paul, MN, $40,000. For summer and school year youth employment and training program. 2002.

1695-63 Trust for Public Land, Saint Paul, MN, $400,000. To protect Mississippi River corridors, tributaries, and watersheds, and to protect open spaces in Twin Cities. 2002.

1695-64 Tulane Educational Fund, New Orleans, LA, $80,000. For legal assistance to low-income individuals and grassroots organizations addressing pollution issues along Mississippi River corridor in Louisiana. 2002.

1695-65 Vietnamese Heritage Institute, Berkeley, CA, $20,000. For revolving credit loan and agriculture and forestry training program for families living near Tram Chim National Park in Vietnam. 2002.

1695-66 Visions for Clarendon, Clarendon, AR, $70,000. To foster river tourism in eastern Arkansas communities. 2002.

1695-67 Wetlands Initiative, Chicago, IL, $150,000. For ecological flood damage reduction plan for Upper Mississippi River basin. 2002.

1695-68 White Earth Land Recovery Project, Ponsford, MN, $50,000. For American Indian conservation and preservation initiative in Mississippi headwaters. 2002.

1695-69 Wisconsin Wetlands Association, Madison, WI, $35,000. For general operating support. 2002.

1695-70 Wolf River Conservancy, Memphis, TN, $75,000. To expand education programs on Mississippi River tributary. 2002.

1696
The McNeely Foundation
444 Pine St.
St. Paul, MN 55101 (651) 228-4503
Contact: Karen M. Reynolds

Established in 1981 in MN.
Donor(s): Lee and Rose Warner Foundation.
Grantmaker type: Independent foundation
Financial data (yr. ended 12/31/01): Assets, $18,156,157 (M); expenditures, $671,391; qualifying distributions, $1,353,567; giving activities include $1,333,946 for 186 grants (high: $450,000; low: $50; average: $1,000–$50,000) and $125,000 for loans/program-related investments.
Purpose and activities: Support for economics and business education; grants also for selected community projects, environmental programs and for arts education. Specific interest in funding projects that benefit the St. Paul area, especially the East Side neighborhoods.
Fields of interest: Business school/education; Education; Environment; Health care; Children/youth, services; Community development; Economics.
Types of support: Program development; Curriculum development; Program evaluation; Employee matching gifts.
Limitations: Giving primarily in the Minneapolis-St. Paul Metro area, especially in East Side St. Paul neighborhoods. No grants to individuals.
Publications: Application guidelines.
Application information: Accepts Minnesota Common Grant Application Form. Application form not required.
Initial approach: Proposal
Copies of proposal: 1
Deadline(s): None

Board meeting date(s): As necessary
Trustees: Armar A. Archbold; W.E. Barness; Gregory McNeely; Harry G. McNeely III; Shannon McNeely Whitaker.
Number of staff: 1 part-time professional.
EIN: 411392221

1697
Meadowood Foundation
5140 Wells Fargo Ctr.
90 S. 7th St.
Minneapolis, MN 55402-4139

Established in 1968.
Donor(s): Douglas J. Dayton.
Grantmaker type: Independent foundation
Financial data (yr. ended 12/31/02): Assets, $10,113,118 (M); expenditures, $715,801; qualifying distributions, $594,190; giving activities include $586,558 for 67 grants (high: $126,000; low: $100).
Purpose and activities: Funding primarily for land and natural resource conservation, arts and culture, and human services.
Fields of interest: Arts; Education; Natural resources; Hospitals (general); Human services; Community development.
Types of support: General/operating support; Building/renovation.
Limitations: Applications not accepted. Giving primarily in Minneapolis, MN. No grants to individuals.
Application information: Contributes only to pre-selected organizations.
Officers and Directors:* Douglas J. Dayton,* Pres. and Treas.; Wendy W. Dayton,* V.P.; James M. Karges, Secy.; Bruce C. Dayton; David D. Dayton; Steven J. Melander-Dayton.
EIN: 410943749

1698
The Laura Jane Musser Fund
(formerly The Musser Fund)
3109 W. 50th St., PMB 119
Minneapolis, MN 55410 (612) 825-5442
Contact: Judith K. Healey, Managing Consultant
FAX: (612) 825-0323; E-mail: jkhealey@aol.com; URL: http://www.musserfund.org/

Established in 1990 in MN.
Donor(s): Laura J. Musser.‡
Grantmaker type: Independent foundation
Financial data (yr. ended 12/31/02): Assets, $16,889,436 (M); expenditures, $751,108; qualifying distributions, $746,401; giving activities include $607,420 for grants.
Purpose and activities: Primary areas of interest include children, the arts, inter-cultural harmony, rural life, the environment and rural leadership development.
Fields of interest: Arts; Environment; Children/youth, services; Race/intergroup relations; Rural development.
Types of support: Program development; Seed money.
Limitations: Giving primarily in CO, HI, MN, OH, and WY. No grants for general operating support, or for ongoing programs, or for capital projects.
Publications: Application guidelines, Program policy statement.

Application information: Application form required.
Initial approach: Letter of intent to apply
Copies of proposal: 2
Deadline(s): May 1 for general program; Sept. 15 for Environmental/Community Initiative grants
Board meeting date(s): Biannually
Final notification: Jan.
Directors: Lisa Duke; Joseph S. Micallef; Walter S. Rosenberry III; Robert Strasburg; Jane Thronas; Drew Walker; Huntingdon Walker; Meg Walker.
Trustee: U.S. Bank, N.A.
Number of staff: None.
EIN: 416334475

1699
Nash Foundation
c/o Lowry Hill, N9305-530
6th and Marquette
Minneapolis, MN 55479
Contact: Jeffrey P. Norton, Pres.
URL: http://www.nashfoundation.org

Established in 1922 in MN.
Grantmaker type: Independent foundation
Financial data (yr. ended 06/30/02): Assets, $4,088,074 (M); gifts received, $427; expenditures, $299,036; qualifying distributions, $261,666; giving activities include $239,190 for 116 grants (high: $20,000; low: $50).
Purpose and activities: Funding primarily for arts and cultural programs, children and youth services, environment and community services.
Fields of interest: Arts; Environment; Human services; Youth, services.
Types of support: General/operating support; Continuing support; Annual campaigns; Capital campaigns; Program development.
Limitations: Giving primarily in the Twin Cities, MN, metropolitan area.
Publications: Application guidelines.
Application information: Application form not required.
Initial approach: Request guidelines
Deadline(s): Sept. 1
Board meeting date(s): May
Final notification: June 1
Officers and Trustees:* Jeffrey P. Norton,* Pres.; Barbara Atwood,* V.P.; Amy Nash Henriksen,* Secy.; Lucinda Walker,* Treas.; Nicholas Atwood; Christine B. Evans; John M. Nash; Nicholas D. Nash; Rebecca Nash.
Number of staff: 1 part-time professional.
EIN: 416019142

1700
National Wildlife Rehabilitators Association
14 N. 7th Ave.
St. Cloud, MN 56303 (320) 259-4086
Contact: Lisa Borgia, Exec. Dir.
E-mail: nwra@nwrawildlife.org; URL: http://www.nwrawildlife.org

Established in 1984.
Grantmaker type: Public charity
Financial data (yr. ended 12/31/02): Revenue, $169,424; assets, $326,499 (M); gifts received, $12,654; expenditures, $203,711; program services expenses, $166,800; giving activities

include $1,300 for 2 grants (high: $1,200; low: $100) and $5,916 for 24 grants to individuals (high: $3,800; low: $20).
Purpose and activities: The association improves and promotes the profession of wildlife rehabilitation and its contributions to preserving natural ecosystems.
Fields of interest: Animals/wildlife, preservation/protection.
Limitations: Giving on a national and international basis.
Publications: Application guidelines, Annual report, Informational brochure, Newsletter.
Application information: See Web site for application and deadline information. Application form required.
Copies of proposal: 1
Deadline(s): Varies
Board meeting date(s): Nov. and Mar.
Officers and Directors:* Erica A. Miller, DVM,* Pres.; Curtiss J. Clumpner,* Pres.-Elect; Lessie Davis,* V.P.; Diane Nickerson,* V.P.; Florina S. Tseng, DVM,* V.P.; Sandra Woltman,* Secy.; Barbara Suto,* Treas.; Lisa Borgia, Exec. Dir.; Di Conger; Jennifer Convy; and 8 additional directors.
Number of staff: 2 full-time professional.
EIN: 371143442

1701
Nicholson Family Foundation
(formerly Richard H. and Nancy B. Nicholson Foundation)
336 Robert St. N., Ste. 1220
St. Paul, MN 55101-1506
Contact: Mary B. Elsholtz, Admin.

Established in 1986 in MN.
Donor(s): Richard H. Nicholson, Nancy B. Nicholson, David O. Nicholson, Ford J. Nicholson, Todd S. Nicholson.
Grantmaker type: Independent foundation
Financial data (yr. ended 06/30/02): Assets, $6,126,700 (M); gifts received, $747,346; expenditures, $323,377; qualifying distributions, $240,721; giving activities include $231,895 for 170 grants (high: $18,000; low: $10).
Purpose and activities: Giving primarily for the arts, education, health, and human services.
Fields of interest: Arts; Education; Natural resources; Health organizations, association; Human services; Christian agencies & churches.
Limitations: Applications not accepted. Giving primarily in MN. No grants to individuals.
Application information: Contributes only to pre-selected organizations. Unsolicited requests for funds not accepted.
Officers: Richard H. Nicholson, Pres.; Todd S. Nicholson, V.P. and Secy.; David O. Nicholson, V.P.; Ford J. Nicholson, Treas.
Number of staff: 1 part-time professional.
EIN: 411572346

1702
Northwest Area Foundation ▼
60 Plato Blvd. East, Ste. 400
St. Paul, MN 55107 (651) 224-9635
Contact: Karl N. Stauber, Pres.
FAX: (651) 225-7701; E-mail: info@nwaf.org; URL: http://www.nwaf.org

Incorporated in 1934 in MN as Lexington Foundation; name changed to Louis W. and Maud Hill Family Foundation in 1950; present name adopted 1975.
Donor(s): Louis W. Hill, Sr.,‡ Maud Hill.‡
Grantmaker type: Independent foundation
Financial data (yr. ended 03/31/02): Assets, $424,599,397 (M); expenditures, $33,515,830; qualifying distributions, $27,822,979; giving activities include $24,964,629 for 35 grants (high: $20,000,000; low: $100; average: $40,000–$400,000) and $21,883 for 1 foundation-administered program.
Purpose and activities: The foundation is seeking to help communities in its eight-state region reduce poverty.
Fields of interest: Community development.
Limitations: Applications not accepted. Giving limited to IA, ID, MN, MT, ND, OR, SD, and WA. No support for lobbying activities. No grants to individuals.
Publications: Annual report, Informational brochure.
Application information: The foundation does not accept proposals.
Officers and Directors:* Bruce M. Brooks,* Chair.; Karl N. Stauber,* Pres.and Secy.-Treas.; Jean Adams, V.P., Oper.; Gregg J. Bourland; Dorothy Bridges; Elouise Cobell; Cornelia Butler Flora; Humberto Fuentes; Patricia A. Jensen; Daniel Kemmis; Antone Minthorn; Nick Smith; Sandra Vargas.
Trustees: Terrence Glarner; James J. Hill III; Louis Fors Hill; Linda L. Hoeschler; Rodney Jordan.
Number of staff: 16 full-time professional; 2 part-time professional; 20 full-time support; 3 part-time support.
EIN: 410719221
Recent environmental and animal welfare grants:
1702-1 Indian Land Tenure Foundation, Saint Paul, MN, $20,000,000. For long-term Partnership initiatives. 2002.
1702-2 Indian Land Tenure Foundation, Saint Paul, MN, $204,550. For planning activities to complete requirements necessary to enter into partnership agreement with Northwest Area Foundation. 2002.

1703
Open Door Foundation
1660 S. Hwy. 100, Ste. 426
St. Louis Park, MN 55416-1533
Contact: David B. Hartwell, Pres.

Established in 1996 in MN.
Donor(s): Charles H. Bell.
Grantmaker type: Independent foundation
Financial data (yr. ended 12/31/02): Assets, $1,251,088 (M); expenditures, $129,813; qualifying distributions, $120,412; giving activities include $120,433 for 23 grants (high: $50,000; low: $100).
Purpose and activities: Giving primarily for the environment, health, and human services.
Fields of interest: Environment; Health care; Human services.
Types of support: General/operating support; Program development.
Limitations: Applications not accepted. Giving primarily in MN. No grants to individuals.

Application information: Contributes only to pre-selected organizations.
Officers: David B. Hartwell, Pres. and Treas.; Elizabeth Debaut, V.P. and Secy.
Number of staff: None.
EIN: 411859476

1704
OSilas Foundation
2545 Manitou Island
White Bear Lake, MN 55110
Contact: Silas M. Ford, III, Pres.
Application address: 309 Pondfield Road, Bronxville, NY 10708, tel.: (914) 337-4044

Established in 1999 in MN.
Donor(s): Silas M. Ford III.
Grantmaker type: Independent foundation
Financial data (yr. ended 12/31/02): Assets, $6,405,713 (M); gifts received, $5,849; expenditures, $345,400; qualifying distributions, $344,419; giving activities include $342,400 for 32 grants (high: $207,500; low: $200).
Fields of interest: Higher education; Education; Environment.
Limitations: Giving on a national basis, with emphasis on MN.
Application information:
Initial approach: Letter
Deadline(s): None
Officers and Directors:* Silas M. Ford III,* Pres.; Durand G. Ford, V.P.; Kimberly Ford-Werling,* V.P.; Olivia C. Ford,* Secy.-Treas; Francios Bertschy; Nannette Bertschy; Christopher Ford; David C. Ford; Margaret Ford; Bruce Genereaux; Olivia J. "Jovine" Genereaux; Robert Werling.
EIN: 411955001

1705
Otter Tail Power Company Contributions Program
215 S. Cascade St.
Fergus Falls, MN 56537
Contact: Cris King, Dir., Public Rels.

Grantmaker type: Corporate giving program
Purpose and activities: Otter Tail makes charitable contributions to nonprofit organizations involved with arts and culture, education, the environment, health and human services, mental health, disease, medical research, crime, recreation, youth development, community development, civic affairs, minorities, disabled people, senior citizens, and economically disadvantaged people. Support is given primarily in areas of company operations.
Fields of interest: Visual arts; Museums; Performing arts; Music; Historic preservation/historical societies; Arts; Education, fund raising; Child development, education; Secondary school/education; Business school/education; Libraries/library science; Education; Environment; Hospitals (general); Health care; Mental health/crisis services; Cancer; Heart & circulatory diseases; Health organizations; Cancer research; Heart & circulatory research; Medical research; Crime/law enforcement; Recreation; Youth development; Children/youth, services; Child development, services; Hospices; Human services; Community development; Leadership

development; Public affairs; Minorities; Disabled; Aging; Economically disadvantaged.
Types of support: Continuing support; Annual campaigns; Building/renovation; Equipment; Endowments; Conferences/seminars; Employee volunteer services; Use of facilities; Sponsorships; Employee matching gifts; Donated equipment; In-kind gifts; Matching/challenge support.
Limitations: Giving primarily in areas of company operations, particularly MN, ND, and SD.
Application information: The Public Relations and Customer Service Department handles giving. A contributions committee reviews all requests. Application form not required.
Initial approach: Proposal to headquarters
Copies of proposal: 1
Deadline(s): None
Final notification: 1 to 4 weeks

1706
The Irwin Andrew Porter Foundation
P.O. Box 580057
Minneapolis, MN 55458-0057
(612) 343-5994
Contact: Amy Hubbard, Chair.
E-mail: iapfoundation@iapfoundation.org; URL: http://www.iapfoundation.org

Established in 1996 in MN.
Donor(s): Amy L. Hubbard.
Grantmaker type: Independent foundation
Financial data (yr. ended 08/31/02): Assets, $3,152,449 (M); expenditures, $137,643; qualifying distributions, $129,193; giving activities include $118,786 for 22 grants (high: $22,200; low: $375).
Purpose and activities: Giving primarily for social programs and the arts; support also for international micro lending.
Fields of interest: Arts; Education; Environment; Human services.
International interests: Africa; Central America.
Types of support: Matching/challenge support.
Limitations: Giving on a national and international basis, with emphasis on IL, MI, MN, and WI. No grants to individuals, or for operating expenses, capital campaigns, endowments, political organizations, or religious programs.
Publications: Application guidelines.
Application information: Application form not required.
Initial approach: Proposal
Copies of proposal: 2
Deadline(s): May 1 for June, Aug. 1 for Sept., Nov. 1 for Dec., and Feb. 1 for Mar.
Board meeting date(s): Quarterly
Officer and Board Members:* Amy L. Hubbard,* Chair. and Pres.; Kari Luther Carlson; Susan A. Clarey; Dipankar Mukherjee; Glenn Morehouse Olson; Justin Williams.
EIN: 411852392

1707
Rahr Foundation
P.O. Box 15186
Minneapolis, MN 55415-0186
(612) 332-5161
Contact: Frederich W. Rahr, Pres.
FAX: (612) 332-6841

Incorporated in 1942 in WI.
Donor(s): Rahr Malting Co.
Grantmaker type: Company-sponsored foundation
Financial data (yr. ended 12/31/02): Assets, $4,487,512 (M); expenditures, $362,665; qualifying distributions, $310,024; giving activities include $271,685 for 69 grants (high: $25,500; low: $100).
Purpose and activities: Support for charitable and educational institutions and public welfare, higher and secondary education, youth agencies, social services, cultural programs, and a scholarship program for children of company employees.
Fields of interest: Arts; Secondary school/education; Higher education; Education; Natural resources; Human services; Children/youth, services.
Types of support: General/operating support; Continuing support; Annual campaigns; Capital campaigns; Land acquisition; Emergency funds; Employee-related scholarships.
Limitations: Giving primarily in MN. No grants for endowment funds or research programs; no loans.
Application information: Application form not required.
　Initial approach: Letter
　Copies of proposal: 1
　Deadline(s): Mar. 15
　Board meeting date(s): June and Nov.
Officers and Directors:* Frederich W. Rahr,* Pres.; Guido R. Rahr, Jr.,* V.P.; Mary Gresham,* Secy.; George D. Gackle,* Treas.; Jack D. Gage.
Number of staff: None.
EIN: 396046046

1708
Reell Precision Manufacturing Corporation Contributions Program
c/o Corp. Contribs.
1259 Wolters Blvd.
St. Paul, MN 55110 (651) 484-2447
FAX: (651) 484-3867

Grantmaker type: Corporate giving program
Purpose and activities: Reell makes charitable contributions to nonprofit organizations involved with arts and culture, education, the environment, human services, and religion. Support is given on an international basis.
Fields of interest: Arts; Education; Environment; Human services; Religion.
Types of support: General/operating support; Employee volunteer services.
Limitations: Giving on an international basis, particularly in MN. No support for political organizations or candidates. No grants to individuals; no loans.
Application information: A contributions committee reviews all requests. Application form not required.
　Initial approach: Proposal to headquarters
　Copies of proposal: 1

Deadline(s): Sept. 1
Final notification: Oct. 31

1709
The Robert and Helen Remick Charitable Foundation
P. O. Box 929
Lakefield, MN 56150-0929

Established in 1998 in MN.
Donor(s): Robert Remick.‡
Grantmaker type: Independent foundation
Financial data (yr. ended 12/31/02): Assets, $4,937,596 (M); gifts received, $500,063; expenditures, $203,509; qualifying distributions, $177,540; giving activities include $171,700 for 12 grants (high: $60,000; low: $850).
Fields of interest: Environmental education; Youth, services; Family services; Protestant agencies & churches.
Limitations: Applications not accepted. Giving primarily in MN. No grants to individuals.
Application information: Contributes only to pre-selected organizations.
Trustees: Howard C. Davis; Lynel Rae Nelson; John D. Remick; Cheryl Holthe Rients.
EIN: 411950527

1710
Rice Family Foundation
2524 Keller Pkwy.
Maplewood, MN 55109
Contact: Carol R. Bowditch, Dir.

Established in 1986 in IL.
Donor(s): Arthur L. Rice, Jr.‡
Grantmaker type: Independent foundation
Financial data (yr. ended 11/30/02): Assets, $3,548,815 (M); expenditures, $307,915; qualifying distributions, $297,471; giving activities include $300,000 for 56 grants (high: $33,000; low: $1,000).
Fields of interest: Humanities; Arts; Education, fund raising; Higher education; Education; Natural resources; Health care; Health organizations, association; Federated giving programs; Protestant agencies & churches.
Limitations: Applications not accepted. Giving primarily in, but not limited to, IL, MN, and WI. No grants to individuals.
Application information: Contributes only to pre-selected organizations.
Directors: Carol R. Bowditch; James A. Bowditch; Emily R. Douglass; John P. Douglass; Arthur Rice III; Carol F. Rice; Lynn D. Rice.
Number of staff: None.
EIN: 363529826

1711
Margaret Rivers Fund
P.O. Box 197
Stillwater, MN 55082 (651) 430-3935
Contact: David F. Pohl, Pres.

Incorporated in 1948 in MN.
Donor(s): Robert E. Slaughter.‡
Grantmaker type: Independent foundation
Financial data (yr. ended 12/31/01): Assets, $33,152,702 (M); expenditures, $1,765,794; qualifying distributions, $1,638,407; giving

activities include $1,599,000 for 190 grants (high: $100,000; low: $200; average: $2,000–$25,000).
Purpose and activities: Grants primarily for hospitals, church support, youth agencies, aid to the handicapped, and care of the aged; support also for cultural programs and conservation.
Fields of interest: Arts; Natural resources; Hospitals (general); Youth, services; Aging, centers/services; Christian agencies & churches; Disabled; Aging.
Types of support: General/operating support.
Limitations: Giving primarily in MN. No grants to individuals.
Application information: Application form not required.
　Initial approach: Letter
　Deadline(s): None
　Board meeting date(s): Monthly
Officers and Trustees:* David F. Pohl,* Pres. and Treas.; Robert G. Briggs,* V.P.; Lawrence Severson, Secy.; Jean Barry.
EIN: 416017102

1712
Rochester Area Foundation
21 1st St. S.W., Ste. 350
Rochester, MN 55902-3007 (507) 282-0203
Contact: Steve Thornton, Exec. Dir.
FAX: (507) 282-4938; E-mail: info@rochesterarea.org; URL: http://www.rochesterarea.org

Established in 1944 in MN by resolution of trust.
Grantmaker type: Community foundation
Financial data (yr. ended 12/31/02): Assets, $24,043,000 (M); gifts received, $3,195,000; expenditures, $3,289,000; giving activities include $582,000 for grants.
Purpose and activities: To help launch new projects which represent innovative approaches to community needs, support special purposes of established organizations, promote volunteer and citizen involvement in the community, respond to current human needs in the community, and support projects without other sources of support; giving in areas of health, education, human services, and development and assistance of community affairs. The foundation administers donor-advised funds.
Fields of interest: Arts; Child development, education; Higher education; Education; Environment; Housing/shelter, development; Human services; Child development, services; Aging, centers/services; Minorities/immigrants, centers/services; Civil rights; Community development; Voluntarism promotion; Government/public administration; Public affairs; Minorities; Disabled; Aging.
Types of support: Building/renovation; Emergency funds; Seed money; Technical assistance; Consulting services; Matching/challenge support.
Limitations: Giving limited to the greater Rochester, MN, area. No support for religious organizations for sectarian purposes. No grants to individuals, or for endowment funds, annual campaigns, operating budgets, continuing support, land acquisition, deficit financing, scholarships, fellowships, or research.
Publications: Application guidelines, Annual report, Informational brochure (including application guidelines), Newsletter.

Application information: Application form required.

Initial approach: Pre-application form
Copies of proposal: 7
Deadline(s): Jan. 1, May 1, and Sept. 1
Board meeting date(s): Feb., Apr., May, Aug., Sept., Oct., Nov., and Dec.
Final notification: 4 months

Officers and Trustees:* Alan De Boer,* Chair.; Alan Schafer,* Vice-Chair.; David Stenhaug,* Vice-Chair.; Sheryl Tasler, Secy.; Charles Elliott, Treas.; Michael Bue; Nancy Brubaker; Joe Duffy; Paul Harkess; Marianne Hockema; Carol Kamper; Mary Jo Kelly; Ronald Seeger; John Wade; Craig Wendland.
Number of staff: 4 full-time professional; 1 full-time support.
EIN: 416017740

1713
Carl and Verna Schmidt Foundation
P.O. Box 638
Rochester, MN 55903-0638 (507) 285-2517

Established in 1958 in MN.
Donor(s): Carl Schmidt, Verna Schmidt.
Grantmaker type: Independent foundation
Financial data (yr. ended 11/30/02): Assets, $19,387,248 (M); expenditures, $2,525,649; qualifying distributions, $2,374,114; giving activities include $2,301,971 for 66 grants (high: $1,383,044; low: $250).
Purpose and activities: Giving primarily for public libraries, health associations, including a children's hospital, volunteer fire departments and human services; funding also for the arts, natural resource conservation, and animals and wildlife.
Fields of interest: Historic preservation/historical societies; Arts; Libraries (public); Natural resources; Animals/wildlife; Hospitals (specialty); Health organizations, association; Housing/shelter, development; Disasters, fire prevention/control; Human services; Children, services.
Limitations: Giving primarily in MN. No grants to individuals.
Application information: Telephone applications not accepted. Application form required.

Initial approach: Letter only
Deadline(s): None

Trustees: Alan C. Anderson; Jonathan S. Anderson.
EIN: 237423942

1714
Schott Foundation
1000 Parkers Lake Rd.
Wayzata, MN 55391 (952) 475-1173
Contact: Owen W. Schott, C.E.O.

Established in 1981.
Donor(s): Schott Corp.
Grantmaker type: Company-sponsored foundation
Financial data (yr. ended 03/31/02): Assets, $4,473,012 (M); expenditures, $290,352; qualifying distributions, $262,701; giving activities include $253,630 for 22 grants (high: $86,000; low: $1,000).

Purpose and activities: Provides assistance toward obtaining and/or disseminating education, knowledge, and learning, or for the preservation of natural heritage and the humanities.
Fields of interest: Television; Museums; Higher education; Education; Natural resources.
Types of support: General/operating support; Scholarship funds.
Limitations: Giving primarily in MN.
Application information: Application form not required.

Initial approach: Letter
Deadline(s): None

Officers and Directors:* Owen W. Schott,* C.E.O. and Pres.; Wendell Schott,* V.P.; D. James Nielsen,* Secy.
EIN: 411390214

1715
Sexton Foundation
P.O. Box 178, R.R. No. 1
Grey Eagle, MN 56336-9801
Contact: M. Yvonne Sexton, Pres.

Established in 1977.
Donor(s): American Trailers, Inc., James Sexton.
Grantmaker type: Independent foundation
Financial data (yr. ended 11/30/02): Assets, $7,448,661 (M); expenditures, $494,300; qualifying distributions, $493,217; giving activities include $494,300 for 41 grants (high: $100,000; low: $300).
Fields of interest: Elementary/secondary education; Water pollution; Environment; Food services; Housing/shelter; Human services; Women; Economically disadvantaged.
Limitations: Giving primarily in MN. No support for private foundations. No grants to individuals.
Application information: Application form not required.

Deadline(s): None

Officers: M. Yvonne Sexton, Pres.; Thomas P. Sexton, V.P.; James Sexton, Secy.-Treas.
Number of staff: None.
EIN: 411312086

1716
Smikis Foundation
Parkdale Plz., Ste. 426
1660 S. Hwy., 100
St. Louis Park, MN 55416-1533
(952) 512-1165
Contact: Brenda Jones

Established in 1993 in MN.
Donor(s): Charles H. Bell.
Grantmaker type: Independent foundation
Financial data (yr. ended 12/31/02): Assets, $6,829,082 (M); expenditures, $485,497; qualifying distributions, $453,825; giving activities include $453,800 for 86 grants (high: $25,000; low: $500; average: $500–$25,000).
Fields of interest: Education; Environment; Housing/shelter, services; Youth development, services; Community development, neighborhood development.
Types of support: General/operating support; Capital campaigns; Program development; Seed money; Scholarship funds.

Limitations: Giving limited to MN, with emphasis on Minneapolis. No grants to individuals, or for membership drives.
Publications: Application guidelines.
Application information: Application form not required.

Initial approach: Proposal
Copies of proposal: 1
Deadline(s): None
Board meeting date(s): Monthly

Officers and Directors:* John M. Hartwell,* Co-Pres.; Lucy B. Hartwell,* Co-Pres.
Number of staff: None.
EIN: 411742700

1717
Somerset Foundation, Inc.
c/o U.S. Bank, N.A.
P.O. Box 64713
St. Paul, MN 55164-0713 (651) 291-5164
Contact: Bradley Klein, Secy.-Treas.
Application address: 800 Nicollet Mall, Minneapolis, MN 55402, tel.: (612) 303-3002

Established in 1960 in MN.
Donor(s): Norman B. Mears.‡
Grantmaker type: Independent foundation
Financial data (yr. ended 12/31/02): Assets, $1,155,382 (M); expenditures, $233,545; qualifying distributions, $227,117; giving activities include $225,932 for 11 grants (high: $200,932; low: $1,000).
Purpose and activities: Giving for cultural programs, including performing arts groups and arts councils; support also for education and educational research and community affairs.
Fields of interest: Performing arts; Arts; Education, research; Education; Environment; Government/public administration; Protestant agencies & churches.
Types of support: General/operating support.
Limitations: Giving primarily in MN.
Application information: Application form not required.

Initial approach: Letter
Copies of proposal: 1
Deadline(s): None

Officers: Hella L. Mears Hueg, Pres.; William F. Hueg, Jr., V.P.; Bradley Klein, Secy.-Treas.
Number of staff: None.
EIN: 416029569

1718
The Harold W. Sweatt Foundation
P.O. Box 43476
Brooklyn Park, MN 55443-0476
Contact: Karen McGlynn
FAX: (763) 560-9106

Established in 1968 in MN as successor in part to The Sweatt Foundation, established in 1951.
Donor(s): Harold W. Sweatt.‡
Grantmaker type: Independent foundation
Financial data (yr. ended 02/28/03): Assets, $3,159,498 (M); expenditures, $210,117; qualifying distributions, $191,967; giving activities include $172,587 for 111 grants (high: $25,000; low: $25).
Purpose and activities: Giving primarily for wildlife conservation and animal protection, with some support for education and human rights.

Fields of interest: Arts; Secondary school/education; Higher education; Environment; Animals/wildlife; Human services; Christian agencies & churches.
Types of support: General/operating support.
Limitations: Applications not accepted. Giving on a national basis. No grants to individuals.
Application information: Unsolicited requests for funds not accepted.
   Board meeting date(s): July
Trustees: A. Lachlan Reed; Harold S. Reed; Lachlan W. Reed; Martha S. Reed; William S. Reed.
Number of staff: 1 part-time professional.
EIN: 416075860

1719
Tamarack Foundation
5140 Wells Fargo Ctr.
90 S. Seventh St.
Minneapolis, MN 55402

Established around 1995 in MN.
Donor(s): Duncan N. Dayton.
Grantmaker type: Independent foundation
Financial data (yr. ended 12/31/02): Assets, $3,543,745 (M); expenditures, $179,127; qualifying distributions, $145,850; giving activities include $142,500 for 16 grants (high: $50,000; low: $1,000).
Purpose and activities: Giving for higher education, family planning and women's services, and for environmental preservation.
Fields of interest: Arts; College; Libraries/library science; Education; Natural resources; Federated giving programs; Women.
Limitations: Applications not accepted. No grants to individuals.
Application information: Contributes only to pre-selected organizations.
Officers: Duncan N. Dayton, Pres.; Katharine L. Kelly, V.P.; James M. Karges, Secy.-Treas.
EIN: 411796504

1720
Tennant Foundation
(formerly Tennant Company Foundation)
701 N. Lilac Dr.
P.O. Box 1452
Minneapolis, MN 55440 (763) 540-1209
Contact: Carol A. Van Lith, Admin.
FAX: (763) 540-1616

Established in 1973 in MN.
Donor(s): Tennant Co.
Grantmaker type: Company-sponsored foundation
Financial data (yr. ended 12/31/02): Assets, $735,639 (M); expenditures, $357,961; qualifying distributions, $357,641; giving activities include $328,944 for grants (average: $1,000–$2,500).
Purpose and activities: Giving for community funds, social service and youth agencies, higher education, and cultural programs, including the arts and public broadcasting; limited support for conservation and health; employee-related scholarships paid through Scholarship Management Services.
Fields of interest: Media/communications; Arts; Higher education; Natural resources; Health care; Health organizations, association; Human

services; Children/youth, services; Community development; Federated giving programs.
Types of support: General/operating support; Continuing support; Capital campaigns; Employee matching gifts; Employee-related scholarships.
Limitations: Giving primarily in areas where Tennant Co. employees live and work; support depends on the extent to which the applicant offers its services to Tennant Co. communities in the Minneapolis and Hennepin County, MN, areas. No support for agencies funded through umbrella organizations, religious organizations for religious purposes, national organizations without active local chapters, or elementary or secondary schools. No grants to individuals (except for employee-related scholarships), or for travel, benefit tickets, or courtesy advertising.
Publications: Annual report (including application guidelines).
Application information: Employee-related scholarships are administered by Scholarship Management Services. Application form not required.
   Initial approach: Call or write for guidelines.
   Copies of proposal: 1
   Deadline(s): 4 weeks prior to board meetings
   Board meeting date(s): Mar., June, Aug., and Dec.
   Final notification: 4 weeks
Officer and Directors:* Roger L. Hale,* Pres.; Richard M. Adams; Barbara A. Clarity; John T. Pain; William R. Strang.
Number of staff: 1 part-time professional; 1 part-time support.
EIN: 237297045

1721
Terhuly Foundation
2565 Walnut St.
Roseville, MN 55113

Established in 1995 in MN.
Donor(s): Hugh K. Schilling.
Grantmaker type: Independent foundation
Financial data (yr. ended 12/31/02): Assets, $2,586,240 (M); expenditures, $202,218; qualifying distributions, $166,274; giving activities include $164,000 for 61 grants (high: $10,000; low: $1,000).
Purpose and activities: Giving primarily for education, children's services, and senior citizens.
Fields of interest: Education, public education; Education; Zoos/zoological societies; Children, services; Foundations (community); Aging.
Limitations: Giving primarily in MN. No grants to individuals.
Application information:
   Board meeting date(s): June 10 and Dec. 10
Officers: Hugh K. Schilling, Pres.; Lynn M. Schilling Brown, V.P.; Terryl Schilling Elwell, Secy.; Hugh K. Schilling, Jr., Treas.
Director: Margaret S. Schilling.
Number of staff: 1 part-time professional; 1 part-time support.
EIN: 411818562

1722
James R. Thorpe Foundation
333 Washington Ave. N., Ste. 322
Minneapolis, MN 55401 (612) 373-9484
Contact: Edith D. Thorpe, Pres., or Jane M. Stamstad, Exec. Dir.

Incorporated in 1974 in MN.
Donor(s): James R. Thorpe.‡
Grantmaker type: Independent foundation
Financial data (yr. ended 11/30/02): Assets, $8,132,766 (M); expenditures, $585,304; qualifying distributions, $529,884; giving activities include $465,750 for 81 grants (high: $25,000; low: $300).
Purpose and activities: Primary areas of interest include the disadvantaged, youth, the elderly, education, and cultural programs. Giving for social service agencies and higher and secondary education; support also for community health care and AIDS services.
Fields of interest: Performing arts; Arts; Education; Environment; Health care; Mental health/crisis services; AIDS; Housing/shelter, development; Human services; Children/youth, services; Family services; Aging, centers/services; Homeless, human services; Disabled; Aging; Economically disadvantaged.
Types of support: General/operating support; Capital campaigns; Equipment; Program development; Internship funds; Scholarship funds.
Limitations: Giving limited to Hennepin County, MN, with emphasis on Minneapolis. No grants to individuals, or for continuing support, emergency or endowment funds, deficit financing, land acquisition, matching gifts, publications, seminars, benefits, or conferences; no loans.
Publications: Annual report (including application guidelines).
Application information: Minnesota Common Grant Application Form accepted. Application form not required.
   Initial approach: Telephone or letter of inquiry (no more than 8 pages)
   Copies of proposal: 1
   Deadline(s): Mar. 1 and Sept. 1
   Board meeting date(s): May and Nov.
   Final notification: 1 week after grants meeting
Officers and Directors:* Edith D. Thorpe,* Pres.; Leonard M. Addington,* V.P.; Mary C. Boos,* V.P.; Elizabeth A. Kelly,* V.P.; Timothy D. Thorpe, V.P.; Samuel A. Cote,* Secy.; Samuel S. Thorpe III,* Treas.; Jane M. Stamstad, Exec. Dir.
Number of staff: 1 part-time professional.
EIN: 416175293

1723
The Toro Company Contributions Program
8111 Lyndale Ave. S.
Bloomington, MN 55420-1196
Contact: Ellen Watson

Grantmaker type: Corporate giving program
Purpose and activities: As a complement to its foundation, Toro also makes charitable contributions to nonprofit organizations directly. Support is given primarily in areas of company operations.
Fields of interest: Education; Environment.
Types of support: General/operating support; Scholarship funds; Employee volunteer services;

Employee matching gifts; Employee-related scholarships; In-kind gifts.
Limitations: Giving primarily in areas of company operations.
Application information: Application form not required.
> *Initial approach:* Proposal to headquarters
> *Copies of proposal:* 1
> *Final notification:* Following review

1724
The Traverse Foundation
c/o William J. Brody
4000 Pillsbury Cnt.
Minneapolis, MN 55402-3397

Established in 1992 in MN.
Donor(s): Norman W. Harris III.
Grantmaker type: Independent foundation
Financial data (yr. ended 12/31/02): Assets, $1,408,052 (M); expenditures, $104,740; qualifying distributions, $99,565; giving activities include $99,763 for 16 grants (high: $25,000; low: $1,000).
Purpose and activities: Giving for education, wildlife conservation, international cultural centers, and children's medical services.
Fields of interest: Arts; Higher education; Education; Animal welfare; Health care; Camps; Foundations (public).
Limitations: Applications not accepted. Giving primarily in MN. No grants to individuals.
Application information: Contributes only to pre-selected organizations.
Officers and Directors:* Norman W. Harris III,* Pres. and Treas.; Norman W. Harris IV,* V.P.; Linda B. Harris,* Secy.; Blake C. Harris.
EIN: 411734297

1725
Unity Avenue Foundation
c/o SRI
342 5th Ave. N.
Bayport, MN 55003 (651) 439-1557
Contact: Sarah J. Andersen, Grant Consultant
Additional tel.: (888) 439-9508; FAX: (651) 439-9480; E-mail: unityavefdtn@srinc.biz

Established in 1985 in MN.
Donor(s): members of the Cowles family.
Grantmaker type: Independent foundation
Financial data (yr. ended 05/31/03): Assets, $1,718,318 (M); expenditures, $119,452; qualifying distributions, $141,126; giving activities include $100,200 for 10 grants (high: $16,700; low: $4,500).
Purpose and activities: The mission is to foster responsible human interaction with the natural environment. Grants for smaller organizations that are visionary and creative, which anticipate and focus on potential future critical concerns rather than react to current conditions.
Fields of interest: Natural resources; Environment.
Types of support: Equipment; Program development; Conferences/seminars; Publication; Seed money; Research.
Limitations: Giving limited to funding projects in the Western Hemisphere. No grants to individuals.
Publications: Application guidelines.

Application information: Contact SRI for specific application information. Application form required.
> *Initial approach:* One-page (one-sided) proposal summary in (12 point font)
> *Copies of proposal:* 12
> *Deadline(s):* Jan. 8
> *Board meeting date(s):* Feb. and Aug.
> *Final notification:* Dec. 15
Officers: Charles Fuller Cowles, Pres.; Ira S. Goldstein, Secy.; Page Knudsen Cowles, Treas.
Directors: Constance M. Cowles; John Cowles, Jr.; John Cowles III; Sage Fuller Cowles; Tessa Sage Flores; Ann Maria Stephens.
Number of staff: None.
EIN: 363409701

1726
The Von Blon Family Charitable Foundation
c/o U.S. Trust
730 2nd Ave. S., Ste. 1400
Minneapolis, MN 55402-3395
Application address: 601 2nd Ave. S., Ste. 5000, Minneapolis, MN 55402, tel.: (612) 332-1544

Established in 1992 in MN.
Donor(s): Philip Von Blon, Joanne Von Blon.
Grantmaker type: Independent foundation
Financial data (yr. ended 12/31/02): Assets, $376,354 (M); gifts received, $25,485; expenditures, $160,635; qualifying distributions, $156,062; giving activities include $155,600 for 28 grants (high: $25,000; low: $500).
Fields of interest: Arts; Education; Environment; Health care; Human services; Federated giving programs.
Limitations: Giving primarily in the Minneapolis-St. Paul, MN, area. No grants to individuals.
Application information:
> *Deadline(s):* None
Officers: Philip Von Blon, Pres.; Joanne Von Blon, V.P.
Trustee: U.S. Trust.
EIN: 416362685

1727
W.M. Foundation
5140 Wells Fargo Ctr.
90 S. 7th St.
Minneapolis, MN 55402-4139

Donor(s): Wallace C. Dayton.
Grantmaker type: Independent foundation
Financial data (yr. ended 12/31/02): Assets, $10,601,564 (M); gifts received, $100,000; expenditures, $812,776; qualifying distributions, $707,694; giving activities include $700,000 for 3 grants (high: $350,000; low: $100,000).
Fields of interest: Natural resources; Animals/wildlife, preservation/protection.
Limitations: Applications not accepted. Giving primarily in the Minneapolis-St. Paul, MN, area. No grants to individuals.
Application information: Contributes only to pre-selected organizations.
Officers: Mary L. Dayton, Pres. and Treas.; James M. Karges, Secy.
Directors: Sally D. Clement; Elizabeth D. Dovydenas; Katherine D. Nielsen; Ellen D. Sturgis.

EIN: 416080486

1728
Lee and Rose Warner Foundation
2501 Rosegate
St. Paul, MN 55113-2717 (651) 604-4200
Contact: Malcolm W. McDonald, Tr.

Incorporated in 1959 in MN.
Donor(s): Rose Warner.‡
Grantmaker type: Independent foundation
Financial data (yr. ended 12/31/01): Assets, $14,130,016 (M); gifts received, $178,947; expenditures, $2,280,548; qualifying distributions, $1,684,170; giving activities include $1,682,466 for 7 grants (high: $1,602,052; low: $1,000).
Purpose and activities: Giving primarily for education.
Fields of interest: Education; Environment.
Limitations: Giving primarily in MN. No grants to individuals, or for endowment funds, research programs, scholarships, or fellowships; no loans.
Application information: Application form not required.
> *Initial approach:* Letter
> *Copies of proposal:* 1
> *Deadline(s):* None
> *Board meeting date(s):* Sept. and Dec.
Officers and Trustees:* Donald G. McNeely,* Chair.; J. Michael Miles,* Secy.; Paul Puerzer,* Treas.; Chas Arend; Cheryl Granlund; Malcolm W. McDonald; Gregory McNeely; Kevin McNeely; Nora McNeely; Michael A. Urbanos.
Number of staff: None.
EIN: 416011523

1729
Frederick O. Watson Foundation
c/o Watson Centers, Inc.
3100 W. Lake St., Ste. 420
Minneapolis, MN 55416 (952) 920-4077
Contact: Douglas F. Watson, Pres.
FAX: (952) 920-5438

Established in 1989 in MN.
Donor(s): Frederick O. Watson.‡
Grantmaker type: Independent foundation
Financial data (yr. ended 12/31/02): Assets, $3,229,108 (M); gifts received, $50,174; expenditures, $624,002; qualifying distributions, $624,002; giving activities include $621,500 for 70 grants (high: $140,000; low: $1,000).
Purpose and activities: Giving primarily for health and human services.
Fields of interest: Arts; Education; Natural resources; Environment; Hospitals (general); Cancer; Human services.
Limitations: Giving primarily in MN.
Application information: Application form not required.
> *Initial approach:* Letter
> *Copies of proposal:* 1
> *Deadline(s):* None
> *Board meeting date(s):* Annually
Officers: Douglas F. Watson, Pres.; Stephen M. Watson, V.P.
Number of staff: None.
EIN: 411625546

1730
Warren F. Weck, Jr. Charitable Trust
c/o Wells Fargo Bank Minnesota, N.A.
625 Marquette Ave.
Minneapolis, MN 55479

Established in 2001 in MN.
Donor(s): Warren F. Weck.
Grantmaker type: Independent foundation
Financial data (yr. ended 12/31/02): Assets,
$4,784,190 (M); gifts received, $12,161;
expenditures, $244,928; qualifying distributions,
$208,925; giving activities include $200,700 for
25 grants (high: $51,000; low: $700).
Fields of interest: Higher education;
Environment; Human services; Religion.
Limitations: Applications not accepted. Giving
primarily in MN. No grants to individuals.
Application information: Contributes only to
pre-selected organizations.
Directors: Bunny Jacobson; Jacqueline Kelly;
Lauren Weck; Warren Weck III.
Trustee: Wells Fargo Bank Minnesota, N.A.
EIN: 416486803

1731
Wedum Foundation
3191 Shorewood Dr.
Arden Hills, MN 55112
Contact: Jim Cooper, Pres.
FAX: (651) 633-0312; E-mail:
kathleenhansen@attbi.com

Established in 1959 in MN.
Donor(s): Maynard C. Wedum,‡ John A.
Wedum.
Grantmaker type: Independent foundation
Financial data (yr. ended 12/31/01): Assets,
$85,877,915 (M); gifts received, $140;
expenditures, $11,506,469; qualifying
distributions, $265,115; giving activities include
$216,331 for 6 grants (high: $160,000; low:
$131) and $13,900 for grants to individuals.
Purpose and activities: Giving primarily for
higher education, including scholarships;
support also for social services.
Fields of interest: Business school/education;
Education, services; Education; Animals/wildlife,
preservation/protection; Health organizations,
association; Alcoholism; Human services; Youth,
services.
Types of support: Seed money; Program-related
investments/loans; Scholarships—to individuals;
Matching/challenge support.
Limitations: Giving primarily in MN.
Application information: Student aid support
beyond existing programs available through
local Dollars for Scholars units. Application
form required.
  Copies of proposal: 1
  Deadline(s): None
  Board meeting date(s): Fall
  Final notification: Late fall
Officers and Directors:* Jim Cooper,* Pres. and
Treas.; Gary Slette, V.P.; John Wedum,* V.P.;
Kathleen Hansen, Secy.; Dan Lindh; Frank
Starke; Dale Vesledahl; Mary Beth Wedum.
Number of staff: 1 part-time professional; 1
part-time support.
EIN: 416025661

1732
Donald Weesner Charitable Trust
c/o U.S. Bank, N.A.
P.O. Box 64713
St. Paul, MN 55164-0713

Established in 1999 in MN.
Grantmaker type: Independent foundation
Financial data (yr. ended 12/31/01): Assets,
$13,935,500 (M); expenditures, $1,234,875;
qualifying distributions, $1,144,852; giving
activities include $1,093,002 for 10 grants (high:
$309,296; low: $5,000).
Purpose and activities: Giving primarily for arts,
culture, nature conservation, and social services.
Fields of interest: Museums
(science/technology); Arts; Natural resources;
Zoos/zoological societies; Human services;
Federated giving programs.
Limitations: Applications not accepted. Giving
primarily in MN. No grants to individuals.
Application information: Contributes only to
pre-selected organizations.
Trustee: U.S. Bank, N.A.
EIN: 416463406

1733
Weyerhaeuser Family Foundation, Inc.
(formerly Weyerhaeuser Foundation)
332 Minnesota St., Ste. 2100
St. Paul, MN 55101 (651) 228-0935
Contact: Judith K. Healey, Prog. Consultant
FAX: (651) 228-0776; E-mail:
jmo@fidcouns.com; URL: http://
www.wfamilyfoundation.org

Incorporated in 1950 in MN.
Donor(s): Members of the Weyerhaeuser family.
Grantmaker type: Independent foundation
Financial data (yr. ended 12/31/02): Assets,
$13,350,805 (M); gifts received, $162,226;
expenditures, $695,513; qualifying distributions,
$687,633; giving activities include $608,619 for
grants (average: $10,000–$20,000).
Purpose and activities: The Weyerhaeuser
Family Foundation supports programs of
national and international significance that
promote the welfare of human and natural
resources. These efforts will enhance the
creativity, strengths and skills already possessed
by those in need and reinforce the sustaining
processes inherent in nature.
Fields of interest: Natural resources;
Environment; Children, services.
Types of support: Program development; Seed
money.
Limitations: Giving for international programs
only through U.S.-based organizations. No
support for elementary or secondary education.
No grants to individuals, or for building or
endowment funds, annual campaigns, operating
budgets, equipment, scholarships, fellowships,
travel, or matching gifts; no loans.
Publications: Application guidelines, Annual
report (including application guidelines).
Application information: Application form
required.
  Initial approach: Letter of intent
  Copies of proposal: 2
  Deadline(s): Submit proposal from Jan.
    through Apr.; deadline May 1

Board meeting date(s): Program committee
  meets annually in early summer to review
  proposals; board usually meets in Nov.
Officers and Trustees:* Kathleen McGoldrick,*
Pres.; Frederick W. Titcomb, V.P. and Secy.;
Margaret R. King,* Secy.; Edward W. Pharis,*
Treas.; Susan Bonsall; John B. Driscoll; Margaret
L. Driscoll; Lisa M. Fremont; Peter E. Heymann;
Brenda C. Jewett; Lucy R. Jones; Jane W. McFee;
Samuel J. Pascoe; Charles W. Rasmussen;
Thomas F. Rasmussen; Philip R. Rosenburg;
Amy W. Stried; Justin H. Weyerhaeuser.
Number of staff: 1 part-time professional.
EIN: 416012062

1734
**The Charles A. Weyerhaeuser Memorial
Foundation**
2100 First National Bank Bldg.
St. Paul, MN 55101 (651) 228-0935
Contact: Lucy Rosenberry Jones, Pres.
FAX: (651) 228-0776

Incorporated in 1959 in MN.
Donor(s): Carl A. Weyerhaeuser Trusts,
Sarah-Maud W. Sivertsen Trusts.
Grantmaker type: Independent foundation
Financial data (yr. ended 02/28/02): Assets,
$6,482,340 (M); gifts received, $77,659;
expenditures, $403,085; qualifying distributions,
$397,128; giving activities include $392,525 for
7 grants (high: $300,000; low: $2,000).
Fields of interest: Arts; Higher education;
Natural resources.
Types of support: Continuing support; Annual
campaigns.
Limitations: Giving primarily in MN. No grants
to individuals.
Application information: Application form not
required.
  Initial approach: Letter
  Copies of proposal: 1
  Deadline(s): None
  Board meeting date(s): As required
  Final notification: 3 months
Officers and Directors:* Lucy R. Jones,* Pres.;
Robert J. Sivertsen,* V.P.; Joseph S. Micallef,*
Secy.-Treas.; Elise R. Donohue; Charles W.
Rosenberry II.
Number of staff: None.
EIN: 416012063

1735
Winona Community Foundation
(formerly Greater Winona Area Community
Foundation)
51 E. 4th St., Ste. 314
Winona, MN 55987-6203 (507) 454-6511
Contact: Sue Cornwell, Pres.
FAX: (507) 454-0441; E-mail:
wincomf@hbci.com

Established in 1987 in MN.
Grantmaker type: Community foundation
Financial data (yr. ended 12/31/01): Assets,
$6,073,908 (M); gifts received, $2,206,810;
expenditures, $844,497; giving activities include
$732,243 for 30+ grants (high: $129,398).
Purpose and activities: The foundation seeks,
accepts, and administers contributions to meet
the charitable needs of the Winona area
community in MN. Preference is for

organizations that have demonstrated actual and potential operating success. The foundation administers a donor-advised fund.

Fields of interest: Multipurpose centers/programs; Elementary/secondary education; Education; Environment; Health care; Recreation; Human services; Religion.

Types of support: General/operating support; Continuing support; Annual campaigns; Equipment; Endowments; Program development; Conferences/seminars; Program-related investments/loans; Matching/challenge support.

Limitations: Giving primarily in Winona, MN, and its surrounding community.

Publications: Application guidelines, Annual report, Grants list, Informational brochure (including application guidelines), Newsletter.

Application information: Application form required.
 Initial approach: Telephone
 Copies of proposal: 6
 Deadline(s): Apr. 1 and Oct. 1
 Board meeting date(s): 4th Tues. of each month

Officers: Bob Gilbertsons, Chair.; Sue Cornwell, Pres.; Kevin Mahoney, V.P.; Joyce Woodworth, Secy.; Carol Heineman, Treas.

Directors: Chris Arnold; Bud Baechler; Sara Brandon; David Bue; Bro. Louis DeThomasis; Rev. William Flesch; Margaret S. Johnson; Jerry Kellum; Darrell Kraeger; Bill McNeil.

Number of staff: 2 part-time professional; 1 part-time support.

EIN: 363500853

MISSISSIPPI

1736
Community Foundation of Greater Jackson

(formerly Greater Jackson Foundation)
525 E. Capitol St., Ste. 2B
Jackson, MS 39201 (601) 974-6044
Contact: Linda Montgomery, Pres.
FAX: (601) 974-6045; E-mail: greaterjackson@bellsouth.net; URL: http://www.greaterjacksonfoundation.com

Established in 1994 in MS.

Grantmaker type: Community foundation

Financial data (yr. ended 03/31/03): Assets, $10,554,703 (M); gifts received, $3,923,359; expenditures, $3,745,031; giving activities include $3,376,014 for 280 grants (average: $50–$600,000).

Purpose and activities: Giving for the arts, education, health, and human services. The foundation administers donor-advised funds.

Fields of interest: Museums; Performing arts; Elementary/secondary education; Higher education; Environment; Health organizations, association; Children/youth, services; Family services; Community development, neighborhood development.

Types of support: General/operating support; Continuing support; Annual campaigns; Capital campaigns; Building/renovation; Endowments; Program development; Conferences/seminars;

Professorships; Curriculum development; Scholarship funds; Scholarships—to individuals; Matching/challenge support.

Limitations: Giving primarily in Hinds, Madison, and Rankin counties, MS.

Publications: Annual report (including application guidelines), Informational brochure (including application guidelines), Newsletter, Occasional report.

Application information: Application form required.
 Initial approach: Letter
 Copies of proposal: 10
 Deadline(s): Mid-Feb.
 Board meeting date(s): Feb., Apr., June, Aug., Oct., and Dec.
 Final notification: Mid-Apr.

Officers and Trustees:* Red Moffat,* Chair.; David Grishman,* Chair.-Elect; Linda Montgomery, Pres.; Fred Banks,* Secy.; Betty Lou Reeves,* Treas.; Duane Gordon, Comm. Devel. Officer.

Number of staff: 2 full-time professional; 1 part-time professional.

EIN: 640845750

1737
Mississippi Chemical Corporation Contributions Program

P.O. Box 388
Yazoo City, MS 39194 (662) 746-4131
Contact: Melinda B. Hood, Dir., Corp. Comm.

Grantmaker type: Corporate giving program

Purpose and activities: Mississippi Chemical makes charitable contributions to nonprofit organizations involved with arts and culture, education, the environment, agriculture, rural development, and engineering. Support is given primarily in areas of company operations.

Fields of interest: Visual arts; Performing arts; Arts; Vocational education; Higher education; Engineering school/education; Education; Natural resources; Environment; Agriculture; Rural development; Engineering.

Types of support: General/operating support; Sponsorships; Donated products; In-kind gifts.

Limitations: Giving primarily in areas of company operations in MS.

Application information: Application form not required.
 Initial approach: Proposal to headquarters
 Copies of proposal: 1
 Final notification: Following review

1738
Walker Foundation

(formerly W. E. Walker Foundation)
2829 Lakeland Dr.
Mirror Lake Plz., Ste. 1600
Jackson, MS 39232-8880 (601) 939-3003
Contact: John S. Jenkins, Dir.

Established in 1972 in MS.

Donor(s): W.E. Walker, Jr.,‡ The Walker Cos., His Way Homes.

Grantmaker type: Independent foundation

Financial data (yr. ended 12/31/01): Assets, $10,309,772 (M); gifts received, $40,000; expenditures, $1,176,817; qualifying distributions, $1,035,450; giving activities include $1,027,337 for 58 grants (high:

$205,000; low: $100; average: $1,000–$15,000) and $5,500 for 3 employee matching gifts.

Purpose and activities: Giving primarily for the arts, education, including Episcopal schools, natural resource conservation, health, youth, and social services, federated giving programs, and religion.

Fields of interest: Museums (art); Performing arts; Arts; Education; Natural resources; Health care; Medical research, institute; Boys & girls clubs; Boy scouts; Human services; Federated giving programs; Protestant agencies & churches.

Types of support: General/operating support; Annual campaigns; Capital campaigns.

Limitations: Giving primarily in MS. Generally no grants for deficit reduction, operating budgets, endowment programs, personnel costs, welfare agencies, physical plant construction, or individual scholarships.

Publications: Annual report.

Application information: Application form required for scholarships.
 Deadline(s): None
 Board meeting date(s): As needed

Officers: James H. Daughdrill III, Pres.; Leigh B. Allen III, Secy.

Trustee: W.E. Walker III.

Director: John S. Jenkins.

Number of staff: 1 part-time professional.

EIN: 237279902

MISSOURI

1739
Ameren Corporation Contributions Program

(formerly Union Electric Company Contributions Program)
1 Ameren Plz., 1901 Chouteau Ave.
P.O. Box 66149, M.C. 100
St. Louis, MO 63166-6149 (314) 554-4740
Contact: Otis Cowan, Mgr., Community Rels.
Additional application addresses: Donna Bailey, Legislative and Community Rels. Supvr., AmerenCIPS, c/o Govt. Affairs Dept., 607 E. Adams St., C1301, Springfield, IL 62739, tel.: (217) 535-5025, Neal Johnson, Dir., Community Affairs, AmerenCILCO, 300 Liberty St., Peoria, IL 61602-1404, tel.: (309) 677-5516; Additional tel.: (314) 554-2789; FAX: (314) 554-2888; E-mail: ocowan@ameren.com; URL: http://www.ameren.com/community/adc_com_homepage.asp

Grantmaker type: Corporate giving program

Financial data (yr. ended 12/31/02): Total giving, $832,609; giving activities include $759,509 for grants and $73,100 for in-kind gifts.

Purpose and activities: As a complement to its foundation, Ameren also makes charitable contributions to nonprofit organizations directly. Support is given primarily in areas of company operations.

Fields of interest: Education; Environment; Youth development; Human services; Aging.

Types of support: General/operating support; Annual campaigns; Capital campaigns; Building/renovation; Equipment; Endowments;

Emergency funds; Program development; Seed money; Curriculum development; Cause-related marketing; Employee volunteer services; Use of facilities; Sponsorships; Program evaluation; Donated equipment; In-kind gifts; Matching/challenge support.
Limitations: Giving primarily in areas of company operations in IL and MO. No support for political organizations or candidates or religious, fraternal, veterans', social, or similar organizations. No grants to individuals; no electric or natural gas service donations.
Publications: Application guidelines, Corporate giving report (including application guidelines).
Application information: Proposals should be submitted using organization letterhead. The Corporate Communications and Public Policy Department handles giving. A contributions committee reviews all requests of over $25,000. Application form not required.
  Initial approach: Proposal to nearest company facility
  Copies of proposal: 1
  Deadline(s): None
  Board meeting date(s): 2 to 3 times per year for requests of over $25,000
  Final notification: 3 to 4 months
Administrators: Donna Bailey, Legislative and Community Rels. Supvr., AmerenCIPS; Susan M. Bell, Sr. Supvr., Community Rels., AmerenUE; Otis Cowan, Mgr., Community Rels.; Neal Johnson, Dir., Community Affairs, AmerenCILCO.
Number of staff: 5 full-time professional; 1 full-time support.

1740
American Lung Association of Eastern Missouri
1118 Hampton Ave.
St. Louis, MO   63139-3196   (314) 645-5505
Contact: Pat Williams, Admin. Asst.
FAX: (314) 645-7128; E-mail: pwilliams@alaem.org; URL: http://www.lungusa.org/easternmissouri/

Established in 1907 in MO.
Grantmaker type: Public charity
Financial data (yr. ended 06/30/02): Revenue, $2,544,973; assets, $3,012,076 (M); gifts received, $1,809,300; expenditures, $2,562,329; program services expenses, $2,033,958; giving activities include $161,203 for 1 grant and $43,885 for 3 grants to individuals (high: $17,500; low: $10,135).
Purpose and activities: The association seeks to prevent lung disease and promote lung health, through education, advocacy and research.
Fields of interest: Environment, air pollution; Smoking; Lung diseases; Asthma; Lung research.
Types of support: Research; Grants to individuals.
Limitations: Giving primarily in MO.
Application information:
  Board meeting date(s): Quarterly
Officers and Directors:* Mario Castro, M.D.,* Pres.; Frank H. Hackmann,* Pres.-Elect; Lisa M. Wood, M.D.,* V.P.; Lori C. Pickens,* Secy.; Bradley F. Baker,* Treas.; Francis L. Barkofske; Carlos C. Daughaday, M.D.; Edwin B. Fisher, Jr., Ph.D.; George M. Matuschak.
Number of staff: 10 full-time professional; 2 part-time professional.

EIN: 430662525

1741
Anheuser-Busch Companies, Inc. Corporate Giving Program
1 Busch Pl.
St. Louis, MO   63118-1852   (314) 577-7368
Contact: Carol Hennemann, Asst. Mgr., Charitable Contribs.

Grantmaker type: Corporate giving program
Purpose and activities: As a complement to its foundation, Anheuser-Busch also makes charitable contributions to nonprofit organizations directly. Support is given primarily in areas of company and theme park operations.
Fields of interest: Arts; Education; Environment; Health care; Youth development; Human services; Minorities.
Types of support: General/operating support; Employee volunteer services; Sponsorships; Employee matching gifts; Employee-related scholarships; In-kind gifts.
Limitations: Giving primarily in areas of company and theme park operations. No support for political, religious, social, fraternal, or athletic organizations. No grants to individuals (except for employee-related scholarships), or for hospital operating expenses.
Publications: Application guidelines.
Application information: The company has a staff that only handles contributions. Application form not required.
  Initial approach: Proposal to headquarters
  Copies of proposal: 1
  Deadline(s): None
  Final notification: 2 months
Administrator: Cynthia Garrone, Mgr., Charitable Contribs.
Number of staff: 1 full-time professional; 1 part-time professional.

1742
Anheuser-Busch Foundation ▼
c/o Anheuser-Busch Cos., Inc.
1 Busch Pl.
St. Louis, MO   63118   (314) 577-7368
Contact: Carol Hennemann, Asst. Mgr., Char. Contribus.

Established in 1975 in MO.
Donor(s): Anheuser-Busch Cos., Inc.
Grantmaker type: Company-sponsored foundation
Financial data (yr. ended 12/31/02): Assets, $28,139,664 (M); gifts received, $10,016,918; expenditures, $17,609,426; qualifying distributions, $17,568,685; giving activities include $16,501,081 for 154 grants (high: $1,500,000; low: $200; average: $1,000–$200,000) and $1,075,577 for 448 employee matching gifts.
Purpose and activities: Giving to United Way agencies and higher education; support for youth, community development, the arts, and health agencies.
Fields of interest: Arts; Higher education; Natural resources; Health care; Human services; Children/youth, services; Community development.
Types of support: Continuing support; Capital campaigns; Building/renovation; Program

development; Scholarship funds; Employee matching gifts; Matching/challenge support.
Limitations: Giving primarily in areas of major company operations of its breweries and theme parks: St. Louis, MO, Newark, NJ, Los Angeles, Fairfield, and San Diego, CA, Houston and San Antonio, TX, Jacksonville, Tampa, and Orlando, FL, Merrimack, NH, Baldwinsville, NY, Fort Collins, CO, Cartersville, GA, and Williamsburg, VA. No support for organizations whose activities are primarily religious in nature, social or fraternal groups, or political or athletic organizations. No grants to individuals, or for hospital operating budgets.
Publications: Application guidelines, Informational brochure.
Application information: Application form not required.
  Initial approach: Letter
  Copies of proposal: 1
  Deadline(s): None
  Board meeting date(s): Approximately every 3 months
  Final notification: Following board meetings
Directors: JoBeth G. Brown; August A. Busch III; John E. Jacob.
Trustee Bank: U.S. Bank, N.A.
Number of staff: None.
EIN: 510168084
Recent environmental and animal welfare grants:
1742-1 Animal Protective Association of Missouri, Saint Louis, MO, $50,000. For general support. 2002.
1742-2 Florida Aquarium, Tampa, Fl, $33,333. For general support. 2002.

1743
Arthur & Helen Baer Charitable Foundation
c/o Grace Advisors, Inc.
3117 S. Big Bend Blvd.
St. Louis, MO   63143

Established around 1984.
Donor(s): Helen K. Baer.‡
Grantmaker type: Independent foundation
Financial data (yr. ended 12/31/02): Assets, $8,542,812 (M); expenditures, $667,547; qualifying distributions, $487,709; giving activities include $455,167 for 21 grants (high: $72,000; low: $3,000).
Purpose and activities: Support for museums and other cultural programs, human services, animal welfare, and education.
Fields of interest: Museums (art); Arts; Elementary/secondary education; Education; Animals/wildlife; Human services; Children/youth, services.
Types of support: Building/renovation; Equipment; Program development; Scholarship funds; Program-related investments/loans.
Limitations: Applications not accepted. Giving primarily in St. Louis, MO. No grants to individuals.
Application information: Contributes only to pre-selected organizations.
Officers: Richard T. Fisher, Pres.; Stephen C. Casagrande, V.P.; Patrick E. Stark, Secy.-Treas.
EIN: 431353474

1744
Donald L. Barnes Foundation
61 Overhills Dr.
St. Louis, MO 63124

Established in 1990 in MO.
Grantmaker type: Independent foundation
Financial data (yr. ended 12/31/01): Assets,
$1,645,417 (M); expenditures, $113,214;
qualifying distributions, $105,692; giving
activities include $94,523 for 27 grants (high:
$42,268; low: $50).
Fields of interest: Child development,
education; Higher education; Education;
Environment; Human services; Children,
services; Christian agencies & churches.
Limitations: Applications not accepted. Giving
on a national basis, with emphasis on IL, IN,
and the greater St. Louis, MO, area. No grants to
individuals.
Application information: Contributes only to
pre-selected organizations.
Officers and Directors:* Thomas E. Phelps,*
Pres.; Trent B. Phelps, Secy.; Mark J. Lincoln,*
Treas.; Natalie B. Phelps; Valier Phelps Stewart.
EIN: 431531070

1745
The Bellwether Foundation, Inc.
c/o University Club Twr.
1034 S. Brentwood Blvd., Ste. 850
St. Louis, MO 63117-1291
Contact: Sally Duffield, Pres.

Established in 1985 in MO.
Donor(s): Robert B. Smith, Nancy M. Smith,
Wallace H. Smith.‡
Grantmaker type: Independent foundation
Financial data (yr. ended 12/31/02): Assets,
$16,726,247 (M); gifts received, $516,820;
expenditures, $887,612; qualifying distributions,
$497,932; giving activities include $400,700 for
11 grants (high: $250,000; low: $2,500).
Purpose and activities: Primarily supports
projects which anticipate the future in the areas
of the arts, computer science, education,
finance, health care, medicine, and the social
sciences, including research in any of these
areas.
Fields of interest: Arts; Higher education;
Natural resources; Botanical gardens; Medical
research, institute.
Types of support: Program development;
Research.
Limitations: Applications not accepted. Giving
primarily in St. Louis, MO. No grants to
individuals.
Application information: Contributes only to
pre-selected organizations. Unsolicited requests
for funds not considered.
Board meeting date(s): Apr. and Dec.
Officers: Robert B. Smith, Chair. and C.E.O.;
Sally Duffield, Pres. and C.O.O.; Robert B.
Smith II, V.P.; Mary Frances Balmer, Secy.-Treas.
Trustees: Edwin J. Putzell; Robert B. Smith III.
EIN: 222635309

1746
Boeing-McDonnell Foundation ▼
(formerly McDonnell Douglas Foundation)
P.O. Box 516, M.C. S100-3462
St. Louis, MO 63166
Contact: Karen A. Bedell, Pres.
FAX: (314) 234-0980; URL: http://
www.boeing.com

Incorporated in 1947 in MO.
Donor(s): McDonnell Douglas Corp.
Grantmaker type: Company-sponsored
foundation
Financial data (yr. ended 12/31/02): Assets,
$11,500,000 (M); expenditures, $4,500,000;
qualifying distributions, $4,500,000; giving
activities include $4,500,000 for 43 grants.
Purpose and activities: Emphasis on education;
support also for engineering, the environment,
health and human services, civic, and cultural
affairs.
Fields of interest: Arts; Education; Environment;
Health care; Human services; Children/youth,
services; Community development; Federated
giving programs.
Types of support: General/operating support;
Continuing support; Annual campaigns; Capital
campaigns; Program development.
Limitations: Giving limited to the St. Louis, MO,
region. No support for sectarian,
denominational, fraternal, social, religious, or
labor organizations, or for university, industry
affiliates, or associates programs. No grants to
individuals (except for employee-related
scholarships), or for advertisements, fundraisers,
or sporting events; no loans.
Publications: Application guidelines.
Application information: Web-based
application process. Application form required.
Copies of proposal: 1
Deadline(s): None
Board meeting date(s): Quarterly
Final notification: 60 to 120 days
Officers and Directors:* John F. McDonnell,*
Chair.; Karen A. Bedell, Pres.; Gerald Daniels;
Patrick Finneran; Samuel Jenkins; William
Stowers.
Number of staff: 1 full-time professional.
EIN: 431128093
**Recent environmental and animal welfare
grants:**
1746-1 Missouri Botanical Garden, Saint Louis,
MO, $50,000. For general support. 2002.

1747
Boswell Foundation, Inc.
1078 S. Jefferson
Lebanon, MO 65536
Contact: Paul Walker, Secy.

Established in 1985 in MO.
Donor(s): Independent Stave Co., Inc., Amie
Boswell Foundation, Joe Boswell Foundation,
Johnathon Boswell Foundation, Julie Boswell
Foundation, The Lois K. Boswell Charitable
Lead Trust.
Grantmaker type: Company-sponsored
foundation
Financial data (yr. ended 11/30/00): Assets,
$15,511 (M); gifts received, $585,000;
expenditures, $843,001; qualifying distributions,
$819,814; giving activities include $819,814 for
23 grants (high: $549,390; low: $100).

Purpose and activities: Giving primarily for
education and human services.
Fields of interest: Arts; Elementary/secondary
education; Education; Zoos/zoological societies;
Health organizations, association; Human
services.
Types of support: Scholarship funds.
Limitations: Giving primarily in the Palm Beach,
FL, area, and Lebanon, MO. No grants to
individuals.
Application information: Application form not
required.
Initial approach: Proposal
Deadline(s): None
Final notification: Within 3 months
Officers: John J. Boswell, Pres.; Tiffany Boswell,
V.P.; Paul Walker, Secy.
EIN: 431409051

1748
The Stephen F. and Camilla T. Brauer
Charitable Trust
c/o Bank of America
800 Market St., 1 Bank of America Plz., Ste.
1900
St. Louis, MO 63101

Established in 1997.
Donor(s): Stephen F. Brauer.
Grantmaker type: Independent foundation
Financial data (yr. ended 12/31/02): Assets,
$160,370 (M); gifts received, $481,593;
expenditures, $386,207; qualifying distributions,
$373,914; giving activities include $376,398 for
23 grants (high: $57,500; low: $1,000).
Purpose and activities: Giving for the arts and
education.
Fields of interest: Museums (art); Theater;
Opera; Arts; Higher education; University;
Education; Zoos/zoological societies; Health
organizations, association; Human services;
Children/youth, services; Federated giving
programs.
Limitations: Applications not accepted. Giving
primarily in St. Louis, MO. No grants to
individuals.
Application information: Contributes only to
pre-selected organizations.
Officer and Trustee:* Stephen F. Brauer,* Mgr.
EIN: 311534822

1749
Dana Brown Charitable Trust ▼
c/o U.S. Bank, N.A.
12935 N. Outer Forty Dr.
St. Louis, MO 63141-8695
Application address: c/o David M. Diener, Trust
Off., U.S. Bank, P.O. Box 387, St. Louis, MO
63166

Established in 1994 in MO.
Donor(s): Dana Brown.
Grantmaker type: Independent foundation
Financial data (yr. ended 06/30/02): Assets,
$69,736,595 (M); expenditures, $3,946,807;
qualifying distributions, $3,473,070; giving
activities include $3,411,223 for 65 grants (high:
$500,000; low: $2,000; average:
$5,000-$100,000).
Purpose and activities: Giving primarily for
health care and youth clubs; support also for the
arts and human services.

Fields of interest: Education; Animals/wildlife, research; Animal welfare; Hospitals (general); Human services; Children/youth, services.
Limitations: Giving primarily in St. Louis, MO. No grants to individuals.
Application information: Application form not required.
Initial approach: Letter
Deadline(s): None
Trustees: Lela G. Rice; U.S. Bank, N.A.
EIN: 436531876

1750
The G. A., Jr. and Kathryn M. Buder Charitable Foundation
c/o Jack Barsanti
1 Metropolitan Sq., Ste. 2600
St. Louis, MO 63102

Established in 1991 in MO.
Donor(s): Kathryn M. Buder.
Grantmaker type: Independent foundation
Financial data (yr. ended 12/31/01): Assets, $20,372,222 (M); gifts received, $4,376,182; expenditures, $1,171,680; qualifying distributions, $940,471; giving activities include $898,786 for 56 grants (high: $459,000; low: $500).
Purpose and activities: Giving primarily for the arts, education and health care.
Fields of interest: Music; Orchestra (symphony); Arts; Higher education; Education; Animal welfare; Hospitals (specialty); Health organizations, association; Human services; Christian agencies & churches.
Limitations: Applications not accepted. Giving primarily in MO. No grants to individuals.
Application information: Contributes only to pre-selected organizations.
Trustees: John R. Barsanti, Jr.; G.A. Buder IV; Marshall O. Buder; Theodore A. Buder; Rev. Robert Dorhauer; Shanti K. Khinduda; David Kinsman.
EIN: 431582356

1751
August A. Busch III Charitable Trust
911 Washington Ave., 7th Fl.
St. Louis, MO 63101 (314) 231-2800
Contact: Thomas E. Lowther

Established in 1986 in MO.
Donor(s): August A. Busch III.
Grantmaker type: Independent foundation
Financial data (yr. ended 12/31/02): Assets, $1,306,660 (M); expenditures, $540,494; qualifying distributions, $539,838; giving activities include $540,494 for 44 grants (high: $72,000; low: $450).
Purpose and activities: Giving primarily for health and human services.
Fields of interest: Education; Animal welfare; Hospitals (general); Youth development; Human services; Aging, centers/services; Roman Catholic federated giving programs; Roman Catholic agencies & churches.
Limitations: Giving primarily in FL and St. Louis, MO. No grants to individuals.
Application information: Application form not required.
Deadline(s): None
Trustee: August A. Busch III.

EIN: 431435400

1752
The Coovert Foundation
2 Deacon Dr.
St. Louis, MO 63131

Established in 1983 in MO.
Donor(s): Sander H. Coovert.
Grantmaker type: Independent foundation
Financial data (yr. ended 05/31/02): Assets, $1,437,144 (M); expenditures, $108,582; qualifying distributions, $97,282; giving activities include $93,000 for 7 grants (high: $65,000; low: $2,500).
Purpose and activities: Giving to symphony, human services, Christian agencies and churches.
Fields of interest: Theater; Zoos/zoological societies; Human services.
Limitations: Applications not accepted. Giving primarily in St. Louis, MO. No grants to individuals.
Application information: Contributes only to pre-selected organizations.
Officers: Isabelle S. Coovert, Pres.; Sander H. Coovert II, Secy.
Director: Nicole L. Coovert-Miller.
EIN: 431300565

1753
Deer Creek Foundation
720 Olive St., Ste. 1975
St. Louis, MO 63101 (314) 241-3228
Contact: Mary Stake Hawker

Established in 1964 in MO.
Donor(s): Aaron Fischer,‡ Teresa M. Fischer.‡
Grantmaker type: Independent foundation
Financial data (yr. ended 12/31/02): Assets, $50,276,479 (M); expenditures, $3,181,031; qualifying distributions, $2,642,974; giving activities include $2,252,777 for 68 grants (high: $150,000; low: $74; average: $25,000–$100,000).
Purpose and activities: Support primarily for programs that preserve and advance majority rule in this society and government accountability, with civil liberties protection provided by the Constitution and the Bill of Rights, and to promote education about democracy; grants primarily to 'action programs' with promise of making a significant national or regional impact; some preference to projects in MO.
Fields of interest: Media/communications; Environment; Race/intergroup relations; Civil liberties, advocacy; Reproductive rights; Civil rights; Public policy, research; Public affairs, citizen participation; Public affairs; Minorities; Women.
Types of support: Program development; Seed money.
Limitations: Giving on a national basis, with some emphasis on MO. No grants to individuals, or for building or endowment funds, equipment, or operating budgets.
Publications: Informational brochure (including application guidelines).
Application information: Application form not required.
Initial approach: Proposal

Copies of proposal: 1
Deadline(s): Mar. 15 and Sept. 15
Board meeting date(s): June and Dec.
Final notification: Within 2 weeks after board meeting
Trustees: Lattie F. Coor; Lois B. De Fleur; M. Peter Fischer; Martha C. Fischer; James C. Kautz.
Number of staff: 2 full-time professional; 1 full-time support; 1 part-time support.
EIN: 436052774

1754
Deramus Foundation, Inc.
(formerly Southern Foundation, Inc.)
c/o Shughart Thomason & Kilroy, P.C.
120 W. 12th St., Ste. 1600
Kansas City, MO 64105 (816) 421-3355
Contact: David N. Zimmerman

Established in 1966 in MO.
Grantmaker type: Independent foundation
Financial data (yr. ended 12/31/02): Assets, $11,463,443 (M); expenditures, $682,437; qualifying distributions, $652,850; giving activities include $652,850 for 12 grants (high: $260,000; low: $5,000).
Fields of interest: Higher education; Education; Zoos/zoological societies; Animals/wildlife; Boys & girls clubs; Human services; Aging, centers/services; Public policy, research.
Limitations: Giving primarily in MO, with emphasis on Kansas City. No grants to individuals.
Application information:
Initial approach: Letter
Deadline(s): None
Officers and Directors:* William N. Deramus IV,* Pres. and Secy.; Patricia D. Bunch,* V.P. and Treas.; Jill D. Dean,* V.P.; Jean D. Wagner,* V.P.
EIN: 436066776

1755
Caleb C. and Julia W. Dula Educational and Charitable Foundation
112 S. Hanley Rd.
St. Louis, MO 63105-3418 (314) 726-2800
Contact: James F. Mauze
FAX: (314) 863-3821

Established in 1995 in MO.
Grantmaker type: Independent foundation
Financial data (yr. ended 12/31/01): Assets, $41,603,432 (M); expenditures, $2,622,620; qualifying distributions, $2,259,317; giving activities include $1,970,000 for 86 grants (high: $150,000; low: $2,000; average: $5,000–$50,000).
Purpose and activities: Grants to charities which the Dulas supported during their lifetime, with emphasis on education, hospitals, libraries, social service agencies, child welfare, church support, cultural programs, and historic preservation.
Fields of interest: Historic preservation/historical societies; Arts; Libraries/library science; Education; Environment; Health organizations, association; Human services.
Types of support: General/operating support.
Limitations: No grants to individuals.
Application information:
Initial approach: Letter
Deadline(s): Apr. 1 and Oct. 1

Trustees: Margaret W. Kobusch; Nicholas Kobusch; Letitia W. Scott; Sage Wightman.
EIN: 431716767

1756
Employees Community Fund of Boeing-St. Louis
P.O. Box 516, M.C. S100-1510
St. Louis, MO 63166 (314) 232-7256
Contact: Angela Most, Secy.-Treas.
FAX: (314) 232-7654

Established in 1947 in MO.
Grantmaker type: Public charity
Financial data (yr. ended 12/31/00): Revenue, $2,355,385; assets, $4,899,680 (M); gifts received, $2,066,531; expenditures, $2,252,006; program services expenses, $2,245,337; giving activities include $2,245,337 for 361 grants (high: $1,000,000; low: $1; average: $1–$1,000,000).
Purpose and activities: The McDonnell Douglas Corporation, the Employees Community Fund of Boeing-St. Louis is administered under the Boeing Company and supports the communities where St. Louis-based employees live and work. Charitable contributions are made to nonprofit organizations involved with arts and culture, education, the environment, health care, human and social services, and youth development.
Fields of interest: Arts; Education; Environment; Health care; Youth development; Human services.
Types of support: General/operating support; Continuing support; Capital campaigns; Building/renovation; Equipment; Emergency funds; Program development; Publication; Curriculum development; Scholarship funds; Program evaluation.
Limitations: Giving limited to the St. Louis, MO, area.
Publications: Application guidelines, Annual report (including application guidelines), Grants list, Informational brochure.
Application information: Application form required.
> *Initial approach:* Letter to Boeing's St. Louis, MO, headquarters requesting application form and guidelines
> *Copies of proposal:* 1
> *Deadline(s):* Jan. 31
> *Board meeting date(s):* Monthly
> *Final notification:* Sept. 30
Officers: Karen Bedell, Pres.; Bonnie Brandt, V.P.; Angela Most, Secy.-Treas.
Number of staff: 1 full-time professional; 1 part-time professional; 1 part-time support.
EIN: 436023034

1757
Fischer-Bauer-Knirps Foundation
c/o Commerce Bank, N.A.
P.O. Box 11356
Clayton, MO 63105
Contact: Katherine Gebhard, Pres.
Application address: P.O. Box 19882, Brentwood, MO 63144, tel.: (314) 746-7335

Incorporated in 1959 in IL.
Grantmaker type: Independent foundation
Financial data (yr. ended 12/31/02): Assets, $2,722,913 (M); expenditures, $167,446;

qualifying distributions, $159,167; giving activities include $152,500 for 125 grants (high: $5,000; low: $500).
Fields of interest: Elementary/secondary education; Higher education; Environment, pollution control; Animal welfare; Hospitals (general); Health care; Disasters, 9/11/01; Human services; YM/YWCAs & YM/YWHAs; Children/youth, services; Christian agencies & churches.
Limitations: Giving primarily in St. Louis, MO. No grants to individuals.
Application information: Application form not required.
> *Initial approach:* Letter
> *Deadline(s):* None
Officers: Katherine Gebhard, Pres. and Treas.; Gary True, Secy.
Directors: Carol Bauer Gebhard; Fritz Gebhard.
Trustee: Commerce Bank, N.A.
EIN: 436036524

1758
The Harry & Flora D. Freund Memorial Foundation
101 S. Hanley Rd., 16th Fl.
St. Louis, MO 63105
Contact: Sigmund E. Freund, Pres.

Donor(s): S.E. Freund.
Grantmaker type: Independent foundation
Financial data (yr. ended 12/31/02): Assets, $486,752 (M); expenditures, $141,009; qualifying distributions, $115,374; giving activities include $115,374 for 9 grants (high: $103,149; low: $250).
Fields of interest: Museums; Higher education; Environment; Urban/community development.
Types of support: General/operating support.
Limitations: Giving primarily in St. Louis, MO.
Application information:
> *Initial approach:* Letter
> *Deadline(s):* None
Officers and Directors:* Sigmund E. Freund,* Pres. and Treas.; Frank Susman,* V.P. and Secy.; Hugh J. Freund,* V.P.; Julie B. Cowhey; Betsy F. Perry.
EIN: 436029916

1759
The Gaea Foundation
22 Muirfeld Ln.
St. Louis, MO 63141
Contact: Karen Gupta, Pres.

Established in 2000 in MO.
Donor(s): Karen Gupta, Surendra Gupta.
Grantmaker type: Independent foundation
Financial data (yr. ended 12/31/01): Assets, $338,312 (M); gifts received, $75,000; expenditures, $113,115; qualifying distributions, $112,850; giving activities include $112,850 for 75 grants (high: $20,500; low: $20).
Fields of interest: Environment; Animals/wildlife; Human services.
Limitations: Giving on a national basis.
Application information:
> *Initial approach:* Letter
> *Deadline(s):* None
Officers and Director:* Karen Gupta,* Pres. and Secy.; Jay Gupta, V.P.; Surendra Gupta, Treas.
EIN: 431889980

1760
Allen P. & Josephine B. Green Foundation
222 S. Jefferson, Rm. 108
P.O. Box 523
Mexico, MO 65265 (573) 581-5568
Contact: Walter G. Staley, Jr., Secy.-Treas.
FAX: (573) 581-1714; E-mail: wstaley@greenfdn.org; additional E-mail: nrcox@greenfdn.org; URL: http://www.greenfdn.org

Trust established in 1941 in MO.
Donor(s): Allen P. Green,‡ Josephine B. Green.‡
Grantmaker type: Independent foundation
Financial data (yr. ended 12/31/02): Assets, $10,040,766 (M); expenditures, $674,513; qualifying distributions, $560,430; giving activities include $528,366 for 56 grants (high: $100,000; low: $2,000) and $10,000 for 2 grants to individuals of $5,000 each.
Purpose and activities: Giving for human services, with emphasis on child development and the family, women, and the elderly; health services, including rehabilitation programs for drug and alcohol abuse, cancer care, and nursing; arts and humanities, especially fine and performing arts groups and historic preservation; education, including early childhood, elementary and secondary, adult and vocational, theological and medical, and other higher educational institutions, and libraries; community development and civic affairs; and environmental conservation and animal welfare.
Fields of interest: Performing arts; History/archaeology; Historic preservation/historical societies; Arts; Early childhood education; Child development, education; Elementary school/education; Secondary school/education; Vocational education; Higher education; Theological school/education; Adult/continuing education; Adult education—literacy, basic skills & GED; Libraries/library science; Reading; Natural resources; Environment; Animal welfare; Medical care, rehabilitation; Nursing care; Health care; Mental health/crisis services; Health organizations, association; Eye diseases; Crime/violence prevention, youth; Nutrition; Human services; Children/youth, services; Child development, services; Hospices; Aging, centers/services; Women, centers/services; Aging; Women; Economically disadvantaged.
Types of support: Capital campaigns; Building/renovation; Equipment; Land acquisition; Endowments; Emergency funds; Program development; Conferences/seminars; Seed money; Curriculum development; Scholarship funds; Matching/challenge support.
Limitations: Giving primarily in MO, with special emphasis on the Mexico area; no giving outside the continental U.S. No grants for operating budgets, or for loans.
Publications: Annual report (including application guidelines), Grants list.
Application information: Application form not required.
> *Initial approach:* Letter
> *Copies of proposal:* 1
> *Deadline(s):* Mar. 15 or Sept. 15
> *Board meeting date(s):* May and Nov.
> *Final notification:* 1 month
Officers and Directors:* Carl D. Fuemmeler,* Pres.; Nancy White,* V.P.; Walter G. Staley, Jr.,* Secy.-Treas.; A.D. Bond III; Christopher S. Bond;

Robert R. Collins; Nancy A. Ekern; Robert E. McIntosh; Andrea Bond Wilson; Robert A. Wood.
Number of staff: 1 part-time support.
EIN: 436030135

1761
Hall Family Foundation ▼
c/o Charitable & Crown Investment-323
P.O. Box 419580
Kansas City, MO   64141-6580   (816) 274-8516
Contact: Jeanne Bates, V.P., John Laney, V.P., or Sally Groves, Prog. Off.

Hallmark Educational Foundation incorporated in 1943 in MO; Hallmark Educational Foundation of KS incorporated in 1954 in KS; combined funds formerly known as Hallmark Educational Foundations; current name adopted due to absorption of Hall Family Foundation of Kansas in 1993.
Donor(s): Hallmark Cards, Inc., Joyce C. Hall,‡ E.A. Hall,‡ R.B. Hall.‡
Grantmaker type: Independent foundation
Financial data (yr. ended 12/31/02): Assets, $611,394,790 (M); gifts received, $38,752,427; expenditures, $41,954,535; qualifying distributions, $39,812,363; giving activities include $38,752,427 for 122 grants (high: $12,375,000; low: $5,000) and $259,575 for 179 grants to individuals (high: $2,250; low: $750).
Purpose and activities: Giving within four main areas of interest: 1) the performing and visual arts; 2) education - all levels; 3) children, youth and families; and 4) community development.
Fields of interest: Performing arts; Arts; Early childhood education; Child development, education; Elementary school/education; Secondary school/education; Higher education; Education; Housing/shelter, development; Human services; Youth, services; Child development, services; Family services; Minorities/immigrants, centers/services; Homeless, human services; Urban/community development; Community development; Minorities; Homeless.
Types of support: General/operating support; Capital campaigns; Building/renovation; Equipment; Land acquisition; Emergency funds; Program development; Seed money; Technical assistance; Program evaluation; Program-related investments/loans.
Limitations: Giving limited to Kansas City, MO. No support for international or religious organizations or for political purposes. No grants to individuals (except for employee-related scholarships), or for travel, operating deficits, conferences, scholarly or medical research, or fundraising campaigns such as telethons.
Publications: Annual report, Informational brochure (including application guidelines).
Application information: Scholarships are for the children and close relatives of Hallmark Cards employees only. Only eligible applicants should apply. Application form not required.
Initial approach: Letter
Copies of proposal: 1
Deadline(s): 6 weeks before board meetings
Board meeting date(s): Mar., June, Sept., and Dec.
Final notification: 6 to 8 weeks

Officers: Donald J. Hall, Chair.; William A. Hall, Pres.; John A. MacDonald, V.P. and Treas.; Jeanne Bates, V.P.; John Laney, V.P.; Danita M.H. Robinson, Secy.
Directors: Irvine O. Hockaday, Jr.; David H. Hughes; Robert A. Kipp; Sandra Lawrence; John P. Mascotte; Margaret Hall Pence; Morton I. Sosland.
Number of staff: 2 full-time professional; 1 part-time professional; 1 full-time support.
EIN: 446006291
Recent environmental and animal welfare grants:
1761-1 Friends of the Zoo, Kansas City, MO, $750,000. For Visitor Transportation Improvements. 2002.
1761-2 Mid-America Regional Council, Kansas City, MO, $260,000. For MetroGreen operating support. 2002.
1761-3 Midwest Research Institute, Kansas City, MO, $3,000,000. For capital campaign. 2002.
1761-4 Wildwood Outdoor Education Center, La Cygne, KS, $10,000. For strategic planning. 2002.

1762
Jane and Whitney Harris Foundation
2818 Stonington Pl.
St. Louis, MO   63131

Established in 1993 in MO.
Donor(s): The Eugene A. & Adlyne Freund Foundation.
Grantmaker type: Independent foundation
Financial data (yr. ended 12/31/02): Assets, $402,288 (M); gifts received, $35,800; expenditures, $205,532; qualifying distributions, $201,662; giving activities include $202,204 for 31 grants (high: $50,000; low: $25).
Purpose and activities: Giving for the arts, education, health, and Jewish organizations.
Fields of interest: Arts; Education; Botanical gardens; Health care; Health organizations, association; Human services; Federated giving programs; Jewish federated giving programs; Jewish agencies & temples.
Limitations: Applications not accepted. Giving primarily in St. Louis, MO. No grants to individuals.
Application information: Contributes only to pre-selected organizations.
Trustee: Whitney Harris.
EIN: 431633702

1763
Lilly Christy Busch Hermann Charitable Foundation
7701 Forsyth Blvd., 10th Fl.
St. Louis, MO   63105   (314) 692-3000
Contact: Robert R. Hermann, Jr., or Carlota H. Holton, Trustees

Established in 1995 in MO.
Donor(s): Harbor Fund.
Grantmaker type: Independent foundation
Financial data (yr. ended 12/31/02): Assets, $3,521,502 (M); expenditures, $228,000; qualifying distributions, $197,161; giving activities include $197,250 for 183 grants (high: $25,000; low: $40).

Purpose and activities: Giving for art and cultural programs, including theatres, museums, and orchestras; giving also for education, environmental conservation and human services.
Fields of interest: Elementary/secondary education; Higher education; Environment; Protestant agencies & churches.
Limitations: Giving primarily in St. Louis, MO. No support for political organizations. No grants to individuals.
Application information:
Initial approach: Proposal
Deadline(s): None
Trustees: Robert R. Hermann, Jr.; Carlota H. Holton.
EIN: 436543271

1764
The Hermann Foundation
7701 Forsyth Blvd., 10th Fl.
St. Louis, MO   63105   (314) 863-9200
Contact: Robert R. Hermann, Sr., Dir.

Established in 1992 in MO.
Donor(s): Robert R. Hermann, Hermann Cos., Inc.
Grantmaker type: Company-sponsored foundation
Financial data (yr. ended 12/31/02): Assets, $1,860,660 (M); expenditures, $367,935; qualifying distributions, $343,193; giving activities include $353,946 for 40 grants (high: $100,000; low: $40) and $98 for 1 grant to an individual.
Purpose and activities: Giving only to local charitable and civic institutions.
Fields of interest: Education; Botanical gardens; Animals/wildlife; Recreation.
Limitations: Giving limited to St. Louis, MO.
Application information:
Initial approach: Proposal
Deadline(s): None
Directors: Dolores Frank; Mary Lee Hermann; Robert R. Hermann, Sr.; Robert R. Hermann, Jr.; Carlota Hermann Holton.
EIN: 431616989

1765
The Holekamp Foundation
c/o William F. Holekamp
5 Barclay Woods
St. Louis, MO   63124

Established in 1998 in MO.
Donor(s): Kerry L. Holekamp, William F. Holekamp.
Grantmaker type: Independent foundation
Financial data (yr. ended 12/31/02): Assets, $5,792,532 (M); expenditures, $475,827; qualifying distributions, $421,029; giving activities include $421,625 for 45 grants (high: $100,000; low: $500).
Purpose and activities: Giving primarily to education and human services.
Fields of interest: Museums; Historical activities, war memorials; Elementary/secondary education; Botanical gardens; Zoos/zoological societies; Science, public education.
Limitations: Applications not accepted. Giving primarily in St. Louis, MO. No grants to individuals.

Application information: Contributes only to pre-selected organizations.
Officer: William F. Holekamp, Mgr.
EIN: 436800541

1766
Intoximeters, Inc. Corporate Giving Program

431D N. Polo Dr.
St. Louis, MO 63105-2631
Contact: Gretta Forrester, Corp. Secy.
FAX: (314) 862-0649

Grantmaker type: Corporate giving program
Purpose and activities: Intoximeters makes charitable contributions to nonprofit organizations involved with arts and culture, education, and the environment. Support is limited to St. Louis, Missouri.
Fields of interest: Arts; Education; Environment.
Types of support: General/operating support; Capital campaigns; Endowments; Program development.
Limitations: Applications not accepted. Giving limited to St. Louis, MO. No grants to individuals.
Application information: Contributes only to pre-selected organizations. The company's board of directors handles giving.

1767
The Jackes Foundation

c/o TIAA-CREF
211 N. Broadway, Ste. 1000
St. Louis, MO 63102
Contact: Martin E. Galt III, Tr.

Established in 1967 in MO.
Donor(s): Dorothy J. Miller,‡ Stanley F. Jackes, Margaret F. Naylor.
Grantmaker type: Independent foundation
Financial data (yr. ended 12/31/02): Assets, $2,020,755 (M); expenditures, $189,536; qualifying distributions, $167,055; giving activities include $166,715 for 71 grants (high: $30,000; low: $75).
Purpose and activities: Giving primarily for education and the arts.
Fields of interest: Arts; Elementary/secondary education; Higher education; Animals/wildlife; Hospitals (general); Medical research; Human services; Religion.
Limitations: Giving primarily in the St. Louis, MO, area. No grants to individuals.
Application information: Application form not required.
  Deadline(s): None
Trustees: Alexander M. Cornwell, Jr.; Martin E. Galt III; Margaret F. Naylor.
EIN: 436074447

1768
Kansas City Power & Light Company Contributions Program

c/o Corp. Contribs.
P.O. Box 418679
Kansas City, MO 64141-9679 (816) 556-2200

Grantmaker type: Corporate giving program

Purpose and activities: Kansas City Power & Light makes charitable contributions to nonprofit organizations involved with youth and education, the environment, diversity, and civic affairs. Support is given primarily in areas of company operations.
Fields of interest: Elementary/secondary education; Environment; Civil rights, equal rights; Public affairs.
Types of support: General/operating support; Employee volunteer services.
Limitations: Giving primarily in areas of company operations. No support for political organizations, religious organizations, fraternal organizations, labor organizations, health-related organizations (except for the March of Dimes and Corporate Challenge), or social organizations. No grants to individuals, or for journal advertising or research or development.
Publications: Informational brochure.
Application information: A contributions committee reviews all requests. Application form not required.
  Initial approach: Proposal to headquarters
  Copies of proposal: 1
  Deadline(s): None
  Board meeting date(s): Monthly

1769
Stanley and Lucy Lopata Foundation

c/o Lopata, Flegel & Co., LLP
600 Mason Ridge Ctr. Dr., Ste. 100
St. Louis, MO 63141

Established in 1968.
Donor(s): Stanley Lopata,‡ Lucy Lopata, Lopata Charitable Lead Trust No. 4.
Grantmaker type: Independent foundation
Financial data (yr. ended 12/31/02): Assets, $7,202,504 (M); gifts received, $61,424; expenditures, $382,221; qualifying distributions, $329,105; giving activities include $331,513 for 212 grants (high: $125,000; low: $20).
Purpose and activities: Giving primarily for Jewish welfare funds and temple support; support also for higher education.
Fields of interest: Arts; Higher education; Zoos/zoological societies; Human services; Jewish federated giving programs; Jewish agencies & temples; Disabled; Aging; Homeless.
Types of support: General/operating support; Annual campaigns; Capital campaigns; Endowments; Emergency funds; Program development.
Limitations: Applications not accepted. Giving primarily in St. Louis, MO. No grants to individuals.
Application information: Contributes only to pre-selected organizations.
  Board meeting date(s): June 15, Dec. 15, and as needed
Trustees: James R. Lopata; Lucy Lopata.
Number of staff: None.
EIN: 436099972

1770
John Allan Love Charitable Foundation

1 Metropolitan Sq., Ste. 2600
St. Louis, MO 63102-2740 (314) 621-5070
Contact: John T. Sant, Jr.

Established in 1966 in MO.
Donor(s): John Allan Love Trusts.
Grantmaker type: Independent foundation
Financial data (yr. ended 12/31/02): Assets, $3,429,784 (M); expenditures, $225,395; qualifying distributions, $190,624; giving activities include $190,000 for 28 grants (high: $25,000; low: $4,000).
Purpose and activities: Grants for medical research concerning the handicapped, cultural programs, education, community funds, and the promotion of good citizenship.
Fields of interest: Arts; Education; Zoos/zoological societies; Medical research, institute; Youth development; Human services; Federated giving programs; Disabled.
Limitations: Giving primarily in St. Louis, MO.
Application information: Application form not required.
  Deadline(s): None
Officers: John McKinney, Pres.; Rumsey Ewing, V.P.; W. Anderson Payne, V.P.; Robert H. Quenon, Treas.
Directors: Parker B. Condie; Charles A. Dill.
EIN: 436066121

1771
Macklanburg Foundation

c/o Betty Littleton
1402 Rollins Rd.
Columbia, MO 65203

Established in 1998 in MO.
Donor(s): Pauline Macklanburg.‡
Grantmaker type: Independent foundation
Financial data (yr. ended 12/31/01): Assets, $3,880,702 (M); gifts received, $101,491; expenditures, $271,365; qualifying distributions, $222,091; giving activities include $223,500 for 17 grants (high: $50,000; low: $1,000).
Purpose and activities: Giving primarily to public charities in the Oklahoma City, OK, area.
Fields of interest: Multipurpose centers/programs; Natural resources; Housing/shelter, development; Boys clubs; American Red Cross.
Limitations: Applications not accepted. Giving primarily in Oklahoma City, OK, and surrounding area. No grants to individuals.
Application information: Contributes only to pre-selected organizations.
Trustees: Charlene Lingo; Betty Littleton.
EIN: 436411670

1772
Monsanto Company Contributions Program

800 N. Lindbergh Blvd.
St. Louis, MO 63167 (314) 694-4391
Contact: Deborah J. Patterson
FAX: (314) 694-7658; E-mail: monsanto.fund@monsanto.com

Grantmaker type: Corporate giving program
Financial data (yr. ended 12/31/01): Total giving, $2,300,000; giving activities include $2,300,000 for grants.
Purpose and activities: As a complement to its foundation, Monsanto also makes charitable contributions to nonprofit organizations directly. Support is given on a national and international basis.

Fields of interest: Education; Environment; Agriculture; Community development; Science.
Types of support: General/operating support; Annual campaigns; Capital campaigns; Emergency funds; Curriculum development; Scholarship funds; Sponsorships; Donated products.
Limitations: Applications not accepted. Giving on a national and international basis in areas of company operations. No grants to individuals.
Publications: Corporate giving report.
Application information: Contributes only to pre-selected organizations. The Global Contributions Department handles giving. The company has a staff that only handles contributions.
Number of staff: 2 full-time professional; 1 part-time professional; 1 full-time support; 1 part-time support.

1773
Monsanto Fund ▼
800 N. Lindbergh Blvd.
St. Louis, MO   63167   (314) 694-4391
Contact: Deborah J. Patterson, Pres.
FAX: (314) 694-7658; E-mail:
monsanto.fund@monsanto.com; URL: http://
www.monsantofund.org/

Incorporated in 1964 in MO as successor to Monsanto Charitable Trust.
Donor(s): Monsanto Co.
Grantmaker type: Company-sponsored foundation
Financial data (yr. ended 12/31/02): Assets, $7,385,607 (M); gifts received, $24,670; expenditures, $14,479,142; qualifying distributions, $14,477,912; giving activities include $13,857,666 for 220 grants (high: $7,500,000; low: $240; average: $500–$100,000) and $550,534 for 734 employee matching gifts.
Purpose and activities: Monsanto Fund operates as the philanthropic arm of Monsanto Company. Its giving priorities include agricultural abundance, the environment, science education, and communities.
Fields of interest: Arts; Environment; Agriculture; Science.
International interests: Canada; Europe; Africa; Latin America; Asia.
Types of support: Equipment; Program development; Conferences/seminars; Curriculum development; Program evaluation; Employee matching gifts; In-kind gifts; Matching/challenge support.
Limitations: Giving primarily in areas where company employees live and work. No support for religious institutions or national organizations. No grants to individuals, or for endowment funds.
Publications: Application guidelines, Annual report.
Application information: See Web site for application requirements.
   Board meeting date(s): 4 times per year
   Final notification: June and Dec.
Officers and Directors:* Carl M. Casale,* Chair.; Deborah J. Patterson, Pres.; Sonya Meyers Davis, Secy.; Robert A. Paley, Treas.; Hakan Astrom; Phillip C. Cara; Francisco Diaz; Kathryn S. Kissam.

Number of staff: 2 full-time professional; 1 part-time professional; 1 full-time support; 1 part-time support.
EIN: 436044736
Recent environmental and animal welfare grants:
1773-1 Alliance for a Livable World, Saint Louis, MO, $15,475. 2002.
1773-2 Ducks Unlimited, Southern Regional Office, Ridgeland, MS, $20,000. 2002.
1773-3 Lake Pontchartrain Basin Foundation, Metairie, LA, $10,000. 2002.
1773-4 Nature Conservancy, Saint Louis, MO, $135,000. 2002.
1773-5 Saint Louis Zoo, Saint Louis, MO, $600,000. For Insectarium. 2002.

1774
Johnny Morris Foundation
c/o Sportsman Park Ctr.
2500 E. Kearney
Springfield, MO   65804

Donor(s): Johnny L. Morris, Bass Pro Trademark, LP, Bass Pro, Inc.
Grantmaker type: Independent foundation
Financial data (yr. ended 12/31/01): Assets, $33,600 (M); gifts received, $90,600; expenditures, $116,095; qualifying distributions, $116,095; giving activities include $115,000 for 6 grants (high: $60,000; low: $5,000).
Fields of interest: Animals/wildlife, preservation/protection; Animals/wildlife, fisheries.
Limitations: Applications not accepted. Giving on a national basis, with emphasis on Washington, DC, MO, SC, and VA. No grants to individuals.
Application information: Contributes only to pre-selected organizations.
Officers: Johnny L. Morris, Pres.; Susie Henry, V.P.; Joe C. Greene, Secy.
EIN: 431512191

1775
Velma A. Neiman Charitable Foundation
c/o Walter L. Wittenberg
6434 Cecil Ave.
Clayton, MO   63105-2225

Established in 1988 in MO.
Donor(s): Velma A. Neiman.‡
Grantmaker type: Independent foundation
Financial data (yr. ended 12/31/01): Assets, $6,105,147 (M); expenditures, $357,387; qualifying distributions, $350,490; giving activities include $321,000 for 8 grants (high: $100,000; low: $21,000).
Purpose and activities: Giving primarily for Roman Catholic education.
Fields of interest: Secondary school/education; Education; Zoos/zoological societies; Housing/shelter, development; Roman Catholic agencies & churches.
Limitations: Applications not accepted. Giving primarily in MO. No grants to individuals.
Application information: Contributes only to pre-selected organizations.
Trustee: Walter L. Wittenberg.
EIN: 436362412

1776
Nestle Purina PetCare Company Contributions Program
(formerly Ralston Purina Company Contributions Program)
Checkerboard Sq., 1-C
St. Louis, MO   63164-0001   (314) 982-1607
Contact: Kasey Bergh, Mgr., Community Affairs

Grantmaker type: Corporate giving program
Purpose and activities: As a complement to its foundation, Nestle Purina also makes charitable contributions to nonprofit organizations directly. Support is given primarily in areas of company operations.
Fields of interest: Animal welfare; Economically disadvantaged.
Types of support: General/operating support; Employee volunteer services; In-kind gifts.
Limitations: Giving primarily in areas of company operations, particularly the St. Louis, MO, area. No support for religious or political organizations or veterans' or fraternal organizations not of direct benefit to the entire community. No grants to individuals, or for investment funds, deficit reduction, advertising, or research; no loans.
Publications: Application guidelines.
Application information: Application form not required.
   Initial approach: Proposal to headquarters
   Copies of proposal: 1
   Deadline(s): None
   Final notification: 2 to 3 months
Number of staff: 1 full-time professional; 1 full-time support.

1777
The No Frills Foundation
c/o Greensfelder, Hemker & Gale, PC
10 S. Broadway
St. Louis, MO   63102

Established in 1998 in MO.
Donor(s): Paula Weil.
Grantmaker type: Independent foundation
Financial data (yr. ended 12/31/02): Assets, $3,629,771 (M); expenditures, $209,014; qualifying distributions, $196,889; giving activities include $197,500 for 10 grants (high: $120,000; low: $2,500).
Purpose and activities: Giving primarily for higher education.
Fields of interest: Arts councils; Higher education; Natural resources; Environment, beautification programs; Family planning; Parasitic diseases; Medical research, institute.
Limitations: Applications not accepted. Giving primarily in New York, NY. No grants to individuals.
Application information: Contributes only to pre-selected organizations.
Director: Edward F. Reilly.
Trustee: Paula Weil.
EIN: 436801427

1778
Spencer T. and Ann W. Olin Foundation ▼
Pierre Laclede Bldg.
7701 Forsyth Blvd., Ste. 1040
St. Louis, MO 63105 (314) 727-6202
Contact: Warren M. Shapleigh, Pres.

Incorporated in 1957 in DE.
Donor(s): Spencer T. Olin,‡ Ann W. Olin.‡
Grantmaker type: Independent foundation
Financial data (yr. ended 12/31/02): Assets,
$21,940,807 (M); expenditures, $8,924,817;
qualifying distributions, $8,647,355; giving
activities include $8,578,915 for 45 grants
(high: $1,500,085; low: $2,500; average:
$25,000–$350,000).
Purpose and activities: Giving primarily for
higher education, medical education, research,
health services and facilities, and environmental
conservation; support also for community
service agencies in the metropolitan St. Louis
area, including cultural, civic, and welfare
programs.
Fields of interest: Higher education; Medical
school/education; Environment; Health care;
Medical research, institute.
Types of support: General/operating support;
Annual campaigns; Research.
Limitations: No support for national health or
welfare organizations, religious groups, or
generally for secondary education, projects that
are substantially financed by public tax funds, or
private foundations or projects that require
expenditure responsibility. No grants to
individuals, or for building or endowment funds,
deficit financing, operating budgets,
conferences, seminars, workshops, travel,
exhibits, scholarships, fellowships, or matching
gifts; no loans.
Officers and Trustees:* Warren M. Shapleigh,*
Pres.; Mary Olin Pritzlaff,* V.P.; Eunice Olin
Higgins,* Secy.; William W. Higgins; John Peters
MacCarthy; John C. Pritzlaff, Jr.; Barbara Olin
Taylor; F. Morgan Taylor, Jr.
Number of staff: 1 part-time professional; 1
part-time support.
EIN: 376044148
**Recent environmental and animal welfare
grants:**
1778-1 EcoLogic Enterprise Ventures,
Cambridge, MA, $265,500. 2002.
1778-2 Missouri Botanical Garden, Saint Louis,
MO, $27,500. 2002.
1778-3 Nature Conservancy, Arlington, VA,
$40,000. 2002.
1778-4 World Resources Institute, DC,
$350,000. 2002.

1779
Pershing Place Foundation
c/o Greensfelder, Hemker & Gale
10 S. Broadway
St. Louis, MO 63102
Contact: Edward F. Reilly

Established in 1998 in MO.
Donor(s): John D. Weil.
Grantmaker type: Independent foundation
Financial data (yr. ended 12/31/02): Assets,
$6,603,042 (M); expenditures, $370,585;
qualifying distributions, $349,022; giving
activities include $350,135 for 30 grants (high:
$114,500; low: $100).

Purpose and activities: Giving primarily to an
institute for the deaf, a theater company, and an
art museum, as well as for education and
human services, and to federated giving
programs, and a college in Amherst, MA.
Fields of interest: Multipurpose
centers/programs; Museums (art); Theater;
Elementary/secondary education; Education,
special; College; Natural resources; Family
planning; Human services; Federated giving
programs; Jewish agencies & temples.
Limitations: Applications not accepted. Giving
primarily in St. Louis, MO. No grants to
individuals.
Application information: Contributes only to
pre-selected organizations.
Director: Edward F. Reilly.
Trustees: Anabeth Calkins; Joseph D. Lehrer;
John D. Weil.
EIN: 436795985

1780
Porthouse Foundation
128 Ridgecrest Rd.
Chesterfield, MO 63017
Contact: J. David Porthouse, Pres.

Donor(s): C.R. Porthouse.
Grantmaker type: Independent foundation
Financial data (yr. ended 12/31/00): Assets,
$1,207,507 (M); expenditures, $106,350;
qualifying distributions, $106,350; giving
activities include $106,350 for 26 grants (high:
$10,000; low: $200).
Purpose and activities: Giving primarily for
higher education; support also for fishing and
game organizations and community funds.
Fields of interest: Higher education;
Animals/wildlife, preservation/protection;
Recreation; Federated giving programs.
Types of support: General/operating support.
Limitations: Giving on a national basis. No
grants to individuals.
Application information: Application form not
required.
Initial approach: Letter
Officers: J. David Porthouse, Pres.; David R.
Porthouse, V.P.
EIN: 346525861

1781
Harry Portman Charitable Trust
2345 Grand Blvd., Ste. 2600
Kansas City, MO 64108-2684 (816) 460-5628

Established in 1991 in MO.
Donor(s): Harry Portman.‡
Grantmaker type: Independent foundation
Financial data (yr. ended 12/31/01): Assets,
$3,342,456 (M); expenditures, $203,005;
qualifying distributions, $182,984; giving
activities include $154,675 for 25 grants (high:
$25,000; low: $1,000).
Purpose and activities: Giving primarily for the
arts and community services.
Fields of interest: University;
Scholarships/financial aid; Education; Botanical
gardens; Environmental education; Hospitals
(specialty); Big Brothers/Big Sisters; Salvation
Army; Neighborhood centers; Jewish agencies &
temples.

Types of support: General/operating support;
Building/renovation; Equipment; Endowments;
Program development; Scholarship funds.
Limitations: Applications not accepted. Giving
primarily in Kansas City, MO. No grants to
individuals.
Application information: Contributes only to
pre-selected organizations.
Trustees: Abraham E. Margolin; UMB Bank, N.A.
EIN: 436406877

1782
Pulitzer Foundation
(formerly Pulitzer Publishing Company
Foundation)
900 N. Tucker Blvd.
St. Louis, MO 63101-1069 (314) 340-8440
Contact: Alan G. Silverglat, Secy.-Treas.

Incorporated in 1963 in MO.
Donor(s): Pulitzer Publishing Co., Star
Publishing Co., Pulitzer Inc., St. Louis
Post-Dispatch LLC.
Grantmaker type: Company-sponsored
foundation
Financial data (yr. ended 12/31/02): Assets,
$644,704 (M); gifts received, $391,350;
expenditures, $423,411; qualifying distributions,
$418,257; giving activities include $418,100 for
29 grants (high: $125,000; low: $250).
Purpose and activities: Giving primarily to
federated giving programs, and higher
education; funding also for the arts and human
services.
Fields of interest: Journalism/publishing;
Museums (art); Arts; Higher education;
Zoos/zoological societies; Disasters, 9/11/01;
Boy scouts; Human services; Federated giving
programs.
Types of support: General/operating support;
Annual campaigns; Capital campaigns;
Building/renovation; Equipment; Endowments;
Professorships; Scholarship funds; Research.
Limitations: Giving primarily in MO, with
emphasis on the St. Louis area. No grants to
individuals.
Application information:
Initial approach: Letter
Deadline(s): None
Board meeting date(s): Varies
Officers and Directors:* Michael E. Pulitzer,*
Chair.; Robert C. Woodworth,* Pres.; Alan G.
Silverglat,* Secy.-Treas.; Terrance C.Z. Egger.
EIN: 436052854

1783
The Ceil & Michael E. Pulitzer
Foundation, Inc.
(formerly The Michael E. Pulitzer Foundation,
Inc.)
900 N. Tucker Blvd.
St. Louis, MO 63101 (314) 340-8000
Contact: Michael E. Pulitzer, Pres.

Established in 1993 in MO.
Donor(s): Michael E. Pulitzer.
Grantmaker type: Independent foundation
Financial data (yr. ended 10/31/02): Assets,
$8,556,929 (M); gifts received, $4,093,990;
expenditures, $281,975; qualifying distributions,
$281,554; giving activities include $277,844 for
37 grants (high: $65,000; low: $500).

Fields of interest: Higher education; Environment; Human services; Religion; African Americans/Blacks.
Limitations: Giving primarily in MO.
Application information:
  Initial approach: Letter
  Deadline(s): None
Officers and Directors:* Michael E. Pulitzer,* Pres.; James V. Maloney,* V.P. and Secy.; Ceil Pulitzer, V.P.
EIN: 431659437

1784
Sachs Fund
400 Chesterfield Ctr., Ste. 600
Chesterfield, MO 63017

Established in 1957 in MO.
Donor(s): Samuel C. Sachs, Sachs Electric Corp.
Grantmaker type: Independent foundation
Financial data (yr. ended 04/30/02): Assets, $1,336,116 (M); gifts received, $1,000,000; expenditures, $737,643; qualifying distributions, $724,189; giving activities include $724,000 for 13 grants (high: $300,000; low: $1,000).
Purpose and activities: Giving primarily for arts, education, conservation, Jewish federated giving programs, and Protestant agencies and churches.
Fields of interest: Arts; Higher education; Animal welfare; Federated giving programs; Protestant agencies & churches; Jewish agencies & temples.
Limitations: Applications not accepted. Giving primarily in MO. No grants to individuals.
Application information: Contributes only to pre-selected organizations.
Trustees: Louis S. Sachs; Mary L. Sachs; Susan E. Sachs.
EIN: 436032385

1785
Singing for Change
(formerly SFC Charitable Foundation)
P.O. Box 7210
Kansas City, MO 64113
Contact: Judith Ranger Smith, Exec. Dir.
FAX: (816) 363-1290; E-mail singingforchange@compuserve.com

Established in 1995.
Grantmaker type: Independent foundation
Financial data (yr. ended 12/31/00): Assets, $535,673 (M); gifts received, $739,297; expenditures, $733,719; qualifying distributions, $636,257; giving activities include $636,500 for 56 grants (high: $50,000; low: $2,500).
Purpose and activities: Funding primarily for human services.
Fields of interest: Education; Environmental education; Human services; Children/youth, services.
Types of support: General/operating support; Continuing support.
Limitations: Giving on a national basis. No support for religious organizations, or other grant-making operations. No grants to individuals, or for art, music, or recreational purposes.
Publications: Application guidelines.
Application information:
  Deadline(s): None

Officers and Trustees:* Howard Kaufman,* Pres.; Joel A. Katz,* Secy.; Irwin L. Rennert,* Treas.; Sunshine Smith.
Number of staff: 1 full-time professional.
EIN: 650565248

1786
Donald Slavik Family Foundation
9648 Olive Blvd., No. 103
St. Louis, MO 63132 (314) 991-8020
Contact: Susan S. Williams, Pres.
E-mail: sswilliams@stlnet.com

Established in 1997 in CA and MO.
Donor(s): Ann A. Slavik, Donald S. Slavik.
Grantmaker type: Independent foundation
Financial data (yr. ended 12/31/02): Assets, $1,986,029 (M); gifts received, $118,050; expenditures, $110,954; qualifying distributions, $107,291; giving activities include $107,500 for 8 grants (high: $25,000; low: $500).
Purpose and activities: U.S. charities involved in conservation of wildlife and nature.
Fields of interest: Animals/wildlife, preservation/protection.
Limitations: Giving primarily in CA.
Application information:
  Deadline(s): None
Officers: Susan Slavik Williams, Pres.; Ann A. Slavik, Secy.-Treas.
Director: Felix Noble Williams III.
EIN: 431778633

1787
St. Louis Community Foundation
319 N. 4th St., Ste. 501
St. Louis, MO 63102 (314) 588-8200
Contact: David R. Luckes, C.E.O. and Pres.
FAX: (314) 588-8088; E-mail: David@stlcf.org;
URL: http://www.stlcf.org

Established in 1915 in MO.
Grantmaker type: Community foundation
Financial data (yr. ended 12/31/02): Assets, $62,965,106 (M); gifts received, $10,181,500; expenditures, $7,356,029; giving activities include $5,952,633 for grants.
Purpose and activities: Improve the quality of life in the greater St. Louis metropolitan area by facilitating the philanthropy of individuals, families and businesses in, but not limited to, the areas of arts and culture, community building, education, environment, health, and human services. The foundation administers donor-advised funds.
Fields of interest: Arts; Education; Environment; Health care; Human services; Nonprofit management; Community development; Philanthropy/voluntarism; Government/public administration.
Types of support: General/operating support; Management development; Program development; Seed money; Scholarship funds; Technical assistance; Consulting services; Program-related investments/loans; Matching/challenge support.
Limitations: Giving primarily in IL, and the metropolitan St. Louis, MO, area. No support for sectarian religious programs, or private elementary or secondary schools. No grants to individuals (except through scholarship funds), or for deficit financing, or endowment or

building funds; grants for operating expenses only during an organization's start-up.
Publications: Application guidelines, Annual report, Informational brochure, Newsletter.
Application information: Contact foundation for specific guidelines and special grant initiative guidelines. Application form required.
  Deadline(s): Applications accepted throughout the year. Deadlines and application criteria for special grant initiatives vary depending on grant program or individual fund specifications
  Board meeting date(s): Mar., June, Sept., and Dec.
  Final notification: Within 2 weeks of board meetings
Officers and Directors:* Albert E. Suter,* Chair.; Lester J. Buechele,* Vice-Chair.; David R. Luckes, Pres. and C.E.O.; H. Douglas Adams, V.P. and C.F.O.; Dennis J. Jacknewitz,* Secy.; Charles Stewart, Jr.,* Treas.
Trustee Banks: Commerce Bank, N.A.; A.G. Edwards Trust Co.; The Guaranty Trust Co. of Missouri; U.S. Bank, N.A.; Merrill Lynch Trust Co.; Bank of America; Union Planters Trust and Investment Co.
Number of staff: 6 full-time professional; 2 full-time support.
EIN: 436023126

1788
Sugar Lakes Foundation
c/o MHM Business Svcs.
420 Nichols Rd.
Kansas City, MO 64112
Contact: Roger M. Crouch, Tr.

Established in 1987 in MO.
Donor(s): Roger M. Crouch.
Grantmaker type: Independent foundation
Financial data (yr. ended 12/31/02): Assets, $1,702,706 (M); expenditures, $212,669; qualifying distributions, $173,473; giving activities include $172,350 for 19 grants (high: $50,000; low: $250).
Purpose and activities: Giving for the prevention of cruelty to animals and charitable giving.
Fields of interest: Animal welfare; Health organizations, association; Cancer; Cancer research; Food services; Human services.
Limitations: Giving primarily in MO and Seattle, WA.
Application information: Application form required.
  Initial approach: Proposal
  Deadline(s): Nov. 1
Trustees: Catherine Crouch; Roger M. Crouch; Rosalie Crouch Sisson.
EIN: 431480264

1789
John S. Swift Company Charitable Trust, Inc.
c/o U.S. Bank, N.A.
P.O. Box 66734
St. Louis, MO 63166-0387
Contact: Bryan M. Swift, Tr.
Application address: 1248 Research Dr., St. Louis, MO 63122, tel.: (314) 991-4300

Trust established in 1952 in MO.

Donor(s): John S. Swift Co., Inc.
Grantmaker type: Company-sponsored foundation
Financial data (yr. ended 12/31/01): Assets, $2,071,103 (M); expenditures, $95,612; qualifying distributions, $89,934; giving activities include $90,050 for 85 grants (high: $7,500; low: $100).
Fields of interest: Museums; Arts; Higher education; Aquariums; Hospitals (general); Children/youth, services.
Limitations: Giving primarily in IL and MO. No grants to individuals.
Application information:
  Initial approach: Letter
  Deadline(s): None
Trustees: Bryan M. Swift; Hampden M. Swift; U.S. Bank, N.A.
EIN: 436020812

1790
Bess Spiva Timmons Foundation, Inc.
c/o U.S. Bank, N.A., Trust Dept.
P.O. Box 8
Joplin, MO 64802-0008
Application address: P.O. Box 271669, Fort Collins, CO 80527-1669

Established in 1967 in MO.
Donor(s): Bess Spiva Timmons.‡
Grantmaker type: Independent foundation
Financial data (yr. ended 12/31/02): Assets, $5,108,641 (M); expenditures, $352,873; qualifying distributions, $306,791; giving activities include $312,070 for 44 grants (high: $28,000; low: $1,000).
Purpose and activities: Primary area of interest is education programs for minorities; support also for health and medical research, the arts, social services, and ecology. Small, tax-exempt organizations, which have little or no federal, state, or local financial assistance, are favored for grants. Awards range from $1000 to $10,000.
Fields of interest: Arts; Higher education; Animals/wildlife, preservation/protection; Hospitals (general); Health care; Children/youth, services; Minorities; Native Americans/American Indians.
Types of support: Equipment; Program development; Seed money; Scholarship funds.
Limitations: Giving primarily in the central and western states. No support for foreign organizations. No grants to individuals; or for operating funds, endowments, building projects, or major acquisitions.
Publications: Annual report.
Application information: Application form not required.
  Initial approach: Letter with application information
  Copies of proposal: 1
  Deadline(s): July 1
  Board meeting date(s): 3rd weekend in July
  Final notification: 30 days after annual meeting
Officers and Directors:* Susan T. Timmons, Pres.; Catherine S. Spillman,* V.P.; Jill Larson, Secy.; Tim Spears, Treas.; JoAnn Kimball; Duane Lawellin; Judith Spears; George Timmons; Robert Timmons.
Trustee: U.S. Bank, N.A.
Number of staff: None.
EIN: 436075014

1791
Trio Foundation of St. Louis
(formerly Trio Foundation)
8029 Forsyth Blvd., No. 201
St. Louis, MO 63105   (314) 725-3040
Contact: Wendy Jaffe, Fdn. Exec.
FAX: (314) 725-2603; E-mail: trio@triostl.org

Established in 1990 in MO.
Donor(s): Dorothy Moog.
Grantmaker type: Independent foundation
Financial data (yr. ended 12/31/02): Assets, $9,964,806 (M); expenditures, $804,076; qualifying distributions, $734,680; giving activities include $689,000 for 74 grants (high: $60,000; low: $1,000).
Fields of interest: Arts; Education; Environment; Youth development; Human services; Civil rights; Jewish agencies & temples; Women.
Types of support: General/operating support; Capital campaigns; Program development; Seed money.
Limitations: Giving primarily in St. Louis, MO. No grants to individuals, or for medical/science research.
Publications: Application guidelines.
Application information: Contact staff for most current application forms. Application form required.
  Initial approach: Telephone or E-mail for guidelines
  Copies of proposal: 3
  Deadline(s): Sept. 1
  Final notification: Dec.
Officers and Directors:* Donna L. Moog,* Pres.; James R. Moog,* V.P. and Secy.; Thomas H. Moog,* Treas.; Wendy Jaffe, Fdn. Exec.
Number of staff: 1 part-time professional.
EIN: 431553538

1792
Two Mauds, Inc.
P.O. Box 381
Mount Vernon, MO 65712   (417) 466-4213
Contact: Jim Mason, Secy.
FAX: (417) 466-0256; E-mail: jbmason@mntvernon.net

Established in 1994.
Donor(s): Dallas Pratt.‡
Grantmaker type: Independent foundation
Financial data (yr. ended 12/31/02): Assets, $3,181,052 (M); gifts received, $8,325; expenditures, $189,152; qualifying distributions, $180,869; giving activities include $125,000 for 19 grants (high: $10,000; low: $2,500).
Purpose and activities: Grants to support animal welfare and prevention of cruelty to animals, especially spay/neutering programs.
Fields of interest: Animal welfare.
Types of support: General/operating support; Continuing support; Building/renovation; Equipment; Publication; Seed money.
Limitations: Giving primarily to mid-America and the southeastern United States. No grants to individuals.
Publications: Program policy statement.
Application information: Application form not required.
  Initial approach: E-mail (preferred) or letter
  Deadline(s): Aug.
  Board meeting date(s): Oct.
  Final notification: Dec.

Officers and Directors:* Linda L. Hackett,* Pres.; David Finkbeiner,* V.P.; James B. Mason,* Secy.; Mark E. Haranzo, Treas.; Nancy Abraham; Melinda Hackett-Hutchins.
Number of staff: 2 part-time professional; 2 part-time support.
EIN: 132665313

1793
Tyco Healthcare/Mallinckrodt Corporate Giving Program
(formerly Mallinckrodt Inc. Corporate Giving Program)
c/o Community Partnership Prog.
P.O. Box 5840
St. Louis, MO 63134   (314) 654-5200
Additional application address: 675 James S. McDonnell Blvd., Hazelwood, MO 63042-2301; FAX: (314) 654-5381; URL: http://www.mallinckrodt.com/corpprofile/cp-citizen.html

Grantmaker type: Corporate giving program
Purpose and activities: Tyco Healthcare/Mallinckrodt makes charitable contributions to nonprofit organizations involved with education, the environment, health, youth development, community development, science, and civic affairs. Support is given on a national and international basis.
Fields of interest: Education; Environment; Health care; Youth development; Community development; Science; Public affairs.
Types of support: General/operating support; Employee volunteer services; Employee matching gifts; Employee-related scholarships.
Limitations: Giving on a national and international basis in areas of company operations. No support for K-12 Schools.

1794
University Lane Foundation
c/o Greensfelder, Hemker & Gale, PC
10 S. Broadway
St. Louis, MO 63102

Established in 1998 in MO.
Donor(s): Mark S. Weil.
Grantmaker type: Independent foundation
Financial data (yr. ended 12/31/02): Assets, $2,866,910 (M); expenditures, $239,091; qualifying distributions, $231,385; giving activities include $231,900 for 17 grants (high: $104,950; low: $1,000).
Purpose and activities: Giving primarily for higher education.
Fields of interest: Museums (art); Arts; Higher education; Education; Botanical gardens; Family planning; Roman Catholic agencies & churches; Jewish agencies & temples.
Limitations: Applications not accepted. Giving primarily in St. Louis, MO. No grants to individuals.
Application information: Contributes only to pre-selected organizations.
Director: Edward F. Reilly.
Trustees: John D. Weil; Mark S. Weil; Phoebe Dent Weil.
EIN: 436795986

1795
James H. Woods Foundation
6425 W. Florissant Ave.
St. Louis, MO 63136-4999 (314) 679-1310
Contact: Becky Power, Exec. Secy.
Additional address: c/o John R. Woods, Jr., 4
Layton Terr., St. Louis, MO 63124; E-mail:
powers@stoutmarketing.com

Trust established in 1958 in MO.
Donor(s): James H. Woods.‡
Grantmaker type: Independent foundation
Financial data (yr. ended 11/30/02): Assets,
$13,917,349 (M); expenditures, $1,263,176;
qualifying distributions, $1,010,208; giving
activities include $1,019,100 for 154 grants
(high: $200,000; low: $500).
Purpose and activities: Funding primarily for
education, federated giving programs, and
human services.
Fields of interest: Elementary/secondary
education; Education; Natural resources;
Human services; Federated giving programs;
Religion.
Types of support: General/operating support;
Building/renovation; Endowments; Seed money;
Scholarship funds.
Limitations: Applications not accepted. Giving
primarily in the midwestern states.
Application information: Giving generally to
pre-selected organizations.
Trustees: Elizabeth Bradbury; Jeff Clark; David L.
Woods; James H. Woods, Jr.; John R. Woods;
Bank of America.
Number of staff: None.
EIN: 436024866

MONTANA

1796
Broadbent Family Foundation, Inc.
P.O. Box 1019
Livingston, MT 59047
Contact: John P. Bailey, Exec. Dir.

Established in 1989 in MT.
Donor(s): Robert R. Broadbent, William S.
Broadbent.
Grantmaker type: Independent foundation
Financial data (yr. ended 12/31/01): Assets,
$2,452,831 (M); gifts received, $1,500;
expenditures, $137,407; qualifying distributions,
$121,000; giving activities include $121,000 for
17 grants (high: $25,000; low: $500).
Purpose and activities: Giving primarily for
education and wildlife preservation.
Fields of interest: Arts; Education;
Animals/wildlife, preservation/protection;
Children/youth, services; Protestant agencies &
churches.
Limitations: Applications not accepted. Giving
primarily in MT and Cleveland, OH. No grants
to individuals.
Application information: Contributes only to
pre-selected organizations.
Officers and Directors:* Robert R. Broadbent,*
Chair.; William S. Broadbent,* Pres.; Mary K.
Broadbent,* V.P.; James A. Posewitz,* Secy.;

Camille W. Broadbent,* Treas.; John P. Bailey,
Exec. Dir.
EIN: 810161642

1797
The Cinnabar Foundation
P.O. Box 5088
Helena, MT 59604 (406) 449-2795
Contact: James Posewitz, Secy.
Application address: 219 Vawter St., Helena,
MT 59601; FAX: (406) 449-9985; E-mail:
cinnabar@mt.net

Established in 1982 in MT.
Donor(s): Leonard Sargent,‡ members of the
Kelsey family.
Grantmaker type: Independent foundation
Financial data (yr. ended 12/31/02): Assets,
$8,452,482 (M); gifts received, $1,115;
expenditures, $351,643; qualifying distributions,
$338,257; giving activities include $312,000 for
61 grants (high: $12,000; low: $1,000).
Purpose and activities: Giving primarily to
promote environmental protection and
conservation in the state of MT.
Fields of interest: Natural resources;
Environment; Animals/wildlife,
preservation/protection; Animals/wildlife,
fisheries.
Types of support: General/operating support;
Land acquisition; Conferences/seminars;
Research; Scholarships—to individuals;
Matching/challenge support.
Limitations: Giving limited to MI and the
Yellowstone area.
Publications: Annual report.
Application information: Application form not
required.
  Initial approach: Proposal (no more than 2
    pages)
  Copies of proposal: 1
  Deadline(s): Generally, Mar. 15
  Board meeting date(s): Quarterly
  Final notification: May 31
Officers and Directors:* Robin Tawney,* Pres.;
William Madden,* V.P.; James Posewitz,* Secy.;
Ernest J. Turner,* Treas.
Member: Rick Hubbard-Sargent.
Number of staff: 1 part-time professional.
EIN: 810415045

1798
The K.L.T. Foundation
3219 N. Reserve St.
Missoula, MT 59808-1527

Established in 1998 in MT.
Donor(s): Karl Tyler, Donna Tyler.
Grantmaker type: Public charity
Financial data (yr. ended 12/31/00): Revenue,
$27,475; assets, $703,702 (M); expenditures,
$24,981; program services expenses, $23,888;
giving activities include $23,888 for 6 grants
(high: $13,650; low: $63).
Fields of interest: Higher education;
Environment, water resources; Mormon
agencies & churches.
Limitations: Applications not accepted. Giving
primarily in MT. No grants to individuals.
Application information: Contributes only to
pre-selected organizations.

Trustees: Marcus A. Christensen; Miles E.
Lignell; Rick L. Linville; Donna F. Tyler; Karl T.
Tyler.
EIN: 810522436

1799
Leaw Family Foundation, Inc.
P.O. Box 1629
Missoula, MT 59806
Contact: Jan Parks

Established in 1996 in DE.
Donor(s): Linda E.A. Wachtmeister.
Grantmaker type: Independent foundation
Financial data (yr. ended 12/31/02): Assets,
$2,838,196 (M); gifts received, $6,986;
expenditures, $200,301; qualifying distributions,
$171,975; giving activities include $166,717 for
8 grants (high: $107,000; low: $2,300).
Purpose and activities: Giving primarily for
children, the arts and environment.
Fields of interest: Arts; Environment; Human
services; Children, services.
Types of support: General/operating support.
Limitations: Giving primarily in Missoula, MT,
and Charlottesville and Sweet Briar, VA. No
grants to individuals.
Application information:
  Initial approach: Letter
  Copies of proposal: 1
  Deadline(s): None
Officers: Linda E.A. Wachtmeister, Pres.; Robert
L. Strini, V.P.; Jan Parks, Secy.-Treas.
Number of staff: 1 part-time support.
EIN: 364003981

1800
Montana Community Foundation
101 N. Last Chance Gulch, Ste. 211
Helena, MT 59601 (406) 443-8313
Contact: Sidney Armstrong, Exec. Dir.
Additional tel.: (800) 443-8314; E-mail:
mtcf@mt.net; URL: http://www.mtcf.org

Incorporated in 1988 in MT.
Grantmaker type: Community foundation
Financial data (yr. ended 06/30/02): Assets,
$39,376,485 (M); gifts received, $6,718,711;
expenditures, $2,426,245; giving activities
include $1,030,016 for 261 grants (high:
$246,250; low: $9) and $117,568 for 116 grants
to individuals (high: $5,000; low: $75).
Purpose and activities: The foundation
administers a donor-advised fund.
Fields of interest: Arts; Education; Natural
resources; Human services; Economic
development.
Limitations: Giving limited to MT. No support
for religious purposes. Generally no grants for
annual or capital campaigns, endowment funds,
debt retirement, or lobbying.
Publications: Annual report, Informational
brochure (including application guidelines),
Newsletter.
Application information: Contact foundation for
current guidelines. Application form required.
  Initial approach: Application with proposal
  Deadline(s): Feb. 15, May 15, Aug. 15 and
    Nov. 15
  Board meeting date(s): Quarterly
  Final notification: Within 30 days

Officers and Directors:* Melvin McNea,*
Chair.; Marie Nopper,* Secy.; Obert Undem,*
Treas.; Mary Ann Gorsich, C.F.O.; Sidney O.
Armstrong, Exec. Dir.; Linda E. Reed, Exec. Dir.;
and 6 additional directors.
Number of staff: 1 full-time professional; 1
full-time support.
EIN: 810450150

1801
The Montana Power Foundation, Inc.
(formerly MPCo/Entech Foundation, Inc.)
40 E. Broadway
Butte, MT 59701-9394 (406) 497-2602
Contact: Bill Cain
FAX: (406) 497-2451; E-mail:
bcain@mtpower.com

Established in 1985 in MT.
Donor(s): The Montana Power Co.,
Independent Power Group, Inc., Entech, Inc.
Grantmaker type: Company-sponsored
foundation
Financial data (yr. ended 12/31/01): Assets,
$3,477 (M); gifts received, $303,699;
expenditures, $314,166; qualifying distributions,
$313,936; giving activities include $253,223 for
22 grants (high: $35,565; low: $250) and
$60,713 for 33 employee matching gifts.
Purpose and activities: Support for colleges and
universities through grants and an employee
matching gift program; primary areas of interest
also include hospital building funds, civic
affairs, and cultural programs.
Fields of interest: Performing arts; Arts;
Elementary/secondary education; Higher
education; Libraries/library science; Education;
Natural resources; Health care; Human services;
Children/youth, services; Community
development.
Types of support: General/operating support;
Annual campaigns; Capital campaigns;
Building/renovation; Equipment; Endowments;
Conferences/seminars; Scholarship funds;
Employee matching gifts; In-kind gifts.
Limitations: Giving primarily in areas of
company operations in MT. No support for
individual United Way agencies (except for
capital funds), fraternal, service, veterans', or
social groups, political activities or
organizations established primarily to influence
legislation, religious activities, economic or
commercial development projects, or national
health organizations. No grants to individuals
(except for scholarships), or for operating funds
(except for organizations such as the United
Way), sporting events, medical equipment,
research, or multi-year requests.
Publications: Annual report (including
application guidelines), Financial statement.
Application information: Application form
required.
   Initial approach: Letter or telephone
   Copies of proposal: 1
   Deadline(s): None
   Board meeting date(s): Apr., Aug., and Dec.
   Final notification: 8 weeks
Officers and Directors:* Robert P. Gannon,*
Chair., C.E.O., and Pres.; Pat Fleming, Secy.;
Ellen M. Senechal, Treas.; A.F. Cain; J.D. Haffey;
Carl Lehrkind III; M.J. Meldahl; J.P. Pederson.
Number of staff: 1 full-time professional.
EIN: 810432484

1802
National Center for Appropriate
Technology, Inc.
3040 Continental Dr.
Butte, MT 59701 (406) 494-4572
Contact: Kathleen L. Hadley, Exec. Dir.
FAX: (406) 494-2905; E-mail: info@ncat.org;
URL: http://www.ncat.org

Established in 1976 in MT.
Grantmaker type: Public charity
Financial data (yr. ended 09/30/02): Revenue,
$4,606,631; assets, $1,706,691; gifts received,
$3,264,593; expenditures, $4,477,078; program
services expenses, $3,534,158.
Purpose and activities: The center seeks to
champion sustainable technologies and
community-based approaches that protect
national resources and assist people, especially
the economically disadvantaged, in becoming
more self-reliant.
Fields of interest: Environment; Agriculture;
Economically disadvantaged.
Types of support: Conferences/seminars;
Technical assistance; Consulting services.
Limitations: Applications not accepted.
Publications: Annual report, Informational
brochure, Newsletter, Program policy statement.
Application information: Contributes only to
pre-selected organizations; unsolicited requests
for funds not considered or acknowledged.
   Board meeting date(s): Quarterly
Officers and Directors:* Adolfo G. Alayon,*
Chair.; George Ortiz,* Vice-Chair.; Jeannie
Jertson,* Secy.; Gene Brady,* Treas.; Allen C.
Bjergo, M.D.; John T. Brown, Jr.; Randall
Chapman; Charles Ederdt; Moses Freeman; Tina
Hobson; Jacqueline Hutchinson; Henry Knowls;
Anthony Maggiore; Charles Prejean; Lolita Ross;
H. Jack Young.
Number of staff: 40 full-time professional; 10
part-time professional; 10 full-time support; 5
part-time support.
EIN: 810361047

1803
Owl Research Institute, Inc.
P.O. Box 39
Charlo, MT 59824-0036 (406) 644-3412
Contact: Denver Holt, Pres.
URL: http://www.owlinstitute.org

Established in 1988 in MT.
Grantmaker type: Public charity
Financial data (yr. ended 12/31/00): Revenue,
$189,437; assets, $287,992; gifts received,
$177,936; expenditures, $148,842; program
services expenses, $102,881; giving activities
include $3,200 for 2 grants to individuals (high:
$2,200; low: $1,000).
Purpose and activities: The Institute seeks to
understand the ecological progresses and
interactions between owls and their
communities, share its findings with the
scientific community, and make scientific
research available to the general public.
Fields of interest: Animals/wildlife,
preservation/protection; Animals/wildlife, bird
preserves.
Types of support: Research.
Limitations: Giving on a national basis.
Officers: Denver Holt, Pres.; Dale Becker, V.P.;
John Boyle, Secy.; Robert Erickson, Treas.

EIN: 810453479

1804
Rocky Mountain Elk Foundation, Inc.
2291 W. Broadway
P.O. Box 8249
Missoula, MT 59807-8249 (406) 523-4500
Contact: Jon S. Fossel, Chair.
Additional tel.: (800) 225-5355; FAX: (406)
523-4550; E-mail: info@rmef.org; URL: http://
www.rmef.org

Established in 1984 in MT.
Grantmaker type: Public charity
Financial data (yr. ended 12/31/00): Revenue,
$30,484,160; assets, $31,396,304; gifts
received, $22,149,255; expenditures,
$29,628,789; program services expenses,
$25,462,967; giving activities include $20,000
for 10 grants to individuals of $2,000 each.
Purpose and activities: The foundation works to
ensure the future of elk, other wildlife, and their
habitats. Program areas include habitat
enhancement, management, research,
conservation education, land acquisition and
protection, and hunting heritage. Grants are
awarded for "on the ground" activities,
undergraduate wildlife management
scholarships, conservation education, and
related programs.
Fields of interest: Natural resources;
Environmental education; Animals/wildlife,
preservation/protection.
Types of support: Land acquisition;
Conferences/seminars; Seed money; Scholarship
funds; Grants to individuals; Scholarships—to
individuals; Matching/challenge support.
Limitations: Giving on a national basis for
educational programs; other giving limited to
regions where elk and other free-ranging
wildlife habitats exist, including Canada. No
support for organizations that lack other funding
sources.
Publications: Application guidelines, Annual
report.
Application information: Scholarship applicants
must be junior or senior undergraduates in a
recognized wildlife program. Application form
required.
   Initial approach: Telephone Conservation
      Programs Office
   Deadline(s): Mar. 1 for Wildlife Leadership
      Awards
   Board meeting date(s): Feb., June, and Dec.
   Final notification: Apr. for Leadership Awards
Officers and Directors:* Jon S. Fossel,* Chair.;
Thomas M. Baker,* Vice-Chair.; Cheryl
Haralson,* Vice-Chair.; Rich Lane, Pres. and
C.E.O., U.S. and Canada; Stacey Christopher,
V.P., Finance and Admin., C.F.O.; David
Ledford, V.P., Conservation Prog. and Opers.,
Western U.S.; Grant Parker, V.P., Legal Affairs
and General Counsel; Gary West, V.P.,
Conservation Opers., Eastern U.S. and Canada;
Dan Walker, V.P., Conservation Lands; Tony
Schoonen, V.P., Marketing and Comm.; Bruce
Alexander, V.P., Devel.; Bill Alexander; Richard
Briskin; Norm Bruce; Larry Bucher; Bill Kiefer;
Jack Ward Thomas, Ph.D.; and 15 additional
directors.
Number of staff: 107.
EIN: 810421425

1805
Sands Memorial Foundation, Inc.
P.O. Box 1127
Havre, MT 59501 (406) 265-4271
Contact: LuAnn McLain, Exec. Dir.
Additional address: 306 3rd Ave., No. 210,
Havre, MT 59501; FAX: (406) 265-4271; E-mail:
smf@hi-line.net

Established in 1977 in MT.
Donor(s): Gordon C. Sands,‡ Nina B. Sands.‡
Grantmaker type: Independent foundation
Financial data (yr. ended 12/31/01): Assets,
$2,666,949 (L); gifts received, $90;
expenditures, $142,622; qualifying distributions,
$139,498; giving activities include $97,278 for
grants (high: $10,000).
Purpose and activities: Support for the care and
protection of companion animals, including
spay/neuter, and cruelty prevention programs.
Fields of interest: Animal welfare; Animal
population control.
Types of support: General/operating support;
Continuing support; Building/renovation;
Equipment; Emergency funds; Seed money.
Limitations: Giving primarily in MT. No grants
to individuals.
Publications: Application guidelines, Annual
report, Grants list, Newsletter.
Application information: Application form
required.
   Initial approach: Letter; FAX applications are
      not accepted
   Copies of proposal: 1
   Deadline(s): Oct. 30
   Board meeting date(s): Last 2 weeks of Mar.
      and Dec.
   Final notification: Dec.
Officers: Cynthia Bryson, Pres.; Cathy
Jamruszka, V.P.; Virginia Reynolds, Secy.;
Leonard Deppmeier, Treas.; LuAnn McLain,
Exec. Dir.
Director: Herman L. Clack.
Number of staff: 1 part-time professional.
EIN: 810368589

NEBRASKA

1806
Ethel S. Abbott Charitable Foundation
P.O. Box 81407
Lincoln, NE 68501-1407 (402) 435-4369
Contact: Del Lienemann, Sr., Pres.

Established in 1989 in NE.
Donor(s): Ethel S. Abbott.‡
Grantmaker type: Independent foundation
Financial data (yr. ended 09/30/02): Assets,
$15,943,487 (M); expenditures, $1,017,516;
qualifying distributions, $1,016,195; giving
activities include $806,300 for 34 grants (high:
$100,000; low: $200; average: $500–$50,000).
Purpose and activities: Giving for arts and
culture, education, health, federated giving
programs and human services.
Fields of interest: Arts; Higher education;
Botanical gardens; Hospitals (general); Health
organizations, association; Human services;
Human services; Community development;

Foundations (community); Federated giving
programs.
Limitations: Giving primarily in NE, with
emphasis on Lincoln and Omaha. No grants to
individuals.
Application information: Application form
required.
   Initial approach: Letter or telephone
      requesting application form
   Deadline(s): Within 90 days after contacting
      the Fdn. Mgr.
Officers: Del Lienemann, Sr., Pres.; Denise
Scholz, 1st V.P.; Daniel Lienemann, 2nd V.P.;
Ruth Cummings, Secy.; Del Lienemann, Jr., Treas.
EIN: 237265876

1807
The Abel Foundation
P.O. Box 80268
Lincoln, NE 68501-0268 (402) 434-1212
Contact: J. Ross McCown, V.P. and Secy.

Trust established in 1951.
Donor(s): Constructors, Inc., NEBCO, Inc.
Grantmaker type: Company-sponsored
foundation
Financial data (yr. ended 12/31/02): Assets,
$2,840,225 (M); gifts received, $205,000;
expenditures, $681,985; qualifying distributions,
$678,940; giving activities include $678,940 for
102 grants (high: $60,000; low: $50).
Purpose and activities: Giving primarily for the
environment, post-secondary education, health
and human services.
Fields of interest: Higher education; Natural
resources; Human services; Federated giving
programs; Protestant agencies & churches.
Types of support: General/operating support;
Capital campaigns; Building/renovation;
Program development.
Limitations: Giving limited to NE, with emphasis
on Lincoln and southeast NE. No grants to
individuals.
Application information: Application form
required.
   Initial approach: Telephone or letter
   Copies of proposal: 1
   Deadline(s): Apr. 20 and Nov. 20
   Board meeting date(s): May and Dec.
   Final notification: Mid-Jan. and mid-June.
Officers: James P. Abel, Pres.; J. Ross McCown,
V.P. and Secy.; James W. Hewitt, V.P. and Treas.
Directors: Alice Abel; Elizabeth N. Abel; Mary
C. Abel.
EIN: 476041771

1808
Cooper Foundation
304 Cooper Plz.
211 N. 12th St.
Lincoln, NE 68508-1411 (402) 476-7571
Contact: E. Arthur Thompson, Pres.
FAX: (402) 476-2356; E-mail:
info@cooperfoundation.org; URL: http://
fdncenter.org/grantmaker/cooper/

Incorporated in 1934 in NE.
Donor(s): Joseph H. Cooper.‡
Grantmaker type: Independent foundation
Financial data (yr. ended 12/31/02): Assets,
$15,018,967 (M); gifts received, $2,100;
expenditures, $2,508,920; qualifying

distributions, $816,386; giving activities include
$584,613 for 36 grants (high: $125,000; low:
$50; average: $50–$50,000).
Purpose and activities: Primary area of interest
is education, including projects recognizing
global inter-relationships, human services, and
the arts and humanities.
Fields of interest: Humanities; Arts; Education;
Environment; Human services.
Types of support: Program development; Seed
money; Technical assistance;
Matching/challenge support.
Limitations: Giving limited to NE, with emphasis
on Lincoln and Lancaster County. No support
for religious or health purposes, private
foundations, businesses, or travel. No grants to
individuals, or for endowment funds; no loans.
Publications: Application guidelines, Biennial
report.
Application information: Contact foundation for
application guidelines. Application form
required.
   Initial approach: Discussion of idea followed
      by letter detailing purpose, audience, and
      budget
   Copies of proposal: 1
   Deadline(s): 15th day of month, for
      consideration at following monthly meeting
   Board meeting date(s): Monthly
   Final notification: 1 month
Officers and Trustees:* Jack D. Campbell,*
Chair.; Norton E. Warner,* Vice-Chair.; E. Arthur
Thompson,* Pres.; Victoria Kovar,* Secy.;
Richard J. Vierk,* Treas.; Richard Knudsen, Genl.
Counsel; Kathryn Druliner; Jane Renner Hood;
John Olsson; Sue K. Renken; John White.
Number of staff: 2 full-time professional; 1
part-time professional.
EIN: 470401230

1809
Robert B. Daugherty Foundation
c/o Valmont Industries, Inc.
1 Valmont Plz.
Omaha, NE 68154 5215

Established in 1968.
Donor(s): Robert B. Daugherty.
Grantmaker type: Independent foundation
Financial data (yr. ended 12/31/02): Assets,
$1,162,694 (M); gifts received, $750,000;
expenditures, $803,348; qualifying distributions,
$804,333; giving activities include $804,417 for
20 grants (high: $416,667; low: $100).
Purpose and activities: Giving primarily to
federated giving programs, and for human
services.
Fields of interest: Education; Animal welfare;
Arthritis research; Human services; YM/YWCAs
& YM/YWHAs; Children, services; Federated
giving programs; Protestant agencies & churches.
Limitations: Applications not accepted. Giving
primarily in NE. No grants to individuals.
Application information: Contributes only to
pre-selected organizations.
Trustees: Mogens Bay; Clarice Barnhill; Frank J.
Daugherty, M.D.; James T. Daugherty; Robert B.
Daugherty; Robert B. Daugherty III; Bruce
Rohde.
EIN: 476059029

1810
William E. & Rose Marie Davis Foundation
2391 Davis Mountain Ln.
Omaha, NE 68112-5159

Established in 1997 in Nebraska.
Donor(s): Rose Marie Davis, William E. Davis.
Grantmaker type: Independent foundation
Financial data (yr. ended 12/31/01): Assets,
$1,015,874 (M); expenditures, $251,637;
qualifying distributions, $248,085; giving
activities include $198,342 for 10 grants (high:
$74,313; low: $1,000) and $49,096 for 23
grants to individuals (high: $5,176; low: $304).
Purpose and activities: Giving to Lutheran
agencies, churches, and schools.
Fields of interest: Scholarships/financial aid;
Animals/wildlife, preservation/protection;
Protestant agencies & churches.
Limitations: Giving primarily in NE.
Application information: Application form
required.
  Initial approach: Write for scholarship
    application form
  Deadline(s): Mar. 28
Officers and Directors:* William E. Davis,*
Pres.; Rose Marie Davis,* V.P. and Secy.-Treas.;
Heather M. Davis,* Secy.
EIN: 911787066

1811
deStwolinski Family Foundation
17330 W. Center Rd., Ste. 110, PMB No. 173
Omaha, NE 68130
Contact: T. Geoffrey Lieben
Additonal address: 100 Scoular Bldg., 2027
Dodge St., Omaha, NE 68102, tel.: (402)
344-4000

Established in 1998 in NE.
Donor(s): Lance deStwolinski.
Grantmaker type: Independent foundation
Financial data (yr. ended 05/31/02): Assets,
$2,445,706 (M); expenditures, $124,663;
qualifying distributions, $122,088; giving
activities include $111,288 for 11 grants (high:
$31,827; low: $5,000) and $10,800 for 1 grant
to an individual.
Purpose and activities: Giving for the
betterment of society though the support of
educational endeavors, community activities
and organizations that better the lives of those in
need. Giving also to the improvement of quality
of life for those living with major medical
conditions. In all areas, preference will be given
to children and those living in communities of
the foundation's board members, or attending
institutions of which they are alumni.
Fields of interest: Higher education; Animal
welfare; Human services; Children, services;
Federated giving programs.
Types of support: Endowments.
Limitations: Applications not accepted. Giving
primarily in AZ, IA, NE, and NM.
Application information: Unsolicited requests
for funds not accepted.
  Board meeting date(s): Nov. and May
Officers: Lance W. deStwolinski, Pres.; Elizabeth
H. deStwolinski, V.P. and Secy.-Treas.
Directors: Matthew deStwolinski; Kimberly
Sealy; Patrick Sealy.
Number of staff: None.
EIN: 470812539

1812
Paul and Oscar Giger Foundation, Inc.
500 Energy Plz., 409 S. 17th St.
Omaha, NE 68102-2663 (402) 341-6000

Established in 1985 in NE.
Donor(s): Ruth Giger.‡
Grantmaker type: Independent foundation
Financial data (yr. ended 12/31/02): Assets,
$2,427,782 (M); expenditures, $166,076;
qualifying distributions, $134,831; giving
activities include $115,940 for 26 grants (high:
$20,000; low: $500).
Purpose and activities: The four major areas of
interest are: musical endeavors and music
education; natural resources; Christian-related
giving; and senior citizens.
Fields of interest: Arts; Natural resources;
Human services; Christian agencies & churches;
Aging.
Limitations: Giving primarily in the Omaha, NE,
area. No support for private foundations. No
grants to individuals.
Application information: Application form
required.
  Initial approach: Letter requesting application
  Copies of proposal: 4
  Deadline(s): May 15 and Oct. 1
  Board meeting date(s): Quarterly
Officers: Frank A. Blazek, Pres.; Beverly Ingram,
V.P.; Janet Acker, Secy.
EIN: 470682708

1813
Bill and Berniece Grewcock Foundation ▼
2123 Mullen Rd.
Omaha, NE 68124-1848

Established in 1990 in NE.
Donor(s): Berniece Grewcock, William L.
Grewcock.
Grantmaker type: Independent foundation
Financial data (yr. ended 12/31/01): Assets,
$13,615,483 (M); expenditures, $3,367,043;
qualifying distributions, $3,298,466; giving
activities include $3,335,000 for 39 grants
(high: $2,000,000; low: $2,000; average:
$5,000–$30,000).
Purpose and activities: Giving primarily for a
state game and parks foundation, and wildlife
preservation; support also for Christian
organizations.
Fields of interest: Elementary/secondary
education; Secondary school/education;
Animals/wildlife, preservation/protection;
Recreation; Human services; Public affairs;
Christian agencies & churches.
Types of support: General/operating support.
Limitations: Applications not accepted. Giving
on a national basis. No grants to individuals.
Application information: Contributes only to
pre-selected organizations.
Officers and Directors:* W. L. Grewcock,* Pres.
and Treas.; Berniece Grewcock,* V.P. and Secy.;
Bruce Grewcock; Douglas Grewcock.
EIN: 470742438

1814
Hastings Community Foundation, Inc.
P.O. Box 703
Hastings, NE 68902 (402) 462-5152
Contact: Susan Poppe, Off. Mgr.
FAX: (402) 462-5171; E-mail:
hcf@inebraska.com

Established in 1987 in NE.
Grantmaker type: Community foundation
Financial data (yr. ended 12/31/02): Assets,
$2,950,000 (M); gifts received, $259,100;
expenditures, $260,568; giving activities
include $214,700 for 23 grants (high: $1,600;
low: $300).
Purpose and activities: Giving primarily for
community development, children, youth and
social services including equipment for a
playground for handicapped youth, and
Christian, Episcopal, Lutheran, Methodist and
Presbyterian churches and organizations. The
foundation also manages a scholarship fund
benefiting the graduates of the Hastings, NE
public school systems. The Watley Scholarship
Fund will be awarded to a graduate of Hastings
Senior High School, who will further his or her
education in the study of business; and the
Osborne Scholarship Fund will be awarded to
any male or female graduate of Hastings High
School who excels in athletics, scholarship and
leadership. The foundation's new Clyde
Sachtleben Scholarship will be awarded to
Hastings College students who go on to
graduate school to study physics or engineering.
Fields of interest: Scholarships/financial aid;
Animal welfare; Crime/law enforcement;
Disasters, fire prevention/control; Recreation;
Human services; Children/youth, services;
Human services; Community development;
Foundations (community); Christian agencies &
churches.
Types of support: Continuing support; Capital
campaigns; Building/renovation; Endowments;
Program development; Curriculum
development; Fellowships; Scholarship funds;
Consulting services; Scholarships—to
individuals; Matching/challenge support.
Limitations: Giving primarily in Hastings, NE,
and the surrounding Adams County.
Publications: Annual report, Informational
brochure, Occasional report.
Application information: Occasionally makes
grants in the fall if funds are available.
Application form required.
  Initial approach: Telephone call requesting an
    application
  Copies of proposal: 2
  Deadline(s): Jan. 31
  Board meeting date(s): 3rd Tues. of each
    month
  Final notification: May 1
Officers: Michael A. Walenz, Pres.; Gayle
McClure, V.P.; D. Charles Shoemaker, Secy.;
Marilyn Nielsen, Treas.
Trustees: Gary Anderson; Lafe Anderson; Paula
Beirow; Martha Boyd; John Crowley; Don
Foote; Charles Hastings; Jerrold Kerr; Hal
Lainson; Chris Oppliger; John C. Osborne;
Robert Portwood; John Quirk; Marilyn
Sachtleben; James Thom; Gretchen Vondrak.
Number of staff: 1 full-time support; 1 part-time
support.
EIN: 363569968

1815
Hickey Family Foundation
13310 I St.
Omaha, NE 68137

Established in 1997.
Donor(s): Bonnie Hickey.
Grantmaker type: Independent foundation
Financial data (yr. ended 05/31/02): Assets, $1,506,995 (M); gifts received, $50,000; expenditures, $242,656; qualifying distributions, $233,591; giving activities include $234,050 for 26 grants (high: $75,000; low: $1,000).
Purpose and activities: Funding primarily for conservation, Roman Catholic agencies and churches, education, and human services.
Fields of interest: Education; Natural resources; Children/youth, services; Roman Catholic agencies & churches.
Limitations: Applications not accepted. No grants to individuals.
Application information: Contributes only to pre-selected organizations.
Officers: Bonnie Hickey, Pres.; Michael Kozlik, Secy.; Mary Jewell, Treas.
EIN: 396658959

1816
The Holland Foundation
1501 S. 80th St.
Omaha, NE 68124 (402) 397-5500
Contact: Richard D. Holland, Pres.

Established in 1996 in NE.
Donor(s): Marilyn M. Holland, Richard D. Holland.
Grantmaker type: Independent foundation
Financial data (yr. ended 12/31/01): Assets, $51,580,702 (M); gifts received, $17,664,000; expenditures, $3,306,761; qualifying distributions, $3,090,543; giving activities include $3,276,758 for 12 grants (high: $1,015,158; low: $5,000; average: $100,000–$500,000).
Purpose and activities: Giving primarily for youth services, and arts and culture.
Fields of interest: Opera; Arts; Early childhood education; Education; Zoos/zoological societies; Children/youth, services; Religion.
Limitations: Giving primarily in NE. No grants to individuals.
Application information:
   Initial approach: Proposal
   Deadline(s): None
Officers: Richard D. Holland, Pres.; Marilyn M. Holland, V.P.; Thomas R. Pansing, Secy.
Director: Wallace R. Weitz.
EIN: 470804949

1817
Lawrence R. & Jeanette James Foundation
9974 Bloomfield Dr.
Omaha, NE 68114
Contact: Lawrence R. James, Pres.
Additional address: 11550 W. Dodge Rd., Omaha, NE 68114, tel.: (402) 496-9600

Established in 1966 in NE.
Donor(s): Sweetbriar Syndicate.
Grantmaker type: Independent foundation
Financial data (yr. ended 06/30/02): Assets, $3,471,804 (M); gifts received, $116,218; expenditures, $233,594; qualifying distributions, $233,311; giving activities include $233,592 for 51 grants (high: $60,550; low: $20).
Purpose and activities: Giving primarily for the arts, and higher education.
Fields of interest: Museums; Performing arts; Higher education; Environment; Health organizations, association; Children/youth, services; Christian agencies & churches.
Types of support: General/operating support.
Limitations: Applications not accepted. Giving primarily in Omaha, NE. No grants to individuals.
Officer: Lawrence R. James, Pres.
EIN: 476040364

1818
Kearney Area Community Foundation
1007 2nd Ave.
P.O. Box 607
Kearney, NE 68847-7305 (308) 237-3114
Contact: Margery Lauer, Exec. Dir.

Grantmaker type: Community foundation
Financial data (yr. ended 12/31/00): Assets, $4,651,180 (M); gifts received, $1,971,054; expenditures, $1,362,044; giving activities include $1,175,270 for grants.
Purpose and activities: To provide support for programs that enhance civic leadership, education, health and human services, and the environment. The foundation administers a donor-advised fund.
Fields of interest: Arts; Education; Horticulture/garden clubs; Health care; Human services; Community development.
Limitations: Giving limited to the Kearney, NE area.
Officers: Steve Chatelain, Chair.; Jerry Colvert, Vice-Chair.; Jackie Rosenlof, Secy.; Al Oldfather, Treas.; Margery Lauer, Exec. Dir.
Directors: Carol Cope; Nancy Etzelmiller; Marilyn Hadley; Lance Hehner; Dan Lindstrom; Sherry Morrow; Dale Pohlman; Janice Wiebusch.
EIN: 470786586

1819
Peter Kiewit Foundation ▼
Guarantee Centre II
8805 Indian Hills Dr., Ste. 225
Omaha, NE 68114 (402) 344-7890
Contact: Lyn Wallin Ziegenbein, Secy.
FAX: (402) 344-8099

Established in 1975 in NE.
Donor(s): Peter Kiewit.‡
Grantmaker type: Independent foundation
Financial data (yr. ended 06/30/02): Assets, $349,247,678 (M); expenditures, $28,714,882; qualifying distributions, $27,268,147; giving activities include $22,295,513 for 172 grants (high: $5,000,000; low: $452; average: $5,000–$500,000) and $3,360,917 for grants to individuals (average: $1,000–$20,000).
Purpose and activities: Giving primarily for cultural programs, including the arts, civic affairs, community development, higher and other education, health and social service agencies, and youth programs. Contributions almost always made as challenge or matching grants.

Fields of interest: Arts; Higher education; Education; Health care; Human services; Youth, services; Rural development; Community development; Government/public administration.
Types of support: General/operating support; Capital campaigns; Building/renovation; Equipment; Land acquisition; Program development; Seed money; Program-related investments/loans; Scholarships—to individuals; Matching/challenge support.
Limitations: Giving limited to Rancho Mirage, CA, western IA, NE, and Sheridan, WY; college scholarships available to high school students in the Omaha, NE-Council Bluffs, IA, area only. No support for elementary or secondary schools, churches, or religious groups. No grants to individuals (except for scholarships), or for endowment funds or annual campaigns.
Publications: Application guidelines, Annual report, Informational brochure (including application guidelines).
Application information: Application form required.
   Initial approach: Letter or telephone
   Copies of proposal: 3
   Deadline(s): Apr. 1 and Oct. 1 for organizations seeking grants greater than $10,000 and Mar. 1, June 1, Sept. 1, and Dec. 1 for grants less than $10,000; Feb. 1 for Teacher Achievement Awards; Mar. 1 for scholarships
   Board meeting date(s): Mar., June, Sept., and Dec.
   Final notification: Within 6 months
Officers and Trustees: G. Richard Russell,* Chair.; John W. Hancock, Vice-Chair.; Lyn Wallin Ziegenbein,* Secy. and Exec. Dir.; Mogens C. Bay; Michael L. Gallagher; Eve Kiewit; U.S. Bank, N.A.
Number of staff: 4 full-time professional; 3 full-time support.
EIN: 476098282
Recent environmental and animal welfare grants:
1819-1 Fontenelle Forest Association, Bellevue, NE, $10,000. For capital construction. 2002.
1819-2 Keep Omaha Beautiful, Omaha, NE, $10,000. For program support. 2002.
1819-3 National Arbor Day Foundation, Lincoln, NE, $17,500. For capital construction. 2002.
1819-4 Nature Conservancy, Omaha, NE, $750,000. For capital construction. 2002.
1819-5 Nebraska Game and Parks Foundation, Omaha, NE, $1,929,408. For capital construction. 2002.
1819-6 Nebraska Trails Foundation, Lincoln, NE, $100,000. For capital construction. 2002.
1819-7 Omaha Zoological Society, Omaha, NE, $500,000. For aquarium. 2002.
1819-8 Omaha, City of, Omaha, NE, $144,211. For improvements to D. F. Lanoha Landscape Nursery in Abbott Drive/Elmwood Park area. 2002.

1820
Lincoln Community Foundation, Inc.
(formerly Lincoln Foundation, Inc.)
215 Centennial Mall S., Ste. 200
Lincoln, NE 68508-1813 (402) 474-2345
Contact: Debra Shoemaker, Dir., Prog. and Dist.
FAX: (402) 476-8532; E-mail: lcf@lcf.org; URL:
http://www.lcf.org/

Incorporated in 1955 in NE.
Grantmaker type: Community foundation
Financial data (yr. ended 12/31/02): Assets,
$39,446,591 (M); gifts received, $1,142,780;
expenditures, $4,182,241; giving activities
include $2,457,378 for 1,366 grants (high:
$345,000; low: $25; average: $50–$50,000).
Purpose and activities: To enrich the quality of
life in the greater Lincoln, NE, area by
responding to emerging and changing needs
and sustaining existing organizations and
institutions through grants for education, arts
and culture, health, social services, economic
development, and civic affairs in
Lincoln/Lancaster County, NE. Primary areas of
interest include family issues, children's issues,
older adults, environmental enhancement,
higher education, and basic needs. The
foundation administers donor-advised funds.
Fields of interest: Museums (marine/maritime);
Arts; Child development, education; Higher
education; Environment; Human services; Child
development, services; Family services; Aging,
centers/services; Aging.
Types of support: General/operating support;
Capital campaigns; Building/renovation;
Emergency funds; Program development; Seed
money; Scholarship funds; Research; Employee
matching gifts; Matching/challenge support.
Limitations: Giving limited to the
Lincoln-Lancaster County, NE, area. No support
for religious or political purposes. No grants to
individuals (except for scholarships), or for
endowments, large capital expenditures, budget
deficits, or projects with long future
commitments.
Publications: Application guidelines, Annual
report, Informational brochure (including
application guidelines), Newsletter, Program
policy statement.
Application information: Application form
required.
 Initial approach: Telephone or letter
 requesting application form
 Copies of proposal: 14
 Deadline(s): June 1 and Dec. 1 for program
 grants; Sept. 1 for capital improvement
 grants
 Board meeting date(s): 3rd Thurs. of Feb.,
 May, Aug., and Nov.
 Final notification: Day of board meeting
Officers and Directors:* Al Hamersky,* Chair.;
Dawson Dowty, Pres.; Marilyn Harris, Ph.D.,*
Secy.; Tom Henning,* Treas.; Deon Bahr; Tom
Ball; Marshall Borchardt; Loel Brooks; Peggy
Chesen; Rich Claussen; M. Doug Deitchler; C.
John Guenzel; Nancy Haessler; Bruce Hocking;
Kathy LeBaron; Janet Labenz; Meg Merchant
Lauerman; Beatrice "Mike" Seacrest; Christie
Schwartzkopf Schroff; Steve Sands; Jose Soto;
Michelle Suarez; Barbara Tolliver-Haskins; Sue
Wilkins; Donna Woods.
Number of staff: 4 full-time professional; 4
full-time support; 1 part-time support.
EIN: 470458128

1821
Lozier Foundation ▼
6336 Pershing Dr.
Omaha, NE 68110-1100 (402) 457-8160
Contact: Robert Braun, Jr.
E-mail: bob.braun@lozier.biz

Established in 1986 in WA.
Donor(s): Allan Gordon Lozier.
Grantmaker type: Independent foundation
Financial data (yr. ended 12/31/02): Assets,
$90,535,000 (M); expenditures, $3,682,844;
qualifying distributions, $3,618,811; giving
activities include $3,618,811 for 156 grants
(high: $1,046,000; low: $100; average:
$1,000–$500,000).
Purpose and activities: Giving primarily for
higher education, domestic violence prevention,
human and youth services, women centers,
homeless, African Americans, and economically
disadvantaged.
Fields of interest: Higher education; Domestic
violence; Human services; Youth, services;
Women, centers/services; Homeless, human
services; African Americans/Blacks; Women;
Economically disadvantaged; Homeless.
Types of support: General/operating support;
Continuing support; Annual campaigns; Capital
campaigns; Building/renovation; Employee
matching gifts; Matching/challenge support.
Limitations: Applications not accepted. Giving
primarily in Omaha, NE. No grants to
individuals.
Application information: Contributes only to
pre-selected organizations.
Trustees: Sheri L. Andrews; Vickey Kleinsmith;
Dianne Seeman Lozier; Allan Gordon Lozier.
Number of staff: None.
EIN: 943027928
**Recent environmental and animal welfare
grants:**
1821-1 Fontenelle Forest Association, Bellevue,
 NE, $25,000. For general operating support.
 2001.
1821-2 Omaha Zoological Society, Omaha, NE,
 $2,183,400. For general operating support.
 2001.
1821-3 Omaha Zoological Society, Omaha, NE,
 $21,000. For general operating support.
 2001.

1822
Armstrong McDonald Foundation
121 S. 13th St., Ste. 201
Lincoln, NE 68508
Contact: Laurie L. Bouchard, Pres.
Application address: P.O. Box 900, Cortaro, AZ
85652-0900, tel.: (520) 878-9627; FAX: (520)
797-3866; E-mail: armmcdfdn@aol.com

Established in 1987 in NE.
Donor(s): J.M. McDonald, Sr.‡
Grantmaker type: Independent foundation
Financial data (yr. ended 12/31/02): Assets,
$15,346,444 (M); expenditures, $917,124;
qualifying distributions, $850,750; giving
activities include $847,250 for 37 grants (high:
$75,000; low: $1,000).
Purpose and activities: Giving primarily for
health education, handicapped, and human
services; giving also for religious organizations
and child welfare.

Fields of interest: Higher education; Animal
welfare; Animals/wildlife, endangered species;
Health care; Health organizations, association;
Human services; Children/youth, services;
Disabled.
Types of support: General/operating support;
Continuing support; Building/renovation;
Equipment; Program development; Research.
Limitations: Giving to states west of MS. No
grants to individuals, or for salaries, or for
capital campaigns.
Publications: Application guidelines.
Application information: Application form not
required.
 Initial approach: Proposal
 Copies of proposal: 1
 Deadline(s): Sept. 30
 Board meeting date(s): Oct.
Officers: Laurie L. Bouchard, Pres.; Ryan M.
Bouchard, V.P.; James M. McDonald IV, V.P.;
Michael J. Bouchard, Secy.-Treas.
Number of staff: None.
EIN: 363458711

1823
Midlands Community Foundation
11111 S. 84th St.
Papillion, NE 68046
Contact: Cora Robinson

Established in 1998 in NE.
Grantmaker type: Independent foundation
Financial data (yr. ended 06/30/02): Assets,
$5,020,346 (M); gifts received, $2,481;
expenditures, $204,025; qualifying distributions,
$167,923; giving activities include $110,700 for
10 grants (high: $25,000; low: $2,000).
Purpose and activities: Giving primarily for
human services.
Fields of interest: Historic
preservation/historical societies; Libraries/library
science; Environment; Health organizations,
association; YM/YWCAs & YM/YWHAs; Aging,
centers/services.
Limitations: Giving limited to NE. No grants to
individuals.
Application information: Application form not
required.
 Initial approach: Letter
 Deadline(s): None
Officers: Jeff Renner, Pres.; Keith Barkley, V.P.;
Mary Gawecki, V.P.; John Sheehan, Secy.-Treas.
EIN: 510191738

1824
Nebraska Statewide Arboretum
P.O. Box 830715
Lincoln, NE 68583-0715 (402) 472-2971
Contact: David Stock, Pres.

Established in 1983.
Grantmaker type: Public charity
Financial data (yr. ended 06/30/02): Revenue,
$297,475; assets, $671,228; gifts received,
$271,215; expenditures, $449,325; program
services expenses, $409,257; giving activities
include $285,037 for 5 grants (high: $273,604;
low: $430).
Purpose and activities: The organization
promotes knowledge, appreciation and use of
indigenous and introduced flora of Nebraska for

the benefit of the citizens and governmental entities of Nebraska.
Fields of interest: Botanical/horticulture/landscape services; Landscaping.
Limitations: Giving limited to NE.
Officers and Directors:* David Stock,* Pres.; Jeff Culbertson,* V.P.; Barton Barcel,* Secy.; Vicki Wohlers,* Treas.; Jane Diesen; Pappy Khouri; Addie Kinghom; Dick Meyer.
EIN: 470600702

1825
Karl H. & Wealtha H. Nelson Family Foundation
c/o Leta Harshman
1901 1st Ave.
Nebraska City, NE 68410

Established in 1993 in NE.
Donor(s): Wealtha H. Nelson.‡
Grantmaker type: Independent foundation
Financial data (yr. ended 12/31/02): Assets, $3,611,489 (M); expenditures, $174,498; qualifying distributions, $116,500; giving activities include $116,500 for 14 grants (high: $50,000; low: $500).
Purpose and activities: Giving primarily for federated giving programs; funding also for education, and human services.
Fields of interest: Historic preservation/historical societies; Arts; Higher education; Environment; Health care; Disasters, fire prevention/control; Human services; Community development; Federated giving programs.
Types of support: Matching/challenge support.
Limitations: Applications not accepted. Giving primarily in Nebraska City, NE.
Application information: Unsolicited requests for funds not accepted.
Officers: Karen Nelson, Pres.; Nicholas Nelson, V.P.; George Blazek, Secy.; Andrew Grier, Treas.
Trustee: Sara Cook; Keith Rohwer; Susie Worth.
Number of staff: 1 part-time support.
EIN: 363879767

1826
Leland J. & Dorothy H. Olson Charitable Foundation
2019 S. 85th Ave.
Omaha, NE 68124
Contact: Leland Olson, Dir.

Established in 1991 in NE.
Donor(s): Leland Olson, Dorothy Olson.
Grantmaker type: Independent foundation
Financial data (yr. ended 12/31/02): Assets, $4,057,367 (M); expenditures, $327,034; qualifying distributions, $288,760; giving activities include $288,800 for 9 grants (high: $100,000; low: $500).
Purpose and activities: Giving primarily for higher education.
Fields of interest: Higher education; Animal welfare; YM/YWCAs & YM/YWHAs.
Limitations: Giving primarily in NE.
Application information:
Initial approach: Letter
Deadline(s): None
Directors: David Olson; Dorothy Olson; Karen Olson; Leland Olson; Nancy Olson.

EIN: 470748772

1827
Omaha Community Foundation ▼
1623 Farnam St., Ste. 600
Omaha, NE 68102 (402) 342-3458
Contact: Michael E. Leighton, Pres. and C.E.O.
FAX: (402) 342-3582; E-mail: sara@omahacf.org; URL: http://www.omahacf.org

Established in 1982 in NE.
Grantmaker type: Community foundation
Financial data (yr. ended 12/31/02): Assets, $302,376,086 (M); gifts received, $6,625,312; expenditures, $46,535,126; giving activities include $31,520,337 for grants.
Purpose and activities: Support primarily for cultural programs, education, neighborhood development, civic affairs, health, and social services, programs for women.
Fields of interest: Arts; Education; Health care; Health organizations, association; Human services; Children/youth, services; Community development; Government/public administration; General charitable giving.
Types of support: Continuing support; Building/renovation; Equipment; Emergency funds; Program development; Conferences/seminars; Publication; Seed money; Scholarship funds; Technical assistance; Matching/challenge support.
Limitations: Giving primarily in the metropolitan Omaha, NE, area including southwest IA. No support for tax-supported institutions, religious organizations for religious purposes, organizations funded by the United Way, arts groups, social clubs, or veterans', labor, or fraternal organizations. No grants to individuals, or for endowments, capital campaigns, deficit financing, annual drives, fundraising events, dinners, or tickets.
Publications: Application guidelines, Annual report (including application guidelines), Grants list, Informational brochure.
Application information: Application form required.
Initial approach: Letter of intent (no more than 2 pages)
Copies of proposal: 1
Deadline(s): Mar. 1 and Sept.1 for letter of intent
Board meeting date(s): Mar., June, Sept., and Dec.
Final notification: May and Nov.
Officers and Directors:* Michael McCarthy,* Chair.; Diane Landen, Vice-Chair.; Michael E. Leighton, Pres. and C.E.O.; John Scott, Secy.; Thomas Whitson,* Treas.; Sara Russell Boyd, V.P.; and 17 additional directors.
Number of staff: 7 full-time professional; 1 part-time professional; 3 full-time support; 2 part-time support.
FIN: 470645958
Recent environmental and animal welfare grants:
1827-1 Audubon Nebraska, Denton, NE, $12,500. 2002.
1827-2 Humane Society of Nebraska, Omaha, NE, $15,000. 2002.
1827-3 Missouri River Basin Lewis and Clark Interpretative Trail and Visitor Center, Nebraska City, NE, $25,000. 2002.

1827-4 Nebraska Game and Parks Foundation, Omaha, NE, $10,000. 2002.

1828
The Omaha World-Herald Foundation
c/o Omaha World-Herald Co.
1334 Dodge St.
Omaha, NE 68114-3732 (402) 444-1000
Contact: John Gottschalk, Pres.
Application address: c/o World Herald Sq., Omaha, NE 68102-1138

Trust established in 1968 in NE.
Donor(s): Omaha World-Herald Co.
Grantmaker type: Company-sponsored foundation
Financial data (yr. ended 12/31/02): Assets, $48,159 (M); gifts received, $528,435; expenditures, $876,994; qualifying distributions, $875,370; giving activities include $875,370 for 34 grants (high: $155,200; low: $1,805).
Purpose and activities: Giving primarily for education, children's services, and arts and culture.
Fields of interest: Journalism/publishing; Historic preservation/historical societies; Arts; Education; Natural resources; Youth, services.
Types of support: Building/renovation; Equipment; Program development; Seed money; Internship funds; Scholarship funds; Matching/challenge support.
Limitations: Giving limited to western IA, and to NE. No grants to individuals, or for operating endowments, research, seminars, or dinners.
Application information: Application form not required.
Initial approach: Letter
Copies of proposal: 1
Deadline(s): None
Board meeting date(s): As required
Final notification: 2 months
Officer and Distribution Committee:* John Gottschalk,* Pres.; A. William Kernen.
Trustee: Wells Fargo Bank Nebraska, N.A.
EIN: 476058691

1829
Morrison Roberts Foundation
12th and Brentwood
P.O. Box 609
Hastings, NE 68902-0609
Contact: Susan M. Morrison Roberts, Secy.-Treas.

Established around 1994.
Donor(s): Kenneth Morrison.
Grantmaker type: Independent foundation
Financial data (yr. ended 08/31/02): Assets, $2,735,147 (M); gifts received, $2,100,000; expenditures, $372,807; qualifying distributions, $370,263; giving activities include $370,263 for 13 grants (high: $125,800; low: $133).
Purpose and activities: Giving to colleges and their foundations, animal welfare organizations and human service organizations.
Fields of interest: Elementary/secondary education; Higher education; Animal welfare; Human services; Foundations (community).
Limitations: Giving primarily in KS and NE. No grants to individuals.
Application information: Preference given to organizations recommended by the officers and directors. Application form not required.

Deadline(s): None
Officers: Kenneth Morrison, Pres.; Susan M. Morrison Roberts, Secy.-Treas.
Director: Gretchen Roberts.
EIN: 363988367

1830
Edward & Lida Robinson Charitable Trust
P.O. Box 241021
Omaha, NE 68124-5021

Established in 1995 in NE.
Grantmaker type: Independent foundation
Financial data (yr. ended 12/31/02): Assets, $4,818,759 (M); expenditures, $394,507; qualifying distributions, $391,681; giving activities include $381,000 for 58 grants (high: $75,000; low: $2,500).
Purpose and activities: Giving primarily for education, and health and human services.
Fields of interest: Arts; Higher education; Education; Zoos/zoological societies; Hospitals (general); Burn centers; Health care; Health organizations; Human services; Children/youth, services; Family services; Federated giving programs.
Limitations: Applications not accepted. Giving primarily in NE, with emphasis on Omaha. No grants to individuals.
Application information: Contributes only to pre-selected organizations.
Trustees: J.J. Exon; Roma Randall; James Roubal.
EIN: 470767603

1831
Rogers Foundation
1311 M St., Ste. A
Lincoln, NE 68508-2539 (402) 477-3725
Contact: Richard W. Agee, Pres. and Treas.

Established in 1954 in NE.
Donor(s): Richard H. Rogers.‡
Grantmaker type: Independent foundation
Financial data (yr. ended 12/31/02): Assets, $8,477,150 (M); expenditures, $561,088; qualifying distributions, $533,751; giving activities include $519,897 for 42 grants (high: $40,000; low: $1,000).
Purpose and activities: Giving primarily for programs that fulfill immediate and practical needs in the community.
Fields of interest: Performing arts; Animals/wildlife, preservation/protection; Health care; Human services; Children/youth, services; Youth, services; Community development.
Limitations: Giving primarily in Lincoln and Lancaster County, NE. No support for religious activities, national organizations, or organizations supported by government agencies. No grants to individuals, or for fundraising benefits, program advertising, endowments, or continuing support; no loans.
Publications: Application guidelines.
Application information:
Initial approach: Proposal
Deadline(s): None
Officers: Richard W. Agee, Pres. and Treas.; Eloise R. Agee, V.P. and Secy.; Rex Marquart, V.P.
EIN: 476026897

1832
Leonard J. & Angeleen E. Stransky Charitable Trust
c/o First Nebraska Trust Co.
P.O. Box 81667
Lincoln, NE 68501-1667

Established in 2000.
Donor(s): Angeleen E. Stransky.
Grantmaker type: Independent foundation
Financial data (yr. ended 12/31/02): Assets, $2,025 (M); gifts received, $140,190; expenditures, $170,116; qualifying distributions, $167,329; giving activities include $167,315 for 7 grants (high: $89,000; low: $461).
Fields of interest: Television; Animal welfare; Human services.
Limitations: Applications not accepted. Giving primarily in Lincoln, NE. No grants to individuals.
Application information: Contributes only to pre-selected organizations.
Trustee: First Nebraska Trust Co.
EIN: 470825670

1833
Stuart Foundation
852 Wells Fargo Ctr.
Lincoln, NE 68508
Contact: James Stuart, Pres.

Established in 1948 in NE.
Grantmaker type: Independent foundation
Financial data (yr. ended 12/31/02): Assets, $2,819,517 (M); expenditures, $107,626; qualifying distributions, $94,903; giving activities include $90,978 for 55 grants (high: $27,168; low: $25).
Purpose and activities: Giving for religion, education, community foundations, environmental conservation, and medical services.
Fields of interest: Higher education; Animal welfare; Hospitals (general); Youth development, services; Leadership development; Christian agencies & churches.
Types of support: Conferences/seminars.
Limitations: Giving primarily in MN and NE.
Application information: Application form not required.
Deadline(s): None
Final notification: 2 months
Officers and Trustees:* Helen C. Stuart,* Chair.; James Stuart,* Pres.; James Stuart III,* V.P.; Scott Stuart,* V.P.
Number of staff: 1.
EIN: 476024642

1834
James Stuart, Jr. Foundation
2001 Pine Lake Rd., Ste. 400
Lincoln, NE 68512-3631
Contact: James Stuart, Jr., Pres.
Application address: 2425 Ridge Rd., Lincoln, NE 68512, tel.: (402) 423-0969

Established in 1997 in NE.
Donor(s): James Stuart, Jr.
Grantmaker type: Independent foundation
Financial data (yr. ended 12/31/02): Assets, $1,797,879 (M); expenditures, $170,603; qualifying distributions, $166,448; giving

activities include $166,448 for 48 grants (high: $51,250; low: $100).
Fields of interest: Orchestra (symphony); Natural resources; Christian agencies & churches.
Limitations: Giving primarily in Lincoln, NE.
Application information:
Initial approach: Letter
Deadline(s): None
Officers: James Stuart, Jr., Pres. and Treas.; Susan S. Stuart, V.P. and Secy.
Director: James Stuart III.
EIN: 911801338

1835
Union Pacific Foundation ▼
1416 Dodge St., Rm. 802
Omaha, NE 68179 (402) 271-5600
Contact: Ms. Darlynn Herweg, Dir.
FAX: (402) 271-5477; E-mail: upf@up.com; URL: http://www.up.com/found

Incorporated in 1959 in UT.
Donor(s): Union Pacific Corp.
Grantmaker type: Company-sponsored foundation
Financial data (yr. ended 12/31/02): Assets, $244,358 (M); gifts received, $7,642,101; expenditures, $7,041,041; qualifying distributions, $6,887,000; giving activities include $6,887,000 for grants.
Purpose and activities: The foundation's signature giving program is the Principal's Partnership. The smaller giving programs contribute to community and civic organizations.
Fields of interest: Museums; Historic preservation/historical societies; Arts; Libraries/library science; Natural resources; Environment; Hospitals (general); Medical care, rehabilitation; Community development.
Types of support: General/operating support; Capital campaigns; Building/renovation; Equipment; Program development.
Limitations: Giving primarily in areas of company operations, with emphasis on the midwestern and western U.S.: AR, AZ, CA, CO, IA, ID, IL, KS, LA, MN, MO, MT, NE, NM, NV, OK, OR, TX, UT, WA, WI, and WY. No support for specialized national health and welfare organizations, religious or labor groups, social clubs, or fraternal or veterans' organizations; support for United Way-affiliated organizations restricted to capital projects. No grants to individuals, or for sponsorship of dinners, benefits, seminars, or other special events.
Application information: If the project is judged to be within the foundation's fields of interest, the applicant will be sent a URL link to application on-line. The foundation acknowledges receipt of proposals. Application form required.
Initial approach: Complete preliminary application form on Web site
Deadline(s): Aug. 15 for consideration in the following calendar year
Board meeting date(s): Late Jan. for consideration for year
Final notification: Feb. through Apr.
Officers and Trustees:* Richard K. Davidson,* Chair.; R.W. Turner,* Pres.; J.J. Koraleski,* V.P., Finance; Carl W. von Bernuth,* Genl. Counsel; I.J. Evans.

Number of staff: 1 full-time professional.
EIN: 136406825
Recent environmental and animal welfare grants:
1835-1 Fontenelle Forest Association, Bellevue, NE, $12,500. 2001.
1835-2 Iowa Natural Heritage Foundation, Des Moines, IA, $10,000. 2001.
1835-3 Nature Conservancy, Sacramento, CA, $10,000. 2001.
1835-4 Omaha Botanical Center, Omaha, NE, $10,000. 2001.
1835-5 Omaha Zoo Foundation, Omaha, NE, $18,000. 2001.
1835-6 Omaha Zoological Society, Omaha, NE, $10,000. 2001.
1835-7 Peregrine Fund, Boise, ID, $10,000. 2001.
1835-8 Saint Louis Zoo Foundation, Saint Louis, MO, $37,500. 2001.

1836
Pamela K. Watanabe-Gerdes/Kyle E. Gerdes Charitable Foundation
P.O. Box 3524
Omaha, NE 68103-0524

Established in 2000 in NE.
Donor(s): Pamela K. Watanabe-Gerdes, Kyle E. Gerdes.
Grantmaker type: Independent foundation
Financial data (yr. ended 12/31/02): Assets, $406,242 (M); expenditures, $193,744; qualifying distributions, $183,164; giving activities include $183,246 for 19 grants (high: $52,646; low: $100).
Fields of interest: Arts; Education; Environment; Human services; Religion.
Limitations: Applications not accepted. Giving primarily in Omaha, NE. No grants to individuals.
Application information: Contributes only to pre-selected organizations.
Officers and Directors:* Pamela K. Watanabe-Gerdes,* Pres. and Treas.; Kyle E. Gerdes,* V.P. and Secy.; Gordon T. Watanabe.
EIN: 470837289

NEVADA

1837
Bing Fund Corporation ▼
990 N. Sierra St.
Reno, NV 89503
Contact: Peter S. Bing, Pres.
Additional address: 9700 W. Pico Blvd., Los Angeles, CA 90035

Established in 1920 in NY; incorporated in 1978 in NV as partial successor to Bing Fund, Inc.
Donor(s): Leo S. Bing,‡ Anna Bing Arnold, Peter S. Bing.
Grantmaker type: Independent foundation
Financial data (yr. ended 05/31/02): Assets, $57,179,452 (M); expenditures, $6,474,828; qualifying distributions, $6,401,899; giving activities include $6,421,982 for 26 grants (high:

$3,007,982; low: $5,000; average: $25,000–$100,000).
Purpose and activities: Giving primarily for higher education, museums, the arts, secondary education, hospitals, and family planning.
Fields of interest: Museums; Arts; Secondary school/education; Higher education; Hospitals (general); Family planning.
Limitations: Applications not accepted. No grants to individuals.
Application information: Contributes only to pre-selected organizations.
Officers and Trustees:* Peter S. Bing,* Pres. and Treas.; Robert D. Burch,* V.P. and Secy.
EIN: 942476169
Recent environmental and animal welfare grants:
1837-1 Earthwatch Expeditions, Maynard, MA, $50,000. For general support. 2002.
1837-2 Monterey Bay Aquarium, Monterey, CA, $3,007,982. For general support. 2002.

1838
Constance H. Bishop Foundation
1880 Gentry Way
Reno, NV 89502   (775) 825-6400
Contact: Leonard H. McIntosh, Pres.

Established in 1966 in NV.
Grantmaker type: Independent foundation
Financial data (yr. ended 12/31/01): Assets, $2,473,837 (M); expenditures, $263,843; qualifying distributions, $138,980; giving activities include $129,300 for 23 grants (high: $50,000; low: $500).
Purpose and activities: Giving for the arts, education, and human services.
Fields of interest: Arts; Education; Animals/wildlife, preservation/protection; Health care; Children/youth, services.
Limitations: Giving on a national basis.
Application information: Application form not required.
   Deadline(s): None
Officers: Leonard H. McIntosh, Pres.; H.P. McIntosh IV, V.P.; Dennes L. Simkins, Secy.-Treas.
EIN: 886006804

1839
The Bretzlaff Foundation, Inc.
c/o Avansino, Melarkey, Knobel & Mulligan
165 W. Liberty St.
Reno, NV 89501   (775) 333-0330
Contact: Michael J. Melarkey, Secy.

Established in 1988 in NV.
Donor(s): Hazel C. Van Allen.
Grantmaker type: Independent foundation
Financial data (yr. ended 06/30/02): Assets, $16,808,454 (M); gifts received, $14,053; expenditures, $1,305,414; qualifying distributions, $1,202,551; giving activities include $1,175,409 for 58 grants (high: $200,000; low: $2,000).
Purpose and activities: Primary interests are (in this order): higher education, youth, the arts, health care, and the environment.
Fields of interest: Arts; Higher education; Environment; Health care; Youth, services.
Types of support: General/operating support; Building/renovation; Equipment; Endowments; Scholarship funds.

Limitations: Applications not accepted. Giving primarily in Honolulu, HI and Reno, NV. No grants to individuals.
Application information: Foundation does its own research and solicitation for applicants.
   Board meeting date(s): Apr., July, and Oct.
Officers and Directors:* William G. Van Allen,* Pres.; Michael J. Melarkey,* Secy.; Richard Gilbert,* Treas.
Number of staff: None.
EIN: 880241424

1840
Helen Close Charitable Foundation
c/o Barnard, Vogler, & Co.
100 W. Liberty St., Ste. 1100
Reno, NV 89501-1959
Contact: Kenneth E. Stieha, Jr., Pres.

Established in 1985 in NV.
Donor(s): Helen Close.‡
Grantmaker type: Independent foundation
Financial data (yr. ended 11/30/02): Assets, $6,269,057 (M); expenditures, $244,803; qualifying distributions, $174,843; giving activities include $151,585 for 10 grants (high: $58,000; low: $3,000).
Purpose and activities: Giving primarily for education, human services, and community improvement.
Fields of interest: Higher education; Animal welfare; Disasters, fire prevention/control; Human services; Community development.
Types of support: General/operating support; Equipment; Internship funds; Scholarship funds.
Limitations: Giving primarily in Reno, NV. No grants to individuals.
Application information: Application form required.
   Initial approach: Request application form
   Deadline(s): None
Officers and Trustees:* Kenneth E. Stieha, Jr.,* Pres.; John Mayer,* V.P.; Carol Matheson,* Secy.; Betty Vogler,* Treas.
EIN: 880214245

1841
Crescere Foundation
4570 S. Eastern Ave., Ste. C-25
Las Vegas, NV 89119

Established in 1997 in NV.
Donor(s): Beverly O. Hamman, Stephen R. Hamman.
Grantmaker type: Independent foundation
Financial data (yr. ended 12/31/01): Assets, $545,969 (M); expenditures, $2,238,972; qualifying distributions, $2,221,522; giving activities include $2,222,000 for 16 grants (high: $2,050,000; low: $500).
Purpose and activities: Giving primarily for wildlife preservation and to Christian agencies and churches.
Fields of interest: Animals/wildlife, preservation/protection; Christian agencies & churches.
Limitations: Applications not accepted. Giving primarily in Las Vegas, NV. No grants to individuals.
Application information: Contributes only to pre-selected organizations.
Officer: Beverly O. Hamman, Pres.

EIN: 860877267

1842
The Nathan & Violet David Foundation
(formerly The Nathan H. David Foundation)
P.O. Box 3303
Incline Village, NV 89450 (775) 831-5615
Contact: Benjamin Solomon, Tr.

Established in 1988 in NV.
Donor(s): Nathan H. David,‡ Violet S. David.‡
Grantmaker type: Independent foundation
Financial data (yr. ended 12/31/02): Assets,
$6,144,683 (M); expenditures, $487,137;
qualifying distributions, $325,253; giving
activities include $327,800 for 23 grants (high:
$126,000; low: $1,000).
Purpose and activities: Giving primarily for
education, the arts, and medical research.
Fields of interest: Arts; Secondary
school/education; Higher education;
Environment; Medical research, institute.
Types of support: Continuing support; Capital
campaigns; Scholarship funds; Research.
Limitations: Giving primarily in CA and NV.
Application information:
Initial approach: Letter
Deadline(s): None
Trustees: Donald L. Blumenthal; Benjamin J.
Solomon.
EIN: 943081320

1843
The Fairweather Foundation
(formerly The Hall Family Foundation)
P.O. Box 1479
Minden, NV 89423-1479
Contact: Joanne Hall, Secy.-Treas.

Established in 1983 in NV.
Donor(s): Joanne Hall.
Grantmaker type: Independent foundation
Financial data (yr. ended 12/31/02): Assets,
$14,652,624 (M); expenditures, $723,504;
qualifying distributions, $637,557; giving
activities include $628,645 for 54 grants (high:
$50,000; low: $750).
Purpose and activities: Giving primarily for
higher education, conservation of wilderness
areas, cancer research and a facility that
provides temporary lodging for families of
cancer patients on a cost-free basis, and a child
welfare organization; support also for health,
including medical education, and the biological
sciences, and nursing.
Fields of interest: Performing arts; Music; Arts;
Higher education; Education; Natural resources;
Environment; Hospitals (general); Family
planning; Speech/hearing centers; Nursing care;
Health care; Substance abuse, services; Health
organizations, association; Cancer; Heart &
circulatory diseases; AIDS; Alcoholism;
Biomedicine; Medical research, institute; Cancer
research; Heart & circulatory research; AIDS
research; Human services; Children/youth,
services; Aging, centers/services; Biological
sciences; Disabled; Aging; Economically
disadvantaged.
Types of support: General/operating support;
Continuing support; Capital campaigns;
Building/renovation; Emergency funds;
Research; Matching/challenge support.

Limitations: Applications not accepted. Giving
primarily in CA and NV. No grants to individuals.
Application information: Contributes only to
pre-selected organizations.
Board meeting date(s): Fall
Officers and Directors:* Arthur E. Hall,* Chair.;
Joanne Hall,* Secy.-Treas.; William H.T. Bush.
EIN: 880193741

1844
The William H. and Mattie Wattis Harris Foundation
(also known as The Harris Foundation)
6655 W. Sahara, Ste. B118
Las Vegas, NV 89146 (702) 253-1317
Contact: Karen H. Winnefeld, Admin. Secy.
FAX: (702) 253-0548; E-mail:
harrisfoundation@lvcm.com

Trust established in 1960 in UT.
Donor(s): Mattie Wattis Harris,‡ William H.
Harris,‡ Ruth Harris Hite.‡
Grantmaker type: Independent foundation
Financial data (yr. ended 12/31/02): Assets,
$6,061,241 (M); expenditures, $605,107;
qualifying distributions, $516,004; giving
activities include $431,174 for 98 grants (high:
$45,000; low: $500; average: $350–$50,000).
Purpose and activities: Giving primarily for
worldwide conservation and conservation
education programs, and for global population
control.
Fields of interest: Arts; Secondary
school/education; Higher education; Natural
resources; Environment; Animals/wildlife,
preservation/protection; Human services;
Engineering/technology; Science.
Types of support: General/operating support;
Continuing support; Annual campaigns;
Equipment; Land acquisition; Endowments;
Program development; Conferences/seminars;
Publication; Curriculum development;
Scholarship funds; Research.
Limitations: Giving primarily in the western
U.S., with emphasis on CO, NM, NV, and UT.
No support for religious or tax-supported
organizations, or private foundations. No grants
to individuals, or for scholarships, building
funds, or road improvements; no loans.
Publications: Informational brochure, Program
policy statement.
Application information: Application form
required.
Initial approach: Letter of intent
Copies of proposal: 1
Deadline(s): July 1 for letter of intent, Sept. 1
for application
Board meeting date(s): June and Nov.
Final notification: Nov. 1
Officers and Trustees:* Marilyn Harris Hite,*
Pres.; Darryl Lewis, Exec. V.P.; Cassidy Harrison,
V.P., Grants Mgmt.; Henry Hite, Secy. and Treas.;
William Rohrbach, Cont.; James W. Hite,*
Grants Mgr.; RuthAnne Anderson, Resource Mgr.
Number of staff: 1 part-time professional.
EIN: 870405724

1845
Robert Z. Hawkins Foundation
1 E. Liberty St., Ste. 509
Reno, NV 89501 (775) 786-1105
Contact: William H. Wallace, Chair.

Established in 1980 in NV.
Donor(s): Kathryn Ackley Hawkins Trust, Robert
Z. Hawkins.‡
Grantmaker type: Independent foundation
Financial data (yr. ended 12/31/02): Assets,
$20,338,632 (M); expenditures, $819,391;
qualifying distributions, $751,262; giving
activities include $628,830 for 62 grants (high:
$125,000; low: $250; average:
$1,000–$25,000).
Purpose and activities: Giving primarily to
charitable and social services in NV.
Fields of interest: Media/communications;
Museums (art); Performing arts; Orchestra
(symphony); Arts; Higher education; Education;
Animal welfare; Health care; Human services;
Children/youth, services; Roman Catholic
agencies & churches.
Types of support: Building/renovation;
Equipment; Program development; Scholarship
funds; Matching/challenge support.
Limitations: Giving limited to NV. No grants to
individuals.
Publications: Informational brochure (including
application guidelines).
Application information: Application form
required.
Initial approach: Proposal
Copies of proposal: 6
Deadline(s): None
Board meeting date(s): 2nd Tues. of every
month
Officer and Trustees:* William H. Wallace,*
Chair.; Carolyn K. Bernard; Prince A. Hawkins;
Bill A. Ligon, Jr.; Roy Powers.
Number of staff: 1 full-time support.
EIN: 880162645

1846
Conrad N. Hilton Foundation ▼
100 W. Liberty St., Ste. 840
Reno, NV 89501 (775) 323-4221
Contact: Steven M. Hilton, Pres.
FAX: (775) 323-4150; E-mail:
foundation@hiltonfoundation.org; URL: http://
www.hiltonfoundation.org

Established in 1944; incorporated in 1950 in
CA; incorporated in 1989 in NV.
Donor(s): Conrad N. Hilton.‡
Grantmaker type: Independent foundation
Financial data (yr. ended 02/28/03): Assets,
$591,884,963 (M); gifts received, $14,285,878;
expenditures, $30,970,528; qualifying
distributions, $26,394,781; giving activities
include $26,367,977 for 184 grants (high:
$2,867,500; low: $1,000; average:
$1,000–$300,000) and $26,804 for 40
employee matching gifts.
Purpose and activities: The greater part of the
foundation's giving is devoted to several major
long-term projects; funding for smaller scale
miscellaneous grants is very limited. Special
areas of interest are: 1) Works of Catholic Sisters
funded through Conrad N. Hilton Fund for
Sisters; 2) Substance abuse prevention education
funded through the BEST Foundation for a

Drug-Free Tomorrow; 3) Multi-handicapped blind services funded through Perkins School for the Blind; and 4) Water development in West Africa, funded through World Vision and multiple entities.
Fields of interest: Environment, water resources; Substance abuse, prevention; Eye diseases; Children/youth, services.
International interests: Africa.
Types of support: General/operating support; Continuing support; Capital campaigns; Building/renovation; Equipment; Endowments; Program development; Publication; Seed money; Curriculum development; Scholarship funds; Research; Technical assistance; Program-related investments/loans; Employee matching gifts; Matching/challenge support.
Limitations: No support for political organizations. No grants to individuals.
Publications: Informational brochure.
Application information: The foundation accepts applications primarily from its specified beneficiaries; unsolicited proposals generally not considered.
   Initial approach: Letter
   Copies of proposal: 1
   Board meeting date(s): Quarterly
Officers and Directors:* Donald H. Hubbs,* Chair. and C.E.O.; Steven M. Hilton,* Pres.; Patrick Modugno, V.P., Admin. and C.F.O.; Dyanne M. Hayes, V.P., Prog.; Conrad N. Hilton III,* V.P., Information Technology & Special Projects; Judy Miller, V.P. and Dir., Humanitarian Prize; Deborah Kerr, Secy.-Treas.; Robert Buckley, M.D.; Gregory R. Dillon; James R. Galbraith; Barron Hilton; Eric M. Hilton; William B. Hilton, Jr.
Number of staff: 10 full-time professional; 1 part-time professional; 6 full-time support.
EIN: 943100217
Recent environmental and animal welfare grants:
1846-1 Alternativas y Procesos de Participacion Social, Tehuacan, Mexico, $333,300. For Water Forever Project to develop potable water sources and supply in impoverished areas of southern Mexico. 2002.
1846-2 Alternativas y Procesos de Participacion Social, Tehuacan, Mexico, $200,000. For Water Forever Project to develop potable water sources and supply in impoverished areas of southern Mexico. 2002.
1846-3 Cornell University, Ithaca, NY, $50,000. For Water Development program. 2002.
1846-4 Synergos Institute, New York, NY, $25,000. For Water Development program. 2002.
1846-5 Wild Salmon Center, Portland, Oregon, $20,000. 2002.

1847
The Oakmead Foundation
622 Centerville Ln.
Gardnerville, NV 89410

Established in 1979.
Donor(s): Lon F. Israel, Mary Israel.
Grantmaker type: Independent foundation
Financial data (yr. ended 11/30/01): Assets, $2,364,234 (M); gifts received, $855,937; expenditures, $304,487; qualifying distributions, $297,613; giving activities include $290,716 for 28 grants (high: $252,166; low: $100).

Purpose and activities: Giving primarily for higher education, and federated giving programs; funding also for the arts and animal welfare.
Fields of interest: Historic preservation/historical societies; Arts; Higher education; Education; Animal welfare; Federated giving programs.
Types of support: Building/renovation; Equipment; Publication; Internship funds; Scholarship funds.
Limitations: Applications not accepted. Giving primarily in CA. No grants to individuals.
Application information: Contributes only to pre-selected organizations.
Officers: Lon F. Israel, Pres.; John Guilliams, V.P.; Mary M. Israel, Secy.
Board Member: Martha Guilliams.
Trustee: Maxwell Steinhardt.
EIN: 942650919

1848
Palm Fund
990 N. Sierra St.
Reno, NV 89503

Established in 1999 in NV.
Grantmaker type: Independent foundation
Financial data (yr. ended 05/31/01): Assets, $537,664 (M); expenditures, $1,327,515; qualifying distributions, $1,313,742; giving activities include $1,326,980 for 3 grants (high: $1,000,000; low: $75,738).
Fields of interest: Museums (art); Natural resources; Public affairs, single organization support.
Limitations: Applications not accepted. Giving primarily in Los Angeles, CA, Washington, DC, and New York, NY. No grants to individuals.
Application information: Contributes only to pre-selected organizations.
Officers and Directors:* Steven L. Bing,* Pres.; Robert D. Burch,* Secy.; Peter S. Bing,* Treas.
EIN: 911962206

1849
Sierra Pacific Resources Charitable
Foundation
P.O. Box 30150
Reno, NV 89520   (775) 579-1589
URL: http://www.sierrapacific.com/comenv/comrel/foundation/

Established in 1987 in NV.
Donor(s): Sierra Pacific Resources.
Grantmaker type: Company-sponsored foundation
Financial data (yr. ended 12/31/01): Assets, $265,939 (M); gifts received, $320,000; expenditures, $327,753; qualifying distributions, $327,661; giving activities include $327,750 for 198 grants.
Purpose and activities: Giving in the following areas: Youth—-Support of programs and/or organizations which provide strong prevention and/or intervention, and which empower young people to gain personal development; Civic—community service organizations, programs and activities that benefit a broad range of citizens and civic improvement interests; Arts and Culture—activities which broaden public exposure to cultural events and ideas. Health and Welfare— Provide direct

services to people whose needs are unmet by human services agencies; Education— support of higher education institutions, education development, and economic and business education programs; Environmental— programs and organizations which address environmental concerns such as air and water quality, wildlife habitat, open space and waste recycling.
Fields of interest: Arts; Higher education; Environment; Children/youth, services; Youth, services; Public affairs, citizen participation.
Types of support: General/operating support; Continuing support; Capital campaigns; Program development; Employee matching gifts.
Limitations: Giving limited to corporate service area within northern NV. No support for private foundations, full participation members of the United Way, or religious organizations. No grants to individuals, or for sponsorship of teams or sporting events, conferences, seminars, trips, or tours.
Publications: Application guidelines.
Application information: Application guidelines available on foundation Web site. Telephone requests will not be considered. Application form not required.
   Initial approach: Letter
   Copies of proposal: 1
   Deadline(s): None
   Board meeting date(s): Monthly
Officers: Jeff Ceccarelli, Chair.; Karen C. Foster, Secy.-Treas.; Greg Lambert, Admin.; Kim Mazeres, Admin.; Sandy Walsh, Admin.
Number of staff: 1 part-time professional; 1 part-time support.
EIN: 880244735

1850
Southwest Gas Corporation Contributions
Program
5241 Spring Mountain Rd.
P.O. Box 98510
Las Vegas, NV 89193-8510   (702) 876-7247
Contact: Suzanne Farinas, Asst. Secy.
FAX: (702) 876-7037

Grantmaker type: Corporate giving program
Financial data (yr. ended 12/31/02): Total giving, $30,163; giving activities include $16,214 for 168 grants (high: $100; low: $25) and $13,949 for 54 in-kind gifts.
Purpose and activities: As a complement to its foundation, Southwest Gas also makes charitable contributions to nonprofit organizations directly. Support is given primarily in areas of company operations.
Fields of interest: Arts; Education; Environment; Health care; Youth development; Human services; Community development.
Types of support: General/operating support; Continuing support; Annual campaigns; Building/renovation; Research; Public relations services; Donated equipment; Donated products; In-kind gifts.
Limitations: Giving primarily in areas of company operations, with emphasis on the Phoenix and Tucson, AZ, Barstow, Big Bear, and Victorville, CA, and Carson City and Las Vegas, NV, areas. No support for churches. No grants to individuals.
Publications: Application guidelines.
Application information: The Consumer and Community Affairs Department handles giving.

A contributions committee at each company location reviews all requests originating from that particular area. Application form not required.

   Initial approach: Proposal to nearest company facility
   Copies of proposal: 1
   Deadline(s): None
   Board meeting date(s): Monthly
   Final notification: 2 weeks
Administrators: Kate Foreman, Admin., Consumer Affairs, Phoenix; Marty Looney, Admin., Consumer Affairs, Tucson; Al O'Neal, Admin., Consumer Affairs, Las Vegas.

1851
The Southwest Gas Corporation Foundation
P.O. Box 98510
Las Vegas, NV 89193-8510 (702) 876-7247
Contact: Suzanne Farinas

Established in 1985 in NV.
Donor(s): Southwest Gas Corp.
Grantmaker type: Company-sponsored foundation
Financial data (yr. ended 12/31/02): Assets, $498,838 (M); gifts received, $450,000; expenditures, $643,577; qualifying distributions, $632,961; giving activities include $643,148 for 353 grants (high: $50,000; low: $25).
Purpose and activities: Giving primarily to health and welfare associations, and for youth, education, human services, and arts and culture.
Fields of interest: Arts; Education; Environment; Health organizations, association; Human services; Children/youth, services.
Types of support: General/operating support; Continuing support; Annual campaigns; Capital campaigns; Emergency funds; Program development; Research; Employee matching gifts.
Limitations: Giving limited to service territories in AZ, San Bernardino County, CA, and NV. No support for religious organizations. No grants to individuals.
Publications: Informational brochure (including application guidelines).
Application information: Application form required.
   Initial approach: Letter
   Copies of proposal: 1
   Deadline(s): None
Directors: George C. Biehl; Michael O. Maffie; Thomas R. Sheets.
Number of staff: None.
EIN: 942988564

1852
Timken-Sturgis Foundation
1525 Foothill Rd.
Gardnerville, NV 89410
Contact: Judy Sturgis, Secy.-Treas.
FAX: (775) 782-2440

Incorporated in 1949 in CA; incorporated in 1995 in NV.
Donor(s): William T. Sturgis, Valerie Timken Whitney,‡ and members of the Sturgis family.
Grantmaker type: Independent foundation
Financial data (yr. ended 11/30/02): Assets, $4,054,766 (M); expenditures, $245,699;

qualifying distributions, $226,611; giving activities include $227,067 for 32 grants (high: $121,067; low: $500).
Purpose and activities: Support for education, including elementary education; medical research and health services, including family planning; arts and culture, including fine arts; programs relating to the environment, conservation and ecology; programs for the aged; and general charitable giving.
Fields of interest: Visual arts; Performing arts; Arts; Education; Natural resources; Environment; Family planning; Health organizations, association; Medical research, institute; Human services.
Types of support: Continuing support; Equipment; Scholarship funds; Research.
Limitations: Applications not accepted. Giving primarily in southern CA and NV. No grants to individuals; no loans.
Application information: Contributes only to pre-selected organizations. Unsolicited requests for funds not considered.
   Board meeting date(s): Nov.
Officers and Trustees:* William T. Sturgis,* Pres.; Judy Sturgis,* Secy.-Treas.; Jason T. Sturgis.
Number of staff: None.
EIN: 943227435

1853
Tuscany Research Institute
4495 S. Polaris Ave.
Las Vegas, NV 89103
Contact: Robert C. Anderson, Tr.
FAX: (702) 739-9897

Established in 1986 in NV.
Donor(s): CCRC Farms, Anthony A. Marnell II.
Grantmaker type: Operating foundation
Financial data (yr. ended 09/30/01): Assets, $14,875,849 (M); expenditures, $496,032; qualifying distributions, $438,659; giving activities include $287,000 for 2 grants (high: $250,000; low: $37,000) and $151,659 for 1 foundation-administered program.
Purpose and activities: Giving to protect and enhance waterfowl habitats.
Fields of interest: Environment, water resources; Animals/wildlife, preservation/protection.
Types of support: Research.
Limitations: Giving primarily in CA. No grants to individuals.
Application information: Application form required.
   Initial approach: Letter requesting application
   Copies of proposal: 8
   Deadline(s): None
   Board meeting date(s): Dec.
   Final notification: June
Trustees: Robert C. Anderson; James A. Barrett, Jr.; Christopher L. Kaempfer; Alisa A. Marnell; Anthony A. Marnell II; Anthony A. Marnell III; John Stuart.
Number of staff: None.
EIN: 943025713

1854
Wendy's of Montana Foundation, Inc.
1349 Galleria Dr.
Henderson, NV 89014
Contact: Sam E. McDonald, Jr., Dir.

Established in 1998 in NV.
Donor(s): Wendy's of Montana, Inc.
Grantmaker type: Company-sponsored foundation
Financial data (yr. ended 12/31/02): Assets, $257,601 (M); gifts received, $200,000; expenditures, $153,010; qualifying distributions, $139,480; giving activities include $125,950 for 33 grants (high: $15,000; low: $1,000).
Purpose and activities: Giving primarily for the arts, education, and youth services.
Fields of interest: Museums (art); Arts; Elementary/secondary education; Higher education; Scholarships/financial aid; Education; Veterinary medicine; YM/YWCAs & YM/YWHAs.
Types of support: General/operating support; Equipment; Program development; Scholarship funds.
Limitations: Giving primarily in MT.
Application information:
   Initial approach: Letter
   Deadline(s): None
Directors: Deborah V. McDonald, Exec. Dir.; Gregory C. McDonald; Judith C. McDonald; Sam E. McDonald, Jr.
EIN: 880393923

NEW HAMPSHIRE

1855
The Butler Foundation
(formerly Neslab Charitable Foundation)
c/o Charter Trust Co.
P.O. Box 2530
Concord, NH 03302-2530

Established in 1985 in NH.
Donor(s): Clara W. Butler Trust, Thomas Butler Trust.
Grantmaker type: Independent foundation
Financial data (yr. ended 12/31/02): Assets, $6,321,804 (M); expenditures, $299,883; qualifying distributions, $287,900; giving activities include $275,340 for 10 grants (high: $155,408; low: $1,000) and $12,886 for 6 grants to individuals (high: $5,000; low: $500).
Purpose and activities: Giving primarily for environmental conservation.
Fields of interest: Arts; Education; Natural resources; Animals/wildlife.
Types of support: General/operating support; Program development; Research; Scholarships—to individuals.
Limitations: Applications not accepted. Giving on a national basis.
Application information: Unsolicited requests for funds not accepted.
Trustees: Bonnie B. Bunning; Barbara Butler; Clara W. Butler; Marjorie W. Butler; Thomas Butler.
EIN: 222701588

1856
Grace Butnam Foundation
1758 Maine St.
P.O. Box 60
Center Conway, NH 03813-0060

Established in 1985 in NH.
Donor(s): Marilyn L. Goodreau.
Grantmaker type: Independent foundation
Financial data (yr. ended 12/31/01): Assets,
$3,535,143 (M); gifts received, $3,223,053;
expenditures, $188,594; qualifying distributions,
$185,431; giving activities include $181,100 for
13 grants (high: $175,000; low: $100).
Fields of interest: Animal welfare.
Types of support: General/operating support.
Limitations: Applications not accepted. Giving
primarily in ME. No grants to individuals.
Application information: Contributes only to
pre-selected organizations.
Officers: Marilyn L. Goodreau, Pres.; Freda Ellis,
Secy.; Nancy Proctor, Treas.
Directors: David Hawkes; Erlon Jones; Dawn
Smith.
EIN: 222672858

1857
The Michael and Elizabeth Dingman Foundation
(formerly Michael D. Dingman Foundation)
1 Liberty Ln.
Hampton, NH 03842 (603) 929-2203
Contact: Lenore Jennings

Established in 1986 in NH.
Donor(s): Michael D. Dingman, Henley
Manufacturing Charitable Foundation, Inc.,
Winthrop, Inc.
Grantmaker type: Independent foundation
Financial data (yr. ended 12/31/02): Assets,
$409,631 (M); gifts received, $32,000;
expenditures, $371,113; qualifying distributions,
$368,646; giving activities include $367,550 for
41 grants (high: $50,000; low: $1,000; average:
$5,000–$50,000).
Purpose and activities: Giving primarily to
cultural institutions and for education.
Fields of interest: Museums; Arts; Higher
education; Animal welfare; Human services.
International interests: Bahamas.
Types of support: Building/renovation.
Limitations: Giving on a national basis; some
giving also in the Bahamas.
Application information:
 Initial approach: Letter
 Deadline(s): None
Officers: Michael D. Dingman, Pres.; Richard
N. Dupuis, V.P. and Secy.-Treas.; Edward
Kavanaugh, V.P. and Secy.-Treas.; Elizabeth T.
Dingman, V.P.
EIN: 943080164

1858
The Fuller Foundation, Inc.
P.O. Box 479
Rye Beach, NH 03871 (603) 964-6998
Contact: John T. Bottomley, Exec. Dir.
E-mail: ATfuller@aol.com; URL: http://
www.agmconnect.org/fuller1.html

Incorporated in 1936 in MA.
Donor(s): Alvan T. Fuller, Sr.‡

Grantmaker type: Independent foundation
Financial data (yr. ended 12/31/02): Assets,
$12,536,429 (M); expenditures, $828,459;
qualifying distributions, $688,393; giving
activities include $599,700 for 135 grants (high:
$30,000; low: $200).
Purpose and activities: The purpose of the
foundation is to support non-profit agencies
which improve the quality of life for people,
animals and the environment. The Foundation
also funds the Fuller Foundation of New
Hampshire which supports horticultural and
educational programs for the public at Fuller
Gardens.
Fields of interest: Arts education; Museums;
Performing arts; Arts; Education; Natural
resources; Animals/wildlife,
preservation/protection; Substance abuse,
services; Youth development.
Types of support: General/operating support;
Continuing support; Program development;
Seed money; Matching/challenge support.
Limitations: Giving primarily in the greater
Boston, MA, area, and the immediate seacoast
area of NH. No grants to individuals, capital
projects, or conferences; no loans.
Publications: Application guidelines.
Application information: Contact foundation for
current guidelines; FAX requests not accepted.
Application form not required.
 Initial approach: Proposal
 Copies of proposal: 1
 Deadline(s): Jan. 15 and June 15
 Board meeting date(s): May and Oct.
 Final notification: 30 to 60 days
Officers and Trustees:* Peter D. Fuller, Jr.,*
Pres.; James O. Henderson II,* Treas.; John T.
Bottomley,* Exec. Dir.; Miranda Fuller Bocko;
Peter Fuller; James D. Henderson II; Suzanne
Fuller MacDonald; Melinda Fuller vanden
Heuvel.
Number of staff: 1 full-time professional; 1
full-time support.
EIN: 042241130

1859
Kingsbury Fund
c/o Kingsbury Corp.
80 Laurel St.
Keene, NH 03431 (603) 352-5212
Contact: William G. Cogger, Exec. Tr.

Trust established in 1952 in NH.
Donor(s): Kingsbury Corp.
Grantmaker type: Company-sponsored
foundation
Financial data (yr. ended 12/31/02): Assets,
$3,096,210 (M); expenditures, $177,096;
qualifying distributions, $158,536; giving
activities include $126,143 for 139 grants (high:
$15,000; low: $25), $12,000 for 12 grants to
individuals of $1,000 each and $14,317 for 7
employee matching gifts.
Purpose and activities: Giving for higher and
other education, including scholarships for
children of employees; support also for youth
agencies and social services and other
charitable activities. Giving primarily to
organizations in which employees are involved
or from which they derive benefit.
Fields of interest: Dance; Arts; Education,
association; Education, research; Education,
fund raising; Early childhood education; Child

development, education; Elementary
school/education; Higher education;
Adult/continuing education; Education; Natural
resources; Environment; Youth development,
citizenship; Human services; Children/youth,
services; Child development, services; Aging,
centers/services; Community development;
Federated giving programs; Public affairs, citizen
participation; Aging.
Types of support: Capital campaigns;
Equipment; Program development; Seed money;
Employee matching gifts; Employee-related
scholarships; Matching/challenge support.
Limitations: Giving limited to Keene, Cheshire
County, and the Monadnock region of NH. No
support for religious or political purposes.
Application information: Application form
required for scholarships only.
 Deadline(s): Mar. 30 for registration for
 scholarships
 Board meeting date(s): Spring, summer, and
 fall
 Final notification: May 5 for scholarships
Trustees: William G. Cogger, Exec. Tr.; Richard
Dugger; Dixie Gurian; Joy Koontz; Priscilla K.
Maynard; Iris A. Mitropoulis; James O'Neil, Jr.
EIN: 026004465

1860
Mascoma Savings Bank Foundation
c/o Mascoma Savings Bank
67 N. Park St.
Lebanon, NH 03766-1317
Application address: c/o Thomas F. Terry,
Mascoma Savings Bank, P.O. Box 435, Lebanon,
NH 03766-0435

Established in 1988 in NH.
Donor(s): Mascoma Savings Bank.
Grantmaker type: Company-sponsored
foundation
Financial data (yr. ended 12/31/02): Assets,
$2,406,436 (M); gifts received, $186,569;
expenditures, $125,456; qualifying distributions,
$112,876; giving activities include $112,276 for
grants.
Purpose and activities: Grants for community
trusts and medical centers; support also for
community development, the disadvantaged,
welfare, and general charitable giving, including
the arts, adult education, the aged, programs
concerning the environment and conservation,
animal welfare, hospices, and the homeless.
Fields of interest: Arts; Adult/continuing
education; Natural resources; Environment;
Animal welfare; Hospitals (general); Human
services; Hospices; Aging, centers/services;
Homeless, human services; Community
development; Aging; Economically
disadvantaged; Homeless.
Types of support: General/operating support;
Continuing support; Annual campaigns; Capital
campaigns; Building/renovation; Equipment;
Land acquisition; Endowments; Program
development; Publication; Seed money;
Matching/challenge support.
Limitations: Giving primarily in Canaan, Enfield,
Hanover, Lebanon, Lyme, Meriden, and West
Lebanon, NH, and Bethel, Chelsea, Hartford,
Norwich, Plainfield, and Thetford, VT, but not
outside the central western NH and central
eastern VT communities. No grants to
individuals.

Publications: Application guidelines, Grants list, Informational brochure.
Application information: Application form not required.

> *Initial approach:* 1- to 3-page letter
> *Copies of proposal:* 1
> *Deadline(s):* Apr. 1 and Oct. 1
> *Board meeting date(s):* Varies
> *Final notification:* 10 weeks after deadline

Officers and Trustees:* Elizabeth L. Crory,* Chair.; Nancy J. Reardon, Secy.; Charles M. Harrington; Raymond A. Lagasse; Joseph M. Longacre; Thomas F. Terry; Charter Trust Co.
EIN: 222816632

1861
National Grange Mutual Charitable Foundation
55 West St.
Keene, NH 03431-3348
Contact: Richard Hyatt, Tr.

Established in 1972.
Donor(s): National Grange Mutual Insurance Co.
Grantmaker type: Company-sponsored foundation
Financial data (yr. ended 12/31/02): Assets, $2,014,992 (M); expenditures, $133,229; qualifying distributions, $133,029; giving activities include $133,030 for 38 grants (high: $50,000; low: $100).
Purpose and activities: Giving primarily for higher education and the United Way.
Fields of interest: Arts; Elementary/secondary education; Higher education; Natural resources; Health organizations, association; Cancer; Food services; Human services; Hospices; Community development, neighborhood development; Federated giving programs.
Types of support: General/operating support.
Limitations: Giving on a national basis. No grants to individuals, or for scholarships.
Application information:

> *Initial approach:* Proposal
> *Deadline(s):* None

Trustees: Jeanne Eddy; Richard Hyatt; Philip D. Koerner; Thomas M. Von Berkel.
Number of staff: 1 part-time support.
EIN: 237228264

1862
The New Hampshire Charitable Foundation ▼
37 Pleasant St.
Concord, NH 03301-4005 (603) 225-6641
Contact: Racheal Stuart, V.P., Progs.
FAX: (603) 225-1700; E-mail: info@nhcf.org, or rs@nhcf.org; URL: http://www.nhcf.org

Incorporated in 1962 in NH.
Grantmaker type: Community foundation
Financial data (yr. ended 12/31/02): Assets, $213,476,114 (M); gifts received, $22,899,131; expenditures, $20,449,095; giving activities include $13,055,621 for 2,306 grants (high: $348,462; low: $25; average: $5,000–$15,000), $2,240,096 for grants to individuals (average: $500–$2,500) and $474,464 for loans to individuals.

Purpose and activities: Giving for charitable and educational purposes including the arts, humanities, the environment and conservation, health, and social and community services; grants primarily to inaugurate new programs and strengthen existing charitable organizations, with emphasis on programs rather than capital needs; support also for college scholarships.
Fields of interest: Humanities; Arts; Education; Natural resources; Environment; Health care; Health organizations, association; Human services.
Types of support: Program development; Seed money; Fellowships; Scholarship funds; Technical assistance; Program-related investments/loans; Scholarships—to individuals; Student loans—to individuals.
Limitations: Giving limited to NH. No support for sectarian or religious purposes. No grants to individuals (except for student aid and special awards); generally no grants for building funds, endowments, operating support, deficit financing, capital campaigns for acquisition of land or renovations to facilities, purchase of major equipment, academic research, out-of-state travel, or to replace public funding or for purposes which are a public responsibility.
Publications: Application guidelines, Annual report, Financial statement, Grants list, Informational brochure, Informational brochure (including application guidelines), Newsletter, Program policy statement.
Application information: Application form required.

> *Initial approach:* Telephone or letter
> *Copies of proposal:* 2
> *Deadline(s):* 1st of Apr., Sept., and Dec.; 3rd Friday in Apr. for student aid applicants for upcoming school year
> *Board meeting date(s):* Feb., June, Nov., and Dec.
> *Final notification:* 10 to 12 weeks

Officers and Directors:* Mary Susan Leahy,* Chair.; Stephen P. Barba,* Vice-Chair.; Stuart Comstock-Gay, C.O.O.; Lewis M. Feldstein,* Pres.; Thomas Deans, Sr. V.P.; Mike Lyons, V.P., Fin. and C.F.O.; Helen Goodman, V.P.; Peter Lamb, V.P.; Racheal Stuart, V.P., Progs.; Harold W. Janeway,* Treas.; Barry L. Brensinger; Jameson S. French; Ann McLane Kuster; Donna Sytek; James W. Varnum; Elizabeth Story Wright.
Number of staff: 23 full-time professional; 6 part-time professional; 6 full-time support; 2 part-time support.
EIN: 026005625
Recent environmental and animal welfare grants:
1862-1 Amherst, Town of, Peabody Mill Environmental Center, Amherst, NH, $14,000. For Phase I and II of facility improvement project. 2002.
1862-2 Antioch New England Graduate School, Keene, NH, $40,000. Toward salary of Switzer Fellow to implement new master's degree program in environmental advocacy and organizing. 2002.
1862-3 Antioch New England Graduate School, Antioch New England Institute, Keene, NH, $40,000. For establishment of Project CO-SEED site in Upper Valley region. 2002.
1862-4 Antioch New England Graduate School, Antioch New England Institute, Keene, NH, $15,000. For Project CO-SEED. 2002.

1862-5 Antrim, Town of, Antrim Conservation Commission, Antrim, NH, $15,000. For acquisition of land to become Antrim Woods. 2002.
1862-6 Appalachian Mountain Club, Boston, MA, $15,000. For development of web-based GIS mapping site. 2002.
1862-7 Appalachian Mountain Club, Boston, MA, $10,000. For production of map and guide to Upper Connecticut Lakes Region. 2002.
1862-8 Appalachian Trail Conference, Harpers Ferry, WV, $15,000. Fo environmental monitoring program along Appalachian Trail. 2002.
1862-9 Association of Vermont Conservation Commissions, Adamant, VT, $10,000. For three-year program to expand community capacity and skills for environmental education and stewardship. 2002.
1862-10 Audubon Society of New Hampshire, Concord, NH, $20,000. For analysis of current state laws and policies which impact green infrastructure and biological diversity. 2002.
1862-11 Audubon Society of New Hampshire, Loon Preservation Committee, Concord, NH, $40,000. For Loon Preservation Committee in Moultanborough. 2002.
1862-12 Caledonia County Natural Resources Conservation District, Saint Johnsbury, VT, $23,285. For work with landowners along two-mile stretch of East Branch of Passumpsic River from northern Lyndonville to East Burke to reestablish natural stream corridor. 2002.
1862-13 Center for Wildlife, Cape Neddick, ME, $10,000. For expanded development efforts. 2002.
1862-14 Clean Water Action, Portsmouth, NH, $15,000. For Zero Mercury Campaign's effort to expand constituency for public health and natural resource protection in New Hampshire. 2002.
1862-15 Connecticut River Watershed Council, Easthampton, MA, $14,500. For community education program on benefits of removal of unused, unusable dams to river habitat restoration. 2002.
1862-16 Conservation Law Foundation, Boston, MA, $50,000. For work related to transportation policy and planning, downtown revitalization, and challenge grant. 2002.
1862-17 Conservation Law Foundation, Boston, MA, $25,000. For campaign to support New Hampshire Chapter endowment. 2002.
1862-18 Container Recycling Institute, Alexandria, VA, $84,000. For full-time employment for Switzer Fellow, into position of executive director, including development and leadership training. 2002.
1862-19 Coos County Human Services, West Stewartstown, NH, $10,000. To stabilize eroding riverbank at County Farm in West Stewartstown. 2002.
1862-20 Copper Cannon Corporation, Franconia, NH, $13,000. To increase staffing for program development. 2002.
1862-21 Fall Mountain Regional School District, Charlestown, NH, $12,000. For outdoor education programs at Walpole Elementary and Fall Mountain Regional High School. 2002.

1862-22 Friends of Odiorne Point, Rye, NH, $15,438. For educational and interpretive programs at Odiorne State Park. 2002.

1862-23 Gibson Center for Senior Services, Conway, NH, $10,990. For environmental education and field experiences for seniors. 2002.

1862-24 Great Works Regional Land Trust, South Berwick, ME, $20,000. For hiring part-time Project Specialists to train, support, and coordinate volunteers for Mount Agamenticus land conservation initiative. 2002.

1862-25 Green Mountain Conservation Group, Effingham, NH, $20,000. For water quality monitoring project. 2002.

1862-26 Harris Center for Conservation and Education, Hancock, NH, $50,000. For two-year challenge grant to apply green technologies in facility renovation project. 2002.

1862-27 Harris Center for Conservation and Education, Hancock, NH, $20,000. For building fund. 2002.

1862-28 Harris Center for Conservation and Education, Hancock, NH, $10,000. To hire Youth Programs Coordinator for expansion of nature-based youth program. 2002.

1862-29 Hubbard Brook Research Foundation, Campton, NH, $15,000. For challenge grant to engage major donors and secure support from foundations outside New England region. 2002.

1862-30 Institute for Sustainable Communities, Montpelier, VT, $10,000. To expand smart growth and sustainable development work in New England. 2002.

1862-31 Jordan Institute, Stratham, NH, $50,000. For second year support of Minimum Impact Development Partnership. 2002.

1862-32 Jordan Institute, Stratham, NH, $17,970. For Pesticides in School Project. 2002.

1862-33 Lake Wentworth Foundation, Wolfeboro, NH, $50,000. For Endowment Fund. 2002.

1862-34 Lyndon State College, Lyndonville, VT, $21,681. For comprehensive inventory of plants and selected insect groups of northern Connecticut River valley for use with other information to guide restoration of streambed and streambank. 2002.

1862-35 Maine Lakes Conservancy and Institute, Nobleboro, ME, $33,333. For general support. 2002.

1862-36 Maine Lakes Conservancy and Institute, Nobleboro, ME, $28,000. For hiring of part-time development person. 2002.

1862-37 Marsh-Billings-Rockefeller National Historic Park, Woodstock, VT, $12,000. For initiative entitled A Forest in Every Classroom. 2002.

1862-38 Monadnock Conservancy, Keene, NH, $11,500. For work with Southwest Regional Planning Commission to develop Open Space Priorities Plan with a pilot community. 2002.

1862-39 Moose Mountains Regional Greenways, Union, NH, $10,000. Toward Executive Director's contract salary. 2002.

1862-40 Nature Conservancy, Concord, NH, $75,000. For Powwow River Watershed project. 2002.

1862-41 Nature Conservancy, Concord, NH, $30,000. Toward Great Bay Stewardship Ecologist position. 2002.

1862-42 Nature Conservancy, Concord, NH, $11,000. For general support. 2002.

1862-43 Nature Museum at Grafton, Grafton, VT, $19,000. For Connecticut River Watershed - Children and Stewardship program in schools. 2002.

1862-44 New England Forestry Foundation, Groton, MA, $35,000. Toward Spednic Lake and Saint Croix River Conservation project. 2002.

1862-45 New England Grassroots Environment Fund, Montpelier, VT, $20,000. For general operating support. 2002.

1862-46 New Hampshire Lakes Association, Concord, NH, $19,500. For Phase III of study of economic value of surface waters in New Hampshire. 2002.

1862-47 New Hampshire Public Interest Research Group Education Fund, Concord, NH, $14,000. For research on range of options for environmental fees. 2002.

1862-48 New York City Environmental Justice Alliance, New York, NY, $34,000. For employment of current Director of Open Space Equity Campaign. 2002.

1862-49 Newbury, Town of, Newbury, VT, $40,000. For plan to restore North Bank of Wells River. 2002.

1862-50 North Country Council, Littleton, NH, $24,000. For inventory of vernal pools along Connecticut River floodplain, and to develop curriculum about vernal pools. 2002.

1862-51 Northern Forest Heritage Park Trust, Berlin, NH, $10,000. For second year of funding for Programs and Interpretation staff position. 2002.

1862-52 Ocean Conservancy, DC, $200,000. For general support. 2002.

1862-53 Passumpsic Valley Land Trust, Saint Johnsbury, VT, $25,000. For feasibility and engineering study of possible removal of East Burke milldam. 2002.

1862-54 Passumpsic Valley Land Trust, Saint Johnsbury, VT, $10,250. For inventory of current owners of shorelands on Passumpsic River mainstem and East Branch from Newark downstream to East Barnet. 2002.

1862-55 Peterborough, Town of, New Common Pathway Committee, Peterborough, NH, $20,000. For construction of multipurpose recreational pathway, specifically for purchase of light poles to be installed along pathway. 2002.

1862-56 Peterborough, Town of, Recreation Department, Peterborough, NH, $10,000. For park beautification plans for Adams Playground. 2002.

1862-57 Peterborough, Town of, Recreation Department, Peterborough, NH, $10,000. For park beautification plans for Adams Playground. 2002.

1862-58 Poore Family Foundation for North Country Conservancy, Colebrook, NH, $11,400. For summer youth employment program. 2002.

1862-59 Rockingham Land Trust, Exeter, NH, $20,000. For operating support. 2002.

1862-60 Seacoast Land Trust, Portsmouth, NH, $10,000. For public outreach and education for land protection in Berry's Brook and Sagamore Creek watersheds. 2002.

1862-61 Seacoast Land Trust, Portsmouth, NH, $10,000. For general support. 2002.

1862-62 Society for the Protection of New Hampshire Forests, Concord, NH, $25,000. For general support. 2002.

1862-63 Society for the Protection of New Hampshire Forests, Concord, NH, $25,000. For new Seacoast Land Protection Specialist. 2002.

1862-64 Society for the Protection of New Hampshire Forests, Center for Land Conservation Assistance, Concord, NH, $60,000. For general support. 2002.

1862-65 Student Conservation Association, Charlestown, NH, $40,000. To build Connecticut River Youth Conservation Coalition. 2002.

1862-66 Tin Mountain Conservation Center, Jackson, NH, $21,594. For general support. 2002.

1862-67 Trust for Public Land, Montpelier, VT, $100,000. Toward expenses for interest and holdings, due diligence, additional easement overlays on phase one property, staff costs and management endowments. 2002.

1862-68 Tufts University, Medford, MA, $17,579. For student aid for New Hampshire residents at School of Veterinary Medicine in North Grafton. 2002.

1862-69 University of New Hampshire, Office of Sponsored Research, Durham, NH, $10,000. For research on sheep-grazing project, which uses sheep to rid parks, historic sites, and land under transmission lines of unwanted plants in environmentally-friendly manner. 2002.

1862-70 Upper Valley Land Trust, Hanover, NH, $150,000. For permanent conservation of prime and ecology-sensitive farmland along Connecticut River in Bath, Haverhill and Piermont. 2002.

1862-71 Upper Valley Land Trust, Hanover, NH, $10,000. For general support. 2002.

1862-72 Vermont Institute of Natural Science, Woodstock, VT, $40,000. For three-year program for development and support of community mapping projects in Upper Valley. 2002.

1862-73 Vermont Leadership Center, Island Pond, VT, $16,145. For Sleepers River Restoration Project to restore forested riparian buffer and provide resting areas for fish in box culbert. Grant made through Northeast Kingdom Conservation Service Corps. 2002.

1862-74 Vinalhaven Land Trust, Vinalhaven, ME, $25,000. Toward purchase of Isle au Haut Mountain property. 2002.

1862-75 Vital Communities of the Upper Valley, White River Junction, VT, $12,373. For Valley Quest program which will work with New Hampshire schools and disseminate materials statewide. 2002.

1862-76 West Virginia Rivers Coalition, Buckhannon, WV, $55,000. To continue support to develop and expand water quality permit analysis in West Virginia. 2002.

1862-77 White River Partnership, Rochester, VT, $23,074. For Riparian restoration projects on Middle and First Branches of White River. 2002.

1862-78 Wilderness Society, Boston, MA, $10,000. For protection of Sandwich Range. 2002.

1862-79 World Media Foundation, Cambridge, MA, $40,000. For Ecological Literacy Project in schools in Upper Valley. 2002.

1863
Northern Utilities, Inc. Corporate Giving Program
325 West Rd.
Portsmouth, NH 03801-5638
URL: http://www.northernutilities.com/incomm/index.htm

Grantmaker type: Corporate giving program
Purpose and activities: Northern Utilities makes charitable contributions to nonprofit organizations involved with arts and culture, education, the environment, human services, and community development. Support is given primarily in areas of company operations.
Fields of interest: Arts; Education; Environment; Human services; Community development.
Types of support: General/operating support; Employee volunteer services.
Limitations: Giving primarily in areas of company operations in ME and NH.
Application information: Contributions generally do not exceed $3,000. Application form not required.
Initial approach: Proposal to headquarters
Copies of proposal: 1
Deadline(s): None

1864
The Dennis A. O'Toole Family Foundation
c/o Albert P. Stowe
200 Marcy St.
Portsmouth, NH 03801

Established in 1997 in NH.
Grantmaker type: Independent foundation
Financial data (yr. ended 12/31/02): Assets, $1,856,542 (M); expenditures, $138,145; qualifying distributions, $120,116; giving activities include $120,185 for 20 grants (high: $45,000; low: $250).
Purpose and activities: Giving primarily for higher education.
Fields of interest: Historic preservation/historical societies; Higher education; Natural resources; Christian agencies & churches.
Limitations: Applications not accepted. Giving on a national basis. No grants to individuals.
Application information: Contributes only to pre-selected organizations.
Trustees: Dennis A. O'Toole; Gertrude L. O'Toole.
EIN: 043371817

1865
The Penates Foundation
1 Liberty Ln.
Hampton, NH 03842 (603) 926-5911
Contact: Michele M. Cogan, V.P.

Established in 1984 in NH.
Donor(s): Paul M. Montrone, Sandra G. Montrone, Prestolite Wire Corp., Latona Associates Inc., Chatam, Inc., Winthrop, Inc., The Oxford League, Inc.

Grantmaker type: Independent foundation
Financial data (yr. ended 09/30/02): Assets, $16,565,786 (M); gifts received, $321,000; expenditures, $1,141,870; qualifying distributions, $955,589; giving activities include $906,835 for 64 grants (high: $175,000; low: $1,000).
Fields of interest: Arts; Secondary school/education; Higher education; Education; Natural resources; Environment; Medical research, institute; Human services; Hospices; Roman Catholic agencies & churches; Economically disadvantaged.
Types of support: Continuing support; Annual campaigns; Capital campaigns; Building/renovation; Land acquisition; Emergency funds; Scholarship funds.
Limitations: Giving on a national basis. No grants to individuals.
Application information: Application form not required.
Initial approach: Letter
Copies of proposal: 1
Deadline(s): None
Board meeting date(s): Nov.
Officers and Directors:* Sandra G. Montrone,* Pres.; Michele M. Cogan,* V.P. and Secy.-Treas.; Matthew R. Friel; Theodore Kurz; Paul Meister; Paul M. Montrone.
Number of staff: None.
EIN: 222536075

1866
PSNH Corporate Giving Program
c/o Mgr., Community Rels.
P.O. Box 330
Manchester, NH 03105-0330
URL: http://www.psnh.com/community/default.asp

Grantmaker type: Corporate giving program
Purpose and activities: PSNH makes charitable contributions to nonprofit organizations involved with environmental stewardship, human services, and economic opportunity. Support is given primarily in New Hampshire.
Fields of interest: Environment; Human services; Economic development.
Types of support: Program development; Employee volunteer services; Sponsorships.
Limitations: Giving primarily in NH. No support for discriminatory organizations, religious, fraternal, or political organizations, or sports leagues or teams. No grants to individuals, or for sporting events, hospital, higher education, or K-12 annual campaigns, or debt reduction.
Application information: The company may request additional information at a later date. An application form is available online. The Community Relations Department handles giving. Application form required.
Initial approach: Download application form and mail to headquarters or complete online application form
Copies of proposal: 1
Deadline(s): None
Final notification: 6 weeks

1867
Putnam Foundation
P.O. Box 323
Keene, NH 03431-0323 (603) 352-2448
Contact: David F. Putnam, Tr.

Trust established in 1952 in NH.
Donor(s): David F. Putnam.
Grantmaker type: Independent foundation
Financial data (yr. ended 10/31/02): Assets, $7,103,225 (M); gifts received, $30,020; expenditures, $541,908; qualifying distributions, $460,397; giving activities include $461,662 for 62 grants (high: $50,000; low: $250).
Fields of interest: Historic preservation/historical societies; Arts; Education; Environment; Children/youth, services; Government/public administration.
Types of support: General/operating support; Capital campaigns; Endowments.
Limitations: Giving limited to NH.
Application information: Application form not required.
Initial approach: Letter
Copies of proposal: 1
Deadline(s): None
Board meeting date(s): Monthly
Officer: Thomas P. Putnam, Secy.
Trustees: David F. Putnam; James A. Putnam; Rosamond P. Putnam.
EIN: 026011388

1868
The Randolph Foundation
P.O. Box 283
Gorham, NH 03581 (603) 643-6640
Contact: John Mudge, Pres.

Established in 1962 in NH.
Grantmaker type: Public charity
Financial data (yr. ended 06/30/02): Assets, $385,419 (M); expenditures, $28,800; program services expenses, $28,800; giving activities include $28,800 for grants to individuals.
Purpose and activities: The foundation promotes support for land conservation and provides scholarships and funding to individuals for other worthwhile experiences.
Fields of interest: Education; Natural resources.
Types of support: Annual campaigns; Capital campaigns; Scholarships—to individuals.
Limitations: Giving limited to NH.
Publications: Annual report, Newsletter.
Application information: Application form not required.
Copies of proposal: 1
Officers and Directors:* John Mudge,* Pres.; Guy Stever, Jr.,* Secy.; Roberta Arbree,* Treas.; Bill Demers; Judy Kenison; Scot Meiklejohn; David Tomlinson; Edith Tucker; Roger Wilson.
Number of staff: None.
EIN: 026009502

1869
Sanders Corporate Giving Program
65 Spitbrook Rd.
Nashua, NH 03061 (603) 885-4558
Contact: Nancy Huntley
FAX: (603) 885-2813

Grantmaker type: Corporate giving program

Purpose and activities: Sanders makes charitable contributions to nonprofit organizations involved with arts and culture, education, the environment, health and human services, youth development, and government. Support is given primarily in areas of company operations.
Fields of interest: Arts; Education; Environment; Health care; Youth development; Human services; Government/public administration.
Types of support: General/operating support; Employee volunteer services; Sponsorships; In-kind gifts.
Limitations: Giving primarily in areas of company operations, particularly in NH. No support for religious, sectarian, or political organizations. No grants to individuals, or for continuing support.
Application information: Application form not required.
   Initial approach: Proposal to headquarters
   Copies of proposal: 1
   Deadline(s): Fall
   Final notification: Following review

1870
Helmut Wolfgang Schumann Foundation
c/o Stebbins, Bradley, Wood & Harvey
41 S. Park St., P.O. Box 382
Hanover, NH   03755

Established in 1983.
Donor(s): Helmut Wolfgang Schumann.†
Grantmaker type: Independent foundation
Financial data (yr. ended 10/31/02): Assets, $2,143,178 (M); gifts received, $100,000; expenditures, $176,835; qualifying distributions, $133,020; giving activities include $133,020 for 51 grants (high: $40,000; low: $500).
Purpose and activities: Giving for the arts, education, hospitals, recreation, and religious organizations.
Fields of interest: Arts; Education; Natural resources; Hospitals (general); Food banks; Recreation; Human services; Religion.
Limitations: Applications not accepted. No grants to individuals.
Application information: Contributes only to pre-selected organizations.
Trustees: Claudia Jacobson; Alexandra Schumann Patchan; Daniel Schumann; Eric R. Schumann; Petra Schumann; Mary Schumann Wheary.
EIN: 222573793

1871
Stonyfield Farm, Inc. Corporate Giving Program
10 Burton Dr.
Londonderry, NH   03053   (603) 437-4040
Contact: Mary Townsend, Dir., Office of the Pres.
Contact for product donations: Jason Kekac, E-mail: jkekac@stonyfield.com; FAX: (603) 437-7594; URL: http://www.stonyfield.com/ldo/index.htm

Grantmaker type: Corporate giving program
Purpose and activities: Stonyfield Farm makes charitable contributions to nonprofit organizations involved with K-12 education, the environment, women's health, disease,

sustainable agriculture, and nutrition. Support is given on a national basis.
Fields of interest: Elementary/secondary education; Environmental education; Environment; Health care; Health organizations; Agriculture, farmlands; Nutrition; Women.
Types of support: General/operating support; Sponsorships; Donated products.
Limitations: Giving on a national basis.
Application information: Proposals should be limited to 2 pages in length. Telephone calls are not encouraged. An application form is required for product donations; application form available online. Product donations are limited to 3 years in length.
   Initial approach: Mail or fax proposal to headquarters; download application form and fax to headquarters for product donations
   Deadline(s): 6 weeks prior to need for product donations
   Board meeting date(s): 2 weeks for product donations

1872
The Timberland Company Contributions Program
c/o Social Enterprise/Grant Review; or Social Enterprise/Product Request
200 Domain Dr.
Stratham, NH   03885
E-mail: csr@timberland.com; URL: http://www.timberland.com/cgi-bin/timberland/timberland/make_a_difference.jsp

Grantmaker type: Corporate giving program
Purpose and activities: Timberland makes charitable contributions to nonprofit organizations involved with natural resources conservation and protection, equal opportunity and access, and volunteerism promotion. Project Grants are grants of under $2,000; Strategic Grants are grants of over $2,000. Support is given primarily in areas of company operations.
Fields of interest: Natural resources; Civil rights, equal rights; Voluntarism promotion.
Types of support: General/operating support; Employee volunteer services; Donated products.
Limitations: Giving primarily in areas of company operations. No support for fraternal, veterans', labor, or political organizations, sectarian or religious organizations, sports teams, or discriminatory organizations. No grants to individuals, or for academic research, sponsorships or advertising, conferences or exhibits, trips or tours, capital campaigns, or sports tournaments.
Publications: Corporate giving report.
Application information: Telephone calls, faxes, E-mail messages, and videotape submissions are not encouraged. An application form is required for Project Grants and Strategic Grants; application forms available online. Requests for product donations should be submitted using organization letterhead.
   Initial approach: Download application form for Project Grants and Strategic Grants; proposal to headquarters for product donations
   Deadline(s): Nov. 1, Feb. 1, May 1, and Aug. 1 for Project Grants; Apr. 1 and Sept. 1 for Strategic Grants

Final notification: Mid-Jan., Mid-Apr., Mid-July, and Mid-Oct. for Project Grants; late July and late Dec. for Strategic Grants; 2 months for product donations

1873
Gilbert Verney Foundation
117 Antrim Rd.
Bennington, NH   03442
Contact: Richard G. Verney, Pres.
Application address: c/o Monadnock Paper Mills, Bennington, NH 03442, tel.: (603) 588-3311

Established in 1947 in MA.
Donor(s): Monadnock Paper Mills, Inc.
Grantmaker type: Company-sponsored foundation
Financial data (yr. ended 12/31/02): Assets, $2,696,339 (M); expenditures, $387,050; qualifying distributions, $336,397; giving activities include $334,900 for 64 grants (high: $125,000; low: $250).
Purpose and activities: Giving primarily for the arts, education and youth programs.
Fields of interest: Arts; Education; Natural resources; Animals/wildlife, preservation/protection; Children/youth, services; Religion.
Types of support: General/operating support; Annual campaigns; Capital campaigns; Equipment.
Limitations: Giving primarily in New England.
Application information: Application form not required.
   Deadline(s): None
Officer: Richard G. Verney, Pres.
Trustees: Lumina V. Greenway; E. Geoffrey Verney.
EIN: 026007363

NEW JERSEY

1874
Actus Foundation
P.O. Box 95
Convent Station, NJ   07961
Contact: Chris Wilkerson, Secy.

Established in 1997.
Donor(s): John Wilkerson.
Grantmaker type: Independent foundation
Financial data (yr. ended 12/31/02): Assets, $1,562,345 (M); expenditures, $124,056; qualifying distributions, $106,977; giving activities include $106,977 for 6 grants (high: $53,500; low: $500).
Purpose and activities: Giving for the arts, community services, health services and nature preservation.
Fields of interest: Arts, services; Natural resources; Health care; Community development.
Types of support: Continuing support; Program development; Internship funds; Research; In-kind gifts.
Limitations: Giving primarily in NJ, NY, and PA.

Application information: Application form not required.
> *Initial approach:* Letter
> *Copies of proposal:* 1
> *Deadline(s):* None
> *Board meeting date(s):* Dec. 20
> *Final notification:* Jan. 15

Officers: John Wilkerson, Pres.; Chris Wilkerson, Secy.
EIN: 223500124

1875
Bernice Barbour Foundation, Inc.

130 Main St.
Hackensack, NJ 07601-7152
Contact: Eve Lloyd Thompson, Tr.
Application address: 14434 Laurel Trail, Wellington, FL 33414, tel.: (561) 791-0861, FAX: (561) 753-9153; E-mail: eve@bernicebarbour.org; URL: http://www.bernicebarbour.org

Established in 1987 in NJ; funded in 1990.
Donor(s): Bernice Barbour.‡
Grantmaker type: Independent foundation
Financial data (yr. ended 12/31/02): Assets, $23,188,651 (M); expenditures, $1,778,714; qualifying distributions, $1,341,960; giving activities include $1,315,475 for 84 grants (high: $300,000; low: $1,000; average: $5,000–$50,000).
Purpose and activities: Giving primarily for the preservation and care of animals and for the prevention of cruelty to animals in the United States.
Fields of interest: Animals/wildlife.
Types of support: General/operating support; Continuing support; Building/renovation; Equipment; Program development; Research; Technical assistance; Matching/challenge support.
Limitations: Giving on a national basis. No support for organizations that do not spay/neuter animals before adopting them out. No grants to individuals, or for indirect costs, litigation, or for costs relating to animals which are not indigenous to the United States.
Publications: Application guidelines, Informational brochure.
Application information: Application form required.
> *Initial approach:* Letter requesting application form
> *Copies of proposal:* 2
> *Deadline(s):* Aug. 10
> *Final notification:* After Dec. 1

Officers and Trustees:* Frank V.D. Lloyd,* Pres.; Jacqueline Little,* V.P.; Eve Lloyd Thompson,* Secy.-Treas.; Gregory Little; Judith Little; Kristina Lloyd Sample.
Number of staff: 2 full-time professional.
EIN: 222779967

1876
BMW of North America, LLC Corporate Giving Program

(formerly BMW of North America, Inc. Corporate Giving Program)
300 Chestnut Ridge Rd.
Woodcliff Lake, NJ 07677 (201) 307-4000
Additional tel.: (201) 307-4289; URL: http://www.bmwusa.com/site_layout/about/philanthropy.html

Grantmaker type: Corporate giving program
Purpose and activities: BMW makes charitable contributions to nonprofit organizations involved with education, the environment, road safety, and community development. Support is given primarily in areas of company operations.
Fields of interest: Education; Environment; Safety, automotive safety; Community development.
Types of support: General/operating support; Employee volunteer services; Scholarships—to individuals; In-kind gifts.
Limitations: Giving primarily in areas of company operations.

1877
The Mary Owen Borden Memorial Foundation

160 Hodge Rd.
Princeton, NJ 08540-3014 (609) 252-9492
Contact: Thomas A. Borden, Exec. Dir.
FAX: (609) 252-9472; URL: http://fdncenter.org/grantmaker/borden/

Incorporated in 1934 in NJ.
Donor(s): Bertram H. Borden,‡ Victory Memorial Park Foundation.
Grantmaker type: Independent foundation
Financial data (yr. ended 12/31/01): Assets, $17,525,107 (M); expenditures, $1,420,780; qualifying distributions, $1,252,344; giving activities include $1,243,200 for 76 grants (high: $50,000; low: $200; average: $5,000–$25,000).
Purpose and activities: The foundation's special focus will be on programs in New Jersey's Mercer and Monmouth counties, addressing the needs of economically disadvantaged youth and their families. This will include health, family planning, education, counseling, child care, substance abuse, and delinquency. Other areas of interest include affordable housing, conservation and the environment, and the arts.
Fields of interest: Arts; Early childhood education; Child development, education; Education; Natural resources; Environment; Family planning; Health care; Substance abuse, services; Mental health/crisis services; Health organizations, association; Alcoholism; Crime/violence prevention, youth; Housing/shelter, development; Human services; Children/youth, services; Child development, services; Family services; Women, centers/services; Homeless, human services; Women; Economically disadvantaged; Homeless.
Types of support: General/operating support; Continuing support; Capital campaigns; Building/renovation; Equipment; Program development; Seed money; Program-related investments/loans; Matching/challenge support.

Limitations: Giving limited to Monmouth and Mercer counties, NJ. No grants to individuals, or for scholarships, fellowships, or multi-year grants.
Publications: Application guidelines, Annual report (including application guidelines).
Application information: Maximum grant award is $25,000, unless trustees determine circumstances warrant larger award for program with a projected major impact in the foundation's area of interest. Application form required.
> *Initial approach:* Write for form; if request meets foundation guidelines and funds are available, application will be sent
> *Copies of proposal:* 1
> *Deadline(s):* Jan. 15, Apr. 15, and Sept. 15
> *Board meeting date(s):* Mar., June, and Nov.
> *Final notification:* 2 months

Officers and Trustees:* Linda B. McKean,* Pres.; Lois Broder,* V.P.; John C. Borden, Jr.,* Secy.; Quinn McKean III,* Treas.; Thomas A. Borden,* Exec. Dir.; Gordon Litwin; Jerri Morrison; Renard Smoots.
Number of staff: 1 part-time professional.
EIN: 136137137

1878
The Bunbury Company

2 Railroad Pl.
Hopewell, NJ 08525 (609) 333-8800
Contact: Samuel W. Lambert III, Treas.
FAX: (609) 333-8900; E-mail: bunburyco@aol.com; URL: http://www.bunburycompany.org

Incorporated in 1952 in NY.
Donor(s): Dean Mathey.‡
Grantmaker type: Independent foundation
Financial data (yr. ended 12/31/02): Assets, $20,529,819 (M); expenditures, $1,330,783; qualifying distributions, $897,333; giving activities include $897,333 for 88 grants (high: $40,000; low: $200).
Purpose and activities: Grants primarily for disadvantaged youth and families, ecology and the natural world, education in the broadest sense, and promotion of the arts.
Fields of interest: Music; Arts; Education; Environment; Children/youth, services; Family services.
Types of support: General/operating support; Capital campaigns; Endowments; Program development; Matching/challenge support.
Limitations: Giving limited to NJ, with emphasis on Mercer County, as well as Burlington, Camden, Hunterdon, Middlesex, Monmouth, Ocean, and Somerset counties. No grants to individuals, or for building funds or fellowships; no loans.
Publications: Application guidelines, Annual report.
Application information: Please follow submission requirements as outlined in guidelines. Application forms available on Web site. Application form required.
> *Initial approach:* Letter
> *Copies of proposal:* 7
> *Deadline(s):* Apr. 4, May 23, Sept. 5, and Dec. 6
> *Board meeting date(s):* Jan., May, July, and Oct.
> *Final notification:* 8-10 weeks after deadline

Officers and Directors:* Edward J. Toohey,*
Pres.; Jamie Kyte Sapoch,* V.P.; Robert M.
Olmsted,* Secy.; Samuel W. Lambert III,* Treas.;
Elizabeth Bankowski; Stephan A. Morse; Charles
C. Townsend, Jr.; Edward J. Zuccaro.
Number of staff: 1 full-time professional; 8
part-time professional.
EIN: 136066172

1879
Nancy and Herbert Burns Foundation

c/o Dorothy Eccleston
2 Golf Ave.
Maywood, NJ 07607
Contact: Nancy Burns, Pres.
Application address: 3 Bridle Way, Saddle River,
NJ 07458, tel.: (201) 327-0396

Established in 1998 in NJ.
Donor(s): Nancy Burns.
Grantmaker type: Operating foundation
Financial data (yr. ended 12/31/02): Assets,
$1,549,777 (M); expenditures, $164,336;
qualifying distributions, $162,000; giving
activities include $162,000 for 13 grants (high:
$20,000; low: $1,000).
Purpose and activities: Giving primarily to
libraries, human services and children's
services, particularly for food.
Fields of interest: Libraries (public); Animal
welfare; Food services; Human services;
American Red Cross; Children, services.
Types of support: General/operating support.
Limitations: Giving on a national basis. No
grants to individuals.
Application information:
 Initial approach: Proposal
 Deadline(s): None
Officers: Nancy Burns, Pres.; Dorothy
Eccleston, V.P. and Treas.; Susan Lenahon, Secy.
EIN: 223583333

1880
Caesar Puff Foundation

c/o Merrill Lynch Trust Co.
P.O. Box 1525
Pennington, NJ 08534

Established in 2000 in PA.
Donor(s): Virginia A. Campana.
Grantmaker type: Independent foundation
Financial data (yr. ended 03/31/02): Assets,
$589,103 (M); expenditures, $171,483;
qualifying distributions, $162,718; giving
activities include $154,661 for 9 grants (high:
$145,661; low: $150).
Fields of interest: Higher education;
Libraries/library science; Animals/wildlife;
Christian agencies & churches.
Limitations: Applications not accepted. Giving
primarily in PA. No grants to individuals.
Application information: Contributes only to
pre-selected organizations.
Trustees: Virginia A. Campana; Merrill Lynch
Trust Co.
EIN: 226866488

1881
Cape Branch Foundation

c/o Danser, Balaam & Frank
5 Independence Way
Princeton, NJ 08540
Contact: Dorothy Frank

Established in 1964 in NJ.
Grantmaker type: Independent foundation
Financial data (yr. ended 12/31/01): Assets,
$23,068,840 (M); expenditures, $1,621,998;
qualifying distributions, $1,085,750; giving
activities include $1,536,060 for 21 grants (high:
$500,000; low: $1,000).
Purpose and activities: Support for secondary
education, conservation, museums, and a
university.
Fields of interest: Museums; Secondary
school/education; Education; Natural resources.
Types of support: General/operating support;
Building/renovation; Land acquisition;
Scholarship funds; Research.
Limitations: Giving primarily in NJ. No grants to
individuals.
Application information: Application form not
required.
 Initial approach: Brief letter
 Deadline(s): None
 Board meeting date(s): Annually
Directors: Gretchen W. Johnson; James L.
Johnson.
Trustees: G.O. Danser; F.J. Hoenemeyer; S.G.
Snow-Johnson.
Number of staff: None.
EIN: 226054886

1882
Celanese Americas Foundation

(formerly Hoechst Corporation Foundation)
c/o Celanese Americas Corp.
86 Morris Ave.
Summit, NJ 07901
Contact: Andrea Stine, Dir., Comm. Svcs.

Established in 1984 in NJ.
Donor(s): Hoechst Corp., Celanese Americas
Corp.
Grantmaker type: Company-sponsored
foundation
Financial data (yr. ended 12/31/01): Assets,
$431,458 (M); expenditures, $664,110;
qualifying distributions, $609,961; giving
activities include $609,961 for 1,113 employee
matching gifts.
Purpose and activities: Giving for education,
particularly the sciences; health and hospitals;
and welfare and youth organizations. Support
also for civic and public affairs, museums and
other cultural programs, and the environment.
Grants are based on an organization's influence
on the community and the level of Celanese
employee involvement.
Fields of interest: Museums; Performing arts;
Theater; Arts; Education, fund raising; Higher
education; Medical school/education; Adult
education—literacy, basic skills & GED;
Reading; Education; Environment; Hospitals
(general); Biomedicine; Medical research,
institute; Human services; Youth, services;
Minorities/immigrants, centers/services;
Community development; Chemistry;
Engineering/technology; Biological sciences;

Science; Government/public administration;
Public affairs; Minorities.
Types of support: General/operating support;
Continuing support; Capital campaigns;
Program development; Research; Employee
matching gifts.
Limitations: Giving primarily in headquarters
city and national operating locations; national
organizations also considered. No support for
religious or fraternal organizations. No grants to
individuals, or for operating expenses of United
Way recipients; special projects of hospitals
have low priority.
Application information: Currently, the
foundation is not making any new commitments
and is in the process of phasing down
operations. Application form not required.
 Board meeting date(s): Feb., May, Aug., and
 Nov.
Officers: Michael E. Grom, Chair. and Pres.;
Susan P. Engleman-Volkert, V.P.; Edmond A.
Collins, Secy.; Terry W. Denzer, Treas.
Number of staff: 1 full-time professional; 1
part-time professional.
EIN: 222577170

1883
Ann Clark Foundation

c/o Merrill Lynch Trust Co.
P.O. Box 1525
Pennington, NJ 08534-1525

Established in 1998 in NJ.
Donor(s): Ann Clark.‡
Grantmaker type: Independent foundation
Financial data (yr. ended 06/30/02): Assets,
$3,582,010 (M); expenditures, $275,662;
qualifying distributions, $218,585; giving
activities include $213,135 for 10 grants (high:
$150,000; low: $1,950).
Purpose and activities: Giving primarily for
education.
Fields of interest: Engineering school/education;
Education; Animals/wildlife; Athletics/sports,
fishing/hunting; Philanthropy/voluntarism.
Types of support: General/operating support.
Limitations: Applications not accepted. Giving
primarily in MI and NJ. No grants to individuals.
Application information: Contributes only to
pre-selected organizations.
Trustees: Mary Lezak; Brian Nunes-Vais;
Maryann Nunes-Vais; Merrill Lynch Trust Co.
EIN: 226742257

1884
The Manny and Ruthy Cohen Foundation, Inc.

231 Chestnut Ave.
Marlton, NJ 08053
Contact: Stephen Morgan, V.P.

Established in 1986 in CT.
Donor(s): Ruth Cohen.‡
Grantmaker type: Independent foundation
Financial data (yr. ended 12/31/02): Assets,
$4,884,895 (M); expenditures, $360,888;
qualifying distributions, $336,643; giving
activities include $221,754 for 104 grants (high:
$14,000; low: $50).
Fields of interest: Arts; Performing arts; Higher
education; Zoos/zoological societies; Health
organizations, association; Human services;

Federated giving programs; Jewish federated giving programs; Jewish agencies & temples.
Limitations: Giving primarily in Washington, DC, Miami, FL, MD, NJ, and Philadelphia, PA. No grants to individuals.
Application information: Application form not required.
Deadline(s): None
Officers: Alvin Morgenstein, Pres.; Steve Morgan, V.P.; Melvin Morgenstern, Secy.
EIN: 592744621

1885
Colton Family Foundation, Inc.
232 Hartshorn Dr.
Short Hills, NJ   07078

Established in 1983 in NJ.
Donor(s): Judith S. Colton, Stewart M. Colton.
Grantmaker type: Independent foundation
Financial data (yr. ended 11/30/02): Assets, $4,275,266 (M); gifts received, $2,500; expenditures, $280,583; qualifying distributions, $259,215; giving activities include $260,395 for 15 grants (high: $135,000; low: $75).
Purpose and activities: Giving for Jewish organizations, higher education and cultural organizations.
Fields of interest: Music; Higher education; Medical school/education; Environment; Health organizations, association; Human services; Jewish federated giving programs; Jewish agencies & temples.
Limitations: Giving on a national basis. No support for private foundations. No grants to individuals.
Officers: Judith S. Colton, Mgr.; Stewart M. Colton, Mgr.; Irving C. Marcus, Mgr.
EIN: 222520918

1886
Community Foundation of New Jersey
35 Knox Hill Rd.
P.O. Box 300
Morristown, NJ   07963-0338   (973) 267-5533
Contact: Hans Dekker, Pres.
FAX: (973) 267-2903; E-mail: cfnj@bellatlantic.net; URL: http://www.cfnj.org

Incorporated in 1979 in NJ.
Grantmaker type: Community foundation
Financial data (yr. ended 04/30/03): Assets, $92,598,215 (M); gifts received, $15,799,500; expenditures, $12,606,970; giving activities include $10,918,020 for 2,905 grants (high: $1,112,000; low: $100; average: $100–$1,112,000).
Purpose and activities: Support for innovative programs which can exert a multiplier effect or through which research may contribute to the solution or easing of important community problems.
Fields of interest: Arts; Education; Environment; Health care; Health organizations, association; AIDS; AIDS research; Youth development, services; Human services; Family services; Urban/community development; Community development; Leadership development; Public affairs; Economically disadvantaged.
Types of support: Program development; Seed money; Scholarship funds; Program-related investments/loans; Matching/challenge support.

Limitations: Giving on a national basis for the benefit of NJ. No grants to individuals, or for continuing support, emergency funds, or deficit financing.
Publications: Annual report (including application guidelines), Informational brochure, Newsletter.
Application information: Application form required.
Initial approach: Telephone
Copies of proposal: 1
Deadline(s): Nov.
Board meeting date(s): 4 times per year
Officers and Trustees:* Stuart D. Sendell,* Chair.; Hans Dekker, C.E.O. and Pres.; Marilyn M. Pfaltz,* Secy.; Susan I. Soldivieri, C.F.O.; Scot R. Guempel,* Treas.; Faith A. Krueger, C.A.O.; Thomas W. Berry; Geoffrey M. Conner; John P. Duffy; Kenneth L. Estabrook; Dan Gaby; Lynn S. Glasser; Michael M. Horn; Robert B. Jones, Ph.D.; Russell J. Lucas; James H. Lynch, Jr.; Ingrid W. Reed; Mark J. Sandler; Stephen A. Tyler; Florence P. Williams; Virginia H. Worden.
Number of staff: 8 full-time professional; 1 part-time professional; 1 full-time support.
EIN: 222281783

1887
The Cowles Charitable Trust
P.O. Box 219
Rumson, NJ   07760   (732) 936-9826
Contact: Gardner Cowles, III, Pres.

Trust established in 1948 in NY.
Donor(s): Gardner Cowles.‡
Grantmaker type: Independent foundation
Financial data (yr. ended 12/31/02): Assets, $19,399,203 (M); expenditures, $1,165,296; qualifying distributions, $915,500; giving activities include $915,500 for 136 grants (high: $35,000; low: $1,000).
Purpose and activities: Grants largely for arts and culture, including museums and the performing arts, education, including early childhood, higher, and secondary, hospitals and AIDS programs, social services, including family planning, and community funds.
Fields of interest: Visual arts; Museums; Performing arts; Dance; Theater; Music; Historic preservation/historical societies; Arts; Education, research; Education, fund raising; Early childhood education; Child development, education; Secondary school/education; Higher education; Medical school/education; Adult/continuing education; Adult education—literacy, basic skills & GED; Libraries/library science; Reading; Education; Natural resources; Environment; Animal welfare; Hospitals (general); Family planning; Health care; Substance abuse, services; Mental health/crisis services; Health organizations, association; Cancer; AIDS; Medical research, institute; Cancer research; AIDS research; Food services; Youth development, services; Human services; Children/youth, services; Child development, services; Family services; Hospices; Aging, centers/services; Women, centers/services; Minorities/immigrants, centers/services; Homeless, human services; Race/intergroup relations; Civil rights; Federated giving programs; Population studies; Leadership development; General charitable giving; Minorities; Disabled; Aging; Women; Homeless.

Types of support: General/operating support; Continuing support; Annual campaigns; Capital campaigns; Building/renovation; Equipment; Endowments; Emergency funds; Program development; Professorships; Seed money; Matching/challenge support.
Limitations: Giving primarily along the Eastern Seaboard, with emphasis on FL and NY. No grants to individuals; no loans.
Publications: Application guidelines, Annual report.
Application information: Applications from any organizations submitted more than once every 12 months not considered. Telephone inquiries are not considered. Application form required.
Initial approach: Letter requesting proposal cover sheet and guidelines
Copies of proposal: 1
Deadline(s): Dec. 1, Mar. 1, June 1, and Sept. 1
Board meeting date(s): Jan., Apr., July, and Oct.
Final notification: Within 2 weeks of board meeting
Officers and Trustees:* Gardner Cowles III,* Pres.; Mary Croft, Secy.-Treas.; Charles Cowles; Jan Cowles; Lois Cowles Harrison; Lois Eleanor Harrison; Kate Cowles Nichols; Virginia Cowles Schroth.
Number of staff: 1 full-time professional.
EIN: 136090295

1888
Degussa-Huls Corporation Contributions Program
65 Challenger Rd.
Ridgefield Park, NJ   07660
Contact: Charles Story, V.P., Govt. and Public Affairs
Application address: P.O. Box 606, Theodore, AL 36590, tel.: (334) 443-4000

Grantmaker type: Corporate giving program
Purpose and activities: Degussa-Huls makes charitable contributions to nonprofit organizations involved with engineering school, the environment, public safety, chemistry, and engineering. Support is given primarily in areas of company operations.
Fields of interest: Engineering school/education; Natural resources; Environment; Safety/disasters; Chemistry; Engineering.
Types of support: Equipment; Conferences/seminars; Internship funds; Consulting services.
Limitations: Giving primarily in areas of company operations. No support for religious or political organizations.
Application information: The Public Relations Department handles giving. Application form not required.
Initial approach: Proposal to headquarters
Copies of proposal: 1
Deadline(s): None
Final notification: Following review
Administrators: Charles Story, V.P., Govt. and Public Affairs; Penny Roman, Mgr., Public Rels.

1889
Geraldine R. Dodge Foundation, Inc. ▼
163 Madison Ave., 6th Fl.
P.O. Box 1239
Morristown, NJ 07962-1239 (973) 540-8442
Contact: David N.W. Grant, III, Exec. Dir.
FAX: (973) 540-1211; E-mail: info@grdodge.org;
URL: http://www.grdodge.org

Incorporated in 1974 in NJ.
Donor(s): Geraldine R. Dodge.‡
Grantmaker type: Independent foundation
Financial data (yr. ended 12/31/01): Assets,
$306,376,880 (M); expenditures, $24,719,277;
qualifying distributions, $23,578,175; giving
activities include $19,852,079 for 605 grants
(high: $600,000; low: $200; average:
$30,000–$50,000), $152,667 for grants to
individuals, $28,779 for 133 employee
matching gifts and $656,291 for 7
foundation-administered programs.
Purpose and activities: The mission of the
foundation is to support and encourage those
educational, cultural, social and environmental
values that contribute to making our society
more human and our world more livable.
Fields of interest: Media/communications;
Visual arts; Museums; Performing arts; Dance;
Theater; Music; Humanities;
Language/linguistics; Literature; Arts; Education,
research; Elementary school/education;
Secondary school/education; Natural
resources; Energy; Environment; Animal welfare;
Animals/wildlife, preservation/protection; Family
planning; Population studies; Leadership
development.
Types of support: General/operating support;
Continuing support; Program development;
Conferences/seminars; Publication; Seed
money; Curriculum development; Research;
Technical assistance; Program evaluation;
Employee matching gifts; Matching/challenge
support; Grants to individuals.
Limitations: Giving primarily in NJ, with support
for the arts and local humane groups limited to
NJ, and support for other local projects limited
to the Morristown-Madison area; some giving in
the other Middle Atlantic states and New
England, and to national organizations. No
support for religious, higher education, health,
or conduit organizations. No grants for capital
projects, equipment purchases, indirect costs,
endowment funds, deficit financing, or
scholarships.
Publications: Application guidelines, Annual
report (including application guidelines).
Application information: Proposal limited to 6
pages plus attachments specified (two-sided
copying preferred). Binders not accepted;
accepts the NYRAG Common Application Form.
Proposal via FAX or E-mail not considered.
Application form not required.
Initial approach: Letter or proposal
Copies of proposal: 2
Deadline(s): Jan. 15 for welfare of animals;
  Mar. 1 for arts; May 1 for Morris County;
  June 1 for environment; and Nov. 1 for
  education
Board meeting date(s): Mar. 15 for
  precollegiate education, June 15 for arts,
  Sept. 15 for local projects, and Nov. 15 for
  critical issues and welfare of animals
Final notification: End of months in which
  board meets

Officers and Trustees:* Robert LeBuhn,* Chair.;
Christopher J. Elliman,* Pres.; James W.
Stevens,* Treas.; John E. Yingling, Jr., C.F.O. and
C.A.O.; David N.W. Grant III, Exec. Dir.; Robert
H.B. Baldwin; Barbara Knowles Debs; John
Lloyd Huck; Betsy S. Michel; Paul J. O'Donnell.
Number of staff: 10 full-time professional; 3
part-time professional; 8 full-time support; 1
part-time support.
EIN: 237406010
**Recent environmental and animal welfare
grants:**
1889-1 Alliance for Contraception in Cats and
  Dogs, Auburn, AL, $20,000. For International
  Symposium on Non-Surgical Methods for Pet
  Population Control. 2002.
1889-2 American Bird Conservancy, The Plains,
  VA, $60,000. For New Jersey and national
  Cats Indoors campaign. 2002.
1889-3 American Kennel Club Museum of the
  Dog, Saint Louis, MO, $22,000. For general
  operating support. 2002.
1889-4 American Littoral Society, Highlands, NJ,
  $60,000. For preservation and restoration of
  New Jersey's coastal areas. 2002.
1889-5 Animal Welfare Association, Voorhees,
  NJ, $50,000. For South Jersey Shelter
  Partnering project and mobile spay/neuter
  clinic for Camden. 2002.
1889-6 Animal Welfare Federation of New
  Jersey, Montclair, NJ, $25,000. For general
  support. 2002.
1889-7 Appalachian Mountain Club, Boston,
  MA, $75,000. To protect natural treasures of
  Highlands. 2002.
1889-8 Association of New Jersey
  Environmental Commissions, Mendham, NJ,
  $250,000. For administering Smart Growth
  Assistance planning and design grants for
  New Jersey municipalities. 2002.
1889-9 Auburn University, College of Veterinary
  Medicine, Scott-Ritchey Research Center,
  Auburn, AL, $80,000. For development of
  immunocontraceptive vaccine. 2002.
1889-10 Audubon Society of New Jersey,
  Bernardsville, NJ, $50,000. To protect bird
  habitat and species diversity in New Jersey.
  2002.
1889-11 Cape May County Animal Shelter,
  Cape May, NJ, $100,000. To construct
  full-service animal shelter facility. 2002.
1889-12 Center for Resource Economics/Island
  Press, DC, $50,000. For production of
  environmental publications. 2002.
1889-13 Clean Ocean Action, Highlands, NJ,
  $75,000. For efforts to ensure protection of
  marine ecosystem off Jersey coast. 2002.
1889-14 Clean Water Fund, Belmar, NJ,
  $75,000. To reduce environmental toxins and
  contaminants in drinking water. 2002.
1889-15 Clean Water Fund, Belmar, NJ,
  $50,000. For Stop the Sprawl media
  campaign. 2002.
1889-16 Coalition for Affordable Housing and
  the Environment, Trenton, NJ, $45,000. To
  promote affordable housing. 2002.
1889-17 Conserve Wildlife Foundation of New
  Jersey, Trenton, NJ, $50,000. For landscape
  projects and Citizen Scientist program. 2002.
1889-18 Defenders of Wildlife, DC, $60,000. To
  analyze economic impacts of designating
  critical lynx habitat areas in North America.
  2002.

1889-19 Delaware and Raritan Greenway,
  Princeton, NJ, $75,000. For land preservation
  activities in central New Jersey. 2002.
1889-20 Delaware Riverkeeper Network,
  Washington Crossing, PA, $55,000. For
  efforts to ensure Delaware River's ecological
  well-being. 2002.
1889-21 Eastern Environmental Law Center,
  Newark, NJ, $200,000. For general operating
  support of legal services to New Jersey's
  environmental community. 2002.
1889-22 Ecological Research and Development
  Group, Milton, DE, $17,300. To engage
  public in conservation of horseshoe crabs.
  2002.
1889-23 Educational Information and Resource
  Center, Sewell, NJ, $120,000. For Earth
  Education program and New Jersey Teachers
  for Biodiversity network. 2002.
1889-24 Environmental Defense, New York, NY,
  $175,000. For environmental protection
  efforts throughout New Jersey/New York
  metropolitan region. 2002.
1889-25 Environmental Leadership Program,
  Cambridge, MA, $100,000. For fellowship
  programs to develop emerging environmental
  leaders. 2002.
1889-26 Environmental Media Services, DC,
  $50,000. For media coverage of major
  environmental issues. 2002.
1889-27 Focus on Animals, West Windsor, NJ,
  $12,500. To complete ventilation system at
  Township of Ewing Animal Shelter. 2002.
1889-28 Friends of the Homeless Animals of
  Trenton-Mercer County, Princeton, NJ,
  $25,000. To establish low-cost spay/neuter
  clinic in Blawenberg. 2002.
1889-29 Fund for a Better Waterfront, Hoboken,
  NJ, $15,000. To secure continuous waterfront
  park and waterfront access in Hoboken.
  2002.
1889-30 Garden State EnviroNet, Boonton, NJ,
  $25,000. For Internet-based environmental
  news and information service. 2002.
1889-31 Genesis Farm, Blairstown, NJ,
  $35,000. For Foodshed Alliance in Ridge and
  Valley region. 2002.
1889-32 Great Swamp Watershed Association,
  New Vernon, NJ, $25,000. To promote sound
  watershed management practices and
  policies. 2002.
1889-33 Greater Newark Conservancy, Newark,
  NJ, $100,000. For Community Greening,
  Education, and Environmental Justice
  programs. 2002.
1889-34 Hackensack Riverkeeper, Teaneck, NJ,
  $25,000. For efforts to protect Hackensack
  River Watershed. 2002.
1889-35 Highlands Coalition, Titusville, NJ,
  $75,000. To protect open space and manage
  growth in New Jersey's Highlands. 2002.
1889-36 Humane Society of Atlantic County,
  Atlantic City, NJ, $30,000. To purchase and
  renovate spay/neuter trailer that will serve
  Atlantic and Cumberland counties. 2002.
1889-37 Humane Society of Ocean City, Ocean
  City, NJ, $20,000. To purchase and equip
  new spay/neuter clinic and education center.
  2002.
1889-38 Humane Society of the United States,
  Humane Society University, DC, $20,000. To
  create cadre of Animal Care Compassion
  Fatigue Specialists in New Jersey. 2002.

1889-39 Isles, Trenton, NJ, $110,000. For Healthy Cities Initiative in Greater Trenton. 2002.

1889-40 Jersey City Municipal Animal Pound-Shelter, Jersey City, NJ, $25,000. For manager for new Jersey City animal shelter. 2002.

1889-41 Jersey Shore Animal Center, Brick, NJ, $25,000. For building expansion and renovations. 2002.

1889-42 Land Institute, Salina, KS, $100,000. For Natural Systems Agriculture graduate research fellowships. 2002.

1889-43 Living Classrooms Foundation, Baltimore, MD, $100,000. For land/sea and shipboard environmental education programs for at-risk students from Paterson, New Jersey. 2002.

1889-44 Marine Mammal Stranding Center, Brigantine, NJ, $15,000. To help center care for stranded and injured marine mammals. 2002.

1889-45 Metropolitan Waterfront Alliance, New York, NY, $60,000. For public education and outreach initiatives that engender waterfront revitalization. 2002.

1889-46 Morris Parks and Land Conservancy, Boonton, NJ, $50,000. For Partners for Greener Communities program. 2002.

1889-47 Mount Pleasant Animal Shelter, East Hanover, NJ, $10,000. To hire full-time dog behaviorist. 2002.

1889-48 National Public Radio (NPR), DC, $125,000. For environmental reporting about land development and sprawl-related issues. 2002.

1889-49 Natural Lands Trust, Media, PA, $100,000. For Delaware Bayshore land protection and stewardship activities. 2002.

1889-50 Natural Resources Defense Council, New York, NY, $150,000. For environmental protection activity in New Jersey. 2002.

1889-51 NatureRail, New York, NY, $25,000. For design of urban wilderness park in Secaucus, New Jersey. 2002.

1889-52 New Jersey Conservation Foundation, Far Hills, NJ, $225,000. For Garden State Greenways Initiative. 2002.

1889-53 New Jersey Department of Environmental Protection, Trenton, NJ, $70,000. To build environmental education programs in New Jersey schools. 2002.

1889-54 New Jersey Future, Trenton, NJ, $75,000. For efforts to curb sprawl and advance smart growth. 2002.

1889-55 New Jersey Institute of Technology, York Center for Environmental Engineering and Science, New Jersey Higher Education Partnership for Sustainability, Newark, NJ, $125,000. To bring environmentally sustainable practices to New Jersey university and college campuses. 2002.

1889-56 New Jersey Network (NJN), Trenton, NJ, $125,000. For regular programs and special productions addressing New Jersey environmental issues. 2002.

1889-57 New Jersey Network (NJN), Trenton, NJ, $20,000. For Homeless Tails, show that profiles animal shelters and their adoptable pets. 2002.

1889-58 New Jersey Public Interest Research Group, Trenton, NJ, $50,000. For Clean Air and Clean Water programs. 2002.

1889-59 New York-New Jersey BayKeeper, Highlands, NJ, $70,000. For efforts aimed at cleaning up lower Passaic River and Newark Bay. 2002.

1889-60 Northeast Organic Farming Association of New Jersey, Pennington, NJ, $65,000. For general support of organic farmer education, advocacy, and outreach. 2002.

1889-61 Open Space Institute, New York, NY, $100,000. For administrative support of New Jersey Conservation Loan Fund. 2002.

1889-62 Passaic County Coalition of Shelter and Rescue Groups, Little Falls, NJ, $150,000. To purchase, equip, and operate low-cost mobile spay/neuter unit in Passaic County. 2002.

1889-63 Passaic River Coalition, Basking Ridge, NJ, $50,000. To preserve and restore Passaic River. 2002.

1889-64 People for Animals, Hillside, NJ, $25,000. For general operating support for Neuter Scooter project. 2002.

1889-65 Pet Savers Foundation, Port Washington, NY, $40,000. For New Jersey Feral Cat Subsidy Program. 2002.

1889-66 Pinelands Preservation Alliance, Pemberton, NJ, $180,000. For work to preserve New Jersey Pinelands. 2002.

1889-67 Preservation New Jersey, Trenton, NJ, $25,000. For Heritage Partnership project, which protects New Jersey's natural and cultural resources. 2002.

1889-68 Prince of Peace Catholic Community, Plano, TX, $20,000. For Resurrection Garden. 2002.

1889-69 Rainforest Alliance, New York, NY, $10,000. For general operating support. 2002.

1889-70 Ramapo-Bergen Animal Refuge, Oakland, NJ, $10,000. For construction of dog isolation runs. 2002.

1889-71 Raptor Trust, Millington, NJ, $15,000. For general operating support. 2002.

1889-72 Regional Plan Association, New York, NY, $100,000. To develop intermunicipal conservation compacts in New Jersey's Highlands. 2002.

1889-73 Regional Planning Partnership, Princeton, NJ, $100,000. To develop and implement regional planning project for Mercer County, New Jersey. 2002.

1889-74 Rockaway River Watershed Cabinet, Cedar Knolls, NJ, $20,000. To improve water quality and to moderate flow of Rockaway River. 2002.

1889-75 Rocky Mountain Institute, Snowmass, CO, $100,000. For general support of programs aimed at creating sustainable societies. 2002.

1889-76 Rutgers, The State University of New Jersey, Cook College, Grant F. Walton Center for Remote Sensing and Spatial Analysis, New Brunswick, NJ, $45,000. For Web site to improve land use planning by citizens in New Jersey's Highlands. 2002.

1889-77 Saint Huberts Giralda, Madison, NJ, $35,000. For Shelter Partner program and new First Grade Humane Education initiative. 2002.

1889-78 Save the Animals Rescue Team Association, Little Falls, NJ, $10,000. For spay/neuter, humane education, and shelter rescue programs. 2002.

1889-79 Science and Conservation Center, Billings, MT, $40,000. For wildlife contraceptive program. 2002.

1889-80 Second Nature, Boston, MA, $60,000. To produce book promoting sustainability among institutions of higher education. 2002.

1889-81 Skylands CLEAN, Ringwood, NJ, $35,000. For protection of open space in New Jersey's Skylands region. 2002.

1889-82 Society for the Prevention of Cruelty to Animals of Atlantic County, Linwood, NJ, $10,000. For low cost spay/neuter clinics and Cat Overpopulation Protection program. 2002.

1889-83 Society for the Prevention of Cruelty to Animals of Cumberland County, Vineland, NJ, $12,000. To purchase and renovate trailer as recovery area for sterilized animals. 2002.

1889-84 Society for the Prevention of Cruelty to Animals of Monmouth County, Eatontown, NJ, $30,000. For renovation and expansion of shelter's animal holding areas. 2002.

1889-85 South Branch Watershed Association, Lebanon, NJ, $20,000. For environmental education programs in schools throughout watershed. 2002.

1889-86 Spay, Neuter and Protect Strays (SNAPS), Oakhurst, NJ, $15,000. For low-cost spay/neuter procedures and medical care for feral cats. 2002.

1889-87 Stony Brook-Millstone Watershed Association, Pennington, NJ, $175,000. To help towns control sprawl through technical assistance, and to strengthen New Jersey watershed groups. 2002.

1889-88 Stony Brook-Millstone Watershed Association, Pennington, NJ, $100,000. For Project for Municipal Excellence. 2002.

1889-89 Sussex County Friends of Animals, Lafayette, NJ, $15,000. To complete ventilation system at Sussex County animal shelter. 2002.

1889-90 Ten Towns Great Swamp Watershed Committee, Cedar Knolls, NJ, $30,000. For improved water monitoring, smart growth education programs and lake monitoring. 2002.

1889-91 Tri-State Transportation Campaign, New York, NY, $100,000. For efforts to improve transportation policy in Greater New York/New Jersey metropolitan area. 2002.

1889-92 Trust for Public Land, New York, NY, $250,000. For work of New Jersey Field Office. 2002.

1889-93 Tufts University, Medford, MA, $75,000. To monitor ecological health of northeastern coastal corridor. 2002.

1889-94 Unity Charter School, Morristown, NJ, $15,000. To educate community about Morristown Greenway Project. 2002.

1889-95 University of Illinois at Urbana-Champaign, College of Veterinary Medicine, Department of Veterinary Biosciences, Urbana, IL, $50,000. For Envirovet Summer Institute. 2002.

1889-96 Wayne Animal Shelter, Friends of the, Wayne, NJ, $15,000. For training of staff and volunteers and for spay/neuter program. 2002.

1889-97 Wilderness Society, DC, $25,000. For Protecting and Connecting Appalachian Highlands program. 2002.

1889-98 Wilderness Society, DC, $25,000. For general operating support. 2002.
1889-99 Wildlife Conservation Society, Bronx, NY, $52,700. For research on conservation of Red Knot, threatened shore bird. 2002.
1889-100 Woodlands Wildlife Refuge, Pittstown, NJ, $10,000. Toward renovation costs of barn, and for equipment. 2002.
1889-101 Work Environment Council of New Jersey, Trenton, NJ, $50,000. For efforts to reduce and prevent air pollution. 2002.
1889-102 World Media Foundation, Cambridge, MA, $75,000. For Living On Earth radio program. 2002.

1890
The Dun & Bradstreet Corporation Foundation

103 JFK Pkwy.
Short Hills, NJ 07078 (973) 921-5605
Contact: Eileen Baker, Prog. Mgr.
FAX: (908) 665-5084; E-mail: bakere@dnb.com

Incorporated in 1953 in DE.
Donor(s): The Dun & Bradstreet Corp.
Grantmaker type: Company-sponsored foundation
Financial data (yr. ended 12/31/02): Assets, $520,010 (M); gifts received, $732,310; expenditures, $704,408; qualifying distributions, $704,357; giving activities include $556,415 for grants and $147,993 for employee matching gifts.
Purpose and activities: The foundation is committed to making a difference in the communities where Dun & Bradstreet has a presence. Contributions are made to support a variety of nonprofit organizations in the areas of education, health and human services, civic and community initiatives, arts and culture, and the environment.
Fields of interest: Arts; Higher education; Environment; Health care; Health organizations, association; Human services; Children/youth, services; Federated giving programs.
Types of support: General/operating support; Continuing support; Annual campaigns; Employee matching gifts; Employee-related scholarships.
Limitations: No grants to individuals (except for employee-related scholarships), or for building or endowment funds, or research; no loans.
Application information: Application form not required.
  Initial approach: Letter
  Board meeting date(s): Semiannually
Officers and Trustees:* David J. Lewinter,* Pres.; Roxanne E. Parker,* V.P. and Treas.; Joanne B. Carson, V.P., Comms.; Chester J. Geveda, Jr., V.P.; Daniel S. Miller,* V.P.; David J. Slobodein, Secy.; Peter J. Ross.
Number of staff: 2.
EIN: 136148188

1891
Eckert Family Foundation

c/o GSC Partners
500 Campus Dr., Ste. 220
Florham Park, NJ 07932

Established in 1985 in NY.
Donor(s): Alfred C. Eckert III.

Grantmaker type: Independent foundation
Financial data (yr. ended 07/31/02): Assets, $1,437,881 (M); gifts received, $229,427; expenditures, $232,878; qualifying distributions, $379,655; giving activities include $379,655 for 49 grants (high: $50,000; low: $500).
Purpose and activities: Giving primarily for the arts, education, health care and to Catholic churches.
Fields of interest: Museums; Elementary/secondary education; Higher education; Animals/wildlife, preservation/protection; Hospitals (general); Human services; Roman Catholic agencies & churches.
Limitations: Applications not accepted. Giving primarily in New York, NY. No grants to individuals; no loans.
Application information: Contributes only to pre-selected organizations.
Trustees: Alfred C. Eckert, Jr.; Alfred C. Eckert III; Kevin W. Kennedy.
EIN: 133318138

1892
Mitzi & Warren Eisenberg Family Foundation

c/o Rockdale Capital
650 Liberty Ave.
Union, NJ 07083

Established in 1992 in NJ.
Donor(s): Warren Eisenberg, Bed Bath & Beyond, Inc.
Grantmaker type: Independent foundation
Financial data (yr. ended 06/30/02): Assets, $81,816,847 (M); gifts received, $2,533,970; expenditures, $2,814,242; qualifying distributions, $2,593,856; giving activities include $2,593,856 for 322 grants (high: $300,000; low: $20; average: $500–$50,000).
Purpose and activities: Giving primarily to Jewish organizations and temples; giving also for the arts, medical research, and human services.
Fields of interest: Arts; Environment; Medical research, institute; Human services; Jewish agencies & temples.
Limitations: Applications not accepted. Giving primarily in NJ and NY. No grants to individuals.
Application information: Contributes only to pre-selected organizations.
Officers: Warren Eisenberg, Pres.; Maxine Eisenberg, Secy.; Ronald Eisenberg, Treas.
EIN: 521798583

1893
The Robert G. & Jane V. Engel Foundation, Inc.

80 Wearimus Rd.
P.O. Box 42
Ho-Ho-Kus, NJ 07423-0042
Contact: Jane V. Engel, Pres.

Established in 1986 in NJ.
Donor(s): Robert G. Engel.
Grantmaker type: Independent foundation
Financial data (yr. ended 09/30/02): Assets, $1,475,718 (M); expenditures, $239,701; qualifying distributions, $232,323; giving activities include $230,000 for 51 grants (high: $40,000; low: $250).

Purpose and activities: Giving for higher education, wildlife conservation, and health care.
Fields of interest: Higher education; Animals/wildlife; Health care; Christian agencies & churches.
Limitations: Giving primarily in NJ and NY. No grants to individuals.
Application information: Application form not required.
  Initial approach: Letter
  Deadline(s): None
Officer: Jane V. Engel, Pres.
Trustees: Robert A. Engel; Jennifer E. Young.
EIN: 222764445

1894
Environmental Endowment for New Jersey, Inc.

P.O. Box 3446
Trenton, NJ 08619-0446 (609) 737-9698
Contact: Richard J. Sullivan, Pres.
Additional tel.: (609) 631-7324

Established in 1991 in NJ.
Grantmaker type: Independent foundation
Financial data (yr. ended 04/30/02): Assets, $5,987,917 (M); gifts received, $45,000; expenditures, $291,791; qualifying distributions, $279,393; giving activities include $265,000 for 29 grants (high: $15,000; low: $500).
Purpose and activities: Giving for innovative environmental projects or programs.
Fields of interest: Environment.
Types of support: Program development; Seed money.
Limitations: Giving limited to the Delaware River Basin, NJ, with exception of the Atlantic Coastal Basin and Wallkill Basin. No grants to individuals, or for continuing support, capital projects, or endowment funds.
Publications: Informational brochure (including application guidelines).
Application information: Application form required.
  Initial approach: 2-page letter
  Copies of proposal: 8
  Deadline(s): Dec. 15
  Final notification: Apr. 22
Officers and Trustees:* Richard J. Sullivan,* Pres.; Jane Nogaki,* V.P.; Joan Burkholtz, Secy.; Ronald Sprague,* Treas.; Abigail Fair; Curtis Fisher; Nancy K. Hedinger; Cindy Zipf.
EIN: 223107878

1895
Fanwood Foundation

c/o King, King and Goldsack
P.O. Box 5244
Plainfield, NJ 07061

Grantmaker type: Independent foundation
Financial data (yr. ended 12/31/01): Assets, $13,883,748 (M); expenditures, $1,042,200; qualifying distributions, $887,355; giving activities include $860,250 for 197 grants (high: $51,000; low: $250).
Purpose and activities: Giving primarily for the arts, education, natural resource conservation, animal welfare, hospitals and health care, human services, and Baptist, Presbyterian and Lutheran churches.

Fields of interest: Arts; Higher education; Education, alumni groups; Education; Natural resources; Environment, land resources; Animal welfare; Animals/wildlife, preservation/protection; Hospitals (general); Health care; Human services; Protestant agencies & churches.
Limitations: Giving on a national basis, with some emphasis on MT.
Trustees: Victor R. King; J. Whitney Stevens; Robert T. Stevens, Jr.; Whitney Stevens.
EIN: 226051922

1896
Feline Friends, Inc.
96 Oval Rd.
Essex Fells, NJ 07021

Established in 2001 in NJ.
Donor(s): Gary Schaedel, Sharon Schaedel.
Grantmaker type: Independent foundation
Financial data (yr. ended 12/31/02): Assets, $3,419 (M); gifts received, $141,716; expenditures, $139,476; qualifying distributions, $139,346; giving activities include $139,346 for grants (high: $92,111).
Purpose and activities: Giving primarily for abused and abandoned animals.
Fields of interest: Veterinary medicine, hospital; Animals/wildlife.
Trustees: Stacey L. Frangella; Kimberly Hoover; Sharon E. Schaedel.
EIN: 223767315

1897
Foster-Karney Trust Fund
P.O. Box 856
Ocean City, NJ 08226 (609) 399-0011
Contact: Byron T. Mercer, Chair., Dist. Comm.

Established in 1988 in NJ.
Grantmaker type: Independent foundation
Financial data (yr. ended 12/31/02): Assets, $2,456,479 (M); expenditures, $136,098; qualifying distributions, $133,015; giving activities include $128,650 for 50 grants (high: $44,000; low: $500).
Purpose and activities: Giving primarily for education.
Fields of interest: Performing arts; Arts; Secondary school/education; Scholarships/financial aid; Environment; Hospitals (general); Children/youth, services.
Types of support: General/operating support; Equipment; Scholarship funds.
Limitations: Giving limited to residents of Cape May County, NJ.
Application information:
Initial approach: Letter
Deadline(s): None
Final notification: Within 2 months
Officers: William K. Grauer, Chair., Fin. Comm.; Byron T. Mercer, Chair., Dist. Comm.; John M. Milne, Secy.; William O. Kruger, Treas., Dist. Comm.; James Cartlidge, Fin. Comm.; Donald E. Rose, Fin. Comm.; Robert Clark, Dist. Comm.
EIN: 226441627

1898
The Fund for New Jersey ▼
94 Church St., Ste. 303
New Brunswick, NJ 08901 (732) 220-8656
Contact: Mark M. Murphy, Exec. Dir.
FAX: (732) 220-8654; *URL:* http://www.fundfornj.org

Incorporated in 1969 in NJ as successor to The Florence Murray Wallace Fund established in 1958.
Donor(s): Charles F. Wallace,‡ and members of his family.
Grantmaker type: Independent foundation
Financial data (yr. ended 12/31/01): Assets, $70,882,033 (M); expenditures, $4,397,228; qualifying distributions, $3,869,636; giving activities include $3,275,365 for 115 grants (high: $150,000; low: $107; average: $30,000–$75,000).
Purpose and activities: Emphasis on projects which provide the basis for public action on state or local problems by way of research, litigation, citizen action, or supervision of government in the areas of social and economic opportunity, environment and land use, and public policy in New Jersey.
Fields of interest: Education; Environment, land resources; Environment; AIDS; Minorities/immigrants, centers/services; Community development; Public policy, research; Government/public administration; Public affairs; Minorities.
Types of support: General/operating support; Continuing support; Program development; Conferences/seminars; Publication; Seed money; Research; Matching/challenge support.
Limitations: Giving primarily in NJ or to regional programs that benefit NJ. No support for recreation, day care centers, drug treatment programs, health care delivery, curricular changes in educational institutions, or arts programs. No grants to individuals, or for capital projects, equipment, endowment funds, scholarships, or fellowships.
Publications: Annual report (including application guidelines).
Application information: Application form not required.
Initial approach: Letter
Copies of proposal: 1
Deadline(s): None
Board meeting date(s): Mar., June, Sept., and Dec.
Final notification: 2 weeks after board meeting
Officers and Trustees:* Leonard Lieberman,* Chair.; Clement A. Price,* Pres.; Candace McKee Ashmun,* V.P.; Mark M. Murphy, Secy. and Exec. Dir.; Gary D. Rose,* Treas.; William O. Baker; John W. Cornwall; Joseph C. Cornwall; Hon. Dickinson R. Debevoise; Linda Dennery; Susan H. Fuhrman; Hon. John J. Gibbons; Gustav Heningburg; Lawrence S. Lustberg; Melvin R. Primas, Jr.; Richard J. Sullivan; Jane W. Thorne, Tr. Emeritus; Richard L. Wright.
Number of staff: 2 full-time professional; 1 part-time professional; 1 full-time support.
EIN: 221895028
Recent environmental and animal welfare grants:
1898-1 Association of New Jersey Environmental Commissions, Mendham, NJ, $50,000. For renewed support to provide

environmental commissions, local officials and interested citizens with training and tools that protect natural resources and promote good environmental planning. 2002.
1898-2 Clean Ocean Action, Highlands, NJ, $30,000. For renewed operating support for Changing Tides campaign to address legal challenges involved in attacking water quality impacts from wastewater treatment facilities and non-point source pollution. 2002.
1898-3 Clean Water Fund, Belmar, NJ, $50,000. For renewed support to expand programs state-wide, recruit new leaders, and diversify grassroots fundraising base. 2002.
1898-4 Clean Water Fund, Belmar, NJ, $40,000. For renewed support to implement crafted, targeted Stop Sprawl paid media campaign. 2002.
1898-5 Coalition for Affordable Housing and the Environment, Trenton, NJ, $75,000. For renewed operational support to promote goals of protecting environment, providing affordable housing and revitalizing urban communities. 2002.
1898-6 Delaware Riverkeeper Network, Washington Crossing, PA, $30,000. For renewed support to advocate for alternative methods of storm water runoff to lessen impact on Delaware River watershed. 2002.
1898-7 Eastern Environmental Law Center, Rutgers School of Law, Newark, NJ, $100,000. For renewed operational support to provide legal counsel to New Jersey environmental organizations. 2002.
1898-8 Hackensack Riverkeeper, Teaneck, NJ, $30,000. For renewed operational support to protect and defend environmental quality of ecosystem of estuary, river, and watershed. 2002.
1898-9 Isles, Trenton, NJ, $25,000. For Mercer Regional Project to educate citizens and community leaders on social and economic trends in county, and work on solutions to address housing, tax reform, education and land use issues. 2002.
1898-10 New Jersey Academy for Aquatic Sciences, Camden, NJ, $25,000. For renewed operational support for CAUSE, exemplary science education program for Camden city youth. 2002.
1898-11 New York-New Jersey BayKeeper, Highlands, NJ, $30,000. For renewed support to protect, preserve and restore ecological integrity and productivity of Hudson-Raritan Estuary through education of public and decision-makers, and advocacy of Public Trust Doctrine. 2002.
1898-12 Pinelands Preservation Alliance, Pemberton, NJ, $50,000. For renewed operational support to protect Pinelands resources and monitor work of Pinelands Commission. 2002.
1898-13 Skylands CLEAN, Ringwood, NJ, $30,000. For renewed operating support to organize communities in Skylands region of Highlands to counter environmentally destructive development threats and advocate for preservation of region's water resources. 2002.
1898-14 Stony Brook-Millstone Watershed Association, Pennington, NJ, $70,000. For renewed operational support for Natural Lands Network and Geographic Information

Service Center projects aimed at combating sprawl, including developing model for management of municipal water resources. 2002.

1898-15 Tri-State Transportation Campaign, New York, NY, $65,000. For renewed operational support to advocate for state policies and priorities that favor public transportation and fix-it first anti-sprawl infrastructure investments. 2002.

1898-16 Work Environment Council of New Jersey, Trenton, NJ, $25,000. For renewed operational support to advocate for strong worker and community right-to-know laws regarding toxic chemical plants. 2002.

1899
The Bulova Gale Foundation
c/o Maurice Silberman
7 Orchid Ct.
Princeton, NJ 08540

Established in 1997 in NY.
Grantmaker type: Independent foundation
Financial data (yr. ended 12/31/01): Assets, $2,484,245 (M); expenditures, $222,175; qualifying distributions, $211,687; giving activities include $205,800 for 16 grants (high: $40,000; low: $3,600).
Purpose and activities: Giving primarily for education, health care, the arts, and Jewish organizations.
Fields of interest: Arts; Elementary/secondary education; Education; Animal welfare; Hospitals (general); Health organizations, association; Parks/playgrounds; Human services; Jewish agencies & temples.
Limitations: Applications not accepted. Giving primarily in CA, NM, and NY. No grants to individuals.
Application information: Contributes only to pre-selected organizations.
Officers and Directors:* Peter Gale,* Pres.; Lynn Gale,* V.P. and Secy.; Barbara Maisel,* V.P. and Treas.
EIN: 133866091

1900
Gibson Family Foundation, Inc.
58 Lyons Pl.
Basking Ridge, NJ 07920

Established in 1993 in NJ.
Donor(s): James G. Gibson.
Grantmaker type: Independent foundation
Financial data (yr. ended 12/31/02): Assets, $2,857,920 (M); expenditures, $388,603; qualifying distributions, $350,037; giving activities include $350,037 for 32 grants (high: $100,000; low: $1,000).
Purpose and activities: Giving for environmental conservation, higher education, and human services.
Fields of interest: Natural resources; Housing/shelter, development; General charitable giving.
Limitations: Applications not accepted. Giving primarily in NJ. No grants to individuals.
Application information: Contributes only to pre-selected organizations.
Officers and Trustees:* James G. Gibson,* Pres.; Jill R. Gibson,* Secy.

EIN: 223197727

1901
Salvatore Giordano Foundation, Inc.
154-4 Mountview Ln.
Bernardsville, NJ 07924

Established in 1949.
Donor(s): Salvatore Giordano, Sr., Salvatore Giordano, Jr., Joseph Giordano.
Grantmaker type: Independent foundation
Financial data (yr. ended 07/31/02): Assets, $1,884,388 (M); gifts received, $141,500; expenditures, $142,619; qualifying distributions, $131,235; giving activities include $132,000 for 4 grants (high: $100,000; low: $2,000).
Fields of interest: Higher education; Natural resources.
Limitations: Applications not accepted. Giving primarily on the East Coast, with emphasis on MA and NY. No grants to individuals.
Application information: Contributes only to pre-selected organizations.
Officers: Salvatore Giordano, Sr., Pres. and Treas.; Joseph Giordano, V.P.; Salvatore Giordano, Jr., V.P.
EIN: 116003606

1902
The Goldring Family Foundation, Inc.
51 J.F.K. Parkway, 4th Fl.
Short Hills, NJ 07078

Established in 1995 in NJ.
Donor(s): Education for Youth Society, Gary F. Goldring.
Grantmaker type: Independent foundation
Financial data (yr. ended 09/30/02): Assets, $12,895,953 (M); gifts received, $4,174,554; expenditures, $546,260; qualifying distributions, $522,853; giving activities include $522,793 for grants (high: $250,000).
Purpose and activities: Giving primarily for education, community, children and Jewish organizations.
Fields of interest: Higher education; Graduate/professional education; Environment, land resources; Recreation, formal/general education; Camps; Children/youth, services; Foundations (community); Jewish agencies & temples.
Limitations: Applications not accepted. Giving primarily in NJ and NY. No grants to individuals.
Application information: Contributes only to pre-selected organizations.
Officers: Gary F. Goldring, Pres. and Treas.; Paul Wolansky, V.P. and Secy.
EIN: 223407792

1903
The Goldsmith Family Charitable Foundation, Inc.
125 Half Mile Rd., Ste. 202
Red Bank, NJ 07701

Established in 1996 in NJ.
Donor(s): Bernard M. Goldsmith III.
Grantmaker type: Independent foundation
Financial data (yr. ended 12/31/02): Assets, $305,614 (M); expenditures, $121,968;

qualifying distributions, $120,573; giving activities include $120,553 for 24 grants (high: $25,803; low: $250).
Fields of interest: Natural resources; Public health.
Types of support: General/operating support.
Limitations: Applications not accepted. No grants to individuals.
Application information: Contributes only to pre-selected organizations.
Officer and Trustees:* Bernard M. Goldstein III,* Pres.; David Goldsmith; Nadine Goldsmith; Sarah R. Goldsmith; Daphne Amanda Kennedy.
EIN: 223482670

1904
E. J. Grassmann Trust
P.O. Box 4470
Warren, NJ 07059   (908) 753-2440
Contact: William V. Engel, Exec. Dir.

Trust established in 1979 in NJ.
Donor(s): Edward J. Grassmann.‡
Grantmaker type: Independent foundation
Financial data (yr. ended 12/31/01): Assets, $33,319,460 (M); expenditures, $1,916,880; qualifying distributions, $1,869,149; giving activities include $1,762,444 for 191 grants (high: $110,000; low: $2,000; average: $5,000–$20,000).
Purpose and activities: Grants for educational institutions, local hospitals and health organizations, organizations engaged in ecological endeavors, and social welfare organizations, particularly those helping children. Preference given to organizations with low administration costs, and which show efforts to achieve a broad funding base.
Fields of interest: Historic preservation/historical societies; Education, fund raising; Secondary school/education; Higher education; Education; Natural resources; Environment; Hospitals (general); Health care; Health organizations, association; Human services; Children/youth, services.
Types of support: Capital campaigns; Building/renovation; Equipment; Land acquisition; Endowments.
Limitations: Giving primarily in GA, primarily middle GA, and in NJ, with emphasis on Union County. No grants to individuals, or for operating expenses, current scholarship funds, conferences, or workshops.
Publications: Application guidelines.
Application information: Application form not required.
   Initial approach: Letter, no more than 4 pages
   Copies of proposal: 1
   Deadline(s): Apr. 20 and Oct. 15
   Board meeting date(s): May or June and Nov.
   Final notification: After May or June meeting by July 31; after Nov. meeting by Dec. 31
Officer and Trustees:* William V. Engel,* Exec. Dir.; Hunter W. Carbin; Suzanne B. Engel; Haydn H. Murray; Henry S. Patterson II.
Number of staff: 1 part-time professional; 2 part-time support.
EIN: 226326539

1905
Harbourton Foundation
47 Hulfish St., Ste. 305
Princeton, NJ 08542

Established in 1982 in NJ.
Donor(s): James S. Regan.
Grantmaker type: Independent foundation
Financial data (yr. ended 06/30/02): Assets, $3,628,007 (M); expenditures, $852,912; qualifying distributions, $667,285; giving activities include $668,675 for 20 grants (high: $189,000; low: $2,000).
Purpose and activities: Support for educational associations, including those seeking to identify learning disabilities of economically disadvantaged children.
Fields of interest: Education, association; Natural resources; Children/youth, services.
Types of support: General/operating support.
Limitations: Applications not accepted. Giving primarily in NJ. No grants to individuals.
Application information: Contributes only to pre-selected organizations.
Officers: James S. Regan, Pres.; Sanford B. Bing, Exec. V.P.; Amy H. Regan, V.P.
EIN: 222436112

1906
The Harris Foundation for the Living Environment, Inc.
c/o Robert & Stephanie Harris
163 Hopewell-Wertsville Rd.
Hopewell, NJ 08525

Established in 1992 in NJ.
Donor(s): Robert H. Harris, Stephanie G. Harris.
Grantmaker type: Independent foundation
Financial data (yr. ended 06/30/02): Assets, $1,916,169 (M); expenditures, $111,290; qualifying distributions, $102,396; giving activities include $103,514 for 7 grants (high: $26,250; low: $2,000).
Purpose and activities: Giving primarily for education and the environment.
Fields of interest: Education; Natural resources.
Types of support: General/operating support.
Limitations: Applications not accepted. Giving primarily in New York, NY. No grants to individuals.
Application information: Contributes only to pre-selected organizations.
Officers: Robert H. Harris, Pres.; Stephanie G. Harris, Treas.
Director: Alexander Harris.
EIN: 521743475

1907
Hickory Foundation
P.O. Box 281
Lambertville, NJ 08530

Established in 1997 in NY.
Donor(s): Virginia Manheimer.
Grantmaker type: Independent foundation
Financial data (yr. ended 12/31/01): Assets, $12,037,892 (M); gifts received, $1,796,445; expenditures, $1,763,614; qualifying distributions, $2,144,551; giving activities include $1,669,865 for 56 grants (high: $257,000; low: $780; average: $1,000–$100,000).

Purpose and activities: Giving primarily for education, federated giving programs, and public affairs.
Fields of interest: Media/communications; Historic preservation/historical societies; Arts; Education; Environment; Hospitals (general); Human services; Children, services; Federated giving programs; Social sciences, public policy; Public affairs.
Limitations: Applications not accepted. Giving primarily in NY.
Application information: Contributes only to pre-selected organizations.
Officer: Virginia Manheimer, Pres.
EIN: 223472805

1908
The Hilfiger Family Foundation, Inc.
c/o Graham, Curtin & Sheridan
P.O. Box 1991
Morristown, NJ 07962-1991

Established in 1999 in CT.
Donor(s): Thomas J. Hilfiger, Susan D. Hilfiger.
Grantmaker type: Independent foundation
Financial data (yr. ended 12/31/02): Assets, $17,379 (M); gifts received, $780,000; expenditures, $775,699; qualifying distributions, $770,994; giving activities include $771,000 for 8 grants (high: $600,000; low: $1,000).
Purpose and activities: Giving primarily for the arts, education, natural resource conservation, children and social services, and Roman Catholic churches and organizations.
Fields of interest: Arts; Higher education; Education; Natural resources; Cancer; Human services; Children, services; Roman Catholic agencies & churches.
Limitations: Applications not accepted. Giving primarily in NY. No grants to individuals.
Application information: Contributes only to pre-selected organizations.
Officers and Directors:* Thomas R. Curtin,* Pres.; Susan D. Hilfiger,* Secy.; Joseph M. Lamastra,* Treas.; Thomas J. Hilfiger.
EIN: 223626164

1909
Thomas A. and Joan M. Holmes Foundation, Inc.
200 Chestnut Ridge Rd.
Woodcliff Lake, NJ 07677-7703

Established in 1986 in NJ.
Donor(s): Thomas A. Holmes, Joan M. Holmes.
Grantmaker type: Independent foundation
Financial data (yr. ended 11/30/01): Assets, $741,594 (M); gifts received, $99,875; expenditures, $110,924; qualifying distributions, $110,924; giving activities include $107,916 for 23 grants (high: $75,000; low: $150).
Purpose and activities: Giving for Christian churches and higher education.
Fields of interest: Arts; Higher education; Natural resources; Human services; Christian agencies & churches.
Limitations: Applications not accepted. Giving on a national basis. No grants to individuals.
Application information: Contributes only to pre-selected organizations.
Officers: Thomas A. Holmes, Pres.; Joan M. Holmes, Secy.

Trustee: G. Burtt Holmes.
EIN: 222766121

1910
Honeywell Foundation
101 Columbia Rd.
Morristown, NJ 07962 (973) 455-5876
Contact: Andre Lewis, Exec. Dir.
FAX: (612) 951-0433; URL: http://www.honeywell.com/about/foundation.html

Incorporated in 1958 in MN.
Donor(s): Honeywell Inc.
Grantmaker type: Company-sponsored foundation
Financial data (yr. ended 12/31/00): Assets, $759,628 (M); gifts received, $5,365,151; expenditures, $7,083,690; qualifying distributions, $7,077,326; giving activities include $6,491,648 for 238 grants (high: $1,589,981; low: $39; average: $1,000–$25,000), $20,727 for 36 grants to individuals (high: $4,000; low: $93; average: $250–$500) and $551,129 for employee matching gifts.
Purpose and activities: Grants primarily for higher education, community funds, cultural programs, and youth agencies.
Fields of interest: Visual arts; Museums; Performing arts; Dance; Theater; Music; Arts; Early childhood education; Child development, education; Elementary school/education; Secondary school/education; Higher education; Adult education—literacy, basic skills & GED; Reading; Education; Energy; Environment; Employment; Housing/shelter, development; Youth development, services; Human services; Children/youth, services; Child development, services; Family services; Women, centers/services; Minorities/immigrants, centers/services; Community development; Voluntarism promotion; Leadership development; Minorities; Women.
Types of support: General/operating support; Continuing support; Annual campaigns; Capital campaigns; Program development; Seed money; Employee matching gifts; Grants to individuals.
Limitations: Giving limited to cities where the company has major facilities, with emphasis on Minneapolis, MN; support also in AZ, FL, IL, and NM. No support for religious denominations for support of denominational causes; or political, fraternal, veterans', or professional organizations. No grants to individuals (except for Teacher Mini-Grants), or for general endowment funds, deficit financing, fundraising, land acquisition, matching or challenge grants, research, demonstration projects, conferences, testimonial events, athletic scholarships, advertising, publications, or production of films or special broadcasts; no loans.
Publications: Application guidelines, Informational brochure (including application guidelines).
Application information: Application form required for Educational Mini-Grants only.
Initial approach: Proposal; local agencies should send proposals to nearest company manufacturing facility
Copies of proposal: 1
Deadline(s): None
Board meeting date(s): July and Dec.

Final notification: 2 to 3 months
Officers and Directors: Kevin J. Gilligan,*
Chair.; Andre Lewis, Pres.; Gerald C.
Vandevoort,* V.P.; Sarah Hernandez, Secy.; Rita
Williams, Treas.; Kris Burhardt; Brad Morton;
Albrecht Weiss.
Number of staff: 5 part-time professional; 2
full-time support; 3 part-time support.
EIN: 416023933

1911
The Hyde and Watson Foundation ▼
437 Southern Blvd.
Chatham, NJ 07928 (973) 966-6024
Contact: Hunter W. Corbin, Pres.
FAX: (973) 966-6404; E-mail:
Hcorbin@HydeandWatson.org; URL: http://
fdncenter.org/grantmaker/hydeandwatson

The Lillia Babbitt Hyde Foundation incorporated
in 1924 in NY; The John Jay and Eliza Jane
Watson Foundation incorporated in 1949;
consolidation of two foundations into Hyde and
Watson Foundation in 1983.
Donor(s): Lillia Babbitt Hyde,‡ Eliza Jane
Watson.‡
Grantmaker type: Independent foundation
Financial data (yr. ended 12/31/02): Assets,
$99,604,186 (M); expenditures, $5,258,472;
qualifying distributions, $5,241,946; giving
activities include $4,497,750 for 307 grants
(high: $150,000; low: $3,500; average:
$5,000–$25,000).
Purpose and activities: Support for capital
projects such as purchase or relocation of
facilities, building improvements, capital
equipment, instructive materials development,
and certain medical research areas. Broad fields
include health, education, religion, social
services, arts, and humanities.
Fields of interest: Performing arts; Humanities;
Arts; Early childhood education; Child
development, education; Elementary
school/education; Secondary school/education;
Medical school/education; Education; Natural
resources; Environment; Hospitals (general);
Medical care, rehabilitation; Health care;
Substance abuse, services; Mental health/crisis
services; Health organizations, association;
Cancer; Medical research, institute; Cancer
research; AIDS research; Human services;
Children/youth, services; Child development,
services; Family services; Aging,
centers/services; Minorities/immigrants,
centers/services; Homeless, human services;
Religion; Minorities; Disabled; Aging;
Economically disadvantaged; Homeless.
Types of support: Capital campaigns;
Building/renovation; Equipment; Land
acquisition; Debt reduction; Emergency funds;
Research; Technical assistance;
Matching/challenge support.
Limitations: Giving includes the metropolitan
New York, NY, region, and primarily Essex,
Union and Morris counties in NJ. No giving
outside the U.S. No grants to individuals, or
generally for operating budgets, continuing
support, annual campaigns, general
endowments, deficit financing, scholarships, or
fellowships.
Publications: Application guidelines, Annual
report (including application guidelines),
Program policy statement.

Application information: Supplemental
information may be required if proposal is
considered by grants committee. The foundation
also accepts the New York/New Jersey Area
Common Application Form but prefers its own
application procedure. Application form
required.
 Initial approach: Letter with grant application
  information sheet, which is available by fax
  or at the foundation's Web site, and
  attachments
 Copies of proposal: 1
 Deadline(s): Submit letter of appeal with
  completed grant application information
  sheet and attachments by Feb. 15 for spring
  meeting and by Sept. 15 for fall meeting.
  There is an ongoing preliminary review of
  proposals, therefore, early submission is
  encouraged
 Board meeting date(s): Apr./May and
  Nov./Dec.
 Final notification: After grant or board meeting
Officers and Directors:* John W. Holman, Jr.,*
Chair.; Hunter W. Corbin,* Pres.; Thomas M.
Moriarty, V.P.; William V. Engel,* Secy.; Thomas
W. Berry,* Treas.; Elizabeth R. Curry; H. Corbin
Day; Jennifer Chandler Hauge; John W. Holman
III; Robert W. Parsons, Jr.; Roger B. Parsons; Kate
B. Wood.
Number of staff: 6 full-time professional.
EIN: 222425725

1912
The International Foundation
271 Rte. 46 West G110
Fairfield, NJ 07004 (973) 227-6107
Contact: Dr. Edward A. Holmes, Grants Chair.
Additional tel.: (973) 227-6618; FAX: (973)
227-6821

Incorporated in 1948 in DE.
Grantmaker type: Independent foundation
Financial data (yr. ended 12/31/02): Assets,
$24,692,142 (M); expenditures, $1,713,510;
qualifying distributions, $1,203,300; giving
activities include $1,203,300 for 102 grants.
Purpose and activities: Giving to help people of
developing nations in their endeavors to solve
some of their problems, to attain a better
standard of living, and to obtain a reasonable
degree of self-sufficiency. Grants are made in
general areas: 1) Agriculture: research and
production, 2) Health: medical, nutrition, and
water, 3) Education: formal at all levels research,
4) Social Development: cultural, economic,
community, and entrepreneurial activity, and
some aid to refugees, and grants for population
planning are given, and 5) Environment.
Fields of interest: Arts; Libraries/library science;
Education; Natural resources; Environment;
Hospitals (general); Medical care, rehabilitation;
Health care; Health organizations, association;
AIDS; Biomedicine; Medical research, institute;
AIDS research; Agriculture; Food services;
Human services; International economic
development; Urban/community development;
Rural development; Voluntarism promotion;
Marine science; Engineering/technology;
Science; Roman Catholic agencies & churches.
International interests: Caribbean; Southern
Africa; Latin America; Oceania; Middle East;
Philippines.

Types of support: Building/renovation;
Equipment; Emergency funds; Program
development; Seed money; Matching/challenge
support.
Limitations: Giving primarily in Asia, the
Caribbean, Latin America, the Middle East, the
Philippines, the South Pacific, and Southern
Africa through U.S.-based philanthropies. No
grants to individuals, or for endowment funds,
operating budgets, scholarships, fellowships,
matching gifts, video productions, or
conferences; no loans.
Publications: Informational brochure (including
application guidelines).
Application information: Application should
include a SASE for reply. Application form
required.
 Initial approach: Letter requesting descriptive
  brochure
 Copies of proposal: 2
 Deadline(s): None
 Board meeting date(s): Jan., Apr., July, and Oct.
 Final notification: 6 months; grants paid in
  Dec.
Officers and Trustees:* Edward A. Holmes,*
Grants Chair.; Gary Dicovitsky,* Fin. Chair.;
Frank Madden,* Pres.; David S. Bate,* V.P.; John
D. Carrico,* Secy.-Treas.; Duncan W. Clark,
M.D.; William McCormack, M.D.
Number of staff: 1 part-time professional; 1
part-time support.
EIN: 131962255

1913
The James Family Charitable Foundation
c/o DLJ Asset Mgmt. Group
1 Pershing Plz., 10th Fl.
Jersey City, NJ 07399
Contact: Mike Cappiccille

Established in 1994 in DE and NY.
Donor(s): Amabel B. James, Hamilton E. James.
Grantmaker type: Independent foundation
Financial data (yr. ended 12/31/00): Assets,
$9,749,088 (M); gifts received, $258,146;
expenditures, $1,012,690; qualifying
distributions, $921,434; giving activities include
$941,113 for 65 grants (high: $250,000; low:
$45).
Fields of interest: Secondary school/education;
Animals/wildlife, preservation/protection;
Hospitals (general); Diabetes research; Boys
clubs; Boy scouts; Christian agencies &
churches.
Limitations: Applications not accepted. No
grants to individuals.
Application information: Contributes only to
pre-selected organizations.
Officers: Hamilton E. James, Pres. and Treas.;
Amabel B. James, V.P. and Secy.
EIN: 137051493

1914
The Jaqua Foundation
100 Campus Dr.
P.O. Box 944
Florham Park, NJ 07932-0944 (973) 593-7000
Contact: Eli Hoffman, Chair.
URL: http://fdncenter.org/grantmaker/jaqua/

Established in 1977.
Donor(s): George R. Jaqua.‡

Grantmaker type: Independent foundation
Financial data (yr. ended 12/31/01): Assets, $11,466,113 (M); expenditures, $3,689,356; qualifying distributions, $3,566,959; giving activities include $3,567,199 for 80 grants (high: $500,000; low: $500; average: $2,500–$100,000).
Purpose and activities: Giving primarily for the arts and for education.
Fields of interest: Performing arts; Elementary/secondary education; Higher education; Animal welfare; Health care.
Limitations: No support for private foundations. No grants to individuals.
Application information: Application form not required.
  Initial approach: Letter
  Deadline(s): None
  Board meeting date(s): 4 times a year
Officers: Eli Hoffman, Chair.; W. Fletcher Hock, Jr., Secy.
Number of staff: 1 part-time support.
EIN: 222086399
Recent environmental and animal welfare grants:
1914-1 Animal Medical Center, New York, NY, $200,000. For endowment fund. 2001.
1914-2 Animal Medical Center, New York, NY, $50,000. For general support. 2001.
1914-3 Newark Beth Israel Medical Center, Newark, NJ, $25,000. For general support of animal lab. 2001.

1915
Clara L. D. Jeffery Charitable Trust
c/o Fleet National Bank, NJRP47402C
1125 Rt. 22 W.
Bridgewater, NJ 08807 (908) 253-4863
Contact: Cindy Leip

Trust established in 1969.
Donor(s): Clara L.D. Jeffery.‡
Grantmaker type: Independent foundation
Financial data (yr. ended 12/31/02): Assets, $7,291,095 (M); expenditures, $385,588; qualifying distributions, $367,524; giving activities include $317,000 for grants.
Purpose and activities: Giving primarily for education, conservation, and animal welfare.
Fields of interest: Education; Natural resources; Animals/wildlife.
Limitations: Giving on a national basis. No grants to individuals.
Application information: Application form not required.
  Initial approach: Letter
  Copies of proposal: 1
  Deadline(s): None
  Final notification: Varies
Trustees: Coleman P. Burke, Jr.; Daniel Burke II; Mary B. Partridge; Fleet National Bank.
EIN: 226138410

1916
The Jockey Hollow Foundation, Inc.
P.O. Box 462
Bernardsville, NJ 07924
Contact: Betsy S. Michel, Pres.

Incorporated in 1960 in NJ.
Donor(s): Carl Shirley,‡ Mrs. Carl Shirley.
Grantmaker type: Independent foundation

Financial data (yr. ended 03/31/02): Assets, $23,626,946 (M); expenditures, $1,146,964; qualifying distributions, $1,033,335; giving activities include $1,026,819 for 136 grants (high: $50,000; low: $35).
Purpose and activities: Giving primarily for the arts, education, and health programs.
Fields of interest: Arts; Education; Natural resources; Hospitals (general).
Limitations: Giving primarily in MA and NJ. No grants to individuals.
Application information: Application form not required.
  Initial approach: Proposal
  Copies of proposal: 1
  Deadline(s): None
  Board meeting date(s): Feb. and June
Officers and Trustees:* Betsy S. Michel,* Pres. and Secy.; Clifford L. Michel,* V.P. and Treas.; Joanne S. Gill,* V.P.; Thomas Gill, V.P.; Betsy B. Shirley, V.P.
EIN: 221724138

1917
Johnson & Johnson Corporate Giving Program
c/o Corp. Contribs. Dept.
1 Johnson & Johnson Plz.
New Brunswick, NJ 08933 (732) 524-3061
Contact: Helen M. Hughes, Dir., Corp. Contribs.
Application address for Community Health Care Prog.: Sierra Veale, Johnson & Johnson Community Health Care Prog., 615 N. Wolfe St., Ste. E2100, Baltimore, MD 21205, tel.: (443) 287-5138, FAX: (410) 510-1974; Additional contacts: International Programs and Product Donations: Conrad Person, Dir., Intl. Progs./Product Giving, Arts/Culture, K-12 Education, and Employee Volunteer Services: Michael J. Bzdak, Dir., Corp. Contribs., FAX: (732) 524-3300; URL: http://www.jnj.com/community/index.htm

Grantmaker type: Corporate giving program
Purpose and activities: Johnson & Johnson makes charitable contributions to nonprofit organizations involved with arts and culture, education, the environment, health and human services, substance abuse, medical research, employment, international relief, and disabled people. Support is given on a national and international basis.
Fields of interest: Arts; Nursing school/education; Education; Environment; Public health; Health care, cost containment; Health care; Substance abuse, services; Medical research; Employment, services; Children, services; Human services; International relief; Disabled.
Types of support: Program development; Fellowships; Internship funds; Research; Sponsorships; Employee matching gifts; Donated products.
Limitations: Giving on a national and international basis; giving limited to AL, Los Angeles, CA, GA, Baltimore, MD, NJ, and TX for Community Health Care Program. No support for sectarian religious organizations not of direct benefit to the entire community or political, fraternal, or athletic organizations; no support for foundations or universities for Community Health Care Program. No grants to individuals, or for general operating support, scholarships,

trips or tours, endowments, or capital campaigns; no loans.
Publications: Corporate giving report.
Application information: Unsolicited requests other than through the Community Health Care Program are not accepted. An application form is required for the Community Health Care Program; application form available online. The Corporate Contributions Department handles giving. The company has a staff that only handles contributions. A selection panel reviews all requests for Community Health Care Program.
  Initial approach: Complete online application form and fax letter of support from organization Chairman or C.E.O., collaborating or endorsing letter of support, and IRS determination letter to application address fax number for Community Health Care Program
  Deadline(s): Oct. 31 for Community Health Care Program
Number of staff: 10 full-time professional; 3 part-time professional.

1918
Barbara Piasecka Johnson Foundation
c/o Danser Balaam & Frank
5 Independence Way
Princeton, NJ 08540 (609) 688-1030
Contact: Beata Piasecka

Established in 1976 in DE.
Donor(s): Barbara Piasecka Johnson, J. Seward Johnson, Sr.‡
Grantmaker type: Independent foundation
Financial data (yr. ended 12/31/02): Assets, $3,074,800 (M); gifts received, $358,637; expenditures, $227,112; qualifying distributions, $182,448; giving activities include $123,898 for 11 grants (high: $47,513; low: $500) and $38,414 for 8 grants to individuals (high: $20,617; low: $300).
Purpose and activities: To support institutions which promote human rights in Poland, promote institutions of Polish character in the U.S. and abroad, and support artists and scientists, primarily those who are Polish or of Polish extraction, and institutions which support such individuals.
Fields of interest: Journalism/publishing; Visual arts; Museums; Performing arts; Language/linguistics; Literature; Arts; Higher education; Medical school/education; Adult/continuing education; Libraries/library science; Education; Natural resources; Environment; Heart & circulatory diseases; Medical research, institute; Heart & circulatory research; International human rights; International affairs; Civil rights; Engineering/technology; Biological sciences; Science; International studies; Religion; Economically disadvantaged.
International interests: Monaco; Poland.
Limitations: Giving limited for the benefit of Poland.
Publications: Application guidelines.
Application information: Contributes generally only to pre-selected organizations. Scholarships and fellowships are for graduate, doctoral and postgraduate education only; no undergraduate programs considered. Application form required.
  Initial approach: Letter or telephone

Copies of proposal: 1
Deadline(s): Mar. 30 and Sept. 1; all
   considered within 3-month basis
Board meeting date(s): July
Trustees: Barbara Piasecka Johnson; Beata P.
Piasecka; Christopher Piasecki; Gregory
Piasecki; Wojciech Piasecki.
Number of staff: 1 part-time professional; 1
part-time support.
EIN: 510201795

1919
The Joyce and Seward Johnson
Foundation, Inc.
P.O. Box 369
Hopewell, NJ 08525
Contact: J. Seward Johnson, Jr., Pres.
Application address: c/o Matthews & Co., 331
Madison Ave., New York, NY 10017

Established in 1990 in NJ.
Donor(s): J. Seward Johnson, Jr., J. Seward
Johnson, Jr. Charitable Annuity Lead Trust.
Grantmaker type: Independent foundation
Financial data (yr. ended 12/31/02): Assets,
$2,851,992 (M); gifts received, $328,876;
expenditures, $411,310; qualifying distributions,
$409,712; giving activities include $409,712 for
49 grants (high: $50,000; low: $250).
Purpose and activities: Giving primarily for
education and the arts.
Fields of interest: Theater; Arts; Higher
education; Education; Natural resources;
Hospitals (general).
Limitations: Giving primarily in Key West, FL,
Nantucket, MA, and New York, NY. No grants to
individuals.
Application information: Application form not
required.
   Deadline(s): None
Officers: J. Seward Johnson, Jr., Pres. and Treas.;
Joyce H. Johnson, V.P. and Secy.
Trustees: Garrett M. Heher; Robert S. Matthews.
EIN: 223048720

1920
JSY Foundation, Inc.
65 Livingston Ave.
Roseland, NJ 07068

Established in 1998 in NJ.
Donor(s): Rhonda Management, LLC.
Grantmaker type: Independent foundation
Financial data (yr. ended 11/30/01): Assets,
$42,554,845 (M); gifts received, $36,000,000;
expenditures, $263,000; qualifying distributions,
$233,830; giving activities include $250,000 for
1 grant.
Fields of interest: Environment.
Limitations: Applications not accepted. Giving
primarily in Oak Glen, CA. No grants to
individuals.
Application information: Contributes only to
pre-selected organizations.
Officers and Trustees: Kenneth J. Slutsky,*
Pres.; Allen Levithan,* V.P.
EIN: 223692917

1921
Kap Foundation, Inc.
c/o Andrew Kogan
P.O. Box K
Whippany, NJ 07981

Established in 1998 in NJ.
Donor(s): Richard J. Kogan.
Grantmaker type: Independent foundation
Financial data (yr. ended 12/31/01): Assets,
$2,079,312 (M); expenditures, $139,055;
qualifying distributions, $127,730; giving
activities include $119,000 for 17 grants (high:
$17,000; low: $1,000).
Fields of interest: Higher education; Education;
Animals/wildlife; Religion.
Limitations: Giving primarily in NJ.
Officers: Andrew Kogan, Pres.; Pamela Kogan,
Secy.-Treas.
Trustee: Thomas J. Ross.
EIN: 223592670

1922
The Kemmerer Family Foundation, Inc.
c/o Kemmerer Resources Corp.
323 Main St.
Chatham, NJ 07928

Established in 2000 in NJ.
Grantmaker type: Independent foundation
Financial data (yr. ended 12/31/02): Assets,
$45,137,302 (M); expenditures, $1,691,740;
qualifying distributions, $1,556,160; giving
activities include $1,548,000 for 15 grants (high:
$500,000; low: $15,000).
Fields of interest: Higher education; University;
Education; Natural resources; Hospitals
(general); Foundations (community); Christian
agencies & churches; Protestant agencies &
churches.
Limitations: Applications not accepted. Giving
primarily in NJ and WY. No grants to individuals.
Application information: Contributes only to
pre-selected organizations.
Officers: John L. Kemmerer, III, Pres.; Constance
A. Kemmerer, Secy.; Elizabeth K. Gray, Treas.
EIN: 223706044

1923
The William A. Kerr Foundation
P.O. Box 1525
Pennington, NJ 08534-1525

Established in 1998 in WA.
Grantmaker type: Independent foundation
Financial data (yr. ended 12/31/02): Assets,
$14,814,003 (M); expenditures, $1,046,792;
qualifying distributions, $877,894; giving
activities include $863,000 for 31 grants (high:
$100,000; low: $1,000).
Purpose and activities: Support primarily for the
fine and performing arts, Jewish synagogues and
other religious organizations, mental health
services, and higher education, including
medical schools; giving also for community
services and recreation.
Fields of interest: Museums; Performing arts;
Theater; Arts; Higher education; Medical
school/education; Natural resources;
Animals/wildlife, preservation/protection; Jewish
agencies & temples.
Types of support: General/operating support.

Limitations: Applications not accepted. Giving
primarily in CA and MO, with emphasis on
Walnut Creek and St. Louis. No grants to
individuals.
Application information: Contributes only to
pre-selected organizations.
Trustees: John H.K. Sweet; William R. Sweet.
EIN: 431770857

1924
F. M. Kirby Foundation, Inc. ▼
17 DeHart St.
P.O. Box 151
Morristown, NJ 07963-0151 (973) 538-4800
Contact: F.M. Kirby, Pres.
URL: http://www.fdncenter.org/grantmaker/kirby

Incorporated in 1931 in DE.
Donor(s): F.M. Kirby,‡ Allan P. Kirby, Sr.‡
Grantmaker type: Independent foundation
Financial data (yr. ended 12/31/02): Assets,
$342,067,001 (M); expenditures, $22,251,484;
qualifying distributions, $19,965,583; giving
activities include $19,766,828 for 344 grants
(high: $1,200,000; low: $1,000; average:
$15,000–$60,000).
Purpose and activities: Support for higher and
secondary education, health and hospitals,
community programs, historic preservation,
church support and church-related
organizations, social services, conservation,
public policy organizations, and family
planning. Grants generally limited to
organizations associated with personal interests
of present or former family members.
Fields of interest: Performing arts; Humanities;
Historic preservation/historical societies; Arts;
Education; Natural resources; Family planning;
Health care; Health organizations, association;
AIDS; Biomedicine; Medical research, institute;
AIDS research; Recreation; Youth development,
services; Youth, services; Economics; Public
policy, research; Government/public
administration; Leadership development;
Religion.
Types of support: General/operating support;
Continuing support; Annual campaigns; Capital
campaigns; Building/renovation; Equipment;
Endowments; Emergency funds; Program
development; Conferences/seminars; Seed
money; Research.
Limitations: Giving primarily in
Raleigh-Durham, NC, Morris County, NJ, and
eastern PA. No grants to individuals, or for
fundraising benefits, dinners, theater, or sporting
events; no loans or pledges.
Publications: Informational brochure (including
application guidelines).
Application information: Application form not
required.
   Initial approach: Proposal with cover letter;
      telephone solicitations not considered
   Copies of proposal: 1
   Deadline(s): Proposals received throughout
      the year; requests received after Oct. 31 are
      held over to the following year
   Board meeting date(s): Three times per year
   Final notification: Monthly for positive
      responses only
Officers and Directors: F.M. Kirby,* Pres.; S.
Dillard Kirby,* Exec. V.P. and Exec. Dir.; Walker
D. Kirby,* V.P.; Thomas J. Bianchini,*

Secy.-Treas.; Alice Kirby Horton; Jefferson W. Kirby.
Number of staff: 2 full-time professional; 1 part-time professional; 1 full-time support; 1 part-time support.
EIN: 516017929
Recent environmental and animal welfare grants:
1924-1 Adirondack Council, Elizabethtown, NY, $30,000. For Acid Rain Awareness Campaign. 2002.
1924-2 Adirondack Nature Conservancy and Adirondack Land Trust, Keene Valley, NY, $65,000. For endowment components only of Headwater's Capital Campaign. 2002.
1924-3 Adirondack Nature Conservancy and Adirondack Land Trust, Keene Valley, NY, $25,000. For general operating support. 2002.
1924-4 Animal Medical Center, New York, NY, $15,000. Toward Guide Dog Program. 2002.
1924-5 Audubon Society of New Jersey, Bernardsville, NJ, $77,500. For construction costs at Scherman-Hoffman Wildlife Sanctuary Education Center. 2002.
1924-6 Brandywine Conservancy, Chadds Ford, PA, $20,000. For Building for a New Century capital campaign for museum construction. 2002.
1924-7 Carrying Capacity Network (CCN), DC, $40,000. For general operating support. 2002.
1924-8 Central Park Conservancy, New York, NY, $17,500. For general operating support. 2002.
1924-9 Duke University, Sarah P. Duke Gardens, Durham, NC, $58,400. Toward construction and upfitting of garden cottage food service courtyard. 2002.
1924-10 Environmental Defense, New York, NY, $75,000. For activities to reduce nitrogen pollution in Adirondacks. 2002.
1924-11 Great Swamp Watershed Association, New Vernon, NJ, $10,000. For general operating support. 2002.
1924-12 Greater Newark Conservancy, Newark, NJ, $25,000. For Community Greening Program. 2002.
1924-13 Morris Parks and Land Conservancy, Boonton, NJ, $15,000. For general operating support. 2002.
1924-14 Nature Conservancy, Chester, NJ, $100,000. Toward Saving Last Great Places of New Jersey campaign. 2002.
1924-15 Negative Population Growth, DC, $45,000. For general operating support. 2002.
1924-16 New Jersey Conservation Foundation, Far Hills, NJ, $75,000. For farmland protection initiatives. 2002.
1924-17 New York Botanical Garden, Bronx, NY, $35,000. For general operating support. 2002.
1924-18 North Carolina Outward Bound School, Asheville, NC, $12,000. For general operating support. 2002.
1924-19 Outward Bound, Garrison, NY, $10,000. For general operating support. 2002.

1924-20 Pinelands Preservation Alliance, Pemberton, NJ, $30,000. For general operating support. 2002.
1924-21 Population-Environment Balance, DC, $40,000. For general operating support. 2002.
1924-22 Rails to Trails Conservancy, DC, $27,500. For Rail-trail projects and New Jersey Initiative. 2002.
1924-23 Residents Committee to Protect the Adirondacks, North Creek, NY, $10,000. For Adirondack Park Sustainable Forestry Project. 2002.
1924-24 Seeing Eye, Morristown, NJ, $45,000. For general operating support. 2002.
1924-25 Trout Unlimited, Arlington, VA, $27,500. For general operating support. 2002.
1924-26 Trust for Public Land, New Jersey Field Office, Morristown, NJ, $50,000. For New Jersey Programs only. 2002.
1924-27 Wilderness Society, DC, $10,000. For general operating support. 2002.
1924-28 Wildlife Conservation Society, Bronx, NY, $22,500. For general operating support. 2002.
1924-29 Winterthur Museum, Garden & Library, Winterthur, DE, $40,000. For general operating support. 2002.

1925
The Thomas D. Klingenstein and Nancy D. Perlman Family Fund, Inc.
c/o E. Martin Davidoff
P.O. Box 835
Dayton, NJ 08810-0835

Established in 1999 in DE.
Donor(s): Thomas D. Klingenstein, Nancy D. Perlman, Nancy K. Simpkins.
Grantmaker type: Independent foundation
Financial data (yr. ended 12/31/00): Assets, $2,285,172 (M); gifts received, $1,557,478; expenditures, $205,720; qualifying distributions, $167,479; giving activities include $182,040 for 5 grants (high: $100,000; low: $5,000).
Fields of interest: Education; Natural resources.
Limitations: Applications not accepted. Giving primarily in NY. No grants to individuals.
Application information: Contributes only to pre-selected organizations.
Officers: Nancy D. Perlman, Pres. and Treas.; Nancy K. Simpkins, V.P. and Secy.
Director: Thomas D. Klingenstein.
EIN: 061524760

1926
Ernest Christian Klipstein Foundation
Village Rd.
New Vernon, NJ 07976   (973) 538-4445
Contact: Marion C. White, Secy.

Established in 1954 in NJ.
Donor(s): Kenneth H. Klipstein.‡
Grantmaker type: Independent foundation
Financial data (yr. ended 12/31/02): Assets, $3,064,843 (M); expenditures, $285,534; qualifying distributions, $247,412; giving

activities include $159,800 for 52 grants (high: $29,000; low: $100).
Fields of interest: Elementary/secondary education; Secondary school/education; Higher education; Education; Natural resources; Health care.
Types of support: General/operating support; Annual campaigns; Capital campaigns; Endowments; Fellowships; Scholarship funds.
Limitations: Giving primarily in NJ. No grants to individuals.
Application information: Application form not required.
  Deadline(s): None
Officers: David H. Klipstein, Pres.; David C. Klipstein, V.P.; Marion C. White, Secy.; Pamela Klipstein, Treas.
Number of staff: 1 full-time support.
EIN: 226028529

1927
Faith & James Knight Foundation, Inc.
c/o R.J. Gaughran
P.O. Box 143
Middletown, NJ 07748

Established in 1999 in NJ.
Grantmaker type: Independent foundation
Financial data (yr. ended 06/30/02): Assets, $5,527,963 (M); gifts received, $40,553; expenditures, $332,086; qualifying distributions, $272,849; giving activities include $253,500 for 7 grants (high: $199,000; low: $2,500).
Purpose and activities: Giving primarily for women's and animal issues, education, and health care.
Fields of interest: Education; Animal welfare; Health care; Women, centers/services; Women.
Limitations: Applications not accepted. Giving primarily in MI and NJ. No grants to individuals.
Application information: Contributes only to pre-selected organizations.
Trustees: Donna Balon; Robert J. Gaughran; Adrian Giuliani; Lisa Knight Giuliani; Frances Lobl; Margot R. McCord.
Number of staff: None.
EIN: 223656542

1928
Koven Foundation
P.O. Box 340
Chester, NJ 07930
Contact: Theodore Koven, Dir.
FAX: (908) 879-7960

Established in 1952.
Grantmaker type: Independent foundation
Financial data (yr. ended 12/31/02): Assets, $1,871,587 (M); expenditures, $150,210; qualifying distributions, $136,288; giving activities include $131,800 for grants (high: $20,000; low: $100).
Fields of interest: Historic preservation/historical societies; Education; Natural resources; Health organizations, association.
International interests: Saint Vincent & the Grenadines.
Limitations: Giving primarily in NJ and NY.

Application information:
Initial approach: Letter
Deadline(s): None
Directors: Gustav Koven; Jane C. Koven;
Theodore Koven.
Number of staff: None.
EIN: 226028758

1929
The Lautenberg Foundation
(formerly The L. Family Foundation)
P.O. Box 960
Cliffside Park, NJ 07010
Contact: E. Rigolosi, Asst. Secy.

Established in 1967 in NJ.
Donor(s): Frank R. Lautenberg Charitable Trusts.
Grantmaker type: Independent foundation
Financial data (yr. ended 12/31/01): Assets,
$12,589,548 (M); expenditures, $704,937;
qualifying distributions, $581,950; giving
activities include $605,887 for 125 grants (high:
$228,000; low: $100).
Purpose and activities: Grants largely for Jewish
welfare funds, education, and cultural programs
locally; some support also for educational and
cultural institutions in Israel.
Fields of interest: Television; Museums; Arts;
Higher education; Education; Environment;
Hospitals (general); Animals/wildlife,
preservation/protection; Cancer; Medical
research, institute; Cancer research; Human
services; Minorities/immigrants, centers/services;
Jewish federated giving programs; Jewish
agencies & temples; Minorities.
International interests: Israel.
Types of support: Annual campaigns; Capital
campaigns; Building/renovation; Endowments;
Emergency funds; Program development;
Scholarship funds; Research.
Limitations: Applications not accepted. Giving
on a national basis, with some emphasis on the
greater metropolitan New York, NY, area,
including NJ. No grants to individuals.
Application information: Contributes only to
pre-selected organizations.
Officers: Frank R. Lautenberg, Pres.; Lois
Lautenberg, V.P.; Fred S. Lafer, Secy.
Number of staff: 1 part-time support.
EIN: 226102734

1930
The Leavens Foundation, Inc.
c/o Nancy Leavens
P.O. Box 673
Long Valley, NJ 07853 (908) 876-1355
Contact: William B. Leavens III, Secy.-Treas.
E-mail: gofly@nac.net

Established in 1991 in NJ as successor to The
Leavens Foundation.
Grantmaker type: Independent foundation
Financial data (yr. ended 12/31/02): Assets,
$3,364,524 (M); expenditures, $411,668;
qualifying distributions, $399,476; giving
activities include $353,500 for 41 grants (high:
$20,000; low: $1,000; average: $200–$5,000).
Purpose and activities: Giving primarily for the
environment and for social services.
Fields of interest: Performing arts; Historic
preservation/historical societies; Arts; Natural
resources; Family planning; Health care.

Types of support: General/operating support;
Continuing support; Capital campaigns;
Building/renovation; Equipment; Program
development; Seed money; Matching/challenge
support.
Limitations: Giving primarily in Morris and
Essex counties, NJ. No support for religious
organizations (unless a board member has a
direct affiliation). No grants to individuals.
Application information:
Copies of proposal: 1
Deadline(s): Apr. 15 and Sept. 15
Board meeting date(s): May and Oct.
Officers and Board Members:* Nancy
Leavens,* Pres.; William L. Gibson,* V.P.;
William B. Leavens III,* Secy.-Treas.; Douglas
Leavens; Treece Tappan.
Number of staff: None.
EIN: 521754606

1931
The Lipper Family Charitable Foundation
c/o A. Michael Lipper
85 Hobart Ave.
Summit, NJ 07901

Established in 1999 in NJ.
Donor(s): A. Michael Lipper, Ruth C. Lipper.
Grantmaker type: Independent foundation
Financial data (yr. ended 11/30/00): Assets,
$1,268,620 (M); gifts received, $1,480,638;
expenditures, $151,968; qualifying distributions,
$138,821; giving activities include $149,275 for
27 grants (high: $25,000; low: $100).
Fields of interest: Museums (art); Performing arts
centers; Elementary/secondary education;
University; Natural resources; Children/youth,
services.
Limitations: Applications not accepted. Giving
primarily in NJ. No grants to individuals.
Application information: Contributes only to
pre-selected organizations.
Trustees: A. Michael Lipper; Ruth C. Lipper.
EIN: 137152755

1932
The Luckow Family Foundation, Inc.
c/o Robert W. Luckow
461 Old Post Rd.
Wyckoff, NJ 07481-1550

Established in 1996 in NJ.
Donor(s): The Robert W. Luckow Corp.,
Education for Youth Society.
Grantmaker type: Independent foundation
Financial data (yr. ended 09/30/02): Assets,
$4,734,189 (M); expenditures, $1,490,201;
qualifying distributions, $1,477,297; giving
activities include $1,473,663 for grants.
Purpose and activities: Giving primarily for
hospitals; some giving also for health
organizations and education.
Fields of interest: Education; Natural resources;
Hospitals (general); Health organizations,
association; Parks/playgrounds; Athletics/sports,
Olympics; Christian agencies & churches.
International interests: New Zealand.
Limitations: Applications not accepted. Giving
on a national basis. No grants to individuals.
Application information: Contributes only to
pre-selected organizations.

Officers: Robert W. Luckow, Pres.; Audrey
Luckow, V.P. and Secy.; Michael Luckow, V.P.;
Stephanie Luckow, V.P.
EIN: 223479153

1933
The Magowan Family Foundation, Inc.
c/o Merrill Lynch & Co., Inc.
100 Union Ave.
Cresskill, NJ 07626

Incorporated in 1954 in NY.
Donor(s): Charles E. Merrill, Sr.,‡ Robert A.
Magowan, Sr.,‡ Doris M. Magowan, Merrill L.
Magowan, Robert A. Magowan, Jr.
Grantmaker type: Independent foundation
Financial data (yr. ended 10/31/01): Assets,
$8,960,971 (M); gifts received, $1,175,808;
expenditures, $1,396,501; qualifying
distributions, $1,302,042; giving activities
include $1,253,298 for 230 grants (high:
$100,000; low: $250).
Fields of interest: Television; Museums
(children's); Arts; Education; Horticulture/garden
clubs; Environment; Zoos/zoological societies;
Hospitals (general); Human services; Christian
agencies & churches.
Limitations: Applications not accepted. Giving
on a national basis. No grants to individuals.
Application information: Contributes only to
pre-selected organizations.
Directors: Mark E. Magowan; Merrill L.
Magowan; Peter A. Magowan; Robin Magowan;
Stephen C. Magowan.
EIN: 136085999

1934
Mallinckrodt Baker, Inc. Corporate Giving Program
c/o Human Resources Dept.
222 Red School Ln.
Phillipsburg, NJ 08865 (908) 859-2151
Contact: Doreen Rounsaville

Grantmaker type: Corporate giving program
Purpose and activities: Mallinckrodt Baker
makes charitable contributions to nonprofit
organizations involved with education, the
environment, science, and to hospitals. Support
is given primarily in the Phillipsburg, New
Jersey, and Easton, Pennsylvania, areas.
Fields of interest: Education; Environment;
Medical care, in-patient care; Science.
Types of support: General/operating support;
Scholarship funds; Employee volunteer services;
Employee matching gifts.
Limitations: Giving primarily in the Phillipsburg,
NJ, and Easton, PA, areas.
Application information: Application form not
required.
Initial approach: Proposal to headquarters
Copies of proposal: 1
Final notification: Following review

1935
Helen and William Mazer Foundation
140 Kent Dr.
Berkeley Heights, NJ 07922

Grantmaker type: Independent foundation

Financial data (yr. ended 09/30/02): Assets, $8,392,958 (M); expenditures, $498,812; qualifying distributions, $468,424; giving activities include $418,450 for 79 grants (high: $50,000; low: $100).
Fields of interest: Arts; Education; Environment; Health organizations, association; Economics.
International interests: Africa.
Limitations: Applications not accepted. No grants to individuals.
Application information: Contributes only to pre-selected organizations.
Officers: Linda Berkowitz, Pres.; Steven Bercu, Secy.; Leonard Berkowitz, Treas.
Directors: Alan Berkowitz; David Berkowitz.
Number of staff: None.
EIN: 020511160

1936
The McCutchen Foundation
c/o United Trust Bank
1130 Rte. 22 E.
Bridgewater, NJ 08807
Contact: Charles W. McCutchen, Tr.
Application address: 209 W. 2nd St., Plainfield, NJ 07061, tel.: (908) 756-0042

Trust established in 1956 in NJ.
Donor(s): Brunson S. McCutchen, Charles W. McCutchen, Margaret W. McCutchen.
Grantmaker type: Independent foundation
Financial data (yr. ended 12/31/02): Assets, $13,769,930 (M); gifts received, $488,877; expenditures, $786,657; qualifying distributions, $738,138; giving activities include $732,000 for 49 grants (high: $100,000; low: $2,000).
Purpose and activities: Giving primarily for education, human services, and health associations.
Fields of interest: Orchestra (symphony); Arts; Higher education; Education; Animal welfare; Hospitals (general); Health organizations, association; Human services; Hospices.
Limitations: Giving primarily in NJ and NY; some funding nationally. No grants to individuals.
Application information:
  Initial approach: Letter
  Deadline(s): Dec. 1
Trustees: Ben Chapman; Charles W. McCutchen; Anne Terry.
EIN: 226050116

1937
The Curtis W. McGraw Foundation
c/o Drinker, Biddle & Reath, LLP
P.O. Box 627
Princeton, NJ 08542-0627 (609) 716-6511
Contact: Samuel W. Lambert III, Secy.-Treas.
FAX: (609) 799-7000

Established in 1964 in NJ.
Donor(s): Elizabeth McGraw Webster.
Grantmaker type: Independent foundation
Financial data (yr. ended 12/31/02): Assets, $18,718,021 (M); expenditures, $1,324,990; qualifying distributions, $1,193,390; giving

activities include $1,159,000 for 112 grants (high: $100,000; low: $1,000; average: $1,000-$100,000).
Purpose and activities: Support primarily for hospitals, mental health, AIDS research, elementary and other educational institutions, the arts, social services, and churches. Grants usually made to charities which are of interest to the officers.
Fields of interest: Performing arts; Arts; Elementary school/education; Education; Natural resources; Environment; Hospitals (general); Substance abuse, services; Mental health/crisis services; AIDS; AIDS research; Human services; Religion.
Types of support: General/operating support; Continuing support; Annual campaigns.
Limitations: Giving limited to the Vail, CO, Sun Valley, ID, and Princeton, NJ, areas. No grants to individuals, or for endowment funds, research, scholarships, fellowships, or matching gifts; no loans.
Application information: Application form not required.
  Initial approach: Letter
  Copies of proposal: 1
  Deadline(s): Oct. 15
  Board meeting date(s): Nov. or Dec., and as required
  Final notification: By Dec. 31
Officers and Trustees:* Elizabeth McGraw Webster,* Pres.; Curtis M. Webster,* Exec. V.P.; Lisette S. Edmond,* V.P.; Marian S. Paen,* V.P.; Samuel W. Lambert III,* Secy.-Treas.; Theo M. Webster.
Number of staff: None.
EIN: 221761678

1938
The McLaughlin Foundation
c/o J.H. Cohn
75 Eisenhower Pkwy.
Roseland, NJ 07068-1697

Established in 1984 in NY.
Donor(s): Anthony P. McLaughlin, Bill Keller.
Grantmaker type: Independent foundation
Financial data (yr. ended 12/31/01): Assets, $426,392 (M); gifts received, $7,000; expenditures, $96,497; qualifying distributions, $92,489; giving activities include $92,489 for 55 grants (high: $39,811; low: $50).
Purpose and activities: Giving for public charities, for education, Roman Catholic charities and organizations, art and cultural organizations, and for human services.
Fields of interest: Education; Animal welfare; Human services; Roman Catholic agencies & churches.
Limitations: Applications not accepted. Giving primarily in NY. No grants to individuals.
Application information: Contributes only to pre-selected organizations.
  Board meeting date(s): Varies
Officer and Directors:* Anthony P. McLaughlin,* Pres.; Patricia McLaughlin.
EIN: 133225925

1939
The Merck Company Foundation ▼
1 Merck Dr.
P.O. Box 100
Whitehouse Station, NJ 08889-0100
(908) 423-2042
FAX: (908) 423-1987; URL: http://www.merck.com/about/cr/policies_performance/social/philanthropy.html

Incorporated in 1957 in NJ.
Donor(s): Merck & Co., Inc.
Grantmaker type: Company-sponsored foundation
Financial data (yr. ended 12/31/01): Assets, $267,205,920 (L); expenditures, $45,508,217; qualifying distributions, $40,345,036; giving activities include $35,726,564 for 389 grants (high: $3,210,195; low: $1,000; average: $1,500-$100,000) and $4,224,877 for 3,445 employee matching gifts.
Purpose and activities: Support of education, primarily medical, including the Merck Sharp & Dohme International Fellowships in Clinical Pharmacology; community programs, hospitals, medical, biological, and physical sciences, health agencies, public and civic organizations, and colleges in localities where the company has major operations; and an employee matching gift program for colleges, secondary schools, hospitals, public broadcasting and public libraries.
Fields of interest: Elementary school/education; Secondary school/education; Higher education; Business school/education; Medical school/education; Engineering school/education; Education; Environment; Hospitals (general); Pharmacy/prescriptions; Nursing care; Health care; Health organizations, association; Eye diseases; Heart & circulatory diseases; Biomedicine; Medical research, institute; Eye research; Heart & circulatory research; Aging, centers/services; Minorities/immigrants, centers/services; Physical/earth sciences; Chemistry; Engineering/technology; Engineering; Biological sciences; Science; Public policy, research; Minorities; Disabled; Aging.
International interests: Japan.
Types of support: Equipment; Program development; Seed money; Fellowships; Employee matching gifts.
Limitations: Giving primarily in areas of company operations, including CA, GA, NJ, PA, and VA. No support for political, fraternal, veterans', labor or sectarian groups, or elementary/secondary education. No grants to individuals (except for fellowships in clinical pharmacology), or for operating budgets, continuing support, annual campaigns, emergency or endowment funds, deficit financing, land acquisition, travel, conferences, publications, media productions or research; no loans.
Publications: Corporate giving report.
Application information: Grants usually made at the initiative of the foundation. Application form not required.
  Initial approach: Letter
  Copies of proposal: 1

Deadline(s): Feb. 1 or Aug. 1 for health care grants; Aug. 31 for fellowships in clinical pharmacology; no set deadline for other grants

Board meeting date(s): Semiannually and as required

Final notification: 2 months

Officers and Directors:* Raymond V. Gilmartin,* Chair.; Joan Wainwright,* Pres.; Leslie M. Hardy, V.P.; Shuang Ruy Huang, Ph.D., V.P.; Celia A. Colbert, Secy.; Caroline Dorsa, Treas.; Lawrence A. Bossidy; William G. Bowen, Ph.D.; Johnnetta B. Cole, Ph.D.; William M. Daley; Niali FitzGerald; William B. Harrison, Jr.; William N. Kelley, M.D.; Heidi Miller; Edward M. Scolnick; Thomas E. Shenk, Ph.D.; Anne M. Tatlock; Samuel O. Thier, M.D.

Number of staff: 3 full-time professional; 3 full-time support.

EIN: 226028476

Recent environmental and animal welfare grants:

1939-1 Mississippi State University, College of Vetennary Medicine, Mississippi State, MS, $28,494. 2001.

1939-2 Steering Commitee for Environmental Quality (COTICAM), Manati, PR, $10,000. 2001.

1940
The Merrill Family Charitable Foundation, Inc.

100 Union Ave.
Cresskill, NJ 07626
Contact: Paul Merrill, Pres.
Application address: 381 Morrell Rd., Worchester, NY 12197

Established in 1997 in NY.
Donor(s): Charles A. Merrill, Jr.
Grantmaker type: Independent foundation
Financial data (yr. ended 12/31/02): Assets, $2,048,384 (M); gifts received, $100,000; expenditures, $124,482; qualifying distributions, $120,895; giving activities include $120,895 for 88 grants (high: $13,000; low: $30).
Purpose and activities: Giving for the arts, education, the environment, and community development.
Fields of interest: Dance; Music; Historical activities; Education; Environment; Human services; Community development.
Limitations: Giving on a national basis. No grants to individuals.
Application information:
Initial approach: Letter
Deadline(s): None
Officers: Paul Merrill, Pres.; Amy Merrill, V.P.; Bruce Merrill, Secy.
EIN: 223494040

1941
Jay R. Monroe Memorial Foundation

P.O. Box 897
Millburn, NJ 07041-0897
Contact: Jay R. Monroe V, Pres.

Established in 1959 in NJ.
Donor(s): Malcolm Monroe,‡ Ethlyn Monroe.‡
Grantmaker type: Independent foundation
Financial data (yr. ended 12/31/01): Assets, $2,560,736 (M); expenditures, $114,929;

qualifying distributions, $109,254; giving activities include $102,975 for 62 grants (high: $10,000; low: $100).
Purpose and activities: Giving primarily for the arts, including the performing arts and historic preservation; education, especially secondary and early childhood education and programs for minorities; social services, child welfare and development, youth programs, family planning, and issues of law and justice and human rights, especially concerning Native Americans and other minorities; health organizations, hospitals, and health services, including rehabilitative programs for the mentally or physically handicapped; and associations concerned with ecology and wildlife.
Fields of interest: Historic preservation/historical societies; Early childhood education; Child development, education; Animal welfare; Animals/wildlife, preservation/protection; Health organizations; Crime/law enforcement; Children/youth, services; Child development, services; Minorities/immigrants, centers/services; Native Americans/American Indians; Disabled.
Types of support: General/operating support; Continuing support; Annual campaigns.
Limitations: Applications not accepted. Giving primarily in NH, NJ, and VT. No grants to individuals.
Application information: Contributes only to pre-selected organizations.
Board meeting date(s): 2nd Mon. in Jan.
Officers: Jay R. Monroe V, Pres.; Martha M. Morrow, V.P.; Celia M. Byrne, Treas.
Number of staff: None.
EIN: 226050156

1942
Benjamin Moore & Co. Contributions Program

51 Chestnut Ridge Rd.
Montvale, NJ 07645 (201) 573-9600

Grantmaker type: Corporate giving program
Purpose and activities: Benjamin Moore makes charitable contributions to nonprofit organizations involved with artistic design, education, the environment, housing, and community development. Support is given on a national basis.
Fields of interest: Design; Education; Environment; Housing/shelter; Community development.
Types of support: General/operating support; Scholarship funds; Employee matching gifts; In-kind gifts.
Limitations: Giving on a national basis.
Application information: Application form not required.
Initial approach: Proposal to headquarters
Copies of proposal: 1
Final notification: Following review

1943
NUI Corporation Contributions Program

550 Rte. 202-206
P.O. Box 760
Bedminster, NJ 07921-0760 (908) 781-0500
Contact: Joseph P. Coughlin, Sr. V.P. and Secy.

Grantmaker type: Corporate giving program

Purpose and activities: NUI makes charitable contributions to nonprofit organizations involved with energy resource conservation and development, telecommunications, and on a case by case basis. Support is given primarily in areas of company operations.
Fields of interest: Energy; Telecommunications; General charitable giving.
Types of support: General/operating support; Employee volunteer services; Employee matching gifts; In-kind gifts.
Limitations: Giving primarily in areas of company operations.
Application information: Application form not required.
Initial approach: Proposal to headquarters
Copies of proposal: 1
Final notification: Following review

1944
OceanFirst Foundation

(formerly Ocean Federal Foundation)
1027 Hooper Ave., Bldg. 1
Toms River, NJ 08753 (732) 341-4676
Contact: Katherine Durante, Exec. Dir.
FAX: (732) 473-9641; E-mail: info@oceanfirstfdn.org; URL: http://www.oceanfirstfdn.org

Established in 1996 in NJ.
Donor(s): Ocean Financial Corp., Ocean Federal Savings Bank, OceanFirst Financial Corp.
Grantmaker type: Company-sponsored foundation
Financial data (yr. ended 12/31/02): Assets, $38,193,905 (M); expenditures, $1,590,974; qualifying distributions, $1,547,986; giving activities include $1,409,597 for 148 grants (high: $125,000; low: $100; average: $1,500–$150,000).
Purpose and activities: Giving primarily for youth education, nonprofit medical services, housing, and quality of life.
Fields of interest: Arts; Higher education; Natural resources; Hospitals (general); Health care; Housing/shelter; Youth development; Human services; Children/youth, services.
Types of support: Annual campaigns; Capital campaigns; Building/renovation; Equipment; Program development; Seed money; Matching/challenge support.
Limitations: Giving primarily in southern Middlesex, southern Monmouth, and Ocean counties, NJ.
Publications: Application guidelines.
Application information: Application form required.
Initial approach: Telephone or letter
Copies of proposal: 1
Deadline(s): None
Board meeting date(s): Quarterly
Officer: Katherine Durante, Exec. Dir.
Directors: John W. Chadwick; Thomas F. Curtin; Anthony J. DiCroce II; Reginald Dryzga; Carl Feltz, Jr.; John R. Garbarino; Anita M. Kneeley; Rev. Msgr. Casimir H. Ladzinski; Amy W. Lotano; Donald F. McLaughlin; Samuel T. Melillo; Diane Rhine; Frederick E. Schlosser; James T. Snyder; John E. Walsh; David C. Wintrode; David W. Wolfe.
Number of staff: 1 full-time professional; 1 part-time support.
EIN: 223465454

1945
The Patchett Foundation, Inc.
P.O. Box 426
Westfield, NJ 07091-3727

Established in 1998 in NJ.
Donor(s): Arthur A. Patchett.
Grantmaker type: Independent foundation
Financial data (yr. ended 06/30/02): Assets,
$1,833,004 (M); gifts received, $292,660;
expenditures, $113,906; qualifying distributions,
$90,000; giving activities include $90,000 for 8
grants (high: $25,000; low: $5,000).
Purpose and activities: Giving primarily for
education and human services.
Fields of interest: Higher education; Education;
Animal welfare; Hospitals (specialty); Human
services; Christian agencies & churches.
Limitations: Giving primarily in MA, NJ, and
NY. No grants to individuals.
Application information:
    Initial approach: Proposal
    Deadline(s): None
Officers: Arthur A. Patchett, Chair.; Lois McNeil
Patchett, Vice-Chair.; Steven Edward Patchett,
Secy.; Thomas John Patchett, Treas.
EIN: 223590125

1946
F. Mason Perkins Trust
c/o Fleet National Bank, NJRP47402C
1125 Rte. 22 W.
Bridgewater, NJ 08807 (908) 253-4863
Contact: Cindy Leip

Established in 1955.
Donor(s): F. Mason Perkins.‡
Grantmaker type: Independent foundation
Financial data (yr. ended 12/31/02): Assets,
$3,447,911 (M); expenditures, $95,083;
qualifying distributions, $95,083; giving
activities include $93,633 for 3 grants (high:
$40,000; low: $15,000; average:
$1,000–$5,000).
Purpose and activities: Giving exclusively to
charities in Italy for aid to the poor and less
fortunate, particularly children and the aged,
and for the protection of animals; first
consideration for grants is given to organizations
providing for the poor, orphans, children and
sisters of charity.
Fields of interest: Animal welfare; Nursing care;
Human services; Children/youth, services;
Aging, centers/services; Disabled; Aging;
Economically disadvantaged.
International interests: Italy.
Types of support: Continuing support;
Endowments; Emergency funds; Program
development; Curriculum development;
Fellowships; Scholarship funds; Research.
Limitations: Giving limited to Italy. No grants to
individuals.
Publications: Application guidelines.
Application information: Application form
required.
    Initial approach: Grant request on requesting
    organization's letterhead
    Copies of proposal: 3
    Deadline(s): May 1 and Nov. 1
    Final notification: June 30 and Dec. 31
Trustee: Fleet National Bank.
EIN: 226040411

1947
Pharmacia Corporation Contributions Program
(formerly Monsanto Company Contributions
Program)
100 Rte. 206 N.
Peapack, NJ 07977
Contact: Erica Ferry, Dir., Community Rels. and
Contribs. Progs.

Grantmaker type: Corporate giving program
Financial data (yr. ended 12/31/01): Total giving,
$3,061,000; giving activities include
$3,061,000 for 180 grants (high: $1,500,000;
low: $500; average: $5,000–$400,000).
Purpose and activities: As a complement to its
foundation, Pharmacia also makes charitable
contributions to nonprofit organizations directly.
Support is given on a national and international
basis.
Fields of interest: Environment; Community
development; Science.
Types of support: General/operating support;
Capital campaigns; Sponsorships; Donated
equipment; In-kind gifts.
Limitations: Giving on a national and
international basis in areas of company
operations.
Publications: Corporate giving report.
Application information: The Corporate
Citizenship Department handles giving. The
company has a staff that only handles
contributions. Application form not required.
    Initial approach: Proposal to headquarters
    Copies of proposal: 1
    Final notification: Following review
Number of staff: 1 part-time professional; 1
full-time support.

1948
Pheasant Hill Foundation, Inc.
c/o R.E. Ingram
410 George St.
New Brunswick, NJ 08901

Established in 1996 in NJ.
Donor(s): Robert N. Wilson.
Grantmaker type: Independent foundation
Financial data (yr. ended 08/31/02): Assets,
$3,056,287 (M); gifts received, $90,000;
expenditures, $137,631; qualifying distributions,
$136,371; giving activities include $135,946 for
37 grants (high: $15,000; low: $60).
Purpose and activities: Giving primarily for
education, the environment and federated
giving programs.
Fields of interest: Museums; Arts; Higher
education; Natural resources; Environment,
water resources; Animals/wildlife, fund raising;
Animals/wildlife, preservation/protection;
Multiple sclerosis; Federated giving programs.
Types of support: General/operating support.
Limitations: Applications not accepted. No
grants to individuals.
Application information: Contributes only to
pre-selected organizations.
Officers and Trustees:* Robert N. Wilson,*
Pres.; Anne Wright Wilson,* Secy.-Treas.; Eileen
H. Roan.
EIN: 311481806

1949
Howard Phipps Foundation
c/o Bessemer Trust Co., N.A.
100 Woodbridge Ctr. Dr.
Woodbridge, NJ 07095-0983
Contact: Austin J. Power, Jr.
Application address: c/o Bessemer Trust Co.,
N.A., 630 5th Ave., New York, NY 10111, tel.:
(212) 708-9242

Established in 1967 in NJ.
Donor(s): Harriet Phipps.‡
Grantmaker type: Independent foundation
Financial data (yr. ended 06/30/01): Assets,
$15,467,177 (M); gifts received, $1,528,545;
expenditures, $1,752,055; qualifying
distributions, $1,664,000; giving activities
include $1,664,000 for 54 grants (high:
$400,000; low: $2,000; average:
$5,000–$25,000).
Purpose and activities: Support for
conservation, cultural programs, and
educational organizations.
Fields of interest: Arts; Education; Natural
resources.
Limitations: Giving primarily in New York, NY.
Application information:
    Initial approach: Letter
    Deadline(s): None
Trustees: Howard Phipps, Jr.; Anne P.
Sidamon-Eristoff; Bessemer Trust Co., N.A.
EIN: 226095226

1950
C. Northrop & A. Marder Pond Foundation
c/o United Trust Bank
1130 Rte. 22 E.
Bridgewater, NJ 08807
Contact: Grace Pond Fisher, Tr.

Established in 1997 in NJ.
Donor(s): Alethea Marder Pond.‡
Grantmaker type: Independent foundation
Financial data (yr. ended 04/30/02): Assets,
$6,170,181 (M); gifts received, $4,000,000;
expenditures, $124,596; qualifying distributions,
$108,409; giving activities include $104,500 for
22 grants (high: $30,000; low: $1,000).
Purpose and activities: The foundation supports
activities in charity, education, health care,
conservation and the environment.
Fields of interest: Education; Environment;
Health care; Human services; American Red
Cross.
Limitations: Giving primarily in NJ.
Trustees: Grace Pond Fisher; Charles N. Pond,
Jr.; United Trust Bank.
EIN: 226727894

1951
PSE&G Corporate Giving Program
c/o Corp. Contribs.
80 Park Plz.
Newark, NJ 07101 (973) 430-5763
Contact: William J. Walsh, Jr.
Additional tel.: (973) 430-7842; URL: http://
www.pseg.com/community/overview.html

Grantmaker type: Corporate giving program
Purpose and activities: As a complement to its
foundation, PSE&G also makes charitable

contributions to nonprofit organizations directly. Support is given primarily in areas of company operations.
Fields of interest: Environment; Children, services; Family services; Economic development.
Types of support: General/operating support; Employee volunteer services; Employee matching gifts.
Limitations: Giving primarily in areas of company operations, with emphasis on NJ. No support for United Way-supported organizations. No grants to individuals.
Application information: The Corporate Responsibility Department handles giving. Application form required.
> *Initial approach:* Contact headquarters for application form
> *Copies of proposal:* 1
> *Deadline(s):* None
> *Final notification:* Following review
Number of staff: 3 full-time professional; 2 full-time support.

1952
PSEG Foundation, Inc.
(formerly Public Serivce Electric and Gas Company Foundation, Inc.)
80 Park Plz., T-10
Newark, NJ 07101   (973) 430-7842
Contact: William J. Walsh, Jr., Pres.
Additional tel.: (973) 430-5763

Established in 1991 in NJ.
Donor(s): Public Service Electric and Gas Co.
Grantmaker type: Company-sponsored foundation
Financial data (yr. ended 12/31/02): Assets, $6,453,651 (M); gifts received, $320,689; expenditures, $3,621,146; qualifying distributions, $3,617,126; giving activities include $3,617,126 for 1,013 grants (high: $500,000; low: $100; average: $1,000–$50,000).
Purpose and activities: Support for federated giving, education, and human service organizations.
Fields of interest: Environment; Children/youth, services; Family services; Economic development.
Types of support: General/operating support; Annual campaigns; Capital campaigns.
Limitations: Giving primarily in NJ. No support for religious, political, athletic, labor, or fraternal organizations, or organizations that address single health issues. No grants to individuals, or for endowments.
Publications: Corporate report, Multi-year report.
Application information: Application form required.
> *Initial approach:* Written request
> *Copies of proposal:* 1
> *Deadline(s):* None
Officers and Trustees:* William J. Walsh, Jr.,* Pres.; Edward J. Biggins, Jr., Secy.; Morton A. Plawner, Treas.; Patricia A. Rado,* Cont.; James Foran, Genl. Counsel; Patrick M. Burke; Frank Cassidy; Frederick D. DeSanti; Robert J. Dougherty, Jr.; Mark G. Kahrer; Alfred C. Koeppe; Robert C. Murray; Thomas M. O'flynn; Ardeshir Rostami; R. Edwin Selover.
EIN: 223125880

Recent environmental and animal welfare grants:
1952-1 Greater Newark Conservancy, Newark, NJ, $20,000. 2002.
1952-2 Hackensack Riverkeeper, Teaneck, NJ, $12,500. 2002.
1952-3 Nature Conservancy, Chester, NJ, $12,500. 2002.

1953
Jessie Reid Foundation, Inc.
65 Livingston Ave.
Roseland, NJ 07068

Established in 1994 in NJ.
Donor(s): C. Fred Taylor.
Grantmaker type: Independent foundation
Financial data (yr. ended 11/30/00): Assets, $19,970,772 (M); expenditures, $4,557,225; qualifying distributions, $4,290,000; giving activities include $4,290,000 for 4 grants (high: $2,500,000; low: $240,000).
Purpose and activities: Support for a Jewish elementary school and a wildlands conservancy.
Fields of interest: Elementary/secondary education; Natural resources.
Limitations: Applications not accepted. No grants to individuals.
Application information: Contributes only to pre-selected organizations.
Officers and Trustees:* Kenneth O. Slutsky,* Pres. and Treas.; Allen Levithan,* V.P. and Secy.; George Mazin,* V.P.; Rhett Holdings, LLC.
EIN: 223366357

1954
Roxiticus Fund
P.O. Box 5359
North Branch, NJ 08876   (908) 707-0724
Contact: John P. De Neufville, Tr.

Established in 1961 in NJ.
Donor(s): Hugo De Neufville.‡
Grantmaker type: Independent foundation
Financial data (yr. ended 12/31/02): Assets, $1,533,918 (M); expenditures, $110,979; qualifying distributions, $98,781; giving activities include $98,975 for 61 grants (high: $20,000; low: $25).
Purpose and activities: Giving for higher education, economic development, historic and environmental conservation, family services, international relief services and federated giving programs.
Fields of interest: Education; Natural resources; Family planning; Human services; International development; Federated giving programs.
Limitations: Giving primarily in NJ and NY. No grants to individuals, or for scholarships or fellowships; no loans.
Application information:
> *Initial approach:* Proposal
> *Deadline(s):* None
Trustee: John P. De Neufville.
EIN: 226041443

1955
Schering-Plough Corporation Contributions Program
2000 Galloping Hill Rd.
Kenilworth, NJ 07033
Contact: Andrew F. Hageman, Mgr., Corp. Philanthropy

Grantmaker type: Corporate giving program
Purpose and activities: As a complement to its foundation, Schering-Plough also makes charitable contributions to nonprofit organizations directly.
Fields of interest: Museums; Theater; Music; Arts; Business school/education; Adult/continuing education; Adult education—literacy, basic skills & GED; Reading; Education; Environment; Hospitals (general); Health care; Substance abuse, services; Alcoholism; Health organizations; Medical research; Food services; Youth development, citizenship; Children/youth, services; Human services; International relief; International affairs; Rural development; Engineering/technology; Science; Public affairs, citizen participation; Public affairs; General charitable giving; Minorities; Women; Homeless.
International interests: Canada; Austria; Belgium; France; Greece; Netherlands; Ireland; Italy; United Kingdom; Portugal; Spain; Switzerland; Germany; Denmark; Norway; Sweden; Bulgaria; Czech Republic; Slovakia; Hungary; Poland; Romania; Russia; Croatia; Slovenia; Egypt; South Africa; Mexico; Panama; Argentina; Bolivia; Brazil; Colombia; Chile; Ecuador; Peru; Venezuela; Turkey; India; Indonesia; Malaysia; Philippines; Singapore; Thailand; China; Taiwan; South Korea; Japan; Hong Kong; Australia; New Zealand.
Types of support: General/operating support; Continuing support; Program development; Conferences/seminars; Employee volunteer services; Use of facilities; Sponsorships; Employee matching gifts; Donated equipment; Donated products; In-kind gifts.
Limitations: Giving primarily in areas of company operations, particularly in CA, FL, IL, NE, NJ, PR, TN, and TX, and in Argentina, Australia, Austria, Belgium, Bolivia, Brazil, Bulgaria, Canada, Chile, China, Colombia, Croatia, the Czech Republic, Denmark, Ecuador, Egypt, France, Germany, Greece, Hong Kong, Hungary, India, Indonesia, Ireland, Italy, Japan, Malaysia, Mexico, the Netherlands, New Zealand, Norway, Panama, Peru, the Philippines, Poland, Portugal, Romania, Russia, Singapore, Slovakia, Slovenia, South Africa, South Korea, Spain, Sweden, Switzerland, Taiwan, Thailand, Turkey, the United Kingdom, and Venezuela. No grants to individuals.
Publications: Corporate giving report, Newsletter.
Application information: The Public Affairs Department handles giving; local management handles giving outside the U.S. Application form required.
> *Initial approach:* Contact headquarters for application form; letter of inquiry to nearest company facility for organizations located outside the U.S
> *Copies of proposal:* 1
> *Final notification:* Following review
Number of staff: 6 full-time professional; 3 full-time support; 1 part-time support.

1956
The Schumann Fund for New Jersey, Inc.
21 Van Vleck St.
Montclair, NJ 07042 (973) 509-9883
Contact: Barbara Reisman, Exec. Dir.
URL: http://fdncenter.org/grantmaker/schumann/

Established in 1988 in NJ.
Donor(s): Florence Schumann,‡ John
Schumann,‡ Florence and John Schumann
Foundation.
Grantmaker type: Independent foundation
Financial data (yr. ended 12/31/01): Assets,
$34,682,456 (M); expenditures, $2,442,258;
qualifying distributions, $2,019,615; giving
activities include $2,019,615 for 57 grants
(high: $100,000; low: $1,500; average:
$15,000–$50,000).
Purpose and activities: Support primarily for 1)
early childhood development; 2) environmental
protection; 3) public policy; and 4) local
activities directed at solving community
problems within Essex County, with emphasis
on social services, children, and education.
Fields of interest: Early childhood education;
Education; Environment; Human services;
Children/youth, services; Public affairs.
Types of support: General/operating support;
Continuing support; Program development;
Seed money.
Limitations: Giving limited to NJ, with emphasis
on Essex County. No grants to individuals, or for
capital campaigns, annual giving, or
endowments.
Publications: Application guidelines, Annual
report, Grants list.
Application information: NY/NJ Common
Application Form encouraged. Application form
not required.
  Initial approach: Proposal
  Copies of proposal: 1
  Deadline(s): Jan. 15, Apr. 15, July 15, and
    Oct. 15
  Board meeting date(s): Mar., June, Sept., and
    Dec.
  Final notification: 4 to 8 weeks
Officers and Trustees:* Christopher J. Daggett,*
Chair.; Leonard S. Coleman, Jr.,* Vice-Chair.;
Aubin Z. Ames,* Secy.; Andrew C. Halvorsen,
Treas.; Barbara Reisman, Exec. Dir.; George R.
Harris; John R. Noonan.
Number of staff: 2 full-time professional.
EIN: 521556076

1957
The Scire Family Foundation, Inc.
5 Cook Pl.
Middletown, NJ 07748

Established in 1998 in NJ.
Donor(s): Patrick Scire.
Grantmaker type: Independent foundation
Financial data (yr. ended 09/30/02): Assets,
$3,044,670 (M); gifts received, $2,500;
expenditures, $192,354; qualifying distributions,
$188,396; giving activities include $186,954 for
76 grants (high: $25,000; low: $35).
Fields of interest: University;
Scholarships/financial aid; Education;
Environment; Religion.
Limitations: Applications not accepted. No
grants to individuals.

Application information: Contributes only to
pre-selected organizations.
Officers: Patrick Scire, Pres. and Treas.; Jennifer
Scire, V.P. and Secy.; Salvatore Scire, V.P.
EIN: 223650428

1958
Sierra Foundation, Inc. ▼
(formerly S. T. Grim Foundation)
33 Witherspoon St., 3rd Fl.
Princeton, NJ 08542
Contact: Martin J. Deitchman, Tr.

Established in 1994 in NJ.
Donor(s): Sierra Enterprises Group LLC, Andrew
Schechtel, C. Fred Taylor.
Grantmaker type: Independent foundation
Financial data (yr. ended 10/31/02): Assets,
$20,296,623 (M); gifts received, $30,721,866;
expenditures, $23,837,145; qualifying
distributions, $23,809,033; giving activities
include $23,809,033 for 20 grants (high:
$7,179,537; low: $500; average:
$10,000–$1,100,000).
Purpose and activities: Giving primarily for
educational purposes.
Fields of interest: Elementary/secondary
education; Law school/education.
Limitations: Applications not accepted. Giving
primarily in NY. No grants to individuals.
Application information: Contributes only to
pre-selected organizations. Unsolicited requests
for funds not accepted.
Trustees: Martin J. Deitchman; Andrew J.
Shechtel; Raquel Shechtel.
EIN: 223331554
**Recent environmental and animal welfare
grants:**
1958-1 Delaware and Raritan Greenway,
  Princeton, NJ, $10,000. For general support.
  2001.
1958-2 Wild Lands Conservancy, Yucaipa, CA,
  $1,109,195. For general support. 2001.
1958-3 Wildlands Endowment Fund, San
  Francisco, CA, $7,209,765. For general
  support. 2001.

1959
Silver Mountain Foundation for the Arts
c/o William E. Simon & Sons, Inc., LLC
310 South St., P.O. Box 1913
Morristown, NJ 07962-1913
Contact: Donald Gummer or M. S. Gummer,
Trustees

Established in 1983.
Donor(s): Donald Gummer, Meryl S. Gummer.
Grantmaker type: Independent foundation
Financial data (yr. ended 10/31/02): Assets,
$1,317,135 (M); gifts received, $257,650;
expenditures, $306,280; qualifying distributions,
$294,801; giving activities include $295,000 for
89 grants (high: $50,000; low: $250).
Purpose and activities: Giving primarily for the
performing arts, environmental conservation
and education.
Fields of interest: Performing arts; Theater;
Education; Natural resources; Housing/shelter,
development; International relief.
Limitations: Giving primarily in CT and NY. No
loans or program-related investments.
Application information:

Initial approach: Letter
Deadline(s): None
Trustees: Donald Gummer; M.S. Gummer.
EIN: 133157286

1960
The Stern Family Foundation
(formerly Leonard N. Stern Foundation)
c/o F. Roscitt
400 Plaza Dr., P.O. Box 1515
Secaucus, NJ 07096-1515

Established in 1963 in NY.
Donor(s): Leonard N. Stern, Hartz Mountain
Industries, Inc.
Grantmaker type: Independent foundation
Financial data (yr. ended 12/31/02): Assets,
$942 (M); gifts received, $182,500;
expenditures, $182,610; qualifying distributions,
$182,610; giving activities include $182,500 for
3 grants (high: $150,000; low: $7,500).
Purpose and activities: Giving primarily for
wildlife conservation; also giving for health and
human services.
Fields of interest: Elementary/secondary
education; Libraries (public); Zoos/zoological
societies; Health organizations, association;
Human services; Jewish federated giving
programs; Jewish agencies & temples.
Types of support: General/operating support;
Continuing support; Building/renovation;
Equipment; Program development; Seed money;
Matching/challenge support.
Limitations: Applications not accepted. Giving
primarily in the metropolitan New York, NY,
area. No grants to individuals.
Application information: Contributes only to
pre-selected organizations.
Officers and Directors:* Leonard N. Stern,*
Pres.; Edward Stern,* V.P.; Emanuel Stern,* V.P.;
Curtis Schwartz, Secy.-Treas.; Andrea Stern.
Number of staff: 1 full-time professional; 1
full-time support.
EIN: 136149990

1961
The Stone Foundation of New Jersey
180 Ave. of the Commons
Shrewsbury, NJ 07702
Contact: Caroline P. Huber, Pres.

Established in 1997 in DE.
Donor(s): Caroline Huber.
Grantmaker type: Independent foundation
Financial data (yr. ended 06/30/02): Assets,
$1,688,415 (M); gifts received, $59,906;
expenditures, $126,715; qualifying distributions,
$99,834; giving activities include $100,000 for
6 grants (high: $20,000; low: $10,000).
Purpose and activities: Giving for arts, social
services, women, the environment and for
education.
Fields of interest: Theater; Education;
Environment; Women, centers/services.
Types of support: General/operating support;
Continuing support; Capital campaigns;
Building/renovation.
Limitations: Giving primarily in Monmouth, NJ.
Application information: Application form not
required.
  Initial approach: Letter
  Copies of proposal: 3

Deadline(s): Apr. 1
Board meeting date(s): Apr.
Final notification: June 1
Officers: Caroline P. Huber, Pres. and Treas.;
Eleanor H. Huber, V.P.; Samuel G. Huber, Secy.
EIN: 133947516

1962
Judi and Howard Strauss Foundation
9 Broadmoor Dr.
Rumson, NJ 07760-1202
Contact: Howard E. Strauss, Pres.

Established in 1989.
Donor(s): Howard E. Strauss.
Grantmaker type: Independent foundation
Financial data (yr. ended 06/30/02): Assets,
$2,859,872 (M); expenditures, $184,240;
qualifying distributions, $178,508; giving
activities include $180,720 for 51 grants (high:
$10,000; low: $20).
Purpose and activities: Giving primarily for
animal welfare, health care, health associations,
and community development.
Fields of interest: Animal welfare; Hospitals
(general); Health care; Health organizations,
association; Human services; Community
development.
Limitations: Giving primarily in FL, NJ, and NY.
No grants to individuals.
Application information:
Initial approach: Written proposal
Deadline(s): Sept. 1
Officers: Howard E. Strauss, Pres.; Judith
Strauss, V.P.
EIN: 222987092

1963
Ann Earle Talcott Fund
c/o Wachovia Bank, N.A.
190 River Rd.
Summit, NJ 07901
Contact: Gale Sykes

Trust established in 1972 in NJ.
Donor(s): Ann Earle Talcott.‡
Grantmaker type: Independent foundation
Financial data (yr. ended 10/31/02): Assets,
$1,924,541 (M); expenditures, $136,619;
qualifying distributions, $128,383; giving
activities include $128,800 for 55 grants (high:
$5,000; low: $1,000).
Purpose and activities: Interests include: 1)
human service activities for disadvantaged
families and the mentally ill; specific areas of
interest include day care and independence
promotion; 2) program support for unique
projects that complement the educational
system at the primary school level; specific areas
of interest include literacy, health awareness and
the developmentally disabled; and 3) projects
and programs that prevent cruelty to animals.
Fields of interest: Child development,
education; Elementary school/education; Adult
education—literacy, basic skills & GED;
Reading; Education; Animal welfare; Health
care; Mental health/crisis services; Human
services; Children/youth, services; Child
development, services; Family services;
Economically disadvantaged.
Types of support: Program development; Seed
money; Matching/challenge support.

Limitations: Giving limited to NJ based
organizations or to NJ chapters of national
organizations. No grants to individuals, or for
endowments, or general operating support; no
loans.
Publications: Application guidelines.
Application information: Must submit Common
Grant Application Form (available upon request)
with proposal. Application form required.
Initial approach: Proposal
Copies of proposal: 1
Deadline(s): Jan. 15 and July 15
Board meeting date(s): Mar. and Sept.
Final notification: 1 month after board meeting
Trustee: Wachovia Bank, N.A.
EIN: 226203894

1964
The Thomas Charitable Foundation
c/o John C. Pretto
P.O. Box 93
Berkeley Heights, NJ 07922
Contact: Karen Kriendler Nelson, Exec. Dir.
Application address: 277 West End Ave., Ste.
11A, New York, NY 10023-2681, tel.: (212)
496-5154

Established in 1997 in CT.
Donor(s): Wilmer J. Thomas, Jr.
Grantmaker type: Independent foundation
Financial data (yr. ended 12/31/01): Assets,
$1,683,514 (M); gifts received, $201,554;
expenditures, $255,124; qualifying distributions,
$186,640; giving activities include $141,640 for
38 grants (high: $20,000; low: $100) and
$45,000 for 3 grants to individuals of $15,000
each.
Purpose and activities: Giving primarily for the
arts, including the enrichment and
encouragement of promising careers of
exceptionally talented native-born or
naturalized American opera singers; funding
also for cancer research.
Fields of interest: Opera; Performing arts
centers; Arts; Natural resources; Cancer research.
Types of support: General/operating support;
Grants to individuals.
Limitations: Giving primarily in New York, NY;
some funding nationally.
Application information:
Initial approach: Letter of no more than 2
pages
Deadline(s): Jan. 15 and July 15
Officer: Karen Kriendler Nelson, Exec. Dir.
Trustees: William D. Porteous; Douglas D.
Thomas; Wilmer J. Thomas, Jr.
EIN: 066444610

1965
The Thomas Foundation
c/o Edward D. Thomas
757 Cherry Valley Rd.
Princeton, NJ 08540-7920

Established in 1989 in NJ.
Donor(s): Edward D. Thomas, Millicent B.
Thomas.
Grantmaker type: Independent foundation
Financial data (yr. ended 12/31/01): Assets,
$24,467 (M); gifts received, $88,284;
expenditures, $208,791; qualifying distributions,

$208,728; giving activities include $208,736 for
66 grants (high: $30,000; low: $500).
Purpose and activities: Emphasis on
conservation and the environment.
Fields of interest: Arts; Education; Natural
resources; Health care; Housing/shelter,
development; Safety/disasters; Children/youth,
services; Family services; International human
rights.
Types of support: General/operating support;
Continuing support; Annual campaigns; Capital
campaigns; Land acquisition; Endowments.
Limitations: Applications not accepted. Giving
primarily in AK, CA, ID, MA, and NJ. No grants
to individuals.
Application information: Contributes only to
pre-selected organizations; unsolicited requests
for funds not accepted.
Board meeting date(s): Annually in Nov. or
Dec.
Officers: Edward D. Thomas, Pres.; Millicent B.
Thomas, V.P.
Trustees: Christopher J. Henderson; Kimberly T.
Henderson; Edward C. Thomas; Gerald O.
Thomas; Paige P. Thomas; Rebecca S. Thomas;
Timothy B. Thomas.
Number of staff: None.
EIN: 222998017

1966
Todino Family Foundation
2133 Bridge Ave.
Point Pleasant Beach, NJ 08742

Established in 1997 in NJ.
Donor(s): Joseph R. Todino.
Grantmaker type: Independent foundation
Financial data (yr. ended 12/31/01): Assets,
$1,889,208 (M); gifts received, $1,300;
expenditures, $100,025; qualifying distributions,
$98,000; giving activities include $98,000 for
15 grants (high: $50,000; low: $1,000).
Purpose and activities: Giving for animal
welfare and social services.
Fields of interest: Higher education; Education;
Animals/wildlife; Human services; Homeless.
Limitations: Applications not accepted. Giving
primarily in NJ. No grants to individuals.
Application information: Contributes only to
pre-selected organizations.
Trustees: Kathryn Casey; Sheila Gagliano;
Rosemary Irre; Christine Todino; Joseph R.
Todino; Rosemary Todino.
EIN: 223515394

1967
Gary & Tamar Tolchin Foundation, Inc.
10 Black Walnut Way
Marlboro, NJ 07746

Established in 1997 in NJ.
Donor(s): Gary Tolchin.
Grantmaker type: Independent foundation
Financial data (yr. ended 09/30/02): Assets,
$2,362,583 (M); expenditures, $346,179;
qualifying distributions, $325,769; giving
activities include $319,749 for 141 grants (high:
$36,000; low: $36).
Fields of interest: Theater; Arts; Early childhood
education; Environment; Health care; Substance
abuse, treatment; Cancer research; Food banks;

Human services; Jewish federated giving programs; Jewish agencies & temples.
Limitations: Applications not accepted. No grants to individuals.
Application information: Contributes only to pre-selected organizations.
Officers: Gary Tolchin, Pres. and Treas.; Tamar Tolchin, V.P. and Secy.; Sam Tolchin, V.P.
EIN: 133986712

1968
Mark Torrance Foundation
c/o Merrill Lynch Trust Co.
P.O. Box 1525, Tax Svcs., MSC 06-03
Pennington, NJ 08534

Established in 2000 WA.
Donor(s): Mark Torrance.
Grantmaker type: Independent foundation
Financial data (yr. ended 09/30/02): Assets, $3,153,465 (M); expenditures, $151,514; qualifying distributions, $124,800; giving activities include $119,372 for 5 grants (high: $50,000; low: $1,000).
Fields of interest: Education; Environment; Human services.
Limitations: Applications not accepted. Giving primarily in Seattle, WA. No grants to individuals.
Application information: Contributes only to pre-selected organizations.
Officers: Mark Torrance, Pres.; Susan Summers Torrance, V.P.; M. Edward Spring, Secy.; Steve Gattis, Treas.
EIN: 911939909

1969
Twin Chimney, Inc.
80 Westcott Rd.
Princeton, NJ 08540

Established in 1986 in NJ.
Donor(s): F. Helmut Weymar, Caroline Weymar.
Grantmaker type: Independent foundation
Financial data (yr. ended 11/30/02): Assets, $5,104,715 (M); expenditures, $564,321; qualifying distributions, $558,865; giving activities include $557,926 for 48 grants (high: $168,231; low: $1,000).
Purpose and activities: Giving primarily for education.
Fields of interest: Arts; Elementary/secondary education; Higher education; Animals/wildlife; Health organizations, association; Human services; Foundations (private grantmaking); Protestant agencies & churches.
Limitations: Applications not accepted. Giving primarily in MA, NJ, NY, and PA. No grants to individuals.
Application information: Contributes only to pre-selected organizations.
Officers: F. Helmut Weymar, Pres.; Caroline Weymar, Secy.
Trustees: Emily Weymar; Mathew Weymar.
EIN: 222787076

1970
John Tyler Foundation
c/o United National Bank
1130 Rte. 22 E.; P.O. Box 6000
Bridgewater, NJ 08807 (908) 429-2316
Contact: Dawn Avallone, Trust Off., United National Bank

Established in 1984 in NJ; funded in 1990.
Grantmaker type: Independent foundation
Financial data (yr. ended 12/31/02): Assets, $2,316,047 (M); expenditures, $152,748; qualifying distributions, $131,892; giving activities include $126,433 for grants (high: $31,564; low: $2,105).
Purpose and activities: Giving for medical services and research, education, homeless and housing services and for the arts.
Fields of interest: Elementary/secondary education; Environment; Heart & circulatory diseases; Cancer research; Human services.
Types of support: Capital campaigns; Building/renovation; Equipment; Emergency funds.
Limitations: Giving primarily in NJ, with emphasis on Plainfield. No grants to individuals.
Application information: Application form not required.
Copies of proposal: 5
Deadline(s): None
Board meeting date(s): July and Dec.
Trustees: Norman Carter; Margaret B. Tyler; United National Bank.
Number of staff: 1 part-time support.
EIN: 226499512

1971
Victoria Foundation, Inc. ▼
946 Bloomfield Ave., 2nd Fl.
Glen Ridge, NJ 07028 (973) 748-5300
Contact: Catherine M. McFarland, Exec. Off.
FAX: (973) 748-0016; E-mail: CatherineMcFarland@victoriafoundation.org;
URL: http://www.victoriafoundation.org

Incorporated in 1924 in NJ.
Donor(s): Hendon Chubb.‡
Grantmaker type: Independent foundation
Financial data (yr. ended 12/31/02): Assets, $171,022,683 (M); expenditures, $9,845,239; qualifying distributions, $9,638,712; giving activities include $8,827,840 for 125 grants (high: $650,000; low: $500; average: $5,000–$100,000).
Purpose and activities: Within Newark, NJ, grants primarily for urban activities and education programs, including early childhood and elementary education; support also for urban problems, leadership development, youth agencies, and certain statewide environmental projects.
Fields of interest: Arts education; Early childhood education; Elementary school/education; Education; Environment; Family planning; Substance abuse, services; AIDS; Alcoholism; Crime/violence prevention, youth; Domestic violence; Housing/shelter, development; Youth development, services; Human services; Children/youth, services; Minorities/immigrants, centers/services; Civil rights, minorities; Urban/community development; Community development; Marine science; Leadership development; Public affairs;

Minorities; African Americans/Blacks; Hispanics/Latinos; Immigrants/refugees; Economically disadvantaged; Homeless.
Types of support: General/operating support; Continuing support; Capital campaigns; Building/renovation; Land acquisition; Emergency funds; Program development; Seed money; Curriculum development; Technical assistance; Consulting services; Program-related investments/loans; Matching/challenge support.
Limitations: Giving limited to greater Newark, NJ; environmental grants limited to NJ. No support for organizations dealing with specific diseases or afflictions, geriatric needs, or day care. No grants to individuals, or for publications or conferences.
Publications: Application guidelines, Annual report, Grants list.
Application information: Request application guidelines. Application form required.
Initial approach: Proposal or 2-page letter of introduction
Copies of proposal: 1
Deadline(s): Submit proposal prior to Feb. 1 or Aug. 1; Mar. 1 for schools only
Board meeting date(s): June and Dec.
Final notification: Within 3 weeks after board meeting if accepted
Officers and Trustees:* Percy Chubb III,* Pres.; Margaret H. Parker,* V.P.; Catherine M. McFarland, Secy. and Exec. Off.; Kevin Shanley,* Treas.; Charles M. Chapin III; Sally Chubb; Robert Curvin; Charles E. Hance; Gordon A. Millspaugh, Jr.; Franklin E. Parker IV; John F. Parker; Helen Parr; Sarah Chubb Sauvayre; Nina Wells; A. Zachary Yamba.
Number of staff: 3 full-time professional; 3 full-time support.
EIN: 221554541
Recent environmental and animal welfare grants:
1971-1 Association of New Jersey Environmental Commissions, Mendham, NJ, $60,000. For general support. 2002.
1971-2 Audubon Society of New Jersey, Bernardsville, NJ, $20,000. For Newark students in School of Ecology, exposing students to environmental education, careers in environmental sciences, and solutions to environmental problems. 2002.
1971-3 Environmental Defense, New York, NY, $30,000. Toward activities in New Jersey, particularly in Highlands, Pinelands, Hudson/Raritan Estuary, and Hackensack Meadowlands. 2002.
1971-4 Greater Newark Conservancy, Newark, NJ, $75,000. For environmental education programs for students. 2002.
1971-5 Hackensack Riverkeeper, Teaneck, NJ, $30,000. For general operating support. 2002.
1971-6 Hudson River Sloop Clearwater, Poughkeepsie, NY, $15,000. For sails on Hudson River for Newark children, Classroom of the Waves. 2002.
1971-7 Morris Parks and Land Conservancy, Boonton, NJ, $10,000. For seed money to develop conservation easement stewardship model for municipalities in New Jersey. 2002.
1971-8 Natural Resources Defense Council, New York, NY, $25,000. For work in New Jersey, chiefly on coastal fisheries and water quality, and on issues surrounding development threats to Hackensack

Meadowlands, important wetlands habitat. 2002.

1971-9 Nature Conservancy, Chester, NJ, $605,880. Toward campaign to preserve acres of natural lands in New Jersey. 2002.

1971-10 New Jersey Conservation Foundation, Far Hills, NJ, $75,000. For financing gap on purchase of acres in New Jersey Highlands. 2002.

1971-11 New Jersey Conservation Foundation, Far Hills, NJ, $40,000. For Conservation Assistance Program. 2002.

1971-12 New Jersey Future, Trenton, NJ, $25,000. For research and analysis activities. 2002.

1971-13 New Jersey Public Interest Research Group, Trenton, NJ, $20,000. For continued support for New Jersey Community Water Watch. 2002.

1971-14 Pinelands Preservation Alliance, Pemberton, NJ, $40,000. For general operating support. 2002.

1971-15 Project USE-Urban Suburban Environments, Red Bank, NJ, $35,000. For services to Newark youth. 2002.

1971-16 Raritan BayKeeper, Raritan, NJ, $70,000. For Baykeeper's activities that are related to open space preservation. 2002.

1971-17 Trust for Public Land, Trenton, NJ, $200,000. For playgrounds for Newark children. 2002.

1971-18 Trust for Public Land, Trenton, NJ, $40,000. 2002.

1971-19 Whippany River Watershed Action Committee, Newark, NJ, $10,500. For beginning of lakes management strategy. 2002.

1972
Johanette Wallerstein Institute
Llewellyn Park
1 Elm Court Way
West Orange, NJ 07052 (973) 731-1394
Contact: Bernard Wallerstein, Pres.
FAX: (973) 731-1395; E-mail: bwallerstein@comcast.net

Established in 1967 in NJ.
Donor(s): Julian Wallerstein,‡ Jane Wallerstein, Bernard Wallerstein.
Grantmaker type: Independent foundation
Financial data (yr. ended 06/30/03): Assets, $9,630,310 (M); gifts received, $121,634; expenditures, $435,427; qualifying distributions, $423,520; giving activities include $423,520 for 49 grants (high: $75,000; low: $250; average: $10,000–$25,000).
Purpose and activities: Primary interests are the environment and environmental justice.
Fields of interest: Environment.
Types of support: Annual campaigns; Building/renovation; Publication; Seed money; Research; Program evaluation; Matching/challenge support.
Limitations: Giving primarily in northern NJ.
Publications: Informational brochure (including application guidelines), Program policy statement.
Application information: Application form not required.
   Initial approach: Letter
   Copies of proposal: 4
   Deadline(s): None

Board meeting date(s): July
Officers and Trustee:* Bernard Wallerstein,* Pres.; Jane Wallerstein, V.P.
Number of staff: None.
EIN: 226042908

1973
Michelle R. Weiss Charitable Foundation, Inc.
2038 83rd St.
North Bergen, NJ 07047

Established in 1997.
Donor(s): John Weiss, Sonia Weiss.
Grantmaker type: Operating foundation
Financial data (yr. ended 07/31/02): Assets, $329,248 (M); gifts received, $71,331; expenditures, $237,745; qualifying distributions, $237,440; giving activities include $237,440 for 12 grants (high: $105,000; low: $100).
Purpose and activities: Giving primarily for education and health care.
Fields of interest: Scholarships/financial aid; Education; Health care; Natural resources.
Types of support: General/operating support; Scholarship funds.
Limitations: Giving primarily in NJ. No grants to individuals.
Officers: John Weiss, Pres.; Sonia Weiss, V.P.
Trustees: Robert Weiss; Steven Weiss.
EIN: 223538607

1974
The Harold Wetterberg Foundation
P.O. Box 30
Princeton, NJ 08542
Contact: Gene R. Korf, Secy.
Application address: c/o Korf & Rosenblatt, 89 Headquarters Plz., North Tower, 14th Fl., Morristown, NJ 07960, tel.: (973) 993-1738

Incorporated in 1961 in NJ.
Donor(s): Harold Wetterberg.‡
Grantmaker type: Independent foundation
Financial data (yr. ended 11/30/02): Assets, $2,855,894 (M); expenditures, $242,065; qualifying distributions, $234,151; giving activities include $190,758 for 34 grants (high: $22,000; low: $1,000).
Purpose and activities: Grants primarily for higher educational institutions and science organizations, with emphasis on research and education programs in the veterinary sciences, including cattle and agriculture, as well as arts and cultural programs, community services and others.
Fields of interest: Arts; Education, research; Higher education; Animal welfare; Veterinary medicine; Agriculture, livestock issues; Community development, service clubs; Biological sciences.
Types of support: General/operating support; Capital campaigns; Scholarship funds.
Limitations: Giving primarily in NJ. No grants to individuals.
Application information: Contact foundation for application guidelines for scholarships. Application form required.
   Initial approach: Applications in the form required by foundation's guidelines
   Copies of proposal: 1
   Deadline(s): None

Board meeting date(s): Varies
Officers and Trustees:* Albert G. Besser,* Pres.; Gene R. Korf,* Secy.; Samuel R. Hoffer,* Treas.
Number of staff: None.
EIN: 226042915

1975
The Winn Feline Foundation
(formerly Robert H. Winn Foundation for Cat Research, Inc.)
1805 Atlantic Ave.
P.O. Box 1005
Manasquan, NJ 08736-0805 (732) 528-9797
Contact: Janet Wolf, Exec. Dir.
E-mail: winn@winnfelinehealth.org; *URL:* http://www.winnfelinehealth.org

Established in 1968.
Grantmaker type: Public charity
Financial data (yr. ended 04/30/02): Revenue, $155,966; assets, $599,651; gifts received, $125,714; expenditures, $169,922; program services expenses, $143,874; giving activities include $143,874 for 11 grants to individuals (high: $15,000; low: $6,354).
Purpose and activities: The foundation promotes awareness of feline health and welfare issues by helping to advance veterinary knowledge and care.
Fields of interest: Veterinary medicine.
Types of support: Research.
Limitations: Giving on a national basis. No support for salaries of principal investigators, expenditures, travel, or indirect costs. No grants for major equipment.
Application information: See Web site for complete application information. Application form required.
   Copies of proposal: 14
   Deadline(s): Dec. 1
   Final notification: Mar.
Officers and Directors:* Hilary Helmrich,* Pres.; Gayle Hand,* V.P.; Betty White,* Secy.; Thomas H. Dent,* Treas.; Janet Wolf, Exec. Dir.; Susan Little.
EIN: 237138699

1976
J. A. & H. G. Woodruff, Jr. Charitable Trust
c/o Merrill Lynch Trust Co.
P.O. Box 1525, MSC06-03
Pennington, NJ 08534-1525

Established in 1998 in FL.
Donor(s): Merrill Lynch Trust Co.
Grantmaker type: Independent foundation
Financial data (yr. ended 05/31/03): Assets, $5,362,395 (M); expenditures, $258,841; qualifying distributions, $204,835; giving activities include $204,835 for 21 grants (high: $27,500; low: $1,500).
Purpose and activities: Giving primarily for education, natural resource conservation, particularly a tree commission, and youth and social services.
Fields of interest: Education; Botanical gardens; Boys & girls clubs; Human services; Children/youth, services.
Limitations: Applications not accepted. Giving primarily in FL and GA. No grants to individuals.
Application information: Contributes only to pre-selected organizations.

Trustees: James Woodruff III; Thomas Woodruff.
EIN: 656246750

1977
YPI Charitable Trust
c/o J. Harvey
6 Revere Ct.
Princeton Junction, NJ 08550

Established in 1991.
Donor(s): John T. Dorrance III, Charles A.
Dorrance.
Grantmaker type: Independent foundation
Financial data (yr. ended 05/31/02): Assets,
$12,181,219 (M); expenditures, $665,110;
qualifying distributions, $614,086; giving
activities include $617,500 for 31 grants (high:
$60,000; low: $5,000).
Fields of interest: Arts; Education;
Animals/wildlife; Health care.
International interests: Bahamas.
Limitations: Applications not accepted. Giving
in the U.S. and the Bahamas. No grants to
individuals.
Application information: Contributes only to
pre-selected organizations.
Trustees: Charles A. Dorrance; Gunda S.
Dorrance; John T. Dorrance III; John T. Dorrance
IV.
EIN: 237675355

NEW MEXICO

1978
Eugene M. Adler Family Fund
2704 Campbell Rd. N.W.
Albuquerque, NM 87104
Contact: Constance Adler, Pres.
E-mail: cadler@earthlink.net

Established in 1969 in IL.
Grantmaker type: Independent foundation
Financial data (yr. ended 04/30/02): Assets,
$3,880,253 (M); gifts received, $3,000,000;
expenditures, $177,042; qualifying distributions,
$159,268; giving activities include $159,998 for
10 grants (high: $25,000; low: $1,000).
Fields of interest: Education; Environment; Civil
rights.
Types of support: General/operating support;
Annual campaigns; Building/renovation;
Equipment; Land acquisition; Program
development; Conferences/seminars; Seed
money; Curriculum development;
Matching/challenge support.
Limitations: Giving primarily in Chicago, IL,
NM, and Providence, RI.
Application information: Application form not
required.
  Initial approach: Letter
  Copies of proposal: 1
  Deadline(s): None
Officers and Directors:* Constance Adler,*
Pres.; Eugenie Adler,* V.P.; Linda Adler-Kassner;
William Meyer; Jacqueline Thurman.
Number of staff: None.
EIN: 366063024

1979
Albuquerque Community Foundation
3301 Menaul Blvd. N.E., Ste. 2
P.O. Box 36960
Albuquerque, NM 87176-6960
(505) 883-6240
Contact: Laura Hueter Bass, Exec. Dir.
FAX: (505) 883-3629; E-mail:
acf@albuquerquefoundation.org; URL: http://
www.albuquerquefoundation.org

Established in 1981 in NM.
Grantmaker type: Community foundation
Financial data (yr. ended 06/03/02): Assets,
$27,578,666 (M); gifts received, $2,912,434;
expenditures, $1,894,278; giving activities
include $1,392,830 for 218 grants (high:
$299,700; low: $250; average: $1,000–$5,000).
Purpose and activities: Giving primarily to a
pool of charitable funds whose income is used
to benefit the community in grants to local
nonprofits. The foundation administers
donor-advised funds.
Fields of interest: Historic
preservation/historical societies; Arts; Education;
Natural resources; Health care; Human services.
Types of support: Continuing support; Program
development; Publication; Seed money;
Scholarship funds; Technical assistance;
Scholarships—to individuals.
Limitations: Giving primarily in the greater
Albuquerque, NM, area. No support for political
or religious purposes or for grantmaking
organizations. Generally, no grants to
individuals (except for scholarship funds), or for
debt retirement, annual campaigns,
endowments, emergency funding or interest or
tax payments.
Publications: Annual report (including
application guidelines), Newsletter.
Application information: Application form not
required.
  Initial approach: Visit Web site
  Deadline(s): May 1
  Board meeting date(s): Quarterly
  Final notification: Annually in Sept.
Officers and Trustees:* Douglas M. Brown,*
Pres.; S. Michael Walker,* V.P. and Treas.; Maria
Griego-Raby,* Secy.; Laura Hueter Bass, Exec.
Dir.; and 14 additional trustees.
Number of staff: 2 full-time professional; 3
part-time professional; 1 full-time support.
EIN: 850295444

1980
BF Foundation
607 Cerrillos Rd., Ste. D-2
Santa Fe, NM 87501
Contact: Katherine Lee Chase, Pres.

Established in 1965 in AZ.
Donor(s): Harvey W. Branigar, Jr.‡
Grantmaker type: Independent foundation
Financial data (yr. ended 06/30/02): Assets,
$4,820,819 (M); expenditures, $432,336;
qualifying distributions, $424,777; giving
activities include $346,563 for 25 grants (high:
$101,600; low: $250).
Purpose and activities: Giving primarily to
individuals through Financial Aid Department.
Awards scholarship grants for Northern Arizona
University. Awards made to institutions on
behalf of named recipients. Students must be

U.S. citizens enrolled full-time at the
undergraduate level, and must maintain a 2.5
G.P.A. Some internships in qualified cultural
organizations.
Fields of interest: Museums; Higher education;
Education; Botanical gardens; Environment;
Foundations (community); Astronomy.
Types of support: Internship funds;
Scholarships—to individuals.
Limitations: Applications not accepted. Giving
primarily to residents of AZ.
Application information: Unsolicited requests
for funds not accepted.
Officers and Directors:* David D. Chase,
Chair.; Katherine Lee Chase,* Pres.; Sarah Lee
Branigar,* V.P.; Sara Chase Shaw,* Secy-Treas;
Richard W. Shaw.
Number of staff: 1 full-time professional; 1
part-time professional.
EIN: 366141070

1981
The Frost Foundation, Ltd.
511 Armijo St., Ste. A
Santa Fe, NM 87501 (505) 986-0208
Contact: Mary Amelia Whited-Howell, Pres.
FAX: (505) 986-0430

Incorporated in 1959 in LA.
Donor(s): Virginia C. Frost.‡
Grantmaker type: Independent foundation
Financial data (yr. ended 12/31/01): Assets,
$37,870,989 (M); expenditures, $2,596,746;
qualifying distributions, $2,248,446; giving
activities include $2,138,093 for 109 grants
(high: $142,857; low: $1,000; average:
$15,000–$25,000).
Purpose and activities: Focus on the following
areas: 1) Social service and humanitarian needs
including, but not limited to, violence in the
streets, domestic violence, child abuse, specific
public health issues such as alcohol and drug
abuse, homelessness, and problems of the
elderly; 2) Environment - consideration given to
programs in research, education, and action to
conserve and protect the environment for the
well-being and safety of plants, animals, and
human beings; and 3) Education - focus on new,
innovative, creative, practical programs to
address students' and society's needs today, and
which recognize our changing sociological
structure and concerns.
Fields of interest: Higher education; Business
school/education; Education; Natural resources;
Environment; Animal welfare; Health care;
Substance abuse, services; Mental health/crisis
services; Health organizations, association;
AIDS; AIDS research; Food services; Human
services; Children/youth, services; Family
services; Hospices; Aging, centers/services;
Women, centers/services; Minorities/immigrants,
centers/services; Homeless, human services;
Minorities; Native Americans/American Indians;
Aging; Women; Homeless.
Types of support: Continuing support; Capital
campaigns; Equipment; Program development;
Conferences/seminars; Publication; Seed
money; Curriculum development; Fellowships;
Technical assistance; Matching/challenge
support.
Limitations: Giving primarily in LA and NM. No
support for animal experimentation. No grants
to individuals, or for building funds,

sponsorships for special events, endowment funds, medical research, or scholarships; no loans.
Publications: Application guidelines, Biennial report.
Application information: Application form not required.
 Initial approach: Telephone or letter; full proposal at foundation's request
 Copies of proposal: 1
 Deadline(s): Dec. 1 and June 1
 Board meeting date(s): Mar. and Sept.
 Final notification: 7 to 10 days
Officers and Directors:* Mary Amelia Whited-Howell,* Pres.; Philip B. Howell,* Exec. V.P.; Taylor F. Moore, Secy.-Treas.; Ann Rogers Gerber; John A. LeVan; Edwin F. Whited.
Number of staff: 1 full-time professional; 1 part-time professional; 1 full-time support.
EIN: 720520342

1982
Grasslans Charitable Foundation
c/o James Weaver
P.O. Box 23
Causey, NM 88113

Established in 2000 in IL.
Grantmaker type: Independent foundation
Financial data (yr. ended 12/31/02): Assets, $3,037,001 (M); gifts received, $1,230; expenditures, $192,635; qualifying distributions, $150,949; giving activities include $151,585 for 5 grants (high: $50,085; low: $1,500).
Purpose and activities: Giving primarily to bird conservation.
Fields of interest: Natural resources; Animals/wildlife, bird preserves.
Limitations: Applications not accepted. Giving primarily in ID and NM. No grants to individuals.
Application information: Contributes only to pre-selected organizations.
Officers: Willard Heck, Exec. Secy.; Chris Weaver, Treas.; James Weaver, Exec. Dir.
EIN: 364375884

1983
Grace and John T. Harrington Foundation
c/o First National Bank of Santa Fe, Trust Dept.
P.O. Box 609
Santa Fe, NM 87504-0609

Established in 1954 in OH.
Grantmaker type: Independent foundation
Financial data (yr. ended 12/31/02): Assets, $1,289,189 (M); expenditures, $110,831; qualifying distributions, $93,000; giving activities include $93,000 for 15 grants (high: $37,500; low: $1,000).
Fields of interest: Historic preservation/historical societies; Higher education; Natural resources; Animals/wildlife, preservation/protection; Health care; Federated giving programs.
Types of support: General/operating support.
Limitations: Applications not accepted. Giving on a national basis. No grants to individuals.
Application information: Contributes only to pre-selected organizations.
Officers: William W. Thornton, Jr., Pres.; John W. Thornton, V.P.; Patricia Thornton, Secy.-Treas.
Trustee: First National Bank of Santa Fe.

EIN: 346514087

1984
The Healy Foundation
c/o Edmund Healy
P.O. Box 767
Taos, NM 87571

Established in 2002 in NM.
Donor(s): M.A. Healy Family Foundation, Inc.
Grantmaker type: Independent foundation
Financial data (yr. ended 12/31/02): Assets, $7,534,498 (M); gifts received, $7,433,826; expenditures, $424,538; qualifying distributions, $424,538; giving activities include $396,500 for 27 grants (high: $50,000; low: $5,000).
Fields of interest: Arts; Natural resources.
Limitations: Applications not accepted. No grants to individuals.
Application information: Contributes only to pre-selected organizations.
Advisors: Edmond Healy; Wilmington Trust Co.
EIN: 030466977

1985
Lannan Foundation ▼
313 Read St.
Santa Fe, NM 87501 (505) 986-8160
Contact: Ruth Simms, Cont.
FAX: (505) 986-8195; URL: http://www.lannan.org

Established in 1960 in IL.
Donor(s): J. Patrick Lannan.‡
Grantmaker type: Independent foundation
Financial data (yr. ended 12/31/02): Assets, $200,648,528 (M); expenditures, $16,135,273; qualifying distributions, $17,734,309; giving activities include $7,973,055 for 132 grants (high: $500,000; low: $500; average: $500–$500,000), $1,775,925 for 26 grants to individuals (high: $350,000; low: $5,925), $11,870 for 11 employee matching gifts, $1,141,501 for 3 foundation-administered programs and $25,000 for 1 loan/program-related investment.
Purpose and activities: The foundation is a family foundation dedicated to cultural freedom, diversity and creativity through projects which support exceptional contemporary artists and writers, as well as inspired Native activists in rural indigenous communities. The foundation recognizes the profound and often unquantifiable value of the creative process and is willing to take risks and make substantial investments in ambitious and experimental thinking. Understanding that globalization threatens all cultures and ecosystems, the foundation is particularly interested in projects that encourage freedom of inquiry, imagination, and expression. The foundation supports this mission with long-term special projects requiring multi-year commitments of funding and technical assistance in the areas of contemporary visual art, literature, indigenous communities, and issues of cultural freedom.
Fields of interest: Visual arts; Museums; Literature; Historic preservation/historical societies; Arts; Native Americans/American Indians.
Types of support: General/operating support; Building/renovation; Equipment; Land

acquisition; Endowments; Publication; Fellowships; Technical assistance; Program-related investments/loans; Employee matching gifts; Grants to individuals; Matching/challenge support.
Limitations: Applications not accepted. No grants to individuals (except for Lannan Literary Awards), or for documentary film or video projects, performing arts or theater, or crafts or decorative arts.
Application information:
 Board meeting date(s): Three times per year
Officers and Directors:* J. Patrick Lannan, Jr.,* Pres.; Frank C. Lawler,* V.P. and Dir., Opers.; Ruth Simms, Cont.; Marian P. Day; Meghan Ferrill; Sharon A. Ferrill; William E. Johnston; Sharron Lannan Korybut; John J. Lannan; John R. Lannan; Lawrence P. Lannan, Jr.; Mary M. Plauche.
Number of staff: 8 full-time professional; 4 full-time support; 2 part-time support.
EIN: 366062451
Recent environmental and animal welfare grants:
1985-1 Collective Heritage Institute, Santa Fe, NM, $40,000. 2002.
1985-2 David Suzuki Foundation, Vancouver, Canada, $250,000. For Pacific Salmon Forests Project. 2002.
1985-3 Environmental-Aboriginal Guardianship through Law and Education (EAGLE), Surrey, Canada, $200,000. For Haida Aboriginal title case. 2002.
1985-4 Environmental-Aboriginal Guardianship through Law and Education (EAGLE), Surrey, Canada, $25,000. For tree farm license appeal. 2002.
1985-5 Families Against Incinerator Risk (FAIR), Salt Lake City, UT, $20,000. For Skull Valley Goshute Nuclear Waste Dump project. 2002.
1985-6 Fort Yuma-Quechan Indian Tribe, Yuma, AZ, $200,000. For initiative to stop gold mine. 2002.
1985-7 Hawk Mountain Sanctuary Association, Kempton, PA, $11,000. 2002.
1985-8 Intertribal Sinkyone Wilderness Council, Ukiah, CA, $50,000. For general support. 2002.
1985-9 Pueblo of Picuris, Penasco, NM, $100,000. For legal challenge to mica mining. 2002.
1985-10 Pueblo of Zuni, Zuni, NM, $200,000. For legal support to stop coal mine and protect sacred lake. 2002.
1985-11 Red Bay Stronghold Foundation, West Palm Beach, FL, $50,000. For operating support. 2002.
1985-12 Seventh Generation Fund for Indian Development, Arcata, CA, $50,000. For general support for Western Shoshone Defense Project in Crescent Valley, NV. 2002.
1985-13 Southwest Research and Information Center, Albuquerque, NM, $30,000. For general support of Eastern Navajo Dine Against Uranium Mining (ENDAUM). 2002.
1985-14 Southwest Research and Information Center, Albuquerque, NM, $10,000. For education program for Eastern Navajo Dine Against Uranium Mining (ENDAUM). 2002.
1985-15 Tides Foundation, San Francisco, CA, $130,000. For tractor for Instituto Terra reforestation project. 2002.

1985-16 White Earth Land Recovery Project, Ponsford, MN, $50,000. For Wild Rice Protection Campaign. 2002.

1985-17 Yukon River Inter-Tribal Watershed Council, Anchorage, AK, $60,000. For mapping project. 2002.

1986
The Frederick H. Leonhardt Foundation, Inc.

(also known as FHL Foundation, Inc.)
P.O. Box 27650
Albuquerque, NM 87125 (505) 247-2400
Contact: Frederick H. Leonhardt II, Pres.
FAX: (505)247-2300; E-mail:
fhlfound@thuntek.net; URL: http://
www.fhlfoundation.org

Established in 1953; incorporated in 1954 in NY; reorganized in 1989; divided in 1997.
Donor(s): Frederick H. Leonhardt.‡
Grantmaker type: Independent foundation
Financial data (yr. ended 07/31/03): Assets, $7,506,856 (M); expenditures, $301,138; qualifying distributions, $216,378; giving activities include $101,570 for 11 grants (high: $22,570; low: $1,000).
Purpose and activities: Interests include programs that strengthen the family, education, human services, and the environment that have a focus on attachment relationships, system, and research.
Fields of interest: Medical school/education; Education; Animal welfare; Health care; Mental health, treatment; Mental health/crisis services, hot-lines; Rape victim services; Abuse prevention; Domestic violence; Child abuse; Human services; Family services; Civil rights, women; Reproductive rights.
Types of support: General/operating support; Program development; Conferences/seminars; Research; Technical assistance; Consulting services; Matching/challenge support.
Limitations: Giving primarily in NM, with emphasis on Albuquerque. Support for certain model programs or research at the national level. No grants to individuals.
Publications: Application guidelines, Grants list, Program policy statement.
Application information: Unsolicited requests for funds not accepted. Applications by invitation only following a review of initial contact private message. Application form required.
  Initial approach: Leave private message at Web site
  Board meeting date(s): Quarterly
Officers and Directors:* Frederick H. Leonhardt II,* Pres. and Treas.; Barbara Rowe Mintz,* V.P. and Secy.; Julie Kilpatrick.
Number of staff: 2 part-time professional; 1 part-time support.
EIN: 136123271

1987
Max and Anna Levinson Foundation

P.O. Box 6309
Santa Fe, NM 87502-6309 (505) 995-8802
Contact: Charlotte Talberth, Exec. Dir.
FAX: (505) 995-8982; E-mail:
info@levinsonfoundation.org; URL: http://
www.levinsonfoundation.org

Incorporated in 1956 in DE.
Donor(s): Max Levinson,‡ Carl A. Levinson.
Grantmaker type: Independent foundation
Financial data (yr. ended 09/30/02): Assets, $15,608,847 (M); gifts received, $5,000; expenditures, $1,228,108; qualifying distributions, $1,012,739; giving activities include $815,565 for grants (average: $5,000–$10,000).
Purpose and activities: Funding is allocated among three categories: 1) Environment - including preservation of ecosystems and biological diversity, alternative energy and efficiency; toxins, alternative agriculture, environmental restoration, natural resource conservation, and sustainable communities; 2) Social - including urban and rural community economic development, multiculturalism, human rights, youth leadership and empowerment, conflict resolution, and aid to survivors of violence, and health care; and 3) Jewish/Israel - including Jewish culture and spirituality, history and education, eastern and world Jewry, the Israeli peace movement, and social and environmental issues in Israel. Whatever the specific area of interest, the foundation encourages projects which are concerned with promoting community, social justice, a healthy environment and a sustainable economy, either by developing alternatives to the status quo or by responsibly modifying existing systems, institutions, conditions, and attitudes which block promising innovation. Support for large organizations given a lower priority.
Fields of interest: Environment; International human rights; Jewish agencies & temples.
International interests: Israel.
Types of support: General/operating support; Equipment; Program development; Conferences/seminars; Publication; Seed money; Grants to individuals.
Limitations: Giving on a national basis. No grants for capital or endowment funds, building programs, travel, projects of primarily local community significance, expansion of existing services, matching gifts, scholarships, or fellowships; no loans.
Publications: Grants list, Informational brochure (including application guidelines).
Application information: Application form available on foundation Web site. Application form required.
  Initial approach: Letter of inquiry or proposal (2-to 6-pages)
  Copies of proposal: 1
  Deadline(s): Apr. 1
  Board meeting date(s): Varies
  Final notification: 2 weeks after board meeting
Officers: Carol Doroshow, Pres.; Charlotte Talberth, V.P. and Exec. Dir.; Carl A. Levinson, Secy.
Directors: Robin Beck; Helen Doroshow; James Doroshow; Douglas Levinson; Gordon Levinson; Julian Levinson.

Number of staff: 1 full-time professional.
EIN: 236282844

1988
McCune Charitable Foundation ▼

(formerly Marshall L. & Perrine D. McCune Charitable Foundation)
345 E. Alameda St.
Santa Fe, NM 87501-2229 (505) 983-8300
Contact: Frances R. Sowers, Assoc. Dir.
FAX: (505) 983-7887; E-mail:
fsowers@swcp.com; URL: http://
www.nmmccune.org

Established in 1992 in NM.
Donor(s): Perrine Dixon McCune,‡ Marshall L. McCune.‡
Grantmaker type: Independent foundation
Financial data (yr. ended 12/31/01): Assets, $132,635,861 (M); expenditures, $9,654,385; qualifying distributions, $8,935,811; giving activities include $7,686,800 for 455 grants (high: $150,000; low: $900; average: $5,000–$50,000) and $370,566 for 2 loans/program-related investments.
Purpose and activities: Primary areas of interest include the arts, education, youth, health, social services and environment.
Fields of interest: Visual arts; Museums; Performing arts; Dance; Theater; Music; History/archaeology; Historic preservation/historical societies; Arts; Early childhood education; Child development, education; Elementary school/education; Secondary school/education; Vocational education; Higher education; Adult/continuing education; Adult education—literacy, basic skills & GED; Libraries/library science; Reading; Education; Natural resources; Environment; Animal welfare; Animals/wildlife, preservation/protection; Hospitals (general); Family planning; Medical care, rehabilitation; Health care; Substance abuse, services; Mental health/crisis services; Health organizations, association; Cancer; Heart & circulatory diseases; AIDS; Alcoholism; Crime/violence prevention, youth; Crime/law enforcement; Employment; Agriculture; Food services; Nutrition; Housing/shelter, development; Youth development, services; Youth development, citizenship; Human services; Children/youth, services; Child development, services; Family services; Hospices; Aging, centers/services; Women, centers/services; Minorities/immigrants, centers/services; Homeless, human services; Rural development; Community development; Federated giving programs; Public affairs, citizen participation; Leadership development; Public affairs; Minorities; Native Americans/American Indians; Disabled; Aging; Women; Gays/lesbians; Economically disadvantaged; Homeless.
Types of support: General/operating support; Continuing support; Annual campaigns; Building/renovation; Equipment; Emergency funds; Program development; Conferences/seminars; Seed money; Scholarship funds; Technical assistance; Program-related investments/loans; Matching/challenge support.
Limitations: Giving limited to NM. No grants to individuals, or for endowments, research, voter registration drives, or to cover deficits.

Publications: Application guidelines, Biennial report.

Application information: See Web site for current cycle dates for initial approach and deadlines; submissions received by FAX not accepted. Application form not required.

Initial approach: On-line application only
Deadline(s): Changes annually
Board meeting date(s): Changes annually
Final notification: Changes annually

Officers and Directors:* Sarah McCune Losinger,* Chair.; Owen M. Lopez, Exec. Dir.; Frances R. Sowers, Assoc. Dir.; James M. Edwards; John R. McCune VI.

Number of staff: 1 full-time professional; 1 full-time support.

EIN: 850429439

Recent environmental and animal welfare grants:

1988-1 1000 Friends of New Mexico, Albuquerque, NM, $50,000. To expand Albuquerque-based Transportation and Neighborhoods project to create healthier growth patterns, support New Mexico Natez project, and increase membership. 2001.

1988-2 1000 Friends of New Mexico, Albuquerque, NM, $50,000. 2001.

1988-3 All Species Project, Santa Fe, NM, $15,000. To expand skill-based ecological educational outreach to students throughout New Mexico. 2001.

1988-4 Amigos Bravos, Taos, NM, $25,000. For general operating support associated with conservation of water resources and mining issues in state of New Mexico. 2001.

1988-5 Angel Fire, Village of, Angel Fire, NM, $15,000. For leak detector for community's water system. 2001.

1988-6 Animal Protection of New Mexico, Albuquerque, NM, $10,000. For Wildlife Diversity Campaign which seeks to identify and establish alternative funding sources for wildlife conservation programs aimed at preserving diversity of state's wildlife. 2001.

1988-7 Audubon Society, National, Santa Fe, NM, $15,000. For operating support and capital improvements. 2001.

1988-8 Canine Companions for Independence, Oceanside, CA, $25,000. To establish free of charge dormitory facility for individuals with disabilities who are receiving team training and follow-up workshops. 2001.

1988-9 Center for Biological Diversity, Tucson, AZ, $10,000. For continuation of New Mexico Forest Program intended to help restore ecological integrity of state's forested ecosystems. 2001.

1988-10 Center for Science in Public Participation, Bozeman, MT, $15,000. To provide technical assistance to New Mexico public interest groups assessing mining environmental issues to ensure good reclamation plans and bonds at all New Mexico mines. 2001.

1988-11 Cimarron Elementary School, Cimarron, NM, $15,000. For salary of teacher to facilitate environmental education curriculum. 2001.

1988-12 Coalition for Clean Affordable Energy, Albuquerque, NM, $10,000. For operating support associated with programs offered to New Mexico citizens concerning deregulation of New Mexico's electric utility industry. 2001.

1988-13 Daylight Productions, Santa Fe, NM, $25,000. To produce video concerning threatened Rio Grande. 2001.

1988-14 Defenders of Wildlife, Albuquerque, NM, $25,000. For preparation of Western Water Policy Transition Project's transition report addressing long term coordinated strategies for more sustainable and equitable uses of western water. 2001.

1988-15 Dixon Animal Protection Society, Dixon, NM, $10,000. For operating support associated with no kill animal shelter services to Dixon, Mora, Taos, Penasco, Las Vegas, Santa Fe, and Espanola communities. 2001.

1988-16 Dreamtree Project, Taos, NM, $12,000. For Wilderness Therapy Summer Program for Taos area children and youth, ages 8-21 years, who have experienced abuse or neglect. 2001.

1988-17 Earth Works Institute, Santa Fe, NM, $10,000. For continuation of environmental educational services to area schools, and for production of video featuring watershed rehabilitation. 2001.

1988-18 Earths Birthday Project, Santa Fe, NM, $10,000. For Blue Morpho Project 2002 linking northern New Mexico fourth and fifth grade students with like students in Belize to share life science learning through intercultural exchange. 2001.

1988-19 Environmental Defense, Boulder, CO, $12,000. To reduce pollutants from Four Corners Power Plant, located on tribal lands in northern New Mexico. 2001.

1988-20 Foothills Trails Trust, Cochiti Lake, NM, $90,000. For design and construction of foothills trails northeast of Santa Fe to serve hikers and bicyclists. 2001.

1988-21 Forest Guardians, Santa Fe, NM, $15,000. For continued mentoring of water resources in Rio Grande. 2001.

1988-22 Forest Trust, Santa Fe, NM, $40,000. For general operating support. 2001.

1988-23 Gila Resources Information Project, Silver City, NM, $12,000. For continuation of air quality monitoring of Hurley copper smelter and to promote smart growth policies at county level. 2001.

1988-24 Hawks Aloft, Albuquerque, NM, $12,500. For continuation of Living with the Landscape-Building a Future for Communities and Wildlife program presented in northern New Mexico. 2001.

1988-25 Jubilados Corporation, Tesuque, NM, $35,000. For development of affordable senior community. 2001.

1988-26 La Jicarita News, Chamisal, NM, $10,000. For monthly publication. 2001.

1988-27 Land Trust Coalition, Santa Fe, NM, $26,250. For consulting to state land trusts. 2001.

1988-28 Malpai Borderlands Group, Douglas, AZ, $10,000. For technical assistance to grass bank program in southern New Mexico. 2001.

1988-29 National Outdoor Leadership School, Lander, WY, $10,000. To identify interested, deserving, and qualified New Mexico student applicants for wilderness skills and leadership program. 2001.

1988-30 National Parks Conservation Association, DC, $15,000. For general operating support for Southwest Region Office. 2001.

1988-31 Nature Conservancy, Santa Fe, NM, $25,000. For matching grant for development of Santa Fe Canton Preserve. 2001.

1988-32 Nature Conservancy, Santa Fe, NM, $15,000. To establish offices in Las Cruces. 2001.

1988-33 New Mexico Acequia Association, Santa Cruz, NM, $12,000. For operating support. 2001.

1988-34 New Mexico Association of Soil and Water Conservation Districts, Carlsbad, NM, $10,000. For general operating support. 2001.

1988-35 New Mexico Bureau of Mines and Mineral Resources, Socorro, NM, $15,000. For annual New Mexico Decision-Makers Earth Science Field Conference to be held in Santa Fe addressing water, watershed, and land use issues. 2001.

1988-36 New Mexico Environmental Law Center, Santa Fe, NM, $35,000. For continuation of free or low cost legal representation and advice to citizens trying to protect their communities from environmental degradation and waste of resources. 2001.

1988-37 New Mexico Forestry Division, Bernalillo, NM, $10,000. For Forest Re-Leaf Program to assist schools, cities and counties by providing trees to plant throughout New Mexico. 2001.

1988-38 New Mexico Mining Act Network, Santa Fe, NM, $50,000. For enforcement of New Mexico Mining Act. 2001.

1988-39 New Mexico Mining Act Network, Santa Fe, NM, $11,000. For operating support associated with enforcement of New Mexico Mining Act and to establish highest possible standards of interpretation of its environmental criteria. 2001.

1988-40 New Mexico Solar Energy Association, Santa Fe, NM, $12,000. For operating support. 2001.

1988-41 New Mexico Water Dialogue, Santa Fe, NM, $12,000. For operating support. 2001.

1988-42 New Mexico Wilderness Alliance, Albuquerque, NM, $10,000. For proactive measures, dedicated to protection and restoration of wild lands and wilderness areas. 2001.

1988-43 New Mexico Wildlife Association, Edgewood, NM, $20,000. For salary of Executive Director to continue to provide wildlife education services statewide. 2001.

1988-44 Northern New Mexico Legal Services, Santa Fe, NM, $24,000. For salary and expenses of coordinator to provide access to legal education and free or low-cost legal assistance for the elderly in rural counties, and legal services for low-income rural Hispanic and Native American communities in northern New Mexico to engage in sustainable economic development relating to agriculture natural resource use, and other community-based activities. 2001.

1988-45 Northern New Mexico Stockmans Association, Taos, NM, $20,000. For establishment of organization. 2001.

1988-46 Quivira Coalition, Santa Fe, NM, $25,000. For general operating support. 2001.

1988-47 Rio Grande Community Farms, Albuquerque, NM, $15,000. For operating support and to match funding for purchase of drip irrigation system and other garden supplies used by community farms. 2001.

1988-48 Rio Grande Restoration, El Prado, NM, $20,000. For river protection, advocacy, and educational outreach to primary and secondary school students. 2001.

1988-49 Santa Fe Mountain Center, Santa Fe, NM, $20,000. For general operating support. 2001.

1988-50 Sawmill Community Land Trust, Albuquerque, NM, $20,000. For general operating support associated with mixed use affordable housing development in historic Sawmill/Old Town community in Albuquerque. 2001.

1988-51 Singing River Field Center, Questa, NM, $30,000. For collaborative program with California Cisneros Youth and Families Center for educational youth program. 2001.

1988-52 Southern Rockies Agricultural Land Trust, Capitan, NM, $12,500. To provide education outreach concerning conservation easements to control development of agricultural lands. 2001.

1988-53 Southwest Desert Sustainability Project, Deming, NM, $10,000. To establish living school to teach skills in sustainable design and building. 2001.

1988-54 Southwest Environmental Center, Las Cruces, NM, $20,000. For general operating support. 2001.

1988-55 Southwest Research and Information Center, Albuquerque, NM, $15,000. For operating support for continuation of environmental education outreach. 2001.

1988-56 Talking Talons Youth Leadership, Tijeras, NM, $10,000. For continuation of middle school program for highest risk youth, and summer program. 2001.

1988-57 Taos Land Trust, Taos, NM, $12,000. For general operating support. 2001.

1988-58 Taos Valley Acequia Association, Taos, NM, $15,000. For general operating support. 2001.

1988-59 TAP Water Santa Fe, Santa Fe, NM, $25,000. For education outreach concerning present water crisis in Santa Fe. 2001.

1988-60 Trust for Public Land, Santa Fe, NM, $40,000. For salary of state director and GIS for land and water conservation purposes. 2001.

1988-61 United States Fish and Wildlife Service, Tule Lake, CA, $15,000. For salary of seasonal employee at Sevilleta National Wildlife Refuge in Socorro to act as liaison to New Mexico schools. 2001.

1988-62 Upper Gila Watershed Alliance, Gila, NM, $10,000. For capacity building to work more effectively on issues and projects affecting long term health of watershed. 2001.

1988-63 Vecinos Del Rio, San Juan Pueblo, NM, $10,000. For general operating services associated with citizens' initiative for responsible mining. 2001.

1988-64 Western Environmental Law Center, Taos, NM, $12,000. For general operating support. 2001.

1988-65 Western Resource Advocates, Boulder, CO, $20,000. To continue to provide technical assistance to New Mexico land trusts. 2001.

1988-66 Wholly Rags, Ranchos de Taos, NM, $12,000. For general operating support. 2001.

1988-67 Wilderness Society, Denver, CO, $10,000. To strengthen and expand local coalition to effectively advocate for preservation of New Mexico through protection of cultural and natural resources. 2001.

1989
Messengers of Healing Winds Foundation
P.O. Box 32360
Santa Fe, NM 87594-2360 (505) 954-4702
Contact: Steven Rasmussen, Exec. Dir.

Established in 1998 in DE and NM.
Donor(s): Andrea Waitt Carlton, Norman W. Waitt, Kind World Foundation.
Grantmaker type: Independent foundation
Financial data (yr. ended 12/31/01): Assets, $37,012,780 (M); gifts received, $235,305; expenditures, $2,313,236; qualifying distributions, $1,777,799; giving activities include $1,830,105 for 75 grants (high: $350,000; low: $100).
Fields of interest: Education; Natural resources; Environmental education; Animal welfare; Animals/wildlife, preservation/protection; Zoos/zoological societies; Human services.
Types of support: Annual campaigns; Capital campaigns; Building/renovation; Equipment; Endowments; Debt reduction; Program development; Matching/challenge support.
Limitations: Giving primarily in the lake region of northwest IA, FL, ND, SD, Santa Fe, NM, and the Southwest. Giving on a national basis for environmental concerns. No grants to individuals.
Application information:
 Initial approach: Written application
 Deadline(s): None
 Final notification: Within 60 days of receipt of proposal
Officers and Directors:* Andrea Waitt Carlton,* Pres.; Donald Poppen,* V.P.; Jennifer Kronebusch,* Secy.-Treas.; Steven Rasmussen, Exec. Dir.
EIN: 860910220
Recent environmental and animal welfare grants:
1989-1 Alliance for the Rio Grande Heritage, Santa Fe, NM, $25,000. For operating support. 2001.
1989-2 American Rivers, DC, $25,000. For mobile display on Lewis and Clark. 2001.
1989-3 Animal Alliance, Santa Fe, NM, $60,000. For Spay-Neuter program. 2001.
1989-4 Candy Kitchen Rescue Ranch, Ramah, NM, $10,000. For land acquisition. 2001.
1989-5 Canine Companions for Independence, Santa Rosa, CA, $10,000. For capital campaign. 2001.
1989-6 Center for Captive Chimpanzee Care, Fort Pierce, FL, $15,000. For construction. 2001.
1989-7 Friends of Lakeside Lab, Milford, IA, $50,000. For capital campaign. 2001.
1989-8 Iowa Natural Heritage Foundation, Des Moines, IA, $35,000. For capital support. 2001.
1989-9 Iowa State University, Veterinary Administration, Ames, IA, $12,500. For operating support for Wildlife Care Clinic. 2001.

1989-10 Lake Area Zoological Society, Watertown, SD, $15,000. For Bramble Park Zoo. 2001.
1989-11 Randall Davey Audubon Center, Santa Fe, NM, $25,000. For renovation project. 2001.
1989-12 Sanibel-Captiva Conservation Foundation, Sanibel, FL, $100,000. For land acquisition. 2001.
1989-13 Santa Fe Animal Shelter, Santa Fe, NM, $14,000. For campaign study. 2001.
1989-14 Santa Fe Childrens Museum, Santa Fe, NM, $10,000. For environmental education program. 2001.
1989-15 Spearfish Canyon Foundation, Spearfish Canyon, SD, $25,000. For land acquisition. 2001.
1989-16 Trust for Public Land, Santa Fe, NM, $10,000. For operating support. 2001.
1989-17 Zoological Society of San Diego, San Diego, CA, $125,000. For Wildlife Vet Hospital. 2001.

1990
Pond Foundation
1447 Seville Rd.
Santa Fe, NM 87505-4647

Established in 1997 in NM.
Donor(s): Georgia Lloyd, Lola Maverick Berndt.
Grantmaker type: Independent foundation
Financial data (yr. ended 12/31/01): Assets, $11,609,261 (M); expenditures, $2,844,585; qualifying distributions, $2,747,845; giving activities include $2,398,873 for 95 grants (high: $648,000; low: $1,800).
Fields of interest: Environment; Animal welfare; Animals/wildlife, preservation/protection; Food services; Housing/shelter, development; International peace/security; Civil rights.
Limitations: Applications not accepted. Giving on a national basis. No grants to individuals.
Application information: Contributes only to pre-selected organizations.
Officers and Directors:* Lola Maverick Berndt, Pres.; Frederick S. Brown,* V.P. and Treas.; Robert Allen Rikoon,* Secy.; Sandra Ingerman.
EIN: 860892601

1991
Santa Fe Community Foundation
516 Alto St.
Santa Fe, NM 87501 (505) 988-9715
Contact: Billie Blair, Pres.
Application address: P.O. Box 1827, Santa Fe, NM 87504-1827; FAX: (505) 988-1829; E-mail: foundation@santafecf.org; URL: http://www.santafecf.org

Incorporated in 1981 in NM.
Grantmaker type: Community foundation
Financial data (yr. ended 12/31/02): Assets, $11,979,480 (M); gifts received, $2,554,631; expenditures, $2,008,113; giving activities include $1,362,469 for 247 grants (high: $84,000; low: $10; average: $10–$84,000).
Purpose and activities: Giving in the following areas: 1) Arts, to support opportunities for young and emerging artists; innovative arts education efforts, including exposure to new technologies, and outreach to and development of new audiences; 2) Civic Affairs, to support

neighborhoods and community, promotion of civic dialogue participation in and access to the political process, and animal welfare; 3) Education, to support early childhood and parenting education, school drop-out prevention and innovative approaches to employment readiness; 4) Environment, for the protection and conservation of water, preservation of open space, and region-wide planning and coordination; and 5) Health and Human Services, for the well-being of children, youth and families, increased access to health care and human services, and integrated methods of delivery services.

Fields of interest: Visual arts; Performing arts; Music; Humanities; Arts; Child development, education; Elementary school/education; Education; Natural resources; Environment; Animal welfare; Animals/wildlife, preservation/protection; Health care; Mental health/crisis services; Health organizations, association; Cancer; AIDS; Alcoholism; Domestic violence; Food services; Human services; Children/youth, services; Child development, services; Aging, centers/services; Homeless, human services; Civil rights, immigrants; Civil rights, minorities; Civil rights, disabled; Civil rights, women; Civil rights, aging; Civil rights, gays/lesbians; Race/intergroup relations; Community development; Science; Public affairs; Minorities; Asians/Pacific Islanders; African Americans/Blacks; Hispanics/Latinos; Native Americans/American Indians; Disabled; Aging; Women; People with AIDS (PWAs); Gays/lesbians; Immigrants/refugees; Economically disadvantaged; Homeless.

Types of support: General/operating support; Continuing support; Management development; Annual campaigns; Endowments; Emergency funds; Program development; Publication; Seed money; Scholarship funds; Technical assistance; Matching/challenge support.

Limitations: Giving limited to northern NM counties, including Santa Fe, Rio Arriba, Los Alamos, Taos, Mora, and San Miguel. No support for religious or political purposes. No grants to individuals; or for capital campaigns; no technical assistance grants for travel, conferences, start-up costs, or staff salaries or functions.

Publications: Annual report, Newsletter.

Application information: Application form required.

   Copies of proposal: 1
   Deadline(s): July 1
   Board meeting date(s): Bimonthly

Officers and Directors:* Joe Allocca,* Chair.; Felice Gonzales,* Vice-Chair.; Fran Mullin, Vice-Chair.; Billie Blair, Pres.; Sandra Brick, Secy.; Sarah Sawtell, C.F.O.; Thomas Bustamante,* Treas.; and 20 additional directors.

Number of staff: 5 full-time professional; 2 part-time professional; 1 full-time support.

EIN: 850303044

1992
SB Foundation

c/o Daniel A. Sisk
500 4th St. N.W., Ste. 100
Albuquerque, NM 87102-2186

Established in 1997 in NM.

Donor(s): Daniel A. Sisk.
Grantmaker type: Independent foundation
Financial data (yr. ended 12/31/02): Assets, $2,282,527 (M); expenditures, $136,754; qualifying distributions, $134,930; giving activities include $135,000 for 17 grants (high: $25,000; low: $5,000).
Purpose and activities: Giving primarily for environmental conservation.
Fields of interest: Education; Water pollution; Natural resources; Environment, water resources; Environment, forests; Human services.
Limitations: Applications not accepted. Giving on a national basis. No grants to individuals.
Application information: Contributes only to pre-selected organizations.
Officers: Daniel A. Sisk, Pres.; Katharine B. Sisk, Secy.-Treas.
Directors: Alan Hamilton; Sara Sisk Hamilton; Mary Pat Schilly; John B. Sisk; Thomas D. Sisk; Helen R. Sparrow.
EIN: 742857008

1993
Lydia B. Stokes Foundation

721 Don Diego Ave.
Santa Fe, NM 87505
URL: http://www.lydiabstokesfoundation.org

Established in 1959 in NJ.
Donor(s): Lydia B. Stokes.‡
Grantmaker type: Independent foundation
Financial data (yr. ended 06/30/03): Assets, $3,710,711 (M); expenditures, $201,653; qualifying distributions, $156,598; giving activities include $133,000 for 20 grants (high: $10,000; low: $5,000).
Purpose and activities: Support for the environment and conservation, education, community funds, and women's and children's issues.
Fields of interest: Education; Natural resources; Environment; Human services; Children/youth, services; Family services; Women, centers/services; Community development; Federated giving programs; Women.
Types of support: General/operating support; Program development; Seed money; Consulting services; Program-related investments/loans; Matching/challenge support.
Limitations: Applications not accepted. Giving in the U.S., with emphasis on CO, New England, FL, and NM. No grants to individuals.
Application information: Unsolicited requests for funds not accepted.
Trustees: Nancy V. Deren; Ann R. Stokes; Sally S. Venerable; Thomas R. Willits.
Number of staff: None.
EIN: 216016107

1994
Taos Community Foundation

229 Camino de la Placita
P.O. Box 1925
Taos, NM 87571 (505) 737-9300
FAX: (505) 751-7130; E-mail foundation@taoscf.org; URL: http://www.taoscf.org

Established in 1998 in NM.
Grantmaker type: Community foundation

Financial data (yr. ended 06/30/02): Assets, $821,596 (M); gifts received, $261,712; expenditures, $378,632; giving activities include $182,648 for 144 grants (high: $21,446; low: $9).
Purpose and activities: Giving primarily in the areas of health and human services; education and activities for youth; visual, literary, and performing arts; community and economic development; natural environment; and historic preservation. The foundation administers donor-advised funds.
Fields of interest: Historic preservation/historical societies; Arts; Education; Natural resources; Health care; Children/youth, services; Human services; Community development.
Limitations: Giving limited to Taos and western Colfax counties, NM. No grants to individuals.
Application information: See Web site for guidelines.
   Deadline(s): May 5
   Board meeting date(s): Feb.
Officers: Wes Patterson, Chair.; Edy Anderson, Vice-Chair.; Maggie Evans-Rael, Secy.; Fred Winter, Treas.
Board Members: Betsy Carey; Rebecca McCracken; Angel Reyes; John Speirs; Bill Stevens.
EIN: 850425147

1995
Eugene V. & Clare E. Thaw Charitable Trust ▼

P.O. Box 2422
Santa Fe, NM 87504-2422 (505) 982-7023
Contact: Sherry Thompson, Exec. Dir.
FAX: (505) 982-7027; E-mail: sherryt@thawtrust.org

Established in 1981 in NY as a private operating foundation; status changed to an independent grantmaking foundation in 1994 in NM.
Donor(s): Eugene Victor Thaw, Clare Eddy Thaw.
Grantmaker type: Independent foundation
Financial data (yr. ended 12/31/02): Assets, $46,243,790 (M); expenditures, $4,516,779; qualifying distributions, $4,250,744; giving activities include $3,912,740 for 96 grants (high: $1,000,000; low: $850; average: $5,000–$50,000).
Purpose and activities: Support for the arts, ecology and the environment, and animal rights and protection. The trust prefers to make challenge grants that are conditional on recipients matching the funds in an agreed-upon proportion.
Fields of interest: Arts; Environment; Animal welfare.
International interests: United Kingdom; Russia.
Types of support: Program development; Conferences/seminars; Publication; Seed money; Research; Technical assistance; Matching/challenge support.
Limitations: Applications not accepted. Giving on a national basis. No grants to individuals or operating support.
Publications: Biennial report.
Application information: Contributes only to pre-selected organizations.
   Board meeting date(s): Fall
Officers and Directors:* Eugene Victor Thaw,* Pres.; Sherry Thompson, Exec. Dir.; William

Acquavella; Jeffrey L. Fornaciari; Patricia Tang; Clare Eddy Thaw.
Number of staff: 2 full-time professional.
EIN: 133081491
Recent environmental and animal welfare grants:
1995-1 1000 Friends of New Mexico, Albuquerque, NM, $25,000. For general support. 2001.
1995-2 1000 Friends of New Mexico, Albuquerque, NM, $15,000. For general support. 2001.
1995-3 1000 Friends of New Mexico, Albuquerque, NM, $15,000. For general support. 2001.
1995-4 Bard College, Annandale on Hudson, NY, $10,000. Toward publication of book, Landscape Design: A Cultural and Architectural History, at Graduate Center for Studies in the Decorative Arts in New York City. 2001.
1995-5 Cherry Valley Historical Association, Cherry Valley, NY, $10,000. Toward development of 19th century garden and park at Cherry Valley Museum. 2001.
1995-6 Food Animal Concerns Trust (FACT), New York, NY, $20,000. For general support. 2001.
1995-7 James A. Baker Institute for Animal Health, Ithaca, NY, $100,000. Toward construction of new auditorium. 2001.
1995-8 Malpai Borderlands Group, Douglas, AZ, $25,000. Toward fire and grazing studies and community outreach. 2001.
1995-9 Malpai Borderlands Group, Douglas, AZ, $25,000. Toward fire and grazing studies and community outreach. 2001.
1995-10 Northern New Mexico Animal Protection Society, Espanola, NM, $15,000. Toward spay and neuter program. 2001.
1995-11 Quivira Coalition, Santa Fe, NM, $50,000. For organizational expansion. 2001.
1995-12 Randall Davey Audubon Center, Santa Fe, NM, $10,000. For Birds of the Rio Grande school classroom program and teacher training workshops. 2001.
1995-13 Santa Fe Institute, Santa Fe, NM, $40,000. Toward research on scaling in biology. 2001.
1995-14 Santa Fe Institute, Santa Fe, NM, $40,000. Toward research on scaling in biology. 2001.
1995-15 Santa Fe Institute, Santa Fe, NM, $25,000. For program to study recovery of species diversity after extinctions. 2001.
1995-16 Santa Fe Watershed Association, Santa Fe, NM, $15,000. For challenge grant to coordinate and monitor thinning of Santa Fe watershed to lessen fire danger. 2001.
1995-17 Science and Conservation Center, Billings, MT, $10,000. Toward research and testing of contraceptive vaccine for mammals. 2001.
1995-18 Staten Island Botanical Garden, New York Chinese Scholars Garden, Staten Island, NY, $30,000. Toward benefit dinner for educational programs about cultural history and traditions of China. 2001.
1995-19 Taos Land Trust, Taos, NM, $25,000. For Northern New Mexico expansion. 2001.
1995-20 Wildlife Conservation Society, Bronx, NY, $100,000. Toward construction and presentation of Congo Gorilla Forest. 2001.

1996
J. E. & Lillian Tipton Foundation
324 Paseo De Peralta
Santa Fe, NM 87501

Established in 1997.
Donor(s): J.E. Tipton.
Grantmaker type: Independent foundation
Financial data (yr. ended 12/31/02): Assets, $4,143,981 (M); expenditures, $1,023,086; qualifying distributions, $937,169; giving activities include $937,169 for 7 grants (high: $500,000; low: $10,000).
Purpose and activities: Giving primarily for religious purposes.
Fields of interest: Elementary/secondary education; Higher education; Botanical gardens; Christian agencies & churches.
Limitations: Applications not accepted. Giving primarily in CA. No grants to individuals.
Application information: Contributes only to pre-selected organizations.
Officers: J.E. Tipton, Chair.; Joseph Byrne, Pres.; Nancy J. Byrne, V.P.; L. Nelle Byrne, Secy.-Treas.
EIN: 911868563

1997
The Wyss Foundation
600 Agua Fria St.
Santa Fe, NM 87501 (505) 466-4616
Contact: Terry Odendahl
FAX: (505) 466-4644; E-mail: email@wyssfoundation.org; URL: http://www.wyssfoundation.org

Established in 1990 in PA.
Donor(s): Hansjoerg Wyss.
Grantmaker type: Independent foundation
Financial data (yr. ended 12/31/02): Assets, $45,000,000 (M); expenditures, $5,120,000; qualifying distributions, $4,300,000; giving activities include $4,300,000 for 85 grants (high: $410,000; low: $250).
Purpose and activities: The purpose of the foundation is to preserve, protect, and restore public lands, waters, and open spaces of the American west to achieve ecological health across the landscape.
Fields of interest: Natural resources.
Types of support: General/operating support; Program development; Seed money; Research.
Limitations: Applications not accepted. Giving primarily in the western U.S. (AZ, CO, ID, MT, NV, NM, UT, WY). No grants to individuals.
Application information: Unsolicited requests for funds not accepted. Proposals by requests only.
Board meeting date(s): Varies
Officers: Hansjoerg Wyss, Chair.; Joseph M. Fisher, Mgr.
Number of staff: 5 full-time professional.
EIN: 251823874

NEW YORK

1998
The Abelard Foundation, Inc.
c/o White & Case
1155 Ave. of the Americas
New York, NY 10036

Incorporated in 1958 in NY as successor to Albert B. Wells Charitable Trust established in 1950 in MA.
Donor(s): Members of the Wells family.
Grantmaker type: Independent foundation
Financial data (yr. ended 12/31/02): Assets, $4,243,507 (M); gifts received, $252,000; expenditures, $634,374; qualifying distributions, $577,626; giving activities include $475,000 for 45 grants (high: $17,500; low: $9,000).
Purpose and activities: Giving especially for seed money to new organizations and model projects, with emphasis on protection of civil rights and civil liberties; support for programs designed to achieve social, political, and economic equality for urban and rural poor, including giving them a voice in decisions about their environment.
Fields of interest: Natural resources; Crime/law enforcement; Labor unions/organizations; Human services; Women, centers/services; Minorities/immigrants, centers/services; International human rights; Civil rights, advocacy; Civil liberties, advocacy; Urban/community development; Rural development; Public policy, research; Public affairs; Minorities; Native Americans/American Indians; Women; Immigrants/refugees; Economically disadvantaged.
Types of support: General/operating support; Program development; Publication; Seed money; Technical assistance; Matching/challenge support.
Limitations: Giving limited to New York, NY, the western states, and the southern states, including the Appalachia region. No support for medical, educational, cultural institutions, or government sponsored programs. No grants to individuals, or for building or endowment funds, continuing support, annual campaigns, emergency funds, scholarships, fellowships, research, or video or film production; no loans.
Publications: Grants list, Informational brochure (including application guidelines).
Application information: Application form not required.
Initial approach: Letter
Copies of proposal: 1
Deadline(s): None
Board meeting date(s): May and Nov.
Final notification: Immediately following board meeting
Officers and Trustee:* Susan Collins, Pres.; Steven Bernhard, V.P.; Melissa Blessing, V.P.; Charles Schreck, V.P.; George B. Wells II, V.P.; Malcolm J. Edgerton, Jr.,* Secy.; Charles R. Schreck, Treas.
Number of staff: 1 part-time professional; 2 part-time support.
EIN: 136064580

1999
The Abraham Foundation, Inc.
c/o B. Strauss Assoc., Ltd.
307 5th Ave., 8th Fl.
New York, NY 10016-8775
Contact: Alexander Abraham, Pres.

Established in 1945.
Donor(s): Alexander Abraham.
Grantmaker type: Independent foundation
Financial data (yr. ended 09/30/02): Assets, $2,660,582 (M); gifts received, $1,806,032; expenditures, $511,906; qualifying distributions, $510,265; giving activities include $501,022 for 57 grants (high: $100,000; low: $250).
Purpose and activities: Giving primarily for education. Funding also for human services, and animals and wildlife.
Fields of interest: Museums; Arts; Education; Natural resources; Animals/wildlife; Human services; Women; Economically disadvantaged.
Limitations: Applications not accepted. Giving primarily in NY. No grants to individuals.
Application information: Contributes only to pre-selected organizations.
Officers: Alexander Abraham, Pres.; Nancy Abraham, V.P.; Helene Abraham, Secy.; James Abraham, Treas.
EIN: 136065944

2000
Louis and Anne Abrons Foundation, Inc. ▼
c/o First Manhattan Co.
437 Madison Ave.
New York, NY 10017 (212) 756-3376
Contact: Richard Abrons, Pres.

Incorporated in 1950 in NY.
Donor(s): Anne S. Abrons,‡ Louis Abrons.‡
Grantmaker type: Independent foundation
Financial data (yr. ended 12/31/02): Assets, $52,799,519 (M); expenditures, $3,755,470; qualifying distributions, $3,746,229; giving activities include $3,735,500 for 185 grants (high: $370,000; low: $750; average: $5,000–$60,000).
Purpose and activities: Giving primarily to social welfare agencies, Jewish charities, major New York, NY, institutions, civic improvement programs, education, and environmental and cultural projects.
Fields of interest: Museums; Arts; Dental school/education; Libraries/library science; Education; Environment; Hospitals (general); Family planning; Legal services; Employment; Human services; Children/youth, services; Family services; Aging, centers/services; Minorities/immigrants, centers/services; Community development; Jewish agencies & temples; African Americans/Blacks; Aging; Economically disadvantaged; Homeless.
Types of support: Continuing support; Annual campaigns; Building/renovation; Program development; Scholarship funds; Research; Technical assistance; Consulting services; Program-related investments/loans.
Limitations: Applications not accepted. Giving primarily in the metropolitan New York, NY, area. No grants to individuals.
Application information: Contributes only to pre-selected organizations. Telephone calls not accepted. Unsolicited applications not considered or acknowledged.

Board meeting date(s): Feb., June, and Oct.
Officers and Directors:* Richard Abrons,* Pres.; Herbert L. Abrons,* V.P.; Rita Aranow,* V.P.; Anne S. Abrons,* Secy.-Treas.; Adam Abrons; Alix Abrons; Henry Abrons; John Abrons; Leslie Abrons; Peter Abrons; Judith Aranow; Stephanie DeChristina; Vicki Feiner; Jennifer Schwartz.
Number of staff: None.
EIN: 136061329

2001
The Achelis Foundation
767 3rd Ave., 4th Fl.
New York, NY 10017 (212) 644-0322
Contact: Joseph S. Dolan, Secy. and Exec. Dir.
FAX: (212) 759-6510; E-mail: main@achelis-bodman-fnds.org; URL: http://fdncenter.org/grantmaker/achelis-bodman/

Incorporated in 1940 in NY.
Donor(s): Elisabeth Achelis.‡
Grantmaker type: Independent foundation
Financial data (yr. ended 12/31/02): Assets, $31,256,185 (M); expenditures, $1,901,760; qualifying distributions, $1,665,000; giving activities include $1,665,000 for 51 grants (high: $150,000; low: $15,000; average: $15,000–$100,000).
Purpose and activities: Giving for social services, including child welfare and youth, the disabled, and issues of health, including hospitals, medical research, drug abuse, and rehabilitation programs, literacy projects and other educational agencies, with preference for school reforms, school choice, and charter school projects rather than nonprofits that provide direct services in public schools, and the arts, culture, and the media. Other interests include voluntarism, entrepreneurship, strengthening the two-parent family, fatherhood (and father absence), private sector job placement, self-help and self-reliance, economic development, promoting the institution of marriage, faith-based programs, and prevention and early intervention. The foundation prefers programs that emphasize measurable participant outcomes and program results, innovations and new cost-saving approaches, consumer choice, and parental involvement.
Fields of interest: Arts; Elementary/secondary school reform; Adult education—literacy, basic skills & GED; Education; Natural resources; Medical care, rehabilitation; Health care; Substance abuse, prevention; Alcoholism; Medical research, institute; Children/youth, services; Family services; Religion; Disabled; Homeless.
Types of support: General/operating support; Program development; Conferences/seminars; Publication; Seed money; Curriculum development; Fellowships; Internship funds; Scholarship funds; Research; Technical assistance; Program evaluation; Matching/challenge support.
Limitations: Giving primarily in the New York, NY, area. Generally, no support for colleges and universities, small art, dance, music, or theater groups, national health or mental health organizations, housing, international projects, government agencies, public schools, or nonprofit programs and services significantly funded or wholly reimbursed by the government. No grants to individuals, or for

annual appeals, dinner functions, fundraising events, capital campaigns, deficit financing, or film or travel; no loans.
Publications: Biennial report (including application guidelines), Financial statement, Grants list.
Application information: Do not send CDs, DVDs, discs or tapes, or proposals through the internet unless requested. Application form not required.
   Initial approach: Letter or short proposal
   Copies of proposal: 1
   Deadline(s): None
   Board meeting date(s): Usually in May, Sept., and Dec.
   Final notification: 3 to 4 weeks
Officers and Trustees:* John N. Irwin III,* Chair., C.E.O. and Treas.; Russell P. Pennoyer,* Pres.; Peter Frelinghuysen,* V.P.; Mary S. Phipps,* V.P.; Joseph S. Dolan, Secy. and Exec. Dir.; Guy G. Rutherfurd, Chair. Emeritus; Horace I. Crary; Hon. Walter J.P. Curley; Anthony Drexel Duke; Sarah Henry Lederman; Leslie Lenkowsky.
Number of staff: 3 shared staff (shared with The Bodman Foundation).
EIN: 136022018

2002
Acquavella Family Foundation
c/o William R. Acquavella
18 E. 79th St.
New York, NY 10021

Established in 1997 in NY.
Donor(s): William Acquavella, H. Anthony Ittleson.
Grantmaker type: Independent foundation
Financial data (yr. ended 12/31/02): Assets, $201,945 (M); expenditures, $112,949; qualifying distributions, $111,496; giving activities include $110,000 for 6 grants (high: $50,000; low: $5,000).
Purpose and activities: Giving primarily for education and animal services.
Fields of interest: Education; Veterinary medicine.
Limitations: Applications not accepted. Giving primarily in NY. No grants to individuals.
Application information: Contributes only to pre-selected organizations.
Trustees: Donna Jo Acquavella; William Acquavella.
EIN: 137140356

2003
Acriel Foundation
c/o U.S. Trust
P.O. Box 2004
New York, NY 10109-1910

Established in 1994 in NY.
Grantmaker type: Operating foundation
Financial data (yr. ended 11/30/00): Assets, $3,865,195 (M); gifts received, $981,967; expenditures, $163,292; qualifying distributions, $125,861; giving activities include $105,000 for 6 grants (high: $30,000; low: $5,000).
Fields of interest: Higher education; Environment, legal rights; Natural resources; Family planning.
Limitations: Applications not accepted. No grants to individuals.

Application information: Contributes only to pre-selected organizations.
Trustee: U.S. Trust.
EIN: 133802863

2004
Adirondack Community Trust
105 Saranac Ave.
Lake Placid, NY 12946 (518) 523-9904
Contact: Cali Brooks, Exec. Dir.
E-mail: info@generousact.org; URL: http://www.generousact.org

Established in 1997 in NY.
Grantmaker type: Community foundation
Financial data (yr. ended 06/30/02): Assets, $3,805,797 (M); gifts received, $1,199,920; expenditures, $375,176; giving activities include $195,980 for grants (high: $75,250).
Purpose and activities: Giving to enhance the quality of life for the people of the Adirondack, NY, area. The trust administers donor-advised funds.
Fields of interest: Historic preservation/historical societies; Arts; Libraries/library science; Education; Environment; Health care; Recreation; Human services; Children/youth, services; Community development.
Types of support: General/operating support; Continuing support; Annual campaigns; Capital campaigns; Building/renovation; Land acquisition; Endowments; Program development; Publication; Seed money; Curriculum development; Scholarship funds; Technical assistance; Scholarships—to individuals; Matching/challenge support.
Limitations: Giving focused in the Adirondack region of NY.
Publications: Annual report, Informational brochure, Newsletter.
Application information: Application form not required.
 Board meeting date(s): Feb., May, Sept. and Dec.
Officers and Trustees:* Meredith Prime, Chair.; David Johnson,* Vice-Chair.; Ann Merkel,* Secy. and Exec. Dir.; Roderic Giltz, Treas.; Gary Benware; Adele Connors; Janet Decker; Michael O'Connor; Craig Randall; Carol Ann Young.
Number of staff: 1 full-time professional; 1 part-time professional.
EIN: 161535724

2005
The Afognak Foundation
c/o U.S. Trust
114 W. 47th St.
New York, NY 10036
Contact: Linda Franciscovich, Managing Dir., or Carolyn Larke, V.P., U.S. Trust
FAX: (212) 852-3377

Established in 1998 in MA.
Grantmaker type: Independent foundation
Financial data (yr. ended 12/31/02): Assets, $15,913,289 (M); expenditures, $685,850; qualifying distributions, $663,809; giving activities include $667,750 for grants.
Fields of interest: Arts; Elementary/secondary education; Natural resources; Agriculture, soil/water issues; International relief; Science,

formal/general education; Native Americans/American Indians.
Limitations: Applications not accepted. No grants to individuals.
Application information: Contributes only to pre-selected organizations.
Trustee: Elizabeth King.
EIN: 061521981

2006
Agrilink Foods/Pro-Fac Foundation
(formerly Curtice-Burns/Pro-Fac Foundation)
90 Linden Oaks
P.O. Box 20670
Rochester, NY 14602-0670 (716) 383-1850
Contact: Susan C. Riker, Secy.
URL: http://www.agrilinkfoods.com/corp/about/community

Established in 1966 in NY.
Donor(s): Agrilink Foods, Inc.
Grantmaker type: Company-sponsored foundation
Financial data (yr. ended 06/30/02): Assets, $114,244 (M); gifts received, $375,000; expenditures, $301,322; qualifying distributions, $301,154; giving activities include $301,007 for 142 grants (high: $20,593; low: $200).
Purpose and activities: Primary areas of interest include community funds, agriculture, and youth and child development and welfare. Emphasis on education, including higher education, building and scholarship funds, literacy and programs for minorities, and libraries; health agencies, hospital building funds, hospices, medical research, drug abuse and alcoholism, and rehabilitation; human services, including women, the elderly, minorities, the handicapped and the disadvantaged, and housing; community development; and cultural programs including the fine and performing arts.
Fields of interest: Visual arts; Museums; Performing arts; Theater; Arts; Education, fund raising; Early childhood education; Child development, education; Higher education; Adult education—literacy, basic skills & GED; Libraries/library science; Reading; Education; Environment; Hospitals (general); Family planning; Medical care, rehabilitation; Health care; Substance abuse, services; Mental health/crisis services; Health organizations, association; Alcoholism; Medical research, institute; Agriculture; Housing/shelter, development; Human services; Children/youth, services; Child development, services; Hospices; Minorities/immigrants, centers/services; Homeless, human services; Community development; Voluntarism promotion; Federated giving programs; Minorities; Disabled; Economically disadvantaged; Homeless.
Types of support: General/operating support; Continuing support; Annual campaigns; Capital campaigns; Building/renovation; Equipment; Endowments; Program development; Conferences/seminars; Professorships; Fellowships; Scholarship funds; Research.
Limitations: Giving primarily in areas of company operations. No support for religious or political organizations. No grants to individuals, or for seed money, emergency funds, deficit financing, land acquisition, matching gifts, or publications; no loans.

Application information: Application form not required.
 Initial approach: Proposal
 Copies of proposal: 1
 Deadline(s): None
 Board meeting date(s): Usually in Jan., Mar., June, Aug., and Nov.
Officers and Trustees:* Paul Roe,* Chair.; Susan C. Riker,* Secy.; Virginia Ford; William Rice.
Number of staff: 1 part-time support.
EIN: 166071142

2007
AKC Fund, Inc.
67A E. 77th St.
New York, NY 10021
Contact: Ann Brownell Sloane, Admin.

Incorporated in 1955 in NY.
Donor(s): Members of the Childs and Lawrence families.
Grantmaker type: Independent foundation
Financial data (yr. ended 12/31/02): Assets, $5,068,095 (M); expenditures, $297,011; qualifying distributions, $279,713; giving activities include $247,162 for 56 grants (average: $1,000–$25,000).
Purpose and activities: Grants largely for secondary and higher education; support also for conservation, health services, family planning, and the arts.
Fields of interest: Historic preservation/historical societies; Arts; Secondary school/education; Higher education; Natural resources; Animals/wildlife, preservation/protection; Family planning; Health care; Human services.
Types of support: Continuing support; Annual campaigns; Capital campaigns.
Limitations: Applications not accepted. Giving primarily in CT, Washington, DC, MA, NY and VA. No grants to individuals.
Application information: Currently supporting trustee-sponsored projects only.
 Board meeting date(s): Fall and spring
Officers and Directors:* Elisabeth C. Gill, Pres.; Alice Childs Anderson,* V.P.; Susannah L. Wood,* Secy.; John Davenport Childs,* Treas.; Hope Stewart Childs; Starling Winston Childs II; Alexander C. Garside; Adair Mali; Taylor Mali.
Number of staff: 4 shared staff (shared with Sloane & Hinshaw, Inc.)
EIN: 136091321

2008
Alfiero Family Charitable Foundation
2150 Elmwood Ave.
Buffalo, NY 14207 (716) 689-4972
Contact: Salvatore H. Alfiero, Chair.

Established in 1989 in NY.
Grantmaker type: Independent foundation
Financial data (yr. ended 12/31/02): Assets, $7,528,154 (M); expenditures, $607,265; qualifying distributions, $602,450; giving activities include $602,450 for 14 grants (high: $333,333; low: $800).
Purpose and activities: Giving for higher education and for human services.
Fields of interest: Education; Environment, forests; Camps; Human services.
Limitations: Giving limited to NY.

Application information:
Initial approach: Proposal
Deadline(s): Nov. 30
Officers: Salvatore H. Alfiero, Chair.; Victor S. Alfiero, Pres.; Charles C. Alfiero, V.P.; James J. Alfiero, Secy.
EIN: 110036051

2009
Allen Brothers Foundation
711 5th Ave.
New York, NY 10022
Contact: Howard Felson

Established about 1983 in NY.
Grantmaker type: Independent foundation
Financial data (yr. ended 12/31/01): Assets, $40,258 (M); expenditures, $3,222,393; qualifying distributions, $3,201,340; giving activities include $3,200,000 for 2 grants of $1,600,000 each.
Fields of interest: Libraries (public); Natural resources; Substance abuse, treatment; Children/youth, services.
Types of support: General/operating support; Research.
Limitations: Giving on a national basis, with some emphasis on NY. No grants to individuals.
Application information: Application form not required.
Deadline(s): None
Officers and Directors:* Herbert A. Allen,* Pres.; Robert H. Cosgriff, V.P.; Paul A. Gould,* V.P.; Irwin H. Kramer, V.P.; Robert H. Werbel,* Secy.; Richard M. Crooks; James W. Quinn; Philip Scaturro; Enrique Senior; Stanley S. Shuman; John Simon; Harold Wit.
EIN: 133202281

2010
The Herbert Allen Foundation
711 5th Ave.
New York, NY 10022-3194
Contact: Howard Felson, Asst. Treas.

Established in 1994 in NY.
Grantmaker type: Independent foundation
Financial data (yr. ended 12/31/02): Assets, $12,072,252 (M); expenditures, $693,593; qualifying distributions, $680,601; giving activities include $681,000 for 24 grants (high: $200,000; low: $2,000).
Purpose and activities: Funding primarily for education, human services, and the environment.
Fields of interest: Education; Natural resources; Human services.
Types of support: General/operating support.
Limitations: Giving primarily in New York, NY. No grants to individuals.
Application information:
Initial approach: Letter
Deadline(s): None
Officers and Directors:* Susan K. Allen, Pres.; Bradley A. Roberts,* V.P. and Secy.; Herbert A. Allen III,* V.P. and Treas.
EIN: 133791176

2011
Alpern Family Foundation, Inc.
c/o Weitzman & Rubin, PC
400 Jericho Tpke., Ste. 205
Jericho, NY 11753

Established in 1952.
Donor(s): Bernard E. Alpern.‡
Grantmaker type: Independent foundation
Financial data (yr. ended 12/31/02): Assets, $9,304,687 (M); gifts received, $550,655; expenditures, $790,498; qualifying distributions, $666,542; giving activities include $576,000 for 30 grants (high: $375,000; low: $1,000).
Purpose and activities: Support for medical research, including cancer and cerebral palsy, as well as to hospitals and health associations, and for children and youth services.
Fields of interest: Medical school/education; Environment; Hospitals (general); Cancer; Medical research, institute; Cerebral palsy research; Cancer research; Human services; Children/youth, services; Federated giving programs.
Types of support: Research.
Limitations: Applications not accepted. Giving primarily in New York, NY. No grants to individuals.
Application information: Contributes only to pre-selected organizations.
Officers and Directors:* Lloyd J. Alpern,* Pres.; Martin H. Schneider,* Sr. V.P. and Secy.; Steven I. Rubin,* Treas.; Rochelle A. Rubin.
EIN: 136100302

2012
Altria Group, Inc. Corporate Giving Program
(formerly Philip Morris Companies Inc. Corporate Giving Program)
c/o Contribs. Dept.
120 Park Ave.
New York, NY 10017 (917) 663-4000
Contact: Jennifer Goodale, V.P., Contribs.
Application address for Shared Solutions: Katherine Trent, Dir., Agricultural Rels., Altria Corporate Services, Inc., 2000 Bells Rd., Gate S/Door 100, Richmond, VA 23234, tel.: (804) 274-3329; FAX: (917) 663-5396; URL: http://www.altria.com/responsibility/04_05_contributions.asp; http://www.altria.com/shared_solutions/shared_solutions_main.asp

Grantmaker type: Corporate giving program
Financial data (yr. ended 12/31/02): Total giving, $138,300,000; giving activities include $100,400,000 for 4,000 grants (high: $1,300,000; low: $100,000), $12,900,000 for employee matching gifts and $25,000,000 for in-kind gifts.
Purpose and activities: Altria makes charitable contributions to nonprofit organizations involved with arts and culture, the environment, agriculture, hunger relief, humanitarian aid, youth development, domestic violence prevention, and human services. Support is given on a national and international basis.
Fields of interest: Arts; Environment; Agriculture; Food services; Disasters, preparedness/services; Youth development; Domestic violence; Human services.
Types of support: General/operating support; Continuing support; Equipment; Emergency funds; Program development; Employee volunteer services; Employee matching gifts; Donated products; In-kind gifts; Matching/challenge support.
Limitations: Giving on a national and international basis in areas of company operations. No support for political or lobbying organizations, religious, fraternal, or veterans' organizations, or discriminatory organizations. No grants to individuals, or for capital campaigns, endowments, building fund drives, television, film, or video production, or athletic or sports-related activities.
Application information: Support for specific programs is limited to 2 years in length for Shared Solutions; multi-year funding is not automatic. An application form is required for Shared Solutions; an application form is available online. The Contributions Department handles giving. The company has a staff that only handles contributions. A contributions committee reviews all requests. An advisory board of agricultural leaders reviews all requests for Shared Solutions.
Initial approach: Visit Web site for application information; download application form for Shared Solutions
Deadline(s): Aug. 15 for Shared Solutions
Final notification: Dec. 2 for Shared Solutions
Administrators: Sandra Blau, Dir., Contribs.; Marilynn Donini, Mgr., Contribs.; Diane Eidman, Dir., Contribs.; Jennifer Goodale, V.P., Contribs.; Lisa Walker, Dir., Contribs.
Number of staff: 15 full-time professional; 3 part-time professional; 8 full-time support; 1 part-time support.

2013
American Conservation Association, Inc.
30 Rockefeller Plz., Rm. 5600
New York, NY 10112
Contact: Charles M. Clusen, Exec. Dir.

Incorporated in 1958 in NY.
Donor(s): Laurance S. Rockefeller, Laurance Rockefeller, Rockefeller Brothers Fund, Jackson Hole Preserve, Inc.
Grantmaker type: Operating foundation
Financial data (yr. ended 12/31/00): Assets, $863,426 (M); gifts received, $500,000; expenditures, $577,031; qualifying distributions, $569,388; giving activities include $237,500 for 40 grants (high: $50,000; low: $1,000) and $97,391 for 4 foundation-administered programs.
Purpose and activities: A private operating foundation organized to advance knowledge and understanding of conservation; to preserve the beauty of the landscape and the natural and living resources in areas of the U.S. and elsewhere; and to educate the public in the proper use of such areas.
Fields of interest: Natural resources.
Types of support: General/operating support; Continuing support; Program development; Conferences/seminars; Publication; Technical assistance; Consulting services; Program-related investments/loans.
Limitations: Giving on a national basis, with emphasis on Washington, DC. No grants to individuals, or for building funds, endowments, scholarships, or fellowships.

Application information: Application form not required.

    Initial approach: Letter or proposal
    Copies of proposal: 1
    Deadline(s): None
    Board meeting date(s): Sept. or Oct.;
      Executive Committee meets as needed
    Final notification: Varies

Officers and Trustees:* Laurance Rockefeller,* Pres.; R. Scott Greathead,* Secy.; Carmen Reyes, Treas.; Charles M. Clusen, Exec. Dir.; John H. Adams; Frances G. Beinecke; Nash Castro; William G. Conway; Henry L. Diamond; Fred I. Kent III; W. Barnabas McHenry; Patrick F. Noonan; Story Clark Resor; David S. Sampson; Cathleen Douglas Stone; Russell E. Train; William H. Whyte, Jr.
Number of staff: 2 part-time professional; 2 part-time support.
EIN: 131874023

2014
American Society for the Prevention of Cruelty to Animals

(also known as ASPCA)
424 E. 92nd St.
New York, NY 10128 (212) 876-7700
Contact: Julie Morris, Sr. V.P.,Natl Shelter Outreach
Application address: 345 Park Ave., 9th Fl., New York, NY 10010; FAX: (212) 860-3435 for Julie Morris; E-mail: juliem@aspca.org; URL: http://www.aspca.org

Founded in 1866.
Grantmaker type: Public charity
Financial data (yr. ended 12/31/02): Revenue, $41,263,102; assets, $62,514,797 (M); gifts received, $32,746,227; expenditures, $41,357,094; program services expenses, $34,633,889; giving activities include $565,657 for 203 grants (high: $58,876; low: $1,000; average: $2,000–$10,000).
Purpose and activities: The organization promotes humane principles, prevents cruelty, and alleviates fear, pain, and suffering in animals. Occasional grants are to organizations that are involved in the development and maintenance of shelters and animal care facilities.
Fields of interest: Animal welfare; Veterinary medicine; Veterinary medicine, hospital; Safety/disasters.
Types of support: Program development; In-kind gifts.
Publications: Annual report, Financial statement, Informational brochure.
Application information: Application form not required.
    Initial approach: Letter
    Deadline(s): None
Officers and Directors:* Hoyle C. Jones,* Chair. and C.E.O.; Linda Lloyd Lambert,* Vice-Chair.; Edwin J. Savres,* Pres.; William Secord,* Secy.; James W. Gerard,* Treas.; and 21 additional directors.
Number of staff: 248 full-time support; 40 part-time support.
EIN: 131623829

2015
The Antz Foundation

c/o Goldman Sachs & Co.
85 Broad St., Tax Dept.
New York, NY 10004

Established in 1989 in NY.
Donor(s): John A. Thain.
Grantmaker type: Independent foundation
Financial data (yr. ended 01/31/02): Assets, $10,232,291 (M); gifts received, $3,373,655; expenditures, $453,092; qualifying distributions, $453,092; giving activities include $449,762 for 24 grants (high: $251,000; low: $250).
Purpose and activities: Giving for day schools, art and culture, the environment, and youth services.
Fields of interest: Museums; Dance; Theater; Arts; Elementary/secondary education; Botanical gardens; Hospitals (general); Health organizations, association; Medical research, institute; Human services; Community development, neighborhood development; Foundations (public).
Limitations: Applications not accepted. Giving primarily in NY. No grants to individuals.
Application information: Contributes only to pre-selected organizations.
Trustees: Carmen M. Thain; John A. Thain.
EIN: 133536523

2016
The Stanley J. Arkin Foundation, Inc.

c/o Rose Ridge Mgmt. Co.
230 Park Ave., 9th Fl.
New York, NY 10169
Contact: Stanley J. Arkin, Pres.

Established in 1982 in NY.
Donor(s): Stanley J. Arkin.
Grantmaker type: Independent foundation
Financial data (yr. ended 09/30/02): Assets, $414,101 (M); gifts received, $20,362; expenditures, $137,385; qualifying distributions, $124,386; giving activities include $115,218 for 44 grants (high: $45,990; low: $150).
Purpose and activities: Giving to the arts, marine conservation, and public services.
Fields of interest: Performing arts; History/archaeology; Higher education; Animal welfare; Health care; Health organizations, association.
Limitations: Applications not accepted. Giving primarily in New York, NY. No grants to individuals.
Application information: Contributes only to pre-selected organizations.
Officers and Directors:* Stanley J. Arkin,* Pres.; Harold Cohen,* V.P.; Barbara D. Arkin,* Secy.-Treas.
Number of staff: 1 shared staff.
EIN: 133105382

2017
The Roone Arledge Charitable Foundation

778 Park Ave., 15th Fl.
New York, NY 10021-3554

Established in 1997 in NY.
Donor(s): Roone Arledge.
Grantmaker type: Independent foundation

Financial data (yr. ended 12/31/00): Assets, $1,996,369 (M); gifts received, $1,003,832; expenditures, $104,728; qualifying distributions, $83,561; giving activities include $92,690 for 35 grants (high: $27,750; low: $250).
Purpose and activities: Giving primarily for health care, particularly a hospital, and human services.
Fields of interest: Education; Veterinary medicine, hospital; Hospitals (general); Brain disorders; Alzheimer's disease; Immunology research; Children/youth, services; International affairs; Foundations (public).
Types of support: General/operating support.
Limitations: Applications not accepted. Giving primarily in Southampton and New York, NY. No grants to individuals.
Application information: Contributes only to pre-selected organizations.
Trustees: Gigi Arledge; Roone Arledge; Ronald S. Konecky.
EIN: 133922166

2018
Arnhold Foundation, Inc.

c/o Joel E. Sammet & Co.
20 Exchange Pl.
New York, NY 10005 (212) 208-4600

Established in 1988 in NY.
Donor(s): Henry H. Arnhold, John P. Arnhold, Bruder-Stiftung.
Grantmaker type: Independent foundation
Financial data (yr. ended 12/31/01): Assets, $22,367,223 (M); gifts received, $235,581; expenditures, $2,596,593; qualifying distributions, $2,508,074; giving activities include $2,519,047 for 195 grants (high: $562,776; low: $50; average: $1,000–$25,000).
Purpose and activities: Giving primarily to arts and cultural programs, education, natural resource conservation and protection, animal welfare and human services.
Fields of interest: Arts; Education; Natural resources; Animal welfare; Human services.
Limitations: Applications not accepted. Giving primarily in New York, NY. No grants to individuals.
Application information: Contributes only to pre-selected organizations.
Officers: Henry H. Arnhold, Pres.; John P. Arnhold, Secy.-Treas.
Number of staff: None.
EIN: 133456684

2019
The Aronovitz Family Foundation, Inc.

c/o Weiler Arnow Mgmt. Co., Inc.
1114 Ave. of the Americas, Ste. 3400
New York, NY 10036

Donor(s): The Weiler-Arnow Investment Co., David Arnow, Joshua Arnow, The JWA Investment Co., Joan Arnow, Robert Arnow.
Grantmaker type: Independent foundation
Financial data (yr. ended 09/30/02): Assets, $358,754 (M); gifts received, $325,000; expenditures, $278,658; qualifying distributions, $278,051; giving activities include $278,086 for 67 grants (high: $110,769; low: $100).
Purpose and activities: Giving primarily for education and Jewish organizations.

Fields of interest: Higher education; Education; Environment; Jewish federated giving programs; Science; Jewish agencies & temples.
Limitations: Applications not accepted. Giving on a national basis. No grants to individuals.
Application information: Contributes only to pre-selected organizations.
Officers: Ruth Arnow, Pres.; Kathi Arnow, V.P.; Joshua Arnow, Secy.
Directors: David Arnow; Kevin Bannon; Raphaelle Haimowitz.
EIN: 133219383

2020
AT&T Foundation ▼
32 Ave. of the Americas, 6th Fl.
New York, NY 10013 (212) 387-6555
Contact: Marilyn Reznick, V.P., Education Progs. and Exec. Dir.
FAX: (212) 387-4882; E-mail: Reznick@att.com;
URL: http://www.att.com/foundation

Established in 1984 in NY.
Donor(s): American Telephone and Telegraph Co., Western Electric Fund, AT&T Corp.
Grantmaker type: Company-sponsored foundation
Financial data (yr. ended 12/31/01): Assets, $48,824,236 (M); gifts received, $25,199,987; expenditures, $43,160,785; qualifying distributions, $43,889,285; giving activities include $40,467,213 for 1,543+ grants (high: $1,299,200; average: $10,000–$250,000) and $3,728,867 for employee matching gifts.
Purpose and activities: The foundation invests globally in projects that are at the intersection of community needs and AT&T's business interests. Emphasis is placed on programs that serve the needs of people in communities where AT&T has a significant business presence; initiatives that use technology in innovative ways; and programs that AT&T employees are actively involved with as contributors and/or volunteers.
Fields of interest: Arts, alliance; Multipurpose centers/programs; Cultural/ethnic awareness; Arts councils; Media/communications; Visual arts; Museums; Performing arts; Performing arts centers; Dance; Music; Arts, services; Elementary/secondary education; Higher education; Teacher school/education; Engineering school/education; Continuing education; Libraries/library science; Education, community/cooperative; Natural resources; Public health; AIDS; Safety/disasters, volunteer services; Disasters, preparedness/services; Disasters, 9/11/01; Youth development; Human services; Women, centers/services; International exchange; International affairs; Civil rights; Economic development; Community development; Philanthropy/voluntarism; Science; Public affairs.
International interests: Canada; France; United Kingdom; Germany; Mexico; India; China; Taiwan; Japan; Australia.
Types of support: General/operating support; Emergency funds; Program development; Conferences/seminars; Curriculum development; Technical assistance; Employee matching gifts; Matching/challenge support.
Limitations: Applications not accepted. Giving on a national and international basis, primarily to Los Angeles and San Francisco, CA; Denver, CO; Washington, DC; Miami, FL; Chicago, IL;

NJ; NY; Pittsburgh and Philadelphia, PA; and Seattle, WA. No support for religious organizations for sectarian purposes, political campaigns, or disease-related health associations other than AIDS-related programs, child care and elder care centers, sports teams, or sports-related activities, planetariums, zoos, or historic buildings or villages. No grants to individuals, or for capital development, scholarships, endowments, deficit financing, medical research projects, operating expenses or capital campaigns of local health or human service agencies other than hospitals, wiring or other equipment, construction or renovation, competitions, land acquisition, or advertising or sponsorship purchases; no equipment donations.
Application information: Unsolicited applications not considered.
Board meeting date(s): Monthly
Officers and Trustees:* Mirian Graddick-Weir,* Chair.; Constance Weaver,* Vice-Chair.; Esther Silver-Parker,* Pres.; Marilyn Reznick, V.P., Education Prog. and Exec. Dir.; Mitzi Vaimberg, V.P., Civic and Community Svc. Prog.; Robert E. Angelica, Treas.; David Condit; Curt Fields; R. Reed Harrison; Barbara Peda.
Number of staff: 7 full-time professional; 1 full-time support.
EIN: 133166495
Recent environmental and animal welfare grants:
2020-1 Ball State University Foundation, Muncie, Indiana, $25,000. For Industrial Ecology Faculty Fellowship Program. 2002.
2020-2 Carnegie Mellon University, Pittsburgh, PA, $25,000. For Industrial Ecology Faculty Fellowship. 2002.
2020-3 Clean Beaches Council, Fredericksburg, VA, $15,000. For Blue Wave educational program. 2002.
2020-4 Denver Zoological Foundation, Denver, CO, $30,000. For Do at the Zoo and Wildlights. 2002.
2020-5 Environmental Law Institute, DC, $25,000. For Corporate Program. 2002.
2020-6 Environmental Literacy Council, DC, $10,000. For Web site enhancements. 2002.
2020-7 Environmentors Project, DC, $25,000. For environmental mentoring program for teens. 2002.
2020-8 Friends of Lead Free Children, New York, NY, $20,000. For general operating support. 2002.
2020-9 Garfield Park Conservatory Alliance, Chicago, IL, $10,000. For operating support. 2002.
2020-10 High School for Environmental Studies, Friends of the, New York, NY, $10,000. For Environmental Internship Program. 2002.
2020-11 Keep America Beautiful, Stamford, CT, $25,000. For web-based and hard-copy environmental education resources. 2002.
2020-12 National Aquarium in Baltimore, Baltimore, MD, $20,000. For exhibit, SharkQuest Virtual Behind the Scenes of Sharks. 2002.
2020-13 National Environmental Education and Training Foundation, DC, $15,000. For Green Business Network. 2002.
2020-14 New England Aquarium, Boston, MA, $25,000. For Boston Kids and Families program. 2002.

2020-15 New Jersey Higher Education Partnership for Sustainability, Newark, NJ, $10,000. For Sustainability Internship. 2002.
2020-16 New York Academy of Sciences, New York, NY, $25,000. For research project Industrial Ecology, Pollution Prevention and the New York/New Jersey Harbor. 2002.
2020-17 Pennsylvania Horticultural Society, Philadelphia, PA, $14,300. For general operating support. 2002.
2020-18 Piedmont Park Conservancy, Atlanta, GA, $15,000. For park maintenance budget. 2002.
2020-19 Rainforest Alliance, New York, NY, $15,000. For Save It-Connecting Kids to Conservation, domestic education program for children in the U.S. 2002.
2020-20 Resources for the Future, DC, $25,000. For program support. 2002.
2020-21 Trinity Commons Foundation, Trinity River Commission Foundation, Dallas, TX, $130,000. For Trinity Fest. 2002.
2020-22 University of California, Berkeley, CA, $25,000. For Industrial Ecology Faculty Fellowship. 2002.
2020-23 University of Leiden, Leiden, Netherlands, $25,000. For AT&T Industrial Ecology Faculty Fellowship. 2002.
2020-24 University of Massachusetts, Amherst, MA, $25,000. For Industrial Ecology Faculty Fellowship. 2002.
2020-25 University of Missouri, Rolla, MO, $25,000. For Industrial Ecology Faculty Fellowship. 2002.
2020-26 Volunteers for Outdoor Colorado, Denver, CO, $15,000. For program support. 2002.
2020-27 Wildlife Conservation Society, Bronx, NY, $75,000. For annual Holiday Lights celebration at the Bronx Zoo. 2002.
2020-28 World Resources Institute, DC, $20,000. For Green Business Letter project. 2002.
2020-29 Yale University, New Haven, CT, $19,500. For Laudise Medal for Industrial Ecology. 2002.
2020-30 Zoological Society of Philadelphia, Philadelphia, PA, $25,000. For general operating support. 2002.

2021
The AYCO Charitable Foundation
1 Wall St.
Albany, NY 12205 (518) 881-7981
Contact: Barry Hamerling, Pres.

Grantmaker type: Public charity
Financial data (yr. ended 06/30/02): Revenue, $75,266,955; assets, $205,489,447; gifts received, $72,576,400; expenditures, $49,506,468; program services expenses, $46,916,337; giving activities include $46,916,337 for grants.
Purpose and activities: The foundation administers a donor-advised fund by contributing to public charities in the United States in the areas of higher education, human services, the arts, health, the environment, and wildlife preservation.
Fields of interest: Multipurpose centers/programs; Museums; Performing arts; Higher education; Graduate/professional education; Natural resources; Animals/wildlife;

Health care; Health organizations; Medical research; Youth development; Human services; International human rights; Community development; Federated giving programs.
Limitations: Applications not accepted. Giving on a national basis.
Application information: Contributes only to pre-selected organizations; unsolicited requests for funds not considered or acknowledged.
Officers and Directors:* Barry Hamerling,* Pres.; Peter Heerwagen,* V.P.; Larry Wyngowski,* V.P.; Peter R. Martin,* Secy.; John J. Collins III,* Treas.; Howard Clark; Anthony DePaula; Paul O'Neill; Vincent Sarni.
EIN: 141782466

2022
Babbitt Family Charitable Trust
c/o Davis & Graber
150 E. 58th St., 22nd Fl.
New York, NY 10155

Established in 1991 in NY.
Donor(s): Edward Babbitt.
Grantmaker type: Independent foundation
Financial data (yr. ended 06/30/02): Assets, $6,028,835 (M); expenditures, $357,667; qualifying distributions, $353,044; giving activities include $351,200 for 87 grants (high: $20,000; low: $100).
Purpose and activities: Funding primarily for arts and culture, human services, health associations, and federated giving programs.
Fields of interest: Performing arts; Theater; Arts; Education; Environment; Animal welfare; Health organizations, association; Disasters, 9/11/01; Human services; Children/youth, services; Federated giving programs; Economically disadvantaged.
Limitations: Applications not accepted. Giving primarily in NY. No grants to individuals.
Application information: Contributes only to pre-selected organizations.
Trustee: Susan Babbitt.
EIN: 136975951

2023
T. Backer Fund, Inc.
P.O. Box 364
Chatham, NY 12037-0364

Donor(s): Judith B. Grunberg, Daniel Grunberg.
Grantmaker type: Operating foundation
Financial data (yr. ended 12/31/02): Assets, $6,781,736 (M); gifts received, $1,649,809; expenditures, $251,528; qualifying distributions, $202,482; giving activities include $172,000 for 17 grants (high: $50,000; low: $1,000).
Purpose and activities: Giving primarily for conservation, medical research, the arts, and education.
Fields of interest: Museums; Education; Natural resources; Hospitals (general); Medical research, institute.
Limitations: Applications not accepted. Giving primarily in NY. No grants to individuals.
Application information: Contributes only to pre-selected organizations.
Officers: Judith Grunberg, Pres.; Daniel Grunberg, V.P.
Director: David Grunberg.
EIN: 141640994

2024
The William O. & Carole P. Bailey Family Foundation
c/o US Trust Co. of NY
114 W. 47th St., TAXRGR
New York, NY 10036

Established in 1997 in VA.
Donor(s): William O. Bailey, Carole P. Bailey, George P. Bailey, Carolyn Bailey Akers, Janet Bailey Faude.
Grantmaker type: Independent foundation
Financial data (yr. ended 12/31/01): Assets, $1,018,569 (M); expenditures, $119,557; qualifying distributions, $103,915; giving activities include $101,000 for 26 grants (high: $17,500; low: $500).
Fields of interest: Arts; Education; Environment; Health organizations, association; Girl scouts; Children/youth, services.
Limitations: Applications not accepted. No grants to individuals.
Application information: Contributes only to pre-selected organizations.
Officers: William O. Bailey, Pres.; Carole P. Bailey, 1st V.P. and Treas.; George P. Bailey, 2nd V.P.; Carolyn Bailey Akers, 2nd V.P.; Janet Bailey Faude, 2nd V.P.
EIN: 541860572

2025
The Cameron Baird Foundation
120 Delaware Ave., 6th Fl.
Buffalo, NY 14202 (716) 845-6000
Contact: Brian D. Baird, Tr.

Trust established in 1960 in NY.
Donor(s): Members of the family of Cameron Baird.
Grantmaker type: Independent foundation
Financial data (yr. ended 12/31/01): Assets, $50,196,994 (M); expenditures, $2,149,555; qualifying distributions, $2,012,391; giving activities include $2,003,286 for 64 grants (high: $600,000; low: $665; average: $10,000–$100,000).
Purpose and activities: Emphasis on music and cultural programs, higher and secondary education, social services, family planning, conservation, and civil rights.
Fields of interest: Music; Arts; Secondary school/education; Higher education; Natural resources; Family planning; Civil rights.
Limitations: Applications not accepted. Giving primarily in the Buffalo, NY, area. No support for religious organizations. No grants to individuals.
Application information: Contributes only to pre-selected organizations. Unsolicited requests for funds not considered or acknowledged.
    Board meeting date(s): Annually
Trustees: Brian D. Baird; Bridget B. Baird; Bruce C. Baird; Jane D. Baird; Peter C. Clauson; Brenda Baird Senturia.
Number of staff: None.
EIN: 166029481

2026
The Baird Foundation
11 Summer St.
Buffalo, NY 14209 (716) 883-2429
Contact: Catherine F. Schweitzer, Mgr.
Application address: P.O. Box 1210, Ellicott Sta., Buffalo, NY 14205

Trust established in 1947 in NY.
Donor(s): Flora M. Baird,‡ Frank B. Baird, Jr.,‡ Cameron Baird,‡ William C. Baird.‡
Grantmaker type: Independent foundation
Financial data (yr. ended 12/31/02): Assets, $9,966,017 (M); expenditures, $803,669; qualifying distributions, $692,816; giving activities include $561,106 for grants (average: $1,000–$10,000).
Purpose and activities: Primary areas of interest include the environment, hospitals, and medical research.
Fields of interest: Museums; Performing arts; Historic preservation/historical societies; Arts; Education; Environment; Hospitals (general); Medical research, institute; Human services; Children/youth, services; Disabled; Economically disadvantaged.
International interests: South Africa.
Types of support: General/operating support; Capital campaigns; Equipment; Research; Matching/challenge support.
Limitations: Giving primarily in the western NY area. No grants to individuals.
Publications: Grants list.
Application information: Application form not required.
    Initial approach: Letter
    Copies of proposal: 5
    Deadline(s): None
    Board meeting date(s): About 3 times a year
    Final notification: Variable
Officer: Catherine F. Schweitzer, Mgr.
Trustees: Arthur W. Cryer; Robert J.A. Irwin; William B. Irwin.
Number of staff: 1 part-time professional; 1 part-time support.
EIN: 166023080

2027
The George F. Baker Trust
477 Madison Ave., Ste., 1650
New York, NY 10022 (212) 755-1890
Contact: Miss Rocio Suarez, Exec. Dir.
FAX: (212) 319-6316; E-mail: rocio@bakernye.com

Trust established in 1937 in NY.
Donor(s): George F. Baker.‡
Grantmaker type: Independent foundation
Financial data (yr. ended 12/31/01): Assets, $18,205,680 (M); expenditures, $3,299,011; qualifying distributions, $2,939,231; giving activities include $2,279,800 for 49 grants (high: $450,000; low: $3,100; average: $10,000–$100,000).
Purpose and activities: Giving primarily for higher and secondary education, hospitals, social services, civic affairs, and religious and international affairs.
Fields of interest: Secondary school/education; Higher education; Natural resources; Hospitals (general); Human services; International affairs; Government/public administration; Religion.

Types of support: General/operating support; Matching/challenge support.
Limitations: Giving primarily in the eastern U.S., with some emphasis on the New York, NY, area. No grants to individuals, or for scholarships; no loans.
Publications: Annual report.
Application information: Application form not required.
  Initial approach: Letter with brief outline of proposal
  Copies of proposal: 1
  Deadline(s): None
  Board meeting date(s): June and Nov.
  Final notification: Up to 6 months
Officer: Rocio Suarez, Exec. Dir.
Trustees: Anthony K. Baker; George F. Baker III; Kane K. Baker; Citibank, N.A.
Number of staff: 1 full-time professional.
EIN: 136056818

2028
Barbash Family Fund, Inc.
265 W. Main St.
Babylon, NY 11702-3419

Established in 1993 in NY.
Donor(s): Maurice Barbash, Lillian Barbash.
Grantmaker type: Independent foundation
Financial data (yr. ended 12/31/01): Assets, $1,238,420 (M); gifts received, $782,287; expenditures, $137,900; qualifying distributions, $137,900; giving activities include $137,450 for 38 grants (high: $27,000; low: $150).
Purpose and activities: Giving primarily for arts and culture and education.
Fields of interest: Opera; Music; Elementary/secondary education; Hospitals (general); Animal welfare.
Limitations: Applications not accepted. Giving primarily in NY. No grants to individuals.
Application information: Contributes only to pre-selected organizations.
Officers: Maurice Barbash, Pres.; Lillian Barbash, V.P.; Susan Barbash, Secy.
Directors: Cathy Barbash; Shepard Barbash.
EIN: 113184479

2029
J. M. R. Barker Foundation
530 5th Ave., 26th Fl.
New York, NY 10036-5101 (212) 398-8700
Contact: Maureen Hopkins, Secy. and Admin.
FAX: (212) 398-2042

Established in 1968 in NY.
Donor(s): James M. Barker,‡ Margaret R. Barker,‡ Robert R. Barker.
Grantmaker type: Independent foundation
Financial data (yr. ended 12/31/01): Assets, $37,200,851 (M); expenditures, $1,607,111; qualifying distributions, $1,412,316; giving activities include $1,337,000 for 37 grants (high: $250,000; low: $1,000; average: $5,000–$10,000).
Purpose and activities: Support primarily for organizations that are well-known to one or more directors, with some emphasis on the areas of higher education, cultural programs, and scientific research.
Fields of interest: Arts; Higher education; Education; Natural resources; Science.

Types of support: General/operating support; Continuing support; Annual campaigns; Capital campaigns; Building/renovation; Endowments; Program development; Seed money; Research; Matching/challenge support.
Limitations: Giving primarily in the greater Boston, MA, area, and the greater New York, NY, area. No grants to individuals, or for scholarships, fellowships, or matching gifts; no loans.
Application information: Application form not required.
  Copies of proposal: 1
  Deadline(s): Nov. 1
  Board meeting date(s): June and Dec.
  Final notification: 3 months
Officers and Directors:* Margaret B. Clark,* Pres.; James R. Barker, V.P. and C.F.O.; W.B. Barker,* V.P.; Maureen A. Hopkins, Secy. and Admin.; Robert P. Connor,* Treas.; Ann S. Barker; Margaret S. Barker; Robert R. Barker; William S. Barker; John W. Holman, Jr.; Richard D. Kahn; Troy Y. Murray.
Number of staff: 1 part-time support.
EIN: 136268289

2030
The Barker Welfare Foundation
P.O. Box 2
Glen Head, NY 11545 (516) 759-5592
Contact: Mrs. Sarane H. Ross, Pres.
FAX: (516) 759-5497

Incorporated in 1934 in IL.
Donor(s): Mrs. Charles V. Hickox.‡
Grantmaker type: Independent foundation
Financial data (yr. ended 09/30/01): Assets, $60,278,364 (M); expenditures, $3,446,876; qualifying distributions, $2,925,252; giving activities include $2,627,607 for 232 grants (high: $50,000; low: $500; average: $7,500–$15,000).
Purpose and activities: Grants to established organizations and charitable institutions, with emphasis on youth and families, museums and the fine and performing arts, child welfare and youth agencies, health services and rehabilitation, welfare, aid to the handicapped, family planning, libraries, the environment, recreation, and programs for the elderly.
Fields of interest: Visual arts; Museums; Arts; Libraries/library science; Environment; Health care; Mental health/crisis services; Recreation; Human services; Children/youth, services; Disabled.
Types of support: General/operating support; Continuing support; Annual campaigns; Capital campaigns; Building/renovation; Equipment.
Limitations: Giving primarily in Chicago, IL, Michigan City, IN, and New York, NY. No support for political activities, start-up organizations, national health, welfare, or education agencies, institutions or funds. No grants to individuals, or for endowment funds, seed money, emergency funds, deficit financing, scholarships, fellowships, medical or scientific research, films or videos, or conferences; no loans.
Publications: Application guidelines, Annual report (including application guidelines).
Application information: Proposals must be completed according to the foundation's guidelines and grants process in order to be

considered for funding. Grants to Chicago agencies are by invitation only. Proposals sent by FAX not considered. Application form required.
  Initial approach: 2- to 3-page letter of inquiry
  Copies of proposal: 2
  Deadline(s): Feb. 1 and Aug. 1
  Board meeting date(s): May and Oct.
  Final notification: After board meeting for positive response; any time for negative response
Officers and Directors:* Mrs. Sarane H. Ross,* Pres.; Katrina H. Becker,* V.P. and Secy.; Thomas P. McCormick,* Treas.; Diane Curtis; Danielle A. Hickox; John B. Hickox; Mary Lou Linnen; Alline Matheson; Sarane R. O'Connor; Alexander B. Ross.
Number of staff: 2 full-time professional; 1 part-time support.
EIN: 366018526
Recent environmental and animal welfare grants:
2030-1 Aiken County Open Land Trust, Aiken, SC, $10,000. To install irrigation system in Winthrop Polo Field. 2002.
2030-2 Central Park Conservancy, New York, NY, $15,000. For Environmental Education Program. 2002.
2030-3 Fidelco Guide Dog Foundation, Bloomfield, CT, $10,000. To place Fidelco dogs in New York City. 2002.
2030-4 Hitchcock Foundation, Aiken, SC, $10,000. For Hitchcock Woods. 2002.
2030-5 Little Traverse Conservancy, Harbor Springs, MI, $18,000. Toward purchase of Fochtman Property. 2002.
2030-6 New York Botanical Garden, Bronx, NY, $15,000. For Children's Adventure Garden. 2002.
2030-7 New York City Outward Bound Center, Long Island City, NY, $10,000. For general operating support. 2002.
2030-8 Trust for Public Land, New York, NY, $10,000. For New York City Land Project. 2002.
2030-9 Wave Hill, Bronx, NY, $25,000. To construct new Visitor's Center. 2002.
2030-10 Wave Hill, Bronx, NY, $10,000. For Environmental Science Camp for Girls. 2002.
2030-11 Wildlife Conservation Society, Bronx, NY, $60,000. For Tiger Kingdom. 2002.

2031
Theodore H. Barth Foundation, Inc.
45 Rockefeller Plz., 20th Fl., Ste. 2006
New York, NY 10111 (212) 332-3466
Contact: Ellen S. Berelson, Pres.
E-mail: barthfoundation@earthlink.net

Incorporated in 1953 in DE.
Donor(s): Theodore H. Barth.‡
Grantmaker type: Independent foundation
Financial data (yr. ended 12/31/01): Assets, $28,963,033 (M); expenditures, $1,670,939; qualifying distributions, $1,471,926; giving activities include $1,337,563 for 107 grants (high: $225,000; low: $750; average: $5,000–$10,000).
Purpose and activities: Grants for higher education, health, the performing and other arts, cultural organizations, and social services; support also for aid to the handicapped and conservation.

Fields of interest: Performing arts; Arts; Higher education; Environment; Health care; Human services; Disabled.
Types of support: General/operating support; Continuing support; Annual campaigns; Endowments; Program development; Seed money.
Limitations: Giving limited to the northeastern U.S. and to MD, NJ, PA, and VA. No grants to individuals, or for capital projects.
Publications: Application guidelines.
Application information: Telephone inquiries will not be accepted. Application form not required.
Initial approach: Letter
Copies of proposal: 1
Deadline(s): None
Final notification: Dec.
Officers and Directors:* Ellen S. Berelson,* Pres. and Treas.; Lois Herrmann, V.P.; Lawrence Franks,* Secy.
EIN: 136103401

2032
The Sandra Atlas Bass & Edythe & Sol G. Atlas Fund, Inc. ▼
185 Great Neck Rd.
Great Neck, NY 11021 (516) 487-9030
Contact: Sandra A. Bass, Pres.

Established in 1962 in NY.
Donor(s): Sol G. Atlas.
Grantmaker type: Independent foundation
Financial data (yr. ended 12/31/01): Assets, $14,420,811 (M); gifts received, $8,149,797; expenditures, $2,112,107; qualifying distributions, $2,074,272; giving activities include $2,071,850 for 142 grants (high: $132,000; low: $250; average: $5,000–$25,000).
Purpose and activities: Giving primarily for social services, health, animal welfare, and Jewish welfare.
Fields of interest: Animal welfare; Health organizations, association; Human services; Jewish federated giving programs.
Limitations: Applications not accepted. Giving primarily in the metropolitan New York, NY, area, with emphasis on Long Island.
Application information: Unsolicited requests for funds not accepted.
Officers: Sandra A. Bass, Pres.; Morton M. Bass, V.P.; Robert Zabelle, Secy.; Richard J. Cunningham, Treas.
EIN: 116036928
Recent environmental and animal welfare grants:
2032-1 American Society for the Prevention of Cruelty to Animals, New York, NY, $14,500. For unrestricted support. 2001.
2032-2 Animal Haven, Flushing, NY, $17,000. For unrestricted support. 2001.
2032-3 Animal Rescue Force, Forest Hills, NY, $18,000. For unrestricted support. 2001.
2032-4 Associated Humane Societies, Newark, NJ, $16,000. For unrestricted support. 2001.
2032-5 BeingKind, Guilford, NY, $15,000. For unrestricted support. 2001.
2032-6 Canine Companions for Independence, Santa Rosa, CA, $22,500. For unrestricted support. 2001.

2032-7 Cornell University, College of Veterinary Medicine, Ithaca, NY, $50,000. For unrestricted support. 2001.
2032-8 Defenders of Animal Rights, Phoenix, MD, $13,500. For unrestricted support. 2001.
2032-9 Dogs for the Deaf, Chicago, IL, $20,000. For unrestricted support. 2001.
2032-10 Fidelco Guide Dog Foundation, Bloomfield, CT, $23,000. For unrestricted support. 2001.
2032-11 Friends of Animals, New York, NY, $16,000. For unrestricted support. 2001.
2032-12 Fund for Animals, New York, NY, $17,000. For unrestricted support. 2001.
2032-13 Guide Dog Foundation for the Blind, Smithtown, NY, $23,000. For unrestricted support. 2001.
2032-14 Guiding Eyes for the Blind, Yorktown Heights, NY, $23,000. For unrestricted support. 2001.
2032-15 Humane Society of Long Island, Freeport, NY, $20,000. For unrestricted support. 2001.
2032-16 Humane Society of New York, New York, NY, $22,500. For unrestricted support. 2001.
2032-17 Humane Society of the United States, DC, $13,500. For unrestricted support. 2001.
2032-18 Humane Society of Washington, DC, $16,000. For unrestricted support. 2001.
2032-19 Humane Urban Group, Great Neck, NY, $12,500. For unrestricted support. 2001.
2032-20 International Hearing Dog, Henderson, CO, $21,000. For unrestricted support. 2001.
2032-21 International Society for Animal Rights, Clarks Summit, PA, $10,500. For unrestricted support. 2001.
2032-22 Kent Animal Shelter, Carmel, NY, $27,500. For unrestricted support. 2001.
2032-23 Little Shelter Animal Rescue, Huntington, NY, $19,000. For unrestricted support. 2001.
2032-24 Mid Hudson Animal Aid, Newburgh, NY, $18,500. For unrestricted support. 2001.
2032-25 Millennium Guild, New York, NY, $36,000. For unrestricted support. 2001.
2032-26 Muffins Pet Connection, Brooklyn, NY, $12,500. For unrestricted support. 2001.
2032-27 National Humane Education Society, Leesburg, VA, $11,500. For unrestricted support. 2001.
2032-28 North Shore Animal League, Port Washington, NY, $25,250. For unrestricted support. 2001.
2032-29 Racing Dog Rescue Project, Sarasota, FL, $16,500. For unrestricted support. 2001.
2032-30 Sanctuary for Animals, Westtown, NY, $12,500. For unrestricted support. 2001.
2032-31 Seeing Eye, Morristown, NJ, $23,000. For unrestricted support. 2001.
2032-32 Tree House Animal Foundation, Chicago, IL, $19,000. For unrestricted support. 2001.

2033
The Bay Foundation, Inc.
(formerly Charles Ulrick and Josephine Bay Foundation, Inc.)
17 W. 94th St., 1st Fl.
New York, NY 10025 (212) 663-1115
Contact: Robert W. Ashton, Secy.
FAX: (212) 932-0316

Incorporated in 1950 in NY.
Donor(s): Charles Ulrick Bay,‡ Josephine Bay.‡
Grantmaker type: Independent foundation
Financial data (yr. ended 12/31/02): Assets, $15,812,591 (M); expenditures, $1,570,165; qualifying distributions, $1,089,089; giving activities include $625,878 for 132 grants (high: $35,000; low: $60; average: $1,000–$15,000) and $150,000 for 6 grants to individuals (high: $30,000; low: $15,000; average: $15,000–$30,000).
Purpose and activities: Support for collections care, preservation and restoration in museums, libraries, and at historic sites; pre-collegiate education in math, science, and writing; conserving biodiversity and intervention on behalf of endangered species and ecological studies; and projects of native Americans.
Fields of interest: Art conservation; Early childhood education; Elementary school/education; Secondary school/education; Natural resources; Science; Biological sciences; Native Americans/American Indians.
Types of support: General/operating support; Program development; Seed money; Research; Grants to individuals; Matching/challenge support.
Limitations: Giving limited to the New England states, NJ, and NY for educational grants. No support for sectarian religious projects. No grants to individuals (except for Biodiversity Leadership Awards Program), or for endowments, building construction or maintenance, scholarships, fellowships, or for travel, film, television, or video production, programs consisting primarily of conferences or annual fund appeals; no loans.
Publications: Annual report (including application guidelines).
Application information: New York Regional Common Application Form accepted (preferably by regular mail). Applications not accepted for Biodiversity Leadership Awards Program. Application form not required.
Initial approach: Proposal
Copies of proposal: 1
Deadline(s): Must be postmarked by Mar. 1, Sept. 1, and Dec. 1
Board meeting date(s): Feb., May, and Oct.
Final notification: 3 months
Officers and Directors:* Frederick Bay,* Chair.; Synnova B. Hayes,* Pres. and Treas.; Hans A. Ege,* V.P.; Robert W. Ashton,* Secy. and Exec. Dir.; Rebecca Adamson; Corinne Steel.
Number of staff: 1 full-time professional; 2 part-time professional; 2 part-time support.
EIN: 135646283

2034
The Howard Bayne Fund
c/o Simpson Thacher & Bartlett
425 Lexington Ave.
New York, NY 10017-3909

Incorporated in 1960 in NY.
Donor(s): Louise Van Beuren Bayne Trust.
Grantmaker type: Independent foundation
Financial data (yr. ended 12/31/02): Assets, $14,457,759 (M); expenditures, $1,105,165; qualifying distributions, $950,064; giving activities include $935,000 for 155 grants (high: $48,500; low: $2,000).

Purpose and activities: Giving primarily for education and the arts.
Fields of interest: Museums; Museums (art); Theater; Music; Orchestra (symphony); Historic preservation/historical societies; Arts; Higher education; Education; Natural resources; Hospitals (general); Human services; Family services; Federated giving programs; Religion.
Types of support: Annual campaigns; Capital campaigns.
Limitations: Applications not accepted. Giving primarily in CT, NJ, and NY, with some emphasis on the New York, NY, area, and RI. No grants to individuals.
Application information: Contributes only to pre-selected organizations.
Officers and Directors: Gurdon B. Wattles,* Pres.; Daphne B. Shih,* V.P.; Victoria B. Bjorklund, Secy.-Treas.; Diana de Vegh; Pierre J. de Vegh; Daisy Paradis; Elizabeth W. Wilkes.
EIN: 136100680

2035
Hildegarde D. Becher Foundation, Inc.
P.O. Box 11
Hartsdale, NY 10530
Contact: Lawrence Dix, Treas.

Established in 1995 in NY.
Grantmaker type: Independent foundation
Financial data (yr. ended 12/31/02): Assets, $3,807,235 (M); expenditures, $330,122; qualifying distributions, $275,284; giving activities include $241,730 for 21 grants (high: $65,000; low: $1,000; average: $1,500–$32,250).
Fields of interest: Environment; Medical research, institute; Children/youth, services.
Types of support: General/operating support; Continuing support; Annual campaigns; Building/renovation; Scholarship funds; Research.
Limitations: Giving on a national basis.
Application information: Application form not required.
  Initial approach: Letter
  Deadline(s): None
  Board meeting date(s): Varies
Officers: Herbert Kroner, Pres.; Jack Geoghegan, Secy.; Lawrence Dix, Treas.
EIN: 133744010

2036
Frederick H. Bedford, Jr. and Margaret S. Bedford Charitable Foundation
2 Wall St.
New York, NY 10005

Established in 1989 in DE; funded in fiscal 1990.
Donor(s): Victaulic Co.
Grantmaker type: Company-sponsored foundation
Financial data (yr. ended 09/30/02): Assets, $2,932,442 (M); gifts received, $250,000; expenditures, $197,043; qualifying distributions, $194,977; giving activities include $192,180 for 61 grants (high: $65,000; low: $100).
Fields of interest: Arts; Elementary/secondary education; Education; Environment; Hospitals (general); Health organizations, association; Human services; Children/youth, services;

Federated giving programs; General charitable giving.
Limitations: Applications not accepted. Giving in the U.S., primarily in PA. No grants to individuals.
Application information: Contributes only to pre-selected organizations.
Officers and Directors: J.M. Trachtenberg,* Pres.; Pierre D'Arenberg,* V.P.; Muffie B. Murray,* Secy.-Treas.; Thomas M. Bancroft, Jr.; George Naumann.
EIN: 133544702

2037
The Bedminster Fund, Inc.
1330 Ave. of the Americas, 27th Fl.
New York, NY 10019-5490
Contact: Dorothy Davis, Secy.

Incorporated in 1948 in NY.
Grantmaker type: Independent foundation
Financial data (yr. ended 06/30/02): Assets, $10,654,674 (M); expenditures, $715,738; qualifying distributions, $679,722; giving activities include $663,500 for 38 grants (high: $100,000; low: $2,000).
Purpose and activities: Emphasis on education, hospitals, the arts, and welfare agencies. Grants only to present beneficiary organizations and to special proposals developed by the directors; additional requests seldom considered.
Fields of interest: Arts; Education; Environment; Hospitals (general); Human services.
Types of support: General/operating support; Continuing support; Annual campaigns; Capital campaigns; Building/renovation; Conferences/seminars.
Limitations: Applications not accepted. Giving on a national basis, with some emphasis on NJ and NY. No grants to individuals; no loans.
Application information: Contributes only to pre-selected organizations.
  Board meeting date(s): Nov. and as required
Officers and Directors: Philip D. Allen,* Pres.; Martin C. Zetterberg,* V.P.; Dorothy Davis, Secy.; James J. Ruddy, Treas.; A. Christine Allen; Alexandra J. Allen; Andrew D. Allen; Christopher D. Allen; Douglas E. Allen; Elisabeth F. Allen; Nicholas E. Allen; Dorothy D. Caplow; Theodore Caplow; Dorothy Dillon Eweson; Judith S. Leonard; David H. Peipers.
Number of staff: 1 part-time professional.
EIN: 136083684

2038
Beldon Fund ▼
(also known as Beldon II Fund)
99 Madison Ave. 8th Fl.
New York, NY 10016 (800) 591-9595
Contact: Holeri Faruolo, Grants Admin.
Additional tel.: (212) 616-5600; FAX: (212) 616-5656; E-mail: info@beldon.org; URL: http://www.beldon.org

Established in 1987 in MI.
Donor(s): John R. Hunting.
Grantmaker type: Independent foundation
Financial data (yr. ended 12/31/01): Assets, $87,613,861 (M); expenditures, $14,757,818; qualifying distributions, $13,621,195; giving activities include $11,574,645 for 95 grants

(high: $500,000; low: $1,000; average: $5,000–$25,000).
Purpose and activities: By supporting effective nonprofit advocacy organizations, the Beldon Fund seeks to build a national consensus to achieve and sustain a healthy planet. To attain this goal, the fund plans to invest its entire principal and earnings by 2009. The fund focuses support in three programs: Human Health and the Environment, Corporate Campaigns, and Key States.
Fields of interest: Environment, management/technical aid; Environment, toxics.
Types of support: General/operating support; Program development; Conferences/seminars; Technical assistance; Consulting services; Employee matching gifts.
Limitations: Giving on a national basis. No support for forest, wildlife habitat/refuges, land, marine, river, lake, wilderness preservation, protection or restoration, arts and culture, international programs, service delivery programs, academic or university projects, school- or classroom-based environmental education. No grants to individuals, or for land acquisition, endowment or capital campaigns, scholarships, research, film, video and radio projects, deficit reduction, or museums or collections acquisitions.
Publications: Annual report (including application guidelines).
Application information: Applications submitted through Beldon Fund; the foundation encourages applicants to use environmentally sensitive applications. See program guidelines and grant application procedures posted on Web site. Application form not required.
  Initial approach: Letter of inquiry (see letter of inquiry checklist posted on Web site)
  Copies of proposal: 2
  Deadline(s): Due dates posted on Web site and updated regularly
  Board meeting date(s): Winter, Spring, and Fall
Officers and Trustees: John R. Hunting,* Chair., Pres. and Treas.; Azade Ardali, C.O.O.; Hally Schadler,* Secy. and Gen. Counsel; William J. Roberts, Exec. Dir.; Patricia Bauman; Wade Greene; Ruth Henning; Gene Karpinski; Lael Stegall; Ann Fowler Wallace.
Number of staff: 9 full-time professional; 5 full-time support.
EIN: 382756784
Recent environmental and animal welfare grants:
2038-1 1000 Friends of Wisconsin Land Use Institute, Madison, WI, $100,000. For Wisconsin Conservation Voters Institute program in Watertown. 2002.
2038-2 Alliance for Justice, DC, $300,000. For Nonprofit Advocacy Project and Foundation Advocacy Initiative, providing workshops on legal rights and obligations governing advocacy to environmental groups in key Beldon states. 2002.
2038-3 Amigos Bravos, Taos, NM, $50,000. For general support of programs. 2002.
2038-4 Arab Community Center for Economic and Social Services (ACCESS), Dearborn, MI, $25,000. For Environmental Program protecting community health in southeastern Michigan. 2002.
2038-5 Audubon Society, National, New York, NY, $100,000. For Audubon Minnesota Birds to Ballots capacity-building project, seeding

policy director position within organization to ensure chapter engagements in related work, and active memberships in Minnesota Environmental Partnership. 2002.

2038-6 Catawba River Foundation, Charlotte, NC, $60,000. For general support to staff and expand volunteer network and other programs. 2002.

2038-7 Center for Health, Environment and Justice, Falls Church, VA, $200,000. For Child Proofing Our Communities, national healthy schools campaign. 2002.

2038-8 Center for Public Interest Research, Boston, MA, $300,000. For work of PIRG organizations based in Florida, Michigan, New Mexico, North Carolina, and Wisconsin, deepening state's ability to deliver advocacy on environmental issues, through State Action for a Clean and Healthy Environment project. 2002.

2038-9 Childrens Environmental Health Network, DC, $150,000. For project, Augmenting Minority Health Professional Participation in Children's Health Concerns and Policy. 2002.

2038-10 Citizens Environmental Coalition, Albany, NY, $40,000. For Right to Know Environmental Hazards Project, building advocates for policies, toxic use reduction and good neighbor agreements. 2002.

2038-11 Clean Water Fund, Minneapolis, MN, $150,000. For program support. 2002.

2038-12 Clean Water Fund, Minneapolis, MN, $15,000. For Strategic Planning and Development Initiatives project, developing grassroots capacity and building in-house opinion research capacity for Minnesota and regional advocates. 2002.

2038-13 Clean Water Network, DC, $100,000. For Florida Clean Water Campaign. 2002.

2038-14 Communities for a Better Environment, Oakland, CA, $75,000. For general support to provide local communities with tools to fight toxic health threats. 2002.

2038-15 Earth Share of North Carolina, Durham, NC, $100,000. For general support to expand environmental community funding access through increased workplace giving. 2002.

2038-16 Earthjustice Legal Defense Fund, Oakland, CA, $100,000. For Florida Sustainable Waters Program, ensuring environmental community and local network access to legal support enforcing clean water regulations. 2002.

2038-17 Ecology Center of Ann Arbor, Ann Arbor, MI, $40,000. For environmental health project, eliminating persistent bioaccumulative toxins in automobile, health care, and chemical industries. 2002.

2038-18 Environmental Advocates, Albany, NY, $50,000. For general support of programs. 2002.

2038-19 Environmental Defense, DC, $100,000. For Keep Antibiotics Working, campaign ending overuse. 2002.

2038-20 Environmental Grantmakers Association, New York, NY, $10,000. For Fall Retreat. 2002.

2038-21 Environmental Health Coalition, San Diego, CA, $50,000. For general support helping border region residents expose links between exposure to toxins and health, and

advocate for local, state, and national protections. 2002.

2038-22 Environmental Leadership Program, Cambridge, MA, $50,000. For general support of programs. 2002.

2038-23 Environmental Media Services, DC, $75,000. To develop Scientists' Support Network, training and expanding number of medical experts and scientists prepared for advocacy. 2002.

2038-24 Environmental Research Foundation, Princeton, NJ, $50,000. For general support to inform community-based activists, journalists, government officials, health affected groups, and medical professionals on relationship between health and environmental deterioration and policies to reverse trend. 2002.

2038-25 Environmental Support Center, DC, $200,000. For general support of programs. 2002.

2038-26 Environmental Working Group, DC, $200,000. For Toxic Chemical Policy Project, including use of body burden data and tort organizing to reduce human exposure. 2002.

2038-27 Federation of State Conservation Voter Leagues, Seattle, WA, $120,000. For program support. 2002.

2038-28 Florida Wildlife Federation, Tallahassee, FL, $35,000. For Constituent Advocacy project, effort organizing business owners, recreational users, and outdoor sports enthusiasts in southern Florida. 2002.

2038-29 Generation Green Fund, Evanston, IL, $40,000. For Illinois Healthy Schools Campaign, coalition for comprehensive policy and coordinated agenda to ensure schools are healthy environments. 2002.

2038-30 Green Corps, Boston, MA, $350,000. For general support of programs. 2002.

2038-31 Health Care Without Harm, DC, $150,000. 2002.

2038-32 Indigenous Environmental Network, Bemidji, MN, $75,000. For Native Youth Program. 2002.

2038-33 Institute for Childrens Environmental Health, Freeland, WA, $15,000. For Partnership for Children's Health and the Environment Meeting in San Francisco, CA. 2002.

2038-34 Institute for Conservation Leadership, Takoma Park, MD, $35,000. For partnership with Environmental Support Center in Rightsize, Don't Capsize: Managing in Hard Times project. 2002.

2038-35 League of Conservation Voters Education Fund, DC, $450,000. For general support of programs. 2002.

2038-36 Legal Environmental Assistance Foundation (LEAF), Tallahassee, FL, $150,000. For general support of programs. 2002.

2038-37 Louisiana Bucket Brigade, New Orleans, LA, $50,000. For general support for work to provide air quality monitoring tools to communities adjacent to petrochemical plants in Louisiana. 2002.

2038-38 Lymphoma Research Foundation, New York, NY, $20,000. For Pesticides Research Project and to distribute and advocate Do Pesticides Cause Lymphoma report. 2002.

2038-39 Maurice and Jane Sugar Law Center for Economic and Social Justice, Detroit, MI, $100,000. For Environmental Justice Project

Community Education and Training Program, increasing number of leaders capable of identifying and organizing residents to mount strategies protecting neighborhood environmental health and supporting statewide advocacy efforts. 2002.

2038-40 Midwest Environmental Advocates, Madison, WI, $300,000. For general support of programs, including Impact Litigation, reaching out to pro-bono lawyers and environmental groups to link litigation and advocacy. 2002.

2038-41 Minnesota Center for Environmental Advocacy, Saint Paul, MN, $50,000. For Children's Environmental Health Initiative. 2002.

2038-42 Mount Sinai School of Medicine of New York University, Center for children's Health and the Environment, New York, NY, $150,000. For Reduction of Children's Exposure to Pesticides project, program of policy development and advocacy on behalf of children's health. 2002.

2038-43 National Black Environmental Justice Network, Detroit, MI, $150,000. For Healthy and Safe Communities Campaign, enhancing awareness within African-American communities of connection between pollution and health. 2002.

2038-44 National Environmental Trust, DC, $150,000. For general support of programs. 2002.

2038-45 National Wildlife Federation, Ann Arbor, MI, $70,000. For Clean the Rain State Mercury Project in Michigan, Minnesota, and Wisconsin. 2002.

2038-46 National Wildlife Federation, Reston, VA, $75,000. For general support of programs, including partnership with Collaborative Defense Campaign, amplifying public voice on environmental issues. 2002.

2038-47 Natural Resources Council, Augusta, ME, $50,000. For Clean Maine, Healthy Communities Project: Increasing Awareness of and Reducing Exposure to Toxic Chemicals. 2002.

2038-48 New Mexico Environmental Law Center, Santa Fe, NM, $75,000. For general support of programs. 2002.

2038-49 North Carolina Coastal Federation, Newport, NC, $100,000. To expand Cape Hatteras CoastKeeper program and engage greater number of communities along state coast in public education and advocacy, resulting in stronger enforcement of clean water laws in state and region. 2002.

2038-50 North Carolina Conservation Network (NC ConNet), Raleigh, NC, $60,000. For legacy project, increasing donor and event revenue and diversifying foundation support. 2002.

2038-51 Ohio Citizen Action Education Fund, Cleveland, OH, $50,000. For good neighbor campaign, mobilizing affected citizenry to advocate for pollution reductions at local and state levels through monitoring and outreach. 2002.

2038-52 Ohio Environmental Council, Columbus, OH, $50,000. For outreach to public health officials as part of Factory Farm Enforcement Project-Part II. 2002.

2038-53 Ohio Valley Environmental Coalition, Huntington, WV, $50,000. For general support of programs, including grassroots organizing and leadership development and efforts to halt mountaintop removal strip mining. 2002.

2038-54 Oregon Environmental Council, Portland, Oregon, $100,000. For Healthy Environment Initiative, organizing health professionals to advocate for policies and programs reducing pollutants adversely impacting health. 2002.

2038-55 Pamlico-Tar River Foundation, Washington, NC, $100,000. For general support of partnership with Neuse River Foundation, advocating for protection and clean-up of state watersheds and stronger enforcement of related laws. 2002.

2038-56 Partnership Project, DC, $250,000. For general support of programs. 2002.

2038-57 Partnership Project, DC, $66,000. For general support of programs, including conducting of opinion research. 2002.

2038-58 Physicians for Social Responsibility, DC, $200,000. To build constituency of physicians and health care providers active in environmental health policy. 2002.

2038-59 Physicians for Social Responsibility, DC, $40,000. For Maryland Pesticide Network in Annapolis, MD, monitoring compliance of existing Integrated Pest Management laws in schools, educating professionals and other stakeholders on poisoning, and creating system for tracking injuries. 2002.

2038-60 River Alliance of Wisconsin, Madison, WI, $150,000. For general support of programs. 2002.

2038-61 Rockefeller Family Fund, New York, NY, $75,000. For Task Force for Environmental Integrity project, addressing national crisis in enforcement. 2002.

2038-62 Science and Environmental Health Network, Windsor, ND, $25,000. For Science Analysis and Direction for the Collaborative on Health and the Environment project in Ames, IA. 2002.

2038-63 Sierra Club Foundation, San Francisco, CA, $240,000. For general support of programs including National Education Project, informing public and training activists. 2002.

2038-64 Sierra Club Foundation, San Francisco, CA, $100,000. For continued support of North Carolina Chapter Clean Water Campaign, fighting hog farm pollution and advocating for stronger laws. 2002.

2038-65 Southwest Network for Environmental and Economic Justice, Albuquerque, NM, $50,000. For Environmental Justice Youth Leadership Project. 2002.

2038-66 Sustain, Chicago, IL, $75,000. For Midwest Communications Initiative, providing media services to Beldon grantees in Michigan, Minnesota, and Wisconsin. 2002.

2038-67 Texas Fund for Energy and Environmental Education, Austin, TX, $80,000. For Empowering Democracy Annual Training, event for grassroots and corporate campaign activists. 2002.

2038-68 Texas Fund for Energy and Environmental Education, Austin, TX, $60,000. For Empowering Democracy Annual Training, event for grassroots and corporate campaign activists. 2002.

2038-69 Texas Fund for Energy and Environmental Education, Austin, TX, $25,000. For Sustainable Energy and Economic Development (SEED) Coalition Refinery Reform Program, using community monitoring efforts to increase awareness of impact of toxic oil refinery pollution on public health, and involve and train people to take action in monitoring and prevention. 2002.

2038-70 Tides Center, San Francisco, CA, $50,000. For Community Toolbox for Children's Environmental Health in Seattle, WA. 2002.

2038-71 United States Public Interest Research Group Education Fund, DC, $200,000. For Environmental Health Program, increase public awareness on of use and release of industrial chemicals. 2002.

2038-72 University of Maryland Foundation, School of Nursing, Baltimore, MD, $100,000. For Environmental Health Education Center, sponsoring Building Environmental Health Advocacy Capacity in the Nursing Community project. 2002.

2038-73 Washington Environmental Alliance for Voter Education, Seattle, WA, $50,000. For general support of programs. 2002.

2038-74 Washington Toxics Coalition, Seattle, WA, $110,000. For general support for various programs, including Toxic-Free Legacy Campaign to address persistent bioaccumulative toxics. 2002.

2038-75 West Harlem Environmental Action, New York, NY, $100,000. For Environmental Health Leadership Campaign, enlisting advocates in movement to reduce toxic exposure. 2002.

2038-76 Western Environmental Law Center, Taos, NM, $75,000. For New Mexico Land Use Initiative, effort to work collaboratively with residents in selected counties to envision, enact, and defend ordinances. 2002.

2038-77 Western Organization of Resource Councils Education Project, Billings, MT, $100,000. For general support of programs. 2002.

2038-78 Wisconsins Environmental Decade Institute, Madison, WI, $550,000. For Drinkable, Fishable, Swimmable Water in the Heartland, multi-year opinion research and communications training project for Wisconsin environmental advocates enhancing capacity to engage public in multi-year campaign. 2002.

2038-79 Wisconsins Environmental Decade Institute, Madison, WI, $150,000. For Wisconsin Stewardship Network program. 2002.

2038-80 Wisconsins Environmental Decade Institute, Madison, WI, $40,000. For Membership Development project to create membership and fundraising plan. 2002.

2038-81 Womens Voices for the Earth, Missoula, MT, $50,000. For Coming Clean Collaboration, coordinating and incubating policy efforts and mode of national campaigns among diverse array of groups and individuals changing national mode of chemical production and regulation. 2002.

2038-82 Work Environment Council of New Jersey, Trenton, NJ, $100,000. For general support of programs, including Healthy School Environments and Right-to-Know projects. 2002.

2038-83 Youth United for Community Action (YUCA), East Palo Alto, CA, $50,000. For Fighting Injustice and Regulating Equality Fellowship Program, training diverse youth as leaders and organizers for environmental justice. 2002.

2039
Robert A. and Renee E. Belfer Family Foundation
c/o Belfer Mgmt., LLC
767 5th Ave., 46th Fl.
New York, NY 10153

Established in 1990 in NY.
Donor(s): Robert A. Belfer, Jack Resnick & Sons, Inc.
Grantmaker type: Independent foundation
Financial data (yr. ended 12/31/00): Assets, $31,902,572 (M); gifts received, $1,713,056; expenditures, $1,634,983; qualifying distributions, $1,462,707; giving activities include $1,486,835 for 90 grants (high: $563,125; low: $40).
Purpose and activities: Giving primarily for the arts, education and Jewish causes.
Fields of interest: Museums (art); Museums (ethnic/folk arts); Opera; Performing arts centers; Arts; Higher education; Medical school/education; Natural resources; Hospitals (general); Health organizations; Jewish federated giving programs; Jewish agencies & temples; Economically disadvantaged.
Limitations: Applications not accepted. Giving primarily in NY. No grants to individuals.
Application information: Contributes only to pre-selected organizations.
Officer: Robert A. Belfer, Pres. and Secy.
Trustees: Laurence D. Belfer; Renee E. Belfer.
EIN: 136935616

2040
The Bender Family Foundation
c/o The Community Foundation for the Capital Region
Executive Park Dr.
Albany, NY 12203 (518) 446-9638
Contact: Jackie Mahoney, Dir. of Grantmaking and Donor Svcs.
URL: http://www.cfcr.org

Established in 1997 in NY.
Donor(s): Matthew Bender IV.
Grantmaker type: Independent foundation
Financial data (yr. ended 12/31/02): Assets, $2,204,754 (M); gifts received, $137,000; expenditures, $295,752; qualifying distributions, $260,070; giving activities include $260,400 for 33 grants (high: $25,000; low: $200).
Purpose and activities: Funding primarily to foster, preserve, and fund the arts, culture, education, history and environment of the New York State Capital Region.
Fields of interest: History/archaeology; Arts; Education; Natural resources; Environment; Youth development.
Types of support: Capital campaigns; Building/renovation; Equipment; Program development; Seed money.

Limitations: Giving primarily in Albany County, NY.
Publications: Application guidelines.
Application information: Contact Community Foundation for the Capital Region for application procedures. Application guidelines also available on foundation Web site. Application form required.
Initial approach: Telephone
Copies of proposal: 1
Deadline(s): Mar. 15 and Sept. 15
Board meeting date(s): Quarterly
Final notification: May 15 and Dec. 1
Officers: Matthew Bender IV, Pres.; Phoebe P. Bender, V.P.; M. Christian Bender, Secy.; Jeffrey P. Bender, Treas.
EIN: 161526228

2041
Bentley Holden Fund
223 Creamery Rd.
Roxbury, NY 12474
Contact: Carol Adams, Dir.
FAX: (607) 326-2819

Established in 1966 in NY.
Grantmaker type: Independent foundation
Financial data (yr. ended 12/31/02): Assets, $2,646,275 (M); expenditures, $159,596; qualifying distributions, $125,991; giving activities include $120,500 for 26 grants (high: $12,100; low: $1,000).
Purpose and activities: Giving to the arts and education.
Fields of interest: Media/communications; Higher education; Environment.
Types of support: Continuing support.
Limitations: Applications not accepted. Giving limited to NY; communications grants limited to Dutchess County. No grants to individuals.
Application information: Contributes only to pre-selected organizations. Unsolicited applications not accepted or acknowledged.
Directors: Carol Adams; Jon H. Adams.
Number of staff: 1 part-time support.
EIN: 146018221

2042
The Bernhill Fund
c/o Siegel, Sacks
630 3rd Ave.
New York, NY 10017
FAX: (212) 605-0222

Incorporated in 1977 in NY as partial successor to The Bernhard Foundation, Inc.
Donor(s): The Bernhard Foundation, Inc.
Grantmaker type: Independent foundation
Financial data (yr. ended 10/31/02): Assets, $440,920 (M); expenditures, $273,789; qualifying distributions, $265,455; giving activities include $267,416 for 178 grants (high: $25,000; low: $220).
Purpose and activities: Grants to urban community organizations and service delivery projects; support also for institutions of particular interest to the trustees, including the fine and performing arts, higher and other education, the environment and ecology, wildlife and animal welfare, the homeless, hospices, and AIDS programs.

Fields of interest: Media/communications; Museums; Performing arts; Arts; Higher education; Education; Natural resources; Animals/wildlife; AIDS; Human services; Public affairs.
Types of support: General/operating support; Continuing support; Program development; Seed money.
Limitations: Applications not accepted. Giving primarily in New York, NY; some giving in CT and FL. No grants to individuals, or for annual campaigns, emergency funds, deficit financing, matching gifts, scholarships, fellowships, demonstration projects, publications, or conferences; no loans.
Application information: Contributes only to pre-selected organizations.
Officers: William L. Bernhard, Pres.; Catherine G. Cahill, V.P.
Number of staff: None.
EIN: 132988599

2043
Berol Foundation, Inc.
c/o Trainor Wortham, Inc.
845 3rd Ave.
New York, NY 10022

Established in 1950.
Donor(s): Kenneth R. Berol.‡
Grantmaker type: Independent foundation
Financial data (yr. ended 02/28/02): Assets, $2,008,948 (M); expenditures, $128,545; qualifying distributions, $105,330; giving activities include $100,000 for 2 grants (high: $75,000; low: $25,000).
Purpose and activities: Giving primarily for the arts, education and health care.
Fields of interest: Theater; Historic preservation/historical societies; Education; Environment; Hospitals (general).
Limitations: Applications not accepted. Giving primarily in CA. No grants to individuals.
Application information: Contributes only to pre-selected organizations. Unsolicited requests for funds not considered or acknowledged.
Officers: John A. Berol, Pres.; Margaret B. Beattie, V.P.; A. Alexander Arnold III, Secy.-Treas.
Number of staff: None.
EIN: 136084214

2044
Margaret T. Biddle Foundation
c/o Cusack & Stiles, LLP
61 Broadway, Rm. 2100
New York, NY 10006

Incorporated in 1952 in NY.
Donor(s): Margaret T. Biddle.‡
Grantmaker type: Independent foundation
Financial data (yr. ended 12/31/02): Assets, $4,454,281 (M); expenditures, $312,372; qualifying distributions, $307,109; giving activities include $300,000 for 6 grants (high: $200,000; low: $15,000).
Fields of interest: Natural resources; Hospitals (general); Medical care, rehabilitation; Children/youth, services; Foundations (community).
Types of support: General/operating support.
Limitations: Applications not accepted. Giving on a national basis. No grants to individuals.

Application information: Contributes only to pre-selected organizations.
Officers and Directors:* Christian C. Hohenlohe,* Pres.; Peter B. Schulze,* V.P. and Secy.; Richard A. Smith,* V.P. and Treas.; Catherine H. Jacobus,* V.P.; Charles T. Schulze.
EIN: 131936016

2045
William Bingham 2nd Betterment Fund
c/o U.S. Trust
114 W. 47th St.
New York, NY 10036
Contact: Linda Franciscovich, Sr. V.P., U.S. Trust
FAX: (212) 852-3377; Application address: 330 Madison Ave., Rm. 3500, New York, NY 10017

Grantmaker type: Independent foundation
Financial data (yr. ended 12/31/01): Assets, $40,174,713 (M); expenditures, $2,712,721; qualifying distributions, $2,289,540; giving activities include $1,977,055 for 70 grants (high: $150,000; low: $2,500; average: $2,500–$50,000).
Purpose and activities: Giving primarily for the advancement of medicine in the state of ME.
Fields of interest: Secondary school/education; Higher education; Environment.
Types of support: General/operating support; Capital campaigns; Scholarship funds.
Limitations: Giving limited to ME. No grants to individuals.
Application information: Application form not required.
Initial approach: Letter
Copies of proposal: 1
Deadline(s): None
Trustees: William P. Clough; Carol Berg Geist; William M. Throop, Jr.; William Winship; Carolyn S. Wollen; U.S. Trust.
EIN: 136072625

2046
Leon Black Family Foundation, Inc.
1301 Ave. of the Americas, 38th Fl.
New York, NY 10019-6022

Established in 1997 in DE and NY.
Grantmaker type: Independent foundation
Financial data (yr. ended 12/31/01): Assets, $21,989 (M); gifts received, $2,472,519; expenditures, $2,568,987; qualifying distributions, $2,568,903; giving activities include $2,568,968 for 32 grants (high: $500,000; low: $2,500; average: $25,000–$100,000).
Purpose and activities: Giving primarily for arts and culture, museums, secondary education, human services, and youth development.
Fields of interest: Museums; Performing arts centers; Historical activities; Arts; Libraries/library science; Education; Animals/wildlife, preservation/protection; Hospitals (specialty); Boy scouts; Youth development; Children, services; Residential/custodial care; Federated giving programs.
Limitations: Applications not accepted. No grants to individuals.
Application information: Contributes only to pre-selected organizations.

Officers: Leon D. Black, Pres. and Treas.; Debra R. Black, V.P. and Secy.
Director: Jeffrey Epstein.
EIN: 133947890

2047
Black River Environmental Improvement Association, Inc.
c/o Butler Capital
745 5th Ave., No. 1702
New York, NY 10151 (212) 980-0606
Contact: Gilbert Butler, Pres.

Donor(s): Gilbert Butler.
Grantmaker type: Public charity
Financial data (yr. ended 04/30/00): Revenue, $209,178; assets, $1,110,198 (M); gifts received, $200,438; expenditures, $159,360; program services expenses, $88,328; giving activities include $14,000 for 3 grants (high: $5,000; low: $4,000).
Purpose and activities: Support for the benefit of the Adirondack Land Trust and other organizations which operate to preserve and enhance the scenic, historical wilderness, wildlife, open space and outdoor recreation values of the Adirondack area.
Fields of interest: Natural resources; Animals/wildlife, preservation/protection.
Limitations: Giving limited to the Adirondack area of NY.
Application information: Application form not required.
  Deadline(s): None
Officers and Trustees:* Gilbert Butler,* Pres. and Treas.; Edward D. Earl, Secy.; Bruce R. Carpenter; Dean D'Amore; Terrence Fitch; R. Bradley Malt; Robert R. Quinn.
EIN: 133243285

2048
John N. Blackman, Sr. Foundation
10 E. 40th St., Ste. 2710
New York, NY 10016-0340 (212) 679-0380
Contact: Howard Schain, Pres.

Established in 1988 in NY.
Donor(s): Mutual Marine Office, Inc.
Grantmaker type: Independent foundation
Financial data (yr. ended 08/31/02): Assets, $2,489,414 (M); expenditures, $309,838; qualifying distributions, $259,500; giving activities include $259,500 for 65 grants (high: $50,000; low: $1,000).
Purpose and activities: Giving primarily for health and human services.
Fields of interest: Arts; Animals/wildlife; Health organizations, association; Youth development; Human services; Religion.
Limitations: Giving primarily in NY. No grants to individuals.
Application information:
  Initial approach: Letter
  Deadline(s): None
Officer: Howard Schain, Pres.
Trustees: John N. Blackman, Jr.; Mark Blackman.
EIN: 222938619

2049
Blacksmith Institute, Inc.
c/o Richard Fuller
2 Park Ave., 29th Fl.
New York, NY 10016 (212) 779-4757
FAX: (212) 779-8044; E-mail: applications@blacksmithinstitute.org; URL: http://www.blacksmithinstitute.org

Grantmaker type: Public charity
Financial data (yr. ended 12/31/02): Revenue, $318,386; assets, $92,221 (M); gifts received, $318,386; expenditures, $360,851; program services expenses, $299,648; giving activities include $131,180 for 1 grant.
Purpose and activities: The institute supports local start-up initiatives solving environmental problems in the developing world.
Fields of interest: Environment, pollution control; International affairs.
International interests: Developing countries.
Types of support: General/operating support; Research; Technical assistance; Consulting services.
Limitations: Giving on an international basis to less developed countries (LDC's). No support for stand alone research studies, foreign consultants, or budgets that indicate northern wage levels.
Publications: Newsletter.
Application information: See Web site for recommended application format. Application form not required.
  Deadline(s): None
  Board meeting date(s): Quarterly
Officer and Directors:* Richard Fuller,* Chair. and Pres.; Elisa Dumitrescu, Admin.; Brij Anand; Allen Barnett; Joshua Ginsberg; Pradeep Kapadia; Richard Bruce Shepard; Alice Slater; Hume Steyer; Chet Tchozewski.
EIN: 134075779

2050
Cornelius N. Bliss Memorial Fund
c/o Boyce, Hughes & Farrell, LLP
1025 Northern Blvd., Ste. 300
Roslyn, NY 11576

Incorporated in 1917 in NY.
Donor(s): Cornelius N. Bliss,‡ Elizabeth M. Bliss, Lizzie P. Bliss, William B. Markell.
Grantmaker type: Independent foundation
Financial data (yr. ended 12/31/01): Assets, $2,599,956 (M); expenditures, $195,095; qualifying distributions, $170,032; giving activities include $165,000 for 29 grants (high: $24,000; low: $1,000).
Fields of interest: Museums; Performing arts; Arts; Secondary school/education; Animals/wildlife; Hospitals (general).
Limitations: Applications not accepted. Giving primarily in NY. No grants to individuals.
Application information: Contributes only to pre-selected organizations.
Officers: John Parkinson III, Pres.; Barbara B. Mestre, V.P.; Cornelius N. Bliss III, Treas.
Number of staff: None.
EIN: 136400075

2051
Freya & Richard Block Family Foundation
c/o DDK & Co.
1500 Broadway, 12th Fl.
New York, NY 10036

Established in 1999 in NY.
Donor(s): Richard H. Block, Freya Block.
Grantmaker type: Independent foundation
Financial data (yr. ended 07/31/02): Assets, $322,806 (M); gifts received, $50,000; expenditures, $116,130; qualifying distributions, $112,248; giving activities include $106,650 for 66 grants (high: $15,000; low: $100).
Fields of interest: Arts; Education; Environment; Human services; Federated giving programs; Jewish agencies & temples.
Limitations: Applications not accepted. Giving primarily in NY. No grants to individuals.
Application information: Contributes only to pre-selected organizations.
Directors: Freya Block; Richard H. Block.
EIN: 134092442

2052
The Bobolink Foundation
(formerly Henry M. & Wendy J. Paulson, Jr. Foundation)
c/o Goldman Sachs & Co.
85 Broad St., Tax Dept.
New York, NY 10004

Established in 1985 in IL.
Donor(s): Henry M. Paulson, Jr., Goldman, Sachs & Co.
Grantmaker type: Independent foundation
Financial data (yr. ended 03/31/01): Assets, $18,181,242 (M); gifts received, $3,708,995; expenditures, $2,205,825; qualifying distributions, $1,952,516; giving activities include $1,948,500 for 93 grants (high: $400,000; low: $500).
Purpose and activities: Support primarily for Christian Science churches, environmental conservation and wildlife preservation, and higher education.
Fields of interest: Higher education; Business school/education; Natural resources; Animals/wildlife, preservation/protection; Children, services; Protestant agencies & churches.
Limitations: Applications not accepted. Giving on a national basis, with some emphasis on New York, NY, Washington, DC, Arlington, VA, and Boston, MA. No grants to individuals; no loans.
Application information: Contributes only to pre-selected organizations.
Trustees: Amanda Clark Paulson; Henry M. Paulson, Jr.; Henry Merritt Paulson III; Wendy J. Paulson.
EIN: 942988627

2053
The Albert C. Bostwick Foundation
Hillside Ave. and Bacon Rd.
P.O. Box 440
Old Westbury, NY 11568
Contact: Eleanor P. Bostwick, Tr.

Established in 1958 in NY.
Donor(s): Albert C. Bostwick.‡

Grantmaker type: Independent foundation
Financial data (yr. ended 12/31/02): Assets,
$3,527,206 (M); expenditures, $235,364;
qualifying distributions, $215,862; giving
activities include $207,500 for 25 grants (high:
$30,000; low: $1,000).
Purpose and activities: Giving primarily for
medical care and medical research
organizations.
Fields of interest: Veterinary medicine;
Hospitals (general); Health care; Health
organizations, association; Medical research,
institute; Human services.
Types of support: Research.
Limitations: Giving primarily in NY. No grants to
individuals.
Application information:
    Initial approach: Letter
    Deadline(s): None
    Board meeting date(s): Annually
Trustees: Albert C. Bostwick, Jr.; Eleanor P.
Bostwick; Andrew G.C. Sage III.
EIN: 116003740

2054
The Brand Foundation of New York, Inc.
(formerly The Martha and Regina Brand
Foundation, Inc.)
521 5th Ave., Ste. 1805
New York, NY   10175-1899   (212) 687-3505

Established in 1962 in NY.
Donor(s): Martha Brand,‡ Marjorie D. Kogan.
Grantmaker type: Independent foundation
Financial data (yr. ended 12/31/02): Assets,
$2,353,643 (M); expenditures, $288,224;
qualifying distributions, $262,501; giving
activities include $236,700 for 32 grants (high:
$45,000; low: $500).
Purpose and activities: Giving primarily for arts
and culture, higher education, human services,
Jewish agencies and temples, as well as for
other religious purposes.
Fields of interest: Theater; Arts; Higher
education; Animal welfare; Human services;
Federated giving programs; Jewish agencies &
temples; Religion.
Limitations: Applications not accepted. Giving
primarily in CA, New York, NY and SC. No
grants to individuals.
Application information: Contributes only to
pre-selected organizations.
Officers: Marjorie D. Kogan, Pres.; Michael S.
Kogan, V.P. and Secy.; Barton H. Kogan, V.P. and
Treas.
EIN: 136159106

2055
Henry & Wendy Breck Foundation
550 Park Ave.
New York, NY   10021
Contact: Henry Breck, Pres.

Established in 1993 in NY.
Donor(s): Henry Breck.
Grantmaker type: Independent foundation
Financial data (yr. ended 12/31/01): Assets,
$939,846 (M); expenditures, $104,756;
qualifying distributions, $102,562; giving
activities include $102,562 for 8 grants (high:
$71,412; low: $250).

Fields of interest: Arts; Elementary/secondary
education; University; Natural resources;
Hospitals (general); Christian agencies &
churches.
Limitations: Applications not accepted. Giving
primarily in MA and New York, NY. No grants to
individuals.
Application information: Contributes only to
pre-selected organizations.
Officers: Henry Breck, Pres. and Treas.; Wendy
Breck, V.P. and Secy.
Director: Christopher Breck.
EIN: 133669369

2056
The Bridgewater Fund, Inc.
c/o Paul Kaplan
40 5th Ave.
New York, NY   10011

Established in 1971 in NY and DE.
Donor(s): Ursula Lerse, Reginald Fullerton,
Charles A. Rivkin, Paul J. Sperry, Paul D. Kaplan.
Grantmaker type: Independent foundation
Financial data (yr. ended 11/30/02): Assets,
$423,585 (M); gifts received, $132,727;
expenditures, $94,534; qualifying distributions,
$91,986; giving activities include $92,030 for
102 grants (high: $15,000; low: $30).
Purpose and activities: Giving primarily for the
arts and education.
Fields of interest: Arts; Elementary
school/education; Secondary school/education;
Higher education; Education; Animals/wildlife,
preservation/protection; Jewish agencies &
temples.
Types of support: General/operating support.
Limitations: Applications not accepted. Giving
in the East, with emphasis on NY and RI. No
grants to individuals.
Application information: Contributes only to
pre-selected organizations.
Officers and Directors:* Paul D. Kaplan,* Pres.;
Robert Tofel, Secy.; Patricia Kaplan.
EIN: 237442465

2057
Brokaw Family Foundation
c/o Starr & Co.
350 Park Ave.
New York, NY   10022

Established in 1990 in NY.
Donor(s): Thomas J. Brokaw, Fast Track
Productions, Inc.
Grantmaker type: Independent foundation
Financial data (yr. ended 12/31/01): Assets,
$75,955 (M); gifts received, $460,000;
expenditures, $447,428; qualifying distributions,
$447,349; giving activities include $447,350 for
74 grants (high: $50,000; low: $500).
Fields of interest: Arts; Education; Natural
resources; Human services.
Limitations: Applications not accepted. Giving
on a national basis. No grants to individuals.
Application information: Contributes only to
pre-selected organizations.
Trustee: Thomas J. Brokaw.
EIN: 133594435

2058
The Andrea and Charles Bronfman
Philanthropies, Inc. ▼
375 Park Ave., 4th Fl.
New York, NY   10152-0192

Established in 1998 in DE and NY.
Grantmaker type: Independent foundation
Financial data (yr. ended 12/31/01): Assets,
$4,646,406 (M); gifts received, $12,794,088;
expenditures, $11,669,674; qualifying
distributions, $11,492,384; giving activities
include $4,922,410 for 96 grants (high:
$786,362; low: $1,000; average:
$1,000–$50,000) and $4,998,642 for 4
foundation-administered programs.
Purpose and activities: The foundation's mission
is to encourage young people to strengthen their
knowledge and appreciation of their history,
heritage and cultural identity. The foundation
has four program areas: 1) Jewish Peoplehood- a
range of initiatives from travel to exchange
programs designed to support the shared Jewish
identity; 2) Project involvement- an educational
reform program in Israel; 3) Education for the
environment- support to research a variety of
community initiatives to raise Israelis knowledge
of environmental issues; 4) Education for
Co-operation and Co-existence- encourages
greater knowledge and understanding between
Israelis and Palestinians.
Fields of interest: Education; Human services;
Jewish agencies & temples.
International interests: Israel.
Types of support: General/operating support;
Program development; Conferences/seminars;
Seed money; Curriculum development;
Research; Technical assistance; Consulting
services; Employee matching gifts.
Limitations: Applications not accepted. Giving
in the U.S. and Israel. No grants to individuals.
Application information: Contributes only to
pre-selected organizations.
Officers and Directors:* Charles R. Bronfman,*
Chair.; Andrea M. Bronfman,* Dep.-Chair.;
Jeffrey Solomon,* Pres.; Janet Aviad, Sr. V.P.,
Israel Prog.; Ann Dadson, Sr. V.P., Admin.; Roger
Bennett, V.P., Strategic Initiatives; Barry Chazan,
V.P., Ed.; Simon Klarfeld, V.P.; Nancy Rosenfeld,
V.P., Canada; G.F. Craig, Secy.; Andrew Parsons,
Treas.
Number of staff: 47.
EIN: 133984936
Recent environmental and animal welfare
grants:
2058-1 Arava Institute for Environmental
    Studies, Kibbutz Ketura, Israel, $20,000. For
    Water Crisis paper, research to involve
    evaluation of existing water management and
    policies around the world. 2001.
2058-2 Heschel Center for Environmental
    Learning and Leadership, Tel Aviv, Israel,
    $100,000. For Green Network of
    Environmental Schools to promote
    environmental programs and community
    involvement in elementary schools. 2001.
2058-3 Heschel Center for Environmental
    Learning and Leadership, Tel Aviv, Israel,
    $70,000. For organization of seminars and
    study of environmental policy in Israel. 2001.
2058-4 Israel Union for Environmental Defense
    (Adam Teva V Din), Tel Aviv, Israel, $50,000.
    For consultation with groups active in
    environmental legal issues and training new

lawyers to be active in area of environmental concerns. 2001.

2058-5 Israel Union for Environmental Defense (Adam Teva V Din), Tel Aviv, Israel, $15,000. For Project Ramat Hanadiv to promote sustainable agriculture projects and conservation strategies. 2001.

2058-6 Kiryat Tivon Regional Council, Kiryat Tivon, Israel, $20,000. For Recycling project, to design special waste containers designated for recycling. 2001.

2058-7 Law of Nature, Haifa, Israel, $15,000. To help professional volunteers organize their services pro bono to grassroots organizations active in environmental concerns. 2001.

2058-8 Middle East Nature Conservation Association, Tel Aviv, Israel, $12,000. For communication on environmental issues. 2001.

2058-9 Society for the Protection of Nature in Israel, Tel Aviv, Israel, $60,000. For Echo to inform national and local environmental representatives on various issues of public concern and facilitate information exchange. 2001.

2058-10 Society for the Protection of Nature in Israel, Tel Aviv, Israel, $20,000. For research into legal, scientific, public, and planning aspects of preservation of Eilat Bay. 2001.

2058-11 Society for the Protection of Nature in Israel, Tel Aviv, Israel, $18,000. To promote awareness of importance of Persian fallow deer as endangered species and important environmental contributor to area. 2001.

2058-12 Society for the Protection of Nature in Israel, Tel Aviv, Israel, $18,000. To form coalition of active groups of environmentalists in neighborhood of Haifa. 2001.

2058-13 Society for the Protection of Nature in Israel, Tel Aviv, Israel, $15,000. For Project Ramat Hanadiv to promote sustainable agriculture projects and conservation strategies. 2001.

2058-14 Society for the Protection of Nature in Israel, Tel Aviv, Israel, $10,000. To create basis for new comprehensive environmental strategic plan with hope of linking Sustainable Jerusalem grass-roots programs to municipal strategies. 2001.

2058-15 Sustainable Development for the Negev, Omer, Israel, $15,000. To encourage environmental education of citizens in southern part of Israel. 2001.

2059
The Brunckhorst Foundation
24 Rock St.
Brooklyn, NY 11206-3886

Established in 1968.
Donor(s): Barbara Brunckhorst.
Grantmaker type: Independent foundation
Financial data (yr. ended 12/31/01): Assets, $24,695,035 (M); expenditures, $1,548,800; qualifying distributions, $1,511,960; giving activities include $1,530,000 for 17 grants (high: $160,000; low: $10,000).
Purpose and activities: Giving primarily for environmental conservation.
Fields of interest: Education; Natural resources; Animal welfare; Animals/wildlife, preservation/protection; Family planning.

Limitations: Applications not accepted. No grants to individuals.
Application information: Contributes only to pre-selected organizations.
Trustees: Barbara Brunckhorst; Frank Brunckhorst III; Richard Todd Stravitz.
EIN: 237000850

2060
The 1994 Sheila Johnson Brutsch Charitable Trust
c/o The Johnson Co., Inc.
630 5th Ave., Ste. 1510
New York, NY 10111

Established in 1994 in NY.
Donor(s): Betty W. Johnson.
Grantmaker type: Independent foundation
Financial data (yr. ended 12/31/02): Assets, $5,300,860 (M); expenditures, $286,163; qualifying distributions, $279,406; giving activities include $282,000 for 9 grants (high: $75,000; low: $10,000).
Fields of interest: Media/communications; Higher education; Natural resources; Animals/wildlife, preservation/protection.
Limitations: Applications not accepted. Giving primarily in FL. No grants to individuals.
Application information: Contributes only to pre-selected organizations.
Trustees: Sheila Johnson Brutsch; Betty W. Johnson.
EIN: 137046312

2061
Gilbert & Ildiko Butler Foundation, Inc.
(formerly Butler Foundation, Inc.)
c/o Butler Capital Corp.
745 5th Ave., Ste. 1702
New York, NY 10151-1706

Established in 1988 in MA.
Donor(s): Gilbert Butler, Butler Capital Corp.
Grantmaker type: Company-sponsored foundation
Financial data (yr. ended 12/31/01): Assets, $21,506,270 (M); gifts received, $4,453,266; expenditures, $742,281; qualifying distributions, $679,015; giving activities include $674,089 for 128 grants (high: $50,000; low: $80).
Purpose and activities: Giving primarily for the arts, education, natural resource conservation, wildlife, health and health associations, human services and federated giving programs. The foundation also implements the Let's Build America Awards Program, which provides funds for the education of employees and/or children of employees of Butler Capital's portfolio companies.
Fields of interest: Museums; Theater (playwriting); Opera; Historic preservation/historical societies; Arts; Higher education; Education; Natural resources; Botanical gardens; Animals/wildlife; Health care; Health organizations, association; Eye diseases; Human services; Federated giving programs.
Types of support: General/operating support; Capital campaigns; Research; Employee-related scholarships.

Limitations: Applications not accepted. Giving on a national basis, with emphasis on NY and the New England region, primarily MA and ME.
Application information: Unsolicited requests for funds not considered.
Officers and Directors:* Gilbert Butler,* Pres. and Treas.; R. Bradford Malt, V.P. and Clerk; Ildiko Butler; Emily Rafferty; Winthrop Rutherford, Jr.
EIN: 043032409

2062
The Bydale Foundation
11 Martine Ave.
White Plains, NY 10606 (914) 683-3519
Contact: Milton D. Solomon, V.P.

Incorporated in 1965 in DE.
Donor(s): James P. Warburg.‡
Grantmaker type: Independent foundation
Financial data (yr. ended 12/31/02): Assets, $12,826,964 (M); expenditures, $838,328; qualifying distributions, $781,487; giving activities include $742,750 for 69 grants (high: $55,000; low: $1,250; average: $2,000–$10,000).
Purpose and activities: Emphasis on international understanding, public policy research, the environment, cultural programs, the law and civil rights, social services, higher education, and economics.
Fields of interest: Arts; Higher education; Natural resources; Environment; Gun control; Crime/law enforcement; Human services; International affairs; Civil rights, women; Reproductive rights; Civil rights; Economics; Political science; Public policy, research; African Americans/Blacks; Women; Economically disadvantaged.
Types of support: General/operating support; Continuing support; Program development; Conferences/seminars; Publication; Seed money; Research; Matching/challenge support.
Limitations: Giving on a national basis. No grants to individuals, or for annual campaigns, emergency funds, deficit financing, endowment funds, demonstration projects, capital funds, scholarships, or fellowships; no loans.
Application information: Application form not required.
Initial approach: Letter or proposal
Copies of proposal: 1
Deadline(s): Submit proposal preferably in July or Aug.; deadline Nov. 1
Board meeting date(s): Dec.
Final notification: 2 or 3 weeks
Officers and Trustees:* Joan M. Warburg,* Pres.; Milton D. Solomon,* V.P. and Secy.; Frank J. Kick, Treas.; Sarah W. Bliumis; James P. Warburg, Jr.; Jennifer Warburg; Philip N. Warburg.
Number of staff: 1 part-time professional; 1 part-time support.
EIN: 136195286

2063
Byrne Foundation
240 Oneida St.
Syracuse, NY 13202

Established in 1960 in NY.

Donor(s): Byrne Dairy, Inc., Sonbyrne Sales, Inc., McMahon's of Central Square, Inc.
Grantmaker type: Independent foundation
Financial data (yr. ended 04/30/02): Assets, $100,236 (M); gifts received, $78,000; expenditures, $102,869; qualifying distributions, $102,178; giving activities include $102,204 for 40 grants (high: $20,000; low: $250).
Purpose and activities: Giving for higher education, hospitals, and Catholic organizations.
Fields of interest: Higher education; Zoos/zoological societies; Hospitals (general); Human services; Roman Catholic agencies & churches; Aging.
Types of support: General/operating support.
Limitations: Applications not accepted. Giving primarily in Syracuse, NY. No grants to individuals.
Application information: Contributes only to pre-selected organizations.
Officer: William M. Byrne, Jr., Mgr.
EIN: 166052248

2064
Cabbage Hill Farm Foundation, Inc.
c/o KISCO Mgmt. Corp.
111 Radio Cir.
Mount Kisco, NY 10549

Established in 1997 in NY.
Donor(s): Jerome Kohlberg.
Grantmaker type: Operating foundation
Financial data (yr. ended 12/31/00): Assets, $9,844,133 (M); gifts received, $225,000; expenditures, $1,126,184; qualifying distributions, $896,685; giving activities include $240,692 for 13 grants (high: $225,000; low: $26) and $730,350 for foundation-administered programs.
Fields of interest: Elementary/secondary education; Natural resources.
Limitations: Applications not accepted. Giving primarily in MA, NY, and PA. No grants to individuals.
Application information: Contributes only to pre-selected organizations.
Officers and Directors:* Nancy S. Kohlberg,* Pres.; Walter W. Farley,* V.P. and Secy.; Eileen M. Capone,* Treas.; Anne Farrell; Jerome Kohlberg; Pamela Kohlberg; Nancy Mccabe; Wilkes Mcclave III.
EIN: 133914519

2065
The Andrew Cader & Deborah Reich Foundation, Inc.
c/o Spear, Leeds & Kellogg
120 Broadway
New York, NY 10271

Established in 1995 in NY.
Donor(s): Education For Youth Society, Andrew Cader.
Grantmaker type: Independent foundation
Financial data (yr. ended 09/30/02): Assets, $10,235,069 (M); gifts received, $820,924; expenditures, $1,124,778; qualifying distributions, $892,433; giving activities include $866,363 for 26 grants (high: $200,000; low: $100).
Purpose and activities: Giving primarily for the arts, education, and human services.

Fields of interest: Orchestra (symphony); Opera; Arts; Education; Botanical gardens; Children/youth; services.
Limitations: Applications not accepted. Giving primarily in NY. No grants to individuals.
Application information: Contributes only to pre-selected organizations.
Officers: Andrew Cader, Pres. and Treas.; Deborah Reich, V.P. and Secy.; Seth J. Lapidow, V.P.
EIN: 133860405

2066
CAL Foundation, Inc.
c/o Siegel, Sacks & Co.
630 3rd Ave.
New York, NY 10017

Established in 1957.
Donor(s): Linda L. Hackett.
Grantmaker type: Independent foundation
Financial data (yr. ended 12/31/02): Assets, $2,456,649 (M); expenditures, $124,188; qualifying distributions, $114,000; giving activities include $114,000 for grants.
Fields of interest: Arts; Environment; Animal welfare; Religion.
Limitations: Applications not accepted. Giving primarily in the metropolitan New York, NY, area. No grants to individuals.
Application information: Contributes only to pre-selected organizations.
Officers: Linda Hackett, Pres.; Melinda Hackett, V.P.; Montague H. Hackett, Jr., Secy.
EIN: 136083347

2067
Camp Fire Conservation Fund, Inc.
230 Camp Fire Rd.
Chappaqua, NY 10514-2419 (914) 941-0199
Contact: J.P. Bigotte, Pres.

Established in 1976.
Grantmaker type: Public charity
Financial data (yr. ended 06/30/03): Revenue, $76,171; assets, $870,615 (M); gifts received, $61,785; expenditures, $34,657; program services expenses, $25,220; giving activities include $22,220 for 7 grants (high: $6,000; low: $1,000).
Purpose and activities: The fund promotes the conservation and preservation of wilderness, wildlife and other natural recreational resources.
Fields of interest: Natural resources; Environment; Animals/wildlife, preservation/protection.
Application information: Application form required.
Officers and Directors:* J.P. Bigotte,* Pres.; Hugh C. Wiley,* V.P. and Treas.; Mark L. Hintsa,* Secy.; George J. Whiting,* Treas.; Charles G. Banks; Thomas J. Fisher; Steven G. Torborg.
EIN: 510192291

2068
The Carson Family Charitable Trust ▼
c/o U.S. Trust Co. of New York
114 W. 47th St.
New York, NY 10036

Established in 1990 in NY.
Donor(s): Russell L. Carson, Judith M. Carson.
Grantmaker type: Independent foundation
Financial data (yr. ended 12/31/02): Assets, $26,485,070 (M); gifts received, $18,877,935; expenditures, $18,857,229; qualifying distributions, $18,804,208; giving activities include $18,798,988 for 71 grants (high: $5,000,000; low: $1,000; average: $20,000–$200,000).
Purpose and activities: Funding primarily for an art museum and higher education. Some funding also for land conservation and public health.
Fields of interest: Museums (art); Higher education; Natural resources; Public health.
Types of support: General/operating support; Capital campaigns.
Limitations: Applications not accepted. Giving primarily in New York, NY. No grants to individuals.
Application information: Contributes only to pre-selected organizations.
Trustees: Cecily M. Carson; Edward S. Carson; Judith M. Carson; Russell L. Carson; William A. Goodloe; U.S. Trust Co. of New York.
EIN: 136957038
Recent environmental and animal welfare grants:
2068-1 Central Park Conservancy, New York, NY, $50,000. 2001.

2069
Mary Flagler Cary Charitable Trust ▼
122 E. 42nd St., Rm. 3505
New York, NY 10168 (212) 953-7700
Contact: Edward A. Ames, Tr. and Dir., Conservation; Gayle Morgan, Prog. Dir., Music; Lois M. Regan, Prog. Dir., Urban Environment
FAX: (212) 953-7720; E-mail: info@carytrust.org; URL: http://www.carytrust.org/

Trust established in 1968 in NY.
Donor(s): Mary Flagler Cary.‡
Grantmaker type: Independent foundation
Financial data (yr. ended 06/30/02): Assets, $102,635,915 (M); expenditures, $9,818,141; qualifying distributions, $9,155,542; giving activities include $8,140,089 for 107 grants (high: $3,671,159; low: $3,500; average: $5,000–$50,000).
Purpose and activities: The trust considers grant proposals in three areas: for music in New York City (directed toward community music schools and small- to medium-sized professional music institutions, with an emphasis on the commissioning, performance, and recording of contemporary music); for the conservation of natural resources (focused on the preservation of coastal wetlands and estuaries in the southern states from Maryland to Florida, primarily for programs to protect selected regional ecosystems); and for urban environmental programs in New York City (focused on support for community initiatives and to help develop local leadership to work on environmental problems within low-income neighborhoods of

the city). The balance of the trust's grant budget is devoted to special commitments undertaken for reasons relating to its history and origin, but no additional, unrelated support is offered in these fields. These include support for the Institute of Ecosystem Studies, Inc. at the Mary Flagler Cary Arboretum in Millbrook, NY; the Rockefeller University Field Research Center for Ecology and Ethnology in Millbrook, NY; and the Rochester Institute of Technology School of Printing.

Fields of interest: Performing arts; Music; Environment, reform; Natural resources; Environment; Leadership development.

Types of support: General/operating support; Continuing support; Land acquisition; Program development; Matching/challenge support.

Limitations: Giving limited to New York, NY, for music and the urban environment; and the southeastern coastal states for conservation. No support for private foundations, hospitals, religious organizations, primary or secondary schools, colleges and universities, libraries, or museums. No grants to individuals, or for scholarships, fellowships, capital funds, annual campaigns, seed money, emergency funds, deficit financing, or endowment funds; no loans to individuals.

Publications: Annual report, Financial statement, Grants list.

Application information: Application form not required.

Initial approach: Letter with brief proposal
Copies of proposal: 1
Deadline(s): None
Board meeting date(s): Monthly
Final notification: 2 months

Trustees: Edward A. Ames, Prog. Dir., Conservation; Paul B. Guenther; Phyllis J. Mills.

Number of staff: 2 full-time professional; 2 full-time support.

EIN: 136266964

Recent environmental and animal welfare grants:

2069-1 Audubon Society, National, New York, NY, $24,000. For support for Audubon of Florida in its work toward implementation of Comprehensive Everglades Restoration Plan. 2002.

2069-2 Audubon Society, National, New York, NY, $15,000. For National Audubon Society in South Carolina. 2002.

2069-3 Chesapeake Bay Foundation, Annapolis, MD, $150,000. For conservation of natural resources on Eastern Shore of Maryland and Virginia. 2002.

2069-4 Chinese Progressive Association, New York, NY, $15,000. For Chinatown environmental health and justice project. 2002.

2069-5 Citizens for NYC, New York, NY, $286,000. For Neighborhood Environmental Action Program and Neighborhood Environmental Leadership Institute. 2002.

2069-6 Ducks Unlimited, Memphis, TN, $40,000. For Ducks Unlimited's Lowcountry Initiative. 2002.

2069-7 Dutchess Land Conservancy, Millbrook, NY, $20,000. For general operating support. 2002.

2069-8 Environmental and Land Use Law Center, Fort Lauderdale, FL, $20,000. For general support for public interest advocacy

to protect southern Everglades and Upper Keys regional ecosystems. 2002.

2069-9 Environmental Defense, New York, NY, $30,000. For initiative to protect and restore marine resources in North Carolina. 2002.

2069-10 Green Guerillas, New York, NY, $28,000. For general support. 2002.

2069-11 Green Guerillas, New York, NY, $15,000. For Youth Environmental Fellowship program. 2002.

2069-12 Institute of Ecosystem Studies, Millbrook, NY, $10,458,477. For general support for Institute of Ecosystem Studies and for stewardship of Mary Flagler Cary Arboretum. 2002.

2069-13 Mothers on the Move, Bronx, NY, $12,000. For leadership development to address environmental problems in the South Bronx. 2002.

2069-14 Nanticoke River Watershed Conservancy, Seaford, DE, $10,000. To participate in collaborative efforts to protect Nanticoke River Watershed. 2002.

2069-15 Nanticoke Watershed Alliance, Tyaskin, MD, $15,000. For general support of work to restore Nanticoke River in Delaware and Maryland. 2002.

2069-16 National Parks Conservation Association, DC, $20,000. For Everglades Restoration Campaign. 2002.

2069-17 Nature Conservancy, Arlington, VA, $450,000. For final support for work to restore regional ecosystems encompassing Everglades and Florida Bay. 2002.

2069-18 Nature Conservancy, Arlington, VA, $300,000. For protection of South Carolina coastal ecosystems. 2002.

2069-19 Nature Conservancy, Arlington, VA, $200,000. For general support for Virginia Coast Reserve. 2002.

2069-20 Neighbors Against Garbage (NAG), Brooklyn, NY, $12,000. For general support. 2002.

2069-21 Neuse River Foundation, New Bern, NC, $15,000. For general support. 2002.

2069-22 New York City Environmental Justice Alliance, New York, NY, $13,000. For general support for Organization of Waterfront Neighborhoods. 2002.

2069-23 North Carolina Coastal Federation, Newport, NC, $30,000. For efforts to protect estuaries of North Carolina. 2002.

2069-24 North Carolina Coastal Land Trust, Wilmington, NC, $20,000. For general support. 2002.

2069-25 North Carolina Conservation Network (NC ConNet), Raleigh, NC, $15,000. For Coastal Outreach Project, which works to strengthen coastal environmental community's ability to influence state and local environmental policy. 2002.

2069-26 Outstanding Renewal Enterprises, New York, NY, $10,000. For general support. 2002.

2069-27 Pamlico-Tar River Foundation, Washington, NC, $15,000. For general support for work to protect Pamlico-Tar River Estuary in North Carolina. 2002.

2069-28 Point Community Development Corporation, Bronx, NY, $22,000. For general support of environmental programs. 2002.

2069-29 Red Hook GAGS, Brooklyn, NY, $12,000. For general support. 2002.

2069-30 Reverend Linnette C. Williamson Memorial Park Association, New York, NY, $12,000. For general support. 2002.

2069-31 Rockefeller University, New York, NY, $75,000. For Field Research Scholars program at University's Field Research Center for Ecology and Ethology in Millbrook, New York. 2002.

2069-32 South Carolina Coastal Conservation League, Charleston, SC, $20,000. For general support to protect coastal resources in South Carolina. 2002.

2069-33 Trust for Public Land, New York, NY, $131,000. For Neighborhood Open Space Management Program. 2002.

2069-34 UPROSE (United Puerto Rican Organization of Sunset Park), Brooklyn, NY, $20,000. For Sunset Park Environmental Justice Community Organizing Initiative. 2002.

2069-35 We Stay/Nos Quedamos, Bronx, NY, $14,000. For outreach component of South Bronx Air Quality Study. 2002.

2069-36 World Wildlife Fund/Conservation Foundation, DC, $25,000. For South Florida/Everglades Program. 2002.

2070
Central New York Community Foundation, Inc.

500 S. Salina St., Ste. 428
Syracuse, NY 13202 (315) 422-9538
Contact: Margaret G. Ogden, Pres.
FAX: (315) 471-6031; URL: http://www.cnycf.org

Incorporated in 1927 in NY; reorganized in 1951.

Grantmaker type: Community foundation

Financial data (yr. ended 03/31/03): Assets, $72,200,412 (M); gifts received, $3,377,470; expenditures, $4,835,178; giving activities include $3,608,285 for grants.

Purpose and activities: Grants primarily to existing agencies for health, welfare, educational, recreational, or cultural purposes. The foundation administers donor-advised funds.

Fields of interest: Humanities; Historic preservation/historical societies; Arts; Child development, education; Education; Environment; Health care; Recreation; Human services, Child development, services; Homeless, human services; Homeless.

Types of support: Capital campaigns; Building/renovation; Equipment; Program development; Publication; Seed money; Scholarship funds; Research; Technical assistance; Matching/challenge support.

Limitations: Giving limited to Onondaga and Madison counties, NY, for general grants; giving in a wider area for donor-advised funds. No support for religious purposes. No grants to individuals, or for conferences and seminars, deficit financing, consulting services, endowment funds, fellowships, operating budgets, or travel expenses.

Publications: Annual report (including application guidelines), Informational brochure (including application guidelines), Newsletter.

Application information: Application form required.

Initial approach: Letter or telephone
Copies of proposal: 1
Deadline(s): 7 weeks before board meetings

Board meeting date(s): Mar., May, Sept., and Dec.
Final notification: Immediately following board meetings
Officers and Directors:* Ronald R. Young,* Chair.; Margaret G. Ogden, C.E.O. and Pres.; Dorothy R. Irish, V.P. and Secy.; Lisa Moore, V.P.; Kimberly S. Scott, V.P.; Dirk E. Sonneborn, Treas.; David Barclay; Sanford A. Belden; Sharon A. Brangman, M.D.; Michael J. Connor; Marion Hancock Fish; John M. Frantz, Jr.; Gary R. Germain; Gloria Hooper-Rasberry; Cydney M. Johnson; John B. McCabe, M.D.; Anne Messenger; John C. Mott; Eric Mower; Michael E. O'Connor; Marilyn L. Pinsky; William L. Pollard, Ph.D.; Jeffrey M. Rubenstein; Mary Ann Shaw; Harold H. Wanamaker, M.D.
Number of staff: 7 full-time professional; 1 part-time professional; 6 full-time support.
EIN: 150626910
Recent environmental and animal welfare grants:
2070-1 ESF College Foundation, Syracuse, NY, $31,980. To design contemporary science-based curriculum for conservation education to be used by Syracuse City School District. 2002.

2071
Dorothy Jordan Chadwick Fund
c/o U.S. Trust of New York
114 W. 47th St.
New York, NY 10036
Contact: Berkeley D. Johnson, Jr., Tr.
Application address: c/o Davidson Dawson & Clark, 36 Grove St., New Canaan, CT 06840; FAX: (203) 966-7894

Trust established in 1957 in NY.
Donor(s): Dorothy J. Chadwick,‡ Dorothy R. Kidder.‡
Grantmaker type: Independent foundation
Financial data (yr. ended 05/31/02): Assets, $20,828,301 (M); expenditures, $1,520,400; qualifying distributions, $1,432,119; giving activities include $1,381,800 for 72 grants (high: $125,600; low: $5,000; average: $5,000–$50,000).
Purpose and activities: Giving primarily to organizations of interest to the family, with emphasis on purposes initiated by the fund. These interests include wildlife conservation and non-traditional developmental education.
Fields of interest: Education; Animals/wildlife, preservation/protection.
Types of support: General/operating support; Continuing support; Capital campaigns; Building/renovation; Program development; Seed money; Research.
Limitations: Giving primarily along the Eastern Seaboard (Boston to Washington). No grants to individuals.
Publications: Application guidelines.
Application information: Application form not required.
 Initial approach: Letter
 Copies of proposal: 1
 Deadline(s): Feb. 1
 Board meeting date(s): As required
 Final notification: May or June
Trustees: Berkeley D. Johnson, Jr.; U.S. Trust.
Number of staff: None.
EIN: 136069950

2072
Chapman Family Fund
P.O. Box 194
Scarborough, NY 10510-0694
Contact: Max C. Chapman, Jr., Tr.

Established in 1987 in NY.
Donor(s): Max C. Chapman, Jr.
Grantmaker type: Independent foundation
Financial data (yr. ended 12/31/01): Assets, $6,566,823 (M); expenditures, $1,159,482; qualifying distributions, $1,124,656; giving activities include $1,110,765 for 50 grants (high: $600,000; low: $50).
Purpose and activities: Giving for diabetes, animal welfare, education, and the arts.
Fields of interest: Arts; Education; Animals/wildlife, preservation/protection; Diabetes.
Limitations: Applications not accepted. Giving primarily in NC and NY. No grants to individuals.
Application information: Contributes only to pre-selected organizations.
Trustees: Katharine M. Chapman; Max C. Chapman, Jr.
EIN: 133388410

2073
The Charitable Foundation of the Burns Family, Inc.
c/o Allen & Brown
60 E. 42nd St., Ste. 1760
New York, NY 10165

Established in 1962 in NY.
Donor(s): Randal B. Borough.
Grantmaker type: Independent foundation
Financial data (yr. ended 11/30/02): Assets, $3,057,743 (M); expenditures, $208,380; qualifying distributions, $165,335; giving activities include $122,000 for 46 grants (high: $20,000; low: $250).
Purpose and activities: Giving primarily to Christian churches and for education.
Fields of interest: Elementary/secondary education; Education; Animal welfare; Medical research, association; Human services; Christian agencies & churches.
Types of support: Building/renovation.
Limitations: Applications not accepted. Giving primarily in Charlotte, NC, NJ, NY, and Sheridan, WY. No grants to individuals.
Application information: Contributes only to pre-selected organizations.
Officers: D. Bruce Burns, Pres.; John B. Goldsborough, V.P.; William J. Ennis, Secy.; Jeremiah E. Brown, Treas.
EIN: 136114052

2074
The Michael J. Charles Foundation, Inc.
c/o CF Partners
126 E. 56th St.
New York, NY 10022

Established in 1993 in NY.
Donor(s): Michael J. Charles.
Grantmaker type: Independent foundation
Financial data (yr. ended 12/31/01): Assets, $11,527 (M); expenditures, $207,376; qualifying distributions, $206,575; giving activities include

$206,094 for 21 grants (high: $100,000; low: $50).
Purpose and activities: Giving for education, human services, health and medical services, and Jewish organizations.
Fields of interest: Arts; Elementary/secondary education; Secondary school/education; University; Education; Natural resources; Hospitals (general); Food services; Human services; Homeless, human services.
Limitations: Applications not accepted. Giving primarily in the metropolitan New York, NY, area. No grants to individuals.
Application information: Contributes only to pre-selected organizations.
Officer: Michael J. Charles, Pres.
EIN: 133746799

2075
Charlpeg Foundation, Inc.
c/o Meyer Handelman Co.
P.O. Box 817
Purchase, NY 10577

Incorporated in 1958 in NY.
Donor(s): Charles M. Grace.
Grantmaker type: Independent foundation
Financial data (yr. ended 10/31/02): Assets, $294,406 (M); gifts received, $176,440; expenditures, $114,351; qualifying distributions, $109,180; giving activities include $108,450 for 16 grants (high: $20,000; low: $200).
Fields of interest: Television; Elementary/secondary education; Higher education; Natural resources; Youth development, centers/clubs; Roman Catholic agencies & churches.
Limitations: Applications not accepted. Giving on a national basis. No grants to individuals, or for endowment funds or operating budgets.
Application information: Contributes only to pre-selected organizations.
Officers and Directors:* Charles M. Grace,* Pres.; Margaret V. Grace,* V.P.; John R. Young,* Secy.; Donald E. Handelman,* Treas.; William R. Handelman.
Number of staff: None.
EIN: 136076805

2076
Citizens Committee for New York City, Inc.
305 7th Ave., 15th Fl.
New York, NY 10001-6008 (212) 989-0909
Contact: Michael Clark, Pres.
FAX: (212) 989-0983; E-mail: info@citizensnyc.org

Established in 1975 in NY.
Donor(s): Jacob K. Javits.‡
Grantmaker type: Public charity
Financial data (yr. ended 09/30/01): Revenue, $2,015,745; assets, $3,049,392; gifts received, $1,921,605; expenditures, $2,831,564; program services expenses, $1,905,289; giving activities include $494,527 for 343 grants (high: $44,761; low: $50).
Purpose and activities: The committee seeks to improve the communities and the city by involving and supporting young people in grassroots projects to make life more livable. Neighborhood volunteers are given the support,

know-how, and recognition they need to succeed through practical programs of training, technical assistance, self-help publications, information, referrals, and hundreds of small cash grants.
Fields of interest: Environment; Human services; Community development, neighborhood associations; Community development.
Types of support: Program development; Publication; Technical assistance.
Limitations: Giving limited to residents of New York, NY.
Publications: Application guidelines, Annual report, Newsletter.
Application information: Applications are reviewed on an ongoing basis. Application form required.
　　Deadline(s): Mar. 15 for Neighborhood Environmental Action; Mar. 31 for Youth for Youth Program; Apr. 3 for Drug and Crime Prevention Awards; others 1st of each month
　　Final notification: Apr. or May for Neighborhood Environmental Action; varies for others
Officers and Trustees:* Osborn Elliot,* Chair.; Michael E. Clark,* Pres.; Bill Chong,* V.P., Progs.; Michael Rosen,* V.P., Fin. and Admin.; John M. Aerni; Christopher Allen; Theodore S. Chapin; Henry Cornell; Evelyn Cunningham; Henry P. Davison II; Peter Duchin; Victor Gotbaum; and 21 additional trustees.
EIN: 510171818

2077
Liz Claiborne & Art Ortenberg Foundation
(formerly The Ortenberg Foundation)
650 5th Ave., 15th Fl.
New York, NY　10019　(212) 333-2536
Contact: James Murtaugh, Dir.
FAX: (212) 956-3531; E-mail: lcaof@fcc.net; URL: http://www.LCAOF.org,orhttp://www.redlodgeworkshop.org

Established in 1984 in NY.
Donor(s): Arthur Ortenberg, Elisabeth Claiborne Ortenberg.
Grantmaker type: Independent foundation
Financial data (yr. ended 12/31/02): Assets, $44,515,016 (M); gifts received, $800,000; expenditures, $3,755,388; qualifying distributions, $3,030,145; giving activities include $2,778,258 for 104 grants (high: $401,464; low: $250; average: $1,000–$50,000).
Purpose and activities: The board of directors has identified two primary program interests for the foundation: 1) Mitigation of conflict between the land and resource needs of rural communities and conservation of biological diversity; and 2) Implementation of field-based scientific, technical and practical training programs in conservation biology for local people. The foundation typically funds modest, carefully designed field activities—primarily in developing countries and in the northern Rocky Mountains region of the United States—in which local communities have substantial proprietary interest.
Fields of interest: Natural resources; Animals/wildlife, preservation/protection.

International interests: Africa; Central America; South America; Developing countries; Oceania.
Types of support: Continuing support; Seed money; Matching/challenge support.
Limitations: Giving primarily in Third World countries in the Tropics and in the Northern Rocky Mountain region of the U.S. No grants for general support, or for underwriting of overhead.
Publications: Informational brochure (including application guidelines).
Application information: Application form not required.
　　Initial approach: Letter
　　Copies of proposal: 1
　　Deadline(s): None
　　Board meeting date(s): Spring and fall
　　Final notification: As soon as possible
Directors: William Conway; William DeBuys; Robert Dewar; James Murtaugh; Arthur Ortenberg; Elisabeth Claiborne Ortenberg; Alison Richard; David Western.
Number of staff: 2 full-time professional; 1 part-time support.
EIN: 133200329

2078
David C. Clapp Foundation
c/o BCRS Assocs., LLC
100 Wall St., 11th Fl.
New York, NY　10005

Established in 1985 in NY.
Donor(s): David C. Clapp.
Grantmaker type: Independent foundation
Financial data (yr. ended 06/30/02): Assets, $221,692 (M); gifts received, $50,000; expenditures, $327,648; qualifying distributions, $327,394; giving activities include $327,468 for grants.
Fields of interest: Television; Theater; Higher education; Education; Natural resources; Hospitals (general); Cancer; Arthritis; Health organizations; Human services; Community development; Federated giving programs.
Limitations: Applications not accepted. Giving primarily in New York, NY. No grants to individuals.
Application information: Contributes only to pre-selected organizations.
Trustees: Constance L. Clapp; David C. Clapp.
EIN: 133318134

2079
Clark Family Foundation, Inc.
1633 Broadway, 30th Fl.
New York, NY　10019

Established in 1986 in NY.
Donor(s): John Sheldon Clark, Valer Clark Austin.
Grantmaker type: Independent foundation
Financial data (yr. ended 12/31/02): Assets, $3,073,490 (M); expenditures, $194,472; qualifying distributions, $159,600; giving activities include $159,600 for 39 grants (high: $10,000; low: $500).
Fields of interest: Elementary/secondary education; Higher education; Natural resources; Disasters, 9/11/01; Human services; Community development; Federated giving programs.

Limitations: Applications not accepted. Giving on a national basis, with emphasis on FL. No grants to individuals.
Application information: Contributes only to pre-selected organizations.
Officers and Trustees:* John Sheldon Clark,* Pres.; Valer Clark Austin,* Treas.; Josia T. Austin.
EIN: 133322083

2080
Robert Sterling Clark Foundation, Inc. ▼
135 E. 64th St.
New York, NY　10021　(212) 288-8900
Contact: Margaret C. Ayers, Exec. Dir.
FAX: (212) 288-1033; URL: http://www.fdncenter.org/grantmaker/rsclark

Incorporated in 1952 in NY.
Donor(s): Robert Sterling Clark.‡
Grantmaker type: Independent foundation
Financial data (yr. ended 10/31/02): Assets, $85,486,855 (M); expenditures, $7,204,552; qualifying distributions, $6,354,694; giving activities include $5,719,144 for 119 grants (high: $325,000; low: $1,000; average: $20,000–$100,000), $8,064 for 26 employee matching gifts and $125,000 for 1 loan/program-related investment.
Purpose and activities: The foundation supports projects that: 1) strengthen cultural institutions in New York City; 2) support arts advocacy; 3) ensure the effectiveness and accountability of public agencies in New York City and State; and 4) ensure access to comprehensive reproductive health information and services.
Fields of interest: Visual arts; Museums; Performing arts; Dance; Theater; Music; Arts; Education; Environment; Family planning; Human services; Family services; Reproductive rights; Urban/community development; Community development; Public policy, research; Government/public administration; Public affairs; Aging; Economically disadvantaged; Homeless.
Types of support: General/operating support; Continuing support; Income development; Program development; Publication; Research; Technical assistance; Consulting services; Employee matching gifts.
Limitations: Giving primarily in New York State for the Public Institutions Program and in New York City for the Cultural Program; giving nationally for reproductive freedom projects. No grants to individuals, or for annual campaigns, seed money, emergency funds, deficit financing, capital or endowment funds, matching gifts, scholarships, fellowships, conferences, or films.
Publications: Application guidelines, Annual report (including application guidelines).
Application information: Application form not required.
　　Initial approach: Proposal (not exceeding 15 pages) and a one-page proposal summary
　　Copies of proposal: 1
　　Deadline(s): None
　　Board meeting date(s): Jan., Apr., July, and Oct.
　　Final notification: 1 to 6 months
Officers and Directors:* Winthrop R. Munyan,* Pres.; Miner D. Crary, Jr.,* Secy.; John Hoyt Stookey,* Treas.; Margaret C. Ayers, Exec. Dir.; James Allen Smith; Virginia Hayes Sibbison; Joanna D. Underwood.

Number of staff: 3 full-time professional; 1 full-time support.
EIN: 131957792
Recent environmental and animal welfare grants:
2080-1 Environmental Advocates, Albany, NY, $65,000. For advocacy, assistance to policymakers, and public education on New York State solid waste management policies, and for Regulatory Watch Project to examine state implementation and enforcement of environmental mandates. 2002.
2080-2 Environmental Defense, New York, NY, $50,000. For policy research and advocacy to improve solid waste management planning. 2002.
2080-3 Healthy Schools Network, Albany, NY, $40,000. To monitor and report on implementation of New York State's school environmental health and safety regulations, and advocate for needed improvements. 2002.
2080-4 INFORM, New York, NY, $50,000. For advocacy and assistance to New York City and New York State government agencies to promote implementation of effective waste prevention strategies. 2002.
2080-5 New York Conservation Education Fund, New York, NY, $30,000. To produce environmental profiles of New York City Council districts and create web-based legislative tracking system that will summarize and monitor progress of key environmental bills introduced in the City Council. 2002.
2080-6 New York Law School, New York, NY, $35,000. To publish monthly newsletter on New York City land use decisions and matters under consideration by various government bodies. 2002.
2080-7 New York Public Interest Research Group (NYPIRG) Fund, Clean Drinking Water Coalition, New York, NY, $50,000. To monitor implementation and enforcement of New York City watershed protection programs, educate the public, and advocate with government officials. 2002.

2081
The Clark Foundation ▼
1 Rockefeller Plz., 31st Fl.
New York, NY 10020 (212) 977-6900
Contact: Charles H. Hamilton, Exec. Dir.

Incorporated in 1931 in NY; merged with Scriven Foundation, Inc. in 1973.
Donor(s): Members of the Clark family.
Grantmaker type: Independent foundation
Financial data (yr. ended 06/30/02): Assets, $469,042,395 (M); gifts received, $400; expenditures, $23,757,434; qualifying distributions, $20,705,141; giving activities include $17,939,478 for grants (high: $1,055,000; low: $1,200; average: $20,000–$200,000).
Purpose and activities: Support for a hospital and museums in Cooperstown, NY; grants also for charitable and educational purposes, including undergraduate scholarships to students residing in the Cooperstown area. Support also for health, educational, youth, cultural, environmental, and community organizations and institutions. The foundation

owns and supports the Clark Sports Center, which is located in Cooperstown, NY.
Fields of interest: Museums; Education; Environment; Health care; Health organizations, association; AIDS; Health organizations; AIDS research; Employment; Human services; Children/youth, services; General charitable giving; Economically disadvantaged.
Types of support: General/operating support; Continuing support; Annual campaigns; Capital campaigns; Building/renovation; Equipment; Emergency funds; Program development; Seed money; Scholarships—to individuals.
Limitations: Giving primarily in Cooperstown, NY and New York City; scholarships restricted to students residing in the Cooperstown, NY, area. No grants to individuals (except as specified in restricted funds), or for deficit financing or matching gifts.
Publications: Application guidelines, Program policy statement.
Application information: Accepts NYRAG Common Application Form. Application form not required.
  Initial approach: Letter
  Copies of proposal: 1
  Deadline(s): Jan. 15, April 15, July 15, and Oct. 15
  Board meeting date(s): Mar., June, Oct., and Dec.
  Final notification: 2 to 6 months
Officers and Directors:* Jane Forbes Clark,* Pres.; Alexander F. Treadwell,* V.P.; Charles H. Hamilton, Secy. and Exec. Dir.; Kevin S. Moore,* Treas.; Kent L. Barwick; Felicia H. Blum; William M. Evarts; Gates Helms Hawn; Archie F. MacAllaster; Mrs. Edward B. McMenamin; Thomas Q. Morris, M.D.; Anne L. Peretz; Edward W. Stack; John Hoyt Stookey; Clifton R. Wharton, Jr.
Number of staff: 4 full-time professional; 3 part-time professional; 43 full-time support; 20 part-time support.
EIN: 135616528
Recent environmental and animal welfare grants:
2081-1 Hurricane Island Outward Bound School, Rockland, ME, $82,100. For Clark Scholarships. 2003.
2081-2 New York City Outward Bound Center, Long Island City, NY, $50,000. For general support. 2003.
2081-3 Otsego County Conservation Association, Cooperstown, NY, $75,000. For general support. 2003.
2081-4 Otsego County Conservation Association, Cooperstown, NY, $57,000. For Otsego Lake Watershed Management Plan. 2003.
2081-5 Outward Bound West, Golden, CO, $19,200. For teacher practicum course. 2003.
2081-6 Trust for Public Land, New York, NY, $60,000. For general support. 2003.

2082
Louis & Virginia Clemente Foundation, Inc.
c/o Kelley, Drye, & Warren LLP
101 Park Ave.
New York, NY 10178
Contact: C. Caufield

Established in 1975.

Grantmaker type: Independent foundation
Financial data (yr. ended 12/31/02): Assets, $4,119,234 (M); expenditures, $193,782; qualifying distributions, $153,467; giving activities include $152,000 for 18 grants (high: $20,000; low: $1,000).
Purpose and activities: Giving primarily for health and human services.
Fields of interest: Arts; Education; Environment; Health care; Health organizations, association; Human services.
Limitations: Applications not accepted. Giving primarily in NY. No grants to individuals.
Application information: Contributes only to pre-selected organizations.
Officers and Directors:* Harry A. LeBien,* Pres. and Treas.; Mary Ellen LeBien,* Secy.; Laurent C. LeBien; Michele LeBien; Thomas E. LeBien.
EIN: 510163549

2083
Cleveland Amory Trust
c/o Vedder Price
805 Third Ave., 23rd Fl.
New York, NY 10022-2203

Grantmaker type: Independent foundation
Financial data (yr. ended 12/31/02): Assets, $3,510,296 (M); expenditures, $233,903; qualifying distributions, $186,655; giving activities include $188,730 for 1 grant.
Fields of interest: Animals/wildlife.
Limitations: Applications not accepted. Giving primarily in New York, NY. No grants to individuals.
Application information: Contributes only to pre-selected organizations.
Trustees: Marian Probst; Edward J. Walsh, Jr.
EIN: 137208650

2084
Cloud Mountain Foundation
c/o Louis Sternbach & Co.
1333 Broadway, Ste. 516
New York, NY 10018

Established in 1999 in MA.
Donor(s): Benjamin Friedman.
Grantmaker type: Independent foundation
Financial data (yr. ended 12/31/01): Assets, $5,430,610 (M); expenditures, $138,265; qualifying distributions, $126,808; giving activities include $127,000 for 14 grants (high: $40,000; low: $1,000).
Fields of interest: Environment.
Limitations: Applications not accepted. No grants to individuals.
Application information: Contributes only to pre-selected organizations.
Officer: Benjamin Friedman, Pres.
EIN: 043493352

2085
The Coach Dairy Goat Farm Foundation
c/o The Coach Farm
105 Mill Hill Rd.
Pine Plains, NY 12567

Established in 1990 in NY.
Donor(s): Lillian Cahn, Miles Cahn.

Grantmaker type: Independent foundation
Financial data (yr. ended 06/30/02): Assets, $55,704 (M); expenditures, $122,130; qualifying distributions, $122,077; giving activities include $122,000 for 47 grants (high: $25,000; low: $500).
Fields of interest: Museums; Performing arts; Natural resources; Health care; Jewish federated giving programs.
Limitations: Applications not accepted. Giving primarily in NY. No grants to individuals.
Application information: Contributes only to pre-selected organizations.
Trustees: Lillian Cahn; Miles Cahn.
EIN: 223075602

2086
The Cohen Family Foundation, Inc.
c/o The Ayco Company, LLP
P.O. Box 8019
Ballston Spa, NY   12020-8019
Contact: W. Michael Reickert

Incorporated in 1986 in NY.
Donor(s): Florence Cohen, Peter A. Cohen, William L. Cohen, and other members of the Cohen family.
Grantmaker type: Independent foundation
Financial data (yr. ended 12/31/00): Assets, $102,066 (M); gifts received, $82,925; expenditures, $94,605; qualifying distributions, $90,311; giving activities include $90,311 for grants.
Purpose and activities: Giving to Jewish institutions, higher education, and hospitals.
Fields of interest: Arts; Elementary/secondary education; Higher education; Environment; Hospitals (general); Jewish agencies & temples.
Limitations: Applications not accepted. Giving primarily in New York, NY. No grants to individuals.
Application information: Contributes only to pre-selected organizations.
Officers: Peter A. Cohen, Pres. and Treas.; William L. Cohen, V.P. and Secy.
Director: Michelle Cohen.
EIN: 133183001

2087
The Pamela Cole Charitable Trust
c/o Holland & Knight, LLP
195 Broadway, 24th Fl.
New York, NY   10007

Established in 1988 in NY.
Donor(s): Pamela Cole,‡ Augustine Properties.
Grantmaker type: Independent foundation
Financial data (yr. ended 02/28/02): Assets, $352,711 (M); gifts received, $882; expenditures, $106,634; qualifying distributions, $100,100; giving activities include $100,000 for 1 grant.
Purpose and activities: Giving primarily for higher education, natural resource conservation and protection, animal welfare, and veterinary education.
Fields of interest: Higher education; Natural resources; Animal welfare.
Types of support: General/operating support; Building/renovation; Program development; Research.

Limitations: Applications not accepted. Giving primarily in New York, NY and Philadelphia, PA. No grants to individuals.
Application information: Contributes only to pre-selected organizations.
Trustees: Charles Bernheim; Charles F. Gibbs.
EIN: 136901088

2088
Kenneth Cole Foundation
c/o TAG Assocs.
75 Rockefeller Plz., Ste. 900
New York, NY   10019

Established in 1994 in NY.
Donor(s): Kenneth Cole.
Grantmaker type: Independent foundation
Financial data (yr. ended 04/30/02): Assets, $5,809,818 (M); expenditures, $366,375; qualifying distributions, $358,824; giving activities include $364,980 for 28 grants (high: $100,000; low: $50).
Purpose and activities: Giving primarily for higher education, as well as for hospitals and health associations, and Jewish agencies and temples.
Fields of interest: Elementary school/education; Higher education; Education; Botanical gardens; Hospitals (general); Health organizations, association; Gun control; Philanthropy/voluntarism; Jewish agencies & temples.
Limitations: Applications not accepted. Giving primarily in Atlanta, GA, and NY. No grants to individuals.
Application information: Contributes only to pre-selected organizations.
Trustees: Kenneth Cole; Maria Cuomo Cole.
EIN: 133799161

2089
Beatrice R. & Joseph A. Coleman Foundation
130 E. 59th St.
New York, NY   10022   (212) 836-1358
Contact: Lauren Katzowitz, Exec. Dir.

Established in 1998 in NY.
Donor(s): Ida & William Rosenthal Foundation, Inc.
Grantmaker type: Independent foundation
Financial data (yr. ended 12/31/02): Assets, $2,602,028 (M); expenditures, $194,795; qualifying distributions, $156,131; giving activities include $120,100 for 11 grants (high: $30,000; low: $250).
Purpose and activities: Giving for education and women's services, and the environment.
Fields of interest: Higher education; Law school/education; Natural resources; Legal services; Human services; Children, services; Women, centers/services.
Types of support: General/operating support; Continuing support; Annual campaigns; Capital campaigns; Program development; Scholarship funds.
Limitations: Applications not accepted. Giving primarily on the East Coast. No grants to individuals.
Application information: Contributes only to pre-selected organizations.

Officers: Elizabeth Coleman, Pres.; Robert Stroup, V.P.
Trustee: Kristin M. Houser.
EIN: 133981351

2090
Coles Family Foundation
c/o BCRS Assocs., LLC
100 Wall St., 11th Fl.
New York, NY   10005

Established in 1980 in NY.
Donor(s): Michael H. Coles, Joan C. Coles.‡
Grantmaker type: Independent foundation
Financial data (yr. ended 03/31/02): Assets, $3,753,835 (M); expenditures, $469,365; qualifying distributions, $413,590; giving activities include $404,340 for 113 grants (high: $30,000; low: $100).
Purpose and activities: Grants for Christian giving, child welfare, higher and other education, theater, cultural programs, and foreign policy.
Fields of interest: Theater; Arts; Higher education; Education; Natural resources; Hospitals (general); Children/youth, services; Foreign policy; Christian agencies & churches.
Types of support: General/operating support; Endowments.
Limitations: Applications not accepted. Giving primarily in the greater metropolitan New York, NY, area. No grants to individuals.
Application information: Contributes only to pre-selected organizations.
Trustees: Alison Aldredge; Isobel Coles; Michael C. Coles; Michael H. Coles; Richard Coles; Caroline Scudder; Roy C. Smith.
Number of staff: 1 part-time support.
EIN: 133050747

2091
Common Cents New York, Inc.
570 Columbus Ave.
New York, NY   10024   (212) 579-0579
Contact: Teddy Gross, Exec. Dir.
FAX: (212) 579-3488; E-mail: info@commoncents.org; URL: http://www.commoncents.org

Established in 1991.
Grantmaker type: Public charity
Financial data (yr. ended 06/30/02): Revenue, $2,024,025; assets, $1,071,658 (L); gifts received, $2,018,057; expenditures, $1,676,095; program services expenses, $1,361,054; giving activities include $626,952 for 750 grants (high: $3,000; low: $100) and $2,000 for 2 loans to individuals.
Purpose and activities: The organization empowers young people (K-12) to mobilize resources (pennies), implement service projects and provides grants to address community needs, thus creating a generation of community activists and good citizens. Each year, approximately one million students in NYC recycle half a million dollars in pennies into service projects and grants.
Fields of interest: Education; Environment, beautification programs; Animal welfare; Health care; Crime/violence prevention; Food services; Youth, services; Family services; Homeless,

human services; International affairs; Women; Economically disadvantaged.

Types of support: General/operating support; Continuing support; Emergency funds; Program development; Publication; Seed money; Curriculum development; Grants to individuals; Scholarships—to individuals.

Limitations: Applications not accepted. Giving limited through participating Penny Harvest schools and SCAF program.

Application information: See Web site for further information; funding is given out through participating Penny Harvest School and Student Committee Action Fund (SCAF) only.

Board meeting date(s): Quarterly

Officers and Directors:* John Hobbs,* Pres.; Ira Wolfman,* Secy.; Karen Kohler,* Treas.; Teddy Gross, Exec. Dir.; Neetu Bhatia; Nora Gross; Colin Greer; Gary Horowitz; Al Leiter; Bill Lynch; Donna Mercurio; Margaret Williams.

Number of staff: 12 full-time professional; 1 part-time professional.

EIN: 133613229

2092
Community Foundation for Greater Buffalo ▼

(formerly The Buffalo Foundation)
712 Main St.
Buffalo, NY 14202-1720 (716) 852-2857
Contact: Myra Lawrence, V.P., Finance and Admin.
FAX: (716) 852-2861; E-mail: mail@cfgb.org;
URL: http://www.cfgb.org

Established in 1919 in NY by resolution and declaration of trust; corporate version established in 1985.

Grantmaker type: Community foundation
Financial data (yr. ended 12/31/01): Assets, $113,327,275 (M); gifts received, $6,847,699; expenditures, $7,245,672; giving activities include $5,528,600 for 257+ grants (high: $347,167).

Purpose and activities: To support creative and innovative responses to existing or emerging community problems; and to support efforts that recognize and build on the community's strengths and assets.

Fields of interest: Arts; Education; Environment; Hospitals (general); Health care; AIDS; Medical research, institute; AIDS research; Human services; Children/youth, services; Family services; Community development; Science; Leadership development.

Types of support: Building/renovation; Equipment; Emergency funds; Program development; Conferences/seminars; Seed money; Scholarship funds; Research; Technical assistance; Program evaluation; Matching/challenge support.

Limitations: Giving limited to western NY; scholarships awarded to students primarily from Erie County. No support for religious purposes, or schools not registered with the State Education Department. No grants to individuals (except from designated scholarship funds) or for annual campaigns, deficit financing, or endowment; no loans.

Publications: Application guidelines, Annual report (including application guidelines), Informational brochure, Newsletter, Program policy statement.

Application information: Application forms required for scholarships, and must be requested in writing between Mar. 1 and May 1 and include a SASE. Application form required.

Initial approach: Telephone or letter
Copies of proposal: 15
Deadline(s): Mar. 1 for humanities and civic needs and environment/science; June 1 for health, and scholarships; Sept. 1 for social needs; Dec. 1 for education
Board meeting date(s): Mar., May, Aug., and Nov.
Final notification: Within 2 weeks of meeting

Officers and Directors:* Ruth D. Bryant,* Chair.; Joseph F. Crangle,* Vice-Chair.; Gail E. Johnstone, C.E.O. and Pres.; Myra Lawrence, V.P. Finance and Admin.; Richard Tobe, V.P., Prog.; Kathryn L. Chatmon, Compt.; Joseph J. Castiglia; Anthony J. Colucci, Jr.; Clotilde Perez-Bode Dedecker; Sue Gardner; Robert D. Gioia; William G. Gisel, Jr.; Andrew J. Rudnick; David Zebro; Howard Zemsky.

Trustee Banks: Fleet National Bank; HSBC Bank USA; KeyBank N.A.; Manufacturers and Traders Trust Co.

Number of staff: 9 full-time professional; 2 part-time professional; 4 full-time support.

EIN: 160743935

Recent environmental and animal welfare grants:

2092-1 Nature Conservancy, Central and Western New York Chapter, Rochester, NY, $20,250. 2001.

2093
The Community Foundation for the Capital Region, Inc.

Executive Park Dr.
Albany, NY 12203 (518) 446-9638
Contact: Judith Lyons, Exec. Dir.
FAX: (518) 446-9708; E-mail: info@cfcr.org;
URL: http://www.cfcr.org

Incorporated in 1968 in NY.

Grantmaker type: Community foundation
Financial data (yr. ended 12/31/02): Assets, $21,098,161 (M); gifts received, $3,540,846; expenditures, $2,347,275; giving activities include $1,691,442 for 618 grants (high: $50,000; low: $100; average: $100–$50,000) and $600 for 1 in-kind gift.

Purpose and activities: The general policy of the foundation is to make grants to innovative, creative projects and programs that are responsive to changing community needs. The purpose of the foundation is to use, apply and devote the foundations properties and funds exclusively for charitable, scientific, cultural and educational purposes, through the making of grants or otherwise extending financial assistance and support to duly authorized persons, institutions and organizations. The foundation administers donor-advised funds.

Fields of interest: Adult education—literacy, basic skills & GED; Environment; Art & music therapy; Health care; AIDS; Abuse prevention; Employment; Children/youth, services; Aging, centers/services; Homeless, human services.

Types of support: General/operating support; Income development; Management development; Program development; Seed money; Technical assistance; Employee-related scholarships.

Limitations: Giving primarily in the Capital Area region, including Albany, Renssalear, Schenectady and Saratoga, NY. No support for sectarian religious purposes. No grants to individuals (except scholarships), or for endowment or building funds, deficit financing, consulting services, continuing support, emergency funds, land acquisition, annual campaigns, or fellowships; no loans; capital campaign grants only to health organizations.

Publications: Application guidelines, Annual report, Financial statement, Informational brochure, Newsletter.

Application information: Grant guidelines available on Web site. Application form required.

Initial approach: Letter or telephone
Copies of proposal: 1
Deadline(s): Mar. 31 for June decision, Oct. 17 for Dec. decision
Board meeting date(s): Bimonthly
Final notification: Quarterly

Officers and Directors:* Barbara K. Hoehn,* Pres.; John H. Lavelle,* 1st V.P.; Phoebe P. Bender,* 2nd V.P.; Roy M. Hershey,* Secy.; Frank M. Lasch,* Treas.; Judith Lyons, Exec. Dir.; Thomas Healey, Fin. Dir.; and 16 additional directors.

Number of staff: 5 full-time professional; 1 part-time professional.

EIN: 141505623

2094
The Community Foundation of Herkimer & Oneida Counties, Inc.

(formerly Utica Foundation, Inc.)
270 Genesee St.
Utica, NY 13502 (315) 735-8212
Contact: Susan D. Smith, Sr. Prog. Off. or Margaret Anne O'Shea
FAX: (315) 735-9363; E-mail: commfdn@borg.com

Incorporated in 1952 in NY.

Grantmaker type: Community foundation
Financial data (yr. ended 12/31/02): Assets, $43,676,660 (L); gifts received, $1,337,836; expenditures, $2,428,193; giving activities include $1,498,035 for grants (high: $107,000).

Purpose and activities: Giving to programs and projects that: offer the greatest opportunity for positive and significant change in the community; identify and enhance local strengths to address and provide creative solutions for important existing or emerging community issues; develop organizational and/or individual self-sufficiency; focus on identifiable outcomes that will make a difference; leverage investment of other community resources; and improve the quality or scope of charitable works in the community. The foundation administers a donor-advised fund.

Fields of interest: Arts; Higher education; Libraries/library science; Education; Environment; Hospitals (general); Health care; Human services; Children/youth, services; Family services; Aging, centers/services; Public affairs; Disabled.

Types of support: General/operating support; Capital campaigns; Building/renovation; Equipment; Endowments; Emergency funds; Program development; Seed money;

Fellowships; Scholarship funds; Technical assistance; Consulting services; Program-related investments/loans; Matching/challenge support.
Limitations: Giving limited to Oneida and Herkimer counties, NY. No support for religious purposes or government agencies and organizations. No grants to individuals, or for ongoing operating support.
Publications: Application guidelines, Annual report, Newsletter.
Application information: Application form not required.
> *Initial approach:* 1-2 page letter of intent
> *Copies of proposal:* 10
> *Deadline(s):* None
> *Board meeting date(s):* Grants committees for each county meet 5 to 6 times per year
> *Final notification:* 4 to 6 weeks

Officers and Directors:* Milton Bloch,* Pres.; Jane A. Halbritter,* V.P.; Richard Hanna,* V.P.; Camille T. Kahler,* Secy.; Lauren E. Bull,* Treas.; Gordon M. Hayes, Exec. Dir.; Harold T. Clark, Jr.; Timothy Foley; Judith B. Gorman; Mary K. Griffith; Joseph H. Hobika, Sr.; John Livingston; Grace McLaughlin; Mary Morse; Earle C. Reed; Faye Short; Sheila Smith; William Stevens.
Trustee Banks: Fleet National Bank; HSBC Bank USA.
Number of staff: 5 full-time professional; 1 full-time support.
EIN: 156016932

2095
The Community Foundation of the Elmira-Corning Area
(formerly The Community Foundation of the Chemung County Area and Corning Community Foundation)
307B, E. Water St.
Elmira, NY 14901-3402 (607) 734-6412
FAX: (607)734-7335; E-mail: info@communityfund.org; URL: http://www.communityfund.org

Established in 1977 in NY as Chemung County; Corning established in 1972 in NY; reincorporated in 1993 under current name after merger of Community Foundation of Chemung County Area and Corning Community Foundation.
Grantmaker type: Community foundation
Financial data (yr. ended 06/30/02): Assets, $11,524,975 (M); gifts received, $1,286,187; expenditures, $841,922; giving activities include $483,480 for 99 grants (high: $72,700; low: $200), $72,600 for 42 grants to individuals (high: $12,000; low: $150) and $10,825 for 4 employee matching gifts.
Purpose and activities: The foundation's unrestricted endowment supports organizations that benefit the Chemung and southeastern Steuben counties, NY, as a whole, especially those that need seed money for pilot projects and innovative solutions to problems, and which promote self-help for individuals and groups. Giving within Chemung County and southeastern Steuben County only. The foundation administers a donor-advised fund.
Fields of interest: Historic preservation/historical societies; Arts; Education; Environment; Health care; Health organizations, association; Human services.

Types of support: General/operating support; Building/renovation; Equipment; Program development; Publication; Seed money; Scholarship funds; Research; Employee-related scholarships; Scholarships—to individuals; Matching/challenge support.
Limitations: Giving only in Chemung and southeastern Steuben counties, NY. No support for religious activities. No grants for annual campaigns, or for trips, or deficit funding; no loans.
Publications: Application guidelines, Annual report (including application guidelines), Newsletter.
Application information: Call or write for guidelines. Scholarship applications and guidelines (for residents of Chemung and southeastern Steuben counties only) available each year on Dec. 15; other grant applications available on Aug. 15. Application form required.
> *Initial approach:* Letter
> *Copies of proposal:* 1
> *Deadline(s):* Varies
> *Board meeting date(s):* Varies
> *Final notification:* Varies

Officers and Trustees:* G. Thomas Tranter, Sr., Chair.; Suzanne H. Lee, Pres.; Richard Bessey,* V.P.; Linda J. Gudas,* V.P.; Clover M. Drinkwater, Secy.; Steve Albertalli,* Treas.; Donald B. Beck; Jane H. Cadwallader; Dalton Cates; Thomas Connelly; Robert Crede; Elizabeth Dalrymple; Kevin Geoghan; John V. Goff; John Gough; John Loose; Robert B. McKinnon; Patricia Powers; Mary Booth Roberts; Ginger Schirmer; Thomas Snow; Rowland Stebbins III; Ann Weiland.
Number of staff: 1 full-time professional; 2 full-time support; 1 part-time support.
EIN: 161100837

2096
Con Edison Corporate Giving Program
c/o Strategic Partnerships
4 Irving Pl., Rm. 1650-S
New York, NY 10003 (212) 460-6942

Grantmaker type: Corporate giving program
Financial data (yr. ended 12/31/02): Total giving, $7,510,509; giving activities include $7,000,000 for 686 grants and $510,509 for 353 employee matching gifts.
Purpose and activities: Con Edison makes charitable contributions to nonprofit organizations involved with arts and culture, education, the environment, health and human services, community development, and civic affairs. Support is given primarily in New York, New York.
Fields of interest: Arts; Education; Environment; Health care; Human services; Community development; Public affairs.
Types of support: General/operating support; Scholarship funds; Employee volunteer services; Sponsorships; Employee matching gifts; In-kind gifts.
Limitations: Giving primarily in New York, NY; giving on a national basis to universities. No support for United Way-supported organizations, labor organizations, houses of worship, K-12 schools, or private foundations. No grants to individuals, or for endowments.
Publications: Application guidelines.
Application information: Support is limited to 1 contribution per organization during any given

year. The Strategic Partnerships Department handles giving. The company has a staff that only handles contributions. A contributions committee reviews all requests. Application form not required.
> *Initial approach:* Proposal to headquarters
> *Copies of proposal:* 1
> *Deadline(s):* Feb. 1 and Oct. 15
> *Final notification:* Following review

2097
Connemara Fund
c/o James D. Miller & Co.
350 5th Ave, Rm. 5019
New York, NY 10118-5019
Contact: Herrick Jackson, Tr.

Established in 1968 in NC.
Donor(s): Mary R. Jackson.‡
Grantmaker type: Independent foundation
Financial data (yr. ended 06/30/02): Assets, $7,647,989 (M); expenditures, $594,156; qualifying distributions, $459,438; giving activities include $440,000 for 68 grants (high: $50,000; low: $2,000).
Purpose and activities: Grants primarily for church support and religious welfare associations; support also for social services, cultural programs, and education.
Fields of interest: Historic preservation/historical societies; Arts; Higher education; Education; Environment; Hospitals (general); Legal services; Human services; Children/youth, services; Federated giving programs; Religious federated giving programs; Religion, equal rights; Religion, formal/general education; Christian agencies & churches; Religion, interfaith issues.
Types of support: General/operating support; Continuing support.
Limitations: Giving primarily in New England. No grants to individuals.
Application information:
> *Initial approach:* Proposal
> *Deadline(s):* None
> *Board meeting date(s):* As required

Trustees: Herrick Jackson; Polly B. Jackson; Alison J. Van Dyk.
Number of staff: 1 shared staff.
EIN: 566096063

2098
The Frank L. and Sarah Miller Coulson Foundation
c/o Goldman Sachs & Co., Tax Dept.
85 Broad St.
New York, NY 10004

Established in 2000 in PA.
Donor(s): Frank L. Coulson, Jr.
Grantmaker type: Independent foundation
Financial data (yr. ended 10/31/02): Assets, $2,749,521 (M); gifts received, $1,861,000; expenditures, $462,444; qualifying distributions, $456,444; giving activities include $453,350 for 58 grants (high: $100,000; low: $250; average: $1,000–$25,000).
Purpose and activities: Giving primarily for higher education, and to performing arts centers.
Fields of interest: Performing arts centers; Arts; Higher education; Education; Animals/wildlife; Philanthropy/voluntarism.

Limitations: Applications not accepted. Giving primarily in New York, NY and Philadelphia, PA. No grants to individuals or for scholarships; no loans.
Application information: Contributes only to pre-selected organizations.
Trustees: Frank L. Coulson, Jr.; Sarah Miller Coulson.
EIN: 134148044

2099
Cranshaw Corporation
c/o White and Case, LLP
1155 Ave. of the Americas, Ste. 3436
New York, NY   10036-2787

Incorporated in 1954 in DE.
Donor(s): Helen Babbott Sanders.‡
Grantmaker type: Independent foundation
Financial data (yr. ended 12/31/02): Assets, $3,703,745 (M); expenditures, $305,615; qualifying distributions, $287,330; giving activities include $283,500 for 25 grants (high: $74,500; low: $1,000).
Purpose and activities: Giving primarily for education and health care.
Fields of interest: Arts; Higher education; Education; Natural resources; Hospitals (general); Disasters, 9/11/01; Human services.
Limitations: Applications not accepted. Giving primarily in MO and NY. No grants to individuals.
Application information: Contributes only to pre-selected organizations.
Officers: Robert MacDonald, Pres.; Edward F. Rover, V.P.
EIN: 136110555

2100
Arthur & Barbara Crocker Charitable Trust
c/o The Bank of New York, Tax Dept.
1 Wall St., 28th Fl.
New York, NY   10286
Contact: Arthur M. Crocker, Tr.
Application address: 126 Mooring Park Dr., Naples, FL 33942

Established in 1967.
Donor(s): Arthur M. Crocker, Barbara S. Crocker.
Grantmaker type: Independent foundation
Financial data (yr. ended 12/31/02): Assets, $210,900 (M); gifts received, $118,140; expenditures, $156,936; qualifying distributions, $152,164; giving activities include $151,673 for grants.
Purpose and activities: Giving for environmental conservation and Christian churches.
Fields of interest: Television; Music; Education; Environment; Animal welfare; Hospitals (general); Children/youth, services; Christian agencies & churches.
Limitations: No grants to individuals.
Application information:
Initial approach: Letter
Deadline(s): None
Trustees: Arthur M. Crocker; Barbara S. Crocker.
EIN: 116103376

2101
Louise B. & Edgar M. Cullman Foundation
641 Lexington Ave., 29th Fl.
New York, NY   10022-4599   (212) 838-0211
Contact: Edgar M. Cullman, Sr., Chair.
Application address: 387 Park Ave. S., New York, NY 10016

Established in 1956 in NY.
Donor(s): Edgar M. Cullman.
Grantmaker type: Independent foundation
Financial data (yr. ended 12/31/02): Assets, $11,187,520 (M); gifts received, $2,500; expenditures, $1,812,280; qualifying distributions, $1,786,230; giving activities include $1,787,729 for 65 grants (high: $827,970; low: $200).
Fields of interest: Museums; Arts; Higher education; Education; Animals/wildlife, preservation/protection; Hospitals (general); Health care; Human services.
Types of support: Annual campaigns; Capital campaigns; Professorships.
Limitations: Giving primarily in CT and NY. No grants to individuals.
Application information: Application form required.
Copies of proposal: 1
Deadline(s): None
Board meeting date(s): Dec.
Officers: Edgar M. Cullman, Sr., Chair.; Louise B. Cullman, V.P.
Number of staff: 1 part-time professional; 1 part-time support.
EIN: 136100041

2102
The Nathan Cummings Foundation ▼
475 10th Ave., 14th Fl.
New York, NY   10018   (212) 787-7300
Contact: Lance E. Lindblom, Pres.
FAX: (212) 787-7377; E-mail: info@nathancummings.org; URL: http://www.nathancummings.org

Established in 1949 in IL.
Donor(s): Nathan Cummings.‡
Grantmaker type: Independent foundation
Financial data (yr. ended 12/31/02): Assets, $350,542,326 (M); expenditures, $23,992,000; qualifying distributions, $21,200,000; giving activities include $19,738,302 for 346 grants (high: $850,000; low: $5,000; average: $20,000–$150,000) and $20,698 for in-kind gifts.
Purpose and activities: The foundation's core programs are the arts, environment, health, Jewish life, and values/contemplative practice. Several basic themes run through all of these programs and inform the foundation's approach to grantmaking: concern for the poor, disadvantaged, and underserved; respect for diversity; promotion of understanding across cultures; empowerment of communities in need.
Fields of interest: Arts; Environment; Health care; Health organizations, association; Human services; Jewish agencies & temples.
International interests: Israel.
Types of support: General/operating support; Continuing support; Program development; Seed money; Research; Program evaluation; In-kind gifts.

Limitations: Giving primarily in the U.S. and Israel. No grants for endowments, debt reduction, capital campaigns, capital construction, equipment, or museum collections acquisitions.
Publications: Application guidelines, Annual report, Grants list.
Application information: Application form required.
Initial approach: 2- to 3-page letter of inquiry
Copies of proposal: 1
Deadline(s): None
Board meeting date(s): 2 times a year, Spring and Fall
Final notification: 60 days
Officers and Trustees:* Ruth Cummings Sorensen,* Chair.; James K. Cummings,* Vice-Chair.; Lance E. Lindblom,* C.E.O. and Pres.; Robert N. Mayer,* Treas.; Caroline Williams, C.F.O.; Adam N. Cummings; Stephen P. Durchslag; Bevis Longstreth; Beatrice Cummings Mayer; Sonia Simon-Cummings; Albert Sui.
Number of staff: 9 full-time professional; 11 full-time support; 1 part-time support.
EIN: 237093201
Recent environmental and animal welfare grants:
2102-1 Center for a New American Dream, Takoma Park, MD, $50,000. To raise public awareness of damaging impacts of excessive consumption and promote positive behavior change among targeted constituencies. 2001.
2102-2 Center for Resource Economics/Island Press, DC, $50,000. For Phase II of project to implement strategy developed from Phase I of Environmental Teaching and Learning Project; and to address shortcomings in environmental education at university level. 2001.
2102-3 Clark Atlanta University, Environmental Justice Resource Center, Atlanta, GA, $50,000. To build and strengthen collaborations among university-based environmental justice resource centers and legal clinics for communities fighting instances of environmental racism. 2001.
2102-4 Commission on Religion in Appalachia, Knoxville, TN, $50,000. To establish National Field Coordinator for State Interfaith Global Climate Change Campaigns efforts. 2001.
2102-5 Community Rights Counsel, DC, $50,000. To raise awareness among state and national policymakers about procedural reform initiatives accompanying partial taking campaigns, and to provide technical assistance to attorneys fighting takings claims and communities engaged in sustainable environmental planning. 2001.
2102-6 Consultative Group on Biological Diversity, San Francisco, CA, $30,000. For Health and Environmental Funders Network (HEFN) to maintain coordinator, upgrade website, listserve and other vehicles for continuing to develop new collaborations between health and environmental funders. 2001.
2102-7 Edith Kanaka Ole Foundation, Hilo, HI, $20,000. For Ke Ana La'ahana Public Charter School Hula Ensemble, which uses traditional art form of hula as means for multi-faceted environmental education experience. 2001.

2102-8 Environmental Defense, New York, NY, $200,000. For Antibiotics Resistance Coalition (ARC) in bringing together wide array of public-interest groups to coordinate their resources and strategies to eliminate overuse of antibiotics in animal agriculture. 2001.

2102-9 Environmental Health Fund, Jamaica Plain, MA, $150,000. To engage U.S. Healthcare industry in adopting environmentally sustainable practices and, over time, allies in encouraging other industries to adopt environmentally sustainable practices. 2001.

2102-10 Environmental Leadership Program, Cambridge, MA, $300,000. For general support for selection and training of annual cohorts of culturally and intellectually diverse future environmental leaders. 2001.

2102-11 Foundation for Jewish Camping, New York, NY, $175,000. To renew and expand Nathan Cummings Environmental Fellowship initiative, program for recruiting, training, and placing top-rate Jewish environmental educators in senior positions at Jewish camps throughout North America. 2001.

2102-12 Green Restaurant Association, San Diego, CA, $20,000. For efforts focused specifically on restaurants and environment. 2001.

2102-13 Harvard University, Cambridge, MA, $286,000. For Senior Associate to further develop Boston's Center for Health and the Global Environment's projects: Biodiversity: It's Importance to Human Health; Consortium for Conservation Medicine; Climate Change, the Oceans and Human Health; and West Nile Virus Surveillance. 2001.

2102-14 Ike Aina, Honolulu, HI, $50,000. To implement strategic plan for land conservation that views land and resources holistically, including function of people on land, and place's relationship to history, art, spiritual beliefs, genealogy, and resources. 2001.

2102-15 Interdenominational Theological Center, Atlanta, GA, $150,000. To substantially and measurably enhance role of Black church in promoting environmental stewardship, in cooperation with National Council of Churches of Christ in the USA. 2001.

2102-16 Jewish Council for Public Affairs, New York, NY, $25,000. To enable Coalition on the Environment and Jewish Life to produce and distribute anniversary report, and to conduct and disseminate findings of survey of rapidly growing field of Jewish environmental education. 2001.

2102-17 Jewish Council for Public Affairs, New York, NY, $13,000. For Coalition on the Environment and Jewish Life to conduct wilderness kayak trip in Alaska for leaders of Jewish environmental movement. 2001.

2102-18 Lawyers Committee for Civil Rights Under Law, DC, $50,000. For Environmental Justice Project to work collaboratively with grassroots groups to address disproportionate burden of environmental hazards borne by low-income and minority communities. 2001.

2102-19 NetCorps, Eugene, Oregon, $10,000. For developing capacity and program building tools and support for nonprofit environmental sector. 2001.

2102-20 New Israel Fund, DC, $780,000. For projects in Israel on environmental protection and Jewish pluralism. 2001.

2102-21 New Israel Fund, DC, $60,000. For staffing of Religious Pluralism and Environmental initiatives. 2001.

2102-22 New Yorkers for Parks, New York, NY, $10,000. For completion of educational learning center within Roy Wilkins Park in Southern Queens to include environmental learning classroom. 2001.

2102-23 Orion Society, Great Barrington, MA, $10,000. For creation of culture and network of activists working to promote values that go beyond economic as essential for healthy culture. 2001.

2102-24 Public Health Institute, New York, NY, $75,000. For Blue-Green Working Group on Climate Change (BGWG), alliance of unions and environmental organizations. 2001.

2102-25 Rudolf Steiner Foundation, San Francisco, CA, $15,300. For project of Jerusalem Waldorf Adam School to transform community around school regarding waste solutions via children's education. 2001.

2102-26 Rutgers, The State University of New Jersey Foundation, Piscataway, NJ, $60,000. For Community/University Consortium for Regional Environmental Justice (CUCREJ) to continue to build network of Greater New York City region's universities, colleges, and research institutions to serve needs of community-based environmental justice organizations. 2001.

2102-27 Sempervirens Fund, Los Altos, CA, $15,000. To preserve and protect natural character of California's Santa Cruz Mountains. 2001.

2102-28 Sierra Club Foundation, San Francisco, CA, $75,000. For Concentrated Animal Feeding Operation (CAFO) Campaign to make livestock corporations accountable to public and government. 2001.

2102-29 Southwest Research and Information Center, Albuquerque, NM, $10,000. For joint project with community-based group, Eastern Navajo Dine Against Uranium Mining (ENDAUM), designed to stop new uranium solution mines in sole source of drinking water for people living in Eastern Navajo Agency in northwestern New Mexico. 2001.

2102-30 TreePeople, Beverly Hills, CA, $15,000. For Campus Forestry program that plants trees on school campuses. 2001.

2102-31 Trust for Public Land, San Francisco, CA, $30,000. To lay foundation for transforming land conservation into more potent force for cultural change by developing thought and new practices that will also revitalize communities. 2001.

2102-32 U.S. Foundation for the Inspiration and Recognition of Science and Technology (U.S. FIRST), Manchester, NH, $20,000. For evaluation of FIRST Robotics Competition. 2001.

2102-33 United States Catholic Conference, DC, $300,000. For Common Good of Creation: Integrating Justice, Ecology and Community, project of Environmental Justice Program, to educate and mobilize clergy and lay leaders to work closely with citizen action groups and draw upon Church's relationships with governments in order to develop and implement constructive

approaches to resolving ecological issues. 2001.

2102-34 University of Washington Foundation, Seattle, WA, $15,000. For Higher Education on the New Commons: Sustainability, Technology, Contemplation project, which seeks ways to make such explorations visible and legitimate at institutions. 2001.

2102-35 Vallecitos Mountain Refuge, Taos, NM, $17,000. For gathering of Environmental Leadership Program (ELP) fellows, young environment leaders from diverse backgrounds and experience, to promote mutual understanding among most recent cohort. 2001.

2102-36 Waterkeeper Alliance, White Plains, NY, $50,000. For Campaign Against Industrialized Hog Farming. 2001.

2102-37 West Harlem Environmental Action, New York, NY, $75,000. For Campus Environmental Advocacy Project which will train college students to become environmental leaders prepared to support communities that bear disproportionate burden of environmental health threats. 2001.

2102-38 Whidbey Institute, Clinton, WA, $10,000. For development of Inside Passages, means of documenting and institutionalizing experience and change of participants in wilderness retreats to extend reach of program. 2001.

2102-39 Wilderness Society, DC, $210,000. For efforts to increase power of land conservation movement by bringing to bear scientifically sound, socially far-reaching, and popularly accessible definitions and applications of land ethic in fight for expansion of land under full protection, and conservation-centered land management policies. 2001.

2103
Cypress Foundation, Inc.

c/o Sandler O'Neill & Partners, LP
919 3rd Ave., 6th Fl.
New York, NY 10022
Contact: James Dunne

Established in 1992 in NY.
Donor(s): Herman Sandler, James Dunne III.
Grantmaker type: Independent foundation
Financial data (yr. ended 12/31/02): Assets, $710,995 (M); expenditures, $667,019; qualifying distributions, $638,673; giving activities include $638,673 for 69 grants (high: $113,012; low: $100).
Purpose and activities: Giving primarily for arts and culture, education, health, social services, Jewish agencies, temples, and federated giving programs, and religious purposes.
Fields of interest: Music; Orchestra (symphony); Arts; Higher education; Education; Natural resources; Health care; Health organizations, association; Human services; Federated giving programs; Jewish federated giving programs; Jewish agencies & temples.
International interests: Israel.
Limitations: Applications not accepted. Giving primarily in the metropolitan New York, NY, area. Some giving also in Israel. No grants to individuals.
Application information: Contributes only to pre-selected organizations.

Officers: James Dunne, Chair.; Jonathan Doyle, V.P.; Fred D. Price, V.P.; May Della Pietra, Secy.-Treas.
EIN: 133667026

2104
The Robert N. DeBenedictis Foundation
227 E. 56th St., Ste. 400
New York, NY 10022 (212) 753-2357
FAX: (212) 888-6828; Additional address: 1400 N.E. 14th St., Fort Lauderdale, FL 33304, FAX: (954) 766-2655; E-mail: robert.debenedictis@verizon.net; URL: http://fdncenter.org/grantmaker/rnd/

Incorporated in 1997 in NY.
Donor(s): Robert N. DeBenedictis.
Grantmaker type: Independent foundation
Financial data (yr. ended 12/31/02): Assets, $2,788 (M); gifts received, $100,500; expenditures, $103,222; qualifying distributions, $89,515; giving activities include $89,515 for 7 grants (high: $36,765; low: $1,500).
Fields of interest: Animal welfare; Human services.
Types of support: Scholarship funds.
Limitations: Applications not accepted. Giving primarily in PA. No grants to individuals.
Application information: Contributes only to pre-selected organizations.
Officers: Robert N. DeBenedictis, Chair. and Pres.; George S. Trisciuzzi, Vice-Chair. and V.P.; Paul Galluccio, Secy.; Julie Martino, Treas.; Ariana Testamarck, Exec. Dir.
EIN: 133989370

2105
Sarah K. deCoizart Article TENTH Perpetual Charitable Trust
(formerly Sarah K. deCoizart Perpetual Charitable Trust)
345 Park Ave., 4th Fl.
New York, NY 10154 (212) 464-2439
Contact: Jacqueline Elias, V.P., JPMorgan Chase Bank
FAX: (212) 464-2305; E-mail: elias_jacqueline@jpmorgan.com; URL: http://fdncenter.org/grantmaker/decoizart/

Established in 1992 in NY.
Grantmaker type: Independent foundation
Financial data (yr. ended 01/31/02): Assets, $35,401,842 (M); expenditures, $1,997,409; qualifying distributions, $1,807,448; giving activities include $1,681,305 for 125 grants (high: $40,000; low: $1,000).
Purpose and activities: Giving primarily for the environment, including conservation, research, and education; and for blindness-related services and research.
Fields of interest: Natural resources; Environmental education; Environment; Eye diseases; Eye research.
Types of support: Program development.
Limitations: Giving limited to New York City for blindness funding; giving primarily in NY and the Northeast for the environment. No support for organizations lacking 501(c)(3) status. No grants to individuals, or for matching gifts; no loans.

Application information: See foundation Web site for application guidelines and requirements. Application form not required.
Deadline(s): Apr. 30 and Sept. 30
Final notification: Jan. and July
Trustees: Carl S. Forsythe III; JPMorgan Chase Bank.
EIN: 137046581

2106
Margarita Victoria Delacorte Foundation
c/o U.S. Trust
114 W. 47th St.
New York, NY 10036
Contact: Margarita V. Delacorte

Established in 1966 in NY.
Donor(s): Margarita V. Delacorte.
Grantmaker type: Independent foundation
Financial data (yr. ended 12/31/02): Assets, $205,052 (M); expenditures, $106,473; qualifying distributions, $104,944; giving activities include $101,800 for 46 grants (high: $6,000; low: $250).
Purpose and activities: Support for private higher and secondary educational institutions.
Fields of interest: Music; Higher education; Libraries/library science; Education; Natural resources; Human services; Aging, centers/services; Christian agencies & churches.
Limitations: Giving primarily in New York, NY. No grants to individuals.
Application information:
Initial approach: Letter
Deadline(s): None
Trustee: U.S. Trust.
EIN: 136197777

2107
Nelson B. Delavan Foundation
c/o JPMorgan Chase Bank
P.O. Box 31412
Rochester, NY 14603
Contact: Janis Mosher, Trust Off.
Application address: 130 S. Main St., Canandaigua, NY 14424-1904, tel.: (315) 394-7675

Established in 1983 in NY.
Grantmaker type: Independent foundation
Financial data (yr. ended 12/31/02): Assets, $5,914,502 (M); expenditures, $459,307; qualifying distributions, $443,887; giving activities include $444,592 for grants.
Purpose and activities: Primary areas of interest include the performing arts and other cultural programs, health, and social services.
Fields of interest: Performing arts; Arts; Medical school/education; Animal welfare; Health care; Health organizations, association; Human services; Children/youth, services; Women, centers/services; International affairs; Women.
Types of support: General/operating support.
Limitations: Giving primarily in NY, with emphasis on the Seneca Falls region. No grants to individuals.
Application information: Application form not required.
Initial approach: Letter
Copies of proposal: 2
Deadline(s): None
Trustee: JPMorgan Chase Bank.

EIN: 166260274

2108
Demartini Family Foundation
9 W. 57th St., 48th Fl.
New York, NY 10019

Established in 2001 in NY.
Donor(s): Richard M. Demartini.
Grantmaker type: Independent foundation
Financial data (yr. ended 09/30/02): Assets, $5,303,316 (M); gifts received, $5,576,500; expenditures, $302,300; qualifying distributions, $185,150; giving activities include $185,150 for 31 grants (high: $44,050; low: $100).
Fields of interest: Arts; Education; Animals/wildlife, preservation/protection; Health care; Cancer; Human services.
Limitations: Applications not accepted. No grants to individuals.
Application information: Contributes only to pre-selected organizations.
Trustees: Jennifer L. Brorsen; Richard M. Demartini.
EIN: 946781245

2109
Deutsche Bank Americas Foundation ▼
(formerly BT Foundation)
60 Wall St., NYC60-2110
New York, NY 10005-2858 (212) 250-0555
Contact: Gary S. Hattem, Pres.
FAX: (212) 797-2255; E-mail: Gary.S.Hattem@db.com; URL: http://www.db.com/community

Established as the BT Foundation in 1986 in NY; changed to Deutsche Bank Americas Foundation in 1999.
Donor(s): Bankers Trust Co., BT Capital Corp., Deutsche Bank Americas Holding Corp.
Grantmaker type: Company-sponsored foundation
Financial data (yr. ended 12/31/01): Assets, $1,767,338 (M); gifts received, $11,526,836; expenditures, $13,143,939; qualifying distributions, $13,133,467; giving activities include $9,807,843 for 327 grants (high: $1,000,000; low: $200; average: $5,000–$30,000) and $3,326,836 for employee matching gifts.
Purpose and activities: The foundation administers the philanthropic activities of Deutsche Bank within the United States, Latin America, and Canada. Together with its Community Development Group, the foundation carries out the firm's corporate citizenship commitments through a program of loans, investments, and grants. Based in New York City, where the majority of grants are awarded, the foundation supports nonprofit organizations that concentrate on community development, education, the arts, and the environment. Deutsche Bank works in partnership with local nonprofit organizations to provide distressed communities and disadvantaged individuals with opportunities for economic advancement. The foundation seeks to enrich these communities by providing access to the arts, and encouraging the exchange of creative expression between diverse communities. In addition, the bank

relies on the talents of its personnel and
leadership of its management to leverage its
financial commitments in addressing local
needs.
Fields of interest: Arts; Education; Environment;
Housing/shelter, development; Economic
development; Urban/community development;
Community development.
International interests: Canada; Latin America.
Types of support: General/operating support;
Continuing support; Capital campaigns;
Program development; Internship funds;
Technical assistance; Employee matching gifts.
Limitations: Giving primarily in areas of
company operations in the U.S., Canada and
Latin America. No support for religious
purposes, veterans' and fraternal organizations,
United Way agencies unless they provide a
fundraising waiver, political parties or their
candidates, or legal advocacy. No grants to
individuals, or for endowment campaigns.
Publications: Application guidelines, Annual
report, Grants list, Newsletter.
Application information: Application form not
required.
  Initial approach: Letter, not to exceed three
    pages
  Deadline(s): None
Officers and Directors:* Rose Tobin, C.O.O.and
Treas.; Gary S. Hattem,* Pres.; Robyn Brady
Ince, V.P.; Sandra West, Secy.; E. Robert Cotter;
Michael Hoelz; Grant Kvalheim; Alexander
Labak; John A. Ross; Seth Waugh.
Number of staff: 3 full-time professional; 3
full-time support.
EIN: 133321736
**Recent environmental and animal welfare
grants:**
2109-1 American Society for the Prevention of
Cruelty to Animals, New York, NY, $10,000.
For disaster relief. 2001.
2109-2 Central Park Conservancy, New York,
NY, $15,000. For Summer Youth Employment
Program. 2001.
2109-3 Green Map System, New York, NY,
$10,000. For general operating support. 2001.
2109-4 Horticultural Society of New York, New
York, NY, $15,000. For GreenBranches
Initiative. 2001.
2109-5 New England Aquarium, Boston, MA,
$10,109. For Opening Night Gala. 2001.
2109-6 Trust for Public Land, New York, NY,
$25,000. For housing and open space
initiative. 2001.
2109-7 World Wildlife Fund/Conservation
Foundation, DC, $100,000. For Center for
Conservation Finance. 2001.

2110
Philip & Gussie Diamond Foundation, Inc.
c/o Cummings & Carroll, PC
175 Great Neck Rd., Ste. 405
Great Neck, NY 11021

Established around 1948 in NY.
Grantmaker type: Independent foundation
Financial data (yr. ended 12/31/02): Assets,
$2,793,825 (M); expenditures, $181,556;
qualifying distributions, $165,704; giving
activities include $168,400 for 13 grants (high:
$75,000; low: $100).
Purpose and activities: Giving primarily for
Jewish causes.

Fields of interest: Animals/wildlife; Hospitals
(general); Human services; Jewish federated
giving programs; Jewish agencies & temples.
Limitations: Applications not accepted. Giving
primarily in the greater New York, NY, area. No
grants to individuals.
Application information: Contributes only to
pre-selected organizations.
Officers: Marvin R. Neuwirth, Pres.; Felice
Neuwirth, V.P.; Barbara Braun, Secy.
EIN: 136116411

2111
Harriet Ford Dickenson Foundation ▼
c/o JPMorgan Chase Bank
345 Park Ave.
New York, NY 10154 (212) 464-1937
Contact: James Largey, V.P., JPMorgan Chase
Bank

Established about 1958 in NY.
Donor(s): Harriet Ford Dickenson.‡
Grantmaker type: Independent foundation
Financial data (yr. ended 12/31/01): Assets,
$43,626,741 (M); expenditures, $1,663,151;
qualifying distributions, $1,477,896; giving
activities include $1,458,000 for 75 grants (high:
$330,000; low: $500; average:
$1,000–$25,000).
Purpose and activities: Giving primarily for the
arts, botanical gardens, hospitals, and human
services.
Fields of interest: Museums; Performing arts;
Arts; Botanical gardens; Hospitals (general);
Human services.
Limitations: Giving limited to Broome County,
NY. No grants to individuals.
Application information: Application form
required.
  Initial approach: Letter
  Deadline(s): None
Trustee: JPMorgan Chase Bank.
Advisory Committee: Gillian Attfield; Ann
Hubbard; David Hubbard; Tom Hubbard; John
Keeler; Shirley Keeler.
Number of staff: None.
EIN: 136047225
**Recent environmental and animal welfare
grants:**
2111-1 Adirondack Council, Elizabethtown, NY,
$25,000. For general support. 2002.
2111-2 Audubon Society, National - Northeast
Regional Office, Albany, NY, $25,000. For
general support. 2002.
2111-3 Nature Conservancy, New York, NY,
$25,000. For general support. 2002.
2111-4 New York Botanical Garden, Bronx, NY,
$2,305,000. For general support. 2002.
2111-5 New York Parks and Conservation
Association, Albany, NY, $25,000. For
general support. 2002.
2111-6 Peconic Land Trust, Southampton, NY,
$15,000. For general support. 2002.
2111-7 Scenic Hudson, Poughkeepsie, NY,
$10,000. For general support. 2002.

2112
The Dillard Foundation
c/o Lazard
30 Rockefeller Plaza
New York, NY 10020 (212) 632-1308
Contact: David B. Dillard, V.P.

Donor(s): David B. Dillard.
Grantmaker type: Independent foundation
Financial data (yr. ended 12/31/02): Assets,
$2,162,740 (M); gifts received, $46,068;
expenditures, $126,204; qualifying distributions,
$124,941; giving activities include $105,772 for
20 grants (high: $52,801; low: $250).
Fields of interest: College; Law
school/education; Natural resources; Legal
services.
Application information:
  Initial approach: Letter
  Deadline(s): None
Officers and Directors:* Christopher Dillard,*
Pres.; David B. Dillard,* V.P.; James Dillard,
Secy.; Patrick Dillard, Treas.
EIN: 133318226

2113
The DiMenna Foundation, Inc.
(formerly The DiMenna Family Foundation, Inc.)
1049 5th Ave., Rm. P3
New York, NY 10028

Established in 1998 in CT and NY.
Donor(s): Joseph A. DiMenna.
Grantmaker type: Independent foundation
Financial data (yr. ended 12/31/00): Assets,
$3,271,931 (M); expenditures, $167,161;
qualifying distributions, $123,509; giving
activities include $127,000 for 4 grants (high:
$50,000; low: $12,000).
Fields of interest: Performing arts centers;
Environment; Health organizations, association;
Cancer.
Limitations: Applications not accepted. Giving
primarily in New York, NY. No grants to
individuals.
Application information: Contributes only to
pre-selected organizations.
Officers: Joseph A. DiMenna, Pres.; Maureen
DiMenna, Secy.
Director: Kevin P. Cannon.
EIN: 061534269

2114
The DJR Trust
c/o Bessemer Trust Co., N.A.
630 5th Ave.
New York, NY 10111

Established in 1998 in NY.
Donor(s): Dan I. Rather, Jean G. Rather.
Grantmaker type: Independent foundation
Financial data (yr. ended 12/31/02): Assets,
$1,857,180 (M); expenditures, $116,158;
qualifying distributions, $98,419; giving
activities include $93,500 for 10 grants (high:
$50,000; low: $2,500).
Fields of interest: University; Environment, plant
conservation; Food distribution, meals on
wheels; Protestant agencies & churches.
Limitations: Applications not accepted. Giving
primarily in New York, NY and TX. No grants to
individuals.

Application information: Contributes only to pre-selected organizations.
Trustees: Dan I. Rather; Jean G. Rather; Bessemer Trust Co., N.A.
EIN: 137148229

2115
The Dobson Foundation, Inc.
4 E. 66th St., Ste. 1E
New York, NY 10021

Incorporated in 1961 in NY.
Donor(s): Walter M. Jeffords, Jr.‡
Grantmaker type: Independent foundation
Financial data (yr. ended 12/31/00): Assets, $5,173,101 (M); expenditures, $253,434; qualifying distributions, $245,284; giving activities include $235,550 for 21 grants (high: $50,000; low: $100).
Purpose and activities: Support for higher education, the performing arts, and museums, including those pertaining to the arts, animals, and sports.
Fields of interest: Museums; Performing arts; Higher education; Animal welfare; Recreation.
Limitations: Applications not accepted. Giving primarily on the East Coast, with emphasis on New York and Saratoga Springs, NY. No grants to individuals.
Application information: Contributes only to pre-selected organizations.
Officers: Kathleen McLaughlin Jeffords, Pres.; George Jeffords, V.P.; Sarah Jeffords Radcliff, Secy.
EIN: 136168259

2116
Cleveland H. Dodge Foundation, Inc. ▼
670 W. 247th St.
Bronx, NY 10471   (718) 543-1221
Contact: Phyllis M. Criscuoli, Exec. Dir.
FAX: (718) 543-0737

Incorporated in 1917 in NY.
Donor(s): Cleveland H. Dodge.‡
Grantmaker type: Independent foundation
Financial data (yr. ended 12/31/01): Assets, $49,217,356 (M); expenditures, $3,064,210; qualifying distributions, $2,684,507; giving activities include $1,938,645 for 104 grants (high: $250,000; low: $175; average: $100–$25,000) and $396,260 for 216 employee matching gifts.
Purpose and activities: To promote the well-being of mankind throughout the world. Grants for a selected list of international organizations in the Near East, including those working toward reversing global overpopulation; grants also to a selected few national agencies in the U.S., the balance directed to organizations located in New York City. Most grants in the U.S. for higher and secondary education, youth agencies and child welfare, and cultural programs.
Fields of interest: Arts; Secondary school/education; Higher education; Children/youth, services; Population studies.
International interests: Middle East.
Types of support: Building/renovation; Equipment; Endowments; Matching/challenge support.

Limitations: Giving primarily in New York, NY, the Near East, and to national organizations. No support for health care, or schools, colleges, and universities, except those that the foundation has consistently supported. No grants to individuals, including scholarships and fellowships, or for general purposes, medical and other research; no loans.
Publications: Annual report, Program policy statement.
Application information: Application form not required.
  Initial approach: Letter
  Copies of proposal: 1
  Deadline(s): Submit letter prior to the 15th of Jan., Apr., or Oct.
  Board meeting date(s): 3 times a year
  Final notification: Within 3 months of submitting the proposal
Officers and Directors:* Cleveland E. Dodge, Jr.,* Pres.; William Dodge Rueckert,* V.P.; Gilbert Kerlin,* Secy.; Phyllis M. Criscuoli, Treas. and Exec. Dir.; Nancy Lee Coughlin; Bayard Dodge; Cornelia W. Dodge; David S. Dodge; Robert Garrett; Sally Dodge Mole; Bayard D. Rea; C. Cary Rea; Ingrid R. Warren; Mary Rea Weidlein.
Number of staff: 1 full-time professional.
EIN: 136015087
Recent environmental and animal welfare grants:
2116-1 American Farm School, Thessaloniki, Greece, $20,000. For Natural History Room Project. 2001.
2116-2 New York Botanical Garden, Bronx, NY, $200,000. For campaign. 2001.
2116-3 New York Botanical Garden, Bronx, NY, $15,000. For fundraiser. 2001.
2116-4 Wave Hill, Bronx, NY, $15,000. For annual support. 2001.
2116-5 Wave Hill, Bronx, NY, $10,000. For fundraiser. 2001.

2117
Oliver S. and Jennie R. Donaldson Charitable Trust
c/o U.S. Trust
114 W. 47th St.
New York, NY 10036-1530
Contact: Linda R. Franciscovich, Sr. V.P., U.S. Trust; or Carolyn L. Larke, Asst. V.P., U.S. Trust
FAX: (212) 852-3377

Trust established in 1969 in NY.
Donor(s): Oliver S. Donaldson.‡
Grantmaker type: Independent foundation
Financial data (yr. ended 12/31/01): Assets, $28,833,712 (M); expenditures, $1,926,619; qualifying distributions, $1,837,083; giving activities include $1,760,250 for grants.
Purpose and activities: Interests include cancer research and treatment, child welfare and youth agencies, hospitals and health agencies, elementary, secondary, and higher education; support also for wildlife preservation, and the town of Pawling, NY; 11 named institutions are given first consideration.
Fields of interest: Elementary school/education; Secondary school/education; Higher education; Animals/wildlife, preservation/protection; Hospitals (general); Health care; Cancer; Medical research, institute; Cancer research; Children/youth, services.

Limitations: Giving primarily in the Northeast, with emphasis on MA and NY. No grants to individuals.
Publications: Application guidelines.
Application information: NY Common Application Form required. Application form required.
  Initial approach: Letter or FAX requesting guidelines
  Copies of proposal: 1
  Deadline(s): 40 days prior to board meeting
  Board meeting date(s): Semiannually
Trustees: Marjorie Atwood; Elizabeth Lawrence, M.D.; William E. Murray; John F. Sisk; Pamela C. Smith; U.S. Trust.
EIN: 046229044

2118
The William H. Donner Foundation, Inc. ▼
60 E. 42nd St., Ste. 1651
New York, NY 10165   (212) 949-5292
Contact: Rachel Gregg, Prog. Off.
FAX: (212) 949-6022; E-mail: whdf@donner.org; URL: http://www.donner.org

Incorporated in 1961 in DC.
Donor(s): William H. Donner.‡
Grantmaker type: Independent foundation
Financial data (yr. ended 10/31/01): Assets, $135,032,057 (M); expenditures, $13,276,265; qualifying distributions, $11,778,469; giving activities include $10,909,100 for 295 grants (high: $500,000; low: $1,000; average: $5,000–$100,000).
Purpose and activities: The foundation is in a period of transition and no longer states a funding preference.
Types of support: General/operating support; Program development.
Limitations: Applications not accepted.
Application information: Only applications invited by the foundation will be considered.
  Board meeting date(s): Sept.
Officers and Trustees:* William Roosevelt,* Pres.; Hon. Curtin Winsor, Jr.,* V.P.; Joseph W. Donner, Jr.,* Secy.; Deborah Donner,* Treas.; Alexander B. Donner; Timothy E. Donner; Stephanie Hanson; Robert D. Spencer.
Number of staff: 1 full-time professional; 3 part-time professional; 1 full-time support; 1 part-time support.
EIN: 231611346
Recent environmental and animal welfare grants:
2118-1 A Grassroots Aspen Experience, Aspen, CO, $10,000. For general support. 2002.
2118-2 African Wildlife Foundation, DC, $75,000. For general support. 2002.
2118-3 African Wildlife Foundation, DC, $55,000. For Mountain Gorilla Conservation Trust Fund. 2002.
2118-4 Audubon Society, National, New York, NY, $12,000. For strengthening Cockscomb Jaguar Reserve in Belize. 2002.
2118-5 Busch Wildlife Sanctuary, Jupiter, FL, $40,000. For Supervisor of Veterinary Services and Director of Amphitheater Education Programs. 2002.
2118-6 Caribbean Marine Research Center (CMRC), Lee Stocking Island, Bahamas, $70,000. For general support. 2002.

2118-7 Caribbean Marine Research Center (CMRC), Lee Stocking Island, Bahamas, $40,029. For general support. 2002.

2118-8 Caribbean Marine Research Center (CMRC), Lee Stocking Island, Bahamas, $40,000. For general support. 2002.

2118-9 Cherokee Ranch and Castle Foundation, Sedalia, CO, $55,200. For Tweet Kimball Bedroom foundation stabilization. 2002.

2118-10 Cherokee Ranch and Castle Foundation, Sedalia, CO, $35,000. For general support. 2002.

2118-11 Cherokee Ranch and Castle Foundation, Sedalia, CO, $22,400. For phase II of structural remediation to west and south walls of castle. 2002.

2118-12 Dogs for the Deaf, Central Point, Oregon, $20,000. For general support. 2002.

2118-13 Dolphin Research Center, Marathon Shores, FL, $10,000. For general support. 2002.

2118-14 Environmental Literacy Council, DC, $25,000. For general support. 2002.

2118-15 Foundation for Research on Economics and the Environment (FREE), Bozeman, MT, $50,000. For general support. 2002.

2118-16 Hidden Harbor Marine Environmental Project, Marathon, FL, $35,000. For general support. 2002.

2118-17 Horse Protection Association of Florida, Micanopy, FL, $40,000. For general support. 2002.

2118-18 Humane Society of Yates County, Penn Yan, NY, $15,000. For general support. 2002.

2118-19 In-Sync Exotics Wildlife Rescue and Educational Center, Wylie, TX, $10,000. For general support. 2002.

2118-20 Nature Conservancy, Minneapolis, MN, $50,000. For general support. 2002.

2118-21 Nature Conservancy, Minneapolis, MN, $50,000. For general support. 2002.

2118-22 Nature Conservancy, Minneapolis, MN, $50,000. For general support. 2002.

2118-23 North Hills Landscape Committee, Oakland, CA, $25,000. For Gateway Emergency Preparedness Exhibit Center and Garden. 2002.

2118-24 Nushagak Mulchatna Wood Tikchik Land Trust, Dillingham, AK, $25,000. For general support. 2002.

2118-25 Paws 2 Help, West Palm Beach, FL, $35,000. For general support. 2002.

2118-26 Performing Animal Welfare Society, Galt, CA, $150,000. For Ark 2000 phase 1 elephant habitat. 2002.

2118-27 Potomac School, McLean, VA, $100,000. For renovation of nature trails and ponds. 2002.

2118-28 Rare Species Conservatory Foundation, Loxahatchee, FL, $150,000. For general support. 2002.

2118-29 United Animals Nations-USA, Sacramento, CA, $70,000. For Emergency Animal Rescue Service (EARS) and Lifeline programs. 2002.

2118-30 United Animals Nations-USA, Sacramento, CA, $30,000. 2002.

2118-31 Yellowstone Park Foundation, Bozeman, MT, $100,000. For general support. 2002.

2119
Doran Family Charitable Trust

c/o U.S. Trust, Tax Dept.
114 W. 47th St.
New York, NY   10036

Established in 1986 in MA.
Donor(s): Robert W. Doran.
Grantmaker type: Independent foundation
Financial data (yr. ended 12/31/02): Assets, $4,628,455 (M); expenditures, $891,081; qualifying distributions, $837,287; giving activities include $838,287 for 22 grants (high: $399,006; low: $3).
Purpose and activities: Giving primarily for education, the environment, the arts, and health and human services.
Fields of interest: Museums; Arts; Elementary/secondary education; Higher education; Education; Botanical gardens; Environment; Hospitals (general); Human services.
Limitations: Applications not accepted. Giving primarily in MA. No grants to individuals.
Application information: Contributes only to pre-selected organizations.
Trustees: Evelyn H. Doran; Robert W. Doran.
EIN: 226424850

2120
Charles H. Douglas Charitable Trust

c/o Trustco Bank, N.A.
P.O. Box 380
Schenectady, NY   12301

Established in 1999 in NY.
Donor(s): Stephanie Bugden.
Grantmaker type: Independent foundation
Financial data (yr. ended 12/31/02): Assets, $4,199,831 (M); expenditures, $351,273; qualifying distributions, $336,714; giving activities include $328,398 for 13 grants (high: $33,762; low: $16,761).
Fields of interest: Natural resources; Animals/wildlife; Health organizations, association; Cancer.
Limitations: Applications not accepted. Giving primarily in Washington, DC, and NY. No grants to individuals.
Application information: Contributes only to pre-selected organizations.
Trustees: John Van Norden; Trustco Bank, N.A.
EIN: 141814550

2121
Drasner Family Foundation

450 W. 33rd St.
New York, NY   10001-2603

Established in 1996 in NY.
Donor(s): Fred Drasner.
Grantmaker type: Independent foundation
Financial data (yr. ended 12/31/00): Assets, $1,324,176 (M); gifts received, $1,480; expenditures, $102,880; qualifying distributions, $101,000; giving activities include $101,000 for 2 grants (high: $100,000; low: $1,000).
Fields of interest: Animal welfare; Hospitals (general).
Limitations: Applications not accepted. Giving primarily in NY. No grants to individuals.

Application information: Contributes only to pre-selected organizations.
Directors: Fred Drasner; Kenneth Drasner; Martin D. Krall.
EIN: 133924566

2122
Doris Duke Charitable Foundation ▼

650 5th Ave., 19th Fl.
New York, NY   10019   (212) 974-7000
Contact: Office of Grants Admin.
Additional tel.: (212) 974-7100; FAX: (212) 974-7590; URL: http://fdncenter.org/grantmaker/dorisduke/

Established in 1996 in NY.
Donor(s): Doris Duke.‡
Grantmaker type: Independent foundation
Financial data (yr. ended 12/31/02): Assets, $1,274,858,594 (M); expenditures, $95,614,292; qualifying distributions, $62,846,690; giving activities include $82,034,936 for 198 grants, $5,000 for employee matching gifts and $456,728 for 3 foundation-administered programs.
Purpose and activities: The mission of the foundation is to improve the quality of people's lives by nurturing the arts, protecting and restoring the environment, seeking cures for diseases, and helping to protect children from abuse and neglect. In addition to its grantmaking activities, the foundation will support three affiliated operating foundations: Duke Farms Foundation, the Doris Duke Foundation for Islamic Art, and the Newport Restoration Foundation.
Fields of interest: Performing arts; Natural resources; Medical research, institute; Child abuse; Disasters, 9/11/01.
Limitations: Giving on a national basis. No support for water or aquatic issues, air or climate change issues, toxic issues, litigation, the visual arts, museums or galleries, or arts programs for rehabilitative or therapeutic purposes. No grants to individuals (except through special foundation programs) or for conferences or publications.
Application information: The foundation staff responds to all letters of inquiry, however, it should be noted that very few grants result from unsolicited letters of inquiry. Do not send binders, books, CDs, videotapes, or audiotapes.
Initial approach: Two-page letter of inquiry
Officers and Trustees:* James F. Gill,* Chair.; Marion Oates Charles,* Vice-Chair.; Joan E. Spero, Pres.; Alan Altschuler, C.F.O.; Harry B. Demopoulos, M.D.; Anthony S. Fauci, M.D.; Nannerl O. Keohane; John J. Mack; John H.T. Wilson.
EIN: 137043679
Recent environmental and animal welfare grants:
2122-1 Bridgespan Group, Boston, MA, $50,000. For Assessment of Forest Certification. 2002.
2122-2 Conservation Fund, Arlington, VA, $200,750. To coordinate Doris Duke Conservation Fellowship Program at five universities. 2002.
2122-3 Consultative Group on Biological Diversity, San Francisco, CA, $15,000. For Partnerships among Conservation Funders. 2002.

2122-4 Duke University, Nicholas School of the Environment, Durham, NC, $550,000. To administer Doris Duke Conservation Fellowships for two additional classes of fellows. 2002.

2122-5 Ecotrust, Portland, Oregon, $20,000. For development of full proposal to conserve biodiversity in large, forested landscape (Central Pacific Coastal Forests). 2002.

2122-6 Environmental Defense, New York, NY, $5,000,000. To establish Center for Conservation Incentives to promote more efficient and effective approaches to conservation of biodiversity on nation's private lands. 2002.

2122-7 Land Trust Alliance, DC, $25,000. To develop three-year action plan for significantly improving stewardship of conservation easements and easement-protected land. 2002.

2122-8 Nature Conservancy, Arlington, VA, $20,000. For development of full proposal to conserve biodiversity in large, forested landscape in Hawaii, Hawaii Moist and Dry Forests. 2002.

2122-9 Nature Conservancy, Arlington, VA, $20,000. For development of full proposal to conserve biodiversity in large, forested landscape in South Carolina, Mid-Atlantic Coastal Forest. 2002.

2122-10 Sustainable Northwest, Portland, Oregon, $20,000. For development of full proposal to conserve biodiversity in large, forested landscape, Klamath Siskiyou Forests. 2002.

2122-11 University of Michigan, Ann Arbor, MI, $550,000. To administer Doris Duke Conservation Fellowships for two additional classes of fellows. 2002.

2122-12 University of Montana, Environmental Studies Program, Missoula, MT, $230,000. To administer Doris Duke Conservation Fellowships for two additional classes of fellows. 2002.

2122-13 University of Wisconsin, Institute for Environmental Studies, Madison, WI, $230,000. To administer Doris Duke Conservation Fellowships for two additional classes of fellows. 2002.

2122-14 Yale University, School of Forestry and Environmental Studies, New Haven, CT, $550,000. To administer Doris Duke Conservation Fellowships for two additional classes of fellows. 2002.

2123
Dexter & Carol Earle Foundation
c/o Citrin Cooperman & Co., LLP
529 5th Ave., 10th Fl.
New York, NY 10017-4667

Established in 1989 in NY.
Donor(s): Dexter D. Earle.
Grantmaker type: Independent foundation
Financial data (yr. ended 01/31/02): Assets, $1,678,188 (M); expenditures, $137,033; qualifying distributions, $124,546; giving activities include $124,296 for 34 grants (high: $34,950; low: $100).
Purpose and activities: Funding primarily for education. Some funding also for human services, health care, and arts and culture.

Fields of interest: Theater; Music; Elementary/secondary education; Higher education; Natural resources; Medical research, institute; Human services.
Limitations: Applications not accepted. Giving primarily in NJ. No grants to individuals.
Application information: Contributes only to pre-selected organizations.
Trustees: Carol A. Earle; Dexter D. Earle.
EIN: 133532028

2124
East Hill Foundation
6500 Main St., Ste. 6
Williamsville, NY 14221 (716) 204-0204
Contact: Michele R. Schmidt, Admin. Dir.
FAX: (716) 204-0208; E-mail:
easthill@easthillfdn.org

Established in 1986 in NY.
Donor(s): Wilson Greatbatch, Eleanor Greatbatch.
Grantmaker type: Independent foundation
Financial data (yr. ended 12/30/02): Assets, $12,297,790 (M); gifts received, $4,398; expenditures, $590,711; qualifying distributions, $504,837; giving activities include $376,107 for 44 grants (high: $32,135; low: $576).
Purpose and activities: Giving for community needs and opportunities, social services, arts and culture, education, and health and social needs.
Fields of interest: Multipurpose centers/programs; Education; Animal welfare; Health care; Youth development.
Types of support: Building/renovation; Equipment; Program development; Program-related investments/loans; Matching/challenge support.
Limitations: Giving primarily in western NY. No support for religious organizations for direct religious purposes. No grants to individuals.
Publications: Informational brochure (including application guidelines).
Application information: Only 1 application per grant cycle. Application form required.
  Initial approach: Letter or telephone
  Copies of proposal: 2
  Deadline(s): Aug. 15
  Board meeting date(s): Semiannually
  Final notification: By letter
Directors: Ami Greatbatch; Eleanor Greatbatch; Warren Greatbatch; Stanton H. Hudson, Jr.; Michele R. Schmidt; John E. Siegel.
Number of staff: 1 full-time professional.
EIN: 161441497

2125
Eastman Kodak Charitable Trust ▼
c/o JPMorgan Chase Bank
P.O. Box 31412
Rochester, NY 14603 (585) 724-2434
Contact: Essie Calhoun, Dir., Corp. Contribs. Prog.
Application address: 343 State St., Rochester, NY 14650

Trust established in 1952 in NY.
Donor(s): Eastman Kodak Co.
Grantmaker type: Company-sponsored foundation

Financial data (yr. ended 12/31/02): Assets, $251,228 (M); gifts received, $7,051,603; expenditures, $6,821,635; qualifying distributions, $6,819,812; giving activities include $6,819,700 for 303 grants (high: $1,100,000; low: $300; average: $1,000–$50,000).
Purpose and activities: Support primarily for the United Way, precollege, higher and minority education, and environmental affairs.
Fields of interest: Arts; Higher education; Education; Environment; Federated giving programs; Minorities.
Types of support: General/operating support; Continuing support; Fellowships; Scholarship funds.
Limitations: Giving primarily in high employment locations, including Windsor, CO, Rochester, NY, and Kingsport, TN; giving nationally only for higher education. No grants to individuals, or for matching gifts; low priority given to building or endowment funds; no loans.
Publications: Corporate giving report.
Application information: Application form not required.
  Initial approach: Letter
  Deadline(s): None
  Board meeting date(s): Monthly
Trustee: JPMorgan Chase Bank.
Number of staff: None.
EIN: 166015274
Recent environmental and animal welfare grants:
2125-1 Global Environmental Management Initiative (GEMI), DC, $10,000. For general support. 2002.
2125-2 South Wedge Planning Committee, Rochester, NY, $10,000. For Genesee River Docks. 2002.

2126
Eastman Kodak Company Contributions Program
343 State St.
Rochester, NY 14650-0517 (716) 724-1980
Contact: Essie L. Calhoun, Dir., Community Rels. and Contribs.
URL: http://www.kodak.com/US/en/corp/community.shtml

Grantmaker type: Corporate giving program
Financial data (yr. ended 12/31/01): Total giving, $16,585,088; giving activities include $16,585,088 for 500 grants (high: $2,400,000; low: $300; average: $300–$2,400,000).
Purpose and activities: As a complement to its foundation, Eastman Kodak also makes charitable contributions to nonprofit organizations directly. Support is given on a national and international basis.
Fields of interest: Arts; Elementary/secondary education; Higher education; Engineering school/education; Education; Environment; Health care; Youth, services; Human services; Community development; Computer science; Engineering; Science; Public policy, research; Public affairs; Minorities; Women.
International interests: Canada; Europe; Russia; South Africa; Latin America; India; China; Japan; Australia.
Types of support: General/operating support; Continuing support; Annual campaigns; Emergency funds; Program development; Seed

money; Curriculum development; Fellowships; Employee volunteer services; Sponsorships; Donated equipment; Donated products.
Limitations: Giving on a national and international basis in areas of company operations, including in Australia, Canada, China, Europe, India, Japan, Latin America, Russia, and South Africa. No support for sectarian organizations, political organizations, or United Way-supported organizations. No grants to individuals or legislators, or for endowed chairs, university capital campaigns, event sponsorships, or political campaigns.
Publications: Corporate giving report (including application guidelines), Grants list.
Application information: Proposals should be no longer than 5 pages in length. Support is limited to 3 years in length. The Community Relations and Contributions Department handles giving. Application form not required.
   Initial approach: Proposal to headquarters
   Copies of proposal: 1
   Deadline(s): Jan. to Apr. 30
   Final notification: 45 days
Number of staff: 1 full-time professional; 1 full-time support.

2127
Echoing Green
(formerly Echoing Green Foundation)
60 E. 42nd St., Ste. 2901
New York, NY   10165   (212) 689-1165
Contact: Cheryl L. Dorsey, Pres.
FAX: (212) 689-9010; E-mail:
general@echoinggreen.org; URL: http://
www.echoinggreen.org

Established in 1987 in DE.
Donor(s): The Atlantic Philanthropies, General Atlantic Partners.
Grantmaker type: Independent foundation
Financial data (yr. ended 06/30/02): Assets, $1,317,108 (M); gifts received, $2,250,000; expenditures, $1,959,287; qualifying distributions, $710,526; giving activities include $710,526 for 40 grants to individuals (high: $30,000; low: $3,750; average: $7,500–$10,000) and $634,642 for 1 foundation-administered program.
Purpose and activities: The Echoing Green offers fellowships to individuals. Through Echoing Green's Public Service Fellowship, seed money and technical support are provided to social entrepreneurs starting innovative public service organizations and projects that seek to catalyze positive social change. Echoing Green invests in entrepreneurs' organizations and projects at an early stage, before most funders are willing to do so, and then provides them with support to help them grow beyond start-up. The Echoing Green network currently includes over 350 fellows working domestically and internationally in a wide range of issue areas, including human rights, the environment, the arts, education, criminal justice, and community development.
Fields of interest: Education; Environment; Health care; Housing/shelter; Children/youth, services; International economic development; International relief; International human rights; Civil rights; Economic development; Community development; Public affairs.
Types of support: Seed money; Fellowships.

Limitations: Giving on a national and international basis.
Publications: Application guidelines, Grants list.
Application information: Initial application available on Web site as of Oct./Nov. annually. Application form required.
   Initial approach: Application form
   Copies of proposal: 1
   Deadline(s): Jan. for initial application; Mar. for final application
   Final notification: Mid-May
Officers and Directors:* David C. Hodgson, Chair.; Cheryl L. Dorsey,* Pres.; Lara Galinsky, V.P., Strategy; Heather McGrew, V.P., Fellow and Alumni Programs; Maya Ajmera; Carter Bales; Betsy Fader; William Ford; Adam Janovic; Kary Preston; Billy Shore; Bill Shutkin; Anthony So; Reggie Stanley.
Number of staff: 3 full-time professional; 2 part-time professional; 1 full-time support; 2 part-time support.
EIN: 133424419

2128
Joseph H. & Barbara I. Ellis Foundation
c/o BCRS Assocs., LLC
100 Wall St., 11th Fl.
New York, NY   10005

Established in 1987 in NY.
Donor(s): Joseph H. Ellis.
Grantmaker type: Independent foundation
Financial data (yr. ended 06/30/02): Assets, $5,579,004 (M); expenditures, $994,118; qualifying distributions, $986,004; giving activities include $985,830 for 61 grants (high: $200,000; low: $300).
Purpose and activities: Giving primarily for environmental conservation, higher education, Jewish organizations, and community services.
Fields of interest: Higher education; Education; Environment, plant conservation; Environment; Animals/wildlife, preservation/protection; Food services; Human services; Jewish agencies & temples.
Types of support: General/operating support.
Limitations: Applications not accepted. Giving primarily in New York, NY. No grants to individuals.
Application information: Contributes only to pre-selected organizations.
Trustees: Leon Cooperman; Barbara I. Ellis; Joseph H. Ellis.
EIN: 133437916

2129
The Lincoln Ellsworth Foundation
c/o Morris & McVeigh, LLP
767 3rd Ave.
New York, NY   10017-2023

Established in 1943.
Grantmaker type: Independent foundation
Financial data (yr. ended 12/31/02): Assets, $3,478,763 (M); gifts received, $3,000; expenditures, $256,085; qualifying distributions, $232,335; giving activities include $219,000 for 14 grants (high: $37,000; low: $2,500).
Fields of interest: Museums (natural history); Arts; Education; Animal welfare; Animals/wildlife; Salvation Army.

Limitations: Applications not accepted. Giving primarily in the metropolitan New York, NY, area. No grants to individuals.
Application information: Contributes only to pre-selected organizations.
Officers: MacDonald Budd, Pres. and Secy.; Guy G. Rutherfurd, V.P.
EIN: 136022017

2130
EMSA Fund, Inc.
c/o Norman Foundation, Inc.
147 E. 48th St.
New York, NY   10017
Contact: Alice Franklin, Pres.

Incorporated in 1962 in GA.
Donor(s): Phoebe Weil Lundeen,‡ and members of the Franklin family.
Grantmaker type: Independent foundation
Financial data (yr. ended 12/31/00): Assets, $5,053,907 (M); gifts received, $1,410,059; expenditures, $228,339; qualifying distributions, $197,234; giving activities include $191,680 for 101 grants (high: $47,500; low: $25).
Purpose and activities: Giving primarily for culture, public policy, race relations, rural development, civil rights, community development, and women's programs, particularly for those who have been neglected or hard to reach in the provision of such programs; support also for environmental programs and educational programs for minorities.
Fields of interest: Museums; Education; Natural resources; Hospitals (general); Children/youth, services; Community development, neighborhood development; Federated giving programs; Jewish agencies & temples.
Types of support: General/operating support; Continuing support; Annual campaigns; Capital campaigns; Endowments; Emergency funds; Program development; Seed money.
Limitations: Giving primarily in CO. No grants to individuals; no loans.
Publications: Grants list.
Application information: Application form not required.
   Initial approach: Letter
   Copies of proposal: 1
   Deadline(s): None
   Board meeting date(s): Annually
   Final notification: 2-4 weeks
Officers: Alice Franklin, Pres.; Audrey Franklin, V.P.; Andrew D. Franklin, Secy.
Number of staff: None.
EIN: 586043282

2131
Emwiga Foundation
(formerly Overlock Family Foundation)
c/o BCRS Assocs., LLC
100 Wall St., 11th Fl.
New York, NY   10005

Established in 1984 in NY.
Donor(s): Willard J. Overlock.
Grantmaker type: Independent foundation
Financial data (yr. ended 02/28/03): Assets, $4,630,895 (M); gifts received, $2,405,100; expenditures, $1,420,132; qualifying distributions, $1,342,125; giving activities

include $1,350,389 for 84 grants (high: $400,000; low: $100).
Purpose and activities: Giving primarily for juvenile diabetes, education, and for children, youth and social services.
Fields of interest: Performing arts centers; Arts; Higher education; Business school/education; Education; Natural resources; Hospitals (general); Health organizations, association; Diabetes research; Human services; Children/youth, services; Philanthropy/voluntarism.
Limitations: Applications not accepted. Giving primarily in CT, MA, and New York, NY. No grants to individuals, or for scholarships; no loans.
Application information: Contributes only to pre-selected organizations.
Trustees: Emily Phelps Overlock; Katharine Overlock; Willard J. Overlock, Jr.; William J. Overlock III.
EIN: 133247601

2132
Blanche T. Enders Charitable Trust
c/o JPMorgan Chase Bank, Global Foundations Group
345 Park Ave., 4th Fl.
New York, NY 10154
Contact: Jacqueline Elias, V.P., JPMorgan Chase Bank
URL: http://fdncenter.org/grantmaker/enders/

Established in 1964.
Grantmaker type: Independent foundation
Financial data (yr. ended 12/31/02): Assets, $6,261,111 (M); expenditures, $441,869; qualifying distributions, $380,259; giving activities include $375,000 for 16 grants (high: $50,000; low: $10,000).
Purpose and activities: Funding interests include K-12 education, animal welfare, and care for the blind, elderly, or disabled. Education grants are made primarily to groups working in the New York City public school system. The trust also provides annual grants to four organizations named in the trust instrument.
Fields of interest: Elementary/secondary education; Animal welfare; Aging, centers/services; Disabled; Aging.
Types of support: Program development.
Limitations: Giving primarily in New York City. No support for organizations lacking 501(c)(3) status. No grants to individuals.
Application information: See foundation Web site for full application guidelines and requirements.
Deadline(s): Sept. 1
Board meeting date(s): Nov.
Final notification: Dec.
Trustee: JPMorgan Chase Bank.
EIN: 136164229

2133
The Charles Engelhard Foundation ▼
645 5th Ave., Ste. 712
New York, NY 10022 (212) 935-2433
Contact: Mary F. Ogorzaly, Secy.

Incorporated in 1940 in NJ.
Donor(s): Charles Engelhard,‡ Engelhard Hanovia, Inc., and others.

Grantmaker type: Independent foundation
Financial data (yr. ended 12/31/01): Assets, $106,537,073 (M); expenditures, $10,490,884; qualifying distributions, $10,022,217; giving activities include $9,880,734 for 274 grants (high: $800,000; low: $100; average: $1,000–$50,000).
Purpose and activities: Emphasis on higher and secondary education, and cultural, medical, religious, wildlife, and conservation organizations.
Fields of interest: Arts; Secondary school/education; Higher education; Natural resources; Animals/wildlife, preservation/protection; Biomedicine; Medical research, institute; Religion.
Types of support: General/operating support; Continuing support; Annual campaigns; Capital campaigns; Building/renovation; Endowments; Program development; Conferences/seminars; Publication; Research; Matching/challenge support.
Limitations: Applications not accepted. Giving on a national basis. No support for international organizations. No grants to individuals.
Application information: Giving only to organizations known to the trustees. Unsolicited requests for funds not considered.
Board meeting date(s): Quarterly
Officers and Trustees: * Charlene B. Engelhard,* Pres.; Mary F. Ogorzaly, Secy.; Edward G. Beimfohr,* Treas.; Sophie Engelhard Craighead; Anne E. de la Renta; Anthony J. Gostkowski; Susan O'Connor; Sally E. Pingree.
Number of staff: 1 full-time professional; 2 part-time professional.
EIN: 226063032

2134
Richard C. & Susan B. Ernst Foundation
c/o Bloomingdale Properties, Inc.
641 Lexington Ave., 29th Fl.
New York, NY 10022-4599 (212) 838-0211
Contact: John L. Ernst, Pres.

Established in 1957 in NY.
Grantmaker type: Independent foundation
Financial data (yr. ended 12/31/02): Assets, $2,153,295 (M); gifts received, $2,500; expenditures, $251,521; qualifying distributions, $216,585; giving activities include $216,250 for 18 grants (high: $50,000; low: $250).
Purpose and activities: Giving primarily to health associations, for education, and for conservation.
Fields of interest: Museums (ethnic/folk arts); Arts; Higher education; Education; Natural resources; Health organizations, association; Native Americans/American Indians.
Limitations: Giving on a national basis. No grants to individuals.
Application information:
Deadline(s): None
Board meeting date(s): Quarterly
Officers: John L. Ernst, Pres.; John Fletcher, V.P.
Number of staff: None.
EIN: 136153761

2135
The Armand G. Erpf Fund, Inc.
c/o Condon, O'Meara, McGinty, and Donnelly, LLP
3 New York Plz., 18th Fl.
New York, NY 10004
Application address: c/o Grant Admin., 640 Park Ave., New York, NY 10021

Incorporated in 1951 in NY.
Donor(s): Armand G. Erpf,‡ Erpf Charitable Trust.
Grantmaker type: Independent foundation
Financial data (yr. ended 11/30/02): Assets, $10,342,549 (M); gifts received, $289,260; expenditures, $192,736; qualifying distributions, $685,721; giving activities include $566,598 for 97 grants (high: $50,000; low: $50).
Purpose and activities: Giving primarily for wildlife conservation, arts and culture, hospitals, and human services.
Fields of interest: Performing arts; Arts; Higher education; Environment; Animals/wildlife, preservation/protection; Hospitals (general); Human services.
Limitations: Giving primarily in New York, NY; funding also in Washington, DC. No grants to individuals, or for endowment funds.
Application information: Application form not required.
Initial approach: Proposal
Copies of proposal: 1
Deadline(s): None
Board meeting date(s): Quarterly
Officers: Sue Erpf Van de Bovenkamp, Pres.; Gina Caimi, Secy.; Armand B. Erpf, Treas.
Directors: Louis Auchincloss; Cornelia A. Erpf; Robert B. Oxnam; Roger D. Stone; Sophie Marr Verons.
EIN: 136085594

2136
R. S. Evans Foundation, Inc.
(formerly Evans Family Foundation, Inc.)
c/o Deutsche Bank Trust Co.
P.O. Box 1297, Church St. Sta.
New York, NY 10008

Established in 1997 in CT.
Donor(s): Robert S. Evans.
Grantmaker type: Independent foundation
Financial data (yr. ended 12/31/02): Assets, $6,262,317 (M); expenditures, $381,792; qualifying distributions, $322,792; giving activities include $315,000 for 25 grants (high: $50,000; low: $1,000).
Purpose and activities: Giving primarily for education.
Fields of interest: Education; Environment.
Limitations: Applications not accepted. No grants to individuals.
Application information: Contributes only to pre-selected organizations.
Officers: Robert S. Evans, Pres.; Susan C. Evans, Secy.
Directors: Ashley Reid Evans; Jonathan Perry Evans; Michael Robinson.
Trustee: Deutsche Bank Trust Co.
EIN: 061480414

2137
Richard & Rebecca Evans Foundation
c/o Lee Dyeing Co.
111 Woodside Ave.
Gloversville, NY 12078

Established in 1955 in NY.
Donor(s): Rebecca M. Evans,‡ Richard Evans II.‡
Grantmaker type: Independent foundation
Financial data (yr. ended 03/31/02): Assets,
$1,930,222 (M); expenditures, $123,822;
qualifying distributions, $100,391; giving
activities include $100,951 for 127 grants (high:
$22,045; low: $10).
Purpose and activities: Giving for the arts,
education, the environment, health, community
development, and religious organizations.
Fields of interest: Arts; Education; Environment;
Health care; Health organizations, association;
Community development; Religion.
Limitations: Applications not accepted. Giving
primarily in CT, MA, and NY. No grants to
individuals.
Application information: Contributes only to
pre-selected organizations.
Officers and Directors:* Morris Evans,* Pres.;
Alexandra E. Willard, V.P.; Nancy Evans Hays,*
Secy.-Treas.
EIN: 146016221

2138
The William Ewing Foundation
c/o U.S. Trust, Tax Dept.
114 W. 47th St.
New York, NY 10036
Contact: William Ewing, Jr.
Application address: c/o Isabelle Fitzpatrick, 342
Madison Ave., Ste. 702, New York, NY
10173-0799; FAX: (212) 852-3377

Established in 1957 in NY.
Donor(s): Moore P. Huffman.
Grantmaker type: Independent foundation
Financial data (yr. ended 12/31/01): Assets,
$2,736,583 (M); expenditures, $187,877;
qualifying distributions, $170,358; giving
activities include $152,375 for grants.
Purpose and activities: Giving primarily for
education, animal welfare and religion.
Fields of interest: Elementary/secondary
education; Education; Animal welfare; Roman
Catholic agencies & churches; General
charitable giving.
Limitations: Giving primarily in the greater
metropolitan New York, NY, area, including
Long Island.
Application information:
  Initial approach: Letter
  Deadline(s): None
Trustees: Grace E. Huffman; Jessie E. Phillips;
U.S. Trust.
EIN: 136065580

2139
F. & J.S. Fund, Inc.
c/o Amex TBS
1185 Ave. of the Americas
New York, NY 10036

Established in 1969.
Donor(s): David W. and Sadie Klau Foundation.
Grantmaker type: Independent foundation

Financial data (yr. ended 12/31/02): Assets,
$9,899,979 (M); gifts received, $55,500;
expenditures, $843,736; qualifying distributions,
$732,259; giving activities include $699,302 for
210 grants (high: $250,000; low: $100).
Purpose and activities: Giving primarily for
education and health care.
Fields of interest: Higher education; Law
school/education; Animals/wildlife, fisheries;
Hospitals (general).
Limitations: Applications not accepted. Giving
primarily in NY. No grants to individuals.
Application information: Contributes only to
pre-selected organizations.
Officers: Felice K. Shea, Pres. and Treas.; Steven
J.C. Shea, V.P.
EIN: 237042425

2140
Falconwood Foundation, Inc.
565 5th Ave.
New York, NY 10017 (212) 984-1444
Contact: Stanley Lefkowitz, V.P.

Established in 1987 in NY.
Donor(s): Henry G. Jarecki.
Grantmaker type: Independent foundation
Financial data (yr. ended 12/31/02): Assets,
$774,045 (M); gifts received, $50,300;
expenditures, $587,095; qualifying distributions,
$586,915; giving activities include $586,600 for
40 grants (high: $100,000; low: $250).
Purpose and activities: Giving primarily for
education and conservation.
Fields of interest: Higher education; Education;
Natural resources; Philanthropy/voluntarism.
Limitations: Giving on a national basis.
Application information: Application form not
required.
  Initial approach: Proposal
  Deadline(s): None
Officers and Directors:* Henry G. Jarecki,*
Pres. and Treas.; Stanley Lefkowitz, V.P. and
Secy.; Andrew R. Jarecki.
EIN: 133456475

2141
Marianne G. Faulkner Trust
(formerly Marianne Galliard Faulkner Trust)
c/o JPMorgan Chase Bank
345 Park Ave., 4th Fl.
New York, NY 10154 (212) 464-2443
Contact: Monica Neal, V.P., JPMorgan Bank
FAX: (212) 464-2305; E-mail:
neal_monica@jpmorgan.com

Trust established in 1959 in VT.
Donor(s): Marianne Gaillard Faulkner.‡
Grantmaker type: Independent foundation
Financial data (yr. ended 03/31/02): Assets,
$9,112,857 (M); expenditures, $537,034;
qualifying distributions, $473,521; giving
activities include $445,916 for 22 grants (high:
$85,923; low: $2,500).
Purpose and activities: Annual funding for
groups identified by the donor; limited funding
available to other groups primarily near or in
Woodstock, VT within program areas.
Fields of interest: Education; Environment;
Aging, centers/services.
Types of support: General/operating support;
Program development.

Limitations: Giving primarily in the Woodstock,
VT, area. No grants to individuals, or for
endowment funds.
Application information: Prefer matching or
1-time grants.
  Initial approach: Proposal
  Copies of proposal: 1
  Deadline(s): June 1st
  Board meeting date(s): As required
  Final notification: Dec. 31
Trustee: JPMorgan Chase Bank.
Number of staff: 2 full-time support.
EIN: 136047458

2142
Ferguson Foundation, Inc.
333 Ellicott St.
Buffalo, NY 14203-1678 (716) 852-2010
Contact: Whitworth Ferguson, Jr., Pres.

Established in 1954 in NY.
Donor(s): Ferguson Construction Co.
Grantmaker type: Independent foundation
Financial data (yr. ended 12/31/02): Assets,
$1,672,763 (M); gifts received, $73,000;
expenditures, $99,291; qualifying distributions,
$96,057; giving activities include $94,317 for
53 grants (high: $12,300; low: $300).
Purpose and activities: Giving for art school,
youth services, higher education, federated
giving programs, and human services.
Fields of interest: Arts; Education, fund raising;
Education; Natural resources; Animal welfare;
Hospitals (general); Health organizations,
association; Youth development, centers/clubs;
Human services; Federated giving programs;
Christian agencies & churches; General
charitable giving.
Types of support: Annual campaigns; Capital
campaigns; Endowments.
Limitations: Giving limited to Buffalo, NY.
Application information: Application form not
required.
  Initial approach: Letter or proposal
  Copies of proposal: 1
  Deadline(s): None
  Board meeting date(s): Quarterly
Officers: Whitworth Ferguson, Jr., Pres. and
Treas.; Donald R. Ferguson, Secy.
Trustee: Dorothy Ferguson.
Number of staff: 1 part-time support.
EIN: 166043861

2143
John J. Flemm Foundation, Inc.
c/o Sidney Horn
208 W. 30th St., Ste. 1105
New York, NY 10001

Established in 1974 in NY.
Donor(s): John J. Flemm.‡
Grantmaker type: Independent foundation
Financial data (yr. ended 01/31/03): Assets,
$2,980,795 (M); expenditures, $182,073;
qualifying distributions, $178,324; giving
activities include $157,500 for 111 grants (high:
$13,300; low: $100).
Purpose and activities: Giving primarily for
Jewish organizations and temples.
Fields of interest: Arts; Elementary/secondary
education; Education; Environment; Animal
welfare; Animals/wildlife,

preservation/protection; Hospitals (general); Health care; Health organizations, association; Medical research, association; Human services; Jewish federated giving programs; Science; Jewish agencies & temples.
Limitations: Applications not accepted. Giving on a national basis.
Application information: Contributes only to pre-selected organizations.
Officers and Trustees:* Daniel Harris,* Pres.; Judith Post,* V.P. and Secy.; Michael Harris,* Treas.; Avery Harris; Leona Post.
EIN: 237348789

2144
Fludzinski Foundation
c/o Thales
140 Broadway, 45th Fl.
New York, NY 10005

Donor(s): Marek T. Fludzinski.
Grantmaker type: Independent foundation
Financial data (yr. ended 12/31/02): Assets, $0 (M); expenditures, $651,010; qualifying distributions, $651,010; giving activities include $651,010 for 10 grants (high: $350,000; low: $1,000).
Purpose and activities: Giving primarily for international relief, as well as for the training and use of assistance dogs; funding also for social services.
Fields of interest: Animals/wildlife; Disasters, search/rescue; Human services; Human services; International relief.
Limitations: Giving primarily in CA and NY; some funding nationally.
Trustees: Marek T. Fludzinski; Laurel Galgano.
EIN: 134147622

2145
The Roger W. Follett Foundation, Inc.
c/o Lee, Emerson & Ferrarese, LLP
35 W. Main St.
Norwich, NY 13815 (607) 334-2247
Contact: Thomas C. Emerson, V.P.

Established in 1995 in NY.
Donor(s): Roger Follet.‡
Grantmaker type: Independent foundation
Financial data (yr. ended 12/31/01): Assets, $4,749,535 (M); expenditures, $441,509; qualifying distributions, $384,443; giving activities include $387,462 for 18 grants (high: $155,396; low: $500).
Purpose and activities: Giving primarily for a YMCA, a hospital, and a classic car museum; funding also for education, animal welfare, social services, and religion.
Fields of interest: Museums (specialized); Education; Animal welfare; Hospitals (general); Human services; YM/YWCAs & YM/YWHAs; Protestant agencies & churches; Roman Catholic agencies & churches.
Limitations: Giving primarily in Chenango County, NY. No grants to individuals.
Application information: Application form required.
Deadline(s): None
Officers: Peter V. Smith, Pres.; Thomas C. Emerson, V.P.; Edward J. Lee, Secy.-Treas.
EIN: 223270901

2146
The Ford Foundation ▼
320 E. 43rd St.
New York, NY 10017 (212) 573-5000
Contact: Secy.
FAX: (212) 351-3677; E-mail: office-secretary@fordfound.org; URL: http://www.fordfound.org

Incorporated in 1936 in MI.
Donor(s): Henry Ford,‡ Edsel Ford.‡
Grantmaker type: Independent foundation
Financial data (yr. ended 09/30/02): Assets, $9,345,030,447 (M); expenditures, $640,007,274; qualifying distributions, $620,392,481; giving activities include $505,738,032 for 2,892 grants (high: $8,000,000; low: $9), $1,212,508 for 77 grants to individuals (high: $103,271; low: $17), $1,381,093 for employee matching gifts and $14,300,000 for 8 loans/program-related investments.
Purpose and activities: The foundation's mission is to serve as a resource for innovative people and institutions worldwide. Its goals are to: strengthen democratic values, reduce poverty and injustice, promote international cooperation, and advance human achievement. Grants are made primarily within three broad categories: (1) asset building and community development; (2) knowledge, creativity, and freedom; and (3) peace and social justice. Local needs and priorities, within these subject areas, determine program activities in individual countries.
Fields of interest: Media/communications; Film/video; Museums; Performing arts; Dance; Theater; Music; Arts; Education, research; Early childhood education; Elementary school/education; Secondary school/education; Higher education; Education; Natural resources; Environment; Reproductive health; Reproductive health, sexuality education; Public health, STDs; AIDS; Abuse prevention; Legal services; Employment; Agriculture; Housing/shelter, development; Youth development; Human services; Women, centers/services; Minorities/immigrants, centers/services; International economic development; Arms control; Foreign policy; International human rights; International affairs; Race/intergroup relations; Civil rights; Urban/community development; Rural development; Community development; Philanthropy/voluntarism; Social sciences; Economics; Law/international law; International studies; Public policy, research; Government/public administration; Public affairs, citizen participation; Leadership development; Religion, interfaith issues; Minorities; Women; Immigrants/refugees; Economically disadvantaged.
International interests: Caribbean; Eastern Europe; Russia; Africa; Latin America; Asia; Middle East; Southeast Asia.
Types of support: General/operating support; Continuing support; Endowments; Program development; Conferences/seminars; Professorships; Publication; Seed money; Curriculum development; Fellowships; Internship funds; Research; Technical assistance; Consulting services; Program evaluation; Program-related investments/loans; Employee

matching gifts; Grants to individuals; Exchange programs; Matching/challenge support.
Limitations: Giving on an international basis, including the U.S., Eastern Europe, Africa and the Middle East, Asia, Russia, Latin America and the Caribbean. No support for programs for which substantial support from government or other sources is readily available, or for religious sectarian activities as such. No grants for routine operating costs, construction or maintenance of buildings, or undergraduate scholarships; graduate fellowships generally channeled through grants to universities or other organizations; no grants for purely personal or local needs.
Publications: Annual report (including application guidelines), Informational brochure (including application guidelines), Newsletter, Occasional report.
Application information: Prospective applicants are advised to review the foundation's Web site for information or current funding guidelines. Foreign applicants should contact foundation for addresses of its overseas offices, through which they must apply. Application form not required.
Initial approach: Brief letter of inquiry
Copies of proposal: 1
Deadline(s): None
Board meeting date(s): Jan., May, and Sept.
Final notification: Initial indication as to whether proposal falls within program interests within 6 weeks
Officers and Trustees:* Paul A. Allaire,* Chair.; Susan V. Berresford,* Pres.; Barron M. Tenny, Exec. V.P., Genl. Counsel, and Secy.; Barry D. Gaberman, Sr. V.P.; Linda B. Strumpf, V.P. and C.I.O.; Alison R. Bernstein, V.P., Knowledge, Creativity, and Freedom; Melvin L. Oliver, V.P., Asset Bldg. and Community Devel.; Bradford K. Smith, V.P., Peace and Social Justice; Alexander Wilde, V.P., Comm.; Nicholas M. Gabriel, Treas. and Dir., Financial Svcs.; Nancy P. Feller, Assoc. Genl. Counsel; Alain J.P. Belda; Afsaneh M. Beschloss; Anke A. Ehrhardt; Kathryn S. Fuller; Juliet V. Garcia; Wilmot G. James; Yolanda Kakabadse; Wilma P. Mankiller; Richard Moe; Yolanda T. Moses; Luis G. Nogales; Deval L. Patrick; Ratan N. Tata; Carl B. Weisbrod; W. Richard West.
Number of staff: 317 full-time professional; 1 part-time professional; 295 full-time support; 2 part-time support.
EIN: 131684331
Recent environmental and animal welfare grants:
2146-1 Africa Resources Trust, Johannesburg, South Africa, $41,000. To facilitate attendance and participation of community representatives from countries in Southern Africa at World Summit on Sustainable Development. 2002.
2146-2 African Conservation Centre, Nairobi, Kenya, $200,000. For technical assistance, networking and asset-building activities to help communities managing natural resources in East Africa. 2002.
2146-3 African Conservation Centre, Nairobi, Kenya, $15,000. To publish proceedings of March 2002 East African Regional Conference on Ecotourism and book on ecotourism in East Africa. 2002.
2146-4 African Wildlife Foundation, DC, $150,000. For community conservation centers and other activities to increase

cooperation in management of shared resources in transboundary regions of Southern Africa. 2002.

2146-5 Alliance for Metropolitan Stability, Minneapolis, MN, $75,000. To promote environmentally sound and socially equitable land-use practices and affordable housing reform in Minneapolis/Saint Paul metropolitan region. 2002.

2146-6 Alternatives for Community and Environment (ACE), Roxbury, MA, $75,000. For strategic planning and organizational development and to expand base of community leadership and environmental justice activism in low-income areas and communities of color in Greater Boston. 2002.

2146-7 Amazon Alliance for Indigenous and Traditional Peoples of the Amazon Basin, DC, $300,000. For general support for partnership between indigenous organizations in the Amazon and environmental and human rights organizations in global North. 2002.

2146-8 Appalachian Mountain Club, Boston, MA, $100,000. To participate in and provide technical assistance to Bronx River Alliance, community-based partnership to restore, protect and improve Bronx River corridor and greenway. 2002.

2146-9 Arid Lands Information Network-Eastern Africa, Nairobi, Kenya, $81,000. For training workshop and technical support to community-based organizations on use of satellite broadcasting technology to expand access to information resources. 2002.

2146-10 Ashoka Trust for Research in Ecology and the Environment, Bangalore, India, $500,000. For endowment support to strengthen social science research capacity and to support innovative action research in Eastern Himalayas. 2002.

2146-11 Aspen Institute, DC, $550,000. To serve as managing partner of Community-Based Forestry Demonstration Project. 2002.

2146-12 Association for Rural Advancement, Pietermaritzburg, South Africa, $100,000. For staff development and to conduct research on land tenure in KwaZulu Natal. 2002.

2146-13 Association for the Protection of the Environment, Cairo, Egypt, $100,000. To improve environmental and health conditions and economic opportunities for Zabaleen community providing informal solid waste management services in Cairo. 2002.

2146-14 Association for the Renewal of the Community and Ecology-Based Law (HuMa), Jakarta, Indonesia, $154,500. To promote legal literacy and research on land and other natural resources in Indonesia. 2002.

2146-15 Association of Uganda Professional Women in Agriculture and the Environment, Kampala, Uganda, $50,000. For capacity building of women as strategy to alleviate poverty and ensure food security in Uganda. 2002.

2146-16 Bank Information Center, DC, $200,000. To monitor response of international financial institutions to September 11th. 2002.

2146-17 Bethel New Life, Chicago, IL, $300,000. For asset-based community development that combines environmental

restoration and brownfields redevelopment with workforce development and smart growth in metropolitan Chicago. 2002.

2146-18 Bharatiya Kisan Sangh, Ranchi, India, $45,506. For program of environmental awareness and livelihood development in mining areas of Lohardagga and Gumla districts of Jharkhand. 2002.

2146-19 Bluefields Indian and Caribbean University, Bluefields, Nicaragua, $100,000. To help multi-ethnic and indigenous communities of Nicaragua's Atlantic Coast map land-use, develop management plans for protected areas and create community networks to advocate for local development. 2002.

2146-20 Brazilian Biodiveristy Fund (FUNBIO), Rio de Janeiro, Brazil, $1,000,000. To create endowment fund for core support. 2002.

2146-21 Bumi Manira Foundation, Bandung, Indonesia, $150,000. To develop participatory methodologies and media services for community-based natural resources management in eastern Indonesia. 2002.

2146-22 Canopy Productions, Brooklyn, NY, $20,000. To complete Daughters of the Canopy, documentary on two Amazonian women's organizations and their struggle to protect the environment for their survival. 2002.

2146-23 CEE Bankwatch Network, Krakow, Poland, $200,000. For strategic planning to promote public participation and increase access to information on policies of international financial institutions in Central and Eastern Europe. 2002.

2146-24 Center for Biodiversity and Indigenous Knowledge, Yunnan, China, $51,800. To host Third Montane Mainland Southeast Asia Symposium. 2002.

2146-25 Center for Biodiversity and Indigenous Knowledge, Yunnan, China, $10,000. For Vietnamese participation in Third Montane Mainland Southeast Asia Symposium. 2002.

2146-26 Center for Community Development Studies, Kunming, China, $190,000. For institutional development and long-term study of poverty dynamics in upland villages in Yunnan Province. 2002.

2146-27 Center for International Environmental Law, DC, $500,000. For partnerships with public interest environmental and human rights law groups in developing countries. 2002.

2146-28 Center for International Environmental Law, DC, $400,000. For activities of Geneva office to expand understanding of global trade and environmental processes among representatives of poor communities and build their capacity to influence processes. 2002.

2146-29 Center for International Forestry Research, Bogor, Indonesia, $415,000. For workshops, research support, sabbaticals and other activities to build capacity among Indonesian forestry professionals. 2002.

2146-30 Center for International Forestry Research, Bogor, Indonesia, $130,000. To strengthen operations of grassroots organizations in Latin America focused on natural resource management, particularly forest resources. 2002.

2146-31 Center for Natural Resources and Environmental Studies, Hanoi, Vietnam, $10,000. To survey graduates of center's short courses on Human Dimensions of Sustainable Uplands Development, conducted between 1995 and 2001. 2002.

2146-32 Center for Neighborhood Technology, Chicago, IL, $65,700. For Faith in Place, woman-led innovative model of inter-religious engagement in environmental, economic and community sustainability. 2002.

2146-33 Center of Alternative Technologies for the Atlantic Forest, Vicosa, Brazil, $175,000. For research, technical assistance and training on sustainable development, with special attention to needs of small-scale producers in Atlantic Forest region of Minas Gerais state. 2002.

2146-34 Centre for Applied Social Sciences Trust, Harare, Zimbabwe, $45,000. To produce play for World Summit on Sustainable Development depicting community experiences of environmental governance in 10 years since Rio Earth Summit. 2002.

2146-35 Centre for Applied Social Sciences Trust, Harare, Zimbabwe, $35,000. For Theatre for Africa to produce play for World Summit on Sustainable Development depicting community experiences of environmental governance in 10 years since Rio Earth Summit. 2002.

2146-36 Centre for World Solidarity, Secunderabad, India, $99,953. To establish regional resource centers for and produce training materials on joint forest management. 2002.

2146-37 Centro por la Justicia, San Antonio, TX, $100,000. To develop and implement community-driven process to assist in clean-up and redevelopment of decommissioned Kelly Airforce Base in San Antonio, Texas. 2002.

2146-38 Certified Forest Products Council, Portland, Oregon, $300,000. For general support for activities to build markets for certified forest products in the U.S. and Canada. 2002.

2146-39 China Agricultural University, Beijing, China, $89,100. For informal forum on forestry governance and local participation. 2002.

2146-40 Chinese Academy of Forestry, Beijing, China, $48,800. To assess potential impact of proposed reforms of Chinese forest taxation system. 2002.

2146-41 Chinese Academy of Sciences, Beijing, China, $19,636. For training course on natural resource management in a market economy. 2002.

2146-42 Chinese Academy of Social Sciences, Beijing, China, $30,000. For international conference on improving management of natural and cultural heritage resources in China. 2002.

2146-43 Chinese Academy of Social Sciences, Center for Environment and Development, Beijing, China, $45,000. To create platform for strengthening public participation in environmental policymaking in China. 2002.

2146-44 Coalition for Womens Economic Development and Global Equality, DC, $200,000. To strengthen grassroots understanding of women's issues in trade, environment, and globalization. 2002.

2146-45 Coalition of Black Trade Unionists, DC, $100,000. To expand Community Action and Response Against Toxics (CARAT) program to promote environmental quality in communities of color. 2002.

2146-46 College of the Southern Border, San Cristobal de las Casas, Mexico, $250,000. To create two academic networks that expand research, technical services and advocacy to strengthen and diversify coffee production and forest management by communities in southern Mexico. 2002.

2146-47 College of the Southern Border, San Cristobal de las Casas, Mexico, $60,000. To explore key elements necessary for successful promotion of in situ conservation of maize genetic diversity in southern Mexico. 2002.

2146-48 Collins Center for Public Policy, Miami, FL, $400,000. For Growth Partnership to promote equitable, environmentally sustainable communities in South Florida and for Funders Network for Smart Growth and Livable Communities to diversify its membership. 2002.

2146-49 Commonweal, Bolinas, CA, $50,000. For publication of Fair Growth: Building Mixed Income Communities. 2002.

2146-50 Communities for a Better Environment, Oakland, CA, $150,000. For Environmental Justice Leadership Program and to implement its communications and organizational capacity-building plan. 2002.

2146-51 Community Conservation and Development Initiative, Lagos, Nigeria, $268,000. For technical assistance to community-based environmental enterprises and to coordinate Nigerian civil society participation in World Summit on Sustainable Development. 2002.

2146-52 Community Forestry Indigenous-Campesino Coordinating Association, San Jose, Costa Rica, $350,000. For field exchanges and to develop management plans in agroecological farming and community forestry for indigenous, black and peasant groups throughout Central America. 2002.

2146-53 Community Forestry Indigenous-Campesino Coordinating Association, San Jose, Costa Rica, $50,000. To help indigenous, black and peasant organizations conduct debates, formulate proposals and design strategies for their participation in World Summit on Sustainable Development. 2002.

2146-54 Community Resource Group, Fayetteville, AR, $200,000. For ShelterHome project to demonstrate feasibility of developing affordable homes for families in Texas colonias. 2002.

2146-55 Community Resource Group, Fayetteville, AR, $105,000. To evaluate impact of receivership program that provides homeowners in Texas colonias with clear titles to their properties. 2002.

2146-56 Community Resources, Baltimore, MD, $200,000. For core support for Greening-Green Jobs-Strong Communities Project to improve total environment of Shaw and Anacostia neighborhoods of Washington, D.C. through community-based urban forestry. 2002.

2146-57 Conference Board, New York, NY, $700,000. For Business Enterprises for Sustainable Travel (BEST), initiative designed to promote sustainable tourism in developing countries and in low-income communities in the U.S. 2002.

2146-58 Conservation Fund, Arlington, VA, $450,000. For Resourceful Communities Program to build grassroots capacity to blend economic and social improvement with environmental conservation in tackling rural poverty in North Carolina. 2002.

2146-59 Consortium for Study and Development of Participation, Lombok, Indonesia, $55,000. To promote collaborations among communities, nongovernmental organizations and government with respect to natural resource management in Nusa Tenggara. 2002.

2146-60 Coordinating Body for the Indigenous Peoples Organizations of the Amazon Basin, Quito, Ecuador, $100,000. To enhance participation of Amazonian indigenous peoples in World Summit for Sustainable Development (WSSD). 2002.

2146-61 Council for Human Ecology Kenya, Nairobi, Kenya, $100,000. To bring together traditional healers and foresters to identify, cultivate, and market indigenous medicinal plants in Western Kenya. 2002.

2146-62 Development Initiatives Network, Lagos, Nigeria, $150,000. For general support to strengthen institutional capacity and to expand public interest law and environment programs. 2002.

2146-63 Development Research Communication and Services Centre, Calcutta, India, $33,456. For research and documentation on local biological resources and local resource management practices to maintain biodiversity. 2002.

2146-64 Development Support Centre, Ahmadabad, India, $350,000. For endowment support to consolidate and institutionalize role as resource organization for other research and advocacy NGOs in field of natural resources management. 2002.

2146-65 Development Training Institute, Baltimore, MD, $50,000. To convene roundtable discussion on sustainable communities and brownfields redevelopment. 2002.

2146-66 Earth Action Network, Norwalk, CT, $50,000. For special issue of e/The Environment Magazine on ecotourism, to be published in conjunction with World Ecotourism Summit. 2002.

2146-67 Earth Council, Earth Council Foundation, San Jose, Costa Rica, $275,000. For multi-stakeholder analysis in eight former Soviet economies of consistency between World Trade Organization agreements and equitable, sustainable national development. 2002.

2146-68 EarthRights International, DC, $400,000. To train minority community members to represent themselves in global forums. 2002.

2146-69 East African Wildlife Society, Nairobi, Kenya, $50,000. To administer feasibility study for proposed East African Conservation Trust. 2002.

2146-70 Eco-Friends Society, Kanpur, India, $62,710. To reduce pollution and restore ecological health of Kanpur stretch of river Ganga. 2002.

2146-71 ECOA-Ecology and Action, Rio de Janeiro, Brazil, $108,000. For applied research, public consultation and publications activities of Rios Vivos Coalition and to hold coalition's International Congress of Affiliates. 2002.

2146-72 Ecotrust Canada, Vancouver, Canada, $200,000. For technical support to monitor and evaluate Iisaak Forest Resources and other activities to strengthen involvement of Canadian First Nations communities in forest management certification. 2002.

2146-73 Education and Training Board of East Kalimantan, Samarinda, Indonesia, $57,000. To develop learning agenda for public servants and legislators on community-based natural resource management in provincial Education and Training Agency. 2002.

2146-74 Education and Training Board of East Kalimantan, Samarinda, Indonesia, $55,000. For action research, planning and dissemination of information regarding community-based natural resource management in Nunukan, East Kalimantan. 2002.

2146-75 Education and Training Board of East Kalimantan, Samarinda, Indonesia, $50,000. For action research on hand-over of natural resource management to local communities in East Kalimantan Regional Planning Board. 2002.

2146-76 Energy Programs Consortium, DC, $49,170. To plan national demonstration program to build capacity of providers of home improvement products and services to serve low-income and disadvantaged homeowners at significant scale. 2002.

2146-77 Environmental Foundation Limited, Colombo, Sri Lanka, $265,347. To initiate activities and address injustices faced by disadvantaged groups and communities in Sri Lanka. 2002.

2146-78 Environmental Grantmakers Association, New York, NY, $122,000. To improve diversity among environmental grantmakers and strengthen Funders Network on Trade and Globalization and for general support. 2002.

2146-79 Environmental Justice Networking Forum, Braamfontein, South Africa, $165,000. For activities to enable members to effectively participate in World Summit on Sustainable Development and to host Soweto-based international week of environmental justice activities. 2002.

2146-80 Environmental Law Alliance Worldwide (E-LAW) Indonesia Foundation, Jakarta, Indonesia, $15,000. To strengthen legal literacy on natural resources management in Indonesia. 2002.

2146-81 Environmental Media Services, DC, $120,000. To provide media and communications services for foundation grantees attending World Summit on Sustainable Development. 2002.

2146-82 Environmental Quality International, London, England, $18,000. To help Arab journalists prepare for and participate in World Summit on Sustainable Development in Johannesburg and related meetings. 2002.

2146-83 Environmental Research Institute of Amazonia, Belem, Brazil, $175,000. For core support for research, advocacy, public forums and education on forest conservation, sustainable development and climate change in the Amazon. 2002.

2146-84 Federal University of Acre Foundation, Rio de Janeiro, Brazil, $85,000. For start-up support for Center for Indigenous Studies and to strengthen sustainable development initiative with indigenous communities of western Amazon. 2002.

2146-85 Federal University of Para, Belem, Brazil, $115,000. To strengthen program of applied research, public forums, training and dissemination on sustainable development, public policy and local governance in eastern Amazon. 2002.

2146-86 Federation of Agencies of Social and Educational Assistance, Rio de Janeiro, Brazil, $190,000. For applied research, public forums, publications and dissemination on sustainable development and democratic governance in Brazil. 2002.

2146-87 Federation of Southern Cooperatives and Land Assistance Fund (FSC/LAF), Epes, AL, $160,000. For Black Belt Legacy Forestry Program to help African-American farmers realize potential of their forest asset base. 2002.

2146-88 Fenton Communications, DC, $150,000. For outreach activities to increase viewership and public awareness of Bill Moyers' special report, NAFTA's Powerful Little Secret, report on NAFTA's Chapter 11 and its impact upon local communities. 2002.

2146-89 Fideicomiso Fondo para la Biodiversidad (Trust Fund for Biodiversity), Mexico City, Mexico, $400,000. To generate innovative models for collective and sustainable management, harvesting and marketing of non-conventional natural products and in situ conservation of biological diversity. 2002.

2146-90 Find Aid for the Aged, Project FIND, New York, NY, $20,000. For Gardening For Life, horticultural therapy program provided semi-weekly for seniors at Woodstock Hotel, residence for low-income seniors located in midtown Manhattan. 2002.

2146-91 Florida International University, Miami, FL, $20,000. To design and implement prototype database and information system for registering and monitoring ongoing community-based forestry activities throughout Mexico. 2002.

2146-92 Forest Trends Association, DC, $500,000. For activities to strengthen community-based natural asset building through Forest Stewardship Council certification and payments for environmental services. 2002.

2146-93 Forest Trends Association, DC, $20,000. To conduct intensive, facilitated eight-week structured electronic conference on future goals and governance structure of FSC worldwide. 2002.

2146-94 Forest Trust, Santa Fe, NM, $200,000. To integrate community forestry into new national fire management plan. 2002.

2146-95 Forum for Justice, Kathmandu, Nepal, $500,000. To improve environmental governance in Nepal through research and training programs on environmental justice issues. 2002.

2146-96 Friends of the Earth International, Amsterdam, Netherlands, $155,000. To improve governance structure and strengthen international network to address global environmental policy issues. 2002.

2146-97 Friends of the Earth Nigeria, Benin City, Nigeria, $250,000. For start-up support for community resource center in Bayelsa State to serve as repository of information on environmental issues affecting Niger Delta for all stakeholders and to develop and implement new media strategy. 2002.

2146-98 Galilee Society: The Arab National Society for Health Research and Services, Shefa-Amr, Israel, $1,000,000. To expand environmental and public health programs for Palestinian Israelis. 2002.

2146-99 Global Village of Beijing, Beijing, China, $20,000. For meeting for Chinese NGOs to reflect on outcomes of World Summit on Sustainable Development. 2002.

2146-100 GLOBE USA, DC, $100,000. To produce pre- and post-conference publications on World Summit on Sustainable Development, ensure high-level participation by legislative leaders and develop post-Summit work program. 2002.

2146-101 Gramin Vikas Pratishthan, Raipur, India, $205,000. For activities to improve local governance and promote environmental, economic and social justice in Madhya Pradesh and Chattisgarh. 2002.

2146-102 Gramin Vikas Pratishthan, Raipur, India, $62,000. For research, awareness, advocacy and legal literacy programs on people's rights over natural resources. 2002.

2146-103 Greater Yellowstone Coalition, Bozeman, MT, $100,000. For activities to reduce rural sprawl development, promote conservation and enhanced environmental quality and improve social equity and livelihoods. 2002.

2146-104 Group for Environmental Monitoring, Braamfontein, South Africa, $220,000. For final support for Conservation and Development Program and for organizational and program development and endowment feasibility study. 2002.

2146-105 Grupo de Estudios Ambientales, Mexico City, Mexico, $130,000. To implement water and soil conservation program with indigenous communities and document program experiences to expand learning and training resources for sustainable natural resource management. 2002.

2146-106 Guizhou Academy of Agricultural Sciences, Guiyang, China, $143,600. To explore new approaches to scaling up successful experiences in community-based natural resource management. 2002.

2146-107 Guizhou Academy of Social Sciences, Guiyang, China, $41,000. To facilitate and document participatory village planning process for conversion of agricultural land to grassland or forest in uplands of Guizhou Province. 2002.

2146-108 Guizhou Normal University, Guiyang, China, $26,100. For Guizhou Participatory Reflection and Action (PRA) Network to conduct capacity-building training workshops for its members on issues of environment and development. 2002.

2146-109 Gujarat Ecological Educational and Research (GEER) Foundation, Ahmadabad, India, $122,000. To expand and strengthen Joint Forest Management program in Gujarat. 2002.

2146-110 Gujarat Institute of Development Research, Ahmadabad, India, $197,759. To facilitate systematic consultations among key individuals and institutions in West and Central region and to develop consensus on common development concerns and priorities for future. 2002.

2146-111 Hanoi Agricultural University, Hanoi, Vietnam, $200,000. For research on asset building in Vietnam's northern uplands in social sciences at University. 2002.

2146-112 Himalayan Consortium for Himalayan Conservation (HIMCON), New Delhi, India, $66,000. For activities to regenerate natural resource base and revitalize economy of newly formed state of Uttaranchal. 2002.

2146-113 Honduran Federation of Agroforestry Cooperatives, Honduras, $120,000. To establish learning program among Honduran community forestry leaders and member organizations to broaden their vision on natural resource management, market access and organizational capacity. 2002.

2146-114 Hue University, College of Agriculture and Forestry, Hue, Vietnam, $137,000. To develop, test and extend participatory strategies through which ethnic minority communities in Vietnam's central uplands can build natural and human assets. 2002.

2146-115 Humane Society of the United States, DC, $185,000. To optimize participation of foundation grantees in World Summit on Sustainable Development by creating linkages between Summit's formal and informal events. 2002.

2146-116 Indian National Trust for Art and Cultural Heritage, New Delhi, India, $39,388. For activities to enforce environmental rights of citizens of Dahanu Taluka, predominantly tribal area in Thane district of Maharashtra. 2002.

2146-117 Indigenous Community Enterprises, Flagstaff, AZ, $40,000. To plan and develop staff capacity to implement programs combining community-based forestry strategies with culturally appropriate enterprises and technology in Navajo Nation. 2002.

2146-118 Indonesian Environmental Forum, Jakarta, Indonesia, $620,000. To maximize involvement and participation of civil society institutions in World Summit on Sustainable Development. 2002.

2146-119 Indonesian Environmental Forum, Jakarta, Indonesia, $15,000. For community workshop on Forest Stewardship Council's certification principles. 2002.

2146-120 Institute for Local Self-Reliance, DC, $125,000. For core support for Waste to Wealth Program to help communities design and implement environmentally sustainable waste management plans that also promote economic development. 2002.

2146-121 Institute for Management and Certification of Agriculture and Forestry, Sao Paulo, Brazil, $280,000. For general support to strengthen programs of research, advocacy and training that promote conservation-based community development in the Amazon region. 2002.

2146-122 Institute for Socio-Economic Studies, Brasilia, Brazil, $75,000. For core support for activities of Brazil Network on Multilateral Financial Institutions. 2002.

2146-123 Institute for Sustainable Forestry, Redway, CA, $150,000. For core support for Collaborative Learning Circle to promote sustainable development strategies and community-based forestry. 2002.

2146-124 Institute of Development Studies, Jaipur, India, $250,000. To promote alternative ecologically sensitive, people-friendly development interventions. 2002.

2146-125 Institute of Environment and Development, Beijing, China, $2,068,700. To implement Pathways for Higher Education program in China. 2002.

2146-126 Institute of International Education, New York, NY, $650,000. To provide logistical and administrative support to participants in both final preparatory meeting for World Summit on Sustainable Development and Summit itself. 2002.

2146-127 Institute of International Education, New York, NY, $430,000. To provide logistical and administrative support to participants in World Summit on Sustainable Development and related Global Forum. 2002.

2146-128 Institute of International Education, New York, NY, $200,000. To facilitate participation of foundation grantees and partners in preparatory meetings for World Summit on Sustainable Development. 2002.

2146-129 Institute of Man and Environment in the Amazon, Belem, Brazil, $150,000. For applied research, assessments and technical assistance to enhance sustainable economic alternatives for traditional forest peoples. 2002.

2146-130 Institute on Taxation and Economic Policy, DC, $250,000. For research, education and outreach to build constituency for Smart Growth practices within organized labor. 2002.

2146-131 International Association for the Study of Common Property, Gary, Indiana, $159,000. For travel and related support for developing country participants in IASP's biennial conference, regional programming and general support. 2002.

2146-132 International Centre for Environment and Development, Switzerland, $150,000. To establish electronic network and provide training to enable Egyptian nongovernmental organizations to exchange information and experiences and strengthen their development efforts. 2002.

2146-133 International Centre for Integrated Mountain Development, Kathmandu, Nepal, $365,700. To develop information packages on best practices learned from its research and demonstration projects for its partners in Hindu Kush utilizing traditional and indigenous forms of communications. 2002.

2146-134 International City/County Management Association, DC, $125,000. To document and assess federal environmental demonstration projects, facilitate conversations among stakeholders and

provide research and technical assistance to demonstration communities. 2002.

2146-135 International Development Research Centre of Canada, Ottawa, Canada, $100,000. To convene 2003 International Forum on Ecosystem Approaches to Human Health in Montreal, Canada. 2002.

2146-136 International Fund for Chinas Environment, DC, $38,500. For second NGO Forum on U.S.-China Environmental Cooperation. 2002.

2146-137 International Institute for Environment and Development, London, England, $42,944. For applied research to improve livelihoods of women cashew workers affected by import liberalization in Kerala and Tamil Nadu. 2002.

2146-138 International Network for Bamboo and Rattan, Beijing, China, $80,000. For community-based bamboo development project in Guizhou Province. 2002.

2146-139 International Possibilities Unlimited, Silver Spring, MD, $225,000. To ensure participation of marginalized groups in World Summit on Sustainable Development held in Barbados. 2002.

2146-140 International Rivers Network, Berkeley, CA, $600,000. For core support for International Committee on Dams, Rivers and People to implement and follow up on recommendations of World Commission on Dams. 2002.

2146-141 International Union for Conservation of Nature and Natural Resources, Gland, Switzerland, $295,000. To prepare case studies and other materials to argue for special status for sacred places at Fifth World Parks Congress. 2002.

2146-142 International Union for Conservation of Nature and Natural Resources, Gland, Switzerland, $100,000. For activities to help its Southern African network articulate relationship among conservation, poverty and sustainable development at World Summit on Sustainable Development. 2002.

2146-143 International Union for Conservation of Nature and Natural Resources, Gland, Switzerland, $60,000. To unravel enigmas of enterprises and challenge some myths about how ordinary people survive macro-economic failure and famine of kind that afflict African continent today. 2002.

2146-144 ISA-Socio-Environmental Institute, Sao Paulo, Brazil, $75,000. For applied research, public consultations, seminars and publications to enhance civic participation at World Summit for Sustainable Development. 2002.

2146-145 Jaagriti, India, $26,738. To promote cultivation of threatened indigenous agricultural varieties and apply and preserve associated indigenous knowledge about them. 2002.

2146-146 Jefferson Center for Education and Research, Wolf Creek, Oregon, $90,000. To conduct community organizing and capacity-building activities for contingent workers in natural resource management in Pacific Northwest. 2002.

2146-147 Jose Bonifacio University Foundation, Rio de Janeiro, Brazil, $150,000. For comparative study on impact of international environment networks on local management of industrial pollution. 2002.

2146-148 Kabaka Foundation, Kampala, Uganda, $75,000. For planning activities to develop institution-building, grantmaking and asset development strategies. 2002.

2146-149 Kahublagan Sang Panimalay, Iloilo, Philippines, $200,000. For technical support to teams of watershed managers and program of public education for communities living and farming in watersheds. 2002.

2146-150 Kapwa Upliftment Foundation, Davao, Philippines, $200,000. For general support for activities to help upland communities within Mount Apo Natural Park gain tenure to land they till and employ more sustainable forms of agroforestry. 2002.

2146-151 Kathmandu University, Kathmandu, Nepal, $250,000. To endow chair in environmental science. 2002.

2146-152 Kelola, Sulawesi, Indonesia, $63,000. To strengthen organizational skills and advocacy capacity of coastal people in North Sulawesi. 2002.

2146-153 Kenya Forestry Research Institute, Nairobi, Kenya, $200,000. For applied research network on community-based forest management and technical assistance to help communities implement forest management plans. 2002.

2146-154 Kibale Forest Foundation, DC, $25,000. To build capacity of rural communities around Kibale National Park in Uganda to support marketing of Wild Coffee Project brand. 2002.

2146-155 Labor Community Strategy Center, Los Angeles, CA, $100,000. For general support for activities to promote environmental health and justice in Los Angeles County. 2002.

2146-156 Land Access Movement of South Africa (LAMOSA), Marshalltown, South Africa, $100,000. To implement land rights and land access program for farm workers and labour tenants in Transvaal. 2002.

2146-157 Lembaga Aliansi Relawan Untuk Penyelamatan Alam, Yogyakarta, Indonesia, $25,000. For conflict mediation between forest-dependent communities and Java State Forest Corporation and to foster development of collaborative community forest management. 2002.

2146-158 Liberty Hill Foundation, Santa Monica, CA, $500,000. For grant-making activities of Environmental Justice Fund and to expand Environmental Justice Institute. 2002.

2146-159 Lijiang Culture and Gender Research Center, China, $20,000. For general support for research on gender and development among minority communities in northwest Yunnan. 2002.

2146-160 M.C. Mehta Environmental Foundation, New Delhi, India, $452,000. For environmental legal and policy research program and to build capacity of members of Panchayati Raj institutions, nongovernmental organizations and young public interest lawyers. 2002.

2146-161 Maasailand Preservation Trust, Nairobi, Kenya, $50,000. For planning activities to develop effective structural and management systems. 2002.

2146-162 Mediterranean Information Office for Environment, Culture and Sustainable Development, Athens, Greece, $50,000. To help Middle Eastern and North African civil society organizations prepare for and participate in 2002 World Summit on Sustainable Development and related meetings. 2002.

2146-163 Methodus Consulting, Oaxaca, Mexico, $75,000. To foster learning, strengthen community technical and organizational capacities and design advocacy strategies to support community-based management of non-timber forest products in Southern Mexico. 2002.

2146-164 Ministry of Health of Vietnam, 10-80 Committee, Hanoi, Vietnam, $243,000. To locate, assess and prioritize dioxin-contaminated areas in southern Vietnam and develop strategies to protect high-risk groups from exposure. 2002.

2146-165 Missouri Botanical Garden, Saint Louis, MO, $100,000. To collaborate with Kunming Institute of Botany on activities to strengthen capacity for and policy relevance of ethnobotany practice in Yunnan Province in China. 2002.

2146-166 Moscow State University, Moscow, Russia, $10,000. To develop and implement communications and outreach program to increase public demand for and access to university's Botanic Garden. 2002.

2146-167 Mountain Association for Community Economic Development, Berea, KY, $50,000. For strategic planning and organizational development in Appalachia areas. 2002.

2146-168 Mountain Institute, DC, $175,000. To develop interpretive and educational materials drawing upon diverse views of cultural and spiritual significance of mountains for U.S. national parks. 2002.

2146-169 National Black Environmental Justice Network, Detroit, MI, $75,000. For Healthy and Safe Communities Campaign to build awareness among African-Americans and other communities of color on link between pollution and poor health. 2002.

2146-170 National Environmental Trust, DC, $50,000. To develop national trade policy campaign. 2002.

2146-171 National Forest Foundation, DC, $160,000. For small grants program in community forestry. 2002.

2146-172 National Land Committee, Braamfontein, South Africa, $200,000. To plan, coordinate and host South African, African and international civil society and NGO activities with respect to World Summit on Sustainable Development. 2002.

2146-173 National Land Committee, Braamfontein, South Africa, $100,000. To host and support senior south African scholar while he completes manuscript on land reform in region. 2002.

2146-174 National Land Committee, Braamfontein, South Africa, $100,000. To ensure participation of landless and other marginalized Southern African groups in World Summit on Sustainable Development. 2002.

2146-175 National Multipurpose Development Society, Ranchi, India, $35,774. To evaluate groundwater quality and conduct awareness and advocacy programs around groundwater issues in Ranchi district of Jharkhand. 2002.

2146-176 National Studies Center on Alternative Development (CENDA), Santiago, Chile, $63,600. For inter-regional workshop, Social Protection in an Insecure Era: South-South Exchange on Alternative Social Policy. 2002.

2146-177 National Wildlife Federation, Reston, VA, $300,000. For core support for Vermont Family Forests Partnerships to use certification, labeling and marketing to increase value of forest products and develop community-equity forestland ownership model. 2002.

2146-178 National Wildlife Federation, Reston, VA, $20,000. To research and develop video documentary on certified wood and fair trade coffee. 2002.

2146-179 Native Action, Lame Deer, MT, $150,000. To protect area water resources and ensure long-term supply of clean water for area residents. 2002.

2146-180 Natural Resources and Environment Foundation, Buenos Aires, Argentina, $45,000. To promote use of existing institutional and legal mechanisms for defense of environmental rights in Argentina. 2002.

2146-181 Natural Resources Law Institute, Jakarta, Indonesia, $100,000. For general support for research and technical assistance with respect to legal and policy aspects of natural resources management. 2002.

2146-182 Nature Conservancy, Arlington, VA, $100,000. For small grants fund to support environmental initiatives in indigenous reserves in Brazilian Amazon and strengthen resource management capacities of indigenous organizations. 2002.

2146-183 Nautilus of America, Berkeley, CA, $300,000. For final support to develop and promote new approach to global economic governance that balances private investor rights with greater societal objectives. 2002.

2146-184 Nautilus of America, Berkeley, CA, $275,000. For core support for East Asia Initiative to Reduce Global Insecurity, to increase security and reduce dangers of war, including nuclear war in region. 2002.

2146-185 Nav Bharat Jagriti Kendra, Hazaribag, India, $35,564. For research, awareness and intervention program to rehabilitate environment in Hazaribag. 2002.

2146-186 Nepal Water Conservation Foundation, Kathmandu, Nepal, $300,000. For endowment support for program to build social capacity through interdisciplinary research on resource management issues including capacity of women and Dalits to participate in social dialogues. 2002.

2146-187 Network for Environmental and Sustainable Development in Africa, Abidjan, Ivory Coast, $200,000. To coordinate activities of Civil Society Organization-Africa Steering Committee for World Summit on Sustainable Development. 2002.

2146-188 New School University, New York, NY, $75,000. For planning process to establish interdisciplinary environmental studies program. 2002.

2146-189 Ngong Road Forest Sanctuary Trust, Nairobi, Kenya, $30,000. To develop environmental education program and design tourist facilities. 2002.

2146-190 Nkuzi Development Association, Pietersburg, South Africa, $200,000. For general support for activities to promote land reform and tenure security in Northern Province. 2002.

2146-191 North Carolina Association of Black Lawyers, Land Loss Prevention Project, Durham, NC, $200,000. For legal assistance to poor, primarily non-white rural communities facing environmental threats. 2002.

2146-192 North Carolina State University, Natural Resources Leadership Institute, Raleigh, NC, $200,000. For initiative, Building Community Leadership on Environmental Justice Issues in North Carolina. 2002.

2146-193 Northern Arizona University, Center for Sustainable Environments, Flagstaff, AZ, $350,000. To develop, implement and evaluate initiative, Promoting Sustainable Cultural Solutions to Life on the Colorado Plateau. 2002.

2146-194 Northern Forest Center, Concord, NH, $120,000. To explore and document lessons learned from developing proposals for two innovative funds to encourage sustainable forestry and from changing market conditions that prevented implementation. 2002.

2146-195 Occidental College, Los Angeles, CA, $20,000. For community building initiatives for transportation, environment, land use, and cultural change. 2002.

2146-196 Oxfam America, Boston, MA, $250,000. For Mexico-based pilot program to increase supply of high quality Fair Trade Certified coffee. 2002.

2146-197 Partnership for Indigenous Peoples Environment (PIPE), New York, NY, $100,000. For general support. 2002.

2146-198 Partnership for Indigenous Peoples Environment (PIPE), New York, NY, $50,000. To publish conference report from its worldwide meeting on constructing indigenous people's networks and global directory of indigenous people's organization and for regional workshops in Africa. 2002.

2146-199 Peoples Commission on Environment and Development, New Delhi, India, $80,000. To conduct series of public hearings on environmental injustice issues. 2002.

2146-200 Perhimpunan Pengembangan Pesantren dan Masyarakat, Jakarta, Indonesia, $42,000. To help local government, communities and institutions develop collaborative agreements in furtherance of sustainable and equitable natural resources management in Sumbawa District, West Nusa Tenggara. 2002.

2146-201 Pro-Natura USA, Vienna, VA, $125,000. For applied and policy research, extension and dissemination to promote sustainable development in Atlantic Forest of Rio de Janeiro state. 2002.

2146-202 Pronatura, Mexico, $70,000. To develop statewide plan for Community-Based Forestry (CBF), consolidate model CBF project and facilitate communication among key stakeholders in forestry sector of Chiapas. 2002.

2146-203 Public Interest Law Foundation, Colombo, Sri Lanka, $102,400. To formulate, advocate and assist in implementing environmental justice strategy in Sri Lanka. 2002.

2146-204 Puerto Rican Legal Defense and Education Fund, New York, NY, $200,000. For start-up support for Latino Environmental Justice Project. 2002.

2146-205 Rainforest Action Network, San Francisco, CA, $290,000. For advocacy among forest products producers and retailers to give preference to FSC certified products. 2002.

2146-206 Regional Community Forestry Training Center for Asia and the Pacific, Bangkok, Thailand, $810,000. For general support to develop and implement mechanisms for identifying, enhancing and sharing practices and ideas for promoting community forestry on regional basis. 2002.

2146-207 Regional Community Forestry Training Center for Asia and the Pacific, Bangkok, Thailand, $300,000. To promote community forestry in Asia in context of World Summit for Sustainable Development. 2002.

2146-208 Rehabilitation of Arid Environments Charitable Trust, Nairobi, Kenya, $300,000. For general support for activities to improve livelihoods and reduce poverty by developing and implementing practical strategies for reclamation and sustainable management of drylands. 2002.

2146-209 Resources Conflict Institute, Nakuru, Kenya, $100,000. For seminars and research on sustaining dialogue for peace in Great Lakes Region. 2002.

2146-210 Rural Action, Trimble, OH, $300,000. To create opportunities for low-income rural residents in Appalachia to generate economic returns from their woodland parcels by cultivating, managing and marketing non-timber forest products. 2002.

2146-211 Rural Action Committee, Nelspruit, South Africa, $190,000. For land rights and capacity-building programs in Mpumalanga and Northwest provinces. 2002.

2146-212 Rural Research and Farmer Consultancy, Oaxaca, Mexico, $100,000. To consolidate community land use and natural resource management programs and develop schemes for sustainable use of biodiversity through payment for environmental services. 2002.

2146-213 School of Desert Sciences, Jodhpur, India, $49,253. To improve working conditions and health status of mine workers in Rajasthan and develop capacities of mine workers to set up cooperatives. 2002.

2146-214 Seventh Generation Fund for Indian Development, Arcata, CA, $75,000. To organize, support and coordinate participation of North American indigenous peoples in World Summit on Sustainable Development. 2002.

2146-215 Shorebank Enterprise Group Pacific, Ilwaco, WA, $500,000. For ongoing efforts to build conservation economy by providing access to capital, development services, information and knowledge to community institutions and community-based entrepreneurs. 2002.

2146-216 Silver City Grant County Economic Development Corporation, Silver City, NM, $150,000. For core support for Jobs and Biodiversity coalition to foster viable local economies using by-products of forest restoration. 2002.

2146-217 Sobrevivencia, Asuncion, Paraguay, $200,000. To train local civic leaders in cross-border regions of South America to engage in global governance forums and civil society discussions and for general support. 2002.

2146-218 Society of Hill Resource Management School, Bihar, India, $250,000. For general support for village-based training and demonstration programs on management of common property resources and for staff development. 2002.

2146-219 Society of Pollution and Environmental Conservation Scientists, Dehra Dun, India, $38,814. To promote equitable, community-based ecotourism in Nanda Devi Biosphere Reserve. 2002.

2146-220 Soil and Water Conservation Foundation, Cebu, Philippines, $150,000. For public education and coordination of citizen participation in management of critical watersheds and Rajah Sikatuna National Park in Bohol, Philippines. 2002.

2146-221 Southern University and A & M College, Baton Rouge, LA, $50,000. For National Forestry Minority Outreach and Education Conference. 2002.

2146-222 Stichting Fern, Fern Foundation, Moreton-in-Marsh, England, $100,000. To strengthen support for Forest Stewardship Councils' certification standards and disseminate information on differences between FSC standards and industry-based alternatives. 2002.

2146-223 Stichting Forest Peoples Programme, Moreton-in-Marsh, England, $150,000. For activities to integrate indigenous people in global policy dialogues. 2002.

2146-224 Sustainable Development Forum, Mexico, $130,000. For technical, financial and marketing innovations to strengthen agricultural production and sustainability in marginalized indigenous communities of Chiapas. 2002.

2146-225 Sustainable Development Forum, Mexico, $25,000. For start-up support for Intercultural Education Collective of Chiapas indigenous educational organizations. 2002.

2146-226 Sustainable Development Forum, Mexico, $20,000. For strategic planning for program to improve finance and marketing for indigenous peasant agro-ecological and craft enterprises. 2002.

2146-227 Sustainable Northwest, Portland, Oregon, $300,000. For core support for Healthy Forests Healthy Communities partnership. 2002.

2146-228 Tanzania Association of Women Leaders in Agriculture and the Environment, Dar es Salaam, Tanzania, $50,000. For general support for training and technical assistance to build women's capacity to participate in formulation of agricultural, natural resource and environmental policy. 2002.

2146-229 Tarun Bharat Sangh, Alwar, India, $300,000. For endowment support for water harvesting initiatives in desert areas of Rajasthan. 2002.

2146-230 Tata Energy Research Institute, School of Advanced Studies, New Delhi, India, $420,000. For endowed chair and for start-up research on contemporary issues in resource management. 2002.

2146-231 Tebtebba Foundation, Baguio, Philippines, $70,000. For Indigenous Peoples Summit to prepare for World Summit on Sustainable Development. 2002.

2146-232 Tellus Institute for Resource and Environmental Strategies, Boston, MA, $25,000. For conference on bridging gaps in global public policy networks. 2002.

2146-233 Third World Institute of Ecological Studies, Quito, Ecuador, $60,000. For conference on Free Trade of Americas Agreement and role of parliamentarians. 2002.

2146-234 Tides Center, San Francisco, CA, $125,000. For CorpWatch Climate Justice Initiative, which seeks to redefine climate change debate in U.S. from discussion of energy use to one of human rights and environmental justice. 2002.

2146-235 Tides Foundation, San Francisco, CA, $50,000. To complete Forest Stewardship Council certification standards for British Columbia. 2002.

2146-236 Toxic Comedy Pictures, New York, NY, $150,000. To complete production on Blue Vinyl, documentary on relationship between consumers and industry, and launch My House is Your House, accompanying community and civic education campaign. 2002.

2146-237 Training and Community Development Alternatives, Chihuahua, Mexico, $100,000. To ensure participation by small civil society organizations in United Nations Financing for Development Conference. 2002.

2146-238 Transfair USA, Oakland, CA, $200,000. For general support for activities to expand Certified Fair Trade movement in United States. 2002.

2146-239 Transportation Alternatives, New York, NY, $20,000. For Midtown Bicycle, Pedestrian and Transit Campaign. 2002.

2146-240 Tudor City Greens, New York, NY, $15,000. For general support for operation and maintenance of Tudor City Parks. 2002.

2146-241 United Nations Development Programme, New York, NY, $60,000. For Equator Initiative to promote and facilitate community participation in World Summit on Sustainable Development. 2002.

2146-242 United Nations Educational, Scientific and Cultural Organization (UNESCO), Paris, France, $200,000. For multidisciplinary research on links between land-use/land-cover changes and watershed services in India. 2002.

2146-243 University of California, Berkeley, CA, $328,500. For visiting scholar on community-based natural management. 2002.

2146-244 University of California, Berkeley, CA, $75,000. For Just Forest Initiative to document preliminary community and faith-based meetings and organize Just Forest Summit on equity and justice in forestry and forest management. 2002.

2146-245 University of California, Santa Cruz, CA, $185,000. For convening of grassroots community groups on globalization. 2002.

2146-246 University of Michigan, School of Natural Resources and Environment, Ann

Arbor, MI, $250,000. For newly instituted environmental justice initiative. 2002.

2146-247 University of Namibia, Windhoek, Namibia, $55,000. To host international workshop on Strategies for Sustainable Resources Development. 2002.

2146-248 University of Oregon, Eugene, Oregon, $200,000. For technical assistance, facilitation and research activities of Ecosystem Workforce Program with respect to restoration forestry. 2002.

2146-249 University of Pretoria, Centre for Indigenous Knowledge, Pretoria, South Africa, $100,000. To develop foundation for establishment of household-based commercially viable projects in partnership with rural communities. 2002.

2146-250 University of Quintana Roo, Chetumal, Mexico, $120,000. To develop mechanisms for outreach and collaboration between University and community-based forestry organizations in Mayan Zone. 2002.

2146-251 University of Sao Paulo, Sao Paulo, Brazil, $180,000. For Nucleus for Research on Brazilian Wetlands to strengthen program of research, extension and publications in support of community-based sustainable development in Atlantic Forest. 2002.

2146-252 University of Stellenbosch, Stellenbosch, South Africa, $100,000. For research on indigenous plant commercialization and domestication. 2002.

2146-253 University of the Autonomous Regions of the Caribbean Coast of Nicaragua, Managua, Nicaragua, $50,000. To help multi-ethnic and indigenous communities of Nicaragua's Atlantic Coast map land-use, develop management plans for protected areas and create community networks to advocate for local development. 2002.

2146-254 University of the Witwatersrand, Johannesburg, South Africa, $50,000. For exploratory study of community preparedness for wildfires in Southern Africa. 2002.

2146-255 Uruguayan Study Center of Appropriate Technologies, Montevideo, Uruguay, $165,000. To strengthen and promote collaboration among Latin American groups on issues of globalization and economic integration and to increase and diversify Latin American voices in global arena. 2002.

2146-256 Utthan Development Action Planning Team, Ahmadabad, India, $100,000. For eco-restoration and medicinal plant-based enterprise development in Uttar Pradesh. 2002.

2146-257 Vallecitos Mountain Refuge, Taos, NM, $300,000. To host series of retreats for environmental justice leaders and activists. 2002.

2146-258 Vitae Civilis Institute for Development, Environment and Peace, Sao Paulo, Brazil, $180,000. For applied research, public consultations, workshops and publications to enhance civic participation at World Summit for Sustainable Development (WSSD). 2002.

2146-259 Vitae Civilis Institute for Development, Environment and Peace, Sao Paulo, Brazil, $66,000. For multimedia public information campaign at World Summit for Sustainable Development and concurrent NGO Global Forum. 2002.

2146-260 Vitoria Amazonica Foundation, Manaus, Brazil, $285,000. For general support for research, advocacy and education on conservation-based community development in northern Amazon and to train youth in lutemaking and woodworking. 2002.

2146-261 Watershed Research and Training Center, Hayfork, CA, $300,000. For community forestry activities integrating forest restoration on public lands, community capacity building for sustainable livelihoods and job training. 2002.

2146-262 Weaver Press, Harare, Zimbabwe, $10,000. To import, distribute and promote scholarly volume to inform civil society debate about Zimbabwe's economic future. 2002.

2146-263 West Harlem Environmental Action, New York, NY, $125,000. For Young Women of Color Reproductive and Environmental Health Project and to participate in national, cross-cultural reproductive rights collective. 2002.

2146-264 West Harlem Environmental Action, New York, NY, $125,000. To produce and disseminate publications and video arising from conference, Human Genetics, Environment, and Communities of Color: Ethical and Social Implications. 2002.

2146-265 West Harlem Environmental Action, New York, NY, $75,000. For Whom Shall I Fear, multimedia, historical survey of environmental justice movement. 2002.

2146-266 West Kutai Regency, East Kalimantan, Indonesia, $125,000. To coordinate decentralized, community-based natural resource planning and management in East Kalimantan. 2002.

2146-267 Wildlands Trust, Hilton, South Africa, $150,000. For core support for Species, People and Conservation of Environment program in KwaZulu/Natal Province. 2002.

2146-268 Winrock International Institute for Agricultural Development (WIIAD) India, New Delhi, India, $109,041. To improve capacity of local communities in India to manage state forest lands. 2002.

2146-269 Women Acting Together for Change (WATCH), Kathmandu, Nepal, $25,000. For targeted program to build awareness and encourage dialogue on community forestry issues in Nepal's Terai region. 2002.

2146-270 World Agroforestry Centre, Nairobi, Kenya, $280,000. For collaborative project on watershed management in Yunnan Province. 2002.

2146-271 World Resources Institute, DC, $425,000. For research and communications on globalization, environment and development issues. 2002.

2146-272 World Resources Institute, DC, $115,000. To help NGOs and funders participate strategically in World Summit on Sustainable Development. 2002.

2146-273 World Summit on Sustainable Development (WSSD) Civil Society Company, Johannesburg, South Africa, $500,000. To host Global Forum of civil society organizations being held in conjunction with United Nations World Summit on Sustainable Development. 2002.

2146-274 World Wide Fund for Nature-Brazil, Amazon Protected Areas Program, Brazil, $1,000,000. To expand network of protected and sustainable use areas in world's largest rainforest and establish Protected Areas Endowment Fund. 2002.

2146-275 World Wide Fund for Nature-Eastern Africa, Nairobi, Kenya, $225,000. To develop region-wide strategy for community-based conservation encompassing coastal forests of Kenya, Tanzania and northern Mozambique. 2002.

2146-276 World Wildlife Fund/Conservation Foundation, DC, $300,000. For competitive conservation fund to support local initiatives for sustainable development in Valdivian Temperate Forest for technical and networking assistance to selected projects. 2002.

2146-277 Worldwide Indigenous Science Network, Lahaina, HI, $458,000. To convene international meetings of traditional elders and their apprentices at sacred sites to discuss global issues. 2002.

2146-278 Yayasan Agro Ekonomika, Jakarta, Indonesia, $225,000. For national secretariat of Forum for Popular Participation and for Forum's activities to further participatory approaches to rural development and local-level democracy. 2002.

2146-279 Yayasan Bina Usaha Lingkungan, Jakarta, Indonesia, $85,150. To communicate success stories on community-based environmental conservation. 2002.

2146-280 Yayasan Gita Pertiwi, Solo, Indonesia, $100,000. For community forestry and poverty alleviation programs in Central Java. 2002.

2146-281 Yayasan Kemala, Jakarta, Indonesia, $100,000. For technical assistance to regional and district-level local intermediary organizations with respect to decentralized natural resources management. 2002.

2146-282 Yayasan Lembaga Binakelola Lingkungan (BIKAL), Indonesia, $50,000. For participatory community-based natural resources management planning in East Kalimantan. 2002.

2146-283 Yayasan Peduli Sesama, Kupang, Indonesia, $94,000. For civic education and training in natural resource management for village leaders in East Nusa Tenggara. 2002.

2146-284 Yunnan University, Rural Development Research Center, Kunming, China, $151,000. To conduct action research on building community assets for community development. 2002.

2147

Fortis Foundation

(formerly AMEV Foundation)
1 Chase Manhattan Plz., 41st Fl.
New York, NY 10005 (212) 859-7000
Contact: Jacqueline Gentile

Established in 1982 in NY.

Donor(s): Time Insurance Co., Fortis Insurance Co., Fortis, Inc., Fortis Benefits Insurance Co.

Grantmaker type: Company-sponsored foundation

Financial data (yr. ended 12/31/02): Assets, $662,514 (M); gifts received, $5,236; expenditures, $320,072; qualifying distributions,

$320,072; giving activities include $318,866 for grants.
Purpose and activities: Funding primarily for college scholarships only for children of individuals who have been employed by Fortis, Inc., or one of its subsidiaries for at least two years. There is also limited funding for New York, NY-based charities concerning education and human services.
Fields of interest: Arts; Higher education; Scholarships/financial aid; Education; Natural resources; Health care; Health organizations, association; Human services; Federated giving programs.
Types of support: General/operating support; Employee matching gifts; Employee-related scholarships.
Application information: Application form not required.
Initial approach: Letter requesting guidelines
Copies of proposal: 1
Deadline(s): None
Trustees: Kerry Clayton; Robert Pollock; Lesley Silvester.
EIN: 133156497

2148
Max & Clara Fortunoff Foundation
70 Charles Lindbergh Blvd.
Uniondale, NY 11553
Contact: Helene Fortunoff, Pres.

Established in 1959 in NY.
Donor(s): Max Fortunoff, Alan Fortunoff,‡ Marjorie Mayrock.‡
Grantmaker type: Independent foundation
Financial data (yr. ended 12/31/02): Assets, $42,114 (M); gifts received, $118,000; expenditures, $150,245; qualifying distributions, $150,240; giving activities include $150,150 for 15 grants (high: $75,000; low: $100).
Purpose and activities: Giving for education, health associations, and Jewish organizations.
Fields of interest: Higher education; Botanical gardens; Health organizations, association; Jewish federated giving programs; Jewish agencies & temples.
Limitations: Giving primarily in NY. No grants to individuals.
Application information:
Initial approach: Letter on organization letterhead
Deadline(s): None
Officer: Helene Fortunoff, Pres.
EIN: 116036903

2149
Evan Frankel Foundation
P.O. Box 5072
East Hampton, NY 11937 (631) 329-2833
Contact: Nancy Wendell
FAX: (631) 329-7102; E-mail: frankelfound@hamptons.com

Established in 1978.
Donor(s): Evan M. Frankel.‡
Grantmaker type: Independent foundation
Financial data (yr. ended 09/30/02): Assets, $4,638,679 (M); expenditures, $3,563,033; qualifying distributions, $3,476,042; giving activities include $3,397,760 for 78 grants

(high: $1,018,400; low: $250; average: $500–$100,000).
Purpose and activities: Giving primarily for higher education in the humanities and the environment.
Fields of interest: Humanities; Higher education; Environment, land resources; Environment.
Types of support: General/operating support; Continuing support; Annual campaigns; Capital campaigns; Building/renovation; Equipment; Land acquisition; Endowments; Professorships; Fellowships; Scholarship funds; Research; Matching/challenge support.
Limitations: Applications not accepted. Giving primarily in Manhattan and Suffolk County, NY and Los Angeles, CA. No grants to individuals.
Application information:
Board meeting date(s): Varies
Officers and Directors:* Ernest Frankel,* Pres.; C. Leonard Gordon,* Secy.; Andrew E. Sabin,* Treas.
Number of staff: 1 full-time professional.
EIN: 132998402

2150
The Regina Frankenberg Foundation
(formerly The Regina Bauer Frankenberg Foundation)
c/o JPMorgan Private Bank, Global Foundations Group
345 Park Ave., 4th Fl.
New York, NY 10154 (212) 464-2443
Contact: Lisa Philip, V.P., JPMorgan Private Bank
FAX: (212) 464-2305; E-mail: neal_monica@JPMorgan.com; URL: http://fdncenter.org/grantmaker/frankenberg/

Established in 1994 in NY.
Donor(s): Regina Bauer Frankenberg.‡
Grantmaker type: Independent foundation
Financial data (yr. ended 12/31/02): Assets, $20,129,244 (M); expenditures, $1,059,826; qualifying distributions, $852,266; giving activities include $865,000 for 18 grants (high: $100,000; low: $20,000).
Purpose and activities: Giving exclusively for animal welfare, particularly for the protection of endangered wild animals or threatened species by supporting conservation and research, and for strengthening the capacity of organizations working to reduce the homelessness, mistreatment and euthanasia of companion animals through adoption, training, spaying/neutering, and other programs.
Fields of interest: Animal welfare; Animals/wildlife, preservation/protection.
Types of support: Capital campaigns; Building/renovation; Program development.
Limitations: Giving primarily in NY, with respect to companion animals; broader focus with respect to wildlife. No grants to individuals.
Application information: Application form not required.
Initial approach: Letter of inquiry or proposal
Copies of proposal: 1
Deadline(s): July 1
Final notification: Dec. 31
Trustee: JPMorgan Chase Bank.
Number of staff: 2 full-time support.
EIN: 133741659

2151
The Freeman Foundation ▼
c/o JPMorgan Private Bank
345 Park Ave., 4th Fl.
New York, NY 10154 (212) 464-2487
Contact: Elizabeth Wong, Prog. Off.
FAX: (212) 464-2305; E-mail: wong_elizabeth@jpmorgan.com

Established in 1978 in VT.
Donor(s): Houghton Freeman, Mansfield Freeman,‡ members of the Freeman family.
Grantmaker type: Independent foundation
Financial data (yr. ended 12/31/02): Assets, $1,112,676,408 (M); expenditures, $85,627,685; qualifying distributions, $82,095,314; giving activities include $81,920,471 for 322 grants (high: $3,554,997; low: $5,000; average: $50,000–$2,000,000).
Purpose and activities: Support primarily for the promotion of international understanding and farmland preservation projects in the state of VT.
Fields of interest: Education, public education; Natural resources; International affairs, goodwill promotion; International studies.
International interests: Asia.
Types of support: General/operating support; Land acquisition; Program development; Fellowships; Exchange programs; Matching/challenge support.
Limitations: Giving primarily in VT for environment and special interest grants; Asian studies grants awarded nationally. No grants to individuals.
Publications: Annual report.
Application information: Application form not required.
Initial approach: Letter
Copies of proposal: 6
Deadline(s): One month before meetings
Board meeting date(s): Quarterly
Officer: Graeme Freeman, Exec. Dir.
Trustees: Doreen Freeman; Houghton Freeman; George B. Snell.
Number of staff: 1 full-time professional; 1 part-time professional.
EIN: 132965090
Recent environmental and animal welfare grants:
2151-1 Catamount Trail Association, Burlington, VT, $20,000. For Trail Protection program. 2002.
2151-2 Garden Conservancy, Cold Spring, NY, $20,600. For Bringing the Japanese garden to the Classroom. 2002.
2151-3 Vermont Land Trust, Montpelier, VT, $5,000,000. For farm and land conservation projects and general support. This grant represents an aggregate total paid throughout the year. 2002.
2151-4 Vermont Leadership Center, Island Pond, VT, $268,000. For Northern Woodlands Magazine/Vermont Leadership Center partnership and Ecosystem Management project. 2002.
2151-5 Vermont Youth Conservation Corps, Waterbury, VT, $150,000. For Youth Corps program. 2002.

2152
Michael Fuchs Charitable Foundation
c/o Michael Fuchs
9 W. 57th St., Ste. 4220
New York, NY 10019

Established in 1997 in NY.
Donor(s): Michael Fuchs.
Grantmaker type: Independent foundation
Financial data (yr. ended 12/31/01): Assets, $1,935,217 (M); expenditures, $605,695; qualifying distributions, $590,142; giving activities include $590,380 for 33 grants (high: $250,000; low: $80).
Purpose and activities: Giving primarily for Jewish organizations, as well as for the arts and social services.
Fields of interest: Museums (art); Arts; Environment, beautification programs; Alzheimer's disease research; Human services; Jewish federated giving programs; Jewish agencies & temples.
Limitations: Applications not accepted. Giving primarily in New York, NY; funding also in Los Angeles, CA. No grants to individuals.
Application information: Contributes only to pre-selected organizations.
Trustee: Michael Fuchs.
EIN: 137068909

2153
Fuji Photo Film U.S.A., Inc. Corporate Giving Program
c/o Corp. Contribs. Dept.
200 Summit Lake Dr.
Valhalla, NY 10595-1356 (800) 755-3854
Additional tel.: (914) 789-8100; URL: http://www.fujifilm.com/JSP/fuji/epartners/AboutResponsibility.jsp

Grantmaker type: Corporate giving program
Purpose and activities: Fuji makes charitable contributions to nonprofit organizations involved with arts and culture, education, the environment, and health and human services. Support is given primarily in areas of company operations.
Fields of interest: Arts; Education; Environment; Health care; Human services.
Types of support: Program development; Scholarship funds; Employee volunteer services; Donated products.
Limitations: Giving primarily in areas of company operations; giving on a national basis for environmental organizations and product donations. No support for political organizations or candidates, legislative advocacy organizations, religious organizations, military agencies, or fraternal, veterans', or social organizations. No grants to individuals, or for continuing support or tickets.
Application information: An application form is available online. Monetary contributions generally do not exceed $5,000; product donations generally do not exceed $1,000 in value. Support is limited to 1 contribution per organization during any given year. Organizations receiving product donations are asked to submit a final report. The Corporate Contributions Department handles giving. A contributions committee reviews all requests. Application form required.

Initial approach: Complete online application form
Copies of proposal: 1
Deadline(s): None
Final notification: 6 to 8 weeks for monetary contributions; 3 months for product donations

2154
The Fund for Animals, Inc.
200 W. 57th St., Ste. 705
New York, NY 10019 (212) 246-2096
Contact: Marian Probst, Pres.
Additional tel.: (888)405-FUND; FAX: (212) 246-2633; E-mail: fundinfo@fund.org; URL: http://www.fund.org

Founded in 1967.
Grantmaker type: Public charity
Financial data (yr. ended 12/31/00): Revenue, $6,890,478; assets, $17,757,676; gifts received, $6,071,777; expenditures, $5,386,201; program services expenses, $4,325,491; giving activities include $793,563 for 32 grants (high: $317,863; low: $50).
Purpose and activities: The fund seeks to alleviate the fear, prevention of pain and the relief of suffering of animals everywhere and to foster humane conduct toward animals and encourage and support the cooperation among all persons interested in humane activities.
Fields of interest: Animal welfare; Animals/wildlife.
Limitations: No support for organizations with annual budgets of more than $250,000.
Officers and Directors:* Marian Probst,* Pres.; Michael Markarian,* Exec. V.P.; Judith Ney,* V.P.; Barbara Brack; Del Donati; Neil Fang; Michael Kilian; Edgar Smith; Kathryn Walker.
EIN: 136218740

2155
Fund for the City of New York, Inc.
121 Ave. of the Americas, 6th Fl.
New York, NY 10013-1590 (212) 925-6675
Contact: Amy Shore, Dir., Comm. and Grants
FAX: (212) 925-5675; URL: http://www.fcny.org

Incorporated in 1968 in NY.
Donor(s): The Ford Foundation.
Grantmaker type: Public charity
Financial data (yr. ended 09/30/00): Assets, $35,834,620 (M); gifts received, $12,235,456; expenditures, $24,966,805; program services expenses, $23,266,154; giving activities include $3,927,759 for grants and $7,996,655 for loans/program-related investments.
Purpose and activities: The Fund of the City of New York, now a public charity, was launched as a private operating foundation by the Ford Foundation in 1968 with the mandate to improve the quality of life for all New Yorkers by improving the performance of government and nonprofit organizations. Through centers on youth, government, and technology, as well as core organizational assistance programs, the fund introduces and helps to implement innovations in policy, programs, practice, and technology that advance the functioning of the public and nonprofit sectors throughout New York City and beyond.

Fields of interest: Environment; Disasters, 9/11/01; Government/public administration.
Types of support: General/operating support; Continuing support; Emergency funds; Program development; Seed money; Technical assistance; Consulting services.
Limitations: Giving limited to New York, NY. No grants to individuals, (except for Public Service Awards), or for academic research, building or endowment funds, scholarships, fellowships, matching gifts, or studies that do not show promise of leading directly to policy or program improvement.
Publications: Application guidelines, Informational brochure, Informational brochure (including application guidelines), Occasional report.
Application information: Accepts NYRAG Common Grant Application Form. Application form not required.
Initial approach: Proposal
Copies of proposal: 2
Deadline(s): None
Board meeting date(s): Approximately 3 times a year in Jan., May, and Oct.
Officers and Directors:* Matina Horner,* Chair.; Mary McCormick, Pres.; Barbara J. Cohn, V.P.; Peter Kleinbard, V.P.; Alfonso Wyatt, V.P.; Abraham Biderman; Allen Boston; Amanda M. Burden; Geoffrey Canada; Robert Caro; Benjamin K. Chu, M.D.; Robert Curvin; Sally Hernandez-Pinero; Robert G.M. Keating; John M.B. O'Connor; Michael J. O'Neill; Judith Shapiro; Daniel Yankelovich.
Number of staff: 151 full-time professional; 6 part-time professional; 17 full-time support; 4 part-time support.
EIN: 132612524

2156
Funding Exchange, Inc.
666 Broadway, Ste. 500
New York, NY 10012 (212) 529-5300
Contact: Charlene Allen, Dir., Grantmaking
FAX: (212) 982-9272; E-mail: Charlene.allen@fex.org; URL: http://www.fex.org

Established in 1979.
Grantmaker type: Public charity
Financial data (yr. ended 06/30/03): Revenue, $6,300,942; assets, $31,836,006 (M); gifts received, $5,062,503; expenditures, $7,207,671; program services expenses, $6,381,278; giving activities include $5,193,150 for grants.
Purpose and activities: The organization is a donor consortium committed to building a permanent institutional and financial base for progressive social change in the U.S. Social change is defined as the process of enabling and encouraging community people to become part of an organization which works on social and economic injustices and educates and challenges the broader community. Social change also means changing the circumstances and the social and institutional systems that lead to oppression.
Fields of interest: Media/communications; Film/video; Environment; Crime/law enforcement; Labor unions/organizations; Safety/disasters; Youth development; International peace/security; Civil rights, gays/lesbians; Race/intergroup relations;

Reproductive rights; Economic development; Community development; Minorities; Native Americans/American Indians; Women.
International interests: Dominican Republic; South Africa; Central America; South America; Israel.
Types of support: General/operating support; Emergency funds; Program development; Publication; Seed money; Technical assistance.
Limitations: Giving on a national and international basis, including the U.S., PR, Central and South America, South Africa, Israel, the Caribbean, Philippines, and Dominican Republic. No support for organizations with access to traditional or mainstream funding sources, community groups with budgets exceeding $500,000, cultural projects or publications not directly connected to organizing campaigns or used as tools for social change organizing, other foundations, or for social services that do not have a capacity for organizing recipients around specific issues. No grants to individuals, or for capital campaigns, equipment, endowments, deficit financing, research projects, or fellowships.
Publications: Application guidelines, Annual report, Grants list, Informational brochure (including application guidelines), Newsletter, Occasional report.
Application information: Accepts NNG Common Grant Application. Application form required.
　Initial approach: See Web site for application information; telephone
　Deadline(s): Postmarked by Mar. 1 for general program; Mar. 15 for Martin-Boro; May 15 for Paul Robeson
　Board meeting date(s): Varies
Directors: Ellen Gurzinsky, Exec. Dir.; Ronald Hanft, Assoc. Dir.
Number of staff: 10 full-time professional; 1 part-time professional; 3 full-time support.
EIN: 133002025

2157
The Ganlee Fund
c/o Lawrence O. Sneag, CPA
20 Windsor Rd.
Great Neck, NY 11021

Established in 1966 in NY.
Grantmaker type: Independent foundation
Financial data (yr. ended 12/31/02): Assets, $1,652,185 (M); expenditures, $95,175; qualifying distributions, $93,091; giving activities include $94,250 for 19 grants (high: $40,000; low: $250).
Purpose and activities: Giving for nature conservation, art and cultural programs, family services and education.
Fields of interest: Museums; Education; Environment; Family planning; Human services; Foundations (private operating).
Limitations: Applications not accepted. Giving primarily in NY. No grants to individuals.
Application information: Contributes only to pre-selected organizations.
Trustee: Sandra I. Van Heerden.
Number of staff: 1 part-time professional; 1 part-time support.
EIN: 136069298

2158
Gerry Charitable Trust
(formerly Peggy N. & Robert G. Gerry Charitable Trust)
c/o McLauglin & Stern, LLP
260 Madison Ave.
New York, NY 10016
Contact: Huyler C. Held, Tr.
FAX: (212) 448-0066; E-mail: hheld@mclaughlinstern.com

Established in NY in 1978.
Donor(s): Roger G. Gerry,‡ Peggy N. Gerry.‡
Grantmaker type: Independent foundation
Financial data (yr. ended 12/31/02): Assets, $2,362,041 (M); gifts received, $3,733,083; expenditures, $907,998; qualifying distributions, $892,998; giving activities include $868,521 for 6 grants (high: $307,621; low: $900; average: $900–$307,621).
Fields of interest: Music; Historic preservation/historical societies; Arts; Higher education; College (community/junior); Botanical gardens; Botany.
Limitations: Applications not accepted. Giving primarily in Long Island, NY; some giving elsewhere in NY. No grants to individuals.
Application information: Unsolicited requests for funds strongly discouraged.
Trustees: Huyler C. Held; The Bank of New York.
Advisory Committee: Huyler C. Held; Robert B. Mackay; Theodore S. Wickersham.
Number of staff: None.
EIN: 136753033

2159
Laurent and Alberta Gerschel Foundation
P.O. Box 42, Planetarium Sta.
New York, NY 10024
Contact: Laurent Gerschel, Pres.

Established in 1981 in NY.
Donor(s): Laurent Gerschel.
Grantmaker type: Independent foundation
Financial data (yr. ended 12/31/01): Assets, $7,167,870 (M); expenditures, $1,134,352; qualifying distributions, $737,639; giving activities include $628,930 for 25 grants (high: $125,000; low: $100).
Purpose and activities: Giving primarily for medical research, particularly nuclear medicine; funding also for Jewish organizations, the arts, the environment and social services.
Fields of interest: Arts; Education; Environment; Zoos/zoological societies; Human services; Hospitals (general); Hospitals (specialty); Health organizations; Medical research, institute; Jewish federated giving programs; Jewish agencies & temples.
Limitations: Giving primarily in NY. No grants to individuals.
Application information:
　Initial approach: Proposal
　Deadline(s): None
Officers: Laurent Gerschel, Pres.; Alberta Gerschel, V.P.; Allan Eagleshan, Mgr.
EIN: 133098507

2160
Patrick A. Gerschel Foundation
720 5th Ave., 10th Fl.
New York, NY 10019-4107 (212) 399-4278

Established in 1986 in NY.
Donor(s): Patrick A. Gerschel.
Grantmaker type: Independent foundation
Financial data (yr. ended 12/31/02): Assets, $5,639,450 (M); expenditures, $538,881; qualifying distributions, $496,748; giving activities include $500,000 for 6 grants (high: $250,000; low: $10,000).
Fields of interest: Museums (art); Historic preservation/historical societies; Arts; Higher education; Natural resources; Botanical gardens; International affairs, goodwill promotion; International affairs.
Types of support: Research.
Limitations: Applications not accepted. Giving primarily in the New York, NY, area. No grants to individuals.
Application information: Unsolicited requests for funds not accepted.
Officer and Director:* Patrick A. Gerschel,* Pres.
EIN: 133317180

2161
Gifford Rudin Foundation, Inc.
47-50 30th St.
Long Island City, NY 11101-3404
(718) 784-5900
Contact: Stephen Rudin, Pres.

Established in 1974.
Donor(s): Milton Paper Co., Inc.
Grantmaker type: Independent foundation
Financial data (yr. ended 04/30/02): Assets, $790,149 (M); gifts received, $5,885; expenditures, $103,493; qualifying distributions, $93,762; giving activities include $94,445 for 51 grants (high: $21,000; low: $500).
Purpose and activities: Giving to Jewish organizations, education and culture.
Fields of interest: Orchestra (symphony); Higher education; Animals/wildlife; Hospitals (general); Cancer; Jewish federated giving programs; Jewish agencies & temples.
Limitations: Giving primarily in NY.
Application information:
　Initial approach: Letter
　Deadline(s): None
Officers: Stephen Rudin, Pres.; Stephen Verp, Secy.
EIN: 237375850

2162
Howard Gilman Foundation, Inc. ▼
111 W. 50th St., 40th Fl.
New York, NY 10020 (212) 307-1073
Contact: Harry Brown, Prog. Assoc.
FAX: (212) 262-4108; E-mail: hbrown@gilman.com; URL: http://www.howardgilman.org

Incorporated in 1981 in DE.
Donor(s): Gilman Investment Co., Gilman Paper Co., Gilman Securities Corp., Howard Gilman,‡ Sylvia P. Gilman.‡
Grantmaker type: Independent foundation

Financial data (yr. ended 12/31/02): Assets, $57,230,970 (M); gifts received, $3,000,000; expenditures, $21,685,567; qualifying distributions, $9,064,133; giving activities include $7,790,750 for 119 grants (average: $1,000-$100,000).

Purpose and activities: The mission of the foundation is to preserve the legacy of Howard Gilman by supporting philanthropic programs in his primary areas of interest: performing arts, wildlife conservation and cardiovascular diseases. The foundation accomplishes its mission through three major activities: 1) managing White Oak Plantation as a refuge for wildlife conservation and a center for residencies by performing artists, and a conference facility for professionals to explore critical issues in the foundation's fields of interest; 2) awarding grants to support creative talent and leadership in the performing arts in New York City; and 3) sustaining research at the Howard Gilman Institute for Valvular Heart Diseases at Weill Medical College of Cornell University.

Fields of interest: Performing arts; Dance; Theater; Music; Arts; Animals/wildlife, preservation/protection; AIDS; Medical research, institute; AIDS research.

Types of support: General/operating support; Continuing support; Building/renovation; Endowments; Program development; Seed money; Curriculum development; Fellowships; Internship funds; Research; Matching/challenge support.

Limitations: Giving primarily in the metropolitan New York, NY, area with emphasis on the arts. No support for political or religious organizations. No grants to individuals, capital investments, fellowships, scholarships, or deficit operations.

Publications: Informational brochure, Program policy statement.

Application information: Applicants must call before submitting letter of inquiry. Application form not required.

> Copies of proposal: 1
> Deadline(s): Varies
> Board meeting date(s): Applications reviewed on a rolling basis
> Final notification: By letter

Officers and Directors:* Isabella Rossellini,* Pres.; Jeffrey Borer, M.D.,* V.P.; Stephen Cropper,* V.P.; Arlene Shuler, Exec. Dir.; Norman Alexander; Pierre Apraxine; Gwendolyn Baker; Bernard D. Bergreen; Donald Bruce; J.D. Campbell; Justin Feldman; John J. Kennedy; Harvey Lichtenstein; William H. Luers; John Lukas; Raymond McGuire; Natalie Moody.

Number of staff: 3 full-time professional.

EIN: 133097486

Recent environmental and animal welfare grants:

2162-1 Audubon Canyon Ranch, Stinson Beach, CA, $20,000. For general support. 2001.

2162-2 Conservation Breeding Specialist Group, Apple Valley, MN, $15,000. For general support. 2001.

2162-3 Fauna and Flora International, San Francisco, CA, $10,000. For general support. 2001.

2162-4 International Rhinoceros Foundation, Columbus, OH, $200,000. For general support. 2001.

2162-5 Marine Biological Laboratory, Woods Hole, MA, $20,000. For general support. 2001.

2163
Peter R. Gimbel & Elga Andersen-Gimbel Memorial Trust

c/o Paneth, Haber & Zimmerman, LLP
622 3rd Ave.
New York, NY 10017

Established in 1996 in NY.

Grantmaker type: Independent foundation

Financial data (yr. ended 12/31/02): Assets, $2,045,502 (M); expenditures, $153,403; qualifying distributions, $114,983; giving activities include $110,000 for 6 grants (high: $25,000; low: $12,500).

Purpose and activities: Giving primarily for environmental causes and social services.

Fields of interest: Natural resources; Environment; AIDS; Human services.

Limitations: Applications not accepted. Giving primarily in New York, NY. No grants to individuals.

Application information: Contributes only to pre-selected organizations.

Trustees: Leslie Gimbel; Thomas S.T. Gimbel; Russell Kagen.

EIN: 137055292

2164
Bernard F. and Alva B. Gimbel Foundation, Inc.

271 Madison Ave., Ste. 606
New York, NY 10016 (212) 895-8050
Contact: Leslie Gimbel, Exec. Dir.
FAX: (212) 895-8052; URL: http://www.gimbelfoundation.org

Incorporated in 1943 in NY.

Donor(s): Bernard F. Gimbel,‡ Alva B. Gimbel.‡

Grantmaker type: Independent foundation

Financial data (yr. ended 12/31/02): Assets, $53,205,272 (M); expenditures, $3,808,560; qualifying distributions, $3,769,553; giving activities include $3,597,400 for 104 grants (high: $100,000; low: $500; average: $1,000-$50,000).

Purpose and activities: Support for education, human services organizations, reproductive rights, the environment, and for advocacy in these areas.

Fields of interest: Elementary/secondary education; Environment; Crime/violence prevention; Offenders/ex-offenders, prison alternatives; Courts/judicial administration; Employment, services; Housing/shelter; Day care; Reproductive rights; Community development, neighborhood development; Economic development; Homeless.

Types of support: General/operating support; Continuing support; Program development.

Limitations: Giving primarily in New York, NY. No grants for scholarships, or for fellowships, no loans.

Application information: Accepts NY/NJ Area Common Application Form or similar format. Application form not required.

> Initial approach: Letter
> Copies of proposal: 1

Deadline(s): Second Wed. in Jan. and first Wed. in Aug. for new grants; second Fri. in Sept. and first Fri. in Feb. for renewals
Board meeting date(s): Dec. and June
Final notification: Varies

Officers and Directors:* Caral G. Lebworth,* Hon. Chair.; Hope G. Solinger,* Hon. Chair.; Leslie Gimbel,* Pres. and Exec. Dir.; Lynn Stern,* V.P.; Stephen D. Greenberg,* Treas.; Judy Mendelsund; Nicholas Stern.

Number of staff: 2 full-time professional; 1 full-time support.

EIN: 136090843

Recent environmental and animal welfare grants:

2164-1 Conservation International, DC, $50,000. For general operating support. 2001.

2164-2 Environmental Defense, New York, NY, $50,000. For general operating support. 2001.

2164-3 Natural Resources Defense Council, New York, NY, $50,000. For general operating support. 2001.

2165
The Herbert & Kitty Glantz Charitable Foundation

16 Court St., 30th Fl.
Brooklyn, NY 11241 (718) 488-9400
Contact: Herbert Glantz, Tr.

Established in 1990 in NY.

Donor(s): Herbert T. Glantz, Kitty Glantz, N. Glantz & Son, Inc.

Grantmaker type: Independent foundation

Financial data (yr. ended 12/31/00): Assets, $24,764 (M); gifts received, $75,000; expenditures, $92,188; qualifying distributions, $88,918; giving activities include $88,920 for 16 grants (high: $38,500; low: $250).

Purpose and activities: Support for arts and culture and hospitals.

Fields of interest: Museums; Arts; Botanical gardens; Hospitals (general); Human services; Christian agencies & churches; Jewish agencies & temples.

Limitations: Giving primarily in Brooklyn, NY.

Application information:
> Initial approach: Letter
> Deadline(s): None

Trustees: Herbert T. Glantz; Kitty Glantz; Joseph C. Hartman.

EIN: 113032861

2166
The Anne and Eric Gleacher Foundation

c/o Gleacher & Co., LLC
660 Madison Ave.
New York, NY 10021
Contact: Eric J. Gleacher, Pres.

Established in 1990 in DE and NY.

Donor(s): Eric J. Gleacher.

Grantmaker type: Independent foundation

Financial data (yr. ended 12/31/02): Assets, $10,368,482 (M); expenditures, $1,909,065; qualifying distributions, $1,755,581; giving activities include $1,755,051 for 55 grants (high: $850,000; low: $500; average: $1,000-$25,000).

Purpose and activities: Giving primarily for secondary and higher education, for health services including family planning, and for social services.

Fields of interest: Elementary/secondary education; Higher education; Environment; Hospitals (general); Reproductive health; Human services; Children/youth, services.

Limitations: Giving primarily in NY. No grants to individuals.

Application information: Application form not required.

Initial approach: Letter
Deadline(s): None

Officers: Eric J. Gleacher, Pres.; Anne G. Gleacher, V.P.

EIN: 133597695

2167
Joseph & Carson Gleberman Foundation
c/o Goldman Sachs & Co.
85 Broad St., Tax Dept.
New York, NY 10004

Established in 1991 in NY.

Donor(s): Joseph H. Gleberman.

Grantmaker type: Independent foundation

Financial data (yr. ended 03/31/02): Assets, $7,433,275 (M); gifts received, $1,733,784; expenditures, $516,122; qualifying distributions, $483,874; giving activities include $481,044 for 81 grants (high: $100,000; low: $250).

Purpose and activities: Giving primarily for arts and cultural programs, education, natural resource conservation and protection, health associations, and human services.

Fields of interest: Arts; Education; Natural resources; Health organizations, association; Human services; Jewish agencies & temples.

Limitations: Applications not accepted. Giving on a national basis, with emphasis on New York, NY. No grants to individuals.

Application information: Contributes only to pre-selected organizations.

Trustees: Carson Gleberman; Joseph H. Gleberman.

EIN: 133632753

2168
The Glickenhaus Foundation
6 E. 43rd St.
New York, NY 10017 (212) 953-7867
Contact: Maddy Wehle

Incorporated in 1960 in NY.

Donor(s): Seth M. Glickenhaus.

Grantmaker type: Independent foundation

Financial data (yr. ended 11/30/01): Assets, $14,495,770 (M); gifts received, $1,175,167; expenditures, $1,475,092; qualifying distributions, $1,364,182; giving activities include $1,364,182 for 319 grants (high: $100,000; low: $20; average: $1,000–$10,000).

Purpose and activities: Support for general charitable activities.

Fields of interest: Humanities; Arts; Education, association; Child development, education; Education; Natural resources; Environment; Hospitals (general); Family planning; Health care; Substance abuse, services; Mental health/crisis services; Cancer; AIDS; Biomedicine; Medical research, institute; Cancer research; AIDS research; Crime/violence prevention, youth; Human services;

Children/youth, services; Child development, services; Family services; Aging, centers/services; Arms control; Civil rights; Community development; Minorities; Disabled; Aging.

Types of support: Endowments; Emergency funds; Research.

Limitations: Applications not accepted. Giving primarily in the greater metropolitan New York, NY, area, including Westchester County.

Application information: Unsolicited requests for funds not accepted.

Officers: Nancy G. Pier, Pres.; James Glickenhaus, V.P.; Alfred Feinman, Secy.-Treas.

Number of staff: 1 full-time support.

EIN: 136160941

2169
The Bradley L. Goldberg Charitable Trust
P.O. Box 737
Mamaroneck, NY 10543

Established in 1984 in NY.

Donor(s): Jennison Assocs. Capital Corp., Bradley L. Goldberg.

Grantmaker type: Independent foundation

Financial data (yr. ended 12/31/02): Assets, $5,377,556 (M); expenditures, $308,472; qualifying distributions, $281,285; giving activities include $280,950 for 27 grants (high: $200,000; low: $200).

Purpose and activities: Giving for animal welfare.

Fields of interest: Museums (art); Animals/wildlife, preservation/protection; Veterinary medicine.

Limitations: Applications not accepted. Giving primarily in New York, NY. No grants to individuals.

Application information: Contributes only to pre-selected organizations.

Trustee: Bradley L. Goldberg.

EIN: 136847767

2170
Morris & Arlene Goldfarb Family Foundation, Inc.
21 Fairway Dr.
Mamaroneck, NY 10543

Established in 1996 in DE & NY.

Donor(s): Morris Goldfarb.

Grantmaker type: Independent foundation

Financial data (yr. ended 08/31/02): Assets, $1,790,105 (M); gifts received, $1,728,000; expenditures, $224,488; qualifying distributions, $222,440; giving activities include $222,100 for 18 grants (high: $200,000; low: $25).

Fields of interest: Law school/education; Animal welfare; Jewish agencies & temples.

Types of support: General/operating support.

Limitations: Applications not accepted. Giving primarily in NY. No grants to individuals.

Application information: Contributes only to pre-selected organizations.

Officers: Morris Goldfarb, Pres.; Arlene Goldfarb, Secy.

EIN: 133925695

2171
The Lionel Goldfrank III Foundation
667 Madison Ave., 20th Fl.
New York, NY 10021-8029

Established in 1999 in NY.

Donor(s): Lionel Goldfrank III.

Grantmaker type: Independent foundation

Financial data (yr. ended 04/30/01): Assets, $355,164 (M); gifts received, $832,710; expenditures, $529,097; qualifying distributions, $523,734; giving activities include $523,734 for 8 grants (high: $250,000; low: $5,000).

Fields of interest: Multipurpose centers/programs; Museums; Higher education; Natural resources; Botanical gardens.

Types of support: General/operating support.

Limitations: Applications not accepted. No grants to individuals.

Application information: Contributes only to pre-selected organizations.

Officer: Lionel Goldfrank III, Pres.

EIN: 316623852

2172
Horace W. Goldsmith Foundation ▼
375 Park Ave., Ste. 1602
New York, NY 10152 (212) 319-8700
Contact: James C. Slaughter, C.E.O.

Incorporated in 1955 in NY.

Donor(s): Horace W. Goldsmith.‡

Grantmaker type: Independent foundation

Financial data (yr. ended 12/31/02): Assets, $719,985,690 (M); expenditures, $43,605,609; qualifying distributions, $41,506,311; giving activities include $41,360,501 for 522 grants (high: $750,000; low: $5,000; average: $10,000–$250,000).

Purpose and activities: Support for cultural programs, including the performing arts and museums; Jewish welfare funds and temple support; hospitals and a geriatric center; and education, especially higher education.

Fields of interest: Visual arts; Museums; Performing arts; Dance; Theater; Music; Arts; Education, research; Higher education; Business school/education; Libraries/library science; Education; Natural resources; Hospitals (general); Family planning; Medical care, rehabilitation; Cancer; AIDS; Medical research, institute; Cancer research; AIDS research; Crime/law enforcement; Human services; Aging, centers/services; Homeless, human services; International relief; Jewish federated giving programs; Jewish agencies & temples; Disabled; Aging; Homeless.

International interests: Israel.

Types of support: General/operating support; Continuing support; Capital campaigns; Building/renovation; Endowments; Scholarship funds; Research; Matching/challenge support.

Limitations: Applications not accepted. Giving primarily in AZ, MA, and New York, NY. No grants to individuals.

Application information: Foundation depends almost exclusively on internally initiated grants.

Board meeting date(s): 6 times a year

Managing Directors: James C. Slaughter, C.E.O.; Richard L. Menschel; Robert B. Menschel; Thomas R. Slaughter; William A. Slaughter.

Number of staff: 1 full-time support.

EIN: 136107758

Recent environmental and animal welfare grants:
2172-1 Breckenridge Outdoor Education Center, Breckenridge, CO, $100,000. 2001.
2172-2 Council on the Environment, New York, NY, $100,000. 2001.
2172-3 Environmental Traveling Companions, San Francisco, CA, $150,000. 2001.
2172-4 Natural Resources Defense Council, New York, NY, $100,000. 2001.
2172-5 Nature Conservancy, Long Island Chapter, Cold Spring Harbor, NY, $100,000. 2001.
2172-6 Pacific Institute for Studies in Development, Environment and Security, Oakland, CA, $100,000. 2001.
2172-7 Shackleton Schools, Boston, MA, $50,000. 2001.
2172-8 Sierra Club Foundation, New York, NY, $100,000. 2001.
2172-9 Strong Wings Adventure School, Nantucket, MA, $50,000. 2001.

2173
The Gordon Fund ▼
(formerly The Gordon/Rousmaniere/Roberts Fund)
c/o Sullivan & Cromwell
125 Broad St.
New York, NY 10004-2498
Contact: James I. Black III
FAX: (212) 558-3064

Established in 1985 in NY.
Donor(s): Albert H. Gordon.
Grantmaker type: Independent foundation
Financial data (yr. ended 12/31/01): Assets, $12,438,349 (M); gifts received, $1,287,563; expenditures, $3,566,478; qualifying distributions, $2,557,000; giving activities include $3,557,000 for 69 grants (high: $1,000,000; low: $1,000; average: $1,000–$50,000).
Purpose and activities: Giving primarily for higher, secondary, and elementary education, including theological education; support also for a medical center and health associations, cultural programs and a historic preservation foundation, international relations, and environmental programs.
Fields of interest: Historic preservation/historical societies; Arts; Elementary school/education; Secondary school/education; Higher education; Theological school/education; Environment; Hospitals (general); Health organizations, association; International affairs.
Limitations: Giving primarily in CA, CT, MA, and NY. No grants to individuals.
Application information:
  Initial approach: Proposal
  Deadline(s): None
Trustee: Mary Gordon Roberts.
EIN: 133257793

2174
The Oliver R. Grace Charitable Foundation
c/o Waldman, Hirsch, & Co., LLP
855 Ave. of the Americas, Ste. 623
New York, NY 10001
Contact: Lorraine G. Grace, Dir.

Established in 1992 in NY.
Donor(s): Lorraine G. Grace.
Grantmaker type: Independent foundation
Financial data (yr. ended 12/31/00): Assets, $685,316 (M); expenditures, $118,148; qualifying distributions, $112,845; giving activities include $112,845 for 43 grants (high: $10,000; low: $35).
Purpose and activities: Funding for medical and cancer research, science institutes, and youth services.
Fields of interest: Arts; Animal welfare; Cancer research; Women, centers/services; Women.
Types of support: Research.
Limitations: Applications not accepted. Giving primarily in Washington, DC, and NY. No grants to individuals.
Application information: Contributes only to pre-selected organizations.
Director: Lorraine G. Grace.
EIN: 113105739

2175
Eugene and Emily Grant Family Foundation
277 Park Ave., 47th Fl.
New York, NY 10172 (212) 688-4700
Contact: Eugene M. Grant, Tr.

Established in 1998 in NY.
Donor(s): Eugene M. Grant, Terry E. Grant.
Grantmaker type: Independent foundation
Financial data (yr. ended 12/31/01): Assets, $1,510,178 (M); gifts received, $1,050,000; expenditures, $1,414,161; qualifying distributions, $1,408,420; giving activities include $1,409,087 for 311 grants.
Purpose and activities: Giving primarily to Jewish agencies, the arts and health care; support also to American and Israeli universities, environmental conservation, intermarriage, and holocaust studies.
Fields of interest: Music; Orchestra (symphony); Opera; History/archaeology; Arts; University; Natural resources; Health care; Health organizations, association; Jewish federated giving programs; Jewish agencies & temples.
International interests: Israel.
Limitations: Giving in the U.S. and Israel.
Application information:
  Initial approach: Letter
  Deadline(s): None
Trustees: Emily Grant; Eugene M. Grant.
Number of staff: None.
EIN: 133997005

2176
Mary A. & Thomas F. Grasselli Endowment Foundation
c/o Fiduciary Trust Co. International
600 Fifth Ave.
New York, NY 10020 (212) 632-3000
Contact: Grace Grasselli Fowler, Pres.

Established in 1965 in DE.
Grantmaker type: Independent foundation
Financial data (yr. ended 12/31/02): Assets, $1,759,969 (M); expenditures, $133,597; qualifying distributions, $117,307; giving activities include $113,660 for 40 grants (high: $12,500; low: $500).

Purpose and activities: Giving primarily for education and the environment.
Fields of interest: Museums; Elementary/secondary education; Higher education; Environment.
Limitations: Giving primarily in NJ and NY. No grants to individuals.
Application information:
  Initial approach: Letter
  Deadline(s): None
Officers: Grace Grasselli Fowler, Pres.; W. Timothy Cashman, V.P.; Robert A. Fowler, Secy.
EIN: 516018870

2177
Grayson-Jockey Club Research Foundation
40 E. 52nd St.
New York, NY 10022 (212) 371-5970
Contact: Edward L. Bowen, Pres.
Application address: 821 Corporate Dr., Lexington, KY 40503, Tel.: (859) 224-2840; E-mail: grayson@jockeyclub.com; URL: http://www.grayson-jockeyclub.org

Established in 1940.
Grantmaker type: Public charity
Financial data (yr. ended 12/31/01): Revenue, $1,088,935; assets, $18,233,851 (M); gifts received, $1,075,913; expenditures, $1,937,455; program services expenses, $1,442,222; giving activities include $1,027,668 for 16 grants (high: $181,064; low: $3,378).
Purpose and activities: The foundation supports equine medical research.
Fields of interest: Animals/wildlife, research; Veterinary medicine.
Types of support: Research.
Limitations: Giving on a national basis.
Application information: See Web site for complete application information. Application form required.
  Deadline(s): Oct. 1
Officers and Directors:* John Hettinger,* Chair.; A. Gary Lavin,* Vice-Chair.; Edward L. Bowen,* Pres.; Nancy C. Kelly,* V.P.; James Liao,* Secy.-Treas.; Josephine Abercrombie; William M. Backer; and 14 additional directors.
EIN: 616031750

2178
Great Island Foundation
c/o U.S. Trust Co. of NY
114 W. 47th St., Ste. TAXRGR
New York, NY 10036

Established in 1994 in DE.
Donor(s): Eliot Chace Nolen, Wilson Nolen, National Indemnity Co.
Grantmaker type: Independent foundation
Financial data (yr. ended 12/31/01): Assets, $13,576,766 (M); gifts received, $199,895; expenditures, $676,118; qualifying distributions, $664,840; giving activities include $661,945 for 92 grants (high: $200,000; low: $250).
Purpose and activities: Giving primarily for art museums and botanical gardens; funding also for human services.
Fields of interest: Museums (art); Arts; Education; Botanical gardens; Human services; Federated giving programs.

Limitations: Applications not accepted. Giving primarily in New York, NY. No grants to individuals.
Application information: Contributes only to pre-selected organizations. Unsolicited requests for funds not accepted.
Directors: Eliot Chace Nolen; Wilson Nolen.
EIN: 134049061

2179
The David J. Greene Foundation, Inc.
599 Lexington Ave., No. 12
New York, NY 10022-6303

Incorporated in 1966 in NY.
Donor(s): David J. Greene,‡ and members of the Greene family.
Grantmaker type: Independent foundation
Financial data (yr. ended 12/31/02): Assets, $15,485,239 (M); gifts received, $59,540; expenditures, $993,130; qualifying distributions, $982,644; giving activities include $979,920 for 139 grants (high: $503,100; low: $100).
Fields of interest: Music; Secondary school/education; Higher education; Education; Environment; Hospitals (general); Eye diseases; Eye research; Human services; Children/youth, services; Aging, centers/services; Jewish federated giving programs; Aging.
Types of support: General/operating support.
Limitations: Applications not accepted. Giving primarily in the metropolitan New York, NY, area. No grants to individuals.
Application information: Contributes only to pre-selected organizations.
  Board meeting date(s): Mar., June, Sept., and Dec.
Officers: Alan I. Greene, Pres.; Michael C. Greene, V.P.; Robert Ravitz, V.P.; James Greene, Treas.
Number of staff: None.
EIN: 136209280

2180
Greentree Foundation
400 Madison Ave., Ste. 1001
New York, NY 10017 (212) 888-7755
Contact: George Patterson, Grants Mgr.

Established in 1982 in NY.
Donor(s): Betsey C. Whitney.‡
Grantmaker type: Independent foundation
Financial data (yr. ended 12/31/01): Assets, $278,015,722 (M); expenditures, $7,719,164; qualifying distributions, $8,387,460; giving activities include $2,105,939 for 79 grants (high: $256,939; low: $7,500; average: $10,000–$25,000).
Purpose and activities: Supports focused projects initiated by local community groups that provide clearly defined participatory roles for schools, parents, children and community-based organizations in order to enhance educational achievements and lessen social and cultural tensions. Giving also for the furtherance of peace, human rights, international cooperation and the preservation of the environment.
Fields of interest: Museums; Arts; Higher education; Education; Environment; Human services; Children/youth, services; International peace/security; International terrorism.

Types of support: Program development.
Limitations: Giving primarily in the metropolitan New York, NY, area. No grants to individuals.
Application information: Application form not required.
  Initial approach: Letter
  Copies of proposal: 1
  Board meeting date(s): Mar., June, Sept., and Dec.
Officers and Trustees:* Robert Curvin, Pres.; Kate R. Whitney,* V.P.; Sara R. Wilford,* V.P.; Robert Carswell,* Treas.; Franklin A. Thomas; Ronald A. Wilford.
Number of staff: 6 full-time professional; 24 full-time support; 2 part-time support.
EIN: 133132117

2181
The Greer Family Foundation
c/o Weiss, Peck & Greer
1 New York Plz., 30th Fl.
New York, NY 10004 (212) 908-9500
Contact: Philip Greer, Pres.

Established in 1985 in IL and NY.
Donor(s): Philip Greer.
Grantmaker type: Independent foundation
Financial data (yr. ended 12/31/00): Assets, $5,680,175 (M); gifts received, $413,083; expenditures, $743,742; qualifying distributions, $733,392; giving activities include $737,742 for 56 grants (high: $271,367; low: $125).
Purpose and activities: Giving primarily for education; funding also for human services, health organizations, and the arts.
Fields of interest: Arts; Higher education; Education; Animals/wildlife; Health organizations, association; Human services; Children/youth, services; Human services.
Types of support: General/operating support; Capital campaigns.
Limitations: Giving primarily in CA, CT, and NY. No grants to individuals.
Application information:
  Initial approach: Proposal in writing
  Deadline(s): None
Officers: Philip Greer, Pres. and Treas.; Norman M. Gold, V.P. and Secy.; Nancy Greer, V.P.; Stephen Weiss, V.P.
Number of staff: None.
EIN: 133321858

2182
The William and Mary Greve Foundation, Inc.
630 5th Ave., Ste. 1750
New York, NY 10111 (212) 307-7850
Contact: Anthony C.M. Kiser, Pres.

Incorporated in 1964 in NY.
Donor(s): Mary P. Greve.‡
Grantmaker type: Independent foundation
Financial data (yr. ended 12/31/02): Assets, $35,691,933 (M); expenditures, $2,911,508; qualifying distributions, $2,382,988; giving activities include $2,081,210 for 44 grants (high: $500,000; low: $5,000; average: $5,000–$50,000).
Purpose and activities: Grants largely for education and related fields, U.S.-Eastern

European relations, the performing arts, and the environment.
Fields of interest: Education; Environment; International affairs, goodwill promotion.
Types of support: General/operating support; Continuing support; Endowments; Matching/challenge support.
Limitations: Applications not accepted. No grants to individuals, or for scholarships or fellowships; no loans.
Application information:
  Board meeting date(s): Varies
Officers and Directors:* John W. Kiser III,* Chair.; Anthony C.M. Kiser,* Pres.; Victoria B. Bjorklund, Secy.; Robert E. Cohen; James W. Sykes, Jr.
Number of staff: 1 full-time professional; 1 part-time professional; 1 part-time support.
EIN: 136020724

2183
The William R. Gruver Foundation
c/o Oscar Capital Management
900 3rd Ave., No. 200
New York, NY 10022
Contact: Anthony Scaramucci, Tr.

Established in 1989 in NJ.
Donor(s): William R. Gruver, Joan L. Gruver.
Grantmaker type: Independent foundation
Financial data (yr. ended 02/28/03): Assets, $2,602,810 (M); expenditures, $161,771; qualifying distributions, $135,047; giving activities include $133,325 for grants (high: $50,100).
Purpose and activities: Giving primarily for education, canine health, and medical research.
Fields of interest: Secondary school/education; Higher education; Education; Animal welfare; Medical research, institute.
Types of support: Endowments; Scholarship funds; Research.
Limitations: Applications not accepted. Giving on a national basis. No grants to individuals.
Application information: Contributes only to pre-selected organizations.
Trustees: Joan L. Gruver; William R. Gruver; Jill G. Puleo; Anthony Scaramucci.
Number of staff: None.
EIN: 133531965

2184
The Gullquist Family Charitable Trust
c/o Lazard Freres & Co., LLC
30 Rockefeller Plz.
New York, NY 10020
Contact: Herbert Gullquist, Tr.

Established in 1991 in NY.
Donor(s): Herbert W. Gullquist.
Grantmaker type: Independent foundation
Financial data (yr. ended 12/31/01): Assets, $1,616,816 (M); expenditures, $138,155; qualifying distributions, $133,155; giving activities include $132,825 for 39 grants (high: $63,000; low: $25).
Fields of interest: Museums; Arts; Education; Natural resources; Health organizations, association; Human services; Salvation Army.
Limitations: Giving primarily in CT. No grants to individuals.
Application information:

Initial approach: Letter
Deadline(s): None
Trustees: Anne K. Gullquist; Herbert W.
Gullquist; Charles Stieglitz.
EIN: 136982699

2185
The Helen Hotze Haas Foundation, Inc.
c/o Blank Rome Tenzer Greenblatt LLP
405 Lexington Ave., 14th Fl.
New York, NY 10174 (212) 885-5000
Contact: Robert H. Haines, Pres.

Established in 1995 in DE and NY.
Grantmaker type: Independent foundation
Financial data (yr. ended 12/31/00): Assets,
$25,698,215 (M); expenditures, $2,076,175;
qualifying distributions, $1,146,016; giving
activities include $1,085,000 for 37 grants (high:
$335,000; low: $5,000).
Purpose and activities: Giving primarily for
education, hospitals, children and social
services, federated giving programs, a
community fund, and a park conservancy.
Fields of interest: Orchestra (symphony); Higher
education; Education; Natural resources;
Hospitals (general); Human services; Children,
services; Federated giving programs.
Limitations: Giving primarily in NY. No grants to
individuals.
Application information:
Initial approach: Letter
Deadline(s): None
Officers and Directors:* Stanley S. Shuman,*
Chair.; Robert H. Haines,* Pres.
EIN: 133836626

2186
Charlotte Cuneen Hackett Charitable Trust
c/o HSBC Bank USA
452 5th Ave., 17th Fl.
New York, NY 10018 (212) 525-2417
Contact: Stephen B. Boics, V.P., HSBC Bank USA

Established in 1971 in NY.
Donor(s): Charlotte Cuneen Hackett.‡
Grantmaker type: Independent foundation
Financial data (yr. ended 12/31/02): Assets,
$2,671,575 (M); expenditures, $207,072;
qualifying distributions, $156,590; giving
activities include $153,000 for 2 grants (high:
$103,000; low: $50,000).
Purpose and activities: Giving for the arts,
education, and religious organizations.
Fields of interest: Music; Historic
preservation/historical societies; Arts; College;
Education; Natural resources; Religion.
Types of support: Continuing support;
Building/renovation; Curriculum development.
Limitations: Applications not accepted. Giving
limited to Dutchess County, NY. No grants to
individuals.
Application information: Contributes only to
pre-selected organizations.
Trustees: John J. Gartland, Jr.; HSBC Bank USA.
Number of staff: None.
EIN: 237215233

2187
Hagedorn Fund
c/o JPMorgan Private Bank, Global Foundations
Group
345 Park Ave., 4th Fl.
New York, NY 10154 (212) 464-2443
Contact: Monica Neal, V.P., JPMorgan Private
Bank
E-mail: neal_monica@jpmorgan.com; URL:
http://fdncenter.org/grantmaker/hagedorn/

Trust established in 1953 in NY.
Donor(s): William Hagedorn.‡
Grantmaker type: Independent foundation
Financial data (yr. ended 12/31/02): Assets,
$29,615,648 (M); expenditures, $1,956,476;
qualifying distributions, $1,787,631; giving
activities include $1,630,000 for 83 grants (high:
$90,000; low: $1,000; average:
$5,000–$25,000).
Purpose and activities: Support for health
(including cancer, HIV/AIDS, blindness),
gardens, social services, youth, education,
senior services, and housing and community
development.
Fields of interest: Education; Botanical gardens;
Health care; Cancer; AIDS; Housing/shelter;
Youth development; Human services;
Community development; Aging.
Types of support: General/operating support;
Building/renovation; Program development.
Limitations: Giving primarily in New York, NY.
No grants to individuals, or for continuing
support, seed money, emergency funds, deficit
financing, endowment funds, matching gifts,
scholarships, fellowships, research, special
projects, publications, or conferences; no loans.
Application information: Almost all grants
represent renewed support for previous
grantees; few new grantees may be considered
each year. Application form not required.
Initial approach: Proposal
Copies of proposal: 1
Deadline(s): Sept. 15
Board meeting date(s): Dec.
Final notification: Dec. 31
Trustees: John J. Kindred III; JPMorgan Chase
Bank.
Number of staff: 5 shared staff.
EIN: 136048718

2188
Hahn Family Foundation
1807 Elmwood Ave., Office 287
Buffalo, NY 14207 (716) 447-7828
Contact: Charles D. Hahn, Tr.

Established in 1965.
Donor(s): Charles Hahn,‡ Charles J. Hahn.
Grantmaker type: Independent foundation
Financial data (yr. ended 12/31/02): Assets,
$4,478,571 (M); gifts received, $22,471;
expenditures, $248,388; qualifying distributions,
$245,429; giving activities include $168,500 for
103 grants (high: $20,400; low: $100).
Purpose and activities: Emphasis on ecology,
particularly in the areas of renewable energy
sources, sustainable farming, preservation of
farmland, and waste management; support also
for local organizations of various types.
Fields of interest: Arts; Education; Natural
resources; Energy; Environment; Agriculture;
Food services; Human services.

Types of support: General/operating support;
Program development; Seed money;
Matching/challenge support.
Limitations: Giving primarily in Buffalo and Erie
County, NY. No support for organizations
eligible for membership in, but not belonging to,
the United Way. No grants to individuals, or for
overhead expenses.
Publications: Application guidelines.
Application information: Application form not
required.
Initial approach: Letter or proposal with
1-page summary
Copies of proposal: 1
Deadline(s): None
Trustees: Anne H. Hahn-Baker; Charles D.
Hahn; Charles J. Hahn; Eric S. Hahn.
Number of staff: 1 part-time support.
EIN: 166128499

2189
Evelyn A. J. Hall Charitable Trust
c/o JPMorgan Chase Bank
345 Park Ave.
New York, NY 10154
Contact: Mary C. Dickens, V.P., JPMorgan Chase
Bank

Trust established in 1952 in NY.
Donor(s): Evelyn A. Hall.
Grantmaker type: Independent foundation
Financial data (yr. ended 12/31/02): Assets,
$6,812,581 (M); expenditures, $1,081,105;
qualifying distributions, $1,035,751; giving
activities include $1,034,777 for 43 grants (high:
$330,000; low: $250; average: $75–$100,000).
Purpose and activities: Primary areas of interest
include cultural programs, hospitals, and
medical research.
Fields of interest: Museums; Historic
preservation/historical societies; Arts; Higher
education; Natural resources; Hospitals
(general); Medical research, institute; Human
services; Children/youth, services; Community
development.
Types of support: General/operating support.
Limitations: Applications not accepted. Giving
primarily in FL and New York, NY. No grants to
individuals.
Application information:
Board meeting date(s): Varies
Trustee: JPMorgan Chase Bank.
Number of staff: None.
EIN: 236286760

2190
Harding Charitable Trust
(formerly The Harding Educational and
Charitable Foundation)
c/o JPMorgan Chase Bank
1211 6th Ave., 34th Fl.
New York, NY 10036

Trust established in 1945 in NY.
Donor(s): Henry J. Harding, Robert L. Harding,
Martha Harding.‡
Grantmaker type: Independent foundation
Financial data (yr. ended 12/31/02): Assets,
$5,260,587 (M); expenditures, $440,032;
qualifying distributions, $373,652; giving
activities include $364,000 for 46 grants (high:
$15,000; low: $500).

Purpose and activities: Giving primarily for wilderness and wildlife conservation, education, and human services.
Fields of interest: Museums; Arts; Higher education; Education; Natural resources; Animals/wildlife; Hospitals (general); Human services; Children/youth, services.
Limitations: Applications not accepted. Giving primarily in MA and NY. No grants to individuals.
Application information: Contributes only to pre-selected organizations.
Trustees: Timothy L. Thompson; JPMorgan Chase Bank.
EIN: 136083440

2191
The Hartley Corporation
c/o St. Philip's Church
1101 Rte. 9D, P.O. Box 158
Garrison, NY 10524

Established in 1921 in CT.
Grantmaker type: Independent foundation
Financial data (yr. ended 05/31/02): Assets, $2,551,923 (M); expenditures, $278,059; qualifying distributions, $246,666; giving activities include $250,250 for 46 grants (high: $131,000; low: $500).
Purpose and activities: Giving for education, arts, human services and community development.
Fields of interest: Arts; Education; Natural resources; Human services; Children/youth, services; Community development.
Types of support: General/operating support; Scholarship funds.
Limitations: Applications not accepted. Giving primarily in CT. No grants to individuals.
Application information: Contributes only to pre-selected organizations.
Officers: Robert H. Mead, Jr., Pres.; Nicholas W. Platt, Treas.
EIN: 066036296

2192
Merrill G. and Emita E. Hastings Foundation
c/o John T. Ablamsky
63 Reid Ave.
Port Washington, NY 11050

Trust established in 1966 in NY.
Donor(s): Emita E. Hastings.‡
Grantmaker type: Independent foundation
Financial data (yr. ended 02/28/02): Assets, $4,067,894 (M); expenditures, $212,534; qualifying distributions, $179,572; giving activities include $114,250 for 72 grants (high: $6,000; low: $250).
Fields of interest: Museums; Arts; Education; Natural resources.
Limitations: Giving primarily in the New York, NY, area. No grants to individuals, or for endowment funds.
Application information: Application form not required.
  Initial approach: Letter
  Copies of proposal: 1
  Deadline(s): None
  Board meeting date(s): As required

Trustees: Janice Haggerty; Elizabeth H. Peterfreund; Joshua Peterfreund; Lisa Peterfreund.
EIN: 136203465

2193
Charles Hayden Foundation ▼
140 Broadway, 51st Fl.
New York, NY 10005 (212) 785-3677
Contact: Kenneth D. Merin, C.E.O. and Pres.
FAX: (212) 785-3689; URL: http://www.fdncenter.org/grantmaker/hayden/

Incorporated in 1937 in NY.
Donor(s): Charles Hayden.‡
Grantmaker type: Independent foundation
Financial data (yr. ended 06/30/02): Assets, $286,069,116 (M); expenditures, $15,624,648; qualifying distributions, $14,758,381; giving activities include $13,197,000 for 150 grants (high: $1,000,000; low: $1,000; average: $15,000–$225,000).
Purpose and activities: To promote the mental, moral and physical development of children and youth ages three to eighteen, especially low-income youth, in the Boston and New York metropolitan areas. Program support grants are available for the expansion of programs with well-defined goals that are expected to be met in a specified time frame. "Bricks and mortar" capital support grants are available for renovation, expansion, construction, and acquisition of physical facilities and purchase of non-expendable equipment.
Fields of interest: Museums (children's); Elementary school/education; Secondary school/education; Vocational education; Education; Children/youth, services.
Types of support: Continuing support; Capital campaigns; Building/renovation; Equipment; Land acquisition; Program development; Matching/challenge support.
Limitations: Giving limited to the metropolitan Boston, MA, and the metropolitan New York, NY (including northern NJ), areas. No support for fraternal groups, religious organizations other than community youth-related projects, arts exposure programs, institutions of higher education except to support work on precollegiate programs (other than recruitment programs for a particular college), hospitals, hospices, or projects essentially medical in nature. No grants to individuals, or for endowment funds, operating budgets, fellowships, annual campaigns, emergency funds, deficit financing, publications, or conferences; no loans.
Application information: Accepts NYRAG and AGM Common Grant Application forms; Boston area, 2 copies of proposal (one copy sent to NYC and one copy sent to Boston); NY and NJ, 1 copy of proposal. Application form not required.
  Initial approach: Proposal
  Copies of proposal: 1
  Deadline(s): None
  Board meeting date(s): 10 times per year
  Final notification: Approximately 2 months
Officers and Trustees:* Kenneth D. Merin,* C.E.O. and Pres.; Carol Van Atten, V.P., Progs.; Kristen J. McCormack,* V.P.; Dean H. Steeger,* Secy.; Robert Howitt,* Treas.; Howard G. Wachenfeld.

Number of staff: 4 full-time professional; 1 part-time professional; 1 full-time support.
EIN: 135562237
Recent environmental and animal welfare grants:
2193-1 New York Botanical Garden, Bronx, NY, $100,000. Toward construction of new School Group Entrance. 2002.
2193-2 New York City Outward Bound Center, Long Island City, NY, $250,000. For programmatic logistics center at new headquarters facility. 2002.
2193-3 Wildlife Conservation Society, Bronx, NY, $1,000,000. Toward permanent exhibits, Tiger Mountain at the Bronx Zoo and Alien Stingers at the New York Aquarium. 2002.

2194
The Heckscher Foundation for Children ▼
17 E. 47th St.
New York, NY 10017 (212) 371-7775
Contact: Virginia Sloane, Pres.
FAX: (212) 371-7787; URL: http://fdncenter.org/grantmaker/heckscher/

Incorporated in 1921 in NY.
Donor(s): August Heckscher.‡
Grantmaker type: Independent foundation
Financial data (yr. ended 12/31/02): Assets, $126,283,004 (M); expenditures, $5,701,645; qualifying distributions, $5,470,700; giving activities include $5,029,887 for 236 grants (high: $250,000; low: $236; average: $1,849–$50,000).
Purpose and activities: To promote the welfare of children; grants particularly for child welfare and family service agencies, education, recreation, music and the performing arts, health, summer youth programs and camps, and aid to the handicapped.
Fields of interest: Museums; Performing arts; Arts; Early childhood education; Child development, education; Libraries/library science; Education; Environment; Health care; Substance abuse, services; Health organizations, association; Recreation; Human services; Youth, services; Child development, services; Family services; Homeless, human services; Minorities; Disabled; Economically disadvantaged.
Types of support: Equipment; Program development; Curriculum development; Scholarship funds.
Limitations: Giving primarily in the greater New York, NY, area. No grants to individuals, or for operating budgets, annual campaigns, deficit financing, fellowships, or endowment funds; no loans.
Publications: Application guidelines, Informational brochure.
Application information: Application form not required.
  Initial approach: Letter or proposal
  Copies of proposal: 1
  Deadline(s): None
  Board meeting date(s): Jan., Mar., May, July, Sept., and Nov.
  Final notification: 2 months
Officers and Trustees:* Howard G. Sloane,* Chair.; Virginia Sloane,* Pres.; William D. Hart, Jr.,* Secy.; Phyllis Fannan; Carole S. Landman; Gail Meyers; Fred Obser; Howard Rosenbaum; Marlene Shyer; Arthur J. Smadbeck; Louis Smadbeck, Jr.; Paul Smadbeck; David Tillson.

Number of staff: 2 full-time professional; 1 part-time professional.
EIN: 131820170

2195
Heilbrunn Foundation
c/o Herbert Paul
450 7th Ave., Ste. 3000
New York, NY 10123

Established in 1960.
Donor(s): Robert Heilbrunn,‡ Berkshire Hathaway Inc.
Grantmaker type: Independent foundation
Financial data (yr. ended 12/31/02): Assets, $275,476 (M); gifts received, $235,030; expenditures, $126,904; qualifying distributions, $126,904; giving activities include $120,320 for 55 grants (high: $25,000; low: $100; average: $1,000–$5,000).
Purpose and activities: Giving primarily for museums, environmental issues, and services for the blind.
Fields of interest: Media/communications; Museums; Higher education; Libraries (public); Natural resources; Human services; Jewish federated giving programs; General charitable giving.
Limitations: Applications not accepted. Giving primarily in New York, NY. No grants to individuals.
Application information: Contributes only to pre-selected organizations.
Officers: Harriet Heilbrunn, Pres.; Helaine Lerner, Secy.-Treas.
EIN: 136138257

2196
Heineman Foundation for Research, Educational, Charitable and Scientific Purposes, Inc.
c/o Brown Brothers Harriman Trust Co.
63 Wall St.
New York, NY 10005

Incorporated in 1947 in DE.
Donor(s): Dannie N. Heineman.‡
Grantmaker type: Independent foundation
Financial data (yr. ended 12/31/01): Assets, $16,047,282 (M); expenditures, $910,918; qualifying distributions, $823,661; giving activities include $797,030 for 31 grants (high: $128,000; low: $2,500).
Purpose and activities: Primary areas of interest include the medical sciences and physics. Support for research programs in mathematical sciences and medicine; grants for higher education, specialized libraries (including the Heineman Library of Rare Books and Manuscripts given to the Pierpont Morgan Library, New York), music schools, and two annual physics awards.
Fields of interest: Visual arts; Performing arts; Dance; Theater; Music; Language/linguistics; Literature; Arts; Education, research; Early childhood education; Child development, education; Elementary school/education; Higher education; Adult/continuing education; Adult education—literacy, basic skills & GED; Libraries/library science; Reading; Education; Natural resources; Energy; Environment;

Animals/wildlife, preservation/protection; Health care; Health organizations, association; Heart & circulatory diseases; Biomedicine; Medical research, institute; Heart & circulatory research; Food services; Human services; Children/youth, services; Child development, services; Women, centers/services; Race/intergroup relations; Civil rights; Physical/earth sciences; Chemistry; Mathematics; Physics; Engineering/technology; Biological sciences; Science; Minorities; Women; Economically disadvantaged.
Types of support: General/operating support; Endowments; Program development; Publication; Seed money; Fellowships; Research; Technical assistance.
Limitations: Giving on a national basis. No grants to individuals.
Application information: Application form not required.
  Copies of proposal: 1
  Board meeting date(s): Apr. and Nov.
Officers and Directors:* Ann R. Podlipny, Pres.; Maria Heineman Bergendahl, V.P.; Andrew Podlipny, Secy.; Agnes Gautier,* Treas.; Anders Bergendahl; Edith Fehr; Marilyn Heineman; June Heineman-Morris; Joan Heineman-Schur; Glen Morris; David Heineman Rose; James A. Rose; Marian Heineman Rose; Simon Rose.
Number of staff: None.
EIN: 136082899

2197
Elizabeth Wakeman Henderson Foundation
c/o Fiduciary Trust Co. International
600 5th Ave.
New York, NY 10020
Contact: William H. Eshbaugh, Tr.
Application address: 209 McKee Ave., Oxford, OH 45056

Established in 1997 in OH.
Donor(s): William H. Eshbaugh, E.W. Henderson.‡
Grantmaker type: Independent foundation
Financial data (yr. ended 12/31/02): Assets, $3,142,918 (M); gifts received, $30,000; expenditures, $248,784; qualifying distributions, $192,135; giving activities include $180,000 for 13 grants (high: $58,500; low: $1,000).
Purpose and activities: Giving for education, the environment, wildlife, and health care.
Fields of interest: Education; Natural resources; Animals/wildlife, preservation/protection; Hospitals (general).
Application information:
  Initial approach: Formal letter
  Deadline(s): None
Trustees: E. Wendy Brown; David C. Eshbaugh; Stephen H. Eshbaugh; William H. Eshbaugh; Alan Van Coller; Ian Van Coller; Margaret E. Van Coller.
EIN: 656234202

2198
Hettinger Foundation
c/o Oberfest & Assocs.
P.O. Box 318
Chappaqua, NY 10514

Trust established in 1961 in NY.
Donor(s): Albert J. Hettinger, Jr.,‡ John Hettinger.

Grantmaker type: Independent foundation
Financial data (yr. ended 12/31/01): Assets, $16,150,631 (M); expenditures, $961,385; qualifying distributions, $897,833; giving activities include $902,000 for 27 grants (high: $370,000; low: $1,000; average: $1,000–$175,000).
Purpose and activities: Giving primarily for education, health care, and children, youth, and social services; funding also for the welfare of thoroughbred racehorses.
Fields of interest: Education; Animal welfare; Hospitals (general); Health care; Cancer research; Athletics/sports, equestrianism; Human services; American Red Cross; Salvation Army; Children/youth, services.
Types of support: General/operating support; Scholarship funds.
Limitations: Applications not accepted. Giving primarily in NY, with emphasis on New York City; funding also nationally, particularly in CT and KY. No grants to individuals.
Application information: Contributes only to pre-selected organizations.
Trustees: Betty Hettinger; John Hettinger; William R. Hettinger.
EIN: 136097726

2199
Tommy Hilfiger Corporate Foundation, Inc.
25 W. 39th St., 11th Fl.
New York, NY 10018 (212) 840-8888

Established in 1996 in NY.
Donor(s): Tommy Hilfiger U.S.A., Inc.
Grantmaker type: Company-sponsored foundation
Financial data (yr. ended 03/31/02): Assets, $837,594 (M); gifts received, $2,255,508; expenditures, $1,477,315; qualifying distributions, $1,477,215; giving activities include $1,477,215 for 60 grants (high: $248,650; low: $100).
Purpose and activities: Giving primarily for educational youth organizations; support also for health, environment, human services, and the arts.
Fields of interest: Museums; Arts; Education; Environment; Hospitals (general); Health organizations, association; Youth development; Human services; Children/youth, services.
Types of support: In-kind gifts.
Limitations: Giving on a national basis. No grants to individuals.
Application information: Application form not required.
  Deadline(s): None
  Final notification: Proposals are reviewed within 90 days of receipt
Directors: Steven R. Gursky; Joel H. Newman; Guy Vickers.
EIN: 133856562

2200
Hilliard Foundation, Inc.
100 W. 4th St.
Elmira, NY 14901-2190 (607) 733-7121
Contact: Nelson Mooers van den Blink, Pres.

Donor(s): The Hilliard Corp.

Grantmaker type: Company-sponsored foundation
Financial data (yr. ended 04/30/02): Assets, $1,134,803 (M); expenditures, $194,183; qualifying distributions, $190,855; giving activities include $189,800 for 26 grants (high: $30,000; low: $100).
Purpose and activities: Giving for the arts, education, and human services.
Fields of interest: Museums; Historical activities; Higher education; Environment; Hospitals (general); Human services; Federated giving programs.
Types of support: General/operating support; Building/renovation; Program development.
Limitations: Giving primarily in Elmira, NY. No grants to individuals.
Application information:
Initial approach: Letter
Deadline(s): None
Officers and Trustees:* Nelson Mooers van den Blink,* Pres.; Mary Welles Mooers Smith,* V.P.; Gordon Webster,* Treas.; George L. Howell; Gerald F. Schichtel; Paul H. Schweizer; Allen C. Smith; Finley M. Steele; Richard W. Swan; Jan van den Blink.
EIN: 161176159

2201
Hitachi America, Ltd. Corporate Giving Program
50 Prospect Ave.
Tarrytown, NY 10591-4698 (914) 332-5800
Contact: Susan Crucy-Brocard, Community Rels. Off.

Grantmaker type: Corporate giving program
Purpose and activities: As a complement to its foundation, Hitachi America also makes charitable contributions to nonprofit organizations directly. Support is given primarily in areas of company operations.
Fields of interest: Education; Environment; Human services; General charitable giving.
Types of support: General/operating support; Employee volunteer services; Use of facilities; Sponsorships; Donated equipment; Donated products.
Limitations: Giving primarily in areas of company operations. No support for religious or political organizations or labor organizations. No grants for special events or endowments.
Application information: Application form not required.
Initial approach: Proposal to nearest company facility
Deadline(s): None

2202
HKH Foundation ▼
521 5th Ave., Ste. 1612
New York, NY 10175-1699
Contact: Harriet Barlow
E-mail: hkh@hkhfdn.org; URL: http://www.hkhfdn.org

Foundation established in 1980 in NY.
Grantmaker type: Independent foundation
Financial data (yr. ended 12/31/01): Assets, $36,147,910 (M); expenditures, $2,517,928; qualifying distributions, $2,143,203; giving activities include $1,991,032 for 49 grants

(high: $433,341; low: $1,500; average: $5,000–$25,000) and $125,000 for 2 loans/program-related investments.
Purpose and activities: Funding considered only in the following areas: 1) disarmament and the prevention of war; 2) civil liberties; and 3) environmental protection.
Fields of interest: Natural resources; Environment; International peace/security; Arms control; Civil liberties, advocacy; Civil rights.
Types of support: General/operating support; Program development; Program-related investments/loans.
Limitations: Applications not accepted. Giving limited to the U.S. No grants to individuals.
Application information: Unsolicited requests for funds not accepted.
Board meeting date(s): Spring and fall (actual dates vary each year)
Trustees: Hermann Hatzfeldt; Adam Hochschild; David Hochschild; Frederick A. Terry, Jr.; Robert R. Worth.
Number of staff: 2 part-time professional; 1 part-time support.
EIN: 136784950

2203
Homeland Foundation, Inc. ▼
c/o Amco
505 Park Ave., 20th Fl.
New York, NY 10022-1106
Contact: E. Lisk Wyckoff, Jr., Treas.
Application address: c/o Wethersfield, 214 Pugsley Hill Rd., Amenia, NY 12501

Incorporated in 1938 in NY.
Donor(s): Chauncey Stillman.‡
Grantmaker type: Independent foundation
Financial data (yr. ended 04/30/02): Assets, $85,969,144 (M); gifts received, $385; expenditures, $5,317,179; qualifying distributions, $4,230,539; giving activities include $2,191,120 for 55 grants (high: $600,000; low: $1,000; average: $10,000–$100,000) and $1,345,263 for 2 foundation-administered programs.
Purpose and activities: Giving predominantly for Roman Catholic church support, including welfare organizations in the U.S. and abroad and educational institutions.
Fields of interest: Arts; Education; Animals/wildlife, preservation/protection; Human services; Roman Catholic federated giving programs; Roman Catholic agencies & churches.
Types of support: General/operating support; Curriculum development; Scholarship funds.
Limitations: Giving on a national and international basis. No grants to individuals.
Application information: Application form not required.
Initial approach: Letter
Deadline(s): None
Officers and Board Members:* E. Lisk Wyckoff, Jr.,* Pres. and Treas.; Rev. Msgr. Eugene V. Clark,* V.P. and Secy.; Robert B. MacKay,* V.P.; Rev. Rafael F. Caamano; Lucy Fleming-McGrath; Dr. Carl Schmitt; Charles Scribner III.
EIN: 136113816

2204
Helen Thomas Howland Testamentary Trust Foundation
c/o M&T Bank, Tax Dept.
P.O. Box 22900
Rochester, NY 14692-2900
Application address: c/o M&T Bank, 2 Court St., Binghamton, NY 13901

Established in 1991 in NY.
Grantmaker type: Independent foundation
Financial data (yr. ended 06/30/02): Assets, $1,827,722 (M); expenditures, $133,417; qualifying distributions, $114,127; giving activities include $115,690 for 17 grants (high: $43,000; low: $1,000).
Fields of interest: Environment; Animals/wildlife, public education; Animals/wildlife, preservation/protection; Children/youth, services; Aging.
Types of support: Capital campaigns; Program development.
Limitations: Giving primarily in Broome and Tompkins counties, NY. No support for churches or organizations for religious purposes. No grants to individuals.
Application information:
Initial approach: Write for guidelines
Board meeting date(s): June
Trustee: M&T Bank.
EIN: 166353030

2205
HSBC Bank USA Corporate Giving Program
(formerly Republic New York Corporation Contributions Program)
452 5th Ave.
New York, NY 10018 (212) 525-8239
Contact: Kristen Alvanson, Asst. V.P., Group Public Affairs
URL: http://us.hsbc.com/inside/community/communities.asp

Grantmaker type: Corporate giving program
Purpose and activities: As a complement to its foundation, HSBC also makes charitable contributions to nonprofit organizations directly. Support is given primarily in areas of company operations.
Fields of interest: Education; Environment.
Types of support: General/operating support; Management development; Land acquisition; Program development; Conferences/seminars; Curriculum development; Scholarship funds; Use of facilities; Sponsorships; Employee matching gifts; Donated equipment; Donated land; In-kind gifts.
Limitations: Giving primarily in areas of company operations, with emphasis on CA, FL, NY, and PA. No support for political organizations. No grants to individuals.
Publications: Application guidelines, Program policy statement.
Application information: Publications are available online. The Group Public Affairs Department handles giving. The company has a staff that only handles contributions. Application form not required.
Initial approach: Proposal to headquarters
Copies of proposal: 1
Deadline(s): None
Final notification: 1 month

Number of staff: 2 full-time professional; 1 full-time support.

2206
HSBC in the Community USA Inc. Foundation

c/o HSBC, Group Public Affairs
452 5th Ave.
New York, NY 10018 (212) 525-8239
Contact: Kristen Alvanson
URL: http://us.hsbc.com/inside/community/HSBCfoundation.asp

Established in 2000 in NY.
Donor(s): HSBC Bank USA.
Grantmaker type: Company-sponsored foundation
Financial data (yr. ended 12/31/02): Assets, $4,532,995 (M); gifts received, $1,050,036; expenditures, $1,046,352; qualifying distributions, $1,044,481; giving activities include $1,043,225 for 72 grants (high: $100,000; low: $2,000).
Purpose and activities: Giving primarily for education and the environment. The focus is on K-12 public schools and post-secondary institutions as well as for adult education, public library programs and welfare-to-work programs. K-12 education may target students, teachers, and/or parents. Higher education support will give precedence to scholarship programs primarily for disadvantaged students. Giving also to organizations that have programs targeting conservation, sustainable development, or environmental education. The foundation will consider support for programs that promote good environmental practices, and programs that increase public awareness. They will also welcome proposals for programs which strive to prevent potential environmental degradation, those that focus on scientific research on environmental issues, and activities promoting energy conservation, recycling, preservation of green spaces, waste reduction, and ecological concerns.
Fields of interest: Education; Natural resources.
Limitations: Giving primarily in areas of company operations. No support for non-educational or non-environmental organizations. No grants to individuals directly.
Application information:
Initial approach: Proposal
Deadline(s): None
Officers: Linda Stryker, Pres.; Robert H. Muth, V.P. and Treas.; Philip S. Toohey, Secy.
EIN: 161593742

2207
Hudson River Foundation

40 W. 20th St., 9th Fl.
New York, NY 10011-4211 (212) 924-8290
Contact: Dennis Suszkowski, Science Dir.
FAX: (212) 924-8325; *E-mail:* info@hudsonriver.org; *URL:* http://www.hudsonriver.org

Established in 1981 in NY.
Grantmaker type: Public charity
Financial data (yr. ended 12/31/00): Revenue, $10,337,525; assets, $40,703,171; gifts received, $370,743; expenditures, $5,082,300; program services expenses, $4,515,766; giving

activities include $1,247,656 for grants and $2,318,386 for 33 grants to individuals (high: $112,288; low: $6,669).
Purpose and activities: The foundation seeks to provide leadership and support for an integrated program of research, monitoring, modeling, synthesis, and education related to the management of the resources of the Hudson River.
Fields of interest: Natural resources; Environment, water resources.
Application information: See Web site for further application information and programs.
Initial approach: Letter or telephone
Deadline(s): Varies
Final notification: Varies
Officers and Directors:* Edward A. Ames,* Chair.; Henry C. Hiles, Exec. Dir.; John G. Boreman, Ph.D.; Robert H. Boyle; Joan K. Davidson; Christopher F. D'Elia, Ph.D.; L.F. Boker Doyle; Robert W. Elliott; Gerald E. Galloway, Jr., Ph.D.; Ashok Gupta; and 13 additional directors.
EIN: 133089956

2208
Huggy Bears, Inc.

c/o Forstmann Little & Co.
767 5th Ave., 44th Fl.
New York, NY 10153

Established in 1998 in NY.
Donor(s): Nicholas C. Forstmann, Theodore J. Forstmann.
Grantmaker type: Independent foundation
Financial data (yr. ended 12/31/01): Assets, $0 (M); gifts received, $1,270,252; expenditures, $3,852,625; qualifying distributions, $2,784,531; giving activities include $1,837,334 for 18 grants (high: $506,934; low: $20,000).
Purpose and activities: Giving primarily for education, and human services, including services for disadvantaged youth.
Fields of interest: Law school/education; Education; Natural resources; Hospitals (specialty); Human services; Children/youth, services; Family services; Foundations (community); Economically disadvantaged.
Limitations: Applications not accepted. Giving on a national basis, with some emphasis on NY. No grants to individuals.
Application information: Contributes only to pre-selected organizations.
Officers: Theodore J. Forstmann, Pres.; Margot McGinniss, Secy.; Kathleen Broderick, Treas.
EIN: 133998844

2209
Geoffrey C. Hughes Foundation, Inc.

c/o Cahill Gordon & Reindel
80 Pine St., Ste. 1736
New York, NY 10005 (212) 701-3400
Contact: John R. Young, Pres.

Established in 1991 in NY.
Donor(s): Geoffrey C. Hughes.‡
Grantmaker type: Independent foundation
Financial data (yr. ended 03/31/03): Assets, $27,472,573 (M); expenditures, $2,325,814; qualifying distributions, $2,164,948; giving activities include $2,128,900 for 24 grants (high:

$300,000; low: $1,000; average: $25,000–$200,000).
Purpose and activities: Support primarily for environmental protection, opera, and ballet, with preference given to organizations which the donor supported during his lifetime or indicated should be supported after his death.
Fields of interest: Ballet; Opera; Natural resources.
Limitations: No grants to individuals.
Application information: Application form not required.
Initial approach: Letter of inquiry or telephone
Deadline(s): None
Final notification: Varies
Officers and Directors:* John R. Young,* Pres.; Ursula Cliff,* V.P. and Secy.; Walter C. Cliff,* V.P. and Treas.; Mary K. Young,* V.P.; June McCandless.
Number of staff: None.
EIN: 133622255

2210
The Charles Evans Hughes Memorial Foundation, Inc.

c/o Foundation Service
130 E. 59th St., 12th Fl.
New York, NY 10022-1302 (212) 836-1798
Contact: Lauren Katzowitz, Secy.

Incorporated in 1962 in NY.
Donor(s): Catherine Hughes Waddell,‡ Chauncey L. Waddell.‡
Grantmaker type: Independent foundation
Financial data (yr. ended 07/31/02): Assets, $20,711,285 (M); expenditures, $1,665,864; qualifying distributions, $1,535,425; giving activities include $1,477,000 for 56 grants (high: $90,000; low: $2,500).
Purpose and activities: Giving primarily to organizations engaged in: 1) education, including legal education, the social sciences, and technical education, with certain emphasis on assisting minorities; 2) combating prejudice based on race, color, or religious belief; 3) protecting the environment, including population aspects and AIDS prevention; and 4) the arts.
Fields of interest: Arts; Law school/education; Education; Environment; Family planning; AIDS; Legal services; Crime/law enforcement; Civil rights.
Types of support: Continuing support; Annual campaigns; Scholarship funds.
Limitations: Applications not accepted. Giving primarily in New York, NY; some giving also in Washington, DC, MA, and NM. No grants to individuals.
Application information: Unsolicited requests for funds not accepted.
Board meeting date(s): Oct. and June
Officers and Directors:* Theodore H. Waddell,* Pres.; William G. Kirkland,* V.P. and Treas.; Lauren Katzowitz, Secy.; Christopher Angell; Anthony C. Howkins; Marjory Hughes Johnson; Karen A.G. Loud; Betty J. Stebman; Brewster Waddell; Wendy J. Williamson.
Number of staff: 2 part-time professional; 1 full-time support.
EIN: 136159445

2211
Lawrence S. Huntington Fund
46 E. 70th St., 4th Fl.
New York, NY 10021 (212) 717-8633
Contact: Lawrence S. Huntington, Dir.

Established in 1997 in NY.
Donor(s): Lawrence S. Huntington.
Grantmaker type: Independent foundation
Financial data (yr. ended 12/31/02): Assets,
$86,380 (M); gifts received, $1,614;
expenditures, $889,841; qualifying distributions,
$860,526; giving activities include $806,714 for
43 grants (high: $500,000; low: $49).
Fields of interest: Higher education; Law
school/education; Education; Animals/wildlife;
Hospitals (general); Human services.
Limitations: Giving primarily in NY.
Application information: Application form not
required.
  Deadline(s): None
Director: Lawrence S. Huntington.
EIN: 133985928

2212
IBM Corporate Giving Program
New Orchard Rd.
Armonk, NY 10504 (914) 499-1900
Contact: Stanley S. Litow, V.P., Corp.
Community Rels.
E-mail: ibmgives@vnet.ibm.com; URL: http://
www.ibm.com/ibm/ibmgives

Grantmaker type: Corporate giving program
Purpose and activities: As a complement to its
foundation, IBM also makes charitable
contributions to nonprofit organizations directly.
Support is given on a national basis.
Fields of interest: Elementary/secondary
education; Early childhood education;
Elementary/secondary school reform; Higher
education; Adult/continuing education;
Education; Environment, research; Environment;
Health organizations; Employment, equal rights;
Employment, services; Employment, retraining;
Employment.
International interests: Canada; Europe; Latin
America; Asia; Australia.
Types of support: General/operating support;
Equipment; Program development; Curriculum
development; Fellowships; Research; Technical
assistance; Employee volunteer services; Loaned
talent; Employee matching gifts; Donated
equipment; Donated products; In-kind gifts;
Matching/challenge support.
Limitations: Giving on a national basis,
particularly in areas of company operations,
including Armonk, NY, and on an international
basis in areas of company operations, including
in Asia, Australia, Canada, Europe, and Latin
America; giving also to national organizations.
No support for political, religious, fraternal, or
animal welfare organizations. No grants to
individuals, or for telethons, walkathons,
sponsorships, raffles, auctions, capital
campaigns, construction or renovation projects,
endowments, academic chairs or scholarships,
or athletic or competitive events.
Publications: Application guidelines, Corporate
giving report (including application guidelines),
Program policy statement.
Application information: National organizations
should contact headquarters. The Corporate
Community Relations Department handles
giving. The company has a staff that only
handles contributions. Application form not
required.
  Initial approach: Proposal to nearest company
    facility
  Copies of proposal: 1
  Deadline(s): None
  Final notification: 2 to 3 weeks
Number of staff: 16 full-time professional.

2213
IBM International Foundation
(formerly IBM South Africa Projects Fund)
c/o International Business Machines Corp.
New Orchard Rd.
Armonk, NY 10504-1709 (914) 766-1900
Contact: Prog. Mgr.
URL: http://www.ibm.com/ibm/ibmgives/

Established in 1985 in NY.
Donor(s): International Business Machines Corp.
Grantmaker type: Company-sponsored
foundation
Financial data (yr. ended 12/31/01): Assets,
$153,475,604 (M); gifts received, $28,100,000;
expenditures, $12,365,048; qualifying
distributions, $12,020,407; giving activities
include $2,861,646 for grants, $1,644,327 for
grants to individuals and $6,786,823 for
employee matching gifts.
Purpose and activities: Giving worldwide for
education with a focus on K-12, adult training,
and projects that address environmental
problems.
Fields of interest: Education, reform;
Environment; Science.
Types of support: Employee matching gifts.
Limitations: Giving on an international basis.
No support for fraternal, labor, political, or
religious organizations, or private or parochial
schools. No grants to individuals (except for
fellowships), or for scholarships, capital
campaigns, fundraising, construction or
renovation projects, chairs, endowments,
conferences, symposia, or sports competitions.
Publications: Application guidelines,
Informational brochure.
Application information: Limited funding is
available for unsolicited proposals that fall
within the foundation's fields of interest. Priority
is placed on projects that include a role for
technology and offer a potential for replication.
The foundation's grantmaking decisions are not
controlled by the corporation. Application form
required.
  Initial approach: Letter of inquiry (2 pages);
    for local projects contact local IBM office
    for name and address of Local External
    Programs Manager
  Copies of proposal: 1
  Deadline(s): None
  Final notification: 1 month
Officers and Directors:* Louis V. Gerstner, Jr.,*
Chair.; Abby F. Kohnstamm,* Vice-Chair.;
Stanley S. Litow,* Pres.; Paula W. Baker, V.P.; A.
Bonzani, Secy.; Cassio A. Calil, Treas.; Richard J.
Carroll, Cont.; Robin G. Willner; Robert F.
Woods.
Number of staff: 1 full-time professional.
EIN: 133267906

2214
IF Hummingbird Foundation, Inc.
(formerly The Iscol Family Foundation, Inc.)
63 Lyndel Rd.
Pound Ridge, NY 10576 (914) 764-8479
Contact: Jill W. Iscol, Pres.
FAX: (203) 972-5237

Established in 1990 in NY.
Donor(s): Kenneth H. Iscol.
Grantmaker type: Independent foundation
Financial data (yr. ended 06/30/02): Assets,
$3,033,075 (M); expenditures, $758,802;
qualifying distributions, $719,635; giving
activities include $388,445 for 108 grants (high:
$80,000; low: $25).
Fields of interest: Elementary/secondary
education; Higher education; Natural resources;
Health organizations, association; Human
services; Children/youth, services; Civil liberties,
advocacy; Public affairs.
Types of support: General/operating support;
Continuing support; Annual campaigns;
Endowments; Conferences/seminars;
Curriculum development; Scholarship funds;
Matching/challenge support.
Limitations: Giving primarily in CT and NY. No
grants to individuals.
Application information:
  Initial approach: Letter
  Deadline(s): None
Officers and Directors:* Jill Iscol,* Pres. and
Treas.; Kenneth Iscol,* V.P. and Secy.
Number of staff: 1 part-time professional; 2
part-time support.
EIN: 061314468

2215
O'Donnell Iselin Foundation, Inc.
c/o John F. Walsh
230 Park Ave, Ste. 1550
New York, NY 10169
Contact: Peter Iselin, Pres.

Established in 1946.
Donor(s): Peter Iselin, Emilie I. Wiggin.
Grantmaker type: Independent foundation
Financial data (yr. ended 12/31/02): Assets,
$3,900,394 (M); expenditures, $308,730;
qualifying distributions, $264,805; giving
activities include $266,250 for 43 grants (high:
$20,000; low: $500).
Fields of interest: Arts; Secondary
school/education;
Botanical/horticulture/landscape services;
Health organizations, association.
Limitations: Applications not accepted. Giving
primarily in NY. No grants to individuals.
Officers: Peter Iselin, Pres. and Treas.; Emilie I.
Wiggin, V.P.; John F. Walsh, Secy.
EIN: 516016471

2216
Ittleson Foundation, Inc.
15 E. 67th St., 5th Fl.
New York, NY 10021 (212) 794-2008
Contact: Anthony C. Wood, Exec. Dir.
FAX: (212) 794-0351; URL: http://
www.ittlesonfoundation.org

Trust established in 1932 in NY.

Donor(s): Henry Ittleson,‡ Blanche F. Ittleson,‡ Henry Ittleson, Jr.,‡ Lee F. Ittleson,‡ Nancy S. Ittleson.‡
Grantmaker type: Independent foundation
Financial data (yr. ended 12/31/01): Assets, $21,710,168 (M); expenditures, $1,531,205; qualifying distributions, $1,281,729; giving activities include $969,021 for 59+ grants (high: $250,000; low: $50; average: $10,000–$40,000).
Purpose and activities: The foundation provides seed money for start-up programs and pilot, model, and demonstration projects with a plan for dissemination, whose significance goes beyond the local area of implementation, in the fields of AIDS, mental health, and the environment, with a special interest in youth and adolescents. The foundation seeks to play a leverage role and is willing to take risks on new ideas and inspired yet untested new leaders, in addition to supporting proven professionals.
Fields of interest: Environment; Mental health/crisis services; AIDS.
Types of support: Program development; Publication; Seed money; Research; Technical assistance; Matching/challenge support.
Limitations: Giving on a national basis. No support for the humanities or cultural projects, general education, social service agencies offering direct service to people in local communities, or projects or organizations that are international in scope or purpose. No grants to individuals, or for continuing support, scholarships, fellowships, internships, annual or capital campaigns, travel, emergency or endowment funds, biomedical research, or deficit financing; no loans.
Publications: Annual report (including application guidelines).
Application information: Application form not required.
Initial approach: Letter
Copies of proposal: 1
Deadline(s): Apr. 1 and Sept. 1
Board meeting date(s): June and Dec.
Final notification: 3 weeks to 3 months
Officers and Directors:* H. Anthony Ittleson,* Chair. and Pres.; Pamela Lee Syrmis,* V.P.; Anthony C. Wood,* Secy. and Exec. Dir.; Lionel I. Pincus; Victor Syrmis, M.D.
Number of staff: 1 full-time professional; 1 part-time support.
EIN: 510172757

2217
Ivor Foundation
c/o Saunders, Karp & Megrue, LP
667 Madison Ave., 5th Fl.
New York, NY 10021

Established in 1989 in NY.
Donor(s): Thomas A. Saunders III.
Grantmaker type: Independent foundation
Financial data (yr. ended 12/31/02): Assets, $3,453,782 (M); expenditures, $547,470; qualifying distributions, $512,417; giving activities include $511,518 for 74 grants (high: $104,232; low: $50).
Fields of interest: Museums (art); Arts; Higher education; Education; Natural resources; Hospitals (general); Health care; Health organizations, association; Human services;

Children/youth, services; Federated giving programs; Protestant agencies & churches.
Limitations: Applications not accepted. Giving primarily in NY and VA. No grants to individuals.
Application information: Contributes only to pre-selected organizations.
Officers: Thomas A. Saunders III, Pres. and Treas.; Mary Jordan Saunders, Secy.
Directors: Joanne Saunders Berkley; Calvert S. Moore; Thomas A. Saunders IV.
EIN: 133506932

2218
J.I. Foundation, Inc.
c/o Patterson, Belknap, Webb & Tyler, LLP
1133 Ave. of the Americas, Ste. 2200
New York, NY 10036-6710

Established in 1954.
Grantmaker type: Independent foundation
Financial data (yr. ended 12/31/01): Assets, $5,397,275 (M); expenditures, $417,811; qualifying distributions, $376,085; giving activities include $364,125 for 23 grants (high: $104,875; low: $1,000).
Purpose and activities: Giving primarily to fish/wildlife organizations, Presbyterian organizations, and human services.
Fields of interest: Museums (natural history); Arts; Law school/education; Theological school/education; Education; Aquariums; Health organizations, association; Cancer research; YM/YWCAs & YM/YWHAs; Children/youth, services; Federated giving programs; Protestant agencies & churches.
Types of support: Research.
Limitations: Applications not accepted. Giving primarily in Baltimore, MD, and New York, NY; funding also in NJ. No grants to individuals.
Application information: Contributes only to pre-selected organizations.
Officers and Trustees:* Herbert H. Chaice,* Pres.; Jane W.I. Droppa,* V.P.; Larry D. Droppa,* V.P.; Antonia M. Grumbach,* Secy.; Stephen W. Schwarz,* Treas.
EIN: 136149199

2219
Jackson Hole Preserve, Inc.
30 Rockefeller Plz., Rm. 5600
New York, NY 10112 (212) 649-5819
Contact: Carmen Reyes, Treas.

Incorporated in 1940 in NY.
Donor(s): John D. Rockefeller, Jr.,‡ Laurance S. Rockefeller, Rockefeller Brothers Fund.
Grantmaker type: Independent foundation
Financial data (yr. ended 12/31/00): Assets, $5,463,408 (M); expenditures, $1,402,828; qualifying distributions, $1,374,810; giving activities include $1,044,210 for 18 grants (high: $500,000; low: $10,000) and $60,000 for 2 foundation-administered programs.
Purpose and activities: Grants to restore, protect, and preserve for the benefit of the public the primitive grandeur and natural beauties of the landscape in areas notable for picturesque scenery; and to promote, encourage, and conduct other activities germane to these purposes.

Fields of interest: Historic preservation/historical societies; Natural resources; Environment; Recreation.
Types of support: General/operating support; Land acquisition; Program development; Publication; Consulting services; Matching/challenge support.
Limitations: Giving primarily in the Hudson River Valley, NY, area and Jackson Hole, WY. No grants to individuals, or for building or endowment funds, scholarships, or fellowships; no loans.
Application information: Application form not required.
Initial approach: Letter
Copies of proposal: 1
Deadline(s): None
Board meeting date(s): Oct. or Nov.; executive committee meets frequently
Officers and Trustees:* Clayton W. Frye, Jr.,* Chair. and Pres.; Antonia M. Grumbach,* Secy.; Carmen Reyes, Treas.; Nash Castro; Henry L. Diamond; Donal C. O'Brien, Jr.; Ellen R.C. Pomeroy; Laurance S. Rockefeller.
Number of staff: 2 part-time professional; 1 part-time support.
EIN: 131813818

2220
The Jaffe Family Foundation
c/o Elliot S. Jaffe, The Dress Barn, Inc.
30 Dunnigan Dr.
Suffern, NY 10901

Established in 1986 in NY.
Donor(s): Elliot Jaffe, Roslyn Jaffe.
Grantmaker type: Independent foundation
Financial data (yr. ended 12/31/01): Assets, $52,230,210 (M); expenditures, $3,084,421; qualifying distributions, $2,490,606; giving activities include $2,461,326 for 174 grants (high: $501,000; low: $45; average: $1,000–$50,000).
Purpose and activities: Giving primarily for the arts, higher education, and Jewish support organizations.
Fields of interest: Museums; Performing arts; Arts; Higher education; Education; Natural resources; Hospitals (general); Food services; Youth development, services; Human services; Community development, neighborhood development; Jewish agencies & temples.
Limitations: Applications not accepted. Giving on a national basis. No grants to individuals.
Application information: Contributes only to pre-selected organizations.
Officer and Directors:* Elliot S. Jaffe,* Pres.; David R. Jaffe; Elise P. Jaffe; Richard E. Jaffe; Roslyn Jaffe.
EIN: 222827692

2221
JCT Foundation
c/o Junction Advisors, Inc.
9 W. 57th St.
New York, NY 10019
Contact: Jeff C. Tarr, Dir.

Established in 1984 in NY.
Donor(s): Jeff C. Tarr.
Grantmaker type: Independent foundation

Financial data (yr. ended 12/31/01): Assets, $19,800,605 (M); expenditures, $1,066,423; qualifying distributions, $933,148; giving activities include $934,500 for 43 grants (high: $500,000; low: $300).
Purpose and activities: Giving primarily for the arts, education, nature conservancy, animal welfare, health care, human services, and federated giving programs; major support for the September 11th Fund.
Fields of interest: Media/communications; Museums (art); Dance; Theater; Arts; Higher education; Natural resources; Animal welfare; Health care; Human services; Federated giving programs; Disasters, 9/11/01.
Limitations: Applications not accepted. Giving primarily in New York, NY. No grants to individuals.
Application information: Contributes only to pre-selected organizations.
Directors: Jeff C. Tarr; Patricia G. Tarr.
Trustees: Jeff Tarr, Jr.; Jennifer Tarr.
EIN: 133237111

2222
JJJ Charitable Foundation
c/o U.S. Trust
114 W. 47th St.
New York, NY 10036

Established in 1997 in CT.
Donor(s): Hillside Capital, Inc.
Grantmaker type: Independent foundation
Financial data (yr. ended 12/31/00): Assets, $13,436,471 (M); gifts received, $839,612; expenditures, $966,409; qualifying distributions, $854,401; giving activities include $852,701 for 11 grants (high: $266,667; low: $5,000).
Fields of interest: Higher education; Teacher school/education; Education; Environment; Health care; Roman Catholic agencies & churches.
Limitations: Applications not accepted. Giving primarily in NJ and NY.
Application information: Contributes only to pre-selected organizations.
Officers and Directors:* John N. Irwin III,* Pres. and Treas.; Robert H.M. Ferguson, Secy.; Jane W.I. Droppa; Jeanet E. Irwin; John N. Irwin II.
EIN: 133932002

2223
JNT Foundation
c/o JPMorgan Chase Bank
345 Park Ave., 5th Fl.
New York, NY 10154

Established in 1999 in IA.
Donor(s): Vesta Hanson.
Grantmaker type: Independent foundation
Financial data (yr. ended 08/31/02): Assets, $5,370,214 (M); expenditures, $271,334; qualifying distributions, $252,416; giving activities include $198,000 for 12 grants (high: $22,000; low: $6,000).
Fields of interest: Higher education; Natural resources; Health care; Agriculture, farmlands; Human services; Domestic violence; International affairs.
Limitations: Applications not accepted. Giving primarily in IA. No grants to individuals.

Application information: Contributes only to pre-selected organizations.
Trustees: Carolyn R. Hansen; Lucy E. Hansen; Vesta Hansen; Walter E. Hansen; James E. Kasper; Robert W. Seery.
EIN: 421493980

2224
The Joelson Foundation
1780 Broadway, 10th Fl.
New York, NY 10019

Established in 1966 in NY.
Donor(s): Julius Joelson.‡
Grantmaker type: Independent foundation
Financial data (yr. ended 03/31/02): Assets, $17,803,321 (M); gifts received, $200,206; expenditures, $1,239,925; qualifying distributions, $1,145,309; giving activities include $1,049,811 for 246 grants (high: $100,000; low: $100).
Purpose and activities: Giving primarily for the arts, health and human services, and education.
Fields of interest: Museums; Performing arts; Arts; Higher education; Education; Natural resources; Health care; Human services; Children/youth, services; Jewish agencies & temples.
Limitations: Applications not accepted. Giving primarily in New York, NY. No grants to individuals.
Application information: Contributes only to pre-selected organizations.
Officers: Barbara J. Fife, Pres.; Joseph C. Mitchell, Secy.-Treas.
Director: Stephen Fife.
EIN: 136220799

2225
The Howard Johnson Foundation
c/o U.S. Trust
114 W. 47th St.
New York, NY 10036
Contact: Carolyn L. Larke, Asst. V.P., U.S. Trust or Linda Franciscovich, Sr. V.P.
FAX: (212) 852-3377

Trust established in 1961 in MA.
Donor(s): Howard D. Johnson,‡ Dorothy J. Henry.
Grantmaker type: Independent foundation
Financial data (yr. ended 12/31/01): Assets, $4,608,713 (M); gifts received, $15,500; expenditures, $272,071; qualifying distributions, $256,874; giving activities include $253,500 for 46 grants (high: $28,000; low: $1,000).
Purpose and activities: Giving primarily for higher and secondary education and health and hospitals; support also for museums, churches, religious welfare agencies, the environment, and animal welfare.
Fields of interest: Museums; Secondary school/education; Higher education; Education; Environment; Animal welfare; Hospitals (general); Health care; Health organizations, association; Human services; Religious federated giving programs; Religion.
Types of support: General/operating support.
Limitations: Giving primarily in CT, MA, and NY. No grants to individuals.
Publications: Application guidelines.

Application information: Application form not required.
  Initial approach: Mail or FAX letter requesting guidelines
  Copies of proposal: 1
  Board meeting date(s): Varies
Trustees: Marissa J. Brock; Patricia Johnson Crawford; Dorothy J. Henry; Howard Bates Johnson; Howard Brennan Johnson; Joshua J. Weeks; William H. Weeks.
Number of staff: 1 part-time support.
EIN: 046060965

2226
John Alfred & Oscar Johnson Memorial Trust
c/o M&T Bank
1 M&T Plz., 8th Fl.
Buffalo, NY 14203
Contact: Carole W. Sellstrom, Fdn. Coord.
Application address: 9-11 E. 4th St., P.O. Box 50, Jamestown, NY 14702-0050, tel: (716) 484-7190

Established in 1996 in NY.
Grantmaker type: Independent foundation
Financial data (yr. ended 01/31/03): Assets, $5,962,216 (M); expenditures, $507,385; qualifying distributions, $456,624; giving activities include $410,700 for 22 grants (high: $205,000; low: $100).
Purpose and activities: Consideration will be given to applications from charitable, religious, and educational organizations that benefit the citizens of Jamestown, NY and the surrounding area. Consideration will also be given to charitable, religious, and educational organizations which promote the appreciation and enrichment of the Swedish language.
Fields of interest: Natural resources; Hospitals (general); Health organizations; Human services; Salvation Army; YM/YWCAs & YM/YWHAs; Community development.
Limitations: Giving limited to Jamestown, NY. No grants to individuals.
Application information:
  Initial approach: Proposal
  Deadline(s): June 1 and Dec. 1
Trustees: John L. Sellstrom; M&T Bank.
EIN: 166438291

2227
The Kandell Fund
59 E. 54th St.
New York, NY 10022-4211

Established in 1952.
Donor(s): Leslie Friedberg, Alice Joseph, Florence Kandell, Leonard Kandell.‡
Grantmaker type: Independent foundation
Financial data (yr. ended 12/31/02): Assets, $251,010 (M); gifts received, $225,000; expenditures, $233,187; qualifying distributions, $232,946; giving activities include $232,795 for 274 grants (high: $6,500; low: $75).
Fields of interest: Arts; Natural resources; Hospitals (general); Human services; Jewish federated giving programs.
Limitations: Applications not accepted. Giving primarily in New York, NY. No grants to individuals.

Application information: Contributes only to pre-selected organizations.
Officers and Directors:* Donald Gordon,* Pres. and Treas.; Debbie Fechter, Secy.; Alice Kandell; Florence Kandell; Leslie Kandell.
Number of staff: None.
EIN: 136117648

2228
Kane Lodge Foundation, Inc.
c/o The Bank of New York, Tax Dept.
1 Wall St., 28th Fl.
New York, NY 10286
Contact: John Stichter, Pres.
Application address: 641 Lexington Ave., 18th Fl., New York, NY 10022

Established in 1960 in NY.
Grantmaker type: Independent foundation
Financial data (yr. ended 09/30/02): Assets, $1,877,435 (M); expenditures, $136,654; qualifying distributions, $118,964; giving activities include $110,000 for 14 grants (high: $25,000; low: $1,500).
Purpose and activities: Giving for art and cultural institutes, education, and children's services.
Fields of interest: Museums; Historic preservation/historical societies; Education; Animals/wildlife; Religion.
Limitations: Giving primarily in NY.
Application information:
   Initial approach: Letter
   Deadline(s): None
Officers: John Stichter, Pres.; Herman E. Muller, Jr., V.P.; John R. Ahlgren, Secy.; Peter Sulick, Jr., Treas.
Directors: P. Michael Puleo; Victor G. Webb; Rodney I. Woods.
EIN: 136105390

2229
The J. M. Kaplan Fund, Inc. ▼
261 Madison Ave., 19th Fl.
New York, NY 10016 (212) 767-0630
Contact: William P. Falahee, Cont.
FAX: (212) 767-0639; Application address for publication program: Furthermore, P.O. Box 667, Hudson, NY 12534; tel.: (518) 828-8900; URL: http://www.jmkfund.org

Incorporated in 1948 in NY as Faigel Leah Foundation, Inc.; The J.M. Kaplan Fund, Inc., a DE corporation, merged with it in 1975 and was renamed The J.M. Kaplan Fund, Inc.
Donor(s): Members of the J.M. Kaplan family.
Grantmaker type: Independent foundation
Financial data (yr. ended 12/31/02): Assets, $128,069,918 (M); expenditures, $12,110,533; qualifying distributions, $9,980,478; giving activities include $8,766,428 for 343 grants (high: $550,000; low: $75; average: $5,000–$150,000).
Purpose and activities: Giving primarily in three areas: environment, historic preservation, and human migrations. The fund offers program-related investments to encourage ventures of particular interest. The fund also has a trustee-initiated grants program that considers grant requests invited by the trustees.
Fields of interest: Historic preservation/historical societies; Natural resources; Environment;

Human services; International migration/refugee issues; Community development.
Types of support: General/operating support; Continuing support; Program development; Publication; Seed money; Research; Technical assistance; Program-related investments/loans.
Limitations: Giving primarily in New York City, NY; cross-borders of North America; and worldwide. No grants to individuals, including scholarships and fellowships, or for construction or building programs, endowment funds, operating budgets of educational or medical institutions, film or video, or sponsorship of books, dances, plays, or other works of art.
Publications: Annual report (including application guidelines).
Application information: Proposals received by FAX not considered.
   Initial approach: 2- to 3-page letter of inquiry
   Copies of proposal: 1
   Deadline(s): None; requests received after Oct. 1 will be carried over to next year
   Board meeting date(s): Quarterly
   Final notification: Formal letter
Officers and Trustees:* Peter W. Davidson,* Chair.; Conn Nugent,* Secy. and Exec. Dir.; William P. Falahee, Cont.; Betsy Davidson; G. Bradford Davidson; J. Matthew Davidson; Joan K. Davidson; Caio Fonseca; Elizabeth K. Fonseca; Isabel Fonseca; Quina Fonseca; Richard D. Kaplan; Mary E. Kaplan.
Number of staff: 4 full-time professional; 1 full-time support.
EIN: 136090286
Recent environmental and animal welfare grants:
2229-1 Adirondack Council, Elizabethtown, NY, $10,000. For capital campaign. 2001.
2229-2 American Farmland Trust, DC, $10,000. For general support for efforts to protect and preserve state's farmland and to promote farming practices that lead to healthy environment. 2001.
2229-3 American Farmland Trust, DC, $10,000. For New York State policy efforts. 2001.
2229-4 Americans for Equitable Climate Solutions, DC, $150,000. For From Symbolism to Reality: Building a Consensus for Carbon Reduction Policies Project that aims to find effective carbon reduction policies and build consensus for those policies. 2001.
2229-5 ANAI Association, Limon, Costa Rica, $20,000. For planning grant to consolidate stream biomonitoring program in canton of Talamanca, Costa Rica and province of Bocas del Toro, Panama. 2001.
2229-6 Audubon Society, National, New York, NY, $75,000. For Ocean Refugees Program and to initiate new targets to expand and strengthen marine protected area (MPA) movement. 2001.
2229-7 Bronx River Restoration, Bronx, NY, $25,000. For transition and development of Bronx River Restoration Alliance that aims to protect, improve and restore Bronx River Watershed. 2001.
2229-8 Brooklyn Bridge Park Coalition, Brooklyn, NY, $15,000. For general operating support to continue efforts to convert downtown Brooklyn's waterfront into self-financed regional park. 2001.
2229-9 Citizens for the Hudson Valley, Hudson, NY, $10,000. For general support. 2001.

2229-10 City Parks Foundation, New York, NY, $10,000. For information boxes for Narrows Botanical Garden that identify and describe various aspects of plants, shrubs, and trees to educate visitors on horticulture and environmental issues. 2001.
2229-11 Columbia Land Conservancy, Chatham, NY, $12,000. For challenge grant for Operating Endowment Campaign. 2001.
2229-12 Community Consulting Services, Brooklyn, NY, $10,000. For Comprehensive Bicycle/Pedestrian Pilot Program with Access Measures for Brooklyn Bridge Park. 2001.
2229-13 Congress for the New Urbanism, San Francisco, CA, $10,000. For general support. 2001.
2229-14 Conservation Law Foundation, Boston, MA, $350,000. For Marine Protected Areas Initiative in the Gulf of Maine. 2001.
2229-15 Council on the Environment, New York, NY, $20,000. For general support for Greenmarket. 2001.
2229-16 Cunningham Park, Friends of, Fresh Meadows, NY, $15,000. To landscape and maintain entrances and areas of Cunningham Park. 2001.
2229-17 Design Trust for Public Space, New York, NY, $20,000. For Public Space Makers, discussion series that brings city builders and architectural thinkers together in exceptional venues to discuss New York's built environment with invited guests. 2001.
2229-18 Environmental Defense, New York, NY, $200,000. To conserve biodiversity linkages in northern Caribbean marine protected areas and for sustainable development in Cuba. 2001.
2229-19 Envision Environmental Media Center, Sag Harbor, NY, $10,000. For treatment development for public awareness program on national energy policy. 2001.
2229-20 ETV Endowment of South Carolina, Spartanburg, SC, $30,000. For documentary series entitled Life Well Lived featuring life and work of Jane Goodall. 2001.
2229-21 Fort Tryon Park, Friends of, New York, NY, $20,000. For rehabilitation, landscaping, and programming in Fort Tryon Park. 2001.
2229-22 Fuerza Ambiental, Chihuahua, Mexico, $200,000. For integrated conservation of Madera Region. 2001.
2229-23 Fuerza Ambiental, Chihuahua, Mexico, $20,000. For strategic planning for conservation and preservation of Madera Region, Mimbres-Paquime Corridor. 2001.
2229-24 Green Guerillas, New York, NY, $15,000. For community gardens. 2001.
2229-25 Heritage Trails New York Fund, New York, NY, $75,000. For integration of Heritage Trails and Alliance for Downtown New York. 2001.
2229-26 Heritage Trails New York Fund, New York, NY, $25,000. For general support. 2001.
2229-27 Horticultural Society of New York, New York, NY, $20,000. For GreenBranches Program, partnership program with New York City's library systems and borough botanical gardens to design, install and maintain gardens around branch libraries. 2001.
2229-28 Hudson River Foundation for Science and Environmental Research, New York, NY, $10,000. For general support. 2001.

2229-29 Hudson River Heritage, Rhinebeck, NY, $25,000. For Hudson River Preservation Coalition. 2001.

2229-30 Hudson River Heritage, Rhinebeck, NY, $20,000. For Hudson River Valley Map. 2001.

2229-31 Idea Wild, Fort Collins, CO, $25,000. For general support. 2001.

2229-32 Jefferson Market Garden, New York, NY, $10,000. For planning stage and development phase for lighting. 2001.

2229-33 Land Institute, Salina, KS, $39,000. For Prairie Writers Circle. 2001.

2229-34 Land Trust Alliance, DC, $10,000. For general support. 2001.

2229-35 Malpai Borderlands Group, Douglas, AZ, $120,000. To complete purchase of conservation easement to protect open space in biologically important part of the United States. 2001.

2229-36 Marine Conservation Biology Institute, Redmond, WA, $75,000. For multi-faceted program aimed at designating networks of fully protected marine reserves in U.S., Canadian and Mexican waters. 2001.

2229-37 Natural Resources Defense Council, New York, NY, $25,000. For planning grant to support research and investigation into opportunities for involvement in energy issues in Mexico, including their relationship with Mexican/US environmental issues. 2001.

2229-38 Natural Resources Defense Council, New York, NY, $25,000. For Amicus Journal. 2001.

2229-39 Natural Resources Defense Council, New York, NY, $10,000. For magazine, On Earth. 2001.

2229-40 Nature Conservancy, East Hampton, NY, $30,000. For site work at Center for Conservation. 2001.

2229-41 Nature Conservancy, Arlington, VA, $115,000. For Phase II Cuatro Esquinas Project. 2001.

2229-42 Nature Conservancy, Arlington, VA, $30,000. To implement strategies that will ensure long-term conservation of Cuatro Esquinas region's biodiversity. 2001.

2229-43 New York League of Conservation Voters, New York, NY, $10,000. For general support. 2001.

2229-44 Northern Arizona University Foundation, Flagstaff, AZ, $48,000. For Integrating Farm and Ranch Lands Functioning Movement Corridors for Pollinators and Carnivores in the Mexico/US Border Region. 2001.

2229-45 Open Space Institute, New York, NY, $29,000. To develop an explicitly political effort to educate and mobilize elected officials, civic leaders and public to increase funding for parks and open spaces in New York City. 2001.

2229-46 Preservation League of New York State, Albany, NY, $10,000. For Rural Landscape Project. 2001.

2229-47 Prospect Park Alliance, Brooklyn, NY, $40,000. For information technology component of public information efforts planned for Prospect Park Audubon Center. 2001.

2229-48 Rainforest Alliance, New York, NY, $10,000. For general support. 2001.

2229-49 Riverdale Nature Preservancy, Bronx, NY, $15,000. To develop community garden

Endor as model to demonstrate aesthetic and ecological potential of parkland and bridges of Henry Hudson Parkway in Riverdale. 2001.

2229-50 Rocky Mountain Institute, Snowmass, CO, $150,000. For Hypercar and Hypercar Center whose vehicles are designed to maximize efficiency. 2001.

2229-51 Rocky Mountain Institute, Snowmass, CO, $35,000. To create and disseminate core information tools necessary to create new secure national energy strategy. 2001.

2229-52 Scenic Hudson, Poughkeepsie, NY, $10,000. For Land Trust's Clermont Buffer and Trail Project. 2001.

2229-53 SeaWeb, DC, $250,000. To develop necessary tools to assume leadership role in environmental community and communicate need for marine reserves. 2001.

2229-54 Transportation Alternatives, New York, NY, $83,000. For partnership with New York Public Interest Group (NYPIRG) Straphangers campaign to win substantially improved and expanded local and express bus service in New York City. 2001.

2229-55 Trust for Public Land, San Francisco, CA, $50,000. For Housing and Open Space Initiative that develops community-managed gardens and parks as integral parts of new housing construction and rehabilitation projects. 2001.

2229-56 Union of Concerned Scientists, Cambridge, MA, $150,000. For work to advance renewable energy and fuel economy solutions to climate change. 2001.

2229-57 Universidad Nacional Autonoma de Mexico, Mexico City, Mexico, $120,000. For conservation of prairie dog ecosystem in northwestern Mexico. 2001.

2229-58 University of Hawaii, Honolulu, HI, $250,000. For Biodiversity, Species Ranges, and Gene Flow in the Abyssal Pacific Nodule Province Predicting and Managing the Impacts of Deep Seabed Mining. 2001.

2229-59 University of South Florida Research Foundation, Saint Petersburg, FL, $120,000. For Pilot Study of Larval Linkages between western Caribbean, Central America, Cuba and South Florida: Critical Information for the Design of a Marine Reserve Network. 2001.

2229-60 Wildlands Project, Tucson, AZ, $150,000. For Peloncillo Mountains Protection Project. 2001.

2229-61 World Wildlife Fund Canada, Toronto, Canada, $125,000. For marine conservation that straddles the Canada-US border in Gulf of Maine. 2001.

2229-62 World Wildlife Fund/Conservation Foundation, DC, $25,000. For conservation efforts to protect native prairie habitat in United States and Canada. 2001.

2230
Henry & Elaine Kaufman Foundation, Inc.
660 Madison Ave., 15th Fl.
New York, NY 10021
Contact: Dr. Henry Kaufman, Pres., or Elaine Kaufman, V.P.

Established in 1969.
Donor(s): Elaine Kaufman, Henry Kaufman, Henry Kaufman Charitable Lead Trust.
Grantmaker type: Independent foundation

Financial data (yr. ended 12/31/01): Assets, $37,509,341 (M); expenditures, $4,062,644; qualifying distributions, $3,574,707; giving activities include $3,589,798 for 149 grants (high: $1,000,000; low: $100; average: $1,000–$100,000).

Purpose and activities: Support primarily for Jewish organizations, museums and other cultural institutions, and education.
Fields of interest: Multipurpose centers/programs; Museums; Arts; Higher education; Business school/education; Education; Animal welfare; Human services; Jewish federated giving programs; Jewish agencies & temples.
Types of support: General/operating support; Annual campaigns.
Limitations: Giving primarily in the metropolitan New York, NY, area, including portions of NJ.
Application information:
Initial approach: Letter
Deadline(s): None
Officers and Directors:* Henry Kaufman,* Pres. and Treas.; Elaine Kaufman,* V.P.; Daniel Kaufman,* Secy.; Craig S. Kaufman; Glenn D. Kaufman.
Number of staff: None.
EIN: 237045903
Recent environmental and animal welfare grants:
2230-1 Animal Medical Center, New York, NY, $100,000. 2001.
2230-2 Animal Medical Center, New York, NY, $23,500. 2001.
2230-3 Animal Medical Center, New York, NY, $10,000. 2001.

2231
Kealy Family Foundation
c/o Goldman Sachs & Co., Tax Dept.
85 Broad St.
New York, NY 10004
Contact: William J. Kealy, Tr.
Additional address: 120 N. Baum Trail, Duck, NC 27949, tel.: (252) 261-0233; E-mail: BEKRI@aol.com

Established in 1985.
Donor(s): William F. Kealy, William J. Kealy, Ellen M. Kealy.
Grantmaker type: Independent foundation
Financial data (yr. ended 05/31/02): Assets, $3,331,003 (M); expenditures, $478,881; qualifying distributions, $476,825; giving activities include $465,385 for 52 grants (high: $50,000; low: $135).

Purpose and activities: Giving primarily for education; support also for the arts, conservation, mental health, and social services.
Fields of interest: Arts; Education; Natural resources; Environment, water resources; Environment, land resources; Mental health/crisis services; Human services; Children/youth, services; Family services; Race/intergroup relations; Marine science; Minorities.
Types of support: General/operating support; Annual campaigns; Capital campaigns; Land acquisition.
Limitations: Applications not accepted. Giving primarily in the Outer Banks, NC area, and New York City. No grants to individuals.

Application information: Contributes only to pre-selected organizations.
Trustees: Maureen K. Jacquelin; Roger A. Jacquelin; Alexandra Kealy; Daniel M. Kealy; Ellen M. Kealy; Tracey E. Kealy; William J. Kealy; William K. Kealy.
Number of staff: 1 part-time support.
EIN: 133318124

2232
Keefe Family Foundation
375 Park Ave., Ste. 2301
New York, NY 10152

Established in 1989 in NY.
Donor(s): Harry V. Keefe, Jr.
Grantmaker type: Independent foundation
Financial data (yr. ended 12/31/01): Assets, $3,912,616 (M); expenditures, $221,482; qualifying distributions, $220,857; giving activities include $219,332 for 12 grants (high: $60,000; low: $1,957).
Purpose and activities: Giving primarily for education.
Fields of interest: Adult education—literacy, basic skills & GED; Reading; Education; Environment; Animals/wildlife, preservation/protection; Hospitals (general); Disabled.
Types of support: General/operating support; Capital campaigns; Program development.
Limitations: Applications not accepted. Giving on a national basis. No support for private foundations. No grants to individuals.
Application information: Contributes only to pre-selected organizations. Unsolicited requests for funds not accepted.
Officers: Harry V. Keefe, Pres. and Treas.; Kathleen Keefe Raffel, V.P. and Secy.; Anita L. Keefe, V.P.; Harry V. Keefe, Jr., V.P.
EIN: 133520397

2233
Keeper Springs Corporate Giving Program
96 Spring St.
New York, NY 10012
URL: http://www.keepersprings.com/donations.html

Grantmaker type: Corporate giving program
Purpose and activities: Keeper Springs makes charitable contributions of bottled water to nonprofit organizations involved with the environment. Support is given primarily on the East Coast.
Fields of interest: Environment.
Types of support: Donated products.
Limitations: Giving primarily on the East Coast, with emphasis on the New York, NY, area.

2234
Ellsworth Kelly Foundation, Inc.
c/o Ellsworth M. Kelly
P.O. Box 220
Spencertown, NY 12165
Contact: Jack Shear, Secy.-Treas.

Established in 1991 in NY.
Donor(s): Ellsworth Kelly.
Grantmaker type: Independent foundation

Financial data (yr. ended 12/31/01): Assets, $11,448,191 (M); gifts received, $2,000,000; expenditures, $522,973; qualifying distributions, $452,810; giving activities include $450,000 for 8 grants (high: $100,000; low: $25,000; average: $5,000–$50,000).
Fields of interest: Arts; Higher education; Natural resources; Animals/wildlife, bird preserves.
Limitations: Applications not accepted. Giving on a national basis, with some emphasis on the East Coast. No grants to individuals.
Application information: Contributes only to pre-selected organizations.
Officers: Ellsworth Kelly, Pres.; Jack Shear, Secy.-Treas.
Directors: Roberta Bernstein; Emily Pulitzer.
EIN: 223132379

2235
The Philip J. and Anne M. Kemper Charitable Foundation
c/o Owl Wire & Cable
P.O. Box 187
Canastota, NY 13032

Established in 1999 in NY.
Donor(s): Philip J. Kemper, Anne M. Kemper.
Grantmaker type: Independent foundation
Financial data (yr. ended 12/31/01): Assets, $2,156,063 (M); expenditures, $107,167; qualifying distributions, $103,928; giving activities include $105,000 for 13 grants (high: $25,000; low: $5,000).
Purpose and activities: Giving for education, medicine, social welfare, the arts, historic preservation, religion, and the environment.
Fields of interest: Arts; Education; Natural resources; Human services; YM/YWCAs & YM/YWHAs; Hospices; Religion.
Limitations: Applications not accepted. Giving primarily in NY. No grants to individuals.
Application information: Contributes only to pre-selected organizations.
Trustees: Anne M. Kemper; Philip J. Kemper.
EIN: 161562659

2236
Thomas L. Kempner, Jr. Foundation
885 3rd Ave., Ste. 3300
New York, NY 10022

Established in 1987 in NY.
Donor(s): Thomas L. Kempner, Jr.
Grantmaker type: Independent foundation
Financial data (yr. ended 12/31/02): Assets, $10,667,985 (M); gifts received, $715,413; expenditures, $467,935; qualifying distributions, $361,136; giving activities include $359,136 for 33 grants (high: $25,000; low: $1,000).
Purpose and activities: Giving for the arts, education, the environment, housing, and youth programs.
Fields of interest: Arts; Education; Environment; Housing/shelter; Children/youth, services.
Limitations: Applications not accepted. No grants to individuals.
Application information: Contributes only to pre-selected organizations.
Officers: Thomas L. Kempner, Jr., Pres.; Dean C. Berry, Secy.; Katheryn C. Patterson, Treas.
Number of staff: None.

EIN: 133407819

2237
The Kenlou Foundation, Inc.
P.O. Box 25300
Rochester, NY 14625

Established in 2000 in NY.
Donor(s): Mary E. Swierkos, John K. Williams, Richard E. Williams, Robert M. Williams.
Grantmaker type: Independent foundation
Financial data (yr. ended 12/31/02): Assets, $3,069,729 (M); expenditures, $214,330; qualifying distributions, $184,162; giving activities include $185,000 for 27 grants (high: $30,000; low: $250).
Fields of interest: Arts; Animals/wildlife; Human services.
Limitations: Applications not accepted. No grants to individuals.
Application information: Contributes only to pre-selected organizations.
Officers: Richard E. Williams, Pres.; John K. Williams, V.P.; Robert M. Williams, Secy.; Mary E. Swierkos, Treas.
EIN: 161596738

2238
Karen A. & Kevin W. Kennedy Foundation
c/o Goldman Sachs & Co.
85 Broad St., Tax Dept.
New York, NY 10004

Established 1985 in NY.
Donor(s): Kevin W. Kennedy.
Grantmaker type: Independent foundation
Financial data (yr. ended 04/30/02): Assets, $2,049,166 (M); gifts received, $1,870,662; expenditures, $984,833; qualifying distributions, $945,333; giving activities include $942,274 for 110 grants (high: $150,000; low: $250; average: $500–$50,000).
Purpose and activities: Giving primarily for the arts, conservation, education, health care and human services.
Fields of interest: Opera; Arts; Higher education; Medical school/education; Nursing school/education; Natural resources; Health care; Human services.
Types of support: Continuing support; Annual campaigns; Capital campaigns; Building/renovation; Endowments; Professorships; Scholarship funds.
Limitations: Applications not accepted. Giving primarily in MA, NJ, and NY. No grants to individuals, or for scholarships; no loans.
Application information: Contributes only to pre-selected organizations.
Trustees: Coleman W. Kennedy; Karen A. Kennedy; Kevin W. Kennedy; William F. Kennedy.
Number of staff: None.
EIN: 133318161

2239
Kenner Foundation, Inc.
437 Madison Ave., No. 2001
New York, NY 10021 (212) 319-2300
Contact: Jeffrey L. Kenner, Dir.

Established in 1996 in NY.
Donor(s): Jeffrey L. Kenner.
Grantmaker type: Independent foundation
Financial data (yr. ended 12/31/01): Assets, $1,527,726 (M); gifts received, $163,460; expenditures, $355,386; qualifying distributions, $354,400; giving activities include $354,400 for 12 grants (high: $150,000; low: $2,000).
Fields of interest: Education; Natural resources.
Application information:
Initial approach: Letter
Directors: Jeffrey L. Kenner; Patricia Kenner.
EIN: 133928876

2240
The KeySpan Foundation
175 E. Old Country Rd.
Hicksville, NY 11801 (516) 545-6100
Contact: David M. Okorn, Exec. Dir.
URL: http://www.keyspanenergy.com/corpinfo/community/foundation_all_all.jsp

Established in 1998 in NY.
Donor(s): MarketSpan Corp., KeySpan Corp.
Grantmaker type: Company-sponsored foundation
Financial data (yr. ended 12/31/01): Assets, $24,913,152 (M); gifts received, $51,033; expenditures, $2,430,663; qualifying distributions, $2,123,425; giving activities include $2,029,023 for 128 grants (high: $150,000; low: $800; average: $5,000–$25,000).
Purpose and activities: The foundation seeks to identify opportunities to take meaningful efforts to enhance the well-being of the people and communities where it does business. Primary areas of focus are arts and culture, education, environmental preservation, health, human services, and community development.
Fields of interest: Arts; Education; Natural resources; Health care; Human services; Community development.
Limitations: Giving primarily in Brooklyn, Queens, Staten Island, and Nassau and Suffolk counties, NY. Some giving also internationally in areas of company operations. No support for religious, political, or fraternal organizations. No grants to individuals, or for fundraisers.
Publications: Application guidelines, Annual report.
Application information: The foundation accepts the New York Area Common Application Form. Application guidelines available on foundation Web site. Application form not required.
Initial approach: Letter
Copies of proposal: 1
Board meeting date(s): Quarterly
Officers and Directors:* Vicki Fuller,* Chair.; Colin Watson,* V.P.; Ronald Jendras, Treas.; David Okorn, Exec. Dir.; Donald Elliot; Kathleen Hearn; Brian McCaffrey; Basil Paterson; Maurice Shaw.
Number of staff: 1 full-time professional; 1 full-time support.
EIN: 113466416

2241
The Peter and Eaddo Kiernan Foundation
c/o BCRS Assoc., LLC
100 Wall St., 11th Fl.
New York, NY 10005

Established in 1991 in NY.
Donor(s): Peter D. Kiernan.
Grantmaker type: Independent foundation
Financial data (yr. ended 05/31/02): Assets, $1,569,758 (M); gifts received, $195,909; expenditures, $199,410; qualifying distributions, $198,260; giving activities include $196,750 for 10 grants (high: $80,000; low: $250; average: $2,500–$20,000).
Purpose and activities: Giving primarily for education; funding also for athletic associations.
Fields of interest: Education; Natural resources; Recreation; Human services; Economically disadvantaged.
Limitations: Applications not accepted. Giving primarily in New York, NY; some giving in CT. No grants to individuals.
Application information: Contributes only to pre-selected organizations.
Trustees: Eaddo H. Kiernan; Peter D. Kiernan.
EIN: 133637705

2242
King Baudouin Foundation United States, Inc.
315 W. 33rd St., Apt. 31-i
New York, NY 10001 (212) 643-8645
Contact: Jean-Paul Warmoes, Exec. Secy.
E-mail: jeanpaul@kbfus.org; *URL:* http://www.kbfus.org

Established in 1997 in GA by the King Baudouin Foundation, Belgium.
Grantmaker type: Public charity
Financial data (yr. ended 12/31/02): Revenue, $1,338,338; assets, $410,599 (M); gifts received, $1,334,910; expenditures, $1,520,265; program services expenses, $1,197,142; giving activities include $964,309 for 26 grants (high: $200,000; low: $288).
Purpose and activities: KBFUS seeks to increase understanding between the United States and Europe through the development and implementation of transatlantic exchange programs. The organization also enables U.S.-based individuals to support people and causes throughout Europe in a tax-efficient and cost-effective way, and helps corporations shape their corporate contributions programs in continental Europe.
Fields of interest: Cultural/ethnic awareness; Education; Environment; Health care; Human services; International affairs.
International interests: Europe.
Types of support: Program-related investments/loans.
Limitations: Applications not accepted. Giving on an international basis.
Application information: Contributes only to pre-selected organizations; unsolicited requests for funds not considered or acknowledged.
Board meeting date(s): Biannually
Officers and Directors:* Baron Jacobs,* Pres.; Hon. Alan John Blinken,* V.P.; Hon. Herman Portocarero,* Secy.; Baron Luc Tayart de Borms,* Treas.; Jean-Paul Warmoes, Exec. Secy.; Baron Buysee; Hon. Anne Cox-Chambers;

Jacques de Vaucheroy; Gregory A. Dexter; Al Mays; Richard C. Notebaert; Cedric Suzman; Baron Herman Vanden Berghe.
Number of staff: 1 full-time professional.
EIN: 582277856

2243
Mark and Anla Cheng Kingdon Fund
c/o Peter J. Cobos
152 W. 57th St., 50th Fl.
New York, NY 10019

Established in 1997 in NY.
Grantmaker type: Independent foundation
Financial data (yr. ended 12/31/01): Assets, $25,318,376 (M); gifts received, $13,350,000; expenditures, $2,644,589; qualifying distributions, $2,644,073; giving activities include $2,644,073 for 109 grants (high: $1,000,000; low: $110; average: $500–$25,000).
Purpose and activities: Giving primarily for the arts, education, and human services.
Fields of interest: Arts; Education; Environment; Hospitals (general); Health organizations, association; Human services; Jewish agencies & temples.
Limitations: Applications not accepted. Giving primarily in NY. No grants to individuals.
Application information: Contributes only to pre-selected organizations.
Officers: Mark Kingdon, Chair.; Peter J. Cobos, Secy.
EIN: 133948023

2244
The Conrad and Virginia Klee Foundation, Inc.
700 Security Mutual Bldg.
80 Exchange St.
Binghamton, NY 13901 (607) 231-6717
Contact: Clayton M. Axtell, III, Pres.

Incorporated in 1957 in NY.
Donor(s): Conrad C. Klee,‡ Virginia Klee.‡
Grantmaker type: Independent foundation
Financial data (yr. ended 12/31/02): Assets, $15,950,372 (M); expenditures, $984,093; qualifying distributions, $913,418; giving activities include $919,693 for 54 grants (high: $115,566; low: $1,263).
Purpose and activities: Giving primarily for the arts, health care, and human services.
Fields of interest: Arts; Animal welfare; Hospitals (general); Health care; Human services; Children/youth, services; Federated giving programs; Christian agencies & churches.
Types of support: General/operating support; Capital campaigns.
Limitations: Giving primarily in Broome County and Guilford, NY. No grants to individuals.
Application information: Application form not required.
Initial approach: Letter
Copies of proposal: 1
Deadline(s): None
Board meeting date(s): Apr. and Nov.
Officers: Clayton M. Axtell, Jr., Pres.; David Birchenough, V.P. and Treas.; David Patterson, Secy.

Directors: Wells Allen, Jr.; Clayton M. Axtell III; Linda Biemer; John E. Gwyn; Floyd Lawson; Robert Nash.
EIN: 156019821

2245
Klingenstein Fund
(formerly Clara Buttenwieser Unger Memorial Foundation)
31 Oxford Rd.
Scarsdale, NY 10583
Contact: Lee P. Klingenstein, Pres.

Established in 1940 in NY.
Donor(s): Alan Klingenstein, Lee Paul Klingenstein, Paul H. Klingenstein, Joanne Ziesing.
Grantmaker type: Independent foundation
Financial data (yr. ended 12/31/02): Assets, $4,476,163 (M); expenditures, $320,215; qualifying distributions, $292,999; giving activities include $288,813 for grants.
Purpose and activities: Support primarily for education including a wilderness education program, as well as for arts, health, and human services.
Fields of interest: Arts; Education; Environmental education; Environment; Hospitals (general); Human services; Jewish agencies & temples.
Limitations: Giving primarily in CT and NY. No grants to individuals.
Application information:
Initial approach: Letter
Deadline(s): None
Officers: Lee Paul Klingenstein, Pres.; Paul H. Klingenstein, V.P.; Joanne K. Ziesing, Secy.; Alan Klingenstein, Treas.
EIN: 136077894

2246
Frederick & Sharon Klingenstein Fund
c/o Tanton & Co., LLP
37 W. 57th St., 5th Fl.
New York, NY 10019-3411
Contact: Frederick A. Klingenstein, Tr.
Application address: 787 7th Ave., 6th Fl., New York, NY 10019-6016

Established in 1997 in NY.
Donor(s): Frederick A. Klingenstein.
Grantmaker type: Independent foundation
Financial data (yr. ended 12/31/01): Assets, $4,155,638 (M); gifts received, $39; expenditures, $1,013,781; qualifying distributions, $943,952; giving activities include $947,120 for 77 grants (high: $425,000; low: $100).
Purpose and activities: Giving primarily to cultural institutions, including a museum of natural history, hospitals, and social services.
Fields of interest: Museums (natural history); Arts; Education; Animal welfare; Hospitals (general); Parks/playgrounds; Human services; Children/youth, services; Community development.
Limitations: Giving primarily in New York, NY.
Application information: Application form not required.
Deadline(s): None
Trustees: Frederick A. Klingenstein; Sharon Klingenstein.

EIN: 061471980

2247
Knafel Family Foundation
810 7th Ave., 41st Fl.
New York, NY 10019-5818

Established in 1994 in NY.
Grantmaker type: Independent foundation
Financial data (yr. ended 12/31/00): Assets, $17,866,990 (M); expenditures, $763,723; qualifying distributions, $725,355; giving activities include $738,750 for 36 grants (high: $350,000; low: $250).
Purpose and activities: Giving primarily for education, and for human services.
Fields of interest: Higher education; Education; Environment; Health organizations, association; Human services.
Limitations: Applications not accepted. Giving primarily in MA and NY. No grants to individuals.
Application information: Contributes only to pre-selected organizations.
Officers: Sidney R. Knafel, Pres.; Andrew G. Knafel, Treas.
Director: Douglas R. Knafel.
EIN: 133779562

2248
The Knapp Fund
c/o James C. Edwards & Co., Inc.
570 Lexington Ave.
New York, NY 10022

Incorporated in 1917 in NY.
Donor(s): George O. Knapp.‡
Grantmaker type: Independent foundation
Financial data (yr. ended 08/31/02): Assets, $3,377,554 (M); expenditures, $236,614; qualifying distributions, $206,873; giving activities include $207,500 for 27 grants (high: $53,000; low: $2,000).
Purpose and activities: Giving primarily for education, land and environmental preservation, health associations, medical research, and human services.
Fields of interest: Elementary/secondary education; Scholarships/financial aid; Education; Environment; Medical research, institute; Human services.
Types of support: General/operating support; Continuing support; Annual campaigns; Building/renovation; Program development; Scholarship funds; Research.
Limitations: Applications not accepted. Giving primarily in CT, FL, NY and PA. No grants to individuals, or for matching gifts; no loans.
Application information: Contributes only to pre-selected organizations.
Board meeting date(s): Sept.
Officers: George O. Knapp III, Pres.; Frank Jared Sprole, V.P. and Treas.; David MacNeil, V.P.; Margaret Hanlon, Secy.
Directors: Wendy Sprole Bangs; Thomas R. Knapp; W. Jared Knapp III; Louise Knapp Page; Jared K. Sprole.
Number of staff: None.
EIN: 136068384

2249
Knight Vision Foundation, Inc.
c/o Schwartz & Co
2580 Sunrise Hwy.
Bellmore, NY 11710-3608
Contact: Peter Kleinknecht, V.P.

Established in 1998 in FL.
Donor(s): Peter Kleinknecht, Maureen Kleinknecht.
Grantmaker type: Independent foundation
Financial data (yr. ended 12/31/01): Assets, $4,301,353 (M); expenditures, $396,969; qualifying distributions, $375,988; giving activities include $376,852 for 22 grants (high: $150,000; low: $112).
Purpose and activities: Giving primarily for education, health care and hospitals, and human services.
Fields of interest: Education, single organization support; Higher education; Natural resources; Animal welfare; Hospitals (general); Health care; Housing/shelter, volunteer services; Housing/shelter; Human services; Philanthropy/voluntarism; Marine science; Economically disadvantaged.
Limitations: Giving on a national basis, with some emphasis on NY.
Application information: Application form not required.
Deadline(s): None
Officers: Maureen Kleinknecht, Pres.; Peter Kleinknecht, V.P. and Secy.
Trustees: Gavin Kleinknecht; Keir Kleinknecht; Sabrina Kleinknecht.
EIN: 650829583

2250
The Seymour H. Knox Foundation
1 HSBC Ctr., Ste. 3840
Buffalo, NY 14203

Incorporated in 1945 in NY.
Donor(s): Seymour H. Knox,‡ Marjorie K.C. Klopp,‡ Dorothy K.G. Rogers.‡
Grantmaker type: Independent foundation
Financial data (yr. ended 12/31/02): Assets, $17,484,825 (M); expenditures, $1,247,232; qualifying distributions, $901,457; giving activities include $779,919 for 116 grants (high: $125,650; low: $100).
Purpose and activities: Giving primarily for the arts, education and human services.
Fields of interest: Arts education; Arts; Education; Zoos/zoological societies; Health care; Human services; YM/YWCAs & YM/YWHAs; Federated giving programs.
Types of support: General/operating support.
Limitations: Giving primarily in the Buffalo, NY, area; some funding nationally. No grants to individuals.
Application information:
Initial approach: Letter
Deadline(s): None
Officers and Directors:* Hazard K. Campbell, Chair.; Northrup R. Knox, Jr.,* Pres.; Seymour H. Knox IV,* V.P. and Secy.; Benjamin K. Campbell,* V.P. and Treas.; Charles W. Banta; Randolph A. Marks; Henry Z. Urban.
EIN: 160839066

2251
The Kohlberg Foundation, Inc. ▼
111 Radio Cir.
Mount Kisco, NY 10549
Contact: Nancy White McCabe, Exec. Dir.
FAX: (914) 241-1195; E-mail:
dehaan@Kfound.org

Established in 1989 in NY.
Donor(s): The Kohlberg Foundation.
Grantmaker type: Independent foundation
Financial data (yr. ended 12/31/01): Assets,
$263,503,097 (M); gifts received, $33,124,048;
expenditures, $13,335,339; qualifying
distributions, $12,123,602; giving activities
include $11,964,504 for 133+ grants (high:
$2,000,000; average: $1,000–$25,000).
Purpose and activities: Support for
environmental programs, integrative medicine,
community, educational and cultural
organizations.
Fields of interest: Environmental education;
Health organizations, association; Medical
research, institute; Children/youth, services.
Types of support: Annual campaigns; Land
acquisition; Program development; Seed
money; Program evaluation.
Limitations: Applications not accepted. Giving
primarily in the U.S., with emphasis on CA and
MA. No grants to individuals.
Publications: Annual report.
Application information: Contributes only to
pre-selected organizations.
  Board meeting date(s): Spring and fall
Officers and Trustees:* Jerome Kohlberg,* Pres.;
Walter J. Farley, V.P. and Treas.; Eileen Capone,
Secy.; Nancy W. McCabe, Exec. Dir.; Karen K.
Davis; Andrew Kohlberg; Karen B. Kohlberg;
Pamela Kohlberg; Alfred C. Viebranz.
Number of staff: 3 full-time professional; 1
full-time support.
EIN: 133496263
**Recent environmental and animal welfare
grants:**
2251-1 Environmental Careers Organization
  (ECO), Boston, MA, $61,244. 2001.
2251-2 Environmental Careers Organization
  (ECO), Boston, MA, $10,000. 2001.
2251-3 Forest Stewardship Council, DC,
  $50,000. 2001.
2251-4 Great Pond Foundation, Edgartown,
  MA, $10,000. 2001.
2251-5 Jane Goodall Institute for Wildlife
  Research, Education and Conservation, Silver
  Spring, MD, $85,000. 2001.
2251-6 Nature Conservancy, Boston, MA,
  $15,000. 2001.
2251-7 Nature Conservancy, Arlington, VA,
  $1,000,000. 2001.
2251-8 San Dieguito River Valley Land
  Conservancy, Del Mar, CA, $35,000. 2001.
2251-9 Teatown Lake Reservation, Ossining,
  NY, $11,000. 2001.
2251-10 Zoological Society of San Diego, San
  Diego, CA, $380,900. 2001.

2252
The H. Frederick Krimendahl II Foundation
c/o BCRS Assocs., LLC
100 Wall St., 11th Fl.
New York, NY 10005

Established in 1968 in NY.
Donor(s): H. Frederick Krimendahl II.
Grantmaker type: Independent foundation
Financial data (yr. ended 05/31/02): Assets,
$8,653,233 (M); expenditures, $459,483;
qualifying distributions, $455,310; giving
activities include $455,259 for 118 grants (high:
$60,000; low: $116).
Purpose and activities: Giving primarily for
education, the arts, and animal welfare.
Fields of interest: Performing arts; Theater;
Music; Arts; Libraries/library science; Education;
Animal welfare; Hospitals (general); Health
organizations, association; Children/youth,
services.
Limitations: Applications not accepted. Giving
primarily in New York, NY. No grants to
individuals.
Application information: Contributes only to
pre-selected organizations.
Trustees: Elizabeth K. Krimendahl; H.F.
Krimendahl II; Nancy C. Krimendahl; James S.
Marcus; Emilia A. Saint-Amand.
EIN: 237000391

2253
Elroy and Terry Krumholz Foundation, Inc.
P.O. Box 640085
Oakland Gardens, NY 11364

Established in 1992 in NY.
Donor(s): Terry Krumholz,‡ Roy Krumholz.‡
Grantmaker type: Independent foundation
Financial data (yr. ended 12/31/02): Assets,
$4,207,785 (M); expenditures, $288,487;
qualifying distributions, $254,737; giving
activities include $248,020 for 49 grants (high:
$35,000; low: $1,000).
Purpose and activities: Primary areas of interest
include animal welfare, the arts, community
services, education, cancer patient/family
support services, social services, including
special camping and community services, and
Jewish community programs.
Fields of interest: Arts education; Arts;
Education; Animal welfare; Human services;
Community development; Jewish federated
giving programs; Jewish agencies & temples.
Types of support: Equipment; Seed money;
Curriculum development; Internship funds;
Scholarship funds.
Limitations: Giving primarily in NY. No support
for political or fraternal organizations. No grants
to individuals, or for endowment funds, private
foundations, publications, or conferences; no
salary, operating support, deficit financing,
capital financing, or non-humane organizations;
no loans.
Publications: Application guidelines.
Application information: Application must be
on Krumholz form only. Application form
required.
  Initial approach: Letter
  Copies of proposal: 1
  Deadline(s): June 30
  Board meeting date(s): 3 to 4 times per year,
    as needed
  Final notification: Sept. 1
Officers and Trustees:* Rosalind Sackoff,* Pres.;
Richard S. Becker,* V.P.; Sanford E. Becker,* V.P.;
Harriet Krantz,* V.P.; Diane Razzano,* V.P.
Number of staff: None.
EIN: 133641606

2254
The Kupferberg Foundation
131-38 Sanford Ave.
Flushing, NY 11352

Established in 1961 in NY.
Donor(s): Jesse Kupferberg, Max Kupferberg,
Kepco, Inc., and members of the Kupferberg
family.
Grantmaker type: Company-sponsored
foundation
Financial data (yr. ended 11/30/02): Assets,
$9,790,569 (M); expenditures, $393,180;
qualifying distributions, $348,603; giving
activities include $346,200 for 50 grants (high:
$50,000; low: $500).
Purpose and activities: Giving primarily for
education, health, children, youth and social
services, and Jewish organizations.
Fields of interest: Museums
(science/technology); Education; Botanical
gardens; Hospitals (general); Health
organizations, association; Human services;
YM/YWCAs & YM/YWHAs; Children/youth,
services; Jewish federated giving programs;
Jewish agencies & temples.
Limitations: Applications not accepted. Giving
primarily in Queens, NY. No grants to
individuals.
Application information: Contributes only to
pre-selected organizations.
Officers: Max Kupferberg, Pres.; Jesse
Kupferberg, V.P.
Trustees: Martin Kupferberg; Saul Kupferberg.
EIN: 116008915

2255
The Kurz Family Foundation, Ltd.
69 Lydecker St.
Nyack, NY 10960-2103 (845) 358-2300
Contact: Herbert Kurz

Established in 1992 in NY.
Donor(s): Herbert Kurz.
Grantmaker type: Independent foundation
Financial data (yr. ended 12/31/02): Assets,
$7,160,672 (M); gifts received, $496,500;
expenditures, $459,768; qualifying distributions,
$459,454; giving activities include $341,250 for
grants.
Fields of interest: Higher education; Natural
resources; Hospitals (general); Human services;
Children/youth, services; International
peace/security; Community development;
Jewish agencies & temples.
Limitations: Giving primarily in NY. No grants to
individuals.
Application information:
  Initial approach: Letter
  Deadline(s): None
Directors: Ellen Kurz; Leonard Kurz; Brenda
Neal; Lewis Wechsler.
EIN: 133680855

2256
The Lagemann Foundation
c/o Diamond, Wohl, Fried, & Leonard
1775 Broadway, Ste. 419
New York, NY 10019-1903

Established in 1944 in NY.
Grantmaker type: Independent foundation

Financial data (yr. ended 12/31/01): Assets, $2,260,615 (M); expenditures, $205,619; qualifying distributions, $194,180; giving activities include $188,000 for 18 grants (high: $35,000; low: $3,000).
Fields of interest: Arts; Elementary/secondary education; Environment; Human services; Children/youth, services; Christian agencies & churches.
Limitations: Applications not accepted. Giving primarily in NY. No grants to individuals.
Application information: Contributes only to pre-selected organizations.
Officers: Peter J. Lagemann, Pres.; Carter S. Bacon, Jr., Secy.; Franklyn E. Parker, Treas.
EIN: 136115306

2257
The Landreth Family Foundation
(formerly William C. Landreth Foundation)
c/o BCRS Assocs., LLP
100 Wall St., 11th Fl.
New York, NY 10005

Established in 1985 in NY.
Donor(s): William C. Landreth.
Grantmaker type: Independent foundation
Financial data (yr. ended 05/31/02): Assets, $3,416,883 (M); expenditures, $262,715; qualifying distributions, $262,715; giving activities include $261,717 for 42 grants (high: $79,700; low: $100).
Purpose and activities: Giving primarily for nature conservancy; funding also for human services and education.
Fields of interest: Arts; Education; Natural resources; Animals/wildlife, preservation/protection; Health care; Human services; Community development; Foundations (community); Federated giving programs.
Limitations: Applications not accepted. Giving primarily in CA. No grants to individuals, or for scholarships; no loans.
Application information: Contributes only to pre-selected organizations.
Trustees: Keith Howard; Jeanne Murphy Landreth; Kerry Cathryn Landreth; Peter William Landreth; William C. Landreth.
EIN: 133318159

2258
James M. Large, Jr. Family Foundation
14 Underhill Rd.
Locust Valley, NY 11560

Established in 1997 in NY.
Donor(s): James M. Large, Jr.
Grantmaker type: Independent foundation
Financial data (yr. ended 12/31/00): Assets, $564,058 (M); expenditures, $112,521; qualifying distributions, $102,976; giving activities include $103,341 for grants (high: $33,875).
Fields of interest: Secondary school/education; Natural resources; Environment; Human services; Salvation Army.
Limitations: Applications not accepted. No grants to individuals.
Application information: Contributes only to pre-selected organizations.
Officer: James M. Large, Jr., Pres.
EIN: 113382951

2259
W. & J. Larson Family Foundation
c/o Kavinoky & Cook
120 Delaware Ave., 6th Fl.
Buffalo, NY 14202

Established in 1985 in NY.
Donor(s): Joan J. Larson, Wilfred J. Larson.
Grantmaker type: Independent foundation
Financial data (yr. ended 10/31/02): Assets, $2,125,703 (M); gifts received, $226,656; expenditures, $136,281; qualifying distributions, $134,165; giving activities include $132,700 for 29 grants (high: $27,000; low: $500).
Purpose and activities: Giving for higher education, federated giving programs, nature preservation organizations, and for the arts, including symphonies.
Fields of interest: Arts; Education; Natural resources; Athletics/sports, Special Olympics; Human services; Federated giving programs.
Limitations: Applications not accepted. Giving on a national basis. No grants to individuals.
Application information: Contributes only to pre-selected organizations.
Trustees: Brian D. Baird; Joan J. Larson; Wilfred J. Larson; Joseph D. Mitchell; Larry J. Nelson.
EIN: 166281709

2260
LaSalle Adams Fund
c/o Rockefeller Fin. Svcs.
30 Rockefeller Plz., 56th Fl.
New York, NY 10112
Contact: Chris Page, Philanthropic Advisor

Established in 1953 in IL; incorporated in 1999 in NY.
Donor(s): Sydney Stein, Jr.‡
Grantmaker type: Independent foundation
Financial data (yr. ended 12/31/01): Assets, $30,905,327 (M); expenditures, $2,258,186; qualifying distributions, $2,068,654; giving activities include $1,834,850 for 15 grants (high: $500,000; low: $25,000; average: $50,000–$150,000).
Purpose and activities: Giving primarily for conservation and wildlife preservation; funding also for violence prevention.
Fields of interest: Natural resources; Animals/wildlife, bird preserves.
International interests: Canada; Mexico.
Types of support: Land acquisition; Program development; Seed money; Program evaluation; Matching/challenge support.
Limitations: Applications not accepted. Giving primarily in the Rocky Mountain States and the Grand Traverse Bay region, MI. No grants to individuals.
Application information: Contributes only to pre-selected organizations.
Board meeting date(s): 3 times a year
Officer and Directors:* Carol Stein,* Pres.; Craig Kennedy.
EIN: 161562907

2261
The Estee Lauder Companies Inc.
Corporate Giving Program
c/o Corp. Contribs.
767 5th Ave.
New York, NY 10153-0003 (212) 572-4600
URL: http://www.elcompanies.com/company/philanthropic.html

Grantmaker type: Corporate giving program
Purpose and activities: Estee Lauder makes charitable contributions to nonprofit organizations involved with arts and culture, education, the environment, and health and human services. Support is given primarily in areas of company operations.
Fields of interest: Arts; Education; Environment; Health care; Human services.
Types of support: General/operating support; Employee volunteer services.
Limitations: Giving primarily in areas of company operations.
Application information: Application form not required.
Initial approach: Proposal to headquarters
Copies of proposal: 1
Final notification: Following review

2262
The Leonard and Evelyn Lauder Foundation
c/o Joan Krupskas, Estee Lauder Inc.
767 5th Ave., 40th Fl.
New York, NY 10153

Established in 2001 in DE.
Donor(s): The Lauder Foundation.
Grantmaker type: Independent foundation
Financial data (yr. ended 12/31/01): Assets, $1,644,205 (M); gifts received, $3,700,000; expenditures, $2,129,340; qualifying distributions, $2,126,078; giving activities include $2,113,986 for 149 grants (high: $219,630; low: $230).
Fields of interest: Arts education; Museums; Performing arts; Performing arts centers; Arts; Higher education; Environment; Health care; Health organizations, association; Breast cancer research; Parks/playgrounds; Human services; Foundations (community); Jewish agencies & temples.
Limitations: Applications not accepted. Giving primarily in New York, NY; funding also in Aspen, CO. No grants to individuals.
Application information: Contributes only to pre-selected organizations.
Officers: Leonard A. Lauder, Pres.; Evelyn H. Lauder, V.P.; Joan Krupskas, Secy.-Treas.
EIN: 134139448

2263
LBC Foundation
c/o Lewis B. Cullman
767 3rd Ave., 36th Fl.
New York, NY 10017

Established in 2001 in NY.
Donor(s): Lewis B. Cullman.
Grantmaker type: Independent foundation
Financial data (yr. ended 06/30/02): Assets, $4,459,596 (M); gifts received, $5,000,100;

expenditures, $268,530; qualifying distributions, $251,143; giving activities include $251,000 for 4 grants (high: $100,000; low: $1,000).
Purpose and activities: Giving primarily to a museum and a botanical garden.
Fields of interest: Museums (art); Botanical gardens; Civil rights.
Limitations: Applications not accepted. Giving primarily in NY. No grants to individuals.
Application information: Contributes only to pre-selected organizations.
Trustee: Lewis B. Cullman.
EIN: 316665976

2264
Charles Henry Leach II Foundation

c/o The Bank of New York, Tax Dept.
1 Wall St., 28th Fl.
New York, NY 10286
Contact: Willis J. Pruitt, V.P., The Bank of New York
Application address: 1290 Ave. of the Americas, New York, NY 10019

Established in 1992 in NY.
Donor(s): Charles Henry Leach II.‡
Grantmaker type: Independent foundation
Financial data (yr. ended 12/31/01): Assets, $16,728,541 (M); expenditures, $1,478,627; qualifying distributions, $1,421,179; giving activities include $1,389,500 for 52 grants (high: $200,000; low: $5,000).
Purpose and activities: Giving primarily for care of underprivileged or emotionally damaged children, prevention of cruelty to animals, environmental protection, and promotion of science research.
Fields of interest: Child development, education; Natural resources; Animal welfare; Human services; Children/youth, services; Child development, services; Economically disadvantaged.
Types of support: Research.
Limitations: Giving primarily in FL and NY.
Application information:
  Initial approach: Letter
  Deadline(s): None
Trustees: Jennifer B. Jordan; Philip E. Leone; The Bank of New York.
EIN: 133651713

2265
The Marvin & Annette Lee Foundation, Inc.

543 Cayuga Heights Rd.
Ithaca, NY 14850
Contact: David M. Lee, Pres.

Established in 1959 in NY.
Donor(s): Marvin Lee,‡ Annette Lee.
Grantmaker type: Independent foundation
Financial data (yr. ended 12/31/02): Assets, $2,505,063 (M); expenditures, $153,707; qualifying distributions, $150,194; giving activities include $149,300 for grants.
Purpose and activities: Giving primarily for hospitals and higher education, as well as to Oxfam, UNICEF and Amnesty International.
Fields of interest: Higher education; University; Environment; Hospitals (general); Health care; Health organizations, association; Federated giving programs; General charitable giving.

Types of support: Continuing support.
Limitations: Applications not accepted. Giving primarily in Ithaca and Tompkins County, NY. No grants to individuals, or for scholarships; no loans.
Application information: Contributes only to pre-selected organizations.
  Board meeting date(s): Annually
Officers and Directors:* David M. Lee,* Pres. and Treas.; Annette Lee,* Secy.
Number of staff: None.
EIN: 066034414

2266
Stephen & May Cavin Leeman Foundation, Inc.

471 W. 22nd St.
New York, NY 10011-2548
Contact: Gina Holland Waldo, Admin.

Established in 1969 in NY.
Donor(s): Stephen Leeman,‡ May Cavin Leeman.‡
Grantmaker type: Independent foundation
Financial data (yr. ended 06/30/03): Assets, $2,481,188 (M); expenditures, $215,835; qualifying distributions, $181,675; giving activities include $159,000 for grants.
Purpose and activities: Giving primarily to relatively small programs serving disadvantaged children and youth.
Fields of interest: Arts; Education; Environment; Health care; Human services; Children/youth, services; International peace/security.
Limitations: Giving primarily in New York, NY. No grants to individuals.
Publications: Annual report.
Application information: New York/New Jersey Common Application Form as modified by the foundation. Application form required.
  Initial approach: Letter
  Copies of proposal: 2
  Deadline(s): None
Officers and Directors:* Cavin P. Leeman, M.D.,* Pres. and Treas.; Diane L. Zimmerman,* V.P. and Secy.; Gina Trent.
Number of staff: 1 part-time professional.
EIN: 237057183

2267
Edith and Herbert Lehman Foundation, Inc.

151 E. 79th St.
New York, NY 10021-0417
Contact: Wendy Lehman Lash, Pres.
FAX: (212) 744-2065

Incorporated in 1952 in NY.
Donor(s): Edith A. Lehman,‡ Herbert H. Lehman.‡
Grantmaker type: Independent foundation
Financial data (yr. ended 09/30/02): Assets, $4,959,367 (M); expenditures, $385,499; qualifying distributions, $374,123; giving activities include $347,500 for 42 grants (high: $100,000; low: $250).
Purpose and activities: Giving primarily for the arts and education.
Fields of interest: Arts; Higher education; Education; Animals/wildlife; Health care; Human services; Children, services.

International interests: United Kingdom.
Types of support: General/operating support; Continuing support; Annual campaigns; Capital campaigns; Building/renovation; Endowments; Emergency funds; Professorships; Seed money; Curriculum development.
Limitations: Applications not accepted. Giving primarily in NY. No grants to individuals.
Publications: Annual report.
Application information: Proposals are accepted by invitation only. Preference is given to organizations which historically have been of interest to the Lehman family and to those in which the family is personally involved.
  Board meeting date(s): Quarterly
Officers and Directors:* Wendy Lehman Lash,* Pres.; Robert C. Graham, Jr., V.P. and Treas.; Abigail S. Lash; Herbert Rosenkid; Deborah Sheridan; Catherine J. Wise.
Number of staff: None.
EIN: 136094015

2268
The Leir Foundation, Inc.

641 Lexington Ave.
New York, NY 10022-4503

Established in 1996 in CT.
Donor(s): Henry J. Leir,‡ Louis Lipton, The Ridgefield Foundation.
Grantmaker type: Operating foundation
Financial data (yr. ended 02/28/02): Assets, $10,569,717 (M); gifts received, $1,000; expenditures, $1,287,256; qualifying distributions, $1,143,705; giving activities include $260,070 for 16 grants (high: $100,000; low: $500) and $723,443 for foundation-administered programs.
Purpose and activities: Giving primarily for a French museum of modern art, as well as for social services, animals and wildlife, Jewish organizations, and to a children's organization in Luxemburg.
Fields of interest: Museums (art); Animals/wildlife; Disasters, 9/11/01; Human services; Children, services; Jewish federated giving programs; Jewish agencies & temples.
International interests: Luxembourg.
Limitations: Applications not accepted. Giving primarily in Ridgefield, CT, and New York, NY. No grants to individuals.
Application information: Contributes only to pre-selected organizations.
Officers: Arthur S. Hoffman, Pres. and Treas.; Fred M. Lowenfels, Secy.
Directors: Mary-Ann Fribourg; Margot Gibis.
EIN: 061466481

2269
Reginald A. & Elizabeth S. Lenna Foundation, Inc.

P.O. Box 407
Lakewood, NY 14750
Contact: Elizabeth S. Lenna, Pres.
E-mail: lennacre@alltel.net

Established in 1985 in NY.
Donor(s): Reginald A. Lenna.‡
Grantmaker type: Independent foundation
Financial data (yr. ended 12/31/02): Assets, $7,753,894 (M); expenditures, $428,200; qualifying distributions, $418,303; giving

activities include $409,000 for 9 grants (high: $200,000; low: $2,000).
Purpose and activities: Giving primarily to a hospital and for children's services.
Fields of interest: Animal welfare; Hospitals (general); YM/YWCAs & YM/YWHAs; Day care; Community development.
Types of support: General/operating support.
Limitations: Giving primarily in southwestern NY. No grants to individuals.
Application information:
  Initial approach: Letter or proposal
  Deadline(s): None
Officers: Elizabeth S. Lenna, Pres.; Joseph Johnson, V.P.; Samuel P. Price, Secy.; Randy Ordines, Treas.
Director: Florence Cass.
Number of staff: 1 part-time professional.
EIN: 112800733

2270
David M. Leuschen Foundation
c/o BCRS Associates, LLC
100 Wall St., 11th Fl.
New York, NY 10005-3720

Established in 1988 in CT.
Donor(s): David M. Leuschen.
Grantmaker type: Independent foundation
Financial data (yr. ended 04/30/02): Assets, $352,263 (M); expenditures, $378,622; qualifying distributions, $362,676; giving activities include $362,871 for 21 grants (high: $50,000; low: $500).
Purpose and activities: Giving primarily for natural resources conservation, and human services, including fire departments.
Fields of interest: Natural resources; Disasters, fire prevention/control; Recreation; Human services; Philanthropy/voluntarism.
Limitations: Applications not accepted. Giving primarily in MT. No grants to individuals.
Application information: Contributes only to pre-selected organizations.
Trustees: Jonathan L. Cohen; David M. Leuschen; Patricia A. Napoli.
EIN: 133501179

2271
The Barbara J. & Gerald M. Levin Family Foundation
(formerly The Levin Family Foundation)
c/o Tag Assocs., Ltd.
75 Rockefeller Plz., Ste. 900
New York, NY 10019 (212) 275-1500

Established in 1993 in NY.
Donor(s): Gerald M. Levin, Barbara J. Levin.
Grantmaker type: Independent foundation
Financial data (yr. ended 04/30/02): Assets, $3,987,132 (M); expenditures, $5,108,290; qualifying distributions, $5,024,830; giving activities include $5,062,680 for 24 grants (high: $1,705,630; low: $250).
Purpose and activities: Giving primarily for the performing arts and sports centers.
Fields of interest: Performing arts; Animal welfare; Veterinary medicine, hospital; Athletics/sports, baseball; Athletics/sports, winter sports.
Limitations: Applications not accepted. Giving on a national basis. No grants to individuals.

Application information: Contributes only to pre-selected organizations.
Trustees: Barbara J. Levin; Gerald M. Levin.
EIN: 113158926

2272
Levitt Foundation
c/o The Philanthropic Group
630 5th Ave., 20th Fl.
New York, NY 10111 (212) 501-7785
Contact: Barbara R. Greenberg
URL: http://fdncenter.org/grantmaker/levitt/

Incorporated in 1949 in NY.
Donor(s): Levitt and Sons, Inc., Abraham Levitt,‡ Alfred Levitt,‡ William Levitt.
Grantmaker type: Independent foundation
Financial data (yr. ended 04/30/02): Assets, $16,255,106 (M); expenditures, $953,908; qualifying distributions, $759,177; giving activities include $705,705 for 49 grants (high: $218,905; low: $500).
Purpose and activities: To enhance the abilities of children and youth in New York City, and Nassau and Suffolk counties on Long Island, NY, to understand and value their environment and to take action to improve and protect the built and natural environments in their own neighborhoods.
Fields of interest: Environment; Children/youth, services; Community development, neighborhood development.
Types of support: Program development.
Limitations: Applications not accepted. Giving limited to Long Island and New York, NY. No grants to individuals.
Application information: Applications accepted by invitation only.
  Board meeting date(s): 3 times per year
Officers and Trustees:* Farrell Jones,* Pres.; Stephen J. Mathes,* Secy.; Robert J. Appel,* Treas.; Prudence Brown; Barbara R. Greenberg; May W. Newburger.
Number of staff: 2 shared staff (shared with The Philanthropic Group).
EIN: 136128226

2273
The Lifebridge Foundation, Inc.
Times Sq. Station
P.O. Box 793
New York, NY 10108
Contact: Larry Elwood Auld, Prog. Dir.
FAX: (212) 757-0246; *E-mail:* lifebridgenyc@aol.com; *URL:* http://www.lifebridge.org

Established in 1992 in CT.
Donor(s): Paul M. Hancock.‡
Grantmaker type: Independent foundation
Financial data (yr. ended 12/31/02): Assets, $5,110,716 (M); gifts received, $445; expenditures, $621,457; qualifying distributions, $558,352; giving activities include $262,500 for 51 grants (high: $12,000; low: $250) and $59,000 for 6 grants to individuals (high: $25,000; low: $5,000; average: $5,000–$25,000).
Purpose and activities: Giving to cutting edge, forward-looking approaches to the arts, education, scientific research, and the environment; also giving for world goodwill.

Fields of interest: Arts; Environment; International affairs, goodwill promotion; Paranormal/mystic studies.
Types of support: General/operating support; Conferences/seminars; Seed money; Research; Program evaluation; Matching/challenge support.
Limitations: Applications not accepted. Giving on a national and international basis.
Publications: Newsletter, Occasional report.
Application information: Unsolicited applications not considered; applicants must be invited to submit proposal.
  Board meeting date(s): Varies
Officers and Directors:* Evelyn W. Hancock,* Chair.; Barbara L. Valocore,* Pres.; Jane A. Southall,* V.P.; Larry Elwood Auld,* Secy. and Prog. Dir.; Nancy Roof, Secy.
Number of staff: 1 full-time professional.
EIN: 061356766

2274
Albert A. & Bertram N. Linder Foundation, Inc.
305 E. 40th St., PH-C
New York, NY 10016
Contact: Bertram N. Linder, Pres.

Incorporated in 1947 in NY.
Donor(s): Bertram N. Linder, Albert A. Linder.‡
Grantmaker type: Independent foundation
Financial data (yr. ended 05/31/02): Assets, $2,193,050 (M); expenditures, $186,552; qualifying distributions, $135,155; giving activities include $129,315 for 186 grants (high: $15,000; low: $25).
Purpose and activities: Emphasis on civil rights, higher education, AIDS programs, and the arts.
Fields of interest: Visual arts; Museums; Performing arts; Arts; Higher education; Education; Natural resources; Environment; Hospitals (general); Family planning; Health care; Mental health/crisis services; Health organizations, association; AIDS; AIDS research; Family services; International affairs; Civil rights; Jewish agencies & temples.
Types of support: General/operating support; Continuing support; Annual campaigns; Capital campaigns; Endowments; Emergency funds; Seed money; Research.
Limitations: Giving primarily in New York, NY, and Scranton, PA. No grants to individuals, or for scholarships, fellowships, or matching gifts; no loans.
Application information: Telephone calls will not be considered. Application form not required.
  Initial approach: Letter
  Copies of proposal: 1
  Deadline(s): Submit application preferably in Apr. or early May; deadline May 15
  Board meeting date(s): May and Dec.
Officers and Trustees:* Bertram N. Linder,* Pres. and Treas.; Mary Ellen Linder,* V.P. and Secy.; Denise Dunbar,* V.P.
Number of staff: 1 part-time support.
EIN: 136100590

2275
The Link Foundation
c/o Binghamton University Fdn.
P.O. Box 6005
Binghamton, NY 13902-6005
Contact: Thomas F. Kelly, Tr.

Established in 1953 in NY.
Donor(s): Edwin A. Link,‡ Mrs. Edwin A. Link,‡
Lawrence Clayton, Link Div. of CAE.
Grantmaker type: Independent foundation
Financial data (yr. ended 06/30/03): Assets,
$10,908,908 (M); gifts received, $3,685;
expenditures, $606,926; qualifying distributions,
$571,439; giving activities include $547,250 for
16 grants (high: $175,000; low: $2,000) and
$15,000 for 8 employee matching gifts.
Purpose and activities: Sponsors research,
development, and simulation of all facets of
aviation, space technology, and oceanography,
and supports research on development of
energy resources.
Fields of interest: Higher education; Energy;
Marine science; Engineering/technology;
Engineering; Science; Public policy, research.
Types of support: Continuing support;
Fellowships; Research.
Limitations: Giving primarily in FL and NY. No
grants to individuals.
Publications: Informational brochure (including
application guidelines).
Application information: Application form
required.
  Initial approach: Letter
  Copies of proposal: 1
  Deadline(s): Jan. 15
  Board meeting date(s): Feb. and June
  Final notification: March
Officers and Trustees:* David M. Gouldin,*
Chair.; Thomas F. Kelly,* Secy.; Douglas R.
Johnson, Treas.; Jon Forbes; Ronald N.
Hendricks.
Special Advisors: Frank Cardullo; Andrew Clark;
Barry Kelly; Marilyn Link; Lee Lynd; Stuart
McCarty; Richard Murray; Robert Sproull; Brian
J. Thompson; William D. Turner.
Number of staff: 1 part-time professional.
EIN: 536011109

2276
The Lipton Foundation
c/o Wachtell, Lipton, Rosen & Katz
51 W. 52nd St.
New York, NY 10019

Established in 2001 in NY.
Donor(s): Wachtell, Lipton, Rosen & Katz.
Grantmaker type: Company-sponsored
foundation
Financial data (yr. ended 12/31/01): Assets,
$8,881,145 (M); gifts received, $5,000,000;
expenditures, $431,971; qualifying distributions,
$427,000; giving activities include $427,000 for
14 grants (high: $100,000; low: $2,000).
Purpose and activities: Giving primarily to law
schools and other educational institutions, the
arts, and Jewish organizations and temples.
Fields of interest: Arts education; Museums
(ethnic/folk arts); Arts; Early childhood
education; Law school/education;
Animals/wildlife, preservation/protection; Jewish
agencies & temples.

Limitations: Applications not accepted. Giving
on a national basis. No grants to individuals.
Application information: Contributes only to
pre-selected organizations.
Officers: Martin Lipton, Pres.; Susan L. Lipton,
V.P. and Secy.; Katherine B. Lipton, V.P.;
Constance Monte, Treas.
EIN: 582629617

2277
The Lucius N. Littauer Foundation, Inc.
60 E. 42nd St., Ste. 2910
New York, NY 10165 (212) 697-2677
Contact: William Lee Frost, Pres.

Incorporated in 1929 in NY.
Donor(s): Lucius N. Littauer.‡
Grantmaker type: Independent foundation
Financial data (yr. ended 12/31/01): Assets,
$41,011,478 (M); gifts received, $3,332,084;
expenditures, $1,774,535; qualifying
distributions, $1,535,297; giving activities
include $1,335,746 for 151 grants (high:
$50,000; low: $100; average: $1,000–$10,000)
and $1,650 for 4 employee matching gifts.
Purpose and activities: Support primarily for
scholarly research on Jewish studies; grants also
for the endowment of Judaica book funds at
university libraries, and for medical ethics and
environmental projects.
Fields of interest: Humanities;
History/archaeology; Language/linguistics;
Literature; Higher education; Environment;
Bioethics; Social sciences; Political science;
Jewish agencies & temples; Religion.
International interests: Israel.
Types of support: Endowments; Program
development; Conferences/seminars;
Publication; Seed money; Research; Employee
matching gifts; Matching/challenge support.
Limitations: Giving primarily in NY for medical
ethics and environmental projects. No support
for synagogues. No grants to individuals, or for
capital projects or operating funds.
Publications: Application guidelines.
Application information: Application form not
required.
  Initial approach: Proposal
  Copies of proposal: 1
  Deadline(s): None
  Board meeting date(s): Annually and as
  required
  Final notification: 3 months
Officers and Directors:* William Lee Frost,*
Pres. and Treas.; Henry A. Lowett,* V.P. and
Secy.; Charles Berlin; Berthold Bilski; Mark A.
Bilski; Robert D. Frost; George Harris; Noah
Perlman; Peter J. Solomon.
Number of staff: 2 full-time professional.
EIN: 131688027

2278
The Wm. Brian & Judith A. Little Charitable Trust
630 5th Ave., Ste. 2620
New York, NY 10111

Established in 1992 in NY.
Donor(s): Wm. Brian Little.‡
Grantmaker type: Independent foundation
Financial data (yr. ended 12/31/01): Assets,
$3,721,813 (M); expenditures, $237,077;

qualifying distributions, $158,132; giving
activities include $156,500 for 24 grants (high:
$50,000; low: $250).
Purpose and activities: Giving for the arts and
community services.
Fields of interest: Museums (art); Historical
activities; Elementary/secondary education;
Higher education; Environment; Hospitals
(general); Human services.
Limitations: Applications not accepted. Giving
primarily in New York, NY. No grants to
individuals.
Application information: Contributes only to
pre-selected organizations.
Trustees: Gregory Little; Jacqueline Little; Judith
A. Little.
EIN: 136995435

2279
Little River Foundation
c/o Curtis, Mallet-Prevost, Colt, & Mosle
101 Park Ave., Ste. 3500
New York, NY 10178-0061

Established in 1972 in VA.
Donor(s): Ohrstrom Foundation.
Grantmaker type: Independent foundation
Financial data (yr. ended 11/30/02): Assets,
$624,590 (M); gifts received, $1,116,800;
expenditures, $1,228,993; qualifying
distributions, $1,228,942; giving activities
include $1,224,900 for 132 grants (high:
$175,000; low: $100).
Fields of interest: Museums (specialized); Arts;
Libraries (special); Education; Natural resources;
Environment; Animal welfare; Health
organizations, association; Athletics/sports,
equestrianism; Human services.
International interests: Africa.
Types of support: General/operating support;
Annual campaigns; Building/renovation;
Endowments; Conferences/seminars; Research.
Limitations: Applications not accepted. Giving
primarily in NY and VA; some giving in CA. No
grants to individuals.
Application information: Contributes only to
pre-selected organizations.
Officers: George L. Ohrstrom, Jr., Pres.; Magalen
O. Bryant, V.P.; Peter A. Kalat, Secy.; Dorothy A.
Barry, Treas.
Number of staff: 2 shared staff (shared with
Ohrstrom Foundation).
EIN: 237218919

2280
William & Marion Littleford Foundation, Inc.
c/o Bryan Cave, LLP
1290 Ave. of the Americas
New York, NY 10104
Contact: John F. Walsh, Jr., Secy.

Established in 1991 in NY.
Donor(s): William D. Littleford, Marian
Littleford.
Grantmaker type: Independent foundation
Financial data (yr. ended 12/31/02): Assets,
$1,014,926 (M); expenditures, $152,969;
qualifying distributions, $138,785; giving
activities include $137,100 for 26 grants (high:
$50,000; low: $100).

Fields of interest: Education; Natural resources; Health organizations, association; Human services; Foundations (community); Philanthropy/voluntarism; Federated giving programs.
Limitations: Applications not accepted. Giving primarily in NY. No grants to individuals.
Application information: Contributes only to pre-selected organizations.
Officers: William D. Littleford, Pres.; John F. Walsh, Jr., Secy.; Marian Littleford, Treas.
EIN: 133633150

2281
The Litwin Foundation
1200 Union Tpke.
New Hyde Park, NY 11040
Contact: Leonard Litwin, Pres.

Established in 1989 in NY.
Donor(s): Leonard Litwin.
Grantmaker type: Independent foundation
Financial data (yr. ended 12/31/01): Assets, $41,003,975 (M); gifts received, $10,000,000; expenditures, $3,066,209; qualifying distributions, $3,019,252; giving activities include $3,066,209 for 283 grants (high: $386,000; low: $250).
Fields of interest: Museums; Education; Natural resources; Hospitals (general); Health organizations, association; Medical research, institute; Human services; Children/youth, services; Jewish agencies & temples; Disabled; Aging; Homeless.
Types of support: General/operating support; Research.
Limitations: Giving primarily in New York, NY. No grants to individuals.
Application information:
Initial approach: Letter
Deadline(s): None
Officers and Directors:* Leonard Litwin,* Pres.; Diane Miller,* V.P.; Ruth Litwin,* Secy.; Carole Pittelman,* Treas.; Howard Kalka; Morton Sanders.
EIN: 133501980

2282
John L. Loeb, Jr. Foundation
c/o B. Strauss Assoc., Ltd.
307 5th Ave., 8th Fl.
New York, NY 10016-6517

Established in 1964.
Donor(s): John L. Loeb, Jr.
Grantmaker type: Independent foundation
Financial data (yr. ended 12/31/01): Assets, $18,996,498 (M); expenditures, $941,191; qualifying distributions, $914,591; giving activities include $909,628 for 105 grants (high: $180,923; low: $75).
Purpose and activities: Giving primarily for the arts, education, and Jewish organizations.
Fields of interest: Arts; Education; Environment; Health organizations, association; Human services; International affairs, U.N.; International affairs; Jewish federated giving programs; Jewish agencies & temples.
Limitations: Applications not accepted. Giving primarily in NY. No grants to individuals.
Application information: Contributes only to pre-selected organizations.

Officer: John L. Loeb, Jr., Pres.
EIN: 136142345

2283
The Lone Rock Foundation, Inc.
(formerly Herring Creek Foundation, Inc.)
635 Madison Ave., 18th Fl.
New York, NY 10022

Established in 1994 in NY.
Donor(s): Susan Scheuer.
Grantmaker type: Independent foundation
Financial data (yr. ended 12/31/00): Assets, $696,694 (M); gifts received, $75,250; expenditures, $98,697; qualifying distributions, $94,264; giving activities include $95,222 for 25 grants (high: $50,000; low: $85).
Fields of interest: Arts; Education; Natural resources; Jewish agencies & temples.
Limitations: Applications not accepted. Giving primarily in MA and NY. No grants to individuals.
Application information: Contributes only to pre-selected organizations.
Officers: Susan Scheuer, Pres.; Jonathan Lipnick, Secy.
Director: Judith Scheuer.
EIN: 133783380

2284
Lostand Foundation, Inc.
c/o Jonathan F.P. Rose
33 Katonah Ave.
Katonah, NY 10536

Established in 1997 in NY.
Donor(s): Jonathan F.P. Rose.
Grantmaker type: Independent foundation
Financial data (yr. ended 10/31/01): Assets, $3,003,422 (M); gifts received, $250,000; expenditures, $276,647; qualifying distributions, $259,306; giving activities include $255,006 for 87 grants (high: $25,000; low: $250).
Purpose and activities: Giving primarily for the arts, education, and Jewish organizations.
Fields of interest: Performing arts; Music; Arts; Higher education; Education; Natural resources; Domestic violence; Jewish federated giving programs; Jewish agencies & temples; Religion.
Limitations: Applications not accepted. Giving primarily in Brooklyn, NY. No grants to individuals.
Application information: Contributes only to pre-selected organizations.
Officers: Jonathan F.P. Rose, Pres.; Diana C. Rose, V.P.; Michael Sullivan, Treas.
Director: Charles L. Mandelstam.
EIN: 133945705

2285
The Low Wood Fund, Inc.
(formerly Lefteria Foundation, Inc.)
c/o 61 Assocs.
350 5th Ave., Ste. 1413
New York, NY 10118-1413

Established in 1984 in NY.
Donor(s): Eli S. Garber, Helen S. Cohen, Thomas Cohen, Amy Cohen, Gail Schorsch, Carolyn Cohen, Daniel Cohen.

Grantmaker type: Independent foundation
Financial data (yr. ended 11/30/02): Assets, $259,303 (M); gifts received, $780,000; expenditures, $646,192; qualifying distributions, $645,938; giving activities include $645,500 for 114 grants (high: $100,000; low: $250).
Purpose and activities: Giving primarily for a community organization providing support to grassroots organizing projects and higher education. Also give to Jewish groups and for preventive psychiatry.
Fields of interest: Arts; Higher education; Education; Environment; Mental health, clinics; Philanthropy/voluntarism; Jewish agencies & temples.
Limitations: Applications not accepted. Giving on a national basis. No grants to individuals.
Application information: Contributes only to pre-selected organizations.
Officer: David Zahner, Pres.
EIN: 133337436

2286
LSR Fund ▼
30 Rockefeller Plz., Rm. 5600
New York, NY 10112
Contact: Mary Haldi

Established in 1994 in NY.
Donor(s): Laurance S. Rockefeller.
Grantmaker type: Independent foundation
Financial data (yr. ended 12/31/02): Assets, $20,585,041 (M); expenditures, $4,049,865; qualifying distributions, $4,049,865; giving activities include $3,917,700 for 45 grants (high: $500,000; low: $2,000; average: $10,000–$100,000).
Purpose and activities: Giving primarily for environmental support, health care, and historic preservation.
Fields of interest: Historic preservation/historical societies; Environment; Health care.
Limitations: Applications not accepted. Giving on a national basis.
Application information: Giving only to pre-selected organizations. Does not accept unsolicited requests for funds.
Trustees: Clayton W. Frye, Jr.; Donal C. O'Brien, Jr.; Ellen R.C. Pomeroy; Laurance S. Rockefeller; James S. Sligar.
Number of staff: 1 part-time support.
EIN: 137039108

2287
The Lubin Family Foundation
c/o DDK & Co., LLP
1500 Broadway
New York, NY 10036-4015
Contact: Sara L. Schupf, Tr.

Established in 1993 in NY.
Donor(s): Tillie K. Lubin.
Grantmaker type: Independent foundation
Financial data (yr. ended 12/31/01): Assets, $3,522,212 (M); gifts received, $203,050; expenditures, $115,460; qualifying distributions, $95,947; giving activities include $94,782 for 10 grants (high: $25,000; low: $1,000).
Purpose and activities: Giving primarily for education and to Sept. 11th-related funds.
Fields of interest: Museums (science/technology); Elementary/secondary

education; Environment; Disasters, 9/11/01; Science.

Types of support: General/operating support.
Limitations: Applications not accepted. Giving on a national basis, with some emphasis on New York, NY. No grants to individuals.
Application information: Contributes only to pre-selected organizations.

Board meeting date(s): Dec.
Trustee: Sara L. Schupf.
EIN: 136991626

2288
Lubo Fund, Inc.
c/o Norman Foundation Inc.
147 E. 48th St.
New York, NY 10017
Contact: Lucinda W. Bunnen, Pres.

Incorporated in 1958 in GA.
Donor(s): Belinda Reusch, members of the Bunnen family.
Grantmaker type: Independent foundation
Financial data (yr. ended 12/31/01): Assets, $7,591,230 (M); gifts received, $79,978; expenditures, $302,439; qualifying distributions, $249,201; giving activities include $243,778 for 253 grants (high: $70,650; low: $25).
Purpose and activities: Giving primarily for cultural programs, including museums, performing and visual arts, with an emphasis on photography; support also for education.
Fields of interest: Photography; Performing arts; Arts; Education; Environment; Health organizations, association; Civil liberties, advocacy; Jewish agencies & temples.
Types of support: General/operating support; Continuing support; Annual campaigns; Emergency funds; Program development; Publication; Seed money; Matching/challenge support.
Limitations: Giving primarily in GA, with emphasis on Atlanta. No grants to individuals, or for land acquisition, renovation projects, endowment funds, scholarships, fellowships, research, or conferences; no loans.
Application information: Application form not required.

Initial approach: Letter or proposal
Copies of proposal: 1
Deadline(s): None
Board meeting date(s): July
Final notification: 1 to 3 months
Officers: Lucinda W. Bunnen, Pres.; Robert L. Bunnen, Sr., V.P. and Secy.
Number of staff: None.
EIN: 586043631

2289
The Henry Luce Foundation, Inc. ▼
111 W. 50th St., Ste. 4601
New York, NY 10020 (212) 489-7700
Contact: Michael Gilligan, Pres.
FAX: (212) 581-9541; E-mail: hlf@hluce.org; URL: http://www.hluce.org

Incorporated in 1936 in NY.
Donor(s): Henry R. Luce,‡ Clare Boothe Luce.‡
Grantmaker type: Independent foundation
Financial data (yr. ended 12/31/02): Assets, $650,000,000 (M); expenditures, $38,840,108; qualifying distributions, $38,472,729; giving

activities include $32,398,093 for 553+ grants (high: $2,000,000; low: $2,000), $489,663 for 35 grants to individuals (average: $22,000–$27,000) and $441,137 for 250 employee matching gifts.

Purpose and activities: Grants for specific projects in the broad areas of Asian affairs, American art, public policy and the environment, theology, advancement of women in science and engineering, and higher education. The Luce Scholars Program gives a select group of young Americans, not Asian specialists, a year's work experience in East and Southeast Asia. Asia grants support the creation of new scholarly and public resources on East and Southeast Asia as well as innovative cultural and intellectual exchange between the Asia-Pacific and the United States. The Henry R. Luce Professorship Program, which supports innovative programs at private colleges and universities, no longer accepts proposals for new grants. The Clare Boothe Luce Program is designed to enhance the careers of women in science and engineering through scholarships, fellowships, and professorships at invited institutions. Funding in the arts focuses on research, scholarship and exhibitions in American art; direct support for specific projects at major museums and service organizations; dissertation support for topics in American art history through the American Council of Learned Societies. Theology grants are made primarily to seminaries and divinity schools for educational purposes. The Henry Luce III Theology Fellows Program is administered through the Association of Theological Schools. Public Policy and the Environment grants are made to support the study of critical issues and environmental training and research.
Fields of interest: Visual arts; Museums; Humanities; Theology; Higher education; Theological school/education; Environment; Engineering/technology; Social sciences; International studies; Public policy, research.
International interests: Asia; Southeast Asia; China; Mongolia; Korea; Japan.
Types of support: Program development; Professorships; Fellowships; Internship funds; Scholarship funds; Employee matching gifts; Matching/challenge support.
Limitations: Giving on a national and international basis; international activities limited to East and Southeast Asia. No support for journalism, medical or media projects. No grants to individuals (except for specially designated programs), or for endowments, domestic building campaigns, general operating support, annual fund drives; no loans (except for program-related investments).
Publications: Biennial report (including application guidelines), Grants list, Informational brochure, Newsletter.
Application information: Nominees for Luce Scholars Program accepted from invited institutions only; Clare Boothe Luce Program by invitation to institutions only, individual applications cannot be considered; American Art Program requires prior inquiry by Mar.1. Application form not required.

Initial approach: Letter
Copies of proposal: 1
Deadline(s): June 15, Luce Fund in American Art; 1st Mon. in Dec., Luce Scholars

nominations; all others, no specific deadlines
Board meeting date(s): Mar., June, Oct., and Dec.
Officers and Directors:* Margaret Boles Fitzgerald,* Chair.; Michael Gilligan,* Pres.; Terrill E. Lautz, V.P. and Secy.; John C. Evans,* V.P. and Treas.; John P. Daley, V.P., Finance and Admin.; Helene E. Redell, V.P. and Prog. Dir., Luce Scholars; Robert E. Armstrong; Anne d'Harnoncourt; Claire L. Gaudiani; Kenneth T. Jackson; James T. Laney; H. Christopher Luce; Henry Luce III; Thomas L. Pulling; David V. Ragone.
Number of staff: 11 full-time professional; 9 full-time support.
EIN: 136001282
Recent environmental and animal welfare grants:
2289-1 Allegheny College, Meadville, PA, $240,000. For French Creek Environmental Program. 2002.
2289-2 College of the Atlantic, Bar Harbor, ME, $200,000. For Coastal Ecology and Integrated Marine Studies program. 2002.
2289-3 Duke University, Durham, NC, $800,000. For Continental Environmental Leadership Program. 2002.
2289-4 Environmental Defense, New York, NY, $250,000. To conserve North Caribbean Biodiversity through Marine Protected Areas and Sustainable Development in Cuba. 2002.
2289-5 Fauna and Flora International, San Francisco, CA, $250,000. To save Asia's Lost World: Renewal of Wildlife Conservation and Sustainable Development in Cambodia's Cardamom Mountains. 2002.
2289-6 Hubbard Brook Research Foundation, Campton, NH, $240,000. For Science Links Program. 2002.
2289-7 International Crane Foundation, Baraboo, WI, $240,000. To preserve Wetland Management in China. 2002.
2289-8 Oberlin College, Oberlin, OH, $700,000. For program on International Perspectives in Environmental Studies. 2002.
2289-9 Royal Oak Foundation, New York, NY, $22,000. For chairman's discretionary grant for Leila Hadley Luce Garden Lecture Series, annual lecture series on role of historic gardens and English design concepts. 2002.
2289-10 Tufts University, Medford, MA, $900,000. For Graduate Education for International Environmental Solutions Governance. 2002.
2289-11 University of Puget Sound, Tacoma, WA, $560,000. For Environmental Decision-Making and Policy Initiative. 2002.

2290
M & T Charitable Foundation ▼
1 M & T Plz., 6th Fl.
Buffalo, NY 14240 (716) 848-3804
Contact: Debbie Pringle
FAX: (716) 848-7318

Established in 1993 in NY.
Donor(s): Manufacturers and Traders Trust Co.
Grantmaker type: Company-sponsored foundation
Financial data (yr. ended 12/31/01): Assets, $29,790,816 (M); expenditures, $7,182,850; qualifying distributions, $7,152,850; giving

activities include $7,152,850 for 1,102 grants (high: $645,621; low: $50; average: $100–$50,000).
Purpose and activities: Giving primarily to performing arts organizations, elementary and secondary education, environmental programs, animal-related activities, community funds and federated giving programs, and Christian and Jewish organizations.
Fields of interest: Performing arts; Elementary/secondary education; Environment; Animals/wildlife; Federated giving programs; Christian agencies & churches; Jewish agencies & temples.
Limitations: Applications not accepted. Giving in the U.S., with emphasis on NY, PA, and Washington, DC. No grants to individuals.
Application information: Contributes only to pre-selected organizations.
Officers and Directors:* Shelley C. Drake,* Chair. and Pres.; Edward L. Beideck, V.P.; Keith M. Belanger, V.P.; R. Carlos Carballada, V.P.; John A. Carmichael,* V.P.; Scott E. Dagenais, V.P.; Edward Gajewski, V.P.; Brian E. Hickey, V.P.; Jeffrey M. Levy, V.P.; Kevin J. Pearson, V.P.; Michael S. Piemonte, V.P.; Marie King, Secy.; Michael P. Pinto,* Treas.; Richard A. Lammert; Robert E. Sadler, Jr.
EIN: 161448017

2291
Bernard L. & Ruth Madoff Foundation
885 3rd Ave., 18th Fl.
New York, NY 10022-4834

Established in 1997 in NY.
Donor(s): Bernard L. Madoff, Ruth Madoff.
Grantmaker type: Independent foundation
Financial data (yr. ended 12/31/02): Assets, $20,245,876 (M); expenditures, $539,057; qualifying distributions, $521,750; giving activities include $521,750 for 18 grants (high: $100,000; low: $1,750).
Purpose and activities: Giving primarily for education.
Fields of interest: Education; Natural resources; Health care; Human services.
Limitations: Applications not accepted. Giving primarily in NY. No grants to individuals.
Application information: Contributes only to pre-selected organizations.
Officers: Bernard L. Madoff, Pres.; Ruth Madoff, Secy.-Treas.
EIN: 133934626

2292
The Russell Maguire Foundation, Inc.
c/o Hecht and Assoc., LLP
10 E. 40th St., Rm. 710
New York, NY 10016

Incorporated in 1941 in NY.
Donor(s): Russell Maguire.‡
Grantmaker type: Operating foundation
Financial data (yr. ended 12/31/01): Assets, $3,219,506 (M); expenditures, $244,769; qualifying distributions, $189,031; giving activities include $157,500 for grants.
Purpose and activities: Giving primarily for human services and family services.
Fields of interest: Arts; Education; Botanical gardens; Horticulture/garden clubs; Human

services; Children/youth, services; Federated giving programs; Christian agencies & churches.
Limitations: Applications not accepted. Giving primarily in CT and NY. No grants to individuals.
Application information: Contributes only to pre-selected organizations.
Directors: F. Richards Ford III; Natasha B. Ford; Tina Grayson.
EIN: 136162698

2293
The Mai Family Foundation
c/o Mahoney Cohen & Co.
1065 Ave. of the Americas
New York, NY 10018

Established in 1996 in NY.
Donor(s): Vincent A. Mai.
Grantmaker type: Independent foundation
Financial data (yr. ended 12/31/02): Assets, $2,571,371 (M); expenditures, $135,260; qualifying distributions, $129,295; giving activities include $130,000 for 9 grants (high: $25,000; low: $5,000).
Fields of interest: Arts; Higher education; Natural resources; Family planning; Mental health/crisis services; Human services; Children/youth, services; Civil rights.
International interests: South Africa.
Limitations: Applications not accepted. Giving primarily in the U.S., including organizations benefiting South Africa. No grants to individuals.
Application information: Contributes only to pre-selected organizations.
Officers and Directors:* Vincent A. Mai,* Pres. and Treas.; Anne Mai,* V.P.; Lisa Moore, Secy.; Sanford Krieger.
EIN: 133915987

2294
The Mailman Foundation, Inc.
150 E. 58th St., 14th Fl.
New York, NY 10155
Contact: Joseph V. Hastings, Secy.-Treas.
FAX: (212) 421-3163

Incorporated in 1943 in DE.
Donor(s): Joseph L. Mailman,‡ Joseph S. Mailman.‡
Grantmaker type: Independent foundation
Financial data (yr. ended 12/31/01): Assets, $42,329,465 (M); expenditures, $1,433,563; qualifying distributions, $1,138,292; giving activities include $1,104,559 for 65 grants (high: $546,562; low: $125).
Purpose and activities: Giving primarily for education, public health, child welfare, the environment and natural resource conservation, performing arts, and for medical research.
Fields of interest: Arts; Education; Natural resources; Environment; Public health, epidemiology; Health care; Mental health, association; Medical research, institute.
Limitations: Applications not accepted. Giving on a national basis. No grants to individuals.
Application information: Contributes only to pre-selected organizations.
Officers and Trustees:* Phyllis Mailman,* Pres.; Joshua L. Mailman,* V.P.; Jody Wolfe,* V.P.; Judson A. Wolfe,* V.P.; Joseph V. Hastings, Secy.-Treas.
Number of staff: None.

EIN: 136161556

2295
Major League Baseball Players Trust
12 E. 49th St.
New York, NY 10017 (212) 826-0808

Grantmaker type: Public charity
Financial data (yr. ended 12/31/00): Revenue, $1,110,974; assets, $1,905,329; gifts received, $1,071,800; expenditures, $857,596; program services expenses, $830,568; giving activities include $816,725 for 35 grants (high: $150,000; low: $500).
Purpose and activities: The organization operates exclusively for charitable, scientific, literary or educational purposes or for the prevention of cruelty to children or animals.
Fields of interest: Animal welfare; Child abuse; Children, services; Human services.
Trustees: Donald Fehr; Thomas Glavine; Rick Helling.
EIN: 133843389

2296
Marble Fund, Inc.
c/o Rosenberg Selsman and Co., LLP
655 3rd. Ave., Ste. 1610
New York, NY 10017
Contact: Marion H. Levy, Pres.

Established in 1952 in NY.
Donor(s): M. William Levy,‡ Marion H. Levy, Caryn L. Magid, William Guy Levy.
Grantmaker type: Independent foundation
Financial data (yr. ended 12/31/02): Assets, $2,475,432 (M); expenditures, $294,103; qualifying distributions, $260,792; giving activities include $260,581 for 26 grants (high: $15,000; low: $100).
Fields of interest: Arts; Education; Animals/wildlife; Hospitals (general); Alzheimer's disease; Human services.
Types of support: General/operating support; Annual campaigns; Capital campaigns; Building/renovation; Seed money; Research; Technical assistance.
Limitations: Giving primarily in NY. No grants to individuals.
Application information:
Initial approach: Letter
Deadline(s): None
Officers: Marion H. Levy,* Pres.; Caryn L. Magid, Secy.; William G. Levy, Treas.
Number of staff: None.
EIN: 136084387

2297
Grace R. and Allan D. Marcus Foundation
7 W. 81st St., Apt. 5B
New York, NY 10024-6049
Contact: Daniel Soba, Tr.

Established in 1990 in NY.
Donor(s): Grace R. Marcus.‡
Grantmaker type: Independent foundation
Financial data (yr. ended 12/31/02): Assets, $2,684,630 (M); expenditures, $184,636; qualifying distributions, $148,020; giving

activities include $145,800 for 56 grants (high: $15,000; low: $500).
Purpose and activities: Giving for Jewish organizations, hospitals, art institutes, and social services.
Fields of interest: Arts; Higher education; Natural resources; Hospitals (general); Health organizations, association; Human services; Jewish federated giving programs; Jewish agencies & temples.
Limitations: Applications not accepted. Giving primarily in NY. No grants to individuals.
Application information: Contributes only to pre-selected organizations.
Trustees: Jonathan J. Halperin; Daniel Soba; Geraldine Soba; Amy Halperin Wood.
EIN: 136928240

2298
James S. Marcus Foundation
c/o BCRS Assocs., LLC
100 Wall St., 11th Fl.
New York, NY 10005-3101

Established in 1969 in NY.
Donor(s): James S. Marcus.
Grantmaker type: Independent foundation
Financial data (yr. ended 05/31/02): Assets, $5,604,804 (M); gifts received, $115,424; expenditures, $420,553; qualifying distributions, $413,892; giving activities include $414,214 for 75 grants (high: $50,000; low: $100).
Purpose and activities: Giving primarily for health and human services, the arts, and education.
Fields of interest: Music; Arts; Higher education; Natural resources; Hospitals (general); Human services.
Limitations: Applications not accepted. Giving primarily in New York, NY. No grants to individuals.
Application information: Contributes only to pre-selected organizations.
Trustees: H. Frederick Krimendahl II; Ellen F. Marcus; James S. Marcus.
EIN: 237044611

2299
The Marks Family Foundation
369 Franklin St., Ste. 100
Buffalo, NY 14202 (716) 854-0425
Contact: Debra Kull

Established in 1990 in NY.
Donor(s): Randolph A. Marks.
Grantmaker type: Independent foundation
Financial data (yr. ended 06/30/03): Assets, $2,049,211 (M); expenditures, $217,967; qualifying distributions, $196,510; giving activities include $196,720 for grants (high: $15,000; low: $25).
Purpose and activities: Giving primarily for education and conservation in Buffalo, NY.
Fields of interest: Education; Natural resources; Environment; Children/youth, services; Minorities.
Types of support: General/operating support; Program development; Scholarship funds; Program-related investments/loans; Matching/challenge support.
Limitations: Giving primarily in Buffalo, NY. No grants to individuals.

Application information: Application form required.
Initial approach: Letter
Copies of proposal: 6
Deadline(s): Apr.
Board meeting date(s): Semiannually
Officer and Trustees:* Randolph A. Marks,* Mgr.; Wendelyn W. Duquette; Joshua R. Marks; Sally Marks; Theodore E. Marks; Heather M. Palmer.
Number of staff: 1 part-time support.
EIN: 161385716

2300
Virginia Cretella Mars Foundation
c/o Brown Brothers Harriman Trust Co.
140 Broadway
New York, NY 10005 (212) 493-8000
Contact: Anna T. Korniczky, Acct.
FAX: (212) 493-8206

Established in 1994.
Grantmaker type: Independent foundation
Financial data (yr. ended 12/31/02): Assets, $6,337,227 (M); gifts received, $445,561; expenditures, $366,579; qualifying distributions, $340,360; giving activities include $333,516 for 10 grants (high: $100,000; low: $5,000).
Purpose and activities: Giving primarily for education.
Fields of interest: Visual arts; Performing arts; Elementary school/education; Secondary school/education; Higher education; Environment.
Types of support: General/operating support; Land acquisition; Seed money; Curriculum development.
Limitations: Applications not accepted. Giving primarily in NY. No grants to individuals.
Application information: Contributes only to pre-selected organizations.
Officers: Pamela M. Wright, Pres.; Marijke E. Mars, V.P.; Valerie A. Mars, Secy.; Victoria B. Mars, Treas.
Number of staff: None.
EIN: 133798973

2301
The Margot Marsh Biodiversity Foundation
c/o Trainer Wortham & Co.
1230 Ave. of the Americas
New York, NY 10020

Established in 1996 in CA.
Grantmaker type: Independent foundation
Financial data (yr. ended 12/31/02): Assets, $8,767,239 (M); expenditures, $874,659; qualifying distributions, $803,737; giving activities include $713,190 for 38 grants (high: $75,000; low: $5,000).
Purpose and activities: Support for wildlife and conservation protection on a worldwide basis.
Fields of interest: Natural resources; Animals/wildlife, preservation/protection.
Types of support: Program development; Research.
Limitations: Applications not accepted. Giving on a national basis. No grants to individuals.
Application information: Contributes only to pre-selected organizations.

Officers: Russell Mittermeier, Pres.; Karl Zobell, V.P. and Secy.; H. Williamson Ghriskey, Jr., V.P. and C.F.O.
Director: William Konstant.
EIN: 330683174

2302
The James Harper Marshall Foundation, Inc.
c/o M.R. Weiser & Co., LLP
3000 Marcus Ave.
New Hyde Park, NY 11042-1066

Established in 1982 in NY and DE.
Donor(s): James Harper Marshall, John H. Peace.
Grantmaker type: Independent foundation
Financial data (yr. ended 12/31/02): Assets, $2,412,541 (M); gifts received, $5,000; expenditures, $161,015; qualifying distributions, $150,155; giving activities include $150,900 for 37 grants (high: $25,000; low: $200).
Purpose and activities: Giving for higher education, medical centers, the arts, federated giving programs, and wildlife conservation.
Fields of interest: Arts; Education; Natural resources; Hospitals (general); Athletics/sports, golf; Youth development; Federated giving programs.
Types of support: Scholarship funds.
Limitations: Applications not accepted. Giving primarily in NY. No grants to individuals.
Application information: Contributes only to pre-selected organizations.
Officers and Director:* James Harper Marshall, Chair.; Lee Harper Marshall, Pres.; Edward G. Beimfohr,* Secy.-Treas.
EIN: 133157280

2303
Ann M. Martin Foundation, Inc.
P.O. Box 430
Boiceville, NY 12412
Contact: Elisa Geliebter, Secy.
FAX: (845) 657-8002

Established in 1991 in NY.
Donor(s): Ann M. Martin.
Grantmaker type: Independent foundation
Financial data (yr. ended 12/31/01): Assets, $567,136 (M); gifts received, $3,308; expenditures, $251,419; qualifying distributions, $251,127; giving activities include $250,533 for 52 grants (high: $17,000; low: $35).
Purpose and activities: Giving support for children and literacy programs, homeless people, and animal welfare.
Fields of interest: Reading; Animal welfare; Children/youth, services; Homeless, human services.
Limitations: Giving on a national basis, with some emphasis on New York City.
Publications: Grants list, Informational brochure (including application guidelines), Occasional report.
Application information: Application form not required.
Initial approach: Request brochure for application procedures
Copies of proposal: 5
Deadline(s): June 15
Board meeting date(s): Feb.

Officers and Directors:* Ann M. Martin, Pres.; Jane Reed Martin, V.P.; Elisa Geliebter,* Secy.; Catherine Gordon, Treas.; Laura Godwin.
EIN: 133620569

2304
The Mary A. and John M. McCarthy Foundation
c/o KCG Capital Advisors
880 3rd Ave., 8th Fl.
New York, NY 10022

Established in 1985 in NY.
Donor(s): Mary A. McCarthy, John M. McCarthy.
Grantmaker type: Independent foundation
Financial data (yr. ended 11/30/02): Assets, $4,227,764 (M); expenditures, $322,782; qualifying distributions, $296,451; giving activities include $255,000 for 20 grants (high: $25,000; low: $6,000; average: $10,000–$15,000).
Purpose and activities: Giving primarily for the arts, particularly theatre, and animal welfare; funding also for education, social services, and children and youth services, including a children's hospital.
Fields of interest: Theater; Historic preservation/historical societies; Arts; Education; Environment; Animal welfare; Hospitals (specialty); Human services; Children/youth, services.
Types of support: General/operating support; Annual campaigns; Capital campaigns; Building/renovation; Program development; Fellowships; Scholarship funds; Matching/challenge support.
Limitations: Applications not accepted. Giving primarily in the Mid-Atlantic and Northeast regions, with emphasis on the greater Washington, DC, area, Boston, MA, and New York, NY. No grants to individuals.
Publications: Multi-year report.
Application information: Contributes only to pre-selected organizations.
Board meeting date(s): Semiannually
Trustees: John M. McCarthy; Laurette E. McCarthy; Mary A. McCarthy; Neil M. McCarthy; Stephen J. McCarthy; Tara A. McCarthy.
Number of staff: 1 part-time professional.
EIN: 136863980

2305
Neil A. McConnell Foundation, Inc.
183 Jerome Ave.
Staten Island, NY 10305 (718) 981-1949
Contact: C. Matranga, Exec. Dir.

Incorporated in 1960 in NY.
Donor(s): Neil A. McConnell.
Grantmaker type: Independent foundation
Financial data (yr. ended 03/31/02): Assets, $1,663,331 (M); expenditures, $355,858; qualifying distributions, $338,271; giving activities include $292,251 for 21 grants (high: $50,000; low: $2,500).
Purpose and activities: Giving for special educational projects identified or developed by the foundation; interests include the arts, medical sciences, child development, and religion.

Fields of interest: Museums (art); Performing arts; Education; Natural resources; Health care; Human services.
Types of support: General/operating support; Annual campaigns; Program development; Conferences/seminars; Research.
Limitations: Giving limited to the northeastern U.S., with emphasis on the metropolitan New York, NY, area. No grants to individuals; no loans or program-related investments.
Application information: Application form not required.
Initial approach: Letter
Copies of proposal: 1
Deadline(s): None
Board meeting date(s): Annually and as required
Officers: B. Scott McConnell, Pres.; James G. Niven, V.P. and Treas.; Peter Brimelow, V.P.; Sandra McConnell, V.P.; Douglas F. Williamson, Jr., Secy.
Number of staff: 1 full-time professional.
EIN: 136114121

2306
Meehan Foundation
c/o M.J. Meehan & Co.
39 Broadway, 36th Fl.
New York, NY 10006

Established in 1996 in NY.
Donor(s): Emily Souvaine Meehan, Terence Meehan.
Grantmaker type: Independent foundation
Financial data (yr. ended 12/31/02): Assets, $5,462,763 (M); gifts received, $1,267,966; expenditures, $560,438; qualifying distributions, $409,834; giving activities include $375,988 for 69 grants (high: $50,000; low: $100).
Fields of interest: Arts; Higher education; Environment.
Limitations: Applications not accepted. Giving limited to New York, NY. No grants to individuals.
Application information: Contributes only to pre-selected organizations.
Trustees: Emily Souvaine Meehan; Terence S. Meehan.
EIN: 137099577

2307
William M. & Miriam F. Meehan Foundation, Inc.
1192 Park Ave., Ste. 3A
New York, NY 10128 (212) 534-8607
Contact: John D. O'Leary, Exec. Dir.
FAX: (212) 426-7472

Established in 1951.
Donor(s): Terence S. Meehan, Miriam F. Meehan, Maureen M. O'Leary, Joanne M. Berghold.
Grantmaker type: Independent foundation
Financial data (yr. ended 12/31/01): Assets, $8,364,101 (M); gifts received, $1,807,886; expenditures, $5,266,167; qualifying distributions, $652,481; giving activities include $626,350 for grants.
Purpose and activities: Giving primarily to Roman Catholic agencies, and for human services and education.

Fields of interest: Arts; Education; Environment; Children/youth, services; Roman Catholic agencies & churches.
Types of support: General/operating support; Continuing support; Annual campaigns; Capital campaigns.
Limitations: Applications not accepted. Giving primarily in New York, NY. No grants to individuals.
Application information: Contributes only to pre-selected organizations.
Board meeting date(s): May and Nov.
Officers and Directors:* Miriam F. Meehan,* Pres.; Maureen Meehan O'Leary,* V.P.; Terence S. Meehan,* Treas.; John D. O'Leary,* Exec. Dir.; Elisabetta Berghold; Joanne M. Berghold; Wm. Mark Berghold; Jennifer Kellogg; Emily Souvaine Meehan; William M. Meehan, Ph.D.; Laura Roebuck, M.D.; Tad Sennott.
Number of staff: 1 part-time professional; 2 part-time support.
EIN: 136062834

2308
The Andrew W. Mellon Foundation ▼
140 E. 62nd St.
New York, NY 10021 (212) 838-8400
Contact: Michele S. Warman, Secy. and Genl. Counsel
URL: http://www.mellon.org

Trust established in 1940 in DE as Avalon Foundation; incorporated in 1954 in NY; merged with Old Dominion Foundation and renamed the Andrew W. Mellon Foundation in 1969.
Donor(s): Ailsa Mellon Bruce,‡ Paul Mellon.‡
Grantmaker type: Independent foundation
Financial data (yr. ended 12/31/02): Assets, $3,600,620,000 (M); gifts received, $235,000; expenditures, $234,244,000; qualifying distributions, $222,427,386; giving activities include $222,662,386 for grants.
Purpose and activities: Grants on a selective basis for higher education; cultural affairs, including the humanities, museums, art conservation, and performing arts; population; conservation and the environment; and public affairs. Graduate fellowship program in the humanities administered by the Woodrow Wilson National Fellowship Foundation, which makes all awards.
Fields of interest: Museums; Performing arts; Humanities; Arts; Higher education; Natural resources; Environment; Population studies; Public policy, research; Public affairs.
Types of support: Continuing support; Endowments; Program development; Fellowships; Research; Matching/challenge support.
Limitations: No support for primarily local organizations. No grants to individuals (including scholarships and fellowships); no loans.
Publications: Annual report.
Application information: Application form not required.
Initial approach: Descriptive letter or proposal with cover letter
Copies of proposal: 1
Deadline(s): None
Board meeting date(s): Mar., June, Sept., and Dec.

Final notification: After board meetings
Officers and Trustees:* Hanna Holborn Gray,* Chair.; William G. Bowen,* Pres.; Harriet Zuckerman, Sr. V.P.; Mary Patterson McPherson, V.P.; Glenda Burkhart, V.P., Opers. and Plan.; Ira H. Fuchs, V.P., Research in Inf.Tech. and Prog. Off.; John E. Hull, V.P., Finance; Michele S. Warman, Secy. and Genl. Counsel; Eileen M. Scott, Treas.; Lewis W. Bernard; Paul LeClerc; Colin Lucas; Walter E. Massey; Timothy Mellon; W. Taylor Reveley III; Anne M. Tatlock.
Number of staff: 19 full-time professional; 25 full-time support; 14 part-time support.
EIN: 131879954
Recent environmental and animal welfare grants:

2308-1 Alley Pond Environmental Center, Douglaston, NY, $75,000. For disaster recovery relief. 2002.

2308-2 Associated Colleges of the South, Atlanta, GA, $230,000. For Environmental Studies. 2002.

2308-3 Barnes Foundation, Merion, PA, $300,000. For core institutional support. 2002.

2308-4 Brooklyn Botanic Garden, Brooklyn, NY, $300,000. For disaster recovery relief. 2002.

2308-5 Carnegie Mellon University, Pittsburgh, PA, $85,000. For environmental regulation program. 2002.

2308-6 Central Park Conservancy, New York, NY, $300,000. For disaster recovery relief. 2002.

2308-7 Cornell University, Ithaca, NY, $486,000. For ecosystems research and training. 2002.

2308-8 Council on the Environment, New York, NY, $30,000. For waste prevention and recycling service. 2002.

2308-9 Duke University, Durham, NC, $500,000. For ecological research and training. 2002.

2308-10 Duke University, Durham, NC, $330,000. For ecological research and training. 2002.

2308-11 Ecological Society of America, DC, $850,000. For Minorities in Ecology-SEEDS program. 2002.

2308-12 Ecological Society of America, DC, $109,000. For JSTOR. 2002.

2308-13 Environmental Law Institute, DC, $200,000. For environmental regulation. 2002.

2308-14 Fideicomiso Fondo para la Biodiversidad (Trust Fund for Biodiversity), Mexico City, Mexico, $340,000. For ecosystems research and training. 2002.

2308-15 Florida International University, Miami, FL, $440,000. For ecosystems research and training. 2002.

2308-16 Green Guerillas, New York, NY, $80,000. For disaster recovery relief. 2002.

2308-17 Greenbelt Conservancy, Staten Island, NY, $60,000. For disaster recovery relief. 2002.

2308-18 Harvard University, Cambridge, MA, $500,000. For ecosystems research and training, Harvard Forest program. 2002.

2308-19 Harvard University, Cambridge, MA, $338,000. For ecosystems research and training. 2002.

2308-20 Institute of Ecosystem Studies, Millbrook, NY, $15,000. For ecosystems

research and training at Hubbard Brook Research Foundation. 2002.

2308-21 Johns Hopkins University, Baltimore, MD, $150,000. For ecosystems research and training on the Arctic. 2002.

2308-22 Marine Biological Laboratory, Woods Hole, MA, $850,000. For ecological research. 2002.

2308-23 Marine Biological Laboratory, Woods Hole, MA, $500,000. For Universal Biological Indexer and Organizer (UBIO). 2002.

2308-24 Michigan State University, East Lansing, MI, $340,000. For ecosystems research and training. 2002.

2308-25 Missouri Botanical Garden, Saint Louis, MO, $400,000. For WWW portal for TROPICOS program. 2002.

2308-26 Missouri Botanical Garden, Saint Louis, MO, $279,000. For Integrated Library System, in collaboration with Missouri Historical Society and St. Louis Art Museum. 2002.

2308-27 Missouri Botanical Garden, Saint Louis, MO, $200,000. For digitization of rare books. 2002.

2308-28 New York Botanical Garden, Bronx, NY, $650,000. For disaster recovery relief. 2002.

2308-29 New York Restoration Project, New York, NY, $300,000. For disaster recovery relief. 2002.

2308-30 Organization for Tropical Studies, Durham, NC, $1,300,000. For South African undergraduate program at Kruger National Park. 2002.

2308-31 Organization for Tropical Studies, Durham, NC, $300,000. For Revolving Operating Reserve Fund. 2002.

2308-32 Princeton University, Princeton, NJ, $650,000. For ecosystems research and training. 2002.

2308-33 Queens Botanical Garden Society, Flushing, NY, $150,000. For disaster recovery relief. 2002.

2308-34 Royal Botanic Gardens, Richmond, England, $340,000. For fellowships for ecosystems research and training in Latin America. 2002.

2308-35 Smithsonian Institution, DC, $850,000. For ecosystems research and training at the Smithsonian Tropical Research Institute. 2002.

2308-36 South African National Parks, Pretoria, South Africa, $42,000. For planning grant for Kruger National Park. 2002.

2308-37 Staten Island Botanical Garden, Staten Island, NY, $100,000. For disaster recovery relief. 2002.

2308-38 Staten Island Zoological Society, Staten Island, NY, $25,000. For disaster recovery relief. 2002.

2308-39 Trust for Public Land, San Francisco, CA, $1,500,000. For land conservation program. 2002.

2308-40 Trust for Public Land, San Francisco, CA, $1,000,000. For land conservation program. 2002.

2308-41 United Negro College Fund, Fairfax, VA, $288,000. For Minorities in Ecology-SEEDS 2 program. 2002.

2308-42 University of Alaska, Fairbanks, AK, $260,000. For ecosystems research and training program. 2002.

2308-43 University of California, Santa Barbara, CA, $700,000. For ecosystems research and training program. 2002.

2308-44 University of California, Santa Barbara, CA, $450,000. For ecosystems research and training program. 2002.

2308-45 University of California, Santa Barbara, CA, $30,000. For ecosystems research and training program. 2002.

2308-46 University of Colorado, Boulder, CO, $260,000. For ecosystems research and training program. 2002.

2308-47 University of Florida, Gainesville, FL, $340,000. For ecological research and training program. 2002.

2308-48 University of Florida, Gainesville, FL, $300,000. For ecological research and training program. 2002.

2308-49 University of Fort Hare, Alice, South Africa, $36,000. For ecological research and training program. 2002.

2308-50 University of KwaZulu-Natal, Durban, South Africa, $150,000. For ecological research and training program. 2002.

2308-51 University of Maine, Orono, ME, $67,000. For ecosystems research and training program in the Arctic. 2002.

2308-52 University of Minnesota, Minneapolis, MN, $275,000. For ecosystems research and training program. 2002.

2308-53 University of Minnesota, Minneapolis, MN, $70,000. For ecological research and training program. 2002.

2308-54 University of Pennsylvania, Philadelphia, PA, $440,000. For ecosystems research and training program. 2002.

2308-55 University of Washington, Seattle, WA, $420,000. For ecological research and training program. 2002.

2308-56 University of Wisconsin, Madison, WI, $650,000. For ecosystems research and training program. 2002.

2308-57 Wave Hill, Bronx, NY, $200,000. For disaster recovery relief. 2002.

2308-58 Wildlife Conservation Society, Bronx, NY, $300,000. For disaster recovery relief. 2002.

2309
The Memton Fund, Inc.
515 Madison Ave., Ste. 3702
New York, NY 10022
Contact: Lillian I. Daniels, Exec. Dir.

Incorporated in 1936 in NY.
Donor(s): Albert G. Milbank,‡ Charles M. Cauldwell.‡
Grantmaker type: Independent foundation
Financial data (yr. ended 12/31/02): Assets, $9,227,461 (M); expenditures, $633,441; qualifying distributions, $503,361; giving activities include $389,000 for 135 grants (high: $15,000; low: $500; average: $1,000–$5,000).
Purpose and activities: Giving primarily for education.
Fields of interest: Museums; Performing arts; Historic preservation/historical societies; Arts; Adult education—literacy, basic skills & GED; Libraries/library science; Education; Natural resources; Environment; Animal welfare; Animals/wildlife; Health care; AIDS; Youth development, citizenship; Human services;

Children/youth, services; Family services; Public affairs, citizen participation.
Types of support: General/operating support; Continuing support; Annual campaigns; Capital campaigns; Building/renovation; Endowments; Program development; Curriculum development; Internship funds; Scholarship funds.
Limitations: Applications not accepted. Giving limited to the U.S. and U.S. Pacific Islands. No grants to individuals.
Application information: Contributes only to pre-selected organizations.
    Board meeting date(s): Spring and fall
Officers and Directors:* Samuel L. Milbank, Pres.; Elenita M. Drumwright,* V.P.; Lillian I. Daniels,* Secy.-Treas.; Elizabeth R.M. Drumwright; Robert V. Edgar; E. Shepard Farrar; Olivia Farrar-Wellman; Alexandra Giordano; Michelle R. Milbank; Thomas Milbank; Debbie Piccone; Karen M. Quackenbush; Pamela White.
Number of staff: 1 full-time professional; 1 part-time support.
EIN: 136096608

2310
Janis and Alan Menken Foundation, Inc.
c/o JH Cohn LLP
1212 6th Ave., 24th Fl.
New York, NY 10036
Contact: Alan Menken, Pres.

Established in 1996 in NY.
Donor(s): Alan Menken.
Grantmaker type: Independent foundation
Financial data (yr. ended 12/31/02): Assets, $87,678 (M); gifts received, $50,000; expenditures, $103,765; qualifying distributions, $103,758; giving activities include $102,520 for 130 grants (high: $10,000; low: $100).
Fields of interest: Arts; Education; Hospitals (general); Environment; Alzheimer's disease; Human services; Children/youth, services; Jewish agencies & temples.
Limitations: Giving primarily in NY. No grants to individuals.
Officers and Directors:* Alan Menken,* Pres.; Janis Menken,* V.P.; Eric Kunis, Secy.; David Gotterer.
EIN: 133920424

2311
Mertz Gilmore Foundation ▼
(formerly Joyce Mertz-Gilmore Foundation)
218 E. 18th St.
New York, NY 10003-3694 (212) 475-1137
Contact: Jay Beckner, Exec. Dir.
FAX: (212) 777-5226; E-mail: info@mertzgilmore.org; URL: http://www.mertzgilmore.org

Incorporated in 1959 in NY.
Donor(s): Robert Gilmore,‡ Joyce Mertz.‡
Grantmaker type: Independent foundation
Financial data (yr. ended 12/31/02): Assets, $89,700,287 (M); expenditures, $6,477,596; qualifying distributions, $5,734,830; giving activities include $4,314,552 for 144 grants.
Purpose and activities: Current concerns include human rights, the environment, peace and security issues in the Middle East, and New York City cultural, social, and civic concerns.

Fields of interest: Dance; Energy; International peace/security; International human rights; Civil rights, immigrants; Civil rights, gays/lesbians; Community development, equal rights; Community development, citizen coalitions; Community development.
International interests: Israel; West Bank/Gaza.
Types of support: General/operating support; Continuing support; Program development; Seed money; Technical assistance; Matching/challenge support.
Limitations: Giving on a national and international basis, with the exception of the New York City Program. No support for sectarian religious concerns. No grants to individuals, or for endowments, annual fund appeals, fundraising events, conferences, workshops, publications, film or media projects, scholarships, research, fellowships, or travel; no loans (except for program-related investments).
Publications: Application guidelines, Biennial report (including application guidelines), Informational brochure.
Application information: The foundation will send an application form to those it feels fall within its guidelines based on the initial inquiry letter. The foundation prefers to receive all inquiries by regular mail. Grantseekers outside the United States may submit inquiry letters via E-mail. Do not submit videos, CDs, audiocassettes, press clippings, books, or other materials unless they are requested. Application form required.
    Initial approach: Letter
    Copies of proposal: 1
    Deadline(s): None
    Board meeting date(s): May and Nov. for grant decisions
    Final notification: Within 3 weeks of board meeting
Officers and Directors:* Larry E. Condon,* Chair.; Elizabeth Burke Gilmore,* Vice-Chair. and Secy.; Denise Nix Thompson,* Treas.; Jay Beckner, Exec. Dir.; Harlan Cleveland; Robert Crane; Hal Harvey; Patricia Ramsay; Peggy Saika; Mikki Shepard; Franklin W. Wallin.
Number of staff: 5 full-time professional; 1 part-time professional; 5 full-time support; 2 part-time support.
EIN: 132872722

2312
Metropolitan Philanthropic Fund, Inc.
(formerly Jane P. & Charles D. Klein Foundation)
666 3rd Ave., 29th Fl.
New York, NY 10017-4011
Contact: Charles D. Klein, V.P.

Established in 1982.
Donor(s): Charles D. Klein, Laila Hafner.
Grantmaker type: Independent foundation
Financial data (yr. ended 06/30/02): Assets, $6,592,147 (M); gifts received, $125,487; expenditures, $895,353; qualifying distributions, $848,507; giving activities include $852,440 for 97 grants (high: $204,400; low: $250).
Purpose and activities: Giving to museums, higher education, and religion, including Jewish and Christian organizations.
Fields of interest: Ballet; Elementary/secondary education; Higher education; Natural resources; Human services; Christian agencies & churches.
Types of support: General/operating support.

Limitations: Giving primarily in New York, NY. No grants to individuals.
Application information: Application form not required.
    Initial approach: Proposal
    Deadline(s): None
Officers and Directors:* Jane P. Klein,* Pres.; Charles D. Klein,* V.P.; David P. Steinmann,* Secy.-Treas.; Alex Anagnos.
EIN: 133128811

2313
Edward & Sandra Meyer Foundation, Inc.
c/o Philip Pollak
432 Park Ave. S., Ste. 400
New York, NY 10016-8013

Established in 1966.
Donor(s): Edward H. Meyer.
Grantmaker type: Independent foundation
Financial data (yr. ended 12/31/00): Assets, $2,913,468 (M); gifts received, $578,440; expenditures, $354,267; qualifying distributions, $346,383; giving activities include $348,820 for 25 grants (high: $100,000; low: $50).
Purpose and activities: Giving primarily for Jewish agencies and federated giving programs, health care and health associations, museums, and education.
Fields of interest: Museums; Historical activities; Arts; Elementary/secondary education; Natural resources; Hospitals (general); Health organizations, association; Jewish federated giving programs; Jewish agencies & temples.
Limitations: Applications not accepted. Giving primarily in the New York, NY, area. No grants to individuals.
Application information: Contributes only to pre-selected organizations.
Officers: Edward H. Meyer, Pres. and Treas.; Sandra Meyer, Secy.
EIN: 136204325

2314
Roger and Barbara Michaels Family Fund, Inc.
c/o Elliott, Tarlow & Co., CPA's
7 Penn Plz., Ste. 804
New York, NY 10001

Established in 1980.
Grantmaker type: Independent foundation
Financial data (yr. ended 12/31/02): Assets, $3,167,643 (M); expenditures, $190,625; qualifying distributions, $149,708; giving activities include $146,760 for 89 grants (high: $65,000; low: $35).
Purpose and activities: Giving primarily for human services, community, education, and health.
Fields of interest: Museums; Performing arts; Arts; Higher education; Education; Environment; Hospitals (general); Health organizations, association; Human services; Community development; Foundations (community).
Limitations: Giving primarily in NY.
Application information:
    Initial approach: Letter
    Deadline(s): None
Directors: Alice M. Ginandes; Barbara R. Michaels; Roger A. Michaels.
EIN: 133022845

2315
Mitsubishi International Corporation Foundation

c/o Mitsubishi International Corp.
520 Madison Ave.
New York, NY 10022 (212) 605-1111
Contact: Reilly Starr., Prog. Off.
E-mail: mic.foundation@org.mitsubishicorp.com

Established in 1992 in NY.
Donor(s): Mitsubishi Corp., Mitsubishi International Corp.
Grantmaker type: Company-sponsored foundation
Financial data (yr. ended 12/31/02): Assets, $3,932,154 (M); gifts received, $300,000; expenditures, $301,086; qualifying distributions, $298,450; giving activities include $298,450 for 9 grants (high: $91,250; low: $1,700).
Fields of interest: Natural resources; Environmental education; Financial services.
International interests: Canada; Latin America.
Types of support: Continuing support; Program development; Curriculum development; Scholarship funds; Research.
Limitations: Giving primarily in the Americas. No grants to individuals.
Application information: Application form not required.
Initial approach: Concept paper
Copies of proposal: 3
Deadline(s): Spring
Board meeting date(s): Fall
Final notification: Summer
Officers: Motoatsu Sakurai, Chair.; James E. Brumm, Pres.; Shunichiro Kimpara, Treas.; Tracy Austin, Exec. Dir.
Number of staff: 3 full-time professional; 3 full-time support.
EIN: 133676166

2316
MJPM Foundation

c/o McLaughlin & Stern, LLP
260 Madison Ave.
New York, NY 10016

Established in 1999 in NY.
Donor(s): Mary J.P. Moore.
Grantmaker type: Independent foundation
Financial data (yr. ended 12/31/01): Assets, $14,900,949 (M); gifts received, $4,859,754; expenditures, $546,399; qualifying distributions, $473,805; giving activities include $489,442 for 8 grants (high: $284,442; low: $10,000).
Purpose and activities: Giving primarily to a community foundation, and to land and other natural resource conversation; funding also for human services.
Fields of interest: Historic preservation/historical societies; Natural resources; Environment, land resources; Food services; Human services; Foundations (community).
Limitations: Applications not accepted. No grants to individuals.
Application information: Contributes only to pre-selected organizations.
Officers: Mary J.P. Moore, Pres.; Samuel F. Posey, Jr., V.P.; Nicholas J. Moore, Secy.; David W. Moore, Treas.
EIN: 134043598

2317
The Ambrose Monell Foundation ▼

c/o Fulton, Rowe, & Hart
1 Rockefeller Plz., Ste. 301
New York, NY 10020-2002 (212) 586-0700
Contact: George Rowe, Jr., Pres.
FAX: (212) 245-1863; *E-mail:* info@monellvetlesen.org; *URL:* http://www.monellvetlesen.org/

Incorporated in 1952 in NY.
Donor(s): Maude Monell Vetlesen.‡
Grantmaker type: Independent foundation
Financial data (yr. ended 12/31/02): Assets, $197,154,217 (M); expenditures, $11,107,780; qualifying distributions, $10,597,444; giving activities include $10,472,500 for 140 grants (high: $625,000; low: $2,500; average: $5,000–$500,000).
Purpose and activities: For the improvement of the physical, mental, and moral condition of humanity throughout the world. Giving largely for hospitals and health services, scientific research, museums, performing arts, and other cultural activities, and higher and secondary education; support also for social services, research in political science, mental health, and aid to the handicapped.
Fields of interest: Secondary school/education; Higher education; Education; Animal welfare; Hospitals (general); Health care; Mental health/crisis services; Health organizations, association; AIDS; Alcoholism; Medical research, institute; AIDS research; Human services; Aging, centers/services; Physical/earth sciences; Political science; Public policy, research; Disabled; Aging.
Types of support: General/operating support; Continuing support; Annual campaigns; Capital campaigns; Building/renovation; Equipment; Endowments; Curriculum development; Scholarship funds; Research.
Limitations: No grants to individuals.
Application information: Application form not required.
Initial approach: Letter of inquiry
Copies of proposal: 1
Deadline(s): Apr. 30 and Oct. 31
Board meeting date(s): June and Dec.
Officers and Directors:* George Rowe, Jr.,* Pres.; Maurizio J. Morello, Secy.; Gary K. Beauchamp, Ph.D.; Eugene P. Grisanti; Ambrose K. Monell.
Number of staff: None.
EIN: 131982683
Recent environmental and animal welfare grants:
2317-1 Animal Medical Center, New York, NY, $25,000. 2001.
2317-2 Brooklyn Botanic Garden, Brooklyn, NY, $50,000. 2001.
2317-3 Central Park Conservancy, New York, NY, $100,000. 2001.
2317-4 New York Botanical Garden, Bronx, NY, $500,000. 2001.

2318
The Moore Charitable Foundation, Inc.

1251 Ave. of the Americas, 53rd Fl.
New York, NY 10020
Contact: Ann Colley, Mgr.

Established in 1992 in NY; funded in 1993.

Donor(s): One to One Charitable Foundation.
Grantmaker type: Independent foundation
Financial data (yr. ended 12/31/01): Assets, $1,082,607 (M); gifts received, $1,680,503; expenditures, $1,952,805; qualifying distributions, $1,931,282; giving activities include $1,626,851 for 172 grants (high: $200,000; low: $50; average: $1,000–$50,000).
Purpose and activities: The mission of the foundation is land and water conservation.
Fields of interest: Environment.
Limitations: Applications not accepted. Giving on a national basis. No grants to individuals.
Application information: Contributes only to pre-selected organizations. Unsolicited requests for funds not considered.
Officer: Ann Colley, Mgr.
Directors: Louis M. Bacon; Larry Noe.
EIN: 133741954

2319
The William C. and Susan F. Morris Foundation

c/o J & W Seligman & Co.
100 Park Ave., 8th Fl.
New York, NY 10017

Established in 2000 in DE.
Donor(s): William Morris.
Grantmaker type: Independent foundation
Financial data (yr. ended 12/31/01): Assets, $7,763,132 (M); expenditures, $2,753,793; qualifying distributions, $2,635,302; giving activities include $2,635,000 for 3 grants (high: $1,675,000; low: $10,000).
Fields of interest: Higher education; Business school/education; Education; Environment, water resources; Environment; Hospitals (general).
Limitations: Applications not accepted. Giving primarily in NY. No grants to individuals.
Application information: Contributes only to pre-selected organizations.
Officers: William Morris, Chair., Pres. and Treas.; Susan Morris, V.P. and Secy.
EIN: 134128044

2320
The Mosaic Fund

c/o Satterlee, Stephens Burke & Burke
230 Park Ave., Ste. 1130
New York, NY 10169-1599

Established in 1994 in NY.
Donor(s): Clattesad Trust.
Grantmaker type: Independent foundation
Financial data (yr. ended 12/31/02): Assets, $201,589 (M); gifts received, $5,555,096; expenditures, $5,552,645; qualifying distributions, $5,446,032; giving activities include $5,446,032 for 45 grants (high: $1,536,380; low: $320).
Purpose and activities: Giving primarily for environmental conservation and protection, including urban parks and gardens; some support also for secondary education and the arts.
Fields of interest: Natural resources; Environment.
Limitations: Applications not accepted. Giving primarily in NY. No grants to individuals.

Application information: Contributes only to pre-selected organizations.
Trustees: Howard G. Seitz; Richard T. Watson.
EIN: 137045257

2321
Henry and Lucy Moses Fund, Inc.
c/o Moses and Singer
1301 Ave. of the Americas
New York, NY 10019
Contact: Irving Sitnick, Esq.

Incorporated in 1942 in NY.
Donor(s): Henry L. Moses,‡ Lucy G. Moses.‡
Grantmaker type: Independent foundation
Financial data (yr. ended 12/31/01): Assets, $1,580,794 (M); gifts received, $1,280,000; expenditures, $1,432,081; qualifying distributions, $1,406,603; giving activities include $1,395,250 for 88 grants (high: $100,000; low: $2,000; average: $1,000–$25,000).
Purpose and activities: Support for hospitals; Jewish and other welfare funds; higher and legal education and educational programs for minorities; social service agencies, including those for youth, child welfare, minorities, the aged, and the handicapped; arts and cultural programs, including dance; and environmental concerns, including Central Park in New York City.
Fields of interest: Performing arts; Dance; Music; Arts; Higher education; Environment; Hospitals (general); Human services; Children/youth, services; Aging, centers/services; Jewish federated giving programs; Disabled.
Types of support: General/operating support; Continuing support; Annual campaigns; Endowments; Professorships; Scholarship funds; Research; Matching/challenge support.
Limitations: Giving primarily in the New York, NY, area. No grants to individuals; no loans.
Application information: Support generally limited to previous grant recipients. Application form not required.
   Initial approach: Letter
   Copies of proposal: 1
   Deadline(s): None
   Board meeting date(s): Usually in Feb., May, Aug., and Oct.
Officers and Directors:* Irving Sitnick,* Pres.; Joseph Fishman,* V.P. and Secy.; Jacqueline Schneider, V.P.
Number of staff: None.
EIN: 136092967

2322
Mostyn Foundation, Inc.
c/o James C. Edwards & Co., Inc.
570 Lexington Ave., 29th Fl.
New York, NY 10022
Contact: Arthur B. Choate, Pres.

Trust established in 1949 in NY; incorporated in 1965.
Donor(s): Harvey D. Gibson,‡ Mrs. Harvey D. Gibson,‡ Whitney Bourne Atwood.
Grantmaker type: Independent foundation
Financial data (yr. ended 12/31/02): Assets, $4,623,218 (M); expenditures, $330,009; qualifying distributions, $282,692; giving

activities include $285,000 for 30 grants (high: $50,000; low: $1,000).
Fields of interest: Higher education; Natural resources; Health care; Human services; Protestant agencies & churches.
Types of support: General/operating support; Endowments.
Limitations: Applications not accepted. Giving in the U.S., with emphasis on FL and NY. No grants to individuals.
Application information: Contributes only to pre-selected organizations.
Officers: Arthur B. Choate, Pres.; Rev. Charles Newbery, V.P.; Peter Megargee Brown, Secy.-Treas.
EIN: 136171217

2323
The Hilda Mullen Foundation
c/o Simpson Thacher & Bartlett
425 Lexington Ave.
New York, NY 10017

Established in 1997 in NY.
Donor(s): Lois Q. Whitman, Martin J. Whitman.
Grantmaker type: Independent foundation
Financial data (yr. ended 12/31/01): Assets, $7,770,674 (M); expenditures, $608,338; qualifying distributions, $606,463; giving activities include $599,500 for 129 grants (high: $200,000; low: $100).
Purpose and activities: Giving primarily for human rights, education, health services, and Jewish agencies.
Fields of interest: Education; Environment; Health care; Human services; Civil rights; Jewish agencies & temples.
Limitations: Applications not accepted. No grants to individuals.
Application information: Contributes only to pre-selected organizations.
Trustees: Lois Q. Whitman; Martin J. Whitman.
EIN: 137120449

2324
Charles & Constance Murcott Charitable Trust
10 Matinecock Farms Rd.
Glen Cove, NY 11542

Established in 1986 in NY.
Donor(s): Charles Murcott.
Grantmaker type: Independent foundation
Financial data (yr. ended 08/31/02): Assets, $195,815 (M); expenditures, $434,850; qualifying distributions, $432,417; giving activities include $432,500 for 29 grants (high: $160,000; low: $50).
Purpose and activities: Giving primarily to health associations and hospitals, as well as for education; funding for a nature conservancy, and social services.
Fields of interest: Education; Natural resources; Hospitals (general); Medical care, rehabilitation; Health organizations, association; Human services.
Limitations: Applications not accepted. Giving primarily in the New York, NY, metropolitan area, including Long Island; some funding also in Tucson, AZ. No grants to individuals.
Application information: Contributes only to pre-selected organizations.

Trustees: Charles Murcott; Constance Murcott.
EIN: 112826619

2325
Muzio Family Foundation
c/o BCRS Assoc., LLC
67 Wall St., 8th Fl.
New York, NY 10005

Established in 1991 in NY.
Donor(s): Gaetano J. Muzio.
Grantmaker type: Independent foundation
Financial data (yr. ended 03/31/02): Assets, $1,133,093 (M); expenditures, $127,075; qualifying distributions, $98,979; giving activities include $97,167 for 43 grants (high: $25,000; low: $250).
Purpose and activities: Giving primarily for arts and culture, educational purposes, and health and human services.
Fields of interest: Museums; Arts; Higher education; Education; Zoos/zoological societies; Health organizations, association; Parks/playgrounds; Human services; Children/youth, services.
Limitations: Applications not accepted. Giving on a national basis, with some emphasis on CA. No grants to individuals; no loans or scholarships.
Application information: Contributes only to pre-selected organizations.
Trustees: Gaetano J. Muzio; Maria T. Muzio; James R. Rosencranz.
EIN: 133632761

2326
The Nadler Family Foundation
260 Madison Ave., 3rd Fl.
New York, NY 10016 (212) 309-9898
Contact: Donna Nadler

Established in 2001 in NY and DE.
Donor(s): David Nadler.
Grantmaker type: Independent foundation
Financial data (yr. ended 12/31/02): Assets, $6,867 (M); gifts received, $106,000; expenditures, $101,934; qualifying distributions, $101,934; giving activities include $101,250 for 7 grants (high: $85,000; low: $125).
Fields of interest: Education; Animal welfare.
Limitations: Giving primarily in New York, NY.
Application information:
   Initial approach: Letter on organization letterhead
   Deadline(s): None
Officers and Directors:* David Nadler,* Pres.; Francesca Nadler,* V.P.; Amy Nadler,* Secy.; Cara Nadler,* Treas.
EIN: 134168889

2327
Daniel M. Neidich & Brooke Garber Foundation
c/o Goldman Sachs & Co.
85 Broad St., Tax Dept.
New York, NY 10004

Established in 1985 in NY.
Donor(s): Daniel M. Neidich.
Grantmaker type: Independent foundation

Financial data (yr. ended 01/31/02): Assets, $9,347,198 (M); gifts received, $1,118,550; expenditures, $553,438; qualifying distributions, $519,841; giving activities include $515,716 for 168 grants (high: $30,000; low: $10).
Purpose and activities: Funding primarily for education. Some funding also for arts and culture, human services, and Jewish agencies.
Fields of interest: Museums; Performing arts; Arts; Elementary/secondary education; Higher education; Education; Natural resources; Hospitals (general); Children/youth, services; Jewish federated giving programs; Protestant agencies & churches; Jewish agencies & temples.
Limitations: Applications not accepted. Giving primarily in New York, NY. No grants to individuals.
Application information: Contributes only to pre-selected organizations.
Trustees: Brooke Garber; Daniel M. Neidich.
EIN: 133318126

2328
The John L. Neu Family Foundation, Inc.
79 5th Ave., 18th Fl.
New York, NY 10003-3034

Established in 1990 in NY.
Donor(s): Hugo Neu Corp.
Grantmaker type: Independent foundation
Financial data (yr. ended 12/31/02): Assets, $4,201,733 (M); gifts received, $1,250,000; expenditures, $539,416; qualifying distributions, $537,738; giving activities include $537,550 for 28 grants (high: $240,000; low: $100).
Purpose and activities: Giving primarily for animal welfare and population control.
Fields of interest: Museums; Higher education; Animal welfare; Animal population control; Hospitals (general); Youth development; Homeless, human services; Federated giving programs; Roman Catholic federated giving programs; Religion.
Limitations: Applications not accepted. Giving primarily in NJ and NY. No grants to individuals.
Application information: Contributes only to pre-selected organizations.
Officers and Directors:* John L. Neu,* Pres.; Donald Hamaker, Secy.-Treas.; Robert T. Neu; Wendy K. Neu.
EIN: 133731089

2329
Neuwirth Foundation, Inc.
c/o Cummings & Carroll
175 Great Neck Rd.
Great Neck, NY 11021

Established in 1991 in NY.
Donor(s): Marvin R. Neuwirth.
Grantmaker type: Independent foundation
Financial data (yr. ended 08/31/02): Assets, $3,921,859 (M); expenditures, $366,884; qualifying distributions, $352,184; giving activities include $357,350 for 16 grants (high: $107,500; low: $100).
Purpose and activities: Giving primarily to health associations, and to a hospital; funding also for museums as well as for a horse show, natural resource conservation, children services, and Jewish and other federated giving programs.

Fields of interest: Museums (art); Natural resources; Hospitals (general); Cancer; Alzheimer's disease research; Athletics/sports, equestrianism; Children, services; Federated giving programs; Jewish federated giving programs.
Limitations: Applications not accepted. Giving primarily in NY. No grants to individuals.
Application information: Contributes only to pre-selected organizations.
Officers and Directors:* Marvin R. Neuwirth,* Pres.; Barbara Braun,* V.P.; Felice Neuwirth,* Secy.; Anthony Braun,* Treas.
EIN: 113048776

2330
The New York Community Trust ▼
2 Park Ave., 24th Fl.
New York, NY 10016-9385 (212) 686-0010
Contact: Lorie A. Slutsky, Pres. and Dir.
FAX: (212) 532-8528; URL: http://www.nycommunitytrust.org

Established in 1924 in NY by resolution and declaration of trust.
Grantmaker type: Community foundation
Financial data (yr. ended 12/31/02): Assets, $1,550,847,559 (M); gifts received, $83,021,663; expenditures, $199,176,458; giving activities include $126,484,987 for grants.
Purpose and activities: A grantmaking community foundation. Priority given to applications for projects having particular significance for the New York City area. Program areas of major interest are: 1) Children, Youth, and Families - includes issues of hunger and homelessness, social services, substance abuse, youth development, girls and young women; 2) Community Development and the Environment - includes civic affairs, community development, conservation, environment, and technical assistance; 3) Education, Arts, and the Humanities - includes arts and culture, education, historic preservation, and human justice; and 4) Health and People With Special Needs - includes health services and policy, biomedical research, AIDS, visual handicaps, children and youth with disabilities, the elderly, and mental health and retardation. In addition, the trust has established divisions that reach out to the greater New York metropolitan area: the Westchester Community Foundation and the Long Island Community Foundation.
Fields of interest: Historic preservation/historical societies; Arts; Education, public education; Child development, education; Environment; Health care; Substance abuse, services; Mental health/crisis services; Health organizations, association; Cancer; AIDS; Domestic violence; Legal services; Employment; Food services; Housing/shelter, development; Human services; Children/youth, services; Family services; Aging, centers/services; Women, centers/services; Homeless, human services; Civil rights, immigrants; Civil rights, minorities; Civil rights, disabled; Civil rights, women; Civil rights, aging; Civil rights, gays/lesbians; Reproductive rights; Community development; Government/public administration.
Types of support: Income development; Management development; Program development; Publication; Seed money;

Fellowships; Scholarship funds; Research; Technical assistance; Consulting services; Program evaluation; Employee matching gifts.
Limitations: Giving limited to the metropolitan New York, NY, area. No support for religious purposes. No grants to individuals, or for deficit financing, emergency funds, building campaigns, endowment funds, capital projects or general operating support.
Publications: Application guidelines, Annual report, Financial statement, Grants list, Informational brochure (including application guidelines), Newsletter, Occasional report.
Application information: Accepts NYRAG Common Application Form. Applicants for support from the Long Island Community Foundation should call (516) 681-5085; those wishing to apply to the Westchester Community Foundation should call (914) 948-5166. Application form required.
  Initial approach: Proposal with cover letter
  Copies of proposal: 1
  Deadline(s): None
  Board meeting date(s): Feb., Apr., June, July, Oct., and Dec.
  Final notification: Up to 25 weeks
Officers and Distribution Committee:* Anne Sidamon-Eristoff,* Chair.; Robert M. Kaufman, Vice-Chair.; Lorie A. Slutsky,* Pres. and Dir.; Joyce M. Bove, V.P., Progs. and Projects; Mercedes M. Leon, V.P., Admin.; Jane L. Wilton, Secy. and Genl. Counsel; Kathryn Conroy, C.F.O.; Mary Greenebaum, C.I.O.; Heidi Hotzler, Cont.; Barbara H. Block; Ernest J. Collazo; Charlynn Goins; Jeh Charles Johnson; Anne Moore, M.D.; Samuel S. Polk; Estelle "Nicki" Newman Tanner; Carroll L. Wainwright, Jr.; Lulu C. Wang.
Trustees: The Bank of New York; Bessemer Trust Co., N.A.; Brown Brothers Harriman Trust Co.; Citibank, N.A.; Deutsche Bank Americas; Fiduciary Trust Co. International; Fleet National Bank; HSBC Bank USA; JPMorgan Chase Bank; Merrill Lynch Trust Co., FSB; Neuberger Berman Trust Co.; Rockefeller Trust Co.; U.S. Trust Co. of New York; Winthrop Trust Co.
Number of staff: 22 full-time professional; 2 part-time professional; 15 full-time support.
EIN: 133062214
Recent environmental and animal welfare grants:
2330-1 Adirondack Council, Elizabethtown, NY, $10,000. For Forever Wild Fund. 2002.
2330-2 American Farmland Trust, DC, $75,000. To increase public resources for farmland preservation in New York and Southern New England. 2002.
2330-3 American Littoral Society, Highlands, NJ, $100,000. To establish bi-state Hudson Raritan Conservancy. 2002.
2330-4 American Museum of Natural History, New York, NY, $200,000. To provide teaching materials for environmentalists in developing and tropical countries. 2002.
2330-5 American Oceans Campaign, DC, $30,000. To educate fishermen and media about destruction of sensitive marine habitat in mid-Atlantic region. 2002.
2330-6 American Rivers, DC, $20,000. For general support. 2002.
2330-7 American Society for the Prevention of Cruelty to Animals, New York, NY, $25,000. For general support. 2002.

2330-8 American Society for the Prevention of Cruelty to Animals, New York, NY, $20,000. For general support. 2002.

2330-9 American Society for the Prevention of Cruelty to Animals, New York, NY, $10,000. For general support. 2002.

2330-10 Americans for Equitable Climate Solutions, DC, $100,000. To promote market-based strategies to curb domestic carbon dioxide emissions and distribute costs equitably. 2002.

2330-11 Animal Medical Center, New York, NY, $300,000. For general support. 2002.

2330-12 Animal Rescue Fund of the Hamptons, Wainscott, NY, $25,000. For general support. 2002.

2330-13 Animal Rescue Fund of the Hamptons, Wainscott, NY, $25,000. For general support. 2002.

2330-14 Association of New Jersey Environmental Commissions, Mendham, NJ, $25,000. For High Ground, quarterly newsletter for Highlands Coalition. 2002.

2330-15 Audubon Partnership for Economic Development Local Development Corporation, New York, NY, $10,000. For strategic planning process. 2002.

2330-16 Black Rock Forest Consortium, Cornwall, NY, $147,000. To develop science and environmental education program for New York City public school children. 2002.

2330-17 Botanical Garden, Naples, FL, $100,000. For general support. 2002.

2330-18 Canine Companions for Independence, Oceanside, CA, $10,000. For general support. 2002.

2330-19 Canine Companions for Independence, Oceanside, CA, $10,000. For general support. 2002.

2330-20 Center for Resource Economics/Island Press, DC, $20,000. For general support. 2002.

2330-21 Center for the Biology of Natural Systems, Flushing, NY, $75,000. To study airborne migration of PCBs from Hudson River to New York watershed. 2002.

2330-22 Central Park Conservancy, New York, NY, $30,000. For general support. 2002.

2330-23 Central Park Conservancy, New York, NY, $10,000. For general support. 2002.

2330-24 Central Park Conservancy, New York, NY, $10,000. For general support. 2002.

2330-25 Christodora, Inc., New York, NY, $50,000. For general support. 2002.

2330-26 Citizens Advisory Panel, Bridgehampton, NY, $12,500. For general support. 2002.

2330-27 Citizens Environmental Research Institute, Farmingdale, NY, $30,000. For general support. 2002.

2330-28 Clean Air Cool Planet-A Northeast Alliance, Portsmouth, NH, $100,000. To promote climate change solutions to individuals and institutions in Northeast. 2002.

2330-29 Clean Water Fund, DC, $100,000. To expand local efforts to protect drinking water quality. 2002.

2330-30 Co-op America Foundation, DC, $20,000. For general support. 2002.

2330-31 Co-op America Foundation, DC, $13,500. For general support. 2002.

2330-32 Columbia University, School of Public Health, New York, NY, $100,000. To study

toxic exposure of children in upper Manhattan. 2002.

2330-33 Commonweal, Bolinas, CA, $100,000. To study methods for lowering levels of toxic chemicals in nursing mothers. 2002.

2330-34 Consumers Union of United States, Yonkers, NY, $45,000. To promote sustainable and equitable waste management practices in New York City. 2002.

2330-35 Earth Pledge Foundation, New York, NY, $13,000. For general support. 2002.

2330-36 East Coast Greenway Alliance, Wakefield, RI, $30,000. To bring East Coast Greenway through New York City. 2002.

2330-37 East Coast Greenway Alliance, Wakefield, RI, $10,000. For general support. 2002.

2330-38 Environmental Advocates, Albany, NY, $15,000. For general support. 2002.

2330-39 Environmental and Energy Study Institute, DC, $75,000. To promote development of renewable energy from agricultural resources. 2002.

2330-40 Environmental Defense, New York, NY, $125,000. To continue focus on urban environmental issues in New York metropolitan region. 2002.

2330-41 Environmental Defense, New York, NY, $75,000. For Keep Antibiotics Working: The Campaign to End Antibiotic Overuse to advocate for reduction in use of antibiotics in animal feed. 2002.

2330-42 Environmental Defense, New York, NY, $10,000. For Keep Antibiotics Working: The Campaign to End Antibiotic Overuse invitational meetings. 2002.

2330-43 Environmental Defense, New York, NY, $10,000. For general support. 2002.

2330-44 Environmental Defense, New York, NY, $10,000. For general support. 2002.

2330-45 Environmental Health Fund, Jamaica Plain, MA, $50,000. To promote safer petrochemical plants. 2002.

2330-46 Environmental Law and Policy Center of the Midwest, Chicago, IL, $50,000. To involve corporate leadership in global warming issues. 2002.

2330-47 Federated Conservationists of Westchester County, Purchase, NY, $30,000. For general support. 2002.

2330-48 Federated Conservationists of Westchester County, Purchase, NY, $10,000. For general support. 2002.

2330-49 Fish America Foundation, Alexandria, VA, $10,000. For general support. 2002.

2330-50 Free the Planet, DC, $50,000. To engage college students in campaigns to curb global warming. 2002.

2330-51 Freedom Guide Dogs for the Blind, Cassville, NY, $10,000. To provide mobility training to people who use guide dogs in NYC. 2002.

2330-52 Friends of Animals, Darien, CT, $12,500. For general support. 2002.

2330-53 Friends of the Bay, Oyster Bay, NY, $25,000. For general support. 2002.

2330-54 Funders Network for Smart Growth and Livable Communities, Coral Gables, FL, $75,000. To help community foundations address environmental issues related to sprawl. 2002.

2330-55 Greater Newark Conservancy, Newark, NJ, $75,000. For Capital Campaign for Urban Environmental and Ecological Center. 2002.

2330-56 Greater Yellowstone Coalition, Bozeman, MT, $50,000. To use scientific data in advocacy for conservation of specific areas in Yellowstone region. 2002.

2330-57 Green Corps, Boston, MA, $50,000. To provide enhanced support for and outreach to minorities in environmental career training program. 2002.

2330-58 Green Guerillas, New York, NY, $25,000. To help neighborhood groups preserve and protect community gardens. 2002.

2330-59 Green Guide Institute, New York, NY, $31,300. For general support. 2002.

2330-60 Groundwork Yonkers, Yonkers, NY, $29,750. For general support. 2002.

2330-61 Groundwork Yonkers, Yonkers, NY, $12,300. For general support. 2002.

2330-62 Group for the South Fork, Bridgehampton, NY, $38,000. For general support. 2002.

2330-63 Group for the South Fork, Bridgehampton, NY, $25,000. For general support. 2002.

2330-64 High School for Environmental Studies, Friends of the, New York, NY, $40,000. To provide local, regional and national outdoors experiences to students at High School for Environmental Studies. 2002.

2330-65 Highlands Coalition, Titusville, NJ, $100,000. To continue regional campaign to secure federal funding and national recognition. 2002.

2330-66 Highlands Coalition, Titusville, NJ, $65,000. To mount regional campaign to secure federal funding and national recognition for Highlands. 2002.

2330-67 Homeless Animal Rescue Team of Maine, Cumberland Center, ME, $12,425. For general support. 2002.

2330-68 Hudson Highlands Land Trust, Garrison, NY, $10,000. For general support and for programs relating to Putnam Valley. 2002.

2330-69 Hudson River Sloop Clearwater, Poughkeepsie, NY, $15,000. For general support. 2002.

2330-70 Hurricane Island Outward Bound School, Rockland, ME, $250,000. For general support. 2002.

2330-71 Hurricane Island Outward Bound School, Rockland, ME, $50,000. For general support. 2002.

2330-72 INFORM, New York, NY, $30,000. For residential and municipal waste prevention and materials re-use initiative. 2002.

2330-73 Isles, Trenton, NJ, $500,000. For general support. 2002.

2330-74 Johns Hopkins University, School of Hygiene and Public Health, Baltimore, MD, $85,000. To study relationship between deforestation in Amazon and spread of malaria. 2002.

2330-75 Long Island Aquarium, Bay Shore, NY, $100,000. For general support. 2002.

2330-76 Long Island Pine Barrens Society, Manorville, NY, $15,000. For general support. 2002.

2330-77 Mohonk Preserve, New Paltz, NY, $15,000. For general support. 2002.

2330-78 Municipal Art Society of New York, New York, NY, $45,000. For Metropolitan Waterfront Alliance to create print and electronic versions of maps for trails along waterways of Lower Hudson, Kill van Kull and Upper New York Bay regions of Highlands. 2002.

2330-79 National Environmental Trust, DC, $100,000. To conduct public education campaign on global warming. 2002.

2330-80 National Forest Foundation, DC, $50,000. For general support of program in Missoula, MT. 2002.

2330-81 National Forest Foundation, DC, $20,000. For general support of programs in Missoula, MT. 2002.

2330-82 National Museum of Wildlife Art, Jackson, WY, $50,000. For general support. 2002.

2330-83 Natural Resources Council, Augusta, ME, $20,000. For general support. 2002.

2330-84 Natural Resources Defense Council, New York, NY, $100,000. To protect drinking water quality nationally and in New York City. 2002.

2330-85 Natural Resources Defense Council, New York, NY, $15,000. For general support. 2002.

2330-86 Natural Resources Defense Council, New York, NY, $10,000. For general support. 2002.

2330-87 Nature Conservancy, Cold Spring Harbor, NY, $40,000. For general support. 2002.

2330-88 Nature Conservancy, Cold Spring Harbor, NY, $15,000. For general support. 2002.

2330-89 Nature Conservancy, Cold Spring Harbor, NY, $10,000. For general support. 2002.

2330-90 Nature Conservancy, East Hampton, NY, $25,000. For general support. 2002.

2330-91 Nature Conservancy, Arlington, VA, $70,000. For general support. 2002.

2330-92 Nature Conservancy, Arlington, VA, $50,000. For general support. 2002.

2330-93 Nature Conservancy, Arlington, VA, $35,000. For general support. 2002.

2330-94 Nature Conservancy, Adirondack Chapter, Keene Valley, NY, $10,000. For general support. 2002.

2330-95 Nature Conservancy, Long Island Chapter, Cold Spring Harbor, NY, $100,000. For general support. 2002.

2330-96 Nature Conservancy, Long Island Chapter, Cold Spring Harbor, NY, $25,000. For general support. 2002.

2330-97 Nature Conservancy, Long Island Chapter, Cold Spring Harbor, NY, $10,000. For general support. 2002.

2330-98 Nature Conservancy, Lower Hudson Chapter, Mount Kisco, NY, $10,000. For Wilson Challenge Grant. 2002.

2330-99 Neighborhood Network Research Center, Massapequa, NY, $25,000. For general support. 2002.

2330-100 Neighborhood Network Research Center, Massapequa, NY, $22,000. For general support. 2002.

2330-101 Neighborhood Network Research Center, Massapequa, NY, $10,000. For general support. 2002.

2330-102 New York Botanical Garden, Bronx, NY, $500,000. For general support. 2002.

2330-103 New York Botanical Garden, Bronx, NY, $300,000. For general support. 2002.

2330-104 New York Botanical Garden, Bronx, NY, $47,300. For general support. 2002.

2330-105 New York Botanical Garden, Bronx, NY, $17,000. For general support. 2002.

2330-106 New York Botanical Garden, Bronx, NY, $13,500. For general support. 2002.

2330-107 New York Botanical Garden, Bronx, NY, $10,000. For general support. 2002.

2330-108 New York Botanical Garden, Bronx, NY, $10,000. For general support. 2002.

2330-109 New York Botanical Garden, Bronx, NY, $10,000. For general support. 2002.

2330-110 New York Botanical Garden, Bronx, NY, $10,000. For general support. 2002.

2330-111 New York Botanical Garden, Bronx, NY, $10,000. For general support. 2002.

2330-112 New York City Outward Bound Center, Long Island City, NY, $100,000. For general support. 2002.

2330-113 New York Law School, New York, NY, $10,000. To help make information on land use decisions available to public. 2002.

2330-114 New York Lawyers for the Public Interest, New York, NY, $40,000. To provide technical assistance to low-income community organizations on environmental issues and promote renewable energy use. 2002.

2330-115 New York Public Interest Research Group (NYPIRG) Fund, New York, NY, $50,000. To raise public awareness about pesticide hazards and promote pesticide policy reform. 2002.

2330-116 New York Restoration Project, New York, NY, $10,000. For general support. 2002.

2330-117 New York Restoration Project, New York, NY, $10,000. For general support. 2002.

2330-118 New York-New Jersey Trail Conference, Mahwah, NJ, $50,000. To train volunteer hikers to document ecological change on corridors in New York metropolitan region. 2002.

2330-119 Outdoor Explorations, Cambridge, MA, $10,000. For general support. 2002.

2330-120 Pine Creek Valley Watershed Association, Oley, PA, $50,000. For general support. 2002.

2330-121 Polly Hill Arboretum, West Tisbury, MA, $135,000. For general support. 2002.

2330-122 Polly Hill Arboretum, West Tisbury, MA, $100,000. For general support. 2002.

2330-123 Pratt Institute, Brooklyn, NY, $90,000. To help community organizations plan for redevelopment of brownfields and major public infrastructure improvements. 2002.

2330-124 Public Health Institute, New York, NY, $100,000. For collaboration between labor and environmental groups on climate protection and other issues. 2002.

2330-125 Queens Botanical Garden Society, Flushing, NY, $35,000. For public programs that explore cultural uses of plants in Southeast Asian communities of Queens. 2002.

2330-126 Rails to Trails Conservancy, DC, $15,000. For general support. 2002.

2330-127 Rainforest Alliance, New York, NY, $100,000. To develop business plan and market analysis for agricultural conservation program in Latin America. 2002.

2330-128 Redefining Progress, Oakland, CA, $75,000. To bring environmental justice issues into climate change debate. 2002.

2330-129 Restore Americas Estuaries, Arlington, VA, $75,000. To develop and promote protecting and restoring habitat and

biodiversity of estuaries as national priority. 2002.

2330-130 Restore Americas Estuaries, Arlington, VA, $10,000. For general support. 2002.

2330-131 Riverdale Nature Preservancy, Bronx, NY, $10,000. For community engagement activities to support designation of Henry Hudson Parkway as New York State Scenic Byway. 2002.

2330-132 Rocking the Boat, Bronx, NY, $250,000. For general support. 2002.

2330-133 Roxbury Land Trust, Roxbury, CT, $10,000. For general support. 2002.

2330-134 Scenic Hudson, Poughkeepsie, NY, $75,000. To provide technical support and ensure coordinated oversight of Hudson River PCB cleanup. 2002.

2330-135 Scenic Hudson, Poughkeepsie, NY, $40,000. For general support. 2002.

2330-136 Scenic Hudson, Poughkeepsie, NY, $30,000. For general support. 2002.

2330-137 Scenic Hudson, Poughkeepsie, NY, $30,000. For general support. 2002.

2330-138 Scenic Hudson, Poughkeepsie, NY, $25,000. For general support. 2002.

2330-139 Scenic Hudson, Poughkeepsie, NY, $10,000. For general support. 2002.

2330-140 Sea Research Foundation, Mystic, CT, $100,000. For general support. 2002.

2330-141 Seeing Eye, Morristown, NJ, $16,000. For general support. 2002.

2330-142 Silicon Valley Toxics Coalition, San Jose, CA, $75,000. For national campaign to ensure that technology companies take responsibility for their obsolete computer products. 2002.

2330-143 Siskiyou Regional Educational Project, Cave Junction, Oregon, $10,000. For general support. 2002.

2330-144 Society for the Prevention of Cruelty to Animals of Massachusetts, Boston, MA, $150,000. For general support. 2002.

2330-145 Standing for Truth About Radiation, East Hampton, NY, $12,500. For general support. 2002.

2330-146 Staten Island Botanical Garden, Staten Island, NY, $10,000. To expand education program for public school children in New York Chinese Scholar's Garden. 2002.

2330-147 Sustainable Long Island, Huntington, NY, $125,000. For general support. 2002.

2330-148 Sustainable Long Island, Huntington, NY, $58,000. For general support. 2002.

2330-149 Sustainable Long Island, Huntington, NY, $45,000. For general support. 2002.

2330-150 Sustainable Long Island, Huntington, NY, $10,000. For general support. 2002.

2330-151 Teatown Lake Reservation, Ossining, NY, $10,000. For general support. 2002.

2330-152 Theodore Roosevelt Sanctuary, Oyster Bay, NY, $200,000. For general support. 2002.

2330-153 Theodore Roosevelt Sanctuary, Oyster Bay, NY, $12,000. For general support. 2002.

2330-154 Toxics Action Center, Boston, MA, $50,000. For campaign to clean up dirtiest power plants in New England. 2002.

2330-155 Transportation Alternatives, New York, NY, $25,000. To increase community support for noise reduction efforts in Queens neighborhoods. 2002.

2330-156 Tri-State Transportation Campaign, New York, NY, $99,000. To reform transportation investments, policies, and projects in New York City. 2002.

2330-157 Trust for Public Land, New York, NY, $10,000. For general support. 2002.

2330-158 University of Illinois at Urbana-Champaign, Urbana, IL, $65,000. To train veterinarians from around world about healthy ecosystems. 2002.

2330-159 Vermont Land Trust, Montpelier, VT, $25,000. For general support. 2002.

2330-160 Wave Hill, Bronx, NY, $30,000. To expand arts and nature program for disabled young people. 2002.

2330-161 Wave Hill, Bronx, NY, $25,000. For general support. 2002.

2330-162 Westchester Land Trust, Bedford Hills, NY, $30,000. For general support. 2002.

2330-163 Westchester Land Trust, Bedford Hills, NY, $10,000. For general support. 2002.

2330-164 Westchester Land Trust, Bedford Hills, NY, $10,000. For general support. 2002.

2330-165 Wilderness Society, DC, $20,000. For general support. 2002.

2330-166 Wildlands Endowment Fund, San Francisco, CA, $500,000. For general support. 2002.

2330-167 Wildlands Endowment Fund, San Francisco, CA, $84,000. For general support. 2002.

2330-168 Wildlife Conservation Society, Bronx, NY, $150,000. For general support. 2002.

2330-169 Wildlife Conservation Society, Bronx, NY, $80,000. For general support. 2002.

2330-170 Wildlife Conservation Society, Bronx, NY, $57,250. For general support. 2002.

2330-171 Wildlife Conservation Society, Bronx, NY, $50,000. For general support. 2002.

2330-172 Wildlife Conservation Society, Bronx, NY, $10,620. For general support. 2002.

2330-173 Wildlife Conservation Society, Bronx, NY, $10,000. For general support. 2002.

2330-174 Wildlife Trust, Prospect Park, PA, $75,000. To conserve biodiversity and endangered habitats by demonstrating connection between human, wildlife, and ecological health in New York City region. 2002.

2330-175 Wildlife Trust, Prospect Park, PA, $50,000. For New York Bioscape initiatives. 2002.

2330-176 Woods Hole Research Center, Woods Hole, MA, $100,000. To document efforts of developing countries to decrease greenhouse gas emissions. 2002.

2330-177 World Wildlife Fund/Conservation Foundation, DC, $1,000,000. For general support. 2002.

2330-178 World Wildlife Fund/Conservation Foundation, DC, $45,000. For general support. 2002.

2330-179 Yale University, School of Forestry and Environmental Studies, New Haven, CT, $16,860. For graduate or advanced students of forestry and agriculture in United States and for advanced musical education. 2002.

2330-180 Yale University, School of Forestry and Environmental Studies, New Haven, CT, $16,860. For graduate or advanced students of forestry and agriculture in the United States and for advanced musical education. 2002.

2331
The New York Times Company Foundation, Inc. ▼
229 W. 43rd St.
New York, NY 10036-3959 (212) 556-1091
Contact: Jack Rosenthal, Pres.
FAX: (212) 556-4450; URL: http://www.nytco.com/foundation

Incorporated in 1955 in NY.
Donor(s): The New York Times Co.
Grantmaker type: Company-sponsored foundation
Financial data (yr. ended 12/31/02): Assets, $1,854,144 (M); gifts received, $7,000,000; expenditures, $6,861,585; qualifying distributions, $6,906,184; giving activities include $4,495,578 for grants and $1,313,655 for employee matching gifts.
Purpose and activities: Grants primarily for higher and secondary education, including minority education, cultural programs, and an employee matching gift program; support also for urban affairs, journalism, and environmental concerns.
Fields of interest: Journalism/publishing; Museums; Performing arts; Arts; Education, association; Secondary school/education; Higher education; Environment; Human services; Community development; Minorities.
Types of support: General/operating support; Continuing support; Annual campaigns; Program development; Seed money; Fellowships; Internship funds; Scholarship funds; Research; Employee matching gifts; Matching/challenge support.
Limitations: Giving primarily in the New York, NY, metropolitan area and in localities served by business units of the company. No support for sectarian religious institutions or for health, drug or alcohol therapy purposes; grants for urban affairs seldom made on the neighborhood level. No grants to individuals, or for capital and building funds; no loans.
Publications: Annual report (including application guidelines).
Application information: Application form required.
  Initial approach: Letter
  Copies of proposal: 1
  Deadline(s): Submit proposal by Dec. 1 or by June 1
  Board meeting date(s): Apr. and Sept.
  Final notification: Varies
Officers and Directors:* Jacqueline H. Dryfoos,* Chair.; Jack Rosenthal,* Pres.; Russell T. Lewis,* Exec. V.P.; Leonard P. Forman, Sr. V.P.; Michael Golden,* Sr. V.P.; Solomon B. Watson IV, Sr. V.P.; Rhonda L. Brauer, Secy.; R. Anthony Benton, Treas.; Ellen R. Marram; Donald M. Stewart; Arthur O. Sulzberger, Jr.
Number of staff: 2 full-time professional; 5 full-time support; 1 part-time support.
EIN: 136066955
Recent environmental and animal welfare grants:

2331-1 American Museum of Natural History, New York, NY, $100,000. For BioBulletin in Hall of Biodiversity. 2001.

2331-2 Argus Community, Bronx, NY, $20,000. For expansion of greenhouse work-training for recovering substance abusers. 2001.

2331-3 Audubon Society, National, New York, NY, $10,000. For environmental writing

workshop at new Audubon Center in Prospect Park. 2001.

2331-4 Brooklyn Botanic Garden, Brooklyn, NY, $15,000. For educational science programs for teachers and children. 2001.

2331-5 Central Park Conservancy, New York, NY, $10,000. For educational programs at Charles A. Dana Discovery Center on Harlem Meer. 2001.

2331-6 City Parks Foundation, New York, NY, $20,000. For nature program for first and second graders and pilot programs for neighborhood parks. 2001.

2331-7 Columbia University, Center for Children's Environmental Health, New York, NY, $15,000. For programs to educate low-income communities in effects of air pollution on children. 2001.

2331-8 Council on the Environment, New York, NY, $10,000. For general operating support. 2001.

2331-9 Horticultural Society of New York, New York, NY, $10,000. For gardens at community libraries. 2001.

2331-10 New York Botanical Garden, Bronx, NY, $30,000. For curriculums for public school children. 2001.

2331-11 New York City Outward Bound Center, Long Island City, NY, $35,000. For continuing mentoring program for young students. 2001.

2331-12 New Yorkers for Parks, New York, NY, $10,000. For urban conservation corps summer program, and sustained public education campaign. 2001.

2331-13 Rainforest Alliance, New York, NY, $10,000. For publication of environmental newsletters. 2001.

2331-14 Wildlife Conservation Society, Bronx, NY, $50,000. For Congo habitat for apes at the Bronx Zoo. 2001.

2332
The New-Land Foundation, Inc.
1114 Ave. of the Americas
New York, NY 10036-7798 (212) 479-6162

Incorporated in 1941 in NY.
Donor(s): Muriel M. Buttinger.‡
Grantmaker type: Independent foundation
Financial data (yr. ended 12/31/01): Assets, $33,734,911 (M); expenditures, $2,037,707; qualifying distributions, $1,774,953; giving activities include $1,658,603 for 119 grants (high: $76,500; low: $792; average: $5,000–$25,000).
Purpose and activities: Grants for child development, civil rights and justice, family planning, environmental preservation, peace, and arms control and disarmament.
Fields of interest: Child development, education; Environment; International peace/security; Arms control; Civil rights; Population studies.
Types of support: General/operating support; Continuing support; Annual campaigns; Program development; Seed money; Research; Matching/challenge support.
Limitations: No support for educational institutions, medicine, religion and general social programs. No grants to individuals or for capital campaigns, publications, films,

endowment campaigns, building campaigns, or conferences; no loans.
Publications: Application guidelines.
Application information: Application form required.
 Initial approach: Letter requesting guidelines
 Copies of proposal: 1
 Deadline(s): Feb. 1 and Aug. 1
 Board meeting date(s): Spring and fall
 Final notification: For positive responses only
Officers and Directors:* Hal Harvey,* Pres.; Constance Harvey,* V.P.; Renee G. Schwartz,* Secy.-Treas.; Ann Harvey; Joan Harvey; George Perkovich, Ph.D.; Albert Solnit.
Number of staff: None.
EIN: 136086562

2333
The Niagara Mohawk Foundation, Inc.
300 Erie Blvd. W.
Syracuse, NY 13202 (315) 474-1511
Contact: Carolyn A. May, Dir.
URL: http://www.niagaramohawk.com/nimotod/community/community.html

Established in 1992 in NY.
Donor(s): Niagara Mohawk Power Corp.
Grantmaker type: Company-sponsored foundation
Financial data (yr. ended 12/31/01): Assets, $2,915,556 (M); gifts received, $1,843,037; expenditures, $1,960,652; qualifying distributions, $1,941,873; giving activities include $1,938,438 for 358 grants (high: $131,903; low: $25; average: $1,000–$25,000).
Purpose and activities: Giving for welcoming neighborhoods, creative learning, urban renaissance, and environmental stewardship programs.
Fields of interest: Arts; Education; Environment; Health care; Health care; Human services; Economic development; Federated giving programs.
Types of support: General/operating support; Continuing support; Annual campaigns; Capital campaigns; Building/renovation; Equipment; Emergency funds; Program development; Employee matching gifts.
Limitations: Giving limited to areas of company operations in upstate NY.
Publications: Annual report, Informational brochure (including application guidelines).
Application information: Application form required.
 Initial approach: Apply online only
 Copies of proposal: 1
 Deadline(s): Legacy grants deadline Feb. 15; Volunteer Connection matching gift program deadline Nov. 30
 Board meeting date(s): Quarterly
Officers and Directors:* Christina M. Moran,* Secy.; Ralph Modugno, Treas.; Carolyn A. May.
Trustees: William E. Davis, Chair.; David J. Arrington; Thomas H. Baron; Albert J. Budney, Jr.; Edward J. Dienst; William F. Edwards; J. Philip Frazier; Darlene D. Kerr; Gary J. Lavine; John H. Mueller.
Number of staff: 1 part-time professional.
EIN: 223132237

2334
Niagara Mohawk Power Corporation Contributions Program
300 Erie Blvd. W.
Syracuse, NY 13202 (315) 428-5691
Contact: Christina Moran
URL: http://www.niagaramohawk.com/nimotod/community/community.html

Grantmaker type: Corporate giving program
Purpose and activities: As a complement to its foundation, Niagara Mohawk also makes charitable contributions to nonprofit organizations directly. Support is given primarily in areas of company operations.
Fields of interest: Historic preservation/historical societies; Arts; Education; Environment; Parks/playgrounds; Youth development; Human services; Community development.
Types of support: General/operating support; Continuing support; Annual campaigns; Capital campaigns; Building/renovation; Equipment; Program development; Publication; Seed money; Research; Technical assistance; Cause-related marketing; Employee volunteer services; Loaned talent; Use of facilities; Sponsorships; Donated equipment; In-kind gifts; Matching/challenge support.
Limitations: Giving primarily in areas of company operations in NY. No support for religious, fraternal, athletic, social, or veterans' organizations, discriminatory organizations, United Way-supported organizations, or political organizations. No grants to individuals, or for debt reduction, endowments, advertising, travel, or fundraising.
Application information: Application form required.
 Initial approach: Complete online application form

2335
Nicholas Family Charitable Trust
c/o Nicholas J. Nicholas, Jr.
88 Central Park W.
New York, NY 10023-6028

Established in 1992 in NY.
Donor(s): Nicholas J. Nicholas, Jr., Llewellyn J. Nicholas.
Grantmaker type: Independent foundation
Financial data (yr. ended 12/31/01): Assets, $2,078,754 (M); expenditures, $1,447,601; qualifying distributions, $1,388,354; giving activities include $1,388,523 for 58 grants (high: $500,000; low: $125).
Purpose and activities: Giving for higher and other education, cultural programs, and for health and human services.
Fields of interest: Arts; Higher education; Education; Natural resources; Environment; Hospitals (general); Mental health, treatment; Human services.
Types of support: General/operating support; Capital campaigns.
Limitations: Applications not accepted. Giving primarily in NY. No grants to individuals.
Application information: Contributes only to pre-selected organizations.
Trustees: Llewellyn J. Nicholas; Nicholas J. Nicholas, Jr.
EIN: 136990536

2336
Nichols Foundation, Inc.
600 5th Ave.
New York, NY 10020 (212) 632-3000
Contact: Peter Coxhead, Pres.
E-mail: gscotto@ftcl.com

Incorporated in 1923 in NY.
Donor(s): Members of the Nichols family.
Grantmaker type: Independent foundation
Financial data (yr. ended 12/31/01): Assets, $17,859,392 (M); gifts received, $270,000; expenditures, $1,640,796; qualifying distributions, $1,501,121; giving activities include $1,389,630 for 51 grants (high: $25,000; low: $1,000).
Purpose and activities: Giving primarily for education, health care, and human services.
Fields of interest: Secondary school/education; Higher education; Reading; Education; Natural resources; Environment; Animals/wildlife, preservation/protection; Hospitals (general); Family planning; Cancer; Biomedicine; Cancer research; Human services; Children/youth, services; Family services; Disabled; Economically disadvantaged.
Types of support: Continuing support; Annual campaigns; Capital campaigns; Building/renovation; Equipment; Land acquisition; Program development; Scholarship funds; Research; Matching/challenge support.
Limitations: Applications not accepted. Giving primarily in Santa Barbara, CA, Hinsdale County, CO, FL, and the metropolitan New York, NY area. No support for religious institutions. No grants to individuals, or for individual scholarships or general support; no loans.
Application information: Contributes only to pre-selected organizations. Unsolicited requests for funds not considered.
 Board meeting date(s): Jan. and June
Officers and Directors:* Peter Coxhead,* Pres.; David H. Nichols,* V.P.; Gina Scotto, Secy.; C. Walter Nichols III, Treas.; Marguerite D.R. Buttrick; Ralph N. Coxhead; Kathleen C. Moseley.
Number of staff: None.
EIN: 136400615

2337
Edward John Noble Foundation, Inc. ▼
32 E. 57th St.
New York, NY 10022-2513 (212) 759-4212
Contact: June Noble Larkin, Chair.

Trust established in 1940 in CT; incorporated in 1982.
Donor(s): Edward John Noble.‡
Grantmaker type: Independent foundation
Financial data (yr. ended 12/31/02): Assets, $122,453,270 (M); expenditures, $8,498,124; qualifying distributions, $7,475,222; giving activities include $6,591,253 for 40 grants (high: $2,000,000; low: $7,000; average: $10,000–$150,000).
Purpose and activities: Grants to major cultural organizations in New York City, especially for educational programs and management training internships. Selected projects concerned with conservation and ecology primarily related to activities on an island off the coast of GA. Supports programs to improve educational

opportunities for gifted and talented disadvantaged children in NY. Programs in health education efforts related to family planning and population education.
Fields of interest: Music; Arts; Education; Natural resources; Environment; Family planning.
Types of support: General/operating support; Continuing support; Endowments; Program development; Internship funds; Matching/challenge support.
Limitations: Giving primarily in the metropolitan New York, NY, area for arts organizations; St. Catherine's Island, GA, and the eastern states for conservation projects and family planning; and the Northeast for private colleges and universities. No grants to individuals, or for publications, building funds, equipment, television, films, or performances; no loans.
Publications: Biennial report (including application guidelines).
Application information: Application form not required.
> *Initial approach:* Brief letter
> *Copies of proposal:* 1
> *Deadline(s):* None
> *Board meeting date(s):* Dec.
> *Final notification:* 3 months
Officers and Directors:* June Noble Larkin,* Chair.; Frank Y. Larkin,* Vice-Chair.; E.J. Noble Smith,* Pres.; Deborah A. Menton-Nightlinger, Secy. and Exec. Dir; E. Mary Heffernan, Treas.; William G. Conway; Ellen V. Futter; Harold B. Johnson; Daniel L. Mosley; Howard Phipps, Jr.; Joseph W. Polisi; Bradford D. Smith; David Smith; Jeremy T. Smith; Malcolm L. Stein; Carroll L. Wainwright, Jr.
Number of staff: 3 full-time professional; 1 full-time support; 1 part-time support.
EIN: 061055586

2338
Norcross Wildlife Foundation, Inc.
Caller Box No. 611
250 W. 88th St., Ste. 806
New York, NY 10024 (212) 362-4831
Contact: Richard S. Reagan, Pres., or John McMurray, Prog. Off.
Additional tel.: (718) 791-2094; Application address: Grants Admin., P.O. Box 269, Wales, MA 01081; URL: http://www.norcrossws.org

Established in 1964 in NY.
Donor(s): Arthur D. Norcross,‡ June Norcross Webster.‡
Grantmaker type: Independent foundation
Financial data (yr. ended 12/31/01): Assets, $67,553,653 (M); gifts received, $102,000; expenditures, $4,419,058; qualifying distributions, $5,892,376; giving activities include $1,869,461 for 272 grants (high: $55,000; low: $750; average: $5,000–$10,000) and $699,000 for 4 loans/program-related investments.
Purpose and activities: Support primarily for conservation, including environmental and wildlife organizations, and historical preservation; extremely limited support also for health organizations, assistance for the handicapped, drug abuse programs, and education.

Fields of interest: Natural resources; Environment; Animals/wildlife, preservation/protection.
Types of support: Building/renovation; Equipment; Land acquisition; Publication.
Limitations: Giving primarily in North America. No grants to individuals, or for operating support, overhead expenses, research endowments, conferences, matching gifts, or multi-year grants.
Publications: Application guidelines, Annual report (including application guidelines), Multi-year report.
Application information: FAX, express mail applications or proposals without an attached application form not accepted; no 990-PF forms or annual reports required; only 1 copy of IRS letter is required. Application form required.
> *Initial approach:* 1-paragraph letter on organization letterhead requesting guidelines and application form; guidelines and application form also available on website
> *Copies of proposal:* 1
> *Deadline(s):* None
> *Board meeting date(s):* Quarterly
Officers and Directors:* Richard S. Reagan,* Pres.; Joseph A. Catalano,* V.P. and Secy.; Karen Outlaw, Treas.; Warren Balgooyen; Albia Dugger; Edward Gallagher; Arthur D. Norcross, Jr.; Michael D. Patrick; Denise Schlener; Christof von Strasser; Ted Williams.
Number of staff: 3 full-time professional; 1 full-time support.
EIN: 132041622

2339
Norman Foundation, Inc.
147 E. 48th St.
New York, NY 10017 (212) 230-9830
Contact: June Makela, Prog. Dir.
FAX: (212) 230-9849; E-mail: info@normanfdn.org; URL: http://www.normanfdn.org/

Incorporated in 1935 in NY.
Donor(s): Aaron E. Norman,‡ and directors of the foundation.
Grantmaker type: Independent foundation
Financial data (yr. ended 12/31/01): Assets, $23,016,587 (M); expenditures, $1,517,229; qualifying distributions, $1,307,662; giving activities include $1,115,311 for 99 grants (high: $25,000; low: $1,000; average: $1,000–$25,000).
Purpose and activities: The foundation funds in three broad areas: economic justice, environmental justice and civil rights. The current priorities for the civil rights program are education equity and criminal justice reform. The foundation is interested in community-based organizing projects that could have a potentially national impact as well as provide potential models for social change. Collaborative projects welcome.
Fields of interest: Environment, legal rights; Employment; Civil rights; Economic development; Community development; Public affairs; Minorities; Economically disadvantaged.
Types of support: General/operating support; Continuing support; Program development; Seed money; Matching/challenge support.

Limitations: Giving limited to the U.S. No support for universities or direct social service agencies. No grants to individuals, or for building or endowment funds, publications, conferences, capital funding projects, fundraising, research, scholarships, films, and arts projects or fellowships.
Application information: Accepts NYRAG Common Application Form. Updated guidelines available on Web site. Application form not required.
> *Initial approach:* A short 2- to 3- page letter of inquiry
> *Copies of proposal:* 1
> *Deadline(s):* Mar. 1, Aug. 1, and Dec. 1
> *Board meeting date(s):* 3 times per year
> *Final notification:* 1 month to 1 year
Officers and Directors:* Honor Lassalle,* Pres.; Alice Franklin,* V.P.; Amanda Weil,* V.P.; Margaret Norman,* Secy.; Melissa Bunnen,* Treas.; Robert L. Bunnen, Jr.; Andrew D. Franklin; Deborah W. Harrington; Philip E. Lassalle; Abigail Norman; Rebecca Norman; Sarah Norman; Belinda Bunnen Reusch; Diana Lassalle Turner; Sandison E. Weil; William S. Weil.
Number of staff: 1 part-time professional; 1 part-time support.
EIN: 131862694

2340
North Star Fund, Inc.
305 7th Ave., 5th Fl.
New York, NY 10001-6008 (212) 620-9110
Contact: Hugh Hogan, Exec. Dir.
FAX: (212) 620-8178; E-mail: info@northstarfund.org; URL: http://www.northstarfund.org

Established in 1979 in NY.
Grantmaker type: Public charity
Financial data (yr. ended 06/30/02): Revenue, $540,584; assets, $2,005,763 (L); gifts received, $444,128; expenditures, $793,749; program services expenses, $622,283; giving activities include $367,325 for 97 grants (high: $14,000; low: $300).
Purpose and activities: The fund is a partnership of donors and activists which administers a donor-advised fund and makes grants to community-based groups in New York, NY, that are organizing around issues of social, economic, and political justice. The fund particularly encourages groups composed of people of color and multiracial organizations to submit proposals. The fund also encourages applications from new organizations, especially those that are working on emerging issues.
Fields of interest: Media/communications; Film/video; Performing arts; Arts; Environment; Health care; Health organizations; Housing/shelter, development; Youth, services; International peace/security; Civil rights, minorities; Civil rights, disabled; Civil rights, women; Civil rights; Community development; Disabled; Women; Gays/lesbians; Economically disadvantaged.
Types of support: General/operating support; Emergency funds; Seed money; Technical assistance; Program-related investments/loans.
Limitations: Giving limited to New York, NY. No support for projects that have large budgets, or groups with sufficient access to traditional

funding sources. No grants to individuals, or for conferences outside of New York, NY.
Publications: Application guidelines, Annual report (including application guidelines), Financial statement, Grants list, Informational brochure, Newsletter.
Application information: Accepts NYRAG Common Application Form. Application form required.
Initial approach: Telephone
Copies of proposal: 4
Deadline(s): Oct. 7
Board meeting date(s): Ongoing
Final notification: Status notification 1 month after deadline; final notification 4 months after deadline
Officers and Directors:* Iris Morales,* Chair.; Lillian Jimenez,* Vice-Chair.; Linda Cronin-Gross,* Secy.; Madeline deLone, Esq.,* Treas.; Hugh Hogan, Exec. Dir.; John Martin Green; Kathy Goldman; Mark Hannay; Arva Rice; Alvin Starks; Amy Wagner.
Number of staff: 4 full-time professional; 1 part-time support.
EIN: 132950801

2341
Northern Chautauqua Community Foundation, Inc.
212 Lake Shore Dr. W.
Dunkirk, NY 14048 (716) 366-4892
Contact: Diane Hannum, Exec. Dir.
FAX: (716) 366-4276; E-mail: nccf@nccfoundation.org; URL: http://www.nccfoundation.org

Incorporated in 1986 in NY.
Grantmaker type: Community foundation
Financial data (yr. ended 12/31/02): Assets, $8,192,633 (M); gifts received, $1,079,232; expenditures, $530,919; giving activities include $944,598 for grants (average: $25–$8,000).
Purpose and activities: Primary areas of interest include education, libraries, family services, community funds, cultural programs, and other general charitable activities. The foundation administers donor-advised funds.
Fields of interest: Arts; Higher education; Adult education—literacy, basic skills & GED; Libraries/library science; Reading; Education; Environment; Hospitals (general); Substance abuse, services; Recreation; Family services; Hospices; Aging, centers/services; Community development; Voluntarism promotion; Federated giving programs; Aging.
Types of support: Building/renovation; Equipment; Endowments; Program development; Seed money; Scholarship funds; Scholarships—to individuals; Matching/challenge support.
Limitations: Giving limited to northern Chautauqua County, NY. No support for religious organizations. No grants to individuals (except for designated scholarship funds), or for capital campaigns, general operating budgets, publication of books, conferences, or annual fundraising campaigns.
Publications: Application guidelines, Annual report (including application guidelines), Newsletter.

Application information: Applications are considered in the spring and fall. Application form required.
Initial approach: Letter or telephone
Copies of proposal: 1
Deadline(s): Mar. 15 and Sept. 15
Board meeting date(s): Quarterly
Final notification: 10 days following board meeting
Officers and Directors:* R. Bard Schaack,* Pres.; James H. Mintun, Jr.,* V.P.; Terry Clifton, Secy.; Susan Marsh,* Treas.; Rosemary Banach; Michael Brunecz; Andrew W. Dorn; Donald Eno; Wendy Heinz; George Pete Holt; Richard Ketcham; David Larson; Kurt Maytum; Robert Miller, Jr.; Jeffrey G. Passafaro; John Potter; Gerard Rocque; J. Carter Rowland, Ph.D.
Number of staff: 2 full-time professional; 1 part-time professional; 1 full-time support.
EIN: 161271663

2342
Northern New York Community Foundation, Inc.
(formerly Watertown Foundation, Inc.)
120 Washington St.
Watertown, NY 13601 (315) 782-7110
Contact: Alex C. Velto, Exec. Dir.
FAX: (315) 782-0047; E-mail: info@nnycf.org; URL: http://www.nnycf.org

Incorporated in 1929 in NY.
Grantmaker type: Community foundation
Financial data (yr. ended 12/31/02): Assets, $20,595,656 (M); gifts received, $419,665; expenditures, $1,305,471; giving activities include $1,049,737 for grants.
Purpose and activities: To promote charitable, educational, cultural, recreational, and health programs through grants to community organizations and agencies, and through a student scholarship program in Jefferson and Lewis counties, NY. The foundation administer a donor-advised fund.
Fields of interest: Historic preservation/historical societies; Arts; Education, fund raising; Child development, education; Adult/continuing education; Libraries/library science; Education; Environment; Hospitals (general); Nursing care; Health care; Substance abuse, services; Health organizations, association; AIDS; Food services; Housing/shelter, development; Recreation; Human services; Children/youth, services; Child development, services; Family services; Hospices; Aging, centers/services; Homeless, human services; Community development; Federated giving programs; Government/public administration; Disabled; Aging; Economically disadvantaged; Homeless.
Types of support: Annual campaigns; Capital campaigns; Building/renovation; Equipment; Land acquisition; Program development; Conferences/seminars; Publication; Seed money; Scholarship funds; Technical assistance; Scholarships—to individuals; Matching/challenge support.
Limitations: Giving limited to organizations and individuals in Jefferson and Lewis counties, NY. No grants for endowment funds or deficit financing.
Publications: Annual report, Newsletter.

Application information: Application form not required.
Initial approach: Letter
Copies of proposal: 1
Deadline(s): Feb. 1, May 1, Aug. 1, and Nov. 1
Board meeting date(s): Mar., June, Sept., and Dec.
Final notification: 1 to 2 months
Officers and Directors:* Janet L. George,* Pres.; Philip J. Sprague, V.P.; James R. Kanik,* Secy.-Treas.; Alex C. Velto, Exec. Dir.; Donald C. Alexander; Douglas Brodie; Lee Clary; Mary Mascott; Tony Morgia; Anderson Wise; and 4 additional directors.
Number of staff: 1 full-time professional; 1 full-time support; 1 part-time support.
EIN: 156020989

2343
The Greater Norwich Foundation
c/o NBT Bank, N.A.
52 S. Broad St.
Norwich, NY 13815 (607) 337-6193

Established in 1965 in NY.
Grantmaker type: Independent foundation
Financial data (yr. ended 03/31/02): Assets, $4,623,859 (M); gifts received, $33,662; expenditures, $271,025; qualifying distributions, $266,217; giving activities include $256,850 for 31 grants (high: $100,000; low: $200).
Fields of interest: Historic preservation/historical societies; Arts; Education; Animal welfare; YM/YWCAs & YM/YWHAs; Children/youth, services.
Types of support: Capital campaigns; Building/renovation; Equipment; Program development; Scholarship funds; Scholarships—to individuals.
Limitations: Giving primarily in the Norwich, NY, area.
Publications: Informational brochure.
Application information: Application form required.
Initial approach: Letter or pre-grant application
Copies of proposal: 1
Deadline(s): Apr. 15 and Oct. 15
Board meeting date(s): May and Nov.
Trustees: James I. Dunne; Jane E. Eaton; Esther C. Flanagan; Everett A. Gilmour; James A. Hoy; Edward J. Lee; Frederic B. Miers; H. William Smith, Jr.; Jacob K. Weinman; NBT Bank, N.A.
EIN: 166064927

2344
A. B. & J. Noyes Foundation, Inc.
50 Broad St.
New York, NY 10004-2307

Established in 1957 in NY.
Grantmaker type: Independent foundation
Financial data (yr. ended 12/31/02): Assets, $966,473 (M); expenditures, $100,929; qualifying distributions, $90,312; giving activities include $90,000 for 18 grants (high: $17,000; low: $500).
Fields of interest: Museums; Education; Natural resources; Breast cancer; Youth development, centers/clubs; Parks/playgrounds; Human services.
Limitations: Applications not accepted. Giving on a national basis. No grants to individuals.

Application information: Contributes only to pre-selected organizations.
Officers: Jansen Noyes III, Pres. and Treas.; Marie L. Cusic, Secy.
Directors: Alfred F. King III; Shirley N. Lathrop; Margaret T. Noyes.
EIN: 136161124

2345
Jessie Smith Noyes Foundation, Inc. ▼
6 E. 39th St., 12th Fl.
New York, NY 10016-0112 (212) 684-6577
Contact: Victor De Luca, Pres.
FAX: (212) 689-6549; E-mail: noyes@noyes.org;
URL: http://www.noyes.org

Incorporated in 1947 in NY.
Donor(s): Charles F. Noyes.‡
Grantmaker type: Independent foundation
Financial data (yr. ended 12/31/01): Assets, $70,230,823 (M); expenditures, $5,918,770; qualifying distributions, $5,560,156; giving activities include $4,389,689 for 225 grants (high: $100,000; low: $250; average: $10,000–$35,000).
Purpose and activities: The foundation views the Earth as one community, an indivisible web of life with human society an integral part. The foundation seeks to protect and restore the planet's capacity for renewal by supporting grassroots organizations and movements whose work promotes healthy, just and sustainable social and natural systems. The foundation's grantmaking addresses two general themes: 1) healthy, just and sustainable environments and communities; and 2) reproductive rights.
Fields of interest: Environment, toxics; Environment; Agriculture; Reproductive rights; Community development, citizen coalitions.
Types of support: General/operating support; Continuing support; Program development; Seed money.
Limitations: Giving limited to the U.S. No grants to individuals, or for scholarships, fellowships, endowment funds, deficit financing, capital construction funds, or general fundraising drives; generally no support for conferences, research, or media; no loans (except for program-related investments).
Application information: Applications not accepted for discretionary or founder-designated funds. Accepts NNG Common Application Form. Full proposal will be requested after review of letter of intent, background of organization, summary of activities for funding and expected outcome. Application form required.
   Initial approach: 1- or 2-page letter of inquiry, including budget estimate
   Copies of proposal: 1
   Deadline(s): None
   Board meeting date(s): Spring, summer and fall
   Final notification: Within 6 weeks of receipt of letters; within 2 weeks of board meetings for final proposals
Officers and Directors:* Steven Carbo,* Chair.; Heather Findlay,* Vice-Chair.; Victor De Luca, Pres.; Dorceta Taylor,* Secy.; Nicholas Jacangelo,* Treas.; Dorothy Anderson; Miriam Ballert; Peter Bedell, Jr.; Stephen Falci; Michael Hamm; Laurel Kearns; Fred Kirschenmann; Leslie Lowe; Dorothy E. Muma; Edith N. Muma; Linda Singer; Ann Wiener.

Number of staff: 3 full-time professional; 1 part-time professional; 1 full-time support; 2 part-time support.
EIN: 135600408
Recent environmental and animal welfare grants:
2345-1 Arkansas Public Policy Panel, Little Rock, AR, $50,000. For technical assistance and organizing for community-based groups working on environmental issues, with special focus on people of color and underrepresented areas of southern and eastern Arkansas. 2002.
2345-2 Asian Pacific Environmental Network (APEN), Oakland, CA, $25,000. For network of Asian-American and Pacific Islander communities working to achieve environmental justice and involve grassroots organizations in movement building. 2002.
2345-3 Center for Health, Environment and Justice, Falls Church, VA, $25,000. To train and assist people in protecting their communities from environmental threats, and to build strong local organizations by providing scientific and technical information, organizing assistance and networking with other groups and resources. 2002.
2345-4 Chinese Progressive Association, New York, NY, $20,000. To train core group of Chinatown residents to research, organize, and advocate around Chinatown's environmental health problems. 2002.
2345-5 Citizens Coal Council, DC, $25,000. To protect people, water and land from harm caused by mining and use of coal at every stage of energy cycle, by organizing affected communities into grassroots-based, democratically controlled movement. 2002.
2345-6 Citizens Environmental Coalition, Albany, NY, $20,000. To launch sustainable agriculture and water quality project that will bring together sustainable agriculture activists with environmentalists in statewide network to address problems stemming from spread of CAFOs and use of toxins in fertilizer. 2002.
2345-7 Coal River Mountain Watch, Whitesville, WV, $15,000. To organize communities to stop environmental destruction caused by mountaintop removal mining. 2002.
2345-8 Colorado Peoples Environmental and Economic Network, Denver, CO, $15,000. To organize and provide technical assistance to people of color and low-income communities in Colorado affected by environmental pollution. 2002.
2345-9 Communities by Choice, Berea, KY, $15,000. For national network of communities, organizations, and individuals engaged in sustainable community development efforts. 2002.
2345-10 Community Environmental Legal Defense Fund, Chambersburg, PA, $15,000. For efforts by community groups throughout Pennsylvania and other parts of country to limit spread of factory farming by asserting democratic control over corporations. 2002.
2345-11 Community Farm Alliance, Frankfort, KY, $20,000. To promote sustainable agriculture in Kentucky by organizing on state and national issues that address environmental and economic sustainability

of state's family farms and rural communities. 2002.
2345-12 Consumer Policy Institute, Yonkers, NY, $15,000. To provide technical assistance to New York City community groups working on solid waste issues. 2002.
2345-13 Croton Watershed Clean Water Coalition, Bedford, NY, $10,000. To protect purity of drinking water derived from Croton Watershed by bringing together residents of New York City and watershed towns in order to press for pollution prevention at source. 2002.
2345-14 DataCenter, Oakland, CA, $25,000. For environmental justice component of ImpactResearch project, providing research and information to community-based organizations working for social, environmental and economic justice. 2002.
2345-15 Dine Citizens Against Ruining our Environment, Dilkon Chapter, Winslow, AZ, $25,000. To address environmental and health consequences of uranium mining and processing on Navajo lands, and to organize Navajo residents to address these and other environmental insults. 2002.
2345-16 Environmental and Economic Justice Project, Los Angeles, CA, $20,000. To increase capacity and effectiveness of environmental and economic justice movement through training and support for organizational development and strategic planning. 2002.
2345-17 Environmental Community Action (ECO-Action), Atlanta, GA, $25,000. For general support for work on environmental and health threats from toxic chemicals. 2002.
2345-18 Environmental Health Coalition, San Diego, CA, $25,000. For environmental justice work in San Diego/Tijuana region through organizing, education and technical assistance to community groups. 2002.
2345-19 Families Against Incinerator Risk (FAIR), Salt Lake City, UT, $25,000. For work with Healthy Environment Alliance of Utah to address industrial pollution, and toxic and nuclear waste disposal. 2002.
2345-20 Healthy Schools Network, Albany, NY, $20,000. To recruit and train parent organizers to implement parent-to-parent education, technical assistance, and advocacy initiative to ensure environmental health and safety of schools in New York Metropolitan Region, with emphasis on Long Island. 2002.
2345-21 Jobs with Justice Education Fund, DC, $25,000. To involve community environmental justice groups in movement to control corporate power and corporate-led globalization. 2002.
2345-22 Just Transition Alliance, DC, $20,000. For partnership among labor, community and environmental justice networks to develop policies to protect workers and communities as toxic chemicals are phased out. 2002.
2345-23 Louisiana Labor Neighbor Project, Gonzales, LA, $20,000. To work with communities, churches and labor groups in Mississippi River parishes of Louisiana to organize for clean environment, better public services and accountability in local government. 2002.

2345-24 Make the Road By Walking, Brooklyn, NY, $20,000. For neighborhood-based initiative that organizes residents of Bushwick to collectively address environmental problems, make public officials accountable for local enforcement of environmental regulations and improve citywide policies. 2002.

2345-25 Military Toxics Project, Lewiston, ME, $25,000. For general support for network of community groups and activists working to document environmental, economic and health consequences of military pollution, and to hold Pentagon accountable for cleanup and Department of Defense accountable. 2002.

2345-26 Mision Industrial de Puerto Rico, San Juan, PR, $20,000. For organizing work on environmental justice issues in Puerto Rico. 2002.

2345-27 Missouri Rural Crisis Center, Columbia, MO, $20,000. To promote sustainable agriculture in Missouri by building linkages between consumers and pork producers who use sustainable practices and by advocating for policies that support family farms and environmental stewardship. 2002.

2345-28 Mothers on the Move, Bronx, NY, $20,000. To organize residents in Hunts Point, Longwood, Morrisania and Port Morris to fight environmental racism, increase green open space, improve community health and work in coalition with other environmental justice groups. 2002.

2345-29 National Campaign for Sustainable Agriculture, Pine Bush, NY, $25,000. For grassroots network of organizations from across the country, which advocates for national public policies that promote ecologically viable, environmentally sound, and socially just food and agriculture system in U.S. 2002.

2345-30 National Family Farm Coalition, DC, $40,000. To coalesce grassroots organizations representing family farmers and rural communities from across the country to advocate for policies and practices that support family farm-based and environmentally sound food and agriculture system. 2002.

2345-31 Native Action, Lame Deer, MT, $25,000. To address environmental justice issues on Northern Cheyenne Indian Reservation in Montana. 2002.

2345-32 New York City Environmental Justice Alliance, New York, NY, $20,000. To provide technical assistance, organizing support, networking opportunities, coalition building and training to member groups and constituents working to improve environmental health of their communities. 2002.

2345-33 New York City Organizing Support Center, New York, NY, $10,000. To provide training and technical assistance to grassroots organizations working in low-income communities throughout city in order to strengthen their constituency building, organizing and collaborative work. 2002.

2345-34 North Carolina Waste Awareness and Reduction Network (NC WARN), Durham, NC, $25,000. To provide organizing, advocacy and technical assistance to groups working on hazardous and nuclear waste issues in North Carolina. 2002.

2345-35 Northeast Sustainable Agriculture Working Group, Belchertown, MA, $25,000. To promote more sustainable and secure food system in Northeast. 2002.

2345-36 Northern Plains Resource Council, Billings, MT, $50,000. For Montana Toxics Action Project. 2002.

2345-37 Northwest Environmental Justice Alliance, Seattle, WA, $25,000. For Northwest Network for Environmental Justice, emerging network for people of color and indigenous peoples in Northwest United States. 2002.

2345-38 Outstanding Renewal Enterprises, Lower East Side Ecology Center, New York, NY, $15,000. To foster environmentally sound management of New York City's solid waste by demonstrating potential of in-vessel composting as way to reduce export of waste and attendant truck pollution, and building public support for recycling and composting. 2002.

2345-39 Pennsylvania Association for Sustainable Agriculture, Millheim, PA, $15,000. To promote sustainable agriculture in Pennsylvania through farmer-based education, community-based market strategies and policy advocacy. 2002.

2345-40 Powder River Basin Resource Council, Sheridan, WY, $25,000. To empower Wyoming citizens through community organizing and leadership development to protect land and resources of their state. 2002.

2345-41 Power U Center for Social Change, Miami, FL, $20,000. For work on environmental justice issues in Miami, unincorporated Dade County and surrounding areas. 2002.

2345-42 Project Underground, Berkeley, CA, $25,000. For Indigenous Mining Campaign Project. 2002.

2345-43 RAFI-USA, Pittsboro, NC, $50,000. To promote sustainable agriculture in North and South Carolina by advocating for agricultural policies and practices that are environmentally sound and economically viable, and by engaging in projects that reduce pesticide use by peanut farmers. 2002.

2345-44 Research and Education Project of Long Island, Massapequa, NY, $20,000. To promote ecologically sound and economically sustainable future on Long Island through community organizing and advocacy on public policies. 2002.

2345-45 Rural Vermont, Montpelier, VT, $20,000. To empower Vermont family farmers to advocate for policies that increase support for sustainable agriculture, remove regulatory barriers that impede small-scale processing and support sustainable economic development. 2002.

2345-46 Southern Echo, Jackson, MS, $25,000. To create environmental coalitions that promote healthy, sustainable living for poor people and people of color in Mississippi and surrounding southern region. 2002.

2345-47 Southern Organizing Committee (SOC) for Economic and Social Justice, Atlanta, GA, $25,000. To organize communities in Southeast around issues of health and environmental justice. 2002.

2345-48 Southern Sustainable Agriculture Working Group, Elkins, AR, $50,000. To promote sustainable agriculture in Southeastern and Southcentral United States through network of family farm, agriculture, consumer, and environmental organizations from 13 states. 2002.

2345-49 Southwest Network for Environmental and Economic Justice, Albuquerque, NM, $25,000. For general support for network of grassroots community groups based in Southwest and working to build regional movement focused on environmental and economic justice. 2002.

2345-50 Southwest Organizing Project, Albuquerque, NM, $25,000. For general support for grassroots organizing work on environmental and economic justice issues in New Mexico. 2002.

2345-51 Southwest Research and Information Center, Albuquerque, NM, $25,000. For general support to provide technical assistance to communities in Southwest on health and environmental issues. 2002.

2345-52 Sustainable South Bronx, Bronx, NY, $20,000. To advocate for and implement development projects in South Bronx that are defined by community input and based on principles of environmental justice. 2002.

2345-53 Tufts University, School of Nutrition Science and Policy; Agriculture, Food, and Environment Program, Medford, MA, $20,000. For New Entry Sustainable Farming Project to help immigrants who have farming experience from their countries of origin re-enter farming in Massachusetts and Rhode Island as way to stem loss of family farming in region and build community food security. 2002.

2345-54 United Church of Christ, Cleveland, OH, $30,000. For planning, organizing, and inclusion of new groups and constituencies in Second People of Color Summit, and for development of collaborative work plans for implementing Summit priorities. 2002.

2345-55 Valley Interfaith Project, Phoenix, AZ, $25,000. To reduce threats posed by polluting industries and hazardous waste facilities in low-income communities and communities of color in Arizona, with primary focus on Phoenix area. 2002.

2345-56 Wallowa Resources, Enterprise, Oregon, $25,000. To create new job and business opportunities that result in long-term sustainable management of natural resources. 2002.

2345-57 Washington Sustainable Food and Farming Network, Bellingham, WA, $20,000. For statewide alliance that mobilizes farmers, residents and organizations in order to create sustainable food and farming system. 2002.

2345-58 We Stay/Nos Quedamos, Bronx, NY, $20,000. To educate residents of community boards in South Bronx about level of air pollution in their neighborhoods, its relationship to community health problems like asthma, and its causes. 2002.

2345-59 Western Shoshone Defense Project, Crescent Valley, NV, $20,000. For Cultural Preservation Program to protect land and water resources from effects of gold mining and maintain health of traditional Western Shoshone land base. 2002.

2345-60 White Earth Land Recovery Project, Ponsford, MN, $20,000. For sustainable agriculture value-added production activities on White Earth Reservation and organizing campaigns to combat groundwater pollution from industrial potato farming and bio-piracy threats posed by mapping of wild rice gene. 2002.

2345-61 Womens Voices for the Earth, Missoula, MT, $20,000. To provide women with skills, resources and support to create sustainable environment and socially just society. 2002.

2345-62 Work Environment Council of New Jersey, Trenton, NJ, $40,000. To build common ground between labor unions and environmental/community organizations in northern New Jersey in order to address issues of jobs and environment and to promote community and worker safety and health. 2002.

2345-63 YouthAction, Albuquerque, NM, $50,000. To involve young people in community organizing on environmental and environmental justice issues. 2002.

2346
Jane W. Nuhn Charitable Trust

c/o Van DeWater & Van DeWater
P.O. Box 112
Poughkeepsie, NY 12602
Contact: Noel De Cordova, Jr., Tr.

Established in 1988 in NY.
Grantmaker type: Independent foundation
Financial data (yr. ended 12/31/01): Assets, $11,380,879 (M); expenditures, $424,479; qualifying distributions, $465,770; giving activities include $412,800 for 21 grants (high: $357,710; low: $300).
Purpose and activities: Areas of support include the arts, music, and prevention of cruelty to animals.
Fields of interest: Arts; Animal welfare; Community development; Federated giving programs.
Types of support: General/operating support; Building/renovation; Equipment; Endowments; Matching/challenge support.
Limitations: Applications not accepted. Giving primarily in Dutchess County, NY. No grants to individuals.
Publications: Annual report.
Application information: Unsolicited requests for funds not accepted.
Board meeting date(s): Monthly
Trustees: Edward V.K. Cunningham, Jr.; Michael De Cordova; Noel De Cordova, Jr.
Number of staff: None.
EIN: 146134057

2347
A. Lindsay and Olive B. O'Connor Foundation

P.O. Box D
Hobart, NY 13788   (607) 538-9248
Contact: Donald F. Bishop II, Exec. Dir.
FAX: (607) 538-9136

Trust established in 1965 in NY.
Donor(s): Olive B. O'Connor.‡
Grantmaker type: Independent foundation

Financial data (yr. ended 12/31/01): Assets, $72,766,636 (M); expenditures, $3,588,125; qualifying distributions, $3,179,363; giving activities include $2,981,839 for 312 grants (high: $200,000; low: $27; average: $500–$20,000).
Purpose and activities: Emphasis on quality of life, including hospitals, libraries, community centers, higher education, nursing and other vocational education, child development and youth agencies, religious organizations, museums, and historic restoration; support also for civic affairs and town, village, and environmental conservation and improvement.
Fields of interest: Architecture; Museums; Performing arts; History/archaeology; Historic preservation/historical societies; Arts; Early childhood education; Child development, education; Vocational education; Higher education; Business school/education; Libraries/library science; Natural resources; Environment; Animal welfare; Animals/wildlife, preservation/protection; Hospitals (general); Nursing care; Substance abuse, services; Alcoholism; Crime/violence prevention, youth; Employment; Agriculture; Housing/shelter, development; Human services; Children/youth, services; Child development, services; Women, centers/services; Rural development; Community development; Federated giving programs; Religious federated giving programs; Biological sciences; Economics; Government/public administration; Christian agencies & churches; Protestant agencies & churches; Religion; Women; Economically disadvantaged.
Types of support: Continuing support; Annual campaigns; Capital campaigns; Building/renovation; Equipment; Land acquisition; Endowments; Emergency funds; Program development; Conferences/seminars; Publication; Seed money; Scholarship funds; Research; Technical assistance; Program-related investments/loans; Matching/challenge support.
Limitations: Giving primarily in Delaware County, NY, and 7 contiguous rural counties in upstate NY. No grants to individuals, or for operating budgets or deficit financing.
Publications: Multi-year report, Program policy statement.
Application information: Application form required.
Initial approach: Letter or telephone
Copies of proposal: 1
Deadline(s): Apr. 1 and Sept. 1; 1st of each month for grants under $5,000
Board meeting date(s): May or June and Sept. or Oct.; committee meets monthly to consider grants under $5,000
Final notification: 7 to 10 days after semiannual meeting
Officers: Donald F. Bishop II, Pres. and Exec. Dir.; Pamela Hill, Secy.-Treas.
Advisory Committee: Robert L. Bishop II, Chair.; Charlotte Bishop Hill, Vice-Chair.; Lawrence C. Anderson; Suzanne Hill; William J. Murphy.
Trustee: BSB Bank & Trust.
Number of staff: 2 full-time professional.
EIN: 166063485

2348
Sylvan and Ann Oestreicher Foundation, Inc.

c/o Marks Paneth & Shron, LLP
622 3rd Ave.
New York, NY 10017
Contact: Ann Oestreicher, Pres.
Application address: Lenox Hill Sta., P.O. Box 2365, New York, NY 10021

Incorporated in 1948 in NY.
Donor(s): Sylvan Oestreicher.‡
Grantmaker type: Independent foundation
Financial data (yr. ended 04/30/02): Assets, $12,244,009 (M); expenditures, $419,039; qualifying distributions, $399,785; giving activities include $392,950 for 157 grants (high: $51,000; low: $200).
Purpose and activities: Grants primarily for religious welfare funds, hospitals, and higher education; support also for youth agencies, religious associations, and cultural programs.
Fields of interest: Museums; Arts; Higher education; Natural resources; Environment; Hospitals (general); Health care; Health organizations, association; Cancer; Medical research, institute; Cancer research; Human services; Children/youth, services; Protestant federated giving programs; Religious federated giving programs; Religion; Minorities; Native Americans/American Indians.
Limitations: Giving primarily in Chicago, IL and NY.
Application information: Application form not required.
Deadline(s): None
Officers: Ann Oestreicher, Pres.; Robert F. Welch, Secy.
EIN: 136085974

2349
The Ohrstrom Foundation, Inc. ▼

c/o Curtis Mallet
101 Park Ave., 35th Fl.
New York, NY 10178-0061

Incorporated in 1953 in DE.
Donor(s): Members of the Ohrstrom family.
Grantmaker type: Independent foundation
Financial data (yr. ended 05/31/02): Assets, $61,159,491 (M); expenditures, $3,198,245; qualifying distributions, $3,086,463; giving activities include $2,826,480 for 101 grants (high: $1,095,300; low: $500; average: $1,000–$50,000).
Purpose and activities: Emphasis on elementary, secondary, and higher education; support also for civic affairs, conservation, hospitals and medical research, and museums.
Fields of interest: Museums; Education, fund raising; Elementary/secondary education; Elementary school/education; Secondary school/education; Higher education; Libraries/library science; Natural resources; Environment; Hospitals (general); Alcoholism; Medical research, institute; Government/public administration; Religion; General charitable giving.
Types of support: General/operating support; Continuing support; Annual campaigns; Building/renovation; Equipment; Land acquisition; Endowments; Emergency funds;

Program development; Seed money; Matching/challenge support.
Limitations: Applications not accepted. Giving primarily in NY and VA. No grants to individuals, or for deficit financing, scholarships, fellowships, research, special projects, publications, or conferences; no loans.
Application information: Contributes only to pre-selected organizations.
Officers and Directors:* George L. Ohrstrom, Jr.,* Pres.; George F. Ohrstrom,* Exec. V.P.; Magalen O. Bryant,* V.P.; Peter A. Kalat,* Secy.; Dorothy Barry, Treas.; Kristiane C. Graham; George L. Ohrstrom II; Winifred E.A. Ohrstrom.
Number of staff: 1 part-time support.
EIN: 546039966
Recent environmental and animal welfare grants:
2349-1 Brandywine Conservancy, Chadds Ford, PA, $15,000. 2002.
2349-2 Cause for Paws, Harpers Ferry, WV, $10,000. 2002.
2349-3 Equine Rescue League Foundation, Leesburg, VA, $15,000. 2002.
2349-4 National Fish and Wildlife Foundation, DC, $153,891. 2002.
2349-5 Piedmont Environmental Council, Warrenton, VA, $60,891. 2002.
2349-6 Shenandoah University, Environmental Science Department, Winchester, VA, $10,000. 2002.
2349-7 Southern Environmental Law Center, Charlottesville, VA, $30,000. 2002.
2349-8 Yellowstone Park Foundation, Bozeman, MT, $60,000. 2002.

2350
Oneida Nation Foundation
223 Genesee St.
Oneida, NY   13421
URL: http://oneida-nation.net/foundation/

Grantmaker type: Public charity
Purpose and activities: The foundation is intended to enhance the quality of life of the Haudenosaunee people as well as members and friends who live and work for the empowerment of American Indians on Turtle Island. Areas of special interest include youth, health, education, environment, and community development/governance.
Fields of interest: Education; Environment; Health care; Youth development; Community development; Native Americans/American Indians.
Types of support: General/operating support; Building/renovation; Equipment; Program development; Conferences/seminars; Publication; Curriculum development; Scholarship funds; Research.
Limitations: Applications not accepted. No grants to individuals, or for dinners, dances, advertising journals, fundraising contests, raffles, booster clubs, endowments, deficit financing, travel expenses; no loans.
Application information: Contributes only to pre-selected organizations; unsolicited requests for funds not considered.

2351
Orange and Rockland Utilities, Inc. Corporate Giving Program
1 Blue Hill Plz.
Pearl River, NY   10965   (845) 577-2147
Contact: Neil Winter, Mgr., Corp. Progs.
FAX: (845) 577-6913; E-mail: nwinter@oru.com;
URL: http://www.oru.com/aboutoru/communitysupport/index.html

Grantmaker type: Corporate giving program
Purpose and activities: Orange and Rockland makes charitable contributions to nonprofit organizations involved with arts and culture, education, the environment, mental health, public safety, minorities, disabled people, and on a case by case basis and to hospitals. Support is limited to areas of company operations.
Fields of interest: Visual arts; Performing arts; Arts; Elementary/secondary education; Higher education; Education; Natural resources; Environment; Hospitals (general); Mental health/crisis services; Crime/law enforcement; Safety/disasters; General charitable giving; Minorities; Disabled.
Types of support: Capital campaigns; Program development; Curriculum development; Scholarship funds; Employee volunteer services; Sponsorships; Employee matching gifts; Scholarships—to individuals.
Limitations: Giving limited to areas of company operations in Bergen, Passaic, and Sussex counties, NJ, Orange, Rockland, and Sullivan counties, NY, and Pike County, PA.
Publications: Application guidelines, Grants list, Newsletter.
Application information: The Public Affairs Department handles giving. The company has a staff that only handles contributions. A contributions committee reviews all requests. Application form required.
   Initial approach: Contact headquarters for application form
   Copies of proposal: 1
   Deadline(s): None
   Board meeting date(s): Monthly
   Final notification: 5 weeks
Number of staff: 1 full-time support.

2352
The Orentreich Family Foundation
909 5th Ave.
New York, NY   10021-1415

Established in 1986 in NY.
Donor(s): David Orentreich, Norman Orentreich, Orentreich Medical Group.
Grantmaker type: Independent foundation
Financial data (yr. ended 09/30/02): Assets, $13,297,709 (M); expenditures, $300,385; qualifying distributions, $270,160; giving activities include $266,325 for grants (high: $45,000).
Purpose and activities: Support primarily for an affiliated medical research facility. Funding also for the arts and city parks.
Fields of interest: Arts; Education; Natural resources; Botanical gardens; Hospitals (general); Health organizations, association; Biomedicine research; Parks/playgrounds; Jewish federated giving programs; Jewish agencies & temples.

Limitations: Applications not accepted. Giving primarily in New York, NY. No grants to individuals.
Application information: Contributes only to pre-selected organizations.
Trustees: David Orentreich; Norman Orentreich.
EIN: 136879797

2353
Edward B. Osborn Charitable Trust
c/o U.S. Trust
114 W. 47th St.
New York, NY   10036

Trust established in 1961 in NY.
Donor(s): Edward B. Osborn.
Grantmaker type: Independent foundation
Financial data (yr. ended 10/31/02): Assets, $6,185,486 (M); expenditures, $308,326; qualifying distributions, $287,642; giving activities include $278,375 for grants.
Fields of interest: Museums; Arts; Higher education; Environment; Cancer; Boys clubs; Children/youth, services; Federated giving programs.
Limitations: Giving primarily in FL and NY. No grants to individuals.
Application information: Application form not required.
   Initial approach: Letter
   Deadline(s): None
Trustee: U.S. Trust.
EIN: 136071296

2354
Osceola Foundation, Inc.
c/o Brooks & Cantor
3000 Marcus Ave., No. 2E4
New Hyde Park, NY   11042
Contact: Ann B. Oliver, Pres.
Additional address: 408 Cove View Pt., Columbia, SC 29212

Incorporated in 1963 in NY.
Donor(s): Katherine Sperry Beinecke Trust.‡
Grantmaker type: Independent foundation
Financial data (yr. ended 12/31/01): Assets, $4,816,638 (M); expenditures, $293,637; qualifying distributions, $219,938; giving activities include $221,980 for 45 grants (high: $50,000; low: $94).
Purpose and activities: Giving primarily for education, the arts, and social services.
Fields of interest: Music; Historic preservation/historical societies; Higher education; Education; Natural resources; Human services.
Types of support: General/operating support; Capital campaigns; Program development.
Limitations: Applications not accepted. Giving primarily in MA, NY, OH, and SC. No grants to individuals.
Application information: Contributes only to pre-selected organizations.
Officers: Ann B. Oliver, Pres.; Perry Ashley, Secy.; Barbara B. Spitler, Treas.
Directors: Deborah B. Beale; Walter Beinecke, Jr.; Walter Beinecke III.
Number of staff: None.
EIN: 136094234

2355
The Ottinger Foundation
80 Broad St., 17th Fl.
New York, NY 10004 (212) 764-3878
Contact: Michele Lord, Exec. Dir.
FAX: (212) 764-4298; E-mail:
info@ottingerfoundation.org; URL: http://
www.ottingerfoundation.org

Incorporated in 1945 in NY.
Donor(s): Lawrence Ottinger.‡
Grantmaker type: Independent foundation
Financial data (yr. ended 12/31/01): Assets,
$7,322,920 (M); gifts received, $371,716;
expenditures, $571,392; qualifying distributions,
$503,581; giving activities include $435,000 for
17 grants (high: $50,000; low: $1,000; average:
$5,000–$10,000).
Purpose and activities: Supports selected
projects designed to advance democracy, social
and economic justice, citizen activism, and
environmental protection. The foundation is
implementing a program area focusing on
economic security issues.
Fields of interest: Environment.
Types of support: General/operating support;
Program development; Seed money;
Matching/challenge support.
Limitations: Giving on a national basis. No
support for local organizations, human services,
or for organizations which typically receive
popular support like universities, museums or
schools. No grants to individuals, or for capital
or annual campaigns, deficit financing, building
or endowment funds, equipment and materials,
land acquisition, publications, conferences, film
or video projects or academic research.
Application information: Guidelines available
on Web site. Accepts NNG Common Grant
Application Form. Proposals for the
environment and democratic participation by
solicitation only. Application form not required.
  Initial approach: Letter of inquiry
  Copies of proposal: 1
  Board meeting date(s): Biannually
  Final notification: 1 month after board meeting
Officers and Trustees:* Lawrence Ottinger,*
Chair.; Richard L. Ottinger,* V.P.; Kim Baptiste,*
Secy.-Treas.; Michael Goldberg; Karen Heath;
Jennifer Ottinger; June Godfrey Ottinger; Lea
Anne Ottinger; Randy Ottinger; Ronald Ottinger;
Cinthia Schuman; Peter Smith; Betsy Taylor.
Number of staff: 2 shared staff.
EIN: 136118423

2356
The Overbrook Foundation ▼
122 E. 42nd St., Ste. 2500
New York, NY 10168-2500 (212) 661-8710
Contact: M. Sheila McGoldrick
FAX: (212) 661-8664; URL: http://
www.overbrook.org

Incorporated in 1948 in NY.
Donor(s): Frank Altschul,‡ Helen G. Altschul,‡
Arthur G. Altschul,‡ Margaret A. Lang.‡
Grantmaker type: Independent foundation
Financial data (yr. ended 12/31/01): Assets,
$162,019,025 (M); gifts received, $124,367;
expenditures, $10,907,620; qualifying
distributions, $8,885,389; giving activities
include $8,154,939 for 244 grants (high:

$600,000; low: $500; average:
$1,000–$25,000).
Purpose and activities: Giving primarily for
conservation and the environment; grants also
for arts and cultural programs, child welfare,
civil rights, community funds, elementary,
secondary, and higher education, hospitals,
international affairs, medical research,
museums, and social services.
Fields of interest: Museums; Arts; Elementary
school/education; Secondary school/education;
Higher education; Natural resources;
Environment; Human services; Children/youth,
services; International affairs; Civil rights.
Types of support: General/operating support.
Limitations: Giving primarily in New York, NY.
No grants to individuals.
Application information:
  Initial approach: Letter of inquiry
  Board meeting date(s): Varies
Officers and Directors:* Vincent McGee,* Pres.;
Stephen F. Altschul,* Secy.; Robert C. Graham,
Jr.,* Treas.; Steven A. Foster, Exec. Dir.; Arthur G.
Altschul, Jr.; Charles Altschul; Julie Graham;
Kathryn C. Graham; Kathryn G. Graham; Cecily
Kooijman; Frances Labaree; Isaiah Lang; Emily
Altschull Miller.
Number of staff: 1 part-time professional; 1
full-time support.
EIN: 136088860
**Recent environmental and animal welfare
grants:**
2356-1 Amazon Conservation Association, DC,
  $50,000. For general support. 2001.
2356-2 Amazon Conservation Team, Arlington,
  VA, $125,000. For general support. 2001.
2356-3 Animal Support, Kindness and Kinship,
  Palm Beach, FL, $20,500. For general
  support. 2001.
2356-4 Center for International Forestry
  Research, Bogor, Indonesia, $75,000. For
  general support for Biodiversity Conservation
  for Local Livelihoods in the Brazilian
  Amazon. 2001.
2356-5 Center for Resource Economics/Island
  Press, DC, $75,000. For general support.
  2001.
2356-6 Center for the Support of Native Lands,
  Arlington, VA, $20,000. For general support.
  2001.
2356-7 Columbia University, Center for
  Environmental Research and Conservation,
  New York, NY, $100,000. For general
  support. 2001.
2356-8 Conservacion y Desarrollo, Quito,
  Ecuador, $25,000. For general support for
  Eco-Chocolate: Promotion of New Solar
  Dryers in Sustainable Cocoa Farming. 2001.
2356-9 Conservation Fund, New York, NY,
  $10,000. For general support. 2001.
2356-10 Earthjustice Legal Defense Fund,
  Oakland, CA, $25,000. For general support.
  2001.
2356-11 EcoLogic Enterprise Ventures,
  Cambridge, MA, $60,000. For general
  support. 2001.
2356-12 Environmental Defense, New York, NY,
  $100,000. For general support. 2001.
2356-13 Environmental Law Institute, DC,
  $45,000. For general support. 2001.
2356-14 Fideicomiso para la Conservacion en
  Guatemala (FCG), Guatemala City,
  Guatemala, $27,500. For general support for

Small Grants Program, supporting applied
  plant conservation projects. 2001.
2356-15 Foundation for Self-Sufficiency (Central
  America), Round Rock, TX, $125,000. For
  general support. 2001.
2356-16 Fundacion Jocotoco, Ecuador,
  $50,000. For general support to purchase
  land at Yanacocha and Buenaventura
  projects. 2001.
2356-17 Green Guide Institute, New York, NY,
  $25,000. For general support. 2001.
2356-18 INFORM, New York, NY, $35,000. For
  general support. 2001.
2356-19 Institute for Management and
  Certification of Agriculture and Forestry, Sao
  Paulo, Brazil, $40,000. For general support
  for Small Grants Program and Agroforestry
  Program. 2001.
2356-20 Mexican Nature Conservation Fund,
  Mexico City, Mexico, $30,000. For general
  support. 2001.
2356-21 Natural Resources Defense Council,
  New York, NY, $153,000. For general
  support. 2001.
2356-22 Nature Conservancy, New York, NY,
  $80,000. For general support. 2001.
2356-23 New York Botanical Garden, Bronx,
  NY, $102,000. For general support. 2001.
2356-24 New York City Outward Bound Center,
  Long Island City, NY, $20,000. For general
  support. 2001.
2356-25 Rainforest Alliance, New York, NY,
  $105,500. For general support. 2001.
2356-26 RARE Center for Tropical Conservation,
  Arlington, VA, $50,000. For general support.
  2001.
2356-27 RARE Center for Tropical Conservation,
  Arlington, VA, $25,437. For general support.
  2001.
2356-28 Rocky Mountain Institute, Snowmass,
  CO, $70,000. For general support. 2001.
2356-29 Rocky Mountain Institute, Snowmass,
  CO, $35,000. For general support. 2001.
2356-30 Shackleton Schools, Boston, MA,
  $35,500. For general support. 2001.
2356-31 SoundWaters, Stamford, CT, $30,000.
  For general support. 2001.
2356-32 Stamford Land Conservation Trust,
  Stamford, CT, $102,500. For general support.
  2001.
2356-33 Thompson Island Outward Bound
  Education Center, Boston, MA, $35,500. For
  general support. 2001.
2356-34 Trout Unlimited, New York, NY,
  $25,000. For general support. 2001.
2356-35 World Wildlife Fund/Conservation
  Foundation, DC, $50,000. For general
  support. 2001.

2357
Overhills Foundation
380 Madison Ave.
New York, NY 10017

Established in 2000 in DE.
Donor(s): Omnibus Charitable Trust, Underhill
Foundation, Wild Wings Foundation.
Grantmaker type: Independent foundation
Financial data (yr. ended 11/30/00): Assets,
$6,426,334 (M); gifts received, $2,804,277;
expenditures, $262,212; qualifying distributions,
$228,753; giving activities include $230,000 for
23 grants (high: $25,000; low: $1,000).

Purpose and activities: Giving primarily for nature conservancies and the environment.
Fields of interest: Museums (specialized); Law school/education; Environment, land resources; Environment, forests; Environment; Employment, services; Human services; Children/youth, services.
Limitations: Applications not accepted. Giving primarily in NY. No grants to individuals.
Application information: Contributes only to pre-selected organizations.
Officers and Directors:* Ann R. Elliman,* Pres.; Lucia R. Brown,* V.P.; Edward H. Elliman,* V.P.; Christopher J. Elliman,* Secy.-Treas.
EIN: 133922745

2358
The Palmer Foundation, Inc.
635 Madison Ave., 18th Fl.
New York, NY 10022
Contact: Barbara R. Palmer, Pres.

Established in 1988 in PA.
Donor(s): James R. Palmer.
Grantmaker type: Independent foundation
Financial data (yr. ended 12/31/02): Assets, $2,884,717 (M); gifts received, $70; expenditures, $1,111,391; qualifying distributions, $792,641; giving activities include $794,690 for 51 grants (high: $100,000; low: $100).
Purpose and activities: Giving primarily to universities. Some funding also for research purposes and the arts.
Fields of interest: Museums; Higher education; Natural resources; Family planning; Heart & circulatory diseases; Cancer research; YM/YWCAs & YM/YWHAs.
Types of support: General/operating support; Grants to individuals.
Limitations: Giving primarily in NY and PA.
Application information: Application form not required.
   Deadline(s): None
Officers: Barbara R. Palmer, Pres.; Wayne Reisner, Secy.-Treas.
Directors: Janet Lipson; Charles Palmer; David Palmer.
EIN: 251568606

2359
The Panaphil Foundation
c/o U.S. Trust
114 W. 47th St.
New York, NY 10036
Contact: Barry Waldorf

Established in 1990 in PA and NY.
Donor(s): Frances A. Velay.
Grantmaker type: Independent foundation
Financial data (yr. ended 12/31/01): Assets, $31,146,076 (M); expenditures, $2,033,999; qualifying distributions, $1,825,256; giving activities include $1,840,000 for 54 grants (high: $350,000; low: $10,000; average: $10,000–$50,000).
Purpose and activities: Giving primarily for environmental concerns, preservation of animal and plant species threatened with extinction, and prevention of cruelty to animals.

Fields of interest: Natural resources; Animal welfare; Family planning; Native Americans/American Indians.
Limitations: Giving primarily on the East Coast. No grants to individuals.
Application information:
   Initial approach: Proposal
   Deadline(s): None
Trustees: Barbara Paul Robinson; Christophe J. Velay; Frances A. Velay.
EIN: 136959472

2360
Park Foundation, Inc. ▼
P.O. Box 550
Ithaca, NY 14851 (607) 272-9124
Contact: Linda Madeo, Exec. Dir.
FAX: (607) 272-6057

Established in 1966.
Donor(s): RHP, Inc., Roy H. Park.‡
Grantmaker type: Independent foundation
Financial data (yr. ended 12/31/02): Assets, $451,536,939 (M); expenditures, $27,359,400; qualifying distributions, $24,198,141; giving activities include $23,201,703 for 356 grants (high: $1,248,506; low: $15; average: $10,000–$100,000) and $2,005 for 30 employee matching gifts.
Purpose and activities: Giving primarily for public television, higher education, the environment, and animal welfare.
Fields of interest: Television; Higher education; Education; Environment; Animal welfare.
Types of support: General/operating support; Program development; Professorships; Seed money; Fellowships; Scholarship funds; Research; Employee matching gifts; Matching/challenge support.
Limitations: Giving limited to the East Coast (primarily in central NY) and the southeastern U.S. No grants to individuals.
Publications: Informational brochure (including application guidelines).
Application information: Application form required.
   Initial approach: Letter
   Copies of proposal: 1
   Deadline(s): None
   Board meeting date(s): Mar., June, Aug., Oct., and Dec.
Officers and Board Members:* Dorothy D. Park,* Pres.; Roy H. Park, Jr., 1st V.P.; Adelaide P. Gomer,* 2nd V.P. and Secy.; Elizabeth P. Fowler,* Treas.; Linda Madeo, Exec. Dir.; Jerome B. Libin; Richard G. Robb.
Junior Advisors: Alicia P. Gomer; Roy H. Park III.
Number of staff: 3 full-time professional; 4 full-time support.
EIN: 166071043
Recent environmental and animal welfare grants:
2360-1 Adirondack Council, Elizabethtown, NY, $30,000. For continued support for Pure Waters Campaign. 2001.
2360-2 Amazon Conservation Association, DC, $100,000. For general operating support. 2001.
2360-3 American Bird Conservancy, The Plains, VA, $10,000. For continued support for technology-based solutions to eliminate or minimize impact of cell towers on migratory birds. 2001.

2360-4 American Chestnut Foundation, Bennington, VT, $25,000. For work to compare European, Chinese, and American Chestnut genetic maps. 2001.
2360-5 American Humane Association, Englewood, CO, $29,713. For education of special audiences, development of profiles, and presentation of Link Training. 2001.
2360-6 Animal Rights Network, Baltimore, MD, $10,000. For general operating support. 2001.
2360-7 Arts of Peace, Mainstream Media Project, Arcata, CA, $30,000. For providing public education on radio stations nationwide, focusing on biological diversity, transportation/conservation/livable communities, and energy issues. 2001.
2360-8 Audubon Society of Massachusetts, Programme for Belize, Lincoln, MA, $15,000. For internship program for students to work at Hill Bank and La Milpa Field Stations in Belize. 2001.
2360-9 Audubon Society, National, New York, NY, $55,000. For research and public education component of New York State Forests Initiative. 2001.
2360-10 Audubon Society, National, New York, NY, $25,000. For full-time coordinator for New York State Important Bird Area program. 2001.
2360-11 Audubon Society, National, Wilmington, NC, $30,000. For Phase II of Important Bird Areas Program. 2001.
2360-12 Audubon Society, National, Project Puffin, New York, NY, $10,000. For Gulf of Maine Seabird Restoration Project. 2001.
2360-13 Aussie Rescue and Placement Helpline, New Wilmington, PA, $10,000. For general operating support of adoption and referral services. 2001.
2360-14 Beyond Pesticides/NCAMP, DC, $35,000. For Center for Community Pesticide and Alternatives Information. 2001.
2360-15 Boca Grande Art Alliance, Boca Grande, FL, $12,000. For production of series of books for fundraising efforts on wildlife of Boca Grande. 2001.
2360-16 Boyce Thompson Institute for Plant Research, Ithaca, NY, $270,000. For Biodiversity Program. 2001.
2360-17 Boyce Thompson Institute for Plant Research, Ithaca, NY, $270,000. For Biodiversity Program. 2001.
2360-18 Boyce Thompson Institute for Plant Research, Ithaca, NY, $75,000. To initiate Development Program. 2001.
2360-19 Boyce Thompson Institute for Plant Research, Ithaca, NY, $75,000. To initiate development program. 2001.
2360-20 Burnet Park Zoo, Friends of the, Syracuse, NY, $100,000. For conditional grant for campaign, specifically for Conservation Education Wing. 2001.
2360-21 Burnet Park Zoo, Friends of the, Syracuse, NY, $45,000. For expansion and improvement of habitats for primates and elephants, and to enable staff to travel to other zoological institutions. 2001.
2360-22 Canine Assistants, Alpharetta, GA, $15,000. For individuals to attend training camp. 2001.
2360-23 Canine Working Companions, Liverpool, NY, $60,000. For creation of

education campaign to heighten awareness. 2001.

2360-24 Carnivore Preservation Trust, Pittsboro, NC, $30,000. For general operating support. 2001.

2360-25 Cats Cradle, Morganton, NC, $10,000. For general operating support. 2001.

2360-26 Cayuga Lake Watershed Network, Ithaca, NY, $37,732. For Watershed Steward for Cayuga Lake. 2001.

2360-27 Cayuga Lake Watershed Network, Ithaca, NY, $37,732. For Watershed Steward for Cayuga Lake. 2001.

2360-28 Cayuga Nature Center, Ithaca, NY, $30,400. For Pee Wee House Calls: Natural Science on Wheels Program. 2001.

2360-29 Cayuga Nature Center, Ithaca, NY, $10,000. For educational programs and toward scholarships for children from low-income families. 2001.

2360-30 Center for a New American Dream, Takoma Park, MD, $40,000. For general operating support. 2001.

2360-31 Center for Captive Chimpanzee Care, Fort Pierce, FL, $50,000. Toward hiring additional caretaker for chimpanzees and to cover expenses not foreseen in budget. 2001.

2360-32 Center for Food Safety and Applied Nutrition, College Park, MD, $25,000. For campaign against genetically engineered fish. 2001.

2360-33 Center for Independent Documentary, Sharon, MA, $25,000. For completion of documentary, Blue Vinyl. 2001.

2360-34 Center for Public Integrity, DC, $135,000. For challenge grant for Water for Sale: How the World's Lifesource is Being Sold to the Highest Bidder. 2001.

2360-35 Center for Public Integrity, DC, $50,000. For challenge grant for Water for Sale: How the World's Lifesource is Being Sold to the Highest Bidder. 2001.

2360-36 Center for Public Integrity, DC, $50,000. For challenge grant for Water for Sale: How the World's Lifesource is Being Sold to Highest Bidder. 2001.

2360-37 CERES, Boston, MA, $25,000. For Green Hotels Initiative. 2001.

2360-38 Chamber of Commerce Foundation, Tompkins County, Ithaca, NY, $25,000. For planning of Cayuga Waterfront Trail Initiative. 2001.

2360-39 Charlotte Country Day School, Charlotte, NC, $35,000. For conditional grant for establishment of Imagination Garden at school. 2001.

2360-40 Cold Mountain, Cold Rivers, Missoula, MT, $10,000. For general support for programs of Buffalo Field Campaign. 2001.

2360-41 Concerned Citizens of Tillery, Tillery, NC, $10,000. For communities' struggle for social and environmental justice. 2001.

2360-42 Conservation Trust for North Carolina, Raleigh, NC, $10,000. For general operating support. 2001.

2360-43 Cornell Cooperative Extension of Tompkins County, Ithaca, NY, $25,000. For Ithaca Children's Garden Odyssey. 2001.

2360-44 Cornell University, College of Agriculture and Life Sciences, Ithaca, NY, $75,000. For housing needs of hawks, eagles, falcons, and owls in Cornell Raptor Program. 2001.

2360-45 Cornell University, Laboratory of Ornithology, Ithaca, NY, $100,000. For expansion of BirdSource. 2001.

2360-46 Cornell University, Laboratory of Ornithology, Ithaca, NY, $100,000. For expansion of BirdSource. 2001.

2360-47 Dogwood Alliance, Brevard, NC, $25,000. To establish moratorium on new chip mills and expansion of industrial forestry in southern states, help institute legal protections, and shift markets from forestry to recycled and alternative products. 2001.

2360-48 Ducks Unlimited, Memphis, TN, $75,000. For Roanoke Island Marshes Restoration. 2001.

2360-49 Eagles Nest Foundation, Pisgah Forest, NC, $25,000. To provide scholarship assistance to students to attend Outdoor Academy of Southern Appalachian and Eagle's Nest Camp. 2001.

2360-50 Eagles Nest Foundation, Pisgah Forest, NC, $10,000. To purchase land adjacent to Eagle's Nest Camp. 2001.

2360-51 Earth Action Network, Norwalk, CT, $18,500. For printing of extra copies of E Magazine on America's most endangered rivers. 2001.

2360-52 Earth Pledge Foundation, New York, NY, $10,000. For FarmToTable.org. 2001.

2360-53 East Coast Greenway Alliance, Wakefield, RI, $30,000. For development of urban multi-use trail, reaching from Maine's Canadian border to Key West, Florida. 2001.

2360-54 Educational Broadcasting Corporation, New York, NY, $750,000. For Nature and American Masters programs. 2001.

2360-55 Educational Broadcasting Corporation, New York, NY, $750,000. To underwrite Nature and American Masters. 2001.

2360-56 Environmental Defense, New York, NY, $125,000. For conditional grant for environmental initiatives in North Carolina. 2001.

2360-57 Environmental Health Fund, Jamaica Plain, MA, $32,217. For Health Care Without Harm program to phase out PVC and DEHP from medical supplies. 2001.

2360-58 Essential Information, DC, $25,000. For Resource Conservation Alliance Project to increase support and use of products made from agricultural fibers for conservation of forests. 2001.

2360-59 Evangelical Committee for Aid and Development (CEPAD)-USA, Brightwood, Oregon, $25,000. For Lamanai Field Research Center. 2001.

2360-60 Farm Sanctuary, Watkins Glen, NY, $10,000. For matching grant for public awareness, education, and other program support. 2001.

2360-61 Farm Sanctuary, Watkins Glen, NY, $10,000. For public awareness, education, and other program support. 2001.

2360-62 Finger Lakes Land Trust, Ithaca, NY, $10,000. For start-up support for Western MidAtlantic Grassroots Environmental Fund to serve New York and Pennsylvania. 2001.

2360-63 Friends of the Earth, DC, $35,000. For campaign to stop genetically engineered salmon. 2001.

2360-64 Fund for Animals, New York, NY, $125,000. For campaign to ban canned hunting in US. 2001.

2360-65 Global Greengrants Fund, Boulder, CO, $15,000. To strengthen global grassroots environmental movement by making small grants to grassroots environmental activist groups around the world. Grant made through Tides Foundation. 2001.

2360-66 Global Greengrants Fund, Boulder, CO, $15,000. To strengthen global grassroots environmental movement by making small grants to grassroots environmental activist groups around the world. Grant made through Tides Foundation. 2001.

2360-67 Hudson River Sloop Clearwater, Poughkeepsie, NY, $50,000. For Urban Outreach Initiative. 2001.

2360-68 Humane Society of Charlotte, Charlotte, NC, $55,000. For maintenance and equipment for shelter. 2001.

2360-69 International Ecotourism Society, DC, $54,250. For Ecotourism Internet News Service, The Ecotourism Observer. 2001.

2360-70 International Primate Protection League, Summerville, SC, $10,000. For general operating support. 2001.

2360-71 Ithacare Center Service, Ithaca, NY, $25,000. To create and establish intergenerational outdoor gardening, ecology, science, and nature study program. 2001.

2360-72 Keeping Track, Jericho, VT, $15,000. For technical support program. 2001.

2360-73 Land Trust for the Little Tennessee, Franklin, NC, $37,500. For conditional grant for development of protection plan for Needmore Tract and purchase of land in immediate area. 2001.

2360-74 Marie Selby Botanical Gardens, Sarasota, FL, $25,000. For conditional grant to expand education and research programs on orchids. 2001.

2360-75 Marine Stewardship Council, Seattle, WA, $10,000. For International Boston Seafood Show. 2001.

2360-76 Mingan Island Cetacean Study, Saint Lambert, Canada, $50,000. For conditional grant for Group for Research and Education on Marine Mammals (GREMM) projects studying beluga whale, its activity and reactions to human generated noises in the ocean. 2001.

2360-77 Mote Marine Laboratory, Sarasota, FL, $20,000. For video project, Ocean Expedition. 2001.

2360-78 National Parks Conservation Association, DC, $75,000. For fourth and final phase of Business Plan Initiative and development of National Park Funding Campaign and Loan Buy-Down program. 2001.

2360-79 National Parks Conservation Association, DC, $50,000. For fourth and final phase of Business Plan Initiative and development of National Park Funding Campaign and Loan Buy-Down program. 2001.

2360-80 Natural Resources Defense Council, New York, NY, $139,000. For priorities in areas of Forests, Water, and Wildlife Protection. 2001.

2360-81 Natural Resources Defense Council, New York, NY, $95,000. For priorities in areas of Forests, Water, and Wildlife Protection. 2001.

2360-82 Neuse River Foundation, New Bern, NC, $10,000. For Neuse Riverkeeper/River Protection Program. 2001.

2360-83 North Carolina Aquarium Society, Raleigh, NC, $75,000. For continuing expansion program of North Carolina Aquarium at Pine Knoll Shores. 2001.

2360-84 North Carolina Coastal Federation, Newport, NC, $60,000. For program of CLEAN-NC (Children Linking with the Environment Across the Nation-North Carolina). 2001.

2360-85 North Carolina Outward Bound School, Asheville, NC, $15,000. To continue tuition support for at-risk South Bronx High School students in summer program. 2001.

2360-86 North Carolina Zoological Society, Asheboro, NC, $50,000. To add pre-release spaces to wildlife rehabilitation facility. 2001.

2360-87 Oasis Sanctuary, New York, NY, $10,000. For efforts to promote public awareness, no-fee adoption, spay/neuter program, and volunteer program. 2001.

2360-88 Ocean Conservancy, DC, $50,000. For research and public education efforts to achieve full protection for Archie Carr National Wildlife Refuge for Sea Turtles. 2001.

2360-89 Ocean Conservancy, DC, $50,000. For research and public education efforts to achieve full protection for Archie Carr National Wildlife Refuge for Sea Turtles. 2001.

2360-90 Outer Banks Wildlife Shelter, Pine Knoll Shores, NC, $12,500. For conditional grant to provide veterinary care and housing to injured, orphaned, and sick native birds, mammals, and reptiles each year and to educate children and adults about cruelty to wildlife and habitat destruction. 2001.

2360-91 Outer Banks Wildlife Shelter, Pine Knoll Shores, NC, $12,500. For conditional grant for general operating support. 2001.

2360-92 Pacific Crest Outward Bound School, Portland, Oregon, $27,500. For Pinnacle Scholarship Program for students. 2001.

2360-93 Peace River Refuge and Ranch, Zolfo Springs, FL, $10,000. For tiger enclosure with pond. 2001.

2360-94 Pets Are Loving Support (PALS), Atlanta, GA, $35,000. For financial support to hire fundraiser and miscellaneous start-up supplies for office. 2001.

2360-95 Primarily Primates, San Antonio, TX, $80,000. For general operating support. 2001.

2360-96 Primate Rescue Center, Nicholasville, KY, $10,000. For general operating support. 2001.

2360-97 Public Broadcasting Service (PBS), DC, $25,000. For production of The Sacred Balance, television series on intimate connectedness of humans to all life on earth. 2001.

2360-98 Raccoon Rescue, Jacksonville, FL, $10,000. For expansion of field rescue, rehabilitation, and relocation services and to develop major wildlife rehabilitation facility. 2001.

2360-99 Rachels Network, DC, $10,000. For operating support. 2001.

2360-100 RAFI-USA, Pittsboro, NC, $25,000. For eco-labeling project. 2001.

2360-101 Raptor Trust, Millington, NJ, $40,000. For remediation of new property, upgraded equipment, and new utility vehicle. 2001.

2360-102 Refuge House of Leon County, Tallahassee, FL, $10,000. For construction of kennel where pets may be housed for short-term basis before they are transferred to animal shelter. 2001.

2360-103 Science and Conservation Center, Billings, MT, $10,000. For development of one-inoculation form of contraception for wildlife. 2001.

2360-104 Seeing Eye, Morristown, NJ, $10,000. For scholarships for puppy raisers to attend college. 2001.

2360-105 Smithsonian Environmental Research Center, Edgewater, MD, $22,000. For Internship Program. 2001.

2360-106 Society for the Prevention of Cruelty to Animals of Tompkins County, Ithaca, NY, $300,000. For development of model no-kill shelter. 2001.

2360-107 Society for the Prevention of Cruelty to Animals of Tompkins County, Ithaca, NY, $100,000. For capital and program campaign for building of model no-kill shelter. 2001.

2360-108 Society for the Prevention of Cruelty to Animals of Tompkins County, Ithaca, NY, $50,000. For development of model no-kill shelter. 2001.

2360-109 South Carolina Coastal Conservation League, Beaufort, SC, $25,000. For land use planning and protection of open space. 2001.

2360-110 Southern Environmental Law Center, Charlottesville, VA, $125,000. For work on Southern Appalachian Mountain Forests, Industrial Hog Pollution, and South Atlantic Coast. 2001.

2360-111 Southern Environmental Law Center, Charlottesville, VA, $125,000. For work on Southern Appalachian Mountain Forests, Industrial Hog Pollution, and South Atlantic Coast. 2001.

2360-112 Student Conservation Association, Charlestown, NH, $37,500. For New York Junior Rangers Environmental Education Initiative. 2001.

2360-113 Student Conservation Association, Charlestown, NH, $17,500. For New York Junior Rangers Environmental Education Initiative. 2001.

2360-114 Third Sector New England, Boston, MA, $40,000. For research, grantmaking, publication, distribution, internet strategy, and program evaluation of Environmental Justice Youth Initiative project. 2001.

2360-115 Tribe of Heart, Ithaca, NY, $37,500. For completion of documentary video anthology entitled, Animal People. 2001.

2360-116 Tribe of Heart, Ithaca, NY, $37,500. For completion of documentary video anthology entitled, Animal People. 2001.

2360-117 Tufts University, School of Veterinary Medicine, Medford, MA, $10,000. For research and educational efforts on humane resolution of conflicts with urban and suburban populations of white-tailed deer in Grafton, MA. 2001.

2360-118 United States Public Interest Research Group Education Fund, Atlanta, GA, $10,000. For work on environmental defense and proposed energy plan. 2001.

2360-119 Utica Zoological Society, Utica, NY, $16,830. For Butterfly/Songbird exhibit and Summer Camp scholarships. 2001.

2360-120 Warren Wilson College, Asheville, NC, $125,000. For Environment Leadership Center. 2001.

2360-121 Warren Wilson College, Asheville, NC, $100,000. For Environment Leadership Center. 2001.

2360-122 Warren Wilson College, Asheville, NC, $40,000. For continued support of internships in environmental research coordinated by Environmental Leadership Center. 2001.

2360-123 Wildlife Care Center of the Blue Ridge, Jonas Ridge, NC, $10,000. For general operating support. 2001.

2360-124 Wildlife Conservation Society, Bronx, NY, $125,000. For teacher training in K-12 life science curricula, Expanding Horizons. 2001.

2360-125 Womens Voices for the Earth, Missoula, MT, $30,000. For Coming Clean Campaign. 2001.

2360-126 Working Films, Wilmington, NC, $40,000. For education and outreach of film, Blue Vinyl. 2001.

2360-127 World Wildlife Fund/Conservation Foundation, DC, $30,000. For emergency support for clean up efforts of oil spill off coast of San Cristobal Island. 2001.

2360-128 Yellowstone Park Foundation, Bozeman, MT, $25,433. For Lynx Population Study. 2001.

2361
The Martin Paskus Foundation, Inc.
c/o Richard M. Danziger
720 5th Ave., 15th Fl.
New York, NY 10019

Established in 1950 in NY.
Donor(s): Elsie Paskus,‡ D. Danziger, Richard M. Danziger.
Grantmaker type: Independent foundation
Financial data (yr. ended 12/31/02): Assets, $1,520,053 (M); expenditures, $442,951; qualifying distributions, $426,586; giving activities include $426,322 for 123 grants (high: $40,000; low: $100).
Purpose and activities: Giving primarily for arts and culture and education.
Fields of interest: Museums; Arts; Higher education; Environment; Human services; Religion.
Limitations: Applications not accepted. Giving primarily in CT, MA, and NY. No grants to individuals.
Application information: Contributes only to pre-selected organizations.
Officers: Richard M. Danziger, Pres.; Frederick M. Danziger, Treas.
EIN: 510166266

2362
Josephine Bay Paul and C. Michael Paul Foundation, Inc.
P.O. Box 20218
Park W. Finance Sta.
New York, NY 10025 (212) 932-0408
Contact: Frederick Bay, Chair. and Exec. Dir.
FAX: (212) 932-0316

Incorporated in 1962 in NY.
Donor(s): Josephine Bay Paul.‡

Grantmaker type: Independent foundation
Financial data (yr. ended 12/31/01): Assets, $50,418,380 (M); expenditures, $2,911,309; qualifying distributions, $2,458,462; giving activities include $1,889,850 for 135 grants (high: $400,000; low: $100; average: $1,000–$100,000) and $150,000 for 6 grants to individuals (high: $30,000; low: $15,000; average: $15,000–$30,000).
Purpose and activities: Support for organizations demonstrating or developing pre-collegiate educational restructuring; support of the professional development of chamber ensembles and their membership organizations; support projects which reinforce the centrality of the arts in pre-collegiate curricula. The foundation also has an interest in projects seeking to sustain the earth's biodiversity. In this area, no unsolicited proposals will be accepted.
Fields of interest: Arts education; Music; Education, research; Elementary school/education; Secondary school/education; Education; Environment.
Types of support: General/operating support; Continuing support; Program development; Conferences/seminars; Seed money; Research; Technical assistance; Matching/challenge support.
Limitations: Giving on a national basis. No support for sectarian religious programs, or to other than publicly recognized charities. No grants to individuals (other than the Bio diversity Leadership Awards) or for building campaigns.
Publications: Program policy statement.
Application information: Application form not required.
  Initial approach: Proposal
  Copies of proposal: 1
  Deadline(s): Postmarked Mar. 1, Sept. 1, and Dec. 1
  Board meeting date(s): Feb., May, and Oct.
  Final notification: Within 30 days following board meeting
Officers and Directors:* Frederick Bay,* Chair. and Exec. Dir.; Synnova B. Hayes,* Pres. and Treas.; Hans A. Ege,* V.P.; Robert Ashton, Secy.; Rebecca Adamson; Corinne Steel.
Number of staff: 1 full-time professional; 2 part-time professional; 2 part-time support.
EIN: 131991717

2363
Pearson-Rappaport Foundation
c/o The Ayco Co., LP
P.O. Box 15014
Albany, NY 12212-5014

Established in 1997 in CT.
Donor(s): Andrall E. Pearson, Jill P. Rappaport, Joanne P. Pearson.
Grantmaker type: Independent foundation
Financial data (yr. ended 12/31/02): Assets, $2,041,420 (M); expenditures, $207,272; qualifying distributions, $205,983; giving activities include $206,110 for 49 grants (high: $38,685; low: $225).
Purpose and activities: Giving primarily for education, animal welfare, and cancer.
Fields of interest: Education; Veterinary medicine, hospital; Health organizations, association; Human services; Women.
Limitations: Applications not accepted. Giving on a national basis. No grants to individuals.

Application information: Contributes only to pre-selected organizations.
Trustees: Andrall E. Pearson; Joanne P. Pearson; Alan H. Rappaport; Jill P. Rappaport.
EIN: 061484929

2364
Peco Foundation
c/o DDK & Co.
1500 Broadway
New York, NY 10036
Contact: Jeffrey S. Feinman, C.P.A.

Established in 1969.
Donor(s): Catherine G. Curran.
Grantmaker type: Independent foundation
Financial data (yr. ended 12/31/02): Assets, $8,431,064 (M); expenditures, $183,239; qualifying distributions, $175,210; giving activities include $173,035 for grants.
Purpose and activities: Giving for arts and culture, education, health associations and human services.
Fields of interest: Arts; Education; Botanical/horticulture/landscape services; Health organizations, association; Human services; Children, services; Women.
Types of support: General/operating support.
Limitations: Applications not accepted. Giving primarily in New York, NY. No grants to individuals.
Application information: Contributes only to pre-selected organizations.
  Board meeting date(s): Dec.
Trustee: Catherine G. Curran.
Number of staff: None.
EIN: 237031675

2365
Donald A. Pels Charitable Trust
c/o Pelsco, Inc.
375 Park Ave., Ste. 3303
New York, NY 10152

Established in 1992 in NY.
Donor(s): Donald A. Pels.
Grantmaker type: Independent foundation
Financial data (yr. ended 12/31/02): Assets, $27,443,309 (M); gifts received, $2,065,177; expenditures, $1,425,388; qualifying distributions, $1,302,688; giving activities include $1,331,524 for 124 grants (high: $300,000; low: $100).
Purpose and activities: Giving primarily to cultural institutions and for education.
Fields of interest: Media/communications; Performing arts; Arts; Higher education; Natural resources; Hospitals (general); Human services.
Types of support: General/operating support.
Limitations: Applications not accepted. Giving primarily in NY. No grants to individuals.
Application information: Contributes only to pre-selected organizations.
Trustee: Donald A. Pels.
EIN: 136998091

2366
Albert Penick Fund
c/o JPMorgan Chase Bank
1211 6th Ave., 34th Fl.
New York, NY 10036
Contact: K. Philip Dresdner, Tr.
Application address: 65 S. Main St., Pennington, NJ 08534

Trust established in 1951 in NY.
Donor(s): A.D. Penick,‡ Mrs. Albert D. Penick.
Grantmaker type: Independent foundation
Financial data (yr. ended 12/31/02): Assets, $3,424,856 (M); expenditures, $446,245; qualifying distributions, $389,380; giving activities include $379,250 for 40 grants (high: $100,000; low: $1,000).
Purpose and activities: Giving primarily for higher education, including pharmacy and nursing schools.
Fields of interest: Higher education; Education; Natural resources; Animal welfare; Health care.
Limitations: Giving primarily in CT, MA, NJ, and NY.
Application information: Application form not required.
  Initial approach: Letter
  Deadline(s): None
Trustees: K. Philip Dresdner; V. Susan Penick.
EIN: 136161137

2367
Penzance Foundation ▼
237 Park Ave., 21st Fl.
New York, NY 10017 (212) 551-3559
Contact: John M. Emery, V.P.

Established in 1981 in DE.
Donor(s): Edna McConnell Clark.‡
Grantmaker type: Independent foundation
Financial data (yr. ended 04/30/02): Assets, $56,087,767 (M); expenditures, $3,325,453; qualifying distributions, $3,052,192; giving activities include $3,008,250 for 23 grants (high: $810,750; low: $1,000; average: $5,000–$100,000).
Purpose and activities: The foundation's grantmaking reflects personal preferences of donor.
Fields of interest: Elementary/secondary education; Higher education; Environment, land resources; Environmental education; Hospitals (general); Marine science.
Types of support: General/operating support.
Limitations: Applications not accepted. No grants to individuals.
Officers and Trustees:* Hays Clark,* Pres.; John M. Emery,* V.P. and Secy.; James McConnell Clark,* V.P. and Treas.
Number of staff: 1.
EIN: 133081557

2368
The Perkin Fund
c/o Morris & McVeigh
767 3rd Ave.
New York, NY 10017
Contact: Robert S. Perkin, Tr.
Application address: 200 Connecticut Ave., 5th Fl., Norwalk, CT 06854

Established in 1967 in NY.

Donor(s): Richard S. Perkin.‡
Grantmaker type: Independent foundation
Financial data (yr. ended 12/31/01): Assets, $30,132,342 (M); expenditures, $1,952,668; qualifying distributions, $1,525,796; giving activities include $1,489,795 for 24 grants (high: $300,000; low: $10,000).
Purpose and activities: Support for advanced scientific education, especially for astronomy, optics and bio-medicine, medical research, especially in bio-medicine, and giving for the performing arts.
Fields of interest: Performing arts; Music; Arts; Higher education; Animal welfare; Hospitals (general); Biomedicine; Medical research, institute; Physical/earth sciences; Astronomy; Biological sciences.
Types of support: General/operating support; Continuing support; Annual campaigns; Capital campaigns; Building/renovation; Equipment; Emergency funds; Program development; Conferences/seminars; Fellowships; Matching/challenge support.
Limitations: Giving primarily in CT, MA, and NY. No grants to individuals; no loans.
Publications: Annual report, Financial statement, Informational brochure (including application guidelines).
Application information: Application form not required.
  Initial approach: Letter
  Copies of proposal: 2
  Deadline(s): Mar. 15 or Sept. 15
  Board meeting date(s): May and Nov.
Trustees: James G. Baker; Kristina P. Davison; John M. Gray; Matthew E.P. Gray; Winifred P. Gray; Peter W. Oldershaw; Christopher T. Perkin; Nicolas R. Perkin; Robert S. Perkin; Howard Phipps, Jr.
Number of staff: 1 part-time professional.
EIN: 136222498

2369
The Pesky Family Foundation, Inc.
59 E. 54th St.
New York, NY 10022 (212) 339-7745
Contact: Wendy Pesky or Alan Pesky, Trustees
Application address: 437 Madison Ave., New York, NY 10022

Established in 1989 in NY.
Donor(s): Wendy Pesky.
Grantmaker type: Independent foundation
Financial data (yr. ended 10/31/02): Assets, $1,447,220 (M); gifts received, $49,664; expenditures, $250,017; qualifying distributions, $175,014; giving activities include $175,014 for 44 grants (high: $116,267; low: $50).
Purpose and activities: Giving to the arts, education, and human services.
Fields of interest: Arts; Education; Natural resources; Health organizations, association; Human services.
Limitations: Giving primarily in CT, ID, and New York, NY. No grants to individuals.
Trustees: Alan Pesky; Gregory Pesky; Wendy Pesky; Heidi Worcester.
EIN: 223008373

2370
The Pevaroff Cohn Family Foundation
c/o Goldman Sachs & Co.
85 Broad St., Tax Dept.
New York, NY 10004

Donor(s): Gary D. Cohn.
Grantmaker type: Independent foundation
Financial data (yr. ended 08/31/02): Assets, $5,755,405 (M); gifts received, $1,178,428; expenditures, $216,040; qualifying distributions, $183,491; giving activities include $180,661 for 28 grants (high: $50,000; low: $100).
Fields of interest: Museums; Education; Natural resources; Family planning; Health organizations; Jewish federated giving programs; Jewish agencies & temples.
Limitations: Applications not accepted. Giving primarily in NY. No grants to individuals; no loans or scholarships.
Application information: Contributes only to pre-selected organizations.
Trustees: Gary D. Cohn; Lisa Pevaroff Cohn; James Riley, Jr.
EIN: 133797393

2371
The Picheny Charitable Trust
322 Central Park West, Ste. 6B
New York, NY 10025-7629

Established in 1997 in NY.
Donor(s): Stanley Picheny, Vivian Picheny.
Grantmaker type: Independent foundation
Financial data (yr. ended 12/31/01): Assets, $700,548 (M); expenditures, $108,419; qualifying distributions, $108,348; giving activities include $108,419 for 18 grants (high: $50,518; low: $400).
Fields of interest: Education; Animals/wildlife, preservation/protection; Children/youth, services.
Limitations: Applications not accepted. No grants to individuals.
Application information: Contributes only to pre-selected organizations.
Trustees: Lonn Berney; Stanley Picheny; Vivian Picheny.
EIN: 137114720

2372
Allen F. Pierce Foundation
33 Gates Cir., Apt. A
Buffalo, NY 14209
Contact: Jean M. Elfvin, Pres.

Grantmaker type: Independent foundation
Financial data (yr. ended 12/31/02): Assets, $1,757 (M); expenditures, $97,248; qualifying distributions, $96,303; giving activities include $97,237 for 31 grants (high: $15,000; low: $250).
Purpose and activities: Giving for the arts, animal welfare, hospitals, and human services.
Fields of interest: Arts; Libraries/library science; Animals/wildlife; Hospitals (general); Human services; Christian agencies & churches.
Limitations: Giving limited to Bradford County, PA. No grants to individuals.
Application information: Application form not required.
  Deadline(s): None

Officer and Directors:* Jean Margaret Elfvin,* Pres.; Ann D. DiLauro; Carole DiLauro; Hon. John T. Elfvin; Janet A. Knapp.
Agent: Wachovia Bank, N.A.
Number of staff: None.
EIN: 232044356

2373
Pinewood Foundation
c/o Rockefeller & Co.
30 Rockefeller Plz., Rm. 5600
New York, NY 10112

Incorporated in 1956 in NY as Celeste and Armand Bartos Foundation.
Donor(s): Celeste G. Bartos, D.S. and R.H. Gottesman Foundation.
Grantmaker type: Independent foundation
Financial data (yr. ended 09/30/02): Assets, $423,051 (M); expenditures, $2,138,817; qualifying distributions, $2,084,444; giving activities include $2,037,368 for 35 grants (high: $271,620; low: $250).
Purpose and activities: Giving primarily for the arts and cultural organizations, early childhood development, and environment.
Fields of interest: Film/video; Museums (art); Higher education; Medical school/education; Natural resources; Medical research, institute; Youth development, services; Children/youth, services.
Limitations: Applications not accepted. Giving on a national basis, with some emphasis on the greater metropolitan New York, NY, area. No grants to individuals.
Application information: Contributes only to pre-selected organizations.
Officers and Directors:* Celeste G. Bartos,* Pres.; Jonathan Altman, V.P.; Kathleen Altman, V.P.; Adam Bartos, V.P.; Michael Lerner, V.P.; Penny Fujiko Willgerodt, Secy.-Treas.
Number of staff: None.
EIN: 136101581

2374
Henry B. Plant Memorial Fund, Inc.
c/o U.S. Trust
114 W. 47th St., 8th Fl.
New York, NY 10036-1532
Contact: Andrew D. Lane, V.P.
FAX: (212) 852-3377

Incorporated in 1947 in NY.
Donor(s): Amy P. Statter.
Grantmaker type: Independent foundation
Financial data (yr. ended 12/31/02): Assets, $10,097,883 (M); expenditures, $663,497; qualifying distributions, $612,611; giving activities include $619,500 for 47 grants (high: $25,000; low: $250).
Purpose and activities: Giving primarily for arts and culture, education, health, and human services.
Fields of interest: Museums; Performing arts; Music; Arts; Higher education; Law school/education; Education; Environment; Health organizations, association; Human services; Children/youth, services; Family services; Federated giving programs.
Limitations: Applications not accepted. No grants to individuals.

Application information: Contributes only to pre-selected organizations.
Officers and Directors:* Mrs. J. Phillip Lee,* Pres.; Mrs. David C. Oxman,* V.P.
Advisor: U.S. Trust.
EIN: 136077327

2375
Plymouth Hill Foundation
P.O. Box 687
Millbrook, NY 12545
Contact: Robert Goodstein, Pres.

Established in 1993 in NY.
Grantmaker type: Independent foundation
Financial data (yr. ended 09/30/02): Assets, $2,993,792 (M); expenditures, $187,351; qualifying distributions, $118,562; giving activities include $120,000 for 22 grants (high: $17,500; low: $1,000).
Purpose and activities: Giving primarily for education, and for medical and community services.
Fields of interest: Museums (natural history); Historic preservation/historical societies; Education; Environment, research; Health care; Housing/shelter; Community development; Science, research.
Types of support: General/operating support; Continuing support; Annual campaigns; Capital campaigns; Building/renovation; Endowments; Seed money; Research.
Limitations: Applications not accepted. Giving primarily in Dutchess County, NY. No grants to individuals.
Application information: Unsolicited requests for funds not accepted.
Officers and Directors:* Robert Goodstein,* Pres.; Gillian Goodwin,* V.P. and Secy.; Jeanne Goodwin,* V.P.; Andrew Goodwin,* Treas.
Number of staff: None.
EIN: 223136685

2376
The Mrs. Cheever Porter Foundation
c/o Adams & Becker, CPAs
22 Oakwood Rd.
Huntington, NY 11743
Contact: Clifford E. Starkins, Dir.

Established in 1962 in NY.
Grantmaker type: Independent foundation
Financial data (yr. ended 06/30/02): Assets, $2,787,892 (M); expenditures, $437,277; qualifying distributions, $393,465; giving activities include $386,500 for 63 grants (high: $40,000; low: $1,000).
Purpose and activities: Giving primarily for higher education with emphasis on veterinary schools; support also for services for the blind, cultural programs, and animal welfare.
Fields of interest: Arts; Higher education; Animal welfare; Hospitals (general); Human services; Disabled.
Limitations: Giving primarily in NY.
Application information:
Initial approach: Letter
Deadline(s): None
Directors: George Marchese; Elizabeth Peters; Clifford E. Starkins.
EIN: 136093181

2377
Victor H. Potamkin Charitable Trust
798 11th Ave.
New York, NY 10019

Established in 1995 in NY.
Donor(s): Victor Potamkin.‡
Grantmaker type: Independent foundation
Financial data (yr. ended 05/31/02): Assets, $13,340,261 (M); expenditures, $1,664,847; qualifying distributions, $1,547,487; giving activities include $1,552,252 for 92 grants (high: $650,000; low: $200).
Purpose and activities: Funding primarily for federated giving programs. Funding also for arts and culture, human services, health care, and religious organizations.
Fields of interest: Arts; Animal welfare; Health care; Medical research, institute; Human services; Federated giving programs; Religion.
Limitations: Applications not accepted. Giving on a national basis, with emphasis on FL, and PA. No grants to individuals.
Application information: Contributes only to pre-selected organizations.
Trustees: Peter Paris; Alan Potamkin; Robert Potamkin.
EIN: 137066009

2378
The Prospect Hill Foundation, Inc. ▼
99 Park Ave., Ste. 2220
New York, NY 10016-1601 (212) 370-1165
FAX: (212) 599-6282; URL: http://fdncenter.org/grantmaker/prospecthill/

Incorporated in 1960 in NY; absorbed The Frederick W. Beinecke Fund in 1983.
Donor(s): William S. Beinecke.
Grantmaker type: Independent foundation
Financial data (yr. ended 06/30/03): Assets, $60,591,056 (M); expenditures, $4,419,042; qualifying distributions, $3,426,851; giving activities include $3,132,250 for grants and $129,889 for 216 employee matching gifts.
Purpose and activities: The foundation has a broad range of philanthropic interests, including education, environmental protection, arts and culture, international affairs, wildlife preservation, and health care.
Fields of interest: Natural resources; Family planning; Arms control.
International interests: Latin America.
Types of support: General/operating support; Continuing support; Capital campaigns; Program development; Seed money; Consulting services; Employee matching gifts; Matching/challenge support.
Limitations: Giving primarily in the northeastern U.S., including NY and RI. No support for religious activities. No grants to individuals, or for research.
Publications: Grants list, Informational brochure (including application guidelines).
Application information: Accepts NYRAG Common Application Form. Application form not required.
Initial approach: Letter (no more than 3 pages)
Copies of proposal: 2
Deadline(s): None
Board meeting date(s): 4 times annually
Final notification: 4 weeks

Officers and Directors:* William S. Beinecke,* Chair.; Elizabeth G. Beinecke,* Pres.; Frederick W. Beinecke,* V.P.; John B. Beinecke,* V.P.; Robert J. Barletta, Treas.; Frances Beinecke Elston; Sarah Beinecke Richardson.
Number of staff: 1 full-time professional; 2 full-time support.
EIN: 136075567
Recent environmental and animal welfare grants:
2378-1 Adirondack Council, Elizabethtown, NY, $50,000. Toward Forever Wild capital campaign. 2002.
2378-2 Audubon Society, National, New York, NY, $35,000. Toward Important Bird Areas Program. 2002.
2378-3 Bank Information Center, DC, $15,000. To improve multi-lateral lending institutions' policies and projects in the Caribbean and Latin America. 2002.
2378-4 Cape Cod Commercial Hook Fishermens Association, S.S. Shanty Community Fisheries Action Center, West Chatham, MA, $20,000. 2002.
2378-5 Center for Coastal Studies, Provincetown, MA, $15,000. To monitor impact of Boston Outfall on water quality in Cape Cod Bay. 2002.
2378-6 Central Park Conservancy, New York, NY, $25,000. Toward salary of zone gardener to maintain Harlem Meer. 2002.
2378-7 Columbia Land Conservancy, Chatham, NY, $15,000. Toward staff salaries. 2002.
2378-8 Conservation Law Foundation, Boston, MA, $20,000. Toward Brayton Point Clean-Up Campaign. 2002.
2378-9 Darien Nature Center, Darien, CT, $12,500. Toward construction of nature center. 2002.
2378-10 Environmental Leadership Program, Cambridge, MA, $25,000. For general support. 2002.
2378-11 Environmental League of Massachusetts, Boston, MA, $12,500. To improve implementation of Rivers Protection Act. 2002.
2378-12 Global Forest Policy Project, DC, $10,000. For salary of coordinator of Global Forest Watch in Venezuela. 2002.
2378-13 Greater Newark Conservancy, Newark, NJ, $50,000. Toward creation of Outdoor Learning Center. 2002.
2378-14 Hawk Mountain Sanctuary Association, Kempton, PA, $50,000. For Internship Endowment Fund. 2002.
2378-15 Hawk Mountain Sanctuary Association, Kempton, PA, $10,000. For general support. 2002.
2378-16 Horticultural Society of New York, New York, NY, $25,000. For general support. 2002.
2378-17 Island Conservation and Ecology Group, Davenport, CA, $20,000. Toward protection of island ecosystems in northwest Mexico. 2002.
2378-18 Land Trust Alliance, Saratoga Springs, NY, $12,000. To promote private land conservation. 2002.
2378-19 Natural Resources Defense Council, New York, NY, $35,000. Toward Ocean Protection Initiative. 2002.
2378-20 Natural Resources Defense Council, New York, NY, $30,000. Toward Nuclear

Conflict Simulation and Education Project. 2002.

2378-21 Nature Conservancy, Arlington, VA, $50,000. Toward acquisition of Round Lake, Bog Lake and Clear Pond, and Shingle Shanty Pond in Adirondacks, New York. 2002.

2378-22 New York Botanical Garden, Bronx, NY, $25,000. Toward Institute of Economic Botany. 2002.

2378-23 New York Conservation Education Fund, New York, NY, $30,000. For participation in planning efforts to rebuild lower Manhattan. 2002.

2378-24 New York Conservation Education Fund, New York, NY, $20,000. Toward administrative expenses of Waterfront Park Coalition. 2002.

2378-25 New York Conservation Education Fund, New York, NY, $20,000. Toward administrative expenses of Waterfront Park Coalition. 2002.

2378-26 Nuclear Control Institute, DC, $25,000. To discourage international use of plutonium and highly enriched uranium in civilian power and research programs. 2002.

2378-27 Open Space Institute, New York, NY, $12,500. For Friends of Hudson to challenge proposed Saint Lawrence Cement facility in Greenport, New York. 2002.

2378-28 Rainforest Alliance, New York, NY, $10,000. Toward business plan for Conservation Agriculture Program in Central and South America. 2002.

2378-29 RARE Center for Tropical Conservation, Arlington, VA, $15,000. To advance conservation education programs in Sierra de Manantlan Biosphere and El Triunfo Biosphere in Mexico. 2002.

2378-30 Save the Bay, Providence, RI, $15,000. Toward protection of Narragansett Bay and its watershed. 2002.

2378-31 Scenic Hudson, Poughkeepsie, NY, $12,500. For challenge grant for Saint Lawrence Cement facility in Greenport, New York. 2002.

2378-32 Trust for Public Land, New York, NY, $10,000. Toward expanding protected land in Hudson Highlands. 2002.

2378-33 University of New Hampshire, Durham, NH, $15,000. To evaluate impact of intensive, rotational sheep grazing on eradicating target plant species under power lines. 2002.

2378-34 University of Rhode Island Foundation, Narragansett, RI, $25,000. To foster sustainable development on Aquidneck Island. 2002.

2378-35 Wave Hill, Bronx, NY, $25,000. For general support. 2002.

2378-36 West Harlem Environmental Action, New York, NY, $25,000. Toward institutional development. 2002.

2378-37 Wilderness Society, DC, $15,000. Toward Northern Forest Campaign. 2002.

2378-38 Wildlife Conservation Society, Bronx, NY, $50,000. Toward Geographic Information and Analysis Program. 2002.

2378-39 World Resources Institute, DC, $30,000. Toward carbon-sequestration sustainability project. 2002.

2378-40 Yale University, School of Forestry and Environmental Studies, New Haven, CT, $100,000. 2002.

2379
Rainforest Alliance, Inc.

665 Broadway, Ste. 500
New York, NY 10012-2331 (212) 677-1900
Contact: Tensie Whelan, Exec. Dir.
Additional tel.: (888) MY-EARTH; FAX: (212) 677-2187; E-mail: canopy@ra.org; URL: http://www.rainforest-alliance.org

Established in 1987 in NY.
Grantmaker type: Public charity
Financial data (yr. ended 06/30/00): Revenue, $4,144,926; assets, $1,931,578 (L); gifts received, $2,448,296; expenditures, $4,091,850; program services expenses, $3,282,975; giving activities include $141,273 for 22 grants.
Purpose and activities: The mission of the alliance is to protect ecosystems and the people and wildlife that live within them by implementing better business practices for biodiversity conservation and sustainability companies, cooperatives, and landowners that participate in our programs meet strict standards for protecting the environment, wildlife, workers, and local communities.
Fields of interest: Environment, research; Environment, public education; Natural resources; Environment, forests; Environment.
Types of support: General/operating support; Land acquisition; Emergency funds; Program development; Seed money; Fellowships; Program-related investments/loans.
Limitations: Giving on an international basis, with emphasis on the Selva Maya of Belize, Guatemala, and Mexico.
Application information: See Web site for application form and guidelines. Application form required.
Officers and Directors:* Daniel R. Katz,* Chair.; Labeeb M. Abboud,* Vice-Chair.; Tensie Whelan, Exec. Dir.; Kerri Anderson-Corn; Jill Blanchard; Noel Brown, Ph.D.; Henry P. Davison II; Robert M. Hallman; David L. Hendrickson; Diane Jukofsky; and 12 additional directors.
EIN: 133377893

2380
The Harold K. Raisler Foundation, Inc.

c/o Eisner & Lubin, LLP
444 Madison Ave.
New York, NY 10022

Incorporated in 1957 in NY.
Grantmaker type: Independent foundation
Financial data (yr. ended 12/31/02): Assets, $2,006,552 (M); expenditures, $98,846; qualifying distributions, $93,357; giving activities include $90,375 for 59 grants (high: $10,000; low: $100).
Purpose and activities: Giving for Jewish federated giving programs, higher education, performing art centers, children and human services, and for environmental conservation.
Fields of interest: Performing arts; Arts; Higher education; Environment; Health care; Human services; Children/youth, services; Jewish federated giving programs; Jewish agencies & temples.
Types of support: General/operating support; Capital campaigns.

Limitations: Applications not accepted. Giving primarily in New York, NY. No grants to individuals.
Application information: Contributes only to pre-selected organizations.
Board meeting date(s): May
Directors: Aline Raisler; Jeanne Raisler.
EIN: 136094406

2381
Rauch Foundation

229 7th St., Ste. 306
Garden City, NY 11530-5766 (516) 873-9808
Contact: John McNally
FAX: (516) 873-0708; E-mail: info@rauchfoundation.org; URL: http://www.rauchfoundation.org

Incorporated in 1960 in NY.
Donor(s): Philip Rauch, Louis J. Rauch,‡ Ruth T. Rauch, Philip J. Rauch, Nancy R. Douzinas.
Grantmaker type: Independent foundation
Financial data (yr. ended 11/30/02): Assets, $35,098,121 (M); gifts received, $331,690; expenditures, $2,257,535; qualifying distributions, $2,112,038; giving activities include $1,690,975 for 84 grants (high: $102,405; low: $250).
Purpose and activities: The foundation concentrates the majority of its grantmaking on prevention programs that benefit young children (ages birth to 6) and their families in Nassau County, NY. The foundation has small programs on Long Island, NY, concerning the environment and community development. The foundation also has an environmental program in MD.
Fields of interest: Early childhood education; Environment; Family services; Community development.
Types of support: Program development; Conferences/seminars; Seed money; Technical assistance; Consulting services; Program evaluation; Matching/challenge support.
Limitations: Giving primarily in Nassau and Suffolk counties, NY; some giving also in MD. Generally, no grants to individuals, or for operating expenses, capital expenditures, annual campaigns, or endowment funds.
Publications: Annual report (including application guidelines), Grants list.
Application information: NYRAG Common Application form accepted. The foundation requests that organizations not send videotapes. Application form not required.
Initial approach: Concept paper (1 to 2 pages)
Copies of proposal: 1
Deadline(s): None
Board meeting date(s): Feb., June, and Oct.
Final notification: Within 3 months
Officers and Directors:* Nancy R. Douzinas,* Pres.; Philip Rauch, V.P. and Secy.-Treas.; Gerald I. Lustig,* V.P.; Philip J. Rauch, V.P.; Lance E. Lindblom; Brooke W. Mahoney; Lisa Mars; Ruth T. Rauch; John Wenzel.
Number of staff: 1 full-time professional; 1 part-time professional; 2 full-time support.
EIN: 112001717

2382
John & Cynthia Reed Foundation
c/o U.S. Trust
114 W. 47th St., 8th Fl.
New York, NY 10036
Contact: Andrew Lane, V.P.

Established in 2000 in NY.
Donor(s): John S. Reed.
Grantmaker type: Independent foundation
Financial data (yr. ended 12/31/02): Assets,
$72,824,800 (M); gifts received, $2,455,277;
expenditures, $4,291,610; qualifying
distributions, $4,155,730; giving activities
include $4,155,730 for 28 grants (high:
$1,000,000; low: $10,000).
Purpose and activities: Giving primarily for
education and arts and culture.
Fields of interest: Museums (art); Theater;
Higher education; University; Animals/wildlife,
preservation/protection; Parks/playgrounds; Big
Brothers/Big Sisters.
Types of support: General/operating support;
Continuing support; Annual campaigns; Capital
campaigns; Building/renovation; Land
acquisition; Program development.
Limitations: Applications not accepted. Giving
on a national basis, with some emphasis on
Princeton, NJ, and the greater metropolitan New
York, NY, area.
Application information: Unsolicited requests
for funds not accepted.
Trustees: Cynthia Reed; John S. Reed.
Number of staff: 1 part-time professional; 1
part-time support.
EIN: 137219392

2383
Reiss Family Foundation
c/o Georgica Advisors, LLC
152 W. 57th St., 46th Fl.
New York, NY 10019
Contact: Richard Reiss, Jr., Tr.

Established in 1987 in NY.
Donor(s): Richard Reiss.
Grantmaker type: Independent foundation
Financial data (yr. ended 12/31/02): Assets,
$2,136,222 (M); expenditures, $137,531;
qualifying distributions, $131,464; giving
activities include $125,396 for 76 grants (high:
$15,000; low: $100).
Fields of interest: Arts; Higher education;
Education; Natural resources; Health
organizations, association; Jewish agencies &
temples.
Limitations: Giving primarily in New York, NY.
No grants to individuals.
Application information:
   Initial approach: Letter
Trustees: Bonnie Reiss; Richard Reiss, Jr.
EIN: 133383095

2384
The Resource Foundation, Inc.
P.O. Box 3006
Larchmont, NY 10538 (914) 834-5810
Contact: Loren Finnell, Exec. Dir.
E-mail: info@resourcefnd.org,
resourcefnd@msn.com; URL: http://
www.resourcefnd.org

Established in 1987.
Grantmaker type: Public charity
Financial data (yr. ended 12/31/02): Revenue,
$2,010,212; assets, $364,758 (M); gifts
received, $1,854,436; expenditures,
$2,073,837; program services expenses,
$1,904,054; giving activities include
$1,596,263 for 62 grants (high: $214,000; low:
$2,500).
Purpose and activities: The foundation
administers donor-advised funds as well as
provides representation, networking, training,
technical assistance and fundraising to Latin
American private development organizations
(PDOs) that implement self-help projects in the
areas of microenterprise, environmental
conservation, sustainable agriculture, basic
education, low-cost housing and primary
healthcare.
Fields of interest: Education; Health care;
Natural resources; Agriculture; Housing/shelter;
International development; International
agricultural development; International
economic development; Community
development, small businesses.
International interests: Latin America.
Types of support: Technical assistance.
Limitations: Giving limited to Latin America.
Publications: Financial statement, Informational
brochure (including application guidelines),
Newsletter.
Application information:
   Board meeting date(s): 5 times a year
Officers and Directors:* Pedro Lichtings,*
Chair.; Daryl Hunt,* Secy.; Larry Prince,* Treas.;
Loren Finnell, Exec. Dir.; and 18 additional
directors.
Number of staff: 4 full-time professional; 1
part-time professional.
EIN: 133421446

2385
Anne S. Richardson Fund
(formerly Anne S. Richardson Charitable Trust)
c/o JPMorgan Chase Bank
345 Park Ave., 4th Fl.
New York, NY 10154 (212) 464-2443
Contact: Monica Neal, V.P., JPMorgan Chase
Bank
FAX: (212) 464-2305; URL: http://fdncenter.org/
grantmaker/richardson/

Trust established in 1965 in CT.
Donor(s): Anne S. Richardson.‡
Grantmaker type: Independent foundation
Financial data (yr. ended 07/31/02): Assets,
$12,069,996 (M); expenditures, $749,730;
qualifying distributions, $678,536; giving
activities include $675,000 for grants (high:
$25,000; low: $1,000).
Purpose and activities: Funding interests include
1) eight organizations recommended by the
donor; 2) programs in Ridgefield, CT, that assist
lower-income people or are of broad interest to
the community; and 3) programs in Fairfield
County, CT, that promote the independence of
women, support the lesbian and gay
community, foster youth development, or
enhance the natural beautification of
communities through parks or gardens.
Fields of interest:
Botanical/horticulture/landscape services;
Parks/playgrounds; Youth development;

Community development; Women;
Gays/lesbians; Economically disadvantaged.
Types of support: General/operating support;
Capital campaigns; Program development.
Limitations: Giving primarily in western CT. No
support for private foundations or organizations
lacking 501(c)(3) status. No grants to
individuals; no loans.
Application information: See foundation Web
site for application guidelines and requirements.
Application form not required.
   Initial approach: Proposal
   Copies of proposal: 1
   Deadline(s): Mar. 1
   Board meeting date(s): June
   Final notification: July 31
Trustee: JPMorgan Chase Bank.
Number of staff: 2 full-time support.
EIN: 136192516

2386
The Riggio Foundation ▼
c/o Robinson, Silverman, Pearce, et. al.
1290 Ave. of the Americas
New York, NY 10104
Contact: J. Levin

Established in 1994 in NY.
Donor(s): Leonard Riggio.
Grantmaker type: Independent foundation
Financial data (yr. ended 08/31/01): Assets,
$52,064,951 (M); expenditures, $5,257,112;
qualifying distributions, $5,142,048; giving
activities include $5,142,048 for 107 grants
(high: $3,775,000; low: $30; average:
$1,000–$100,000).
Purpose and activities: Giving primarily for the
welfare of children, the protection and welfare
of animals, and to health associations including
hospitals and research centers; some giving to
the arts and civil liberties.
Fields of interest: Multipurpose
centers/programs; Natural resources; Animal
welfare; Hospitals (general); Health
organizations, association; Housing/shelter;
Athletics/sports, Special Olympics; Human
services; Children/youth, services; Family
services; Civil liberties, advocacy; Mutual aid
societies.
Types of support: General/operating support;
Capital campaigns.
Limitations: Applications not accepted. Giving
primarily in NY. No grants to individuals.
Application information: Contributes only to
pre-selected organizations.
Trustees: Leonard Riggio; Louise Riggio.
EIN: 137039631

2387
The Ripple Foundation
c/o Wien & Malkin, LLP
60 E. 42nd St.
New York, NY 10165
Contact: Richard Shapiro

Established in 1999 in DE.
Donor(s): Anthony E. Malkin, Rachelle B.
Malkin.
Grantmaker type: Independent foundation
Financial data (yr. ended 12/31/02): Assets,
$1,157,104 (M); gifts received, $72,238;
expenditures, $208,469; qualifying distributions,

$205,551; giving activities include $206,200 for 31 grants (high: $80,000; low: $250).

Fields of interest: Arts; Elementary/secondary education; Higher education; Education; Natural resources; Children/youth, services; Federated giving programs.

Application information:
Initial approach: Letter
Deadline(s): None

Officer: Anthony E. Malkin, Pres.

Director: Rachelle B. Malkin.

EIN: 134081347

2388
Ripplewood Foundation, Inc.
1 Rockefeller Plz., 32nd Fl.
New York, NY 10020

Established in 1997 in DE and NY.

Donor(s): Ripplewood Holdings LLC.

Grantmaker type: Company-sponsored foundation

Financial data (yr. ended 12/31/00): Assets, $771,361 (M); expenditures, $540,903; qualifying distributions, $498,903; giving activities include $508,725 for 57 grants (high: $50,000; low: $125).

Purpose and activities: Giving primarily for education, health associations, social services, and children and youth services.

Fields of interest: Arts; Higher education; Education; Natural resources; Health organizations, association; Human services; Children/youth, services.

Limitations: Applications not accepted. Giving on a national basis, with some emphasis on NY. No grants to individuals.

Application information: Contributes only to pre-selected organizations.

Officers: Timothy C. Collins, Pres.; John M. Duryea, Secy.

EIN: 522036080

2389
RMF Family Fund, Inc.
c/o W. Michael Reickert, The Ayco Co. LP
P.O. Box 8019
Ballston Spa, NY 12020-8019

Established in 1997 in NY.

Donor(s): Richard M. Furlaud.

Grantmaker type: Independent foundation

Financial data (yr. ended 12/31/02): Assets, $1,214,211 (M); expenditures, $274,105; qualifying distributions, $272,502; giving activities include $272,550 for 26 grants (high: $150,750; low: $100).

Purpose and activities: Giving primarily for arts and education and to medical organizations.

Fields of interest: Performing arts; Arts; Higher education; Education; Animal welfare; Hospitals (general).

Limitations: Applications not accepted. Giving primarily in FL and NY. No grants to individuals.

Application information: Contributes only to pre-selected organizations.

Officers: Richard M. Furlaud, Pres.; Isabel P. Furlaud, V.P.; Therese A. Ninesling, Secy.

Director: Tamsin Rachofsky.

EIN: 133931623

2390
The Evelyn & Paul Robinson Family Foundation
c/o Bessemer Trust Co., N.A.
630 5th Ave., 34th Fl.
New York, NY 10111
Contact: Kathleen J. Fraher, Tr.
Application address: 395 Bay Rd., Queensbury, NY 12804

Established in 1999 in NY.

Donor(s): Evelyn M. Robinson Trust, E.M. Robinson Charitable Lead Annuity Trust.

Grantmaker type: Independent foundation

Financial data (yr. ended 04/30/02): Assets, $249,247 (M); gifts received, $680,045; expenditures, $581,946; qualifying distributions, $578,768; giving activities include $567,900 for 24 grants (high: $248,000; low: $500).

Purpose and activities: Giving primarily for Lutheran and other Protestant churches and agencies; support also for health organizations, animal welfare, and human services.

Fields of interest: Animal welfare; Animals/wildlife, special services; Health organizations; Human services; Protestant agencies & churches.

Limitations: Giving primarily in upstate NY, with emphasis on Amersterdam, Glens Falls, Albany, and Syracuse. No grants to individuals.

Application information:
Initial approach: Letter
Deadline(s): None

Trustees: Kathleen J. Fraher; Phillip K. Whittemore.

EIN: 141814054

2391
Rochester Area Community Foundation
(formerly Rochester Area Foundation)
500 East Ave.
Rochester, NY 14607-1912 (585) 271-4100
Contact: Deborah A. Ellwood, V.P.
FAX: (518) 271-4292; E-mail: jleonard@racf.org; URL: http://www.racf.org

Incorporated in 1972 in NY.

Grantmaker type: Community foundation

Financial data (yr. ended 03/31/03): Assets, $143,456,539 (M); gifts received, $14,642,318; expenditures, $15,227,450; giving activities include $22,009,858 for grants.

Purpose and activities: Giving for broad purposes related to community betterment, including education, the environment, cultural programs, health services, especially for youth, community development and responsibility, and social services, including family and legal services, minorities, women, and youth. Scholarship recipients are chosen by institutions. Primary interests include early childhood education, community development, including leadership programs for young people, and strengthening families and children through expansion of housing counseling and resource management counseling to low-income families. The foundation also provides management guidance to area nonprofit organizations for capacity building. The foundation administers donor-advised funds.

Fields of interest: Arts; Early childhood education; Child development, education; Adult education—literacy, basic skills & GED; Natural resources; Environment; Legal services; Housing/shelter, development; Recreation; Youth development, services; Human services; Children/youth, services; Child development, services; Family services; Women, centers/services; Minorities/immigrants, centers/services; Community development; Voluntarism promotion; Leadership development; Minorities; Aging; Women.

Types of support: General/operating support; Management development; Building/renovation; Equipment; Program development; Conferences/seminars; Publication; Seed money; Scholarship funds; Technical assistance; Consulting services; Program evaluation; Program-related investments/loans; Scholarships—to individuals.

Limitations: Giving limited to Monroe, Livingston, Ontario, Orleans, Genesee, and Wayne counties, NY, except for donor-designated funds. No support for partisan political organizations or religious projects. No grants to individuals (except from restricted funds), or for annual campaigns, deficit financing, land acquisition, or endowment or emergency funds.

Publications: Annual report (including application guidelines), Financial statement, Informational brochure, Newsletter, Program policy statement.

Application information: Scholarship recipients chosen by institutions. Application form required.
Initial approach: Letter
Copies of proposal: 1
Deadline(s): Dec. 12
Board meeting date(s): Jan., Feb., Mar., May, June, July, Oct., and Nov.
Final notification: Ongoing

Officers: Michael J. Cooney, Chair.; Bruce B. Bates, Vice-Chair.; Patricia S. Burns, Vice-Chair.; James V. D'Amico, Vice-Chair.; Marvin J. Hoffman, Vice-Chair.; Margaret A. Sanchez, Vice-Chair.; Jeffrie B. Leahy, C.O.O. and V.P.; Jennifer Leonard, Pres. and Exec. Dir.; J. Charmaine Bennett, Secy.; Ray H. Hutch, Treas.

Board Members: Edward Adams; Francis R. Antonelli; Dennis Bassett; Ted Boucher; James B. Brush; Michael F. Buckley; Robert C. Silver; and 23 additional board members.

Number of staff: 6 full-time professional; 3 part-time professional; 5 full-time support.

EIN: 237250641

Recent environmental and animal welfare grants:

2391-1 Genesee Land Trust, Pittsford, NY, $10,000. For design and development of urban trail on unused railroad bed. 2002.

2391-2 Rochester Landscape Technicians Program, Rochester, NY, $10,000. For training and jobs for youth in green industry. Grant made through Joan and Harold Feinbloom Supporting Foundation. 2002.

2392
Rockefeller Brothers Fund, Inc. ▼
437 Madison Ave., 37th Fl.
New York, NY 10022-7001 (212) 812-4200
Contact: Benjamin R. Shute, Jr., Secy.
FAX: (212) 812-4299; General E-mail: info@rbf.org; E-mail for annual report: anreport@rbf.org; URL: http://www.rbf.org

Incorporated in 1940 in NY.

Donor(s): John D. Rockefeller, Jr.,‡ Martha Baird Rockefeller,‡ Abby Rockefeller Mauze,‡ David Rockefeller, John D. Rockefeller III,‡ Laurance S. Rockefeller, Nelson A. Rockefeller,‡ Winthrop Rockefeller.‡

Grantmaker type: Independent foundation

Financial data (yr. ended 12/31/02): Assets, $622,583,676 (M); expenditures, $26,507,024; qualifying distributions, $22,945,764; giving activities include $22,916,744 for grants, $29,020 for employee matching gifts and $4,017,081 for foundation-administered programs.

Purpose and activities: The Rockefeller Brothers Fund promotes social change that contributes to a more just, sustainable, and peaceful world. Through its grantmaking, the Fund supports efforts to expand knowledge, clarify values and critical choices, nurture creative expression, and shape public policy. The Fund's programs are intended to develop leaders, strengthen institutions, engage citizens, build community, and foster partnerships that include government, business, and civil society. Respect for cultural diversity and ecological integrity pervades the Fund's activities.

Fields of interest: Cultural/ethnic awareness; Arts; Global warming; Natural resources; Environment; Health care; International peace/security; Leadership development.

International interests: Serbia; South Africa.

Types of support: General/operating support; Continuing support; Program development; Conferences/seminars; Seed money; Internship funds; Technical assistance; Consulting services; Program evaluation; Program-related investments/loans; Employee matching gifts; Matching/challenge support.

Limitations: Giving on a national basis, and in Central and Eastern Europe, East and Southeast Asia, and South Africa. No grants to individuals (including research, graduate study, or the writing of books or dissertations by individuals, with 3 exceptions: the RBF Fellowships under the education program, which are limited to those students nominated by the colleges that have been selected to participate in this program, the Ramon Magsaysay Awards through the Program for Asian Projects), and the Culpeper Medical Scholarships, or land acquisitions or building funds.

Publications: Annual report (including application guidelines), Grants list, Informational brochure, Occasional report.

Application information: Application form not required.

  Initial approach: Letter (not exceeding 2 to 3 pages) except for Arts and Culture

  Copies of proposal: 1

  Deadline(s): From Jan. 15 to Mar. 15 for Arts and Culture; all others, none

  Board meeting date(s): Mar., June, Oct., and Dec.

  Final notification: 3 months

Officers and Trustees:* Steven C. Rockefeller,* Chair.; Neva R. Goodwin,* Vice-Chair.; Stephen B. Heintz,* Pres.; William F. McCalpin, C.O.O. and Exec. V.P.; Benjamin R. Shute, Jr., Secy.; Boris A. Wessely, Treas.; Geraldine F. Watson, Compt.; David J. Callard; Richard Chasin; Peggy Dulany; Jessica P. Einhorn; Jonathan F. Fanton, Advisory Tr.; William H. Luers, Advisory Tr.; James E. Moltz; John Morning; Abby M. O'Neill,

Advisory Tr.; Robert B. Oxnam; Richard D. Parsons, Advisory Tr.; Joseph A. Pierson; David Rockefeller, Advisory Tr.; David Rockefeller, Jr.; Laurance S. Rockefeller, Advisory Tr.; Richard G. Rockefeller; Edmond D. Villani; Frank G. Wisner; Tadataka Yamada, M.D.

Number of staff: 20 full-time professional; 2 part-time professional; 22 full-time support.

EIN: 131760106

Recent environmental and animal welfare grants:

2392-1 Brooklyn Bridge Park Coalition, Brooklyn, NY, $90,000. For efforts to maintain and expand political, financial, and community support. 2002.

2392-2 CAB International, Wallingford, England, $84,000. For harmonizing provisions of rules of World Trade Organization with the Cartagena Biosafety Protocol. 2002.

2392-3 Center for Economic and Environmental Partnership, Albany, NY, $40,000. To convene, plan and run High Performance Buildings Initiative in response to the events of September 11th, aiming to advance high-performance building into mainstream of real estate development, construction, and management in New York City, by identifying and addressing practical issues that impede opportunities for green building, through broad-based, multi-stakeholder process that will engender incremental change and gradually widen acceptance and commitment to green building; first, working to demystify notion that high performance building initiatives necessarily increase building costs and rely on untested innovations; persuading stakeholders that change is inevitable, and that if they work collaboratively, they will be able to manage process in order to maximize benefits on all sides; and demonstrating through fact-based value equations that, in many situations, high-performance building and renovating is good business for all stakeholders; then focusing on details such as building codes, work rules, costs, and accounting methods, in order to develop shared and objective body of knowledge and identify changes that are needed to remove impediments. 2002.

2392-4 Center for International Environmental Law, DC, $150,000. For capacity-building for Southern countries and civil society groups seeking more transparent, democratic, and balanced international trade policymaking. 2002.

2392-5 Earth Share, Bethesda, MD, $80,000. To implement partnerships with affiliated state and regional environmental federations. 2002.

2392-6 Ecologists Linked for Organizing Grassroots Initiatives and Action (ECOLOGIA), Middlebury, VT, $10,000. For strategic assessment of work to reform standard setting processes. 2002.

2392-7 Friends of the Earth Japan, Tokyo, Japan, $200,000. For Export Credit Agency Reform Campaign. 2002.

2392-8 GLOBE USA, DC, $200,000. For reform of export credit agencies. 2002.

2392-9 Greater Jamaica Development Corporation, Jamaica, NY, $125,000. To develop Neighborhood Brownfields Pilot-Reclaiming Jamaica's Brownfields. 2002.

2392-10 Green Network of Vojvodina, Novi Sad, Serbia, $96,000. For general operating support. 2002.

2392-11 H. John Heinz III Center for Science, Economics and the Environment, DC, $50,000. For project, Alerting Americans to Global Challenges, to explore different initiatives that could help Americans understand the world as an interdependent system, to educate them on key issues, and to counter widely-held misperceptions that inhibit progress (for instance, the belief that official U.S. foreign aid is a major budget outlay and largely wasted, or that no scientific consensus has crystallized on climate change). 2002.

2392-12 Institute for Sustainable Communities, Montpelier, VT, $50,000. For community and youth action project in Serbia. 2002.

2392-13 International Institute of Rural Reconstruction, Cavite, Philippines, $10,000. For Strengthening Local Capacities for Community-based Integrated Watershed Management in the Bicol Region, Philippines. 2002.

2392-14 Municipal Art Society of New York, New York, NY, $50,000. For Metropolitan Waterfront Alliance project, helping New York and New Jersey reclaim and reconnect harbors, rivers, and estuaries. 2002.

2392-15 National Environmental Trust, DC, $300,000. For creating a positive vision for U.S. trade policymaking, and developing a communications strategy. 2002.

2392-16 United Nations, New York, NY, $52,000. For projects of United Nations Development Programme in Montenegro to promote an ecological state. 2002.

2392-17 Wildlife Conservation Society, Bronx, NY, $100,000. For Wild Achievements: Wildlife Integrated for Language Development and Achievement program. 2002.

2393

Rockefeller Family Fund, Inc.

437 Madison Ave., 37th Fl.
New York, NY 10022-7001 (212) 812-4252
Contact: Lee Wasserman, Secy. and Dir.
FAX: (212) 812-4299; E-mail:
mmccarthy@rffund.org; URL: http://www.rffund.org

Incorporated in 1967 in NY.

Donor(s): Members of the Rockefeller family.

Grantmaker type: Public charity

Financial data (yr. ended 12/31/01): Revenue, $3,659,644; assets, $60,735,104 (M); gifts received, $4,671,678; expenditures, $9,912,436; program services expenses, $9,120,076; giving activities include $6,324,940 for grants.

Purpose and activities: The fund makes grants to support advocacy programs that are action-oriented and likely to yield tangible results in five program areas: 1) Citizen Participation and Government Accountability - encourages the organized participation of citizens in government, and seeks to make government more accountable and responsive. This program supports the efforts of nonpartisan organizations to help citizens exercise the right to vote, advocate for structural improvement to systems of government, and otherwise increase opportunities to participate in public policy formation; 2) Economic Justice for Women-supports projects that seek to provide women with equitable employment opportunities and the improvement of their work lives; 3) Environment- emphasizes conservation of natural resources, protection of health as affected by the environment, the cessation of pollution caused by the Department of Energy and military services, and domestic efforts to broaden the definition of national security and global stability to include environmental security; 4) Institutional Responsiveness-traditionally the most open-ended of the fund's program areas, its purpose is to provide individuals and organizations with the means to influence the policies and actions of public and private institutions; and 5) Self-Sufficiency-which emerged out of a recognition that advocacy groups need help in developing renewable sources of funding, rather than depending too heavily on support from private foundations. This program supports efforts to increase and diversify organizational support.

Fields of interest: Natural resources; Environment; Employment, equal rights; Women.

Types of support: General/operating support; Continuing support; Program development; Seed money.

Limitations: Giving on a national basis. No support for international programs, domestic programs dealing with international issues, or for social or human services programs. No grants to individuals, or for building funds, renovation, construction or restoration projects, deficit financing, research, endowment funds, scholarships, or fellowships.

Publications: Annual report (including application guidelines).

Application information: The fund does not ordinarily consider projects which pertain to a single city, except in the rare instance where a project is unique and might clearly serve as a national model. Those applicants asked to submit a full proposal will be provided with guidelines for material to include. Application form not required.

　Initial approach: Letter of inquiry (no more than 2 pages)
　Copies of proposal: 1
　Deadline(s): None
　Board meeting date(s): June and Dec.; executive committee usually meets 2 additional times a year
　Final notification: 1 to 3 months

Officers and Trustees:* Peter M. O'Neill,* Pres.; David W. Kaiser,* V.P.; Julia S. Robbins,* V.P.; Wendy G. Rockefeller,* V.P.; Theodore Spencer,* V.P.; Lee Wasserman, Secy. and Dir.; Leah A. D'Angelo, Treas.; James S. Sligar, Counsel; Peter Case; Paul Growald; Miranda Kaiser; Alida R. Messinger; Stuart A. Rockefeller; Emily Rockefeller; Geoffrey Strawbridge.

Number of staff: 10 full-time professional; 3 full-time support.
EIN: 136257658

2394
The David Rockefeller Fund, Inc.
30 Rockefeller Plz., Rm. 5600
New York, NY 10112 (212) 649-5600
Contact: Marnie Pillsbury, Exec. Dir.

Established in 1989 in NY.
Donor(s): David Rockefeller.
Grantmaker type: Independent foundation
Financial data (yr. ended 12/31/02): Assets, $7,316,060 (M); gifts received, $558,982; expenditures, $772,088; qualifying distributions, $690,886; giving activities include $659,100 for grants.
Purpose and activities: Giving primarily for conservation and historic preservation, community services, and health services; minor support also for the arts, local fire departments, and recreation.
Fields of interest: Historic preservation/historical societies; Arts; Education; Natural resources; Environment; Health care; Recreation; Community development.
Types of support: Continuing support; Annual campaigns.
Limitations: Giving limited to Seal Harbor and Mount Desert Island, ME, the Pocantico communities in Westchester County, NY, and the Livingston communities of Columbia County.
Publications: Annual report.
Application information: Application form not required.
　Copies of proposal: 1
　Deadline(s): None
　Board meeting date(s): Spring and fall
　Final notification: Positive replies only
Officers and Directors:* Richard Rockefeller,* Pres.; Richard E. Salomon,* Secy.-Treas.; Marnie S. Pillsbury, Exec. Dir.; Colin G. Campbell; Peggy Dulany; Neva Goodwin; Paul Growald; Christopher Lindstrom; Ariana Rockefeller; Clayton Rockefeller; Diana Rockefeller; James Sligar.
Number of staff: 1 part-time professional; 1 part-time support.
EIN: 133533359

2395
The Roe Foundation, Inc.
(formerly G.R.M. Foundation, Inc.)
c/o Pan Am Equities, Inc.
3 New York Plz.
New York, NY 10004

Donor(s): Greg Manocherian, Jed Manocherian, Fraydun Foundation.
Grantmaker type: Independent foundation
Financial data (yr. ended 12/31/01): Assets, $506,585 (M); gifts received, $600,571; expenditures, $203,416; qualifying distributions, $173,484; giving activities include $112,750 for 9 grants (high: $65,000; low: $250).
Fields of interest: Animals/wildlife, preservation/protection; Human services.
Limitations: Applications not accepted. Giving primarily in NY. No grants to individuals.
Application information: Contributes only to pre-selected organizations.
Officers and Directors:* Greg Manocherian,* Pres.; John Manocherian, V.P.; Jed Manocherian,* Secy.; Jerome H. Katz, Treas.; Fred Manocherian.
EIN: 133840700

2396
Rohauer Collection Foundation, Inc.
c/o E Grainger
125 Park Ave., 3rd Fl.
New York, NY 10017 (212) 697-2710

Established in 1990 in NY.
Donor(s): Raymond Rohauer.‡
Grantmaker type: Independent foundation
Financial data (yr. ended 07/31/02): Assets, $2,953,755 (M); expenditures, $145,233; qualifying distributions, $169,989; giving activities include $101,200 for 18 grants (high: $10,000; low: $1,200).
Purpose and activities: Support primarily for the arts, animal welfare, and the environment.
Fields of interest: Film/video; Museums (specialized); Environment; Animal welfare.
Limitations: Applications not accepted. Giving on a national basis, with emphasis on nonprofits in NY and CA. No grants to individuals.
Application information: Contributes only to pre-selected organizations.
Officer and Trustees:* Edmund C. Grainger, Jr.,* Pres.; Richard Gordon; Edmund C. Grainger III.
EIN: 133578176

2397
Lee Romney Foundation, Inc.
c/o M.A. Romney & Co.
200 Park Ave. S., Ste. 1018
New York, NY 10003 (212) 982-1405
Contact: Mark A. Romney, Treas.
FAX: (212) 982-2045

Established in 1988.
Donor(s): Mark A. Romney, Vera J. Tucker, Leonor Romney Charitable Lead Trust.
Grantmaker type: Independent foundation
Financial data (yr. ended 11/30/02): Assets, $1,598,149 (M); gifts received, $19,135; expenditures, $174,403; qualifying distributions, $165,124; giving activities include $158,742 for 71 grants (high: $35,320; low: $50).
Purpose and activities: Giving for music, education, and natural resource conservation and protection.
Fields of interest: Music; Education; Natural resources.
Types of support: Annual campaigns; Capital campaigns; Endowments.
Limitations: Applications not accepted. Giving primarily in NY. No grants to individuals.
Application information: Contributes only to pre-selected organizations.
　Board meeting date(s): Dec.
Officers and Directors:* Sharon Rosenfeld Scott,* Pres.; Michael H. Romney,* V.P.; Mark A. Romney,* Treas.; Martin E. Greif.
Number of staff: None.
EIN: 133187997

2398
Rose Family Foundation
c/o Brown Brothers Harriman Trust Co.
63 Wall St.
New York, NY 10005-2831

Established in 1998 in DE and NY.
Grantmaker type: Independent foundation
Financial data (yr. ended 12/31/00): Assets, $6,272,556 (M); expenditures, $184,649;

---

qualifying distributions, $142,825; giving activities include $133,537 for 3 grants (high: $65,000; low: $28,537).
Purpose and activities: Giving primarily to an institute of science, and a community foundation.
Fields of interest: Cultural/ethnic awareness; Water pollution; Science.
Limitations: Applications not accepted. Giving primarily in NY. No grants to individuals.
Application information: Contributes only to pre-selected organizations.
Officers: Marian H. Rose, Pres.; Ann R. Podlipny, V.P.; David H. Rose, Secy.; Simon M. Rose, Treas.
EIN: 134016964

2399
Adam R. Rose Foundation
200 Madison Ave., 5th Fl.
New York, NY 10016

Established in 1996 in DE.
Donor(s): Adam Rose.
Grantmaker type: Independent foundation
Financial data (yr. ended 12/31/01): Assets, $54,261 (M); gifts received, $400,000; expenditures, $515,885; qualifying distributions, $515,569; giving activities include $515,575 for 69 grants (high: $100,000; low: $200).
Purpose and activities: Giving for education, music, human rights, lesbian and gay services, and public gardens.
Fields of interest: Music; Education; Botanical gardens; International human rights; Gays/lesbians.
Limitations: Applications not accepted. Giving primarily in NY. No grants to individuals.
Application information: Contributes only to pre-selected organizations.
Officers: Adam M. Rose, Pres.; Michael D. Sullivan, Secy.
EIN: 137095495

2400
The Rosenthal Fund
784 Park Ave., Apt. 19B
New York, NY 10021

Established in 1996 in NY.
Donor(s): Charles Rosenthal.
Grantmaker type: Independent foundation
Financial data (yr. ended 09/30/02): Assets, $2,847,280 (M); gifts received, $648,425; expenditures, $520,751; qualifying distributions, $511,490; giving activities include $514,370 for 64 grants (high: $25,000; low: $25).
Purpose and activities: Giving primarily for higher education.
Fields of interest: Arts; Higher education; Animals/wildlife; Human services; Jewish agencies & temples.
Types of support: General/operating support.
Limitations: Applications not accepted. Giving primarily in NY and RI. No grants to individuals.
Application information: Contributes only to pre-selected organizations.
Officers: Charles Rosenthal, Pres.; Phyllis Rosenthal, Secy.
EIN: 133919545

2401
Arthur Ross Foundation, Inc.
20 E. 74th St., 4-C
New York, NY 10021 (212) 737-7311
Contact: Arthur Ross, Pres.

Incorporated in 1955 in NY.
Donor(s): Arthur Ross.
Grantmaker type: Independent foundation
Financial data (yr. ended 12/31/01): Assets, $9,410,450 (M); gifts received, $1,643,858; expenditures, $3,171,983; qualifying distributions, $3,035,722; giving activities include $2,932,551 for 128+ grants (high: $400,000; average: $25,000–$100,000).
Purpose and activities: Giving for higher education and cultural institutions, especially museums and parks; support also for environmental organizations and historic preservation.
Fields of interest: Museums; Historic preservation/historical societies; Arts; Higher education; Medical school/education; Environment; Disabled; Aging; Homeless.
Types of support: Continuing support; Capital campaigns; Endowments; Conferences/seminars; Scholarship funds; Matching/challenge support.
Limitations: Giving primarily in NY.
Application information:
Initial approach: Letter
Officers and Directors:* Arthur Ross,* Pres. and Treas.; Janet C. Ross,* Exec. V.P.; George J. Gillespie III,* Secy.; Gail Lloyd, Exec. Dir.; William T. Golden; Hon. William J. vanden Heuvel; Edgar Wachenheim III.
Number of staff: 2.
EIN: 136121436

2402
Joan Rothenberg Family Foundation, Inc.
(formerly Rothenberg Family Foundation, Inc.)
1111 Lac De Ville Blvd., Ste. 302
Rochester, NY 14618
Contact: Sandra Rothenberg, Treas.
E-mail: rothenberg@rothenbergfamilyfoundation.org;
URL: http://www.rothenbergfamilyfoundation.org

Established in 1998 in NY.
Donor(s): Martin Rothenberg.
Grantmaker type: Independent foundation
Financial data (yr. ended 12/31/01): Assets, $1,478,547 (M); expenditures, $112,848; qualifying distributions, $106,888; giving activities include $103,360 for 10 grants (high: $48,233; low: $100).
Purpose and activities: Supports women's welfare, children and environmental organizations.
Fields of interest: Environment; Family planning; Youth development; Women.
Types of support: General/operating support; Continuing support; Annual campaigns; Capital campaigns; Building/renovation; Equipment; Land acquisition; Emergency funds; Program development; Conferences/seminars; Professorships; Seed money; Curriculum development; Internship funds; Research; Employee-related scholarships; Matching/challenge support.
Limitations: Giving primarily in central and western NY.
Application information:

Initial approach: Proposal
Deadline(s): None
Officers: Sandra Rothenberg, Pres. and Treas.; Marcia Rothenberg, Secy.
Directors: Larry Rothenberg; Martin Rothenberg.
Number of staff: 1 part-time professional.
EIN: 133940229

2403
Royal Oak Foundation
26 Broadway, Ste. 950
New York, NY 10004 (212) 480-2889
Contact: Damaris S. Horan, Exec. Dir.
Additional tel.: (800) 913-6565; FAX: (212) 785-7234; E-mail: general@royal-oak.org; URL: http://www.royal-oak.org

Established in 1973 in NY.
Grantmaker type: Public charity
Financial data (yr. ended 12/31/01): Revenue, $1,748,035; assets, $1,886,235 (M); expenditures, $1,680,910; program services expenses, $1,402,026; giving activities include $438,288 for 7 grants (high: $150,000; low: $3,500) and $34,995 for 6 grants to individuals (high: $15,000; low: $3,500).
Purpose and activities: The foundation raises funds for the conservation of areas of historic properties, including houses and gardens in Britain and elsewhere. It sponsors educational programs which address issues in conservation and preservation.
Fields of interest: Architecture; Historic preservation/historical societies; Arts; Environment; Animals/wildlife.
International interests: United Kingdom.
Types of support: General/operating support; Continuing support; Annual campaigns; Program development; Publication; Scholarship funds; Employee-related scholarships; Scholarships—to individuals; In-kind gifts.
Limitations: Giving on an international basis, England, Wales, Scotland, and Northern Ireland, and on a national basis.
Publications: Application guidelines, Financial statement, Grants list, Informational brochure, Newsletter.
Application information: Application form not required.
Initial approach: Letter or telephone
Deadline(s): None
Board meeting date(s): Mar., June, Sept., and Dec.
Officers and Directors:* Betsy Shack Barbanell,* Chair.; Herbert F. Aspbury,* Vice-Chair.; Dandridge L. Ince,* Vice-Chair.; Wendell D. Garrett,* Secy.; Damaris S. Horan, Exec. Dir.; Pamela K. Armour; Pamela S. Banker; David C. Beal; Martyn S. Belmont; Marica E. Brocklebank; Danforth P. Fales; J. Dudley Fishburn; Fayal Greene; William M. Lese; Thomas D. Mullins; Charles K.R. Nunneley; Christine V. Ness; Fiona Reynolds; Renny Reynolds; Marjorie G. Rosen; Richards F. Sammons; J. Thomas Savage; Suzanne C. Schutz; Patricia T. Smalley; Molly K. Smith; John E. Young; Mrs. Henry J. Heinz II,* Hon. Chair.
Number of staff: 8 full-time professional; 2 part-time support.
EIN: 237349380

2404
Mary A. H. Rumsey Foundation
c/o Brown Brothers Harriman Trust Co.
140 Broadway, 4th Fl.
New York, NY 10005

Established in 1984 in NY.
Donor(s): Mary A.H. Rumsey.‡
Grantmaker type: Independent foundation
Financial data (yr. ended 09/30/02): Assets,
$7,996,665 (M); expenditures, $691,220;
qualifying distributions, $636,413; giving
activities include $611,200 for 109 grants (high:
$60,000; low: $500).
Purpose and activities: Giving primarily for
education, wildlife, and nature preservation,
and the arts.
Fields of interest: Arts; Secondary
school/education; Higher education; Natural
resources; Animals/wildlife,
preservation/protection; Medical care, in-patient
care; Health organizations, association; Human
services; Children/youth, services; Christian
agencies & churches.
Limitations: Applications not accepted. Giving
primarily in the greater metropolitan New York,
NY, area. No grants to individuals.
Application information: Contributes only to
pre-selected organizations.
Officers and Directors:* Charles Cary Rumsey,*
Pres.; Mary M. Rumsey,* V.P.; William F.
Hibberd, Secy.; Anna T. Korniczky, Treas.; Edwin
R. Ward; Douglas F. Williamson, Jr.
EIN: 133244314

2405
Richard Nelson Ryan Foundation
787 7th Ave.
New York, NY 10019-6099
Contact: Augusta L. Packer, Secy.

Established in 1950 in NY.
Grantmaker type: Independent foundation
Financial data (yr. ended 12/31/02): Assets,
$1,330,822 (M); expenditures, $143,427;
qualifying distributions, $140,519; giving
activities include $140,000 for 9 grants (high:
$40,000; low: $2,000).
Purpose and activities: Giving for museums,
animal welfare, and youth services.
Fields of interest: Museums;
Elementary/secondary education; Animal
welfare; Animals/wildlife,
preservation/protection; Human services;
Children/youth, services.
Limitations: Giving primarily in Seattle, WA. No
grants to individuals.
Application information: Application form not
required.
Deadline(s): None
Officers: Richard N. Ryan, Jr., Pres.; Hope R.
Garrett, V.P. and Treas.; Hope Farnell, V.P.;
Augusta L. Packer, Secy.
EIN: 136161617

2406
The Peter M. Sacerdote Foundation
c/o BCRS Assocs., LLC
67 Wall St., 8th Fl.
New York, NY 10005 (212) 902-6897

Established in 1981.

Donor(s): Peter M. Sacerdote, P.M. Sacerdote
Charitable Lead Trust.
Grantmaker type: Independent foundation
Financial data (yr. ended 02/28/01): Assets,
$15,318,014 (M); expenditures, $1,965,325;
qualifying distributions, $1,832,794; giving
activities include $1,830,775 for 32 grants
(high: $521,625; low: $200).
Purpose and activities: Funding primarily for
education and health care. Some funding also
for human services and religion.
Fields of interest: Secondary school/education;
Higher education; Business school/education;
Education; Environment; Hospitals (general);
Health care; Human services; Religion.
Limitations: Applications not accepted. Giving
primarily in New York, NY. No grants to
individuals.
Application information: Contributes only to
pre-selected organizations.
Trustee: Peter M. Sacerdote.
EIN: 133102940

2407
Salute to the Seasons Fund, Inc.
110 E. 42nd St., Ste. 1300
New York, NY 10017

Classified as a private operating foundation in
1971.
Donor(s): Mary W. Lasker.‡
Grantmaker type: Operating foundation
Financial data (yr. ended 12/31/02): Assets,
$1,848,703 (M); gifts received, $49,980;
expenditures, $301,644; qualifying distributions,
$280,861; giving activities include $250,000 for
1 grant and $298,708 for
foundation-administered programs.
Purpose and activities: Provides for the planting
and maintenance of trees, flowers, and other
landscaping throughout New York City.
Fields of interest: Landscaping; Environment,
beautification programs.
Limitations: Applications not accepted. Giving
primarily in New York, NY. No grants to
individuals.
Publications: Newsletter.
Application information: Contributes only to
pre-selected organizations.
Officer and Directors: Margaret Ternes, Exec.
Dir.; Anne Boardman Fordyce; James W.
Fordyce; James E. Hughes, Jr.; Ronald D.
Spencer.
Number of staff: 1 full-time professional; 1
part-time support.
EIN: 136162773

2408
Ernest & Rose Samuels Foundation, Inc.
c/o Feldheim
8 Hillcrest Ln.
Woodbury, NY 11797

Established around 1977 in FL.
Donor(s): Ernest Samuels.
Grantmaker type: Independent foundation
Financial data (yr. ended 12/31/02): Assets,
$2,395,566 (M); expenditures, $218,839;
qualifying distributions, $146,470; giving
activities include $127,400 for 16 grants (high:
$12,500; low: $3,700).

Fields of interest: Museums; Natural resources;
Housing/shelter, development; Human services.
Limitations: Applications not accepted. No
grants to individuals.
Application information: Contributes only to
pre-selected organizations.
Officers: Herbert D. Feldheim, Pres.; Deborah
Feldheim, Secy.
EIN: 591733119

2409
Sandpiper Fund, Inc.
c/o Hecht and Co., PC
111 W. 40th St.
New York, NY 10018

Established in 1990 in NY.
Donor(s): Daniel Scheuer, Shelley Leizman.
Grantmaker type: Independent foundation
Financial data (yr. ended 12/31/01): Assets,
$2,875,627 (M); gifts received, $100,000;
expenditures, $176,861; qualifying distributions,
$152,008; giving activities include $150,500 for
122 grants (high: $10,000; low: $250).
Fields of interest: Arts; Environment;
Animals/wildlife; AIDS; Human services; Youth,
services; Human services.
Limitations: Applications not accepted. Giving
primarily in New York, NY. No grants to
individuals.
Application information: Contributes only to
pre-selected organizations.
Officers: Daniel Scheuer, Pres.; Shelley
Leizman, V.P.
EIN: 133557069

2410
Mac and Sally Sands Foundation, Inc.
c/o Constellation Brands, Inc.
300 Willowbrook Office Park
Fairport, NY 14450

Established in 1959 in NY.
Donor(s): Robert Sands, Richard Sands.
Grantmaker type: Independent foundation
Financial data (yr. ended 12/31/02): Assets,
$1,986,264 (M); gifts received, $202,551;
expenditures, $223,949; qualifying distributions,
$211,515; giving activities include $211,515 for
18 grants (high: $100,000; low: $50).
Purpose and activities: Giving primarily for
education, Jewish organizations, and social
services.
Fields of interest: Arts; Education; Environment;
Health organizations; Human services;
Federated giving programs; Jewish federated
giving programs.
Limitations: Applications not accepted. Giving
primarily in NY. No grants to individuals.
Application information: Contributes only to
pre-selected organizations.
Officers: Robert Sands, Pres. and Treas.; Richard
Sands, V.P. and Secy.
EIN: 546052978

2411
Sansom Foundation, Inc.
c/o Sanford E. Becker
1430 Broadway, 6th Fl.
New York, NY 10018

Established in 1958.
Donor(s): Ira D. Glackens.‡
Grantmaker type: Independent foundation
Financial data (yr. ended 12/31/01): Assets,
$21,106,764 (M); expenditures, $575,950;
qualifying distributions, $575,956; giving
activities include $299,700 for 3 grants (high:
$264,700; low: $15,000).
Purpose and activities: Donates and loans
works of art to museums and galleries.
Fields of interest: Museums (art); Animal welfare.
Limitations: Applications not accepted. Giving
primarily in FL. No grants to individuals.
Application information: Contributes only to
pre-selected organizations.
Directors: Sanford E. Becker; Frank Buscaglia;
Rev. Edward M. DePaoli; C. Richard Hilker;
Donald G. Hilker; Jorge H. Santis; Lawrence
Thompson.
EIN: 136136127

2412
Sasco Foundation
67A E. 77th St.
New York, NY 10021-1813
Contact: Ann Brownell Sloane, Admin.

Trust established in 1951 in NY.
Donor(s): Leila E. Riegel,‡ Katherine R. Emory.‡
Grantmaker type: Independent foundation
Financial data (yr. ended 12/31/02): Assets,
$5,600,846 (M); expenditures, $280,470;
qualifying distributions, $280,470; giving
activities include $259,500 for grants.
Purpose and activities: Giving for the arts,
education, the environment, health, and human
services.
Fields of interest: Arts; Natural resources; Health
care; Human services; Family services; Women.
Types of support: Continuing support.
Limitations: Giving primarily in CT, ME, and NY.
No grants to individuals.
Application information: Currently supporting
trustee-sponsored projects only. Application
form not required.
Copies of proposal: 1
Deadline(s): Sept. 1
Board meeting date(s): Fall
Trustees: Lucy E. Ambach; Benjamin Riegel
Emory; Katherine Emory Stookey.
Number of staff: 4 shared staff (shared with
Sloane & Hinshaw, Inc.)
EIN: 136046567

2413
Schafer Family Foundation
c/o Executive Monetary Mgmt.
220 E. 42nd St., 32nd Fl.
New York, NY 10017 (212) 536-9700

Established in 1986 in NY.
Donor(s): Oscar S. Schafer.
Grantmaker type: Independent foundation
Financial data (yr. ended 12/31/02): Assets,
$668,113 (M); expenditures, $164,068;
qualifying distributions, $140,900; giving

activities include $141,566 for 37 grants (high:
$25,000; low: $100).
Purpose and activities: Giving primarily for
social services.
Fields of interest: Television; Performing arts;
Historic preservation/historical societies;
Education; Animal welfare; Health care;
Children/youth, services; Christian agencies &
churches; Jewish agencies & temples.
Limitations: Applications not accepted. Giving
primarily in the metropolitan New York, NY,
area. No grants to individuals.
Application information: Contributes only to
pre-selected organizations.
Officer: Oscar S. Schafer, Pres.
Director: Myer Berlow; Sigrid U. Schafer;
Michael Stein.
EIN: 133382931

2414
The Schenectady Foundation
c/o United Way of Schenectady County
P.O. Box 916
Schenectady, NY 12301
Contact: Robert A. Carreau, Secy.

Established in 1963 in NY.
Donor(s): Eleanor F. Green,‡ Mabel Birdsall,‡
Agnes Macdonald,‡ Laura Ayer,‡ S. Wells
Corbin,‡ John N. Erbacher,‡ Kathryn Rice,‡
Martin Rice,‡ Willis R. Whitney,‡ Herman
Blumer,‡ Patrick Garey,‡ Irving Handelman,‡
Sara Handelman,‡ Adelaide Parker,‡ Alice
Stackpole,‡ Charles W. Carl, Jr.,‡ Edna Wood,‡
General Electric Foundation.
Grantmaker type: Community foundation
Financial data (yr. ended 12/31/02): Assets,
$9,744,976 (M); gifts received, $704,627;
expenditures, $732,149; giving activities include
$667,479 for 5 grants.
Purpose and activities: Support for general
charitable purposes; awards scholarships to
graduating seniors of Schenectady County, NY,
high schools planning to enter the teaching
profession.
Fields of interest: Animals/wildlife,
preservation/protection; Engineering/technology.
Types of support: Capital campaigns;
Building/renovation; Equipment; Land
acquisition; Seed money; Research;
Matching/challenge support.
Limitations: Giving limited to Schenectady
County, NY. No grants for operating budgets,
continuing support, annual campaigns,
emergency or deficit financing, general or
special endowments, demonstration projects,
publications, or conferences or seminars; no
loans.
Publications: Application guidelines, Annual
report, Grants list, Informational brochure.
Application information: Contact foundation for
current deadline. Application form required.
Initial approach: Proposal
Copies of proposal: 1
Board meeting date(s): Mar., June, Sept., Dec.
Officers: Joann E. Paulsen, Chair.; Robert A.
Carreau, Secy.; Robert T. Cushing, Treas.
Number of staff: None.
EIN: 146019650

2415
The Schenker Family Foundation
c/o Curtis Schenker
1175 Park Ave., Apt. 8A
New York, NY 10128

Established in 1998 in NY.
Donor(s): Curtis Schenker, Leo Schenker.
Grantmaker type: Independent foundation
Financial data (yr. ended 12/31/01): Assets,
$923,315 (M); gifts received, $716,180;
expenditures, $727,066; qualifying distributions,
$701,783; giving activities include $701,783 for
grants.
Purpose and activities: Giving primarily for
education, health, children and youth services,
human services, and Jewish organizations.
Fields of interest: Arts; Education;
Animals/wildlife; Hospitals (general); Health
organizations, association; Human services;
Children/youth, services; Jewish federated giving
programs; Jewish agencies & temples.
Types of support: General/operating support.
Limitations: Applications not accepted. No
grants to individuals.
Application information: Contributes only to
pre-selected organizations.
Officer: Livia Schenker, Secy.
Directors: Curtis Schenker; Leo Schenker; Jeffrey
Schwarz.
EIN: 133992998

2416
The Scherman Foundation, Inc. ▼
16 E. 52nd St., Ste. 601
New York, NY 10022-5306 (212) 832-3086
Contact: Sandra Silverman, Pres. and Exec. Dir.
FAX: (212) 838-0154; E-mail:
info@scherman.org; URL: http://
www.scherman.org

Incorporated in 1941 in NY.
Donor(s): Members of the Scherman family.
Grantmaker type: Independent foundation
Financial data (yr. ended 12/31/02): Assets,
$68,569,280 (M); expenditures, $6,149,430;
qualifying distributions, $5,774,598; giving
activities include $5,224,700 for 144 grants
(high: $100,000; low: $1,000; average:
$5,000–$100,000).
Purpose and activities: Grants largely for
environment, peace and security, reproductive
rights and services, human rights and liberties,
the arts and social welfare. In the social welfare
field, grants are made to organizations
concerned with social justice, housing,
community organizing, and community
self-help.
Fields of interest: Performing arts; Theater;
Music; Arts; Libraries/library science; Natural
resources; Environment; Family planning; Legal
services; Housing/shelter, development; Human
services; International peace/security; Arms
control; International human rights; Civil rights,
minorities; Reproductive rights; Civil rights;
Community development; Economically
disadvantaged; Homeless.
Types of support: General/operating support;
Continuing support; Annual campaigns;
Program development; Technical assistance;
Matching/challenge support.
Limitations: Giving in NY and nationally in all
areas, except for the arts and social welfare,

which are primarily in New York City. No support for colleges, universities, or other higher educational institutions. No grants to individuals, or for building or endowment funds, scholarships, fellowships, conferences or symposia, specific media or arts production, or medical, science or engineering research.
Publications: Annual report (including application guidelines).
Application information: Application form not required.
  Initial approach: Letter
  Copies of proposal: 1
  Deadline(s): None
  Board meeting date(s): Quarterly
  Final notification: 8 to 10 weeks
Officers and Directors:* Karen R. Sollins, Chair.; Axel G. Rosin,* Chair. Emeritus; Sandra Silverman, Pres. and Exec. Dir.; Susanna Bergtold,* Secy.; Mitchell C. Pratt, Treas. and Prog. Off.; Hillary Brown; Gordon N. Litwin; John J. O'Neil; Katharine S. Rosin; Anthony M. Schulte; Marcia Thompson; John Wroclawski.
Number of staff: 2 full-time professional; 1 full-time support; 1 part-time support.
EIN: 136098464
Recent environmental and animal welfare grants:
2416-1 Conservation Law Foundation, Boston, MA, $90,000. For general support. 2002.
2416-2 Council on the Environment, New York, NY, $10,000. For education, open space and waste prevention programs. 2002.
2416-3 Earthjustice Legal Defense Fund, San Francisco, CA, $75,000. For general support. 2002.
2416-4 Environmental Advocates, Albany, NY, $50,000. For general support. 2002.
2416-5 Environmental Advocates, Albany, NY, $10,000. For Climate Change program. 2002.
2416-6 Environmental Defense, New York, NY, $30,000. For general support. 2002.
2416-7 Green Corps, Boston, MA, $20,000. For general support. 2002.
2416-8 Green Guerillas, New York, NY, $40,000. For general support. 2002.
2416-9 League of Conservation Voters Education Fund, DC, $40,000. For general support. 2002.
2416-10 League of Conservation Voters Education Fund, DC, $25,000. For Energy Policy program. 2002.
2416-11 Mineral Policy Center, DC, $40,000. For general support. 2002.
2416-12 Natural Resources Defense Council, New York, NY, $75,000. For general support. 2002.
2416-13 Natural Resources Defense Council, New York, NY, $25,000. For Climate Change program. 2002.
2416-14 New York City Environmental Justice Alliance, New York, NY, $20,000. For general support. 2002.
2416-15 New York City Street Tree Consortium, New York, NY, $20,000. For Tress New York. 2002.
2416-16 New York Public Interest Research Group (NYPIRG) Fund, New York, NY, $40,000. For Clean Drinking Water Coalition. 2002.
2416-17 Ocean Conservancy, DC, $50,000. For general support. 2002.
2416-18 Partnership Project, DC, $75,000. For Collaborative Defense Campaign. 2002.

2416-19 Pratt Institute, Center for Community and Environmental Development, Brooklyn, NY, $35,000. For general support. 2002.
2416-20 Public Employees for Environmental Responsibility (PEER), DC, $40,000. For general support. 2002.
2416-21 Sustainable South Bronx, Bronx, NY, $15,000. For general support. 2002.
2416-22 Tri-State Transportation Campaign, New York, NY, $50,000. For New York City activities. 2002.
2416-23 Tri-State Transportation Campaign, New York, NY, $10,000. For special one-time grant. 2002.
2416-24 Trustees for Alaska, Anchorage, AK, $50,000. For general support. 2002.
2416-25 United States Public Interest Research Group Education Fund, Atlanta, GA, $50,000. For Environmental Defense Campaign. 2002.
2416-26 UPROSE (United Puerto Rican Organization of Sunset Park), Brooklyn, NY, $15,000. For general support. 2002.

2417
Richard J. & Joan G. Scheuer Family Foundation, Inc.
c/o TAG Assocs., Ltd.
75 Rockefeller Plz., Ste. 900
New York, NY 10019

Established in 1966 in NY.
Donor(s): Joan G. Scheuer, Richard J. Scheuer.
Grantmaker type: Independent foundation
Financial data (yr. ended 10/31/02): Assets, $2,143 (M); gifts received, $382,956; expenditures, $358,360; qualifying distributions, $353,673; giving activities include $352,610 for 106 grants (high: $56,700; low: $50).
Purpose and activities: Giving primarily for the arts, and for archaeological research; funding also for social services and Jewish organizations and temples.
Fields of interest: Museums (ethnic/folk arts); Theater; History/archaeology; Arts; Education, association; Higher education; Environment, land resources; Human services; Jewish agencies & temples.
Limitations: Applications not accepted. Giving primarily in MA, NY, and OH. No grants to individuals.
Application information: Contributes only to pre-selected organizations.
Officers and Directors:* Richard J. Scheuer,* Pres. and Treas.; Joan G. Scheuer,* V.P. and Secy.
EIN: 136197447

2418
Sarah I. Schieffelin Residuary Trust
c/o The Bank of New York
1 Wall St., 28th Fl.
New York, NY 10286   (212) 635-1520
Contact: Grace Allen
Application address: c/o The Bank of New York, 1290 6th Ave., New York, NY 10104

Established in 1976.
Donor(s): Sarah I. Schieffelin.‡
Grantmaker type: Independent foundation
Financial data (yr. ended 03/31/02): Assets, $14,386,990 (M); expenditures, $817,522; qualifying distributions, $737,000; giving

activities include $699,580 for 33 grants (high: $200,000; low: $1,000).
Purpose and activities: Giving primarily to the American Red Cross, and for a historical society, human services, and animals and wildlife.
Fields of interest: Historic preservation/historical societies; Arts; Libraries (public); Education; Natural resources; Animals/wildlife, preservation/protection; Health care; Health organizations, association; Human services; American Red Cross; Children/youth, services; Christian agencies & churches; Roman Catholic agencies & churches.
Types of support: Continuing support.
Limitations: Giving primarily in New York, NY. No grants to individuals.
Application information: Application form not required.
  Initial approach: Letter
  Copies of proposal: 1
  Deadline(s): Mar. 31
  Board meeting date(s): May 31
  Final notification: June 30
Trustees: Thomas B. Fenlon; The Bank of New York.
EIN: 136724459

2419
The Schiff Foundation
50 Rockefeller Plz., 15th Fl.
New York, NY 10020-1605   (212) 655-7044
Contact: David T. Schiff, Pres.
FAX: (212)259-3896

Incorporated in 1946 in NY.
Donor(s): John M. Schiff,‡ Edith B. Schiff,‡ David T. Schiff, Peter G. Schiff.
Grantmaker type: Independent foundation
Financial data (yr. ended 12/31/02): Assets, $10,082,555 (M); expenditures, $693,656; qualifying distributions, $622,690; giving activities include $625,486 for 98 grants (high: $100,000; low: $100; average: $100–$100,000).
Purpose and activities: Giving for special medical programs, certain youth and social service agencies, museums, animal welfare, and education; funds substantially committed to organizations of interest to the donors.
Fields of interest: Museums; Arts; Education; Animal welfare; Health care; Human services; Children/youth, services.
Types of support: General/operating support; Annual campaigns; Capital campaigns; Program development.
Limitations: Applications not accepted. Giving primarily in NY. No grants to individuals.
Application information: Contributes only to pre-selected organizations.
Officers and Directors:* David T. Schiff,* Pres.; Peter G. Schiff,* V.P.; Sandra Frey Davies, Secy.; Andrew N. Schiff,* Treas.
Number of staff: None.
EIN: 136088221

2420
The Schloss Family Foundation, Inc.
c/o Walter J. Schloss
350 Park Ave., 9th Fl.
New York, NY 10022

Established in 1997 in NY.
Donor(s): Walter J. Schloss.

Grantmaker type: Independent foundation
Financial data (yr. ended 12/31/02): Assets, $4,499,934 (M); expenditures, $253,087; qualifying distributions, $237,881; giving activities include $242,000 for 21 grants (high: $55,000; low: $1,000).
Purpose and activities: Giving for art and cultural programs, and for education.
Fields of interest: Media/communications; Television; Museums (art); Education; Natural resources; Family planning; Residential/custodial care, special day care; Civil rights.
Limitations: Applications not accepted. Giving limited to Washington, DC, and NY. No grants to individuals.
Application information: Contributes only to pre-selected organizations.
Officers: Walter J. Schloss, Pres. and Treas.; Edwin W. Schloss, V.P.; Stephanie Cassel Scott, Secy.
EIN: 133935646

2421
The Marvin and Donna Schwartz Foundation
c/o Neuberger & Berman
605 3rd Ave.
New York, NY   10158-3698

Established in 1997 in NY.
Donor(s): Donna Schwartz, Marvin C. Schwartz.
Grantmaker type: Independent foundation
Financial data (yr. ended 04/30/01): Assets, $43,528,578 (M); expenditures, $3,879,426; qualifying distributions, $3,458,150; giving activities include $3,531,895 for 134 grants (high: $1,600,000; low: $25; average: $1,000–$25,000).
Purpose and activities: Giving primarily to a university; some funding also for the arts, health, and medical research.
Fields of interest: Arts; Higher education; Natural resources; Health organizations, association; Medical research, institute; Human services; Community development; Religion.
Limitations: Applications not accepted. No grants to individuals.
Application information: Contributes only to pre-selected organizations.
Trustees: Donna Schwartz; Marvin C. Schwartz.
EIN: 137114848

2422
William P. & Gertrude Schweitzer Foundation, Inc.
c/o Theodore R. Shiffman
317 Madison Ave., Ste. 1410
New York, NY   10017

Established in 1961 in NY.
Donor(s): Gertrude Schweitzer.‡
Grantmaker type: Independent foundation
Financial data (yr. ended 12/31/01): Assets, $2,206,381 (M); expenditures, $127,782; qualifying distributions, $117,407; giving activities include $118,000 for 9 grants (high: $25,000; low: $6,500).
Purpose and activities: Giving to museums, performing arts, and hospitals.

Fields of interest: Museums; Orchestra (symphony); Arts; Animal welfare; Jewish agencies & temples.
Limitations: Applications not accepted. Giving primarily in New York, NY; some giving also in Washington, DC. No grants to individuals.
Application information: Contributes only to pre-selected organizations.
Officer: Peter W. Schweitzer, C.E.O. and Pres.
EIN: 136160772

2423
Nathan & Lena Seiler Family Foundation, Inc.
c/o Lenat Co.
315 Westchester Ave.
Port Chester, NY   10573

Established in 1981 in NY.
Donor(s): Lena Seiler,‡ Nathan Seiler.
Grantmaker type: Independent foundation
Financial data (yr. ended 12/31/02): Assets, $3,850,844 (M); expenditures, $371,937; qualifying distributions, $330,426; giving activities include $330,885 for 73 grants (high: $100,000; low: $75).
Purpose and activities: Giving primarily to Jewish agencies and temples, and for social services.
Fields of interest: Education; Animal welfare; End of life care; Health organizations, association; Human services; International affairs; Jewish federated giving programs; Jewish agencies & temples.
Limitations: Applications not accepted. Giving primarily in the greater New York, NY, area. No grants to individuals.
Application information: Contributes only to pre-selected organizations.
Officer: Irving Kaplan, V.P. and Secy.
EIN: 133106906

2424
The Jack & Muriel Seiler Foundation, Inc.
c/o Lenat Co.
315 Westchester Ave.
Port Chester, NY   10573

Established in 1981 in FL.
Donor(s): Jack M. Seiler.
Grantmaker type: Independent foundation
Financial data (yr. ended 12/31/02): Assets, $3,010,262 (M); expenditures, $376,040; qualifying distributions, $334,731; giving activities include $335,000 for 9 grants (high: $135,000; low: $5,000).
Purpose and activities: Giving primarily to hospitals, conservation, and education.
Fields of interest: Education; Environment; Hospitals (general); Jewish agencies & temples.
Limitations: Giving on a national basis. No grants to individuals.
Officers: John Heffer, Pres.; Jane H. Julius, V.P.; Elaine A. Seiler, V.P.; Lewis Seiler, V.P.
EIN: 581473401

2425
Selz Foundation, Inc.
230 Park Ave.
New York, NY   10169
Contact: Bernard T. Selz, Pres.

Established in 1983 in NY.
Donor(s): Bernard T. Selz.
Grantmaker type: Independent foundation
Financial data (yr. ended 12/31/01): Assets, $19,232,423 (M); gifts received, $184,583; expenditures, $1,008,264; qualifying distributions, $984,399; giving activities include $938,547 for 58 grants (high: $300,600; low: $90).
Purpose and activities: Giving primarily to activities relating to pre-Columbian art.
Fields of interest: Museums; Arts; Education; Animals/wildlife; Children/youth, services.
Types of support: General/operating support; Program development; Professorships.
Limitations: Giving on a national basis.
Application information: Application form not required.
   Copies of proposal: 1
   Deadline(s): None
Officers and Directors:* Bernard T. Selz,* Pres.; Lisa Selz, Secy.-Treas.; Arnold Sytop.
Number of staff: 3 part-time support.
EIN: 133180806

2426
Semlitz/Glaser Foundation
1 Gracie Sq., Apt. 11
New York, NY   10028

Established in 1991 in NY.
Donor(s): Stephen M. Semlitz, Cathy Glaser.
Grantmaker type: Independent foundation
Financial data (yr. ended 04/30/03): Assets, $402,329 (M); expenditures, $122,971; qualifying distributions, $121,558; giving activities include $121,570 for 34 grants (high: $15,000; low: $50).
Purpose and activities: Giving for children's health, education, welfare and medical research.
Fields of interest: Child development; education; Higher education; Natural resources; Health care; Medical research, institute; Food distribution, meals on wheels; Children/youth, services; Jewish agencies & temples.
Types of support: Continuing support; Annual campaigns; Capital campaigns; Building/renovation; Equipment; Emergency funds; Curriculum development; Scholarship funds; Research.
Limitations: Applications not accepted. Giving primarily in New York, NY. No grants to individuals.
Application information: Contributes only to pre-selected organizations.
Trustees: Cathy Glaser; Stephen M. Semlitz.
EIN: 133632754

2427
The Peter Jay Sharp Foundation ▼
(formerly Sharp Foundation)
545 Madison Ave., 11th Fl.
New York, NY   10022   (212) 397-6060
Contact: Barry Tobias, Treas.

Established in 1984 in NY.

Donor(s): Peter J. Sharp.‡
Grantmaker type: Independent foundation
Financial data (yr. ended 12/31/01): Assets, $111,471,837 (M); gifts received, $58,686,231; expenditures, $17,741,275; qualifying distributions, $17,358,326; giving activities include $17,204,837 for 60 grants (high: $1,800,000; low: $3,000; average: $25,000–$300,000).
Purpose and activities: Support primarily for museums; giving also for the performing arts, with emphasis on music.
Fields of interest: Museums; Performing arts; Music; Education.
Limitations: Applications not accepted. Giving primarily in New York, NY. No grants to individuals.
Application information: Contributes only to pre-selected organizations.
Officers: Norman Peck, Pres.; Barry Tobias, Treas.
Directors: Edmund Duffy; Dan Lufkin; Jack Nash.
EIN: 133253731
Recent environmental and animal welfare grants:
2427-1 Conservation Fund, New York, NY, $500,000. For easements. 2001.
2427-2 Conservation Fund, New York, NY, $200,000. For land conservation program. 2001.
2427-3 Conservation International, DC, $85,000. 2001.
2427-4 International Crane Foundation, Baraboo, WI, $250,000. 2001.
2427-5 National Environmental Education and Training Foundation, DC, $75,000. 2001.
2427-6 New York Restoration Project, New York, NY, $50,000. 2001.
2427-7 Peconic Land Trust, Southampton, NY, $1,000,000. 2001.
2427-8 Quebec-Labrador Foundation/Atlantic Center for the Environment, Ipswich, MA, $50,000. 2001.

2428
The Sharpe Family Foundation
c/o Fiduciary Trust Co.
600 5th Ave.
New York, NY 10020 (212) 466-4100
Contact: Henry D. Sharpe, Jr., Tr.

Established in 1966 in RI.
Donor(s): Mary Elizabeth Sharpe.‡
Grantmaker type: Independent foundation
Financial data (yr. ended 12/31/01): Assets, $23,480,562 (M); gifts received, $600,000; expenditures, $1,300,366; qualifying distributions, $786,789; giving activities include $786,739 for 162 grants (high: $100,000; low: $100; average: $1,000–$50,000).
Purpose and activities: Giving primarily for art and culture, education, nature conservation and health.
Fields of interest: Media/communications; Arts; Secondary school/education; Higher education; Education; Natural resources; Health organizations, association; General charitable giving.
Limitations: Giving primarily in RI. No grants to individuals.
Application information:
Initial approach: Letter

Deadline(s): None
Trustees: Henry D. Sharpe, Jr.; Peggy B. Sharpe; Fiduciary Trust Co.
EIN: 136208422

2429
Eric P. Sheinberg Foundation
c/o Goldman Sachs & Co.
85 Broad St., Tax Dept.
New York, NY 10004

Established in 1971.
Donor(s): Eric P. Sheinberg.
Grantmaker type: Independent foundation
Financial data (yr. ended 06/30/02): Assets, $9,912,876 (M); expenditures, $488,752; qualifying distributions, $482,430; giving activities include $482,550 for 56 grants (high: $106,000; low: $100).
Fields of interest: Libraries (public); Education; Environment; Hospitals (general); Health organizations; Crime/law enforcement, police agencies; Human services; Community development; Federated giving programs.
Types of support: General/operating support.
Limitations: Applications not accepted. Giving primarily in CT and New York, NY. No grants to individuals.
Application information: Contributes only to pre-selected organizations.
Trustees: Eric P. Sheinberg; Michael Steinhardt.
EIN: 137004291

2430
Ralph C. Sheldon Foundation, Inc.
P.O. Box 417
Jamestown, NY 14702-0417 (716) 664-9890
Contact: Miles L. Lasser, Exec. Dir.
Application address: 7 E. 3rd St., Jamestown, NY 14701; FAX: (716) 483-6116

Incorporated in 1948 in NY.
Donor(s): Julia S. Livengood,‡ Isabell M. Sheldon.‡
Grantmaker type: Independent foundation
Financial data (yr. ended 05/31/03): Assets, $9,509,420 (M); gifts received, $1,849,119; expenditures, $1,681,627; qualifying distributions, $1,642,302; giving activities include $1,621,590 for 59 grants (high: $500,000; low: $100; average: $500–$50,000).
Purpose and activities: Support for youth development organizations, community improvement, cultural organizations, hospitals, social service organizations, and education.
Fields of interest: Visual arts; Performing arts; Theater; Arts; Libraries/library science; Education; Environment; Hospitals (general); Human services; Youth, services; Community development.
Types of support: General/operating support; Annual campaigns; Capital campaigns; Building/renovation; Equipment; Emergency funds.
Limitations: Giving limited to southern Chautauqua County, NY. No support for religious organizations. No grants to individuals.
Publications: Application guidelines.
Application information: Contact foundation for deadlines. Application form required.
Initial approach: Letter or telephone for application

Copies of proposal: 6
Deadline(s): None
Board meeting date(s): Varies, approx. 5 times a year
Final notification: Immediately after determination
Officers and Directors:* Jane E. Sheldon,* Pres.; Mark Hampton,* V.P.; Barclay O. Wellman,* V.P.; Miles L. Lasser,* Secy. and Exec. Dir.; Peter B. Sullivan,* Treas.; Betsy Shults; Alexis Theofilactidis.
Number of staff: 1 part-time professional; 1 part-time support.
EIN: 166030502

2431
The Sherrill Foundation
c/o H. Virgil Sherrill
1 Sutton Pl. S.
New York, NY 10022

Established around 1980.
Donor(s): H. Virgil Sherrill, Betty S. Sherrill.
Grantmaker type: Independent foundation
Financial data (yr. ended 10/31/02): Assets, $3,023,747 (M); expenditures, $256,205; qualifying distributions, $253,724; giving activities include $254,355 for 135 grants (high: $35,000; low: $100).
Fields of interest: Museums; Education; Animal welfare; Health care; Cancer; Medical research, institute; Human services; Children/youth, services; Christian agencies & churches.
Limitations: Applications not accepted. Giving primarily in Hobe Sound, FL, and NY. No grants to individuals.
Application information: Contributes only to pre-selected organizations.
Officers and Trustees:* H. Virgil Sherrill,* Pres.; Ann Sherrill Pyne, V.P.; Betty S. Sherrill,* V.P.; Stephen Sherrill, V.P.; Helen T. Harrison, Secy.
EIN: 136112730

2432
The Shoreland Foundation
1 Comac Loop
Ronkonkoma, NY 11779
Contact: Carol-Ann Mealy

Established in 1994 in NY.
Donor(s): Anthony W. Wang.
Grantmaker type: Independent foundation
Financial data (yr. ended 12/31/01): Assets, $46,960,392 (M); expenditures, $5,972,914; qualifying distributions, $5,950,289; giving activities include $5,958,516 for 51 grants (high: $4,602,615; low: $100; average: $1,000–$20,000).
Purpose and activities: Giving to human services, horticulture and garden clubs, education and museums.
Fields of interest: Museums; University; Horticulture/garden clubs; Children/youth, services; Philanthropy/voluntarism.
Types of support: General/operating support; Endowments.
Limitations: Applications not accepted. Giving primarily in NY. No grants to individuals.
Application information: Contributes only to pre-selected organizations.
Officers: Anthony W. Wang, Pres.; Lulu C. Wang, V.P.; Gary E. Martinelli, Secy.-Treas.

EIN: 113241828
Recent environmental and animal welfare grants:
2432-1 Winterthur Museum, Garden & Library, Winterthur, DE, $10,000. For general support for Collectors Circle. 2001.

2433
Siemens Corporation Contributions Program
Citicorp Ctr.
153 E. 53rd St.
New York, NY   10022-4611   (800) 743-6367

Grantmaker type: Corporate giving program
Purpose and activities: As a complement to its foundation, Siemens also makes charitable contributions to nonprofit organizations directly. Support is given on a national basis.
Fields of interest: Arts; Higher education; Education; Environment; Health care; Community development.
Types of support: General/operating support; Employee matching gifts; Employee-related scholarships.
Limitations: Giving on a national basis.
Application information: Application form required.
   Initial approach: Contact headquarters for application form
   Copies of proposal: 1
   Deadline(s): None
   Final notification: Following review

2434
The Sigety Family Foundation, Inc.
1760 3rd Ave.
New York, NY   10029
Contact: Elizabeth Sigety Marcus, Exec. Dir.

Established in 1994 in NJ.
Donor(s): Charles Sigety, Katharine Sigety.
Grantmaker type: Independent foundation
Financial data (yr. ended 02/28/02): Assets, $1,176,270 (M); expenditures, $125,948; qualifying distributions, $117,894; giving activities include $118,666 for 29 grants (high: $25,000; low: $100).
Fields of interest: Higher education; Law school/education; Natural resources; Human services; Children, services; Jewish agencies & temples.
Limitations: Giving primarily in CA, NY, and PA.
Application information:
   Initial approach: Proposal
   Deadline(s): Feb. 1, May 15 or Sept. 15
Officers and Trustees:* Charles Sigety,* Co-Chair.; Katharine Sigety,* Co-Chair.; Elizabeth S. Marcus,* Secy. and Exec. Dir.; Cornelius Sigety,* Treas.
EIN: 223287292

2435
Esther Simon Charitable Trust
c/o JPMorgan Chase Bank
345 Park Ave.
New York, NY   10154
Contact: Mary C. Dickens, V.P.

Trust established in 1952 in NY.

Donor(s): Esther Simon.‡
Grantmaker type: Independent foundation
Financial data (yr. ended 12/31/02): Assets, $7,377,083 (M); expenditures, $388,281; qualifying distributions, $360,109; giving activities include $353,500 for 86 grants (high: $27,500; low: $1,000).
Purpose and activities: Primary areas of interest include cultural programs and the arts, education, social services, and medical research.
Fields of interest: Historic preservation/historical societies; Arts; Education; Natural resources; Hospitals (general); Medical research, institute; Human services; Children/youth, services; Community development.
Types of support: General/operating support; Annual campaigns.
Limitations: Applications not accepted. Giving primarily in Washington, DC, and New York, NY. No grants to individuals.
Application information: Contributes only to pre-selected organizations. Unsolicited requests for funds not accepted.
Trustees: Stephen Simon; JPMorgan Chase Bank.
Number of staff: None.
EIN: 236286763

2436
The C. F. Roe Slade Foundation
c/o U.S. Trust Co. of NY
114 W. 47th St.
New York, NY   10016

Established in 1969 in NY.
Donor(s): Marie-Antoinette Slade.‡
Grantmaker type: Independent foundation
Financial data (yr. ended 06/30/02): Assets, $3,265,621 (M); gifts received, $741,334; expenditures, $340,658; qualifying distributions, $320,279; giving activities include $275,000 for 8 grants (high: $210,000; low: $5,000).
Purpose and activities: Giving for cultural institutes, botanical gardens, medical institutes, and animal care.
Fields of interest: Arts; Higher education; Botanical gardens; Hospitals (general); Public affairs, government agencies.
Types of support: General/operating support; Building/renovation; Research.
Limitations: Applications not accepted. Giving primarily in NY. No grants to individuals.
Application information: Contributes only to pre-selected organizations.
Trustees: John H. Bell, Jr.; W. Macy Johnson; Susan Porter.
EIN: 136205873

2437
Mary Jean & Frank P. Smeal Foundation
c/o Tom Burke, The Ayco Co., LP
P.O. Box 8019
Ballston Spa, NY   12020-8019

Established in 1985 in NY.
Donor(s): Frank P. Smeal.‡
Grantmaker type: Independent foundation
Financial data (yr. ended 02/28/01): Assets, $2,433,905 (M); gifts received, $1,043,952; expenditures, $1,284,441; qualifying distributions, $1,246,416; giving activities include $1,254,889 for 3 grants (high: $1,004,889; low: $125,000).

Fields of interest: Natural resources.
Types of support: General/operating support; Scholarship funds.
Limitations: Applications not accepted. Giving primarily in New York, NY. No grants to individuals; no loans or program-related investments.
Application information: Contributes only to pre-selected organizations.
Trustees: Henry F. Smeal; Mary Margaret Smeal.
EIN: 133318167

2438
The Randall & Kathryn Smith Foundation
c/o Smith Mgmt., LLC
885 3rd Ave., 34th Fl.
New York, NY   10022
Contact: John W. Adams

Established in 1982 in NJ.
Donor(s): John W. Adams, Randall Smith.
Grantmaker type: Independent foundation
Financial data (yr. ended 12/31/01): Assets, $1,765,900 (M); expenditures, $352,985; qualifying distributions, $315,927; giving activities include $316,671 for grants (high: $133,000).
Purpose and activities: Giving primarily for higher education, as well as for the environment, health associations and hospitals, and the arts.
Fields of interest: Museums (art); Higher education; Environment, air pollution; Hospitals (general); Health organizations, association; Human services.
Types of support: General/operating support; Annual campaigns; Research.
Limitations: Giving primarily in NC and NY.
Application information:
   Initial approach: Letter
   Deadline(s): None
Officers: Randall D. Smith, Pres.; Jeffrey A. Smith, Secy.
Trustee: Robert Haribson.
EIN: 222422965

2439
The John Ben Snow Foundation, Inc.
50 Presidential Plz., Ste. 106
Syracuse, NY   13202
Contact: Jonathan L. Snow, Treas.
FAX: (315) 471-5256

Incorporated in 1948 in NY.
Donor(s): John Ben Snow.‡
Grantmaker type: Independent foundation
Financial data (yr. ended 12/31/02): Assets, $5,881,747 (M); gifts received, $200; expenditures, $348,996; qualifying distributions, $279,196; giving activities include $212,300 for 21 grants (high: $30,000; low: $150).
Purpose and activities: The mission of the foundation is to make grants within specific focus areas to enhance the quality of life in central and northern NY state. The focus areas are: Arts and Culture, Community, Education, and Journalism.
Fields of interest: Journalism/publishing; Historic preservation/historical societies; Higher education; Libraries/library science; Education; Environment; Children/youth, services; Community development; Disabled.

Types of support: Building/renovation;
Equipment; Program development; Publication;
Seed money; Fellowships; Scholarship funds;
Matching/challenge support.
Limitations: Giving limited to central NY, with
emphasis on Onondaga and Oswego counties.
No support for religious organizations or
for-profit groups. No grants to individuals, or for
operating budgets, endowment funds, or
contingency financing.
Publications: Annual report (including
application guidelines), Financial statement.
Application information: All inquiries by mail.
Application form required.
 Initial approach: Letter of inquiry
 Copies of proposal: 1
 Deadline(s): Jan. 1 for letters of inquiry;
  submit inquiry preferably from July through
  Dec.; submit application by Apr. 1; either a
  final report after project is completed by
  Apr. 1 or a progress report by Apr. 1
 Board meeting date(s): June
 Final notification: July 1
Officers and Directors:* David H. Snow,* Pres.;
Jonathan L. Snow,* V.P. and Treas.; Emelie
Melton-Williams,* Secy.; Valerie A. Macfie;
Allen R. Malcolm; Bruce Malcolm.
Number of staff: 1 part-time support.
EIN: 136112704

2440
John Ben Snow Memorial Trust
50 Presidential Plz., Ste. 106
Syracuse, NY 13202
Contact: Jonathan L. Snow, Tr. (NY), Emelie M.
Williams, Tr. (NV), or Allen R. Malcom, Tr. (MD)
Regional offices: c/o Allen R. Malcom, 104
Church Alley, Chestertown, MD 21620; c/o
Emelie M. Williams, 2975 Knight Rd., Reno, NV
89509

Trust established in 1975 in NY.
Donor(s): John Ben Snow.‡
Grantmaker type: Independent foundation
Financial data (yr. ended 12/31/02): Assets,
$24,038,200 (M); expenditures, $1,474,898;
qualifying distributions, $1,291,590; giving
activities include $1,182,420 for 62 grants
(high: $50,000; low: $1,000; average:
$5,000–$25,000).
Purpose and activities: Support primarily for
higher education, scholarship funds, the
humanities and cultural institutions, especially
libraries, the performing arts, theater, and
historical preservation; environmental groups;
media and communications; and community
development. Support also for the handicapped,
and science and technology.
Fields of interest: Performing arts; Theater; Arts;
Higher education; Libraries/library science;
Environment; Health organizations, association;
Children/youth, services; Community
development; Disabled.
Types of support: Building/renovation;
Equipment; Program development; Publication;
Seed money; Scholarship funds;
Matching/challenge support.
Limitations: Giving primarily in MD, NV, and
central NY. No support for unspecified projects,
religious organizations, or for-profit groups. No
grants to individuals, or for operating budgets,
endowment funds, or contingency financing; no
loans.

Publications: Annual report (including
application guidelines).
Application information: Contact closest
regional office. Application form required.
 Initial approach: Letter of inquiry by Jan. 1 of
  the year for which funding is requested
 Copies of proposal: 1
 Deadline(s): Submit proposal preferably from
  July through Feb.; deadline Apr. 1
 Board meeting date(s): June
 Final notification: July 1
Trustees: Allen R. Malcolm; Jonathan L. Snow;
Emelie M. Williams; The Bank of New York.
Number of staff: 1 shared staff (shared with John
Ben Snow Foundation).
EIN: 136633814

2441
Society of International Cultural Exchange (SICE), Inc.
150 E. 52nd St., 34th Fl.
New York, NY 10022

Established in 1994 in FL and NY.
Donor(s): Fujisankei Communications
International, Inc.
Grantmaker type: Company-sponsored
foundation
Financial data (yr. ended 03/31/02): Assets,
$1,284,776 (M); gifts received, $300,000;
expenditures, $311,106; qualifying distributions,
$302,991; giving activities include $283,149 for
6 grants (high: $209,419; low: $1,000).
Purpose and activities: Giving primarily for art
and culture.
Fields of interest: Museums; Museums (art);
Agriculture, farmlands; Human services;
International affairs.
International interests: Japan.
Limitations: Giving primarily in New York, NY.
Application information: Application form not
required.
 Deadline(s): None
Officers: Hisashi Hieda, Chair. and C.E.O.;
Takashi Hoga, Co-Pres.; Koichi Murakami,
Co-Pres.; Atsuo Nakahara, Sr. V.P. and Secy.; Yuji
Itoyama, Treas.
Director: John J. Parker.
EIN: 133244953

2442
Sheldon H. Solow Foundation, Inc.
9 W. 57th St., Ste. 4500
New York, NY 10019-2601 (212) 754-0284
Contact: Rosalie S. Wolff, V.P.

Incorporated in 1986 in DE.
Donor(s): Sheldon H. Solow.
Grantmaker type: Independent foundation
Financial data (yr. ended 11/30/01): Assets,
$6,244,815 (M); gifts received, $1,756,000;
expenditures, $1,869,203; qualifying
distributions, $1,864,996; giving activities
include $1,866,050 for 22 grants (high:
$1,000,000; low: $250).
Purpose and activities: Giving primarily for the
arts, including visual arts organizations and
programs.
Fields of interest: Visual arts;
History/archaeology; Arts; Animals/wildlife,
preservation/protection; Human services; Jewish
federated giving programs.

Types of support: General/operating support;
Continuing support; Endowments;
Professorships; Fellowships.
Limitations: Giving on a national basis. No
grants to individuals.
Application information: Application form not
required.
 Initial approach: Letter
 Copies of proposal: 1
 Deadline(s): None
Officers: Sheldon H. Solow, Pres.; Steven
Cherniak, V.P.; Rosalie Wolff, V.P.
EIN: 133386646

2443
Martin and Toni Sosnoff Foundation
(formerly Martin T. Sosnoff Foundation)
P.O. Box 135
Rhinebeck, NY 12572

Established in 1978.
Donor(s): Martin T. Sosnoff.
Grantmaker type: Independent foundation
Financial data (yr. ended 11/30/02): Assets,
$2,272,330 (M); expenditures, $122,036;
qualifying distributions, $114,989; giving
activities include $113,331 for 35 grants (high:
$25,000; low: $50).
Purpose and activities: Giving primarily for
higher education, services for dogs, the arts, and
children and social services.
Fields of interest: Museums (art); Performing
arts; Higher education; Animal welfare; Human
services; Children/youth, services.
Types of support: General/operating support;
Building/renovation.
Limitations: Applications not accepted. Giving
primarily in NY. No support for private
foundations. No grants to individuals.
Application information: Contributes only to
pre-selected organizations.
Trustees: Martin T. Sosnoff; Toni Sosnoff.
EIN: 222231640

2444
The SPIA Foundation
(formerly Dorinda Pell and Mark Winkelman
Foundation)
780 3rd Ave., 16th Fl.
New York, NY 10017-2024

Established in 1985 in NY.
Donor(s): Mark O. Winkelman, Dorinda Pell,
Marius O. Winkelman.
Grantmaker type: Independent foundation
Financial data (yr. ended 02/28/02): Assets,
$5,021,567 (M); expenditures, $383,359;
qualifying distributions, $270,095; giving
activities include $268,515 for 30 grants (high:
$50,000; low: $40).
Purpose and activities: Giving primarily for
education, health care, and the arts.
Fields of interest: Arts; Elementary/secondary
education; Higher education; Natural resources;
Hospitals (general); Health organizations,
association; Food distribution, meals on wheels;
Human services.
Limitations: Applications not accepted. Giving
primarily in NY. No grants to individuals.
Application information: Contributes only to
pre-selected organizations.

Trustees: Dorinda P. Winkelman; Marius O. Winkelman.
EIN: 133318172

2445
The Seth Sprague Educational and Charitable Foundation ▼
c/o U.S. Trust
114 W. 47th St.
New York, NY 10036-1532
Contact: Carolyn L. Larke, Asst. V.P., U.S. Trust, or Linda R. Francisocovich, V.P., U.S. Trust
FAX: (212) 852-3377

Trust established in 1939 in NY.
Donor(s): Seth Sprague.‡
Grantmaker type: Independent foundation
Financial data (yr. ended 12/31/02): Assets, $54,663,473 (M); expenditures, $3,034,802; qualifying distributions, $2,769,869; giving activities include $2,390,571 for 346 grants (high: $50,000; low: $500; average: $1,000–$10,000).
Purpose and activities: Emphasis on health and human services, education, culture and the arts, and civic affairs and community development.
Fields of interest: Performing arts; Arts; Secondary school/education; Higher education; Education; Hospitals (general); Health care; Human services; Children/youth, services; Community development; Government/public administration.
Types of support: General/operating support; Program development; Matching/challenge support.
Limitations: Giving primarily in MA and NY. No grants to individuals, or for building funds; no loans.
Publications: Application guidelines.
Application information: Application form not required.
  Initial approach: Mail or fax letter requesting guidelines
  Copies of proposal: 1
  Deadline(s): Apr. 15
  Board meeting date(s): Mar., June, Sept., and Dec. (grants awarded at June and Dec. meetings)
  Final notification: Letter
Trustees: Patricia Dunnington; Arline Ripley Greenleaf; Jacqueline D. Simpkins; U.S. Trust.
Number of staff: None.
EIN: 136071886
Recent environmental and animal welfare grants:
2445-1 Association for the Preservation of Cape Cod, Orleans, MA, $15,000. 2001.
2445-2 Barnstable Land Trust, Cotuit, MA, $10,000. 2001.
2445-3 Cape Outdoor Discovery, Falmouth, MA, $10,000. 2001.
2445-4 Cape Outdoor Discovery, Falmouth, MA, $10,000. 2001.
2445-5 Center for Coastal Studies, Provincetown, MA, $50,000. 2001.
2445-6 Center for Coastal Studies, Provincetown, MA, $15,000. 2001.
2445-7 Central Park Conservancy, New York, NY, $10,000. 2001.
2445-8 Environmental and Land Use Law Center, Fort Lauderdale, FL, $10,000. 2001.
2445-9 Marine Biological Laboratory, Woods Hole, MA, $20,000. 2001.

2445-10 Marine Biological Laboratory, Woods Hole, MA, $20,000. 2001.
2445-11 National Marine Life Center, Buzzards Bay, MA, $20,000. 2001.
2445-12 National Marine Life Center, Buzzards Bay, MA, $10,000. 2001.
2445-13 Natural Resources Defense Council, New York, NY, $15,000. 2001.
2445-14 Natural Resources Defense Council, New York, NY, $10,000. 2001.
2445-15 New York Botanical Garden, Bronx, NY, $15,000. 2001.
2445-16 New York Botanical Garden, Bronx, NY, $15,000. 2001.
2445-17 Wilderness Society, DC, $10,000. 2001.

2446
John and Dorothy Sprague Foundation
770 Park Ave., Apt. 7D
New York, NY 10021

Established in 1994 in NY.
Grantmaker type: Independent foundation
Financial data (yr. ended 11/30/02): Assets, $889,763 (M); expenditures, $206,205; qualifying distributions, $173,920; giving activities include $172,845 for 27 grants (high: $130,470; low: $30).
Purpose and activities: Giving for education, environmental conservation, and family services.
Fields of interest: Arts; Education; Environment; Hospitals (general); Cancer; Recreation; Human services; Federated giving programs; Roman Catholic agencies & churches.
Limitations: Applications not accepted. Giving primarily in NY. No grants to individuals.
Application information: Contributes only to pre-selected organizations.
Trustees: John A. Sprague; Dorothy S. Whitmarsh.
EIN: 137053818

2447
The Stainman Family Foundation, Inc.
c/o Arthur J. Stainman
320 E. 72nd St.
New York, NY 10021-4769

Donor(s): Arthur J. Stainman, Lois Stainman.
Grantmaker type: Independent foundation
Financial data (yr. ended 12/31/02): Assets, $1,845,548 (M); gifts received, $395,406; expenditures, $109,823; qualifying distributions, $98,990; giving activities include $98,990 for 42 grants (high: $15,000; low: $150).
Fields of interest: Museums (art); Animals/wildlife, preservation/protection; Food services.
Officers: Arthur J. Stainman, Pres.; Lois Stainman, V.P.; Evan Stainman, Secy.
EIN: 133980213

2448
Staritch Foundation, Inc.
c/o W.A. Sweeney
P.O. Box 1355
Saranac Lake, NY 12983-7355

Donor(s): Charles L. Ritchie, Jr., James M. Ritchie, Mary Anne Ritchie.
Grantmaker type: Independent foundation
Financial data (yr. ended 12/31/01): Assets, $1,162,353 (M); gifts received, $249,391; expenditures, $103,244; qualifying distributions, $103,244; giving activities include $100,900 for grants (high: $40,000).
Fields of interest: Theater; Animals/wildlife, preservation/protection; Youth development, centers/clubs; Human services.
Limitations: Applications not accepted. Giving primarily in NY. No grants to individuals.
Application information: Contributes only to pre-selected organizations.
Officers: Charles L. Ritchie, Jr., Pres.; William A. Sweeney, V.P.; Mary Anne Ritchie, Secy.; James M. Ritchie, Treas.
EIN: 141827670

2449
The Starr Foundation ▼
70 Pine St.
New York, NY 10270 (212) 770-6881
Contact: Florence A. Davis, Pres.
FAX: (212) 425-6261; E-mail: grants@starrfoundation.org; URL: http://fdncenter.org/grantmaker/starr/

Incorporated in 1955 in NY.
Donor(s): Cornelius V. Starr.‡
Grantmaker type: Independent foundation
Financial data (yr. ended 12/31/02): Assets, $3,322,102,520 (M); gifts received, $89,531; expenditures, $212,770,168; qualifying distributions, $211,532,404; giving activities include $203,647,041 for 869 grants (high: $15,000,000; low: $1,000; average: $25,000–$125,000) and $5,654,369 for 980 grants to individuals (high: $16,280; low: $250; average: $2,000–$12,000).
Purpose and activities: Grants largely for education with emphasis on higher education, including scholarships under specific programs; support also for culture, health, welfare, and social sciences.
Fields of interest: Arts; Higher education; Education; Health care; Health organizations, association; Human services; Social sciences.
Types of support: General/operating support; Continuing support; Capital campaigns; Endowments; Professorships; Fellowships; Scholarship funds; Scholarships—to individuals.
Limitations: No grants to individuals (except through foundation's scholarship programs), or for matching gifts; no loans.
Application information: Application form not required.
  Initial approach: Letter
  Copies of proposal: 1
  Deadline(s): None
  Board meeting date(s): Feb. and Sept.
  Final notification: Varies
Officers and Directors:* Maurice R. Greenberg,* Chair.; Florence A. Davis,* Pres.; Gladys R. Thomas, V.P. and Secy.; Marion I. Breen,* V.P.; H.I. Smith,* Treas.; T.C. Hsu; Edwin A.G. Manton; E.E. Matthews; John J. Roberts; Ernest E. Stempel; E.S. Tse.
Number of staff: 2 full-time professional; 3 full-time support; 1 part-time support.
EIN: 136151545

Recent environmental and animal welfare grants:

2449-1 American Society for the Prevention of Cruelty to Animals, New York, NY, $10,000. For general support. 2002.

2449-2 Brooklyn Botanic Garden, Brooklyn, NY, $50,000. For program and general operating support. 2002.

2449-3 Central Park Conservancy, New York, NY, $100,000. For installation of irrigation system. 2002.

2449-4 Central Park Conservancy, New York, NY, $25,000. For Annual Frederick Law Olmsted Luncheon. 2002.

2449-5 Environmental Concern, Saint Michaels, MD, $12,000. For scholarships for seminars in wetlands management. 2002.

2449-6 Horticultural Society of New York, New York, NY, $25,000. For GreenWays community outreach initiative. 2002.

2449-7 Huntington Library, Art Collections and Botanical Gardens, San Marino, CA, $500,000. For Chinese Garden project. 2002.

2449-8 Nature Conservancy, Arlington, VA, $1,000,000. For site conservation planning, alternative energy and tourism in China. 2002.

2449-9 New York Botanical Garden, Bronx, NY, $2,000,000. For Virtual Herbarium project. 2002.

2449-10 New York Botanical Garden, Bronx, NY, $50,000. For table at Founders Award Dinner honoring Mr. and Mrs. Maurice R. Greenberg. 2002.

2449-11 New York Botanical Garden, Bronx, NY, $25,000. For Founders Award Dinner. 2002.

2449-12 Outward Bound, Garrison, NY, $50,000. For general support. 2002.

2449-13 Rainforest Alliance, New York, NY, $100,000. For micro-grants in developing countries. 2002.

2449-14 Riverkeeper, Garrison, NY, $10,000. For Benefit Dinner. 2002.

2449-15 Staten Island Botanical Garden, Staten Island, NY, $100,000. To match NEH challenge grant for general support. 2002.

2449-16 Wildlife Conservation Society, Bronx, NY, $5,000,000. For Year of the Tiger initiative. 2002.

2450
The Stebbins Fund, Inc.
P.O. Box 545
Cedarhurst, NY 11516
Contact: Brian M. Duftler, Secy.

Incorporated in 1947 in NY.
Donor(s): Members of the Stebbins family.
Grantmaker type: Independent foundation
Financial data (yr. ended 12/31/01): Assets, $4,407,781 (M); expenditures, $331,642; qualifying distributions, $243,663; giving activities include $239,950 for 59 grants (high: $25,000; low: $250).
Purpose and activities: Giving primarily for education, including higher education and art education; support also for museums and historical preservation.
Fields of interest: Museums; Historic preservation/historical societies; Arts; Higher education; Education; Environment; Animal welfare.

Types of support: General/operating support; Annual campaigns; Capital campaigns.
Limitations: Applications not accepted. Giving primarily in NY. No grants to individuals, or for endowment funds; no loans.
Application information: Contributes only to pre-selected organizations. Unsolicited requests for funds not accepted.
  Board meeting date(s): June
Officers: Theodore E. Stebbins, Pres.; Jane S. Sykes, V.P.; James F. Stebbins, V.P.; Brian M. Duftler, Secy.
Directors: Victoria Stebbins Greenleaf; J. Wright Rumbough, Jr.; Edwin E.F. Stebbins; Michael Morgan Stebbins.
EIN: 116021709

2451
The Steele-Reese Foundation
32 Washington Sq. W.
New York, NY 10011 (212) 505-2696
Contact: William T. Buice III, Tr. (in NY for general matters), Ms. Jane B. Stephenson (for southern Appalachian applicants) or Ms. Jeanne E. Wolverton (for Idaho and Montana)
Application addresses: 3121 Grantham Way, Lexington, KY 40509, tel.: (859) 263-5313 (for Appalachia), and P.O. Box 249, Alberton, MT 59820, tel.: (406) 722-4564 (for Idaho and Montana); URL: http://www.Steele-Reese.org

Trust established in 1955 in NY.
Donor(s): Eleanor Steele Reese,‡ Emmet P. Reese.‡
Grantmaker type: Independent foundation
Financial data (yr. ended 08/31/02): Assets, $40,025,927 (M); expenditures, $2,822,566; qualifying distributions, $2,438,237; giving activities include $2,267,750 for 78 grants (high: $80,000; low: $6,000; average: $10,000–$50,000).
Purpose and activities: Principally to aid organized charities in southern Appalachia, Idaho and Montana. Support for education (primarily elementary and secondary), health and hospices, welfare, including programs for drug abuse and youth, conservation, and the humanities, with a strong preference for rural projects; student aid only to students of Lemhi and Custer counties, Idaho, administered autonomously by institutions.
Fields of interest: Humanities; Elementary/secondary education; Education; Natural resources; Environment; Health care; Substance abuse, services; Health organizations, association; Human services; Children/youth, services; Family services; Hospices; Rural development.
Types of support: General/operating support; Equipment; Endowments; Professorships; Scholarship funds; Matching/challenge support.
Limitations: Giving primarily in ID, MT, and the Appalachian Mountain region of GA, KY, NC, and TN; scholarship program limited to students from Lemhi and Custer counties, ID. No support for community chests, efforts to influence school board and other elections, recreational facilities, athletic or academic competitions, or efforts to promulgate religious or political beliefs. No grants for continuing support, annual campaigns, conferences or workshops, seed money, emergency or building funds, deficit financing, research, endowments for small

organizations, computers or other technology used for instruction in schools, or land acquisition; no loans; grants to individuals confined to scholarships and paid through institutions.
Publications: Annual report (including application guidelines).
Application information: High school seniors in Lemhi and Custer counties, ID, should apply for scholarships through their schools. Application form not required.
  Initial approach: Letter to regional office
  Copies of proposal: 3
  Deadline(s): Apr. 1 for payment during current fiscal year; payments are generally made in Aug. and Sept.
  Board meeting date(s): Monthly
  Final notification: 3 to 6 months
Trustees: Charles U. Buice; William T. Buice III; J.P. Morgan & Co. Incorporated.
Number of staff: 3 part-time professional; 3 part-time support.
EIN: 136034763

2452
The Judy and Michael Steinhardt Foundation ▼
650 Madison Ave., 17th Fl
New York, NY 10022

Established in 1986 in NY.
Grantmaker type: Independent foundation
Financial data (yr. ended 09/30/02): Assets, $17,964,923 (M); gifts received, $1,500; expenditures, $7,042,455; qualifying distributions, $6,888,726; giving activities include $6,848,688 for 150 grants (high: $500,000; low: $50; average: $1,000–$25,000).
Purpose and activities: Support for Jewish giving and Jewish welfare, including organizations supporting Israel; support also for higher and other education and a botanical garden.
Fields of interest: Higher education; Education; Natural resources; Human services; Jewish federated giving programs; Jewish agencies & temples.
International interests: Israel.
Limitations: Applications not accepted. No grants to individuals.
Application information: Contributes only to pre-selected organizations.
Trustees: Judith Steinhardt; Michael Steinhardt.
EIN: 133357500
Recent environmental and animal welfare grants:
2452-1 Wildlife Conservation Society, Bronx, NY, $275,000. For unrestricted support. 2002.
2452-2 Wildlife Conservation Society, Bronx, NY, $15,000. For unrestricted support. 2002.

2453
W. P. Stewart & Co. Foundation, Inc.
527 Madison Ave.
New York, NY 10022

Established in 1998 in NY and DE.
Donor(s): W.P. Stewart & Co., Inc.
Grantmaker type: Company-sponsored foundation
Financial data (yr. ended 12/31/02): Assets, $31,957 (M); expenditures, $467,609; qualifying distributions, $464,733; giving

activities include $462,705 for 90 grants (high: $50,000; low: $100).
Purpose and activities: Giving for art and cultural programs, higher education, Jewish federated giving programs, environmental and wildlife conservation and for health and medical services.
Fields of interest: Museums; Arts; College; Natural resources; Animals/wildlife; Health care, research; Hospitals (general); Human services; Federated giving programs.
International interests: Bermuda.
Types of support: General/operating support.
Limitations: Applications not accepted. Giving on a national and international basis. No grants to individuals.
Application information: Contributes only to pre-selected organizations.
Officers: William P. Stewart, Chair.; John C. Russell, Pres.; Sandra Coleman, Treas.
Directors: Marilyn G. Breslow; Robert L. Rohn; Harry W. Segalas.
EIN: 134034704

2454
The Stony Point Foundation
c/o BCRS Assocs., LLC
100 Wall St., 11th Fl.
New York, NY 10005
E-mail: greenjn56@aol.com

Established in 1993 in NY.
Donor(s): John O. Downing.
Grantmaker type: Independent foundation
Financial data (yr. ended 01/31/03): Assets, $7,989,584 (M); gifts received, $1,843,741; expenditures, $295,608; qualifying distributions, $258,635; giving activities include $257,005 for 53 grants (high: $75,000; low: $25).
Fields of interest: Higher education; Natural resources; Hospitals (general).
Limitations: Applications not accepted. Giving primarily in NJ. No grants to individuals or for scholarships; no loans.
Application information: Contributes only to pre-selected organizations.
Trustees: Frances V.S. Downing; John O. Downing.
EIN: 133766973

2455
Stowe Family Foundation
1088 Park Ave., No. 16F
New York, NY 10128-1132
Contact: Virginia K. Stowe, Tr.

Established in 1996.
Donor(s): Richard H. Stowe, Virginia K. Stowe.
Grantmaker type: Independent foundation
Financial data (yr. ended 09/30/02): Assets, $1,026,841 (M); expenditures, $286,108; qualifying distributions, $284,195; giving activities include $284,392 for 42 grants (high: $150,000; low: $200).
Purpose and activities: Giving primarily for community development and higher education; the arts, natural resource conservation, children, youth, and social services and Christian churches.
Fields of interest: Arts; Higher education; Natural resources; Mental health/crisis services; Human services; Children/youth, services;

Community development; Christian agencies & churches.
Limitations: Giving primarily in Brunswick, ME, New York, NY, and PA.
Application information:
Initial approach: Letter requesting information
Trustees: Douglas Stowe; Richard H. Stowe; Virginia K. Stowe.
EIN: 137104307

2456
The Melville Straus Charitable Trust
c/o B. Strauss Assoc., Ltd.
307 5th Ave., 8th Fl.
New York, NY 10016-6517

Established in 1986 in NY.
Donor(s): Melville Straus.
Grantmaker type: Independent foundation
Financial data (yr. ended 02/28/02): Assets, $164,557 (M); gifts received, $385,147; expenditures, $476,425; qualifying distributions, $475,829; giving activities include $477,394 for 86 grants (high: $130,202; low: $200).
Purpose and activities: Giving primarily for arts and culture and educational purposes; some support also for health and human services.
Fields of interest: Museums; Museums (art); Performing arts; Arts; Higher education; Environment; Health care; Women, centers/services.
Limitations: Applications not accepted. Giving primarily in New York, NY. No grants to individuals.
Application information: Contributes only to pre-selected organizations.
Trustees: Richard Reiss; Melville Straus; Eugene Zuriff.
EIN: 136881724

2457
Strong Foundation of New York
30 E. 71st St.
New York, NY 10021-4956   (212) 249-1253
Contact: Roger L. Strong, Pres.
E-mail: vicki.lee@worldnet.att.net

Established in 1961 in NY.
Donor(s): Marguerite Strong,‡ Roger L. Strong, Jeffrey Strong, Lee Strong, Roger L. Strong, Jr., Thomas Strong.
Grantmaker type: Independent foundation
Financial data (yr. ended 03/31/02): Assets, $5,471,620 (M); gifts received, $110,580; expenditures, $302,543; qualifying distributions, $266,625; giving activities include $266,122 for 142 grants (high: $28,500; low: $100).
Purpose and activities: Giving primarily for primary and secondary education and the arts, and to Jewish agencies.
Fields of interest: Arts; Education, fund raising; Higher education; Libraries/library science; Natural resources; Jewish agencies & temples.
Types of support: General/operating support; Continuing support; Annual campaigns; Capital campaigns; Building/renovation; Land acquisition; Endowments; Emergency funds; Internship funds; Matching/challenge support.
Limitations: Applications not accepted. Giving primarily in New York, NY. No grants to individuals.
Publications: Annual report.

Application information: Contributes only to pre-selected organizations.
Board meeting date(s): Quarterly
Officers: Roger L. Strong, Pres.; Roger L. Strong, Jr., V.P.; Lee Strong, Secy.
Directors: Jeffrey Strong; Thomas Strong.
Number of staff: None.
EIN: 136093147

2458
C. H. Stuart Foundation
c/o JPMorgan Chase Bank
P.O. Box 31412
Rochester, NY 14603-1412
Contact: Janis Mosher, V.P., JPMorgan Chase Bank

Trust established in 1951 in NY.
Donor(s): Emmons Jewelers, Inc., Sarah Coventry, Inc.
Grantmaker type: Independent foundation
Financial data (yr. ended 12/31/02): Assets, $1,134,830 (M); expenditures, $124,981; qualifying distributions, $114,836; giving activities include $113,617 for 20 grants (high: $10,000; low: $250).
Purpose and activities: Giving for historical societies, Christian churches, and social services.
Fields of interest: Historic preservation/historical societies; Arts; Education; Animal welfare; Youth development, centers/clubs; Human services; Children/youth, services; Federated giving programs; Christian agencies & churches.
Types of support: Continuing support.
Limitations: Applications not accepted. Giving primarily in Wayne County and Newark, NY. No grants to individuals, or for endowment funds.
Application information: Contributes only to pre-selected organizations.
Board meeting date(s): May and Nov.
Trustee: JPMorgan Chase Bank.
Number of staff: None.
EIN: 166015254

2459
The Sulzberger Foundation, Inc.
229 W. 43rd St., Ste. 1031
New York, NY 10036   (212) 556-1755
Contact: Marian S. Heiskell, Pres.

Incorporated in 1956 in NY.
Donor(s): Arthur Hays Sulzberger,‡ Iphigene Ochs Sulzberger,‡ Marian S. Heiskell, Ruth S. Holmberg, Judith P. Sulzberger, Arthur Ochs Sulzberger.
Grantmaker type: Independent foundation
Financial data (yr. ended 12/31/01): Assets, $48,476,548 (M); gifts received, $2,000; expenditures, $2,987,371; qualifying distributions, $2,653,309; giving activities include $2,563,708 for 222 grants (high: $265,758; low: $100; average: $500–$15,000).
Purpose and activities: Giving primarily to arts/cultural programs, education, natural resource conservation and protection, hospitals, and human services.
Fields of interest: Arts; Education; Natural resources; Hospitals (general); Human services.
Types of support: General/operating support; Continuing support; Annual campaigns; Building/renovation; Endowments; Emergency funds; Program development; Scholarship funds.

Limitations: Giving on a national basis, with emphasis on NY, Chattanooga, TN, CA, and Washington, DC. No grants to individuals, or for matching gifts; no loans.
Application information: Application form not required.
  Initial approach: Letter
  Copies of proposal: 1
  Deadline(s): None
  Board meeting date(s): Jan. and as required
Officers and Directors:* Marian S. Heiskell,* Pres.; Arthur Ochs Sulzberger,* V.P. and Secy.-Treas.; Ruth S. Holmberg,* V.P.; Judith P. Sulzberger,* V.P.
Number of staff: 1 part-time professional; 2 part-time support.
EIN: 136083166

2460
Surdna Foundation, Inc. ▼
330 Madison Ave., 30th Fl.
New York, NY 10017-5001   (212) 557-0010
Contact: Edward Skloot, Exec. Dir.
FAX: (212) 557-0003; E-mail:
request@surdna.org; URL: http://www.surdna.org

Incorporated in 1917 in NY.
Donor(s): John E. Andrus.‡
Grantmaker type: Independent foundation
Financial data (yr. ended 06/30/02): Assets, $602,254,356 (M); gifts received, $1,479,199; expenditures, $38,867,479; qualifying distributions, $37,037,269; giving activities include $33,091,855 for 493 grants (high: $500,000; low: $100; average: $50,000–$150,000).
Purpose and activities: The foundation's guidelines focus on five areas: 1) The Environment, specifically transportation and energy, urban and suburban issues, and biological and cultural diversity; 2) Community Revitalization, which takes a comprehensive and holistic approach to restoring communities in America; 3) Building an Effective Citizenry, to advance social and emotional learning, enhance conflict resolution theory, practice and expand opportunities for service and citizenship, and support character development and ethical behavior; 4) The Arts; and 5) The Nonprofit Sector. The foundation is particularly interested in fostering catalytic, entrepreneurial programs that offer solutions to difficult systemic problems.
Fields of interest: Arts education; Natural resources; Energy; Environment; Dispute resolution; Housing/shelter, development; Disasters, 9/11/01; Economic development; Urban/community development; Community development; Philanthropy/voluntarism, association; Public affairs, citizen participation.
Types of support: General/operating support; Continuing support; Program development; Technical assistance.
Limitations: No support for international projects, or programs addressing toxics, hazardous waste, environmental education, sustainable agriculture, food production and distribution. No grants to individuals, or for capital campaigns, building funds, endowments, or land acquisition.
Publications: Annual report (including application guidelines).
Application information: Application form not required.

  Initial approach: Letter of inquiry and preliminary outline
  Copies of proposal: 1
  Deadline(s): None
  Board meeting date(s): Sept., Feb., and May
  Final notification: 90 days
Officers and Directors:* Elizabeth H. Andrus,* Chair.; John F. Hawkins, Vice-Chair.; John J. Lynagh,* Secy.; Marc de Venoge, C.F.O. and C.A.O.; Frederick F. Moon III,* Treas.; Edward Skloot, Exec. Dir.; John E. Andrus III, Chair. Emeritus; Alice Andrus; Peter B. Benedict; Pamela Brill, Ed.D.; Christopher F. Davenport; Lawrence S.C. Griffith, M.D.; Sandra T. Kaupe; J. Michael Pakradooni; Michael S. Spensley; Edith D. Thorpe; Samuel S. Thorpe III.
Number of staff: 11 full-time professional; 5 full-time support.
EIN: 136108163
Recent environmental and animal welfare grants:
2460-1 1000 Friends of New Mexico, Albuquerque, NM, $680,000. To work with partner organizations and statewide smart growth coalition to implement campaign and related projects at local, regional and state level to change direction of growth management in New Mexico. 2002.
2460-2 Alaska Marine Conservation Council, Anchorage, AK, $40,000. For fisheries management reform in North Pacific marine ecosystem at local, regional, and federal levels. 2002.
2460-3 Alaska Wilderness League, DC, $50,000. To facilitate and act as clearinghouse for broad-based campaign to defend Arctic Refuge and to educate public and build base of activist support for its protection. 2002.
2460-4 Alternatives for Community and Environment (ACE), Roxbury, MA, $50,000. For convening and facilitating new regional alliance for environmental and transportation justice in Boston. 2002.
2460-5 American Oceans Campaign, DC, $75,000. For continued support for initiative to promote fish habitat protection in New England. 2002.
2460-6 Americans for Equitable Climate Solutions, DC, $100,000. For common assets policy proposal that would reduce U.S. greenhouse gas emissions without diminishing economic growth or violating principles of fairness. 2002.
2460-7 Baltimore Regional Partnership, Baltimore, MD, $60,000. For core budget of partnership of organizations that work on smart growth issues in Baltimore region. 2002.
2460-8 Bay Area Transportation and Land Use Coalition, San Francisco, CA, $100,000. For reforming transportation investment and land use planning in Bay Area. 2002.
2460-9 California Association of Nonprofits, Los Angeles, CA, $50,000. For efforts to encourage California nonprofit groups to greatly reduce energy consumption. 2002.
2460-10 Cape and Islands Self-Reliance Corporation, East Falmouth, MA, $40,000. For public and decision-maker education campaign on economic, environmental, and health benefits of renewable energy. 2002.
2460-11 Cape Cod Commercial Hook Fishermens Association, West Chatham, MA,

$45,000. For continued support for campaign of commercial fishermen and other concerned coastal residents for reform of New England ground fisheries management to make it environmentally sustainable. 2002.
2460-12 Center for a New American Dream, Takoma Park, MD, $300,000. For general support for addressing scale and patterns of American consumption and working to improve quality of life by fostering more sustainable behaviors and lifestyles. 2002.
2460-13 Center for Neighborhood Technology, Chicago, IL, $150,000. To implement transportation reform in Chicago area. 2002.
2460-14 Center for Public Interest Research, Boston, MA, $200,000. For activities of state public interest research group activists in New Mexico and Maryland to craft meaningful policy solutions to sprawl problem and build grassroots support for reform at state level. 2002.
2460-15 Chesapeake Bay Foundation, Annapolis, MD, $600,000. For collaboration with Baltimore Regional Partnership for promotion and implementation of land use and transportation plan for Baltimore Region and for smart growth advocacy statewide. 2002.
2460-16 Citizens for Pennsylvanias Future, Harrisburg, PA, $75,000. For development of marketing and outreach program to increase consumer demand for renewable energy power in Pittsburgh area. 2002.
2460-17 Clean Energy Group, Montpelier, VT, $100,000. For operating support of national network of state-based clean energy funds. 2002.
2460-18 Climate Neutral Network, Lake Oswego, Oregon, $100,000. For pilot project in Oregon that aims to develop new market mechanism to fund innovative, climate-neutral transportation projects and raise awareness about climate change. 2002.
2460-19 Coastal Conservation Association-Florida, Winter Park, FL, $80,000. For initiative to document problems with federal management of fisheries in Southeastern United States and financial conflicts of interest on federal fishery management councils; and to develop and advocate management approaches that address these problems through systematic change in Florida and federal fishery management processes, including transfer of some management authority to states. 2002.
2460-20 College of the Atlantic, Bar Harbor, ME, $30,000. For ECO-ECO Smart Growth Forum for process of education and engagement of Maine's lay planners, civic leaders, and activists in application of best smart growth practices. 2002.
2460-21 Community Rights Counsel, DC, $75,000. For public interest law firm that is helping communities defend critical health and environmental protections, particularly in area of land use. 2002.
2460-22 Connecticut Clean Air Through Renewable Energy (Connecticut CAREs), Rocky Hill, CT, $125,000. To establish broad education and marketing campaign that brings together wide range of community and business organizations to help improve Connecticut's air quality by promoting renewable energy power. 2002.

2460-23 Conservation Fund, Arlington, VA, $100,000. For program to use development as tool for conservation through partnerships with private sector, especially real estate development industry; and to advance concept of green infrastructure as new strategic approach to land conservation that brings conservation biology into smart growth arena. 2002.

2460-24 Consumers Choice Council, DC, $100,000. To encourage more sustainable forest management through procurement initiatives that promote use of certified and other environmentally preferable building materials. 2002.

2460-25 Council on the Environment, New York, NY, $25,000. To administer and implement key aspects of professional development, student research, and enrichment programs of Friends of the New York High School for Environmental Studies. 2002.

2460-26 Development Training Institute, Baltimore, MD, $160,000. To launch national training program that will educate community development leaders about smart growth development and sponsor regional demonstration programs. 2002.

2460-27 E and Co, Bloomfield, NJ, $40,000. For feasibility study to evaluate models of successful market interventions in area of renewable energy finance, project development, and market support, and to assess new role for nonprofit sector in clean energy implementation in U.S. 2002.

2460-28 Endangered Species Coalition, DC, $60,000. For campaign to mobilize grassroots to protect endangered species, to educate public and opinion leaders on biodiversity and endangered species issues, and to uphold and increase funding for Endangered Species Act. 2002.

2460-29 Environmental Leadership Program, Cambridge, MA, $110,000. For leadership development program that trains and supports new generation of environmental leaders, characterized by diversity, innovative thinking, coalition building, and effective communication. 2002.

2460-30 Environmental Support Center, DC, $150,000. For ongoing work as intermediary to enhance organizational effectiveness of grassroots environmental advocacy organizations in United States; and for its continual oversight of State Environmental Leadership Program that enhances effectiveness and strengthens network between lead state environmental organizations. 2002.

2460-31 Envision Utah, Salt Lake City, UT, $400,000. Toward continued implementation of growth strategy for Greater Wasatch Area surrounding Salt Lake City. 2002.

2460-32 Forest Stewards Guild, Santa Fe, NM, $100,000. For organization that provides forum and support system for practicing foresters and other resource management professionals working to advance ecologically responsible forest management. 2002.

2460-33 Funders Network for Smart Growth and Livable Communities, Coral Gables, FL, $75,000. For Surdna's continued membership and for projects, funders'

working group on transportation and strategic assessment of field. 2002.

2460-34 Georgetown University, Environmental Law and Policy Institute, DC, $100,000. For general support to launch Georgetown Environmental Law and Policy Institute, which focuses on legal and policy arguments in support of public efforts to protect environment. 2002.

2460-35 Glynwood Center, Cold Spring, NY, $75,000. For evaluation and business plan to improve quality of community decision-making on linked issue of conservation and economic development. 2002.

2460-36 Growth Management Leadership Alliance, DC, $40,000. For building organizational, outreach and collaborative capacity of national network of state and regional smart growth advocacy organizations. 2002.

2460-37 Gulf Restoration Network, New Orleans, LA, $40,000. For project to reform key elements of fisheries management in Gulf of Mexico region. 2002.

2460-38 Habitat Media, San Rafael, CA, $50,000. For completion of two part PBS documentary series called Empty Oceans, Empty Nets, which examines state of marine fisheries worldwide and efforts being made to restore and sustain them. 2002.

2460-39 Institute for Community Economics, Springfield, MA, $250,000. To launch major capacity building effort targeting community land trust movement. 2002.

2460-40 Jane Goodall Institute for Wildlife Research, Education and Conservation, Silver Spring, MD, $100,000. For Conflict and Conservation: African Pilot Study and Information Acquisition-Lessons for Reconciliation. 2002.

2460-41 Michigan Land Use Institute, Beulah, MI, $30,000. For communications project that is supporting smart growth movement with series of nationally syndicated opinion articles by prominent writers. 2002.

2460-42 Mountain Association for Community Economic Development, Berea, KY, $15,000. For strategic planning. 2002.

2460-43 National Council for Science and the Environment, DC, $1,000,000. For new national commission designed to strengthen scientific understanding of impact of applied forestry on biodiversity as well as to communicate that information to broad group of practitioners and other stakeholders. 2002.

2460-44 National Environmental Trust, DC, $75,000. To mobilize supplementary media outreach, public education, and organizing on behalf of key marine conservation initiatives. 2002.

2460-45 National League of Cities Institute, DC, $150,000. For program which will educate, provide information, and help local municipal officials analyze and reform state and local land use policies that contribute to sprawl and disinvestment in historically urban areas. 2002.

2460-46 National Network of Forest Practitioners, Providence, RI, $40,000. For expanding efforts to mobilize and strengthen community forestry practitioners at grassroots level. 2002.

2460-47 National Religious Partnership for the Environment, Amherst, MA, $150,000. For strategic initiative to deepen and institutionalize engagement and commitment of American religious community to connections between environmental protection and religion. 2002.

2460-48 Natural Resources Defense Council, New York, NY, $75,000. To assess environmental impact of the World Trade Center disaster. 2002.

2460-49 Nature Conservancy, Rochester, NY, $180,000. For program to promote sustainable forestry certification within largest conservation organization in United States. 2002.

2460-50 New Ecology, Cambridge, MA, $125,000. For planning and implementation of initiative that is engaging Massachusetts' community development corporations in green development. 2002.

2460-51 New Jersey Future, Trenton, NJ, $300,000. For process of policy development, refinement, and advocacy to strengthen smart growth in New Jersey. 2002.

2460-52 Noise Pollution Clearinghouse, Montpelier, VT, $75,000. To create Washington Watchdog, online information searching tool that will enable environmental activists and others to quickly and cheaply search vast federal databases for information about legislative and regulatory developments. 2002.

2460-53 Northern Forest Alliance, Montpelier, VT, $240,000. For work to promote forest certification and to ensure high quality working forest easements as part of conservation deals currently being executed in Northern Forest. 2002.

2460-54 Northern Forest Center, Concord, NH, $100,000. To continue development of innovative regional investment funds which will target sustainable forestry land deals as well as opportunities to build or strengthen enterprises that support distribution and use of sustainable forest products. 2002.

2460-55 Northwest Atlantic Marine Alliance, Saco, ME, $65,000. For general support. 2002.

2460-56 Oceana, DC, $200,000. To assist with formation and operation of new marine conservation organization that will be focused on protecting ocean resources in United States and around the world. 2002.

2460-57 Oregon League of Conservation Voters Education Fund, Portland, Oregon, $25,000. For research and public education activities related to property rights and land use in Oregon. 2002.

2460-58 Organizing Project, Portland, Oregon, $60,000. For process of education of leaders of institutions (schools, congregations, unions, and civic groups) and families about potential of environmentally-centered economic development to create significant number of living wage jobs for families in Portland, OR and Seattle, WA metropolitan areas, and for negotiations between these institutions and private and government sources of capital to begin to create jobs. 2002.

2460-59 Pacific Rivers Council, Eugene, Oregon, $50,000. For project that will focus on strengthening sustainable forestry certification standards as they apply to aquatic biodiversity and on extending certification as tool to improve management on forestlands currently managed through federal habitat conservation plans that are inadequate for maintaining healthy aquatic biodiversity. 2002.

2460-60 Piedmont Environmental Council, Warrenton, VA, $50,000. To adapt, for multiple audiences, presentation on exemplary approach to smart growth in Washington, DC metropolitan region, disseminate it nationally, and facilitate its roll out in region. 2002.

2460-61 Redefining Progress, Oakland, CA, $150,000. For initiative to build coalition that will shape and implement policy agenda to connect common assets to our everyday lives in a way that best serves interests of America's common prosperity and health. 2002.

2460-62 Regional Plan Association, New York, NY, $75,000. For organizational and strategic evaluation and plan for New York metropolitan area's leading land use and transportation policy and advocacy organization. 2002.

2460-63 Regional Plan Association, New York, NY, $50,000. For broad civic alliance to develop world class consensus vision for rebuilding downtown Manhattan that will represent best practices in urban planning, transit systems, energy efficiency, communications, green building, and public safety. 2002.

2460-64 Renewable Energy Policy Project, DC, $75,000. For second phase of project to identify and advocate opportunities for development of renewable energy in Southeast. 2002.

2460-65 Resource Renewal Institute, San Francisco, CA, $50,000. For continued support for campaign to advance concept and implementation of green planning - an approach to environmental planning and recovery that is comprehensive, integrated, and long term. 2002.

2460-66 Scenic America, DC, $15,000. To hire consultant to develop corporate fundraising program and build individual donor support to assist in planned growth of organization. 2002.

2460-67 Southern Alliance for Clean Energy, Knoxville, TN, $40,000. To strengthen policies in Southeast that support renewable energy and energy efficiency and to continue moving Tennessee Valley Authority to position of social and environmental leadership. 2002.

2460-68 Sustainability Institute, Hartland, VT, $150,000. To assist move to full scale program of training and technical support for systems thinking about sustainability. 2002.

2460-69 Sustainable Northwest, Portland, Oregon, $100,000. For project that seeks to make forest restoration more viable for rural Northwest communities by better commercializing by-products of forest ecosystem management. 2002.

2460-70 Theodore Roosevelt Conservation Partnership, Millersville, MD, $50,000. For general support for motivating hunters and fishermen to participate more actively in national forest management decision-making. 2002.

2460-71 Tides Center, San Francisco, CA, $100,000. For Green Media Toolshed project for cooperatively run national Internet-based clearinghouse of media related tools and information that are being used by member local, regional, and national nonprofit environment, conservation and preservation groups. 2002.

2460-72 Turtle Bay Museums and Arboretum on the River, Redding, CA, $500,000. For mobile forestry education exhibit that will bring information on sustainable forestry to rural communities in northern California, southern Oregon and western Nevada. 2002.

2460-73 Western Resource Advocates, Boulder, CO, $150,000. For expansion of capacity of leading regional group in West in efforts to respond to issues of growth and sprawl as they relate to energy, water, and land use. 2002.

2460-74 Youth Ministries for Peace and Justice, Bronx, NY, $150,000. For youth organizing focused on environmental concerns, reclaiming only neighborhood park for residents, and cleaning polluted Bronx River in River/Soundview neighborhood. 2002.

2461
Edna Bailey Sussman Fund

c/o Boyce, Hughes & Farrell, LLP
1025 Northern Blvd., Ste. 300
Roslyn, NY 11576-1587
Contact: Dorothy Bertine, Admin.

Established in 1984 in NY.
Donor(s): Arthur H. Dean,‡ Edward S. Miller.
Grantmaker type: Independent foundation
Financial data (yr. ended 04/30/02): Assets, $5,551,639 (M); expenditures, $277,342; qualifying distributions, $252,813; giving activities include $234,920 for 8 grants (high: $64,740; low: $4,095).
Purpose and activities: To further the preservation of wildlife, the control of pollution, and the preservation of natural land and resources by funding internships for individuals in a field of study at an institution of higher learning in an area that significantly impacts the environment.
Fields of interest: Higher education; Environment.
Types of support: Internship funds.
Limitations: Giving on a national basis.
Application information: The fund only accepts applications from colleges and universities with whom it has established relationships. It does not accept applications from individuals. Stipends are disbursed to institution on behalf of intern selected by fund trustees. Application form required.
  Initial approach: Application process must conform with host institution's general procedures
  Deadline(s): None
Trustees: Robert H. Frey; Edward S. Miller.
Number of staff: None.
EIN: 133187064

2462
Sweetgrass Foundation

170 Newell Rd.
Hammond, NY 13646
Contact: Allan P. Newell, Pres.

Established in 1992 in NY.
Donor(s): Allan P. Newell, Jean Newell.‡
Grantmaker type: Independent foundation
Financial data (yr. ended 12/31/02): Assets, $8,622,254 (M); expenditures, $685,168; qualifying distributions, $679,878; giving activities include $678,679 for 32 grants (high: $133,000; low: $500; average: $500–$133,000).
Fields of interest: Arts; Education; Environment, water resources; Environment; Youth development, services; Human services; Government/public administration.
Types of support: Capital campaigns; Building/renovation; Endowments; Program development; Conferences/seminars; Publication; Seed money; Matching/challenge support.
Limitations: Applications not accepted. Giving limited to St. Lawrence County and the St. Lawrence River Valley, NY, areas. No grants to individuals.
Application information: Contributes only to pre-selected organizations. Unsolicited requests for grants not accepted.
Officers and Directors:* Allan P. Newell,* Pres. and Treas.; Catherine B. Newell,* V.P. and Secy.; Mark Scarlett.
Number of staff: None.
EIN: 161414871

2463
Sykes Family Foundation

c/o Goldman Sachs & Co., Tax Dept.
85 Broad St.
New York, NY 10004

Established in 1993 in CA.
Donor(s): Gene T. Sykes.
Grantmaker type: Independent foundation
Financial data (yr. ended 06/30/02): Assets, $5,104,573 (M); gifts received, $2,500; expenditures, $149,343; qualifying distributions, $117,603; giving activities include $115,500 for 46 grants (high: $25,000; low: $250).
Purpose and activities: Giving for higher education, and human services.
Fields of interest: Elementary/secondary education; Higher education; Scholarships/financial aid; Environment; Human services.
Types of support: General/operating support.
Limitations: Applications not accepted. Giving on a national basis. No grants to individuals; no loans or scholarships.
Application information: Contributes only to pre-selected organizations.
Trustee: Gene T. Sykes.
EIN: 133748075

2464
Tamarind Foundation, Inc.

(formerly Helaine Heilbrunn Lerner Fund, Inc.)
175 E. 74th St.
New York, NY 10021

Established in 1999 in DE and NY.

Donor(s): Robert Heilbrunn, Helaine Lerner.
Grantmaker type: Independent foundation
Financial data (yr. ended 12/31/01): Assets, $68,419,611 (M); gifts received, $998,976; expenditures, $2,925,626; qualifying distributions, $2,925,626; giving activities include $2,907,412 for 122 grants (high: $1,638,000; low: $25; average: $100–$25,000).
Fields of interest: Higher education; Environment; Human services.
Limitations: Applications not accepted. No grants to individuals.
Application information: Contributes only to pre-selected organizations. Unsolicited requests for funds not accepted.
Officer: Helaine Lerner, Pres.
EIN: 134082873

2465
Task Foundation, Inc.
(formerly Consumer Action Council on Collective Purchasing, Inc.)
c/o Phil Weinper
20 S. Bayles Ave.
Port Washington, NY 11050 (516) 883-7711
Contact: Theodore W. Kheel, Pres.

Established around 1992.
Donor(s): Ann S. Kheel,‡ Theodore W. Kheel.
Grantmaker type: Independent foundation
Financial data (yr. ended 12/31/01): Assets, $9,315,214 (M); expenditures, $1,763,209; qualifying distributions, $1,769,893; giving activities include $1,415,441 for 37 grants (high: $590,000; low: $100; average: $1,000–$20,000).
Purpose and activities: Giving primarily for higher education.
Fields of interest: Higher education; Natural resources; Environment; Health care; Health organizations, association; Youth, services; Community development; Public affairs.
Limitations: Giving primarily in NY. No grants to individuals.
Application information: Application form not required.
Officers: Theodore W. Kheel, Pres.; Robert Kheel, Secy.
EIN: 131968353

2466
Milton Tenenbaum Charitable Foundation
c/o The Bank of New York, Tax Dept.
1 Wall St., 28th Fl.
New York, NY 10286
Contact: Patricia Healy
Application address: c/o The Bank of New York, 235 Main St., White Plains, NY 10601

Established in 1999 in NY.
Grantmaker type: Independent foundation
Financial data (yr. ended 05/31/02): Assets, $1,484,377 (M); expenditures, $157,226; qualifying distributions, $140,106; giving activities include $132,500 for 31 grants (high: $10,000; low: $1,000).
Fields of interest: Theater; Animals/wildlife; Health organizations, association; Human services; Jewish agencies & temples; Public affairs, volunteer services.
Application information:
Initial approach: Letter

Deadline(s): None
Trustee: The Bank of New York.
EIN: 137209332

2467
Thanksgiving Foundation
c/o Fiduciary Trust Co.
600 5th Ave.
New York, NY 10020
Contact: Alexandra von Stackelberg
Application addresses: c/o Thomas H. Stine, 380 Claremont Rd., Bernardsville, NJ 07924; or c/o Marc C. Winmill, 672 Tower Hill Rd., Millbrook, NY 12545

Established in 1985 in NJ.
Donor(s): Thomas M. Peters, Marion Post Peters.
Grantmaker type: Independent foundation
Financial data (yr. ended 07/31/02): Assets, $7,867,952 (M); expenditures, $656,277; qualifying distributions, $589,029; giving activities include $497,550 for 236 grants (high: $47,653; low: $23).
Purpose and activities: Giving primarily for elementary and secondary education and human services, including child welfare; some support also for museums and the fine arts, hospitals, and environmental conservation, including reforestation and wildlife preservation.
Fields of interest: Arts; Elementary/secondary education; Higher education; Environment; Animals/wildlife, preservation/protection; Hospitals (general); Human services; Children/youth, services.
Limitations: Giving primarily in NJ and New York, NY. No grants to individuals.
Application information:
Initial approach: Letter
Deadline(s): None
Officers: Marc C. Winmill, Chair.; Thomas H. Stine, Pres.
Trustee: Fiduciary Trust Co.
EIN: 136861874

2468
Thayer Family Scholarship Trust
c/o KeyBank N.A.
P.O. Box 1965
Albany, NY 12201-1965

Grantmaker type: Independent foundation
Financial data (yr. ended 07/31/02): Assets, $2,113,146 (M); expenditures, $161,074; qualifying distributions, $144,094; giving activities include $144,425 for grants to individuals.
Purpose and activities: Giving primarily for higher education. Scholarships awarded only to graduates of Cooperstown High School.
Fields of interest: Higher education; Medical school/education; Animals/wildlife, preservation/protection; Veterinary medicine; Agriculture; Biological sciences.
Types of support: Scholarships—to individuals.
Limitations: Applications not accepted. Giving primarily in Cooperstown, NY.
Trustee: KeyBank N.A.
EIN: 146134451

2469
Theobald Foundation
c/o Bessemer Trust
630 5th Ave., 34th Fl.
New York, NY 10111

Established in 1993 in IL.
Donor(s): Regina Mahon, Thomas C. Theobald.
Grantmaker type: Independent foundation
Financial data (yr. ended 10/31/02): Assets, $5,307,192 (M); expenditures, $247,409; qualifying distributions, $234,527; giving activities include $219,178 for 45 grants (high: $106,768; low: $500).
Purpose and activities: Giving primarily for education.
Fields of interest: Museums; Higher education; Education; Zoos/zoological societies; Human services.
Limitations: Applications not accepted. Giving primarily in Chicago, IL. No grants to individuals.
Application information: Unsolicited requests for funds not accepted.
Trustees: Regina Mahon; Thomas C. Theobald.
EIN: 367085378

2470
The Daniel K. Thorne Foundation, Inc.
c/o Stroock & Stroock
142 W. 57th St., 16th Fl.
New York, NY 10019

Established in 1996 in NY.
Donor(s): Daniel K. Thorne.
Grantmaker type: Independent foundation
Financial data (yr. ended 12/31/00): Assets, $11,300,365 (M); expenditures, $842,426; qualifying distributions, $785,427; giving activities include $769,892 for 37 grants (high: $339,392; low: $500).
Purpose and activities: Giving for natural resource conservation.
Fields of interest: Natural resources.
Types of support: Continuing support; Emergency funds; Matching/challenge support.
Limitations: Applications not accepted. Giving on a national basis.
Application information: Unsolicited requests for funds not accepted.
Board meeting date(s): Mar., June, Oct. and Dec. 15
Officers and Directors:* Daniel K. Thorne,* Pres. and Treas.; Theodore S. Lynn,* Secy.; Alexandra T. Thorne.
Number of staff: 1 part-time support.
EIN: 133857951

2471
The Thorne Foundation
435 E. 52nd St.
New York, NY 10022 (212) 758-2425
Contact: Miriam Thorne Gilpatric, Pres.

Incorporated in 1930 in NY.
Donor(s): Landon K. Thorne,‡ Julia L. Thorne.‡
Grantmaker type: Independent foundation
Financial data (yr. ended 12/31/01): Assets, $1,317,358 (M); expenditures, $190,186; qualifying distributions, $176,050; giving activities include $176,050 for 87 grants (high: $25,000; low: $50).

Purpose and activities: Emphasis on wildlife and conservation, education, museums, cultural programs, and health organizations; support also for hospitals and libraries.
Fields of interest: Arts; Education; Natural resources; Animals/wildlife; Hospitals (general); Health organizations, association; Human services; YM/YWCAs & YM/YWHAs.
Limitations: Applications not accepted. Giving primarily in NY. No grants to individuals.
Application information: Contributes only to pre-selected organizations.
Officers: Miriam Thorne Gilpatric, Pres.; John B. Jessup, V.P.; David H. Thorne, V.P.
EIN: 136109955

2472
The Tiffany & Co. Foundation
727 5th Ave.
New York, NY 10022 (212) 230-6591
Contact: Fernanda M. Kellogg, V.P.

Established in 2000 in NY.
Donor(s): Tiffany & Co.
Grantmaker type: Company-sponsored foundation
Financial data (yr. ended 01/31/03): Assets, $5,869,234 (M); expenditures, $440,913; qualifying distributions, $440,913; giving activities include $440,000 for grants.
Purpose and activities: The foundation's efforts are focused on two areas: 1) Arts, especially in the areas of crafts education, arts education, preservation and conservation, decorative arts, performing arts, and visual arts, and 2) Environmental conservation.
Fields of interest: Arts education; Visual arts; Museums; Arts; Natural resources.
Types of support: Program development.
Limitations: Giving on a national basis. No support for religious, social, or fraternal groups, athletic teams or events, or organizations lacking 501(c)(3) status. No grants to individuals, or for capital campaigns or fundraising events.
Application information: Application form not required.
 Initial approach: Letter of inquiry
 Copies of proposal: 1
 Deadline(s): May 15 and Nov. 15
 Board meeting date(s): Jan. and July
Officers: Michael J. Kowalski, Pres.; James N. Fernandez, Exec. V.P.; James Quinn, Exec. V.P.; Fernanda M. Kellogg, V.P.; Patrick B. Dorsey, Secy.; Michael W. Connolly, Treas.
EIN: 134096178

2473
The Tinker Foundation Inc. ▼
55 E. 59th St., 21st Fl.
New York, NY 10022 (212) 421-6858
Contact: Renate Rennie, Pres.
FAX: (212) 223-3326; E-mail: tinker@tinker.org;
URL: http://fdncenter.org/grantmaker/tinker

Trust established in 1959 in NY; incorporated in 1975 in NY.
Donor(s): Edward Larocque Tinker.‡
Grantmaker type: Independent foundation
Financial data (yr. ended 12/31/02): Assets, $65,515,377 (M); expenditures, $3,849,964; qualifying distributions, $3,550,606; giving

activities include $2,741,690 for 58 grants (high: $150,000; low: $4,650; average: $20,000–$75,000).
Purpose and activities: Broadly, to promote better understanding among the peoples of the U.S., Latin America, Portugal and Spain. More specifically, grants are awarded in the areas of: 1) environmental issues, particularly incentive-based environmental activities, and those projects supporting the collaboration of NGO (Nongovernmental Organization) groups and corporate interests; 2) projects on governance including the reform of the judicial sector, decentralization, anti-violence and anti-corruption programs, and, in general, assistance to groups promoting transparency and accountability; and 3) economic policy programs concerned with modernization, liberalization and privatization issues.
Fields of interest: Natural resources; Environment; Foreign policy; International affairs; Marine science; Economics; Political science; Public policy, research; Government/public administration.
International interests: Portugal; Spain; Latin America; Mexico; Antarctica.
Types of support: Program development; Conferences/seminars; Seed money; Research; Matching/challenge support.
Limitations: Giving limited to projects related to Latin America, Spain, Portugal, and Antarctica. No support for projects concerned with health or medical issues or the arts and humanities. No grants to individuals, or for building or endowment funds, equipment, annual campaigns, operating budgets, annual appeals of community funds, or production costs for film, television, and radio projects.
Publications: Application guidelines, Annual report.
Application information: Application form required.
 Initial approach: Letter requesting application procedures
 Copies of proposal: 2
 Deadline(s): Institutional grants: Mar. 1 for summer meeting and Sept. 1 for winter meeting; Field Research Grants: Oct. 1
 Board meeting date(s): Institutional grants: June and Dec.; Field Research Grants: Dec.
 Final notification: Institutional and Field Research grants: 2 weeks after board meetings
Officers and Directors:* Martha T. Muse,* Chair.; Renate Rennie,* Pres.; Richard de J. Osborne,* Secy.; John A. Luke, Jr.,* Treas.; William R. Chaney; Sally Grooms Cowal; Charles McC. Mathias, Jr.; Kenneth R. Maxwell; Susan L. Segal; Alan Stoga.
Number of staff: 4 full-time professional; 1 part-time professional; 2 full-time support.
EIN: 510175449

2474
John & Daniel Tishman Fund, Inc.
(formerly Rose & John Tishman Fund, Inc.)
666 5th Ave.
New York, NY 10103-0001
Contact: John L. Tishman, Pres.

Established in 1957 in NY.
Donor(s): Rose F. Tishman, John Tishman, Daniel Tishman.

Grantmaker type: Independent foundation
Financial data (yr. ended 12/31/01): Assets, $5,830,568 (M); gifts received, $750,000; expenditures, $2,761,108; qualifying distributions, $2,718,728; giving activities include $2,700,000 for 29 grants (high: $1,537,000; low: $250).
Purpose and activities: Giving primarily for education, and the arts.
Fields of interest: Museums (natural history); Performing arts; Theater; Arts; Higher education; Education; Environment; Health care; Human services; Jewish federated giving programs.
Limitations: Giving primarily in NY.
Application information:
 Initial approach: Proposal
 Deadline(s): None
Officers: John L. Tishman, Pres.; Daniel Tishman, V.P. and Treas.; Katherine Blacklock, V.P.; Kathleen E. Kotoun, Secy.
EIN: 136151766

2475
Tompkins County Foundation, Inc.
P.O. Box 97
Ithaca, NY 14851
Contact: Janet Hewitt, Recording Secy.

Established in 1945 in NY.
Grantmaker type: Independent foundation
Financial data (yr. ended 12/31/02): Assets, $1,924,138 (M); gifts received, $275,999; expenditures, $199,628; qualifying distributions, $171,088; giving activities include $171,299 for 21 grants (high: $25,000; low: $964).
Purpose and activities: Giving for the arts, education, environment, and human services.
Fields of interest: Humanities; Arts; Education; Environment; Health care; Mental health/crisis services; Housing/shelter; Human services; Children/youth, services; Community development.
Types of support: Capital campaigns; Building/renovation; Equipment; Program development; Seed money; Grants to individuals; Matching/challenge support.
Limitations: Giving limited to the Tompkins County, NY, area.
Publications: Application guidelines, Annual report, Informational brochure.
Application information: Application form not required.
 Initial approach: Proposal
 Copies of proposal: 1
 Deadline(s): None
 Board meeting date(s): May and Oct.
 Final notification: June 15 and Nov. 15
Officers and Directors:* Larry Baum,* Pres.; Arthur W. Pearce,* V.P.; James Byrnes,* Secy.-Treas.; James Brown; R. Davis Cutting; Anthony C. Digiacomo; Bonnie Howell; Patricia Johnson; Bruce Kane; Charles W. Treman, Jr.
Number of staff: 2 part-time support.
EIN: 156018481

2476
Topol Foundation
825 Orienta Ave.
Mamaroneck, NY 10543-4314
(914) 698-3532
Contact: Robert M. Topol, Pres.

Established in 1968 in DE and NY.
Donor(s): Robert M. Topol, D'Vera Topol.
Grantmaker type: Independent foundation
Financial data (yr. ended 12/31/02): Assets,
$159,989 (M); gifts received, $37,480;
expenditures, $113,455; qualifying distributions,
$117,020; giving activities include $112,956 for
95 grants (high: $37,500; low: $15).
Purpose and activities: Giving primarily for the
arts, education, health, and Jewish organizations.
Fields of interest: Museums; Arts; Higher
education; Education; Natural resources;
Hospitals (general); Health care; Health
organizations, association; Geriatrics research;
Human services; Day care; Jewish federated
giving programs; Jewish agencies & temples.
Limitations: Giving primarily in the greater New
York, NY, area. No grants to individuals.
Application information: Application form not
required.
> *Initial approach:* Letter on organization
> letterhead
> *Copies of proposal:* 1
> *Deadline(s):* None
> *Board meeting date(s):* Jan., May, and Sept.
Officers: Robert M. Topol, Pres.; D'Vera Topol,
V.P.; Martha Kirby, Secy.; Clifford Topol, Treas.
Directors: Gail Topol; Phyllis Topol.
Number of staff: None.
EIN: 237002556

2477
Tortuga Foundation
c/o Siegel, Sacks & Co.
630 3rd Ave., 22nd Fl.
New York, NY 10017

Established in 1979 in NY.
Donor(s): William C. Breed III, J.L. Tweedy.
Grantmaker type: Independent foundation
Financial data (yr. ended 09/30/02): Assets,
$16,495,513 (M); expenditures, $1,227,442;
qualifying distributions, $1,068,917; giving
activities include $1,070,000 for 39 grants (high:
$70,000; low: $10,000).
Purpose and activities: Support primarily for
land preservation, the environment, and
women's and family planning groups; support
also for health organizations and education.
Fields of interest: Education; Natural resources;
Environment; Health organizations, association;
Human services; Women, centers/services;
Women.
Limitations: Applications not accepted. Giving
on a national basis. No grants to individuals.
Application information: Contributes only to
pre-selected organizations.
Officers: Mildred Siceloff, Pres.; Patricia
Livingston, Secy.
Number of staff: 2 shared staff.
EIN: 510245279

2478
Towbin Fund
1010 5th Ave., Apt. 11B
New York, NY 10028

Trust established in 1955 in NY.
Donor(s): A. Robert Towbin, Belmont Towbin.
Grantmaker type: Independent foundation
Financial data (yr. ended 06/30/02): Assets,
$14,697 (M); gifts received, $138,390;

expenditures, $129,864; qualifying distributions,
$125,346; giving activities include $125,346 for
45 grants (high: $40,938; low: $200).
Purpose and activities: Giving primarily for
human services, children services, conservation,
the arts, and education.
Fields of interest: Arts; Elementary/secondary
education; Higher education; Natural resources;
Human services; Children/youth, services.
Types of support: General/operating support.
Limitations: Applications not accepted. Giving
primarily in NY. No grants to individuals.
Application information: Contributes only to
pre-selected organizations.
Trustee: A. Robert Towbin.
Number of staff: None.
EIN: 136158005

2479
Toyota Motor North America, Inc.
Corporate Giving Program
9 W. 57th St., Ste. 4900
New York, NY 10019 (212) 715-7470
Contact: Jennifer Rochkind, Asst. Mgr., Corp.
Philanthropy
Additional tel.: (212) 223-0303; FAX: (212)
750-3564; E-mail:
jennifer_rochkind@tma.toyota.com; URL: http://
www.toyota.com/about/community

Grantmaker type: Corporate giving program
Purpose and activities: Toyota Motor North
America makes charitable contributions to
nonprofit organizations involved with K-12
education and the environment. Support is
given primarily in the New York, New York,
metropolitan area.
Fields of interest: Elementary/secondary
education; Environment.
Types of support: Program development.
Limitations: Giving primarily in the New York,
NY, metropolitan area. No support for religious
or political organizations. No grants to
individuals.
Application information: The Community
Relations Department handles giving.
Application form not required.
> *Initial approach:* Proposal to headquarters
> *Copies of proposal:* 1
> *Deadline(s):* None
> *Final notification:* 2 to 3 weeks

2480
The Treetops Foundation
c/o Reminick Aarons & Co., LLP
1430 Broadway, 17th Fl.
New York, NY 10018

Established in 1999 in NY.
Donor(s): Lisa Belzberg, Matthew Bronfman.
Grantmaker type: Independent foundation
Financial data (yr. ended 12/31/01): Assets,
$103,292 (M); gifts received, $811,002;
expenditures, $717,367; qualifying distributions,
$685,904; giving activities include $689,912 for
70 grants (high: $160,063; low: $47).
Purpose and activities: Giving primarily for
education, depression research, and Jewish
organizations.
Fields of interest: Arts; Education; Botanical
gardens; Environment; Human services;
Women, centers/services; Civil rights;

Foundations (public); Public affairs; Jewish
agencies & temples.
Limitations: Applications not accepted. Giving
primarily in NY. No grants to individuals.
Application information: Contributes only to
pre-selected organizations.
Trustees: Lisa Belzberg; Matthew Bronfman.
EIN: 134093466

2481
The Trust for Mutual Understanding ▼
30 Rockefeller Plz., Rm. 5600
New York, NY 10112 (212) 632-3405
Contact: Richard S. Lanier, Dir.
FAX: (212) 632-3409; E-mail: tmu@tmuny.org;
URL: http://www.tmuny.org

Established in 1984 in NY.
Grantmaker type: Independent foundation
Financial data (yr. ended 12/31/01): Assets,
$64,089,842 (M); gifts received, $356;
expenditures, $5,030,588; qualifying
distributions, $4,539,283; giving activities
include $3,837,807 for 184 grants (high:
$75,000; low: $23; average: $5,000–$50,000).
Purpose and activities: Support to American
nonprofit organizations for professional
exchanges in the arts and in environmental
conservation between the United States, Russia,
and Eastern and Central Europe. Approximately
75 percent of grant funds are allocated for
cultural projects and approximately 25 percent
for environmental projects. Support is provided
primarily for travel and related expenses for
exchange projects in which professional
interaction plays a major role and in which
there is a significant degree of collaborative
effort.
Fields of interest: Visual arts; Museums;
Performing arts; Dance; Theater; Music; Historic
preservation/historical societies; Arts; Natural
resources; Environment; Animals/wildlife,
preservation/protection; International exchange.
International interests: Albania; Bulgaria; Czech
Republic; Slovakia; Hungary; Poland; Romania;
Belarus; Georgia (Republic of); Moldova; Russia;
Ukraine; Bosnia-Herzegovina; Croatia;
Macedonia; Slovenia; Mongolia.
Types of support: Exchange programs.
Limitations: Giving for exchanges between the
U.S. and the countries of Central and Eastern
Europe, primarily the Czech Republic, Hungary,
Poland, Russia, and Slovakia. Support is also
provided, to a lesser extent, for exchanges
involving Albania, Belarus, Bosnia and
Herzegovina, Bulgaria, Croatia, Georgia,
Macedonia, Moldova, Mongolia, Romania,
Serbia and Montenegro, Slovenia, and Ukraine.
No support for large-scale institutional programs
lacking an individual exchange component,
youth or undergraduate exchanges, economic
development, medicine, public health,
agricultural issues, or activities pertaining to
nuclear weapons and arms control. No grants to
individuals, or for fellowships, capital
campaigns, deficit financing, endowments,
general program and operating costs, salaries,
honoraria, publications, library and equipment
purchases, film, media, or one-person
exhibitions or performance tours.
Publications: Annual report (including
application guidelines), Grants list.

Application information: Grants are made only to tax-exempt organizations in the United States for exchange projects involving Eastern and Central Europe. Application form required.

Initial approach: Letter; initial contact should be established at least 3 months prior to anticipated date of project implementation
Copies of proposal: 1
Deadline(s): Feb. 1 and Aug. 1
Board meeting date(s): Fall and spring
Final notification: Directly following board meeting

Director and Trustees:* Richard S. Lanier,* Dir.; Elizabeth J. McCormack; Donal C. O'Brien, Jr.
Board of Advisors: Ruth Adams; Wade Greene; William H. Luers; Joseph Polisi; Blair Ruble; Isaac Shapiro.
Number of staff: 2 full-time professional; 2 full-time support; 1 part-time support.
EIN: 133212724

Recent environmental and animal welfare grants:

2481-1 Academy of Natural Sciences of Philadelphia, Philadelphia, PA, $30,000. For exchange of environmental specialists from Mongolia and the U.S. participating in Mongolian Long-Term Ecological Research Project at Lake Hovsgol. 2002.

2481-2 Alaska Marine Conservation Council, Anchorage, AK, $11,000. To enable indigenous leader and environmentalist from Russia to participate in North Pacific Fisheries Management Council Meeting in Unalaska. 2002.

2481-3 Association for the Protection of the Adirondacks, Schenectady, NY, $30,000. To enable American cultural and environmental specialists and representatives of native communities in the Adirondacks to travel to Russia and Mongolia as part of Russian-American-Mongolian exchange program entitled Beyond the Boundaries. 2002.

2481-4 Atlantic States Legal Foundation, Syracuse, NY, $40,000. To enable American specialists in nutrient reduction techniques to travel to Bulgaria, Georgia, Romania, Russia, and Ukraine in connection with Foundation's training program entitled, Black Sea Recovery Project: NGO Technical Facilitation Program. 2002.

2481-5 Brushy Fork Institute, Berea, KY, $20,000. To enable American specialists to travel to Russian Far East to conduct sustainable development workshops for indigenous communities. 2002.

2481-6 Center for Democracy, DC, $35,000. For international travel and related support of Russian environmental specialists in conference co-organized with Center for Russian Environmental Policy in Moscow entitled, The Health of the Environment, at White Oak Plantation in Jacksonville, FL. 2002.

2481-7 Earth Day Network, DC, $30,000. To enable environmentalists from Eastern and Central Europe to participate in Fellowship Program in the U.S. 2002.

2481-8 Earth Island Institute, San Francisco, CA, $35,000. For international exchange component of Center for Safe Energy's Sustainable Energy Project in Russia and Ukraine. 2002.

2481-9 Ecologists Linked for Organizing Grassroots Initiatives and Action (ECOLOGIA), Middlebury, VT, $17,000. To enable representatives of ECOLOGIA from the U.S. and Russia to participate in World Summit on Sustainable Development in Johannesburg. 2002.

2481-10 Ecology Center, Missoula, MT, $40,000. For international travel and related support in conjunction with exchange programs designed to increase capacity of organizations in Russia to use geographic information systems to monitor and assess environmental issues. 2002.

2481-11 Environmental Defense, New York, NY, $25,000. To enable American energy specialists to travel to Moscow in connection with project entitled, Business Workshop on Climate Change and New Environmental Markets. 2002.

2481-12 Environmental Health Network, Chesapeake, VA, $30,000. Toward international travel between the U.S. and the Caspian region in connection with program entitled, Developing and Strengthening Public Voices in the Call for Corporate Responsibility: Empowerment Workshops on the CPC Pipeline, organized by Crude Accountability, organization focused on oil and gas-related environmental health and justice issues in the Caspian basin. 2002.

2481-13 Environmental Law Alliance Worldwide (E-LAW), Eugene, Oregon, $14,000. To enable environmental lawyers from Czech Republic, Russia, Slovak Republic, and Ukraine to participate in fellowship programs in the U.S. and to attend E-LAW's Annual International Meeting and the 21st Annual Public Interest Environmental Law Conference. 2002.

2481-14 Global Forest Watch, DC, $30,000. For international travel and related support of Russian and American environmental scientists participating in exchange project to map boreal forests in Russia. 2002.

2481-15 Global Green USA, Santa Monica, CA, $25,000. For international travel and related support for Russian-American exchanges associated with Legacy Program: Building Public Participation in Russian and American Decision-Making for Toxic Waste Clean-Up and Environmentally Responsible Chemical Weapons Destruction. 2002.

2481-16 Government Accountability Project (GAP), DC, $15,000. For Russian-American exchanges associated with program entitled, Confronting the Legacies of Nuclear Weapons: Russia Project of Mutual Support and Exchange. 2002.

2481-17 Greenpeace International, DC, $22,000. For international travel and related support for American participants in project entitled, Discover Lake Baikal: Next Steps in Developing an Eco-Tourism Industry. 2002.

2481-18 Initiative for Social Action and Renewal in Eurasia (ISAR), DC, $75,000. For international travel and related support for environmental activists from Russia, Georgia, and the U.S. participating in project entitled, Educating for Change: Environmental Exchange and the Caspian Basin. 2002.

2481-19 Institute for Agriculture and Trade Policy, Minneapolis, MN, $20,000. To enable American environmental specialists to participate in workshop entitled, The Role of Biodiversity Conservation in the Transition to Rural Sustainability in Krakow and to attend follow-up meeting in Poland. 2002.

2481-20 Institute for Sustainable Communities, Montpelier, VT, $30,000. To allow grassroots activists from Russian Far East to undertake study tour of state of Washington, and to enable environmental experts from the U.S. to participate in ISC's Community Action Conference in Macedonia. 2002.

2481-21 Institute for Sustainable Communities, Montpelier, VT, $10,000. To enable representatives of NGOs and government officials in Romania to visit the U.S. in connection with ISC's Sustainable Rural Development in Romania program. 2002.

2481-22 International Crane Foundation, Baraboo, WI, $25,000. For international travel and related support for Russian and American representatives of Foundation and of Russia's Crane Working Group of Eurasia. 2002.

2481-23 Nature Conservancy, New York, NY, $10,000. To enable specialist from Conservancy to discuss environmental issues and priorities with government officials and scientists in Mongolia. 2002.

2481-24 New York Botanical Garden, Bronx, NY, $40,000. For international travel and related support associated with collaborative training program conducted jointly with Georgian Academy of Sciences in Tblisi. 2002.

2481-25 Northern Forum, Anchorage, AK, $30,000. To enable wildlife specialists from Russia to travel to Alaska for Brown Bear Management Workshop. 2002.

2481-26 Pacific Environment and Resources Center, Oakland, CA, $75,000. For international travel and related support associated with exchange programs designed to promote effective citizen participation in environmental protection activities in Siberia and the Russian Far East involving logging, biodiversity, marine conservation, and oil and gas exploration. 2002.

2481-27 Peregrine Fund, Boise, ID, $20,000. For international travel and related support associated with training program at Boise State University and at Raptor Research Center of the U.S. Geological Survey for raptor specialist from Mongolia. 2002.

2481-28 Quebec-Labrador Foundation/Atlantic Center for the Environment, Ipswich, MA, $30,000. For international travel and related support for exchange projects developed as part of Foundation's Central European Stewardship Program in Belarus, the Czech Republic, Poland, Romania, and Ukraine. 2002.

2481-29 Rails to Trails Conservancy, DC, $25,000. For international travel and related support for Eastern and Central European participants in international conference, TrailLink 2003: Designing for the Future. Conference will be held in Providence, RI. 2002.

2481-30 Ramapo College of New Jersey, Mahwah, NJ, $40,000. For international exchange component of project entitled, Empowering Russian and American NGOs to Address Issues of Future Sustainability. 2002.

2481-31 Sacred Earth Network, Petersham, MA, $50,000. For international exchange component of Russian Environmental Partnership Program focusing on Altai region of Siberia. 2002.

2481-32 Tahoe-Baikal Institute, South Lake Tahoe, CA, $20,000. For international travel and related support associated with Russian-American exchange component of Tahoe-Baikal Institute Summer Program and of Executive Director Exchange. 2002.

2481-33 University of Montana, Missoula, MT, $35,000. For research in Kamchatka by American salmon specialists as part of Kamchatka Wild Salmon Sanctuary Project. Research conducted by Flathead Lake Biological Station in Polson, MT. 2002.

2481-34 Wild Salmon Center, Portland, Oregon, $30,000. To enable Russian and American scientists, environmentalists, and policy makers to attend North Pacific Salmon Protected Areas Workshop in Khabarovsk. 2002.

2481-35 Woods Hole Research Center, Woods Hole, MA, $30,000. To enable environmental scientists and specialists from Russia to participate in Russian Visiting Scholars Program. 2002.

2482
The Ungar Foundation
P.O. Box 752
Copake, NY   12516
Contact: Mrs. Aine Ungar, Tr.

Grantmaker type: Independent foundation
Financial data (yr. ended 11/30/02): Assets, $1,624,220 (M); expenditures, $521,088; qualifying distributions, $512,970; giving activities include $463,200 for 13 grants (high: $130,000; low: $1,200).
Purpose and activities: Giving to education, Native American organizations, human services and Jewish agencies.
Fields of interest: Visual arts; Museums; Performing arts; Dance; Theater; Music; Historic preservation/historical societies; Arts; Education, fund raising; Early childhood education; Libraries/library science; Natural resources; Environment; Animal welfare; Animals/wildlife, preservation/protection; Hospitals (general); Health organizations, association; Marine science; Engineering/technology; Science; Native Americans/American Indians.
International interests: Israel.
Types of support: Continuing support; Annual campaigns; Building/renovation; Program development; Professorships; Internship funds; Scholarship funds; Research.
Limitations: Giving primarily in New York, NY. No grants to individuals.
Application information:
  Initial approach: Letter
  Deadline(s): None
Trustee: Mrs. Aine Ungar.
Number of staff: 1 part-time support.
EIN: 136937282

2483
Unilever United States Foundation
390 Park Ave.
New York, NY   10022   (212) 888-1260
Contact: Paul W. Wood, Pres.

Incorporated in 1952 in NY.
Donor(s): Unilever United States, Inc., Lever Bros. Co., Van den Bergh Foods Co., Unilever Research.
Grantmaker type: Company-sponsored foundation
Financial data (yr. ended 12/31/01): Assets, $12,192,310 (L); gifts received, $17,069,266; expenditures, $5,824,352; qualifying distributions, $5,775,994; giving activities include $5,775,994 for 424 grants (high: $1,500,000; low: $100; average: $500–$20,000).
Purpose and activities: Giving primarily for education emphasizing early childhood and elementary education, environment, health care/associations, housing, homeless, community development, minorities, and human services.
Fields of interest: Early childhood education; Elementary school/education; Education; Environment; Health care; Health organizations, association; Housing/shelter, development; Homeless, human services; Community development; Minorities; Homeless.
Types of support: General/operating support; Employee matching gifts; Employee-related scholarships; In-kind gifts.
Limitations: Giving primarily in areas of company operations. No support for religious, labor, political, or veterans organizations. No grants to individuals (except for employee-related scholarships), or goodwill advertising; fundraising events, capital fund campaigns; no loans.
Application information: Application form not required.
  Initial approach: Proposal
  Copies of proposal: 1
  Deadline(s): None
  Board meeting date(s): May, Oct., and Dec.
  Final notification: 1 month after meeting
Officers and Directors:* Paul W. Wood,* Pres.; A. Peter Harwich, Secy.; Maureen A. Collins; John W. Rice; Ronald M. Soiefer; Neal P. Vorchheimer; C. Perry Yeatman.
Number of staff: 1 part-time professional.
EIN: 136122117

2484
United States-Japan Foundation ▼
145 E. 32nd St., 12th Fl.
New York, NY   10016   (212) 481-8753
FAX: (212) 481-8762; E-mail: info@US-JF.org; Tokyo, Japan office address: Reinanzaka Bldg. 1F, 1-14-2 Akasaka, Minato-ku, Tokyo 107-0052, Japan, tel.: (03) 3586-0541; FAX: (03) 3586-1128; E-mail: JDU05456@nifty.ne.jp; URL: http://www.us-jf.org

Foundation incorporated in 1980 in NY.
Donor(s): The Nippon Foundation.
Grantmaker type: Independent foundation
Financial data (yr. ended 12/31/01): Assets, $86,979,675 (M); expenditures, $7,658,733; qualifying distributions, $6,621,910; giving activities include $4,770,126 for 88 grants (high:

$253,850; low: $5,000; average: $50,000–$150,000).
Purpose and activities: The United States-Japan Foundation is committed to promoting stronger ties between Americans and Japanese by supporting projects that foster mutual knowledge and education, deepen understanding, create effective channels of communication, and address common concerns in an increasingly interdependent world. The current focus of grantmaking activities is in the areas of communication/public opinion, precollege education and policy studies.
Fields of interest: Elementary school/education; Secondary school/education; Education; Energy; Environment; International economic development; Foreign policy; International affairs; Economics; Public policy, research; Government/public administration.
International interests: Asia; Japan.
Types of support: Program development; Publication; Curriculum development; Research; Matching/challenge support.
Limitations: Giving primarily in the U.S. and Japan. No support for projects in the arts involving performances, exhibitions, or productions, or for sports exchanges or student exchanges. No grants to individuals, or for building or endowment funds, capital campaigns, deficit operations.
Publications: Annual report.
Application information: The foundation is reviewing its program areas. Application form not required.
  Initial approach: Letter (no longer than 4 pages)
  Copies of proposal: 2
  Deadline(s): Feb. and Aug.
  Board meeting date(s): Apr. and Oct.
  Final notification: 1 to 3 months
Officers and Trustees:* Thomas S. Johnson, Chair.; Shinji Fukukawa,* Vice-Chair.; George R. Packard,* Pres.; Takeo Takuma,* V.P. and Dir., Tokyo office; Yusuke Saraya,* Board Secy.; Christine Manapat-Sims, Treas.; John Brademas; Gerald L. Curtis; Robin Chandler Duke; Thomas S. Foley; William Frenzel; Shinichi Kitaoka; Yotaro Kobayashi; T. Timothy Ryan, Jr.; Yohei Sasakawa; Thomas W. Strauss; Jiro Ushio.
Number of staff: 8 full-time professional; 1 part-time support.
EIN: 133054425

2485
Universal Studios Foundation, Ltd.
(formerly MCA Foundation, Ltd.)
P.O. Box 5023
New York, NY   10150
Contact: Helene Giambone
Application address: 100 Universal City Plz., Universal City, CA 91608, tel.: (818) 777-1208

Incorporated in 1956 in CA.
Donor(s): Universal Studios, Inc.
Grantmaker type: Company-sponsored foundation
Financial data (yr. ended 06/30/01): Assets, $13,897,052 (M); expenditures, $887,870; qualifying distributions, $879,662; giving activities include $887,870 for 24 grants (high: $100,000; low: $2,500; average: $5,000–$50,000).

Fields of interest: Film/video; Theater; Arts; Higher education; Education; Zoos/zoological societies; Hospitals (general); Cystic fibrosis research; Human services; Federated giving programs.
Types of support: General/operating support; Annual campaigns; Capital campaigns; Building/renovation; Endowments; Program development; Seed money; Fellowships; Scholarship funds; Employee matching gifts.
Limitations: Giving primarily in the Los Angeles, CA, and New York, NY, areas. No grants to individuals.
Publications: Application guidelines.
Application information: Application form not required.
> *Initial approach:* Proposal (not exceeding 3 pages)
> *Copies of proposal:* 1
> *Deadline(s):* None
Officers and Directors:* Ron Meyer,* Pres.; Karen Randall,* Exec. V.P. and Secy.; Deborah S. Rosen,* Sr. V.P.; Kevin Conway, V.P.; H. Stephen Gorden, V.P.; Marc Palotay, V.P.; John R. Preston, V.P.
Number of staff: 2 full-time professional.
EIN: 136096061

2486
USA Networks Foundation, Inc.
152 W. 57th St., 42nd Fl.
New York, NY 10019
Contact: William Severance, Dir.

Established in 1998 in NY.
Donor(s): USA Networks, Inc., USA Interactive, InterActiveCorp.
Grantmaker type: Company-sponsored foundation
Financial data (yr. ended 12/31/01): Assets, $6,383,099 (M); expenditures, $697,220; qualifying distributions, $695,579; giving activities include $625,830 for 98 grants (high: $25,000; low: $80; average: $1,000–$15,000).
Purpose and activities: Giving primarily for arts and culture, education, health associations, social and children's services, and international organizations.
Fields of interest: Arts; Higher education; Education; Natural resources; Health organizations, association; Human services; Children/youth, services; International development; International affairs.
Limitations: Giving on a national basis.
Application information: Application form not required.
> *Deadline(s):* None
Officers: Victor Kaufman, Pres.; Julius Genachowski, Secy.
Director: William Severance.
EIN: 133994361

2487
The Vanderbilt Family Foundation
(formerly The William H. & Helen C. Vanderbilt Foundation)
c/o U.S. Trust Co.
114 W. 47th St., Ste. C-1
New York, NY 10036-1594
Contact: Andrew Lane, Asst. V.P.

Donor(s): William H. Vanderbilt Charitable Trust.

Grantmaker type: Independent foundation
Financial data (yr. ended 02/28/02): Assets, $5,489,739 (M); gifts received, $3,500; expenditures, $386,914; qualifying distributions, $336,160; giving activities include $334,000 for 31 grants (high: $30,000; low: $1,000).
Purpose and activities: Giving for education and the environment.
Fields of interest: Education; Environment; Health care; Human services; International affairs.
Limitations: Applications not accepted. Giving on a national basis, with emphasis on the Northeast. No grants to individuals.
Application information: Contributes only to pre-selected organizations.
Trustees: Ellen F. Vanderbilt Aidnoff; Anne C. Vanderbilt Hartwell; William Henry Vanderbilt, Jr.; Emily Vanderbilt Wade.
EIN: 042743143

2488
The G. Unger Vetlesen Foundation ▼
c/o Fulton, Rowe, Hart & Coon
1 Rockefeller Plz., Ste. 301
New York, NY 10020-2002 (212) 586-0700
Contact: George Rowe, Jr., Pres.
E-mail: info@monellvetlesen.org; URL: http://www.monellvetlesen.org/

Incorporated in 1955 in NY.
Donor(s): George Unger Vetlesen.‡
Grantmaker type: Independent foundation
Financial data (yr. ended 12/31/01): Assets, $86,579,908 (M); expenditures, $5,255,421; qualifying distributions, $4,755,610; giving activities include $4,730,000 for 25 grants (high: $1,100,000; low: $2,500; average: $20,000–$150,000).
Purpose and activities: Established a biennial international science award for discoveries in the earth sciences; grants for biological, geophysical, and environmental research, including scholarships, and cultural organizations, including those emphasizing Norwegian-American relations and maritime interests. Support also for public policy research and libraries.
Fields of interest: Arts; Libraries/library science; Environment; Marine science; Physical/earth sciences; Engineering/technology; Biological sciences; Science; Public policy, research.
Types of support: General/operating support; Continuing support; Annual campaigns; Capital campaigns; Building/renovation; Equipment; Endowments; Program development; Professorships; Scholarship funds; Research.
Limitations: No grants to individuals.
Publications: Application guidelines, Annual report.
Application information: Application form not required.
> *Initial approach:* Letter
> *Copies of proposal:* 1
> *Deadline(s):* None
> *Board meeting date(s):* June and Dec.
Officers and Directors:* George Rowe, Jr.,* Pres. and Treas.; Maurizio J. Morello, Secy.; Gary K. Beauchamp; Eugene P. Grisanti; Ambrose K. Monell.
Number of staff: None.
EIN: 131982695

Recent environmental and animal welfare grants:
2488-1 Atlantic Salmon Federation, New York, NY, $40,000. 2001.
2488-2 Black Rock Forest Consortium, Cornwall, NY, $25,000. 2001.
2488-3 Cape Eleuthera Island School, Bahamas, $50,000. 2001.
2488-4 Marine Biological Laboratory, Woods Hole, MA, $250,000. For Center for Comparative Molecular Biology and Evolution and Marine Biomedical Institute. 2001.
2488-5 Marine Biological Laboratory, Woods Hole, MA, $100,000. Toward retention of marine veterinarian. 2001.
2488-6 Massachusetts Institute of Technology, Cambridge, MA, $100,000. For Joint Program on the Science and Policy of Global Change. 2001.
2488-7 Open Space Institute, New York, NY, $50,000. For Hudson Valley Program. 2001.
2488-8 Resources for the Future, DC, $50,000. For Climate Economics and Policy Program. 2001.
2488-9 Scenic Hudson, Poughkeepsie, NY, $75,000. 2001.
2488-10 Scripps Institution of Oceanography, La Jolla, CA, $900,000. For Global Change Program. 2001.
2488-11 Wildlife Conservation Society, Bronx, NY, $75,000. 2001.

2489
The Vidda Foundation
c/o Carter, Rupp & Roberts
10 E. 40th St., Ste. 3808
New York, NY 10016 (212) 696-4050
Contact: Gerald E. Rupp, Mgr.

Established in 1979 in NY.
Donor(s): Ursula Corning.
Grantmaker type: Independent foundation
Financial data (yr. ended 05/31/02): Assets, $3,185,552 (M); gifts received, $1,200,000; expenditures, $1,291,187; qualifying distributions, $1,186,902; giving activities include $1,053,500 for 41 grants (high: $100,000; low: $1,500; average: $1,000–$250,000).
Purpose and activities: Giving primarily to higher education and educational projects, cultural programs, including fine arts and museums, church music funds, animal welfare, the environment and conservation, hospitals, and social services, including child welfare and the elderly.
Fields of interest: Visual arts; Museums; Performing arts; Dance; Theater; Music; Arts; Higher education; Education; Natural resources; Environment; Animal welfare; Animals/wildlife, preservation/protection; Hospitals (general); Human services; Children/youth, services; Aging, centers/services; Community development; Protestant agencies & churches; Aging; Economically disadvantaged.
Types of support: General/operating support; Continuing support; Building/renovation; Endowments; Program development; Seed money; Research.
Limitations: Giving primarily in NY. No grants to individuals.
Publications: Financial statement.

Application information: Application form not required.

Initial approach: Letter or proposal
Copies of proposal: 1
Deadline(s): None
Board meeting date(s): Dec. and May
Final notification: Approximately 3 months

Officer and Trustees:* Gerald E. Rupp,* Mgr.; John A. Downey, M.D.; Helen C. Evarts; Ian Fraser.

Number of staff: 2 shared staff (shared with Civitella Ranieri Foundation).

EIN: 132981105

2490
Geraldine S. Violet Charitable Foundation

c/o JPMorgan Chase Bank
1211 Ave. of The Americas, 34th Fl.
New York, NY   10036

Established in 1996 in NY.

Grantmaker type: Independent foundation

Financial data (yr. ended 08/31/02): Assets, $2,915,380 (M); expenditures, $265,309; qualifying distributions, $194,883; giving activities include $180,000 for 2 grants of $90,000 each.

Fields of interest: Environment, public education; Hospitals (general).

Limitations: Applications not accepted. No grants to individuals.

Application information: Contributes only to pre-selected organizations.

Trustees: Eugene E. Ressler; JPMorgan Chase Bank.

EIN: 136952499

2491
Geraldine S. Violett Charitable Foundation

(formerly Charles Schleussner Charitable Trust)
c/o JPMorgan Private Bank
345 Park Ave., 4th Fl.
New York, NY   10154
Contact: Jacqueline Elias, V.P., JPMorgan Private Bank
FAX: (212) 464-2305

Established in 1996 in NY.

Grantmaker type: Independent foundation

Financial data (yr. ended 08/31/00): Assets, $4,524,898 (M); expenditures, $239,745; qualifying distributions, $126,951; giving activities include $100,000 for 2 grants of $50,000 each.

Purpose and activities: Giving primarily to a hospital and a wilderness society.

Fields of interest: Natural resources; Hospitals (general).

Limitations: Applications not accepted. No grants to individuals.

Application information: Contributes only to pre-selected organizations.

Trustees: Eugene E. Ressler; JPMorgan Chase Bank.

EIN: 136852499

2492
Voelker-Orth Museum

149-19 38th Ave.
Flushing, NY   11354
Contact: Catherine Abrams, Dir.

Established in 1999 in NY.

Donor(s): Elisabeth Catherine Orth.

Grantmaker type: Independent foundation

Financial data (yr. ended 07/31/02): Assets, $5,633,291 (M); expenditures, $181,787; qualifying distributions, $90,000; giving activities include $90,000 for 3 grants of $30,000 each.

Fields of interest: Historic preservation/historical societies; Botanical gardens; Animals/wildlife, bird preserves.

Limitations: Giving primarily in New York, NY.

Application information:

Initial approach: Letter

Directors: Lee Cogan; Stanley Cogan; Anthony DiBrita; Catherine Fitts; Paul Kerson; Joan S. Kingsley; Barbara Levin; Chun Soo Pyn; Rolan G. Wade.

EIN: 113498583

2493
Wainscott Charitable Trust

c/o Argonaut Capital Mgmt.
780 3rd Ave., 9th Fl.
New York, NY   10017

Established in 1997 in NY.

Donor(s): David E. Gerstenhaber.

Grantmaker type: Independent foundation

Financial data (yr. ended 12/31/01): Assets, $76,409 (M); gifts received, $15,000; expenditures, $170,750; qualifying distributions, $170,750; giving activities include $170,750 for 12 grants (high: $131,100; low: $225).

Fields of interest: Animals/wildlife, preservation/protection; Cancer; Jewish federated giving programs; Jewish agencies & temples.

Limitations: Applications not accepted. Giving primarily in New York, NY. No grants to individuals.

Application information: Contributes only to pre-selected organizations.

Trustee: David E. Gerstenhaber.

EIN: 137135370

2494
The Walbridge Fund

c/o William S. Phillips, C.P.A.
26 Firemans Memorial Dr., Ste. 110
Pomona, NY   10970-3569

Established in 1997 in NY.

Grantmaker type: Independent foundation

Financial data (yr. ended 12/31/02): Assets, $14,590,465 (M); expenditures, $1,161,683; qualifying distributions, $1,046,222; giving activities include $1,051,500 for 63 grants (high: $100,000; low: $4,000).

Purpose and activities: Giving primarily for environmental programs.

Fields of interest: Museums; Elementary/secondary education; Higher education; Natural resources; Environment; Human services.

Limitations: Applications not accepted. Giving primarily in NY and UT. No grants to individuals.

Application information: Contributes only to pre-selected organizations.

Officers: George W. Perkins, Jr., Pres.; Jennifer P. Speers, V.P.; Arthur V. Savage, Secy.; William S. Phillips, Treas.

Trustees: Arthur Yorke Allen; Nancy F. Perkins; Randon W. Wilson.

EIN: 133936131

2495
The Rosalind P. Walter Foundation

509 Madison Ave., Ste. 1216
New York, NY   10022

Established in 1951 as the Walter Foundation.

Donor(s): Henry G. Walter, Jr.,‡ Rosalind P. Walter.

Grantmaker type: Independent foundation

Financial data (yr. ended 12/31/02): Assets, $2,018,243 (M); expenditures, $175,487; qualifying distributions, $172,271; giving activities include $170,686 for grants (high: $55,000).

Purpose and activities: Giving primarily for television and media, wildlife conservation, tennis organizations, and human services.

Fields of interest: Media/communications; Television; Museums (natural history); Animals/wildlife; Athletics/sports, racquet sports; Boys & girls clubs; Human services; Federated giving programs.

Limitations: Applications not accepted. Giving primarily in NY. No grants to individuals.

Application information: Contributes only to pre-selected organizations.

Trustee: Rosalind P. Walter.

EIN: 136177284

2496
The Honore T. Wamsler Foundation, Inc.

c/o Robert Morse, Mgr.
230 Park Ave., Ste. 1635
New York, NY   10169

Established in 1998 in DE.

Donor(s): Honore T. Wamsler.

Grantmaker type: Independent foundation

Financial data (yr. ended 03/31/02): Assets, $567,094 (M); gifts received, $12,320; expenditures, $517,212; qualifying distributions, $500,275; giving activities include $500,000 for 1 grant.

Fields of interest: Botanical gardens.

Limitations: Applications not accepted. Giving primarily in New York, NY. No grants to individuals.

Application information: Contributes only to pre-selected organizations.

Officer: Robert Morse, Mgr.

Directors: Pauline Joerger; Susanne Redetzki; Caroline Wamsler; Irene Wamsler-Snow; Bettina Wamsler-Weithauer.

EIN: 134011655

2497
Patrick J. Ward and Family Foundation
c/o Goldman Sachs & Co., Tax Dept.
85 Broad St.
New York, NY 10004

Established in 1991 in IL.
Donor(s): Patrick J. Ward.
Grantmaker type: Independent foundation
Financial data (yr. ended 03/31/02): Assets,
$799,537 (M); expenditures, $266,055;
qualifying distributions, $225,912; giving
activities include $226,025 for 15 grants (high:
$200,000; low: $100).
Fields of interest: Education; Animals/wildlife,
preservation/protection; Disabled.
International interests: United Kingdom;
Southern Africa.
Types of support: General/operating support.
Limitations: Applications not accepted. Giving
primarily in London, England. No grants to
individuals.
Application information: Contributes only to
pre-selected organizations.
Trustees: Robert K. Steel; Kathleen M. Ward;
Patrick J. Ward.
EIN: 133639293

2498
Albert and Bessie Warner Fund
P.O. Box 2580
Sag Harbor, NY 11963
Application address: c/o Funding Exchange, 666
Broadway, Ste. 500, New York, NY 10012

Trust established in 1955 in NY.
Grantmaker type: Independent foundation
Financial data (yr. ended 12/31/02): Assets,
$5,511,641 (L); expenditures, $203,965;
qualifying distributions, $174,000; giving
activities include $174,000 for 26 grants (high:
$66,500; low: $1,000).
Purpose and activities: Primary areas of giving
include advancing civil rights and civil liberties;
strengthening the movement toward peace and
disarmament; empowering young people; and
preserving the environment.
Fields of interest: Environment; Health care;
Legal services; Crime/law enforcement; Labor
unions/organizations; Children/youth, services;
International peace/security; Arms control;
International human rights; Race/intergroup
relations; Civil rights; Native
Americans/American Indians;
Immigrants/refugees.
Types of support: General/operating support;
Land acquisition; Program development; Seed
money; Technical assistance.
Limitations: Giving primarily in New York City
and Suffolk County, NY. No grants to
individuals, or for building or endowment funds.
Publications: Annual report.
Application information:
  Initial approach: Letter
  Deadline(s): None
  Board meeting date(s): Feb., May, Aug., and
    Nov.
Trustees: John Steel; Kitty Steel; Lewis M. Steel;
Ruth M. Steel.
Number of staff: 1 part-time support.
EIN: 136095213

2499
Waterfowl Research Foundation, Inc.
c/o Milbank, Tweed, Hadley & McCloy
1 Chase Manhattan Plz.
New York, NY 10005
Contact: Carroll L. Wainwright, Jr., Pres.
Application address: 57 Dunemere Ln., East
Hampton, N.Y. 11937

Established in 1955 in NY.
Donor(s): M.E. Davis.‡
Grantmaker type: Independent foundation
Financial data (yr. ended 12/31/02): Assets,
$8,142,394 (M); expenditures, $615,036;
qualifying distributions, $530,518; giving
activities include $521,000 for 4 grants (high:
$200,000; low: $50,000).
Purpose and activities: To support waterfowl
preservation programs.
Fields of interest: Animals/wildlife, research;
Animals/wildlife, preservation/protection.
Types of support: Land acquisition; Research.
Limitations: Giving primarily in the U.S. and
Canada. No grants to individuals.
Application information: Application form not
required.
  Board meeting date(s): Apr. and Dec.
Officers: Carroll L. Wainwright, Jr., Pres.;
Lincoln P. Lyman, Secy.
Number of staff: 1 part-time support.
EIN: 136122167

2500
The Waterwheel Foundation
c/o BG & Co.
156 W. 56th St., Ste. 1803
New York, NY 10019
URL: http://www.phunky.com/twwsit/wwf.html

Established in 1997 in VT.
Donor(s): Ben & Jerry's Homemade, Inc.
Grantmaker type: Independent foundation
Financial data (yr. ended 12/31/01): Assets,
$483,605 (M); gifts received, $297,727;
expenditures, $230,201; qualifying distributions,
$228,547; giving activities include $225,601 for
21 grants (high: $100,000; low: $150).
Purpose and activities: Giving primarily for
conservation.
Fields of interest: Environment, legal rights;
Natural resources; Legal services, public interest
law; Human services.
Types of support: General/operating support.
Limitations: Applications not accepted. Giving
on a national basis, with some emphasis on VT.
No grants to individuals.
Application information: Contributes only to
pre-selected organizations.
Officers: Ernest Anastasio III, Pres.; Jonathan
Fishman, V.P.; Page McConnell, Secy.; Michael
Gordon, Treas.
EIN: 133948773

2501
The Watts Family Foundation
c/o Bessemer Trust Co., N.A.
630 5th Ave.
New York, NY 10111

Established in 1997 in MA.
Donor(s): Beverly Watts, David B. Watts.
Grantmaker type: Operating foundation

Financial data (yr. ended 06/30/02): Assets,
$6,567,480 (M); gifts received, $2,000,000;
expenditures, $320,693; qualifying distributions,
$274,438; giving activities include $275,000 for
17 grants (high: $200,000; low: $1,000).
Purpose and activities: Giving primarily for
higher education.
Fields of interest: Arts; Higher education;
University; Environment; Federated giving
programs.
Limitations: Applications not accepted. Giving
primarily in MA and VI. No grants to individuals.
Application information: Contributes only to
pre-selected organizations.
Trustees: Beverly Watts; David B. Watts.
EIN: 043402936

2502
Weeden Foundation
(formerly Frank Weeden Foundation)
747 3rd Ave., 34th Fl.
New York, NY 10017   (212) 888-1672
Contact: Donald A. Weeden, Exec. Dir.
FAX: (212) 888-1354; E-mail:
weedenfdn@weedenfdn.org; URL: http://
www.weedenfdn.org

Established 1963 in CA.
Donor(s): Frank Weeden,‡ Alan N. Weeden,
Donald E. Weeden, John D. Weeden, William F.
Weeden.
Grantmaker type: Independent foundation
Financial data (yr. ended 06/30/02): Assets,
$29,913,217 (M); expenditures, $3,106,172;
qualifying distributions, $2,712,686; giving
activities include $2,529,483 for 265 grants
(high: $50,000; low: $175; average:
$5,000–$50,000).
Purpose and activities: Giving primarily to
environmental organizations working to
preserve biological diversity. Program interests
also include organizations working to stabilize
human population and organizations working to
address the over consumption of the earth's
resources.
Fields of interest: Natural resources;
Environment; Population studies.
International interests: Russia; Bolivia; Chile.
Types of support: General/operating support;
Continuing support; Land acquisition; Program
development; Seed money.
Limitations: Giving on a national and
international basis, primarily in northern CA, the
Pacific Northwest, Latin America (Chile and
Bolivia), and Central Siberia. No grants to
individuals; generally no funding for films,
conferences, or scientific research.
Application information: Application form not
required.
  Initial approach: Letter of inquiry 1 month
    before proposal deadline
  Copies of proposal: 2
  Deadline(s): 6 weeks prior to each board
    meeting; telephone or check Web site for
    dates
  Board meeting date(s): 3 times a year
Officers and Directors:* Norman Weeden,
Ph.D.,* Pres.; William F. Weeden, M.D.,* V.P.;
John D. Weeden,* Secy.-Treas.; Donald A.
Weeden, Exec. Dir.; David Davies; Christina
Roux; Alan N. Weeden; Donald E. Weeden;
Leslie Weeden.
Number of staff: 2 full-time professional.

EIN: 946109313

2503
Weiksner Family Foundation
(formerly The Sandra & George Weiksner
Foundation)
c/o Cleary Gottlieb
1 Liberty Plz., 43rd Fl.
New York, NY 10006

Established in 1986 in NY.
Donor(s): George B. Weiksner, Jr.
Grantmaker type: Independent foundation
Financial data (yr. ended 12/31/02): Assets,
$608,892 (M); gifts received, $272,688;
expenditures, $108,910; qualifying distributions,
$108,650; giving activities include $108,550 for
45 grants (high: $45,000; low: $25).
Fields of interest: Performing arts; Arts;
Elementary/secondary education; Higher
education; Medical school/education;
Theological school/education; Environment;
Human services; Foundations (public); Public
affairs, political organizations; Religion.
Limitations: Applications not accepted. Giving
primarily in New York, NY. No grants to
individuals.
Application information: Contributes only to
pre-selected organizations.
Trustees: George B. Weiksner; Sandra S.
Weiksner.
EIN: 133398052

2504
Sidney J. Weinberg, Jr. Foundation
c/o BCRS Associates, LLC
100 Wall St., 11th Fl.
New York, NY 10005

Established in 1979 in NY.
Donor(s): Sidney J. Weinberg, Jr.
Grantmaker type: Independent foundation
Financial data (yr. ended 05/31/01): Assets,
$46,758,950 (M); gifts received, $1,366,875;
expenditures, $3,362,134; qualifying
distributions, $3,127,780; giving activities
include $3,137,350 for 80 grants (high:
$1,000,000; low: $100; average:
$10,000–$50,000).
Purpose and activities: Giving primarily for
education, health, human services, and
churches.
Fields of interest: Arts; Higher education;
Education; Environment; Health organizations,
association; Children/youth, services;
Community development; Federated giving
programs; Christian agencies & churches.
Types of support: General/operating support.
Limitations: Applications not accepted. Giving
primarily in the eastern U.S., with emphasis on
New York, NY. No grants to individuals; no
loans or scholarships.
Application information: Contributes only to
pre-selected organizations.
Trustees: Elizabeth W. Smith; Peter A. Weinberg;
Sidney J. Weinberg, Jr.; Sydney H. Weinberg.
Number of staff: None.
EIN: 132998603

2505
The Stephen and Cathy Weinroth
Charitable Trust
700 W. 247th St.
Riverdale, NY 10471

Established in 1998 in NY.
Donor(s): Stephen D. Weinroth.
Grantmaker type: Independent foundation
Financial data (yr. ended 12/31/00): Assets,
$1,542,708 (M); gifts received, $775,000;
expenditures, $255,311; qualifying distributions,
$249,285; giving activities include $245,611 for
42 grants (high: $153,000; low: $25).
Purpose and activities: Giving primarily for
dance and human services.
Fields of interest: Dance; Natural resources;
Medical research, institute; Human services.
Types of support: General/operating support.
Limitations: Applications not accepted. Giving
primarily in New York, NY. No grants to
individuals.
Application information: Contributes only to
pre-selected organizations.
Trustee: Stephen D. Weinroth.
EIN: 137131559

2506
Weissman Family Foundation, Inc.
81 Manursing Way
Rye, NY 10580
Contact: George Weissman, Chair.

Established in 1992 in NY.
Donor(s): George Weissman.
Grantmaker type: Independent foundation
Financial data (yr. ended 12/31/02): Assets,
$7,437,392 (M); expenditures, $576,283;
qualifying distributions, $477,300; giving
activities include $477,300 for 153 grants (high:
$200,000; low: $50; average: $100–$10,000).
Purpose and activities: Giving primarily for
education and for human services.
Fields of interest: Arts; Education; Environment;
Human services; Jewish agencies & temples.
International interests: Israel.
Types of support: General/operating support;
Continuing support; Annual campaigns; Capital
campaigns; Endowments; Emergency funds;
Publication; Seed money.
Limitations: Applications not accepted. Giving
primarily in New York, NY; some giving also in
Israel. No grants to individuals.
Application information: Contributes only to
pre-selected organizations.
  Board meeting date(s): Annually
Officers: George Weissman, Chair.; Mildred
Weissman, Pres.; Daniel Weissman, V.P.; Ellen
Weissman, Secy.; Paul Weissman, Treas.
Number of staff: 1 part-time support.
EIN: 133688122

2507
Wellington Foundation, Inc.
14 Wall St., Ste. 1702
New York, NY 10005

Incorporated in 1955 in NY.
Donor(s): Herbert G. Wellington,‡ Herbert G.
Wellington, Jr., Elizabeth D. Wellington.‡
Grantmaker type: Independent foundation

Financial data (yr. ended 12/31/02): Assets,
$1,057,427 (M); expenditures, $105,740;
qualifying distributions, $103,227; giving
activities include $102,000 for 19 grants (high:
$30,000; low: $1,000).
Purpose and activities: Giving for higher
education, health and medical services, and
youth services.
Fields of interest: Television;
Elementary/secondary education; Higher
education; Natural resources; Hospitals
(general); Boys & girls clubs; Human services;
Foundations (public).
Limitations: Applications not accepted. Giving
primarily in NY. No grants to individuals.
Application information: Contributes only to
pre-selected organizations.
Officers: Charles H. Wellington, Pres. and
Treas.; Patricia B. Wellington, V.P.; Thomas D.
Wellington, Secy.
EIN: 136110175

2508
The Wendling Foundation
80 Broad St., 17th Fl.
New York, NY 10004
Contact: Michelle Lord
FAX: (212) 764-4298

Established in 1984 in FL.
Donor(s): Helen C. Vanderbilt.‡
Grantmaker type: Independent foundation
Financial data (yr. ended 12/31/02): Assets,
$8,572,917 (M); gifts received, $63,597;
expenditures, $766,647; qualifying distributions,
$646,236; giving activities include $563,000 for
34 grants (high: $100,000; low: $500; average:
$1,000–$50,000).
Purpose and activities: Giving primarily for
educational reform, the environment,
organizational and leadership development,
including job development, and international
rights and women's rights.
Fields of interest: Education, reform;
Environment; Employment; International human
rights; Civil rights, women; Community
development; Leadership development.
Types of support: General/operating support;
Continuing support; Program development;
Conferences/seminars; Seed money; Research;
Technical assistance.
Limitations: Applications not accepted. Giving
on a national basis, with emphasis on
Washington, DC, and the New England states,
especially ME. No grants to individuals.
Publications: Grants list.
Application information: Application process,
initiated by the board of directors, includes
completion of application in Apr. and Nov. (1
month prior to board meeting). Grantees must
be invited to submit proposals; unsolicited
requests not accepted.
  Board meeting date(s): 2 weeks following
    board meetings for board-initiated
    application process
Officers and Directors:* Averill Cook,*
Co-Chair.; John Cook, Jr.,* Co-Chair.; Heleny
Cook,* Pres.; Rebecca Cook,* Secy.; Willard
Cook,* Treas.; Warren C. Cook.
Number of staff: None.
EIN: 133249448

2509
The Margaret L. Wendt Foundation
40 Fountain Plz., Ste. 277
Buffalo, NY 14202-2220 (716) 855-2146
Contact: Robert J. Kresse, Secy.-Treas.

Trust established in 1956 in NY.
Donor(s): Margaret L. Wendt.‡
Grantmaker type: Independent foundation
Financial data (yr. ended 01/31/02): Assets,
$118,168,880 (M); expenditures, $8,166,966;
qualifying distributions, $7,677,173; giving
activities include $6,611,610 for 152 grants
(high: $750,000; low: $300; average:
$5,000–$50,000) and $1,000,000 for 1
loan/program-related investment.
Purpose and activities: Emphasis on education,
the arts, and social services; support also for
churches and religious organizations, health
associations, public interest organizations, and
youth agencies.
Fields of interest: Visual arts; Museums;
Performing arts; Theater; History/archaeology;
Historic preservation/historical societies; Arts;
Education, fund raising; Early childhood
education; Higher education; Libraries/library
science; Education; Natural resources; Hospitals
(general); Substance abuse, services; Mental
health/crisis services; Health organizations,
association; Cancer; AIDS; Alcoholism;
Biomedicine; Medical research, institute; Cancer
research; AIDS research; Legal services;
Crime/law enforcement; Human services;
Children/youth, services; Hospices; Aging,
centers/services; Minorities/immigrants,
centers/services; International human rights;
Community development; Federated giving
programs; Political science; Government/public
administration; Public affairs; Religion;
Minorities; Disabled; Aging; Economically
disadvantaged.
Types of support: Program-related
investments/loans.
Limitations: Giving primarily in Buffalo and
western NY. No grants to individuals, or for
scholarships.
Publications: Application guidelines.
Application information: Application form not
required.
Initial approach: Letter or application form
Copies of proposal: 4
Deadline(s): 1 month prior to board meeting
Board meeting date(s): Quarterly; no fixed
dates
Final notification: Usually 4 to 6 months
Officer and Trustees:* Robert J. Kresse,*
Secy.-Treas.; Janet L. Day; Thomas D. Lunt.
Number of staff: 1 part-time support.
EIN: 166030037
**Recent environmental and animal welfare
grants:**
2509-1 Buffalo Olmsted Parks Conservancy,
Buffalo, NY, $33,750. For matching funds
toward Lila Wallace-Reader's Digest Fund's
Urban Parks Initiative. 2002.
2509-2 Buffalo Olmsted Parks Conservancy,
Buffalo, NY, $33,750. For matching funds
toward Lila Wallace-Reader's Digest Fund's
Urban Parks Initiative. 2002.
2509-3 Buffalo Olmsted Parks Conservancy,
Buffalo, NY, $33,750. For matching funds
toward Lila Wallace-Reader's Digest Fund's
Urban Parks Initiative. 2002.

2509-4 League of Women Voters of the Greater
Buffalo Area, Buffalo, NY, $15,000. Toward
educational campaign in Erie and Niagara
Counties on cost of urban sprawl and
possible remedies. 2002.
2509-5 Medaille College, Buffalo, NY,
$100,000. For construction of two-story
addition to expand Veterinary Technology
and Science facilities. 2002.

2510
Whalesback Foundation
1 Pierrepont St.
Brooklyn, NY 11201

Established in 1996 in PA.
Donor(s): Theodore Roosevelt III, Theodore
Roosevelt IV.
Grantmaker type: Independent foundation
Financial data (yr. ended 12/31/02): Assets,
$4,499,880 (M); expenditures, $202,459;
qualifying distributions, $194,575; giving
activities include $196,500 for 15 grants (high:
$76,000; low: $100).
Fields of interest: Museums (art); Business
school/education; Animals/wildlife; International
affairs.
Limitations: Applications not accepted. Giving
primarily in NY. No grants to individuals.
Application information: Contributes only to
pre-selected organizations.
Officer and Trustees:* Theodore Roosevelt IV,*
Pres. and Secy.-Treas.; Constance Roosevelt.
EIN: 311478498

2511
Idalia Whitcomb Charitable Trust
c/o JPMorgan Private Bank
345 Park Ave., 4th Fl.
New York, NY 10154 (212) 464-2467
Contact: Lisa Philp, V.P.
FAX: (212) 464-2305

Established in 1989 in NY.
Grantmaker type: Independent foundation
Financial data (yr. ended 06/30/03): Assets,
$1,952,399 (M); expenditures, $126,562;
qualifying distributions, $103,767; giving
activities include $96,759 for 6 grants (high:
$25,000; low: $14,000).
Purpose and activities: Giving for higher
education, animal welfare, and cultural centers.
Fields of interest: Multipurpose
centers/programs; Higher education; Animal
welfare; Human services.
Limitations: Applications not accepted. Giving
primarily in Warren, RI. No grants to individuals.
Application information: Contributes only to
pre-selected organizations.
Trustees: Thomas E. Wright; JPMorgan Chase
Bank.
EIN: 136912627

2512
The Whitehead Foundation
65 E. 55th St.
New York, NY 10022 (212) 755-3131
Contact: Denise Emmett

Established in 1982 in NY.

Donor(s): John C. Whitehead.
Grantmaker type: Independent foundation
Financial data (yr. ended 06/30/02): Assets,
$4,356,849 (M); gifts received, $1,830,727;
expenditures, $2,269,540; qualifying
distributions, $2,267,515; giving activities
include $2,264,387 for 323 grants (high:
$35,000; low: $45; average: $1,000–$25,000).
Purpose and activities: Primary categories of
interest are international affairs, higher
education, and youth; support also for the arts,
civic affairs, and public policy.
Fields of interest: Arts; Higher education;
Natural resources; Children/youth, services;
International affairs; Public policy, research.
International interests: Eastern Europe.
Types of support: Annual campaigns; Capital
campaigns; Program-related investments/loans.
Limitations: Applications not accepted. Giving
primarily in NY. No grants to individuals.
Application information: Unsolicited proposals
are rarely approved.
Board meeting date(s): Quarterly
Trustees: Anne Whitehead Crawford; Wade
Greene; John C. Whitehead; John Gregory
Whitehead.
Number of staff: None.
EIN: 133119344

2513
The Wiegers Family Foundation
c/o Barry Strauss Assoc., Ltd.
307 5th Ave., 8th Fl.
New York, NY 10016-6517

Established in 1992 in CO.
Donor(s): George A. Wiegers.
Grantmaker type: Independent foundation
Financial data (yr. ended 02/28/02): Assets,
$3,772,702 (M); expenditures, $382,212;
qualifying distributions, $273,736; giving
activities include $268,680 for 24 grants (high:
$100,000; low: $100).
Fields of interest: Arts; Higher education;
Business school/education; Environment;
Animals/wildlife, preservation/protection.
Limitations: Applications not accepted. Giving
primarily in CO and NY. No grants to
individuals.
Application information: Contributes only to
pre-selected organizations.
Trustees: Hans P. Utsch; E. Alexander Wiegers;
Elizabeth C. Wiegers; George A. Wiegers.
EIN: 841214070

2514
Wildlife Conservation Society
2300 Southern Blvd.
Bronx, NY 10460-1099 (718) 220-5100
Contact: Steven E. Sanderson, Pres. and C.E.O.
URL: http://www.wcs.org

Established in 1895 in NY as the New York
Zoological Society; name changed in 1994.
Grantmaker type: Public charity
Financial data (yr. ended 06/30/02): Revenue,
$97,774,032; assets, $550,070,491; gifts
received, $73,422,898; expenditures,
$128,184,025; program services expenses,
$111,138,745; giving activities include
$2,397,303 for 323 grants to individuals (high:
$77,000; low: $15).

Purpose and activities: The society saves wildlife and wild lands through careful science, international conservation, education, and the management of the world's largest system of urban wildlife parks.
Fields of interest: Animals/wildlife, preservation/protection; Animals/wildlife, sanctuaries.
Officers and Trustees: David T. Schiff,* Chair.; Edith McBean,* Vice-Chair.; Mrs. Gordon P. Pattee,* Vice-Chair.; Mrs. Leonard Stern,* Vice-Chair.; Steven E. Sanderson,* Pres. and C.E.O.; Patricia Calabrese,* Sr. V.P. and C.F.O.; Annette Berkovits,* Sr. V.P., Edu.; John Calvelli,* Sr. V.P., Gov. Affairs; Richard Lattis,* Sr. V.P., Living Institutions; W.B. McKeown,* Sr. V.P., General Counsel; John Robinson,* Sr. V.P., International Conservation; Robert Wood Johnson IV,* Secy.; John N. Irwin III,* Treas.; Jane Alexander; and 40 additional trustees.
EIN: 131740011

2515
Robert W. Wilson Foundation, Inc.
520 83rd St., Ste. 3R
Brooklyn, NY 11209

Established in 1992 in NY.
Donor(s): Robert Wilson.
Grantmaker type: Independent foundation
Financial data (yr. ended 12/31/00): Assets, $150,113,233 (M); gifts received, $130,960,376; expenditures, $22,382,260; qualifying distributions, $20,480,922; giving activities include $20,471,051 for 73 grants (high: $5,200,000; low: $50).
Purpose and activities: Giving primarily for the arts and the environment.
Fields of interest: Historic preservation/historical societies; Arts; Libraries (public); Natural resources; Environment; Animals/wildlife, preservation/protection; Animals/wildlife, sanctuaries.
Limitations: Applications not accepted. Giving primarily in New York, NY. No grants to individuals.
Application information: Contributes only to pre-selected organizations.
Officer: Robert W. Wilson, Pres.
EIN: 133686884

2516
The Winfield Foundation
c/o Hollyer, Brady
551 5th Ave., 27th Fl.
New York, NY 10176
Contact: Helen Hooke, Tr.

Incorporated in 1941 in NY.
Grantmaker type: Independent foundation
Financial data (yr. ended 12/31/01): Assets, $2,144,056 (M); expenditures, $136,867; qualifying distributions, $111,032; giving activities include $107,000 for 28 grants (high: $60,000; low: $2,000).
Purpose and activities: Giving for the arts, higher education, the environment, health, and human services.
Fields of interest: Historical activities; Arts; Environment; Health care; Higher education; Human services.

Limitations: Giving primarily in NY. No grants to individuals, or for research-related programs, scholarships, fellowships, or matching gifts; no loans.
Application information: Application form not required.
Initial approach: Letter
Copies of proposal: 1
Board meeting date(s): Annually
Officers and Trustees: Franklin W. McCann,* Pres. and Treas.; D. Chase Troxell,* V.P. and Secy.; Jonathan W. McCann,* V.P.; Margaret M. Fenhagen; Helen Hooke; Douglas Irwin.
EIN: 136158017

2517
Winley Foundation
2303 Salt Point Tpke.
Clinton Corners, NY 12514 (845) 266-3065
Contact: Anna M. Barone, Treas.

Grantmaker type: Independent foundation
Financial data (yr. ended 12/31/02): Assets, $20,562,918 (M); gifts received, $5,229,344; expenditures, $514,344; qualifying distributions, $464,000; giving activities include $464,000 for 7 grants (high: $140,000; low: $10,000).
Purpose and activities: Giving is limited to the benefit of animals.
Fields of interest: Animal welfare.
Limitations: Giving primarily in Washington, DC and New York, NY. No grants to individuals.
Application information:
Initial approach: Letter
Deadline(s): None
Officers: Cathy Liss, Pres.; Heidi Prescott, V.P.; Edward J. Walsh, Jr., Secy.; Anna M. Barone, Treas.
EIN: 521230146

2518
Robert Winthrop Charitable Trust
c/o Bonnie Mgmt. Co., Inc.
53 N. Park Ave., Ste. 53
Rockville Centre, NY 11570

Donor(s): Robert Winthrop,‡ Cornelia W. Bonnie.
Grantmaker type: Independent foundation
Financial data (yr. ended 11/30/02): Assets, $666,401 (M); expenditures, $278,232; qualifying distributions, $275,806; giving activities include $275,970 for 63 grants (high: $44,270; low: $100).
Fields of interest: Arts, fund raising; Historic preservation/historical societies; Higher education; Environment, legal rights; Human services; Federated giving programs.
Limitations: Applications not accepted. Giving on a national basis. No grants to individuals.
Application information: Contributes only to pre-selected organizations.
Trustee: Cornelia W. Bonnie.
EIN: 237441147

2519
WJS Foundation, Inc.
c/o Tag Associates, LLC
75 Rockefeller Plz., 9th Fl.
New York, NY 10019

Established in 1997 in NJ.
Donor(s): Walter J. Shipley.
Grantmaker type: Independent foundation
Financial data (yr. ended 12/31/02): Assets, $2,364,538 (M); expenditures, $211,798; qualifying distributions, $203,522; giving activities include $204,500 for 30 grants (high: $100,000; low: $1,000).
Purpose and activities: Funding primarily for arts and culture and historical preservation; funding also for human services.
Fields of interest: Television; Arts; Education; Natural resources; Hospitals (general).
Limitations: Applications not accepted. Giving primarily in NJ and NY. No grants to individuals.
Application information: Contributes only to pre-selected organizations.
Officers and Directors: Walter J. Shipley,* Pres.; Judith L. Shipley,* V.P. and Secy.; Allison P. Shipley, Treas.; Barbara S. Pandoli; John P. Shipley; Pamela J. Shipley; Dorothy S. Stabolepszy.
EIN: 223514762

2520
Wolfensohn Family Foundation
1350 Ave. of the Americas, Ste. 2900
New York, NY 10019 (212) 974-0111
Contact: Bridget Batson, Asst. Dir.
FAX; 212 97414371; *E-mail:* info@wolfensohn.org; URL: http://www.wolfensohn.org

Established in 1995 in NY.
Grantmaker type: Independent foundation
Financial data (yr. ended 12/31/01): Assets, $23,348,998 (M); gifts received, $1,000,000; expenditures, $3,212,108; qualifying distributions, $1,859,623; giving activities include $1,859,623 for 256 grants (high: $200,000; low: $25; average: $1,000–$50,000).
Purpose and activities: Giving primarily to arts and cultural programs, environment and community.
Fields of interest: Arts; Education; Environment; Cancer research; Community development, neighborhood development; Jewish agencies & temples.
Types of support: General/operating support; Continuing support; Annual campaigns; Capital campaigns; Program development; Seed money; Research; Technical assistance.
Limitations: Applications not accepted. Giving primarily on the East Coast, with emphasis on NY and Washington, DC. Giving for environmental programs in AK and WY. Giving for religious pluralism and Jewish-Arab coexistence in Israel; giving also in Australia and England. No grants to individuals.
Application information: Contributes only to pre-selected organizations.
Director and Trustees: Sara R. Wolfensohn,* Dir.; Adam R. Wolfensohn; Elaine R. Wolfensohn; James D. Wolfensohn; Naomi R. Wolfensohn.
Number of staff: 2 full-time professional.
EIN: 133781581

2521
Louis S. & Molly B. Wolk Foundation
1600 East Ave., Ste. 701
Rochester, NY 14610 (716) 442-6900
Contact: Grants Committee

Established in 1982.
Donor(s): Louis S. Wolk.
Grantmaker type: Independent foundation
Financial data (yr. ended 12/31/02): Assets,
$23,137,323 (M); expenditures, $1,521,973;
qualifying distributions, $1,331,782; giving
activities include $1,264,304 for 58 grants
(high: $350,000; low: $500; average:
$1,000–$50,000).
Purpose and activities: Giving primarily to
organizations in the greater Rochester area
whose goals are focused on health related,
educational, geriatric and social issues.
Fields of interest: Zoos/zoological societies;
Health care; Health organizations; Youth
development, scouting agencies (general);
Human services; Domestic violence; Jewish
agencies & temples.
Limitations: Giving primarily in Rochester, NY.
No grants to individuals.
Application information: Application form
required.
Copies of proposal: 2
Deadline(s): Mar. 1
Board meeting date(s): May and Oct.
Final notification: June 1
Officer and Trustees:* Alvin L. Ureles, M.D.,*
Chair.; Michael B. Berger; Audrey P. Cooke;
Leon Germanow; Harold Samloff; David M.
Wolk; Marvin L. Wolk.
EIN: 222405596

2522
The Woodcock Foundation
437 Madison Ave., 37th Fl.
New York, NY 10022
Contact: Alexandra Christy, Exec. Dir.

Established in 1988 in NY.
Donor(s): Polly Guth, John H.J. Guth.
Grantmaker type: Independent foundation
Financial data (yr. ended 11/30/02): Assets,
$37,000,000 (M); expenditures, $2,000,000;
qualifying distributions, $1,600,000; giving
activities include $1,600,000 for grants.
Fields of interest: Education; Natural resources;
Health care; Youth, services; Women.
Types of support: General/operating support;
Continuing support; Income development;
Program development.
Limitations: Applications not accepted. No
grants to individuals.
Application information: Contributes only to
pre-selected organizations.
Trustees: Stuart Davidson; Jeremy Guth; John
H.J. Guth; Polly Guth; Virginia Montgomery;
Holly Davidson Nagy; Herschel Post; Lindsay
Davidson Shea; Richard T. Watson.
Number of staff: 1 full-time professional.
EIN: 341606085

2523
The Woods Foundation
(formerly The Ward W. Woods Foundation)
c/o Bessemer Trust Co., N.A., Tax Dept.
630 5th Ave.
New York, NY 10111
Contact: Ward W. Woods, Jr., Pres.

Established in 1985 in NY.
Donor(s): Ward W. Woods, Jr., Priscilla B.
Woods, Katherine Weld Bacon.
Grantmaker type: Independent foundation
Financial data (yr. ended 09/30/02): Assets,
$291,642 (M); gifts received, $10,980;
expenditures, $1,014,466; qualifying
distributions, $999,295; giving activities include
$988,540 for 30 grants (high: $380,000; low:
$100; average: $1,000–$50,000).
Purpose and activities: Giving primarily for
wildlife conservation, the arts and cultural
programs, higher education, health care, and
human services.
Fields of interest: Cultural/ethnic awareness;
Museums (art); Secondary school/education;
Higher education; Environment;
Animals/wildlife, preservation/protection;
Hospitals (general); Children/youth, services;
Religion; Asians/Pacific Islanders.
International interests: Asia.
Limitations: Giving on a national basis. No
grants to individuals.
Application information:
Initial approach: Letter
Deadline(s): None
Officers and Directors:* Ward W. Woods, Jr.,*
Pres.; Priscilla B. Woods,* V.P.; Robert Roriston,*
Secy.-Treas.; Katherine Woods Emerick;
Alexandra Woods.
EIN: 133314966

2524
Woodshouse Foundation
(formerly The Biggs Foundation)
c/o Josephine Glass
1221 Ave. of the Americas
New York, NY 10020
Contact: Wende Biggs Ratcliffe, Tr.
Application address: Les Chetifs Champs, St.
Aubin Le Monial, France 03160

Established in 1992 in CT.
Grantmaker type: Independent foundation
Financial data (yr. ended 12/31/02): Assets,
$4,092,698 (M); expenditures, $254,979;
qualifying distributions, $198,059; giving
activities include $200,000 for 23 grants (high:
$30,000; low: $1,000).
Purpose and activities: Giving primarily for
animal welfare, environmental conservation,
and Waldorf education.
Fields of interest: Education; Environment;
Animal welfare.
International interests: France.
Limitations: Giving primarily in the U.S. and
France.
Application information:
Initial approach: Letter
Deadline(s): None
Board meeting date(s): Jan. and June
Trustees: Barton W. Biggs; Gretchen Biggs;
Wende Biggs Ratcliffe.
Number of staff: None.
EIN: 136983078

2525
The Woodward Charitable Foundation
c/o Condon O'Meara, McGinty & Donnelly, LLP
3 New York Plz., 18th Fl.
New York, NY 10004-2442

Established in 1953 in NY.
Grantmaker type: Independent foundation
Financial data (yr. ended 04/30/02): Assets,
$1,431,222 (M); expenditures, $138,812;
qualifying distributions, $124,605; giving
activities include $96,856 for 7 grants (high:
$75,246; low: $50).
Purpose and activities: Giving for primary and
secondary education, and for children and
youth services.
Fields of interest: Arts; Education; Environment;
Children/youth, services; Federated giving
programs.
Types of support: General/operating support;
Equipment.
Limitations: Applications not accepted. Giving
primarily in New York, NY. No grants to
individuals.
Application information: Contributes only to
pre-selected organizations.
Trustee: Lisa Woodward.
EIN: 136117375

2526
Ann Eden Woodward Foundation
c/o J. Lapatin
977 6th Ave., No. 810
New York, NY 10018

Established in 1963 in NY.
Donor(s): Ann Eden Woodward.‡
Grantmaker type: Independent foundation
Financial data (yr. ended 05/31/02): Assets,
$640,283 (M); gifts received, $320,000;
expenditures, $326,698; qualifying distributions,
$316,500; giving activities include $316,500 for
36 grants (high: $25,000; low: $1,500).
Purpose and activities: Giving for the arts,
including museums, and for hospitals,
environmental and wildlife preservation, and
public libraries.
Fields of interest: Museums; Arts;
Libraries/library science; Natural resources;
Animals/wildlife, preservation/protection;
Hospitals (general).
Limitations: Applications not accepted. Giving
primarily in New York, NY. No grants to
individuals.
Application information: Grants awarded at
discretion of managers.
Managers: J. Lapatin; J.A. Wood.
EIN: 136126021

2527
The Wright Family Foundation, Inc.
P.O. Box 1046
Schenectady, NY 12301 (518) 347-4530
Contact: Adeline W. Graham, Chair.
FAX: (518) 370-3105; E-mail:
info@wrightfamilyfoundation.org; URL: http://
www.wrightfamilyfoundation.org

Established in 1997 in Schenectady, NY.
Donor(s): Schenectady International, Inc.
Grantmaker type: Independent foundation

Financial data (yr. ended 09/30/02): Assets, $20,000,000 (M); expenditures, $960,100; qualifying distributions, $960,100; giving activities include $960,000 for 40 grants (high: $5,000; low: $1,000).
Purpose and activities: Funding for community, education, health, social needs, and the arts.
Fields of interest: Museums; Arts; Higher education; Environment; Health care; Community development; Human services.
Types of support: Capital campaigns; Building/renovation; Equipment; Matching/challenge support.
Limitations: Giving limited to the Schenectady, NY, area and Brazoria County, TX. No support for religious nor political organizations. No grants to individuals.
Application information: Application form available online. Application form required.
  Initial approach: Applications must be submitted thru Web site
  Copies of proposal: 1
  Deadline(s): Jan. 31, May 31, Aug. 31, and Nov. 30
  Board meeting date(s): Quarterly
Officers: Adeline W. Graham, Chair.; A. Malcolm MacCormick, Vice-Chair.; Heather M. Ward, Secy.; Robert D. McQueen, Treas.
Trustees: Gregg W. Brown; Ashley G. Gardner.
EIN: 141792255

2528
Yaron Foundation, Inc.
201 E. 37th St., Lobby Ste.
New York, NY 10016-3142
Contact: Norman Horowitz, Exec. Dir.

Established in 1984.
Donor(s): Isaac Steven Herschkopf, Debrah Lee Charatan, Robert Durst, Martin L. Markowitz, Leon Miller, Charles Ramat, Jay Susman, Charles Yassky.
Grantmaker type: Independent foundation
Financial data (yr. ended 12/31/00): Assets, $579,217 (M); gifts received, $107,879; expenditures, $166,351; qualifying distributions, $162,904; giving activities include $163,079 for 116 grants (high: $10,000; low: $18).
Purpose and activities: Giving to Jewish agencies, cultural institutes, public services and youth services.
Fields of interest: Film/video; Museums; Theater; Music; Arts; Education, research; Education, fund raising; Higher education; Medical school/education; Adult/continuing education; Adult education—literacy, basic skills & GED; Libraries/library science; Reading; Education; Natural resources; Environment; Animals/wildlife, preservation/protection; Hospitals (general); Health care; Health organizations, association; Biomedicine; Medical research, institute; Human services; Youth, services; Hospices; Aging, centers/services; Women, centers/services; Minorities/immigrants, centers/services; International peace/security; International

human rights; Jewish federated giving programs; Psychology/behavioral science; Jewish agencies & temples; Minorities; Disabled; Aging; Women.
International interests: Israel.
Types of support: Annual campaigns; Building/renovation; Equipment; Emergency funds; Curriculum development; Research.
Limitations: Giving primarily in New York, NY.
Application information: Academic qualifications required for individual applicants; proposal required for research grants. Application form not required.
  Copies of proposal: 1
  Deadline(s): None
  Board meeting date(s): Monthly
  Final notification: 2 months
Officers: Isaac Steven Herschkopf, Pres.; Norman Horowitz, Exec. Dir.
Number of staff: 1 full-time professional; 1 part-time support.
EIN: 133209791

2529
Zenkel Foundation
15 W. 53rd St.
New York, NY 10019-5410
Contact: Lois Zenkel, Pres.

Established in 1987 in NY.
Grantmaker type: Independent foundation
Financial data (yr. ended 12/31/02): Assets, $3,286,597 (M); expenditures, $367,139; qualifying distributions, $350,377; giving activities include $335,755 for 61 grants (high: $100,700; low: $100).
Purpose and activities: Giving primarily for Jewish welfare, the arts, higher education, the environment, and human rights.
Fields of interest: Photography; Museums (art); Arts; Higher education; Environment; Hospitals (general); Health organizations, association; Medical research, institute; Human services; International human rights; Race/intergroup relations; Community development; Jewish federated giving programs; Jewish agencies & temples.
Types of support: General/operating support; Annual campaigns; Capital campaigns; Building/renovation; Professorships; Scholarship funds.
Limitations: Applications not accepted. No grants to individuals.
Application information: Contributes only to pre-selected organizations.
  Board meeting date(s): Apr.
Officers and Directors:* Lois S. Zenkel,* Pres.; Daniel R. Zenkel,* Secy.; Gary B. Zenkel,* Treas.; Lisa Z. Sheldon; Bruce L. Zenkel.
Number of staff: None.
EIN: 133380631

2530
Zeron Foundation
200 Theatre Pl.
Buffalo, NY 14202

Established in 1993 in NY.
Donor(s): Jessica Enstice, members of the Jacobs family.
Grantmaker type: Independent foundation
Financial data (yr. ended 12/31/02): Assets, $2,250,603 (M); expenditures, $258,018; qualifying distributions, $247,158; giving activities include $247,158 for 23 grants (high: $55,000; low: $200).
Purpose and activities: Giving for education, community foundations, and human services.
Fields of interest: Arts; Education; Animals/wildlife, preservation/protection; Youth development; Human services; Children/youth, services; Foundations (community); Christian agencies & churches.
Limitations: Giving primarily in IN and western NY. No grants to individuals.
Application information:
  Initial approach: Proposal, no more than 4 pages
  Copies of proposal: 2
  Deadline(s): Sept. 15
  Board meeting date(s): Last week of Nov.
Trustees: Jessica H. Enstice; Matthew Enstice; Christopher L. Jacobs; Danielle Jacobs; Elizabeth R. Jacobs; Lawrence D. Jacobs, Jr.; Luke T. Jacobs; Pamela R. Jacobs.
EIN: 161429495

2531
The Daniel M. Ziff Foundation
c/o Ziff Bros. Investments
153 E. 53rd St., 43rd Fl.
New York, NY 10022

Donor(s): Ziff Investment Partnership II.
Grantmaker type: Independent foundation
Financial data (yr. ended 12/31/01): Assets, $3,049,920 (M); expenditures, $645,262; qualifying distributions, $624,672; giving activities include $629,978 for 32 grants (high: $333,333; low: $200).
Purpose and activities: Giving primarily to higher education, health, human services, federated giving programs, and to a tropical garden in FL.
Fields of interest: Higher education; Natural resources; Botanical gardens; Health organizations, association; Medical research, institute; Human services; Foundations (private operating); Federated giving programs; Jewish federated giving programs.
Limitations: Applications not accepted. Giving primarily in FL and NY. No grants to individuals.
Application information: Contributes only to pre-selected organizations.
Officers: Daniel M. Ziff, Pres.; David Moody, V.P. and Secy.; Mark Beaudoin, V.P.; Peter Cawley, V.P.; Timothy Mitchell, Treas.
EIN: 134083253

2532
The Robert D. Ziff Foundation
c/o Ziff Bros. Investments
153 E. 53rd St., 43rd Fl.
New York, NY 10022

Established in 2000 in DE.
Donor(s): Ziff Investment Partnership LP II.
Grantmaker type: Independent foundation
Financial data (yr. ended 12/31/01): Assets,
$2,809,635 (M); expenditures, $977,524;
qualifying distributions, $958,439; giving
activities include $962,333 for 25 grants (high:
$427,000; low: $333).
Purpose and activities: Giving primarily for
international causes, as well as to organizations
for the economically disadvantaged; funding
also for natural resource conservation, health
associations, human services, and Jewish and
other federated giving programs.
Fields of interest: Natural resources; Health
organizations, association; Diabetes research;
Human services; International affairs; Federated
giving programs; Jewish federated giving
programs; Economically disadvantaged.
Limitations: Applications not accepted. Giving
primarily in New York, NY. No grants to
individuals.
Application information: Contributes only to
pre-selected organizations.
Officers: Robert D. Ziff, Pres.; David Moody,
V.P. and Secy.; Mark Beaudoin, V.P.; Peter
Cawley, V.P.; Timothy Mitchell, Treas.
EIN: 134083712

2533
Charlotte & Arthur Zitrin Foundation
56 Ruxton Rd.
Great Neck, NY 11023
Application address: 32 Lockerman Sq., Ste.
L-100, Dover, DE 19901

Established in 1991 in DE.
Donor(s): Arthur Zitrin, Charlotte Zitrin.
Grantmaker type: Independent foundation
Financial data (yr. ended 10/31/02): Assets,
$5,440,126 (M); gifts received, $100,000;
expenditures, $261,780; qualifying distributions,
$244,962; giving activities include $243,200 for
81 grants (high: $41,000; low: $250).
Purpose and activities: Giving for the arts,
education, the environment, housing, and
human services.
Fields of interest: Arts; Higher education;
Education; Environment; Legal services;
Housing/shelter; Human services; Jewish
federated giving programs.
Types of support: Scholarship funds.
Limitations: Giving primarily in New York, NY.
No grants to individuals.
Application information: Application form not
required.
   Initial approach: Letter or proposal
   Deadline(s): None
Officers: Arthur Zitrin, Pres.; Charlotte Zitrin, V.P.
Number of staff: None.
EIN: 510337212

2534
The Donald & Barbara Zucker Foundation, Inc.
103 W. 55th St.
New York, NY 10019

Established in 1998.
Donor(s): Donald Zucker, Barbara Zucker.
Grantmaker type: Independent foundation
Financial data (yr. ended 09/30/01): Assets,
$3,521 (M); gifts received, $1,055,000;
expenditures, $1,058,528; qualifying
distributions, $1,058,528; giving activities
include $1,058,428 for 175 grants (high:
$175,000; low: $10).
Purpose and activities: Giving primarily to
Jewish organizations, and to hospitals; funding
also for arts and culture, education, wildlife
preservation, and youth and social services.
Fields of interest: Arts; Higher education;
Education; Animals/wildlife,
preservation/protection; Hospitals (general);
Human services; Youth, services; Jewish
federated giving programs; Jewish agencies &
temples.
Limitations: Applications not accepted. Giving
primarily in NY. No grants to individuals.
Application information: Contributes only to
pre-selected organizations.
Officers: Donald Zucker, Pres.; Barbara Zucker
Albinder, V.P.; Laurie Zucker, V.P.; Barbara
Hrbek Zucker, Secy.-Treas.
EIN: 134032142

2535
Roberta L. Zuhlke Trust
c/o JPMorgan Chase Bank
1211 Ave. of the Americas
New York, NY 10036

Established in 1972.
Grantmaker type: Public charity
Financial data (yr. ended 11/30/01): Revenue,
$3,638,675; assets, $32,488,131; expenditures,
$1,419,701; program services expenses,
$1,217,166; giving activities include
$1,217,166 for 10 grants (high: $243,433; low:
$73,029).
Purpose and activities: The trust exists for the
sole benefit of the American Red Cross, National
Association of Mental Health, New York
Presbyterian Hospital, Lincoln Center, the
Salvation Army, International Center for the
Disabled, The Humane Society of the USA, and
Planned Parenthood.
Fields of interest: Arts, single organization
support; Animal welfare; Hospitals (general);
Family planning; Mental health/crisis services,
single organization support; American Red
Cross; Salvation Army; Developmentally
disabled, centers & services.
Limitations: Applications not accepted.
Application information: Contributes only to
pre-selected organizations; unsolicited requests
for funds not considered or acknowledged.
Trustee: JPMorgan Chase Bank.
EIN: 136374227

NORTH CAROLINA

2536
Arthur F. and Alice E. Adams Charitable Foundation
c/o Wachovia Bank, N.A.
401 S. Tryon St., NC1159
Charlotte, NC 28288
Application address: c/o Wachovia Bank, N.A.,
Attn.: Susan Best, 200 S. Biscayne Blvd., 14th
Fl., Miami, FL 33131

Established in 1987 in FL.
Donor(s): Alice E. Adams.‡
Grantmaker type: Independent foundation
Financial data (yr. ended 09/30/02): Assets,
$19,594,932 (M); expenditures, $1,918,771;
qualifying distributions, $1,907,307; giving
activities include $1,901,441 for 71 grants
(high: $600,000; low: $1,000).
Fields of interest: Opera; Performing arts; Arts;
Higher education; Libraries/library science;
Botanical gardens.
Limitations: Giving primarily in FL and TN. No
grants to individuals.
Application information:
   Initial approach: Letter
   Deadline(s): None
   Board meeting date(s): May and Nov.
Governors: R. Grady Barrs; Virginia Clark;
Renee Clark Guibao.
Trustees: William B. Warren; Wachovia Bank,
N.A.
EIN: 656003785

2537
American Kennel Club Canine Health Foundation, Inc.
P.O. Box 37941
Raleigh, NC 27627-7941 (919) 334-4010
Contact: D.D. DiLalla, Exec. Dir.
Additional tel.: (888) 682-9696; FAX: (919)
334-4011; E-mail: takcchf@aol.com; URL: http://
www.akcchf.org

Founded in 1995.
Grantmaker type: Public charity
Financial data (yr. ended 12/31/01): Revenue,
$2,606,464; assets, $4,642,439; gifts received,
$2,640,985; expenditures, $2,553,296; program
services expenses, $1,776,608; giving activities
include $1,329,137 for grants.
Purpose and activities: The foundation develops
significant resources for basic and applied
health programs with emphasis on canine
genetics to improve the quality of life for dogs
and their owners.
Fields of interest: Veterinary medicine;
Veterinary medicine, hospital; Disasters, 9/11/01.
International interests: Canada; Europe; France;
United Kingdom.
Types of support: Annual campaigns; Program
development; Conferences/seminars; Research;
Matching/challenge support.
Limitations: No grants to individuals, or for
capital equipment.
Publications: Application guidelines, Annual
report, Grants list, Informational brochure
(including application guidelines), Newsletter.

Application information: Application form not required.

Initial approach: Pre-proposal
Copies of proposal: 10
Deadline(s): Apr. 17 for pre-proposal; Aug. 11 for full proposals
Board meeting date(s): Quarterly
Final notification: Jan. 1

Officers and Directors:* John A. Studebaker,* Pres.; Wayne Ferguson,* V.P.; Catherine Bell,* 2nd V.P.; Lee Arnold,* Secy.; Robert Kelly,* Treas.; D.D. DiLatta, Exec. Dir.; Sheldon B. Adler, M.D.; Pamela Stephens Buckles; Duane Butherus; Thomas Millner; and 11 additional directors.

Number of staff: 3 full-time professional; 2 full-time support.
EIN: 133813813

2538
American Lung Association of North Carolina

P.O. Box 27895
Raleigh, NC 27611-7985 (919) 832-8326
Contact: Deborah Bryan, Pres. and C.E.O.
Additional tel.: (800)-LUNGUSA; E-mail: dbryan@lungnc.org; URL: http://lungnc.org/

Established in 1904.
Grantmaker type: Public charity
Financial data (yr. ended 06/30/02): Revenue, $2,665,620; assets, $2,465,058; gifts received, $2,206,102; expenditures, $3,076,700; program services expenses, $2,214,827; giving activities include $424,075 for grants and $115,925 for grants to individuals.
Purpose and activities: The organization seeks to prevent lung disease and promote lung health through education, research, and advocacy.
Fields of interest: Environment, air pollution; Smoking; Lung diseases; Asthma; Lung research; Asthma research; Transportation.
Types of support: Research.
Publications: Annual report, Financial statement, Newsletter, Occasional report.
Application information:
Board meeting date(s): Mar., July, Sept., and Dec.
Officers and Directors:* Rebecca Logan,* Chair.; John O'Neil,* Chair.-Elect; Deborah C. Bryan,* Pres. and C.E.O.; Lois Colbert,* Secy.-Treas.
Number of staff: 15 full-time professional; 3 full-time support; 2 part-time support.
EIN: 560547515

2539
The Anonymous Fund

c/o Joseph M. Bryan, Jr.
P.O. Box 9908
Greensboro, NC 27429

Established in 1995 in NC.
Grantmaker type: Independent foundation
Financial data (yr. ended 12/31/01): Assets, $22,398,659 (M); expenditures, $2,099,490; qualifying distributions, $2,053,395; giving activities include $1,952,500 for 22 grants (high: $250,000; low: $12,500).
Purpose and activities: Giving primarily for the arts and human services.

Fields of interest: Arts; Natural resources; Human services; Children, services; Hospices; Roman Catholic agencies & churches.
Limitations: Applications not accepted. Giving on a national basis, with emphasis on NC. No grants to individuals.
Application information: Contributes only to pre-selected organizations.
Officers: Joseph M. Bryan, Jr., Pres.; Ronald P. Johnson, Secy.
Trustee: William P. Massey.
EIN: 562152734

2540
The Bailey Wildlife Foundation

10223 Bushveld Ln.
Raleigh, NC 27612
Contact: H. Whitney Bailey, Tr.
Application address: 30 Gray Rd., Andover, MA 01810, tel.: (978) 901-3471

Established in 1987.
Grantmaker type: Independent foundation
Financial data (yr. ended 12/31/02): Assets, $6,060,991 (M); expenditures, $210,302; qualifying distributions, $167,177; giving activities include $100,685 for 5 grants (high: $50,000; low: $35).
Purpose and activities: Support for wildlife and environmental conservation.
Fields of interest: Natural resources; Environment; Animals/wildlife, preservation/protection.
Types of support: Research.
Limitations: Giving primarily in the eastern U.S. No grants to individuals.
Application information:
Initial approach: Letter
Deadline(s): None
Trustees: Gordon M. Bailey; H. Whitney Bailey; Merritt P. Bailey; William H. Bailey; Margaret B. Barbabella.
EIN: 546037402

2541
Erwin Bauer Charitable Trust

c/o Wachovia Bank, N.A.
401 S. Tryon St., 4th Fl.
Charlotte, NC 28288-1159

Established in 1997 in CT.
Donor(s): Erwin Bauer.‡
Grantmaker type: Independent foundation
Financial data (yr. ended 10/31/02): Assets, $1,686,814 (M); expenditures, $128,160; qualifying distributions, $102,361; giving activities include $101,013 for 8 grants (high: $27,900; low: $2,000).
Fields of interest: Education; Environment, land resources; Human services.
Limitations: Applications not accepted. No grants to individuals.
Application information: Contributes only to pre-selected organizations.
Trustee: Catherine Carroll Petroni.
Agent: Wachovia Bank, N.A.
EIN: 256620895

2542
The Beattie Foundation

(formerly Frances and William H. Beattie Foundation)
c/o Wachovia Bank, N.A.
P.O. Box 3099
Winston-Salem, NC 27150-6732

Donor(s): William H. Beattie.‡
Grantmaker type: Independent foundation
Financial data (yr. ended 12/31/01): Assets, $6,939,682 (M); expenditures, $389,126; qualifying distributions, $364,769; giving activities include $358,200 for 38 grants (high: $15,000; low: $1,000; average: $2,000–$10,000).
Purpose and activities: Giving primarily for higher education; also giving for the performing arts and conservation.
Fields of interest: Performing arts; Higher education; Education; Natural resources; Housing/shelter, development.
Limitations: Applications not accepted. Giving primarily in the Greenville, SC, area. No grants to individuals.
Application information: Contributes only to pre-selected organizations.
Trustee: Wachovia Bank, N.A.
Advisory Committee: Dorothy B. Hamill; Joel B. Adams, Jr.; Mrs. Joel B. Adams, Jr.
EIN: 576113645

2543
The Blumenthal Foundation

P.O. Box 34689
Charlotte, NC 28234 (704) 377-9237
Contact: Philip Blumenthal, Tr.
Additional tel.: (704) 377-6555, ext. 2305; URL: http://www.blumenthalfoundation.org/index.htm

Trust established in 1953 in NC.
Donor(s): I.D. Blumenthal,‡ Herman Blumenthal, Radiator Specialty Co.
Grantmaker type: Independent foundation
Financial data (yr. ended 12/31/01): Assets, $20,747 (M); gifts received, $13,206; expenditures, $3,214,694; qualifying distributions, $1,892,015; giving activities include $1,771,607 for 191 grants (high: $100,000; low: $60; average: $1,000–$50,000).
Purpose and activities: Giving for higher education, Jewish welfare organizations, and programs in the arts and humanities; also supports Wildacres, a conference center in NC, which invites nonprofit groups with planned educational programs in a variety of disciplines to use its facilities.
Fields of interest: Humanities; Arts; Higher education; Environment; Human services; Jewish federated giving programs.
Types of support: General/operating support; Annual campaigns; Capital campaigns; Building/renovation; Equipment; Endowments; Emergency funds; Program development; Conferences/seminars; Professorships; Publication; Seed money; Research; Matching/challenge support.
Limitations: Giving primarily in NC, with emphasis on Charlotte and Mecklenburg County. No grants to individuals, or for scholarships or fellowships; no loans.
Publications: Application guidelines, Annual report, Grants list, Multi-year report.

Application information: Application form not required.

Initial approach: Letter or telephone
Copies of proposal: 1
Board meeting date(s): Mar., June, Sept., and Dec.

Trustees: Alan Blumenthal; Anita Blumenthal; Philip Blumenthal; Samuel Blumenthal, Ph.D.
Number of staff: 2 full-time professional; 1 part-time professional.
EIN: 560793667

2544
R. A. Bryan Foundation, Inc.
400 Patetown Rd.
P.O. Drawer 919
Goldsboro, NC 27533-0919 (919) 734-8400
Contact: R.A. Bryan, Jr., Pres.

Established in 1956 in NC.
Donor(s): R.A. Bryan, Jr., Ruby M. Bryan,‡ Aviation Fuel Terminals, Inc., Ridgewood, Inc., T.A. Loving Co.
Grantmaker type: Independent foundation
Financial data (yr. ended 12/31/02): Assets, $12,533,006 (M); expenditures, $770,030; qualifying distributions, $684,275; giving activities include $675,625 for 50 grants (high: $121,400; low: $100).
Purpose and activities: Giving to public day schools, higher education, youth services, and health and medical organizations.
Fields of interest: Arts; Higher education; Animals/wildlife, preservation/protection; Health care; Health organizations, association; Cancer; Medical research, institute; Cancer research; Human services; Christian agencies & churches.
Types of support: General/operating support; Continuing support; Annual campaigns; Capital campaigns; Building/renovation; Endowments; Program development; Scholarship funds; Research.
Limitations: Applications not accepted. Giving primarily in NC. No grants to individuals.
Application information: Contributes only to pre-selected organizations.
Officers: R.A. Bryan, Jr., Pres.; Stephen C. Bryan, V.P.; Thomas R. Howell, Treas.
Number of staff: None.
EIN: 566044320

2545
Robert Lee Chastain and Thomas M. Chastain Charitable Foundation
c/o Wachovia Bank, N.A.
401 S. Tryon St., 4th Fl.
Charlotte, NC 28202-1934

Trust established in 1966 in FL.
Donor(s): Robert Lee Chastain.‡
Grantmaker type: Independent foundation
Financial data (yr. ended 12/31/02): Assets, $3,613,481 (L); expenditures, $256,317; qualifying distributions, $220,000; giving activities include $220,000 for 20 grants (high: $70,000; low: $6).
Purpose and activities: Grants policy confined to community and publicly-managed agencies with emphasis given to public higher education, programs in the humanities, arts, and sciences, and environmental resource management

projects offering benefits to the general population. A few trustee-initiated contributions may exceed these limits.
Fields of interest: Humanities; Arts; Higher education; Environment; Engineering/technology; Science.
Limitations: Applications not accepted. Giving primarily in the Palm Beach and Martin County, FL, area. No support for church-related groups or national charities. No grants to individuals, or for building or endowment funds or appeals in mass circulation.
Application information: Contributes only to pre-selected organizations.
Board meeting date(s): Quarterly
Trustee: Wachovia Bank, N.A.
Number of staff: None.
EIN: 596171294

2546
The Thomas B. and Robertha K. Coleman Foundation, Inc.
c/o Katherine C. Haroldson
P.O. Box 1169
New Bern, NC 28563-1169

Established in 1998 in NC.
Donor(s): Robertha K. Coleman.
Grantmaker type: Independent foundation
Financial data (yr. ended 12/31/02): Assets, $1,716,674 (M); expenditures, $146,281; qualifying distributions, $119,594; giving activities include $119,134 for 41 grants (high: $33,000; low: $25).
Fields of interest: Historic preservation/historical societies; Arts; Education; Environment; Health care; Human services; Christian agencies & churches.
Limitations: Applications not accepted. Giving primarily in New Bern, NC. No grants to individuals.
Application information: Contributes only to pre-selected organizations.
Officers: Katherine C. Haroldson, Pres. and Secy.; Robertha K. Coleman, V.P.; Thomas Brooks Coleman III, V.P.; John O. Haroldson, Treas.
EIN: 562086113

2547
Community Foundation of Burke County
P.O. Box 1156
Morganton, NC 28680-1156 (828) 437-7105

Established in 1999 in NC.
Grantmaker type: Community foundation
Financial data (yr. ended 12/31/02): Assets, $1,394,089 (M); gifts received, $268,409; expenditures, $173,301; giving activities include $122,511 for 9+ grants.
Purpose and activities: Giving primarily for a public library, as well as for the environment, education, health, human services, and an Episcopal church. The foundation administers a donor-advised fund.
Fields of interest: Early childhood education; Libraries (public); Environment, association; Health care; Human services; Protestant agencies & churches.
Types of support: Annual campaigns; In-kind gifts.

Limitations: Giving primarily in Burke County, NC.
Publications: Annual report, Informational brochure.
Officers: James H. Rostan, Pres.; C. Michael Fulenwider, V.P.; John W. Ervin, Jr., Secy.; John F. Black, Jr., Treas.; Caroline Avery, Exec. Dir.
Directors: John T. Branstrom; Sterling R. Collett III; P. Pual Deaton; Elisabeth C. Ervin; Charles E. Horton; Jack B. Kirksey; James E. Lowdermilk; Nettie M. McIntosh; W. Harold Mitchell; Barbara C. Norvell; Otto H. Woerner.
EIN: 562170220

2548
The Community Foundation of Henderson County, Inc.
401 N. Main St., 3rd Fl.
P.O. Box 1108
Hendersonville, NC 28793 (828) 697-6224
Contact: Priscilla Cantrell, Exec. Dir., or Crystal Reese, Fin. Dir.
FAX: (828) 696-4026; E-mail: info@cfhendersoncounty.org; URL: http://www.cfhendersoncounty.org

Incorporated in 1982 in NC.
Grantmaker type: Community foundation
Financial data (yr. ended 06/30/02): Assets, $38,701,171 (M); gifts received, $18,270,183; expenditures, $2,383,440; giving activities include $1,436,479 for 406 grants (high: $70,000; low: $25; average: $200–$5,000) and $261,816 for grants to individuals (average: $500–$3,000).
Purpose and activities: The foundation exists to enrich the quality of life in the greater Henderson County, NC, area, through building and increasing endowments in perpetuity. The foundation administers donor-advised funds.
Fields of interest: Arts; Child development, education; Education; Environment; Health care; Human services; Child development, services; Aging, centers/services; Homeless, human services; Community development; Aging; Homeless.
Types of support: Equipment; Emergency funds; Program development; Publication; Seed money; Curriculum development; Scholarship funds; Technical assistance; Scholarships—to individuals; Matching/challenge support.
Limitations: Giving limited to the Henderson County, NC, area. No support for religious or political organizations. No grants for endowment funds, capital campaigns, annual campaigns, or fundraising events; no loans.
Publications: Application guidelines, Annual report, Informational brochure, Newsletter.
Application information: Scholarship availability is announced in Nov. Application form required.
Initial approach: Letter or telephone
Copies of proposal: 2
Deadline(s): Mar. 1, June 1, Sept. 1, and Dec. 1; Apr. 1 for scholarships
Board meeting date(s): Monthly
Final notification: 3 months
Officers and Directors:* Sherri Metzger,* Pres.; Bill Smith,* V.P., Distrib.; Sue Ballard Gilliam,* V.P., Development; Ronald Rosenburger,* Secy.; F. Lee Thomas,* Treas.; Priscilla Cantrell,* Exec. Dir.; Sally Boyd; Katie Hunter; Fair Johnson; Sam Leftwich; Bernie Linder; Bob Ogden; David

Reeves; Jan Shefter; Alice Soder; Art Stuenkel; and 4 additional directors.
Number of staff: 4 full-time professional; 2 full-time support.
EIN: 561330792

2549

The Community Foundation of Western North Carolina, Inc.
1 W. Pack Sq., Ste. 1600
Asheville, NC 28802 (828) 254-4960
Contact: Pat Smith, Exec. Dir.
Mailing address: P.O. Box 1888, Asheville, NC 28802; FAX: (828) 251-2258; URL: http://www.cfwnc.org

Incorporated in 1978 in NC as the Community Foundation of Greater Asheville, Inc.
Grantmaker type: Community foundation
Financial data (yr. ended 06/30/02): Assets, $85,739,721 (M); gifts received, $16,594,262; expenditures, $17,759,185; giving activities include $11,160,708 for grants.
Purpose and activities: To increase philanthropy and work within the community to find solutions to pressing needs; to create opportunities to make the western NC, area, a better place to live. The foundation administers donor-advised funds.
Fields of interest: Arts; Education; Environment; Health care; Human services; Children/youth, services; Community development.
Types of support: Income development; Management development; Program development; Seed money; Curriculum development; Scholarship funds; Technical assistance; Consulting services; Program evaluation; Program-related investments/loans; Employee-related scholarships; Scholarships—to individuals; Matching/challenge support.
Limitations: Giving limited to western NC. No support for religious organizations or sectarian purposes (except from designated funds). No grants to individuals (except for scholarships), or for capital campaigns, endowment funds, start-up funds, fundraising activities, debt retirement, or general operating support.
Publications: Application guidelines, Annual report, Informational brochure (including application guidelines), Newsletter.
Application information: Application form required.
  Initial approach: Telephone or letter
  Copies of proposal: 1
  Deadline(s): Feb. 1 and Aug. 15
  Board meeting date(s): Quarterly, 2nd Wed. in Feb., May, Aug., and Nov.
  Final notification: Within 3 months of each deadline
Officers and Directors:* James B. Powell II,* Chair.; Eleanor Owen,* Vice-Chair.; Isabel Nichols,* Secy.; Charles Nesbitt,* Treas.; Pat Smith, Exec. Dir.; and 30 additional directors.
Number of staff: 10 full-time professional; 1 part-time professional; 3 full-time support; 1 part-time support.
EIN: 561223384

2550

Edward E. Crutchfield Family Foundation
401 S. Tryon St., Ste. 2880
Charlotte, NC 28288-0001

Established in 2000 in NC.
Donor(s): Edward E. Crutchfield.
Grantmaker type: Independent foundation
Financial data (yr. ended 12/31/02): Assets, $3,719,049 (M); gifts received, $611,802; expenditures, $295,437; qualifying distributions, $289,000; giving activities include $282,000 for 14 grants (high: $154,000; low: $500).
Fields of interest: Environment; Human services; Religion.
Limitations: Applications not accepted. Giving primarily in NC. No grants to individuals.
Application information: Contributes only to pre-selected organizations.
Officers: Edward E. Crutchfield, Chair. and Pres.; Sarah Crutchfield Davis, V.P.; Edward E. Crutchfield, Jr., Secy.-Treas.
EIN: 562220389

2551

Cumberland Community Foundation, Inc.
P.O. Box 2345
Fayetteville, NC 28302 (910) 483-4449
Contact: Mary Holmes, Exec. Dir.
FAX: (910) 483-2905; URL: http://www.cumberlandcf.org

Established in 1980 in NC.
Donor(s): Lucile Hutaff.‡
Grantmaker type: Community foundation
Financial data (yr. ended 06/30/02): Assets, $19,729,047 (M); gifts received, $4,118,139; expenditures, $2,445,747; giving activities include $1,947,448 for 857 grants (high: $279,606; low: $50).
Purpose and activities: Support primarily for innovative and collaborative projects. As part of its general discretionary grantmaking, the foundation frequently funds capacity-building efforts by nonprofits. The foundation administers a donor-advised fund.
Fields of interest: Museums; Performing arts; Dance; Humanities; History/archaeology; Language/linguistics; Literature; Arts; Early childhood education; Child development, education; Vocational education; Higher education; Adult/continuing education; Libraries/library science; Education; Natural resources; Environment; Animals/wildlife, preservation/protection; Family planning; Medical care, rehabilitation; Health care; Substance abuse, services; Mental health/crisis services; AIDS; Crime/violence prevention, youth; Crime/law enforcement; Employment; Nutrition; Housing/shelter, development; Recreation; Youth development, services; Human services; Children/youth, services; Child development, services; Family services; Hospices; Women, centers/services; Minorities/immigrants, centers/services; Homeless, human services; Race/intergroup relations; Civil rights; Urban/community development; Rural development; Community development; Voluntarism promotion; Population studies; Military/veterans' organizations; Leadership development; Minorities; Native Americans/American Indians;

Disabled; Women; Economically disadvantaged; Homeless.
Types of support: General/operating support; Income development; Management development; Endowments; Program development; Conferences/seminars; Publication; Seed money; Scholarship funds; Technical assistance; Scholarships—to individuals; In-kind gifts; Matching/challenge support.
Limitations: Giving limited to southeastern NC.
Publications: Application guidelines, Annual report, Financial statement, Grants list, Informational brochure, Newsletter, Occasional report, Program policy statement.
Application information: Competitive grants are awarded in the county of the donor. Application form required.
  Initial approach: Letter
  Copies of proposal: 1
  Deadline(s): Spring and fall; see Web site for dates
  Board meeting date(s): 2nd Thurs. of every other month
  Final notification: See Web site
Officers and Directors:* Leslie A. Griffin,* Pres.; Robert W. Drake,* V.P.; Anthony G. Chavonne,* Secy.; Sammy Short,* Treas.; Kamal M. Bakri; Mildred Braxton; Mary Lynn M. Bryan; Elaine M. Bryant; Alfred E. Cleveland; Margaret H. Dickson; Ellie Fleishman; Loleta Wood Foster; Aston L. Fox; J. "Mac" Healey; John T. Henley, Jr.; J. Wes Jones; J.S. McFadyen, Jr.; Samuel H. Meares; Donald Porter; Robert G. Ray; Dot Wyatt.
Number of staff: 2 full-time professional; 1 full-time support; 2 part-time support.
EIN: 581406831

2552

Nancy Sayles Day Foundation
c/o Wachovia Bank, N.A.
401 S. Tryon St., 4th Fl.
Charlotte, NC 28288-5709
Contact: John Small
Application address: c/o Wachovia Bank, N.A., 10 State House Sq., 2nd Fl., Hartford, CT 06103

Trust established in 1964 in CT.
Donor(s): Nancy Sayles Day,‡ Mrs. Lee Day Gillespie.
Grantmaker type: Independent foundation
Financial data (yr. ended 09/30/02): Assets, $12,315,545 (M); expenditures, $795,057; qualifying distributions, $655,401; giving activities include $661,500 for 37 grants (high: $250,000; low: $2,000).
Fields of interest: Opera; Music; Arts; Higher education; Education; Natural resources; Youth, services.
Types of support: General/operating support; Continuing support.
Limitations: Giving primarily in MA. No grants to individuals, or for building or endowment funds, research, or matching gifts; no loans.
Application information: Application form not required.
  Initial approach: Letter
  Copies of proposal: 1
  Deadline(s): None
Trustee: Wachovia Bank, N.A.
Number of staff: None.
EIN: 066071254

2553
The Dover Foundation, Inc.
P.O. Box 208
Shelby, NC 28151 (704) 487-8888
Contact: Hoyt Q. Bailey, Pres.
FAX: (704) 482-6818; E-mail:
doverfnd@shelby.net

Incorporated in 1944 in NC.
Grantmaker type: Independent foundation
Financial data (yr. ended 08/31/02): Assets,
$20,041,011 (M); expenditures, $1,612,351;
qualifying distributions, $1,440,619; giving
activities include $1,351,850 for 151 grants
(high: $100,000; low: $100; average:
$500–$25,000).
Purpose and activities: Giving for museums,
education, environment, health care, and youth
development, religion, and human services.
Fields of interest: Museums; Secondary
school/education; Higher education; Education;
Environment; Health care; Youth development,
services; Human services; Public affairs;
Religion.
Types of support: General/operating support;
Continuing support; Annual campaigns; Capital
campaigns; Building/renovation; Endowments;
Emergency funds; Professorships; Fellowships;
Scholarship funds; Research;
Matching/challenge support.
Limitations: Giving primarily in Cleveland
County, NC.
Publications: Informational brochure (including
application guidelines).
Application information: Application form not
required.
 Initial approach: Letter
 Copies of proposal: 9
 Board meeting date(s): Jan., April, July, and
  Oct.
Officers and Directors:* Hoyt Q. Bailey,* Pres.;
Kathleen D. Hamrick,* V.P.; Harvey B.
Hamrick,* Secy.; J. Linton Suttle,* Treas.; Nancy
T. Moore, Exec. Dir.; Cynthia B. Buckingham;
Harvey B. Hamrick, Jr.; Melanie A. Knight;
Kathleen H. Wilson.
Number of staff: 1 full-time professional.
EIN: 560769897

2554
Foundation for the Carolinas ▼
217 South Tryon St.
Charlotte, NC 28202 (704) 973-4500
Contact: Don Jonas, Sr. V.P., Community
Philanthropy
Additional tel.: (888) 335-9541; FAX: (704)
973-4599; URL: http://www.fftc.org

Incorporated in 1958 in NC.
Grantmaker type: Community foundation
Financial data (yr. ended 12/31/01): Assets,
$254,010,245 (M); gifts received, $46,769,081;
expenditures, $44,798,558; giving activities
include $34,937,758 for 1,753+ grants (high:
$1,574,424; average: $5,000–$200,000).
Purpose and activities: Support primarily for
education, environment, human services, and
health.
Fields of interest: Historic
preservation/historical societies; Arts; Education;
Environment; Health care; Health organizations,
association; Human services; Children/youth,

services; Aging, centers/services; Public affairs;
Religion.
Types of support: Seed money; Scholarship
funds; Matching/challenge support.
Limitations: Giving primarily to organizations
serving the citizens of NC and SC, with
emphasis on the greater Charlotte, NC, region.
No grants to individuals (except for
scholarships), or for deficit financing, capital
campaigns, operating budgets, publications,
conferences, videos, travel, equipment, or
endowment funds.
Publications: Application guidelines, Annual
report (including application guidelines),
Newsletter.
Application information: The foundation is
currently undertaking an internal study and
review of grantmaking program areas.
Applications are not being accepted at this time.
Application form required.
 Initial approach: Letter or telephone
 Copies of proposal: 1
 Deadline(s): Varies
 Board meeting date(s): Distribution
  Committee meets 3 times per year
 Final notification: 2 months
Officers and Directors:* Peter B. Ridder,*
Chair.; Michael Marsicano, C.E.O. and Pres.;
Laura L. Meyer, Exec. V.P.; McCray V. Benson,
Sr. V.P., Regional Initiatives; Don Jonas, Sr. V.P.,
Community Philanthropy; Judy L. Kerns, Sr. V.P.,
Finance and Admin.; C. Barton Landess, Sr. V.P.,
Devel. and Donor Svcs.; Sharon Carr
Harrington, V.P., Donor Svcs.; Charity L.
Perkins,* V.P., Comm. and Donor Svcs.; Debra
S. Watt, V.P., Finance; Holly K. Welch, V.P.,
Devel. and Legal Affairs; and 15 additional
directors.
Number of staff: 17 full-time professional; 10
full-time support; 1 part-time support.
EIN: 566047886
**Recent environmental and animal welfare
grants:**
2554-1 Allison Woods Foundation, Statesville,
 NC, $25,700. 2001.
2554-2 American Chestnut Foundation,
 Bennington, VT, $130,100. 2001.
2554-3 Appalachian Voices, Boone, NC,
 $165,000. 2001.
2554-4 Blue Ridge Environmental Defense
 League, Glendale Springs, NC, $30,000.
 2001.
2554-5 Carolina Raptor Center, Charlotte, NC,
 $20,627. 2001.
2554-6 Catawba Lands Conservancy, Charlotte,
 NC, $34,300. 2001.
2554-7 Conservation Council of North Carolina
 Foundation, Raleigh, NC, $10,000. 2001.
2554-8 Conservation Trust for North Carolina,
 Raleigh, NC, $1,751,850. This grant
 represents aggregate totals of grants from
 different funds. It is not a single grant and
 should not be construed as such. 2001.
2554-9 Daniel Jonathan Stowe Conservancy,
 Belmont, NC, $16,900. 2001.
2554-10 Dogwood Alliance, Brevard, NC,
 $61,500. 2001.
2554-11 Earth Island Institute, San Francisco,
 CA, $10,000. For program in Pasadena. 2001.
2554-12 Environmental Defense, Raleigh, NC,
 $226,750. 2001.
2554-13 Friends of the Earth, DC, $10,000.
 2001.

2554-14 High Country Conservancy, Boone,
 NC, $10,000. 2001.
2554-15 Humane Society of Richmond County,
 Rockingham, NC, $125,000. 2001.
2554-16 Land Trust for Central North Carolina,
 Salisbury, NC, $411,000. 2001.
2554-17 Long Branch Environmental Education
 Center, Leicester, NC, $12,000. 2001.
2554-18 National Parks and Conservation
 Association, Norris, TN, $100,000. 2001.
2554-19 Nature Conservancy, Durham, NC,
 $1,533,550. This grant represents aggregate
 totals of grants from different funds. It is not a
 single grant and should not be construed as
 such. 2001.
2554-20 Nature Conservancy, Columbia, SC,
 $27,000. 2001.
2554-21 Neuse River Foundation, New Bern,
 NC, $25,000. 2001.
2554-22 North Carolina Coastal Federation,
 Newport, NC, $126,100. 2001.
2554-23 North Carolina Coastal Land Trust,
 Wilmington, NC, $90,000. 2001.
2554-24 North Carolina John Muir Foundation,
 Winston-Salem, NC, $26,000. 2001.
2554-25 North Carolina Outward Bound
 School, Asheville, NC, $116,050. 2001.
2554-26 North Carolina Solar Energy
 Association, Raleigh, NC, $12,500. 2001.
2554-27 North Carolina Veterinary Medical
 Foundation, Raleigh, NC, $25,000. 2001.
2554-28 North Carolina Waste Awareness and
 Reduction Network (NC WARN), Durham,
 NC, $14,000. 2001.
2554-29 North Carolina Zoological Society,
 Asheboro, NC, $43,594. 2001.
2554-30 Palmetto Conservation Foundation,
 Columbia, SC, $12,500. 2001.
2554-31 Riverlink, Asheville, NC, $100,000.
 2001.
2554-32 Save Our State, Raleigh, NC, $28,700.
 2001.
2554-33 Sierra Club Foundation, San Francisco,
 CA, $125,000. 2001.
2554-34 South Carolina Aquarium, Charleston,
 SC, $30,000. 2001.
2554-35 South Carolina Coastal Conservation
 League, Charleston, SC, $10,000. 2001.
2554-36 South Carolina Waterfowl Association
 (SWCA), Pinewood, SC, $25,000. 2001.
2554-37 Southern Appalachian Biodiversity
 Project, Asheville, NC, $65,000. 2001.
2554-38 Southern Appalachian Highlands
 Conservancy, Asheville, NC, $246,050. 2001.
2554-39 Southern Environmental Law Center,
 Charlottesville, VA, $564,000. 2001.
2554-40 Trips for Kids, Mill Valley, CA,
 $17,050. 2001.
2554-41 Trust for Public Land, Charlotte Field
 Office, Charlotte, NC, $27,000. 2001.
2554-42 Western North Carolina Alliance,
 Asheville, NC, $20,000. 2001.
2554-43 Wing Haven Foundation, Charlotte,
 NC, $18,687. 2001.
2554-44 World Stewardship Institute, Santa
 Rosa, CA, $10,000. 2001.
2554-45 Yadkin-Pee Dee Lakes Project, Badin,
 NC, $10,000. 2001.

2555
GlaxoSmithKline Holdings (Americas) Inc. Corporate Giving Program
(formerly Glaxo Wellcome Americas Inc. Corporate Giving Program)
5 Moore Dr.
Research Triangle Park, NC 27709-3398
(919) 483-2719
Contact: William A. Shore, Dir., U.S. Community Partnerships
Application address: P.O. Box 13398, Research Triangle Park, NC 27709; FAX: (919) 483-8765

Grantmaker type: Corporate giving program
Financial data (yr. ended 12/31/02): Total giving, $365,486,066; giving activities include $144,526,066 for grants and $220,960,000 for in-kind gifts.
Purpose and activities: As a complement to its foundation, GlaxoSmithKline Holdings (Americas) also makes charitable contributions to nonprofit organizations directly. Support is given on a national and international basis.
Fields of interest: Arts; Education; Environment; Health care; Children, services; Human services; Community development; Public affairs; Aging.
Types of support: Program development; Conferences/seminars; Seed money; Curriculum development; Employee matching gifts; Donated products; In-kind gifts; Matching/challenge support.
Limitations: Giving on a national and international basis in areas of company operations, with emphasis on Research Triangle Park, NC; giving also to national and international organizations. No support for political or religious organizations. No grants to individuals.
Publications: Corporate giving report (including application guidelines).
Application information: Application form not required.
Initial approach: Proposal to headquarters
Copies of proposal: 1
Deadline(s): None
Final notification: 8 to 12 weeks

2556
The Carrie E. & Lena V. Glenn Foundation
1552 Union Rd., Ste. D
Gastonia, NC 28054-5582 (704) 867-0296
Contact: Barbara H. Voorhees, Exec. Dir.
FAX: (704) 867-4496; E-mail: glennfnd@bellsouth.net

Established in 1971 in NC.
Donor(s): Carrie Eugenia Glenn,‡ Lena Viola Glenn.‡
Grantmaker type: Independent foundation
Financial data (yr. ended 09/30/02): Assets, $7,238,854 (M); expenditures, $490,848; qualifying distributions, $437,393; giving activities include $359,425 for 32 grants (high: $100,000; low: $1,500; average: $500–$50,000).
Purpose and activities: Giving primarily for education, the arts, human services and for religious purposes.
Fields of interest: Arts; Elementary/secondary education; Environment; Human services; Children/youth, services; Christian agencies & churches.

Types of support: General/operating support; Building/renovation; Equipment; Program development; Seed money; Matching/challenge support.
Limitations: Giving limited to Gaston County, NC. No grants to individuals; no multi-year grants, scholarships, planning grants, capital campaigns, or fund-raising campaigns.
Publications: Application guidelines, Grants list.
Application information: Application form required.
Initial approach: Letter
Copies of proposal: 9
Deadline(s): Mar. 1
Board meeting date(s): Quarterly
Final notification: June 30
Officers and Directors:* W. Alex Hall,* Chair.; Ernest W. Sumner,* Vice-Chair.; Caroline H. Garrison,* Secy.; George L. Hodges III,* Treas.; David Stoker; Mayor Jennifer T. Stultz.
Trustee: BB&T.
Number of staff: 1 part-time professional.
EIN: 237140170

2557
Guzenhauser-Chapin Fund
c/o Piedmont Financial Co., Inc.
P.O. Box 20124
Greensboro, NC 27420
Contact: Chester F. Chapin, V.P.

Established in 1998 in NC.
Grantmaker type: Independent foundation
Financial data (yr. ended 12/31/00): Assets, $7,542,776 (M); gifts received, $4,015,954; expenditures, $209,077; qualifying distributions, $179,991; giving activities include $186,100 for 15 grants (high: $37,500; low: $3,000).
Purpose and activities: Giving for health and family planning services, and for recreation.
Fields of interest: Animal welfare; Family planning; Health care; Athletics/sports, equestrianism; Human services.
Limitations: Giving primarily in CA.
Application information:
Initial approach: Written proposal
Deadline(s): None
Officers and Directors:* Charles S. Chapin,* Pres.; Chester F. Chapin,* V.P.; Lynn R. Chapin Guzenhauser,* V.P.; Lisa Vinson Beaman,* Secy.; Samuel C. Chapin,* Treas.
EIN: 562089195

2558
The John W. and Anna H. Hanes Foundation
c/o Wachovia Bank N.A.
P.O. Box 3099, MC-NC6732
Winston-Salem, NC 27150 (336) 732-5372
Contact: Linda G. Tilley, Sr. V.P., Wachovia Bank, N.A.

Trust established in 1947 in NC.
Grantmaker type: Independent foundation
Financial data (yr. ended 12/31/01): Assets, $28,253,555 (M); expenditures, $1,582,075; qualifying distributions, $1,470,184; giving activities include $1,447,902 for 55 grants (high: $200,000; low: $1,000; average: $1,000–$200,000).
Purpose and activities: Giving primarily for the arts.

Fields of interest: Historic preservation/historical societies; Arts; Education; Natural resources; Environment; Health care; Human services; Children/youth, services.
Types of support: Annual campaigns; Capital campaigns; Building/renovation; Equipment; Land acquisition; Endowments; Emergency funds; Program development; Seed money; Matching/challenge support.
Limitations: Giving limited to NC, with emphasis on Forsyth County. No grants to individuals, or for operating expenses.
Publications: Application guidelines, Program policy statement.
Application information: Application form required.
Initial approach: Telephone or letter
Copies of proposal: 1
Deadline(s): 15th day of month preceding board meeting
Board meeting date(s): Jan., Apr., July, and Oct.
Final notification: 10 days
Trustees: Frank Borden Hanes, Sr.; Frank Borden Hanes, Jr.; R. Philip Hanes, Jr.; Drewry H. Nostitz; Ralph H. Womble; Wachovia Bank, N.A.
Number of staff: None.
EIN: 566037589

2559
James G. Hanes Memorial Fund
(formerly James G. Hanes Memorial Fund/Foundation)
c/o Wachovia Bank, N.A.
401 S. Tryon St., 4th Fl.
Charlotte, NC 28288-0001
Contact: Matt Johnson
FAX: (704) 374-2242

Established in 1957 in NC. The James G. Hanes Memorial Fund reincorporated under its current name following the formal merger and transfer of all foundation assets to the fund in Dec. 1991. The foundation terminated in 1992.
Grantmaker type: Independent foundation
Financial data (yr. ended 10/31/02): Assets, $19,185,019 (M); expenditures, $1,196,705; qualifying distributions, $1,108,040; giving activities include $1,114,917 for 45 grants (high: $73,220; low: $5,000).
Purpose and activities: Giving primarily for arts and culture, with emphasis on a contemporary art center.
Fields of interest: Museums (art); Arts; Natural resources; Health care; Health organizations; Community development.
Types of support: General/operating support; Annual campaigns; Capital campaigns; Building/renovation; Equipment; Land acquisition; Endowments; Emergency funds; Program development; Conferences/seminars; Publication; Seed money; Research; Matching/challenge support.
Limitations: Giving primarily in NC, with emphasis on Winston-Salem. No grants to individuals, or for maintenance purposes, or salary requests or funding on a recurring basis.
Publications: Application guidelines, Informational brochure.
Application information: Application form required.
Initial approach: Proposal
Copies of proposal: 1

Deadline(s): Jan. 1, Apr. 1, July 1, and Oct. 1
Board meeting date(s): Jan., Apr., Aug., and Oct.
Final notification: 10 business days
Trustee: Wachovia Bank, N.A.
Number of staff: None.
EIN: 566036987

2560
The Leonard G. Herring Family Foundation, Inc.
310 Coffey St.
North Wilkesboro, NC 28659
Contact: Leonard G. Herring, Pres.

Established in 1994 in NC.
Donor(s): Leonard G. Herring.
Grantmaker type: Independent foundation
Financial data (yr. ended 12/31/02): Assets, $7,495,781 (M); gifts received, $2,300; expenditures, $380,006; qualifying distributions, $339,312; giving activities include $340,303 for 35 grants (high: $75,000; low: $250).
Fields of interest: Higher education; Natural resources; Zoos/zoological societies; Health organizations, association; YM/YWCAs & YM/YWHAs; Children/youth, services; Federated giving programs; Protestant agencies & churches.
Limitations: Applications not accepted. No grants to individuals.
Application information: Contributes only to pre-selected organizations.
Officers: Leonard G. Herring, Pres.; Rozelia S. Herring, V.P.; Sandra Herring Gaddy, Secy.; Albert Lee Herring, Treas.
EIN: 561881015

2561
Janirve Foundation ▼
1 N. Pack Sq., Ste. 416
Asheville, NC 28801 (828) 258-1877
Contact: Met R. Poston, Chair.
FAX: (828) 258-1837

Established in 1954 in FL.
Donor(s): Irving J. Reuter,‡ Jeannett M. Reuter.‡
Grantmaker type: Independent foundation
Financial data (yr. ended 12/31/01): Assets, $62,766,930 (M); expenditures, $7,643,045; qualifying distributions, $7,318,070; giving activities include $7,093,457 for 89 grants (high: $1,250,000; low: $334; average: $10,000–$100,000).
Purpose and activities: Giving primarily for colleges and universities and human services, including child welfare, family services, and housing programs; some support also for hospitals and health associations and community development projects.
Fields of interest: Higher education; Hospitals (general); Health organizations, association; Housing/shelter, development; Human services; Children/youth, services; Family services; Community development; General charitable giving.
Types of support: Capital campaigns; Building/renovation.
Limitations: Giving primarily in western NC. No support for public and private elementary schools, or churches and religious programs. No grants to individuals (except for scholarship

program), or generally for operating budgets, endowments or for research programs, publication of books or printed material, theatrical productions, videos, radio or television programs; no loans.
Publications: Application guidelines, Annual report.
Application information: Applicants should contact Asheville, NC, office for application procedures. Application form required.
Initial approach: Telephone or letter
Copies of proposal: 5
Deadline(s): Dec. 1 for first quarter; Mar. 1 for the second quarter; June 1 for the third quarter; and Sept. 1 for the fourth quarter
Board meeting date(s): At least monthly
Final notification: Within 4 months
Directors: Met R. Poston, Chair.; E. Charles Dyson; John W. Erichson; James Woolcott; Richard B. Wynne.
Trustee: First National in Palm Beach.
Number of staff: 1 full-time professional.
EIN: 596147678

Recent environmental and animal welfare grants:
2561-1 Carolina Kids Conservancy, Columbus, NC, $25,000. For general support. 2002.
2561-2 Carolina Mountain Land Conservancy, Hendersonville, NC, $25,000. For general support. 2002.
2561-3 Foothills Conservancy of North Carolina, Morganton, NC, $40,000. For general support. 2002.
2561-4 Genesis Wildlife Sanctuary, Beech Mountain, NC, $15,000. For general support. 2002.
2561-5 Humane Society of Valley River, Marble, NC, $13,234. For general support. 2002.
2561-6 National Committee for the New River, Jefferson, NC, $10,000. For general support. 2002.
2561-7 Nature Conservancy, North Carolina Chapter, Durham, NC, $167,000. For general support. 2002.
2561-8 North Carolina Outward Bound School, Asheville, NC, $24,000. For general support. 2002.
2561-9 Quality Forward, Asheville, NC, $100,000. For general support. 2002.
2561-10 Riverlink, Asheville, NC, $150,000. For general support. 2002.

2562
Earl Johnson, Jr. & Margery Scott Johnson Endowment Trust
P.O. Box 26262
Greensboro, NC 27402

Established in 1960 in NC.
Donor(s): Margery Scott Johnson, Earl Johnson, Jr.
Grantmaker type: Independent foundation
Financial data (yr. ended 12/31/02): Assets, $577,344 (M); expenditures, $131,883; qualifying distributions, $123,784; giving activities include $122,390 for 72 grants (high: $30,000; low: $25).
Purpose and activities: Giving for the arts, education, the environment, human services, and Christian organizations.
Fields of interest: Orchestra (symphony); Arts; Education; Environment; Boys & girls clubs;

Human services; Federated giving programs; Christian agencies & churches.
Types of support: General/operating support; Continuing support; Annual campaigns; Endowments.
Limitations: Applications not accepted. Giving primarily in Raleigh, NC. No grants to individuals.
Application information: Contributes only to pre-selected organizations.
Trustees: Earl Johnson, Jr.; Margery Scott Johnson.
Number of staff: None.
EIN: 546048452

2563
Keep North Carolina Clean and Beautiful, Inc.
(also known as NC Beautiful)
P.O. Box 12943
Raleigh, NC 27605-2943 (919) 787-1693
Contact: Stephen W. Earp, Pres.
E-mail: ncbeautiful@bellsouth.net

Grantmaker type: Public charity
Financial data (yr. ended 12/31/01): Revenue, $201,379; assets, $389,367 (M); gifts received, $2,593; expenditures, $117,120; program services expenses, $30,003; giving activities include $21,669 for 9 grants to individuals (high: $5,000; low: $998).
Purpose and activities: The organization improves North Carolina's environmental resources through education and environmental stewardship.
Fields of interest: Education; Environment.
Limitations: Giving limited to NC.
Application information: Contact organization for application information. Application form required.
Deadline(s): Sept. 19 for Windows of Opportunity Grants
Officers: Stephen W. Earp, Pres.; Sherry Duvall, V.P.; H. Glenn Dunn, Secy.; Constance C. Leaman, Treas.
EIN: 560932528

2564
John R. and Carolyn J. Maness Family Foundation
c/o U.S. Trust Co. of North Carolina
P.O. Box 26262
Greensboro, NC 27402

Established in 1995 in NC.
Donor(s): John R. Maness, Carolyn J. Maness.
Grantmaker type: Independent foundation
Financial data (yr. ended 12/31/02): Assets, $2,313,607 (M); expenditures, $158,531; qualifying distributions, $141,694; giving activities include $137,200 for 31 grants (high: $63,000; low: $500).
Fields of interest: Education; Natural resources; Animals/wildlife, preservation/protection; Human services.
Limitations: Applications not accepted. Giving primarily in NC. No grants to individuals.
Application information: Contributes only to pre-selected organizations.
Officers: John R. Maness, Pres.; Carolyn J. Maness, Secy.

EIN: 561949954

2565
Martin Marietta Materials, Inc. Corporate Giving Program
2710 Wycliff Rd.
Raleigh, NC 27607-3033
Contact: Anne Lloyd

Grantmaker type: Corporate giving program
Purpose and activities: As a complement to its foundation, Martin Marietta Materials also makes charitable contributions to nonprofit organizations directly. Support is given primarily in areas of divisional offices.
Fields of interest: Arts; Education; Natural resources.
Types of support: General/operating support; Employee volunteer services; In-kind gifts.
Limitations: Giving primarily in areas of divisional offices.
Application information: Application form not required.
  Initial approach: Proposal to headquarters

2566
Martin Marietta Philanthropic Trust
(formerly Martin Marietta Materials, Inc. Philanthropic Trust)
c/o Wachovia Bank, N.A.
401 S. Tryon St., 4th Fl.
Charlotte, NC 28288-1159
Contact: Rebecca Gomez
Application address: 2710 Wycliff Rd., Raleigh, NC 27607

Trust established in 1952 in NC.
Donor(s): Martin Marietta Materials, Inc., Superior Stone Co.
Grantmaker type: Company-sponsored foundation
Financial data (yr. ended 12/31/02): Assets, $206,931 (M); expenditures, $321,006; qualifying distributions, $312,517; giving activities include $311,250 for 126 grants (high: $50,000; low: $500).
Purpose and activities: Grants for community funds, social services, youth and child welfare agencies, rural and civic affairs, community development, higher and other education, health services and associations, and cultural programs, including museums and the performing arts. Support for building funds for education.
Fields of interest: Museums; Performing arts; Arts; Education, association; Education, research; Education, fund raising; Higher education; Natural resources; Hospitals (general); Health organizations, association; Parks/playgrounds; Youth development; Children/youth, services; Rural development; Community development; Federated giving programs; Christian agencies & churches.
Types of support: General/operating support; Continuing support; Annual campaigns; Capital campaigns; Building/renovation; Endowments; Emergency funds; Program development; Fellowships; Scholarship funds; In-kind gifts.
Limitations: Giving limited to areas of company operations in 13 states in the Southeast and the Midwest. No grants to individuals, or for courtesy advertising, tickets for fundraising, or

memberships in local chambers of commerce or other civic groups.
Application information: Application form not required.
  Initial approach: Letter
  Copies of proposal: 1
  Deadline(s): None
Trustee: Wachovia Bank, N.A.
Number of staff: 1 part-time professional.
EIN: 566035971

2567
Percy & Elizabeth Meekins Charitable Trust
P.O. Box 2537
5 W. Hargett St., Ste. 500
Raleigh, NC 27602 (919) 833-7744
Contact: William A. Alexander, Mgr.
Application address: 201 Ananias Dare St., Manteo, NC 27954-9576

Established in 1996 in NC.
Grantmaker type: Independent foundation
Financial data (yr. ended 12/31/01): Assets, $1,743,598 (M); gifts received, $138,677; expenditures, $182,689; qualifying distributions, $124,532; giving activities include $125,000 for 6 grants (high: $60,000; low: $5,000).
Fields of interest: Museums; Theater; Natural resources; YM/YWCAs & YM/YWHAs.
Limitations: Giving limited to Dare County, NC. No grants to individuals.
Application information: Application form not required.
  Deadline(s): July 15
Officer: William Alexander, Mgr.
Trustees: Myrtle E. Alexander; Charles Evans.
EIN: 566484256

2568
Melba Bayers Meyer Charitable Trust
c/o Wachovia Bank, N.A.
401 S. Tryon St., NC1159
Charlotte, NC 28288
Contact: Connie Cox
Application address: c/o Wachovia Bank, N.A., 21 E. Garden St., Pensacola, FL 32501

Established in 1995 in PA.
Donor(s): Melba Bayers Meyer.‡
Grantmaker type: Independent foundation
Financial data (yr. ended 05/31/02): Assets, $5,356,056 (M); expenditures, $369,364; qualifying distributions, $329,162; giving activities include $330,638 for 29 grants (high: $125,000; low: $100).
Purpose and activities: The foundation gives primarily to charities devoted to needs of children, indigent Native Americans, and neglected animals.
Fields of interest: Animal welfare; Human services; Children/youth, services; Native Americans/American Indians.
Limitations: Giving primarily in Pensacola, FL. No grants to individuals.
Application information: Application form not required.
  Initial approach: Letter
  Deadline(s): None
Trustee: Wachovia Bank, N.A.
EIN: 656192782

2569
Mills Family Foundation, Inc.
P.O. Box 8100
Asheville, NC 28814-8100
Contact: Pamela M. Turner, Pres.

Established around 1963.
Grantmaker type: Independent foundation
Financial data (yr. ended 05/31/03): Assets, $476,337 (M); expenditures, $96,421; qualifying distributions, $94,712; giving activities include $94,447 for 52 grants (high: $56,666; low: $12).
Purpose and activities: Giving primarily for arts and culture, education, and health and human services.
Fields of interest: Arts; Education; Natural resources; Health care; Health organizations, association; Human services; YM/YWCAs & YM/YWHAs; Federated giving programs.
Types of support: General/operating support; Continuing support; Annual campaigns; Capital campaigns; Building/renovation; Equipment; Endowments; Emergency funds; Seed money; Scholarship funds; Matching/challenge support.
Limitations: Applications not accepted. Giving primarily in Asheville, Buncombe, and Madison counties, NC. No grants to individuals.
Application information: Unsolicited requests for funds not accepted.
Officers and Directors:* Pamela M. Turner,* Pres.; James W. Turner,* V.P.; Robin Turner Oswald; Brian Mills Turner.
EIN: 566060644

2570
J. Leonard & Dorothy B. Moore Foundation
c/o Wachovia Bank, N.A.
401 S. Tryon St., 4th Fl.
Charlotte, NC 28288-8709

Established in 2000 in NC.
Grantmaker type: Independent foundation
Financial data (yr. ended 12/31/02): Assets, $4,876,429 (M); expenditures, $217,482; qualifying distributions, $171,944; giving activities include $171,206 for 11 grants (high: $20,455; low: $4,158).
Fields of interest: Environment; Human services.
Limitations: Applications not accepted. Giving primarily in Richmond, VA. No grants to individuals.
Application information: Contributes only to pre-selected organizations.
Trustee: Wachovia Bank, N.A.
EIN: 566558952

2571
Nickel Producers Environmental Research Association, Inc.
2605 Meridian Pkwy., Ste. 200
Durham, NC 27713-2203 (919) 544-8500
Contact: Hudson K. Bates, Exec. Dir.
FAX: (919) 544-7724

Established in 1980.
Grantmaker type: Independent foundation
Financial data (yr. ended 12/31/02): Assets, $2,856,997 (M); gifts received, $2,066,701; expenditures, $3,085,198; qualifying

distributions, $1,480,022; giving activities include $591,488 for grants (high: $424,908; low: $1,203) and $1,256,875 for 4 foundation-administered programs.
Purpose and activities: Giving primarily for research investigations, studies, and surveys relating to occupational health and safety aspects of the nickel producing industries and related environmental matters.
Fields of interest: Higher education; Environment; Health care; Health organizations, association; Safety/disasters; Engineering/technology; Science.
International interests: Canada; Europe; Japan.
Types of support: Fellowships; Research.
Limitations: Giving primarily in the U.S., Europe, Canada, and Japan.
Application information:
  Initial approach: Proposal
  Board meeting date(s): Sept.
Officers: John L. Nixon, Chair.; Toshiharu Kanai, Vice-Chair.; Scott Grove, Secy.; David Griffiths, Treas.; Hudson K. Bates, Exec. Dir.
Board Members: Tim E. Aiken; L.J.G. Nacken.
EIN: 133070077

2572
North Carolina Community Foundation
200 S. Salisbury St.
Raleigh, NC 27602-2828   (919) 828-4387
Contact: Elizabeth C. Fentress, Exec. Dir.
FAX: (919) 828-5495; E-mail: general@nccommf.org; Western Regional Office: P.O. Box 2148, Sylva, NC 28779, tel.: (828) 586-4616, FAX: (828) 631-3951, E-mail: slelivre@earthlink.net; Northeastern Regional Office: Harbinger Ctr., Ste. 4, Point Harbor, NC 27964, tel.: (252) 491-8166, FAX: (252) 491-5714, E-mail: pbirknccommf@mindspring.com; Hickory, NC office: P.O. Box 2851, Hickory, NC 28603, tel.: (828) 328-1237, FAX: (828) 328-3948, E-mail: cvcf@earthlink.net; Newborn office: P.O. Box 13276, Newborn, NC 28651, tel.:(252) 635-1001; FAX: (252) 635-3265; E-mail: jadcock@nccomf.org; URL: http://www.nccommf.org

Established in 1985 in NC.
Grantmaker type: Community foundation
Financial data (yr. ended 03/31/03): Assets, $59,556,500 (M); gifts received, $11,295,000; expenditures, $3,445,500; giving activities include $1,907,000 for 550 grants (high: $213,100; low: $100; average: $100–$213,100).
Purpose and activities: Primary areas of interest include higher and other education, conservation, community funds, and other general charitable activities. The foundation administers a donor-advised fund.
Fields of interest: Museums; Performing arts; Historic preservation/historical societies; Higher education; Adult education—literacy, basic skills & GED; Reading; Education; Natural resources; Environment; Health care; Substance abuse, services; Health organizations, association; Children/youth, services; Hospices; Aging, centers/services; Women, centers/services; Homeless, human services; Federated giving programs; Christian agencies & churches; Aging; Women; Homeless.

Types of support: Endowments; Program development; Conferences/seminars; Technical assistance; Consulting services.
Limitations: Applications not accepted. Giving primarily in NC.
Publications: Annual report, Informational brochure, Newsletter.
Application information:
  Board meeting date(s): June and Nov.
Officers and Directors: Charles W. Gaddy, V.P.; Billy T. Woodard, Secy.; C. Ronald Scheeler, Treas.; Elizabeth C. Fentress, Exec. Dir.; and 33 additional directors.
Number of staff: 10 full-time professional; 1 part-time professional; 4 full-time support; 1 part-time support.
EIN: 581661700

2573
Anna Oschwald Trust
c/o Wachovia Bank, N.A.
401 S. Tryon St., 4th Fl.
Charlotte, NC 28288-5709

Established in 2000 in NJ.
Donor(s): Anna Oschwald.‡
Grantmaker type: Independent foundation
Financial data (yr. ended 12/31/02): Assets, $7,460,798 (M); gifts received, $248,845; expenditures, $349,702; qualifying distributions, $282,942; giving activities include $282,942 for grants.
Fields of interest: Higher education; Animal welfare; Animal population control; Hospitals (general); Health organizations, association; Cancer research; Salvation Army.
Limitations: Applications not accepted. Giving primarily in Red Bank, NJ, and NY, with emphasis on New York City and Port Washington; funding also in Washington, DC and Philadelphia, PA. No grants to individuals.
Application information: Contributes only to pre-selected organizations.
Trustees: Stephen J. Oppenheim; Wachovia Bank, N.A.
EIN: 256626923

2574
Outer Banks Community Foundation, Inc.
P.O. Box 1100
Kill Devil Hills, NC 27948-1100
(252) 261-8839
Contact: Barbara A. Bingham, Exec. Dir.
FAX: (252) 261-0371; E-mail: info@obcf.org; URL: http://www.obcf.org

Incorporated in 1982 in NC.
Donor(s): David Stick, Andy Griffith, Edward Greene, W. Ray White, Jack Adams, George S. Crocker,‡ Martin Kellogg, Jr.‡
Grantmaker type: Community foundation
Financial data (yr. ended 12/31/02): Assets, $2,268,385 (M); gifts received, $141,510; expenditures, $193,857; giving activities include $73,109 for 22 grants (high: $12,500; low: $250; average: $250–$12,500) and $39,650 for 42 grants to individuals (high: $2,000; low: $200; average: $200–$2,000).
Purpose and activities: Giving to the arts, education and human services. The foundation administers donor-advised funds.

Fields of interest: Historic preservation/historical societies; Arts; Education; Environment; Youth development; Human services.
Types of support: Building/renovation; Equipment; Endowments; Seed money; Scholarship funds; Scholarships—to individuals.
Limitations: Giving limited to the Outer Banks, NC, area. No grants to individuals (except through designated scholarship funds), or for annual operating expenses.
Publications: Application guidelines, Annual report, Financial statement, Grants list, Informational brochure, Newsletter.
Application information: Application form required.
  Initial approach: Letter or telephone
  Copies of proposal: 5
  Deadline(s): Feb. 10, May 10, Aug. 10, and Nov. 10
  Board meeting date(s): Mar., June, Sept., and Dec.
  Final notification: Mar. 10, June 10, Sept. 10, and Dec. 10
Officers and Directors: T. Olin Davis, Pres.; Bob Oakes, V.P.; Nonie Booth, Secy.; Helen Ford, Treas.; Barbara A. Bingham, Exec. Dir.; Cashar Evans; William J. Fields; Bobby Harrell; John F. Hughes; Michael Kelly; Ken Mann; Dorothy Toolan; Sue Woolard.
Number of staff: 1 part-time professional.
EIN: 581516313

2575
The Polk County Community Foundation, Inc.
(formerly Polk Community Foundation)
255 S. Trade St.
Tryon, NC 28782-3707   (828) 859-5314
Contact: Elizabeth Nager, Exec. Dir.
FAX: (828) 859-6122; E-mail: foundation@polkccf.org; URL: http://www.polkccf.org

Incorporated in 1975 in NC.
Grantmaker type: Community foundation
Financial data (yr. ended 12/31/02): Assets, $14,924,616 (M); gifts received, $867,325; expenditures, $1,131,598; giving activities include $592,126 for 18+ grants.
Purpose and activities: Improve the quality of life in Polk County, NC, and surrounding areas.
Fields of interest: Arts; Education; Natural resources; Health care; Community development.
Types of support: Capital campaigns; Building/renovation; Equipment; Program development; Conferences/seminars; Publication; Seed money; Internship funds; Scholarship funds; Scholarships—to individuals; Matching/challenge support.
Limitations: Giving limited to Polk County, NC, and its surrounding areas.
Publications: Application guidelines, Annual report, Financial statement, Informational brochure (including application guidelines), Newsletter.
Application information: Application form required.
  Initial approach: Letter
  Copies of proposal: 1
  Deadline(s): Call for deadline

Board meeting date(s): 3rd Thurs. in Feb., Apr., June, Sept., Nov., and Dec.
Final notification: Immediately following board meetings
Officers and Directors:* Betty Knopp,* Pres.; Larry Wassong,* V.P.; Cathie A. Campbell,* Secy.; Peggy C. Woodward,* Treas.; Elizabeth Nager, Exec. Dir.; Holland Brady, Jr.; Arthur Brown; Donald Eifert; Laura Fields; Ann McCown; Renee McDermott; David Slater; Alice Tennant; B.G. Woodham; Robert Worsnop.
Number of staff: 1 full-time professional; 2 part-time professional; 1 full-time support.
EIN: 510168751

2576
Mary Norris Preyer Fund
c/o Piedmont Financial Co. Inc.
P.O. Box 20124
Greensboro, NC 27420-0124 (336) 274-5471
Contact: Jane Preyer, Admin.

Established in 1965 in NC.
Donor(s): members of the Preyer family.
Grantmaker type: Independent foundation
Financial data (yr. ended 06/30/02): Assets, $3,809,244 (M); expenditures, $219,400; qualifying distributions, $197,114; giving activities include $188,500 for 33 grants (high: $10,000; low: $5,000).
Purpose and activities: Giving mainly for art, the environment, youth services and community development; general charitable support.
Fields of interest: Museums; Environment; Youth, services; Community development.
Types of support: General/operating support; Continuing support; Annual campaigns; Capital campaigns; Program development; Seed money.
Limitations: Giving primarily in NC. No grants to individuals.
Publications: Application guidelines.
Application information: Application form not required.
Initial approach: Written proposal
Copies of proposal: 1
Deadline(s): Apr. 1
Board meeting date(s): Summer
Trustees: Ellen Preyer Davis; Mary Norris Preyer Oglesby; Frederick L. Preyer; Norris W. Preyer, Sr.; Robert O. Preyer.
Number of staff: 1 shared staff.
EIN: 566068167

2577
The Julian Price Family Foundation
c/o Wachovia Bank, N.A.
401 S. Tryon St., 4th Fl.
Charlotte, NC 28288-5709

Established in 1996 in NC.
Grantmaker type: Independent foundation
Financial data (yr. ended 12/31/02): Assets, $15,265,782 (M); expenditures, $1,238,974; qualifying distributions, $1,169,906; giving activities include $1,126,970 for 214 grants (high: $50,000; low: $400).
Purpose and activities: Giving primarily for environmental conservation programs, as well as for education, the arts, community development, and health and human services.
Fields of interest: Television; Arts; Education; Natural resources; Environment; Hospitals

(general); Human services; Community development; Christian agencies & churches; Protestant agencies & churches.
Limitations: Applications not accepted. Giving primarily in NC. No grants to individuals.
Application information: Contributes only to pre-selected organizations.
Trustees: Laura Deboisfeuillet Edwards; Susan Jarrell Edwards; Melaine Taylor Farland; Mary P.T. Harrison; J.M. Bryan Taylor; John Guest Taylor; Ray Howard Taylor III.
EIN: 311665269

2578
Progress Energy Foundation, Inc. ▼
(formerly CP&L Foundation, Inc.)
P.O. Box 2591
Raleigh, NC 27602-2591 (919) 546-6441
Contact: Merrilee Jacobson, Contrib. Specialist
URL: http://www.progress-energy.com/community/foundation/index.asp

Established in 1990 in NC.
Donor(s): Carolina Power & Light Co., Progress Energy, Inc., Florida Progress Corp.
Grantmaker type: Company-sponsored foundation
Financial data (yr. ended 12/31/02): Assets, $5,436,475 (M); gifts received, $5,844,402; expenditures, $9,495,091; qualifying distributions, $9,444,057; giving activities include $9,441,876 for 219 grants (high: $500,000; low: $87; average: $10,000–$110,000) and $72,800 for 1 in-kind gift.
Purpose and activities: The foundation supports programs and activities that benefit Progress Energy's customers and employees. The foundation focuses its attention on three main areas: 1) education (primarily in math and science), 2) the environment, and 3) economic development.
Fields of interest: Elementary/secondary education; Teacher school/education; Engineering school/education; Education; Environment, association; Water pollution; Environment; Economic development.
Types of support: General/operating support; Continuing support; Annual campaigns; Capital campaigns; Building/renovation; Program development; Conferences/seminars; Curriculum development; Scholarship funds; Research; Employee matching gifts; In-kind gifts.
Limitations: Giving primarily in Progress Energy service areas of NC, SC, and FL. No support for fraternal, veterans', or labor organizations, athletic teams, religious organizations for religious purposes, or for individual K-12 schools. No grants to individuals, or for memberships or courtesy advertising.
Publications: Application guidelines, Annual report.
Application information: Grant proposal required. Application form required.
Initial approach: Letter or telephone request for informational brochure
Copies of proposal: 1
Deadline(s): Feb. 1, May 1, Aug. 1, and Nov. 1
Board meeting date(s): Quarterly
Final notification: Within 2 weeks of meeting
Officers and Directors:* William Cavanaugh III, Pres.; William "Skip" Orser,* V.P.; Tammy S.

Brown, Secy.; Fred Day; William Habermeyer; William Johnson; Robert McGehee; Peter Scott.
Trustee: Wachovia Bank, N.A.
Number of staff: None.
EIN: 561720636
Recent environmental and animal welfare grants:
2578-1 Asheville Parks and Greenways Foundation, Asheville, NC, $25,000. For general support. 2002.
2578-2 Blue Ridge Parkway Foundation, Winston-Salem, NC, $16,000. For general support. 2002.
2578-3 Environmental Education Fund, Raleigh, NC, $25,000. For general support. 2002.
2578-4 Fisheries Development Foundation of North Carolina, New Bern, NC, $10,000. For general support. 2002.
2578-5 Friends of Weedon Island, Saint Petersburg, FL, $50,000. For general support. 2002.
2578-6 Nature Conservancy, Arlington, VA, $250,000. For general support. 2002.
2578-7 North Carolina Big Sweep, Zebulon, NC, $10,000. For general support. 2002.
2578-8 North Carolina Coastal Federation, Newport, NC, $11,528. For general support. 2002.
2578-9 North Carolina Zoological Society, Asheboro, NC, $150,000. For general support. 2002.
2578-10 Quality Forward, Asheville, NC, $20,000. For general support. 2002.

2579
Progress Energy, Inc. Corporate Giving Program
(formerly CP&L Corporate Giving Program)
P.O. Box 1551, M.C. PEB-14A
Raleigh, NC 27602-1551 (919) 546-6441
Contact: Merrilee Jacobson, Contribs. Specialist
Application address in FL: Sandra Tabor, 100 Central Ave., P.O. Box 14042, M.C. CX 2H, St. Petersburg, FL 33733, tel.: (727) 820-5348;
URL: http://www.progress-energy.com/community/index.asp

Grantmaker type: Corporate giving program
Financial data (yr. ended 12/31/02): Total giving, $4,488,534; giving activities include $3,997,654 for 1,781 grants (high: $38,000; low: $250; average: $5,000–$10,000) and $490,880 for 682 employee matching gifts.
Purpose and activities: As a complement to its foundation, Progress Energy also makes charitable contributions to nonprofit organizations directly. Support is given primarily in areas of company operations.
Fields of interest: Education; Environment; Economic development.
Types of support: General/operating support; Capital campaigns; Building/renovation; Program development; Conferences/seminars; Scholarship funds; Research; Employee volunteer services; Sponsorships; Employee matching gifts.
Limitations: Giving primarily in areas of company operations in FL, NC, and SC. No support for religious, fraternal, veterans', or labor organizations. No grants to individuals, or for advertising, memberships, or athletic activities.
Publications: Application guidelines.

Application information: The Corporate Community Relations Department handles giving. A contributions committee reviews all requests of over $10,000. Application form not required.

Initial approach: Proposal to nearest company facility
Copies of proposal: 1
Deadline(s): None
Final notification: Following review

Administrators: Tammy Brown, Mgr., Corp. Community Rels.; Merrilee Jacobson, Contribs. Specialist.

2580
Provident Benevolent Foundation

(formerly Providence Charitable Foundation)
c/o Wachovia Bank, N.A.
P.O. Box 3099
Winston-Salem, NC 27150-7131
Contact: Jesse J. Thompson
Application address: 4500 Cameron Valley Pkwy., Ste. 450, Charlotte, NC 28211

Established in 1989 in NC.
Donor(s): Jesse J. Thompson.
Grantmaker type: Independent foundation
Financial data (yr. ended 06/30/01): Assets, $14,913,814 (M); expenditures, $908,741; qualifying distributions, $846,392; giving activities include $851,000 for grants.
Purpose and activities: Giving primarily for education, health, and human services.
Fields of interest: Arts; Education; Natural resources; Hospitals (general); Human services; Children/youth, services.
Types of support: General/operating support.
Limitations: Giving limited to NC. No grants for endowments or deficit financing.
Application information:
Initial approach: Letter not to exceed 2 pages
Deadline(s): Mar. 31, June 30, Sept. 30, and Dec. 31

Trustees: Jesse J. Thompson; Wachovia Bank, N.A.
EIN: 581881092

2581
The Reese Foundation

P.O. Box 69
Hickory, NC 28603 (828) 465-3431

Established in 1985 in NC.
Donor(s): Thomas W. Reese.
Grantmaker type: Independent foundation
Financial data (yr. ended 09/30/02): Assets, $336,751 (M); gifts received, $50,961; expenditures, $124,921; qualifying distributions, $124,039; giving activities include $124,100 for grants.
Fields of interest: Historic preservation/historical societies; Arts; Higher education; Education; Natural resources.
Limitations: Applications not accepted. Giving primarily in NC. No grants to individuals.
Officers: Thomas W. Reese, Pres.; Jeffrey A. Hale, V.P.; Sallie A. Martin, Secy.-Treas.
Director: Elizabeth Watts.
EIN: 581627279

2582
Z. Smith Reynolds Foundation, Inc. ▼

14 S. Cherry St., Ste. 200
Winston-Salem, NC 27101-5287
(336) 725-7541
Contact: Thomas W. Ross, Exec. Dir.
Additional tel.: (800) 443-8319; FAX: (336) 725-6069; E-mail: info@zsr.org; URL: http://www.zsr.org

Incorporated in 1936 in NC.
Donor(s): Nancy S. Reynolds,‡ Mary Reynolds Babcock,‡ Richard J. Reynolds, Jr.,‡ William N. Reynolds.‡
Grantmaker type: Independent foundation
Financial data (yr. ended 12/31/02): Assets, $332,612,438 (M); gifts received, $20,816,201; expenditures, $25,627,049; qualifying distributions, $25,627,845; giving activities include $23,356,266 for 371 grants (high: $2,000,000; low: $100; average: $5,000–$75,000) and $577,460 for 3 foundation-administered programs.
Purpose and activities: The goals of the foundation are: 1) to promote social, economic and environmental justice; 2) to strengthen democracy, through an educated and informed populace; 3) to encourage innovation and excellence in a dynamic nonprofit sector; 4) to support progressive public policy and social change; 5) to foster cooperation and respect among all racial, ethnic, and socio-economic groups; and 6) to build strong, vibrant, economically sound, and peaceful communities. To accomplish its purpose, the foundation currently gives special attention to certain focus areas: community building and economic development; environment; governance, public policy and civic engagement; pre-collegiate education; and social justice and equity.
Fields of interest: Early childhood education; Child development, education; Elementary school/education; Secondary school/education; Adult education—literacy, basic skills & GED; Reading; Education; Natural resources; Environment; Crime/violence prevention, youth; Gun control; Domestic violence; Legal services; Housing/shelter, development; Youth development, services; Youth development, citizenship; Human services; Children/youth, services; Child development, services; Family services; Women, centers/services; Minorities/immigrants, centers/services; Civil rights, minorities; Civil rights, women; Race/intergroup relations; Reproductive rights; Civil rights; Rural development; Community development; Voluntarism promotion; Public policy, research; Public affairs, citizen participation; Leadership development; Public affairs; Minorities; African Americans/Blacks; Hispanics/Latinos; Native Americans/American Indians; Women; Economically disadvantaged.
Types of support: General/operating support; Continuing support; Program development; Publication; Seed money; Technical assistance; Matching/challenge support.
Limitations: Giving limited to NC. No grants to individuals (except for Nancy Susan Reynolds Awards for community leadership and sabbatical program), endowment funds, equipment purchases, fraternal groups, or for research; no loans or program-related investments.

Publications: Annual report (including application guidelines), Informational brochure, Occasional report.
Application information: Application form required.
Initial approach: Letter or telephone for specifics
Copies of proposal: 1
Deadline(s): For grants, Feb. 1 and Aug. 1; for Sabbatical Program, Dec. 1; for Nancy Susan Reynolds Awards, June 1
Board meeting date(s): 3rd Fri. in May and Nov.
Final notification: 4 months after deadline
Officers and Trustees:* Mary Mountcastle,* Pres.; Lloyd P. Tate, Jr.,* V.P.; Thomas W. Ross, Secy. and Exec. Dir.; Jane S. Patterson,* Treas.; Nancy R. Bagley; Smith W. Bagley; Daniel G. Clodfelter; Anita Brown Graham; R. Darrell Hancock; John O. McNairy; Katharine B. Mountcastle; Stephen L. Neal; Zachary T. Smith.
Number of staff: 7 full-time professional; 5 full-time support.
EIN: 586038145
Recent environmental and animal welfare grants:

2582-1 Agricultural Resources Center, Carrboro, NC, $20,000. To reduce use of pesticides and protect public and environment from toxic waste. 2001.

2582-2 Appalachian Voices, Boone, NC, $25,000. To mobilize network of North Carolina citizens for support of clean air and for Clean Smokestacks Plan and comprehensive Energy Blueprint. 2001.

2582-3 Blue Ridge Resource Conservation and Development Council, Sugar Grove, NC, $35,000. For Project Branch Out and planning and construction at Avery Landfill Gas Project and Maryland Community College Greenhouse and Regional Horticultural Center. 2001.

2582-4 Blue Ridge Rural Land Trust, Sugar Grove, NC, $25,000. To monitor easements held by Trust. 2001.

2582-5 Canary Coalition, Whittier, NC, $25,000. For community education on problem of air pollution in western region of North Carolina and for discussing potential long-term solutions to region-wide problem. 2001.

2582-6 Catawba-Wateree Relicensing Coalition, Charlotte, NC, $35,000. To facilitate open process involving stakeholders to protect, enhance, and restore natural, cultural, recreational, and economic resources of operations on river basin in conjunction with Duke Power's efforts to secure new license for its hydropower operation. 2001.

2582-7 Clean Water Fund of North Carolina, Asheville, NC. For programs and activities to work for clean, safe communities and for enforcement of strong environmental regulations to protect North Carolina citizens from environmental hazards threatening drinking water and public health in the state. 2001.

2582-8 Conservation Fund, Chapel Hill, NC, $140,000. To strengthen and expand Resourceful Communities Program, which is helping rural communities in most significant natural areas of North Carolina create new economies. 2001.

2582-9 Conservation Trust for North Carolina, Raleigh, NC, $75,000. For comprehensive public awareness campaign on behalf of local land trusts in North Carolina to let public know who they are, what they do, and how land trusts help landowners and general public protect natural resources. 2001.

2582-10 Conservation Trust for North Carolina, Raleigh, NC, $25,000. For Northeast Tarheel Conservancy, new land trust in northeastern portion of North Carolina. 2001.

2582-11 Core Sound Waterfowl Museum, Harkers Island, NC, $25,000. For support and expansion of environmental and cultural educational programs. 2001.

2582-12 Dogwood Alliance, Brevard, NC, $25,000. To protect North Carolina's forests from proliferation of chip mills and expansion of industrial forestry. 2001.

2582-13 Earth Share of North Carolina, Durham, NC, $35,000. To support workplace solicitation efforts. 2001.

2582-14 Environmental Defense, Raleigh, NC, $150,000. For collaborative effort by North Carolina Coastal Federation and North Carolina Environmental Defense to achieve smarter growth on North Carolina coast. 2001.

2582-15 Environmental Defense, Raleigh, NC, $25,000. For North Carolina Air Quality Initiative to analyze air pollution problems and potential solutions, empower North Carolina Clean Air Coalition to influence key decisions, develop North Carolina Clean Smokestack Plan, broker dialogue with utilities, and encourage North Carolina leadership with upwind states. 2001.

2582-16 Fisheries Development Foundation of North Carolina, New Bern, NC, $15,000. To conduct studies, create artificial reefs, and train fishermen. 2001.

2582-17 Forest Trust, Santa Fe, NM, $20,000. To increase Forest Stewards Guild membership in North Carolina and to boost capacity of member foresters to provide North Carolina landowners with ecologically responsible and economically viable forestry services. 2001.

2582-18 High Country Conservancy, Boone, NC, $20,000. For land preservation and sensible growth in mountains of western North Carolina. 2001.

2582-19 Land Trust for Central North Carolina, Salisbury, NC, $50,000. For operating support and for South Yadkin River Wildlife Refuge capital campaign. 2001.

2582-20 Legal Services of North Carolina, Raleigh, NC, $40,000. For North State Legal Services' Environmental Poverty Law Project to help low-income residents in North Carolina fight environmental hazards in their communities, on the job, and in their homes. 2001.

2582-21 Little Tennessee Watershed Association, Franklin, NC, $20,000. To protect biodiversity of Little Tennessee River and its tributaries. 2001.

2582-22 Lower Neuse Initiative, New Bern, NC, $15,000. For Collectively Defining Smart Growth in Your Community Symposium, which will focus on equipping attendees with broader understanding of many facets that complete smart growth initiatives. 2001.

2582-23 Nature Conservancy, Durham, NC, $300,000. For long-term protection of Sandhills Longleaf Pine and Roanoke River landscapes. 2001.

2582-24 Neuse River Foundation, New Bern, NC, $25,000. For Neuse River Watershed Protection-Phase II, to work with local governments and others in target subbasins of Neuse River Basin to increase number of riparian land restoration and conservation projects. 2001.

2582-25 Neuse River Foundation, New Bern, NC, $20,000. For Nancy Susan Reynolds Award designated by Rick Dove. 2001.

2582-26 New River Foundation, Jacksonville, NC, $35,000. For New Riverkeeper Project designed to improve water quality by recognizing pollutants and polluters and taking aggressive actions to remedy situations that are not healthy to river and its wildlife. 2001.

2582-27 North Carolina Coastal Federation, Newport, NC, $150,000. For collaborative effort by Federation and North Carolina Environmental Defense to achieve smarter growth on North Carolina coast. 2001.

2582-28 North Carolina Coastal Land Trust, Wilmington, NC, $65,000. To protect rapidly vanishing coastal habitats — barrier island beach, non-riverine hardwood forest, native plant savanna, and maritime forest. 2001.

2582-29 North Carolina Conservation Network (NC ConNet), Raleigh, NC, $40,000. To build capacity of statewide conservation community to strengthen environmental community's ability to impact local and state environmental policy. 2001.

2582-30 North Carolina Foundation for Soil and Water Conservation Districts, Raleigh, NC, $25,000. For implementation of first slate of programs through soil and water conservation districts across North Carolina. 2001.

2582-31 North Carolina John Muir Foundation, Winston-Salem, NC, $80,000. For North Carolina Clean Water Campaign to build lasting network of members of faith communities and residents of rural communities who are committed to environmental protection and social justice. 2001.

2582-32 North Carolina Public Interest Research Group Education Fund, Chapel Hill, NC, $25,000. For Clean Air Program, to frame debate on clean air in North Carolina and increase public scrutiny of link between old power plants and air pollution. 2001.

2582-33 North Carolina Smart Growth Alliance, Carrboro, NC, $35,000. For general operating support. 2001.

2582-34 North Carolina Waste Awareness and Reduction Network (NC WARN), Durham, NC, $30,000. For general support to work with state and local citizens to help oversee safe clean-up of failing Warren County PCB Landfill. 2001.

2582-35 Pamlico-Tar River Foundation, Washington, NC, $25,000. For Defending a Treasure at Risk, for multitude of strategic activities to protect, preserve, and promote environmental quality of Pamlico-Tar River. 2001.

2582-36 Pantego Area Community Developers, Pantego, NC, $15,000. For community-wide sewage treatment facility. 2001.

2582-37 Piedmont Land Conservancy, Greensboro, NC, $25,000. For full-time Development Director position. 2001.

2582-38 RAFI-USA, Pittsboro, NC, $35,000. For general support for Peanut Project and Tobacco Project. 2001.

2582-39 Save Our State, Raleigh, NC, $225,000. For operating support to continue to perform primary mission of policy development, education, and advocacy. 2001.

2582-40 Smart Growth Partners of Western North Carolina, Asheville, NC, $30,000. For operating support to increase donor base, expand technical capabilities, create collaborative network of smart growth partners in Western North Carolina, and provide useful database of smart growth research. 2001.

2582-41 Southern Appalachian Biodiversity Project, Asheville, NC, $25,000. For National Forest Protection and Restoration, to protect nationally significant ecosystems in Southeast through education, community organizing, and legal advocacy. 2001.

2582-42 Southern Appalachian Highlands Conservancy, Asheville, NC, $70,000. For land conservation in Highlands of western North Carolina. 2001.

2582-43 Southern Environmental Law Center, Chapel Hill, NC, $400,000. For general support for North Carolina office for environmental protection of natural resources. 2001.

2582-44 Southwestern North Carolina Resource Conservation and Development Council, Waynesville, NC, $20,000. For general support and expansion of Watershed Association for Tuckasegee River. 2001.

2582-45 Tar River Land Conservancy, Louisburg, NC, $25,000. For operating support to build capacity and continue operations of newly launched land trust serving Upper Tar River Basin. 2001.

2582-46 Triangle Growth Strategies, Raleigh, NC, $30,000. To promote smart growth by building support and capacity for region building in Greater Triangle Area. 2001.

2582-47 University of North Carolina, Chapel Hill, NC, $50,000. For Carolina Smart Growth Training Program to provide local planners, elected officials, developers, realtors, lenders, and conservationists with knowledge, understanding, and tools necessary to promote smart growth in their communities. 2001.

2582-48 University of North Carolina, Chapel Hill, NC, $30,000. For Building Capacity: The Next Step in North Carolina's Smart Growth Agenda, to build capacity of state, local, and regional decision-makers and citizens to participate effectively in debates about impact of North Carolina's rapid and uneven growth. 2001.

2582-49 University of North Carolina, Wilmington, NC, $25,000. For Lower Cape Fear River Program, to develop understanding of processes which control and influence Cape Fear River in order to preserve capacity of river to sustain economic development and to protect its natural resource values. 2001.

2582-50 Voices and Choices of the Central Carolinas, Charlotte, NC, $30,000. For Quality of Life Initiative, to build economic and environmental sustainability in central Carolinas. 2001.

2582-51 Walthour Moss Foundation, Southern Pines, NC, $20,000. To apply existing objectives and management priorities of Foundation lands to Firestone land to preserve its endangered longleaf pine communities and manage land in balance with compatible public use. 2001.

2582-52 Warren Wilson College, Asheville, NC, $25,000. For Environmental Leadership Center as place for environmental re-thinking and as problem-solving center. 2001.

2582-53 West End Revitalization Association, Mebane, NC, $30,000. For Environmental Justice for African Americans, legal and technical assistance for Title VI of Civil Rights Act for Administrative Complaints filed in February 1999 regarding the 119 Bypass. 2001.

2582-54 Western North Carolina Alliance, Asheville, NC, $25,000. To become stronger, more diverse and self-reliant organization to preserve natural resources of western North Carolina. 2001.

2582-55 Western North Carolina Tomorrow, Cullowhee, NC, $35,000. For Quality Growth and Management: The Work of Mountain Communities, to increase number of citizens with awareness and commitment necessary to accelerate adoption of appropriate land use strategies. 2001.

2582-56 Yadkin-Pee Dee Lakes Project, Badin, NC, $25,000. For organizational development to strengthen board, focus and develop program efforts, and devise fund-raising and income generation strategies. 2001.

2583
Grace Jones Richardson Trust

c/o Piedmont Financial Co.
P.O. Box 20124
Greensboro, NC 27420-0124
Contact: P.L. Richardson, Tr.

Trust established in 1962 in CT.
Donor(s): Grace Jones Richardson.‡
Grantmaker type: Independent foundation
Financial data (yr. ended 12/31/01): Assets, $59,949,928 (M); gifts received, $1,462,190; expenditures, $1,841,201; qualifying distributions, $1,539,870; giving activities include $1,306,000 for 333 grants (high: $40,000; low: $250).
Purpose and activities: Giving primarily for the arts, education, and human services.
Fields of interest: Arts; Higher education; Natural resources; Health care; Human services; Federated giving programs; Christian agencies & churches.
Types of support: General/operating support.
Limitations: Giving on a national basis. No grants to individuals.
Application information:
   Initial approach: Proposal
   Deadline(s): None
   Board meeting date(s): As required

Trustees: P.L. Richardson; S.S. Richardson.
Number of staff: 1 shared staff.
EIN: 066023003

2584
The Blanche and Julian Robertson Family Foundation, Inc.

P.O. Box 4242
Salisbury, NC 28145-4242 (704) 637-0511
Contact: David Setzer, Exec. Dir.
FAX: (704) 637-0177

Established in 1997 in NC.
Donor(s): Julian H. Robertson, Jr., Wyndham Robertson.
Grantmaker type: Independent foundation
Financial data (yr. ended 12/31/02): Assets, $12,704,631 (M); gifts received, $1,000,000; expenditures, $1,107,428; qualifying distributions, $1,091,878; giving activities include $1,049,923 for 44 grants (high: $250,000; low: $1,200; average: $5,000–$75,000).
Purpose and activities: The foundation, committed to improving the quality of life in Salisbury, NC, and its surrounding area, is interested in funding programs that address social, family, educational, health, and neighborhood issues, and those which enrich lives through cultural, arts, and recreational opportunities. Preference is given to projects that encourage constructive change, strive toward achieving excellence, and have a significant component of public service.
Fields of interest: Arts; Education; Environment; Health care; Recreation; Human services; Youth, services; Family services; Community development.
Types of support: General/operating support; Continuing support; Capital campaigns; Building/renovation; Equipment; Land acquisition; Emergency funds; Program development; Conferences/seminars; Curriculum development; Technical assistance; Program evaluation; Matching/challenge support.
Limitations: Giving limited to Salisbury, NC, and its surrounding area.
Publications: Application guidelines, Grants list, Informational brochure (including application guidelines), Occasional report.
Application information: Application form required.
   Initial approach: Telephone, personal visit, or letter
   Copies of proposal: 1
   Deadline(s): Determined by board
   Board meeting date(s): Determined by board
   Final notification: Upon board's decision and action
Officers and Directors:* James F. Hurley,* Chair.; James G. Whitton,* Vice-Chair.; Margaret H. Kluttz,* Secy.; Catrelia Hunter; B. Clay Lindsay, Jr.; R. Scott Maddox; Lillian L. Morgan; Alex Robertson; Spencer Robertson; Wyndham Robertson; Fred J. Stanback, Jr.
Number of staff: 1 part-time professional.
EIN: 562027907

2585
The Florence Rogers Charitable Trust

P.O. Box 36006
Fayetteville, NC 28303-1006 (910) 484-2033
Contact: Nolan P. Clark, Tr.

Trust established in 1961 in NC.
Donor(s): Florence L. Rogers.‡
Grantmaker type: Independent foundation
Financial data (yr. ended 03/31/02): Assets, $4,687,481 (M); expenditures, $371,462; qualifying distributions, $241,334; giving activities include $186,093 for 48 grants (high: $30,000; low: $90).
Purpose and activities: Support for music and the arts, education, recreation, hunger programs, youth and child welfare, nursing and hospices, wildlife, and the general quality of life in the area. Preference is given to seed money for new ideas.
Fields of interest: Museums; Arts; Elementary/secondary education; Higher education; Botanical gardens; Human services; Protestant agencies & churches.
Types of support: General/operating support; Equipment; Emergency funds; Program development; Conferences/seminars; Publication; Seed money; Scholarship funds; Research; Matching/challenge support.
Limitations: Giving primarily in Fayetteville, Cumberland County, and southeastern NC. No grants to individuals, or for building or endowment funds, scholarships, or fellowships; no loans.
Publications: Informational brochure (including application guidelines).
Application information: Application form required.
   Initial approach: Letter or telephone
   Copies of proposal: 1
   Deadline(s): Last day of each month
   Board meeting date(s): Monthly
   Final notification: By the end of the following month
Trustees: Nolan P. Clark; John C. Tally.
Number of staff: 2 full-time professional; 1 part-time professional; 2 full-time support; 1 part-time support.
EIN: 566074515

2586
Sall Family Foundation, Inc.

201 Vineyard Ln.
Cary, NC 27513-3067 (919) 677-8000
Contact: John Phillip Sall, Pres.

Established in 1993.
Donor(s): John Phillip Sall, Virginia B. Sall.
Grantmaker type: Independent foundation
Financial data (yr. ended 12/31/02): Assets, $9,286,479 (M); gifts received, $1,000,000; expenditures, $2,201,328; qualifying distributions, $2,166,322; giving activities include $2,138,000 for 2 grants (high: $2,000,000; low: $138,000).
Purpose and activities: Giving primarily for health, education, environmental protection, and community development.
Fields of interest: Education; Natural resources; Health care; Community development.
Limitations: Giving on a national basis. No grants to individuals.
Application information:

Initial approach: Letter
Deadline(s): Sept. 30
Officers: John Phillip Sall, Pres.; Virginia B. Sall, Treas.
EIN: 582016050

2587
The Schechter Foundation, Inc.
1204 Perry Park Dr.
Kinston, NC 28501-3550   (252) 527-1128
Contact: Sol Schechter, Pres.

Established in 1982 in NC.
Donor(s): Sol Schechter.
Grantmaker type: Independent foundation
Financial data (yr. ended 12/31/02): Assets, $1,665,612 (M); expenditures, $110,785; qualifying distributions, $103,032; giving activities include $103,848 for 144 grants (high: $15,000; low: $24).
Purpose and activities: Giving primarily to Jewish agencies, with support for various human service organizations.
Fields of interest: Arts; Education; Animal welfare; Health organizations, association; Youth development, centers/clubs; Human services; Jewish federated giving programs; Jewish agencies & temples.
Limitations: Giving primarily in NC.
Application information: Application form not required.
Initial approach: Letter of proposal
Deadline(s): None
Officers: Sol Schechter, Pres. and Treas.; Arielle C. Schechter, V.P.; Arnold M.C. Schechter, V.P.; Pearl F. Schechter, Secy.
EIN: 561318527

2588
Slick Family Foundation
P.O. Box 5958
Winston-Salem, NC 27113

Established in 1997 in NC.
Donor(s): Earl F. Slick.
Grantmaker type: Independent foundation
Financial data (yr. ended 12/31/02): Assets, $6,353,619 (M); expenditures, $492,977; qualifying distributions, $472,586; giving activities include $436,000 for 18 grants (high: $82,500; low: $1,000).
Purpose and activities: Giving for the arts, the environment, human services, and education.
Fields of interest: Arts; Education; Environment; Human services.
Limitations: Applications not accepted. Giving primarily in NC. No grants to individuals.
Application information: Contributes only to pre-selected organizations.
Officers and Directors:* Earl F. Slick,* Pres.; Phyllis S. Cowell,* V.P.; Jane P. Slick,* V.P.; Mary Caroline Gamble,* Secy.-Treas.; R. Elaine Addison; John Cowell; John L.W. Garrou; Lynn C. Ives.
EIN: 311500854

2589
C. Hamilton Sloan Foundation
P.O. Box 26006
Raleigh, NC 27611
Contact: Ann C. Sloan, Tr.

Established in 1994 in NC.
Grantmaker type: Independent foundation
Financial data (yr. ended 12/31/02): Assets, $271,218 (M); gifts received, $247,226; expenditures, $290,970; qualifying distributions, $282,324; giving activities include $278,100 for 65 grants (high: $50,000; low: $400).
Fields of interest: Dance; Higher education; Zoos/zoological societies; Cancer; Multiple sclerosis research; Food distribution, meals on wheels; Boys & girls clubs; Boy scouts; Salvation Army; YM/YWCAs & YM/YWHAs; Protestant agencies & churches.
Limitations: Applications not accepted. Giving on a national basis. No grants to individuals.
Application information: Unsolicited requests for funds not accepted.
Trustees: Ann C. Sloan; O. Temple Sloan, Jr.; W. Gerald Thornton.
EIN: 561870847

2590
Edward C. Smith, Jr. & Christopher B. Smith Foundation, Inc.
P.O. Box 1527
Greenville, NC 27835

Established in 1993 in NC.
Donor(s): Edward C. Smith, Jr., Christopher B. Smith, C & E Enterprises.
Grantmaker type: Independent foundation
Financial data (yr. ended 06/30/02): Assets, $14,128,621 (M); gifts received, $3,601,313; expenditures, $659,080; qualifying distributions, $528,087; giving activities include $537,712 for 112 grants (high: $50,000; low: $100).
Purpose and activities: Giving primarily for the arts, education, natural resource conservation, health, children, youth and social services, federated giving programs, and Baptist and Episcopal churches.
Fields of interest: Museums; Museums (science/technology); Opera; Arts; Higher education; Education; Natural resources; Animals/wildlife, fisheries; Hospitals (general); Health organizations, association; Human services; Children/youth, services; Family services; Foundations (community); Federated giving programs; Protestant agencies & churches.
Limitations: Applications not accepted. Giving primarily in NC; some funding nationally, particularly FL, TX, VA, and Washington, DC. No grants to individuals.
Application information: Contributes only to pre-selected organizations.
Directors: Christopher B. Smith; Edward C. Smith, Jr.; Jo A. Smith.
EIN: 561844198

2591
The Sprinkle Family Foundation, Inc.
c/o U.S. Trust Co. of North Carolina
P.O. Box 26262
Greensboro, NC 27420

Established in 1994 in NC.

Donor(s): R. David Sprinkle.
Grantmaker type: Independent foundation
Financial data (yr. ended 12/31/02): Assets, $533,491 (M); expenditures, $116,794; qualifying distributions, $109,636; giving activities include $109,050 for 9 grants (high: $102,850; low: $200).
Purpose and activities: Giving primarily for higher education.
Fields of interest: Higher education; Natural resources; Animals/wildlife, preservation/protection; Human services.
Types of support: Scholarship funds.
Limitations: Applications not accepted. No grants to individuals.
Application information: Contributes only to pre-selected organizations.
Officers and Directors:* R. David Sprinkle,* Pres.; Pamela P. Sprinkle,* V.P. and Treas.; David Phelps Sprinkle; Ellen Sprinkle Thomas.
EIN: 561900911

2592
Robert Lee Stowe, Jr. Foundation, Inc.
P.O. Box 351
Belmont, NC 28012   (704) 825-1340
Contact: Robert L. Stowe III, Pres. or Daniel Harding Stowe, V.P.

Incorporated in 1945 in NC.
Donor(s): Robert Lee Stowe, Jr.,‡ Robert Lee Stowe III, R.L. Stowe Mills, Inc.
Grantmaker type: Independent foundation
Financial data (yr. ended 12/31/02): Assets, $1,257,159 (M); expenditures, $188,856; qualifying distributions, $180,321; giving activities include $180,321 for 33 grants (high: $110,000; low: $100).
Purpose and activities: Giving primarily for human services and to Protestant agencies and churches.
Fields of interest: Elementary/secondary education; Higher education; Botanical gardens; Human services; Protestant agencies & churches.
Limitations: Giving primarily in NC, with emphasis on the Charlotte area. No grants to individuals.
Application information:
Initial approach: Letter
Deadline(s): None
Officers: Robert Lee Stowe III, Pres.; Daniel Harding Stowe, V.P.; Richmond H. Stowe, V.P.; Jean H. Gibson, Secy.-Treas.
EIN: 566034773

2593
Edward B. Timmons, Jr. Charitable Trust
c/o Bank of America
101 S. Tryon St., NC1-002-11-18
Charlotte, NC 28255-0001   (704) 388-2837
Contact: Michael W. Lowrance, Tr. and H. Dewain Herring, Tr.

Established in 1991 in SC.
Grantmaker type: Independent foundation
Financial data (yr. ended 08/31/02): Assets, $2,383,877 (M); expenditures, $122,875; qualifying distributions, $105,110; giving activities include $99,347 for 4 grants (high: $24,837; low: $24,836).

Purpose and activities: Limited grantmaking to organizations that provide services for children and youth in the central midland region of SC.
Fields of interest: Museums (art); University; Animal welfare.
Limitations: Giving limited to the central midland region of SC. No grants to individuals.
Application information: Contributes mostly to pre-selected organizations.
   Initial approach: Letter
   Deadline(s): Oct. 15
   Board meeting date(s): Fall
Trustees: H. Dewain Herring, Jr.; Michael W. Lowrance; Bank of America.
EIN: 576137580

2594
Triangle Community Foundation
4813 Emperor Blvd., Ste. 130
P.O. Box 12834
Research Triangle Park, NC 27709
(919) 549-9840
Contact: Krystin Jorgenson, Fin. Assoc.
FAX: (919) 941-9208; E-mail: info@trianglecf.org; E-mail for application: jan@trianglecf.org; URL: http://www.trianglecf.org

Incorporated in 1983 in NC.
Grantmaker type: Community foundation
Financial data (yr. ended 06/30/02): Assets, $81,001,164 (M); gifts received, $11,499,761; expenditures, $10,682,927; giving activities include $9,364,092 for 2,359 grants (high: $500,000; low: $56).
Purpose and activities: The foundation administers donor-advised funds.
Fields of interest: Visual arts; Museums; Performing arts; Dance; Theater; Music; Humanities; Historic preservation/historical societies; Arts; Early childhood education; Child development, education; Elementary school/education; Vocational education; Higher education; Adult/continuing education; Adult education—literacy, basic skills & GED; Libraries/library science; Reading; Education; Natural resources; Energy; Environment; Animal welfare; Animals/wildlife, preservation/protection; Family planning; Medical care, rehabilitation; Health care; Substance abuse, services; Mental health/crisis services; Health organizations, association; AIDS; Alcoholism; Crime/violence prevention, youth; Legal services; Crime/law enforcement; Food services; Housing/shelter, development; Recreation; Youth development, services; Human services; Children/youth, services; Child development, services; Family services; Hospices; Aging, centers/services; Women, centers/services; Minorities/immigrants, centers/services; Homeless, human services; International peace/security; Race/intergroup relations; Urban/community development; Rural development; Community development; Voluntarism promotion; Government/public administration; Leadership development; Public affairs; Minorities; Native Americans/American Indians; Disabled; Aging; Women; Gays/lesbians; Economically disadvantaged; Homeless.
Types of support: Continuing support; Annual campaigns; Emergency funds; Program development; Seed money; Scholarship funds;

Technical assistance; Program-related investments/loans; Employee matching gifts; Employee-related scholarships; Scholarships—to individuals; In-kind gifts.
Limitations: Giving limited to Durham, Orange, Chatham and Wake counties, NC. No grants for annual campaigns or operating budgets.
Publications: Application guidelines, Annual report (including application guidelines), Financial statement, Grants list, Newsletter.
Application information: Application form required.
   Initial approach: Letter, telephone or E-mail for application
   Copies of proposal: 6
   Deadline(s): Feb. 1 and Aug. 1
   Board meeting date(s): Feb., May, Aug., and Nov.
   Final notification: June 15 and Dec. 1
Officers and Directors:* Fred D. Hutchinson,* Chair.; Peter J. Meehan, Vice-Chair.; Ronald A. Strom,* Chair., Fin. Comm. and Treas.; Sara Brooks Strassle, Chair., Philanthropic Svcs. Comm.; R. Peyton Woodson III,* Chair., Fdn. Leadership Council; Shannon E. St. John, Pres.; Keith Burwell, Exec. V.P.; Jean Gordon Carter, Secy.; Richard T. "Stick" Williams; and 11 additional directors.
Number of staff: 9.
EIN: 561380796

2595
The Wachovia Foundation, Inc. ▼
c/o Wachovia Corp.
301 S. College St., Ste. 2525
Charlotte, NC 28288-0143 (704) 374-4085
Contact: Shannon W. McFayden, Dir.
Community Affairs Contacts: CT, NJ, NY: Yvonne Calcagno, 370 Scotch Rd., Trenton, NJ 08628, tel.: (609) 530-7357, FL: Connie Smith, 225 Water St., 7th Fl., FL0670, Jacksonville, FL 32202, tel.: (904) 489-3268, DC, MD, VA: Anita Wynn, 102 E. Cary St., VA9603, Richmond, VA 23219, tel.: (804) 697-7231, DE, PA: Kevin Dow, 1339 Chestnut St., 13th Fl., Philadelphia, PA 19107, tel.: (267) 321-7664, Wachovia Securities, Inc.: Tim Holtz, 901 E. Byrd St., Richmond, VA 23219, tel.: (804) 782-4140, NC, SC: Joseph D. Crocker, GA: Ben Boswell; FAX: (704) 374-2484; URL: http://www.wachovia.com/inside/page/0,,139_414_430,00.html

Incorporated in NC.
Donor(s): Wachovia Corp.
Grantmaker type: Company-sponsored foundation
Financial data (yr. ended 12/31/02): Assets, $5,184,818 (M); expenditures, $20,637,545; qualifying distributions, $20,633,898; giving activities include $19,316,098 for grants.
Purpose and activities: Support primarily for education, community development, health and human services, and arts and culture.
Fields of interest: Arts councils; Visual arts; Museums; Performing arts; Dance; Music; Education, fund raising; Elementary/secondary education; Early childhood education; Child development, education; Elementary school/education; Secondary school/education; Higher education; Business school/education; Adult/continuing education; Adult education—literacy, basic skills & GED;

Libraries/library science; Reading; Education; Natural resources; Environment; Hospitals (general); Medical care, rehabilitation; Health care; Substance abuse, services; Health organizations, association; Heart & circulatory diseases; Alcoholism; Heart & circulatory research; Youth development, citizenship; Human services; Children/youth, services; Child development, services; Family services; Hospices; Aging, centers/services; Minorities/immigrants, centers/services; Homeless, human services; Urban/community development; Community development; Voluntarism promotion; Federated giving programs; Economics; Public affairs; Minorities; Disabled; Economically disadvantaged.
Types of support: General/operating support; Annual campaigns; Capital campaigns; Building/renovation; Endowments; Program development; Scholarship funds; Employee matching gifts.
Limitations: Giving primarily in CT, DE, Washington, DC, FL, GA, MD, NC, NJ, NY, PA, SC, and VA. No support for political, religious, veterans', or fraternal organizations, retirement homes, precollege level private schools except through employee matching gifts, organizations supported through the United Way, except for approved capital campaigns, international organizations or intermediary organizations or agents. No grants to individuals, or for travel or conferences, or capital projects.
Publications: Annual report.
Application information: Application form required.
   Initial approach: Applications available on foundation's Web site
   Copies of proposal: 1
   Deadline(s): None
   Board meeting date(s): Semi-annually
Directors: G. Kennedy Thompson, Chair.; Stephen C. Bentley; Steve Cummings; Jean E. Davis; Malcolm E. Everett III; Barnes Hauptfuhrer; Benjamin P. Jenkins III; Stanhope A. Kelly; Shannon W. McFayden; Donald McMullen, Jr.
Trustee: Wachovia Bank, N.A.
Number of staff: None.
EIN: 581485946
Recent environmental and animal welfare grants:
2595-1 Chesapeake Bay Foundation, Annapolis, MD, $15,000. 2002.
2595-2 Clean Air Campaign, Atlanta, GA, $10,000. 2002.
2595-3 Georgia Forestry Foundation, Norcross, GA, $50,000. 2002.
2595-4 Jacksonville Zoological Society, Jacksonville, FL, $50,000. 2002.
2595-5 National Aquarium in Baltimore, Baltimore, MD, $20,000. 2002.
2595-6 Nature Conservancy, Arlington, VA, $20,000. 2002.
2595-7 North Carolina Zoological Society, Asheboro, NC, $240,000. For Revitalized African Entry Plaza. 2002.
2595-8 PATH Foundation, Atlanta, GA, $50,000. 2002.
2595-9 Riverbanks Zoological Park Society, Columbia, SC, $16,667. For expansion program. 2002.
2595-10 South Carolina Aquarium, Charleston, SC, $20,000. 2002.

2596
Walrath Trust
c/o Wachovia Bank, N.A.
401 S. Tryon St., 4th Fl.
Charlotte, NC 28288-1159

Established in 2000 in PA.
Grantmaker type: Independent foundation
Financial data (yr. ended 12/31/02): Assets, $4,714,242 (L); expenditures, $285,448; qualifying distributions, $258,870; giving activities include $258,692 for 5 grants (high: $63,423; low: $5,000).
Purpose and activities: Giving primarily for the arts and human services.
Fields of interest: Opera; Historic preservation/historical societies; Zoos/zoological societies; Housing/shelter, aging; Human services.
Types of support: General/operating support.
Limitations: Applications not accepted. Giving primarily in Wilmington, DE. No grants to individuals.
Application information: Contributes only to pre-selected organizations.
Trustee: Wachovia Bank, N.A.
EIN: 516179755

2597
Weaver Foundation, Inc.
324 W. Wendover Ave., Ste. 300
Greensboro, NC 27408 (336) 378-7910
Contact: Richard L. Moore, Pres.
Application address: P.O. Box 26040, Greensboro, NC 27420-6040; FAX: (336) 275-9602; E-mail: RLM@weaverfoundation.com; URL: http://www.weaverfoundation.com

Incorporated in 1967 in NC.
Donor(s): W.H. Weaver,‡ E.H. Weaver, H. Michael Weaver.
Grantmaker type: Independent foundation
Financial data (yr. ended 12/31/02): Assets, $17,933,124 (M); gifts received, $175,457; expenditures, $1,766,407; qualifying distributions, $1,563,833; giving activities include $1,355,036 for 46 grants (high: $316,000; low: $100; average: $1,000–$25,000).
Purpose and activities: The purpose of the foundation is to help the Greater Greensboro, NC, community enhance and improve the quality of life and the economic environment for its citizens while developing a sense of philanthropy, civic education, and commitment in current and future generations of the founders' families. Focus areas include education, children and youth, environment, reducing poverty, advancement of civil rights, and economic development.
Fields of interest: Arts; Early childhood education; Higher education; Education; Natural resources; Environment; Housing/shelter, development; Human services; Children/youth, services; Homeless, human services; Leadership development; Economically disadvantaged.
Types of support: Management development; Capital campaigns; Building/renovation; Equipment; Land acquisition; Endowments; Program development; Professorships; Seed money; Consulting services; Employee matching gifts; Matching/challenge support.

Limitations: Applications not accepted. Giving limited to the greater Greensboro, NC, area. No support for fraternal organizations. No grants to individuals, or for conferences, travel or group trips, or video productions.
Publications: Annual report, Grants list.
Application information: Unsolicited requests for funds not accepted.
Board meeting date(s): Quarterly
Officers and Trustees:* H.M. Weaver,* Chair.; Ashley W. Hodges, Vice-Chair.; Richard L. Moore, Pres.; Katherine Weaver, Secy.; William Stone, Treas.; Greg Shutter.
Number of staff: 1 full-time professional.
EIN: 566093527

2598
W. S. Wellons Foundation
P.O. Box 766
Spring Lake, NC 28390
Contact: W.S. Wellons, Jr., Chair.

Donor(s): W.S. Wellons, Sr., Florence Wellons, William S. Wellons, Jr., David Wellons.
Grantmaker type: Independent foundation
Financial data (yr. ended 12/31/02): Assets, $1,814,338 (M); gifts received, $243,000; expenditures, $237,966; qualifying distributions, $96,005; giving activities include $96,005 for 30 grants (high: $17,800; low: $25).
Fields of interest: Botanical gardens; Education; Human services; Christian agencies & churches.
Limitations: Giving primarily in Fayetteville, NC. No grants to individuals.
Application information: Contact foundation for requirements.
Deadline(s): None
Officers: W.S. Wellons, Jr., Chair.; Florence C. Wellons, Secy.-Treas.
EIN: 581537766

2599
Margaret C. Woodson Foundation, Inc.
201 W. Council St.
Salisbury, NC 28145-0829
Contact: Beulah Hillard, Dir.
Application address: P.O. Box 829, Salisbury, NC 28145-0829

Incorporated in 1954 in NC.
Donor(s): Margaret C. Woodson.‡
Grantmaker type: Independent foundation
Financial data (yr. ended 12/31/02): Assets, $618,393 (M); gifts received, $635,171; expenditures, $1,075,755; qualifying distributions, $1,072,864; giving activities include $1,023,050 for 45 grants (high: $150,000; low: $500).
Purpose and activities: Giving primarily for education and human services.
Fields of interest: Arts, association; Museums; Performing arts; Historic preservation/historical societies; Arts; Secondary school/education; Higher education; Theological school/education; Libraries (public); Animal welfare; Hospitals (general); Food distribution, meals on wheels; Parks/playgrounds; Youth development, services; Human services; YM/YWCAs & YM/YWHAs; Children/youth, services; Family services; Family services, counseling; Residential/custodial care.
Types of support: General/operating support.

Limitations: Giving primarily in Davie and Rowan counties, NC. No grants for research.
Application information: Application form not required.
Initial approach: Letter with 2 years' accounting statements
Deadline(s): Mar. 1
Officers and Directors:* Mary H. Woodson,* Pres.; Mary Anne Woodson,* V.P.; Paul B. Woodson, Jr.,* Secy.; Donald D. Sayers,* Treas.; Paul Leake Bernhardt; John B.E. Cunningham; Beulah H. Hillard; William G. Johnson; Robert P. Shay, Jr.
EIN: 566064938

NORTH DAKOTA

2600
North Dakota Natural Resources Trust, Inc.
(formerly North Dakota Wetlands Trust, Inc.)
1605 E. Capitol Ave., Ste. 101
Bismarck, ND 58501-2102 (701) 223-8501
Contact: Keith Trego

Established in 1987 in ND.
Grantmaker type: Independent foundation
Financial data (yr. ended 12/31/02): Assets, $16,513,876 (M); gifts received, $616,225; expenditures, $1,164,241; qualifying distributions, $1,112,862; giving activities include $281,821 for 21 grants (high: $88,000; low: $1,929).
Purpose and activities: Giving for natural resource conservation.
Fields of interest: Natural resources.
Limitations: Applications not accepted. Giving limited to ND.
Application information: Contributes only to pre-selected organizations.
Officers: Dick Kroger, V.P.; Scott Peterson, Secy.-Treas.
Directors: Bruce Adams; Dean Hildebrand; Duane Liffirg; Jack Olin; Genevieve Thompson.
Number of staff: 4 full-time professional; 2 part-time professional.
EIN: 363512179

OHIO

2601
The 1525 Foundation
1111 Superior Ave., Ste. 1000
Cleveland, OH 44114-2507 (216) 696-4200
Contact: Dorothy Yoder, Asst. Secy.
FAX: (216) 696-7303

Incorporated in 1971 in OH.
Donor(s): Kent H. Smith.‡
Grantmaker type: Independent foundation
Financial data (yr. ended 12/31/02): Assets, $10,389,449 (M); gifts received, $2,988,131; expenditures, $2,429,523; qualifying distributions, $2,304,365; giving activities

include $2,195,014 for 29 grants (high: $1,014,859; low: $3,000; average: $5,000–$150,000).

Purpose and activities: Emphasis on higher and other education, environmental quality and conservation of natural resources, and social service agencies; charities of interest to the founder during his lifetime are favored.

Fields of interest: Higher education; Education; Natural resources; Environment.

Types of support: General/operating support; Continuing support; Capital campaigns; Building/renovation; Equipment; Endowments; Professorships; Seed money; Matching/challenge support.

Limitations: Giving primarily in OH, with emphasis on Cuyahoga County.

Application information: Application form not required.

> *Initial approach:* Proposal
> *Copies of proposal:* 1
> *Deadline(s):* None
> *Board meeting date(s):* As required - at least monthly
> *Final notification:* Within 1 month of receipt

Officers and Trustees:* Thelma G. Smith,* Pres.; William B. LaPlace,* V.P.; Phillip A. Ranney,* Secy.-Treas.

Number of staff: 1 part-time professional; 1 full-time support.

EIN: 341089206

2602
The Alpaugh Foundation

525 Vine St., 21st Fl.
Cincinnati, OH 45202-3121

Established in 1986 in OH.
Donor(s): Peter A. Alpaugh.
Grantmaker type: Independent foundation
Financial data (yr. ended 06/30/02): Assets, $2,603,576 (M); gifts received, $56,213; expenditures, $119,366; qualifying distributions, $119,366; giving activities include $114,300 for 103 grants (high: $15,000; low: $75).

Purpose and activities: Giving for art and culture, education, and human services and community development.

Fields of interest: Arts; Education; Environment; Health organizations, association; Medical research; Disasters, fire prevention/control; Recreation; Human services; Community development; Federated giving programs; Religion.

Limitations: Giving on a national basis.
Application information: Application form not required.

> *Deadline(s):* None

Officer: Peter A. Alpaugh, Mgr.
EIN: 316314074

2603
The American Foundation Corporation

720 National City Bank Bldg.
Cleveland, OH 44114 (216) 241-6664

Incorporated in 1974 as successor to trust established in 1944 in OH.
Donor(s): Members of the Corning family, and members of the Murfey family.
Grantmaker type: Independent foundation

Financial data (yr. ended 12/31/02): Assets, $28,758,668 (M); gifts received, $9,744; expenditures, $2,449,475; qualifying distributions, $2,367,984; giving activities include $2,312,059 for 120 grants (high: $518,349; low: $27; average: $500–$25,000).

Purpose and activities: Emphasis on an arboretum, the arts, higher and secondary education, child welfare, and community funds.

Fields of interest: Museums; Arts; Secondary school/education; Higher education; Environment; Hospitals (general); Children/youth, services; Federated giving programs; Engineering/technology; Science.

Types of support: General/operating support; Continuing support; Annual campaigns.

Limitations: Applications not accepted. Giving primarily in CA and in the Cleveland, OH, area. No grants to individuals, or for capital or endowment funds, special projects, research, scholarships, fellowships, or matching gifts; no loans.

Publications: Annual report.

Application information: Contributes only to pre-selected organizations. Funds presently committed.

> *Board meeting date(s):* As necessary

Officers and Trustees:* William W. Murfey,* Pres.; Spencer L. Murfey, Jr., V.P.; Maria G. Muth, Secy.-Treas.; Dwight B. Corning; Spencer Murfey.

Number of staff: None.
EIN: 237348126

2604
William P. Anderson Foundation

c/o PNC Advisors, Ohio
P.O. Box 1198
Cincinnati, OH 45273-9631
Contact: Paul D. Myers, Secy.

Incorporated in 1941 in OH.
Grantmaker type: Independent foundation
Financial data (yr. ended 10/31/02): Assets, $5,337,273 (M); expenditures, $380,593; qualifying distributions, $340,051; giving activities include $331,000 for 57 grants (high: $22,000; low: $1,000).

Purpose and activities: Giving primarily for the arts, health care and for AIDS research.

Fields of interest: Visual arts; Performing arts; Arts; Education; Natural resources; Hospitals (general); Health care; AIDS; AIDS research; Crime/violence prevention, youth; Children/youth, services; Federated giving programs.

Types of support: Annual campaigns; Capital campaigns; Building/renovation; Equipment; Seed money.

Limitations: Giving primarily in Cincinnati, OH. No grants to individuals.

Application information: The foundation no longer awards scholarships to individual students; existing commitments will be paid out. Application form required.

> *Initial approach:* Letter
> *Copies of proposal:* 1
> *Deadline(s):* Oct. 1
> *Board meeting date(s):* Nov.

Officers and Trustees:* William P. Anderson V,* Pres.; Vachael Anderson Coombe,* V.P.; Harry W. Whittaker,* V.P.; Greenville Anderson,* Treas.; Eva Jane Coombe; Michael A. Coombe;

Tucker J. Coombe; James A. Myers; Polly W. Rosenkrantz.
Number of staff: None.
EIN: 316034059

2605
The Mildred Andrews Fund

925 Euclid Ave., Ste. 2000
Cleveland, OH 44115-1407

Established in 1972 in OH.
Donor(s): Peter Putnam.‡
Grantmaker type: Operating foundation
Financial data (yr. ended 12/31/02): Assets, $721,204 (M); expenditures, $296,857; qualifying distributions, $290,869; giving activities include $290,000 for 2 grants (high: $225,000; low: $65,000).

Fields of interest: Natural resources.

Limitations: Applications not accepted. Giving primarily in Washington, DC. No grants to individuals.

Application information: Contributes only to pre-selected organizations.

Trustee: Eugene A. Kratus.
EIN: 237158695

2606
The Evenor Armington Fund

c/o The Huntington National Bank
917 Euclid Ave.
Cleveland, OH 44115 (216) 515-6798
Contact: William E. Babis, V.P.
E-mail: bill.babis@huntington.com

Established in 1954 in OH.
Donor(s): Everett Armington, and members of the Armington family.
Grantmaker type: Independent foundation
Financial data (yr. ended 06/30/02): Assets, $5,709,022 (M); expenditures, $785,319; qualifying distributions, $749,332; giving activities include $734,800 for 26 grants (high: $160,000; low: $6,000).

Purpose and activities: Grants primarily for special projects, usually short-term, in education, child welfare, medical research, health, the arts, the environment, and public policy organizations, including human rights, peace and justice, and the struggle against poverty.

Fields of interest: Arts; Education; Natural resources; Environment; Health care; Medical research, institute; Human services; Children/youth, services; International peace/security; International human rights; Civil rights; Public policy, research.

Types of support: General/operating support; Continuing support; Annual campaigns; Emergency funds; Program development; Publication; Research; Consulting services.

Limitations: Applications not accepted. Giving on a national basis. No grants to individuals, or for deficit financing or general purposes.

Application information: Contributes only to pre-selected organizations. Unsolicited requests for funds not considered or acknowledged.

> *Board meeting date(s):* Summer

Advisors: David E. Armington; Paul Armington; Peter Armington.

Trustee: The Huntington National Bank.
Number of staff: None.

EIN: 346525508

2607
The Austin Memorial Foundation
251 W. Garfield Rd., Ste. 230
Aurora, OH 44202-8856
Contact: Donald G. Austin, Jr., Pres.

Incorporated in 1961 in OH.
Donor(s): Members of the Austin family.
Grantmaker type: Independent foundation
Financial data (yr. ended 12/31/02): Assets,
$10,331,037 (M); expenditures, $852,138;
qualifying distributions, $799,593; giving
activities include $713,576 for 44 grants (high:
$150,000; low: $500).
Fields of interest: Education, fund raising;
Environment; Hospitals (general); Human
services; Religion.
Limitations: Applications not accepted. No
grants to individuals.
Application information: Contributes only to
pre-selected organizations. Unsolicited requests
for funds not accepted.
Board meeting date(s): Semiannually
Officers and Trustees:* Donald G. Austin, Jr.,*
Pres.; Colette F. Mylott, Secy.; David A.
Rodgers,* Treas.; James W. Austin; John C.
Austin; Paul W. Austin; Richard C. Austin;
Samuel H. Austin; Stewart G. Austin, Sr.; Stewart
G. Austin, Jr.; Thomas G. Austin; Winifred N.
Austin; Margaret C. Chiles; Sarah R. Cole;
Gretchen Cole-Corona; Alexandra R. Loeffler;
Ann R. Loeffler; Ellen Austin Smith.
Number of staff: 1 part-time professional.
EIN: 346528879

2608
The John C. Bates Foundation
2401 Front St.
Toledo, OH 43605

Established in 1993 in OH.
Donor(s): Heidtman Steel Products, Inc.,
Centaur, Inc., HS Processing, LP.
Grantmaker type: Company-sponsored
foundation
Financial data (yr. ended 03/31/02): Assets,
$4,681 (M); gifts received, $431,700;
expenditures, $428,448; qualifying distributions,
$428,419; giving activities include $423,917 for
26 grants (high: $255,000; low: $500).
Purpose and activities: Giving primarily for
education, health, a community foundation, and
a zoological society.
Fields of interest: Elementary/secondary
education; Higher education; Education;
Zoos/zoological societies; Cancer; Human
services; Family services; Foundations
(community); Christian agencies & churches;
Roman Catholic agencies & churches.
Types of support: Capital campaigns.
Limitations: Applications not accepted. Giving
primarily in MI and OH. No grants to
individuals.
Application information: Contributes only to
pre-selected organizations.
Officers and Trustees:* Darlene B. Dotson,*
Pres.; John M. Carey,* Secy.; Mark E. Ridenour,*
Treas.
EIN: 341749094

2609
The Molly Bee Fund
c/o Thomas F. Allen
20325 Center Ridge Rd., Ste. 629
Rocky River, OH 44116

Established in 1995 in OH.
Donor(s): Elizabeth B. Blossom.
Grantmaker type: Independent foundation
Financial data (yr. ended 12/31/02): Assets,
$4,966,541 (M); expenditures, $476,850;
qualifying distributions, $465,025; giving
activities include $405,000 for 12 grants (high:
$100,000; low: $10,000) and $50,000 for 1
employee matching gift.
Purpose and activities: Giving primarily for the
arts as well as for education, human services, a
nature center, and a wheelchair sports fund.
Fields of interest: Arts, association; Performing
arts; Ballet; Music; Arts; Education; Natural
resources; Recreation; Human services;
Foundations (community).
Types of support: General/operating support;
Capital campaigns; Building/renovation;
Equipment; Endowments; Program-related
investments/loans.
Limitations: Applications not accepted. Giving
primarily in Palm Beach and West Palm Beach,
FL, and Cleveland, OH. No grants to individuals.
Application information: Contributes only to
pre-selected organizations. Unsolicited requests
for funds not accepted.
Officers and Trustees:* Mary E. Gale,* Pres.;
Benjamin Gale,* V.P.; Thomas F. Allen,
Secy.-Treas.; Thomas H. Gale; Kevin R. Kneisly.
EIN: 341812998

2610
The William Bingham Foundation
20325 Center Ridge Rd., Ste. 629
Rocky River, OH 44116 (440) 331-6350
Contact: Laura H. Gilbertson, Dir.
E-mail: info@WBinghamFoundation.org; URL:
http://fdncenter.org/grantmaker/bingham/

Incorporated in 1955 in OH.
Donor(s): Elizabeth B. Blossom.‡
Grantmaker type: Independent foundation
Financial data (yr. ended 12/31/02): Assets,
$20,458,042 (M); expenditures, $523,795;
qualifying distributions, $403,950; giving
activities include $265,000 for 10 grants (high:
$50,000; low: $3,000).
Purpose and activities: Support for a wide
variety of programs. Grants reflect the interests
of the trustees and the needs of the communities
in which they reside.
Fields of interest: Arts; Education; Environment.
Types of support: General/operating support;
Continuing support; Management development;
Capital campaigns; Building/renovation;
Equipment; Endowments; Program
development; Conferences/seminars;
Curriculum development; Technical assistance;
Matching/challenge support.
Limitations: Giving primarily in the eastern U.S.
and the West Coast, with emphasis on
communities in which the trustees reside. No
grants to individuals; no loans.
Publications: Informational brochure (including
application guidelines).
Application information: Full proposals
accepted only by request in response to

applicant's initial letter; many of the grant
proposals are initiated by trustees. FAX and
E-mail proposals not accepted. Application form
not required.
Initial approach: Letter of 2 pages or less; no
attachments
Copies of proposal: 1
Deadline(s): None
Board meeting date(s): Usually Feb. and Aug.
Officers and Trustees:* C. Bingham Blossom,*
Pres.; Rebecca B. Kovacik,* V.P.; Thomas F.
Allen, Secy.; C. Perry Blossom,* Treas.; David B.
Blossom; Jonathan B. Blossom; Laurel Blossom;
Robin Dunn Blossom; Virginia O. Blossom;
Elizabeth B. Heffernan.
Director: Laura H. Gilbertson.
Number of staff: 1 full-time professional; 1
part-time support.
EIN: 346513791

2611
Bishop Fund
c/o KeyBank N.A.
127 Public Sq., 17th Fl.
Cleveland, OH 44114 (216) 689-4651
Contact: Cyndi Clifton

Established about 1964.
Grantmaker type: Independent foundation
Financial data (yr. ended 12/31/02): Assets,
$1,727,678 (M); expenditures, $144,785;
qualifying distributions, $131,050; giving
activities include $127,300 for 48 grants (high:
$12,000; low: $500).
Purpose and activities: Primary interest in
organizations with a scientific or environmental
orientation.
Fields of interest: Education; Environment;
Engineering/technology; Science; General
charitable giving.
Limitations: Applications not accepted. Giving
on a national basis. No grants to individuals.
Application information: Contributes only to
pre-selected organizations. Unsolicited requests
for funds not considered or acknowledged.
Director: Jonathan S. Bishop.
Trustee: KeyBank N.A.
Number of staff: None.
EIN: 346513612

2612
Robert Rogan Burchenal Foundation
c/o Fifth Third Bank
38 Fountain Sq. Plz.
Cincinnati, OH 45263
Contact: Heroi Jork

Established in 1972 in OH.
Donor(s): Robert R. Burchenal.
Grantmaker type: Independent foundation
Financial data (yr. ended 11/30/02): Assets,
$2,543,861 (M); expenditures, $213,829;
qualifying distributions, $199,396; giving
activities include $197,573 for 19 grants (high:
$38,782; low: $1,000).
Purpose and activities: Giving to medical
services for children, education, and Catholic
inner city schools.
Fields of interest: Museums; Education;
Environment; Hospitals (general); Human
services; Federated giving programs.

Limitations: Giving primarily in MO, MT, and OH.
Application information:
Initial approach: Letter or proposal
Deadline(s): None
Trustees: Catherine J. Bournstein; Cooper L. Burchenal; James J. Burchenal; Martha L. Burchenal; Beth B. Jones; William H. Kreidler II.
EIN: 237231471

2613
The Camden Foundation
c/o Fifth Third Bank
38 Fountain Sq. Plz., Trust Tax Dept.
Cincinnati, OH 45263 (513) 579-5472
Contact: David Garber

Established in 1952 in OH.
Grantmaker type: Independent foundation
Financial data (yr. ended 09/30/02): Assets, $2,459,282 (M); expenditures, $175,351; qualifying distributions, $158,667; giving activities include $152,000 for 23 grants (high: $25,000; low: $1,000).
Purpose and activities: Giving primarily for the arts, education, environmental conservation, and federated giving programs.
Fields of interest: Museums; Elementary/secondary education; Natural resources; Federated giving programs.
Limitations: Giving primarily in the Cincinnati, OH, area.
Application information: Application form required.
Initial approach: Letter or telephone
Deadline(s): None
Trustee: Fifth Third Bank.
EIN: 316024141

2614
Castellini Foundation
312 Elm St., Ste. 2600
Cincinnati, OH 45202
Contact: Christopher L. Fister, Secy.-Treas.

Established in 1991 in OH.
Donor(s): Robert H. Castellini, Susan F. Castellini.
Grantmaker type: Independent foundation
Financial data (yr. ended 03/31/03): Assets, $8,466,691 (M); expenditures, $1,518,691; qualifying distributions, $1,478,829; giving activities include $1,462,969 for 118 grants (high: $250,000; low: $50).
Purpose and activities: Giving primarily for education, health care, and the arts.
Fields of interest: Arts; Higher education; Education; Botanical gardens; Animal welfare; Hospitals (general); Health organizations, association; Human services; Federated giving programs; Religion.
Limitations: Giving limited to the greater Cincinnati, OH, area. No grants to individuals or for religious purposes.
Application information: Application form not required.
Initial approach: Letter
Deadline(s): None
Officers and Trustees:* Robert H. Castellini,* Chair. and Pres.; Christopher L. Fister,* Secy.-Treas.; Susan F. Castellini.
Agent: Fifth Third Bank.

EIN: 316429763

2615
Charities Foundation
1 Seagate, 5-OSG
Toledo, OH 43666 (419) 247-2929
Contact: Cher Johnson, Contribs. Admin.
Additional tel.: (419) 247-1386

Trust established in 1937 in OH.
Donor(s): Owens-Illinois, Inc., William E. Levis,‡ Harold Boeschenstein,‡ and others.
Grantmaker type: Company-sponsored foundation
Financial data (yr. ended 12/31/02): Assets, $646,228 (M); gifts received, $1,523,500; expenditures, $2,598,821; qualifying distributions, $2,587,638; giving activities include $2,113,487 for 42 grants (high: $250,000; low: $500; average: $5,000–$25,000) and $474,361 for 121 employee matching gifts.
Purpose and activities: Contributions from the foundation are initiated internally, with emphasis on higher and other education, community funds, hospitals, cultural programs, including museums and performing arts, conservation, youth and social service agencies, and civic and public affairs organizations.
Fields of interest: Visual arts; Museums; Performing arts; Arts; Education, fund raising; Higher education; Business school/education; Education; Natural resources; Hospitals (general); Health organizations, association; Human services; Children/youth, services; Federated giving programs; Government/public administration; Public affairs.
Types of support: General/operating support; Employee matching gifts.
Limitations: Applications not accepted. Giving primarily in OH, with emphasis on Toledo. No grants to individuals, or for scholarships.
Publications: Annual report.
Application information: Contributes only to pre-selected organizations. All funds presently committed.
Board meeting date(s): Jan. 26, Apr. 27, Aug. 3, and Oct. 26
Trustees: Jeffrey Denker; Henry Page; Carter Smith; Lee A. Wesselmann.
Number of staff: 1 part-time support.
EIN: 346554560

2616
Chiquita Brands International Foundation
(formerly United Brands Foundation)
250 E. 5th St., 27th Fl., Tax Dept.
Cincinnati, OH 45202
Contact: Stephanie Krummert, Corp. Affairs

Incorporated in 1954 in IL.
Donor(s): Chiquita Brands International, Inc.
Grantmaker type: Company-sponsored foundation
Financial data (yr. ended 12/31/02): Assets, $35,114 (M); gifts received, $70,500; expenditures, $131,327; qualifying distributions, $131,327; giving activities include $131,304 for 41 grants (high: $25,000; low: $8).
Purpose and activities: Giving for education, environmental and wildlife conservation, health associations and human services.

Fields of interest: Elementary/secondary education; Higher education; Business school/education; Natural resources; Health organizations, association; Agriculture; Human services; Children/youth, services.
Types of support: General/operating support.
Limitations: Giving on a national basis.
Application information: Application form not required.
Deadline(s): None
Officers and Directors:* Joseph W. Bradley, V.P.; James B. Riley, V.P.; Jeffrey M. Zalla,* V.P.; Robert W. Olson, Secy.; William A. Tsacalis,* Treas.
EIN: 366051081

2617
The Greater Cincinnati Foundation ▼
200 W. 4th St.
Cincinnati, OH 45202-2602 (513) 241-2880
Contact: E. Miles Wilson, V.P., Grants and Progs.
FAX: (513) 852-6888; E-mail: info@greatercincinnatifdn.org; URL: http://www.greatercincinnatifdn.org

Established in 1963 in OH by bank resolution and declaration of trust.
Grantmaker type: Community foundation
Financial data (yr. ended 12/31/02): Assets, $314,916,701 (M); gifts received, $30,032,025; expenditures, $39,237,676; giving activities include $30,432,000 for grants (average: $5,000–$1,000,000).
Purpose and activities: Grants for a broad range of both new and existing activities in general categories of arts and culture, community progress, environmental needs, education, health, and social and human services, including youth agencies. The foundation actively seeks to promote access, equity and diversity, and to end discrimination based on race, ethnicity, gender, disability or age.
Fields of interest: Arts; Early childhood education; Education; Environment; Health care; Housing/shelter, home owners; Human services; Children/youth, services; Community development; Voluntarism promotion; African Americans/Blacks; Disabled; Aging; Economically disadvantaged; Homeless.
Types of support: Capital campaigns; Building/renovation; Equipment; Emergency funds; Program development; Seed money; Technical assistance; Program-related investments/loans; Matching/challenge support.
Limitations: Giving limited to southeastern IN, northern KY, and the greater Cincinnati, OH area. No support for sectarian religious purposes, schools, hospitals, nursing homes, or retirement centers. No grants to individuals, or for operating budgets, annual campaigns, deficit financing, scholarships, endowments, travel grants, fellowships, internships, exchange programs, or scholarly or medical research.
Publications: Application guidelines, Annual report (including application guidelines), Informational brochure (including application guidelines), Newsletter.
Application information: Common Grant Application form used after invitation. Application form required.
Initial approach: Letter or telephone, followed by interview with foundation staff and volunteers

Copies of proposal: 1
Deadline(s): 90 days prior to board meetings
Board meeting date(s): Feb., Mar., May, June,
Sept., and Dec.
Final notification: Immediately following
board meetings
Officers: Kathryn E. Merchant, C.E.O. and Pres.;
Amy L. Cheney, V.P., Advancement; Scott
McReynolds, V.P., Finance and Admin.; E. Miles
Wilson, V.P., Grants and Progs.
Governing Board: John A. Stith, Chair.; Barbara
Lewis, Vice-Chair.; Richard J. Ruebel, Legal
Counsel; Thomas A. Brennan; Lee A. Carter;
Paul W. Chellgren; Cathy Crain; Johnathan M.
Holifield; Bert Huff; William C. Portman III;
Myrtis Powell, Ph.D.; Carole Rigaud; Marvin H.
Rorick, M.D.
Trustee Banks: Bank One, N.A.; Fifth Third
Bank; The Huntington National Bank; KeyBank
N.A.; The Lebanon Citizens National Bank;
North Side Bank & Trust Co.; PNC Bank, N.A.;
The Provident Bank; U.S. Bank, N.A.
Number of staff: 15 full-time professional; 9
full-time support; 1 part-time support.
EIN: 310669700
**Recent environmental and animal welfare
grants:**
2617-1 Audubon Society, National, New York,
NY, $15,000. For Important Bird Areas
program in Southwest Ohio. 2001.
2617-2 Better Housing League of Greater
Cincinnati, Cincinnati, OH, $30,000. For
ClearCorps program expansion. 2001.
2617-3 League of Women Voters of Cincinnati
Area Education Fund, Cincinnati, OH,
$50,000. For Sustainable Cincinnati, A
Regional Indicators Project. 2001.
2617-4 Northern Kentucky Area Development
District, Florence, KY, $10,000. For Solid
Waste Education Program. 2001.
2617-5 Three Valley Conservation Trust, Oxford,
OH, $30,000. For executive director
position. 2001.
2617-6 WAVE Foundation, Newport, KY,
$15,000. For volunteer program training and
education. 2001.
2617-7 Western Wildlife Corridor, Cincinnati,
OH, $25,000. For expanded staff. 2001.

2618
The Cleveland Foundation ▼
1422 Euclid Ave., Ste. 1300
Cleveland, OH 44115-2001 (216) 861-3810
Contact: Ronald B. Richard, Pres.
FAX: (216) 589-9039; TTY: (216) 861-3806;
E-mail: ldunford@clevefdn.org; URL: http://
www.clevelandfoundation.org

Established in 1914 in OH by bank resolution
and declaration of trust.
Grantmaker type: Community foundation
Financial data (yr. ended 12/31/02): Assets,
$1,312,166,868 (M); gifts received,
$34,962,985; expenditures, $73,443,672; giving
activities include $63,144,990 for 1,756 grants.
Purpose and activities: The Cleveland
Foundation is the nation's first community
foundation and model for community
foundations nationwide and around the world.
Its purpose is to enhance the quality of life for
all the citizens of greater Cleveland by building
community endowment, addressing needs
through grantmaking, and providing leadership

on key community issues. The foundation
awards grants in seven program areas: arts and
culture, civic affairs, economic development,
education, the environment, health, and social
services. Special cross-functional grantmaking
initiatives include neighborhoods and housing,
strengthening the arts and cultural community,
downtown redevelopment and other projects of
scale, public school improvement, strengthening
the quality of life in early childhood, combating
persistent poverty.
Fields of interest: Visual arts; Performing arts;
Arts; Elementary school/education; Secondary
school/education; Higher education; Medical
school/education; Environment; Health care;
Health organizations, association; AIDS;
Medical research, institute; AIDS research;
Housing/shelter, development; Human services;
Youth, services; Aging, centers/services;
Urban/community development; Community
development; Economics; Government/public
administration; Aging.
Types of support: Capital campaigns; Program
development; Seed money; Scholarship funds;
Research; Technical assistance; Consulting
services; Program-related investments/loans;
Matching/challenge support.
Limitations: Giving limited to the greater
Cleveland, OH, area, with primary emphasis on
Cleveland, Cuyahoga, Lake, and Geauga
counties, unless specified by donor. No support
for sectarian or religious activities, community
services such as fire and police protection, and
library and welfare services. No grants to
individuals, or for endowment funds, operating
costs, debt reduction, fundraising campaigns,
publications, films and audiovisual materials
(unless they are an integral part of a program
already being supported), memberships, travel
for bands, sports teams, classes and similar
groups; no capital support for planning,
construction, renovation, or purchase of
buildings, equipment and materials, land
acquisition, or renovation of public space unless
there is strong evidence that the program is of
priority to the foundation.
Publications: Application guidelines, Annual
report (including application guidelines),
Financial statement, Informational brochure,
Newsletter, Occasional report.
Application information: Application available
on foundation's Web site. Application form
required.
Initial approach: Letter
Copies of proposal: 2
Deadline(s): None
Board meeting date(s): Distribution committee
meets in Mar., June, Sept., and Dec.
Final notification: 1 month
Officers: Ronald B. Richard, Pres.; J.T. Mullen,
Sr. V.P., Treas. and C.F.O.; Richard Batyko, V.P.,
Comm.; Marlene Casini, V.P., Gift Planning and
Donor Rels.; Robert E. Eckardt, V.P., Prog.; Lynn
M. Sargi, V.P., Admin. and Human Resources;
Leslie A. Dunford, Corp. Secy., and C.O.S.
Directors: John Sherwin, Jr., Chair.; Jerry Sue
Thorton, Vice-Chair.; James E. Bennett III; Terri
Hamilton Brown; Tana N. Carney; David
Goldberg; Ric Harris; Joseph P. Keithley; Benson
Lee; Catherine Monroe Lewis; Alex Machaskee;
Rev. Otis Moss, Jr.; Maria Jose Pujana, M.D.;
Alayne L. Reitman; Jacqueline F. Woods.

Trustees: Bank One, N.A.; FirstMerit Bank, N.A.;
The Huntington National Bank; KeyBank N.A.;
National City Bank.
Number of staff: 41 full-time professional; 18
full-time support; 1 part-time support.
EIN: 340714588
**Recent environmental and animal welfare
grants:**
2618-1 Cleveland Botanical Garden, Cleveland,
OH, $450,000. For Phase II of Family
Learning Project. 2002.
2618-2 Cleveland Botanical Garden, Cleveland,
OH, $25,000. For equipment and furniture
for Hershey Children's Classroom. 2002.
2618-3 Cleveland Botanical Garden, Cleveland,
OH, $20,000. For capital campaign. 2002.
2618-4 Cleveland Botanical Garden, Cleveland,
OH, $10,000. For underwriting members for
Green Corps program. 2002.
2618-5 Cleveland Metroparks System,
Cleveland, OH, $10,500. For Floating Water
Quality Lab. 2002.
2618-6 Cleveland Zoological Society,
Cleveland, OH, $100,000. For renovation
and expansion of Center for Zoological
Medicine. 2002.
2618-7 EcoCity Cleveland, Cleveland Heights,
OH, $30,000. For operating support of
website. 2002.
2618-8 Environmental Health Watch,
Cleveland, OH, $30,000. For
community-based education program
focusing on reducing environmental triggers
for asthma. 2002.
2618-9 Foundation for Environmental Research,
Cleveland, OH, $450,000. For general
support. 2002.
2618-10 Foundation for Environmental
Research, Cleveland, OH, $80,000. For
general support. 2002.
2618-11 Foundation for Environmental
Research, Cleveland, OH, $50,000. For
general support. 2002.
2618-12 Grand River Partners, Painesville, OH,
$65,000. For operating support. 2002.
2618-13 Grand River Partners, Painesville, OH,
$20,000. For operating support. 2002.
2618-14 Great Lakes Museum of Science,
Environment and Technology, Cleveland,
OH, $15,000. For general support. 2002.
2618-15 Humane Society of Lake County,
Mentor, OH, $20,000. For humane
education program. 2002.
2618-16 Humane Society, Geauga County,
Novelty, OH, $26,000. For salary support for
veterinary technician at Sarah's Place,
medical clinic at Rescue Village. 2002.
2618-17 Lake Metroparks, Concord, OH,
$17,000. For bronze sculpture for Kevin P.
Clinton Wildlife Center at Penitentiary Glen.
2002.
2618-18 Lincoln Institute of Land Policy,
Cambridge, MA, $50,000. For land reform
documentary project called, Making Sense of
Place. 2002.
2618-19 Neighborhood Progress, Cleveland,
OH, $38,500. For Developing Sustainability
and Neighborhood Impact Plan. 2002.
2618-20 North Cuyahoga Valley Corridor,
Cleveland, OH, $50,000. For development of
Ohio and Erie Canal National Heritage
Corridor and other related projects. 2002.
2618-21 Ohio City Near West Development
Corporation, Cleveland, OH, $40,000. For

development of Cleveland Environmental Center. 2002.

2618-22 Ohio League of Conservation Voters Education Fund, Columbus, OH, $15,000. For program activities in Northeast Ohio. 2002.

2618-23 ParkWorks, Cleveland, OH, $250,000. For creation of public space at Huron Point. 2002.

2618-24 ParkWorks, Cleveland, OH, $125,000. For strategic work related to refining Downtown Green Space Plan. 2002.

2618-25 ParkWorks, Cleveland, OH, $30,000. For staffing and consulting costs associated with downtown greenspace project. 2002.

2618-26 Second Growth Institute, Chagrin Falls, OH, $90,000. For Five Points Initiative project. 2002.

2618-27 Shaker Lakes Regional Nature Center, Cleveland, OH, $145,000. For campaign to expand and enhance facilities and operations. 2002.

2618-28 Shaker Lakes Regional Nature Center, Cleveland, OH, $100,000. For capital project. 2002.

2618-29 Shaker Lakes Regional Nature Center, Cleveland, OH, $100,000. For renovation and new construction project. 2002.

2618-30 Shaker Lakes Regional Nature Center, Cleveland, OH, $25,000. For completion of capital renovation and expansion campaign. 2002.

2618-31 Shaker Lakes Regional Nature Center, Cleveland, OH, $13,805. For general support. 2002.

2618-32 Shaker Lakes Regional Nature Center, Cleveland, OH, $10,000. For capital campaign. 2002.

2618-33 Shaker Lakes Regional Nature Center, Cleveland, OH, $10,000. For general support. 2002.

2618-34 Trust for Public Land, Cleveland, OH, $45,000. For Ohio Field Office. 2002.

2618-35 Trust for Public Land, Cleveland, OH, $20,000. For Ohio Field Office's acquisition of 574-acre Bass Lake Sanctuary in Geauga County. 2002.

2618-36 West Creek Preservation Committee, Parma, OH, $25,000. For Watershed Coordinator and associated expenses. 2002.

2619
The Columbus Foundation and Affiliated Organizations ▼

(formerly The Columbus Foundation)
1234 E. Broad St.
Columbus, OH 43205-1453 (614) 251-4000
Contact: Raymond J. Biddiscombe, V.P., Finance and Admin.
FAX: (614) 251 4009; E-mail: info@columbusfoundation.org, rbiddisc@columbusfoundation.org; URL: http://www.columbusfoundation.org

Established in 1943 in OH by resolution and declaration of trust.
Grantmaker type: Community foundation
Financial data (yr. ended 12/31/02): Assets, $628,139,633 (M); gifts received, $77,564,524; expenditures, $56,063,055; giving activities include $50,179,800 for 5,386 grants (high: $1,500,000; low: $25; average: $100–$25,000).

Purpose and activities: A public charitable foundation for receiving funds for distribution to charitable organizations mainly in the central OH region. Grants made to strengthen existing agencies or to initiate new programs in the following categories: arts and humanities, urban affairs, conservation and environmental protection, education, health, mental health and the developmentally disabled, and social service agencies.

Fields of interest: Performing arts; Humanities; Historic preservation/historical societies; Arts; Education, association; Child development, education; Adult education—literacy, basic skills & GED; Reading; Education; Natural resources; Energy; Environment; Family planning; Health care; Mental health/crisis services; Health organizations, association; AIDS; AIDS research; Human services; Youth, services; Child development, services; Women, centers/services; Homeless, human services; Race/intergroup relations; Community development; Government/public administration; Public affairs; Disabled; Women; Economically disadvantaged; Homeless.

Types of support: Continuing support; Capital campaigns; Building/renovation; Land acquisition; Program development; Publication; Seed money; Scholarship funds; Technical assistance; Matching/challenge support.

Limitations: Giving limited to Franklin County, OH, from unrestricted and other discretionary funds. No support for religious purposes, or for projects normally the responsibility of a public agency. No grants to individuals, or generally for budget deficits, conferences, scholarly research, or endowment funds.

Publications: Application guidelines, Annual report, Informational brochure (including application guidelines), Newsletter.

Application information: Grant requests to the Columbus Youth Foundation must be submitted by the 1st Fri. in Feb. and Oct. for consideration at meetings held in Apr. and Dec.; requests to the Ingram-White Castle Foundation must be submitted by the 1st Fri. in Feb. and Sept. for consideration in Apr. and Nov. Application form required.

Initial approach: Meeting with staff
Copies of proposal: 4
Deadline(s): Usually as follows: Education, Feb.; Health, Apr.; Social Services, July; Urban Affairs, Sept.; and Arts and Conservation, Nov. Contact foundation for exact dates
Board meeting date(s): Feb., Apr., May, July, Sept., Oct., and Dec.
Final notification: Approximately 3 months after the given deadline

Officers: Douglas F. Kridler, Pres.; Raymond J. Biddiscombe, V.P., Finance and Admin.; Lisa S. Courtice, Ph.D., V.P., Community Research and Grants Mgmt.; Philip T. Schavone, V.P., Advancement.

Governing Committee: Abigail Wexner, Chair.; Bill Ingram, Vice-Chair.; John B. Gellach, Jr.; Archie Griffin; David R. Meuse; Ann Pizzuti; Lewis R. Smott, Sr.; Ann Isaly Wolfe.

Trustee Banks: Bank One Trust Co., N.A.; The Huntington National Bank; KeyBank N.A.; National City Bank, Columbus.

Number of staff: 23 full-time professional; 14 full-time support; 3 part-time support.
EIN: 316044264

Recent environmental and animal welfare grants:

2619-1 Audubon Society of Columbus, Columbus, OH, $17,000. For Important Bird Areas project for protection and preservation of bird habitats in central Ohio. 2002.

2619-2 Canine Companions for Independence, Delaware, OH, $15,000. For general operating support. 2002.

2619-3 Clear Creek Farm, Piqua, OH, $140,000. To support operations. 2002.

2619-4 Clear Creek Farm, Piqua, OH, $140,000. To support operations. 2002.

2619-5 Clear Creek Farm, Piqua, OH, $15,869. 2002.

2619-6 Clear Creek Farm, Piqua, OH, $11,647. 2002.

2619-7 Columbus Neighborhood Design Assistance Center, Columbus, OH, $60,000. To hire case managers and for patient education components of Prescription for Care program. 2002.

2619-8 Columbus Neighborhood Design Assistance Center, Columbus, OH, $23,000. To produce and publish illustrated book highlighting progress and potential of inner-city communities in Columbus. 2002.

2619-9 Columbus Zoological Park Association, Powell, OH, $25,000. To support creation of zoo geographic region encompassing Australia and Islands of Southeast Asia. 2002.

2619-10 Columbus Zoological Park Association, Powell, OH, $20,000. To support operations. 2002.

2619-11 Columbus Zoological Park Association, Powell, OH, $20,000. For sculpture. 2002.

2619-12 Columbus Zoological Park Association, Powell, OH, $16,962. For Sara Bennett's Wattled Curassow Research Project. 2002.

2619-13 Columbus Zoological Park Association, Powell, OH, $12,000. For Pony Ride project. 2002.

2619-14 Columbus Zoological Park Association, Powell, OH, $10,000. To support operations. 2002.

2619-15 Columbus Zoological Park Association, Powell, OH, $10,000. For Tiger Pass. 2002.

2619-16 Denison University, Department of Environmental Studies, Granville, OH, $12,000. 2002.

2619-17 Firstlink, Columbus, OH, $11,000. To provide laboratory service to Franklin County Dental OPTIONS clients who do not have dental insurance. 2002.

2619-18 Franklin Park Conservatory and Botanical Garden, Columbus, OH, $20,000. To support Ants in Your Plants fall education exhibit, active inquiry-based hands-on learning experience. 2002.

2619-19 Franklin Park Conservatory and Botanical Garden, Columbus, OH, $20,000. To support operations. 2002.

2619-20 Franklin Park Conservatory and Botanical Garden, Columbus, OH, $10,000. To support Hat Day Luncheon. 2002.

2619-21 Franklin Park Conservatory and Botanical Garden, Columbus, OH, $10,000. 2002.

2619-22 Franklin Park Conservatory and Botanical Garden, Columbus, OH, $10,000. 2002.

2619-23 Franklin Park Conservatory and Botanical Garden, Columbus, OH, $10,000. 2002.
2619-24 Green Energy Ohio, Columbus, OH, $15,000. To support public education campaign in Greater Columbus to promote clean, renewable energy. 2002.
2619-25 Highlands Nature Sanctuary, Bainbridge, OH, $84,831. 2002.
2619-26 Inniswood Garden Society, Westerville, OH, $25,000. To provide plant materials, interpretive signage, and classroom-based activities for children visiting Sisters' Garden at Inniswood. 2002.
2619-27 Inniswood Garden Society, Westerville, OH, $22,500. For Secret Garden. 2002.
2619-28 Inniswood Garden Society, Westerville, OH, $10,000. 2002.
2619-29 Lancaster Parks and Recreation, Friends of, Lancaster, OH, $20,000. To support Lancaster Loop of Fairfield Heritage Trail. 2002.
2619-30 Little Traverse Conservancy, Harbor Springs, MI, $20,000. For Offield Family Foundation Conservancy Challenge - Harbor Springs Green Belt Project. 2002.
2619-31 MiraCit Development Corporation, Columbus, OH, $32,250. To construct picnic shelter and related landscaping improvements. 2002.
2619-32 Mote Marine Laboratory, Sarasota, FL, $37,500. 2002.
2619-33 Mote Marine Laboratory, Sarasota, FL, $31,000. To support Mason Scholarship Fund for Teacher Professional Development in Marine Sciences. 2002.
2619-34 Ohio Environmental Council, Columbus, OH, $20,000. To support efforts to increase citizen participation in local watershed restoration projects. 2002.
2619-35 Pilot Dogs, Columbus, OH, $10,000. To support operations. 2002.
2619-36 Sierra Club Foundation, San Francisco, CA, $10,000. To support Sierra Club of Ohio Chapter's campaign for sustainable transportation. 2002.
2619-37 Westerville City Schools, Westerville, OH, $26,500. To support Kids and Canines Program for severely emotionally disturbed students at Walnut Springs Middle School. 2002.

2620
The Community Foundation of Greater Lorain County ▼
1865 N. Ridge Rd. E., Ste. A
Lorain, OH 44055 (440) 277-0142
Contact: Brian R. Frederick, C.E.O. and Pres.
Additional tel.: (440) 323-4445; FAX: (440) 277-6955; E-mail: Foundation@cfglc.org; URL: http://www.cfglc.org

Incorporated in 1980 in OH.
Grantmaker type: Community foundation
Financial data (yr. ended 12/31/02): Assets, $53,280,183 (M); gifts received, $3,038,545; expenditures, $4,166,703; giving activities include $3,438,322 for 376 grants (high: $640,218; low: $50) and $237,603 for 207 grants to individuals (high: $3,000; low: $250; average: $250–$3,000).
Purpose and activities: The foundation seeks to improve the quality of life and to instill a greater

sense of unity in the Greater Lorain County community by mobilizing individuals to become active partners in building a better community; providing a permanent instrument for receiving and managing charitable gifts and bequests; supporting innovative programs and acting as a catalyst in identifying problems and sharing information with individuals, other foundations, corporations, and organizations; and exercising and promoting leadership in meeting the changing needs and opportunities of the entire community.
Fields of interest: Arts; Education; Environment; Health care; Health organizations, association; Human services; Community development, neighborhood development; Economic development; Asians/Pacific Islanders; African Americans/Blacks; Hispanics/Latinos; Women.
Types of support: General/operating support; Endowments; Program development; Seed money; Scholarship funds; Technical assistance; Consulting services; Scholarships—to individuals; Matching/challenge support.
Limitations: Giving limited to Lorain County and Huron County, OH, and immediate vicinity. No support for religious purposes, street repair, government services, public or non-public school services required by law, or self-help clubs that meet the needs of a small population. No grants to individuals (except for scholarships), or for annual campaigns, medical research, deficit financing, membership fees, equipment, group travel, or capital campaigns.
Publications: Application guidelines, Annual report (including application guidelines), Informational brochure (including application guidelines), Newsletter, Program policy statement.
Application information: Grant seekers should contact the Prog. Off. to discuss the proposal before submitting an application. Application form required.
  Initial approach: Proposal, letter, or telephone
  Copies of proposal: 1
  Deadline(s): Mar. 1 and Aug. 1
  Board meeting date(s): Monthly
  Final notification: 1 to 2 weeks following board meeting
Officers and Directors:* Rita Canfield,* Chair.; Jim Park,* Vice-Chair.; Brian R. Frederick,* C.E.O. and Pres.; John Keyse-Walker,* Secy.; Don Arnold,* Treas.; Cheryl McKenna, C.F.O.; Bob Bowman; Jim Bucci; Andy Culberson; Leonard DeLuca; Maria Escuro; Kevin Flanigan; Terry Goode; Michael Goodman; E. Jean Harper, Ph.D.; Charles Horton; Jane Norton; Rigoberto Reveron; Lou Suarez; Helen Woodward.
Number of staff: 9 full-time professional.
EIN: 341322781
Recent environmental and animal welfare grants:
2620-1 Animal Protective League of Lorain County, Elyria, OH, $15,390. For Subsidized Spay/Neuter Community Program. 2002.

2621
Community Foundation of Mount Vernon & Knox County
(formerly The Mount Vernon/Knox County Community Trust)
c/o The First-Knox National Bank
1 S. Main St., P.O. Box 1270
Mount Vernon, OH 43050 (740) 392-3270
Contact: Sam Barone, Exec. Dir.
FAX: (740) 399-5296; E-mail: thefoundation@firstknox.com

Established in 1944 in OH by declaration of trust.
Grantmaker type: Community foundation
Financial data (yr. ended 12/31/02): Assets, $21,726,362 (M); gifts received, $1,455,445; expenditures, $974,910; giving activities include $582,720 for 130 grants (high: $75,522; low: $10), $187,667 for 148 grants to individuals (high: $10,000; low: $250) and $75,522 for 1 in-kind gift.
Purpose and activities: To assist public, educational, charitable or benevolent enterprises. Grants, in accordance with the donors' wishes, for student loan and scholarship funds, community funds, youth agencies, nursing and the health profession, and museums. The foundation administers a donor-advised fund.
Fields of interest: Museums; Education; Natural resources; Nursing care; Health care; Health organizations, association; Parks/playgrounds; Children/youth, services; Federated giving programs.
Types of support: Capital campaigns; Building/renovation; Equipment; Program development; Conferences/seminars; Seed money; Scholarship funds; Program evaluation; Scholarships—to individuals; Matching/challenge support.
Limitations: Giving primarily in Knox County, OH. No support for religious purposes. No grants for endowment funds or research; no loans.
Publications: Application guidelines, Annual report, Informational brochure, Occasional report.
Application information: Application form required.
  Initial approach: Letter
  Copies of proposal: 1
  Deadline(s): Varies with projects
  Board meeting date(s): Bi-monthly
  Final notification: Following next board meeting
Officers: Mark A. Ramser, Chair.; John D. Ellis, Vice-Chair.; Robert L. Rauzi, Secy.; Sally A. Nelson, Treas.
Board Members: Douglas O. Brenneman; E. LeBron Fairbanks; Thomas R. Fosnaught; Ronald G. Godfrey; Joan E. Jones; L. Bruce Levering; Deborah J. Reeder; Dennis L. Snyder.
Investment Manager: The First-Knox National Bank.
Number of staff: 1 part-time professional; 1 part-time support.
EIN: 311768219

2622
Community Foundation of the Mahoning Valley

1600 Metropolitan Twr.
1 Federal Plz. W.
Youngstown, OH 44503   (330) 743-5555
Contact: Patricia Brozik
FAX: (330) 746-0330; E-mail: info@cfmv.org;
URL: http://www.cfmv.org

Established in 1999 in OH.
Grantmaker type: Community foundation
Financial data (yr. ended 06/30/03): Assets,
$10,911,073 (M); gifts received, $6,080,407;
expenditures, $318,900; giving activities
include $277,802 for grants (average:
$1,000–$5,000).
Purpose and activities: Giving primarily for
health, education, economic development,
human services, and historical, cultural, and
environmental activities. The foundation
administers a donor-advised fund.
Fields of interest: Arts; Education; Environment;
Health care; Human services; Economic
development.
Limitations: Giving limited to Mahoning Valley,
OH.
Publications: Application guidelines, Financial
statement, Informational brochure.
Application information: Grant guidelines
available on Web site. Application form
required.
   Copies of proposal: 10
   Deadline(s): Feb. 1, May 1, Aug. 1, and Nov. 1
   Board meeting date(s): Mar., June, Sept. and
   Dec.
Officers: John L. Pogue, Chair.; Janice E.
Strasfeld, Secy.; Frank Dixon, Treas.
Directors: Franklin Bennett; William J.
Bresnahan; Donald Cagigas; Earnest Perry;
William R. Powell; Molly Steals.
EIN: 341904353

2623
Community Foundations, Inc.

1234 E. Broad St.
Columbus, OH 43205-1463   (614) 251-4000
Contact: Raymond J. Biddiscomse, V.P., Fin. and
Admin.

Established in 1985 in OH.
Grantmaker type: Community foundation
Financial data (yr. ended 12/31/02): Assets,
$18,869,205 (M); gifts received, $2,560,043;
expenditures, $1,310,352; giving activities
include $1,162,437 for 250 grants (high:
$50,000; low: $100; average: $250–$10,000).
Purpose and activities: Entrusted with the
responsibility to improve the quality of life of
each county where a particular fund is focused,
Community Foundations, Inc. has a five-part
mission: to serve as a leader, catalyst, and
resource for charitable giving, to preserve and
grow an endowment to address changing
community needs in partnership with all
stakeholders, to strive for measurable
community improvement through strategic
grantmaking in the arts, education, community
development, health, social services, and other
community needs, to promote and participate in
partnerships on evolving community issues and
leverage resources to meet major needs, and to
provide a flexible and cost-effective way for

donors to improve their community now and for
all time. The foundation administers a
donor-advised fund.
Fields of interest: Arts; Education; Natural
resources; Health care; Human services;
Urban/community development; Religion.
Types of support: General/operating support;
Capital campaigns; Seed money; Scholarship
funds.
Limitations: Applications not accepted. Giving
primarily in OH. No grants to individuals.
Publications: Annual report.
Application information: Unsolicited requests
for funds not accepted.
   Board meeting date(s): Feb., Apr., May, Jul.,
   Oct., and Dec.
Officers and Trustees:* Abigail S. Wexner,*
Chair.; Bill Ingram, Vice-Chair.; Dimon R.
McFerson, Vice-Chair.; Douglas F. Kridler, Pres.;
Raymond J. Biddiscombe, V.P., Fin. and Admin.;
Philip T. Schavone, V.P., Advancement; John B.
Gellach, Jr.; Archie Griffin; David R. Meuse; Ann
Pizzuti; Lewis R. Smoot, Sr.; Ann Isaly Wolfe.
Number of staff: None.
EIN: 311197385

2624
Justin F. Coressel Charitable Trust

c/o Terry L. Melton
101 Clinton St., Ste. 2000
Defiance, OH 43512
Contact: Justin F. Coressel, Dir.
Application address: 500 E. High St., Defiance,
OH 43512, tel.: (419) 782-6677

Established around 1969.
Donor(s): Justin F. Coressel.
Grantmaker type: Independent foundation
Financial data (yr. ended 12/31/02): Assets,
$2,674,689 (M); expenditures, $164,128;
qualifying distributions, $160,708; giving
activities include $162,000 for 20 grants (high:
$50,000; low: $500).
Purpose and activities: Giving primarily for
higher education and religious institutions.
Fields of interest: Higher education;
Animals/wildlife, association; Health care;
Human services; Community development;
Roman Catholic agencies & churches.
Types of support: Building/renovation.
Limitations: Giving primarily in Defiance, OH.
No grants to individuals.
Application information: Application form not
required.
   Deadline(s): None
Director: Justin F. Coressel.
Trustees: Mark Hench; Terry L. Melton; Paul L.
Moser.
EIN: 237022234

2625
The Cotswold Foundation

c/o Fifth Third Bank
38 Fountain Sq. Plz., Trust Tax Dept.,
MD1COM31
Cincinnati, OH 45263   (513) 579-6034
Contact: Stephanie A. Smith, Fdn. Dir.
Application address: Fifth Third Bank, MD
1090CA, Cincinnati, OH, 45263

Established in 1998 in OH.
Donor(s): Beth B. Jones.

Grantmaker type: Independent foundation
Financial data (yr. ended 12/31/02): Assets,
$3,304,824 (M); expenditures, $225,307;
qualifying distributions, $211,490; giving
activities include $207,500 for 12 grants (high:
$30,000; low: $5,000).
Purpose and activities: Giving primarily for the
preservation of wilderness areas, the prevention
of cruelty to animals and to promote the welfare
of children.
Fields of interest: Education; Natural resources;
Animals/wildlife, preservation/protection;
Aquariums.
Types of support: General/operating support.
Limitations: Giving primarily in FL, MT and OH.
No grants to individuals.
Application information:
   Initial approach: Letter
   Deadline(s): None
Trustees: Catherine J. Bournstein; Martha L.
Burchenal; Beth B. Jones; Fifth Third Bank.
EIN: 316611702

2626
James M. Cox, Jr. Foundation, Inc.

4th and Ludlow Sts.
Dayton, OH 45402   (678) 645-0602
Contact: Leigh Ann Launius, Asst. Secy.
Application address: c/o Cox Enterprises, Inc.,
P.O. Box 105720, Atlanta, GA 30348

Established in 1969 in GA.
Donor(s): James M. Cox, Jr.‡
Grantmaker type: Independent foundation
Financial data (yr. ended 12/31/02): Assets,
$43,126,340 (M); expenditures, $2,587,697;
qualifying distributions, $2,448,792; giving
activities include $2,458,500 for 26 grants
(high: $1,750,000; low: $2,000; average:
$2,000–$100,000).
Purpose and activities: Support for
environmental conservation, higher education
(through scholarship program), including
schools of journalism and media
communications, and social services.
Fields of interest: Journalism/publishing; Higher
education; Natural resources; Environment;
Human services.
Types of support: Capital campaigns;
Building/renovation.
Limitations: Giving limited to cities where Cox
Enterprises does business.
Publications: Application guidelines.
Application information: Application form not
required.
   Initial approach: Letter
   Copies of proposal: 3
   Deadline(s): One month before meeting
   Board meeting date(s): Quarterly
Officers and Trustees:* Barbara Cox Anthony,*
Chair.; Timothy W. Hughes,* V.P.; Andrew A.
Merdek, Secy.; John G. Bayette, Treas.; Richard
Braunstein; James Cox Kennedy; Leigh Ann
Launius.
Number of staff: 1 shared staff (shared with
James M. Cox Foundation).
EIN: 237256190

2627
The Davey Company Foundation
1500 N. Mantua St.
P.O. Box 5193
Kent, OH 44240-5193 (330) 673-9511
Contact: David Adante, Pres.
FAX: (330) 673-7089

Established in 1957 in OH.
Donor(s): The Davey Tree Expert Co.
Grantmaker type: Company-sponsored foundation
Financial data (yr. ended 12/31/02): Assets, $701,554 (M); gifts received, $50,000; expenditures, $199,473; qualifying distributions, $185,099; giving activities include $185,099 for 211 grants (high: $3,388; low: $333).
Purpose and activities: Giving primarily for the study of trees.
Fields of interest: College; Environment, forests.
International interests: Canada.
Types of support: General/operating support; Research; Employee matching gifts; Employee-related scholarships.
Limitations: Giving primarily in the U.S.; some giving also in Canada.
Application information: Scholarship grants made only to students who are children of employees of the Davey Tree Expert Co. and who have academic qualifications and financial need. Application form not required.
   Initial approach: Letter
   Copies of proposal: 1
Officers: R. Douglas Cowan, Chair.; David E. Adante, Pres.; Howard Bowles, V.P.; C. Kenneth Celmer, V.P.; Roger C. Funk, V.P.; Richard Ramsey, V.P.; Karl J. Warnke, V.P.; Marjorie L. Conner, Secy.
EIN: 346555132

2628
John and Shirley Davies Foundation
(formerly Bishopric Foundation)
8044 Montgomery Rd., Ste. 163
Cincinnati, OH 45236-2923
Contact: S. John Davies, Jr., Pres.

Established in 1991 in OH.
Donor(s): S. John Davies, Jr., Shirley Davies,‡ Enerfab.
Grantmaker type: Independent foundation
Financial data (yr. ended 12/31/02): Assets, $1,308,486 (M); gifts received, $550,016; expenditures, $924,246; qualifying distributions, $904,655; giving activities include $894,179 for 127 grants (high: $375,000; low: $60).
Purpose and activities: Giving primarily for education and health and human services.
Fields of interest: Arts; Higher education; Animals/wildlife, preservation/protection; Zoos/zoological societies; Health organizations, association.
Types of support: General/operating support; Grants to individuals; Scholarships—to individuals.
Limitations: Giving primarily in Cincinnati, OH.
Application information: Scholarship awards limited to Goshen school district students and are paid directly to the college or university on behalf of the named recipient. Application form not required.
   Initial approach: Letter
   Deadline(s): None

Officers: S. John Davies, Jr., Pres.; Ashley Davies, V.P.; Shirl Moran, Secy.; Darla Davies, Treas.
EIN: 311335126

2629
The Dayton Foundation
2300 Kettering Twr.
Dayton, OH 45423-1395 (937) 222-0410
Contact: Michael M. Parks, Pres.
Toll-free tel.: (877) 222-0410; FAX: (937) 222-0636; E-mail: info@daytonfoundation.org; URL: http://www.daytonfoundation.org

Established in 1921 in OH by resolution and declaration of trust.
Grantmaker type: Community foundation
Financial data (yr. ended 06/30/02): Assets, $214,291,797 (M); gifts received, $60,440,693; expenditures, $64,124,532; giving activities include $28,433,217 for 13,128 grants (high: $2,327,722; low: $25) and $18,023,384 for 594 grants to individuals (high: $10,000; low: $1,000).
Purpose and activities: To assist public charitable, benevolent and educational purposes which benefit local citizens and respond to a wide variety of community needs, including the arts, race relations, social services, and youth as primary areas of interest. Also, to help launch new projects which represent a unique and unduplicated opportunity for the community. The foundation administers donor-advised funds.
Fields of interest: Humanities; Arts; Education; Environment; Health care; Human services; Children/youth, services; Race/intergroup relations.
Types of support: Capital campaigns; Building/renovation; Equipment; Land acquisition; Program development; Publication; Seed money; Technical assistance; Consulting services.
Limitations: Giving limited to the greater Dayton and Miami Valley, OH, area. No support for religious organizations for religious purposes. No grants to individuals (except for specific scholarships and award programs), or for operating budgets, exchange programs, professorships, continuing support, annual campaigns, or deficit financing; no loans or program-related investments. Generally, no endowments.
Publications: Application guidelines, Annual report (including application guidelines), Informational brochure (including application guidelines), Newsletter, Program policy statement.
Application information: Application form required.
   Initial approach: Letter or telephone
   Copies of proposal: 1
   Deadline(s): Jan. 6, Mar. 21, June 20, and Sept. 19
   Board meeting date(s): Mar., June, Sept., and Dec.
   Final notification: 4 to 6 weeks
Officers and Governing Board:* Robert S. Neff,* Chair.; Michael M. Parks, Pres. and Secy.; John N. Taylor, Jr.,* Treas.; Thomas G. Breitenbach; Douglas L. Hawthorne; Franz J. Hoge; Charles A. Jones; Helen Jones-Kelley; Jamie King; Leo Knight, Jr.; Paula J. MacIlwaine; Judy D.

McCormick; Laura Pannier; Douglas Scholz; Fred C. Setzer, Jr.; Fred E. Weber.
Trustees: Bank One Trust Co., N.A.; Fifth Third Bank; KeyBank N.A.; Merrill Lynch Pierce Fenner & Smith; National City Bank; PNC Bank, N.A.
Number of staff: 17 full-time professional; 2 part-time professional; 6 full-time support; 2 part-time support.
EIN: 316027287
Recent environmental and animal welfare grants:
2629-1 Society for the Improvement of Conditions for Stray Animals, Dayton, OH, $25,000. Toward construction of new center in Kettering that will meet ongoing demands for animal care and shelter. 2002.

2630
The Dayton Power and Light Company Foundation
1065 Woodman Dr.
Dayton, OH 45432 (937) 259-7924
Contact: Ginny Strausburg, Exec. Dir.
FAX: (937) 259-7923

Established in 1985 in OH.
Donor(s): The Dayton Power and Light Co.
Grantmaker type: Company-sponsored foundation
Financial data (yr. ended 12/31/02): Assets, $30,492,307 (M); expenditures, $1,833,150; qualifying distributions, $1,138,345; giving activities include $1,111,953 for 73 grants (high: $350,000; low: $500; average: $1,000–$20,000).
Purpose and activities: The foundation makes contributions to charitable and educational organizations that greatly impact the well-being and general welfare of the communities it serves. The majority of the foundation's contributions are made to programs in support of education and charitable activities in communities where Dayton Power and Light people live.
Fields of interest: Museums; Arts; Engineering school/education; Adult education—literacy, basic skills & GED; Reading; Education; Energy; Environment; Health care; Health organizations, association; Human services; Race/intergroup relations; Community development; Engineering; Government/public administration; General charitable giving.
Types of support: General/operating support.
Limitations: Giving primarily in west central OH. No support for fraternal organizations, religious organizations, veterans' organizations, or sports leagues. No grants to individuals, or for endowments, development funds, capital campaigns, college fundraising associations, or hospital operating needs.
Publications: Informational brochure (including application guidelines).
Application information: Application form not required.
   Initial approach: Letter requesting guidelines
   Copies of proposal: 1
   Deadline(s): None
   Board meeting date(s): Quarterly
Officers and Trustees:* Stephen F. Kozair,* Pres.; Judy Wyatt,* Secy.; Caroline E. Muhlenkamp,* Treas.; Virginia M. Strausburg, Exec. Dir.; Peter H. Forster*; Allen M. Hill*.

Number of staff: 1 full-time professional.
EIN: 311138883

2631
Deupree Family Foundation
1242 E. Lytle-Five Points Rd.
Dayton, OH 45458
Contact: Caleb T. Deupree, Treas.
E-mail: Ctdeupree@sbcglobal.net

Established in 2000 in OH.
Donor(s): Ann T. Deupree.
Grantmaker type: Independent foundation
Financial data (yr. ended 06/30/02): Assets, $2,814,164 (M); expenditures, $161,759; qualifying distributions, $134,452; giving activities include $134,856 for 14 grants (high: $22,000; low: $1,000).
Fields of interest: History/archaeology; Environment; Hospitals (general); Employment; Parks/playgrounds; Children/youth, services; Christian agencies & churches.
Types of support: General/operating support; Program development.
Limitations: Giving on a national basis.
Application information: Application form required.
  Initial approach: Letter
  Copies of proposal: 5
  Deadline(s): May 1
  Board meeting date(s): June annually
  Final notification: By July 15
Officers and Trustees:* Ann T. Deupree,* Pres.; Susan D. Jones,* V.P.; Thomas R. Deupree,* Secy.; Caleb T. Deupree,* Treas.; Richard R. Deupree III.
EIN: 311746946

2632
Dominion East Ohio Corporate Giving Program
(formerly The East Ohio Gas Company Contributions Program)
P.O. Box 5759
Cleveland, OH 44101-0759 (216) 736-6503
Contact: Theresa C. Bishop, Sr. Philanthropy Coord.
FAX: (216) 736-5385; E-mail: terry_c_bishop@dom.com

Grantmaker type: Corporate giving program
Purpose and activities: Dominion East Ohio makes charitable contributions to nonprofit organizations involved with arts and culture, education, the environment, health and human services, and community development. Support is given primarily in areas of company operations.
Fields of interest: Arts; Education; Environment; Health care; Human services; Economic development; Community development.
Types of support: General/operating support; Employee volunteer services; Sponsorships; Employee matching gifts; In-kind gifts.
Limitations: Giving primarily in areas of company operations. No support for political, religious, fraternal, labor, or advocacy organizations. No grants to individuals, or for advertising.
Publications: Application guidelines, Program policy statement.

Application information: The Corporate Philanthropy Department handles giving. Application form not required.
  Initial approach: Proposal to headquarters
  Copies of proposal: 1
  Deadline(s): None
  Final notification: Following review
Number of staff: 1 full-time professional; 1 full-time support.

2633
Helen G., Henry F. & Louise T. Dornette Foundation
c/o Fifth Third Bank
38 Fountain Sq. Plz., Dept. 00858
Cincinnati, OH 45263

Established in 1991 in OH.
Donor(s): Helen G. Dornette.‡
Grantmaker type: Independent foundation
Financial data (yr. ended 03/31/02): Assets, $14,166,602 (M); gifts received, $2,713,916; expenditures, $698,977; qualifying distributions, $634,760; giving activities include $607,500 for 21 grants (high: $100,000; low: $7,500).
Fields of interest: Media/communications; Museums; Arts; Botanical gardens; Zoos/zoological societies; Health organizations, association; Human services; American Red Cross; Salvation Army.
Limitations: Applications not accepted. Giving primarily in OH. No grants to individuals.
Application information: Contributes only to pre-selected organizations.
Trustee: Fifth Third Bank.
EIN: 316425317

2634
The Cyrus Eaton Foundation
24200 Chagrin Blvd., Ste. 233
Beachwood, OH 44122-5531 (216) 360-9550
Contact: Henry W. Gulick, Treas.
FAX: (216) 464-6647; URL: http://www.deepcove.org

Established in 1955 in DE.
Grantmaker type: Independent foundation
Financial data (yr. ended 12/31/01): Assets, $3,702,842 (M); expenditures, $255,935; qualifying distributions, $203,022; giving activities include $177,300 for 52 grants (high: $15,000; low: $750).
Purpose and activities: Giving primarily for Cleveland-based, little-known or supported cultural programs, public affairs, social services, and international peace studies (through support of the Pugwash Conferences of Scientists); limited support also for ecological and environmental programs.
Fields of interest: Arts; Education; Natural resources; Environment; Human services; International peace/security; Community development; Public affairs.
International interests: Canada.
Types of support: General/operating support; Endowments; Program development; Seed money.
Limitations: Giving primarily in OH, with emphasis on Cleveland. No support for municipalities or organizations lacking 501(c)(3) status. No grants to individuals, or for tickets or tables for events.

Application information: Application form required.
  Initial approach: Cover letter no more than 2 pages
  Copies of proposal: 1
  Deadline(s): May 1 and Nov. 1
  Board meeting date(s): Oct.
  Final notification: Following board meeting
Officers and Trustees:* Raymond Szabo,* Pres.; Mary Stephens Eaton,* V.P.; Alice J. Gulick,* V.P.; Ralph P. Higgins,* Secy.; Henry W. Gulick,* Treas.; Barring Coughlin; Catherine I. Eaton.
Number of staff: 1 part-time support.
EIN: 237440277

2635
Elisha-Bolton Foundation
c/o Advisory Svcs., Inc.
1422 Euclid Ave., 1010 Hanna Bldg.
Cleveland, OH 44115-2078
Contact: James C. Sekerak, Treas.

Established in 1986 in OH.
Donor(s): Betsy Bolton Schafer.
Grantmaker type: Independent foundation
Financial data (yr. ended 12/31/02): Assets, $3,770,411 (M); expenditures, $308,461; qualifying distributions, $265,533; giving activities include $254,000 for 57 grants (high: $20,000; low: $500).
Purpose and activities: Emphasis on health, higher education, and Christian religious organizations; support also for disaster relief.
Fields of interest: Visual arts; Performing arts; Elementary/secondary education; Higher education; Natural resources; Environment; Health care; Health organizations, association; Federated giving programs; Christian agencies & churches; Religion.
Types of support: General/operating support; Continuing support; Annual campaigns; Program development; Scholarship funds.
Limitations: No grants to individuals.
Application information: Application form not required.
  Initial approach: Proposal
  Copies of proposal: 1
  Deadline(s): None
  Board meeting date(s): Aug.
Officers and Trustees:* Betsy Bolton Schafer,* Pres.; Kenneth G. Hochman,* V.P.; Gilbert P. Schafer III,* V.P.; Paulette Kitko, Secy.; James C. Sekerak, Treas.
Number of staff: None.
EIN: 341500135

2636
John F. and Doris E. Ernsthausen Charitable Foundation
c/o Citizens National Bank
12 E. Main St.
Norwalk, OH 44857-1542
Contact: Frederick F. Waugh
Application address: 13 E. Main St., Ste. B, Norwalk, OH 44857, tel.: (419) 668-2067

Trust established in 1956 in OH.
Donor(s): John F. Ernsthausen, Doris E. Ernsthausen.
Grantmaker type: Independent foundation
Financial data (yr. ended 06/30/02): Assets, $7,282,393 (M); expenditures, $1,516,349;

qualifying distributions, $1,450,456; giving activities include $1,451,730 for 10 grants (high: $1,229,130; low: $1,000).
Purpose and activities: Giving primarily for a United Methodist church, and education.
Fields of interest: Historic preservation/historical societies; Elementary/secondary education; Higher education; Animal welfare; Housing/shelter, development; Human services; Federated giving programs; Protestant agencies & churches; Aging.
Limitations: Giving primarily in OH. No loans or program-related investments.
Application information: Application form not required.
   Deadline(s): None
Trustee: Citizens Banking Corp.
EIN: 346501908

2637
The Fairfax Foundation
29425 Chagrin Blvd., Ste. 203
Pepper Pike, OH 44122
Contact: Gerald A. Conway, Tr.; Kevin C. Conway, Tr.; or Martine V. Conway, Tr.
Application address: 30195 Chagrin Blvd., Ste. 350W., Cleveland, OH 44124

Established in 1986 in OH.
Donor(s): Gerald A. Conway, Martine V. Conway.
Grantmaker type: Independent foundation
Financial data (yr. ended 12/31/02): Assets, $2,224,664 (M); gifts received, $510; expenditures, $203,949; qualifying distributions, $161,015; giving activities include $162,600 for 23 grants (high: $35,000; low: $100).
Purpose and activities: Giving for environmental protection, religion and education.
Fields of interest: Education; Environment, forests; Brain research; Human services; International affairs; Christian agencies & churches; General charitable giving.
International interests: Central America.
Types of support: Annual campaigns; Capital campaigns; Research; Matching/challenge support.
Limitations: Giving primarily in OH. No grants to individuals.
Application information: Contributes primarily to pre-selected organizations. Application form required.
   Initial approach: Telephone
   Copies of proposal: 1
   Deadline(s): None
   Board meeting date(s): Varies
   Final notification: 2 months
Officer and Trustees:* Gerald A. Conway,* Chair.; Gerald A. Conway, Jr.; Kevin C. Conway; Martine V. Conway.
Number of staff: 1 part-time professional.
EIN: 341553708

2638
Richard J. Fasenmyer Foundation
c/o Lawrence N. Schultz
3875 Embassy Pkwy.
Fairlawn, OH 44333-8330

Established in 1989 in OH.
Donor(s): RJF International Corp.

Grantmaker type: Independent foundation
Financial data (yr. ended 12/31/02): Assets, $446,714 (M); gifts received, $301,020; expenditures, $336,362; qualifying distributions, $335,000; giving activities include $335,000 for 9 grants (high: $150,000; low: $5,000).
Fields of interest: Performing arts centers; Arts; Higher education; Animal welfare; Health care, clinics/centers; Health organizations, association; Human services.
Types of support: General/operating support.
Limitations: Applications not accepted. Giving primarily in Cleveland, OH; some funding in University Park, PA, and Fort Lauderdale, FL. No grants to individuals.
Application information: Contributes only to pre-selected organizations.
Officers and Trustees:* Richard J. Fasenmyer,* Pres. and Treas.; Haven J. Hood,* V.P. and Secy.; John L. Baechle; James Berlin; Walter R. Collins, Jr.; Gordon Hartnett; Lawrence N. Schultz.
EIN: 341627457

2639
Leonard C. & Mildred F. Ferguson Foundation
c/o FirstMerit Bank, N.A.
121 S. Main St., Ste. 200
Akron, OH 44308   (330) 384-7304
Contact: Joseph Wojcik

Established in 1998 in FL.
Donor(s): Mildred F. Ferguson Irrevocable Trust.
Grantmaker type: Independent foundation
Financial data (yr. ended 01/31/03): Assets, $11,058,411 (M); expenditures, $555,610; qualifying distributions, $521,173; giving activities include $509,740 for 21 grants (high: $75,000; low: $400).
Purpose and activities: Giving primarily for education, medicine, social welfare, historic preservation, religion, the environment, and the arts.
Fields of interest: Museums (specialized); Historic preservation/historical societies; Arts; Theological school/education; Education; Natural resources; Hospitals (general); Human services; Youth, services; Community development; Science, single organization support; Christian agencies & churches.
Types of support: Annual campaigns; Capital campaigns; Building/renovation; Land acquisition; Program development; Seed money; Scholarship funds; Matching/challenge support.
Limitations: Giving primarily in FL, IL, and in home territory where board members live (CA, ME and VT). No grants to individuals.
Application information: Application form not required.
   Initial approach: Letter
   Deadline(s): None
   Board meeting date(s): Last week of July
Officers and Directors:* Nancy Seeley,* Pres.; Lynne Seeley,* V.P.
Trustee: FirstMerit Bank, N.A.
Number of staff: None.
EIN: 656245247

2640
The Ferry Family Foundation
1422 Euclid Ave., Ste. 1030
Cleveland, OH 44115-2001

Established in 2002 in OH.
Grantmaker type: Independent foundation
Financial data (yr. ended 12/31/02): Assets, $4,682,272 (M); gifts received, $5,085,943; expenditures, $172,111; qualifying distributions, $158,702; giving activities include $155,350 for 16 grants (high: $25,000; low: $600).
Purpose and activities: Giving primarily for education, human services, and Christian and Methodist churches.
Fields of interest: Higher education; Law school/education; Botanical gardens; Human services; Christian agencies & churches; Protestant agencies & churches.
Limitations: Applications not accepted. Giving primarily in OH. No grants to individuals.
Application information: Contributes only to pre-selected organizations.
Trustees: Carolyn P. Ferry; Richard Ferry; Carroll Wiener.
EIN: 326000096

2641
Firman Fund
c/o H & I Advisors
1422 Euclid Ave., 1030 Hanna Bldg.
Cleveland, OH 44115-2078   (216) 363-1030
Contact: Royal Firman, III, Pres.

Incorporated in 1951 in OH.
Donor(s): Pamela H. Firman.‡
Grantmaker type: Independent foundation
Financial data (yr. ended 12/31/02): Assets, $10,256,239 (M); expenditures, $565,213; qualifying distributions, $502,209; giving activities include $493,000 for 24 grants (high: $150,000; low: $500; average: $100–$50,000).
Purpose and activities: Giving primarily for the arts, education, health care, the environment, and human services.
Fields of interest: Performing arts; Arts; Secondary school/education; Higher education; Natural resources; Health care; Human services; Government/public administration.
Types of support: General/operating support; Annual campaigns; Capital campaigns; Building/renovation; Scholarship funds.
Limitations: Applications not accepted. Giving primarily in Denver, CO, Tallahassee, FL, Thomasville, GA, and Cleveland, OH. No grants to individuals, or for research; no loans.
Application information: Unsolicited requests for funds not accepted.
   Board meeting date(s): Apr. and Nov.
Officers and Trustees:* Royal Firman III, Pres.; Cynthia F. Webster,* V.P.; Neil A. Brown, Secy.; Carole M. Nowak, Treas.; Stephanie Firman; Robert Webster, Jr.
EIN: 346513655

2642
FirstEnergy Foundation
(formerly Centerior Energy Foundation)
76 S. Main St.
Akron, OH 44308-1890 (330) 761-4246
Contact: Donna Valentine, Dir.
URL: http://www.firstenergycorp.com/community

Incorporated in 1961 in OH.
Donor(s): The Cleveland Electric Illuminating
Co., Centerior Energy Corp., FirstEnergy Corp.,
The Toledo Edison Co., G.P.O. Service Co.,
Met-Ed, JCP&L, Ohio Edison Co., Penelec.
Grantmaker type: Company-sponsored
foundation
Financial data (yr. ended 12/31/02): Assets,
$51,472,660 (M); expenditures, $4,515,528;
qualifying distributions, $4,511,032; giving
activities include $4,462,670 for 733 grants
(high: $484,650; average: $500–$50,000).
Purpose and activities: Emphasis on qualifying
nonprofit organizations in health and human
services, civic, cultural, or educational
endeavors; support also for community funds;
giving generally within the corporation's service
area. The foundation priorities are to ensure the
safety and health of the community, to promote
economic development, to advance
professional development, and to support
employee involvement and investment.
Fields of interest: Museums; Arts; Environment;
Higher education; Crime/law enforcement;
Human services; Federated giving programs.
Types of support: Annual campaigns; Capital
campaigns; Building/renovation; Program
development; Curriculum development;
Employee matching gifts; Matching/challenge
support.
Limitations: Giving limited to areas served in NJ,
OH, and PA. Generally, no grants to individuals,
or for deficit financing, research, equipment,
scholarships, or fellowships; no gifts to other
foundations; no loans.
Publications: Informational brochure, Program
policy statement.
Application information: Application form not
required.
  Initial approach: 1- to 2-page letter; via E-mail
    in 2004
  Copies of proposal: 1
  Deadline(s): None
  Board meeting date(s): Contributions
    Committee meets as needed
  Final notification: 12 to 16 weeks
Officer and Trustees:* Mary Beth Carroll,* Pres.;
H. Peter Burg; Charles E. Jones; Richard Marsh;
Leila Vespoli.
Number of staff: None.
EIN: 346514181

2643
The Fleischmann Foundation
4001 Carew Tower
441 Vine St., Ste. 4001
Cincinnati, OH 45202 (513) 621-1384
Contact: Charles Fleischmann III, Pres.

Incorporated in 1931 in OH.
Donor(s): Julius Fleischmann.‡
Grantmaker type: Independent foundation
Financial data (yr. ended 12/31/02): Assets,
$2,607,331 (M); expenditures, $158,209;
qualifying distributions, $144,326; giving

activities include $145,743 for 22 grants (high:
$41,000; low: $100).
Purpose and activities: Emphasis on arts and the
humanities, especially support for museums and
historic preservation.
Fields of interest: Museums; Museums (history);
Historic preservation/historical societies; Arts;
Natural resources; Foundations (community).
Types of support: General/operating support.
Limitations: Giving primarily in OH. No grants
to individuals.
Application information:
  Deadline(s): None
Officers: Charles Fleischmann III, Pres. and
Treas.; Eric B. Yeiser, V.P.; Blair S. Fleischmann,
Secy.
Trustee: Noah Fleischmann.
EIN: 316025516

2644
The Foster Family Foundation
c/o National City Bank
P.O. Box 94651
Cleveland, OH 44101-4651
Contact: Bonita Rowbotham
Application address: c/o National City Bank,
P.O. Box 5756, Cleveland, OH 44101-0756,
tel.: (216) 575-2420

Established in 1992 in OH.
Donor(s): The Clyde T. and Lyla C. Foster
Foundation.
Grantmaker type: Independent foundation
Financial data (yr. ended 12/31/02): Assets,
$1,525,779 (M); expenditures, $317,248;
qualifying distributions, $291,391; giving
activities include $291,018 for 141 grants (high:
$35,934; low: $50).
Fields of interest: Performing arts; Arts; Higher
education; Natural resources; Botanical gardens;
Alcoholism; Human services; Women,
centers/services; Federated giving programs;
Women.
Types of support: General/operating support.
Limitations: Giving primarily in OH and WI.
Application information:
  Initial approach: Letter
  Deadline(s): None
Trustees: Byron T. Foster; Coleman A. Foster.
Agent: National City Bank.
EIN: 346968228

2645
Friedlander Family Fund
36 E. 4th St., Ste. 400
Cincinnati, OH 45202-3810
Contact: Melissa LaCorte, Secy.-Treas.

Established in 1968 in OH.
Donor(s): William A. Friedlander, Susan S.
Friedlander, Jane K. Steinfirst,‡ Ellen Friedlander.
Grantmaker type: Independent foundation
Financial data (yr. ended 12/31/02): Assets,
$2,891,551 (M); gifts received, $59,784;
expenditures, $144,060; qualifying distributions,
$129,817; giving activities include $130,870 for
123 grants (high: $55,000; low: $50; average:
$50–$5,000).
Purpose and activities: Giving to Jewish
organizations, art and cultural organizations,
environmental and wildlife conservation,

education, and health, family and human
services.
Fields of interest: Arts; Education; Environment;
Human services; Jewish federated giving
programs.
Types of support: General/operating support.
Limitations: Giving limited to the greater
Cincinnati, OH, area. No grants to individuals.
Application information: Application form not
required.
  Initial approach: 1-page letter
  Copies of proposal: 1
  Deadline(s): None
  Board meeting date(s): Mar., June, Sept. and
    Dec.
Officers: William A. Friedlander, Pres.; Susan S.
Friedlander, V.P.; Melissa M. LaCorte, Secy.-Treas.
Number of staff: 1 part-time support.
EIN: 316023791

2646
The Gale Foundation
c/o T.F. Allen
20325 Center Ridge Rd., Ste. 629
Rocky River, OH 44116 (440) 331-8220

Established in 1995 in OH.
Donor(s): Elizabeth B. Blossom, The William
Bingham Foundation.
Grantmaker type: Independent foundation
Financial data (yr. ended 12/31/02): Assets,
$5,221,534 (M); expenditures, $309,915;
qualifying distributions, $297,115; giving
activities include $285,000 for 13 grants (high:
$70,000; low: $1,000).
Purpose and activities: Giving primarily to a
Christian church, as well as for natural resource
conservation, health care, education, and
human services.
Fields of interest: Secondary school/education;
Natural resources; Reproductive health, prenatal
care; Health care; Human services; Christian
agencies & churches.
Types of support: General/operating support;
Capital campaigns; Building/renovation; Land
acquisition.
Limitations: Applications not accepted. Giving
primarily in Brunswick, GA, and VA; some
funding also in Prescott, AZ. No grants to
individuals.
Application information: Contributes only to
pre-selected organizations. Unsolicited requests
for funds not accepted.
Officers and Trustees:* Benjamin Gale,* Pres.;
Deborah B. Gale,* V.P.; Thomas F. Allen,
Secy.-Treas.; Charles L. Freer; Deborah G. Freer;
Mary B. Gale; Thomas V. Gale.
EIN: 341812999

2647
The George Foundation
P.O. Box 21609
Columbus, OH 43221-0609
Contact: Jack George, Pres.

Established in 1982 in OH.
Donor(s): Kaplan Trucking Co., Noel George
Trust.
Grantmaker type: Independent foundation
Financial data (yr. ended 12/31/02): Assets,
$3,963,693 (M); gifts received, $68,214;
expenditures, $227,802; qualifying distributions,

$223,851; giving activities include $226,045 for 71 grants (high: $86,850; low: $25).
Purpose and activities: Emphasis on higher education; some support also for environmental issues and museums and other cultural programs.
Fields of interest: Museums; Arts; Higher education; Environment.
Limitations: Giving on a national basis, with some emphasis on Columbus, OH.
Application information: Application form not required.
Initial approach: Letter
Deadline(s): None
Officers: Jack George,* Pres.; Joan George,* Secy.-Treas.
Trustees: Carol George; Sarah George.
EIN: 311030194

2648
The Gettler Family Foundation
30 Garfield Pl., Ste. 1000
Cincinnati, OH 45202 (513) 621-2850
Contact: Benjamin Gettler, Chair.

Established in 1993 in OH.
Donor(s): Benjamin Gettler.
Grantmaker type: Independent foundation
Financial data (yr. ended 02/28/03): Assets, $925,588 (M); gifts received, $157,884; expenditures, $119,959; qualifying distributions, $116,878; giving activities include $116,878 for 113 grants (high: $44,283; low: $10).
Purpose and activities: Giving primarily for education, conservation, and to Jewish organizations.
Fields of interest: Natural resources; Human services; Jewish federated giving programs; Public affairs; Jewish agencies & temples.
Types of support: General/operating support.
Application information:
Initial approach: Proposal
Deadline(s): None
Officers: Benjamin Gettler, Chair. and Treas.; Delian A. Gettler, Pres. and Secy.; Benjamin R. Gettler, V.P.
Trustee: Thomas D. Gettler.
EIN: 311374350

2649
Walter L. Gross, Jr. Family Foundation
9435 Waterstone Blvd., Ste. 390
Cincinnati, OH 45249 (513) 785-6060
Contact: Jeffrey H. Gross, Tr.

Established in 1997 in OH.
Donor(s): Walter L. Gross, Jr.
Grantmaker type: Independent foundation
Financial data (yr. ended 12/31/02): Assets, $2,561,534 (M); expenditures, $162,277; qualifying distributions, $151,250; giving activities include $151,050 for 20 grants (high: $16,250; low: $1,000).
Purpose and activities: Giving primarily for religion, education, medical and community projects.
Fields of interest: Arts; Higher education; Education; Environment; Animals/wildlife; Health care; Human services; Christian agencies & churches.
Types of support: General/operating support.

Limitations: Giving primarily in the greater Cincinnati, OH, area. No grants to individuals.
Application information: Application form required.
Initial approach: Letter
Deadline(s): None
Trustees: Barbara Gross; Jeffrey H. Gross; Sandra L. Gross; Walter L. Gross III.
EIN: 311571716

2650
The George Gund Foundation ▼
1845 Guildhall Bldg.
45 Prospect Ave., W.
Cleveland, OH 44115-1018 (216) 241-3114
Contact: David Abbott, Exec. Dir.
FAX: (216) 241-6560; URL: http://www.gundfdn.org

Incorporated in 1952 in OH.
Donor(s): George Gund.‡
Grantmaker type: Independent foundation
Financial data (yr. ended 12/31/02): Assets, $397,249,175 (M); expenditures, $21,793,484; qualifying distributions, $21,576,909; giving activities include $19,707,748 for 528 grants (high: $2,000,000; low: $1,000; average: $10,000–$50,000) and $150,000 for 1 loan/program-related investment.
Purpose and activities: Priority to education projects, with emphasis on new concepts and methods of teaching and learning, and on increasing educational opportunities for the disadvantaged; programs advancing economic revitalization and job creation; projects promoting neighborhood development; projects for improving human services, employment opportunities, housing for minority and low-income groups; support also for ecology, civic affairs, and the arts. Preference is given to pilot projects and innovative programs which present prospects for broad replication.
Fields of interest: Arts; Education, research; Early childhood education; Elementary school/education; Secondary school/education; Higher education; Education; Natural resources; Environment; AIDS; AIDS research; Crime/law enforcement; Employment; Housing/shelter, development; Human services; Children/youth, services; Women, centers/services; Minorities/immigrants, centers/services; Race/intergroup relations; Urban/community development; Community development; Government/public administration; Public affairs; Minorities; Women; Economically disadvantaged.
Types of support: General/operating support; Continuing support; Land acquisition; Emergency funds; Program development; Conferences/seminars; Publication; Seed money; Internship funds; Scholarship funds; Research; Technical assistance; Program-related investments/loans; Matching/challenge support.
Limitations: Giving primarily in northeastern OH and the greater Cleveland, OH, area. No support for political groups, services for the physically, mentally or developmentally disabled, or the elderly. Generally, no grants to individuals, or for building or endowment funds, political campaigns, debt reduction, equipment, renovation projects, or to fund benefit events.
Publications: Application guidelines, Annual report (including application guidelines), Grants

list, Informational brochure (including application guidelines).
Application information: Proposals sent by FAX not considered. Please do not submit proposals in notebooks, binders, or plastic folders. Application form not required.
Initial approach: Proposal (including 1-page cover letter)
Copies of proposal: 1
Deadline(s): Mar. 30, June 30, Sept. 30, and Dec. 30
Board meeting date(s): Mar., June, Sept., and Dec.
Final notification: 8 weeks
Officers and Trustees:* Geoffrey Gund,* Pres. and Treas.; Llura A. Gund,* V.P.; Ann L. Gund,* Secy.; David Abbott, Exec. Dir.; Marjorie M. Carlson; Catherine Gund; George Gund III; Zachary Gund; Robert D. Storey.
Number of staff: 6 full-time professional; 5 full-time support.
EIN: 346519769
Recent environmental and animal welfare grants:
2650-1 American Farmland Trust, DC, $70,000. For Ohio office operating support. 2002.
2650-2 Audubon Society, National, New York, NY, $48,000. For bird conservation programs in Ohio. 2002.
2650-3 Buckeye Environmental Network, Grove City, OH, $30,000. For People Power project. 2002.
2650-4 Buckeye Forest Council, The Plains, OH, $25,000. For forest protection on public land. 2002.
2650-5 Center for Health, Environment and Justice, Falls Church, VA, $40,000. For Stop Dioxin Exposure Campaign. 2002.
2650-6 Center for Public Interest Research, Boston, MA, $25,000. For project to ban oil and gas drilling in Lake Erie. 2002.
2650-7 Chagrin River Watershed Partners, Willoughby, OH, $40,000. For operating support. 2002.
2650-8 Clean Air Conservancy, Cleveland Heights, OH, $50,000. For Cleveland ozone database project. 2002.
2650-9 Cleveland Botanical Garden, Cleveland, OH, $100,000. For School Garden Outreach Program. 2002.
2650-10 Cleveland Metroparks System, Cleveland, OH, $50,000. For planning for greenway along the east branch of the Rocky River. 2002.
2650-11 Cleveland Tomorrow, Cleveland, OH, $125,000. For public engagement in Lakefront highway quieting and land use planning. 2002.
2650-12 Cuyahoga Countryside Conservancy, Hudson, OH, $45,000. For reestablishment of farmsteads in Cuyahoga Valley National Park. 2002.
2650-13 Cuyahoga River Community Planning Organization, Cleveland, OH, $25,000. For operating support. 2002.
2650-14 Cuyahoga Valley Environmental Education Center, Peninsula, OH, $85,000. For establishment of Cuyahoga Valley National Park Association. 2002.
2650-15 Delta Institute, Chicago, IL, $45,000. For Lake Erie Fish Consumption Advisory project. 2002.
2650-16 Earth Day Coalition, Cleveland, OH, $120,000. For operating support. 2002.

2650-17 Earth Day Coalition, Cleveland, OH, $30,000. For Northeast Ohio Student Environmental Congress. 2002.

2650-18 EcoCity Cleveland, Cleveland Heights, OH, $110,000. For Building the Livable Urban Edge (BLUE) Project. 2002.

2650-19 EcoCity Cleveland, Cleveland Heights, OH, $65,000. For operating support. 2002.

2650-20 Ecological Design Innovation Center, Oberlin, OH, $15,000. For Northern Ohio Foodshed Alliance. 2002.

2650-21 Environmental and Energy Study Institute, DC, $40,000. For policymaker briefings on energy and smart growth. 2002.

2650-22 Environmental Fund for Ohio, Columbus, OH, $35,000. For operating support through Nonprofit Capacity-Building Initiative. 2002.

2650-23 Environmental Health Watch, Cleveland, OH, $100,000. For Healthy Indoor Environments for Children project. 2002.

2650-24 Environmental Law Institute, DC, $25,000. For federal and state policy research on invasive species control. 2002.

2650-25 Environmental Support Center, DC, $40,000. For operating support. 2002.

2650-26 Environmental Working Group, DC, $45,000. For lead poisoning program in Ohio. 2002.

2650-27 Friends of the Crooked River, Peninsula, OH, $15,000. For organizational planning. 2002.

2650-28 Grand River Partners, Painesville, OH, $30,000. For operating support. 2002.

2650-29 Great Lakes United, Buffalo, NY, $50,000. For Habitat and Biodiversity Task Force. 2002.

2650-30 Green Energy Ohio, Columbus, OH, $25,000. For operating support. 2002.

2650-31 Greene Environmental Coalition, Yellow Springs, OH, $35,000. For Cleanup 2000 Project. 2002.

2650-32 Heartwood, Inc., Bloomington, Indiana, $20,000. For operating support. 2002.

2650-33 Historic Gateway Neighborhood Corporation, Cleveland, OH, $48,000. For commercial and residential development initiatives. 2002.

2650-34 Institute for Conservation Leadership, Takoma Park, MD, $100,000. For Great Lakes Executive Director Training Program. 2002.

2650-35 International Center for the Preservation of Wild Animals, Cumberland, OH, $96,000. For Center for Restoration Ecology. 2002.

2650-36 Lake Erie Nature and Science Center, Bay Village, OH, $20,000. For Resource Center specialist. 2002.

2650-37 Land Trust Alliance, DC, $45,000. For Ohio land trust training and technical assistance. 2002.

2650-38 League of Conservation Voters Education Fund, DC, $50,000. For list enhancement, Soap Project, coalition building, and leadership development in Ohio. 2002.

2650-39 Mid-Ohio Regional Planning Commission, Columbus, OH, $47,067. For policymaker education on smart growth in Ohio. 2002.

2650-40 National Wildlife Federation, Reston, VA, $40,000. For Great Lakes Mercury Phase-out Project. 2002.

2650-41 Natural Resources Council of America, DC, $20,000. For Leadership Roundtable. 2002.

2650-42 North Cuyahoga Valley Corridor, Cleveland, OH, $40,000. For National Heritage Corridor improvements. 2002.

2650-43 Ohio and Erie Canal Corridor Coalition, Akron, OH, $46,000. For operating support. 2002.

2650-44 Ohio League of Conservation Voters Education Fund, Columbus, OH, $50,000. For operating support through Nonprofit Capacity-Building Initiative. 2002.

2650-45 Ohio Parklands Foundation, Columbus, OH, $50,000. For Ohio Greenways project. 2002.

2650-46 Ohio River Advocacy, Cincinnati, OH, $25,000. For Ohio River basin conservation coordination and technical assistance. 2002.

2650-47 Ohio State University Research Foundation, Columbus, OH, $50,000. For urban gardening program. 2002.

2650-48 ParkWorks, Cleveland, OH, $60,000. For program support. 2002.

2650-49 ParkWorks, Cleveland, OH, $15,000. For junior community parks liaisons/Showagon Performing Arts Troupe. 2002.

2650-50 River Network, Portland, Oregon, $30,000. For National River Rally scholarships for Great Lakes river conservation activists and for Clean Water Act online tutorial project. 2002.

2650-51 Rivers Unlimited-Mill Creek Restoration Project, Cincinnati, OH, $25,000. For Ohio Environmental Enforcement Campaign. 2002.

2650-52 Safe Energy Communication Council, DC, $40,000. For operating support. 2002.

2650-53 Saint Clair-Superior Neighborhood Development Association, Cleveland, OH, $35,000. For Environmental Issues Organizing Project. 2002.

2650-54 Second Growth Institute, Chagrin Falls, OH, $30,000. For Five Points Redevelopment Project in Collinwood. 2002.

2650-55 Shorebank Enterprise Group Cleveland, Cleveland, OH, $25,000. For Entrepreneurs for Sustainability. 2002.

2650-56 Sierra Club, San Francisco, CA, $30,000. For Great Lakes Clean Air Program in Ohio. 2002.

2650-57 Surface Transportation Policy Project (STPP), DC, $50,000. For Smart Growth America. 2002.

2650-58 Trust for Public Land, San Francisco, CA, $50,000. For Ohio office operating support. 2002.

2650-59 Union of Concerned Scientists, Cambridge, MA, $25,000. For federal policy research and education on invasive species control. 2002.

2650-60 University of Michigan, Ann Arbor, MI, $25,000. For Great Lakes Radio Consortium training for environmental journalists. 2002.

2650-61 University of Vermont, Burlington, VT, $30,000. For Earth Shareholders Report. 2002.

2650-62 Water Watch of Oregon, Portland, Oregon, $25,000. For operating support. 2002.

2650-63 West Creek Preservation Committee, Parma, OH, $50,000. For operating support. 2002.

2650-64 Western Reserve RC & D, Painesville, OH, $60,000. For Countryside Program to promote residential conservation development. 2002.

2650-65 Western Reserve RC & D, Painesville, OH, $48,000. For Center for Farmland Preservation in Northeast Ohio. 2002.

2650-66 Wildlife Habitat Council, Silver Spring, MD, $20,000. For Cuyahoga Valley Partnership program to restore habitat on corporate land. 2002.

2651
H.C.S. Foundation ▼
1801 E. 9th St., Ste. 1035
Cleveland, OH 44114-3103 (216) 781-3502
Contact: Trustees

Trust established in 1959 in OH.
Donor(s): Harold C. Schott.‡
Grantmaker type: Independent foundation
Financial data (yr. ended 12/31/02): Assets, $77,561,178 (M); expenditures, $4,584,503; qualifying distributions, $4,345,529; giving activities include $4,059,200 for 31 grants (high: $500,000; low: $2,500; average: $5,000–$150,000).
Purpose and activities: Grants primarily for health care, higher education, the arts, a botanical garden, and the United Way.
Fields of interest: Arts; Higher education; Botanical gardens; Hospitals (general); Health care; Human services; Federated giving programs; Roman Catholic agencies & churches.
Types of support: General/operating support; Capital campaigns; Building/renovation; Endowments; Program development; Scholarship funds.
Limitations: Giving limited to OH. No grants to individuals.
Application information: Application form not required.
  Initial approach: Letter
  Copies of proposal: 1
  Deadline(s): None
Trustees: Francie S. Hiltz; L. Thomas Hiltz; Betty Jane Mulcahy; William Dunne Saal; Milton B. Schott, Jr.
Number of staff: 1 full-time professional.
EIN: 346514235
Recent environmental and animal welfare grants:

2651-1 Cleveland Botanical Garden, Cleveland, OH, $500,000. Toward additions and renovations for construction of Environmental Education Center. 2002.

2651-2 Cleveland Zoological Society, Cleveland, OH, $50,000. Toward new Center for Zoological Medicine to create world-class facility for care of rare and endangered species. 2002.

2651-3 Great Lakes Museum of Science, Environment and Technology, Cleveland, OH, $50,000. For Education Sponsorship for China: 7,000 years of Discovery, showcasing historical, astronomy, navigation, medicine and porcelain exhibits. 2002.

2652
Carol Ann and Ralph V. Haile, Jr. Foundation, Inc.
c/o U.S. Bank, N.A.
P.O. Box 1118
Cincinnati, OH 45201-1118

Established in 1997 in OH.
Donor(s): Carol Ann Haile, Ralph V. Haile, Jr.
Grantmaker type: Independent foundation
Financial data (yr. ended 12/31/02): Assets, $326,704 (M); gifts received, $650,000; expenditures, $650,216; qualifying distributions, $649,956; giving activities include $650,000 for 17 grants (high: $500,000; low: $1,000).
Purpose and activities: Giving primarily for higher and other education, health and human services, federated giving programs and for art and cultural programs.
Fields of interest: Education; Zoos/zoological societies; Hospitals (general); Cancer; Human services; Federated giving programs.
Limitations: Applications not accepted. Giving primarily in KY and OH. No grants to individuals.
Application information: Contributes only to pre-selected organizations. Unsolicited requests for funds not accepted.
Officers: Carol Ann Haile, Pres.; Ralph V. Haile, Jr., V.P.; Jennie P. Carlson, Secy.
Trustees: Jerry A. Grundhofer; Timothy J. Maloney; David M. Moffett.
EIN: 311492387

2653
Haskell Fund
c/o Advisory Svcs., Inc.
1422 Euclid Ave., 1010 Hanna Bldg.
Cleveland, OH 44115-2078 (216) 363-6481
Contact: James Sekerak, Treas.

Incorporated in 1955 in OH.
Donor(s): Melville H. Haskell,‡ Coburn Haskell, Melville H. Haskell, Jr., Mark Haskell.
Grantmaker type: Independent foundation
Financial data (yr. ended 12/31/02): Assets, $3,502,626 (M); expenditures, $247,202; qualifying distributions, $219,954; giving activities include $209,000 for 79 grants (high: $16,000; low: $500).
Purpose and activities: Giving locally for community services; national support for education, including building funds, hospitals and health agencies, community funds and social services, and the environment.
Fields of interest: History/archaeology; Education, fund raising; Education; Natural resources; Environment; Animal welfare; Animals/wildlife, preservation/protection; Hospitals (general); Health care; AIDS; AIDS research; Human services; International human rights; Federated giving programs; Marine science.
Types of support: General/operating support; Continuing support; Annual campaigns; Building/renovation; Endowments; Program development; Scholarship funds.
Limitations: Giving on a national basis for education; giving primarily in Cleveland, OH, for community services. No grants to individuals.
Application information: Application form not required.
Initial approach: Proposal

Copies of proposal: 1
Deadline(s): None
Board meeting date(s): Late summer
Officers and Trustees:* Coburn Haskell,* Pres.; Schuyler A. Haskell,* V.P.; Paulette Kitko, Secy.; James C. Sekerak, Treas.; Sarah Haskell Greene; Eric T. Haskell; Mark Haskell; Mary E. Haskell; Melville H. Haskell, Jr.; Mary H. Walker.
Number of staff: None.
EIN: 346513797

2654
Joyce and Paul Heiman Foundation
(formerly Heiman Family Charitable Foundation)
P.O. Box 371805
Cincinnati, OH 45222-1805
Contact: Edward M. Frankel, Treas.

Established in 1994 in OH.
Donor(s): Paul L. Heiman, Joyce E. Heiman.
Grantmaker type: Independent foundation
Financial data (yr. ended 12/31/01): Assets, $246,608 (M); gifts received, $50,000; expenditures, $185,951; qualifying distributions, $185,701; giving activities include $184,240 for 33 grants (high: $30,000; low: $500).
Purpose and activities: Funding primarily for Jewish agencies, and for human and senior services.
Fields of interest: Arts; Education; Zoos/zoological societies; Hospitals (general); Health organizations, association; Medical research, institute; Food services; Housing/shelter; Human services; Day care; Aging, centers/services; Federated giving programs; Jewish federated giving programs; Jewish agencies & temples.
Limitations: Applications not accepted. No grants to individuals.
Application information: Unsolicited requests for funds not accepted.
Officers and Trustees:* Paul L. Heiman,* Pres.; Joyce E. Heiman,* Exec. V.P.; Gary Lee Heiman,* V.P.; Mark J. Heiman,* V.P.; Harry J. Heiman,* Secy.; Edward M. Frankel,* Treas.
EIN: 311423877

2655
The Heymann Foundation
c/o Trust Co. of Toledo, N.A.
6135 Trust Dr.
Holland, OH 43528

Established in 1955 in OH.
Donor(s): Ohio Plate Glass.
Grantmaker type: Independent foundation
Financial data (yr. ended 12/31/02): Assets, $1,852,324 (M); expenditures, $110,998; qualifying distributions, $101,574; giving activities include $100,384 for 106 grants (high: $25,000; low: $100).
Purpose and activities: Giving primarily for arts and culture, human services, youth programs, and federated giving programs.
Fields of interest: Arts; Animal welfare; Human services; Children/youth, services; Federated giving programs.
Types of support: General/operating support; Continuing support; Endowments; Scholarship funds.

Limitations: Applications not accepted. Giving primarily in Toledo, OH. No grants to individuals.
Application information: Contributes only to pre-selected organizations.
Trustee: Trust Co. of Toledo, N.A.
Number of staff: None.
EIN: 346518714

2656
Highfield Foundation
c/o Fifth Third Bank
38 Fountain Sq. Plz., MD 1090HC
Cincinnati, OH 45202-3102
Contact: Francis Fisher

Established in 1990 in OH.
Donor(s): Samuel Benedict.
Grantmaker type: Independent foundation
Financial data (yr. ended 09/30/02): Assets, $3,568,341 (M); expenditures, $261,308; qualifying distributions, $209,276; giving activities include $201,000 for 29 grants (high: $16,000; low: $2,500).
Purpose and activities: Giving primarily for education, conservation, and for Christian and Episcopal churches and organizations.
Fields of interest: Arts; Higher education; Education; Natural resources; Health care; Christian agencies & churches; Protestant agencies & churches.
Types of support: General/operating support; Building/renovation; Endowments; Scholarship funds.
Limitations: Giving on a national basis. No grants to individuals.
Application information: Not currently accepting outside solicitations. Application form required.
Deadline(s): None
Trustee: Fifth Third Bank.
EIN: 316391904

2657
Holden Arboretum Trust
KeyBank N.A.
800 Superior Ave., 4th Fl.
Cleveland, OH 44114-1306

Established in 1988.
Grantmaker type: Public charity
Financial data (yr. ended 12/31/02): Assets, $67,762,045 (M); gifts received, $82,180; expenditures, $4,410,461; program services expenses, $4,191,777; giving activities include $4,191,777 for grants.
Purpose and activities: The organization aims to perform the functions of the charitable, educational and scientific purposes of the Arboretum.
Fields of interest: Education; Environment, plant conservation.
Limitations: Applications not accepted. Giving limited to Kirkland, OH.
Application information: Contributes only to a pre-selected organization; unsolicited requests for funds not considered or acknowledged.
Trustee: KeyBank N.A.
EIN: 346919291

2658
Honda of America Foundation
c/o Comm. Dept., Marysville Motorcycle Plant
24000 Honda Pkwy.
Marysville, OH 43040-9251 (937) 645-8785
Contact: Lourene Hoy, Asst. Mgr.
E-mail: rene_hoy@ham.honda.com; URL: http://
www.ohio.honda.com/info/involvement/
index.asp

Established in 1981 in OH.
Donor(s): Honda of America Mfg., Inc.
Grantmaker type: Company-sponsored
foundation
Financial data (yr. ended 12/31/02): Assets,
$7,412,362 (M); gifts received, $2,000,000;
expenditures, $575,115; qualifying distributions,
$475,776; giving activities include $477,086 for
23 grants (high: $75,000; low: $1,000; average:
$1,600–$50,000).
Purpose and activities: Support for arts and
culture, and education, including a program
sending educators to Japan.
Fields of interest: Arts; Education; Environment;
Health care; Human services; Community
development.
Limitations: Giving primarily in OH, where
Honda of America facilities are located and
associates reside.
Application information: See foundation Web
site for guidelines and downloadable
application form. Application form required.
  Initial approach: Letter with proposal
  Copies of proposal: 1
  Deadline(s): Annually
  Board meeting date(s): Quarterly
Officers and Trustees:* Rick Schostek,* Pres.;
Shaun McCloskey,* Treas.; John Adams; Larry
Jutte; Kay Miller; Ted Noguchi.
Number of staff: 1 full-time professional.
EIN: 311006130

2659
The Herbert W. Hoover Foundation
Unizan Plz.
220 Market Ave. S.
Canton, OH 44702 (330) 453-5555
Contact: Ellen Beidler, Exec. Dir.
FAX: (330) 453-5622; E-mail:
herbertwhoover@neo.rr.com

Established in 1990 in Canton, OH.
Donor(s): The Hoover Foundation.
Grantmaker type: Independent foundation
Financial data (yr. ended 12/31/02): Assets,
$20,294,250 (M); expenditures, $1,070,359;
qualifying distributions, $1,017,108; giving
activities include $831,020 for 35 grants (high:
$100,000; low: $2,500).
Purpose and activities: The focus of the Herbert
W. Hoover Foundation is on children,
education, the environment, and health and
social services. The foundation only contributes
to 501c(3) organizations.
Fields of interest: Education; Environment;
Health care; Human services; Children/youth,
services.
Limitations: Giving primarily in Stark County,
OH. No grants to individuals, or for annual
campaigns, administrative costs, endowments,
start-up funds, or organizational fund drives.
Publications: Application guidelines.
Application information:

Initial approach: Request application
guidelines
Deadline(s): Last day of Feb., June and Sept.
Board meeting date(s): 3 times per year
Trust Committee: Elizabeth Lacey Hoover,
Chair.; Mrs. Carl Good Hoover, Vice-Chair.;
Ruth H. Basner; Robert S. O'Brien; Blair C.
Woodside, Jr.
Trustee: KeyBank N.A.
Number of staff: 1 full-time professional; 1
full-time support.
EIN: 346905388

2660
Letha E. House Foundation
c/o FirstMerit Bank, N.A.
39 Public Sq.
Medina, OH 44256 (330) 764-7251
Contact: Catherine M. Carmany

Established in 1967 in OH.
Grantmaker type: Independent foundation
Financial data (yr. ended 06/30/02): Assets,
$1,307,738 (M); expenditures, $189,276;
qualifying distributions, $173,813; giving
activities include $140,492 for 5 grants (high:
$52,712; low: $1,500).
Purpose and activities: Support primarily for
historical restoration projects.
Fields of interest: Historic
preservation/historical societies; Environment,
government agencies; Environment, plant
conservation; Animal welfare; Cemeteries/burial
services, burial association.
Types of support: General/operating support;
Building/renovation.
Limitations: Giving primarily in the Medina
County, OH, area.
Application information: Application form not
required.
  Initial approach: Letter (not to exceed 2 pages)
  Deadline(s): None
Trustees: Charles Clark Griesinger; Paul M.
Jones, Jr.; FirstMerit Bank, N.A.
EIN: 237025122

2661
Howe Family Foundation
c/o Roger L. Howe
425 Walnut St., Ste. 2120
Cincinnati, OH 45245

Established in 1991 in OH.
Donor(s): Roger L. Howe, Karen C. Howe, R.
Edwin Howe, Mary H. Davis.
Grantmaker type: Independent foundation
Financial data (yr. ended 12/31/02): Assets,
$1,552,338 (M); expenditures, $99,800;
qualifying distributions, $99,550; giving
activities include $99,350 for 16 grants (high:
$25,000; low: $150).
Purpose and activities: Giving for the arts and
conservation.
Fields of interest: Arts; Natural resources;
Federated giving programs.
Types of support: General/operating support.
Limitations: Applications not accepted. Giving
primarily in Cincinnati, OH. No grants to
individuals.
Application information: Contributes only to
pre-selected organizations.

Officers: Karen C. Howe, Pres.; Mary H. Davis,
Secy.; R. Edwin Howe, Treas.
Trustees: Joyce L. Howe; Roger L. Howe.
EIN: 311339302

2662
Humane Society Foundation of Hancock County
4550 Fostoria Ave.
Findlay, OH 45840

Established in 1985.
Grantmaker type: Public charity
Financial data (yr. ended 12/31/02): Assets,
$1,573,794 (M); gifts received, $525;
expenditures, $85,354; program services
expenses, $81,161; giving activities include
$39,551 for grants.
Purpose and activities: The foundation exists for
the sole benefit of the Humane Society and
SPCA of Hancock County, Ohio.
Fields of interest: Animal welfare.
Limitations: Applications not accepted. Giving
limited to Hancock County, OH.
Application information: Contributes only to a
pre-selected organization; unsolicited requests
for funds not considered or acknowledged.
Officers and Board Members:* Kurt Kah,* Pres.;
Jack Crates,* V.P.; C.R. Becket, M.D.,* Secy.;
Diane Kirk,* Treas.; William Alcott, M.D.; Zan
Palmer; George Ranzau; Robert Sprague; Robert
Welker.
EIN: 341467793

2663
The Iams Company Contributions Program
7250 Poe Ave.
Dayton, OH 45414-5801 (937) 264-7322
Contact: Connie McKamey, Mgr., Corp. Contribs.
FAX: (937) 264-7214; E-mail:
connie.mckamey@iams.com

Grantmaker type: Corporate giving program
Financial data (yr. ended 06/30/02): Total giving,
$1,173,000; giving activities include
$1,173,000 for grants.
Purpose and activities: Iams makes charitable
contributions to nonprofit organizations
involved with K-12 education, responsible pet
ownership, service animals, and children.
Special emphasis is directed towards programs
designed to promote best practices where
people and companion animals work together
to benefit one another and programs designed
to make a significant difference in the lives of
children. Support is given primarily in areas of
company operations and on a national basis for
companion animal programs.
Fields of interest: Elementary/secondary
education; Animal welfare; Animals/wildlife,
special services; Children, services; Disabled.
Types of support: General/operating support;
Continuing support; Capital campaigns;
Building/renovation; Program development;
Conferences/seminars; Research; Employee
volunteer services; Use of facilities;
Sponsorships; Donated equipment; Donated
products; In-kind gifts.
Limitations: Giving primarily in areas of
company operations, with emphasis on Dayton,
OH; giving on a national basis for companion
animal programs. No grants to individuals, or

for fundraising (except for organizations already receiving support from Iams) or mass mailings; no grants totaling over 10 percent of an organization's budget.
Publications: Informational brochure (including application guidelines).
Application information: The External Relations Department handles giving. The company has a staff that only handles contributions. A contributions committee reviews all requests. Application form not required.
  Initial approach: Telephone nearest company facility for guidelines; proposal to nearest company facility
  Copies of proposal: 1
  Deadline(s): 15th of each month
  Board meeting date(s): Between the 12th and 20th of each month
  Final notification: Following review
Number of staff: 1 full-time professional; 1 part-time support.

2664
ICF Foundation

4000 Embassy Pkwy., Ste. 330
Akron, OH   44333
Contact: Kate Ong-Landini, Secy.
FAX: (330) 668-3662

Established in 1998 in OH.
Donor(s): John Ong.
Grantmaker type: Independent foundation
Financial data (yr. ended 12/31/02): Assets, $2,153,411 (M); expenditures, $110,160; qualifying distributions, $109,476; giving activities include $95,000 for 5 grants (high: $50,000; low: $5,000).
Purpose and activities: Giving primarily for education.
Fields of interest: Multipurpose centers/programs; Education; Environment; Public health.
Types of support: Capital campaigns; Building/renovation; Land acquisition; Program development; Seed money; Scholarship funds; Matching/challenge support.
Limitations: Giving primarily in OH and western PA. No grants to individuals.
Publications: Application guidelines.
Application information: Application form not required.
  Copies of proposal: 1
  Deadline(s): June 30
  Board meeting date(s): July or Aug.
  Final notification: Sept. 30
Officers: John D. Ong, Pres.; Mary Lee Ong, V.P.; M. Katherine Ong-Landini, Secy.; Richard P.B. Ong, Treas.
Trustee: John F.H. Ong.
EIN: 341826821

2665
The Louise H. and David S. Ingalls Foundation, Inc.

301 Tower E.
20600 Chagrin Blvd.
Shaker Heights, OH   44122   (216) 921-6000
Contact: Jane W. Watson

Incorporated in 1953 in OH.
Donor(s): Louise H. Ingalls,‡ Edith Ingalls Vignos, Louise Ingalls Brown,‡ David S. Ingalls,‡

David S. Ingalls, Jr.,‡ Jane I. Davison, Anne I. Lawrence.
Grantmaker type: Independent foundation
Financial data (yr. ended 12/31/01): Assets, $30,040,199 (M); expenditures, $1,798,973; qualifying distributions, $1,745,308; giving activities include $1,704,625 for 44 grants (high: $396,000; low: $1,625; average: $5,000–$50,000).
Purpose and activities: Support mainly to organizations known to the trustees for the improvement of the physical, educational, mental, and moral condition of humanity primarily in the Cleveland OH area; grants largely for education, fine arts and culture, music, historical preservation, archaeology and anthropology, the environment and conservation, health programs, and hospital building funds, rehabilitation programs, the disadvantaged, and child development.
Fields of interest: Museums; Performing arts; Historic preservation/historical societies; Arts; Higher education; Natural resources; Hospitals (general); Medical care, rehabilitation; Medical research, institute.
Types of support: Capital campaigns; Building/renovation; Program development; Research.
Limitations: Giving on a national basis, primarily in Cleveland, OH. No grants to individuals; or for annual giving.
Application information: Application form not required.
  Initial approach: Proposal
  Copies of proposal: 1
  Deadline(s): None
  Board meeting date(s): As required
Officers and Trustees:* Barbara Brown,* Pres.; Nina S. Ingalls,* V.P.; Caren V. Sturges,* Secy.; John T. Lawrence III, Treas.; E.P. Davison, Jr.; Anne I. Lawrence.
Number of staff: 2 part-time support.
EIN: 346516550

2666
International Partners in Mission

2475 Lee Blvd., Ste. 10
Cleveland Heights, OH   44118   (216) 932-4082
Contact: Janet L. Bullard, Pres.
FAX: (216) 932-4084; E-mail: office@ipm-connections.org; URL: http://www.ipm-connections.org

Established in 1974.
Grantmaker type: Public charity
Financial data (yr. ended 12/31/02): Revenue, $334,981; assets, $160,929 (M); gifts received, $335,076; expenditures, $402,077; program services expenses, $283,190; giving activities include $143,698 for grants.
Purpose and activities: The organization fosters justice, peace and hope around the world by developing partnerships that promote community building, health and environmental justice through the empowerment of women, children and youth.
Fields of interest: Environment; Health care; Children/youth, services; Community development; Women.
Types of support: Income development; Emergency funds; Program development; Seed money; Technical assistance; Program-related investments/loans.

Limitations: Giving on a national and international basis, limited to Cleveland, OH, St. Louis, MO, Eastern Europe, Asia, Africa, South America, and Central America.
Publications: Application guidelines, Annual report, Financial statement, Informational brochure, Newsletter.
Application information: Application form required.
  Initial approach: Letter or e-mail
Officers and Trustees:* Janet L. Bullard,* Pres.; Rev. Jane Sullivan-Davis,* V.P.; Carol Findling,* Secy.; David N. Westcott,* Treas.; J. Matthew Carter; Joseph F. Cistone; Michael B. Congdon, Ph.D.; Nadine Hopwood Feighan*; Christine E. Henry*; and 8 additional trustees.
Number of staff: 3 full-time professional; 2 part-time professional.
EIN: 431487311

2667
Kate Ireland Foundation

1422 Euclid Ave., Ste. 1030
Cleveland, OH   44115-2004

Established in 1994 in OH.
Donor(s): Kate Ireland Charitable Lead Trust No. 1, Ireland Foundation.
Grantmaker type: Independent foundation
Financial data (yr. ended 12/31/02): Assets, $1,259,655 (M); gifts received, $109,400; expenditures, $310,888; qualifying distributions, $284,332; giving activities include $278,000 for 39 grants (high: $46,000; low: $500).
Purpose and activities: Giving primarily for education, animals and wildlife, and the environment; funding also for Episcopal churches.
Fields of interest: Opera; Elementary/secondary education; Higher education; Environment; Animals/wildlife; Health care; Federated giving programs; Protestant agencies & churches.
Types of support: Annual campaigns.
Limitations: Applications not accepted. Giving on a national basis. No grants to individuals.
Application information: Contributes only to pre-selected organizations.
Officers and Trustees:* Kate Ireland,* Pres.; Carole M. Nowak, Secy.; Neil A. Brown, Treas.; DuBose Ausley; Thomas Barron; Richard T. Watson.
EIN: 341786209

2668
Carl Jacobs Foundation

c/o Fifth Third Bank, Trust Dept.
38 Fountain Sq. Plz., MD 1COM31
Cincinnati, OH   45263
Contact: Robert Erickson, V.P., Fifth Third Bank

Established in 1997 in DE.
Donor(s): Carl Jacobs.
Grantmaker type: Independent foundation
Financial data (yr. ended 12/31/02): Assets, $4,588,778 (M); expenditures, $319,308; qualifying distributions, $283,019; giving activities include $268,310 for 109 grants (high: $20,000; low: $500).
Purpose and activities: Giving primarily to the arts; funding also for human services.
Fields of interest: Museums (art); Performing arts; Opera; Ballet; Theater; Arts; Higher

education; Libraries (public); Animals/wildlife; Human services; International affairs.
Limitations: Giving primarily in New York, NY; some funding nationally.
Application information:
Initial approach: Letter
Deadline(s): None
Trustee: Fifth Third Bank.
EIN: 133933000

2669
The Walter and Jean Kalberer Foundation
c/o Walter E. Kalberer
1259 W. Hill Dr.
Gates Mills, OH 44040-9636

Established in 1995 in OH.
Donor(s): Walter E. Kalberer, Jean C. Kalberer, Peter Scheid.
Grantmaker type: Independent foundation
Financial data (yr. ended 12/31/01): Assets, $7,425,729 (M); expenditures, $481,840; qualifying distributions, $476,245; giving activities include $476,700 for 42 grants (high: $105,000; low: $500).
Purpose and activities: Giving primarily for the arts and higher education; funding also for human services.
Fields of interest: Museums; Opera; Theater; Orchestra (symphony); Arts; Higher education; Botanical gardens; Human services.
Limitations: Applications not accepted. Giving primarily in Cleveland, OH. No grants to individuals.
Application information: Contributes only to pre-selected organizations.
Trustees: Jean C. Kalberer; Lori Kalberer; Walter E. Kalberer; Gwenn S. Winkhaus.
EIN: 341817179

2670
Kenridge Fund
c/o Advisory Svcs., Inc.
1422 Euclid Ave., 1010 Hanna Bldg.
Cleveland, OH 44115-2078
Contact: Jackie Horning, Treas.

Established in 1989 in OH as partial successor to Bolton Foundation.
Donor(s): Fanny H. Bolton, Claire H.B. Jonklaas.
Grantmaker type: Independent foundation
Financial data (yr. ended 12/31/02): Assets, $2,694,908 (M); expenditures, $159,472; qualifying distributions, $128,480; giving activities include $117,000 for 28 grants (high: $30,000; low: $1,000; average: $1,000–$5,000).
Fields of interest: Secondary school/education; Higher education; Education; Natural resources; Hospitals (general); Nursing care; Human services; Federated giving programs.
Types of support: General/operating support; Annual campaigns; Capital campaigns; Building/renovation; Scholarship funds; Matching/challenge support.
Limitations: Giving on a national basis, with some emphasis on GA and OH. No grants to individuals.
Application information: Application form not required.
Initial approach: Proposal
Deadline(s): None
Board meeting date(s): June - Sept.

Officers and Trustees:* Claire H.B. Jonklaas,* Pres.; Kenneth G. Hochman,* V.P.; J.A. Horning, Treas.; Claire Hanna Buckley; Anthony Jonklaas.
EIN: 341616683

2671
The Kettering Family Foundation
1560 Kettering Twr.
Dayton, OH 45423
Contact: Charles F. Kettering III, Pres.
Application address: 2833 S. Colorado Blvd., Ste. 2415, Denver, CO 80222; E-mail: Ketteringfamilyf@aol.com; URL: http://www.ketteringfamilyfoundation.org/

Incorporated in 1956 in IL; reincorporated in 1966 in OH.
Donor(s): E.W. Kettering,‡ Virginia W. Kettering, Jane K. Lombard, S.K. Williamson, P.D. Williamson, Richard D. Lombard,‡ B. Weiffenbach,‡ Charles F. Kettering III, Lisa S. Kettering, Leslie G. Williamson, Douglas E. Williamson, Susan S. Kettering, Kyle W. Cox, Mark A. Cox, Douglas J. Cushnie, Karen W. Cushnie, Linda K. Danneberg, William H. Danneberg, Jean S. Kettering, Richard J. Lombard, Debra L. Williamson, Nathalie R. Lombard.
Grantmaker type: Independent foundation
Financial data (yr. ended 12/31/02): Assets, $11,027,406 (M); gifts received, $5,000; expenditures, $574,522; qualifying distributions, $545,937; giving activities include $532,583 for 39 grants (high: $76,000; low: $500; average: $500–$76,000).
Fields of interest: Visual arts; Performing arts; Arts; Higher education; Education; Natural resources; Environment; Health care; Medical research, institute; Human services.
Types of support: General/operating support; Annual campaigns; Capital campaigns; Equipment; Endowments; Program development; Conferences/seminars; Publication; Curriculum development; Research; Technical assistance; Matching/challenge support.
Limitations: Giving on a national basis. No support for foreign purposes, religious organizations for religious purposes, public elementary or secondary schools, or local chapters of national organizations, or conduit organizations. No grants to individuals, or for scholarships, fellowships, memberships, multi-year grants, capital construction, travel expenses, or community drives; no loans.
Publications: Informational brochure (including application guidelines).
Application information: Unsolicited proposals considered after trustee-sponsored requests. Trustee-sponsored requests get priority. Trustees may sponsor requests from generally excluded areas. Only trustee-sponsored requests will be considered for international giving. Grants list available on the foundation's Web site. Application form not required.
Initial approach: 1-page letter of inquiry
Copies of proposal: 1
Deadline(s): Feb. 1 and Aug. 1
Board meeting date(s): Mid-May and mid-Nov.
Final notification: 2 weeks after board meetings
Officers and Trustees:* Charles F. Kettering III, Pres.; Susan S. Kettering,* V.P.; Debra L.

Williamson,* V.P.; Richard J. Lombard,* Secy.-Treas.; Kyle W. Cox; Karen W. Cushnie; Linda K. Danneberg; Jean S. Kettering; Lisa S. Kettering, M.D.; Jane K. Lombard; Douglas E. Williamson, M.D.; P.D. Williamson, M.D.; Susan K. Williamson.
Number of staff: None.
EIN: 310727384

2672
The Klein Foundation
24200 Chagrin Blvd., Rm. 242
Beachwood, OH 44122 (216) 464-5105
Contact: G. Robert Klein, Chair.

Established in 1979 in OH.
Donor(s): George R. Klein, George R. Klein, Jr.
Grantmaker type: Independent foundation
Financial data (yr. ended 09/30/02): Assets, $6,972 (M); gifts received, $109,909; expenditures, $113,790; qualifying distributions, $110,190; giving activities include $109,813 for 70 grants (high: $20,000; low: $50) and $961 for 1 grant to an individual.
Purpose and activities: Support primarily for the arts and museums; support also for higher education, churches, and environmental conservation.
Fields of interest: Museums; Arts; Higher education; Environment; Religion.
Types of support: General/operating support.
Limitations: Giving primarily in Cleveland, OH.
Application information: Application form not required.
Deadline(s): None
Board meeting date(s): Nov. 15
Officers: George R. Klein, Chair.; George R. Klein, Jr., Pres.; Marilyn E. Brown, Secy.
Number of staff: None.
EIN: 341288590

2673
The Lampl Family Foundation
30799 Pinetree Rd., Unit 409
Pepper Pike, OH 44124
Contact: Jack W. Lampl III, Pres.
FAX: (216) 491-3995

Established in 1988 in OH.
Grantmaker type: Independent foundation
Financial data (yr. ended 12/31/01): Assets, $1,843,083 (M); expenditures, $142,738; qualifying distributions, $120,786; giving activities include $114,750 for 34 grants (high: $18,000; low: $1,000).
Purpose and activities: Giving to higher education, Jewish federated programs, medical centers, and organizations promoting peaceful coexistence, protection of the environment, and social justice.
Fields of interest: Museums; Environment; Human services; Jewish agencies & temples.
Types of support: Continuing support; Annual campaigns; Capital campaigns; Endowments; Program development; Scholarship funds; Matching/challenge support.
Limitations: Applications not accepted. Giving primarily in Cleveland, OH. No support for non-traditional religious organizations or sects. No grants to individuals.
Application information: Unsolicited requests for funds not accepted.

Officer and Trustees:* Jack W. Lampl III,* Pres.;
Carolyn C. Lampl; Joshua C. Lampl.
EIN: 341499838

2674
The Lamson & Sessions Foundation
c/o KeyBank N.A.
800 Superior Ave., 4th Fl.
Cleveland, OH 44114-2601
Application address: c/o James J. Abel, The
Lamson & Sessions Co., 25701 Science Dr.,
Cleveland, OH 44122, tel.: (216) 464-3400

Trust established in 1951 in OH.
Donor(s): The Lamson & Sessions Co.
Grantmaker type: Company-sponsored
foundation
Financial data (yr. ended 06/30/02): Assets,
$8,723 (M); gifts received, $100,000;
expenditures, $122,057; qualifying distributions,
$120,557; giving activities include $87,093 for
29 grants (high: $6,743; low: $25) and $32,787
for 48 employee matching gifts.
Purpose and activities: Grants for organizations
whose purposes are religious, educational, or
for prevention of cruelty to children and animals.
Fields of interest: Museums (art); Higher
education; Animal welfare; Federated giving
programs; Religion.
Limitations: Giving primarily in OH. No grants
to individuals; no loans or program-related
investments.
Application information: Application form not
required.
    Deadline(s): None
Trustee: KeyBank N.A.
EIN: 346501823

2675
LeBlond Foundation
7680 Innovation Way
Mason, OH 45040
Contact: Beverly J. Bowser

Established in 1952 in OH.
Donor(s): LeBlond Makino Machine Tool Co.
Grantmaker type: Company-sponsored
foundation
Financial data (yr. ended 12/31/02): Assets,
$606,097 (M); expenditures, $95,366;
qualifying distributions, $89,127; giving
activities include $89,600 for 14 grants (high:
$20,000; low: $1,000).
Purpose and activities: Giving primarily for
community funds and youth programs; support
also for education, community development,
and the fine arts.
Fields of interest: Arts; Education; Environment;
Human services; Community development;
Federated giving programs.
Types of support: General/operating support;
Capital campaigns; Seed money.
Limitations: Giving primarily in the greater
Cincinnati, OH, area. No grants to individuals.
Application information: Application form not
required.
    Initial approach: Letter
    Deadline(s): None
Officers: Daniel W. LeBlond, Chair.; Donald D.
Lane, Vice-Chair.; James M. McVicker, Secy.
EIN: 316036274

2676
The Linnemann Family Foundation
312 Walnut St., Ste. 3150
Cincinnati, OH 45202-4059
Contact: Beth Troendly

Established in 1995 in OH.
Donor(s): Patricia G. Linnemann, Calvin C.
Linnemann.
Grantmaker type: Independent foundation
Financial data (yr. ended 12/31/02): Assets,
$3,150,311 (M); expenditures, $207,877;
qualifying distributions, $196,335; giving
activities include $197,000 for 41 grants (high:
$15,000; low: $1,000).
Purpose and activities: Gives preference to
organizations with activities in the greater
Cincinnati, OH, area. Grants are generally
restricted to the fields of religion, education,
medical and community projects. However, to
the extent funds are available, grants may be
made for other projects.
Fields of interest: Education; Natural resources;
Botanical gardens; Animals/wildlife,
preservation/protection; Zoos/zoological
societies; Children/youth, services; Population
studies.
Limitations: Giving on a national basis.
Application information: Application form not
required.
    Initial approach: Letter
    Deadline(s): None
Officers: Calvin C. Linnemann, Pres.; Patricia G.
Linnemann, Secy.-Treas.
Trustees: Catherine A. Linnemann; Mark D.
Linnemann.
EIN: 311394291

2677
The Katherine Kenyon Lippitt Foundation
c/o National City Bank
P.O. Box 94651
Cleveland, OH 44101-4651
Application address: c/o Tom Gilchrist, National
City Bank, P.O. Box 5756, LOC 2020,
Cleveland, OH 44101, tel.: (216) 222-9272

Established in 1987 in OH.
Donor(s): Esther McEwan Black.‡
Grantmaker type: Independent foundation
Financial data (yr. ended 12/31/02): Assets,
$4,963,108 (M); expenditures, $560,586;
qualifying distributions, $513,697; giving
activities include $490,500 for 30 grants (high:
$102,000; low: $500).
Fields of interest: Performing arts; Arts;
Education; Animals/wildlife,
preservation/protection; Health organizations,
association; Human services; YM/YWCAs &
YM/YWHAs; Federated giving programs.
Types of support: General/operating support;
Continuing support; Annual campaigns; Capital
campaigns; Building/renovation; Land
acquisition.
Limitations: Giving primarily in Mansfield and
Richland County, OH. No grants to individuals.
Application information: Generally contributes
only to pre-selected organizations. Application
form not required.
    Initial approach: Letter
    Copies of proposal: 1
    Deadline(s): None
    Board meeting date(s): July and Dec.

Officers: John B. Black, Pres.; Peter M. Black,
V.P. and Treas.; Kenneth G. Hochman, Secy.
Number of staff: None.
EIN: 341571383

2678
Lowe-Marshall Trust
c/o C. Marshall Lowe
5301 C. Huffman Ln.
Chesterhill, OH 43728-9021
Contact: C. Marshall Lowe, Tr.
E-mail: mblowe@morganco.net

Established in 1968.
Donor(s): James T. Lowe,‡ Constance M. Lowe.‡
Grantmaker type: Independent foundation
Financial data (yr. ended 12/31/02): Assets,
$4,986,308 (M); expenditures, $245,558;
qualifying distributions, $243,837; giving
activities include $245,000 for 23 grants.
Purpose and activities: Primary areas of interest
include peacemaking and conflict resolution
projects, sustainable development in Appalachia
and other economically depressed rural areas.
Funding also for environmental quality,
protection and beautification, and community
improvement and capacity building.
Fields of interest: Natural resources;
Environment; International development;
International conflict resolution; Community
development.
Types of support: General/operating support;
Continuing support; Annual campaigns;
Program development; Seed money;
Program-related investments/loans.
Limitations: Applications not accepted. Giving
primarily in the Appalachian region and in
developing countries by U.S.-based charities.
No grants to individuals.
Publications: Program policy statement.
Application information: Contributes only to
pre-selected organizations.
Officer and Trustees:* C. Marshall Lowe,*
Chair.; Betty M. Lowe; Peter A. Lowe.
Number of staff: None.
EIN: 316084154

2679
The Lubrizol Foundation
29400 Lakeland Blvd., No. 053A
Wickliffe, OH 44092 (440) 347-5080
Contact: K.M. Iwashita, Pres., Secy., and C.O.O.
FAX: (440) 347-1858; *E-mail:* Kmi@lubrizol.com
and Kal@lubrizol.com; *URL:* http://
www.lubrizol.com/foundation/default.asp

Incorporated in 1952 in OH.
Donor(s): The Lubrizol Corp.
Grantmaker type: Company-sponsored
foundation
Financial data (yr. ended 12/31/02): Assets,
$15,465,208 (M); expenditures, $2,272,699;
qualifying distributions, $2,202,982; giving
activities include $1,652,650 for grants and
$553,885 for 1,982 employee matching gifts.
Purpose and activities: Emphasis on higher
education, social services, civic, cultural, and
environmental programs, youth agencies, and
health; the foundation also conducts an
employee matching gift program.
Fields of interest: Visual arts; Performing arts;
Arts; Secondary school/education; Higher

education; Engineering school/education; Adult education—literacy, basic skills & GED; Reading; Education; Environmental education; Hospitals (general); Health care; Health organizations, association; Human services; Children/youth, services; Family services; Engineering/technology; Engineering; Biological sciences; Science.

Types of support: General/operating support; Continuing support; Annual campaigns; Capital campaigns; Building/renovation; Equipment; Fellowships; Scholarship funds; Employee matching gifts; Matching/challenge support.

Limitations: Giving primarily in areas of major company operations, particularly the greater Cleveland, OH, and Houston, TX, areas. No support for religious or political purposes. No grants to individuals, or for seed money, deficit financing, endowment funds, demonstration projects, publications, or conferences; no loans.

Publications: Annual report (including application guidelines).

Application information: Application form not required.

> *Initial approach:* Proposal
> *Copies of proposal:* 1
> *Deadline(s):* None
> *Board meeting date(s):* As required, usually 4 times per year
> *Final notification:* 2 weeks after meeting

Officers and Trustees:* George R. Hill,* Chair. and C.E.O.; Kenneth M. Iwashita,* Pres., Secy., and C.O.O.; Kenneth J. Marr,* Treas.; W.G. Bares; Stephen A. DiBiase; James L. Hambrick; Joe E. Hodge; Kenneth H. Hopping; C.W. Jones; L.K. Naylor; J.L. Petric; J. Robinson; M.F. Salomon; D.L. Sheets; J.M. Sutherland.

Number of staff: 1 part-time professional; 1 part-time support.

EIN: 346500595

Recent environmental and animal welfare grants:

2679-1 Americas River Communities, San Carlos, CA, $30,000. Toward production of PBS documentary on environmental issues surrounding Cuyahoga River. 2002.

2679-2 Houston Arboretum and Nature Center, Houston, TX, $10,000. Toward environmental education programs. 2002.

2679-3 Parks and Wildlife Foundation of Texas, Dallas, TX, $15,000. Toward construction of new Environmental Education Center. 2002.

2680
The Frances R. Luther Charitable Trust
c/o Fifth Third Bank
38 Fountain Sq. Plz., Trust Tax Dept., MD 1090HB
Cincinnati, OH 45263
Contact: Paula Wharton, Trust Off., Fifth Third Bank

Established in 2000 in OH.
Donor(s): Frances R. Luther Trust.
Grantmaker type: Independent foundation
Financial data (yr. ended 12/31/02): Assets, $41,409,425 (M); expenditures, $2,312,135; qualifying distributions, $2,094,319; giving activities include $2,015,500 for 71 grants (high: $200,000; low: $2,000; average: $10,000–$100,000).
Fields of interest: Media/communications; Arts; Zoos/zoological societies; Hospitals (general);

Food banks; Human services; YM/YWCAs & YM/YWHAs; Children/youth, services.
Limitations: Giving primarily in Cincinnati, OH.
Application information: Application form required.

> *Initial approach:* Letter
> *Deadline(s):* Feb. 1, May 1, Aug. 1, and Nov. 1

Trustees: Narley L. Haley; Fifth Third Bank.
EIN: 316646985

2681
LZ Francis Foundation
c/o Mark Mihalik
3550 Lander Rd., Ste. 200
Pepper Pike, OH 44124

Established in 1992 in OH as partial successor to the Nason Foundation.
Donor(s): The Nason Foundation, Katharine Nason Tipper.
Grantmaker type: Independent foundation
Financial data (yr. ended 12/31/02): Assets, $10,331,144 (M); gifts received, $429; expenditures, $527,591; qualifying distributions, $489,260; giving activities include $450,500 for 9 grants (high: $250,000; low: $2,500).
Purpose and activities: Giving primarily for education and conservation.
Fields of interest: Arts; College; Education; Natural resources; Food services; Human services; Federated giving programs.
Limitations: Applications not accepted. Giving primarily in FL and VT. No grants to individuals.
Application information: Contributes only to pre-selected organizations.
Officers: Katharine Nason Tipper, Pres. and Treas.; Charles F. Tipper, V.P. and Secy.; Jessica A. Oski, V.P.
EIN: 341721860

2682
The S. Livingston Mather Charitable Trust
c/o Glenmede Trust Co., N.A.
25825 Science Park Dr., Ste. 110
Beachwood, OH 44122 (216) 514-7862
Contact: Janet W. Havener, V.P., Glenmede Trust Co., N.A.
FAX: (216) 378-2917

Trust established in 1953 in OH.
Donor(s): S. Livingston Mather.‡
Grantmaker type: Independent foundation
Financial data (yr. ended 12/31/02): Assets, $4,563,179 (M); gifts received, $10,855; expenditures, $298,949; qualifying distributions, $243,445; giving activities include $213,320 for 53 grants (high: $12,120; low: $500; average: $1,000–$10,000).
Purpose and activities: Primary areas of interest include cultural programs, education, child welfare, and social services. Support also for youth programs and the environment and natural resources.
Fields of interest: Arts; Education; Natural resources; Environment; Family planning; Children/youth, services; Family services.
Types of support: General/operating support; Continuing support; Annual campaigns; Capital campaigns; Building/renovation; Endowments; Emergency funds; Program development; Seed money; Scholarship funds.

Limitations: Giving primarily in northeastern OH. No support for science and medical research programs, or in areas appropriately supported by the government and/or the United Way. No grants to individuals, or for deficit financing or mass mailing solicitations; no loans.
Publications: Application guidelines.
Application information: Mass mail solicitations not considered. Application form not required.

> *Initial approach:* Letter or telephone
> *Copies of proposal:* 1
> *Deadline(s):* None
> *Board meeting date(s):* Quarterly, and as required
> *Final notification:* 2 months

Officers and Distribution Committee:* Elizabeth M. McMillan,* Pres.; Thomas W. Offutt III,* Secy.; Katharine M. Jeffrey, Ph.D.; Elizabeth H. McMillan, M.D.; Judith K. McMillan; S. Sterling McMillan, Ph.D.
Trustee: The Glenmede Trust Co.
Number of staff: 1 part-time support.
EIN: 346505619

2683
Elizabeth Ring Mather and William Gwinn Mather Fund
1111 Superior Ave., Ste. 1000
Cleveland, OH 44114
Contact: James D. Ireland III, Pres.
FAX: (216) 861-4908

Incorporated in 1954 in OH.
Donor(s): Elizabeth Ring Mather.‡
Grantmaker type: Independent foundation
Financial data (yr. ended 12/31/02): Assets, $7,929,962 (M); gifts received, $241,786; expenditures, $994,373; qualifying distributions, $977,235; giving activities include $932,000 for 32 grants (high: $250,000; low: $2,000).
Purpose and activities: Primary areas of interest include the arts, civic affairs, and higher and secondary education.
Fields of interest: Museums; Historic preservation/historical societies; Secondary school/education; Higher education; Education; Natural resources; Health care; Federated giving programs; Roman Catholic agencies & churches.
Types of support: General/operating support; Annual campaigns; Building/renovation; Endowments; Publication.
Limitations: Giving primarily in OH, with emphasis on the greater Cleveland area. No grants to individuals, or for scholarships or fellowships; no loans.
Application information: The foundation does not encourage new requests for grants. Application form not required.

> *Initial approach:* Letter
> *Copies of proposal:* 1
> *Deadline(s):* None
> *Board meeting date(s):* June and Dec.

Officers and Trustees:* James D. Ireland III,* Pres.; Lucy I. Weller,* V.P.; Cornelia I. Hallinan,* Secy.; George R. Ireland,* Treas.
Number of staff: 1 part-time professional.
EIN: 346519863

2684
Nelson Mead Fund
c/o Rend & Co.
500 Lincoln Park Blvd., Ste. 322
Kettering, OH   45429
Contact: Ruth C. Mead, Tr.
FAX: (937) 395-3568

Established in 1965 in OH.
Donor(s): loka Fund, Ruth C. Mead.
Grantmaker type: Independent foundation
Financial data (yr. ended 11/30/02): Assets,
$4,873,585 (M); expenditures, $319,218;
qualifying distributions, $288,371; giving
activities include $289,197 for 111 grants (high:
$50,000; low: $30).
Purpose and activities: Support primarily for
conservation and wildlife preservation; giving
also for Episcopal churches, civic and cultural
groups, health associations, and educational
institutions.
Fields of interest: Arts; Education; Natural
resources; Animals/wildlife,
preservation/protection; Health organizations,
association; Government/public administration;
Christian agencies & churches; Protestant
agencies & churches.
Types of support: Continuing support; Annual
campaigns; Capital campaigns;
Building/renovation; Equipment; Emergency
funds.
Limitations: Applications not accepted. Giving
on a national basis. No grants to individuals.
Application information: Contributes only to
pre-selected organizations. Unsolicited requests
for funds not considered.
Trustee: Ruth C. Mead.
EIN: 316064591

2685
The Meyers Foundation
c/o Bartlett & Co.
35 E. 4th St.
Cincinnati, OH   45202

Established in 1949 in OH.
Grantmaker type: Independent foundation
Financial data (yr. ended 12/31/01): Assets,
$2,340,764 (M); expenditures, $136,391;
qualifying distributions, $111,828; giving
activities include $110,500 for 25 grants (high:
$50,000; low: $500).
Fields of interest: Higher education;
Zoos/zoological societies.
Limitations: Applications not accepted. Giving
primarily in OH. No grants to individuals.
Application information: Contributes only to
pre-selected organizations.
Officers: Philip M. Meyers III, Pres.; Ann
Meyers, Secy.
Trustees: Susan Falk; Lynne Gordon.
EIN: 316023945

2686
Clement O. Miniger Memorial Foundation
709 Madison Ave., Rm. 205
P.O. Box 1985
Toledo, OH   43603-1985

Incorporated in 1952 in OH.
Donor(s): George M. Jones, Jr.,‡ Eleanor Miniger
Jones.‡

Grantmaker type: Independent foundation
Financial data (yr. ended 12/31/02): Assets,
$9,619,585 (M); expenditures, $664,165;
qualifying distributions, $661,608; giving
activities include $627,031 for 33 grants (high:
$65,000; low: $500).
Fields of interest: Museums; Orchestra
(symphony); Arts; Higher education; Education;
Natural resources; Zoos/zoological societies;
Boys & girls clubs; Human services; Hospices.
Types of support: Capital campaigns;
Equipment; Emergency funds;
Matching/challenge support.
Limitations: Giving primarily in OH, with
emphasis on Toledo. No grants to individuals.
Application information: Application form not
required.
  Copies of proposal: 8
  Deadline(s): 2 weeks prior to board meeting
  Board meeting date(s): Quarterly
Officers and Trustees:* George M. Jones III,*
Pres.; John A. Morse,* V.P.; Thomas DeVilbiss,
Exec. Secy. and Treas.; William F. Buckley;
Severn Joyce; Mark Schaffer; Steve Staellin;
Edward Weber.
EIN: 346523024

2687
A. Malachi Mixon III & Barbara W. Mixon Foundation
Republic Bldg.
25 W. Prospect Ave., Ste.1400
Cleveland, OH   44113

Established in 1991 in OH.
Donor(s): A. Malachi Mixon III, Barbara W.
Mixon.
Grantmaker type: Independent foundation
Financial data (yr. ended 11/30/01): Assets,
$793,412 (M); gifts received, $744,700;
expenditures, $770,618; qualifying distributions,
$759,092; giving activities include $765,918 for
51 grants (high: $201,283; low: $100).
Purpose and activities: Giving primarily for the
arts, education, health care, and human services.
Fields of interest: Performing arts; Orchestra
(symphony); Arts; Business school/education;
Education; Botanical gardens; Health care,
clinics/centers; Health care; Human services;
American Red Cross; Federated giving programs.
Limitations: Applications not accepted. Giving
primarily in Cleveland, OH. No grants to
individuals.
Application information: Contributes only to
pre-selected organizations.
Officer: A. Malachi Mixon III, Pres.
Trustees: Robert N. Gudbranson; Barbara W.
Mixon.
Number of staff: None.
EIN: 341692992

2688
Muskingum County Community Foundation
534 Putnam Ave.
Zanesville, OH   43701   (740) 453-5192
FAX: (740) 453-5734; E-mail: giving@mccf.org;
URL: http://www.mccf.org
Scholarship Central tel.: Joey Osborn, Prog.
Coord., (740) 453-5192

Established in 1985 in OH.
Grantmaker type: Community foundation
Financial data (yr. ended 12/31/01): Assets,
$11,830,271 (M); gifts received, $886,472;
expenditures, $1,092,591; giving activities
include $466,489 for grants (high: $15,742) and
$9,000 for 8 grants to individuals of $1,000
each.
Purpose and activities: The foundation seeks to
support worthwhile organizations and programs
that enhance the quality of life in Muskingum
County, OH. The foundation administers
donor-advised funds.
Fields of interest: Performing arts; Music; Arts;
Elementary/secondary education;
Libraries/library science; Education; Animal
welfare; Animals/wildlife,
preservation/protection; Hospitals (general);
Health care; Recreation; Youth development,
services; Children/youth, services; Hospices;
Community development; Leadership
development; Aging.
Types of support: Capital campaigns;
Building/renovation; Equipment; Land
acquisition; Endowments; Program
development; Conferences/seminars;
Publication; Seed money; Fellowships;
Scholarship funds; Scholarships—to individuals;
Matching/challenge support.
Limitations: Giving limited to Muskingum
County, OH.
Publications: Annual report, Grants list,
Informational brochure, Newsletter.
Application information: See Web site for
application guidelines. Application form
required.
  Initial approach: Proposal
  Deadline(s): Apr. 1 and Oct. 1 (for proposals),
  scholarship application deadlines vary,
  telephone Scholarship Central for
  information
  Board meeting date(s): 4th Wed. of Jan., Apr.,
  July, and Oct.
Officers and Trustee:* James McDonald,* Pres.;
Donna Cole,⁺ V.P.; Sandy Kopf,* Secy.; Frank
Dosch,* Treas.; David P. Mitzel, Exec. Dir.; and
21 additional trustees.
Number of staff: 3 full-time professional; 1
full-time support; 1 part-time support.
EIN: 311147022

2689
L. and L. Nippert Charitable Foundation, Inc.
c/o The Randolph Co.
8255 Spooky Hollow Rd.
Cincinnati, OH   45242-6518   (513) 891-7144
Contact: Carter Randolph, V.P.
E-mail: crandolph@green-acres.org

Established in 1992 in OH as successor to L.
and L. Nippert Charitable Foundation.
Donor(s): Louis Nippert,‡ Louise D. Nippert.
Grantmaker type: Independent foundation
Financial data (yr. ended 12/31/02): Assets,
$10,615,790 (M); expenditures, $715,775;
qualifying distributions, $667,186; giving
activities include $670,000 for 4 grants (high:
$500,000; low: $30,000).
Purpose and activities: Support for the arts,
music (especially vocal, symphonic, and
chamber music), historic preservation,

conservation, environmental education, and parks.

Fields of interest: Music; Historic preservation/historical societies; Arts; Natural resources; Environment; Health care; Medical research, institute; Human services; Religion.

Types of support: General/operating support; Continuing support; Annual campaigns; Capital campaigns; Building/renovation; Endowments; Program development; Seed money; Curriculum development; Internship funds; Scholarship funds; Research.

Limitations: Giving primarily in Hamilton County, OH. No grants to individuals.

Application information: Application form not required.

> *Initial approach:* Letter requesting guidelines
> *Copies of proposal:* 7
> *Deadline(s):* Sept. 15
> *Board meeting date(s):* Annual
> *Final notification:* Jan. of the following year

Officers and Trustees:* Louise D. Nippert,* Pres.; Carter Randolph,* V.P.; Marie Eberhard,* Secy.-Treas.; Tim Johnson; Lawrence Kyte; Guy Randolph; Jane Randolph.

Number of staff: 2 shared staff (shared with Greenacres Foundation).

EIN: 311351011

2690

The Nord Family Foundation ▼
747 Milan Ave.
Amherst, OH 44001 (440) 984-3939
Contact: John Mullaney, Exec. Dir.
Additional tel.: (800) 745-8946; FAX: (440) 984-3934; E-mail: info@nordff.org or execdir@nordff.org; URL: http://www.nordff.org

Trust established in 1952 in OH; reorganized in 1988 under current name.

Donor(s): Walter G. Nord,‡ Mrs. Walter G. Nord,‡ Nordson Corp.

Grantmaker type: Independent foundation

Financial data (yr. ended 12/31/02): Assets, $68,056,989 (M); expenditures, $4,421,559; qualifying distributions, $3,177,497; giving activities include $2,953,910 for 220 grants (high: $125,000; low: $200; average: $10,000–$50,000), $54,270 for employee matching gifts and $169,317 for 2 foundation-administered programs.

Purpose and activities: Emphasis on projects to assist the disadvantaged and minorities, including giving for early childhood, secondary, and higher education, social services, health, cultural affairs, and civic activities. Initiatives included a project to establish a common agenda to address factors which inhibit social and economic progress within the county and a program to strengthen nonprofit organizations which address family issues.

Fields of interest: Arts; Early childhood education; Child development, education; Secondary school/education; Higher education; Education; Environment; Health care; Health organizations, association; Human services; Children/youth, services; Child development, services; Minorities/immigrants, centers/services; Urban/community development; Minorities; Economically disadvantaged.

Types of support: General/operating support; Continuing support; Program development; Publication; Seed money; Technical assistance;

Program-related investments/loans; Employee matching gifts; Matching/challenge support.

Limitations: Giving primarily in the Lorain and Cuyahoga County, OH, areas; also gives secondarily in Denver, CO, Boston, MA, and Columbia, SC. No grants to individuals, or for deficit financing, research, capital campaigns, general operations, scholarships, fellowships, tickets, advertising for fundraising activities, or conferences.

Publications: Annual report (including application guidelines), Informational brochure (including application guidelines).

Application information: Application form required.

> *Initial approach:* One-page abstract of the proposal
> *Copies of proposal:* 1
> *Deadline(s):* Apr. 1, Aug. 1, and Dec. 1
> *Board meeting date(s):* Feb., June, and Oct.
> *Final notification:* 1 to 3 months

Officers and Trustees:* Virginia Barbato, Pres.; Emily McClintock, V.P.; Emily Porter, Secy.; Emma Mason,* Treas.; Sharon White, Cont.; John J. Mullaney, Exec. Dir.; Randall Barbato; Sam Berk; Pam Ignat; Camille Mamlin-Allen; Evan Nord; Shannon Nord; Luis Villarreal.

Number of staff: 3 full-time professional; 1 part-time professional; 1 full-time support.

EIN: 341595929

2691

The Eric and Jane Nord Foundation
P.O. Box 457
Oberlin, OH 44074

Established in 1984 in OH.

Donor(s): Eric T. Nord, Jane B. Nord.

Grantmaker type: Independent foundation

Financial data (yr. ended 06/30/02): Assets, $9,114,712 (M); gifts received, $320,000; expenditures, $483,946; qualifying distributions, $477,719; giving activities include $478,183 for 35 grants (high: $125,000; low: $200).

Purpose and activities: Giving primarily for the arts, particularly an inter-museum association; funding also for education, and human services.

Fields of interest: Arts, association; Museums; Opera; Arts; Education, information services; Higher education; Libraries (public); Botanical gardens; Health care, clinics/centers; Disasters, 9/11/01; Boys & girls clubs; Human services; Community development; Federated giving programs.

Limitations: Applications not accepted. Giving primarily in OH. No grants to individuals.

Application information: Contributes only to pre-selected organizations.

Officers: Eric T. Nord, Pres. and Treas.; Jane B. Nord, V.P.; William D. Ginn, Secy.

Number of staff: None.

EIN: 341465569

2692

The Nordson Corporation Foundation
28601 Clemens Rd.
Westlake, OH 44145-1119 (440) 892-1580
Contact: Constance T. Haqq, Exec. Dir.
Additional tel.: (440) 988-9411; FAX: (216) 892-9253; URL: http://www.nordson.com/corporate/grants.html

Established in 1988 in OH.

Donor(s): Nordson Corp.

Grantmaker type: Company-sponsored foundation

Financial data (yr. ended 10/31/02): Assets, $1,505,043 (M); expenditures, $1,061,628; qualifying distributions, $1,040,120; giving activities include $1,040,540 for 137 grants (high: $100,000; low: $1,000).

Purpose and activities: To provide a source of stable funding for community programs and projects in the areas of education, human welfare, civics, and art and culture. Educational support is generally limited to improving elementary and secondary public schools and certain programs for public and private higher education. The foundation is willing to consider a number of funding areas, including urban affairs, volunteerism, public policy, and literacy.

Fields of interest: Visual arts; Performing arts; Humanities; Education, association; Education, research; Education, fund raising; Early childhood education; Elementary school/education; Secondary school/education; Higher education; Business school/education; Adult/continuing education; Adult education—literacy, basic skills & GED; Reading; Environment; Mental health/crisis services; Health organizations, association; Alcoholism; Employment; Food services; Youth development, services; Youth development, citizenship; Human services; Youth, services; Aging, centers/services; Minorities/immigrants, centers/services; Homeless, human services; International affairs; Race/intergroup relations; Community development; Voluntarism promotion; Federated giving programs; Mathematics; Public policy, research; Government/public administration; Public affairs, citizen participation; Leadership development; Public affairs; Minorities; African Americans/Blacks; Hispanics/Latinos; Disabled; Aging; Women; Economically disadvantaged; Homeless.

Types of support: General/operating support; Continuing support; Annual campaigns; Capital campaigns; Building/renovation; Equipment; Emergency funds; Seed money; Scholarship funds; Technical assistance; Employee matching gifts.

Limitations: Giving limited to San Diego County, CA, Atlanta, GA, northern OH, and the Providence, RI, area.

Publications: Annual report (including application guidelines), Corporate giving report, Grants list.

Application information: Application form required.

> *Initial approach:* Letter or application form
> *Copies of proposal:* 2
> *Deadline(s):* 15th of Nov., Feb., May, and Aug.
> *Board meeting date(s):* Jan., Apr., July, and Oct.
> *Final notification:* Within 1 month after meeting

Officer: Constance T. Haqq, Exec. Dir.

Trustees: Edward P. Campbell; Beverly J. Coen; Mark Gacka; Peter S. Hellman; Donald J. McLane.

Number of staff: 5 full-time professional; 1 full-time support.

EIN: 341596194

2693
Edwin D. Northrup II Fund Trust
c/o National City Bank
P.O. Box 94651
Cleveland, OH 44101-4651
Application address: c/o Michael Galland,
National City Bank, P.O. Box 5756, Cleveland,
OH 44101, tel.: (216) 575-2736

Established in 1984 in OH.
Donor(s): Edwin Northrup II.‡
Grantmaker type: Independent foundation
Financial data (yr. ended 12/31/02): Assets,
$2,132,142 (M); expenditures, $151,304;
qualifying distributions, $142,630; giving
activities include $136,250 for 20 grants (high:
$25,000; low: $2,000).
Fields of interest: Performing arts; Higher
education; Education; Zoos/zoological societies;
Health organizations, association; Human
services; Roman Catholic agencies & churches.
Types of support: General/operating support.
Limitations: Giving primarily in Cleveland, OH.
Application information: Application form not
required.
  Initial approach: Letter
  Copies of proposal: 1
  Deadline(s): None
Trustee: National City Bank.
Number of staff: None.
EIN: 346829894

2694
The Norweb Foundation
c/o KeyBank N.A.
800 Superior Ave., 4th Fl.
Cleveland, OH 44114

Established in 1952 in OH.
Donor(s): Eliz Norweb, R. Henry Norweb, Jr.‡
Grantmaker type: Independent foundation
Financial data (yr. ended 12/31/02): Assets,
$1,405,941 (M); gifts received, $10,000;
expenditures, $177,296; qualifying distributions,
$163,304; giving activities include $159,400 for
138 grants (high: $15,000; low: $100).
Purpose and activities: Giving for the arts, the
environment, education, and youth services.
Fields of interest: Arts; Secondary
school/education; Natural resources; Recreation;
Human services; YM/YWCAs & YM/YWHAs;
Federated giving programs.
Types of support: General/operating support;
Annual campaigns; Capital campaigns.
Limitations: Applications not accepted. Giving
primarily in Cleveland, OH. No grants to
individuals.
Application information: Contributes only to
pre-selected organizations.
  Board meeting date(s): Apr. and Nov.
Trustee: KeyBank N.A.
EIN: 346517914

2695
Charles O'Bleness Foundation No. 3
c/o The Huntington National Bank, Trust Dept.
P.O. Box 1558, EA4E86
Columbus, OH 43216
Application address: Donna Auten, V.P. c/o The
Huntington National Bank, 41 S. High St.,
Columbus, OH 43215, tel.: (614) 480-5453

Established in 1963 in OH.
Donor(s): Charles O'Bleness,‡ Charles
O'Bleness Foundation No. 1.
Grantmaker type: Independent foundation
Financial data (yr. ended 06/30/02): Assets,
$3,240,781 (M); expenditures, $203,771;
qualifying distributions, $179,165; giving
activities include $170,402 for 10 grants (high:
$100,000; low: $75).
Fields of interest: Higher education; Libraries
(public); Environment; Hospitals (general);
Community development.
Types of support: General/operating support;
Building/renovation; Program development;
Scholarship funds.
Limitations: Giving limited to Athens County,
OH. No grants to individuals.
Application information: Application form not
required.
  Copies of proposal: 3
  Deadline(s): Oct. 15
  Board meeting date(s): Mar., June, Sept., and
  Dec.
Advisors: John M. Jones; David Vogt.
Trustee: The Huntington National Bank.
Number of staff: None.
EIN: 316042978

2696
The O'Neill Brothers Foundation
30000 Aurora Rd., Ste. 250
Solon, OH 44139
Contact: Robert K. Healey, Pres.
FAX: (440) 248-2153

Incorporated in 1953 in MI.
Donor(s): William J. O'Neill,‡ P.J. O'Neill,‡
H.M. O'Neill,‡ Francis J. O'Neill,‡ George C.
Fortner,‡ Robert K. Healey, Mrs. Robert K.
Healey.
Grantmaker type: Independent foundation
Financial data (yr. ended 12/31/01): Assets,
$759,765 (M); expenditures, $170,645;
qualifying distributions, $162,286; giving
activities include $153,387 for 101 grants (high:
$20,000; low: $100).
Purpose and activities: Giving primarily to
Roman Catholic agencies, churches, schools,
and hospitals.
Fields of interest: Secondary school/education;
Higher education; Natural resources; Animal
welfare; Health care; Health organizations,
association; Children/youth, services;
Community development; Roman Catholic
agencies & churches.
Types of support: General/operating support.
Limitations: Giving primarily in Cleveland, OH;
giving also in FL. No grants to individuals.
Application information: Application form
required.
  Initial approach: Letter

Deadline(s): None
  Board meeting date(s): 4 times a year
Officers and Trustees:* Robert K. Healey,* Pres.;
Hugh O'Neill,* Secy.
Number of staff: None.
EIN: 346545084

2697
The Olive Branch Foundation, Inc.
P.O. Box 20881
Canton, OH 44701 (330) 456-7900

Established in 1998 in OH.
Donor(s): Marshall B. Belden, Jr.
Grantmaker type: Independent foundation
Financial data (yr. ended 12/31/02): Assets,
$4,964,946 (M); gifts received, $995,346;
expenditures, $521,542; qualifying distributions,
$488,852; giving activities include $488,852 for
19 grants (high: $200,000; low: $100; average:
$1,000–$25,000).
Purpose and activities: Giving for the purpose of
improving the quality of life and scope of
human knowledge in the areas of science,
medicine, literature, philosophy, environmental
science, or sociology.
Fields of interest: Historic preservation/historical
societies; Higher education; Environment;
Health organizations, association.
Limitations: Applications not accepted. Giving
primarily in OH. No grants to individuals.
Application information: Unsolicited requests
for funds not accepted.
Trustees: James Bagnola; Diana Davis Belden;
Marshall B. Belden, Jr.
EIN: 341862239

2698
Jane and Jon Outcalt Foundation
(formerly Outcalt Charitable Fund)
3201 Enterprise Pkwy., Ste. 220
Beachwood, OH 44122

Donor(s): Jon H. Outcalt, Jane Q. Outcalt.
Grantmaker type: Independent foundation
Financial data (yr. ended 12/31/02): Assets,
$5,541,859 (M); gifts received, $382,840;
expenditures, $272,748; qualifying distributions,
$254,754; giving activities include $255,000 for
42 grants (high: $110,000; low: $100).
Fields of interest: Theater; University; Botanical
gardens; Hospitals (general); Federated giving
programs.
Limitations: Applications not accepted. Giving
primarily in Cleveland, OH. No grants to
individuals.
Application information: Contributes only to
pre-selected organizations.
Officers: Kenneth W. Outcalt, Pres.; Jane Q.
Outcalt, V.P.; Jon H. Outcalt, Secy.; Jon H.
Outcalt, Jr., Treas.
EIN: 311194069

2699
Oxford Community Foundation
52 E. Park Pl., Ste. 4
Oxford, OH 45056-1884 (513) 523-0623
Contact: Roger D. Millar, Exec. Dir.
FAX: (513) 524-1026; E-mail:
oxcomfdn@ix.netcom.com; URL: http://
www.oxfordfdn.org/

Established in 1996 in OH.
Grantmaker type: Community foundation
Financial data (yr. ended 06/30/03): Assets,
$2,212,135 (M); gifts received, $150,608;
expenditures, $325,768; giving activities
include $250,787 for grants.
Purpose and activities: To improve the quality of
life in the Oxford, OH, area. Also awards
scholarships to individuals committed to
planning a career in community and public
service. The foundation administers
donor-advised funds.
Fields of interest: Arts; Education; Environment;
Health care; Recreation; Community
development.
Types of support: Building/renovation;
Equipment; Emergency funds; Publication; Seed
money; Technical assistance; Scholarships—to
individuals; Matching/challenge support.
Limitations: Giving limited to the Oxford, OH,
area.
Publications: Financial statement, Grants list,
Informational brochure (including application
guidelines), Newsletter.
Application information: 8 copies required for
any proposal over 5 pages. Application form not
required.
  Initial approach: Telephone
  Copies of proposal: 1
  Board meeting date(s): 4th Wed. of Sept.,
    Nov., Jan., Mar., and May
Officers and Trustees:* Jim Robinsom,* Pres.;
Thomas Collins, V.P.; Ed Demske,* Treas.; K.E.
Smith, Exec. Dir.; Linda Balogh; J. K.
Bhattacharjee; Biz Campbell; Sondra Engel;
John Kirsch; Roberta L. Norman; Harry Ogle;
Tom Peterson; Judy Ramsey; Judith Schiller; Phil
Shriver; Suzanne H. Summers.
Number of staff: 1 full-time professional; 2
part-time professional; 1 part-time support.
EIN: 311428999

2700
P & G Corporate Giving Program
P.O. Box 599
Cincinnati, OH 45201 (513) 983-1100
Contact: Carol G. Talbot, Assoc. Dir., Contribs.
and Community Rels.
FAX: (513) 945-8979; URL: http://www.pg.com/
about_pg/corporate/corp_citizenship_main.jhtml

Grantmaker type: Corporate giving program
Purpose and activities: As a complement to its
foundation, P&G also makes charitable
contributions to nonprofit organizations directly.
Support is given on a national basis.
Fields of interest: Arts; Higher education;
Environment; Health care; Human services;
Public affairs.
Types of support: General/operating support;
Employee volunteer services; Employee

matching gifts; Employee-related scholarships;
In-kind gifts.
Limitations: Giving on a national basis.
Publications: Corporate giving report, Grants
list, Informational brochure.
Application information: The Public Affairs
Department handles giving. Application form
not required.
  Initial approach: Proposal to headquarters
  Copies of proposal: 1
  Deadline(s): None
  Final notification: 2 to 3 weeks
Number of staff: 5 full-time professional.

2701
Holden Parks Trust
c/o KeyBank N.A.
800 Superior Ave., 4th Fl.
Cleveland, OH 44114 (216) 828-9770

Established in 1988.
Grantmaker type: Public charity
Financial data (yr. ended 12/31/01): Revenue,
$627,457; assets, $8,143,002 (M); expenditures,
$463,386; program services expenses,
$419,939; giving activities include $419,939 for
9 grants (high: $133,817; low: $2,895).
Purpose and activities: The trust aims to
improve and beautify the public park system of
Cleveland, OH.
Fields of interest: Environment, beautification
programs; Parks/playgrounds.
Limitations: Giving primarily in Cleveland, OH.
Trustee: KeyBank N.A.
EIN: 346888980

2702
The Payne Fund
2950 Terminal Twr.
50 Public Sq.
Cleveland, OH 44113

Incorporated in 1929 in OH.
Donor(s): Frances P. Bolton.‡
Grantmaker type: Independent foundation
Financial data (yr. ended 12/31/01): Assets,
$4,290,361 (M); gifts received, $979,488;
expenditures, $1,149,865; qualifying
distributions, $1,088,893; giving activities
include $1,034,500 for 37 grants (high:
$207,000; low: $2,500) and $2,064 for
foundation-administered programs.
Purpose and activities: To initiate, assist, or
conduct research and experiments in education
and other activities on behalf of the welfare of
mankind; support also for higher education and
cultural programs.
Fields of interest: Arts, association; Museums;
Theater; Music; Arts; Education, research;
Higher education; Education; Natural resources;
Nursing care.
Types of support: General/operating support;
Capital campaigns; Building/renovation.
Limitations: Applications not accepted. Giving
primarily in San Francisco, CA, Atlanta, GA,
Boston, Cambridge, and Milton, MA, and
Cleveland and Gambier, OH. No grants to
individuals.

Application information: Contributes only to
pre-selected organizations.
  Board meeting date(s): Nov.
Officers: Barbara Bolton Gratry, Pres.; Kenyon
C. Bolton III, V.P.; Thomas C. Bolton, V.P.;
William B. Bolton, V.P.; Mary Bolton Hooper,
V.P.; Charles P. Bolton,* Secy.-Treas.
Directors: John B. Bolton; Philip P. Bolton;
Frederick B. Taylor.
Number of staff: 1 full-time professional.
EIN: 135563006

2703
The Perkins Charitable Foundation
1030 Hanna Bldg.
1422 Euclid Ave.
Cleveland, OH 44115 (216) 621-0465
Contact: Marilyn Best, Secy.-Treas.

Trust established in 1950 in OH.
Donor(s): Leigh H. Perkins, Sallie Sullivan,
Members of the Perkins family.
Grantmaker type: Independent foundation
Financial data (yr. ended 12/31/02): Assets,
$21,478,982 (M); expenditures, $1,586,380;
qualifying distributions, $1,522,567; giving
activities include $1,515,250 for 163 grants
(high: $116,100; low: $250; average:
$250–$15,000).
Fields of interest: Arts; Elementary/secondary
education; Higher education; Natural resources;
Health care; Human services; Federated giving
programs.
Limitations: Giving on a national basis. No
grants to individuals.
Application information: Application form not
required.
  Deadline(s): None
Officer: Marilyn Best, Secy.-Treas.
Trustees: George Oliva III; Leigh H. Perkins;
Sallie P. Sullivan.
EIN: 346549753

2704
The Jesse and Caryl Philips Foundation
3870 Honey Hill Ln.
Dayton, OH 45405
Contact: Christine Pack, Admin. Asst.
FAX: (937) 277-9603

Established in 1990 in OH.
Donor(s): Jesse Philips.‡
Grantmaker type: Independent foundation
Financial data (yr. ended 06/30/02): Assets,
$23,120,872 (M); expenditures, $722,176;
qualifying distributions, $644,789; giving
activities include $641,150 for 36 grants (high:
$150,000; low: $50).
Fields of interest: Museums; Animals/wildlife,
bird preserves; Jewish federated giving programs.
Limitations: Applications not accepted. Giving
primarily in Dayton, OH. No grants to
individuals.
Application information: Contributes only to
pre-selected organizations.
Officer and Trustees:* Caryl Philips,* Pres.;
Benjamin M. Beatty; Mary Dombrowsky Beatty.
EIN: 341656718

2705
Charles M. & Thelma M. Pugliese Charitable Foundation

c/o Sky Bank
P.O. Box 479
Youngstown, OH 44501-0479 (330) 742-7000
Application address: c/o Sky Bank, 23 Federal
Plz., 2nd Fl., Youngstown, OH 44501

Established in 1998 in OH.
Donor(s): Charles M. Pugliese, Thelma M.
Pugliese.
Grantmaker type: Independent foundation
Financial data (yr. ended 12/31/02): Assets,
$7,568,557 (M); expenditures, $275,529;
qualifying distributions, $236,157; giving
activities include $235,300 for 7 grants (high:
$125,000; low: $2,000).
Fields of interest: Education; Animal welfare;
Disasters, fire prevention/control; Human
services; Aging, centers/services; Foundations
(community).
Limitations: Giving primarily in Jefferson
County, OH. No grants to individuals.
Application information:
Initial approach: Letter
Deadline(s): None
Officers: William W. McElwain, Chair.; Douglas
C. Naylor, Sr., Secy.
Trustee: H. Lee Kinney.
Agent: Sky Bank.
EIN: 341784660

2706
P. K. Ranney Foundation

111 Superior Ave., Ste. 1000
Cleveland, OH 44114-2507 (216) 696-4200
Contact: Phillip A. Ranney, Secy.
Application address: 13881 Lake Ave.,
Lakewood, OH 44107-1424; FAX: (216)
696-7303; E-mail: pranney@ssrl.com

Incorporated in 1973 in OH.
Grantmaker type: Independent foundation
Financial data (yr. ended 12/31/01): Assets,
$5,597,321 (M); expenditures, $551,127;
qualifying distributions, $527,963; giving
activities include $506,838 for 31 grants (high:
$181,838; low: $1,000; average:
$5,000–$10,000).
Purpose and activities: Support primarily but
not exclusively to museums, healthcare, the
environment, education and a local community
foundation.
Fields of interest: Environment; Health care;
Marine science.
Types of support: General/operating support;
Continuing support; Endowments; Research.
Limitations: Giving primarily in the greater
Cleveland, OH, area. No grants to individuals.
Application information: Application form not
required.
Initial approach: Proposal
Copies of proposal: 1
Deadline(s): None
Board meeting date(s): As required
Officers: Peter K. Ranney, Pres. and Treas.;
Robert K. Bissell, V.P.; Phillip A. Ranney, Secy.
Number of staff: 1 part-time professional.
EIN: 237343201

2707
The Reinberger Foundation ▼

27600 Chagrin Blvd.
Cleveland, OH 44122 (216) 292-2790
Contact: Robert N. Reinberger, Dir.
FAX: (216) 292-4466

Established in 1968 in OH.
Donor(s): Clarence T. Reinberger,‡ Louise F.
Reinberger.‡
Grantmaker type: Independent foundation
Financial data (yr. ended 12/31/01): Assets,
$78,951,631 (M); expenditures, $5,260,785;
qualifying distributions, $4,773,091; giving
activities include $4,483,473 for 74 grants (high:
$250,000; low: $1,200; average:
$5,000–$100,000).
Purpose and activities: Support for the arts,
social welfare, Protestant churches, higher
education, and medical research.
Fields of interest: Media/communications;
Visual arts; Museums; Performing arts; Dance;
Theater; Music; Historic preservation/historical
societies; Arts; Education, research; Education,
fund raising; Environment; Animals/wildlife,
preservation/protection; Hospitals (general);
Health care; Health organizations, association;
Cancer; Biomedicine; Medical research,
institute; Cancer research; Children/youth,
services; Family services; Aging,
centers/services; Community development;
Aging.
Types of support: General/operating support;
Continuing support; Annual campaigns; Capital
campaigns; Building/renovation; Equipment;
Endowments; Debt reduction; Program
development; Publication; Scholarship funds;
Research; Matching/challenge support.
Limitations: Giving primarily in the Cleveland
and Columbus, OH, metropolitan areas. No
grants to individuals, or for seed money,
emergency funds, land acquisition,
demonstration projects, or conferences; no
loans.
Publications: Application guidelines, Grants list,
Informational brochure (including application
guidelines).
Application information: Application form not
required.
Initial approach: Proposal
Copies of proposal: 1
Deadline(s): None
Board meeting date(s): Feb., May, Aug., and
Nov.
Final notification: 6 months
Officer: Richard H. Oman, Secy.
Directors: Sara R. Dyer; Karen R. Hooser;
Robert N. Reinberger; William C. Reinberger.
Agent: The Glenmede Trust Co.
Number of staff: 2 full-time professional.
EIN: 346574879

2708
The Fran and Warren Rupp Foundation

c/o KeyBank N.A.
42 N. Main St.
Mansfield, OH 44902 (419) 525-7665
Contact: David R. Irvin
FAX: (419) 525-7666

Established in 1977.
Donor(s): Fran R. Christian, Warren Rupp,‡
Suzanne R. Hartung.

Grantmaker type: Independent foundation
Financial data (yr. ended 12/31/02): Assets,
$16,297,090 (M); gifts received, $36,000;
expenditures, $1,461,483; qualifying
distributions, $1,269,267; giving activities
include $1,219,135 for grants (average:
$4,000–$25,000).
Purpose and activities: Giving primarily for arts
and culture, education, conservation and the
environment, and social services.
Fields of interest: Theater; Arts; Natural
resources; Environment; Animal welfare;
Crime/law enforcement; Housing/shelter,
development; Human services.
Types of support: General/operating support;
Capital campaigns; Building/renovation; Land
acquisition; Endowments; Publication;
Matching/challenge support.
Limitations: Giving primarily in Mansfield and
Richland County, OH. No grants to individuals.
Publications: Informational brochure (including
application guidelines).
Application information: Application form
required.
Initial approach: Letter
Copies of proposal: 8
Deadline(s): None
Board meeting date(s): May and Nov.
Officers: Frances R. Christian, Co-Chair.; Sheron
A. Rupp, Co-Chair.; Suzanne R. Hartung, Pres.;
Sheila York, Secy.; B. Gene Hahn, Treas.
Trustee: Arnold Haring.
Number of staff: None.
EIN: 341230690

2709
Sandusky/Erie County Community Foundation

165 E. Washington Row, Ste. 304
Sandusky, OH 44870 (419) 621-9690
Contact: Dee Leibersberger, Pres.
FAX: (419) 621-9691; E-mail:
info@sanduskyfound.org; URL: http://
www.sanduskyfoundation.org/

Established in 1996 in OH.
Grantmaker type: Community foundation
Financial data (yr. ended 12/31/01): Assets,
$8,272,805 (M); gifts received, $2,422,375;
expenditures, $339,508; giving activities include
$181,550 for 45 grants (high: $25,000; low:
$2,000).
Purpose and activities: The foundation
administers donor-advised funds.
Fields of interest: Arts; Education; Environment;
Health organizations, association; Human
services; Economic development.
Types of support: General/operating support;
Continuing support; Capital campaigns;
Building/renovation; Equipment; Endowments;
Program development; Conferences/seminars;
Publication; Curriculum development;
Scholarship funds; Technical assistance;
Consulting services; Program evaluation;
Matching/challenge support.
Limitations: Giving limited to Erie County, OH.
Publications: Application guidelines, Annual
report, Financial statement, Grants list,
Informational brochure (including application
guidelines), Newsletter, Occasional report.
Application information: Application form
required.

Initial approach: Letter, telephone, FAX, or E-mail
Copies of proposal: 1
Deadline(s): Feb. 1 and July 1
Final notification: 6 to 8 weeks
Officers and Directors:* John O. Bacon,* Chair.; Mary Jane Hill, Vice-Chair.; Dee Leibersberger, Pres.; Mel Stauffer, Secy.; Eugene Koby, Treas.; Laurence Bettcher; George Mylander; Ruth Parker; Charles W. Rainger; and 10 additional directors.
Number of staff: 1 full-time professional; 1 part-time professional.
EIN: 341792862

2710
The Sauerland Foundation
P.O. Box 621
Chagrin Falls, OH 44022
Contact: Franz Sauerland, Tr.

Established in 1994 in OH.
Donor(s): Franz L. Sauerland.
Grantmaker type: Independent foundation
Financial data (yr. ended 12/31/02): Assets, $2,468,434 (M); expenditures, $189,234; qualifying distributions, $186,280; giving activities include $187,500 for 9 grants (high: $100,000; low: $1,500).
Fields of interest: Environment, land resources; Crime/violence prevention; Housing/shelter, development; Human services; Federated giving programs.
Types of support: General/operating support.
Limitations: Giving primarily in OH. No grants to individuals.
Application information:
Initial approach: Letter
Deadline(s): None
Trustees: Elizabeth I. Sauerland; Franz Sauerland; Paul Sauerland.
EIN: 341787952

2711
John J. and Mary R. Schiff Foundation
P.O. Box 145496
Cincinnati, OH 45250-5496

Established in 1983 in OH.
Donor(s): John J. Schiff, Mary R. Schiff.
Grantmaker type: Independent foundation
Financial data (yr. ended 06/30/02): Assets, $104,777,087 (M); gifts received, $12,792,385; expenditures, $3,722,088; qualifying distributions, $3,676,200; giving activities include $3,635,500 for 27 grants (high: $700,000; low: $5,000).
Purpose and activities: Support primarily for a historical society; support also for higher education and hospitals.
Fields of interest: Museums (art); Historic preservation/historical societies; Higher education; Animal welfare; Hospitals (general).
Limitations: Applications not accepted. Giving primarily in Cincinnati, OH. No grants to individuals.
Application information: Contributes only to pre-selected organizations.
Officer: John J. Schiff, Jr., Chair.
Trustees: Suzanne Reid; Thomas R. Schiff.
EIN: 311077222

Recent environmental and animal welfare grants:
2711-1 Society for the Prevention of Cruelty to Animals of Hamilton County, Cincinnati, OH, $250,000. For unrestricted support. 2002.

2712
Marge & Charles J. Schott Foundation
30 E. Central Pkwy., Ste. 300
Cincinnati, OH 45202-1147 (513) 721-8400
Contact: Phyllis J. Cartwright, Secy.-Treas.

Established around 1980.
Donor(s): Margaret U. Schott.
Grantmaker type: Independent foundation
Financial data (yr. ended 06/30/02): Assets, $9,049,082 (M); gifts received, $9,644; expenditures, $583,438; qualifying distributions, $574,675; giving activities include $575,816 for 38 grants (high: $500,000; low: $6).
Fields of interest: Zoos/zoological societies; Parks/playgrounds; Boys & girls clubs; Human services; Community development; Christian agencies & churches.
Limitations: Giving primarily in Cincinnati, OH. No grants to individuals.
Application information:
Initial approach: Letter
Deadline(s): None
Officers: Margaret U. Schott, Pres.; Phyllis J. Cartwright, Secy.-Treas.
EIN: 316063407

2713
The Scioto County Area Foundation
National City Bank Bldg., Ste. 801
800 Gallia St.
Portsmouth, OH 45662 (740) 354-4612
Contact: Kimberly E. Cutlip, Exec. Dir.
FAX: (740) 354-4612; URL: http://www.scaf-online.com/main.html

Established in 1974 in OH.
Grantmaker type: Community foundation
Financial data (yr. ended 12/31/02): Assets, $15,240,306 (M); gifts received, $1,875,060; expenditures, $795,030; giving activities include $590,065 for 14+ grants.
Purpose and activities: Giving for charitable purposes to benefit the citizens of Scioto County; primary areas of interest include education, health care, community development, economic development, arts and culture, social services, and civic benefit. The foundation administers donor-advised funds.
Fields of interest: Arts; Education; Natural resources; Health care; Human services; Family services; Economic development; Community development; Public affairs.
Types of support: Management development; Equipment; Program development; Conferences/seminars; Publication; Seed money; Scholarship funds; Research; Technical assistance; Consulting services; Program evaluation; Matching/challenge support.
Limitations: Giving primarily in Scioto County, OH; distributions are regional depending on donor preference. No support for religious organizations for religious programs. No grants to individuals, or for continuing support, annual campaigns, emergency funds, deficit financing,

building funds, land acquisition, endowments, foundation-managed projects, exchange programs, or program support; no loans.
Publications: Application guidelines, Annual report, Informational brochure (including application guidelines), Newsletter.
Application information: Grants accepted on a quarterly basis. See foundation Web site for complete guidelines and downloadable application form. Application form required.
Initial approach: Telephone
Copies of proposal: 6
Deadline(s): Quarterly: Mar. 31, June 30, Sept. 29, and Dec. 29
Board meeting date(s): 3rd Thurs. of each month
Final notification: 1 month
Officers: Charles Wilson, Chair.; Kimberly E. Cuttlip, Exec. Dir.
Number of staff: 2 full-time professional; 1 part-time professional.
EIN: 510157026

2714
Kenneth A. Scott Charitable Trust
c/o KeyBank N.A.
127 Public Sq., 17th Fl.
Cleveland, OH 44114-1306 (216) 556-4062
Contact: H. Richard Obermanns, Exec. Dir.

Established in 1995 in OH.
Grantmaker type: Independent foundation
Financial data (yr. ended 12/31/01): Assets, $19,723,893 (M); expenditures, $2,440,938; qualifying distributions, $2,238,424; giving activities include $2,147,705 for grants.
Purpose and activities: Support only for organizations whose purpose is the prevention of cruelty to animals.
Fields of interest: Animal welfare.
Limitations: Giving primarily in OH for local organizations; giving outside OH only for national organizations. No grants to individuals, or for endowments, general support, capital expenditures, or deficit reduction.
Publications: Application guidelines, Annual report.
Application information:
Initial approach: Letter
Deadline(s): Jan 1, May 1, and Sept. 1
Trustee: KeyBank N.A.
Number of staff: 1 part-time professional.
EIN: 347034544

2715
The Scotts Company Contributions Program
41 S. High St., Ste. 3500
Columbus, OH 43215 (614) 719-5500
Contact: Dianna Keller, Mgr., Community Rels.
Application address: Scotts Give Back to Grow Awards, c/o Weber Shandwick Worldwide, 100 S. 4th St., Ste. 1200, St. Louis, MO 63102, tel.: (800) 551-5971; FAX: (614) 719-5750

Grantmaker type: Corporate giving program
Purpose and activities: Scotts awards grants to individuals involved with gardening. Support is given on a national basis.
Fields of interest: Horticulture/garden clubs.
Types of support: Grants to individuals.
Limitations: Giving on a national basis.

Application information: An application form is required for the Give Back to Grow Awards; application form available online.
Initial approach: Download application form for Give Back to Grow Awards
Deadline(s): Postmarked by Dec. 6 for Give Back to Grow Awards
Final notification: Feb. 10 for Give Back to Grow Awards

2716
The Sears-Swetland Family Foundation
(formerly The Sears-Swetland Foundation)
2700 Eaton Rd.
Cleveland, OH 44118
Contact: Ruth Swetland Eppig, Tr.
FAX: (216) 932-2745

Trust established in 1949 in OH.
Donor(s): Anna L. Sears,‡ Lester M. Sears,‡ Ruth P. Sears,‡ Mary Ann Swetland,‡ David W. Swetland, David S. Swetland, Ruth S. Eppig, Polly S. Jones.
Grantmaker type: Independent foundation
Financial data (yr. ended 12/31/02): Assets, $2,959,634 (M); expenditures, $159,925; qualifying distributions, $149,764; giving activities include $142,500 for 34 grants (high: $60,000; low: $500).
Fields of interest: Visual arts; Museums; Historic preservation/historical societies; Education; Botanical/horticulture/landscape services; Environment; Health care; Human services.
Types of support: General/operating support; Continuing support; Annual campaigns; Capital campaigns; Building/renovation; Equipment; Land acquisition; Program development; Seed money; Curriculum development; Research; Matching/challenge support.
Limitations: Giving primarily in the Cleveland, OH, area. No support for secondary schools. No grants to individuals.
Publications: Application guidelines, Grants list.
Application information: Application form not required.
Initial approach: Letter
Copies of proposal: 1
Deadline(s): Submit proposal preferably before Dec.; and annual fund proposals before Apr.
Board meeting date(s): As needed
Final notification: 60 days
Trustees: Ruth Swetland Eppig; Polly Swetland Jones; David Sears Swetland; David W. Swetland.
Number of staff: 2 part-time support.
EIN: 346522143

2717
Murray and Agnes Seasongood Good Government Foundation
15 E. 8th St., Ste. 200W
Cincinnati, OH 45202
Contact: D. David Altman, Exec. Secy.

Established in 1987 in OH.
Grantmaker type: Independent foundation
Financial data (yr. ended 12/31/02): Assets, $5,273,269 (M); expenditures, $306,895; qualifying distributions, $277,272; giving activities include $210,474 for 24 grants (high: $31,500; low: $900).

Fields of interest: Media/communications; University; Education; Environment; Human services; Community development; neighborhood development; Community development, citizen coalitions; Foundations (community); Government/public administration.
Types of support: Program development; Internship funds; Research.
Limitations: Giving primarily in Cincinnati, OH.
Publications: Informational brochure.
Application information: Application form required.
Initial approach: Request for application
Copies of proposal: 15
Deadline(s): 15th of even-numbered months
Board meeting date(s): Odd-numbered months
Officers: Travis L. Kubale, Pres.; Dean Jay Chatterjee, 1st V.P.; David D. Black, 2nd V.P.; Henry R. Winkler, Secy.; William T. Bahlman, Jr., Treas.
Board Members: Mary Asbury; Arnold L. Bortz; Janet Hoffheimer; Jon Hoffheimer; Bruce I. Petrie, Sr.; Myrtis M. Powell; Jack Sherman, Jr.
Number of staff: 1 part-time professional.
EIN: 311220827

2718
Sedgwick Family Charitable Trust
c/o KeyBank N.A.
800 Superior Ave., 4th Fl.
Cleveland, OH 44114
Additional address: 105 W. Hill Dr., Farmville, VA 23901

Established in 1991 in OH.
Donor(s): Ellery Sedgwick, Jr.‡
Grantmaker type: Independent foundation
Financial data (yr. ended 12/31/02): Assets, $2,970,963 (M); expenditures, $204,994; qualifying distributions, $189,651; giving activities include $188,754 for 83 grants (high: $26,000; low: $50).
Purpose and activities: Giving primarily for education, wildlife protection, and human services.
Fields of interest: Education; Animals/wildlife, preservation/protection; Human services.
Types of support: Annual campaigns; Capital campaigns; Building/renovation; Scholarship funds; Research.
Limitations: Applications not accepted. Giving primarily in south GA. No grants to individuals.
Application information: Contributes only to pre-selected organizations the family has involvement with. Unsolicited requests for funds not accepted.
Trustees: Irene Sedgwick Briedis; Elizabeth W. Sedgwick; Ellery Sedgwick III; Theodore Sedgwick; Walter Cabot Sedgwick; KeyBank N.A.
EIN: 346958569

2719
Ladislas & Vilma Segoe Family Foundation
c/o Lewis G. Gatch
8050 Hosbrook Rd., Ste. 210
Cincinnati, OH 45236 (513) 984-3587
Additional address: c/o David Ellis, 580 Walnut St., Cincinnati, OH 45202, tel.: (513) 579-5941

Established in 1991 in OH.
Donor(s): Vilma Segoe.‡

Grantmaker type: Independent foundation
Financial data (yr. ended 12/31/02): Assets, $3,196,300 (M); expenditures, $215,168; qualifying distributions, $174,375; giving activities include $139,328 for 14 grants (high: $25,000; low: $5,000).
Purpose and activities: Giving primarily in three areas: land planning; arts and museums; and education, all with an emphasis on youth and the elderly.
Fields of interest: Museums; Performing arts; Arts; Higher education; Education; Environment, land resources; Horticulture/garden clubs; Environment.
Types of support: General/operating support; Scholarship funds.
Limitations: Giving limited to the greater Cincinnati, OH, area. No grants to individuals.
Application information:
Initial approach: Letter
Deadline(s): Quarterly
Trustees: David W. Ellis III; Lewis G. Gatch.
EIN: 316369499

2720
The Sendzimir Foundation, Inc.
c/o Clark, Schaefer, Hackett & Co.
105 E. 4th St., Ste. 1600
Cincinnati, OH 45202 (513) 241-3111
Contact: Jan Sendzimir, Pres.

Established in 1994 in MA.
Donor(s): Sendzimir Charitable Lead Trust.
Grantmaker type: Independent foundation
Financial data (yr. ended 06/30/02): Assets, $320,419 (M); gifts received, $121,139; expenditures, $178,842; qualifying distributions, $165,475; giving activities include $91,622 for 10 grants (high: $50,000; low: $1,800) and $59,546 for 8 grants to individuals (high: $12,000; low: $858).
Purpose and activities: Provides scholarships and grants to individuals for the conduct of research to address problems of ecology and the environment, with particular emphasis on the environment of Eastern Europe.
Fields of interest: Environment.
International interests: Eastern Europe; Poland.
Types of support: Research; Grants to individuals; Scholarships—to individuals.
Limitations: Giving in the U.S. and Eastern Europe, with emphasis on Poland.
Application information:
Initial approach: Proposal
Deadline(s): None
Officers: Jan Sendzimir, Pres.; Gisela Bosch, Mgr.
Director: Stanley Sendzimir.
EIN: 223309860

2721
The Harold W. & Mary Louise Shaw Foundation
1700 Courthouse Plz. N.E.
Dayton, OH 45402

Established in 1997 in OH.
Donor(s): Harold Shaw, Louise Shaw.
Grantmaker type: Independent foundation
Financial data (yr. ended 11/30/02): Assets, $4,107,693 (M); expenditures, $270,566; qualifying distributions, $230,000; giving

activities include $230,000 for 7 grants (high: $100,000; low: $5,000).
Fields of interest: Zoos/zoological societies; Recreation; Hospices.
Limitations: Applications not accepted. No grants to individuals.
Application information: Contributes only pre-selected organizations.
Officers: Mary Louise Shaw, Pres. and Treas.; Sally Louise Veitch, V.P.; Ames Gardner, Jr., Secy.
EIN: 311577890

2722
The Kelvin and Eleanor Smith Foundation ▼
26380 Curtiss Wright Pkwy., Ste. 105
Cleveland, OH 44143 (216) 289-5789
Contact: Carol W. Zett, Grants Mgr.
FAX: (216) 289-5948

Incorporated in 1955 in OH.
Donor(s): Kelvin Smith.‡
Grantmaker type: Independent foundation
Financial data (yr. ended 10/31/02): Assets, $121,197,802 (M); expenditures, $5,576,823; qualifying distributions, $5,074,607; giving activities include $4,927,775 for 57 grants (high: $1,000,000; low: $1,500; average: $5,000–$50,000).
Purpose and activities: The foundation's principal interests are in the fields of nonsectarian education, the performing and visual arts, and the environment.
Fields of interest: Arts; Education; Environment; Health care; Human services.
Types of support: General/operating support; Continuing support; Annual campaigns; Capital campaigns; Building/renovation.
Limitations: Giving primarily in the greater Cleveland, OH, area. No grants to individuals, or for endowment funds, scholarships, or fellowships, no loans.
Publications: Application guidelines.
Application information: Application form not required.
  Initial approach: Letter of inquiry
  Copies of proposal: 1
  Deadline(s): None
  Board meeting date(s): No set time
  Final notification: By mail
Officers and Trustees:* Lucia S. Nash,* Co-Chair.; Cara S. Stirn,* Co-Chair.; Ellen S. Mavec,* Pres.; Andrew L. Fabens III, Secy.; William B. LaPlace,* Treas.; Carol W. Zett, Grants Mgr.; Charles P. Bolton; Michael D. Eppig, M.D.; William J. O'Neill, Jr.
Number of staff: 1 full-time professional.
EIN: 346555349
Recent environmental and animal welfare grants:
2722-1 Chagrin River Land Conservancy, Chagrin Falls, OH, $25,000. For annual fund. 2002.
2722-2 Cleveland Botanical Garden, Cleveland, OH, $1,000,000. For capital campaign. 2002.
2722-3 Cleveland Zoological Society, Cleveland, OH, $50,000. For capital campaign. 2002.
2722-4 Cuyahoga Valley Environmental Education Center, Peninsula, OH, $15,000. For general operating support. 2002.
2722-5 Earth Day Coalition, Cleveland, OH, $10,000. For program support. 2002.

2722-6 Great Lakes Museum of Science, Environment and Technology, Great Lakes Science Center, Cleveland, OH, $20,000. For general operating support. 2002.
2722-7 ParkWorks, Cleveland, OH, $10,000. For general operating support. 2002.

2723
Mary C. & Perry F. Spencer Foundation
c/o National City Bank of Indiana
P.O. Box 94651
Cleveland, OH 44101-4651
Application address: c/o Michele Delaney, National City Bank of Indiana, P.O. Box 110, Fort Wayne, IN 46801, tel.: (219) 461-6199

Established in 1981.
Donor(s): Mary Spencer.‡
Grantmaker type: Independent foundation
Financial data (yr. ended 12/31/02): Assets, $3,868,251 (M); expenditures, $264,132; qualifying distributions, $256,275; giving activities include $245,900 for 35 grants (high: $30,000; low: $1,000).
Purpose and activities: Giving primarily for the arts, education, conservation, and human services; some funding also for religious purposes.
Fields of interest: Arts; Education; Natural resources; Human services; Children/youth, services; Family services.
Limitations: Giving primarily in Fort Wayne, IN. No grants to individuals.
Application information:
  Initial approach: Letter
  Deadline(s): None
Directors: D.J. Brandenberger; Homer Harper; Connie Sowers; Don Wolf.
Trustee: National City Bank of Indiana.
EIN: 311016213

2724
The Springfield Foundation
4 W. Main St., Ste. 825
Springfield, OH 45502-1323 (937) 324-8773
Contact: Robin Atwood Pfeil, Exec. Dir.
FAX: (937) 324-1836; URL: http://www.springfieldfoundation.org

Incorporated in 1948 in OH.
Grantmaker type: Community foundation
Financial data (yr. ended 03/31/03): Assets, $24,158,115 (M); gifts received, $2,502,100; expenditures, $1,861,040; giving activities include $1,587,040 for 250 grants (high: $50,000; low: $500; average: $500–$50,000).
Purpose and activities: Giving to organizations which serve Clark County, OH. The foundation administers donor-advised funds.
Fields of interest: Arts; Education; Environment; Health care; Human services; Public affairs.
Types of support: General/operating support; Building/renovation; Equipment; Program development; Publication; Seed money; Curriculum development; Research; Technical assistance; Program evaluation; Scholarships—to individuals.
Limitations: Giving limited to Clark County, OH. No grants to individuals (except for designated scholarships).
Publications: Application guidelines, Annual report, Financial statement, Grants list,

Informational brochure (including application guidelines), Newsletter, Program policy statement.
Application information: Application form required.
  Initial approach: Letters of inquiry are required
  Copies of proposal: 10
  Deadline(s): May 15; Mar. 1 for scholarship applications
  Board meeting date(s): Mar., June, and Nov.
  Final notification: Dec. 30
Officers and Directors:* Peter Noonan,* Pres.; Peter Gus Geil, V.P.; David Sanders,* Treas.; Robin Atwood Pfeil, Exec. Dir.; and 21 additional directors.
Number of staff: 3 full-time professional; 1 full-time support.
EIN: 316030764

2725
Stark Community Foundation
(formerly The Stark County Foundation, Inc.)
Unizan Plz., Ste. 750
220 Market Ave. S.
Canton, OH 44702 (330) 454-3426
Contact: James A. Bower, Pres., and Cynthia M. Lazor, V.P., Progs.
FAX: (330) 454-5855; E-mail: jbower@starkcf.org; Additional E-mail: cmlazer@starkcf.org; URL: http://www.starkcommunityfoundation.org

Established in 1963 in OH by resolution and declaration of trust.
Grantmaker type: Community foundation
Financial data (yr. ended 12/31/02): Assets, $104,500,000 (M); gifts received, $11,122,605; expenditures, $5,963,899; giving activities include $5,119,678 for grants.
Purpose and activities: To enhance the sound health and general welfare of Stark County, OH, citizens through support for civic improvement programs and educational institutions. Primary areas of interest include the arts, education, community development, health and wellness, youth, and social services. The foundation administers donor-advised funds.
Fields of interest: Visual arts; Performing arts; Historic preservation/historical societies; Arts; Early childhood education; Child development, education; Elementary school/education; Higher education; Business school/education; Law school/education; Education; Natural resources; Environment; Health care; Substance abuse, services; AIDS; AIDS research; Crime/law enforcement; Food services; Housing/shelter, development; Recreation; Youth development, services; Human services; Children/youth, services; Child development, services; Family services; Aging, centers/services; Minorities/immigrants, centers/services; Homeless, human services; Urban/community development; Community development; Government/public administration; Leadership development; Minorities; Disabled; Aging; Homeless.
Types of support: General/operating support; Capital campaigns; Building/renovation; Equipment; Land acquisition; Emergency funds; Program development; Seed money; Scholarship funds; Research; Technical assistance; Consulting services; Scholarships—to individuals;

Matching/challenge support; Student loans—to individuals.
Limitations: Giving limited to Stark County, OH. No support for religious organizations for religious purposes. No grants for endowment funds, operating budgets, continuing support, annual campaigns, publications, conferences or deficit financing; no grants or loans to individuals (except to college students who are permanent residents of Stark County, OH).
Publications: Application guidelines, Annual report (including application guidelines), Financial statement, Grants list, Informational brochure, Newsletter, Program policy statement.
Application information: Application form required only for student aid; applicants may telephone foundation for form. Application form not required.
    Initial approach: Letter or proposal
    Copies of proposal: 15
    Deadline(s): Student aid applications accepted Mar. 1 to May 30. No deadline for other grants
    Board meeting date(s): 8 to 10 times per year
    Final notification: 60 to 90 days
Officers: James A. Bower, Pres.; Cynthia M. Lazor, V.P., Progs.; Howard S. Rubin, Jr., V.P., Devel.; Patricia C. Quick, V.P., Fin. and C.F.O.
Distribution Committee: Paul R. Bishop, Chair; Nazamovia "Naz" Adams-Phillips; Lynne S. Dragomier; Jeffrey A. Fisher; Thomas W. Schervish; Candy Wallace; John R. Werren.
Trustee Banks: Bank One Trust Co., N.A.; FirstMerit Bank, N.A.; KeyBank N.A.; National City Bank, Northeast; Unizan Bank; Sky Bank.
Number of staff: 4 full-time professional; 3 part-time professional; 1 full-time support; 3 part-time support.
EIN: 340943665

2726
Helen & Louis Stolier Family Foundation
20102 Chagrin Blvd.
Shaker Heights, OH 44122 4947
(216) 991-6892
Contact: Carl J. Monastra, Tr.
E-mail: stolierfdn@aol.com

Established in 1995 in OH.
Donor(s): Helen Stolier.‡
Grantmaker type: Independent foundation
Financial data (yr. ended 12/31/02): Assets, $2,566,768 (M); expenditures, $254,083; qualifying distributions, $191,845; giving activities include $191,845 for 16 grants (high: $75,000; low: $250).
Fields of interest: Secondary school/education; Higher education; Dental school/education; Animal welfare; AIDS; Day care.
Types of support: General/operating support; Endowments; Program development; Scholarship funds.
Limitations: Giving limited to Cuyahoga County, OH, and its adjacent counties.
Publications: Application guidelines.
Application information: Application form not required.
    Initial approach: Detailed proposal, including cover letter signed by executive director and chairperson
    Copies of proposal: 1
    Deadline(s): Jan. 15, Apr. 15, July 15, and Oct. 15

Board meeting date(s): Jan., Apr., July, and Oct.
    Final notification: Within 1 month
Trustees: Louis P. Castellarin; Carl J. Monastra; Ruth Stolier.
Number of staff: 1 part-time professional.
EIN: 346991709

2727
Thomas C. and Sandra S. Sullivan Foundation
(formerly Thomas C. Sullivan Family Foundation, Inc.)
c/o The Catholic Diocese of Cleveland Foundation
1404 E. 9th St.
Cleveland, OH 44114
Contact: Valerie Raines
Tel: (216) 696-6525, ext. 1630; URL: http://www.cdcf.org

Established in 1986 in OH as an independent foundation; in 2003 became a supporting organization of the Catholic Diocese of Cleveland Foundation.
Donor(s): Margaret Sullivan, Thomas C. Sullivan.
Grantmaker type: Public charity
Financial data (yr. ended 10/31/02): Assets, $3,570,093 (M); gifts received, $17,000; expenditures, $169,861; program services expenses, $155,200; giving activities include $154,000 for 19 grants (high: $20,000; low: $1,000).
Purpose and activities: Preference given to organizations that provide food, shelter, and assistance to the economically disadvantaged.
Fields of interest: Education; Environment; Human services.
Types of support: General/operating support.
Limitations: Giving primarily in northwestern OH.
Application information: Application form required.
    Initial approach: Letter or telephone
    Deadline(s): Sept. 1
    Board meeting date(s): Nov.
Officers: Thomas C. Sullivan, Pres.; Julie Sullivan Graham, V.P.; Anthony F. Lang, Secy.-Treas.
EIN: 341537658

2728
Nelson Talbott Foundation
Hanna Bldg., Ste. 1044
1422 Euclid Ave.
Cleveland, OH 44115
Contact: Nelson Talbott, Tr.

Established in 1947 in OH.
Donor(s): Nelson S. Talbott.
Grantmaker type: Independent foundation
Financial data (yr. ended 09/30/02): Assets, $2,616,445 (M); expenditures, $146,501; qualifying distributions, $130,999; giving activities include $118,424 for 99 grants (high: $10,000; low: $35).
Purpose and activities: Giving primarily for conservation programs and local charities.
Fields of interest: Arts; Higher education; Natural resources; Environment; Human services.

Limitations: Applications not accepted. Giving primarily in Washington, DC, and Cleveland, OH. No grants to individuals.
Application information: Contributes only to pre-selected organizations.
Trustees: Malvin Banks; Josephine L. Talbott; Nelson S. Talbott.
EIN: 316039441

2729
The C. Carlisle and Margaret M. Tippit Charitable Trust
925 Euclid Ave., Ste. 2000
Cleveland, OH 44115-1496

Established in 1989 in OH.
Donor(s): Tippit 1992 Charitable Lead Trust.
Grantmaker type: Independent foundation
Financial data (yr. ended 08/31/02): Assets, $6,363,352 (M); gifts received, $60,000; expenditures, $331,245; qualifying distributions, $312,100; giving activities include $300,000 for 18 grants (high: $60,000; low: $2,000).
Purpose and activities: Giving primarily for education, health and human services.
Fields of interest: Higher education; Environment; Hospitals (general); Health care; Human services.
Limitations: Applications not accepted. Giving primarily in OH, with emphasis on Cleveland. No grants to individuals.
Application information: Contributes only to pre-selected organizations.
Trustees: James R. Bright; Carl J. Tippit.
EIN: 341627297

2730
Toledo Community Foundation, Inc.
608 Madison Ave., Ste. 1540
Toledo, OH 43604-1151   (419) 241-5049
Contact: Virginia F. Keller, Sr. Prog. Off.
FAX: (419) 242-5549; E-mail: fktcf@hotmail.com; URL: http://www.pdgc.net/TOLEDO

Established in 1924 in OH by trust agreement; reactivated in 1973.
Grantmaker type: Community foundation
Financial data (yr. ended 12/31/02): Assets, $77,524,547 (M); gifts received, $4,214,695; expenditures, $6,759,136; giving activities include $5,464,680 for grants.
Purpose and activities: Support for projects which promise to affect a broad segment of the citizens of northwestern OH or which tend to help those living in an area not being adequately served by local community resources. Areas of interest include social services and youth programs, arts and culture, education, natural resources, government and urban affairs, and physical and mental health. The foundation administers donor-advised funds.
Fields of interest: Arts; Child development, education; Education; Natural resources; Health care; Mental health/crisis services; Health organizations, association; Human services; Children/youth, services; Child development, services; Aging, centers/services; Homeless, human services; Community development; Public affairs; Aging; Homeless.
Types of support: Program development; Seed money; Matching/challenge support.

Limitations: Giving primarily in northwestern OH, with emphasis on the greater Toledo area. No grants to individuals, or for annual campaigns, operating budgets, film, video, or TV productions, equipment purchase, or endowment funds.
Publications: Annual report (including application guidelines), Newsletter.
Application information: Application form not required.
Initial approach: Telephone
Copies of proposal: 1
Deadline(s): Varies, consult guidelines
Board meeting date(s): Apr., Sept., and Dec.
Final notification: See guidelines
Officer and Trustees:* Frank D. Jacobs,* Chair.; Charles Doneghy; William Foster; Dennis Johnson; Ed McNeal; Charles Oswald; Elizabeth Ruppert.
Director: Chris Kolasirski, Prog. Off.
Number of staff: 6 full-time professional; 1 part-time professional; 1 full-time support.
EIN: 237284004

2731
The Troy Foundation
c/o U.S. Bank Building
910 W. Main St.
Troy, OH 45373 (937) 335-8513
Contact: Melissa A. Kleptz, Exec. Dir.
FAX: (937) 332-8305; E-mail: info@thetroyfoundation.org

Established in 1924 in OH by bank resolution and declaration of trust.
Donor(s): Nannie Kendall,‡ A.G. Stouder,‡ J.M. Spencer.‡
Grantmaker type: Community foundation
Financial data (yr. ended 12/31/02): Assets, $39,417,793 (M); gifts received, $5,738,197; expenditures, $2,598,494; giving activities include $2,225,254 for 318 grants (high: $300,000; low: $25) and $1,600 for 2 employee matching gifts.
Purpose and activities: To assist, encourage, and promote the well-being of mankind.
Fields of interest: Museums; Historic preservation/historical societies; Arts; Elementary/secondary education; Child development, education; Elementary school/education; Vocational education; Business school/education; Libraries/library science; Education; Natural resources; Environment; Hospitals (general); Health care; Substance abuse, services; Recreation; Human services; Children/youth, services; Child development, services; Hospices; Community development.
Types of support: Capital campaigns; Building/renovation; Equipment; Emergency funds; Program development; Seed money; Curriculum development; Scholarship funds; Matching/challenge support.
Limitations: Giving limited to the Troy City, OH, School District. No support for religious organizations. No grants to individuals, or for endowment funds, operating budgets, continuing support, deficit financing, research, demonstration projects, publications, conferences, or fellowships; no loans.
Publications: Application guidelines, Annual report, Informational brochure, Informational

brochure (including application guidelines), Newsletter.
Application information: Application form required.
Initial approach: Proposal
Copies of proposal: 6
Deadline(s): 15th of the month preceeding board meeting
Board meeting date(s): 3rd Fri. of Mar., June, Sept., and Dec.
Final notification: 1-3 business days
Officer and Trustees:* Ronald B. Scott,* Chair.; Thomas B. Atkinson; R. Daniel Sadlier.
Distribution Committee: Elizabeth A. Earhart, Chair.; Steve M. Baker; Arthur D. Haddad; Joan C. Heidelburg; Cindy Meeker.
Number of staff: 2 full-time professional.
EIN: 316018703

2732
Vesper Foundation
6950 S. Edgerton Rd.
Brecksville, OH 44141-3184

Established in 1961 in OH.
Donor(s): Vesper Corp.
Grantmaker type: Company-sponsored foundation
Financial data (yr. ended 12/31/02): Assets, $7,044,257 (M); gifts received, $300,000; expenditures, $578,274; qualifying distributions, $578,274; giving activities include $583,026 for 72 grants (high: $106,600; low: $100).
Fields of interest: Arts; Elementary/secondary education; Education; Natural resources; Botanical gardens; Horticulture/garden clubs; Athletics/sports, water sports; Human services; Christian agencies & churches.
Types of support: General/operating support; Scholarship funds.
Limitations: Applications not accepted. Giving on a national basis, with emphasis on the Northeast. No grants to individuals.
Application information: Contributes only to pre-selected organizations.
Trustees: James Benenson, Jr.; James Benenson III; John V. Curci.
EIN: 236251198

2733
Vista Foundation
1991 Madison Rd.
Cincinnati, OH 45208 (513) 321-6999
Contact: Helen K. Heekin, Pres.

Established in 1998 in OH.
Grantmaker type: Independent foundation
Financial data (yr. ended 12/31/01): Assets, $2,317,501 (M); gifts received, $751,286; expenditures, $154,431; qualifying distributions, $104,945; giving activities include $104,945 for 47 grants (high: $30,500; low: $100).
Fields of interest: Arts; Education; Environment; YM/YWCAs & YM/YWHAs; Federated giving programs.
Limitations: Giving primarily in Cincinnati, OH.
Application information:
Initial approach: Letter, not to exceed 3 pages
Officers and Trustees:* Helen K. Heekin,* Pres.; Charles L. Heekin III,* V.P.; Peter K. Heekin,* V.P.; R. McShane Heekin,* Secy.; Micaela K. Heekin,* Treas.

EIN: 311347794

2734
Waite-Brand Foundation
c/o KeyBank N.A.
P.O. Box 10099
Toledo, OH 43699-0099
Contact: Gregory G. Alexander, Tr.
Application address: c/o Shumaker, Loop & Kendrick, 1000 Jackson Blvd., Toledo, OH 43624, tel.: (419) 241-9000

Established in 1965 in OH.
Grantmaker type: Independent foundation
Financial data (yr. ended 02/28/03): Assets, $2,971,943 (M); expenditures, $293,859; qualifying distributions, $281,585; giving activities include $244,000 for 26 grants (high: $25,000; low: $1,000).
Purpose and activities: Giving primarily for the arts, health care, and human services.
Fields of interest: Arts; Education; Natural resources; Health care; Health organizations, association; Human services; Youth, services.
Types of support: Capital campaigns; Building/renovation; Program development; Seed money; Matching/challenge support.
Limitations: Giving primarily in the Toledo, OH, area. No grants to individuals.
Application information: Application form not required.
Initial approach: Letter requesting information
Copies of proposal: 1
Deadline(s): None
Board meeting date(s): Feb.
Trustees: Gregory G. Alexander; Gregory S. Shumaker; Hope J. Welles; Philip H. Wolf; KeyBank N.A.
Number of staff: None.
EIN: 346563471

2735
The Warrington Foundation
c/o Fifth Third Bank
38 Fountain Sq. Plz., Trust Tax Dept., MD 1COM31
Cincinnati, OH 45263
Contact: Julie Herbert, Sr. Trust Off., Fifth Third Bank
Application address: c/o Fifth Third Bank, 38 Fountain Sq. Plz., MD 1COM45, Cincinatti, OH 45263

Established in 1997 in OH.
Donor(s): Elsie H. Warrington.
Grantmaker type: Independent foundation
Financial data (yr. ended 12/31/02): Assets, $7,234,049 (M); expenditures, $462,104; qualifying distributions, $412,486; giving activities include $405,634 for 91 grants (high: $20,000; low: $500).
Purpose and activities: Giving primarily for the arts, education, the environment, medical research, including juvenile diabetes, and religion.
Fields of interest: Museums (art); Orchestra (symphony); Arts; Higher education; Education; Environment; Medical research, institute; Diabetes research; Human services; Children/youth, services; Religion.
Limitations: Giving on a national basis.
Application information:

Initial approach: Letter
Deadline(s): None
Trustees: Dan Bailey; John Bailey; Lesley Bailey; Sam Bailey.
Agent: Fifth Third Bank.
EIN: 311582067

2736
Greater Wayne County Foundation, Inc.
133 S. Market St.
P.O. Box 201
Wooster, OH 44691 (330) 262-3877
Contact: B. Diane Gordon, Exec. Dir.
FAX: (330) 262-8057; E-mail: gwcf@earthlink.net; URL: http://www.gwcf.net

Established in 1978 in OH.
Grantmaker type: Community foundation
Financial data (yr. ended 06/30/03): Assets, $21,452,789 (M); gifts received, $2,412,575; expenditures, $3,230,264; giving activities include $3,006,242 for 444 grants (low: $7).
Purpose and activities: Giving primarily for scholarships, community projects, and other charitable purposes throughout Wayne County, OH. The foundation administers a donor-advised fund.
Fields of interest: Arts; Education; Environment; Health care; Human services; Community development; Religion.
Types of support: General/operating support; Continuing support; Capital campaigns; Building/renovation; Equipment; Endowments; Emergency funds; Program development; Seed money; Scholarship funds; Matching/challenge support.
Limitations: Giving limited to Wayne County, OH. No grants for deficit financing for programs or capital expenditures, endowment funds, annual appeals or membership contributions, conferences, or recognition events.
Publications: Application guidelines, Annual report, Financial statement, Informational brochure (including application guidelines).
Application information: Application guidelines available on foundation Web site. FAX or E-mail proposals will not be accepted. Application form required.
Copies of proposal: 3
Deadline(s): Mar.1 (for June decision) and Sept.1 (for December decision)
Board meeting date(s): Quarterly
Final notification: June 1 and Dec. 1
Officer: B. Diane Gordon, Exec. Dir.
Number of staff: 1 part-time professional; 1 part-time support.
EIN: 341281026

2737
The Weatherhead Foundation ▼
730 Ohio Savings Plz.
1801 E. 9th St., Ste. 1300
Cleveland, OH 44114-3103 (216) 771-4000
Contact: Thomas F. Allen, Treas.
FAX: (216) 771-0422

Incorporated in 1953 in OH; foundation is income beneficiary of a perpetual trust; assets reflect assets of both feeder trust and foundation.
Donor(s): Albert J. Weatherhead, Jr.‡
Grantmaker type: Independent foundation

Financial data (yr. ended 12/31/02): Assets, $7,351,349 (M); gifts received, $4,515,118; expenditures, $5,029,986; qualifying distributions, $4,989,595; giving activities include $4,850,186 for 12 grants (high: $2,480,320; low: $2,405; average: $15,000–$270,000).
Purpose and activities: Grants for endowments or programs, principally to universities and research organizations.
Fields of interest: Higher education.
Types of support: General/operating support; Endowments; Program development; Research.
Limitations: Giving on a national basis. No support for religious purposes or for general support of church or denominational institutions. No grants to individuals.
Publications: Application guidelines, Informational brochure.
Application information: Grants are initiated by the trustees. Unsolicited applications are not encouraged.
Initial approach: Letter
Deadline(s): None
Board meeting date(s): Spring, fall, and as required
Officers and Trustees:* Albert J. Weatherhead III,* Pres.; Dr. Eamon M. Kelly,* V.P.; Terry Lacy,* V.P.; Frank M. Rasmussen,* V.P.; Henry Rosovsky,* V.P.; Charles E. Sheedy,* V.P.; Celia J. Weatherhead,* V.P.; Thomas F. Allen,* Secy.-Treas.
Number of staff: 1 full-time professional.
EIN: 132711998
Recent environmental and animal welfare grants:
2737-1 Cleveland Botanical Garden, Cleveland, OH, $488,326. For grant made in form of stock. 2002.

2738
The S. K. Wellman Foundation
P.O. Box 32554
Euclid, OH 44132-0554 (216) 261-7250
Contact: Ethel Pearson, Secy.

Incorporated in 1951 in OH.
Donor(s): S.K. Wellman.‡
Grantmaker type: Independent foundation
Financial data (yr. ended 12/31/02): Assets, $6,326,191 (M); expenditures, $590,843; qualifying distributions, $523,405; giving activities include $500,000 for 74 grants (high: $25,000; low: $1,000).
Fields of interest: Arts; Elementary/secondary education; Higher education; Natural resources; Animals/wildlife, preservation/protection; Health care; Human services; Children/youth, services; Government/public administration; General charitable giving.
Limitations: Giving primarily in OH. No grants to individuals.
Publications: Application guidelines, Grants list.
Application information: Application form not required.
Initial approach: Letter
Deadline(s): June 1
Board meeting date(s): July
Officers: John M. Wilson, Jr., Pres.; Ethel Pearson, Secy.
Trustees: Franklin B. Floyd; Susanne Wellman O'Gara; Patricia Wellman Wilson.
EIN: 346520032

2739
Charles Westheimer Family Fund
36 E. 4th St., Ste. 905
Cincinnati, OH 45202-3810
Contact: Charles Westheimer, Pres. or May O. Westheimer, V.P.
FAX: (513) 421-9343

Established in 1980 in OH.
Donor(s): Charles Westheimer, Irwin F. Westheimer,‡ May O. Westheimer.
Grantmaker type: Independent foundation
Financial data (yr. ended 12/31/01): Assets, $313,202 (M); gifts received, $328,930; expenditures, $148,798; qualifying distributions, $144,268; giving activities include $146,493 for 129 grants (high: $75,000; low: $25).
Purpose and activities: Giving for the arts, education, and human services.
Fields of interest: Visual arts; Museums; Performing arts; Music; History/archaeology; Language/linguistics; Literature; Historic preservation/historical societies; Arts; Early childhood education; Secondary school/education; Higher education; Adult education—literacy, basic skills & GED; Libraries/library science; Reading; Education; Environment; Family planning; Crime/violence prevention, youth; Youth development, citizenship; Hospices; Homeless, human services; International peace/security; Arms control; Foreign policy; Race/intergroup relations; Civil rights; Urban/community development; Community development; Anthropology/sociology; Government/public administration; Public affairs, citizen participation; Minorities; Homeless.
Types of support: Continuing support; Annual campaigns; Capital campaigns; Building/renovation; Emergency funds; Program development; Conferences/seminars; Publication; Seed money; Scholarship funds; Matching/challenge support.
Limitations: Giving primarily in Cincinnati, OH.
Application information: Application form not required.
Initial approach: Letter
Deadline(s): None
Board meeting date(s): Varies
Officers: Charles Westheimer, Pres.; May O. Westheimer, V.P. and Treas.; John R. Westheimer, Secy.
Number of staff: None.
EIN: 311016766

2740
Wodecroft Foundation
1900 Chemed Ctr.
255 E. 5th St.
Cincinnati, OH 45202 (513) 977-8236
Contact: J. Michael Cooney, Chair.

Established in 1958 in OH.
Donor(s): Roger Drackett.‡
Grantmaker type: Independent foundation
Financial data (yr. ended 12/31/02): Assets, $13,559,814 (M); expenditures, $984,819; qualifying distributions, $902,731; giving activities include $906,000 for 37 grants (high: $130,000; low: $1,000).
Purpose and activities: Giving primarily for the arts, particularly a performing arts center; funding also for higher education, conservation,

health and hospitals, including a children's hospital, children, youth and social services, federated giving programs, and Christian churches.
Fields of interest: Museums; Performing arts centers; Orchestra (symphony); Arts; Higher education; Natural resources; Hospitals (general); Health organizations, association; Human services; Children/youth, services; Federated giving programs; Christian agencies & churches.
Types of support: Annual campaigns; Capital campaigns; Building/renovation; Equipment.
Limitations: Giving primarily in southwestern FL, and southwestern OH. No grants to individuals.
Application information: Few unsolicited applications granted. Application form not required.
  Initial approach: Letter
  Deadline(s): Jun. 30
  Board meeting date(s): As required
  Final notification: Prior to Dec. 31
Trustees: William Bahl; J. Michael Cooney; Jeanne Drackett.
EIN: 316047601

2741
Wood Foundation
(also known as Robert S. Wood Foundation)
35 N. High St.
P.O. Box 575
Canal Winchester, OH 43110

Established in 1987 in OH.
Grantmaker type: Independent foundation
Financial data (yr. ended 12/31/02): Assets, $2,041,771 (M); gifts received, $75,848; expenditures, $151,053; qualifying distributions, $140,737; giving activities include $141,000 for 22 grants (high: $72,000; low: $500).
Purpose and activities: Giving for religion, children's medical services, development foundations and veteran's organizations.
Fields of interest: Historic preservation/historical societies; Education; Environment; Hospitals (general); Health organizations, association; Human services; Recreation, community facilities; Christian agencies & churches.
Limitations: Applications not accepted. Giving primarily in OH. No grants to individuals.
Application information: Contributes only to pre-selected organizations.
Officers: Robert S. Wood, Chair. and Pres.; Kitty I. Argobright, V.P.; Robert S. Wood II, V.P.; Cheryl E. Mathias, Secy.; Vicki M. Wood, Treas.
EIN: 311217729

2742
Yellow Springs Community Foundation
P.O. Box 55
Yellow Springs, OH 45387 (937) 767-2655
Contact: Francine Rickenbach, Pres.
E-mail: yscf@juno.com

Chartered in 1974 in OH.
Grantmaker type: Community foundation
Financial data (yr. ended 12/31/02): Assets, $1,851,410 (L); gifts received, $394,450; expenditures, $119,394; giving activities include $92,312 for 49 grants (high: $15,000; low: $50;

average: $50–$15,000) and $2,600 for 4 grants to individuals (high: $1,000; low: $500; average: $500–$1,000).
Purpose and activities: The mission of the foundation is to enhance community life by supporting a broad array of activities which include assisting education, helping the sick and elderly, promoting the arts, supporting public recreation, promoting scientific research, and providing scholarships. The foundation administers a donor-advised fund.
Fields of interest: Multipurpose centers/programs; Literature; Elementary school/education; Education; Natural resources; Environment; Health care; Aging, centers/services.
Types of support: Continuing support; Capital campaigns; Building/renovation; Equipment; Endowments; Program development; Seed money; Grants to individuals; Matching/challenge support.
Limitations: Giving limited to the Yellow Springs and Greene County, OH, areas.
Publications: Application guidelines, Annual report, Grants list, Informational brochure.
Application information: Application form required.
  Initial approach: Submit written request to grants review committee
  Copies of proposal: 9
  Deadline(s): None
  Board meeting date(s): Monthly
Officers and Trustees:* Francine Rickenbach,* Pres.; Bruce Bradtmiller,* V.P.; Evelyn LaMers,* Secy.; Larry Gerthoffer,* Treas.; Jane Baker; Staffan Erickson; John Gudgel; Dorothy O. Scott; Saul Young.
Number of staff: 2 part-time support.
EIN: 237372791

2743
YSI Foundation, Inc.
P.O. Box 279
Yellow Springs, OH 45387 (937) 767-7241
Contact: Deb Stottlemyer, Treas.
E-mail: dturner@ysi.com

Established in 1990 in OH.
Donor(s): YSI Inc.
Grantmaker type: Company-sponsored foundation
Financial data (yr. ended 12/31/02): Assets, $43,390 (M); gifts received, $175,000; expenditures, $163,188; qualifying distributions, $161,810; giving activities include $161,810 for 33 grants (high: $50,000; low: $500).
Purpose and activities: Support for local organizations affecting YSI employees.
Fields of interest: Arts; Education; Environment; Human services; Science.
Types of support: Building/renovation; Equipment; Endowments; Emergency funds; Program development; Publication; Seed money; Curriculum development; Scholarship funds; Technical assistance; Employee-related scholarships; Scholarships—to individuals.
Limitations: Giving primarily in OH. Generally, no support for large national or local organizations. No grants for operating funds, capital funds or campaigns, or for annual funds.
Publications: Application guidelines, Informational brochure.

Application information: Application form not required.
  Initial approach: Letter
  Copies of proposal: 1
  Deadline(s): None
  Board meeting date(s): Quarterly
Officers: Sarah Harris, Chair.; Susan Miller, Secy.; Deb Stottlemyer, Treas.
Number of staff: None.
EIN: 311292180

OKLAHOMA

2744
American Fidelity Corporation Founders Fund, Inc.
2000 N. Classen Blvd.
Oklahoma City, OK 73106
Contact: Jo Ella Ramsey, Secy.
Application address: P.O. Box 25523, Oklahoma City, OK 73125

Established in 1984 in OK.
Donor(s): American Fidelity Assurance Co.
Grantmaker type: Company-sponsored foundation
Financial data (yr. ended 12/31/02): Assets, $3,641,761 (M); expenditures, $221,457; qualifying distributions, $220,134; giving activities include $221,312 for 113 grants (high: $70,000; low: $25).
Purpose and activities: Support for education, including higher education and educational research, health associations and clinics, various arts councils, local cultural events and museums, community and civic affairs groups.
Fields of interest: Museums; Arts; Adult education—literacy, basic skills & GED; Libraries/library science; Reading; Education; Environment; Health care; Health organizations, association; Medical research, institute; Federated giving programs; Government/public administration.
Types of support: General/operating support; Annual campaigns; Capital campaigns; Program development; Research; Employee matching gifts.
Limitations: Giving primarily in OK. No grants to individuals.
Publications: Application guidelines.
Application information: Application form required.
  Initial approach: Letter
  Copies of proposal: 1
  Board meeting date(s): Varies
Officers and Directors:* William M. Cameron,* Pres.; John W. Rex,* Exec V.P. and Treas.; Jo Ella Ramsey,* Secy.; Jo Carol Cameron,* Treas.; Brett Barrowman; Laura Cameron; William E. Durrett.
Number of staff: None.
EIN: 731236059

2745
Hu & Eva Maud Bartlett Foundation
300 S. Oak St.
Sapulpa, OK 74066
Application address: P.O. Box 1368, Sapulpa, OK 74066

Established in 1950 in OK.
Grantmaker type: Independent foundation
Financial data (yr. ended 12/31/02): Assets, $2,033,064 (M); expenditures, $120,447; qualifying distributions, $104,979; giving activities include $104,979 for 6 grants (high: $34,295; low: $1,000).
Purpose and activities: Giving to historical restoration projects and to community support organizations.
Fields of interest: Historical activities; Historic preservation/historical societies; Animal welfare; Hospitals (general).
Limitations: Giving primarily in Sapulpa, OK. No grants to individuals.
Application information:
   Initial approach: Letter or in person
   Deadline(s): None
Trustees: Barbara Benedict; Jerrold Benedict; Cale Sherwood; Sherry Sherwood.
EIN: 736092249

2746
The Mervin Bovaird Foundation
401 S. Boston Ave., Ste. 3300
Tulsa, OK 74103-4070 (918) 592-3300
Contact: R. Casey Cooper, Pres.

Established in 1955.
Donor(s): Mabel W. Bovaird.‡
Grantmaker type: Independent foundation
Financial data (yr. ended 12/31/02): Assets, $37,755,733 (M); expenditures, $1,388,568; qualifying distributions, $1,051,524; giving activities include $720,550 for 48+ grants (high: $62,500; low: $500; average: $5,000–$50,000) and $183,000 for 58 grants to individuals of $3,000 each.
Purpose and activities: Support for social services, health, and education; also funds a scholarship program for Tulsa County High School graduating seniors and graduates of Tulsa Community College at the University of Tulsa (not for graduate or professional study).
Fields of interest: Arts; Education; Environment; Health care; Health organizations, association; Human services; Community development.
Types of support: General/operating support; Continuing support; Annual campaigns; Capital campaigns; Building/renovation; Equipment; Endowments; Program development; Conferences/seminars; Curriculum development; Scholarship funds; Research; Matching/challenge support.
Limitations: Giving limited to the Tulsa, OK, area. No grants to individuals (except for scholarships); no loans.
Publications: Program policy statement.
Application information: Scholarship recipients are chosen by Tulsa public high schools and Tulsa Community College based on need and ability to attend Tulsa University. Application form not required.
   Initial approach: Brief letter
   Copies of proposal: 1

Deadline(s): May 1 (or date established by schools selecting a recipient for scholarships); Nov. 15 for grants
Board meeting date(s): Quarterly
Final notification: Dec. 15 through 20
Officers and Trustees:* R. Casey Cooper,* Pres.; David B. McKinney,* V.P. and Treas.; Alinda F. Jones, Secy.; Tilford H. Eskridge; Lance Stockwell; Thomas H. Trower.
Number of staff: 2 part-time professional; 1 part-time support.
EIN: 736102163

2747
Buford Family Foundation
3310 S. Birmingham Ave.
Tulsa, OK 74105
Contact: Martha C. Buford, Pres.
FAX: (918) 742-8519; *E-mail:* viperz@ibm.net

Established in 1997 in OK.
Donor(s): Martha C. Buford.
Grantmaker type: Independent foundation
Financial data (yr. ended 12/31/02): Assets, $2,061,827 (M); gifts received, $10,000; expenditures, $251,065; qualifying distributions, $241,800; giving activities include $241,500 for 18 grants (high: $50,000; low: $1,000).
Purpose and activities: Giving primarily for the arts and social services.
Fields of interest: Museums (art); Music; Higher education; Zoos/zoological societies; Salvation Army; Children/youth, services; Christian agencies & churches.
Limitations: Applications not accepted. Giving primarily in KS and OK. No grants to individuals.
Application information: Contributes only to pre-selected organizations.
Officers and Directors:* Martha C. Buford,* Pres. and Secy.; Josephine B. Siegfried,* V.P. and Treas.; Anne S. Buford; C. Robert Buford; R.C. Buford.
EIN: 731519009

2748
Communities Foundation of Oklahoma
(formerly Oklahoma Communities Foundation, Inc.)
2932 N.W. 122nd St., Ste. D
Oklahoma City, OK 73102 (405) 218-4080
Contact: Susan R. Graves, Exec. Dir.
FAX: (405) 155-0938; *E-mail:* sgraves@cfok.org

Established in 1992 in OK.
Grantmaker type: Community foundation
Financial data (yr. ended 06/30/03): Assets, $6,598,717 (L); gifts received, $1,710,283; expenditures, $1,033,235; giving activities include $904,905 for 187 grants (high: $50,000; low: $75; average: $75–$50,000).
Purpose and activities: The foundation is statewide with primary service to non-metropolitan donors and charities.
Fields of interest: Historic preservation/historical societies; Arts; Animal welfare; Substance abuse, services; Substance abuse, prevention; Substance abuse, treatment; Medical research, institute; Offenders/ex-offenders, transitional care; Offenders/ex-offenders, rehabilitation; Offenders/ex-offenders, services; Recreation, community facilities; Recreation, centers;

Human services; Human services; Science, research; Poverty studies.
Types of support: Endowments; Seed money; Scholarship funds; Scholarships—to individuals; Matching/challenge support.
Limitations: Applications not accepted. Giving primarily in OK.
Publications: Informational brochure.
Application information: Contributes only to pre-selected organizations.
   Board meeting date(s): Quarterly
Officers: Richard E. Dixon, Chair.; Jenny Hendrick, Vice-Chair.; April Stobbe, Secy.; Susan R. Graves, Exec. Dir.
Directors: Gene Nelson; Ann Powell; Jeannine Rainbolt; Richard Ryerson; Wes Stucky.
Number of staff: 1 full-time professional; 2 part-time professional; 2 full-time support; 1 part-time support.
EIN: 731396320

2749
Inasmuch Foundation
First National Ctr., Ste. 723 W.
120 N. Robinson St.
Oklahoma City, OK 73102 (405) 604-5292
Contact: Nancy Woodson, Prog. Off.
FAX: (405) 604-0297; *E-mail:* foundationoffice@coxinet.net

Established in 1982 in OK.
Donor(s): Edith Gaylord Harper.‡
Grantmaker type: Independent foundation
Financial data (yr. ended 06/30/02): Assets, $22,305,274 (M); gifts received, $16,804,182; expenditures, $2,486,162; qualifying distributions, $2,367,536; giving activities include $520,133 for 79 grants (high: $30,000; low: $100).
Purpose and activities: Grants are made in the following areas: education, cultural affairs, environmental concerns, the performing arts, human or social services, and the health field, including the provision of direct health services, research, and health education.
Fields of interest: Performing arts; Arts; Education; Environment; Health care; Health organizations, association; Medical research, institute; Human services.
Types of support: Program development; Seed money; Curriculum development; Research.
Limitations: Giving primarily in Colorado Springs, CO, and OK. No grants to individuals, or for regular operating expenses or endowments.
Publications: Informational brochure (including application guidelines).
Application information: Application form required.
   Initial approach: Concept paper (up to 3-pages)
   Copies of proposal: 2
   Deadline(s): Feb. 15 and Aug. 15
   Board meeting date(s): Apr. and Oct.
Trustees: David O. Hogan; Andrew W. Roff; J. Hugh Roff, Jr.; Patrick T. Rooney; Robert J. Ross; William J. Ross.
Advisory Committee: Christine Gaylord Everest; Tricia L. Everest; Cathy O. Robbins; Jeanne H. Smith; Barbara L. Yalich.
Number of staff: 2 full-time professional; 2 full-time support.
EIN: 731167188

2750
Kerr-McGee Foundation Corporation
(formerly Kerr-McGee Corporation Foundation)
Kerr-McGee Ctr.
123 Robert S. Kerr Ave., (MT-803)
Oklahoma City, OK 73102 (405) 270-3924
Contact: Martha Brady, Admin., Public Affairs

Established in 1996 in OK.
Donor(s): Kerr-McGee Corp.
Grantmaker type: Company-sponsored foundation
Financial data (yr. ended 12/31/01): Assets, $21,654,715 (M); expenditures, $1,622,387; qualifying distributions, $1,509,048; giving activities include $1,528,111 for 316 grants (high: $250,000; low: $25; average: $100–$250,000).
Purpose and activities: Giving primarily for the arts, education, health care, human services and community development.
Fields of interest: Arts; Elementary/secondary education; Secondary school/education; Higher education; Education; Natural resources; Zoos/zoological societies; Health care; Athletics/sports, Special Olympics; Human services; Community development; Federated giving programs.
Types of support: General/operating support; Continuing support; Employee matching gifts; Employee-related scholarships.
Limitations: Giving primarily in areas of company and affiliate operations, with emphasis on OK. No grants to individuals (except for employee-related scholarships).
Application information: Application form not required.
Initial approach: Letter
Deadline(s): Nov. 30 of year preceding the year requested to be funded
Officers and Directors:* Luke R. Corbett,* Chair. and C.E.O.; Robert M. Wohleber, Sr. V.P.; Gregory F. Pilcher, V.P. and Secy.; John M. Rauh, V.P. and Treas.
EIN: 731496403

2751
Kirkpatrick Foundation, Inc.
P.O. Box 268822
Oklahoma City, OK 73126-8822
(405) 840-2882
Contact: Susan McCalmont, Secy.
FAX: (405) 840-2946; E-mail: kirkpatrickfoundation@msn.com

Incorporated in 1955 in OK.
Donor(s): Eleanor B. Kirkpatrick,‡ John E. Kirkpatrick, Kirkpatrick Oil Co., Joan E. Kirkpatrick, Kathryn T. Blake.‡
Grantmaker type: Independent foundation
Financial data (yr. ended 12/31/02): Assets, $27,724,128 (M); expenditures, $2,041,518; qualifying distributions, $1,858,331; giving activities include $1,635,240 for 57 grants (high: $274,750; low: $1,000; average: $1,000–$75,000).
Purpose and activities: Support primarily for cultural education, the arts, research and conservation of animals, and Oklahoma's natural and built resources.
Fields of interest: Visual arts; Museums; Performing arts; Historic preservation/historical societies; Arts; Education; Animals/wildlife,

research; Animals/wildlife, preservation/protection.
Types of support: General/operating support; Continuing support; Program development; Seed money; Curriculum development.
Limitations: Giving primarily in Oklahoma City, OK. No support for medical and health related causes, social welfare, or lobbying organizations. No grants to individuals or for school trips; no loans.
Publications: Application guidelines.
Application information: Application form required.
Initial approach: Letter
Copies of proposal: 1
Deadline(s): Jan. 15 and July 15
Board meeting date(s): Mar., June, Sept., and Dec.
Officers and Directors:* John E. Kirkpatrick,* Chair.; Joan E. Kirkpatrick,* Pres.; Christian K. Keesee,* 1st V.P.; Anne Hodges Morgan,* 2nd V.P.; Susan McCalmont, Secy.; Mischa Gorkuscha,* Treas.; John L. Belt; Joe Howell; Linda Lambert; George Records; Laura Warriner; Max Weitzenhoffer.
Number of staff: 1 part-time professional.
EIN: 730701736

2752
The McGee Foundation, Inc.
P.O. Box 18127
Oklahoma City, OK 73154
Contact: Marcia McGee Bieber, Pres.

Incorporated in 1963 in OK.
Donor(s): Dean A. McGee.‡
Grantmaker type: Independent foundation
Financial data (yr. ended 06/30/02): Assets, $6,741,569 (M); expenditures, $372,334; qualifying distributions, $362,889; giving activities include $365,000 for 19 grants (high: $100,000; low: $2,500).
Fields of interest: Historic preservation/historical societies; Education; Natural resources; Family planning; Children/youth, services; Women.
Types of support: General/operating support; Annual campaigns; Capital campaigns; Building/renovation; Equipment; Land acquisition; Endowments; Professorships; Scholarship funds; Research; Matching/challenge support.
Limitations: Giving primarily in CA and OK. No grants to individuals.
Publications: Application guidelines.
Application information: Application form not required.
Initial approach: Proposal
Copies of proposal: 1
Deadline(s): None
Board meeting date(s): Early May
Officers and Directors:* Marcia McGee Bieber,* Pres.; Patricia McGee Maino,* V.P.; Charles Bieber, M.D.,* Secy.-Treas.; Jerry Love.
Number of staff: 1 part-time support.
EIN: 736099203

2753
The Samuel Roberts Noble Foundation, Inc. ▼
2510 Sam Noble Pkwy.
P.O. Box 2180
Ardmore, OK 73402 (580) 223-5810
Contact: Michael A. Cawley, C.E.O. and Pres.
Additional tel.: 866 223-5810; URL: http://www.noble.org

Trust established in 1945 in OK; incorporated in 1952.
Donor(s): Lloyd Noble.‡
Grantmaker type: Independent foundation
Financial data (yr. ended 12/31/02): Assets, $908,040,161 (M); expenditures, $11,072,325; qualifying distributions, $10,774,968; giving activities include $10,297,511 for 71 grants (high: $2,822,868; low: $5,000; average: $5,000–$500,000), $367,244 for grants to individuals and $110,213 for employee matching gifts.
Purpose and activities: Support through three operating programs for: 1) enabling individual farmers and ranchers to better understand resource management and achieve their goals through consultation, education, research and demonstration; 2) enhancing plant productivity through fundamental research and applied biotechnology; and 3) assisting community service, health research and delivery systems, educational and other selected nonprofit organizations through grants and employee involvement. The foundation also administers a matching gift program for Noble Co. employees.
Fields of interest: Higher education; Health care; Medical research, institute; Human services.
Types of support: General/operating support; Capital campaigns; Building/renovation; Equipment; Endowments; Professorships; Seed money; Research; Program-related investments/loans; Employee matching gifts; Employee-related scholarships; Matching/challenge support.
Limitations: Giving primarily in the Southwest, with emphasis on OK. No grants to individuals (except through Noble Educational Fund and Sam Noble Scholarship Program); no loans (except for program-related investments).
Publications: Application guidelines, Annual report, Informational brochure.
Application information: Application form required.
Initial approach: Letter; Public policy requests: letter with 2-page summary
Copies of proposal: 1
Deadline(s): 6 weeks prior to board meeting dates
Board meeting date(s): Jan., Apr., July, and Oct.
Final notification: 2 weeks after board meetings
Officers and Trustees:* Michael A. Cawley,* C.E.O. and Pres.; Larry Pulliam, Exec. V.P.; Patrick Jones, V.P., C.F.O. and Treas.; Elizabeth A. Aldridge, Secy.; Ann Noble Brown; D. Randolph Brown; Susan Brown; James C. Day; Vivian N. Dubose; William R. Goddard, Jr.; Shelley Dru Mullins; Edward E. Noble; Maria Noble; Nick Noble; Rusty Noble; Marianne Rooney; William G. Thurman.
Number of staff: 120 full-time professional; 160 full-time support.
EIN: 730606209

Recent environmental and animal welfare grants:
2753-1 Oklahoma State University Foundation, Stillwater, OK, $900,000. For Bovine Respiratory Disease Research. 2002.

2754
The Oxley Foundation
1437 S. Boulder, Ste. 770
Tulsa, OK   74119
Contact: Kyra Prater, Grants Mgr.
FAX: (918) 582-9419; E-mail: kprater@oxleyfdn.com

Established in 1986 in OK.
Donor(s): John T. Oxley.‡
Grantmaker type: Independent foundation
Financial data (yr. ended 12/31/02): Assets, $95,671,311 (M); gifts received, $21,347,690; expenditures, $12,020,597; qualifying distributions, $5,241,415; giving activities include $10,142,781 for 323 grants (high: $700,000; low: $100).
Fields of interest: Museums; Higher education; Natural resources; Health organizations; Athletics/sports, equestrianism; Christian agencies & churches.
Types of support: General/operating support; Annual campaigns; Capital campaigns; Endowments; Scholarship funds.
Limitations: Applications not accepted. Giving primarily in CO, FL, OH and OK. No grants to individuals.
Application information: Contributes only to pre-selected organizations.
Trustees: Russell H. Harbaugh, Jr.; John C. Oxley; Mary Jane Tritsch.
EIN: 736224031

2755
Sarkeys Foundation
530 E. Main
Norman, OK   73071   (405) 364-3703
Contact: Susan C. Frantz, Prog. Off.
FAX: (405) 364-8191; E-mail: Sarkeys@sarkeys.org; URL: http://www.sarkeys.org

Established in 1962 in OK.
Donor(s): S.J. Sarkeys.‡
Grantmaker type: Independent foundation
Financial data (yr. ended 11/30/02): Assets, $82,423,726 (M); expenditures, $5,297,863; qualifying distributions, $5,215,398; giving activities include $3,848,147 for 104 grants (high: $533,000; low: $100; average: $10,000–$50,000).
Purpose and activities: Emphasis on education, health care and medical research, and cultural and humanitarian programs of regional significance. Preference given to project-oriented grants.
Fields of interest: Arts; Education; Environment; Health care; Medical research, institute; Human services.
Types of support: Capital campaigns; Building/renovation; Equipment; Endowments; Program development; Professorships; Research; Matching/challenge support.
Limitations: Giving limited to OK. No support for direct-to-government agencies or individual public or private elementary or secondary

schools, unless they are serving the needs of a special population which are not met elsewhere; generally, no support for hospitals or local programs appropriately financed within the community or for religious institutions and their subsidiaries. No grants to individuals, or for operating support, permanent financing, profitmaking programs, grants which trigger expenditure responsibility, direct mail solicitations, start-up funding for new organizations, feasibility studies, or vehicles.
Publications: Annual report, Informational brochure (including application guidelines).
Application information: Call foundation for guidelines; proposals received by FAX or E-mail not considered. Application form required.
  Initial approach: Proposal (no more than 10 pages)
  Copies of proposal: 1
  Deadline(s): Feb. 1 and Aug. 1
  Board meeting date(s): Jan., Apr., July, and Oct.; grants considered at Apr. and Oct. meeting
  Final notification: Shortly after Apr. and Oct. board meetings
Officers and Trustees:* Joseph W. Morris,* Pres.; Robert S. Rizley,* V.P.; Paul F. Sharp, Secy.-Treas.; Cheri D. Cartwright, Exec. Dir.; Teresa Adwin; Richard Bell; Fred Gipson; Kim Henry; Dan Little; Terry W. West.
Number of staff: 4 full-time professional; 3 full-time support; 3 part-time support.
EIN: 730736496
Recent environmental and animal welfare grants:
2755-1 Second Chance Animal Sanctuary, Norman, OK, $20,000. For outreach programs which include education and adoption programs. 2002.

2756
Harold C. Stuart Foundation
(formerly Harold C. and Joan S. Stuart Foundation)
2431 E. 61st St.
Tulsa, OK   74136-1235
Contact: Harold C. Stuart, Tr.

Established in 1969 in OK.
Donor(s): Harold C. Stuart; Joan S. Stuart.†
Grantmaker type: Independent foundation
Financial data (yr. ended 12/31/02): Assets, $4,843,113 (M); expenditures, $272,247; qualifying distributions, $213,374; giving activities include $154,400 for 10 grants (high: $57,000; low: $1,000).
Purpose and activities: Giving primarily to higher education.
Fields of interest: Higher education; Law school/education; Animals/wildlife, preservation/protection; Foundations (community).
Types of support: General/operating support.
Limitations: Giving primarily in the Tulsa, OK, area.
Application information: Application form not required.
  Deadline(s): None
  Board meeting date(s): Varies
Trustees: Frances Langford Stuart; Harold C. Stuart.
Number of staff: None.
EIN: 237052187

2757
Anna K. Ackerman Trust
c/o U.S. Bank, N.A., Trust Tax Svcs.
P.O. Box 3168
Portland, OR   97208

Established in 1963.
Grantmaker type: Independent foundation
Financial data (yr. ended 12/31/02): Assets, $8,116,728 (M); expenditures, $474,601; qualifying distributions, $431,468; giving activities include $425,421 for 30 grants (high: $101,000; low: $1,000).
Purpose and activities: Giving primarily to federated giving programs, recreation, health associations, children and youth services, and human services.
Fields of interest: Higher education; Animal welfare; Zoos/zoological societies; Health organizations, association; Recreation; Boys & girls clubs; Youth development, scouting agencies (general); Human services; YM/YWCAs & YM/YWHAs; Children/youth, services; Family services; Foundations (community); Federated giving programs.
Types of support: General/operating support; Annual campaigns; Building/renovation; Endowments.
Limitations: Giving limited to CO, with emphasis on Colorado Springs. No grants to individuals.
Application information: Application form not required.
  Initial approach: Letter
  Copies of proposal: 3
  Deadline(s): None
Trustee: U.S. Bank, N.A.
EIN: 846032046

2758
The Autzen Foundation
P.O. Box 3709
Portland, OR   97208   (503) 226-6051
Contact: Robin Stewart, Admin.

Incorporated in 1951 in OR.
Donor(s): Thomas J. Autzen.‡
Grantmaker type: Independent foundation
Financial data (yr. ended 12/31/02): Assets, $1,615,522 (M); expenditures, $991,907; qualifying distributions, $944,494; giving activities include $908,277 for 202 grants (high: $30,000; low: $1,000).
Purpose and activities: Giving primarily for youth services, education, the arts, and nature.
Fields of interest: Performing arts; Arts; Higher education; Environment; Health care; Human services; Children/youth, services.
Types of support: Continuing support; Building/renovation; Program development; Seed money; Matching/challenge support.
Limitations: Giving primarily in OR, with some emphasis on Portland. Giving limited to the Pacific Northwest region. No grants to individuals, or for scholarships or fellowships; no loans.

Application information: Application form not required.

Initial approach: Letter
Copies of proposal: 1
Deadline(s): Apr. 15, Aug. 15, and Nov. 15
Board meeting date(s): May, Sept., and Dec.
Final notification: 3 to 4 months

Officers and Directors:* Henry C. Houser,* Pres.; Christina Grady,* Secy.; Thomas J. Autzen; Gregory Houser; Robert W. Patton III; Wendy Ulman.

Number of staff: 1 part-time professional.
EIN: 936021333

2759
Bay Area Sportsman's Association, Inc.
P.O. Box 1624
Coos Bay, OR 97420-0335 (541) 756-6962
Contact: Larry Garboden, Secy.
FAX: (541) 756-0217

Established in 1986 in OR.
Grantmaker type: Public charity
Financial data (yr. ended 12/31/01): Revenue, $40,931; assets, $50,705; gifts received, $2,424; expenditures, $40,601; program services expenses, $32,320; giving activities include $32,320 for 14 grants (high: $14,425; low: $160).
Purpose and activities: The association supports underfunded local organizations in Coos County, OR.
Fields of interest: Animals/wildlife, preservation/protection; Recreation; Youth development.
Types of support: Annual campaigns; Capital campaigns; Building/renovation; Equipment; Scholarship funds; Matching/challenge support.
Limitations: Giving limited to Coos County, OR. No grants to individuals or for operational costs.
Publications: Application guidelines.
Application information: Application form required.

Initial approach: Telephone
Deadline(s): May 1
Board meeting date(s): 1st Mon. in May
Final notification: End of May

Officers and Board Members:* Anton Dub,* Pres.; Larry Garboden,* Secy.; Mike Helfrich,* Treas.; Steve Auer; Steve Bauder; Howard Gavette; Bill Lilly.
EIN: 943067266

2760
Bechen Family Foundation
15350 S.W. Sequoia Pkwy., Ste. 300
Portland, OR 97224

Established in 1997 in OR.
Donor(s): Peter F. Bechen.
Grantmaker type: Independent foundation
Financial data (yr. ended 12/31/02): Assets, $1,433,483 (M); expenditures, $348,109; qualifying distributions, $342,050; giving activities include $343,850 for 15 grants (high: $300,000; low: $100).
Purpose and activities: Giving primarily for education.
Fields of interest: Education; Animals/wildlife, preservation/protection; Children/youth, services; Protestant agencies & churches.

Limitations: Applications not accepted. Giving primarily in CA and OR. No grants to individuals.
Application information: Contributes only to pre-selected organizations.
Directors: Jane G. Bechen; Peter F. Bechen; Sarah G. Bechen.
EIN: 911811266

2761
Bonneville Environmental Foundation
133 S.W. 2nd Ave., Ste. 410
Portland, OR 97204 (503) 248-1905
Contact: Angus Duncan, Exec. Dir.
FAX: (503) 248-1908; E-mail: info@b-e-f.org;
URL: http://www.bonenvfdn.org

Established in 1998.
Grantmaker type: Public charity
Financial data (yr. ended 12/31/00): Revenue, $5,389,694; assets, $7,219,298 (M); gifts received, $5,335,656; expenditures, $593,416; program services expenses, $278,029; giving activities include $146,189 for 6 grants (high: $38,689; low: $10,000; average: $5,000–$52,000).
Purpose and activities: The foundation encourages and funds projects that develop and/or apply clean environmentally preferred, renewable power and acquire, maintain, preserve, restore, protect, and/or sustain fish and wildlife habitats within the Pacific Northwest.
Fields of interest: Environment, water resources; Energy.
Types of support: General/operating support.
Limitations: Giving primarily in the Pacific Northwest.
Publications: Application guidelines, Annual report, Financial statement, Informational brochure, Multi-year report.
Application information: Renewable Energy Program requires 5 copies of full proposal. Application form not required.

Initial approach: Letter of inquiry
Deadline(s): Oct. 6 for inquiry letter, Jan. 19 for proposals
Final notification: Apr. 15

Officers and Directors:* Hon. Mark O. Hatfield,* Pres.; Ralph Cavanagh,* V.P.; Rachel Shimshak,* Secy.; Brett Wilcox,* Treas.; Angus Duncan, Exec. Dir.; Aldo Benedetti; Don Frisbee; Jim Lichatowich; Jaime Pinkham; Bill Towey.
Number of staff: 5.
EIN: 931248274

2762
The Carpenter Foundation
711 E. Main St., Ste. 10
Medford, OR 97504 (541) 772-5851
Contact: Jane Carpenter, Pres. or Polly Williams, Prog. Off.
Additional tel.: (541) 772-5732; FAX: (541) 773-3970; E-mail: carpfdn@internetcds.com;
URL: http://www.carpenter-foundation.org

Incorporated in 1957 in OR.
Donor(s): Helen Bundy Carpenter,‡ Alfred S.V. Carpenter.‡
Grantmaker type: Independent foundation
Financial data (yr. ended 06/30/03): Assets, $15,195,264 (M); gifts received, $5,000;

expenditures, $750,566; qualifying distributions, $597,421; giving activities include $597,421 for 70 grants (high: $25,000; low: $250).
Purpose and activities: The primary purpose of the Carpenter Foundation is to add opportunity, choice, inclusiveness, enrichment, and a climate for change for those living in the Rogue Valley, OR. Primary areas of interest include the arts, education, public interest, regional planning, and human services, including child welfare and youth.
Fields of interest: Visual arts; Performing arts; Theater; Arts; Early childhood education; Child development, education; Secondary school/education; Higher education; Adult/continuing education; Adult education—literacy, basic skills & GED; Libraries/library science; Reading; Education; Natural resources; Environment; Health care; Substance abuse, services; Mental health/crisis services; Legal services; Housing/shelter, development; Human services; Children/youth, services; Child development, services; Family services; Rural development; Community development; Government/public administration; Economically disadvantaged.
Types of support: General/operating support; Continuing support; Annual campaigns; Capital campaigns; Building/renovation; Equipment; Land acquisition; Program development; Conferences/seminars; Publication; Seed money; Curriculum development; Scholarship funds; Technical assistance; Consulting services; Program evaluation; Matching/challenge support.
Limitations: Giving limited to Jackson and Josephine counties, OR. No grants to individuals, or for deficit financing.
Publications: Annual report (including application guidelines), Financial statement, Grants list, Informational brochure (including application guidelines).
Application information: Contact foundation for latest information. Application form not required.

Initial approach: Letter or telephone for guidelines
Copies of proposal: 1
Deadline(s): Submit proposal 6 weeks before board meeting
Board meeting date(s): Usually in Mar., June, Sept., and Dec.
Final notification: 1 to 2 weeks after board meeting

Officers and Trustees:* Jane H. Carpenter,* Pres.; Emily C. Mostue,* V.P.; Karen C. Allan,* Secy.; Dunbar Carpenter,* Treas.; A. Brian Mostue.
Public Trustees: Susan Cohen; Mary Ellen Fleeger; Burke Raymond; Dan Thorndyke; Polly Williams, Prog. Off.
Number of staff: 1 part-time professional; 1 part-time support.
EIN: 930491360

2763
Earth Share of Oregon
P.O. Box 40333
Portland, OR 97240 (503) 223-9015
Contact: Trudy Toliver, Exec. Dir.
E-mail: info@earthshare-oregon.org; URL: http://www.earthshare-oregon.org/index.html

Established in 1989 in OR.

Grantmaker type: Public charity
Financial data (yr. ended 03/31/03): Revenue, $747,992; assets, $605,090 (L); gifts received, $651,907; expenditures, $513,601; program services expenses, $579,769; giving activities include $302,735 for grants (high: $33,934; low: $5,827).
Purpose and activities: The organization provides financial support for environmental organizations through workplace giving campaigns and grants.
Fields of interest: Natural resources.
Limitations: Giving on a national basis, with some emphasis on OR.
Publications: Annual report, Newsletter.
Application information: Application form required.
  Initial approach: Letter of interest
  Deadline(s): Varies
Officers and Directors:* Deb Furry,* Pres.; Amy Winkelman,* V.P.; Jane Foreman,* Secy.; Beth Brown,* Treas.; Trudy Toliver, Exec. Dir.; Cynthia Beckwith; Rob Guttridge; David Wilkins; and 10 additional directors.
Number of staff: 3 full-time professional; 1 full-time support.
EIN: 931001285

2764
Green Empowerment
2950 S.E. Stark St., Ste. 100
Portland, OR 97214 (503) 284-5774
Contact: Michael Royce, Pres.
FAX: (503) 460-0450; E-mail: info@greenempowerment.org; URL: http://www.greenempowerment.org

Established in 1997 in OR.
Grantmaker type: Public charity
Financial data (yr. ended 12/31/00): Revenue, $97,741; assets, $57,415; gifts received, $96,410; expenditures, $84,286; program services expenses, $49,722; giving activities include $2,547 for 2 grants (high: $1,797; low: $750) and $1,975 for in-kind gifts.
Purpose and activities: The organization seeks to promote community-based renewable energy projects internationally to generate social and environmental progress.
Fields of interest: Energy.
Limitations: Giving on a national and international basis.
Officers and Directors:* Michael Royce,* Pres.; Lisa Adatto,* Treas.; John Paisley; Francie Royce; Alida Thacher.
EIN: 931230409

2765
The Jackson Foundation
c/o U.S. Bank, N.A., Trust Group
P.O. Box 3168
Portland, OR 97208 (503) 275-4414
Contact: Robert H. Depew, V.P., U.S. Bank, N.A.

Trust established in 1960 in OR; Philip Ludwell Jackson Charitable and Residual Trusts were merged into The Jackson Foundation in 1981.
Donor(s): Maria C. Jackson.‡
Grantmaker type: Independent foundation
Financial data (yr. ended 06/30/02): Assets, $11,994,728 (M); expenditures, $742,985; qualifying distributions, $657,966; giving

activities include $582,410 for 120 grants (high: $15,000; low: $1,000; average: $1,000–$25,000).
Purpose and activities: Support for adult care counseling and training, education, children and youth programs, arts and humanities, medical issues, civic affairs and the environment, domestic violence, and food, fuel and shelter.
Fields of interest: Performing arts; Humanities; Arts; Education; Environment; Health care; Substance abuse, services; Health organizations, association; Housing/shelter, development; Human services; Children/youth, services; Aging, centers/services; Women, centers/services; Minorities/immigrants, centers/services; Minorities; Disabled; Aging; Women.
Types of support: Continuing support; Capital campaigns; Endowments; Scholarship funds; Research; Matching/challenge support.
Limitations: Giving limited to OR. No support for churches or temples. No grants to individuals, or for matching gifts, scholarships, fellowships, or building or equipment funds for religious organizations; no loans to individuals.
Publications: Annual report.
Application information: Application form required.
  Initial approach: Request for application form
  Copies of proposal: 3
  Deadline(s): Sept. 30, Dec. 31, Mar. 31, and June 30
  Board meeting date(s): July, Oct., Jan., and Apr.
  Final notification: 4 to 6 weeks
Trustees: Milo E. Ormseth; Julie Vigeland; U.S. Bank, N.A.
Number of staff: 3 part-time professional.
EIN: 936020752

2766
Lora L. & Martin N. Kelley Family Foundation Trust
P.O. Box 23503
Eugene, OR 97402

Established in 1990 in OR.
Donor(s): Martin N. Kelley, Lora L. Kelley.
Grantmaker type: Independent foundation
Financial data (yr. ended 12/31/01): Assets, $20,315,786 (M); expenditures, $5,152,835; qualifying distributions, $4,977,265; giving activities include $4,927,610 for 27 grants (high: $3,700,000; low: $5,000).
Purpose and activities: Giving primarily for the performing arts, education, federated giving programs, the environment and human services.
Fields of interest: Performing arts; Arts; Libraries (public); Education; Environment; Aquariums; Human services; Children, services; Federated giving programs.
Limitations: Applications not accepted. Giving primarily in MT and OR. No grants to individuals.
Application information: Contributes only to pre-selected organizations.
Officers and Trustees:* Bruce R. Kelley,* Vice-Chair.; Craig C. Kelley,* Secy.; Karen D. Kelley; Kent R. Kelley; Mark Kelley; Martin N. Kelley; Stephen S. Kelley.
EIN: 476174269

2767
Kinsman Foundation
43327 S.E. Spaulding Ave.
Milwaukie, OR 97267-3938 (503) 654-1668
Contact: Keith J. Kinsman, C.E.O.
FAX: (503) 654-1759; E-mail: grants@kinsmanfoundation.org

Established in 1983 in OR.
Donor(s): Elizabeth T. Kinsman,‡ John W. Kinsman.‡
Grantmaker type: Independent foundation
Financial data (yr. ended 12/31/02): Assets, $23,238,827 (M); gifts received, $2,167,990; expenditures, $592,042; qualifying distributions, $394,314; giving activities include $277,510 for 11 grants (high: $112,000; low: $3,000).
Purpose and activities: Giving to historical societies, native wildlife rehabilitation and wildlife appreciation, science and medical institutes and health care policy, museums and community service organizations.
Fields of interest: Historical activities; Historic preservation/historical societies; Animals/wildlife; Health care, public policy.
Types of support: General/operating support; Continuing support; Income development; Management development; Annual campaigns; Capital campaigns; Building/renovation; Equipment; Land acquisition; Endowments; Debt reduction; Emergency funds; Program development; Conferences/seminars; Publication; Seed money; Curriculum development; Internship funds; Research; Technical assistance; Consulting services; Program evaluation.
Limitations: Giving primarily in OR and southern WA. No grants to individuals, or for scholarships.
Publications: Annual report (including application guidelines), Grants list, Program policy statement.
Application information: Application form required.
  Initial approach: Letter
  Copies of proposal: 1
  Deadline(s): Aug. 15, no deadline for small grants
  Board meeting date(s): Fall
  Final notification: Nov.
Officers and Directors:* Keith J. Kinsman,* C.E.O. and Pres.; Mary Mitchell,* V.P. and Secy.; Pamela Reynolds,* Treas. and C.F.O.; Jack Schwab.
Number of staff: 2 full-time professional.
EIN: 930861885

2768
Lamb Foundation
(formerly OCRI Foundation)
P.O. Box 1705
Lake Oswego, OR 97035-0575
(503) 635-8010
Contact: Debra Iguchi, Admin.
FAX: (503) 635-6544; E-mail: lambfnd@thelambfoundation.org; URL: http://www.thelambfoundation.org

Established in 1971 in OR.
Donor(s): Members of the Lamb family.
Grantmaker type: Independent foundation
Financial data (yr. ended 12/31/02): Assets, $4,713,649 (M); expenditures, $311,794;

qualifying distributions, $260,529; giving activities include $242,400 for 83 grants (high: $12,000; low: $250).
Purpose and activities: Support for a wide range of creative programs to improve the quality of the human experience. Funding strategy will be changing significantly at the end of 2003 as the foundation will take a more proactive approach in soliciting applications, which may decrease the number of award recipients.
Fields of interest: Arts; Environment; Children/youth, services.
Types of support: Program development; Seed money; Matching/challenge support.
Limitations: Applications not accepted. Giving limited to OR and WA. No grants to individuals, or for scholarships, operating funds (except for start-up projects), production or distribution of books, films, videotapes or web pages, emergency funding, purchase of computer equipment for administrative purposes, capital expenses or campaigns, or for proposals submitted to individual directors.
Application information: The foundation will not accept unsolicited letters of inquiry or proposals. Please see Web site for updated information.
  Board meeting date(s): May and Nov.
Officers and Directors:* Frank Lamb, Pres.; Ben Bailey, V.P.; Jim Lamb, Secy.; Maryann Lamb,* Treas.; Anita Lamb Bailey; Christopher Bailey; Barbara Lamb; Dorothy Lamb; Greg Lamb; Helen Lamb; Paula L. Lamb.
Number of staff: 1 part-time professional.
EIN: 237120564

2769
The Larson Legacy
14404 S.E. Krause Ln.
Portland, OR 97236-6534
Contact: Leland E.G. Larson, Pres.
FAX: (503) 658-5273

Established in 1997 in OR.
Donor(s): Leland E.G. Larson, Kathleen C. Larson.
Grantmaker type: Independent foundation
Financial data (yr. ended 12/31/02): Assets, $3,905,370 (M); gifts received, $650,100; expenditures, $469,406; qualifying distributions, $381,783; giving activities include $383,275 for 40 grants (high: $100,317; low: $50).
Purpose and activities: Giving for the environment, human rights, and civil liberties.
Fields of interest: Education; Environment; Human services; International human rights; Civil liberties, advocacy; Religion.
Types of support: Annual campaigns.
Limitations: Giving primarily in the Northwest.
Publications: Application guidelines, Multi-year report.
Application information: Application form not required.
  Initial approach: Letter
  Copies of proposal: 3
  Deadline(s): None
  Board meeting date(s): Annually
  Final notification: Within 5 months of application
Officers: Leland E.G. Larson, Pres.; Kristen C. Larson, V.P.; Kathleen C. Larson, Secy.-Treas.
Number of staff: None.
EIN: 911859861

2770
The Lazar Foundation
715 S.W. Morrison St., No. 901
Portland, OR 97204 (503) 225-0265
Contact: Irene Vlach
FAX: (503) 225-9620; E-mail: info@lazarfoundation.org; URL: http://www.lazarfoundation.org

Incorporated in 1956 in DE.
Donor(s): Jack Lazar,‡ Helen B. Lazar.‡
Grantmaker type: Independent foundation
Financial data (yr. ended 12/31/01): Assets, $18,878,458 (M); gifts received, $1,341,036; expenditures, $1,569,822; qualifying distributions, $955,378; giving activities include $955,378 for 101 grants (high: $50,000; low: $200).
Purpose and activities: The foundation focuses on preservation of biological diversity and ecosystems; broadening the environmental movement, and message development.
Fields of interest: Environment.
International interests: Canada.
Types of support: General/operating support; Program development; Seed money.
Limitations: Giving primarily in AK, ID, MT, OR, and WA in the U.S., and British Columbia in Canada. No grants to individuals, or for endowments or capital campaigns.
Publications: Application guidelines, Grants list.
Application information: Application form required.
  Initial approach: Letter
  Copies of proposal: 1
  Deadline(s): Feb. 15, June 15, and Oct. 15
  Board meeting date(s): Mar., July, and Nov.
Officers and Trustees:* William B. Lazar,* Pres. and Treas.; Jeanne L. Morency,* Secy.; Anne Lazar; Michael Morency.
Number of staff: 1 part-time professional; 1 part-time support.
EIN: 136088182

2771
The E. L. & B. G. Lightfoot Foundation
c/o U.S. Bank, N.A., Trust Tax
P.O. Box 3168
Portland, OR 97208-3168
Contact: Michael W. Sullivan
Application address: P.O. Box 886, Meridian, ID 83642

Established in 1992 in ID.
Donor(s): Elma Lightfoot Newgen.
Grantmaker type: Independent foundation
Financial data (yr. ended 02/28/03): Assets, $8,581,142 (M); gifts received, $4,120,045; expenditures, $632,676; qualifying distributions, $537,930; giving activities include $178,500 for 18 grants (high: $20,000; low: $1,000) and $414,613 for 221 grants to individuals (high: $4,000; low: $259).
Purpose and activities: Giving for education, housing or environmental purposes.
Fields of interest: Education; Natural resources; Housing/shelter; Human services.
Limitations: Giving limited to southern ID and eastern OR.
Application information: Application form required.
  Initial approach: Letter
  Deadline(s): None

Charitable Committee: Elma Lightfoot Newgen, Chair.; Maureen L. Howe; Kathleen D. Mayhew; Sydney L. Mitchell.
Trustee: U.S. Bank, N.A.
EIN: 820454166

2772
Louisiana-Pacific Corporation Contributions Program
111 S.W. 5th Ave.
Portland, OR 97204-3600 (503) 221-0800

Grantmaker type: Corporate giving program
Purpose and activities: As a complement to its foundation, Louisiana-Pacific also makes charitable contributions to nonprofit organizations directly. Support is given primarily in areas of company operations.
Fields of interest: Education; Environment; Housing/shelter; Community development.
Types of support: General/operating support; Scholarship funds; Employee volunteer services; Employee matching gifts; Scholarships—to individuals; In-kind gifts.
Limitations: Giving primarily in areas of company operations.
Publications: Application guidelines.
Application information: The Corporate Communications Department handles giving. Application form not required.
  Initial approach: Proposal to headquarters
  Copies of proposal: 1
  Final notification: Following review

2773
The McCoy Foundation
211 N. Meridian St., No. 202
Newberg, OR 97132
Application addresses: c/o Arthur H. McCoy, 35150 N.E. Wilsonville Rd., Newburg, OR 97132, c/o Barbara M. Gartner, V.P., 5315 Waterbury Rd., Des Moines, IA 50312, c/o Craig W. McCoy, 4700 S.W. Macadam, Portland, OR 97201; FAX: (503) 538-4421; E-mail: mccoyfnd@easystreet.com

Established in 1979 in CO.
Donor(s): Arthur H. McCoy.
Grantmaker type: Independent foundation
Financial data (yr. ended 11/30/02): Assets, $1,244,384 (M); expenditures, $385,898; qualifying distributions, $376,356; giving activities include $362,360 for 8 grants (high: $200,860; low: $6,000).
Purpose and activities: Giving primarily for the arts, wildlife preservation and health care.
Fields of interest: Arts; Animals/wildlife, fisheries; Hospitals (specialty); Health organizations, association.
Types of support: Capital campaigns; Building/renovation; Program development; Conferences/seminars; Curriculum development; Matching/challenge support.
Limitations: Giving primarily in HI and OR. No grants to individuals, or for operating funds.
Publications: Application guidelines, Annual report.
Application information: Grants limited to organizations where at least 1 trustee has direct, personal knowledge of the work being done and specifics of the project presented. Completion of the Common Grant Application Form by CO

organizations not required. Application form not required.
> *Initial approach:* Brief letter, followed by formal application request within 30 days if the foundation determines the project is within the current scope of its operations
> *Copies of proposal:* 2
> *Board meeting date(s):* Mar. and Nov.
> *Final notification:* 2 to 3 months

Officers: Arthur H. McCoy, Pres.; Barbara M. Gartner, V.P.; Virginia G. McCoy, Secy.; Craig McCoy, Treas.
Number of staff: 1 part-time support.
EIN: 860802889

2774

McGraw Family Foundation, Inc.

707 S.W. Washington St., No. 934
Portland, OR 97205-3531
Contact: Nancie S. McGraw, Pres.

Established in 1986 in OR.
Donor(s): Donald H. McGraw, Nancie S. McGraw.
Grantmaker type: Independent foundation
Financial data (yr. ended 09/30/02): Assets, $1,611,042 (M); expenditures, $115,303; qualifying distributions, $95,601; giving activities include $96,500 for 16 grants (high: $10,000; low: $1,500).
Purpose and activities: Primarily giving to educational, cultural and social service organizations in OR.
Fields of interest: Libraries/library science; Animal welfare; Hospitals (specialty); Children, services.
Limitations: Giving limited to Portland, OR. No grants to individuals.
Application information:
> *Initial approach:* Letter
> *Deadline(s):* None

Officers: Nancie S. McGraw, Pres. and Treas.; Mary M. Richenstein, V.P. and Secy.
EIN: 930934831

2775

McKenzie River Gathering Foundation

(also known as MRG)
P.O. Box 50160
Eugene, OR 97405 (541) 485-2790
Contact: Linda Reymers, Grants Dir.
FAX: (541) 485-7604; Additional address: 2705 E. Burnside, No. 210, Portland, OR 97214, tel.: (503) 289-1517, FAX: (503) 289-1731; E-mail: info@mrgfoundation.org; URL: http://www.mrgfoundation.org

Established in 1976 in OR.
Grantmaker type: Public charity
Financial data (yr. ended 06/30/02): Revenue, $181,017; assets, $3,545,331 (L); gifts received, $482,838; expenditures, $1,010,189; program services expenses, $817,418; giving activities include $691,656 for 186 grants (high: $10,000; low: $1,000; average: $3,000–$5,000).
Purpose and activities: The foundation works for social, economic, and environmental justice, and is dedicated to funding grassroots community activism that can mobilize residents of Oregon to safeguard environmental integrity, fight discrimination, and protect human and civil rights.

Fields of interest: Natural resources; Environment; International peace/security; International affairs; Civil rights.
Types of support: General/operating support; Equipment; Program development; Publication; Seed money; Technical assistance.
Limitations: Giving limited to OR. No support for schools, co-ops, or social services. No grants to individuals.
Publications: Application guidelines, Annual report, Informational brochure, Newsletter.
Application information: Application form not required.
> *Initial approach:* Telephone
> *Copies of proposal:* 17
> *Deadline(s):* Mar. and Oct. for Funding Cycle Grants; mid-June for Lilla Jewel Award
> *Board meeting date(s):* Bimonthly
> *Final notification:* Jan. 1 and June 1 for Funding Cycle Grants; Sept. for Lilla Jewel Award

Officers and Directors:* Debra Connaway,* Chair.; Juan Carlos Ocana,* Vice-Chair; and 6 additional directors.
Number of staff: 4 full-time professional; 2 full-time support.
EIN: 930691187

2776

Meyer Memorial Trust ▼

(formerly Fred Meyer Charitable Trust)
425 N.W. 10th Ave., Ste. 400
Portland, OR 97209 (503) 228-5512
Contact: Doug Stamm, Exec. Dir.
FAX: (503) 228-5840; E-mail: mmt@mmt.org; URL: http://www.mmt.org

Trust established by will in 1978; obtained IRS status in 1982 in OR.
Donor(s): Fred G. Meyer.‡
Grantmaker type: Independent foundation
Financial data (yr. ended 03/31/03): Assets, $402,321,542 (M); expenditures, $19,366,655; qualifying distributions, $16,654,323; giving activities include $16,654,323 for grants and $1,256,000 for 1 loan/program-related investment.
Purpose and activities: The trust provides general purpose grants, primarily in Oregon and Clark County, WA, for education, the arts and humanities, health, and social welfare. Under general purpose, the trust operates the Small Grants Program, which provides awards of $500 to $12,000 for small projects in Oregon. The Support for Teacher Initiatives Program provides awards of up to $7,000 to teachers in Oregon and Clark County, WA.
Fields of interest: Museums; Performing arts; Humanities; Historic preservation/historical societies; Arts; Child development, education; Higher education; Education; Natural resources; Environment; Health care; Health organizations, association; Crime/violence prevention, youth; Housing/shelter, development; Human services; Children/youth, services; Child development, services; Family services; Aging, centers/services; Community development; Aging.
Types of support: General/operating support; Capital campaigns; Building/renovation; Equipment; Program development; Seed money; Technical assistance; Program-related investments/loans; Matching/challenge support.

Limitations: Giving primarily in OR and Clark County, WA. No support for sectarian or religious organizations for religious purposes. No grants to individuals or for endowment funds, annual campaigns, deficit financing, scholarships, fellowships, or indirect or overhead costs, except as specifically and essentially related to the grant project; occasional program-related loans only.
Publications: Application guidelines, Annual report.
Application information: Special guidelines for Small Grants Program and Support for Teacher Initiatives Program. Application guidelines and cover sheet available on the internet. Application form required.
> *Initial approach:* Proposal
> *Copies of proposal:* 1
> *Deadline(s):* Jan. 15, Apr. 15, and Oct. 15 for Small Grants Program; Feb. 1 for Support for Teacher Initiatives; no set deadline for other grants
> *Board meeting date(s):* Monthly
> *Final notification:* 3 to 5 months for General Purpose proposals that pass first screening; 1 to 2 months for those that do not; 12 to 16 weeks for Small Grants; 12 weeks for Support for Teacher Initiatives

Officers and Trustees:* Orcilla Z. Forbes,* Chair.; Wayne G. Pierson, C.F.O. and Treas.; Doug Stamm, Exec. Dir.; Debbie F. Craig; John Emrick; Warne Nunn; Gerry Pratt.
Number of staff: 4 full-time professional; 3 part-time professional; 5 full-time support; 1 part-time support.
EIN: 930806316
Recent environmental and animal welfare grants:

2776-1 1000 Friends of Oregon, Portland, Oregon, $50,000. For series of community workshops that address expansion of urban growth boundary in Damascus area. 2003.

2776-2 Aprovecho Research Center, Cottage Grove, Oregon, $30,000. Toward building community center for education programs at its sustainable campus. 2003.

2776-3 BRING Recycling, Eugene, Oregon, $110,000. For capital campaign to relocate and redesign recycling/reuse program and to develop educational exhibits designed to reduce consumption and encourage sustainable living. 2003.

2776-4 Deschutes Basin Land Trust, Bend, Oregon, $95,000. To hire land steward to monitor and manage sites protected through conservation activities. 2003.

2776-5 Deschutes Resources Conservancy, Bend, Oregon, $170,587. To develop collaborative watershed restoration strategies for Deschutes River Basin to increase water quantity and improve water quality. 2003.

2776-6 Friends of Trees, Portland, Oregon, $12,000. For planting equipment for organization's public stewardship of urban forest. 2003.

2776-7 Headwaters Community Association, Ashland, Oregon, $12,000. To develop ecological guidelines for fire management in Klamath-Siskiyou region. 2003.

2776-8 Johnson Creek Watershed Council, Portland, Oregon, $12,000. For strategic planning to meet community's needs for watershed restoration. 2003.

2776-9 ONE/Northwest, Seattle, WA, $25,000. Toward establishing office in Portland to better assist Oregon conservation organizations with technology improvements. 2003.

2776-10 Oregon Coastal Environments Awareness Network (OCEAN), Coos Bay, Oregon, $11,600. To train elementary and middle school teachers on southern Oregon coast in interdisciplinary environmental learning program. 2003.

2776-11 Oregon State University, Office of Sponsored Programs, Corvallis, Oregon, $600,000. For Willamette Basin Conservation Project, which provides technical information and data about Willamette Basin to conservation groups and members of public. 2003.

2776-12 Oregon Trout, Portland, Oregon, $104,000. To expand membership program. 2003.

2776-13 Oregon Water Trust, Portland, Oregon, $120,000. Toward diversifying and stabilizing organization. 2003.

2776-14 Saint Philip Neri Catholic Church, Portland, Oregon, $12,000. For environmental project to collect runoff from parking lot. 2003.

2776-15 Saint Vincent de Paul Society of Lane County, Eugene, Oregon, $50,000. To add textile recycling facility to waste-based economic development program. 2003.

2776-16 Three Rivers Land Conservancy, Lake Oswego, Oregon, $95,000. For development project to raise more individual donations for land conservation activities in metropolitan area. 2003.

2776-17 World Forestry Center, Portland, Oregon, $400,000. To build covered, elevated walkway to explore tree canopy in forest behind museum. 2003.

2777
Fred Meyer Stores, Inc. Corporate Giving Program

c/o Donations Comm.
P.O. Box 42121
Portland, OR 97242 (503) 797-7155
URL: http://www.fredmeyerstores.com/corpnewsinfo_charitablegiving.htm

Grantmaker type: Corporate giving program
Purpose and activities: As a complement to its foundation, Fred Meyer also makes charitable contributions to nonprofit organizations directly. Support is limited to areas of company operations.
Fields of interest: Environment; Youth development; Human services; Urban/community development; Community development; Economically disadvantaged.
Types of support: Employee volunteer services; In-kind gifts.
Limitations: Giving limited to areas of company operations. No support for sectarian or religious organizations not of direct benfit to the entire community, discriminatory organizations, or external athletic programs. No grants to individuals, or for general operating support of United Way-supported organizations.
Application information: Proposals should be submitted using organization letterhead. Support

is limited to 1 contribution per organization during any given year.
  Initial approach: Proposal to headquarters
  Deadline(s): 4 to 6 weeks prior to need

2778
Arthur E. & Faye G. Munson Charitable Trust

c/o U.S. Bank, N.A.
P.O. Box 3168
Portland, OR 97208

Established in 1999 in WA.
Grantmaker type: Independent foundation
Financial data (yr. ended 12/31/02): Assets, $1,940,651 (M); expenditures, $128,073; qualifying distributions, $108,876; giving activities include $106,404 for 2 grants (high: $79,803; low: $26,601).
Fields of interest: Animal welfare; Human services.
Limitations: Applications not accepted. Giving primarily in Seattle, WA. No grants to individuals.
Application information: Contributes only to pre-selected organizations.
Trustee: U.S. Bank, N.A.
EIN: 916483037

2779
Northwest Natural Gas Company Contributions Program

220 N.W. 2nd Ave.
Portland, OR 97209 (503) 226-4211
Contact: George Richardson, Chair., Contribs. Comm.

Grantmaker type: Corporate giving program
Financial data (yr. ended 12/31/02): Total giving, $725,500; giving activities include $725,500 for grants.
Purpose and activities: Northwest Natural Gas makes charitable contributions to nonprofit organizations involved with arts and culture, education, the environment, housing, children, families, and civic affairs. Support is given primarily in western Oregon and southwestern Washington.
Fields of interest: Arts; Education; Environment; Housing/shelter; Children, services; Family services; Public affairs.
Types of support: Annual campaigns; Program development; Publication; Curriculum development; Scholarship funds; Employee volunteer services; Use of facilities; Sponsorships; In-kind gifts; Matching/challenge support.
Limitations: Giving primarily in western OR and southwestern WA. No support for discriminatory organizations or political or religious organizations. No grants to individuals, or for travel.
Publications: Application guidelines.
Application information: The Public Relations and Communications Department handles giving. Application form not required.
  Initial approach: Proposal to headquarters
  Copies of proposal: 1
  Deadline(s): None
  Final notification: 6 to 8 weeks
Number of staff: 2 part-time professional.

2780
Parks Foundation

(formerly Psychological Research Foundation)
P.O. Box 5669
Beaverton, OR 97006-0669

Established in 1977 as the Psychological Research Foundation.
Donor(s): Loren E. Parks.
Grantmaker type: Independent foundation
Financial data (yr. ended 11/30/02): Assets, $4,243,341 (M); expenditures, $411,831; qualifying distributions, $391,145; giving activities include $191,890 for 9 grants (high: $80,000; low: $250).
Purpose and activities: Giving primarily for breast cancer research, public broadcasting, and organizations providing assistance to the needy.
Fields of interest: Natural resources; Education; Cancer; Medical research, institute; Food services; Human services.
Types of support: Research.
Limitations: Applications not accepted. Giving limited to Portland, OR. No grants to individuals.
Application information: Contributes only to pre-selected organizations.
Officers: Loren E. Parks, Pres.; Gary L. Parks, Secy.
Director: Ray C. Parks.
EIN: 930729614

2781
PGE Corporate Giving Program

121 S.W. Salmon St.
Portland, OR 97204 (503) 464-7618

Grantmaker type: Corporate giving program
Purpose and activities: As a complement to its foundation, PGE also makes charitable contributions to nonprofit organizations directly. Support is given primarily in areas of company operations.
Fields of interest: Arts; Education; Environment; Family services.
Types of support: General/operating support; Donated equipment.
Limitations: Giving primarily in areas of company operations in OR.

2782
Phileo Foundation

220 N.W. 2nd Ave., Ste. 1000
Portland, OR 97209-3953
Contact: James Crabbe, Pres.; or Michael Crabbe, Secy.
Application address: P.O. Box 8783, Portland, OR 97207-8783

Established in 1999 in OR.
Donor(s): James E. Crabbe.
Grantmaker type: Independent foundation
Financial data (yr. ended 12/31/01): Assets, $4,645,907 (M); expenditures, $239,137; qualifying distributions, $103,084; giving activities include $112,450 for 19 grants (high: $15,000; low: $1,000).
Fields of interest: Natural resources; Youth, services.
Types of support: Program development.
Limitations: Giving limited to the Portland, OR, area. No grants to individuals.

Publications: Annual report (including application guidelines), Multi-year report.
Application information: Unsolicited requests for funds not considered. Application form required.
   Deadline(s): May 1 and Oct. 1
Officers: James E. Crabbe, Pres.; Michael D. Crabbe, Secy.; James E. Crabbe, Jr., Treas.
Number of staff: 2 part-time professional.
EIN: 931283076

2783
Charla Richards-Kreitzberg Charitable Foundation

c/o Karen J. Lord
835 Saginaw St. S.
Salem, OR 97302-4121 (503) 391-1814
E-Mail: information@crkfoundation.org; URL: http://www.crkfoundation.org

Grantmaker type: Independent foundation
Financial data (yr. ended 12/31/02): Assets, $1,912,551 (M); expenditures, $122,871; qualifying distributions, $103,000; giving activities include $103,000 for 5 grants (high: $50,000; low: $5,000).
Fields of interest: Education; Environment; Human services; YM/YWCAs & YM/YWHAs.
Limitations: Applications not accepted. Giving primarily in OR.
Application information: Unsolicited requests for funds not accepted.
Officers: Jane Edwards, Pres.; Bonnie Heitsch, V.P.; Meredith Russell, Secy.; Britta Franz, Treas.
Directors: Kathy Evans; Barbara Hanneman; Mary Ann Kaestner; Karen J. Lords; Sally Miller.
EIN: 931255604

2784
The Salem Foundation

c/o Pioneer Trust Bank, N.A.
P.O. Box 2305
Salem, OR 97308 (503) 363-3136
Contact: Carol Herman

Established in 1964 in OR.
Grantmaker type: Community foundation
Financial data (yr. ended 04/30/03): Assets, $12,716,913 (M); gifts received, $302,428; expenditures, $1,072,377; giving activities include $936,707 for 86 grants (high: $137,000; low: $195) and $16,712 for grants to individuals.
Purpose and activities: Scholarships to local students and distributions for the benefit of the community.
Fields of interest: Elementary/secondary education; Education; Botanical gardens; Health care; Parks/playgrounds; Youth development; Human services; Family services; Protestant agencies & churches; Roman Catholic agencies & churches.
Limitations: Giving limited to the Salem, OR, area.
Publications: Financial statement, Informational brochure (including application guidelines).
Application information:
   Initial approach: Letter of intent or telephone call
   Copies of proposal: 1
   Deadline(s): May 1 and Dec. 1
Trustee: Pioneer Trust Bank, N.A.
Number of staff: None.

EIN: 936018523

2785
The J. Frank Schmidt Family Charitable Foundation

P.O. Box 189
Boring, OR 97009

Established in 1986 in OR.
Donor(s): Evelyn Schmidt, J. Frank Schmidt, Jr.
Grantmaker type: Independent foundation
Financial data (yr. ended 09/30/02): Assets, $4,485,148 (M); gifts received, $115,000; expenditures, $188,353; qualifying distributions, $168,288; giving activities include $159,517 for 85 grants (high: $29,666; low: $100).
Purpose and activities: Giving primarily to universities and botanical gardens for horticultural research, and to medical associations for medical research.
Fields of interest: Education, research; Higher education; Education; Botanical/horticulture/landscape services; Hospitals (general); Health care; Health organizations, association; Medical research, institute; Agriculture; Human services; Children/youth, services.
Types of support: Continuing support; Annual campaigns; Endowments; Program development; Scholarship funds; Research; Matching/challenge support.
Limitations: Applications not accepted. No grants to individuals.
Trustees: Jan Schmidt Barkley; John A. Fought, Jr.; Robert Kinen; J. Frank Schmidt, Jr.; J. Frank Schmidt III; Jean Schmidt Webster.
Number of staff: 1 shared staff (shared with Oregon Garden Foundation, Gresham-Barlow Education Foundation, Mt. Hood Community College Education Foundation).
EIN: 931265440

2786
Vera L. Smith Charitable Foundation

2165 S.W. Main St.
Portland, OR 97205

Established in 1992 in OR.
Donor(s): Vera L. Smith.‡
Grantmaker type: Independent foundation
Financial data (yr. ended 06/30/02): Assets, $2,099,436 (M); expenditures, $190,457; qualifying distributions, $146,582; giving activities include $103,500 for 17 grants (high: $20,000; low: $1,500).
Purpose and activities: Giving primarily for health and human services.
Fields of interest: Veterinary medicine, hospital; Hospitals (general); Health care; Food services; Human services; Youth, services; Federated giving programs.
Limitations: Applications not accepted. Giving primarily in Portland, OR. No grants to individuals.
Application information: Contributes only to pre-selected organizations.
Officers: Lynn D. Simpson, Pres.; Lisa A. Joerin, V.P.; Edward L. Joy, Secy.-Treas.
EIN: 931095010

2787
The Standard Corporate Giving Program

P.O. Box 711
Portland, OR 97207 (503) 321-6418
Contact: Kira Higgs, Asst. V.P., Public Affairs and Corp. Comm.
FAX: (503) 321-6776; URL: http://www.stancorpfinancial.com/community.html; Additional URL: http://www.standard.com/the_standard/community.html

Grantmaker type: Corporate giving program
Purpose and activities: The Standard makes charitable contributions to nonprofit organizations involved with arts and culture, education, the environment, and health and human services. Support is given primarily in areas of company operations.
Fields of interest: Arts; Education; Environment; Health care; Human services.
Types of support: General/operating support; Employee volunteer services; Employee matching gifts.
Limitations: Giving primarily in areas of company operations, with emphasis on the Portland, OR, metropolitan area.
Application information: Application form not required.
   Initial approach: Proposal to headquarters
   Copies of proposal: 1
   Final notification: Following review

2788
Rose E. Tucker Charitable Trust

900 S.W. 5th Ave., Ste. 2600
Portland, OR 97204 (503) 224-3380
Contact: Terrence R. Pancoast, or Milo E. Ormseth, Trustees

Trust established in 1976 in OR.
Donor(s): Rose E. Tucker,‡ Max and Rose Tucker Foundation.
Grantmaker type: Independent foundation
Financial data (yr. ended 06/30/02): Assets, $20,250,449 (M); expenditures, $1,185,179; qualifying distributions, $1,094,508; giving activities include $1,023,700 for 194 grants (high: $52,500; low: $1,000; average: $2,500–$20,000).
Fields of interest: Arts; Higher education; Education; Environment; Health care; Human services; Children/youth, services; Community development; Disabled; Economically disadvantaged.
Types of support: General/operating support; Capital campaigns; Building/renovation; Equipment; Land acquisition; Program development; Scholarship funds; Matching/challenge support.
Limitations: Giving limited to organizations and projects in OR, with emphasis on the metropolitan Portland area. No support for religious purposes, private foundations, or conduit organizations. No grants to individuals, or for fellowships; no loans or program-related investments.
Publications: Application guidelines, Annual report (including application guidelines), Grants list.
Application information: Organizations may only apply once within a 12 month period. Application form not required.
   Initial approach: Proposal

Copies of proposal: 2
Deadline(s): None
Board meeting date(s): Approximately every 2
 months
Final notification: Within 15 days of board
 meetings
Trustees: Milo E. Ormseth; Terrence R. Pancoast;
U.S. Bank, N.A.
Number of staff: None.
EIN: 936119091

2789
Paul F. Wenner Charitable Foundation
Trust
3549 S.E. Main St.
Portland, OR 97214 (503) 235-8193
Contact: Giovanni Rosati

Established in 1994 in OR.
Donor(s): Paul F. Wenner.
Grantmaker type: Independent foundation
Financial data (yr. ended 12/31/02): Assets,
$183,614 (M); expenditures, $210,801;
qualifying distributions, $204,135; giving
activities include $204,200 for 2 grants (high:
$203,000; low: $1,200; average:
$1,200–$203,000).
Purpose and activities: Giving for nutritional
and environmental education and research.
Fields of interest: Environmental education;
Medical specialty research; Agriculture/food,
research; Nutrition.
Types of support: Program development;
Research.
Limitations: Applications not accepted. Giving
primarily in OR. No grants to individuals.
Application information: Contributes only to
pre-selected organizations.
Trustee: Paul F. Wenner.
Number of staff: 2 part-time professional.
EIN: 936289211

2790
WF Foundation
c/o K. Evans
280 Court St. N.E., Ste. 1
Salem, OR 97301-3443

Donor(s): Chris G. Wolcott, Guy R. Wolcott.
Grantmaker type: Independent foundation
Financial data (yr. ended 08/31/02): Assets,
$468,665 (M); gifts received, $478,000;
expenditures, $355,922; qualifying distributions,
$355,904; giving activities include $352,000 for
6 grants (high: $290,000; low: $1,000).
Purpose and activities: Giving primarily to a
Protestant ministry and churches.
Fields of interest: Animals/wildlife,
preservation/protection; Children, services;
Protestant agencies & churches.
Limitations: Applications not accepted. Giving
primarily in OR and TX. No grants to individuals.
Application information: Contributes only to
pre-selected organizations.
Officers: Guy R. Wolcott, Pres.; Chris G.
Wolcott, Secy.
Director: Guy R. Wolcott II.
EIN: 931291150

2791
The Woodard Family Foundation
40 S. 6th
Cottage Grove, OR 97424 (541) 942-4113
Contact: Tod C. Woodard, V.P.
E-mail: wff@uci.net

Incorporated in 1952 in OR.
Donor(s): Walter A. Woodard, Carlton Woodard.
Grantmaker type: Independent foundation
Financial data (yr. ended 06/30/02): Assets,
$5,442,283 (M); expenditures, $330,459;
qualifying distributions, $289,134; giving
activities include $222,994 for 101 grants (high:
$42,000; low: $40).
Purpose and activities: Preference is given to
organizations which historically have been of
interest to the Woodard family.
Fields of interest: Arts; Business
school/education; Education; Animal welfare;
Human services; Community development.
Types of support: General/operating support;
Annual campaigns; Capital campaigns;
Building/renovation; Land acquisition; Program
development; Professorships; Seed money;
Consulting services.
Limitations: Giving limited to local
organizations in the greater Cottage
Grove/Eugene, OR, area.
Publications: Application guidelines.
Application information: Application form
required.
 Initial approach: Request application form
 Copies of proposal: 1
 Deadline(s): Jan. 30, May 31, and Sept. 30
 Board meeting date(s): Quarterly
 Final notification: 30 days following board
  meeting
Officers and Directors:* Carlton Woodard,*
Pres.; Tod C. Woodard,* V.P. and Secy.
Number of staff: 1 part-time professional; 2
part-time support.
EIN: 936026550

PENNSYLVANIA

2792
The 1957 Charity Trust
c/o Mellon Financial Corp.
P.O. Box 7236
Philadelphia, PA 19101-7236
Contact: Judith L. Bardes, Mgr.

Trust established in 1957 in PA.
Donor(s): Elizabeth R. Moran.
Grantmaker type: Independent foundation
Financial data (yr. ended 06/30/01): Assets,
$2,193 (M); expenditures, $1,691,440;
qualifying distributions, $1,531,011; giving
activities include $1,325,562 for 245 grants
(high: $35,000; low: $1,000; average:
$1,000–$10,000).
Purpose and activities: Primary areas of interest
include projects benefiting human service and
social welfare organizations, youth, and early
childhood education; giving also for
environmental concerns, health care for the
indigent, education, conservation, and culture.

Fields of interest: Early childhood education;
Child development, education; Elementary
school/education; Adult education—literacy,
basic skills & GED; Reading; Education; Natural
resources; Environment; Medical care,
rehabilitation; Health care; Substance abuse,
services; Health organizations, association;
Housing/shelter, development; Youth
development, services; Human services;
Children/youth, services; Child development,
services; Aging, centers/services; Homeless,
human services; Community development;
Leadership development; Minorities; Disabled;
Aging; Economically disadvantaged; Homeless.
Types of support: General/operating support;
Continuing support; Annual campaigns; Capital
campaigns; Building/renovation; Equipment;
Endowments; Program development; Seed
money.
Limitations: Giving primarily in the five-county
region in southeastern PA. No grants to
individuals; no loans.
Publications: Annual report (including
application guidelines).
Application information: Application form
required.
 Deadline(s): Jan. 15 and Apr. 15
 Board meeting date(s): Feb., June, and Oct.
Trustee: Mellon Financial Corp.
Number of staff: 2 part-time professional.
EIN: 236227603

2793
Acorn Alcinda Foundation, Inc.
c/o Kit C. Kennedy
RR4 Box 710
Mifflintown, PA 17059

Established in 1984 in VA.
Donor(s): Robert J. Kennedy.‡
Grantmaker type: Independent foundation
Financial data (yr. ended 05/31/02): Assets,
$5,111,462 (M); expenditures, $317,763;
qualifying distributions, $283,893; giving
activities include $278,000 for 57 grants (high:
$64,000; low: $1,000).
Purpose and activities: Support for
organizations which 1) promote scientific
research, advancement, and knowledge in
wood chemistry, forestry, and tree farming; or 2)
assist in developing means and procedures for
the recovery, training, and education of the
elderly who have become disabled as the result
of strokes, heart attacks, or disease. Funding also
for the arts, education, religion and social
services, including services for people who are
blind.
Fields of interest: Performing arts; Higher
education; University; Natural resources;
Environment; Hospitals (general); Medical care,
rehabilitation; Health organizations, association;
Human services; Human services; Aging,
centers/services; Christian agencies & churches;
Protestant agencies & churches; Aging.
Types of support: General/operating support.
Limitations: Applications not accepted. Giving
primarily on the East Coast, with some emphasis
on CT, PA and VA. No grants to individuals.
Application information: Contributes only to
pre-selected organizations.
Officers and Directors:* Kit C. Kennedy,* Pres.
and Secy.; Jan B. Kennedy,* V.P.
EIN: 541303250

2794
Alcoa Foundation ▼

Alcoa Corporate Ctr.
201 Isabella St.
Pittsburgh, PA 15212-5858 (412) 553-2348
E-mail: Alcoa.Foundation@alcoa.com; *URL:*
http://www.alcoa.com/global/en/community/
foundation.asp

Trust established in 1952 in PA; incorporated in 1964.

Donor(s): Aluminum Co. of America, Alcoa Inc.

Grantmaker type: Company-sponsored foundation

Financial data (yr. ended 12/31/02): Assets, $391,868,847 (M); expenditures, $19,983,152; qualifying distributions, $18,992,550; giving activities include $17,038,313 for 1,907 grants (high: $250,000; low: $25; average: $1,000–$100,000) and $178,500 for grants to individuals.

Purpose and activities: Five distinct Areas of Excellence provide thematic focus to the global allocation of the foundation's philanthropic resources. The majority of the foundation's grants fit within one of the following areas: conservation and sustainability; safe and healthy children and families; global education in business, engineering science and technology; business and community partnerships; and workforce skills today for tomorrow.

Fields of interest: Higher education; Business school/education; Engineering school/education; Education; Natural resources; Human services; Youth, services; Family services; Community development; Science; Government/public administration.

International interests: Caribbean; Jamaica; Netherlands; Italy; Wales; Spain; Hungary; Mexico; Brazil; Suriname; China; Australia.

Types of support: General/operating support; Continuing support; Annual campaigns; Capital campaigns; Building/renovation; Equipment; Emergency funds; Program development; Conferences/seminars; Seed money; Fellowships; Scholarship funds; Research; Program-related investments/loans; Employee matching gifts; Employee-related scholarships; Matching/challenge support.

Limitations: Giving primarily in areas of company operations, national and international; emphasis on local communities: Davenport, IA, Evansville, IN, Massena, NY, Cleveland, OH, Pittsburgh, PA, Knoxville, TN, and Rockdale, TX. No support for sectarian or religious organizations, or political purposes. No grants to individuals (except for employee-related scholarships), or for endowment funds, deficit reduction, documentaries and videos, tickets, souvenir programs, advertising, golf outings, trips, tours, or student exchange programs.

Publications: Annual report (including application guidelines), Informational brochure (including application guidelines).

Application information: Application form required.

   Initial approach: Letter
   Copies of proposal: 1
   Deadline(s): None
   Board meeting date(s): Monthly
   Final notification: 1 to 4 months

Officers and Directors:* Kathleen W. Buechel,* Pres. and Treas.; Velma Montelro Tribble, Secy.; Ricardo E. Belda; Earnest J. Edwards; Richard B.

Kelson; William E. Leahey, Jr.; Renata de Camargo Nasicmento; Barry C. Owens; G. John Pizzey; Richard L. Siewart.

Corporate Trustee: Mellon Financial Corp.

Number of staff: 6 full-time professional; 1 full-time support.

EIN: 251128857

Recent environmental and animal welfare grants:

2794-1 American Enterprise Institute for Public Policy Research, DC, $30,000. For research on meaning and challenges of globalization, and implications of globalization for international trade, environmental and tax policy. 2002.

2794-2 Ashoka Trust for Research in Ecology and the Environment, Belmont, MA, $10,000. For research, education and outreach programs in India. 2002.

2794-3 Asociacion Civil Hermana Tierra, Lima, Peru, $26,879. For general operating support. 2002.

2794-4 Asociacion Pro-Enfermos Mentales (APEM), La Coruna, Spain, $27,469. For purchase of vehicle to transport patients and materials to Classroom of Nature and Environment in countryside. 2002.

2794-5 Asociacion VIDA de Acuna, Acuna, Mexico, $179,100. For park restoration project under matching grant program provided by State of Coahuila. 2002.

2794-6 Aviles City Council, Aviles, Spain, $30,000. For improvement of French Garden at Ferrera Park. 2002.

2794-7 Chesapeake Bay Foundation, Annapolis, MD, $10,000. For current programs. 2002.

2794-8 Clean Air Force of Central Texas, Austin, TX, $21,500. To reduce emissions of ozone causing pollutants through outreach program to retailers and consumers. 2002.

2794-9 Colexio de Educacion Infantil e Primario (CEIP) Mestre Rivera Casas, Spain, $25,520. For construction of educational plant laboratory/greenhouse. 2002.

2794-10 Conselleria de Medio Ambiente, Centro de Desarrollo Sostenible, Santiago de Compostela, Spain, $39,200. For Plis Plas project to promote non-academic environmental education. 2002.

2794-11 Conservation Fund, Arlington, VA, $25,000. For work to integrate economic development and environmental protection. 2002.

2794-12 Evansvilles Mesker Park Zoo and Gardens, Evansville, Indiana, $10,000. For construction and renovation of Children's Forest area in new children's petting zoo. 2002.

2794-13 Fejer County Organisation of Federation of Technical and Scientific Societies - MTESZ, Szekesfehervar, Hungary, $10,500. For National Environmental Conference and for purchase of projector for House of Technology. 2002.

2794-14 Handy Dog- Associazione Cani dAssitenza e Terapia, Martellago, Italy, $32,000. To purchase equipped minibus to transport people with disabilities. 2002.

2794-15 Ijams Nature Center, Knoxville, TN, $10,000. For Phase II of Meads Quarry Nature Sanctuary clean-up and restoration. 2002.

2794-16 International Commission for the Protection of the Danube River, Vienna,

Austria, $35,000. For purchase of total organic carbon analyzer. 2002.

2794-17 JeunEssor Portneuf, Saint Basile, Canada, $25,000. For construction and expansion of workshop. 2002.

2794-18 Jovonk a Falu Foundation, Szabadbattyan, Hungary, $10,500. For re-cultivation of area, maintenance to flora, and exhibits for public. 2002.

2794-19 Keystone Center, Keystone Science School, Keystone, CO, $30,000. For sponsorship of teachers to attend Key Issues: Bringing Environmental Issues to Classroom professional development program. 2002.

2794-20 Lewis Ginter Botanical Gardens, Richmond, VA, $10,000. For Children's Educational Programming. 2002.

2794-21 Living Lands and Waters Restoration Organization, East Moline, IL, $50,000. For current clean-up projects. 2002.

2794-22 Maymont Foundation, Richmond, VA, $10,000. For Environmental Education programs. 2002.

2794-23 Midewin Tallgrass Prairie Alliance, Joliet, IL, $10,000. For establishment of Midewin Interpretive Association and to provide range of educational programs to visitors and school-age children. 2002.

2794-24 National Wildlife Federation, Reston, VA, $11,000. For one-day workday to promote Backyard Habitats, Community Habitats, Schoolyard Habitats and Workplace Habitats programs. 2002.

2794-25 Pittsburgh Voyager, Pittsburgh, PA, $19,000. For Environmental Science School program for North Side Pittsburgh Public Schools. 2002.

2794-26 Resources for the Future, DC, $12,500. For current programs. 2002.

2794-27 Rotary Club Paramaribo Central, Paramaribo, Suriname, $13,500. For Opo Yu Ay environmental awareness program. 2002.

2794-28 Saint Croix Environmental Association, Christiansted, VI, $20,000. For current programs to encourage environmental action. 2002.

2794-29 Sociedad Espanola de Ornitologia, Spain, $10,000. For disaster relief for oil spill in Spain. 2002.

2794-30 South Spencer County School Corporation, Luce Elementary School, Richland, Indiana, $10,000. For development of Nature Center Recreation Area at Luce Elementary School. 2002.

2794-31 Stichting Hulpcentrum voor Wilde Dieren, Limbricht, Netherlands, $10,000. For re-location of center and for needed materials for animals. 2002.

2794-32 Stichting tot Behoud van de Veluwse Beken en Sprengen, Heerde, Netherlands, $10,000. For publication of book on cultural heritage of springs and streams of Veluwe. 2002.

2794-33 Szekesfehervar, Municipality of, Environmental Department, Szekesfehervar, Hungary, $20,000. For rehabilitation and development of Nature Conservation Area of Szekesfehervar Sosto. 2002.

2794-34 Tennessee Trails Association, Crossville, TN, $20,000. For creation of Cumberland Trail State Park. 2002.

2794-35 Texas Ornithological Society, San Antonio, TX, $14,540. For Magic Ridge Bird Sanctuary in Calhoun County. 2002.

2794-36 Vogel and Zoogdierenopvangcentrum, Heusden-Zolder, Belgium, $16,000. For purchase of rubber boat to clean waterways and treat diseased animals. 2002.

2794-37 Western Pennsylvania Conservancy, Pittsburgh, PA, $26,400. For teacher training activities and materials for Trees of Pittsburgh field guide and educational program. 2002.

2794-38 Whitehall, City of, Whitehall, MI, $10,500. For beautification of walk/bicycle trail. 2002.

2794-39 Wildlife Trust for Lancashire, Manchester, and North Merseyside, Preston, England, $12,000. For installation of solar water heating system for Nature Has Power project. 2002.

2794-40 Winda Mara Aboriginal Corporation, Heywood, Australia, $25,000. For planning and development of Lake Condah Sustainable Development Partnership five-year project. 2002.

2795
The Allerton Foundation, Inc.
(formerly The Diane Lenfest Myer Foundation, Inc.)
5 Tower Bridge
300 Barr Harbor Dr., Ste. 450
West Conshohocken, PA 19428
(610) 828-4510
Contact: Bruce Melgary, Exec. Dir.
FAX: (610) 828-0390

Established in 1999 in PA.
Donor(s): Diane Lenfest Myer.
Grantmaker type: Independent foundation
Financial data (yr. ended 06/30/03): Assets, $54,584,928 (M); expenditures, $2,836,414; qualifying distributions, $2,609,293; giving activities include $2,588,500 for 22 grants (high: $1,000,000; low: $2,000; average: $2,000–$1,000,000).
Fields of interest: Environment, land resources; Animal welfare; Animals/wildlife.
Types of support: General/operating support; Continuing support; Annual campaigns; Capital campaigns; Building/renovation; Seed money.
Limitations: Applications not accepted. Giving primarily in southeastern PA. No grants to individuals.
Application information: Contributes only to pre-selected organizations.
Board meeting date(s): As necessary
Officers and Directors:* Diane Lenfest Myer,* Pres.; Grahame Richards,* Secy.; Joy Tartar, C.F.O.; Marguerite Lenfest,* Treas.; Bruce Melgary,* Exec. Dir.
EIN: 233035225

2796
Amaranth Foundation
c/o Duane, Morris & Heckscher, LLP
1 Liberty Pl.
Philadelphia, PA 19103-7396

Established in 1993 in PA.
Donor(s): Joan M. Moran.
Grantmaker type: Independent foundation
Financial data (yr. ended 12/31/02): Assets, $117,828 (M); gifts received, $284,873; expenditures, $211,293; qualifying distributions,

$208,864; giving activities include $207,400 for 67 grants (high: $15,000; low: $100).
Purpose and activities: Giving for the arts, animal welfare, and religion.
Fields of interest: Performing arts; Music; Animals/wildlife; Human services; Religion.
Limitations: Applications not accepted. Giving primarily in PA, with emphasis on Allentown. No grants to individuals.
Application information: Contributes only to pre-selected organizations.
Trustee: Joan M. Moran.
EIN: 237743235

2797
Harriett Ames Charitable Trust
c/o Hawthorn, PNC Advisors
1600 Market St., 19th Fl.
Philadelphia, PA 19103
Contact: L. Dianne Lomonaco, Trust Admin.

Trust established in 1952 in NY.
Donor(s): Harriett Ames.‡
Grantmaker type: Independent foundation
Financial data (yr. ended 12/31/00): Assets, $9,184,466 (M); expenditures, $689,049; qualifying distributions, $664,772; giving activities include $635,120 for 47 grants (high: $192,220; low: $1,000; average: $1,000–$25,000).
Purpose and activities: Grants to educational and charitable organizations, with emphasis on medical research, education, health associations, and cultural organizations.
Fields of interest: Photography; Museums; Museums (art); Arts; Education; Animals/wildlife, preservation/protection; Health organizations, association; Medical research, institute; Human services; Community development; Jewish federated giving programs; Jewish agencies & temples.
Types of support: General/operating support; Annual campaigns.
Limitations: Applications not accepted. Giving primarily in the metropolitan New York, NY, area. No grants to individuals.
Application information: Contributes only to pre-selected organizations. Unsolicited requests for funds not considered.
Board meeting date(s): Varies
Trustee: Steven Ames.
Number of staff: 6 shared staff (shared with Lita Annenberg Hazen Charitable Trust, Janet A. Hooker Charitable Trust, Polly Annenberg Levee Charitable Trust - Krancer Trust, Polly Annenberg Levee Charitable Trust - Levee Trust, Esther Simon Charitable Trust).
EIN: 236286757

2798
AMETEK Foundation, Inc.
37 N. Valley Rd., Bldg. 4
P.O. Box 1764
Paoli, PA 19301-0801 (610) 647-2121
Contact: Kathryn E. Londra

Incorporated in 1960 in NY.
Donor(s): AMETEK, Inc.
Grantmaker type: Company-sponsored foundation
Financial data (yr. ended 12/31/02): Assets, $6,911,528 (M); expenditures, $1,018,883;

qualifying distributions, $872,815; giving activities include $874,415 for 86 grants (high: $116,231; low: $1,000; average: $1,000–$25,000).
Purpose and activities: Giving primarily for education and health and human services.
Fields of interest: History/archaeology; Arts; Education, fund raising; Elementary school/education; Higher education; Natural resources; Hospitals (general); Cancer; Medical research, institute; Cancer research; Human services; International human rights; Federated giving programs; Jewish agencies & temples.
Types of support: General/operating support; Annual campaigns; Building/renovation; Equipment; Endowments; Scholarship funds; Research; Technical assistance; Exchange programs; Matching/challenge support.
Limitations: Giving on a national basis. No grants to individuals, or for matching funds (except for the United Way); no loans.
Application information: Application form not required.
Initial approach: Letter
Copies of proposal: 1
Deadline(s): None
Board meeting date(s): Apr. and Nov.
Final notification: 2 weeks after board meets
Officers and Directors:* Frank S. Hermance,* Chair. and Pres.; Elizabeth R. Varet,* V.P.; Kathryn E. Londra, Secy. and Treas.; Lewis Cole; Helmut N. Friedlaender.
EIN: 136095939

2799
The Arcadia Foundation ▼
105 E. Logan St.
Norristown, PA 19401-3058 (610) 275-8460
Contact: Marilyn Lee Steinbright, Pres.
FAX: (610) 275-8460

Incorporated in 1964 in PA.
Donor(s): Edith C. Steinbright,‡ Marilyn Lee Steinbright.
Grantmaker type: Independent foundation
Financial data (yr. ended 09/30/03): Assets, $37,573,874 (M); expenditures, $7,528,917; qualifying distributions, $7,256,818; giving activities include $7,290,659 for 222 grants (high: $500,000; low: $1,000; average: $1,000–$25,000).
Purpose and activities: Emphasis on hospitals and hospital building funds, health agencies and services, nursing, hospices, early childhood, adult and higher education, libraries, child development and welfare agencies, youth organizations, and social service and general welfare agencies, including care of the handicapped, aged, and hungry; support also for family services, the environment and conservation, wildlife and animal welfare, religious organizations, historical preservation, and music organizations.
Fields of interest: Music; Historic preservation/historical societies; Early childhood education; Child development, education; Higher education; Adult/continuing education; Libraries/library science; Education; Natural resources; Environment; Animal welfare; Animals/wildlife, preservation/protection; Hospitals (general); Nursing care; Health care; Health organizations, association; Food services; Human services; Children/youth,

services; Child development, services; Family services; Hospices; Aging, centers/services; Christian agencies & churches; Protestant agencies & churches; Religion; General charitable giving; Disabled; Aging; Economically disadvantaged.
Types of support: General/operating support; Continuing support; Annual campaigns; Capital campaigns; Building/renovation; Equipment; Endowments; Program development; Scholarship funds; Research.
Limitations: Giving limited to eastern PA organizations whose addresses have zip codes of 18000 - 19000. Generally, low support for cultural programs. No grants to individuals, or for deficit financing, land acquisition, fellowships, demonstration projects, publications, or conferences; no loans.
Publications: Application guidelines, Annual report.
Application information: Application form not required.
Initial approach: Letter or proposal (not exceeding 2 pages; otherwise entire proposal will be discarded)
Copies of proposal: 1
Deadline(s): Submit proposal only between Sept. 1 and Nov. 1; deadline Nov. 1 for the calendar year
Board meeting date(s): Dec.
Final notification: Up to 3 months after Nov. 1
Officers and Directors:* Marilyn Lee Steinbright,* Pres.; Tanya Hashorva,* V.P.; David P. Sandler,* Secy.; Harvey S.S. Miller,* Treas.; Edward L. Jones, Jr.; Kathleen Shellington.
Number of staff: None.
EIN: 236399772
Recent environmental and animal welfare grants:
2799-1 Conservancy of Montgomery County, Ambler, PA, $10,000. 2002.
2799-2 Elmwood Park Zoo, Norristown, PA, $25,000. 2002.
2799-3 Wissahickon Valley Watershed Association, Ambler, PA, $10,000. 2002.

2800
Asplundh Foundation
708 Blair Mill Rd.
Willow Grove, PA 19090 (215) 784-4200
Contact: Edward K. Asplundh, Pres.

Incorporated in 1953 in PA.
Donor(s): Carl H. Asplundh,‡ Lester Asplundh.‡
Grantmaker type: Independent foundation
Financial data (yr. ended 12/31/02): Assets, $15,372,090 (M); gifts received, $705,000; expenditures, $731,870; qualifying distributions, $731,870; giving activities include $725,000 for 95 grants (high: $100,000; low: $250).
Fields of interest: Historical activities; Arts; Education; Environment; Hospitals (general); Human services; Christian agencies & churches.
Limitations: Giving primarily in PA. No grants to individuals.
Application information:
Initial approach: Letter
Officers: Edward K. Asplundh, Pres.; Christopher B. Asplundh, V.P.; Kurt H. Asplundh, Secy.-Treas.
EIN: 236297246

2801
Frederick A. Bailey Trust
c/o Mellon Financial Corp.
P.O. Box 185
Pittsburgh, PA 15230-0185
Application address: c/o Sandra Brown-McMullen, 1 Boston Pl., Boston, MA 02108, tel.: (617) 722-3891

Established in 1968 in MA.
Grantmaker type: Independent foundation
Financial data (yr. ended 08/31/02): Assets, $1,570,053 (M); expenditures, $110,807; qualifying distributions, $91,791; giving activities include $91,000 for 8 grants (high: $20,000; low: $5,000).
Purpose and activities: Giving for programs that use sports and recreation to address problems facing inner-city youth; access programs for the handicapped, including a school for the blind and a residence for the blind; community organizations; social services; and animal welfare programs.
Fields of interest: Animal welfare; Recreation; Human services; Children/youth, services; Disabled; Economically disadvantaged.
Types of support: General/operating support.
Limitations: Giving limited to the greater Boston, MA, area. No grants to individuals.
Application information: Application form required.
Initial approach: Telephone
Copies of proposal: 1
Deadline(s): Mar. 1
Board meeting date(s): May
Trustees: William G. Cornish; Ronald Garmey; Mellon Financial Corp.
Number of staff: 1 full-time professional.
EIN: 046185933

2802
Bannerot-Lappe Foundation
c/o Mellon Financial Corp.
P.O. Box 185
Pittsburgh, PA 15230-9897 (412) 234-0023
Contact: Laurie A. Moritz, Mellon Financial Corp.

Established in 1994 in PA.
Donor(s): Joanc Lappe Bowman.‡
Grantmaker type: Independent foundation
Financial data (yr. ended 05/31/02): Assets, $6,509,299 (M); expenditures, $404,311; qualifying distributions, $368,372; giving activities include $350,000 for 6 grants (high: $100,000; low: $20,000).
Purpose and activities: Support for organizations that provide guide dogs for the blind.
Fields of interest: Animals/wildlife, special services; Eye diseases.
Limitations: Giving primarily in NY. No grants to individuals.
Application information: Application form required.
Initial approach: Letter
Deadline(s): None
Trustees: G. Donald Gerlach; Mellon Financial Corp.
EIN: 256440597

2803
Bayer Foundation ▼
(formerly Miles Inc. Foundation)
100 Bayer Rd.
Pittsburgh, PA 15205-9741 (412) 777-2000
Contact: Rebecca Lucore, Exec. Dir.
URL: http://www.bayerus.com/search/index.html

Established in 1985 in PA.
Donor(s): Bayer Corp.
Grantmaker type: Company-sponsored foundation
Financial data (yr. ended 12/31/01): Assets, $48,563,325 (M); gifts received, $1,437,053; expenditures, $4,127,006; qualifying distributions, $4,127,006; giving activities include $4,127,006 for 351 grants (high: $360,000; low: $100; average: $500–$100,000).
Purpose and activities: Primary areas of interest include education, including science programs, chemistry, and arts and cultural programs in the communities in which Bayer Corp. operates.
Fields of interest: Arts; Elementary school/education; Higher education; Education; Health care; Community development; Chemistry; Engineering/technology; Science.
Types of support: General/operating support; Continuing support; Capital campaigns; Program development; Curriculum development; Research.
Limitations: Giving primarily in communities where Bayer operations are located. No support for religious or political organizations, or United Way affiliated agencies. No grants to individuals, or for endowment funds, deficit reduction, operating funds, community advertising, athletic sponsorships, telephone solicitations, charitable dinners or events, student trips, or exchange programs.
Publications: Application guidelines.
Application information: Application form required.
Initial approach: 1-page cover letter with a proposal of no more than 6 pages
Copies of proposal: 1
Deadline(s): Varies depending on geographic location; check Web site
Board meeting date(s): Spring and fall
Final notification: After board meeting
Officers and Directors:* Joseph A. Akers,* Pres.; Margo L. Barnes,* V.P.; Thomas E. Kerr,* Secy.; Jon R. Wyne,* Treas.; Rebecca Lucore, Exec. Dir.; Nicholas T. Cullen, Jr.; Helge H. Wehmeier.
Number of staff: None.
EIN: 251508079
Recent environmental and animal welfare grants:
2803-1 Duquesne University, Bayer School of Natural and Environmental Sciences, Pittsburgh, PA, $360,000. 2001.
2803-2 Schooner Sound Learning, New Haven, CT, $10,000. 2001.
2803-3 Zoological Society of Pittsburgh, Pittsburgh, PA, $50,000. 2001.

2804
The Beach Foundation
3 Radnor Corporate Ctr., Ste. 410
Radnor, PA 19087 (610) 225-1100
Contact: Thomas E. Beach, Pres.

Established in 1997 in PA.
Donor(s): Thomas E. Beach.

Grantmaker type: Independent foundation
Financial data (yr. ended 12/31/02): Assets, $1,922,019 (M); expenditures, $153,371; qualifying distributions, $119,609; giving activities include $120,825 for 21 grants (high: $60,000; low: $50).
Purpose and activities: Giving primarily for education and conservation.
Fields of interest: Education; Natural resources; Children/youth, services; Federated giving programs.
Limitations: Giving on a national basis, with emphasis on CA, MA, NH, and PA.
Application information:
  Initial approach: Letter
  Deadline(s): None
Officers and Directors:* Thomas E. Beach,* Pres.; Walter T. Beach,* V.P.; Jonathan T. Beach,* Secy.; Theodore T. Beach,* Treas.
EIN: 232897351

2805
Elaine and Vincent Bell Foundation
7007 Lafayette Ave.
Fort Washington, PA 19034
Contact: Meg Bell Knysh, Exec. Dir.
E-mail: EVBellFoundation@aol.com

Established in 1985 in PA.
Grantmaker type: Independent foundation
Financial data (yr. ended 12/31/02): Assets, $1,080,771 (M); expenditures, $230,007; qualifying distributions, $223,303; giving activities include $204,425 for 48 grants (high: $50,000; low: $300).
Purpose and activities: Giving primarily to improve the quality of life of the community.
Fields of interest: Arts; Education; Environment; Human services.
Types of support: General/operating support; Continuing support; Annual campaigns; Capital campaigns; Building/renovation; Equipment; Land acquisition; Research; Matching/challenge support.
Limitations: Applications not accepted. Giving primarily in AK and PA. No grants to individuals.
Publications: Informational brochure.
Application information: Contributes only to pre-selected organizations. Unsolicited requests for funds not accepted.
  Board meeting date(s): Mar., June, and Nov.
Officers and Trustees:* Vincent G. Bell, Jr.,* Pres.; Meg Bell Knysh,* Exec. Dir.; Elaine V. Bell; Scott Bell; Amy Bell Brody.
Number of staff: 1 part-time professional.
EIN: 232384942

2806
Beneficia Foundation
1 Pitcairn Pl., Ste. 3000
Jenkintown, PA 19046-3593 (215) 887-6700
Contact: Feodor U. Pitcairn, Exec. Secy.

Incorporated in 1953 in PA.
Donor(s): Members of the Feodor Pitcairn Family.
Grantmaker type: Independent foundation
Financial data (yr. ended 04/30/02): Assets, $14,448,322 (M); expenditures, $1,001,933; qualifying distributions, $943,435; giving activities include $925,000 for 36 grants (high:

$85,000; low: $10,000; average: $1,000–$50,000).
Purpose and activities: Solicitations limited to the arts and conservation of the environment, with an emphasis on tropical and marine ecosystems. The foundation does not have a regional focus.
Fields of interest: Arts; Natural resources.
Limitations: No grants to individuals.
Publications: Informational brochure (including application guidelines).
Application information: Small, innovative projects with limited alternative sources of funding are favored. Application form not required.
  Initial approach: Letter
  Copies of proposal: 1
  Board meeting date(s): May
Officers and Directors:* Laren Pitcairn,* Pres.; John D. Mitchell,* V.P.; Feodor U. Pitcairn,* Exec. Secy.; Mark J. Pennink,* Treas.; Deana P. Duncan; Miriam P. Mitchell; Eshowe P. Pennink; Kirstin O. Pitcairn; Mary Eleanor Pitcairn; Sharon R. Pitcairn; Heather D. Reynolds.
Number of staff: None.
EIN: 246015630

2807
Berwind Corporation Contributions Program
3000 West Tower, Centre Sq.
1500 Market St.
Philadelphia, PA 19102 (215) 563-2800
Contact: Mary A. La Rue, Chair., Contribs. Comm.
FAX: (215) 563-8347

Grantmaker type: Corporate giving program
Purpose and activities: Berwind makes charitable contributions to nonprofit organizations involved with arts and culture, education, the environment, health and human services, disease, community development, civic affairs, and minorities. Support is given primarily in areas of company operations.
Fields of interest: Visual arts; Performing arts; Arts; Higher education; Education; Environment; Health care; Health organizations; Human services; Community development; Public affairs; Minorities.
Types of support: General/operating support; Annual campaigns; Employee-related scholarships; Matching/challenge support.
Limitations: Giving primarily in areas of company operations, particularly Philadelphia, PA.
Application information: A contributions committee reviews all requests. Application form not required.
  Initial approach: Proposal to headquarters
  Copies of proposal: 1
  Final notification: Following review
Number of staff: 3.

2808
Bethlehem Steel Foundation
Martin Tower
1170 8th Ave., Rm. 1711
Bethlehem, PA 18016-7699 (610) 694-6940
Contact: James F. Kostecky, Exec. Dir.
FAX: (610) 694-1509; *E-mail:* Kostecky@bethsteel.com

Established in 1993 in PA.
Donor(s): Bethlehem Steel Corp.
Grantmaker type: Company-sponsored foundation
Financial data (yr. ended 12/31/01): Assets, $248,910 (M); gifts received, $243,662; expenditures, $243,662; qualifying distributions, $243,662; giving activities include $190,931 for 24 grants (high: $40,312; low: $300; average: $500–$30,000) and $43,780 for 95 employee matching gifts.
Purpose and activities: Support in the areas of education, human services, including the United Way, health care, economic education, public policy research, culture and the arts, and civic and community development.
Fields of interest: Arts; Business school/education; Education; Environmental education; Health care; Health organizations, association; Human services; Community development, neighborhood development; Federated giving programs; Economics; Public policy, research; Government/public administration.
Types of support: General/operating support; Annual campaigns; Capital campaigns; Employee matching gifts; In-kind gifts; Matching/challenge support.
Limitations: Giving primarily in areas of company operations. No support for religious, political or foreign organizations. No grants to individuals.
Publications: Application guidelines, Annual report.
Application information: Minimal new grantmaking while the parent company undergoes reorganization. Application form not required.
  Initial approach: Brief letter and proposal
  Deadline(s): None
  Board meeting date(s): Apr. of each year
  Final notification: 4 weeks
Officers and Directors:* D.R. Dunham,* Chair.; Stephen G. Donches,* Pres.; A.E. Moffitt, Jr.,* V.P.; C.W. Campbell, Jr., Secy.; G.L. Millenbruch, Treas.; L.A. Arnett,* Cont.; James F. Kostecky, Exec. Dir.; Frank L. Fisher, Admin.; V.R. Reiner.
Number of staff: None.
EIN: 232709041

2809
Bitz Foundation
c/o Francois Bitz
1640 Pleasant Hill Rd.
Baden, PA 15005-2518

Established in 1997 in PA.
Donor(s): Francois Bitz.
Grantmaker type: Independent foundation
Financial data (yr. ended 12/31/00): Assets, $10,694,682 (M); gifts received, $345,750; expenditures, $1,377,485; qualifying distributions, $926,178; giving activities include

$936,524 for 10 grants (high: $815,235; low: $700).
Purpose and activities: Giving primarily for education, health, and the arts.
Fields of interest: Arts; Animals/wildlife; Health care; Health organizations, association; Human services.
Limitations: Applications not accepted. Giving primarily in Pittsburgh, PA. No grants to individuals.
Application information: Contributes only to pre-selected organizations.
Officers: Francois Bitz, Pres.; Graziella Pruiti, Secy.
EIN: 232901971

2810
Peter P. Blanchard III Trust- Dendroica Foundation
(formerly The Dendroica Foundation)
c/o Mellon Financial Corp.
P.O. Box 185
Pittsburgh, PA 15230-0185
Contact: Leonard Richards
Application address: 1 Mellon Bank Ctr., Ste. 3725, Pittsburgh, PA 15258

Established in 1997 in PA.
Donor(s): Peter P. Blanchard, Jr.‡
Grantmaker type: Independent foundation
Financial data (yr. ended 12/31/02): Assets, $23,645,301 (M); gifts received, $14,250,000; expenditures, $651,300; qualifying distributions, $513,168; giving activities include $515,000 for 4 grants (high: $280,000; low: $25,000).
Fields of interest: Natural resources.
Limitations: Giving primarily in NJ and NY.
Application information:
  Initial approach: Contact foundation for application materials and guidelines
Trustee: Mellon Financial Corp.
EIN: 237912826

2811
Blue Mountain Conservation Fund, Inc.
341 East Park St.
Elizabethtown, PA 17022 (717) 731-6634
Contact: Walter W. Wilt, Pres.

Grantmaker type: Public charity
Financial data (yr. ended 06/30/01): Revenue, $39,310; assets, $26,450; expenditures, $28,327; program services expenses, $7,495; giving activities include $7,495 for grants.
Purpose and activities: The organization seeks to engage in activities designed to preserve, protect, and defend the environment.
Fields of interest: Environment.
Officers and Directors:* Walter W. Wilt,* Pres.; Thomas N. Papoutsis,* Secy.; James Papoutsis,* Treas.; Randy Billman; James Costopoulos; Ed Dannels; Bob Dunn; Bill Paule; John Plowman, Jr.
EIN: 251569239

2812
The Bon-Ton Foundation
2801 E. Market St.
York, PA 17402 (717) 751-3247
Contact: Christine De Julis, Fdn. Admin.
Application address: P.O. Box 2821, York, PA 17405

Established in 1991 in PA.
Donor(s): The Bon-Ton Stores, Inc.
Grantmaker type: Company-sponsored foundation
Financial data (yr. ended 01/31/03): Assets, $198,742 (M); gifts received, $168,840; expenditures, $236,194; qualifying distributions, $235,837; giving activities include $185,271 for 102 grants (high: $31,500; low: $25) and $45,944 for employee matching gifts.
Fields of interest: Arts; Education, fund raising; Higher education; Environment; Health care; Human services; Children/youth, services; Community development; Foundations (community); Jewish agencies & temples.
Types of support: Matching/challenge support.
Limitations: Giving primarily in PA. No grants to individuals.
Publications: Informational brochure.
Application information: Application form required.
  Initial approach: Through local Bon-Ton store (except in York, PA)
  Copies of proposal: 1
  Deadline(s): None
  Board meeting date(s): Quarterly
  Final notification: Within 3 months
Officers and Directors:* Ryan J. Sattler,* Pres.; Melinda A. Shue, Secy.-Treas.; Ken Heitz; Mary Kerr; Joseph L. Leahy; Jim Volk; Susan M. Wolfe.
EIN: 232656774

2813
The Florence Lamme Feicht Boyer Family Foundation
c/o R.M. Daniel
11 Stanwix St., 15th Fl.
Pittsburgh, PA 15222-1319

Established in 1996 in PA.
Donor(s): Florence F. Boyer.‡
Grantmaker type: Independent foundation
Financial data (yr. ended 04/30/02): Assets, $1,423,497 (M); gifts received, $10,534; expenditures, $95,325; qualifying distributions, $92,110; giving activities include $90,300 for 30 grants (high: $20,500; low: $200).
Purpose and activities: Giving for federated giving programs, religious organizations, and education.
Fields of interest: Education, single organization support; Natural resources; Federated giving programs; Christian agencies & churches.
Limitations: Applications not accepted. Giving primarily in PA. No grants to individuals.
Application information: Contributes only to pre-selected organizations.
Trustees: Dorothy L. Boyer; John L. Boyer.
EIN: 251801104

2814
Bread and Roses Community Fund
(formerly The People's Fund)
1500 Walnut St., Ste. 1305
Philadelphia, PA 19102 (215) 731-1107
Contact: Christie Balka, Exec. Dir.
FAX: (215) 731-0453; E-mail: info@breadrosesfund.org; URL: http://www.breadrosesfund.org/

Established in 1971 in PA.
Grantmaker type: Public charity
Financial data (yr. ended 06/30/01): Revenue, $809,715; assets, $1,757,868; gifts received, $794,364; expenditures, $614,573; program services expenses, $520,595; giving activities include $364,164 for grants.
Purpose and activities: The Fund is a unique partnership of donors and activists committed to supporting social change in the Delaware Valley. A public foundation, Bread and Roses has distributed nearly $6 million to groups working for access to health care, economic justice, a clean, safe environment, civil and human rights, peace, and other issues.
Fields of interest: Environment; Health care; International peace/security; Civil rights, advocacy; Civil liberties, advocacy; Civil rights.
Types of support: General/operating support; Continuing support; Emergency funds; Program development; Conferences/seminars; Seed money; Technical assistance; Scholarships—to individuals.
Limitations: Giving limited to Philadelphia, Bucks, Chester, Delaware, and Montgomery counties, PA, and Camden County, NJ. No support for direct service organizations, unless involved in social change, or generally for organizations with budgets exceeding $100,000. No grants to individuals (except for scholarships), or for capital campaigns or building projects.
Publications: Application guidelines, Grants list, Informational brochure, Newsletter.
Application information: See Web site for application forms and guidelines. Application form required.
  Initial approach: Letter, telephone, or FAX
  Deadline(s): Jan. 15 for LAX Scholarship Fund for Gay Men; Nov. 2, Dec. 10, and Jan. 14 for Discretionary/Emergency Grants; Sept. 14 for Phoebus Initiative; Jan. 15 for general fund grants
  Board meeting date(s): Jan., Mar., May, June, Sept., Oct., and Nov.
  Final notification: May for LAX Scholarships; within 3 to 4 weeks for Discretionary/Emergency Grants; 2 months for Phoebus Initiative; June for general fund grants
Directors: Christie Balka, Exec. Dir.; Adina Abramowitz; Cathy Coate; Cynthia Fowler; Molly Frantz; Debbie Friedman; Jeri Nutter; Angie Pabon; and 8 additional directors.
Number of staff: 6 full-time professional.
EIN: 232047297

2815
William B. Butz Memorial Fund
(formerly William & Alice Butz Memorial Fund)
220 Long Ln.
Oley, PA 19547
Contact: Ilse Morning

Established in 1954 in PA.
Donor(s): William B. Butz.‡
Grantmaker type: Independent foundation
Financial data (yr. ended 12/31/02): Assets,
$3,255,919 (M); expenditures, $349,002;
qualifying distributions, $305,134; giving
activities include $270,000 for 13 grants (high:
$100,000; low: $1,000).
Purpose and activities: Giving primarily for
cultural programs, including the fine and
performing arts; support for medical centers and
environmental protection.
Fields of interest: Arts; Natural resources;
Hospitals (general); Medical research, institute.
Limitations: Applications not accepted. Giving
on a national basis. No grants to individuals.
Application information: Contributes only to
pre-selected organizations. Unsolicited requests
for funds not considered.
Trustees: Ingrid Morning; Ober Morning II; Scott
R. Stoneback.
Number of staff: None.
EIN: 236259515

2816
Alpin J. and Alpin W. Cameron Memorial
Fund
c/o Ehmann, Van Denbergh & Trainor
2 Penn Ctr. Plz., Ste. 725
Philadelphia, PA 19102
Contact: F.A. Van Denbergh
FAX: (215) 851-9820

Trust established in 1957 in PA.
Donor(s): Alpin W. Cameron,‡ Alpin J.
Cameron.‡
Grantmaker type: Independent foundation
Financial data (yr. ended 09/30/02): Assets,
$3,772,585 (M); expenditures, $141,479;
qualifying distributions, $137,009; giving
activities include $134,500 for 63 grants (high:
$9,500; low: $500).
Purpose and activities: Primary areas of interest
include education, science, literary, and
charitable (aid to the needy).
Fields of interest: Humanities; Literature; Arts;
Higher education; Education; Environment;
Health care; Human services; Youth, services;
Science; Religion.
Limitations: Giving primarily in the
Philadelphia, PA, area.
Application information: Application form not
required.
Initial approach: Letter
Board meeting date(s): 4 to 5 times per year
Trustee: PNC Bank, N.A.
Board Members: Jonathan H. Sprogell;
Frederick A. Van Denbergh, Jr.; Margaret Anne
Van Denbergh; Ross Van Denbergh.
Number of staff: None.
EIN: 236213225

2817
Centre County Community Foundation,
Inc.
2013 Sandy Dr., No. 202
P.O. Box 824
State College, PA 16804-0824 (814) 237-6229
Contact: Barbara Steen, Admin. Asst.
FAX: (814) 237-2624; E-mail:
info@centrecountycf.org; URL: http://
www.centrecountycf.org/

Established in 1981 in PA.
Grantmaker type: Community foundation
Financial data (yr. ended 12/31/02): Assets,
$7,698,000 (M); gifts received, $1,061,000;
expenditures, $1,711,000; giving activities
include $453,000 for 128 grants (high: $40,000;
low: $100).
Purpose and activities: The foundation awards
grants in the following areas of community
service: health and social services, the arts,
education, and the environment. The
foundation administers donor advised funds.
Fields of interest: Arts; Education; Environment;
Health care; Human services.
Types of support: General/operating support;
Income development; Annual campaigns;
Capital campaigns; Building/renovation;
Equipment; Emergency funds; Program
development; Conferences/seminars;
Publication; Seed money; Scholarship funds;
Research; Technical assistance;
Matching/challenge support.
Limitations: Giving limited to Centre County,
PA. No support for religious organizations for
sectarian purposes.
Publications: Application guidelines, Annual
report (including application guidelines),
Informational brochure, Newsletter, Occasional
report.
Application information: See foundation Web
site for guidelines and downloadable
application forms. Application form required.
Copies of proposal: 15
Deadline(s): Mar. 1, June 1, Sept. 1, and Dec.
1
Board meeting date(s): 4th Tues. of Jan., Apr.,
July, and Oct.
Final notification: Within 5 days of board
meeting
Officers and Directors:* Richard L. Kalin,*
Chair.; Jeffrey M. Bower,* 1st Vice-Chair.;
Charles W. Rohrbeck,* 2nd Vice-Chair. and
Treas.; John P. Mandryk,* Secy.; Lydia Abdullah;
Richard L. Campbell; Edward A. Friedman;
Blake Gall; Henry B. Haitz III; Gerald C.
Hartman; Bruce Heim; Larry J. Hofer; William
D. Karch; Norman K. Lathbury; Eileen W.
Leibowtiz; Robert N. Levy; William H. Martin;
Frances E. Mason; Robert McNichol; James M.
Rayback; Martha L. Starling; Helen Dix Steward;
Ralph W. Stewart; Eloise Dunn Stuhr; Dolares
Taricani.
Number of staff: 2 full-time professional.
EIN: 251782197

2818
The Century Fund Trust
462 Walnut St., Ste. 202
Allentown, PA 18102-5497 (610) 434-4000
Contact: Lisa M. Curran

Established in 1985 in PA.

Grantmaker type: Independent foundation
Financial data (yr. ended 12/31/01): Assets,
$32,832,400 (M); gifts received, $4,447;
expenditures, $2,025,991; qualifying
distributions, $1,806,884; giving activities
include $1,816,030 for 105 grants (high:
$125,000; low: $1,500; average:
$2,500–$25,000).
Purpose and activities: Giving primarily to arts
and cultural programs, education, conservation,
human services, and community development.
Fields of interest: Historic
preservation/historical societies; Arts; Education;
Natural resources; Animal welfare; Human
services; YM/YWCAs & YM/YWHAs;
Children/youth, services; Aging,
centers/services; Community development.
Types of support: General/operating support;
Continuing support; Annual campaigns; Capital
campaigns; Building/renovation; Equipment;
Debt reduction; Program development;
Scholarship funds; Matching/challenge support.
Limitations: Giving primarily in the greater
Lehigh Valley, PA, area.
Publications: Application guidelines.
Application information: Application form not
required.
Initial approach: Proposal
Copies of proposal: 6
Deadline(s): Apr. 1 and Oct. 1
Board meeting date(s): 6-10 times per year
Officers and Trustees:* Alice A. Miller,* Pres.;
Rev. Grant E. Harrity,* Secy.; Richard J.
Hummel,* Treas.; David K. Bausch; John H. Leh
II.
Number of staff: 1 part-time support.
EIN: 226404912

2819
Michele and Agnese Cestone Foundation,
Inc.
Two PNC Plz., 25th Fl.
620 Liberty Ave.
Pittsburgh, PA 15222 (412) 762-3502
Contact: Bruce Bickel
FAX: (412) 762-5439; E-mail:
bruce.bickel@pncadvisors.com

Established in 1990 in NJ.
Donor(s): Eclesia J. Cestone, Ralph M. Cestone,
The Remvac Group, Inc., The Marvec Corp.,
Macvest Group, Inc., Maria A. Cestone, Vincent
R. Cestone, Michele J. Cestone.
Grantmaker type: Independent foundation
Financial data (yr. ended 12/31/02): Assets,
$11,956,713 (M); expenditures, $699,720;
qualifying distributions, $595,164; giving
activities include $517,591 for 44 grants (high:
$125,120; low: $150).
Purpose and activities: Giving primarily for the
care and welfare of animals.
Fields of interest: Animal welfare.
Limitations: Giving in the U.S., with some
emphasis on NJ and NY.
Application information:
Initial approach: Letter
Deadline(s): None
Officers and Trustees:* Michele J. Cestone,*
Pres. and Secy.; Vincent Cestone II,* V.P.;
William M. Otterbein,* Treas.; Michael Krick.
Number of staff: 2 full-time professional.
EIN: 521720903

2820
Claneil Foundation, Inc.

630 W. Germantown Pike, Ste. 400
Plymouth Meeting, PA 19462-1059
Contact: Cathy M. Weiss, Exec. Dir.

Incorporated in 1968 in DE.
Donor(s): Henry S. McNeil,‡ Claneil Enterprises, Inc.
Grantmaker type: Independent foundation
Financial data (yr. ended 12/31/01): Assets, $51,265,949 (M); gifts received, $13,078,940; expenditures, $3,030,570; qualifying distributions, $2,956,992; giving activities include $2,948,246 for 233 grants (high: $315,000; low: $1,000; average: $1,000–$25,000).
Purpose and activities: Giving primarily for the arts, education, health, the environment, and community development.
Fields of interest: Visual arts; Historic preservation/historical societies; Arts; Early childhood education; Secondary school/education; Natural resources; Environment, beautification programs; Environment; Family planning; Health care; Domestic violence; Child abuse; Youth development; Human services; Family services; Reproductive rights; Community development; Women; Economically disadvantaged.
Types of support: General/operating support; Capital campaigns; Building/renovation; Equipment; Endowments; Program development; Publication; Seed money; Research; Technical assistance; Exchange programs; Matching/challenge support.
Limitations: Giving primarily in southeastern PA. No grants to individuals.
Publications: Informational brochure (including application guidelines).
Application information: Applications accepted between Jan. 1 and Feb. 15 and July 1 and Aug. 15; grant requests over $10,000 by invitation only. Application form required.
  Initial approach: Letter of inquiry due Jan. 5 or July 5
  Copies of proposal: 1
  Deadline(s): Aug. 15 and Feb. 15
  Board meeting date(s): Nov. and June
  Final notification: Dec. and July
Officers and Directors:* Henry A. Jordan,* Chair.; Marjorie M. Findlay, V.P.; Langhorne B. Smith,* Treas.; Cathy M. Weiss, Exec. Dir.; Geoffrey T. Freeman; Jennifer McNeil; Robert D. McNeil; Gretchen Menzies.
Number of staff: 1 full-time professional; 1 full-time support.
EIN: 236445450

2821
Columbia Gas of Pennsylvania, Inc./Columbia Gas of Maryland, Inc. Corporate Giving Program

650 Washington Rd.
Pittsburgh, PA 15228 (412) 572-7136
Contact: Robert Boulware, Mgr., Corp. Contribs. and Community Rels.
FAX: (412) 572-7165; E-mail: rboulware@nisource.com; URL: http:// www.columbiagaspamd.com/ community_outreach/community_outreach.htm

Grantmaker type: Corporate giving program

Purpose and activities: Columbia Gas of Pennsylvania/Maryland makes charitable contributions to nonprofit organizations involved with education, natural resources, public safety, youth, community development, minorities, disabled people, senior citizens, and women. Support is given primarily in Maryland and Pennsylvania.
Fields of interest: Education; Natural resources; Safety/disasters; Youth, services; Community development; Minorities; Disabled; Aging; Women.
Types of support: Program development; Cause-related marketing; Employee volunteer services; Sponsorships; Donated equipment; In-kind gifts.
Limitations: Giving primarily in MD and PA. No support for fraternal, political, municipal, veterans', or athletic organizations or United Way-supported organizations. No grants to individuals.
Publications: Corporate giving report (including application guidelines), Informational brochure (including application guidelines).
Application information: The common grant application form of the Association of Baltimore Area Grantmakers or Grantmakers of Western Pennsylvania is required. Faxes are not encouraged. The Communications and External Affairs Department handles giving. A contributions committee reviews all requests. Application form required.
  Initial approach: Proposal and application form to headquarters
  Copies of proposal: 1
  Deadline(s): None
  Final notification: Varies

2822
The Community Foundation for the Alleghenies

(formerly The Community Foundation of Greater Johnstown)
216 Franklin St., Ste. 606
Johnstown, PA 15901-1911 (814) 536-7741
Contact: Michael E. Kane, Exec. Dir.
Toll-free tel.: (888) 280-7741; FAX: (814) 536-5859; E-mail: cfalleghenies@charter.net; URL: http://www.CFAlleghenies.org

Established in 1990 in PA.
Grantmaker type: Community foundation
Financial data (yr. ended 06/30/02): Assets, $19,239,613; gifts received, $4,380,069; expenditures, $1,868,665; giving activities include $1,395,859 for 47 grants (high: $400,000; low: $100) and $44,001 for 69 grants to individuals (high: $3,500; low: $100).
Purpose and activities: To obtain permanent endowments to provide benefits to individuals and organizations located in Bedford, Cambria, Indiana and Somerset counties, PA.
Fields of interest: Arts; Education; Natural resources; Health organizations, association; Children/youth, services; Community development.
Types of support: Continuing support; Scholarships—to individuals.
Limitations: Giving primarily in Bedford, Cambria, Indiana and Somerset counties, PA.
Publications: Annual report, Grants list, Informational brochure, Newsletter.

Application information: Accepts Grantmakers of Western Pennsylvania Common Grant Application Format. Application form required.
  Copies of proposal: 2
  Deadline(s): Last Fri. in Jan. and last Fri. in Aug.
  Board meeting date(s): Every 2 months
  Final notification: Mar. 30 and Oct. 30
Officer: Michael E. Kane, Exec. Dir.
Number of staff: 2 full-time professional; 1 part-time professional; 1 full-time support; 1 part-time support.
EIN: 251637373

2823
The Cooper-Siegel Family Foundation

c/o Mellon Financial Corp.
P.O. Box 185
Pittsburgh, PA 15230
Contact: Robert Lepre

Established in 1996 in PA.
Donor(s): Eric C. Cooper, Cooper-Siegel Foundation Charitable Lead Trusts.
Grantmaker type: Independent foundation
Financial data (yr. ended 04/30/02): Assets, $1,061,965 (M); gifts received, $431,672; expenditures, $576,490; qualifying distributions, $569,449; giving activities include $586,000 for grants.
Purpose and activities: Giving primarily for education, health, children's services, including juvenile diabetes and a children's hospital, and social services.
Fields of interest: Media/communications; Literature; Higher education; Education; Environment; Hospitals (general); Cancer research; Diabetes research; Human services; Children, services; Jewish agencies & temples; Economically disadvantaged.
Limitations: Giving primarily in Pittsburgh, PA. No grants to individuals.
Application information: Application form required.
  Initial approach: Letter requesting application form
  Deadline(s): None
Trustees: David Margolis; Mellon Financial Corp.
EIN: 311537177

2824
Cranaleith Foundation, Inc.

c/o N. Allen, ML&B
1701 Market St.
Philadelphia, PA 19103

Established in 1993 in PA.
Donor(s): Francis H. Trainer, Jr., Jeanne A. Trainer.
Grantmaker type: Independent foundation
Financial data (yr. ended 12/31/02): Assets, $11,627,834 (M); gifts received, $600,000; expenditures, $404,176; qualifying distributions, $347,048; giving activities include $345,000 for 5 grants (high: $300,000; low: $5,000).
Purpose and activities: Giving primarily for the shelter of homeless children; funding also for natural resource conservation and social services.
Fields of interest: Natural resources; Parks/playgrounds; Human services; Children, services.

Limitations: Applications not accepted. Giving on a national basis. No grants to individuals.
Application information: Contributes only to pre-selected organizations.
Officers: Francis H. Trainer, Jr., Pres.; Jeanne A. Trainer, V.P.
EIN: 232726952

2825
The Charles B. Degenstein Foundation
c/o Mellon Financial Corp.
P.O. Box 185
Pittsburgh, PA 15230-0185
Application address: c/o Sidney Apfelbaum, 4350 5th St., Sunbury, PA 17801, tel.: (570) 286-1582

Established in 1989.
Donor(s): Charles Degenstein.‡
Grantmaker type: Independent foundation
Financial data (yr. ended 09/30/02): Assets, $1,943,182 (M); expenditures, $478,332; qualifying distributions, $472,652; giving activities include $462,950 for 38 grants (high: $160,000; low: $500).
Purpose and activities: Giving for community and public services; giving also for animal welfare and youth services.
Fields of interest: Education; Natural resources; Hospitals (general); Disasters, fire prevention/control; Recreation; Youth development; American Red Cross; YM/YWCAs & YM/YWHAs; Children/youth, services.
Limitations: Giving within a 75-mile radius of Sunbury, PA.
Publications: Informational brochure (including application guidelines).
Application information: Giving for 501(c)(3) organizations. Application form required.
 Copies of proposal: 12
 Deadline(s): None
 Board meeting date(s): Quarterly
Trustee: Mellon Financial Corp.
EIN: 236971532

2826
The Newell Devalpine Foundation
c/o Bernard Eizen
2001 Market St., Ste. 3410
Philadelphia, PA 19103-7391

Established in 1995 in CT.
Grantmaker type: Independent foundation
Financial data (yr. ended 12/31/01): Assets, $3,613,360 (M); expenditures, $171,754; qualifying distributions, $132,440; giving activities include $132,350 for 32 grants (high: $34,500; low: $250).
Fields of interest: Education; Animals/wildlife; Health organizations, association; Human services; Jewish agencies & temples.
Limitations: Applications not accepted. Giving limited to PA. No grants to individuals.
Application information: Contributes only to pre-selected organizations.
Trustees: Bernard Eizen; The Glenmede Trust Co.
EIN: 237821726

2827
The Anna F. Doell Memorial Trust Fund
c/o Allfirst
21 E. Market St., M/C 402-130
York, PA 17401-1500

Established in 2000 in PA.
Grantmaker type: Independent foundation
Financial data (yr. ended 12/31/02): Assets, $3,629,526 (M); expenditures, $232,899; qualifying distributions, $206,341; giving activities include $207,554 for 4 grants (high: $103,777; low: $25,944).
Fields of interest: Animal welfare; Health organizations, association; Eye diseases; Christian agencies & churches.
Limitations: Applications not accepted. Giving primarily in PA. No grants to individuals.
Application information: Contributes only to pre-selected organizations.
Trustees: Walter C. Flatt, Jr.; Allfirst.
EIN: 256536714

2828
Dolfinger-McMahon Foundation
c/o Duane Morris, LLP
1 Liberty Pl.
Philadelphia, PA 19103-7396 (215) 979-1768
Contact: Sharon Renz, Exec. Secy.

Trust established in 1957 in PA, and originally comprised of four separate trusts: T/W of Henry Dolfinger as modified by will of Mary McMahon; 1935 D/T of Henry Dolfinger as modified by will of Caroline D. McMahon; Residuary T/W of Caroline D. McMahon; Dolfinger-McMahon Trust for Greater Philadelphia. In 1986 the 1935 D/T of H. Dolfinger was merged with the residuary T/W of C. McMahon.
Donor(s): Caroline D. McMahon,‡ Mary M. McMahon.‡
Grantmaker type: Independent foundation
Financial data (yr. ended 09/30/02): Assets, $15,433,292 (M); expenditures, $856,014; qualifying distributions, $751,740; giving activities include $748,000 for 189 grants (high: $25,000; low: $1,000).
Purpose and activities: Primary areas of interest include community development, the disadvantaged, education, the handicapped, and health. Emphasis on experimental, demonstration, or "seed money" projects in race relations, aid to the handicapped, higher and secondary education, social and urban programs, church programs, and health agencies. Emergency funding will be made rarely and, once made, will disqualify the agency from receiving any additional funding for the succeeding three years. Grants limited to $20,000 in any one year to a single project or program.
Fields of interest: Museums; Performing arts; Dance; Theater; Music; Humanities; Arts; Elementary/secondary education; Early childhood education; Child development, education; Elementary school/education; Secondary school/education; Vocational education; Higher education; Theological school/education; Adult/continuing education; Adult education—literacy, basic skills & GED; Reading; Education; Natural resources; Energy; Environment; Animal welfare; Hospitals

(general); Family planning; Nursing care; Health care; Substance abuse, services; Mental health/crisis services; Health organizations, association; AIDS; Alcoholism; AIDS research; Crime/violence prevention, youth; Legal services; Crime/law enforcement; Employment; Food services; Nutrition; Recreation; Youth development, services; Human services; Children/youth, services; Child development, services; Family services; Aging, centers/services; Women, centers/services; Minorities/immigrants, centers/services; Homeless, human services; Race/intergroup relations; Urban/community development; Community development; Voluntarism promotion; Religious federated giving programs; Government/public administration; Transportation; Leadership development; Public affairs; Religion; Minorities; Disabled; Aging; Women; Economically disadvantaged; Homeless.
Types of support: Emergency funds; Program development; Conferences/seminars; Publication; Seed money; Matching/challenge support.
Limitations: Giving limited to the greater Philadelphia, PA, area. No support for private foundations or special interest advocacy through legislative lobbying or solicitation of government agencies. No grants to individuals, or for endowment funds, physical facilities, ordinary operating expenses, renovations or building repairs, building funds, scholarships, medical or scientific research, or fellowships.
Publications: Application guidelines, Annual report (including application guidelines).
Application information: See guidelines for format required for requests. Application form not required.
 Initial approach: Letter requesting guidelines, followed by proposal
 Copies of proposal: 1
 Deadline(s): Submit proposal preferably in Mar. or Sept.; must actually be received on or before Apr. 1 or Oct. 1 (or the preceding Fri. if the 1st falls on a weekend)
 Board meeting date(s): Late spring, late fall, and as required
 Final notification: 2 to 4 weeks following semiannual meeting
Officer: Sharon Renz, Exec. Secy.
Trustees: David E. Loder; Roland Morris.
Number of staff: None.
EIN: 236207346

2829
Dominion Foundation ▼
(formerly Consolidated Natural Gas Company Foundation)
c/o Dominion Tower
625 Liberty Ave., 21st Fl.
Pittsburgh, PA 15222-3199 (412) 690-1430
Contact: James C. Mesloh, Exec. Dir.
FAX: (412) 690-7608; URL: http://www.dom.com/about/community/foundation/index.jsp

Established about 1985 in PA.
Donor(s): Consolidated Natural Gas Co., Dominion Resources, Inc.
Grantmaker type: Company-sponsored foundation

Financial data (yr. ended 12/31/02): Assets, $2,531,780 (M); expenditures, $7,393,920; qualifying distributions, $7,136,345; giving activities include $5,479,296 for 780 grants (high: $112,825; low: $220; average: $2,000–$25,000) and $1,061,231 for 3,901 employee matching gifts.
Purpose and activities: Support for health and human services, education, culture and the arts, community and economic development, and the environment.
Fields of interest: Arts; Education; Environment; Health care; Human services; Community development; Federated giving programs.
Types of support: General/operating support; Continuing support; Annual campaigns; Capital campaigns; Building/renovation; Equipment; Program development; Conferences/seminars; Curriculum development; Employee matching gifts; In-kind gifts; Matching/challenge support.
Limitations: Giving primarily in CT, LA, NC, NY, OH, PA, TX, VA, WV, and areas where the company has business interests. No support for fraternal, political, or labor organizations, or organizations for strictly sectarian purposes. No grants to individuals, or for operating funds of United Way-supported organizations, fundraising activities, or courtesy advertising, magazines, or yearbooks.
Publications: Application guidelines, Informational brochure (including application guidelines).
Application information: Application form not required.
> *Initial approach:* Letter
> *Copies of proposal:* 1
> *Board meeting date(s):* Varies
Officers and Directors:* W.C. Hall, Jr.,* Pres.; M.N. Grier,* V.P.; James C. Mesloh,* Exec. Dir.; T.N. Chewning; T.F. Farrell; E.S. Hardy; J.L. Johnson; Duane Radtke.
Trustee: Mellon Bank, N.A.
Number of staff: 6 full-time professional; 3 full-time support.
EIN: 136077762
Recent environmental and animal welfare grants:
2829-1 Cowanshannock Creek Watershed Association, Rural Valley, PA, $12,000. For operating support. 2001.
2829-2 Earth Day Coalition, Cleveland, OH, $10,000. For operating support. 2001.
2829-3 Great Lakes Museum of Science, Environment and Technology, Great Lakes Science Center, Cleveland, OH, $30,000. For operating support. 2001.
2829-4 James River Association, Richmond, VA, $20,000. For operating support. 2001.
2829-5 Lewis Ginter Botanical Gardens, Richmond, VA, $30,000. For operating support. 2001.
2829-6 ParkWorks, Cleveland, OH, $10,000. For operating support. 2001.
2829-7 Phipps Conservatory and Botanical Gardens, Pittsburgh, PA, $20,000. For operating support. 2001.
2829-8 Rocky Mountain Elk Foundation, Missoula, MT, $15,000. For operating support. 2001.
2829-9 Western Pennsylvania Conservancy, Pittsburgh, PA, $30,000. For renovation at Fallingwater. 2001.

2829-10 Western Pennsylvania Conservancy, Pittsburgh, PA, $15,200. For operating support. 2001.
2829-11 Western Pennsylvania Conservancy, Pittsburgh, PA, $10,000. For operating support. 2001.
2829-12 Wildlife Habitat Council, Silver Spring, MD, $15,000. For operating support. 2001.
2829-13 Zoological Society of Pittsburgh, Pittsburgh, PA, $15,000. For Education program for West Virginia. 2001.

2830
Richard H. Donnell Foundation
P.O. Box 1340
McMurray, PA 15317
Contact: Richard H. Donnell, Pres.
FAX: (724) 746-2309

Established in 1997 in PA.
Donor(s): Richard H. Donnell, Christopher M. Donnell, Marni C. Donnell, David Kresh, Mrs. D. Kresh.
Grantmaker type: Independent foundation
Financial data (yr. ended 12/31/02): Assets, $987,055 (M); gifts received, $15,000; expenditures, $98,755; qualifying distributions, $95,000; giving activities include $95,000 for 4 grants (high: $50,000; low: $5,000).
Purpose and activities: Giving only for religious, charitable, scientific, public safety testing, literary or educational purposes.
Fields of interest: Animal welfare; Health care; Housing/shelter, development; Hospices.
Types of support: General/operating support; Continuing support; Annual campaigns; Program development; Seed money; Matching/challenge support.
Limitations: Giving primarily in Washington County, PA.
Publications: Annual report, Informational brochure.
Application information: Application form required.
> *Initial approach:* Letter
> *Copies of proposal:* 1
> *Deadline(s):* Preferably Apr., but accepted on a continual basis
> *Board meeting date(s):* Jan., Apr., July, and Oct.
Officers and Directors:* Richard H. Donnell,* Pres. and Treas.; Shana M. Donnell,* V.P. and Secy.; Cathi E. Kresh,* Dir. of Opers.; Christopher M. Donnell; Edwin E. Edwards III.
EIN: 232900282

2831
Eden Hall Foundation ▼
600 Grant St., Ste. 3232
Pittsburgh, PA 15219 (412) 642-6697
Contact: Sylvia Fields, Prog. Dir.

Established in 1984 in PA.
Donor(s): Eden Hall Farm.
Grantmaker type: Independent foundation
Financial data (yr. ended 12/31/02): Assets, $141,245,359 (M); expenditures, $10,097,763; qualifying distributions, $9,637,466; giving activities include $9,637,466 for 90 grants (high: $1,000,000; low: $650; average: $5,000–$125,000).
Purpose and activities: Support for higher education, the prevention and alleviation of

sickness and disease, social welfare and the improvement of conditions of the poor and needy.
Fields of interest: Higher education; Health care; Human services; Economically disadvantaged.
Types of support: General/operating support; Management development; Capital campaigns; Building/renovation; Equipment; Endowments; Program development; Scholarship funds; Program evaluation.
Limitations: Giving limited to southwestern PA. No support for private foundations. No grants to individuals, or for operating budgets, deficit financing, or general fundraising campaigns.
Publications: Application guidelines.
Application information: Interviews or visitation may be necessary for additional information. Application form not required.
> *Initial approach:* Letter
> *Copies of proposal:* 5
> *Board meeting date(s):* Quarterly
Officers and Directors:* George C. Greer,* Chair.; Debora Foster, Secy.; John M. Mazur, Treas.; E.H. Shifler.
Number of staff: 1 full-time professional; 1 full-time support; 1 part-time support.
EIN: 251384468
Recent environmental and animal welfare grants:
2831-1 Carnegie Mellon University, Pittsburgh, PA, $250,000. For Green Chemistry Project, research that allows for replacement of chlorine in cleaning agents with more environmentally friendly agents. 2002.
2831-2 Horticultural Society of Western Pennsylvania, Pittsburgh, PA, $20,000. To plan and develop Botanic Garden. 2002.
2831-3 Pittsburgh Parks Conservancy, Pittsburgh, PA, $1,000,000. For capital drive. 2002.
2831-4 Rosedale Block Cluster, Pittsburgh, PA, $110,000. For landscaping program and technological upgrades. 2002.
2831-5 Student Conservation Association, Pittsburgh, PA, $50,000. For Three Rivers Region Program. 2002.
2831-6 Western Pennsylvania School for Blind Children, Pittsburgh, PA, $10,000. For Children's Sensory Garden. 2002.
2831-7 Westminster College, New Wilmington, PA, $15,000. For Traverse Titan Leadership Program. 2002.
2831-8 Zoological Society of Pittsburgh, Pittsburgh, PA, $63,683. For KidScience Project. 2002.

2832
Leon Falk Family Trust
3315 Grant Bldg.
Pittsburgh, PA 15219 (412) 261-5533
Contact: Sigo Falk, Chair.
FAX: (412) 471-7739

Trust established in 1952 in PA.
Donor(s): Leon Falk, Jr.,‡ Marjorie L. Falk.‡
Grantmaker type: Independent foundation
Financial data (yr. ended 12/31/02): Assets, $3,150,065 (M); gifts received, $78,709; expenditures, $482,962; qualifying distributions, $477,067; giving activities include $472,111 for 17 grants (high: $372,211; low: $200; average: $200–$35,000).

Purpose and activities: Giving support for the arts, higher education, human services, civil rights organizations, and land conservation.
Fields of interest: Visual arts; Performing arts; Higher education; Environment, land resources; Human services; Civil rights.
Types of support: General/operating support; Continuing support; Annual campaigns; Capital campaigns; Building/renovation; Land acquisition; Endowments; Program development.
Limitations: Applications not accepted. Giving primarily in Allegheny County, PA. No grants to individuals.
Application information: Contributes only to pre-selected organizations. No new grants currently accepted.
   Board meeting date(s): Fall or early winter
Trustees: Sigo Falk, Chair.; Andrew D. Falk; Margaret F. Steckel.
Number of staff: 1 shared staff (shared with Maurice Falk Medical Fund).
EIN: 256065756

2833
Federated Investors Foundation, Inc.
Federated Investors Tower
Pittsburgh, PA 15222-3779

Established in 1997.
Donor(s): Federated Investors, Inc.
Grantmaker type: Company-sponsored foundation
Financial data (yr. ended 04/30/02): Assets, $1,501,646 (M); gifts received, $175,000; expenditures, $407,629; qualifying distributions, $406,667; giving activities include $406,550 for 59 grants (high: $60,000; low: $100).
Fields of interest: Education; Natural resources; Medical research, institute; Human services; Federated giving programs; Roman Catholic agencies & churches.
Limitations: Applications not accepted. Giving primarily in PA. No grants to individuals.
Application information: Contributes only to pre-selected organizations.
Officers and Directors:* J. Christopher Donahue,* Pres.; John W. McGonigle, Secy.; Thomas R. Donahue, Treas.; John F. Donahue; Thomas J. Donnelly.
EIN: 232913182

2834
Fidelity Bank, PaSB Corporate Giving Program
1009 Perry Hwy.
Pittsburgh, PA 15237 (412) 367-3300
Contact: David Newell, V.P., Public Affairs
FAX: (412) 364-6504

Grantmaker type: Corporate giving program
Purpose and activities: Fidelity Bank makes charitable contributions to nonprofit organizations involved with arts and culture, education, the environment, health and human services, employment, housing, economic development, government and public administration, and economically disadvantaged people. Support is given primarily in areas of company operations.
Fields of interest: Arts; Education; Environment; Hospitals (general); Health care; Employment; Housing/shelter; Youth, services; Human

services; Economic development; Government/public administration; Economically disadvantaged.
Types of support: Employee matching gifts; In-kind gifts.
Limitations: Giving primarily in areas of company operations. No support for political parties, religious, veterans', or fraternal organizations not of direct benefit to the entire community, or government- or national philanthropy-supported organizations. No grants to individuals, or for missionary activities, endowments, or medical research.
Application information: Proposals should be no longer than 2 pages in length. Application form not required.
   Initial approach: Proposal to headquarters
   Deadline(s): Sept. 1

2835
The Fine Family Foundation
(formerly Milton Fine Family Charitable Foundation)
c/o FFC Capital Corp.
Dominion Twr., 625 Liberty Ave., Ste. 3110
Pittsburgh, PA 15222 (412) 444-3500
Contact: Milton Fine, Pres.

Donor(s): Milton Fine, The Milton Fine Irrevocable Trust of 1998, The Milton Fine Irrevocable Trust of 2000.
Grantmaker type: Independent foundation
Financial data (yr. ended 06/30/02): Assets, $359,393 (M); gifts received, $502,708; expenditures, $529,703; qualifying distributions, $529,700; giving activities include $500,868 for 18 grants (high: $118,368; low: $1,500).
Purpose and activities: Giving primarily to the arts, education, including environmental education, human services, and Jewish organizations.
Fields of interest: Museums (art); Museums (ethnic/folk arts); Arts; Higher education; Environment; Health care; Human services; Federated giving programs; Jewish federated giving programs; Jewish agencies & temples.
International interests: England.
Limitations: Giving primarily in MA and PA.
Application information: Application form not required.
   Deadline(s): None
Officer and Directors:* Milton Fine,* Pres. and Secy.-Treas.; David Fine; Sheila Fine; Carolyn Fine Friedman; Sibyl Fine King.
EIN: 256335329

2836
Fleming Foundation
7661 Beryl Rd.
Zionsville, PA 18092

Established in 1990 in PA.
Donor(s): Richard Fleming.
Grantmaker type: Independent foundation
Financial data (yr. ended 12/31/01): Assets, $7,329,967 (M); expenditures, $1,047,452; qualifying distributions, $1,044,578; giving activities include $1,023,055 for 20 grants (high: $384,342; low: $15).
Purpose and activities: Giving for emergency relief services, human services, and for community services.

Fields of interest: Animal welfare; Hospitals (general); Disasters, 9/11/01; Salvation Army; Community development.
Limitations: Applications not accepted. Giving limited to Allentown, PA. No grants to individuals.
Application information: Contributes only to pre-selected organizations.
Trustees: Kathleen Arnold; Richard Fleming; Roberta Fleming.
EIN: 232585510

2837
FMC Foundation
c/o FMC Corp.
1735 Market St., 23rd Fl.
Philadelphia, PA 19103 (215) 299-6000
Contact: Judith Smeltzer, Fdn. Coord.

Incorporated in 1953 in CA.
Donor(s): FMC Corp.
Grantmaker type: Company-sponsored foundation
Financial data (yr. ended 11/30/02): Assets, $420,995 (M); expenditures, $101,101; qualifying distributions, $101,101; giving activities include $101,101 for 120 grants (high: $10,000; low: $25; average: $1,000–$25,000).
Purpose and activities: Giving primarily for higher education and community improvement funds; grants also for public issues, economic education, urban affairs, health and human services, cultural institutions, civic affairs groups, and youth agencies.
Fields of interest: Arts; Higher education; Business school/education; Education; Environment; Agriculture; Youth, services; Public policy, research; Minorities.
Types of support: General/operating support; Continuing support; Capital campaigns; Building/renovation; Equipment; Program development; Scholarship funds; Employee matching gifts.
Limitations: Giving primarily in areas in which company facilities are located. No support for educational institutions below the college or university level, or state or regional associations of independent colleges, national health agencies, or United Way-supported organizations. No grants to individuals, or for endowment funds or hospital operating expenses or research; no loans.
Publications: Application guidelines, Program policy statement.
Application information: Application form not required.
   Initial approach: Letter
   Copies of proposal: 1
   Deadline(s): None
   Board meeting date(s): Quarterly
   Final notification: 6 weeks
Officers and Director:* Ken Garrett,* Pres.; Andrea Utecht, V.P.; Tom Deas, Secy.
Number of staff: 1 full-time professional; 1 part-time support.
EIN: 946063032

2838
The John H. Foster Foundation

c/o Foster Mgmt. Co., Inc.
1018 W. 9th Ave.
King of Prussia, PA 19406

Established in 1984.
Donor(s): John H. Foster.
Grantmaker type: Independent foundation
Financial data (yr. ended 12/31/01): Assets,
$6,856,102 (M); expenditures, $840,723;
qualifying distributions, $475,788; giving
activities include $475,786 for 20 grants (high:
$230,236; low: $100; average:
$1,000–$10,000).
Purpose and activities: Giving primarily for
education, wildlife preservation, and cultural
programs.
Fields of interest: Arts; Higher education;
Education; Animals/wildlife,
preservation/protection.
Limitations: Applications not accepted. Giving
primarily in CT and NY. No grants to individuals.
Application information: Contributes only to
pre-selected organizations.
Officers and Directors: John H. Foster,* Pres.;
Stephen C. Curley,* Treas.
EIN: 133249353

2839
The French Foundation

c/o Mellon Financial Corp.
P.O. Box 185
Pittsburgh, PA 15230-9897
Contact: George E. Coorssen, Jr.
Application address: c/o Mellon Financial Corp.,
1 Boston Pl., Boston, MA 02108

Established in 1947 in MA.
Grantmaker type: Independent foundation
Financial data (yr. ended 12/31/02): Assets,
$4,633,426 (M); expenditures, $302,580;
qualifying distributions, $285,634; giving
activities include $279,222 for 69 grants (high:
$10,000; low: $477).
Purpose and activities: Giving primarily for
conservation and the environment; support also
for the arts and social services.
Fields of interest: Arts; Natural resources;
Environment; Human services.
Limitations: No grants to individuals.
Application information: Application form not
required.
 Initial approach: Letter
 Deadline(s): Feb., May, Aug., and Nov.
 Board meeting date(s): Mar., June, Sept., and
 Dec.
Trustees: Jameson S. French; Robert L.V. French;
Steven B. French; David W. Williams; Edward S.
Williams; Mellon Financial Corp.
EIN: 046053426

2840
Friendship Fund, Inc.

c/o Mellon Financial Corp.
P.O. Box 185
Pittsburgh, PA 15230-0185

Incorporated in 1918 in NY.
Donor(s): Charles R. Crane.‡
Grantmaker type: Independent foundation

Financial data (yr. ended 06/30/02): Assets,
$4,807,239 (M); expenditures, $327,879;
qualifying distributions, $300,074; giving
activities include $290,250 for grants.
Purpose and activities: Giving for the
advancement of the humanities and the sciences
and for the welfare of humanity. Emphasis on
local giving for environmental protection, social
services, and international affairs. Funds largely
committed in advance.
Fields of interest: Education; Environment;
Human services; International affairs.
Types of support: Capital campaigns;
Building/renovation; Equipment; Land
acquisition; Program development; Publication;
Seed money.
Limitations: Applications not accepted. Giving
on a national basis. No grants to individuals
whose needs are not already known to the
trustees.
Application information: Unsolicited requests
for funds not considered.
 Board meeting date(s): Aug.
Officers and Trustees: Ellen D.B.F. Tully,* Pres.;
Thomas S. Crane,* Treas.; Darby Bradley;
Charles M. Crane; Diane Crane; Sylvia E. Crane;
Josephine DeGive; Elizabeth McLane-Bradley;
Mellon Financial Corp.
Number of staff: None.
EIN: 136089220

2841
William F. & Lynn D. Gauss Foundation

c/o PNC Advisors
620 Liberty Ave., P2-PTPP-10-2
Pittsburgh, PA 15222-2705 (412) 762-3189
Contact: W. Brewster Cockrell

Established in 2001 in PA.
Donor(s): William F. Gauss.
Grantmaker type: Independent foundation
Financial data (yr. ended 12/31/02): Assets,
$3,142,386 (M); gifts received, $3,608;
expenditures, $141,705; qualifying distributions,
$104,008; giving activities include $90,000 for
6 grants (high: $30,000; low: $5,000).
Fields of interest: University; Animals/wildlife;
Hospitals (general); Boy scouts; Human services;
Protestant agencies & churches.
Limitations: Giving primarily in Pittsburgh, PA.
No grants to individuals.
Application information: Application form not
required.
 Deadline(s): None
Trustees: R. Michael Daniel; Mary S. Kroll; PNC
Bank, N.A.
EIN: 256784891

2842
Alexander B. Gilfillian Trust

c/o National City Bank of Pennsylvania
20 Stanwix St., National City Ctr.
Pittsburgh, PA 15222-4802
Contact: William M. Schmidt, V.P.

Established in 1997 in PA.
Donor(s): Alexander B. Gilfillian.‡
Grantmaker type: Independent foundation
Financial data (yr. ended 12/31/02): Assets,
$2,422,494 (M); expenditures, $163,560;
qualifying distributions, $152,753; giving

activities include $140,525 for 6 grants (high:
$49,184; low: $14,053).
Purpose and activities: Giving to Presbyterian
churches, historical societies, humane societies,
and educational institutions.
Fields of interest: Historic preservation/historical
societies; Elementary/secondary education;
Animal welfare; Protestant agencies & churches.
Limitations: Applications not accepted. Giving
limited to western PA. No grants to individuals.
Application information: Contributes only to
pre-selected organizations.
 Board meeting date(s): None
Trustee: National City Bank of Pennsylvania.
EIN: 237895267

2843
Sonia Raiziss Giop Charitable Foundation

c/o Mellon Financial Corp.
P.O. Box 185
Pittsburgh, PA 15230-9897

Established in 1994 in PA.
Donor(s): Sonia Giop,‡ Ines Giop Crut.
Grantmaker type: Independent foundation
Financial data (yr. ended 12/31/02): Assets,
$4,204,768 (M); expenditures, $353,903;
qualifying distributions, $349,046; giving
activities include $342,250 for grants.
Purpose and activities: Giving primarily for
education, the arts, particularly for poetry and
other literary organizations, and animal welfare.
Fields of interest: Music; Literature; Arts; Higher
education; Animal welfare.
Limitations: Applications not accepted. Giving
primarily in CT and FL. No grants to individuals.
Application information: Contributes only to
pre-selected organizations.
Trustee: Mellon Financial Corp.
EIN: 256453053

2844
Grandom Institution

366 Roumfort Rd.
Philadelphia, PA 19119
Contact: John N. Childs, Secy.-Treas.

Incorporated in 1841 in PA.
Donor(s): Hartt Grandom.‡
Grantmaker type: Independent foundation
Financial data (yr. ended 06/30/02): Assets,
$1,449,003 (M); expenditures, $94,495;
qualifying distributions, $91,322; giving
activities include $91,635 for 15 grants (high:
$25,190; low: $1,595).
Purpose and activities: Support for fuel aid
programs, furnishing winter fuels to the worthy
poor; some giving also to a YMCA for heating
purposes of a homeless program.
Fields of interest: Energy; Human services.
Types of support: Endowments.
Limitations: Giving limited to the Philadelphia,
PA, area.
Publications: Informational brochure.
Application information: Application form not
required.
 Board meeting date(s): Oct.
 Final notification: Nov.
Officers: F. Preston Buckman, Pres.; John N.
Childs, Secy.-Treas.; Robert C. Bodine, Mgr.;
Mary Buckman, Mgr.; Thomas O. Ely, Mgr.;

Carolyn Moon, Mgr.; Robert Neff, Mgr.; Louise Senopoulos, Mgr.; Gerald van Arkel, Mgr.
Number of staff: None.
EIN: 230640770

2845
Guanacaste Dry Forest Conservation Fund
University of Penn., Biology Dept.
Philadelphia, PA 19104   (215) 898-5636
Contact: Daniel Janzen, Pres.

Grantmaker type: Public charity
Financial data (yr. ended 12/31/00): Revenue, $1,479,762; assets, $2,352,823; gifts received, $1,395,771; expenditures, $144,604; program services expenses, $117,511; giving activities include $33,713 for 2 grants (high: $25,000; low: $8,713).
Purpose and activities: The fund supports organizations that work for wildlife conservation and preservation of the Rincon rainforest in Costa Rica.
Fields of interest: Environment, forests; Animals/wildlife, preservation/protection; Animals/wildlife.
International interests: Costa Rica.
Types of support: Land acquisition.
Limitations: Giving on an international basis, primarily in Costa Rica.
Officers and Director:* Daniel Janzen,* Pres.; Winnie Hallwachs,* Secy. and C.F.O.; George Gorman.
EIN: 943280315

2846
The Hamer Foundation
2470 Fox Hill Rd.
State College, PA 16803   (814) 355-8004
Contact: Donald W. Hamer, Tr.

Established in 1989 in PA.
Donor(s): Donald W. Hamer.
Grantmaker type: Independent foundation
Financial data (yr. ended 12/31/02): Assets, $3,514,837 (M); gifts received, $1,280,000; expenditures, $1,668,921; qualifying distributions, $1,654,981; giving activities include $1,655,550 for 22 grants (high: $1,000,000; low: $1,250; average: $1,250–$1,000,000).
Purpose and activities: Giving primarily for conservation and educational programs.
Fields of interest: Visual arts; Museums; Performing arts; Higher education; Libraries/library science; Natural resources; Animal welfare; Human services; Christian agencies & churches; Religion.
Types of support: General/operating support; Annual campaigns; Capital campaigns; Building/renovation.
Limitations: Giving primarily in Centre County, PA. No grants to individuals.
Application information: Application form not required.
    Initial approach: Proposal
    Copies of proposal: 1
    Deadline(s): None
    Board meeting date(s): As needed
Trustees: Donald W. Hamer; Diane M. Kerly; Edward Matosziuk.
Number of staff: None.
EIN: 251610780

2847
The Hamilton Family Foundation
200 Eagle Rd., Ste. 316
Wayne, PA 19087   (610) 975-0517
Contact: Cynthia Smith, Admin.
FAX: (610) 293-0967

Established in 1992 in PA.
Donor(s): Dorrance H. Hamilton.
Grantmaker type: Independent foundation
Financial data (yr. ended 12/31/01): Assets, $43,305,076 (M); expenditures, $2,370,045; qualifying distributions, $2,116,322; giving activities include $2,121,077 for 340 grants (high: $500,000; low: $25; average: $500–$10,000).
Purpose and activities: Emphasis is on educational endeavors, including teaching and research with a focus on programs in schooling, conservation, historic preservation, medicine and the arts.
Fields of interest: Historic preservation/historical societies; Arts; Higher education; Education; Natural resources; Hospitals (general); Health care.
Types of support: General/operating support; Annual campaigns; Program development; Scholarship funds; Matching/challenge support.
Limitations: Giving primarily in Philadelphia, PA and surrounding counties. No grants to individuals.
Publications: Application guidelines.
Application information: Proposals accepted only once during a 12-month period. Application form required.
    Initial approach: Proposal
    Copies of proposal: 1
    Deadline(s): Approximately 1 month prior to meeting date
    Board meeting date(s): Quarterly
    Final notification: Within 1 month of meeting
Officer and Directors:* Dorrance H. Hamilton,* Pres.; Barbara R. Cobb; Margaret H. Duprey; Nathaniel P. Hamilton; S. Matthews V. Hamilton, Jr.; Francis J. Mirabello.
Number of staff: 1 full-time professional; 1 full-time support.
EIN: 232684976

2848
The Greater Harrisburg Foundation
200 N. 3rd St., 8th Fl.
P.O. Box 678
Harrisburg, PA 17108-0678   (717) 236-5040
Contact: Janice R. Black, C.E.O. and Pres.
FAX: (717) 231-4463; E-mail: info@ght.org; URL: http://www.ghf.org

Established in 1920 in PA; assets first acquired in 1940; grants first made in the mid-1940's.
Grantmaker type: Community foundation
Financial data (yr. ended 12/31/02): Assets, $20,154,823 (M); gifts received, $5,998,258; expenditures, $5,305,184; giving activities include $1,592,996 for grants (high: $60,416) and $346,016 for 221 grants to individuals (high: $8,000; low: $10).
Purpose and activities: Giving for education, health, human services, community development, the arts, and the environment. The foundation administers donor-advised funds.

Fields of interest: Arts; Education; Environment; Health care; Health organizations, association; Human services; Community development.
Types of support: General/operating support; Equipment; Program development; Publication; Seed money; Scholarship funds; Technical assistance; Scholarships—to individuals; Matching/challenge support.
Limitations: Giving primarily in PA, with emphasis on Dauphin, Cumberland, Franklin, Perry, and Lebanon counties. No support for religious organizations for religious purposes, or for private foundations or discretionary funds. No grants to individuals directly.
Publications: Application guidelines, Annual report (including application guidelines), Financial statement, Grants list, Informational brochure (including application guidelines), Newsletter, Program policy statement.
Application information: Call program officer for current application guidelines. Application form available on website. Application form required.
    Initial approach: Letter of interest, or telephone call to Prog. Off.
    Copies of proposal: 13
    Deadline(s): Jan. 17, Apr. 14, July 14, and Sept. 29
    Board meeting date(s): Jan., Mar., Sept., June, and Nov.
    Final notification: Approx. 8 weeks after proposal submission
Officers and Distribution Committee:* William Lehr, Jr.,* Chair.; Janice R. Black, C.E.O. and Pres.; Dorothea Aronson; Raymond L. Gover; Leonardo Herrado; Linda Hicks; Joan R. Holman; Ellen Brody Hughes; Harold McInnes; James Mead; John Oyler; Velma Redmond; David Schankweiler; Hasu P. Shah; Kathleen Smarilli; Jonathan Vipond; Mary Webber; Robert Zuillinger.
Trustee Banks: Allfirst; Citizens Bank of Southern Pennslyvania; Farmers & Merchants Trust Co.; Farmers Trust of Carlisle; Financial Trust Services; First National Bank & Trust of Waynesboro; First National Bank of Greencastle; Wachovia Bank, N.A.; Fulton Bank; GHF, Inc.; Hershey Trust Co.; The Juniata Valley Bank; M&T Bank; Mellon Financial Corp.; PNC Bank, N.A.; Pennsylvania State Bank; Sentry Trust Co.; Valley Bank & Trust Co.
Number of staff: 5 full-time professional; 1 part-time professional; 2 full-time support.
EIN: 010564355

2849
The Hawksglen Foundation
c/o Mellon Financial Corp.
3740 One Mellon Ctr.
Pittsburgh, PA 15258-0001

Established in 2002 in PA.
Donor(s): Rebecca Barclay Humphrey.
Grantmaker type: Independent foundation
Financial data (yr. ended 12/31/02): Assets, $9,920,943 (M); gifts received, $10,025,000; expenditures, $136,915; qualifying distributions, $98,000; giving activities include $98,000 for 20 grants (high: $10,000; low: $2,000).
Fields of interest: Natural resources; Botanical/horticulture/landscape services; Animals/wildlife, preservation/protection.

Limitations: Giving on a national basis, with emphasis on PA. No grants to individuals.
Application information:
  Initial approach: Letter
Trustees: Rebecca Barclay Humphrey; Mellon Financial Corp.
EIN: 256820594

2850
The HBE Foundation
c/o Beucler, Kelly & Irwin Ltd.
125 Strafford Ave., Ste. 116
Wayne, PA 19087 (610) 688-0143
Contact: Bruce Maitland Brown, Tr.
Application address: 350 Pond View, Devon, PA 19333-1732

Established in 1988 in PA.
Donor(s): Bruce Maitland Brown.
Grantmaker type: Independent foundation
Financial data (yr. ended 06/30/03): Assets, $1,260,240 (M); gifts received, $50,535; expenditures, $98,547; qualifying distributions, $94,203; giving activities include $89,924 for 14 grants (high: $50,000; low: $700).
Purpose and activities: Giving for the arts, culture, education, and human services.
Fields of interest: Arts; Libraries (public); Education; Horticulture/garden clubs; Homeless, human services; Philanthropy/voluntarism; Christian agencies & churches.
Types of support: General/operating support; Capital campaigns; Building/renovation; Program development; Publication; Seed money; Scholarship funds; Research; In-kind gifts.
Limitations: Giving primarily in southeastern PA. No grants to individuals, or for debt reduction, emergencies, tickets, tables, or ad books.
Publications: Multi-year report (including application guidelines).
Application information: Unsolicited proposals not acknowledged unless trustee is interested. Application form not required.
  Initial approach: Telephone or letter
  Copies of proposal: 1
  Deadline(s): None
  Board meeting date(s): After site visit
  Final notification: After site visit
Trustee: Bruce Maitland Brown.
Number of staff: 1 shared staff (shared with Hoxie Harrison Smith Foundation).
EIN: 236910944

2851
H. J. Heinz Company Contributions Program
P.O. Box 57
Pittsburgh, PA 15230 (412) 237-5806
Contact: Loretta Oken

Grantmaker type: Corporate giving program
Purpose and activities: As a complement to its foundation, Heinz also makes charitable contributions to nonprofit organizations directly. Support is given on a national basis.
Fields of interest: Animal welfare; Children, services; Family services; Women.
Types of support: General/operating support; In-kind gifts.
Limitations: Giving on a national basis, particularly in areas of company operations. No

support for political organizations or sectarian religious organizations. No grants to individuals, or for general scholarships, fellowships, or travel.
Application information: Application form not required.
  Initial approach: Proposal to nearest company facility
  Copies of proposal: 1
  Deadline(s): None
  Final notification: Following review

2852
Howard Heinz Endowment ▼
30 Dominion Tower
625 Liberty Ave.
Pittsburgh, PA 15222-3115 (412) 281-5777
Contact: Maxwell King, Pres.
FAX: (412) 281-5788; E-mail: info@heinz.org;
URL: http://www.heinz.org

Trust established in 1941 in PA.
Donor(s): Howard Heinz,‡ Elizabeth Rust Heinz.‡
Grantmaker type: Independent foundation
Financial data (yr. ended 12/31/02): Assets, $773,319,000 (M); expenditures, $49,103,000; qualifying distributions, $43,728,288; giving activities include $43,728,288 for grants.
Purpose and activities: The endowment's mission is to help southwestern Pennsylvania thrive as a whole community-economically, ecologically, educationally, and culturally-while advancing the state of knowledge and practice in the fields in which we work. It funds activities in 5 program areas: Arts and Culture; Children, Youth, and Families; Economic Opportunity; Education; and the Environment.
Fields of interest: Arts; Environment; Children/youth, services; Family services; Economic development.
Types of support: General/operating support; Capital campaigns; Building/renovation; Equipment; Program development; Seed money; Research; Technical assistance; Program-related investments/loans; Matching/challenge support.
Limitations: Giving limited to activities which directly benefit the citizens of PA, with emphasis on Pittsburgh and southwestern PA. No grants to individuals.
Publications: Application guidelines, Annual report, Newsletter, Occasional report, Program policy statement.
Application information: Application form not required.
  Initial approach: Letter of inquiry
  Copies of proposal: 1
  Deadline(s): 90 days before meeting date
  Board meeting date(s): May and Oct.
  Final notification: Within several weeks of board meeting
Officers and Directors:* Teresa F. Heinz, Chair.; Maxwell King, Pres.; J.E. Kime, C.F.O.; Ann C. Plunkett, Cont.; Carol R. Brown; Frank V. Cahouet; Judith Davenport; H. John Heinz IV; Howard M. Love; Shirley M. Malcom; William H. Rea; Barbara K. Robinson; Frederick W. Thieman; Mallory Walker.
Number of staff: 32 shared staff (shared with Vira I. Heinz Endowment).
EIN: 251721100
Recent environmental and animal welfare grants:

2852-1 Air and Waste Management Association, Pittsburgh, PA, $128,000. To promote collaboration among environmental organizations and businesses in Pittsburgh and target cities in Central Europe. 2001.
2852-2 American Farmland Trust, DC, $20,000. To develop approach and objectives for comprehensive rural agricultural preservation and sustainable development strategy. 2001.
2852-3 ASSET, Inc., Pittsburgh, PA, $150,000. To develop and implement environmental education curricula in elementary schools. 2001.
2852-4 Audubon Society, National, Harrisburg, PA, $80,000. For research and education in support of White-tailed deer management. 2001.
2852-5 Chemical Strategies Partnership, San Francisco, CA, $100,000. For work with industries in Pennsylvania. Grant made through Tides Center. 2001.
2852-6 Chesapeake Bay Foundation, Harrisburg, PA, $50,000. For reducing nutrient pollution to Pennsylvania waters and Chesapeake Bay. 2001.
2852-7 Citizens for Pennsylvanias Future, Harrisburg, PA, $400,000. For Western Pennsylvania Environmental Communications Resource Center and campaign for land use, and sustainable transportation in southwestern Pennsylvania. 2001.
2852-8 Citizens for Pennsylvanias Future, Harrisburg, PA, $100,000. For Mid-Atlantic Renewable Energy Campaign. 2001.
2852-9 Clean Air Council, Philadelphia, PA, $50,000. For monitoring Pennsylvania's implementation of Clean Air Act. 2001.
2852-10 Clean Air Task Force, Boston, MA, $250,000. For protection of air quality in southwestern Pennsylvania. 2001.
2852-11 Clean Water Fund, Pittsburgh, PA, $75,000. For Pennsylvania's Clean Water Fund's Tap into Watersheds Project. 2001.
2852-12 Clean Water Fund, Pittsburgh, PA, $40,000. To promote environmental quality and reduced emissions by industries on Neville Island. 2001.
2852-13 Community Environmental Legal Defense Fund, Chambersburg, PA, $45,000. For community grassroots litigation support program. 2001.
2852-14 Community Loan Fund of Southwestern Pennsylvania, Pittsburgh, PA, $50,000. To provide technical assistance to Green Business Initiative and Green Building Fund. 2001.
2852-15 Conservation Consultants, Pittsburgh, PA, $350,000. For expansion of Green Neighborhood Initiative. 2001.
2852-16 Conservation Consultants, Pittsburgh, PA, $30,000. For Pennsylvania Wind Map project. 2001.
2852-17 Earth Force, Wyncote, PA, $50,000. For Ginodo Earth Force-Western PA Expansion, Phase One. 2001.
2852-18 Friends of the Riverfront, Pittsburgh, PA, $75,000. For riverfront trail development and public education. 2001.
2852-19 Green Building Alliance, Pittsburgh, PA, $250,000. For continued operating support. 2001.
2852-20 Group Against Smog and Pollution (GASP), Pittsburgh, PA, $50,000. To increase

effectiveness as regional environmental advocate working particularly on air quality and environmental health issues. 2001.

2852-21 PbX, Pittsburgh, PA, $265,000. For CLEARCorps and Lead Safe Pittsburgh Coalition projects. 2001.

2852-22 Pennsylvania Conservation Voters Education League, West Brownsville, PA, $40,000. To carry out voter education programs on environmental issues. 2001.

2852-23 Pennsylvania State University, Center for Sustainability, University Park, PA, $20,000. To develop business/strategic plan. 2001.

2852-24 Phipps Conservatory and Botanical Gardens, Pittsburgh, PA, $1,000,000. For capital campaign, Bringing Phipps into Full Flower. 2001.

2852-25 Pinchot Institute for Conservation, DC, $40,000. For Appalachian Forest Workshop. 2001.

2852-26 Pittsburgh Community Broadcasting Corporation, Pittsburgh, PA, $100,000. For Allegheny Front, environmental radio program. 2001.

2852-27 Safe Energy Communication Council, DC, $20,000. For Pennsylvania Home Power Boosters Project. 2001.

2852-28 Second Nature, Boston, MA, $200,000. For planning grant to evaluate institutional readiness of western Pennsylvania higher education environmental literacy focus. 2001.

2852-29 South Side Local Development Company, Pittsburgh, PA, $50,000. For energy efficient improvements in business district and for public space planning between South Side Works and East Carson Street. 2001.

2852-30 Tides Center - Western Pennsylvania, Pittsburgh, PA, $300,000. For Sustainable Pittsburgh. 2001.

2852-31 University of Pittsburgh, Graduate School of Public Health, Pittsburgh, PA, $130,000. For Phase II of chemical Toxicity Testing Program. 2001.

2852-32 Western Pennsylvania Conservancy, Pittsburgh, PA, $50,000. For Sideling Hill Creek Watershed Outreach Project. 2001.

2853
Vira I. Heinz Endowment ▼

30 Dominion Tower
625 Liberty Ave.
Pittsburgh, PA 15222-3115 (412) 281-5777
Contact: Maxwell King, Pres.
FAX: (412) 281-5788; E-mail: info@heinz.org;
URL: http://www.heinz.org

Trust established in 1986 in PA; incorporated in 1995.
Donor(s): Vira I. Heinz.‡
Grantmaker type: Independent foundation
Financial data (yr. ended 12/31/02): Assets, $399,182,000 (M); expenditures, $20,653,000; qualifying distributions, $17,964,598; giving activities include $17,964,598 for grants.
Purpose and activities: The endowment's mission is to help southwestern Pennsylvania thrive as a whole community - economically, ecologically, educationally, and culturally - while advancing the state of knowledge and practice in the fields in which it works. It funds

activities in 5 program areas: Arts and Culture; Children, Youth and Families; Economic Opportunity; Education; and the Environment.
Fields of interest: Humanities; Arts; Education; Environment; Children/youth, services; Economic development.
Types of support: General/operating support; Capital campaigns; Building/renovation; Equipment; Program development; Seed money; Research; Technical assistance; Program-related investments/loans; Matching/challenge support.
Limitations: Giving primarily directed to Pittsburgh and southwestern PA, although in certain cases support may be considered on a national or international basis. No grants to individuals.
Publications: Application guidelines, Annual report, Newsletter, Occasional report, Program policy statement.
Application information: Please do not send additional supporting materials with the initial letter of inquiry. Applicants should not submit full proposals unless they have been asked to do so by a representative of the foundation. Application form not required.
   Initial approach: Letter of inquiry
   Copies of proposal: 1
   Deadline(s): Jan. 15 (for consideration at spring meeting) and Aug. 1 (for fall meeting)
   Board meeting date(s): May. and Oct.
   Final notification: Within several weeks of board meeting
Officers and Directors:* James M. Walton,* Chair.; Maxwell King, Pres.; Jack E. Kime, C.F.O.; Ann C. Plunkett, Cont.; Andre T. Heinz; Teresa F. Heinz; Wendy MacKenzie; William H. Rea; Barbara K. Robinson; Konrad M. Weis; S. Donald Wiley.
Number of staff: 32 shared staff (shared with Howard Heinz Endowment).
EIN: 251762825
Recent environmental and animal welfare grants:

2853-1 Brookings Institution, DC, $250,000. For Smart Growth education and assistance in southwestern Pennsylvania. 2001.

2853-2 Dollar Energy Fund, Pittsburgh, PA, $150,000. For energy conservation programs in low-income communities. 2001.

2853-3 Earthome, Baldwin, MD, $10,000. To produce documentary film entitled Signal of Intention, the Work and Vision of William McDonough. 2001.

2853-4 Ecologic Development Fund, Cambridge, MA, $10,000. For general operating support. 2001.

2853-5 Enterprising Environmental Solutions, Pittsburgh, PA, $150,000. For continued support of Interfaith Power and Light program. 2001.

2853-6 Enterprising Environmental Solutions, Pittsburgh, PA, $70,000. For Pennsylvania Sustainable Investor's Database. 2001.

2853-7 National Parks Conservation Association, DC, $25,000. For participation of Heinz School in National Parks Business Initiative in Pennsylvania. 2001.

2853-8 Nature Conservancy, Philadelphia, PA, $100,000. For Pennsylvania Aquatic Community Classification Project. 2001.

2853-9 North American Water Trails, DC, $20,000. For water trails development in western Pennsylvania. 2001.

2853-10 PbX, Pittsburgh, PA, $125,000. For Healthy Homes for Families, environmental health collaborative. 2001.

2853-11 Pennsylvania Environmental Council, Philadelphia, PA, $292,000. For continued support of western Pennsylvania watershed protection and education efforts. 2001.

2853-12 Pennsylvania Environmental Defense Foundation, Paoli, PA, $200,000. For Pennsylvania Total Maximum Daily Loadings (TMDL) project. 2001.

2853-13 Pennsylvania Resources Council, Newtown Square, PA, $75,000. For Pittsburgh regional anti-litter campaign and commercial waste reduction program. 2001.

2853-14 Pennsylvania State University, University Park, PA, $50,000. For Maurice K. Goddard Chair for natural resources and environment. 2001.

2853-15 Pittsburgh Parks Conservancy, Pittsburgh, PA, $100,000. For membership development toward implementation of Master Plan for city parks. 2001.

2853-16 Resources for the Future, DC, $25,000. For Scarcity and Growth in the New Millennium Project. 2001.

2853-17 Riverlife Task Force, Pittsburgh, PA, $300,000. For operating support. 2001.

2853-18 Riverlife Task Force, Pittsburgh, PA, $11,500. For consulting. 2001.

2853-19 Rocky Mountain Institute, Snowmass, CO, $10,000. For general operating support. 2001.

2853-20 Three Rivers Wet Weather, Pittsburgh, PA, $200,000. For ecological design of storm water management. 2001.

2853-21 Tides Center, San Francisco, CA, $10,000. For Funders' Forum on environmental education. 2001.

2853-22 Tides Center - Western Pennsylvania, Pittsburgh, PA, $148,000. For completion of Pennsylvania Energy Project. 2001.

2853-23 ULI Foundation, DC, $45,000. To build regional support for sustainable development by conducting national symposium in Pittsburgh. 2001.

2853-24 University of Pennsylvania, Philadelphia, PA, $50,000. For enhancement and expansion of Pennsylvania Flora Database on worldwide web. 2001.

2853-25 Waterkeeper Alliance, White Plains, NY, $12,000. For Water Keeper Conference. 2001.

2853-26 Western Pennsylvania Conservancy, Pittsburgh, PA, $100,000. For continued support of Green Neighborhood Initiative community garden program. 2001.

2853-27 Wildlife Habitat Council, Silver Spring, MD, $20,000. For Three Rivers Habitat Partnership (TRHP). 2001.

2854
Heinz Family Foundation ▼

3200 Dominion Tower
625 Liberty Ave.
Pittsburgh, PA 15222 (412) 497-5775
Contact: Jeffrey R. Lewis, Pres.
FAX: (412) 497-5790

Established in 1984 in PA; incorporated in 1992.
Grantmaker type: Independent foundation
Financial data (yr. ended 12/31/02): Assets, $69,000,000 (M); gifts received, $6,659,935;

expenditures, $7,968,785; qualifying distributions, $4,858,401; giving activities include $3,608,401 for 210 grants (high: $1,000,000; low: $250; average: $250–$250,000) and $1,250,000 for 5 grants to individuals (high: $250,000).

Purpose and activities: Giving primarily for the Heinz Awards, environmental organizations, arts and cultural organizations, and women's health and pension.

Fields of interest: Museums; Arts; Education; Environment.

Types of support: Capital campaigns; Building/renovation; Equipment; Endowments; Grants to individuals.

Limitations: Applications not accepted. Giving only in the U.S. No grants to individuals (except for Heinz Awards).

Application information: Contributes only to pre-selected organizations; unsolicited applications not considered.

Officers and Directors:* Teresa F. Heinz,* Chair. and C.E.O.; Jeffrey R. Lewis, Pres.; Wendy Mackenzie, Secy.; S. Donald Wiley, Treas.; Jack E. Kime, C.F.O.; John R. Taylor, C.I.O.; Andre Heinz.

Number of staff: None.

EIN: 251689382

Recent environmental and animal welfare grants:

2854-1 Blaine County Citizens for Smart Growth, Hailey, ID, $25,000. For general operating support. 2001.

2854-2 H. John Heinz III Center for Science, Economics and the Environment, DC, $50,000. For general operating support. 2001.

2854-3 International Center for Journalists, DC, $60,000. For John Heinz Fellowship in Environmental Reporting. 2001.

2854-4 League of Conservation Voters Education Fund, DC, $10,000. For general operating support. 2001.

2854-5 Pittsburgh Parks Conservancy, Pittsburgh, PA, $20,000. For Spring Hat Luncheon fundraiser. 2001.

2855

Hershey Foods Corporation Contributions Program

c/o Corp. Contribs. and Community Rels. Dept.
100 Crystal A Dr., P.O. Box 810
Hershey, PA 17033-0810
Contact: Jennifer M. Goss, Coord., Corp. Contribs. and Community Rels.
FAX: (717) 534-7015; *URL:* http://www.hersheys.com/about/contributions

Grantmaker type: Corporate giving program

Financial data (yr. ended 12/31/00): Total giving, $2,376,792; giving activities include $1,735,942 for 734 grants (high: $158,000; low: $25; average: $500–$5,000), $625,850 for 786 employee matching gifts and $15,000 for in-kind gifts.

Purpose and activities: Hershey makes charitable contributions to nonprofit organizations involved with arts and culture, education, the environment, health and human services, community development, public affairs, and minorities. Support is given primarily in areas of company operations.

Fields of interest: Arts; Education; Environment; Health care; Human services; Community development; Public affairs; Minorities.

International interests: Canada; Mexico.

Types of support: General/operating support; Capital campaigns; Employee volunteer services; Employee matching gifts; Donated products.

Limitations: Giving primarily in areas of company operations, including in Canada and Mexico; giving also to statewide and national organizations. No support for political or lobbying organizations, churches or religious organizations, fraternal organizations, veterans' organizations, or labor organizations. No grants to individuals, or for general operating support for Allied Arts Fund- or United Way-supported organizations.

Publications: Application guidelines, Corporate giving report (including application guidelines).

Application information: Statewide and national organizations should contact headquarters. Contact headquarters for nearest application address. The Corporate Contributions Department handles giving. The company has a staff that only handles contributions. A contributions committee reviews all requests. Application form required.

Initial approach: Contact nearest company facility for application form
Copies of proposal: 1
Deadline(s): 3 months prior to need
Board meeting date(s): 11 times per year
Final notification: 2 months

Administrators: Jennifer M. Goss, Coord., Corp. Contribs. and Community Rels.; John C. Long, V.P., Corp. Comm.; Susan K. Smith, Corp. Contribs. and Community Rels. Rep.

Number of staff: 2 full-time professional; 1 full-time support.

2856

The Henry L. Hillman Foundation ▼

2000 Grant Bldg.
Pittsburgh, PA 15219 (412) 338-3466
Contact: Ronald W. Wertz, Secy. and Exec. Dir.
FAX: (412) 338-3463; *E-mail:* foundation@hillmanfo.com

Established in 1964 in PA.

Donor(s): Henry L. Hillman.

Grantmaker type: Independent foundation

Financial data (yr. ended 12/31/02): Assets, $82,150,251 (M); gifts received, $96,545; expenditures, $4,586,339; qualifying distributions, $4,583,115; giving activities include $4,541,000 for 94 grants (high: $1,000,000; low: $1,000; average: $1,000–$10,000).

Purpose and activities: Support primarily for art and cultural programs, and higher and secondary education; support also for youth, conservation, civic affairs, community development, social services, and hospitals.

Fields of interest: Arts; Secondary school/education; Higher education; Education; Natural resources; Hospitals (general); Domestic violence; Human services; Children/youth, services; Community development; Government/public administration; Disabled; Aging; Women; People with AIDS (PWAs); Economically disadvantaged; Homeless.

Types of support: General/operating support; Continuing support; Annual campaigns; Capital campaigns; Building/renovation; Equipment; Endowments; Program development; Seed money; Matching/challenge support.

Limitations: Giving primarily in Pittsburgh and southwestern PA. No grants to individuals, or for deficit financing, publications, or conferences; no loans.

Publications: Application guidelines.

Application information: Application form not required.

Initial approach: Letter
Copies of proposal: 1
Deadline(s): None
Board meeting date(s): Mar. and Dec.

Officers and Directors:* Henry L. Hillman,* Pres.; Ronald W. Wertz,* Secy. and Exec. Dir.; Lawrence M. Wagner, Treas.; H. Vaughan Blaxter III.

Number of staff: 1 part-time professional.

EIN: 256065959

Recent environmental and animal welfare grants:

2856-1 Jupiter Island, Town of, Hobe Sound, FL, $100,000. Toward purchase of conservation site. 2001.

2856-2 Phipps Conservatory and Botanical Gardens, Pittsburgh, PA, $300,000. Toward establishing endowed chair for Head of Horticulture. 2001.

2856-3 Squam Lakes Association, Holderness, NH, $50,000. Toward endowment as part of capital campaign. 2001.

2857

The Henry Lea Hillman, Jr. Foundation, Inc.

2000 Grant Bldg.
Pittsburgh, PA 15219 (412) 338-3466
Contact: Ronald W. Wertz, Secy. and Exec. Dir.
FAX: (412) 338-3463; *E-mail:* foundation@hillmanfo.com

Established in 1986 in PA.

Donor(s): Henry Lea Hillman, Jr., Henry Lea Hillman Charitable Lead Trust.

Grantmaker type: Independent foundation

Financial data (yr. ended 12/31/02): Assets, $7,628,357 (M); expenditures, $350,415; qualifying distributions, $309,320; giving activities include $296,000 for 22 grants (high: $50,000; low: $2,500; average: $2,500–$15,000).

Fields of interest: Visual arts; Arts; Higher education; Natural resources; Environment; Health care; Youth development; Economically disadvantaged.

Types of support: General/operating support; Continuing support; Annual campaigns; Capital campaigns; Building/renovation; Program development; Seed money.

Limitations: Giving primarily in Portland, OR.

Publications: Application guidelines.

Application information: Application form not required.

Initial approach: Proposal
Copies of proposal: 1
Deadline(s): None
Board meeting date(s): May and Dec.

Officers and Directors:* Henry Lea Hillman, Jr.,* Pres.; Lawrence M. Wagner,* V.P.; Ronald

W. Wertz,* Secy. and Exec. Dir.; Maurice J. White,* Treas.
Number of staff: 1 part-time professional.
EIN: 251536656

2858
Emma Clyde Hodge Memorial Fund
c/o PNC Advisors, P2-PTPP-25-1
620 Liberty Ave., 2 PNC Plz.
Pittsburgh, PA 15222-2719
Contact: Beatrice A. Lynch, Trust Off., PNC Advisors

Established in 1990 in PA.
Donor(s): Edwin Hodge, Jr.‡
Grantmaker type: Independent foundation
Financial data (yr. ended 06/30/02): Assets, $8,794,226 (M); expenditures, $502,171; qualifying distributions, $454,055; giving activities include $454,206 for 39 grants (high: $53,402; low: $1,500).
Purpose and activities: Giving primarily for natural resource conservation and human services.
Fields of interest: Arts; Natural resources; Human services.
Types of support: Building/renovation.
Limitations: Applications not accepted. Giving primarily in PA. No grants to individuals.
Application information: Unsolicited requests for funds are not accepted.
Trustee: PNC Bank, N.A.
EIN: 256227653

2859
Bob Hoffman Foundation
c/o Fulton Financial Advisors
P.O. Box 3215
Lancaster, PA 17604-3215
Contact: John B. Terpak, Jr., Tr.

Established about 1964 in PA.
Donor(s): York Barbell Co., Inc., and related companies.
Grantmaker type: Company-sponsored foundation
Financial data (yr. ended 03/31/02): Assets, $1,768,394 (M); gifts received, $25,305; expenditures, $165,166; qualifying distributions, $134,801; giving activities include $135,283 for 30 grants (high: $24,000; low: $100).
Purpose and activities: Giving for community, youth, and recreational activities and hospitals.
Fields of interest: Performing arts; Education; Environment; Hospitals (general); Health care; Recreation; Children/youth, services; Community development; Science; General charitable giving.
Types of support: General/operating support; Annual campaigns; Capital campaigns; In-kind gifts.
Limitations: Giving primarily in York County, PA.
Publications: Application guidelines.
Application information: Application form required.
Initial approach: Letter for organizations
Copies of proposal: 1
Deadline(s): 1 month prior to meeting dates
Board meeting date(s): Last week of Jan., Apr., July, and Oct.

Trustees: David J. Fortney; Alda M. Ketterman; George E. MacDonald; Paul Strombaugh; John B. Terpak, Jr.
EIN: 236298674

2860
Holt Family Foundation
1611 Pond Rd., Ste. 300
Allentown, PA 18104-2256
Contact: Leon C. Holt, Jr., Mgr.

Established in 1987 in PA.
Donor(s): Leon C. Holt, Jr.
Grantmaker type: Independent foundation
Financial data (yr. ended 12/31/02): Assets, $4,132,742 (M); gifts received, $10,000; expenditures, $265,113; qualifying distributions, $271,520; giving activities include $215,250 for 48 grants (high: $40,000; low: $250; average: $1,000–$10,000).
Purpose and activities: Giving primarily for the arts, education, and environmental programs.
Fields of interest: Arts; Education; Environment.
Types of support: Annual campaigns; Capital campaigns; Program development; Seed money; Scholarship funds.
Limitations: Giving primarily in Allentown and Lehigh County, PA. No support for political, fraternal, or social organizations; no giving to religious organizations for religious purposes. No grants to individuals, or for endowments, debt reduction, fund raising events, or lobbying.
Publications: Application guidelines.
Application information: Application form not required.
Initial approach: Letter
Copies of proposal: 1
Deadline(s): Apr. 15 and Sept. 15
Board meeting date(s): May and Nov.
Final notification: June and Nov.
Officer and Trustees:* Leon C. Holt, Jr.,* Mgr.; June W. Holt; Richard W. Holt; Deborah Holt Weil.
Number of staff: 1 part-time support.
EIN: 236906143

2861
Janet A. Hooker Charitable Trust ▼
c/o PNC Advisors
1600 Market St., 29th Fl.
Philadelphia, PA 19103 (215) 585-4609

Trust established in 1952 in NY.
Donor(s): Janet A. Neff Hooker.
Grantmaker type: Independent foundation
Financial data (yr. ended 12/31/01): Assets, $3,433,038 (M); expenditures, $1,555,226; qualifying distributions, $1,537,852; giving activities include $1,541,000 for 35 grants (high: $350,000; low: $500; average: $5,000–$100,000).
Purpose and activities: Primary areas of interest include education, community development, and arts and cultural programs. Support for historic preservation, and social service agencies; giving also for animal welfare.
Fields of interest: Opera; Historic preservation/historical societies; Arts; University; Education; Animal welfare; Health care; Medical research, institute; Human services; Community development.

Types of support: General/operating support; Annual campaigns.
Limitations: Applications not accepted. Giving primarily in CA, FL, and NY. No grants to individuals.
Application information: Contributes only to pre-selected organizations. Unsolicited requests for funds not considered.
Board meeting date(s): Varies
Trustees: Donald P. Kahn; Gilbert S. Kahn.
Number of staff: 6 shared staff (shared with Harriet Ames Charitable Trust, Polly A. Levee Charitable Trust - Krancer Trust, Polly A. Levee Charitable Trust - Levee Trust, Esther Simon Charitable Trust, Lita Annenberg Hazen Charitable Trust).
EIN: 236286762
Recent environmental and animal welfare grants:
2861-1 American Kennel Club Museum of the Dog, Saint Louis, MO, $20,000. For unrestricted support. 2001.
2861-2 Animal Welfare Society of South Florida, Coral Gables, FL, $200,000. For building fund. 2001.
2861-3 Animal Welfare Society of South Florida, Coral Gables, FL, $100,000. For general support. 2001.
2861-4 University of Pennsylvania, School of Veterinary Medicine, Philadelphia, PA, $10,000. For Charing Cross Research Fund. 2001.

2862
John M. Hopwood Charitable Trust
c/o PNC Advisors
620 Liberty Ave., 25th Fl., 2 PNC Plz.
Pittsburgh, PA 15222-2719 (412) 762-7076
Contact: Mia Hallet Bernard

Trust established about 1948 in PA.
Donor(s): John M. Hopwood,‡ Mary S. Hopwood,‡ William T. Hopwood, Danforth K. Richardsion, Marge Richardson.
Grantmaker type: Independent foundation
Financial data (yr. ended 12/31/01): Assets, $27,340,796 (M); expenditures, $1,926,686; qualifying distributions, $1,774,590; giving activities include $1,667,284 for 57 grants (high: $205,000; low: $1,000; average: $5,000–$50,000).
Purpose and activities: Primary areas of interest include hospitals, education, and the environment.
Fields of interest: Arts; Higher education; Education; Natural resources; Energy; Environment; Hospitals (general); Health organizations, association; Human services; Youth, services; Religion.
Types of support: General/operating support; Continuing support; Annual campaigns; Capital campaigns; Building/renovation; Endowments; Emergency funds; Program development; Conferences/seminars; Seed money; Scholarship funds; Research; Technical assistance; Program-related investments/loans; Matching/challenge support.
Limitations: Giving primarily in western PA.
Publications: Application guidelines.
Application information: Application form not required.
Initial approach: Letter
Copies of proposal: 1

Deadline(s): None
Board meeting date(s): Varies
Trustees: William T. Hopwood; PNC Bank, N.A.
Number of staff: 2 part-time professional.
EIN: 256022634

2863
Horsehead Community Development Fund, Inc.
P.O. Box 351
Palmerton, PA 18071-0351 (610) 826-2239
Contact: Charles H. Campton, Exec. Consultant
Additional tel.: (610) 826-4377

Established in 1989 in PA.
Donor(s): Horsehead Resource Development Co., Inc.
Grantmaker type: Company-sponsored foundation
Financial data (yr. ended 12/31/01): Assets, $168,594 (M); gifts received, $118,982; expenditures, $136,036; qualifying distributions, $134,891; giving activities include $134,376 for 35 grants (high: $19,500; low: $500).
Purpose and activities: Giving primarily for hospitals and library associations; support also for community development and sports activities for youth.
Fields of interest: Performing arts; Libraries/library science; Natural resources; Environment; Hospitals (general); Recreation; Children/youth, services; Community development; Federated giving programs; Disabled; Aging.
Types of support: Capital campaigns; Building/renovation; Equipment; Emergency funds; Program development.
Limitations: Giving limited to the Palmerton, PA, area. No grants to individuals, or for start-up funds.
Publications: Annual report (including application guidelines), Financial statement, Grants list, Informational brochure (including application guidelines), Occasional report, Program policy statement.
Application information: Grants must be used in same year awarded. Application form required.
Initial approach: Letter or telephone
Copies of proposal: 1
Deadline(s): Apr. 1, July 1, Sept. 1, and Dec. 1
Board meeting date(s): Jan., Apr., July, and Oct.
Final notification: After board meeting
Officers and Directors:* William Bechdolt,* Chair.; Joseph Bechtel,* Vice-Chair.; Richard Hager,* Secy.; Michael Harleman,* Treas.; Charles H. Campton, Exec. Consultant; Mary Elizabeth Cyr; Michael R. Harleman.
Number of staff: 1 part-time professional.
EIN: 232588172

2864
The Houghton-Carpenter Foundation
P.O. Box 930
Valley Forge, PA 19482-0930 (610) 666-4049
Contact: W.F. MacDonald, Jr., Tr.

Established in 1951 in PA.
Donor(s): Aaron E. Carpenter,‡ Edythe A. Carpenter,‡ E.F. Houghton & Co.
Grantmaker type: Independent foundation

Financial data (yr. ended 06/30/03): Assets, $3,277,913 (M); expenditures, $2,687,681; qualifying distributions, $162,950; giving activities include $162,950 for 34 grants (low: $200).
Purpose and activities: Giving primarily for children's services, education, and the arts.
Fields of interest: Arts; Elementary/secondary education; Education; Zoos/zoological societies; Youth development; Human services; Children/youth, services; Disabled.
Types of support: General/operating support; Annual campaigns; Equipment; Emergency funds.
Limitations: Giving primarily in PA. No grants to individuals.
Publications: Application guidelines.
Application information: Application form not required.
Initial approach: Letter
Copies of proposal: 1
Deadline(s): None
Trustees: William F. MacDonald, Jr.; William Streich.
Number of staff: None.
EIN: 236230874

2865
Roy A. Hunt Foundation ▼
1 Bigelow Sq., Ste. 630
Pittsburgh, PA 15219-3030 (412) 281-8734
Contact: Torrence M. Hunt, Jr., Pres.
FAX: (412) 255-0522; E-mail: info@rahuntfdn.org; URL: http://www.rahuntfdn.org

Established in 1966 in PA.
Donor(s): Roy A. Hunt.‡
Grantmaker type: Independent foundation
Financial data (yr. ended 05/31/02): Assets, $81,535,907 (M); expenditures, $4,306,484; qualifying distributions, $4,200,769; giving activities include $3,790,039 for 530 grants (high: $50,000; low: $500; average: $100–$25,000).
Purpose and activities: Grants initiated by the trustees for higher, secondary and elementary education, the arts and cultural programs, social services, the environment, health services, community development, and youth violence prevention.
Fields of interest: Arts; Elementary/secondary education; Secondary school/education; Higher education; Environment; Health organizations, association; Crime/violence prevention, youth; Human services; Community development; Religion.
Types of support: General/operating support; Annual campaigns; Capital campaigns; Building/renovation; Endowments.
Limitations: Giving primarily in the Boston, MA, and Pittsburgh, PA, areas. No grants to individuals.
Application information: See Web site for application information. Application form required.
Initial approach: Letter of inquiry
Deadline(s): Mar.15 and Aug. 15
Board meeting date(s): June and Nov.
Final notification: Mar. and Aug.
Officer and Trustees:* Torrence M. Hunt, Jr., Pres.; Helen Hunt Bouscaren; Susan Hunt Hollingsworth; A. James Hunt; Andrew McQ.

Hunt; Caroline H. Hunt; Cathryn J. Hunt; Christopher M. Hunt; Daniel K. Hunt; John B. Hunt; Richard M. Hunt; Roy A. Hunt III; Torrence M. Hunt, Sr.; William E. Hunt; Marion M. Hunt-Badiner; Rachel Hunt Knowles; Joan F. Scott.
Number of staff: 2 full-time professional; 2 full-time support.
EIN: 256105162
Recent environmental and animal welfare grants:
2865-1 Animal Welfare Institute, DC, $12,500. For general operating support. 2002.
2865-2 Center for Ecoliteracy, Berkeley, CA, $20,000. For food systems project. 2002.
2865-3 Commonweal, Bolinas, CA, $25,000. For Health Care Without Harm program. 2002.
2865-4 Conemaugh Valley Conservancy, Apollo, PA, $20,000. For management staff support. 2002.
2865-5 EarthWays Foundation, Malibu, CA, $10,000. For general operating support. 2002.
2865-6 Environmental Resource Center, Ketchum, ID, $10,000. For general operating support. 2002.
2865-7 Friends of the Earth, DC, $12,000. For general operating support. 2002.
2865-8 Game Conservation International, Fort Worth, TX, $10,000. For general operating support. 2002.
2865-9 Horticultural Society of Western Pennsylvania, Pittsburgh, PA, $12,500. For Botanic Garden of Western Pennsylvania. 2002.
2865-10 National Parks Conservation Association, DC, $75,000. For Business Plan Initiative. 2002.
2865-11 National Parks Conservation Association, DC, $50,000. For Business Plan Initiative. 2002.
2865-12 Natural Step, San Francisco, CA, $15,000. For sustainability education and training for corporate sector. 2002.
2865-13 Ocean Classroom Foundation, Cornwall, NY, $10,000. For sea education program for students of Epiphany School. 2002.
2865-14 Phipps Conservatory and Botanical Gardens, Pittsburgh, PA, $25,000. For capital campaign for Visitors and Education Center. 2002.
2865-15 Phipps Conservatory and Botanical Gardens, Pittsburgh, PA, $10,000. For general operating support. 2002.
2865-16 Pittsburgh Parks Conservancy, Pittsburgh, PA, $10,000. For interactive information kiosk. 2002.
2865-17 Rainforest Action Network, San Francisco, CA, $12,000. For education program. 2002.
2865-18 Rocky Mountain Institute, Snowmass, CO, $10,000. For general operating support. 2002.
2865-19 Shikar-Safari Club International Foundation, Chicago, IL, $10,000. For general operating support. 2002.
2865-20 Student Conservation Association, Pittsburgh, PA, $10,000. For general operating support. 2002.
2865-21 Sustainability Institute, Hartland, VT, $25,000. To support case studies of sustainability practices in commodities industries. 2002.

2865-22 Zoological Society of Pittsburgh, Pittsburgh, PA, $10,000. For Aqua Zoo Capital Campaign. 2002.

2866
Myrtle V. C. Huplits & Woodman E. Huplits Foundation Trust
2 Davis Dr.
Washington Crossing, PA 18977
Contact: Arnold M. Peskin, Tr.

Established in 1990.
Grantmaker type: Independent foundation
Financial data (yr. ended 12/31/02): Assets, $2,373,099 (M); expenditures, $325,265; qualifying distributions, $325,265; giving activities include $270,000 for 5 grants (high: $81,000; low: $13,500).
Fields of interest: Natural resources; Animals/wildlife, alliance; Human services.
Limitations: Applications not accepted. Giving primarily in PA. No grants to individuals.
Application information: Contributes only to pre-selected organizations.
Trustees: Arnold M. Peskin; Marni L. Peskin; Todd E. Peskin.
EIN: 237451411

2867
The Stewart Huston Charitable Trust
50 S. 1st Ave., 2nd Fl.
Coatesville, PA 19320 (610) 384-2666
Contact: Scott G. Huston, Exec. Dir.
FAX: (610) 384-3396; E-mail: admin@stewarthuston.org; URL: http://www.stewarthuston.org

Established in 1989 in PA.
Donor(s): Stewart Huston.‡
Grantmaker type: Independent foundation
Financial data (yr. ended 12/31/01): Assets, $21,066,937 (M); expenditures, $1,827,118; qualifying distributions, $1,733,805; giving activities include $1,105,498 for 95 grants (high: $76,448; low: $1,100; average: $1,000–$30,000).
Purpose and activities: Giving primarily for religion, the arts, education, the environment, health care, substance abuse, human services, community development, and public affairs.
Fields of interest: Performing arts; Historic preservation/historical societies; Arts; Early childhood education; Vocational education; Adult education—literacy, basic skills & GED; Reading; Education; Natural resources; Environment; Medical care, rehabilitation; Health care; Substance abuse, services; Health organizations, association; AIDS; Alcoholism; Employment; Food services; Housing/shelter, development; Recreation; Youth development, services; Human services; Children/youth, services; Family services; Hospices; Aging, centers/services; Homeless, human services; International peace/security; Community development; Voluntarism promotion; Public policy, research; Leadership development; Public affairs; Christian agencies & churches; General charitable giving; Disabled; Aging; Economically disadvantaged; Homeless.
Types of support: General/operating support; Continuing support; Capital campaigns; Building/renovation; Equipment; Emergency

funds; Program development; Seed money; Technical assistance; Employee matching gifts; Matching/challenge support.
Limitations: Giving primarily in the Savannah, GA, area and Coatesville and Chester County, PA. No support for political organizations or volunteer fire companies. No grants to individuals, including scholarships or for endowments.
Publications: Application guidelines, Annual report, Informational brochure.
Application information: Application form required.
  Initial approach: Letter of intent
  Copies of proposal: 1
  Deadline(s): Mar. 1 and Sept. 1
  Board meeting date(s): June and Dec.
  Final notification: June and Dec.
Officer and Trustees:* Scott G. Huston,* Exec. Dir.; Samuel A. Cann; Charles L. Huston III; Louis N. Seltzer.
Number of staff: 1 full-time professional; 1 full-time support; 1 part-time support.
EIN: 232612599

2868
Helen St. John Iverson Trust
c/o PNC Advisors
1600 Market St., 4th Fl.
Philadelphia, PA 19103-7240

Established in 1997 in PA.
Grantmaker type: Public charity
Financial data (yr. ended 12/31/00): Revenue, $223,804; assets, $2,003,596 (M); expenditures, $61,023; program services expenses, $52,057; giving activities include $52,057 for 1 grant.
Purpose and activities: Support only for Seeing Eye Inc., Morrristown, NJ.
Fields of interest: Animals/wildlife, training.
Types of support: General/operating support.
Limitations: Applications not accepted. Giving limited to Morristown, NJ. No grants to individuals.
Application information: Contributes only to a pre-selected organization; unsolicited requests for funds not considered or acknowledged.
Trustee: PNC Bank, N.A.
EIN: 911918474

2869
The J.D.B. Fund
404 S. Swedesford Rd.
P.O. Box 157
Gwynedd, PA 19436-0157 (215) 699-2233
Contact: Paul J. Corr, Mgr.

Established in 1966 in PA.
Donor(s): John Drew Betz,‡ Claire S. Betz.
Grantmaker type: Independent foundation
Financial data (yr. ended 12/31/02): Assets, $2,275,559 (M); gifts received, $19,188; expenditures, $698,420; qualifying distributions, $755,390; giving activities include $756,750 for 30 grants (high: $500,000; low: $200).
Purpose and activities: Giving primarily to Catholic organizations, human services, health care, and wildlife conservation.
Fields of interest: Arts; Education; Natural resources; Environment; Hospitals (general); Medical care, rehabilitation; Health organizations, association; Vocational

rehabilitation; Human services; Children/youth, services; Family services; Human services; Federated giving programs; Roman Catholic agencies & churches.
Types of support: General/operating support; Building/renovation; Equipment; Land acquisition; Matching/challenge support.
Limitations: Applications not accepted. Giving primarily in Montgomery County, PA. No grants to individuals.
Application information: Contributes only to pre-selected organizations.
  Board meeting date(s): Monthly
Officer: Paul J. Corr, Mgr.
Trustee: Claire S. Betz.
Number of staff: 2.
EIN: 236418867

2870
Robert S. and Louise S. Kahn Foundation
c/o Robert J. Lally
5700 Corporate Dr., Ste. 800
Pittsburgh, PA 15237

Established in 2002 in PA.
Donor(s): Louise S. Kahn, Robert S. Kahn.
Grantmaker type: Independent foundation
Financial data (yr. ended 12/31/02): Assets, $2,842,403 (M); gifts received, $3,564,227; expenditures, $195,497; qualifying distributions, $161,260; giving activities include $160,000 for 4 grants (high: $100,000; low: $10,000).
Fields of interest: Arts; Animal welfare; Christian agencies & churches.
Application information: Application form required.
  Deadline(s): None
Officers and Directors:* Robert S. Kahn,* Pres.; Louise S. Kahn,* V.P.; Robert J. Lally,* Secy.-Treas.; D. Grant Peacock.
EIN: 311810008

2871
Katherine H. Keiser Trust
21 E. Market St.
York, PA 17401-1500

Established in 1989.
Grantmaker type: Public charity
Financial data (yr. ended 12/31/02): Revenue, $35,789; assets, $1,306,721 (M); expenditures, $41,296; program services expenses, $38,628; giving activities include $38,628 for 6 grants of $6,438 each.
Purpose and activities: The trust exists for the sole benefit of the six named charitable organizations.
Fields of interest: Orchestra (symphony); Animal welfare; Christian agencies & churches.
Limitations: Applications not accepted. Giving limited to Mohnton and Reading, PA.
Application information: Contributes only to pre-selected organizations; unsolicited requests for funds not considered or acknowledged.
Trustee: Allfirst.
EIN: 236877150

2872
Klorfine Foundation
P.O. Box 128
Gladwyne, PA 19035
Contact: Leonard Klorfine, or Norma Klorfine,
Trustees
E-mail: lklor@comcast.net

Established in 1993 in PA.
Donor(s): Leonard Klorfine, Norma E. Klorfine.
Grantmaker type: Independent foundation
Financial data (yr. ended 11/30/02): Assets,
$11,424,194 (M); gifts received, $1,614,683;
expenditures, $416,226; qualifying distributions,
$390,824; giving activities include $394,786 for
16 grants (high: $177,386; low: $100).
Purpose and activities: Giving for the arts,
medicine, fire prevention, political research, and
the environment.
Fields of interest: Arts; Environment; Health
care, formal/general education; Disasters, fire
prevention/control; Camps.
Types of support: General/operating support;
Continuing support; Annual campaigns; Capital
campaigns; Building/renovation; Endowments;
Emergency funds.
Limitations: Giving primarily in Philadelphia, PA
and Seattle, WA; some giving also in
Washington, DC. No grants to individuals.
Application information: Application form not
required.
  Initial approach: Letter
  Copies of proposal: 1
  Deadline(s): None
  Board meeting date(s): Monthly
Trustees: Leonard Klorfine; Norma E. Klorfine.
Number of staff: None.
EIN: 227743385

2873
Laurel Foundation
2 Gateway Ctr., Ste. 1800
Pittsburgh, PA 15222 (412) 765-2400
Contact: D. Panazzi, V.P.
FAX: (412) 765-2407

Incorporated in 1951 in PA.
Donor(s): C. May.
Grantmaker type: Independent foundation
Financial data (yr. ended 12/31/02): Assets,
$33,709,123 (M); gifts received, $792,992;
expenditures, $2,715,679; qualifying
distributions, $2,488,672; giving activities
include $2,339,900 for 80 grants (high:
$767,000; low: $1,000; average:
$5,000–$25,000).
Purpose and activities: Grants largely to
organizations operating in the fields of
education, the environment, conservation,
family planning, museums and the performing
arts, with concentration in the southwestern
Pennsylvania area.
Fields of interest: Performing arts; Theater;
Literature; Arts; Secondary school/education;
Natural resources; Family planning; Health care;
Medical research, institute; Human services;
Population studies; General charitable giving.
Types of support: General/operating support;
Capital campaigns; Building/renovation;
Equipment; Land acquisition; Program
development; Conferences/seminars;
Publication; Seed money; Curriculum
development; Matching/challenge support.

Limitations: Giving primarily in southwestern
PA. No grants to individuals, or for multi-year
support.
Publications: Annual report (including
application guidelines).
Application information: Common Grant
Application form accepted but not required.
  Initial approach: Proposal, or common grant
  application
  Copies of proposal: 1
  Deadline(s): Apr. 1 and Oct. 1
  Board meeting date(s): June and Dec.
  Final notification: June and Dec.
Officers and Trustees:* C. May,* Chair.; R.
Meyer,* Pres.; D. Panazzi, V.P. and Secy.; T.
Inglis, V.P. and Treas.; N. Fales; C. Scaife; T.
Schmidt.
Number of staff: None.
EIN: 256008073

2874
The Lebovitz Fund
3050 Tremont St.
Allentown, PA 18104 (610) 820-5053
Contact: Herbert C. Lebovitz, Pres.

Established in 1944 in PA.
Donor(s): Beth Ann Segal Trust.
Grantmaker type: Independent foundation
Financial data (yr. ended 07/31/02): Assets,
$3,688,776 (M); gifts received, $70,000;
expenditures, $205,833; qualifying distributions,
$191,208; giving activities include $193,330 for
87 grants (high: $36,000; low: $10).
Purpose and activities: Giving primarily to
Jewish agencies and temples, and for education
and the arts.
Fields of interest: Arts; Education; Natural
resources; Human services; Jewish federated
giving programs; Jewish agencies & temples.
Limitations: Giving primarily in CT,
Minneapolis, MN, New York, NY, and eastern
PA.
Application information: Application form not
required.
  Initial approach: Letter
  Deadline(s): None
Officers and Directors:* Herbert C. Lebovitz,*
Pres. and Treas.; Beth Ann Segal,* V.P. and Secy.;
Jonathan Javitch; James Lebovitz.
EIN: 236270079

2875
Lehigh Valley Community Foundation
(formerly Bethlehem Area Foundation)
961 Marcon Blvd., Ste. 300
Allentown, PA 18109 (610) 266-4284
Contact: Carol Dean Henn, Exec. Dir.
FAX: (610) 266-4285; *E-mail:*
lvcf@lehighvalleyfoundation.org; *URL:* http://
www.lehighvalleyfoundation.org/

Established in 1967 in PA.
Grantmaker type: Community foundation
Financial data (yr. ended 06/30/02): Assets,
$14,453,926 (M); gifts received, $1,867,294;
expenditures, $506,764; giving activities include
$237,017 for 126 grants (high: $75,009; low:
$50; average: $1,500–$5,000).
Purpose and activities: Giving for arts and
culture, history and heritage, community
betterment, education, environment, health

care, human services and science. The
foundation administers donor-advised funds.
Fields of interest: Historic preservation/historical
societies; Arts; Education; Environment; Health
care; Human services; Children, services; Family
services; Community development; Science.
Types of support: Capital campaigns;
Building/renovation; Equipment; Emergency
funds; Program development; Publication; Seed
money; Scholarship funds; Matching/challenge
support.
Limitations: Giving limited to Lehigh, Monroe
and Northampton counties, PA. No support for
sectarian religious purposes. No grants to
individuals, or for operating budgets, continuing
support, annual campaigns, deficit financing,
endowments, foundation scholarships, or
research; no loans.
Publications: Application guidelines, Annual
report (including application guidelines), Grants
list, Informational brochure (including
application guidelines), Newsletter, Program
policy statement.
Application information: Capital funding: must
submit invoice copies when requesting release
of funds. Site visits will be made; mid-year and
final reports required. Application form
available on foundation Web site. Application
form required.
  Initial approach: Letter or telephone
  requesting application brochure
  Copies of proposal: 7
  Deadline(s): Submit proposal from May 1 to
  July 1
  Board meeting date(s): Quarterly
  Final notification: Dec. 1
Officers and Board of Governors:* Robert H.
Littner,* Chair.; Patrick Connell,* Vice-Chair.;
Carol Dean Henn, Secy. and Exec. Dir.; J.
Marshall Wolff,* Treas.; Joseph Boligitz; Llyena
Boylan; Walter W. Buckley, Jr.; Lee A. Butz; Rev.
Douglas Caldwell; Alvina L. Campbell; Maxwell
E. Davison; Lesley H. Fallon; Robert Finn;
Marlene O. Fowler; Fr. Daniel Gambert; Kostas
Kalogeropoulos; Frederick Kutteroff; Cynthia A.
Lambert; Richard G. Lang; Michael Lieberman;
Stephen Link; Robert Margolis; Jack H. McNairy;
Charles M. Meredith III; William K. Murphy;
Elizabeth M. Roberts; Robert D. Romeril;
Barbara Rothkopf; Barbara Tallman; Ferdinand
Thun; John H. Updegrove, M.D.
Investment Management: Dean McDermott &
Co.; Wachovia Bank, N.A.; Fleet National Bank;
Legg Mason; Mellon Financial Corp.; Merrill
Lynch Trust Co.
Number of staff: 2 full-time professional; 2
full-time support.
EIN: 231686634

2876
Lloyd Foundation
c/o PNC Advisors
620 Liberty Ave., 25th Fl.
Pittsburgh, PA 15222-2705 (412) 762-7076
Contact: Mia Hallett Bernard

Established in 1981 in PA.
Grantmaker type: Independent foundation
Financial data (yr. ended 06/30/02): Assets,
$1,509,480 (M); expenditures, $209,197;
qualifying distributions, $201,350; giving
activities include $200,212 for 8 grants (high:
$66,585; low: $1,509).

Purpose and activities: Giving for arts, education, the environment, human services and religion.
Fields of interest: Arts; Higher education; Animals/wildlife, preservation/protection; Animals/wildlife, sanctuaries; Human services; YM/YWCAs & YM/YWHAs; Christian agencies & churches.
Limitations: Giving primarily in Pittsburgh, PA. No grants to individuals.
Application information:
Initial approach: Letter
Deadline(s): None
Trustee: PNC Bank, N.A.
EIN: 256228888

2877
The Luzerne Foundation
613 Baltimore Dr.
Wilkes-Barre, PA 18702 (570) 822-5420
Contact: Charles M. Barber, Exec. Dir.
FAX: (570) 208-9145; E-mail:
Luzernefdn@aol.com; URL: http://
www.luzernefoundation.org

Established in 1994 in PA.
Grantmaker type: Community foundation
Financial data (yr. ended 12/31/02): Assets, $5,000,000 (M); expenditures, $843,453; giving activities include $511,555 for grants.
Purpose and activities: Giving for educational programs, projects benefiting the environment, community arts programs, and community, health and social service projects for the residents of the Luzerne County, PA, area.
Fields of interest: Arts; Education; Environment; Health organizations, association; Human services.
Types of support: Endowments; Program development; Scholarship funds; Technical assistance; Consulting services; Scholarships—to individuals.
Limitations: Giving limited to the Luzerne County, PA, area.
Publications: Application guidelines, Annual report, Financial statement, Grants list, Informational brochure (including application guidelines), Newsletter, Program policy statement.
Application information: Application form required.
Initial approach: Letter
Copies of proposal: 3
Deadline(s): Apr. 1 or Oct. 15
Board meeting date(s): Quarterly
Officer: Charles M. Barber, Exec. Dir.
Number of staff: 2 full-time professional.
EIN: 232765498

2878
Samuel P. Mandell Foundation
1818 Market St., Ste. 3220
Philadelphia, PA 19103 (215) 979-3410
Contact: Seymour Mandell, Tr.

Established in 1955 in PA.
Donor(s): Samuel P. Mandell,‡ Ida S. Mandell.‡
Grantmaker type: Independent foundation
Financial data (yr. ended 12/31/02): Assets, $16,812,916 (M); expenditures, $1,094,756; qualifying distributions, $989,899; giving

activities include $899,791 for 241 grants (high: $110,009; low: $15).
Purpose and activities: Emphasis on religious funds, hospitals, medical research, health associations and services, higher and other education, the fine arts and other cultural programs, community affairs, and the environment.
Fields of interest: Media/communications; Visual arts; Museums; Performing arts; Arts; Higher education; Libraries/library science; Education; Environment; Hospitals (general); Health care; Health organizations, association; Cancer; Medical research, institute; Cancer research; Crime/law enforcement; Human services; Jewish federated giving programs; Religious federated giving programs; Government/public administration; Roman Catholic agencies & churches; Minorities; Disabled.
Types of support: General/operating support; Continuing support; Annual campaigns; Capital campaigns; Building/renovation; Program development; Professorships; Research.
Limitations: Giving primarily in PA. No support for private operating foundations. No grants to individuals.
Application information: Application form not required.
Initial approach: Letter
Copies of proposal: 1
Deadline(s): None
Board meeting date(s): Quarterly
Trustees: Harold Cramer; Gerald Mandell, M.D.; Judith Mandell; Morton Mandell, M.D.; Ronald Mandell; Seymour Mandell.
Number of staff: 2 part-time support.
EIN: 236274709

2879
Maple Hill Foundation
115 Maple Hill Rd.
Gladwyne, PA 19035 (610) 642-5164
Contact: Ella Warren Miller, Dir.

Established in 1986 in PA.
Donor(s): Paul F. Miller, Jr., Ella Warren Miller.
Grantmaker type: Independent foundation
Financial data (yr. ended 07/31/02): Assets, $5,694,153 (M); expenditures, $965,546; qualifying distributions, $960,609; giving activities include $962,372 for 39 grants (high: $155,590; low: $500; average: $1,000–$25,000).
Purpose and activities: Giving for charitable, educational and scientific purposes.
Fields of interest: Arts; Higher education; Education; Natural resources; Animals/wildlife, preservation/protection.
Limitations: Applications not accepted. Giving primarily in Palo Alto CA, MA, NH, and Philadelphia, PA.
Application information: Unsolicited requests for funds not accepted.
Officers and Directors:* Ella Warren Merrill,* Pres.; Katharine S. Miller,* V.P. and Secy.; Paul F. Miller III,* V.P. and Treas.; Ella Warren Miller; Paul F. Miller, Jr.
EIN: 222751182

2880
Richard C. Marquardt Family Foundation
P.O. Box 26
Waverly, PA 18471-0026 (570) 586-9237
Application address: c/o Richard C. Marquardt, B.D.A. Building, Ste. 102, Abington Executive Pk., Clarks Summit, PA 18411

Established in 1997 in PA.
Donor(s): Richard C. Marquardt.
Grantmaker type: Independent foundation
Financial data (yr. ended 12/31/02): Assets, $1,397,382 (M); gifts received, $77,565; expenditures, $156,808; qualifying distributions, $153,754; giving activities include $154,150 for 52 grants (high: $66,500; low: $50).
Purpose and activities: Giving primarily for education, the United Way and religion.
Fields of interest: Theater; Elementary/secondary education; Higher education; Botanical/horticulture/landscape services; Animals/wildlife, fisheries; Health organizations, association; Human services; Federated giving programs; Christian agencies & churches.
Limitations: Giving primarily in PA.
Application information:
Initial approach: Letter or telephone
Deadline(s): None
Officers: Richard C. Marquardt, Pres. and Treas.; Sarah W. Marquardt, V.P. and Secy.
Director: Jeffrey W. Marquardt.
EIN: 232896467

2881
George & Miriam Martin Foundation
1818 Market St., 35th Fl.
Philadelphia, PA 19103 (215) 587-8400
Contact: George Martin, Tr.

Established in 1996 in PA.
Donor(s): George Martin.
Grantmaker type: Independent foundation
Financial data (yr. ended 12/31/02): Assets, $2,425,012 (M); gifts received, $400,000; expenditures, $133,133; qualifying distributions, $129,200; giving activities include $129,200 for grants.
Purpose and activities: Grants are given for charitable river or watershed protection activities, including trails, conservation easements, and wetland protection.
Fields of interest: Environment, research; Environment, water resources.
Types of support: General/operating support; Continuing support; Annual campaigns; Capital campaigns; Land acquisition; Seed money; Matching/challenge support.
Limitations: Giving primarily in southeast PA.
Application information: Application form not required.
Initial approach: Letter
Deadline(s): None
Trustees: Glenn Emery; George Martin; M. Christine Martin; Rebecca Martin; Regis McCann; Carol Martin Strange; H. Lawrence Strange.
Number of staff: None.
EIN: 232828201

2882
Maslow Family Foundation, Inc.

P.O. Box 174, Huntsville Rd.
Dallas, PA 18612 (570) 674-6532
Contact: Marilyn J. O'Boyle, Exec. Dir.
Application address: 147 Hayfield Rd.,
Shavertown, PA 18708-9748

Established in 1994 in PA.
Donor(s): Richard Maslow.
Grantmaker type: Independent foundation
Financial data (yr. ended 12/31/02): Assets,
$3,361,322 (M); gifts received, $70,000;
expenditures, $235,377; qualifying distributions,
$213,149; giving activities include $212,000 for
14 grants (high: $50,000; low: $2,000).
Purpose and activities: Giving for the arts and
the environment, and to improve the overall
quality of life.
Fields of interest: Arts; Education; Environment;
Children, services.
Types of support: Continuing support; Capital
campaigns; Building/renovation; Endowments;
Program development; Seed money; Scholarship
funds; Matching/challenge support.
Limitations: Giving primarily in the greater
Wyoming Valley area, in Luzerne County, PA.
No grants to individuals.
Application information: Application form not
required.
  Initial approach: Letter
  Copies of proposal: 1
  Deadline(s): Aug. 1
  Final notification: Dec.
Officers and Trustees:* Richard Maslow,* Pres.;
Douglas Maslow,* V.P.; Jennifer Maslow
Holtzman,* Secy.; Melanie Maslow Lumia,*
Treas.; Marilyn J. O'Boyle, Exec. Dir.; Allison
Maslow; Leslie Maslow; Hillary Maslow Naud;
Eugene Roth.
Number of staff: 1 part-time support.
EIN: 232791676

2883
Katherine Mabis McKenna Foundation, Inc. ▼

P.O. Box 186
Latrobe, PA 15650 (724) 537-6900
Contact: Linda McKenna Boxx, Chair.

Incorporated in 1969 in PA.
Donor(s): Katherine M. McKenna.‡
Grantmaker type: Independent foundation
Financial data (yr. ended 12/31/01): Assets,
$75,858,517 (M); expenditures, $4,290,271;
qualifying distributions, $3,796,991; giving
activities include $3,796,991 for grants.
Purpose and activities: Giving primarily for
education, the arts and cultural organizations,
philanthropy, and human services. Some
support also for environmental organizations
and community development.
Fields of interest: Arts; Higher education;
Natural resources.
Types of support: General/operating support;
Annual campaigns; Capital campaigns;
Building/renovation; Equipment; Land
acquisition; Endowments; Program
development; Seed money.
Limitations: Giving primarily in Westmoreland
County, PA. No grants to individuals; no loans.
Publications: Program policy statement.

Application information: Application form not
required.
  Initial approach: Letter
  Copies of proposal: 1
  Deadline(s): Submit proposal preferably in
    Jan. through July; deadline Oct. 1
  Board meeting date(s): Mar., June, Sept., and
    Dec.
  Final notification: 3 to 6 months
Officers and Directors:* Linda McKenna Boxx,*
Chair.; Wilma F. McKenna,* Vice-Chair.; Zan
McKenna Rich,* Secy.; T. William Boxx, Treas.
Trustee: Mellon Financial Corp.
Number of staff: 1 full-time professional; 1
part-time support.
EIN: 237042752

2884
The McLean Contributionship

945 Haverford Rd.
Bryn Mawr, PA 19010 (610) 527-6330
Contact: Sandra L. McLean, Exec. Dir.
FAX: (610) 527-9733; URL: http://fdncenter.org/
grantmaker/mclean/

Trust established in 1951 in PA.
Donor(s): William L. McLean, Jr.,‡ Robert
McLean,‡ William L. McLean III, William Clarke
Mason,‡ William L. McLean IV, Sandra McLean,
Lisa McLean, Bulletin Co., Independent
Publication, Inc.
Grantmaker type: Independent foundation
Financial data (yr. ended 12/31/02): Assets,
$42,296,548 (M); gifts received, $88,408;
expenditures, $2,487,606; qualifying
distributions, $2,308,412; giving activities
include $2,240,219 for 108 grants (high:
$100,000; low: $1,000; average:
$10,000–$50,000).
Purpose and activities: Supports understanding
and preservation of the environment,
compassionate and cost effective health care
and improving the quality of life through capital
and other projects. Trustees prefer special
projects rather than continuing programs and
focus on capital projects: bricks and mortar,
endowment, or will provide seed money for
purposes falling within the contributorship's
guidelines.
Fields of interest: Museums; Performing arts;
Historic preservation/historical societies;
Libraries/library science; Education; Natural
resources; Environmental education; Medical
research, institute; Hospitals (general); Nursing
home/convalescent facility; Health care, home
services; Youth development, services;
Children/youth, services; Aging, centers/services.
Types of support: Capital campaigns;
Building/renovation; Equipment; Land
acquisition; Endowments; Program
development; Conferences/seminars;
Publication; Seed money; Internship funds;
Scholarship funds.
Limitations: Giving primarily in southeastern PA.
No grants to individuals.
Publications: Application guidelines.
Application information: Accepts Delaware
Valley Grantmakers Common Grant
Application. Application form not required.
  Initial approach: Proposal
  Copies of proposal: 1
  Board meeting date(s): Quarterly

Officers and Trustees:* William L. McLean III,*
Chair.; William L. McLean IV,* Vice-Chair.;
Charles E. Catherwood, Treas.; Sandra L.
McLean, Exec. Dir.; Jean G. Bodine; Joseph K.
Gordon; Carolyn M. Raymond.
Advisory Committee: Leila Gordon Dyer;
Hunter R. Gordon.
Number of staff: None.
EIN: 236396940

2885
R. K. Mellon Family Foundation

P.O. Box 690
Ligonier, PA 15658-0690 (724) 238-5269
Contact: Michael Watson, Dir.

Incorporated in PA in 1978 through
consolidation of Landfall, Loyalhanna,
Rachelwood, and Cassandra Mellon Henderson
foundations.
Donor(s): Seward Prosser Mellon, Richard P.
Mellon, Constance B. Mellon,‡ Cassandra M.
Milbury.
Grantmaker type: Independent foundation
Financial data (yr. ended 12/31/02): Assets,
$32,682,211 (M); expenditures, $2,043,967;
qualifying distributions, $1,900,222; giving
activities include $1,719,595 for 67 grants (high:
$150,000; low: $500; average:
$5,000–$50,000).
Purpose and activities: Grants largely for
education, health care, social and human
services, and conservation programs.
Fields of interest: Education; Natural resources;
Health care; Human services; Public affairs.
Types of support: General/operating support;
Continuing support; Annual campaigns; Capital
campaigns; Building/renovation; Equipment;
Program development; Seed money; Research.
Limitations: Giving primarily in western PA. No
grants to individuals, or for endowment funds,
scholarships, fellowships, or matching gifts; no
loans.
Publications: Informational brochure (including
application guidelines).
Application information: Application form
required.
  Initial approach: Proposal
  Copies of proposal: 1
  Deadline(s): Submit proposal preferably Jan.
    through Mar. or July through Sept.;
    deadlines Apr. 1 and Oct. 1
  Board meeting date(s): June and Dec.
  Final notification: 1 to 6 months
Officers and Trustees:* Richard P. Mellon,*
Chair.; Scott D. Izzo, Secy.; Robert B. Burr, Jr.,*
Treas.; John Turcik, Cont.; Michael Watson, Dir.;
W. Russell G. Byers, Jr.; Catharine M. Cathey;
Richard A. Mellon; Seward Prosser Mellon.
Number of staff: 4 part-time professional; 9
part-time support.
EIN: 251356145

2886
Richard King Mellon Foundation ▼

1 Mellon Ctr.
500 Grant St., 41st Fl., Ste. 4106
Pittsburgh, PA 15219-2502 (412) 392-2800
Contact: Michael Watson, V.P.
FAX: (412) 392-2837; URL: http://fdncenter.org/
grantmaker/rkmellon

Trust established in 1947 in PA; incorporated in 1971 in PA.

Donor(s): Richard K. Mellon.‡

Grantmaker type: Independent foundation

Financial data (yr. ended 12/31/02): Assets, $1,393,565,202 (M); expenditures, $76,423,092; qualifying distributions, $69,322,864; giving activities include $61,843,303 for grants and $4,577,889 for loans/program-related investments.

Purpose and activities: Local grant programs emphasize conservation, education, families and youth, regional economic development, system reform; support also for conservation of natural areas and wildlife preservation elsewhere in the United States.

Fields of interest: Early childhood education; Education; Natural resources; Environment; Youth development, services; Human services; Children/youth, services; Family services; Urban/community development; Community development.

Types of support: General/operating support; Continuing support; Capital campaigns; Building/renovation; Equipment; Land acquisition; Program development; Seed money; Research; Program evaluation; Program-related investments/loans; Matching/challenge support.

Limitations: Giving primarily in Pittsburgh and southwestern PA, except for nationwide conservation programs. No grants outside the U.S. No grants to individuals, or for fellowships or scholarships, or conduit organizations.

Publications: Annual report (including application guidelines), Informational brochure.

Application information: Electronic requests are not accepted. Video tapes should not be sent unless specifically requested. Application form required.

Initial approach: Proposal
Copies of proposal: 1
Deadline(s): None
Board meeting date(s): Varies
Final notification: 1 to 6 months

Officers and Trustees:* Richard P. Mellon,* Chair.; Seward Prosser Mellon,* Pres.; Arthur D. Miltenberger, V.P.; Michael Watson,* V.P.; Scott D. Izzo, Secy. and Assoc. Dir.; Robert B. Burr, Jr.,* Treas.; John J. Turcik, Cont.; Lawrence S. Busch.

Number of staff: 3 full-time professional; 7 part-time professional; 1 full-time support; 14 part-time support.

EIN: 251127705

Recent environmental and animal welfare grants:

2886-1 Allegheny Conference on Community Development, Pittsburgh, PA, $200,000. For research project on wastewater and water quality in southwestern Pennsylvania. 2002.

2886-2 American Farmland Trust, DC, $100,000. For projects in Pennsylvania that prevent loss of productive farmland and promote best farming practices. 2002.

2886-3 Audubon Society, National, Harrisburg, PA, $250,000. For ecosystem-based deer management program for Commonwealth of Pennsylvania. 2002.

2886-4 Conemaugh Valley Conservancy, Apollo, PA, $225,000. For Stream Team Initiative and general operating support. 2002.

2886-5 Conservation Fund, Arlington, VA, $100,000. For summit meeting of state natural resource agency leadership. 2002.

2886-6 Foundation for California University of Pennsylvania, California, PA, $134,400. To initiate and evaluate ring-necked pheasant restoration project. 2002.

2886-7 Green Building Alliance, Pittsburgh, PA, $300,000. For programs that facilitate environmentally responsible practices in building design, construction, and operation. 2002.

2886-8 Humane Society, Western Pennsylvania, Pittsburgh, PA, $250,000. For capital campaign for new shelter. 2002.

2886-9 Loyalhanna Watershed and Environmental Association, Ligonier, PA, $150,000. Toward purchasing and preventing commercialization of Ligonier Township property. 2002.

2886-10 Mountain Watershed Association, Melcroft, PA, $116,000. For land acquisition to develop water treatment facility to address Acid Mine Drainage. 2002.

2886-11 Outside-In School of Experiential Education, Greensburg, PA, $275,000. To develop Therapeutic Activity Complex and support strategic planning. 2002.

2886-12 Pennsylvania Environmental Council, Pittsburgh, PA, $500,000. For land and water conservation projects. 2002.

2886-13 Pennsylvania Organization for Watersheds and Rivers, Harrisburg, PA, $50,000. To protect, manage, and enhance state's rivers and watersheds. 2002.

2886-14 Pennsylvanians for Responsible Use of Animals, Elizabethtown, PA, $24,000. Toward developing program to enable food banks to obtain harvested venison for distribution to needy families. 2002.

2886-15 Pittsburgh History and Landmarks Foundation, Pittsburgh, PA, $500,000. For rural preservation program encompassing farms and farmland of historic value. 2002.

2886-16 Pittsburgh Parks Conservancy, Pittsburgh, PA, $240,000. Toward establishing position of Director of Park Management and Maintenance Policies. 2002.

2886-17 Quebec-Labrador Foundation/Atlantic Center for the Environment, Ipswich, MA, $250,000. For operating support of resource conservation efforts in rural communities of northern New England. 2002.

2886-18 Riverlife Task Force, Pittsburgh, PA, $450,000. For operating support related to development of Pittsburgh's unique waterfront. 2002.

2886-19 Tides Center - Western Pennsylvania, Pittsburgh, PA, $150,000. For project designed to engage communities in river-related development. 2002.

2886-20 Tides Center - Western Pennsylvania, Pittsburgh, PA, $100,000. For Sustainable Pittsburgh's VO2 (Venture Outdoors 2002) and Ride Rack Roll projects. 2002.

2886-21 Tides Center - Western Pennsylvania, Pittsburgh, PA, $100,000. For Sustainable Pittsburgh's development of regional plan for smart growth, and related conference to address the need for regional planning. 2002.

2886-22 Tides Center - Western Pennsylvania, Pittsburgh, PA, $15,000. For Sustainable

Pittsburgh's development of strategic plan for Amenities Initiative. 2002.

2886-23 University of Pennsylvania, School of Veterinary Medicine, Philadelphia, PA, $1,000,000. Toward capital campaign to construct new teaching and research facility. 2002.

2886-24 University of Pittsburgh, Greensburg, PA, $225,000. Toward operating support for Smart Growth Partnership of Westmoreland County. 2002.

2886-25 Western Pennsylvania School for Blind Children, Pittsburgh, PA, $50,000. To create specially designed, outdoor garden for children who are blind and/or multi-disabled. 2002.

2886-26 Winnie Palmer Nature Reserve, Latrobe, PA, $500,000. For development of nature reserve. 2002.

2887
The Dorothy A. Metcalf Charitable Foundation

c/o PNC Advisors
1600 Market St., Tax Dept.
Philadelphia, PA 19103-7240

Established in 1997 in MD.

Donor(s): Dorothy A. Metcalf.

Grantmaker type: Independent foundation

Financial data (yr. ended 12/31/02): Assets, $22,460 (M); gifts received, $935,650; expenditures, $1,009,172; qualifying distributions, $1,008,603; giving activities include $1,008,000 for 31 grants (high: $350,000; low: $1,000; average: $5,000–$25,000).

Purpose and activities: Giving primarily for historic preservation, wildlife conservation, and health care.

Fields of interest: Museums; Historic preservation/historical societies; Arts; Education; Natural resources; Animal welfare; Animals/wildlife, preservation/protection; Hospitals (general); Human services; Christian agencies & churches.

Limitations: Applications not accepted. Giving on a national basis. No grants to individuals.

Application information: Contributes only to pre-selected organizations.

Trustees: Dorothy A. Metcalf; Robert A. Metcalf; John E. Mullikin.

Agent: PNC Bank, N.A.

EIN: 522053820

2888
Miller-Worley Charitable Foundation

(formerly The Richard B. Worley and Leslie A. Miller Charitable Trust)
1111 Barberry Rd.
Bryn Mawr, PA 19010 (610) 525-3778
Contact: Richard B. Worley and Leslie A. Miller, Trustees

Established in 1996 in PA.

Donor(s): Richard B. Worley.

Grantmaker type: Independent foundation

Financial data (yr. ended 09/30/02): Assets, $8,450,748 (M); expenditures, $456,258; qualifying distributions, $387,232; giving activities include $390,950 for 53 grants (high: $100,000; low: $100).

Purpose and activities: Funding primarily for education and arts and culture. Some funding also for animal welfare and wildlife preservation, and human services.
Fields of interest: Arts; Education; Animals/wildlife; Human services.
Limitations: Giving primarily in PA. No grants to individuals.
Application information: Application form not required.
  Initial approach: Letter
  Deadline(s): None
Trustees: Leslie A. Miller; Richard B. Worley.
EIN: 237862650

2889
Mudge Foundation
c/o PNC Advisors, Trust Dept.
620 Liberty Ave., 33rd Fl.
Pittsburgh, PA 15222-2719 (412) 762-4133
Contact: M. Bradley Dean, V.P.

Established in 1955 in PA.
Grantmaker type: Independent foundation
Financial data (yr. ended 12/31/02): Assets, $3,091,272 (M); expenditures, $206,707; qualifying distributions, $196,448; giving activities include $192,028 for 10 grants (high: $56,300; low: $5,000).
Purpose and activities: Giving primarily for museums, higher education, health associations, federated giving programs, and Episcopal churches.
Fields of interest: Museums; Higher education; Natural resources; Health organizations, association; Federated giving programs; Protestant agencies & churches.
Types of support: Research.
Limitations: Giving primarily in ME, PA, and TX. No grants to individuals.
Application information: Application form not required.
  Initial approach: Letter
  Deadline(s): None
Trustee: PNC Bank, N.A.
Number of staff: None.
EIN: 256023150

2890
National Philanthropic Trust
165 Township Line Rd., Ste. 150
Jenkintown, PA 19046 (215) 277-3010
Contact: Diane L. Fitzgerald, Mgr., Admin. Svcs.
Additional tel.: (888) 878-7900; FAX: (215) 277-3029; E-mail: npt@nptrust.org; URL: http:// www.nptrust.org

Established in 1996 in PA.
Grantmaker type: Public charity
Financial data (yr. ended 06/30/03): Revenue, $98,466,961; assets, $271,364,499 (M); gifts received, $92,313,219; expenditures, $83,540,154; program services expenses, $79,745,120.
Purpose and activities: The trust seeks to make giving more meaningful and effective by granting through its various funds. The fund has established donor-advised funds directly with donors and donors working in partnership with financial service companies while providing educational materials and opportunities for its

donor along with services about philanthropic interests and strategies.
Fields of interest: Arts; Education; Animal welfare; Health care.
Limitations: Applications not accepted. Giving on a national and international basis.
Application information: Contributes only to pre-selected organizations; unsolicited requests for funds not considered or acknowledged.
Officers and Trustees:* Sharon Mueller,* Chair.; Eileen R. Heisman,* Pres.; Sam McClea,* Asst. Secy.; Bruce Boucher, C.F.O.; Catherine Banat; Theodore W. Brickman, Jr.; Elizabeth Wallace Ellers; Charles B. Fancher; Robert B. Hodes; Dirk Junge; Christopher Liedel; Jim Luck; Clark D. Pitcairn.
Number of staff: 11 full-time professional; 1 part-time professional.
EIN: 237825575

2891
Nimick Forbesway Foundation
(formerly Forbesway Foundation)
1 Oxford Ctr., 20th Fl.
Pittsburgh, PA 15219 (412) 562-8879
Contact: Jack J. Kessler, Secy.-Treas.

Established in 1989 in PA.
Donor(s): Thomas H. Nimick, Jr.
Grantmaker type: Independent foundation
Financial data (yr. ended 06/30/02): Assets, $1,410,862 (M); expenditures, $135,372; qualifying distributions, $124,908; giving activities include $125,000 for 12 grants (high: $50,000; low: $1,000).
Purpose and activities: Giving primarily to museums, universities and hospitals.
Fields of interest: University; Natural resources; Hospitals (general); Health care, clinics/centers; Cancer; Cancer research.
Limitations: Applications not accepted. Giving primarily in Pittsburgh, PA. No grants to individuals.
Application information: Unsolicited requests for funds not accepted.
Officers and Directors:* Thomas H. Nimick, Jr.,* Chair.; Theresa L. Nimick,* Vice-Chair.; Jack J. Kessler,* Secy.-Treas.; Victoria Nimick Enright.
EIN: 251597437

2892
Jeffrey P. Orleans Charitable Foundation
c/o Jeffrey P. Orleans
3333 Street Rd., Ste. 101
Bensalem, PA 19020-2051

Donor(s): Jeffrey P. Orleans.
Grantmaker type: Independent foundation
Financial data (yr. ended 12/31/02): Assets, $385,105 (M); gifts received, $593,462; expenditures, $212,025; qualifying distributions, $210,983; giving activities include $209,957 for 42 grants (high: $25,000; low: $20).
Purpose and activities: Giving for art and cultural programs, education, human services, and Jewish organizations.
Fields of interest: Arts; Education; Animals/wildlife; Health organizations, association; Youth development, adult & child programs; Human services; Salvation Army; Federated giving programs; Jewish federated giving programs.

Limitations: Applications not accepted. No grants to individuals.
Application information: Contributes only to pre-selected organizations.
Trustee: Jeffrey P. Orleans.
EIN: 232870134

2893
Oxford Foundation, Inc.
125D Lancaster Ave.
Strasburg, PA 17579 (717) 687-9335
Contact: Philip L. Calhoun, Exec. Dir.
FAX: (717) 687-9336; E-mail: pcalhoun@oxfordfoundation.org; URL: http:// www.oxfordfoundation.org/

Incorporated in 1947 in DE.
Donor(s): John H. Ware III,‡ Marian S. Ware.
Grantmaker type: Independent foundation
Financial data (yr. ended 12/31/02): Assets, $60,406,110 (M); expenditures, $3,641,761; qualifying distributions, $3,446,506; giving activities include $3,250,230 for 240 grants (high: $298,571; low: $500; average: $1,000–$25,000).
Purpose and activities: Emphasis on human services health and health-related research; support also for higher education, early childhood issues, and environmental conservation.
Fields of interest: Historic preservation/historical societies; Higher education; Natural resources; Medical research, institute; Safety/disasters; Human services; Children/youth, services; Child development, services.
Types of support: General/operating support; Annual campaigns; Capital campaigns; Building/renovation; Land acquisition; Endowments; Program development; Conferences/seminars; Professorships; Scholarship funds; Research; Technical assistance; Matching/challenge support.
Limitations: Giving primarily in Lanaster and Chester counties, PA. No grants to individuals, or for scholarships; no loans.
Publications: Application guidelines, Financial statement, Grants list, Occasional report.
Application information: See foundation Web site for application details. Application form not required.
  Initial approach: 1-page Letter
  Copies of proposal: 1
  Deadline(s): Sept. 30
  Board meeting date(s): Quarterly
  Final notification: Letter of approval or denial is sent
Officers and Trustees:* Paul W. Ware,* Chair. and Pres.; John H. Ware IV,* V.P.; Marilyn W. Ware,* Secy.; Carol W. Gates,* Treas.; Philip L. Calhoun, Exec. Dir.; Marian S. Ware, Emeritus Tr.
Number of staff: 2 full-time professional.
EIN: 236278067
Recent environmental and animal welfare grants:
2893-1 American Farmland Trust, DC, $10,000. For educational programs. 2002.
2893-2 Canine Partners for Life, Cochranville, PA, $50,000. For general operating support. 2002.
2893-3 Conservation Fund, Arlington, VA, $100,000. For challenge grant. 2002.
2893-4 Gorilla Foundation, Woodside, CA, $10,000. For general support. 2002.

2893-5 Keystone Center, Keystone, CO, $25,000. For awards dinner. 2002.

2893-6 National Parks Conservation Association, DC, $20,000. For Valley Forge National Historic Park. 2002.

2893-7 Russell Byers Charter School, Philadelphia, PA, $50,000. For Expeditionary Learning Outboard Overview Program. 2002.

2893-8 Strategies for the Global Environment, Arlington, VA, $50,000. For general operating support. 2002.

2893-9 Stroud Water Research Center, Avondale, PA, $10,000. For capital campaign. 2002.

2893-10 Stroud Water Research Center, Avondale, PA, $10,000. For general operating support. 2002.

2893-11 United Disabilities Services, Lancaster, PA, $10,000. For New Life Assistance Dogs program. 2002.

2893-12 Zoological Society of Philadelphia, Philadelphia, PA, $75,000. For Children's Zoo. 2002.

2894
PECO Energy Company Contributions Program

2301 Market St., 7th Fl.
Philadelphia, PA 19103   (215) 841-4393
Contact: Anne Baker, Mgr., Corp. Sponsorship Progs. and Devel.; or Patricia A. Payne, Specialist
FAX: (215) 841-4040; Additional FAX: (215) 841-1614

Grantmaker type: Corporate giving program
Purpose and activities: PECO makes charitable contributions to nonprofit organizations involved with arts and culture, education, the environment, health and human services, disease, crime, economic development, public affairs, disabled people, and senior citizens. Support is given primarily in areas of company operations.
Fields of interest: Cultural/ethnic awareness; Arts; Higher education; Education; Environment; Health care; Health organizations; Crime/law enforcement; Human services; Economic development; Public affairs; Disabled; Aging.
Types of support: General/operating support; Continuing support; Capital campaigns; Emergency funds; Program development; Scholarship funds; Employee volunteer services; Sponsorships; Donated equipment; In-kind gifts.
Limitations: Giving primarily in areas of company operations, particularly Philadelphia, PA. No support for political organizations, lobbying organizations, or individual neighborhood sports teams. No grants to individuals, or for operating budgets, salaries, or political campaigns.
Publications: Corporate giving report (including application guidelines).
Application information: The Corporate and Public Affairs Department handles giving. The company has a staff that only handles contributions. Application form not required.
Initial approach: Proposal to headquarters
Copies of proposal: 1
Deadline(s): None
Final notification: 1 to 2 months
Number of staff: 2 full-time professional; 1 full-time support.

2895
The William Penn Foundation ▼

2 Logan Sq., 11th Fl.
100 N. 18th St.
Philadelphia, PA 19103-2757   (215) 988-1830
Contact: Kathryn Engebretson, Pres.
FAX: (215) 988-1823; E-mail: moreinfo@williampennfoundation.org; URL: http://www.williampennfoundation.org

Incorporated in 1945 in DE.
Donor(s): Otto Haas,‡ Phoebe W. Haas,‡ Otto Haas & Phoebe W. Haas Charitable Trusts.
Grantmaker type: Independent foundation
Financial data (yr. ended 12/31/02): Assets, $904,488,083 (M); gifts received, $15,543,570; expenditures, $72,927,193; qualifying distributions, $64,676,176; giving activities include $63,726,388 for grants and $949,788 for employee matching gifts.
Purpose and activities: The foundation strives to improve the quality of life in the Philadelphia region through efforts that foster rich cultural expression, strengthen children's futures, and deepen connections to nature and community.
Fields of interest: Multipurpose centers/programs; Performing arts; Historic preservation/historical societies; Arts; Child development, education; Elementary school/education; Secondary school/education; Elementary/secondary school reform; Natural resources; Environment, beautification programs; Environment; Youth development; Human services; Children/youth, services; Child development, services; Family services; Community development, neighborhood development; Community development, neighborhood associations; Urban/community development; Economically disadvantaged.
Types of support: General/operating support; Capital campaigns; Building/renovation; Equipment; Land acquisition; Program development; Seed money; Technical assistance; Employee matching gifts; Matching/challenge support.
Limitations: Giving limited to the six-county greater Philadelphia region: Camden County, NJ and Philadelphia, Bucks, Chester, Delaware, and Montgomery counties, PA; environmental giving in expanded region including portions of the Delaware, Schuykill, and Chesapeake Bay watersheds in DE, MD, NJ, and PA. No support for sectarian religious activities, recreational programs, political lobbying or legislative activities, nonpublic schools, pass-through organizations, mental health or retardation treatment programs, or programs focusing on a particular disease, disability, or treatment for addiction, or profit-making enterprises; no support for private foundations. No grants to individuals, or for debt reduction, hospital capital projects, medical research, programs that replace lost government support, housing construction or rehabilitation, scholarships, or fellowships; no loans (except for program-related investments).
Publications: Annual report.
Application information: See foundation's Web site for application instructions and proposal outline. Application form not required.
Initial approach: Letter of inquiry (for Children, Youth and Families); and phone call to Prog. Dir. (for Arts and Culture, and Environment and Communities)

Copies of proposal: 1
Deadline(s): None
Board meeting date(s): Four times per year
Final notification: 3 to 6 months
Officers and Directors:* David W. Haas,* Chair.; Frederick R. Haas,* Vice-Chair. and Secy.; Kathryn J. Engebretson, Ph.D.,* Pres.; Louise M. Foster, C.F.O.; Carol R. Collier; Joseph A. Dworetzky; Nancy B. Haas; Robert E. Hanrahan, Jr.; Ernest E. Jones; Thomas M. McKenna; John P. Mulroney; Hon. Anthony Scirica; Lise Yasui.
Number of staff: 17 full-time professional; 1 part-time professional; 7 full-time support.
EIN: 231503488
Recent environmental and animal welfare grants:

2895-1 Academy of Natural Sciences of Philadelphia, Patrick Center for Environmental Research, Philadelphia, PA, $74,800. Toward development of assessment framework to collect data on important characteristics of restoration projects and to provide basis for evaluating outcomes. 2002.

2895-2 American Littoral Society, Highlands, NJ, $264,000. Toward research and advocacy to advance coastal protection in New Jersey, and toward development of plan for coastal sanctuaries. 2002.

2895-3 American Rivers, DC, $68,750. Toward technical assistance and other guidance to individual dam removal efforts within Delaware River watershed. 2002.

2895-4 Berks County Conservancy, Reading, PA, $605,000. Toward implementing watershed planning projects within Schuylkill River watershed and providing technical assistance to municipalities on smart growth and land use planning issues in Berks County. 2002.

2895-5 Brandywine Conservancy, Environmental Management Center, Chadds Ford, PA, $81,400. Toward completion of scientific studies of Upper East Branch of Brandywine River, to improve understanding of biodiversity, stream flow, groundwater, and stream morphology, for inclusion in water conservation plan. 2002.

2895-6 Camden City Garden Club, Camden, NJ, $82,500. Toward increasing capacity of community greening programs. 2002.

2895-7 Center City District, Philadelphia, PA, $82,500. For planning phase of Center City Green, initiative to consolidate management of open space in Center City Philadelphia in collaboration with Pennsylvania Horticultural Society. 2002.

2895-8 Citizens for Pennsylvanias Future, Harrisburg, PA, $660,000. Toward expansion of PennFutures public policy and technical assistance programs in southeastern Pennsylvania to improve public and private stewardship of watersheds. 2002.

2895-9 Citizens for Pennsylvanias Future, Harrisburg, PA, $43,000. Toward development and implementation of education and outreach program to build voter support for public funding of Growing Greener program. 2002.

2895-10 Clean Ocean Action, Highlands, NJ, $220,000. Toward research and advocacy to advance protection of New Jersey's coastal waters, and toward expanded outreach and education in southern New Jersey. 2002.

2895-11 Clean Water Fund, Philadelphia, PA, $191,400. Toward technical assistance and public education to facilitate implementing recommendations of Schuylkill River Source Water Assessment and Protection report to protect and restore drinking water sources and watersheds in southeastern Pennsylvania. 2002.

2895-12 Collins Center for Public Policy, Miami, FL, $50,000. To Funders' Network for Smart Growth and Livable Communities, providing outreach and education to funders in Greater Philadelphia region. 2002.

2895-13 Conservation Fund, Arlington, VA, $253,000. For re-grant program designed to facilitate implementation of watershed plans and stewardship projects within Pinelands and Delaware River and Barnegat Bay watersheds. 2002.

2895-14 Delaware Valley Regional Planning Commission, Philadelphia, PA, $56,100. Toward developing measurable indicators to track progress in Foundation's Environment and Communities program. 2002.

2895-15 Earth Force, Wyncote, PA, $269,500. Toward building organizational capacity to deliver high quality programs that are policy oriented, have action outcomes, and promote youth development. 2002.

2895-16 Energy Coordinating Agency of Philadelphia, Philadelphia, PA, $165,000. Toward implementation of energy efficient home and nonprofit facility improvements in targeted low- and moderate-income neighborhoods in Philadelphia. 2002.

2895-17 Friends of Philadelphia Parks, Philadelphia, PA, $77,000. Toward building and strengthening citywide constituency for Philadelphia parks. 2002.

2895-18 Friends of the Pennypack, Philadelphia, PA, $29,920. Toward forest recovery monitoring program in Wissahickon and Pennypack parks in Philadelphia. 2002.

2895-19 Friends of the Wissahickon, Philadelphia, PA, $275,000. To build capacity from primarily volunteer to staffed organization in order to restore and preserve Wissahickon Valley in Fairmount Park. 2002.

2895-20 Glen Foerd Conservation Corporation, Philadelphia, PA, $11,000. Toward consultancy to facilitate development of strategic plan. 2002.

2895-21 Hawk Mountain Sanctuary Association, Kempton, PA, $165,000. Toward increasing land holdings for watershed and wildlife protection. 2002.

2895-22 Heritage Conservancy, Doylestown, PA, $495,000. Toward implementation of conservation plans in Cooks Creek watershed, Quakertown Swamp, and Forks of Neshaminy. 2002.

2895-23 Heritage Conservancy, Doylestown, PA, $300,000. Toward protection through acquisition of critical landscapes in Cooks Creek watershed, Quakertown Swamp, and Forks of Neshaminy. 2002.

2895-24 Isles, Trenton, NJ, $143,000. Toward completing study of socioeconomic disparities and development patterns in New Jersey and organizing coalitions to foster smart growth in urban centers and suburbs. 2002.

2895-25 Jenkins Arboretum, Friends of the, Devon, PA, $49,500. Toward increasing and diversifying operating income. 2002.

2895-26 John Bartram Association, Philadelphia, PA, $275,000. Toward improved organizational capacity through construction of administrative offices and enhanced facilities for local community residents and volunteers. 2002.

2895-27 Lancaster Farmland Trust, Lancaster, PA, $150,000. Toward protection through acquisition of prime agricultural land in Lancaster County. 2002.

2895-28 Lancaster Farmland Trust, Lancaster, PA, $66,000. For program work associated with protection of prime agricultural land in Lancaster County. 2002.

2895-29 Land Trust Alliance, DC, $234,300. Toward expanding technical and financial assistance program to build capacity of Pennsylvania land trusts, in collaboration with Pennsylvania Land Trust Association and toward assistance in updating PALTA's strategic plan. 2002.

2895-30 League of Conservation Voters Education Fund, DC, $77,000. Toward building capacity of Pennsylvania field office to expand its programs in southeastern Pennsylvania. 2002.

2895-31 Montgomery County Land Trust, Lederach, PA, $121,000. Toward strengthening capacity to promote smart growth and protect key watershed and greenway lands in Montgomery County, Pennsylvania. 2002.

2895-32 Natural Lands Trust, Media, PA, $300,000. Toward protection through acquisition of regionally significant lands in Pennsylvania Highlands and Delaware River watershed. 2002.

2895-33 Nature Conservancy, Pennsylvania Field Office, Conshohocken, PA, $82,500. Toward Delaware River Invasive Plant Partnership, to increase partner participation and improve planning and implementation. 2002.

2895-34 Neighborhood Gardens, Philadelphia, PA, $38,500. Toward assisting community land trusts in Philadelphia to implement management and improvement plans. 2002.

2895-35 New Jersey Future, Trenton, NJ, $385,000. Toward research, coalition building and advocacy to promote implementation of smart growth policies and systems in New Jersey. 2002.

2895-36 Ocean Conservancy, DC, $82,500. For expansion of grassroots International Coastal Cleanup efforts in Pennsylvania, Delaware and New Jersey. 2002.

2895-37 Partnership for the Delaware Estuary, Wilmington, DE, $330,000. Toward tracking and implementing habitat restoration projects and engaging corporations and businesses in watershed stewardship in Delaware Estuary. 2002.

2895-38 Pennsylvania Economy League, Philadelphia, PA, $165,000. Toward publication of Greater Philadelphia Regional Review, and presentation of smart growth policy forums in Greater Philadelphia. 2002.

2895-39 Pennsylvania Economy League, Philadelphia, PA, $55,000. Toward increasing public awareness of smart growth issues

through IssuesPA e-panel and other communication projects. 2002.

2895-40 Pennsylvania Environmental Council, Harrisburg, PA, $1,265,000. Toward work in southeastern Pennsylvania involving watershed conservation and education, transit-oriented development, GreenSpace Alliance, and North Delaware riverfront. 2002.

2895-41 Pennsylvania Horticultural Society, Philadelphia, PA, $2,000,000. Toward implementation of Philadelphia Greens Green City Strategy, to enhance stewardship of city's key transit corridors, parks, and community-managed open spaces. 2002.

2895-42 Pennsylvania Horticultural Society, Philadelphia, PA, $75,000. Toward development and implementation of Management Information/Decision Support System. 2002.

2895-43 Pennsylvania Land Trust Association, Harrisburg, PA, $150,000. Toward building capacity to expand technical assistance and policy programs. 2002.

2895-44 Pennsylvania Organization for Watersheds and Rivers, Harrisburg, PA, $110,000. Toward building capacity and expanding programs to southeastern Pennsylvania. 2002.

2895-45 Pennypack Ecological Restoration Trust, Huntingdon Valley, PA, $110,000. For challenge grant toward natural resource area master plan to guide protection and restoration of central Pennypack Creek valley, tributary of Delaware River flowing through eastern Montgomery County and Philadelphia. 2002.

2895-46 Pinelands Preservation Alliance, Pemberton, NJ, $264,000. Toward advocacy and public education to advance ecosystem-based land use planning for protection of water resources and threatened ecologically important forest areas. 2002.

2895-47 Project USE-Urban Suburban Environments, Red Bank, NJ, $74,250. Toward expansion of environmental service-learning program into Camden, Gloucester, and Atlantic Counties, providing opportunities to participate in hands-on and policy projects. 2002.

2895-48 Schuylkill Canal Association, Oaks, PA, $66,000. Toward salary of executive director to enhance project implementation and fundraising capacity. 2002.

2895-49 Stony Brook-Millstone Watershed Association, Pennington, NJ, $350,000. For completing, field testing, and documenting model watershed planning program. 2002.

2895-50 Stony Brook-Millstone Watershed Association, Pennington, NJ, $80,300. Toward assessment and report with recommendations on State of New Jersey's watershed management rules. 2002.

2895-51 Temple University, Philadelphia, PA, $330,000. Toward study assessing stormwater and nonpoint source pollution in Pennypack Creek watershed at Ambler College Center for Sustainable Communities. 2002.

2895-52 Ten Thousand Friends of Pennsylvania, Philadelphia, PA, $660,000. Toward efforts to promote implementation of smart growth policies and systems in Pennsylvania, and to build organizational capacity. 2002.

2895-53 Willistown Conservation Trust, Newtown Square, PA, $264,000. Toward building organizational capacity to preserve critical watershed land through planning, acquisition, and easements in Crum, Ridley, and Darby Creek watersheds. 2002.

2895-54 Zoological Society of Philadelphia, Philadelphia, PA, $4,000,000. Toward implementing Strategic Master Plan, strengthening zoo as cultural, education, and environmental institution through creation of new Children's Zoo, Aviary, and Africa exhibit and renovations to Carnivora House. 2002.

2896
The Pennsylvania Fund

100 Four Falls Corp. Ctr., Ste. 205
West Conshohocken, PA   19428
(610) 397-0880
Contact: Peter C. Morse, Tr.

Donor(s): Martha F. Morse, Peter C. Morse.
Grantmaker type: Independent foundation
Financial data (yr. ended 06/30/02): Assets, $795,255 (M); expenditures, $444,374; qualifying distributions, $440,291; giving activities include $440,450 for 41 grants (high: $106,000; low: $500).
Fields of interest: Natural resources; Human services; Christian agencies & churches.
Limitations: Giving primarily in PA. No grants to individuals.
Application information: Generally contributes to pre-selected organizations.
Initial approach: Letter
Deadline(s): None
Trustees: Martha F. Morse; Peter C. Morse.
EIN: 232222176

2897
The Peoples Natural Gas Company
Contributions Program

625 Liberty Ave.
Pittsburgh, PA   15222-3197   (412) 471-5100
Contact: Fran Toohill, Mgr., Community Affairs

Grantmaker type: Corporate giving program
Purpose and activities: Peoples Natural Gas makes charitable contributions to nonprofit organizations involved with education, the environment, health and human services, and community development. Support is limited to Louisiana, New York, North Carolina, Ohio, Pennsylvania, Virginia, and West Virginia.
Fields of interest: Education; Environment; Health care; Human services; Economic development; Community development.
Types of support: General/operating support; Scholarship funds; Employee volunteer services; Employee matching gifts; In-kind gifts.
Limitations: Giving limited to LA, NY, NC, OH, PA, VA, and WV.
Application information: Application form not required.
Initial approach: Proposal to headquarters
Copies of proposal: 1
Final notification: Following review

2898
The Pew Charitable Trusts ▼

1 Commerce Sq.
2005 Market St., Ste. 1700
Philadelphia, PA   19103-7077   (215) 575-9050
Contact: Rebecca W. Rimel, C.E.O. and Pres.
FAX: (215) 575-4939; E-mail: info@pewtrusts.com; URL: http://www.pewtrusts.com

Pew Memorial Trust, J.N. Pew, Jr. Charitable Trust, J. Howard Pew Freedom Trust, Mabel Pew Myrin Trust, Medical Trust, Knollbrook Trust, and Mary Anderson Trust established in 1948, 1956, 1957, 1957, 1979, 1965, and 1957 respectively.
Donor(s): Mary Ethel Pew,‡ Mabel Pew Myrin,‡ J. Howard Pew,‡ Joseph N. Pew, Jr.‡
Grantmaker type: Public charity
Financial data (yr. ended 12/31/02): Assets, $3,753,638,080 (M); expenditures, $264,362,973; program services expenses, $264,362,973; giving activities include $238,151,626 for grants and $383,196 for 649 employee matching gifts.
Purpose and activities: The Pew Charitable Trusts support nonprofit activities in the areas of culture, education, the environment, health and human services, public policy and religion. Based in Philadelphia, the trusts make strategic investments to help organizations and citizens develop practical solutions to difficult problems.
Fields of interest: Journalism/publishing; Visual arts; Museums; Performing arts; Dance; Theater; Music; Humanities; Historic preservation/historical societies; Arts; Education, research; Child development, education; Education; Natural resources; Energy; Environment; Animals/wildlife, preservation/protection; Public health; Health care; Biomedicine; Employment; Housing/shelter, development; Safety/disasters; Youth development, services; Youth development, citizenship; Human services; Children/youth, services; Child development, services; Family services; Aging, centers/services; Minorities/immigrants, centers/services; Homeless, human services; Civil rights; Urban/community development; Rural development; Community development; Voluntarism promotion; Biological sciences; Science; Social sciences; Government/public administration; Public affairs, election regulation; Public affairs, citizen participation; Leadership development; Public affairs; Religion, research; Christian agencies & churches; Protestant agencies & churches; Religion; Minorities; Immigrants/refugees; Economically disadvantaged; Homeless.
Types of support: General/operating support; Continuing support; Program development; Conferences/seminars; Publication; Seed money; Fellowships; Internship funds; Research; Technical assistance; Program-related investments/loans; Employee matching gifts; Matching/challenge support.
Limitations: Giving on a national basis, with a special commitment to the Philadelphia, PA, region. No support for political organizations. No grants to individuals, or for endowment funds, capital campaigns, construction, equipment, deficit financing, scholarships, or fellowships (except those identified or initiated by the trusts).

Publications: Application guidelines, Grants list, Occasional report.
Application information: Contact foundation for specific guidelines and limitations or visit the trusts' Web site; applicants should not send full proposals unless requested by trustee representatives. Application form required.
Initial approach: Letter of inquiry (2 to 3 pages)
Copies of proposal: 1
Deadline(s): None
Board meeting date(s): Mar., June, Sept., and Dec.
Final notification: Approximately 4 to 6 weeks after board meetings
Officer and Board Members:* Rebecca W. Rimel,* C.E.O. and Pres.; Robert H. Campbell; Susan W. Catherwood; Thomas W. Langfitt, M.D.; Arthur E. Pew III; J. Howard Pew II; J.N. Pew III; Joseph N. Pew IV, M.D.; Mary Catherine Pew, M.D.; R. Anderson Pew; Richard F. Pew; Robert G. Williams.
Trustee: The Glenmede Trust Co.
Number of staff: 80 full-time professional; 3 part-time professional; 58 full-time support; 3 part-time support.
EIN: 562307147
Recent environmental and animal welfare grants:

2898-1 American Littoral Society, Highlands, NJ, $331,000. To reverse decline of U.S. fish stocks through effective and strategic conservation advocacy that promotes adoption of improved fishery management plans by regional councils and National Marine Fisheries Service. 2002.

2898-2 American Littoral Society, Marine Fish Conservation Network, Highlands, NJ, $539,000. To expand participation of conservation-minded fishermen in deliberations of regional fishery management councils and in public education efforts within their own communities. 2002.

2898-3 Barnes Foundation, Merion, PA, $1,000,000. For general operating support. 2002.

2898-4 Barnes Foundation, Merion, PA, $500,000. For Phase II of Collections Assessment Project in collaboration with Henry Luce Foundation and Andrew Mellon Foundation. 2002.

2898-5 Barnes Foundation, Merion, PA, $500,000. For specialized technical assistance. 2002.

2898-6 Barnes Foundation, Merion, PA, $350,000. For specialized technical assistance. 2002.

2898-7 Border WaterWorks, Santa Fe, NM, $1,225,000. For final grant to help communities along United States-Mexico border resolve public health and environmental problems related to lack of water and wastewater systems. 2002.

2898-8 Brandywine Conservancy, Chadds Ford, PA, $300,000. For Brandywine River Museum's expansion and renovation project. 2002.

2898-9 Center for Agricultural Partnerships, Asheville, NC, $200,000. To inform and facilitate development of federal programs to reduce environmental and human health risks from pesticide use in agriculture. 2002.

2898-10 Center for Resource Economics/Island Press, DC, $573,000. To produce, disseminate and promote signature series of high-quality research by world-class scientists in support of conservation advocacy. 2002.

2898-11 Conservation Law Foundation, Boston, MA, $200,000. To improve fish stock and protect habitat areas essential to fish development in New England. 2002.

2898-12 Conservation Law Foundation, Boston, MA, $100,000. To build public support for designation of marine protected areas in Gulf of Maine. 2002.

2898-13 Consultative Group on Biological Diversity, San Francisco, CA, $70,000. For continued support to create partnerships among foundations and other nonprofits to strategically address loss of biodiversity. 2002.

2898-14 Ducks Unlimited, Memphis, TN, $4,500,000. For scientifically based, public education campaign supporting permanent protection of wilderness in Canadian boreal forest. 2002.

2898-15 Earthjustice Legal Defense Fund, Oakland, CA, $5,500,000. For American Wilderness Campaign, to coordinate and support public education initiatives to enhance wilderness protection efforts in five states. 2002.

2898-16 Environment Northeast, Hallowell, ME, $150,000. To continue support for Connecticut Green Power Market Project to develop and implement model green power market development project. 2002.

2898-17 Florida State University Research Foundation, Department of Biological Science, Tallahassee, FL, $240,000. To assess impact of recreational fishing on marine stocks of economic importance in United States. 2002.

2898-18 National Environmental Trust, DC, $3,000,000. For general operating support. 2002.

2898-19 National Parks Conservation Association, DC, $1,400,000. For continued support for comprehensive public education effort demonstrating need for increased funding for national park system and for conservation and visitor interpretation programs in national parks. 2002.

2898-20 Natural Resources Council, Augusta, ME, $450,000. To restore Penobscot River system to Atlantic salmon, American shad and other anadromous fish species. 2002.

2898-21 New England Aquarium Corporation, Boston, MA, $1,000,000. To continue support for Pew Fellows Program in Marine Conservation. 2002.

2898-22 New England Aquarium Corporation, Boston, MA, $230,000. For administrative expenses to operate Pew Fellows Program. 2002.

2898-23 Oceana, DC, $4,500,000. For efforts to stop destruction of marine life by curtailing use of destructive fishing practices, assess and reduce amount of fish and other marine life destroyed in pursuit of target species, and reduce ocean pollution. 2002.

2898-24 Pace University, New York, NY, $4,500,000. For efforts to reduce harmful air emissions from nation's power plants. 2002.

2898-25 Pennsylvania Horticultural Society, Philadelphia, PA, $900,000. For general support of Philadelphia Green, which provides leadership in community-greening activities in Philadelphia's low-income neighborhoods and improves landscapes of Philadelphia's landmarks and gateways. 2002.

2898-26 Research Foundation of the State University of New York, Albany, NY, $140,000. To develop plan for communicating findings of pending scientific study. 2002.

2898-27 Save Our Wild Salmon Coalition, Seattle, WA, $1,000,000. To restore salmon populations in Snake/Columbia Rivers through partial removal of dams. 2002.

2898-28 Stanford University, Stanford, CA, $163,000. To undertake comprehensive analysis of management council structure and recommend changes based on that analysis. 2002.

2898-29 Strategies for the Global Environment, Arlington, VA, $4,000,000. For Pew Center on Global Climate Change to educate public and policy makers on climate change, and to encourage domestic and international efforts to reduce emissions of greenhouse gases. 2002.

2898-30 Trout Unlimited, Arlington, VA, $1,250,000. For national alliance of hunters and fishermen working to protect fish and wildlife populations on federal public lands. 2002.

2898-31 Union of Concerned Scientists, Cambridge, MA, $1,000,000. For efforts to increase nation's commitment to energy efficiency and renewable energy as cornerstone of balanced and environmentally sound energy policy. 2002.

2898-32 United Communities Southeast Philadelphia, Philadelphia, PA, $62,000. For Philadelphia Youth Environmental Leadership and Solidarity program to develop leadership and life skills among middle-school youth in Southeast Philadelphia. 2002.

2898-33 University of British Columbia, Fisheries Centre, Vancouver, Canada, $2,000,000. To apply newly developed ecological model to assess overall health of major global marine regions, with particular emphasis on ecosystem impacts of commercial fishing. 2002.

2898-34 University of British Columbia, Fisheries Centre, Vancouver, Canada, $300,000. To disseminate balanced and accurate information to public regarding results of scientific study on contaminant levels in farmed-raised and wild-caught salmon. 2002.

2898-35 Wildlife Conservation Society, Bronx, NY, $427,000. To assemble team of scientists and independent fisheries managers to develop ecosystem-based methodology for managing fisheries. 2002.

2898-36 World Resources Institute, DC, $250,000. To continue support for work of Green Power Market Development Group on procurement of renewable energy resources. 2002.

2899
Pollock Foundation
(formerly S. Wilson & Grace M. Pollock Foundation)
21 E. Market St., MC 402-130
York, PA 17401-1500
Contact: Heath Allen
Application address: P.O. Box 11963, Harrisburg, PA 17108-1963

Established in 1997 in PA.
Donor(s): Grace Pollock, S. Wilson Pollock.
Grantmaker type: Independent foundation
Financial data (yr. ended 04/30/02): Assets, $9,200,024 (M); expenditures, $790,475; qualifying distributions, $754,778; giving activities include $697,700 for 11 grants (high: $180,000; low: $5,000).
Purpose and activities: Giving primarily for a public library; some funding also for education and human services.
Fields of interest: Libraries (public); Education; Animals/wildlife, single organization support; Hospitals (general); Health organizations, association; Human services; Federated giving programs; Protestant agencies & churches.
Limitations: Giving primarily in PA. No grants to individuals.
Application information:
  Deadline(s): None
Directors: Heath Allen; David McLane; Douglas Pollock; Grace M. Pollock; Laureen Elizabeth Pollock.
Trustee: Allfirst.
EIN: 237889770

2900
The Price Foundation
P.O. Box 369
Indianola, PA 15051-0369
Contact: Douglas Schofield, Tr.

Established in 1993.
Donor(s): Wendell Price.
Grantmaker type: Independent foundation
Financial data (yr. ended 12/31/02): Assets, $3,956,762 (M); expenditures, $290,952; qualifying distributions, $288,755; giving activities include $275,000 for 12 grants (high: $48,000; low: $8,000).
Fields of interest: Natural resources; Family planning; AIDS research; Children/youth, services; Population studies.
Types of support: General/operating support; Program development; Research.
Limitations: Applications not accepted. Giving on a national basis. No grants to individuals.
Application information: Contributes only to pre-selected organizations.
Trustees: Wendell Price; Douglas Schofield.
Number of staff: None.
EIN: 251701024

2901
Purple Martin Conservation Association
Edinboro Univ. of PA
Edinboro, PA 16444 (814) 734-4420
Contact: James R. Hill III, Exec. Dir.
FAX: (814) 734-5803; E-mail: pmca@edinboro.edu; URL: http://www.purplemartin.org

Established in 1987 in PA.
Grantmaker type: Public charity
Financial data (yr. ended 12/31/02): Revenue, $261,011; assets, $174,374 (M); gifts received, $33,031; expenditures, $247,907; program services expenses, $169,698; giving activities include $2,500 for 1 grant to an individual.
Purpose and activities: The association is dedicated to the conservation, management, restoration and enhancement of the Purple Martin bird species.
Fields of interest: Natural resources; Animals/wildlife, bird preserves.
Types of support: Research; Grants to individuals.
Limitations: Giving on a national basis. No support for projects testing Martin House design preference; or placement of Martin housing for aesthetic or humanitarian purposes.
Application information: See Web site for application information. Application form not required.
  Copies of proposal: 5
  Deadline(s): Feb. 15
  Final notification: Mar. 15
Director and Trustees: James R. Hill III, Exec. Dir.; Kathy Aranyos; Louise Chambers; Elaine Eppinger; Mary Havican; Susan Smith; Donald B. Snyder, M.D.; William Snyder; Gene F. Sonney; Beth Zewe.
Number of staff: 4 full-time professional; 2 full-time support; 3 part-time support.
EIN: 251555430

2902
The Reidler Foundation
c/o Fleet Private Client Group
101 W. Broad St.
Hazleton, PA 18201
Contact: Diana L. James, Secy.-Treas.

Incorporated in 1944 in PA.
Donor(s): John W. Reidler,‡ Verna C. Reidler,‡ Howard D. Fegan, Ann B. Fegan.
Grantmaker type: Independent foundation
Financial data (yr. ended 10/31/02): Assets, $8,026,173 (M); gifts received, $29,985; expenditures, $534,020; qualifying distributions, $478,376; giving activities include $475,000 for 42 grants (high: $59,500; low: $500).
Fields of interest: Higher education; Environment; Health care; Human services; Youth, services; Protestant agencies & churches.
Types of support: General/operating support; Capital campaigns; Building/renovation; Endowments.
Limitations: Giving primarily in the Ashland, Hazleton, and Lehigh Valley, PA, areas. No grants to individuals.
Application information:
  Initial approach: Letter
  Deadline(s): None
  Board meeting date(s): June and Oct.
Officers and Trustees:* Ann B. Fegan,* Pres.; Robert K. Gicking,* V.P.; Diana L. James, Secy.-Treas.; Howard D. Fegan; John H. Fegan; Eugene C. Fish; Carl J. Reidler; Paul G. Reidler.
EIN: 246022888

2903
The Reinvestment Fund
(also known as Delaware Valley Community Reinvestment Fund)
718 Arch St., Ste. 300 N.
Philadelphia, PA 19106-1591 (215) 925-1130
Contact: Sandra Choukroun, Dir., Investor Rels. and Comm.
FAX: (215) 923-4764; E-mail: sandra.choukroun@trfund.com; URL: http://www.trfund.com

Established in 1985 in PA.
Grantmaker type: Public charity
Financial data (yr. ended 06/30/02): Revenue, $9,599,990; assets, $86,559,714 (M); gifts received, $5,325,685; expenditures, $9,036,145; program services expenses, $8,036,608.
Purpose and activities: The fund is a regional finance corporation dedicated to building wealth and creating economic opportunity for low-wealth communities, and low and moderate income individuals through socially and environmentally responsible development. It accomplishes its mission through its financial support of affordable housing development, community facilities, small businesses, work force development programs, and energy conservation projects.
Fields of interest: Early childhood education; Natural resources; Energy; Housing/shelter, development; Community development, neighborhood development; Community development, small businesses; Community development.
Limitations: Giving primarily in New Castle County, DE, Baltimore, MD, Atlantic, Burlington, Camden, Cape May, Cumberland, Gloucester, Mercer, Middlesex, Monmouth, Ocean, and Salem counties, NJ, Berks, Bucks, Chester, Delaware, Lancaster, Lehigh, Northampton, Philadelphia, and Montgomery counties, PA.
Publications: Annual report, Informational brochure, Newsletter.
Application information:
  Initial approach: Telephone or e-mail
  Deadline(s): None
Officers and Directors:* John K. Ball,* Chair.; Martha Van Cleve,* Vice-Chair.; Jeremy Nowek,* Pres. and C.E.O.; D.L. Wormley,* Secy.; Andrea R. Allon; Robert L. Archie, Jr.; Lawrence H. Berger; Lee A. Casper; Dennis H. Courtright; Joseph Cozza; Scott Jenkins; Robert E. Keith, Jr.; Steve Lazin; and 11 additional directors.
Number of staff: 39 full-time professional; 2 part-time professional; 15 full-time support.
EIN: 232331946

2904
Ralph & Suzanne Roberts Foundation
c/o Comcast Corp.
1500 Market St., 35th Fl.
Philadelphia, PA 19102-4735

Established in 1963.
Donor(s): Ralph J. Roberts, Suzanne F. Roberts.
Grantmaker type: Independent foundation
Financial data (yr. ended 11/30/00): Assets, $20,391,968 (M); expenditures, $1,141,467;

qualifying distributions, $989,650; giving activities include $1,018,349 for grants.
Fields of interest: Museums; Music; Higher education; Natural resources; Human services.
Limitations: Applications not accepted. Giving primarily in PA. No grants to individuals.
Application information: Grants initiated by trustees.
Trustees: Ralph J. Roberts; Suzanne F. Roberts.
EIN: 237015984

2905
Donald & Sylvia Robinson Family Foundation
6507 Wilkins Ave.
Pittsburgh, PA 15217 (412) 661-1200
Contact: Donald M. Robinson, Pres.
FAX: (412) 661-4645

Established in 1970.
Grantmaker type: Independent foundation
Financial data (yr. ended 10/31/02): Assets, $2,911,019 (M); expenditures, $205,891; qualifying distributions, $202,594; giving activities include $201,673 for 195 grants (high: $20,000; low: $18).
Fields of interest: Visual arts; Performing arts; Arts; Natural resources; Environment; Animals/wildlife, preservation/protection; Family planning; Eye diseases; Eye research; Food services; Human services; Arms control; Jewish federated giving programs.
International interests: Israel.
Types of support: General/operating support; Annual campaigns; Capital campaigns; Building/renovation; Emergency funds.
Limitations: Giving on a national basis. No grants to individuals.
Application information: Application form not required.
  Copies of proposal: 1
  Deadline(s): None
Officers and Trustees:* Donald M. Robinson,* Pres.; Sylvia Robinson,* V.P.; Carol L. Robinson; Stephen G. Robinson.
Number of staff: None.
EIN: 237062017

2906
The Rockwell Foundation
c/o PNC Advisors, P2-PTPP-25-1
620 Liberty Ave., 2 PNC Plz.
Pittsburgh, PA 15222-2719 (412) 762-5182
Contact: Bea Lynch, Asst. V.P.

Trust established in 1956 in PA.
Donor(s): Willard F. Rockwell,‡ and family.
Grantmaker type: Independent foundation
Financial data (yr. ended 12/31/02): Assets, $10,873,007 (M); expenditures, $630,440; qualifying distributions, $592,479; giving activities include $577,300 for grants.
Purpose and activities: Giving primarily for higher and secondary education; support also for the fine and performing arts, museums, music and dance organizations, child welfare and family services, conservation, hospitals and health agencies, including drug abuse programs, cancer research, mental illness and hospices, biology, science and technology, historic preservation, and religion.

Fields of interest: Museums; Performing arts; Dance; Music; Historic preservation/historical societies; Arts; Secondary school/education; Higher education; Education; Natural resources; Hospitals (general); Health care; Substance abuse, services; Mental health/crisis services; Health organizations, association; Cancer; Cancer research; Children/youth, services; Family services; Hospices; Engineering/technology; Biological sciences; Science; Religion; Disabled.
Types of support: General/operating support; Continuing support; Annual campaigns; Capital campaigns; Building/renovation; Equipment; Endowments; Seed money; Scholarship funds; Matching/challenge support.
Limitations: Giving primarily in PA. No grants to individuals, or for fellowships; no loans.
Application information: Application form not required.
  Initial approach: Letter or telephone
  Copies of proposal: 1
  Deadline(s): Nov. 1
  Board meeting date(s): As required
Officer and Trustees:* H. Campbell Stuckeman,* Secy.; George Peter Rockwell; Russell A. Rockwell; PNC Bank, N.A.
Number of staff: None.
EIN: 256035975

2907
The Roemer Foundation
(formerly Mary Alice Dorrance Malone Foundation)
c/o B. Rosenfield
1600 Market St., Ste. 3600
Philadelphia, PA 19103-7286

Established in 1996 in PA.
Donor(s): Mary Alice Dorrance Malone.
Grantmaker type: Independent foundation
Financial data (yr. ended 06/30/02): Assets, $7,119,983 (M); gifts received, $50,000; expenditures, $1,084,518; qualifying distributions, $997,800; giving activities include $1,000,000 for 1 grant.
Fields of interest: Natural resources.
Limitations: Applications not accepted. Giving primarily in PA. No grants to individuals.
Application information: Contributes only to pre-selected organizations.
Directors: Mary Alice Malone; James L. McCabe.
EIN: 232870277

2908
Rohm and Haas Company Contributions Program
100 Independence Mall W.
Philadelphia, PA 19106-2399 (215) 592-3644
Contact: Alexandra Samuels, Mgr., Civic and Philanthropic Affairs
Application address in Chicago, IL: Joe Wojtonik, c/o Morton International, Inc., 123 N. Wacker Dr., Chicago, IL 60606; FAX: (215) 592-6808; E-mail: alexandra_samuels@rohmhaas.com; URL: http://www.rohmhaas.com/community/index.htm

Grantmaker type: Corporate giving program
Financial data (yr. ended 12/31/02): Total giving, $4,957,450; giving activities include $4,700,000 for grants (high: $100,000; low:

$250) and $257,450 for employee matching gifts.
Purpose and activities: Rohm and Haas makes charitable contributions to nonprofit organizations involved with arts and culture, education, the environment, health and human services, community development, and civic affairs. Support is given on a national and international basis.
Fields of interest: Arts; Education; Environment; Health care; Human services; Community development; Public affairs.
Types of support: General/operating support; Continuing support; Program development; Consulting services; Employee volunteer services; Employee matching gifts; In-kind gifts; Matching/challenge support.
Limitations: Giving on a national and international basis in areas of company operations, with emphasis on Chicago, IL, and the greater Philadelphia, PA, area. No grants to individuals, or for fundraising, testimonials, or advertising.
Publications: Application guidelines.
Application information: Requests may be submitted using the Delaware Valley Grantmakers Common Grant Application and Common Report Form. Publications are available online. The Corporate Communications Department handles giving. The company has a staff that only handles contributions. Application form required.
  Initial approach: Contact nearest company facility for application form
  Copies of proposal: 1
  Deadline(s): None
  Final notification: 2 months
Administrators: Brian McPeak, Mgr., Contribs. and Site Public Affairs; Alexandra Samuels, Mgr., Civic and Philanthropic Affairs.
Number of staff: 1 full-time professional; 1 part-time support.

2909
The Rosenlund Family Foundation
P.O. Box 297
Haverford, PA 19041
Contact: Hope Rosenlund, Managing Tr.

Established in 1962 in PA.
Donor(s): Arthur O. Rosenlund.‡
Grantmaker type: Independent foundation
Financial data (yr. ended 06/30/02): Assets, $2,779,621 (M); expenditures, $157,657; qualifying distributions, $147,804; giving activities include $145,000 for 40 grants (high: $25,000; low: $1,000).
Purpose and activities: Giving primarily for human services and the arts.
Fields of interest: Museums; Natural resources; Animal welfare; Human services; Community development, neighborhood development.
Limitations: Giving primarily in Philadelphia, PA. No support for political organizations. No grants to individuals.
Application information: Application form not required.
  Initial approach: Letter (no more than 2 pages), including list of funders
  Copies of proposal: 1
  Deadline(s): Mar.-Apr.
  Board meeting date(s): Varies

Trustees: Hope Rosenlund, Managing Tr.; April Rosenlund Ford; Alarik A. Rosenlund; Arthur O. Rosenlund, Jr.; David E. Rosenlund; Mary L. Rosenlund; Stephanie Rosenlund Shim; Kristin Turrill.
Number of staff: None.
EIN: 236243642

2910
The Ross Family Foundation
5 Overlook Rd.
Clarks Green, PA 18411 (570) 587-1365
Contact: Adrian E. Ross, Pres.

Established in 1954 in PA.
Donor(s): Adrian E. Ross, Daniel R. Ross, James A. Ross,‡ James A. Ross.
Grantmaker type: Independent foundation
Financial data (yr. ended 12/31/02): Assets, $2,870,425 (M); gifts received, $24,915; expenditures, $190,117; qualifying distributions, $183,610; giving activities include $178,200 for 78 grants (high: $38,500; low: $100).
Fields of interest: Museums; Music; Higher education; Libraries/library science; Education; Natural resources; Children/youth, services; Federated giving programs; Christian agencies & churches.
Types of support: Annual campaigns; Capital campaigns; Endowments.
Limitations: Giving primarily in the Scranton, PA, area.
Application information:
  Initial approach: Letter
  Deadline(s): None
Officers and Trustees:* Adrian E. Ross,* Pres.; James A. Ross,* V.P.; Daniel R. Ross,* Secy.-Treas.
Number of staff: None.
EIN: 246017499

2911
Ryan Memorial Foundation
P.O. Box 426
Pittsburgh, PA 15230

Established in 1996 in PA.
Grantmaker type: Independent foundation
Financial data (yr. ended 12/31/02): Assets, $9,210,657 (M); expenditures, $594,871; qualifying distributions, $583,616; giving activities include $579,979 for 51 grants (high: $101,367; low: $500).
Fields of interest: Opera; Music (choral); Multipurpose centers/programs; Ballet; Orchestra (symphony); Literature; Secondary school/education; Higher education; Zoos/zoological societies; Hospitals (general); Hospitals (specialty); Youth development, business; Residential/custodial care; International affairs; Federated giving programs; Roman Catholic agencies & churches.
Limitations: Applications not accepted. Giving primarily in PA. No grants to individuals.
Application information: Contributes only to pre-selected organizations.
Trustees: Julia Ryan Parker; Daniel H. Ryan; John T. Ryan III; Mary Irene Ryan; Michael Denis Ryan; William F. Ryan; Irene R. Shaw.
EIN: 251781266

2912
Sansom-Eligator Foundation
105 Fairway Ln.
Pittsburgh, PA 15238

Established in 1996 in PA.
Donor(s): Robert D. Sansom.
Grantmaker type: Independent foundation
Financial data (yr. ended 12/31/00): Assets,
$9,314,695 (M); gifts received, $993,713;
expenditures, $292,605; qualifying distributions,
$200,000; giving activities include $200,000 for
2 grants of $100,000 each.
Purpose and activities: Giving primarily for
recreation centers and conservation.
Fields of interest: Natural resources; Recreation,
centers.
Limitations: Giving primarily in Pittsburgh, PA.
Officers: Robert D. Sansom, Pres.; Edith L.
Eligator, Treas.
Director: John R. Washlick.
EIN: 232870275

2913
The Scranton Area Foundation, Inc.
Bank Towers, Ste. 608
321 Spruce St.
Scranton, PA 18503-1409 (570) 347-6203
Contact: Jeanne A. Bovard, Exec. Dir.
FAX: (717) 347-7587; E-mail: safinfo@safdn.org;
URL: http://www.safdn.org

Established in 1954 in PA by resolution and
declaration of trust; reorganized in 1998.
Grantmaker type: Community foundation
Financial data (yr. ended 12/31/02): Assets,
$16,139,566 (M); gifts received, $277,265;
expenditures, $875,159; giving activities
include $359,267 for 49 grants (high: $65,000;
low: $250; average: $250–$65,000).
Purpose and activities: Encourages and helps to
build community endowment through grants for
new projects and services to address unmet
needs; provides a variety of donor services. The
foundation administers donor-advised funds.
Fields of interest: Historic
preservation/historical societies; Arts; Child
development, education; Vocational education;
Higher education; Libraries/library science;
Education; Natural resources; Health care;
Mental health/crisis services; Health
organizations, association; Youth development,
services; Human services; Children/youth,
services; Child development, services;
International human rights; Community
development; Voluntarism promotion;
Leadership development; Public affairs; Religion.
Types of support: Continuing support;
Endowments; Program development;
Conferences/seminars; Publication; Seed
money; Scholarship funds; Research; Consulting
services; Matching/challenge support.
Limitations: Giving limited to the Scranton and
Lackawanna County, PA, area. No grants for
building funds, annual campaigns, deficit
financing, or emergency funds; generally no
support for operating budgets; no loans.
Publications: Application guidelines, Annual
report, Grants list, Informational brochure,
Informational brochure (including application
guidelines), Newsletter, Occasional report.
Application information: Application form
required.

Initial approach: Letter or telephone
Copies of proposal: 1
Deadline(s): None
Board meeting date(s): Jan., Apr., July, Oct.
and Dec.
Final notification: Jan., Apr., July, Oct. and
Dec.
Officers and Governors:* James W. Reid,*
Chair.; Austin J. Burke, Vice-Chair.; Kathleen
Graff,* Treas.; Jeanne A. Bovard, Exec. Dir.;
Dorrance R. Belin; James F. Bell III; Richard S.
Bishop; Eugene F. Cosgrove; Sr. Jean Coughlin,
I.H.M.; Carlene Gallo; Robert N. Lettieri;
Thomas R. Nealon; Carlon E. Preate; Letha
Reinheimer; and 9 additional Governors.
Investment Managers: PNC Bank, N.A.; Penn
Security; Smith Barney.
Number of staff: 1 full-time professional; 3
full-time support.
EIN: 232890364

2914
Sea Breeze Foundation
c/o Mellon Financial Corp.
P.O. Box 185
Pittsburgh, PA 15230-9897
Application address: c/o Richard Towle, Jr., Trust
Off., Mellon Financial Corp., 1 Boston Pl.,
Boston, MA 02108, tel.: (617) 722-7326

Established in 1997 in MA.
Grantmaker type: Independent foundation
Financial data (yr. ended 12/31/02): Assets,
$1,691,261 (M); expenditures, $112,011;
qualifying distributions, $103,469; giving
activities include $100,000 for 8 grants (high:
$25,000; low: $5,000).
Purpose and activities: Giving for educational,
environmental and medical organizations.
Fields of interest: Education; Natural resources;
Health care, research.
Types of support: General/operating support.
Limitations: Giving primarily in MA. No grants
to individuals.
Trustee: Mellon Financial Corp.
EIN: 043388014

2915
Frances C. Sharp Charitable Foundation
c/o Wachovia Bank, N.A.
P.O. Box 1102, 600 Penn St., PA 6497
Reading, PA 19603-1102
Contact: Hans F. Hass

Established in 1993 in PA.
Donor(s): Frances C. Sharp.‡
Grantmaker type: Independent foundation
Financial data (yr. ended 06/30/02): Assets,
$3,716,748 (M); expenditures, $232,912;
qualifying distributions, $203,988; giving
activities include $204,108 for 3 grants of
$68,036 each.
Purpose and activities: Giving only for spaying
and neutering animals in Lehigh and Berks
counties, PA.
Fields of interest: Animal welfare.
Limitations: Applications not accepted. Giving
limited to Berks and Lehigh counties, PA. No
grants to individuals.
Application information: Contributes only to
pre-selected organizations. Unsolicited requests
for funds not accepted.

Trustee: Wachovia Bank, N.A.
EIN: 237758537

2916
The Thomas H. and Mary Williams Shoemaker Fund
1120 Hagues Mill Rd.
Ambler, PA 19002
Contact: Carolyn R. Moon
Tel./FAX: (215) 542-1340

Established in 1953 in PA.
Donor(s): Mary Williams Shoemaker,‡ Thomas
H. Shoemaker,‡ Thomas H. and Mary Williams
Shoemaker Trust.
Grantmaker type: Independent foundation
Financial data (yr. ended 09/30/02): Assets,
$6,397,209 (M); expenditures, $296,072;
qualifying distributions, $260,842; giving
activities include $244,500 for 67 grants (high:
$20,000; low: $500).
Purpose and activities: Emphasis on religious,
charitable, and educational institutions of the
Religious Society of Friends.
Fields of interest: Education; Environment;
Human services; International peace/security;
Religious federated giving programs; Protestant
agencies & churches.
Types of support: General/operating support;
Continuing support; Capital campaigns;
Building/renovation; Endowments; Program
development; Publication; Seed money;
Curriculum development; Scholarship funds.
Limitations: Giving primarily in PA. No grants to
individuals, or for matching gifts; no loans.
Publications: Application guidelines,
Informational brochure (including application
guidelines).
Application information: Application form not
required.

Initial approach: Brief proposal and cover
letter
Copies of proposal: 6
Deadline(s): Apr. 15 and Oct. 15
Board meeting date(s): May and Nov.
Final notification: 3 weeks after meetings
Trustee: The Glenmede Trust Co.
Number of staff: 1 full-time support.
EIN: 236209783

2917
Arthur & Estelle Sidewater Foundation
c/o Lafayette Financial Svcs.
215 W. Church Rd., Ste. 108
King of Prussia, PA 19406

Established in 1990 in PA.
Donor(s): Arthur Sidewater.
Grantmaker type: Independent foundation
Financial data (yr. ended 12/31/02): Assets,
$2,969,804 (M); expenditures, $144,009;
qualifying distributions, $130,300; giving
activities include $130,300 for 21 grants (high:
$45,000; low: $100).
Fields of interest: Arts; Animals/wildlife; Health
care; Health organizations, association; Human
services; Federated giving programs; Jewish
federated giving programs; Jewish agencies &
temples.
Limitations: Applications not accepted. Giving
primarily in PA. No grants to individuals.

Application information: Contributes only to pre-selected organizations.
Officers: June Wolfson, Pres.; Stephen Wolfson, V.P. and Secy.-Treas.
EIN: 232582882

2918
The Stuart and Jill Siegel Charitable Trust
166 Tinari Ln.
Richboro, PA 18954 (215) 785-0900
Contact: Stuart Siegel, Tr.

Established in 1995 in NY.
Donor(s): Stuart Siegel.
Grantmaker type: Independent foundation
Financial data (yr. ended 12/31/01): Assets, $876,072 (M); expenditures, $103,839; qualifying distributions, $100,123; giving activities include $100,669 for 27 grants (high: $48,815; low: $25).
Fields of interest: Education; Environment; Health organizations, association; Human services; Jewish agencies & temples.
Limitations: Giving on a national basis, with some emphasis on Philadelphia, PA, and New York, NY. No grants to individuals.
Application information: Application form not required.
Deadline(s): None
Trustees: Jill Siegel; Stuart Siegel.
EIN: 113297021

2919
Snee-Reinhardt Charitable Foundation
River Park Commons 2
2425 Sidney St.
Pittsburgh, PA 15203 (412) 390-2690
Contact: Joan E. Szymanski, Fdn. Mgr.

Established in 1987 in PA.
Donor(s): Katherine E. Snee.‡
Grantmaker type: Independent foundation
Financial data (yr. ended 12/31/02): Assets, $19,833,629 (M); gifts received, $500,000; expenditures, $1,309,421; qualifying distributions, $1,186,458; giving activities include $953,846 for grants (average: $500–$25,000).
Fields of interest: Arts; Libraries/library science; Education; Environment; Health care; Substance abuse, services; Health organizations, association; Cancer; Children/youth, services; Aging, centers/services; Community development; Aging.
Types of support: Building/renovation; Equipment; Program development.
Limitations: Giving primarily in northern MD, PA (especially the southwestern region) and northeast WV. No support for sectarian or religious organizations or organizations that promote abortion or euthanasia. No grants to individuals, or for capital improvement, endowment funds, or general operating expenses.
Publications: Application guidelines, Annual report, Grants list, Informational brochure (including application guidelines).
Application information: Application form required.
Initial approach: Telephone for guidelines
Copies of proposal: 1
Deadline(s): Varies

Board meeting date(s): May, Sept., and Nov.
Final notification: 2 weeks after board meeting
Directors: Paul A. Heasley, Chair.; Virginia M. Davis; Christina R. Heasley; Karen L. Heasley; Richard T. Vail.
Trustee: PNC Bank, N.A.
Number of staff: 2 full-time support.
EIN: 256292908

2920
Sordoni Foundation, Inc.
45 Owen St.
Forty Fort, PA 18704-4305 (570) 287-3161
Contact: William B. Sordoni, Secy.-Treas., or Andrew J. Sordoni III, Pres.
FAX: (570) 288-3663

Incorporated in 1946 in PA.
Donor(s): Andrew J. Sordoni, Sr.,‡ Andrew J. Sordoni, Jr.,‡ Andrew J. Sordoni III, Mrs. Andrew J. Sordoni, Sr.,‡ Mrs. Andrew J. Sordoni, Jr.,‡ Mrs. Andrew J. Sordoni III, Helen Mary Sekera, William B. Sordoni, Margaret F. Sordoni.
Grantmaker type: Independent foundation
Financial data (yr. ended 12/31/02): Assets, $11,283,829 (M); expenditures, $509,891; qualifying distributions, $474,040; giving activities include $475,484 for 41 grants (high: $200,000; low: $250; average: $250–$60,000).
Purpose and activities: Giving is restricted regionally with emphasis on arts, culture, economic development, education, health, human services, nature and environment.
Fields of interest: Arts; Education; Environment; Health care; Human services; Economic development.
Types of support: Continuing support; Annual campaigns; Capital campaigns; Building/renovation; Equipment; Program development; Seed money.
Limitations: Giving primarily in northeastern PA. No support for organizations that receive support from governmental agencies. No grants to individuals, or for scholarships.
Application information: The foundation has discontinued the scholarships to individuals program. No new grants will be awarded. Application form not required.
Initial approach: Letter
Copies of proposal: 1
Deadline(s): None
Board meeting date(s): As required
Final notification: By letter
Officers and Directors:* Andrew J. Sordoni III,* Pres.; William B. Sordoni, Secy.-Treas.; Richard Allan; A. William Kelly; John J. Menapace; Patrick Solano; Margaret F. Sordoni; Susan F. Sordoni.
Number of staff: 1 full-time professional; 1 part-time support.
EIN: 246017505

2921
Stackpole-Hall Foundation
44 S. Saint Mary's St.
St. Marys, PA 15857-1667 (814) 834-1845
Contact: William C. Conrad, Exec. Secy.
FAX: (814) 834-1869; E-mail: stackpolehall@alltel.net

Trust established in 1951 in PA.

Donor(s): Lyle G. Hall, Sr.,‡ J. Hall Stackpole,‡ Harrison C. Stackpole,‡ Lyle G. Hall, Jr., Adelaide Stackpole.‡
Grantmaker type: Independent foundation
Financial data (yr. ended 12/31/02): Assets, $20,322,455 (M); expenditures, $1,210,625; qualifying distributions, $1,093,908; giving activities include $870,197 for 92 grants (high: $50,000; low: $200).
Purpose and activities: Support for higher and secondary education, and literacy and vocational projects; Christian agencies and churches; social services, including youth and child welfare agencies; the arts and cultural programs; health services, including mental health and drug abuse issues; and community development, including civic affairs and leadership development, conservation concerns, rural development, and voluntarism.
Fields of interest: Visual arts; Performing arts; Arts; Education, fund raising; Secondary school/education; Vocational education; Higher education; Adult/continuing education; Adult education—literacy, basic skills & GED; Libraries/library science; Reading; Education; Natural resources; Hospitals (general); Nursing care; Health care; Substance abuse, services; Mental health/crisis services; Alcoholism; Recreation; Youth development, services; Human services; Children/youth, services; Hospices; Rural development; Community development; Voluntarism promotion; Government/public administration; Leadership development; Christian agencies & churches; Disabled.
Types of support: Annual campaigns; Capital campaigns; Building/renovation; Equipment; Program development; Seed money; Matching/challenge support.
Limitations: Giving primarily in Elk County, PA. No grants to individuals, or for scholarships or fellowships; generally, no grants for operating budgets or endowment funds; no loans.
Publications: Annual report (including application guidelines).
Application information: Application form not required.
Initial approach: Letter
Copies of proposal: 1
Deadline(s): None
Board meeting date(s): Quarterly
Officers and Trustees:* Lyle G. Hall, Jr.,* Chair.; Douglas R. Dobson, Vice-Chair.; William C. Conrad, Secy.; J.M. Hamlin Johnson; Laurey Nixon; John Saalfield; Alexander Sheble-Hall; R. Dauer Stackpole; Sara-Jane Stackpole; Laurey Stackpole Turner.
Board Members: Heather Conrad; Greta Fredrickson; Cara Hall Liu; Charlotte Hall Perkins.
Number of staff: 1 full-time professional; 2 part-time support.
EIN: 256006650

2922
The Starpoint Charitable Trust
819 Church Rd.
Wayne, PA 19087
Contact: Susan Lyall, Mgr.

Established in 2000.
Donor(s): Susan Lyall.
Grantmaker type: Independent foundation

Financial data (yr. ended 06/30/01): Assets, $84,509 (M); gifts received, $386,000; expenditures, $400,050; qualifying distributions, $399,050; giving activities include $399,050 for 47 grants (high: $250,000; low: $250).
Purpose and activities: Giving primarily to a community center; as well as for education, and human services.
Fields of interest: Arts; Education; Animal welfare; Human services; Children, services; Community development, neighborhood development; Philanthropy/voluntarism.
Limitations: Giving primarily in New York, NY, and Philadelphia, PA.
Application information:
   Initial approach: Letter
   Deadline(s): None
Officer: Susan Lyall, Mgr.
EIN: 137231615

2923
Alexander Stewart, M.D. Foundation
c/o Mellon Financial Corp.
P.O. Box 185
Pittsburgh, PA 15230-9897   (215) 553-8636
Contact: Adelina Martorelli, Trust Off., Mellon Financial Corp.

Established in 1981 in PA.
Grantmaker type: Independent foundation
Financial data (yr. ended 06/30/02): Assets, $7,108,720 (M); expenditures, $437,162; qualifying distributions, $408,053; giving activities include $388,077 for 44 grants (high: $26,000; low: $1,000).
Purpose and activities: Giving primarily for human services and mental health. Support also for historical societies and libraries.
Fields of interest: Historic preservation/historical societies; Libraries/library science; Natural resources; Mental health/crisis services; Safety/disasters, volunteer services; Human services; Salvation Army; YM/YWCAs & YM/YWHAs.
Types of support: General/operating support.
Limitations: Giving limited to Shippensburg, PA, and vicinity, including Cumberland, Franklin, Fulton, and Perry counties. No grants to individuals.
Application information:
   Initial approach: Proposal
   Deadline(s): Apr. 1
Trustee: Mellon Financial Corp.
EIN: 236732616

2924
James M. and Margaret V. Stine Foundation
c/o Robert J. Weinberg
3000 2 Logan Sq.
Philadelphia, PA 19103-2799

Established in 1996 in PA.
Donor(s): James M. Stine, Margaret V. Stine.
Grantmaker type: Independent foundation
Financial data (yr. ended 12/31/02): Assets, $20,410,443 (M); expenditures, $9,729,496; qualifying distributions, $865,281; giving activities include $860,980 for 21 grants (high: $200,000; low: $1,000).

Purpose and activities: Giving primarily to Roman Catholic agencies and churches, including a medical foundation.
Fields of interest: Natural resources; Health organizations, association; Federated giving programs; Roman Catholic federated giving programs; Roman Catholic agencies & churches.
Limitations: Applications not accepted. Giving primarily in MD and PA. No grants to individuals.
Application information: Contributes only to pre-selected organizations.
Officers and Directors:* Margaret V. Stine,* Pres. and Treas.; Sarah Igler,* V.P.; Martha Lee Boyd,* Secy.; Michael Boyd; Thomas Igler; David J. Stine.
EIN: 232834787

2925
Margaret Dorrance Strawbridge Foundation of Pennsylvania I, Inc.
4000 Bell Atlantic Twr.
1717 Arch St.
Philadelphia, PA 19103-2793

Established in 1985 in PA.
Donor(s): Margaret Dorrance Strawbridge Foundation, George Strawbridge, Jr.
Grantmaker type: Independent foundation
Financial data (yr. ended 12/31/02): Assets, $9,227,324 (M); gifts received, $973,327; expenditures, $1,046,221; qualifying distributions, $935,826; giving activities include $943,450 for 16 grants (high: $290,850; low: $15,000).
Purpose and activities: Giving primarily to a museum and for higher education and medical research.
Fields of interest: Museums; Arts; Elementary/secondary education; Higher education; Natural resources; Hospitals (general); Health organizations, association; Cancer; Medical research, institute.
Limitations: Applications not accepted. Giving on a national basis. No grants to individuals, or for endowment funds.
Application information: Contributes only to pre-selected organizations.
Officers: George Strawbridge, Jr., Pres. and Secy.; Nina S. Strawbridge, V.P.
EIN: 232373081

2926
Morris W. Stroud 3rd Trust Pennswood 2
c/o The Glenmede Trust Co.
1650 Market St., Ste. 1200
Philadelphia, PA 19103-7301

Established in 1991.
Grantmaker type: Public charity
Financial data (yr. ended 06/30/01): Revenue, $439,983; assets, $9,350,490; expenditures, $429,192; program services expenses, $405,075; giving activities include $405,075 for 1 grant.
Purpose and activities: The trust exists for the sole benefit of the Stroud Water Research Center.
Fields of interest: Environment, water resources.
Limitations: Applications not accepted. Giving limited to Avondale, PA.

Application information: Contributes only to a pre-selected organization; unsolicited requests for funds not considered or acknowledged.
Trustee: The Glenmede Trust Co.
EIN: 237651476

2927
Sunoco, Inc. Corporate Giving Program
(formerly Sun Company, Inc. Corporate Giving Program)
10 Penn Ctr.
1801 Market St.
Philadelphia, PA 19103-1699   (215) 977-3000
Contact: Ed Hazzouri, Dir., Public Affairs, Delaware Valley

Grantmaker type: Corporate giving program
Purpose and activities: Sunoco makes charitable contributions to nonprofit organizations involved with arts and culture, education, the environment, health and human services, employment, employment training, economic development, and civic affairs. Support is given primarily in areas of company operations.
Fields of interest: Arts; Education; Environment; Health care; Employment, services; Employment, training; Human services; Economic development; Public affairs.
Types of support: Program development; Employee volunteer services; Sponsorships; In-kind gifts.
Limitations: Giving primarily in areas of company operations. Generally, no support for national or international organizations, religious organizations, fraternal organizations, athletic organizations, schools, colleges, or universities, or disease-specific organizations. Generally, no grants to individuals, or for debt reduction, fundraising, endowments, surveys, or studies.
Publications: Informational brochure (including application guidelines).
Application information: Multi-year funding is not automatic. Application form not required.
   Initial approach: Proposal to headquarters
   Copies of proposal: 1
   Deadline(s): None
   Final notification: Following review
Number of staff: 2.

2928
Tasty Baking Foundation
2801 Hunting Park Ave.
Philadelphia, PA 19129-1392   (215) 221-8573
Contact: Marie Mann

Established in 1955 in PA.
Donor(s): Tasty Baking Co.
Grantmaker type: Company-sponsored foundation
Financial data (yr. ended 12/31/02): Assets, $462,942 (M); gifts received, $90,000; expenditures, $89,824; qualifying distributions, $88,650; giving activities include $88,650 for 43 grants (high: $10,000; low: $100).
Purpose and activities: Giving for the arts, education, health, the disadvantaged, general welfare, and low-income housing.
Fields of interest: Museums; Performing arts; Arts; Elementary/secondary education; University; Scholarships/financial aid; Zoos/zoological societies; Hospitals (general);

Diabetes; American Red Cross; Salvation Army; YM/YWCAs & YM/YWHAs; Jewish federated giving programs.
Types of support: General/operating support.
Limitations: Giving limited to the greater Philadelphia, PA, area.
Application information: Application form required.
  Initial approach: Letter
  Copies of proposal: 1
  Deadline(s): 2 days prior to monthly meeting of trustees
  Board meeting date(s): Quarterly
Officers and Trustees:* Philip J. Baur, Jr.,* Chair.; John M. Pettine,* Secy.-Treas.; Nelson G. Harris; Charles P. Pizzi.
Number of staff: None.
EIN: 236271018

2929
Kenneth and Caroline Taylor Family Foundation
R.R. 1, Box 6B
Wyalusing, PA 18853

Established in 2000 in PA.
Donor(s): Caroline E. Taylor, Kenneth H. Taylor, Jr.
Grantmaker type: Independent foundation
Financial data (yr. ended 12/31/02): Assets, $9,778,845 (M); gifts received, $8,086,109; expenditures, $126,354; qualifying distributions, $92,853; giving activities include $92,853 for 17 grants (high: $21,500; low: $500).
Fields of interest: Higher education; Environment, land resources; Health care; Human services; Protestant agencies & churches.
Limitations: Applications not accepted. Giving primarily in PA and WY. No grants to individuals.
Application information: Contributes only to pre-selected organizations.
Trustees: Caroline E. Taylor; Kenneth H. Taylor, Jr.
EIN: 256742004

2930
Teleflex Foundation
630 W. Germantown Pike, Ste. 461
Plymouth Meeting, PA 19462 (610) 834-6378
Contact: Thelma A. Fretz, V.P.
E-mail: foundation@teleflex.com; URL: http://www.teleflex.com/foundation/guidelines.html

Established in 1980 in PA.
Donor(s): Teleflex Inc.
Grantmaker type: Company-sponsored foundation
Financial data (yr. ended 12/31/01): Assets, $3,909,362 (M); gifts received, $480,000; expenditures, $304,812; qualifying distributions, $304,812; giving activities include $281,927 for 99 grants (high: $32,200; low: $100; average: $1,000–$5,000).
Purpose and activities: Support for higher, elementary, and vocational education and literacy programs; hospitals and health, medical research, rehabilitation programs for alcohol and drug abuse, science, and technology; community funds and social services, including women and child welfare, family planning, and the handicapped; public affairs and policies; culture, especially fine and performing arts;

environmental issues; and urban and civic affairs.
Fields of interest: Visual arts; Museums; Performing arts; Dance; Theater; Music; Historic preservation/historical societies; Arts; Elementary school/education; Vocational education; Higher education; Business school/education; Engineering school/education; Adult education—literacy, basic skills & GED; Libraries/library science; Reading; Education; Natural resources; Environment; Animals/wildlife, preservation/protection; Hospitals (general); Family planning; Medical care, rehabilitation; Health care; Substance abuse, services; Mental health/crisis services; Health organizations, association; Cancer; Alcoholism; Crime/law enforcement; Human services; Children/youth, services; Family services; Hospices; Aging, centers/services; Women, centers/services; Minorities/immigrants, centers/services; International human rights; Urban/community development; Community development; Federated giving programs; Engineering/technology; Engineering; Science; Public policy, research; Government/public administration; Public affairs; Minorities; Disabled; Aging; Women; Economically disadvantaged.
Types of support: Program development; Seed money; Curriculum development; Technical assistance; Employee matching gifts.
Limitations: Giving on a national basis. No support for religious organizations (except when a need is provided to the community at large). No grants to individuals, or for scholarships, general operating funds, veterans', labor, athletic or fraternal groups, advertising, fundraising, subscription fees or admission tickets, or trips or tours.
Publications: Application guidelines.
Application information: See Web site for application guidelines. Application form required.
  Initial approach: Proposal and a cover letter of no more than 2 pages
  Copies of proposal: 1
  Deadline(s): Mar. 3 and Sept. 8
  Board meeting date(s): May and Nov.
Officers: Lennox K. Black, Pres.; Thelma A. Fretz, V.P.; John H. Remer, Treas.
Directors: Christopher Black; Thomas Byrne; M.C. Chisholm; Janine Dusossoit; Diane Fukuda; William Haussmann; Stephen Holland; Anita Piacentino; Palmer Retzlaff.
Number of staff: 1 part-time professional.
EIN: 232104782

2931
Edna H. Tompkins Trust
c/o Mellon Financial Corp.
P.O. Box 185
Pittsburgh, PA 15230-0185
Application address: Sandra Brown-McMullen, 1 Boston Pl., Boston, MA 02108, tel.: (617) 722-3891

Established in 1986 in MA.
Grantmaker type: Independent foundation
Financial data (yr. ended 08/31/02): Assets, $1,365,287 (M); expenditures, $164,080; qualifying distributions, $153,229; giving

activities include $152,000 for 5 grants (high: $50,000; low: $14,000).
Fields of interest: Higher education; Law school/education; Animal welfare; Hospitals (general); Health organizations, association; Medical research, institute.
Limitations: Giving limited to the greater Boston, MA, area. No grants to individuals.
Application information: Application form not required.
  Initial approach: Letter requesting guidelines
  Deadline(s): Feb., May, Aug., and Nov.
  Board meeting date(s): Mar., June, Sept., and Dec.
Trustee: Mellon Financial Corp.
EIN: 046423442

2932
United States Steel Foundation, Inc. ▼
(formerly USX Foundation, Inc.)
600 Grant St., Rm. 685
Pittsburgh, PA 15219-4776 (412) 433-5237
Contact: Craig D. Mallick, Genl. Mgr.
FAX: (412) 433-6847; URL: http://www.ussteel.com/corp/ussfoundation/ussfound.htm

Incorporated in 1953 in DE.
Donor(s): United States Steel Corp., and certain subsidiaries.
Grantmaker type: Company-sponsored foundation
Financial data (yr. ended 11/30/02): Assets, $6,929,439 (M); expenditures, $4,120,437; qualifying distributions, $3,726,800; giving activities include $3,250,538 for 92 grants (high: $500,000; low: $500; average: $1,000–$25,000), $223,500 for 39 grants to individuals (high: $10,000; low: $2,500) and $214,459 for 298 employee matching gifts.
Purpose and activities: Giving for capital and operating grants primarily for higher education, including matching gifts and support of educational associations; health and human services, including the United Way; arts and culture; and scientific affairs.
Fields of interest: Museums; Performing arts; Historic preservation/historical societies; Arts; Education, association; Higher education; Business school/education; Law school/education; Engineering school/education; Libraries (public); Natural resources; Energy; Environment; Health care; Substance abuse, services; Mental health/crisis services; Crime/violence prevention, youth; Safety/disasters; Human services; Children/youth, services; Federated giving programs; Engineering/technology; Computer science; Engineering; Science; Economics; Public policy, research; Public affairs; Minorities; Native Americans/American Indians; Disabled; Economically disadvantaged.
Types of support: General/operating support; Capital campaigns; Building/renovation; Equipment; Scholarship funds; Employee matching gifts; Employee-related scholarships.
Limitations: Giving primarily in areas of company operations in the U.S., including AK, AL, CO, IL, IN, LA, MI, MN, OH, OK, western PA, and TX. No support for religious organizations for religious purposes, economic development projects, or preschool to grade 12 education, hospitals or nursing homes. No

grants to individuals (except for employee-related scholarships), or for conferences, seminars, symposia, travel, exhibits, special or fundraising events, fellowships, publication of papers, books or magazines, production of films, videotapes, or other audio-visual materials, or operating support of United Way agencies; no loans.
Publications: Application guidelines, Annual report (including application guidelines).
Application information: Grantmakers of Western PA Common Grant Application Format accepted. Application form not required.
  Initial approach: Letter
  Copies of proposal: 1
  Deadline(s): Jan. 15 for public, cultural, and scientific affairs; Apr. 15 for education; July 15 for health and human services
  Board meeting date(s): Apr., July, and Oct.
  Final notification: Following board meetings
Officers and Trustees:* Thomas J. Usher,* Chair.; Roy G. Dorrance,* Pres.; Gary A. Glynn, V.P., Investments; Gretchen R. Haggerty,* V.P.; Dan D. Sandman,* Secy. and Genl. Counsel; John P. Surma, Jr.,* C.F.O.; Larry G. Schultz, Compt.; Craig D. Mallick,* Genl. Mgr.; Gary W. Walsh, Tax Counsel; Susan M. Kapusta,* Dir.; David H. Lohr.
Number of staff: 1 full-time professional; 1 part-time professional; 2 full-time support.
EIN: 136093185
Recent environmental and animal welfare grants:
2932-1 Birmingham-Southern College, Birmingham, AL, $10,000. For capital support of Birmingham Environmental Center. 2001.
2932-2 Great Lakes Aquarium, Duluth, MN, $20,000. For capital support. 2001.
2932-3 National Aviary in Pittsburgh, Pittsburgh, PA, $50,000. For capital support. 2001.
2932-4 Wildlife Habitat Council, Silver Spring, MD, $10,000. For operating support. 2001.
2932-5 Winnie Palmer Nature Reserve, Latrobe, PA, $100,000. For capital support. 2001.

2933
Up East, Inc.
P.O. Box 48
Chadds Ford, PA 19317

Established in 1995 in DE, PA and ME.
Donor(s): Andrew N. Wyeth, Betsy James Wyeth.
Grantmaker type: Independent foundation
Financial data (yr. ended 06/30/02): Assets, $11,565,618 (M); gifts received, $300,000; expenditures, $528,242; qualifying distributions, $799,976; giving activities include $168,146 for 4 grants (high: $63,048; low: $14,013) and $479,681 for foundation-administered programs.
Fields of interest: Higher education; Environment, research; Animals/wildlife, preservation/protection.
Limitations: Giving primarily in ME.
Application information: Application form not required.
  Initial approach: 2-page letter
  Deadline(s): None
Officer: Betsy James Wyeth, Pres.
Trustees: Gail A. Graham; William Prickett; J. Robinson West; Prof. John Wilmerding; Andrew N. Wyeth; James Browning Wyeth; Nicholas Wyeth.

EIN: 510367586

2934
The Vanguard Group Foundation
100 Vanguard Blvd.
Malvern, PA 19355
Contact: Tami F. Wise, Dir., Corp. Contribs.
Application address: c/o Tami F. Wise, P.O. Box 2600 (V38), Valley Forge, PA 19482, tel.: (610) 669-6331

Established in 1992 in PA.
Donor(s): The Vanguard Group, Inc.
Grantmaker type: Company-sponsored foundation
Financial data (yr. ended 12/31/01): Assets, $3,843,843 (M); gifts received, $3,005,178; expenditures, $3,003,503; qualifying distributions, $3,000,223; giving activities include $2,994,351 for 602 grants (high: $1,551,000; low: $25; average: $100–$2,000).
Purpose and activities: Giving primarily to arts and cultural programs, education, the environment, health and human services, federated giving programs, and community and civic affairs.
Fields of interest: Arts; Elementary/secondary education; Higher education; Environment; Human services; Community development; Federated giving programs; Public affairs.
Types of support: Employee matching gifts.
Limitations: Giving primarily in the greater Philadelphia, PA, metropolitan area. No grants to individuals.
Application information: Accepts Delaware Valley Grantmakers Common Grant Application and Common Report Form. Application form required.
  Initial approach: Proposal
  Deadline(s): None
  Board meeting date(s): Quarterly
  Final notification: Within 4 to 6 weeks
Officers: John J. Brennan, C.E.O.; James H. Gately, V.P.; F. William McNabb, V.P.; Pauline C. Scalvino, Secy.; Ralph K. Packard, Treas.
EIN: 232699769

2935
Richard C. von Hess Foundation
c/o The Glenmede Trust Co.
1650 Market St., Ste. 1200
Philadelphia, PA 19103-7391 (215) 419-6000

Established in 1989 in PA.
Donor(s): Richard C. von Hess.
Grantmaker type: Independent foundation
Financial data (yr. ended 12/31/01): Assets, $29,764,014 (M); gifts received, $880,558; expenditures, $1,641,346; qualifying distributions, $1,500,935; giving activities include $1,398,260 for 28 grants (high: $250,000; low: $2,230).
Purpose and activities: The foundation was created to assist the work of Wright's Ferry Museum, a historic 18th Century house museum in Columbia, PA, as well as to further art education, and other charitable purposes.
Fields of interest: Museums (specialized); Historic preservation/historical societies; Horticulture/garden clubs.
Limitations: Applications not accepted. Giving primarily in PA. No grants to individuals.

Application information: Contributes only to pre-selected organizations.
Trustees: Thomas Hills Cook; Anne Genter; Warren A. Reintzel.
EIN: 236962077

2936
Washington Federal Charitable Foundation
190 N. Main St.
Washington, PA 15301 (724) 222-3120
Contact: Richard L. White, Dir.
E-mail: info@washfed.com; URL: http://www.washfed.com/Community/community.html

Established in 1991 in PA.
Donor(s): Washington Federal Savings Bank.
Grantmaker type: Company-sponsored foundation
Financial data (yr. ended 06/30/02): Assets, $579,086 (M); gifts received, $186,564; expenditures, $135,170; qualifying distributions, $133,464; giving activities include $132,000 for 11 grants (high: $25,000; low: $2,000).
Purpose and activities: Giving primarily for higher education, health, community centers, and youth services.
Fields of interest: Museums (specialized); Higher education; Education; Animal welfare; Hospitals (general); Child abuse; Children/youth, services; Aging, centers/services; Community development; Science.
Types of support: General/operating support; Building/renovation; Equipment; Scholarship funds.
Limitations: Giving limited to southwestern PA, with emphasis on Washington County. No support for religious programs, churches, other sectarian organizations, or political campaigns, parties or candidates. No grants to individuals; no loans.
Publications: Informational brochure (including application guidelines).
Application information: Application form required.
  Initial approach: Proposal
  Copies of proposal: 1
  Deadline(s): First day of second month in each quarter
  Board meeting date(s): Quarterly
Officers: William M. Campbell, Chair.; Mary Lyn Drewitz, Secy.
Directors: David R. Andrews; Martin P. Beichner, Jr.; James H. Boylan; Joseph M. Jefferson; D. Jackson Milhollan; James R. Proudfit; Telford W. Thomas; Louis E. Waller; Richard L. White.
Number of staff: None.
EIN: 256395164

2937
Robert S. Waters Charitable Trust
c/o Mellon Financial Corp.
1 Mellon Ctr., Rm. 151-3825
Pittsburgh, PA 15258 (412) 234-5784
Contact: Barbara K. Robinson, F.V.P., Mellon Financial Corp.

Trust established in 1952 in PA.
Donor(s): Robert S. Waters.‡
Grantmaker type: Independent foundation

Financial data (yr. ended 12/31/02): Assets, $7,150,251 (M); expenditures, $505,530; qualifying distributions, $471,310; giving activities include $452,000 for 22 grants (high: $160,000; low: $1,000).

Fields of interest: Historic preservation/historical societies; Arts; Secondary school/education; Natural resources; Human services.

Limitations: Giving primarily in Johnstown and Pittsburgh, PA. No grants to individuals, or for scholarships or fellowships; no loans.

Application information: Application form required.

  Initial approach: Letter
  Copies of proposal: 2
  Deadline(s): None
  Board meeting date(s): May and Nov.

Trustee: Mellon Financial Corp.

Number of staff: None.

EIN: 256018986

2938
**Westinghouse Electric Company LLC
  Corporate Giving Program**
c/o Charitable Giving Prog.
P.O. Box 355
Pittsburgh, PA 15230-0355
Contact: Lynnann S. Reid, Mgr., Employee Comm. and Community Rels.
URL: http://www.westinghouse.com/e.asp

Grantmaker type: Corporate giving program

Purpose and activities: Westinghouse makes charitable contributions to nonprofit organizations involved with K-12 education, the environment, human services, and community economic development. Special emphasis is directed towards programs designed to help meet the needs of populations such as the disadvantaged, the young, the elderly, minorities, and people with disabilities. Support is given on a national basis.

Fields of interest: Elementary/secondary education; Environment; Children/youth, services; Human services; Urban/community development; Minorities; Disabled; Aging; Economically disadvantaged.

Types of support: General/operating support; Program development; Technical assistance; Employee volunteer services; Donated equipment; Donated products; In-kind gifts.

Limitations: Giving on a national basis in areas of company operations, with emphasis on southwestern PA. No support for political organizations, religious organizations, highly specialized health, medical, or welfare organizations, discriminatory organizations, hospitals, colleges or universities, or United Way-affiliated organizations. No grants to individuals, or for educational capital campaigns, medical education, chairs or professorships, liberal arts, fine arts, or similar education, educational research, graduate education, endowments, tickets, or memberships.

Publications: Application guidelines.

Application information: Proposals should be brief in length. Support is limited to 2 contributions per organization during any given five-year period. Contributions generally do not exceed $5,000. The Employee Communications and Community Relations Department handles

giving. A contributions committee reviews all requests. Application form not required.

  Initial approach: Proposal to headquarters or nearest company facility
  Copies of proposal: 1
  Deadline(s): None
  Board meeting date(s): Quarterly
  Final notification: 6 months

2939
Willary Foundation
c/o PNC Advisors
P.O. Box 937
Scranton, PA 18501-0937 (570) 961-6952
Contact: M. Linda Donovan, Admin. Dir.
FAX: (570) 961-6913; E-mail: info@willary.org;
URL: http://www.willary.org

Established in 1968 in PA.

Donor(s): William W. Scranton, Mary L. Scranton.

Grantmaker type: Independent foundation

Financial data (yr. ended 12/31/02): Assets, $4,275,527 (M); expenditures, $315,444; qualifying distributions, $299,829; giving activities include $281,228 for 11 grants (high: $52,366; low: $3,500) and $300,751 for foundation-administered programs.

Purpose and activities: Giving primarily for arts and culture, community and youth development, and for environmental causes.

Fields of interest: Television; Orchestra (symphony); Arts; Higher education; Environment; Cancer research; Housing/shelter, volunteer services; Housing/shelter, development; Human services.

Types of support: Program development; Matching/challenge support.

Limitations: Giving primarily in northeastern PA. No grants to individuals, or for capital campaigns or annual drives; no loans.

Publications: Application guidelines.

Application information: Application form required.

  Copies of proposal: 4
  Deadline(s): Mar. 25 and Sept. 10
  Board meeting date(s): June and Nov.

Trustees: Susan Scranton Dawson; Joseph C. Scranton; Mary L. Scranton; Peter K. Scranton; William W. Scranton; William W. Scranton III; PNC Bank, N.A.

EIN: 237014785

2940
Williamsport-Lycoming Foundation
(formerly Williamsport Foundation)
220 W. 4th St., Ste. C, 3rd Fl.
Williamsport, PA 17701-6102 (570) 321-1500
Contact: Sheryl Hoff, C.F.O.
FAX: (570) 321-6434; E-mail:
wlf@wlfoundation.org; URL: http://www.wlfoundation.org

Established in 1916 in PA by bank resolution.

Grantmaker type: Community foundation

Financial data (yr. ended 12/31/02): Assets, $39,373,357 (M); gifts received, $1,476,119; expenditures, $3,601,577; giving activities include $2,713,597 for 334 grants (high: $1,000,000; low: $50; average: $1,000–$30,000) and $10,000 for 1 loan/program-related investment.

Purpose and activities: The foundation exists to make Williamsport and Lycoming counties, PA, and the surrounding regions the best possible place to live. The foundation helps people find the most effectual way for "giving back" to help build vibrant communities. The foundation administers donor-advised funds.

Fields of interest: Arts; Education; Health care; Natural resources; Recreation; Human services; Youth, services; Family services; Economic development; Community development.

Types of support: General/operating support; Continuing support; Capital campaigns; Building/renovation; Equipment; Land acquisition; Endowments; Program development; Conferences/seminars; Seed money; Scholarship funds; Program-related investments/loans; Matching/challenge support.

Limitations: Giving primarily to organizations serving Lycoming County, PA. No support for sectarian religious programs. No grants to individuals, or for endowment funds. Generally no grants for ongoing operating support.

Publications: Application guidelines, Annual report, Financial statement, Informational brochure, Program policy statement.

Application information: Application form required.

  Initial approach: Letter or telephone for application guidelines
  Copies of proposal: 15
  Deadline(s): Mar. 1, June 1, Sept. 1, and Dec. 1
  Board meeting date(s): Monthly
  Final notification: 1 to 4 months

Officers and Directors:* Ann M. Alsted,* Chair.; Carol Sides, Vice.-Chair.; Kimberley Pittman-Schulz,* Pres.; Daniel G. Fultz, Secy.-Treas.; Barbara Hudock; Robert More; John C. Schultz; John Young.

Number of staff: 4 full-time professional; 1 part-time professional; 1 full-time support; 1 part-time support.

EIN: 246013117

2941
Willow Grove Foundation
Welsh and Norristown Rds.
P.O. Box 3030
Maple Glen, PA 19002-8030
Contact: C. Harold Schuler, Jr., Exec. Dir.
Application address: 2440 Oaks Cir., Huntingdon Valley, PA 19006

Established in 1998 in PA.

Donor(s): Willow Grove Bank.

Grantmaker type: Independent foundation

Financial data (yr. ended 06/30/02): Assets, $1,233,705 (M); gifts received, $55,800; expenditures, $130,632; qualifying distributions, $128,462; giving activities include $115,868 for 48 grants (high: $25,000; low: $500).

Purpose and activities: Giving primarily for education and health and human services.

Fields of interest: Secondary school/education; Environment; Cancer; American Red Cross; Children/youth, services; Community development.

Types of support: General/operating support; Capital campaigns; Building/renovation; Equipment.

Limitations: Giving primarily in PA. No grants to individuals, fraternal or professional groups,

organizations which discriminate by race, color, creed, gender, sexual orientation, or national origin, or for religious activities.
Application information: Application form required.
  Deadline(s): 2 weeks prior to quarterly board meeting
  Board meeting date(s): Jan., Apr., July, and Oct.
  Final notification: Within 2 weeks following meeting
Officers and Directors:* Charles F. Kremp III, Chair.; William B. Weihenmayer, Vice-Chair. and Treas.; Frederick A. Marcell, Jr.,* Secy.; C. Harold Schuler, Jr., Exec. Dir.; Donald L. Clark; Shirley M. Dennis; Stewart J. Greenleaf; J. Ellwood Kirk.
EIN: 233002286

2942
Peter J. Wood Foundation
55 Crosby Brown Rd.
Gladwyne, PA 19035-1512

Established in 1996.
Grantmaker type: Independent foundation
Financial data (yr. ended 10/31/02): Assets, $112,272 (M); expenditures, $105,826; qualifying distributions, $105,819; giving activities include $104,250 for 6 grants (high: $55,000; low: $250).
Purpose and activities: Giving for federated giving programs and animal welfare.
Fields of interest: Animal welfare; Disasters, 9/11/01; Federated giving programs; Jewish federated giving programs; Jewish agencies & temples.
Limitations: Applications not accepted. Giving on a national basis. No grants to individuals.
Application information: Contributes only to pre-selected organizations.
Officers: Peter J. Wood, Pres.; Michael Krekstein, Secy.
EIN: 232868525

2943
Woodmere Foundation
c/o Robert B. Knutson
300 6th Ave.
Pittsburgh, PA 15222-2514   (412) 562-0900
Contact: Kathy Villalpando, Educ. Mgmt. Corp.

Established in 1993 in PA.
Donor(s): Robert B. Knutson.
Grantmaker type: Independent foundation
Financial data (yr. ended 12/31/00): Assets, $2,588,244 (M); gifts received, $694,376; expenditures, $206,336; qualifying distributions, $179,593; giving activities include $187,448 for 38 grants (high: $57,000; low: $150).
Purpose and activities: Giving for the arts, human services, conservation, education, and medical services and research.
Fields of interest: Museums; Arts; Education; Natural resources; Mental health/crisis services, research; Human services.
Limitations: Giving primarily in PA.
Application information:
  Initial approach: Proposal
  Deadline(s): None
Officer: Robert B. Knutson, Pres.
EIN: 251705913

2944
Wurster Family Foundation
940 Haverford Rd., Ste. 103
Bryn Mawr, PA 19010

Established in 1997 in PA.
Donor(s): William H. Wurster.
Grantmaker type: Independent foundation
Financial data (yr. ended 12/31/02): Assets, $1,795,370 (M); expenditures, $166,253; qualifying distributions, $149,827; giving activities include $149,000 for 6 grants (high: $55,000; low: $1,000).
Fields of interest: Veterinary medicine; Hospitals (specialty); Salvation Army; Children/youth, services; Foreign policy; Community development.
Limitations: Applications not accepted. No grants to individuals.
Application information: Contributes only to pre-selected organizations.
Officers and Trustees:* William H. Wurster,* Pres.; Janine Wurster Putnam,* V.P.; William Glendon Wurster,* V.P.; Donna Ellis, Secy.; Jeanne D. Wurster, Secy.; Anthony Melvin, Treas.
EIN: 237880440

2945
The Wyomissing Foundation, Inc.
12 Commerce Dr.
Wyomissing, PA 19610
Contact: Paul R. Roedel, Pres.
FAX: (610) 372-7626; E-mail: wfbbec@nnl.com

Incorporated in 1929 in DE.
Donor(s): Ferdinand Thun,‡ and family.
Grantmaker type: Independent foundation
Financial data (yr. ended 12/31/01): Assets, $33,641,811 (M); expenditures, $3,381,543; qualifying distributions, $1,439,755; giving activities include $1,385,676 for 25 grants (high: $130,821; low: $1,000; average: $1,000–$25,000).
Purpose and activities: Primary areas of interest include education, building funds, the environment, and community funds. Giving also for hospitals and health services, higher education, civic affairs, youth and social service agencies, child welfare, and family planning and services; support also for the environment and conservation, and the arts, including performing arts and music.
Fields of interest: Performing arts; Music; Arts; Education, fund raising; Higher education; Education; Natural resources; Environment; Hospitals (general); Family planning; Health care; Health organizations, association; Human services; Children/youth, services; Family services; Federated giving programs; Government/public administration.
Types of support: General/operating support; Continuing support; Annual campaigns; Capital campaigns; Building/renovation; Equipment; Endowments; Emergency funds; Seed money; Matching/challenge support.
Limitations: Giving primarily in Berks County, PA, and contiguous counties; limited support also in the mid-Atlantic area. No grants to individuals, or for deficit financing, land acquisition, publications, conferences, scholarships, or fellowships; no loans.
Publications: Application guidelines, Program policy statement.

Application information: Application form not required.
  Initial approach: Proposal (no more than 2 pages, excluding supporting materials)
  Copies of proposal: 1
  Deadline(s): Submit proposal preferably in Feb., May, Aug., or Oct.; deadline 25th of month preceding board meeting
  Board meeting date(s): Mar., June, Sept., and Dec.
  Final notification: 3 months
Officers and Trustees:* Paul R. Roedel,* Pres.; Hildegard Ryals,* V.P.; Ned E. Diefenderfer, Secy.; Thomas A. Beaver,* Treas.; Robert W. Cardy; Toni Lake; Samuel McCollough; Steffan Plehn; David Thun; Michael Thun.
Number of staff: 1 full-time support; 1 part-time support.
EIN: 231980570

2946
Wyss Foundation
c/o Joseph Fisher
1690 Russell Rd.
Paoli, PA 19301
Contact: Geoff Webb, Exec. Dir.
Application address: 21 Ladera Rd., Santa Fe, NM 87505, tel.: (505) 466-4616

Established in 1999 in PA.
Donor(s): Hansjoerg Wyss.
Grantmaker type: Independent foundation
Financial data (yr. ended 12/31/01): Assets, $48,669,272 (M); gifts received, $6,069,456; expenditures, $4,693,437; qualifying distributions, $4,274,220; giving activities include $4,065,252 for 95 grants (high: $450,000; low: $250; average: $1,000–$50,000).
Purpose and activities: Giving primarily to grassroots organizations which work to protect open spaces on public and private lands, from the Rocky Mountains to the west coast and AK.
Fields of interest: Environment, legal rights; Natural resources; Environment; Human services.
Limitations: Giving primarily from the Rocky Mountains to the West Coast, and AK. Large funding in AZ, Washington, DC, and PA; giving also in CA, CO, NM, NY, OR and UT. No grants to individuals.
Officers: Hansjoerg Wyss, Chair.; Joseph Fisher, Secy.; Geoff Webb, Exec. Dir.
EIN: 231823874

2947
York Foundation
20 W. Market St.
York, PA 17401-1203   (717) 848-3733
FAX: (717) 854-7231; E-mail: info@yorkfoundation.org; URL: http://www.yorkfoundation.org

Established in 1961 in PA.
Grantmaker type: Community foundation
Financial data (yr. ended 12/31/02): Assets, $23,128,771 (M); gifts received, $1,629,330; expenditures, $1,494,750; giving activities include $1,235,887 for grants.
Purpose and activities: To promote the betterment of York County, PA, and the enhancement of the quality of life for all its

citizens by attracting and managing funds to build a permanent endowment, serving as a leader in responding to community needs, and by serving as a resource and catalyst for charitable activities. The foundation administers donor-advised funds.

Fields of interest: Arts; Education; Environment, land resources; Energy; Child development, services; Community development; Philanthropy/voluntarism, management/technical aid.

Types of support: Equipment; Program development; Conferences/seminars; Seed money; Scholarship funds; Technical assistance; Consulting services; Matching/challenge support.

Limitations: Giving primarily in York County, PA. No grants to individuals, or for endowments, capital campaigns, annual appeals, scholarships, travel, or for research.

Publications: Application guidelines, Annual report, Informational brochure, Newsletter.

Application information: Guidelines available on Web site. Application form required.

Initial approach: Letter or telephone for guidelines
Copies of proposal: 3
Deadline(s): Sept. 30 and Mar. 31
Board meeting date(s): Quarterly
Final notification: June and Dec.

Officers and Directors:* Thomas C. Norris,* Pres.; Cornelia W. Wolf,* V.P.; John J. Shorb,* Secy.; Stephen H. Klunk,* Treas.; Susan A. Barry, Exec. Dir.; and 27 additional directors.

Number of staff: 2 full-time professional; 1 part-time professional; 1 full-time support.

EIN: 236299868

PUERTO RICO

2948
FNZ Foundation, Inc.
Box 3425
Carolina, PR 00984
Contact: James D. Klau, Pres.
FAX: (787) 762-2115; E-mail: RonadK@prtc.net

Established in 1996 in DE.
Grantmaker type: Independent foundation
Financial data (yr. ended 12/31/02): Assets, $8,922,739 (M); expenditures, $583,325; qualifying distributions, $544,243; giving activities include $544,243 for 108 grants (high: $61,065; low: $36).
Purpose and activities: Giving primarily for Native Americans, Jewish organizations and temples, youth, health care, animals, education and social action.
Fields of interest: Arts; Education; Animals/wildlife; Health care; Urban League; Youth, services; Jewish agencies & temples.
International interests: Israel.
Limitations: Giving on a national basis.
Officer: James D. Klau, Pres.
Member: Susan L. Klau.
EIN: 660535017

2949
Puerto Rico Community Foundation
P.O. Box 70362
San Juan, PR 00936-8362 (787) 721-1037
Contact: Juan J. Reyes, Admin.
FAX: (787) 721-1673; E-mail: fcpr@fcpr.org

Incorporated in 1984 in PR; began operations in 1985.
Grantmaker type: Community foundation
Financial data (yr. ended 12/31/02): Assets, $16,989,749 (M); gifts received, $1,770,036; expenditures, $2,393,625; giving activities include $1,046,750 for grants.
Purpose and activities: The foundation seeks to contribute to the achievement of a healthier economy and enhance quality of life in Puerto Rico; giving in areas such as economic development, educational associations, the elderly, community development, science and technological innovation, health, including AIDS programs, drug and alcohol abuse programs, arts and cultural activities, including dance and fine arts, criminal justice, agriculture, animal welfare, and civic affairs. The foundation administers donor-advised funds.
Fields of interest: Visual arts; Architecture; Performing arts; Dance; Arts; Education, association; Early childhood education; Child development, education; Adult/continuing education; Education; Natural resources; Animal welfare; Health care; Substance abuse, services; Health organizations, association; AIDS; Alcoholism; AIDS research; Crime/violence prevention, youth; Crime/law enforcement; Agriculture; Human services; Child development, services; Aging, centers/services; Civil rights; Community development; Engineering/technology; Computer science; Science; Anthropology/sociology; Economics; Government/public administration; Minorities; Aging; Economically disadvantaged.
Types of support: General/operating support; Continuing support; Building/renovation; Equipment; Emergency funds; Conferences/seminars; Professorships; Publication; Curriculum development; Research; Technical assistance; Consulting services; Program-related investments/loans; Scholarships—to individuals; In-kind gifts; Matching/challenge support.
Limitations: Giving limited to PR. No support for religious organizations or commonly accepted community services. No grants for annual campaigns, seed money, endowments, deficit financing; generally no grants for building funds.
Publications: Application guidelines, Annual report, Financial statement, Informational brochure (including application guidelines), Newsletter, Program policy statement.
Application information: Application form required.
Initial approach: Letter
Deadline(s): None
Board meeting date(s): June, Sept., Mar., and Dec.
Final notification: Within 2 weeks after board meetings
Officers and Directors:* Antonio Escudero Viera,* Chair.; Mabel Burckhart,* V.P.; William Lockwood, Secy.; Alina Herrera, Treas.; and 11 additional directors.
Number of staff: 15 full-time support.
EIN: 660413230

RHODE ISLAND

2950
Bafflin Foundation
1500 Fleet Ctr.
Providence, RI 02903-2319
Contact: Paul A. Silver, Secy.

Established in 1990 in RI.
Donor(s): Lois Orswell.‡
Grantmaker type: Independent foundation
Financial data (yr. ended 12/31/02): Assets, $17,409,795 (M); gifts received, $107,895; expenditures, $938,983; qualifying distributions, $825,484; giving activities include $799,800 for 20 grants (high: $250,000; low: $4,000).
Purpose and activities: Giving primarily for the preservation of land and wildlife; some support also for art museums.
Fields of interest: Museums (art); Natural resources; Animals/wildlife, preservation/protection; Physical therapy; Human services.
Limitations: Giving on a national basis, with some emphasis on the East Coast. No grants to individuals.
Application information: Application form not required.
Deadline(s): None
Officers and Directors:* Paul A. Silver,* Secy.; Michael M. Edwards,* Treas.; Joachim A. Weissfeld.
EIN: 050454795

2951
The Chace Fund, Inc.
1 Providence Washington Plz.
Providence, RI 02903
Contact: Malcolm G. Chace, Pres.

Established in 1947 in RI.
Donor(s): Malcolm G. Chace III, Arnold B. Chace, Berkshire Hathaway Inc., Kathleen Osborne,‡ Beatrice O. Chace,‡ Patricia Kent.
Grantmaker type: Independent foundation
Financial data (yr. ended 12/31/02): Assets, $4,047,500 (M); gifts received, $62,093; expenditures, $989,320; qualifying distributions, $962,189; giving activities include $963,000 for 63 grants (high: $157,300; low: $100; average: $2,000–$10,000).
Fields of interest: Theater; Historic preservation/historical societies; Arts; Education; Natural resources; Cystic fibrosis research; Domestic violence; Human services; Children, services; Women, centers/services; Federated giving programs; Christian agencies & churches.
Types of support: General/operating support.
Limitations: Giving primarily in MA, NY, and RI. No grants to individuals.
Application information:
Initial approach: Letter
Deadline(s): None
Officers and Directors:* Malcolm G. Chace,* Pres.; Arnold B. Chace, Jr.,* V.P.; Thomas E. Gardiner, Secy.-Treas.; Malcolm G. Chace, Jr.
EIN: 056008849

2952
Mary Dexter Chafee Fund
81 Henry Case Way
Wakefield, RI 02879
Contact: Mark H. Chafee, Treas.
Application address: c/o Augusta Haydock, Fleet
National Bank, 100 Federal St., Boston, MA
02110

Established in 1933 in RI.
Grantmaker type: Independent foundation
Financial data (yr. ended 12/31/01): Assets,
$2,445,611 (M); gifts received, $500;
expenditures, $137,407; qualifying distributions,
$123,144; giving activities include $108,900 for
grants (high: $10,000).
Purpose and activities: Giving primarily for the
prevention of cruelty to children and animals.
Fields of interest: Historic
preservation/historical societies; Arts; Education;
Natural resources; Animal welfare; Human
services; Children/youth, services.
Types of support: Capital campaigns;
Building/renovation; Land acquisition; Program
development.
Limitations: Giving primarily in RI. No grants to
individuals.
Application information: Application form
required.
  Initial approach: Proposal, including 1-page
    synopsis
  Deadline(s): None
  Board meeting date(s): Nov.
Officers and Director:* Alexandra Reynolds,
Pres.; Richard S. Chafee,* Secy.; Mark H.
Chafee, Treas.
Agent: Fleet National Bank.
EIN: 056006295

2953
The Champlin Foundations ▼
300 Centerville Rd, Ste. 300S
Warwick, RI 02886-0226 (401) 736-0370
Contact: Keith H. Lang, Exec. Dir.
FAX: (401) 736-7248; E-mail:
champlinfdns@worldnet.att.net; URL: http://
www.fdncenter.org/grantmaker/champlin

Trusts established in 1932, 1947, and 1975 in
DE.
Donor(s): George S. Champlin,‡ Florence C.
Hamilton,‡ Hope C. Neaves.‡
Grantmaker type: Independent foundation
Financial data (yr. ended 12/31/02): Assets,
$351,305,285 (M); expenditures, $20,446,017;
qualifying distributions, $19,187,246; giving
activities include $18,430,271 for 402 grants
(high: $2,300,000; low: $200; average:
$25,000–$65,000).
Purpose and activities: Giving primarily for
conservation; higher, secondary, and other
education, including libraries; health and
hospitals; cultural activities, including historic
preservation; scientific activities; and social and
family services, including programs for youth
and the elderly.
Fields of interest: Historic
preservation/historical societies; Arts; Secondary
school/education; Higher education;
Libraries/library science; Education; Natural
resources; Environment; Animal welfare;
Hospitals (general); Family planning; Health
care; Health organizations, association; Human

services; Youth, services;
Engineering/technology; Science.
Types of support: Capital campaigns;
Building/renovation; Equipment; Land
acquisition.
Limitations: Giving primarily in RI. No support
for religious schools, books, films, videos, or
plays. No grants to individuals, or for general
support, program or operating budgets,
matching gifts, special projects, research,
publications, conferences, or continuing
support; no loans.
Publications: Application guidelines, Annual
report, Grants list, Program policy statement.
Application information: No grants are awarded
on a continuing basis, but applicants may
qualify annually. Application form not required.
  Initial approach: Brief 1-page letter
  Copies of proposal: 1
  Deadline(s): Submit public school requests by
    June 30 if invited; submit all other requests
    between Mar. 1 and June 30
  Board meeting date(s): Nov.
  Final notification: After Nov. meeting
Distribution Committee: Keith H. Lang, Exec.
Dir.; John Gorham; Timothy Gorham; Louis R.
Hampton; Earl W. Harrington, Jr.; Robert W.
Kenyon; Norma B. LaFreniere; John W. Linnell.
Trustee: PNC Bank, N.A.
Number of staff: 2 full-time professional; 2
part-time professional; 1 full-time support; 1
part-time support.
**Recent environmental and animal welfare
grants:**
2953-1 Hope Associates, Hope, RI, $16,000.
  For restroom repairs. 2002.
2953-2 Hope Associates, Hope, RI, $11,600.
  For heating system replacement. 2002.
2953-3 Nature Conservancy of Rhode Island,
  Providence, RI, $2,300,000. For acquisition
  of land for open space and recreation. 2002.
2953-4 Nature Conservancy of Rhode Island,
  Providence, RI, $63,560. Toward start-up
  support for Francis C. Carter Memorial
  Preserve. 2002.
2953-5 Nature Conservancy of Rhode Island,
  Providence, RI, $45,665. For operating
  support for Francis C. Carter Memorial
  Preserve. 2002.
2953-6 Norman Bird Sanctuary, Middletown,
  RI, $50,000. For continued development of
  Environmental Education Center. 2002.
2953-7 Ocean View Foundation, Block Island,
  RI, $18,000. For equipment costs involved in
  expanding education program on Block
  Island ferries. 2002.
2953-8 Potter League for Animals, Middletown,
  RI, $11,000. To update phone system. 2002.
2953-9 Providence Animal Rescue League,
  Providence, RI, $30,000. To replace
  structures covering outdoor kennels. 2002.
2953-10 Providence Animal Rescue League,
  Providence, RI, $12,000. To replace peaked
  shingle roof of building. 2002.
2953-11 Rhode Island Zoological Society,
  Providence, RI, $500,000. Toward
  construction of African Elephant Breeding
  and Exhibit Complex and White Rhino
  Exhibit. 2002.
2953-12 Roger Williams Park, Providence, RI,
  $500,000. Toward construction of Botanical
  Gardens project. 2002.
2953-13 South Providence Development
  Corporation, Providence, RI, $50,000. For

additional capital equipment for Cleanscape.
  2002.
2953-14 University of Rhode Island, Kingston,
  RI, $41,600. For continuation of Ruffed
  Grouse project with Rhode Island
  Department of Environmental Management.
  2002.
2953-15 University of Rhode Island, Kingston,
  RI, $11,046. For Woodvale Farms
  camperships at W. Alton Jones Campus in
  West Greenwich. 2002.
2953-16 Wood-Pawcatuck Watershed
  Association, Hope Valley, RI, $25,000. For
  continued capital improvements to buildings
  on Wood River. 2002.

2954
The Cranston Foundation
c/o Cranston Fdn. Trustees
1381 Cranston St.
Cranston, RI 02920-6789 (401) 943-4800

Trust established in 1960 in RI.
Donor(s): Cranston Print Works Co.
Grantmaker type: Company-sponsored
foundation
Financial data (yr. ended 06/30/02): Assets,
$17,517 (M); gifts received, $208,244;
expenditures, $205,151; qualifying distributions,
$204,177; giving activities include $41,150 for
24 grants (high: $7,500; low: $200), $135,821
for 51 grants to individuals (high: $8,000; low:
$74) and $27,206 for employee matching gifts.
Purpose and activities: Grants largely for higher
education, including a scholarship program for
children of Cranston Print Works Co.
employees. Support also for community funds,
hospitals, cultural programs, the environment,
and textile institutions and organizations.
Fields of interest: Arts; Higher education;
Libraries/library science; Education;
Environment; Hospitals (general); Health care;
Human services; Community development;
Federated giving programs.
Types of support: General/operating support;
Employee matching gifts; Employee-related
scholarships.
Limitations: Giving primarily in MA, NY, and RI.
Application information: Application form
required for scholarships.
  Initial approach: Proposal
  Copies of proposal: 1
  Deadline(s): Feb. 15 for scholarships; Aug. 31
    for grants
  Board meeting date(s): Semiannually
  Final notification: Sept. 30
Trustees: Brian Adriance; B. Grandison; J.
Menzies; G. Nickeson; C. Pietruszka; Frederic L.
Rockefeller; George W. Shuster; S. Wollseiffen.
Number of staff: 1 full-time professional.
EIN: 056015348

2955
Margarette G. Crossman Trust
c/o Fleet Private Clients Group
P.O. Box 6767
Providence, RI 02940-6767

Established in 1972.
Grantmaker type: Public charity
Financial data (yr. ended 12/31/01): Revenue,
$252,588; assets, $3,227,911; expenditures,

$156,905; program services expenses, $143,319; giving activities include $143,319 for 3 grants (high: $141,819; low: $500).
Purpose and activities: The trust exists for the sole benefit of Animal Rescue League of Boston, MA, Mass. Soc. Prev. Cruel Animals, MA, and Laurinburg Normal & Industrial Inst., NC.
Fields of interest: Animal welfare.
Limitations: Applications not accepted. Giving limited to Boston, MA, and Laurinburg, NC.
Application information: Contributes only to a pre-selected organizations; unsolicited requests for funds not considered or acknowledged.
Trustee: Fleet National Bank.
EIN: 046028852

2956
The Sophie & Murray Danforth Foundation

22 Parsonage St.
Providence, RI 02903   (401) 274-1550
Contact: Murray S. Danforth III, Treas.

Established in 1996 in RI.
Donor(s): Sophie F. Danforth, Stephanie D. Chafee.
Grantmaker type: Independent foundation
Financial data (yr. ended 12/31/02): Assets, $3,192,823 (M); gifts received, $360,248; expenditures, $169,098; qualifying distributions, $155,115; giving activities include $159,000 for 16 grants (high: $50,000; low: $1,000).
Purpose and activities: Giving primarily for wildlife conservation.
Fields of interest: Animals/wildlife, preservation/protection.
Limitations: Giving primarily in PA. No grants to individuals.
Application information: Application form not required.
Deadline(s): None
Officers and Directors:* Sophie F. Danforth,* Pres.; Stephanie D. Chafee,* Secy.; Murray S. Danforth III,* Treas.
EIN: 050494224

2957
Dorot Foundation ▼

439 Benefit St.
Providence, RI 02903   (401) 351-8866
Contact: Ernest S. Frerichs, Exec. Dir.
FAX: (401) 351-4975; E-mail: info@dorot.org; URL: http://www.dorot.org

Incorporated in 1958 in NY as Joy and Samuel Ungerleider Foundation.
Donor(s): Joy G. Ungerleider-Mayerson,‡ D.S. and R.H. Gottesman Foundation.
Grantmaker type: Independent foundation
Financial data (yr. ended 03/31/02): Assets, $49,704,771 (M); gifts received, $2,683,030; expenditures, $13,769,532; qualifying distributions, $12,871,442; giving activities include $11,866,252 for 31+ grants (high: $9,000,000).
Purpose and activities: Grants primarily for higher education and educational organizations including fellowships to individuals studying in Israel; support also for Jewish organizations.
Fields of interest: Museums; Education, association; Higher education; Medical school/education; Libraries (public);

Environment, administration/regulation; Human services; Jewish agencies & temples.
International interests: Israel.
Types of support: General/operating support; Endowments; Program development; Professorships; Fellowships.
Limitations: Applications not accepted. Giving primarily in the U.S.; some giving also in Israel.
Application information: Contributes only to pre-selected organizations. Does not accept unsolicited requests for funds.
Officers and Directors:* Jeane Ungerleider,* Pres.; Steven Ungerleider,* V.P.; Steven Baum, Secy. and Treas.; Ernest S. Frerichs, Exec. Dir.
Number of staff: 2 full-time professional; 4 part-time professional; 1 full-time support.
EIN: 136116927
Recent environmental and animal welfare grants:
2957-1 Coalition on the Environment and Jewish Life, New York, NY, $25,000. 2002.

2958
The Doyle Charitable Foundation

c/o Fleet Private Client Group
P.O. Box 6767
Providence, RI 02940-6767
Contact: Sharon M. Driscoll, Trust Off., Fleet National Bank
Application address: c/o Fleet National Bank, Charitable Trusts, 100 Federal St., Boston, MA 02110

Established in 1957 in MA.
Grantmaker type: Independent foundation
Financial data (yr. ended 12/31/02): Assets, $3,868,632 (M); gifts received, $1,150,984; expenditures, $136,686; qualifying distributions, $116,355; giving activities include $100,000 for 2 grants of $50,000 each.
Purpose and activities: Giving for higher education and the prevention of cruelty to animals.
Fields of interest: Education; Animal welfare.
Types of support: General/operating support; Capital campaigns.
Limitations: Giving primarily in the greater Boston, MA, area. No support for private foundations, national organizations, or projects requiring multi-year commitment. No grants to individuals, or for conferences, film production, travel, research projects, publications, or scholarships; no loans.
Application information: Application form not required.
Initial approach: Proposal
Deadline(s): None
Trustees: Louise I. Doyle; Fleet National Bank.
EIN: 046010367

2959
The Dunn Foundation

333 Strawberry Field Rd.
Warwick, RI 02886   (401) 941-3009
Contact: Richard C. Youngken, Exec. Dir.
FAX: (401) 738-1535; E-mail: dunnfndn@tiac.net; URL: http://www.dunnfoundation.org/

Established in 1992 in RI.
Grantmaker type: Public charity

Financial data (yr. ended 12/31/01): Revenue, $50,115; gifts received, $50,000; expenditures, $62,195; program services expenses, $61,050; giving activities include $61,050 for grants (high: $15,000; low: $2,000).
Purpose and activities: The foundation promotes a national ethic for the conservation and enhancement of the visual environment through increasing public understanding of the contribution community appearance makes to our quality of life, and by linking people to the tools they need to make positive aesthetic changes in their environment.
Fields of interest: Environment, beautification programs; Community development.
Types of support: Conferences/seminars; Publication; Curriculum development; Research; Technical assistance; Consulting services; Program evaluation; Matching/challenge support.
Limitations: Applications not accepted. Giving on a national basis.
Publications: Informational brochure, Newsletter.
Application information:
Board meeting date(s): Bimonthly
Officers and Directors:* David Dunn,* Pres.; Kim Dunn,* Secy.; Thomas E. Flynn,* Treas.; Richard C. Youngken, Exec. Dir.
Number of staff: 1 full-time professional; 2 part-time professional.
EIN: 050451095

2960
The Ensworth Charitable Foundation

c/o Fleet Private Clients Group
P.O. Box 6767
Providence, RI 02940-6767
Contact: Marjorie Alexandre Davis, Trust Off.
Application address: 777 Main St., Hartford, CT 06115, tel.: (860) 952-7405

Trust established in 1948 in CT.
Donor(s): Antoinette L. Ensworth.‡
Grantmaker type: Independent foundation
Financial data (yr. ended 05/31/02): Assets, $19,445,431 (M); expenditures, $917,481; qualifying distributions, $870,790; giving activities include $796,819 for 122 grants (high: $25,000; low: $160).
Purpose and activities: Primary areas of interest include health and welfare programs, youth activities, enjoyment of the natural environment, relief of human suffering, education, religion, and the arts, particularly music.
Fields of interest: Arts; Education; Environment; Health care; Health organizations, association; AIDS research; Housing/shelter, development; Human services; Youth, services; Family services; Homeless, human services; Community development.
Types of support: Program development; Seed money; Technical assistance; Matching/challenge support.
Limitations: Giving limited to Hartford, CT, and contiguous surrounding areas. No grants to individuals, or for operating budgets, annual campaigns, deficit financing, building or endowment funds, equipment and materials, land acquisition, scholarships, fellowships, research, or publications; no loans.
Publications: Application guidelines, Program policy statement.

Application information: Application form required.

Initial approach: Letter or full proposal
Copies of proposal: 4
Deadline(s): Jan. 18, Apr. 18, July 18, and Oct. 18
Board meeting date(s): Feb., May, Aug., and Nov.
Final notification: 8 weeks
Trustee: Fleet National Bank.
Number of staff: 1 full-time professional.
EIN: 066026018

2961
FM Global Foundation
(formerly Allendale Insurance Foundation)
1301 Atwood Ave.
P.O. Box 7500
Johnston, RI   02919
Contact: Gail Russell

Established in 1986 in RI.
Donor(s): Allendale Mutual Insurance Co.
Grantmaker type: Company-sponsored foundation
Financial data (yr. ended 12/31/01): Assets, $2,744,522 (M); gifts received, $3,003,000; expenditures, $1,455,731; qualifying distributions, $1,339,404; giving activities include $1,369,058 for grants.
Purpose and activities: Giving primarily for arts and culture, education, animals and wildlife, hospitals and health associations, human services, and the United Way.
Fields of interest: Arts; Higher education; Education; Animals/wildlife; Health care; Health organizations, association; Human services; Federated giving programs.
International interests: Canada.
Types of support: Employee matching gifts.
Limitations: Applications not accepted. Giving on a national basis. No grants to individuals.
Publications: Financial statement.
Application information: Contributes only to pre-selected organizations.
Officers: Shivan S. Subramaniam, Chair., C.E.O. and Pres.; William A. Mekrut, Treas.
Directors: Norman D. Baker, Jr.; John M. Lemieux; Nelson G. Wester.
Trustee: Investors Bank & Trust Co.
Number of staff: 1.
EIN: 222773230

2962
Doris Ellen Frick Trust
P.O. Box 6767
Providence, RI   02940-6767

Established in 2002 in NJ.
Grantmaker type: Independent foundation
Financial data (yr. ended 12/31/02): Assets, $3,531,095 (M); expenditures, $136,538; qualifying distributions, $123,050; giving activities include $104,127 for 5 grants (high: $20,826; low: $20,825).
Fields of interest: Animals/wildlife; Cancer; Eye diseases; Roman Catholic agencies & churches.
Limitations: Applications not accepted. Giving primarily in NY. No grants to individuals.
Application information: Contributes only to pre-selected organizations.
Trustee: Fleet National Bank.

EIN: 526898046

2963
Ira S. and Anna Galkin Charitable Trust
c/o Rosenstein, Halper & Maselli, LLP
27 Dryden Ln.
Providence, RI   02904   (401) 331-6851
Contact: Arnold T. Galkin, Tr.

Established in 1947 in RI.
Donor(s): Ira S. Galkin.
Grantmaker type: Independent foundation
Financial data (yr. ended 12/31/02): Assets, $4,029,130 (M); expenditures, $240,694; qualifying distributions, $234,119; giving activities include $215,461 for 141 grants (high: $50,000; low: $25).
Purpose and activities: Giving primarily to Jewish temples, agencies, and federated giving programs; giving also for education, health associations, human services, animal welfare, and the arts.
Fields of interest: Arts; University; Education; Animal welfare; Hospitals (general); Health organizations, association; Human services; Jewish federated giving programs; Jewish agencies & temples.
Limitations: Giving primarily in RI. No grants to individuals.
Application information:
Initial approach: Letter requesting funds
Deadline(s): None
Trustees: Arnold T. Galkin; Herbert S. Galkin; Irwin S. Galkin.
EIN: 056006231

2964
Hugh Gregg Foundation
c/o Fleet Private Clients Group
P.O. Box 6767
Providence, RI   02940
Contact: Hugh Gregg, Tr.
Application address: R.F.D. 5, Gregg Rd., Nashua, NH 03062

Grantmaker type: Independent foundation
Financial data (yr. ended 12/31/01): Assets, $287,026 (M); expenditures, $128,244; qualifying distributions, $126,680; giving activities include $124,125 for grants (high: $50,000).
Fields of interest: Education; Animal welfare.
Limitations: Giving primarily in NH. No grants to individuals.
Application information:
Initial approach: Letter
Deadline(s): None
Trustees: Catherine Gregg; Hugh Gregg; Fleet National Bank.
EIN: 026004636

2965
Hasbro Charitable Trust, Inc.
(formerly Hasbro Industries Charitable Trust, Inc.)
c/o Hasbro, Inc.
1027 Newport Ave.
Pawtucket, RI   02862   (401) 727-5429
Contact: Karen Davis, Dir.
URL: http://www.hasbro.org

Established in 1984 in RI.
Donor(s): Hasbro, Inc.
Grantmaker type: Company-sponsored foundation
Financial data (yr. ended 12/31/01): Assets, $1,365,927 (M); gifts received, $1,150,200; expenditures, $1,092,517; qualifying distributions, $1,398,793; giving activities include $1,371,085 for 109 grants (high: $166,000; low: $1,000).
Purpose and activities: Giving primarily for education, health, human service organizations, and youth services.
Fields of interest: Arts; Early childhood education; Higher education; Education; Environment; Hospitals (general); Health organizations, association; Human services; Children/youth, services; Federated giving programs.
Types of support: General/operating support; Capital campaigns; Building/renovation; Program development; Employee matching gifts; In-kind gifts.
Limitations: Giving primarily in Vernon Hills, IL, Springfield, MA, RI, Seattle, WA, and areas of major company operations. No grants to individuals, or for scholarships, endowments, fundraising events, conferences, travel stipends, or other special event sponsorships.
Publications: Application guidelines, Corporate giving report, Informational brochure.
Application information: Application form required.
Initial approach: Telephone or letter
Copies of proposal: 1
Deadline(s): Mar. 31
Board meeting date(s): June
Final notification: June 30
Officers: Alan G. Hassenfeld, Pres.; Richard B. Holt, Sr. V.P. and Cont.; Alfred J. Verrecchia, C.O.O.
Director: Karen Davis.
Number of staff: 2 full-time professional; 1 part-time support.
EIN: 222538470

2966
Horace A. Kimball and S. Ella Kimball Foundation
c/o The Washington Trust Co.
23 Broad St.
Westerly, RI   02891   (401) 364-3565
Contact: Thomas F. Black III, Pres.
FAX: (401) 364-7799; *URL:* http://www.hkimballfoundation.org

Incorporated in 1956 in DE.
Donor(s): H. Earle Kimball.‡
Grantmaker type: Independent foundation
Financial data (yr. ended 10/31/02): Assets, $6,637,970 (M); expenditures, $423,751; qualifying distributions, $349,278; giving activities include $341,619 for 36 grants (high: $26,500; low: $100).
Fields of interest: Arts; Secondary school/education; Education; Natural resources; Environment; Animal welfare; Health care; Health organizations, association; Human services; Children/youth, services; Aging, centers/services; Homeless, human services; General charitable giving; Disabled; Aging; Economically disadvantaged; Homeless.

Types of support: General/operating support; Capital campaigns; Building/renovation; Emergency funds; Seed money; Matching/challenge support.
Limitations: Giving limited to RI, with emphasis on South County. No grants to individuals, or for feasibility studies.
Application information: Submit application through website only. Application form required.
Copies of proposal: 3
Deadline(s): None
Board meeting date(s): Varies
Officers and Trustees:* Thomas F. Black III,* Pres.; Norman D. Baker, Jr.,* Secy.-Treas.; F. Thomas Lenihan.
Number of staff: 1 part-time support.
EIN: 056006130

2967
Narragansett Bay Resources Foundation
(formerly Renew the Resources of the Bay Foundation)
461 Water St.
Warren, RI 02885

Established in 1999 in RI.
Donor(s): Luther H. Blount.
Grantmaker type: Operating foundation
Financial data (yr. ended 12/31/02): Assets, $38,198 (M); gifts received, $1,500; expenditures, $968,021; qualifying distributions, $960,000; giving activities include $960,000 for 1 grant.
Fields of interest: Environment.
Limitations: Applications not accepted. Giving primarily in RI. No grants to individuals.
Application information: Contributes only to pre-selected organizations.
Officers: Luther H. Blount, Pres. and Treas.; Julie Blount, Secy.
Directors: Paul Frechette; Pasco Gasbarro, Jr.
EIN: 050505420

2968
The Frank Loomis Palmer Fund
c/o Fleet Private Clients Group
P.O. Box 6767
Providence, RI 02940-6767
Contact: Marjorie Alexandre Davis
Application address: 777 Main St., Hartford, CT 06115, tel.: (860) 952-7405

Trust established in 1936 in CT.
Donor(s): Virginia Palmer.‡
Grantmaker type: Independent foundation
Financial data (yr. ended 07/31/02): Assets, $28,106,239 (M); expenditures, $2,145,365; qualifying distributions, $1,524,118; giving activities include $1,513,369 for 92 grants (high: $150,000; low: $600; average: $2,500–$60,000).
Purpose and activities: Grants to encourage new projects and to provide seed money, with emphasis on child welfare and family services and youth agencies; support also for civic groups, cultural programs, social services, and educational programs.
Fields of interest: Performing arts; Arts; Elementary school/education; Secondary school/education; Higher education; Adult/continuing education; Libraries/library science; Education; Natural resources;

Environment; Hospitals (general); Family planning; Health care; Health organizations, association; AIDS; Alcoholism; AIDS research; Legal services; Safety/disasters; Children/youth, services; Family services; Hospices; Aging, centers/services; Minorities/immigrants, centers/services; Community development; Engineering/technology; Science; Government/public administration; Transportation; Religion; Minorities; Aging.
Types of support: Equipment; Program development; Conferences/seminars; Publication; Seed money; Scholarship funds; Research; Consulting services; Matching/challenge support.
Limitations: Giving limited to New London, CT. No grants to individuals, or for endowment funds.
Publications: Informational brochure (including application guidelines).
Application information: Application form required.
Initial approach: Telephone
Copies of proposal: 1
Deadline(s): May 15 and Nov. 15
Board meeting date(s): Jan. and July
Final notification: Feb. 1 and Aug. 1
Trustee: Fleet National Bank.
Number of staff: None.
EIN: 066026043

2969
The Rhode Island Foundation ▼
1 Union Sta.
Providence, RI 02903 (401) 274-4564
Contact: Karen Voci, Sr. V.P., Prog.
FAX: (401) 331-8085; URL: http://www.rifoundation.org

Incorporated in 1916 in RI (includes The Rhode Island Community Foundation in 1984).
Grantmaker type: Community foundation
Financial data (yr. ended 12/31/01): Assets, $366,346,451 (M); gifts received, $16,087,287; expenditures, $24,430,836; giving activities include $19,486,289 for 1,017 grants (high: $4,087,703; low: $75; average: $5,000–$75,000).
Purpose and activities: To promote educational and charitable activities that tend to improve the living conditions and well-being of the inhabitants of RI; grants for capital and operating purposes principally to agencies working in the fields of education, health care, the arts and cultural affairs, youth, the aged, social services, urban affairs, historic preservation, and the environment. Some restricted grants for scholarships and medical research. The foundation administers a donor-advised fund.
Fields of interest: Performing arts; Historic preservation/historical societies; Arts; Libraries/library science; Education; Natural resources; Environment; Animal welfare; Hospitals (general); Health care; Health organizations, association; AIDS; Alcoholism; AIDS research; Legal services; Food services; Human services; Children/youth, services; Family services; Aging, centers/services; Minorities/immigrants, centers/services; Homeless, human services; Community development; Voluntarism promotion; Government/public administration; Public

affairs; Minorities; Aging; Immigrants/refugees; Economically disadvantaged; Homeless.
Types of support: General/operating support; Capital campaigns; Building/renovation; Equipment; Land acquisition; Emergency funds; Program development; Conferences/seminars; Publication; Seed money; Fellowships; Scholarship funds; Technical assistance; Consulting services; Scholarships—to individuals; Matching/challenge support.
Limitations: Giving limited to RI. No support for religious organizations for sectarian purposes (except as specified by donors). No grants to individuals (except from donor-advised and designated funds), or for endowment funds, research, hospital equipment, capital needs of health organizations, annual campaigns, deficit financing, or educational institutions for general operating expenses; no loans.
Publications: Application guidelines, Annual report (including application guidelines), Informational brochure, Newsletter, Occasional report, Program policy statement.
Application information: Organizations are invited to submit a full application after letter of intent is received. For scholarship information from the designated and donor-advised funds contact the foundation. Application form not required.
Initial approach: 3- to 4-page letter of intent
Copies of proposal: 5
Deadline(s): June 1 for Arts and Education, Oct. 1 for Children and Families, Feb. 1 for Economic/Community Development for letters of intent; Applications after invitativon due Sept. 1 for Arts and Ed., Jan. 1 for Children and Families, May 1 for Eco./Comm. Devel.
Board meeting date(s): Dec., Apr., and Aug.
Final notification: 1 week after board meeting
Officers: Ronald V. Gallo, C.E.O. and Pres.; Carol Golden, Sr. V.P., Devel.; Karen Voci, Sr. V.P., Prog.; Michael Jenkinson, V.P., Finance and Admin.; Jennifer Reid, Cont.
Board of Directors: Pablo Rodriguez, Chair.; Elizabeth Z. Chace; Peter Damon; George Graboys; Carol Grant; Margaret Goddard Leeson; Florence K. Murray; Ruth Simmons; Walter R. Stone; John W. Wall.
Number of staff: 20 full-time professional; 1 part-time professional; 19 full-time support.
EIN: 050208270

2970
Roosa Family Foundation Trust
P.O. Box 6767
Providence, RI 02940-6767
Contact: Cathy Iacovazzi
Application address: 65 LaSalle Rd., West Hartford, CT 06017, tel.: (860) 586-7257

Established in 1994 in CT.
Grantmaker type: Independent foundation
Financial data (yr. ended 12/31/02): Assets, $7,238,231 (M); expenditures, $596,411; qualifying distributions, $556,096; giving activities include $488,339 for 52 grants (high: $100,000; low: $80).
Purpose and activities: Giving primarily for education, historical preservation, conservation, health associations, children, youth and social services, economic development, and Baptist and Presbyterian churches.

Fields of interest: Museums; Museums (children's); Higher education; Education; Natural resources; Health organizations, association; Boys & girls clubs; Human services; Children/youth, services; Economic development; Protestant agencies & churches.
Limitations: Giving primarily in CT and RI.
Application information:
   Initial approach: Proposal
   Deadline(s): None
Trustees: David E. Roosa; Fleet National Bank.
EIN: 223295175

2971
E. J. & V. M. Routhier Foundation
(formerly Edward J. & Virginia M. Routhier Foundation)
c/o Fleet Private Clients Group
P.O. Box 6767
Providence, RI 02940-6767

Established in 1995 in CT.
Grantmaker type: Independent foundation
Financial data (yr. ended 12/31/02): Assets, $15,853,760 (M); gifts received, $4,166,908; expenditures, $580,524; qualifying distributions, $534,025; giving activities include $385,000 for 9 grants (high: $205,000; low: $1,500).
Fields of interest: Elementary/secondary education; Animals/wildlife; Foundations (community); Roman Catholic agencies & churches.
Limitations: Applications not accepted. Giving primarily in RI. No grants to individuals.
Application information: Contributes only to pre-selected organizations.
Trustees: Edward J. Routhier; Dennis C. Dibennedetto; Phyllis Nigris; Fleet National Bank.
EIN: 050485198

2972
The Sachem Foundation
22 Parsonage St.
Providence, RI 02903
Contact: Esther E.M. Mauran, Pres.

Established in 1997 in RI.
Donor(s): Esther E.M. Mauran.
Grantmaker type: Independent foundation
Financial data (yr. ended 12/31/02): Assets, $2,435,993 (M); gifts received, $250,279; expenditures, $154,241; qualifying distributions, $115,557; giving activities include $117,950 for 16 grants (high: $30,000; low: $100).
Purpose and activities: Giving for nature conservation and for art and cultural programs.
Fields of interest: Education; Natural resources; Human services.
Limitations: Giving primarily in ME and RI.
Application information:
   Deadline(s): None
Officers and Trustees:* Esther E.M. Mauran,* Pres.; Frank Mauran IV,* Secy.; Paul W. Whyte, Treas.; Pauline C. Metcalf.
EIN: 061483391

2973
van Beuren Charitable Foundation, Inc.
P.O. Box 4098
Middletown, RI 02842 (401) 846-8167
Contact: Barbara van Beuren, Exec. Dir.
FAX: (401) 849-6859; E-mail: vBCFnd@aol.com;
URL: http://www.vBCF.net

Established in 1986 in RI.
Donor(s): Members of the van Beuren family.
Grantmaker type: Independent foundation
Financial data (yr. ended 12/31/01): Assets, $51,286,298 (M); expenditures, $3,632,381; qualifying distributions, $3,259,175; giving activities include $3,191,464 for grants (average: $1,500–$600,000).
Purpose and activities: The van Beuren Charitable Foundation is a family foundation. It was established in 1986 as a vehicle for the philanthropic activities of John A. and Hope H. van Beuren and their family. The van Beuren Charitable Foundation is primarily interested in promoting the well-being of its community, Newport County, Rhode Island. In recent years, the foundation has made grants mainly in the areas of local social services, historic preservation, and land conservation.
Fields of interest: History/archaeology; Environment, land resources; Human services.
Types of support: General/operating support; Capital campaigns; Building/renovation; Land acquisition; Endowments; Program development; Professorships.
Limitations: Giving primarily in Newport County, RI. No grants to individuals.
Publications: Annual report (including application guidelines), Grants list.
Application information: Call or write for complete guidelines. Application form required.
   Copies of proposal: 1
   Deadline(s): Dec. 15 and June 15
   Board meeting date(s): Spring and fall
Officers and Directors:* John A. van Beuren,* Chair. and Treas.; Barbara van Beuren,* Pres. and Exec. Dir.; Hope Hill van Beuren,* V.P.; Leonard Boehner, Secy.; Andrea van Beuren; Archbold D. van Beuren.
Number of staff: 1 part-time professional; 1 full-time support.
EIN: 222773769

2974
Vigneron Memorial Fund
c/o Fleet Private Client Group
P.O. Box 6767
Providence, RI 02940-6767
Application address: Karen Hibbert, Trust Off., c/o Fleet National Bank, 100 Westminster St., Providence, RI 02903

Grantmaker type: Independent foundation
Financial data (yr. ended 12/31/02): Assets, $2,190,881 (M); expenditures, $138,585; qualifying distributions, $131,947; giving activities include $121,366 for 15 grants (high: $20,000; low: $3,000).
Purpose and activities: Giving primarily for health care for the physically disabled.
Fields of interest: Theater; University; Animals/wildlife, bird preserves; Medical care, rehabilitation; Art & music therapy; Health care, patient services; Vocational rehabilitation; Human services.

Types of support: General/operating support; Equipment; Endowments; Program development; Matching/challenge support.
Limitations: Giving limited to RI. No grants to individuals.
Application information:
   Initial approach: Proposal
   Deadline(s): None
Trustee: Fleet National Bank.
EIN: 056005884

2975
The Woodward Fund
c/o Fleet Private Clients Group
P.O. Box 6767
Providence, RI 02940-6767
Contact: S.A. Curtis, Jr.
Application address: Fleet National Bank, 1 East Ave., Rochester, NY 14638

Established in 1965 in NY.
Donor(s): Florence S. Woodward.
Grantmaker type: Independent foundation
Financial data (yr. ended 11/30/02): Assets, $3,074,623 (M); expenditures, $204,387; qualifying distributions, $202,142; giving activities include $200,000 for 30 grants (high: $50,000; low: $2,000).
Purpose and activities: Funding primarily for higher education, wildlife conservation, human services, and the arts.
Fields of interest: Arts; Higher education; Animals/wildlife, preservation/protection; Human services; Federated giving programs; Native Americans/American Indians.
Limitations: Giving primarily in AZ, CA, and ME. No grants to individuals.
Trustee: Fleet National Bank.
EIN: 166064221

SOUTH CAROLINA

2976
The Arkwright Foundation
P.O. Box 1086
Spartanburg, SC 29304 (864) 585-9213
Contact: Walter S. Montgomery, Jr., Vice-Chair.

Incorporated in 1945 in SC.
Donor(s): Members of the M.L. Cates family, members of the W.S. Montgomery family.
Grantmaker type: Independent foundation
Financial data (yr. ended 12/31/02): Assets, $11,212,743 (M); expenditures, $734,204; qualifying distributions, $659,185; giving activities include $683,990 for 91 grants (high: $390,500; low: $30).
Purpose and activities: Giving primarily for higher education and human services.
Fields of interest: Higher education; Education; Animals/wildlife; Health organizations, association; Human services; Children/youth, services; Community development; Protestant agencies & churches.
Limitations: Giving primarily in SC. No grants to individuals.
Application information:

Initial approach: Letter, personal visit, or telephone
Deadline(s): None
Officers: M.L. Cates, Sr., Chair.; Walter S. Montgomery, Jr., Vice-Chair.
EIN: 576000066

2977
Lucy Hampton Bostick Charitable Trust
c/o H. Simmons Tate, Jr.
P.O. Box 11889
Columbia, SC 29211

Established in 1968 in SC.
Grantmaker type: Independent foundation
Financial data (yr. ended 12/31/02): Assets, $2,153,494 (M); expenditures, $113,478; qualifying distributions, $106,290; giving activities include $106,290 for 7 grants (high: $25,000; low: $1,790).
Purpose and activities: Giving for art and cultural programs, and for higher education.
Fields of interest: Museums (art); Historic preservation/historical societies; Arts; Education; Environment, land resources; Animal welfare; Hospitals (general).
Types of support: General/operating support.
Limitations: Applications not accepted. Giving primarily in SC. No grants to individuals.
Application information: Contributes only to pre-selected organizations.
Trustees: A. Mason Gibbes; H. Simmons Tate, Jr.; George R.P. Walker.
EIN: 576042059

2978
Drs. Bruce and Lee Foundation
181 E. Evans St.
BTC Box 022
Florence, SC 29506 (843) 664-2870
Contact: L. Bradley Callicott, Exec. Dir.
FAX: (843) 664-2815; E-mail: blfound@bellsouth.net

Established in 1995 in SC; converted from the sale of the assets of Carolinas Hospital System to Quorum, Inc.
Grantmaker type: Independent foundation
Financial data (yr. ended 12/31/01): Assets, $145,012,031 (M); gifts received, $350; expenditures, $14,299,623; qualifying distributions, $5,433,445; giving activities include $5,114,697 for 36 grants (high: $2,500,000; low: $4,100).
Purpose and activities: The foundation aims to advance the welfare of people in the Florence, SC, area by providing economic support to organizations and programs which contribute to the area's medical, educational, and cultural resources.
Fields of interest: Arts; Education; Environment; Medical research; Human services.
Types of support: Continuing support; Capital campaigns; Building/renovation; Equipment; Endowments; Debt reduction; Emergency funds; Professorships; Seed money; Scholarship funds; Consulting services; Matching/challenge support.
Limitations: Giving primarily in the Florence, SC, area. No grants to individuals.
Publications: Application guidelines, Annual report (including application guidelines), Grants list, Occasional report.

Application information: Application form required.
Initial approach: Telephone
Copies of proposal: 1
Deadline(s): None
Board meeting date(s): 3rd Tues. monthly except in Dec.
Final notification: Generally within 90 days
Officer and Trustees: L. Bradley Callicott,* Exec. Dir.; Gordon Baker, Jr.; John L. Bruce; Mark Buyck, Jr.; C. Edward Floyd; Thomas C. Griffin; Frank B. Lee, Sr.; Haigh Porter; Henry Swink; John M. Thomason; and 3 additional trustees.
Number of staff: 2 full-time professional.
EIN: 570902483
Recent environmental and animal welfare grants:
2978-1 South Carolina Department of Health and Environmental Control, Lancaster, SC, $60,000. 2002.

2979
The Cart Foundation
1741 Hwy. 56
Spartanburg, SC 29302

Established in 1996 in SC.
Grantmaker type: Independent foundation
Financial data (yr. ended 12/31/02): Assets, $1,945,321 (M); expenditures, $111,651; qualifying distributions, $110,000; giving activities include $110,000 for 39 grants (high: $17,500; low: $500).
Purpose and activities: Giving primarily for environmental conservation.
Fields of interest: Higher education; Natural resources; Family planning; Health organizations, association; Cancer; Food services; Human services.
Limitations: Applications not accepted. Giving on a national basis. No grants to individuals.
Application information: Contributes only to pre-selected organizations.
Officer and Trustees: Joan M. Cart,* Mgr.; Ben M. Cart; Walter M. Cart; Elizabeth M. White.
EIN: 570987085

2980
The Ceres Foundation, Inc.
328 E. Bay St.
Charleston, SC 29401

Established in 1999.
Donor(s): Diane D. Terni.
Grantmaker type: Independent foundation
Financial data (yr. ended 12/31/02): Assets, $29,070,453 (M); expenditures, $2,244,359; qualifying distributions, $2,016,306; giving activities include $1,937,500 for 82 grants (high: $300,000; low: $500).
Purpose and activities: Giving primarily for education, the environment, human services, and arts and cultural programs.
Fields of interest: Arts; Education; Environment, land resources; Human services.
Limitations: Applications not accepted. No grants to individuals.
Application information: Unsolicited requests for funds not considered.

Officers: Diane D. Terni, Pres.; Stephen L. Gavel, V.P.; Linda G. Webb, Secy.; Frank J. Gavel, Jr., Treas.
EIN: 582479387

2981
Chase Wildlife Foundation
C/O Executive Tax
P.O. Box 1769, No. 4103
Pawleys Island, SC 29585 (843) 237-1384
FAX: (212) 213-8232; URL: http://www.lynnchasedesigns.com

Established in 1988 in DE.
Grantmaker type: Public charity
Financial data (yr. ended 12/31/00): Revenue, $69,883; assets, $119,751 (M); gifts received, $23,385; expenditures, $44,703; program services expenses, $44,703; giving activities include $35,150 for grants.
Purpose and activities: The foundation promotes the preservation of wildlife and the environment on a global scale. It operates with two goals: first, to stop the destruction of animal habitats by human growth and expansion; and second, to focus on the survival and re-establishment of key species in that environment. To these ends, the foundation provides individual grants and joins cooperative efforts with other preservation and conservation organizations worldwide.
Fields of interest: Global warming; Environment; Animals/wildlife, preservation/protection.
Types of support: Equipment; Program development; Seed money; Research; Grants to individuals.
Publications: Financial statement, Newsletter.
Application information:
Initial approach: Letter of inquiry
Deadline(s): None
Board meeting date(s): 3 times per year
Final notification: By end of calendar year
Officers and Directors: Marianna Baker,* Chair.; Kathleen Gerard,* Pres.; John E. Eisinger,* Treas.; Lynn Chase; Georgianna Ducas; Botsy Jones; Angelene Pell Wagner.
EIN: 222968708

2982
The Cline Foundation
c/o N.Q. Cline, Sr.
P.O. Box 3768
Greenville, SC 29608

Established in 1983.
Donor(s): The Cline Co., Inc., N.Q. Cline, Sr.
Grantmaker type: Company-sponsored foundation
Financial data (yr. ended 12/31/02): Assets, $1,922,903 (M); expenditures, $319,871; qualifying distributions, $310,142; giving activities include $317,100 for 22 grants (high: $51,000; low: $1,000).
Fields of interest: Animals/wildlife, preservation/protection; Boy scouts; Camps.
Types of support: Endowments; Employee matching gifts.
Limitations: Applications not accepted. Giving primarily in Greenville, SC. No grants to individuals.

Application information: Contributes only to pre-selected organizations.
Officers: Martha Cline, Pres.; David M. Cline, Secy.
EIN: 570752730

2983
Coats & Clark Inc. Corporate Giving Program

c/o Consumer Svcs.
P.O. Box 12229
Greenville, SC 29612-0229 (800) 648-1479
Contact: Billy Chism

Grantmaker type: Corporate giving program
Purpose and activities: Coats & Clark makes charitable contributions to nonprofit organizations involved with education, the environment, youth, rural development, and minorities. Support is given primarily in areas of company operations.
Fields of interest: Education; Environment; Youth, services; Rural development; Minorities.
Types of support: General/operating support; Employee volunteer services; Sponsorships.
Limitations: Giving primarily in areas of company operations.
Application information: Application form not required.
Initial approach: Proposal to headquarters
Deadline(s): None

2984
Community Foundation of Greater Greenville, Inc.

27 Cleveland St., Ste. 101
Greenville, SC 29601 (864) 233-5925
Contact: Robert W. Morris, Pres.
FAX: (864) 242-9292; E-mail: bmorris@cfgg.com; URL: http://www.cfgg.com

Established in 1956 in SC; incorporated in 1970.
Grantmaker type: Community foundation
Financial data (yr. ended 12/31/02): Assets, $24,581,099 (M); gifts received, $9,250,148; expenditures, $8,639,298; giving activities include $4,773,189 for grants.
Purpose and activities: The foundation exists to enhance the quality of life of citizens of Greater Greenville by linking philanthropic leadership, charitable resources and civic influence with needs.
Fields of interest: Arts; Early childhood education; Education; Environment; Health care; Human services.
Types of support: Capital campaigns; Equipment; Emergency funds; Program development; Conferences/seminars; Seed money; Internship funds; Scholarship funds; Technical assistance; In-kind gifts; Matching/challenge support.
Limitations: Giving limited to greater Greenville, SC. No grants to individuals, or for ongoing operational expenses of existing organizations.
Publications: Application guidelines, Annual report, Informational brochure, Newsletter, Program policy statement.
Application information: Application form required.
Initial approach: Telephone or letter
Copies of proposal: 2

Deadline(s): Varies, usually beginning of Mar.
Board meeting date(s): Jan., Mar., May, July, Sept., and Nov.
Final notification: May
Officers and Directors:* Susan Shi, Chair.; Ernest Lathem,* Vice-Chair.; Robert W. Morris, Pres.; Pedrick Lowrey, Secy.; Charles Whitmire, Jr., Treas.; J. Tod Hyche, Legal Counsel; and 25 additional directors.
Number of staff: 5 full-time professional.
EIN: 576019318
Recent environmental and animal welfare grants:
2984-1 Upstate Forever, Greenville, SC, $22,500. 2001.

2985
Community Foundation of the Lowcountry
(formerly Hilton Head Island Foundation, Inc.)
4 Northridge Dr., Ste. A
P.O. Box 23019
Hilton Head Island, SC 29925-3019
(843) 681-9100
Contact: Dianne K. Garnett, C.E.O.
FAX: (843) 681-9101; E-mail: foundation@cf-lowcountry.org; URL: http://www.cf-lowcountry.org

Established in 1983 in SC; converted to a community foundation in 1994 from the proceeds of the sale of Hilton Head Hospital to AMI.
Grantmaker type: Community foundation
Financial data (yr. ended 06/30/03): Assets, $30,259,343 (L); gifts received, $1,657,701; expenditures, $2,099,114; giving activities include $1,029,654 for 187 grants (high: $100,000; low: $100) and $153,700 for 77 grants to individuals (high: $5,000; low: $500).
Purpose and activities: Strengthening the community by connecting people, resources and needs. The foundation administers donor-advised funds.
Fields of interest: Arts; Education; Environment; Health care; Human services; Community development, neighborhood development.
Types of support: Management development; Capital campaigns; Building/renovation; Equipment; Program development; Seed money; Curriculum development; Technical assistance; Consulting services; Program evaluation; Scholarships—to individuals; Matching/challenge support.
Limitations: Giving limited to Beaufort, Colleton, Hampton and Jasper counties, SC.
Publications: Annual report, Grants list, Informational brochure (including application guidelines), Newsletter.
Application information: Application form required.
Initial approach: Letter or telephone
Deadline(s): Apr. 1, Aug. 1, and Dec. 1
Board meeting date(s): Jan., Mar., May, July, Sept., and Nov.
Final notification: Approximately 3 months after deadline
Officers and Trustees:* David W. Ames,* Chair.; Kaye Black,* Vice-Chair.; Dianne K. Garnett, C.E.O., Pres. and Secy.; James L. Elder, Treas.; Charlie H. Brown; Clifford Bush III; Emory Campbell; Joseph B. Fraser III; Elizabeth P. Grace; Bernard Moscovitz; Dorothy G. Perkins;

Julius S. Scott, Jr., Ph.D.; G. Thomas Upshaw; Wade J. Webster.
Number of staff: 6 full-time professional; 1 part-time professional; 1 full-time support.
EIN: 570756987

2986
The Community Foundation Serving Coastal South Carolina
(formerly Trident Community Foundation)
90 Mary St.
Charleston, SC 29403-6230 (843) 723-3635
Contact: Madeleine McGee, Pres.
FAX: (843) 577-3671; E-mail: info@tcfgives.org; URL: http://www.tcfgives.org

Incorporated in 1974 in SC.
Grantmaker type: Community foundation
Financial data (yr. ended 06/30/02): Assets, $88,134,629 (M); gifts received, $7,720,092; expenditures, $5,443,621; giving activities include $3,947,445 for 1,100 grants (high: $175,000; low: $100; average: $100–$175,000) and $143,816 for 5 foundation-administered programs.
Purpose and activities: Giving primarily for education and human services.
Fields of interest: Arts; Child development, education; Education; Environment; Housing/shelter, development; Human services; Children/youth, services; Family services; Homeless, human services; Civil rights; Rural development; Community development; Minorities; Homeless.
Types of support: General/operating support; Capital campaigns; Building/renovation; Equipment; Land acquisition; Emergency funds; Program development; Publication; Seed money; Scholarship funds; Technical assistance; Consulting services.
Limitations: Giving primarily in Beaufort, Berkeley, Charleston, Colleton, Dorchester, Georgetown, Hampton and Jasper counties, SC. No support for religious activities, private foundations, or political organizations. No grants to individuals (except for designated scholarship funds), or for endowments, deficit financing, dinners or other special one-time events, or generally for building funds.
Publications: Application guidelines, Biennial report, Financial statement, Grants list, Informational brochure (including application guidelines), Newsletter, Occasional report.
Application information: Application form required.
Initial approach: Letter of intent (not to exceed 2 pages excluding attachments)
Copies of proposal: 1
Deadline(s): Varies according to program
Board meeting date(s): 2nd Wed. of alternate months
Final notification: Varies according to program
Officers and Directors:* Linda Plunkett,* Chair.; Henry Blackford III, Vice-Chair.; Madeleine McGee, Pres.; Richard Hendry, V.P., Progs.; Brian Hussain, V.P., Finance; George Miller,* Secy.-Treas.; and 22 additional directors.
Number of staff: 8 full-time professional; 4 full-time support; 1 part-time support.
EIN: 237390313

2987
The Laura E. Dupont Foundation
(formerly The Echols-Johnston Family
Foundation)
P.O. Box 8099
Greenville, SC 29604-8099

Established in 1997 in SC.
Donor(s): Laura E. Dupont.
Grantmaker type: Independent foundation
Financial data (yr. ended 04/30/02): Assets,
$1,221,590 (M); expenditures, $188,369;
qualifying distributions, $169,975; giving
activities include $170,059 for 42 grants (high:
$25,610; low: $25).
Purpose and activities: Giving primarily for
wildlife conservation, health associations, and
Christian organizations.
Fields of interest: Animals/wildlife,
preservation/protection; Health organizations,
association; Christian agencies & churches.
Limitations: Applications not accepted. Giving
primarily in SC. No grants to individuals.
Application information: Contributes only to
pre-selected organizations.
Trustees: Laura E. Dupont; Charles P. Johnston;
Ellis M. Johnston II; James S. Johnston, Jr.
EIN: 586340729

2988
The Fat Cat Foundation
c/o Sellars & Cole, LLC
P.O. Box 11878
Columbia, SC 29211-1878

Established in 1998 in SC.
Donor(s): Harriott H. Faucette.
Grantmaker type: Independent foundation
Financial data (yr. ended 12/31/00): Assets,
$409,924 (M); expenditures, $400,769;
qualifying distributions, $388,291; giving
activities include $390,000 for 10 grants (high:
$200,000; low: $5,000).
Purpose and activities: Giving primarily for the
environment, art and cultural organizations, and
higher education.
Fields of interest: Arts; Higher education;
Environment; Children/youth, services.
Limitations: Applications not accepted. Giving
primarily in Columbia, SC. No grants to
individuals.
Application information: Contributes only to
pre-selected organizations.
Trustees: Mary R. Cantey; Harriott H. Faucette;
Martha M. Faucette.
EIN: 582337838

2989
First Citizens Foundation, Inc.
1230 Main St.
Columbia, SC 29201
Contact: Peter Bristow, V.P.

Established in 2000 in SC.
Donor(s): First Citizens Bancorporation of SC.
Grantmaker type: Independent foundation
Financial data (yr. ended 12/31/02): Assets,
$8,233,115 (M); expenditures, $464,393;
qualifying distributions, $338,479; giving
activities include $328,699 for 38 grants (high:
$25,000; low: $1,000).

Fields of interest: Libraries/library science;
Zoos/zoological societies; Federated giving
programs.
Application information: Application form
required.
Deadline(s): None
Officers: Jim Apple, Pres.; Peter Bristow, V.P.;
Charles Cook, Secy.; Craig L. Nix, Treas.
EIN: 571108547

2990
Hilton Head Island Foundation
(formerly Hilton Head Health Service
Corporation)
P.O. Box 21117
Hilton Head Island, SC 29925-1117
(843) 691-9100
Contact: Dianne K. Garnett, Pres. and C.E.O.
URL: http://www.cf-lowcountry.org/
foundation.aspx

Established in 1984.
Grantmaker type: Public charity
Financial data (yr. ended 06/30/02): Assets,
$20,247,946 (M); gifts received, $29,013;
expenditures, $1,752,115; program services
expenses, $1,752,115; giving activities include
$1,559,010 for 42 grants (high: $228,800; low:
$370).
Purpose and activities: The foundation supports
non-profits in arts and culture, community
development, education, the environment,
health, and human services.
Fields of interest: Arts; Education; Environment;
Health care; Human services; Community
development.
Types of support: Seed money.
Limitations: Giving limited to the greater Hilton
Head, SC, area.
Application information: Application form
required.
Deadline(s): Apr. 1, Aug. 1, and Dec. 1 for
Mission Support and Seed Grants; 20th of
each month for Developmental Assistance
Grants
Officers and Trustees:* John T. Brennan, M.D.,*
Chair.; Ronald C. Onorato,* Vice-Chair.; Dianne
K. Garnett,* Pres., C.E.O., and Secy.; Dorothy G.
Perkins,* Treas.; David W. Ames; Kaye Black;
Charlie H. Brown; and 6 additional trustees.
EIN: 570757036

2991
Joanna Foundation
P.O. Box 308
Sullivans Island, SC 29482 (843) 883-9199
Contact: Margaret P. Schachte, Exec. V.P.

Established in 1945 in SC.
Donor(s): Marquette Charitable Organization.
Grantmaker type: Independent foundation
Financial data (yr. ended 12/31/02): Assets,
$3,025,914 (M); expenditures, $302,468;
qualifying distributions, $257,634; giving
activities include $227,500 for 35 grants (high:
$25,000; low: $1,000; average:
$1,000–$25,000).
Purpose and activities: Primary areas of interest
include higher education, youth, the
environment, community development, the arts,
health, and public benefit.

Fields of interest: Historic preservation/historical
societies; Arts; Higher education; Environment;
Health care; Human services; Children/youth,
services; Community development; Public
affairs.
Types of support: General/operating support;
Building/renovation; Program development;
Matching/challenge support.
Limitations: Giving primarily in Berkeley,
Charleston, Dorchester, Laurens and Newberry
counties, SC.
Publications: Informational brochure (including
application guidelines).
Application information: Application form not
required.
Initial approach: Letter
Copies of proposal: 7
Deadline(s): Jan. 10, May 10, and Sept. 10
Board meeting date(s): Feb., June, and Oct.
Final notification: Approx. within 8 weeks of
deadline
Officers and Trustees:* Walter C. Regnery,*
Pres.; Margaret P. Schachte,* Exec. V.P.; Charles
E. Menefee, Jr.,* Secy.-Treas.; Yonge R. Jones;
Eugenie F. Regnery; Patricia Regnery.
Number of staff: 1 part-time professional.
EIN: 570314444

2992
The McNair Law Firm Foundation
P.O. Box 11390
Columbia, SC 29211 (803) 799-9800
Contact: O. Wayne Corley, Chair.
Application address: Bank of America Twr.,
1301 Gervais St., 17th Fl., Columbia, SC 29201

Established in 1999 in SC.
Donor(s): O. Wayne Corley, Richard J. Morgan.
Grantmaker type: Independent foundation
Financial data (yr. ended 12/31/02): Assets,
$33,960 (M); gifts received, $255,200;
expenditures, $142,437; qualifying distributions,
$141,900; giving activities include $141,900 for
36 grants (high: $78,000; low: $200).
Purpose and activities: Giving primarily for the
arts and education.
Fields of interest: Arts; Education;
Zoos/zoological societies; Health organizations,
association.
Types of support: Capital campaigns.
Limitations: Giving primarily in SC.
Application information:
Initial approach: Letter
Deadline(s): None
Board meeting date(s): Apr., Aug., Oct., and
Dec.
Officers and Board Members:* O. Wayne
Corley,* Chair.; Jonathan H. Nason,* Secy.;
Missy Schumpert, Treas.; Erik P. Doerring;
Joseph D. Walker; M. William Youngblood.
EIN: 571090042

2993
Rose & Walter Montgomery Foundation
P.O. Box 5565
Spartanburg, SC 29304 (864) 585-9213
Contact: Walter S. Montgomery, Jr., Tr.

Donor(s): Walter S. Montgomery,‡ Rose C.
Montgomery Trust A.
Grantmaker type: Independent foundation

Financial data (yr. ended 12/31/02): Assets, $16,345,966 (M); expenditures, $1,243,621; qualifying distributions, $788,000; giving activities include $788,000 for 66 grants (high: $230,000; low: $500).
Purpose and activities: Giving primarily for the arts, social services, and Episcopal churches and organizations.
Fields of interest: Arts education; Music; Arts; Higher education; Education; Environment, beautification programs; Animal welfare; Health care; Human services; Federated giving programs; Protestant agencies & churches.
Limitations: Giving primarily in Spartanburg, SC, and Memphis, TN; some funding nationally, particularly in Atlanta, GA. No grants to individuals.
Application information:
  Initial approach: Letter
  Deadline(s): None
Trustees: Rose M. Johnston; Walter S. Montgomery, Jr.
EIN: 570986535

2994
Schuyler & Yvonne Moore Family Foundation
P.O. Box 2044
West Columbia, SC   29171

Established in 1993 in CA.
Donor(s): Schuyler Moore, Yvonne Moore.
Grantmaker type: Independent foundation
Financial data (yr. ended 12/31/02): Assets, $108,531 (L); expenditures, $169,397; qualifying distributions, $151,228; giving activities include $151,228 for 16 grants (high: $45,000; low: $500).
Purpose and activities: Giving primarily for education.
Fields of interest: Higher education; Medical school/education; Animal welfare; Athletics/sports, school programs.
Types of support: Scholarships—to individuals.
Limitations: Applications not accepted. Giving on a national basis.
Application information: Contributes only to pre-selected organizations.
Trustees: Schuyler Moore; Yvonne Moore.
EIN: 943182712

2995
Post and Courier Foundation
134 Columbus St.
Charleston, SC   29403-4800
Contact: J. Douglas Donehue, Admin.

Incorporated in 1951 in SC.
Donor(s): Evening Post Publishing Co.
Grantmaker type: Company-sponsored foundation
Financial data (yr. ended 12/31/00): Assets, $8,338,992 (M); gifts received, $534,825; expenditures, $807,685; qualifying distributions, $770,614; giving activities include $770,644 for 74 grants (high: $80,000; low: $200; average: $500–$10,000).
Fields of interest: Historic preservation/historical societies; Arts; Education, association; Natural resources; Health care; Health organizations, association; Crime/law enforcement; Community development.

Types of support: Continuing support; Capital campaigns; Building/renovation; Program-related investments/loans; Employee-related scholarships.
Limitations: Giving primarily in Charleston, SC.
Application information: Application form not required.
  Initial approach: Proposal
  Deadline(s): None
  Board meeting date(s): As needed, usually twice annually
Officers: Peter Manigault, Pres.; Ivan V. Anderson, Jr., Exec. V.P.; Pierre Manigault, V.P.; James W. Martin, Treas.; J. Douglas Donehue, Admin.
Number of staff: 1 part-time professional.
EIN: 576020356

2996
Callie & John Rainey Foundation
402nd Blvd.
Anderson, SC   29621
Contact: John S. Rainey, Tr.

Established in 1995 in SC.
Grantmaker type: Independent foundation
Financial data (yr. ended 12/31/02): Assets, $5,226,516 (M); expenditures, $419,606; qualifying distributions, $324,730; giving activities include $294,123 for 34 grants (high: $114,000; low: $250).
Purpose and activities: Giving for the community, and for education, including museums and schools.
Fields of interest: Museums; Historical activities; Education; Botanical/horticulture/landscape services; Medical care, rehabilitation.
Limitations: Giving primarily in SC. No grants to individuals.
Application information: Application form not required.
  Initial approach: Letter
  Deadline(s): Sept. 10
Trustees: Mary R. Belser; Nancy R. Crowley; John S. Rainey; Robert M. Rainey.
EIN: 570970656

2997
Adrianne B. Reilly Foundation
c/o John Winthrop & Co., Inc.
1 N. Adgers Wharf
Charleston, SC   29401
Contact: Adrianne B. Reilly, Tr.
Application address: 92 Rockwood Ln., Greenwich, CT 06830, tel.: (203) 869-9837

Established in 1990 in CT and SC.
Donor(s): Adrianne B. Reilly.
Grantmaker type: Independent foundation
Financial data (yr. ended 12/31/02): Assets, $647,499 (M); gifts received, $446,138; expenditures, $180,825; qualifying distributions, $178,689; giving activities include $178,885 for 8 grants (high: $54,000; low: $6,385).
Purpose and activities: Giving for the protection of natural resources, health and medical issues, and human services.
Fields of interest: Natural resources; Health care; Human services; Aging, centers/services; Christian agencies & churches; Religion; Aging.
Types of support: Program development.

Limitations: Giving primarily in CT. No grants to individuals.
Application information:
  Initial approach: Proposal
  Deadline(s): None
Trustees: Adrianne B. Reilly; John Winthrop.
EIN: 223109258

2998
Wilbur S. Smith Foundation, Inc.
P.O. Box 265
Columbia, SC   29202

Established in 1990 in SC as successor foundation to Wilbur Smith Foundation.
Grantmaker type: Independent foundation
Financial data (yr. ended 12/31/02): Assets, $3,131,873 (M); gifts received, $1,078,057; expenditures, $128,297; qualifying distributions, $125,000; giving activities include $125,000 for 31 grants (high: $11,500; low: $500).
Purpose and activities: Giving primarily for historical preservation, education, and social services.
Fields of interest: Theater; Historic preservation/historical societies; Higher education; Education; Animal welfare; Human services; Protestant agencies & churches; Roman Catholic agencies & churches.
Limitations: Applications not accepted. Giving primarily in SC.
Application information: Contributes only to pre-selected organizations.
Officers: Sarah S. Cahalan, Pres.; Stephanie E. Smith-Phillips, V.P.
Trustees: Paul Bartolomeo; James H. Phillips.
EIN: 570916368

2999
TSC Foundation, Inc.
104 E. Springs St.
Lancaster, SC   29720

Established in 2001 in SC.
Grantmaker type: Independent foundation
Financial data (yr. ended 12/31/02): Assets, $989,269 (M); gifts received, $2,403,000; expenditures, $1,714,060; qualifying distributions, $1,714,060; giving activities include $1,711,889 for grants.
Purpose and activities: Giving primarily to public and community foundations, health associations and medical research, particularly for Lou Gehrig's disease and juvenile diabetes, social services, farmworker legal services, Episcopal churches, and a women's shelter; funding also for children's services, education, and the arts.
Fields of interest: Arts; Elementary school/education; Higher education; Animals/wildlife; Health organizations, association; Medical research, institute; Nerve, muscle & bone research; Diabetes research; Legal services; Food banks; Boy scouts; Human services; American Red Cross; Children, services; Hospices; Women, centers/services; Foundations (public); Foundations (community); Protestant agencies & churches.
Limitations: Applications not accepted. Giving primarily in NC and SC. No grants to individuals.
Application information: Contributes only to pre-selected organizations.

Officers: William Taylor, Pres.; Harry Emerson, V.P. and Secy.; Peyton Worley, V.P. and Treas.
EIN: 571124837

SOUTH DAKOTA

3000
The Kind World Foundation
P.O. Box 980
Dakota Dunes, SD   57049   (605) 232-9139
Contact: Arlene T. Curry, Exec. Dir.
FAX: (605) 232-3098; E-mail:
acurry@kindworld.org

Established in 1991 in SD.
Donor(s): Norman W. Waitt, Jr.
Grantmaker type: Independent foundation
Financial data (yr. ended 12/31/02): Assets, $21,018,875 (M); expenditures, $2,380,753; qualifying distributions, $2,211,911; giving activities include $2,054,814 for 44 grants (high: $1,000,000; low: $500; average: $500–$1,000,000).
Purpose and activities: Giving primarily for the environment, education and human services.
Fields of interest: Arts; Education; Natural resources; Children/youth, services; Family services.
Types of support: General/operating support; Continuing support; Annual campaigns; Capital campaigns; Building/renovation; Equipment; Land acquisition; Endowments; Program development; Scholarship funds; Research; Consulting services; Matching/challenge support.
Limitations: Giving primarily in Santa Fe, NM, Sioux City, IA, and nationally for environmental programs and projects.
Publications: Informational brochure (including application guidelines).
Application information: Application form not required.
  Initial approach: Telephone or letter of inquiry
  Copies of proposal: 1
  Deadline(s): 2 weeks before board meetings
  Board meeting date(s): Quarterly, and as needed
  Final notification: Within 90 days of receipt
Officers: Arlene T. Curry, Exec. Dir.; Deb Jesse, Cont.
Directors: David M. Curry; Lee Lysne; Amanda Waitt; Norman W. Waitt, Jr.
Number of staff: 1 full-time professional; 1 part-time professional; 1 part-time support.
EIN: 363776553

3001
NorthWestern Corporation Contributions Program
125 South Dakota Ave.
Sioux Falls, SD   57104
Contact: Linda Wittrock
Application address in MT: Fran Galvin, Accountant, 40 E. Broadway, Butte, MT 59701;
URL: http://www.northwesternonline.com/sub_news_info/community_relations/default.asp;
http://www.northwesternenergy.com/aboutus/grants.htm

Grantmaker type: Corporate giving program
Purpose and activities: NorthWestern makes charitable contributions to nonprofit organizations involved with arts and culture, education, the environment, health and human services, community development, and civic affairs. Support is given primarily in areas of company operations.
Fields of interest: Arts; Education; Natural resources; Environment; Health care; Human services; Community development; Public affairs.
Types of support: Capital campaigns; Building/renovation; Employee matching gifts; In-kind gifts.
Limitations: Giving primarily in areas of company operations, with emphasis on MT, NE, and SD. No support for national health organizations, sports teams, or athletic organizations. No grants to individuals, or for general operating support.
Application information: An application form is available online. A contributions committee reviews all requests. Application form required.
  Initial approach: Submit online application form for organizations located in NE and SD; download application form and mail to application address for organizations located in MT
  Deadline(s): None
  Board meeting date(s): Quarterly

3002
Sioux Falls Area Community Foundation
300 N. Phillips Ave., Ste. 102
Sioux Falls, SD   57104-6035   (605) 336-7055
Contact: Sue Brown, C.E.O.
FAX: (605) 336-0038; E-mail: sbrown@sfacf.org;
URL: http://www.sfacf.org

Established in 1976 in SD.
Grantmaker type: Community foundation
Financial data (yr. ended 06/30/03): Assets, $35,674,643 (M); gifts received, $5,492,031; expenditures, $4,067,854; giving activities include $3,346,264 for grants (high: $100,000; low: $100).
Purpose and activities: The purpose of the foundation is to attract, invest, and distribute charitable gifts for the benefit of donors and charitable institutions in the Sioux Falls, SD, area.
Fields of interest: Arts; Education; Environment; Health care; Human services; Community development; Religion.
Types of support: General/operating support; Building/renovation; Equipment; Endowments; Program development; Conferences/seminars; Seed money; Curriculum development; Scholarship funds; Research; Technical assistance; Program evaluation; Employee-related scholarships; Grants to individuals; Matching/challenge support.
Limitations: Giving generally limited to the Sioux Falls, SD, area.
Publications: Application guidelines, Annual report (including application guidelines), Financial statement, Informational brochure (including application guidelines), Newsletter.
Application information: Scholarship application forms available from high school counseling offices. Application form required.
  Initial approach: Letter or telephone

Copies of proposal: 1
Deadline(s): Varies by grant program; usually Mar. 15 for scholarships
Board meeting date(s): Bimonthly
Officers and Directors:* Jeff Scherschligt,* Chair.; Mary Lynn Myers,* Vice-Chair.; Sue Brown, C.E.O and Pres.; Candy Hanson, V.P., Devel.; Mary Pat Sweetman, Secy.; Jack Carmody,* Treas.; Dave Austad; Larry Bierman; Dick Corcoran; Steve Crim; Caroline Deinema; Steve Garry; Vance Goldammer; Helen Madsen; Paul Schiller; Mary Tidwell; Hugh Venrick.
Number of staff: 5 full-time professional; 1 full-time support.
EIN: 311748533

3003
Watertown Community Foundation
1200 33rd St. S.E., Ste. 309A
P.O. Box 116
Watertown, SD   57201-0116   (605) 882-3731
Contact: Jan DeBerg, Exec. Dir.
FAX: (605) 886-5957; E-mail:
foundation@dailypost.com

Incorporated in 1979 in SD.
Grantmaker type: Community foundation
Financial data (yr. ended 12/31/02): Assets, $5,074,409 (M); gifts received, $167,826; expenditures, $316,389; giving activities include $210,110 for grants (high: $54,000).
Purpose and activities: Giving primarily for civic affairs, arts and culture, human services, education, health and the environment. The foundation administers a donor-advised fund.
Fields of interest: Arts; Education; Natural resources; Housing/shelter, development; Safety/disasters; Recreation; Human services; Family services; Women, centers/services.
Types of support: Capital campaigns; Building/renovation; Emergency funds; Program development; Conferences/seminars; Seed money; Scholarship funds; Consulting services; Scholarships—to individuals.
Limitations: Giving limited to the metropolitan Watertown, SD, area. No support for private foundations. No grants to individuals (except for designated scholarship funds), or for operating expenses.
Publications: Annual report (including application guidelines), Informational brochure, Newsletter.
Application information: Application form required.
  Initial approach: Letter or telephone requesting Grant Application Summary
  Copies of proposal: 8
  Deadline(s): Mar. 15, June 15, Sept. 15, and Dec. 15
  Board meeting date(s): Monthly
  Final notification: Jan., Apr., July, and Oct.
Officers and Directors:* Rick Melmer,* Chair.; John Hopper,* Vice-Chair.; Jan DeBerg, Exec. Dir.; Paul Hinderaker; John Redlinger; Nancy J. Turbak.
Number of staff: 1 full-time professional.
EIN: 460350319

TENNESSEE

3004
Appalachian Community Fund
107 W. Main St., No. 202
Knoxville, TN 37902   (865) 523-5783
Contact: Gaye Evans, Exec. Dir.
FAX: (865) 523-1896; E-mail:
info@appalachiancommunityfund.org; URL:
http://www.appalachiancommunityfund.org

Established in 1987 in TN.
Grantmaker type: Public charity
Financial data (yr. ended 06/30/00): Revenue,
$320,783; assets, $307,135; gifts received,
$310,520; expenditures, $335,363; program
services expenses, $248,389; giving activities
include $215,800 for 44 grants (high: $10,000;
low: $2,400).
Purpose and activities: The fund supports
progressive community change in the central
Appalachian states. Conceived as a unique
partnership of community activists and donors,
it works to leverage money and resources to the
region. The focus of grantmaking is social
change, which is defined as working to
redistribute wealth, power, and resources, and
to eliminate barriers that keep people from
participating fully in society. Social change also
means focusing efforts on changing the
circumstances and the social institutional
systems that create barriers and inequities.
Fields of interest: Environment; Health care;
Civil rights, equal rights; Civil rights, minorities;
Civil rights, gays/lesbians; Economic
development.
Types of support: Seed money; Technical
assistance.
Limitations: Giving limited to central Appalacia:
WV, eastern KY, southwest VA, and eastern TN.
No support for profit-making organizations
(except worker-owned cooperatives) or direct
service groups, unless they are tied to social
change programs, or are likely to empower the
communities served. No grants to individuals, or
for projects that are funded heavily from large
foundations or the government, direct union
organizing, electoral lobbying for initiatives or
public office, or major capital projects, such as
land or buildings.
Publications: Application guidelines, Annual
report, Informational brochure, Occasional
report.
Application information: Application form
required.
Initial approach: Letter or telephone
Copies of proposal: 5
Deadline(s): Nov. 1 for general cycles; June 1
for Leadership Development Program;
None for Mini-grants
Board meeting date(s): Jan., Apr., July and Oct.
Final notification: Late winter
Board Members: Gaye Evans, Exec. Dir.; Darryl
Cannady; Marian Collette; Carol Greene; Lissa
McLeod; Joan Porter; Angel Rubio; Jean Stone;
and 7 additional board members.
Number of staff: 1 full-time professional; 2
part-time support.
EIN: 621316019

3005
The Aslan Foundation
P.O. Box 550
Knoxville, TN 37901-0550   (865) 637-1440
Contact: Debbie Black, Asst. Secy.
FAX: (865) 546-9808

Established in 1995 in TN.
Donor(s): Lindsay Young.
Grantmaker type: Independent foundation
Financial data (yr. ended 12/31/02): Assets,
$11,508,917 (M); expenditures, $831,926;
qualifying distributions, $729,651; giving
activities include $716,500 for 26 grants (high:
$239,000; low: $1,500).
Purpose and activities: Giving for child and
family welfare, health care, and for literacy
programs.
Fields of interest: Literature; Adult
education—literacy, basic skills & GED; Animal
welfare; Health care; Children/youth, services;
Family services.
Limitations: Giving primarily in east TN.
Application information: Application form
required.
Initial approach: Completed application form
Copies of proposal: 5
Deadline(s): None
Board meeting date(s): Mar. and Oct.
Officers and Directors:* Robert S. Young III,*
Pres.; Robert S. Young, Jr.,* V.P.; Mark K.
Williams,* Secy.; Gregory E. Erickson,* Treas.;
Lindsay Y. McDonough; Lindsay Young.
EIN: 621520208

3006
Bays Mountain Park Association
853 Bays Mt. Park Rd.
Kingsport, TN 37660-7599   (423) 229-9447
Contact: Bob Estes, Pres.

Established in 1979.
Grantmaker type: Public charity
Financial data (yr. ended 06/30/02): Revenue,
$65,147; assets, $47,462; gifts received, $3,021;
expenditures, $72,374; program services
expenses, $22,313; giving activities include
$22,313 for grants.
Purpose and activities: The organization is
operated solely for the benefit of The Bays
Mountain Park facility.
Fields of interest: Environment.
Limitations: Applications not accepted. Giving
limited to Kingsport, TN.
Application information: Contributes only to a
pre-selected organization; unsolicited requests
for funds not considered or acknowledged.
Officers and Directors:* Bob Estes,* Pres.; Anita
Greer,* V.P.; Tom Odom,* Secy.; Horace Hall,*
Treas.; Tom Bowman; Mary Cunningham; Lisa
Dishner; John Dodson; and 5 additional
directors.
EIN: 621042329

3007
The Emily & Robert Beasley Charitable Trust
150 4th Ave., N., Ste. 1500
Nashville, TN 37219-2434

Established around 1984.
Grantmaker type: Independent foundation

Financial data (yr. ended 12/31/02): Assets,
$1,190,513 (M); expenditures, $360,795;
qualifying distributions, $318,763; giving
activities include $319,500 for 10 grants (high:
$75,000; low: $4,000).
Purpose and activities: Giving primarily for
human services and community development,
particularly in the city of Sparta, TN.
Fields of interest: Environment, pollution
control; Substance abuse, prevention; Disasters,
fire prevention/control; Human services;
Community development.
Limitations: Applications not accepted. Giving
primarily in Sparta, TN. No grants to individuals.
Application information: Contributes only to
pre-selected organizations.
Trustees: George Elrod; William Johnson.
EIN: 581552213

3008
Benwood Foundation, Inc. ▼
SunTrust Bank Bldg.
736 Market St., Ste. 1600
Chattanooga, TN 37402   (423) 267-4311
Contact: Corinne Allen, Exec. Dir.
FAX: (423) 267-9049; E-mail:
Benwoodfnd@Benwood.org

Incorporated in 1944 in DE, and 1945 in TN.
Donor(s): George Thomas Hunter.‡
Grantmaker type: Independent foundation
Financial data (yr. ended 12/31/02): Assets,
$93,924,813 (M); expenditures, $5,069,586;
qualifying distributions, $4,463,599; giving
activities include $4,209,591 for 107 grants
(high: $1,410,500; low: $500; average:
$1,000–$50,000).
Purpose and activities: Support for secondary
and early childhood education, social welfare,
health agencies, cultural programs, arts and
humanities, including the performing arts, and
the environment, including beautification
programs.
Fields of interest: Performing arts; Humanities;
Arts; Early childhood education; Secondary
school/education; Environment; Health
organizations, association; Human services;
Economic development; Urban/community
development.
Types of support: Continuing support; Capital
campaigns; Building/renovation; Equipment;
Program development; Conferences/seminars;
Seed money; Scholarship funds; Technical
assistance; Matching/challenge support.
Limitations: Giving primarily in the
Chattanooga, TN, area. No support for political
organizations or causes. No grants to
individuals, or for general operating expenses,
financial deficits, fundraising, endowments, or
multi-year grants; no loans (except for program
related investments).
Publications: Application guidelines.
Application information: Application form
required.
Initial approach: Brief 2-page letter
Copies of proposal: 6
Deadline(s): 1st day of month preceding
board meetings
Board meeting date(s): Jan., Apr., July, and Oct.
Final notification: 3 weeks after board
meeting; board reserves privilege of
delaying decision for 3 months

Officer and Trustees:* Robert J. Sudderth, Jr.,* Chair.; Sebert Brewer, Jr.; Paul K. Brock, Jr.; William H. Chapin; Martha T. Robinson.
Number of staff: 3 full-time professional; 1 part-time professional.
EIN: 620476283
Recent environmental and animal welfare grants:
3008-1 Nature Conservancy, Chattanooga, TN, $50,000. 2001.
3008-2 Southern Sustainable Agriculture Working Group, Elkins, AR, $10,000. For conference. 2001.
3008-3 Tennessee River Gardens and Nature Preserve, Lookout Mountain, TN, $19,600. 2001.
3008-4 Tennessee Wildlife Center, Chattanooga, TN, $50,000. 2001.
3008-5 Trust for Public Land, Chattanooga, TN, $50,000. 2001.

3009
Charles H. Boyle Foundation, Inc.
P.O. Box 17800
Memphis, TN 38187

Established in 1972 in TN.
Donor(s): J. Bayard Boyle, Jr., Elizabeth R. Boyle, Snowden B. Morgan, Boyle Investment Co.
Grantmaker type: Independent foundation
Financial data (yr. ended 12/31/02): Assets, $1,177,329 (M); expenditures, $167,412; qualifying distributions, $154,700; giving activities include $154,700 for 38 grants (high: $27,000; low: $1,000).
Purpose and activities: Giving for federated giving programs, religion and for environmental conservation.
Fields of interest: Arts; Higher education; Education; Natural resources; Health organizations, association; Children/youth, services; Federated giving programs; Protestant agencies & churches.
Types of support: General/operating support.
Limitations: Applications not accepted. Giving primarily in Memphis, TN. No grants to individuals.
Application information: Contributes only to pre-selected organizations.
Officers and Directors:* J. Bayard Boyle, Jr.,* Pres.; Henry W. Morgan,* V.P.; J. Roy Taylor, Secy.-Treas.; Snowden B. Morgan.
EIN: 237256010

3010
Bridgestone/Firestone Trust Fund ▼
(formerly The Firestone Trust Fund)
535 Marriott Dr.
Nashville, TN 37214 (615) 937-1415
Contact: Bernice Csaszar, Admin.
FAX: (615) 937-1414; E-mail: bfstrustfund@bfusa.com

Trust established in 1952 in OH.
Donor(s): The Firestone Tire and Rubber Co., Bridgestone/Firestone, Inc.
Grantmaker type: Company-sponsored foundation
Financial data (yr. ended 12/31/02): Assets, $18,854,646 (M); expenditures, $4,857,826; qualifying distributions, $4,669,095; giving

activities include $4,593,895 for 1,121 grants (high: $250,000; low: $50; average: $2,000–$100,000).
Purpose and activities: The major categories in which contributions are considered are: education (including employee matching gifts), health and welfare, civic and community, and culture and the arts. Special consideration is given to organizations to which employees give their money and volunteer their time to improve the communities where they live and work.
Fields of interest: Television; Radio; Museums; Performing arts; Arts; Higher education; Adult/continuing education; Education; Environment; Health care; Substance abuse, services; Crime/law enforcement; Employment, services; Human services; Youth, services; Voter education; Community development, neighborhood development; Federated giving programs.
Types of support: General/operating support; Continuing support; Annual campaigns; Capital campaigns; Building/renovation; Endowments; Emergency funds; Program development; Seed money; Research; Employee matching gifts; Matching/challenge support.
Limitations: Giving primarily in areas of major company operations: AR, CO, CT, FL, IA, IL, IN, KY, LA, MI, NC, OH, OK, PA, SC, TN, TX, UT, and WI. No support for religious or partisan political organizations or organizations that will use funds outside the U.S. No grants to individuals, or for deficit financing, equipment, land acquisition, fellowships, publications, or conferences; no loans.
Publications: Application guidelines.
Application information: Application form not required.
  Initial approach: Letter (no more than 2 pages)
  Copies of proposal: 1
  Deadline(s): None
  Board meeting date(s): As required
Committee Members: Christine Karbowiak, Chair.; Gene Stephens; Ronald Tepner.
Trustee: KeyBank N.A.
Number of staff: 1 full-time support.
EIN: 346505181
Recent environmental and animal welfare grants:
3010-1 Cumberland River Compact, Springfield, TN, $10,000. 2001.
3010-2 Tennessee Conservation League, Nashville, TN, $15,000. 2001.
3010-3 Tennessee Parks and Greenways Foundation, Nashville, TN, $21,000. 2001.
3010-4 Tennessee Wildlife Resources Foundation, Nashville, TN, $50,000. 2001.

3011
The Chazen Family Foundation
1810 Chestnut St.
P.O. Box 6308
Chattanooga, TN 37401-6308

Grantmaker type: Independent foundation
Financial data (yr. ended 11/30/02): Assets, $1,376,669 (M); expenditures, $245,671; qualifying distributions, $231,383; giving activities include $231,600 for 12 grants (high: $60,000; low: $350).
Purpose and activities: Giving for the arts, education, animal welfare, health, and youth programs.

Fields of interest: Museums (art); Education; Zoos/zoological societies; Hospitals (general); YM/YWCAs & YM/YWHAs; Federated giving programs; Jewish agencies & temples.
Limitations: Applications not accepted. Giving primarily in NC and TN. No grants to individuals.
Application information: Contributes only to pre-selected organizations.
Directors: Gary D. Chazen; Robert G. Chazen; Ruth E. Chazen.
EIN: 621722318

3012
Cloud Forest School Foundation
P.O. Box 3223
Sewanee, TN 37375-3223
Contact: Elizabeth Lowell, Chair.
E-mail: info@cloudforestschool.org; URL: http://www.cloudforestschool.org/cfsfoundation.html

Established in 1991.
Grantmaker type: Public charity
Financial data (yr. ended 06/30/03): Assets, $159,838 (M); gifts received, $66,617; expenditures, $124,177; program services expenses, $108,893; giving activities include $107,857 for 1 grant.
Purpose and activities: The foundation exists for the sole benefit of the Centro de Educacion Creativa, a bilingual, environmentally focused, pre-K-11th grade school in Monteverde, Costa Rica.
Fields of interest: Elementary/secondary education; Environment.
International interests: Costa Rica.
Types of support: Annual campaigns; Capital campaigns; Building/renovation; Endowments; Scholarship funds; In-kind gifts.
Limitations: Applications not accepted. Giving limited to Costa Rica.
Publications: Newsletter.
Application information: Contributes only to a pre-selected organization; unsolicited requests for funds not considered or acknowledged.
Officers and Trustees:* Elizabeth M. Lowell,* Chair.; Christopher R. Tompkins,* Vice-Chair.; Mary Susan Cushman,* Secy.; Douglas A. Caves,* Treas.; Jim Richards; Robert G. Shibley; Stephen Watters.
EIN: 621532788

3013
The Community Foundation of Greater Chattanooga, Inc.
1270 Market St.
Chattanooga, TN 37402 (423) 265-0586
Contact: Peter T. Cooper, Pres.
FAX: (423) 265-0587; E-mail: pcooper@cfgc.org; URL: http://www.cfgc.org/

Incorporated in 1963 in TN.
Grantmaker type: Community foundation
Financial data (yr. ended 12/31/02): Assets, $46,991,048 (M); gifts received, $10,648,390; expenditures, $13,475,946; giving activities include $12,134,116 for 2,246 grants (high: $2,000,000; low: $15; average: $200–$50,000).
Purpose and activities: To promote and enhance the well-being of the inhabitants of the greater Chattanooga area. Primary areas of interest include education, community development,

youth and child development, the arts, race relations, and literacy development.

Fields of interest: Performing arts; Dance; Arts; Early childhood education; Child development, education; Elementary school/education; Higher education; Adult education—literacy, basic skills & GED; Reading; Education; Natural resources; Environment; Medical care, rehabilitation; Children/youth, services; Child development, services; Family services; Aging, centers/services; Race/intergroup relations; Urban/community development; Community development; General charitable giving; Minorities; Women.

International interests: Japan.

Types of support: Management development; Capital campaigns; Building/renovation; Equipment; Land acquisition; Program development; Seed money; Scholarship funds; Program evaluation; Scholarships—to individuals; Exchange programs.

Limitations: Giving limited to the greater Chattanooga,TN, area. No support for private schools, religious causes, or political activities, veteran or fraternal organizations, public agencies, state, national or regional organizations. No grants to individuals (except for scholarship programs), endowment campaigns, operating support for existing programs, conferences, advertising, telephone solicitations, fundraising expenses, federated fund drives; no loans.

Publications: Application guidelines, Annual report (including application guidelines), Informational brochure, Informational brochure (including application guidelines).

Application information: The foundation requires a letter of intent 2 months prior to the application deadline; all applicants are by invitation following staff consideration of the letter of intent. Application form required.

 Initial approach: Telephone program staff or letter of intent
 Copies of proposal: 15
 Deadline(s): Apr. 1 and Oct. 1, call for future dates
 Board meeting date(s): Quarterly; program committee meets to award grants in June and Dec.
 Final notification: 5 to 6 weeks after meeting

Officers and Directors:* Grant Law,* Chair.; Ruth S. Holmberg, Vice-Chair.; Spencer McCallie,* Vice-Chair.; Virginia Anna Sharber,* Vice-Chair.; Peter T. Cooper, Pres.; Jennifer R. Jackson, V.P., Prog.; Marty Robinson, V.P., Donor Relations; Amber L. Tappin, V.P., Finance and Admin.; E. Liston Bishop, Secy.; Nick Decosimo, Treas.; Paul K. Brock; Susan Burkett; Paul Campbell; George Clark III; Ann Coulter; Mike Cranford; Jane Harbaugh; Jerry Konahia; Jill Levine; Warren Logan; Kincaid Mills; Tom Montague; Chris Ramsey; Pete Serodino; Edna Varner.

Number of staff: 6 full-time professional; 1 part-time professional; 1 full-time support.

EIN: 626045999

Recent environmental and animal welfare grants:

3013-1 American Hiking Society, DC, $15,000. For Southern Appalachian Initiative to strengthen, build and network hiking and conservation constituency among Southeast's trail volunteers and their clubs. 2002.

3013-2 Reflection Riding, Chattanooga, TN, $10,000. For Facility Improvement Project. 2002.

3014
Community Foundation of Middle Tennessee, Inc.

(formerly Nashville Community Foundation, Inc.)
3833 Cleghorn Ave., No. 400
Nashville, TN 37215-2519   (615) 321-4939
Contact: Ellen Lehman, Pres.
Additional tel.: (888) 540-5200; FAX: (615) 327-2746; E-mail: mail@cfmt.org; URL: http://www.cfmt.org

Established in 1991 in TN.

Grantmaker type: Community foundation

Financial data (yr. ended 12/31/02): Assets, $223,762,419 (M); gifts received, $149,527,705; expenditures, $35,882,955; giving activities include $35,578,163 for 1,899 grants (high: $4,000,000; low: $100).

Purpose and activities: The foundation is dedicated to enriching the quality of life in middle TN. The foundation serves as a leader, catalyst and resource for philanthropy. The foundation strives to build a permanent endowment for the community for now and all time. The foundation administers a donor-advised fund.

Fields of interest: Humanities; Historic preservation/historical societies; Arts; Education; Natural resources; Environment; Health care; Health organizations, association; Employment; Housing/shelter, development; Human services; Aging, centers/services; Community development, neighborhood development; Community development; Aging.

Types of support: Program development; Seed money; In-kind gifts.

Limitations: Giving limited to central TN. No support for private foundations, religious or sectarian purposes, private schools, or biomedical or clinic studies. No grants for fundraising events, debt retirement, annual and capital campaigns, general operations, advertising, trips, conferences, computers or equipment.

Publications: Application guidelines, Annual report, Informational brochure, Newsletter.

Application information: Application form not required.

 Initial approach: Proposal
 Copies of proposal: 1
 Deadline(s): May 1
 Board meeting date(s): Feb., Apr., June, Sept., Nov., and Dec.
 Final notification: Sept. 15

Officers and Directors:* Jack Bovender,* Chair.; John Maupin,* Vice-Chair.; Ellen E. Lehman,* Pres.; Nicki Weaver,* Secy.; Charlie Cook,* Treas.

Number of staff: 12 full-time professional; 1 part-time professional.

EIN: 621471789

3015
Community Shares Knoxville

107 W. Main St., Ste. 201
Knoxville, TN 37902-2126   (865) 522-1604
Contact: Paul Ford, Pres.
FAX: (865) 522-5281; E-mail: cshares@korrnet.com; URL: http://www.korrnet.org/cshares

Established in 1985 in TN.

Grantmaker type: Public charity

Financial data (yr. ended 06/30/01): Revenue, $512,827; assets, $250,327; gifts received, $444,520; expenditures, $493,355; program services expenses, $386,836; giving activities include $338,801 for 41 grants.

Purpose and activities: Funding to Tennessee-area nonprofits for work involving social, economic, and environmental justice.

Fields of interest: Environment; Civil rights; Economic development.

Types of support: General/operating support.

Limitations: Giving limited to TN.

Publications: Annual report, Newsletter.

Application information: Application process is for organizations to become members of the federated fund. Application form required.

 Initial approach: Telephone
 Copies of proposal: 1
 Deadline(s): Nov. 30
 Board meeting date(s): Feb., May, Aug., and Nov.

Officer and Directors:* Paul Ford,* Pres.; Shelley Wascom, Exec. Dir.; Nkechi Ajanaku; Elizabeth Carnahan; Bob Corney; Mary Donovan; and 12 additional directors.

Number of staff: 4 full-time professional.

EIN: 621233685

3016
Mike Curb Family Foundation

47 Music Sq. E.
Nashville, TN 37203

Established in 1998 in TN.

Donor(s): Mike Curb, Leanne Rimes.

Grantmaker type: Independent foundation

Financial data (yr. ended 07/31/02): Assets, $16,596,768 (M); gifts received, $6,512,859; expenditures, $884,975; qualifying distributions, $741,048; giving activities include $743,767 for 2 grants (high: $732,443; low: $11,324).

Fields of interest: Zoos/zoological societies; Hospitals (general).

Limitations: Applications not accepted. Giving primarily in Nashville, TN. No grants to individuals.

Application information: Contributes only to pre-selected organizations.

Officers and Directors:* Mike Curb,* Pres.; Tracy Moore,* Secy.; Linda Curb.

EIN: 954686920

3017
Ducks Unlimited, Inc.

1 Waterfowl Way
Memphis, TN 38120-2350   (901) 758-3825
Contact: Adam Webster, Internal Auditor
FAX: (901) 758-3855; E-mail: awebster@ducks.org; URL: http://www.ducks.org

Established in 1937 in DC.

Grantmaker type: Public charity
Financial data (yr. ended 02/28/02): Revenue, $139,232,266; assets, $73,998,779 (L); gifts received, $129,775,480; expenditures, $146,866,637; program services expenses, $121,982,807; giving activities include $21,644,830 for 2 grants (high: $20,834,408; low: $830,422).
Purpose and activities: The organization conserves, restores, and manages wetlands and associated habitats for North America's waterfowl. These habitats also benefit other wildlife and people. Since its founding, Ducks Unlimited has contributed to the conservation of over 10.3 million acres of wildlife habitat in all 50 states, each of the Canadian Provinces, and in key areas of Mexico.
Fields of interest: Natural resources.
Limitations: Applications not accepted. Giving limited to U.S., Canada, and Mexico.
Publications: Annual report, Financial statement, Informational brochure, Newsletter.
Application information: Contributes only to pre-selected organizations; unsolicited applications are neither considered nor acknowledged.
Officers and Directors:* L.J. Mayeux, Jr., M.D.,* Chair.; John A. Tomka,* Pres.; D. A. "Don" Young,* Exec. Vice Pres.; Robert Berg,* Sr. V.P.; Steve Brown,* Sr. V.P.; Elliot Gassner, Sr. V.P.; Rogers Hoyt,* Sr. V.P.; James "Jim" Hulbert,* Sr. V.P.; Stanley C. Huner,* Sr. V.P.; Roger Mosher,* Sr. V.P.; Fred Taylor,* Sr. V.P.; Jim Wildman,* Sr. V.P.; Stephen C. Reynolds,* Secy.; W. Bruce Lewis,* Treas.; and 8 additional directors.
EIN: 135643799

3018
EBS Foundation
c/o Elizabeth Bullard Stadler, Tr.
2212 Hillsboro Valley Rd.
Brentwood, TN 37027

Established in 1989.
Donor(s): Ella Hayes.
Grantmaker type: Independent foundation
Financial data (yr. ended 12/31/01): Assets, $10,384,083 (M); gifts received, $412,319; expenditures, $1,362,598; qualifying distributions, $1,194,627; giving activities include $1,124,390 for grants.
Purpose and activities: Giving primarily to Christian organizations.
Fields of interest: Arts; Education; Natural resources; Boys & girls clubs; Human services; Christian agencies & churches.
Types of support: Continuing support; Annual campaigns.
Limitations: Applications not accepted. Giving primarily in TN. No grants to individuals.
Application information: Contributes only to pre-selected organizations.
Trustee: Elizabeth Bullard Stadler.
EIN: 581797047

3019
James E. & Katharine B. Harwood Charitable Trust
2670 Union Ave. Ext., Ste. 700
Memphis, TN 38112-4416

Established in 1992 in TN.

Donor(s): James E. Harwood, Jr.
Grantmaker type: Independent foundation
Financial data (yr. ended 12/31/02): Assets, $363,656 (M); expenditures, $91,462; qualifying distributions, $90,063; giving activities include $89,445 for 37 grants (high: $12,000; low: $500).
Purpose and activities: Giving primarily for the arts, education, health, and youth programs.
Fields of interest: Arts; Education; Botanical gardens; Boys & girls clubs; Boy scouts; Christian agencies & churches.
Limitations: Applications not accepted. Giving primarily in TN. No grants to individuals.
Application information: Contributes only to pre-selected organizations.
Trustees: Katherine H. Gooch; James E. Harwood.
EIN: 582025944

3020
Healing Stones Foundation
P.O. Box 50276
Nashville, TN 37205-0276 (615) 269-6663
Contact: George Bullard, Pres.

Grantmaker type: Operating foundation
Financial data (yr. ended 12/31/02): Assets, $1,246,809 (M); gifts received, $255,000; expenditures, $321,967; qualifying distributions, $253,101; giving activities include $96,125 for 8 grants (high: $36,000; low: $320; average: $320–$23,000).
Fields of interest: Environment; Agriculture.
Types of support: Seed money.
Limitations: Applications not accepted. Giving primarily in TN. No grants to individuals.
Application information: Contributes only to pre-selected organizations.
Officer: George Bullard, Pres.
Number of staff: 1 full-time professional; 1 part-time professional.
EIN: 621633499

3021
The Jeniam Foundation
(also known as The Jeniam Clarkson Foundation)
270 Bremington Pl.
Memphis, TN 38111 (901) 454-7080
Contact: Charlotte G. King, Exec. Dir.

Established in 1992 in TN.
Donor(s): Andrew M. Clarkson, Carole G. Clarkson.
Grantmaker type: Independent foundation
Financial data (yr. ended 12/31/01): Assets, $13,134,059 (M); gifts received, $549,850; expenditures, $361,176; qualifying distributions, $352,440; giving activities include $281,150 for 13 grants (high: $76,400; low: $1,000; average: $2,500–$35,000) and $17,650 for 1 loan/program-related investment.
Fields of interest: Museums (children's); Education; Natural resources; Nursing home/convalescent facility; Youth development, services; Aging.
Types of support: Capital campaigns; Building/renovation; Equipment; Seed money; Research; Program-related investments/loans.
Limitations: Giving on a national basis for conservation; in New Canaan, CT, for education and aging; and in Memphis, TN, for the arts. No

grants to individuals, or for ongoing operating support.
Publications: Informational brochure (including application guidelines).
Application information: Contact Exec. Dir. for application guidelines. Application form not required.
Initial approach: 1- to 2-page letter
Copies of proposal: 1
Deadline(s): None
Board meeting date(s): Varies
Officer: Charlotte G. King, Exec. Dir.
Trustees: Andrew M. Clarkson; Carole G. Clarkson; Jennifer M. Clarkson.
Number of staff: 1 full-time professional.
EIN: 621516244

3022
The Joyce Family Foundation
424 Church St., Ste. 2101
Nashville, TN 37219-2305 (615) 256-2556
Contact: Douglas Joyce, Secy.

Established in 1990 in TN.
Donor(s): Kathryn Craig Henry.
Grantmaker type: Independent foundation
Financial data (yr. ended 12/31/02): Assets, $1,745,621 (M); gifts received, $17,124; expenditures, $242,778; qualifying distributions, $227,389; giving activities include $218,000 for grants.
Fields of interest: Libraries/library science; Education; Zoos/zoological societies; Cancer; Food banks; Philanthropy/voluntarism.
Limitations: Giving primarily in AL, SC, and TN. No grants to individuals.
Application information: Application form not required.
Deadline(s): None
Officer: Margaret Henry Wood, Chair.
Directors: Benjamin F. Byrd, Jr.; Douglas Henry; Richard D. Holton; Alexis Jones Joyce.
Trustee: SunTrust Banks, Inc.
EIN: 626225946

3023
Robin & Bill King Family Foundation
3946 Woodlawn Ave.
Nashville, TN 37205

Established in 1997 in TN.
Donor(s): William B. King, Jr.
Grantmaker type: Independent foundation
Financial data (yr. ended 12/31/01): Assets, $1,220,840 (M); expenditures, $160,582; qualifying distributions, $160,582; giving activities include $150,000 for 1 grant.
Fields of interest: Natural resources; Federated giving programs.
Limitations: Applications not accepted. Giving primarily in TN. No grants to individuals.
Application information: Contributes only to pre-selected organizations.
Trustee: William B. King, Jr.
EIN: 626328848

3024
LifeWorks Foundation

(formerly George N. Bullard Foundation)
P.O. Box 50276
Nashville, TN 37205 (615) 269-6663
Contact: George Bullard, Dir.
FAX: (615) 269-7496

Established in 1967 in TN; reorganized in 1988 in FL; name change in 1990.
Donor(s): Ella Hayes Trust.
Grantmaker type: Independent foundation
Financial data (yr. ended 12/31/02): Assets, $8,474,066 (M); gifts received, $275,000; expenditures, $863,530; qualifying distributions, $775,927; giving activities include $607,338 for 61 grants (high: $255,000; low: $40; average: $500–$1,000).
Fields of interest: Animals/wildlife; Agriculture; Food services.
Limitations: Applications not accepted. Giving limited to Nashville, TN. No grants to individuals.
Application information: Unsolicited applications not considered.
Board meeting date(s): Monthly
Director: George Bullard.
Number of staff: 2 full-time professional.
EIN: 621428468

3025
Lyndhurst Foundation ▼

517 E. 5th St.
Chattanooga, TN 37403-1826 (423) 756-0767
Contact: Jack E. Murrah, Pres.
FAX: (423) 756-0770; E-mail: jmurrah@lyndhurstfoundation.org; URL: http://www.lyndhurstfoundation.org

Incorporated in 1938 in DE.
Donor(s): T. Cartter Lupton,‡ Central Shares Corp.
Grantmaker type: Independent foundation
Financial data (yr. ended 12/31/02): Assets, $152,000,000 (M); expenditures, $6,500,000; qualifying distributions, $6,000,000; giving activities include $5,290,285 for 51 grants (high: $1,035,000; low: $2,000; average: $10,000–$50,000), $240,000 for 6 grants to individuals of $40,000 each and $34,886 for 43 employee matching gifts.
Purpose and activities: The current focus of the foundation is on arts and cultural activities, public education and community development in Chattanooga, TN, and environmental improvement in the Southeast.
Fields of interest: Arts; Elementary school/education; Secondary school/education; Environment; Community development.
Types of support: General/operating support; Continuing support; Capital campaigns; Building/renovation; Land acquisition; Program development; Seed money; Technical assistance; Employee matching gifts; Matching/challenge support.
Limitations: Giving limited to the southeastern U.S., with emphasis on Chattanooga, TN.
Publications: Annual report (including application guidelines).
Application information: Application form not required.
Initial approach: Letter (no more than 3 pages)
Copies of proposal: 1

Deadline(s): Dec., Mar., June, and Sept.; Call fdn. for actual dates
Board meeting date(s): Feb., May, Aug., and Nov.
Final notification: 3 months
Officers and Trustees:* Allen L. McCallie,* Chair.; Jack E. Murrah,* Pres.; Benic M. Clark III, V.P. and Secy.; Charles B. Chitty, Treas.; Nelson D. Campbell; George R. Fontaine; Margaret L. Gerber; Katherine L. Juett; T. Cartter Lupton II; L. Thomas Montague; Alice L. Smith.
Number of staff: 4 full-time professional; 1 full-time support.
EIN: 626044177
Recent environmental and animal welfare grants:
3025-1 American Chestnut Foundation, Bennington, VT, $30,000. To advance programs aimed at restoration of American chestnut tree within Southern Appalachian Mountain region. 2001.
3025-2 American Hiking Society, DC, $25,000. For conferencing and staffing expenses in association with development of southeastern regional network of linked hiking trails. 2001.
3025-3 Appalachian Trail Conference, Harpers Ferry, WV, $25,000. Toward acquisition of critical tract that will enhance Appalachian Trail corridor and protect endangered cranberry bogs in Shady Valley community of East Tennessee. 2001.
3025-4 Blue Ridge Rural Land Trust, Sugar Grove, NC, $50,000. For organizational development to enable acceleration of land protection activities in rural northwest North Carolina. 2001.
3025-5 Caesar Kleberg Wildlife Research Institute, Kingsville, TX, $20,000. To advance black bear research and conservation in Texas and northern Mexico. 2001.
3025-6 Chattowah Open Land Trust, Alpharetta, GA, $35,000. For challenge grant to support land protection activities in Ridge and Valley and Cumberland Plateau regions of Georgia, Tennessee, and Alabama. 2001.
3025-7 Foothills Land Conservancy, Maryville, TN, $250,000. To enhance survival of Sandhill cranes and other waterfowl and wildlife through purchase of Smith Bend tract, now designated as wildlife refuge and management area. 2001.
3025-8 Humane Educational Society of Chattanooga, Chattanooga, TN, $10,000. For challenge grant for development of on-site surgery center to reduce number of stray and neglected animals through spaying and neutering procedures. 2001.
3025-9 Kinkaid School, Houston, TX, $50,000. To celebrate life and memory of John Fontaine through memorial contribution to Kinkaid School Backyard nature preserve. 2001.
3025-10 Land Trust Alliance, DC, $10,000. For capacity building project to strengthen skills and effectiveness of land trusts based in Southeast. 2001.
3025-11 Land Trust for Tennessee, Nashville, TN, $50,000. Toward establishing project office to address land conservation opportunities in South Cumberland Plateau and Sequatchie Valley regions. 2001.
3025-12 Land Trust for the Little Tennessee, Franklin, NC, $50,000. For activities leading to protection of farmland, forests, and

riparian zones within Little Tennessee River watershed. 2001.
3025-13 Nature Conservancy, Columbia, SC, $100,000. For comprehensive initiative aimed at protection and preservation of South Carolina's watersheds and ecosystems; additional partners include Low Country Open Land Trust, South Carolina Coastal Conservation League, and Ducks Unlimited. 2001.
3025-14 Pinchot Institute for Conservation, DC, $80,000. To facilitate forest certification pilot project on state forest lands in Tennessee. 2001.
3025-15 RiverCity Company, Chattanooga, TN, $2,025,000. To construct new downtown public elementary schools incorporating energy-efficient lighting technologies into construction process. 2001.
3025-16 Saint Philips Neighborhood Development Corporation, Dallas, TX, $10,000. To enhance community revitalization efforts in Saint Philip's neighborhood of Dallas through establishment of land bank. 2001.
3025-17 Southern Appalachian Forest Coalition, Asheville, NC, $250,000. For development and implementation of science-based plan to protect and restore wildlands, waters, native forests, and ecosystems of Southern Appalachian landscape. 2001.
3025-18 Southern Appalachian Highlands Conservancy, Kingsport, TN, $100,000. For land conservation activities in Highlands region of western North Carolina and eastern Tennessee. 2001.
3025-19 Southern Environmental Law Center, Charlottesville, VA, $100,000. For general support. 2001.
3025-20 Southwings, Chattanooga, TN, $10,000. For matching grant toward building donor base. 2001.
3025-21 Tennessee Parks and Greenways Foundation, Nashville, TN, $60,000. Toward acquisition of Black Mountain, prominent landmark along Cumberland Trail, and for mini-grants program for greenways projects in East Tennessee. 2001.

3026
The Pattee Foundation, Inc.

c/o Dennis McCurry
The Krystal Bldg., Ste. 700
Chattanooga, TN 37402
Contact: Gordon B. Pattee, Pres.

Established in 1989 in TN.
Grantmaker type: Independent foundation
Financial data (yr. ended 06/30/02): Assets, $5,600,487 (M); expenditures, $628,961; qualifying distributions, $424,772; giving activities include $420,000 for 17 grants (high: $140,000; low: $500).
Purpose and activities: Giving primarily for arts and culture, including a children's museum, education, and wildlife.
Fields of interest: Museums (children's); Arts; Higher education; University; Education; Animals/wildlife, preservation/protection; Athletics/sports, equestrianism; Federated giving programs.

Limitations: Giving primarily in CA, Washington, DC, New York, NY, and TN. No grants to individuals.
Application information:
  Initial approach: Letter or proposal
  Deadline(s): None
Officers and Directors:* Gordon B. Pattee,* Pres.; Anne L. Pattee,* Secy.; Dorothy E. Pattee.
EIN: 621376116

3027
Justin & Valere Blair Potter Foundation
c/o Bank of America
1 Bank of America Plz., Ste. M-7
Nashville, TN 37239-1697 (615) 749-3916
Contact: Patrick Nelson, Trust Off., Bank of America

Established in 1953.
Grantmaker type: Independent foundation
Financial data (yr. ended 12/31/01): Assets, $22,764,199 (M); expenditures, $1,819,140; qualifying distributions, $1,659,306; giving activities include $1,610,000 for 10 grants (high: $500,000; low: $10,000; average: $50,000–$350,000).
Purpose and activities: Giving primarily for animal welfare, human services, Roman Catholic agencies, youth organizations, and archives.
Fields of interest: Archives; Animal welfare; Health organizations, association; Athletics/sports, equestrianism; Boy scouts; Human services; Federated giving programs; Roman Catholic agencies & churches.
Limitations: Giving primarily in Nashville, TN.
Application information:
  Initial approach: Letter
  Deadline(s): None
Trustees: Albert L. Menefee, Jr.; Valere Menefee; Bank of America.
EIN: 626306577

3028
Kate Collins Roddy and J. P. Roddy, Sr. Foundation, Inc.
(formerly The Roddy Foundation, Inc.)
6701 Baum Dr., Ste. 250
Knoxville, TN 37919
Contact: Thomas R. Roddy, Exec. Dir.
Application address: 3340 Peachtree Rd., Ste. 1660, Atlanta, GA 30326

Established in 1991 in TN.
Donor(s): J.P. Roddy, Jr.,‡ Roddy Coca-Cola Bottling Co., Inc.
Grantmaker type: Independent foundation
Financial data (yr. ended 12/31/02): Assets, $1,575,388 (M); expenditures, $114,026; qualifying distributions, $94,113; giving activities include $94,500 for 21 grants (high: $8,000; low: $1,000).
Purpose and activities: Giving primarily to projects that build the family; some giving also to those that build needy communities.
Fields of interest: Education; Zoos/zoological societies; Health care, clinics/centers; Youth, services; Roman Catholic agencies & churches.
Types of support: General/operating support.
Limitations: Giving primarily in eastern TN. Generally no giving to governmental agencies,

capital campaigns, endowments, and generally not to churches and no multiple year gifts.
Application information:
  Initial approach: Letter
  Deadline(s): Oct. 31
Officers: Ellen R. Mitchell, Pres.; James P. Roddy III, Secy.; Rev. Thomas R. Roddy, Exec. Dir.
Trustees: William J. Mitchell, Sr.; Alexandra W. Roddy; Dorothy M. Roddy.
EIN: 621464394

3029
The Rose Foundation
6305 Humphrey Blvd., Ste. 110
Memphis, TN 38120-2300

Established in 1990 in TN.
Donor(s): Gayle S. Rose, Michael D. Rose.
Grantmaker type: Independent foundation
Financial data (yr. ended 12/31/00): Assets, $4,254,728 (M); gifts received, $503,500; expenditures, $368,509; qualifying distributions, $326,850; giving activities include $326,850 for 28 grants (high: $125,000; low: $175).
Purpose and activities: Giving primarily for higher education, youth services and the arts.
Fields of interest: Museums; Arts; Higher education; Education; Natural resources; Health care; Health organizations, association; Children/youth, services.
Limitations: Applications not accepted. Giving primarily in Memphis, TN. No grants to individuals.
Application information: Contributes only to pre-selected organizations.
Officers and Directors:* Michael D. Rose,* Pres.; Dale Ericson,* Secy.; Gabrielle E. Rose; Matthew D. Rose.
Number of staff: 1 full-time support.
EIN: 621450062

3030
Margaret F. Shackelford Charitable Trust
c/o NBC, Tr. Div., Attn.: Ken Cain
850 Ridge Lake Blvd., Ste. 101
Memphis, TN 38120
Contact: Paul A. Calame, Jr.
Application address: 326 S. Goodlett St., Memphis, TN 38117, tel.: (901) 458-6654

Established in 1999 in TN.
Grantmaker type: Independent foundation
Financial data (yr. ended 12/31/02): Assets, $8,303,234 (M); expenditures, $805,754; qualifying distributions, $710,244; giving activities include $711,343 for 2 grants (high: $439,754; low: $271,589).
Purpose and activities: Giving primarily for natural resource and wildlife conservation and protection, with particular interest in hardwood trees, (reforestation and management).
Fields of interest: Natural resources; Animals/wildlife, preservation/protection.
Limitations: Giving primarily in MS. No grants to individuals.
Application information: Application form not required.
  Initial approach: Letter
  Copies of proposal: 3
  Deadline(s): None
  Board meeting date(s): Quarterly
Trustee: National Bank of Commerce.

EIN: 626363101

3031
The Thompson Charitable Foundation
P.O. Box 10516
Knoxville, TN 37939
Contact: Monica Luke, Fdn. Mgr.

Established in 1987 in TN.
Donor(s): B.R. Thompson, Sr.‡
Grantmaker type: Independent foundation
Financial data (yr. ended 06/30/02): Assets, $41,377,244 (M); expenditures, $2,034,668; qualifying distributions, $1,847,454; giving activities include $1,780,671 for 62 grants (high: $150,000; low: $1,000).
Purpose and activities: Giving primarily for education, health, and human services.
Fields of interest: Libraries (public); Education; Environment, water resources; Hospitals (general); Health care; Food services; Housing/shelter, development; Human services; Children/youth, services; Foundations (community).
Types of support: General/operating support; Capital campaigns; Program development.
Limitations: Giving limited to Bell, Clay, Laurel, and Leslie counties, KY; Anderson, Blount, Knox, and Scott counties, TN; and Buchanan and Tazewell counties, VA. No grants for budget deficits or endowments.
Application information:
  Initial approach: Letter (no more than 2 pages)
  Deadline(s): Mar. 31, June 30, Sept. 30, and Dec. 31
Officers and Directors:* Merle D. Wolfe,* Pres.; Monica Luke, Mgr.; Carl Ensor, Jr.; Greg Erickson; Jesse J. Thompson; Sylvia M. Thompson; Lindsay Young.
EIN: 581754763

3032
The Tucker Foundation
600 Krystal Bldg.
Chattanooga, TN 37402 (423) 756-1202
Contact: M. Hayne Hamilton, Pres.
FAX: (423) 756-5661

Established in 1996.
Grantmaker type: Independent foundation
Financial data (yr. ended 12/31/02): Assets, $24,517,889 (M); expenditures, $1,211,535; qualifying distributions, $1,084,550; giving activities include $1,084,550 for 73 grants (high: $125,000; low: $100).
Purpose and activities: Giving primarily for the arts, conservation, education, and social services.
Fields of interest: Multipurpose centers/programs; Museums; Theater; Secondary school/education; College; Environment; Youth development; Human services; Federated giving programs.
Types of support: Annual campaigns; Capital campaigns; Building/renovation; Land acquisition; Program development; Scholarship funds; Research; Employee-related scholarships.
Limitations: Giving primarily in Atlanta, GA, Hamilton and Bradley counties, TN, and Sheridan, WY.
Application information: Application form not required.

Initial approach: Letter
Deadline(s): None
Board meeting date(s): June and Dec.
Officers and Trustees:* M. Hayne Hamilton,*
Pres.; Pamela K. Cuzzort,* Treas.; Andrew G.
Cope; Robert T. Johnston; S.K. Johnston, Jr.; S.K.
Johnston III; Lavinia Johnston; Katherine J. Tudor.
Number of staff: 1 full-time professional.
EIN: 621603398

TEXAS

3033
AIM Management Group Inc. Corporate Giving Program
11 Greenway Plz., Ste. 2600
Houston, TX 77046 (713) 830-3400
Contact: Patricia N. Lewis, Dir., Community
Rels.

Grantmaker type: Corporate giving program
Financial data (yr. ended 12/31/01): Total giving,
$250,000; giving activities include $250,000 for
42 grants (high: $13,000; low: $1,000).
Purpose and activities: As a complement to its
foundation, AIM also makes charitable
contributions to nonprofit organizations directly.
Support is limited to the Houston, Texas, area.
Fields of interest: Arts; Education; Environment;
Health care; Human services.
Types of support: General/operating support;
Annual campaigns.
Limitations: Giving limited to the Houston, TX,
area.
Application information: Contributions have
been allocated for 2003. The AIM Foundation
handles giving. The company has a staff that
only handles contributions. A contributions
committee reviews all requests. Application
form not required.
Initial approach: Proposal to headquarters
Copies of proposal: 1
Number of staff: 6.

3034
American Paint Horse Association Youth Development Foundation
P.O. Box 961023
Fort Worth, TX 76161-0023
Tel.: (817) 834-2742, ext. 422; FAX: (817)
834-3152; E-mail: rteate@apha.com; URL: http://
www.apha.com/ydf/

Established in 1980.
Grantmaker type: Public charity
Financial data (yr. ended 12/31/00): Revenue,
$94,002; assets, $536,366; gifts received,
$59,738; expenditures, $32,968; program
services expenses, $28,064; giving activities
include $28,064 for 29 grants to individuals
(high: $1,000; low: $500).
Purpose and activities: The foundation seeks to
support scientific research within the equine
industry, as well as to help reward and educate
young horsemen and women.
Fields of interest: Higher education;
Animals/wildlife, research; Athletics/sports,
equestrianism.

Types of support: Research; Scholarships—to
individuals.
Limitations: Giving on a national basis.
Application information: See Web site for
application information.
Officers and Directors:* Mary Parrott,* Pres.;
Lynn Titlow,* V.P.; Rosemary Teate,* Secy.; Travis
Titlow,* Treas.; Jerry Boomhower; Harry Gilbert;
John Hertner; Diane Hughes; Mark Kuhlwein;
Annette Lindstrom; Connie Nelson; and 4
additional directors.
EIN: 751729447

3035
Josephine Anderson Charitable Trust
c/o Amarillo National Bank
Plz. 1, P.O. Box 1
Amarillo, TX 79105 (806) 378-8342
Contact: James R. Garrison, V.P. and Trust Off.

Established in 1976.
Donor(s): Josephine Anderson.‡
Grantmaker type: Independent foundation
Financial data (yr. ended 02/28/02): Assets,
$7,517,131 (M); expenditures, $447,513;
qualifying distributions, $280,918; giving
activities include $254,500 for 54 grants (high:
$15,000; low: $1,000).
Purpose and activities: Giving primarily for arts,
education, health associations, human services,
and Christian agencies & churches.
Fields of interest: Performing arts; Arts;
Education; Botanical gardens; Health
organizations, association; Food distribution,
meals on wheels; Human services;
Children/youth, services; Family services;
Residential/custodial care; Christian agencies &
churches; Protestant agencies & churches;
Disabled.
Types of support: General/operating support;
Building/renovation.
Limitations: Giving primarily in the TX
Panhandle, with emphasis on Amarillo. No
grants to individuals.
Application information:
Initial approach: Letter
Deadline(s): None
Officer and Trustees:* Imadell Carter,* Mgr.;
Amarillo National Bank.
EIN: 751469596

3036
Aramco Services Company Contributions Program
c/o Corp. Contribs.
9009 W. Loop S.
Houston, TX 77096 (713) 432-4000

Grantmaker type: Corporate giving program
Purpose and activities: Aramco makes
charitable contributions to nonprofit
organizations involved with arts and culture,
education, the environment, and community
development. Support is given primarily in
Houston, Texas.
Fields of interest: Arts; Education; Environment;
Community development.
Types of support: General/operating support;
Sponsorships; In-kind gifts.
Limitations: Giving primarily in Houston, TX.
Application information: Application form not
required.

Initial approach: Proposal to headquarters
Copies of proposal: 1
Final notification: Following review

3037
Aurora Foundation
c/o Jeffrey Bronfman
520 Cypress Creek Ln.
Wimberley, TX 78676

Established in 1993 in TX.
Donor(s): Jeffrey Bronfman.
Grantmaker type: Operating foundation
Financial data (yr. ended 09/30/02): Assets,
$63,998 (M); gifts received, $744,057;
expenditures, $683,392; qualifying distributions,
$683,246; giving activities include $645,754 for
15 grants (high: $361,498; low: $500) and
$24,081 for 1 grant to an individual.
Purpose and activities: Support for projects that
embody the strategic efforts for the preservation
and protection of planetary ecosystems, (i.e. the
environment) as well as efforts that secure the
perpetuation and practice of indigenous cultures
and ancient religious, spiritual and ceremonial
traditions (e.g. certain Native American cultures
and their religious traditions).
Fields of interest: Education; Environment.
International interests: Global programs;
Central America; South America.
Limitations: Giving on a national and
international basis, with emphasis on Santa Fe,
NM, and Central and South America.
Application information:
Deadline(s): None
Officers and Directors:* Jeffrey Bronfman,*
Pres. and Treas.; Duncan E. Osborne,* Secy.;
Irvin F. Diamond.
EIN: 742660772

3038
Perry and Nancy Lee Bass Corporation ▼
201 Main St., Ste. 2300
Fort Worth, TX 76102-3127

Established in 1989 in TX.
Donor(s): Perry R. Bass.
Grantmaker type: Independent foundation
Financial data (yr. ended 06/30/02): Assets,
$49,842,653 (M); expenditures, $11,813,426;
qualifying distributions, $11,773,113; giving
activities include $11,786,770 for 19 grants
(high: $5,000,000; low: $250).
Purpose and activities: Support primarily for the
performing arts and museums.
Fields of interest: Museums; Performing arts;
Animals/wildlife, preservation/protection.
Types of support: General/operating support.
Limitations: Applications not accepted. Giving
primarily in Fort Worth, TX. No grants to
individuals.
Application information: Contributes only to
pre-selected organizations.
Officers and Directors:* Perry R. Bass,* Chair.
and Pres.; Nancy Lee Bass,* Vice-Chair. and
V.P.; W. Robert Cotham, V.P.; Gary W. Reese,
V.P.; Valleau Wilkie, Jr., V.P.; Lee M. Bass,*
Secy.-Treas.
EIN: 752308846
**Recent environmental and animal welfare
grants:**

3038-1 Nature Conservancy of Texas, San Antonio, TX, $10,000. For general support. 2002.
3038-2 World Wildlife Fund/Conservation Foundation, DC, $25,000. For general support. 2002.

3039
Bass Foundation ▼
309 Main St.
Fort Worth, TX 76102 (817) 336-0494
Contact: Valleau Wilkie, Jr., Exec. Dir.

Established in 1945 in TX.
Donor(s): Perry R. Bass, Lee M. Bass, Edward P. Bass, Sid Richardson Carbon and Gasoline Co., Perry R. Bass, Inc.
Grantmaker type: Independent foundation
Financial data (yr. ended 12/31/02): Assets, $5,222,234 (M); expenditures, $1,637,884; qualifying distributions, $1,604,984; giving activities include $1,569,001 for 13 grants (high: $550,000; low: $2,500; average: $2,500–$250,000).
Purpose and activities: Giving primarily for the arts and cultural institutions; some support for conservation.
Fields of interest: Arts; Natural resources.
Types of support: General/operating support; Capital campaigns; Building/renovation.
Limitations: Applications not accepted. Giving primarily in Fort Worth, TX.
Application information: Contributes only to pre-selected organizations.
Board meeting date(s): Feb.
Officers and Directors:* Perry R. Bass,* Pres.; Edward P. Bass,* V.P.; Lee M. Bass,* V.P.; Nancy Lee Bass,* V.P.; Cynthia K. Alexander, Secy.-Treas.; Valleau Wilkie, Jr., Exec. Dir.
Number of staff: 3 part-time professional.
EIN: 756033983

3040
The Anne Hendricks Bass Foundation
1801 Deepdale Dr.
Fort Worth, TX 76107-3517 (817) 735-1863
Contact: Anne H. Bass, Tr.

Established in 1997 in TX.
Donor(s): Anne H. Bass.
Grantmaker type: Independent foundation
Financial data (yr. ended 12/31/02): Assets, $3,837,918 (M); expenditures, $340,255; qualifying distributions, $339,228; giving activities include $339,228 for 36 grants (high: $28,200; low: $350).
Purpose and activities: Giving primarily for the arts and for education.
Fields of interest: Museums; Museums (art); Ballet; Arts; Libraries (public); Education; Environment.
Limitations: Giving primarily in NY. No grants to individuals.
Application information:
Initial approach: Letter
Deadline(s): None
Trustees: Anne H. Bass; Hyatt A. Bass; Samantha S. Bass.
EIN: 137117629

3041
Lee and Ramona Bass Foundation ▼
309 Main St.
Fort Worth, TX 76102 (817) 336-0494
Contact: Valleau Wilkie, Jr., Exec. Dir.
FAX: (817) 332-2176; E-mail: cjohns@sidrichardson.org

Established in 1994 in TX.
Donor(s): Lee M. Bass.
Grantmaker type: Independent foundation
Financial data (yr. ended 12/31/02): Assets, $21,310,198 (M); expenditures, $1,375,465; qualifying distributions, $1,317,447; giving activities include $1,215,000 for 6 grants (high: $500,000; low: $10,000; average: $5,000–$500,000).
Purpose and activities: Giving primarily for arts, higher education, and conservation.
Fields of interest: Arts; Higher education; Environment.
Types of support: General/operating support; Building/renovation; Endowments; Curriculum development.
Limitations: Giving primarily in TX. No grants to individuals.
Publications: Annual report.
Application information: Application form not required.
Initial approach: Brief letter of inquiry
Copies of proposal: 1
Deadline(s): None
Board meeting date(s): Varies
Officers and Directors:* Lee M. Bass,* Pres. and Treas.; Ramona S. Bass,* V.P.; William P. Hallman, Jr.,* Secy.; Valleau Wilkie, Jr.,* Exec. Dir.
Number of staff: 3 full-time support.
EIN: 752495163
Recent environmental and animal welfare grants:
3041-1 Fort Worth Zoological Association, Fort Worth, TX, $5,000,000. For Texas Wild exhibit. 2001.
3041-2 International Elephant Foundation, Azle, TX, $25,000. For general operating support. 2001.
3041-3 Peregrine Fund, Boise, ID, $1,500,000. For efforts to restore Aplomado Falcon and other programs once Aplomado program is fully funded. 2001.

3042
Bat Conservation International
P.O. Box 162603
Austin, TX 78716 (512) 327-9721
Contact: Robb Hankins, Exec. Dir.
FAX: (512) 327-9724; URL: http://www.batcon.org

Grantmaker type: Public charity
Financial data (yr. ended 05/31/02): Revenue, $2,322,808; assets, $3,966,182; gifts received, $1,318,429; expenditures, $2,776,132; program services expenses, $2,402,421; giving activities include $225,336 for 82 grants (high: $36,127; low: $300) and $44,468 for 9 grants to individuals (high: $5,000; low: $32).
Purpose and activities: The organization protects and restores bats and their habitats worldwide.
Fields of interest: Animals/wildlife, preservation/protection.

Limitations: Giving on a national and international basis.
Officer and Director:* Merlin D. Tuttle,* Pres.; Robb Hankins, Exec. Dir.
EIN: 742553144

3043
Behmann Brothers Foundation
P.O. Box 271486
Corpus Christi, TX 78427-1486
Contact: Charles L. Kosarek, Jr., Pres.

Established in 1979.
Donor(s): Arno W. Behmann,‡ Herman W. Behmann.‡
Grantmaker type: Independent foundation
Financial data (yr. ended 06/30/02): Assets, $6,629,155 (M); expenditures, $383,137; qualifying distributions, $334,210; giving activities include $325,065 for 100 grants (high: $40,000; low: $138).
Purpose and activities: Primary areas of interest are farming, education, health, and youth programs.
Fields of interest: Arts; Higher education; Education; Health care; Health organizations, association; Agriculture, farmlands; Human services; Children/youth, services; Community development; Christian agencies & churches.
Types of support: Program development.
Limitations: Giving primarily in southern TX. No grants to individuals.
Application information:
Initial approach: Proposal
Deadline(s): May 1
Final notification: June, positive replies only
Officers and Directors:* Charles L. Kosarek, Jr.,* Pres.; Frances R. Kosarek,* V.P.; Ross Mitchon,* Secy.; Willie J. Kosarek,* Treas.; T. Mark Anderson; John Lloyd Bluntzer; Karen K. Clark; Joshua Kosarek.
EIN: 742146739

3044
The Belo Foundation
(formerly A. H. Belo Corporation Foundation)
400 S. Record St., Ste. 200
Dallas, TX 75202-4841 (214) 977-6661
Contact: Marian Spitzberg, V.P.
Application address: P.O. Box 655237, Dallas, TX 75265-5237

Established in 1995 in TX as successor to The Dallas Morning News - WFAA Foundation.
Donor(s): A.H. Belo Corp., Belo Corp.
Grantmaker type: Company-sponsored foundation
Financial data (yr. ended 12/31/02): Assets, $34,480,889 (M); expenditures, $2,910,579; qualifying distributions, $2,346,738; giving activities include $1,977,875 for 23 grants (high: $1,500,000; low: $2,000).
Purpose and activities: The foundation focuses its giving on capital and endowment campaigns for parks, open space, city planning, public improvement, and journalism education. The foundation also makes community service grants.
Fields of interest: Journalism/publishing; Environment, beautification programs; Parks/playgrounds; Community development;

Government/public administration; Public affairs.
Types of support: Capital campaigns; Endowments.
Limitations: Giving primarily in areas of company operations, including Phoenix and Tucson, AZ, Riverside, CA, Boise, ID, Louisville, KY, New Orleans, LA, Charlotte, NC, Portland, OR, Providence, RI, Austin, Dallas-Fort Worth, Houston, and San Antonio, TX, the Hampton-Norfolk, VA, area, Spokane and the Seattle-Tacoma area, WA.
Publications: Application guidelines, Informational brochure.
Application information: Application form not required.
  Initial approach: Telephone foundation prior to submitting letter of request
  Copies of proposal: 1
  Deadline(s): None
Officers and Trustees:* Burl Osborne,* Chair.; Robert W. Decherd,* Pres.; Marian Spitzberg,* V.P.; Ward L. Huey, Jr.; James M. Moroney, Jr.; Judith Garret Segura.
Number of staff: 2 full-time professional; 1 part-time professional.
EIN: 752564365

3045
BHP Petroleum (Americas) Inc. Corporate Giving Program
BHP Tower
1360 Post Oak Blvd., Ste. 500
Houston, TX 77056-3020
FAX: (713) 961-8680

Grantmaker type: Corporate giving program
Purpose and activities: BHP Petroleum makes charitable contributions to nonprofit organizations involved with arts and culture, education, the environment, health, and youth development. Support is given primarily in areas of company operations.
Fields of interest: Arts; Education; Environment; Health care; Youth development.
Types of support: General/operating support; Employee volunteer services.
Limitations: Giving primarily in areas of company operations.
Application information: Application form not required.

3046
Bodhi Foundation
P.O. Box 4517
Austin, TX 78765-4517

Established in 1998 in TX.
Donor(s): David Lunsford.
Grantmaker type: Independent foundation
Financial data (yr. ended 06/30/01): Assets, $874,560 (M); expenditures, $244,755; qualifying distributions, $164,737; giving activities include $170,053 for 11 grants (high: $71,789; low: $30).
Fields of interest: Animals/wildlife, preservation/protection; Foundations (community); Buddhism.
Limitations: Applications not accepted. Giving on a national basis. No grants to individuals.
Application information: Contributes only to pre-selected organizations.

Manager: David Lunsford.
Directors: Stephanie Lane; Peter Lunsford.
EIN: 742890569

3047
The Boeckman Family Foundation
2911 Turtle Creek Blvd., Ste. 1240
Dallas, TX 75219-6256
Contact: Duncan E. Boeckman, V.P.

Established in 1998 in TX.
Donor(s): Elizabeth Mayer Boeckman, Duncan E. Boeckman.
Grantmaker type: Independent foundation
Financial data (yr. ended 12/31/01): Assets, $4,789,706 (M); expenditures, $242,487; qualifying distributions, $218,881; giving activities include $209,294 for 54 grants (high: $25,000; low: $193).
Fields of interest: Museums; Arts; Elementary/secondary education; Education; Environment.
Types of support: General/operating support; Capital campaigns; Curriculum development.
Limitations: Applications not accepted. Giving primarily in Santa Fe, NM and Dallas, TX. No grants to individuals.
Application information: Unsolicited requests for funds not accepted.
Officers and Trustees:* Elizabeth Mayer Boeckman,* Pres.; Duncan E. Boeckman,* V.P. and Secy.-Treas.; Kathryn Boeckman Howd.
EIN: 752766894

3048
Brandenburg Life Foundation
4545 Biltmore Dr.
Frisco, TX 75034
Contact: David Warren Brandenburg, Pres.
E-mail: davidbra@sprynet.com

Established in 1996 in TX.
Donor(s): David Warren Brandenburg, Inet, Inc., InterVoice, Inc.
Grantmaker type: Independent foundation
Financial data (yr. ended 12/31/01): Assets, $3,148,332 (M); gifts received, $61,686; expenditures, $188,530; qualifying distributions, $183,746; giving activities include $138,075 for 23 grants (high: $32,500; low: $500).
Fields of interest: Higher education; Animal welfare; Human services.
Limitations: Applications not accepted. No grants to individuals.
Application information: Contributes only to pre-selected organizations.
Officers and Directors:* David Warren Brandenburg,* Pres.; Diana Brandenburg,* V.P. and Secy.-Treas.; Geraldine Gurney.
EIN: 752651513

3049
The Bridge Foundation, Inc.
c/o Bruce Petty
201 Main St., Ste. 600
Fort Worth, TX 76102 (817) 339-1156
Contact: Marguerite M. Gordon, Pres.

Donor(s): Anna Melissa Gordon.
Grantmaker type: Independent foundation

Financial data (yr. ended 12/31/02): Assets, $9,821,988 (M); gifts received, $9,999,978; expenditures, $488,211; qualifying distributions, $384,000; giving activities include $384,000 for 4 grants (high: $234,000; low: $10,000).
Fields of interest: Animal welfare.
Limitations: Giving on a national basis.
Application information:
  Initial approach: Letter
  Deadline(s): None
Officers: Marguerite M. Gordon, Pres.; Anna Melissa Gordon, V.P. and Treas.; Bruce Petty, Secy.
EIN: 850476426

3050
Bridgeway Charitable Foundation
5615 Kirby Dr., Ste. 518
Houston, TX 77005
URL: http://www.bridgewayfund.com/aboutChar.asp

Established in 2000 in TX.
Donor(s): Bridgeway Capital Management, Inc.
Grantmaker type: Company-sponsored foundation
Financial data (yr. ended 12/31/02): Assets, $697,263 (M); gifts received, $1,200,000; expenditures, $783,702; qualifying distributions, $775,976; giving activities include $775,976 for 65 grants (high: $150,000; low: $100).
Fields of interest: Environment, radiation control; American Red Cross; Disasters, preparedness/services; Religion.
Types of support: General/operating support.
Limitations: Applications not accepted. No grants to individuals.
Application information: Contributes only to pre-selected organizations.
Officers and Directors:* John N.R. Montgomery,* Pres. and Treas.; Ann M. Montgomery,* V.P.; Joanna R. Schima Barnhill,* Secy.
EIN: 760666069

3051
The Butcher Fund
3733-1 Westheimer Rd., PMB 686
Houston, TX 77027 (713) 629-1381
Contact: Boone Schwartzel, Pres.

Established in 1966.
Donor(s): E.D. Butcher.‡
Grantmaker type: Independent foundation
Financial data (yr. ended 03/31/03): Assets, $2,100,192 (M); expenditures, $123,259; qualifying distributions, $91,369; giving activities include $90,000 for 18 grants of $5,000 each.
Purpose and activities: Giving primarily for community services, with an emphasis on food and health services.
Fields of interest: Elementary/secondary education; Higher education; Natural resources; Human services; Human services; Protestant agencies & churches; Disabled.
Limitations: Giving primarily in Houston, TX. No grants to individuals.
Application information: Application form not required.
  Deadline(s): None
  Board meeting date(s): Mar.

Officers and Directors:* Boone Schwartzel,
Pres.; Allen Butcher,* V.P.; John E. Butcher,* V.P.;
Anna B. Nemeti,* Secy.; R. Ernie Butcher;
Wanda Butcher; Betty Hudson.
Number of staff: None.
EIN: 746074669

3052
Kathleen Cailloux Family Foundation
c/o JPMorgan Chase Bank
P.O. Box 47531
San Antonio, TX 78265-7531 (210) 841-7011
Contact: John D. Rogers

Established in 1998 in TX.
Donor(s): Kathleen C. Cailloux.
Grantmaker type: Independent foundation
Financial data (yr. ended 12/31/01): Assets,
$19,527,865 (M); expenditures, $1,315,065;
qualifying distributions, $1,244,547; giving
activities include $1,250,000 for 12 grants (high:
$475,000; low: $2,500; average:
$10,000–$100,000).
Purpose and activities: Giving primarily for
higher education and hospitals and health
associations; support also for social service
agencies and youth organizations.
Fields of interest: Education; Animal welfare;
Hospitals (general); Health organizations,
association; Human services.
Limitations: Applications not accepted. Giving
primarily in Galveston and Kerr counties, TX.
Application information: Unsolicited requests
for funds not accepted.
Board meeting date(s): Mar.
Trustees: Robert S. Andresakis; Kenneth F.
Cailloux; Sandy Cailloux; Blackie Heileman;
Paula L. Heileman; JPMorgan Chase Bank.
EIN: 742857513

3053
The Gordon and Mary Cain Foundation ▼
8 Greenway Plz., Ste. 702
Houston, TX 77046 (713) 960-9283
Contact: James D. Weaver, Pres.

Established in 1988 in TX.
Donor(s): Gordon A. Cain, Mary H. Cain.
Grantmaker type: Independent foundation
Financial data (yr. ended 12/31/02): Assets,
$101,619,856 (M); gifts received, $333,738;
expenditures, $6,203,004; qualifying
distributions, $5,692,183; giving activities
include $5,620,316 for 110 grants (high:
$525,000; low: $1,000; average:
$5,000–$25,000).
Purpose and activities: Giving primarily for
higher and secondary education, social services,
health associations, arts, and denominational
giving.
Fields of interest: Visual arts; Museums;
Performing arts; Dance; Music; Historic
preservation/historical societies; Arts; Education,
association; Education, fund raising; Elementary
school/education; Secondary school/education;
Higher education; Medical school/education;
Adult education—literacy, basic skills & GED;
Reading; Education; Natural resources;
Environment; Hospitals (general); Family
planning; Nursing care; Substance abuse,
services; Health organizations, association;
Cancer; Heart & circulatory diseases; AIDS;

Alcoholism; Medical research, institute; Cancer
research; Heart & circulatory research; AIDS
research; Youth development, services; Human
services; Children/youth, services; Family
services; Homeless, human services; Chemistry;
Economics; Leadership development; Disabled;
Economically disadvantaged; Homeless.
Types of support: General/operating support;
Continuing support; Annual campaigns; Capital
campaigns; Building/renovation; Professorships;
Scholarship funds; Research.
Limitations: Giving primarily in Houston, TX.
No grants to individuals.
Publications: Application guidelines.
Application information: Application form not
required.
Initial approach: Proposal
Copies of proposal: 1
Deadline(s): None
Board meeting date(s): May, Sept., and Dec.
Officers and Trustee:* Gordon A. Cain,* Chair.
and C.E.O.; James D. Weaver, Pres.; Mary H.
Cain, V.P.; William A. McMinn, V.P.; Margaret
W. Oehmig, V.P.; Sharyn A. Weaver, V.P.;
William C. Oehmig, Secy.-Treas.
Number of staff: 1 full-time professional.
EIN: 760251558

3054
Walter O. Caldwell, Jr. Charitable Trust
c/o Compass Bank
P.O. Box 4886
Houston, TX 77210-4886

Established in 1972.
Grantmaker type: Public charity
Financial data (yr. ended 06/30/01): Revenue,
$414,697; assets, $8,245,423; expenditures,
$324,254; program services expenses,
$264,255; giving activities include $264,255 for
4 grants (high: $66,064; low: $66,063).
Purpose and activities: The trust exists for the
sole benefit of the Depelchin Children's Center,
Shriners Center, Houston SPCA, and Holly Hall,
Inc.
Fields of interest: Animal welfare;
Children/youth, services; Senior continuing care.
Limitations: Applications not accepted. Giving
limited to TX.
Application information: Contributes only to
pre-selected organizations; unsolicited requests
for funds not considered or acknowledged.
Officer and Trustees:* John S. Bace,* Chair.;
Jesse Couch; Harry J. Green, Jr.; William J.
Miller; Robert W. Paddock; David D. Welsh.
EIN: 237166208

3055
Harry S. and Isabel C. Cameron
Foundation
c/o Bank of America
P.O. Box 2518
Houston, TX 77252-2518
Contact: Diane Guiberteau

Established in 1966 in TX.
Donor(s): Isabel C. Cameron.‡
Grantmaker type: Independent foundation
Financial data (yr. ended 06/30/02): Assets,
$30,491,302 (M); gifts received, $129,048;
expenditures, $2,332,634; qualifying
distributions, $2,055,066; giving activities

include $2,042,150 for 154 grants (high:
$225,000; low: $200; average: $1,000–$5,000).
Purpose and activities: Giving primarily for
elementary, secondary, and higher education,
religious organizations, and human services.
Fields of interest: Elementary school/education;
Secondary school/education; Higher education;
Natural resources; Environment; Nursing care;
Health care; Substance abuse, services; Mental
health/crisis services; Health organizations,
association; AIDS; AIDS research; Food services;
Human services; Youth, services; Hospices;
Aging, centers/services; Homeless, human
services; Roman Catholic federated giving
programs; Roman Catholic agencies &
churches; Aging; Homeless.
Types of support: General/operating support;
Building/renovation; Equipment; Research.
Limitations: Giving primarily in TX, with
emphasis on Houston. No grants to individuals,
or for operating support, endowment funds, or
matching gifts; no loans.
Application information: Application form not
required.
Initial approach: Letter
Copies of proposal: 6
Deadline(s): Prior to board meetings
Board meeting date(s): Apr., Aug., and Dec.
Final notification: 2 weeks after board
meetings, when action is favorable
Directors: Priscilla Bormet; David W. Cameron;
Sylvia J. Cameron; Estelle Cameron Maloney;
Frances Cameron Miller.
Trustee: Bank of America.
Number of staff: None.
EIN: 746073312

3056
Carlson Family Foundation, Inc.
113 S. Gardenview St.
San Antonio, TX 78213
Contact: Thomas A. Norton, Treas.

Established in 2000 in NJ.
Grantmaker type: Independent foundation
Financial data (yr. ended 12/31/02): Assets,
$15,205,313 (M); expenditures, $839,726;
qualifying distributions, $724,812; giving
activities include $586,242 for 69 grants (high:
$85,000; low: $500) and $3,345 for employee
matching gifts.
Fields of interest: Education; Natural resources;
Cancer research; Children/youth, services;
Family services.
International interests: Spain; Peru.
Types of support: General/operating support;
Capital campaigns; Matching/challenge support.
Limitations: Applications not accepted. Giving
on a national and international basis.
Application information: Unsolicited requests
for funds not accepted.
Officers: John A. Norton, Pres.; Michael A.
Norton, Secy.; Thomas A. Norton, Treas.
Directors: Elaine Boylen; John Lont; James M.
Norton; Lenore C. Norton; Lenore "Trilby"
Norton; Mary T. Norton; Paul S. Norton.
EIN: 311678303

3057
Catto Charitable Foundation
200 Navarro St., Ste. 200
San Antonio, TX 78205 (210) 222-2161
Contact: Jessica Hobby Catto, Pres.

Established in 1967.
Grantmaker type: Independent foundation
Financial data (yr. ended 12/31/02): Assets,
$23,107,675 (M); expenditures, $1,920,501;
qualifying distributions, $1,727,381; giving
activities include $1,714,455 for 70 grants
(high: $600,000; low: $2,000).
Purpose and activities: Funding primarily for
environmental conservation and education.
Some funding also for arts and culture.
Fields of interest: Arts; Education; Natural
resources; Environment.
Limitations: No grants to individuals.
Application information:
Initial approach: Letter
Deadline(s): None
Officers and Directors:* Jessica Hobby Catto,*
Pres.; Henry E. Catto, Jr.,* V.P.; Susan R.
Farrimond, Secy.-Treas.
EIN: 742773632

3058
Michael and Rebecca Cemo Foundation
4015 Inverness Dr.
Houston, TX 77019

Established in 1997 in TX.
Donor(s): Michael J. Cemo, Rebecca A. Cemo.
Grantmaker type: Independent foundation
Financial data (yr. ended 04/30/02): Assets,
$6,577,723 (M); expenditures, $455,745;
qualifying distributions, $410,077; giving
activities include $381,572 for 27 grants (high:
$60,000; low: $1,000).
Purpose and activities: Giving primarily to the
arts, human services, and education.
Fields of interest: Performing arts; Arts;
University; Education; Animal welfare; Human
services; Religion.
Limitations: Applications not accepted. Giving
primarily in Houston, TX. No grants to
individuals.
Application information: Contributes only to
pre-selected organizations.
Officers and Directors:* Michael J. Cemo,*
Pres. and Treas.; Rebecca A. Cemo,* V.P. and
Secy.; Jason M. Cemo; Stephanie C. Cemo.
EIN: 760537009

3059
The Clayton Fund, Inc.
c/o J.P. Morgan Private Bank
P.O. Box 2558
Houston, TX 77252-8037 (713) 216-4513
Contact: Charlene Slack

Trust established in 1952 in TX.
Donor(s): William L. Clayton,‡ Susan V.
Clayton.‡
Grantmaker type: Independent foundation
Financial data (yr. ended 12/31/01): Assets,
$48,832,420 (M); expenditures, $2,748,501;
qualifying distributions, $2,401,922; giving
activities include $2,353,350 for 88 grants
(high: $180,000; low: $2,000; average:
$5,000–$50,000).

Purpose and activities: Giving primarily to the
needy, especially children, the environment,
family planning, education, agriculture, and arts
and culture organizations.
Fields of interest: Arts; Higher education;
Education; Natural resources; Hospitals
(general); Agriculture; Human services;
Children/youth, services; Family services.
Types of support: General/operating support;
Continuing support; Building/renovation;
Program development; Scholarship funds.
Limitations: Giving primarily in TX. No grants to
individuals.
Publications: Application guidelines.
Application information: Request application
guidelines. Application form not required.
Copies of proposal: 5
Deadline(s): Feb. 1, May 1, Aug. 1, and Nov. 1
Board meeting date(s): Mar., June, Sept., and
Dec.
Final notification: In writing
Officers and Trustees:* Burdine C. Johnson,*
Pres.; William L. Garwood, Jr.,* V.P.; William C.
Baker; J.P. Morgan Private Bank.
Number of staff: 1 full-time professional; 1
full-time support.
EIN: 760285764

3060
Coastal Bend Community Foundation
The Six Hundred Bldg.
600 Leopard St., Ste. 1716
Corpus Christi, TX 78473 (361) 882-9745
Contact: Jim Moloney, Exec. Dir.
FAX: (361) 882-2865; E-mail:
jmoloney@cbcfoundation.org; URL: http://
www.cbcfoundation.org

Established in 1980 in TX.
Grantmaker type: Community foundation
Financial data (yr. ended 12/31/01): Assets,
$29,986,847 (L); gifts received, $3,938,178;
expenditures, $6,508,709; giving activities
include $5,676,561 for grants.
Purpose and activities: Giving primarily for
social services, including alcohol and drug
abuse programs, youth and child welfare, the
disadvantaged, the homeless and hungry, and
welfare; hospitals; voluntarism; community
development; animal welfare; higher and other
education, including scholarship funds, literacy,
and libraries; and arts and culture, including
museums and history.
Fields of interest: Museums;
History/archaeology; Arts; Higher education;
Adult education—literacy, basic skills & GED;
Libraries/library science; Reading; Education;
Animal welfare; Hospitals (general); Substance
abuse, services; Alcoholism; Food services;
Human services; Children/youth, services;
Homeless, human services; Community
development; Voluntarism promotion;
Economically disadvantaged; Homeless.
Types of support: General/operating support;
Equipment; Program development; Seed money;
Fellowships; Scholarship funds.
Limitations: Giving limited to Aransas, Bee, Jim
Wells, Kleberg, Nueces, Refugio, and San
Patricio counties, TX.
Publications: Application guidelines, Annual
report, Grants list, Informational brochure.
Application information: Cover form required.
Application form required.

Initial approach: Letter requesting guidelines
Copies of proposal: 1
Deadline(s): Sept. 1
Board meeting date(s): Feb., May, Aug., and
Nov.
Final notification: Nov.
Officers and Directors:* T.D. Sells, Jr.,* Pres.;
Pat M. Eisenhauer,* V.P. Investments; Ginger D.
Fagen,* V.P.; Lou Adele May, Secy.-Treas.; Jim
Moloney,* Exec. Dir.; Harry Lee Adams, Jr.; Deb
Bauer; Jeff Bell; Susie Bracht Black; Roberto
Bosquez, M.D.; Austin Brown; John Chapman;
Lawrence Cornelius; Patricia Cypher; Joe
DeLeon, Jr.; Tom Dobson; Bill Finley, Jr.; Lucien
Flournoy; Joe Fulton; Paul R. Haas; Ed Harte;
Mark H. Hulings; Dick Messbanger; Patty P.
Mueller; Gorman Ritchie; Robert Rooke; Chela
Storm; Norman P. Wilcox; Ivan Wilson; and 3
additional directors.
Number of staff: 2 full-time professional; 1
part-time professional; 1 full-time support.
EIN: 742190039

3061
Communities Foundation of Texas, Inc. ▼
5500 Caruth Haven Ln.
Dallas, TX 75225-8146 (214) 750-4222
Contact: Jeverley R. Cook, Ph.D., V.P., Grants
FAX: (214) 750-4210; URL: http://
www.cftexas.org

Established in 1953 in TX; incorporated in 1960.
Grantmaker type: Community foundation
Financial data (yr. ended 06/30/03): Assets,
$562,427,000 (M); gifts received, $11,201,000;
expenditures, $61,836,000; giving activities
include $51,806,000 for grants.
Purpose and activities: Grants from unrestricted
funds are generally for education, health, social
services, youth activities, civic improvement,
and arts and culture.
Fields of interest: Arts; Higher education;
Education; Natural resources; Hospitals
(general); Health care; Health organizations,
association; Human services; Youth, services.
Types of support: Capital campaigns;
Building/renovation; Equipment; Land
acquisition; Emergency funds; Program
development; Seed money; Research; Technical
assistance; Matching/challenge support.
Limitations: Giving primarily in the Dallas, TX,
area (for grants from unrestricted funds). No
support for political or religious purposes from
general fund or organizations which redistribute
funds to other organizations. No grants to
individuals, or for continuing support, media
projects or publications, deficit financing,
endowment funds, scholarships, fellowships,
salaries, annual campaigns, or operational
expenses of well-established organizations.
Publications: Application guidelines, Annual
report, Financial statement, Newsletter, Program
policy statement.
Application information: Proposals sent by FAX
are not accepted; E-mail: ABrown@cftexas.org.
Application form not required.
Initial approach: After review of guidelines,
contact Grants Dept. by letter for further
information or submit proposal
Copies of proposal: 1
Deadline(s): Feb. 1, July 1, and Oct. 1

Board meeting date(s): Distribution committee for unrestricted funds meets in Mar., Aug., and Nov.

Final notification: 1 week after distribution committee meeting

Officers and Trustees:* Charles J. Wyly, Jr.,* Chair.; Milton P. Levy, Jr.,* Vice-Chair.; Edward M. Fjordbak,* Pres.; Jeverley R. Cook, Ph.D., V.P., Grants; Marcia Williams Godwin, V.P., Admin.; Cheryl Unis Mansour, V.P., External Affairs; J. Michael Redfearn, V.P., Finance; Thompson H. Sawyer, Jr., V.P., Investments; Philip O'Bryan Montgomery III,* Secy.; Linda Pitts Custard, Treas.; Jack Kinnebrew, Interim Exec. Dir. and Genl. Counsel; Ebby Halliday Acers, Tr. Emeritus; Ruth Sharp Altshuler, Chair. Emeritus; Daniel W. Cook III; Joseph M. Grant, Ph.D.; Linda Brack McFarland; Lydia Haggar Novakov; Jere W. Thompson; Gifford Touchstone; Joel T. Williams III.

Number of staff: 10 full-time professional; 1 part-time professional; 15 full-time support; 4 part-time support.

EIN: 750964565

Recent environmental and animal welfare grants:

3061-1 A Grassroots Aspen Experience, Aspen, CO, $30,500. 2002.

3061-2 Amazon Conservation Team, Arlington, VA, $40,000. 2002.

3061-3 Audubon Society, National, Austin, TX, $10,000. 2002.

3061-4 Botanical Research Institute of Texas, Fort Worth, TX, $200,000. 2002.

3061-5 California Trout Foundation, San Francisco, CA, $15,000. 2002.

3061-6 Climate Institute, DC, $50,000. 2002.

3061-7 Dallas Arboretum and Botanical Society, Dallas, TX, $34,450. 2002.

3061-8 Dallas Zoological Society, Dallas, TX, $28,200. 2002.

3061-9 Ducks Unlimited, Memphis, TN, $10,000. 2002.

3061-10 Fort Worth Garden Club, Fort Worth, TX, $65,309. 2002.

3061-11 Fort Worth Zoological Association, Fort Worth, TX, $18,150. 2002.

3061-12 Furbearers Unlimited, Nacogdoches, TX, $66,977. 2002.

3061-13 Great River Greening, Saint Paul, MN, $10,000. 2002.

3061-14 Humane Society of Dallas County, Dallas, TX, $29,555. 2002.

3061-15 National Museum of Wildlife Art, Jackson, WY, $10,000. 2002.

3061-16 Nature Conservancy, Dallas, TX, $12,000. 2002.

3061-17 Nature Conservancy of Texas, San Antonio, TX, $17,561. 2002.

3061-18 Parks and Wildlife Foundation of Texas, Dallas, TX, $22,250. 2002.

3061-19 River Bend Nature Works, Wichita Falls, TX, $119,000. 2002.

3061-20 Society for the Prevention of Cruelty to Animals of Texas, Dallas, TX, $155,278. 2002.

3061-21 Texas Discovery Gardens, Dallas, TX, $170,860. 2002.

3061-22 Wilderness Inquiry, Minneapolis, MN, $10,000. 2002.

3061-23 Womens Council of the Dallas Arboretum and Botanical Garden, Dallas, TX, $40,420. 2002.

3062
The Community Foundation of Brazoria County, Texas

P.O. Box 2392
Angleton, TX 77516-2392 (979) 848-2628
Contact: Vicki Kirby, Pres.
FAX: (979) 848-0032; E-mail: cfbrzco@brazosport.edu; URL: http://www.cfbr.org

Established in 1994 in TX.

Grantmaker type: Community foundation

Financial data (yr. ended 06/30/02): Assets, $789,883 (L); gifts received, $330,507; expenditures, $253,942; giving activities include $186,850 for 42 grants (high: $50,000; low: $100; average: $1,000–$4,000) and $35,500 for 37 grants to individuals (high: $1,000; low: $500).

Purpose and activities: The foundation administers a donor-advised fund.

Fields of interest: Theater; Arts; Elementary/secondary education; Higher education; Environment; Health care; Human services; Community development.

Types of support: General/operating support; Continuing support; Annual campaigns; Capital campaigns; Building/renovation; Equipment; Endowments; Seed money; Curriculum development; Scholarship funds; Scholarships—to individuals; Matching/challenge support.

Limitations: Applications not accepted. Giving primarily in Brazoria County, TX.

Publications: Informational brochure, Newsletter.

Application information: Unsolicited requests for funds not accepted.

Board meeting date(s): 4th Tues. of each month

Officers: Ron Jones, Chair.; Vicki Kirby, Pres. and Exec. Dir.; Jim Jarvie, V.P., Devel.; Juan Longoria, V.P., Finance; Suzanne Stofor, Secy.; Ken Smith, Treas.

Number of staff: 1 part-time professional.

EIN: 760427068

3063
ConocoPhillips Corporate Giving Program

(formerly Conoco Inc. Corporate Giving Program)
c/o Corp. Contribs., 3132 Marland Bldg.
600 N. Dairy Ashford
Houston, TX 77079-1175 (281) 293-1000
Contact: Clara Bradley
FAX: (281) 293-2767; URL: http://www.conocophillips.com/community/community.asp

Grantmaker type: Corporate giving program

Financial data (yr. ended 12/31/00): Total giving, $2,000,000; giving activities include $2,000,000 for grants.

Purpose and activities: ConocoPhillips makes charitable contributions to nonprofit organizations involved with arts and culture, education, the environment, safety, youth development, human services, and civic affairs. Support is given on a national and international basis.

Fields of interest: Arts; Education; Environment; Safety, education; Youth development; Human services; Public affairs.

Types of support: General/operating support; Emergency funds; Employee volunteer services; Employee matching gifts; Employee-related scholarships.

Limitations: Giving on a national and international basis in areas of company operations, with emphasis on OK and TX. No support for sectarian or religious organization. No grants to individuals, or for sponsorships or advertising or endowments.

Application information: An application form is available online. Application form required.

Initial approach: Download application form and mail proposal and application form to headquarters; download application form and mail proposal and application form to nearest company facility for organizations located outside the U.S.
Copies of proposal: 1
Deadline(s): By Aug. 31 is preferred

3064
Cooper Industries Foundation ▼

600 Travis, Ste. 5800
Houston, TX 77002-1001 (713) 209-8464
Contact: Leonor V. Carrosquilla, Secy. and Mgr., Community Affairs
Application address: P.O. Box 4446, Houston, TX 77210-4446, tel.: (713) 209-8800; FAX: (713) 209-8982; E-mail: info@cooperindustries.com; URL: http://www.cooperindustries.com/about/index.htm

Incorporated in 1964; absorbed Crouse-Hinds Foundation in 1982; absorbed McGraw-Edison Foundation in 1985.

Donor(s): Cooper Industries, Inc., Gerda Kaudisch.‡

Grantmaker type: Company-sponsored foundation

Financial data (yr. ended 12/31/02): Assets, $567,915 (M); expenditures, $2,751,515; qualifying distributions, $2,738,525; giving activities include $2,375,137 for 333 grants (high: $131,598; low: $100; average: $1,000–$50,000) and $363,388 for 628 employee matching gifts.

Purpose and activities: Functions solely as a conduit through which Cooper Industries, Inc. and its operating units throughout the country make contributions to local charities, the United Way, education, civic and community affairs, health services, and cultural programs where company's operations are located; emergency funds are for local organizations only.

Fields of interest: Museums; Performing arts; Arts; Vocational education; Higher education; Natural resources; Environment; Safety, education; Youth, services; Community development.

Types of support: General/operating support; Continuing support; Annual campaigns; Capital campaigns; Building/renovation; Emergency funds; Program development; Seed money; Employee matching gifts; In-kind gifts; Matching/challenge support.

Limitations: Giving in Houston, TX, and other communities of company operations in AL, AR, CA, CO, CT, FL, GA, IL, ME, MI, MO, MS, NC, NV, NY, OH, OR, PA, SC, TX, and WI. No support for religious, political, fraternal, or veterans' organizations, national or state health and welfare organizations (except through the

United Way and the company's matching gift program), public or private elementary and secondary schools or hospitals. No grants to individuals, or for endowment funds, publications, conferences and seminars, or, generally, for hospital capital fund drives or their operating campaigns; no loans.
Publications: Application guidelines, Corporate giving report.
Application information: Requests that are local in nature will be referred to the nearest local operation for recommendation. Application form not required.
> *Initial approach:* Letter
> *Copies of proposal:* 1
> *Deadline(s):* None; however, budgets are compiled annually each fall for the following year
> *Board meeting date(s):* Feb. and Nov.
> *Final notification:* Within 90 days

Officers and Trustees:* H. John Riley, Jr.,* Chair.; Vicki B. Guennewig,* Pres.; Leonor V. Carrosquilla, Secy. and Mgr., Community Affairs.; Terry A. Klebe, Treas.; D.K. Schumacher.
Number of staff: 1 full-time support.
EIN: 316060698

3065
Cooper Industries, Inc. Corporate Giving Program
Chase Tower
600 Travis, 58th Fl.
Houston, TX 77002-1001 (713) 209-8400
Application address: P.O. Box 4446, Houston, TX 77210-4446; FAX: (713) 209-8982; E-mail: info@cooperindustries.com; URL: http://www.cooperindustries.com/about

Grantmaker type: Corporate giving program
Financial data (yr. ended 12/31/00): Total giving, $243,265; giving activities include $238,400 for 31 grants (high: $25,000; low: $150) and $4,865 for 3 in-kind gifts.
Purpose and activities: As a complement to its foundation, Cooper Industries also makes charitable contributions to nonprofit organizations directly. Support is given on an international basis.
Fields of interest: Arts; Education; Environment; Health care; Human services; Community development.
International interests: Canada; Italy; United Kingdom; Germany; Latin America; Mexico; Australia.
Types of support: General/operating support; Employee volunteer services; Loaned talent; Sponsorships; Donated equipment; Donated products; In-kind gifts.
Limitations: Giving on an international basis in areas of company operations, particularly Houston, TX, and in Australia, Canada, Germany, Italy, Latin America, Mexico, and the United Kingdom. No support for discriminatory organizations. No grants to individuals.
Publications: Application guidelines, Corporate giving report (including application guidelines).
Application information: The Public Affairs Department handles giving. The company has a staff that only handles contributions. Application form not required.
> *Initial approach:* Proposal to headquarters
> *Copies of proposal:* 1
> *Deadline(s):* None

Final notification: 3 months
Administrator: Victoria B. Guennewig, V.P., Public Affairs.
Number of staff: 1 full-time professional; 1 full-time support.

3066
Renee C. Crowell f/b/o Charities
c/o Bank of America, N.A.
P.O. Box 831041
Dallas, TX 75283-1041

Established in 1973.
Grantmaker type: Public charity
Financial data (yr. ended 12/31/01): Revenue, $1,060,960; assets, $16,387,047; expenditures, $647,637; program services expenses, $561,861; giving activities include $561,861 for 7 grants (high: $160,529; low: $20,070).
Purpose and activities: The organization exists for the sole benefit of St. Luke's Hospital, Unity School of Christianity, Grace and Holy Trinity Cathedral, Alphapointe Association for the Blind, St. Paul's Episcopal Church, University of Kansas Endowment Association, and the Humane Society of Wyandotte Co.
Fields of interest: University; Animal welfare; Hospitals (general); Eye diseases; Christian agencies & churches.
Limitations: Applications not accepted. Giving limited to Kansas City and Lee's Summit, MO.
Application information: Contributes only to pre-selected organizations; unsolicited requests for funds not considered or acknowledged.
Trustee: Bank of America, N.A.
EIN: 436113386

3067
Andrew Delaney Foundation
2727 Allen Pkwy., Ste. 460
Houston, TX 77019
Contact: Andrew Delaney, Pres.
E-mail: jld215@aol.com

Established in 1988 in TX.
Donor(s): Andrew Delaney.
Grantmaker type: Independent foundation
Financial data (yr. ended 12/31/02): Assets, $3,821,902 (M); expenditures, $144,599; qualifying distributions, $124,063; giving activities include $98,500 for 25 grants (high: $20,000; average: $250–$20,000).
Purpose and activities: Giving to education, and to family, youth and community services.
Fields of interest: Museums; Higher education; Natural resources; Animal welfare; Health care, research; Health organizations, association; Human services; Protestant agencies & churches.
Types of support: Endowments.
Limitations: Applications not accepted. Giving primarily in TX. No grants to individuals.
Application information: Contributes only to pre-selected organizations.
Officers and Trustees:* Andrew Delaney,* Pres.; Janet L. Delaney,* V.P. and Secy.-Treas.; Pauline M. Delaney; James P. Lee; Antoinette R. Stapper.
Number of staff: 1 part-time support.
EIN: 760265537

3068
Denman/Newman Foundation
c/o Linwood Newman
3443 Ella Lee Ln.
Houston, TX 77027-4101

Established in 1998 in TX.
Donor(s): Linwood D. Newman.
Grantmaker type: Independent foundation
Financial data (yr. ended 12/31/01): Assets, $1,192,157 (M); expenditures, $92,030; qualifying distributions, $90,500; giving activities include $90,500 for grants.
Fields of interest: Higher education; Education; Animals/wildlife; Cancer; Human services; Children/youth, services.
Limitations: Applications not accepted. Giving primarily in TX. No grants to individuals.
Application information: Contributes only to pre-selected organizations.
Officer: Linwood D. Newman, Pres.
EIN: 311596627

3069
Dougherty Foundation
P.O. Box 640
Beeville, TX 78104-0640 (361) 358-3560
Contact: Daren R. Wilder, Treas.

Established in 1940 in TX.
Donor(s): Genevieve T. Dougherty,‡ James R. Dougherty.‡
Grantmaker type: Independent foundation
Financial data (yr. ended 07/31/02): Assets, $1,785,159 (M); expenditures, $104,322; qualifying distributions, $100,114; giving activities include $101,000 for 18 grants (high: $15,000; low: $1,000).
Purpose and activities: Giving primarily for education and for health and human services.
Fields of interest: Higher education; Libraries/library science; Environment; Animals/wildlife; Hospitals (general); Human services; Christian agencies & churches.
Types of support: General/operating support; Continuing support; Annual campaigns; Capital campaigns; Building/renovation; Equipment; Endowments; Program development; Conferences/seminars; Scholarship funds; Research.
Limitations: Giving primarily in southern TX. No grants to individuals.
Application information: 3-line executive summary should appear on first page of request. Application form not required.
> *Initial approach:* Letter
> *Copies of proposal:* 1
> *Deadline(s):* None

Officer: Daren R. Wilder, Treas.
Trustees: Molly Dougherty; Frances Carr Tapp; Ben F. Vaughan III.
Number of staff: None.
EIN: 746039859

3070
Anne Duncan & C. W. Duncan, Jr. Foundation
600 Travis St., Ste. 6100
Houston, TX 77002
Contact: Robert J. Faust, Secy.-Treas.

Established in 1964.

Grantmaker type: Independent foundation
Financial data (yr. ended 09/30/02): Assets,
$4,246,504 (M); expenditures, $433,725;
qualifying distributions, $397,222; giving
activities include $428,500 for 26 grants (high:
$239,942; low: $250).
Purpose and activities: Giving primarily for
education and youth services.
Fields of interest: Museums;
Elementary/secondary education; Natural
resources; Children/youth, services.
Limitations: Giving primarily in TX and WY. No
grants to individuals, including scholarships and
loans.
Application information: Application form not
required.
   Initial approach: Letter
   Deadline(s): None
Officers and Directors:* M.A. Dingus,* Chair.;
C.W. Duncan, Jr.,* Pres.; A.S. Duncan,* V.P.;
C.W. Duncan III,* V.P.; R.J. Faust,* Secy.-Treas.
EIN: 746064309

3071
El Paso Community Foundation
310 N. Mesa, 10th Fl.
El Paso, TX   79901   (915) 533-4020
Contact: Janice W. Windle, Pres.
Mailing address: P.O. Box 272, El Paso, TX,
79943-0272; FAX: (915) 532-0716; E-mail:
info@epcf.org; URL: http://www.epcf.org

Incorporated in 1977 in TX.
Grantmaker type: Community foundation
Financial data (yr. ended 12/31/02): Assets,
$83,234,856 (M); gifts received, $2,171,640;
expenditures, $8,335,282; giving activities
include $2,546,832 for 859 grants (high:
$85,000; low: $50).
Purpose and activities: Giving for education,
social services, health and disabilities, arts and
humanities, the environment, and community
benefit and development.
Fields of interest: Arts; Education; Environment;
Health care; Human services; Community
development.
Types of support: Continuing support; Program
development; Seed money; Scholarship funds;
Technical assistance; Matching/challenge
support.
Limitations: Giving limited to the El Paso, TX,
area. No support for medical research, religious
projects or political organizations. No grants to
individuals (except for scholarships), or for
deficit financing, annual campaigns, travel,
capital campaigns, fundraising events, or
ongoing support.
Publications: Application guidelines, Annual
report, Informational brochure, Newsletter.
Application information: Only 1 request per
year per applicant will be considered by the
board. Application form not required.
   Initial approach: Initial letter of inquiry
   Copies of proposal: 1
   Deadline(s): No set deadline; board considers
      requests semiannually
   Board meeting date(s): May and Nov.
   Final notification: Following board
      consideration
Officers and Directors:* Frances R. Axelson,*
Chair.; Margaret Varner Bloss, Vice-Chair.;
Lillian Crouch, Vice-Chair; Janice W. Windle,
Pres.; Virginia Kemendo, Exec. V.P.; Nestor

Valencia, V.P., Plan.; Cathy Hill, V.P.; Carl E.
Ryan, Secy.; Tom Hussmann,* Treas.; Yvonne
Carrillo; Mabel Fayant; Richard H. Feuille;
Susan Gray Kisler; Jose Manuel Mascarenas;
Roger Ortiz; Marylee Warwick; Dorothy White.
Number of staff: 12 full-time professional; 6
full-time support.
EIN: 741839536

3072
Margaret & James A. Elkins, Jr. Foundation
1166 First City Tower
1001 Fannin St.
Houston, TX   77002
Contact: Lauren Baird

Established in 1956 in TX.
Grantmaker type: Independent foundation
Financial data (yr. ended 10/31/02): Assets,
$22,889,538 (M); expenditures, $1,679,938;
qualifying distributions, $1,524,625; giving
activities include $1,524,625 for 15 grants (high:
$500,000; low: $5,000; average:
$10,000–$100,000).
Purpose and activities: Grants primarily for
charitable, religious, scientific, or educational
and literacy programs, including public safety
testing, and the prevention of cruelty to children
and animals.
Fields of interest: Child development,
education; Elementary school/education;
Secondary school/education; Higher education;
Medical school/education; Education; Animal
welfare; Hospitals (general); Health
organizations, association; Medical research,
institute; Safety/disasters; Children/youth,
services; Child development, services;
Engineering/technology; Biological sciences;
Science; Christian agencies & churches;
Religion.
Types of support: Capital campaigns;
Building/renovation; Equipment; Endowments;
Emergency funds; Program development;
Research.
Limitations: Giving primarily in TX, with
emphasis on the metropolitan Houston area. No
grants to individuals, or for deficit financing;
generally no grants for continuing operating
support.
Application information: Application form not
required.
   Initial approach: Letter
   Copies of proposal: 1
   Deadline(s): Aug. 31
   Board meeting date(s): Varies
Trustees: J.A. Elkins, Jr.; James A. Elkins III.
Number of staff: 1 shared staff.
EIN: 746051746

3073
Entergy Gulf States, Inc. Corporate Giving Program
(formerly Gulf States Utilities Company
Contributions Program)
350 Pine St.
Beaumont, TX   77701   (409) 981-2890

Grantmaker type: Corporate giving program
Purpose and activities: Entergy Gulf States
makes charitable contributions to nonprofit
organizations involved with education, the
environment, health and human services,

disease, community development, civic affairs,
and economically disadvantaged people.
Support is given primarily in areas of company
operations.
Fields of interest: Higher education; Education;
Environment; Hospitals (general); Health care;
Health organizations; Human services;
Community development; Public affairs;
Economically disadvantaged.
Types of support: General/operating support;
Employee volunteer services; Sponsorships;
Employee matching gifts; Employee-related
scholarships; Donated equipment; Donated
products; In-kind gifts.
Limitations: Giving primarily in areas of
company operations.
Application information: A contributions
committee reviews all requests. Application
form required.
   Initial approach: Contact headquarters for
      application form
   Deadline(s): None
   Board meeting date(s): Monthly

3074
Exxon Mobil Corporation Contributions Program
(formerly Exxon Corporation Contributions
Program)
c/o Corp. Contribs.
5959 Las Colinas Blvd.
Irving, TX   75039-2298   (972) 444-1000
Contact: Edward F. Ahnert, Mgr., Contribs.; or
Bill Carpenter, Coord., Contribs. Admin.
FAX: (972) 444-1405; URL: http://
www.exxonmobil.com/Corporate/Notebook/
Citizen/Corp_N_CitizenDetails.asp

Grantmaker type: Corporate giving program
Financial data (yr. ended 12/31/02): Total giving,
$25,326,820; giving activities include
$25,326,820 for 1,136 grants (high: $6,213,000;
low: $100).
Purpose and activities: Exxon Mobil makes
charitable contributions to nonprofit
organizations involved with arts and culture,
education, the environment, health, community
development, civic affairs, minorities, and
women. Support is given on a national and
international basis.
Fields of interest: Museums; Historic
preservation/historical societies; Arts; Education;
Environment; Health care; Community
development; Public policy, research; Public
affairs; Minorities; Women.
International interests: Canada; Caribbean;
Europe; Africa; Latin America; Asia; Middle East.
Types of support: General/operating support;
Fellowships; Employee volunteer services;
Sponsorships; Employee matching gifts.
Limitations: Giving on a national and
international basis in areas of company
operations, with emphasis on Baldwin County,
AL, Anchorage, AK, Torrance, CA, Cortez, CO,
Washington, DC, Joliet, IL, Kingman, KS, Baton
Rouge, Chalmette, New Orleans, Plaquemine,
Raceland, and Sunset, LA, Billings and Laurel,
MT, Clinton, East Millstone, Edison, Paulsboro,
and the Linden, NJ, area, Rochester, NY,
Baytown, Dallas-Fort Worth, Longview,
Midland, Mount Belvieu, Odessa, and the
Houston, TX, area, Fairfax County, VA, Lincoln,
Sublette, and Sweetwater counties, WY, and in

Africa, Canada, the Caribbean, Europe, the Far East, Latin America, and the Middle East; giving also to national organizations. No support for political or religious organizations or United Way-supported organizations; low priority for disease-specific organizations. No grants to individuals, or for endowments.

Publications: Application guidelines, Corporate giving report, Grants list.

Application information: Proposals should be no longer than 4 pages in length. Requests may be forwarded by the company to other Exxon Mobil locations when appropriate. The Contributions Department handles giving. The company has a staff that only handles contributions. Application form not required.

Initial approach: Proposal to headquarters
Copies of proposal: 1
Deadline(s): None
Final notification: Following review

Number of staff: 6 full-time professional; 4 full-time support.

3075

ExxonMobil Foundation ▼

(formerly ExxonMobil Education Foundation)
5959 Las Colinas Blvd.
Irving, TX 75039-2298 (972) 444-1104
Contact: Edward F. Ahnert, Pres.
FAX: (972) 444-1405

Incorporated in 1955 in NJ as Esso Education Foundation; name changed to Exxon Education Foundation in 1972; current name adopted in 1999.

Donor(s): Exxon Corp., Exxon Mobil Corp., and affiliated companies.

Grantmaker type: Company-sponsored foundation

Financial data (yr. ended 12/31/02): Assets, $67,890,706 (M); gifts received, $46,689,850; expenditures, $47,527,011; qualifying distributions, $47,555,340; giving activities include $27,911,955 for grants and $19,392,390 for employee matching gifts.

Purpose and activities: To aid education in the United States: 1) by matching gifts made by Exxon Mobil employees and retirees to colleges and universities; 2) by supporting university-based research in areas of science and technology related to the petroleum and chemical industries; 3) by aiding organizations and associations serving significant segments of the educational community; and 4) through project-oriented programs concerned with mathematics education, particularly in the primary grades; elementary and secondary school restructuring and teacher education reform, particularly as they relate to enhancing the success of the educational system with disadvantaged minority students; and undergraduate science, math, and engineering education reform.

Fields of interest: Education, association; Education, research; Elementary school/education; Secondary school/education; Higher education; Engineering school/education; Education; Mathematics; Engineering/technology; Engineering; Science; Minorities.

Types of support: Program development; Seed money; Employee matching gifts.

Limitations: No grants to individuals, or for institutional scholarship or fellowship programs, capital or building funds, land acquisition, equipment, renovation projects, or endowment purposes; no loans.

Publications: Annual report.

Application information: Applications are not encouraged.

Officers and Trustees:* K.P. Cohen,* Chair.; Edward F. Ahnert, Pres.; A.E. Lawson, Exec. Dir.; R.M. Cureton, Secy.; S.B.L. Penrose, Treas.; R. E. Harayda, Cont.; F.W. Bass; S.E. Carter; J.C. Glaubig; B.G. Macklin; F.A. Risch; F.B. Sprow; P.A. Wetz.

Number of staff: 4 full-time professional; 2 full-time support.

EIN: 136082357

Recent environmental and animal welfare grants:

3075-1 Academy of Natural Sciences of Philadelphia, Philadelphia, PA, $20,000. For Environmental Associates Program. 2002.

3075-2 Advancement of Sound Science Center, DC, $10,000. 2002.

3075-3 Alaska Childrens Zoo, Anchorage, AK, $10,000. For Siberian Tiger Exhibit. 2002.

3075-4 Alaska Raptor Rehabilitation Center (ARRC), Sitka, AK, $10,000. 2002.

3075-5 American Forests, DC, $25,000. For reforestation project. 2002.

3075-6 Annapolis Center for Science-Based Public Policy, Annapolis, MD, $70,000. For general support. 2002.

3075-7 Arizona State University, Tempe, AZ, $10,000. For research on methyl tertiary butyl ether (MTBE) in the environment. 2002.

3075-8 Armand Bayou Nature Center, Houston, TX, $27,000. For education programs. 2002.

3075-9 Audubon Nature Institute, New Orleans, LA, $100,000. For Project LEAD. 2002.

3075-10 Baldwin County Board of Education, Mobile, AL, $25,000. For Aquaculture Center. 2002.

3075-11 Baytown, City of, Baytown, TX, $33,000. For Nature Center. 2002.

3075-12 Baytown, City of, Baytown, TX, $10,000. For Trash Off 2002. 2002.

3075-13 Bermuda Biological Station for Research, Ferry Reach, Bermuda, $50,000. For marine carbon cycle research. 2002.

3075-14 Bowdoin College, Brunswick, ME, $15,000. For research on effects of oil spills on the environment. 2002.

3075-15 California Foundation on the Environment and the Economy, San Francisco, CA, $75,000. For Energy Education Program. 2002.

3075-16 Capital Research Center, DC, $25,000. For Green Watch Project. 2002.

3075-17 Carnegie Mellon University, Center for the Study and Improvement of Regulation, Pittsburgh, PA, $300,000. 2002.

3075-18 Chemical Educational Foundation, Arlington, VA, $25,000. For Product Stewardship Bulletins. 2002.

3075-19 Clarkson University, Potsdam, NY, $10,000. For Environmental Manufacturing Management. 2002.

3075-20 Colorado School of Mines Foundation, Golden, CO, $15,000. For International Groundwater Modeling Initiative. 2002.

3075-21 Dallas Zoological Society, Dallas, TX, $20,000. For Zoo Billboard. 2002.

3075-22 Ducks Unlimited, Ridgeland, MS, $25,000. For reforestation project. 2002.

3075-23 Duke University, Center for Environmental Solutions, Durham, NC, $45,000. 2002.

3075-24 East Coast Greenway Alliance, Wakefield, RI, $10,000. 2002.

3075-25 Eddie V. Gray Wetlands Education and Recreation Center, Friends of, Baytown, TX, $30,000. For Wetland Ecology Program. 2002.

3075-26 Environmental Literacy Council, DC, $20,000. 2002.

3075-27 Foundation for Research on Economics and the Environment (FREE), Bozeman, MT, $30,000. 2002.

3075-28 Frontiers of Freedom Institute, Fairfax, VA, $97,000. For global climate change outreach activities. 2002.

3075-29 Frontiers of Freedom Institute, Fairfax, VA, $35,000. For global climate change science projects. 2002.

3075-30 Galveston Bay Foundation, Webster, TX, $15,000. For Calendar Project, fundraising initiative to sell calendars with conservation-themed art drawn by local fifth graders. 2002.

3075-31 George and Freda Chandler Arboretum, Baytown, TX, $20,000. 2002.

3075-32 George C. Marshall Research Foundation, Lexington, VA, $80,000. For Global Climate Change Program. 2002.

3075-33 Houston Arboretum and Nature Center, Houston, TX, $10,000. For exhibits and educational materials. 2002.

3075-34 Institute for Energy Research, Houston, TX, $30,000. 2002.

3075-35 Landmark Legal Foundation, Kansas City, MO, $10,000. For Environmental Accountability Initiative. 2002.

3075-36 Louisiana, State of, Baton Rouge, LA, $10,000. For conservation work at Lake Catahoula. 2002.

3075-37 Marine Biological Laboratory, Woods Hole, MA, $40,000. For Ecosystems Center. 2002.

3075-38 Marine Environmental Sciences Consortium, Dauphin Island, AL, $50,000. For Dauphin Island Sea Lab-BayMobile. 2002.

3075-39 Massachusetts Institute of Technology, Cambridge, MA, $200,000. For joint program on Science and Policy of Global Change. 2002.

3075-40 Massachusetts Institute of Technology, Cambridge, MA, $90,000. For energy policy studies. 2002.

3075-41 Mickey Leland National Urban Air Toxics Research Center, Houston, TX, $30,000. For Air Quality Project. 2002.

3075-42 Midewin Tallgrass Prairie Alliance, Joliet, IL, $10,000. 2002.

3075-43 National Fish and Wildlife Foundation, DC, $1,000,000. For Save the Tiger Fund (STF) Council. 2002.

3075-44 Nature Conservancy, Baton Rouge, LA, $34,800. For restoration work in Grand Isle. 2002.

3075-45 Nature Conservancy, Arlington, VA, $28,000. For International Leadership Council meeting. 2002.

3075-46 NatureServe, Arlington, VA, $10,000. For web site management support. 2002.

3075-47 Openlands Project, Chicago, IL, $10,000. For Midewin Tallgrass Prairie project. 2002.

3075-48 Parks and Wildlife Foundation of Texas, Dallas, TX, $20,000. For Texas Freshwater Fisheries Center. 2002.

3075-49 Peregrine Fund, Boise, ID, $25,000. For bird conservation work. 2002.

3075-50 Point Reyes Bird Observatory, Stinson Beach, CA, $10,000. 2002.

3075-51 Political Economy Research Center, Bozeman, MT, $15,000. 2002.

3075-52 Puerto Rico Conservation Trust Fund, San Juan, PR, $10,000. For education programs. 2002.

3075-53 Recreation and Park Commission for the Parish of East Baton Rouge, Baton Rouge, LA, $75,000. For tiger exhibit at Baton Rouge Zoo. 2002.

3075-54 Rocky Mountain Elk Foundation, Missoula, MT, $10,000. To analyze Piney Front elk heard habitat. 2002.

3075-55 Rutgers, The State University of New Jersey, New Brunswick, NJ, $15,000. For Brownfields Redevelopment Program. 2002.

3075-56 Stanford University, Stanford, CA, $90,000. For energy policy studies. 2002.

3075-57 Texas State Aquarium Association, Corpus Christi, TX, $25,000. For Project WILD/Aquatic WILD. 2002.

3075-58 Tri-State Bird Rescue and Research, Newark, DE, $10,000. For rehabilitation of aquatic wildfowl. 2002.

3075-59 University of Massachusetts, Amherst, MA, $25,000. For Biological Effects of Low-Level Exposure (BELLE) Chemical Hormesis Database, initiative to study effects of low levels of chemical agents and radioactivity on human biology. 2002.

3075-60 University of Texas, Austin, TX, $20,000. For research on Methyl Tertiary Butyl Ether (MTBE) dissolved plumes. 2002.

3075-61 University of Texas, Austin, TX, $10,000. For Environmental Solutions Program. 2002.

3075-62 University of Texas Health Science Center, Houston, TX, $15,000. For study of ethanol preservation. 2002.

3075-63 University of Washington, Seattle, WA, $20,000. For study of Magellanic Penguins, which breed on east and western coasts of Chile and Argentina in South America, and on offshore islands and in the Falkland Islands. 2002.

3075-64 Wildlife Conservation Society, Bronx, NY, $33,000. For Tiger Kingdom exhibit at the Bronx Zoo. 2002.

3076
I. D. & Marguerite Fairchild Foundation
P.O. Box 150143
Lufkin, TX 75915-0143 (936) 634-2771
Contact: C. James Haley, Jr., Pres.

Established in 1977 in TX.
Donor(s): Marguerite Fairchild.‡
Grantmaker type: Independent foundation
Financial data (yr. ended 06/30/02): Assets, $3,907,248 (M); expenditures, $322,365; qualifying distributions, $283,656; giving activities include $252,000 for 9 grants (high: $126,000; low: $2,500).

Purpose and activities: Giving primarily for a college and museums. Giving also for libraries, a zoo, and education.
Fields of interest: Museums; Higher education; Libraries (public); Education; Zoos/zoological societies; Community development.
Types of support: Endowments; Program development; Scholarship funds.
Limitations: Giving limited to the Angelina County, TX, area. No grants to individuals.
Application information: Application form not required.
> *Initial approach:* Letter
> *Copies of proposal:* 9
> *Deadline(s):* None
> *Board meeting date(s):* June
> *Final notification:* June 30
Officers: C. James Haley, Jr., Pres.; Hilda Mitchell, V.P.; Mary Duncan, Secy.
Number of staff: None.
EIN: 751572514

3077
The Johanna A. Favrot Fund
1770 St. James Pl., Ste. 510
Houston, TX 77056-3405 (713) 622-1442
Contact: Julie Richardson

Established in 2000 in TX.
Grantmaker type: Independent foundation
Financial data (yr. ended 12/31/02): Assets, $2,001,740 (M); expenditures, $152,847; qualifying distributions, $129,295; giving activities include $126,000 for 14 grants (high: $14,000; low: $2,000).
Purpose and activities: Support primarily for international affairs; giving also for wildlife preservation, the environment, education, human services, and the arts.
Fields of interest: Museums (children's); Higher education; Education; Natural resources; Animals/wildlife, preservation/protection; Human services; International affairs.
Types of support: General/operating support; Building/renovation; Emergency funds; Program development; Research.
Limitations: Giving on a national basis.
Application information: Application form not required.
Officers and Trustees:* Tatiana Stephens,* Pres.; Thomas Channing Arndt,* V.P.; Michael De Bruyn Arndt,* Secy.; David De Kanter Arndt,* Treas.; Christopher Favrot Arndt; Genevieve Helen Peterson; Joseph Favrot Peterson; Sara Johanna Peterson Pittock; Noel Shepard Stephens.
EIN: 760638641

3078
The Favrot Fund
1770 St. James Pl.
Houston, TX 77056-3405
Contact: Julie Richardson

Grantmaker type: Independent foundation
Financial data (yr. ended 12/31/02): Assets, $20,031,348 (M); expenditures, $1,531,822; qualifying distributions, $1,344,965; giving activities include $1,320,050 for 42 grants (high: $200,000; low: $550).
Fields of interest: Arts; Education; Animals/wildlife; Human services.

Limitations: Giving primarily in CA and TX.
Application information: Application form not required.
Officers and Trustees:* Laurence Favrot,* Pres.; Marcia Favrot,* Secy.; Romelia Favrot,* Treas.; Celestine Favrot Arndt; Leo M. Favrot; Lenior M. Josey; Jeanette F. Peterson.
EIN: 760638639

3079
Field-Day Foundation
10100 Reunion Pl., Ste. 750
San Antonio, TX 78216-4171

Established in 2001 in TX.
Donor(s): Julia N.H. Widdowson.
Grantmaker type: Independent foundation
Financial data (yr. ended 09/30/02): Assets, $886,667 (M); gifts received, $38,187; expenditures, $127,730; qualifying distributions, $126,305; giving activities include $123,675 for 22 grants (high: $45,500; low: $50).
Purpose and activities: Giving primarily to environmental organizations for the protection and conservation of our natural resources.
Fields of interest: Arts; Education; Natural resources; Environment, land resources.
Limitations: Applications not accepted. Giving primarily in NY; some giving also in Washington, DC.
Application information: Contributes only to pre-selected organizations.
Officers and Directors: Julia N.I I. Widdowson,* Pres.; Nigel D. Widdowson,* V.P. and Secy.; David L. Sinak.
EIN: 522364623

3080
Leland Fikes Foundation, Inc. ▼
3050 Lincoln Plz.
500 N. Akard St.
Dallas, TX 75201 (214) 754-0144
Contact: Nancy J. Solana, V.P., Research and Grant Admin.

Incorporated in 1952 in DE.
Donor(s): Leland Fikes,‡ Catherine W. Fikes.‡
Grantmaker type: Independent foundation
Financial data (yr. ended 12/31/02): Assets, $70,942,614 (M); expenditures, $6,225,961; qualifying distributions, $4,929,217; giving activities include $4,581,062 for 68 grants (high: $1,080,000; low: $1,000; average: $5,000–$75,000).
Purpose and activities: Giving primarily for medical research, health, youth, and social services, family planning, public interest groups, and education; grants also for population research and cultural programs.
Fields of interest: Museums; Performing arts; Music; Arts; Elementary school/education; Secondary school/education; Higher education; Medical school/education; Adult education—literacy, basic skills & GED; Reading; Education; Natural resources; Environment; Family planning; Health care; Substance abuse, services; Mental health/crisis services; Health organizations, association; AIDS; Alcoholism; Medical research, institute; AIDS research; Domestic violence; Food services; Housing/shelter, development; Human services; Children/youth, services; Family

services; Homeless, human services; Reproductive rights; Voluntarism promotion; Engineering/technology; Science; Population studies; Public policy, research; Public affairs; Immigrants/refugees; Homeless.
Types of support: General/operating support; Continuing support; Annual campaigns; Capital campaigns; Building/renovation; Equipment; Endowments; Emergency funds; Program development; Professorships; Seed money; Research; Matching/challenge support.
Limitations: Giving primarily in the Dallas, TX, area. No grants to individuals; no loans.
Publications: Application guidelines.
Application information: Submit proposal upon request. Application form not required.
  Initial approach: Letter
  Copies of proposal: 1
  Deadline(s): None
  Board meeting date(s): Bimonthly
  Final notification: By letter
Officers and Trustees:* Lee Fikes,* Pres. and Treas.; Nancy J. Solana, V.P., Research and Grant Admin. and Secy.; Amy L. Fikes,* V.P.; Brendan J. Fikes; Catherine L. Fikes.
Number of staff: 1 full-time professional; 3 part-time professional; 1 full-time support; 1 part-time support.
EIN: 756035984
Recent environmental and animal welfare grants:
3080-1 NumbersUSA, Arlington, VA, $25,000. For Urban Sprawl project. 2001.

3081
FINA Foundation
(formerly American Petrofina Foundation)
P.O. Box 2159
Dallas, TX 75221-2159
Contact: J. Maria Martineau, Secy.

Incorporated in 1974 in TX.
Donor(s): FINA, Inc.
Grantmaker type: Company-sponsored foundation
Financial data (yr. ended 12/31/01): Assets, $3,381,947 (M); expenditures, $101,201; qualifying distributions, $99,348; giving activities include $99,348 for 53 grants (high: $25,000; low: $25).
Purpose and activities: Interests include health, especially hospitals and cancer and other medical research; community funds and civic affairs; the fine and performing arts, museums and other cultural programs; higher and other education; family and social services; and the environment.
Fields of interest: Visual arts; Museums; Performing arts; Arts; Higher education; Education; Environment; Hospitals (general); Health care; Health organizations, association; Cancer; Medical research, institute; Cancer research; Human services; YM/YWCAs & YM/YWHAs; Children/youth, services; Family services; Federated giving programs; Government/public administration.
Types of support: Continuing support; Annual campaigns; Employee matching gifts.
Limitations: Giving primarily in TX, in areas where company employees reside. No support for religious organizations. No grants to individuals.

Application information: Application form required for employee matching gifts. Grants are between $50 and $5,000; special restrictions applied to grants to higher education institutions.
  Initial approach: Proposal
  Copies of proposal: 1
  Deadline(s): None
  Board meeting date(s): Annually
Officers and Directors:* Ronald W. Haddock,* Pres.; Cullen M. Godfrey,* V.P.; Carla H. Meadows,* V.P.; J. Maria Martineau,* Secy.
Number of staff: 1 part-time professional.
EIN: 237391423

3082
Louis and Elizabeth Nave Flarsheim Charitable Foundation
c/o Bank of America
P.O. Box 831041
Dallas, TX 75283-1041
Contact: David P. Ross, Sr. V.P., Bank of America
Application address: c/o Bank of America, 1200 Main St., Kansas City, MO 64105, tel.: (816) 979-7481

Established in 1980.
Donor(s): Louis Flarsheim, Elizabeth Flarsheim.
Grantmaker type: Independent foundation
Financial data (yr. ended 11/30/02): Assets, $3,126,032 (M); expenditures, $615,367; qualifying distributions, $589,911; giving activities include $570,970 for 39 grants (high: $62,000; low: $500).
Purpose and activities: Grants primarily for the performing and visual arts; support also for higher education.
Fields of interest: Performing arts; Arts; Higher education; Education; Zoos/zoological societies; Children/youth, services.
Types of support: Program development; Seed money.
Limitations: Giving primarily in KS, and the Kansas City, MO, area.
Application information: Application form not required.
  Initial approach: Letter (no more than 3 pages)
  Copies of proposal: 1
  Deadline(s): None
  Board meeting date(s): Varies
Trustee: Bank of America.
Number of staff: 1 full-time professional.
EIN: 436223957

3083
Four Cedars Foundation, Inc.
P.O. Box 2950
San Antonio, TX 78299

Established in 1998 in WI.
Donor(s): William P. Rogers.
Grantmaker type: Independent foundation
Financial data (yr. ended 05/31/02): Assets, $1,064,839 (M); expenditures, $97,494; qualifying distributions, $93,227; giving activities include $93,500 for 22 grants (high: $20,000; low: $1,000).
Purpose and activities: Giving for education, the environment, variety of human services, and for religion.
Fields of interest: Higher education; Scholarships/financial aid; Environment; Human

services; Women, centers/services; Federated giving programs; Christian agencies & churches.
Limitations: Applications not accepted. Giving primarily in Duluth, MN. No grants to individuals.
Application information: Contributes only to pre-selected organizations.
Officer: James L. Banks, V.P. and Secy.
Directors: Robert D. Banks, Jr.; Joel S. Cooper; Mark D. Johnson; William P. Rogers.
Agent: Frost National Bank.
EIN: 391945362

3084
C. J. & Syble Fowlston Charitable Trust
P.O. Box 51259
Amarillo, TX 79124-1259   (806) 355-7640
Contact: Joyce Perkins, Tr.

Established in 1981.
Donor(s): Syble E. Fowlston,‡ C.J. Fowlston.‡
Grantmaker type: Independent foundation
Financial data (yr. ended 12/31/02): Assets, $4,918,432 (M); expenditures, $346,785; qualifying distributions, $197,874; giving activities include $176,300 for 7 grants (high: $125,000; low: $2,800).
Purpose and activities: Giving primarily for food distribution.
Fields of interest: Arts; Botanical gardens; Food services.
Types of support: General/operating support; Equipment.
Limitations: Giving limited to the 20 northernmost counties of the TX Panhandle. No grants to individuals.
Application information:
  Initial approach: Letter
  Deadline(s): None
  Final notification: Within 2 months
Trustee: Joyce Perkins.
EIN: 756281596

3085
Friedkin Conservation Fund
7701 Wilshire Place Dr.
Houston, TX 77040   (713) 580-3200
Contact: Charles L. Williams, Pres.

Grantmaker type: Public charity
Financial data (yr. ended 12/31/00): Revenue, $160,534; assets, $29,069; gifts received, $160,534; expenditures, $203,761; program services expenses, $148,329; giving activities include $148,329 for 2 grants (high: $142,968; low: $5,361).
Purpose and activities: The fund seeks to concentrate on the conservation of wildlife, and village assistance such as food, clothing, shelter, and education in Tanzania, Africa.
Fields of interest: Natural resources; Economically disadvantaged.
International interests: Africa; Tanzania.
Limitations: Giving on an international basis, primarily in Tanzania, Africa.
Officers and Directors:* Charles L. Williams,* Pres.; L. Michael Phelps,* Secy.-Treas.; Frank X. Gruen; Jerry H. Pyle.
EIN: 760438974

3086
The Frill Foundation
4200 Chase Twr.
600 Travis St.
Houston, TX 77002
Contact: William R. Lummis, Pres.

Established in 1997 in TX.
Donor(s): France B. Lummis, William R. Lummis.
Grantmaker type: Independent foundation
Financial data (yr. ended 12/31/02): Assets, $2,376,935 (M); gifts received, $200,000; expenditures, $121,568; qualifying distributions, $115,784; giving activities include $110,000 for 14 grants (high: $25,000; low: $5,000).
Purpose and activities: Giving primarily for museums, education, particularly secondary schools, the environment, hospitals, and community services.
Fields of interest: Arts; Education; Environment; Hospitals (general); Community development.
Limitations: Giving primarily in TX.
Application information:
Initial approach: Letter
Deadline(s): None
Officers: William R. Lummis, Pres. and Treas.; France B. Lummis, Sr. V.P. and Secy.; Frederick R. Lummis II, V.P.; Palmer Bradley Lummis, V.P.; Ransom C. Lummis, V.P.
EIN: 311505628

3087
Harry A. and Rose Getz Foundation
1717 St. James Pl., Ste. 245
Houston, TX 77056

Grantmaker type: Independent foundation
Financial data (yr. ended 11/30/02): Assets, $644,180 (M); gifts received, $949,014; expenditures, $320,000; qualifying distributions, $320,000; giving activities include $320,000 for 10 grants (high: $125,000; low: $10,000).
Fields of interest: Natural resources; Hospitals (general); Health organizations, association; Alzheimer's disease; American Red Cross; Children/youth, services; Jewish agencies & temples.
Limitations: Giving primarily in Houston, TX; some funding nationally.
Trustee: Elton S. Lipnick.
EIN: 760678230

3088
The W. K. Gordon, Jr. Foundation
201 Main St., Ste. 600
Fort Worth, TX 76102 (817) 339-1156
Contact: Bruce Petty, Secy.-Treas.

Established in 1997 in TX.
Donor(s): Anna Melissa Gordon.
Grantmaker type: Independent foundation
Financial data (yr. ended 12/31/02): Assets, $3,932,873 (M); expenditures, $266,194; qualifying distributions, $259,613; giving activities include $257,000 for 28 grants (high: $75,000; low: $1,000).
Purpose and activities: Giving primarily for animal welfare, health, and social services.
Fields of interest: Natural resources; Animal welfare; Health care; Health organizations;

Human services; Children, services; Federated giving programs.
Limitations: Giving primarily in Albuquerque, NM, and Fort Worth, TX. No grants to individuals.
Application information: Application form not required.
Deadline(s): None
Officers and Directors:* Anna Melissa Gordon,* Pres.; Marguerite Melissa Gordon,* V.P.; W.K. Gordon III,* V.P.; Bruce Petty,* Secy.-Treas.; Joel A. Gordon.
EIN: 752708533

3089
The Neil and Elaine Griffin Foundation
P.O. Box 291910
Kerrville, TX 78029-1910
Contact: Richard D. Griffin, Managing Tr.
Application address: P.O. Box 1961, Kerrville, TX 78028, tel.: (830) 896-6667

Established in 1994 in TX.
Donor(s): F. O'Neil Griffin.
Grantmaker type: Independent foundation
Financial data (yr. ended 09/30/02): Assets, $5,780,273 (M); expenditures, $602,573; qualifying distributions, $540,618; giving activities include $59,925 for 9 grants (high: $25,000; low: $550) and $480,962 for 57 grants to individuals (high: $15,700; low: $1,456).
Fields of interest: Higher education; Animal welfare; Cancer; Human services.
Types of support: Building/renovation; Scholarships—to individuals.
Limitations: Giving limited to Kerrville, TX.
Application information: Scholarships are restricted to Kerr County High School graduates only. Application form required.
Deadline(s): None
Directors: F. O'Neil Griffin; Richard D. Griffin.
EIN: 742729281

3090
William and Evelyn Griffin Foundation
3207 Groveland
Houston, TX 77019 (713) 827-4870

Established in 1997 in TX.
Donor(s): Evelyn H. Griffin, William A. Griffin.
Grantmaker type: Independent foundation
Financial data (yr. ended 12/31/01): Assets, $1,331,180 (M); expenditures, $95,720; qualifying distributions, $88,285; giving activities include $88,850 for 15 grants (high: $15,000; low: $100).
Purpose and activities: Giving primarily for education, and Christian agencies and churches.
Fields of interest: Higher education; Education; Animals/wildlife, preservation/protection; Protestant agencies & churches.
Limitations: Applications not accepted. Giving primarily in GA; some giving also in CA and TX. No grants to individuals.
Application information: Contributes only to pre-selected organizations.
Officers and Directors:* Evelyn H. Griffin,* Pres.; G. Eyvonne Hairell, Secy.; William A. Griffin III.
EIN: 760538855

3091
Paul and Mary Haas Foundation
P.O. Box 2928
Corpus Christi, TX 78403 (361) 887-6955
Contact: Karen L. Wesson, Exec. Dir.
FAX: (361) 883-5992; E-mail: haasfdn@aol.com

Established in 1954 in TX.
Donor(s): Paul R. Haas, Mary F. Haas.
Grantmaker type: Independent foundation
Financial data (yr. ended 12/31/02): Assets, $2,210,267 (M); gifts received, $285,488; expenditures, $369,054; qualifying distributions, $331,875; giving activities include $171,107 for 52 grants (high: $35,000; low: $100) and $140,500 for 12 grants to individuals (high: $3,000; low: $1,500; average: $750–$3,000).
Purpose and activities: Primary areas of interest include social services, the disadvantaged and the homeless, higher and other education, and civic affairs. Grants also for youth agencies, housing, child development, alcohol abuse programs, early childhood, and adult education, the fine arts and other cultural programs, and community funds; scholarships only to Corpus Christi High School graduates entering freshman year; limited medical support, including cancer and other medical research.
Fields of interest: Visual arts; Performing arts; Dance; Music; Arts; Education, association; Early childhood education; Child development, education; Elementary school/education; Secondary school/education; Higher education; Adult/continuing education; Adult education—literacy, basic skills & GED; Reading; Education; Animal welfare; Hospitals (general); Family planning; Medical care, rehabilitation; Health care; Substance abuse, services; Health organizations, association; Cancer; AIDS; Alcoholism; Cancer research; AIDS research; Crime/violence prevention, youth; Food services; Housing/shelter, development; Youth development, services; Human services; Children/youth, services; Child development, services; Family services; Aging, centers/services; Women, centers/services; Homeless, human services; Civil rights; Community development; Federated giving programs; Government/public administration; Leadership development; Disabled; Aging; Women; Economically disadvantaged; Homeless.
Types of support: General/operating support; Continuing support; Annual campaigns; Equipment; Emergency funds; Program development; Conferences/seminars; Seed money; Matching/challenge support.
Limitations: Giving primarily in the Corpus Christi, TX, area.
Publications: Application guidelines, Financial statement, Grants list, Informational brochure (including application guidelines).
Application information: Application form required.
Initial approach: Proposal for organizations; letter or telephone for scholarship applicants
Copies of proposal: 2
Board meeting date(s): 1st quarter of the year
Final notification: Within a few weeks of receipt of proposal
Officers and Trustees:* Paul R. Haas,* Pres.; Rheta Haas Page,* Secy.; Mary F. Haas; Raymond P. Haas; Rene Haas.
Number of staff: 1 part-time professional.

EIN: 746031614

3092
Antonio Haghenbeck y de La Lama Foundation, Inc.
811 Caroline St.
Montgomery, TX 77356
Contact: Mary Jo Gutierrez, V.P.
Application address: 7134 Las Ventanas Dr.,
Austin, TX 78731, tel.: (512) 795-0450

Established in 1986 in TX.
Donor(s): Antonio Haghenbeck y de La Lama.‡
Grantmaker type: Independent foundation
Financial data (yr. ended 11/30/02): Assets,
$3,445,751 (M); expenditures, $811,412;
qualifying distributions, $91,300; giving
activities include $91,300 for 1 grant.
Purpose and activities: Giving for prevention of
cruelty to animals.
Fields of interest: Animal welfare.
International interests: Mexico.
Limitations: Giving primarily in Mexico. No
grants to individuals.
Application information:
Initial approach: Letter
Deadline(s): None
Officers and Directors:* Carmela Rivero
Jimenez,* Pres.; Mary Jo Gutierrez,* V.P. and
Treas.; Roy Diaz Gonzalez,* Secy.; Cecilia Vega
Leon.
EIN: 760227001

3093
Henderson-Wessendorff Foundation
P.O. Box 669
Richmond, TX 77469
Contact: Loise H. Wessendorff, Pres.

Established in 1956 in TX.
Donor(s): Loise J. Henderson.‡
Grantmaker type: Independent foundation
Financial data (yr. ended 12/31/02): Assets,
$8,101,280 (M); expenditures, $473,276;
qualifying distributions, $467,669; giving
activities include $119,593 for 65 grants (high:
$20,318; low: $50).
Fields of interest: Elementary/secondary
education; Theological school/education;
Animal welfare; Hospitals (general); Mental
health/crisis services; Health organizations,
association; Human services; Protestant
agencies & churches; Religion.
Limitations: Giving primarily in TX. No grants to
individuals.
Application information:
Initial approach: Letter
Deadline(s): None
Officers: Loise H. Wessendorff, Pres. and Treas.;
Joe C. Wessendorff, V.P. and Secy.; James A.
Elkins, Jr., V.P.; Joe Darst Robinson, V.P.
Trustee: Jack Moore.
EIN: 746047149

3094
The Jacob and Terese Hershey Foundation
2121 San Felipe, Ste. 124
Houston, TX 77019 (713) 529-7611
Contact: Judith Boyce, Exec. Dir.
FAX: (713) 529-7613; E-mail: hbar@wt.net

Established in 1961 in TX.
Donor(s): J.W. Hershey,‡ Terese T. Hershey,
Gerald Smith,‡ Dell Butcher,‡ Peter S. Meyer.
Grantmaker type: Independent foundation
Financial data (yr. ended 12/31/02): Assets,
$2,586,940 (M); gifts received, $18,000;
expenditures, $290,325; qualifying distributions,
$250,294; giving activities include $218,000 for
119 grants (high: $5,000; low: $250).
Fields of interest: Museums; Natural resources;
Environmental education; Environment; Animal
welfare; Animals/wildlife,
preservation/protection; Family planning;
Recreation; Reproductive rights.
Types of support: General/operating support;
Continuing support; Annual campaigns; Land
acquisition; Conferences/seminars; Publication;
Seed money; Internship funds.
Limitations: Giving primarily in southwest CO
and Houston, TX. No support for medical or
religious institutions. No grants to individuals, or
for galas.
Publications: Application guidelines.
Application information: Application form not
required.
Initial approach: Letter
Copies of proposal: 1
Deadline(s): May 1 and Oct. 1
Board meeting date(s): June and Nov.
Final notification: July 31 and Dec. 31
Officers and Directors:* Terese T. Hershey,*
Pres.; Ann Hamilton,* V.P.; Amie Rodnick,*
Secy.; Peter S. Meyer,* Treas.; Judith Boyce,
Exec. Dir.; Jeffrey Hershey; Olive S. Hershey;
Arthur L. Storey, Jr.
Number of staff: 1 full-time professional.
EIN: 766039126

3095
Albert & Ethel Herzstein Charitable Foundation
6131 Westview Dr.
Houston, TX 77055-5421 (713) 681-7868
Contact: L. Michael Hajtman, Pres.
E-mail: albertandethel@herzsteinfoundation.org;
URL: http://www.herzsteinfoundation.org

Established in 1965 in TX.
Donor(s): Albert H. Herzstein,‡ Ethel Avis
Herzstein,‡ Sadie Herzstein Smith,‡ and
members of the Herzstein family.
Grantmaker type: Independent foundation
Financial data (yr. ended 12/31/01): Assets,
$69,230,797 (M); gifts received, $24,361,634;
expenditures, $4,863,717; qualifying
distributions, $3,477,008; giving activities
include $3,197,289 for 127 grants (high:
$550,000; low: $500; average:
$5,000–$25,000).
Purpose and activities: The trust was organized
and shall be operated exclusively for religious,
charitable, scientific, literary and/or educational
purposes.
Fields of interest: Arts; Education,
community/cooperative; Education;
Environment; Health care; Youth development;

Human services; Civic centers; Community
development.
Types of support: General/operating support;
Continuing support; Annual campaigns; Capital
campaigns; Building/renovation; Equipment;
Land acquisition; Endowments; Debt reduction;
Seed money; Scholarship funds; Research.
Limitations: Giving primarily in TX.
Publications: Application guidelines,
Informational brochure (including application
guidelines).
Application information: Application form not
required.
Initial approach: Letter or proposal
Copies of proposal: 1
Deadline(s): None
Officer: L. Michael Hajtman, Pres.
Directors: Richard Loewenstern; George W.
Strake, Jr.; Nathan Topek, M.D.
Number of staff: 1 full-time professional; 3
full-time support.
EIN: 746070484

3096
The Tim and Karen Hixon Foundation
315 E. Commerce St., Ste. 300
San Antonio, TX 78205
Contact: George C. Hixon, Pres.

Established in 1994 in TX.
Donor(s): Karen J. Hixon, George C. Hixon.
Grantmaker type: Independent foundation
Financial data (yr. ended 12/31/02): Assets,
$2,748,420 (M); expenditures, $190,595;
qualifying distributions, $173,357; giving
activities include $172,056 for 23 grants (high:
$25,000; low: $1,000).
Purpose and activities: Giving primarily to
support wildlife and zoological organizations
and programs.
Fields of interest: Arts; Higher education;
Education; Natural resources; Animals/wildlife,
research.
Types of support: General/operating support;
Continuing support; Annual campaigns; Capital
campaigns; Land acquisition; Research.
Limitations: Applications not accepted. Giving
primarily in TX. No grants to individuals.
Publications: Financial statement.
Application information: Contributes only to
pre-selected organizations.
Board meeting date(s): Dec.
Officers and Directors:* George C. Hixon,*
Pres.; Karen J. Hixon,* V.P.; Kimberly Owens,
Secy.-Treas.; Bryan S. Hixon; George S. Hixon;
Jack J. Spector.
EIN: 742730275

3097
Hobby Family Foundation ▼
2131 San Felipe
Houston, TX 77019-5620 (713) 521-1163
Contact: Jennifer Cole, Secy.

Established in 1995.
Donor(s): W.P. Hobby.
Grantmaker type: Independent foundation
Financial data (yr. ended 12/31/01): Assets,
$21,330,468 (M); expenditures, $2,373,178;
qualifying distributions, $2,243,753; giving
activities include $2,239,675 for 110 grants

(high: $1,292,866; low: $100; average: $1,000–$100,000).

Purpose and activities: Giving primarily for the arts, health care, community development and social services.

Fields of interest: Orchestra (symphony); Humanities; Elementary school/education; Higher education; Natural resources; Health care, clinics/centers; Medical research, institute; Human services; American Red Cross; Children/youth, services; Community development; Protestant agencies & churches.

Limitations: Giving primarily in TX. No grants to individuals.

Application information: Application form not required.

Deadline(s): None

Officers and Trustees:* W.P. Hobby,* Pres.; Laura H. Beckworth,* V.P.; Diana P. Hobby,* V.P.; Paul W. Hobby, V.P.; Jennifer Cole, Secy.; Cathy Leeson, Treas.

EIN: 760489862

Recent environmental and animal welfare grants:

3097-1 Fort Worth Zoological Association, Fort Worth, TX, $12,500. For operating support of Texas Wild program. 2001.

3098
Houston Endowment Inc. ▼

600 Travis, Ste. 6400
Houston, TX 77002-3007 (713) 238-8100
Contact: H. Joe Nelson III, Pres.
FAX: (713) 238-8101; URL: http://www.houstonendowment.org

Incorporated in 1937 in TX.

Donor(s): Jesse H. Jones,‡ Mrs. Jesse H. Jones.‡

Grantmaker type: Independent foundation

Financial data (yr. ended 12/31/02): Assets, $1,183,628,090 (M); expenditures, $78,038,223; qualifying distributions, $68,413,852; giving activities include $68,413,852 for 552 grants (high: $4,000,000; low: $1,000; average: $25,000–$250,000).

Purpose and activities: For the support of any charitable, educational or religious undertaking.

Fields of interest: Arts; Education; Health care; Human services.

Types of support: General/operating support; Continuing support; Annual campaigns; Capital campaigns; Building/renovation; Equipment; Land acquisition; Endowments; Program development; Conferences/seminars; Professorships; Publication; Curriculum development; Fellowships; Scholarship funds; Research; Employee matching gifts.

Limitations: Giving primarily in Houston, TX; no grants outside the continental U.S. No support for religious organizations for religious purposes, or organizations that are the responsibility of the government. No grants to individuals; or for fundraising activities including galas, grantmaking organizations or charities operated by service clubs, testimonial dinners, or advertising; or the purchase of uniforms, equipment or trips for school related organizations; no loans.

Publications: Annual report, Informational brochure (including application guidelines).

Application information: Proposal materials that are bound or inserted in protective sleeves are discouraged. Application form not required.

Initial approach: Letter
Copies of proposal: 1
Deadline(s): None
Board meeting date(s): 9 to 10 times per year
Final notification: 3 to 6 months

Officers and Directors:* D. Kent Anderson,* Chair.; H. Joe Nelson III,* Pres.; Sheryl L. Johns, V.P., C.F.O., and Treas.; David L. Nelson, V.P. and Grants Dir.; Audrey Jones Beck; Anthony W. Hall, Jr.; Melissa A. Jones; Harold Metts; Laurence E. Simmons; Rosie Zamora.

Number of staff: 13 full-time professional; 10 full-time support.

EIN: 746013920

Recent environmental and animal welfare grants:

3098-1 American Farmland Trust, DC, $225,000. Toward providing information about voluntary measures that keep private land intact and free from development. 2002.

3098-2 Bat Conservation International, Austin, TX, $60,000. Toward documenting and quantifying positive impact of Mexican freetail bats on Texas agriculture. 2002.

3098-3 Buffalo Bayou ArtPark, Houston, TX, $20,000. Toward placing art in public, outdoor places. 2002.

3098-4 Buffalo Bayou Partnership, Houston, TX, $750,000. Toward acquiring land along historic Buffalo Bayou. 2002.

3098-5 Buffalo Bayou Partnership, Houston, TX, $750,000. Toward developing land along historic Buffalo Bayou. 2002.

3098-6 Conservation Fund, Arlington, VA, $200,000. Toward purchasing large tracts of land and significant historic sites in Texas that are transferred to and managed by public agencies. 2002.

3098-7 Gulf Coast Bird Observatory, Houston, TX, $150,000. Toward establishing stopover habitat along Gulf of Mexico for birds that travel twice a year between the United States and Latin America. 2002.

3098-8 Gulf Coast Institute, Houston, TX, $350,000. Toward collaboration with Center for Houston's Future Inc. to convene stakeholders and gather data to build consensual and comprehensive vision of Houston's future. 2002.

3098-9 Hawkwatch International, Salt Lake City, UT, $10,000. Toward monitoring and protecting hawks, eagles, and other birds of prey through research, education, and conservation at south Texas sites. 2002.

3098-10 Houston Advanced Research Center, The Woodlands, TX, $150,000. Toward developing plans to create cleaner, greener Houston through reforestation and reflective building and paving surfaces. 2002.

3098-11 Houston Arboretum and Nature Center, Houston, TX, $15,000. Toward maintaining urban sanctuary for native plants and animals and educating public about natural environment. 2002.

3098-12 Houston Heights Association, Houston, TX, $50,000. Toward planting trees and enhancing Heights Boulevard. 2002.

3098-13 Houston Zoo, Houston, TX, $500,000. Toward fund to assist in Houston Zoo's transition from public to private, nonprofit entity. 2002.

3098-14 International Crane Foundation, Baraboo, WI, $90,000. Toward studying and monitoring whooping cranes and their

primary food supply in and around Aransas National Wildlife Refuge and helping west Texas landowners conserve scarce wetland habitat for sandhill cranes. 2002.

3098-15 Katy Prairie Land Conservancy, Houston, TX, $750,000. Toward acquiring land to preserve Katy Prairie and protect habitat for species of birds, mammals, and reptiles. 2002.

3098-16 Korima Foundation of the Big Bend Ranch, Taylor Lake Village, TX, $50,000. Toward weeklong workshops that expose at-risk high school sophomores from Houston and San Antonio to scientific academic experiences and personal growth opportunities in culturally and environmental rich region of west Texas wilderness. 2002.

3098-17 Land Trust Alliance, Grand Junction, CO, $11,350. Toward sending Texas conservationists and landowners to seminars about conservation easements, land stewardship, and nonprofit management. 2002.

3098-18 National Parks Conservation Association, DC, $20,000. Toward collecting and sharing data about environmental threats to Big Bend National Park. 2002.

3098-19 Nature Conservancy of Texas, San Antonio, TX, $400,000. Toward acquiring land in Bandera Canyonlands of Hill Country to protect watershed integrity and water quality in southern Edward Aquifer, San Antonio's primary source of drinking water. 2002.

3098-20 Rio Grande Rio Bravo Basin Coalition, El Paso, TX, $50,000. Toward building multicultural network of organizations and citizens to help local communities along border restore and sustain environment and economies of area. 2002.

3098-21 San Marcos River Foundation, San Marcos, TX, $75,000. Toward protecting San Marcos River and watershed and tributaries. 2002.

3098-22 Southwest Texas State University, San Marcos, TX, $500,000. Toward developing Institute for Sustainable Freshwater Resources to address issues surrounding local and global freshwater resources. 2002.

3098-23 Special Pals, Houston, TX, $27,000. Toward purchasing mobile adoption unit for use at animal shelter. 2002.

3098-24 Student Conservation Association, Arlington, VA, $75,000. Toward recruiting and training high school and college students from Texas to volunteer at natural resource management sites throughout state. 2002.

3098-25 Texans for Alternatives to Pesticides, Houston, TX, $30,000. Toward monitoring exposure to pesticides, particularly in schools, and informing public, government officials, and pest control companies about harmful effects of pesticides by suggesting alternative methods of pest control. 2002.

3098-26 Texas Center for Policy Studies, Austin, TX, $80,000. Toward updating and expanding Texas Water Matters, Web site that offers information about Texas environment. 2002.

3098-27 Texas Coalition for Conservation, Austin, TX, $125,000. Toward collaborative effort to acquire public parkland and protect natural and cultural resources. 2002.

3098-28 Texas Committee on Natural Resources, Austin, TX, $70,000. Toward protecting Neches River, threatened habitat and surrounding bottomland hardwood forests. 2002.

3098-29 Texas Cooperative Extension, College Station, TX, $150,000. Toward conserving water and ensuring future supplies through WaterSmart Landscaping for Houston, program that promotes sustainable residential, commercial, and community landscapes. 2002.

3098-30 Trees for Houston, Houston, TX, $250,000. Toward planting and maintaining trees along Navigation Avenue in Houston's East End. 2002.

3098-31 Trust for Public Land, San Francisco, CA, $500,000. Toward acquiring land for open spaces and recreational facilities in urban and suburban communities. 2002.

3098-32 Trust for Public Land, San Francisco, CA, $250,000. Toward research, outreach activities, and Houston-Galveston project office. 2002.

3098-33 Turtle Island Restoration Network, Forest Knolls, CA, $100,000. Toward merging programs and opening Texas office to strengthen efforts to protect sea turtles in Gulf of Mexico. 2002.

3098-34 United States Public Interest Research Group Education Fund, DC, $50,000. Toward recruiting and educating Texas college seniors to lead environmental organizations. 2002.

3098-35 Upper Kirby District Foundation, Houston, TX, $150,000. Toward revitalizing Levy Park with community gardens, nature center, wetlands demonstration pond, and arbor and amphitheater. 2002.

3098-36 Urban Forestry Council of Texas, Austin, TX, $45,000. Toward providing tools and expertise communities need to create and preserve forests. 2002.

3098-37 Wildlife Rescue and Rehabilitation, Boerne, TX, $75,000. Toward rescuing, rehabilitating, and releasing orphaned, injured, and displaced wildlife, and toward caring for nonreleasable animals. 2002.

3099
Huffington Foundation

700 Louisiana St., Ste. 2400
Houston, TX 77002 (713) 753-1001
Contact: Roy M. Huffington, Tr.
Application address: P.O. Box 4337, Houston, TX 77210-4337

Established in 1987 in TX.
Donor(s): Terry L. Huffington, Michael Huffington, Roy M. Huffington.
Grantmaker type: Independent foundation
Financial data (yr. ended 12/31/02): Assets, $21,924,801 (M); expenditures, $1,524,611; qualifying distributions, $1,241,243; giving activities include $1,246,000 for 43 grants (high: $450,000; low: $1,000).
Purpose and activities: Giving primarily for medical school education, as well as regular education, including a Baptist school; funding also for the arts, health associations, including a prostate cancer center, and children's services.
Fields of interest: Museums (art); Performing arts centers; Arts; Higher education; Medical

school/education; Education; Natural resources; Hospitals (general); Health organizations, association; Cancer; Children, services.
Types of support: General/operating support; Annual campaigns; Endowments; Scholarship funds.
Limitations: Applications not accepted. Giving primarily in Houston, TX. No grants to individuals.
Application information: Contributes only to pre-selected organizations.
Board meeting date(s): Varies
Trustees: Phyllis Gough Huffington; Roy M. Huffington; Terry L. Huffington.
EIN: 766040840

3100
The i2 Foundation, Inc.

11701 Luna Rd.
Dallas, TX 75234 (469) 357-4200
Contact: Judith Cunningham, Prog. Off.
FAX: (469) 357-7777; URL: http://www.i2foundation.org

Donor(s): i2 Technologies, Inc., John Hogge, Brian Kennedy, Lekha Singh, Hiten Varia.
Grantmaker type: Company-sponsored foundation
Financial data (yr. ended 12/31/02): Assets, $769,406 (M); gifts received, $1,088,448; expenditures, $1,765,973; qualifying distributions, $1,729,170; giving activities include $517,802 for 12 grants (high: $133,208; low: $1,860) and $559,952 for foundation-administered programs.
Purpose and activities: The foundation is dedicated to promoting advancements in education, technology, environmental practices, medicine and economic opportunity through programs that improve quality of life and create a healthier society.
Fields of interest: Education; Environment; Health care; Human services; Children/youth, services.
Limitations: Giving on a national and international basis. No grants to individuals.
Officers: Lekha Singh, Pres.; Robert Donohoo, Secy.; William Beecher, Treas.
Directors: Sarinder Chhabra; Melis Jones; Brian Kennedy; Dave Pace; Austin Thomas; Hiten Varia; Romesh Wadhwani.
EIN: 752764747

3101
i2 Technologies, Inc. Corporate Giving Program

c/o Corp. Contribs.
1 i2 Pl., 11701 Luna Rd.
Dallas, TX 75234

Grantmaker type: Corporate giving program
Purpose and activities: As a complement to its foundation, i2 also makes charitable contributions to nonprofit organizations directly. Support is given primarily in areas of company operations.
Fields of interest: Education; Natural resources; Disasters, preparedness/services; Children, services; Family services; Science.
Types of support: General/operating support.
Limitations: Giving primarily in areas of company operations.

Application information: Unsolicited requests are accepted from i2 employees on behalf of nonprofit organizations only.

3102
Joan and Herb Kelleher Charitable Foundation

110 E. Crockett St.
San Antonio, TX 78205
Contact: Ruth K. Agather, Tr.
FAX: (210) 223-3512; E-mail: tina.pawelek@paisanocattle.com

Established in 1997 in TX.
Donor(s): Herbert D. Kelleher, Joan N. Kelleher.
Grantmaker type: Independent foundation
Financial data (yr. ended 12/31/02): Assets, $10,354,937 (M); expenditures, $673,471; qualifying distributions, $550,321; giving activities include $520,000 for 51 grants (high: $50,000; low: $1,000; average: $1,000–$250,000).
Fields of interest: Historic preservation/historical societies; Arts; Environment; Youth development; Human services.
Types of support: General/operating support; Capital campaigns; Building/renovation.
Limitations: Giving primarily in TX and WY.
Application information: Application form not required.
Initial approach: Letter requesting application guidelines
Copies of proposal: 1
Deadline(s): None
Board meeting date(s): Varies
Trustees: Ruth K. Agather; David N. Kelleher; Herbert D. Kelleher; J. Michael Kelleher; Joan N. Kelleher; Julia K. Stacy.
Number of staff: None.
EIN: 742833381

3103
Dee J. Kelly Foundation

201 Main St., Ste. 2500
Fort Worth, TX 76102

Established in 1990 in TX.
Donor(s): Dee J. Kelly, Sr.
Grantmaker type: Independent foundation
Financial data (yr. ended 07/31/02): Assets, $657,484 (M); expenditures, $269,177; qualifying distributions, $265,613; giving activities include $267,100 for 25 grants (high: $75,000; low: $250).
Fields of interest: Orchestra (symphony); Arts; University; Zoos/zoological societies; Medical care, in-patient care; Philanthropy/voluntarism; Christian agencies & churches.
Limitations: Applications not accepted. Giving primarily in the Fort Worth, TX, area. No grants to individuals.
Application information: Contributes only to pre-selected organizations.
Officers: Dee J. Kelly, Sr., Pres.; Dee J. Kelly, Jr., V.P. and Secy.; Craig Kelly, V.P.
Director: Cynthia Barnes.
EIN: 752363975

3104
Harris and Eliza Kempner Fund, Inc.
2201 Market St., Ste. 601
Galveston, TX 77550-1529   (409) 762-1603
Contact: Elaine R. Perachio, Exec. Dir.
FAX: (409) 762-5435; E-mail:
information@kempnerfund.org; URL: http://
www.kempnerfund.org

Established in 1946 in TX; incorporated in 2001.
Donor(s): Various interests and members of the
Kempner family.
Grantmaker type: Independent foundation
Financial data (yr. ended 12/31/01): Assets,
$41,263,559 (M); gifts received, $6,128;
expenditures, $1,903,883; qualifying
distributions, $2,175,222; giving activities
include $1,373,627 for 146 grants (high:
$180,000; low: $1,000; average:
$1,000–$25,000), $255,877 for 502 employee
matching gifts and $271,339 for 49 loans to
individuals (high: $4,000; low: $1,000; average:
$1,300–$4,000).
Purpose and activities: Support primarily for
human services, arts and humanities, education,
community development, and Jewish issues in
the Galveston, TX area, and a small allocation
for international issues.
Fields of interest: Visual arts; Museums;
Performing arts; Dance; Theater; Humanities;
History/archaeology; Historic
preservation/historical societies; Arts; Early
childhood education; Child development,
education; Elementary school/education;
Secondary school/education; Higher education;
Medical school/education; Adult
education—literacy, basic skills & GED;
Reading; Education; Natural resources;
Environment; Family planning; Health care;
Substance abuse, services; Mental health/crisis
services; Health organizations, association;
Cancer; Heart & circulatory diseases;
Biomedicine; Medical research, institute; Cancer
research; Heart & circulatory research;
Crime/law enforcement; Food services;
Housing/shelter, development; Youth
development, services; Human services; Youth,
services; Child development, services; Hospices;
Minorities/immigrants, centers/services;
Homeless, human services; International
economic development; International relief;
International affairs; Race/intergroup relations;
Community development; Federated giving
programs; Economics; Population studies;
Leadership development; Jewish agencies &
temples; Minorities; Native Americans/American
Indians; Disabled; Economically disadvantaged;
Homeless.
International interests: Africa; Mexico.
Types of support: General/operating support;
Continuing support; Annual campaigns; Capital
campaigns; Building/renovation; Equipment;
Emergency funds; Program development;
Conferences/seminars; Professorships;
Publication; Seed money; Curriculum
development; Fellowships; Scholarship funds;
Research; Matching/challenge support; Student
loans—to individuals.
Limitations: Giving primarily in Galveston
County, TX. No grants to individuals (except for
student loans), non-U.S. based organizations,
fundraising benefits, or for direct mail
solicitations.

Publications: Annual report (including
application guidelines).
Application information: Computerized
solicitations not considered. Student loans are
restricted. Application form not required.
  Initial approach: Letter requesting guidelines
  Copies of proposal: 1
  Deadline(s): For grant program: Mar. 15, June
    15, and Oct. 15; Dec. 1 for
    national/international requests in the areas
    of environment, or family planning
  Board meeting date(s): Usually in Apr., July,
    Dec., and as required
  Final notification: 2 weeks
Officers and Trustees:* Robert L.K. Lynch,*
Chair.; John Thornton Currie,* Vice-Chair.;
Barbara Weston Sasser,* Secy.; Peter Kempner
Thompson, M.D.,* Treas.; Elaine R. Perachio,
Exec. Dir.; Hetta Towler Kempner; Isaac Herbert
Kempner III; James Lee Kempner; Lyda Ann
Quinn Thomas; Daniel Kempner Thorne.
Number of staff: 2 part-time professional; 1
full-time support; 1 part-time support.
EIN: 760680130

3105
Killam Family Foundation
P.O. Box 499
Laredo, TX 78042   (956) 724-7141
Contact: Radcliffe Killam, Tr.

Established in 1998 in TX.
Donor(s): Radcliffe Killam, Sue Killam, Michael
Dileo, Tracy Dileo, David Killam.
Grantmaker type: Independent foundation
Financial data (yr. ended 12/31/02): Assets,
$540,427 (M); gifts received, $175,277;
expenditures, $265,165; qualifying distributions,
$262,100; giving activities include $262,100 for
37 grants (high: $150,000; low: $100).
Purpose and activities: Giving primarily for
higher education, and human services.
Fields of interest: Higher education; Education;
Animals/wildlife; Health care; Human services.
Limitations: Giving primarily in TX, with
emphasis on Laredo.
Application information: Application form not
required.
  Deadline(s): None
Trustees: Radcliffe Killam; Sue Killam.
EIN: 746473230

3106
Kimberly-Clark Foundation, Inc. ▼
P.O. Box 619100
Dallas, TX 75261-9100   (972) 281-1200
Contact: Carolyn A. Mentesana, V.P.

Incorporated in 1952 in WI.
Donor(s): Kimberly-Clark Corp.
Grantmaker type: Company-sponsored
foundation
Financial data (yr. ended 12/31/01): Assets,
$6,019,856 (M); gifts received, $7,398,694;
expenditures, $7,941,253; qualifying
distributions, $7,935,546; giving activities
include $6,795,710 for 75 grants (high:
$1,740,000; low: $200; average:
$1,000–$75,000) and $969,406 for employee
matching gifts.
Purpose and activities: Emphasis on higher
education, community funds, community

development, social services, and cultural
programs.
Fields of interest: Museums; Performing arts;
Arts; Higher education; Engineering
school/education; Education; Natural resources;
Health care; Substance abuse, services; Health
organizations, association; Cancer; Cancer
research; Human services; Youth, services;
Homeless, human services; Community
development; Federated giving programs;
Engineering; Minorities; Homeless.
Types of support: General/operating support;
Continuing support; Annual campaigns; Capital
campaigns; Building/renovation; Equipment;
Land acquisition; Seed money; Scholarship
funds; Research; Employee matching gifts.
Limitations: Giving primarily in communities
where the company has operations; limited
contributions to national organizations. No
support for religious, political, or athletic
organizations. No grants to individuals; no loans.
Publications: Annual report.
Application information: Request must be in
writing, received by mail and addressed to the
foundation's V.P. Application form required.
  Initial approach: Proposal
  Copies of proposal: 1
  Board meeting date(s): Apr.
  Final notification: July
Officers and Directors:* Tina S. Barry, Pres.;
Carolyn A. Mentesana, V.P.; Ron McCray, Secy.;
W. Anthony Gamron,* Treas.; O. George
Everbach; Wayne R. Sanders.
Number of staff: 1 full-time professional; 1
full-time support.
EIN: 396044304
**Recent environmental and animal welfare
grants:**
3106-1 Audubon Society, National, New York,
  NY, $10,000. 2001.
3106-2 Dallas Arboretum and Botanical Society,
  Dallas, TX, $25,000. 2001.
3106-3 Environmental Careers Organization
  (ECO), Boston, MA, $10,000. 2001.
3106-4 National Environmental Education and
  Training Foundation, DC, $15,000. 2001.

3107
Kinder Foundation
(formerly Richard D. Kinder Foundation, Inc.)
3355 Del Monte Dr.
Houston, TX 77019
Contact: Nancy G. Kinder, Pres.
Application address: P.O. Box 130776,
Houston, TX, 77219-0776

Established in 1994 in TX.
Donor(s): Richard D. Kinder.
Grantmaker type: Independent foundation
Financial data (yr. ended 12/31/01): Assets,
$22,925,361 (M); expenditures, $1,559,205;
qualifying distributions, $1,502,242; giving
activities include $1,485,764 for 70 grants (high:
$606,800; low: $100).
Purpose and activities: Giving primarily for
education including teacher appreciation, and
children's issues. Some giving also for the
environment, health, and religious organizations.
Fields of interest: Arts; Higher education;
Environment; Zoos/zoological societies;
Hospitals (general); Health organizations,
association; Human services; Children, services;

Race/intergroup relations; Federated giving programs; Religion.
Types of support: General/operating support; Continuing support; Annual campaigns; Capital campaigns; Building/renovation; Endowments; Program development; Professorships.
Limitations: Applications not accepted. Giving primarily in CO, Washington, DC, MO, NY, and TX. No grants to individuals.
Application information: Contributes only to pre-selected organizations.
Officers: Richard D. Kinder, Chair.; Nancy G. Kinder, Pres.; Katherine Kinder Howes, V.P. and Secy.-Treas.
Director: Peggy B. Menchaca.
Number of staff: 1 part-time professional.
EIN: 760519073

3108
Robert J. Kleberg, Jr. and Helen C. Kleberg Foundation ▼
700 N. St. Mary's St., Ste. 1200
San Antonio, TX 78205   (210) 271-3691
Contact: Robert L. Washington, Grants Coord.

Incorporated in 1950 in TX.
Donor(s): Helen C. Kleberg,‡ Robert J. Kleberg, Jr.‡
Grantmaker type: Independent foundation
Financial data (yr. ended 12/31/02): Assets, $167,063,548 (M); expenditures, $10,640,192; qualifying distributions, $9,665,634; giving activities include $9,673,734 for 46 grants (high: $1,600,000; low: $3,000; average: $10,000–$100,000).
Purpose and activities: Giving on a national basis for medical research, veterinary and animal sciences, wildlife research and preservation, health services, higher education, and arts and humanities; support also for local community organizations.
Fields of interest: Arts; Higher education; Animals/wildlife, preservation/protection; Health care; Health organizations, association; Medical research, institute; Biological sciences.
Types of support: Building/renovation; Equipment; Conferences/seminars; Research; Matching/challenge support.
Limitations: No support for organizations limited by race or religion. No grants for endowments, or for normal operating functions.
Publications: Application guidelines, Annual report.
Application information: Application form not required.
  Initial approach: Letter on organization letterhead
  Copies of proposal: 1
  Deadline(s): None
  Board meeting date(s): Usually in June and Dec.
  Final notification: 6 months
Officers and Directors:* Helen K. Groves,* Pres.; John D. Alexander, Jr.,* V.P. and Secy.; Emory A. Hamilton,* V.P. and Treas.; Helen C. Alexander,* V.P.; John B. Carter, Jr.; Caroline R. Forgason; Henrietta A. George; Dorothy A. Matz; H. Virgil Sherrill.
Number of staff: 1 full-time professional.
EIN: 746044810
Recent environmental and animal welfare grants:

3108-1 Botanical Research Institute of Texas, Fort Worth, TX, $10,000. For general support. 2001.
3108-2 Brandywine Conservancy, Chadds Ford, PA, $500,000. For Building and Endowment Campaign. 2001.
3108-3 North American Butterfly Association (NABA), Morristown, NJ, $50,000. For Butterfly Park in Mission, Texas. 2001.
3108-4 South Texas Public Broadcasting System, Corpus Christi, TX, $30,000. For Nature and Nova programs. 2001.

3109
Caesar Kleberg Foundation for Wildlife Conservation
711 Navarro St., Ste. 535
San Antonio, TX 78205   (361) 592-7174
Contact: Leroy G. Denman, Jr., Tr.
FAX: (210) 223-3657

Trust established about 1951 in TX.
Donor(s): Caesar Kleberg.‡
Grantmaker type: Independent foundation
Financial data (yr. ended 12/31/01): Assets, $42,654,061 (M); gifts received, $2,500; expenditures, $2,724,509; qualifying distributions, $2,176,486; giving activities include $2,130,463 for 2 grants (high: $2,125,463; low: $5,000).
Purpose and activities: Funding for wildlife conservation and studies.
Fields of interest: Animals/wildlife, research; Animals/wildlife, preservation/protection.
Limitations: No grants to individuals, or for building or endowment funds, scholarships, fellowships, or matching gifts; no loans.
Application information: Application form not required.
  Initial approach: Letter
  Copies of proposal: 3
  Deadline(s): None
  Board meeting date(s): As required
  Final notification: 3 months
Trustees: Leroy G. Denman, Jr.; Stephen J. Kleberg; Duane M. Leach.
Number of staff: None.
EIN: 746038766

3110
Kleh Family Foundation
5231 Lymbar Dr.
Houston, TX 77096
Contact: Terri G. Rogers, V.P. and Treas.

Established in 1997 in CO.
Donor(s): William H. Kleh, Patricia M. Kleh.
Grantmaker type: Independent foundation
Financial data (yr. ended 12/31/02): Assets, $1,935,595 (M); expenditures, $177,157; qualifying distributions, $160,349; giving activities include $150,000 for 10 grants (high: $25,000; low: $5,000).
Fields of interest: Elementary/secondary education; College; Education; Environmental education; Animals/wildlife, preservation/protection; Boys clubs; Foundations (public).
Limitations: Giving on a national basis.
Application information:
  Initial approach: Letter
  Deadline(s): None

Officers: William H. Kleh, Chair. and Pres.; Patricia M. Kleh, V.P. and Secy.; Terri G. Rogers, V.P. and Treas.; Erin S. Kleh, V.P.
Directors: Jack Kleh; Jeffrey Steele.
EIN: 911757481

3111
Barney F. and Ellen L. Kogen Charitable Foundation
3131 Eastside, Ste. 120
Houston, TX 77098
Contact: W. Mark Moore, Pres.

Established in 1996 in TX.
Donor(s): Barney F. Kogen, Ellen L. Kogen.
Grantmaker type: Independent foundation
Financial data (yr. ended 12/31/00): Assets, $116,319 (M); expenditures, $114,343; qualifying distributions, $112,399; giving activities include $112,399 for 16 grants (high: $60,000; low: $12).
Purpose and activities: Giving for animal protection, Jewish organizations, and services related to cystic fibrosis.
Fields of interest: Animal welfare; Cystic fibrosis; Diabetes; Jewish agencies & temples.
Limitations: Applications not accepted. Giving primarily in TX. No grants to individuals.
Application information: Contributes only to pre-selected organizations.
Officers: Barney F. Kogen, Chair.; W. Mark Moore, Pres.; Linda Gaines, V.P. and Secy.-Treas.
Director: Ellen L. Kogen.
EIN: 760495253

3112
Albert & Bessie Mae Kronkosky Charitable Foundation ▼
112 E. Pecan, Ste. 830
San Antonio, TX 78205   (210) 475-9000
Contact: Palmer Moe, Managing Dir.
Additional tel.: (888) 309-9001; FAX: (210) 354-2204; E-mail: kronfndn@kronkosky.org; URL: http://www.kronkosky.org

Established in 1991 in TX.
Donor(s): Albert Kronkosky,‡ Bessie Mae Kronkosky.
Grantmaker type: Independent foundation
Financial data (yr. ended 12/31/01): Assets, $294,998,137 (M); expenditures, $20,001,442; qualifying distributions, $18,538,888; giving activities include $16,951,916 for 126 grants (high: $1,500,000; low: $5,000; average: $10,000–$100,000).
Purpose and activities: Support for the arts, museums, libraries, animal welfare, wildlife, medical research, child abuse prevention, parks, youth development, disabled, and aging.
Fields of interest: Multipurpose centers/programs; Museums; Libraries (public); Animal welfare; Animals/wildlife, sanctuaries; Zoos/zoological societies; Medical research, institute; Child abuse; Parks/playgrounds; Youth development, centers/clubs; Family services, parent education; Disabled; Aging.
Types of support: General/operating support; Continuing support; Capital campaigns; Building/renovation; Equipment; Endowments; Program development; Research; Consulting

services; Program evaluation; Matching/challenge support.
Limitations: Giving limited to Bandera, Bexar, Comal, and Kendall counties, TX.
Publications: Application guidelines.
Application information: Application form required.
Initial approach: Letter of Inquiry
Copies of proposal: 1
Deadline(s): None
Board meeting date(s): 6 times annually
Final notification: Within 2 weeks of Dist. Comm. meeting
Officer: Palmer Moe, Managing Dir.
Trustee: Bank of America.
Number of staff: 7 full-time professional; 3 part-time support.
EIN: 746385152
Recent environmental and animal welfare grants:
3112-1 Association of Sanctuaries, Kendalia, TX, $25,000. For Wildlife as Pets: A Strategy for Prevention program. 2001.
3112-2 Parks and Wildlife Foundation of Texas, Dallas, TX, $125,000. For Government Canyon State Natural Area Visitor Center. 2001.
3112-3 San Antonio Wildlife Emergency Center, San Antonio, TX, $45,000. For natural tiger compound. 2001.
3112-4 San Antonio Zoological Society, San Antonio, TX, $1,000,000. For capital support for Early Childhood Project. 2001.
3112-5 San Antonio Zoological Society, San Antonio, TX, $450,000. For design development of Early Childhood Project. 2001.
3112-6 San Antonio Zoological Society, San Antonio, TX, $241,335. For Kid's Place Project. 2001.

3113
Lennox Foundation
P.O. Box 799900
Dallas, TX 75379-9900
Contact: David H. Anderson, Chair.

Incorporated in 1951 in IA.
Grantmaker type: Independent foundation
Financial data (yr. ended 11/30/02): Assets, $19,540,727 (M); gifts received, $120,000; expenditures, $1,373,743; qualifying distributions, $1,208,671; giving activities include $1,208,671 for 28 grants (high: $100,000; low: $5,000).
Purpose and activities: Grants primarily for land conservation, education, health, and human services.
Fields of interest: Education; Environment, land resources; Health care; Human services.
Types of support: General/operating support; Continuing support; Annual campaigns; Capital campaigns; Building/renovation; Equipment; Land acquisition; Program development; Matching/challenge support.
Limitations: Applications not accepted. Giving limited to areas of family involvement in CA, IA, ME, and TX. No grants to individuals.
Application information: Unsolicited requests for funds not accepted.
Board meeting date(s): Mar. and Sept.

Officers and Trustees:* David H. Anderson,* Chair.; Robert W. Norris,* Vice-Chair.; Lynn B. Storey,* Secy.
Number of staff: None.
EIN: 426053380

3114
Martha, David & Bagby Lennox Foundation
228 6th St. S.E.
Paris, TX 75460
Contact: William P. Streng, Pres.
Application address: c/o Bracewell & Patterson, LP, 711 Louisiana St., Ste. 2900, Houston, TX 77002-2781

Established in 1985 in TX.
Donor(s): Martha Lennox,‡ David Lennox,‡ Bagby Lennox.‡
Grantmaker type: Independent foundation
Financial data (yr. ended 12/31/02): Assets, $11,612,662 (M); expenditures, $1,125,979; qualifying distributions, $821,461; giving activities include $791,625 for grants.
Purpose and activities: Giving primarily for education, natural resource conservation, and historical preservation.
Fields of interest: Historic preservation/historical societies; Higher education; Education; Natural resources; Animal welfare; Human services; Children/youth, services; Family services.
Limitations: Giving limited to the northeast TX area. No grants to individuals.
Publications: Application guidelines.
Application information:
Initial approach: Letter
Deadline(s): None
Board meeting date(s): Varies
Officers: William P. Streng, Pres.; Sam L. Hocker, V.P.
Director: Mary Clark.
Number of staff: None.
EIN: 760157945

3115
Lennox International Inc. Corporate Giving Program
2140 Lake Park Blvd.
Richardson, TX 75080-2254 (972) 497-5000
Contact: Karen O'Shea, V.P., Comm. and Public Rels.

Grantmaker type: Corporate giving program
Purpose and activities: Lennox makes charitable contributions to nonprofit organizations involved with arts and culture, education, and the environment.
Fields of interest: Arts; Education; Environment.
Types of support: General/operating support; Employee volunteer services; Employee-related scholarships.
Limitations: Giving on a national basis. No grants to individuals.
Application information: Application form not required.
Initial approach: Proposal to headquarters
Deadline(s): None

3116
The Morris L. Lichtenstein, Jr. Foundation
210 S. Carancahua, Ste. 500
Corpus Christi, TX 78401
Contact: Harry L. Marks, Tr.
Application address: P.O. Box 2888, Corpus Christi, TX 78403, tel.: (512) 884-1961

Established in 1995 in TX.
Donor(s): Morris L. Lichtenstein, Jr.‡
Grantmaker type: Independent foundation
Financial data (yr. ended 12/31/02): Assets, $7,722,549 (M); expenditures, $1,931,342; qualifying distributions, $1,138,502; giving activities include $1,105,500 for 10 grants (high: $695,000; low: $1,000).
Purpose and activities: Grants given primarily to public charities in south TX for medical research, arts, historical landmarks, care of animals, and mental health.
Fields of interest: Historical activities; Arts; Animal welfare; Mental health/crisis services; Medical research; Foundations (community).
Types of support: General/operating support; Research.
Limitations: Giving primarily in Corpus Christi, TX. No support for private foundations. No grants to individuals.
Application information:
Initial approach: Proposal
Deadline(s): None
Trustees: Harry L. Marks; Marcia Marks; Charles W. Thomasson.
EIN: 742757309

3117
Los Trigos Fund
c/o Gayle D. Fogelson
300 Crescent Ct., Ste. 920
Dallas, TX 75201-7851

Established in 1990 in TX.
Donor(s): Gayle D. Fogelson.
Grantmaker type: Independent foundation
Financial data (yr. ended 12/31/00): Assets, $262,057 (M); expenditures, $144,414; qualifying distributions, $132,196; giving activities include $127,184 for 39 grants (high: $42,000; low: $100).
Purpose and activities: Giving primarily for health and human services, education, and to Unitarian Universalist agencies and churches.
Fields of interest: Museums; Arts; Education; Natural resources; Health care; Human services; Population studies; Protestant agencies & churches.
Types of support: General/operating support.
Limitations: Applications not accepted. Giving on a national basis, primarily in NM and TX. No grants to individuals.
Application information: Contributes only to pre-selected organizations.
Officer and Trustee:* Gayle D. Fogelson,* Mgr.
EIN: 752339010

3118
Lubbock Area Foundation, Inc.

1655 Main, Ste. 209
Lubbock, TX 79401 (806) 762-8061
Contact: Kathleen Stocco, Exec. Dir.
FAX: (806) 762-8551; E-mail:
Kathy@lubbockareafoundation.org; URL: http://
www.lubbockareafoundation.org/

Incorporated in 1980 in TX.
Grantmaker type: Community foundation
Financial data (yr. ended 12/31/01): Assets,
$7,515,373 (M); gifts received, $692,362;
expenditures, $554,332; giving activities
include $303,787 for grants (high: $55,500;
low: $150; average: $500–$5,000).
Purpose and activities: Giving primarily for
education, arts, environment, health, civic
affairs, and social services. The foundation
administers donor-advised funds.
Fields of interest: Historic
preservation/historical societies; Arts; Adult
education—literacy, basic skills & GED;
Reading; Education; Environment; Health care;
Substance abuse, services; Health organizations,
association; Human services; Children/youth,
services; Family services; Community
development.
Types of support: General/operating support;
Continuing support; Capital campaigns;
Building/renovation; Equipment; Program
development; Seed money; Scholarship funds;
Matching/challenge support.
Limitations: Giving limited to Lubbock, TX, and
the surrounding South Plains counties. No
grants to individuals, or for debt retirement; no
loans.
Publications: Application guidelines, Financial
statement, Informational brochure, Newsletter.
Application information: Application form not
required.
> *Initial approach:* Telephone or letter
> *Copies of proposal:* 9
> *Deadline(s):* None
> *Board meeting date(s):* Jan., Mar., May, July,
> Sept., and Nov.
Officers and Directors:* Cindy McCuistion,
Pres.; Kathy Smith,* V.P.; Donna Courville,
Treas.; Kathleen Stocco, Exec. Dir.; and 22
additional directors.
Number of staff: 2 full-time professional.
EIN: 751709180

3119
Lyondell Chemical Company
Contributions Program

c/o Public Affairs Dept.
1221 McKinney St., Ste. 700
Houston, TX 77010
Additional application addresses: for
organizations located in Europe: Lyondell
Chemical Europe, Inc., c/o Public Affairs Dept.,
Lyondell House, Bridge Ave., Maidenhead,
Berkshire, United Kingdom SL61YP, for
organizations located in Asia and the Pacific:
Lyondell Asia Pacific, Ltd., c/o Pres., The Lee
Gardens, Rm. 4101, 33 Hysan Ave., Causeway
Bay, Hong Kong, for Explore Science: Equistar
Chemicals, LP, c/o Explore Science Coord., P.O.
Box 2583, Houston, TX 77252-2583; URL:
http://www.lyondell.com/html/social/
social_responsibility.shtml

Grantmaker type: Corporate giving program
Purpose and activities: Lyondell makes
charitable contributions to nonprofit
organizations involved with K-12 education, the
environment, and community development.
Fields of interest: Elementary/secondary
education; Environment; Community
development.
International interests: Belgium; France;
Netherlands; United Kingdom; Indonesia;
Singapore; Taiwan; Japan; Hong Kong.
Types of support: General/operating support;
Employee volunteer services.
Limitations: Giving on an international basis in
areas of company operations, including in
Belgium, France, Hong Kong, Indonesia, Japan,
the Netherlands, Singapore, Taiwan, and the
United Kingdom. No support for political,
religious, labor, or fraternal organizations,
discriminatory organizations, or organizations
receiving United Way support of over 50
percent. No grants to individuals, or for travel
expenses.
Application information: The Public Affairs
Department handles giving. Application form
not required.
> *Initial approach:* Proposal to nearest company
> facility
> *Copies of proposal:* 1
> *Deadline(s):* None
> *Final notification:* Following review

3120
Mays Family Foundation

200 E. Basse Rd.
San Antonio, TX 78209

Established around 1994.
Donor(s): L. Lowry Mays, Mark Mays, Randall
Mays.
Grantmaker type: Independent foundation
Financial data (yr. ended 12/31/02): Assets,
$41,784,475 (M); gifts received, $14,534,964;
expenditures, $1,245,060; qualifying
distributions, $1,229,495; giving activities
include $1,228,619 for 58 grants (high:
$453,003; low: $30).
Fields of interest: Museums; Environment;
Health organizations, association; Human
services; YM/YWCAs & YM/YWHAs; Federated
giving programs.
Limitations: Applications not accepted. Giving
primarily in San Antonio, TX. No grants to
individuals.
Application information: Contributes only to
pre-selected organizations.
Officers and Directors:* Peggy P. Mays,* Pres.;
Kathryn M. Johnson,* V.P.; L. Lowry Mays,*
Treas.; Randall T. Mays; Linda M. McCaul.
EIN: 742691624

3121
The Mazanec Foundation

302 Fall River Ct.
Houston, TX 77024

Established in 1996 in TX.
Donor(s): George L. Mazanec, Elsa B. Mazanec.
Grantmaker type: Independent foundation
Financial data (yr. ended 12/31/02): Assets,
$131,877 (M); expenditures, $117,409;
qualifying distributions, $114,208; giving

activities include $114,228 for 6 grants (high:
$100,000; low: $1,000).
Purpose and activities: Giving for education.
Fields of interest: Higher education;
Scholarships/financial aid; Zoos/zoological
societies; Federated giving programs.
Limitations: Applications not accepted. Giving
primarily in Houston, TX. No grants to
individuals.
Application information: Contributes only to
pre-selected organizations.
Officers and Directors:* George L. Mazanec,
Pres.; Elsa B. Mazanec, V.P. and Secy.; Robert
Andrew Mazanec,* V.P.; John Charles
Mazanec,* Treas.
EIN: 760521836

3122
Hugh A. McAllister, Jr. Charitable
Foundation

2500 City West Blvd., Ste. 1000
Houston, TX 77042

Established in 1997 in TX.
Donor(s): Hugh A. McAllister, Jr.
Grantmaker type: Independent foundation
Financial data (yr. ended 12/31/02): Assets,
$5,061,902 (M); expenditures, $294,529;
qualifying distributions, $235,038; giving
activities include $237,500 for 3 grants (high:
$125,000; low: $12,500).
Purpose and activities: Giving primarily for
health care and wildlife preservation.
Fields of interest: Animals/wildlife; Hospitals
(general).
Limitations: Applications not accepted. Giving
on a national basis, with emphasis on
Washington, DC. No grants to individuals.
Application information: Contributes only to
pre-selected organizations.
Officers: Hugh A. McAllister, Pres.; Angela
McAllister, V.P. and Secy.; Dana Leigh
McAllister, Treas.
EIN: 760556345

3123
Miriam and Emmett McCoy Foundation

P.O. Box 1028
San Marcos, TX 78667-1028

Established in 1993 in TX.
Donor(s): Emmett F. McCoy, Miriam M. McCoy.
Grantmaker type: Independent foundation
Financial data (yr. ended 12/31/02): Assets,
$5,405,894 (M); gifts received, $500,000;
expenditures, $549,850; qualifying distributions,
$533,075; giving activities include $529,311 for
25 grants (high: $118,000; low: $275).
Purpose and activities: Giving primarily to an
animal shelter and for community service.
Fields of interest: Environment;
Animals/wildlife; Diabetes; Women.
Limitations: Applications not accepted. Giving
primarily in TX. No grants to individuals.
Application information: Contributes only to
pre-selected organizations.
Officers and Directors:* Emmett F. McCoy,*
Pres.; Miriam M. McCoy,* V.P. and Treas.;
Brenda M. Remme,* Secy.
EIN: 742686146

3124
McCrea Foundation
c/o Phoebe Muzzy
5005 Woodway Dr., Ste. 210
Houston, TX 77056

Established in 1960 in VA.
Donor(s): Mary Corling McCrea.‡
Grantmaker type: Independent foundation
Financial data (yr. ended 02/28/03): Assets,
$5,567,573 (M); expenditures, $272,599;
qualifying distributions, $272,599; giving
activities include $267,500 for 27 grants (high:
$112,500).
Purpose and activities: Giving primarily for
education and health, including a children's
hospital; funding also for human services and
religion.
Fields of interest: Museums; Secondary
school/education; Education; Animal welfare;
Hospitals (specialty); Cancer research; Human
services; Children/youth, services; Hospices;
Community development; Religion.
Types of support: General/operating support;
Scholarship funds.
Limitations: Applications not accepted. Giving
primarily in Minden, NV, Portland, OR, and
Houston, TX. No grants to individuals.
Application information: Contributes only to
pre-selected organizations.
Officers: Mrs. John L. Welsh, Pres.; Phoebe W.
Muzzy, V.P. and Treas.; David D. Welsh, V.P.;
John L. Welsh III, V.P.; Gray H. Muzzy, Secy.
Director: Edward C. Welsh.
Agent: The Northern Trust Co.
EIN: 546052010

3125
Amy Shelton McNutt Charitable Trust
153 Treeline Park, Ste. 300
San Antonio, TX 78209-1880
Contact: Carol Bruehler, Secy.

Established about 1983 in TX.
Donor(s): Amy Shelton McNutt.‡
Grantmaker type: Independent foundation
Financial data (yr. ended 09/30/02): Assets,
$11,067,115 (M); expenditures, $835,569;
qualifying distributions, $785,833; giving
activities include $724,816 for 127 grants (high:
$100,000; low: $50).
Fields of interest: Museums (art); Arts; Higher
education; Education; Natural resources; Animal
welfare; Zoos/zoological societies; Human
services; Foundations (private grantmaking);
Christian agencies & churches.
Types of support: General/operating support;
Capital campaigns; Building/renovation;
Matching/challenge support.
Limitations: Giving primarily in TX, with
emphasis on San Antonio. No grants to
individuals.
Application information: Application form not
required.
 Initial approach: Proposal
 Deadline(s): None
 Board meeting date(s): Mar. and Aug.
Officer: Carol Bruehler, Secy.
Trustees: R.B. Cutlip; Jack Guenther; Courtney J.
Walker.
Number of staff: None.
EIN: 742298675

3126
The Meadows Foundation, Inc. ▼
Wilson Historic District
3003 Swiss Ave.
Dallas, TX 75204-6090 (214) 826-9431
Contact: Bruce H. Esterline, V.P., Grants
Additional tel.: (800) 826-9431; FAX: (214)
827-7042; E-mail: grants@mfi.org; URL: http://
www.mfi.org

Incorporated in 1948 in TX.
Donor(s): Algur Hurtle Meadows,‡ Virginia
Meadows.‡
Grantmaker type: Independent foundation
Financial data (yr. ended 12/31/02): Assets,
$682,933,409 (M); expenditures, $47,007,951;
qualifying distributions, $31,497,130; giving
activities include $31,417,918 for 335+ grants
(high: $2,500,000; low: $400; average:
$25,000–$250,000), $79,212 for employee
matching gifts and $5,092,756 for 7
loans/program-related investments.
Purpose and activities: Support for the arts,
social services, community and rural
development, health including mental health,
education, and civic and cultural programs.
Operates a historic preservation
investment-related program using a cluster of
Victorian homes as offices for nonprofit agencies.
Fields of interest: Media/communications;
Architecture; Museums; Humanities;
History/archaeology; Historic
preservation/historical societies; Arts; Education,
public education; Early childhood education;
Child development, education; Medical
school/education; Adult/continuing education;
Adult education—literacy, basic skills & GED;
Libraries/library science; Reading; Education;
Natural resources; Environment;
Animals/wildlife, preservation/protection; Dental
care; Medical care, rehabilitation; Nursing care;
Health care; Substance abuse, services; Mental
health/crisis services; AIDS; Alcoholism; AIDS
research; Crime/law enforcement; Employment;
Agriculture; Nutrition; Housing/shelter,
development; Safety/disasters; Recreation; Youth
development, services; Human services;
Children/youth, services; Child development,
services; Family services; Hospices; Aging,
centers/services; Homeless, human services;
Race/intergroup relations; Urban/community
development; Rural development; Community
development; Voluntarism promotion;
Government/public administration;
Transportation; Leadership development; Public
affairs; Christian agencies & churches; Aging;
Economically disadvantaged; Homeless.
Types of support: General/operating support;
Continuing support; Capital campaigns;
Building/renovation; Equipment; Land
acquisition; Endowments; Debt reduction;
Emergency funds; Program development;
Publication; Seed money; Curriculum
development; Research; Technical assistance;
Consulting services; Program evaluation;
Program-related investments/loans; Employee
matching gifts; Matching/challenge support.
Limitations: Giving limited to TX. No grants to
individuals; generally, no grants for annual
campaigns, fundraising events, professional
conferences and symposia, travel expenses for
groups to perform or compete outside of TX, or
construction of churches and seminaries.

Publications: Application guidelines, Annual
report (including application guidelines).
Application information: An on-line grant
application form is available on the foundation's
Web site. Application form not required.
 Initial approach: Proposal
 Copies of proposal: 1
 Deadline(s): None
 Board meeting date(s): Grants review
 committee meets monthly; full board meets
 2 or 3 times a year
 Final notification: 3 to 4 months
Officers and Directors:* Robert A. Meadows,*
Chair. and V.P.; Linda P. Evans,* C.E.O. and
Pres.; Martha L. Benson, V.P., Treas. and C.F.O.;
Michael E. Patrick, V.P. and C.I.O.; Bruce H.
Esterline, V.P., Grants; Robert E. Weiss, V.P.,
Admin.; Emily J. Jones, Corp. Secy.; Evelyn
Meadows Acton, Dir. Emeritus; John W.
Broadfoot; J.W. Bullion, Dir. Emeritus; True
Miller Campbell; Daniel H. Chapman; Judy B.
Culbertson; John A. Hammack; Sally R.
Lancaster, Dir. Emeritus; P. Mike McCullough;
Curtis W. Meadows, Jr., Dir. Emeritus; Eric
Richard Meadows; Mark A. Meadows; Michael
L. Meadows; Sally C. Miller, Dir. Emeritus;
William A. Nesbitt; G. Tomas Rhodus; Evy Kay
Ritzen; Eloise Meadows Rouse, Dir. Emeritus;
Dorothy C. Wilson, Dir. Emeritus; Stephen
Wheeler Wilson.
Number of staff: 23 full-time professional; 1
part-time professional; 21 full-time support; 2
part-time support.
EIN: 756015322
**Recent environmental and animal welfare
grants:**
3126-1 Animal Protection Institute of America,
 Sacramento, CA, $25,000. Toward
 emergency repairs to Snow Monkey
 sanctuary resulting from damage caused by
 recent flooding. 2002.
3126-2 Austin College, Center for
 Environmental Studies, Sherman, TX,
 $138,000. Toward educational staff positions.
 2002.
3126-3 BellNET (Bell County Network for
 Educational Technology), Temple, TX,
 $60,000. Toward developing and
 implementing horticultural curriculum for
 incarcerated juveniles. 2002.
3126-4 Boy Scouts of America, Buffalo Trail
 Council, Midland, TX, $85,000. Toward
 installing water system on Burkitt property to
 support expanded programming in
 wilderness setting. 2002.
3126-5 Brownfields Stewardship Fund, DC,
 $206,000. Toward establishing statewide
 program in Texas to return environmentally
 contaminated property to commercial use.
 2002.
3126-6 Conservation History Association of
 Texas, Austin, TX, $15,000. Toward
 developing oral history of conservation
 movement in Texas and making it accessible
 via Web. 2002.
3126-7 Dallas Arboretum and Botanical Society,
 Dallas, TX, $100,000. Toward emergency
 operating support to replace revenue losses
 suffered as result of difficult economic
 conditions and to meet increasing demand
 for services. 2002.
3126-8 Dallas County Sheriffs Department,
 Dallas, TX, $25,000. To continue waste
 management services in Sandbranch. 2002.

3126-9 Environmental Defense, Austin, TX, $250,000. Toward expanding Black-capped Vireo and Golden-cheeked Warbler habitat restoration program to Chalk Mountain ecosystem. 2002.

3126-10 Lady Bird Johnson Wildflower Center, Austin, TX, $155,500. Toward emergency operating support due to difficult economic conditions. 2002.

3126-11 National Fish and Wildlife Foundation, Dallas, TX, $225,000. Toward additional staff to increase federal and other funding resources for environmental projects. 2002.

3126-12 Nature Conservancy of Texas, San Antonio, TX, $845,000. Toward acquiring and preserving critical watersheds in Texas. 2002.

3126-13 North American Butterfly Association (NABA), Morristown, NJ, $197,000. Toward creating butterfly park in Rio Grande Valley to increase ecotourism. 2002.

3126-14 Northwest Texas Museum Association, Mobeetie, TX, $15,000. Toward travel and educational expenses associated with traveling exhibit on importance of playas in Texas environment. 2002.

3126-15 San Marcos River Foundation, San Marcos, TX, $155,000. Toward acquiring water rights on Guadalupe River to be banked in Water Trust of Texas Department of Parks and Wildlife. 2002.

3126-16 Southwest Texas State University, San Marcos, TX, $375,000. Toward start-up funding of International Institute for Sustainable Water Resources. 2002.

3126-17 Sustainable Food Center, Austin, TX, $25,000. Toward expanding nutrition demonstration series by including train-the-trainers component. 2002.

3126-18 Therapy Dogs of Central Texas, Georgetown, TX, $25,000. Toward start-up expenses associated with training volunteers and service dogs to provide assistance to disabled, elderly and dying clients. 2002.

3126-19 Westcave Preserve Corporation, Round Mountain, TX, $150,000. Toward constructing environmental learning center. 2002.

3126-20 Woodside Trails Wilderness Experience, Smithville, TX, $26,500. Toward purchasing van and truck to transport emotionally disturbed boys from therapeutic camp to off-site services and activities. 2002.

3127
William A. and Elizabeth B. Moncrief Foundation
Moncrief Bldg.
950 Commerce St.
Fort Worth, TX 76102   (817) 336-7232
Contact: W.A. Moncrief, Jr., Pres.

Established in 1954.
Donor(s): W.A. Moncrief,‡ Elizabeth B. Moncrief,‡ W.A. Moncrief, Jr.
Grantmaker type: Independent foundation
Financial data (yr. ended 09/30/02): Assets, $8,648,489 (M); gifts received, $2,813,605; expenditures, $2,403,436; qualifying distributions, $2,425,583; giving activities include $2,428,660 for 15 grants (high: $2,000,000; low: $300).

Purpose and activities: Giving primarily to an art museum, as well as for the arts; funding also for education, health and hospitals and social services.
Fields of interest: Museums (art); Museums (specialized); Arts; Education; Zoos/zoological societies; Hospitals (general); Human services; Federated giving programs.
Types of support: General/operating support.
Limitations: Giving primarily in TX. No grants to individuals.
Application information:
Initial approach: Letter
Deadline(s): None
Officers: W.A. Moncrief, Jr., Pres. and Mgr.; R.W. Moncrief, V.P.; C.B. Moncrief, Secy.-Treas.
Number of staff: None.
EIN: 756036329

3128
The Moody Foundation ▼
2302 Post Office St., Ste. 704
Galveston, TX 77550   (409) 763-5333
Contact: Peter M. Moore, Dir., Grants
FAX: (409) 763-5564; URL: http://www.moodyf.org

Trust established in 1942 in TX.
Donor(s): William Lewis Moody, Jr.,‡ Libbie Shearn Moody.‡
Grantmaker type: Independent foundation
Financial data (yr. ended 12/31/02): Assets, $967,301,681 (M); gifts received, $19,266,170; expenditures, $13,824,801; qualifying distributions, $11,996,713; giving activities include $9,193,456 for 42 grants (high: $3,946,784; low: $1,592; average: $10,000–$100,000) and $135,740 for grants to individuals.
Purpose and activities: Funds to be used for historic restoration projects, performing arts organizations, and cultural programs; promotion of health, science, and education; community and social services; and the field of religion.
Fields of interest: Performing arts; Arts; Medical school/education; Education; Environment; Health care; AIDS; Medical research, institute; AIDS research; Youth development; Human services; Community development; Engineering/technology; Science; Religion; Disabled; Aging; Economically disadvantaged.
Types of support: Capital campaigns; Building/renovation; Equipment; Land acquisition; Program development; Conferences/seminars; Publication; Seed money; Scholarship funds; Research; Technical assistance; Grants to individuals; Matching/challenge support.
Limitations: Giving limited to TX. No grants to individuals (except for students covered by one scholarship program in Galveston County), or for operating budgets (except for start-up purposes), continuing support, annual campaigns, or deficit financing; no loans or program-related investments.
Publications: Application guidelines, Annual report.
Application information: Foundation will send application guidelines if project is of interest. For scholarship application form and submission deadlines contact Sandy Griffin. Application form not required.
Initial approach: Letter or telephone

Copies of proposal: 1
Deadline(s): 6 weeks prior to board meetings
Board meeting date(s): Quarterly
Final notification: 3 weeks after board meetings
Officers and Trustees:* Frances Moody Newman,* Chair.; Robert L. Moody,* Vice-Chair.; Ross Moody, Treas.; Harold C. MacDonald, Compt.; Frances Ann Moody, Exec. Dir.
Number of staff: 10 full-time professional; 5 full-time support.
EIN: 741403105
Recent environmental and animal welfare grants:
3128-1 Lady Bird Johnson Wildflower Center, Austin, TX, $10,000. Toward presenting annual environmental education events for children and families. 2001.
3128-2 West Nueces-Las Moras Soil and Water Conservation District, Brackettville, TX, $35,000. For Phase V research efforts to determine effects on wildlife habitats and Edwards Aquifer watershed resulting from control of Ashe Juniper. 2001.

3129
James D. and Kay Y. Moran Foundation
5500 Preston Rd., Ste. 390
Dallas, TX 75205   (214) 528-6483
Contact: Kay Moran McCord, Pres.

Established in 1989 in TX.
Donor(s): Geary Ellet, Kay Moran McCord.
Grantmaker type: Independent foundation
Financial data (yr. ended 09/30/02): Assets, $1,548,584 (M); expenditures, $113,988; qualifying distributions, $110,741; giving activities include $111,000 for 39 grants (high: $10,000; low: $1,000).
Purpose and activities: Giving primarily for education and youth programs.
Fields of interest: Arts; Higher education; Education; Natural resources; Children/youth, services.
Limitations: Applications not accepted. Giving primarily in OK and TX. No grants to individuals.
Application information: Contributes only to pre-selected organizations.
Officers: Kay Moran McCord, C.E.O. and Pres.; Heather Moran, V.P.; Elberta Washburn, Secy.-Treas.
Director: E.W. Moran, Jr.
EIN: 752303252

3130
Alma Morelock Charitable Trust
c/o Bank of America
P.O. Box 831041
Dallas, TX 75283-1041
Contact: David P. Ross, Sr. V.P., Bank of America
Application address: 1200 Main St., 14th Fl., Kansas City, MO 64105, tel.: (816) 979-7481

Established in 1987 in MO.
Grantmaker type: Independent foundation
Financial data (yr. ended 12/31/01): Assets, $953,269 (M); expenditures, $198,385; qualifying distributions, $187,192; giving activities include $174,350 for 7 grants (high: $63,000; low: $5,000).

Purpose and activities: Support for the Boy Scouts of America, education, and the arts.
Fields of interest: Arts; Education; Zoos/zoological societies; Boy scouts.
Limitations: Giving primarily in Kansas City, MO, and Emory, VA. No grants to individuals.
Application information:
  Initial approach: 3-page letter
  Deadline(s): None
Trustee: Bank of America.
EIN: 446008586

3131
Harry S. Moss Foundation
970 San Jacinto Twr.
2121 San Jacinto St.
Dallas, TX 75201 (214) 754-2984
Contact: Frank S. Ryburn, Pres.

Incorporated in 1952 in TX.
Donor(s): Harry S. Moss, Florence M. Moss, Moss Petroleum Co.
Grantmaker type: Independent foundation
Financial data (yr. ended 11/30/02): Assets, $4,677,799 (M); expenditures, $355,703; qualifying distributions, $319,407; giving activities include $317,500 for 48 grants (high: $41,000; low: $500).
Fields of interest: Museums; Humanities; Education; Animals/wildlife; Human services; Children/youth, services; Community development; Federated giving programs; Religion.
Types of support: General/operating support.
Limitations: Giving primarily in the Dallas, TX, area. No grants to individuals.
Application information: Application form not required.
  Initial approach: Letter
  Deadline(s): None
Officers: Frank S. Ryburn, Pres.; Mary Jane Ryburn, V.P. and Secy.-Treas.
EIN: 756036333

3132
Mary Moody Northen Endowment
P.O. Box 1300
Galveston, TX 77553-1300 (409) 765-9770
Contact: Betty Massey, Exec. Dir.

Established in 1964.
Donor(s): Mary Moody Northen.‡
Grantmaker type: Independent foundation
Financial data (yr. ended 12/31/02): Assets, $62,258,551 (M); expenditures, $3,782,633; qualifying distributions, $1,012,757; giving activities include $547,086 for 8 grants (high: $455,000; low: $2,000) and $3,310,857 for 3 foundation-administered programs.
Purpose and activities: Support for educational institutions, community development and civic affairs, and wildlife and the environment. The foundation has completed restoration of the W.L. Moody residence and currently operates it as a house museum. The foundation also conducts research of the history of 20th century Texas.
Fields of interest: Museums; History/archaeology; Historic preservation/historical societies; Education, research; Higher education; Education; Natural resources; Environment; Animals/wildlife,

preservation/protection; Community development.
Types of support: General/operating support; Continuing support; Capital campaigns; Building/renovation; Program development; Curriculum development; Consulting services.
Limitations: Giving limited to TX and VA.
Application information: Application form not required.
  Initial approach: Letter
  Copies of proposal: 1
  Deadline(s): None
  Board meeting date(s): Monthly
  Final notification: Grants are usually made in the 2nd quarter of each year
Officers and Directors:* Edward L. Protz,* Pres.; G. William Rider,* V.P. and Treas.; Robert L. Moody,* Secy.; Betty Massey, Exec. Dir.
Number of staff: 1 full-time professional; 1 full-time support; 1 part-time support.
EIN: 751171741

3133
Notsew Orm Sands Foundation
50 Briar Hollow Ln., Ste. 590E
Houston, TX 77027

Established around 1995.
Donor(s): Charles Burnett III.
Grantmaker type: Independent foundation
Financial data (yr. ended 12/31/01): Assets, $1,914,059 (M); gifts received, $5,300; expenditures, $111,361; qualifying distributions, $101,016; giving activities include $91,887 for 6 grants (high: $43,876; low: $1,000).
Purpose and activities: Giving primarily for animal welfare, including search and rescue organizations; support also for medical education and research.
Fields of interest: Medical school/education; Animal welfare; Disasters, search/rescue; Human services.
Limitations: Applications not accepted. Giving on a national and international basis, with some emphasis in Houston, TX, and the United Kingdom. No grants to individuals.
Application information: Contributes only to pre-selected organizations.
Officers: Charles Burnett III, Pres. and Secy.; Miriam W. Burnett, V.P. and Treas.
Directors: Garfield Mitchell; Graham Weston.
EIN: 760455176

3134
John M. O'Quinn Foundation
(formerly The O'Quinn Foundation)
3518 Travis, Ste. 200
Houston, TX 77002
Contact: John M. O'Quinn, Pres.
Application address: 440 Louisiana, Houston,TX 77002, tel.: (713) 236-2659

Established in 1986 in TX.
Donor(s): John M. O'Quinn.
Grantmaker type: Independent foundation
Financial data (yr. ended 12/31/01): Assets, $34,494,510 (M); expenditures, $2,744,889; qualifying distributions, $2,641,339; giving activities include $2,543,135 for 27 grants (high: $656,538; low: $300).

Purpose and activities: Giving primarily for education, the environment, and children and youth services.
Fields of interest: Education, fund raising; Law school/education; Natural resources; Environment; Children/youth, services.
Limitations: Giving primarily in Houston, TX. No grants to individuals.
Application information: Application form not required.
  Initial approach: Letter
  Deadline(s): None
Officers: John M. O'Quinn, Pres.; Robert A. Higley, Secy.-Treas.
Trustee: David Griffis.
Number of staff: None.
EIN: 760206844

3135
Once Upon A Time Foundation
(formerly Will E. Coyote Foundation)
301 Commerce St., Ste. 2975
Fort Worth, TX 76102

Established in 1998 in TX.
Donor(s): Geoffrey P. Raynor.
Grantmaker type: Independent foundation
Financial data (yr. ended 12/31/02): Assets, $3,647,975 (M); expenditures, $1,177,224; qualifying distributions, $877,224; giving activities include $857,507 for 69 grants (high: $100,000; low: $1,000).
Purpose and activities: Support primarily for the arts, especially toward the construction of a modern art museum facility; giving also for health care and animal welfare.
Fields of interest: Multipurpose centers/programs; Museums (art); Performing arts; Education; Animal welfare; Hospitals (general); Health care; Health organizations.
Types of support: General/operating support; Capital campaigns; Building/renovation; Equipment; Program development.
Limitations: Applications not accepted. Giving primarily in Fort Worth, TX. No grants to individuals.
Application information: Contributes only to pre-selected organizations.
Officers: Geoffrey P. Raynor, Pres.; Robert McCormick, V.P.; Kim Baldi, Secy.
EIN: 752765224

3136
Otter Island Foundation
700 Louisiana St., Ste. 5000
Houston, TX 77002-2767

Established in 1993 in TX.
Donor(s): Matthew R. Simmons, Ellen Simmons.
Grantmaker type: Independent foundation
Financial data (yr. ended 12/31/02): Assets, $3,023,413 (M); gifts received, $50,000; expenditures, $430,132; qualifying distributions, $418,594; giving activities include $422,139 for 130 grants (high: $25,000; low: $50).
Purpose and activities: Giving primarily for the arts, education, and health and human services.
Fields of interest: Arts; Education; Environment; Health organizations, association; Human services.
Limitations: Applications not accepted. No grants to individuals.

Application information: Contributes only to pre-selected organizations.
Officers and Director:* Matthew R. Simmons,* Pres.; Ellen C.L. Simmons, V.P. and Treas.; Shelly K. Daugherty, Secy.
EIN: 760421104

3137
Alvin and Lucy Owsley Foundation
65 Briar Hollow Ln.
Houston, TX 77027
Contact: Alvin Owsley, Jr., Tr.

Trust established in 1950 in TX.
Donor(s): Alvin M. Owsley,‡ Lucy B. Owsley.‡
Grantmaker type: Independent foundation
Financial data (yr. ended 12/31/02): Assets, $6,234,812 (M); expenditures, $428,658; qualifying distributions, $398,247; giving activities include $390,550 for 53 grants (high: $100,000; low: $100).
Purpose and activities: Giving primarily for the arts, education and human services.
Fields of interest: Arts; Medical school/education; Education; Animal welfare; Family planning; Biomedicine; Medical research, institute; Human services; Reproductive rights.
Types of support: General/operating support; Continuing support; Annual campaigns; Building/renovation; Emergency funds; Seed money; Scholarship funds; Matching/challenge support.
Limitations: Giving limited to TX. No grants to individuals, or for endowment funds; no loans.
Publications: Application guidelines.
Application information: Application form not required.
  Initial approach: Letter not exceeding 2 pages
  Copies of proposal: 1
  Deadline(s): Submit proposal preferably in months when board meets; no set deadline
  Board meeting date(s): Mar., June, Sept., and Dec.
  Final notification: 2 months, positive responses only
Trustees: Wendy Garrett; Alvin Owsley, Jr.; David T. Owsley.
Number of staff: None.
EIN: 756047221

3138
The P Twenty-One Foundation
675 Bering Dr., Ste. 110
Houston, TX 77057 (713) 782-9897
Contact: Joseph W. Ryan, Pres.

Established in 2000 in TX.
Donor(s): Joseph W. Ryan, Yolanda V. Ryan.
Grantmaker type: Independent foundation
Financial data (yr. ended 11/30/02): Assets, $3,864,215 (M); expenditures, $237,244; qualifying distributions, $227,000; giving activities include $227,000 for 11 grants (high: $75,000; low: $5,000).
Purpose and activities: Giving for public health and ecological activities in the south Texas area.
Fields of interest: Environment; Public health.
Limitations: Giving primarily in southern TX.
Application information:
  Initial approach: Letter
  Deadline(s): None

Officers and Directors:* Joseph W. Ryan,* Pres. and Treas.; Yolanda V. Ryan,* V.P. and Secy.; Minerva V. Campos.
EIN: 760628482

3139
The Paulos Foundation
6708 Ashbrook Dr.
Fort Worth, TX 76132

Established in 1990 in TX.
Donor(s): James J. Paulos.
Grantmaker type: Independent foundation
Financial data (yr. ended 12/31/02): Assets, $4,022,480 (M); expenditures, $367,840; qualifying distributions, $361,596; giving activities include $358,480 for 47 grants (high: $50,200; low: $250).
Purpose and activities: Giving for education, youth services and religion.
Fields of interest: Media/communications; Arts; Education; Natural resources; Zoos/zoological societies; Health organizations, association; Human services; Children/youth, services; Protestant federated giving programs; Protestant agencies & churches; Religion.
Limitations: Applications not accepted. Giving limited to Dallas, TX. No grants to individuals.
Application information: Contributes only to pre-selected organizations.
Officers: Flora P. Brewer, Chair. and Pres.; Angela D. Paulos, V.P. and Secy.
Directors: John J. Paulos; Sam G. Paulos.
EIN: 752353196

3140
Perkins-Prothro Foundation
2304 Midwestern Pkwy., Ste. 200
Wichita Falls, TX 76308-2334 (940) 723-7163

Established in 1967.
Donor(s): Lois Perkins,‡ Charles N. Prothro, Elizabeth P. Prothro.
Grantmaker type: Independent foundation
Financial data (yr. ended 12/31/01): Assets, $41,423,487 (M); gifts received, $46,456; expenditures, $3,670,593; qualifying distributions, $3,487,502; giving activities include $3,356,640 for 81 grants (high: $701,098; low: $100; average: $1,000-$100,000).
Purpose and activities: Emphasis on higher education, an aquarium, Protestant organizations, youth development, and social services.
Fields of interest: Higher education; Aquariums; Camp Fire; Human services; Protestant agencies & churches.
Types of support: General/operating support; Building/renovation; Endowments.
Limitations: Applications not accepted. Giving limited to TX, with emphasis on Wichita Falls. No grants to individuals.
Application information: Contributes only to pre-selected organizations.
Officers and Trustees:* Joe N. Prothro,* Pres.; Elizabeth P. Prothro,* V.P.; Kathryn Prothro Yeager,* V.P.; K. Elizabeth Edwards,* Secy.; Mark H. Prothro,* Treas.; David H. Prothro.
EIN: 751247407

3141
Potts and Sibley Foundation
P.O. Box 8907
Midland, TX 79708 (915) 686-7051
Contact: Robert W. Bechtel, Mgr.

Established in 1967 in TX.
Donor(s): Effie Potts Sibley Irrevocable Trust.
Grantmaker type: Independent foundation
Financial data (yr. ended 07/31/02): Assets, $4,432,793 (M); expenditures, $362,045; qualifying distributions, $214,932; giving activities include $204,900 for 28 grants (high: $30,000; low: $2,000).
Fields of interest: Museums; Orchestra (symphony); Literature; Higher education; Natural resources; Hospitals (general); Mental health, association; Medical research, institute; Food services; Human services; Hospices; Protestant agencies & churches.
Limitations: Giving primarily in TX. No support for private foundations. No grants to individuals.
Application information: Application form required.
  Deadline(s): None
Officers and Trustee:* Hiram Sibley, Chair.; Robert W. Bechtel,* Mgr.
Directors: Allen G. McGuire; Tom Scott.
EIN: 756081070

3142
The Powell Foundation
2121 San Felipe, Ste. 110
Houston, TX 77019-5600 (713) 523-7557
Contact: Caroline J. Sabin, Exec. Dir.
FAX: (713) 523-7553; E-mail: info@powellfoundation.org; URL: http://www.powellfoundation.org

Established in 1967 in TX.
Donor(s): Ben H. Powell, Jr.,‡ Kitty King Powell.
Grantmaker type: Independent foundation
Financial data (yr. ended 12/31/02): Assets, $13,653,261 (M); gifts received, $915,162; expenditures, $823,436; qualifying distributions, $770,430; giving activities include $661,223 for 93 grants (high: $25,000; low: $100).
Purpose and activities: Giving primarily for public education.
Fields of interest: Arts; Education, association; Education, research; Early childhood education; Higher education; Education; Environment; Health care; Human services; Minorities; Economically disadvantaged.
Types of support: General/operating support; Program development; Curriculum development.
Limitations: Giving primarily in Harris, Walker, and Travis counties, TX. No support for private foundations, or religious organizations for religious purposes. No grants to individuals, or for testimonial dinners, fundraising events, advertising, or debt retirement.
Publications: Application guidelines, Annual report (including application guidelines).
Application information: Application guidelines available on Web site. Application form not required.
  Initial approach: Letter
  Copies of proposal: 1
  Deadline(s): Varies
  Board meeting date(s): 2 times a year
  Final notification: Positive replies only

Officers and Trustees:* Nancy Powell Moore,* Pres. and Treas.; Eunice Meyer,* V.P. and Secy.; Ben H. Powell V,* V.P.; Marian Moore Casey; Molly N. Kidd; Katherine G. Osborne; Kitty King Powell.
Number of staff: 1 full-time professional; 1 part-time professional; 1 part-time support.
EIN: 746104592

3143
The Prentice Foundation
5100 San Felipe, Ste. 233E
Houston, TX 77056 (713) 850-0346
Contact: Cynthia R. Prentice, V.P.

Established in 1994 in TX.
Donor(s): F. David Prentice, Mrs. F. David Prentice.
Grantmaker type: Independent foundation
Financial data (yr. ended 11/30/02): Assets, $1,280,543 (M); expenditures, $109,468; qualifying distributions, $99,453; giving activities include $100,200 for 9 grants (high: $37,500; low: $200).
Purpose and activities: Providing for animal care.
Fields of interest: Animals/wildlife.
Limitations: Giving primarily in TX.
Application information:
   Initial approach: Proposal
   Deadline(s): None
Officers: F. David Prentice, Pres. and Treas.; Cynthia R. Prentice, V.P. and Secy.
Director: Howard Shylman.
EIN: 760455526

3144
Quicksilver Resources Inc. Corporate Giving Program
c/o Corp. Contribs.
777 W. Rosedale, Ste. 300
Fort Worth, TX 76104
URL: http://www.qrinc.com/environ.htm

Grantmaker type: Corporate giving program
Purpose and activities: Quicksilver makes charitable contributions to nonprofit organizations involved with the environment and youth development. Support is given primarily in Gaylord, Michigan, Cut Bank, Montana, Fort Worth, Texas, and Casper, Wyoming.
Fields of interest: Environment; Youth development.
Types of support: General/operating support; Scholarship funds; Employee volunteer services; Use of facilities.
Limitations: Giving primarily in Gaylord, MI, Cut Bank, MT, Fort Worth, TX, and Casper, WY.
Application information: Application form not required.
   Initial approach: Proposal to headquarters
   Copies of proposal: 1
   Final notification: Following review

3145
Rainforest Cafe Friends of the Future Foundation
c/o Landry's Restaurants, Inc.
1400 Post Oak Blvd., Ste. 1010
Houston, TX 77056 (800) 552-6379
Contact: Brenda Henscey
FAX: (713) 623-5238

Grantmaker type: Public charity
Financial data (yr. ended 12/31/01): Revenue, $250,423; assets, $383,246 (M); gifts received, $226,423; expenditures, $53,432; program services expenses, $49,667; giving activities include $2,500 for 1 grant.
Purpose and activities: The foundation supports environmental causes, as well as causes that enrich the lives of children, their families, and the community in areas which Rainforest Cafe operates.
Fields of interest: Environment.
Limitations: No support for organizations that are not 501(c)(3) or equivalent. No grants to individuals.
Application information: Requests for applications by e-mail or telephone not accepted.
   Initial approach: Letter
Officers and Director:* Kenneth W. Brimmer,* Pres.; Stephen W. Schussler,* V.P.; Kathy Roberts, Dir.
EIN: 411909838

3146
Rockwell Fund, Inc. ▼
1330 Post Oak Blvd., Ste. 1825
Houston, TX 77056 (713) 629-9022
Contact: Carolyn L. Watson, Prog. Off. or Jana Mullins, Prog. Off.
FAX: (713) 629-7702; E-mail: cwatson@rockfund.org or jmullins@rockfund.org; URL: http://www.rockfund.org

Trust established in 1931; incorporated in 1949 in TX; merged with Rockwell Brothers Endowment, Inc. in 1981.
Donor(s): Members of the James M. Rockwell family.
Grantmaker type: Independent foundation
Financial data (yr. ended 12/31/02): Assets, $102,177,274 (M); gifts received, $1,000; expenditures, $6,066,240; qualifying distributions, $5,370,761; giving activities include $4,833,315 for 195 grants (high: $126,000; low: $500; average: $3,000–$126,000).
Purpose and activities: Giving primarily for charitable, human services, educational, health, arts and humanities, environmental, and civic purposes.
Fields of interest: Visual arts; Museums; Performing arts; Theater; Music; Humanities; Historic preservation/historical societies; Arts; Early childhood education; Child development, education; Elementary school/education; Secondary school/education; Higher education; Adult education—literacy, basic skills & GED; Libraries/library science; Reading; Education; Natural resources; Environment; Hospitals (general); Medical care, rehabilitation; Nursing care; Health care; Health organizations, association; AIDS; Biomedicine; Crime/violence

prevention, youth; Crime/law enforcement; Food services; Human services; Children/youth, services; Child development, services; Homeless, human services; Government/public administration; General charitable giving; Minorities; Disabled; Aging; Homeless.
Types of support: General/operating support; Continuing support; Annual campaigns; Capital campaigns; Building/renovation; Equipment; Land acquisition; Endowments; Program development; Professorships; Seed money; Curriculum development; Scholarship funds; Technical assistance; Program-related investments/loans; Matching/challenge support.
Limitations: Giving primarily in TX, with emphasis on Houston. No grants to individuals or for medical or scientific research projects, underwriting benefits, dinners, galas, and fundraising special events, or mass appeal solicitations; grants primarily awarded on a year-to-year basis only.
Publications: Application guidelines, Annual report, Grants list.
Application information: Applicants should not submit more than 1 proposal per year; Applications must include a written narrative, application form, and check list. Application form required.
   Initial approach: Letter requesting application and guidelines
   Copies of proposal: 1
   Deadline(s): None
   Board meeting date(s): Quarterly
   Final notification: After each quarterly meeting
Officers and Trustees:* R. Terry Bell,* C.E.O. and Pres.; Margaret E. McConn,* V.P. and C.F.O.; Barbara Bellatti,* Secy.; Bennie Green,* Treas.; Gene Graham.
Number of staff: 4 full-time professional; 2 full-time support.
EIN: 746040258
Recent environmental and animal welfare grants:
3146-1 Buffalo Bayou Partnership, Houston, TX, $25,000. For project support to continue redevelopment of Allen's Landing. 2001.
3146-2 Environmental Defense, Austin, TX, $10,000. For program support for environmental protection projects in Texas. 2001.
3146-3 Houston Arboretum and Nature Center, Houston, TX, $10,000. For operating support for educational and environmental programs. 2001.
3146-4 Lady Bird Johnson Wildflower Center, Austin, TX, $10,000. For capital support to purchase fencing, gates, and security cameras. 2001.
3146-5 Texas Tech University Foundation, College of Agricultural Sciences and Natural Resources, Lubbock, TX, $50,000. For endowed professorship. 2001.
3146-6 Trees for Houston, Houston, TX, $10,000. For program support for Trees for Schools project. 2001.
3146-7 Trees for Houston, Houston, TX, $10,000. For expansion of Trees for Schools project. 2001.

3147
The Rosewood Foundation
500 Crescent Ct., Ste. 300
Dallas, TX 75201

Established in 2000 in TX.
Donor(s): The Rosewood Corp.
Grantmaker type: Independent foundation
Financial data (yr. ended 12/31/00): Assets,
$21,686 (M); gifts received, $398,163;
expenditures, $386,192; qualifying distributions,
$382,086; giving activities include $383,903 for
77 grants (high: $30,000; low: $25).
Fields of interest: Arts; Education; Environment;
Human services; Children/youth, services.
Limitations: Applications not accepted. Giving
primarily in TX. No grants to individuals.
Application information: Contributes only to
pre-selected organizations.
Officers and Trustees:* David K. Sands,* Pres.;
Don W. Crisp,* V.P.; Patrick B. Sands,* Secy.;
Laurie Sands Harrison,* Treas.; Schuyler B.
Marshall IV; J.B. Sands; Stephen H. Sands.
EIN: 752827470

3148
The Ross Foundation
P.O. Box 78
2121 Kirby Dr.
Houston, TX 77019
Contact: Ellen G. Ross, Dir.

Established in 1989 in TX.
Donor(s): David Ross III, Florence Shutts Ross.‡
Grantmaker type: Independent foundation
Financial data (yr. ended 12/31/02): Assets,
$839,204 (M); expenditures, $137,385;
qualifying distributions, $132,834; giving
activities include $131,120 for 40 grants (high:
$60,000; low: $150).
Purpose and activities: Giving to public service
institutes and agencies for education, the arts
and culture.
Fields of interest: Arts; Education; Animal
welfare; Health care; Human services.
Limitations: Applications not accepted. Giving
primarily in MA and TX. No grants to
individuals.
Application information: Contributes only to
pre-selected organizations.
Directors: David Ross III; David Ross IV; Ellen
G. Ross.
EIN: 760286746

3149
The Salzman-Medica Foundation
8613 Mendocino Dr.
Austin, TX 78735-1420

Established in 1998 in TX.
Donor(s): John K. Medica, Megan S. Medica.
Grantmaker type: Independent foundation
Financial data (yr. ended 12/31/02): Assets,
$258,105 (M); expenditures, $491,873;
qualifying distributions, $487,417; giving
activities include $487,500 for 11 grants (high:
$250,000; low: $2,500).
Fields of interest: Higher education; College;
University; Animal welfare; Human services.
Limitations: Applications not accepted. Giving
on a national basis. No grants to individuals.

Application information: Contributes only to
pre-selected organizations.
Directors: Angela Asbury; John K. Medica;
Megan S. Medica.
EIN: 742881198

3150
Earl C. Sams Foundation, Inc.
101 N. Shoreline Dr., Ste. 602
Corpus Christi, TX 78401 (361) 888-6485
Contact: Bruce S. Hawn, Pres.
FAX: (361) 884-4241

Incorporated in 1946 in NY; reincorporated in
1988 in TX.
Donor(s): Earl C. Sams.‡
Grantmaker type: Independent foundation
Financial data (yr. ended 12/31/02): Assets,
$24,083,496 (M); expenditures, $1,602,099;
qualifying distributions, $1,387,194; giving
activities include $1,160,074 for 60 grants
(high: $120,000; low: $2,000).
Purpose and activities: Giving support for health
care, youth and community development, and
the environment.
Fields of interest: Environment; Health care;
Children/youth, services; Community
development.
Types of support: General/operating support;
Continuing support; Annual campaigns;
Building/renovation; Equipment; Program
development; In-kind gifts; Matching/challenge
support.
Limitations: Giving primarily in southern TX. No
grants to individuals.
Application information: Application form not
required.
  Initial approach: Proposal
  Copies of proposal: 1
  Deadline(s): 4 weeks prior to board meeting
  Board meeting date(s): Quarterly
Officers and Directors:* Susan Hawn Yuras,*
Chair. and V.P.; Bruce Sams Hawn,* C.E.O. and
Pres.; Susan Ohnmacht, Secy.-Treas.; Nancy E.
Hawn.
Number of staff: 4 full-time professional.
EIN: 741463151

3151
Samsung Semiconductor, Inc. Corporate Giving Program
c/o Public Rels. Dept.
12100 Samsung Blvd.
Austin, TX 78754
URL: http://www.sas.samsung.com/
philanthropy.htm

Grantmaker type: Corporate giving program
Purpose and activities: Samsung Semiconductor
makes charitable contributions to nonprofit
organizations involved with arts and culture,
education, the environment, and health and
human services. Support is given primarily in
the Austin, Texas, area.
Fields of interest: Arts; Education; Environment;
Health care; Human services.
Types of support: Program development;
Conferences/seminars; Employee volunteer
services; Sponsorships.
Limitations: Giving primarily in the Austin, TX,
area. No support for organizations not of direct
benefit to the entire community, political or

lobbying organizations, disease-specific
organizations, parent-supported organizations,
or private foundations. No grants to individuals,
or for capital campaigns or endowments or
general operating support.
Application information: Support is limited to 1
contribution per organization during any given
year. An application form is available online. A
site visit may be requested. Multi-year funding is
not automatic. Telephone calls are not
encouraged. Application form required.
  Initial approach: Complete online application
  form
  Copies of proposal: 1
  Deadline(s): Jan. 10, Apr. 10, July 10, and
  Oct. 10
  Final notification: Feb. 14, May 15, Aug. 14,
  and Nov. 14

3152
San Antonio Area Foundation
110 Broadway, Ste. 230
San Antonio, TX 78205 (210) 225-2243
Contact: Clarence R. "Reggie" Williams, C.E.O.
FAX: (210) 225-1980; E-mail: gift@saafdn.org;
URL: http://www.saafdn.org

Established in 1964 in TX.
Grantmaker type: Community foundation
Financial data (yr. ended 12/31/01): Assets,
$106,312,000 (M); gifts received, $13,846,803;
expenditures, $1,778,887; giving activities
include $7,706,229 for grants (average:
$250–$250,000).
Purpose and activities: The foundation
administers donor-advised funds.
Fields of interest: Media/communications;
Visual arts; Museums; Performing arts; Dance;
Theater; Historic preservation/historical
societies; Arts; Education, research; Early
childhood education; Child development,
education; Higher education; Medical
school/education; Nursing school/education;
Adult/continuing education; Adult
education—literacy, basic skills & GED;
Reading; Education; Natural resources;
Environment; Animal welfare; Animals/wildlife,
preservation/protection; Family planning;
Medical care, rehabilitation; Health care;
Substance abuse, services; Health organizations,
association; Cancer; Heart & circulatory
diseases; AIDS; Alcoholism; Medical research,
institute; Cancer research; Heart & circulatory
research; AIDS research; Domestic violence;
Human services; Children/youth, services; Child
development, services; Family services;
Hospices; Aging, centers/services; Homeless,
human services; Community development;
Computer science; Biological sciences;
Government/public administration; Roman
Catholic agencies & churches; Religion;
Minorities; African Americans/Blacks;
Hispanics/Latinos; Disabled; Aging; Women;
Economically disadvantaged; Homeless.
Types of support: General/operating support;
Continuing support; Annual campaigns; Capital
campaigns; Building/renovation; Equipment;
Land acquisition; Emergency funds; Program
development; Professorships; Publication; Seed
money; Curriculum development; Internship
funds; Scholarship funds; Research;
Program-related investments/loans;

Scholarships—to individuals;
Matching/challenge support.
Limitations: Giving limited to Bexar County, TX,
and surrounding counties, except when
otherwise specified by donor. No support for
individual churches, congregations, or parishes
(unless projects benefit community at large). No
grants to individuals (except for designated
scholarship funds), or for debt reduction, deficit
financing, endowment funds, or salaries for
full-time regular employees.
Publications: Application guidelines, Annual
report, Financial statement, Grants list,
Informational brochure, Newsletter.
Application information: Scholarship
applications must be submitted to Bexar County
Scholarship Clearinghouse, unless specifically
designated by donor. Application form required.
   Initial approach: Letter or telephone
      requesting grant guidelines information
   Copies of proposal: 11
   Deadline(s): Nov. 1
   Board meeting date(s): Bimonthly
   Final notification: May
Officers and Directors:* Clarence R. "Reggie"
Williams, C.E.O. and Exec. Dir.; Marvin Forland,
M.D.,* Pres.; Laura McNutt,* V.P.; Barbara
Gentry,* Secy.; Raymond Carvajal,* Treas.; Janet
Irwine, C.F.O.; John E. Banks, Jr.; Michael D.
Beldon; John Brazil, Ph.D.; Rita Elizondo; Cathy
Obriotti Green; Claudia Ladensohn; Joe Linson;
Sherman P. Macdaniel; Lissa Martinez; Ommy
Strauch; Pat L. Wilson; Mollie Zachry.
Trustee Banks: Broadway National Bank;
JPMorgan Chase Bank; Bank of America; Merrill
Lynch Trust Co.; Wells Fargo Bank, N.A.; Frost
National Bank; Bank One, N.A.; UBS
PaineWebber Inc.
Number of staff: 10 full-time professional; 1
part-time professional.
EIN: 746065414

3153
Sarah M. & Charles E. Seay Charitable Trust

300 Crescent Ct., Ste. 1370
Dallas, TX   75201-6923

Established in 1983 in TX.
Donor(s): Charles E. Seay, Sarah M. Seay.
Grantmaker type: Independent foundation
Financial data (yr. ended 12/31/02): Assets,
$3,878,130 (M); expenditures, $1,151,866;
qualifying distributions, $1,146,674; giving
activities include $1,146,674 for 24 grants (high:
$500,000; low: $20).
Purpose and activities: Support primarily for
cultural organizations, and animal welfare.
Fields of interest: Arts; Education; Animal
welfare; Human services; Children/youth,
services; Christian agencies & churches.
Types of support: Building/renovation;
Endowments; Professorships.
Limitations: Applications not accepted. Giving
primarily in TX, with emphasis on Dallas. No
grants to individuals.
Application information: Contributes only to
pre-selected organizations. Unsolicited requests
for funds not considered.
Trustees: Truman Kemper; Charles E. Seay;
Charles E. Seay, Jr.; Sarah M. Seay; Stephen M.
Seay.
EIN: 751894505

3154
Shell Oil Company Contributions Program

P.O. Box 2463
Houston, TX   77252
Contact: Dennis Winkler, Mgr., Public Affairs,
Houston

Grantmaker type: Corporate giving program
Financial data (yr. ended 12/31/00): Total giving,
$2,480,000; giving activities include
$2,480,000 for 480 grants (high: $100,000; low:
$250; average: $1,000–$10,000).
Purpose and activities: As a complement to its
foundation, Shell also makes charitable
contributions to nonprofit organizations directly.
Support is given on a national basis.
Fields of interest: Environment.
Types of support: Conferences/seminars;
Scholarship funds; Employee volunteer services;
Sponsorships.
Limitations: Giving on a national basis,
particularly in areas of company operations,
including Houston, TX; giving also to national
organizations.
Application information: The Corporate Affairs
Department handles giving. A contributions
committee reviews all requests. Application
form not required.
   Initial approach: Proposal to nearest company
      facility
   Copies of proposal: 1
   Board meeting date(s): Weekly
   Final notification: Following review

3155
Shell Oil Company Foundation ▼

(formerly Shell Companies Foundation, Inc.)
910 Louisiana, Ste. 4137
1 Shell Plz., P.O. Box 2999
Houston, TX   77252   (713) 241-4480
Contact: Betty Lynn McHam, V.P.
FAX: (713) 241-3329; E-mail:
socfoundation@shellus.com; Application
Address: National Merit Scholarship Corp., 1
American Plz., Evanston, IL 60201; Scholarship
Mgmt. Sucs., P.O. Box 297, St. Peter, MN
56082; URL: http://www.countonshell.com/
community/involvement/shell_foundation.html

Incorporated in 1953 in NY.
Donor(s): Shell Oil Co., and other participating
companies.
Grantmaker type: Company-sponsored
foundation
Financial data (yr. ended 12/31/02): Assets,
$52,092,395 (M); gifts received, $20,000,000;
expenditures, $27,305,087; qualifying
distributions, $25,714,148; giving activities
include $23,093,281 for 716+ grants (high:
$3,650,000; average: $10,000–$50,000) and
$2,620,086 for employee matching gifts.
Purpose and activities: Preferred areas of giving
are education, civic and public policy,
community involvement, culture and the arts,
environment, and health and human services.
About 48 percent of the budget is channeled
through a number of planned programs that
provide student aid, faculty development, basic
research grants, departmental grants and to a
few national educational organizations. Main
interests in education are math, engineering,
science, and business. The remaining funds are
paid to a limited number of national

organizations concerned with a broad range of
needs and, to a greater extent, to local
organizations in communities where significant
numbers of Shell employees reside.
Fields of interest: Visual arts; Museums;
Performing arts; Dance; Theater; Music; Arts;
Education, association; Elementary
school/education; Secondary school/education;
Higher education; Business school/education;
Law school/education; Engineering
school/education; Libraries/library science;
Education; Natural resources; Energy;
Environment; Animals/wildlife,
preservation/protection; Hospitals (general);
Health care; Substance abuse, services; Health
organizations, association; Cancer; Medical
research, institute; Cancer research; Youth
development, citizenship; Human services;
Children/youth, services; Hospices;
Minorities/immigrants, centers/services;
Business/industry; Federated giving programs;
Chemistry; Mathematics;
Engineering/technology; Computer science;
Engineering; Science; Economics; Public policy,
research; Government/public administration;
Public affairs, citizen participation; Minorities;
Disabled; Economically disadvantaged.
Types of support: General/operating support;
Continuing support; Annual campaigns; Capital
campaigns; Program development;
Professorships; Publication; Curriculum
development; Fellowships; Scholarship funds;
Research; Consulting services; Employee
matching gifts; Matching/challenge support.
Limitations: Giving primarily in areas of
company operations in the U.S. No support for
special requests of colleges, universities, and
college fundraising associations, or hospital
operating expenses. No grants to individuals, or
for endowment funds, capital campaigns of
national organizations, or development funds;
no in-kind or product contributions; no loans.
Publications: Corporate giving report (including
application guidelines).
Application information: See foundation's Web
site for information regarding new initiatives and
activities. Application form not required.
   Initial approach: Letter
   Copies of proposal: 1
   Deadline(s): Sept. before the year for which
      organization requires funding
   Board meeting date(s): Mar. and Dec.
   Final notification: 1 month
Officers and Directors:* R.J. Routs,* Pres.; Betty
Lynn McHam, V.P.; Pat Loman, Secy.; Greg
Hullinger, Treas.; R.J. Decyk; P.M. Dreckman;
J.R. Eagan; E.F. Gibson; M.F. Keeth; C.A.
Lamboley; A.Y. Noojin; R.M. Restucci.
Number of staff: 7.
EIN: 136066583
**Recent environmental and animal welfare
grants:**
3155-1 Audubon Nature Institute, New Orleans,
LA, $35,000. 2001.
3155-2 Audubon Nature Institute, Audubon
Louisiana Nature Center, New Orleans, LA,
$25,000. 2001.
3155-3 Buffalo Bayou Partnership, Houston, TX,
$25,000. 2001.
3155-4 Earthwatch Expeditions, Maynard, MA,
$13,000. 2001.
3155-5 Georgia Conservancy, Atlanta, GA,
$10,000. 2001.

3155-6 Houston Arboretum and Nature Center, Houston, TX, $10,000. 2001.

3155-7 Izaak Walton League of America, Gaithersburg, MD, $10,000. 2001.

3155-8 Marine Environmental Sciences Consortium, Dauphin Island, AL, $12,500. 2001.

3155-9 Mickey Leland National Urban Air Toxics Research Center, Houston, TX, $20,000. 2001.

3155-10 Mid-City Green Project, New Orleans, LA, $25,000. 2001.

3155-11 National Fish and Wildlife Foundation, DC, $1,000,000. 2001.

3155-12 National Wildlife Federation, Reston, VA, $250,000. 2001.

3155-13 Nature Conservancy, Arlington, VA, $250,000. 2001.

3155-14 Nature Conservancy, Arlington, VA, $12,500. 2001.

3155-15 Northlake Nature Center, Covington, LA, $25,000. 2001.

3155-16 Offshore Rig Museum, Houston, TX, $22,000. 2001.

3155-17 Resources for the Future, DC, $10,000. 2001.

3155-18 South Main Center Association, Houston, TX, $15,000. 2001.

3155-19 Student Conservation Association, Charlestown, NH, $10,000. 2001.

3155-20 Zoological Society of Houston, Houston, TX, $200,000. 2001.

3156
Shiloff Family Foundation

c/o Robert M. Shiloff
4171 N. Mesa St., Ste. B-100
El Paso, TX 79902

Established in 1994 in TX.
Grantmaker type: Independent foundation
Financial data (yr. ended 12/31/02): Assets, $2,705,672 (M); expenditures, $196,834; qualifying distributions, $172,998; giving activities include $173,500 for 46 grants (high: $56,000; low: $500).
Purpose and activities: Giving primarily for the arts, wildlife preservation, and human services.
Fields of interest: Arts; Education; Zoos/zoological societies; Human services.
Limitations: Applications not accepted. Giving primarily in the El Paso, TX, area. No grants to individuals.
Application information: Contributes only to pre-selected organizations. Unsolicited requests for funds not accepted.
Officers and Directors:* Robert M. Shiloff,* Pres.; Robyn Shiloff Pragner, V.P.; Bryan Shiloff, V.P.; Stuart Shiloff, V.P.; Martin N. Colton, Secy.; Sara P. Shiloff.
EIN: 742691141

3157
The Virginia and L. E. Simmons Family Foundation

6600 JPMorgan Chase Twr.
Houston, TX 77002-3007

Established in 1994 in TX.
Donor(s): L.E. Simmons, Virginia W. Simmons.
Grantmaker type: Independent foundation

Financial data (yr. ended 12/31/02): Assets, $4,930,422 (M); gifts received, $1,986,233; expenditures, $285,870; qualifying distributions, $275,661; giving activities include $275,842 for 46 grants (high: $50,000; low: $50).
Purpose and activities: Giving for religion, art and culture organizations, education, and for youth and medical associations.
Fields of interest: Museums (ethnic/folk arts); Arts; Education; Environment; Hospitals (general); Health organizations, association; Pediatrics; Cancer research; Human services; Family services; Community development, women's clubs; Foundations (private grantmaking); Federated giving programs; Christian agencies & churches.
Limitations: Applications not accepted. Giving primarily in TX. No grants to individuals.
Application information: Contributes only to pre-selected organizations.
Officers: L.E. Simmons, Pres.; Virginia W. Simmons, V.P.; Anthony F. Deluca, Secy.
EIN: 760453177

3158
James C. and Norma I. Smith Foundation

P.O. Box 190369
Dallas, TX 75219

Established in 1994 in IL and TX.
Grantmaker type: Operating foundation
Financial data (yr. ended 11/30/02): Assets, $4,583,384 (M); expenditures, $265,046; qualifying distributions, $252,635; giving activities include $255,000 for 14 grants (high: $100,000; low: $5,000).
Purpose and activities: Giving for medical organizations, environmental organizations, international medical services, women and children services, and for relief services.
Fields of interest: Television; Museums (art); University; Environment; Human services; Children, services; Women, centers/services.
Limitations: Applications not accepted. Giving primarily in AZ. No grants to individuals.
Application information: Contributes only to pre-selected organizations.
Officers and Directors:* James C. Smith,* Pres.; Norma I. Smith,* Treas.; Joseph E. Whitters.
EIN: 363994810

3159
Ralph L. Smith Foundation

c/o Bank of America
P.O. Box 831041
Dallas, TX 75283-1041
Application address: c/o David P. Ross, Sr. V.P., Bank of America, 1200 Main St., Kansas City, MO 64105, tel.: (816) 979-7481

Trust established in 1952 in MO.
Donor(s): Harriet T. Smith,‡ Ralph L. Smith.‡
Grantmaker type: Independent foundation
Financial data (yr. ended 12/31/02): Assets, $19,485,866 (M); expenditures, $1,331,187; qualifying distributions, $1,185,611; giving activities include $1,181,510 for 160 grants (high: $50,000; low: $500).
Fields of interest: Arts; Higher education; Education; Natural resources; Health care; Human services; Children/youth, services; Women, centers/services; Community

development, neighborhood development; Women.
Limitations: Giving primarily in the metropolitan Kansas City, MO, area. No grants to individuals.
Application information: Applications for grants will not be acknowledged.
Initial approach: Telephone followed by 3-page letter
Copies of proposal: 1
Deadline(s): None
Board meeting date(s): Quarterly
Final notification: 2 months
Managers: Neil T. Dauthat; Harriet H. Dennison; E.M. Douthat III; Paul N. Douthat; Ralph L. Smith.
Trustee Bank: Bank of America.
EIN: 446008508

3160
Marguerite Sours Foundation

P.O. Box 1419
Rockport, TX 78381-1419
Contact: William G. Walston Sr., Pres.
Application address: 1021 N. Hwy. 35, Rockport, TX 78382

Established around 1986.
Grantmaker type: Independent foundation
Financial data (yr. ended 12/31/00): Assets, $3,430,269 (M); expenditures, $201,800; qualifying distributions, $172,200; giving activities include $162,220 for grants (high: $27,000).
Fields of interest: Education; Zoos/zoological societies; Hospitals (general); Cancer; Recreation, community facilities; Human services; Salvation Army; Christian agencies & churches.
Types of support: General/operating support; Scholarship funds.
Limitations: Giving primarily in KS and TX.
Application information:
Initial approach: Letter
Deadline(s): None
Officers: William G. Walston, Sr., Pres.; Dale Stuckey, V.P.; Jackie Bauer, Secy.
EIN: 742425445

3161
Southern Union Company Contributions Program

400 W. 15th St.
Austin, TX 78701 (512) 477-5852
Contact: Bruce Henderson, Asst. General Counsel

Grantmaker type: Corporate giving program
Purpose and activities: Southern Union makes charitable contributions to nonprofit organizations involved with arts and culture, education, the environment, health and human services, minorities, and on a case by case basis. Support is given primarily in areas of company operations.
Fields of interest: Arts; Education; Environment; Health care; Human services; General charitable giving; Minorities.
Types of support: General/operating support; Employee volunteer services; Sponsorships; In-kind gifts.

Limitations: Giving primarily in areas of company operations.
Application information: Application form not required.
  Initial approach: Proposal to headquarters
  Copies of proposal: 1
  Final notification: Following review

3162
Southwest Medical Institute, Inc.
10300 N. Central Expwy., No. 230
Dallas, TX 75231

Donor(s): Kevin Gill.
Grantmaker type: Independent foundation
Financial data (yr. ended 12/31/00): Assets, $0 (M); gifts received, $584,234; expenditures, $157,637; qualifying distributions, $102,310; giving activities include $82,456 for 4 grants (high: $44,500; low: $1,214) and $19,854 for 1 grant to an individual.
Fields of interest: Environment; Medical research, institute.
Types of support: General/operating support.
Limitations: Giving primarily in GA and TX.
Officers: Kevin Gill, M.D., Pres.; John F. Lown, V.P.
EIN: 752281441

3163
Sterling Chemicals, Inc. Corporate Giving Program
1200 Smith St.
Houston, TX 77002 (713) 650-3700
Contact: Richard K. Crump, C.E.O.

Grantmaker type: Corporate giving program
Purpose and activities: Sterling makes charitable contributions to nonprofit organizations involved with waste management, the environment, safety education, and children and youth. Support is given primarily in areas of company operations.
Fields of interest: Waste management; Environment; Safety, education; Children/youth, services.
Types of support: General/operating support; Employee volunteer services.
Limitations: Giving primarily in areas of company operations.
Application information: Application form not required.
  Initial approach: Proposal to headquarters
  Deadline(s): None

3164
Sterling-Turner Foundation
(formerly Turner Charitable Foundation)
815 Walker St., Ste. 1543
Houston, TX 77002-5724 (713) 237-1117
Contact: Patricia Moser, Exec. Asst.
FAX: (713) 223-4638; E-mail: eyvonne@sterlingturnerfoundation.org; URL: http://sterlingturnerfoundation.org

Incorporated in 1960 in TX.
Donor(s): Isla Carroll Turner,‡ P.E. Turner.‡
Grantmaker type: Independent foundation
Financial data (yr. ended 12/31/02): Assets, $37,375,886 (M); expenditures, $2,689,753;

qualifying distributions, $2,570,749; giving activities include $2,497,000 for 100 grants (high: $200,000; low: $500; average: $5,000–$45,000).
Purpose and activities: Giving for higher and secondary education, social services, youth, the elderly, fine and performing arts groups and other cultural programs, Catholic, Jewish, and Protestant church support and religious programs, hospitals, health services, AIDS research, hospices, programs for women and children, minorities, the homeless, the handicapped, urban and community development, civic and urban affairs, libraries, and conservation programs.
Fields of interest: Visual arts; Museums; Performing arts; Theater; Historic preservation/historical societies; Arts, association; Education, research; Education, fund raising; Elementary/secondary education; Child development, education; Secondary school/education; Higher education; Adult education—literacy, basic skills & GED; Libraries/library science; Reading; Natural resources; Hospitals (general); Medical care, rehabilitation; Health care; Substance abuse, services; Mental health/crisis services; Cancer; Heart & circulatory diseases; AIDS; Cancer research; Heart & circulatory research; AIDS research; Domestic violence; Food services; Recreation; Children/youth, services; Child development, services; Family services; Hospices; Minorities/immigrants, centers/services; Homeless, human services; Community development, business promotion; Community development; Protestant agencies & churches; Roman Catholic agencies & churches; Jewish agencies & temples; Religion; Minorities; African Americans/Blacks; Hispanics/Latinos; Aging; Women; People with AIDS (PWAs); Homeless.
Types of support: General/operating support; Continuing support; Annual campaigns; Capital campaigns; Building/renovation; Equipment; Land acquisition; Endowments; Debt reduction; Emergency funds; Program development; Conferences/seminars; Professorships; Publication; Seed money; Curriculum development; Fellowships; Scholarship funds; Research; Matching/challenge support.
Limitations: Giving limited to TX. No grants to individuals.
Publications: Application guidelines, Annual report (including application guidelines).
Application information: Guidelines can be found on Web site. Application form required.
  Initial approach: On-line application
  Copies of proposal: 1
  Deadline(s): Mar. 1 at 5:00 p.m.
  Board meeting date(s): First Tues. in Apr.
Officers and Trustees:* T.R. Reckling III,* Pres.; Bert F. Winston, Jr.,* V.P.; Christiana R. McConn,* Secy.; Isla C. Reckling,* Treas.; Eyvonne Moser, Exec. Dir.; Thomas E. Berry; Carroll R. Goodman; Chaille W. Hawkins; James S. Reckling; John B. Reckling; Stephen M. Reckling; T.R. "Cliff" Reckling IV; Thomas K. Reckling; Blake W. Winston; L. David Winston; Bert F. Winston III.
Number of staff: 2 full-time professional.
EIN: 741460482

3165
The Keith and Mattie Stevenson Foundation
c/o Kanaly Trust Co.
4550 Post Oak Place Dr., Ste. 139
Houston, TX 77027
Contact: David Doll

Established in 1992 in TX.
Donor(s): Keith T. Stevenson, Mattie Stevenson.
Grantmaker type: Independent foundation
Financial data (yr. ended 12/31/01): Assets, $2,871,083 (M); expenditures, $191,667; qualifying distributions, $164,191; giving activities include $165,000 for 20 grants (high: $30,000; low: $1,000).
Purpose and activities: Giving for wildlife conservation, higher education, animal welfare and protection, and health services.
Fields of interest: Higher education; Environment; Animal welfare; Children/youth, services; Federated giving programs.
Types of support: General/operating support.
Limitations: Giving primarily in TX. No grants to individuals.
Application information: Application form not required.
  Deadline(s): None
Trustees: Keith T. Stevenson; Mattie Stevenson; Kanaly Trust Co.
EIN: 760366599

3166
Still Water Foundation
3939 Bee Caves, Ste. C-100
Austin, TX 78746 (512) 328-1184
Contact: Patti O'Meara, Managing Agent
FAX: (512) 327-1940; E-mail: padminc@aol.com

Established in 1982 in NM.
Donor(s): Julia Matthews Wilkinson.
Grantmaker type: Independent foundation
Financial data (yr. ended 12/31/02): Assets, $2,977,169 (M); expenditures, $337,586; qualifying distributions, $299,228; giving activities include $269,882 for 27 grants (high: $44,300; low: $2,000; average: $5,000–$25,000).
Purpose and activities: Giving primarily in the areas of education, the arts, the environment, and spirituality.
Fields of interest: Multipurpose centers/programs; Museums; Higher education; Education; Environment; Religion.
Types of support: General/operating support; Annual campaigns; Capital campaigns; Building/renovation; Endowments; Seed money; Curriculum development; Scholarship funds; Matching/challenge support.
Limitations: Applications not accepted. Giving primarily in TX. No grants to individuals.
Application information: The foundation has instituted a self-directed grantmaking policy, whereby only those organizations invited to submit proposals will be reviewed. Unsolicited requests for funds not accepted.
  Board meeting date(s): Quarterly
Directors: James Flieller; Duncan E. Osborne; Julia Matthews Wilkinson.
Number of staff: 1 part-time professional.
EIN: 850307646

3167
The Summerlee Foundation
5956 Sherry Ln., Ste. 610
Dallas, TX 75225-8025 (214) 363-9000
Contact: Melanie Lambert, V.P., for animal welfare, or John W. Crain, V.P., for Texas history
FAX: (214) 363-1941; E-mail: info@summerlee.org; URL: http://www.summerlee.org/

Established in 1988 in TX.
Donor(s): Annie Lee Roberts.‡
Grantmaker type: Independent foundation
Financial data (yr. ended 06/30/01): Assets, $52,188,414 (M); expenditures, $3,072,176; qualifying distributions, $2,470,288; giving activities include $1,804,225 for 129 grants (high: $125,000; low: $887; average: $1,000–$25,000).
Purpose and activities: Giving limited to 1) the alleviation of pain and suffering and the prevention of cruelty to animals; and 2) for the study, promotion, preservation, and documentation of all facets of TX history.
Fields of interest: History/archaeology; Historic preservation/historical societies; Animal welfare; Animals/wildlife, preservation/protection.
Types of support: Capital campaigns; Building/renovation; Equipment; Land acquisition; Endowments; Emergency funds; Program development; Conferences/seminars; Publication; Seed money; Curriculum development; Fellowships; Internship funds; Research; Technical assistance; Matching/challenge support.
Limitations: Giving primarily in TX. No support for religious purposes. No grants to individuals.
Publications: Application guidelines, Biennial report (including application guidelines), Grants list.
Application information: Application form not required.
   Initial approach: Letter
   Copies of proposal: 1
   Deadline(s): June, May, July, and Sept.
   Board meeting date(s): Quarterly
Officers and Directors:* Hon. David D. Jackson,* Pres.; Melanie Lambert,* V.P. and Treas.; John W. Crain,* V.P.; Lynne Starnes, Secy.; Ron Tyler*.
Number of staff: 3 full-time professional; 1 full-time support.
EIN: 752252355

3168
David L. Tandy Foundation
P.O. Box 126377
Fort Worth, TX 76126
Contact: Erwin C. Whitney, Secy.
Application address: P.O. Box 101477, Fort Worth, TX 76185-1477

Established in 1968 in TX.
Grantmaker type: Independent foundation
Financial data (yr. ended 05/31/02): Assets, $4,104,201 (M); expenditures, $270,574; qualifying distributions, $268,248; giving activities include $267,100 for 45 grants (high: $20,000; low: $1,000).
Purpose and activities: Giving primarily for education and human and children's services.
Fields of interest: Museums; Performing arts; Arts; University; Education; Zoos/zoological societies; Hospitals (general); Health care; Cancer; Brain disorders; Food services; Boys & girls clubs; Big Brothers/Big Sisters; Youth development, business; Youth development; Human services; Family services; Women, centers/services; Protestant agencies & churches.
Limitations: Giving primarily in TX, with emphasis on Fort Worth. No grants to individuals.
Application information:
   Initial approach: Letter
   Deadline(s): None
   Board meeting date(s): 2nd Mon. in July
Officers and Directors:* E.E. Duemke,* Pres.; Bill R. Roland,* V.P. and Treas.; A.R. Tandy, V.P.; Mrs. E.C. Whitney,* V.P.; Paul N. Whitney, V.P.; T.L. Whitney, V.P.; Erwin C. Whitney, Secy.
Number of staff: None.
EIN: 756083140

3169
The Tapeats Fund
P.O. Box 1063
Houston, TX 77251 (713) 830-3400
Contact: Patricia N. Lewis, Exec. Dir.

Established in 1993 in TX.
Donor(s): Robert H. Graham, Laurel A.W. Graham.
Grantmaker type: Independent foundation
Financial data (yr. ended 12/31/02): Assets, $12,133,417 (M); expenditures, $878,082; qualifying distributions, $733,631; giving activities include $659,329 for 53 grants (high: $30,000; low: $2,500).
Purpose and activities: Support for organizations which benefit the health, education, and general welfare of children; support also for zoos, animal shelters and wildlife associations, and organizations which preserve or enrich the environment; and for civic revitalization in Houston, TX.
Fields of interest: Education; Environment; Animals/wildlife; Health care; Human services; Children/youth, services; Federated giving programs.
Types of support: General/operating support; Continuing support; Annual campaigns; Capital campaigns; Building/renovation; Equipment.
Limitations: Giving primarily in TX, with emphasis on Houston.
Publications: Application guidelines.
Application information: Application form not required.
   Initial approach: Letter
   Copies of proposal: 1
   Deadline(s): None
   Board meeting date(s): 4th quarter
Officers: Robert H. Graham, Pres.; Laurel A.W. Graham, Exec. V.P.; David R. Graham, V.P.
Trustee: Whitney Laurel Graham.
Number of staff: 6 full-time support.
EIN: 760412011

3170
T. L. L. Temple Foundation ▼
109 Temple Blvd., Ste. 300
Lufkin, TX 75901 (936) 639-5197
Contact: A. Wayne Corely, Exec. Dir.

Trust established in 1962 in TX.
Donor(s): Georgie T. Munz,‡ Katherine S. Temple.‡
Grantmaker type: Independent foundation
Financial data (yr. ended 11/30/02): Assets, $284,997,443 (M); expenditures, $15,149,442; qualifying distributions, $14,215,839; giving activities include $14,081,293 for 132 grants (high: $2,500,000; low: $50; average: $5,000–$60,000).
Purpose and activities: Support for education, health, and community and social services; support also for civic affairs and cultural programs.
Fields of interest: Arts; Elementary school/education; Higher education; Adult/continuing education; Education; Animal welfare; Hospitals (general); Medical care, rehabilitation; Health care; Substance abuse, services; Mental health/crisis services; Human services; Hospices; Community development; Government/public administration; Economically disadvantaged.
Types of support: General/operating support; Capital campaigns; Building/renovation; Equipment; Emergency funds; Program development; Scholarship funds; Research; Program-related investments/loans; Employee matching gifts; Matching/challenge support.
Limitations: Giving primarily in counties in TX constituting the East Texas Pine Timber Belt. No support for private foundations. No grants to individuals, or for deficit financing.
Publications: Application guidelines, Program policy statement.
Application information: Application form required.
   Initial approach: Letter
   Copies of proposal: 1
   Deadline(s): None
   Board meeting date(s): As required
   Final notification: 2-4 months
Officers and Trustees:* Arthur Temple III,* Chair.; Arthur Temple,* Chair. Emeritus; M.F. Zeagler, Cont.; A. Wayne Corley, Exec. Dir.; Ward R. Burke; Phillip M. Leach; H.J. Shands III; W. Temple Webber, Jr.; W. Temple Webber III.
Number of staff: 4 full-time professional; 2 part-time professional; 1 full-time support; 1 part-time support.
EIN: 756037406
Recent environmental and animal welfare grants:
3170-1 Angelina Beautiful/Clean, Lufkin, TX, $20,000. For general support. 2002.
3170-2 Conservation Fund, Arlington, VA, $10,000. For land in Angelina and Polk counties. 2002.
3170-3 Humane Society of Angelina County, Lufkin, TX, $40,000. For general support. 2002.
3170-4 Huntington Independent School District, Huntington, TX, $22,650. To complete Greenhouse. 2002.
3170-5 Nacogdoches, City of, Nacogdoches, TX, $125,000. To construct animal control facility. 2002.
3170-6 Stephen F. Austin State University, Nacogdoches, TX, $2,000,000. For Temple College of Forestry. 2002.
3170-7 Texas Garden Clubs, San Augustine, TX, $10,000. For improvements to multi-purpose facility. 2002.

3171
Tesoro Petroleum Corporation Contributions Program

300 Concord Plaza Dr.
San Antonio, TX 78216 (210) 283-2864
Contact: Carrol Kurtzman, Admin. Asst.
URL: http://www.tesoropetroleum.com/
community.html

Grantmaker type: Corporate giving program
Purpose and activities: Tesoro makes charitable contributions to nonprofit organizations involved with arts and culture, education, the environment, health, disease, youth development, and community development. Support is given on a national basis.
Fields of interest: Arts; Education; Environment; Health care; Health organizations; Youth development; Community development.
Types of support: General/operating support; Scholarship funds; Employee volunteer services; Sponsorships; Employee matching gifts; Employee-related scholarships; In-kind gifts.
Limitations: Giving on a national basis in areas of company operations, with emphasis on San Antonio, TX. No grants to individuals.
Application information: The Corporate Relations Department handles giving. A contributions committee reviews all requests. Application form not required.
    Initial approach: Mail or E-mail proposal to headquarters
    Copies of proposal: 1
    Deadline(s): None
    Board meeting date(s): Monthly
    Final notification: Following review if approved
Number of staff: 1.

3172
Texas Instruments Foundation ▼

7839 Churchill Way
Dallas, TX 75251 (972) 917-4505
Contact: Ann F. Minnis, Grants Admin.
Application address: P.O. Box 650311, M.S. 3906, Dallas, TX 75265; URL: http://
www.ti.com/corp/docs/company/citizen/
foundation/index.shtml

Trust established in 1951 in TX; incorporated in 1964.
Donor(s): Texas Instruments Inc., and wholly-owned subsidiaries.
Grantmaker type: Company-sponsored foundation
Financial data (yr. ended 12/31/01): Assets, $23,764,464 (M); expenditures, $8,196,284; qualifying distributions, $6,886,599; giving activities include $5,421,066 for 60 grants (high: $1,300,000; low: $1,000; average: $1,000–$50,000), $1,378,519 for employee matching gifts and $93,983 for foundation-administered programs.
Purpose and activities: Giving largely for community funds; grants also for higher and secondary education, including employee matching gifts, hospitals, youth agencies, and cultural programs; Founders' Prize awarded for outstanding achievement in the physical, health, or management sciences, or mathematics.
Fields of interest: Arts; Early childhood education; Secondary school/education; Higher education; Education; Natural resources;

Hospitals (general); Substance abuse, services; Youth, services; Federated giving programs.
Types of support: Continuing support; Capital campaigns; Building/renovation; Research; Employee matching gifts.
Limitations: Giving limited to plant site cities in TX: Attleboro, Austin, Dallas, Houston, Hunt Valley, Lubbock, Sherman, and Versailles. No grants to individuals (except for Founders' Prize award), or for advertising; no product donations; no loans.
Publications: Application guidelines.
Application information: Application for Founders' Prize by nomination only; application forms for Founders' Prize available from Liston M. Rice, Jr., Pres. Application form not required.
    Initial approach: Letter (1 to 2 pages)
    Copies of proposal: 1
    Board meeting date(s): Mar., June, Sept., and Dec.
    Final notification: 3 weeks after board meetings
Officers and Directors:* Liston M. Rice, Jr.,* Pres.; Terri West,* V.P.; Cynthia Stewart, Secy.; William A. Aylesworth,* Treas.; Ann F. Minnis,* Grants Admin.; Richard J. Agnich; Thomas Engibous; Steve Leven; James C. Mitchell; Phil Ritter; Bart Thomas.
Number of staff: 1 full-time professional; 1 part-time professional; 1 full-time support.
EIN: 756038519

3173
The Truchard Foundation

3816 Hunterwood Point
Austin, TX 78746 (512) 327-8558

Established in 1997 in TX.
Donor(s): James J. Truchard, Lee I. Truchard.
Grantmaker type: Independent foundation
Financial data (yr. ended 12/31/02): Assets, $3,548,854 (M); expenditures, $229,346; qualifying distributions, $225,378; giving activities include $223,108 for 2 grants of $111,554 each.
Purpose and activities: Giving for higher education, environmental conservation and Catholic organizations.
Fields of interest: University; Natural resources; Roman Catholic agencies & churches.
Types of support: General/operating support.
Limitations: Applications not accepted. Giving primarily in TX. No grants to individuals.
Application information: Contributes only to pre-selected organizations.
Officers and Directors:* James J. Truchard,* Pres.; Lee I. Truchard, V.P. and Treas.; Aimee C. Truchard, Secy.; Anthony M. Truchard; John-Marcel E. Truchard; Michael James Truchard.
EIN: 742816894

3174
The Trull Foundation

404 4th St.
Palacios, TX 77465 (361) 972-5241
Contact: E. Gail Purvis, Exec. Dir.
FAX: (361) 972-1109; E-mail:
info@trullfoundation.org; URL: http://
www.trullfoundation.org

Established in 1967 in TX.

Donor(s): R.B. Trull, Florence M. Trull,‡ Gladys T. Brooking, Jean T. Herlin, Laura Shiflett.
Grantmaker type: Independent foundation
Financial data (yr. ended 12/31/02): Assets, $21,646,633 (M); expenditures, $1,270,114; qualifying distributions, $1,082,095; giving activities include $1,007,045 for 252 grants (high: $20,000; low: $250).
Purpose and activities: Primary areas of interest include youth, minorities, and education. Giving also for child welfare, the disadvantaged, Protestant church support and welfare programs, denominational giving, higher, elementary, and secondary education with emphasis on religious schools, theological education, and literacy programs, child development, and youth agencies; some support for community development, assistance for immigrants, international relief activities, organizations promoting peace, ecology and the environment, (particularly the TX coast environment), population studies, AIDS research, museums, and the performing arts.
Fields of interest: Museums; Performing arts; History/archaeology; Elementary/secondary education; Child development, education; Elementary school/education; Secondary school/education; Higher education; Theological school/education; Adult education—literacy, basic skills & GED; Libraries/library science; Reading; Education; Natural resources; Environment; Substance abuse, services; Food services; Human services; Children/youth, services; Child development, services; Family services; Minorities/immigrants, centers/services; Homeless, human services; International relief; International peace/security; Community development; Protestant federated giving programs; Population studies; Protestant agencies & churches; Religion; Minorities; Hispanics/Latinos; Immigrants/refugees; Economically disadvantaged; Homeless.
Types of support: General/operating support; Continuing support; Annual campaigns; Equipment; Program development; Conferences/seminars; Publication; Seed money; Curriculum development; Internship funds; Scholarship funds; Technical assistance; Consulting services.
Limitations: Giving primarily in southern TX, with emphasis on the Palacios, TX, area. No grants to individuals directly, and rarely for building or endowment funds; no loans.
Publications: Application guidelines, Biennial report (including application guidelines).
Application information: Proposals submitted by FAX not considered. Application form required.
    Initial approach: Letter, telephone or visit Web site
    Copies of proposal: 4
    Deadline(s): None
    Board meeting date(s): Usually 3 to 5 times a year; contributions committee meets monthly and as required
    Final notification: 6 weeks
Officers and Trustees:* Colleen Claybourn,* Chair.; Rose C. Lancaster,* Vice-Chair.; J. Fred Huitt,* Secy.-Treas.; E. Gail Purvis, Exec. Dir.; Cara P. Herlin; Jean T. Herlin; Sarah H. Olfers; R.B. Trull; R. Scott Trull.
Number of staff: 1 full-time professional; 1 full-time support; 1 part-time support.
EIN: 237423943

3175
TXU Corp. Contributions Program
(formerly Texas Utilities Company Contributions Program)
c/o Corp. Citizenship Dept.
1601 Bryan St., Ste. 19-112
Dallas, TX 75201 (214) 812-3191
Contact: Sharon Neal, Sr. Mgr., Corp. Citizenship

Grantmaker type: Corporate giving program
Financial data (yr. ended 12/31/02): Total giving, $6,255,000; giving activities include $6,255,000 for 1,240 grants (high: $500,000; low: $50; average: $1,500–$5,000).
Purpose and activities: TXU makes charitable contributions to nonprofit organizations involved with education and the environment. Support is given primarily in areas of company operations.
Fields of interest: Education; Environment.
International interests: Australia.
Types of support: General/operating support; Annual campaigns; Program development; Seed money; Curriculum development; Employee volunteer services; Sponsorships; Program-related investments/loans.
Limitations: Giving primarily in areas of company operations, with emphasis on Dallas, TX, and in Australia.
Publications: Application guidelines, Corporate giving report (including application guidelines), Program policy statement.
Application information: The Corporate Citizenship Department handles giving. The company has a staff that only handles contributions. A contributions committee reviews all requests. Application form required.
Initial approach: Contact headquarters for application form
Copies of proposal: 1
Deadline(s): None
Board meeting date(s): Monthly
Number of staff: 4 full-time professional.

3176
Unocal Foundation
14141 S.W. Fwy.
Sugar Land, TX 77478
Contact: Laurie Regelbrugge, Mgr.
Application address: 1150 Connecticut Ave. N.W., Ste. 1025, Washington, DC, tel.: (202) 367-2782

Incorporated in 1962 in CA.
Donor(s): Unocal Corp.
Grantmaker type: Company-sponsored foundation
Financial data (yr. ended 01/31/01): Assets, $2,143,443 (M); gifts received, $636,146; expenditures, $1,045,158; qualifying distributions, $961,521; giving activities include $961,615 for 213+ grants (high: $292,076; low: $10).
Purpose and activities: Giving primarily for higher education and community development organizations.
Fields of interest: Arts; Higher education; Education; Energy; Children/youth, services; Community development; Federated giving programs.
Types of support: Continuing support; Annual campaigns; Equipment; Fellowships;

Scholarship funds; Research; Employee matching gifts; Employee-related scholarships.
Limitations: Giving primarily in areas of parent company operations in CA, IL, and TX. No support for veterans', fraternal, sectarian, social, religious, athletic, choral, band, or similar groups, trade or business associations, state agencies and departments, or elementary or secondary education. No grants to individuals (except for employee-related scholarships), or for general purposes, capital funds for education, endowment funds, courtesy advertising, conferences, supplemental operating support to recipients of United Funds, or for trips or tours; no loans.
Publications: Annual report.
Application information: Application form required for employee-related scholarships.
Initial approach: Letter or printed form for employee child scholarship
Copies of proposal: 1
Deadline(s): Sept. 15
Board meeting date(s): As required
Final notification: 6 to 8 weeks
Officers and Trustees:* George A. Walker,* Chair.; Gregory F. Huger, Pres.; Stephen L. Hayes, V.P.; Carl D. McAulay,* V.P.; Roberta E. Kass, Secy.; Darrell D. Chessum, Treas.; Joe D. Cecil; Andrew L. Fawthrop; Thomas E. Fisher; Brian W. G. Marcotte.
Number of staff: 1 full-time professional; 1 full-time support; 2 part-time support.
EIN: 956071812

3177
Rachael & Ben Vaughan Foundation
P.O. Box 2233
Austin, TX 78768-2233 (512) 477-4726
Contact: William R. Ward, Jr.
Application address: 515 Congress Ave., No. 2060, Austin TX, 78701; FAX: (512) 477-1437; E-mail: rbvf@swbell.net

Established in 1952 in TX.
Donor(s): Ben F. Vaughan, Jr.,‡ Rachael Vaughan.‡
Grantmaker type: Independent foundation
Financial data (yr. ended 11/30/02): Assets, $4,502,547 (M); expenditures, $241,745; qualifying distributions, $223,597; giving activities include $216,734 for 60 grants (high: $10,000; low: $500).
Purpose and activities: Support for educational, cultural, environmental, community, and religious development of central and south TX; support for the needy and disadvantaged in this area.
Fields of interest: Arts; Child development, education; Education; Natural resources; Environment; Animals/wildlife, preservation/protection; Family planning; Health care; Human services; Child development, services; Community development; Roman Catholic federated giving programs; Roman Catholic agencies & churches.
Types of support: General/operating support; Annual campaigns; Capital campaigns; Building/renovation; Equipment; Land acquisition; Endowments; Program development; Conferences/seminars; Professorships; Publication; Seed money; Curriculum development; Fellowships; Internship funds; Scholarship funds; Research;

Technical assistance; Consulting services; Exchange programs; Matching/challenge support.
Limitations: Giving limited to southern and central TX. No grants to individuals; no loans.
Publications: Application guidelines, Grants list.
Application information: Application form not required.
Initial approach: Letter
Copies of proposal: 1
Deadline(s): June 1
Board meeting date(s): Aug.
Final notification: End of 1st week in Sept.
Officers and Trustees:* Ben F. Vaughan III,* Pres.; Ben F. Vaughan IV,* V.P.; Genevieve Vaughan,* V.P.; Daphne duPont Vaughan,* Secy.-Treas.
Number of staff: 1 part-time professional; 1 part-time support.
EIN: 746040479

3178
Susan Vaughan Foundation, Inc.
(formerly McAshan Foundation, Inc.)
c/o J. P. Morgan Private Bank
P.O. Box 2558
Houston, TX 77252-8037 (713) 216-4513
Contact: Charlene D. Slack; or Bill Askey, Trust Off., JP Morgan Private Bank

Trust established in 1952 in TX; reorganized in 1991 under current name.
Donor(s): Susan C. McAshan, Susan Vaughan Clayton Trust No. 1.
Grantmaker type: Independent foundation
Financial data (yr. ended 12/31/01): Assets, $28,239,845 (M); expenditures, $1,726,029; qualifying distributions, $1,442,066; giving activities include $1,426,000 for 53 grants (high: $275,000; low: $2,500; average: $10,000–$50,000).
Purpose and activities: Emphasis on education, population, conservation, and the arts.
Fields of interest: Arts; Higher education; Education; Natural resources; Family planning; Human services.
Types of support: General/operating support; Annual campaigns; Capital campaigns; Building/renovation; Matching/challenge support.
Limitations: Giving limited to Houston and Austin, TX.
Publications: Application guidelines.
Application information: Application form not required.
Initial approach: Letter
Copies of proposal: 1
Deadline(s): Jan. 1, Apr. 1, July 1, and Oct. 1
Board meeting date(s): Quarterly (Feb., May, Aug., and Nov.)
Final notification: Within 3 months
Trustees: Susan C. Garwood; Duncan E. Osborne; Elizabeth B. Osborne.
EIN: 760285765

3179
Von Ehr Foundation
3510 Tree Trunk Trail
Richardson, TX 75082

Established in 1999 in TX.
Donor(s): James R. Von Ehr II.

Grantmaker type: Independent foundation
Financial data (yr. ended 12/31/02): Assets, $2,247,109 (M); expenditures, $226,541; qualifying distributions, $226,131; giving activities include $226,500 for 14 grants (high: $200,000; low: $500).
Fields of interest: Arts; Education; Zoos/zoological societies; Health organizations, association; Cancer; Human services.
Limitations: Applications not accepted. Giving primarily in TX. No grants to individuals.
Application information: Contributes only to pre-selected organizations.
Officer and Directors:* James R. Von Ehr II,* Pres.; James L. Halperin; Gayla Von Ehr.
EIN: 752825954

3180
The Waco Foundation
900 Austin Ave., Ste. 1000
Waco, TX 76701-1949 (254) 754-3404
Contact: Tom H. Collins, Jr., Exec. Dir.
FAX: (254) 753-2887; E-mail: info@wacofoundation.org or tomc@wacofoundation.org; URL: http://www.wacofoundation.org

Established in 1958 in TX.
Grantmaker type: Community foundation
Financial data (yr. ended 03/31/03): Assets, $36,351,497 (L); gifts received, $2,531,517; expenditures, $2,268,521; giving activities include $1,568,839 for 380 grants (high: $50,000; low: $500) and $191,008 for foundation-administered programs.
Purpose and activities: To make a positive difference in the lives and future of the people in Waco and McLennan County through grantmaking, promotion of community philanthropy, and support of the not-for-profit sector. The foundation administers donor-advised funds.
Fields of interest: Arts; Education; Environment; Medical research, institute; Human services; Children/youth, services; Day care; Family services; Women, centers/services; Community development; Women; Economically disadvantaged.
Types of support: Building/renovation; Equipment; Emergency funds; Program development; Seed money; Scholarship funds; Matching/challenge support.
Limitations: Giving limited to McLennan County, TX. No grants to individuals, or for continuing support, deficit financing, endowments, operating budgets, student loans, or technical assistance.
Publications: Application guidelines, Annual report, Grants list, Informational brochure, Program policy statement.
Application information: Application form required.
Initial approach: Letter or telephone
Copies of proposal: 12
Deadline(s): Apr. 1 and Sept. 1
Board meeting date(s): 4th Wed. of each month
Final notification: Mid-June and mid-Nov.
Officers and Directors:* Hal Whitaker,* Chair.; Nancy Callan,* Vice-Chair.; Louis Englander,* Secy.; Tom H. Collins, Jr.,* Exec. Dir.; Rick Bostwick; David Horner; Beth Mayfield; William

R. Pakis; Art Pertile; Nelwyn Reagan; Tom Salome.
Number of staff: 3 full-time professional; 2 full-time support.
EIN: 746054628

3181
Marjorie T. Walthall Perpetual Charitable Trust
112 W. Ridgewood Ct.
San Antonio, TX 78212-2342 (210) 822-5433
Contact: Paul T. Walthall, Tr.

Established in 1976 in TX.
Donor(s): Marjorie T. Walthall.
Grantmaker type: Independent foundation
Financial data (yr. ended 12/31/00): Assets, $4,296,094 (M); expenditures, $137,393; qualifying distributions, $128,068; giving activities include $90,820 for 33 grants (high: $6,000; low: $500).
Purpose and activities: Giving primarily for nursing education, human services, health, and animal welfare.
Fields of interest: Elementary/secondary education; Animal welfare; Eye diseases; Ear & throat diseases; Housing/shelter; Human services; Christian agencies & churches.
Types of support: General/operating support; Scholarship funds.
Limitations: Giving primarily in San Antonio, TX. No grants to individuals.
Application information:
Initial approach: Letter
Deadline(s): Preferably before Oct. 1
Trustees: Marjorie Walthall Fry; Paul T. Walthall; Wilson J. Walthall III.
EIN: 510170313

3182
The Waste Management Charitable Foundation
(formerly Wheelabrator Technologies Rust International Charitable Foundation, Inc.)
c/o Waste Management, Inc.
1001 Fannin St., Ste. 4000
Houston, TX 77002 (713) 512-6200
Contact: Marilyn Brown

Established in 1990 in TX.
Donor(s): Wheelabrator Technologies Inc.
Grantmaker type: Company-sponsored foundation
Financial data (yr. ended 12/31/01): Assets, $8,029,041 (M); expenditures, $2,244,922; qualifying distributions, $376,750; giving activities include $376,750 for 23 grants (high: $55,890; low: $250; average: $5,000–$10,000).
Fields of interest: Education; Environment; Community development.
International interests: Canada.
Types of support: General/operating support; Annual campaigns; Emergency funds; Program development; Seed money.
Limitations: Giving on a national basis, with some emphasis on TX, some funding also in Canada. No grants to individuals.
Publications: Occasional report.
Application information: Application form not required.
Initial approach: Letter

Copies of proposal: 1
Deadline(s): Last day of Mar., June, Sept., and Dec.
Board meeting date(s): Annually
Final notification: Within 30 days of board meeting
Officers and Directors:* Barry Caldwell,* Pres.; Linda Smith, V.P. and Secy.; Ron Jones, V.P. and Treas.; Marilyn Brown, V.P.; Jimmy LaValley, V.P.; Cherie Rice, V.P.; Robert Simpson, V.P.; David Steiner,* V.P.
Number of staff: None.
EIN: 043073733

3183
Waste Management, Inc. Corporate Giving Program
1001 Fannin, Ste. 4000
Houston, TX 77002
Contact: Marilyn Brown, Dir., Community Rels.

Grantmaker type: Corporate giving program
Financial data (yr. ended 12/31/02): Total giving, $2,750,565; giving activities include $2,750,565 for grants (high: $30,000; low: $100; average: $100–$5,000).
Purpose and activities: As a complement to its foundation, Waste Management also makes charitable contributions to nonprofit organizations directly. Support is given on a national basis and in Canada.
Fields of interest: Education; Environment; Community development.
International interests: Canada.
Types of support: General/operating support; Annual campaigns; Emergency funds; Program development; Cause-related marketing; Employee volunteer services; Use of facilities; Sponsorships; Donated equipment; Donated land; In-kind gifts.
Limitations: Giving on a national basis and in Canada in areas of company operations, with emphasis on Houston, TX.
Application information: The Community Relations Department handles giving. A contributions committee at some company locations review all requests originating from that area. Application form not required.
Initial approach: Proposal to nearest company facility
Copies of proposal: 1
Deadline(s): Varies
Board meeting date(s): Varies
Number of staff: 1 full-time professional.

3184
The Watson Charitable Foundation
(formerly The Mark and Kathleen Watson Charitable Foundation)
P.O. Box 6886
San Antonio, TX 78209-0886 (210) 824-4546
Contact: Mark E. Watson, Jr., Pres.

Established in 1997 in TX.
Donor(s): Mark Watson.
Grantmaker type: Independent foundation
Financial data (yr. ended 09/30/02): Assets, $1,570,453 (M); expenditures, $320,719; qualifying distributions, $306,208; giving activities include $306,543 for 34 grants (high: $9,939; low: $100).

Fields of interest: Arts; Higher education; Environment; Zoos/zoological societies; Health organizations, association; Human services; Community development; Federated giving programs; Religion.
Types of support: General/operating support.
Limitations: Giving primarily in San Antonio, TX.
Application information: Application form not required.
Initial approach: Letter
Deadline(s): None
Officer: Mark E. Watson, Jr., Pres.
Trustee: F.B. Lyon III.
EIN: 742825092

3185
Weatherspoon Charitable Foundation
3402 Hillview Dr.
Austin, TX 78703
Contact: Mary Bowden, Treas.

Established in 1988 in IA.
Donor(s): Margaret Weatherspoon.
Grantmaker type: Independent foundation
Financial data (yr. ended 12/31/02): Assets, $2,501,086 (M); expenditures, $147,170; qualifying distributions, $143,830; giving activities include $140,000 for 36 grants (high: $24,000; low: $750).
Purpose and activities: Giving for childhood development and education, Christian services, food services to the needy, aid to the homeless, and environmental conservation.
Fields of interest: Education; Environment; Food services; Children/youth, services; Christian agencies & churches; Homeless.
Limitations: Giving on a national basis, with some emphasis on IA and OR.
Application information: Unsolicited requests for funds not accepted. Application form not required.
Deadline(s): None
Officers: Margaret Weatherspoon, Pres.; Jacqueline Reineke, V.P. and Secy.; Mary Bowden, Treas.
EIN: 421324028

3186
Rob and Bessie Welder Wildlife Foundation
P.O. Box 1400
Sinton, TX 78387-1400 (361) 364-2643
Contact: Dr. D. Lynn Drawe, Dir.
FAX: (361) 364-2650; E-mail: Welderwf@aol.com; URL: http://hometown.aol.com/welderwf/welderweb.html

Trust established in 1954 in TX.
Donor(s): R.H. Welder,‡ Mrs. R.H. Welder,‡ Edward H. & Winnie H. Smith Fellowship Trust Fund.
Grantmaker type: Independent foundation
Financial data (yr. ended 12/31/01): Assets, $26,314,903 (M); gifts received, $64,026; expenditures, $1,425,715; qualifying distributions, $1,271,341; giving activities include $267,858 for 23 grants to individuals (high: $14,609; low: $3,600).
Purpose and activities: Established to further education in wildlife conservation, to support graduate-level research into wildlife problems,

and to develop scientific methods for increasing wildlife populations; operates a wildlife refuge.
Fields of interest: Natural resources; Environment; Animals/wildlife, preservation/protection.
International interests: Canada.
Types of support: Fellowships; Internship funds.
Limitations: Giving primarily in the U.S. No grants for building or endowment funds, work/study programs, or for operating budgets.
Publications: Application guidelines, Biennial report, Informational brochure (including application guidelines).
Application information: Application guidelines available on website. Application form required.
Initial approach: Letter
Copies of proposal: 2
Deadline(s): Submit application preferably in fall; deadline Oct. 1
Board meeting date(s): Usually in Nov. and June
Final notification: Prior to Dec. 15
Director: D. Lynn Drawe.
Trustees: H.C. Weil; John J. Welder V; Patrick H. Welder.
Number of staff: 4 full-time professional; 10 full-time support.
EIN: 741381321

3187
The Wortham Foundation ▼
2727 Allen Pkwy., Ste. 1570
Houston, TX 77019 (713) 526-8849
Contact: Barbara J. Snyder, Grants Admin.
FAX: (713) 526-7222; E-mail: bsnyder@wortham.org

Trust established in 1958 in TX.
Donor(s): Gus S. Wortham,‡ Lyndall F. Wortham.‡
Grantmaker type: Independent foundation
Financial data (yr. ended 09/30/01): Assets, $211,395,002 (M); expenditures, $13,764,529; qualifying distributions, $11,850,666; giving activities include $11,994,500 for 74 grants (high: $1,500,000; low: $4,000; average: $10,000–$100,000).
Purpose and activities: Support primarily for the arts, including the performing arts and museums, and community improvement, including civic beautification projects that benefit the citizens of Houston and Harris County, TX.
Fields of interest: Museums; Performing arts; Historic preservation/historical societies; Arts; Environment, beautification programs.
Types of support: General/operating support; Continuing support; Annual campaigns; Capital campaigns; Endowments; Emergency funds; Seed money; Matching/challenge support.
Limitations: Giving limited to Houston and Harris County, TX. Generally, no grants to colleges, universities, or hospitals. No grants to individuals.
Publications: Annual report, Informational brochure (including application guidelines).
Application information: Please do not send bound copies of proposal. Application form required.
Initial approach: Letter
Copies of proposal: 1
Deadline(s): Submit proposal preferably by the 1st week of Jan., Apr., July, or Oct.

Board meeting date(s): Feb., May, Aug., and Nov.
Final notification: 3 months
Officers and Trustees:* Fred C. Burns,* Chair.; Brady F. Carruth,* Pres.; R.W. Wortham III,* Secy.-Treas.; William V.H. Clarke, Cont.; James A. Elkins III; E.A. Stumpf III.
Number of staff: 2 full-time support.
EIN: 741334356
Recent environmental and animal welfare grants:
3187-1 Armand Bayou Nature Center, Houston, TX, $35,000. For operating support. 2001.
3187-2 Buffalo Bayou Partnership, Houston, TX, $325,000. For capital support. 2001.
3187-3 Houston Arboretum and Nature Center, Houston, TX, $20,000. For general operating support. 2001.
3187-4 Houston Clean City Commission, Houston, TX, $25,000. For general operating support. 2001.
3187-5 Katy Prairie Land Conservancy, Houston, TX, $250,000. For capital support. 2001.
3187-6 Nature Discovery Center, Bellaire, TX, $50,000. For capital support. 2001.
3187-7 Rice University, Houston, TX, $150,000. For Lowery Arboretum. 2001.
3187-8 Scenic Texas, Houston, TX, $60,000. For general operating support. 2001.
3187-9 Trees for Houston, Houston, TX, $150,000. For general operating support. 2001.

3188
Lola Wright Foundation, Inc.
P.O. Box 1138
Georgetown, TX 78627-1138 (512) 869-2574
Contact: Wilford Flowers, Pres.
Austin tel.: (512) 255-5353

Incorporated in 1954 in TX.
Donor(s): Johnie E. Wright.‡
Grantmaker type: Independent foundation
Financial data (yr. ended 12/31/02): Assets, $13,934,447 (M); expenditures, $979,597; qualifying distributions, $780,056; giving activities include $741,652 for 63 grants (high: $30,000; low: $1,500).
Purpose and activities: Emphasis on social services, including drug and alcohol abuse programs, family services and planning, organizations providing assistance to minorities, the aged and youth, legal services, community funds, and health services and hospitals, including rehabilitation programs, AIDS research, diseases of the heart, and organizations serving the handicapped. Support also for the arts and culture, including fine and performing arts, early childhood, adult, higher, and other education, media and communications, and the environment.
Fields of interest: Media/communications; Visual arts; Museums; Performing arts; Arts; Education, association; Early childhood education; Child development, education; Higher education; Adult/continuing education; Adult education—literacy, basic skills & GED; Reading; Education; Environment; Family planning; Medical care, rehabilitation; Health care; Substance abuse, services; Health organizations, association; Heart & circulatory diseases; AIDS; Alcoholism; Heart & circulatory

research; AIDS research; Legal services; Human services; Children/youth, services; Child development, services; Family services; Hospices; Aging, centers/services; Minorities/immigrants, centers/services; Homeless, human services; Federated giving programs; Minorities; Disabled; Aging; Homeless.
Types of support: Continuing support; Building/renovation; Equipment; Program development; Research; Matching/challenge support.
Limitations: Giving limited to within a 50-mile radius of Austin, TX. No grants to individuals; generally no support for operating budgets.
Publications: Application guidelines.
Application information: Application form not required.
>   *Initial approach:* Letter
>   *Copies of proposal:* 9
>   *Deadline(s):* Feb. 28 and Aug. 31
>   *Board meeting date(s):* May and Nov.
>   *Final notification:* May 15 and Nov. 15
Officers and Directors:* Wilford Flowers,* Pres.; Paul Hilgers, V.P.; Vivian E. Todd,* Secy.; Adrian Fowler; James Meyers; Ron Oliveira; Carole Strayhorn.
Number of staff: None.
EIN: 746054717

3189
Roger L. and Laura D. Zeller Charitable Foundation

P.O. Box 13430
San Antonio, TX   78213   (210) 321-0671
Contact: Ronald J. Herrmann, Tr.

Established in 1991 in TX.
Donor(s): Laura D. Zeller,‡ Roger L. Zeller, Zeller Living Trust.
Grantmaker type: Independent foundation
Financial data (yr. ended 12/31/02): Assets, $72,772 (M); gifts received, $660,000; expenditures, $675,231; qualifying distributions, $674,465; giving activities include $673,699 for 18 grants (high: $481,025; low: $1,000).
Purpose and activities: Giving is limited to the following areas: health care, zoo and animal welfare, promotion of education, and charities related to the sport of bowling.
Fields of interest: Education; Animal welfare; Health care; Cancer; Cancer research; Recreation; Human services; Christian agencies & churches.
Types of support: General/operating support; Capital campaigns; Endowments.
Limitations: Giving limited to Bexar County, TX, with emphasis on San Antonio. No grants to individuals.
Application information: Application form required.
>   *Initial approach:* Letter or proposal
>   *Copies of proposal:* 1
>   *Deadline(s):* None
Trustees: David S. Herrmann; Karen H. Hermann; Ronald J. Herrmann.
Number of staff: None.
EIN: 742610755

![UTAH banner]

UTAH

3190
Aquarius Plateau Foundation

c/o Richard T. Beard
10 E. South Temple, Ste. 900
Salt Lake City, UT   84133

Established in 1994 in UT.
Donor(s): David Mock.
Grantmaker type: Independent foundation
Financial data (yr. ended 12/31/02): Assets, $189,797 (M); expenditures, $102,701; qualifying distributions, $102,312; giving activities include $102,000 for grants.
Fields of interest: Environment.
Limitations: Applications not accepted. Giving primarily in MT and UT. No grants to individuals.
Application information: Contributes only to pre-selected organizations.
Officers: David Mock, Pres.; Martin Mock, V.P.
Trustee: Richard T. Beard.
EIN: 870532648

3191
The Ashton Family Foundation

251 River Park Dr., Ste. 350
Provo, UT   84604
Contact: Alan C. Ashton, Tr.
Application address: c/o Ralph Rasmussen, P.O. Box 432, Provo, UT 84603

Established in 1993 in UT.
Donor(s): Alan C. Ashton.
Grantmaker type: Independent foundation
Financial data (yr. ended 12/31/02): Assets, $16,617,723 (M); expenditures, $7,402,852; qualifying distributions, $7,145,415; giving activities include $7,143,125 for 43 grants (high: $5,432,632; low: $1,500; average: $10,000–$100,000) and $2,833 for 2 grants to individuals (high: $2,400; low: $433).
Purpose and activities: Support for religious institutions, as well as education, the arts and health.
Fields of interest: Arts; Education; Health organizations, association; Mormon agencies & churches.
Types of support: General/operating support; Grants to individuals.
Limitations: Giving primarily in UT.
Application information:
>   *Initial approach:* Letter
>   *Deadline(s):* None
Trustees: Alan C. Ashton; Brigham Ashton; Eliza Ashton; Elizabeth Ashton; Karen Ashton; Melissa Ashton; Morgan Ashton; Samuel Ashton; Spencer Ashton; Stephanie Ashton; Traci Ashton; Emily Ann Eddington; Paul Eddington; Allison Norton; Toby Norton; Michael Smith; Amy Jo Young; Chad Young.
EIN: 870480108
Recent environmental and animal welfare grants:
3191-1 Foundation for Anthropological Research and Environmental Studies, Rupert, ID, $30,000. For unrestricted support. 2001.

3191-2 Thanksgiving Point Institute, Provo, UT, $4,153,280. For unrestricted support. 2001.

3192
Brindle Foundation

P.O. Box 628
Salt Lake City, UT   84110-0628

Established in 2002 in DE.
Donor(s): Martha Healy.
Grantmaker type: Independent foundation
Financial data (yr. ended 12/31/02): Assets, $7,127,017 (M); gifts received, $7,389,262; expenditures, $382,177; qualifying distributions, $382,015; giving activities include $381,000 for 27 grants (high: $100,000; low: $2,500).
Fields of interest: Arts; Environment, legal rights; Environment, formal/general education; Animal welfare; Family services.
Limitations: Applications not accepted. Giving primarily in NM. No grants to individuals.
Application information: Contributes only to pre-selected organizations.
Officer: Nancy Healy Schwanfelder, Pres.
Director: Martha A. Healy.
EIN: 030466957

3193
Dr. Ezekiel R. and Edna Wattis Dumke Foundation

P.O. Box 776
Kaysville, UT   84037   (801) 497-9474
Contact: Denise R. Johnsen, Office Mgr.
E-mail: erd@fndtn.org

Incorporated in 1959 in UT.
Grantmaker type: Independent foundation
Financial data (yr. ended 12/31/02): Assets, $10,077,967 (M); expenditures, $1,409,826; qualifying distributions, $1,258,821; giving activities include $1,249,589 for 27 grants (high: $100,000; low: $5,000; average: $5,000–$20,000).
Purpose and activities: Support for organizations involved with arts and culture, education, the environment, and health and human services.
Fields of interest: Arts; Higher education; Natural resources; Hospitals (general); Health care; Children/youth, services.
Types of support: Equipment; Land acquisition; Technical assistance; Matching/challenge support.
Limitations: Giving limited to the western region of the U.S., with emphasis on ID, MT, NM, UT, and WY. No grants to individuals or for scholarships.
Publications: Application guidelines.
Application information: Application form required.
>   *Initial approach:* Telephone, E-mail, or letter requesting application form and deadline
>   *Copies of proposal:* 4
>   *Board meeting date(s):* Approx. Apr. and Aug.
>   *Final notification:* Within 6 weeks after board meeting
Directors: Ezekiel R. Dumke, Jr.; Andrea Dumke Manship; Claire Dumke Ryberg; Nancy Healy Schwanfelder; Betsy Thornton.
Number of staff: None.
EIN: 876119783

3194

Willard L. Eccles Charitable Foundation

P.O. Box 58198
Salt Lake City, UT 84158-0198
(801) 463-9580
Contact: Stephen E. Denkers, Secy.
FAX: (801) 463-9748; E-mail:
wleccles@evoskis.com; URL: http://
www.wleccles.org

Established in 1981 in UT.
Grantmaker type: Independent foundation
Financial data (yr. ended 03/31/02): Assets,
$42,421,980 (M); expenditures, $2,659,157;
qualifying distributions, $2,567,337; giving
activities include $2,433,350 for 60 grants
(high: $255,000; low: $1,000; average:
$5,000–$20,000).
Purpose and activities: Grants primarily for the
environment, medical education, human
services, medical research, and health
organizations.
Fields of interest: Medical school/education;
Environment; Health care; Health organizations,
association; Biomedicine; Medical research,
institute.
Types of support: General/operating support;
Capital campaigns; Building/renovation;
Equipment; Land acquisition; Fellowships;
Scholarship funds; Research;
Matching/challenge support.
Limitations: Giving primarily in UT, with
emphasis in the Ogden area. No grants to
individuals, or for land acquisition,
construction, building purposes, or to endow
medical education positions.
Application information: Application form
required.
Initial approach: Letter
Copies of proposal: 8
Deadline(s): Aug. 5 and Jan. 15
Board meeting date(s): Quarterly
Final notification: Following meeting
Officer and Committee Members:* Stephen E.
Denkers,* Secy.; Susan Coit; William E. Coit,
M.D.; Barbara E. Coit-Yeager; Julie E. Denkers;
Stephen G. Denkers; Susan E. Denkers; Ann
Goss.
Trustees: David Buckmen; First Security Bank of
Utah, N.A.
Number of staff: 1 full-time support.
EIN: 942759395

3195

The Force for Good Foundation

c/o Nu Skin Enterprises
75 W. Center St.
Provo, UT 84601-4432
URL: http://www.forceforgood.org

Established in 1998 in UT.
Donor(s): Diamond Technology Partners Inc.,
Nu Skin Enterprises, Inc.
Grantmaker type: Company-sponsored
foundation
Financial data (yr. ended 12/31/01): Assets,
$515,005 (M); gifts received, $589,279;
expenditures, $484,688; qualifying distributions,
$478,360; giving activities include $478,360 for
18 grants (high: $163,039; low: $3,000).
Purpose and activities: The foundation provides
funds and products to create a better world for
our children by improving human life,

continuing indigenous cultures, and protecting
fragile environments.
Fields of interest: Natural resources; Skin
disorders research; Medical research;
International relief.
Limitations: Giving on a national and
international basis. No support for fraternal
organizations or religious purposes. No grants to
individuals, or for capital campaigns, seed
funding, administrative costs, or for advertising
space in benefit programs.
Application information:
Initial approach: Letter of inquiry; telephone
solicitations not considered
Deadline(s): None
Officers: Blake M. Roney, Chair. and Pres.;
Sandra N. Tillotson, V.P.; Steven J. Lund, Secy.;
Brooke Roney, Treas.; Shannon Anderson,
Compt.
EIN: 870577244

3196

Hayward Family Foundation

(formerly Nancy Eccles & Homer M. Hayward
Foundation)
c/o Wells Fargo Bank Northwest, N.A.
P.O. Box 25491
Salt Lake City, UT 84125
Contact: David L. Buchman

Established in 1993 in UT.
Donor(s): Nancy Eccles Hayward.
Grantmaker type: Independent foundation
Financial data (yr. ended 06/30/02): Assets,
$6,870,803 (M); expenditures, $633,307;
qualifying distributions, $609,215; giving
activities include $608,094 for 17 grants (high:
$125,000; low: $1,000).
Fields of interest: Botanical gardens; Recreation.
Types of support: General/operating support;
Continuing support; Building/renovation;
Research; Program evaluation;
Matching/challenge support.
Limitations: Applications not accepted. Giving
on a national basis. No grants to individuals.
Application information: Contributes only to
pre-selected organizations. Unsolicited requests
for funds not accepted.
Trustee: Wells Fargo Bank Northwest, N.A.
EIN: 876227330

3197

**Huntsman Corporation Contributions
Program**

500 Huntsman Way
Salt Lake City, UT 84108-1235

Grantmaker type: Corporate giving program
Purpose and activities: Huntsman makes
charitable contributions to nonprofit
organizations involved with education, the
environment, health, international relief,
community development, and homeless people.
Support is given on a national and international
basis.
Fields of interest: Education; Environment;
Health care; International development;
Economic development; Business/industry;
Community development; Homeless.
International interests: Armenia.

Types of support: General/operating support;
Employee volunteer services; Employee-related
scholarships.
Limitations: Giving on a national and
international basis in areas of company
operations, including in Armenia.
Application information:
Initial approach: Contact nearest company
facility for application information

3198

The Jones Family Charitable Foundation

344 W. Pleasant View Dr.
Ogden, UT 84414-2118

Established in 1993 in UT.
Donor(s): Leon L. Jones, Judith B. Jones.
Grantmaker type: Independent foundation
Financial data (yr. ended 12/31/01): Assets,
$1,488,237 (M); gifts received, $198,960;
expenditures, $96,365; qualifying distributions,
$94,295; giving activities include $95,000 for
25 grants (high: $20,000; low: $500).
Purpose and activities: Giving primarily for
conservation and the environment.
Fields of interest: Radio; Environment.
Limitations: Applications not accepted. Giving
primarily in UT. No grants to individuals.
Application information: Contributes only to
pre-selected organizations.
Officers and Trustees:* Amelia C. Jones, Mgr.;
Ezra Thomas Jones,* Mgr.; Judith B. Jones, Mgr.;
L.C. Allen Jones, Mgr.; Leon L. Jones,* Mgr.
EIN: 876223972

3199

**Kennecott Utah Copper Corporation
Contributions Program**

P.O. Box 6001
Magna, UT 84044-6001

Grantmaker type: Corporate giving program
Purpose and activities: As a complement to its
foundation, Kennecott also makes charitable
contributions to nonprofit organizations directly.
Support is given primarily in Utah.
Fields of interest: Arts; Education; Environment;
Human services; Youth development;
Community development.
Types of support: General/operating support;
In-kind gifts.
Limitations: Giving primarily in UT.
Application information: Application form not
required.
Initial approach: Proposal to headquarters

3200

Janet Q. Lawson Foundation

P.O. Box 45385
Salt Lake City, UT 84145-0385

Established around 1991 in UT.
Donor(s): Emma Eccles Jones,‡ Janet Q. Lawson.
Grantmaker type: Independent foundation
Financial data (yr. ended 12/31/01): Assets,
$18,341,228 (M); gifts received, $500,000;
expenditures, $1,201,253; qualifying
distributions, $1,156,780; giving activities
include $1,140,000 for 13 grants (high:
$250,000; low: $25,000).

Purpose and activities: Giving primarily for the arts and culture, education, youth organizations, health, human services, and federated giving programs.
Fields of interest: Arts; Higher education; Education; Natural resources; Zoos/zoological societies; Hospitals (general); Health organizations, association; Human services; Children, services; Federated giving programs.
Limitations: Applications not accepted. Giving limited to UT, with emphasis on Salt Lake City. No grants to individuals.
Application information: Contributes only to pre-selected organizations.
Advisory Committee and Trustees:* Frederick Q. Lawson, Advisor; Janet Q. Lawson,* Advisor; Peter Q. Lawson, Advisor; Herbert C. Livsey,* Advisor; JoAnne L. Shrontz, Advisor.
EIN: 870481508

3201
Questar Corporation Contributions Program
180 E. 1st South St.
P.O. Box 45433
Salt Lake City, UT 84145-0433
(801) 324-5435
Contact: Janice Bates, Dir., Community Affairs
FAX: (801) 324-5483; *E-mail:* janb@questar.com

Grantmaker type: Corporate giving program
Financial data (yr. ended 12/31/02): Total giving, $563,000; giving activities include $563,000 for grants.
Purpose and activities: Questar makes charitable contributions to nonprofit organizations involved with arts and culture, education, animal protection, health and human services, food distribution, community development, people with disabilities, senior citizens, economically disadvantaged people, and homeless people. Support is limited to areas of company operations.
Fields of interest: Museums; Performing arts; Humanities; Arts; Higher education; Engineering school/education; Education; Animal welfare; Health care; Food services; Children/youth, services; Family services; Human services; Community development; Disabled; Aging; Economically disadvantaged; Homeless.
Types of support: Continuing support; Annual campaigns; Building/renovation; Equipment; Endowments; Emergency funds; Program development; Scholarship funds; Employee volunteer services; Loaned talent; Use of facilities; Sponsorships; Donated equipment; In-kind gifts.
Limitations: Giving limited to areas of company operations in CO, OK, UT, and WY. No support for religious or fraternal organizations. No grants for trips, exhibitions, or general operating support.
Publications: Newsletter.
Application information: The Community Affairs Department handles giving. A contributions committee reviews all requests. Application form not required.
Initial approach: Proposal to nearest company facility
Copies of proposal: 1
Deadline(s): None
Board meeting date(s): Every 6 to 8 weeks
Final notification: Following review

Number of staff: 1 part-time professional; 1 part-time support.

3202
S. J. & Jessie E. Quinney Foundation ▼
P.O. Box 45385
Salt Lake City, UT 84145-0385
Contact: Herbert C. Livsey, Dir.

Established about 1982 in UT.
Donor(s): S.J. Quinney.‡
Grantmaker type: Independent foundation
Financial data (yr. ended 12/31/01): Assets, $88,777,796 (M); expenditures, $3,577,898; qualifying distributions, $3,222,439; giving activities include $3,100,634 for 87 grants (high: $951,000; low: $300; average: $1,000–$50,000).
Purpose and activities: Giving primarily for higher and other education; support also for social services, cultural programs, including performing arts, and Protestant churches.
Fields of interest: Performing arts; Arts; Elementary/secondary education; Higher education; Environment; Medical care, in-patient care; Health organizations, association; Human services; Christian agencies & churches.
Types of support: General/operating support.
Limitations: Applications not accepted. Giving limited to UT. No grants to individuals.
Application information: Contributes only to pre-selected organizations. The foundation solicits funding requests. Unsolicited requests for funding not considered.
Directors: James W. Freed; Clark P. Giles; Frederick Q. Lawson; Janet Q. Lawson; Peter Q. Lawson; Herbert C. Livsey; Stephen B. Nebeker; David E. Quinney, Jr.; JoAnne L. Shrontz; Alonzo W. Watson, Jr.
EIN: 870389312
Recent environmental and animal welfare grants:
3202-1 Friends of Alta, Alta, UT, $20,000. For general support. 2001.
3202-2 Friends of the Bear River Refuge, Brigham City, UT, $50,000. For general support. 2001.
3202-3 Henrys Fork Foundation, Ashton, ID, $10,000. For general support. 2001.
3202-4 Nature Conservancy, Salt Lake City, UT, $513,500. For general support. 2001.
3202-5 Utah State University, College of Natural Resources, Logan, UT, $50,000. For general support. 2001.

3203
Raymond Family Foundation
c/o Wells Fargo Bank Northwest, N.A.
P.O. Box 25491
Salt Lake City, UT 84125   (801) 246-1436
Contact: David L. Buchman

Established in 1996 in UT.
Donor(s): Mary R. Redmond, Mary R. Raymond Charitable Lead Trust, Robert Raymond Foundation, Inc.
Grantmaker type: Independent foundation
Financial data (yr. ended 12/31/02): Assets, $9,318,344 (M); gifts received, $250,000; expenditures, $434,608; qualifying distributions,

$364,500; giving activities include $364,500 for 79 grants (high: $20,000; low: $250).
Fields of interest: Arts; Higher education; Libraries (public); Education; Animals/wildlife; Hospitals (general); Family planning; Human services; Federated giving programs.
Limitations: Giving on a national basis, with emphasis on CA, ME, NY, PA, and UT.
Application information: Application form not required.
Deadline(s): None
Trustee: Wells Fargo Bank Northwest, N.A.
EIN: 566502391

3204
Charles Redd Foundation
P.O. Box 247
La Sal, UT 84530
Contact: Robert Byron Redd, Tr.
Application address: c/o Beverly Woods, 1425 N. 1200 W., Mapleton, UT 84664

Established in 1971 in UT.
Grantmaker type: Independent foundation
Financial data (yr. ended 12/31/01): Assets, $2,969,675 (M); expenditures, $123,228; qualifying distributions, $97,935; giving activities include $94,250 for 20 grants (high: $25,000; low: $100).
Purpose and activities: Support for agricultural, economic, and historical research at public and private universities in UT.
Fields of interest: History/archaeology; Arts; Higher education; Education; Natural resources; Agriculture; Economics.
Types of support: Equipment; Endowments; Conferences/seminars; Fellowships; Research; Matching/challenge support.
Limitations: Giving primarily in southwestern CO and southeastern UT.
Application information: Application form not required.
Copies of proposal: 15
Deadline(s): Nov. 30
Board meeting date(s): Jan.
Trustees: Robert Clegg; Rebecca Lambert; Regina Mitchell; Katheryn Mullins; Maraley Rasmussen; Regina Rasmussen; Annaley Redd; Charles Hardy Redd; Paul Redd; Robert Byron Redd; Debbie Stevens; Beverly Woods.
Number of staff: None.
EIN: 876148176

3205
William E. Slaughter, Jr. Foundation, Inc.
59 S. Main St., PMB 144
Moab, UT 84532

Incorporated in 1959 in MI.
Donor(s): William E. Slaughter, Jr.‡
Grantmaker type: Independent foundation
Financial data (yr. ended 12/31/02): Assets, $0 (M); expenditures, $162,361; qualifying distributions, $145,000; giving activities include $145,000 for 33 grants (high: $19,000; low: $500).
Purpose and activities: Giving primarily for wildlife and animal preservation, world improvement, and the environment.
Fields of interest: Natural resources; Environment; Animal welfare; International peace/security.

Types of support: General/operating support; Continuing support; Annual campaigns; Seed money.
Limitations: Applications not accepted. Giving primarily in AZ, HI, and UT. No grants to individuals.
Application information: Contributes only to pre-selected organizations.
Officers and Directors:* Kent C. Slaughter,* Pres. and Secy.; Gloria Slaughter,* V.P.; William E. Stillwater,* V.P.; William A. Corbett, C.F.O.
Number of staff: None.
EIN: 386065616

3206
Steiner Foundation, Inc.
505 E. South Temple St.
Salt Lake City, UT 84102-1004
(801) 328-8831
Contact: Kevin K. Steiner, Pres.

Established in 1959 in UT.
Donor(s): Steiner Corp.
Grantmaker type: Company-sponsored foundation
Financial data (yr. ended 06/30/02): Assets, $3,049,132 (M); expenditures, $299,789; qualifying distributions, $284,474; giving activities include $275,008 for 44 grants (high: $100,000; low: $500) and $6,845 for 9 in-kind gifts.
Purpose and activities: Giving primarily for education, the arts and social services.
Fields of interest: Arts; Education; Environment; Human services; Children/youth, services; Religion.
Limitations: Giving primarily in UT.
Application information: Application form not required.
Initial approach: Proposal
Deadline(s): None
Officers: Kevin K. Steiner, Pres.; Timothy L. Weiler, Secy.
EIN: 876119190

3207
Dr. W. C. Swanson Family Foundation, Inc. ▼
2955 Harrison Blvd., Ste. 201
Ogden, UT 84403 (801) 392-0360
Contact: Lynda Murphy, Grants Admin.
Additional tel.: (801) 530-0360; FAX: (801) 392-0429; E-mail: SFF@swanfound.org; Lynda@swanfound.org

Established in 1977; incorporated in 1999.
Donor(s): W.C. Swanson.‡
Grantmaker type: Independent foundation
Financial data (yr. ended 12/31/02): Assets, $37,254,713 (M); gifts received, $2,717,661; expenditures, $6,820,251; qualifying distributions, $552,270; giving activities include $924,142 for 47 grants (high: $496,861; low: $90; average: $1,000–$50,000), $1,035,690 for 4 foundation-administered programs and $3,212,260 for 102 in-kind gifts.
Purpose and activities: Giving primarily for education, arts and culture, human services, and the prevention of cruelty to children and animals.

Fields of interest: Media/communications; Arts; Education; Animal welfare; Children/youth, services; Homeless, human services.
International interests: Cambodia; Mongolia.
Types of support: General/operating support; Continuing support; Capital campaigns; Equipment; Emergency funds; Program development; Conferences/seminars; Scholarship funds; Research; In-kind gifts; Matching/challenge support.
Limitations: Giving primarily in UT, with emphasis on Weber County and Ogden City. No grants to individuals, or for salaries and benefits; limited funding for "bricks and mortar".
Publications: Application guidelines, Informational brochure, Newsletter.
Application information: Must complete application and provide all requested information. Application form required.
Initial approach: Letter
Copies of proposal: 1
Deadline(s): End of the quarter/prior to the quarter when grant request will be considered. Contact Grants Admin. for specific deadline dates, they may vary year to year
Board meeting date(s): Quarterly
Advisory Board and Directors:* W. Charles Swanson,* Chair. and C.E.O.; Cindy Purcell, Pres.; Annabel Hofer,* Exec. V.P.; Lew Costley,* Secy.; Kim Dohrer; Michael Fosmark; Marcy Korgenski; Robert Marguardt; Tami Swanson.
Number of staff: 5 full-time professional; 3 part-time professional; 14 full-time support; 2 part-time support.
EIN: 870578540
Recent environmental and animal welfare grants:
3207-1 Greater Ogden Community Nature Center, Ogden, UT, $25,000. For general operating support of Wildlife on Wheels Program. 2002.
3207-2 Utah Animal-Assisted Therapy Association-People and Animals Working to Serve (UAATA, Salt Lake City, UT, $10,000. For memorial grant. 2002.

3208
Tanner Charitable Trust
1930 S. State St.
Salt Lake City, UT 84115 (801) 486-2430

Incorporated in 1965 in UT.
Donor(s): Obert C. Tanner.
Grantmaker type: Independent foundation
Financial data (yr. ended 12/31/01): Assets, $6,274,914 (M); expenditures, $2,042,453; qualifying distributions, $2,021,762; giving activities include $2,014,600 for 69 grants (high: $1,002,500; low: $100).
Purpose and activities: Giving primarily for arts, education, and social services.
Fields of interest: Performing arts; Orchestra (symphony); Arts; Higher education; Natural resources; Health organizations, association; Human services; Federated giving programs.
Limitations: Applications not accepted. Giving primarily in Salt Lake City, UT. No grants to individuals.
Application information: Contributes only to pre-selected organizations.
Officer and Trustees:* Carolyn T. Irish,* Chair.; Kent H. Murdock; Grace A. Tanner.

EIN: 876125059

3209
Robert I. Wishnick Foundation
(formerly The Witco Foundation)
P.O. Box 681869
Park City, UT 84068
Contact: William Wishnick, Pres.

Incorporated in 1951 in IL.
Donor(s): William Wishnick.
Grantmaker type: Independent foundation
Financial data (yr. ended 12/31/02): Assets, $7,736,358 (M); expenditures, $408,437; qualifying distributions, $380,986; giving activities include $374,700 for 87 grants (high: $50,000; low: $100).
Fields of interest: Performing arts; Arts; Higher education; Natural resources; Animal welfare; Hospitals (general); Human services; Jewish federated giving programs; Jewish agencies & temples.
Types of support: General/operating support; Annual campaigns; Capital campaigns; Endowments; Research.
Limitations: Applications not accepted. Giving on a national basis. No grants to individuals.
Application information: Contributes only to pre-selected organizations.
Board meeting date(s): 4 to 5 times a year
Officers and Directors:* William Wishnick,* Pres.; Lisa Wishnick,* V.P.; Robert L. Bachner,* Secy.; Simeon Brinberg; Ami Jo Gibson; Gina Grossman.
Number of staff: None.
EIN: 136068668

VERMONT

3210
Alcyon Foundation
c/o Frederick H. West
P.O. Box 1015, Prospect St., Ste. 433350
Manchester, VT 05254

Established in 1994 in DE.
Donor(s): Lucile E. Dupont Flint, Frederick H. West, Mrs. Frederick H. West.
Grantmaker type: Independent foundation
Financial data (yr. ended 12/31/02): Assets, $3,044,780 (M); gifts received, $78,720; expenditures, $205,311; qualifying distributions, $196,420; giving activities include $187,683 for 22 grants (high: $75,500; low: $500).
Fields of interest: Museums (history); Arts; Education; Natural resources; Human services.
Limitations: Applications not accepted. Giving primarily in VT. No grants to individuals.
Application information: Contributes only to pre-selected organizations.
Officers: Frederick H. West, Pres. and Treas.; Constance F. West, V.P. and Secy.
EIN: 510355030

3211
Ben & Jerry's Foundation, Inc.
30 Community Dr.
South Burlington, VT 05403 (802) 846-1500
Contact: Debby Kessler, Admin. Asst.
URL: http://www.benjerry.com/foundation/
index.html

Established in 1985 in NY.
Donor(s): Ben & Jerry's Homemade Inc.
Grantmaker type: Company-sponsored
foundation
Financial data (yr. ended 12/31/01): Assets,
$5,864,790 (M); gifts received, $1,429,857;
expenditures, $1,897,574; qualifying
distributions, $1,824,994; giving activities
include $1,824,994 for grants (average:
$250–$15,000).
Purpose and activities: Support for, but not
limited to, projects which facilitate progressive
social change/justice in the following areas:
children and families, disenfranchised groups,
and the environment. Funding primarily for
grassroots organizations and for projects that are
models of systemic change and examples of
creative problem-solving, and that are focused
on strategy rather than on issues or agenda.
Fields of interest: Child development,
education; Natural resources; Environment;
AIDS; Labor unions/organizations; Employment;
Agriculture; Housing/shelter, development;
Youth development, citizenship;
Race/intergroup relations; Civil rights;
Community development; Public affairs, citizen
participation; Minorities; Native
Americans/American Indians; Women;
Gays/lesbians; Immigrants/refugees;
Economically disadvantaged; Homeless.
Types of support: General/operating support;
Program development; Seed money;
Matching/challenge support.
Limitations: Giving limited to the U.S. and its
territories. No support for state agencies, basic
or direct service organizations, religious
projects, or universities. No grants to
individuals, or for research projects,
discretionary or emergency funds, international
or foreign programs, or scholarship funds.
Publications: Application guidelines, Annual
report, Grants list.
Application information: Preliminary
application must be submitted 8 weeks prior to
any deadline to be considered for that deadline.
Full proposals accepted following foundation
invitation only. Accepts NNG Common Grant
Application; however, applicant must contact
foundation before submitting. Do not submit
proposals via FedEx or express mail. Application
form required.
  Initial approach: Call or write for application
    materials or see Web site for application
    material
  Copies of proposal: 2
  Deadline(s): Mar. 1, July 1, and Nov. 1 for
    invited proposals only
  Final notification: Approximately 10 weeks
    after deadline
Officers and Trustees:* Jerry Greenfield,* Pres.;
Elizabeth Bankowski,* Secy.; Jeffrey Furman,*
Treas.; Rebecca Golden, Fdn. Dir.
Number of staff: 1 full-time professional; 1
part-time support.
EIN: 030300865

3212
Ben & Jerry's Homemade Inc. Corporate
Giving Program
30 Community Dr.
South Burlington, VT 05403 (802) 846-1500
Contact: Lisa Pendolino

Grantmaker type: Corporate giving program
Purpose and activities: As a complement to its
foundation, Ben & Jerry's also makes charitable
contributions to nonprofit organizations directly.
Support is given on a national basis.
Fields of interest: Environment; Agriculture/food.
Types of support: General/operating support;
Program development; Seed money; Employee
matching gifts; Donated products.
Limitations: Giving on a national basis. No
support for sports organizations or human
services organizations. No grants for sporting
events.
Application information: The Social Mission
Department handles giving. Application form
not required.
  Initial approach: Proposal to headquarters
  Copies of proposal: 1
  Deadline(s): None
  Final notification: Varies
Number of staff: 1 full-time professional; 1
full-time support.

3213
G.D.S. Legacy Foundation, Inc.
80 Ordway Shore Rd.
Shelburne, VT 05482 (802) 985-2998
Contact: Peter D. Swift, Tr.

Established in 2000 in VT.
Donor(s): Peter D. Swift.
Grantmaker type: Independent foundation
Financial data (yr. ended 12/31/02): Assets,
$3,744,371 (M); gifts received, $300,059;
expenditures, $308,797; qualifying distributions,
$303,406; giving activities include $250,500 for
22 grants (high: $50,000; low: $500).
Fields of interest: Arts; Education; Health care;
Environment; Human services.
Limitations: Giving primarily in Washington,
DC, NY, and VT.
Application information:
  Initial approach: Letter
Trustees: Ted Cronin; William G. Post, Jr.; Peter
D. Swift.
EIN: 030368174

3214
The Kelsey Trust
c/o Vermont Community Foundation
P.O. Box 30
Middlebury, VT 05753 (802) 388-3355
Contact: Judy Dunning, Sr. Prog. Officer
URL: http://www.vermontcf.org/
grants-rounds.html

Established in 1988 in MA.
Donor(s): Sally P. Johnson.
Grantmaker type: Independent foundation
Financial data (yr. ended 06/30/02): Assets,
$3,779,138 (M); expenditures, $227,968;
qualifying distributions, $215,732; giving
activities include $209,150 for 26 grants (high:
$62,500; low: $1,000).

Purpose and activities: Primary areas of interest
include education, health, the environment, and
children and families in the Champlain Basin.
Fields of interest: Child development,
education; Vocational education; Adult
education—literacy, basic skills & GED;
Reading; Education; Natural resources;
Environment; Family planning; Health care;
Nutrition; Children/youth, services; Family
services; Aging.
Types of support: General/operating support;
Continuing support; Land acquisition;
Emergency funds; Program development;
Publication; Seed money; Curriculum
development; Scholarship funds; Program
evaluation; Program-related investments/loans;
Matching/challenge support.
Limitations: Giving limited to the Lake
Champlain Valley Drainage Basin region: the
eastern Adirondacks in NY, and western VT,
north of Rutland. No grants to individuals.
Publications: Application guidelines,
Occasional report, Program policy statement.
Application information: Application form
required.
  Initial approach: Letter requesting application
    material
  Copies of proposal: 1
  Deadline(s): Sept. 1 and Feb. 1
  Board meeting date(s): Nov. and May
  Final notification: Dec. and June
Trustees: Paula D. Johnson; Sally P. Johnson;
Stephen P. Johnson.
Number of staff: None.
EIN: 046609917

3215
Lintilhac Foundation
886 North Gate Rd.
Shelburne, VT 05482 (802) 985-4106
Contact: Crea S. Lintilhac, Pres.
FAX: (802) 985-3725

Established in 1975.
Donor(s): Claire Malcolm Lintilhac.‡
Grantmaker type: Independent foundation
Financial data (yr. ended 12/31/01): Assets,
$17,252,118 (M); gifts received, $702,734;
expenditures, $1,014,268; qualifying
distributions, $892,859; giving activities include
$836,211 for 85 grants (high: $60,000; low:
$300).
Purpose and activities: Support for medical
education programs at specified institutions in
VT; support also for health services, community
development, civic projects and educational
institutions.
Fields of interest: Medical school/education;
Education; Environment; Family planning;
Health care; Family services; Community
development; Marine science;
Government/public administration.
Types of support: General/operating support;
Continuing support; Building/renovation;
Equipment; Land acquisition; Program
development; Conferences/seminars;
Professorships; Seed money; Curriculum
development; Fellowships; Scholarship funds;
Matching/challenge support.
Limitations: Giving primarily in north central
VT, including Chittenden, Lamoille, and
Washington counties. No grants to individuals.
Publications: Biennial report.

Application information: Application form not required.

Initial approach: Proposal
Copies of proposal: 4
Deadline(s): None
Board meeting date(s): Quarterly

Officers and Directors:* Crea S. Lintilhac,* Pres.; Philip M. Lintilhac,* V.P. and Secy.; Raeman P. Sopher,* Treas.

Number of staff: 1 full-time support; 1 part-time support.

EIN: 510176851

3216
Maverick Lloyd Foundation
(formerly Maverick Foundation)
P.O. Box 100
Sharon, VT   05065   (802) 763-5255
Contact: Ann McLaughlin, Admin. Asst.
FAX: (802) 763-5265

Established in 1995 in IL.
Donor(s): Georgia Lloyd.‡
Grantmaker type: Independent foundation
Financial data (yr. ended 12/31/02): Assets, $2,199,638 (M); gifts received, $249,188; expenditures, $121,847; qualifying distributions, $100,460; giving activities include $97,500 for 8 grants (high: $15,000; low: $7,500; average: $7,500–$15,000).
Purpose and activities: Giving for projects which educate, or advocate for the public or particular group, or help sustain and protect the environment. Projects that promote conflict resolution, where applicable, are encouraged.
Fields of interest: Natural resources; Family planning; Agriculture/food, management/technical aid; Civil liberties, advocacy; Civil rights.
Limitations: Giving on a national basis, with emphasis on VT and other New England states. No support for religious organizations. No grants to individuals, or for general operating support, travel, scholarships, new construction or endowments, or to the medical or health-related fields.
Publications: Application guidelines, Grants list.
Application information: Application form not required.

Initial approach: Letter requesting foundation's operating principles and grant guidelines, or a 1-page letter of intent
Copies of proposal: 1
Deadline(s): Apr. 1 for June funding, Oct. 1 for Dec. funding
Board meeting date(s): May 30 and Oct. 30
Final notification: Within 1 month

Trustees: Anne Berndt; Arthur Berndt.
Number of staff: 1 part-time support.
EIN: 367093389

3217
National Gardening Association
1100 Dorset St.
South Burlington, VT   05403   (802) 863-1308
Contact: Susan W. Dixon, Grant Coord.
FAX: (802) 863-5962; *E-mail:* NGA@garden.org;
URL: http://www.garden.org

Established in 1972.
Grantmaker type: Public charity

Financial data (yr. ended 08/31/02): Revenue, $1,337,402; assets, $1,200,437 (M); gifts received, $243,190; expenditures, $1,640,837; program services expenses, $1,378,999; giving activities include $84,221 for grants.
Purpose and activities: The association seeks to support and encourage youth gardening in schools, hospitals, clubs, camps, residential treatment facilities, communities, and intergenerational gardens with children and seniors.
Fields of interest: Horticulture/garden clubs.
Application information:

Deadline(s): Nov. 1 for Youth Garden Grants

Officers and Directors:* Steven Frownie,* Chair.; A. William Miller,* V.P.; Valerie Kelsey, Ph.D.,* V.P., Educ. and Progs.; Larry Sommers,* V.P., Publ. and Info.; William Dredge; David Els; Neil Hamilton; Frederick B. Kieckhefer, Jr.; Renee Shepherd; Catherine Sneed; Kathleen Tierney; Peter Tonge; Alan Vandenburgh; Ramsey Yoder.
EIN: 237346417

3218
The Redducs Chartered Foundation Corp.
c/o Fred Tiballi & Assoc., PC
120 Pine St.
Burlington, VT   05401
Contact: Frederick P. Tiballi, Exec. Dir.

Established in 1998 in FL and VT.
Donor(s): Mary Gale Scudder, Edward Scudder, Jr., Edward Scudder III, Katherine Scudder Tiballi.
Grantmaker type: Independent foundation
Financial data (yr. ended 12/31/02): Assets, $3,804,609 (M); expenditures, $236,158; qualifying distributions, $192,605; giving activities include $143,600 for 18 grants (high: $25,000; low: $400).
Purpose and activities: Giving primarily for social services.
Fields of interest: Natural resources; Animal welfare; Human services.
Types of support: General/operating support; Continuing support; Annual campaigns; Capital campaigns; Land acquisition; Emergency funds; Program development; Curriculum development.
Limitations: Giving primarily in CA and VT.
Application information: Application form not required.

Initial approach: Letter
Board meeting date(s): Mid-July
Final notification: Within 60 days

Officers and Directors:* Edward Scudder, Jr.,* Chair.; Katherine Scudder Tiballi,* Vice-Chair.; Edward Scudder III,* Pres.; Mary Gale Scudder,* V.P.; Robert F. Scudder,* V.P.; Fred Tiballi, Exec. Dir.
Number of staff: 1 part-time professional.
EIN: 650840245

3219
Frank and Brinna Sands Foundation
c/o Conrad Reining
319 Caldwell Rd.
East Thetford, VT   05043

Established in 1996 in VT.
Donor(s): Brinna B. Sands, Frank E. Sands II.
Grantmaker type: Independent foundation

Financial data (yr. ended 11/30/02): Assets, $1,860,456 (M); expenditures, $153,029; qualifying distributions, $145,176; giving activities include $136,400 for 55 grants (high: $45,000; low: $100).
Purpose and activities: Giving for education and alumni associations.
Fields of interest: Higher education; Education, alumni groups; Environment, land resources.
Limitations: Applications not accepted. Giving primarily in CT and VT. No grants to individuals.
Application information: Contributes only to pre-selected organizations.
Officers and Directors:* Brinna B. Sands,* Pres.; Frank E. Sands II,* V.P. and Secy.; Jennifer B. Kitchel; Conrad Reining.
EIN: 043342111

3220
Seventh Generation, Inc. Corporate Giving Program
212 Battery St., Ste. A
Burlington, VT   05401-5281

Grantmaker type: Corporate giving program
Purpose and activities: Seventh Generation makes charitable contributions to nonprofit organizations involved with the environment. Support is given on a national basis and in Canada.
Fields of interest: Environment.
International interests: Canada.
Types of support: General/operating support; Donated products.
Limitations: Giving on a national basis, with emphasis on VT, and in Canada.

3221
Amy E. Tarrant Foundation, Inc.
570 S. Prospect St.
Burlington, VT   05401   (802) 860-6188
Contact: Ron Roberts

Established in 2000 in VT.
Donor(s): Amy E. Tarrant.
Grantmaker type: Independent foundation
Financial data (yr. ended 12/31/00): Assets, $2,951,062 (M); gifts received, $876,584; expenditures, $178,210; qualifying distributions, $157,258; giving activities include $165,500 for 17 grants (high: $25,000; low: $1,500).
Fields of interest: Humanities; Education; Animal welfare; Food services; Housing/shelter, temporary shelter; Family services; Aging, centers/services.
Limitations: Giving primarily in VT.
Application information:

Initial approach: Letter
Deadline(s): None

Directors: Amy E. Tarrant; Brian Tarrant; Jeremiah Tarrant; Richard E. Tarrant, Jr.
EIN: 020514457

3222
Vermont Community Foundation
3 Court St.
P.O. Box 30
Middlebury, VT 05753 (802) 388-3355
Contact: Faith I. Brown
FAX: (802) 388-3398; E-mail:
vcf@vermontcf.org; URL: http://
www.vermontcf.org

Established in 1986 in VT.
Grantmaker type: Community foundation
Financial data (yr. ended 12/31/02): Assets,
$73,413,316 (M); gifts received, $21,890,640;
expenditures, $6,522,481; giving activities
include $5,207,368 for grants.
Purpose and activities: As a developer of
resources, the foundation seeks to build a
permanent accessible endowment of funds for
charitable purposes, and to increase charitable
capital for VT.
Fields of interest: Historic preservation/historical
societies; Arts; Early childhood education; Child
development, education; Elementary
school/education; Secondary school/education;
Higher education; Adult/continuing education;
Libraries/library science; Natural resources;
Environment; Animal welfare; Family planning;
Substance abuse, services; Mental health/crisis
services; AIDS; Alcoholism; Health
organizations; Human services; Children/youth,
services; Youth, services; Child development,
services; Family services; Minorities/immigrants,
centers/services; Homeless, human services;
Civil rights; Community development; Public
affairs; Disabled; Aging; Economically
disadvantaged.
Types of support: Management development;
Program development; Seed money; Scholarship
funds; Technical assistance; Consulting services;
Program-related investments/loans.
Limitations: Giving limited to VT. No support for
religious purposes. No grants for annual
campaigns, or for building funds, continuing
support, debt reduction, equipment and
materials, general endowments, or for operating
budgets.
Publications: Application guidelines, Annual
report, Financial statement, Grants list,
Informational brochure (including application
guidelines), Multi-year report, Occasional
report, Program policy statement.
Application information: Proposal summary
form required. Application form not required.
Initial approach: Proposal
Copies of proposal: 3
Deadline(s): Apr. 1 and Oct. 1
Board meeting date(s): 4 times annually
Final notification: 2 months
Officers and Directors:* Richard C. White,*
Chair.; Vicky Young, Vice-Chair.; Brian T.
Byrnes,* Pres.; Robert Woolmington, Secy.;
Deborah W. Granquist, Treas.; Kevin Harper;
Cornelius D. Hogan; Kathy Hoyt; Ellen Kahler;
Lisa Lorimer; Lawrence H. Mandell; Cheryl
Mitchell; Patricia Motch; Ernest A. Pomerleau;
Albert Perry; John F. Taylor.
Number of staff: 9 full-time professional; 3
part-time professional; 2 full-time support; 2
part-time support.
EIN: 222712160

3223
Vermont Yankee Nuclear Power
Corporation Contributions Program
185 Ferry Rd.
Brattleboro, VT 05301 (802) 258-4118
Contact: Laurence M. Smith, Corp. and
Community Rels. Rep.
FAX: (802) 258-2129

Grantmaker type: Corporate giving program
Purpose and activities: Vermont Yankee Nuclear
Power makes charitable contributions to
nonprofit organizations involved with arts and
culture, education, the environment, youth
development, and to hospitals. Support is given
within a 10-mile emergency planning zone
surrounding the company's nuclear power
station.
Fields of interest: Arts; Education; Environment;
Hospitals (general); Youth development.
Types of support: General/operating support;
Continuing support; Annual campaigns; Capital
campaigns; Building/renovation; Equipment;
Emergency funds; Program development; Seed
money; Scholarship funds; Employee volunteer
services; Public relations services; Sponsorships;
Employee matching gifts; Donated equipment;
Matching/challenge support.
Limitations: Giving within a 10-mile emergency
planning zone surrounding the company's
nuclear power station.
Publications: Corporate report, Corporate giving
report (including application guidelines),
Program policy statement.
Application information: The Public Affairs
Department handles giving. The company has a
staff that only handles contributions. Application
form required.
Initial approach: Contact headquarters for
application form
Copies of proposal: 1
Deadline(s): None
Final notification: Following review
Number of staff: 1 full-time professional; 1
part-time professional; 1 full-time support.

3224
The Windham Foundation, Inc.
P.O. Box 70
Grafton, VT 05146 (802) 843-2211
Contact: Stephan A. Morse, C.E.O.
FAX: (802) 843-2205; E-mail:
winfound@sover.net; URL: http://
www.windham-foundation.org

Incorporated in 1963 in VT.
Donor(s): The Bunbury Co., Inc., Dean Mathey.‡
Grantmaker type: Operating foundation
Financial data (yr. ended 10/31/02): Assets,
$51,648,885 (M); gifts received, $40,000;
expenditures, $3,994,788; qualifying
distributions, $2,767,454; giving activities
include $85,975 for 60 grants (high: $15,000;
low: $500; average: $100–$500), $111,302 for
grants to individuals and $658,835 for
foundation-administered programs.
Purpose and activities: The Windham
Foundation, the largest foundation chartered in
the state, is a not-for-profit organization located
in Grafton, VT. The foundation was established
in 1963 with a three-fold purpose: to restore
buildings and economic vitality in the village of
Grafton; to provide financial support for

education and private charities; and to develop
projects that will benefit the general welfare of
VT and its residents. The foundation supports
projects that assure the preservation of the rural
nature of VT. Such projects include sheep
management, land conservation, forest
management, dairy operations, and recreational
opportunities. The foundation also has a
particular interest in innovative programs and
furthering proven academic programs that could
be replicated in other VT locations and will
assist elementary and secondary education in VT.
Fields of interest: Elementary/secondary
education; Education, services; Education;
Environment, forests; Environment.
Types of support: General/operating support;
Continuing support; Building/renovation;
Equipment; Program development; Seed money;
Curriculum development; Technical assistance;
Scholarships—to individuals;
Matching/challenge support.
Limitations: Giving limited to VT, with emphasis
on Grafton. No grants to individuals (except for
college scholarship program for residents of
Windham County, VT), or for endowment funds;
no loans.
Publications: Application guidelines, Annual
report, Grants list, Informational brochure
(including application guidelines).
Application information: E-mail or FAX requests
will not be accepted. Application form available
on Web site. Application form required.
Initial approach: Letter or telephone for
application and guidelines
Copies of proposal: 7
Deadline(s): Dec. 6, Apr. 4, May 23, and Sept.
5
Board meeting date(s): Quarterly
Final notification: 8-10 weeks
Officers and Trustees:* Samuel W. Lambert III,*
Chair.; Stephan A. Morse,* C.E.O. and Pres.;
Arthur Schubert, V.P.; Edward R. Zuccaro,* V.P.;
Elizabeth Bankowski,* Secy.; Robert M.
Olmsted, Treas.; William H. Bruett; William A.
Gilbert; Jamie Kyte Sapoch; Edward J. Toohey.
Number of staff: 7 full-time professional.
EIN: 136142024

3225
Woodstock Foundation, Inc.
P.O. Box 489
Woodstock, VT 05091 (802) 457-2355
Contact: Marian Koetsier, Secy.
FAX: (802) 457-4663; E-mail:
Mkoetsier@valley.net

Established in 1968 in VT.
Donor(s): Laurance S. Rockefeller, Mary F.
Rockefeller.‡
Grantmaker type: Operating foundation
Financial data (yr. ended 12/31/01): Assets,
$48,132,048 (M); gifts received, $28,135;
expenditures, $2,770,544; qualifying
distributions, $2,575,286; giving activities
include $99,758 for 71 grants (high: $16,100;
low: $100).
Purpose and activities: The principal activity of
the foundation is to operate the Billings Farm &
Museum in the town of Woodstock, VT, for the
benefit of the general public; the Woodstock
Foundation has not made grants to individuals
and it focuses on programs and organizations of
immediate benefit to the Woodstock community

and/or related to the purposes of the Marsh-Billings-Rockefeller National Historical Park.

Fields of interest: Education; Natural resources; Health care; Health organizations, association; Human services; Community development, neighborhood development.

Types of support: General/operating support; Program development; Curriculum development; Scholarship funds; Matching/challenge support.

Limitations: Giving primarily in the immediate Woodstock, VT, area. No grants to individuals.

Publications: Application guidelines.

Application information: Application form not required.

Initial approach: Letter
Copies of proposal: 1
Deadline(s): Aug. 1
Board meeting date(s): Annually in the fall
Final notification: Nov.

Officers and Trustees:* C. Wesley Frye, Jr.,* Chair.; David A. Donath,* Pres.; Marian Koetsier, Secy.; Jeffrey D. Fink, Treas.; and 4 additional trustees and advisory board.

Number of staff: 6 full-time professional; 9 full-time support; 1 part-time support.

EIN: 030221142

VIRGIN ISLANDS

3226
Prosser ICC Foundation, Inc.

P.O. Box 1730
Christiansted, VI 00821-1730 (340) 713-8998
Contact: Bernice D. Knight, Admin.

Grantmaker type: Independent foundation
Financial data (yr. ended 12/31/01): Assets, $235,748 (M); expenditures, $208,611; qualifying distributions, $208,611; giving activities include $197,130 for 39 grants (high: $30,000; low: $75).

Fields of interest: Arts; Animal welfare; Athletics/sports, amateur leagues; Athletics/sports, golf; Boy scouts; Women, centers/services.

Limitations: Giving primarily in VI.

Application information: Application form required.

Deadline(s): None

Officers: Dawn E. Prosser, Pres.; Adrian LaBennett, V.P.; Luz Highfield, Secy.

Director: Dwain Ford.

Trustee: Lillian Ebbesen.

EIN: 660565727

3227
St. Croix Foundation for Community Development

P.O. Box 1128, Christiansted
St. Croix, VI 00821-1128
Contact: Roger W. Dewey, Exec. Dir.
FAX: (809) 773-8727

Established in 1990 in VI.
Donor(s): The Ford Foundation.
Grantmaker type: Community foundation

Financial data (yr. ended 12/31/00): Assets, $1,759,829 (M); gifts received, $1,710,171; expenditures, $1,905,477; giving activities include $232,407 for grants.

Purpose and activities: The foundation administers a donor-advised fund.

Fields of interest: Education; Environment; Health care; Health organizations; Crime/law enforcement; Community development; Government/public administration.

Limitations: Giving limited to the territory of the U.S. Virgin Islands, with emphasis on St. Croix.

Publications: Application guidelines, Annual report, Informational brochure.

Application information: Contact foundation for deadline. Application form required.

Copies of proposal: 5
Board meeting date(s): Quarterly

Officers: Frandelle Gerard, Chair.; Gerville Larsen, Vice-Chair.; Richard Austin, Secy.; Pablo O'Neill, Treas.; Roger W. Dewey, Exec. Dir.

Board Members: Daryl Brow; Valdmar Hill, Jr.; Stephanie Hodge; Robert Koch; Martin Ludington; Brenda Pederson; Lee Rohn; William Taylor; Claudette Young-Hinds.

Number of staff: 1 full-time professional; 3 part-time professional; 2 part-time support.

EIN: 660480131

VIRGINIA

3228
Ashoka

1700 N. Moore St., Ste. 2000
Arlington, VA 22209-1939 (703) 527-8300
Contact: William Drayton, Chair.
FAX: (703) 527-8383; E-mail: info@ashoka.org; URL: http://www.ashoka.org

Established in 1980.
Grantmaker type: Public charity
Financial data (yr. ended 08/31/02): Revenue, $7,721,159; assets, $39,619,158; gifts received, $6,969,089; expenditures, $12,712,306; program services expenses, $11,311,668; giving activities include $4,291,792 for grants.

Purpose and activities: The organization gives fellowships internationally to individuals who possess the innovation and drive to realize social change in education and youth development, health care, environment, human rights, access to technology and economic development.

Fields of interest: Education; Environment; Health care; Employment; Agriculture/food; Youth development.

Types of support: Fellowships.

Limitations: Giving on a national and international basis.

Publications: Newsletter.

Application information: Application by both nomination and unsolicited application.

Officers and Directors:* William Drayton,* Chair.; C. William Carter,* Secy.-Treas.; Gloria de Souza; Fred Hehuwat; William Kelly, Jr.; Julien Phillips; Kyle Zimmer.

Number of staff: 42.

EIN: 510255908

3229
The William M. Backer Foundation, Inc.

7181 Smitten Farm Ln.
The Plains, VA 20198
Contact: William M. Backer, Pres.

Established in 1990 in DE.
Donor(s): William M. Backer.
Grantmaker type: Independent foundation
Financial data (yr. ended 07/31/02): Assets, $3,637,174 (M); gifts received, $54,204; expenditures, $249,034; qualifying distributions, $205,851; giving activities include $207,305 for 36 grants (high: $150,250; low: $35).

Fields of interest: Arts; Education; Environment; Human services; Federated giving programs; Protestant agencies & churches.

Types of support: General/operating support; Continuing support; Capital campaigns; Building/renovation; Land acquisition; Endowments; Scholarship funds; Research.

Limitations: Applications not accepted. Giving in the U.S., with emphasis on VA. No grants to individuals.

Application information: Contributes only to pre-selected organizations.

Officers: William M. Backer, Pres. and Treas.; Philip S. Reiss, Secy.

Number of staff: None.

EIN: 133579157

3230
Bedford Falls Foundation

6501 Menlo Rd.
McLean, VA 22101-3012

Established in 1997 in VA.
Donor(s): William E. Conway, Joanne Conway.
Grantmaker type: Independent foundation
Financial data (yr. ended 12/31/02): Assets, $184,450 (M); gifts received, $144,230; expenditures, $403,332; qualifying distributions, $401,239; giving activities include $399,574 for 32 grants (high: $145,000; low: $162).

Purpose and activities: Giving primarily for animal welfare, and to an art gallery; funding also for education, health associations, children, youth and social services, and Roman Catholic organizations.

Fields of interest: Museums (art); Higher education; Education; Animal welfare; Health organizations, association; Kidney diseases; Big Brothers/Big Sisters; Human services; Children/youth, services; Roman Catholic agencies & churches.

Limitations: Applications not accepted. Giving primarily in Washington, DC, and Nashua, NH. No grants to individuals.

Application information: Contributes only to pre-selected organizations.

Trustees: Joanne Conway; William E. Conway.

EIN: 526834462

3231
The Blocker Foundation

P.O. Box 14219
Norfolk, VA 23518-0219 (757) 583-4040
Contact: S. Frank Blocker, Jr., Pres.

Established in 1982.
Grantmaker type: Independent foundation

Financial data (yr. ended 07/31/02): Assets, $2,507,910 (M); expenditures, $180,081; qualifying distributions, $176,942; giving activities include $177,812 for 90 grants (high: $57,500; low: $50).
Purpose and activities: Giving for higher education, medical services and world peace.
Fields of interest: Higher education; Botanical/horticulture/landscape services; Hospitals (general); Human services; General charitable giving.
Types of support: General/operating support; Capital campaigns; Building/renovation; Endowments; Scholarship funds.
Limitations: Giving primarily in Norfolk, VA.
Application information:
Deadline(s): None
Officers and Directors:* S. Frank Blocker, Jr.,* Pres.; Mariam B. Lawler,* Secy.; M. Ward Cole; Frederick V. Martin.
Number of staff: 1 part-time professional.
EIN: 541217447

3232
Blue Moon Fund, Inc.
(formerly W. Alton Jones Foundation, Inc.)
433 Park St.
Charlottesville, VA 22902 (434) 295-5160
FAX: (434) 295-6894; E-mail:
info@bluemoonfund.org; URL: http://www.bluemoonfund.org

Incorporated in 1944 in NY as W. Alton Jones Foundation. Underwent restructure in 2001, reorganizing as Blue Moon Fund (retaining original EI number) and two new funds, Oak Hill Fund and Edgerton Foundation.
Donor(s): W. Alton Jones.‡
Grantmaker type: Independent foundation
Financial data (yr. ended 12/31/01): Assets, $362,862,472 (M); expenditures, $34,239,333; qualifying distributions, $30,540,924; giving activities include $26,141,156 for 388 grants (high: $550,000; low: $600).
Purpose and activities: The fund supports initiatives that elevate the human condition by comprehensively addressing human consumption, the natural world, and economic advancement, including sponsoring a fellows program aimed at cultivating cutting-edge approaches to these issues.
Fields of interest: Natural resources; International development; Economic development.
Types of support: General/operating support; Program development; Fellowships.
Limitations: Giving on a national and international basis.
Publications: Annual report (including application guidelines).
Application information: See fund Web site for application requirements for BMF Urban Fellowship.
Officers and Directors:* Diane Edgerton Miller,* C.E.O. and Pres.; Ji-Qiang Zhang, V.P., Programs; Ethan A. Miller,* Secy.; Diane Schmidt, C.F.O.; Pat Jones Edgerton,* Treas.; Beverly Lamb, Compt.
EIN: 136034219

3233
Boat US Foundation for Boating Safety and Clean Water
(formerly Boat US Foundation for Boating Safety)
880 S. Pickett St.
Alexandria, VA 22304
Contact: Vanessa Pert, Grant Admin.
Tel.: (703) 823-9550, ext. 3200; Additional tel.: (800) 336-2628; FAX: (703) 461-2855; E-mail: vpert@boatus.com, mpodlich@boatus.com (for Clean Water); URL: http://www.boatus.com/foundation/

Established in 1989 in VA.
Grantmaker type: Public charity
Financial data (yr. ended 12/31/00): Revenue, $1,300,322; assets, $1,105,656; gifts received, $981,691; expenditures, $1,308,232; program services expenses, $919,140; giving activities include $51,336 for 32 grants (high: $7,119; low: $350).
Purpose and activities: The foundation provides safe and environmentally sensitive boating with the purpose of reducing accidents and fatalities while increasing stewardship of our water resources.
Fields of interest: Environment, water resources; Environment; Safety, education; Recreation, administration/regulation; Athletics/sports, water sports; Recreation.
Types of support: Annual campaigns; Equipment; Endowments; Program development; Conferences/seminars; Publication; Seed money; Curriculum development; Technical assistance; In-kind gifts; Matching/challenge support.
Limitations: No support for for-profit businesses, private clubs, or groups not open to the general public. No grants to individuals, or for capital improvement, general operating support, debt reduction, salaries, or travel expenses.
Publications: Application guidelines, Annual report, Grants list, Informational brochure.
Application information: See Web site for application samples. Application form required.
Initial approach: Letter, telephone, or e-mail for application guidelines
Copies of proposal: 1
Deadline(s): Nov. 1 for Grassroots; Feb. 1 for Clean Water
Board meeting date(s): Dec. for Grassroots; Mar. for Clean Water
Final notification: Jan. for Grassroots; Apr. for Clean Water
Officers and Trustees:* Richard Schwartz,* Chair.; James F. Ellis,* Pres.; N. Ruth Wood,* V.P.; Richard Moreland; Ronald Peterson; Robert Putnam.
Number of staff: 8 full-time professional; 3 full-time support.
EIN: 541156448

3234
The Burford Leimenstoll Foundation, Inc.
2956 Hathaway Rd., Apt. 712
Richmond, VA 23225-1734

Established in 1991 in VA.
Donor(s): Betty Sams Christian.
Grantmaker type: Independent foundation
Financial data (yr. ended 12/31/01): Assets, $1,406,607 (M); gifts received, $12,855; expenditures, $116,775; qualifying distributions,

$107,200; giving activities include $103,920 for 63 grants (high: $60,000; low: $100).
Purpose and activities: Giving for education, water and nature conservation, and human and youth services.
Fields of interest: Arts; Education; Environment; Health organizations, association; Housing/shelter; Human services; Children/youth, services.
Limitations: Applications not accepted. Giving on a national basis. No grants to individuals.
Application information: Contributes only to pre-selected organizations.
Officers and Director:* Betty Sams Christian,* Pres.; Ben R. Lacy IV, Secy.
EIN: 541608741

3235
Camp Foundation
P.O. Box 813
Franklin, VA 23851 (757) 562-3439
Contact: Bobby B. Worrell, Exec. Dir.

Incorporated in 1942 in VA.
Donor(s): James L. Camp,‡ P.D. Camp,‡ and their families.
Grantmaker type: Independent foundation
Financial data (yr. ended 12/31/02): Assets, $15,925,683 (M); expenditures, $777,680; qualifying distributions, $757,472; giving activities include $552,959 for 55 grants and $90,000 for 28 grants to individuals (high: $4,500; low: $3,000).
Purpose and activities: To provide or aid in providing, in or near the town of Franklin, VA, parks, playgrounds, recreational facilities, libraries, hospitals, clinics, homes for the aged or needy, refuge for delinquent, dependent or neglected children, training schools, or other like institutions or activities. Grants also to select organizations statewide, with emphasis on youth agencies, safety programs, hospitals, mental illness, and nursing programs, higher and secondary education, including scholarships filed through high school principals, recreation, the environment, historic preservation, and cultural programs.
Fields of interest: Historic preservation/historical societies; Arts; Secondary school/education; Higher education; Libraries/library science; Education; Environment; Hospitals (general); Nursing care; Health care; Mental health/crisis services; Safety/disasters; Recreation; Children/youth, services; Aging, centers/services; Government/public administration; Aging.
Types of support: Annual campaigns; Building/renovation; Equipment; Land acquisition; Emergency funds; Seed money; Scholarship funds; Research; Scholarships—to individuals; Matching/challenge support.
Limitations: Giving primarily in the city of Franklin, and Southampton and Isle of Wight counties, VA.
Publications: Application guidelines.
Application information: 4-year scholarships awarded to graduating high school seniors who are residents of the City of Franklin or the counties of Southampton and Isle of Wight. Application form not required.
Initial approach: Proposal
Copies of proposal: 7

Deadline(s): Submit proposal between June and Aug.; deadline Sept. 1. Scholarship application deadlines: Feb. 26 for filing with high school principals
Board meeting date(s): May and Nov.
Final notification: 3 months
Officers and Directors:* Robert C. Ray,* Chair.; Sol W. Rawls, Jr.,* Pres.; Westbrook Parker,* V.P.; John M. Camp, Jr.,* Treas.; Bobby B. Worrell,* Exec. Dir.; John M. Camp III; W.M. Camp, Jr.; Clifford A. Cutchins III; William W. Cutchins; Randy B. Drake; John R. Marks; Paul Camp Marks; J. Edward Moyler, Jr.; John D. Munford; S. Waite Rawls, Jr.; J.E. Ray III; Richard E. Ray; Toy D. Savage, Jr.
Number of staff: 2 full-time professional; 1 part-time support.
EIN: 546052488

3236
Carrie S. Camp Foundation, Inc.
P.O. Box 557
Franklin, VA 23851-0057
Contact: L. Clay Camp, Jr., Secy.

Incorporated about 1949 in VA.
Donor(s): Edith Clay Camp.
Grantmaker type: Independent foundation
Financial data (yr. ended 12/31/01): Assets, $1,204,432 (M); expenditures, $93,962; qualifying distributions, $90,107; giving activities include $90,500 for 32 grants (high: $20,000; low: $600).
Purpose and activities: To support community development, environmental conservation, historical preservation, and education.
Fields of interest: Historic preservation/historical societies; Education; Natural resources; Animals/wildlife; Health organizations, association; Medical research, institute; Human services; Children/youth, services; Community development; Protestant agencies & churches.
Types of support: General/operating support; Building/renovation; Scholarship funds.
Limitations: Giving primarily in VA.
Application information: Application form not required.
Initial approach: Letter
Deadline(s): None
Officers: L. Clay Camp, Sr., Pres.; Barbara P. Camp, V.P.; L. Clay Camp, Jr., Secy.; Mildred M. Branche, Treas.
Director: Carrie Camp Gibbons.
EIN: 546052446

3237
The Beirne Carter Foundation
1802 Bayberry Ct., Ste. 301
Richmond, VA 23226-3773 (804) 521-0272
FAX: (804) 521-0274; E-mail: bcarterfn@aol.com; URL: http://www.bcarterfdn.org

Established in 1986 in VA.
Donor(s): Beirne B. Carter.‡
Grantmaker type: Independent foundation
Financial data (yr. ended 12/31/01): Assets, $28,373,630 (M); expenditures, $1,692,897; qualifying distributions, $1,480,255; giving activities include $1,293,000 for 55 grants

(high: $250,000; low: $500; average: $500–$50,000).
Purpose and activities: Support primarily for education, the environment, human services, housing, arts and culture, youth development, and health care.
Fields of interest: History/archaeology; Arts; Education; Natural resources; Environment; Health care; Health organizations, association; Children/youth, services.
Types of support: Capital campaigns; Building/renovation; Equipment; Matching/challenge support.
Limitations: Giving primarily in VA. No support for Churches, public secondary schools and colleges and local municipalities. No grants to individuals; endowment funds, existing deficits or debt reduction.
Publications: Informational brochure (including application guidelines).
Application information: See Web site for list of items needed in proposal. Application form required.
Initial approach: Complete proposals
Copies of proposal: 4
Deadline(s): Feb. 1 and August 1 by 12:00 p.m.
Board meeting date(s): May and Oct.
Final notification: After board meeting
Officers: Mary Ross Carter Hutcheson, Pres.; Kenneth Laughon, V.P.; Talfourd H. Kemper, Secy.-Treas.
Number of staff: 2 part-time professional.
EIN: 541397827

3238
The Catesby Foundation
P.O. Box 500
The Plains, VA 20198-0500 (540) 253-5358
Contact: Casey Linehan

Established in 1971 in VA.
Donor(s): Richard R. Ohrstrom.‡
Grantmaker type: Independent foundation
Financial data (yr. ended 12/31/01): Assets, $2,714,148 (M); gifts received, $20,189; expenditures, $155,927; qualifying distributions, $145,646; giving activities include $140,000 for 22 grants (high: $20,000; low: $1,000).
Purpose and activities: Giving primarily for education, the environment, and health.
Fields of interest: Historic preservation/historical societies; Elementary/secondary education; Education; Environment; Health care; Substance abuse, services; Protestant agencies & churches.
Limitations: Applications not accepted. Giving on a national basis. No grants to individuals.
Application information: Contributes only to pre-selected organizations.
Officers: George L. Ohrstrom II, Pres.; Mark J. Ohrstrom, V.P.; Kenneth M. Ohrstrom, Secy.; Barnaby A. Ohrstrom, Treas.
EIN: 237149750

3239
Charlottesville-Albemarle Foundation
114 4th St. S.E.
P.O. Box 1767
Charlottesville, VA 22902 (434) 296-1024
Contact: John R. Redick, Exec. Dir.
FAX: (434) 296-2503; E-mail: cacf@cstone.net; URL: http://www.cacfonline.org

Established in 1967 in VA; first grants distribution in 1972.
Grantmaker type: Community foundation
Financial data (yr. ended 12/31/01): Assets, $4,106,120 (M); gifts received, $1,019,018; expenditures, $1,126,205; giving activities include $864,056 for grants (high: $114,576).
Purpose and activities: To give initial or early assistance to community projects which can be expected to develop other sources of support after a reasonable period of time and to give support to established organizations or groups for projects of special importance or of an experimental nature. The foundation administers donor-advised funds.
Fields of interest: Humanities; Arts; Education; Environment; Health care; Youth development; Human services; Community development; Homeless.
Types of support: Capital campaigns; Building/renovation; Equipment; Conferences/seminars; Publication; Seed money; Matching/challenge support.
Limitations: Giving limited to the Charlottesville and Albemarle, VA, areas, within a fifty-mile radius. No support for religious purposes or for projects normally government-funded. No grants to individuals, or for ongoing operating support, deficit financing, scholarships, fellowships or travel, or equipment.
Publications: Application guidelines, Annual report, Informational brochure (including application guidelines), Newsletter.
Application information: Foundations must wait at least 12 months before reapplying. Application form required.
Initial approach: Letter, telephone, or E-mail requesting guidelines and cover sheet
Copies of proposal: 2
Deadline(s): Feb. 1, May 1, Aug. 1, and Nov. 1
Board meeting date(s): Quarterly
Final notification: Mar., June, Sept., and Dec.
Officers: Shelah Scott, Chair.; James L. Jessup, Jr., Vice-Chair.; John R. Redick, Exec. Dir.
Trustees: RADM. Thomas E. Bass III; Raymond L. Bell; Lucius H. Bracey, Jr.; Edward H. Brownfield; M. Corwith Davis; Rhoda Dreyfus; Ralph L. Feil; Linda K. Ford; Bebe Heiner; John W. Howard; Patricia B. Jensen; Arthur G. Kiser; Christopher McLean; James B. Murray, Jr.; E. Marshall Pryor; Charles M. Rotgin, Jr.; Charlotte H. Scott; Constance M. Waite.
Number of staff: 1 full-time professional; 1 part-time professional; 1 part-time support.
EIN: 546068643

3240
Chelonia Institute, Inc.
3330 Washington Blvd.
Arlington, VA 22201

Donor(s): Chelonian Research Foundation.
Grantmaker type: Operating foundation

Financial data (yr. ended 02/28/02): Assets, $1,464,321 (M); gifts received, $46,773; expenditures, $746,113; qualifying distributions, $734,421; giving activities include $712,000 for 3 grants (high: $612,000; low: $50,000) and $734,696 for foundation-administered programs.
Purpose and activities: Support for protecting and furthering the life expectancy and population of sea turtles. Giving also for horse rescue.
Fields of interest: Animals/wildlife, preservation/protection.
Limitations: Applications not accepted. Giving primarily in Arlington, VA. No grants to individuals.
Application information: Contributes only to pre-selected organizations.
Officers: Robert W. Truland, Pres. and Treas.; Mary W. Truland, Secy.
EIN: 521081407

3241
Chesapeake Corporation Contributions Program
1021 E. Cary St.
Richmond, VA 23219
Contact: Joseph C. Vagi
Application address: P.O. Box 2350, Richmond, VA 23218-2350; FAX: (804) 697-1199

Grantmaker type: Corporate giving program
Financial data (yr. ended 12/31/02): Total giving, $15,000; giving activities include $15,000 for 13 grants.
Purpose and activities: As a complement to its foundation, Chesapeake also makes charitable contributions to nonprofit organizations directly. Support is given primarily in the Richmond, Virginia, area.
Fields of interest: Education; Environmental education.
Types of support: General/operating support.
Limitations: Giving primarily in the Richmond, VA, area. No support for religious or political organizations. No grants to individuals.
Application information: The Corporate Communications Department handles giving. A contributions committee reviews all requests. Application form not required.
Initial approach: Proposal to headquarters
Copies of proposal: 1
Deadline(s): Prior to committee meetings
Board meeting date(s): Quarterly
Final notification: 1 week following committee meetings
Number of staff: 1 part-time support.

3242
Columbia Gas of Virginia, Inc. Corporate Giving Program
9001 Arboretum Pkwy.
Richmond, VA 23235 (804) 323-5323
URL: http://www.columbiagasva.com/community

Grantmaker type: Corporate giving program
Purpose and activities: Columbia Gas of Virginia makes charitable contributions to nonprofit organizations involved with education and the environment. Support is given primarily in areas of company operations.

Fields of interest: Education; Energy; Environment.
Types of support: General/operating support; Employee volunteer services; In-kind gifts.
Limitations: Giving primarily in areas of company operations. No support for political organizations, religious organizations, hospitals, or libraries.
Application information:
Initial approach: Telephone headquarters

3243
The Connors Foundation, Inc.
P.O. Box 7317
Alexandria, VA 22307-0317 (703) 683-4367
Contact: Julia B. Connors, V.P.
E-mail: JConnors@aol.com

Established in 1999.
Donor(s): Michael M. Connors, Julia B. Connors.
Grantmaker type: Independent foundation
Financial data (yr. ended 12/31/02): Assets, $6,603,118 (M); expenditures, $305,603; qualifying distributions, $304,909; giving activities include $293,610 for 23 grants (high: $50,000; low: $250).
Purpose and activities: Giving primarily for children's health and development, environmental protection and development, and the arts.
Fields of interest: Museums (art); Performing arts; Natural resources; Health care; Children/youth, services.
Limitations: Giving primarily in Washington, DC. No grants to individuals.
Application information: Accepts Common Grant Application Form of the National Network of Grantmakers.
Initial approach: Letter (no more than 3 pages)
Deadline(s): None
Board meeting date(s): 4 times per year
Final notification: 1 month for receipt
Officers: Michael M. Connors, Pres.; Julia B. Connors, V.P.
Directors: Patrick E. Connors; Kathleen C. Mueller.
EIN: 522204597

3244
The Conservation Fund
1800 N. Kent St., Ste. 1120
Arlington, VA 22209 (703) 525-6300
Contact: Lawrence A. Selzer, Pres. and C.E.O.
FAX: (703) 525-4610; E-mail: postmaster@conservationfund.org; URL: http://www.conservationfund.org/

Established in 1985.
Grantmaker type: Public charity
Financial data (yr. ended 12/31/01): Revenue, $64,199,053; assets, $217,582,945; gifts received, $57,002,199; expenditures, $30,924,329; program services expenses, $28,469,036; giving activities include $568,866 for grants (high: $50,000; low: $1,000; average: $1,000–$50,000), $22,000 for 2 grants to individuals (high: $12,000; low: $10,000), $5,000,000 for 2 foundation-administered programs and $4,864,507 for 22 loans/program-related investments.
Purpose and activities: The fund seeks to protect America's legacy of land and water resources

through partnerships by land acquisition, sustainable programs, and leadership training, and to demonstrate effective conservation solutions emphasizing the integration of economic and environmental goals.
Fields of interest: Natural resources; Environment.
Types of support: Seed money.
Limitations: Giving on a national basis.
Publications: Application guidelines, Annual report, Corporate giving report, Newsletter.
Application information: Application form required.
Officers and Directors:* Patrick F. Noonan,* Chair.; Charles R. Jordan,* Vice-Chair.; Lawrence A. Selzer,* Pres. and C.E.O.; Richard L. Erdmann,* Exec. V.P.; Hadlai A. Hull,* Treas.; Jessica H. Catto; Norman L. Christensen, Jr.; Sylvia A. Earle; and 8 additional directors.
EIN: 521388917

3245
The Charles Delmar Foundation
2 Skyline Pl., Ste. 1304
5203 Leesburg Pike
Falls Church, VA 22041
Contact: Mareen D. Hughes, Pres.

Established in 1957 in DC.
Donor(s): Charles Delmar,‡ Roland H. Delmar,‡ Elizabeth A. Delmar,‡ Mareen D. Hughes.
Grantmaker type: Independent foundation
Financial data (yr. ended 12/31/02): Assets, $6,996,577 (M); expenditures, $532,789; qualifying distributions, $502,717; giving activities include $493,250 for 177 grants (high: $16,000; low: $1,000; average: $2,000–$5,000).
Purpose and activities: Special interests include inter-American studies, higher, secondary, elementary, and other education, underprivileged youth, the disadvantaged, the aged, the homeless and housing issues, general welfare organizations, and fine and performing arts.
Fields of interest: Visual arts; Museums; Performing arts; Theater; Music; Historic preservation/historical societies; Elementary school/education; Secondary school/education; Higher education; Adult education—literacy, basic skills & GED; Reading; Natural resources; Hospitals (general); Family planning; Substance abuse, services; Health organizations, association; Cancer research; Housing/shelter, development; Human services; Children/youth, services; Family services; Hospices; Aging, centers/services; Homeless, human services; Race/intergroup relations; Native Americans/American Indians; Disabled; Aging; Economically disadvantaged; Homeless.
International interests: Latin America.
Types of support: Continuing support; Annual campaigns; Capital campaigns; Conferences/seminars; Seed money; Internship funds; Scholarship funds.
Limitations: Giving primarily in Washington, DC; giving also in Latin America. No grants to individuals, or for building or endowment funds, or matching gifts; no loans.
Application information: Application form not required.
Initial approach: Letter
Copies of proposal: 1
Deadline(s): None

Board meeting date(s): As required
Officers and Trustees:* Mareen D. Hughes,*
Pres.; R. Bruce Hughes,* Secy.-Treas.
Number of staff: None.
EIN: 526035345

3246
The Overton and Katherine Dennis Fund
c/o SunTrust Banks, Inc.
P.O. Box 85159
Richmond, VA   23285-5159   (804) 782-5230
Contact: Mgr.

Established in 1987 in VA as successor trust to
Dennis Fund.
Grantmaker type: Independent foundation
Financial data (yr. ended 05/31/02): Assets,
$7,480,426 (M); expenditures, $422,519;
qualifying distributions, $383,179; giving
activities include $385,500 for grants.
Purpose and activities: Giving primarily for
education, children and social services,
Episcopal churches, and federated giving
programs.
Fields of interest: Higher education; Education;
Environment; Human services; Children,
services; Federated giving programs; Protestant
agencies & churches.
Types of support: Scholarship funds.
Limitations: Giving primarily in VA, with
emphasis on Richmond. No grants to
individuals.
Application information:
  Initial approach: Letter or proposal
  Deadline(s): None
  Board meeting date(s): Apr.
Officers and Directors:* Overton D. Dennis,
Jr.,* Pres.; Philip H. Webb,* Treas.; Janet D.
Branch; Elizabeth O. Dennis; Janet Jackson
Dennis.
EIN: 541418161

3247
The Dorothy-Ann Foundation
1177 Jamestown Rd.
Williamsburg, VA   23185

Established in 1999 in VA.
Donor(s): Darwin O'Ryan Curtis, Darwin
O'Ryan Curtis Charitable Lead Annunity Trust.
Grantmaker type: Independent foundation
Financial data (yr. ended 12/31/02): Assets,
$1,970,963 (M); gifts received, $179,789;
expenditures, $141,693; qualifying distributions,
$120,120; giving activities include $117,114 for
7 grants (high: $50,000; low: $5,355).
Purpose and activities: Giving primarily for
health, education, and environmental
conservation.
Fields of interest: Higher education; Natural
resources; Health care.
Types of support: General/operating support.
Limitations: Applications not accepted. Giving
primarily in FL, GA, NY, and VA. No grants to
individuals.
Application information: Contributes only to
pre-selected organizations.
Officers: Darwin O'Ryan Curtis, Pres.; Vernon
M. Geddy, Jr., V.P.; Vernon M. Geddy III,
Secy.-Treas.
EIN: 541965966

3248
The George & Grace Dragas Foundation
4538 Bonney Rd.
Virginia Beach, VA   23462-3818
(757) 490-0161
Contact: Helen E. Dragas, Dir.

Established in 1990 in VA.
Donor(s): George Dragas, Jr.
Grantmaker type: Independent foundation
Financial data (yr. ended 12/31/02): Assets,
$2,492,090 (M); gifts received, $300,000;
expenditures, $155,299; qualifying distributions,
$152,984; giving activities include $139,250 for
21 grants (high: $55,000; low: $200).
Purpose and activities: Giving primarily for
education and federated giving programs, giving
also for children's services and the arts.
Fields of interest: Museums; Opera; Arts;
Elementary/secondary education; Higher
education; University; Scholarships/financial
aid; Zoos/zoological societies; Hospitals
(general); Foundations (public).
Limitations: Applications not accepted. Giving
primarily in Norfolk, VA. No grants to
individuals.
Application information: Contributes only to
pre-selected organizations.
Directors: Grace V. Dragas; Helen E. Dragas;
Mary D. Shearin; Jennifer D. Stedfast; Anita D.
Weaver.
EIN: 541569136

3249
Dreaming Hand Foundation
2115 Dogwood Ln.
Charlottesville, VA   22901

Established in 2000 in VA.
Donor(s): Kay F. Bechtel, Stefan D. Bechtel.
Grantmaker type: Independent foundation
Financial data (yr. ended 12/31/02): Assets,
$225,748 (M); gifts received, $143,717;
expenditures, $110,113; qualifying distributions,
$100,200; giving activities include $100,200 for
18 grants (high: $75,000; low: $50).
Purpose and activities: Giving primarily for the
arts.
Fields of interest: Arts; Education; Natural
resources.
Limitations: Applications not accepted. Giving
primarily in Charlottesville, VA. No grants to
individuals.
Application information: Contributes only to
pre-selected organizations.
Officers: Kay F. Bechtel, Pres and Treas.; David
W. Kudravetz, Secy.
EIN: 542014866

3250
Earth Force, Inc.
1908 Mount Vernon Ave., 2nd Fl.
Alexandria, VA   22301   (703) 299-9400
Contact: Thomas D. Martin, Pres.
FAX: (703) 299-9485; *E-mail:*
earthforce@earthforce.org; *URL:* http://
www.earthforce.org

Established in 1992 in DE.
Grantmaker type: Public charity
Financial data (yr. ended 09/30/01): Revenue,
$3,572,231; assets, $2,985,583; gifts received,

$3,347,892; expenditures, $2,572,415; program
services expenses, $2,170,507; giving activities
include $4,400 for 5 grants (high: $2,965; low:
$175).
Purpose and activities: The organization seeks
to provide young people, ages 10-14, with
educational experience in working with their
communities to care for their environments now
while developing life-long habits of active
citizenship and environmental stewardship.
Fields of interest: Environment, formal/general
education; Natural resources; Youth
development.
Types of support: Employee-related scholarships.
Limitations: Applications not accepted. Giving
on a national basis.
Application information:
  Board meeting date(s): Quarterly
Officers and Directors:* Tom Watkins,* Chair.;
Thomas D. Martin,* Pres.; Christine Bates; Susan
J. Colby; James W. Kohlmoos; Robert Light,
Ph.D.; Jack Lorenz; and 8 additional directors.
EIN: 521830873

3251
Andrew H. & Anne O. Easley Trust
(also known as The Easley Foundation)
c/o Wachovia Bank, N.A. Charitable Funds Dept.
P.O. Box 27602
Richmond, VA   23261   (804) 697-6901
Contact: Secy., The Easley Foundation

Established in 1968 in VA.
Donor(s): Andrew H. Easley.‡
Grantmaker type: Independent foundation
Financial data (yr. ended 06/30/01): Assets,
$407,887,389 (M); expenditures, $569,284;
qualifying distributions, $508,031; giving
activities include $508,498 for grants.
Purpose and activities: Giving primarily for the
arts, education and human services.
Fields of interest: Arts; Higher education;
Environment; Recreation; Family services;
Native Americans/American Indians.
Types of support: General/operating support;
Continuing support; Capital campaigns;
Building/renovation; Equipment; Land
acquisition; Endowments; Emergency funds;
Program development; Curriculum
development; Scholarship funds; Technical
assistance; Matching/challenge support.
Limitations: Giving limited to the central VA,
area, within a 30-mile radius of Lynchburg. No
support for religious organizations. No grants to
individuals, or for research, deficit financing,
seed money, annual campaigns, or conferences
and seminars; no loans.
Publications: Application guidelines.
Application information: Application form not
required.
  Initial approach: Proposal not exceeding 2
  pages
  Copies of proposal: 6
  Deadline(s): Apr. 1 and Oct. 1
  Board meeting date(s): June and Dec.
Trustee: Wachovia Bank, N.A.
Number of staff: None.
EIN: 546074720

3252
The Elmwood Fund
P.O. Box 85678
Richmond, VA 23285
Contact: E.A. Rennolds, Jr., Pres.

Established in 1970 in VA.
Grantmaker type: Independent foundation
Financial data (yr. ended 12/31/02): Assets,
$1,543,063 (M); expenditures, $122,452;
qualifying distributions, $117,300; giving
activities include $117,300 for 60 grants (high:
$20,000; low: $500).
Purpose and activities: Giving for historical
preservation, youth services, and park and
recreation services.
Fields of interest: Arts; Education; Natural
resources; Health organizations, association;
Parks/playgrounds; Youth development;
YM/YWCAs & YM/YWHAs.
Limitations: Giving primarily in NY, TN and
Richmond, VA. No grants to individuals.
Application information:
  Initial approach: Letter
  Deadline(s): None
Officers: E.A. Rennolds, Jr., Pres.; Mary Z.
Rennolds, V.P.
Directors: Walter Dotts; Zayde R. Dotts.
EIN: 237075321

3253
Environmental Research and Education Foundation
(formerly EIA Research and Education
Foundation)
120 S. Fayette St.
Alexandria, VA 22314 (703) 299-5139
Contact: Michael J. Cagney, Pres.
FAX: (703) 299-5145; E-mail:
mcagney@erefdn.org; URL: http://
www.erefdn.org

Established in 1993 in DC.
Grantmaker type: Public charity
Financial data (yr. ended 12/31/02): Revenue,
$423,831; assets, $5,668,156 (L); gifts received,
$963,253; expenditures, $2,405,592; program
services expenses, $1,347,579; giving activities
include $1,197,141 for 17 grants.
Purpose and activities: The foundation makes
grants to provide environmental solutions for the
future.
Fields of interest: Education; Environment,
research; Environment.
Types of support: General/operating support;
Conferences/seminars; Publication; Curriculum
development; Fellowships; Scholarship funds;
Research; Technical assistance; Scholarships—to
individuals.
Limitations: Giving on a national and
international basis, primarily in the U.S. and
Europe. No support for religious causes or
organizations that discriminate by race, color,
creed, gender, or national origin. No grants to
individuals (unless affiliated with research
institutions), or for capital campaigns, political
contributions, operating funds, loans, annual
campaigns, or lobbying activities.
Publications: Application guidelines, Annual
report, Financial statement, Grants list,
Informational brochure, Newsletter, Occasional
report.

Application information: See Web site for
additional application information. Application
form not required.
  Initial approach: 2- to 3-page letter
  Copies of proposal: 1
  Deadline(s): None
  Board meeting date(s): Apr., Aug./Sept.,
    Nov./Dec.
  Final notification: 2 weeks following a board
    meeting
Officers and Directors:* Deborah H. Hockman,
Ph.D.,* Chair.; Robert P. Stearns, P.E., D.E.E.,*
Vice-Chair.; Michael J. Cagney,* Pres.; Kevin
Walbridge,* Secy.-Treas.; Leonard Joyce, P.E.;
Frederick Leach; Ronald J. McCracken, J.D.;
Paul R. Mitchener; Jacques Petry; Lonnie C.
Poole, Jr.; Debra R. Reinhart, Ph.D., P.E.; Robert
J. Riethmiller, Jr.; William Terry; Thomas Van
Weelden; Charles Williams.
Number of staff: 2 full-time professional; 4
part-time professional.
EIN: 521804051

3254
Edward P. Evans Foundation
P.O. Box 46, Rte. 602
Casanova, VA 20139
Contact: Edward P. Evans, Tr.

Established in 1983 in VA.
Donor(s): Edward P. Evans.
Grantmaker type: Independent foundation
Financial data (yr. ended 11/30/02): Assets,
$3,169,792 (M); expenditures, $281,485;
qualifying distributions, $277,514; giving
activities include $269,901 for 21 grants (high:
$200,000; low: $112).
Fields of interest: Secondary school/education;
Environment; Hospitals (general); Health care;
Health organizations, association.
Types of support: General/operating support.
Limitations: Giving primarily in MA and VA. No
grants to individuals.
Application information: Application form not
required.
  Deadline(s): None
Trustees: Edward P. Evans; Robert S. Evans;
Dorsey R. Gardner; Charles J. Queenan, Jr.
Number of staff: None.
EIN: 256232129

3255
First Nations Development Institute
The Stores Bldg.
11917 Main St.
Fredericksburg, VA 22408 (540) 371-5615
Contact: Rebecca Sieb, Dir., Grantmaking
FAX: (540) 371-3505; E-mail:
fndi@firstnations.org; URL: http://
www.firstnations.org

Established in 1983 in VA.
Grantmaker type: Public charity
Financial data (yr. ended 06/30/00): Revenue,
$4,301,135; assets, $4,781,574 (M); gifts
received, $4,074,906; expenditures,
$3,600,969; program services expenses,
$2,810,486; giving activities include $990,837
for grants.
Purpose and activities: The institute helps
Native American tribal members to mobilize
enterprises that are reform-minded, culturally

suitable, and economically feasible by
coordinating local grassroots projects with
national program and policy development
initiatives to build capacity for self-reliant
reservation economies.
Fields of interest: Arts; Education; Environment;
Health care; Housing/shelter; Youth
development; Economic development; Rural
development; Community development,
business promotion; Native
Americans/American Indians.
Types of support: Program development;
Conferences/seminars; Seed money; Technical
assistance; Grants to individuals.
Limitations: Giving limited to Native American
reservations and rural Native American
communities. No grants for non-Native
Americans, or for scholarships, fellowships,
construction, renovation, land acquisition,
capital or endowment campaigns, media
campaigns/projects (unless part of an overall
project), or research which has no direct
practical application.
Publications: Application guidelines, Biennial
report, Grants list, Informational brochure,
Newsletter.
Application information: Application form
required.
  Initial approach: Letter or telephone
  Copies of proposal: 1
  Deadline(s): Feb. 15, July 15, and Oct. 15 for
    Working Capital Grants; none for Seed and
    Start-up grants
  Board meeting date(s): Mar., July, and Dec.
  Final notification: Mar. 30, July 30, and Dec.
    30 for Working Capital Grants; within 2
    months for Seed Grants; within 4 months
    for Start-up Grants
Officers and Trustees:* B. Thomas Vigil,* Chair.;
Rebecca Adamson,* Pres.; Sherry Salway
Black,* V.P.; Siobhan Oppenheimer-Nicolau,*
Secy.; Gelvin Stevenson,* Treas.; Joseph Jacobs;
N. Scott Momaday; Michael E. Roberts;
Marguerite Smith; Dagmar Thorpe.
Number of staff: 20 full-time professional; 7
full-time support.
EIN: 541254491

3256
FishAmerica Foundation
225 Reinekers Ln., Ste.420
Alexandria, VA 22315 (703) 519-9691
Contact: Johanna Laderman, Managing Dir.
FAX: (703) 519-1872; E-mail:
fishamerica@asafishing.org; URL: http://
www.fishamerica.org/

Established in 1983 in OK.
Donor(s): Zebco Corp., Brunswick Foundation,
Kmart Corp., Shimano American Corp.,
Wal-Mart Stores, Inc., Outdoor Cap, Grady
White Boats, Mercury Marine, Champion Boats,
Yo-Zuri, Plano Molding Co., Pure Fishing, Top
Line Manufacturing, NOAA Restoration Center,
U.S. Fish and Wildlife Service.
Grantmaker type: Public charity
Financial data (yr. ended 09/30/01): Revenue,
$856,120; assets, $1,795,016 (M); gifts
received, $810,967; expenditures, $888,571;
program services expenses, $751,600; giving
activities include $751,600 for 69 grants (high:
$30,000; low: $500).

Purpose and activities: Support is given primarily for hands-on projects that enhance fish populations, conserve and enhance waterways and fisheries, and promote fish habitat and water quality.
Fields of interest: Natural resources; Animals/wildlife, fisheries; Marine science.
Types of support: Program development; Seed money; Matching/challenge support.
Limitations: Giving limited to the U.S. and Canada. No grants to individuals, or for access, endowments, operating expenses, advertising, or traveling costs; no loans.
Publications: Application guidelines, Grants list, Informational brochure (including application guidelines), Newsletter.
Application information: Application form required.
Initial approach: Proposal
Copies of proposal: 2
Deadline(s): None
Board meeting date(s): Annually
Officers and Directors:* Jerry Calenger,* Chair.; Dave Pfieffer,* Vice-Chair.; James C. Hubbard,* Treas.; Johanna Laderman, Managing Dir.; and 13 additional directors.
Number of staff: 1 full-time professional.
EIN: 363219015

3257
T. David Fitz-Gibbon Charitable Trust
951 E. Byrd St., Ste. 930
Richmond, VA 23219
Contact: Thomas N.P. Johnson III, Tr.

Established in 1983 in VA.
Donor(s): T. David Fitz-Gibbon.‡
Grantmaker type: Independent foundation
Financial data (yr. ended 06/30/02): Assets, $46,447 (M); expenditures, $1,651,782; qualifying distributions, $1,599,293; giving activities include $1,600,100 for 6 grants (high: $640,000; low: $64,000).
Purpose and activities: Giving primarily for higher education, including education building funds, secondary education, architecture, and historic preservation.
Fields of interest: Architecture; Historic preservation/historical societies; Secondary school/education; Higher education; Medical school/education; Nursing school/education; Education; Animal welfare; Hospitals (general); Nursing care; Human services.
Types of support: Continuing support; Capital campaigns; Building/renovation; Endowments; Professorships; Scholarship funds.
Limitations: Giving primarily in VA. No grants to individuals.
Application information: Limited amount of funds available due to long-term commitments. Application form not required.
Initial approach: Letter
Copies of proposal: 1
Deadline(s): None
Board meeting date(s): Feb. and Aug.
Trustees: Thomas Nelson Page Johnson, Jr.; Thomas Nelson Page Johnson III; William M. Walsh, Jr.
Number of staff: None.
EIN: 521272224

3258
The Horace G. Fralin Charitable Trust
P.O. Box 20069
Roanoke, VA 24018   (540) 774-4415
Contact: W. Heywood Fralin, Tr.

Established in 1989 in VA.
Grantmaker type: Independent foundation
Financial data (yr. ended 12/31/01): Assets, $43,788,075 (M); expenditures, $2,956,128; qualifying distributions, $2,138,426; giving activities include $2,138,426 for 37 grants (high: $2,042,874; low: $50; average: $1,000–$15,000).
Fields of interest: Museums (art); Music; Arts; Higher education; Education; Natural resources; Human services; Children/youth, services.
Limitations: Giving primarily in Roanoke, VA.
Application information: Application form not required.
Deadline(s): None
Officer and Trustee: W. Heywood Fralin, Mgr.
EIN: 541509505

3259
Fund for Innovation and Public Service
c/o William Drayton
1200 N. Nash St.
Arlington, VA 22209-3616

Grantmaker type: Independent foundation
Financial data (yr. ended 12/31/01): Assets, $1,755,333 (M); gifts received, $5,933; expenditures, $101,069; qualifying distributions, $94,345; giving activities include $94,345 for 20 grants (high: $60,000; low: $30).
Purpose and activities: Giving to organizations supporting employment opportunities in the U.S., helping young people start their own common service organizations, and encouraging social entrepreneurship globally.
Fields of interest: College; Education; Environment, beautification programs; Environment; Children/youth, services; International economics/trade policy.
International interests: Developing countries.
Types of support: Seed money; Fellowships.
Limitations: Applications not accepted. No grants to individuals.
Publications: Occasional report.
Application information: Contributes only to pre-selected organizations.
Board meeting date(s): As needed
Officer: William Drayton, Pres. and Treas.
Directors: Ann Simon Hadley; Steven Hadley; David C. Oxman.
Number of staff: 1 part-time professional.
EIN: 133384072

3260
Gannett Foundation, Inc. ▼
(formerly Gannett Communities Fund/Gannett Co., Inc.)
7950 Jones Branch Dr.
McLean, VA 22107   (703) 854-6069
Contact: Irma Simpson, Mgr.
FAX: (703) 854-2002; E-mail: isimpson@gannett.com; URL: http://www.gannettfoundation.org

Established in 1991 in VA.
Donor(s): Gannett Co., Inc.

Grantmaker type: Company-sponsored foundation
Financial data (yr. ended 12/31/01): Assets, $36,299,024 (M); gifts received, $12,311,850; expenditures, $17,936,836; qualifying distributions, $17,725,828; giving activities include $17,489,242 for 390 grants (high: $10,102,474; low: $500; average: $1,000–$10,000) and $236,586 for 164 employee matching gifts.
Purpose and activities: The foundation values projects that take a creative approach to such fundamental issues as education and neighborhood improvement, economic development, youth development, community problem-solving, assistance to people who are disadvantaged, environmental conservation, and cultural enrichment. The foundation has an employee matching gift program for all levels of educational institutions in the United States and its territories.
Fields of interest: Arts; Vocational education; Adult education—literacy, basic skills & GED; Reading; Education; Natural resources; Environment; Health care; Housing/shelter, development; Human services; Youth, services; Civil rights, aging; Community development; Voluntarism promotion; Asians/Pacific Islanders; African Americans/Blacks; Hispanics/Latinos; Native Americans/American Indians; Disabled; Aging; Women; People with AIDS (PWAs); Gays/lesbians; Immigrants/refugees; Economically disadvantaged; Homeless.
Types of support: General/operating support; Capital campaigns; Building/renovation; Equipment; Program development; Technical assistance; Employee matching gifts; Employee-related scholarships; Matching/challenge support.
Limitations: Giving limited to organizations in communities served by a local daily Gannett newspaper or TV broadcast station, including the U.S., the U.S. territory of Guam, and the United Kingdom. No support for religious purposes, elementary or secondary schools (except special initiatives not provided by regular school budgets), medical or other research, fraternal, political, or veterans' organizations, athletic teams, bands, volunteer firefighters, or similar groups, or national or regional programs. No grants to individuals, (except for employee-related scholarships), or for endowments or multiple-year pledge campaigns.
Publications: Annual report, Corporate report, Informational brochure (including application guidelines).
Application information: Each local Gannett operation establishes its own priorities depending on local needs, and may have additional guidelines and restrictions. Application form required.
Initial approach: Contact nearest daily Gannett newspaper or broadcast station; one-page letter of inquiry is welcome
Copies of proposal: 2
Deadline(s): Check with local executives for local deadlines
Board meeting date(s): Proposals reviewed 3 times per year, Feb. to Oct.
Final notification: Approximately 60 to 90 days after submission
Officers and Directors:* Douglas H. McCorkindale,* Pres.; Daniel S. Ehrman, V.P.;

Millicent A. Feller, V.P.; Larry F. Miller,* V.P.; Thomas L. Chapple, Secy.; Gracia C. Martore, Treas.
Number of staff: 1 full-time professional; 1 full-time support.
EIN: 541568843
Recent environmental and animal welfare grants:
3260-1 Indiana Canine Assistant and Adolescent Network (ICAAN), Indianapolis, Indiana, $10,000. For Project FETCH, which trains service dogs to assist people with physical disabilities while providing at-risk youth with alternative method to develop communication skills through community service. 2002.
3260-2 Jackson Zoological Park, Jackson, MS, $25,000. For Cougar Exhibit, part of massive renovation project to improve quality of animal housing and visitors center. 2002.
3260-3 Jericho Underhill Land Trust, Jericho, VT, $10,000. Toward purchasing critical wildlife habitat. 2002.
3260-4 Lewa Wildlife Conservancy USA, Park City, UT, $20,000. For general operating support. 2002.
3260-5 Piedmont Environmental Council, Warrenton, VA, $20,000. For general support. 2002.
3260-6 Zoo Atlanta, Atlanta, GA, $11,000. For Zoomobile program, traveling conservation education program that offers live animals encounters. 2002.

3261
Gifts In Kind International
333 N. Fairfax St.
Alexandria, VA   22314-2632   (703) 836-2121
Contact: Susan Corrigan, C.E.O.
FAX: (703) 549-1481; E-mail: productdonations@giftsinkind.org; URL: http://www.giftsinkind.org

Founded in 1984 in VA.
Grantmaker type: Public charity
Financial data (yr. ended 12/31/01): Revenue, $415,088,326; assets, $20,640,577 (M); gifts received, $411,589,203; expenditures, $446,202,464; program services expenses, $443,913,850; giving activities include $440,466,785 for in-kind gifts.
Purpose and activities: The organization assists companies to effectively and efficiently donate top quality products and services to nonprofit organizations worldwide. Contributions include office equipment and supplies, computers and software, building materials including construction materials, appliances, fixtures, and furniture, products for youth programs such as arts and crafts supplies, books, computers labs, and recreational supplies and equipment, and items such as clothing and personal care products used by shelters, nursing homes, and similar facilities.
Fields of interest: Arts; Education; Environment; Health care; Employment, retraining; Youth development; Human services; Community development; Philanthropy/voluntarism; Engineering/technology.
International interests: Canada; Europe; Southern Africa; Latin America; Mexico; Asia.
Types of support: Building/renovation; Equipment; In-kind gifts.

Limitations: Giving worldwide, specifically in the U.S., Canada, Europe, Asia, the Pacific, Mexico, Latin America, and South Africa. No support for for-profit organizations. No grants to individuals.
Publications: Application guidelines, Annual report, Financial statement, Informational brochure (including application guidelines).
Application information: Charities select needed products through weekly notice, monthly update, and quarterly catalog; year-round giving; nominal membership fee. Application form required.
   Initial approach: Letter (including SASE), FAX, or e-mail
   Deadline(s): None
   Board meeting date(s): May and Nov.
Officers and Directors:* Thomas Dowling,* Chair.; Susan Corrigan,* C.E.O. and Pres.; Peter Asimakopoulos,* C.O.O.; Mike Kelly,* C.O.O.; Mark Weinberger,* Secy.; Robert J. Symon,* Treas.; Wael Aburida; Barry Anderson; Rayna Aylward; Paula Baker; Diane J. Brisebois; Sylvia Clark; Ralph Drayer; Keith Fulton; Roger Kallock; Katherine Mance; Walter McHendry; Joseph Norton; Jeffrey Rodek; Amb. Stapleton Roy; Jim Schoenwetter; Steven Spencer; Bess Stephens; Robert Sullivan.
Number of staff: 43 full-time professional.
EIN: 541282616

3262
The Glenstone Foundation
8404 Parham Ct.
McLean, VA   22102

Established in 1995 in VA.
Donor(s): Mitchell P. Rales.
Grantmaker type: Independent foundation
Financial data (yr. ended 12/31/00): Assets, $34,521,605 (M); gifts received, $17,154,844; expenditures, $1,393,829; qualifying distributions, $879,211; giving activities include $876,920 for 28 grants (high: $200,000; low: $800).
Purpose and activities: Support for services for children, including hospitals and human services; giving also for art museums and wildlife conservation.
Fields of interest: Museums (art); Education; Animals/wildlife, preservation/protection; Children, services.
Limitations: Applications not accepted. No grants to individuals.
Application information: Contributes only to pre-selected organizations.
Officers and Director:* Mitchell P. Rales,* Chair.; Michael G. Ryan, Pres.; Joseph O. Bunting III, V.P.; Teresa L.C. Baldwin, Secy.-Treas.
EIN: 541739159

3263
C. W. Gooch, Jr. Charitable Trust
c/o SunTrust Banks, Inc.
P.O. Box 27385
Richmond, VA   23261-7385
Application address: Advisory Comm., c/o SunTrust Banks, Inc., P.O. Box 678, Lynchburg, VA 24505

Established in 1968 in VA.
Grantmaker type: Independent foundation

Financial data (yr. ended 04/30/02): Assets, $2,294,674 (M); expenditures, $144,396; qualifying distributions, $140,908; giving activities include $141,100 for 48 grants (high: $25,000; low: $100).
Fields of interest: University; Education; Natural resources; Human services; YM/YWCAs & YM/YWHAs; Christian agencies & churches.
Types of support: Building/renovation; Equipment; Scholarship funds.
Limitations: Giving primarily in MD and VA. No grants to individuals.
Application information:
   Initial approach: Letter
   Deadline(s): Apr. 1
   Final notification: Prior to Apr. 30
Trustee: SunTrust Banks, Inc.
EIN: 546074371

3264
Gottwald Foundation
P.O. Box 955
Goochland, VA   23063

Established in 1957.
Donor(s): Floyd D. Gottwald, Sr.,‡ Floyd D. Gottwald, Jr.
Grantmaker type: Independent foundation
Financial data (yr. ended 12/31/02): Assets, $11,005,758 (M); expenditures, $566,260; qualifying distributions, $523,293; giving activities include $523,293 for 40 grants (high: $350,000; low: $100; average: $100–$200,000).
Purpose and activities: Giving primarily to a botanical garden, as well as for education, health, human services and federated giving programs.
Fields of interest: Education, alliance; Botanical gardens; Hospitals (specialty); Health care; Health organizations, association; Human services; American Red Cross; Neighborhood centers; Children, services; Federated giving programs.
Types of support: General/operating support; Capital campaigns; Scholarship funds.
Limitations: Applications not accepted. Giving primarily in VA. No grants to individuals.
Application information: Contributes only to pre-selected organizations.
Officers: F.D. Gottwald, Jr., Pres.; James T. Gottwald, V.P.; Bruce C. Gottwald, Secy.-Treas.
Number of staff: None.
EIN: 546040560

3265
The Gradison Foundation
1031 Savile Ln.
McLean, VA   22101
Contact: Willis D. Gradison, Jr., Pres.

Established in 1959.
Donor(s): Willis D. Gradison, Jr.
Grantmaker type: Independent foundation
Financial data (yr. ended 12/31/02): Assets, $1,599,955 (M); gifts received, $106,520; expenditures, $127,450; qualifying distributions, $105,286; giving activities include $106,700 for 76 grants (high: $20,000; low: $50).
Purpose and activities: Giving primarily for the arts and education.

Fields of interest: Arts; Elementary/secondary education; Environment; Human services; Jewish federated giving programs.
Types of support: General/operating support; Continuing support; Annual campaigns; Capital campaigns; Building/renovation.
Limitations: Giving primarily in Washington, DC, Cincinnati, OH, and VA. No grants to individuals.
Application information: Application form not required.
> *Initial approach:* Letter or proposal
> *Copies of proposal:* 1
> *Deadline(s):* None

Officers and Trustees:* Willis D. Gradison, Jr.,* Pres. and Treas.; Margaret Gradison,* V.P. and Secy.; Joan Coe,* V.P.; Robin Gradison,* V.P.; Wendy Gradison,* V.P.; Beth Lyon,* V.P.
Number of staff: None.
EIN: 316032172

3266
Graphic Arts Education and Research Foundation

1899 Preston White Dr.
Reston, VA 20191 (703) 264-7200
FAX: (703) 620-3165; E-mail: gaerf@npes.org;
URL: http://www.gaerf.org

Established in 1984 in VA.
Donor(s): Graphic Arts Show Co., Inc.
Grantmaker type: Independent foundation
Financial data (yr. ended 12/31/01): Assets, $2,164,665 (M); gifts received, $948,044; expenditures, $583,703; qualifying distributions, $116,246; giving activities include $116,246 for 6 grants (high: $36,668; low: $9,590).
Purpose and activities: Support for education and research pertaining to the graphic communications industry.
Fields of interest: Journalism/publishing; Design; Education, research; Higher education; Teacher school/education; Environment; Engineering/technology.
Types of support: Program development; Conferences/seminars; Publication; Curriculum development; Scholarship funds; Research.
Limitations: Giving on a national basis. Generally, no grants for equipment, except under rare and extenuating circumstances.
Publications: Application guidelines, Annual report, Informational brochure.
Application information: Application form required.
> *Initial approach:* Proposal, using GAERF proposal guidelines
> *Copies of proposal:* 3
> *Deadline(s):* Apr.
> *Final notification:* Late Oct.

Officers: J. Kenneth Garner, Chair.; Robert E. Murphy, Vice-Chair.; Regis J. Delmontagne, Pres.; Raymond W. Roper, Secy.; I. Greg Van Wert, Treas.
Directors: James Hyder, Jr.; Raymond W. Lawton; Gerald Nathe.
Number of staff: 2 full-time professional.
EIN: 521321169

3267
Elizabeth Ireland Graves Charitable Trust

1853 Glenarvon Dr.
Bremo Bluff, VA 23022

Established in 1998 in VA.
Grantmaker type: Independent foundation
Financial data (yr. ended 12/31/02): Assets, $11,487,699 (M); expenditures, $514,271; qualifying distributions, $478,050; giving activities include $478,050 for 34 grants (high: $300,000; low: $250).
Purpose and activities: Giving primarily for animal welfare, as well as for the arts, education, social services, and to a Baptist church.
Fields of interest: Museums; Historic preservation/historical societies; Arts; Elementary/secondary education; Higher education; Education; Animal welfare; Human services; Protestant agencies & churches.
Types of support: General/operating support; Equipment; Program development; Publication.
Limitations: Applications not accepted. Giving primarily in VA; some funding nationally. No grants to individuals.
Application information: Contributes only to pre-selected organizations.
Trustee: Sayre O. Graves.
EIN: 546421160

3268
The Hastings Trust

5629 George Washington Hwy., Ste. D
Yorktown, VA 23692
Contact: Robert C. Hastings, Tr.

Established in 1964 in VA.
Donor(s): Charles E. Hastings,‡ Mary C. Hastings.‡
Grantmaker type: Independent foundation
Financial data (yr. ended 12/31/02): Assets, $1,671,857 (M); expenditures, $189,753; qualifying distributions, $188,914; giving activities include $186,035 for 36 grants (high: $48,100; low: $70).
Fields of interest: Arts; Elementary/secondary education; Higher education; Environment; Animals/wildlife; Health organizations, association; Human services; Civil rights; Public affairs.
Limitations: Applications not accepted. Giving primarily in VA. No grants to individuals.
Application information: Contributes only to pre-selected organizations.
Trustees: John A. Hastings; Robert C. Hastings; Carol Sanders.
EIN: 546040247

3269
Hunt Family Fund

5841 Whitehall Rd.
Zanoni, VA 23191

Established in 1998.
Donor(s): William O. & Jeannette P. Hunt Foundation.
Grantmaker type: Independent foundation
Financial data (yr. ended 12/31/02): Assets, $2,266,929 (M); gifts received, $22,992; expenditures, $146,952; qualifying distributions,

$129,494; giving activities include $130,000 for 8 grants (high: $55,000; low: $2,000).
Fields of interest: Education; Environment; Cancer; Human services; Foundations (community); Protestant agencies & churches.
Limitations: Applications not accepted. Giving primarily in VA. No grants to individuals.
Application information: Contributes only to pre-selected organizations.
Officers: Robert P. Hunt, Pres. and Treas.; Barbara B. Hunt, Secy.
EIN: 311604788

3270
The Jackson Foundation

104 Shockoe Slip, Ste. 2B
Richmond, VA 23219-4125 (804) 644-5735
Contact: Linda Buchanan, Admin., or Patricia M. Asch, Exec. Dir.
FAX: (804) 644-5736; E-mail: linda@jacksonf.org or pat@jacksonf.org; URL: http://www.jacksonf.org

Established in 1981 in VA.
Donor(s): Andrew J. Asch, Jr.‡
Grantmaker type: Independent foundation
Financial data (yr. ended 11/30/02): Assets, $13,605,038 (M); expenditures, $1,620,734; qualifying distributions, $1,468,639; giving activities include $1,470,774 for 53 grants (high: $125,000; low: $25; average: $10,000–$30,000).
Purpose and activities: Giving for the betterment of education and the environment in the metropolitan Richmond, VA, area; support also for education of economically disadvantaged children and historical preservation.
Fields of interest: History/archaeology; Historic preservation/historical societies; Education; Environment; Children/youth, services.
Types of support: Building/renovation; Seed money; Scholarship funds; Matching/challenge support.
Limitations: Giving primarily in the metropolitan Richmond, VA, area. No grants to individuals or for endowment funds.
Publications: Informational brochure (including application guidelines).
Application information: Application form required.
> *Initial approach:* See guidelines at www.jacksonf.org
> *Copies of proposal:* 3
> *Deadline(s):* 2nd Fri. of Jan. and 2nd Fri. of June, by noon
> *Final notification:* 2nd Fri. of May and 2nd Fri. of Nov., by noon

Officers and Directors:* Anthony James Asch,* Pres. and Treas.; Thomas A. Asch,* Secy.; Patricia M. Asch, Exec. Dir.; Linda Buchanan; W. Birch Douglass III.
Number of staff: 2 part-time professional.
EIN: 541186114

3271
Janet Stone Jones Foundation

c/o Investors' Records Corp.
614 E. High St.
Charlottesville, VA 22902
Contact: Russell J. Bell, Secy.

Established in 1978 in NY.
Donor(s): Janet Stone Jones Charitable Lead Trust.
Grantmaker type: Independent foundation
Financial data (yr. ended 12/31/00): Assets, $27,315 (M); gifts received, $103,910; expenditures, $217,325; qualifying distributions, $213,559; giving activities include $214,325 for 54 grants (high: $90,000; low: $100).
Fields of interest: Elementary/secondary education; Education; Animals/wildlife; Health care; Human services.
Types of support: General/operating support.
Limitations: Giving primarily in the northeastern U.S. No grants to individuals.
Application information:
    Initial approach: Letter
    Deadline(s): None
Officer: Russell J. Bell, Secy.
Directors: Whitney Brewster Armstrong; Benjamin Brewster; Janet Brewster York.
EIN: 132988287

3272
The Kington Foundation, Inc.
201 N. Union St., Ste. 300
Alexandria, VA   22314-2642   (703) 519-3036
Contact: Allison W. Cryor, Pres.

Established in 1997 in VA.
Donor(s): Ann A. Kington, Mark J. Kington.
Grantmaker type: Independent foundation
Financial data (yr. ended 11/30/02): Assets, $1,381,544 (M); expenditures, $352,205; qualifying distributions, $348,767; giving activities include $348,200 for 29 grants (high: $150,000; low: $500).
Fields of interest: Museums (art); Historic preservation/historical societies; Education; Environment; Protestant agencies & churches.
Types of support: Annual campaigns; Building/renovation.
Limitations: Giving primarily in TN and VA.
Application information: Application form required.
    Initial approach: Letter
    Deadline(s): None
Officers: Allison W. Cryor, Pres.; Mark J. Kington, Secy.
Director: Ann A. Kington.
EIN: 541831668

3273
Koenig Private Foundation, Inc.
64 Wolfe St.
Alexandria, VA   22314

Established in 2000 in VA.
Donor(s): Ann M. Koenig Charitable Trust.
Grantmaker type: Independent foundation
Financial data (yr. ended 12/31/01): Assets, $2,994,900 (M); gifts received, $55,843; expenditures, $206,658; qualifying distributions, $202,455; giving activities include $97,191 for 3 grants (high: $91,191; low: $1,000).
Fields of interest: Botanical/horticulture/landscape services; Cancer; AIDS.
Limitations: Applications not accepted. No grants to individuals.
Application information: Contributes only to pre-selected organizations.

Officers and Directors:* Duane W. Beckhorn,* Pres.; Patrick M. Buehler,* V.P., C.O.O., and Secy.; Kenneth H. Reese,* Treas.
EIN: 542010650

3274
Julian G. Lange Family Foundation II
P.O. Box 5
White Stone, VA   22578
Contact: Julie L. Peyton, Tr.
Application address: 856 Barcarmil Way, Naples, FL 34110

Established in 1999.
Grantmaker type: Independent foundation
Financial data (yr. ended 06/30/01): Assets, $1,907,390 (M); expenditures, $131,763; qualifying distributions, $128,929; giving activities include $108,200 for 7 grants (high: $75,000; low: $1,000).
Fields of interest: Education; Environment; Hospitals (general); Federated giving programs.
Limitations: Giving primarily in the southwest OH area, with emphasis on Dayton and Oxford.
Application information:
    Initial approach: Letter
    Deadline(s): None
Trustee: Julie L. Peyton.
EIN: 311663389

3275
Gordon R. Larson Foundation
c/o G. Larson & Old Dominion Trust Co.
100 E. Main St., Ste. 200
Norfolk, VA   23510

Established in 1998 in VA.
Donor(s): Gordon R. Larson, Old Dominion Trust Co.
Grantmaker type: Independent foundation
Financial data (yr. ended 12/31/01): Assets, $1,717,766 (M); expenditures, $125,534; qualifying distributions, $100,919; giving activities include $101,585 for 10 grants (high: $100,000; low: $50).
Purpose and activities: Giving for education, religion, wildlife conservation, animal welfare and human services.
Fields of interest: Education, fund raising; Secondary school/education; Education; Animal welfare; Animals/wildlife, preservation/protection; Human services.
Limitations: Applications not accepted. Giving primarily in VA. No grants to individuals.
Application information: Contributes only to pre-selected organizations.
Trustees: Gordon R. Larson; Old Dominion Trust Co.
EIN: 541895344

3276
Robert & Dee Leggett Foundation
P.O. Box 240
Great Falls, VA   22066
Contact: Robert N. Leggett, Jr., Pres.
FAX: (703) 430-9608; *E-mail:* rnleggett@aol.com

Established in 1999 in VA.
Donor(s): Robert Leggett, Dee C. Leggett.
Grantmaker type: Operating foundation

Financial data (yr. ended 12/31/01): Assets, $3,857,648 (M); gifts received, $993,910; expenditures, $952,258; qualifying distributions, $1,055,858; giving activities include $385,478 for 35 grants (high: $21,117; low: $1,000) and $115,100 for 1 loan/program-related investment.
Fields of interest: Education; Environment; Christian agencies & churches; Religion; Economically disadvantaged.
Types of support: General/operating support; Land acquisition; Program development.
Limitations: Applications not accepted. Giving primarily in the Blue Ridge region, VA. No grants to individuals.
Publications: Financial statement, Informational brochure.
Application information: Contributes only to pre-selected organizations. Unsolicited requests for funds not accepted.
    Board meeting date(s): Mar. and Nov.
Officers: Robert "Bob" N. Leggett, Jr., Pres.; Dee C. Leggett, V.P.; Donna I. Measell, Secy.-Treas.
Directors: W. James Athearn; David James Chadwick; Laura L. Leggett; David Lillard; Charles W. Sloan.
Number of staff: 3 full-time professional; 1 part-time professional.
EIN: 541921311

3277
The George W. Logan Charitable Foundation
P.O. Box 1190
Salem, VA   24153-1190

Donor(s): George W. Logan.
Grantmaker type: Independent foundation
Financial data (yr. ended 12/31/02): Assets, $333,191 (M); expenditures, $115,537; qualifying distributions, $109,675; giving activities include $108,650 for 50 grants (high: $27,000; low: $50).
Purpose and activities: Giving primarily for education, particularly an Episcopal high school; funding also for the arts, natural conservation, children, and social services, and a marine biological laboratory.
Fields of interest: Arts; Secondary school/education; Higher education; Education; Natural resources; Human services; Children, services; Federated giving programs; Biological sciences; Economically disadvantaged.
Limitations: Applications not accepted. Giving primarily in Roanoke, VA. No grants to individuals.
Application information: Contributes only to pre-selected organizations.
Officers and Director:* George W. Logan,* Pres.; Patra F. Bedwell, Secy.
EIN: 541902872

3278
Ludington, Inc.
P.O. Box 12641
Roanoke, VA   24027

Established in 1984.
Grantmaker type: Independent foundation
Financial data (yr. ended 12/31/02): Assets, $6,499,812 (M); expenditures, $486,697; qualifying distributions, $475,545; giving

activities include $475,000 for 3 grants (high: $240,000; low: $40,000).
Purpose and activities: Giving primarily for natural resource conservation, and family planning.
Fields of interest: Natural resources; Family planning.
Limitations: Applications not accepted. Giving primarily in Washington, DC, and New York, NY. No grants to individuals; no loans.
Application information: Contributes only to pre-selected organizations.
Directors: Philip Abbey; Emily Parrino; Greta Tisdale.
EIN: 311128833

3279
The Mars Foundation
6885 Elm St.
McLean, VA 22101-3810 (703) 821-4900
Contact: Sue Martin, Asst. Secy.
FAX: (703) 448-9678

Incorporated in 1956 in IL.
Donor(s): Mars, Inc.
Grantmaker type: Company-sponsored foundation
Financial data (yr. ended 12/31/02): Assets, $7,692,539 (M); gifts received, $600,000; expenditures, $1,095,017; qualifying distributions, $778,408; giving activities include $759,500 for 99 grants (high: $30,000; low: $1,000).
Fields of interest: Visual arts; Historic preservation/historical societies; Arts; Education; Natural resources; Environment; Animals/wildlife, preservation/protection; Animals/wildlife; Health care; Human services; Children/youth, services.
Types of support: Continuing support; Annual campaigns; Building/renovation; Equipment; Endowments; Research; Matching/challenge support.
Limitations: No grants to individuals, or for scholarships, fundraising or recognition dinners; no loans.
Application information: Application form required.
Initial approach: Request for guidelines and application
Copies of proposal: 1
Deadline(s): Oct. 15
Board meeting date(s): May and Dec.
Final notification: Jan.
Officers: Jacqueline B. Mars, Pres.; Forrest E. Mars, Jr., V.P.; John F. Mars, V.P.; Otis O. Otih, Secy.-Treas.
EIN: 546037592

3280
National Recycling Coalition
1727 King St., Ste. 105
Alexandria, VA 22314-2720
Contact: Kate M. Krebs, Exec. Dir.
Tel.: (703) 683-9025, ext. 201; FAX: (703) 683-9026; E-mail: katek@nrc-recycle.org; URL: http://www.nrc-recycle.org

Established in 1978.
Grantmaker type: Public charity
Financial data (yr. ended 03/31/00): Revenue, $2,009,426; assets, $629,424; gifts received,

$1,169,064; expenditures, $2,002,528; program services expenses, $1,932,557; giving activities include $8,000 for 6 grants to individuals (high: $1,500; low: $1,250).
Purpose and activities: The coalition is dedicated to the advancement and improvement of recycling, source reduction, composting and reuse by providing technical information, education, training, outreach and advocacy services to its members in order to conserve resources and benefit the environment. NRC serves as the national voice of and resource for recycling.
Fields of interest: Environment, public policy; Waste management; Recycling.
Types of support: Conferences/seminars; Scholarships—to individuals.
Limitations: Giving on a national basis.
Publications: Biennial report, Informational brochure, Newsletter.
Application information: Dean of school recommends candidates. Application form required.
Initial approach: Letter or e-mail
Officers and Directors:* Meg Morris,* Chair.; Paul Baldridge,* Pres.; Chris Cloutier,* V.P.; Terry Gilman,* V.P.; Pete Pasterz,* V.P.; Lori Gummow,* Secy.; Bernie Brill,* Treas.; Jim Bosch; Krista Henkels; and 6 additional directors.
Number of staff: 15.
EIN: 132954127

3281
National Wildlife Federation
c/o Devel. Office
8925 Leesburg Pike
Vienna, VA 22184 (703) 790-4028
Contact: Deborah Wallower, Grant Coord.
URL: http://www.nwf.org

Established in 1936.
Grantmaker type: Public charity
Financial data (yr. ended 08/31/01): Assets, $98,967,617 (M); expenditures, $110,248,511; giving activities include $4,920,812 for grants and $26,738 for grants to individuals.
Purpose and activities: Funding to educate, inspire, and assist individuals and organizations of diverse cultures to conserve wildlife and other natural resources and to protect the Earth's environment in order to achieve a peaceful, equitable and sustainable future.
Fields of interest: Natural resources; Environment; Animals/wildlife.
Types of support: Grants to individuals.
Limitations: Applications not accepted. Giving on a national basis.
Application information: Contributes only to pre-selected organizations; unsolicited requests for funds not considered or acknowledged.
Officers and Directors:* Paula J. DelGiudice,* Chair.; Richard J. Baldes,* Vice-Chair.; Edward E. Clark, Jr.,* Vice-Chair.; Becky Scheibelhut,* Vice-Chair.; Mark Van Putten,* Pres. and C.E.O.; James Baldock; Charles T. Brown; Daniel Deeb; Ken Driggers; Judith Espinosa; Faith Gemmill; Tom Gonzales; Mary C. Harris; and 16 additional directors.
EIN: 530204616

3282
Noah's Ark Foundation
P.O. Box 725
Chincoteague Island, VA 23336
(757) 336-0066
Contact: Carole Marchesano, Pres.

Established in 1991.
Donor(s): Carole Marchesano.
Grantmaker type: Public charity
Financial data (yr. ended 12/31/01): Revenue, $76,778; assets, $35,109 (M); gifts received, $73,475; expenditures, $86,821; program services expenses, $80,066; giving activities include $1,475 for 4 grants (high: $1,000; low: $25).
Purpose and activities: The foundation provides food, shelter and medical attention for stray animals, and provides low cost spay and neuter services.
Fields of interest: Animal welfare; Veterinary medicine.
Limitations: Giving primarily in Chincoteague Island, VA.
Application information:
Initial approach: Letter
Deadline(s): None
Officers: Carole Marchesano, Pres.; Norman Goldberg, V.P.; Michelle McCormack, Secy.
EIN: 541592265

3283
The Norfolk Foundation ▼
1 Commercial Pl., Ste 1410
Norfolk, VA 23510-2113 (757) 622-7951
Contact: Angelica D. Light, Pres.
FAX: (757) 622-1751; E-mail: info@norfolkfoundation.org; URL: http://www.norfolkfoundation.org

Established in 1950 in VA by resolution and declaration of trust; the foundation was incorporated in 2002.
Grantmaker type: Community foundation
Financial data (yr. ended 12/31/02): Assets, $114,893,110 (M); gifts received, $2,869,768; expenditures, $6,972,481; giving activities include $6,206,308 for 547 grants (high: $350,000; low: $200; average: $200–$350,000).
Purpose and activities: Support for local hospitals; higher, medical, and other educational institutions; family and child welfare agencies; a community fund; programs for drug abuse, the aged, the homeless, and the handicapped; and cultural and civic programs.
Fields of interest: Museums; Historic preservation/historical societies; Arts; Child development, education; Higher education; Medical school/education; Adult/continuing education; Adult education—literacy, basic skills & GED; Libraries/library science; Reading; Education; Natural resources; Environment; Animal welfare; Hospitals (general); Family planning; Medical care, rehabilitation; Health care; Substance abuse, services; Mental health/crisis services; Health organizations, association; AIDS; Medical research, institute; AIDS research; Youth development, services; Human services; Children/youth, services; Child development, services; Family services; Aging, centers/services; Homeless, human services; Community development; Voluntarism promotion; Government/public administration;

Leadership development; Disabled; Aging; Economically disadvantaged; Homeless.
Types of support: Capital campaigns; Building/renovation; Equipment; Land acquisition; Seed money; Scholarships—to individuals.
Limitations: Giving limited to Norfolk, VA, and a 50-mile area from its boundaries. No support for national or international organizations, or religious organizations for religious purposes, hospitals and similar health care facilities, or projects normally the responsibility of the government. No grants to individuals (except for donor-designated scholarships), or for operating budgets, annual campaigns, research, endowment funds, or deficit financing; no loans.
Publications: Application guidelines, Annual report (including application guidelines), Financial statement, Grants list, Informational brochure, Newsletter.
Application information: Application form required for scholarships only; applications available Dec. 1.
  Initial approach: Letter or telephone
  Copies of proposal: 1
  Deadline(s): Mar. 1 for scholarships; none for other grants
  Board meeting date(s): 4 times a year
  Final notification: 3 to 4 months
Officers and Directors:* Joshua P. Darden, Jr.,* Chair.; Toy D. Savage, Jr.,* Vice-Chair.; Angelica D. Light,* Pres.; John O. Wynne,* Treas.; Jean C. Bruce; Paul Hirschbiel; Kurt M. Rosenbach; Martha M. Williams.
Number of staff: 3 full-time professional; 2 part-time professional; 1 full-time support.
EIN: 542035996
Recent environmental and animal welfare grants:
3283-1 Chesapeake Bay Foundation, Richmond, VA, $25,000. For Virginia Oyster Aquaculture Program. 2001.
3283-2 Humane Society, Chesapeake, Chesapeake, VA, $24,000. For participation in Spay/Neuter Immediately Program. 2001.
3283-3 Norfolk Botanical Garden Society, Norfolk, VA, $10,000. For horticultural education programs. 2001.
3283-4 Society for the Prevention of Cruelty to Animals, Norfolk, VA, $65,000. For van and equipment to expand existing spay/neuter clinic operations. 2001.
3283-5 Society for the Prevention of Cruelty to Animals, Virginia Beach, VA, $60,000. For purchase of medical equipment for spay/neuter clinic. 2001.

3284
Norfolk Southern Foundation

P.O. Box 3040
Norfolk, VA 23514-3040 (757) 629-2881
Contact: Deborah H. Wyld, Exec. Dir.
E-mail: dhwyld@nscorp.com; URL: http://www.nscorp.com/nscorp/html/foundation.html

Established in 1983 in VA.
Donor(s): Norfolk Southern Corp.
Grantmaker type: Company-sponsored foundation
Financial data (yr. ended 12/31/02): Assets, $3,421,809 (M); expenditures, $2,804,058; qualifying distributions, $2,712,490; giving

activities include $2,027,586 for 154 grants and $666,474 for 1,310 employee matching gifts.
Purpose and activities: Giving primarily for cultural programs, including museums and performing arts groups, and higher education, including independent college funds, and environmental programming dealing with land, air, and water conservation. The foundation also sponsors an employee matching gift program to educational and cultural institutions.
Fields of interest: Museums; Performing arts; Arts; Higher education; Natural resources; Federated giving programs.
Types of support: General/operating support; Continuing support; Annual campaigns; Capital campaigns; Building/renovation; Equipment; Emergency funds; Program development; Seed money; Scholarship funds; Employee matching gifts; Employee-related scholarships; In-kind gifts; Matching/challenge support.
Limitations: Giving restricted to 22-state operating territory of Norfolk Southern Corp. No support for health and welfare programs, or for grants/matching gifts to sports or athletic programs, including athletic scholarships. No grants to individuals (except for employee-related scholarships), or for fundraising events.
Publications: Application guidelines, Annual report, Program policy statement.
Application information: Application form not required.
  Initial approach: Letter
  Copies of proposal: 1
  Deadline(s): From July 15 to Sept. 30 for funding in the following calendar year
  Board meeting date(s): As necessary
  Final notification: 90 days
Officers: David R. Goode, Chair., C.E.O. and Pres.; T.L. Ingram, V.P.; Kathryn B. McQuade, V.P.; L.I. Prillaman, Jr., V.P.; Stephen C. Tobias, V.P.; Henry C. Wolf, V.P.; Reginald J. Chaney, Secy.; Marta Stewart, Treas.; Deborah H. Wyld, Exec. Dir.
Number of staff: 1 full-time professional.
EIN: 521328375

3285
North Shore Foundation

c/o Bank of America
1 Commercial Pl.
Norfolk, VA 23510-2103 (757) 627-0611
Contact: Tou D. Savage, Jr., Pres., Bank of America

Established in 1982 in VA.
Donor(s): Constance S. duPont Darden.
Grantmaker type: Independent foundation
Financial data (yr. ended 04/30/02): Assets, $1,164,019 (M); gifts received, $1,320,589; expenditures, $157,400; qualifying distributions, $157,400; giving activities include $157,000 for 7 grants (high: $75,000; low: $2,000).
Purpose and activities: Giving primarily for education and human services.
Fields of interest: Arts; Higher education; Environment; Human services; Federated giving programs.
Types of support: General/operating support; Scholarship funds.
Limitations: Giving primarily in VA. No grants to individuals.

Application information: Application form not required.
  Initial approach: Letter
  Deadline(s): None
Officers and Directors:* Joshua P. Darden, Jr.,* Pres. and Treas.; Irene D. Field,* Secy.; Constance S. duPont Darden.
EIN: 521296293

3286
Elis Olsson Memorial Foundation

c/o Dennis I. Belcher
P.O. Box 397
Richmond, VA 23218-0397 (804) 843-9066
Application address: P.O. Box 151, West Point, VA 23181; tel.: (804) 843-9066

Established in 1966 in VA.
Donor(s): Inga Olsson Nylander,‡ Signe Maria Olsson.‡
Grantmaker type: Independent foundation
Financial data (yr. ended 12/31/02): Assets, $20,107,884 (M); gifts received, $21,801; expenditures, $1,367,612; qualifying distributions, $1,274,190; giving activities include $1,193,875 for 84 grants (high: $200,000; low: $500).
Purpose and activities: Giving primarily for higher and other education, Roman Catholic churches, and the arts, particularly historical activities; funding also for hospitals and health associations, including services for people who are blind, children, youth and social services, and volunteer and fire departments.
Fields of interest: Museums; Historic preservation/historical societies; Arts; Elementary/secondary education; Higher education; Education; Natural resources; Hospitals (general); Health organizations, association; Food services; Disasters, fire prevention/control; Human services; Children/youth, services; Residential/custodial care, group home; Foundations (community); Marine science; Roman Catholic agencies & churches; Economically disadvantaged.
Types of support: Professorships; Fellowships.
Limitations: Giving primarily in VA. No grants to individuals.
Application information:
  Initial approach: Letter
  Deadline(s): None
  Board meeting date(s): Oct. 1
Officers and Directors:* Sture G. Olsson,* Chair.; C. Elis Olsson,* Pres.; Shirley C. Olsson,* V.P.; Lisa O. Armstrong,* Secy.-Treas.; Thelma L. Downey, Exec. Dir.; Anne O. Loebs; Inga O. Rogers.
Number of staff: 1 part-time professional.
EIN: 546062436

3287
The Alison J. & Ella W. Parsons Foundation

999 Waterside Dr., Ste. 1700
Norfolk, VA 23510 (757) 622-3366
Contact: Marie Achtemeier Finch, Admin.
Application address: P.O. Box 3460, Norfolk, VA 23514, additional tel.: (757) 629-0666

Established in 1984 in VA.
Donor(s): Alison J. Parsons,‡ Ella W. Parsons.‡
Grantmaker type: Independent foundation

Financial data (yr. ended 04/30/02): Assets, $7,576,881 (M); expenditures, $472,293; qualifying distributions, $421,705; giving activities include $407,500 for 32 grants (high: $50,000; low: $1,000; average: $1,000–$50,000).
Purpose and activities: Primary areas of interest include the arts, health, higher education, literacy, and social services.
Fields of interest: Arts; Early childhood education; Higher education; Botanical gardens; Hospitals (general); Health organizations, association; Medical research, institute; Human services.
Types of support: Capital campaigns; Building/renovation; Equipment; Professorships; Seed money; Matching/challenge support.
Limitations: Giving limited to the South Hampton Roads area (Portsmouth, Chesapeake, Virginia Beach, Suffolk and Norfolk,) VA. No support for private elementary or secondary schools. No grants to individuals.
Publications: Application guidelines.
Application information: 3-year hiatus between funded grant and new application. Application form not required.
  Initial approach: Letter
  Copies of proposal: 6
  Deadline(s): 30 days before board meeting
  Board meeting date(s): Spring and fall
  Final notification: Within 3 weeks of board meeting
Officers and Directors:* William K. Butler II,* Pres.; Howard L. Brantly,* V.P.; Robert C. Nusbaum,* Secy.-Treas.; Jane P. Batten; Constance C. Laws.
Number of staff: 1 part-time professional.
EIN: 541253938

3288
The Pauley Family Foundation
c/o S.F. Pauley
314 Saint David's Ln.
Richmond, VA 23221

Established in 1993 in VA.
Donor(s): Stanley F. Pauley, Dorothy A. Pauley.
Grantmaker type: Independent foundation
Financial data (yr. ended 12/31/01): Assets, $13,351,223 (M); expenditures, $1,476,551; qualifying distributions, $1,387,812; giving activities include $1,382,500 for 7 grants (high: $1,250,000; low: $12,500; average: $12,500–$25,000).
Purpose and activities: Giving primarily for the arts.
Fields of interest: Museums; Orchestra (symphony); Historic preservation/historical societies; Higher education; Botanical gardens; Boy scouts; American Red Cross.
Limitations: Applications not accepted. Giving primarily in Richmond, VA. No grants to individuals.
Application information: Contributes only to pre-selected organizations.
Officers: Stanley F. Pauley, Chair.; Dorothy A. Pauley, Pres. and Treas.; Katharine Pauley Hickok, V.P.; Lorna Pauley Jordan, V.P.; W. Birch Douglass III, Secy.
EIN: 541685158

3289
Rare Center for Tropical Conservation
1840 Wilson Blvd., Ste. 204
Arlington, VA 22201-3000 (703) 522-5070
Contact: Brett S. Jenks, Pres. and C.E.O,
FAX: (703) 522-5027; E-mail:
rare@rarecenter.org; URL: http://
www.rarecenter.org/

Established in 1973.
Grantmaker type: Public charity
Financial data (yr. ended 09/30/01): Revenue, $2,545,235; assets, $1,415,420; gifts received, $2,511,063; expenditures, $1,896,798; program services expenses, $1,750,547; giving activities include $42,970 for 2 grants (high: $28,538; low: $14,432).
Purpose and activities: The organization seeks to protect wildlands of globally significant biological diversity by empowering local people to benefit from their preservation. Current areas of focus include the Caribbean, Latin America, the Pacific, and South Africa.
Fields of interest: Natural resources.
International interests: Caribbean; South Africa; Latin America; Marianas; Marshall Islands; Micronesia; Indonesia.
Limitations: Giving on an international basis.
Officers and Trustees:* Vadim A. Nikitine,* Chair.; Susan A. Babcock,* Vice-Chair.; Brett S. Jenks,* Pres. and C.E.O.; Thomas McNamee,* Secy.; Peter H. Flint,* Treas.; David Ayer; Peter P. Blanchard III; Howard Brokaw; Katherine Carpenter; Miles Chapin; and 17 additional trustees.
EIN: 237380563

3290
Richard S. Reynolds Foundation
1403 Pemberton Rd., Ste. 102
Richmond, VA 23233 (804) 740-7350
Contact: Victoria Pitrelli, Exec. Dir.
FAX: (804) 740-7807; E-mail:
VPRSRFDN@aol.com

Incorporated in 1955 in VA.
Donor(s): David P. Reynolds, Julia L. Reynolds.‡
Grantmaker type: Independent foundation
Financial data (yr. ended 06/30/01): Assets, $39,562,412 (M); gifts received, $38,526; expenditures, $1,729,962; qualifying distributions, $1,483,979; giving activities include $1,456,780 for 49 grants (high: $125,821; low: $1,000; average: $10,000–$50,000).
Purpose and activities: Support for higher and secondary education, health, museums, cultural organizations, human services, religion, environmental protection, historic preservation, and technological research/education.
Fields of interest: Museums; Historic preservation/historical societies; Secondary school/education; Higher education; Natural resources; Health care; Health organizations, association; Human services; Engineering/technology; Religion.
Types of support: General/operating support; Annual campaigns; Capital campaigns; Building/renovation; Endowments; Professorships; Scholarship funds; Research.
Limitations: Giving primarily in VA. No grants to individuals.

Application information: Application form not required.
  Initial approach: Letter
  Copies of proposal: 1
  Deadline(s): No formal deadline; informal Apr. 30 and Oct. 31
  Board meeting date(s): Mid-May and Mid-Nov.
  Final notification: 2 weeks after board meeting
Officers and Directors:* David P. Reynolds,* Pres.; Mrs. Glenn R. Martin,* V.P.; Richard S. Reynolds III,* Secy.; Victoria Pitrelli, Exec. Dir.
Number of staff: 1 full-time professional.
EIN: 546037003

3291
Rouse-Bottom Foundation
115 Harbor Dr.
Hampton, VA 23661-3301
Contact: Viola K. Wood, Admin. Asst.

Established in 1989 in VA.
Donor(s): Dorothy Bottom.‡
Grantmaker type: Independent foundation
Financial data (yr. ended 12/31/02): Assets, $2,812,674 (M); expenditures, $206,702; qualifying distributions, $180,369; giving activities include $177,850 for 53 grants (high: $13,000; low: $500; average: $500–$5,000).
Fields of interest: Museums; Historic preservation/historical societies; Arts; Higher education; Libraries/library science; Environment.
Limitations: Giving primarily in VA, with emphasis on the Lower Peninsula, Hampton Roads, and Tidewater areas. No support for health, social services, or youth or civic programs. No grants to individuals.
Application information: Giving strictly limited to the foundation's fields of interest; funds are committed mainly to a core group of grantees. Application form not required.
  Initial approach: Letter
  Copies of proposal: 6
  Deadline(s): Aug. 15
  Board meeting date(s): Quarterly
  Final notification: Following board meeting
Officers and Directors:* Raymond B. Bottom, Jr.,* Pres.; Dorothy Rouse-Bottom,* Secy.-Treas.; Lewis T. Booker; Jesse R. Forst; M. Whitney Gilkey; Lester Migdal.
Number of staff: None.
EIN: 541521527

3292
Seagears Family Foundation
9909 Evenstar Ln.
Fairfax Station, VA 22039
Contact: Marilyn Neff Seagears, Pres.

Established in 1998 in VA.
Grantmaker type: Independent foundation
Financial data (yr. ended 12/31/02): Assets, $1,413,255 (M); expenditures, $117,327; qualifying distributions, $104,531; giving activities include $104,700 for 43 grants (high: $25,000; low: $100).
Fields of interest: Education; Natural resources; Cancer; Federated giving programs; Human services; Christian agencies & churches.
Limitations: Giving on a national basis, with emphasis on NY and the greater metropolitan

Washington, DC, area, including MD and VA. No grants to individuals.
Application information:
  Initial approach: Letter
  Deadline(s): None
Officers and Directors:* Marilyn Neff Seagears,* Pres.; Murray W. Seagears,* Secy.-Treas.; Joanne N. Arbaugh.
EIN: 541899835

3293
Staunton Augusta Waynesboro Community Foundation

(also known as SAW Community Foundation)
1100 W. Broad St.
Waynesboro, VA 22980 (540) 932-7878
Contact: Joi E. Brown, Exec. Dir.
FAX: (540) 932-7539; E-mail: sawfdtn@cfw.com; URL: http://www.cfw.com/~sawfdtn

Established in 1992.
Donor(s): H.D. "Buz" Dawbarn.‡
Grantmaker type: Community foundation
Financial data (yr. ended 12/31/02): Assets, $5,647,316 (M); gifts received, $1,395,649; expenditures, $289,043; giving activities include $197,103 for grants.
Purpose and activities: Giving for the arts, education and human services. The foundation administers endowment funds.
Fields of interest: Arts; Education; Environment; Health care; Youth, services; Family services; Community development, neighborhood development.
Types of support: Continuing support; Equipment; Program development.
Limitations: Giving limited to Augusta County, Nelson County, Staunton, and Waynesboro, VA. No support for start-up operations.
Publications: Financial statement, Grants list, Informational brochure, Newsletter.
Application information: Application form required.
  Initial approach: Telephone requesting application
  Copies of proposal: 1
  Deadline(s): Dec. 31
  Board meeting date(s): Mon. following 3rd Wed. of every other odd number month
  Final notification: Apr. or May
Officers and Directors:* David Deering,* Pres.; Beverly S. "Cheri" Moran,* V.P.; P. William Moore, Jr.,* Secy.-Treas.; Joi E. Brown, Exec. Dir.; A. Tracy Aitcheson; C. Phillip Barger; Benham Black; Harold Cook; Timothy C. Hess; Pamela T. Huggins; Carl G. Lind; William McIntyre; E. Ray Murphy; Richard Schilling; Edward Stemmler; Robert A. Sullivan; Jennifer Vela; Wesley Wampler; Marcia J. Winfield.
Number of staff: 1 full-time professional; 1 part-time support.
EIN: 541647385

3294
SunTrust Foundation MidAtlantic ▼

(formerly Crestar Foundation)
c/o SunTrust Banks, Inc.
919 E. Main St.
Richmond, VA 23219 (804) 782-7907
Contact: Brenda L. Skidmore, Pres.

Established in 1973 in VA.

Donor(s): Crestar Bank, and other affiliates of Crestar Financial Corp., SunTrust Bank.
Grantmaker type: Company-sponsored foundation
Financial data (yr. ended 12/31/01): Assets, $6,561,137 (M); gifts received, $4,000,000; expenditures, $3,903,807; qualifying distributions, $3,901,502; giving activities include $3,901,502 for 809 grants (high: $162,500; low: $25; average: $1,000–$20,000).
Purpose and activities: Priority given to community funds and established educational and arts and cultural organizations in the communities served by bank affiliates; grants also for business and health services.
Fields of interest: Arts; Higher education; Environment; Health care; Business/industry; Federated giving programs.
Types of support: Annual campaigns; Capital campaigns; Building/renovation; Equipment; Professorships; Employee matching gifts.
Limitations: Giving limited to VA and communities served by bank affiliates. No support for government-supported, religious, or national agencies. No grants to individuals, or for research, scholarships, or fellowships; no loans.
Publications: Informational brochure.
Application information: Application form not required.
  Initial approach: Letter and proposal
  Copies of proposal: 1
  Deadline(s): Submit proposal before Oct. 15
  Board meeting date(s): Semiannually, and as required
Officers: Brenda L. Skidmore, Pres.; Shirley Swartwout, Secy.-Treas.
Number of staff: 2 full-time professional.
EIN: 237336418
Recent environmental and animal welfare grants:
3294-1 Lewis Ginter Botanical Gardens, Richmond, VA, $20,000. 2002.
3294-2 National Aquarium in Baltimore, Baltimore, MD, $20,000. 2002.
3294-3 Society for the Prevention of Cruelty to Animals, Richmond, VA, $10,000. 2002.

3295
Tara Foundation, Inc.

P.O. Box 1850
Middleburg, VA 20118 (540) 687-8884
Contact: Mary Painter

Donor(s): Magalen O. Bryant.
Grantmaker type: Independent foundation
Financial data (yr. ended 12/31/01): Assets, $4,787,635 (M); gifts received, $600; expenditures, $357,160; qualifying distributions, $342,398; giving activities include $343,156 for 167 grants (high: $60,000; low: $15).
Fields of interest: Arts; Libraries/library science; Education; Natural resources; Human services; Government/public administration; Religion.
Limitations: Giving on a national basis. No grants to individuals.
Application information:
  Deadline(s): None
Officers and Directors:* Magalen C. Webert,* Pres.; John C.O. Bryant,* V.P.; John Gordon,* Secy.-Treas.; Magalen O. Bryant; Michael R. Crane; W. Carey Crane III; Kristiane W. Graham.
Number of staff: 1 shared staff.

EIN: 541596203

3296
The J. Edwin Treakle Foundation, Inc.

P.O. Box 1157
Gloucester, VA 23061 (804) 693-0881
Contact: John Warren Cooke, Pres. and Genl. Mgr.

Incorporated in 1963 in VA.
Donor(s): J. Edwin Treakle.‡
Grantmaker type: Independent foundation
Financial data (yr. ended 04/30/02): Assets, $7,273,959 (M); expenditures, $468,908; qualifying distributions, $413,435; giving activities include $365,000 for 85 grants (high: $24,000; low: $300).
Fields of interest: Arts; Higher education; Education; Animal welfare; Hospitals (general); Cancer; Cancer research; Youth, services; Community development; Protestant agencies & churches.
Types of support: General/operating support; Continuing support; Annual campaigns; Capital campaigns; Building/renovation; Equipment; Scholarship funds.
Limitations: Giving primarily in VA. No grants to individuals.
Application information: Application form required.
  Copies of proposal: 1
  Deadline(s): Submit proposal between Jan. 1 and Apr. 30
  Board meeting date(s): Thurs. after 2nd Mon. in Feb., Apr., June, Aug., Oct., and Dec.
Officers and Directors:* John W. Cooke,* Pres. and General Mgr.; Harry E. Dunn,* V.P. and Treas.; Cynthia B. Horsley,* Secy.; Nancy Powell.
Number of staff: 2 part-time professional; 2 part-time support.
EIN: 546051620

3297
The Truland Foundation

3330 Washington Blvd.
Arlington, VA 22201 (703) 516-2600
Contact: Robert W. Truland, Tr.
E-mail: rtruland@truland.com

Established in 1954 in VA.
Donor(s): Truland Systems Corp., and members of the Truland family.
Grantmaker type: Company-sponsored foundation
Financial data (yr. ended 03/31/02): Assets, $2,293,172 (M); gifts received, $10,500; expenditures, $433,441; qualifying distributions, $420,270; giving activities include $401,216 for 46 grants (high: $50,000; low: $35).
Fields of interest: Arts; Higher education; Natural resources; Hospitals (general); Human services; Children/youth, services.
Types of support: Continuing support; Publication; Matching/challenge support.
Limitations: Giving primarily in VA. No grants to individuals.
Application information: Application form not required.
  Initial approach: Letter
  Deadline(s): None
Trustees: Alice O. Truland; Robert W. Truland.
EIN: 546037172

3298
US Airways Group, Inc. Corporate Giving Program
2345 Crystal Dr.
Arlington, VA 22227
Contact: H. Michael Clark, Dir., Community Rels.

Grantmaker type: Corporate giving program
Purpose and activities: US Airways makes charitable contributions to nonprofit organizations involved with arts and culture, education, the environment, health, job training, and community development. Support is given on an international basis.
Fields of interest: Arts; Education; Environment; Health care; Employment, services; Community development.
Types of support: General/operating support; In-kind gifts.
Limitations: Giving on an international basis in areas of company operations. No support for religious or political organizations. No grants to individuals.
Application information: Application form not required.
Initial approach: Proposal to headquarters
Copies of proposal: 1
Deadline(s): None
Final notification: 3 months

3299
The Virginia Beach Foundation
P.O. Box 4629
Virginia Beach, VA 23454 (757) 422-5249
Contact: Ted Clarkson, Exec. Dir.
Application address: 1604 W. Hilltop Exec. Ctr., Ste. 214A, Virginia Beach, VA 23451; FAX: (757) 422-1849; E-mail: mainoffice@vabeachfoundation.org; URL: http://www.vabeachfoundation.org

Incorporated in 1987 in VA.
Grantmaker type: Community foundation
Financial data (yr. ended 09/30/02): Assets, $9,122,783 (M); gifts received, $992,521; expenditures, $858,237; giving activities include $721,412 for grants and $30,000 for 4 in-kind gifts.
Purpose and activities: Giving to organizations working in human services, health care, education, the environment, animal welfare, and arts and culture in the Virginia Beach, VA, area. The foundation administers donor-advised funds.
Fields of interest: Arts; Education; Environment; Animals/wildlife; Health care; Domestic violence; Human services; Children/youth, services; Disabled; Aging; Economically disadvantaged; Homeless.
Types of support: Emergency funds; Program development; Technical assistance; In-kind gifts; Matching/challenge support.
Limitations: Giving primarily within a 60-mile radius of Virginia Beach, VA. No grants to individuals, or for general operating support, seed money, conferences, seminars, or scholarships.
Publications: Application guidelines, Annual report, Financial statement, Grants list, Informational brochure, Newsletter.

Application information: Project report and site visit for evaluation required. Application form required.
Initial approach: Letter
Copies of proposal: 2
Deadline(s): Mar.
Board meeting date(s): Semiannually
Final notification: June
Officers and Directors:* Robert C. Goodman, Jr.,* Chair.; Macon F. Brock,* 1st Vice-Chair.; Mrs. Robin D. Ray,* 2nd Vice-Chair.; Margaret G. Campbell,* Secy.; Dennis R. Deans,* Treas.; and 7 additional directors.
Number of staff: 1 full-time professional; 1 full-time support.
EIN: 541553631

3300
Virginia Environmental Endowment
3 James Ctr.
1051 E. Cary St., Ste. 1400
Richmond, VA 23219 (804) 644-5000
Contact: Gerald P. McCarthy, Exec. Dir.
Mailing address: P.O. Box 790, Richmond, VA 23218-0790; E-mail: info@vee.org; URL: http://www.vee.org

Incorporated in 1977 in VA.
Donor(s): Allied Chemical Corp., Bethlehem Steel Corp., FMC Corp., Wheeling-Pittsburgh Steel Corp., Hauni Richmond, Inc., IR International, Inc.
Grantmaker type: Independent foundation
Financial data (yr. ended 03/31/03): Assets, $13,285,220 (M); expenditures, $944,997; qualifying distributions, $721,649; giving activities include $721,649 for 36 grants.
Purpose and activities: Virginia Environmental Endowment's mission is to improve the quality of the environment by using its capital to encourage all sectors to work together to prevent pollution, conserve natural resources, and promote environmental literacy. The endowment makes grants to nonprofit, tax-exempt, charitable organizations and institutions, and to government agencies.
Fields of interest: Water pollution; Natural resources; Environment, land resources; Environmental education.
Types of support: Equipment; Program development; Publication; Seed money; Research; Technical assistance; Matching/challenge support.
Limitations: Giving limited to KY and WV for the Ohio and Kanawha River Valleys Program and VA for the Virginia Program and Mini-Grant Program. No grants to individuals, or for overhead, general support, indirect costs, capital projects, building construction or renovation, land purchases, endowments, or for law suits.
Publications: Annual report (including application guidelines).
Application information: Application procedures and proposal requirements listed on Web site and in annual report. Application form not required.
Initial approach: Cover letter with proposal of no more than 5 pages
Copies of proposal: 2
Deadline(s): March 15, August 1, and December 1; March 15 only for Kanawha and Ohio River Valleys Program

Board meeting date(s): Usually in Mar., June, and Nov.
Final notification: 3 months
Officers and Directors:* Dixon M. Butler,* Pres.; Alson H. Smith, Jr.,* Sr. V.P.; Gerald P. McCarthy, Secy. and Exec. Dir.; Paul U. Elbling,* Treas.; Robert M. Freeman; Linwood Holton; Nina Randolph; Robert B. Smith, Jr.
Number of staff: 1 full-time professional; 1 full-time support.
EIN: 541041973
Recent environmental and animal welfare grants:
3300-1 Alliance for the Chesapeake Bay, Baltimore, MD, $45,000. For matching grant for Builders for the Bay. 2003.
3300-2 American Farmland Trust, Culpeper, VA, $65,000. For matching grant for Virginia Rural Lands Program. 2003.
3300-3 Friends of Chesterfields Riverfront, Chesterfield, VA, $23,000. For matching grant for exemplary environmental community pilot study phase I: Chesterfield Watershed Education. 2003.
3300-4 Izaak Walton League of America, Arlington, VA, $15,000. For Virginia Save Our Streams Program. 2003.
3300-5 Kentucky Waterways Alliance, Munfordville, KY, $60,000. For matching grant for Watershed Watch in Kentucky. 2003.
3300-6 League of Conservation Voters Education Fund, DC, $47,650. For testing the viability of a Natural Resources Funding Campaign in Virginia. 2003.
3300-7 Nature Conservancy, Charlottesville, VA, $74,445. For Natural Resources Funding Campaign in Virginia. 2003.
3300-8 New River Land Trust, Blacksburg, VA, $10,000. For challenge grant for New River Easement Education Effort. 2003.
3300-9 Radford University, Radford, VA, $19,210. For matching grant for Small Business Environmental Management Assistance Program. 2003.
3300-10 University of Charleston, Charleston, WV, $30,000. For matching grant for Kanawha River Project: Metal Analysis and the Mobile Education and Research Laboratory. 2003.
3300-11 University of Virginia, Charlottesville, VA, $105,399. For matching grant to create Environmentally Wired Kids through use of wireless technology. 2003.
3300-12 University of Virginia, Institute for Environmental Negotiation, Charlottesville, VA, $40,000. For matching grant for Virginia Environmental Conflict Resolution Project. 2003.
3300-13 Valley Conservation Council, Staunton, VA, $16,000. For matching grant for Botetourt Community Partnership: Expanding the Model. 2003.
3300-14 Virginia Department of Environmental Quality, Richmond, VA, $50,000. For matching grant for Virginia Classroom Grants Program. 2003.
3300-15 Virginia Polytechnic Institute and State University, Blacksburg, VA, $61,554. For matching grant for expanding the soil factors of Virginia Phosphorous Index. 2003.
3300-16 Virginia, Commonwealth of, Richmond, VA, $10,000. For matching grant for Governor's Natural Resources Leadership Summit. 2003.

3300-17 West Virginia Rivers Coalition, Buckhannon, WV, $14,000. For matching grant to promote adoption of scientifically sound and protective nutrient criteria in West Virginia. 2003.

3301
Elbert H., Evelyn J. and Karen H. Waldron Charitable Foundation, Inc.
P.O. Box 20069
Roanoke, VA 24018-0503
Contact: Karen H. Waldron, Pres.

Established in 1982 in VA.
Donor(s): Elbert H. Waldron,‡ Evelyn J. Waldron.
Grantmaker type: Independent foundation
Financial data (yr. ended 12/31/02): Assets, $1,106,644 (M); gifts received, $356,442; expenditures, $213,526; qualifying distributions, $212,346; giving activities include $211,508 for 11 grants (high: $100,000; low: $300).
Purpose and activities: Giving for community and public affairs and service organizations.
Fields of interest: Higher education; Veterinary medicine.
Limitations: Applications not accepted. Giving limited to VA. No grants to individuals.
Application information: Contributes only to pre-selected organizations.
Officers and Director:* Karen H. Waldron,* Pres.; Shawn A. Ricci, V.P.; Rebecca F. Rosenberg, Secy.-Treas.
EIN: 521289232

3302
Water Environment Research Foundation
601 Wythe St.
Alexandria, VA 22314-1994 (703) 684-2470
Contact: Stephanie Llewellyn, Prod. Mgr.
FAX: (703) 299-0742; E-mail: werf@werf.org;
URL: http://www.werf.org

Established in 1989 in VA.
Grantmaker type: Public charity
Financial data (yr. ended 12/31/00): Revenue, $8,050,170; assets, $8,275,356 (M); gifts received, $3,410,027; expenditures, $8,398,069; program services expenses, $7,745,702; giving activities include $5,153,901 for 67 grants (high: $345,967; low: $2,851).
Purpose and activities: The foundation provides a balanced water quality research program addressing current wastewater research needs. This program covers a broad range of water quality issues, including collection and treatment systems, watershed management, human health and environmental effects, and residual management.
Fields of interest: Environment, pollution control; Water pollution; Environment, water resources.
Types of support: Research.
Publications: Annual report, Informational brochure (including application guidelines), Multi-year report (including application guidelines), Newsletter, Occasional report.
Application information: See Web site for application information. Application form required.
Initial approach: Letter
Copies of proposal: 10

Deadline(s): June 1 for Paul L. Borsch Award; July 19 for Solicited Research
Board meeting date(s): Apr. and Dec.
Final notification: Varies
Officers and Directors:* Stephen T. Hayashi,* Chair.; James F. Stahl,* Vice-Chair.; William J. Bertera,* Secy.; Karl W. Mueldener,* Treas.; Glenn Reinhardt, Exec. Dir.; Robert Berger; Gordon R. Garner; Richard D. Kutchenrither, Ph.D.; and 9 additional directors.
Number of staff: 32.
EIN: 541511635

3303
The Tracy Webb Memorial Foundation
1147 Mill Rd.
Woodstock, VA 22664-2321 (540) 459-4613
Contact: Bernard Webb, Pres.

Established in 1998.
Donor(s): Bernard Webb, Patricia Webb.
Grantmaker type: Operating foundation
Financial data (yr. ended 06/30/02): Assets, $327,121 (M); gifts received, $150,000; expenditures, $106,446; qualifying distributions, $106,337; giving activities include $106,164 for 227 grants (high: $1,034; low: $53).
Fields of interest: Medical school/education; Veterinary medicine; Veterinary medicine, hospital.
Types of support: General/operating support.
Limitations: Giving primarily in VA. No grants to individuals.
Application information: Application form required.
Deadline(s): None
Officers and Directors:* Bernard Webb,* Pres.; Bernard C. Webb,* V.P.; Patricia Webb,* Secy.-Treas.; Bruce Costod.
EIN: 541903763

3304
The Wellspring Foundation
(formerly The Stone Foundation)
c/o Investors Records Corp.
614 E. High St.
Charlottesville, VA 22902
Contact: Kelly Seshimo, Secy.
Mailing address: Canal St. Sta., P.O. Box 276, New York, NY 10012, tel./FAX: (212) 226-1992; E-mail: wllsprg@aol.com

Established in 1985 in NY.
Donor(s): Diana B. Clark, James Clark.‡
Grantmaker type: Independent foundation
Financial data (yr. ended 12/31/01): Assets, $3,638,864 (M); gifts received, $171,511; expenditures, $364,201; qualifying distributions, $297,000; giving activities include $297,000 for 21 grants (high: $40,000; low: $5,000).
Fields of interest: Film/video; Education; Environment.
Limitations: Giving primarily in New York, NY. No grants to individuals.
Application information: Application form not required.
Initial approach: Letter or proposal
Deadline(s): Nov. 1
Board meeting date(s): Early Dec.
Final notification: Jan. 31
Officers: Kelly Seshimo, Secy.; Benjamin Brewster, Treas.

Trustees: Ashley S. Pettus; Brewster W. Pettus; Elise S. Pettus.
Number of staff: 1 part-time support.
EIN: 133457878

3305
WestWind Foundation
232 E. High St.
Charlottesville, VA 22902 (434) 977-5762
Contact: Heidi Binko, Prog. Off.
E-mail: binko@westwindfoundation.org; URL: http://www.westwindfoundation.org

Established in 1987 in DC.
Donor(s): Edward M. Miller.
Grantmaker type: Independent foundation
Financial data (yr. ended 12/31/02): Assets, $12,418,281 (M); gifts received, $4,000,000; expenditures, $1,334,624; qualifying distributions, $1,289,065; giving activities include $1,294,093 for 47 grants (high: $200,000; low: $125).
Purpose and activities: Giving primarily for education and human services. Giving also for forest and land conservation, watershed protection, advocacy and policy groups that protect against climate change, as well as for reproductive health services, and family planning.
Fields of interest: Higher education; Environment, land resources; Environment, forests; Environment; Family planning; Youth development; Human services; Biological sciences.
International interests: Caribbean; Latin America; Central America; Bolivia; Brazil.
Types of support: General/operating support; Continuing support; Land acquisition; Program development; Conferences/seminars.
Limitations: Giving on a national level, with emphasis on the Southeast, New England and AK, for environment program. Giving is primarily targeted toward Latin America and the Caribbean for family planning program, although domestic support is available. No grants to individuals.
Publications: Annual report (including application guidelines), Grants list.
Application information: Application form required.
Initial approach: 1- to 2-page letter of inquiry to Prog. Off.
Copies of proposal: 1
Deadline(s): Sept. 2
Board meeting date(s): Varies annually; usually Oct.-Nov.
Final notification: Dec.
Trustees: Edward M. Miller; Janet H. Miller.
Number of staff: 1 full-time professional.
EIN: 526358830

3306
Mark and Catherine Winkler Foundation
4900 Seminary Rd., Ste. 900
Alexandria, VA 22311 (703) 998-0400
Contact: Lynne S. Ball, Asst. Treas.

Established about 1964 in VA.
Donor(s): Catherine Winkler, Mark Winkler,‡ Catherine W. Herman.
Grantmaker type: Independent foundation

Financial data (yr. ended 12/31/01): Assets, $1,103,144 (M); expenditures, $583,191; qualifying distributions, $471,408; giving activities include $458,330 for 33 grants (high: $71,000; low: $500).
Purpose and activities: Giving primarily for social services, particularly for aid to single parents, environmental projects, conservation, and medical research.
Fields of interest: Education, administration/regulation; Higher education; Environment, research; Global warming; Natural resources; Health care; Surgery; Human services; Salvation Army; Children/youth, services; Community development; Social sciences.
Types of support: General/operating support; Annual campaigns; Capital campaigns; Building/renovation; Equipment; Endowments; Emergency funds; Program development; Conferences/seminars; Professorships; Seed money; Fellowships; Research; Matching/challenge support.
Limitations: Giving in a national basis, with some emphasis on the metropolitan Washington, DC, area.
Publications: Application guidelines.
Application information: Accepts WG Common Grant Application Format. Application form required.
  Initial approach: Proposal or letter
  Copies of proposal: 1
  Deadline(s): None
  Board meeting date(s): Nov.
Officers: Catherine W. Herman, Chair.; Kathleen W. Wennesland, Pres.; Margaret Hecht, V.P.; Corolyn W. Thomas, Secy.
Director: Kim S. Wennesland.
Number of staff: 1 part-time professional; 1 part-time support.
EIN: 546054383

3307
Wise Foundation
P.O. Box 557
Marshall, VA 20116-0557
Contact: Lewis B. Pollard, Pres.

Established in 1999 in VA.
Donor(s): Mary L.F. Wiley.
Grantmaker type: Independent foundation
Financial data (yr. ended 12/31/02): Assets, $4,153,831 (M); expenditures, $248,325; qualifying distributions, $226,698; giving activities include $228,000 for 39 grants (high: $23,000; low: $500).
Purpose and activities: Giving to local community projects.
Fields of interest: Education; Animal welfare; Disasters, fire prevention/control; Human services.
Limitations: Giving limited to VA. No grants to individuals.
Application information:
  Initial approach: Letter
  Deadline(s): None
Officers and Directors:* Lewis B. Pollard,* Pres. and Secy.-Treas.; Lewis S. Wiley,* V.P.
Number of staff: None.
EIN: 541942771

3308
Wrinkle in Time Foundation, Inc.
P.O. Box 306
The Plains, VA 20198-0306

Established in 1980 in NY.
Donor(s): A.B. Currier.
Grantmaker type: Independent foundation
Financial data (yr. ended 12/31/02): Assets, $7,924,089 (M); expenditures, $651,885; qualifying distributions, $571,572; giving activities include $576,500 for 17 grants (high: $140,000; low: $1,000).
Purpose and activities: Support primarily for improving the rural and urban environment; including wildlife and wilderness preservation; as well as to gather, preserve and disseminate information about the environment, make productive contributions to either the rural or urban surroundings; restore and maintain historic buildings, sites and antiquities; or encourage, promote and popularize art or design which enhances the rural or urban environment.
Fields of interest: Education; Natural resources; Environment; Animals/wildlife, preservation/protection; Rural development.
Types of support: General/operating support; Program development; Seed money.
Limitations: Applications not accepted. Giving primarily in VA. No grants to individuals; no loans.
Application information: Unsolicited requests for funds not accepted.
  Board meeting date(s): Jan., Apr., July, and Oct.
Officer and Board Member:* Andrea B. Currier,* Chair. and Pres.
Number of staff: None.
EIN: 222351518

WASHINGTON

3309
444S Foundation
(also known as 444 Sierra Foundation)
P.O. Box 1128
Bellevue, WA 98008-1128
Contact: Peggy Ford, Fdn. Admin.

Established in 1998 in WA.
Donor(s): G. James Roush.
Grantmaker type: Independent foundation
Financial data (yr. ended 12/31/02): Assets, $18,845,633 (M); gifts received, $1,957,610; expenditures, $1,111,400; qualifying distributions, $894,440; giving activities include $930,000 for 17 grants (high: $272,500; low: $10,000).
Purpose and activities: Giving for the environment and animal welfare.
Fields of interest: Natural resources; Animals/wildlife, preservation/protection.
Types of support: General/operating support; Program development; Matching/challenge support.
Limitations: Applications not accepted. Giving primarily in the Pacific Northwest, including Western Canada. No grants to individuals.

Application information: Contributes only to pre-selected organizations. Foundation will solicit proposals. Unsolicited requests for funds not accepted.
  Board meeting date(s): Varies
Trustees: Del Langbauer; G. James Roush; William Morgan Roush; Cynthia Wayburn.
Number of staff: 1 part-time support.
EIN: 916468421

3310
A Territory Resource
(also known as ATR)
603 Stewart St., Ste. 1007
Seattle, WA 98101-1229 (206) 624-4081
Contact: Bookda Gheisar, Exec. Dir.
FAX: (206) 382-2640; E-mail: grants@atrfoundation.org; URL: http:// www.atrfoundation.org/

Established in 1978 in WA.
Grantmaker type: Public charity
Financial data (yr. ended 12/31/01): Revenue, $1,115,503; assets, $1,687,519; gifts received, $1,042,155; expenditures, $1,096,146; program services expenses, $746,404; giving activities include $554,330 for grants (high: $3,000; low: $1,000) and $1,289,992 for loans/program-related investments.
Purpose and activities: Support is given for grassroots organizations attempting to establish a society that is politically and economically democratic, equitable, and environmentally sound.
Fields of interest: Environment; Civil rights, immigrants; Civil rights; Community development, ethics; Community development, citizen coalitions; Economic development; Rural development.
Types of support: General/operating support; Continuing support; Emergency funds; Program development; Seed money; Technical assistance.
Limitations: Giving limited to ID, MT, OR, WA, and WY. No support for projects providing only direct services to a client, media events, arts or theater productions, projects sponsored by an individual or governmental agency, or projects which can be funded by traditional funding sources. No grants to individuals, or for litigation, legal expenses, research, scholarships, or publications.
Publications: Application guidelines, Biennial report, Financial statement, Grants list, Informational brochure, Newsletter.
Application information: Accepts NNG Common Application Form; see Web site for grants list. Application form required.
  Initial approach: Telephone
  Copies of proposal: 10
  Deadline(s): Varies
  Board meeting date(s): Jan., Mar., May, Sept., and Nov.
  Final notification: Varies
Officers and Directors:* Jill Arnow,* Chair.; Eric Ward,* Vice-Chair.; Michael Baker,* Treas.; Bookda Gheisar, Exec. Dir.; Barbara Becker; Moira Bowman; Rosemary Bratton; Pat Close; Andy Himes; Ivan Inger; Vince Lemus; Gary Owens; Janet Robideau; Bryony Schwan; Lori Villarosa; Tim Wise.
Number of staff: 2 full-time professional; 2 part-time professional; 1 full-time support.
EIN: 911036971

3311
Alaska Air Group, Inc. Corporate Giving Program
c/o Public Affairs Dept.
P.O. Box 68900
Seattle, WA 98168 (206) 433-3383
Contact: Donna R. Hartman, Admin., Corp.
Contribs.
FAX: (206) 431-5558

Grantmaker type: Corporate giving program
Financial data (yr. ended 12/31/02): Total giving, $196,660; giving activities include $196,660 for grants and $2,587,252 for company-administered programs.
Purpose and activities: Alaska Air makes charitable contributions to nonprofit organizations involved with arts and culture, education, the environment, medical research, and human services. Support is given primarily in areas of company operations.
Fields of interest: Arts; Education; Environment; Medical research; Human services.
Types of support: General/operating support; Employee volunteer services; Employee-related scholarships; In-kind gifts.
Limitations: Giving primarily in areas of company operations, with emphasis on AK, CA, OR, and WA.
Publications: Application guidelines.
Application information: Application form not required.
  Initial approach: Proposal to headquarters
  Copies of proposal: 1
  Deadline(s): 6 weeks prior to need
  Final notification: Following review
Administrators: Susan Bramstedt, Dir., Alaska Public Affairs; Donna R. Hartman, Admin., Corp. Contribs.
Number of staff: 4.

3312
The Albohn Family Foundation
c/o Anita Pennington
6709 Westhill Ct.
Olympia, WA 98512
Contact: Catherine Heay, Pres.

Established in 1992 in WA.
Donor(s): Angela L. Albohn.‡
Grantmaker type: Operating foundation
Financial data (yr. ended 12/31/02): Assets, $2,704,910 (M); expenditures, $147,707; qualifying distributions, $120,519; giving activities include $95,900 for 6 grants (high: $60,000; low: $900).
Purpose and activities: Grants are given to animal welfare organizations.
Fields of interest: Animal welfare; Animals/wildlife, preservation/protection.
Types of support: General/operating support; Equipment; Emergency funds.
Limitations: Giving primarily in Thurston County, WA. No grants to individuals.
Application information: Application form not required.
  Initial approach: Proposal
  Copies of proposal: 4
  Deadline(s): None
  Board meeting date(s): Quarterly
Officers and Directors:* Catherine Heay,* Pres.; Mary Gentry,* Secy.; Anita Pennington,* Treas.; Susan Beauregard.

EIN: 911562963

3313
Alistar International
(formerly Alistar Foundation)
P.O. Box 947
Issaquah, WA 98027-0035

Established in 1995 in WA.
Donor(s): The Alistar Group, Bernard G. Greer, Judith O.A. Greer.
Grantmaker type: Operating foundation
Financial data (yr. ended 12/31/00): Assets, $28,579 (M); gifts received, $941,532; expenditures, $961,454; qualifying distributions, $949,919; giving activities include $668,708 for 5 grants (high: $551,063; low: $17,860).
Purpose and activities: Giving primarily for the relief and rehabilitation of the 64 communities along the Bocay and Coco rivers in northern Nicaragua, by providing food and other supplies, reforestation, agriculture, and medical supplies, assisting 22000 people. In addition, the foundation is assisting the communities in planning for the long-term management of the rainforest in which they live.
Fields of interest: Natural resources; International relief; Community development.
International interests: Nicaragua.
Limitations: Applications not accepted. Giving primarily in Nicaragua; some funding also in Seattle, WA. No grants to individuals.
Application information: Contributes only to pre-selected organizations.
Officers and Directors:* Bernard G. Greer,* Pres.; Nan Marie Greer, V.P.; Judith O.A. Greer,* Secy.-Treas.; Frederic Gregory; Carl Mayers; Anuar Murrar; Anthony Stocks.
EIN: 911672495

3314
The Paul G. Allen Forest Protection Foundation ▼
505 5th Ave. S., Ste. 900
Seattle, WA 98104
Contact: Jo Allen Patton, Exec. Dir.
E-mail: info@pgafoundations.com; URL: http://www.pgafoundations.com/

Established in 1997 in WA.
Donor(s): Paul G. Allen.
Grantmaker type: Independent foundation
Financial data (yr. ended 12/31/01): Assets, $5,116,004 (M); gifts received, $6,715,000; expenditures, $2,371,743; qualifying distributions, $2,596,101; giving activities include $2,371,101 for 7 grants (high: $1,500,000; low: $40,000; average: $40,000–$250,000) and $225,000 for 1 loan/program-related investment.
Purpose and activities: To protect old growth forests and other special forest lands for the preservation of wildlife habitat and, where possible, for the provision of recreational use. Through its grantmaking the Paul G. Allen Forest Protection Foundation seeks to safeguard the beauty, natural resources, and recreational opportunities distinctive to the Pacific Northwest for present and future generations.
Fields of interest: Natural resources; Environment.

Types of support: Land acquisition; Matching/challenge support; Program-related investments/loans.
Limitations: Giving limited to the Pacific Northwest. No support for religious organizations for religious purposes. No grants to individuals or for annual fund drives or federated campaigns.
Publications: Biennial report (including application guidelines).
Application information: Application form required.
  Initial approach: Application
  Copies of proposal: 2
  Deadline(s): Mar. 31 and Sept. 30
  Final notification: Within 120 days of receipt of application
Officers and Directors:* Paul G. Allen,* Chair.; Bert E. Kolde, Pres.; Richard E. Leigh, Jr., V.P. and Secy.; Jo Allen Patton,* V.P. and Exec. Dir.; Nathaniel T. Brown, V.P.
Number of staff: 2 full-time professional; 1 full-time support.
EIN: 911764177

3315
Paul M. Anderson Foundation
c/o Bank of America
P.O. Box 24565, No. CSC-23
Seattle, WA 98124
Contact: Rod Johnson

Established in 1994 in WA.
Donor(s): John Privat, Priscilla Privat.
Grantmaker type: Independent foundation
Financial data (yr. ended 09/30/02): Assets, $2,732,626 (M); expenditures, $166,934; qualifying distributions, $157,831; giving activities include $158,000 for 20 grants (high: $15,000; low: $2,500).
Purpose and activities: Giving primarily for higher education.
Fields of interest: Education; Environment, pollution control; Health organizations, association.
Types of support: Program development; Curriculum development.
Limitations: Applications not accepted. Giving primarily in WA. No grants to individuals.
Application information: Contributes only to pre-selected organizations. Unsolicited requests for funds not accepted.
  Board meeting date(s): Nov.
Officers: John Privat, Pres.; Priscilla Privat, V.P.
Number of staff: None.
EIN: 911697666

3316
Norman Archibald Charitable Foundation
c/o Wells Fargo Bank Northwest, N.A.
P.O. Box 21927, 14th Fl.
Seattle, WA 98111 (206) 343-8367
Contact: Stuart H. Prestrud, Secy. of Board of Managers
Additional tel.: (206) 343-2217

Established in 1976 in WA.
Donor(s): Norman Archibald.‡
Grantmaker type: Independent foundation
Financial data (yr. ended 09/30/02): Assets, $7,942,239 (M); expenditures, $581,025; qualifying distributions, $498,390; giving

activities include $473,100 for 100 grants (high: $50,000; low: $1,000).

Purpose and activities: Support youth and child development programs; support also for medical research, higher education and libraries, museums and the performing arts, social services for the aged and the handicapped, housing programs, and animal welfare and conservation.

Fields of interest: Museums; Performing arts; Theater; Music; History/archaeology; Arts; Child development, education; Higher education; Libraries/library science; Education; Natural resources; Environment; Animal welfare; Hospitals (general); Health care; Health organizations, association; AIDS; Medical research, institute; AIDS research; Housing/shelter, development; Youth development, services; Human services; Children/youth, services; Child development, services; Hospices; Aging, centers/services; Federated giving programs; Engineering/technology; Science; Leadership development; Native Americans/American Indians; Disabled; Aging.

Types of support: General/operating support; Building/renovation; Equipment; Land acquisition; Program development; Seed money; Research.

Limitations: Giving primarily in the Puget Sound region of WA. No support for government entities, private foundations, or religious organizations for religious purposes. No grants to individuals, or for ongoing operational support, deficit financing, endowment funds, or scholarships; no loans.

Publications: Application guidelines, Annual report.

Application information: Application form not required.

   Initial approach: Letter
   Copies of proposal: 3
   Deadline(s): None
Advisory Board: Robert L. Gerth; J. Shan Mullin; Stuart H. Prestrud.
Trustee: Wells Fargo Bank Northwest, N.A.
Number of staff: None.
EIN: 911098014

3317
Attachmate Corporation Contributions Program
c/o Corp. Contribs.
3617 131st Ave. S.E.
Bellevue, WA 98006
URL: http://cooljobs.attachmate.com/cooljobs/community.asp

Grantmaker type: Corporate giving program
Purpose and activities: Attachmate makes charitable contributions to nonprofit organizations involved with arts and culture, education, the environment, health and human services, and on a case by case basis. Support is given primarily in areas of company operations.
Fields of interest: Arts; Education; Environment; Health care; Human services; General charitable giving.
Types of support: General/operating support; Employee volunteer services; Employee matching gifts; Donated equipment; Donated products; In-kind gifts.

Limitations: Giving primarily in areas of company operations.
Application information: A contributions committee reviews all requests. Application form not required.
   Initial approach: Proposal to headquarters
   Copies of proposal: 1
   Final notification: Following review

3318
Clara & Art Bald Trust
P.O. Box 1757
Walla Walla, WA 99362 (509) 527-3500
Contact: Tom Scribner, Tr.

Established in 1985 in WA.
Grantmaker type: Independent foundation
Financial data (yr. ended 03/31/02): Assets, $2,250,998 (M); expenditures, $129,265; qualifying distributions, $95,326; giving activities include $96,275 for 38 grants (high: $5,000; low: $1,000).
Purpose and activities: Giving primarily for veterans' organizations, social services, and agriculture and forestry education.
Fields of interest: Education; Natural resources; Human services; Federated giving programs.
Types of support: General/operating support.
Limitations: Giving limited to Walla Walla, WA. No grants to individuals.
Application information: Application form not required.
   Initial approach: Letter
   Deadline(s): None
Trustee: Tom Scribner.
Number of staff: None.
EIN: 916275061

3319
Eddie Bauer, Inc. Corporate Giving Program
15010 N.E. 36th St.
Redmond, WA 98052-9700
Contact: Lurma Rackley, Dir., Public Affairs and Social Responsibility
FAX: (425) 882-6127; URL: http://www.eddiebauer.com/about/eb_philanthropy.asp

Grantmaker type: Corporate giving program
Purpose and activities: Eddie Bauer makes charitable contributions to nonprofit organizations involved with education, the environment, and equal opportunity and access. Support is given on a national basis.
Fields of interest: Education; Environment; Civil rights, equal rights.
Types of support: General/operating support; Continuing support; Scholarship funds; Cause-related marketing; Employee volunteer services; Loaned talent; Sponsorships; Employee matching gifts; Employee-related scholarships; Donated products; In-kind gifts.
Limitations: Giving on a national basis.
Publications: Application guidelines, Corporate giving report.
Application information: The Corporate Social Responsibility Department handles giving. The company has a staff that only handles contributions. Application form not required.
   Initial approach: Proposal to headquarters or nearest company facility
   Copies of proposal: 1

Deadline(s): None
Final notification: Following review
Administrators: Miranda Bayne, Community and Public Affairs Specialist; Kevin Martinez, Mgr., Community Affairs; Lurma Rackley, Dir., Public and Social Responsibility.
Number of staff: 3 full-time professional.

3320
Beardsley Foundation Trust
(formerly Beardsley Family Foundation Trust)
c/o Union Bank of California, N.A.
P.O. Box 84495
Seattle, WA 98124-5796 (206) 587-3627

Established in 1976 in WA.
Grantmaker type: Independent foundation
Financial data (yr. ended 05/31/02): Assets, $1,961,710 (M); expenditures, $126,023; qualifying distributions, $107,061; giving activities include $100,600 for 25 grants (high: $25,000; low: $1,000).
Purpose and activities: Giving primarily for the arts, children and youth services, and community organizations.
Fields of interest: Arts; Higher education; Education; Animals/wildlife; Youth, services; Philanthropy/voluntarism.
Types of support: Capital campaigns.
Limitations: Applications not accepted. Giving primarily in Seattle, WA. No grants to individuals, or for start-up or operations costs.
Application information: Contributes only to pre-selected organizations.
Trustee: Union Bank of California, N.A.
Number of staff: None.
EIN: 916214189

3321
Blue Mountain Community Foundation
(formerly Blue Mountain Area Foundation)
8 S. 2nd, Ste. 618
P.O. Box 603
Walla Walla, WA 99362 (509) 529-4371
Contact: Lawson F. Knight, Exec. Dir.
FAX: (509) 529-5284; URL: http://www.bluemountainfoundation.org

Incorporated in 1984 in WA.
Grantmaker type: Community foundation
Financial data (yr. ended 06/30/03): Assets, $15,683,946 (M); gifts received, $109,403; expenditures, $1,031,190; giving activities include $316,603 for 51 grants (high: $69,588; low: $125; average: $125–$69,588).
Purpose and activities: Giving primarily for community projects, programs for organizations promoting welfare and education, social services, historical preservation, the arts, health, and animal welfare; support also for higher education through scholarship funds. The foundation administers a donor-advised fund.
Fields of interest: Visual arts; Performing arts; Humanities; Historic preservation/historical societies; Higher education; Adult education—literacy, basic skills & GED; Animal welfare; Family planning; Health care; Human services; Children/youth, services; Child development, services; Family services; Hospices; Aging, centers/services; Homeless, human services.

Types of support: General/operating support; Endowments; Program development; Seed money; Scholarships—to individuals.
Limitations: Giving limited to Umatilla County, OR, and Walla Walla, Columbia, Garfield, Benton, and Franklin counties, WA.
Publications: Application guidelines, Annual report, Grants list, Informational brochure, Newsletter.
Application information: Application guidelines available on foundation Web site. Application form required.
> *Initial approach:* Letter
> *Copies of proposal:* 9
> *Deadline(s):* July 1
> *Board meeting date(s):* Monthly
> *Final notification:* Oct.

Officers and Trustees:* Jane Kreitzberg,* Pres.; Ellen Wolf, V.P.; John M. Reese,* Secy.; Tom Baker; Megan Clubb; Deborah Frol; Michael W. Gillespie; Peter Harvey; Jim Hayner; Jim Hobkirk; Tom Madsen; Judy Mulkerin; Terry Nealey; Bert Nelson; Mark Thompson.
Number of staff: 1 full-time professional; 1 full-time support.
EIN: 911250104

3322
The Brainerd Foundation
1601 2nd Ave., Ste. 610
Seattle, WA 98101 (206) 448-0676
Contact: Ann Krumboltz, Exec. Dir.
FAX: (206) 448-7222; E-mail: info@brainerd.org;
URL: http://www.brainerd.org

Established in 1995 in WA.
Donor(s): Paul Brainerd.
Grantmaker type: Independent foundation
Financial data (yr. ended 12/31/02): Assets, $34,727,158 (M); expenditures, $3,642,252; qualifying distributions, $3,642,252; giving activities include $2,810,000 for 125 grants (high: $140,000; low: $500; average: $1,000–$30,000) and $14,605 for foundation-administered programs.
Purpose and activities: The foundation has two environmental programs: Endangered Ecosystems, and Communications and Capacity Building.
Fields of interest: Natural resources.
International interests: Canada.
Types of support: General/operating support; Continuing support; Income development; Equipment; Emergency funds; Program development; Conferences/seminars; Seed money; Research; Technical assistance; Matching/challenge support.
Limitations: Giving primarily in AK, ID, MT, OR, WA, and British Columbia and the Yukon territory. No grants for school education campaigns, land purchases or easements, endowments, capital campaigns, debt reduction, basic research, fellowships, or books and videos that are not components of a broader strategy.
Publications: Financial statement.
Application information: Proposals are accepted by invitation only. Application form required.
> *Initial approach:* Letter of inquiry
> *Copies of proposal:* 1
> *Deadline(s):* None
> *Board meeting date(s):* Mar., June, and Nov.

Officers and Directors:* Paul Brainerd,* Pres. and Treas.; Sherry Brainerd,* V.P. and Secy.; Ann Krumboltz, V.P. and Exec. Dir., Comm. and Capacity Building.
Number of staff: 2 full-time professional; 1 part-time professional; 1 full-time support; 2 part-time support.
EIN: 911675591

3323
The Bullitt Foundation ▼
1212 Minor Ave.
Seattle, WA 98101-2825 (206) 343-0807
Contact: Denis Hayes, Pres.
FAX: (206) 343-0822; E-mail: info@bullitt.org;
URL: http://www.bullitt.org

Incorporated in 1952 in WA.
Donor(s): Members of the Bullitt family.
Grantmaker type: Independent foundation
Financial data (yr. ended 12/31/02): Assets, $84,399,287 (M); expenditures, $8,196,708; qualifying distributions, $7,838,485; giving activities include $6,552,275 for 166 grants (high: $1,300,000; low: $5,000; average: $10,000–$50,000), $250,497 for 164 employee matching gifts and $192,320 for 1 loan/program-related investment.
Purpose and activities: Giving for the protection and restoration of the environment in the Pacific Northwest, including mountains, forests, rivers, wetlands, coastal areas, soils, fish, and wildlife.
Fields of interest: Environment, radiation control; Environment, toxics; Global warming; Natural resources; Environment, water resources; Environment, land resources; Energy; Environment, Animals/wildlife; Agriculture/food, management/technical aid; Agriculture, soil/water issues; Transportation.
Types of support: General/operating support; Continuing support; Equipment; Emergency funds; Program development; Seed money; Technical assistance; Program-related investments/loans; Employee matching gifts; Matching/challenge support.
Limitations: Giving exclusively in the Pacific Northwest. No support for political organizations. No grants to individuals, or for capital campaigns.
Publications: Application guidelines.
Application information: Applications sent by FAX or other electronic applications are discouraged. Application form required.
> *Initial approach:* Proposal
> *Copies of proposal:* 1
> *Deadline(s):* May 1 and Nov. 1
> *Board meeting date(s):* Apr. and Oct.
> *Final notification:* 5 months

Officers and Trustees:* B. Gerald Johnson,* Chair.; Katherine M. Bullitt,* Vice-Chair.; Denis Hayes,* Pres.; David Buck, Secy.; Tomoko Moriguchi-Matsuno,* Treas.; Harriet Bullitt; Estella Leopold; Hubert G. Locke, Ph.D.; James Youngren.
Number of staff: 5 full-time professional.
EIN: 916027795
Recent environmental and animal welfare grants:
3323-1 1000 Friends of Oregon, Portland, Oregon, $50,000. For operating support. 2001.
3323-2 1000 Friends of Oregon, Portland, Oregon, $25,000. For capacity-building

project to improve effectiveness of citizen groups working on Smart Growth issues in Northwest. 2001.
3323-3 1000 Friends of Washington, Seattle, WA, $75,000. For operating support. 2001.
3323-4 1000 Friends of Washington, Seattle, WA, $20,000. For board challenge grant for new or expanded contributions from individual donors, with Foundation's contribution dedicated to reserve fund. 2001.
3323-5 Alaska Conservation Alliance, Anchorage, AK, $10,000. For board challenge grant for new and expanded contributions from individual donors and member groups. 2001.
3323-6 Alternative Energy Resources Organization, Helena, MT, $30,000. For project in western Montana to increase organization's farmer membership and actively engage farmers as advocates on smart growth, renewable energy, energy conservation, and sustainable agriculture issues. 2001.
3323-7 American Lands Alliance, DC, $25,000. For project to craft and coordinate efforts to protect Northwest old growth forests and roadless lands. 2001.
3323-8 American Rivers, Seattle, WA, $40,000. For work of Northwest office, focusing on river protection issues such as salmon restoration efforts and hydroelectric dam reform. 2001.
3323-9 American Rivers, Seattle, WA, $25,000. For challenge grant for new or increased major donor contributions. 2001.
3323-10 Americans for Our Heritage and Recreation, DC, $20,000. For project to build public and governmental support for open-space protection in the Northwest. 2001.
3323-11 Audubon Society of Portland, Portland, Oregon, $40,000. For project to protect fish and wildlife habitat and water quality in northwestern coastal region of Oregon by promoting improved land-use policies and advocating public support for better protection of land and water. 2001.
3323-12 Audubon Society, Tahoma, Tacoma, WA, $25,000. For project to protect natural environment and quality of life in Pierce County. 2001.
3323-13 Audubon Society, Tahoma, Tacoma, WA, $10,000. For challenge grant for contributions from individual donors and participating groups. 2001.
3323-14 Better Environmentally Sound Transportation Association, Vancouver, Canada, $25,000. For work to promote transportation choices in British Columbia, and project to expand organization's membership and fundraising capacity. 2001.
3323-15 Better Environmentally Sound Transportation Association, Vancouver, Canada, $10,000. For board challenge grant for new or expanded contributions from individual donors, with Foundation's contribution dedicated to reserve fund. 2001.
3323-16 British Columbia Spaces for Nature, Gibsons, Canada, $30,000. For Jobs and Environment campaign, designed to eliminate unsustainable timber practices, protect biodiversity, and promote rural employment as well as efforts to monitor

management of protected lands throughout province. 2001.

3323-17 Center for Environmental Law and Policy, Seattle, WA, $40,000. For operating support. 2001.

3323-18 Center for Science in Public Participation, Bozeman, MT, $20,000. For work in Northwest. 2001.

3323-19 Center for Watershed and Community Health, Springfield, Oregon, $25,000. For project to demonstrate economic benefits of environmental protection to business, government, and community leaders. 2001.

3323-20 Central Cascades Alliance, Hood River, Oregon, $20,000. For project to restore and protect wild lands of Central Cascades and ensure long-term survival of native species through development of long-term conservation biology-based plan. 2001.

3323-21 Citizens for a Better Flathead, Kalispell, MT, $80,000. For smart growth project and efforts to counter anti-environmental rhetoric through expanded public education, outreach to the media, and coordination with other citizen groups, including conservation roundtable. 2001.

3323-22 Citizens for a Healthy Bay, Tacoma, WA, $20,000. For operating support. 2001.

3323-23 Clallam, County of, Department of Community Development, Port Angeles, WA, $14,000. For Streamkeepers of Clallam County's volunteer efforts to provide timely, consistent and credible data on stream health to local officials, planners, tribes, landowners, and public. 2001.

3323-24 Clark Fork Coalition, Missoula, MT, $25,000. For operating support to continue to challenge mining proposals that will further degrade water quality in basin. 2001.

3323-25 Clark Fork Coalition, Missoula, MT, $20,000. For work of Montana Smart Growth Coalition in western Montana. 2001.

3323-26 Climate Solutions, Olympia, WA, $40,000. For operating support, including leading regional climate change initiative and working with farming groups to foster renewable energy resources. Grant made through Earth Island Institute. 2001.

3323-27 Climate Solutions, Olympia, WA, $20,000. For challenge grant for new individual donors. Grant made through Earth Island Institute. 2001.

3323-28 Climate Solutions, Olympia, WA, $15,000. For technology upgrades. Grant made through Earth Island Institute. 2001.

3323-29 Coast Range Association, Corvallis, Oregon, $25,000. For activities focused on state forests, successful watershed protection, and forest conservation in coastal Oregon-especially Tillamook forest-including grassroots education, organizing, economic analysis, and media outreach. 2001.

3323-30 Coast Range Association, Corvallis, Oregon, $10,000. For challenge grant for new or expanded contributions from individual donors. 2001.

3323-31 Columbia Riverkeeper, Hood River, Oregon, $55,000. For operating support, including building its membership and funding base. 2001.

3323-32 CommEn Space, Seattle, WA, $12,000. For project to help environmental organizations in western Washington use

mapping technologies more effectively. Grant made through Tides Center. 2001.

3323-33 Committee for Idahos High Desert, Boise, ID, $15,000. For project to evaluate, monitor, and document degradation of streams, wetlands, and springs in Idaho's arid high desert, to be used in resource damage litigation, site protection, and public education. 2001.

3323-34 Committee for Idahos High Desert, Boise, ID, $10,000. For challenge grant for individual donors. 2001.

3323-35 Conservation Geography, Boise, ID, $25,000. For expansion of capacity to serve Idaho conservation groups, including technical analysis, support for litigation, and public education. 2001.

3323-36 Conservation Leaders Network, Wedderburn, Oregon, $10,000. For project to build visible support among county officials for roadless area and old growth protection, to identify and train conservation-oriented participants in Resource Advisory Committees authorized by recent county payments legislation, and to coordinate Oregon and California Lands Action Network. 2001.

3323-37 Cook Inlet Keeper, Homer, AK, $25,000. For monitoring and advocacy work to hold extractive industries accountable for habitat and water-quality protection in Cook Inlet watershed, including monitoring local waters and reporting violators. 2001.

3323-38 CUB Educational Fund, Portland, Oregon, $40,000. For Fair and Clean Energy Coalition, project to build support for Green Power program, customer-driven approach to electric utility restructuring. 2001.

3323-39 David Suzuki Foundation, Vancouver, Canada, $55,000. For climate change program, including key involvement in new regional coalition. 2001.

3323-40 David Suzuki Foundation, Vancouver, Canada, $30,000. For challenge grant for project of West Coast Sustainability Foundation to develop Aquatic Conservation Trust, mechanism designed to manage sustainable fisheries and protect marine ecosystems on West Coast of Vancouver Island. 2001.

3323-41 Earth Day Network, DC, $50,000. For project to organize Earth Day 2002 events designed to educate public about climate change throughout Northwest and promote greenhouse gas reduction commitments from public and private institutions throughout region. 2001.

3323-42 Earthjustice Legal Defense Fund, San Francisco, CA, $70,000. For Fish-Trees-Water campaign, which will use litigation to enforce environmental statutes in order to protect salmon, restore abundant clean water, and safeguard forest ecosystems throughout Northwest. 2001.

3323-43 East Kootenay Environmental Society, Kimberley, Canada, $25,000. For project to adopt land-use management plan that will protect critical ecosystems in Upper Columbia River Basin, and project to promote climate-change solutions in coordination with regional climate coalition. 2001.

3323-44 Ecotrust Canada, Vancouver, Canada, $50,000. For overall work, including

mapping, providing training and technical assistance to First Nations and others, economic development, and support for environmental entrepreneurs. 2001.

3323-45 Ecotrust Canada, Vancouver, Canada, $15,000. For project to develop strategic and business plan for Rainforest Education Society, rainforest educational and interpretive center that will promote knowledge of natural and cultural environments of Clayoquot Sound region. 2001.

3323-46 Environmental Mining Council of British Columbia, Victoria, Canada, $25,000. For work with local groups, government employees, and mine workers to document concerns, research alternatives, and find sustainable solutions to mining problems. Grant made through British Columbia Spaces for Nature. 2001.

3323-47 Forest Stewardship Council, Nelson, Canada, $30,000. For initiative to develop and implement regional wood certification standards for British Columbia. Grant made through Tides Foundation. 2001.

3323-48 Forest Trust, Santa Fe, NM, $20,000. For operating support of Northwest chapter, including efforts to strengthen link between forestry and conservation biology, advocate progressive forest management policies, build capacity of forestry professionals, and recruit new members in region. 2001.

3323-49 ForestEthics, Berkeley, CA, $30,000. For project to redirect US consumer markets away from British Columbia interior forest products and toward ecologically sound alternatives, and to influence purchasing policies of large corporations and companies in US. 2001.

3323-50 Friends of Clark County, Vancouver, WA, $25,000. For smart growth work throughout county, including activities that result in high-quality urban developments, healthy rural communities, transportation choices, and affordable housing. 2001.

3323-51 Friends of Clark County, Vancouver, WA, $10,000. For board challenge grant for new or expanded contributions from individual donors, with portion dedicated to reserve fund. 2001.

3323-52 Friends of Clayoquot Sound, Tofino, Canada, $20,000. For project of Markets Initiative Coalition to reduce Canadian consumption of ancient forests and create economic and political leverage for their protection by changing the way businesses purchase wood and paper products. 2001.

3323-53 Friends of Skagit County, Mount Vernon, WA, $10,000. For challenge grant for new or expanded contributions from individual donors. 2001.

3323-54 Friends of the Columbia Gorge, Portland, Oregon, $25,000. For work to influence pending revision of management plan for scenic area, including outreach, education, and organizing. 2001.

3323-55 Georgetown University, Law Center, Georgetown Environmental Law and Policy Institute, DC, $25,000. For project to protect wildlife and wildlife habitat on private lands in Oregon and Washington through litigation, legal analysis, and public education. 2001.

3323-56 Georgia Strait Alliance, Nanaimo, Canada, $50,000. For operating support, including promoting marine protected areas, building public support for improved management and operation of salmon farming industry, water monitoring, and reducing toxic chemical discharges from boats, homes, businesses, and municipalities. 2001.

3323-57 Gifford Pinchot Task Force, Vancouver, WA, $20,000. For project to conduct oversight of US Forest Service management decisions and activities and conduct public education and outreach focused on forest protection in region. 2001.

3323-58 Government Accountability Project (GAP), DC, $45,000. For Hanford whistleblower protection work that is conducted by Seattle office. 2001.

3323-59 Gowgaia Institute Society, Queen Charlotte, Canada, $25,000. For project to map Haida Gwaii Forest on Queen Charlotte Islands and promote changes in forest management and decision-making. Grant made through Earthlife Canada Foundation. 2001.

3323-60 Greater Yellowstone Coalition, Bozeman, MT, $25,000. For work to protect national forests in Idaho and western Montana from road construction, oil and gas development, and unsustainable timber practices. 2001.

3323-61 Green Fire Productions, Eugene, Oregon, $15,000. For project to build public support for protecting Northwest ancient forests, endangered species, and critical public wildlands. 2001.

3323-62 Heart of America Northwest Research Center, Seattle, WA, $40,000. For ongoing efforts to ensure cleanup at Hanford Nuclear Reservation. 2001.

3323-63 Hells Canyon Preservation Council, Joseph, Oregon, $25,000. For ongoing advocacy for conservation in region, including public education and work with media. 2001.

3323-64 Idaho Community Action Network (I CAN), Boise, ID, $20,000. For project to reduce contamination caused by elemental phosphorous mine on Fort Hall Reservation, Shoshone-Bannock Tribes, and to improve worker safety at this mining and processing operation. 2001.

3323-65 Idaho Conservation League, Boise, ID, $60,000. For operating support, including protection of selected Idaho rivers and roadless areas in several regional public forests, and efforts to build understanding of impacts of climate change. 2001.

3323-66 Idaho Rivers United, Boise, ID, $50,000. For operating support, including actions to strengthen local watershed groups and improve water allocation and water quality policies in state of Idaho. 2001.

3323-67 Idaho Rural Council, Bliss, ID, $30,000. For work to address environmental problems associated with farming practices such as factory farms, and to influence decisions about future of Idaho's electricity providers, rates, and investments in conservation and renewables. 2001.

3323-68 Idaho Smart Growth, Boise, ID, $30,000. For operating support, including technology improvements. 2001.

3323-69 Idaho Smart Growth, Boise, ID, $20,000. For board challenge grant, with portion dedicated to reserve account. 2001.

3323-70 Idaho Sporting Congress, Boise, ID, $15,000. For program to protect national forests in Idaho, eastern Oregon, and Washington. 2001.

3323-71 Kettle Range Conservation Group, Republic, WA, $30,000. For operating support, including work to protect wilderness areas in eastern Washington. 2001.

3323-72 Klamath-Siskiyou Wildlands Center, Williams, Oregon, $15,000. For projects targeted at monitoring government management of Oregon public lands and gathering scientific evidence in support of legal protection for imperiled species and habitats. 2001.

3323-73 Kooskooskie Commons, Walla Walla, WA, $40,000. For regional Farm Connections project to assist conservation community in improving access to information needed to work on environmental issues related to farming, and project targeted at local farming, environmental, and cultural organizations and businesses to restore salmon habitat and streamflows in Walla Walla River. 2001.

3323-74 Labour Environmental Alliance Society, Vancouver, Canada, $20,000. For efforts to strengthen alliances between workers, worker unions, and environmental organizations in British Columbia. 2001.

3323-75 Land Trust Alliance, Seattle, WA, $30,000. For work with Northwest land trusts through consulting, training, and providing small grants. 2001.

3323-76 Land Trust Alliance, Seattle, WA, $10,000. For challenge grant for new or increased major donor contributions. 2001.

3323-77 Lands Council, Spokane, WA, $40,000. For forest watch program and mining pollution cleanup and prevention project. 2001.

3323-78 League of Conservation Voters Education Fund, DC, $35,000. For general support for work in Northwest. 2001.

3323-79 Leavenworth Audubon Adopt-A-Forest, Peshastin, WA, $10,000. For project to leverage government funding for forest habitation protection and restoration efforts and provide outreach and education to public. 2001.

3323-80 Lewis and Clark College, Pacific Environmental Advocacy Center, Portland, Oregon, $25,000. For work to provide legal support to organizations working to protect endangered species and to reduce adverse impacts of pollution on public health and the environment. 2001.

3323-81 Livable Communities Coalition, Seattle, WA, $10,000. To promote Smart Growth solutions in King County. Grant made through One Thousand Friends of Washington. 2001.

3323-82 Livable Communities Coalition, Seattle, WA, $10,000. For board challenge grant for new and expanded contributions from individual donors and member groups. Grant made through One Thousand Friends of Washington. 2001.

3323-83 Living Oceans Society, Sointula, Canada, $25,000. For project to promote continuing existing moratorium on oil and gas development off British Columbia coast,

including public and government outreach and education. Grant made through Sierra Legal Defense Fund. 2001.

3323-84 Mineral Policy Center, DC, $25,000. For Northwest Circuit Rider project to provide technical, organizational, fundraising, and media outreach assistance to citizen groups in Northwest communities that are faced with environmental problems from hardrock mining. 2001.

3323-85 Montana Conservation Voters Education Fund, Billings, MT, $20,000. For work in western Montana. 2001.

3323-86 Montana Environmental Information Center, Helena, MT, $50,000. For work to promote and support energy, deregulation, renewable energy development, and customer demand for renewable energy. 2001.

3323-87 Montana Wilderness Association, Helena, MT, $15,000. For wildlands project in northwest Montana, seeking to protect some of the largest native ecosystems remaining in contiguous 48 states. 2001.

3323-88 Natural Resources Defense Council, San Francisco, CA, $110,000. For climate change, energy, water, forestry, location-efficient mortgage, and hazardous waste work in Northwest. 2001.

3323-89 Nez Perce Tribe, Lapwai, ID, $25,000. For work to protect fisheries, water quality, and water quantity in Snake River Basin. 2001.

3323-90 Northwest Coalition for Alternatives to Pesticides, Eugene, Oregon, $35,000. For legal work to address harmful impacts of pesticide use on salmon and efforts to encourage policies that restrict pesticide use and promote salmon-friendly pest management practices. 2001.

3323-91 Northwest Ecosystem Alliance, Bellingham, WA, $40,000. For campaign to hold US accountable for environmental impacts of softwood lumber agreements with Canada, and to pressure British Columbia government to establish and enforce meaningful reforms in forest practice regulations. 2001.

3323-92 Northwest Energy Coalition, Seattle, WA, $75,000. For Northwest Climate Response, new initiative that will create broad-based, member-driven, well-financed alliance of public interest groups and others to advance solutions to climate change in region. 2001.

3323-93 Northwest Energy Coalition, Seattle, WA, $50,000. For operating support, including activities aimed at utility restructuring and deregulation. 2001.

3323-94 Northwest Energy Coalition, Seattle, WA, $25,000. For challenge grant for contributions to project from member groups and individual donors. 2001.

3323-95 Northwest Energy Coalition, Seattle, WA, $10,000. To build reserve fund. 2001.

3323-96 Northwest Environment Watch, Seattle, WA, $45,000. For operating support. 2001.

3323-97 Northwest Natural Resource Group, Port Townsend, WA, $15,000. For research on development of regionally based independent verification program for forestry carbon offset projects, to ensure their credibility from policy, scientific, and market perspective. 2001.

3323-98 ONE/Northwest, Seattle, WA, $45,000. For operating support. 2001.

3323-99 ONE/Northwest, Seattle, WA, $35,000. For project to provide digital presentation equipment, training, and resources to environmental groups in region to enhance and amplify their messages. 2001.

3323-100 Oregon Environmental Council, Portland, Oregon, $75,000. For agriculture, transportation reform, and climate change work. 2001.

3323-101 Oregon Environmental Council, Portland, Oregon, $10,000. For technology improvements. 2001.

3323-102 Oregon League of Conservation Voters Education Fund, Portland, Oregon, $50,000. For campaign to help expand participation of Oregon conservation groups in electoral process, focusing on assessment and training. 2001.

3323-103 Oregon Natural Desert Association, Bend, Oregon, $25,000. For litigation challenging water quality violations and failure of federal agencies to adequately protect rivers of Oregon's arid east side under Clean Water Act, Wild and Scenic Rivers Act, and Taylor Grazing Act. 2001.

3323-104 Oregon Natural Resources Council Fund, Portland, Oregon, $25,000. For challenge grant for major donor contributions. 2001.

3323-105 Oregon Natural Resources Council Fund, Portland, Oregon, $20,000. For organizational development efforts and campaign to broaden public support for protection of five million acres of pristine forestland in Oregon. 2001.

3323-106 Oregon Trout, Portland, Oregon, $35,000. For work in salmon recovery, watershed restoration, and development of strategy for fish refuges and protected areas throughout Oregon. 2001.

3323-107 Pacific Biodiversity Institute, Winthrop, WA, $15,000. For landscape research and analysis on Washington State wildlands to inform and educate public agencies, activists, and citizens. 2001.

3323-108 Pacific Crest Biodiversity Project, Seattle, WA, $20,000. For advocacy public education, and media outreach efforts to protect old growth forests in Pacific Northwest. 2001.

3323-109 Pacific Rivers Council, Eugene, Oregon, $30,000. For project to promote forest practice reform in Washington and Oregon, including research, media outreach, and public education. 2001.

3323-110 Pacific Science Center, Seattle, WA, $10,000. For project to engage high school students in production of watershed education guide that will enable other high schools and education centers to create similar program for their community watersheds. 2001.

3323-111 People for Puget Sound, Seattle, WA, $35,000. For challenge grant for new members or increased gifts from major donors. 2001.

3323-112 People for Puget Sound, Seattle, WA, $30,000. For operating support including salmon restoration, oil tanker spill prevention, and restoration of shorelines and estuaries. 2001.

3323-113 Point Reyes Bird Observatory, Stinson Beach, CA, $10,000. For project to monitor resident bird populations on threatened arid shrubsteppe habitat in Columbia basin and use information to target land management and conservation efforts. 2001.

3323-114 Puget Soundkeeper Alliance, Seattle, WA, $50,000. For operating support, including citizen Baykeeper program, plus capacity building and organizational development. 2001.

3323-115 Puget Soundkeeper Alliance, Seattle, WA, $10,000. For board challenge grant for new or expanded contributions from individual donors, with Foundation's contribution dedicated to reserve fund. 2001.

3323-116 Raincoast Conservation Foundation, Canada, $25,000. For development of scientific data to encourage protection of habitat for coastal wolves in British Columbia. 2001.

3323-117 Re Sources, Bellingham, WA, $35,000. For operating support, including citizen water-quality monitoring activities and legal challenges to polluters. 2001.

3323-118 Renewable Northwest Project, Portland, Oregon, $60,000. For operating support, including leadership on regional climate change initiative and efforts to work with farming groups to foster renewable energy resources on farms. 2001.

3323-119 RIDGE, Roslyn, WA, $25,000. For administrative and legal challenges to development proposals in area, aiming to ensure protection of water resources and wildlife habitat. 2001.

3323-120 Rivershed Society of British Columbia, Coquitlam, Canada, $20,000. For educational initiative that uses community-based activities to promote conservation of Fraser Riverhead. 2001.

3323-121 Round River Conservation Studies, Salt Lake City, UT, $25,000. For project to develop conservation design for crucial wildlife conservation areas in Taku River watershed, integrating ecological knowledge of Tlingit peoples and principles of conservation biology to ensure future health of watershed, and work on other transboundary watersheds, and in Muskwa-Kechika region of interior British Columbia. 2001.

3323-122 Salish Sea Expeditions, Bainbridge Island, WA, $15,000. For board challenge grant for new or expanded contributions from individual donors. 2001.

3323-123 Salmonweb, Seattle, WA, $19,000. For operating support, focusing on strategic planning and organizational development. 2001.

3323-124 Salt Spring Island Conservancy, Ganges, Canada, $10,000. For program to protect island's freshwater resources and watershed environments, enhance wildlife habitat, and promote sustainable use of land and water. 2001.

3323-125 Sea Resources, Chinook, WA, $20,000. For implementation of restoration plan for Chinook watershed, including monitoring, education, community outreach, and organizational development. 2001.

3323-126 Sierra Club of British Columbia Foundation, Victoria, Canada, $30,000. For project to preserve last unprotected wildlands

in lower British Columbia, key habitat for grizzly bears, spotted owls, mountain sheep, and anadromous fish. 2001.

3323-127 Sierra Legal Defence Fund, Vancouver, Canada, $50,000. For project to ensure enforcement of environmental laws resulting in greater protection of water, and to provide legal advice to conservation groups in British Columbia who are working for water resource protection. 2001.

3323-128 Sierra Legal Defence Fund, Vancouver, Canada, $20,000. For work of Environmental-Aboriginal Guardianship through Law and Education (EAGLE), environmental law center that provides legal and educational support to First Nations in British Columbia. 2001.

3323-129 Sierra Legal Defence Fund, Vancouver, Canada, $10,000. For challenge grant for individual donors. 2001.

3323-130 Silva Forest Foundation, Slocan Park, Canada, $25,000. For operating support of Harrop-Procter Watershed Protection Society, including public education and outreach targeted at protection of community watersheds in British Columbia. 2001.

3323-131 Siskiyou Regional Educational Project, Cave Junction, Oregon, $25,000. For campaign to gain national monument designation for portion of Siskiyou area and to protect wild lands and rivers of Siskiyou Mountains from adverse impacts of mining, logging, and other land uses. 2001.

3323-132 Smart Growth British Columbia, Vancouver, Canada, $30,000. For communications and media project. Grant made through Institute for New Economics Public Interest Research Association. 2001.

3323-133 Snake River Alliance Education Fund, Boise, ID, $25,000. For operating support. 2001.

3323-134 Snake River Alliance Education Fund, Boise, ID, $10,000. For board challenge grant for contributions from major donors, with Foundation's funds dedicated to technology upgrades and staff training. 2001.

3323-135 Society of Environmental Journalists, Jenkintown, PA, $43,250. For Annual Conference to be held in Portland, Oregon. 2001.

3323-136 Swan View Coalition, Kalispell, MT, $15,000. For forest-watch efforts focused on protecting ecosystems of Flathead National Forest in northwest Montana. 2001.

3323-137 Training Resources for the Environmental Community, Vashon, WA, $75,000. For training services in region, emphasizing services provided to groups working on foundation's program priorities. 2001.

3323-138 Transportation Choices Coalition, Seattle, WA, $60,000. For operating support, including its leadership in advancing climate change initiative such as clean fuels campaign aimed at transportation sector. 2001.

3323-139 Trout Unlimited, Arlington, VA, $35,000. For program to maintain instream flows for healthy coldwater fisheries in western Montana. 2001.

3323-140 Tualatin River Keepers, Sherwood, Oregon, $30,000. For work to monitor state implementation of federal Clean Water Act requirements, targeting enforcement of pollution limits and protection of wetlands and streams. 2001.

3323-141 Valhalla Wilderness Society, New Denver, Canada, $25,000. For project to establish provincial park to protect ancient forest ecosystem that serves as habitat for rare Kermode bear, as well as resident wolves, salmon, and other rainforest species. 2001.

3323-142 Washington Agriculture and Forestry Education Foundation, Spokane, WA, $40,000. For project to expand dialogue between environmental community and farmers about integrating economically viable farming with environmental protection and enhancement. 2001.

3323-143 Washington Environmental Alliance for Voter Education, Seattle, WA, $75,000. For NW Ballot Watch, project to engage in those things that nonprofit educational organization can do to monitor, evaluate, and respond to ballot measures that impact environment in Washington and Oregon. Grant made through the Tides Center. 2001.

3323-144 Washington Environmental Alliance for Voter Education, Seattle, WA, $75,000. For general support. 2001.

3323-145 Washington Environmental Council, Seattle, WA, $75,000. For operating support and work to protect forest habitat, improve water-quality policies, increase habitat protection on agricultural lands, and foster strong land-use management practices. 2001.

3323-146 Washington Tilth Association, Greenbank, WA, $35,000. For work of Tilth Producers, including challenge grant for new or expanded contributions from individual donors. 2001.

3323-147 Washington Tilth Association, Greenbank, WA, $25,000. For work of Washington Sustainable Food and Farming Network, including challenge grant for new or expanded contributions from individual donors or member groups and portion dedicated to reserve fund. 2001.

3323-148 Washington Toxics Coalition, Seattle, WA, $45,000. For operating support, including efforts to reduce or eliminate pesticide use in Washington State cities and counties. 2001.

3323-149 Washington Trout, Duvall, WA, $15,000. For project of Thornton Creek Alliance to challenge new development in Seattle's Thornton Creek watershed, seek commitment to restore watershed as part of any redevelopment, and identify and build alliances with interests of others in watershed to protect its future. 2001.

3323-150 Washington Wilderness Coalition, Seattle, WA, $35,000. For Wild Washington Campaign, project to educate public about value of wild forests and encourage actions that result in long-term protection. 2001.

3323-151 Western Canada Wilderness Committee, Vancouver, Canada, $40,000. For wilderness protection work, which focuses on Clayquot Sound, Stoltmann, Great Bear Rainforest, and Lillooet-Rainshadow wilderness. 2001.

3323-152 Western Mining Action Project, Boulder, CO, $30,000. For continued efforts to provide legal services to Northwest groups that are challenging destructive mining proposals and practices. Grant made through Land and Water Fund of the Rockies. 2001.

3323-153 Western Resource Advocates, Boulder, CO, $45,000. For operating support. 2001.

3323-154 Western Watersheds Project, Hailey, ID, $25,000. For project to improve public land management in Caribou National Forest of southeastern Idaho, focusing on impacts of livestock on sources of fresh water and riparian areas. 2001.

3323-155 Wild Salmon Center, Portland, Oregon, $35,000. For project to identify, map, and restore key habitats for native salmon, steelhead, and cutthroat trout in Tillamook Basin of western Oregon and Hoh River basin of Washington's Olympic Peninsula. 2001.

3323-156 Wild Salmon Center, Portland, Oregon, $30,000. For Tillamook Rainforest Coalition campaign to influence pending decisions by state of Oregon regarding future management of Tillamook and Clatsop state forests. Grant made through Audubon Society of Portland. 2001.

3323-157 Wilderness Society, DC, $60,000. For campaign targeted at securing comprehensive protection for roadless areas in Northwest national forests, and new initiative focused on restoration and protection of Klamath Basin. 2001.

3323-158 Xerces Society, Portland, Oregon, $20,000. For aquatic macroinvertebrate monitoring program designed to promote volunteer aquatic monitoring by giving volunteers knowledge, tools, and information necessary to collect biological stream data that will be used to protect and restore waters. 2001.

3323-159 Yaak Valley Forest Council, Troy, MT, $10,000. For forest watch program focused on conservation, monitoring, community outreach, and education. 2001.

3324
The Burning Foundation

5135 Ballard Ave. N.W.
Seattle, WA 98107 (206) 781-3472
Contact: Therese Ogle, Grants Consultant
FAX: (206) 784-5987; E-mail: OgleFounds@aol.com; URL: http://fdncenter.org/grantmaker/burning/

Established in 1997 in WA.
Donor(s): David Weise.
Grantmaker type: Independent foundation
Financial data (yr. ended 12/31/01): Assets, $6,334,865 (M); gifts received, $3,313,500; expenditures, $238,925; qualifying distributions, $223,750; giving activities include $218,500 for 36 grants (high: $10,000; low: $2,000).
Purpose and activities: Giving in the following areas: to protect the region's rivers, forest, native fish, and land; to help low-income youth become environmental stewards; and to address the impact of overpopulation and to develop effective pregnancy prevention strategies for teens.
Fields of interest: Natural resources; Environment, water resources; Environment, land resources; Environment, forests; Environmental education; Animals/wildlife, fisheries; Youth, pregnancy prevention; Youth, services.

Types of support: General/operating support; Program development.
Limitations: Giving limited to OR and WA for environmental requests, and the Puget Sound area for conservation programs for youth and teen pregnancy prevention programs. No support for private schools. No grants to individuals for research or scholarships, or for capital campaigns for building construction or renovations, computer, software, or office equipment purchases, or book, video, film, or home-page productions, unless the production is an essential component of the funded project.
Application information: See foundation Web site for complete application guidelines. Accepts Philanthropy Northwest Common Grant Application Form. Materials submitted by fax or e-mail not considered.
   Initial approach: 1- to 2-page letter or inquiry; submission of full proposals is by invitation only
   Deadline(s): Spring cycle: 3rd Wed. of Jan. for letter, 1st Wed. of Mar. for invited proposal; Fall cycle: 3rd Wed. of Aug for letter, 1st Wed. of Oct. for invited proposal
   Final notification: 1st Wed. of May and 4th Wed. of Nov.
Officers: David Weise, Pres. and Secy.; Virginia Hadlett, V.P.; Ira Weise, Secy.
EIN: 911815335

3325
Cascade Natural Gas Corporation Contributions Program

c/o Customer Svc. Dept.
222 Fairview Ave. N.
Seattle, WA 98109 (206) 624-3900
Contact: Julie Marshall, Dir., Customer Svc.
FAX: (206) 624-7215; Additional FAX: (206) 654-4069; E-mail: jmarshal@cngc.com

Grantmaker type: Corporate giving program
Financial data (yr. ended 09/30/02): Total giving, $28,500; giving activities include $26,000 for 127 grants (high: $2,000; low: $10), $2,500 for 61 employee matching gifts and $30,000 for 1 company-administered program.
Purpose and activities: Cascade makes charitable contributions to nonprofit organizations involved with arts and culture, education, the environment, health and human services, community development, and civic affairs. Support is given primarily in areas of company operations.
Fields of interest: Arts; Education; Natural resources; Environment; Health care; Human services; Community development; Public affairs.
Types of support: General/operating support; Emergency funds; Program development; Curriculum development; Employee volunteer services; Use of facilities; Employee matching gifts; Donated equipment; In-kind gifts.
Limitations: Giving primarily in areas of company operations in OR and WA. No support for national organizations, political organizations, lobbying organizations, sectarian religious organizations, or fraternal or labor organizations. No grants for fundraising or travel.
Publications: Application guidelines, Program policy statement.
Application information: The Customer Service Department handles giving. A contributions

committee reviews all requests of over $750. Application form required.

Initial approach: Contact nearest company facility for application form
Copies of proposal: 1
Deadline(s): None
Board meeting date(s): As needed
Final notification: Following review
Number of staff: 2 full-time professional.

3326
CGMK Foundation

(formerly King Family Foundation)
c/o FMG, LLC
1000 2nd Ave., 34th Fl.
Seattle, WA 98104-1022
E-mail: cgmk@foundgroup.com

Established in 2000 in WA.
Donor(s): Martin T. King, Cheryl A. Grunbock.
Grantmaker type: Independent foundation
Financial data (yr. ended 12/31/02): Assets, $5,416,157 (M); gifts received, $17,023; expenditures, $177,294; qualifying distributions, $154,148; giving activities include $143,500 for 10 grants (high: $50,000; low: $1,000).
Fields of interest: Animals/wildlife, preservation/protection; Animals/wildlife.
Limitations: Giving primarily in Seattle, WA. No grants to individuals.
Application information: Application form required.

Initial approach: E-mail
Deadline(s): Varies
Final notification: Within 30 days by E-mail
Officer and Trustees:* Martin T. King,* Mgr.; Cheryl A. Grunbock.
EIN: 916500110

3327
Community Foundation of North Central Washington

(formerly Greater Wenatchee Community Foundation)
P.O. Box 3332
Wenatchee, WA 98807-3332 (509) 663-7716
Contact: Beth A. Stipe, Exec. Dir.
FAX: (509) 667-2208; E-mail: foundation@cfncw.org; URL: http://www.cfncw.org/

Incorporated in 1986 in WA.
Grantmaker type: Community foundation
Financial data (yr. ended 06/30/03): Assets, $13,341,000 (M); gifts received, $1,028,000; expenditures, $720,000; giving activities include $366,000 for 352 grants (high: $22,000; low: $500; average: $1,000–$5,000) and $106,000 for 110 grants to individuals (high: $4,000; low: $154; average: $250–$1,000).
Purpose and activities: Primary areas of interest include the arts, education, the environment, and the disadvantaged, with emphasis on child welfare and the elderly. The foundation administers a donor-advised fund.
Fields of interest: Media/communications; Visual arts; Museums; Performing arts; Theater; Music; Humanities; History/archaeology; Historic preservation/historical societies; Arts; Early childhood education; Child development, education; Elementary school/education; Higher education; Adult/continuing education; Adult

education—literacy, basic skills & GED; Libraries/library science; Reading; Education; Natural resources; Environment; Animal welfare; Animals/wildlife, preservation/protection; Hospitals (general); Family planning; Medical care, rehabilitation; Health care; Substance abuse, services; Mental health/crisis services; AIDS; Alcoholism; Food services; Housing/shelter, development; Safety/disasters; Recreation; Human services; Children/youth, services; Child development, services; Family services; Hospices; Aging, centers/services; Women, centers/services; Minorities/immigrants, centers/services; Homeless, human services; Community development; Voluntarism promotion; Minorities; Disabled; Aging; Women; Economically disadvantaged; Homeless.
Types of support: Capital campaigns; Building/renovation; Equipment; Land acquisition; Program development; Seed money; Technical assistance; Scholarships—to individuals; Matching/challenge support.
Limitations: Giving limited to north central WA, especially Chelan, Douglas, Grant, and Okanogan counties. No support for religious sectarian purposes. No grants to individuals (except for designated scholarships), or for continuing support, annual campaigns, general operating budgets, or conferences.
Publications: Application guidelines, Annual report, Grants list, Informational brochure, Occasional report.
Application information: Contact foundation for application guidelines or use the PNGF Common Form. Application form not required.

Initial approach: Telephone or letter
Copies of proposal: 4
Deadline(s): Varies; telephone to verify
Board meeting date(s): Quarterly
Final notification: 2 months
Officers and Trustees:* Terry Sorom,* Chair.; John J. "Jack" Snyder, Jr.,* Vice-Chair.; Mall Boyd,* Secy.-Treas.; Beth A. Stipe, Exec. Dir.; Roger Bumps; Gerald E. Gibbons, M.D.; Courtney Guderian; Dennis S. Johnson; Grant Johnson; Frank Konz; Judith Lurie; Kenneth Martin; Brian Nelson; Christine Scull; Christopher Stahler; Wayne Wright.
Number of staff: 1 full-time professional; 1 part-time professional; 1 part-time support.
EIN: 911349486

3328
Contorer Foundation

1415 2nd Ave., Ste. 2002
Seattle, WA 98101
Contact: Aaron Contorer, Dir.

Established in 2000 in WA.
Donor(s): Aaron Contorer, Rachael E.H. Contorer.
Grantmaker type: Independent foundation
Financial data (yr. ended 09/30/02): Assets, $909,595 (M); expenditures, $204,203; qualifying distributions, $190,080; giving activities include $188,300 for 7 grants (high: $104,000; low: $300).
Fields of interest: Environment.
Limitations: Giving primarily in WA.
Application information:

Initial approach: Letter
Deadline(s): None

Directors: Aaron Contorer; Rachael E.H. Contorer.
EIN: 912045646

3329
De Falco Family Foundation

2205 55th St. Ct. N.W.
Gig Harbor, WA 98335
Contact: Santina De Falco, Pres.

Established in 1992 in CA.
Grantmaker type: Independent foundation
Financial data (yr. ended 09/30/02): Assets, $5,088,237 (M); expenditures, $405,566; qualifying distributions, $320,109; giving activities include $312,900 for 37 grants (high: $50,000; low: $2,000).
Fields of interest: Arts; Scholarships/financial aid; Zoos/zoological societies; Aquariums; Medical care, in-patient care; Health care; Pediatrics; Food distribution, meals on wheels; Parks/playgrounds; Children/youth, services; Homeless, human services; Homeless.
Types of support: General/operating support; Continuing support; Annual campaigns; Scholarship funds; Research.
Limitations: Applications not accepted. Giving primarily in San Diego, CA, and WA. No grants to individuals.
Application information: Contributes only to pre-selected organizations.

Board meeting date(s): June and Sept.
Officers and Trustees:* Santina De Falco,* Pres.; William Beamer,* V.P.; Sue Robertson,* Secy.-Treas.
Number of staff: None.
EIN: 330526533

3330
The Dimmer Family Foundation

1019 Pacific Ave., Ste. 916
Tacoma, WA 98402-4492 (253) 572-4607
Contact: Diane C. Dimmer, Exec. Dir.
FAX: (253) 572-4647

Established in 1994.
Donor(s): John C. Dimmer.
Grantmaker type: Independent foundation
Financial data (yr. ended 12/31/02): Assets, $9,286,360 (M); gifts received, $423,429; expenditures, $771,749; qualifying distributions, $574,772; giving activities include $552,688 for 116 grants (high: $260,200; low: $500).
Purpose and activities: Giving primarily for the arts, education, and for health care and human services.
Fields of interest: Museums; Arts; Higher education; Education; Animal welfare; Hospitals (general); Health care; Medical research, institute; Youth development, centers/clubs; Human services.
Types of support: General/operating support; Continuing support; Annual campaigns; Capital campaigns; Building/renovation; Equipment; Endowments; Program development; Scholarship funds; Research; Matching/challenge support.
Limitations: Giving primarily in Tacoma, WA.
Publications: Grants list, Informational brochure.
Application information: Application form not required.

Initial approach: Grant request

Copies of proposal: 1
Deadline(s): Jan. 30, Apr. 30 and Sept. 30
Board meeting date(s): 4-6 weeks after each deadline
Final notification: Within 2 weeks of each meeting
Officers: John C. Dimmer, Pres.; Carolyn Dimmer, V.P.; Marilyn Dimmer, V.P.; Diane C. Dimmer, Secy. and Exec. Dir.; John B. Dimmer, Treas.
Number of staff: 1 part-time professional.
EIN: 911622059

3331
Discuren Charitable Foundation
c/o Perkins Coie
1201 3rd Ave., 40th Fl.
Seattle, WA 98101-3099 (425) 828-3737
Contact: Greg Coy, Prog. Mgr.
E-mail: gcoy@isomedia.com

Established in 1983 in WA.
Grantmaker type: Independent foundation
Financial data (yr. ended 10/31/02): Assets, $674,757 (M); gifts received, $545,528; expenditures, $1,317,355; qualifying distributions, $1,315,503; giving activities include $1,219,316 for 46 grants (high: $60,000; low: $450).
Purpose and activities: Supports programs related to education, literacy and drop-out prevention.
Fields of interest: Early childhood education; Elementary school/education; Secondary school/education; Drop-out prevention; Education; Environmental education.
Types of support: Continuing support; Program development; Conferences/seminars; Seed money; Curriculum development; Research; Consulting services; Program-related investments/loans.
Limitations: Giving primarily in WA. No support for military efforts, or for religious missionary work or programs only benefiting adherents to specific faiths. No grants to individuals.
Publications: Informational brochure (including application guidelines), Occasional report.
Application information: Application form required.
  Initial approach: E-mail, telephone, or letter
  Copies of proposal: 4
  Deadline(s): 3 weeks prior to board meeting
  Board meeting date(s): Quarterly
  Final notification: 1 week following board meeting
Trustee: Bank of America.
Board of Managers: Fred Bassetti; Greg Coy.
Number of staff: 1 part-time professional.
EIN: 916249597

3332
The Dudley Foundation
609A N. Shore Dr.
Bellingham, WA 98226-4414
Contact: Rick Dudley, Pres.
E-mail: dudleyfdn@yahoo.com; URL: http://www.dudleyfoundation.org

Established in 1990 in WA.
Donor(s): Tilford E. Dudley,‡ Gerric W. Dudley.
Grantmaker type: Independent foundation

Financial data (yr. ended 12/31/02): Assets, $4,272,013 (M); expenditures, $519,063; qualifying distributions, $438,455; giving activities include $437,005 for 45 grants (high: $25,000; low: $100).
Purpose and activities: To alleviate present and future unnecessary suffering of all sentient beings by addressing its social and environmental roots, e.g.: (human) overpopulation, intolerance, excessive consumption (greed), and ecological destruction.
Fields of interest: Environment, pollution control; Natural resources; Environment; Consumer protection; Public affairs; Population studies.
Types of support: General/operating support; Continuing support.
Limitations: Giving on a national basis. No grants to individuals.
Application information: Application guidelines and form available on foundation Web site. Application form required.
  Initial approach: E-mail completed application form
  Deadline(s): Oct. 31
  Board meeting date(s): Nov.
Officers and Board Members:* Gerric W. Dudley,* Pres.; Todd Jones,* V.P.; Eric Dudley,* Secy.-Treas.; Mike Feerer; Bob Keller; Colleen Verdon; Saul Weisberg.
Number of staff: None.
EIN: 911474291

3333
Edwards Mother Earth Foundation
7317 164th Pl. S.W.
Edmonds, WA 98026
Application address: P.O. Box 1120, Patton, CA 92369

Established in 1997 in WA.
Donor(s): Bob Edwards,‡ Jane Edwards.‡
Grantmaker type: Independent foundation
Financial data (yr. ended 12/31/02): Assets, $24,856,282 (M); gifts received, $1,252,995; expenditures, $845,796; qualifying distributions, $750,077; giving activities include $758,300 for 23 grants (high: $80,800; low: $10,000).
Purpose and activities: Giving for youth services, environmental and wildlife conservation, and family planning.
Fields of interest: Natural resources; Children/youth, services; Family services.
Types of support: General/operating support; Continuing support; Capital campaigns; Equipment; Land acquisition; Program development.
Limitations: Giving on a national basis. No grants to individuals.
Application information: Application form required.
  Initial approach: Letter of inquiry
  Copies of proposal: 2
  Deadline(s): Sept. 18
  Board meeting date(s): 3rd weekend in Oct.
  Final notification: Nov. 1
Directors: Sonia Baker; Deborah Bell; Jonathan D. Edwards; Toby Edwards; Johanne B. Luce; Kristie Rayl; Tara Reinartson.
EIN: 911789783

3334
The Martin Fabert Foundation
c/o Foundation Mgmt. Group, LLC
1000 2nd Ave., 34th Fl.
Seattle, WA 98104

Established in 2001 in IL.
Donor(s): Martin Foundation, Elizabeth Martin.
Grantmaker type: Independent foundation
Financial data (yr. ended 06/30/03): Assets, $10,246,015 (M); expenditures, $441,575; qualifying distributions, $334,200; giving activities include $334,200 for 20 grants (high: $100,000; low: $2,500).
Fields of interest: Arts; Environment; Animals/wildlife.
Limitations: Applications not accepted. Giving on a national basis. No grants to individuals.
Application information: Contributes only to pre-selected organizations.
Officers: Elizabeth Martin, Pres.; Kenneth Fabert, V.P.; Daniel Asher, Secy.
EIN: 364437950

3335
Frank B. and Virginia V. Fehsenfeld Charitable Foundation
1107 1st Ave., Ste. 1404
Seattle, WA 98101
Contact: H. Warren Smith, V.P.

Established in 1987 in MI.
Donor(s): Frank B. Fehsenfeld, Virginia V. Fehsenfeld.
Grantmaker type: Independent foundation
Financial data (yr. ended 12/31/01): Assets, $1,789,320 (M); expenditures, $123,524; qualifying distributions, $118,396; giving activities include $119,500 for 48 grants (high: $15,000; low: $500).
Purpose and activities: Giving for the arts, education, and human services.
Fields of interest: Arts; Education; Natural resources; Human services; Children/youth, services.
Types of support: Annual campaigns; Building/renovation.
Limitations: Giving primarily in the Grand Rapids, MI and Seattle, WA, areas. No grants to individuals.
Application information:
  Initial approach: Letter
  Deadline(s): None
Officers: Frank B. Fehsenfeld, Pres. and Treas.; H. Warren Smith, V.P.; Nancy Fehsenfeld Smith, Secy.
Trustees: John A. Fehsenfeld; Thomas V. Fehsenfeld; William S. Fehsenfeld.
EIN: 382775201

3336
The Hugh and Jane Ferguson Foundation
701 5th Ave., No. 6770
Seattle, WA 98104 (206) 781-3472
Contact: Therese Ogle, Prog. Off.
E-mail: OgleFounds@aol.com; URL: http://fdncenter.org/grantmaker/ferguson/

Established in 1986 in WA.
Donor(s): Hugh S. Ferguson, Jane Avery Ferguson.‡
Grantmaker type: Independent foundation

Financial data (yr. ended 09/30/02): Assets, $1,604,982 (M); gifts received, $620,000; expenditures, $1,095,796; qualifying distributions, $1,071,010; giving activities include $1,044,050 for 107 grants (high: $200,000; low: $250; average: $3,000–$7,000).

Purpose and activities: The foundation is dedicated to the preservation and restoration of nature, including wildlife and their required habitats. It also supports the institutions that present nature and the cultural heritage of the greater Puget Sound area to the public—museums, libraries, aquariums, zoos and public media.

Fields of interest: Museums; Higher education; Libraries (public); Education; Natural resources; Zoos/zoological societies; Aquariums; Animals/wildlife; Human services; Federated giving programs.

Types of support: General/operating support; Continuing support; Capital campaigns; Land acquisition; Program development; Seed money; Technical assistance.

Limitations: Giving primarily in AK, OR, and WA, with emphasis on WA. No support for social service agencies, schools or government agencies or collaborations between nonprofits and government agencies in which the government provides majority funding or leadership. No grants to individuals or for research projects, book publications, web or video/film productions, capital campaigns, curriculum development, or scholarships.

Publications: Application guidelines, Grants list.

Application information: The foundation accepts the Common Application Form developed by the Pacific Northwest Grantmakers Forum. Application form not required.

  Initial approach: Telephone, E-mail, or submit 2- page pre-application letter
  Copies of proposal: 1
  Deadline(s): Pre-application letter: Jan. 15 and July 15; Full proposal if requested: Feb. 15 and Aug. 15
  Board meeting date(s): Mar. and Sept.
  Final notification: Mar. and Sept.

Officers and Directors:* Hugh S. Ferguson,* Pres.; Ellen Lee Ferguson,* Secy.
Number of staff: 1 shared staff.
EIN: 911357603

3337
Forest Foundation
820 A St., Ste. 345
Tacoma, WA 98402 (253) 627-1634
Contact: Frank D. Underwood, Exec. Dir.

Incorporated in 1962 in WA.
Donor(s): C. Davis Weyerhaeuser,‡ William T. Weyerhaeuser.
Grantmaker type: Independent foundation
Financial data (yr. ended 10/31/02): Assets, $26,585,122 (M); expenditures, $2,131,489; qualifying distributions, $1,823,020; giving activities include $1,633,583 for 70 grants (high: $200,000; low: $1,000; average: $1,000–$50,000).
Purpose and activities: Giving primarily for arts and culture, environment, human services, and community development.
Fields of interest: Arts; Environment; Human services; Community development.

Types of support: General/operating support; Capital campaigns; Building/renovation; Matching/challenge support.
Limitations: Giving primarily in southwestern WA, with emphasis on Pierce County. Grants given outside Pierce County are for capital projects only. No support for religious organizations to promulgate religion. No grants to individuals, or for endowment funds, debt retirement, annual appeals, research, scholarships, films, publications, or fellowships; no loans.
Publications: Application guidelines.
Application information: Application form required.

  Initial approach: 2-to 3-page letter of inquiry, 2 copies required
  Copies of proposal: 6
  Deadline(s): Check guidelines for specific dates
  Board meeting date(s): 6 times a year
  Final notification: 60 to 90 days

Officers and Directors:* Gail T. Weyerhaeuser,* Pres. and Treas.; Annette B. Weyerhaeuser,* V.P.; Nicholas C. Spika, Secy.; Frank D. Underwood, Exec. Dir.; William T. Weyerhaeuser.
Number of staff: None.
EIN: 916020514

3338
Fries-Tait Foundation
2025 1st Ave., Ste. 600
Seattle, WA 98121

Established in 1998 in WA.
Donor(s): William Rashkov,‡ Richard Tait, Karen Fries.
Grantmaker type: Independent foundation
Financial data (yr. ended 12/31/02): Assets, $1,273,452 (M); expenditures, $122,720; qualifying distributions, $115,931; giving activities include $107,035 for 11 grants (high: $20,000; low: $1,000).
Fields of interest: Radio; Natural resources; Animal welfare; Animals/wildlife, preservation/protection; Human services; International development; International relief.
Limitations: Applications not accepted. Giving on a national basis. No grants to individuals.
Application information: Contributes only to pre-selected organizations.
Trustees: Karen Fries; Richard Tait.
EIN: 916458447

3339
Richard and Janet Geary Foundation, Inc.
c/o Bank of America
P.O. Box 34345, CSC-9
Seattle, WA 98124-1345

Established in 1996 in OR.
Donor(s): Richard Geary, Janet H. Geary.
Grantmaker type: Independent foundation
Financial data (yr. ended 12/31/01): Assets, $7,726,469 (M); expenditures, $760,320; qualifying distributions, $702,476; giving activities include $693,756 for 91 grants (high: $120,000; low: $25).
Purpose and activities: Giving primarily for the arts.
Fields of interest: Museums (art); Arts; Education; Natural resources; Health

---

organizations, association; Children/youth, services.
Limitations: Applications not accepted. Giving primarily in OR and WA. No grants to individuals.
Application information: Contributes only to pre-selected organizations.
Officers and Directors:* Janet H. Geary,* Chair.; Richard Geary,* Pres. and Treas.; Suzanne G. Paymar, Secy.
Trustee: Bank of America.
EIN: 911748475

3340
Glaser Progress Foundation
(formerly The Glaser Foundation)
P.O. Box 91123
Seattle, WA 98111 (206) 728-1050
Contact: Leslie McDonald, Operations Dir.
FAX: (206) 728-1123; E-mail: grants@glaserprogress.org; URL: http://www.glaserprogress.org

Established in 1993 in WA.
Donor(s): Robert D. Glaser.
Grantmaker type: Independent foundation
Financial data (yr. ended 12/31/02): Assets, $28,961,962 (M); expenditures, $2,199,903; qualifying distributions, $2,193,282; giving activities include $1,820,638 for 42 grants (high: $450,000; low: $200; average: $1,000–$25,000) and $47,360 for foundation-administered programs.
Purpose and activities: The foundation focuses on three program areas: 1) Measuring Progress: build a more equitable and sustainable world by improving our understanding and measurement of human progress, 2) Animal Advocacy: make animal treatment a crucial consideration in business, policy and personal decision-making, 3) Independent Media: strengthen democracy by making independent voices heard.
Fields of interest: Media/communications; Animals/wildlife, equal rights; Animal welfare; Civil rights; Community development.
Types of support: General/operating support; Program development; Technical assistance; Matching/challenge support.
Limitations: Giving on a national and international basis. No grants to individuals.
Publications: Application guidelines.
Application information: Guidelines available on website. Application form not required.

  Initial approach: Letter of inquiry
  Copies of proposal: 1
  Deadline(s): None

Officers: Martin Collier, Exec. Dir.; Robert D. Glaser, Mgr.
Number of staff: 3 full-time professional.
EIN: 911626010

3341
Hamalainen Charitable Trust
1076 S. West Camano Dr.
Camano Island, WA 98292

Established in 1994 in WA.
Donor(s): Asko Hamalainen, Karen Hamalainen.
Grantmaker type: Independent foundation
Financial data (yr. ended 12/31/02): Assets, $0 (M); expenditures, $102,639; qualifying

---

distributions, $98,594; giving activities include $99,249 for 50 grants (high: $24,564; low: $25).
Purpose and activities: Giving for the arts, the environment, health, and human services.
Fields of interest: Historic preservation/historical societies; Environment; Health organizations, association; Parks/playgrounds; Human services; Federated giving programs.
Limitations: Applications not accepted. Giving primarily in WA. No grants to individuals.
Application information: Contributes only to pre-selected organizations.
Trustees: Asko Hamalainen; Karen Hamalainen.
EIN: 916376196

3342
The Handsel Foundation

P.O. Box 1322
Freeland, WA 98249 (360) 331-7282
Contact: Diane Johnson, Pres.
E-mail: handselfdn@aol.com

Established in 1990 in CA.
Donor(s): Theodore R. Johnson, Sr.‡
Grantmaker type: Independent foundation
Financial data (yr. ended 12/31/01): Assets, $3,529,053 (M); gifts received, $63,302; expenditures, $180,000; qualifying distributions, $163,706; giving activities include $160,350 for 24 grants (high: $30,000; low: $1,000).
Purpose and activities: Giving primarily for animal welfare.
Fields of interest: Animal welfare; Animals/wildlife, preservation/protection.
Types of support: Equipment; Matching/challenge support.
Limitations: Giving primarily in the western U.S. No grants to individuals.
Publications: Informational brochure, Informational brochure (including application guidelines).
Application information: Application form not required.
  Initial approach: Telephone or letter
  Copies of proposal: 1
  Deadline(s): None
Officers and Directors:* Diane N. Johnson,* Pres.; T.R. Johnson, Jr.,* Secy. and C.F.O.; Hilary Austen Johnson.
Number of staff: None.
EIN: 943112006

3343
Harder Foundation

401 Broadway
Tacoma, WA 98402 (253) 593-2121
Contact: Mary G. Martin, Off. Mgr.

Incorporated in 1955 in MI.
Donor(s): Delmar S. Harder.‡
Grantmaker type: Independent foundation
Financial data (yr. ended 12/31/02): Assets, $25,269,451 (M); gifts received, $335,930; expenditures, $1,501,712; qualifying distributions, $1,199,511; giving activities include $1,040,000 for grants (average: $10,000–$50,000).
Purpose and activities: Giving primarily for environmental awareness and conservation.
Fields of interest: Natural resources; Environment.

Types of support: General/operating support; Continuing support; Annual campaigns; Endowments; Seed money; Matching/challenge support.
Limitations: Giving limited to AK, CO, FL, ID, MT, NV, OR, UT, WA, and WY. No grants to individuals, or for deficit financing, building funds, equipment, renovation projects, scholarships, fellowships, research, publications, or conferences; no loans.
Publications: Application guidelines, Annual report.
Application information: Proposals from LA and the Great Lake states not presently considered. Proposals from FL accepted by invitation only. Application form required.
  Initial approach: Letter requesting application guidelines
  Copies of proposal: 1
  Deadline(s): Late May and late Aug.
  Board meeting date(s): Feb.
  Final notification: 2 months
Officers and Trustees:* Del Langbauer,* Pres.; Jay A. Herbst,* Secy.; Robert Langbauer,* Treas.; John Driggers; William H. Langbauer.
Number of staff: 2 full-time professional; 1 full-time support.
EIN: 386048242

3344
Horizons Foundation

4020 E. Madison St., Ste. 322
Seattle, WA 98112 (206) 323-8061
Contact: Ralph R. Hadac, Exec. Dir.
E-mail: rhadac@aol.com

Established in 1990 in WA as partial successor to the McAshan Foundation, Inc.
Donor(s): The McAshan Foundation, Inc.
Grantmaker type: Independent foundation
Financial data (yr. ended 12/31/02): Assets, $18,571,163 (M); expenditures, $1,026,842; qualifying distributions, $978,286; giving activities include $916,500 for 92 grants (high: $100,000; low: $1,000; average: $5,000–$10,000).
Purpose and activities: Giving primarily to address the social and environmental problems of the Pacific Northwest. Emphasis is on the prevention of problems through educational projects, and citizen education programs aimed at improving the quality of the environment; some support also for arts and culture.
Fields of interest: Natural resources; Environment; Family planning; Domestic violence; Human services; Youth, pregnancy prevention; Domestic violence; Family services, adolescent parents; Family services, counseling; Human services, emergency aid; Women, centers/services.
Types of support: General/operating support; Capital campaigns; Land acquisition; Emergency funds; Program development.
Limitations: Giving primarily in WA. No support for religious organizations. No grants to individuals, or for scholarships, debt retirement, operating deficits, endowment funds; no loans.
Publications: Application guidelines, Program policy statement.
Application information: Full proposal required if foundation accepts synopsis. Application form required.
  Initial approach: 2-page synopsis

  Copies of proposal: 4
  Deadline(s): None
  Board meeting date(s): Monthly
  Final notification: 10 days after board meeting
Officers and Directors:* Lucy J. Hadac,* Pres.; Jerald Forster,* V.P.; Stephen Hadac,* Secy.; Ralph R. Hadac,* Treas. and Exec. Dir.
Number of staff: 1 full-time professional.
EIN: 911493424

3345
The Hyde Foundation

4715 133rd St. N.W.
Gig Harbor, WA 98332
Contact: William B. Hyde, Pres.
Tel.: (253) 858-3278, ext. 7104

Established in 1997.
Donor(s): William B. Hyde.
Grantmaker type: Independent foundation
Financial data (yr. ended 12/31/02): Assets, $2,461,397 (M); expenditures, $238,387; qualifying distributions, $210,000; giving activities include $210,000 for 6 grants (high: $83,000; low: $10,000).
Purpose and activities: Giving primarily for education and conservation.
Fields of interest: Museums (art); Elementary/secondary education; Natural resources; Animal welfare.
Limitations: Giving limited to WA.
Application information: Application form not required.
  Initial approach: 1-page letter
  Deadline(s): None
Officers: William B. Hyde, Pres.; Elizabeth D. Hyde, V.P.; Pamela Hyde Smith, Treas.
EIN: 911797073

3346
The I.F.C. Foundation

P.O. Box 822
Friday Harbor, WA 98250

Established in 1992 in OR.
Donor(s): J. Jerry Inskeep, Jr.
Grantmaker type: Independent foundation
Financial data (yr. ended 12/31/02): Assets, $4,665,199 (M); expenditures, $272,674; qualifying distributions, $275,981; giving activities include $275,981 for 15 grants (high: $106,260; low: $100).
Purpose and activities: Giving primarily for higher education, as well as for health, environmental organizations, and an art museum.
Fields of interest: Museums (art); Higher education; Environment, public education; Natural resources; Health care; Health organizations, association; Federated giving programs.
Limitations: Applications not accepted. Giving primarily in OR. No grants to individuals.
Application information: Contributes only to pre-selected organizations.
Officers: J. Jerry Inskeep, Jr., Pres.; M. Jacqueline Inskeep, V.P.; John J. Inskeep III, Secy.-Treas.
Directors: Martha Inskeep Brandt; Jill Inskeep; Sarah Inskeep-Meling.
Number of staff: None.
EIN: 931098708

3347
Islands Fund
900 4th Ave., Ste. 2925
Seattle, WA 98164-1009

Established in 1995.
Donor(s): Sarah R. Werner.
Grantmaker type: Independent foundation
Financial data (yr. ended 12/31/02): Assets,
$15,447,144 (M); expenditures, $1,105,778;
qualifying distributions, $1,005,626; giving
activities include $1,010,000 for 37 grants
(high: $160,000; low: $5,000).
Purpose and activities: Giving primarily for
conservation and the environment.
Fields of interest: Education; Natural resources;
Children/youth, services.
Limitations: Applications not accepted. No
grants to individuals.
Application information: Contributes only to
pre-selected organizations.
Directors: E. Leeds Gulick; George G. Gulick;
John Munn; Rick S. Werner; Sarah R. Werner.
EIN: 911663838

3348
The Henry M. Jackson Foundation
1001 4th Ave., Ste. 3317
Seattle, WA 98154-1101 (206) 682-8565
Contact: Lara Iglitzin, Exec. Dir.
FAX: (206) 682-8961; E-mail:
foundation@hmjackson.org; URL: http://
www.hmjackson.org

Established in 1983 in DC.
Grantmaker type: Public charity
Financial data (yr. ended 09/30/01): Revenue,
$1,196,070; assets, $17,763,055 (L); gifts
received, $50,321; expenditures, $1,555,840;
program services expenses, $1,316,938; giving
activities include $1,188,328 for 33 grants
(high: $125,000; low: $5,000).
Purpose and activities: The foundation was
established to carry forward the commitment of
the late Senator Henry M. "Scoop" Jackson of
advancing education and public service. Its
mission is to build bridges between the
academic and policy worlds, between the
public and private sectors, and between citizens
and their government. Primary areas of interest
include international affairs, human rights,
public service, and environmental and natural
resources management.
Fields of interest: Natural resources;
Environment; International affairs, research.
Types of support: Program development;
Conferences/seminars; Professorships;
Publication; Fellowships; Internship funds;
Scholarship funds; Research; Program-related
investments/loans; Matching/challenge support.
Limitations: Giving on an international basis.
No support for political campaigns or efforts to
influence legislation other than making
available results of nonpartisan analysis and
research. No grants to individuals, or for
unrestricted operating expenses, operating
deficits, or capital expenditures, except in rare
circumstances.
Publications: Application guidelines, Annual
report, Financial statement, Grants list,
Informational brochure, Newsletter.
Application information: Letters of inquiry or
proposals are not accepted by e-mail; see Web

site for latest grants list. Application form not
required.
  Initial approach: Letter
  Copies of proposal: 1
  Deadline(s): Dec. 1, Mar. 1, June 1, and Sept.
    1
  Board meeting date(s): Annually
  Final notification: Mar., May, Sept., and Dec.
Officers and Directors:* Helen Hardin
Jackson,* Chair.; William J. Van Ness, Jr.,* Pres.;
James Wickwire,* V.P.; Julia P. Cancio,* Secy.;
Keith D. Grinstein,* Treas.; Lara Iglitzin, Exec.
Dir.; Joel C. Merkel, Genl. Counsel.
Number of staff: 5.
EIN: 521313011

3349
The Brian and Traci Janssen Foundation
1000 Lakeside Ave. S.
Seattle, WA 98144

Established in 1999 in WA.
Donor(s): Brian Janssen, Traci Janssen.
Grantmaker type: Independent foundation
Financial data (yr. ended 12/31/02): Assets,
$26,316 (M); gifts received, $41,680;
expenditures, $135,785; qualifying distributions,
$133,369; giving activities include $134,327 for
7 grants (high: $80,840; low: $500).
Fields of interest: Natural resources;
Environment.
Limitations: Giving primarily in Seattle, WA. No
grants to individuals.
Application information:
  Initial approach: Letter
  Deadline(s): None
Officers: Traci Janssen, Pres.; Brian Janssen, V.P.
EIN: 912011011

3350
Jungers Foundation
P.O. Box 3146
Battle Ground, WA 98604
Contact: Gary Jungers, Treas.

Established in 1999 in OR.
Donor(s): Francis Jungers, Gary Jungers, FJF, Inc.
Grantmaker type: Independent foundation
Financial data (yr. ended 12/31/01): Assets,
$2,328,977 (M); expenditures, $310,141;
qualifying distributions, $152,847; giving
activities include $150,951 for 1 grant.
Fields of interest: Natural resources.
Limitations: Applications not accepted. No
grants to individuals.
Application information: Contributes only to
pre-selected organizations.
Officers and Directors:* Frank Jungers,* Chair.;
Julia Jungers,* Secy.; Gary Jungers, Treas. and
Exec. Dir.; Mary Ellen Jungers.
EIN: 931282864

3351
Kaleidoscope Foundation
c/o Richard Leeds
1075 Bellevue Way, N.E., Ste. 366
Bellevue, WA 98004

Established in 1997 in WA.

Donor(s): Gerard Leeds, Liselotte Leeds, Richard
Leeds.
Grantmaker type: Independent foundation
Financial data (yr. ended 11/30/02): Assets,
$16,801,482 (M); expenditures, $3,585,563;
qualifying distributions, $3,539,731; giving
activities include $3,485,712 for 37 grants
(high: $1,391,000; low: $1,000; average:
$1,000–$50,000).
Purpose and activities: Giving for conservation
and wildlife, education, and children's services.
Fields of interest: Education; Environment;
Children/youth, services.
Limitations: Applications not accepted.
Application information: Unsolicited requests
for funds not accepted.
Officers: Anne F. Kroeker, Co-Pres.; Richard
Leeds, Co-Pres.; Robert H. Blais, Secy.
EIN: 911874926

3352
Keller Foundation
c/o Keller Enterprises
1701 S.E. Columbia River Dr., Ste. 100
Vancouver, WA 98661

Established in 1997 in OR.
Grantmaker type: Independent foundation
Financial data (yr. ended 12/31/02): Assets,
$3,008,169 (M); expenditures, $111,566;
qualifying distributions, $109,809; giving
activities include $91,000 for 28 grants (high:
$20,000; low: $250).
Purpose and activities: Giving primarily for
higher education, the arts, and health.
Fields of interest: Orchestra (symphony); Arts;
Early childhood education; Higher education;
Business school/education; Law
school/education; Environment; Health care;
Human services.
Limitations: Applications not accepted. Giving
primarily in Portland, OR. No grants to
individuals.
Application information: Contributes only to
pre-selected organizations.
Officers: Richard B. Keller, Chair. and Pres.;
Ruth E. Keller, V.P.; Elizabeth K. McCaslin, V.P.
EIN: 911811697

3353
Keyes Foundation
P.O. Box 50088
Bellevue, WA 98015
Contact: Doreen Keyes, Pres.

Established in 1998 in WA.
Donor(s): Doreen Keyes, David Keyes.
Grantmaker type: Independent foundation
Financial data (yr. ended 12/31/01): Assets,
$2,506,786 (M); expenditures, $174,593;
qualifying distributions, $171,789; giving
activities include $172,000 for 29 grants (high:
$25,000; low: $250).
Purpose and activities: Giving primarily for
health care and to health associations; support
also for education and religious purposes.
Fields of interest: Cultural/ethnic awareness;
Elementary/secondary education; University;
Animal welfare; Hospitals (general); Health care;
Cancer; Alzheimer's disease; Food banks;
Human services; Foundations (public); Christian
agencies & churches.

Limitations: Applications not accepted.
Application information: Unsolicited requests for grants not accepted.
Officers: Doreen Keyes, Pres.; David Keyes, V.P.
EIN: 911939734

3354
Paul L. King Charitable Foundation
P.O. Box 61669
Vancouver, WA 98666-1669

Established in 1997 in WA.
Donor(s): Paul L. King.
Grantmaker type: Independent foundation
Financial data (yr. ended 12/31/02): Assets, $2,497,632 (M); expenditures, $403,077; qualifying distributions, $399,714; giving activities include $400,290 for 9 grants (high: $85,000; low: $10,000).
Fields of interest: Theater; Music; Environment, forests.
Limitations: Applications not accepted. Giving primarily in Boston, MA, Santa Fe, NM, and Charleston, SC. No grants to individuals.
Application information: Contributes only to pre-selected organizations.
Trustee: Paul L. King.
EIN: 911811633

3355
Kongsgaard-Goldman Foundation
1932 1st Ave., Ste. 602
Seattle, WA 98101 (206) 448-1874
Contact: Martha Kongsgaard, Pres.
FAX: (206) 448-1973; E-mail: kgf@kongsgaard-goldman.org; URL: http://www.kongsgaard-goldman.org

Established in 1988 in WA.
Donor(s): Peter Goldman, Martha Kongsgaard.
Grantmaker type: Independent foundation
Financial data (yr. ended 12/31/02): Assets, $35,727 (M); gifts received, $789,965; expenditures, $870,072; qualifying distributions, $866,830; giving activities include $763,699 for 104 grants (high: $50,000; low: $500; average: $5,000–$15,000) and $11,784 for 2 foundation-administered programs.
Purpose and activities: Primary areas of interest include the arts (in WA only), civil rights, the environment, social change, and civic development.
Fields of interest: Visual arts; Museums; Performing arts; Theater; Music; Arts; Child development, education; Adult education—literacy, basic skills & GED; Education; Environment; Family planning; AIDS; Child development, services; Women, centers/services; International peace/security; Race/intergroup relations; Civil rights; Community development; Jewish federated giving programs; Economics; Jewish agencies & temples; Women; Gays/lesbians; Immigrants/refugees.
International interests: Canada.
Types of support: General/operating support; Continuing support; Annual campaigns; Equipment; Land acquisition; Emergency funds; Program development; Conferences/seminars; Seed money; Technical assistance; Matching/challenge support.

Limitations: Giving limited to AK, ID, MT, OR, and WA, with emphasis on Missoula, MT, Portland, OR, and Seattle, WA; giving also in British Columbia, Canada. No support for institutions of higher learning or medical institutions. No grants to individuals, or for scholarships, fellowships, medical research or general animal welfare; no direct services in the human services sector, or for land acquisition.
Publications: Informational brochure (including application guidelines).
Application information: Accepts Philanthropy Northwest Common Grant Application Form. Application form not required.
  Initial approach: Letter of intent due Mar. 16 or Sept. 16
  Copies of proposal: 1
  Deadline(s): Mar. 16 and Sep. 16
  Board meeting date(s): Contributions made in Feb. and Aug.
  Final notification: Feb. and Aug.
Officers and Directors:* Martha Kongsgaard,* Pres.; Peter Goldman,* V.P.
Number of staff: 1 full-time professional.
EIN: 943088217

3356
Laird Norton Endowment Foundation
801 2nd Ave., Ste. 1300
Seattle, WA 98104 (206) 464-5242
Contact: Patrick S. de Freitas, Prog. Dir.
FAX: (206) 464-5250; E-mail: defreitas@lairdnorton.org; URL: http://www.lairdnorton.org

Incorporated in 1940 in MN.
Donor(s): Founding family members and related businesses.
Grantmaker type: Independent foundation
Financial data (yr. ended 12/31/02): Assets, $4,718,756 (M); gifts received, $59,428; expenditures, $233,316; qualifying distributions, $213,829; giving activities include $150,533 for grants.
Purpose and activities: Giving to fund distinctive programs in conservation and forestry education. Through the year 2004, the foundation will be funding in the area of sustainable forestry.
Fields of interest: Natural resources; Environment, forests; Environmental education.
Types of support: Program development; Publication; Seed money; Curriculum development; Internship funds; Research; Matching/challenge support.
Limitations: Giving on a national basis, with emphasis on the Pacific Northwest. No grants to individuals, or for capital campaigns, annual campaigns, building funds, endowment funds, scholarships, international projects, programs for specific animals, operating budgets, or general expenses; no loans.
Application information: Letters of inquiry must be sent in two forms: via E-mail, and printed copy; See Web site for application guidelines. Application form required.
  Initial approach: 1 to 2-page letter of inquiry
  Copies of proposal: 1
  Deadline(s): 1 month prior to board meetings; initial letter of inquiry due Feb. 6 for spring 2004
  Board meeting date(s): Apr. and Nov.
  Final notification: 2 weeks after board meeting

Officers and Directors:* William Baran-Mickle,* Pres.; Deborah S. Wicks,* V.P.; Bruce Reed,* Secy.; Clint Driver,* Treas.; Samuel Brown; Tori Brown; Elizabeth C. Clark; Linda Henry; Charles C. Richardson, Jr.
Number of staff: None.
EIN: 916339917

3357
The Laurel Foundation ▼
P.O. Box 77630
Seattle, WA 98177-0630
Contact: Jennifer D. Hannibal, Fdn. Admin.

Established in 1995 in WA.
Donor(s): Julia Calhoun.
Grantmaker type: Independent foundation
Financial data (yr. ended 12/31/01): Assets, $7,989,519 (M); gifts received, $800,000; expenditures, $4,315,403; qualifying distributions, $4,303,918; giving activities include $4,294,645 for 128 grants (high: $1,300,000; low: $100; average: $1,000–$25,000).
Purpose and activities: Giving primarily to education, children, health care, and human services.
Fields of interest: Education; Youth development; Human services; Family services.
Types of support: General/operating support; Continuing support.
Limitations: Applications not accepted. Giving primarily in WA. No grants to individuals.
Application information: Contributes only to pre-selected organizations.
Officers: Julia Calhoun, Pres.; Christopher Larson, V.P.; Larry Bailey, Secy.; Jennifer D. Hannibal, Fdn. Admin.
EIN: 911689238
Recent environmental and animal welfare grants:
3357-1 Conservation International, DC, $10,000. For general operating support. 2001.
3357-2 Friends of the Cedar River Watershed, Seattle, WA, $10,000. For Cedar River Watershed Education Center capital campaign. 2001.
3357-3 Pacific Crest Biodiversity Project, Seattle, WA, $10,000. For general operating support. 2001.
3357-4 Progressive Animal Welfare Society, Lynnwood, WA, $20,000. For operating support. 2001.
3357-5 Seattle Chinese Garden Society, Seattle, WA, $250,000. For capital campaign. 2001.
3357-6 Trust for Public Land, Seattle, WA, $10,000. For general operating support. 2001.
3357-7 Woodland Park Zoological Society, Seattle, WA, $500,000. For capital campaign for Learning Center. 2001.
3357-8 Woodland Park Zoological Society, Seattle, WA, $10,000. For Zoo Corps teen internship and job program. 2001.
3357-9 World Wildlife Fund/Conservation Foundation, DC, $10,000. For operating support. 2001.

3358
Leslie Fund, Inc.
7502 E. Greenlake Dr. N.
Seattle, WA 98103
Contact: James W. Leslie, V.P.
Application address: 2400 N.W. 80th St.,
PMB154, Seattle, WA 98117

Incorporated in 1956 in IL.
Donor(s): Virginia A. Leslie Trust, and members of the Leslie family.
Grantmaker type: Independent foundation
Financial data (yr. ended 03/31/02): Assets, $8,482,701 (M); gifts received, $22,947; expenditures, $543,939; qualifying distributions, $507,365; giving activities include $472,500 for 55 grants (high: $100,000; low: $500).
Purpose and activities: Giving primarily for human services, education, the arts, and animal care.
Fields of interest: Arts; Education, gifted students; Education; Environment; Animals/wildlife, preservation/protection; Family planning; Health care; Human services; Children, services.
Limitations: Giving primarily in Chicago, IL, and Seattle, WA. No grants to individuals.
Application information: Application form not required.
  Initial approach: Letter
  Copies of proposal: 1
  Deadline(s): None
  Board meeting date(s): Jan., Apr., July, and Oct.
Officers: James W. Leslie, Pres.; Victoria H. Leslie, Secy.-Treas.
Director: Judith W. McCue.
Number of staff: 1 part-time support.
EIN: 366055800

3359
The LJCPJ Foundation
(formerly The LJCP Foundation)
P.O. Box 21749
Seattle, WA 98111-3749 (425) 828-1815
Contact: Stanley B. McCammon, V.P. and Secy.

Established in 1993.
Donor(s): John E. McCaw, Jr., Donna McCaslin, Bruce R. McCaw.
Grantmaker type: Independent foundation
Financial data (yr. ended 10/31/02): Assets, $50,229 (M); gifts received, $256,201; expenditures, $366,175; qualifying distributions, $355,798; giving activities include $356,000 for 4 grants (high: $250,000; low: $1,000).
Purpose and activities: Giving primarily for community development, education and conservation.
Fields of interest: Arts; Higher education; Natural resources; Civic centers.
Limitations: Applications not accepted. Giving primarily in Atlanta, GA, New York, NY, and Seattle, WA. No grants to individuals.
Application information: Contributes only to pre-selected organizations.
Officers: John E. McCaw, Jr., Pres. and Treas.; Stanley B. McCammon, V.P. and Secy.
EIN: 953192332

3360
Curren Ludwig Foundation
c/o Cornerstone Advisors, Inc.
777 108th Ave. N.E., Ste. 2000
Bellevue, WA 98004
Contact: Ken Hart

Established in 1999 in WA.
Donor(s): Cristi Curren Ludwig, John H. Ludwig.
Grantmaker type: Independent foundation
Financial data (yr. ended 12/31/01): Assets, $2,827,727 (M); expenditures, $185,030; qualifying distributions, $166,311; giving activities include $165,938 for 13 grants (high: $66,144; low: $1,000).
Fields of interest: Education; Animals/wildlife, preservation/protection; Children/youth, services; Economically disadvantaged.
Limitations: Applications not accepted. No grants to individuals.
Application information: Contributes only to pre-selected organizations.
Officers and Directors:* Cristi Curren Ludwig,* Pres.; John H. Ludwig,* Secy.-Treas.
EIN: 912015162

3361
Charlotte Y. Martin Foundation
c/o Bank of America
P.O. Box 34345
Seattle, WA 98124-1345 (206) 365-7892
Contact: Andrea Grosso, V.P.
Application address: 701 5th Ave., Ste. 4700, Seattle, WA 98104-7001; E-mail: info@charlottemartin.org; URL: http://www.charlottemartin.org

Established in 1988 in WA.
Donor(s): Charlotte Y. Martin.‡
Grantmaker type: Independent foundation
Financial data (yr. ended 03/31/02): Assets, $22,290,341 (M); expenditures, $1,457,116; qualifying distributions, $1,418,899; giving activities include $1,288,030 for 83 grants (high: $300,000; low: $1,000).
Purpose and activities: Support for 1) education of youth through the establishment of permanent scholarship funds at several pre-selected educational institutions; 2) youth organizations and organizations providing youth-related programs designed to educate and develop young people's cultural awareness and athletic skills beyond the basics of a formal classroom education; and 3) organizations and agencies dedicated to the preservation, protection, and perpetuation of fish and wildlife and/or their habitats.
Fields of interest: Visual arts; Performing arts; Elementary/secondary education; Higher education; Natural resources; Animals/wildlife, fisheries; Animals/wildlife, sanctuaries; Youth development, centers/clubs; Children/youth, services.
Types of support: General/operating support; Continuing support; Capital campaigns; Building/renovation; Equipment; Land acquisition; Endowments; Program development; Publication; Seed money; Curriculum development; Internship funds; Scholarship funds; Matching/challenge support.
Limitations: Giving primarily in the Pacific Northwest. No support for private foundations. No grants to individuals.

Publications: Application guidelines, Program policy statement.
Application information: Application information available on website. Application form not required.
  Initial approach: 2-page letter of inquiry
  Copies of proposal: 4
  Deadline(s): None
  Board meeting date(s): Quarterly
Managers: Joan Gagliardi; Peter Galloway; Karl D. Guelich; Sheila Kelly; Kermit Rudolf.
Trustee: Bank of America.
Number of staff: 1 part-time professional.
EIN: 916294504

3362
The Craig and Susan McCaw Foundation ▼
P.O. Box 2908
Kirkland, WA 98083

Established in 1998 in WA.
Donor(s): Craig O. McCaw.
Grantmaker type: Independent foundation
Financial data (yr. ended 12/31/01): Assets, $8,657,094 (M); gifts received, $500,000; expenditures, $5,920,407; qualifying distributions, $58,334,914; giving activities include $5,833,555 for 29 grants (high: $1,921,185; low: $50; average: $1,000–$380,000).
Purpose and activities: Giving primarily for community development and community organizations.
Fields of interest: Education; Health care; Community development.
Limitations: Applications not accepted. Giving primarily in Seattle, WA. No grants to individuals.
Application information: Contributes only to pre-selected organizations.
Officers and Directors:* Craig O. McCaw, Pres.; Susan R. McCaw,* Secy.
EIN: 911943269
Recent environmental and animal welfare grants:
3362-1 Ocean Futures Society, Santa Barbara, CA, $570,600. For grant made in form of stock. 2001.
3362-2 Ocean Futures Society, Santa Barbara, CA, $385,000. 2001.
3362-3 Ocean Futures Society, Santa Barbara, CA, $380,000. 2001.
3362-4 Ocean Futures Society, Santa Barbara, CA, $370,000. 2001.
3362-5 Ocean Futures Society, Santa Barbara, CA, $369,338. For grant made in form of stock. 2001.
3362-6 Ocean Futures Society, Santa Barbara, CA, $324,870. For grant made in form of stock. 2001.
3362-7 Ocean Futures Society, Santa Barbara, CA, $308,740. For grant made in form of stock. 2001.
3362-8 Ocean Futures Society, Santa Barbara, CA, $242,500. 2001.
3362-9 Ocean Futures Society, Santa Barbara, CA, $171,435. For grant made in form of stock. 2001.
3362-10 Ocean Futures Society, Santa Barbara, CA, $122,019. For grant made in form of stock. 2001.

3362-11 Ocean Futures Society, Santa Barbara, CA, $29,172. For grant made in form of stock. 2001.

3363
Pendleton and Elisabeth Carey Miller Charitable Foundation
3147 Fairview Ave. E., Ste. 200
Seattle, WA 98102-3019 (206) 329-1019
Contact: Frank Minton, Secy.-Treas.
FAX: (206) 329-8230; E-mail: Plangiv@aol.com

Established in 1995 in WA.
Grantmaker type: Independent foundation
Financial data (yr. ended 12/31/02): Assets, $12,588,254 (M); gifts received, $468,415; expenditures, $452,429; qualifying distributions, $381,648; giving activities include $344,532 for 13 grants (high: $106,339; low: $2,000).
Purpose and activities: Giving primarily for horticulture, education, and Northwest history.
Fields of interest: Museums; Museums (art); Higher education; University; Botanical/horticulture/landscape services.
Types of support: Continuing support; Equipment; Endowments; Program development; Conferences/seminars; Publication; Seed money; Internship funds; Research; Technical assistance; Program evaluation; Program-related investments/loans; Matching/challenge support.
Limitations: Giving primarily in WA.
Publications: Application guidelines, Informational brochure (including application guidelines), Occasional report.
Application information: Application form not required.
    Initial approach: Letter
    Copies of proposal: 1
    Deadline(s): None
    Board meeting date(s): May and Nov.
    Final notification: Apr. 15 and Oct. 15
Officers and Trustees:* Winlock W. Miller,* Pres.; Carey K. Miller,* V.P.; Frank D. Minton,* Secy.-Treas.; Elisabeth A. Bottler; Richard A. Brown; W. Howarth Meadowcroft; Malcolm Moore; Ralph Polumbo; Geoffrey G. Revelle.
Number of staff: 2 part-time professional.
EIN: 911671814

3364
Moccasin Lake Foundation
1405 42nd Ave. E.
Seattle, WA 98112

Established in 1991 in WA.
Donor(s): James C. Pigott, Gaye T. Pigott, Mark Kranwinkle, Sara Kranwinkle.
Grantmaker type: Independent foundation
Financial data (yr. ended 12/31/01): Assets, $867,133 (M); gifts received, $537,741; expenditures, $567,186; qualifying distributions, $545,631; giving activities include $544,186 for 71 grants (high: $130,745; low: $100).
Purpose and activities: Giving primarily for education.
Fields of interest: Arts; Education; Natural resources; Animals/wildlife, preservation/protection; Hospitals (general); Cancer; Religion.
Limitations: Applications not accepted. Giving primarily in WA. No grants to individuals.

Application information: Contributes only to pre-selected organizations.
Officers and Directors:* Frederick Beau Gould,* Pres.; Mark Kranwinkle,* V.P.; Micheal Anderson,* Secy.; Gaye T. Pigott,* Co-Treas.; James C. Pigott,* Co-Treas.; Lisa Anderson; Julie Gould; Sara Kranwinkle; Maureen "Dina" Pigott; Paul Pigott.
EIN: 911545081

3365
Murr Family Foundation
1040 Southview Dr.
Walla Walla, WA 99362 (509) 525-1555
Contact: Neil Follett, Pres.

Established in 1992 in WA.
Donor(s): Eva Murr, Michael Murr.
Grantmaker type: Independent foundation
Financial data (yr. ended 06/30/02): Assets, $100,802 (M); gifts received, $213,375; expenditures, $223,465; qualifying distributions, $222,143; giving activities include $222,150 for 9 grants (high: $50,000; low: $1,150).
Purpose and activities: Giving primarily for higher education, a community foundation, and a golf association.
Fields of interest: Arts, alliance; Higher education; Environment, land resources; Athletics/sports, golf; Foundations (community).
Limitations: Giving primarily in Walla Walla, WA. No grants to individuals.
Application information:
    Initial approach: Letter
    Deadline(s): None
Officers: Neil Follett, Pres.; William Bieloh, V.P.; William Fleenor, Secy.-Treas.
EIN: 911568178

3366
Neukom Family Foundation
2120 Waverly Way E.
Seattle, WA 98112

Established in 1998 in WA.
Donor(s): William H. Neukom.
Grantmaker type: Independent foundation
Financial data (yr. ended 03/31/02): Assets, $34,834,650 (M); gifts received, $166,379; expenditures, $2,275,501; qualifying distributions, $2,055,279; giving activities include $2,053,062 for 7 grants (high: $550,589; low: $150,753).
Fields of interest: Higher education; Libraries (public); Environment; Family planning; Cancer research; AIDS research; YM/YWCAs & YM/YWHAs.
Limitations: Applications not accepted. No grants to individuals.
Application information: Contributes only to pre-selected organizations.
Directors: Gillian Neukom; John McMakin Neukom; Josselyn Neukom; Samantha Neukom; William H. Neukom.
EIN: 911737888

3367
New Priorities Foundation
c/o Community Bldg.
35 W. Main Ave., Ste. 310
Spokane, WA 99201 (509) 456-5977
Contact: Patty Gates, Exec. Dir.
FAX: (509) 835-3867; E-mail: patty@newpriorities.org

Established in 1996 in WA.
Donor(s): Nancy G. Schaub.
Grantmaker type: Independent foundation
Financial data (yr. ended 12/31/01): Assets, $3,254,710 (M); expenditures, $208,186; qualifying distributions, $164,753; giving activities include $167,688 for 20 grants (high: $28,000; low: $250; average: $1,000–$5,000).
Fields of interest: Environment, legal rights; Environment, formal/general education; Natural resources.
Types of support: General/operating support; Continuing support; Land acquisition; Program development; Curriculum development.
Limitations: Giving primarily in the Pacific Northwest and East of the Cascades. No support for religious activities or institutes. No grants to individuals.
Application information: Application form required.
    Initial approach: Letter
    Copies of proposal: 7
    Deadline(s): None
    Board meeting date(s): Spring and fall
Officers and Trustees:* Nancy G. Schaub, Chair. and Treas.; Sally G. Douglas, Vice-Chair.; Patty Gates,* Exec. Dir.; Carole Rolando; Annie Schaub; Dave Schaub; Tim Schaub.
Number of staff: 1 part-time professional.
EIN: 911805939

3368
The Norcliffe Foundation ▼
(formerly The Norcliffe Fund)
First Interstate Ctr.
999 3rd Ave., Ste. 1006
Seattle, WA 98104 (206) 682-4820
Contact: Dana Pigott, Pres.

Incorporated in 1952 in WA.
Donor(s): Theiline M. McCone.‡
Grantmaker type: Independent foundation
Financial data (yr. ended 11/30/02): Assets, $116,059,823 (M); gifts received, $1,639,394; expenditures, $4,806,337; qualifying distributions, $4,709,642; giving activities include $4,622,820 for 181 grants (high: $735,359; low: $50; average: $1,000–$25,000).
Purpose and activities: Emphasis on the arts and cultural activities, Roman Catholic church support and religious associations, hospitals, early childhood, higher and secondary education, and historic preservation; support also for medical research and health associations, hospices, the environment and conservation, and social services, including programs for the disabled, the homeless, child welfare, youth agencies, wildlife organizations, and the aged.
Fields of interest: Visual arts; Architecture; Performing arts; Theater; Music; Historic preservation/historical societies; Arts; Education, association; Education, fund raising; Elementary/secondary education; Vocational

education; Higher education; Adult education—literacy, basic skills & GED; Libraries/library science; Reading; Education; Natural resources; Environment; Animals/wildlife, preservation/protection; Hospitals (general); Dental care; Health care; Substance abuse, services; Mental health/crisis services; Health organizations, association; Cancer; AIDS; Alcoholism; Biomedicine; Medical research, institute; Cancer research; AIDS research; Legal services; Employment; Food services; Nutrition; Housing/shelter, development; Recreation; Human services; Children/youth, services; Child development, services; Family services; Hospices; Human services; Community development; Voluntarism promotion; Federated giving programs; Mathematics; Computer science; Christian agencies & churches; Minorities; Native Americans/American Indians; Disabled; Aging; Women; Economically disadvantaged; Homeless.

Types of support: General/operating support; Capital campaigns.

Limitations: Giving in the Puget Sound region of WA, with emphasis on Seattle. No grants to individuals, or for deficit financing, matching gifts, or scholarships; no loans.

Publications: Application guidelines, Program policy statement.

Application information: Application form not required.

Initial approach: Telephone or submission based on guidelines

Copies of proposal: 1

Deadline(s): None

Board meeting date(s): As required

Final notification: 3 to 6 months

Officers and Trustees:* Dana Pigott,* Pres.; Ann Pigott Wyckoff,* V.P.; Arline Hefferline, Secy.; Theiline P. Scheumann,* Treas.; Lisa Anderson; Theiline Cramer; Mary Ellen Hughes; Charles M. Pigott; James C. Pigott; Susan Pohl; Lee W. Rolfe.

Number of staff: 1 full-time professional.

EIN: 916029352

Recent environmental and animal welfare grants:

3368-1 IslandWood, Inc., Seattle, WA, $166,667. For capital campaign to construct center. 2002.

3368-2 Trust for Public Land, Seattle, WA, $45,000. 2002.

3369
Northwest Fund for the Environment

1904 3rd Ave., Ste. 615
Seattle, WA 98101 (206) 386-7220
Contact: Pamela Fujita-Yuhas, Fund Admin. or Zoe Rothchild, Fund Admin.
FAX: (206) 386-7223; E-mail: staff@nwfund.org; URL: http://www.nwfund.org

Established in 1971 in WA.
Donor(s): Helen May Marcy Johnson.‡
Grantmaker type: Independent foundation
Financial data (yr. ended 12/31/02): Assets, $5,422,860 (M); expenditures, $496,344; qualifying distributions, $495,725; giving activities include $411,868 for 28 grants (high: $20,000; low: $2,500; average: $1,000–$20,000).
Purpose and activities: Giving for environmental purposes, including grants for

stewardship programs, action plans, strategic litigation, and capacity building for conservation organizations. Also giving for protection of wildlife habitats, water quality, and shoreline and wetland environments.

Fields of interest: Environment, alliance; Environment, research; Natural resources; Environment, water resources; Animals/wildlife, preservation/protection.

Types of support: General/operating support; Program development; Seed money; Technical assistance; Matching/challenge support.

Limitations: Giving limited to WA. No support for partisan political activities or purely educational programs. No grants to individuals, or for academic research, endowment funds, or capital projects or debt reduction; no loans.

Publications: Annual report.

Application information: See Web site for application information. Application form required.

Copies of proposal: 3

Officers and Trustees:* Derek Poon,* Pres.; Rodney Brown,* V.P.; Parrish Jones,* Treas.; Dave Mann, Secy.; Mike Fraidenburg; Dave Goeke; Chris Golde; Peter Golde; Kim Moore; Robert Rose; Tom Scribner; Judy Turpin.

Number of staff: 2 part-time professional.

EIN: 237134880

3370
The Osberg Family Trust

c/o Bank of America
P.O. Box 34345
Seattle, WA 98124-1345
Contact: Kevin Fox
Application address: c/o Bank of America, P.O. Box 24565, Seattle, WA 98124, tel.: (206) 358-1652

Established in 1988 in WA.
Donor(s): Hilma Osberg,‡ Axel Osberg.‡
Grantmaker type: Independent foundation
Financial data (yr. ended 12/31/02): Assets, $5,281,678 (M); expenditures, $317,217; qualifying distributions, $298,554; giving activities include $274,450 for 20 grants (high: $70,000; low: $1,000).
Fields of interest: Museums (history); Higher education; Natural resources; Human services; Voluntarism promotion; Federated giving programs.
Limitations: Giving primarily in WA. No grants to individuals.
Application information: Application form not required.
Deadline(s): None
Trustee: Bank of America.
EIN: 943067305

3371
Peach Foundation

1017 Minor Ave., Ste. 1202
Seattle, WA 98104

Established in 2001 in WA.
Donor(s): Priscilla B. Collins.
Grantmaker type: Independent foundation
Financial data (yr. ended 12/31/02): Assets, $5,743,764 (M); gifts received, $836,230; expenditures, $240,522; qualifying distributions,

$236,125; giving activities include $237,000 for 12 grants (high: $60,000; low: $4,000).
Fields of interest: Museums (art); University; Agriculture, farmlands.
Limitations: Applications not accepted. Giving primarily in Seattle, WA. No grants to individuals.
Application information: Contributes only to pre-selected organizations.
Officers and Directors:* Priscilla B. Collins,* Pres.; Delphine Haley,* Secy.; Crane Wright,* Treas.; Jean Gardner.
EIN: 912094325

3372
Pet Care Trust

3951 Leland Valley Rd. W.
Quilcene, WA 98376 (360) 765-3311
Contact: John Pitts, D.V.M., Prog. Coord.
FAX: (360) 765-3399; E-mail: Jlpitts@Olympus.net; URL: http://www.petcaretrust.org

Established in 1990 in DC.
Grantmaker type: Public charity
Financial data (yr. ended 09/30/01): Revenue, $186,084; assets, $1,463,258 (M); gifts received, $113,109; expenditures, $202,221; program services expenses, $147,396; giving activities include $90,540 for 8 grants (high: $19,040; low: $4,500) and $1,500 for 2 grants to individuals of $750 each.
Purpose and activities: The trust promotes public understanding of the value of, and the right to enjoy companion animals; enhances society's knowledge about companion animals; and promotes professionalism among members of the companion animal community. Research grants are given in the areas of research programs to improve the understanding of environmental, humane, social, economic, and medical aspects of the health, care, and possession of companion animals; education programs for preparation and dissemination of materials to enhance society's knowledge about companion animals, and to promote professionalism in the community through forums, lectures, and seminars; and special programs to improve the health and welfare of companion animals through direct assistance.
Fields of interest: Teacher school/education; Veterinary medicine; Animals/wildlife, public education.
Types of support: Program development; Conferences/seminars; Curriculum development; Scholarship funds; Research; Grants to individuals.
Limitations: Giving limited to North America, primarily U.S. and Canada. No support for organizations lacking nonprofit status. No grants for general operating expenses or equipment.
Publications: Application guidelines, Grants list, Informational brochure.
Application information: Application form required.
Initial approach: Telephone, FAX, or e-mail for application guidelines for research grants
Copies of proposal: 3
Deadline(s): lst week in July for full proposal and Jan. for pre-proposal for research grants
Board meeting date(s): 2 times each year
Final notification: Oct.

Officers and Trustees:* Andreas Schmidt,* Pres.; Mark Hagen,* V.P.; Lew Sutton,* Secy.; Carol Frank,* Treas.; Terri Meyer; Brent Weinmann; Jim Wingate.
Number of staff: 1 part-time support.
EIN: 521684353

3373
Plum Creek Foundation
999 3rd Ave., Ste. 2300
Seattle, WA 98104
Contact: Robert J. Jirsa, Pres.
URL: http://www.plumcreek.com/company/foundation.cfm

Established in 1993 in WA.
Donor(s): Plum Creek Timber Co., L.P., Plum Creek Timber Co., Inc.
Grantmaker type: Company-sponsored foundation
Financial data (yr. ended 12/31/01): Assets, $455,821 (M); gifts received, $650,000; expenditures, $197,541; qualifying distributions, $197,410; giving activities include $169,850 for 32 grants (high: $50,000; low: $500) and $27,535 for 74 employee matching gifts.
Purpose and activities: Support for community projects, education, arts, and environmental programs.
Fields of interest: Arts; Elementary/secondary education; Higher education; Environment; Youth, services; Community development.
Limitations: Giving primarily in ID, MT, and WA. No grants to individuals.
Application information: Application form required.
    Deadline(s): None
Officers: James A. Kraft, Chair.; Robert J. Jirsa, Pres.; Art H. Vail, V.P.; Barbara L. Crowe, Secy.; Scott N. Dell'Osso, Treas.
EIN: 911621028

3374
Puget Sound Energy, Inc. Corporate Giving Program
(formerly Puget Sound Power & Light Company Contributions Program)
P.O. Box 97034, OBC-11E
Bellevue, WA 98009-9734 (425) 462-3799
Contact: Heather Wangaard, Coord., Community Progs.
FAX: (425) 462-3355; E-mail: hwanga@puget.com

Grantmaker type: Corporate giving program
Financial data (yr. ended 12/31/00): Total giving, $1,400,000; giving activities include $1,400,000 for 300 grants (high: $500,000; low: $1,000).
Purpose and activities: Puget Sound Energy makes charitable contributions to nonprofit organizations involved with arts and culture, education, the environment, public safety, human services, and economic development. Support is limited to areas of company operations.
Fields of interest: Arts; Higher education; Education; Environment; Safety/disasters; Human services; Economic development.
Types of support: Continuing support; Annual campaigns; Capital campaigns; Emergency funds; Program development; Employee

volunteer services; Sponsorships; Employee matching gifts; Matching/challenge support.
Limitations: Giving limited to areas of company operations. No support for religious organizations not of direct benefit to the entire community, fraternal, political, or labor organizations, grantmaking organizations, or discriminatory organizations. No grants to individuals, or for mass mailings, tickets, advertising, endorsements, endowments, or travel.
Publications: Application guidelines, Program policy statement.
Application information: The Community Relations Department handles giving. Application form not required.
    Initial approach: Proposal to headquarters
    Copies of proposal: 1
    Deadline(s): Quarterly
    Final notification: 2 months following end of quarter
Number of staff: 1 full-time professional.

3375
Quitslund Foundation
c/o Dana Quitslund
13724 Sunrise Dr.
Bainbridge Island, WA 98110 (206) 780-9422
Contact: Nancy Quitslund, Pres.

Established in 1998 in WA.
Donor(s): Dana E. Quitslund, Nancy N. Quitslund.
Grantmaker type: Independent foundation
Financial data (yr. ended 12/31/02): Assets, $1,336,591 (M); expenditures, $151,555; qualifying distributions, $135,452; giving activities include $136,000 for 19 grants (high: $25,000; low: $1,000).
Purpose and activities: Giving to organizations assisting the needy in seeking self-sufficiency, education and preservation of the environment.
Fields of interest: Education; Environment; Human services; Economically disadvantaged.
Limitations: Applications not accepted.
Application information: Unsolicited requests for funds not accepted.
Officers and Directors:* Nancy N. Quitslund,* Pres.; Dana E. Quitslund,* Secy.-Treas.; Beth M. Quitslund; Sarah N. Quitslund.
EIN: 911885633

3376
Quixote Foundation, Inc.
6723 21st Ave. N.W.
Seattle, WA 98117-5746
Contact: Erik M. Hanisch, Pres.

Established in 1998 in WI.
Donor(s): Arthur S. Hanisch.
Grantmaker type: Independent foundation
Financial data (yr. ended 12/31/01): Assets, $7,627,060 (M); gifts received, $2,532,482; expenditures, $427,437; qualifying distributions, $284,703; giving activities include $269,326 for 14 grants (high: $76,606; low: $2,000).
Fields of interest: Higher education; Natural resources; Animals/wildlife.
Types of support: Program development.
Limitations: Giving primarily in WI. No grants to individuals.
Publications: Application guidelines.

Application information: Application form required.
    Copies of proposal: 1
    Deadline(s): Quarterly
    Board meeting date(s): May
Officers: Erik M. Hanisch, Chair. and Pres.; Richard J. Langer, V.P.; Martha Vukelich-Austin, Secy.-Treas.
Directors: Martha V. Austin; Richard J. Lauger; Paul R. Soglin.
Number of staff: 1 part-time support.
EIN: 391916960

3377
Raynier Institute & Foundation
c/o William N. Appel
1904 3rd Ave., Ste. 432
Seattle, WA 98101
FAX: (206) 342-9593

Established in 1994 in WA.
Donor(s): James W. Ray.
Grantmaker type: Operating foundation
Financial data (yr. ended 12/31/01): Assets, $32,353 (M); gifts received, $401,163; expenditures, $380,194; qualifying distributions, $267,978; giving activities include $271,905 for 43 grants (high: $57,000; low: $39).
Purpose and activities: Giving primarily for arts and culture, and to environmental and wildlife organizations.
Fields of interest: Arts; Natural resources; Environment; Animals/wildlife, preservation/protection.
Limitations: Applications not accepted. No grants to individuals.
Application information: Contributes only to pre-selected organizations.
Officer: Harold E. Abbott, V.P.
Director: Edward D. Gardner.
EIN: 911644205

3378
REI Corporate Giving Program
c/o Corp. Contribs.
6750 S. 228th
Kent, WA 98032
URL: http://www.rei.com/reihtml/about_rei/gives.html

Grantmaker type: Corporate giving program
Purpose and activities: REI makes charitable contributions to nonprofit organizations involved with natural resources conservation and protection, recreation, and youth development. Support is given primarily in areas of company operations.
Fields of interest: Natural resources; Recreation; Youth development.
Types of support: General/operating support; Employee volunteer services; Use of facilities; Donated products.
Limitations: Applications not accepted. Giving primarily in areas of company operations.
Application information: Contributes only to pre-selected organizations.

3379
The Russell Family Foundation ▼
P.O. Box 2567
Gig Harbor, WA 98335 (253) 858-5050
Contact: Stephanie Anderson, Grants Mgr.
Toll Free tel: (888) 252-4331; FAX: (253)
851-0460; E-mail: steph@trff.org; URL: http://
www.trff.org

Established in 1994 in WA.
Donor(s): George F. Russell, Jr., Jane T. Russell.‡
Grantmaker type: Independent foundation
Financial data (yr. ended 12/31/01): Assets,
$121,183,928 (M); expenditures, $6,873,272;
qualifying distributions, $6,119,347; giving
activities include $5,373,472 for 163 grants
(high: $332,500; low: $500; average:
$5,000–$50,000).
Purpose and activities: Giving primarily for
education and the environment. The
foundation's main environmental goal is to
protect, restore and enhance the waters of the
Greater Puget Sound.
Fields of interest: Education; Environment.
Types of support: General/operating support;
Program development; Employee matching gifts.
Limitations: Giving primarily in the Puget Sound
region of WA. No support for organizations
lacking 501(c)(3) status. No grants to individuals.
Application information: No unsolicited
education grants in 2003. Application form
required.
> *Initial approach:* Letter of inquiry; full
> proposal by invitation only
> *Copies of proposal:* 1
> *Deadline(s):* See foundation's Web site for
> deadlines
> *Board meeting date(s):* Three times a year
> *Final notification:* After meeting
Officers and Directors:* Sarah R. Cavanaugh,*
Pres.; George F. Russell, Jr.,* V.P.; Dion R.
Rurik,* 2nd V.P.; Eric A. Russell,* Treas.; Richard
Woo, Exec. Dir.; Tim Cavanaugh; Jileen Russell;
Richard F. Russell.
Number of staff: 5 full-time professional.
EIN: 911663336
**Recent environmental and animal welfare
grants:**
3379-1 1000 Friends of Washington, Seattle,
WA, $25,000. For general operating support
for work in Pierce County. 2001.
3379-2 American Farmland Trust, Pacific
Northwest Regional Office, Puyallup, WA,
$20,000. For Solutions for a Growing
Community: Pierce County Farm-City Forum.
2001.
3379-3 Audubon Society, Tahoma, Tacoma,
WA, $20,000. For outreach programs. 2001.
3379-4 Center for Biological Diversity, Tucson,
AZ, $50,000. For Puget Sound Biodiversity
Assessment and Protection Project in Shaw
Island, Washington. 2001.
3379-5 Center for Environmental Law and
Policy, Seattle, WA, $50,000. For general
operating support. 2001.
3379-6 Center for Watershed and Community
Health, Springfield, Oregon, $15,000. For
Washington State Green Planning Initiative.
2001.
3379-7 Citizens for a Healthy Bay, Tacoma, WA,
$35,000. For Clean Boating/Clean Marina
program. 2001.

3379-8 Citizens for a Healthy Bay, Tacoma, WA,
$10,000. For general operating support for
Carolyn Foundation matching grant. 2001.
3379-9 Earth Ministry, Seattle, WA, $30,000. For
The Greening Congregations Handbook.
2001.
3379-10 EarthCorps, Seattle, WA, $50,000. For
new vehicles. 2001.
3379-11 Ecotrust, Portland, Oregon, $25,000.
For GreenTide, section of Tidepool.org
Website, dedicated to providing weekly
green business updates. 2001.
3379-12 Environmental Media Services, Seattle
Center, DC, $50,000. For general operating
support for Western States Office in Seattle,
Washington. Grant made through The Tides
Center. 2001.
3379-13 Environmental Support Center, DC,
$50,000. For general operating support for
work in Washington state. 2001.
3379-14 Environmental Works, Seattle, WA,
$35,000. For Sustaining Affordable
Communities project. 2001.
3379-15 Habitat for Humanity, South Puget
Sound, Olympia, WA, $50,000. For reusable
building materials drop-off site. 2001.
3379-16 Marine Conservation Biology Institute,
Redmond, WA, $35,000. For general
operating support. 2001.
3379-17 North Cascades Institute, Sedro
Woolley, WA, $45,000. For North Cascades
Environmental Learning Center. 2001.
3379-18 ONE/Northwest, Seattle, WA, $25,000.
For general operating support. 2001.
3379-19 Peninsula Neighborhood Association,
Gig Harbor, WA, $11,600. For low impact
development education. 2001.
3379-20 Salish Sea Expeditions, Salish Sea
Expeditions on Bainbridge Island, Bainbridge
Island, WA, $25,000. For general operating
support. 2001.
3379-21 Sea Resources, Chinook, WA,
$24,000. For Watershed Restoration
Education program at Watershed Learning
Center. 2001.
3379-22 Skagitonians to Preserve Farmland,
Mount Vernon, WA, $40,000. For creating
new markets for environmental stewardship
in Skagit Valley agriculture. 2001.
3379-23 Sustainable Seattle, Seattle, WA,
$70,000. For Chinook book. 2001.
3379-24 Tacoma Community College
Foundation, Tacoma, WA, $55,000. For
technology-equipped classroom and learning
resources for environmental science program
for Gig Harbor/Peninsula College Center.
2001.
3379-25 Tacoma Garden Club, Northwest
Native Plant Garden, Tacoma, WA, $10,000.
For general operating support. 2001.
3379-26 Tacoma, City of, Tacoma, WA,
$125,000. For Aquarium/Marine Science
Center feasibility study. 2001.
3379-27 Washington Public Interest Research
Group Foundation, Seattle, WA, $20,000. For
Clean Water Now campaign. 2001.
3379-28 Washington Water Trust, Seattle, WA,
$50,000. For senior water rights project in
the Puget Sound and Western Washington.
2001.

3380
Samis Foundation ▼
208 James St., Ste. C
Seattle, WA 98104 (206) 623-3363
Contact: Eddie I. Hasson, Co-Chair.
FAX: (206) 622-4918; E-mail:
grantsadministrator@samis.com; URL: http://
www.samis.com/Frame_found.html

Established in 1979.
Donor(s): Samuel Israel.
Grantmaker type: Independent foundation
Financial data (yr. ended 12/31/02): Assets,
$122,566,799 (M); expenditures, $18,009,462;
qualifying distributions, $3,728,298; giving
activities include $3,444,629 for 38+ grants
(high: $930,611; low: $1,000; average:
$5,000–$50,000).
Purpose and activities: Support primarily for
Jewish giving, with emphasis on education in
WA; giving also for general support in Israel,
including Jewish welfare, archeology, wildlife
and scholarships.
Fields of interest: History/archaeology;
Elementary/secondary education;
Animals/wildlife, preservation/protection; Jewish
agencies & temples; Religion.
International interests: Israel.
Types of support: General/operating support;
Continuing support; Capital campaigns;
Building/renovation; Emergency funds; Program
development; Publication; Seed money;
Scholarship funds; Research; Technical
assistance; Exchange programs.
Limitations: Giving primarily in WA for Jewish
organizations; some giving also in Israel. No
grants to individuals.
Publications: Application guidelines, Grants list,
Informational brochure (including application
guidelines).
Application information: Application form
required.
> *Initial approach:* Letter
> *Copies of proposal:* 2
> *Deadline(s):* Mar. 1
> *Board meeting date(s):* Quarterly
> *Final notification:* July 1
Officers and Directors:* Eddie I. Hasson,*
Co-Chair. and Pres.; Albert S. Maimon,*
Co-Chair. and V.P.; Irwin Treiger,* Secy.; Victor
D. Alhadeff; Eli J. Almo; Jerome O. Cohen; Barry
D. Ernstoff; David Friedenberg; Eli Genauer;
Rabbi William Greenberg; Mike Israel; Morris
Piha; Lucy Pruzan; Martin Selig; Ernest
Sherman; Alex Sytman.
Number of staff: 2 full-time professional; 1
full-time support.
EIN: 911641746

3381
The Seattle Foundation
425 Pike St., Ste. 510
Seattle, WA 98101 (206) 622-2294
Contact: Phyllis Campbell, Pres.
FAX: (206) 622-7673; E-mail:
info@seattlefoundation.org; URL: http://
www.seattlefoundation.org

Incorporated in 1946 in WA.
Grantmaker type: Community foundation
Financial data (yr. ended 12/30/02): Assets,
$282,557,458 (M); gifts received, $40,528,925;
expenditures, $47,364,361; giving activities

include $38,915,813 for 2,729 grants (high: $1,554,705; low: $250; average: $250-$100,000).

Fields of interest: Arts; Education; Health care; Health organizations, association; Human services; Children/youth, services; Community development.

Types of support: General/operating support; Capital campaigns; Building/renovation; Equipment.

Limitations: Giving limited to the greater Puget Sound region, WA. No support for political or religious organizations. No grants to individuals, or for scholarships, fellowships, endowment funds, research, operating budgets, general purposes, matching gifts, conferences or seminars, exhibits, film or video production, or publications; no loans.

Publications: Application guidelines, Annual report, Grants list, Informational brochure, Program policy statement.

Application information: Application guidelines available on Web site. Application form not required.

Initial approach: Letter requesting guidelines
Copies of proposal: 1
Deadline(s): Jan. 1, Apr. 1, July 1, and Oct. 1
Board meeting date(s): Mar., June, Sept., and Dec.
Final notification: 6 weeks to 2 months

Officers and Trustees:* Irwin Treiger,* Chair.; Stewart Landefeld,* Vice-Chair.; Phyllis Campbell,* C.E.O. and Pres.; Carolyn J. Norton, V.P., Fin. and Admin.; Molly Stearns, Sr. V.P., Progs. and DS; Susan G. Duffy, Secy.; Dan Regis, Treas.; and 26 additional trustees.

Corporate Trustees: Union Bank of California, N.A.; Columbia Management Co.; KeyBank N.A.; Miller Anderson Sherrad; PIMCO; T. Rowe Price Svc.; Bank of America; Sirach Capital Management, Inc.; U.S. Bank of Washington, N.A.; Warburg, Pincus Cansellors, Inc.; Washington Mutual Savings Bank; Wells Fargo Bank Northwest, N.A.

Number of staff: 15 full-time professional; 1 part-time professional; 6 full-time support.

EIN: 916013536

Recent environmental and animal welfare grants:

3381-1 1000 Friends of Washington, Seattle, WA, $25,000. To provide general support. 2002.

3381-2 Alaska Raptor Rehabilitation Center (ARRC), Sitka, AK, $10,000. For Building Fund. 2002.

3381-3 Arboretum Foundation, Seattle, WA, $25,000. For general operating expenses and purchase of computer equipment. 2002.

3381-4 Audubon Society of Washington State, Seattle, WA, $24,000. For general operating expenses. 2002.

3381-5 Cascade Land Conservancy, Seattle, WA, $25,000. To provide operational support for acquisition activity generated by Wildlife Forever Foundation project. 2002.

3381-6 Center for Environmental Law and Policy, Seattle, WA, $20,000. To provide general support. 2002.

3381-7 Center for Environmental Law and Policy, Seattle, WA, $10,000. For general operating expenses and purchase of computer equipment. 2002.

3381-8 CleanScapes, Seattle, WA, $30,792. For dumpster-free alley program and install alley lighting fixtures in Pioneer Square. 2002.

3381-9 CleanScapes, Seattle, WA, $19,408. For football game day clean-up program for South Downtown. 2002.

3381-10 Conservation International, Seattle, WA, $10,000. To provide general support. 2002.

3381-11 Conservation International, Seattle, WA, $10,000. To provide general support. 2002.

3381-12 Delta Society, Renton, WA, $10,000. For computer equipment and training. 2002.

3381-13 Dorobo Fund for Tanzania, Minneapolis, MN, $20,000. To provide general support. 2002.

3381-14 Ducks Unlimited, Memphis, TN, $10,000. To provide general support. 2002.

3381-15 E. B. Dunn Historic Garden Trust, Shoreline, WA, $22,166. For classroom, conservation easement line and for Ruth Hughbanks Memorial Fund. 2002.

3381-16 EarthCorps, Seattle, WA, $100,000. For Youth Engagement at Cheasty Greenspace project. 2002.

3381-17 First Place, Seattle, WA, $10,000. For workshop for children at Puget Sound Environmental Learning Center, art and play therapy supplies and library books. 2002.

3381-18 Friends of P-Patch, Seattle, WA, $15,000. For purchase of Judkins Park P-Patch. 2002.

3381-19 High Mountain Institute, Leadville, CO, $16,239. To provide general support. 2002.

3381-20 International Fund for Animal Welfare, Yarmouth Port, MA, $20,000. To provide general support. 2002.

3381-21 International Snow Leopard Trust, Seattle, WA, $25,000. To provide general support. 2002.

3381-22 IslandWood, Inc., Seattle, WA, $150,000. For capital campaign. 2002.

3381-23 IslandWood, Inc., Seattle, WA, $100,000. For campaign to Build PSELC. 2002.

3381-24 IslandWood, Inc., Seattle, WA, $83,000. For Campaign to Build IslandWood. 2002.

3381-25 IslandWood, Inc., Seattle, WA, $33,583. For Building and Construction Fund. 2002.

3381-26 IslandWood, Inc., Seattle, WA, $10,000. To provide general support. 2002.

3381-27 IslandWood, Inc., Seattle, WA, $10,000. For campaign to build IslandWood. 2002.

3381-28 Livable Communities Coalition, Seattle, WA, $10,000. For general operating expenses. 2002.

3381-29 Long Live the Kings, Seattle, WA, $15,000. To provide general support. 2002.

3381-30 Mountains to Sound Greenway Trust, Seattle, WA, $15,000. To provide general support. 2002.

3381-31 North Seattle Community College Foundation, Seattle, WA, $10,000. For general operating expenses of Thornton Creek/Homewaters Project. 2002.

3381-32 Northwest Ecosystem Alliance, Bellingham, WA, $30,308. For Cascade Conservation Partnerships for protection of wildlife corridors. 2002.

3381-33 Northwest Organization for Animal Help, Stanwood, WA, $400,000. To provide general support. 2002.

3381-34 Northwest Organization for Animal Help, Stanwood, WA, $200,000. To provide general support. 2002.

3381-35 ONE/Northwest, Seattle, WA, $20,000. For Next Generation E-Mail List Hosting project. 2002.

3381-36 Passages Northwest, Seattle, WA, $15,000. For scholarships. 2002.

3381-37 Pigs Peace Sanctuary, Arlington, WA, $250,000. To help purchase new home for sanctuary. 2002.

3381-38 Puget Sound Restoration Fund, Bainbridge Island, WA, $10,000. For general operating expenses for Seattle/King County projects. 2002.

3381-39 Puget Soundkeeper Alliance, Seattle, WA, $10,000. For general operating expenses. 2002.

3381-40 Resource Media, Seattle, WA, $50,000. To provide general support for programs taking place primarily in Pacific Northwest. 2002.

3381-41 Salish Sea Expeditions, Bainbridge Island, WA, $20,000. For general operating expenses. 2002.

3381-42 Saras Sanctuary, Redmond, WA, $10,000. For general operating expenses. 2002.

3381-43 Seattle Youth Garden Works, Seattle, WA, $40,000. To provide general support. 2002.

3381-44 Training Resources for the Environmental Community, Vashon, WA, $325,000. To provide general support. 2002.

3381-45 Training Resources for the Environmental Community, Vashon, WA, $200,000. To provide general support. 2002.

3381-46 Vashon-Maury Island Land Trust, Vashon, WA, $100,000. For Judd Properties Land Acquisition Fund. 2002.

3381-47 Vashon-Maury Island Land Trust, Vashon, WA, $10,000. For general operating expenses. 2002.

3381-48 Washington Environmental Alliance for Voter Education, Seattle, WA, $50,000. For Youth Project, Engagement Initiative, and Planning Cycle Overhaul. 2002.

3381-49 Washington Environmental Alliance for Voter Education, Seattle, WA, $20,000. To provide general operational support. 2002.

3381-50 Washington Environmental Alliance for Voter Education, Seattle, WA, $15,000. For general operating expenses. 2002.

3381-51 Washington Environmental Council, Seattle, WA, $11,000. For new phone system and computers. 2002.

3381-52 Washington Toxics Coalition, Seattle, WA, $50,000. For Clean Water for Salmon and Health campaign and Leaving Toxic Free Legacy Campaign. 2002.

3381-53 Washington Water Trails Association, Seattle, WA, $10,000. For general operating support. 2002.

3381-54 Washington Water Trust, Seattle, WA, $50,000. To provide general support and for program expansion in Western Washington. 2002.

3381-55 Woodland Park Zoological Society, Seattle, WA, $100,000. To provide general support. 2002.

3381-56 Woodland Park Zoological Society, Seattle, WA, $50,000. For purchase of zoo vehicles. 2002.

3381-57 Woodland Park Zoological Society, Seattle, WA, $35,000. To provide general support. 2002.

3381-58 Woodland Park Zoological Society, Seattle, WA, $23,560. To provide general support. 2002.

3382
The Seattle Times Company Contributions Program
c/o Corp. Contribs.
P.O. Box 70
Seattle, WA 98111-0070 (206) 464-2119

Grantmaker type: Corporate giving program
Purpose and activities: The Seattle Times Company makes charitable contributions to nonprofit organizations involved with journalism and publishing, higher education, the environment, youth development, minorities, and women. Support is given primarily in areas of company operations.
Fields of interest: Journalism/publishing; Higher education; Environment; Youth development; Minorities; Women.
Types of support: Continuing support; Capital campaigns; Program development; Scholarship funds; Sponsorships; In-kind gifts.
Limitations: Giving primarily in areas of company operations. No support for United Way-, Corporate Council for the Arts-, or Independent Colleges of Washington-supported organizations, agencies with a combined administrative and fundraising cost of over 15 percent, discriminatory organizations, political campaigns, organizations, or committees, lobbying efforts or organizations funnelling money to such causes, religious institutions or organizations other than community-wide services or projects with no theological focus, national organizations not pertinent to the company's industry or special interests, or government agencies or programs primarily funded by the public sector. No grants to individuals, or for development or start-up needs, travel expenses, operating deficits, conferences or seminars outside the newspaper industry not pertinent to the company's interests as a grantmaker within the community, publication, film, or video production, or advertising.
Application information: An application form is required for all requests of over $500. Requests may be submitted using the Pacific Northwest Grantmakers Forum's Common Grant Application Form. Multi-year funding is not automatic. The Public Relations Department handles giving.
 Initial approach: Proposal to headquarters; contact headquarters for application form for requests of over $500
 Deadline(s): None
 Final notification: Following review

3383
Charles See Foundation
1 Lake Bellevue Dr., Ste. 112
Bellevue, WA 98005 (425) 635-7250
Contact: Anne R. See, Pres.

Incorporated in 1960 in CA.
Donor(s): Charles B. See.
Grantmaker type: Independent foundation
Financial data (yr. ended 12/31/02): Assets, $1,888,681 (M); expenditures, $173,163; qualifying distributions, $144,662; giving activities include $117,000 for 35 grants (high: $5,000; low: $500).
Purpose and activities: Emphasis on education and hospitals; giving also for mental health, church support, conservation, cultural programs, and international affairs.
Fields of interest: Arts; Education; Natural resources; Animal welfare; Hospitals (general); Mental health/crisis services; Human services; International affairs; Religion.
Limitations: Giving primarily in CA and WA. No grants to individuals.
Application information: Application form not required.
 Initial approach: Letter
 Copies of proposal: 1
 Deadline(s): Nov. 15
 Board meeting date(s): Around Dec. 1
Officers: Anne R. See, Pres. and Treas.; Harry A. See, V.P. and Secy.; Richard W. See, V.P.
Directors: Bruce M. Pym; Stephen D. Varon.
Number of staff: None.
EIN: 956038358

3384
Simpson Fund
(formerly Simpson Investment Company Contributions Program)
1301 5th Ave., Ste. 2800
Seattle, WA 98101-2613 (206) 224-5198
Contact: Colleen Musgrave, Corp. Giving Admin.; or Maureen S. Frisch, V.P., Public Affairs
FAX: (206) 436-1852; E-mail: cmusgra@simpson.com; URL: http://www.simpson.com/communitymain.cfm

Grantmaker type: Corporate giving program
Financial data (yr. ended 12/31/02): Total giving, $1,145,036; giving activities include $1,026,905 for 400 grants (high: $50,000; low: $25; average: $100–$5,000), $75,000 for 25 grants to individuals (high: $3,000), $15,000 for 75 employee matching gifts and $28,131 for 36 in-kind gifts.
Purpose and activities: Through the Simpson Fund, a direct corporate giving program, Simpson makes charitable contributions to nonprofit organizations involved with education, the environment, health and human services, and community development. Support is given primarily in areas of company operations.
Fields of interest: Education; Environment; Health care; Human services; Community development.
Types of support: General/operating support; Continuing support; Capital campaigns; Endowments; Emergency funds; Seed money; Research; Employee volunteer services; Sponsorships; Employee matching gifts; Employee-related scholarships; Donated

equipment; Donated products; In-kind gifts; Matching/challenge support.
Limitations: Giving primarily in areas of company operations in Del Norte and Humboldt counties, CA, Lincoln and Tillamook counties, OR, and Grays Harbor, King, Mason, Pierce, Tacoma, and Thurston counties, WA.
Publications: Application guidelines, Informational brochure (including application guidelines).
Application information: The Public Affairs Department handles giving. The company has a staff that only handles contributions. A contributions committee reviews all requests. Application form not required.
 Initial approach: Proposal to headquarters or nearest company facility
 Copies of proposal: 1
 Deadline(s): None
 Board meeting date(s): As needed
 Final notification: Following review
Number of staff: 1 part-time professional.

3385
Sportsmen for Conservation Fund
P.O. Box 159
Wapato, WA 98951 (509) 877-3260
Contact: Bill Harrison, Pres.

Grantmaker type: Public charity
Financial data (yr. ended 06/30/00): Revenue, $27,706; assets, $138,421; gifts received, $1,250; expenditures, $32,841; program services expenses, $27,502; giving activities include $19,178 for 6 grants (high: $11,070; low: $250) and $7,665 for 3 grants to individuals of $2,555 each.
Purpose and activities: The fund seeks to conserve the wildlife and habitat of WA. It supports efforts to educate the public about such issues, and also provides scholarships to students at Washington State University (WSU) in the Fish and Wildlife Program.
Fields of interest: Animals/wildlife, public education; Animals/wildlife, formal/general education; Animals/wildlife, preservation/protection; Animals/wildlife, fisheries.
Types of support: Scholarships—to individuals.
Limitations: Giving primarily in WA.
Officers and Directors:* Bill Harrison,* Pres.; Don Morin,* V.P.; John Lecky,* Secy.; Gary Tennison,* Treas.; Dan Bonnell; Robert Brisebois; Dick Gates; Jack Gooch; Don Jefferson; Velle Kolde; and 4 additional directors.
EIN: 911160596

3386
Winifred L. Stevens Foundation
c/o John V. Stevens, Sr.
1184 Schwartz Rd.
Nordland, WA 98358

Established in 1996 in CA.
Donor(s): Linda S. Spady.
Grantmaker type: Independent foundation
Financial data (yr. ended 12/31/02): Assets, $24,181,495 (M); gifts received, $70,000; expenditures, $671,860; qualifying distributions, $801,642; giving activities include $816,000 for 1 grant.

Purpose and activities: Funding primarily for a Seventh Day Adventist church and other religious organizations.
Fields of interest: Animals/wildlife, preservation/protection; Human services; Protestant agencies & churches; Religion.
Limitations: Applications not accepted. Giving primarily in CA. No grants to individuals.
Application information: Contributes only to pre-selected organizations.
Officers and Directors:* John V. Stevens, Sr.,* Pres.; Linda S. Spady,* V.P.; John V. Stevens, Jr.,* Secy.
EIN: 954505998

3387
Suskin Foundation
618 Priest Point Dr. N.W.
Marysville, WA 98271-6825

Established in 1999 in WA.
Donor(s): Margie Suskin.
Grantmaker type: Independent foundation
Financial data (yr. ended 12/31/02): Assets, $2,903,731 (M); expenditures, $178,275; qualifying distributions, $177,500; giving activities include $177,500 for 8 grants (high: $45,000; low: $12,500).
Fields of interest: Animal welfare; Hospitals (general); Cancer; Children/youth, services.
Limitations: Applications not accepted. Giving primarily in WA. No grants to individuals.
Application information: Contributes only to pre-selected organizations.
Trustees: Jon G. Bowman; James M. Hayes; Margie Suskin; Steven C. Suskin.
EIN: 912015382

3388
Sustainable Solutions Foundation
189 Coulter Rd.
Sequim, WA 98382-9362

Established in 1997 in WA.
Grantmaker type: Independent foundation
Financial data (yr. ended 12/31/00): Assets, $2,560,358 (M); expenditures, $135,547; qualifying distributions, $129,483; giving activities include $130,000 for 7 grants (high: $40,000; low: $10,000).
Fields of interest: Environment; Animals/wildlife, preservation/protection.
Types of support: General/operating support.
Limitations: Applications not accepted. Giving on a national basis. No grants to individuals.
Application information: Contributes only to pre-selected organizations.
Officers: Steve Clapp, Pres.; Robert L. Sander, Treas.
Trustees: Joe Bowen; Booth Gardner.
EIN: 911817420

3389
T.E.W. Foundation
506 2nd Ave., Ste. 2900
Seattle, WA 98104-2343

Established in 1997 in WA.
Donor(s): T. Evans Wyckoff.‡
Grantmaker type: Independent foundation

Financial data (yr. ended 12/31/02): Assets, $7,723,517 (M); expenditures, $375,143; qualifying distributions, $316,931; giving activities include $312,305 for 49 grants (high: $65,000; low: $100).
Purpose and activities: Giving primarily for education.
Fields of interest: Performing arts; Elementary/secondary education; Secondary school/education; University; Natural resources; Zoos/zoological societies; Cancer; Human services; Family services, counseling; Foundations (public); Roman Catholic agencies & churches.
Limitations: Applications not accepted. Giving primarily in WA. No grants to individuals.
Application information: Contributes only to pre-selected organizations.
Officers: Alison Wyckoff Milliman, Co-Chair.; Paul L. Wyckoff, Co-Chair.
Trustees: Theiline Wyckoff Cramer; Susan Wyckoff Pohl; Ann P. Wyckoff; Martha Wyckoff-Byrne; Sheila Wyckoff-Dickey.
EIN: 911817398

3390
The Greater Tacoma Community Foundation
1019 Pacific Ave.
P.O. Box 1995
Tacoma, WA 98401-1995 (253) 383-5622
Contact: Lynne Rumball, Prog. Off.
FAX: (253) 272-8099; E-mail: lrumball@gtcf.org;
URL: http://www.tacomafoundation.org

Incorporated in 1977 in WA.
Grantmaker type: Community foundation
Financial data (yr. ended 06/30/02): Assets, $37,283,207 (M); gifts received, $12,744,060; expenditures, $15,155,535; giving activities include $14,032,141 for 713 grants (high: $2,795,000; low: $30) and $13,940 for 13 grants to individuals (high: $1,313; low: $196).
Purpose and activities: The foundation improves the quality of life in the community by promoting private giving, maximizing donor benefits and grantmaking for the public good.
Fields of interest: Museums; Performing arts; Theater; Historic preservation/historical societies; Arts; Child development, education; Higher education; Adult/continuing education; Libraries/library science; Education; Natural resources; Environment; Hospitals (general); Health care; Substance abuse, services; Mental health/crisis services; Health organizations, association; AIDS; AIDS research; Food services; Housing/shelter, development; Recreation; Youth development, services; Human services; Children/youth, services; Child development, services; Family services; Hospices; Aging, centers/services; Homeless, human services; Community development; Voluntarism promotion; Government/public administration; Leadership development; Disabled; Aging; Economically disadvantaged; Homeless.
Types of support: General/operating support; Continuing support; Capital campaigns; Building/renovation; Equipment; Land acquisition; Emergency funds; Program development; Seed money; Technical assistance; Consulting services; Program-related investments/loans; Matching/challenge support.

Limitations: Giving limited to Pierce County, WA. No support for religious or political activities. No grants for annual campaigns, fellowships, seminars, meetings or travel, or publications, unless specified by donor.
Publications: Application guidelines, Annual report, Informational brochure (including application guidelines), Newsletter.
Application information: Application form available on Web site. Application form required.
   Initial approach: Letter of intent due 1 month prior to deadlines
   Copies of proposal: 2
   Deadline(s): Mar. 15, July 15, and Nov. 15
   Board meeting date(s): 5 times yearly
   Final notification: Within 3 months
Officers and Directors:* Tom Hosea,* Chair.; James Walton,* Vice-Chair.; Margy McGroarty, Pres.; James Brown,* Secy.; James P. Dawson,* Treas.; Richard S. DeVine; Wendy Gray; Tammis Greene; Linda Gutman; Dennis Hanberg; John S. Larsen; Mary Long; Claude A. Remy; Barbara Skinner; Terry Stone; Pamela Transue.
Number of staff: 4 full-time professional; 1 full-time support.
EIN: 911007459

3391
The Tamaki Foundation
4603 University Way N.E., Ste. 37
Seattle, WA 98105

Established in 1988 in WA.
Donor(s): Meriko Tamaki.
Grantmaker type: Independent foundation
Financial data (yr. ended 12/31/02): Assets, $3,273,198 (M); gifts received, $5,000; expenditures, $215,089; qualifying distributions, $191,781; giving activities include $190,211 for 8 grants (high: $73,936; low: $275).
Purpose and activities: Giving primarily for education and social services.
Fields of interest: Higher education; Environment, research; Human services; Roman Catholic agencies & churches.
Limitations: Giving on a national basis, with emphasis on CA.
Application information:
   Initial approach: Letter
   Deadline(s): None
Officers: Meriko Tamaki, Pres.; Fr. John Martin, V.P.; Kozo Yamamura, Secy.; John H. Hopkins, Treas.
EIN: 943099647

3392
Van Waters & Rogers Foundation
(formerly Univar Foundation)
P.O. Box 34325
Seattle, WA 98124-1325 (425) 889-3400
Contact: Nancy Johnson, Pres.

Established in 1967.
Donor(s): Van Waters & Rogers Inc., Vopak USA Inc.
Grantmaker type: Company-sponsored foundation
Financial data (yr. ended 12/31/01): Assets, $33 (M); gifts received, $386; expenditures, $96,124; qualifying distributions, $96,000; giving

activities include $96,000 for 28 grants (high: $5,000; low: $500).

Purpose and activities: Primary areas of giving include the arts, education, the environment, and human services.

Fields of interest: Arts; Education, fund raising; Higher education; Business school/education; Environment; Health care; Human services; Youth, services; Community development.

Types of support: Continuing support; Annual campaigns; Capital campaigns; Building/renovation; Emergency funds; Program development.

Limitations: Giving primarily in the Seattle, WA, area. No grants to individuals.

Application information: Application form not required.

Initial approach: Letter or telephone
Copies of proposal: 1
Board meeting date(s): Quarterly

Officer: Nancy Johnson, Pres.

Trustees: William A. Butler; Linda Holman; Gary Pruitt.

Number of staff: None.

EIN: 910826180

3393

Warm Foundation

(formerly Wayne M. Abramson Foundation)
204 W. Benton St.
Leavenworth, WA 98826
Contact: Leslie Hontou, V.P.

Established in 1980 in TX.

Donor(s): A.D. Abramson.‡

Grantmaker type: Independent foundation

Financial data (yr. ended 12/31/02): Assets, $1,006,052 (M); expenditures, $123,570; qualifying distributions, $115,685; giving activities include $115,000 for 2 grants (high: $100,000; low: $15,000).

Purpose and activities: Giving for substance abuse services, domestic violence programs and womens issues.

Fields of interest: Animal welfare; Substance abuse, prevention; Children/youth, services; Domestic violence; Women, centers/services.

Types of support: General/operating support; Continuing support; Building/renovation; Program development; Seed money; Technical assistance; Matching/challenge support.

Limitations: Giving primarily in CA and WA. No grants to individuals.

Publications: Informational brochure.

Application information:

Initial approach: Proposal
Deadline(s): June 1

Officers: Kim Tieken, Pres.; Lon Abramson, V.P.; Leslie Hontou, Secy.-Treas.

Director: Edith Abramson.

EIN: 760064293

3394

Washington Women's Foundation

1325 4th Ave.
Seattle, WA 98101 (206) 340-1710
Contact: Emily Parker, Deputy Exec. Dir.
FAX: (206) 340-1936; E-mail: info@wawomensfoundation.org; URL: http://www.wawomensfoundation.org

Established in 1995 in WA.

Grantmaker type: Public charity

Financial data (yr. ended 06/30/01): Revenue, $90,018; assets, $33,015; expenditures, $86,214.

Purpose and activities: Funding to charitable organizations primarily for projects that address at least one of the following criteria: responses to urgent and critical need; bold new ventures; and/or new approaches to time-worn problems.

Fields of interest: Arts; Education; Environment; Health care; Human services; Women.

Types of support: General/operating support; Capital campaigns.

Limitations: Giving limited to Seattle, WA. No support for organizations lacking 501(c)(3) designation. No grants for endowments.

Application information: See Web site for program information and guidelines.

Initial approach: Letter of inquiry
Deadline(s): Jan. 1

Officer and Directors:* Colleen S. Willoughby,* Pres.; Emily Parker, Deputy Exec. Dir.; Rhoda Altom; Judi Beck; Anne Farrell; Sue Lile Hunter; Faye Sarkowsky; Margaret Walker.

EIN: 911754933

3395

The Wellworth Foundation

11055 204th Ave. N.E.
Redmond, WA 98053

Established in 1997 in WA.

Donor(s): David J. Thacher, Nancy C. Thacher.

Grantmaker type: Independent foundation

Financial data (yr. ended 12/31/02): Assets, $2,300,674 (M); gifts received, $306,589; expenditures, $205,456; qualifying distributions, $202,120; giving activities include $201,335 for 21 grants (high: $60,000; low: $200).

Fields of interest: Higher education; Environment; Federated giving programs.

Limitations: Applications not accepted. Giving primarily in WA. No grants to individuals.

Application information: Contributes only to pre-selected organizations.

Trustees: David J. Thacher; Nancy C. Thacher.

EIN: 916438273

3396

Weyerhaeuser Company Foundation ▼

EC2-2A8
P.O. Box 9777
Federal Way, WA 98063-9777
(253) 924-3159
Contact: Elizabeth Crossman, Pres.
FAX: (253) 924-3658; URL: http://www.weyerhaeuser.com/citizenship/philanthropy/weyerfoundation.asp

Incorporated in 1948 in WA.

Donor(s): Weyerhaeuser Co.

Grantmaker type: Company-sponsored foundation

Financial data (yr. ended 12/31/02): Assets, $16,295,728 (M); gifts received, $16,601,000; expenditures, $8,846,930; qualifying distributions, $7,789,659; giving activities include $7,134,179 for 957+ grants (high: $226,780; low: $1,000; average: $1,000-$10,000) and $270,085 for employee matching gifts.

Purpose and activities: Grants are awarded for two purposes: to improve the quality of life in areas where Weyerhaeuser Co. has a major presence, and to increase understanding of the importance and sustainability of forests and the products they provide that meet human needs. Support also for employee-related scholarships administered by Scholarship America, Inc. and a matching gift program for higher education.

Fields of interest: Arts; Education, research; Elementary/secondary education; Elementary school/education; Higher education; Education; Waste management; Natural resources; Environment, forests; Environment; Human services; International affairs, goodwill promotion; Rural development; Community development; Federated giving programs.

Types of support: General/operating support; Capital campaigns; Building/renovation; Equipment; Land acquisition; Emergency funds; Program development; Conferences/seminars; Publication; Seed money; Curriculum development; Research; Technical assistance; Employee matching gifts; Employee-related scholarships.

Limitations: Giving limited to areas of company operations, especially AL, AR, GA, LA, MS, NC, southeastern OK, western OR, and western WA (including Tacoma, Seattle, and Federal Way); giving to national organizations in fields related to the forest products industry. No support for religious organizations for religious purposes, operating funds for United Way-supported organizations, political campaigns, or for the influence of legislation. No grants to individuals (except for employee-related scholarships), or for deficit financing, indirect costs, conferences outside the forest products industry, endowments, or memorials.

Publications: Biennial report (including application guidelines).

Application information: Requests received in the fall may be considered for the following year's budget. The foundation will acknowledge inquiries as soon as possible (normally within 30 days). If further consideration is warranted, additional information or a formal proposal may be requested. Personal meetings or site visits are normally arranged only for projects that have passed initial screening. Application form not required.

Initial approach: Letter
Copies of proposal: 1
Deadline(s): None
Board meeting date(s): Feb. and mid-year
Final notification: 2 to 3 months

Officers and Trustees:* Mack L. Hogans,* Chair.; Elizabeth Crossman, Pres.; Karen L. Veitenhans, V.P. and Secy.; Dick Taggart, Treas.; Steve Hillyard, Cont.; William R. Corbin; Dan Fulton; R.E. Hanson; James R. Keller; Susan M. Mersereau; Mick Onustock; Steven R. Rogel; George Weyerhaeuser, Jr.

Number of staff: None.

EIN: 916024225

Recent environmental and animal welfare grants:

3396-1 Agriculture and Forestry Education Foundation, Spokane, WA, $20,000. 2002.

3396-2 American Bird Conservancy, The Plains, VA, $10,000. 2002.

3396-3 American Forest Foundation, DC, $123,860. 2002.

3396-4 American Forest Foundation, DC, $25,000. 2002.

3396-5 California Resource Management Institute, Sacramento, CA, $10,400. 2002.

3396-6 Friends of Trees, Portland, Oregon, $25,000. 2002.

3396-7 Georgia Forestry Foundation, Norcross, GA, $100,000. 2002.

3396-8 Institute for Forest Biotechnology, Research Triangle Park, NC, $25,000. 2002.

3396-9 Mississippi Forestry Foundation, Jackson, MS, $20,000. 2002.

3396-10 Mountains to Sound Greenway Trust, Seattle, WA, $25,000. 2002.

3396-11 National Recycling Coalition, Alexandria, VA, $10,000. 2002.

3396-12 Nature Conservancy, Arlington, VA, $15,000. 2002.

3396-13 Nature Conservancy, Seattle, WA, $10,000. 2002.

3396-14 North Carolina Forestry Foundation, Raleigh, NC, $10,125. 2002.

3396-15 Oregon Zoo Foundation, Portland, Oregon, $10,000. 2002.

3396-16 Resources for the Future, DC, $50,000. 2002.

3396-17 San Joaquin River Parkway and Conservation Trust, Fresno, CA, $10,000. 2002.

3396-18 Trout Unlimited, Aberdeen, WA, $12,000. 2002.

3396-19 University of Washington, College of Forest Resources, Seattle, WA, $30,000. 2002.

3396-20 West Virginia University, Davis College of Agriculture, Forestry, and Consumer Sciences, Morgantown, WV, $22,500. 2002.

3396-21 World Forestry Congress, Quebec, Canada, $75,000. 2002.

3396-22 World Resources Institute, DC, $10,000. 2002.

3396-23 Yale University, School of Forestry and Environmental Studies, New Haven, CT, $50,000. 2002.

3397
Whatcom Community Foundation

119 Grand Ave., Ste. A
Bellingham, WA 98225 (360) 671-6463
Contact: Don Drake, Pres.
FAX: (360) 671-6437; E-mail:
wcf@whatcomcf.org; URL: http://whatcomcf.org

Established in 1996 in WA.
Grantmaker type: Community foundation
Financial data (yr. ended 06/30/02): Assets, $3,404,323 (M); gifts received, $504,701; expenditures, $500,510; giving activities include $195,711 for 112 grants (high: $19,411; low: $25; average: $100–$2,000).
Purpose and activities: Giving for the arts, education, the environment, youth, families, and community organizations. The foundation administers a donor-advised fund.
Fields of interest: Arts; Education; Environment; Children/youth, services; Family services; Foundations (community).
Types of support: General/operating support; Program development; Scholarship funds; Consulting services.
Limitations: Giving limited to Whatcom County, WA. No support for capital grants.

Publications: Application guidelines, Annual report, Grants list, Informational brochure, Newsletter.
Application information: Application form required.
  Initial approach: Telephone
  Copies of proposal: 7
  Deadline(s): Feb. 1 and Sept. 1
  Board meeting date(s): 3rd Wed. of each month
  Final notification: 6 weeks after application deadline
Officers and Directors:* Tom Hunter, Chair.; Mary Boire, Vice-Chair.; Don Drake,* Pres.; Paul Tholfsen,* Treas.; Randy Bode; Sue Cole; Paul B. Hanson; Marge Laidlow; D.C. Morse; Charles Self; Sue Sharpe; Tom Thornton; Sue Webber.
Number of staff: 1 full-time professional; 2 part-time support.
EIN: 911726410

3398
The Wilburforce Foundation ▼

3601 Fremont Ave. N., Ste. 304
Seattle, WA 98103 (206) 632-2325
Contact: Timothy Greyhavens, Exec. Dir.
Additional tel.: (800) 201-0148 (Seattle office), (800) 317-8180 (Montana office); FAX: (206) 632-2326; E-mail: grants@wilburforce.org; URL: http://www.wilburforce.org

Established in 1990 in WA.
Grantmaker type: Independent foundation
Financial data (yr. ended 12/31/01): Assets, $16,713,670 (M); expenditures, $5,821,834; qualifying distributions, $5,785,980; giving activities include $4,905,860 for 185 grants (high: $175,000; low: $500; average: $5,000–$50,000).
Purpose and activities: The foundation is dedicated to protecting nature's richness and diversity through funding programs that help preserve our remaining wild places.
Fields of interest: Natural resources; Environment.
International interests: Canada.
Types of support: General/operating support; Capital campaigns; Equipment; Program development; Seed money; Technical assistance; Consulting services; Matching/challenge support.
Limitations: Giving primarily in western U.S. and western Canada, particularly AK, AZ, NM, NV, OR, UT, WA, British Columbia, and the Yellowstone to Yukon region of U.S.-Canada. No support for family planning, health, medical, clinical, social service or AIDS awareness programs, schools or universities, or governmental agencies. No grants to individuals, or for fellowships or scholarships, endowment funds, operating budgets, or deficit financing or indirect costs; no loans.
Application information: Application form required.
  Initial approach: 1- to 2-page letter or telephone
  Copies of proposal: 1
  Deadline(s): Given upon invitation
  Board meeting date(s): Spring, summer, and fall
  Final notification: 4 months
Officers and Directors:* Rosanna Letwin,* Chair.; James G. Letwin,* Pres.; Gary Austin,

Secy.; Tim Greyhavens, Exec. Dir.; William S. Holder; Stephanie Nichols-Young.
Number of staff: 9 full-time professional.
EIN: 943137894
Recent environmental and animal welfare grants:

3398-1 Alaska Center for the Environment, Anchorage, AK, $30,000. For membership and capacity building. 2001.

3398-2 Alaska Conservation Alliance, Anchorage, AK, $20,000. For general support. 2001.

3398-3 Alaska Wilderness League, DC, $50,000. For general support. 2001.

3398-4 Alberta Wilderness Association, Calgary, Canada, $25,000. For Wildcanada.net. 2001.

3398-5 Alliance for the Wild Rockies, Missoula, MT, $30,000. For general support. 2001.

3398-6 American Wildlands, Bozeman, MT, $35,000. For Corridors of Life outreach program. 2001.

3398-7 American Wildlands, Bozeman, MT, $16,000. For assessing river system integrity. 2001.

3398-8 Audubon Society, National, New York, NY, $15,000. For project, Conservation Strategy for Western Arctic Alaska. 2001.

3398-9 British Columbia Spaces for Nature, Gibsons, Canada, $35,000. For Conservation Forest program. 2001.

3398-10 Canadian Parks and Wilderness Society, Ottawa, Canada, $120,000. For Yellowstone to Yukon (Y2Y) initiative in Alberta and British Columbia and technical assistance. 2001.

3398-11 Canadian Parks and Wilderness Society, Ottawa, Canada, $29,000. For security analysis for grizzly bear. 2001.

3398-12 Canadian Parks and Wilderness Society, Ottawa, Canada, $25,000. For Geographic Information Systems (GIS) modeling of animal corridors. 2001.

3398-13 Castle-Crown Wilderness Coalition, Pincher Creek, Canada, $11,500. For general support. 2001.

3398-14 Center for Science in Public Participation, Bozeman, MT, $15,000. For Alaska Technical Support Project. 2001.

3398-15 Citizens for a Better Flathead, Kalispell, MT, $20,000. For CommUnity Campaign. 2001.

3398-16 Conservation Biology Institute, Corvallis, Oregon, $25,000. For Web site updates and audit. 2001.

3398-17 Craighead Environmental Research Institute, Moose, WY, $15,000. For CERI/Beringia South Geographic Information Systems (GIS) Research. 2001.

3398-18 David Suzuki Foundation, Vancouver, Canada, $120,000. For Pacific Salmon Forests Project. 2001.

3398-19 Defenders of Wildlife, DC, $17,000. For wolf habitat analysis. 2001.

3398-20 Earthjustice Legal Defense Fund, Oakland, CA, $75,000. For Public Lands Protection Campaign. 2001.

3398-21 East Kootenay Environmental Society, Kimberley, Canada, $40,000. For implementation of Conservation Biology Principles for British Columbia. 2001.

3398-22 East Kootenay Environmental Society, Kimberley, Canada, $28,000. For Purcell Grizzly Bear/DNA Project. 2001.

3398-23 East Kootenay Environmental Society, Kimberley, Canada, $13,000. To increase technical capacity. 2001.

3398-24 Ecology Center, Missoula, MT, $10,000. For general support. 2001.

3398-25 Ecotrust Canada, Vancouver, Canada, $40,000. For Sustaining the Tree of Life: A Heiltsuk Cedar Strategy. 2001.

3398-26 Environmental Media Services, DC, $45,000. For Rapid Response Media Outreach. 2001.

3398-27 Forest Conservation Council, Santa Fe, NM, $35,000. For Roadless Area and Timber Safe Challenges. 2001.

3398-28 Forest Guardians, Santa Fe, NM, $20,000. For Geographic Information Systems (GIS) staff position. 2001.

3398-29 Forest Service Employees for Environmental Ethics, Eugene, Oregon, $45,000. For creation of British Columbia FSEEE. 2001.

3398-30 Friends of Nevada Wilderness, Las Vegas, NV, $41,000. For general support. 2001.

3398-31 Friends of the Clearwater, Moscow, ID, $10,000. For general support. 2001.

3398-32 Gifford Pinchot Task Force, Vancouver, WA, $15,000. For general support. 2001.

3398-33 Glacier Institute, Kalispell, MT, $17,000. For Crown of the Continent Ecosystem Education Consortium. 2001.

3398-34 Grand Canyon Trust, Flagstaff, AZ, $35,000. For Monument Management and Reducing Habitat Fragmentation projects. 2001.

3398-35 Grand Canyon Wildlands Council, Flagstaff, AZ, $25,000. For general support. 2001.

3398-36 Great Basin Mine Watch, Reno, NV, $12,000. For Pristine Lands Protection Project. 2001.

3398-37 Great Bear Foundation of Montana, Bozeman, MT, $22,000. For connectivity studies in Kakwa Provincial Park. 2001.

3398-38 Greater Yellowstone Coalition, Bozeman, MT, $50,000. For Anchoring Yellowstone to Yukon (Y2Y) at Yellowstone. 2001.

3398-39 Green Fire Productions, Eugene, Oregon, $25,000. For general support. 2001.

3398-40 Greenpeace Fund, DC, $30,000. For Consolidating the Win in British Columbia. 2001.

3398-41 Hells Canyon Preservation Council, Joseph, Oregon, $30,000. For general support. 2001.

3398-42 Hornocker Wildlife Institute, Bozeman, MT, $24,000. For project, Wolverine Ecology in Northern Rockies. 2001.

3398-43 Idaho Conservation League, Boise, ID, $40,000. For Yellowstone to Yukon (Y2Y) Wild Forest Defense. 2001.

3398-44 Institute for Conservation Leadership, Takoma Park, MD, $45,000. For capacity development for Crown of the Continent. 2001.

3398-45 Kettle Range Conservation Group, Republic, WA, $35,000. For Wild Washington Campaign. 2001.

3398-46 Land Trust Alliance, DC, $150,000. For Northern Rockies Initiative. 2001.

3398-47 Land Trust Alliance, DC, $150,000. For Western Programs and Regrant Program. 2001.

3398-48 Land Trust Alliance, DC, $150,000. For Western Programs and Regrant Program. 2001.

3398-49 Lands Council, Spokane, WA, $15,000. For Selkirks Project. 2001.

3398-50 Leavenworth Audubon Adopt-A-Forest, Peshastin, WA, $10,000. For Adopt-A-Roadless Area program in Wenatchee National Forest. 2001.

3398-51 Mineral Policy Center, DC, $50,000. For general support. 2001.

3398-52 Mineral Policy Center, DC, $25,000. For Stop the Rollbacks Campaign. 2001.

3398-53 Montana Environmental Information Center, Helena, MT, $23,000. For general support. 2001.

3398-54 Montana Environmental Information Center, Helena, MT, $10,000. For Montana Old Growth Project. 2001.

3398-55 Montana Wilderness Association, Helena, MT, $35,000. For Crown of the Continent Transboundary Organizing Campaign. 2001.

3398-56 National Fish and Wildlife Foundation, DC, $10,000. For Grizzly Monitoring in Yellowstone. 2001.

3398-57 National Parks Conservation Association, DC, $50,000. For Crown of the Continent Campaign. 2001.

3398-58 National Parks Conservation Association, DC, $20,000. For Greater Yellowstone Business Council. 2001.

3398-59 Nature Conservancy, Arlington, VA, $100,000. To build capacity to achieve large-scale conservation in key areas in Yellowstone to Yukon (Y2Y) region: Swan/Blackfoot Valleys, North Fork of the Flathead River, and Centennial Valley. 2001.

3398-60 New Mexico Wilderness Alliance, Albuquerque, NM, $45,000. For general support. 2001.

3398-61 New Mexico Wilderness Alliance, Albuquerque, NM, $15,000. For technology upgrade. 2001.

3398-62 Northern Alaska Environmental Center, Fairbanks, AK, $40,000. For Arctic Campaign. 2001.

3398-63 Northern Rockies Conservation Cooperative, Jackson, WY, $10,000. For general support. 2001.

3398-64 Northwest Ecosystem Alliance, Bellingham, WA, $30,000. For Watchdogging the National Forests of Washington. 2001.

3398-65 ONE/Northwest, Seattle, WA, $50,000. For general support. 2001.

3398-66 Oregon League of Conservation Voters Education Fund, Portland, Oregon, $15,000. For training program. 2001.

3398-67 Oregon Natural Desert Association, Bend, Oregon, $25,000. For Wildlands ReSearch and Rescue project. 2001.

3398-68 Oregon Natural Resources Council Fund, Portland, Oregon, $50,000. For general support to evaluate pilot project. 2001.

3398-69 Oregon Student Public Interest Research Group, Portland, Oregon, $30,000. For Oregon Wilds Project. 2001.

3398-70 Pacific Crest Biodiversity Project, Seattle, WA, $22,750. For Northwest Ancient Forests Campaign. 2001.

3398-71 Pacific Rivers Council, Eugene, Oregon, $30,000. For project, Forest Service Roads Policy: Next Steps. 2001.

3398-72 Predator Conservation Alliance, Bozeman, MT, $30,000. For Forest Predator Ecosystem Protection Program. 2001.

3398-73 Predator Conservation Alliance, Bozeman, MT, $21,000. For project on cougar pathogens in Central Rockies Corridor. 2001.

3398-74 Predator Conservation Alliance, Bozeman, MT, $10,000. For capacity-building, including computers and Web site. 2001.

3398-75 Predator Conservation Alliance, Bozeman, MT, $10,000. For grizzly bear conservation program. 2001.

3398-76 Raincoast Conservation Foundation, Canada, $30,000. For Coast Wolf Research Project. 2001.

3398-77 Red Rock Forests, Moab, UT, $10,000. For general support. 2001.

3398-78 Round River Conservation Studies, Salt Lake City, UT, $20,000. For Taku River Tlingit Wildlife Conservation Project. 2001.

3398-79 Selkirk-Priest Basin Association, Coolin, ID, $20,000. For Selkirk Mountains Conservation Area Design. 2001.

3398-80 Selkirk-Priest Basin Association, Coolin, ID, $10,000. For general support. 2001.

3398-81 Sierra Club Foundation, San Francisco, CA, $40,000. For Arctic Wilderness Defense Campaign. 2001.

3398-82 Sierra Club of British Columbia Foundation, Victoria, Canada, $50,000. For general support. 2001.

3398-83 Sierra Club of British Columbia Foundation, Victoria, Canada, $40,000. For Environmental Mining Council of British Columbia. 2001.

3398-84 Sierra Club of British Columbia Foundation, Victoria, Canada, $15,000. For Wilderness Protection in Fraiser Headwaters Region. 2001.

3398-85 Sierra Club of British Columbia Foundation, Victoria, Canada, $12,000. For Northern Rockies Regional Coordinator. 2001.

3398-86 Sierra Legal Defence Fund, Vancouver, Canada, $10,000. For EAGLE (Environmental-Aboriginal Guardianship through Law) program. 2001.

3398-87 Siskiyou Regional Educational Project, Cave Junction, Oregon, $30,000. For Wild Siskiyou Program. 2001.

3398-88 Sky Island Alliance, Tucson, AZ, $50,000. For Rewilding Program. 2001.

3398-89 Soda Mountain Wilderness Council, Ashland, Oregon, $20,000. For general support. 2001.

3398-90 Sonoran Institute, Tucson, AZ, $40,000. For project on Community Stewardship in the Canadian Rockies. 2001.

3398-91 Southeast Alaska Conservation Council, Juneau, AK, $30,000. For general support. 2001.

3398-92 Southern Utah Wilderness Alliance, Salt Lake City, UT, $50,000. For America Redrock Wilderness Campaign. 2001.

3398-93 Southwest Forest Alliance, Flagstaff, AZ, $20,000. For Kaibab Plateau Old Growth Campaign. 2001.

3398-94 Training Resources for the Environmental Community, Vashon, WA, $175,000. For general support. 2001.

3398-95 Training Resources for the Environmental Community, Vashon, WA, $175,000. For general support. 2001.

3398-96 Training Resources for the Environmental Community, Vashon, WA, $50,000. For Southwest capacity-building. 2001.

3398-97 Trustees for Alaska, Anchorage, AK, $50,000. For project, Protecting America's Arctic. 2001.

3398-98 Umpqua Watersheds, Roseburg, Oregon, $20,000. For general support. 2001.

3398-99 United States Public Interest Research Group Education Fund, DC, $40,000. For Arctic Refuge Campaign. 2001.

3398-100 Utah Environmental Congress, Salt Lake City, UT, $20,000. For Forest Monitoring Program. 2001.

3398-101 Utah Wilderness Coalition, Salt Lake City, UT, $25,000. For general support. 2001.

3398-102 Valhalla Wilderness Society, New Denver, Canada, $17,500. For capacity-building for Spirit Bear Program. 2001.

3398-103 Washington Environmental Alliance for Voter Education, Seattle, WA, $40,000. For general support. 2001.

3398-104 Washington Wilderness Coalition, Seattle, WA, $30,000. For Wild Washington Campaign. 2001.

3398-105 Washington Wilderness Coalition, Seattle, WA, $25,000. For Adopt-A-Wilderness Network. 2001.

3398-106 Washington Wildlife and Recreation Foundation, Seattle, WA, $20,000. For Great Outdoors Washington 2010 outreach campaign. 2001.

3398-107 Western Environmental Law Center, Eugene, Oregon, $30,000. For Wild and Scenic Rivers Initiative. 2001.

3398-108 Western Land Exchange Project, Seattle, WA, $35,000. For general support. 2001.

3398-109 Western Resource Advocates, Boulder, CO, $33,800. For Utah Grazing Policy Reform. 2001.

3398-110 Western Resource Advocates, Boulder, CO, $25,000. For Western Mining Action Project. 2001.

3398-111 Wilderness Society, DC, $100,000. For Alaska Coalition on the Arctic National Wildlife Refuge. 2001.

3398-112 Wilderness Society, DC, $40,000. For Wilderness Support Center. 2001.

3398-113 Wilderness Society, DC, $40,000. For project, Protecting Wildlands in the Northern Rockies. 2001.

3398-114 Wildlands Center for Preventing Roads, Missoula, MT, $30,000. For Motorized Recreation Program. 2001.

3398-115 Wildlands Center for Preventing Roads, Missoula, MT, $15,000. For Road Removal Research. 2001.

3398-116 Wildlands Project, Richmond, VT, $40,000. For general support and capacity-building for Nevada Wilderness Project. 2001.

3398-117 Wildlands Project, Richmond, VT, $20,000. For general support for Wild Utah Project. 2001.

3398-118 Wildlife Conservation Society, Bronx, NY, $125,000. For Crowsnest Pass Carnivore Study. 2001.

3398-119 Wildlife Trust, Greenwich, CT, $30,000. For Yellowstone to Yukon (Y2Y) Wildlife Health Program. 2001.

3398-120 Wolf Awareness, Canmore, Canada, $15,000. For wildlife corridors around Canmore. 2001.

3398-121 Yellowstone to Yukon Conservation Initiative, Canmore, Canada, $150,000. For general support. 2001.

3398-122 Yellowstone to Yukon Conservation Initiative, Canmore, Canada, $38,000. For capacity-building for outreach program. 2001.

3398-123 Yellowstone to Yukon Conservation Initiative, Canmore, Canada, $28,000. For Conservation Science Symposium. 2001.

3398-124 Yukon Conservation Society, Whitehorse, Canada, $10,000. For general support. 2001.

3399
Howard S. Wright Family Foundation
(formerly Howard S. Wright Foundation)
1264 Eastlake Ave. E.
Seattle, WA 98102
Contact: Sally S. Wright, Pres.

Established in 1984 in WA.
Donor(s): Howard S. Wright.‡
Grantmaker type: Independent foundation
Financial data (yr. ended 12/31/01): Assets, $8,036,410 (M); expenditures, $507,358; qualifying distributions, $408,326; giving activities include $400,000 for 26 grants (high: $100,000; low: $500; average: $1,000–$10,000).
Purpose and activities: Primary areas of interest include the arts, education, and health.
Fields of interest: Arts; Higher education; Education; Environment; Health care; Health organizations, association; Christian agencies & churches.
Types of support: Annual campaigns; Capital campaigns; Building/renovation; Endowments.
Limitations: Applications not accepted. Giving primarily in the Pacific Northwest, with emphasis on Seattle, WA. No grants to individuals.
Application information: Unsolicited requests for funds not accepted.
Board meeting date(s): Quarterly
Officers and Directors:* Sally S. Wright,* Pres.; Katherine A. Janeway,* Treas.; Theiline W. Rolfe; Korynne H. Wright.
EIN: 911276047

3400
Beckley Area Foundation, Inc.
129 Main St., Ste. 203
Beckley, WV 25801 (304) 253-3806
Contact: Chair., Grants Comm.
FAX: (304) 253-7304; E-mail: funds@beckleyareafoundation.com; URL: http://beckleyareafoundation.com/

Established in 1985 in WV.
Donor(s): Dr. Thomas Walker Memorial Health Foundation.
Grantmaker type: Community foundation
Financial data (yr. ended 03/31/03): Assets, $12,961,346 (M); gifts received, $1,657,768; expenditures, $456,042; giving activities include $298,091 for 250 grants (high: $10,000; low: $300).
Purpose and activities: The foundation focuses its grantmaking on the arts, health and human services, public recreation, education, and civic beautification. The foundation administers a donor-advised fund.
Fields of interest: Arts; Education; Environment, beautification programs; Health organizations, association; Recreation; Human services; Community development, neighborhood development.
Types of support: Building/renovation; Equipment; Program development; Conferences/seminars; Seed money; Scholarship funds; Technical assistance; Consulting services; Matching/challenge support.
Limitations: Giving limited to the Beckley and Raleigh County, WV, area. No support for sectarian religious programs. No grants for operating budgets, annual campaigns, or endowments.
Publications: Application guidelines, Annual report, Financial statement, Grants list, Informational brochure, Newsletter, Occasional report.
Application information: See foundation Web site for application requirements and guidelines. Application form required.
Initial approach: Letter (no more than 3 pages)
Copies of proposal: 1
Deadline(s): Dec. 15
Board meeting date(s): Sept., Dec., Mar., and June
Final notification: Mar.
Officers: Ned Eller, Pres.; Roslyn Clark-Payne, V.P.; Nancy Kissinger, Secy.; Dan Calfee, Treas.; Susan S. Landis, Exec. Dir.
Number of staff: 1 full-time support; 1 part-time support.
EIN: 311125328

3401
Brier Patch Charitable Trust
c/o Alice Ann W. Mills
P.O. Box T
Shepherdstown, WV 25443-1113

Established in 1996 in IN.
Donor(s): Alice Ann W. Mills, Howard S. Mills, Jr.

Grantmaker type: Independent foundation
Financial data (yr. ended 09/30/02): Assets, $509,061 (M); expenditures, $96,834; qualifying distributions, $96,729; giving activities include $96,500 for 5 grants (high: $75,000; low: $500).
Fields of interest: Historic preservation/historical societies; Higher education; Environmental education.
Types of support: General/operating support.
Limitations: Applications not accepted. Giving primarily in IN and WV. No grants to individuals.
Application information: Contributes only to pre-selected organizations.
Trustees: Alice Ann W. Mills; Howard S. Mills.
EIN: 352000005

3402
The Greater Kanawha Valley Foundation
Huntington Sq., Ste. 1600
900 Lee St. E.
Charleston, WV 25301 (304) 346-3620
Contact: Rebecca C. Cain
FAX: (304) 346-3640; E-mail: tgkvf@tgkvf.org; URL: http://www.tgkvf.org

Established in 1962 in WV.
Grantmaker type: Community foundation
Financial data (yr. ended 12/31/02): Assets, $82,588,315 (M); expenditures, $5,273,815; giving activities include $3,430,433 for grants and $880,594 for grants to individuals.
Purpose and activities: Primary areas of interest include higher and other education, youth, recreation, the arts, and the social sciences. Support also for child welfare and family services, women, housing, the medical sciences, including research on AIDS, heart disease, and cancer, ecology and the environment, and community development programs. The foundation administers a donor-advised fund.
Fields of interest: Museums; Performing arts; Dance; Humanities; Historic preservation/historical societies; Arts; Early childhood education; Elementary school/education; Higher education; Libraries/library science; Education; Natural resources; Environment; Dental care; Nursing care; Health care; Substance abuse, services; Housing/shelter, development; Recreation; Human services; Children/youth, services; Family services; Hospices; Women, centers/services; Homeless, human services; Community development; Social sciences; Disabled; Women; Homeless.
Types of support: General/operating support; Continuing support; Capital campaigns; Building/renovation; Equipment; Emergency funds; Program development; Publication; Seed money; Scholarship funds; Research; Technical assistance; Program evaluation; Scholarships—to individuals; Matching/challenge support.
Limitations: Giving limited to the greater Kanawha Valley, WV, area, except scholarships which are limited to residents of WV. No support for religious, sectarian programs, or video programs. No grants to individuals (except for designated scholarship funds); no loans; no support for annual campaigns, or uniforms.
Publications: Application guidelines, Annual report (including application guidelines),

Financial statement, Grants list, Informational brochure, Occasional report.
Application information: Application available on foundation Web site. Application form required.
Initial approach: Letter, telephone, FAX, or E-mail
Copies of proposal: 3
Deadline(s): Varies; contact foundation for information; Feb. 15 for scholarships
Board meeting date(s): Quarterly, usually in Mar., June, Sept., and Dec.
Final notification: Immediately after board action
Officers and Trustees:* T. Randolph Cox,* Chair.; Mary Anne Michael,* Vice-Chair.; Lesley A. Russo, Secy.; Hazo Carter; Stephan R. Crislip; Kim Foster; Rebecca B. Goldman; Judith N. McJunkin; Rick Morgan; David Rollins; Barbara Rose; Arthur Standish.
Advisory Committee: Paul Arbogast; G. Thomas Battle; Frederick H. Belden, Jr.; Charles L. Capito, Jr.; Elsie P. Carter; William D. Chambers; Elizabeth E. Chilton; William M. Davis; Deborah A. Faber; Charles R. McElwee; Thomas N. McJunkin; Harry Moore; William E. Mullett, Ph.D.; Sandra Murphy; Virginia Rugeley; Mark H. Schaul; Dolly Sherwood; K. Richard C. Sinclair; Olivia R. Singleton; Louis B. Southworth; L. Newton Thomas, Jr.; Adeline J. Voorhees.
Trustee Banks: Bank One, West Virginia, N.A.; City National Bank of Charleston; The Huntington National Bank; United National Bank; WesBanco Bank, Inc.; BB&T.
Number of staff: 8 full-time professional; 2 part-time support.
EIN: 556024430

3403
Parkersburg Area Community Foundation
501 Avery St.
P.O. Box 1762
Parkersburg, WV 26102-1762 (304) 428-4438
Contact: Judy Sjostedt, Exec. Dir.
Toll-free tel.: 1-866-428-4438; FAX: (304) 428-1200; E-mail: info@pacfwv.com; URL: http://www.pacfwv.com

Established in 1963 in WV.
Donor(s): Albert Wolfe,‡ The Keystone Foundation, members of the Wolfe family.
Grantmaker type: Community foundation
Financial data (yr. ended 06/30/02): Assets, $9,234,029 (M); gifts received, $1,372,697; expenditures, $864,479; giving activities include $395,690 for grants (average: $500–$5,000) and $202,805 for 195 grants to individuals (average: $80–$5,000).
Purpose and activities: Support for programs leading toward the improvement or fulfillment of charitable, educational, cultural, health, and welfare activities, including direct human services and scholarships to individuals. The foundation administers donor-advised funds.
Fields of interest: Museums; Historic preservation/historical societies; Arts; Child development, education; Higher education; Adult education—literacy, basic skills & GED; Libraries/library science; Reading; Education; Health care; Animal welfare; Mental health/crisis services; Health organizations, association; Human services; Children/youth,

services; Child development, services; Family services; Community development; Disabled.
Types of support: Building/renovation; Equipment; Emergency funds; Program development; Seed money; Scholarship funds; Scholarships—to individuals; Matching/challenge support; Student loans—to individuals.
Limitations: Giving limited to the Mid-Ohio Valley communities of Calhoun, Doddridge, Gilmer, Wirt, Wood, Jackson, Pleasants, Ritchie, and Roane counties, WV, and Washington County, OH. No grants for travel, meetings, seminars, conferences, student exchange programs, annual campaigns, endowment funds, operating budgets, debt reduction, or maintenance needs.
Publications: Application guidelines, Annual report, Informational brochure, Newsletter.
Application information: Application form required.
Initial approach: Letter, E-mail, telephone, or see Web site for guidelines
Copies of proposal: 10
Deadline(s): Mar. 1 and Sept. 1 for local grants; Apr. 1 for the Ruth Hornbrook Memorial Fund
Board meeting date(s): 3rd Fri. in Jan., Mar., May, Sept., and Nov.
Final notification: May/Nov.; will consider emergency grants at other times
Officers and Governors:* Barbara N. Fish, Chair.; Walt Auvil, Vice-Chair.; Judy Sjostedt,* Exec. Dir.; and 15 additional members.
Trustee Banks: BB&T; Peoples Bank; United National Bank; WesBanco Bank, Inc.
Number of staff: 2 full-time professional; 2 part-time professional; 1 full-time support.
EIN: 556027764

WISCONSIN

3404
Allerton Gardens Trust
c/o Bank One Trust Co., N.A.
P.O. Box 1308
Milwaukee, WI 53201

Donor(s): John Wyatt Gregg Allerton.‡
Grantmaker type: Independent foundation
Financial data (yr. ended 04/30/02): Assets, $25,039,359 (M); expenditures, $1,166,588; qualifying distributions, $1,014,903; giving activities include $967,878 for 1 grant.
Fields of interest: Botanical gardens.
Limitations: Applications not accepted. Giving primarily in HI. No grants to individuals.
Application information: Contributes only to pre-selected organizations.
Trustee: Bank One, N.A.
EIN: 366836626

3405
Jacqueline G. Archer Charitable Trust
c/o Bank One Trust Co., N.A.
P.O. Box 1308
Milwaukee, WI 53201

Established in 2002 in CO.
Grantmaker type: Independent foundation
Financial data (yr. ended 12/31/02): Assets,
$13,345,947 (M); gifts received, $14,996,048;
expenditures, $190,481; qualifying distributions,
$170,144; giving activities include $163,275 for
51 grants (high: $29,097; low: $178).
Fields of interest: Education; Animal welfare;
Youth development, services; Human services;
Christian agencies & churches.
Limitations: Applications not accepted. Giving
primarily in CO. No grants to individuals.
Application information: Contributes only to
pre-selected organizations.
Trustee: Bank One Trust Co., N.A.
EIN: 686218949

3406
Norman Bassett Foundation - Wisconsin
P.O. Box 3037
Madison, WI 53704 (608) 242-5265
Contact: J. Reed Coleman, Pres.
FAX: (608) 242-5320; E-mail:
jscott@madison-kipp.com

Established in 1954 in WI.
Grantmaker type: Independent foundation
Financial data (yr. ended 03/31/02): Assets,
$2,319,904 (M); expenditures, $528,273;
qualifying distributions, $501,953; giving
activities include $500,000 for 54 grants (high:
$50,000; low: $500; average: $500–$50,000).
Purpose and activities: Giving primarily for the
arts, education, environment and human
services.
Fields of interest: Museums; Theater; Orchestra
(symphony); Arts; Higher education; Education;
Natural resources; Environment; Youth
development, services; Human services;
Children/youth, services; Community
development, neighborhood development;
Aging.
Types of support: General/operating support;
Continuing support; Emergency funds;
Professorships; Seed money; Research.
Limitations: Giving primarily in Madison and
Dane County, WI. No grants to individuals.
Publications: Financial statement.
Application information: Application form not
required.
  Initial approach: Letter
  Copies of proposal: 5
  Deadline(s): None
  Board meeting date(s): Quarterly
Officers: J. Reed Coleman, Pres.; Thomas
Ragatz, Secy.; Thomas R. Johnson, Treas.
Board Member: Milton McPike.
Number of staff: None.
EIN: 396043890

3407
Lucy & Emily Beasley Charitable Trust
c/o Bank One Trust Co., N.A.
P.O. Box 1308
Milwaukee, WI 53201
Contact: Thomas D. Barsody
Application address: 50 S. Main St., Akron, OH
44308

Established in 1981.
Donor(s): Robert P. Beasley Trust.
Grantmaker type: Independent foundation

Financial data (yr. ended 09/30/02): Assets,
$6,685,794 (M); gifts received, $49,680;
expenditures, $458,767; qualifying distributions,
$415,409; giving activities include $403,000 for
17 grants (high: $75,000; low: $2,000).
Purpose and activities: Giving primarily for
education.
Fields of interest: Education; Zoos/zoological
societies; Youth development, scouting agencies
(general); Human services; Christian agencies &
churches.
Limitations: Giving primarily in Akron, OH.
Application information:
  Initial approach: Letter
  Deadline(s): None
Advisory Committee: Howard W. Cable, Jr.;
Robert E. Hissong; A. Russell Smith.
Trustee: Bank One, N.A.
EIN: 341350747

3408
Bleser Family Foundation, Inc.
P.O. Box 328
Shawano, WI 54166

Established in 1986 in WI.
Donor(s): Clarence P. Bleser.‡
Grantmaker type: Independent foundation
Financial data (yr. ended 12/31/02): Assets,
$25,136,729 (M); gifts received, $283,288;
expenditures, $1,654,004; qualifying
distributions, $1,294,129; giving activities
include $1,288,000 for 27 grants (high:
$500,000; low: $500).
Fields of interest: Higher education; Education;
Environment; Health organizations, association;
Human services.
Limitations: Applications not accepted. Giving
primarily in WI. No grants to individuals.
Application information: Contributes only to
pre-selected organizations.
Officers and Directors:* Mary B. Hayes,* Pres.;
Carol A. Bleser,* V.P. and Secy.; James F. Bleser,*
Treas.
EIN: 391585269

3409
Eugenie Mayer Bolz Family Foundation
P.O. Box 8100
Madison, WI 53708-8100 (608) 257-6761

Established in 1976 in WI and IL.
Donor(s): Eugenie M. Bolz, Eugenie M. Bolz
Charitable Lead Trust.
Grantmaker type: Independent foundation
Financial data (yr. ended 12/31/01): Assets,
$6,257,018 (M); gifts received, $421,700;
expenditures, $1,452,146; qualifying
distributions, $1,385,547; giving activities
include $1,384,100 for 48 grants (high:
$421,700; low: $1,000).
Purpose and activities: Giving primarily to arts
organizations; some support also for higher
education and social services.
Fields of interest: Museums; Arts; Higher
education; Natural resources; Human services;
Children/youth, services.
Types of support: General/operating support.
Limitations: Applications not accepted. Giving
primarily in Madison, WI. No grants to
individuals.

Application information: Contributes only to
pre-selected organizations.
Officers: Robert M. Bolz, Pres.; Julia M. Bolz,
V.P.; Sara L. Bolz, V.P.; John A. Bolz, Secy.-Treas.
EIN: 237428561

3410
The Brico Fund, Inc.
205 E. Wisconsin Ave., Ste. 200
Milwaukee, WI 53202 (414) 272-2747
Contact: Anne E. Summers, Exec. Dir.
FAX: (414) 272-2036; E-mail:
bricofund@bricofund.org; URL: http://
www.bricofund.org/

Established in 1989 in WI.
Donor(s): Lynde B. Uihlein.
Grantmaker type: Independent foundation
Financial data (yr. ended 12/31/02): Assets,
$6,717,766 (M); gifts received, $4,235,000;
expenditures, $2,772,793; qualifying
distributions, $2,648,371; giving activities
include $2,648,371 for 51 grants (high:
$500,000; low: $3,000; average:
$3,000–$500,000).
Purpose and activities: The foundation supports
programs for women and girls that focus on
reproductive rights, leadership skills and
advocacy, and opportunities. The foundation
also funds targeted environmental programs,
and programs designed to promote a just and
equitable society. Brico seeks to encourage
innovators by supporting pioneering approaches
in a range of program areas; these grants are
made to nourish the creative spirit in all of its
manifestations.
Fields of interest: Environment, water resources;
Reproductive health; Community development,
equal rights; Women.
Types of support: General/operating support;
Continuing support; Annual campaigns; Capital
campaigns; Building/renovation; Endowments;
Program development; Seed money; Research;
Technical assistance; Matching/challenge
support.
Limitations: Giving primarily in southeastern
WI. No support for religious activities,
disease-specific programs, educational, medical,
or zoological institutions or media projects. No
grants to individuals, or for
conferences/meetings.
Publications: Application guidelines, Program
policy statement.
Application information: Application form
required.
  Initial approach: Letter/Application
  Copies of proposal: 1
  Deadline(s): Jan. 15 and Aug. 15
  Board meeting date(s): May and Nov.
  Final notification: June and Dec.
Officers and Directors:* Lynde B. Uihlein,*
Pres. and Treas.; Sue Hitler, V.P.; Miriam
Reading, Secy.; Sarah O. Zimmerman.
Number of staff: 2 full-time professional.
EIN: 391656190

3411
Cavaliere Foundation, Inc.
1716 Jefferson St.
Madison, WI 53711
Contact: James A. Knight, Dir.
Application address: 211 S. Patterson St.,
Madison, WI 53703, tel.: (608) 260-9500

Established in 1999 in WI.
Donor(s): James A. Knight, Jr.
Grantmaker type: Independent foundation
Financial data (yr. ended 12/31/01): Assets,
$5,442,372 (M); expenditures, $257,401;
qualifying distributions, $219,937; giving
activities include $193,225 for 10 grants (high:
$35,000; low: $2,000).
Fields of interest: Environment.
Limitations: Giving primarily in WI. No grants
to individuals.
Application information:
Initial approach: Letter
Deadline(s): None
Directors: Audrey Arner; Linda Halley; James A.
Knight; Tom Mosgaller; Richard Pirog.
EIN: 391960035

3412
**Community Foundation of Portage
County, Inc.**
(formerly Stevens Point Area Foundation, Inc.)
1501 Clark St.
P.O. Box 968
Stevens Point, WI 54481-0968
(715) 342-4454
Contact: Shannon K. Semmerling, Exec. Dir.
FAX: (715) 342-5560; E-mail: cfpcwi@g2a.net;
URL: http://www.cfpcwi.org

Established in 1982 in WI.
Grantmaker type: Community foundation
Financial data (yr. ended 06/30/02): Assets,
$2,181,435 (M); gifts received, $703,626;
expenditures, $256,627; giving activities
include $119,782 for grants.
Purpose and activities: Giving to assist the
needy, hungry, and underprivileged.
Scholarships to individuals pursuing careers in
health care. The foundation administers
donor-advised funds.
Fields of interest: Arts; Education; Environment;
Health care; Human services; Women.
Types of support: Continuing support;
Building/renovation; Equipment; Land
acquisition; Program development;
Conferences/seminars; Seed money; Curriculum
development; Scholarship funds; Research;
Matching/challenge support.
Limitations: Giving limited to Portage County,
WI.
Publications: Application guidelines, Annual
report, Informational brochure, Newsletter.
Application information: Unsolicited requests
for funds not accepted. Application form
required.
Initial approach: Telephone
Copies of proposal: 10
Deadline(s): May 1
Board meeting date(s): Monthly
Final notification: Mid-June
Officers: Brian Formella, Pres.; John Buzza, V.P.;
Fred Kreul, Secy.; Robert Taylor, Treas.; Shannon
Semmerling, Exec. Dir.

Board Members: Judy Cable Anderson; Kathy
Davies; Nancy Dolce; Karen Engelhard; Meg
Erler; and 16 additional board members.
Number of staff: 1 part-time professional; 1
part-time support.
EIN: 390827885

3413
Community Trust
c/o Marshall & Ilsley Trust Company, N.A.
P.O. Box 1980
West Bend, WI 53095-7980
Contact: Stephen Zimmel

Established in 1953 in WI.
Donor(s): Norman A. Schowalter.‡
Grantmaker type: Independent foundation
Financial data (yr. ended 12/31/02): Assets,
$1,245,209 (M); expenditures, $102,146;
qualifying distributions, $95,773; giving
activities include $96,700 for 32 grants (high:
$10,000; low: $1,000).
Purpose and activities: Giving primarily for
local programs with emphasis on theological
and other higher education, social services, and
youth; support also for conservation, cultural
programs, and public affairs.
Fields of interest: Arts; Higher education;
Theological school/education; Natural
resources; Human services; Children/youth,
services; Public affairs.
Types of support: General/operating support;
Continuing support; Building/renovation;
Scholarship funds.
Limitations: Giving primarily in Washington
County, WI. No grants to individuals.
Application information: Contributes primarily
to pre-selected organizations. Application form
not required.
Initial approach: Letter or proposal
Copies of proposal: 1
Board meeting date(s): Spring and late fall
Trustees: Thomas R. Bast; Eldor Kannenberg;
Thomas A. Schowalter.
Number of staff: 3 full-time professional.
EIN: 396040395

3414
Courtier Foundation, Inc.
P.O. Box 1497
Madison, WI 53701-1497 (608) 258-4224
Contact: David W. Reinecke, Secy.-Treas.

Established in 1999 in WI.
Donor(s): Veryl F. Courtier Survivor's Trust,
Wilma W. Courtier Residual Trust.
Grantmaker type: Independent foundation
Financial data (yr. ended 12/31/02): Assets,
$3,575,981 (M); expenditures, $177,576;
qualifying distributions, $142,464; giving
activities include $105,773 for 14 grants (high:
$35,000; low: $1,000).
Purpose and activities: Giving primarily to
organizations which provide services for
children, and housing and other services for
elderly individuals in financial need.
Fields of interest: Environment; Children/youth,
services; Aging, centers/services.
Limitations: Giving limited to WI. No grants to
individuals.
Application information: Application form
required.

Initial approach: Request application form
Deadline(s): None
Officers and Directors:* Thomas G. Ragatz,*
Pres.; Ronald M. Wanek,* V.P.; David W.
Reinecke,* Secy.-Treas.
EIN: 391935038

3415
Michael J. Cudahy Foundation
c/o Kevin L. Lindsey, Tr.
10850 W. Park Pl., Ste. 980
Milwaukee, WI 53224

Established in 1999 in WI.
Donor(s): Michael J. Cudahy.
Grantmaker type: Independent foundation
Financial data (yr. ended 12/31/01): Assets,
$71,034,342 (M); expenditures, $4,245,146;
qualifying distributions, $3,705,883; giving
activities include $3,721,542 for 17 grants
(high: $1,003,000; low: $200; average:
$20,000–$700,000).
Fields of interest: Education; Health care;
Housing/shelter, development; Human services;
Children/youth, services.
Limitations: Applications not accepted. Giving
primarily in Milwaukee, WI. No grants to
individuals.
Application information: Contributes only to
pre-selected organizations.
Trustees: Joanna D. Hamadi; Julia D. Hamadi;
Kevin L. Lindsey; John W. Linnen.
EIN: 396720806
**Recent environmental and animal welfare
grants:**
3415-1 Wisconsin Lake Schooner Education
Association, Milwaukee, WI, $1,003,000.
2001.

3416
Patrick and Anna M. Cudahy Fund
P.O. Box 11978
Milwaukee, WI 53211 (414) 271-6020
Contact: Judith L. Borchers, Exec. Dir.
IL address: 1007 Church St., Ste. 414, Evanston,
IL, 60201; IL tel.: (847) 866-0760; FAX: (847)
475-0679; E-mail: secretary@cudahyfund.org or
jborcher@cudahyfund.org; URL: http://
www.cudahyfund.org

Incorporated in 1949 in WI.
Donor(s): Michael F. Cudahy.‡
Grantmaker type: Independent foundation
Financial data (yr. ended 12/31/02): Assets,
$19,148,027 (M); expenditures, $2,187,534;
qualifying distributions, $2,051,526; giving
activities include $1,924,996 for 188 grants
(high: $30,000; low: $500).
Purpose and activities: Primary areas of interest
include the arts, education, youth, international
relief, and social services. Support for the
homeless, family services, and international
development programs; support also for
national programs concerned with
environmental and public interest issues, and
cultural and civic affairs programs.
Fields of interest: Arts; Adult/continuing
education; Adult education—literacy, basic
skills & GED; Reading; Education; Environment;
Food services; Housing/shelter, development;
Human services; Youth, services; Family
services; Homeless, human services;

International economic development; International relief; International human rights; Rural development; Public affairs; Roman Catholic agencies & churches; Disabled; Aging; Women; Immigrants/refugees; Economically disadvantaged; Homeless.
International interests: Africa.
Types of support: General/operating support; Continuing support; Annual campaigns; Building/renovation; Equipment; Program development; Seed money; Technical assistance; Matching/challenge support.
Limitations: Giving limited to Chicago, IL, and WI for local programs and for international (U.S.-based) programs. No grants to individuals, or for endowments; no loans.
Publications: Application guidelines, Grants list.
Application information: See Web site for Summary of Request Form. Application form required.
> *Initial approach:* Proposal
> *Copies of proposal:* 1
> *Deadline(s):* Jan. 5, Apr. 5, July 5, and Oct. 5 (for full proposal)
> *Board meeting date(s):* Usually in Mar., June, Sept., and Dec.
> *Final notification:* 2 weeks after meetings
Officers and Directors:* Richard D. Cudahy,* Chair.; Janet S. Cudahy,* Pres.; Dudley J. Godfrey, Jr.,* Secy.; Judith L. Borchers, Exec. Dir.; James Bailey; Michaela Cudahy; Molly Cudahy; Jean Holtz; Wesley Scott; Annette Stoddard-Freeman.
Number of staff: 1 part-time professional; 1 part-time support.
EIN: 390991972

3417
Mae E. Demmer Charitable Trust
c/o Bank One Trust Co., N.A.
P.O. Box 1308
Milwaukee, WI 53201
Contact: Lynn Paull
Application address: c/o Bank One Trust Co., N.A., 111 E. Wisconsin Ave., Milwaukee, WI 53202

Established in 1998 in WI.
Donor(s): Mae E. Demmer.‡
Grantmaker type: Independent foundation
Financial data (yr. ended 12/31/02): Assets, $8,065,868 (M); expenditures, $511,625; qualifying distributions, $426,334; giving activities include $400,000 for 26 grants (high: $55,000; low: $5,000).
Purpose and activities: Giving primarily to the arts and human services.
Fields of interest: Arts education; Museums; Performing arts; Arts; Elementary/secondary education; Higher education; Environmental education; Zoos/zoological societies; Hospitals (general); Cerebral palsy; Arthritis; Food services; Human services; Foundations (public); Federated giving programs; Protestant agencies & churches.
Limitations: Giving primarily in Milwaukee, WI.
Application information:
> *Initial approach:* Proposal
> *Deadline(s):* None
Trustees: Richard Goisman; Harrold McComas; Bank One, N.A.
EIN: 311576907

3418
Derse Foundation
(formerly Derse Family Foundation)
36058 N. Beach Rd.
Oconomowoc, WI 53066
Contact: Judith Derse Langenbach, Pres.
E-mail: jderse@wi.rr.com

Established in 1986 in WI.
Grantmaker type: Independent foundation
Financial data (yr. ended 12/31/02): Assets, $2,371,780 (M); expenditures, $261,896; qualifying distributions, $142,100; giving activities include $142,100 for 42 grants (high: $21,000; low: $50).
Purpose and activities: The foundation provides technology equipment for conservation-related causes, including procuring, delivering, and installing the equipment, and related education.
Fields of interest: Arts; Education; Environment; Health care; Health organizations, association.
International interests: Kenya; Belize.
Types of support: General/operating support; Continuing support; Equipment; Program development; Technical assistance.
Limitations: Giving primarily in WI, with emphasis on Milwaukee and Waukesha counties.
Application information: Application form required.
> *Initial approach:* Proposal
> *Copies of proposal:* 1
> *Deadline(s):* None
> *Board meeting date(s):* Jan. and June
Officers: Judith Derse Langenbach, Pres.; Diane K. Dressler, V.P.
Directors: Michelle Derse Langenbach; Lisa K. Rader.
Number of staff: 1 full-time professional.
EIN: 391540822

3419
Louise Head Duncan Trust
(also known as The Peyton Samuel Head Family Trust)
c/o Bank One Trust Co., N.A.
P.O. Box 1308
Milwaukee, WI 53201
Application address: c/o The Peyton Samuel Head Family Trust, P.O. Box 248, LaGrange, KY 40031

Established in 1991.
Donor(s): Louise Head Duncan.‡
Grantmaker type: Independent foundation
Financial data (yr. ended 12/31/02): Assets, $7,951,387 (M); expenditures, $322,293; qualifying distributions, $254,285; giving activities include $236,586 for 23 grants (high: $50,000; low: $300).
Fields of interest: Historic preservation/historical societies; Education; Natural resources; Disasters, fire prevention/control; Human services; American Red Cross; Community development.
Types of support: General/operating support.
Limitations: Giving limited to Oldham County, KY. No grants to individuals.
Application information: Application form required.
> *Copies of proposal:* 3
> *Board meeting date(s):* July and Nov.

Advisory Committee: Thomas W. Gaines, Jr.; Joseph William Hall; Rose Ethel Hall; Annette Paine; John F. Payne.
Trustee: Bank One, N.A.
Number of staff: None.
EIN: 616183556

3420
Albert J. & Flora H. Ellinger Foundation, Inc.
1000 N. Water St., 13th Fl.
Milwaukee, WI 53202 (414) 287-7177
Contact: William T. Gaus, Pres.
FAX: (414) 287-7025

Established in 1956 in WI.
Donor(s): Albert J. Ellinger,‡ Flora H. Ellinger.‡
Grantmaker type: Independent foundation
Financial data (yr. ended 07/31/02): Assets, $1,978,328 (M); expenditures, $119,399; qualifying distributions, $96,900; giving activities include $96,900 for 69 grants (high: $10,000; low: $400).
Purpose and activities: Giving for arts and culture, higher education, the environment, medical and health related services, and family and youth services.
Fields of interest: Arts; Higher education; Natural resources; Environment; Animals/wildlife, preservation/protection; Hospitals (general); Health organizations, association; Medical research, institute; Human services; Children/youth, services; Family services.
Types of support: General/operating support; Continuing support; Annual campaigns; Capital campaigns.
Limitations: Giving primarily in Milwaukee, WI.
Application information: Application form not required.
> *Initial approach:* 1-page letter
> *Copies of proposal:* 1
> *Deadline(s):* 30 days prior to board meeting
> *Board meeting date(s):* June and Dec.
Officers and Directors:* William T. Gaus,* Pres.; John U. Schmid, Jr.,* Secy.
Board Member: Thomas N. Tuttle, Jr.
Number of staff: None.
EIN: 237098671

3421
The Evjue Foundation, Inc.
1901 Fish Hatchery Rd.
P.O. Box 8060
Madison, WI 53708 (608) 252-6401
Contact: Arlene Hornung

Incorporated in 1958 in WI.
Donor(s): William T. Evjue.‡
Grantmaker type: Community foundation
Financial data (yr. ended 02/28/03): Assets, $21,005,133 (M); gifts received, $1,427,363; expenditures, $3,749,515; giving activities include $3,628,206 for 154 grants (high: $100,000; low: $280; average: $1,000–$10,000).
Purpose and activities: Support for education, including higher education; grants also for mental health, youth, and social service agencies, and for cultural programs.
Fields of interest: Journalism/publishing; Arts; Higher education; Education; Animal welfare;

Hospitals (general); Family planning; Substance abuse, services; Mental health/crisis services; Alcoholism; Food services; Human services; Children/youth, services; Family services; Aging, centers/services; Aging.
Types of support: Continuing support; Annual campaigns; Capital campaigns; Endowments; Emergency funds; Program development; Conferences/seminars; Professorships; Publication; Seed money; Internship funds; Scholarship funds.
Limitations: Giving primarily in Dane County, WI. No support for medical or scientific research. No grants to individuals, or for building funds, equipment, land acquisition, renovation projects, or operating expenses; no loans.
Publications: Application guidelines, Informational brochure (including application guidelines), Program policy statement.
Application information: Application form required.
  Initial approach: Letter or telephone inquiry
  Copies of proposal: 1
  Deadline(s): Submit proposal preferably in Oct., Feb., or Apr.
  Board meeting date(s): Mar. May, Nov. and as required
  Final notification: 3 months
Officers and Directors:* John H. Lussier,* Pres.; Nancy Brooke Gage,* V.P.; Clayton Frink,* Secy.; Frederick W. Miller,* Treas.; Marion F. Brown; W. Jerome Frautschi; Virginia Henderson; James D. Lussier; Laura J. Lussier; Hal Mayer; Steve Mixtacki; Melany Newby; Marianne D. Pollard; Andrew A. Wilcox; John Wiley.
Number of staff: 1 part-time support.
EIN: 396073981

3422
The Four-Four Foundation, Inc.
c/o Provident Investors
N27W23957 Paul Rd.
Pewaukee, WI 53072
Contact: Sally S. Manegold, Pres.

Established in 1994 in WI.
Grantmaker type: Independent foundation
Financial data (yr. ended 12/31/02): Assets, $19,172,554 (M); gifts received, $8,639,202; expenditures, $544,361; qualifying distributions, $455,160; giving activities include $451,000 for 27 grants (high: $114,000; low: $1,200).
Fields of interest: Arts; Education; Natural resources; Medical care, rehabilitation; Public health.
Types of support: Continuing support; Annual campaigns; Capital campaigns; Building/renovation; Endowments; Professorships.
Limitations: Applications not accepted. Giving primarily in Milwaukee, WI. No grants to individuals.
Application information: Contributes only to pre-selected organizations. Unsolicited requests for funds not accepted.
  Board meeting date(s): Sept. or Oct.
Officers and Directors:* Sally S. Manegold,* Pres.; Lynee M. Rix, Secy.; Robert L. Manegold,* Treas.; Katherine M. Biersach; Joan M. Dukes; Robert H. Manegold.
EIN: 391867243

3423
Philip M. Gelatt Foundation, Inc.
P.O. Box 17
Sparta, WI 54656-0017 (608) 269-6911
Contact: Rita A. Forbes, V.P.

Established in 1985 in WI.
Donor(s): PMG, Inc., Northern Engraving Corp., NECO Corp.
Grantmaker type: Independent foundation
Financial data (yr. ended 06/30/02): Assets, $2,131,573 (M); gifts received, $65,318; expenditures, $254,834; qualifying distributions, $245,808; giving activities include $242,500 for 12 grants (high: $75,000; low: $500).
Purpose and activities: Giving primarily for education, natural resource conservation, and human services.
Fields of interest: Theater; Libraries/library science; Education; Environment, formal/general education; Natural resources; Human services.
Limitations: Giving primarily in WI, with emphasis on the Sparta-La Crosse area.
Application information: Application form not required.
  Deadline(s): None
Officers and Directors:* Philip M. Gelatt, Pres. and Treas.; Rita A. Forbes,* V.P. and Secy.; Robert J. Wood.
EIN: 391568547

3424
Donald A. Gordon Foundation
c/o North Central Trust Co.
311 Main St.
La Crosse, WI 54601

Grantmaker type: Independent foundation
Financial data (yr. ended 12/31/02): Assets, $4,227,661 (M); expenditures, $249,030; qualifying distributions, $199,497; giving activities include $200,491 for 11 grants (high: $58,098; low: $7,525).
Fields of interest: Libraries (public); Animal welfare; Hospitals (general); Health care; Boys & girls clubs; Human services; Salvation Army; Foundations (community); Federated giving programs.
Limitations: Applications not accepted. Giving primarily in La Crosse, WI. No grants to individuals.
Application information: Contributes only to pre-selected organizations.
Trustee: North Central Trust Co.
EIN: 316672086

3425
Gertrude S. Gordon Foundation
c/o North Central Trust Co.
311 Main St.
La Crosse, WI 54601

Grantmaker type: Independent foundation
Financial data (yr. ended 12/31/02): Assets, $8,148,612 (M); expenditures, $867,136; qualifying distributions, $786,855; giving activities include $788,926 for 10 grants (high: $244,464; low: $33,381).
Fields of interest: Libraries (public); Education; Hospitals (general); Animal welfare; Boys & girls clubs; Salvation Army; Foundations

(community); Federated giving programs; Protestant agencies & churches.
Limitations: Applications not accepted. Giving primarily in La Crosse, WI. No grants to individuals.
Application information: Contributes only to pre-selected organizations.
Trustee: North Central Trust Co.
EIN: 316672080

3426
Greater Green Bay Community Foundation
302 N. Adams St., Ste. 100
Green Bay, WI 54301 (920) 432-0800
Contact: Steve Schumeisser, Treas.
FAX: (920) 432-5577; *URL:* http://www.ggbcf.org

Established in 1991 in WI.
Grantmaker type: Community foundation
Financial data (yr. ended 06/30/02): Assets, $29,842,516 (M); gifts received, $2,986,000; expenditures, $3,399,043; giving activities include $2,814,238 for 173 grants (high: $656,000; low: $100) and $59,700 for 33 grants to individuals (high: $10,000; low: $200).
Purpose and activities: The foundation administers donor-advised funds.
Fields of interest: Historic preservation/historical societies; Arts; Education; Environment; Health care; Youth development; Human services; Aging.
Types of support: Emergency funds; Equipment; Program development; Conferences/seminars; Seed money; Curriculum development; Scholarship funds; Technical assistance; Program evaluation; Scholarships—to individuals; Matching/challenge support.
Limitations: Giving limited to Brown, Door, Kewaunee and Oconto counties, WI.
Publications: Application guidelines, Annual report, Informational brochure, Newsletter.
Application information: Scholarship application forms available through Northeast, WI high schools. Application form required for scholarships; scholarship recipients must be residents of Brown, Door, Kewaunee or Oconto counties, WI. Application form required.
  Initial approach: Telephone
  Copies of proposal: 1
  Deadline(s): Jan. 1, Apr. 1, July 1, and Oct. 1
  Board meeting date(s): Mar., June, Sept., and Dec.
  Final notification: Within 4 weeks of application deadline
Officers and Directors:* Charles Johnson,* Chair.; Kenneth D. Strmiska,* Pres.; Richard Beuerstein,* V.P.; Paul Meinke,* V.P.; Jeff Ottum,* V.P.; Sheri Prosser,* V.P.; Diane Conway,* Secy.; Tim Day,* Treas.
Number of staff: 3 full-time professional; 1 part-time professional; 1 part-time support.
EIN: 391699966

3427
Green Bay Packers Foundation
1265 Lombardi Ave.
Green Bay, WI 54304-3928 (920) 496-5700
Contact: Phillip Pionek, Secy.
URL: http://www.packers.com/community/packers_foundation/

Established in 1986 in WI.
Donor(s): Green Bay Packers, Inc.
Grantmaker type: Company-sponsored foundation
Financial data (yr. ended 03/31/03): Assets, $1,858,643 (M); gifts received, $305,642; expenditures, $167,104; qualifying distributions, $145,663; giving activities include $146,125 for 52 grants (high: $5,000; low: $600; average: $600–$5,000).
Purpose and activities: Giving primarily for library services, botanical gardens, and youth services.
Fields of interest: Libraries/library science; Botanical gardens; Substance abuse, services; Children/youth, services; Domestic violence.
Types of support: Continuing support.
Limitations: Applications not accepted. Giving limited to WI. No grants to individuals.
Publications: Annual report, Financial statement.
Application information: Contributes only to pre-selected organizations.
  Board meeting date(s): Aug. and Dec.
Officers and Trustees:* Carl W. Kuehne,* Chair.; Phillip Pionek, Secy.; Andrew E. Farah; C. Patricia LaViolette; Michael R. Reese; Gary M. Rotherham; James A. Temp; Associated Banc-Corp.
Number of staff: None.
EIN: 391577137

3428
H. J. Hagge Foundation, Inc.
500 3rd St., Ste. 506
Wausau, WI 54403-4896 (715) 845-1818
Contact: Carol M. Krieg

Established in 1956 in WI.
Donor(s): H.J. Hagge,‡ Helen S. Hagge.‡
Grantmaker type: Independent foundation
Financial data (yr. ended 12/31/02): Assets, $1,707,814 (M); expenditures, $114,693; qualifying distributions, $107,412; giving activities include $103,010 for 81 grants (high: $6,000; low: $100; average: $500–$1,000).
Purpose and activities: Giving for education, civic projects, community and human services.
Fields of interest: Arts; Education, association; Libraries/library science; Animals/wildlife, preservation/protection; Health organizations, association; Cancer; Cancer research; Human services; Protestant agencies & churches; Religion; Minorities.
Types of support: General/operating support; Continuing support; Annual campaigns; Capital campaigns; Emergency funds.
Limitations: Giving primarily in WI. No grants to individuals.
Application information: Application form not required.
  Initial approach: Letter
  Copies of proposal: 1
  Deadline(s): None
  Board meeting date(s): July
Officers and Directors:* Robert S. Hagge, Jr.,* Pres. and Treas.; Kristin Single Hagge,* V.P.; Leigh Hagge Tuckey,* Secy.; A. Woodson Hagge; Daniel L. Hagge, Jr.
Number of staff: 1 shared staff (shared with Robert S. and Betsy Hagge Foundation, Inc.)
EIN: 396037112

3429
Joseph & Sally Handleman Charitable Foundation Trust C
c/o Bank One Trust Co., N.A.
P.O. Box 1308
Milwaukee, WI 53201
Contact: Gary W. Gomoll, Mgr.
Application address: c/o Bank One Trust Co., N.A., 3399 PGA Blvd., Ste. 100, Palm Beach Gardens, FL 33410, tel.: (561) 627-9400

Grantmaker type: Independent foundation
Financial data (yr. ended 12/31/02): Assets, $5,175,461 (M); expenditures, $339,011; qualifying distributions, $301,757; giving activities include $288,400 for grants (high: $50,000).
Purpose and activities: Giving primarily for human services.
Fields of interest: Education, special; Education; Animal welfare; Human services; Salvation Army; Children/youth, services; Jewish agencies & temples.
Limitations: Giving primarily in FL and NY. No grants to individuals.
Application information: Application form not required.
  Initial approach: Proposal
  Deadline(s): None
Trustees: Joyce Ann Muller; Arne R. Themmen; Bank One, N.A.
EIN: 656263328

3430
Ann E. & Joseph F. Heil, Jr. Charitable Trust
7560 N. River Rd.
River Hills, WI 53217-3323

Established in 1999 in WI.
Donor(s): Marjorie Heil.‡
Grantmaker type: Independent foundation
Financial data (yr. ended 12/31/02): Assets, $3,162,660 (M); expenditures, $168,997; qualifying distributions, $148,816; giving activities include $146,500 for 18 grants (high: $50,000; low: $1,000).
Fields of interest: Visual arts; Performing arts; Ballet; Natural resources; Botanical gardens; Health care; Boys & girls clubs; Human services; Federated giving programs.
Limitations: Applications not accepted. Giving primarily in Milwaukee, WI. No grants to individuals.
Application information: Contributes only to pre-selected organizations.
Trustee: Ann E. Heil.
EIN: 396713764

3431
The Richard & Ethel Herzfeld Foundation, Inc. ▼
219 N. Milwaukee St., 7th fl.
Milwaukee, WI 53202 (414) 727-1136
Contact: Mark Warhus, Prog. Mgr.
E-mail: mail@herzfeldfoundation.org

Established around 1973 in WI.
Donor(s): Ethel D. Herzfeld,‡ Richard P. Herzfeld.‡
Grantmaker type: Independent foundation

Financial data (yr. ended 12/31/02): Assets, $63,374,353 (M); expenditures, $3,329,801; qualifying distributions, $3,599,801; giving activities include $2,259,968 for 55 grants (high: $468,330; low: $250; average: $1,000–$50,000).
Purpose and activities: Giving primarily to museums, arts organizations, and education.
Fields of interest: Museums; Arts; Education; Urban/community development.
Types of support: General/operating support; Continuing support; Capital campaigns; Building/renovation; Endowments; Program development.
Limitations: Giving primarily in WI, with emphasis on the greater Milwaukee area. No grants to individuals.
Publications: Application guidelines.
Application information: Application form required.
  Initial approach: Letter or telephone
  Copies of proposal: 1
  Deadline(s): Feb. 1, May. 1, and Aug. 1
  Board meeting date(s): Spring, summer, and fall
  Final notification: Approximately 3 months
Officer: F. William Haberman, Pres. and Treas.
Directors: Edward Hinshaw; Roy C. LaBudde.
Number of staff: 1 full-time professional; 2 part-time professional.
EIN: 237230686
Recent environmental and animal welfare grants:
3431-1 Wisconsin Lake Schooner Education Association, Milwaukee, WI, $500,000. For Pier Wisconsin. 2002.

3432
Ralph J. Huiras Family Foundation, Inc.
2560 Hwy. 32
P.O. Box 366
Port Washington, WI 53074-0366
Contact: Ralph J. Huiras, Pres.

Established in 1996 in WI.
Donor(s): Ralph J. Huiras.
Grantmaker type: Operating foundation
Financial data (yr. ended 12/31/02): Assets, $2,970,210 (M); gifts received, $697,130; expenditures, $184,382; qualifying distributions, $164,243; giving activities include $148,000 for 31 grants (high: $28,500; low: $1,000).
Purpose and activities: Giving primarily for a land trust, education, human services, and religious organizations.
Fields of interest: Orchestra (symphony); Education; Environment, land resources; Health care, single organization support; Human services; Roman Catholic agencies & churches.
Limitations: Giving primarily in WI.
Application information: Application form not required.
  Initial approach: Letter
  Deadline(s): None
Officer: Ralph J. Huiras, Pres.
Directors: William J. Farrell; Margaret Schreiner.
EIN: 391844576

3433
Frieda & William Hunt Memorial Trust
c/o Wayne Lueders
777 E. Wisconsin Ave., Ste. 3500
Milwaukee, WI 53202-5302 (414) 297-5786

Established in 1988 in WI.
Donor(s): Frieda E. Hunt.‡
Grantmaker type: Independent foundation
Financial data (yr. ended 12/31/02): Assets,
$5,631,340 (M); expenditures, $365,456;
qualifying distributions, $334,283; giving
activities include $291,000 for 32 grants (high:
$35,000; low: $1,000).
Fields of interest: Performing arts; Arts;
Education; Natural resources; Animals/wildlife,
preservation/protection; Health care; Human
services.
Types of support: General/operating support;
Annual campaigns; Capital campaigns;
Building/renovation; Equipment; Emergency
funds; Program development; Seed money.
Limitations: Applications not accepted. Giving
primarily in Milwaukee, WI. No grants to
individuals.
Application information: Contributes only to
pre-selected organizations.
Trustees: Wayne R. Lueders; John T. Seaman, Jr.;
John T. Seaman III; Patricia G. Seaman.
Number of staff: None.
EIN: 391642918

3434
Dorothy Inbusch Foundation, Inc.
(formerly Charles E. & Dorothy Watkins Inbusch
Foundation, Inc.)
660 E. Mason St.
Milwaukee, WI 53202
Contact: Thomas J. Drought, Secy.-Treas.

Established in 1964.
Grantmaker type: Independent foundation
Financial data (yr. ended 12/31/02): Assets,
$3,444,757 (M); expenditures, $258,001;
qualifying distributions, $239,390; giving
activities include $204,725 for 48 grants (high:
$10,000; low: $1,000).
Purpose and activities: Funding primarily for
arts and culture, health and human services,
education, environmental and historic
preservation.
Fields of interest: Historic
preservation/historical societies; Arts; Education;
Natural resources; Health care; Human services.
Types of support: General/operating support;
Continuing support; Capital campaigns;
Building/renovation; Program development;
Seed money.
Limitations: Giving primarily in the greater
Milwaukee, WI, area. No grants to individuals.
Application information: Use Donor's Forum
Common Grant Application. Application form
required.
   Copies of proposal: 1
   Deadline(s): Oct. 31
   Board meeting date(s): Varies
Officers and Directors:* Robert E. Cook,* Pres.;
Harry F. Franke,* V.P.; Thomas J. Drought,*
Secy.-Treas.
EIN: 396084238

3435
J.P.C. Foundation
c/o William B. Vogt
P.O. Box 1148
Janesville, WI 53547-1148

Established in 1991 in WI.
Donor(s): J.P. Cullen & Sons, Inc., John P. Cullen.
Grantmaker type: Company-sponsored
foundation
Financial data (yr. ended 05/31/02): Assets,
$1,515,565 (M); gifts received, $342,330;
expenditures, $253,324; qualifying distributions,
$240,676; giving activities include $240,804 for
53 grants (high: $67,000; low: $250).
Purpose and activities: Giving primarily to
YMCAs and to a botanical garden; funding also
for higher education, health associations and
hospitals, children, youth and social services,
and Roman Catholic churches.
Fields of interest: Higher education; Botanical
gardens; Hospitals (general); Health
organizations, association; Human services;
YM/YWCAs & YM/YWHAs; Children/youth,
services; Federated giving programs; Roman
Catholic agencies & churches.
Types of support: Scholarship funds.
Limitations: Applications not accepted. Giving
limited to Platteville, WI. No grants to
individuals.
Application information: Contributes only to
pre-selected organizations.
Trustees: J.P. Cullen; Mark A. Cullen.
EIN: 391703739

3436
Janesville Foundation, Inc.
121 N. Parker Dr.
P.O. Box 8123
Janesville, WI 53547-8123 (608) 752-1032
Contact: Bonnie Lynne Robinson, Pres. and
Exec. Dir.
FAX: (608) 752-1952

Incorporated in 1944 in WI.
Donor(s): The Parker Pen Co.
Grantmaker type: Independent foundation
Financial data (yr. ended 12/31/02): Assets,
$7,527,561 (M); expenditures, $381,957;
qualifying distributions, $443,129; giving
activities include $304,538 for 14 grants (high:
$100,000; low: $500) and $61,500 for grants to
individuals (high: $3,500; low: $1,500).
Purpose and activities: Primary areas of interest
include secondary and elementary education,
including scholarships for local high school
graduates; emphasis on youth, and community
development.
Fields of interest: Elementary/secondary
education; Education; Environmental education;
Children/youth, services; Community
development; Federated giving programs.
Types of support: Capital campaigns;
Building/renovation; Equipment; Land
acquisition; Program development;
Conferences/seminars; Seed money;
Scholarships—to individuals;
Matching/challenge support.
Limitations: Giving limited to the Janesville, WI,
area; scholarships limited to Janesville high
school students. No grants to individuals (except
for scholarships), or for operating budgets or
endowment funds.

Publications: Informational brochure (including
application guidelines).
Application information: Application form not
required.
   Initial approach: Letter with brief outline of
proposal, or by telephone
   Copies of proposal: 2
   Deadline(s): None
   Board meeting date(s): Varies
   Final notification: After board meetings
Officers and Directors:* George Parker,* Chair.;
Alan W. Dunwiddie,* Vice-Chair.; Bonnie Lynne
Robinson,* Pres. and Exec. Dir.; Roger E.
Axtell,* V.P.; Alfred P. Diotte,* V.P.; Dolores M.
Dilley, Secy.; Ronald K. Ochs,* Treas.; Rowland
J. McClellan.
Number of staff: 1 full-time professional; 2
part-time support.
EIN: 396034645

3437
SC Johnson Fund, Inc. ▼
(formerly SC Johnson Wax Fund Inc.)
1525 Howe St.
Racine, WI 53403 (262) 260-4855
Contact: Colleen Cribari, Prog. Admin.
URL: http://www.scjohnson.com/community/

Incorporated in 1959 in WI.
Donor(s): S.C. Johnson & Son, Inc.
Grantmaker type: Company-sponsored
foundation
Financial data (yr. ended 06/30/02): Assets,
$7,781,185 (M); gifts received, $11,301,798;
expenditures, $10,387,742; qualifying
distributions, $10,350,608; giving activities
include $8,795,047 for 77 grants (high:
$1,512,500; low: $2,000; average:
$5,000–$250,000) and $1,339,726 for
employee matching gifts.
Purpose and activities: Scholarships for children
of company employees through Scholarship
America, Inc.; scholarships and fellowships in
specific areas of interest, i.e., chemistry, biology,
marketing, and business; grants to local
colleges; support for local welfare, cultural, and
civic organizations; grants also for
environmental protection, health, and
education; seed funding for new programs that
address high-priority human service needs.
Fields of interest: Arts; Higher education;
Business school/education; Education;
Environment; Health care; Health organizations,
association; Human services; Chemistry;
Biological sciences; Government/public
administration; Minorities.
Types of support: Capital campaigns;
Building/renovation; Equipment; Seed money;
Fellowships; Scholarship funds; Employee
matching gifts; Employee-related scholarships;
Grants to individuals; Scholarships—to
individuals.
Limitations: Giving primarily in headquarters
community of Racine, WI. No support for
national health organizations or religious or
social groups, organizations receiving support
from the United Way, or veterans', labor,
political or fraternal organizations. No grants to
individuals (except for scholarship and
fellowship programs), or for operating budgets,
emergency funds, deficit financing,
demonstration projects, or conferences; no
loans.

Publications: Annual report.
Application information: Application form required.
   Initial approach: Telephone
   Copies of proposal: 1
   Deadline(s): Mar. 1, July 1, and Nov. 1
   Board meeting date(s): Feb., June, and Oct.
   Final notification: 3 to 4 months
Officers and Trustees:* Samuel C. Johnson,* Chair. and Pres.; William D. Perez,* Vice-Chair.; Jane M. Hutterly, Exec. V.P.; Thomas J. Reigle, V.P., Secy., and Exec. Dir.; Jeffrey M. Waller,* Treas.; Richard S. Hutchings; H. Fisk Johnson; S. Curtis Johnson; Helen P. Johnson-Leipold; J. Gary Raley; Thomas M. Wierzba.
Number of staff: 2 full-time professional; 2 part-time professional; 2 part-time support.
EIN: 396052089
Recent environmental and animal welfare grants:
3437-1 Caledonia Conservancy, Racine, WI, $50,000. 2002.
3437-2 Conservation International, DC, $250,000. 2002.
3437-3 International Crane Foundation, Baraboo, WI, $12,000. 2002.
3437-4 Keystone Center, Keystone Science School, Keystone, CO, $28,000. 2002.
3437-5 Sustainable Racine, Racine, WI, $330,000. 2002.
3437-6 Sustainable Racine, Racine, WI, $157,700. 2002.

3438
Johnson Wax Professional Corporate Giving Program

8310 16th St.
P.O. Box 902
Sturtevant, WI 53177-0902

Grantmaker type: Corporate giving program
Purpose and activities: Johnson Wax Professional makes charitable contributions to nonprofit organizations involved with education, the environment, and youth development. Support is given primarily in southeastern Wisconsin.
Fields of interest: Education; Environment; Youth development.
Types of support: General/operating support; Scholarship funds; Employee volunteer services; Sponsorships; Employee matching gifts; Employee-related scholarships; In-kind gifts.
Limitations: Giving primarily in southeastern WI.
Application information: Application form not required.
   Initial approach: Proposal to headquarters
   Copies of proposal: 1
   Final notification: Following review

3439
Greater Kenosha Area Foundation, Inc.

P.O. Box 1829
Kenosha, WI 53141 (262) 654-2412
Contact: Peter Walcott, Exec. Dir.
FAX: (262) 654-2615; E-mail: email@kenoshafoundation.org; URL: http://www.kenoshafoundation.org

Established in 1926 in WI.
Grantmaker type: Community foundation

Financial data (yr. ended 12/31/02): Assets, $2,990,304 (M); expenditures, $1,107,707; giving activities include $812,370 for 81 grants (high: $50,000; low: $500).
Purpose and activities: The foundation administers donor-advised funds.
Fields of interest: Arts; Education; Environment; Health care; Human services.
Types of support: General/operating support; Seed money; Scholarship funds; Matching/challenge support.
Limitations: Giving primarily in Kenosha County, WI.
Application information: Application form required.
   Copies of proposal: 12
   Deadline(s): Varies
   Board meeting date(s): Quarterly
Officers: Alan R. Schaefer, Pres.; Kenneth L. Fellman, V.P.; Peter Walcott, Exec. Dir.
Directors: Constance M. Ferwerda; Neil F. Guttormsen; Jack S. Harris.
Board of Advisors: Mary Frost Ashley; George R. Connolly; Robert A. Cornog; Mary P. Euroth; Jerold P. France; A. Allan Jankus; Ralph J. Tenuta.
Number of staff: 1 full-time professional; 1 part-time support.
EIN: 396045289

3440
Kohler Co. Contributions Program

444 Highland Dr.
Kohler, WI 53044 (920) 457-4441
Contact: Lynn M. Kulow, Sr. Comm. Specialist, Corp. Giving and Civic Svcs.
FAX: (920) 457-9064

Grantmaker type: Corporate giving program
Financial data (yr. ended 12/31/01): Total giving, $1,900,000; giving activities include $1,602,000 for 250 grants (high: $200,000; low: $10), $103,000 for 57 grants to individuals, $33,000 for employee matching gifts and $162,000 for in-kind gifts.
Purpose and activities: Kohler makes charitable contributions to nonprofit organizations involved with arts and culture, education, the environment, disease, medical research, housing, youth citizenship, human services, community development, disabled people, women, and homeless people. Support is given primarily in areas of company operations.
Fields of interest: Visual arts; Performing arts; Humanities; History/archaeology; Historic preservation/historical societies; Arts; Education, fund raising; Child development, education; Higher education; Adult education—literacy, basic skills & GED; Reading; Education; Natural resources; Environment; Cancer; Organ diseases; Heart & circulatory diseases; AIDS; Health organizations; Cancer research; Heart & circulatory research; AIDS research; Medical research; Housing/shelter; Youth development, citizenship; Children/youth, services; Child development, services; Human services; Community development; Disabled; Women; Homeless.
Types of support: General/operating support; Building/renovation; Equipment; Endowments; Internship funds; Scholarship funds; Employee volunteer services; Loaned talent; Employee-related scholarships; Scholarships—to

individuals; Donated equipment; Donated products; In-kind gifts.
Limitations: Giving primarily in areas of company operations, with emphasis on the Spartanburg, SC, Brownwood, TX, and Kohler, WI, areas.
Application information: The Civic Services Department handles giving. Application form not required.
   Initial approach: Proposal to nearest company facility
   Copies of proposal: 1
   Final notification: Before Dec. 31
Number of staff: 1 full-time professional; 1 part-time support.

3441
Kohler Trust for Preservation

7254 Woodlake Rd.
Kohler, WI 53044-1521

Established in 1990.
Grantmaker type: Public charity
Financial data (yr. ended 01/31/02): Revenue, $3,379,941; assets, $4,398,280 (M); gifts received, $2,969,800; expenditures, $784,059; program services expenses, $759,989; giving activities include $741,373 for 2 grants (high: $721,500; low: $19,873).
Purpose and activities: Funds are largely committed to the State Historical Society and to the Eagle Valley Preserve.
Fields of interest: Natural resources; Environment.
Limitations: Applications not accepted. Giving limited to WI.
Application information: Contributes only to pre-selected organizations; unsolicited requests for funds not considered or acknowledged.
Officers and Trustees:* Herbert V. Kohler, Jr.,* Chair.; William Reiss, Jr.,* Secy.; Jeffrey Cheney,* Treas.; Susan Flader; Thomas Hayssen; K. David Kohler; Ruth Deyoung Kohler; Lois Pauls.
EIN: 391579803

3442
Krause Family Foundation

(formerly Charles A. Krause Foundation)
c/o Krause Consultants, Ltd.
700 N. Water St., Ste. 1246
Milwaukee, WI 53202-4206
Contact: Charles A. Krause III, Secy.-Treas.

Incorporated in 1952 in WI.
Grantmaker type: Independent foundation
Financial data (yr. ended 12/31/02): Assets, $5,126,943 (M); expenditures, $307,960; qualifying distributions, $274,822; giving activities include $274,822 for 78 grants (high: $25,000; low: $100).
Fields of interest: Museums; Arts; Secondary school/education; Higher education; Education; Natural resources.
Types of support: General/operating support; Continuing support; Annual campaigns; Capital campaigns; Building/renovation; Endowments.
Limitations: Giving limited to southeastern WI. No grants to individuals, or for medical research.
Application information: Employee-related scholarship program has been discontinued. Previous commitments honored; no new awards to individuals. Application form not required.

Copies of proposal: 1
Deadline(s): Nov. 15
Board meeting date(s): Mid-Dec.
Officers and Directors:* Carol Krause Wythes,*
Pres.; Eleanor T. Sullivan,* V.P.; Charles A.
Krause III,* Secy.-Treas.; Victoria K. Mayer.
Number of staff: None.
EIN: 396044820

3443
Frank and Mary Lamberson Foundation

c/o Bank One Trust Co., N.A.
P.O. Box 1308
Milwaukee, WI 53201
Application address: c/o Gary W. Gomoll, Bank
One Trust Co., N.A., 3399 PGA Blvd., Ste.100,
Palm Beach, FL 33410, tel.: (561) 627-9400

Established in 1997.
Grantmaker type: Independent foundation
Financial data (yr. ended 12/31/01): Assets,
$1,619,291 (M); expenditures, $135,441;
qualifying distributions, $110,252; giving
activities include $101,000 for 7 grants (high:
$25,000; low: $1,000).
Purpose and activities: Giving primarily to
museums and education.
Fields of interest: Museums; Higher education;
Environment; Zoos/zoological societies.
Limitations: Giving primarily in FL, MI,
Asheville, NC, and Poughkeepsie, NY. No grants
to individuals.
Application information: Application form
required.
Initial approach: Letter
Deadline(s): None
Trustees: Frank A. Lamberson; Mary T.
Lamberson; Bank One Trust Co., N.A.
EIN: 597096409

3444
Jean Thomas Lambert Foundation

c/o Bank One Trust Co., N.A.
P.O. Box 1308
Milwaukee, WI 53201

Established in 1999 in OH.
Grantmaker type: Independent foundation
Financial data (yr. ended 12/31/02): Assets,
$609,515 (M); gifts received, $400,000;
expenditures, $249,212; qualifying distributions,
$232,502; giving activities include $225,000 for
5 grants (high: $75,000; low: $25,000).
Purpose and activities: Giving primarily for
education; support also for conservation.
Fields of interest: Historic
preservation/historical societies; Education;
Natural resources; Hospitals (general).
Limitations: Applications not accepted. Giving
primarily in CT and OH. No grants to
individuals.
Application information: Contributes only to
pre-selected organizations.
Trustees: Jean Thomas Lambert; Thomas
Lambert; Nancy Reymann.
Agent: Bank One Trust Co., N.A.
EIN: 341897221

3445
Lands' End, Inc. Corporate Giving Program

2 Lands' End Ln.
Dodgeville, WI 53595 (608) 935-4221
Contact: Ginnie Helin, Mgr., Corp. Giving
Application address for sponsorships: c/o Mktg.
Dept., 5 Lands' End Ln., Dodgeville, WI 53595;
FAX: (608) 935-6432

Grantmaker type: Corporate giving program
Purpose and activities: Lands' End makes
charitable contributions to nonprofit
organizations involved with education, the
environment, health and human services, and
community development. Support is given
primarily in Illinois, Iowa, Minnesota, Rochester,
New York, and Wisconsin.
Fields of interest: Education; Environment;
Health care; Human services; Community
development.
Types of support: General/operating support;
Employee volunteer services; In-kind gifts.
Limitations: Giving primarily in IL, IA, MN,
Rochester, NY, and WI. No support for political
organizations or candidates or lobbying
organizations. No grants to individuals, or for
advertising, endowments, testimonial or award
dinners, or political campaigns; no loans.
Publications: Application guidelines,
Informational brochure.
Application information: The company has a
staff that only handles contributions. Application
form not required.
Initial approach: Proposal to headquarters
Copies of proposal: 1
Deadline(s): 3 months prior to need
Final notification: Following review
Number of staff: 1 full-time professional; 1
full-time support.

3446
Leaf, Ltd.

125 S. 84th St., Ste. 100
Milwaukee, WI 53214-1498 (414) 272-3146
Contact: Bruce A. Findley, Pres.

Established in 1999 in WI.
Donor(s): Foundation of Faith.
Grantmaker type: Independent foundation
Financial data (yr. ended 12/31/02): Assets,
$3,241,691 (M); expenditures, $246,562;
qualifying distributions, $181,800; giving
activities include $180,000 for 15 grants (high:
$40,000; low: $2,000).
Purpose and activities: Giving primarily for
wildlife and other conservation efforts; support
also for education.
Fields of interest: Higher education; Education;
Animals/wildlife, preservation/protection.
Limitations: Giving primarily in WI.
Application information: Application form not
required.
Initial approach: Letter
Deadline(s): None
Officers and Directors:* Bruce A. Findley,*
Pres. and Treas.; Ellen V. Findley,* V.P. and Secy.;
Holly T. Brown.
EIN: 391938591

3447
LUX Foundation, Inc.

c/o Foley & Lardner
777 E. Wisconsin Ave.
Milwaukee, WI 53202-5367

Established in 1988 in WI.
Donor(s): Barbara E. Manger, William H. Lynch,
Edmund B. Manger.
Grantmaker type: Independent foundation
Financial data (yr. ended 12/31/02): Assets,
$5,691,662 (M); gifts received, $275,001;
expenditures, $333,625; qualifying distributions,
$286,938; giving activities include $284,000 for
29 grants (high: $25,000; low: $1,000).
Purpose and activities: Giving primarily to a
botanical garden, as well as for education,
natural resource conservation, wildlife, boys
and girls clubs, and social services.
Fields of interest: Higher education; Nursing
school/education; Education; Natural resources;
Botanical gardens; Animals/wildlife,
preservation/protection; Boys & girls clubs;
Human services; Human services.
Types of support: General/operating support.
Limitations: Applications not accepted. Giving
primarily in WI, with emphasis on Green Bay
and Milwaukee. No grants to individuals.
Application information: Contributes only to
pre-selected organizations.
Officers and Directors:* Robert E. Manger,*
Pres. and Treas.; Stephen M. Fisher,* V.P. and
Secy.; Edmund B. Manger.
EIN: 391618778

3448
Madison Community Foundation

2 Science Ct.
P.O. Box 5010
Madison, WI 53705-0010 (608) 232-1763
Contact: Kathleen Woit, Pres.
FAX: (608) 232-1772; E-mail:
frontdesk@madisoncommunityfoundation.org;
URL: http://
www.madisoncommunityfoundation.org

Established in 1942 in WI.
Grantmaker type: Community foundation
Financial data (yr. ended 12/31/02): Assets,
$63,254,956 (M); gifts received, $14,406,146;
expenditures, $5,714,303; giving activities
include $5,480,782 for grants (average:
$5,000–$125,000).
Purpose and activities: To enhance the quality
of life in Dane County, WI, in the areas of arts
and culture, economic and community
development, education, the environment, the
elderly, families, and youth. The foundation
makes capacity-building grants to area
nonprofits to hire key personnel or expand the
core business of the organization. The
foundation administers donor-advised funds.
Fields of interest: Performing arts; Arts;
Education; Environment; Youth, services; Family
services; Community development; Aging.
Types of support: Management development;
Building/renovation; Equipment; Land
acquisition; Program development; Seed
money; Technical assistance;
Matching/challenge support.
Limitations: Applications not accepted. Giving
limited to Dane County, WI. No support for
religious purposes, political campaigns, or

substance abuse treatment. Generally, no grants to individuals, or for annual campaigns, operating expenses, conferences, endowment funds, deficit financing.
Publications: Annual report.
Application information: Unsolicited requests for funds not accepted.
  Board meeting date(s): 6 times a year
Officers and Board of Governors:* Melany Newby,* Chair.; James Burgess,* Vice-Chair.; Kathleen Woit,* Pres.; Ann Casey, V.P., Fin. and Admin.; Wendy Coe, V.P., Donor Rels.; Amy T. Overby, V.P., Prog.; George Nelson,* Treas.; and 12 additional members.
Number of staff: 4 full-time professional; 1 part-time professional; 2 full-time support; 1 part-time support.
EIN: 396038248

3449
Maihaugen Foundation, Inc.
311 Main St.
La Crosse, WI 54601
Contact: Julia B. Faulkner, Dir.
Application address: 18380 Astor Ct., Apt. 201, Brookfield, WI 53405

Established in 1996 in WI.
Donor(s): Frances May, Merrydelle May.‡
Grantmaker type: Independent foundation
Financial data (yr. ended 12/31/02): Assets, $2,268,458 (M); expenditures, $136,166; qualifying distributions, $120,884; giving activities include $121,000 for 13 grants (high: $50,000; low: $1,000).
Purpose and activities: Focusing on historic preservation, cultural activities, and environmental issues.
Fields of interest: Environment, formal/general education; Animals/wildlife, sanctuaries.
Types of support: Capital campaigns; Building/renovation; Equipment; Land acquisition; Endowments; Program development; Seed money; Curriculum development; Scholarship funds; Research; Matching/challenge support.
Limitations: Giving primarily in Door County and Milwaukee, WI. No grants to individuals, or for scholarships.
Application information: No international applications accepted. Application form not required.
  Initial approach: Pre-proposal letter not exceeding 2 pages
  Copies of proposal: 1
  Deadline(s): None
  Board meeting date(s): Biannually
  Final notification: Within 1 month of application
Directors: Michael R. Burton; Paul R. Burton; Julia B. Faulkner; Frances May.
Investment Trustee: North Central Trust Co.
EIN: 391857836

3450
Marshfield Area Community Foundation
P.O. Box 456
Marshfield, WI 54449 (715) 384-9029
Contact: Dean Markwardt, Exec. Dir.
FAX: (715) 384-9029; *E-mail:* macf@tznet.com

Established in 1993 in WI.

Donor(s): Harry Chronquist,‡ Gladys Chronquist,‡ G. Stanley Custer,‡ Violet Custer,‡ Leonard L. Hartl,‡ Margaret Quirt Heck,‡ Melvin A. Hintz,‡ LaVerne R. Kohs,‡ Patrice LeGrand,‡ J.P. Leonard,‡ George Mac Kinnon,‡ and 15 additional donors.
Grantmaker type: Community foundation
Financial data (yr. ended 12/31/01): Assets, $1,824,924 (M); gifts received, $405,582; expenditures, $297,207; giving activities include $230,848 for 25 grants (high: $93,005; low: $37; average: $38–$51,215) and $22,084 for 34 grants to individuals (high: $1,500; low: $205; average: $205–$1,500).
Purpose and activities: Giving primarily for education, the arts, and community recreation. The foundation administers a donor-advised fund.
Fields of interest: Arts; Education; Environment; Recreation; Community development, neighborhood development.
Types of support: General/operating support; Capital campaigns; Equipment; Endowments; Program development; Conferences/seminars; Publication; Scholarship funds; Technical assistance; Grants to individuals; Scholarships—to individuals; In-kind gifts.
Limitations: Giving limited to Marshfield, WI and surrounding areas.
Publications: Annual report, Financial statement, Grants list, Informational brochure (including application guidelines).
Application information: Application form required.
  Initial approach: Letter (no more than 2 pages)
  Copies of proposal: 7
  Deadline(s): Sept. 1
  Board meeting date(s): Last Tues. in Jan., Mar., May, July, Sept., and Nov.
  Final notification: Following Sept. board meeting
Officers and Trustees:* Dennis DeVetter,* Chair.; Deborah Janz,* Chair., Allocations; John Bujalski, Chair., Devel.; James Bartelt, Chair., Investments; Jane Wagner,* Chair., Promotions; Georgette Frazer,* Chair., Fin. and Mgmt.; Pat Anderson,* Vice-Chair.; Terri Malueg, Secy.; Anne Adler; Elizabeth Adler; Michelle Boernke; Steve Johnson; John Adam Kruse; Rev. Dean Pingle; Terri Richards; Aaron Staab; Connie Willfahrt.
Number of staff: 1 part-time professional; 1 part-time support.
EIN: 396578767

3451
Menasha Corporation Contributions Program
P.O. Box 367
Neenah, WI 54957
Contact: Roger Ackerman, Mgr., Corp. Purchasing

Grantmaker type: Corporate giving program
Purpose and activities: As a complement to its foundation, Menasha also makes charitable contributions to nonprofit organizations directly. Support is given primarily in areas of company operations.
Fields of interest: Arts; Education; Environment; Health care; Human services; Public affairs.

Types of support: Scholarship funds; Employee volunteer services; Sponsorships; Employee matching gifts.
Limitations: Giving primarily in areas of company operations.
Application information: Application form not required.
  Initial approach: Proposal to headquarters
  Copies of proposal: 1
  Deadline(s): None
  Final notification: Following review

3452
Menasha Corporation Foundation
P.O. Box 367
Neenah, WI 54957-0367 (920) 751-1000
Contact: Steven S. Kromholz, Pres.

Established in 1953 in WI.
Donor(s): Menasha Corp.
Grantmaker type: Company-sponsored foundation
Financial data (yr. ended 12/31/02): Assets, $690,998 (M); gifts received, $317,000; expenditures, $552,061; qualifying distributions, $548,265; giving activities include $412,553 for grants, $53,500 for grants to individuals and $60,016 for employee matching gifts.
Purpose and activities: Grants primarily for health, welfare, community funds, cultural, environmental, and higher educational organizations in areas of company operations; giving also for employee-related scholarships and an employee matching gift program.
Fields of interest: Media/communications; Arts; Higher education; Business school/education; Education; Natural resources; Environment; Hospitals (general); Health care; Health organizations, association; Human services; Community development; Federated giving programs; Economics.
Types of support: General/operating support; Continuing support; Annual campaigns; Capital campaigns; Building/renovation; Equipment; Emergency funds; Program development; Curriculum development; Fellowships; Scholarship funds; Research; Employee matching gifts; Employee-related scholarships; Matching/challenge support.
Limitations: Giving primarily in areas of company operations. No grants to individuals (except for employee-related scholarships).
Publications: Application guidelines.
Application information: Application form required.
  Initial approach: Proposal
  Copies of proposal: 1
  Deadline(s): 15th day of month preceding board meeting
  Board meeting date(s): Feb., May, Sept., and Dec.
Officers: Oliver C. Smith, Chair.; Steven S. Kromholz, Pres.; Kristine A. Pavletich, V.P.; Angie Burns, Secy.; Kevin Schuh, Treas.
Number of staff: None.
EIN: 396047384

3453
The Merrill Foundation, Inc.
312 E. Wisconsin Ave., Ste. 402
Milwaukee, WI 53201 (414) 765-5668
Contact: Marion C. Read, Pres.

Established in 1997 in WI.
Donor(s): Marion C. Read.
Grantmaker type: Independent foundation
Financial data (yr. ended 12/31/02): Assets,
$1,123,757 (M); gifts received, $219,950;
expenditures, $299,985; qualifying distributions,
$284,688; giving activities include $286,997 for
32 grants (high: $101,000; low: $200).
Fields of interest: University; Natural resources;
Botanical gardens; Zoos/zoological societies;
Christian agencies & churches.
Limitations: Giving primarily in Milwaukee, WI.
Application information: Application form not
required.
Deadline(s): None
Officers and Directors:* Marion Chester Read,*
Pres.; Verne R. Read,* V.P.; Alice E. Read,* Secy.;
V. Ross Read III,* Treas.; Alexander R. Read;
Thomas Merrill Read.
Trustee: U.S. Bank, N.A.
EIN: 391892801

3454
Robert T. Meyer Foundation
(formerly Robert T. and Betty Rose Meyer Family
Foundation)
469 Security Blvd.
Green Bay, WI 54313
Contact: Mark McMullen, Tr.
Application address: P.O. Box 19006, Green
Bay, WI 54307-9006, tel.: (920) 433-3102

Established in 1985 in WI.
Donor(s): Janet E. Meyer.
Grantmaker type: Independent foundation
Financial data (yr. ended 12/31/02): Assets,
$3,079,539 (M); expenditures, $116,162;
qualifying distributions, $95,500; giving
activities include $95,500 for 19 grants (high:
$10,000; low: $1,000).
Fields of interest: Museums; Higher education;
Natural resources; Environmental education;
Youth development, centers/clubs; Human
services; Federated giving programs.
Limitations: Giving primarily in Green Bay, WI.
Application information: Application form not
required.
Initial approach: Letter or proposal
Copies of proposal: 1
Deadline(s): None
Trustees: Mark McMullen; Janet E. Meyer; John
M. Rose.
EIN: 396413619

3455
Greater Milwaukee Foundation ▼
(formerly Milwaukee Foundation)
1020 N. Broadway, Ste. 112
Milwaukee, WI 53202 (414) 272-5805
Contact: Douglas M. Jansson, Exec. Dir.
FAX: (414) 272-6235; E-mail: info@mkefdn.org;
URL: http://
www.greatermilwaukeefoundation.org

Established in 1915 in WI by declaration of trust.
Grantmaker type: Community foundation

Financial data (yr. ended 12/31/02): Assets,
$279,978,699 (M); gifts received, $29,605,291;
expenditures, $25,364,406; giving activities
include $21,130,356 for 2,092 grants (high:
$1,000,000; low: $100).
Purpose and activities: Present funds include
many discretionary funds and some funds
designated by the donors to benefit specific
institutions or for special purposes, including
educational institutions, the arts and cultural
programs, community development, social
services, and health care; support also for
conservation and historic preservation.
Fields of interest: Visual arts; Performing arts;
Dance; Historic preservation/historical societies;
Arts; Early childhood education; Child
development, education; Elementary
school/education; Secondary school/education;
Higher education; Adult/continuing education;
Education; Natural resources; Family planning;
Health care; Substance abuse, services; Mental
health/crisis services; Health organizations,
association; AIDS; Alcoholism; AIDS research;
Crime/violence prevention, youth; Legal
services; Employment, training; Employment;
Food services; Nutrition; Housing/shelter,
development; Recreation; Human services;
Children/youth, services; Child development,
services; Family services; Aging,
centers/services; Women, centers/services;
Homeless, human services; Race/intergroup
relations; Urban/community development;
Community development; Public policy,
research; Government/public administration;
Minorities; Disabled; Aging; Women;
Economically disadvantaged; Homeless.
Types of support: Capital campaigns;
Building/renovation; Equipment; Land
acquisition; Program development; Seed
money; Technical assistance;
Matching/challenge support.
Limitations: Giving primarily in Milwaukee,
Waukesha, Ozaukee, and Washington counties
of WI. No support for the general use of
churches or for sectarian religious purposes, or
for specific medical or scientific projects, except
from components of the foundation established
for such purposes. No grants to individuals
(except for established awards), or for operating
budgets, continuing support, annual campaigns,
endowment funds, or deficit financing.
Publications: Application guidelines, Annual
report (including application guidelines), Grants
list, Informational brochure (including
application guidelines), Newsletter, Program
policy statement.
Application information: The foundation uses
the Common Application Form used by many
Milwaukee-area foundations. Capital requests
are reviewed at Dec. board meeting.
Application form required.
Initial approach: Letter of intent
Copies of proposal: 1
Deadline(s): Submit preferably 10 weeks
before board meetings; deadlines Jan. 2,
Apr. 1, July 1, and Oct. 1
Board meeting date(s): Mar., June, Sept., Dec.,
and as needed
Final notification: 1 week after board meetings
Officers: Douglas M. Jansson, Pres., Secy., and
Exec. Dir.; James A. Marks, V.P.; Wendy Horton,
C.F.O.
Directors: Linda T. Mellowes, Chair.; Stephen H.
Marcus, Vice-Chair.; Ned W. Bechthold;

Franklyn M. Gimbel; Stephen N. Graff; George
Kaiser; Patricia McKeithan; Jose A. Olivieri; Joan
Marie Prince, Ph.D.; Augustas A. Ramirez;
Blaine E. Rieke; Frederick P. Stratton, Jr.
Trustees: Bank One Investment Advisors
Corporation; Firstar Investment Research and
Management Company; Marshall & Ilsley Bank;
The Northern Trust Co.; U.S. Bank, N.A.
Number of staff: 24 full-time professional; 1
part-time professional; 5 full-time support.
EIN: 396036407

3456
Outagamie Charitable Foundation, Inc.
100 W. Lawrence St.
P.O. Box 727
Appleton, WI 54912-0727

Established in 1985 in WI.
Donor(s): Fox Valley Corp.
Grantmaker type: Independent foundation
Financial data (yr. ended 03/31/02): Assets,
$7,206,642 (M); expenditures, $455,343;
qualifying distributions, $400,024; giving
activities include $405,000 for 18 grants (high:
$100,000; low: $3,000).
Purpose and activities: Giving primarily for the
arts, education, nature conservancy, human
services, children and youth services, federated
giving programs, and the YMCA.
Fields of interest: Arts; Higher education;
Natural resources; Human services; YM/YWCAs
& YM/YWHAs; Federated giving programs.
Limitations: Applications not accepted. Giving
on a national basis. No grants to individuals.
Application information: Contributes only to
pre-selected organizations.
Officers and Directors:* Linda Jacob,* Pres.;
David Buchanan,* V.P.; Lyle H. Richter,
Secy.-Treas.; Betsey Aalfs; Charlie Buchanan;
John Buchanan; Wendy Buchanan; Caroline
Fey; James Lenfestey.
EIN: 391526589

3457
The Pangburn Foundation
c/o Bank One Trust Co., N.A.
P.O. Box 1308
Milwaukee, WI 53201
Contact: Robert Lansford
Application address: c/o Bank One, Texas, N.A.,
P.O. Box 2050, Fort Worth, TX 76113, tel.: (817)
884-4151

Established in 1962 in TX.
Grantmaker type: Independent foundation
Financial data (yr. ended 03/31/02): Assets,
$8,114,631 (M); expenditures, $498,261;
qualifying distributions, $429,072; giving
activities include $414,500 for 12 grants (high:
$100,000; low: $1,000).
Purpose and activities: Emphasis on cultural
programs, especially music and the performing
arts.
Fields of interest: Museums
(science/technology); Performing arts;
Education; Zoos/zoological societies; Boys &
girls clubs; Big Brothers/Big Sisters; Human
services; Foundations (public); Christian
agencies & churches.
Limitations: Giving primarily in the Fort Worth,
TX, area. No grants to individuals.

Application information:
  Initial approach: Letter
  Copies of proposal: 1
  Deadline(s): Sept. 30
  Board meeting date(s): Oct. or Nov.
Trustee: Bank One, N.A.
EIN: 756042630

3458
Edwin E. Perkins Foundation
c/o Bank One Trust Co., N.A.
P.O. Box 1308
Milwaukee, WI 53201
Contact: Gary A. Cueno

Established in 1961 in IL.
Donor(s): Edwin E. Perkins.‡
Grantmaker type: Independent foundation
Financial data (yr. ended 01/31/02): Assets,
$4,265,671 (M); expenditures, $424,761;
qualifying distributions, $331,753; giving
activities include $320,000 for 12 grants (high:
$50,000; low: $5,000).
Purpose and activities: Giving for animal
welfare, treatment of alcoholism, human
services, and the economically disadvantaged.
Fields of interest: Animal welfare; Alcoholism;
Human services; Children/youth, services;
Economically disadvantaged.
Types of support: General/operating support.
Limitations: Giving primarily on the West Coast.
Application information: Application form not
required.
  Initial approach: Letter
  Copies of proposal: 1
  Deadline(s): None
Trustees: Thomas J. O'Neil; Catherine O.
Williford; Bank One, N.A.
EIN: 366090223

3459
R. D. and Linda Peters Foundation, Inc.
c/o Bank One Trust Co., N.A.
P.O. Box 1308
Milwaukee, WI 53201 (414) 765-2445
Contact: Richard G. Hugo, Dir.

Established in 1965.
Donor(s): R.D. Peters,‡ Linda Peters.‡
Grantmaker type: Independent foundation
Financial data (yr. ended 12/31/02): Assets,
$5,447,565 (M); expenditures, $375,755;
qualifying distributions, $331,064; giving
activities include $317,006 for 26 grants (high:
$100,006; low: $1,000).
Purpose and activities: Emphasis normally
restricted to conservation endeavors, an
educational scholarship fund, and youth
activities; support also for a medical college.
Fields of interest: Medical school/education;
Engineering school/education; Education;
Natural resources; Youth, services.
Types of support: General/operating support;
Capital campaigns; Equipment; Research.
Limitations: Giving primarily in the Brillion, WI,
area.
Application information: Application form not
required.
  Initial approach: Proposal
  Copies of proposal: 4
  Deadline(s): None
  Board meeting date(s): Quarterly

Directors: F. William Haberman; Richard G.
Hugo; Lowell O. Reese; Harold Wolf.
Trustee: Bank One Trust Co., N.A.
EIN: 396097994

3460
Ellsworth and Carla Peterson Charitable Foundation
55 Utopia Cir.
Sturgeon Bay, WI 54235
Contact: Ellsworth L. Peterson, or Carla J.
Peterson, Trustees

Established in 1992 in WI.
Donor(s): Ellsworth L. Peterson, Carla J.
Peterson.
Grantmaker type: Independent foundation
Financial data (yr. ended 10/31/02): Assets,
$2,445,493 (M); expenditures, $281,537;
qualifying distributions, $276,900; giving
activities include $265,176 for 101 grants (high:
$50,000; low: $10).
Purpose and activities: Giving primarily for the
arts, the environment, and human services.
Fields of interest: Historical activities; Arts;
Environment; Hospitals (general); Human
services; YM/YWCAs & YM/YWHAs;
Community development; Federated giving
programs.
Limitations: Giving primarily in WI.
Application information:
  Initial approach: Letter
  Deadline(s): None
Trustees: Carla J. Peterson; Ellsworth L. Peterson.
EIN: 396566719

3461
Jane Bradley Pettit Foundation ▼
(formerly Jane and Lloyd Pettit Foundation, Inc.)
660 E. Mason St.
Milwaukee, WI 53202 (414) 227-1266
Contact: Margaret T. Lund, V.P.
URL: http://www.jbpf.org

Incorporated in 1986 in WI.
Donor(s): Jane Bradley Pettit.‡
Grantmaker type: Independent foundation
Financial data (yr. ended 12/31/01): Assets,
$7,474,339 (M); gifts received, $19,158,388;
expenditures, $15,149,308; qualifying
distributions, $15,017,160; giving activities
include $14,575,848 for 185 grants (high:
$1,000,000; low: $280; average:
$10,000–$500,000).
Purpose and activities: Giving to projects which
promote the welfare of families, children, the
elderly and disadvantaged of the greater
Milwaukee area. The foundation supports
charitable organizations in the arts, community
and social welfare, education, and community
health.
Fields of interest: Secondary school/education;
Higher education; Hospitals (general); Health
care; Health organizations, association; Human
services; Children/youth, services; Children,
services; Aging, centers/services; Women,
centers/services.
Types of support: General/operating support;
Annual campaigns; Capital campaigns;
Building/renovation; Program development;
Research.

Limitations: Giving primarily in the greater
Milwaukee, WI, area. No grants to individuals.
Publications: Application guidelines.
Application information: The foundation will
not consider requests for additional support for
the period in which an organization currently
has a grant in effect.
  Initial approach: Letter of inquiry
  Copies of proposal: 1
  Deadline(s): Jan. 15, May 15, and Sept. 15
  Board meeting date(s): Varies
  Final notification: Following board meeting
Officers and Directors:* Francis R. Croak,*
Pres.; Margaret T. Lund,* V.P.; JoAnn C.
Youngman,* Secy.-Treas.
Number of staff: None.
EIN: 391574123
**Recent environmental and animal welfare
grants:**
3461-1 Boerner Botanical Gardens, Hales
  Corners, WI, $500,000. 2001.
3461-2 Conservancy of Southwest Florida,
  Naples, FL, $25,400. 2001.
3461-3 Growing Power, Milwaukee, WI,
  $50,000. 2001.
3461-4 Humane Society, Wisconsin,
  Milwaukee, WI, $50,000. 2001.
3461-5 International Crane Foundation,
  Baraboo, WI, $50,000. 2001.
3461-6 International Crane Foundation,
  Baraboo, WI, $50,000. 2001.
3461-7 Pets Helping People, New Berlin, WI,
  $10,000. 2001.
3461-8 Rachels Network, DC, $10,000. 2001.
3461-9 Riveredge Nature Center, Milwaukee,
  WI, $250,000. 2001.
3461-10 Riveredge Nature Center, Milwaukee,
  WI, $250,000. 2001.
3461-11 Riveredge Nature Center, Milwaukee,
  WI, $75,000. 2001.
3461-12 Schlitz Audubon Center, Milwaukee,
  WI, $250,000. 2001.
3461-13 Schlitz Audubon Center, Milwaukee,
  WI, $250,000. 2001.
3461-14 Schlitz Audubon Center, Milwaukee,
  WI, $18,946. 2001.
3461-15 Urban Ecology Center, Milwaukee, WI,
  $20,000. 2001.

3462
Anthony Petullo Foundation, Inc.
312 E. Buffalo St., Ste. 200
Milwaukee, WI 53202

Established in 1999 in WI.
Donor(s): Anthony Petullo.
Grantmaker type: Independent foundation
Financial data (yr. ended 09/30/02): Assets,
$1,941,683 (M); expenditures, $186,016;
qualifying distributions, $164,408; giving
activities include $124,100 for 38 grants (high:
$17,000; low: $250).
Purpose and activities: Giving primarily for the
visual and performing arts, and for education.
Fields of interest: Arts; Education; Animal
welfare.
Limitations: Giving primarily in southeastern WI.
Application information: Donors Forum of
Wisconsin Common Application Form must be
used. Application form required.
  Deadline(s): Feb., June, and Oct.
  Final notification: Mar., July, and Nov.

Officers: Anthony Petullo, Pres.; Amy Cesarz, Exec. Dir.
Directors: Henry Loos; Katherine Minerath; Meg Petullo.
EIN: 311656951

3463
Robert W. & Josephine Pieper Foundation, Inc.
14425 Westover Rd.
Elm Grove, WI 53122-1634

Established in 1963 in WI.
Donor(s): Isabel Schendel.‡
Grantmaker type: Independent foundation
Financial data (yr. ended 12/31/02): Assets, $61,610 (M); gifts received, $112,125; expenditures, $134,377; qualifying distributions, $133,500; giving activities include $133,500 for 8 grants (high: $33,500; low: $5,000).
Fields of interest: Secondary school/education; Higher education; Natural resources; Boys & girls clubs.
Limitations: Applications not accepted. Giving primarily in WI. No grants to individuals.
Application information: Contributes only to pre-selected organizations.
Directors: Harold Emch, Jr.; William R. Law; Richard A. Sachs; Richard A. Sachs, Jr.
EIN: 396083875

3464
Pollybill Foundation, Inc.
111 E. Kilbourn Ave., 19th Fl.
Milwaukee, WI 53202-6622

Incorporated in 1960 in WI.
Donor(s): William D. Van Dyke, Polly H. Van Dyke.
Grantmaker type: Independent foundation
Financial data (yr. ended 12/31/01): Assets, $4,408,684 (M); gifts received, $1,457,000; expenditures, $1,725,714; qualifying distributions, $1,641,874; giving activities include $1,656,350 for 63 grants (high: $350,000; low: $500).
Purpose and activities: Giving primarily for arts and culture, particularly for the symphony, and institute of art and design, resource conservation, particularly a botanical garden and the Audubon Society, hospitals, family planning, social services, and federated giving programs.
Fields of interest: Arts education; Museums (art); Orchestra (symphony); Higher education; Natural resources; Botanical gardens; Hospitals (general); Family planning; Human services; Children, services; Federated giving programs.
Limitations: Applications not accepted. Giving primarily in Milwaukee, WI. No grants to individuals.
Application information: Contributes only to pre-selected organizations.
Officers and Directors:* Polly H. Van Dyke,* Pres. and Treas.; William D. Van Dyke III,* V.P.; Paul F. Meissner,* Secy.; Leonard C. Campbell.
EIN: 396078550

3465
Puelicher Foundation, Inc.
1000 N. Water St.
Milwaukee, WI 53202 (414) 287-7184
Contact: James B. Wigdale, Pres.

Established in 1956.
Donor(s): John A. Puelicher.
Grantmaker type: Independent foundation
Financial data (yr. ended 12/31/01): Assets, $10,953,035 (M); expenditures, $1,387,694; qualifying distributions, $1,341,865; giving activities include $1,345,500 for 28 grants (high: $500,000; low: $5,000; average: $1,000–$250,000).
Purpose and activities: Funding primarily for a university and for wildlife conservation.
Fields of interest: Arts; Higher education; Natural resources; Animals/wildlife, preservation/protection; Human services.
Types of support: General/operating support; Scholarship funds.
Limitations: Giving primarily in Milwaukee, WI.
Application information:
  Initial approach: Letter, including expected community benefits
  Deadline(s): None
Officers and Director:* James B. Wigdale, Pres.; Mary P. Uihlein,* V.P.; Diane L. Sebion, Secy.-Treas.
EIN: 396055461

3466
Kailas J. & Becky L. Rao Foundation
5270 N. Lake Dr.
Milwaukee, WI 53217
Contact: Kailas J. Rao, Tr.

Established in 1993 in WI.
Donor(s): Carol V. Jackley.
Grantmaker type: Independent foundation
Financial data (yr. ended 12/31/02): Assets, $701,993 (M); expenditures, $197,113; qualifying distributions, $187,290; giving activities include $187,290 for 22 grants (high: $50,000; low: $250).
Fields of interest: Cultural/ethnic awareness; Higher education; Animal welfare; Boys & girls clubs; Religion.
Types of support: Scholarships—to individuals.
Limitations: Giving primarily in WI.
Application information: Application form not required.
  Initial approach: Letter
  Deadline(s): None
Trustees: Becky L. Rao; Kailas J. Rao.
EIN: 396584791

3467
Reiman Charitable Foundation, Inc. ▼
115 S. 84th St., No. 221
Milwaukee, WI 53214

Established in 1986 in WI.
Donor(s): Roy J. Reiman, Roberta M. Reiman, Scott J. Reiman, Joni R. Winston, Cynthia A. Lambert, Julia M. Ellis, Terrin S. Riemer.
Grantmaker type: Independent foundation
Financial data (yr. ended 12/31/01): Assets, $129,220,590 (M); gifts received, $7,500,000; expenditures, $12,543,105; qualifying distributions, $11,482,528; giving activities

include $11,482,528 for 107 grants (high: $4,062,801; low: $100; average: $5,000–$100,000).
Purpose and activities: Giving primarily for education, health care, and human services.
Fields of interest: Arts; Education; Animal welfare; Hospitals (general); Health organizations, association; Human services; Religion.
Limitations: Applications not accepted. No grants to individuals.
Application information: Contributes only to pre-selected organizations.
Officers and Directors:* Scott J. Reiman,* Pres.; Brian F. Fleischmann,* V.P.; Roberta M. Reiman,* V.P.; Roy J. Reiman,* V.P.; Michael J. Hipp,* Secy.; Troy G. Hildebrandt.
EIN: 391570264
Recent environmental and animal welfare grants:
3467-1 Colorado State University, Fort Collins, CO, $100,000. For Animal Cancer Center Building Fund. 2001.
3467-2 Colorado State University, Fort Collins, CO, $100,000. For Animal Cancer Building Fund. 2001.
3467-3 Colorado State University, Fort Collins, CO, $100,000. For Animal Cancer Center Building Fund. 2001.
3467-4 Colorados Ocean Journey, Denver, CO, $20,000. For general operating support. 2001.
3467-5 Denver Dumb Friends League-Humane Society of Denver, Denver, CO, $20,000. For general operating support. 2001.
3467-6 Denver Dumb Friends League-Humane Society of Denver, Denver, CO, $10,000. For general operating support. 2001.
3467-7 Denver Dumb Friends League-Humane Society of Denver, Denver, CO, $10,000. For general operating support. 2001.
3467-8 Denver Dumb Friends League-Humane Society of Denver, Denver, CO, $10,000. For general operating support. 2001.
3467-9 Denver Dumb Friends League-Humane Society of Denver, Denver, CO, $10,000. For general operating support. 2001.
3467-10 Greendale Park and Recreation Department, Greendale, WI, $31,577. For birdhouse workshop. 2001.
3467-11 Iowa State University, Ames, IA, $455,200. For Reiman Gardens Conservatory Building Fund. 2001.
3467-12 Iowa State University, Ames, IA, $315,122. For Reiman Gardens. 2001.
3467-13 Iowa State University Foundation, Ames, IA, $40,000. For Reiman Gardens Conservatory. 2001.
3467-14 Iowa State University Foundation, Ames, IA, $20,000. For Reiman Gardens. 2001.

3468
The Oscar Rennebohm Foundation, Inc.
P.O. Box 5187
Madison, WI 53719 (608) 274-5991
Contact: Steven F. Skolaski, Pres. and Treas.

Incorporated in 1949 in WI.
Donor(s): Oscar Rennebohm.‡
Grantmaker type: Independent foundation
Financial data (yr. ended 12/31/01): Assets, $58,078,906 (M); expenditures, $2,935,145;

qualifying distributions, $2,502,000; giving activities include $2,502,000 for 4 grants (high: $2,062,000; low: $100,000; average: $100,000–$2,062,000).
Purpose and activities: Emphasis on higher education; support also for the arts, conservation, and health and social service agencies.
Fields of interest: Multipurpose centers/programs; Higher education; Environmental education; Medical care, rehabilitation.
Types of support: Building/renovation; Equipment; Research.
Limitations: Giving primarily in WI.
Application information: Application form not required.
  Initial approach: Letter
  Deadline(s): None
Officers: Steven F. Skolaski, Pres. and Treas.; William H. Young, V.P.; Leona A. Sonderegger, Secy.
Directors: Patrick E. Coyle; Curtis F. Hastings; Robert B. Rennebohm.
EIN: 396039252

3469
Rexnord Foundation Inc.
P.O. Box 2191
Milwaukee, WI 53201-2191
Scholarship address: c/o Scholarship Admin., Rexnord Corp., 4701 W. Greenfield Ave., Milwaukee, WI 53214, tel.: (414) 643-2505

Incorporated in 1953 in WI.
Donor(s): Rexnord Corp.
Grantmaker type: Company-sponsored foundation
Financial data (yr. ended 10/31/02): Assets, $3,553,401 (M); expenditures, $139,363; qualifying distributions, $135,035; giving activities include $74,250 for grants and $60,629 for employee matching gifts.
Purpose and activities: Awards scholarships to children or dependents of Rexnord employees who have scored 20 on the ACT or 1000 on the SAT. Funding also for the arts, education, health associations and hospitals, animal welfare, children, youth and social services, and the United Way.
Fields of interest: Performing arts; Arts; Elementary/secondary education; Higher education; Animal welfare; Hospitals (general); Health organizations; Human services; Children/youth, services; Family services; Federated giving programs.
Types of support: Building/renovation; Program development; Employee matching gifts; Employee-related scholarships.
Limitations: Giving primarily in areas of company operations, with some emphasis on Milwaukee, WI. No support for religious organizations. No grants to individuals (except for employee-related scholarships), or for endowment funds.
Publications: Application guidelines.
Application information: Application form not required.
  Initial approach: Letter or proposal
  Copies of proposal: 1
  Deadline(s): June 12
  Board meeting date(s): 2 or 3 times per year
  Final notification: 6 months

Officers and Directors:* C.R. Roy,* Pres. and Treas.; J.R. Swenson,* V.P. and Secy.; P.C. Wallace,* V.P.; R.M. MacQueen; W.E. Schauer; D. Taylor; R.R. Wallis.
Number of staff: None.
EIN: 396042029

3470
Ripples, Inc.
P.O. Box 128
Townsend, WI 54175-0128

Established in 1999.
Grantmaker type: Independent foundation
Financial data (yr. ended 12/31/02): Assets, $3,440,523 (M); expenditures, $206,680; qualifying distributions, $185,280; giving activities include $180,000 for 5 grants (high: $75,000; low: $15,000).
Purpose and activities: Giving primarily for natural resource conservation, and higher education.
Fields of interest: Higher education; Natural resources.
Limitations: Applications not accepted. Giving primarily in FL and WI. No grants to individuals.
Application information: Contributes only to pre-selected organizations.
Officers: Harold Petraske, Pres. and Treas.; Gretchen Petraske, V.P. and Secy.
Director: Susan Rose.
EIN: 391938912

3471
Sand County Foundation, Inc.
1955 Atwood Ave.
P.O. Box 3186
Madison, WI 53704

Classified as a private operating foundation in 1987.
Donor(s): Nash Williams, Wisconsin Dept. of Natural Resources, Norman Basset Foundation, US Fish and Wildlife, Ed Warner, Wisconsin Dept. of Transportation.
Grantmaker type: Operating foundation
Financial data (yr. ended 12/31/02): Assets, $3,493,790 (M); gifts received, $377,883; expenditures, $1,732,842; qualifying distributions, $1,266,157; giving activities include $334,183 for 11 grants (high: $92,852; low: $2,500) and $1,114,279 for foundation-administered programs.
Purpose and activities: Primary support for ecology of body waters and rivers; some giving to seminar on water and land restoration.
Fields of interest: Environment, water resources; Environment, land resources; Education.
International interests: Southern Africa.
Types of support: General/operating support; Program development; Conferences/seminars; Research.
Limitations: Applications not accepted. No grants to individuals.
Application information: Contributes only to pre-selected organizations.
Officers: Reed Coleman, Chair.; Brent M. Haglund, Pres.; Howard W. Mead, V.P.; David J. Hanson, Secy.-Treas.
Directors: Helen Alexander; Thomas Bourland; Craig Kennedy; Scott Klug; Paul Risser; Toby

Sherry; Peter Stent; Nash Williams; James Wood; and 7 additional directors.
EIN: 396089450

3472
Douglas and Eleanor Seaman Charitable Foundation
5205 N. Ironwood Ln., Ste. 101
Milwaukee, WI 53217-4907 (414) 964-6310
Contact: Douglas Seaman, Tr.

Established in 1997 in WI.
Donor(s): Douglas Seaman.
Grantmaker type: Independent foundation
Financial data (yr. ended 12/31/02): Assets, $1,692,025 (M); expenditures, $141,579; qualifying distributions, $123,202; giving activities include $123,202 for 66 grants (high: $10,650; low: $50).
Purpose and activities: Giving for human services, education, medical centers, arts, and women's associations.
Fields of interest: Arts; Medical school/education; Education; Botanical gardens; Health care; Health organizations, research; Human services; Christian agencies & churches; Women.
Limitations: Applications not accepted. Giving on a national basis. No grants to individuals.
Application information: Contributes only to pre-selected organizations.
Trustees: Harry V. Carlson; Gerald L. Hestekin; Douglas Seaman; Eleanor R. Seaman; Joseph B. Tyson, Jr.
EIN: 396636617

3473
Seeds of Faith, Inc.
P.O. Box 197
Hartland, WI 53029 (262) 367-1990
Contact: William Rose, Pres.

Established in 1999 in WI.
Grantmaker type: Independent foundation
Financial data (yr. ended 12/31/02): Assets, $3,101,791 (M); expenditures, $215,014; qualifying distributions, $179,758; giving activities include $180,000 for 6 grants (high: $50,000; low: $20,000).
Fields of interest: Education; Environment, pollution control; Human services; Christian agencies & churches.
Limitations: Giving primarily in WI.
Application information: Application form not required.
  Initial approach: Letter
  Deadline(s): None
Officers: William Rose, Pres. and Treas.; Susan Rose, V.P. and Secy.
Director: Gretchen Petraske.
EIN: 391938697

3474
Shockley Foundation
401 Charmany Dr., Ste. 200
Madison, WI 53719 (608) 288-3040
Contact: Terry K. Shockley, Tr.

Established 2001 in WI.
Donor(s): Terry Shockley, Sandy Shockley.

Grantmaker type: Independent foundation
Financial data (yr. ended 12/31/01): Assets, $1,006,558 (M); gifts received, $1,105,000; expenditures, $99,000; qualifying distributions, $98,994; giving activities include $99,000 for 17 grants (high: $25,000; low: $100).
Purpose and activities: Giving primarily for education and human services.
Fields of interest: Higher education; Aquariums; Health care; Athletics/sports, amateur leagues; Boy scouts; Human services.
Types of support: General/operating support.
Limitations: Applications not accepted. Giving primarily in IL, KS, MN, and WI. No grants to individuals.
Application information: Contributes only to pre-selected organizations.
Board meeting date(s): Jan. and Sept.
Trustees: Toni K. Peterson; Sandra K. Shockley; Terry K. Shockley; Todd L. Shockley.
EIN: 396764154

3475
Silverman Family Foundation
P.O. Box 2980
Milwaukee, WI 53201

Established in 1993 in WI.
Donor(s): Albert A. Silverman, Francie H. Silverman.
Grantmaker type: Independent foundation
Financial data (yr. ended 12/31/02): Assets, $1,894,227 (M); gifts received, $500,000; expenditures, $160,139; qualifying distributions, $149,662; giving activities include $150,600 for 52 grants (high: $45,000; low: $600).
Fields of interest: Higher education; Animals/wildlife; Hospitals (general); Food services; Protestant agencies & churches; Jewish agencies & temples; Religion.
Limitations: Applications not accepted. Giving primarily in WI. No grants to individuals.
Application information: Contributes only to pre-selected organizations.
Trustees: William T. Gaus; Francie H. Silverman.
EIN: 396577946

3476
Frances C. & William P. Smallwood Foundation
(also known as Smallwood Foundation)
c/o Bank One Trust Co., N.A.
P.O. Box 1308
Milwaukee, WI 53201
Contact: Rick S. Piersall
Application address: c/o Bank One, Texas, N.A., P.O. Box 2050, Fort Worth, TX 76113

Established in 1968.
Donor(s): William P. Smallwood Trust.
Grantmaker type: Independent foundation
Financial data (yr. ended 12/31/02): Assets, $8,366,034 (M); expenditures, $510,167; qualifying distributions, $463,835; giving activities include $444,552 for 28 grants (high: $50,000; low: $3,000).
Purpose and activities: Giving primarily for medical research, education, the arts, and human services.
Fields of interest: Historical activities; Arts; Libraries (public); Education; Natural resources; Medical research, institute.

Limitations: Giving primarily in Chapel Hill, NC, NV and Tarrant County, TX. No grants to individuals.
Application information: Requirements vary depending on type of grant requested.
Initial approach: Request guidelines
Deadline(s): None
Trustees: Saul Baker; Harry Bartel; Sally Muller; Rick Piersall; Suzy Stockdale.
Agent: Bank One Trust Co., N.A.
EIN: 237000306

3477
Nancy Woodson Spire Foundation, Inc.
P.O. Box 65
Wausau, WI 54402-0065 (715) 845-9201
Contact: San W. Orr, Jr., Pres.

Grantmaker type: Independent foundation
Financial data (yr. ended 06/30/02): Assets, $34,295,348 (M); gifts received, $16,210,356; expenditures, $1,590,427; qualifying distributions, $1,521,476; giving activities include $1,505,000 for 4 grants (high: $500,000; low: $275,000).
Fields of interest: Museums; Higher education; Environment.
Limitations: Giving primarily in Wausau, WI.
Application information: Application form not required.
Deadline(s): None
Officers and Directors:* San W. Orr, Jr.,* Pres.; Ann M. Dubore,* Secy.; Julie A. Williams,* Treas.; Daryl E. Gebhart.
EIN: 391367383

3478
St. Croix Valley Community Foundation
516 2nd St., Ste. 214
P.O. Box 39
Hudson, WI 54016 (715) 386-9490
Contact: David H. Griffith, Pres.
FAX: (715) 386-1250; E-mail: info@scvcf.org; URL: http://www.scvcf.org

Established in 1995.
Grantmaker type: Community foundation
Financial data (yr. ended 06/30/02): Assets, $3,703,071 (L); gifts received, $2,450,078; expenditures, $600,241; giving activities include $364,993 for 189 grants (high: $100,000; low: $100; average: $500–$3,000) and $8,500 for 10 grants to individuals (high: $1,500; low: $250; average: $250–$1,500).
Purpose and activities: Giving for the arts, education, the environment, human services, and civic projects. The foundation administers donor-advised funds.
Fields of interest: Arts; Education; Environment; Human services; Community development.
Limitations: Giving primarily in Chisago and Washington counties, MN and Pierce, Polk and St. Croix counties, WI.
Publications: Annual report, Financial statement, Informational brochure.
Application information: Applications required for art grants. Application form not required.
Initial approach: Letter
Copies of proposal: 1
Deadline(s): None
Board meeting date(s): 2nd Fri. of each month

Final notification: Within 2 months of submission
Officers and Directors: Orville Johnson,* Chair.; Peter Kilde, Vice-Chair.; David H. Griffith, Pres.; Rita Lawson,* Secy.; John M. Coughlin,* Treas.; Sarah Andersen; John B. Baird; James H. Bradshaw; David H. Brandt; William E. Campbell; Heidi Smith Erspamer; Karen Hansen; Larry Horsch; Marilyn McCarty; Erv Neff; Lynn Shafer; John R. Tunheim; Dan Willius.
Number of staff: 1 full-time professional; 1 part-time support.
EIN: 411817315

3479
The Stateline Community Foundation
(formerly The Greater Beloit Community Foundation)
121 W. Grand Ave.
Beloit, WI 53511 (608) 362-4228
Contact: Tara Tinder, Exec. Dir.
FAX: (608) 362-0056; E-mail: statelinecf@aol.com

Established in 1986 in WI.
Grantmaker type: Community foundation
Financial data (yr. ended 12/31/01): Assets, $4,427,117 (M); expenditures, $362,846; giving activities include $161,253 for 56 grants (high: $11,934; low: $50) and $49,652 for grants to individuals (high: $5,600; low: $250; average: $250–$5,600).
Purpose and activities: The foundation administers a donor-advised fund.
Fields of interest: Performing arts; Arts; Early childhood education; Higher education; Environment; Recreation; Youth development, services; Human services; Children/youth, services; Homeless, human services; Urban/community development; Leadership development; General charitable giving; Minorities; Disabled; Homeless.
Types of support: Equipment; Emergency funds; Program development; Seed money; Curriculum development; Scholarship funds; Program evaluation; Scholarships—to individuals; Matching/challenge support.
Limitations: Applications not accepted. Giving limited to the greater Stateline area encompassing Rock County, WI, and northern Winnebago County, IL. No grants to individuals (except for designated scholarship funds), or for operating budgets, endowment funds, deficit reduction, or medical or scientific research.
Publications: Annual report.
Application information: Unsolicited requests for funds not accepted.
Officers and Directors:* John Erikson,* Chair.; D. Richard Barder, 1st Vice-Chair.; Charldene Schnier,* Secy.; Bruce Lans,* Treas.; Tara Tinder, Exec. Dir.; Joanne Acomb; Richard Bastian; Sally Burris; Tracy Dudkewicz; Diane Hendricks; Diane Henry; Samuel Paddock.
Number of staff: 3 full-time professional.
EIN: 391585271

3480
Jack & Joan Stein Foundation, Inc.
5400 S. 27th St.
Milwaukee, WI 53221

Established in 1994 in WI.

Donor(s): Jack Stein.
Grantmaker type: Independent foundation
Financial data (yr. ended 12/31/02): Assets, $434,366 (M); gifts received, $325,000; expenditures, $746,675; qualifying distributions, $746,596; giving activities include $744,825 for 71 grants (high: $400,000; low: $20).
Purpose and activities: Giving for the arts, education, and health and medical concerns.
Fields of interest: Museums; Arts; Higher education; Education; Natural resources; Family planning; Medical care, rehabilitation; Health organizations, association; Boys & girls clubs; American Red Cross.
Limitations: Applications not accepted. Giving on a national basis. No grants to individuals.
Application information: Contributes only to pre-selected organizations.
Officers: Jack Stein, Mgr.; Joan Stein, Mgr.
EIN: 391805213

3481
R. A. Stevens Family Foundation
P.O. Box 310
Genesee Depot, WI 53127-0310
(414) 303-7285
Contact: Paul Fleckenstein, Tr.

Established in 1999 in WI.
Donor(s): Andrew J. Fleckenstein, Rita A. Stevens.
Grantmaker type: Independent foundation
Financial data (yr. ended 12/31/02). Assets, $4,436,904 (M); expenditures, $395,695; qualifying distributions, $365,240; giving activities include $364,370 for 29 grants (high: $50,000; low: $2,000).
Purpose and activities: Giving primarily for higher education and human services.
Fields of interest: Arts; Education; Environment, plant conservation; Health care; Breast cancer; Human services.
Limitations: Giving primarily in SC, and Milwaukee, WI.
Application information: Application form required.
  Initial approach: Letter
  Deadline(s): None
Trustees: John Fleckenstein; Paul Fleckenstein; Rita A. Stevens.
EIN: 396711913

3482
H. Chase Stone Trust B
c/o Bank One Trust Co., N.A.
P.O. Box 1308
Milwaukee, WI 53201
Application address: c/o Bank One Trust Co., N.A., 30 E. Pikes Peak, Colorado Springs, CO 80942

Established in 1974 in CO.
Grantmaker type: Independent foundation
Financial data (yr. ended 12/31/02): Assets, $3,258,910 (M); expenditures, $166,086; qualifying distributions, $146,974; giving activities include $142,700 for 18 grants (high: $25,000; low: $1,700).
Fields of interest: Arts; Libraries (public); Education; Zoos/zoological societies; Hospitals (general); Children, services.

Types of support: Building/renovation; Equipment.
Limitations: Giving limited to El Paso County, CO. No grants to individuals.
Publications: Application guidelines.
Application information: Application form not required.
  Initial approach: Letter
  Copies of proposal: 1
  Deadline(s): Apr. 30 and Oct. 31
  Board meeting date(s): Quarterly
Trustee: Bank One Trust Co., N.A.
EIN: 846066113

3483
Paul E. Stry Foundation, Inc.
311 Main St.
La Crosse, WI 54601

Established in 1988 in WI.
Donor(s): Paul E. Stry.‡
Grantmaker type: Independent foundation
Financial data (yr. ended 12/31/02): Assets, $4,325,306 (M); expenditures, $219,387; qualifying distributions, $202,838; giving activities include $157,575 for 19 grants (high: $75,000; low: $405).
Fields of interest: Historic preservation/historical societies; Arts; Higher education; Natural resources; Children/youth, services.
Types of support: Land acquisition; Program development; Conferences/seminars; Publication; Curriculum development.
Limitations: Applications not accepted. Giving primarily in WI. No grants to individuals.
Application information: Unsolicited requests for funds not accepted.
Officers: Robert Swartz, Pres.; Robert Skemp, V.P.; Erv Albrecht, Secy.-Treas.
Number of staff: None.
EIN: 391598681

3484
E.C. Styberg Foundation, Inc.
1600 Gould St.
P.O. Box 788
Racine, WI 53401-0788
Contact: E.C. Styberg, Jr., Pres.

Established in 1981 in WI.
Donor(s): E.C. Styberg, Jr., Bernice M. Styberg.
Grantmaker type: Independent foundation
Financial data (yr. ended 06/30/02): Assets, $5,706,125 (M); gifts received, $237,615; expenditures, $273,179; qualifying distributions, $197,940; giving activities include $197,630 for 85 grants (high: $25,000; low: $100; average: $500–$10,000).
Purpose and activities: Support primarily for a theological seminary, community development, education, and youth and health organizations.
Fields of interest: Arts; Theological school/education; Education; Natural resources; Health organizations, association; Human services; Youth, services; Community development; Federated giving programs; Protestant agencies & churches.
Types of support: General/operating support; Capital campaigns.
Limitations: Giving primarily in southeastern WI; giving also in Evanston, IL. No grants to individuals.

Application information: Application form required.
  Deadline(s): None
  Final notification: Within 90 days
Officers: E.C. Styberg, Jr., Pres.; Bernice M. Styberg, V.P. and Secy.; Paul L. Guenther, Treas.
EIN: 391410323

3485
James A. Taylor Family Foundation, Inc.
1222 W. Venture Ct.
Mequon, WI 53092-3437 (262) 367-7999
Contact: James A. Taylor, Pres.

Established in 1959 in WI.
Donor(s): James A. Taylor, Taylor Electric Co.
Grantmaker type: Independent foundation
Financial data (yr. ended 06/30/03): Assets, $442,503 (M); expenditures, $140,599; qualifying distributions, $137,795; giving activities include $137,795 for 106 grants (high: $100,000; low: $50).
Fields of interest: Museums; Performing arts; Arts; Elementary/secondary education; Higher education; Environment; Animal welfare; Hospitals (general); Health care; Mental health/crisis services; Health organizations, association; Medical research, institute; Crime/violence prevention, youth; Human services; Family services, Aging, centers/services; Federated giving programs; Christian agencies & churches; Religion; General charitable giving; Disabled; Aging; Economically disadvantaged.
Types of support: General/operating support; Continuing support; Annual campaigns; Capital campaigns; Building/renovation; Emergency funds; Seed money; Research.
Limitations: Giving primarily in WI.
Application information: Giving to new applicants is very limited. Application form not required.
  Deadline(s): None
Officers and Directors: James A. Taylor,* Pres.; James A. Taylor, Jr.,* V.P.; John W. Taylor,* Secy.-Treas.; Barbara T. Mans.
Number of staff: None.
EIN: 396045247

3486
Trostel Foundation, Ltd.
800 N. Marshall St.
Milwaukee, WI 53202-3911 (414) 273-3421
Contact: Elizabeth H. Perry, Pres.

Established in 1986 in WI.
Donor(s): Albert Trostel and Sons Co.
Grantmaker type: Independent foundation
Financial data (yr. ended 11/30/02): Assets, $7,013 (M); gifts received, $150,000; expenditures, $156,790; qualifying distributions, $156,790; giving activities include $149,200 for 22 grants (high: $25,000; low: $1,000) and $6,250 for 3 grants to individuals (high: $2,500; low: $1,250).
Purpose and activities: Giving primarily for youth services and health organizations.
Fields of interest: Elementary/secondary education; Higher education; Natural resources; Health care; Parks/playgrounds; Human services; Children/youth, services; Federated giving programs; Christian agencies & churches.

Types of support: General/operating support; Scholarships—to individuals.
Limitations: Giving primarily in WI.
Application information: The foundation's present plans preclude extensive consideration of unsolicited requests for funds. Application form not required.
  Initial approach: Letter
  Deadline(s): None
Officers and Directors:* Elizabeth H. Perry,* Pres. and Treas.; Anders Segerdahl,* V.P.; Ellen R. Ludwig,* Secy.; Kim Harter; Thomas Hauske, Jr.; Charles D. Krull.
EIN: 391550227

3487
Robert A. Uihlein Foundation
735 N. Water St., Ste. 712
Milwaukee, WI 53202-4104

Established in 1942 in WI.
Donor(s): Robert A. Uihlein III, James J. Uihlein.
Grantmaker type: Independent foundation
Financial data (yr. ended 12/31/02): Assets, $3,085,412 (M); expenditures, $227,251; qualifying distributions, $219,663; giving activities include $220,200 for 31 grants (high: $50,000; low: $200).
Purpose and activities: Support for the environment, education, medical care, welfare services, and religion; giving also to youth and arts groups.
Fields of interest: Arts; Education; Natural resources; Health care; Health organizations, association; Children/youth, services; Christian agencies & churches.
Limitations: Applications not accepted. Giving primarily in Milwaukee, WI. No grants to individuals.
Application information: Contributes only to pre-selected organizations.
Officers and Directors:* Lorraine G. Uihlein,* Pres.; Thomas F. Lechner,* V.P. and Secy.-Treas.
EIN: 396033236

3488
Dorothy Kopmeier Vallier Foundation, Inc.
c/o Edwin P. Wiley
231 W. Wisconsin Ave., Ste. 805
Milwaukee, WI 53203

Established in 1974 in WI.
Donor(s): Dorothy K. Vallier.
Grantmaker type: Independent foundation
Financial data (yr. ended 06/30/02): Assets, $1,425,342 (M); expenditures, $134,813; qualifying distributions, $125,353; giving activities include $122,848 for 2 grants (high: $62,848; low: $60,000).
Fields of interest: Higher education; Natural resources.
Limitations: Applications not accepted. Giving primarily in WI. No grants to individuals.
Application information: Contributes only to pre-selected organizations.
Officers and Directors:* Dorothy K. Vallier,* Pres.; William G. Kummer,* V.P.; Michael A. Gehl,* Secy.-Treas.
EIN: 237417554

3489
John & Janet Van Den Wymelenberg Foundation, Inc.
1570 Mesa Dr.
Green Bay, WI 54313

Donor(s): John Van Den Wymelenberg.
Grantmaker type: Independent foundation
Financial data (yr. ended 08/31/02): Assets, $2,133,166 (M); gifts received, $413,499; expenditures, $93,332; qualifying distributions, $89,656; giving activities include $90,500 for 29 grants (high: $28,000; low: $100).
Fields of interest: Botanical gardens; Boys & girls clubs; Salvation Army; Christian agencies & churches.
Limitations: Applications not accepted. Giving primarily in WI. No grants to individuals.
Application information: Contributes only to pre-selected organizations.
Officer and Directors:* Kathy McAllister,* Pres.; Linda Boss; Mary Ann Hunt; Susan Marten.
EIN: 391392405

3490
Waukesha County Community Foundation
2727 N. Grandview Blvd., Ste. 122
Waukesha, WI 53188 (262) 513-1861
Contact: Valerie J. Brown, Exec. Dir.
E-mail: wccf@waukeshafoundation.org; URL: http://www.waukeshafoundation.org

Established in 1999 in WI.
Grantmaker type: Community foundation
Financial data (yr. ended 12/31/02): Assets, $2,946,781 (M); gifts received, $842,499; expenditures, $181,868; giving activities include $101,148 for grants.
Purpose and activities: Giving primarily to benefit the people and programs throughout the Waukesha County, WI, community. The foundation administers donor-advised, designated, field of interest and unrestricted endowment funds.
Fields of interest: Historic preservation/historical societies; Arts; Education; Environment; Health care; Human services; Community development.
Types of support: General/operating support; Continuing support; Annual campaigns; Capital campaigns; Building/renovation; Program development; Curriculum development; Scholarship funds; Technical assistance.
Limitations: Giving primarily in Waukesha County, WI.
Publications: Annual report, Informational brochure, Newsletter.
Application information: Application form required.
  Initial approach: Letter
  Copies of proposal: 5
  Deadline(s): Aug. 1
  Board meeting date(s): Aug. and Nov.
  Final notification: Nov.
Officers and Directors:* Bryce P. Styza,* Pres.; Donald Fundingsland,* V.P.; Ronald L. Bertieri,* Secy.; Peter J. Lettenberger,* Treas.; Betty Arndt; Andrea B. Bryant; Beverly Chappie; Thomas E. Dalum; Jill M. Haupt; E. John Raasch; Keith Rupple; T. Michael Schober; Donald J. Stephens.
Number of staff: 1 part-time professional.
EIN: 391969122

3491
West Bend Mutal Charitable Trust
1900 S. 18th Ave.
West Bend, WI 53095
Contact: John R. Dedrick, Tr.

Established in 1995 in WI.
Grantmaker type: Independent foundation
Financial data (yr. ended 12/31/02): Assets, $4,558,037 (M); expenditures, $312,266; qualifying distributions, $272,826; giving activities include $274,200 for 53 grants (high: $35,000; low: $500).
Purpose and activities: Giving primarily for education and youth services.
Fields of interest: Performing arts; Higher education; Scholarships/financial aid; Animal welfare; Zoos/zoological societies; Hospitals (general); Health care, blood supply; Heart & circulatory diseases; Athletics/sports, baseball; Boy scouts; Human services; YM/YWCAs & YM/YWHAs; Federated giving programs.
Limitations: Giving primarily in WI, with emphasis on West Bend.
Application information: Application form not required.
  Initial approach: Letter
  Deadline(s): None
Trustees: John R. Dedrick; John F. Duwell; James J. Pauly; Larry G. Roth; Anthony J. Warren; Sharon S. Ziegler.
EIN: 396591551

3492
Frank L. Weyenberg Charitable Trust
c/o Quarles & Brady
411 E. Wisconsin Ave.
Milwaukee, WI 53202 (414) 277-5000
Contact: Henry J. Loos, Tr.

Established in 1983 in WI.
Grantmaker type: Independent foundation
Financial data (yr. ended 07/31/02): Assets, $4,595,458 (M); expenditures, $343,824; qualifying distributions, $306,358; giving activities include $285,000 for 22 grants (high: $50,000; low: $1,000; average: $5,000–$10,000).
Purpose and activities: Giving primarily for education, health, and the arts.
Fields of interest: Arts; Education; Environment; Hospitals (general); Human services.
Limitations: Applications not accepted. Giving on a national basis. No grants to individuals.
Application information: Contributes only to pre-selected organizations.
Trustees: Henry J. Loos; First National in Palm Beach.
EIN: 391461670

3493
Wisconsin Community Fund
1202 Williamson St., Ste. D
Madison, WI 53703 (608) 251-6834
Contact: Steve Starkey, Exec. Dir.
FAX: (608) 251-6846; E-mail: info@wcfund.org; URL: http://www.wcfund.org/
Additional address: 1442 N. Farwell Ave., Ste. 100, Milwaukee, WI 53202, tel.: (414) 225-9965, FAX: (414) 225-9964

Established in 1982 in WI.

Grantmaker type: Public charity
Financial data (yr. ended 06/30/03): Revenue, $491,741; assets, $369,111 (L); gifts received, $458,584; expenditures, $476,992; program services expenses, $321,977; giving activities include $193,816 for 39 grants (high: $28,750; low: $250) and $3,000 for 10 in-kind gifts.
Purpose and activities: Funding to progressive groups, with budgets under $400,000, working for democracy, diversity, justice, and social and economic equality in Wisconsin. The fund also supports grassroots activism through outreach and education, technical assistance, in-kind donations, and coalition-building.
Fields of interest: Environment, legal rights; Health care; Labor unions/organizations; International peace/security; International human rights; Civil rights, gays/lesbians; Race/intergroup relations; Civil rights; Minorities; Native Americans/American Indians; Women.
International interests: Central America; South America.
Types of support: General/operating support; Income development; Management development; Equipment; Emergency funds; Program development; Conferences/seminars; Publication; Seed money; Scholarship funds; Technical assistance; Consulting services; Program evaluation; In-kind gifts; Matching/challenge support.
Limitations: Giving primarily in WI. No support for social service, research organizations, or groups with budgets over $200,000. No grants for academic, cultural, or religious projects, annual fund drives, endowments, or capital campaigns.
Publications: Application guidelines, Annual report (including application guidelines), Grants list, Informational brochure, Multi-year report, Newsletter, Program policy statement.
Application information: General Fund Grants are limited to WI and are only granted to social change organizations. Application form required.
   Initial approach: Letter or telephone
   Copies of proposal: 16
   Deadline(s): Vary annually; contact fund for updates
   Board meeting date(s): 8 times per year
   Final notification: Mar.
Officers and Directors:* Dwain Berry,* Pres.; Nan Cheney, V.P.; Caitlin Skinner, Secy.; Yvonne Nair,* Treas.; Steve Starkey, Exec. Dir.; Marsha Dymzarov; Becky Glass.
Number of staff: 2 full-time professional; 2 part-time professional; 1 part-time support.
EIN: 391398124

3494
John H. Witte, Jr. Foundation
c/o U.S. Bank, N.A.
P.O. Box 2043, Ste. LC4NE
Milwaukee, WI 53201-9116
Contact: Terri Dowell
Application address: c/o U.S. Bank, N.A., 201 Jefferson St., Burlington, IA 52601-5250

Established in 1979 in IA.
Donor(s): John H. Witte, Jr.‡
Grantmaker type: Independent foundation
Financial data (yr. ended 08/31/02): Assets, $6,840,770 (M); expenditures, $456,433; qualifying distributions, $417,224; giving

activities include $399,275 for 27 grants (high: $64,000; low: $500).
Purpose and activities: Giving primarily for education and social services.
Fields of interest: Arts; Elementary/secondary education; Higher education; Natural resources; Human services; Children/youth, services; Community development; Federated giving programs.
Types of support: Building/renovation; Equipment; Program development.
Limitations: Giving primarily in the Burlington, IA, area. No grants to individuals.
Application information:
   Initial approach: Letter
   Deadline(s): None
Trustee: U.S. Bank, N.A.
EIN: 426297940

3495
WPS Foundation, Inc.
(formerly Wisconsin Public Service Foundation, Inc.)
700 N. Adams St.
Green Bay, WI 54301
Contact: P.J. Reinhard
Application address: P.O. Box 19001, Green Bay, WI 54307-9001; URL: http://www.wpsr.com/foundat/wpscfoun.html
Scholarship application address: c/o Scholarship Prog., Scholarship Assessment Svc., P.O. Box 5189, Appleton, WI 54913-5189

Incorporated in 1964 in WI.
Donor(s): Wisconsin Public Service Corp.
Grantmaker type: Company-sponsored foundation
Financial data (yr. ended 12/31/02): Assets, $15,360,269 (M); gifts received, $25,000; expenditures, $1,000,382; qualifying distributions, $992,850; giving activities include $752,736 for 165 grants (high: $90,000; low: $500; average: $500–$90,000), $171,400 for grants to individuals (average: $500–$2,000) and $65,345 for 845 employee matching gifts.
Purpose and activities: Primary areas of interest include cultural programs, higher education, health, and social services.
Fields of interest: Museums; Performing arts; Historic preservation/historical societies; Arts; Higher education; Education; Natural resources; Hospitals (general); Health care; Health organizations, association; Human services; Family services.
Types of support: General/operating support; Continuing support; Annual campaigns; Capital campaigns; Building/renovation; Equipment; Program development; Scholarship funds; Research; Employee matching gifts; Scholarships—to individuals.
Limitations: Giving generally limited to upper MI and northeastern WI. Generally, no grants for endowment funds.
Publications: Application guidelines, Informational brochure.
Application information: Application form required for grants and scholarships can be downloaded at foundation Web site. Application form required.
   Initial approach: Letter
   Copies of proposal: 1
   Deadline(s): Dec. 15 for scholarships
   Board meeting date(s): May and as required

Final notification: Feb.
Officers: L.L. Weyers, Pres.; T.P. Meinz, V.P.; B.J. Wolf, Secy.; J.P. O'Leary, Treas.
Number of staff: None.
EIN: 396075016

WYOMING

3496
Archie W. and Grace Berry Foundation
1122 Soldier Creek Rd.
Wolf, WY 82844

Established in 1988 in PA.
Donor(s): Archie W. Berry, Sr.
Grantmaker type: Independent foundation
Financial data (yr. ended 06/30/02): Assets, $7,569,346 (M); expenditures, $612,091; qualifying distributions, $555,774; giving activities include $556,500 for 26 grants (high: $100,000; low: $1,000).
Purpose and activities: Giving primarily for the arts, conservation, and human services.
Fields of interest: Education; Environment; Animals/wildlife; Human services.
Limitations: Applications not accepted. Giving primarily in PA and WY. No grants to individuals.
Application information: Contributes only to pre-selected organizations.
Trustees: Archie Berry, Jr.; Robert B. Berry; Louis F. Rivituso.
EIN: 236951678

3497
C & N Foundation
P.O. Box 767
Wilson, WY 83014-0767

Established in 1987 in MI.
Donor(s): Norman H. Hofley, Carole S. Hofley.
Grantmaker type: Independent foundation
Financial data (yr. ended 05/31/02): Assets, $2,954,580 (M); expenditures, $113,397; qualifying distributions, $101,983; giving activities include $101,600 for 31 grants (high: $15,000; low: $100).
Fields of interest: Music; Orchestra (symphony); Historic preservation/historical societies; Arts; Natural resources; Foundations (community).
Types of support: General/operating support.
Limitations: Applications not accepted. Giving primarily in WY. No grants to individuals.
Application information: Contributes only to pre-selected organizations.
Officers: Norman H. Hofley, Pres. and Treas.; Carole S. Hofley, V.P. and Secy.
EIN: 382746657

3498
Community Foundation of Jackson Hole
255 E. Simpson St.
P.O. Box 574
Jackson, WY 83001 (307) 739-1026
Contact: Clare Payne Symmons, Pres.
FAX: (307) 734-2841; E-mail:
info@cfjacksonhole.org; URL: http://
www.cfjacksonhole.org

Established in 1989 in WY as a component fund
of Wyoming Community Foundation; in 1995
became a separate entity.
Grantmaker type: Community foundation
Financial data (yr. ended 12/31/02): Assets,
$34,239,062 (M); gifts received, $10,400,419;
expenditures, $17,464,079; giving activities
include $12,071,699 for 1,231 grants (high:
$1,000,000; low: $240; average:
$240–$1,000,000).
Purpose and activities: To enhance philanthropy
and strengthen the sense of community in the
Jackson Hole, WY, area, by providing a
permanent source of funding and other support
for non-profit organizations and scholarship
recipients. The foundation administers a
donor-advised fund.
Fields of interest: Arts; Education; Environment;
Health care; Human services; Community
development, neighborhood development.
Types of support: General/operating support;
Continuing support; Capital campaigns;
Building/renovation; Equipment; Endowments;
Emergency funds; Program development;
Conferences/seminars; Publication; Seed
money; Curriculum development; Scholarship
funds; Technical assistance; Consulting services;
Program evaluation; Program-related
investments/loans; Grants to individuals;
Scholarships—to individuals; In-kind gifts;
Matching/challenge support.
Limitations: Giving primarily in the Jackson
Hole, WY, area.
Publications: Application guidelines, Annual
report (including application guidelines), Grants
list, Informational brochure, Newsletter.
Application information: Guidelines available
on Web site. Application form required.
  Initial approach: Proposal
  Copies of proposal: 17
  Deadline(s): Last business day of each
    calendar quarter
  Board meeting date(s): 4 times annually
  Final notification: Within following quarter
Officer: Clare Payne Symmons, Pres.
Number of staff: 6 full-time professional.
EIN: 830308856

3499
The Dunoir Fund Trust
c/o Stephen Gordon
P.O. Box 25009
Jackson, WY 83001

Established in 1991 in WY.
Grantmaker type: Independent foundation
Financial data (yr. ended 12/31/00): Assets,
$1,538,713 (M); expenditures, $136,443;
qualifying distributions, $116,250; giving
activities include $116,250 for 12 grants (high:
$50,000; low: $250).
Purpose and activities: Giving primarily for
education.

Fields of interest: Museums; Performing arts;
Theater; Arts; Education; Natural resources;
Family planning.
Limitations: Applications not accepted. Giving
on a national basis. No grants to individuals.
Application information: Contributes only to
pre-selected organizations.
Trustee: Stephen Gordon.
EIN: 830294737

3500
Norman Hirschfield Foundation
P.O. Box 7443
Jackson, WY 83001

Established in 1957.
Donor(s): Alan J. Hirschfield, Bert E. Hirschfield.
Grantmaker type: Independent foundation
Financial data (yr. ended 11/30/02): Assets,
$3,798,709 (M); expenditures, $215,478;
qualifying distributions, $206,612; giving
activities include $191,340 for 24 grants (high:
$57,000; low: $100).
Purpose and activities: Giving for art and
cultural programs, education, health care and
youth services.
Fields of interest: Arts; Higher education;
Education; Environment; Health organizations,
association; Human services; Children/youth,
services; Foundations (community).
Limitations: Applications not accepted. Giving
primarily in Jackson, WY. No grants to
individuals.
Application information: Contributes only to
pre-selected organizations.
Officers: Alan J. Hirschfield, Pres.; Bert E.
Hirschfield, V.P. and Secy.-Treas.
EIN: 736092984

3501
The Robert S. and Grayce B. Kerr
Foundation, Inc.
P.O. Box, 20000, PMB 25106
Jackson, WY 83001-7000
Contact: William G. Kerr, Pres., or Sarah J. Lacy,
Admin. Asst.

Chartered in 1986 in OK.
Donor(s): Grayce B. Kerr Flynn.‡
Grantmaker type: Independent foundation
Financial data (yr. ended 12/31/00): Assets,
$36,748,229 (M); expenditures, $1,650,864;
qualifying distributions, $1,758,938; giving
activities include $1,240,458 for grants
(average: $5,000–$10,000) and $330,169 for 5
loans/program-related investments.
Purpose and activities: Giving limited to
organizations that benefit the specified fields of
interest and geographic affiliations of the
foundation.
Fields of interest: Arts education; Natural
resources; Animals/wildlife,
preservation/protection.
Types of support: General/operating support;
Building/renovation; Equipment; Emergency
funds; Matching/challenge support.
Limitations: Applications not accepted. Giving
primarily in OK and WY; some giving also in
OH. No grants to individuals, or for
endowments, annual campaigns, memberships,
or medical or scientific research.

Application information: Unsolicited proposals
not considered.
  Board meeting date(s): June and Dec.
Officers and Trustees:* William G. Kerr,* Chair.
and Pres.; Joffa Kerr, Sr.,* V.P.; Mara Kerr,* Secy.;
James G. Anderson,* Treas.
Number of staff: 1 part-time professional.
EIN: 731256123

3502
Lightner Sams Foundation of Wyoming
P.O. Box 429
Teton Village, WY 83025 (307) 733-9619
Contact: Robin H. Lightner, V.P. and Secy.
FAX: (307) 733-0843

Established in 1990 in WY.
Grantmaker type: Independent foundation
Financial data (yr. ended 12/31/00): Assets,
$7,640,971 (M); expenditures, $540,373;
qualifying distributions, $409,735; giving
activities include $279,630 for grants (average:
$200–$55,000).
Fields of interest: Arts; Education;
Animals/wildlife; Human services.
Types of support: General/operating support;
Continuing support; Annual campaigns; Capital
campaigns; Building/renovation; Equipment;
Matching/challenge support.
Limitations: Giving primarily in WY.
Application information:
  Initial approach: Letter
  Board meeting date(s): Quarterly
Directors and Trustees:* Earl Sams Lightner,
Sr.,* Pres. and Treas.; Robin H. Lightner,* V.P.
and Secy.; Camille M. Lightner; Earl Sams
Lightner, Jr.; Larry F. Lightner; Sue B. Lightner.
Number of staff: 3.
EIN: 830309453

3503
S & G Foundation, Inc.
P.O. Box 20000, No. 25185
Jackson, WY 83001 (307) 733-7707

Established around 1995.
Donor(s): Gale L. Davis, Shelby M.C. Davis.
Grantmaker type: Independent foundation
Financial data (yr. ended 06/30/01): Assets,
$188,353,011 (M); gifts received, $64,707,495;
expenditures, $5,029,080; qualifying
distributions, $3,650,281; giving activities
include $3,650,281 for 67 grants (high:
$1,237,500; low: $100).
Fields of interest: Arts; Higher education;
Education; Environment; Christian agencies &
churches.
Types of support: General/operating support.
Limitations: Applications not accepted. Giving
primarily on the East Coast, with emphasis on
FL, ME, NJ, and NY; some giving also in NM.
No grants to individuals.
Application information: Contributes only to
pre-selected organizations.
Officers: Shelby M.C. Davis, Pres.; Mary Ann
McGrath, V.P.; Gale L. Davis, Secy.-Treas.
EIN: 364193183
**Recent environmental and animal welfare
grants:**
3503-1 Jackson Hole Land Trust, Jackson, WY,
  $250,000. For general operating support.
  2002.

3503-2 Maine Coast Heritage Trust, Topsham, ME, $200,000. For general operating support. 2002.
3503-3 National Museum of Wildlife Art, Jackson, WY, $22,500. For general operating support. 2002.

3504
Newell B. Sargent Foundation
P.O. Box 50581
Casper, WY 82605-0581
Contact: Charles W. Smith, Tr.

Established in 1984 in UT and WY.
Donor(s): Newell B. Sargent.
Grantmaker type: Independent foundation
Financial data (yr. ended 10/31/02): Assets, $12,637,662 (M); gifts received, $212,786; expenditures, $956,696; qualifying distributions, $739,019; giving activities include $679,019 for 21 grants (high: $273,569; low: $500).
Purpose and activities: Giving primarily to a humane society, and for human services.
Fields of interest: Museums; Education; Animal welfare; Hospitals (general); Human services; Children/youth, services.
Types of support: General/operating support; Building/renovation; Land acquisition.
Limitations: Giving primarily in WY, with emphasis on Worland.
Application information: Application form not required.
Initial approach: Letter
Deadline(s): None
Trustees: Ron Hansen; Douglas W. Morrison; Charles W. Smith.
EIN: 830271536

3505
The Arthur B. Schultz Foundation
620 Table Rock West Rd.
Alta, WY 83414 (307) 413-2273
Contact: Erik B. Schultz, Exec. Dir.
FAX: (307) 353-2273; E-mail: info@absfoundation.org; URL: http://www.absfoundation.org

Established in 1985 in CA.
Donor(s): Arthur B. Schultz.
Grantmaker type: Independent foundation
Financial data (yr. ended 11/30/02): Assets, $5,053,282 (M); gifts received, $1,001,000; expenditures, $467,171; qualifying distributions, $466,091; giving activities include $357,250 for 21 grants (high: $30,000; low: $5,000).
Purpose and activities: Giving primarily for international microenterprise, global understanding, environmental conservation, and disabled recreation and mobility.
Fields of interest: Natural resources; Animals/wildlife, preservation/protection; Physical therapy; International relief; Economic development; Disabled.
Types of support: General/operating support; Continuing support; Building/renovation; Equipment; Land acquisition; Endowments; Program development; Seed money; Scholarship funds; Research; Matching/challenge support.
Limitations: Giving in western North America for disabled recreation, the Yellowstone to Yukon eco-region of the U.S. and Canada for environmental conservation, and the Third

World for disabled mobility. No geographic preference for international microenterprise. No grants to individuals.
Publications: Application guidelines, Financial statement, Informational brochure (including application guidelines).
Application information: No plastic folders or binders. Grants list, program policy statement and application on Web site. Application form not required.
Initial approach: Letter, FAX, or E-mail
Copies of proposal: 1
Deadline(s): None
Board meeting date(s): Jan., May, and Sept.
Final notification: After meetings
Officer and Trustees: Erik B. Schultz,* Exec. Dir.
Number of staff: 1 full-time professional.
EIN: 953980014

3506
The Seeley Foundation
P.O. Box 513
Wilson, WY 83014
Contact: Ellen Fales Roberts, V.P. and Secy.

Incorporated in 1945 in MI.
Donor(s): Halsted H. Seeley,‡ Laurel H. Seeley.‡
Grantmaker type: Independent foundation
Financial data (yr. ended 12/31/02): Assets, $2,556,148 (M); expenditures, $230,805; qualifying distributions, $215,318; giving activities include $216,250 for 19 grants (high: $36,000; low: $1,000).
Purpose and activities: Giving primarily for the arts, the environment and renewable energy research, mental health treatment, human services, particularly for pathways for cycling and pedestrians.
Fields of interest: Arts; Energy; Environment; Mental health, treatment; Human services.
Types of support: General/operating support; Continuing support; Annual campaigns; Capital campaigns; Equipment; Endowments; Seed money; Research.
Limitations: Applications not accepted. Giving primarily in CO, CT, KS, MO, NM, VA, and WY. No grants to individuals.
Application information: The foundation engages in objective grantmaking. Unsolicited requests or proposals are not considered or acknowledged.
Board meeting date(s): Oct.
Officers and Trustees: Judith S. Fales,* Co-Pres. and Treas.; Miles P. Seeley,* Co-Pres.; Ellen F. Roberts,* V.P. and Secy.; Eugene Fales; Dana M. Seeley; Laura M. Seeley.
Number of staff: None.
EIN: 366049991

3507
The George B. Storer Foundation, Inc. ▼
P.O. Box 1270
Saratoga, WY 82331
Contact: Peter Storer, Pres.
Application address (from Jan. 1 to May 15:)
P.O. Box 1907, Islamorada, FL 33036, tel.: (305) 664-4822

Incorporated in 1955 in FL.
Grantmaker type: Independent foundation
Financial data (yr. ended 12/31/02): Assets, $81,665,017 (M); expenditures, $5,066,798;

qualifying distributions, $4,489,076; giving activities include $4,520,000 for 149 grants (high: $600,000; low: $2,000; average: $10,000–$100,000).
Purpose and activities: Grants for higher education, social services, particularly for the blind, youth organizations, conservation, hospitals, and cultural programs.
Fields of interest: Arts; Higher education; Natural resources; Hospitals (general); Human services; Children/youth, services; Disabled.
Types of support: General/operating support; Building/renovation; Endowments; Research; Matching/challenge support.
Limitations: Giving primarily in FL. No grants for scholarships or fellowships; no loans.
Publications: Grants list.
Application information: Application form not required.
Initial approach: Letter and proposal
Copies of proposal: 1
Deadline(s): Send proposal between Oct. 15 and Nov. 15
Board meeting date(s): Dec.
Officers and Directors: Peter Storer,* Pres. and Treas.; William Michaels,* V.P.; James P. Storer,* Secy.
EIN: 596136392
Recent environmental and animal welfare grants:
3507-1 1000 Friends of Florida, Tallahassee, FL, $50,000. 2002.
3507-2 American Rivers, DC, $75,000. 2002.
3507-3 Audubon Society of Wyoming, Casper, WY, $50,000. 2002.
3507-4 Best Friends Animal Sanctuary, Kanab, UT, $20,000. 2002.
3507-5 Billfish Foundation, Fort Lauderdale, FL, $10,000. 2002.
3507-6 Camp Fire Conservation Fund, Chappaqua, NY, $10,000. 2002.
3507-7 Coastal Conservation Association, Houston, TX, $75,000. 2002.
3507-8 Ducks Unlimited, Memphis, TN, $50,000. 2002.
3507-9 Everglades Foundation, Islamorada, FL, $20,000. 2002.
3507-10 Florida Keys Land and Sea Trust, Marathon, FL, $25,000. 2002.
3507-11 Florida Keys Wild Bird Rehabilitation Center, Tavernier, FL, $20,000. 2002.
3507-12 Gates Mills Garden Club, Gates Mills, OH, $15,000. 2002.
3507-13 Grand River Partners, Painesville, OH, $45,000. 2002.
3507-14 Greater Yellowstone Coalition, Bozeman, MT, $10,000. 2002.
3507-15 Humane Society of San Antonio, San Antonio, TX, $50,000. 2002.
3507-16 Idaho Rivers United, Boise, ID, $10,000. 2002.
3507-17 Izaak Walton League of America, Gaithersburg, MD, $30,000. 2002.
3507-18 National Bighorn Sheep International Association, DuBois, WY, $12,000. 2002.
3507-19 National Fish and Wildlife Foundation, DC, $25,000. 2002.
3507-20 Pigeon Key Foundation, Marathon, FL, $25,000. 2002.
3507-21 Powder River Basin Resource Council, Sheridan, WY, $25,000. 2002.
3507-22 Reef Relief, Key West, FL, $30,000. 2002.
3507-23 River Network, DC, $10,000. 2002.

3507-24 Rocky Mountain Elk Foundation, Missoula, MT, $25,000. 2002.

3507-25 Seeing Eye, Morristown, NJ, $25,000. 2002.

3507-26 Texas Hearing and Service Dogs, Austin, TX, $10,000. 2002.

3507-27 Trout Unlimited, Arlington, VA, $50,000. For Coldwater Conservation Fund, supporting scientific and economic research and analysis and science-based watershed restoration projects. 2002.

3507-28 Trout Unlimited, Arlington, VA, $50,000. For Western Water Plan. 2002.

3507-29 Trout Unlimited, Jackson, WY, $10,000. 2002.

3507-30 Trustees of Reservations, Beverly, MA, $10,000. 2002.

3507-31 University of South Carolina, Spartanburg, SC, $10,000. For Predatory Bird Research Fund. 2002.

3507-32 University of Wyoming, Institute for Environment and Natural Resources, Laramie, WY, $25,000. 2002.

3507-33 Ventana Wilderness Sanctuary, Carmel Valley, CA, $10,000. 2002.

3507-34 Vineyard Open Land Foundation, West Tisbury, MA, $15,000. For cranberry bog. 2002.

3507-35 Vineyard Open Land Foundation, West Tisbury, MA, $10,000. 2002.

3507-36 World Wildlife Fund/Conservation Foundation, DC, $27,000. 2002.

3507-37 Wyoming Outdoor Council, Lander, WY, $20,000. 2002.

3507-38 Wyoming Wildlife Federation, Cheyenne, WY, $25,000. 2002.

3507-39 Zoological Society of Florida, Miami, FL, $10,000. 2002.

3508
William E. Weiss Foundation, Inc.
P.O. Box 14270
Jackson, WY 83002 (307) 739-8330
Contact: Liz D. Hutchinson
FAX: (307) 733-7545

Incorporated in 1955 in NY.
Donor(s): William E. Weiss, Jr.,‡ Helene K. Brown.‡
Grantmaker type: Independent foundation
Financial data (yr. ended 03/31/03): Assets, $8,054,380 (M); expenditures, $630,150; qualifying distributions, $567,867; giving activities include $566,910 for 35 grants (high: $50,000; low: $2,500).
Purpose and activities: Giving primarily to museums and for arts and cultural programs.
Fields of interest: Museums; Arts; Education; Environment; Human services; Family services; Homeless.
Types of support: General/operating support; Continuing support; Capital campaigns; Building/renovation; Program development.
Limitations: Applications not accepted. Giving limited to CA, NY, TN, and WY. No grants to individuals.
Application information: Contributes only to pre-selected organizations. Unsolicited requests for funds not considered.
  Board meeting date(s): Mar.
Officers and Directors:* Daryl B. Uber,* Pres.; Monte Brown,* V.P.; William D. Weiss, Secy.; Dwyer Brown, Treas.; Katrina D. Weiss; William U. Weiss.
Number of staff: 1 part-time support.
EIN: 556016633

3509
Wiancko Charitable Foundation, Inc.
P.O. Box 459
Teton Village, WY 83025

Established in 1989 in WY.
Donor(s): Thomas H. Wiancko, Sibyl S. Wiancko.
Grantmaker type: Independent foundation
Financial data (yr. ended 12/31/02): Assets, $5,026,866 (M); expenditures, $259,254; qualifying distributions, $228,418; giving activities include $222,900 for 18 grants (high: $20,000; low: $5,000).
Purpose and activities: Giving primarily for environmental and wildlife conservation.
Fields of interest: Natural resources; Environment; Animals/wildlife, preservation/protection; Family planning.
Limitations: Applications not accepted. Giving on a national basis. No grants to individuals.
Application information: Contributes only to pre-selected organizations.
Officers: Thomas H. Wiancko, Pres.; Richard D. Wiancko, V.P.; Judith W. Parker, Secy.-Treas.
Trustees: Paul Chasman; Bradley Parker; Anna K. Wiancko-Chasman.
EIN: 830291490

3510
Wyoming Community Foundation
221 Ivinson Ave., Ste. 202
Laramie, WY 82070-3038 (307) 721-8300
Contact: George H. Gault, Pres.
Additional tel.: toll free (866) 708-7878; FAX: (307) 721-8333; E-mail: wcf@wycf.org; URL: http://www.wycf.org

Incorporated in 1989 in WY.
Grantmaker type: Community foundation
Financial data (yr. ended 12/31/02): Assets, $29,488,704 (M); gifts received, $3,127,646; expenditures, $2,276,364; giving activities include $1,676,121 for 423 grants (high: $45,000).
Purpose and activities: Current statewide areas of need from the foundation's unrestricted funds are children and youth and civic projects. The foundation administers a donor-advised fund.
Fields of interest: Arts; Education; Natural resources; Health care; Health organizations, association; Children/youth, services; Community development, public/private ventures; Rural development; Community development; Voluntarism promotion.
Types of support: General/operating support; Continuing support; Management development; Program development; Conferences/seminars; Seed money; Technical assistance; Program evaluation; Scholarships—to individuals; Matching/challenge support.
Limitations: Giving primarily in WY. No support for lobbying efforts. Generally, no support for block grants, capital campaigns, annual campaigns, or debt retirement.
Publications: Application guidelines, Annual report, Grants list, Informational brochure (including application guidelines), Newsletter, Program policy statement.
Application information: Application form required.
  Initial approach: Letter
  Copies of proposal: 10
  Deadline(s): Mar. 1, July 3, and Nov. 1
  Board meeting date(s): Quarterly
  Final notification: June 15, Oct. 15 and Mar. 15
Officers and Directors:* Tad Daly,* Chair.; Patti MacMillan,* Vice-Chair.; George H. Gault, Pres.; Lollie Benz Plank,* Secy.; Jim Moses,* Treas.; and 18 additional directors.
Number of staff: 4 full-time professional; 1 part-time professional; 1 full-time support.
EIN: 830287513

INDEX TO DONORS, OFFICERS, TRUSTEES

3M Co., 1653
A & B Properties, Inc., 896
Aalfs, Betsey, 3456
Aaroe & Assocs., John, 66
Aaron, Susan, 1160
Abbey, Philip, 3278
Abbott, David, 2650
Abbott, Ethel S., 1806
Abbott, Harold E., 3377
Abbott, Richard, 1587
Abboud, Labeeb M., 2379
Abdalla, Ken, 117
Abdullah, Lydia, 2817
Abel, Alice, 1807
Abel, Elizabeth N., 1807
Abel, James P., 1807
Abel, Mary C., 1807
Abel-Smith, Mary Mills, 623
Abele, Alexander T., 1349
Abele, Christopher S., 1349
Abele, Jennifer L., 1349
Abele, John E., 1349
Abele, Mary S., 1349
Abell Co., A.S., 1268
Abell, W. Shepherdson, 1268
Abelson, Hope A., 921
Abelson, Katherine A., 921
Abelson, Lester S., 921
Abercrombie, Josephine, 2177
Abercrombie, Josephine E., 1206
Abraham, Alexander, 1999
Abraham, Helene, 1999
Abraham, James, 1999
Abraham, Nancy, 1792, 1999
Abramowitz, Adina, 2814
Abramson, A.D., 3393
Abramson, Edith, 3393
Abramson, Lon, 3393
Abrons, Adam, 2000
Abrons, Alix, 2000
Abrons, Anne S., 2000
Abrons, Henry, 2000
Abrons, Herbert L., 2000
Abrons, John, 2000
Abrons, Leslie, 2000
Abrons, Louis, 2000
Abrons, Peter, 2000
Abrons, Richard, 2000
Aburida, Wael, 3261
Acadia Trust, N.A., 1245
Acers, Ebby Halliday, 3061
Achelis, Elisabeth, 2001
Acheson, James C., 1525
Acker, Frederick G., 1050
Acker, Janet, 1812
Ackerley, Margaret, 707
Ackerson, Robert L., 1220
Acmaro Securities Corp., The, 892
Acomb, Joanne, 3479
Acosta, Frank, 280
Acquavella, Donna Jo, 2002
Acquavella, William, 1995, 2002
Acree, Lucy, 870
Acton, Evelyn Meadows, 3126
Acton, Jean, 1118

Acuff, A. Marshall, Jr., 1619
Adam, Milton F., 912
Adams, Alice E., 2536
Adams, Bruce, 2600
Adams, C., 831
Adams, Carol, 2041
Adams, Cindy, 654
Adams, Donnalyn Frey, 1270
Adams, Edith M., 1422
Adams, Edward, 2391
Adams, Frederick M., Jr., 1548
Adams, H. Douglas, 1787
Adams, Harry Lee, Jr., 3060
Adams, Jack, 2574
Adams, Jean, 1702
Adams, Joel B., Jr., 2542
Adams, Joel B., Jr., Mrs., 2542
Adams, John, 2658
Adams, John H., 2013
Adams, John W., 2438
Adams, Jon H., 2041
Adams, Michael, 198
Adams, Richard, 1270
Adams, Richard L., Jr., 1270
Adams, Richard M., 1720
Adams, Rob, 1423
Adams, Ruth, 513, 2481
Adams, Sara Trillo, 1523
Adams, Susan C., 1423
Adams-Phillips, Nazamovia "Naz", 2725
Adamson, Rebecca, 2033, 2362, 3255
Adante, David E., 2627
Adatto, Lisa, 2764
Addington, Leonard M., 1722
Addis, D., 831
Addison, R. Elaine, 2588
Adelmann, Gerald W., 967
Adkins, Ruth F., 1222
Adler, Anne, 3450
Adler, Constance, 1978
Adler, Elizabeth, 3450
Adler, Eugenie, 1978
Adler, Sheldon B., 2537
Adler-Kassner, Linda, 1978
Admire, Jack G., 794
Admire, John G., 794
Admire, Ruth S., 794
Adriance, Brian, 2954
Adwin, Teresa, 2755
Aerni, John M., 2076
Agather, Ruth K., 3102
Agee, Bob, 1285
Agee, Eloise R., 1831
Agee, Richard W., 1831
Agger, David, 325
AGL Foundation, 814
AGL Resources Inc., 814
Agnich, Richard J., 3172
Agrilink Foods, Inc., 2006
Ahlgren, John R., 2228
Ahmed, Mohamed, 1563
Ahn, Alison D., 537
Ahn, Laura, 537
Ahn, Sangwoo, 537
Ahnert, Edward F., 3075

Aichenbrenner, John, 1182
Aidnoff, Ellen F. Vanderbilt, 2487
Aiken, Tim E., 2571
Ainsworth, Maryan, 545
Aircraft Gear Corp., 960
Aitcheson, A. Tracy, 3293
Ajanaku, Nkechi, 3015
Ajmera, Maya, 2127
Akers, Carolyn Bailey, 2024
Akers, Joseph A., 2803
Akestam, Sten A., 1305
Al-Abdulla, Rania, Queen, 1305
Alayon, Adolfo G., 1802
Albano, Mary, 1345
Alberding, Ellen S., 1023
Alberghini, John, 1344
Albert, Jack, 657
Albertalli, Steve, 2095
Albinder, Barbara Zucker, 2534
Albohn, Angela L., 3312
Albrecht, Erv, 3483
Albrecht, Henry, 741
Albrecht, Mike, 408
Albregts, Stijn, 1424
Albright, Adam, 691, 924
Albright, Joseph P., 691
Albright, Rachel, 924
Albro, Les, 1122
Alcoa Inc., 2794
Alcott, William, 2662
Alden, A.F. Drew, 552
Aldredge, Alison, 2090
Aldrich, Hope, 1334
Aldridge, David P., 971
Aldridge, Elizabeth A., 2753
Alexander & Baldwin, Inc., 896
Alexander, Bill, 1804
Alexander, Bruce, 1804
Alexander, Cynthia K., 3039
Alexander, Donald C., 2342
Alexander, Duncan, 1205
Alexander, Emily H., 1097
Alexander, Gregory G., 2734
Alexander, Helen, 3471
Alexander, Helen C., 3108
Alexander, Helen Campbell, 688
Alexander, Jane, 2514
Alexander, Jodi Tara, 708
Alexander, John, 1097
Alexander, John D., Jr., 3108
Alexander, Leslie L., 708
Alexander, Myrtle E., 2567
Alexander, Nanci B., 708
Alexander, Nick, 362
Alexander, Norman, 2162
Alexander, Susan, 1361
Alexander, Ted, 816
Alexander, Thomas S., 1097
Alexander, W. Robert, 495
Alexander, William, 2567
Alexandrowski, Muriel, 1592
Alfiero, Charles C., 2008
Alfiero, James J., 2008
Alfiero, Salvatore H., 2008
Alfiero, Victor S., 2008

Alfond, Peter G., 1246
Alfond, William, 1246
Alfs, Barbara, 1005
Alhadeff, Victor D., 3380
Alistar Group, The, 3313
Allaire, Paul A., 2146
Allan, Karen C., 2762
Allan, Richard, 2920
Allen, A. Christine, 2037
Allen, Alexandra F., 2037
Allen, Andrew D., 2037
Allen, Andrew E., 71
Allen, Arthur Yorke, 2494
Allen, B. David, 1536
Allen, C. Donald, 89
Allen, Calvin, 744
Allen, Christopher, 2076
Allen, Christopher D., 2037
Allen, Donald C., 1140
Allen, Douglas E., 2037
Allen, Elisabeth F., 2037
Allen, Harry B., 71
Allen, Heath, 2899
Allen, Herbert A., 2009
Allen, Herbert A. III, 2010
Allen, Howard B., 71
Allen, Jack G., 19
Allen, Jack W., 867
Allen, James A., 71
Allen, Joelle, 785
Allen, Lee Barclay Patterson, Mrs., 867
Allen, Leigh B. III, 1738
Allen, Lucy R., 1634
Allen, M.H., 869
Allen, Nicholas E., 2037
Allen, Paul G., 3314
Allen, Paul J., 1294
Allen, Philip D., 2037
Allen, Samuel R., 962
Allen, Susan K., 2010
Allen, Thomas F., 2609, 2610, 2646, 2737
Allen, Wells, Jr., 2244
Allen, Winifred, 71
Allenby, Brandon R., 687
Allendale Mutual Insurance Co., 2961
Allerton, John Wyatt Gregg, 3404
Allesee, Maggie, 1548
Alley, Steven E., 34
Allfirst, 2827, 2848, 2871, 2899
Allied Chemical Corp., 3300
Allison, Diane M., 558, 559
Allison, Don M., 1127
Allocca, Joe, 1991
Allon, Andrea R., 2903
Allred, Ron, 527
Allred, S.E., 831
Allsop, Theresa, 592
Allsop, Theresa H., 589
Almo, Eli J., 3380
Alms, Dean M., 177
Alpaugh, Peter A., 2602
Alpe, Debbie, 536
Alpern, Bernard E., 2011
Alpern, Lloyd J., 2011

Ben & Jerry's Homemade, Inc., 2500
Bender, Bob, 1532
Bender, Christine, 914
Bender, Jeffrey P., 2040
Bender, M. Christian, 2040
Bender, Matthew IV, 2040
Bender, Peter A., 1470
Bender, Phoebe P., 2040, 2093
Benedetti, Aldo, 2761
Benedict, Barbara, 2745
Benedict, Jerrold, 2745
Benedict, Peter B., 2460
Benedict, Samuel, 2656
Benenson, James III, 2732
Benenson, James, Jr., 2732
Benes, Carl, 1594
Benjamin, Adelaide Wisdom, 1243
Benjamin, Edward Wisdom, 1243
Benjamin, Stuart Minor, 1243
Benjamin, Thomas P., 1293
Bennett, Evelyn Jane, 94
Bennett, Franklin, 2622
Bennett, J. Charmaine, 2391
Bennett, James E. III, 2618
Bennett, Joanna, 1445
Bennett, John R., 870
Bennett, M.K., 341
Bennett, Roger, 2058
Bennett, S.W., 341
Bennett, Vera, 335
Benson, Bill W., 1333
Benson, Bruce D., 465
Benson, David, 465
Benson, Geof, 1158
Benson, Marguerite, 465
Benson, Martha L., 3126
Benson, McCray V., 2554
Benson, Nancy, 478
Benson, P. Bruce, 465
Benson-Brown, Polly, 465
Bentley, Judy, 586
Bentley, Stephen C., 2595
Benton, R. Anthony, 2331
Benware, Gary, 2004
Bercow, Elizabeth S., 1399
Bercu, Steven, 1935
Berde, Carol, 1695
Berelson, Ellen S., 2031
Berg, Robert, 3017
Bergen, Hunt, 1344
Bergen, Roger V.D., 1391
Bergendahl, Anders, 2196
Bergendahl, Maria Heineman, 2196
Berger, Alan H., 77
Berger, Lawrence H., 2903
Berger, Michael B., 2521
Berger, Robert, 3302
Bergeron, Ellen, 1179
Bergesen, Todd, 301
Berghold, Elisabetta, 2307
Berghold, Joanne M., 2307
Berghold, Wm. Mark, 2307
Bergkamp, Vicki, 1203
Bergman, Marilyn, 418
Bergreen, Bernard D., 2162
Bergsund, Joan, 408
Bergtold, Susanna, 2416
Beringer, David P., 331
Berk, Sam, 2690
Berkley, Amy C., 496
Berkley, Joanne Saunders, 2217
Berkovits, Annette, 2514
Berkowitz, Alan, 1935
Berkowitz, David, 1935
Berkowitz, Leonard, 1935
Berkowitz, Linda, 1935
Berkshire Hathaway Inc., 1246, 2195, 2951
Berlanti, Donald V., 479
Berlanti, Karen L., 479
Berlanti, Matthew D., 479
Berlanti, McKenna L., 479
Berlanti, Merryl A., 480

Berlanti, Richard A., 480
Berlanti, Todd A., 480
Berlin, Charles, 2277
Berlin, James, 2638
Berlow, Myer, 2413
Berman, Harriet, 1165
Berman, Herbert, 384
Berman, Joseph, 1165
Berman, Ronald, 1405
Berman, Stuart, 384
Berman, Warren, 1165
Bernard, Carolyn K., 1845
Bernard, Lewis W., 2308
Berndt, Anne, 3216
Berndt, Arthur, 3216
Berndt, Lola Maverick, 1990
Berndt, Richard O., 1273
Berney, Jaques, 1293
Berney, Lonn, 2371
Bernhard Foundation, Inc., The, 2042
Bernhard, Steven, 1998
Bernhard, William L., 2042
Bernhardson, Ivy S., 1665
Bernhardt, Paul Leake, 2599
Bernheim, Charles, 2087
Berning, Larry D., 1054
Bernstein, Alison R., 2146
Bernstein, Leslie S., 96
Bernstein, Philip L., 96
Bernstein, Roberta, 2234
Bernstein, Sanford, 370
Bernthal, Bethany M., 1634
Berol, John A., 2043
Berol, Kenneth R., 2043
Berrard, Steven R., 761
Berresford, Susan V., 2146
Berry, Archie, Jr., 3496
Berry, Archie W., Jr., 1265
Berry, Archie W., Sr., 3496
Berry Charitable Trust, 1265
Berry, Dean C., 2236
Berry, Dwight H., 3493
Berry, John, 688
Berry, Jon W., 1265
Berry, Mark, 1265
Berry, Marla, 1265
Berry, Myra M., 468
Berry, Nan, 1265
Berry, Nathanel W., 1265
Berry, Robert B., 3496
Berry, Suphaporn V., 1265
Berry, Thomas E., 3164
Berry, Thomas W., 1886, 1911
Berry, William S., 789
Berryhill, John, 274
Bersted, Alfred, 1049
Bersted, Grace A., 931
Bertain, Lisa M., 263
Bertera, William J., 3302
Bertieri, Ronald L., 3490
Bertschy, Francios, 1704
Bertschy, Nannette, 1704
Berwick, Keith, 370
Bescherer, Edwin A., Jr., 560
Beschloss, Afsaneh M., 2146
Bessemer Trust Co., N.A., 665, 1949, 2114, 2330
Besser, Albert G., 1974
Bessey, Richard, 2095
Best, Marilyn, 2703
Bethel, Jim, 827
Bethlehem Steel Corp., 2808, 3300
Betlach, Charles J., 97
Betlach, Melanie C., 97
Betley, Leonard J., 1130
Bettcher, Laurence, 2709
Bettigole, Bruce J., 1427
Betts, Kirk H., 1311
Betts, Richard, 527
Betz, Claire S., 2869
Betz, John Drew, 2869
Beuche, James R., 1618
Beuerstein, Richard, 3426

Beusse, Margaret, 1629
Beuthin, Lucille M., 1634
Beveridge, Frank Stanley, 723
Beverly, Joseph E., 890
Beyer, Don, Jr., 663
Bhatia, Neetu, 2091
Bhattacharjee, J. K., 2699
Bianchini, Thomas J., 1924
Bibber, Richard V., 1258
Bibby, Douglas, 699
Bibby, Douglas M., 663
Bickham, Brad, 476
Biddiscombe, Raymond J., 2619, 2623
Biddle, Margaret T., 2044
Biderman, Abraham, 2155
Bieber, Charles, 2752
Bieber, Marcia McGee, 2752
Biedenharn, R.Z., 1224
Biehl, George C., 1851
Biehl, Larry, 573
Bieloh, William, 3365
Biemer, Linda, 2244
Bierman, Larry, 3002
Biersach, Katherine M., 3422
Bigenho, Bruce, 201
Biggins, Edward J., Jr., 1952
Biggs, Alison, 462
Biggs, Barton W., 2524
Biggs, Gretchen, 2524
Bigotte, J.P., 2067
Bilas, Richard A., 142
Bilezikion, Doreen, 1434
Billing, Christie, 131
Billman, Randy, 2811
Bills, Mary, 1394
Bilodeau, Kenneth D., 1550
Bilski, Berthold, 2277
Bilski, Mark A., 2277
Bilski, Nanine, 655
Bilson, Ira E., 417
bin Ra'ad, Prince Firas, H.R.H., 677
Binda, Elizabeth H., 1538
Binda, Guido A., 1538
Binda, Robert, 1538
Bing, Kenneth, 1552
Bing, Leo S., 1837
Bing, Peter S., 1837, 1848
Bing, Sanford B., 1905
Bing, Steven L., 1848
Binger, Ben, 1695
Binger, Erika, 1695
Binger, James H., 1695
Binger, James M., 1695
Binger, Patricia S., 1695
Binger, Virginia M., 1695
Bingham, Barbara A., 2574
Bingham, Darcy C., 365
Bingham Foundation, William, The, 2646
Bingham, William II, 546
Binswanger, Suzanne H., 660
Binz, Margaret R., 725
Birchenough, David, 2244
Birck, Michael, 1102
Bird, Carolyn G., 1482
Bird, Walter M. III, 1482
Bird, Walter M., Jr., 1482
Birdsall, Mabel, 2414
Birdsey, Barbara U., 1470
Birk, Jeffrey H., 1148
Birk, Peggy J., 1695
Bisgrove, Gerald, 29
Bishop, Brad, 1140
Bishop, Donald F. II, 2347
Bishop, E. Liston, 3013
Bishop, Jonathan S., 2611
Bishop, Leah M., 255
Bishop, Lillian H., 619
Bishop, Nancy, 1119
Bishop, Paul R., 2725
Bishop, Richard S., 2913
Bishop, Robert L. II, 2347
Bissell, Robert K., 2706

Bisson, Keith, 1260
Biszantz, Frances B., 99
Biszantz, Gary E., 99
Bittner, Ilana, 1289
Bittner, R. Richard, 1163
Bitz, Francois, 2809
Bjergo, Allen C., 1802
Bjorklund, Victoria B., 2034, 2182
Bjornson, Donald R., 912
Black, Allida, 668
Black, Benham, 3293
Black, Carl O., 10
Black, Charles, 864
Black, Christopher, 2930
Black, Dameron III, 862
Black, David D., 2717
Black, Debra R., 2046
Black, Esther McEwan, 2677
Black, Gary, Jr., 1268
Black, Gary, Sr., 1268
Black, Harry C., 1268
Black, Janice R., 2848
Black, Jerry B., 1205
Black, John B., 2677
Black, John F., 2547
Black, Kaye, 2985, 2990
Black, Lennox K., 2930
Black, Leon D., 2046
Black, Lynne, 1586
Black, Marilyn S., 10
Black, Paula Cooper, 536
Black, Pete, 2
Black, Peter M., 2677
Black, Sherry Salway, 3255
Black, Susie Bracht, 3060
Black, Thomas F. III, 2966
Blackford, Henry III, 2986
Blacklock, Katherine, 2474
Blackman, John N., Jr., 2048
Blackman, Mark, 2048
Blackmon, Elaine O., 820
Blackwell, Anna D., 901
Blaine, Joan S., 651
Blair, Audrey R., 581
Blair, Billie, 1991
Blair, Dorothy S., 932
Blair, Peter H., 581
Blais, Robert H., 3351
Blake, Jeanne, 1472
Blake, Jon R., 676
Blake, Kathryn T., 2751
Blake, Lucy, 155
Blakley, Bruce G., 365
Blalock, Robert, 619
Blalock, Robert G., 643
Blanchard, Jill, 2379
Blanchard, Lisa G., 1627
Blanchard, Peter P. III, 3289
Blanchard, Peter P., Jr., 2810
Blank, A.H., 1166
Blank, Andrew, 726
Blank, Arthur M., 821
Blank, Danielle, 821
Blank, Dena, 821
Blank, Jacqueline N., 1166
Blank, Jerome, 726
Blank, Kenny, 821
Blank, Mark, 726
Blank, Myron N., 1166
Blank, Stephanie, 821
Blank, Tony, 726
Blankenship, Robert P., 300
Blankfort, Lowell A., 660
Blasdale, R. William, 1341
Blasdale, R. William, Mrs., 1341
Blattmachr, Jonathan, 22
Blau, Sandra, 2012
Blaxter, H. Vaughan III, 2856
Blazek, Diane, 1573
Blazek, Frank A., 1812
Blazek, George, 1825
Blecke, Janalou, 1534
Bleser, Carol A., 3408

Gelman, Michael C., 221, 1318
Gelman, Susan, 219
Gelman, Susan R., 221, 1318
Gemmill, Faith, 3281
Gemple, Nylda, 335
Genachowski, Julius, 2486
Genauer, Eli, 3380
General Atlantic Partners, 2127
General Electric Co., 567
General Electric Foundation, 2414
Genereaux, Bruce, 1704
Genereaux, Olivia J. "Jovine", 1704
Genn, Jonathan, 1300
GenRad, Inc., 1407
Genter, Anne, 2935
Genter, Beth H., 796
Gentry, Barbara, 3152
Gentry, Mary, 3312
Geoghan, Kevin, 2095
Geoghegan, Jack, 2035
George, Anton Hulman, 1137
George, Bonnie, 210
George, Carol, 2647
George, Deborah, 1207
George, Henrietta A., 3108
George, Jack, 2647
George, Janet L., 2342
George, Joan, 2647
George, Mari Hulman, 1137
George, Sarah, 2647
George Trust, Noel, 2647
Georgehead, Kit, 1211
Georgia Gas Co., 814
Georgia Power Co., 836
Georgia-Pacific Corp., 837
Gerard, C.H. Coster, 634
Gerard, Diane, 223
Gerard, Frandelle, 3227
Gerard, Hariet C., 634
Gerard, James W., 2014
Gerard, Kathleen, 2981
Gerard, Sumner, 634
Gerber, Ann Rogers, 1981
Gerber, Margaret L., 3025
Gerbode, Frank A., 209
Gerdes, Kyle E., 1836
Geremia, Timothy V., 1401
Gerhard, Lang, 210
Gerhard, Melissa, 210
Gerlach, G. Donald, 2802
Gerlinger, Charles D., 1361
Germain, Gary R., 2070
Germanow, Leon, 2521
Germany, Federal Republic of, 670
Geronime, Karen, 1677
Gerrish, Allan M., 487
Gerrish, Gail S., 487
Gerrity, Dottie, 741
Gerry, Peggy N., 2158
Gerry, Roger G., 2158
Gerschel, Alberta, 2159
Gerschel, Laurent, 2159
Gerschel, Patrick A., 2160
Gershen, William, 527
Gershon Fund, Ben-Ephraim, 684
Gersie, Mike, 1182
Gerstenhaber, David E., 2493
Gerstle, Allan, 527
Gerstner, Louis V., Jr., 2213
Gerth, Robert L., 3316
Gerthoffer, Larry, 2742
Gertler, Larry, 280
Gettelfinger, Dale L., 1159
Gettler, Benjamin, 2648
Gettler, Benjamin R., 2648
Gettler, Delian A., 2648
Gettler, Thomas D., 2648
Getz, Bert A., 29, 41
Getz, Bert A., Jr., 41
Getz, Emma, 986
Getz, George F., 41
Getz, George F., Jr., 41
Getz, Oscar, 986

Getz, William M., 986
Getz-Schmidt, Lynn, 41
Geveda, Chester J., Jr., 1890
Ghafari, Yousif B., 1548
Gheisar, Bookda, 3310
GHF, Inc., 2848
Ghriskey, H. Williamson, Jr., 2301
Giacomini, Gary T., 292
Gianas, Peter T., 53
Gianelli, Jim, 408
Gibbard, Mary, 940
Gibbes, A. Mason, 2977
Gibbings, Sandra, 1529
Gibbons, Carrie Camp, 3236
Gibbons, Gerald E., 3327
Gibbons, John J., Hon., 1898
Gibbons, Joseph M., 1488
Gibbs, Charles F., 2087
Gibbs, James R., 403
Gibis, Margot, 2268
Gibson, Ami Jo, 3209
Gibson, E.F., 3155
Gibson, Harvey D., 2322
Gibson, Harvey D., Mrs., 2322
Gibson, James G., 1900
Gibson, Jean H., 2592
Gibson, Jill R., 1900
Gibson, Marshall, 549
Gibson, Mary Jane, Hon., 1363
Gibson, Sloan D. IV, 3
Gibson, William L., 1930
Gicking, Robert K., 2902
Giesen, Richard A., 1050
Giffin, John D., 263
Gifford, Carolyn DeSwarte, 973
Giger, Ruth, 1812
Gilbert, Harry, 3034
Gilbert, Richard, 1839
Gilbert, William A., 3224
Gilbertson, Laura H., 2610
Gilbertsons, Bob, 1735
Gildea, Barry Y., 1298
Gildea, Brian W., 1298
Gildea, Gertrude S., 1298
Gildea, Phillis A., 1298
Gildea, Ray M., 1298
Gildea, Ray Y., Jr., 1298
Gildenhorn, Joseph B., 704
Gile, Rob, 470
Giles, Clark P., 3202
Giles, Pat R., 897
Gilfillian, Alexander B., 2842
Gilkerson, George N., Jr., 971
Gilkey, M. Whitney, 3291
Gill, Elisabeth C., 2007
Gill, James F., 2122
Gill, Joanne S., 1916
Gill, Kevin, 3162
Gill, Thomas, 1916
Gillespie, Deborah, 1023
Gillespie, George J. III, 2401
Gillespie, Lee Day, Mrs., 2552
Gillespie, Michael W., 3321
Gillett, Will M., 971
Gilliam, Linda J., 628
Gilliam, Sue Ballard, 2548
Gilligan, Kevin J., 1910
Gilligan, Michael, 2289
Gilman, Dave, 476
Gilman, Howard, 2162
Gilman Investment Co., 2162
Gilman, Martha, 628
Gilman Paper Co., 2162
Gilman Securities Corp., 2162
Gilman, Sylvia P., 2162
Gilman, Terry, 3280
Gilmartin, Raymond V., 1939
Gilmore, Charlotte, 988
Gilmore Co., A.F., 212
Gilmore, Elizabeth Burke, 2311
Gilmore, John F., Jr., 988
Gilmore, Marie Dent, 212
Gilmore, Robert, 2311

Gilmore, William G., 213
Gilmore, William G., Mrs., 213
Gilmour, Allan D., 1548, 1580
Gilmour, Everett A., 2343
Gilpatric, Miriam Thorne, 2471
Gilstrap, Frank E., 1295
Giltz, Roderic, 2004
Gilzean, Larry, 362
Gimbel, Alva B., 2164
Gimbel, Bernard F., 2164
Gimbel, Franklyn M., 3455
Gimbel, Leslie, 2163, 2164
Gimbel, Thomas S.T., 2163
Gimon, Eleanor, 191
Gimon, Eleanor H., 238
Gimon, Marianne, 191
Gimpel, William, 1295
Ginandes, Alice M., 2314
Ginden, Charles B., 892
Ginn, William D., 2691
Ginsberg, Bertrand I., 255
Ginsberg, Joshua, 2049
Ginsberg, Marc, 553
Ginsberg, William W., 552
Ginzberg, Abigail, 245
Gioia, Robert D., 2092
Giop, Sonia, 2843
Giordano, Alexandra, 2309
Giordano, Joseph, 1901
Giordano, Salvatore, Jr., 1901
Giordano, Salvatore, Sr., 1901
Gipson, Fred, 2755
Gisel, William G., Jr., 2092
Gitlin, Bruce, 654
Giuliani, Adrian, 1927
Giuliani, Lisa Knight, 1927
Given, Robert, 106
Glackens, Ira D., 2411
Glancy, Alfred R. III, 1548, 1583
Glancy, Alfred R. IV, 1583
Glancy, Joan C., 1583
Glancy, Ruth R., 1583
Glantz & Son, N., Inc., 2165
Glantz, Herbert T., 2165
Glantz, Kitty, 2165
Glarner, Terrence, 1702
Glaser, Cathy, 2426
Glaser, Robert D., 3340
Glass, Becky, 3493
Glass, Michael, 1550
Glassen, Harold, 1584
Glasser, Lynn S., 1886
Glassman, Jeffrey, 441
Glaubig, J.C., 3075
Glavine, Thomas, 2295
Glazer, Bradford A., 1235
Glazer, Jerome S., 1235
Gleacher, Anne G., 2166
Gleacher, Eric J., 2166
Gleason, Ann, 1107
Gleaves, Vernon, 87
Gleberman, Carson, 2167
Gleberman, Joseph H., 2167
Glenmede Trust Co., The, 2682, 2707, 2826, 2898, 2916, 2926
Glenn, Carrie Eugenia, 2556
Glenn, Constance, 250
Glenn, Donald J., 1203
Glenn, Lena Viola, 2556
Glennon, Victoria P., 946
Gless, Michael M., 263
Glick, Carrie, 1594
Glick, Lawrence J., 1523
Glickenhaus, James, 2168
Glickenhaus, Seth M., 2168
Glide, Katrina D., 215
Globetti, Steven "Chip", 19
Glore, Frederick H., 989
Glore, Robert Hixon, 989
Glossberg, Joseph, 1081
Glynn, Gary A., 2932
Godbersen, Gary, 1170
Godbersen, Leone L., 1170

Godbersen, Sharon, 1170
Godchaux, Charles R., 1237
Godchaux, Frank A. III, 1237
Godchaux, Frank K., 1237
Godchaux, Frank M., 1237
Godchaux, Leslie K., 1237
Goddard, Deborah M., 382
Goddard, Samuel P., Jr., 53
Goddard, William R., Jr., 2753
Godfrey, Cullen M., 3081
Godfrey, David L., 558, 559
Godfrey, Dudley J., Jr., 3416
Godfrey, Ronald G., 2621
Godwin, Laura, 2303
Godwin, Marcia Williams, 3061
Goebel, Chris, 1203
Goebel, J. Martin, 698
Goeke, Dave, 3369
Goergen, Pamela M., 568
Goergen, Robert B., 568
Goergen, Robert B., Jr., 568
Goergen, Todd A., 568
Goff, John V., 2095
Goguen, June, 1401
Goins, Charlynn, 2330
Goisman, Richard, 3417
Gold, David B., 218
Gold, Elaine, 218
Gold, Emily, 218
Gold Kist Inc., 831
Gold, Mark S., 1357
Gold, Norman M., 2181
Gold, Steven A., 218
Gold-Bubier, Diane, 218
Gold-Lurie, Barbara, 218
Goldammer, Vance, 3002
Goldberg, Bradley L., 2169
Goldberg, Brian L., 671
Goldberg, David, 2618
Goldberg, Diana L., 671
Goldberg, Joel, 871
Goldberg, Kim Glazer, 1235
Goldberg, Lauren B., 671
Goldberg, Michael, 2355
Goldberg, Norman, 3282
Goldberg, Stephen A., 671
Goldberg, Stuart W., 671
Goldblatt, Stanford J., 1029
Goldblum, Israela, 690
Golde, Chris, 3369
Golde, Peter, 3369
Golden, Carol, 2969
Golden, Connie, 915
Golden, Michael, 2331
Golden, Morley, 915
Golden, Rebecca, 3211
Golden, Terence, 661
Golden, William T., 2401
Goldfarb, Arlene, 2170
Goldfarb, Morris, 2170
Goldfrank, Lionel III, 2171
Goldman 1997 Charitable Lead Annuity Trust, Richard, 1318
Goldman, Douglas E., 219, 220, 221, 229
Goldman, Guido, 670
Goldman, John D., 219, 221, 229
Goldman, Kathy, 2340
Goldman, Lisa M., 220, 221
Goldman, Marcia L., 221
Goldman, Peter, 3355
Goldman, Rebecca B., 3402
Goldman, Rhoda H., 219, 221
Goldman, Richard N., 219, 221
Goldman, Robert, 1308
Goldman, Roger, 281
Goldman, Sachs & Co., 2052
Goldring, Gary F., 1902
Goldring, William, 1244
Goldsborough, John B., 2073
Goldschmidt, Neil, Hon., 688
Goldsmith, Bernard M. III, 1903
Goldsmith, David, 1903

Markell, William B., 2050
MarketSpan Corp., 2240
Markline, Judith Woods, 370
Markowitz, Martin L., 2528
Markquart, Edward F., Rev., 1311
Marks, Harry L., 3116
Marks, Howard S., 255
Marks, James A., 3455
Marks, John R., 3235
Marks, Joshua R., 2299
Marks, Kevin S., 203
Marks, Lowell, 113
Marks, M.J., 896
Marks, Marcia, 3116
Marks, Paul Camp, 3235
Marks, Randolph A., 2250, 2299
Marks, Sally, 2299
Marks, Theodore E., 2299
Marks, Walter N., Jr., 280
Markus, Ann, 156
Markus Charitable Lead Trust, Eva, The, 279
Marley, Ethel, 46
Marley Trust, Kemper, 46
Marn, Rudy, 744
Marnell, Alisa A., 1853
Marnell, Anthony A. II, 1853
Marnell, Anthony A. III, 1853
Maroney, Eleanor S., 627
Marotta, Justin, 1573
Marquardt, Jeffrey W., 2880
Marquardt, Richard C., 2880
Marquardt, Sarah W., 2880
Marquart, Rex, 1831
Marquet, Kay M., 145
Marquette Charitable Organization, 2991
Marr, Kenneth J., 2679
Marram, Ellen R., 2331
Mars, Inc., 3279
Mars, Forrest E., Jr., 3279
Mars, Jacqueline B., 3279
Mars, John F., 3279
Mars, Lisa, 2381
Mars, Marijke E., 2300
Mars, Robert, Jr., 1678
Mars, Valerie A., 2300
Mars, Victoria B., 2300
Marsden, K. Gerald, 1553
Marsh, Charles Edward, 695
Marsh, Dayle P., 519
Marsh, Hattie Heller, 237
Marsh, Richard, 2642
Marsh, Susan, 2341
Marshall & Ilsley Bank, 3455
Marshall, Colin S., 1453, 1513
Marshall, Gene, 743
Marshall, James Harper, 2302
Marshall, John D., 1056
Marshall, John E. III, 1606
Marshall, Lee Harper, 2302
Marshall, Robert S., 1373
Marshall, Schuyler B. IV, 3147
Marshall, Shauna, 245
Marshall, Stephanie P., 1102
Marshall, Thomas O., Hon., 851
Marshall, Thurgood, Jr., 688
Marsicano, Michael, 2554
Marten, Susan, 3489
Martin, Ann M., 2303
Martin, Anne Marie, 253
Martin, Atherton, 1424
Martin, Casper, 1144, 1403
Martin, Charlotte Y., 3361
Martin, Elizabeth, 3334
Martin, Esther, 1144
Martin Foundation, 3334
Martin Foundation, Inc., 1403
Martin, Frederick V., 3231
Martin, George, 2881
Martin, Geraldine F., 1144
Martin, Glenn R., Mrs., 3290
Martin, Holly, 1342

Martin, Jack, 1548
Martin, James W., 2995
Martin, Jane Reed, 2303
Martin, Jeffrey S., 253
Martin, Jennifer L., 1144
Martin, Jim, 1677
Martin, John, 1527
Martin, John, Fr., 3391
Martin, Joseph, 656
Martin, Joseph W., Jr., 398
Martin, Kenneth, 3327
Martin, Kenneth C., 630
Martin, Lee, 1144
Martin, Leonard C., 468
Martin, Lisa, 1144
Martin, M. Christine, 2881
Martin Marietta Materials, Inc., 2566
Martin, Nancy E., 1203
Martin, Patricia, 461
Martin, Peter R., 2021
Martin, Rebecca, 2881
Martin, Richard L., 253
Martin, Ross, 1144
Martin, Sallie E., 2581
Martin, Susan M., 1052
Martin, Thomas D., 3250
Martin, Webb F., 1619
Martin, William H., 2817
Martinat, Linda, 1041
Martineau, J. Maria, 3081
Martineau, Steve, 1620
Martinelli, Gary E., 2432
Martinenza, Stephen A., 626
Martinez, Frank, 28
Martinez, Julie Quiroz, 139
Martinez, Kevin, 3319
Martinez, Lissa, 3152
Martinez, Manuell, 478
Martinez, Olivia G., 335
Martinez, Ronald P., 938
Martinez, Steven F., 923
Martinez, Vilma S., 121
Martino, Julie, 2104
Marton, Steve, 49
Martore, Gracia C., 3260
Marvec Corp., The, 2819
Marvin, Elise, 78
Marx, Ruth M., 294
Mascarenas, Jose Manuel, 3071
Mascoma Savings Bank, 1860
Mascott, Mary, 2342
Mascotte, John P., 1761
Maslow, Allison, 2882
Maslow, Douglas, 2882
Maslow, Leslie, 2882
Maslow, Richard, 2882
Mason, Cheryl White, 247
Mason, Emma, 2690
Mason, Frances E., 2817
Mason, Howard E., Jr., 171
Mason, James B., 1792
Mason, Lawrence N., 1293
Mason, William Clarke, 2884
Masowitz Trust, Aaron, 225
Masselink, Carla, 1552
Massey, Betty, 3132
Massey, Catherine Andrea, 959
Massey, Christopher, 959
Massey, Richard S., 959
Massey, Walter E., 2308
Massey, William P., 2539
Massie, Michael M., Mrs., 642
Mastropieri, Robert W., 1312
Masuda, Hideki, 1068
Masumoto, David Mas, 247
Matchett, David, 435
Matheny, N. Dale, 403
Mather, Elizabeth Ring, 2683
Mather, S. Livingston, 2682
Matherne, Lee J., 1238
Mathes, Stephen J., 2272
Matheson, Alline, 2030
Matheson, Bonnie B., 1564

Matheson, Carol, 1840
Mathew, Kay, 1483
Mathews, Mary, 1671
Mathey, Dean, 1878, 3224
Mathias, Charles McC., Jr., 2473
Mathias, Cheryl E., 2741
Mathiasen, Karl, 684
Mathis, Bradford, 1567
Mathis, James E., Jr., 864
Mathison, William A., 1679
Mathot, H., 831
Matikan, Ann, 669
Matlock, Kent, 833
Matos, Maria M., 628
Matosziuk, Edward, 2846
Matson Navigation Co., Inc., 896
Matsumoto, Marilynn, 907
Matta, Anne H.G., 227
Mattar, Helio, 1305
Matteson, Duncan L., 89
Matthews, Dave, 1396
Matthews, E.E., 2449
Matthews, George G., 644
Matthews, Janice C., 912
Matthews, Peggy, 878
Matthews, Robert S., 1919
Matthews, William, 739
Matuschak, George M., 1740
Matuska, Karen, 374
Matwiczyk, Peter, 739
Matz, Dorothy A., 3108
Mauer, Julie, 429
Mauger, Deborah N., 260
Maupin, Emily, 346
Maupin, John, 3014
Mauran, Esther E.M., 2972
Mauran, Frank IV, 2972
Mauritz, William W., 1049
Maus, Blair Collins, 1047
Mausshardt, Theodore, 1314
Mauze, Abby Rockefeller, 2392
Mavec, Ellen S., 2722
Mawby, Russell G., 1599
Maxon Corp., 1145
Maxwell, Kenneth R., 2473
May, Barbara V., 807
May, C., 2873
May, Carolyn A., 2333
May, Frances, 3449
May, Irenee duPont, 638
May, Jeff, 1677
May, Joan, 527
May, Linda, 1528
May, Lou Adele, 3060
May, Merrydelle, 3449
May, T. Michael, 905
Mayeda, Mari, 245
Mayer, Beatrice Cummings, 2102
Mayer, Charles B., 1225
Mayer, Frank, Jr., 994
Mayer, Hal, 3421
Mayer, John, 1840
Mayer, Robert N., 2102
Mayer, Roger, 823
Mayer, Victoria K., 3442
Mayers, Carl, 3313
Mayerson, Arlene, 245
Mayeux, L.J., Jr., 3017
Mayfield, Beth, 3180
Mayhew, Kathleen D., 2771
Maynard, Olivia P., 1619
Maynard, Priscilla K., 1859
Mayne, Kate, 364
Mayo, Andy, 1256
Mayo, Z.B., Jr., 1295
Mayrock, Marjorie, 2148
Mays, Al, 2242
Mays, L. Lowry, 3120
Mays, Mark, 3120
Mays, Peggy P., 3120
Mays, Randall, 3120
Mays, Randall T., 3120
Maytag, Fred II, 1179

Maytag, Frederick L. III, 1179
Maytag, Kenneth P., 1179
Maytum, Kurt, 2341
Mazanec, Elsa B., 3121
Mazanec, George L., 3121
Mazanec, John Charles, 3121
Mazanec, Robert Andrew, 3121
Mazar, Anne, 1447
Mazar, Brian, 1447
Mazda Motor of America, 681
Mazda North American Opers., 681
Mazda Research & Development of North America, 681
Maze, Judith, 1595
Mazeres, Kim, 1849
Mazin, George, 1953
Mazur, John M., 2831
McAllister, Angela, 3122
McAllister, Dana Leigh, 3122
McAllister, Hugh A., 3122
McAllister, Hugh A., Jr., 3122
McAllister, Kathy, 3489
McAshan Foundation, Inc., The, 3344
McAshan, Susan C., 3178
McAulay, Carl D., 3176
McBean, Alletta Morris, 296
McBean, Atholl, 297
McBean, Edith, 297, 2514
McBean, Judith, 297
McBean, Nancy, 297
McBean, Peter, 297
McBride, John P., 460
McBride, John P., Jr., 460
McBride, Katherine H., 460
McBride, Laurie M., 460
McBride, Peter, 460
McBride, Peter M., 460
McBurney, Wendell, 1118
McCabe, James L., 2907
McCabe, John B., 2070
Mccabe, Nancy, 2064
McCabe, Nancy W., 2251
McCaffrey, Brian, 2240
McCain, John, 42
McCall, John R., 1216
McCallie, Allen L., 3025
McCallie, Spencer, 3013
McCallion, Timothy J., 437
McCallister, Betsy, 1527
McCallum, Elkin, 1444
McCalmont, Susan, 2751
McCalpin, William F., 2392
McCamish, Henry F., Jr., 853
McCammon, Stanley B., 3359
McCance, Allison J., 1448
McCance, Henry F., 1448
Mccandless, Elizabeth T., 1263
McCandless, June, 2209
McCann, Franklin W., 2516
McCann, Jennifer, 550
McCann, Jonathan W., 2516
McCann, Regis, 2881
McCarter, Fred, 1126
McCarter, Jerry, 1671
McCarthy, Edwin J., 600
McCarthy, Gerald P., 3300
McCarthy, John M., 2304
McCarthy, Laurette E., 2304
McCarthy, Mary A., 2304
McCarthy, Michael, 1827
McCarthy, Neil M., 1357, 2304
McCarthy, Roger, 525
McCarthy, Stephen J., 2304
McCarthy, Susan B., 600
McCarthy, Tara A., 2304
McCarty, Marilyn, 3478
McCarty, Stuart, 2275
McCarty-Houser, Mary, 1271
McCarvel, Cynthia, 1202
McCarville, Mark, 973
McCaslin, Donna, 3359
McCaslin, Elizabeth K., 3352
McCaul, Linda M., 3120

Meader, Mary U., 1644
Meadowcroft, W. Howarth, 3363
Meadows, Algur Hurtle, 3126
Meadows, Carla H., 3081
Meadows, Curtis W., Jr., 3126
Meadows, Eric Richard, 3126
Meadows, Mark A., 3126
Meadows, Michael L., 688, 3126
Meadows, Robert A., 3126
Meadows, Virginia, 3126
Means, T. Sam, 651
Meara, Jackie, 1048
Meares, Samuel H., 2551
Mears, Norman B., 1717
Measell, Donna I., 3276
Medica, John K., 3149
Medica, Megan S., 3149
Medrud, Mariagnes, 476
Meehan, Emily Souvaine, 2306, 2307
Meehan, Miriam F., 2307
Meehan, Peter J., 2594
Meehan, Terence, 2306
Meehan, Terence S., 2306, 2307
Meehan, William M., 2307
Meek, Samuel W., Jr., 583
Meeker, Cindy, 2731
Mees, Philip, 414
Meier, Anne R., 717
Meier, Linda, 335
Meier, Linda R., 89
Meier, Walter C., 717
Meijer, Inc., 1615
Meijer, Frederik G.H., 1615
Meijer, Mark, 1586
Meikel, Teresa, Ms., 377
Meiklejohn, Scot, 1868
Meinke, Paul, 3426
Meinz, T.P., 3495
Meissner, Paul F., 3464
Meissner, Rose, 1123
Meister, Paul, 1865
Mekrut, William A., 2961
Melander-Dayton, Steven J., 1697
Melarkey, Michael J., 1839
Meldahl, M.J., 1801
Mele, Patrick J., Jr., 1357
Melgary, Bruce, 2795
Melican, James P., Jr., 575
Melillo, Samuel T., 1944
Mellam, Laura M., 304
Mellano, H. Michael, Sr., 923
Mellencamp, John, 1396
Mellon Bank, N.A., 2829
Mellon, Constance B., 2885
Mellon Financial Corp., 745, 1443,
    2792, 2794, 2801, 2802, 2810,
    2823, 2825, 2839, 2840, 2843,
    2848, 2849, 2875, 2883, 2914,
    2923, 2931, 2937
Mellon, Paul, 2308
Mellon, Richard A., 2885
Mellon, Richard K., 2886
Mellon, Richard P., 2885, 2886
Mellon, Seward Prosser, 2885, 2886
Mellon, Timothy, 2308
Mellowes, Linda T., 3455
Melmer, Rick, 3003
Melton, Terry L., 2624
Melton-Williams, Emelie, 2439
Melvin, Anthony, 2944
Melvoin, Hugo J., 1052
Melvoin, Jeffrey D., 1052
Melvoin, Lois G., 1052
Melvoin, Richard I., 1052
Memmen, Ava-Liisa, 1504
Menapace, John J., 2920
Menasha Corp., 3452
Menchaca, Peggy B., 3107
Mendelsund, Judy, 2164
Mendicina, Frank J., 385
Menefee, Albert L., Jr., 3027
Menefee, Charles E., Jr., 2991
Menefee, Valere, 3027

Menken, Alan, 2310
Menken, Janis, 2310
Menschel, Richard L., 47, 2172
Menschel, Robert B., 2172
Mensching, Jack E., 971
Mentesana, Carolyn A., 3106
Menton-Nightlinger, Deborah A., 2337
Menzel, Scott, 1592
Menzie, Robert, 1127
Menzies, Gretchen, 2820
Menzies, J., 2954
Mercantile-Safe Deposit & Trust Co.,
    1280, 1281, 1309
Mercer, Byron T., 1897
Mercer, Debbie, 1118
Mercer, Marty Hansen, 1594
Merchant, Kathryn E., 2617
Merck & Co., Inc., 1939
Merck, Antony M., 1449
Merck, Josephine, 613
Merck, Josephine A., 1449
Merck, Serena S., 1450
Merck, Wilhelm M., 1449
Mercurio, Donna, 2091
Mercury Marine, 3256
Merdek, Andrew A., 2626
Meredith, Charles M. III, 2875
Meredith, E.T. III, 1181
Meredith, Katherine C., 1181
Meredith Publishing Co., 1181
Merin, Kenneth D., 2193
Meriwether, Heath J, 1548
Merkel, Ann, 2004
Merkel, Joel C., 3348
Merlin, H. Stephen, 853
Merriam, Dena, 514
Merrick, Anne M., 1297
Merrick, Robert G. III, 1297
Merrick, Robert G., Jr., 1297
Merrick, Robert G., Sr., 1297
Merrifield, Peggy, 180
Merrifield, Roger, 1534
Merrill, Amy, 1940
Merrill, Bruce, 1940
Merrill, Charles A., Jr., 1940
Merrill, Charles E., Sr., 1933
Merrill, Eleanor, 1283
Merrill, Ella Warren, 2879
Merrill, Holly, 744
Merrill, Jane Ann, 856
Merrill Lynch & Co., Inc., 809
Merrill Lynch Pierce Fenner & Smith,
    2629
Merrill Lynch Trust Co., 1787, 1880,
    1883, 1976, 2875, 3152
Merrill Lynch Trust Co., FSB, 2330
Merrill, Michelle Christy, 856
Merrill, Paul, 1940
Merrill, Philip, 1283
Merrill, T. Randolph, 856
Merrill, Thomas, 230
Merrill, Tracy Louis, 1035
Merriman, M. Heminway, 616
Mersereau, Susan M., 3396
Mershon, Marianne, 56
Merthan, Claudia Boettcher, 466
Mertz, Joyce, 2311
Mertz-Gilmore Foundation, Joyce, 182
Meserve, Hamilton W., 1357
Meserve, William G., 1391
Mesloh, James C., 2829
Messbanger, Dick, 3060
Messenger, Anne, 2070
Messina, Sal, 1255
Messinger, Alida R., 1334, 2393
Mestre, Barbara B., 2050
Met-Ed, 2642
Metcalf, Dorothy A., 2887
Metcalf, Pauline C., 2972
Metcalf, Robert A., 2887
Metcalfe, Stacie, 824
Metts, Harold, 3098
Metz, Christie M., 779

Metz, Henry J., 779
Metzger, Sherri, 2548
Metzger, William L., 940
Metzner, David A., 704
Meuse, David R., 2619, 2623
Meyer, Adolph H., 1526
Meyer, Bruce, 819
Meyer, Carla E., 1491
Meyer, David, 244
Meyer, Dick, 1824
Meyer, Edward H., 2313
Meyer, Eunice, 3142
Meyer, Fred F., 1533
Meyer, Fred G., 2776
Meyer, Ida M., 1526
Meyer, James, 519
Meyer, Janet E., 3454
Meyer, Jerome H., 552
Meyer, Laura L., 2554
Meyer, Lyle L., 1019
Meyer, Melba Bayers, 2568
Meyer, Orin H., 1419
Meyer, Paul, 365
Meyer, Peter S., 3094
Meyer, R., 2873
Meyer, Ron, 2485
Meyer, Sandra, 2313
Meyer, Ted A., 1551
Meyer, Terri, 3372
Meyer, William, 1978
Meyers, Ann, 2685
Meyers, David R., 1053
Meyers, Frederick C., 1053
Meyers, Gail, 2194
Meyers, Hannes, 1552
Meyers, James, 3188
Meyers, N. Marshall, 1293
Meyers, Philip M. III, 2685
Miami Corp., 963, 987
Miani, Philip, 744
Micallef, Joseph S., 1698, 1734
Michael, Mary Anne, 3402
Michaels, Barbara R., 2314
Michaels, Gilbert N., 146
Michaels, J. Patrick, Jr., 780
Michaels, Kimberly L., 780
Michaels, Roger A., 2314
Michaels, William, 3507
Michaud, David N., 1291
Michel, Betsy S., 1889, 1916
Michel, Clifford L., 1916
Michel, Sally J., 1268
Michelfelder, David, 360
Mickelton, Mike, 1285
Mickle, Catherine E., 884
Middendorf, Alice C., 1316
Middendorf, J. William, Jr., 1316
Middleton, Carole, 307
Middleton, Fred A., 307
Midkiff, Robert F., 897
Miers, Frederic B., 2343
Migdal, Lester, 3291
Mikkelsen, Chris D., 33
Milavetz, Diane, 141
Milbank, Albert G., 2309
Milbank, Michelle R., 2309
Milbank, Samuel L., 2309
Milbank, Thomas, 2309
Milbury, Cassandra M., 2885
Miles, Cliff, 1617
Miles, J. Michael, 1728
Miles, J.C. Vernor, 266
Miles, Serena, 1315
Miles, Wilfred Vernor, 266
Milfs, Audrey L., 328
Milhollan, D. Jackson, 2936
Millard, Mary E., 1678
Millard, Philip H., 1627
Millares, Maria R., 787
Millenbruch, G.L., 2808
Miller, A. William, 3217
Miller, Alice A., 2818
Miller Anderson Sherrad, 3381

Miller, Anne W., 1340
Miller, C. Richard, Jr., 1290
Miller, Carey K., 3363
Miller, Charles D., 827
Miller, Craig R., 1674
Miller, Daniel S., 1890
Miller, David J., 478
Miller, Diane, 2281
Miller, Diane Edgerton, 3232
Miller, Dorothy J., 1767
Miller, Edward J., 1548
Miller, Edward M., 3305
Miller, Edward S., 2461
Miller, Ella Warren, 2879
Miller, Emily Altschull, 2356
Miller, Erica A., 1700
Miller, Ethan A., 3232
Miller, Eugene A., 1548
Miller, Frances Cameron, 3055
Miller, Frederick W., 3421
Miller, George, 2986
Miller, George D., Jr., 1649
Miller, Glen, 1077, 1584
Miller, Gordon E., 105
Miller, Harvey S.S., 2799
Miller, Heidi, 1939
Miller, Heidi G., 926
Miller, Herman, 1452
Miller, J. Jefferson, 1340
Miller, Janet H., 3305
Miller, Jennifer L., 448
Miller, John F., Jr., 1556
Miller, Joshua M., 1340
Miller, Judy, 1846
Miller, Katharine S., 2879
Miller, Kay, 2658
Miller, Larry F., 3260
Miller, Leon, 2528
Miller, Leslie A., 2888
Miller, Lucy, 611
Miller, Marc, 1483
Miller, Margaret Mary, 308
Miller, Mark, 1536
Miller, Maurie J., 1054
Miller, Myron, 1452
Miller, O'Malley M., 308
Miller, Owens O., 308
Miller, Paul F. III, 2879
Miller, Paul F., Jr., 2879
Miller, Paul J., 984
Miller, R.M., 1653
Miller Revocable Trust, Josepha S., 1340
Miller, Robert, 26
Miller, Robert, Jr., 2341
Miller, Sally, 2783
Miller, Sally C., 3126
Miller, Stuart A., 774
Miller, Susan, 2743
Miller, Terry L., 95
Miller, W. Owens, 308
Miller, William J., 3054
Miller, Winlock W., 3363
Milligan, Alex B., 1150
Milligan, Cynthia H., 1599
Milligan, Suanne, 1148
Milliken, Ann E., 633
Milliken, John W., 633
Milliken, Peter, 641
Milliken, Phoebe, 641
Milliken, Roger, 637, 641
Milliman, Alison Wyckoff, 3389
Millkey, John M., 894
Millkey, Linda, 894
Millner, Thomas, 2537
Mills, Alice Ann W., 3401
Mills, Alice duPont, 623
Mills, David W., 311
Mills, Howard S., 3401
Mills, Howard S., Jr., 3401
Mills, Kincaid, 3013
Mills, Phyllis J., 2069
Mills, Suzanne, 1543
Millspaugh, Gordon A., Jr., 1971

Newman, Linwood D., 3068
Newman, Richard A., 640
Newnum, Kenneth, 1148
Newquist, Dana E., 87
Newson, Eddie, 1147
Newton, Jane Norton, 1217
Newton, Jerry, 1078
Ney, Judith, 2154
Neydon, Peter, 1552
Nguyen, Minh-Tram, 1469
Niagara Mohawk Power Corp., 2333
Nicholas, Llewellyn J., 2335
Nicholas, Nicholas J., Jr., 2335
Nicholls-Payne, Naoma, 117
Nichols, C. Walter III, 2336
Nichols, David H., 2336
Nichols, Horace S., 1490
Nichols, Isabel, 2549
Nichols, James R., 1351, 1354, 1474
Nichols, Kate Cowles, 1887
Nichols, Mary, 183
Nichols, Wendell I., 727
Nichols-Young, Stephanie, 3398
Nicholson, David O., 1701
Nicholson, Ford J., 1701
Nicholson, James B., 1548
Nicholson, Maureen N., 1627
Nicholson, Nancy B., 1701
Nicholson, Richard H., 1701
Nicholson, Susan V., 1211
Nicholson, Todd S., 1701
Nickerson, Diane, 1700
Nickerson, Joshua A., Jr., 1434
Nickerson, Stuart J., 1373
Nickeson, G., 2954
Nicklin, F. Oliver, 977
Nicoll, Jill D., 689
Nicrosi, WIlliam K. II, 10
Nielsen, D. James, 1714
Nielsen, Kate, 7
Nielsen, Katherine D., 1727
Nielsen, Marilyn, 1814
Nielsen, Patricia, 476
Nielson, Karen, 109
Nieman, Beth, 1147
Nienhueser, Helen, 22
Niester, Donna M., 1525
Nigris, Phyllis, 2971
Nikitine, Vadim A., 3289
Niles, Clayton E., 53
Niles, Clayton N., 53
Nimcrut, Shirley Sieg, 1635
Nimick, Theresa L., 2891
Nimick, Thomas H., Jr., 2891
Ninesling, Therese A., 2389
Nippert, Louis, 2689
Nippert, Louise D., 2689
Nippon Foundation, The, 2484
Niven, James G., 2305
Nix, Craig L., 2989
Nix, J. Kenneth, 864
Nix, John M., 864
Nixon, John L., 2571
Nixon, Laurey, 2921
Nixon, P. Andrews, 1257
NOAA Restoration Center, 3256
Nobil, John, 461
Noble, Edward E., 2753
Noble, Edward John, 2337
Noble, Lloyd, 2753
Noble, Maria, 2753
Noble, Nick, 2753
Noble, Rusty, 2753
Nodar, Rudy P., 253
Noe, Larry, 2318
Nogaki, Jane, 1894
Nogales, Luis G., 2146
Noguchi, Ted, 2658
Noland, Mariam C., 1548
Noland, Virginia B., 1223
Nolen, Eliot Chace, 2178
Nolen, Wilson, 2178
Noojin, A.Y., 3155

Noonan, John R., 1956
Noonan, Patrick F., 2013, 3244
Noonan, Peter, 2724
Nopper, Marie, 1800
Norcross, Arthur D., 2338
Norcross, Arthur D., Jr., 2338
Nord, Eric T., 2691
Nord, Evan, 2690
Nord, Jane B., 2691
Nord, Shannon, 2690
Nord, Walter G., 2690
Nord, Walter G., Mrs., 2690
Nordson Corp., 2690, 2692
Nordstrom, John, 1552
Norfolk Southern Corp., 3284
Norman, Aaron E., 2339
Norman, Abigail, 2339
Norman, Ajulo, 833
Norman, Andrew, 322
Norman, Margaret, 2339
Norman, Rebecca, 2339
Norman, Roberta L., 2699
Norman, Sarah, 2339
Norrington, Margaret, 331
Norrington, Ralph, 331
Norris, David E., 601
Norris, Paul J., 1299
Norris, Robert W., 3113
Norris, Thomas C., 2947
North Central Trust Co., 3424, 3425, 3449
North Side Bank & Trust Co., 2617
North, Walter, 1553
Northeast Nuclear Energy Co., 589
Northeast Utilities, 589
Northen, Mary Moody, 3132
Northenor, Jean, 1140
Northern Arkansas Telephone Co., 62
Northern Engraving Corp., 3423
Northern Trust Bank of Florida, N.A., 745
Northern Trust Co., The, 910, 932, 970, 983, 999, 1032, 1070, 3124, 3455
Northey, Lyle W., 1678
Northrup, Edwin II, 2693
Norton, Allison, 3191
Norton, Carolyn J., 3381
Norton, Gale, Hon., 689
Norton, George W., Mrs., 1217
Norton, James M., 3056
Norton, Jane, 2620
Norton, Jeffrey P., 1699
Norton, John A., 3056
Norton, Joseph, 3261
Norton, Lenore "Trilby", 3056
Norton, Lenore C., 3056
Norton, Mary T., 3056
Norton, Michael A., 3056
Norton, Paul S., 3056
Norton, Thomas A., 3056
Norton, Toby, 3191
Norvell, Barbara C., 2547
Norweb, Eliz, 2694
Norweb, R. Henry, Jr., 2694
Nostitz, Drewry H., 2558
Notebaert, Richard C., 2242
Novak, Kristin C., 1167
Novakov, Lydia Haggar, 3061
Nowak, Carole M., 2641, 2667
Nowek, Jeremy, 2903
Noyes, Charles F., 2345
Noyes, Jansen III, 2344
Noyes, Margaret T., 2344
Nu Skin Enterprises, Inc., 3195
Nugen, J. Bryan, 1127
Nugent, Conn, 2229
Nulsen, Carol, 1661
Nunes, Mary Louise, 1374
Nunes-Vais, Brian, 1883
Nunes-Vais, Maryann, 1883
Nunn, Warne, 2776
Nunneley, Charles K.R., 2403
Nusbaum, Robert C., 3287
Nutter, Jeri, 2814

Nutter, W.L., 789
Nye, Homer E., 1544
Nye, Michael, 1592
Nylander, Inga Olsson, 3286
Nystrom, William B., 300

O'Bleness, Charles, 2695
O'Bleness Foundation No. 1, Charles, 2695
O'Boyle, Marilyn J., 2882
O'Brien, Arthur R., 964
O'Brien, Donal C., Jr., 2219, 2286, 2481
O'Brien, Michael, 964
O'Brien, Robert S., 2659
O'Connell, Brian, 1373
O'Connell, Michael, 1424
O'Connor, James J., 935
O'Connor, Janet M., 539
O'Connor, John M.B., 2155
O'Connor, Michael, 2004
O'Connor, Michael E., 2070
O'Connor, Olive B., 2347
O'Connor, Robert, 182
O'Connor, Sarane R., 2030
O'Connor, Susan, 2133
O'Connor, Thomas E., 539
O'Donnell, Paul J., 1889
O'flynn, Thomas M., 1952
O'Gara, Susanne Wellman, 2738
O'Grady, J.P., 789
O'Grady, John B., 1327
O'Hara, Margaret E., 926
O'Hara, S., 530
O'Keefe, Mary, 1182
O'Keefe, William, 1057
O'Leary, J.P., 3495
O'Leary, John D., 2307
O'Leary, Maureen M., 2307
O'Leary, Maureen Meehan, 2307
O'Neal, Al, 1850
O'Neal, Solon F., Jr., 795
O'Neil, Abby McCormick, 1047
O'Neil, James, Jr., 1859
O'Neil, John, 2538
O'Neil, John J., 2416
O'Neil, Thomas J., 3458
O'Neill, Abby M., 2392
O'Neill, David J., 1286
O'Neill, Francis J., 2696
O'Neill, H.M., 2696
O'Neill, Hugh, 2696
O'Neill, Michael J., 2155
O'Neill, P.J., 2696
O'Neill, Pablo, 3227
O'Neill, Paul, 2021
O'Neill, Peter M., 2393
O'Neill, William J., 2696
O'Neill, William J., Jr., 2722
O'Quinn, John M., 3134
O'Regan, Frederick, 1424
O'Rourke, Eileen M., 1268
O'Sullivan, Erin, 1344
O'Toole, Dennis A., 1864
O'Toole, Gertrude L., 1864
Oak Tree Racing Assn., 323
Oak Trust, The, 1460
Oakes, Bob, 2574
Oakford, Arthur, 957
Oates, William A., Jr., 1459
Oatman, Michael, 1203
Oberfest, Bruce D., 758
Oberlie, Stephanie, 1147
Obser, Fred, 2194
Ocana, Juan Carlos, 2775
Ocean Federal Savings Bank, 1944
Ocean Financial Corp., 1944
OceanFirst Financial Corp., 1944
Ochs, Devra, 523
Ochs, Ronald K., 3436
Odell, Steve, 681
Odom, Tom, 3006
Oehmig, Margaret W., 3053

Oehmig, William C., 3053
Oestreicher, Ann, 2348
Oestreicher, Sylvan, 2348
Oetinger, Judith F., 1114
Offield, Chase, 1065
Offield, Dorothy Wrigley, 1065
Offield, James S., 1065
Offield, Meighan, 1065
Offield, Paxson H., 1065
Offutt, Thomas W. III, 2682
Ogaz, Brian, 317
Ogden, Bob, 2548
Ogden, Doug, 182
Ogden, Margaret G., 2070
Ogle, Harry, 2699
Oglesby, Mary Norris Preyer, 2576
Oglesby, Myrna, 108
Ogorzaly, Mary F., 2133
Ogstrup-Pedersen, Anne-Margrete, 1479
Ohio Edison Co., 2642
Ohio Plate Glass, 2655
Ohlmansiek, Jane, 1126
Ohlsen, Ronald, 1064
Ohnmacht, Susan, 3150
Ohrstrom, Barnaby A., 3238
Ohrstrom Foundation, 2279
Ohrstrom, George F., 2349
Ohrstrom, George L. II, 2349, 3238
Ohrstrom, George L., Jr., 2279, 2349
Ohrstrom, Kenneth M., 3238
Ohrstrom, Mark J., 3238
Ohrstrom, Richard R., 3238
Ohrstrom, Winifred E.A., 2349
Okamoto, Melanie, 69
Okorn, David, 2240
Okubo, Setsu, 906
Olavarrieta-Coker, Trudie, 885
Old Dominion Trust Co., 3275
Old National Trust Co., 1137
Oldershaw, Peter W., 2368
Oldfather, Al, 1818
Olds, Ransom E., 1630
Oleson, Donald W., 1624
Oleson, Frances M., 1624
Oleson, Gerald E., 1624
Oleson, Gerald W., 1624
Olfers, Sarah H., 3174
Olin, Ann W., 1778
Olin Corp., 14, 591
Olin, Jack, 2600
Olin, Kent O., 484
Olin, Spencer T., 1778
Olincy, Dan, 322
Olinger, Jan, 1141
Oliva, George III, 2703
Olivarez, Juan R., 1586
Oliveira, Gilbert C., 1401
Oliveira, Ron, 3188
Oliver, Ann B., 2354
Oliver, John T., Jr., 19
Oliver, Julia, 1543
Oliver, Melvin L., 2146
Olivera, Joseph A., Jr., 370
Olivieri, Jose A., 3455
Ollila, Paul, 1602
Olmes, James, 1295
Olmsted, Robert M., 1878, 3224
Olney, Richard III, 1522
Olsen, Eeva-Liisa Aulikki, 1504
Olsen, Kenneth H., 1504
Olsen, Michael J., 41
Olsen, Patricia, 49
Olsen, Thomas S., 1434
Olson, Amy, 960
Olson, David, 1826
Olson, Dorothy, 1826
Olson, Glenn Morehouse, 1706
Olson, Jim, 1673
Olson, Karen, 1826
Olson, Karen Van Hoesen, 335
Olson, Katherine L., 1066
Olson, Leland, 1826
Olson, Nan R., 1678

Rubin, Rochelle A., 2011
Rubin, Steven I., 2011
Rubio, Angel, 3004
Ruble, Blair, 2481
Ruby, Burton B., 1160
Rudawsky, Leslie Robbins, 1026
Ruddy, James J., 2037
Rudgis, Justine, 1345
Rudin, Stephen, 2161
Rudman, Edward I., 1431
Rudnick, Andrew J., 2092
Rudolf, Kermit, 3361
Rudolph, Alexander S., 1097
Rudolph, Geoffrey E., 1097
Ruebel, Richard J., 2617
Rueckert, William Dodge, 2116
Ruegsegger, Brian D., 1127
Ruehle, Judi A., 251
Ruehle, William J., 251
Ruffin, John W., Jr., 740
Rugeley, Virginia, 3402
Rumbough, J. Wright, Jr., 2450
Rumbough, Nina Craig, 693
Rummel, Jack R., 1634
Rummer, Sheila, 1587
Rumsey, Charles Cary, 2404
Rumsey, Mary A.H., 2404
Rumsey, Mary M., 2404
Rupp, Gerald E., 2489
Rupp, Sheron A., 2708
Rupp, Warren, 2708
Ruppel, John, 1634
Ruppert, Elizabeth, 2730
Rupple, Keith, 3490
Rurik, Dion R., 3379
Ruskin, Florita, 452
Russell, Charles P., 138
Russell, Christine H., 138, 204
Russell, Eric A., 3379
Russell, Frank E., 1152
Russell, G. Richard, 1819
Russell, George F., Jr., 3379
Russell, Gordon, 335
Russell, H.M., 51
Russell, Jane T., 3379
Russell, Jenny, 1449
Russell, Jileen, 3379
Russell, John C., 2453
Russell, Madeleine H., 138
Russell, Meredith, 2783
Russell, Nancy M., 1152
Russell, Richard F., 3379
Russell, Scott, 1661
Russell-Shapiro, Alice C., 138
Russo, Joan, 730
Russo, Lesley A., 3402
Russom, Mary S., 18
Rust, Margaret Dole, 767
Ruszin, Thomas E., Jr., 1294
Rutherford, Winthrop, Jr., 2061
Rutherfurd, Guy G., 2001, 2129
Rutledge, David, 1527
Rutman, Michael, 456
Rutter, Vicki J., 33
Ryals, Hildegard, 2945
Ryan, Carl E., 3071
Ryan, Cynthia J., 1491
Ryan, Daniel H., 2911
Ryan, John T. III, 2911
Ryan, Joseph W., 3138
Ryan, Mary Irene, 2911
Ryan, Michael Denis, 2911
Ryan, Michael G., 3262
Ryan, Richard N., Jr., 2405
Ryan, Scott, 429
Ryan, T. Timothy, Jr., 2484
Ryan, Vincent J., 1491
Ryan, William F., 2911
Ryan, Yolanda V., 3138
Ryberg, Claire Dumke, 3193
Rybnick, William, 202
Ryburn, Frank S., 3131
Ryburn, Mary Jane, 3131

Rycenga, Charles, 1585
Ryerson, Richard, 2748
Ryker, Debra B., 148, 193
Rymec, Dave, 295
Rysavy, Jirka, 488

Saal, Harry J., 267
Saal, William Dunne, 2651
Saalfield, John, 2921
Sabin, Andrew E., 2149
Sabin, Paul, 1394
Sacerdote Charitable Lead Trust, P.M., 2406
Sacerdote, Peter M., 2406
Saces, Jeffrey, 164
Sachs Electric Corp., 1784
Sachs, Louis S., 1784
Sachs, Mary L., 1784
Sachs, Ned, 741
Sachs, Richard A., 3463
Sachs, Richard A., Jr., 3463
Sachs, Samuel C., 1784
Sachs, Susan E., 1784
Sachtleben, Marilyn, 1814
Sack, Michael, 441
Sackett, John I., 912
Sackoff, Rosalind, 2253
Sadler, Dorothy C., 876
Sadler, Phillip E., 876
Sadler, Robert E., Jr., 2290
Sadler, Shannon G., 739
Sadlier, R. Daniel, 2731
Sadowsky, William, 1375
Saehz-Ackerman, Elizabeth, 364
Sage, Andrew G.C. III, 2053
Sahs, Tim, 1608
Saika, Peggy, 2311
Saint James, Susan, 527
Saint-Amand, Emilia A., 2252
Saito, Kazuo, 1068
Sajdak, Robert, 1638
Sajdak, Robert A., 1544
Sakrison, James M., 39, 53
Sakurai, Motoatsu, 2315
Salant, Anthony, 202
Salant, Dorothy, 202
Salant, Peter, 202
Sale, Josh, 527
Salem Five Cents Savings Bank, 1488
Salisbury, Alicia, 1199
Sall, John Phillip, 2586
Sall, Virginia B., 2586
Salome, Tom, 3180
Salomon, M.F., 2679
Salomon, Richard E., 2394
Salter, Lee W., 300
Saltonsall, Richard, 1489
Salzman, Philip, 1472
Samaniego, Sandy, 23
Samloff, Harold, 2521
Sammons, Richards F., 2403
Sammuels, Sherwin, 141
Sample, Kristina Lloyd, 1875
Sampson, David S., 2013
Sampson, Holly C., 1678
Sams, Earl C., 3150
Samsky, Scott B., 437
Samson, Ellery, 917
Samson, Helen Leidy, 917
Samson, Leidy Sue, 917
Samson, Meagan, 917
Samuel, Roger, 1549
Samuelian, Karl M., 212
Samuels, Alexandra, 2908
Samuels, Ernest, 2408
Samuelson, Carole W., 7
Sanchez, Ada, 1458
Sanchez, Margaret A., 2391
Sanchez, Miren duPont, 639
Sanchez, Tawna, 1469
Sand, Carolyn, 702
Sandalow, David, 707

Sander, Robert L., 3388
Sanders, Cam III, 1338
Sanders, Carol, 3268
Sanders, David, 2724
Sanders, Helen Babbott, 2099
Sanders, Malika, 878
Sanders, Morton, 2281
Sanders, Steven, 62
Sanders, Wayne R., 3106
Sanderson, Steven E., 2514
Sandler, David P., 2799
Sandler, Herman, 2103
Sandler, Mark J., 1886
Sandman, Dan D., 2932
Sands, Brinna B., 2219
Sands, David K., 3147
Sands, Frank E. II, 3219
Sands, Gordon C., 1805
Sands, J.B., 3147
Sands, John L., Jr., 819
Sands, Jon F., 462
Sands, Nina B., 1805
Sands, Patrick B., 3147
Sands, Richard, 2410
Sands, Robert, 2410
Sands, Stephen H., 3147
Sands, Steve, 1820
Sandstrom, Frederick H., 769
Sanford, Laraine M., 369
Sanford, Robert V., 369
Sannino, Louis J., 1239
Sansom, Robert D., 2912
Sanson, Jean, 1026
Sant, Alexis, 698
Sant, Michael, 698
Sant, Roger, 707
Sant, Roger W., 698, 699
Sant, Vicki, 699
Sant, Victoria P., 663, 698
Santa, S. George, 549
Santiago, Felipe R., 169
Santis, Jorge H., 2411
Saperstein, Guy, 395
Saperstein, Shira, 684, 698
Sapoch, Jamie Kyte, 1878, 3224
Saraya, Yusuke, 2484
Sargent, Leonard, 1797
Sargent, Newell B., 3504
Sargent Trust, Gladys W., 374
Sargi, Lynn M., 2618
Sarkeys, S.J., 2755
Sarkowsky, Faye, 3394
Sarmiento, Gil, 1023
Sarni, Vincent, 2021
Sarow, Robert D., 1596
Sarpy, Maxine, 1230
Sas, Marc, 101
Sasakawa, Yohei, 2484
Sasaki, R.K., 896
Sasiela, Joseph, 1596
Sasser, Barbara Weston, 3104
Sasso, Greg, 1140
Satco., Inc., 284
Satterlee, Ellen, 1647
Sattler, Ryan J., 2812
Satz, Joseph, 443
Sauerland, Elizabeth I., 2710
Sauerland, Franz, 2710
Sauerland, Franz L., 2710
Sauerland, Paul, 2710
Saul Charitable Annuity Trust, 375
Saul, Faye E. Batten, 375
Saul, George W., 375
Saul, Jane Wynne, 375
Saunders, Eve McClatchey, 854
Saunders, J. Harvey, 854
Saunders, Mary Jordan, 2217
Saunders, Ruby Lee, 795
Saunders, Ruth, 553
Saunders, Shawn E., 89
Saunders, Thomas A. III, 2217
Saunders, Thomas A. IV, 2217
Saunders, William N., 795

Sauvayre, Sarah Chubb, 1971
Sauve, Brad, 1563
Savage, Arthur V., 2494
Savage, Carol, 19
Savage, J. Thomas, 2403
Savage, Toy D., Jr., 3235, 3283
Savala, Rudy L., 198
Savitt, Charles, 427
Savlov, Simone, 255
Savres, Edwin J., 2014
Sawtell, Sarah, 1991
Sawyer, Alden H., Jr., 1250
Sawyer, Thompson H., Jr., 3061
Saxon, Andrew, 330
Saxon, Ken, 370
Sayers, Donald D., 2599
Sazerac Co., Inc., 1244
Scaife, C., 2873
Scaife, Jennie K., 796
Scaife, Sarah Mellon, 796
Scalvino, Pauline C., 2934
Scanlon, Diane, 1362
Scanlon, Thomas J., 695
Scaramucci, Anthony, 2183
Scarlett, Charles E., Jr., 1277
Scarlett, Mark, 2462
Scaturro, Philip, 2009
Schaack, R. Bard, 2341
Schaaf, David, 1546
Schachet, Carol, 1483
Schachte, Margaret P., 2991
Schadewald, Shelly, 1594
Schadler, Hally, 2038
Schaedel, Gary, 1896
Schaedel, Sharon, 1896
Schaedel, Sharon E., 1896
Schaefer, Alan R., 3439
Schaefer, Robert, 1160
Schaefer, Robert J., 1160
Schaefer, Robert W., 1297
Schaeneman, Lewis G. III, 598
Schaeneman, Lewis G., Jr., 598
Schafer, Alan, 1712
Schafer, Betsy Bolton, 2635
Schafer, Gilbert P. III, 2635
Schafer, Oscar S., 2413
Schafer, Sigrid U., 2413
Schafer, Suzie, 1529
Schaffer, Mark, 2686
Schaffer, Susan J., 1594
Schaible, Kenneth, 552
Schain, Howard, 2048
Schankweiler, David, 2848
Schastok, Sara L., 973
Schatt, Carol P., 1152
Schaub, Annie, 3367
Schaub, Benson, 31
Schaub, Benson L., 26
Schaub, Benson S., 26
Schaub, Dave, 3367
Schaub, Nancy G., 3367
Schaub, Tim, 3367
Schauer, W.E., 3469
Schaul, Mark H., 3402
Schavone, Philip T., 2619, 2623
Schechtel, Andrew, 1958
Schechter, Arielle C., 2587
Schechter, Arnold M.C., 2587
Schechter, Pearl F., 2587
Schechter, Sol, 2587
Schechtman, Nancy, 982
Scheeler, C. Ronald, 2572
Schehr, Barry, 75
Scheibel, Elizabeth D., 1375
Scheibelhut, Becky, 3281
Scheid, Peter, 2669
Scheifla, Jacqueline C., 732
Schendel, Isabel, 3463
Schenectady International, Inc., 2527
Schenker, Curtis, 2415
Schenker, Leo, 2415
Schenker, Livia, 2415
Scher, Abbey, 1483

Simmons, Matthew R., 3136
Simmons, Ruth, 2969
Simmons, Sylvia, 1498
Simmons, Virginia W., 3157
Simms, Ruth, 1985
Simon, Esther, 2435
Simon, John, 2009
Simon, Peter, 991
Simon, R. Matthew, 935
Simon, Raymond F., 935
Simon, Stephen, 2435
Simon-Cummings, Sonia, 2102
Simons, Louise M., 736
Simonson, Ann Larsen, 577
Simonson, Todd, 408
Simpkins, Jacqueline D., 2445
Simpkins, Nancy K., 1925
Simpson, Deborah, 586
Simpson, Howard B., 972
Simpson, James IV, 972
Simpson, Jon, 1532
Simpson, Lynn D., 2786
Simpson, Rita Price, 1140
Simpson, Robert, 3182
Simpson, William M., 972
Sims, Howard F., 1548, 1599
Sims, Joanne, 1536
Sims, Linda L., 1634
Sinak, David L., 3079
Sinclair, K. Richard C., 3402
Sindelar, Nancy E., 971
Singer, Andrew, 648
Singer, Gordon, 648
Singer, Linda, 648, 2345
Singer, Paul E., 648
Singh, Lekha, 3100
Singletary, Julia, 877
Singletary, Karen L., 877
Singletary, Lewis Hall II, 877
Singletary, Rebecca, 877
Singletary, Richard L., 877
Singletary, Richard L., Jr., 877
Singletary, Tim, 877
Singleton, Olivia R., 3402
Sink, Adelaide, 743
Sinnett, Clifford H., 1249
Sinskey, Robert M., 397
Sion, L. Gilles, 545
Sioukas, Lillian, 362
Sirach Capital Management, Inc., 3381
Siragusa, Alexander, 1092
Siragusa, John R., 1092
Siragusa, Martha P., 1092
Siragusa, Richard D., 1092
Siragusa, Ross D., 1092
Siragusa, Ross D. III, 1092
Siragusa, Ross D., Jr., 1092
Siragusa, Sinclair C., 1092
Sirota, Wilbert H., 1283
Sisk, Daniel A., 1992
Sisk, John B., 1992
Sisk, John F., 2117
Sisk, Katharine B., 1992
Sisk, Thomas D., 1992
Siske, John, 22
Sissel, Mary, 478
Sisson, Rosalie Crouch, 1788
Sitnick, Irving, 2321
Sivertsen, Robert J., 1734
Sivertsen Trusts, Sarah-Maud W., 1734
Sizelove, Paul, 156
Sizer, Stephen, 1536
Sjostedt, Judy, 3403
Skaggs, L.J., 398
Skaggs, L.S., 910
Skaggs, Mary C., 398
Skaggs, Sam, 22
Skarlatos, Candy, 295
Skeel, Earl, 917
Skemp, Robert, 3483
Skerker, Susan F., 1646
Skidmore, Brenda L., 3294
Skilling, Hazel D., 1636

Skilling Trust, Hugh H., 1636
Skinner, Barbara, 3390
Skinner, Caitlin, 3493
Skinner, Franklin, 883
Skinner, Julie, 1121
Skinner, William L., 1114
Skloot, Edward, 2460
Skolaski, Steven F., 3468
Skoll, Jeff, 144
Skurka, Robert A., 1401
Sky Bank, 2705, 2725
Slade, Arthur, 1482
Slade, Marie-Antoinette, 2436
Sladen, Frank J., Jr., 1589
Slagle, Frederick, 861
Slater, Alice, 2049
Slater, David, 2575
Slater, Gilbert M., 1368
Slaughter, Gloria, 3205
Slaughter, James C., 2172
Slaughter, Kent C., 3205
Slaughter, Robert E., 1711
Slaughter, Thomas R., 2172
Slaughter, William A., 2172
Slaughter, William E., Jr., 3205
Slavik, Ann A., 1786
Slavik, Donald S., 1786
Slavitt, Lesley D., 926
Sleazak, Mark, 1038
Sleet, Gregory M., 628
Slette, Gary, 1731
Slick, Earl F., 2588
Slick, Jane P., 2588
Sligar, James, 2394
Sligar, James S., 2286, 2393
Sloan, Ann C., 2589
Sloan, Barbara M., 796
Sloan, Charles W., 3276
Sloan, O. Temple, Jr., 2589
Sloane, Howard G., 2194
Sloane, Virginia, 2194
Slobodein, David J., 1890
Slocum, Claran, 801
Slonecker, Jean, 142
Sloss, Anthony, 400
Sloss, Karen, 400
Sloss, Louis, Jr., 400
Slosser, Charles O., 370
Slutsky, Kenneth J., 1920
Slutsky, Kenneth O., 1953
Slutsky, Lorie A., 2330
Slye, Terry, 1656
Smadbeck, Arthur J., 2194
Smadbeck, Louis, Jr., 2194
Smadbeck, Paul, 2194
Small, George L., 1319
Small, Malinda B., 1294
Smalley, Patricia T., 2403
Smallwood, Edward, 645
Smallwood, Guy, 645
Smallwood Trust, William P., 3476
Smallwood, Valerie, 645
Smarilli, Kathleen, 2848
Smart, David A., 602
Smart, John, 602
Smart, Mary, 602
Smart, Raymond L., 602
Smeal, Frank P., 2437
Smeal, Henry F., 2437
Smeal, Mary Margaret, 2437
Smeby, K.S., 341
Smith, A. Russell, 3407
Smith, Aaron A., 731
Smith, Alice L., 3025
Smith, Allen C., 2200
Smith, Allyson Dupree, 739
Smith, Alson H., Jr., 3300
Smith, Andrea, 1147
Smith, Anne, 370
Smith Barney, 2913
Smith, Betty, 62
Smith, Betty Denny, 374
Smith, Bill, 1592, 2548

Smith, Boyd C., 144
Smith, Bradford D., 2337
Smith, Bradford K., 2146
Smith, Brenda J., 484
Smith, Carter, 2615
Smith, Charles M., 628
Smith, Charles W., 3504
Smith, Christopher B., 929, 2590
Smith, Christopher L., 740
Smith, Coy, 295
Smith, David, 2337
Smith, David B., 929
Smith, Dawn, 1856
Smith, Dawn M., 1600
Smith, E.J. Noble, 2337
Smith, Edgar, 2154
Smith, Edward C., Jr., 2590
Smith, Elizabeth W., 2504
Smith, Ellen Austin, 2607
Smith, Farwell, 1062
Smith Fellowship Trust Fund, Edward H. & Winnie H., 3186
Smith, Geoffrey T., 940
Smith, Gerald, 3094
Smith, Gilbert H., 628
Smith, Gloria, 198
Smith, H. Warren, 3335
Smith, H. William, Jr., 2343
Smith, H.I., 2449
Smith, Harold Byron, 929
Smith, Harold Byron, Jr., 929
Smith, Harriet T., 3159
Smith, Herbert, 1122
Smith, James Allen, 2080
Smith, James C., 3158
Smith, Jeanne H., 2749
Smith, Jeffrey A., 2438
Smith, Jeremy T., 2337
Smith, Jim, 553
Smith, Jo A., 2590
Smith, Joan Irvine, 402
Smith, John, 1167
Smith, K.E., 2699
Smith, Kathryn "Kathy", 697
Smith, Kathryn H., 582
Smith, Kathy, 3118
Smith, Kay A., 1620
Smith, Kelvin, 2722
Smith, Ken, 3062
Smith, Kent H., 2601
Smith, Langhorne B., 2820
Smith, Leslie K., 692
Smith, Linda, 3182
Smith, Margaret J., 637
Smith, Marguerite, 3255
Smith Marital Trust, Omer, 404
Smith, Marschall I., 940
Smith, Marsha J., 1632
Smith, Mary Welles Mooers, 2200
Smith, Matt, Jr., 1546, 1553
Smith, May, 403
Smith, Michael, 3191
Smith, Molly K., 2403
Smith, Nancy Fehsenfeld, 3335
Smith, Nancy M., 1745
Smith, Nick, 1702
Smith, Nora Stone, 1062
Smith, Norma I., 3158
Smith, Oliver C., 3452
Smith, Ora K., 637
Smith, Pamela C., 2117
Smith, Pamela Hyde, 3345
Smith, Pat, 2549
Smith, Peter, 2355
Smith, Peter V., 2145
Smith, Ralph L., 3159
Smith, Randall, 2438
Smith, Randall D., 2438
Smith, Richard A., 2044
Smith, Richard J., 1232
Smith, Rita M., 1327
Smith, Robert B., 1745
Smith, Robert B. II, 1745

Smith, Robert B. III, 1745
Smith, Robert B., Jr., 3300
Smith, Roy C., 2090
Smith, S.W., 1559
Smith, Sadie Herzstein, 3095
Smith, Sheila, 2094
Smith, Sidney W., Jr., 37, 1559
Smith, Stanley, 1592
Smith, Stephen B., 929
Smith, Steve C., 89
Smith, Sunshine, 1785
Smith, Susan, 2901
Smith, Susan K., 2855
Smith, Ted, 22, 1242
Smith, Thelma G., 2601
Smith, Theodore M., 1435
Smith, Timothy R., 10
Smith, Vera L., 2786
Smith, Verne, 534
Smith, W. Sidney, 1620
Smith, Wallace H., 1745
Smith, William E., Jr., 7
Smith, Zachary T., 2582
Smith-Phillips, Stephanie E., 2998
Smitson, Robert M., 1115, 1145
Smoot, Lewis R., Sr., 2623
Smoots, Renard, 1877
Smott, Lewis R., Sr., 2619
Smout, Joanne, 800
Smout, Judy, 800
Smout, Les, 800
Smurfit-Stone Container Corp., 1019
Smykal, Ralph, 971
Smysor, Dorothy, 40
Smyth, Maureen H., 1619
Snee, Katherine E., 2919
Sneed, Catherine, 3217
Snell, George B., 2151
Snell, Richard "Dick", 42
Snider, Eliot I., 739
Snider, Jody Binswager, 660
Snoddy, Marsha, 73
Snow, David H., 2439
Snow, Heide, 902
Snow, John Ben, 2439, 2440
Snow, Jonathan L., 2439, 2440
Snow, Thomas, 2095
Snow-Johnson, S.G., 1881
Snowdon, Edward W., Jr., 674
Snowdon, Marguerite H., 674
Snowdon, Richard W., 674
Snowdon, Roger S., 1130
Snyder, Dennis L., 2621
Snyder, Donald B., 2901
Snyder, James T., 1944
Snyder, Jennifer C., 1378
Snyder, John J. "Jack", Jr., 3327
Snyder, Linda, 1358
Snyder, William, 2901
So, Anthony, 2127
Soba, Daniel, 2297
Soba, Geraldine, 2297
Soboleff, Walter A., 23
Soda, Hiroshi, 73
Soder, Alice, 2548
Soglin, Paul R., 3376
Soiefer, Ronald M., 2483
Solana, Nancy J., 3080
Solano, Patrick, 2920
Solari, Mary C., 406
Solari, Richard C., 406
Soldano, Patricia M., 114
Soldivieri, Susan I., 1886
Soler, Ana, 473
Solesbee, John D., 864
Solinger, Hope G., 2164
Sollins, Karen R., 2416
Solnit, Albert, 2332
Solomon, Benjamin J., 1842
Solomon, Daniel, 662
Solomon, David, 662
Solomon, Jeffrey, 2058
Solomon, Joel, 427

Swanson, Tami, 3207
Swanson, W. Charles, 3207
Swanson, W.C., 3207
Swartwout, Shirley, 3294
Swartz, Robert, 3483
Sweatt, Blaine III, 746
Sweatt, Harold W., 1718
Sweeney, Aileen, 292
Sweeney, Patrick, 666
Sweeney, William A., 2448
Sweet, John H.K., 1923
Sweet, Lawrence, 1529
Sweet, William R., 1923
Sweetbriar Syndicate, 1817
Sweetman, Mary Pat, 3002
Swegler, Jeffrey F., 1507
Swenson, J.R., 3469
Swensrud, Anthony S., 1507
Swensrud, Leslie R., 1507
Swensrud, S. Blake II, 1507
Swensrud, Stephen B., 1507
Swetland, David S., 2716
Swetland, David Sears, 2716
Swetland, David W., 2716
Swetland, Mary Ann, 2716
Swierkos, Mary E., 2237
Swift, Bryan M., 1789
Swift, Byron, 706
Swift Co., John S., Inc., 1789
Swift, E. Clinton, 1473
Swift, Hampden M., 1789
Swift, Peter D., 3213
Swift, Sara Taylor, 526
Swinden, James I., 402
Swink, Henry, 2978
Switzer, Mark, 1266
Switzer, Patricia, 1266
Switzer, Patricia D., 1266
Switzer, Peter, 1266
Switzer, Robert, 1266
Swope, Jeffrey, 1363
Sykes, Gene T., 2463
Sykes, James W., Jr., 2182
Sykes, Jane S., 2450
Sylvia, Anthony L., 1401
Symmons, Clare Payne, 3498
Symon, Robert J., 3261
Synovus Trust Co., 844
Syrmis, Pamela Lee, 2216
Syrmis, Victor, 2216
Sytek, Donna, 1862
Sytman, Alex, 3380
Sytop, Arnold, 2425
Szabo, Raymond, 2634
Szapary, Gladys, 296
Szekely, Deborah, 422

Tabankin, Margery, 418
Tabola, Lara, 529
Tabola, Toby, 529
Tabor, Ann Irish, 1585
Tabor, Gary, 1424
Taft, John E., 1505
Taggart, Dick, 3396
Taiclet, Gordon, 1143
Tait, Richard, 3338
Tait, Thomas, 42
Takemoto, Helene, 904
Takuma, Takeo, 2484
Takvorian, Katherine U., 1508
Takvorian, Ronald W., 1508
Talberth, Charlotte, 1987
Talbot, Nancy F., 967
Talbott, Josephine L., 2728
Talbott, Nelson S., 2728
Talcott, Ann Earle, 1963
Tall, Joann, 388
Talley, G. Tyler, Jr., 828
Tallman, Barbara, 2875
Tally, John C., 2585
Tamaki, Meriko, 3391
Tamminen, Terry, 183

Tandy, A.R., 3168
Tanenbaum, Allan J., 812
Tang, Patricia, 1995
Tanner, Derry, 1505
Tanner, Estelle "Nicki" Newman, 2330
Tanner, Grace A., 3208
Tanner, Obert C., 3208
Taper, S. Mark, 423
Tapp, Frances Carr, 3069
Tappan, Treece, 1930
Tappin, Amber L., 3013
Taricani, Dolares, 2817
Tarola, Robert M., 1299
Tarpoff, Diane M., 1630
Tarr, Jeff C., 2221
Tarr, Jeff, Jr., 2221
Tarr, Jennifer, 2221
Tarr, Patricia G., 2221
Tarrant, Amy E., 3221
Tarrant, Brian, 3221
Tarrant, Jeremiah, 3221
Tarrant, Jr., Richard E., 3221
Tartar, Joy, 2795
Tasler, Sheryl, 1712
Tasty Baking Co., 2928
Tata, Ratan N., 2146
Tate, Atwood B., 1335
Tate, Creston G., 1335
Tate, H. Simmons, Jr., 2977
Tate, J. Kenneth, 740
Tate, Lloyd P., Jr., 2582
Tateisi, Yoshio, 1068
Tatlock, Anne M., 1939, 2308
Tauscher, Shehla, 1666
Taviner, Gloria, 266
Tawney, Robin, 1797
Tayart de Borms, Luc, Baron, 2242
Tayer, John, 476
Taylor, Anna Diggs, Hon., 1548
Taylor, Annamarie, 1345
Taylor, Barbara Olin, 974, 1778
Taylor, Betsy, 1337, 2355
Taylor, Bonnie, 1214
Taylor, C. Fred, 1953, 1958
Taylor, Caroline E., 2929
Taylor Charitable Trust, Galen D., 804
Taylor, D., 3469
Taylor, Dorceta, 2345
Taylor, Edna May, 1101
Taylor Electric Co., 3485
Taylor, Elizabeth F., 805
Taylor, F. Morgan, Jr., 974, 1778
Taylor, Frances B., 1106
Taylor, Fred, 478, 3017
Taylor, Frederick B., 2702
Taylor, Frederick M. III, 974
Taylor, Galen D., 804
Taylor, Gerald, 804
Taylor, J., 263
Taylor, J. Roy, 3009
Taylor, J.M. Bryan, 2577
Taylor, James A., 3485
Taylor, James A., Jr., 3485
Taylor, James C., 526
Taylor, James W., 974
Taylor, John F., 3222
Taylor, John Guest, 2577
Taylor, John N., Jr., 2629
Taylor, John R., 2854
Taylor, John W., 3485
Taylor, John W. III, 1106
Taylor, John W., Jr., 1106
Taylor, Jonathan V., 1509
Taylor, Kaari T., 1106
Taylor, Kenneth H., Jr., 2929
Taylor, Lois, 1373
Taylor, Margaret L., 290
Taylor, Peter J., 247
Taylor, Ray Howard III, 2577
Taylor, Robert, 3412
Taylor, S. Martin, 1565
Taylor, Sandra, 744
Taylor, Spencer O., 974

Taylor, Timothy A., 1371
Taylor, Trudie, 903
Taylor, Vernon F., Jr., 526
Taylor, William, 2999, 3227
Taylor, William F., 1509
Tchen, Christine M., 977
Tchozewski, Chet, 2049
Teate, Rosemary, 3034
Tedder, Steve, 42
Teichert, Inc., 425
Teichert & Son, A., Inc., 425
Teichert, Fred, 362
Teichert, Frederick A., 425
Teichert, Melita M., 425
Teixeira, Lisa, 348
Teleflex Inc., 2930
Tellabs, Inc., 1102
Temp, James A., 3427
Temple, Arthur, 3170
Temple, Arthur III, 3170
Temple, Katherine S., 3170
Tennant, Alice, 2575
Tennant Co., 1720
Tennille, Jocelyn D., 963
Tennison, Gary, 3385
Tenny, Barron M., 2146
Tenuta, Ralph J., 3439
Tepner, Ronald, 3010
Tepp, Tracy, 819
Termondt, M. James, 942
Ternan, Lawrence, 1550
Ternes, Margaret, 2407
Terni, Diane D., 2980
Terpak, John B., Jr., 2859
Terrazas, Alfredo, 177
Terre Haute Gas Corp., 1137
Terrelonge, Marsha, 1344
Terrill, J.E., 1019
Terry, Anne, 1936
Terry, Frederick A., Jr., 682, 2202
Terry, Richard E., 656
Terry, Thomas F., 1860
Terry, Wade, 73
Terry, William, 3253
Testa, Florence H., 949
Testa, Richard J., 1504
Testamarck, Ariana, 2104
Texas Instruments Inc., 3172
Thacher, Alida, 2764
Thacher, Carter P., 449
Thacher, David J., 3395
Thacher, Gladys, 367
Thacher, Nancy C., 3395
Thain, Carmen M., 2015
Thain, John A., 2015
Thaw, Clare Eddy, 1995
Thaw, Eugene Victor, 1995
Thaxter, Sidney St. F., 1259
Thayer, Brooks S., 1373
Themmen, Arne R., 3429
Theobald, Thomas C., 2469
Theobold, Thomas C., 1039
Theofilactidis, Alexis, 2430
Therrien, Mary Banghart, 1567
Thiede, James, 1101
Thieman, Frederick W., 2852
Thier, Samuel O., 1939
Thoelecke, Timothy N., 1050
Tholfsen, Paul, 3397
Thom, James, 1814
Thomas, Austin, 3100
Thomas, Bart, 3172
Thomas, Corolyn W., 3306
Thomas, Dennis, 575
Thomas, Douglas D., 1964
Thomas, Edward C., 1965
Thomas, Edward D., 1965
Thomas, Ellen Sprinkle, 2591
Thomas, Erin, 1546
Thomas, F. Lee, 2548
Thomas, Franklin A., 2180
Thomas, Gerald O., 1965
Thomas, Gladys R., 2449

Thomas, Jack Ward, 1804
Thomas, Jonathan, 1526
Thomas, L. Newton, Jr., 3402
Thomas, Lance M., 528
Thomas, Lyda Ann Quinn, 3104
Thomas, Mary Hager, 755
Thomas, Millicent B., 1965
Thomas, Paige P., 1965
Thomas, Paul A., 1573
Thomas, Paula, 145
Thomas, Raymond V., 365
Thomas, Rebecca, 1140
Thomas, Rebecca S., 1965
Thomas, Roger M., 1417
Thomas, Telford W., 2936
Thomas, Timothy B., 1965
Thomas, Todd E., 528
Thomas, V. Marc, 528
Thomas, Victor C., 528
Thomas, Wilmer J., Jr., 1964
Thomason, John M., 2978
Thomasson, Charles W., 3116
Thomasson, Jeffrey H., 1117, 1151
Thompson, Angela E., 605
Thompson, Anne H., 74
Thompson, B.R., Sr., 3031
Thompson, Brian J., 2275
Thompson, Charles A.Y., 605
Thompson, Connie, 1665
Thompson, Denise Nix, 2311
Thompson, E. Arthur, 1808
Thompson, Eve Lloyd, 1875
Thompson, Frederic, 1250
Thompson, G. Kennedy, 2595
Thompson, Genevieve, 2600
Thompson, Jere W., 3061
Thompson, Jesse J., 2580, 3031
Thompson, Laird L., 1150
Thompson, Lawrence, 2411
Thompson, Marcia, 2416
Thompson, Margaret E., 1564
Thompson, Mark, 3321
Thompson, Mary Cobb, 1224
Thompson, Peter Kempner, 3104
Thompson, Sandra S., 1084
Thompson, Sherry, 1995
Thompson, Sylvia M., 3031
Thompson, Timothy L., 2190
Thompson, Wade F.B., 605
Thomsen, George E., 1298
Thorn, Craig III, 1357
Thorndyke, Dan, 2762
Thorne, Alexandra T., 2470
Thorne, Barbara, 19
Thorne, Daniel K., 2470
Thorne, Daniel Kempner, 3104
Thorne, David H., 2471
Thorne, Jane W., 1898
Thorne, Julia L., 2471
Thorne, Landon K., 2471
Thornton, Betsy, 3193
Thornton, Charles, 529
Thornton, Dawn, 529
Thornton, George, 529
Thornton, John W., 1983
Thornton, Louise F., 529
Thornton, Patricia, 1983
Thornton, Tom, 3397
Thornton, W. Gerald, 2589
Thornton, William W., Jr., 1983
Thorpe, Dagmar, 3255
Thorpe, Edith D., 1722, 2460
Thorpe, James R., 1722
Thorpe, Samuel S. III, 1722, 2460
Thorpe, Timothy D., 1722
Thorsen, Dorothy, 989
Thorson, Dorothy W., 1103
Thorson, Reuben, 1103
Thorson, Robert D., 1103
Thorton, Jerry Sue, 2618
Throckmorton, Timothy, 586
Thronas, Jane, 1698
Throop, William M., Jr., 2045

Willems, Jacques, 545
Willfahrt, Connie, 3450
Willgerodt, Penny Fujiko, 2373
William C., Pauli, 70
Williams, Arthur A., 1520
Williams, Barbara, 1122
Williams, Benjamin, Jr., 1382
Williams, Bennie G., 890
Williams, Betty A., 891
Williams, Caroline, 1202, 2102
Williams, Carolyn, 366
Williams, Charles, 3253
Williams, Charles L., 3085
Williams, Clarence R. "Reggie", 3152
Williams, Constance, 1363
Williams, David, 1546
Williams, David W., 2839
Williams, Diane Simmons, 699
Williams, Edward S., 2839
Williams, Emelie M., 2440
Williams, Felix Noble III, 1786
Williams, Florence P., 1886
Williams, Gary, 1547
Williams, James B., 888, 891, 892
Williams, Jane H., 335
Williams, Jerome, 1203
Williams, Joel T. III, 3061
Williams, John K., 2237
Williams, Julie A., 3477
Williams, Justin, 1706
Williams, Lamar Harper, 1000
Williams, Linda, 1587
Williams, Luis, 11
Williams, M., 451
Williams, Margaret, 2091
Williams, Marguerite N., 890
Williams, Mark K., 3005
Williams, Martha M., 3283
Williams, Michael C., 695
Williams, Nash, 3471
Williams, Nate, 1147
Williams, Paul, 266
Williams, Polly, 2762
Williams, R., 451
Williams, Ray, 388
Williams, Richard E., 2237
Williams, Richard T. "Stick", 2594
Williams, Rita, 1910
Williams, Robert G., 2898
Williams, Robert M., 2237
Williams, Stephen J., 1154
Williams, Steve, 688
Williams, Susan Slavik, 1786
Williams, Ted, 2338
Williams, Thomas, 466
Williams, Thomas L. III, 890
Williams, Webster, 442
Williamson, Anne, 1598
Williamson, Brett J., 402
Williamson, Debra L., 2671
Williamson, Douglas E., 2671
Williamson, Douglas F., Jr., 2305, 2404
Williamson, Jack, 1204
Williamson, Leslie G., 2671
Williamson, P.D., 2671
Williamson, S.K., 2671
Williamson, Susan K., 2671
Williamson, Wendy J., 2210
Williard, David, 1365
Williford, Catherine O., 3458
Willingham, Pat, 19
Willis, Dudley H., 1489
Willis, Mary, 316
Willis, Sally S., 1489
Willits, Thomas R., 1993
Willius, Dan, 3478
Willmore, Richard H., 1125
Willner, Robin G., 2213
Willoughby, Colleen S., 3394
Willow Grove Bank, 2941
Wilmans, Ann Carlie, 136
Wilmerding, John, Prof., 2933

Wilmington Trust Co., 619, 620, 633, 637, 643, 1984
Wilsen, Oscar, Rev., 716
Wilsey, Alfred, 325
Wilson, Alfred G., 1649
Wilson, Andrea Bond, 1760
Wilson, Anne Wright, 1948
Wilson, Charles, 2713
Wilson, Christina, 69
Wilson, Dennis, 142
Wilson, Diane Wenger, 1648
Wilson, Donald A., 805
Wilson, Dorothy C., 3126
Wilson, E. Miles, 2617
Wilson, Faye, 213
Wilson, Howard O., 417
Wilson, Ivan, 3060
Wilson, James, 1162
Wilson, James B., 1092
Wilson, Jane T., 1162
Wilson, Jennifer J., 1162
Wilson, Jill, 143
Wilson, John, 1643
Wilson, John D., 1162
Wilson, John H.T., 548, 2122
Wilson, John, Mr., Jr., 2738
Wilson, Kathleen H., 2553
Wilson, Kenneth, 135
Wilson, Matilda R., 1649
Wilson, Pat L., 3152
Wilson, Patricia Wellman, 2738
Wilson, Peter A., 1504
Wilson, Randon W., 2494
Wilson, Robert, 2515
Wilson, Robert B., 1050
Wilson, Robert L., 288
Wilson, Robert N., 1948
Wilson, Robert W., 2515
Wilson, Roger, 1868
Wilson, Sandra W., 548
Wilson, Serena S., 805
Wilson, Stephen Wheeler, 3126
Wilson, Steven, 1547
Wilson, Thomas D., 1162
Wilt, Walter W., 2811
Wilton, Jane L., 2330
Wiltshire, Kimery, 264
Windle, Janice W., 3071
Windley, David, 1119
Windsor, James H. IV, 1186
Windsor, Mary Belle H., 1186
Winfield, Marcia J., 3293
Wingate, Jim, 3372
Winkelman, Amy, 2763
Winkelman, Dorinda P., 2444
Winkelman, Marius O., 2444
Winkelman, Mark O., 2444
Winkelman, Stuart A., 173
Winkenwerder, Mary Pride, 15
Winkhaus, Gwenn S., 2669
Winkler, Catherine, 3306
Winkler, Henry R., 2717
Winkler, Mark, 3306
Winmill, Marc C., 2467
Winn, John C., 809
Winn, Mary E., 809
Winn, Mary Lou, 809
Winship, William, 2045
Winslow, Julia D., 705
Winslow, Nancy M., 1251
Winsor, Curtin, Jr., Hon., 2118
Winston, Bert F. III, 3164
Winston, Bert F., Jr., 3164
Winston, Blake W., 3164
Winston, Joni R., 3467
Winston, L. David, 3164
Winter, Barbara Ecke, 178
Winter, Cynthia A., 1175
Winter, Fred, 1994
Winter, Larry, 827
Winter, Nancy C.H., 998
Winters, Richard H., 1634
Winthrop, Inc., 1857, 1865

Winthrop, Clara B., 1522
Winthrop, John, 2997
Winthrop, Phoebe Jane, 1334
Winthrop, Robert, 2518
Winthrop Trust Co., 2330
Winton, David M., 1660
Winton, Sarah R., 1660
Wintriss, Lynn, 1328
Wintrode, David C., 1944
Wirth, Timothy E., 700
Wirth, Wren Winslow, 705
Wisconsin Dept. of Natural Resources, 3471
Wisconsin Dept. of Transportation, 3471
Wisconsin Public Service Corp., 3495
Wisdom, Arthur Mitteer, 1243
Wisdom, Betty, 1243
Wisdom, Helen H., 1243
Wisdom, Mary Freeman, 1243
Wisdom, Matthew Morgan, 1243
Wise, Anderson, 2342
Wise, Bradford A., 1256
Wise, Catherine J., 2267
Wise, Tim, 3310
Wishnick, Lisa, 3209
Wishnick, William, 3209
Wisner, Frank G., 2392
Wisniewski, Carisa, 365
Wisniewski, Suzanne, 1674
Wit, Harold, 2009
Witek, Lucy, 906
Witherbee, Victoria, 452
Witherspoon, Douglas C., 1088
Withington, Lothrop III, 1419
Withington, Nathan N., 1419
Witmer, Wilma, 374
Witt, Jocelyn S., 1310
Witte, John H., Jr., 3494
Wittenberg, Walter L., 1775
Witter & Co., Dean, 453
Witter, Dean, 453
Witter, Dean, Mrs., 453
Witter, Dean III, 453
Witter, Jill, 789
Witter, Malcolm G., 453
Witter, William D., 453
Witter, William P., 453
Woerner, Otto H., 2547
Wohleber, Robert M., 2750
Wohlers, Vicki, 1824
Woit, Kathleen, 3448
Wolanksy, Paul, 1902
Wolcott, Chris G., 2790
Wolcott, Guy R., 2790
Wolcott, Guy R. II, 2790
Woldenberg, Malcolm, 1244
Wolf, B.J., 3495
Wolf, Cornelia W., 2947
Wolf, Don, 2723
Wolf, Ellen, 3321
Wolf, Harold, 3459
Wolf, Henry C., 3284
Wolf, Janet, 1975
Wolf, Mollie, 1592
Wolf, Philip H., 2734
Wolfe, Albert, 3403
Wolfe, Ann Isaly, 2619, 2623
Wolfe, David W., 1944
Wolfe, Jack, 525
Wolfe, Jody, 2294
Wolfe, Judson A., 2294
Wolfe, Merle D., 3031
Wolfe, Robert, 346
Wolfe, Susan M., 2812
Wolfensohn, Adam R., 2520
Wolfensohn, Elaine R., 2520
Wolfensohn, James D., 2520
Wolfensohn, Naomi R., 2520
Wolfensohn, Sara R., 2520
Wolff, J. Marshall, 2875
Wolff, Paula, 1023
Wolff, Rosalie, 2442
Wolfman, Ira, 2091

Wolford, Kathryn F., 1311
Wolfson, June, 2917
Wolfson, Stephen, 2917
Wolk, David M., 2521
Wolk, Louis S., 2521
Wolk, Marvin L., 2521
Wollen, Carolyn S., 2045
Wollseiffen, S., 2954
Wolters, Kate Pew, 1639
Woltman, Sandra, 1700
Wolverine Sign Works, 1555
Wolverton, Karolyn C., 60
Womack, Christopher, 836
Womble, Ralph H., 2558
Woo, Richard, 3379
Woo, Timothy, 401
Wood, Amy Halperin, 2297
Wood, Anthony C., 2216
Wood, Edna, 2414
Wood, J.A., 2526
Wood, James, 3471
Wood, Kate B., 1911
Wood, Lisa M., 1740
Wood, Margaret Henry, 3022
Wood, N. Ruth, 3233
Wood, Paul W., 2483
Wood, Peter J., 2942
Wood, R. Lyman, 1375
Wood, Robert A., 1760
Wood, Robert J., 3423
Wood, Robert S., 2741
Wood, Robert S. II, 2741
Wood, Steven J., 715
Wood, Susannah L., 2007
Wood, Vicki M., 2741
Woodall, Fredna, 824
Woodard, Billy T., 2572
Woodard, Carlton, 2791
Woodard, Elizabeth G., 1464
Woodard, Mike, 337
Woodard, Tod C., 2791
Woodard, Walter A., 2791
Woodham, B.G., 2575
Woodruff, Barbara, 298
Woodruff, James III, 1976
Woodruff, Robert W., 892
Woodruff, Thomas, 1976
Woods, Alexandra, 2523
Woods, Beverly, 3204
Woods, David F., 723
Woods, David L., 1795
Woods, Donna, 1820
Woods, Jacqueline F., 2618
Woods, James H., 1795
Woods, James H., Jr., 1795
Woods, John, 1046
Woods, John R., 1795
Woods, Patrick, 292
Woods, Priscilla B., 2523
Woods, Robert F., 2213
Woods, Rodney I., 2228
Woods, Steven H., 740
Woods, Ward W., 688
Woods, Ward W., Jr., 2523
Woodside, Blair C., Jr., 2659
Woodson, Margaret C., 2599
Woodson, Mary Anne, 2599
Woodson, Mary H., 2599
Woodson, Paul B., Jr., 2599
Woodson, R. Peyton III, 2594
Woodsum, Harold E., Jr., 601
Woodward, Ann Eden, 2526
Woodward, Florence S., 2975
Woodward, Frank, 1264
Woodward, Helen, 2620
Woodward, Helen W., 457
Woodward, Jane, 345
Woodward, Lisa, 2525
Woodward, O. James III, 198
Woodward, Peggy C., 2575
Woodward, Susan S., 484
Woodwell, George, 42
Woodworth, Joyce, 1735

GEOGRAPHIC INDEX

Grantmakers in boldface type make grants on a national, regional, or international basis; the others generally limit giving to the city or state in which they are located. For local funders with a history of giving in another state, consult the "see also" references at the end of each state section.

ALABAMA

Birmingham: Abahac 1, AmSouth 3, Anderson 4, Barber 5, Brock 6, Community 7, Founders 10, Linn 13, Schuler 15, Strain 16, **Vulcan 18,** Webb 20, **Whatley 21**
Dothan: Community 8, Dove 9
Jasper: Walker 19
McIntosh: McIntosh 14
Mobile: Hearin 11, Larkins 12
Montgomery: Alabama 2, Viro 17

see also 591, 686, 828, 855, 1007, 1639, 3022, 3025

ALASKA

Anchorage: Alaska 22
Juneau: **Sealaska 23**

see also 303, 336, 507, 530, 682, 1965, 2770, 2805, 3311, 3314, 3322, 3323, 3336, 3343, 3398

ARIZONA

Cortaro: **T & E 56**
Flagstaff: Grand 42
Gilbert: Johnson 44
Paradise Valley: Estes 37
Patagonia: Cadeau 33
Phoenix: A.P.S. 24, America 25, **American 26,** APS 27, Arizona 28, Arizona 29, Benlei 31, Burns 32, du Bois 36, Marley 46, Ottosen 48, **PETsMART 49,** SRP 54
Prescott: **Kieckhefer 45,** Morris 47
Rio Verde: Zicarelli 59
Scottsdale: Arizona 30, Fleischer 38, **Globe 41,** Reese 50, **Schumann 52,** Weatherup 58
Sedona: Haldan 43
Tempe: Crown 35
Tucson: Community 34, Foundation 39, **Furrow 40,** Russell 51, Spalding 53, Stang 55, TEP 57

see also 222, 235, 250, 288, 328, 813, 821, 926, 969, 1065, 1100, 1133, 1152, 1184, 1307, 1482, 1563, 1688, 1811, 1850, 1851, 1910, 1980, 1997, 2172, 2324, 2646, 2975, 3158, 3205, 3398

ARKANSAS

Arkadelphia: Ross 61
Bentonville: Wal 64
Fayetteville: Bradberry 60
Flippin: Southshore 62
McGehee: Wallace 65

Pine Bluff: Trinity 63

CALIFORNIA

Agoura Hills: Community 141
Alameda: Chintu 134, **Maddie's 290**
Aptos: Solari 406
Arcadia: Oak 323, Sai 363, **Stans 413**
Arcata: **Seventh 388**
Atherton: Urbanek 432
Bakersfield: Raskind 351
Belvedere: Allen 71
Berkeley: Center 128, Epstein 184, **Impact 245,** La Fetra 271, Otter 326, Peradam 336, **PowerBar 347, Rosengarten 361, South 409**
Beverly Hills: Bridges 111, Casden 124, Chais 129, Cheeryble 132, Corwin 150, Daly 159, **DJ & T 168, G.T.R. 203,** Greenberg 224, Laffin 272, **Mohn 312, PADI 330,** Shapiro 391
Bolinas: Kapor 260
Bonsall: Schmidt 379
Brea: **VPI 440**
Burbank: **Disney 166,** Disney 167, Lantz 273
Camarillo: Ventura 437
Carlsbad: Ecke 178
Carmel: McElvany 301, McMahan 302, Sanford 369, Segal 384
Carmichael: Pfund 343
Concord: Farallon 187, Hofmann 240
Corte Madera: Springcreek 412
Costa Mesa: Brown 114
Crockett: Crockett 156
Culver City: **Compassion 146**
Cupertino: Seven 387
Cypress: **Mitsubishi 310**
Daly City: Doelger 171
Danville: **Sargent 374**
Davis: Chapman 131, Glide 215
East Palo Alto: Romic 359
Encinitas: G.A.G. 202
Encino: Horn 242
Escondido: Namaste 319
Foster City: Saul 375
Fresno: Fresno 198, Peters 338, Peters 339
Gardena: **Nissan 321**
Glendale: Freeberg 197, Lund 288
Glendora: Ludwick 286
Gold River: Harvego 231
Goleta: Raintree 350
Greenbrae: Fullerton 200, Gerhard 210
Healdsburg: Crabb 152, Ducommun 175
Irvine: Aaroe 66
Irwindale: Select 385
Kentfield: Morris 316
La Canada: Crawford 154

La Jolla: Berlin 95, Rivkin 356, Scripps 382
Lafayette: Llagas 282
Laguna Beach: **Foundation 194, Homeland 241**
Lake Forest: McBeth 298
Larkspur: Middleton 307
Linden: Webster 442
Long Beach: Keesal 263, Miller 308, Reid 352
Los Altos: Byers 119, Moore 313, Morgan 315, **Packard 329,** Vadasz 433
Los Angeles: Argonaut 78, Booth 102, Broad 112, Brotman 113, Burkle 117, California 121, Chandler 130, Collins 137, David 161, **DiCaprio 164,** Frankel 196, Friesen 199, Garen 205, Gilmore 212, **Howard 243,** James 248, Janssen 250, Jewish 255, **JL 256,** King 265, Lavine 276, Lowitz 285, Metropolitan 306, Morton 317, Mudd 318, Naturganic 320, Norman 322, Petersen 340, Resnick 353, **Richter 354,** Sheinberg 393, Skylark 399, SoCalGas 405, Sprague 411, Taper 423, Taub 424, Tyler 431, Vanoff 436, Von Hagen 439, Wallis 441, Weisz 444, Whitecap 447, Windfall 451, Wouk 455, Wunderkinder 456, Zilber 458, Zilkha 459
Los Gatos: JWS 258, **K.L. 259**
Malibu: **Luster 289, Smith 404**
Marina Del Rey: Jud 257
Menlo Park: **Compton 147,** Flora 191, Hewlett 238, Stephenson 416
Mill Valley: Katz 261
Milpitas: **Solectron 407**
Modesto: Great 223
Monterey: Community 140
Mountain View: **Beagle 90,** SGI 389
Napa: Mead 303
Newport Beach: Crummer 157, **Environment 183,** Pacific 328, Smith 402
Newport Coast: Jay 251
Nicasio: Endurance 181
Novato: Birkenstock 98, Marin 292
Oakland: **Acorn 67,** Braddock 107, **Common 139,** Doelger 172, **Earthjustice 176,** East 177, Give 214, Hazen 235, **Philanthropic 345,** Rose 360, Skaggs 398, Valley 434
Orinda: Ark 79, **Barth 88,** Dahl 158
Pacific Palisades: **Global 216,** Stern 417
Palo Alto: Bay 89, **Christensen 135,** Country 151, **Hewlett 239,** Katz 262, **Ludwick 287**
Pasadena: Boswell 104, Flintridge 190, Garland 206, Pasadena 331, Ridder 355
Pebble Beach: Vital 438
Pilot Hill: Whittier 448
Pleasanton: ProAction 348, Shaklee 390
Portola Valley: Blue 100, Diller 165, Lipman 281
Poway: Gateway 207, Wells 445
Rancho Mirage: Barker 87, Conte 149, Mirada 309

NORTH CAROLINA

NORTH DAKOTA

OHIO

OKLAHOMA

OREGON

TYPES OF SUPPORT INDEX

Grantmakers in boldface type make grants on a national, regional, or international basis; the others generally limit giving to the city or state in which they are located.

Annual campaigns: any organized effort by a nonprofit to secure gifts on an annual basis; also called annual appeals.

Building/renovation: money raised for construction, renovation, remodeling, or rehabilitation of buildings; may be part of an organization's capital campaign.

Capital campaigns: a campaign, usually extending over a period of years, to raise substantial funds for enduring purposes, such as building or endowment funds.

Cause-related marketing: linking gifts to charity with marketing promotions. This may involve donating products which will then be auctioned or given away in a drawing with the proceeds benefiting a charity. The advertising campaign for the product will be combined with the promotion for the charity. In other cases it will be advertised that when a customer buys the product a certain amount of the proceeds will be donated to charity. Often gifts made to charities stemming from cause-related marketing are not called charitable donations and may be assigned as expenses to the department in charge of the program. Public affairs and marketing are the departments usually involved.

Conferences/seminars: a grant to cover the expenses of holding a conference or seminar.

Consulting services: professional staff support provided by the foundation to a nonprofit to consult on a project of mutual interest or to evaluate services (not a cash grant).

Continuing support: a grant that is renewed on a regular basis.

Curriculum development: grants to schools, colleges, universities, and educational support organizations to develop general or discipline-specific curricula.

Debt reduction: also known as deficit financing. A grant to reduce the recipient organization's indebtedness; frequently refers to mortgage payments.

Donated equipment: surplus furniture, office machines, paper, appliances, laboratory apparatus, or other items that may be given to charities, schools, or hospitals.

Donated land: land or developed property. Institutions of higher education often receive gifts of real estate; land has also been given to community groups for housing development or for parks or recreational facilities.

Donated products: companies giving away what they make or produce. Product donations can include periodic clothing donations to a shelter for the homeless or regular donations of pharmaceuticals to a health clinic resulting in a reliable supply.

Emergency funds: a one-time grant to cover immediate short-term funding needs on an emergency basis.

Employee matching gifts: a contribution to a charitable organization by a corporate employee which is matched by a similar contribution from the employer. Many corporations support employee matching gift programs in higher education to stimulate their employees to give to the college or university of their choice. In addition, many foundations support matching gift programs for their officers and directors.

Employee volunteer services: an ongoing coordinated effort through which the company promotes involvement with nonprofits on the part of employees. The involvement may be during work time or after hours. (Employees may also volunteer on their own initiative; however, that is not described as corporate volunteerism). Many companies honor their employees with awards for outstanding volunteer efforts. In making cash donations, many favor the organizations with which their employees have worked as volunteers. Employee volunteerism runs the gamut from school tutoring programs to sales on work premises of employee-made crafts or baked goods to benefit nonprofits. Management of the programs can range from fully-staffed offices of corporate volunteerism to a part-time coordinating responsibility on the part of one employee.

Employee-related scholarships: a scholarship program funded by a company-sponsored foundation usually for children of employees; programs are frequently administered by the National Merit Scholarship Corporation which is responsible for selection of scholars.

Endowments: a bequest or gift intended to be kept permanently and invested to provide income for continued support of an organization.

Equipment: a grant to purchase equipment, furnishings, or other materials.

Exchange programs: usually refers to funds for educational exchange programs for foreign students.

Fellowships: usually indicates funds awarded to educational institutions to support fellowship programs. A few foundations award fellowships directly to individuals.

General/operating support: a grant made to further the general purpose or work of an organization, rather than for a specific purpose or project; also called unrestricted grants.

Grants to individuals: awards made directly by the foundation to individuals rather than to nonprofit organizations; includes aid to the needy. (See also "Fellowships," "Scholarships—to individuals," and "Student loans—to individuals.")

In-kind gifts: a contribution of equipment, supplies, or other property as distinct from a monetary grant. Some organizations may also donate space or staff time as an in-kind contribution.

Income development: grants for fundraising, marketing, and to expand audience base.

Internship funds: usually indicates funds awarded to an institution or organization to support an internship program rather than a grant to an individual.

Land acquisition: a grant to purchase real estate property.

Lectureships: see "Curriculum development."

Loaned talent: an aspect of employee volunteerism. It differs from the usual definition of such in that it usually involves loaned professionals and executive staff who are helping a nonprofit in an area involving their particular skills. Loaned talents can assist a nonprofit in strategic planning, dispute resolution or negotiation services, office administration, real estate technical assistance, personnel policies, lobbying, consulting, fundraising, and legal and tax advice.

Loans: see "Program-related investments/loans" and "Student loans —to individuals.")

Management development: grants for salaries, staff support, staff training, strategic and long-term planning, budgeting and accounting.

Matching/challenge support: a grant which is made to match funds provided by another donor. (See also "Employee matching gifts.")

Operating budgets: see "General/operating support."

Professorships: a grant to an educational institution to endow a professorship or chair.

Program development: grants to support specific projects or programs as opposed to general purpose grants.

Program evaluation: grants to evaluate a specific project or program; includes awards both to agencies to pay for evaluation costs and to research institutes and other program evaluators.

Program-related investments/loans: a loan is any temporary award of funds that must be repaid. A program-related investment is a loan or other investment (as distinguished from a grant) made by a foundation to another organization for a project related to the foundation's stated charitable purpose and interests.

Public relations services: may include printing and duplicating, audio-visual and graphic arts services, helping to plan special events such as festivals, piggyback advertising (advertisements that mention a company while also promoting a nonprofit), and public service advertising.

Publication: a grant to fund reports or other publications issued by a nonprofit resulting from research or projects of interest to the foundation.

Renovation projects: see "Building/renovation."

Research: usually indicates funds awarded to institutions to cover costs of

investigations and clinical trials. Research grants for individuals are usually referred to as fellowships.

Scholarship funds: a grant to an educational institution or organization to support a scholarship program, mainly for students at the undergraduate level. (See also "Employee-related scholarships.")

Scholarships—to individuals: assistance awarded directly to individuals in the form of educational grants or scholarships. (See also "Employee-related scholarships.")

Seed money: a grant or contribution used to start a new project or organization. Seed grants may cover salaries and other operating expenses of a new project. Also known as "start-up funds."

Special projects: see "Program development."

Sponsorships: endorsements of charities by corporations; or corporate contributions to all or part of a charitable event.

Student aid: see "Fellowships," "Scholarships—to individuals," and "Student loans—to individuals."

Student loans—to individuals: assistance awarded directly to individuals in the form of educational loans.

Technical assistance: operational or management assistance given to nonprofit organizations; may include fundraising assistance, budgeting and financial planning, program planning, legal advice, marketing, and other aids to management. Assistance may be offered directly by a foundation staff member or in the form of a grant to pay for the services of an outside consultant.

Use of facilities: this may include rent free office space for temporary periods, dining and meeting facilities, telecommunications services, mailing services, transportation services, or computer services.

Annual campaigns

Alabama: Brock 6, **Vulcan 18,** Webb 20
Arizona: **Globe 41, Kieckhefer 45,** Zicarelli 59
California: Angelica 76, **Autodesk 82,** Bannerman 86, **Barth 88,** Bear 91, Bechtel 92, Boswell 104, Corwin 150, Disney 167, Eucalyptus 186, Flora 191, Foothills 192, Garland 206, Gilmore 213, Gruber 228, **Impact 245, JL 256, K.L. 259,** McMahan 302, Moore 313, Morgan 315, **Paws 333,** Reid 352, Rocca 358, **Schlinger 377,** Schmidt 379, **Schwab 381, Sempra 386,** Seven 387, **Seventh 388, Stans**

413, Steiner 414, Stern 417, Surfrider 421, Taper 423, **Tides 427,** Wilbur 449, **Wilkinson 450**
Colorado: Boettcher 466, Colorado 474, Community 476, Duncan 481, Goodwin 489, Hughes 495, Leighty 507, Myhren 520, Sterne 524, Summit 525, Telluride 527, Thornton 529, Yampa 536
Connecticut: Baldwin 543, Garden 565, Larsen 577, Olin 591, Patricelli 593, Sewall 601, Thompson 605
Delaware: Cawley 622, Conectiv 625, Crestlea 626, Longwood 638
District of Columbia: Cohen 662, Himmelfarb 675, Landscape 678, Raiser 696

Florida: Banbury 717, Beveridge 723, Gubelmann 757, **Hope 759,** Maltz 776, Peacock 785, Rayonier 789
Georgia: Blank 821, Cash 824, Georgia 836, Georgia 837, Marshall 851, Oxford 865, Patterson 867, Rich 871, Sapelo 874, Weber 887, Zeist 895
Hawaii: Alexander 896, Atherton 897, Bank 899, Hawaiian 905
Illinois: Ameren 922, BANK 926, **Brach 935,** Cain 945, Chicago 951, DAO 960, Deere 962, Donnelley 968, Field 976, Haffner 996, Halligan 997, Harris 1001, Hedberg 1003, Jocarno 1021, Louis 1035, Lumpkin 1037, MACFUND 1041, McGraw 1049,

Building/renovation

Capital campaigns

Cause-related marketing

Conferences/seminars

Consulting services

Continuing support

Employee matching gifts

Employee volunteer services

Employee-related scholarships

Endowments

Equipment

Exchange programs

Fellowships

General/operating support

Grants to individuals

In-kind gifts

Income development

Internship funds

1470, Sheehan 1493, Stearns 1498, Stevens 1500, Stevens 1501, Stoddard 1503, Sudbury 1505, Sweet 1506, Wallace 1516, Worcester 1523

Michigan: Americana 1526, Ann Arbor 1527, Barry 1532, Battle Creek 1533, Berrien 1536, Branch 1539, Capital 1543, Community 1546, Community 1547, Community 1549, Community 1550, Community 1551, Consumers 1554, Dart 1557, Dow 1564, **Ford 1580,** Four 1581, Grand Haven 1585, Grand Rapids 1586, Great 1588, Hillsdale 1592, Jackson 1594, Kalamazoo 1595, Kantzler 1596, Keller 1598, **Kellogg 1599,** Keweenaw 1602, **Kresge 1606,** Midland 1617, **Mott 1619,** Mount Pleasant 1620, Oleson 1624, Petoskey 1627, Porter 1629, Ransom 1630, Rotary 1632, Saginaw 1634, Steelcase 1639, Wege 1647, Wilson 1649

Minnesota: **3M 1652,** Bush 1665, **Cottonwood 1674,** Griggs 1685, Larsen 1689, Lilly 1691, Marbrook 1693, McKnight 1695, Otter 1705, **Porter 1706,** Rochester 1712, Wedum 1731, Winona 1735

Mississippi: Community 1736

Missouri: Ameren 1739, **Anheuser 1742,** Green 1760, **Monsanto 1773,** St. Louis 1787

Montana: Cinnabar 1797, **Rocky 1804**

Nebraska: Cooper 1808, Hastings 1814, Kiewit 1819, Lincoln 1820, Lozier 1821, Nelson 1825, Omaha 1827, Omaha 1828

Nevada: Fairweather 1843, Hawkins 1845, **Hilton 1846**

New Hampshire: Fuller 1858, Kingsbury 1859, Mascoma 1860

New Jersey: **Barbour 1875,** Borden 1877, Bunbury 1878, Community 1886, Cowles 1887, Dodge 1889, Fund 1898, Hyde 1911, **International 1912,** Leavens 1930, OceanFirst 1944, Stern 1960, Talcott 1963, Victoria 1971, Wallerstein 1972

New Mexico: Adler 1978, Frost 1981, **Lannan 1985,** Leonhardt 1986, McCune 1988, Messengers 1989, Santa Fe 1991, Stokes 1993, **Thaw 1995**

New York: **Abelard 1998,** Achelis 2001, Adirondack 2004, **Altria 2012, AT&T 2020,** Baird 2026, **Baker 2027,** Barker 2029, Bay 2033, **Bydale 2062,** Cary 2069, Central 2070, **Claiborne 2077,** Community 2092, Community 2094, Community 2095, **Dodge 2116,** East 2124, **Engelhard 2133, Ford 2146, Frankel 2149,** Freeman 2151, Gilman 2162, Goldsmith 2172, **Greve 2182,** Hahn 2188, Hayden 2193, **IBM 2212,** IF 2214, **Ittleson 2216,** Jackson Hole 2219, **LaSalle 2260, Lifebridge 2273,** Littauer 2277, Lubo 2288, **Luce 2289,** Marks 2299, McCarthy 2304, **Mellon 2308, Mertz 2311,** Moses 2321, **New 2332,** New York 2334, Niagara 2334, Nichols 2336, **Noble 2337, Norman 2339,** Northern 2341, Northern 2342, Nuhn 2346, O'Connor 2347, Ohrstrom 2349, **Ottinger 2355,** Park 2362, **Paul 2362,** Perkin 2368, Prospect 2378, Rauch 2381, **Rockefeller 2392,** Ross 2401, Rothenberg 2402, Schenectady 2414, Scherman 2416, Snow 2439, Snow 2440, Sprague 2445, Steele 2451, Strong 2457, Sweetgrass 2462, **Thorne 2470, Tinker 2473,** Tompkins 2475, **United 2484,** Wright 2527

North Carolina: American 2537, Blumenthal 2543, Community 2548, Community 2549, Cumberland 2551, Dover 2553, Foundation 2554, **GlaxoSmithKline 2555,** Glenn 2556, Hanes 2558, Hanes 2559, Mills 2569, Polk 2575, Reynolds 2582, Robertson 2584, Rogers 2585, Weaver 2597

Ohio: 1525 2601, **Bingham 2610,** Cincinnati 2617, Cleveland 2618, Columbus 2619, Community 2620, Community 2621, Fairfax 2637, Ferguson 2639, FirstEnergy 2642, Gund 2650, ICF 2664, **Kenridge 2670, Kettering 2671,** Lampl 2673, Lubrizol 2679, Miniger 2686, Muskingum 2688, Nord 2690, Oxford 2699, Reinberger 2707, Rupp 2708, Sandusky 2709, Scioto 2713, Sears 2716, Stark 2725, Toledo 2730, Troy 2731, Waite 2734, Wayne 2736, Westheimer 2739, Yellow Springs 2742

Oklahoma: Bovaird 2746, Communities 2748, McGee 2752, Noble 2753, Sarkeys 2755

Oregon: Autzen 2758, Bay 2759, Carpenter 2762, Jackson 2765, Lamb 2768, McCoy 2773, Meyer 2776, Northwest 2779, **Schmidt 2785,** Tucker 2788

Pennsylvania: **Alcoa 2794, AMETEK 2798,** Bell 2805, Berwind 2807, Bethlehem 2808, Bon 2812, Centre 2817, Century 2818, Claneil 2820, Dolfinger 2828, Dominion 2829, Donnell 2830, Hamilton 2847, Harrisburg 2848, Heinz 2852, Heinz 2853, Hillman 2856, Hopwood 2862, Huston 2867, J.D.B. 2869, Laurel 2873, Lehigh Valley 2875, Martin 2881, Maslow 2882, Mellon 2886, Oxford 2893, Penn 2895, **Pew 2898,** Rockwell 2906, **Rohm 2908,** Scranton 2913, Stackpole 2921, Willary 2939, Williamsport 2940, Wyomissing 2945, York 2947

Puerto Rico: Puerto Rico 2949

Rhode Island: **Dunn 2959,** Ensworth 2960, Kimball 2966, Palmer 2968, Rhode Island 2969, Vigneron 2974

South Carolina: Bruce 2978, Community 2984, Community 2985, Joanna 2991

South Dakota: Kind 3000, Sioux Falls 3002

Tennessee: Benwood 3008, **Bridgestone 3010,** Lyndhurst 3025

Texas: **Carlson 3056,** Communities 3061, Community 3062, **Cooper 3064,** El Paso 3071, Fikes 3080, Haas 3091, Kempner 3104, **Kleberg 3108,** Kronkosky 3112, Lennox 3113, Lubbock 3118, McNutt 3125, Meadows 3126, Moody 3128, Owsley 3137, Rockwell 3146, Sams 3150, San Antonio 3152, **Shell 3155,** Sterling 3164, Still 3166, Summerlee 3167, Temple 3170, Vaughan 3177, Vaughan 3178, Waco 3180, Wortham 3187, Wright 3188

Utah: Dumke 3193, Eccles 3194, **Hayward 3196,** Redd 3204, Swanson 3207

Vermont: **Ben 3211,** Kelsey 3214, Lintilhac 3215, Vermont 3223, Windham 3224, Woodstock 3225

Virginia: **Boat 3233,** Camp 3235, Carter 3237, Charlottesville 3239, Easley 3251, **FishAmerica 3256, Gannett 3260,** Jackson 3270, Mars 3279, Norfolk 3284, Parsons 3287, Truland 3297, Virginia 3300, Virginia Beach 3299, **Winkler 3306**

Washington: **444S 3309,** Allen 3314, Brainerd 3322, Bullitt 3323, Community 3327, Dimmer 3330, Forest 3331, **Glaser 3340, Handsel 3342,** Harder 3343, **Jackson 3348, Kongsgaard 3355, Laird 3356,** Martin 3361, Miller 3363, Northwest 3369, Puget 3374, Simpson 3384, Tacoma 3390, Warm 3393, Wilburforce 3398

West Virginia: Beckley 3400, Kanawha 3402, Parkersburg 3403

Wisconsin: Brico 3410, Community 3412, Cudahy 3416, Green Bay 3426, Janesville 3436, Kenosha 3439, Madison 3448, Maihaugen 3449, Menasha 3452, Milwaukee 3455, Stateline 3479, Wisconsin 3493

Wyoming: Community 3498, Kerr 3501, Lightner 3502, **Schultz 3505,** Storer 3507, Wyoming 3510

Professorships

Arizona: **Globe 41**

California: Flora 191, **Schlinger 377**

Connecticut: Larsen 577

Delaware: Rowland 645, **Seraph 646**

Florida: Duckwall 747, Opler 783

Georgia: AEC 811, Lane 848, Tull 883

Illinois: **Boeing 934,** Harris 1001, McGraw 1049, Tellabs 1102

Indiana: Ball 1114, Ball 1115, Fairbanks 1130

Iowa: Blank 1166, Maytag 1179, McElroy 1180, Principal 1182

Louisiana: Booth 1225

Maryland: Middendorf 1316, Richmond 1325

Massachusetts: Stoddard 1503

Michigan: DeVlieg 1560

Minnesota: **3M 1652,** Marbrook 1693

Mississippi: Community 1736

Missouri: Pulitzer 1782

New Jersey: Cowles 1887

New York: Agrilink 2006, Cullman 2101, **Ford 2146, Frankel 2149,** Kennedy 2238, Lehman 2267, **Luce 2289,** Moses 2321, Park 2360, Rothenberg 2402, **Selz 2425, Solow 2442, Starr 2449,** Steele 2451, Ungar 2482, **Vetlesen 2488, Zenkel 2529**

North Carolina: Blumenthal 2543, Dover 2553, Weaver 2597

Ohio: 1525 2601

Oklahoma: McGee 2752, Noble 2753, Sarkeys 2755

Oregon: Woodard 2791

Pennsylvania: Mandell 2878, Oxford 2893

Puerto Rico: Puerto Rico 2949

Rhode Island: **Dorot 2957,** van Beuren 2973

South Carolina: Bruce 2978

Texas: Cain 3053, Fikes 3080, Houston 3098, Kempner 3104, Kinder 3107, Rockwell 3146, San Antonio 3152, Seay 3153, **Shell 3155,** Sterling 3164, Vaughan 3177

Vermont: Lintilhac 3215

Virginia: Fitz-Gibbon 3257, Olsson 3286, Parsons 3287, Reynolds 3290, SunTrust 3294, **Winkler 3306**

Washington: **Jackson 3348**

Wisconsin: Bassett 3406, Evjue 3421, Four 3422

Program development

Alabama: Community 7, **Vulcan 18,** Walker 19, Webb 20

Alaska: Alaska 22

Arizona: **American 26,** Arizona 29, Community 34, **Globe 41, Kieckhefer 45,** Morris 47, **PETsMART 49**

Arkansas: Ross 61

California: **Altman 72, American 73,** Ark 79, Arntz 80, **Autodesk 82,** Bannerman 86, Barker 87, Bay 89, Bechtel 92, Bella 93, Blue 100, California 121, Castagnola 126, Center 131, **Christensen 135,** Cleo 136, Columbia 138, Community 140, Community 142, Community 143, Community 144, Community 145, **Compton 147,** Crocker 155, Crockett 156, **Damien 160, Delano 163, Disney 166,** Disney 167, Downing 173, East 177, Eldorado 180, **Energy 182,** Firedoll 188, Flintridge 190, Flora 191, **Foundation 193, Foundation 194,** Fox 195, Gaia 204, Gellert 208, Gerbode 209, **Global 216,** Godric 217, Gold 218, Goldman 220, Goldman 221, Great 223, Gruber 228, Haas 229, Heller 236, Heller 237, Hewlett 238, **Hewlett 239,** Hofmann 240, **Homeland 241,** Irvine 247, Jamieson 249, Jewett 254, Jewish 255, **JL 256, K.L. 259,** Katz 261, **Kenney 264,** Laurel 275, Looker 284, Marin 292, **Marra 293,** McMahan 302, Mead 303, Mental 305, Metropolitan 306, Moore 313, Morgan 315, Norman 322, Osher 325, Pacific 328, **Packard 329,** Peninsula 335, PG&E 344, **Philanthropic 345,** Plum 346, **Rainforest 349,** Roberts 357, Romic 359, Rose 360, Sacramento 362, San Diego 365, San Diego 366, San Francisco 367, Santa Barbara 370, SANYO 372, Schmidt 379, **Sempra 386,** Seven 387, **Seventh 388,** Shaklee 390, Skaggs 398, Skylark 399, **Smith 403,** SoCalGas 405, Sonora 408, **South 409, Steiner 414,** Stern 417, **Streisand 418,** Surfrider 421, Taper 423, Tides 426, **Tides 427,** Truckee 429, Valley 434, Ventura 437, Whitecap 447, **Wilkinson 450,** Witter 453, WWW 457

Colorado: American 461, Animal 462, Chamberlain 472, Chinook 473, Community 476, Denver 478, Duncan 481, Edmondson 483, El Pomar 484, Hughes 495, **Janus 499,** Johns 500, Leighty 507, Maki 513, Myhren 520, Nielsen 521, Summit 525, True 530, Yampa 536

Connecticut: Bodenwein 547, Bridgeport 549, CL&P 551, Community 552, Community 553, Connecticut 554, Dibner 557, **Educational 558, Ettinger 559,** Fairfield 560, **GE 567, Huisking 574,** International 575, **Iselin 576,** Larsen 577, Long 580, **McKenzie 582,** New Canaan 586, Olin 591, Patricelli 593, Perrin 594, **Praxair 595, Prentice 596,** Schumann 599, **Tremaine 607, Valentine 611,** Vanderbilt 612

Delaware: Cawley 622, **DuPont 629**

District of Columbia: American 657, **Bauman 658, Butler 660,** Cafritz 661, Community 663, **Moriah 684,** Munson 686, **National 687, National 688, National 689,** New 690, **Public 695,** Spring 697, **Summit 698, United 700, Wallace 702, Wallace 703, Winslow 705, World 707**

Florida: Archibald 710, Bank 718, Beveridge 723, Community 739, Community 740, Community 741,

3436, Madison 3448, Maihaugen 3449, Marshfield 3450, Menasha 3452, Milwaukee 3455, Pettit 3461, Rexnord 3469, Sand 3471, Stateline 3479, Stry 3483, Waukesha 3490, Wisconsin 3493, Witte 3494, WPS 3495
Wyoming: Community 3498, **Schultz 3505,** Weiss 3508, Wyoming 3510

Program evaluation

Alaska: Alaska 22
California: Bear 91, Bechtel 92, California 121, **Christensen 135,** Community 145, East 177, Firedoll 188, Flora 191, Fund 201, Great 223, Heller 236, Irvine 247, Jewish 255, Marin 292, Morgan 315, Morris 316, **Packard 329,** Reid 352, Sacramento 362, San Diego 365, Sonora 408, **Steiner 414,** Tides 426, Ventura 437
Colorado: Summit 525
Connecticut: Bridgeport 549, Community 552
District of Columbia: Cohen 662, Community 663, **Summit 698, United 700, World 707**
Florida: Community 741
Georgia: Community 828, Zeist 895
Hawaii: Cooke 901
Illinois: Grand 991
Indiana: Community 1119, Community 1124
Iowa: Principal 1182
Kansas: **Koch 1194**
Maryland: **International 1305, Lutheran 1311,** Rathmann 1324
Massachusetts: Barr 1355, Berkshire 1357, Horizon 1418, **Oak 1460, Pegasus 1470,** Sheehan 1493, Worcester 1523
Michigan: Barry 1532, Battle Creek 1533, Berrien 1536, Community 1549, Community 1552, **Mott 1619**
Minnesota: Beim 1661, Beverly 1664, Duluth 1678, McNeely 1696
Missouri: Ameren 1739, Employees 1756, Hall 1761, **Monsanto 1773**
New Jersey: Dodge 1889, Wallerstein 1972
New York: Achelis 2001, Community 2092, **Cummings 2102, Ford 2146,** Kohlberg 2251, **LaSalle 2260, Lifebridge 2273,** New York 2330, Rauch 2381, Rochester 2391, **Rockefeller 2392**
North Carolina: Community 2549, Robertson 2584
Ohio: Community 2621, Sandusky 2709, Scioto 2713, Springfield 2724
Oregon: Carpenter 2762, Kinsman 2767
Pennsylvania: Eden 2831, Mellon 2886
Rhode Island: **Dunn 2959**
South Carolina: Community 2985
South Dakota: Sioux Falls 3002
Tennessee: Community 3013
Texas: Kronkosky 3112, Meadows 3126
Utah: **Hayward 3196**
Vermont: Kelsey 3214
Washington: Miller 3363
West Virginia: Kanawha 3402
Wisconsin: Green Bay 3426, Stateline 3479, Wisconsin 3493
Wyoming: Community 3498, Wyoming 3510

Program-related investments/loans

California: Agape 69, California 121, Community 144, Community 145, **Compton 147,** Firedoll 188, Fresno 198, Gerbode 209, Irvine 247, Jamieson 249, Marin 292, McMahan 302, Morris 316, Norman 322, **Packard 329, Paws 333,** Peninsula 335, San Diego 365, San Francisco 367, Save 376, Scripps 382, Skylark 399, **Steiner 414,** Taper 423
Colorado: Community 476, Denver 478, El Pomar 484, Island 498, **Weaver 533**
Connecticut: Community 552, New Canaan 586, **Smart 602**
District of Columbia: **Butler 660,** Cohen 662, **Gaea 668, Moriah 684**
Florida: Archibald 710, Dade 745
Georgia: Lanier 849, North 864, TBS 881
Illinois: **MacArthur 1039,** Prince 1076

Indiana: Community 1118
Louisiana: Baton Rouge 1223, Brown 1227
Maryland: Abell 1268, Columbia 1289, Rathmann 1324
Massachusetts: Haymarket 1412, Island 1425, Parker 1467, Stevens 1500, Sweet 1506, Worcester 1523
Michigan: Battle Creek 1533, Binda 1538, Community 1547, Grand Rapids 1586, Jackson 1594, Kalamazoo 1595
Minnesota: Central 1671, Greycoach 1684, McKnight 1695, Wedum 1731, Winona 1735
Missouri: Baer 1743, Hall 1761, St. Louis 1787
Nebraska: Kiewit 1819
Nevada: **Hilton 1846**
New Hampshire: New Hampshire 1862
New Jersey: Borden 1877, Community 1886, Victoria 1971
New Mexico: **Lannan 1985,** McCune 1988, Stokes 1993
New York: Abrons 2000, **American 2013,** Community 2094, East 2124, **Ford 2146, HKH 2202,** Kaplan 2229, **King 2242,** Marks 2299, North 2340, O'Connor 2347, **Rainforest 2379,** Rochester 2391, **Rockefeller 2392,** Wendt 2509, Whitehead 2512
North Carolina: Community 2549, Triangle 2594
Ohio: Bee 2609, Cincinnati 2617, Cleveland 2618, Gund 2650, **International 2666, Lowe 2678,** Nord 2690
Oklahoma: Noble 2753
Oregon: Meyer 2776
Pennsylvania: **Alcoa 2794,** Heinz 2852, Heinz 2853, Hopwood 2862, Mellon 2886, **Pew 2898,** Williamsport 2940
Puerto Rico: Puerto Rico 2949
South Carolina: Post 2995
Tennessee: **Jeniam 3021**
Texas: Meadows 3126, Rockwell 3146, San Antonio 3152, Temple 3170, **TXU 3175**
Vermont: Kelsey 3214, Vermont 3222
Washington: Allen 3314, Bullitt 3323, Discuren 3331, **Jackson 3348,** Miller 3363, Tacoma 3390
Wyoming: Community 3498

Public relations services

California: **Mitsubishi 310,** San Diego 366, **Sempra 386,** SoCalGas 405
Colorado: Colorado 474
Florida: **AutoNation 711**
Illinois: **Boeing 934**
Kentucky: Ashland 1207
Nevada: Southwest 1850
Vermont: Vermont 3223

Publication

Alabama: Community 7, Webb 20
Alaska: Alaska 22
Arizona: Arizona 29, **Kieckhefer 45**
Arkansas: Ross 61
California: Ark 79, Castagnola 126, Columbia 138, Firedoll 188, Flora 191, **Foundation 193, Foundation 194,** Gellert 208, Great 223, Heller 236, Mental 305, Sacramento 362, San Diego 365, Save 376, **Seventh 388,** Skaggs 398, **Smith 403, Steiner 414,** Surfrider 421, Taper 423, **Tides 427,** Truckee 429, Witter 453
Colorado: Leighty 507
Connecticut: Beinecke 544, Bodenwein 547, **GE 567, Tremaine 607**
District of Columbia: **Bauman 658, German 670**
Florida: Dade 745, Opler 783
Georgia: AEC 811
Hawaii: People's 906
Idaho: Reed 918
Illinois: **Brach 935, Farm 975,** Henry 1006, Mahoney 1042
Indiana: Ball 1114, Marshall 1143
Iowa: Cedar Rapids 1167, Maytag 1179
Kentucky: Community 1211
Louisiana: Booth 1225
Maine: Burnham 1249

Maryland: **International 1305,** Macht 1312, Marpat 1313, Snyder 1333
Massachusetts: Berkshire 1357, Boston 1358, Community 1375, **Cricket 1383, International 1424, Merck 1450, New 1458, RESIST 1483,** Sweet 1506, Wharton 1518
Michigan: Americana 1526, Ann Arbor 1527, Battle Creek 1533, Community 1547, Consumers 1554, Dart 1557, Dyer 1567, **Ford 1580,** Hillsdale 1592, Michigan 1616, Mount Pleasant 1620, Saginaw 1634
Minnesota: Andersen 1656, **Cottonwood 1674,** Duluth 1678, Lilly 1691, **Unity 1725**
Missouri: Employees 1756, **Two 1792**
Nebraska: Omaha 1827
Nevada: Harris 1844, **Hilton 1846,** Oakmead 1847
New Hampshire: Mascoma 1860
New Jersey: Dodge 1889, Fund 1898, Wallerstein 1972
New Mexico: Albuquerque 1979, Frost 1981, **Lannan 1985, Levinson 1987,** Santa Fe 1991, **Thaw 1995**
New York: **Abelard 1998,** Achelis 2001, Adirondack 2004, **American 2013,** Bydale 2062, Central 2070, Citizens 2076, Clark 2080, Common 2091, Community 2095, **Engelhard 2133, Ford 2146, Funding 2156, Heineman 2196, Ittleson 2216,** Jackson Hole 2219, Kaplan 2229, Littauer 2277, Lubo 2288, New York 2330, Niagara 2334, **Norcross 2338,** Northern 2342, O'Connor 2347, Oneida 2350, Rochester 2391, **Royal 2403,** Snow 2439, Snow 2440, Sweetgrass 2462, **United 2484,** Weissman 2506
North Carolina: Blumenthal 2543, Community 2548, Cumberland 2551, Hanes 2559, Polk 2575, Reynolds 2582, Rogers 2585
Ohio: **Armington 2606,** Columbus 2619, Dayton 2629, Gund 2650, **Kettering 2671,** Mather 2683, Muskingum 2688, Nord 2690, Oxford 2699, Reinberger 2707, Rupp 2708, Sandusky 2709, Scioto 2713, Springfield 2724, Westheimer 2739, YSI 2743
Oregon: Carpenter 2762, Kinsman 2767, McKenzie 2775, Northwest 2779
Pennsylvania: Centre 2817, Claneil 2820, Dolfinger 2828, **Friendship 2840,** Harrisburg 2848, HBE 2850, Laurel 2873, Lehigh Valley 2875, McLean 2884, **Pew 2898,** Scranton 2913, Shoemaker 2916
Puerto Rico: Puerto Rico 2949
Rhode Island: **Dunn 2959,** Palmer 2968, Rhode Island 2969
South Carolina: Community 2986
Texas: Hershey 3094, Houston 3098, Kempner 3104, Meadows 3126, Moody 3128, San Antonio 3152, **Shell 3155,** Sterling 3164, Summerlee 3167, Trull 3174, Vaughan 3177
Vermont: Kelsey 3214
Virginia: **Boat 3233,** Charlottesville 3239, **Environmental 3253, Graphic 3266,** Graves 3267, Truland 3297, Virginia 3300
Washington: **Jackson 3348, Laird 3356,** Martin 3361, Miller 3363, Samis 3380, **Weyerhaeuser 3396**
West Virginia: Kanawha 3402
Wisconsin: Evjue 3421, Marshfield 3450, Stry 3483, Wisconsin 3493
Wyoming: Community 3498

Research

Alabama: Brock 6, Linn 13
Arizona: Arizona 29, **Globe 41, Kieckhefer 45,** Zicarelli 59
Arkansas: Ross 61
California: **Autodesk 82,** Bechtel 92, Blue 100, Brotman 113, Byers 119, California 121, Castagnola 126, Center 128, **Christensen 135,** Columbia 138, **Compton 147,** Downing 173, Flora 191, Fox 195, Garland 206, Great 223, Heller 236, Heller 237, Hofmann 240, **Impact 245,** Jamieson 249, Jewett 254, **K.L. 259,** Laffin 272, Marin 292, McBean 297, Mead 303, Mental 305, **Packard 329, PADI 330,** Rocca 358, Rose 360, Sacramento 362, Save 376, **Schlinger 377,** Schmidt 379, Scripps 382, Seven 387, **Sierra 395,** Skylark 399, Smith 402, **Smith 403, Stans 413, Steiner 414,** Stern 417, Surfrider

Scholarship funds

Scholarships—to individuals

Seed money

Sponsorships

Student loans—to individuals

Technical assistance

Use of facilities

INDEX TO GRANTMAKERS BY SUBJECT

Terms used in this index are listed below and conform to the Foundation Center's Grants Classification System. In the index itself, grantmakers are arranged under each term by state location, abbreviated name, and sequence number. Grantmakers in boldface type make grants on a national, regional, or international basis. The others generally limit their giving to the state or city in which they are located. For a subject index to the individual grants in this volume, see the Index to Grants by Subject.

Agriculture, farmlands

Massachusetts: **Farm 1396**
New Hampshire: **Stonyfield 1871**
New York: JNT 2223, Society 2441
Texas: Behmann 3043
Washington: Peach 3371

Agriculture, soil/water issues

Connecticut: **Valentine 611**
New York: Afognak 2005
Washington: Bullitt 3323

Animal population control

California: Bennett 94, **DJ & T 168, Luster 289**

Colorado: Animal 462
Georgia: Singletary 877
Massachusetts: **Pegasus 1470**
Montana: Sands 1805
New York: Neu 2328
North Carolina: Oschwald 2573

Animal welfare

Alabama: Schuler 15, Viro 17
Arizona: Arizona 30, Cadeau 33, Crown 35, du Bois 36, Fleischer 38, Morris 47, **PETsMART 49,** Reese 50
California: **Animal 77,** Balin 85, Boeing 101, Boudjak-dji 106, Broad 112, Bruhn 115, Byers 119, California 121, Cameron 122, **Compassion 146,** Conte 149, Corwin 150, Crummer 157, Dmarlou 169, Doelger 171, Doelger 172, Firth 189, Foothills 192,

Fox 195, Fullerton 200, **G.T.R. 203,** Glide 215, Grand 222, Greenberg 224, Harden 230, **Humane 244,** Janssen 250, Jud 257, **Kinnoull 266,** Knowles 269, Laffin 272, Latkin 274, Laurel 275, Lavine 276, Lee 278, Ludwick 286, Lund 288, **Luster 289, Maddie's 290,** Mental 305, Middleton 307, **MLB 311,** Naturganic 320, Petco 337, Pfleger 342, **Richter 354,** Roberts 357, **Rosengarten 361,** San Diego 365, Sandercock 368, **Sargent 374, Seebe 383,** Segal 384, Select 385, Sheinberg 393, Sonora 408, **Stans 413, Stuart 419,** Vanoff 436, Vital 438, Webster 442, Weisz 444, Wells 445, Wouk 455, WWW 457
Colorado: **Airport 460,** American 461, Animal 462, Boogies 467, **Domanica 479,** Duncan 481, **Horizon 494,** Iselin 497, Keesling 503, Nielsen 521, Sterne 524, Wann 532, Wild 535

Animals/wildlife

Animals/wildlife, alliance

Animals/wildlife, association

Animals/wildlife, bird preserves

Rhode Island: Vigneron 2974

Animals/wildlife, endangered species

California: **Delano 163, Oracle 324**
Colorado: Keesling 503
District of Columbia: **World 707**
Florida: Chingos 733
Maryland: **Shared 1332**
Massachusetts: **International 1424**
Michigan: **Arcus 1528**
Nebraska: **McDonald 1822**

Animals/wildlife, equal rights

Washington: **Glaser 3340**

Animals/wildlife, fisheries

California: **Maher 291, Packard 329**
District of Columbia: Munson 686, **National 688**
Florida: Taylor 805
Illinois: Melvoin 1052
Michigan: Great 1588
Missouri: Morris 1774
Montana: Cinnabar 1797
New York: F. & J.S. 2139
North Carolina: Smith 2590
Oregon: McCoy 2773
Pennsylvania: Marquardt 2880
Virginia: **FishAmerica 3256**
Washington: Burning 3324, Martin 3361, Sportsmen 3385

Animals/wildlife, formal/general education

Illinois: Swanson 1100
Maryland: **American 1271**
Massachusetts: Overly 1463
Washington: Sportsmen 3385

Animals/wildlife, fund raising

New Jersey: Pheasant 1948

Animals/wildlife, information services

Arizona: **T & E 56**

Animals/wildlife, management/technical aid

Arizona: **T & E 56**

Animals/wildlife, preservation/protection

Alabama: Barber 5
Alaska: Alaska 22
Arizona: **Furrow 40, T & E 56**
California: **Acorn 67,** Allen 71, Bannerman 86, Bechtel 92, Byers 119, Chapman 131, Collins 137, Columbia 138, Davies 162, **Delano 163, Disney 166,** Dmarlou 169, **Foundation 193,** Glide 215, Hofmann 240, **Howard 243,** Katz 262, **Kinnoull 266,** Long 283, **Luster 289,** McBean 297, McCaw 299, Mental 305, **MLB 311,** Payden 334, Peradam 336, Petersen 340, Plum 346, Roberts 357, Rocca 358, Sanford 369, Saul 375, **Seebe 383,** Skaggs 398, Truckee 429, **VPI 440, Wilkinson 450,** Witherbee 452
Colorado: Barish 464, **Brown 469, Hawley 493,** Keesling 503, Kenney 504, **Oak 522**
Connecticut: Baldwin 543, Foster 563, **Greenfield 570,** Larsen 577, **Mad 581,** Olin 591, Schumann 599, Sewall 601
Delaware: **Fair 631,** Relgalf 644
District of Columbia: Alaska 654, **Conservation 664, National 688**

Florida: Alexander 708, **Anderson 709,** Dunn 748, Henderson 758, KBR 767, Michaels 780, Opler 783, Weiler 808, **Winn 809**
Georgia: Anncox 817, **Bancker 820,** Cooper 829, CRJ 830, Gaines 834, Hardaway 841, Illges 844, Lane 848, McCamish 853, Patterson 867, Sapelo 874, **Turner 884,** Williams 890
Idaho: **ALSAM 910**
Illinois: **Clemens 952,** Community 957, Donnelley 966, Donnelley 968, Field 976, Grohne 992, Haffner 996, **Harvey 1002,** Henry 1006, Huntington 1012, JYN 1024, Kinship 1028, Love 1036, McCormack 1046, **McGraw 1050,** Meyers 1053, **Norwell 1062,** OMRON 1068, Pioneer 1072, Rosenthal 1081, Rothschild 1083, Salwil 1085, **Shifting 1091**
Indiana: Indiana 1137, Marshall 1143, Martin 1144, Met 1146
Iowa: **Krause 1176**
Louisiana: **Entergy 1232**
Maine: Aldermere 1245
Maryland: **Knapp 1306,** Koch 1307, Lapides 1308, **Mpala 1319, Shared 1332,** Snyder 1333
Massachusetts: Arnold 1350, Bright 1359, Chelonian 1369, Childs 1370, **Clark 1371,** Cogan 1372, Community 1375, **Conservation 1376, International 1424,** Island 1425, Killam 1437, Lingos 1442, Morse 1453, Orchard 1461, **Pegasus 1470,** Red 1482, **Sacharuna 1487,** Silver 1496, Sweet 1506, Wharton 1518, Windsor 1521, Yawkey 1524
Michigan: Consumers 1554, Devereaux 1559, Foley 1574, Foley 1575, Frey 1582, Great 1588, Kellogg's 1600, Saddle 1633, Turner 1643
Minnesota: Beim 1661, Bell 1662, Bell 1663, Federated 1682, **National 1700,** W.M. 1727, Wedum 1731
Missouri: Morris 1774, **Porthouse 1780,** Slavik 1786, **Timmons 1790**
Montana: Broadbent 1796, Cinnabar 1797, **Owl 1803, Rocky 1804**
Nebraska: Davis 1810, **Grewcock 1813,** Rogers 1831
Nevada: **Bishop 1838,** Crescere 1841, Harris 1844, Tuscany 1853
New Hampshire: Fuller 1858, Verney 1873
New Jersey: Dodge 1889, Eckert 1891, **Fanwood 1895, James 1913,** Kerr 1923, **Lautenberg 1929,** Monroe 1941, Pheasant 1948
New Mexico: **Harrington 1983,** McCune 1988, Messengers 1989, **Pond 1990,** Santa Fe 1991
New York: AKC 2007, Black 2046, Black River 2047, **Bobolink 2052,** Bridgewater 2056, Brunckhorst 2059, Brutsch 2060, Camp 2067, Chadwick 2071, Chapman 2072, **Claiborne 2077,** Cullman 2101, Demartini 2108, Donaldson 2117, Ellis 2128, **Engelhard 2133,** Erpf 2135, **Flemm 2143,** Frankenberg 2150, Gilman 2162, Goldberg 2169, **Heineman 2196,** Henderson 2197, **Homeland 2203,** Howland 2204, **Keefe 2232,** Landreth 2275, **Lipton 2276, Marsh 2301,** Nichols 2336, **Norcross 2338,** O'Connor 2347, Picheny 2371, **Reed 2382,** Roe 2395, Rumsey 2404, Ryan 2405, Schenectady 2414, Schieffelin 2418, **Solow 2442,** Stainman 2447, Staritch 2448, Thanksgiving 2467, Thayer 2468, **Trust 2481,** Ungar 2482, Vidda 2489, Wainscott 2493, **Ward 2497, Waterfowl 2499,** Wiegers 2513, Wildlife 2514, Wilson 2515, **Woods 2523,** Woodward 2526, Yaron 2528, Zeron 2530, Zucker 2534
North Carolina: **Bailey 2540,** Bryan 2544, Cumberland 2551, Maness 2564, Sprinkle 2591, Triangle 2594
Ohio: Cotswold 2625, Davies 2628, **Haskell 2653, Linnemann 2676,** Lippitt 2677, **Mead 2684,** Muskingum 2688, Reinberger 2707, Sedgwick 2718, Wellman 2738
Oklahoma: Kirkpatrick 2751, Stuart 2756
Oregon: Bay 2759, Bechen 2760, WF 2790
Pennsylvania: Ames 2797, Arcadia 2799, Foster 2838, **Guanacaste 2845,** Hawksglen 2849, Lloyd 2876, Maple 2879, **Metcalf 2887, Pew 2898, Robinson 2905, Teleflex 2930,** Up 2933
Rhode Island: **Bafflin 2950,** Danforth 2956, Woodward 2975
South Carolina: Chase 2981, Cline 2982, Dupont 2987
Tennessee: Pattee 3026, Shackelford 3030

Texas: Bass 3038, **Bat 3042, Bodhi 3046, Favrot 3077,** Griffin 3090, Hershey 3094, **Kleberg 3108, Kleberg 3109, Kleh 3110,** Meadows 3126, Northen 3132, San Antonio 3152, **Shell 3155,** Summerlee 3167, Vaughan 3177, **Welder 3186**
Virginia: Chelonia 3240, **Glenstone 3262,** Larson 3275, Mars 3279, Wrinkle 3308
Washington: **444S 3309,** Albohn 3312, CGMK 3326, Community 3327, **Fries 3338, Handsel 3342,** Leslie 3358, Ludwig 3360, Moccasin 3364, Norcliffe 3368, Northwest 3369, Raynier 3377, Samis 3380, Sportsmen 3385, Stevens 3386, **Sustainable 3388**
Wisconsin: Ellinger 3420, Hagge 3428, Hunt 3433, Leaf 3446, LUX 3447, Puelicher 3465
Wyoming: Kerr 3501, **Schultz 3505, Wiancko 3509**

Animals/wildlife, public education

New York: Howland 2204
Washington: **Pet 3372,** Sportsmen 3385

Animals/wildlife, research

Arizona: **T & E 56**
California: Mirada 309, Whittier 448
Florida: Bacardi 713
Kentucky: **AAEP 1205**
Maryland: Entomological 1295
Massachusetts: **Schooner 1491**
Missouri: Brown 1749
New York: **Grayson-Jockey 2177, Waterfowl 2499**
Oklahoma: Kirkpatrick 2751
Texas: **American 3034,** Hixon 3096, **Kleberg 3109**

Animals/wildlife, sanctuaries

Alaska: Alaska 22
Colorado: Botkins 468
Hawaii: **Ungar 908**
Illinois: WD 1107
Louisiana: Matherne 1238
Michigan: **Arcus 1528,** Foley 1574
New York: Wildlife 2514, Wilson 2515
Pennsylvania: Lloyd 2876
Texas: Kronkosky 3112
Washington: Martin 3361
Wisconsin: Maihaugen 3449

Animals/wildlife, single organization support

Indiana: Perelman 1151
Michigan: Foley 1574
Pennsylvania: Pollock 2899

Animals/wildlife, special services

California: Jay 251, Steiner 415
Colorado: McKee 516
Michigan: **Arcus 1528,** Duffy 1566, Farago 1570
New York: Robinson 2390
Ohio: **Iams 2663**
Pennsylvania: Bannerot 2802

Animals/wildlife, training

Arizona: Johnson 44
Pennsylvania: Iverson 2868

Aquariums

California: Keesal 263, Kriens 270
Colorado: Magness 512
Connecticut: Worthington 617
Florida: Eckerd 749, Free 754, Saunders 795
Illinois: Bartholomay 927, Bellebyron 929, Buehler 942, Front 984, Mason 1045, Stewart 1097
Massachusetts: Henderson 1414, Jordan 1430, Karp 1432, Keane 1433
Missouri: Swift 1789

3013, Community 3014, Community 3015, Healing 3020, Lyndhurst 3025, Tucker 3032

Texas: AIM 3033, Aramco 3036, **Aurora 3037,** Bass 3040, Bass 3041, BHP 3045, Boeckman 3047, Cain 3053, Cameron 3055, **Catto 3057,** Community 3062, **ConocoPhillips 3063, Cooper 3064, Cooper 3065,** Dougherty 3069, El Paso 3071, Entergy 3073, **Exxon 3074,** Fikes 3080, FINA 3081, Four 3083, Frill 3086, Hershey 3094, Herzstein 3095, **i2 3100,** Kelleher 3102, Kempner 3104, Kinder 3107, **Lennox 3115,** Lubbock 3118, **Lyondell 3119,** Mays 3120, McCoy 3123, Meadows 3126, Moody 3128, Northen 3132, O'Quinn 3134, Otter 3136, P 3138, Powell 3142, Quicksilver 3144, Rainforest 3145, Rockwell 3146, Rosewood 3147, Sams 3150, Samsung 3151, San Antonio 3152, **Shell 3154, Shell 3155,** Simmons 3157, Smith 3158, Southern 3161, Southwest 3162, Sterling 3163, Stevenson 3165, Still 3166, Tapeats 3169, Tesoro 3171, Trull 3174, **TXU 3175,** Vaughan 3177, Waco 3180, **Waste 3182, Waste 3183,** Watson 3184, **Weatherspoon 3185,** Welder 3186, Wright 3188

Utah: Aquarius 3190, Eccles 3194, **Huntsman 3197,** Jones 3198, Kennecott 3199, Quinney 3202, Slaughter 3205, Steiner 3206

Vermont: **Ben 3211, Ben 3212,** G.D.S. 3213, Kelsey 3214, Lintilhac 3215, **Seventh 3220,** Vermont 3222, Vermont 3223, Windham 3224

Virgin Islands: St. Croix 3227

Virginia: **Ashoka 3228,** Backer 3229, **Boat 3233, Burford 3234,** Camp 3235, Carter 3237, **Catesby 3238,** Charlottesville 3239, Columbia 3242, **Conservation 3244,** Dennis 3246, Easley 3251, **Environmental 3253,** Evans 3254, **First 3255,** Fund 3259, **Gannett 3260, Gifts 3261,** Gradison 3265, **Graphic 3266,** Hastings 3268, Hunt 3269, Jackson 3270, Kington 3272, Lange 3274, Leggett 3276, Mars 3279, **National 3281,** Norfolk 3283, North 3285, Rouse 3291, Staunton 3293, SunTrust 3294, **US 3298,** Virginia Beach 3299, Wellspring 3304, **WestWind 3305,** Wrinkle 3308

Washington: A Territory 3310, Alaska 3311, Allen 3314, Archibald 3316, Attachmate 3317, **Bauer 3319,** Bullitt 3323, Cascade 3325, Community 3327, Contorer 3328, **Dudley 3332, Fabert 3334,** Forest 3337, Hamalainen 3341, Harder 3343, Horizons 3344, **Jackson 3348,** Janssen 3349, Kaleidoscope 3351, Keller 3352, Leslie 3358, Neukom 3366, Norcliffe 3368, Plum 3373, Puget 3374, Quitslund 3375, Raynier 3377, Russell 3379, Seattle 3382, Simpson 3384, **Sustainable 3388,** Tacoma 3390, Van Waters 3392, Washington 3394, Wellworth 3395, **Weyerhaeuser 3396,** Whatcom 3397, Wilburforce 3398, Wright 3399

West Virginia: Kanawha 3402

Wisconsin: Bassett 3406, Bleser 3408, Cavaliere 3411, Community 3412, Courtier 3414, Cudahy 3416, Derse 3418, Ellinger 3420, Green Bay 3426, Johnson 3437, Johnson 3438, Kenosha 3439, Kohler 3440, Kohler 3441, Lamberson 3443, Lands' 3445, Madison 3448, Marshfield 3450, Menasha 3451, Menasha 3452, Peterson 3460, Spire 3477, St. Croix 3478, Stateline 3479, Taylor 3485, Waukesha 3490, **Weyenberg 3492**

Wyoming: Berry 3496, Community 3498, Hirschfield 3500, S & G 3503, Seeley 3506, Weiss 3508, **Wiancko 3509**

Environment, administration/regulation

Rhode Island: **Dorot 2957**

Environment, air pollution

Colorado: Colorado 474
Georgia: AGL 813, Sapelo 874
Michigan: Asthma 1529
Missouri: American 1740
New York: Smith 2438
North Carolina: American 2538

Environment, alliance

Maine: **Golden 1255**
Washington: Northwest 3369

Environment, association

Florida: Schultz 798
Iowa: Hubbell 1172
Massachusetts: Towards 1510
North Carolina: Community 2547, Progress 2578

Environment, beautification programs

Alabama: Hearin 11
California: Jewett 254, **Oracle 324**
Colorado: McStain 517
Connecticut: Community 552
District of Columbia: Garden 669, Landscape 678, **Mountain 685**
Georgia: AGL 813, McAliley 852
Illinois: GATX 985
Maryland: Tate 1335
Massachusetts: Babson 1354
Missouri: No 1777
New York: Common 2091, Fuchs 2152, Salute 2407
Ohio: Parks 2701
Pennsylvania: Claneil 2820, Penn 2895
Rhode Island: **Dunn 2959**
South Carolina: Montgomery 2993
Texas: Belo 3044, Wortham 3187
Virginia: Fund 3259
West Virginia: Beckley 3400

Environment, forests

Alabama: Alabama 2
California: **Conservation 148, Delano 163,** Flintridge 190, Jeangerard 252
Colorado: **Botkins 468,** Merlin 518
Connecticut: **Tyrrell 609**
District of Columbia: Post 693, **Wallace 703**
Florida: Simons 799
Georgia: AGL 813, Sapelo 874
Illinois: Melvoin 1052
Maine: North 1264
Massachusetts: Cardinal 1366, DiMaura 1387, Hoffman 1417, King 1439, **New 1457**
New Mexico: **SB 1992**
New York: Alfiero 2008, Overhills 2357, **Rainforest 2379**
Ohio: **Davey 2627,** Fairfax 2637
Pennsylvania: **Guanacaste 2845**
Vermont: Windham 3224
Virginia: **WestWind 3305**
Washington: Burning 3324, King 3354, **Laird 3356, Weyerhaeuser 3396**

Environment, formal/general education

California: King 265
Connecticut: Perrin 594
Massachusetts: Perfect 1472
Utah: Brindle 3192
Virginia: **Earth 3250**
Washington: **New 3367**
Wisconsin: Gelatt 3423, Maihaugen 3449

Environment, government agencies

Louisiana: Wiener 1242
Ohio: House 2660

Environment, land resources

Arizona: Arizona 28
California: Bear 91, Crabb 152, Diller 165, Ducommun 175, **Foundation 193,** Glide 215, Hazen 235, Jewett 254, Levy 279, Materials 295, McBean 296, Miller 308, Segal 384, Siebel 394, Springcreek 412

Colorado: Joy 501, MacAllister 509, Merlin 518, RLC 523
Connecticut: Anderson 538
Delaware: Gerard 634
Georgia: Morgens 859, Poe 869
Illinois: Froehlich 983, Getz 986, MACFUND 1041, Mason 1045
Indiana: Igo 1136, Met 1146
Maryland: Chesapeake 1286, **Conservation 1293,** Feldman 1296, Helena 1303, Middle 1317, **Shared 1332**
Massachusetts: Gateway 1406, Hornblower 1419, Howell 1421, Narada 1455, Pardoe 1466, Radley 1476, Raymond 1480, Sweet 1506, Takvorian 1508
Michigan: Ford 1576, Herrington 1591
New Jersey: **Fanwood 1895,** Fund 1898, Goldring 1902
New York: **Frankel 2149,** Kealy 2231, MJPM 2316, Overhills 2357, **Penzance 2367,** Scheuer 2417
North Carolina: Bauer 2541
Ohio: Sauerland 2710, Segoe 2719
Pennsylvania: Allerton 2795, Falk 2832, Taylor 2929, York 2947
Rhode Island: van Beuren 2973
South Carolina: Bostick 2977, Ceres 2980
Texas: Field 3079, Lennox 3113
Vermont: Sands 3219
Virginia: Virginia 3300, **WestWind 3305**
Washington: Bullitt 3323, Burning 3324, Murr 3365
Wisconsin: Huiras 3432, Sand 3471

Environment, legal rights

California: **Earthjustice 176**
Connecticut: **Valentine 611**
Georgia: Brewer 822
Massachusetts: **Peace 1469**
New York: Acriel 2003, **Norman 2339, Waterwheel 2500,** Winthrop 2518
Pennsylvania: **Wyss 2946**
Utah: Brindle 3192
Washington: **New 3367**
Wisconsin: Wisconsin 3493

Environment, management/technical aid

Alaska: **Sealaska 23**
Michigan: Rotary 1632
New York: **Beldon 2038**

Environment, plant conservation

California: Naturganic 320, Save 376
Connecticut: Sewall 601
Georgia: **Foundation 831**
Michigan: **Floriculture 1573**
New York: DJR 2114, Ellis 2128
Ohio: Holden 2657, House 2660
Wisconsin: Stevens 3481

Environment, pollution control

California: Agricultural 70, Kapor 260, Lawrence 277, McCaw 299
Connecticut: Middlesex 585
District of Columbia: **Bellona 659**
Florida: Gubelmann 757
Georgia: **Turner 884**
Maine: Kenduskeag 1257
Maryland: **Adams 1270,** Community 1290
Michigan: Hunting 1593, **Mott 1619**
Missouri: Fischer 1757
New York: **Blacksmith 2049**
Tennessee: Beasley 3007
Virginia: Water 3302
Washington: Anderson 3315, **Dudley 3332**
Wisconsin: Seeds 3473

Environment, public education

California: Center 128, Doe 170, **Foundation 194,** Heller 236
Colorado: Denver 478

District of Columbia: **National 687**
Maryland: **International 1305,** Snyder 1333
Massachusetts: Argosy 1349
Michigan: Great 1588
New York: **Rainforest 2379,** Violet 2490
Washington: I.F.C. 3346

Environment, public policy

California: Flora 191, Heller 236, **Impact 245**
District of Columbia: **International 676**
Georgia: Sapelo 874
Virginia: **National 3280**

Environment, radiation control

Texas: Bridgeway 3050
Washington: Bullitt 3323

Environment, reform

Louisiana: Wiener 1242
New York: Cary 2069

Environment, research

Alaska: Alaska 22
California: **Christensen 135,** Downing 173, **Foundation 194,** Heller 236, **Smith 403,** Tyler 431
District of Columbia: **Summit 698**
Florida: Katcher 766, POLE 787, Simons 799
Georgia: **Money 857**
Illinois: Lurie 1038
Maryland: Gudelsky 1300
Massachusetts: Earthwatch 1391
Michigan: Great 1588
New York: **IBM 2212,** Plymouth 2375, **Rainforest 2379**
Pennsylvania: Martin 2881, Up 2933
Virginia: **Environmental 3253, Winkler 3306**
Washington: Northwest 3369, Tamaki 3391

Environment, single organization support

California: **Foundation 194,** Suisun 420

Environment, toxics

California: **Acorn 67, Homeland 241,** Kapor 260
Georgia: Sapelo 874, **Turner 884**
Maine: **Golden 1255**
Massachusetts: Garfield 1405
New York: **Beldon 2038, Noyes 2345**
Washington: Bullitt 3323

Environment, water resources

Arizona: Arizona 28
California: Agricultural 70, **Conservation 148,** Flintridge 190, **Homeland 241,** McCaw 299, Metropolitan 306, Namaste 319, Otter 326, Rivkin 356, Sai 363, West 446, Whitecap 447
Delaware: **Fair 631**
District of Columbia: Hanley 673, Munson 686, **National 687**
Florida: Cobin 735, Taylor 805
Georgia: Sapelo 874
Illinois: Froehlich 983, Melvoin 1052, Schneider 1087
Iowa: Kehl 1175
Maryland: Chesapeake 1286
Massachusetts: Kahn 1431, **New 1457, Oak 1460,** Sweet 1506
Michigan: Great 1588
Montana: K.L.T. 1798
Nevada: **Hilton 1846,** Tuscany 1853
New Jersey: Pheasant 1948
New Mexico: **SB 1992**
New York: Hudson 2207, Kealy 2231, Morris 2319, Sweetgrass 2462
Oregon: Bonneville 2761
Pennsylvania: Martin 2881, Stroud 2926

Tennessee: Thompson 3031
Virginia: **Boat 3233,** Water 3302
Washington: Bullitt 3323, Burning 3324, Northwest 3369
Wisconsin: Brico 3410, Sand 3471

Environmental education

Alabama: Alabama 2
Alaska: Alaska 22
Arizona: TEP 57
California: Center 128, Chintu 134, Cleo 136, Jewett 254, **Oracle 324,** Osher 325, Small 401
Colorado: **Horizon 494,** Island 498, McStain 517
Connecticut: Leever 578, Olin 591, **Praxair 595**
District of Columbia: **America 655,** Garden 669, Mazda 681, **Mountain 685, National 687, Wallace 702**
Florida: Peacock 785
Georgia: Atlanta 819, Singletary 877
Hawaii: Garden 903
Illinois: **American 923,** ComEd 954
Kentucky: Yeager 1222
Louisiana: Coypu 1231
Maryland: PG&E 1323
Massachusetts: American 1343, Horizon 1418, **Peppercorn 1471**
Michigan: Cook 1555, **Floriculture 1573,** Knight 1604, Michigan 1616
Minnesota: Remick 1709
Missouri: Portman 1781, **Singing 1785**
Montana: **Rocky 1804**
New Hampshire: **Stonyfield 1871**
New Mexico: Messengers 1989
New York: deCoizart 2105, Klingenstein 2245, Kohlberg 2251, **Mitsubishi 2315, Penzance 2367**
Ohio: Lubrizol 2679
Oregon: Wenner 2789
Pennsylvania: Bethlehem 2808, McLean 2884
Texas: Hershey 3094, **Kleh 3110**
Virginia: Chesapeake 3241, Virginia 3300
Washington: Burning 3324, Discuren 3331, **Laird 3356**
West Virginia: Brier 3401
Wisconsin: Demmer 3417, Janesville 3436, Meyer 3454, Rennebohm 3468

Global warming

District of Columbia: **Butler 660, Wallace 703**
Massachusetts: **Oak 1460**
New York: **Rockefeller 2392**
South Carolina: Chase 2981
Virginia: **Winkler 3306**
Washington: Bullitt 3323

Horticulture/garden clubs

Alabama: Larkins 12
District of Columbia: Garden 669
Florida: Colen 738
Georgia: American 816
Hawaii: Garden 903
Illinois: Grunsfeld 994, Lebus 1032, McLamore 1051, Winona 1112
Massachusetts: Fessenden 1397
Michigan: **Floriculture 1573,** Meijer 1615
Nebraska: Kearney 1818
New Jersey: **Magowan 1933**
New York: Maguire 2292, Shoreland 2432
Ohio: **Scotts 2715,** Segoe 2719, **Vesper 2732**
Pennsylvania: HBE 2850, von Hess 2935
Vermont: **National 3217**

Landscaping

District of Columbia: **Mountain 685**
Hawaii: Garden 903
Minnesota: Bank 1660
Nebraska: Nebraska 1824
New York: Salute 2407

Natural resources

Alabama: Barber 5, Brock 6, **Whatley 21**
Alaska: Alaska 22, **Sealaska 23**
Arizona: Arizona 28, Arizona 29, Burns 32, Cadeau 33, Estes 37, **Furrow 40,** Grand 42, **Kieckhefer 45, Schumann 52,** Weatherup 58
Arkansas: Ross 61, Wallace 65
California: Aaroe 66, **Acorn 67,** Agricultural 70, Allen 71, **American 73,** Barker 87, **Barth 88, Beagle 90,** Bella 93, Berlin 95, **Betlach 97, Borun 103,** Braddock 107, Bradford 108, Brewster 110, Broad 112, Capecchio 123, Casner 125, Chais 129, Chandler 130, **Cheeryble 132, ChevronTexaco 133,** Chintu 134, **Christensen 135,** Columbia 138, **Compton 147, Conservation 148,** Crawford 154, Crocker 155, **Damien 160,** Davies 162, **Delano 163, Disney 166,** Earthjustice 176, Eldorado 180, **Environment 183,** Epstein 184, Eriksen 185, Firedoll 188, Flintridge 190, **Foundation 193, Foundation 194,** Friesen 199, G.A.G. 202, Garen 205, Gateway 207, Gellert 208, Gerhard 210, Gilmore 212, Gilmore 213, Gold 218, Great 223, Haas 229, Haynes 234, Hazen 235, Heller 236, Heller 237, Hewlett 238, Hofmann 240, **Homeland 241,** Irvine 247, James 248, Jeangerard 252, **JL 256,** JWS 258, King 265, Klein 268, Lee 278, Lipman 281, **Looker 284, Luster 289,** McCaw 299, McElvany 301, Mead 303, Mellam 304, **Mohn 312,** Moore 313, Morton 317, Mudd 318, Otter 326, **Packard 329, PADI 330, Patagonia 332,** Peradam 336, Peterson 341, Pfleger 342, PG&E 344, **PowerBar 347,** ProAction 348, **Rainforest 349,** Raintree 350, Reid 352, Rose 360, Sacramento 362, San Diego 364, San Francisco 367, Sapling 373, **Schlinger 377,** Schmidt 379, **Schwab 381,** Segal 384, Seven 387, **Seventh 388,** Shapiro 391, Sheinberg 393, **Sierra 395, Sinskey 397,** Skaggs 398, Skylark 399, Smith 402, Sprague 411, **Stuart 419, Tides 427,** Vanoff 436, Ventura 437, Von Hagen 439, Wallis 441, Webster 442, Wilbur 449, **Wilkinson 450,** Windfall 451, Witter 453, Wunderkinder 456, Zilkha 459
Colorado: **Airport 460, Benson 465,** Boettcher 466, **Brown 469,** Caulkins 471, Chamberlain 472, Chinook 473, Dominic 480, **Ecumenical 482,** El Pomar 484, **Fergus 485,** Gates 486, Green 490, **Hamilton 492, Hawley 493, Horizon 494,** Hunter 496, Iselin 497, Island 498, Joy 501, Koelbel 506, Maki 513, Manitou 514, McGrath 515, McStain 517, Merlin 518, **Oak 522,** Summit 525, Taylor 526, True 530
Connecticut: Ahn 537, Baldwin 543, Beinecke 544, **Belgian 545,** Community 553, Connecticut 554, Connecticut 555, **Educational 558,** Flinn 562, Garden 565, Grant 569, **Greenfield 570, Huisking 574, Iselin 576,** Larsen 577, Meek 583, **October 590,** Olin 591, Patricelli 593, Schumann 599, **Scrooby 600, Sun 604,** Tsunami 608, Vanderbilt 612, Walker 614
Delaware: Buckner 621, Cawley 622, Chichester 623, Cohen 624, Crestlea 626, Crystal 627, Ederic 630, Four 633, **Jade 635,** Kent 636, Marmot 639, Rowland 645, **Seraph 646,** Shrieking 647, Singer 648, Starrett 649, **Stroud 651,** Struthers 652, **Syngenta 653**
District of Columbia: **America 655,** Cafritz 661, Community 663, Friedman 667, Leon 679, LWH 680, Mazda 681, McIntosh 682, McNamara 683, **Moriah 684,** Munson 686, **National 688, National 689, Patterson 691, Peet 692,** Post 693, Raiser 696, Spring 697, **Summit 698,** Summit 699, **United 700, Wallace 702, Winslow 705, World 706**
Florida: Bailey 714, Bank 718, Batchelor 720, Blank 726, **Brabson 728,** Chingos 733, Cole 737, Community 739, Community 741, Darden 746, Dunn 748, Flaherty 750, GSB 756, **Hope 759, Hufty 760,** Jelks 764, **Johnson 765,** KBR 767, Landmark 771, Lastinger 772, Lattner 773, Maltz 776, Marden 777, Opler 783, Rayonier 789, **Regan 790,** Rosenberg 794, **Vanneck 807, Winn 809**
Georgia: AGL 813, **Bancker 820,** Community 828, Cooper 829, Gaines 834, Goddard 839, Hardaway 841, McCamish 853, **Money 857,** Montgomery 858, Morgens 859, Morris 860, Newland 863, Patterson 867, Price 870, **Turner 884, Wardlaw 885,** Williams 890,

Texas: Bass 3039, Butcher 3051, Cain 3053, Cameron 3055, **Carlson 3056, Catto 3057,** Clayton 3059, Communities 3061, **Cooper 3064,** Delaney 3067, Duncan 3070, **Favrot 3077,** Field 3079, Fikes 3080, **Friedkin 3085,** Getz 3087, Gordon 3088, Hershey 3094, Hixon 3096, Hobby 3097, Huffington 3099, i2 3101, Kempner 3104, Kimberly 3106, Lennox 3114, Los 3117, McNutt 3125, Meadows 3126, Moran 3129, Northen 3132, O'Quinn 3134, Paulos 3139, Potts 3141, Rockwell 3146, San Antonio 3152, **Shell 3155,** Smith 3159, Sterling 3164, Texas 3172, Truchard 3173, Trull 3174, Vaughan 3177, Vaughan 3178, **Welder 3186**

Utah: Dumke 3193, **Force 3195,** Lawson 3200, Redd 3204, Slaughter 3205, Tanner 3208, **Wishnick 3209**

Vermont: Alcyon 3210, **Ben 3211,** Kelsey 3214, **Maverick 3216,** Redducs 3218, Vermont 3222, Woodstock 3225

Virginia: **Blue 3232,** Camp 3236, Carter 3237, Connors 3243, **Conservation 3244,** Delmar 3245, Dorothy 3247, Dreaming 3249, **Earth 3250,** Elmwood 3252, **FishAmerica 3256,** Fralin 3258, **Gannett 3260,** Gooch 3263, Logan 3277, Ludington 3278, Mars 3279, **National 3281,** Norfolk 3283, **Norfolk 3284,** Olsson 3286, **Rare 3289,** Reynolds 3290, Seagears 3292, **Tara 3295,** Truland 3297, Virginia 3300, **Winkler 3306,** Wrinkle 3308

Washington: **444S 3309, Alistar 3313,** Allen 3314, Archibald 3316, Bald 3318, Brainerd 3322, Bullitt 3323, Burning 3324, Cascade 3325, Community 3327, **Dudley 3332, Edwards 3333,** Fehsenfeld 3335, Ferguson 3336, **Fries 3338,** Geary 3339, Harder 3343, Horizons 3344, Hyde 3345, I.F.C. 3346, Islands 3347, **Jackson 3348,** Janssen 3349, Jungers 3350, **Laird 3356,** LJCPJ 3359, Martin 3361, Moccasin 3364, **New 3367,** Norcliffe 3368, Northwest 3369, Osberg 3370, Quixote 3376, Raynier 3377, REI 3378, See 3383, T.E.W. 3389, Tacoma 3390, **Weyerhaeuser 3396,** Wilburforce 3398

West Virginia: Kanawha 3402

Wisconsin: Bassett 3406, Bolz 3409, Community 3413, Duncan 3419, Ellinger 3420, Four 3422, Gelatt 3423, Heil 3430, Hunt 3433, Inbusch 3434, Kohler 3440, Kohler 3441, Krause 3442, Lambert 3444, LUX 3447, Menasha 3452, Merrill 3453, Meyer 3454, Milwaukee 3455, **Outagamie 3456,** Peters 3459, Pieper 3463, Pollybill 3464, Puelicher 3465, Ripples 3470, Smallwood 3476, **Stein 3480,** Stry 3483, Styberg 3484, Trostel 3486, Uihlein 3487, Vallier 3488, Witte 3494, WPS 3495

Wyoming: C & N 3497, **Dunoir 3499,** Kerr 3501, **Schultz 3505,** Storer 3507, **Wiancko 3509,** Wyoming 3510

Recycling

Colorado: McStain 517
Virginia: **National 3280**

Veterinary medicine

California: Arques 81, Craig 153, McBeth 298
Kansas: **Morris 1197**
Maine: Narragansett 1263
Michigan: Muntwyler 1623
Nevada: Wendy's 1854
New Jersey: Wetterberg 1974, **Winn 1975**
New York: Acquavella 2002, American 2014, Bostwick 2053, Goldberg 2169, **Grayson-Jockey 2177,** Thayer 2468
North Carolina: American 2537
Pennsylvania: Wurster 2944
Virginia: Noah's 3282, Waldron 3301, Webb 3303
Washington: **Pet 3372**

Veterinary medicine, hospital

California: Solari 406
Delaware: Kent 636
New Jersey: Feline 1896
New York: American 2014, Arledge 2017, **Levin 2271, Pearson 2363**
North Carolina: American 2537
Oregon: Smith 2786
Virginia: Webb 3303

Waste management

California: Agricultural 70, Kapor 260
Minnesota: **Lindbergh 1692**
Texas: Sterling 3163
Virginia: **National 3280**
Washington: **Weyerhaeuser 3396**

Water pollution

California: Agricultural 70, Doe 170
Florida: Schultz 798
Georgia: Turner 884
Minnesota: Sexton 1715
New Mexico: **SB 1992**
New York: Rose 2398
North Carolina: Progress 2578
Virginia: Virginia 3300, Water 3302

Zoos/zoological societies

Alabama: Dove 9, Linn 13
Arizona: Haldan 43, Marley 46, Stang 55
California: Amerman 74, Bundy 116, Casden 124, Doelger 171, Freeberg 197, Harvego 231, Llagas 282, McBeth 298, Outhwaite 327, Peters 338, Peters 339, Tuney 430, Von Hagen 439, Weiss 443, Witherbee 452
Colorado: **Hawley 493,** Keesling 503, Thomas 528
Connecticut: **Scrooby 600**
Florida: Bell 722, Boyer 727, Eckerd 749, Jacarlene 762, Kirk 769, Kislak 770, Lennar 774, Lowry 775,

McNulty 778, Osiason 784, Rooms 793, Saunders 795, Schultz 798, Stein 803
Georgia: **Morris 861,** Weber 887
Illinois: Bellebyron 929, Block 933, Bramsen 936, Chicago 951, Comer 956, Delta 964, Douglass 969, EBR 972, Fischer 979, Gilmore 988, Goodyear 990, Grumhaus 993, Harris 1001, **Harvey 1002,** Hoellen 1008, Hogan 1009, Kovler 1030, **Levin 1033,** Levine 1034, McCormick 1047, Meyers 1053, Pitzman 1073, Staley 1094, Stewart 1097, Warwick 1106, Wilemal 1110, Wilson 1111
Indiana: Burris 1117, Custer 1125, Fields 1132, Hilbert 1135, Igo 1136, Indiana 1137, Jones 1139, Michigan 1147, Perelman 1151, Reilly 1155, Rotary 1157
Iowa: Blank 1166, Iowa 1174, Windsor 1186
Kansas: Coleman 1190, Wagnon 1201
Kentucky: Frazier 1213, Friends 1214, Juilfs 1215, Schneider 1220
Louisiana: Woldenberg 1244
Maryland: **Brown 1279, Head 1302,** Schweizer 1331
Massachusetts: Janci 1427, Quinque 1475
Michigan: Farbman 1571, Ford 1577, Ford 1578, Glancy 1583, Hartwick 1589, Keller 1598, Klopcic 1603, Korman 1605, Mardigian 1613, Polk 1628, Porter 1629, Rosenthal 1631, Stoker 1642
Minnesota: **Collins 1672,** McGuire 1694, Terhuly 1721, Weesner 1732
Missouri: Boswell 1747, Brauer 1748, Coovert 1752, Deramus 1754, Holekamp 1765, Lopata 1769, Love 1770, Neiman 1775, Pulitzer 1782
Nebraska: Holland 1816, Robinson 1830
New Jersey: Cohen 1884, **Magowan 1933,** Stern 1960
New Mexico: Messengers 1989
New York: Byrne 2063, Gerschel 2159, Knox 2250, **Muzio 2325,** Theobald 2469, Universal 2485, Wolk 2521
North Carolina: Herring 2560, **Sloan 2589,** Walrath 2596
Ohio: Bates 2608, Davies 2628, Dornette 2633, Haile 2652, Heiman 2654, **Linnemann 2676,** Luther 2680, Meyers 2685, Miniger 2686, Northrup 2693, Schott 2712, Shaw 2721
Oklahoma: Buford 2747, Kerr 2750
Oregon: Ackerman 2757
Pennsylvania: Houghton 2864, Ryan 2911, Tasty 2928
South Carolina: First 2989, McNair 2992
Tennessee: Chazen 3011, Curb 3016, Joyce 3022, Roddy 3028
Texas: Fairchild 3076, Flarsheim 3082, Kelly 3103, Kinder 3107, Kronkosky 3112, Mazanec 3121, McNutt 3125, Moncrief 3127, Morelock 3130, Paulos 3139, Shiloff 3156, Sours 3160, Tandy 3168, Von Ehr 3179, Watson 3184
Utah: Lawson 3200
Virginia: Dragas 3248
Washington: De Falco 3329, Ferguson 3336, T.E.W. 3389
Wisconsin: Beasley 3407, Demmer 3417, Lamberson 3443, Merrill 3453, Pangburn 3457, Stone 3482, West Bend 3491

INDEX TO GRANTS BY SUBJECT

For each subject term, grants are listed first by grantmaker entry number, then by grant number within the grantmaker entry. When known, type of support is also included. For a general subject index to the environment or animal welfare-based purposes and activities of the grantmakers in this volume, see the Index to Grantmakers by Subject.

Animals/wildlife, sanctuaries, faculty/staff development 370-10, 370-12, 2118-5
Animals/wildlife, sanctuaries, income development 935-28
Animals/wildlife, sanctuaries, internship funds 2378-14
Animals/wildlife, sanctuaries, land acquisition 627-5, 935-6, 2895-21
Animals/wildlife, sanctuaries, management development 1988-43, 2619-17
Animals/wildlife, sanctuaries, research 2360-88, 2360-89, 2481-33
Animals/wildlife, sanctuaries, seed money 2953-4
Animals/wildlife, seed money 314-18, 884-101
Animals/wildlife, single organization support 144-13, 478-12, 478-13, 486-5, 499-1, 542-58, 773-17, 926-7, 926-16, 926-18, 1047-6, 1077-4, 1077-5, 1088-7, 1182-2, 1835-5, 1835-8, 2020-4, 2360-83, 2617-6, 2619-9, 2619-10, 2619-12, 2619-13, 2619-14, 2619-15, 3010-4, 3061-5, 3202-2, 3260-4, 3396-15
Animals/wildlife, South Africa 1599-16, 2146-267
Animals/wildlife, South America 884-248, 3075-63
Animals/wildlife, Southeast Asia 329-87, 2619-9
Animals/wildlife, Southern Africa 2146-4
Animals/wildlife, Soviet Union (Former) 884-187
Animals/wildlife, Spain 2392-2, 2794-29
Animals/wildlife, special services 29-3, 92-5, 206-1, 288-2, 292-18, 335-12, 335-29, 335-38, 365-14, 367-75, 441-18, 441-19, 486-6, 542-44, 739-1, 796-4, 796-9, 796-10, 796-11, 821-9, 883-1, 935-4, 1038-2, 1088-1, 1088-9, 1152-12, 1182-1, 1468-5, 1548-13, 1924-24, 1988-8, 1989-5, 2030-3, 2032-6, 2032-9, 2032-10, 2032-13, 2032-14, 2032-31, 2118-12, 2330-18, 2330-19, 2330-51, 2330-141, 2360-22, 2360-23, 2360-94, 2619-2, 2619-35, 2619-37, 2893-2, 2893-11, 3126-18, 3207-2, 3260-1, 3461-7, 3507-25, 3507-26
Animals/wildlife, special services, aging 796-10, 1088-9, 3126-18, 3461-7
Animals/wildlife, special services, blind/visually impaired 292-18, 335-29, 365-14, 486-6, 796-11, 1548-13, 1924-24, 2030-3, 2032-10, 2032-13, 2032-14, 2032-31, 2330-51, 2330-141, 2619-35, 3507-25
Animals/wildlife, special services, building/renovation 883-1
Animals/wildlife, special services, capital campaigns 1989-5
Animals/wildlife, special services, children/youth 821-9, 2619-37, 3461-7
Animals/wildlife, special services, crime/abuse victims 3461-7
Animals/wildlife, special services, deaf/hearing impaired 2032-9, 2118-12
Animals/wildlife, special services, disabled 29-3, 92-5, 206-1, 288-2, 335-12, 542-44, 739-1, 796-4, 821-9, 883-1, 935-4, 1088-1, 1088-9, 1468-5, 1988-8, 1989-5, 2032-6, 2330-18, 2330-19, 2360-22, 2619-2, 2893-2, 2893-11, 3126-18, 3207-2, 3461-7, 3507-26
Animals/wildlife, special services, economically disadvantaged 367-75, 1088-9
Animals/wildlife, special services, electronic media/online services 367-75
Animals/wildlife, special services, equipment 1088-9, 1468-5, 2360-94
Animals/wildlife, special services, faculty/staff development 2360-94, 3126-18
Animals/wildlife, special services, income development 2360-94
Animals/wildlife, special services, mentally disabled 2619-37
Animals/wildlife, special services, offenders/ex-offenders 796-11, 1152-12, 3260-1
Animals/wildlife, special services, People with AIDS (PWAs) 367-75, 441-18, 441-19, 1038-2, 2360-94
Animals/wildlife, special services, physically disabled 1152-12, 2360-23, 3260-1
Animals/wildlife, special services, scholarship funds 2360-22
Animals/wildlife, special services, seed money 1988-8, 3126-18

Animals/wildlife, special services, technical assistance 1548-13
Animals/wildlife, special services, youth 1152-12, 3260-1
Animals/wildlife, substance abusers 2360-87
Animals/wildlife, Tanzania 1039-9, 2229-20
Animals/wildlife, technical assistance 2898-1, 2898-11, 2898-26
Animals/wildlife, training 1889-47, 1924-4
Animals/wildlife, training, blind/visually impaired 1924-4
Animals/wildlife, training, faculty/staff development 1889-47
Animals/wildlife, Uganda 1039-56
Animals/wildlife, volunteer services 1889-17, 1889-96, 2360-87
Animals/wildlife, Western Africa 313-9
Antarctica, animals/wildlife 884-32
Antarctica, environment 884-32
Antarctica, international affairs/development 884-32
Anthropology/sociology 329-138, 2895-24, 3191-1
Anthropology/sociology, economically disadvantaged 2895-24
Anthropology/sociology, minorities 2895-24
Anthropology/sociology, research 329-138, 2895-24
Aquariums 92-3, 92-12, 135-4, 138-2, 140-1, 140-2, 144-13, 221-17, 314-4, 325-2, 329-84, 335-6, 335-7, 335-8, 335-37, 367-13, 367-58, 441-1, 557-3, 567-3, 575-26, 621-11, 821-41, 935-9, 935-18, 1038-1, 1076-28, 1077-3, 1092-2, 1092-3, 1355-32, 1355-33, 1355-34, 1429-2, 1460-5, 1606-10, 1742-2, 1819-7, 1837-2, 1898-10, 2020-2, 2020-14, 2109-5, 2193-3, 2330-75, 2330-140, 2360-83, 2445-11, 2445-12, 2554-34, 2595-5, 2595-10, 2617-6, 2898-21, 2898-22, 2932-2, 3075-57, 3294-2, 3379-26, 3467-4
Aquariums, building/renovation 935-18, 1606-10, 2932-2
Aquariums, children/youth 135-4, 1092-3, 2020-14
Aquariums, curriculum development 1092-3
Aquariums, endowments 1092-2
Aquariums, equipment 135-4, 935-18
Aquariums, exhibitions 135-4, 314-4, 335-37, 935-9, 1606-10, 2020-12, 2193-3
Aquariums, faculty/staff development 2617-6
Aquariums, fellowships 2898-21, 2898-22
Aquariums, management development 329-84
Aquariums, research 1092-2, 3379-26
Aquariums, technical assistance 3379-26
Aquariums, youth 1898-10
Arctic Region, environment 2308-21, 2308-51
Argentina, animals/wildlife 884-150, 884-374, 884-375
Argentina, community improvement/development 884-150, 2146-180
Argentina, crime/courts/legal services 2146-180
Argentina, environment 193-7, 193-48, 238-12, 238-72, 241-64, 884-150, 884-374, 884-375, 1599-7, 2146-180
Argentina, food/nutrition/agriculture 1599-7
Argentina, international affairs/development 238-12, 238-72, 241-64
Argentina, social sciences 2146-180
Armenia, environment 2146-67
Armenia, international affairs/development 2146-67
Art & music therapy 2146-90, 3381-17
Art & music therapy, aging 2146-90
Art & music therapy, children/youth 3381-17
Art & music therapy, conferences/seminars 3381-17
Art & music therapy, disabled 3381-17
Art & music therapy, economically disadvantaged 2146-90, 3381-17
Art & music therapy, equipment 3381-17
Art & music therapy, homeless 3381-17
Art history 1995-4
Art history, publication 1995-4
Arts 2146-42
Arts education 147-18, 1182-4, 1599-6, 1606-8, 1988-51, 3075-30
Arts education, awards/prizes/competitions 147-18
Arts education, building/renovation 1606-8
Arts education, children 3075-30

Arts education, children/youth 147-18, 1599-6, 1988-51
Arts education, girls 1606-8
Arts education, income development 3075-30
Arts education, management development 1599-6
Arts, artist's services 329-203
Arts, artist's services, building/renovation 329-203
Arts, artist's services, children/youth 329-203
Arts, conferences/seminars 2146-42
Arts, cultural/ethnic awareness 121-2, 221-5, 227-1, 227-6, 238-39, 241-1, 241-138, 313-1, 335-17, 1985-6, 1985-12, 1995-18, 2102-7, 2146-193, 2146-277, 2356-2, 2481-3, 3061-2
Arts, folk arts 1182-4, 2146-226, 2146-260
Arts, formal/general education 2582-11
Arts, management/technical aid 2650-60
Arts, multipurpose centers/programs 135-7, 135-11, 209-8, 367-104, 575-45, 1695-15, 1695-19, 2146-168, 2146-195
Arts/culture/humanities, Africa 2146-9, 2146-35
Arts/culture/humanities, Asia 314-19
Arts/culture/humanities, Australia 314-19
Arts/culture/humanities, Brazil 227-1, 313-1, 2146-260, 2356-2, 3061-2
Arts/culture/humanities, Canada 3323-132
Arts/culture/humanities, Central America 684-13
Arts/culture/humanities, China 1995-18, 2146-42
Arts/culture/humanities, Colombia 221-5, 227-1, 241-1, 2356-2, 3061-2
Arts/culture/humanities, Costa Rica 227-1, 2356-2, 3061-2
Arts/culture/humanities, England 193-21, 2146-82
Arts/culture/humanities, Europe 884-163
Arts/culture/humanities, Germany 884-163
Arts/culture/humanities, Global programs 193-21, 221-47, 238-97, 238-101, 367-84, 698-7, 884-183, 884-330, 1450-75, 1580-26, 1619-48, 1619-61, 2146-34, 2146-42, 2146-81, 2146-82, 2146-141, 2146-178, 2146-277, 2392-15
Arts/culture/humanities, Italy 1619-61
Arts/culture/humanities, Japan 884-265
Arts/culture/humanities, Kenya 2146-9
Arts/culture/humanities, Mexico 227-1, 1599-23, 2146-88, 2146-226, 2356-2, 3061-2
Arts/culture/humanities, Middle East 2146-82
Arts/culture/humanities, Mongolia 2481-3
Arts/culture/humanities, Netherlands 1619-48
Arts/culture/humanities, New Zealand 314-19
Arts/culture/humanities, Oceania 314-19
Arts/culture/humanities, Philippines 698-24
Arts/culture/humanities, Russia 2481-3
Arts/culture/humanities, South Africa 2146-82
Arts/culture/humanities, Suriname 227-1, 2356-2, 3061-2
Arts/culture/humanities, Switzerland 2146-141
Arts/culture/humanities, Tanzania 2229-20
Arts/culture/humanities, United Kingdom 2289-9
Arts/culture/humanities, Zimbabwe 2146-34, 2146-35
Asia, animals/wildlife 167-9, 314-19, 367-82, 2162-4, 2356-26, 2356-27, 2449-16, 2481-22, 3381-21
Asia, arts/culture/humanities 314-19
Asia, community improvement/development 221-11, 2146-207, 2481-12
Asia, environment 221-11, 238-59, 241-84, 329-21, 329-74, 329-110, 329-129, 329-130, 329-149, 329-194, 367-82, 1039-8, 1619-19, 1619-43, 1619-95, 2146-29, 2146-206, 2146-207, 2356-26, 2356-27, 2481-12, 3381-21
Asia, health—general 329-129, 2481-12
Asia, international affairs/development 221-11, 238-59, 1039-8, 1450-61, 1619-19, 1619-43, 1619-95, 2146-29, 2146-184, 2146-206, 2146-207, 2481-12, 2481-22
Asia, public affairs/government 1450-61, 1619-19, 1619-43, 2481-12
Asians/Pacific Islanders, arts/culture/humanities 209-5, 209-8, 2102-7, 2102-14
Asians/Pacific Islanders, civil rights 367-3, 2069-4, 2345-2
Asians/Pacific Islanders, community improvement/development 227-2, 2345-2, 2345-4
Asians/Pacific Islanders, crime/courts/legal services 2069-4, 2345-2

Community improvement/development, Peru
1039-46, 1599-29
Community improvement/development, Philippines
2146-149, 2146-150, 2146-220
Community improvement/development, Poland
1619-59, 2481-19, 2481-28
Community improvement/development, Romania
1619-29, 2481-21, 2481-28
Community improvement/development, Russia
2481-17, 2481-20
Community improvement/development, South Africa
147-83, 191-1, 1599-1, 1599-12, 1599-16,
1619-74, 2146-1, 2146-12, 2146-104, 2146-156,
2146-172, 2146-173, 2146-174, 2146-190,
2146-211, 2146-249, 2146-252, 2146-254,
2146-267
Community improvement/development, South
America 2146-60, 2146-85, 2146-121, 2146-176
Community improvement/development, Southeast
Asia 2146-24, 2146-25
Community improvement/development, Southern
Africa 1599-58, 2146-1, 2146-142, 2146-174
Community improvement/development, Soviet Union
(Former) 238-33, 2481-12
Community improvement/development, Sri Lanka
2146-77
Community improvement/development, Switzerland
2146-142
Community improvement/development, Tanzania
1695-24, 2146-228, 2146-275
Community improvement/development, Thailand
2146-207
Community improvement/development, Turkey
703-16
Community improvement/development, Uganda
2146-15, 2146-148, 2146-154
Community improvement/development, Ukraine
2481-28
Community improvement/development, Vietnam
1695-65, 2146-25, 2146-31, 2146-111, 2146-114,
2146-164
Community improvement/development, Yugoslavia
2481-12
Community improvement/development, Zimbabwe
1599-52, 1599-58, 2146-34, 2146-35, 2146-262
Computer systems/equipment, animals/wildlife
292-27, 627-6, 2229-47, 3381-12, 3398-74
Computer systems/equipment, community
improvement/development 2831-4, 3323-68
Computer systems/equipment, crime/courts/legal
services 1606-7
Computer systems/equipment, education 3379-24
Computer systems/equipment, environment 623-13,
627-3, 742-2, 884-18, 1039-58, 1450-3, 1450-4,
1450-6, 1468-11, 1606-7, 2229-47, 2831-4,
2895-42, 3323-28, 3323-68, 3323-101, 3323-134,
3379-24, 3381-3, 3381-7, 3381-51, 3398-23,
3398-61
Computer systems/equipment, health—general
3381-12
Computer systems/equipment, international
affairs/development 1039-58, 1450-3
Computer systems/equipment, public
affairs/government 884-18, 3398-74
Computer systems/equipment,
recreation/sports/athletics 2229-47
Computer systems/equipment, science 292-27
Computer systems/equipment, social sciences 884-18
Congo, animals/wildlife 1039-56
Congo, environment 1039-56
Consumer protection 182-7, 182-53, 182-59, 182-68,
182-110, 182-137, 182-177, 182-195, 193-47,
209-2, 241-57, 241-58, 241-62, 241-79, 329-47,
329-204, 558-3, 558-4, 684-39, 695-12, 698-3,
698-17, 698-22, 703-4, 884-80, 884-95, 884-265,
884-268, 884-274, 884-328, 1023-5, 1449-19,
1450-23, 1450-28, 1450-48, 1599-32, 1599-55,
2146-236, 2146-238, 2330-59, 2345-27, 2345-48,
2356-17, 2360-32, 2360-63, 2360-100, 2460-16,
2460-24, 2650-15, 3323-38
Consumer protection, conferences/seminars 1023-5
Consumer protection, economically disadvantaged
182-137, 182-177, 2360-100

Consumer protection, electronic media/online
services 884-95
Consumer protection, film/video/radio 2146-236
Consumer protection, research 182-7, 182-59,
182-68, 558-4, 684-39, 698-22, 1450-48
Consumer protection, seed money 182-195
Consumer protection, technical assistance 182-53
Costa Rica, arts/culture/humanities 227-1, 2356-2,
3061-2
Costa Rica, community improvement/development
147-8, 313-5, 1039-30, 2146-52, 2146-53
Costa Rica, environment 147-8, 227-1, 313-5,
1039-30, 2146-52, 2146-53, 2146-67, 2229-5,
2356-2, 3061-2
Costa Rica, food/nutrition/agriculture 313-5
Costa Rica, international affairs/development
1039-30, 2146-52, 2146-53, 2146-67
Courts/judicial administration 684-36, 884-367,
1268-2, 2038-59, 2038-81
Courts/judicial administration, children/youth 2038-59
Courts/judicial administration, research 2038-59
Courts/judicial administration, women 2038-81
Crime/abuse victims, animals/wildlife 2360-5,
2360-102, 3461-7
Crime/abuse victims, environment 1988-16
Crime/abuse victims, human services—multipurpose
1988-16, 2360-5, 3461-7
Crime/courts/legal services, Africa 221-45
Crime/courts/legal services, Argentina 2146-180
Crime/courts/legal services, Bolivia 1039-18
Crime/courts/legal services, Canada 221-70, 329-157,
329-158, 884-294, 884-295, 1985-3, 1985-4,
3323-83, 3323-127, 3323-128, 3323-129, 3398-86
Crime/courts/legal services, Central America 147-50
Crime/courts/legal services, Chile 241-47, 241-52
Crime/courts/legal services, Czech Republic 2481-13
Crime/courts/legal services, Developing countries
2146-27
Crime/courts/legal services, Europe 884-231
Crime/courts/legal services, Global programs 147-21,
558-18, 884-231, 1450-34, 1450-92, 1619-34,
2038-59, 2460-40, 2481-13
Crime/courts/legal services, India 2146-102, 2146-160
Crime/courts/legal services, Indonesia 2146-80,
2146-157
Crime/courts/legal services, Israel 2058-4, 2058-7
Crime/courts/legal services, Kenya 2146-209
Crime/courts/legal services, Latin America 221-70
Crime/courts/legal services, Mexico 238-17, 238-18,
241-25, 698-5, 698-6, 2229-22, 2229-23
Crime/courts/legal services, Nepal 2146-95
Crime/courts/legal services, Nigeria 2146-62
Crime/courts/legal services, Peru 1039-49
Crime/courts/legal services, Russia 884-367, 2481-13
Crime/courts/legal services, Slovakia 1619-16,
2481-13
Crime/courts/legal services, South Africa 2146-156
Crime/courts/legal services, Sri Lanka 2146-203
Crime/courts/legal services, Ukraine 2481-13
Crime/law enforcement, information services 558-18
Crime/law enforcement, management/technical aid
698-5
Crime/law enforcement, minorities 558-18
Crime/law enforcement, police agencies 796-9,
1268-2
Crime/law enforcement, seed money 698-5
Crime/violence prevention 1268-2
Cuba, animals/wildlife 884-43, 2229-18, 2289-4
Cuba, environment 2229-18, 2229-59, 2289-4
Cuba, international affairs/development 2229-18,
2289-4
Cuba, science 2229-59
Czech Republic, community
improvement/development 1619-26, 2481-28
Czech Republic, crime/courts/legal services 2481-13
Czech Republic, environment 1619-26, 1619-27,
2481-13, 2481-28
Czech Republic, international affairs/development
2481-13, 2481-28
Czech Republic, social sciences 2481-13
Deaf/hearing impaired, animals/wildlife 206-4,
1152-11, 2032-9, 2032-20, 2118-12

Deaf/hearing impaired, human
services—multipurpose 206-4, 1152-11, 2032-9,
2032-20, 2118-12
Developing countries, animals/wildlife 167-6, 241-80,
313-3, 314-5, 335-14, 353-1, 367-25, 602-1,
1039-42, 1077-1, 1580-6, 1580-8, 1580-9,
1580-10, 1580-11, 2164-1, 2229-31, 2427-3,
3357-1, 3381-10, 3381-11, 3437-2
Developing countries, civil rights 2146-44
Developing countries, community
improvement/development 182-219, 695-21,
703-23, 703-28, 1619-109, 2146-57, 2146-60,
2146-233, 2449-13
Developing countries, crime/courts/legal services
2146-27
Developing countries, education 135-14
Developing countries, environment 135-14, 167-6,
182-219, 182-220, 221-62, 221-63, 241-80,
241-92, 313-3, 314-5, 335-14, 353-1, 367-25,
567-14, 575-46, 602-1, 658-40, 663-18, 684-26,
695-5, 695-14, 695-21, 698-8, 698-34, 703-1,
703-5, 703-10, 703-21, 703-23, 703-26, 703-27,
703-28, 884-44, 884-182, 884-331, 884-379,
935-30, 1039-34, 1039-42, 1039-58, 1077-1,
1460-10, 1479-21, 1580-6, 1580-8, 1580-9,
1580-10, 1580-11, 1580-49, 1599-14, 1619-1,
1619-2, 1619-15, 1619-17, 1619-30, 1619-37,
1619-40, 1619-47, 1619-64, 1619-79, 1619-93,
1619-109, 1619-110, 1778-4, 1846-4, 2146-27,
2146-28, 2146-44, 2146-57, 2146-60, 2146-68,
2146-79, 2146-126, 2146-128, 2146-131,
2146-223, 2146-231, 2146-233, 2146-241,
2146-271, 2146-272, 2164-1, 2229-31, 2330-4,
2330-176, 2378-39, 2427-3, 2449-13, 2460-27,
2776-2, 2898-36, 3357-1, 3381-10, 3381-11,
3396-22, 3437-2
Developing countries, health—general 703-26
Developing countries, international
affairs/development 135-14, 182-219, 182-220,
221-62, 221-63, 241-92, 567-14, 575-46, 658-40,
684-26, 695-14, 695-21, 698-8, 703-1, 703-5,
703-10, 703-21, 703-26, 703-27, 884-44, 884-182,
884-331, 935-30, 1039-34, 1039-42, 1039-58,
1460-10, 1479-21, 1580-49, 1599-14, 1619-1,
1619-2, 1619-15, 1619-17, 1619-30, 1619-37,
1619-40, 1619-47, 1619-64, 1619-79, 1619-93,
1619-109, 1619-110, 1778-4, 1846-4, 2146-27,
2146-28, 2146-44, 2146-57, 2146-60, 2146-68,
2146-79, 2146-126, 2146-128, 2146-131,
2146-223, 2146-231, 2146-233, 2146-241,
2146-271, 2146-272, 2229-31, 2392-4, 2449-13,
2460-27, 3396-22
Developing countries, public affairs/government
684-26, 695-5, 703-5, 703-10, 703-21, 884-44,
884-182, 884-379, 1599-14, 1619-1, 1619-2,
1619-15, 1619-17, 1619-30, 1619-37, 1619-40,
1619-47, 1619-64, 1619-79, 1619-93, 2146-44,
2146-223, 2146-233, 2392-4, 2898-36
Developing countries, science 313-3, 703-28,
2229-31
Developing countries, social sciences 703-1, 703-26,
1619-15, 1619-17, 1619-64, 1619-110, 2146-27,
2146-231
Developmentally disabled, centers & services 2794-4
Developmentally disabled, centers & services,
equipment 2794-4
Disabled, animals/wildlife 29-3, 92-5, 206-1, 288-2,
335-12, 542-44, 739-1, 796-4, 821-9, 883-1,
935-4, 1088-1, 1088-9, 1468-5, 1988-8, 1989-5,
2032-6, 2330-18, 2330-19, 2360-22, 2619-2,
2893-2, 2893-11, 3126-18, 3207-2, 3461-7,
3507-26
Disabled, arts/culture/humanities 2330-160
Disabled, education 2886-25, 3381-17
Disabled, environment 221-51, 227-8, 325-3, 335-20,
367-109, 552-7, 1468-8, 1580-47, 2172-3,
2330-119, 2330-160, 2886-25, 3061-22, 3381-17
Disabled, health—general 3207-2, 3381-17
Disabled, human services—multipurpose 29-3, 92-5,
206-1, 288-2, 335-12, 542-44, 739-1, 796-4,
821-9, 883-1, 935-4, 1088-1, 1088-9, 1468-5,
1468-8, 1988-8, 1989-5, 2032-6, 2330-18,

703-21, 720-1, 745-3, 758-7, 773-2, 773-8, 773-9, 773-10, 773-11, 773-12, 773-13, 773-14, 773-15, 773-16, 773-24, 821-2, 821-11, 821-13, 821-22, 821-24, 821-25, 821-26, 821-27, 821-39, 821-42, 821-45, 836-4, 836-5, 836-6, 836-8, 836-10, 836-11, 837-7, 837-8, 837-13, 837-14, 837-19, 883-2, 884-1, 884-2, 884-4, 884-5, 884-7, 884-13, 884-16, 884-18, 884-22, 884-40, 884-44, 884-47, 884-48, 884-49, 884-52, 884-55, 884-58, 884-62, 884-63, 884-65, 884-89, 884-94, 884-95, 884-96, 884-97, 884-99, 884-101, 884-102, 884-105, 884-109, 884-115, 884-116, 884-119, 884-120, 884-121, 884-122, 884-124, 884-130, 884-133, 884-138, 884-143, 884-144, 884-145, 884-147, 884-154, 884-163, 884-164, 884-167, 884-169, 884-172, 884-175, 884-176, 884-180, 884-187, 884-197, 884-198, 884-199, 884-203, 884-204, 884-205, 884-212, 884-216, 884-219, 884-220, 884-221, 884-224, 884-227, 884-228, 884-229, 884-234, 884-237, 884-240, 884-241, 884-245, 884-246, 884-250, 884-251, 884-252, 884-253, 884-261, 884-273, 884-276, 884-277, 884-280, 884-284, 884-287, 884-288, 884-295, 884-296, 884-300, 884-303, 884-312, 884-313, 884-315, 884-321, 884-325, 884-326, 884-331, 884-339, 884-342, 884-343, 884-346, 884-353, 884-356, 884-359, 884-364, 884-368, 884-370, 884-371, 884-374, 884-375, 884-380, 884-382, 884-384, 892-2, 892-6, 897-1, 897-2, 897-6, 926-2, 926-20, 991-2, 991-4, 991-7, 991-16, 991-17, 991-19, 1023-6, 1023-10, 1023-13, 1023-14, 1023-17, 1023-19, 1023-20, 1023-21, 1023-25, 1023-43, 1039-1, 1039-3, 1039-4, 1039-6, 1039-8, 1039-9, 1039-10, 1039-12, 1039-14, 1039-15, 1039-16, 1039-17, 1039-20, 1039-21, 1039-25, 1039-26, 1039-27, 1039-30, 1039-31, 1039-32, 1039-33, 1039-34, 1039-37, 1039-38, 1039-44, 1039-47, 1039-48, 1039-49, 1039-50, 1039-53, 1039-58, 1039-60, 1039-62, 1047-1, 1047-2, 1047-7, 1065-14, 1071-4, 1076-4, 1076-5, 1076-6, 1076-11, 1076-12, 1076-14, 1076-20, 1076-22, 1076-30, 1076-34, 1076-43, 1076-49, 1076-51, 1076-52, 1076-54, 1077-1, 1088-3, 1088-8, 1088-10, 1114-3, 1115-1, 1115-5, 1115-6, 1115-7, 1152-2, 1152-3, 1152-4, 1152-14, 1152-17, 1182-3, 1184-2, 1184-3, 1184-6, 1184-7, 1184-8, 1184-10, 1184-11, 1223-3, 1223-5, 1265-3, 1265-4, 1268-4, 1268-7, 1297-1, 1297-2, 1355-4, 1355-12, 1355-17, 1355-18, 1355-23, 1355-27, 1355-28, 1355-29, 1355-30, 1355-31, 1355-47, 1355-48, 1357-3, 1357-4, 1357-6, 1404-2, 1415-1, 1415-2, 1449-9, 1449-18, 1449-19, 1449-22, 1449-25, 1449-27, 1449-39, 1449-45, 1449-52, 1449-53, 1449-58, 1449-63, 1449-65, 1449-66, 1449-67, 1450-8, 1450-12, 1450-26, 1450-27, 1450-30, 1450-36, 1450-40, 1450-56, 1450-62, 1450-64, 1450-66, 1450-69, 1450-75, 1450-82, 1450-85, 1450-89, 1460-2, 1460-4, 1460-6, 1468-3, 1468-4, 1468-6, 1479-2, 1479-6, 1479-11, 1479-13, 1479-14, 1479-17, 1479-19, 1479-20, 1479-21, 1479-26, 1479-28, 1479-29, 1479-31, 1479-33, 1479-37, 1479-41, 1504-1, 1504-2, 1504-3, 1548-24, 1564-4, 1564-8, 1580-3, 1580-4, 1580-5, 1580-6, 1580-7, 1580-8, 1580-9, 1580-10, 1580-11, 1580-16, 1580-17, 1580-18, 1580-20, 1580-30, 1580-31, 1580-32, 1580-37, 1580-39, 1580-42, 1580-44, 1580-45, 1580-48, 1582-4, 1582-5, 1586-2, 1586-5, 1586-6, 1599-1, 1599-4, 1599-7, 1599-10, 1599-12, 1599-13, 1599-14, 1599-15, 1599-16, 1599-18, 1599-20, 1599-21, 1599-23, 1599-26, 1599-27, 1599-28, 1599-29, 1599-31, 1599-32, 1599-35, 1599-38, 1599-41, 1599-45, 1599-46, 1599-47, 1599-48, 1599-49, 1599-52, 1599-55, 1599-58, 1619-1, 1619-2, 1619-6, 1619-8, 1619-9, 1619-10, 1619-11, 1619-13, 1619-14, 1619-15, 1619-17, 1619-18, 1619-19, 1619-22, 1619-24, 1619-26, 1619-27, 1619-28, 1619-29, 1619-30, 1619-31, 1619-32, 1619-36, 1619-37, 1619-38, 1619-40, 1619-41, 1619-42, 1619-43, 1619-45, 1619-47, 1619-48, 1619-50, 1619-56, 1619-61, 1619-62, 1619-66, 1619-71, 1619-72, 1619-73, 1619-75, 1619-79, 1619-87, 1619-89, 1619-93, 1619-94, 1619-95,

1619-96, 1619-100, 1619-101, 1619-103, 1619-104, 1619-105, 1619-108, 1619-110, 1647-7, 1647-8, 1647-9, 1647-12, 1653-7, 1653-8, 1665-11, 1666-6, 1695-8, 1695-13, 1695-21, 1695-23, 1695-25, 1695-30, 1695-31, 1695-37, 1695-39, 1695-40, 1695-42, 1695-56, 1773-1, 1773-4, 1778-3, 1819-4, 1819-6, 1827-1, 1835-2, 1835-3, 1837-1, 1862-2, 1862-5, 1862-6, 1862-7, 1862-8, 1862-9, 1862-10, 1862-12, 1862-16, 1862-17, 1862-22, 1862-26, 1862-27, 1862-30, 1862-41, 1862-42, 1862-47, 1862-65, 1862-69, 1862-72, 1889-4, 1889-7, 1889-8, 1889-10, 1889-12, 1889-15, 1889-16, 1889-23, 1889-25, 1889-26, 1889-29, 1889-33, 1889-35, 1889-39, 1889-50, 1889-54, 1889-55, 1889-61, 1889-66, 1889-67, 1889-72, 1889-75, 1889-80, 1889-81, 1889-93, 1889-95, 1889-97, 1889-98, 1889-102, 1898-1, 1898-5, 1898-12, 1924-3, 1924-7, 1924-14, 1924-15, 1924-20, 1924-22, 1924-27, 1952-1, 1952-3, 1958-3, 1971-2, 1971-14, 1985-3, 1985-6, 1985-8, 1985-9, 1985-10, 1985-12, 1988-1, 1988-4, 1988-7, 1988-10, 1988-19, 1988-23, 1988-24, 1988-30, 1988-31, 1988-32, 1988-34, 1988-35, 1988-44, 1988-53, 1988-54, 1988-60, 1988-67, 1989-8, 1989-11, 1989-12, 1995-8, 1995-9, 2020-7, 2020-15, 2020-16, 2020-19, 2020-29, 2038-1, 2038-5, 2038-15, 2038-22, 2038-23, 2038-27, 2038-28, 2038-32, 2038-34, 2038-35, 2038-45, 2038-46, 2038-49, 2038-50, 2038-56, 2038-57, 2038-63, 2038-66, 2038-77, 2038-79, 2038-80, 2058-4, 2058-5, 2058-8, 2058-9, 2058-12, 2058-13, 2058-14, 2069-1, 2069-2, 2069-12, 2069-13, 2069-16, 2069-18, 2069-19, 2069-22, 2069-25, 2069-28, 2069-31, 2069-32, 2069-36, 2070-1, 2080-5, 2081-3, 2092-1, 2102-6, 2102-10, 2102-13, 2102-15, 2102-17, 2102-20, 2102-21, 2102-23, 2102-33, 2102-35, 2102-38, 2109-7, 2111-1, 2111-2, 2111-3, 2111-5, 2118-20, 2118-21, 2118-22, 2122-2, 2122-3, 2122-4, 2122-6, 2122-11, 2122-12, 2122-13, 2122-14, 2125-1, 2146-1, 2146-2, 2146-3, 2146-4, 2146-7, 2146-8, 2146-10, 2146-14, 2146-17, 2146-18, 2146-19, 2146-20, 2146-21, 2146-22, 2146-26, 2146-27, 2146-28, 2146-31, 2146-32, 2146-33, 2146-34, 2146-35, 2146-41, 2146-43, 2146-44, 2146-48, 2146-50, 2146-51, 2146-53, 2146-56, 2146-57, 2146-58, 2146-59, 2146-60, 2146-62, 2146-63, 2146-64, 2146-65, 2146-66, 2146-67, 2146-68, 2146-71, 2146-73, 2146-74, 2146-75, 2146-77, 2146-79, 2146-80, 2146-81, 2146-82, 2146-83, 2146-84, 2146-85, 2146-86, 2146-88, 2146-89, 2146-96, 2146-97, 2146-99, 2146-101, 2146-102, 2146-103, 2146-104, 2146-105, 2146-106, 2146-108, 2146-110, 2146-111, 2146-112, 2146-113, 2146-115, 2146-116, 2146-118, 2146-120, 2146-122, 2146-124, 2146-126, 2146-127, 2146-128, 2146-129, 2146-130, 2146-131, 2146-132, 2146-133, 2146-135, 2146-136, 2146-138, 2146-139, 2146-141, 2146-142, 2146-144, 2146-146, 2146-147, 2146-148, 2146-152, 2146-158, 2146-159, 2146-160, 2146-161, 2146-162, 2146-167, 2146-168, 2146-172, 2146-176, 2146-178, 2146-180, 2146-181, 2146-182, 2146-186, 2146-187, 2146-193, 2146-195, 2146-200, 2146-212, 2146-214, 2146-215, 2146-218, 2146-219, 2146-225, 2146-226, 2146-231, 2146-233, 2146-236, 2146-237, 2146-238, 2146-241, 2146-243, 2146-245, 2146-247, 2146-249, 2146-253, 2146-254, 2146-255, 2146-256, 2146-258, 2146-259, 2146-262, 2146-266, 2146-267, 2146-271, 2146-272, 2146-273, 2146-277, 2146-279, 2146-281, 2146-282, 2146-283, 2146-284, 2151-4, 2151-5, 2162-1, 2162-2, 2164-1, 2164-3, 2172-4, 2172-5, 2172-8, 2229-1, 2229-9, 2229-13, 2229-18, 2229-22, 2229-23, 2229-25, 2229-26, 2229-29, 2229-30, 2229-31, 2229-33, 2229-38, 2229-39, 2229-40, 2229-41, 2229-42, 2229-43, 2229-49, 2229-57, 2229-60, 2229-62, 2251-1, 2251-2, 2251-6, 2251-7, 2251-9, 2289-1, 2289-3, 2289-5,

2289-8, 2289-10, 2289-11, 2308-5, 2308-7, 2308-9, 2308-10, 2308-11, 2308-12, 2308-13, 2308-14, 2308-15, 2308-17, 2308-19, 2308-20, 2308-21, 2308-22, 2308-24, 2308-30, 2308-32, 2308-34, 2308-35, 2308-36, 2308-41, 2308-42, 2308-43, 2308-44, 2308-45, 2308-46, 2308-47, 2308-48, 2308-49, 2308-50, 2308-51, 2308-52, 2308-53, 2308-54, 2308-55, 2308-56, 2330-1, 2330-3, 2330-4, 2330-14, 2330-15, 2330-20, 2330-30, 2330-31, 2330-47, 2330-48, 2330-54, 2330-55, 2330-56, 2330-60, 2330-61, 2330-62, 2330-63, 2330-65, 2330-66, 2330-73, 2330-76, 2330-77, 2330-78, 2330-83, 2330-85, 2330-86, 2330-87, 2330-88, 2330-89, 2330-90, 2330-91, 2330-92, 2330-93, 2330-94, 2330-95, 2330-96, 2330-97, 2330-98, 2330-99, 2330-100, 2330-101, 2330-126, 2330-131, 2330-143, 2330-147, 2330-148, 2330-149, 2330-150, 2330-151, 2330-158, 2330-162, 2330-163, 2330-164, 2330-165, 2330-166, 2330-167, 2330-177, 2330-178, 2330-179, 2331-1, 2331-12, 2345-5, 2345-7, 2345-9, 2345-11, 2345-15, 2345-27, 2345-29, 2345-30, 2345-35, 2345-39, 2345-44, 2345-45, 2345-48, 2345-52, 2345-53, 2345-56, 2345-57, 2349-1, 2356-1, 2356-2, 2356-5, 2356-7, 2356-8, 2356-9, 2356-15, 2356-20, 2356-21, 2356-22, 2356-26, 2356-27, 2356-35, 2360-2, 2360-7, 2360-8, 2360-38, 2360-40, 2360-42, 2360-59, 2360-62, 2360-65, 2360-66, 2360-69, 2360-72, 2360-78, 2360-79, 2360-80, 2360-81, 2360-84, 2360-90, 2360-99, 2360-110, 2360-111, 2360-112, 2360-113, 2360-118, 2360-120, 2360-121, 2360-122, 2378-1, 2378-8, 2378-10, 2378-17, 2378-21, 2378-23, 2378-29, 2378-34, 2378-40, 2392-2, 2392-3, 2392-5, 2392-10, 2392-12, 2392-16, 2416-1, 2416-9, 2416-12, 2416-18, 2416-19, 2416-21, 2427-1, 2427-3, 2445-1, 2445-13, 2445-14, 2445-17, 2449-8, 2460-1, 2460-3, 2460-7, 2460-20, 2460-26, 2460-29, 2460-30, 2460-31, 2460-33, 2460-34, 2460-35, 2460-40, 2460-42, 2460-43, 2460-47, 2460-50, 2460-58, 2460-60, 2460-65, 2460-68, 2460-71, 2481-1, 2481-3, 2481-5, 2481-6, 2481-7, 2481-9, 2481-10, 2481-13, 2481-18, 2481-19, 2481-20, 2481-21, 2481-23, 2481-26, 2481-28, 2481-29, 2481-30, 2481-31, 2481-32, 2509-4, 2554-3, 2554-7, 2554-8, 2554-9, 2554-13, 2554-18, 2554-19, 2554-20, 2554-22, 2554-24, 2554-30, 2554-33, 2554-35, 2554-37, 2554-43, 2554-44, 2561-1, 2561-7, 2578-3, 2578-5, 2578-6, 2578-8, 2582-8, 2582-13, 2582-14, 2582-22, 2582-23, 2582-27, 2582-29, 2582-40, 2582-43, 2582-44, 2582-47, 2582-48, 2582-51, 2582-52, 2582-53, 2582-55, 2595-6, 2617-3, 2617-5, 2618-7, 2618-12, 2618-13, 2618-19, 2618-22, 2618-26, 2619-25, 2650-2, 2650-16, 2650-18, 2650-19, 2650-20, 2650-22, 2650-28, 2650-29, 2650-35, 2650-38, 2650-41, 2650-43, 2650-44, 2650-45, 2650-54, 2650-56, 2650-57, 2650-60, 2650-61, 2650-64, 2650-66, 2722-5, 2776-2, 2776-3, 2776-7, 2776-11, 2794-2, 2794-3, 2794-10, 2794-11, 2794-13, 2794-15, 2794-23, 2794-24, 2794-28, 2794-33, 2794-37, 2794-40, 2799-1, 2829-2, 2829-9, 2829-10, 2829-11, 2829-12, 2831-3, 2831-5, 2852-4, 2852-7, 2852-13, 2852-14, 2852-17, 2852-22, 2852-23, 2852-28, 2852-30, 2853-1, 2853-3, 2853-7, 2853-15, 2853-23, 2853-27, 2854-4, 2854-5, 2856-1, 2856-3, 2865-4, 2865-5, 2865-6, 2865-7, 2865-10, 2865-11, 2865-12, 2865-16, 2865-20, 2865-21, 2886-3, 2886-4, 2886-5, 2886-9, 2886-12, 2886-16, 2886-17, 2886-20, 2886-21, 2886-22, 2886-24, 2886-26, 2893-3, 2895-1, 2895-4, 2895-5, 2895-9, 2895-12, 2895-14, 2895-15, 2895-17, 2895-19, 2895-20, 2895-24, 2895-30, 2895-38, 2895-39, 2895-40, 2895-46, 2895-52, 2898-1, 2898-2, 2898-10, 2898-11, 2898-13, 2898-15, 2898-19, 2898-28, 2898-30, 2932-4, 2932-5, 2953-3, 2957-1, 2984-1, 3008-1, 3010-2, 3013-1, 3013-2, 3025-2, 3025-3, 3025-13, 3025-17, 3025-20, 3038-1, 3038-2, 3061-2, 3061-3, 3061-16, 3061-17, 3075-1, 3075-17, 3075-19, 3075-23, 3075-30, 3075-37,

182-129, 182-130, 182-132, 182-134, 182-135,
182-136, 182-138, 182-142, 182-143, 182-146,
182-147, 182-148, 182-149, 182-150, 182-152,
182-153, 182-154, 182-155, 182-156, 182-158,
182-161, 182-169, 182-170, 182-171, 182-172,
182-173, 182-174, 182-175, 182-176, 182-177,
182-178, 182-179, 182-183, 182-184, 182-185,
182-186, 182-187, 182-188, 182-189, 182-191,
182-192, 182-193, 182-194, 182-195, 182-196,
182-197, 182-199, 182-200, 182-201, 182-202,
182-205, 182-206, 182-208, 182-209, 182-210,
182-211, 182-212, 182-213, 182-215, 182-216,
182-217, 182-219, 182-220, 182-224, 182-225,
209-6, 209-12, 209-15, 221-2, 221-21, 221-131,
221-137, 221-145, 238-3, 238-7, 238-8, 238-30,
238-42, 238-43, 238-44, 238-48, 238-49, 238-52,
238-53, 238-54, 238-72, 238-87, 238-88, 238-90,
238-91, 238-102, 241-50, 241-79, 247-2, 247-3,
247-4, 292-31, 314-15, 329-3, 329-63, 329-74,
329-80, 329-92, 329-97, 329-107, 329-108,
329-111, 329-135, 329-136, 329-137, 329-138,
329-167, 329-168, 329-188, 367-2, 367-10,
367-22, 367-39, 367-40, 367-41, 367-61, 367-68,
367-110, 558-52, 567-2, 567-4, 567-7, 567-9,
575-37, 658-10, 658-19, 658-20, 658-31, 661-3,
684-11, 684-27, 684-51, 695-32, 698-6, 698-25,
702-21, 702-31, 703-1, 703-2, 703-5, 703-9,
703-11, 703-13, 703-15, 703-17, 703-20, 703-23,
703-25, 703-26, 703-28, 773-8, 821-26, 837-5,
837-17, 837-18, 884-1, 884-2, 884-3, 884-6,
884-20, 884-24, 884-26, 884-30, 884-52, 884-53,
884-56, 884-68, 884-72, 884-76, 884-77, 884-78,
884-80, 884-87, 884-89, 884-91, 884-97, 884-101,
884-102, 884-111, 884-121, 884-122, 884-123,
884-127, 884-131, 884-133, 884-139, 884-145,
884-148, 884-157, 884-172, 884-175, 884-177,
884-197, 884-205, 884-211, 884-213, 884-214,
884-220, 884-228, 884-233, 884-234, 884-238,
884-240, 884-254, 884-264, 884-274, 884-275,
884-278, 884-288, 884-289, 884-294, 884-297,
884-302, 884-306, 884-309, 884-316, 884-340,
884-341, 884-343, 884-357, 884-359, 884-366,
884-368, 884-370, 884-374, 884-379, 884-380,
991-11, 1023-2, 1023-4, 1023-7, 1023-10,
1023-12, 1023-13, 1023-15, 1023-18, 1023-20,
1023-21, 1023-27, 1023-28, 1023-29, 1023-30,
1023-33, 1023-35, 1023-38, 1023-41, 1039-4,
1039-6, 1039-11, 1039-20, 1039-22, 1039-28,
1039-39, 1039-42, 1039-49, 1076-17, 1184-11,
1268-1, 1268-9, 1355-4, 1449-9, 1449-14,
1449-18, 1449-22, 1449-37, 1449-48, 1449-50,
1449-53, 1449-65, 1449-66, 1449-67, 1449-70,
1450-4, 1450-9, 1450-16, 1450-18, 1450-19,
1450-22, 1450-35, 1450-39, 1450-54, 1450-55,
1450-57, 1450-67, 1450-70, 1450-76, 1450-83,
1479-3, 1479-5, 1479-28, 1479-30, 1580-40,
1580-41, 1599-17, 1619-5, 1619-7, 1619-20,
1619-21, 1619-23, 1619-25, 1619-28, 1619-30,
1619-32, 1619-33, 1619-39, 1619-49, 1619-55,
1619-59, 1619-63, 1619-66, 1619-68, 1619-70,
1619-72, 1619-76, 1619-77, 1619-78, 1619-80,
1619-81, 1619-82, 1619-83, 1619-84, 1619-85,
1619-88, 1619-92, 1619-94, 1619-95, 1619-96,
1619-97, 1619-99, 1619-100, 1619-107, 1619-110,
1619-111, 1665-4, 1665-8, 1695-12, 1695-18,
1695-27, 1695-37, 1695-43, 1695-44, 1695-59,
1862-10, 1862-47, 1889-58, 1898-11, 1971-1,
1971-12, 1988-10, 1988-14, 1988-36, 1988-38,
1988-39, 1988-41, 2020-5, 2020-20, 2038-18,
2038-26, 2038-48, 2038-62, 2058-1, 2058-3,
2058-9, 2058-10, 2058-14, 2069-25, 2080-1,
2080-2, 2080-4, 2080-5, 2080-6, 2080-7, 2102-3,
2102-4, 2102-5, 2102-33, 2102-35, 2102-37,
2102-39, 2118-15, 2146-15, 2146-21, 2146-40,
2146-43, 2146-45, 2146-95, 2146-96, 2146-97,
2146-100, 2146-114, 2146-121, 2146-134,
2146-147, 2146-150, 2146-155, 2146-157,
2146-160, 2146-181, 2146-209, 2146-228,
2146-232, 2146-251, 2146-271, 2229-3, 2229-4,
2229-19, 2229-51, 2289-6, 2289-11, 2330-27,
2330-38, 2330-46, 2330-50, 2330-72, 2330-115,
2330-129, 2345-44, 2356-13, 2356-19, 2360-47,
2360-118, 2360-120, 2360-121, 2378-11, 2416-4,

2416-10, 2416-11, 2416-25, 2460-6, 2460-17,
2460-34, 2460-51, 2460-52, 2460-64, 2460-65,
2460-67, 2460-70, 2481-6, 2481-7, 2481-8,
2481-14, 2481-23, 2481-29, 2481-34, 2481-35,
2582-15, 2582-29, 2582-39, 2618-18, 2650-5,
2650-21, 2650-24, 2650-26, 2650-39, 2650-50,
2650-53, 2650-59, 2776-2, 2794-1, 2794-26,
2852-9, 2853-16, 2854-2, 2893-5, 2893-8, 2895-2,
2895-5, 2895-8, 2895-10, 2895-11, 2895-35,
2895-38, 2895-43, 2895-45, 2895-46, 2895-50,
2895-52, 2898-9, 2898-10, 2898-12, 2898-13,
2898-27, 2898-28, 2898-29, 2898-31, 3075-2,
3075-6, 3075-16, 3075-17, 3075-20, 3075-23,
3075-27, 3075-28, 3075-29, 3075-32, 3075-35,
3075-40, 3075-51, 3075-56, 3128-2, 3155-17,
3300-16, 3323-6, 3323-7, 3323-10, 3323-11,
3323-17, 3323-24, 3323-33, 3323-34, 3323-36,
3323-40, 3323-41, 3323-42, 3323-43, 3323-48,
3323-49, 3323-52, 3323-55, 3323-60, 3323-66,
3323-67, 3323-72, 3323-80, 3323-83, 3323-84,
3323-86, 3323-90, 3323-91, 3323-92, 3323-97,
3323-103, 3323-121, 3323-138, 3323-145,
3323-156, 3323-157, 3379-5, 3379-6, 3379-27,
3381-6, 3381-7, 3396-5, 3396-16, 3398-8,
3398-20, 3398-21, 3398-25, 3398-51, 3398-52,
3398-63, 3398-64, 3398-69, 3398-71, 3398-109
Environment, publication   138-5, 182-28, 182-50,
182-65, 182-75, 182-128, 182-185, 182-211,
193-50, 221-153, 238-19, 241-99, 329-104,
365-23, 365-24, 365-45, 884-34, 884-381,
1023-20, 1023-32, 1268-1, 1268-6, 1450-37,
1988-14, 2058-1, 2080-5, 2080-6, 2146-36,
2146-66, 2146-100, 2146-198, 2146-251,
2146-264, 2229-38, 2229-39, 2331-13, 2360-114,
2650-61, 2895-38, 2898-10, 2898-34
Environment, radiation control   147-31, 147-46,
227-3, 558-44, 884-10, 884-90, 884-149, 884-191,
884-243, 884-317, 884-353, 1450-4, 1450-5,
1450-6, 1450-14, 1450-15, 1450-24, 1450-25,
1450-31, 1450-34, 1450-35, 1450-41, 1450-50,
1450-53, 1450-73, 1450-79, 1450-92, 1985-5,
1985-13, 1985-14, 2330-145, 2345-15, 2345-19,
2345-34, 2378-26, 2481-16, 2650-52, 2852-27,
3323-62
Environment, radiation control, children/youth
1985-5, 2345-19
Environment, radiation control, computer
systems/equipment   1450-4, 1450-6
Environment, radiation control, conferences/seminars
1450-4, 1450-35
Environment, radiation control, economically
disadvantaged   2345-15
Environment, radiation control, electronic media/online
services   1450-24
Environment, radiation control, equipment   1450-6
Environment, radiation control, management
development   1450-4, 1450-24
Environment, radiation control, Native
Americans/American Indians   884-353, 1985-5,
1985-13, 1985-14, 2345-15
Environment, radiation control, research   884-90,
1450-50, 1450-92
Environment, recycling   138-10, 147-17, 191-3,
191-9, 221-65, 221-85, 221-86, 292-42, 329-25,
329-135, 335-74, 367-72, 367-85, 367-99, 552-7,
558-12, 684-25, 698-14, 739-6, 884-79, 884-97,
884-112, 884-140, 884-142, 884-165, 884-166,
884-178, 884-271, 884-329, 1265-1, 1449-14,
1449-26, 1580-1, 1666-4, 1862-18, 1988-66,
2020-28, 2058-6, 2069-26, 2080-4, 2146-37,
2308-8, 2345-38, 2360-30, 2360-47, 2460-12,
2776-3, 2776-15, 2953-13, 3155-10, 3379-15,
3396-11
Environment, reform   182-29, 221-106, 221-137,
661-3, 661-11, 884-145, 884-179, 884-203,
884-343, 1023-30, 1023-35, 1619-77, 1619-78,
2080-2, 2102-31, 2330-115, 2330-154, 2460-14,
3323-91, 3323-109
Environment, research   147-12, 147-27, 147-73,
147-120, 182-1, 182-3, 182-7, 182-11, 182-11,
182-12, 182-14, 182-15, 182-16, 182-26, 182-28,
182-30, 182-38, 182-41, 182-43, 182-47, 182-52,
182-56, 182-57, 182-58, 182-59, 182-62, 182-63,

182-65, 182-66, 182-67, 182-68, 182-69, 182-70,
182-72, 182-73, 182-75, 182-79, 182-84, 182-88,
182-91, 182-96, 182-107, 182-108, 182-111,
182-112, 182-113, 182-128, 182-142, 182-148,
182-152, 182-154, 182-154, 182-156, 182-158,
182-171, 182-176, 182-184, 182-185, 182-189,
182-192, 182-198, 182-206, 182-209, 182-210,
182-213, 182-213, 182-218, 182-220, 182-223,
182-223, 193-56, 221-49, 238-14, 238-21, 238-21,
238-22, 238-30, 238-36, 238-37, 238-46, 238-47,
238-60, 238-61, 238-62, 238-100, 238-102,
241-50, 241-108, 241-110, 241-124, 247-6,
313-11, 313-17, 314-5, 314-12, 314-15, 329-16,
329-86, 329-110, 329-133, 329-138, 329-147,
329-152, 329-152, 329-167, 329-168, 335-35,
335-36, 335-84, 365-5, 365-26, 365-34, 365-36,
367-1, 367-2, 367-11, 367-15, 367-40, 367-41,
367-68, 367-77, 367-86, 367-88, 367-101,
367-116, 552-9, 557-6, 558-43, 558-57, 567-14,
575-46, 627-1, 658-2, 663-18, 684-30, 684-39,
684-51, 695-13, 695-25, 695-26, 698-25, 698-34,
698-35, 702-8, 703-27, 703-29, 782-1, 821-44,
837-12, 884-3, 884-20, 884-31, 884-34, 884-56,
884-90, 884-104, 884-131, 884-133, 884-150,
884-183, 884-230, 884-237, 884-240, 884-277,
884-297, 884-305, 884-313, 884-316, 884-318,
884-318, 884-322, 884-337, 884-337, 884-345,
884-355, 884-366, 884-373, 884-374, 884-375,
884-378, 884-381, 892-3, 935-30, 1023-7, 1023-7,
1023-14, 1023-15, 1023-23, 1023-23, 1023-31,
1023-32, 1023-38, 1023-44, 1039-3, 1039-11,
1039-21, 1039-25, 1039-30, 1039-41, 1039-42,
1039-48, 1039-58, 1065-1, 1065-12, 1065-13,
1065-20, 1184-7, 1268-4, 1355-26, 1429-1,
1449-6, 1449-14, 1449-30, 1449-30, 1449-41,
1449-41, 1449-53, 1449-71, 1450-40, 1450-50,
1460-9, 1460-10, 1468-12, 1479-11, 1479-42,
1580-24, 1580-49, 1582-3, 1582-3, 1599-3,
1599-51, 1619-20, 1619-21, 1619-25, 1619-30,
1619-66, 1619-68, 1619-74, 1619-77, 1619-78,
1619-83, 1619-84, 1619-94, 1619-95, 1619-99,
1619-99, 1665-1, 1761-3, 1778-4, 1862-10,
1862-29, 1862-35, 1862-36, 1862-47, 1862-50,
1862-76, 1971-12, 1995-13, 1995-14, 2038-8,
2038-12, 2038-24, 2038-26, 2038-29, 2038-42,
2038-62, 2038-78, 2058-1, 2058-3, 2058-10,
2058-10, 2069-35, 2080-1, 2080-2, 2080-5,
2118-6, 2118-7, 2118-8, 2146-23, 2146-33,
2146-40, 2146-51, 2146-72, 2146-74, 2146-75,
2146-95, 2146-100, 2146-104, 2146-110,
2146-114, 2146-121, 2146-129, 2146-134,
2146-147, 2146-153, 2146-160, 2146-185,
2146-222, 2146-228, 2146-248, 2146-251,
2146-252, 2146-271, 2146-271, 2146-275,
2146-276, 2162-5, 2172-6, 2229-4, 2229-19,
2229-28, 2289-1, 2289-2, 2289-3, 2289-8,
2289-10, 2289-11, 2308-7, 2308-7, 2308-9,
2308-9, 2308-10, 2308-10, 2308-14, 2308-14,
2308-15, 2308-18, 2308-19, 2308-20, 2308-21,
2308-22, 2308-24, 2308-31, 2308-32, 2308-32,
2308-34, 2308-35, 2308-35, 2308-42, 2308-42,
2308-43, 2308-43, 2308-44, 2308-44, 2308-45,
2308-45, 2308-46, 2308-46, 2308-47, 2308-47,
2308-48, 2308-48, 2308-49, 2308-49, 2308-50,
2308-50, 2308-51, 2308-51, 2308-52, 2308-52,
2308-53, 2308-53, 2308-54, 2308-54, 2308-55,
2308-55, 2308-56, 2308-56, 2330-16, 2330-21,
2330-32, 2330-39, 2330-74, 2330-118, 2330-129,
2330-129, 2330-176, 2356-7, 2356-18, 2356-28,
2356-29, 2360-77, 2360-105, 2360-114, 2360-122,
2378-5, 2445-5, 2445-6, 2445-9, 2445-10,
2460-14, 2460-18, 2460-48, 2460-57, 2481-1,
2481-4, 2481-6, 2481-8, 2481-10, 2481-14,
2481-17, 2481-23, 2481-24, 2481-34, 2481-35,
2481-35, 2582-15, 2618-9, 2618-10, 2618-11,
2619-32, 2650-8, 2650-24, 2650-35, 2650-59,
2794-1, 2794-2, 2831-1, 2852-25, 2853-19,
2865-18, 2893-9, 2893-10, 2895-2, 2895-5,
2895-5, 2895-10, 2895-24, 2895-35, 2895-49,
2895-50, 2895-51, 2898-10, 2898-28, 2898-29,
2898-33, 2898-34, 3061-6, 3075-7, 3075-13,
3075-14, 3075-17, 3075-20, 3075-23, 3075-28,
3075-29, 3075-32, 3075-40, 3075-56, 3075-60,

300-5, 300-6, 313-11, 313-12, 313-16, 313-20,
314-7, 314-10, 329-1, 329-3, 329-5, 329-6, 329-9,
329-12, 329-13, 329-14, 329-20, 329-32, 329-33,
329-34, 329-37, 329-45, 329-48, 329-54, 329-58,
329-60, 329-68, 329-73, 329-77, 329-83, 329-85,
329-87, 329-88, 329-89, 329-90, 329-92, 329-93,
329-96, 329-100, 329-102, 329-103, 329-104,
329-105, 329-106, 329-107, 329-109, 329-110,
329-112, 329-113, 329-116, 329-118, 329-121,
329-123, 329-124, 329-136, 329-144, 329-146,
329-148, 329-149, 329-150, 329-151, 329-152,
329-162, 329-167, 329-168, 329-169, 329-170,
329-173, 329-175, 329-181, 329-185, 329-187,
329-189, 329-190, 329-192, 329-193, 329-194,
329-195, 329-196, 329-199, 329-201, 329-204,
329-205, 329-206, 329-207, 329-211, 329-212,
329-213, 335-2, 335-23, 335-40, 335-43, 365-2,
365-15, 365-19, 365-20, 365-21, 365-22, 365-26,
367-2, 367-9, 367-10, 367-11, 367-12, 367-19,
367-27, 367-40, 367-41, 367-51, 367-59, 367-63,
367-64, 367-69, 367-71, 367-84, 367-86, 367-88,
367-92, 367-93, 367-98, 367-99, 367-105, 370-5,
370-1, 441-2, 441-23, 478-14, 478-20, 484-6,
484-10, 542-47, 552-4, 552-6, 552-10, 557-1,
557-6, 558-1, 558-2, 558-8, 558-15, 558-17,
558-22, 558-38, 558-42, 575-7, 575-13, 602-6,
621-3, 621-10, 623-3, 638-3, 638-5, 658-37,
661-2, 661-3, 661-9, 661-16, 661-17, 661-18,
661-19, 661-20, 661-24, 663-1, 663-2, 663-8,
684-2, 684-14, 684-33, 684-35, 684-36, 684-38,
684-41, 684-43, 684-47, 684-52, 695-4, 695-50,
698-2, 698-17, 698-20, 702-3, 702-6, 702-47,
709-1, 709-3, 773-1, 773-6, 773-19, 773-23,
821-37, 821-51, 837-6, 837-11, 884-3, 884-6,
884-11, 884-12, 884-14, 884-23, 884-24, 884-25,
884-26, 884-28, 884-29, 884-31, 884-32, 884-33,
884-34, 884-38, 884-39, 884-41, 884-50, 884-51,
884-64, 884-66, 884-67, 884-68, 884-70, 884-74,
884-75, 884-77, 884-81, 884-82, 884-98, 884-100,
884-104, 884-108, 884-110, 884-134, 884-137,
884-141, 884-146, 884-148, 884-151, 884-158,
884-160, 884-173, 884-186, 884-189, 884-192,
884-200, 884-207, 884-215, 884-226, 884-233,
884-235, 884-238, 884-242, 884-244, 884-249,
884-259, 884-260, 884-270, 884-272, 884-279,
884-281, 884-282, 884-285, 884-286, 884-301,
884-307, 884-316, 884-318, 884-320, 884-332,
884-333, 884-335, 884-336, 884-338, 884-347,
884-348, 884-349, 884-354, 884-355, 884-358,
884-361, 884-363, 884-369, 926-10, 962-1, 962-2,
991-12, 991-18, 1023-3, 1023-8, 1023-15,
1023-23, 1023-25, 1023-28, 1023-29, 1023-30,
1023-32, 1039-23, 1039-43, 1039-55, 1047-3,
1065-10, 1065-15, 1065-17, 1065-18, 1076-19,
1076-37, 1076-38, 1076-45, 1076-46, 1088-4,
1152-6, 1152-9, 1265-7, 1268-5, 1355-7, 1355-8,
1355-13, 1355-25, 1355-42, 1355-43, 1449-7,
1449-34, 1449-46, 1449-47, 1449-56, 1468-9,
1468-10, 1479-25, 1548-1, 1548-23, 1564-2,
1564-3, 1580-12, 1580-23, 1580-34, 1580-35,
1580-43, 1582-2, 1582-3, 1582-15, 1582-20,
1599-42, 1606-12, 1619-3, 1619-7, 1619-12,
1619-23, 1619-25, 1619-33, 1619-51, 1619-52,
1619-64, 1619-67, 1619-68, 1619-69, 1619-70,
1619-74, 1619-76, 1619-77, 1619-78, 1619-80,
1619-81, 1619-82, 1619-83, 1619-84, 1619-85,
1619-88, 1619-91, 1619-92, 1619-97, 1619-98,
1619-99, 1619-106, 1619-107, 1619-111, 1647-1,
1647-2, 1647-3, 1647-11, 1653-2, 1653-4, 1665-1,
1665-2, 1666-1, 1666-3, 1666-7, 1695-3, 1695-4,
1695-5, 1695-6, 1695-7, 1695-12, 1695-13,
1695-14, 1695-17, 1695-20, 1695-22, 1695-26,
1695-27, 1695-29, 1695-32, 1695-33, 1695-35,
1695-36, 1695-45, 1695-46, 1695-47, 1695-48,
1695-50, 1695-51, 1695-54, 1695-55, 1695-58,
1695-60, 1695-61, 1695-63, 1695-64, 1695-66,
1695-67, 1695-68, 1695-69, 1695-70, 1773-2,
1773-3, 1862-15, 1862-19, 1862-25, 1862-33,
1862-34, 1862-35, 1862-36, 1862-40, 1862-43,
1862-44, 1862-46, 1862-49, 1862-50, 1862-52,
1862-53, 1862-54, 1862-73, 1862-76, 1862-77,
1889-13, 1889-20, 1889-32, 1889-34, 1889-59,
1889-63, 1889-74, 1889-87, 1889-88, 1889-90,

1898-6, 1898-8, 1898-13, 1898-14, 1924-2,
1924-11, 1924-25, 1952-2, 1971-5, 1971-6,
1971-8, 1971-13, 1971-16, 1971-19, 1985-17,
1988-13, 1988-14, 1988-17, 1988-21, 1988-33,
1988-41, 1988-48, 1988-58, 1988-59, 1988-62,
1989-1, 1989-2, 1995-16, 2038-3, 2038-6,
2038-16, 2038-55, 2038-60, 2038-64, 2038-78,
2058-1, 2058-10, 2069-3, 2069-6, 2069-9,
2069-14, 2069-15, 2069-21, 2069-23, 2069-27,
2080-7, 2081-4, 2125-2, 2146-70, 2146-105,
2146-140, 2146-149, 2146-175, 2146-179,
2146-220, 2146-229, 2146-242, 2146-270, 2229-5,
2229-6, 2229-7, 2229-14, 2229-36, 2229-53,
2229-58, 2229-59, 2229-61, 2251-4, 2289-2,
2289-4, 2289-7, 2330-5, 2330-6, 2330-53,
2330-69, 2330-120, 2330-129, 2330-130, 2345-6,
2345-13, 2356-34, 2360-26, 2360-27, 2360-34,
2360-35, 2360-36, 2360-48, 2360-51, 2360-67,
2360-75, 2360-80, 2360-81, 2360-82, 2378-5,
2378-11, 2378-19, 2378-30, 2392-13, 2392-14,
2416-17, 2445-5, 2445-6, 2449-5, 2449-14,
2460-2, 2460-38, 2460-44, 2460-55, 2460-56,
2460-59, 2481-2, 2481-4, 2481-17, 2554-21,
2554-31, 2554-45, 2561-6, 2561-10, 2582-6,
2582-15, 2582-21, 2582-24, 2582-25, 2582-26,
2582-31, 2582-35, 2582-44, 2582-49, 2582-56,
2595-1, 2618-36, 2619-34, 2650-6, 2650-7,
2650-27, 2650-34, 2650-40, 2650-46, 2650-50,
2650-51, 2650-62, 2679-1, 2776-5, 2776-8,
2776-13, 2776-14, 2794-7, 2794-32, 2794-36,
2799-3, 2829-1, 2829-4, 2852-11, 2852-32,
2853-8, 2853-9, 2853-11, 2853-17, 2853-18,
2853-25, 2865-13, 2886-4, 2886-10, 2886-12,
2886-13, 2886-18, 2886-19, 2893-9, 2893-10,
2895-2, 2895-3, 2895-4, 2895-8, 2895-11,
2895-13, 2895-21, 2895-22, 2895-23, 2895-31,
2895-32, 2895-36, 2895-37, 2895-40, 2895-44,
2895-45, 2895-48, 2895-49, 2895-50, 2895-53,
2898-7, 2898-12, 2898-20, 2898-23, 2898-27,
2953-16, 3010-1, 3025-12, 3061-9, 3075-10,
3075-20, 3075-25, 3075-36, 3075-38, 3075-39,
3098-4, 3098-5, 3098-7, 3098-14, 3098-19,
3098-21, 3098-22, 3098-28, 3098-29, 3126-12,
3126-15, 3126-16, 3128-2, 3146-1, 3155-3,
3155-8, 3187-2, 3202-3, 3283-1, 3300-1, 3300-3,
3300-4, 3300-5, 3300-17, 3323-8, 3323-9,
3323-11, 3323-17, 3323-22, 3323-23, 3323-24,
3323-29, 3323-31, 3323-33, 3323-37, 3323-40,
3323-50, 3323-56, 3323-65, 3323-66, 3323-83,
3323-89, 3323-103, 3323-106, 3323-110,
3323-111, 3323-112, 3323-114, 3323-115,
3323-119, 3323-120, 3323-121, 3323-123,
3323-124, 3323-125, 3323-127, 3323-130,
3323-136, 3323-139, 3323-145, 3323-149,
3323-154, 3323-155, 3323-158, 3357-2, 3362-1,
3362-2, 3362-3, 3362-4, 3362-5, 3362-6, 3362-7,
3362-8, 3362-9, 3362-10, 3362-11, 3379-4,
3379-5, 3379-7, 3379-8, 3379-21, 3379-28,
3381-6, 3381-7, 3381-14, 3381-31, 3381-38,
3381-39, 3381-52, 3381-53, 3381-54, 3396-18,
3398-7, 3398-107, 3507-2, 3507-7, 3507-8,
3507-9, 3507-16, 3507-22, 3507-23, 3507-27,
3507-28, 3507-29

Environment, water resources, African
  Americans/Blacks 695-50
Environment, water resources,
  awards/prizes/competitions 484-6, 2582-25
Environment, water resources, boys 241-13
Environment, water resources, building/renovation
  313-20, 661-16, 1468-10, 1582-20, 1606-12,
  2125-2, 2953-16, 3146-1, 3187-2
Environment, water resources, capital campaigns
  1076-45, 2893-9, 3357-2
Environment, water resources, children/youth 147-3,
  221-1, 229-1, 367-9, 367-51, 367-84, 884-66,
  1862-43, 1971-6, 1988-17, 1988-48, 2865-13,
  3075-10
Environment, water resources, computer
  systems/equipment 3381-7
Environment, water resources, conferences/seminars
  241-118, 241-129, 329-100, 329-149, 658-37,
  702-47, 1023-8, 1695-33, 2449-5, 2481-2, 2853-25

Environment, water resources, curriculum
  development 229-1, 1862-50, 2289-2, 2865-13,
  3075-10
Environment, water resources, economically
  disadvantaged 367-51, 661-9, 1265-7, 1619-64,
  1619-74, 1695-64, 2146-105, 2146-149, 2146-179,
  2392-13, 3323-50
Environment, water resources, electronic media/online
  services 884-354, 1268-5, 1619-99, 2650-50
Environment, water resources, endowments 370-5,
  1862-33, 1924-2, 2146-229
Environment, water resources, equipment 135-13,
  2794-36, 3075-38
Environment, water resources, exhibitions 884-34,
  1989-2
Environment, water resources, faculty/staff
  development 241-95, 329-68, 1449-46, 1862-36,
  2360-26, 2360-27, 2481-4
Environment, water resources, fellowships 558-17
Environment, water resources, film/video/radio
  147-106, 209-15, 329-13, 661-17, 1988-13,
  1988-17, 2460-38, 2679-1
Environment, water resources, Hispanics/Latinos
  238-73
Environment, water resources, income development
  329-68, 329-146, 329-193, 884-200, 1862-36,
  2449-14, 2895-48, 3323-9, 3323-111, 3323-115
Environment, water resources, land acquisition
  884-108, 884-134, 884-151, 884-200, 884-336,
  1468-9, 1619-23, 2886-10, 2895-21, 2895-23,
  2895-32, 3098-4, 3098-19, 3126-12
Environment, water resources, management
  development 238-53, 329-60, 329-121, 329-146,
  329-162, 329-193, 365-19, 365-20, 365-21,
  367-93, 558-42, 702-47, 1152-9, 1619-98,
  1695-29, 1695-48, 1988-62, 2229-5, 2229-53,
  2392-13, 2582-56, 2618-36, 2650-27, 2776-8,
  2895-44, 2895-48, 2895-53, 3323-114
Environment, water resources, minorities 241-80,
  367-51, 661-9, 1619-64, 2146-105, 2481-2
Environment, water resources, Native
  Americans/American Indians 238-73, 558-42,
  884-286, 884-355, 884-363, 1695-68, 1985-17,
  2146-179, 3323-89, 3323-121
Environment, water resources, program evaluation
  1023-15, 1619-99, 2895-50
Environment, water resources, publication 241-22,
  241-128, 329-104, 558-22, 884-34, 1023-32,
  1268-5, 1619-64, 1988-14, 2058-1, 2360-34,
  2360-35, 2360-36, 2360-51, 2794-32, 3323-110
Environment, water resources, research 147-12,
  147-14, 147-82, 221-94, 238-36, 238-37, 238-46,
  238-47, 241-23, 241-104, 241-108, 241-130,
  313-11, 329-110, 329-152, 329-167, 329-168,
  365-26, 367-2, 367-11, 367-40, 367-41, 367-86,
  367-88, 684-35, 884-3, 884-31, 884-38, 884-81,
  884-104, 884-270, 884-281, 884-316, 884-318,
  884-347, 884-355, 1023-3, 1023-23, 1023-32,
  1039-43, 1039-55, 1548-1, 1582-3, 1599-42,
  1619-25, 1619-64, 1619-68, 1619-74, 1619-77,
  1619-78, 1619-83, 1619-84, 1619-99, 1665-1,
  1862-34, 1862-46, 1862-50, 1862-53, 1862-54,
  1862-76, 2038-78, 2058-1, 2058-10, 2146-105,
  2146-175, 2146-242, 2229-59, 2289-2, 2330-129,
  2378-5, 2481-4, 2481-17, 2895-2, 2895-49,
  2895-50, 2898-23, 3075-20, 3075-39, 3098-14,
  3128-2, 3300-3, 3300-17, 3323-155, 3323-158,
  3379-4, 3398-7, 3507-27
Environment, water resources, scholarship funds
  2449-5, 2650-50
Environment, water resources, seed money 329-113,
  884-286, 884-318, 1582-2, 1971-19, 2460-56,
  3126-16
Environment, water resources, technical assistance
  329-88, 552-6, 1619-70, 1619-76, 1619-82,
  1619-88, 1889-87, 2146-149, 2853-18
Environment, water resources, women 1619-74
Environment, water resources, youth 575-7, 575-13,
  661-9, 884-12, 3323-110
Environment, West Bank/Gaza 221-57
Environment, Western Africa 313-9, 1039-4
Environment, women 221-87, 221-152, 658-38,
  661-11, 703-26, 884-125, 884-131, 884-377,

GRANTMAKER NAME INDEX

Dornette Foundation, Helen G., Henry F. & Louise T., OH, 2633
Dorot Foundation, RI, 2957
Dorothy-Ann Foundation, The, VA, 3247
Dougherty Foundation, TX, 3069
Douglas Charitable Trust, Charles H., NY, 2120
Douglass Family Foundation, IL, 969
Dove Foundation, G. Mack and Nancy R., The, AL, 9
Dove Foundation, The see 9
Dover Foundation, Inc., The, NC, 2553
Dow AgroSciences LLC Corporate Giving Program, IN, 1129
Dow Corning Corporation Contributions Program, MI, 1562
Dow Corning Foundation, MI, 1563
Dow Foundation, Herbert H. and Grace A., The, MI, 1564
Downing Foundation, Barry L. & Paula M., KS, 1192
Downing Foundation, J. C., The, CA, 173
Doyle Charitable Foundation, The, RI, 2958
Doyle Charitable Trust, Mildred & Bernard, IL, 970
Dragas Foundation, George & Grace, The, VA, 3248
Dragon Foundation, Inc., The, MA, 1388
Draper Foundation, The, CA, 174
Drasner Family Foundation, NY, 2121
Dreaming Hand Foundation, VA, 3249
DSN Foundation, The see 863
DTE Energy Foundation, MI, 1565
du Bois Foundation, Inc., E. Blois, AZ, 36
Dub Foundation, Carlton, The, MA, 1389
Duckwall Foundation, Inc., Frank E., FL, 747
Ducommun & Gross Foundation, CA, 175
Dudley Foundation, The, WA, 3332
Duffield Family Foundation, The see 290
Duffy Foundation, The, MI, 1566
Duke Charitable Foundation, Doris, NY, 2122
Dula Educational and Charitable Foundation, Caleb C. and Julia W., MO, 1755
Duluth-Superior Area Community Foundation, MN, 1678
Dumke Foundation, Dr. Ezekiel R. and Edna Wattis, UT, 3193
Dun & Bradstreet Corporation Foundation, The, NJ, 1890
Duncan Trust, John G., CO, 481
Duncan Trust, Louise Head, WI, 3419
Duncan, Jr. Foundation, Anne Duncan & C. W., TX, 3070
Dunn Foundation, Inc., Elizabeth Ordway, FL, 748
Dunn Foundation, The, RI, 2959
Dunoir Fund Trust, The, WY, 3499
DuPage Community Foundation, The, IL, 971
DuPont Corporate Giving Program, DE, 629
Dupont Foundation, Laura E., The, SC, 2987
Dusky Foundation, The, MA, 1390
Dyer-Ives Foundation, MI, 1567

Earle Foundation, Dexter & Carol, NY, 2123
Earth Force, Inc., VA, 3250
Earth Share of Oregon, OR, 2763
Earthjustice Legal Defense Fund, Inc., CA, 176
Earthwatch Expeditions, Inc., MA, 1391
Earthwatch Institute see 1391
Easley Foundation, The see 3251
Easley Trust, Andrew H. & Anne O., VA, 3251
East Bay Community Foundation, The, CA, 177
East Hill Foundation, NY, 2124
East Ohio Gas Company Contributions Program, The see 2632
Eastman Kodak Charitable Trust, NY, 2125
Eastman Kodak Company Contributions Program, NY, 2126
Eaton Foundation, Cyrus, The, OH, 2634
EBR Foundation, IL, 972
EBS Foundation, TN, 3018
Eccles & Homer M. Hayward Foundation, Nancy see 3196
Eccles Charitable Foundation, Willard L., UT, 3194
Echoing Green, NY, 2127
Echoing Green Foundation see 2127
Echols-Johnston Family Foundation, The see 2987

Ecke Poinsettia Foundation, Paul & Magdalena, CA, 178
Eckerd Family Foundation, Inc., FL, 749
Eckert Family Foundation, NJ, 1891
Eco-Logic Development Fund, MA, 1392
Ecolab Foundation, MN, 1679
Ecotrust Foundation, MN, 1680
Ecumenical Project for International Cooperation, Inc., CO, 482
Eden Foods, Inc. Corporate Giving Program, MI, 1568
Eden Hall Foundation, PA, 2831
Ederic Foundation, Inc., DE, 630
Edison International Corporate Giving Program, CA, 179
Edmondson Foundation, Joseph Henry, The, CO, 483
Educational Foundation of America, The, CT, 558
Edwards Mother Earth Foundation, WA, 3333
EIA Research and Education Foundation see 3253
Eisenberg Family Foundation, Mitzi & Warren, NJ, 1892
El Paso Community Foundation, TX, 3071
El Pomar Foundation, CO, 484
Eldorado Foundation, CA, 180
Elfers Foundation, Inc., MA, 1393
Elisha-Bolton Foundation, OH, 2635
Elkins, Jr. Foundation, Margaret & James A., TX, 3072
Ellinger Foundation, Inc., Albert J. & Flora H., WI, 3420
Ellis Foundation, Joseph H. & Barbara I., NY, 2128
Ellsworth Foundation, Lincoln, The, NY, 2129
Elmwood Fund, The, VA, 3252
Employees Community Fund of Boeing-St. Louis, MO, 1756
EMSA Fund, Inc., NY, 2130
Emwiga Foundation, NY, 2131
Enders Charitable Trust, Blanche T., NY, 2132
Endurance Fund, The, CA, 181
Energy Foundation, CA, 182
Engel Foundation, Inc., Robert G. & Jane V., The, NJ, 1893
Engelhard Foundation, Charles, The, NY, 2133
Ensworth Charitable Foundation, The, RI, 2960
Entergy Charitable Foundation, LA, 1232
Entergy Corporation Contributions Program, LA, 1233
Entergy Gulf States, Inc. Corporate Giving Program, TX, 3073
Entomological Foundation, MD, 1295
Environment Now Foundation, CA, 183
Environmental Endowment for New Jersey, Inc., NJ, 1894
Environmental Leadership Program, Inc., MA, 1394
Environmental Research and Education Foundation, VA, 3253
Environmental Support Center, Inc., DC, 666
EPIC see 482
Epstein/Roth Foundation, CA, 184
Eriksen Trust Fund, T. R., CA, 185
Ernst Foundation, Richard C. & Susan B., NY, 2134
Ernsthausen Charitable Foundation, John F. and Doris E., OH, 2636
Erpf Fund, Inc., Armand G., The, NY, 2135
ESB Charitable Trust, MA, 1395
Estes Foundation, Elliott M. & Constance L., AZ, 37
Ettinger Foundation, Inc., The, CT, 559
Eucalyptus Foundation, The, CA, 186
Evans Family Foundation, Inc. see 2136
Evans Foundation, Edward P., VA, 3254
Evans Foundation, Inc., R. S., NY, 2136
Evans Foundation, Richard & Rebecca, NY, 2137
Evanston Community Foundation, IL, 973
Evinrude Foundation, Ole, The see 1067
Evjue Foundation, Inc., The, WI, 3421
Ewing Foundation, William, The, NY, 2138
Excelsior! Foundation, The, IL, 974
Exxon Corporation Contributions Program see 3074
Exxon Mobil Corporation Contributions Program, TX, 3074
ExxonMobil Education Foundation see 3075
ExxonMobil Foundation, TX, 3075

F. & J.S. Fund, Inc., NY, 2139
Fabert Foundation, Martin, The, WA, 3334
Fabiano Foundation, MI, 1569
Fair Play Foundation, DE, 631
Fairbanks Foundation, Inc., Richard M., IN, 1130

Fairbanks Foundation, Inc. see 1130
Fairchild Foundation, I. D. & Marguerite, TX, 3076
Fairfax Foundation, The, OH, 2637
Fairfield County Community Foundation, Inc., CT, 560
Fairview Foundation, MN, 1681
Fairweather Foundation, The, NV, 1843
Falcon Charitable Foundation, The, ME, 1252
Falconwood Foundation, Inc., NY, 2140
Falk Family Trust, Leon, PA, 2832
Fanwood Foundation, NJ, 1895
Farago Foundation Trust, Paul, The, MI, 1570
Farallon Islands Foundation, CA, 187
Farbman Foundation, Burton and Susan see 1571
Farbman Foundation, The, MI, 1571
Farm Aid, MA, 1396
Farm Foundation, IL, 975
Farmor Foundation, DE, 632
Fasenmyer Foundation, Richard J., OH, 2638
Fat Cat Foundation, The, SC, 2988
Faulkner Trust, Marianne G., NY, 2141
Faulkner Trust, Marianne Galliard see 2141
Favrot Fund, Johanna A., The, TX, 3077
Favrot Fund, The, TX, 3078
Fayette County Foundation, IN, 1131
FCCF see 560
Federated Insurance Foundation, Inc., MN, 1682
Federated Investors Foundation, Inc., PA, 2833
Fehsenfeld Charitable Foundation, Frank B. and Virginia V., WA, 3335
Feldman Private Foundation, Inc., Gretchen V. & Samuel M., MD, 1296
Feline Friends, Inc., NJ, 1896
Fergus Foundation, Robert & Elizabeth, CO, 485
Ferguson Foundation, Hugh and Jane, The, WA, 3336
Ferguson Foundation, Leonard C. & Mildred F., OH, 2639
Ferguson Foundation, Inc., NY, 2142
Ferry Family Foundation, The, OH, 2640
Fessenden Charitable Foundation, Elizabeth T., The, MA, 1397
FHL Foundation, Inc. see 1986
Fidelity Bank, PaSB Corporate Giving Program, PA, 2834
Fiduciary Charitable Foundation, MA, 1398
Field Foundation, Jamee and Marshall, IL, 976
Field Foundation of Illinois, Inc., The, IL, 977
Field-Day Foundation, TX, 3079
Fields Foundation Trust see 1132
Fields Pond Foundation, Inc., MA, 1399
Fields Trust Foundation, John Anna & Martha Jane, IN, 1132
Fieldstone Foundation, Inc., MA, 1400
Fikes Foundation, Inc., Leland, TX, 3080
FINA Foundation, TX, 3081
Fine Family Foundation, The, PA, 2835
Fink Foundation, Betsy and Jesse, CT, 561
Finkl Foundation, Inc., C. W., IL, 978
Firedoll Foundation, CA, 188
Firestone Trust Fund, The see 3010
Firman Fund, OH, 2641
First Citizens Foundation, Inc., SC, 2989
First National Bank of Chicago Foundation see 926
First Nations Development Institute, VA, 3255
FirstEnergy Foundation, OH, 2642
FIRSTFED Charitable Foundation, The, MA, 1401
Firth Testamentary Trust, Clara Helen see 189
Firth Trust, Clara Helen, CA, 189
Fischer Foundation, Sonja and F. Conrad, IL, 979
Fischer-Bauer-Knirps Foundation, MO, 1757
FishAmerica Foundation, VA, 3256
Fisher Charitable Foundation, ME, 1253
Fisher Charitable Foundation, Dean L. see 1253
Fitz-Gibbon Charitable Trust, T. David, VA, 3257
Flaherty Family Foundation, The, FL, 750
Flanagan Family Foundation, IL, 980
Flarsheim Charitable Foundation, Louis and Elizabeth Nave, TX, 3082
Fleischer Foundation, M. H., The see 38
Fleischer Foundation, The, AZ, 38
Fleischmann Foundation, The, OH, 2643
Fleming Family Foundation, IA, 1168
Fleming Family Foundation, The, MA, 1402
Fleming Foundation, PA, 2836

Flemm Foundation, Inc., John J., NY, 2143
Flinn, Jr. Charitable Trust, Lawrence, The, CT, 562
Flint Foundation, Mary G. & Robert H., MI, 1572
Flintridge Foundation, CA, 190
Flora Family Foundation, CA, 191
Floriculture Industry Research and Scholarship Trust, MI, 1573
Florida Power & Light Company Contributions Program, FL, 751
Fludzinski Foundation, NY, 2144
FM Global Foundation, RI, 2961
FMC Foundation, PA, 2837
FNZ Foundation, Inc., PR, 2948
Foley & M. H. Frischkorn Wildlife & Conservation Fund I, L. H., MI, 1574
Foley & M. H. Frischkorn Wildlife & Conservation Fund II, L. H., MI, 1575
Follett Foundation, Inc., Roger W., The, NY, 2145
Foothills Foundation, The, CA, 192
Forbesway Foundation see 2891
Force for Good Foundation, The, UT, 3195
Ford Foundation, William & Lisa, MI, 1576
Ford Foundation, The, NY, 2146
Ford Fund, William and Martha, MI, 1577
Ford II Fund, Edsel B., MI, 1578
Ford Motor Company Contributions Program, MI, 1579
Ford Motor Company Fund, MI, 1580
Fore River Foundation, ME, 1254
Foreman Family Foundation, Peter and Virginia, IL, 981
Foreman Foundation, Peter and Virginia see 981
Forest Foundation, WA, 3337
Fortis Foundation, NY, 2147
Fortunoff Foundation, Max & Clara, NY, 2148
Foster Family Foundation, The, OH, 2644
Foster Foundation, John H., The, PA, 2838
Foster-Davis Foundation, Inc., CT, 563
Foster-Karney Trust Fund, NJ, 1897
Foulds Foundation, Claiborne and Ned see 752
Foulds Foundation Trust, Claiborne F., FL, 752
Foundation Carinoso, AZ, 39
Foundation for Agronomic Research, Inc., GA, 831
Foundation for Animal Information & Pet Services, Inc. see 1333
Foundation for Deep Ecology, CA, 193
Foundation for Sustainability and Innovation, The, CA, 194
Foundation for the Carolinas, NC, 2554
Foundation for the National Capital Region, The see 663
Foundation M, MA, 1403
Founders Charitable Foundation, Inc., AL, 10
Four Cedars Foundation, Inc., TX, 3083
Four County Community Foundation, MI, 1581
Four County Foundation see 1581
Four Daughters Foundation, DE, 633
Four-Four Foundation, Inc., The, WI, 3422
Fowlston Charitable Trust, C. J. & Syble, TX, 3084
Fox Foundation, John H. see 195
Fox Foundation, Samuel I. & John Henry, CA, 195
FPL Foundation, Inc. see 753
FPL Group Foundation, Inc., FL, 753
Fralin Charitable Trust, Horace G., The, VA, 3258
France-Merrick Foundation, MD, 1297
Frank Family Foundation, Inc., The, GA, 832
Frank Fund, Mrs. Zollie S., IL, 982
Frank Fund, Zollie and Elaine see 982
Frankel Foundation, Evan, NY, 2149
Frankel Foundation, The, CA, 196
Frankenberg Foundation, Regina Bauer, The see 2150
Frankenberg Foundation, Regina, The, NY, 2150
Frazier Family Foundation, Inc., Owsley Brown, KY, 1213
Free Family Foundation Corp., FL, 754
Freeberg Foundation, Don and Lorraine, The, CA, 197
Freeman Foundation, Ella West, The, LA, 1234
Freeman Foundation, The, NY, 2151
French Foundation, The, PA, 2839
Fresno Regional Foundation, CA, 198
Freund Memorial Foundation, Harry & Flora D., The, MO, 1758
Frey Foundation, MI, 1582
Frick Trust, Doris Ellen, RI, 2962
Friedkin Conservation Fund, TX, 3085

Friedlander Family Fund, OH, 2645
Friedman-French Foundation, Inc., DC, 667
Friends of the Louisville Zoo, Inc., KY, 1214
Friendship Fund, Inc., PA, 2840
Fries-Tait Foundation, WA, 3338
Friesen Foundation, Gilbert B., CA, 199
Frill Foundation, The, TX, 3086
Froehlich Foundation, Helen V., IL, 983
Front Family Charitable Foundation, Marshall B., IL, 984
Frost Foundation, Ltd., The, NM, 1981
FSB Foundation, Inc., CT, 564
Fuchs Charitable Foundation, Michael, NY, 2152
Fuji Photo Film U.S.A., Inc. Corporate Giving Program, NY, 2153
Fuller Company Contributions Program, H. B., MN, 1683
Fuller Foundation, George F. and Sybil H., MA, 1404
Fuller Foundation, Inc., The, NH, 1858
Fullerton Family Charitable Trust, The, CA, 200
Fund for Animals, Inc., The, NY, 2154
Fund for Innovation and Public Service, VA, 3259
Fund for New Jersey, The, NJ, 1898
Fund for Santa Barbara, Inc., CA, 201
Fund for Southern Communities, GA, 833
Fund for the City of New York, Inc., NY, 2155
Funding Exchange, Inc., NY, 2156
Furrow Foundation, Virginia Sugg, AZ, 40

G.A.G. Charitable Corporation, CA, 202
G.D.S. Legacy Foundation, Inc., VT, 3213
G.R.M. Foundation, Inc. see 2395
G.T.R. & B. Charitable Foundation, CA, 203
Gaea Foundation, Inc., The, DC, 668
Gaea Foundation, The, MO, 1759
Gaia Fund, CA, 204
Gaines Foundation, Courtney Knight, GA, 834
Gainesville Community Foundation see 864
Gale Foundation, Bulova, The, NJ, 1899
Gale Foundation, The, OH, 2646
Galkin Charitable Trust, Ira S. and Anna, RI, 2963
Ganlee Fund, The, NY, 2157
Gannett Communities Fund/Gannett Co., Inc. see 3260
Gannett Foundation, Inc., VA, 3260
Garden Club of Honolulu, The, HI, 903
Garden Homes Fund, CT, 565
Garden of Eatin' Foundation see 320
Garden Resources of Washington, DC, 669
Garen Family Foundation, CA, 205
Garfield Foundation, The, MA, 1405
Garland Foundation, John Jewett & H. Chandler, CA, 206
Gates Family Foundation, CO, 486
Gates Foundation see 486
Gateway 2000 Foundation, Inc. see 207
Gateway Foundation, CA, 207
Gateway Fund, The, MA, 1406
GATX Corporation Contributions Program, IL, 985
Gauntlett Foundation, Inc., Barbara, The see 163
Gauss Foundation, William F. & Lynn D., PA, 2841
GE Corporate Giving Program, CT, 566
GE Foundation, CT, 567
GE Fund see 567
Geary Foundation, Inc., Richard and Janet, WA, 3339
Gelatt Foundation, Inc., Philip M., WI, 3423
Gellert Family Foundation, Fred, The, CA, 208
GenRad Foundation, MA, 1407
George Foundation, The, OH, 2647
Georgia Power Company Contributions Program, GA, 835
Georgia Power Foundation, Inc., GA, 836
Georgia-Pacific Foundation, Inc., GA, 837
Gerard Foundation, Sumner, DE, 634
Gerbode Foundation, Wallace Alexander, CA, 209
Gerhard Family Foundation, CA, 210
German Marshall Fund of the United States, The, DC, 670
Gerrish Foundation, CO, 487
Gerry Charitable Trust, NY, 2158
Gerry Charitable Trust, Peggy N. & Robert G. see 2158
Gerschel Foundation, Laurent and Alberta, NY, 2159
Gerschel Foundation, Patrick A., NY, 2160

Gettler Family Foundation, The, OH, 2648
Getz Foundation, Emma & Oscar see 986
Getz Foundation, Harry A. and Rose, TX, 3087
Getz Foundation, The, IL, 986
Giannini Fund, Claire A., CA, 211
Gibbet Hill Foundation, IL, 987
Gibson Family Foundation, Inc., NJ, 1900
Gifford Rudin Foundation, Inc., NY, 2161
Gifts In Kind International, VA, 3261
Giger Foundation, Inc., Paul and Oscar, NE, 1812
Gilchrist Foundation, IA, 1169
Gildea Foundation, Inc., MD, 1298
Gilfillian Trust, Alexander B., PA, 2842
Gilman Foundation, Inc., Howard, NY, 2162
Gilmore Foundation, Earl B., CA, 212
Gilmore Foundation, John and Charlotte, The, IL, 988
Gilmore Foundation, William G., The, CA, 213
Gimbel & Elga Andersen-Gimbel Memorial Trust, Peter R., NY, 2163
Gimbel Foundation, Inc., Bernard F. and Alva B., NY, 2164
Giop Charitable Foundation, Sonia Raiziss, PA, 2843
Giordano Foundation, Inc., Salvatore, NJ, 1901
Give Something Back, LLC Corporate Giving Program, CA, 214
Glancy Foundation, Inc., Lenora and Alfred, GA, 838
Glancy Foundation, Inc., The, MI, 1583
Glantz Charitable Foundation, Herbert & Kitty, The, NY, 2165
Glaser Foundation, The see 3340
Glaser Progress Foundation, WA, 3340
Glassen Memorial Foundation, Hal & Jean, MI, 1584
Glaxo Wellcome Americas Inc. Corporate Giving Program see 2555
GlaxoSmithKline Holdings (Americas) Inc. Corporate Giving Program, NC, 2555
Glazer Foundation, Inc., Jerome S., LA, 1235
Gleacher Foundation, Anne and Eric, The, NY, 2166
Gleberman Foundation, Joseph & Carson, NY, 2167
Glenn Foundation, Carrie E. & Lena V., The, NC, 2556
Glenstone Foundation, The, VA, 3262
Glickenhaus Foundation, The, NY, 2168
Glide Foundation, Thornton S. Glide, Jr. and Katrina D., CA, 215
Global Environment Project Institute, Inc., CA, 216
Globe Foundation, AZ, 41
Glore Fund, IL, 989
Godbersen Family Foundation, Harold W. and Leone L., IA, 1170
Godchaux Foundation, Frank & Mary see 1237
Goddard Foundation, Inc., John N., The, GA, 839
Godric Foundation, The, CA, 217
Goergen Foundation, Inc., The, CT, 568
Gold Foundation, David B., The, CA, 218
Goldberg Charitable Trust, Bradley L., The, NY, 2169
Goldberg Foundation, Stephen A. and Diana L., DC, 671
Golden Foundation, Robert M., ID, 915
Golden Light Foundation, The, IN, 1133
Golden Rule Foundation, Inc., The, ME, 1255
Golden Rule, Inc., CO, 488
Goldfarb Family Foundation, Inc., Morris & Arlene, NY, 2170
Goldfrank III Foundation, Lionel, The, NY, 2171
Goldman Environmental Foundation, CA, 219
Goldman Fund, Lisa and Douglas, CA, 220
Goldman Fund, Richard & Rhoda, CA, 221
Goldring Family Foundation, Inc., The, NJ, 1902
Goldsmith Family Charitable Foundation, Inc., The, NJ, 1903
Goldsmith Foundation, Horace W., NY, 2172
Gooch, Jr. Charitable Trust, C. W., VA, 3263
Goode Residuary Trust, Edith J., DC, 672
Goodwin Foundation, CO, 489
Goodyear Foundation, William and Karen, IL, 990
Gordon Foundation, Donald A., WI, 3424
Gordon Foundation, Gertrude S., WI, 3425
Gordon Fund, The, NY, 2173
Gordon, Jr. Foundation, W. K., The, TX, 3088
Gordon/Rousmaniere/Roberts Fund, The see 2173
Gottesman Family Foundation, LA, 1236
Gottwald Foundation, VA, 3264
Grace Charitable Foundation, Oliver R., The, NY, 2174

Lehman Foundation, Inc., Edith and Herbert, NY, 2267

Leidy Foundation, Inc., Joan, ID, 917

Leighty Foundation, The, CO, 507

Leir Foundation, Inc., The, NY, 2268

Lenna Foundation, Inc., Reginald A. & Elizabeth S., NY, 2269

Lennar Foundation, Inc., The, FL, 774

Lennox Foundation, TX, 3113

Lennox Foundation, Martha, David & Bagby, TX, 3114

Lennox International Inc. Corporate Giving Program, TX, 3115

Leon Foundation, The, DC, 679

Leonhardt Foundation, Inc., Frederick H., The, NM, 1986

Lerner Fund, Inc., Helaine Heilbrunn *see* 2464

Leslie Fund, Inc., WA, 3358

Leuschen Foundation, David M., NY, 2270

Leuthold Family Foundation, Steven C., MN, 1690

Leverett Memorial Fund, Hollis Declan, MA, 1441

Levin Family Foundation, Barbara J. & Gerald M., The, NY, 2271

Levin Family Foundation, Donald, IL, 1033

Levin Family Foundation, The *see* 2271

Levine Family Foundation, Inc., Stuart & Sheri, IL, 1034

Levinson Foundation, Max and Anna, NM, 1987

Levitt Foundation, NY, 2272

Levy-Markus Foundation, Inc., The, CA, 279

Lewis Foundation, Inc., Jonathan D. *see* 787

LG&E Energy Foundation, Inc., KY, 1216

Liberty Hill Foundation, CA, 280

Lichtenstein, Jr. Foundation, Morris L., The, TX, 3116

Lifebridge Foundation, Inc., The, NY, 2273

LifeWorks Foundation, TN, 3024

Lightfoot Foundation, E. L. & B. G., The, OR, 2771

Lightner Sams Foundation of Wyoming, WY, 3502

Lilly Foundation, Richard Coyle, MN, 1691

Lincoln Community Foundation, Inc., NE, 1820

Lincoln Foundation, Inc. *see* 1820

Lindbergh Foundation, Charles A. and Anne Morrow, The, MN, 1692

Linder Foundation, Inc., Albert A. & Bertram N., NY, 2274

Lingos Family Foundation, John and Sonia, MA, 1442

Link Foundation, The, NY, 2275

Linke Foundation, Gordon F. and Jocelyn B., MD, 1310

Linn-Henley Charitable Trust, AL, 13

Linnemann Family Foundation, The, OH, 2676

Lintilhac Foundation, VT, 3215

Lipman Family Foundation, Inc., The, CA, 281

Lipman Foundation, Inc., Howard and Jean *see* 281

Lipper Family Charitable Foundation, The, NJ, 1931

Lippitt Foundation, Katherine Kenyon, The, OH, 2677

Lipton Foundation, The, NY, 2276

Littauer Foundation, Inc., Lucius N., The, NY, 2277

Little Charitable Trust, Wm. Brian & Judith A., The, NY, 2278

Little Family Foundation, The, MA, 1443

Little River Foundation, NY, 2279

Littleford Foundation, Inc., William & Marion, NY, 2280

LittleJohn Family Foundation, The, CT, 579

Litwin Foundation, The, NY, 2281

Live Oak Foundation, LA, 1237

LJCP Foundation, The *see* 3359

LJCPJ Foundation, The, WA, 3359

Llagas Foundation, CA, 282

Lloyd Foundation, PA, 2876

Loeb, Jr. Foundation, John L., NY, 2282

Logan Charitable Foundation, George W., The, VA, 3277

Lone Rock Foundation, Inc., The, NY, 2283

Long Foundation *see* 283

Long Foundation, George A. and Grace L., CT, 580

Long Foundation, J. M., The, CA, 283

Longwood Foundation, Inc., DE, 638

Looker Foundation, The, CA, 284

Looney Foundation, Inc., Martha and Wilton, The, GA, 850

Lopata Foundation, Stanley and Lucy, MO, 1769

Los Trigos Fund, TX, 3117

Lostand Foundation, Inc., NY, 2284

Louis Foundation, Josephine P. & John J., IL, 1035

Louis, Jr. Foundation, John J. *see* 1035

Louisiana-Pacific Corporation Contributions Program, OR, 2772

Louisville Community Foundation, Inc. *see* 1211

Louisville Zoological Society, Inc. *see* 1214

Love Charitable Foundation, John Allan, MO, 1770

Love Conservation Foundation, Edward K., IL, 1036

Low Wood Fund, Inc., The, NY, 2285

Lowe-Marshall Trust, OH, 2678

Lowell Community Foundation, Greater, MA, 1444

Lowitz Foundation, CA, 285

Lowry Foundation, Inc., Sumter and Ivilyn, The, FL, 775

Lozier Foundation, NE, 1821

LSR Fund, NY, 2286

Lubbock Area Foundation, Inc., TX, 3118

Lubin Family Foundation, The, NY, 2287

Lubo Fund, Inc., NY, 2288

Lubrizol Foundation, The, OH, 2679

Luce Foundation, Inc., Henry, The, NY, 2289

Luckow Family Foundation, Inc., The, NJ, 1932

Ludington, Inc., VA, 3278

Ludlow-Griffith Foundation, CO, 508

Ludwick Family Foundation, CA, 286

Ludwick Family Foundation, The, CA, 287

Ludwig Foundation, Curren, WA, 3360

Lumpkin Family Foundation, The, IL, 1037

Lund Foundation, CA, 288

Lurie Family Foundation, Ann and Robert H., IL, 1038

Luster Family Foundation, Inc., CA, 289

Luther Charitable Trust, Frances R., The, OH, 2680

Lutheran World Relief, MD, 1311

LUX Foundation, Inc., WI, 3447

Luyckx Trust, Jeanne McMurchy, MI, 1609

Luzerne Foundation, The, PA, 2877

LWH Family Foundation, The, DC, 680

Lyndhurst Foundation, TN, 3025

Lyondell Chemical Company Contributions Program, TX, 3119

LZ Francis Foundation, OH, 2681

M & T Charitable Foundation, NY, 2290

MacAllister Foundation, Jack and Marilyn, CO, 509

MacArthur Foundation, John D. and Catherine T., IL, 1039

MacDonald Foundation, Inc., Marquis George, IL, 1040

MacDonald Foundation, Peter Lloyd, The, CO, 510

MACFUND, IL, 1041

Macht Foundation, Inc., Morton and Sophia, MD, 1312

Macklanburg Foundation, MO, 1771

Mad River Foundation, CT, 581

Maddie's Fund, CA, 290

Madigan Foundation, Edward, CO, 511

Madison Community Foundation, WI, 3448

Madoff Foundation, Bernard L. & Ruth, NY, 2291

Magness Foundation, Bob & Sharon, CO, 512

Magowan Family Foundation, Inc., The, NJ, 1933

Maguire Foundation, Inc., Russell, The, NY, 2292

Maher Family Foundation, John F., CA, 291

Mahoney Foundation, J. Edward, IL, 1042

Mai Family Foundation, The, NY, 2293

Maihaugen Foundation, Inc., WI, 3449

Mailman Foundation, Inc., The, NY, 2294

Main Charitable Trust, Anna, MI, 1610

Maine Community Foundation, Inc., The, ME, 1259

Maine Initiatives, Inc., ME, 1260

Major League Baseball Players Trust, NY, 2295

Makepeace Family Foundation, Maurice and Anne, The, MA, 1445

Maki Foundation, CO, 513

Makray Family Foundation, IL, 1043

Mallinckrodt Baker, Inc. Corporate Giving Program, NJ, 1934

Mallinckrodt Inc. Corporate Giving Program *see* 1793

Malloure Family Foundation, MI, 1611

Malone Foundation, Mary Alice Dorrance *see* 2907

Malott Family Foundation, IL, 1044

Maltz Family Foundation, Inc., Milton and Tamar, The, FL, 776

Mandell Foundation, Samuel P., PA, 2878

Maness Family Foundation, John R. and Carolyn J., NC, 2564

Manitou Foundation, Inc., CO, 514

Maple Hill Foundation, PA, 2879

Marble Fund, Inc., NY, 2296

Marbrook Foundation, MN, 1693

Marcks Foundation, Oliver Dewey, MI, 1612

Marcus Foundation, Grace R. and Allan D., NY, 2297

Marcus Foundation, James S., NY, 2298

Marden Foundation, Bernard A. & Chris, FL, 777

Mardigian Foundation, Edward & Helen, MI, 1613

Mariel Foundation, MI, 1614

Marin Community Foundation, CA, 292

Marino Charitable Foundation, Roger M., The, MA, 1446

Marks Family Foundation, The, NY, 2299

Marley Foundation, Kemper and Ethel, The, AZ, 46

Marmot Foundation, The, DE, 639

Marpat Foundation, Inc., MD, 1313

Marquardt Family Foundation, Richard C., PA, 2880

Marra Foundation, CA, 293

Mars Foundation, Virginia Cretella, NY, 2300

Mars Foundation, The, VA, 3279

Marsh Biodiversity Foundation, Margot, The, NY, 2301

Marshall County Community Foundation, Inc., IN, 1143

Marshall Foundation, Inc., James Harper, The, NY, 2302

Marshall Foundation, Mattie H. *see* 851

Marshall Foundation Trust, Mattie H., GA, 851

Marshall Reynolds Foundation, The, DE, 640

Marshfield Area Community Foundation, WI, 3450

Martin Foundation, Inc., Ann M., NY, 2303

Martin Foundation, Charlotte Y., WA, 3361

Martin Foundation, George & Miriam, PA, 2881

Martin Foundation, Inc., The, IN, 1144

Martin Marietta Materials, Inc. Corporate Giving Program, NC, 2565

Martin Marietta Materials, Inc. Philanthropic Trust *see* 2566

Martin Marietta Philanthropic Trust, NC, 2566

Marvin Foundation, The, MD, 1314

Marx Foundation, Dr. Harry Z. & Ruth M., CA, 294

Mascoma Savings Bank Foundation, NH, 1860

Maslow Family Foundation, Inc., PA, 2882

Mason Charitable Foundation *see* 1045

Mason Foundation, Inc., IL, 1045

Materials for the Future Foundation, The, CA, 295

Mather Charitable Trust, S. Livingston, The, OH, 2682

Mather Fund, Elizabeth Ring Mather and William Gwinn, OH, 2683

Matherne Family Foundation, Lee, The, LA, 1238

Maverick Foundation *see* 3216

Maverick Lloyd Foundation, VT, 3216

Max Charitable Foundation *see* 456

Maxon Charitable Foundation, Inc., The, IN, 1145

Mays Family Foundation, TX, 3120

Maytag Family Foundation, F., The, IA, 1179

Maytag Family Foundation, Fred, The *see* 1179

Mazanec Foundation, The, TX, 3121

Mazar Family Charitable Foundation, MA, 1447

Mazda Foundation (USA), Inc., The, DC, 681

Mazer Foundation, Helen and William, NJ, 1935

MCA Foundation, Ltd. *see* 2485

McAliley Endowment Fund, GA, 852

McAllister, Jr. Charitable Foundation, Hugh A., TX, 3122

McAshan Foundation, Inc. *see* 3178

McBean Charitable Trust, Alletta Morris, CA, 296

McBean Family Foundation, CA, 297

McBean Foundation, Atholl, The *see* 297

McBeth Foundation, CA, 298

McCamish Foundation, GA, 853

McCance Foundation, The, MA, 1448

McCarthy Foundation, Mary A. and John M., The, NY, 2304

McCaw Foundation, Craig and Susan, The, WA, 3362

McCaw Foundation, Wendy P., CA, 299

McClatchey Foundation, Inc., Devereaux F. and Dorothy, The, GA, 854

McConnell Foundation, Inc., Neil A., NY, 2305

McConnell Foundation, The, CA, 300

McCormack Foundation, Anne Beverly, The, IL, 1046

McCormick Foundation, Chauncey and Marion Deering, IL, 1047

McCoy Foundation, Miriam and Emmett, TX, 3123

McCoy Foundation, The, OR, 2773

McCrea Foundation, TX, 3124

McCune Charitable Foundation, NM, 1988

National Fish and Wildlife Foundation, DC, 688
National Gardening Association, VT, 3217
National Grange Mutual Charitable Foundation, NH, 1861
National Park Foundation, The, DC, 689
National Philanthropic Trust, PA, 2890
National Recycling Coalition, VA, 3280
National Wildlife Federation, VA, 3281
National Wildlife Rehabilitators Association, MN, 1700
Naturganic Foundation, CA, 320
NC Beautiful see 2563
NEB Corporate Giving Program, MA, 1456
Nebraska Statewide Arboretum, NE, 1824
Neidich & Brooke Garber Foundation, Daniel M., NY, 2327
Neiman Charitable Foundation, Velma A., MO, 1775
Nelson Family Foundation, Karl H. & Wealtha H., NE, 1825
Nelson Foundation, James & Aune, IL, 1059
Neslab Charitable Foundation see 1855
Nestle Purina PetCare Company Contributions Program, MO, 1776
Neu Family Foundation, Inc., John L., The, NY, 2328
Neukom Family Foundation, WA, 3366
Neuman Family Foundation, IL, 1060
Neuwirth Foundation, Inc., NY, 2329
New Canaan Community Foundation, Inc., CT, 586
New England Biolabs Foundation, MA, 1457
New Hampshire Charitable Foundation, The, NH, 1862
New Haven Foundation, The see 552
New Israel Fund, DC, 690
New Priorities Foundation, WA, 3367
New Tudor Foundation, The, MA, 1458
New York Community Trust, The, NY, 2330
New York Times Company Foundation, Inc., The, NY, 2331
New-Land Foundation, Inc., The, NY, 2332
Newland Family Foundation, Inc., The, GA, 863
Newman's Own, Inc. Corporate Giving Program, CT, 587
Newmark Foundation, Lawrence S. Newmark and Gloria, IL, 1061
Niagara Mohawk Foundation, Inc., The, NY, 2333
Niagara Mohawk Power Corporation Contributions Program, NY, 2334
Nicholas Family Charitable Trust, NY, 2335
Nichols Foundation, Inc., NY, 2336
Nicholson Family Foundation, MN, 1701
Nicholson Foundation, Richard H. and Nancy B. see 1701
Nickel Producers Environmental Research Association, Inc., NC, 2571
Nielsen Foundation, Aksel, The, CO, 521
Niles Foundation, Laura J., CT, 588
Nimick Forbesway Foundation, PA, 2891
Nippert Charitable Foundation, Inc., L. and L., OH, 2689
Nissan North America, Inc. Corporate Giving Program, CA, 321
No Frills Foundation, The, MO, 1777
Noah's Ark Foundation, VA, 3282
Noble Foundation, Inc., Edward John, NY, 2337
Noble Foundation, Inc., Samuel Roberts, The, OK, 2753
Norcliffe Foundation, The, WA, 3368
Norcliffe Fund, The see 3368
Norcross Wildlife Foundation, Inc., NY, 2338
Nord Family Foundation, The, OH, 2690
Nord Foundation, Eric and Jane, The, OH, 2691
Nordson Corporation Foundation, The, OH, 2692
Norfolk Foundation, The, VA, 3283
Norfolk Southern Foundation, VA, 3284
Norman Foundation, Andrew, CA, 322
Norman Foundation, Inc., NY, 2339
North American Rockwell Employees Donate Once Club see 101
North Carolina Community Foundation, NC, 2572
North Dakota Natural Resources Trust, Inc., ND, 2600
North Dakota Wetlands Trust, Inc. see 2600
North Georgia Community Foundation, GA, 864
North Manchester Community Foundation see 1124
North Shore Foundation, VA, 3285
North Star Fund, Inc., NY, 2340
North Woods Wilderness Trust, ME, 1264

Northeast Charitable Trust, MA, 1459
Northeast Michigan Community Foundation see 1547
Northeast Utilities Foundation, Inc., CT, 589
Northen Endowment, Mary Moody, TX, 3132
Northern Chautauqua Community Foundation, Inc., NY, 2341
Northern New York Community Foundation, Inc., NY, 2342
Northern Utilities, Inc. Corporate Giving Program, NH, 1863
Northrup II Fund Trust, Edwin D., OH, 2693
Northwest Area Foundation, MN, 1702
Northwest Fund for the Environment, WA, 3369
Northwest Natural Gas Company Contributions Program, OR, 2779
NorthWestern Corporation Contributions Program, SD, 3001
Norton Foundation, Inc., George W., The see 1217
Norton Foundation, Inc., The, KY, 1217
Norweb Foundation, The, OH, 2694
Norwell Fund, IL, 1062
Norwich Foundation, Greater, The, NY, 2343
Norwottock Charitable Trust, IL, 1063
Notsew Orm Sands Foundation, TX, 3133
Noyes Foundation, Inc., A. B. & J., NY, 2344
Noyes Foundation, Inc., Jessie Smith, NY, 2345
NRZ Foundation see 1133
Nuhn Charitable Trust, Jane W., NY, 2346
NUI Corporation Contributions Program, NJ, 1943

O'Bleness Foundation No. 3, Charles, OH, 2695
O'Connor Foundation, A. Lindsay and Olive B., NY, 2347
O'Neill Brothers Foundation, The, OH, 2696
O'Quinn Foundation, John M., TX, 3134
O'Quinn Foundation, The see 3134
O'Toole Family Foundation, Dennis A., The, NH, 1864
Oak Foundation U.S.A., The, MA, 1460
Oak Lodge Foundation, CO, 522
Oak Tree Charitable Foundation, CA, 323
Oakmead Foundation, The, NV, 1847
Oberweiler Foundation, IL, 1064
Ocean Federal Foundation see 1944
OceanFirst Foundation, NJ, 1944
OCRI Foundation see 2768
October Hill Foundation, The, CT, 590
Oestreicher Foundation, Inc., Sylvan and Ann, NY, 2348
Offield Family Foundation, The, IL, 1065
Ohrstrom Foundation, Inc., The, NY, 2349
Oklahoma Communities Foundation, Inc. see 2748
Oleson Foundation, MI, 1624
Olin Corporation Charitable Trust, CT, 591
Olin Foundation, Spencer T. and Ann W., MO, 1778
Olive Branch Foundation, Inc., The, OH, 2697
Olson Charitable Foundation, Katherine L., IL, 1066
Olson Charitable Foundation, Leland J. & Dorothy H., NE, 1826
Olsson Memorial Foundation, Elis, VA, 3286
Omaha Community Foundation, NE, 1827
Omaha World-Herald Foundation, The, NE, 1828
OMC Foundation, The, IL, 1067
OMRON Foundation, Inc., IL, 1068
On Top of the World Foundation, Inc., The see 738
Once Upon A Time Foundation, TX, 3135
Oneida Nation Foundation, NY, 2350
Open Door Foundation, MN, 1703
Open Spaces, Sacred Places see 1336
Operation Fuel, Inc., CT, 592
Opler Foundation, Scott, FL, 783
Oppenheimer Family Foundation, The, IL, 1069
Oracle Corporation Contributions Program, CA, 324
Orange and Rockland Utilities, Inc. Corporate Giving Program, NY, 2351
Orange Tree Foundation, The, DE, 642
Orchard Foundation, The, MA, 1461
Orentreich Family Foundation, The, NY, 2352
Orleans Charitable Foundation, Jeffrey P., PA, 2892
Ortenberg Foundation, The see 2077
Osberg Family Trust, The, WA, 3370
Osborn Charitable Trust, Edward B., NY, 2353
Osceola Foundation, Inc., NY, 2354

Oschwald Trust, Anna, NC, 2573
Osher Foundation, Bernard, CA, 325
Osiason Educational Foundation, Inc., The, FL, 784
OSilas Foundation, MN, 1704
Osram Sylvania Inc. Corporate Giving Program, MA, 1462
Otter Cove Foundation, CA, 326
Otter Island Foundation, TX, 3136
Otter Tail Power Company Contributions Program, MN, 1705
Ottinger Foundation, The, NY, 2355
Ottley Trust-Watertown, Marian W. see 616
Ottosen Family Foundation, The, AZ, 48
Outagamie Charitable Foundation, Inc., WI, 3456
Outcalt Charitable Fund see 2698
Outcalt Foundation, Jane and Jon, OH, 2698
Outer Banks Community Foundation, Inc., NC, 2574
Outhwaite Charitable Trust, June G., CA, 327
Overbrook Foundation, The, NY, 2356
Overhills Foundation, NY, 2357
Overlock Family Foundation see 2131
Overly Foundation, Edith H., MA, 1463
Overton Research Institute, Inc., MT, 1803
Owsley Foundation, Alvin and Lucy, TX, 3137
Oxford Community Foundation, OH, 2699
Oxford Foundation, Inc. see 849
Oxford Foundation, Inc., PA, 2893
Oxford Industries Foundation, Inc., GA, 865
Oxley Foundation, The, OK, 2754

P & G Corporate Giving Program, OH, 2700
P Twenty-One Foundation, The, TX, 3138
Pacer Foundation, The, MA, 1464
Pacific Life Foundation, CA, 328
Pacific Mutual Charitable Foundation see 328
Packard Foundation, David and Lucile, The, CA, 329
PADI Foundation, CA, 330
Paducah Area Community Foundation see 1212
Palm Beach County Community Foundation see 739
Palm Fund, NV, 1848
Palmer Foundation, Inc., The, NY, 2358
Palmer Fund, Frank Loomis, The, RI, 2968
Panaphil Foundation, The, NY, 2359
Pangburn Foundation, The, WI, 3457
Pappas Foundation, Arthur M. & Martha R., MA, 1465
Pardoe Foundation, Samuel P., MA, 1466
Parfet Family Foundation, Donald and Ann, MI, 1625
Parish Foundation, Preston S., MI, 1626
Park Foundation, Inc., NY, 2360
Parke County Community Foundation, Inc., IN, 1150
Parker Family Foundation, IL, 1070
Parker Foundation, Mary E., The, DE, 643
Parker Foundation, Theodore Edson, The, MA, 1467
Parkersburg Area Community Foundation, WV, 3403
Parks Foundation, OR, 2780
Parks Trust, Holden, OH, 2701
Parsons Foundation, Alison J. & Ella W., The, VA, 3287
Pasadena Foundation, CA, 331
Paskus Foundation, Inc., Martin, The, NY, 2361
Patagonia Environmental Grants Program, CA, 332
Patchett Foundation, Inc., The, NJ, 1945
Patricelli Family Foundation, Robert & Margaret, The, CT, 593
Pattee Foundation, Inc., The, TN, 3026
Patterson Endowment Trust, Abreu, GA, 866
Patterson Foundation, Cissy, The, DC, 691
Patterson-Barclay Memorial Foundation, Inc., GA, 867
Paul Foundation, Inc., Josephine Bay Paul and C. Michael, NY, 2362
Pauley Family Foundation, The, VA, 3288
Paulos Foundation, The, TX, 3139
Paulson, Jr. Foundation, Henry M. & Wendy J. see 2052
Paws Up Foundation, CA, 333
Payden Foundation, Mary R. Payden & Joseph R., CA, 334
Payne Foundation, Frank E. Payne and Seba B., IL, 1071
Payne Fund, The, OH, 2702
Peabody Charitable Fund, Amelia, MA, 1468
Peace Development Fund, MA, 1469
Peach Foundation, WA, 3371
Peacock Foundation, Inc., FL, 785
Pearson-Rappaport Foundation, NY, 2363

Richmond Foundation, Inc., Frederick W., The, MD, 1325
Richter Charitable Trust, Adam, CA, 354
Ridder Foundation, Georgia B., The, CA, 355
Riepe Charitable Foundation, James S. & Gail P., MD, 1326
Riggio Foundation, The, NY, 2386
Ringoen Family Trust, Richard and Joan, IN, 1156
Ripple Foundation, The, NY, 2387
Ripples, Inc., WI, 3470
Ripplewood Foundation, Inc., NY, 2388
River Branch Foundation, FL, 791
Rivers Fund, Margaret, MN, 1711
Rivkin Family Foundation, CA, 356
RLC Foundation, CO, 523
RMF Family Fund, Inc., NY, 2389
Robbins-De Beaumont Foundation, The, MA, 1484
Roberts Family Foundation, IL, 1079
Roberts Foundation, Morrison, NE, 1829
Roberts Foundation, Ralph & Suzanne, PA, 2904
Roberts Foundation, The, CA, 357
Robertson Family Foundation, Inc., Blanche and Julian, The, NC, 2584
Robins, Jr. Foundation, Anne Carter Robins and Walter R., The, MD, 1327
Robinson Charitable Trust, Edward & Lida, NE, 1830
Robinson Family Foundation, Donald & Sylvia, PA, 2905
Robinson Family Foundation, Evelyn & Paul, The, NY, 2390
Rocca, Jr. Foundation, B. T., CA, 358
Rochester Area Community Foundation, NY, 2391
Rochester Area Community Foundation, Greater see 1550
Rochester Area Foundation see 2391
Rochester Area Foundation, MN, 1712
Rock-Tenn Company Contributions Program, GA, 873
Rockefeller Brothers Fund, Inc., NY, 2392
Rockefeller Family Fund, Inc., NY, 2393
Rockefeller Fund, Inc., David, The, NY, 2394
Rockwell Foundation, The, PA, 2906
Rockwell Fund, Inc., TX, 3146
Rocky Mountain Elk Foundation, Inc., MT, 1804
Roddy Foundation, Inc., The see 3028
Roddy, Sr. Foundation, Inc., Kate Collins Roddy and J. P., TN, 3028
Roe Foundation, Inc., The, NY, 2395
Roehr Family Foundation, Inc., MA, 1485
Roemer Foundation, The, PA, 2907
Rogers Charitable Trust, Florence, The, NC, 2585
Rogers Foundation, NE, 1831
Rogers, Jr. Family Foundation, Inc., J. Carlisle Rogers, Ruth G. Rogers & James Carlisle, FL, 792
Rohauer Collection Foundation, Inc., NY, 2396
Rohlen Foundation, IL, 1080
Rohm and Haas Company Contributions Program, PA, 2908
Romic Environmental Technologies Corp. Contributions Program, CA, 359
Romney Foundation, Inc., Lee, NY, 2397
Rooms to Go Children's Fund, FL, 793
Roosa Family Foundation Trust, RI, 2970
Rose Family Foundation, NY, 2398
Rose Foundation, Adam R., NY, 2399
Rose Foundation for Communities and the Environment, CA, 360
Rose Foundation, The, TN, 3029
Roseman Foundation, Inc., Ephraim, KY, 1219
Rosenberg Foundation, William J. & Tina, FL, 794
Rosengarten Horowitz Fund, CA, 361
Rosenlund Family Foundation, The, PA, 2909
Rosenthal Family Foundation see 1631
Rosenthal Family Foundation, Ann & Mike, MI, 1631
Rosenthal Foundation, Benjamin J., IL, 1081
Rosenthal Fund, The, NY, 2400
Rosewood Foundation, The, TX, 3147
Ross Family Foundation, The, PA, 2910
Ross Foundation, Inc., Arthur, NY, 2401
Ross Foundation, The, AR, 61
Ross Foundation, The, TX, 3148
Rossetter Foundation, IL, 1082
Roswell Foundation, Inc., Elizabeth B. and Arthur E., MD, 1328

Rotary Charities of Traverse City, MI, 1632
Rotary Foundation of Indianapolis, Inc., IN, 1157
Rothenberg Family Foundation, Inc., Joan, NY, 2402
Rothenberg Family Foundation, Inc. see 2402
Rothschild Fund, A. Frank and Dorothy B., IL, 1083
Rouse-Bottom Foundation, VA, 3291
Routhier Foundation, E. J. & V. M., RI, 2971
Routhier Foundation, Edward J. & Virginia M. see 2971
Rowland Foundation, Inc., DE, 645
Roxiticus Fund, NJ, 1954
Royal Oak Foundation, NY, 2403
RREEF Outreach, IL, 1084
Rumsey Foundation, Mary A. H., NY, 2404
Rupp Foundation, Fran and Warren, The, OH, 2708
Russell Charitable Trust, AZ, 51
Russell Family Foundation, The, WA, 3379
Ryan Family Charitable Foundation see 1491
Ryan Foundation, Richard Nelson, NY, 2405
Ryan Memorial Foundation, PA, 2911
Ryerson Charitable Trust, John B. & Jane M., MA, 1486

S & G Foundation, Inc., WY, 3503
Sacerdote Foundation, Peter M., The, NY, 2406
Sacharuna Foundation, MA, 1487
Sachem Foundation, The, RI, 2972
Sachs Fund, MO, 1784
Sacramento Regional Foundation, CA, 362
Saddle Foundation, MI, 1633
Saginaw Community Foundation, MI, 1634
Sai Foundation of America, Sathya, CA, 363
Salem Five Charitable Foundation, Inc., MA, 1488
Salem Foundation, The, OR, 2784
Sall Family Foundation, Inc., NC, 2586
Saltonstall Charitable Foundation, Richard, MA, 1489
Salute to the Seasons Fund, Inc., NY, 2407
Salwil Foundation, IL, 1085
Salzman-Medica Foundation, The, TX, 3149
Samis Foundation, WA, 3380
Sams Foundation, Inc., Earl C., TX, 3150
Samsung Semiconductor, Inc. Corporate Giving Program, TX, 3151
Samuels Foundation, Inc., Ernest & Rose, NY, 2408
San Antonio Area Foundation, TX, 3152
San Diego Community Foundation see 365
San Diego Foundation for Change, CA, 364
San Diego Foundation, The, CA, 365
San Diego Gas & Electric Company Contributions Program, CA, 366
San Francisco Foundation, The, CA, 367
Sand County Foundation, Inc., WI, 3471
Sandercock Trust, Marian, CA, 368
Sanders Corporate Giving Program, NH, 1869
Sandpiper Fund, Inc., NY, 2409
Sands Foundation, Frank and Brinna, VT, 3219
Sands Foundation, Inc., Mac and Sally, NY, 2410
Sands Memorial Foundation, Inc., MT, 1805
Sandusky/Erie County Community Foundation, OH, 2709
Sandy River Charitable Foundation, The, ME, 1265
Sanford Charitable Foundation, Robert V. Sanford and Laraine M., CA, 369
Sansom Foundation, Inc., NY, 2411
Sansom-Eligator Foundation, PA, 2912
Santa Barbara Foundation, CA, 370
Santa Cruz County Community Foundation, Greater see 143
Santa Cruz Island Foundation, CA, 371
Santa Fe Community Foundation, NM, 1991
SANYO North America Corporation Contributions Program, CA, 372
Sapelo Foundation, Inc., The, GA, 874
Sapelo Island Research Foundation, Inc. see 874
Sapling Foundation, The, CA, 373
Saquish Foundation, MA, 1490
Sarasota County Community Foundation, Inc., The see 742
Sargent Foundation, Gladys W., The, CA, 374
Sargent Foundation, Newell B., WY, 3504
Sarkeys Foundation, OK, 2755
Sasco Foundation, NY, 2412
Sauerland Foundation, The, OH, 2710
Saul Family Fund, CA, 375

Saul Family Fund, George W. & Faye Batten see 375
Saunders Foundation, The, FL, 795
Savannah Electric and Power Company Contributions Program, GA, 875
Save the Dunes Conservation Fund, IN, 1158
Save-the-Redwoods League, CA, 376
SAW Community Foundation see 3293
SB Foundation, NM, 1992
Scaife Family Foundation, FL, 796
SCEcorp Contributions Program see 179
Schaeneman, Jr. Foundation, Inc., Lewis G., CT, 598
Schafer Family Foundation, NY, 2413
Schechter Foundation, Inc., The, NC, 2587
Schenectady Foundation, The, NY, 2414
Schenker Family Foundation, The, NY, 2415
Schering-Plough Corporation Contributions Program, NJ, 1955
Scherman Foundation, Inc., The, NY, 2416
Scheuer Family Foundation, Inc., Richard J. & Joan G., NY, 2417
Schieffelin Residuary Trust, Sarah I., NY, 2418
Schiff Foundation, John J. and Mary R., OH, 2711
Schiff Foundation, The, NY, 2419
Schiff, Hardin & Waite Foundation, IL, 1086
Schifter Family Foundation, MD, 1329
Schimmel Foundation, Inc., Stephen Harold, The, FL, 797
Schleussner Charitable Trust, Charles see 2491
Schlinger Foundation, CA, 377
Schloss Family Foundation, William & Jane, CA, 378
Schloss Family Foundation, Inc., The, NY, 2420
Schmidt Family Charitable Foundation, J. Frank, The, OR, 2785
Schmidt Foundation, Carl and Verna, MN, 1713
Schmidt Foundation, Marjorie Mosher, CA, 379
Schneider Foundation, Robert E., IL, 1087
Schneider Foundation Corporation, Al J., KY, 1220
Schoeneman-Halle Foundation, Inc., The, MD, 1330
Schoeneman-Weiler Fund, Inc., The see 1330
Scholl Foundation, Dr., IL, 1088
Schooner Foundation, The, MA, 1491
Schott Foundation, MN, 1714
Schott Foundation, Marge & Charles J., OH, 2712
Schow Foundation, The, CA, 380
Schuler Foundation, Doris M., AL, 15
Schuller Fund, Inc. see 500
Schultz Foundation, Arthur B., The, WY, 3505
Schultz Foundation, Inc., FL, 798
Schumann Foundation, Helmut Wolfgang, NH, 1870
Schumann Foundation, Robert F. & Marilyn H., CT, 599
Schumann Foundation, W. Ford, The, AZ, 52
Schumann Fund for New Jersey, Inc., The, NJ, 1956
Schwab Corporation Foundation, Charles, The, CA, 381
Schwartz Foundation, Marvin and Donna, The, NY, 2421
Schweitzer Foundation, Inc., William P. & Gertrude, NY, 2422
Schweizer Foundation, Inc., Tim and Barbara, MD, 1331
Scioto County Area Foundation, The, OH, 2713
Scire Family Foundation, Inc., The, NJ, 1957
Scott Charitable Trust, Kenneth A., OH, 2714
Scotts Company Contributions Program, The, OH, 2715
Scranton Area Foundation, Inc., The, PA, 2913
Scripps Foundation, Ellen Browning, The, CA, 382
Scrooby Foundation, The, CT, 600
Sea Breeze Foundation, PA, 2914
Seagears Family Foundation, VA, 3292
Sealaska Heritage Foundation, AK, 23
Seaman Charitable Foundation, Douglas and Eleanor, WI, 3472
Sears-Swetland Family Foundation, The, OH, 2716
Sears-Swetland Foundation, The see 2716
Seasongood Good Government Foundation, Murray and Agnes, OH, 2717
Seattle Foundation, The, WA, 3381
Seattle Times Company Contributions Program, The, WA, 3382
Seay Charitable Trust, Sarah M. & Charles E., TX, 3153
Sedgwick Family Charitable Trust, OH, 2718
See Foundation, Charles, WA, 3383
Seebe Trust, Frances, CA, 383
Seeds of Faith, Inc., WI, 3473

Seeley Foundation, The, WY, 3506
Segal Charitable Trust, Barnet, CA, 384
Segoe Family Foundation, Ladislas & Vilma, OH, 2719
Sehgal Family Foundation, IA, 1183
Seiler Family Foundation, Inc., Nathan & Lena, NY, 2423
Seiler Foundation, Inc., Jack & Muriel, The, NY, 2424
Select Copy System of Southern California Foundation see 385
Select Office Solutions Foundation, CA, 385
Selz Foundation, Inc., NY, 2425
Semlitz/Glaser Foundation, NY, 2426
Sempra Energy Corporate Giving Program, CA, 386
Sendzimir Foundation, Inc., The, OH, 2720
Septimus Foundation II, MA, 1492
Seraph Foundation, The, DE, 646
Seven Springs Foundation, The, CA, 387
Seventh Generation Fund, CA, 388
Seventh Generation Fund for Indian Development, Inc. see 388
Seventh Generation, Inc. Corporate Giving Program, VT, 3220
Sewall Foundation, Elmina B., CT, 601
Sexton Foundation, MN, 1715
SF Foundation II, The, GA, 876
SFC Charitable Foundation see 1785
SGI Corporate Giving Program, CA, 389
Shackelford Charitable Trust, Margaret F., TN, 3030
Shaklee Corporation Contributions Program, CA, 390
Shapiro Family Charitable Foundation, CA, 391
Shapiro Family Foundation, Inc., Soretta & Henry, IL, 1089
Shared Earth Foundation, The, MD, 1332
Sharp Charitable Foundation, Frances C., PA, 2915
Sharp Foundation see 2427
Sharp Foundation, Peter Jay, The, NY, 2427
Sharpe Family Foundation, The, NY, 2428
Shasta Regional Community Foundation, CA, 392
Shaw Foundation, Harold W. & Mary Louise, The, OH, 2721
Sheehan Family Foundation, MA, 1493
Sheinberg Foundation, Eric P., NY, 2429
Sheinberg Foundation, The, CA, 393
Sheldon Foundation, Inc., Ralph C., NY, 2430
Shell Companies Foundation, Inc. see 3155
Shell Oil Company Contributions Program, TX, 3154
Shell Oil Company Foundation, TX, 3155
Sherman Fund, Saul & Devorah, IL, 1090
Sherrill Foundation, The, NY, 2431
Shifting Foundation, The, IL, 1091
Shiloff Family Foundation, TX, 3156
Shine Foundation, Inc., Sam, IN, 1159
Shipley Family Foundation, Inc., The, MA, 1494
Shockley Foundation, WI, 3474
Shoemaker Fund, Thomas H. and Mary Williams, The, PA, 2916
Sholley Foundation, Inc., MA, 1495
Shoreland Foundation, The, NY, 2432
Shrieking Meadow Foundation, DE, 647
Sidewater Foundation, Arthur & Estelle, PA, 2917
Siebel Foundation, Thomas and Stacey, The, CA, 394
Sieg Foundation, Louis & Nellie, MI, 1635
Siegel Charitable Trust, Stuart and Jill, The, PA, 2918
Siemens Corporation Contributions Program, NY, 2433
Sierra Club Foundation, The, CA, 395
Sierra Foundation, Inc., NJ, 1958
Sierra Pacific Foundation, CA, 396
Sierra Pacific Resources Charitable Foundation, NV, 1849
Sigety Family Foundation, Inc., The, NY, 2434
Silver Mountain Foundation for the Arts, NJ, 1959
Silver Tie Fund, Inc., The, MA, 1496
Silverman Family Foundation, WI, 3475
Simmons Family Foundation, Virginia and L. E., The, TX, 3157
Simon Charitable Trust, Esther, NY, 2435
Simons Charitable Trust, Richard H., FL, 799
Simpson Fund, WA, 3384
Simpson Investment Company Contributions Program see 3384
Singer Family Foundation, Paul, The, DE, 648
Singer Foundation, Paul & Linda, The see 648
Singing for Change, MO, 1785

Singletary Foundation, Inc., Lewis Hall & Mildred Sasser, GA, 877
Sinskey Foundation, Robert M., The, CA, 397
Sioux Falls Area Community Foundation, SD, 3002
Siragusa Foundation, The, IL, 1092
Skaggs Foundation, L. J. Skaggs and Mary C., CA, 398
Skilling and Andrews Foundation, MI, 1636
Skylark Foundation, The, CA, 399
Slade Foundation, C. F. Roe, The, NY, 2436
Slaughter, Jr. Foundation, Inc., William E., UT, 3205
Slavik Family Foundation, Donald, MO, 1786
Slick Family Foundation, NC, 2588
Sloan Foundation, C. Hamilton, NC, 2589
Sloss Foundation, Margaret K., CA, 400
Small Change Foundation, The, CA, 401
Smallwood Foundation see 3476
Smallwood Foundation, Frances C. & William P., WI, 3476
Smart Family Foundation, CT, 602
Smeal Foundation, Mary Jean & Frank P., NY, 2437
Smikis Foundation, MN, 1716
Smith & Athalie R. Clarke Foundation, Joan Irvine, CA, 402
Smith Charitable Foundation, Vera L., OR, 2786
Smith Foundation, Inc., Edward C. Smith, Jr. & Christopher B., NC, 2590
Smith Foundation, James C. and Norma I., TX, 3158
Smith Foundation, Kelvin and Eleanor, The, OH, 2722
Smith Foundation, Ralph L., TX, 3159
Smith Foundation, Randall & Kathryn, The, NY, 2438
Smith Foundation, Inc., Wilbur S., SC, 2998
Smith Horticultural Trust, Stanley, The, CA, 403
Smith-Welsh Foundation, CA, 404
Smout Foundation, Inc., Les and Judy, FL, 800
Snee-Reinhardt Charitable Foundation, PA, 2919
Snow Foundation, Inc., John Ben, The, NY, 2439
Snow Memorial Trust, John Ben, NY, 2440
Snyder Foundation for Animals, Inc., The, MD, 1333
SoCalGas Corporate Giving Program, CA, 405
Society of International Cultural Exchange (SICE), Inc., NY, 2441
Solari Charitable Trust, Richard & Mary, CA, 406
Solectron Corporation Contributions Program, CA, 407
Solid Waste Management Foundation see 1557
Solow Foundation, Inc., Sheldon H., NY, 2442
Somerset Foundation, Inc., MN, 1717
Sonken Charitable Trust, Joe, FL, 801
Sonoma County Community Foundation, The see 145
Sonora Area Foundation, CA, 408
Sontheimer Foundation, Inc., The, CT, 603
Sordoni Foundation, Inc., PA, 2920
Sosnoff Foundation, Martin and Toni, NY, 2443
Sosnoff Foundation, Martin T. see 2443
Sours Foundation, Marguerite, TX, 3160
South Coast Foundation, Inc., CA, 409
Southern Foundation, Inc. see 1754
Southern Partners Fund, GA, 878
Southern Union Company Contributions Program, TX, 3161
Southshore Foundation, AR, 62
Southwest Gas Corporation Contributions Program, NV, 1850
Southwest Gas Corporation Foundation, The, NV, 1851
Southwest Medical Institute, Inc., TX, 3162
Southwire Company Contributions Program, GA, 879
Spalding Family Foundation, CA, 410
Spalding Foundation, Eliot, AZ, 53
Speckhard-Knight Charitable Foundation, MI, 1637
Spencer Foundation, Mary C. & Perry F., OH, 2723
Spencer Fund, Benjamin, The, MD, 1334
SPIA Foundation, The, NY, 2444
Spire Foundation, Inc., Nancy Woodson, WI, 3477
Spitz Foundation, Joel & Maxine see 1093
Spitz-Nebenzahl Foundation, Inc., IL, 1093
Sportsmen for Conservation Fund, WA, 3385
Sprague Educational and Charitable Foundation, Seth, The, NY, 2445
Sprague Foundation, John and Dorothy, NY, 2446
Sprague, Jr. Foundation, Norman F., CA, 411
Spring Creek Foundation, The, DC, 697
Springcreek Foundation, CA, 412
Springfield Foundation, The, OH, 2724
Springhouse Foundation see 261

Sprinkle Family Foundation, Inc., The, NC, 2591
SRP Corporate Giving Program, AZ, 54
St. Croix Foundation for Community Development, VI, 3227
St. Croix Valley Community Foundation, WI, 3478
St. Deny's Foundation, Inc., MI, 1638
St. Louis Community Foundation, MO, 1787
Stackpole-Hall Foundation, PA, 2921
Stainman Family Foundation, Inc., The, NY, 2447
Staley Foundation, Bill and Orli, The, IL, 1094
Staley, Jr. Foundation, A. E., IL, 1095
Stamps Family Charitable Foundation, Inc., MA, 1497
Standard Corporate Giving Program, The, OR, 2787
Stang Foundation, Fred W., AZ, 55
Stans Foundation, The, CA, 413
Staritch Foundation, Inc., NY, 2448
Stark Community Foundation, OH, 2725
Stark County Foundation, Inc., The see 2725
Starpoint Charitable Trust, The, PA, 2922
Starr Foundation, The, NY, 2449
Starrett Foundation, The, DE, 649
Stateline Community Foundation, The, WI, 3479
Staton Foundation, Jocelyn Botterell see 846
Stauffer Communications Foundation see 860
Staunton Augusta Waynesboro Community Foundation, VA, 3293
Steadley Memorial Trust, Kent D. & Mary L., IL, 1096
Stearns Charitable Foundation, Inc., Anna B., MA, 1498
Stearns Charitable Foundation, MA, 1499
Stearns Charitable Trust, Janet Upjohn, DE, 650
Stebbins Fund, Inc., The, NY, 2450
Steelcase Foundation, MI, 1639
Steelcase Inc. Corporate Giving Program, MI, 1640
Steele-Reese Foundation, The, NY, 2451
Steere Foundation, William & Lynda, FL, 802
Stein Family Foundation see 803
Stein Foundation, Inc., David A., The, FL, 803
Stein Foundation, Inc., Jack & Joan, WI, 3480
Steiner Foundation, Inc., Rudolf, CA, 414
Steiner Foundation, Inc., UT, 3206
Steiner Trust, Lionel, CA, 415
Steinhardt Foundation, Judy and Michael, The, NY, 2452
Stephenson Foundation, CA, 416
Sterling Chemicals, Inc. Corporate Giving Program, TX, 3163
Sterling-Turner Foundation, TX, 3164
Stern Family Foundation, The, NJ, 1960
Stern Foundation, Helmut, The, MI, 1641
Stern Foundation, Leonard N. see 1960
Stern Memorial Trust, Sidney, CA, 417
Sterne-Elder Memorial Trust, CO, 524
Stevens Family Foundation, R. A., WI, 3481
Stevens Foundation, Abbot and Dorothy H., The, MA, 1500
Stevens Foundation, Nathaniel and Elizabeth P., The, MA, 1501
Stevens Foundation, Winifred L., WA, 3386
Stevens Point Area Foundation, Inc. see 3412
Stevenson Family Charitable Trust, MA, 1502
Stevenson Foundation, Keith and Mattie, The, TX, 3165
Stewart & Co. Foundation, Inc., W. P., NY, 2453
Stewart Foundation, IL, 1097
Stewart, M.D. Foundation, Alexander, PA, 2923
Sticht Foundation, Paul and Ferne, GA, 880
Still Water Foundation, TX, 3166
Stine Foundation, James M. and Margaret V., PA, 2924
Stoddard Charitable Trust, The, MA, 1503
Stoker Charitable Trust, Margaret Jane, MI, 1642
Stokes Foundation, Lydia B., NM, 1993
Stolier Family Foundation, Helen & Louis, OH, 2726
Stone Family Foundation, KS, 1198
Stone Foundation of New Jersey, The, NJ, 1961
Stone Foundation, The see 3304
Stone Trust B, H. Chase, WI, 3482
Stony Point Foundation, The, NY, 2454
Stonyfield Farm, Inc. Corporate Giving Program, NH, 1871
Storer Foundation, Inc., George B., The, WY, 3507
Stowe Family Foundation, NY, 2455
Stowe, Jr. Foundation, Inc., Robert Lee, NC, 2592
Strain Foundation, AL, 16